# HANDBOOK OF
# CHILD PSYCHOLOGY

# HANDBOOK OF CHILD PSYCHOLOGY

## SIXTH EDITION

Volume Two:    Cognition, Perception, and Language

*Volume Editors*

DEANNA KUHN and ROBERT SIEGLER

*Editors-in-Chief*

WILLIAM DAMON and RICHARD M. LERNER

**WILEY**

John Wiley & Sons, Inc.

Published by John Wiley & Sons, Inc., Hoboken, New Jersey.
Published simultaneously in Canada.

*Library of Congress Cataloging-in-Publication Data:*

Handbook of child psychology / editors-in-chief, William Damon & Richard M. Lerner.—
  6th ed.
    p.  cm.
  Includes bibliographical references and indexes.
  Contents: v. 1. Theoretical models of human development / volume editor,
Richard M. Lerner — v. 2. Cognition, perception, and language / volume editors,
Deanna Kuhn, Robert Siegler — v. 3. Social, emotional, and personality development /
volume editor, Nancy Eisenberg — v 4. Child psychology in practice / volume editors, K.
Ann Renninger, Irving E. Sigel.
  ISBN 0-471-27287-6 (set : cloth)
  — ISBN 0-471-27288-4 (v. 1 : cloth) — ISBN 0-471-27289-2 (v. 2 : cloth)
  — ISBN 0-471-27290-6 (v. 3 : cloth) — ISBN 0-471-27291-4 (v. 4 : cloth)
  1. Child psychology.   I. Damon, William, 1944–   II. Lerner, Richard M.
BF721.H242    2006
155.4—dc22
                                                              2005043951

Printed in the United States of America.
10  9  8  7  6  5  4  3  2  1

In memory of Paul Mussen, whose generosity of spirit
touched our lives and helped build a field.

# Contributors

**Karen E. Adolph**
Department of Psychology
New York University
New York, New York

**Glenda Andrews**
Department of Psychology
Griffith University
Queensland, Australia

**Martha E. Arterberry**
Department of Psychology
Gettysburg College
Gettysburg, Pennsylvania

**Patricia J. Bauer**
Department of Psychological and Brain Sciences
Duke University
Durham, North Carolina

**Sarah E. Berger**
Department of Psychology
City University of New York
College of Staten Island
Staten Island, New York

**Cara H. Cashon**
Department of Psychological and Brain Sciences
University of Louisville
Louisville, Kentucky

**Leslie B. Cohen**
Department of Psychology
University of Texas
Austin, Texas

**Michael Cole**
Department of Communication
University of California, San Diego
La Jolla, California

**Michelle de Haan**
Cognitive Neuroscience Unit
Institute of Child Health
London, England

**Sam Franklin**
Department of Human Development
Columbia University Teachers College
New York, New York

**Howard Gardner**
Graduate School of Education
Harvard University
Cambridge, Massachusetts

**David C. Geary**
Department of Psychological Sciences
University of Missouri
Columbia, Missouri

**Susan A. Gelman**
Department of Psychology
University of Michigan
Ann Arbor, Michigan

**Susan Goldin-Meadow**
Department of Psychology
University of Chicago
Chicago, Illinois

**Graeme S. Halford**
School of Psychology
University of Queensland
Brisbane, Australia

**Paul L. Harris**
Graduate School of Education
Harvard University
Cambridge, Massachusetts

**Katherine Hilden**
Department of Counseling,
   Educational Psychology,
   and Special Education
Michigan State University
East Lansing, Michigan

**Janellen Huttenlocher**
Center for Early Childhood Research
University of Chicago
Chicago, Illinois

**Charles W. Kalish**
Department of Educational Psychology
University of Michigan
Ann Arbor, Michigan

**Frank Keil**
Department of Psychology
Yale University
New Haven, Connecticut

**Philip J. Kellman**
Department of Psychology
University of California
Los Angeles, California

**Deanna Kuhn**
Department of Human Development
Columbia University Teachers College
New York, New York

**Jeffrey L. Lidz**
University of Maryland
College Park, Maryland

**Seana Moran**
Graduate School of Education
Harvard University
Cambridge, Massachusetts

**Yuko Munakata**
Department of Psychology
University of Colorado
Boulder, Colorado

**Charles A. Nelson III**
Richard David Scott Chair in Pediatrics
Boston Children's Hospital
Developmental Medicine Center Laboratory
   of Cognitive Neuroscience
Harvard Medical School
Boston, Massachusetts

**Nora S. Newcombe**
Department of Psychology
Temple University
Philadelphia, Pennsylvania

**Michael Pressley**
College of Education
Michigan State University
East Lansing, Michigan

**Jenny R. Saffran**
Department of Psychology
University of Wisconsin
Madison, Wisconsin

**Robert S. Siegler**
Department of Psychology
Carnegie-Mellon University
Pittsburgh, Pennsylvania

**Kathleen M. Thomas**
Institute of Child Development
University of Minnesota
Minneapolis, Minnesota

**Michael Tomasello**
Max Planck Institute for Evolutionary Anthropology
Leipzig, Germany

**Sandra R. Waxman**
Department of Psychology
Northwestern University
Evanston, Illinois

**Janet F. Werker**
Department of Psychology
University of British Colombia
Vancouver, British Colombia, Canada

**Lynne A. Werner**
Department of Speech and Hearing Sciences
University of Washington
Seattle, Washington

**Ellen Winner**
Department of Psychology
Boston College
Chestnut Hill, Massachusetts

# *Preface to* Handbook of Child Psychology, *Sixth Edition*

WILLIAM DAMON

Scholarly handbooks play several key roles in their disciplines. First and foremost, they reflect recent changes in the field as well as classic works that have survived those changes. In this sense, all handbooks present their editors' and authors' best judgments about what is most important to know in the field at the time of publication. But many handbooks also influence the fields that they report on. Scholars—especially younger ones—look to them for sources of information and inspiration to guide their own work. While taking stock of the shape of its field, a handbook also shapes the stock of ideas that will define the field's future. It serves both as an indicator and as a generator, a pool of received knowledge and a pool for spawning new insight.

## THE *HANDBOOK*'S LIVING TRADITION

Within the field of human development, the *Handbook of Child Psychology* has served these key roles to a degree that has been exceptional even among the impressive panoply of the world's many distinguished scholarly handbooks. The *Handbook of Child Psychology* has had a widely heralded tradition as a beacon, organizer, and encyclopedia of developmental study for almost 75 years—a period that covers the vast majority of scientific work in this field.

It is impossible to imagine what the field would look like if it had not occurred to Carl Murchison in 1931 to assemble an eclectic assortment of contributions into the first *Handbook of Child Psychology*. Whether or not Murchison realized this potential (an interesting speculation in itself, given his visionary and ambitious nature), he gave birth to a seminal publishing project that

not only has endured over time but has evolved into a thriving tradition across a number of related academic disciplines.

All through its history, the *Handbook* has drawn on, and played a formative role in, the worldwide study of human development. What does the *Handbook*'s history tell us about where we, as developmentalists, have been, what we have learned, and where we are going? What does it tell us about what has changed and what has remained the same in the questions that we ask, in the methods that we use, and in the theoretical ideas that we draw on in our quest to understand human development? By asking these questions, we follow the spirit of the science itself, for developmental questions may be asked about any endeavor, including the enterprise of studying human development. To best understand what this field has to tell us about human development, we must ask how the field itself has developed. In a field that examines continuities and changes, we must ask, for the field itself, what are the continuities and what are the changes?

The history of the *Handbook* is by no means the whole story of why the field is where it is today, but it is a fundamental part of the story. It has defined the choices that have determined the field's direction and has influenced the making of those choices. In this regard, the *Handbook*'s history reveals much about the judgments and other human factors that shape a science.

## THE CAST OF CHARACTERS

Carl Murchison was a scholar/impresario who edited *The Psychological Register;* founded and edited key psychological journals; wrote books on social psychology,

xii  Preface to *Handbook of Child Psychology,* Sixth Edition

politics, and the criminal mind; and compiled an assortment of handbooks, psychology texts, autobiographies of
renowned psychologists, and even a book on psychic beliefs (Sir Arthur Conan Doyle and Harry Houdini were
among the contributors). Murchison's initial *Handbook
of Child Psychology* was published by a small university
press (Clark University) in 1931, when the field itself
was still in its infancy. Murchison wrote:

> Experimental psychology has had a much older scientific
> and academic status [than child psychology], but at the
> present time it is probable that much less money is being
> spent for pure research in the field of experimental psy-
> chology than is being spent in the field of child psychol-
> ogy. In spite of this obvious fact, many experimental
> psychologists continue to look upon the field of child psy-
> chology as a proper field of research for women and for
> men whose experimental masculinity is not of the maxi-
> mum. This attitude of patronage is based almost entirely
> upon a blissful ignorance of what is going on in the
> tremendously virile field of child behavior. (Murchison,
> 1931, p. ix)

Murchison's masculine allusion, of course, is from another era; it could furnish some good material for a social
history of gender stereotyping. That aside, Murchison
was prescient in the task that he undertook and the way
that he went about it. At the time Murchison wrote the
preface to his *Handbook,* developmental psychology was
known only in Europe and in a few forward-looking
American labs and universities. Nevertheless, Murchison
predicted the field's impending ascent: "The time is not
far distant, if it is not already here, when nearly all competent psychologists will recognize that one-half of the
whole field of psychology is involved in the problem of
how the infant becomes an adult psychologically"
(Murchison, 1931, p. x).

For his original 1931 *Handbook,* Murchison looked to
Europe and to a handful of American centers (or "field
stations") for child research (Iowa, Minnesota, the University of California at Berkeley, Columbia, Stanford,
Yale, Clark). Murchison's Europeans included a young
"genetic epistemologist" named Jean Piaget, who, in an
essay on "Children's Philosophies," quoted extensively
from interviews with 60 Genevan children between the
ages of 4 and 12 years. Piaget's chapter would provide
American readers with an introduction to his seminal
research program on children's conceptions of the
world. Another European, Charlotte Bühler, wrote a
chapter on children's social behavior. In this chapter,

which still is fresh today, Bühler described intricate
play and communication patterns among toddlers, patterns that developmental psychology would not rediscover until the late 1970s. Bühler also anticipated the
critiques of Piaget that would appear during the sociolinguistics heyday of the 1970s:

> Piaget, in his studies on children's talk and reasoning, em-
> phasizes that their talk is much more egocentric than so-
> cial . . . that children from 3 to 7 years accompany all their
> manipulations with talk which actually is not so much in-
> tercourse as monologue . . . [but] the special relationship
> of the child to each of the different members of the house-
> hold is distinctly reflected in the respective conversations.
> (Buhler, 1931, p. 138)

Other Europeans included Anna Freud, who wrote on
"The Psychoanalysis of the Child," and Kurt Lewin,
who wrote on "Environmental Forces in Child Behavior
and Development."

The Americans whom Murchison chose were equally
notable. Arnold Gesell wrote a nativistic account of his
twin studies, an enterprise that remains familiar to us
today, and Stanford's Louis Terman wrote a comprehensive account of everything known about the "gifted
child." Harold Jones described the developmental effects of birth order, Mary Cover Jones wrote about children's emotions, Florence Goodenough wrote about
children's drawings, and Dorothea McCarthy wrote
about language development. Vernon Jones's chapter on
"children's morals" focused on the growth of *character,*
a notion that was to become lost to the field during the
cognitive-developmental revolution, but that reemerged
in the 1990s as the primary concern in the study of
moral development.

Murchison's vision of child psychology included an
examination of cultural differences as well. His *Handbook* presented to the scholarly world a young anthropologist named Margaret Mead, just back from her tours of
Samoa and New Guinea. In this early essay, Mead wrote
that her motivation in traveling to the South Seas was to
discredit the views that Piaget, Levy-Bruhl, and other
nascent "structuralists" had put forth concerning "animism" in young children's thinking. (Interestingly,
about a third of Piaget's chapter in the same volume was
dedicated to showing how Genevan children took years
to outgrow animism.) Mead reported some data that she
called "amazing": "In not one of the 32,000 drawings
(by young 'primitive' children) was there a single case
of personalization of animals, material phenomena, or

inanimate objects" (Mead, 1931, p. 400). Mead parlayed these data into a tough-minded critique of Western psychology's ethnocentrism, making the point that animism and other beliefs are more likely to be culturally induced than intrinsic to early cognitive development. This is hardly an unfamiliar theme in contemporary psychology. Mead also offered a research guide for developmental fieldworkers in strange cultures, complete with methodological and practical advice, such as the following: Translate questions into native linguistic categories; don't do controlled experiments; don't do studies that require knowing ages of subjects, which are usually unknowable; and live next door to the children whom you are studying.

Despite the imposing roster of authors that Murchison assembled for the 1931 *Handbook of Child Psychology,* his achievement did not satisfy him for long. Barely 2 years later, Murchison put out a second edition, of which he wrote: "Within a period of slightly more than 2 years, this first revision bears scarcely any resemblance to the original *Handbook of Child Psychology.* This is due chiefly to the great expansion in the field during the past 3 years and partly to the improved insight of the editor" (Murchison, 1933, p. vii). The tradition that Murchison had brought to life was already evolving.

Murchison saw fit to provide the following warning in his second edition: "There has been no attempt to simplify, condense, or to appeal to the immature mind. This volume is prepared specifically for the scholar, and its form is for his maximum convenience" (Murchison, 1933, p. vii). It is likely that sales of Murchison's first volume did not approach textbook levels; perhaps he received negative comments regarding its accessibility.

Murchison exaggerated when he wrote that his second edition bore little resemblance to the first. Almost half of the chapters were virtually the same, with minor additions and updating. (For the record, though, despite Murchison's continued use of masculine phraseology, 10 of the 24 authors in the second edition were women.) Some of the authors whose original chapters were dropped were asked to write about new topics. So, for example, Goodenough wrote about mental testing rather than about children's drawings, and Gesell wrote a general statement of his maturational theory that went well beyond the twin studies.

But Murchison also made some abrupt changes. He dropped Anna Freud entirely, auguring the marginalization of psychoanalysis within academic psychology. Leonard Carmichael, who was later to play a pivotal role

in the *Handbook* tradition, made an appearance as author of a major chapter (by far the longest in the book) on prenatal and perinatal growth. Three other physiologically oriented chapters were added as well: one on neonatal motor behavior, one on visual-manual functions during the first 2 years of life, and one on physiological "appetites" such as hunger, rest, and sex. Combined with the Goodenough and Gesell shifts in focus, these additions gave the 1933 *Handbook* more of a biological thrust, in keeping with Murchison's long-standing desire to display the hard science backbone of the emerging field.

Leonard Carmichael was president of Tufts University when he organized Wiley's first edition of the *Handbook.* The switch from a university press to the long-established commercial firm of John Wiley & Sons was commensurate with Carmichael's well-known ambition; indeed, Carmichael's effort was to become influential beyond anything that Murchison might have anticipated. The book (one volume at that time) was called the *Manual of Child Psychology,* in keeping with Carmichael's intention of producing an "advanced scientific manual to bridge the gap between the excellent and varied elementary textbooks in this field and the scientific periodical literature" (Carmichael, 1946, p. viii).

The publication date was 1946, and Carmichael complained that "this book has been a difficult and expensive one to produce, especially under wartime conditions" (Carmichael, 1946, p. viii). Nevertheless, the project was worth the effort. The *Manual* quickly became the bible of graduate training and scholarly work in the field, available virtually everywhere that human development was studied. Eight years later, now head of the Smithsonian Institution, Carmichael wrote, in the preface to the 1954 second edition, "The favorable reception that the first edition received not only in America but all over the world is indicative of the growing importance of the study of the phenomena of the growth and development of the child" (Carmichael, 1954, p. vii).

Carmichael's second edition had a long life: Not until 1970 did Wiley bring out a third edition. Carmichael was retired by then, but he still had a keen interest in the book. At his insistence, his own name became part of the title of the third edition; it was called, improbably, *Carmichael's Manual of Child Psychology,* even though it had a new editor and an entirely different cast of authors and advisors. Paul Mussen took over as the editor, and once again the project flourished. Now a two-volume set, the third edition swept across the social sciences, generating widespread interest in developmental psychology and its related disciplines. Rarely had a scholarly compendium become both so dominant in its own field and so familiar in related disciplines. The set became an essential source for graduate students and advanced scholars alike. Publishers referred to *Carmichael's Manual* as the standard against which other scientific handbooks were compared.

The fourth edition, published in 1983, was now redesignated by John Wiley & Sons to become once again the *Handbook of Child Psychology.* By then, Carmichael had passed away. The set of books, now expanded to four volumes, became widely referred to in the field as "the Mussen handbook."

## WHAT CARMICHAEL CHOSE FOR THE NOW EMERGENT FIELD

Leonard Carmichael, who became Wiley's editor for the project in its now commercially funded and expanded versions (the 1946 and 1954 *Manuals*), made the following comments about where he looked for his all-important choices of content:

> Both as editor of the *Manual* and as the author of a special chapter, the writer is indebted . . . [for] extensive excerpts and the use of other materials previously published in the *Handbook of Child Psychology, Revised Edition.* (1946, p. viii)

> Both the *Handbook of Child Psychology* and the *Handbook of Child Psychology, Revised Edition,* were edited by Dr. Carl Murchison. I wish to express here my profound appreciation for the pioneer work done by Dr. Murchison in producing these handbooks and other advanced books in psychology. The *Manual* owes much in spirit and content to the foresight and editorial skill of Dr. Murchison. (1954, p. viii)

The first quote comes from Carmichael's preface to the 1946 edition, the second from his preface to the 1954 edition. We shall never know why Carmichael waited until the 1954 edition to add the personal tribute to Carl Murchison. Perhaps a careless typist dropped the laudatory passage from a handwritten version of the 1946 preface and its omission escaped Carmichael's notice. Or perhaps 8 years of further adult development increased Carmichael's generosity of spirit. (It also may be possible that Murchison or his family com-

plained.) In any case, Carmichael acknowledged the roots of his *Manuals,* if not always their original editor. His choice to start with those roots is a revealing part of the *Handbook*'s history, and it established a strong intellectual legacy for our present-day descendants of the early pioneers who wrote for the Murchison and Carmichael editions.

Although Leonard Carmichael took the 1946 *Manual* in much the same direction established by Murchison back in 1931 and 1933, he did bring it several steps further in that direction, added a few twists of his own, and dropped a couple of Murchison's bolder selections. Carmichael first appropriated five Murchison chapters on biological or experimental topics, such as physiological growth, scientific methods, and mental testing. He added three new biologically oriented chapters on animal infancy, physical growth, and motor and behavioral maturation (a tour de force by Myrtal McGraw that instantly made Gesell's chapter in the same volume obsolete). Then he commissioned Wayne Dennis to write an adolescence chapter that focused exclusively on physiological changes associated with puberty.

On the subject of social and cultural influences in development, Carmichael retained five of the Murchison chapters: two chapters on environmental forces on the child by Kurt Lewin and by Harold Jones, Dorothea McCarthy's chapter on children's language, Vernon Jones's chapter on children's morality (now entitled "Character Development—An Objective Approach"), and Margaret Mead's chapter on "primitive" children (now enhanced by several spectacular photos of mothers and children from exotic cultures around the world). Carmichael also stayed with three other Murchison topics (emotional development, gifted children, and sex differences), but he selected new authors to cover them. But Carmichael dropped Piaget and Bühler.

Carmichael's 1954 revision, his second and final edition, was very close in structure and content to the 1946 *Manual.* Carmichael again retained the heart of Murchison's original vision, many of Murchison's original authors and chapter topics, and some of the same material that dated all the way back to the 1931 *Handbook.* Not surprisingly, the chapters that were closest to Carmichael's own interests got the most significant updating. Carmichael leaned toward the biological and physiological whenever possible. He clearly favored experimental treatments of psychological processes. Yet he still kept the social, cultural, and psychological analyses by Lewin, Mead, McCarthy, Terman, Harold Jones, and

Vernon Jones, and he even went so far as to add one new chapter on social development by Harold and Gladys Anderson and one new chapter on emotional development by Arthur Jersild.

The Murchison and Carmichael volumes make for fascinating reading, even today. The perennial themes of the field were there from the start: the nature-nurture debate; the generalizations of universalists opposed by the particularizations of contextualists; the alternating emphases on continuities and discontinuities during ontogenesis; and the standard categories of maturation, learning, locomotor activity, perception, cognition, language, emotion, conduct, morality, and culture—all separated for the sake of analysis, yet, as authors throughout each of the volumes acknowledged, all somehow inextricably joined in the dynamic mix of human development.

These things have not changed. Yet, much in the early editions is now irrevocably dated. Long lists of children's dietary preferences, sleeping patterns, elimination habits, toys, and somatic types look quaint and pointless through today's lenses. The chapters on children's thought and language were written prior to the great contemporary breakthroughs in neurology and brain/behavior research, and they show it. The chapters on social and emotional development were ignorant of the processes of social influence and self-regulation that soon would be revealed through attribution research and other studies in social psychology. Terms such as *cognitive neuroscience, neuronal networks, behavior genetics, social cognition, dynamic systems,* and *positive youth development* were of course unknown. Even Mead's rendition of the "primitive child" stands as a weak straw in comparison to the wealth of cross-cultural knowledge available in today's *cultural psychology.*

Most telling, the assortments of odd facts and normative trends were tied together by very little theory throughout the Carmichael chapters. It was as if, in the exhilaration of discovery at the frontiers of a new field, all the facts looked interesting in and of themselves. That, of course, is what makes so much of the material seem odd and arbitrary. It is hard to know what to make of the lists of facts, where to place them, which ones were worth keeping track of and which ones are expendable. Not surprisingly, the bulk of the data presented in the Carmichael manuals seems not only outdated by today's standards but, worse, irrelevant.

By 1970, the importance of theory for understanding human development had become apparent. Looking back

on Carmichael's last *Manual,* Paul Mussen wrote, "The 1954 edition of this *Manual* had only one theoretical chapter, and that was concerned with Lewinian theory which, so far as we can see, has not had a significant lasting impact on developmental psychology" (Mussen, 1970, p. x). The intervening years had seen a turning away from the norm of psychological research once fondly referred to as "dust-bowl empiricism."

The Mussen 1970 edition—or *Carmichael's Manual,* as it was still called—had a new look and an almost entirely new set of contents. The two-volume edition carried only one chapter from the earlier books, Carmichael's updated version of his own long chapter on the "Onset and Early Development of Behavior," which had made its appearance under a different title in Murchison's 1933 edition. Otherwise, as Mussen wrote in his preface, "It should be clear from the outset . . . that the present volumes are not, in any sense, a *revision* of the earlier editions; this is a completely new *Manual"* (Mussen, 1970, p. x).

And it was. In comparison to Carmichael's last edition 16 years earlier, the scope, variety, and theoretical depth of the Mussen volumes were astonishing. The field had blossomed, and the new *Manual* showcased many of the new bouquets that were being produced. The biological perspective was still strong, grounded by chapters on physical growth (by J. M. Tanner) and physiological development (by Dorothy Eichorn) and by Carmichael's revised chapter (now made more elegant by some excerpts from Greek philosophy and modern poetry). But two other cousins of biology also were represented, in an ethological chapter by Eckhard Hess and a behavior genetics chapter by Gerald McClearn. These chapters were to define the major directions of biological research in the field for at least the next 3 decades.

As for theory, Mussen's *Handbook* was thoroughly permeated with it. Much of the theorizing was organized around the approaches that, in 1970, were known as the "three grand systems": (1) Piaget's cognitive-developmentalism, (2) psychoanalysis, and (3) learning theory. Piaget was given the most extensive treatment. He reappeared in the *Manual,* this time authoring a comprehensive (and, some say, definitive) statement of his entire theory, which now bore little resemblance to his 1931/1933 sortings of children's intriguing verbal expressions. In addition, chapters by John Flavell, by David Berlyne, by Martin Hoffman, and by William Kessen, Marshall Haith, and Philip Salapatek all gave major treatments to one or another aspect of Piaget's body of work. Other approaches were represented as well. Herbert and Ann Pick explicated Gibsonian theory in a chapter on sensation and perception, Jonas Langer wrote a chapter on Werner's organismic theory, David McNeill wrote a Chomskian account of language development, and Robert LeVine wrote an early version of what was soon to become "culture theory."

With its increased emphasis on theory, the 1970 *Manual* explored in depth a matter that had been all but neglected in the book's previous versions: the mechanisms of change that could account for, to use Murchison's old phrase, "the problem of how the infant becomes an adult psychologically." In the process, old questions such as the relative importance of nature versus nurture were revisited, but with far more sophisticated conceptual and methodological tools.

Beyond theory building, the 1970 *Manual* addressed an array of new topics and featured new contributors: peer interaction (Willard Hartup), attachment (Eleanor Maccoby and John Masters), aggression (Seymour Feshback), individual differences (Jerome Kagan and Nathan Kogan), and creativity (Michael Wallach). All of these areas of interest are still very much with us in the new millennium.

If the 1970 *Manual* reflected a blossoming of the field's plantings, the 1983 *Handbook* reflected a field whose ground cover had spread beyond any boundaries that could have been previously anticipated. New growth had sprouted in literally dozens of separate locations. A French garden, with its overarching designs and tidy compartments, had turned into an English garden, a bit unruly but glorious in its profusion. Mussen's two-volume *Carmichael's Manual* had now become the four-volume Mussen *Handbook,* with a page-count increase that came close to tripling the 1970 edition.

The grand old theories were breaking down. Piaget was still represented by his 1970 piece, but his influence was on the wane throughout the other chapters. Learning theory and psychoanalysis were scarcely mentioned. Yet the early theorizing had left its mark, in vestiges that were apparent in new approaches, and in the evident conceptual sophistication with which authors treated their material. No return to dust bowl empiricism could be found anywhere in the set. Instead, a variety of classical and innovative ideas were coexisting: Ethology, neurobiology, information processing, attribution theory, cultural approaches, communications theory, behavioral genetics, sensory-perception models, psycholinguistics, sociolinguistics, discontinuous stage theories, and continuous memory theories all took their places, with none

quite on center stage. Research topics now ranged from children's play to brain lateralization, from children's family life to the influences of school, day care, and disadvantageous risk factors. There also was coverage of the burgeoning attempts to use developmental theory as a basis for clinical and educational interventions. The interventions usually were described at the end of chapters that had discussed the research relevant to the particular intervention efforts, rather than in whole chapters dedicated specifically to issues of practice.

This brings us to the efforts under the present editorial team: the *Handbook*'s fifth and sixth editions (but really the seventh and eighth editions, if the germinal two pre-Wiley Murchison editions are counted). I must leave it to future commentators to provide a critical summation of what we have done. The volume editors have offered introductory and/or concluding renditions of their own volumes. I will add to their efforts here only by stating the overall intent of our design and by commenting on some directions that our field has taken in the years from 1931 to 2006.

We approached our editions with the same purpose that Murchison, Carmichael, and Mussen before us had shared: "to provide," as Mussen wrote, "a comprehensive and accurate picture of the current state of knowledge—the major systematic thinking and research—in the most important research areas of the psychology of human development" (Mussen, 1983, p. vii). We assumed that the *Handbook* should be aimed "specifically for the scholar," as Murchison declared, and that it should have the character of an "advanced text," as Carmichael defined it. We expected, though, that our audiences may be more interdisciplinary than the readerships of previous editions, given the greater tendency of today's scholars to cross back and forth among fields such as psychology, cognitive science, neurobiology, history, linguistics, sociology, anthropology, education, and psychiatry. We also believed that research-oriented practitioners should be included under the rubric of the "scholars" for whom this *Handbook* was intended. To that end, for the first time in 1998 and again in the present edition, we devoted an entire volume to child psychology in practice.

Beyond these very general intentions, we have let chapters in the *Handbook*'s fifth and sixth editions take their own shape. We solicited the chapters from authors who were widely acknowledged to be among the leading experts in their areas of the field, although we know that, given an entirely open-ended selection process and no limits of budget, we would have invited a large number of other leading researchers whom we did not have the space—and thus the privilege—to include. With very few exceptions, every author whom we invited agreed to accept the challenge. Our only real, and great, sadness was to hear of the passing of several authors from the 1998 edition prior to our assembly of the present edition. Where possible, we arranged to have their collaborators revise and update their chapters.

Our directive to authors was simple: Convey your area of the field as you see it. From then on, the authors took center stage—with, of course, much constructive feedback from reviewers and volume editors. No one tried to impose a perspective, a preferred method of inquiry, or domain boundaries on any of the chapters. The authors expressed their views on what researchers in their areas attempt to accomplish, why they do so, how they go about it, what intellectual sources they draw on, what progress they have made, and what conclusions they have reached.

The result, in my opinion, is still more glorious profusion of the English garden genre, but perhaps contained a bit by some broad patterns that have emerged over the past decade. Powerful theoretical models and approaches—not quite unified theories, such as the three grand systems—have begun once again to organize much of the field's research and practice. There is great variety in these models and approaches, and each is drawing together significant clusters of work. Some have been only recently formulated, and some are combinations or modifications of classic theories that still have staying power.

Among the formidable models and approaches that the reader will find in this *Handbook* are the dynamic system theories, the life span and life course approaches, cognitive science and neuronal models, the behavior genetics approach, person-context interaction theories, action theories, cultural psychology, and a wide assortment of neo-Piagetian and neo-Vygotskian models. Although some of these models and approaches have been in the making for some time, they have now come into their own. Researchers are drawing on them directly, taking their implied assumptions and hypotheses seriously, using them with specificity and control, and exploiting their implications for practice.

Another pattern that emerges is a rediscovery and exploration of core processes in human development that had been underexamined by the generation of researchers just prior to the present one. Scientific interest has a way of moving in alternating cycles (or spirals, for those who wish to capture the progressive nature of scientific development). In our time, developmental study has cycled away from classic topics such as motivation and learning—not in the sense that they were entirely forgotten, or that good work ceased to be done in such areas, but in the sense that they no longer were the most prominent subjects of theoretical reflection and debate. Some of the relative neglect was intentional, as scholars got caught up in controversies about whether psychological motivation was a "real" phenomenon worthy of study or whether learning could or should be distinguished from development in the first place. All this has changed. As the contents of our current edition attest, developmental science always returns, sooner or later, to concepts that are necessary for explaining the heart of its concerns, progressive change in individuals and social groups over time, and concepts such as learning and motivation are indispensable for this task. Among the exciting features of this *Handbook* edition are the advances it presents in theoretical and empirical work on these classic concepts.

The other concept that has met some resistance in recent years is the notion of development itself. For some social critics, the idea of progress, implicit in the notion of development, has seemed out of step with principles such as equality and cultural diversity. Some genuine benefits have accrued from that critique; for example, the field has worked to better appreciate diverse developmental pathways. But, like many critique positions, it led to excesses. For some, it became questionable to explore issues that lie at the heart of human development. Growth, advancement, positive change, achievement, and standards for improved performance and conduct, all were questioned as legitimate subjects of investigation.

Just as in the cases of learning and motivation, no doubt it was inevitable that the field's center of gravity sooner or later would return to broad concerns of development. The story of growth from infancy to adulthood is a developmental story of multifaceted learning, acquisitions of skills and knowledge, waxing powers of attention and memory, growing neuronal and other biological capacities, formations and transformations of character and personality, increases and reorganizations in the understanding of self and others, advances in emotional and behavioral regulation, progress in communicating and collaborating with others, and a host of other achievements documented in this edition. Parents, teachers, and other adults in all parts of the world recognize and value such developmental achievements in children, although they do not always know how to understand them, let alone how to foster them.

The sorts of scientific findings that the *Handbook*'s authors explicate in their chapters are needed to provide such understanding. The importance of sound scientific understanding has become especially clear in recent years, when news media broadcast story after story based on simplistic and biased popular speculations about the causes of human development. The careful and responsible discourse found in these chapters contrasts sharply with the typical news story about the role of parents, genes, or schools in children's growth and behavior. There is not much contest as to which source the public looks to for its information and stimulation. But the good news is that scientific truth usually works its way into the public mind over the long run. The way this works would make a good subject for developmental study some day, especially if such a study could find a way to speed up the process. In the meantime, readers of this edition of the *Handbook of Child Psychology* will find the most solid, insightful

and current set of scientific theories and findings available in the field today.

February 2006
*Palo Alto, California*

## REFERENCES

Bühler, C. (1931). The social participation of infants and toddlers. In C. Murchison (Ed.), *A handbook of child psychology.* Worcester, MA: Clark University Press.

Carmichael, L. (Ed.). (1946). *Manual of child psychology.* New York: Wiley.

Carmichael, L. (Ed.). (1954). *Manual of child psychology* (2nd ed.). New York: Wiley.

Mead, M. (1931). The primitive child. In C. Murchison (Ed.), *A handbook of child psychology.* Worcester, MA: Clark University Press.

Murchison, C. (Ed.). (1931). *A handbook of child psychology.* Worcester, MA: Clark University Press.

Murchison, C. (Ed.). (1933). *A handbook of child psychology* (2nd ed.). Worcester, MA: Clark University Press.

Mussen, P. (Ed.). (1970). *Carmichael's manual of child psychology.* New York: Wiley.

Mussen, P. (Ed.). (1983). *Handbook of child psychology.* New York: Wiley.

# Acknowledgments

A work as significant as the *Handbook of Child Psychology* is always produced by the contributions of numerous people, individuals whose names do not necessarily appear on the covers or spines of the volumes. Most important, we are grateful to the more than 150 colleagues whose scholarship gave life to the Sixth Edition. Their enormous knowledge, expertise, and hard work make this edition of the *Handbook* the most important reference work in developmental science.

In addition to the authors of the chapters of the four volumes of this edition, we were fortunate to have been able to work with two incredibly skilled and dedicated editors within the Institute for Applied Research in Youth Development at Tufts University, Jennifer Davison and Katherine Connery. Their "can-do" spirit and their impressive ability to attend to every detail of every volume were invaluable resources enabling this project to be completed in a timely and high quality manner.

It may be obvious, but we want to stress also that without the talent, commitment to quality, and professionalism of our editors at John Wiley & Sons, this edition of the *Handbook* would not be a reality and would not be the cutting-edge work we believe it to be. The breadth of the contributions of the Wiley staff to the *Handbook* is truly enormous. Although we thank all these colleagues for their wonderful contributions, we wish to make special note of four people in particular: Patricia Rossi, Senior Editor, Psychology, Linda Witzling, Senior Production Editor, Isabel Pratt, Associate Editor, and Peggy Alexander, Vice President and Publisher. Their creativity, professionalism, sense of balance and perspective, and unflagging commitment to the tradition of quality of the *Handbook* were vital ingredients for any success we may have with this edition. We are also deeply grateful to Pam Blackmon and her colleagues at Publications Development Company for undertaking the enormous task of copy editing and producing the thousands of pages of the Sixth Edition. Their professionalism and commitment to excellence were invaluable resources and provided a foundation upon which the editors' work was able to move forward productively.

Child development typically happens in families. So too, the work of editors on the *Handbook* moved along productively because of the support and forbearance of spouses, partners, and children. We thank all of our loved ones for being there for us throughout the several years on which we have worked on the Sixth Edition.

Numerous colleagues critiqued the chapters in manuscript form and provided valuable insights and suggestions that enhanced the quality of the final products. We thank all of these scholars for their enormous contributions.

William Damon and Richard M. Lerner thank the John Templeton Foundation for its support of their respective scholarly endeavors. In addition, Richard M. Lerner thanks the National 4-H Council for its support of his work. Nancy Eisenberg thanks the National Institute of Mental Health, the Fetzer Institute, and The Institute for Research on Unlimited Love—Altruism, Compassion, Service (located at the School of Medicine, Case Western Reserve University) for their support. K. Ann Renninger and Irving E. Sigel thank Vanessa Ann Gorman for her editorial support for Volume 4. Support from the Swarthmore College Provost's Office to K. Ann Renninger for editorial assistance on this project is also gratefully acknowledged.

Finally, in an earlier form, with Barbara Rogoff's encouragement, sections of the preface were published in *Human Development* (April 1997). We thank Barbara for her editorial help in arranging this publication.

# Preface to Volume Two
# Cognition, Perception, and Language

DEANNA KUHN and ROBERT S. SIEGLER

When we were approached about beginning work on the sixth edition of the *Handbook of Child Psychology,* the two of us had the same startled reaction: "What?" It seemed not that long ago that we had regained our stride after the rush of attention devoted to completing the fifth edition, and we couldn't believe it was time to start again. Now, another 3 years has passed, and once again we are in the final phases of completing the manuscript for the volume, this time the sixth edition; at this point, we have greater appreciation for the timeliness and value of a new edition that will appear 8 years after the previous one.

The field is growing at a prodigious rate. The number of specialized journals has increased as the field itself not only grows but becomes more segmented and specialized. New journals target a much narrower range of authors and readers than do the traditional journals *Child Development* and *Developmental Psychology.* Few researchers claim expertise and a command of the relevant literature in more than a very few subfields.

In this climate, high-quality *Handbook* chapters, written by leaders in their specialties, serve a very important function. They offer an efficient and effective means to escape the tunnel vision that has become an academic occupational hazard. The danger is that of becoming increasingly focused on one's own narrow specialty until it absorbs all one's awareness. Access to broad, integrative *Handbook* chapters reduces the likelihood of the field becoming a collection of diligent scholars who know more and more about less and less, their own work ultimately diminished by lack of nourishment from analogous themes, insights, and questions that emerge in other areas.

The present volume offers such a set of broad, integrative contributions. Although the interval between

publication of the 5th and 6th editions of the *Handbook* is only half as long as the interval between the 4th and 5th editions, there certainly seemed to be as much new material to be examined in this edition as there had in the previous one, again perhaps a reflection of the rapidly growing field but also a reflection of the new perspectives that are introduced. As volume editors we had a critical decision to make at the outset of planning the sixth edition—whether to ask authors of chapters in the fifth edition to update their chapters or whether to commission new chapters. We decided that we would commission all new chapters because there were so many important topics that had not been covered in the earlier edition and so many leading authorities with unique and important perspectives who had not previously contributed a chapter to this *Handbook.* Soliciting entirely new chapters also guaranteed freshly construed integrations from an early twenty-first-century vantage point for all chapters.

The Cognition, Language, and Perception volume of the sixth edition of the *Handbook of Child Psychology* contains 22 chapters, compared to 19 in the fifth edition. In a number of cases, chapters in the sixth edition represent new perspectives on literatures that were also included in the fifth edition—for example the chapters by Nelson, Thomas, and de Haan on neural bases of cognition, Kellman and Arterberry on infant visual perception, Adolph and Berger on motor development, Waxman and Lidz on early word learning, Halford and Andrews on problem solving and reasoning, and Cole on cognition in cultural context. Comparison of the corresponding chapters from the 1998 and current editions makes clear the value of offering readers a different perspective on the same research area. Comparison of the two editions also makes clear that the chapters in the fifth edition are by no means obsolete; they continue to offer unique insights and integrative visions.

Soliciting new chapters also allowed us to include new topics that had not been the focus of chapters in the corresponding volume of the previous *Handbook* but that represent areas of growing importance in the field. These include Goldin-Meadow's chapter on noverbal communication, Geary's chapter on mathematical development, Winner's chapter on development in the arts, Newcombe and Huttenlocher's chapter on spatial cognition, and Siegler's chapter on microgenetic studies of learning. The rapid growth of these areas, and the many intriguing theoretical debates within them, attests to the vigor of the field of child development.

Other differences between the current and the previous volume reflect a variety of other currents within the field and within the *Handbook*. We chose to omit two topics that were the subject of chapters in the previous edition: representation and individual differences. Both topics have become so fundamental that they warranted treatment within the context of almost all of the individual chapters, rather than being limited to a single chapter. We divided another topic—memory—into two chapters because a clear division has arisen between event memory, which is dominant in infancy and early childhood, and intentional, strategic memory, which becomes of critical interest in later childhood. Finally, chapters by two other authors—one on cognitive science and cognitive development by Frank Keil and one on exceptional cognitive development by Seana Moran and Howard Gardner—are new to the volume, although Keil and Gardner each contributed chapters to other volumes of the fifth edition of the *Handbook*.

We asked authors in the sixth edition to emphasize five themes. These themes help to unify the diverse topics covered in the volume. They are:

1. *The history of the area.* How has the study of your topic evolved over the years?
2. *The contemporary status of the topic.* Here you should feel free to express your own appropriately supported opinions, while acknowledging that others exist.
3. *An emphasis on mechanisms of change.* The time has passed when it is sufficient to describe development, and we must now seek to understand how this development occurs.

4. *An emphasis on individual differences.* How do children become so different from each other?
5. *Predictions and recommendations for the future with respect to your topic.*

All of our authors were conscientious and good humored about meeting deadlines and responding to suggestions for modifications, with the result that we had a final set of manuscripts in hand while all were still fresh and timely. This favorable set of circumstances gave us the opportunity to react to them as a whole. In this respect we would like to share several reactions. The major one connects to a remark that appeared in our earlier commentary in connection with the fifth edition, and that was the detection of a growing dissatisfaction with "task-bound" paradigms on the part of the chapters' authors—in other words, lines of work whose explanatory power derives from a single experimental task. Such paradigms leave unanswered the question of whether their explanatory power extends at all beyond that particular research context.

In the present volume, we see more pronounced and multiple kinds of evidence of advances regarding task-bound paradigms. One form of evidence is the fact that the authors of many of the chapters bring multiple levels of explanation to bear on their topic and their more specific claims—neurological, biographical, anthropological, evolutionary, species comparative, and historical comparative, as well as behaviors amenable to more traditional examination in a laboratory. None of the authors looks to a single narrow form of evidence as exhaustive input for addressing the questions at hand. Tomasello, for example, emphasizes the impossibility of studying language development apart from the context of developing cognitive and social skills, and Cohen and Cashon argue that infant cognition research must incorporate neuroscience. And certainly, the combination of experimental and naturalistic methodologies is no longer unusual. At the level of the entire volume, the chapters added to the sixth edition are signs of a broadened perspective: Both nonverbal and aesthetic dimensions of cognitive development are included as offering valuable insight into what develops.

A second form of evidence is the number of authors who take an explicitly historical view. They decline to view their topic only in terms of the research paradigms most popular at the moment and instead ask how these paradigms connect to ones in use at earlier times. Harris, for example, asks how current theory-of-mind research (and the particular false-belief task from which it arose) connects to research of several decades ago on role-taking and perspective-taking. Cohen and Cashon suggest that recent infant cognition research continues the study of object permanence and causality associated with Piaget's early work. Pressley and Hilden probe the connections between the current research they examine and early memory strategy research, while Kuhn and Franklin, Siegler, and Geary examine relations between contemporary and earlier classical learning research, and Kuhn and Franklin do the same with respect to adolescent cognition. Other authors, for example Tomasello, Newcombe and Huttenlocher, and Munakata, make explicit note of the limited explanatory power of constrained task formats.

A third and related form of evidence is the number of authors who take an extended view ontogenetically, as well as historically. In other words, even if their own area of investigation is largely limited to the early years of life, they ask what the later implications are or what further developmental course the investigated competencies may follow. Kuhn and Franklin's chapter explicitly takes the perspective of this later development, as does Moran and Gardner's, but the authors of a number of other chapters reflect their awareness that development does not stop, or cease to be interesting at age 3, or 5, or 10. Authors who have characteristically focused their attention on early development, such as Gelman and Kalish, Harris, and Bauer, now ask what might be expected in the years following early childhood. New-combe and Huttenlocher remind us in their chapter of the value of this extended ontogenetic perspective—a value that is often overlooked in the current focus on searching for cognitive origins of competencies in the earliest years of life. Ultimately, we can only fully understand a competency to the extent that we understand where it is headed, that is, understand its mature state. As Saffran, Werker, and Werner make clear, this often entails research investigating the nature of adult competencies.

Fourth, and finally, we see in these chapters an awareness that new, enriched perspectives, and new forms of evidence, brought to bear on a topic have the potential to provide new insights into old questions, questions that may have been regarded as at a standstill. Keil makes this point explicitly in his chapter in arguing for an expanded interdisciplinary approach. But this same awareness is reflected in other chapters as well. Like Tomasello, who draws our attention to individual differences, Newcombe and Huttenlocher note that individual differences, long regarded by many simply as nuisance variance to be avoided, to the contrary stand to provide insight into the fundamental nature of the common competencies and developmental pathways that are of interest.

We are privileged to have worked with this exceptional set of authors and thank them for their dedication to their task and their contribution to the final product. We have said enough that we should at this point conclude our own remarks and let the authors speak for themselves.

# Contents

## Section One: Foundations

1 | **NEURAL BASES OF COGNITIVE DEVELOPMENT**   3
Charles A. Nelson III, Kathleen M. Thomas, and Michelle de Haan

2 | **THE INFANT'S AUDITORY WORLD: HEARING, SPEECH, AND THE BEGINNINGS OF LANGUAGE**   58
Jenny R. Saffran, Janet F. Werker, and Lynne A. Werner

3 | **INFANT VISUAL PERCEPTION**   109
Philip J. Kellman and Martha E. Arterberry

4 | **MOTOR DEVELOPMENT**   161
Karen E. Adolph and Sarah E. Berger

5 | **INFANT COGNITION**   214
Leslie B. Cohen and Cara H. Cashon

## Section Two: Cognition and Communication

6 | **ACQUIRING LINGUISTIC CONSTRUCTIONS**   255
Michael Tomasello

7 | **EARLY WORD LEARNING**   299
Sandra R. Waxman and Jeffrey L. Lidz

8 | **NONVERBAL COMMUNICATION: THE HAND'S ROLE IN TALKING AND THINKING**   336
Susan Goldin-Meadow

# Section Three: Cognitive Processes

9 | **EVENT MEMORY**   373
Patricia J. Bauer

10 | **INFORMATION PROCESSING APPROACHES TO DEVELOPMENT**   426
Yuko Munakata

11 | **MICROGENETIC ANALYSES OF LEARNING**   464
Robert S. Siegler

12 | **COGNITIVE STRATEGIES**   511
Michael Pressley and Katherine Hilden

13 | **REASONING AND PROBLEM SOLVING**   557
Graeme S. Halford and Glenda Andrews

14 | **COGNITIVE SCIENCE AND COGNITIVE DEVELOPMENT**   609
Frank Keil

15 | **CULTURE AND COGNITIVE DEVELOPMENT IN PHYLOGENETIC, HISTORICAL, AND ONTOGENETIC PERSPECTIVE**   636
Michael Cole

# Section Four: Conceptual Understanding and Achievements

16 | **CONCEPTUAL DEVELOPMENT**   687
Susan A. Gelman and Charles W. Kalish

17 | **DEVELOPMENT OF SPATIAL COGNITION**   734
Nora S. Newcombe and Janellen Huttenlocher

18 | **DEVELOPMENT OF MATHEMATICAL UNDERSTANDING**   777
David C. Geary

19 | **SOCIAL COGNITION**   811
Paul L. Harris

20 | **DEVELOPMENT IN THE ARTS: DRAWING AND MUSIC**   859
Ellen Winner

21 | **EXTRAORDINARY ACHIEVEMENTS: A DEVELOPMENTAL AND SYSTEMS ANALYSIS**   905
Seana Moran and Howard Gardner

## Section Five: The Perspective beyond Childhood

22 | **THE SECOND DECADE: WHAT DEVELOPS (AND HOW)**   953
Deanna Kuhn and Sam Franklin

**Author Index**   995

**Subject Index**   1029

# Foundations

CHAPTER 1

# Neural Bases of Cognitive Development

CHARLES A. NELSON III, KATHLEEN M. THOMAS, and MICHELLE DE HAAN

WHY DEVELOPMENTAL PSYCHOLOGISTS SHOULD
  BE INTERESTED IN NEUROSCIENCE  4
BRAIN DEVELOPMENT AND NEURAL
  PLASTICITY: A PRÉCIS TO
  BRAIN DEVELOPMENT  5
Brain Development  5
Summary  12
NEURAL PLASTICITY  13
Developmental Plasticity  14
Adult Plasticity  16
What Are the Effects of Enriched Environments on
  Brain Development and Function?  17
What Is the Difference between Development
  and Plasticity?  17
THE NEURAL BASES OF
  COGNITIVE DEVELOPMENT  19
Memory  19
Disorders of Memory  26
Nondeclarative Memory  27
SPATIAL COGNITION  31
Mental Rotation  31
Spatial Pattern Processing  32

Visuospatial Working Memory  33
Visuospatial Recognition and Recall Memory  34
Spatial Navigation  35
OBJECT RECOGNITION  35
Face/Object Recognition  35
Occipito-Temporal Cortex  35
Amygdala  38
Role of Experience  38
Is There a Visuospatial Module?  39
EXECUTIVE FUNCTIONS  39
Domains of Executive Function  40
Working Memory Revisited  40
Inhibitory Control  41
Attentional Control  41
NONEXECUTIVE ASPECTS OF ATTENTION  43
Alerting, Vigilance, or Arousal  43
Orienting  43
THE FUTURE OF DEVELOPMENTAL
  COGNITIVE NEUROSCIENCE  44
REFERENCES  45

The goal of this chapter is to review what is known about the neural bases of cognitive development. We begin by discussing why developmental psychologists might be interested in the neural bases of behavior (with particular reference to cognitive development). Having established the value of viewing child development through the lens of the developmental neurosciences, we provide an overview of brain development. This is followed by a

The writing of this chapter was made possible, in part, by grants from the NIH to the first author (NS34458, NS329976), and from the John D. and Catherine T. MacArthur Foundation (through their funding of a research network on *Early Experience and Brain Development*) and to the second author from the NIMH (MH02024). The first author wishes to thank Lisa Benz for assistance in literature reviews, Eric Knudsen for sharing his insights into neural plasticity, and members of the Laboratory of Developmental Cognitive Neuroscience.

discussion of how experience influences the developing—and when appropriate, developed—brain. Within this discussion on experience-dependent changes in brain development, we briefly touch on two issues we consider to be essential for all developmental psychologists: whether the mechanisms that underlie developmental plasticity differ from those that underlie adult plasticity, and more fundamentally, what distinguishes plasticity from development.

With this basic neuroscience background behind us, we turn our attention to specific content areas, limiting ourselves to domains in which there is a corpus of knowledge about the neural underpinnings of cognitive development. We discuss learning and memory, face/object recognition, attention/executive functions, and spatial cognition, including illustrative examples from both typical and atypical development. We conclude the chapter with a discussion of the future of developmental cognitive neuroscience.

## WHY DEVELOPMENTAL PSYCHOLOGISTS SHOULD BE INTERESTED IN NEUROSCIENCE

Prior to the ascendancy of Piagetian theory, the field of cognitive development, such as it was, was dominated by behaviorism (for discussion, see Goldman-Rakic, 1987; Nelson & Bloom, 1997). As students of the history of psychology are well aware, behaviorism eschewed the nonobservable; therefore, the study of the neural bases of behavior was not pursued for the simple reason that neural processes could not be observed. Through the 1950s and 1960s, Piagetian theory gradually came to replace behaviorism as the dominant theory of cognitive development. Despite being a biologist by training, Piaget and, subsequently, his followers primarily concerned themselves with developing a richly detailed cognitive architecture of the mind—albeit a brainless mind. We do not mean this in a pejorative sense, but rather, to imply that the zeitgeist of the time was to develop elegant models of cognitive structures, with little regard for (a) whether such structures were biologically plausible or (b) the neurobiological underpinnings of such structures. (At that time, there was no way to observe the living child's brain directly.) Throughout the late 1970s and into the last decade of the twentieth century, neo- and non-Piagetian approaches came into favor. Curiously, a prominent theme of a number of investigators writing during this time was that of *nativism;* we say curiously because inherent in nativism is the notion of biological determinism, yet those touting a nativist perspective rarely if ever grounded their models and data in biological reality. It was not until the mid-1990s that neurobiology began to be inserted into a discussion of cognitive development, as reflected in Mark Johnson's eloquent contribution to this *Handbook*'s fifth edition (Johnson, 1998). This perspective has become more commonplace, although the field of developmental cognitive neuroscience is still in its infancy. (For recent overviews of this field generally, see de Haan & Johnson, 2003a; Nelson & Luciana, 2001.) Moreover, we have observed that it is still not clear to many developmental psychologists why they should be interested in the brain. This is the topic to which we next direct our attention.

Our major argument in this regard is that our understanding of cognitive development will improve as the mechanisms that underlie development are elucidated. This, in turn, should permit us to move beyond the descriptive, black box level to the level at which the actual cellular, physiologic, and eventually, genetic machinery will be understood—the mechanisms that underlie development. An example follows.

A number of distinguished cognitive developmentalists and cognitive theorists have proposed or at least implied that elements of number concept (Wynn, 1992; Wynn, Bloom, & Chiang, 2002), object permanence (Baillargeon, 1987; Baillargeon, Spelke, & Wasserman, 1985; Spelke, 2000), and perhaps face recognition (Farah, Rabinowitz, Quinn, & Liu, 2000) reflect what we refer to as experience-independent functions; that is, they reflect inborn traits (presumably coded in the genome) that do not require experience to emerge. We see several problems with this perspective. First, these arguments seem biologically implausible because they represent sophisticated cognitive abilities; if they were coded in the genome, they would surely be polygenic traits and would not reflect the action of a single gene. Given that we now know the human genome consists of approximately 30,000 to 40,000 genes, it seems highly unlikely that we could spare the genes to separately code for number concept, object permanence, or face recognition. After all, those 40,000 genes must be involved in myriad other events (e.g., the general operation of the body as a whole) far more important than subserving these aspects of cognitive development.

A second concern about this nativist perspective is that it is not developmental. To say something is innate essentially closes the door to any discussion of mechanism. More problematic is that genes do not cause behaviors; rather, genes express proteins that in turn work their magic through the brain. It seems unlikely that behaviors that are not absolutely essential to survival (of the species, not the individual) have been directly coded in the genome, given the limited number of genes that are known to exist. Far more likely is that these behaviors are subserved by discrete or distributed neural circuits in the brain. And, these circuits, in turn, most likely vary in the extent to which they depend on experience or activity for their subsequent elaboration.

We make three general points: (1) The "value added" of thinking about behavior in the context of neurobiology is that doing so provides biological plausibility to our models of behavior (to be discussed further later).

(2) Viewing behavioral development through the lens of neuroscience may shed light on the mechanism(s) underlying behavior and behavioral development, thereby moving us beyond the descriptive level to the process level. (3) When we insert the molecular biology of brain development into the equation, a more holistic view of the child becomes possible—genes, brain, and behavior. This, in turn, permits us to move beyond simplistic notions of gene-environment interactions to talk about the influence of specific experiences on specific neural circuits, which in turn influence the expression of particular genes, which influence how the brain functions and how the child behaves.

## BRAIN DEVELOPMENT AND NEURAL PLASTICITY: A PRÉCIS TO BRAIN DEVELOPMENT

Before discussing the details of neural development, it is important to understand that brain development, at the species level, has been shaped over many thousands of generations by selective pressures that drive evolution. According to Knudsen (2003b), this portion of biological inheritance is responsible for nearly all the genetic influences that shape the development and function of the nervous system, the majority of which have proven to be adaptive for the success of any given species. These influences determine both the properties of individual neurons and the patterns of neural connections. As a result, these selective pressures delimit an individual's cognitive, emotional, sensory, and motor capabilities.

There is, however, a small portion of biological inheritance that is unique to the individual, resulting from the novel combination of genes that the child receives from the parents. Because there is no history to this gene pattern, any new phenotype that is produced has never been subjected to the forces of natural selection and is unlikely to confer any selective advantage for that individual. However, this small portion of biological inheritance is particularly important for driving evolutionary change, as novel combinations of genes or mutations that do confer a selective advantage will increase in the gene pool, while those that result in maladaptive phenotypes will die out (Knudsen, 2003a, 2003b).

The brain develops according to a complex array of genetically programmed influences. These include both molecular and electrical signals that arise spontaneously in growing neural networks. By *spontaneously,* we mean signals that are inherent in the circuitry and are entirely independent of any outside influence. These molecular and electrical signals establish neural pathways and patterns of connections that are remarkably precise and that make it possible for animals to carry out discrete behaviors beginning immediately after birth. They also underlie instinctive behaviors that may appear much later in life, often associated with emotional responses, foraging, sex, and social interactions. Beyond the scope of this chapter, but certainly worth considering, is which human behaviors fall into this category of "instinctive." Our bias is that these are most likely going to be behaviors that have enormous implications for survival or reproductive fitness, such as the ability to experience fear, to avoid predators or to experience pleasure and conversely, the reduction of displeasure, to become attached to a caregiver.

To return to our discussion of nativism, there is no question that genetics has an enormous influence over who we are. To a large extent, human characteristics reflect evolutionary learning, which is exhibited in patterns of neural connections and interactions that have been shaped adaptively by evolution over thousands of generations. In addition to adaptive capacities, however, genetics (through mutations) can lead to deficits in brain function, such as impairments of sensation, cognition, emotion, and movement. We provide examples of both in subsequent sections of this chapter.

Genes specify the properties of neurons and neural connections to different degrees in different pathways and at different computational levels. On one hand, the extent of genetic determination reflects the degree to which the information processed at a particular connection is predictable from one generation to the next. On the other hand, because many aspects of an individual's world are not predictable, the brain's circuitry must rely on experience to customize connections to serve the needs of the individual. Experience shapes these neural connections and interactions but always within the constraints imposed by genetics.

### Brain Development

The construction and development of the human brain occurs over a very protracted period beginning shortly after conception and, depending on how we view the end of

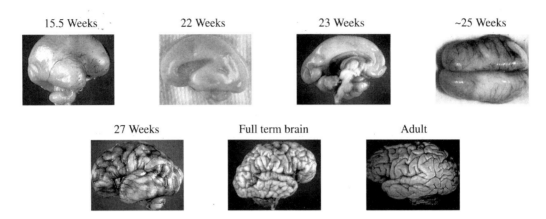

**Figure 1.1**   Overview of human brain development, beginning the 15th prenatal week and continuing to term and then adult.

development, continuing through at least the end of adolescence (for overviews, see Figure 1.1 and Table 1.1).

Shortly after conception, embryonic tissue forms from the two-celled zygote (specifically, from the blastocyst, the ball of cells created through multiplying cells). The outer layer of the embryo gives rise to, among other things, the central (brain and spinal cord) and peripheral nervous systems. It is this outermost layer we will be concerned with in this chapter.

### Neural Induction and Neurulation— Typical Development

The process of transforming the undifferentiated tissue lining the dorsal side of the ectoderm into nervous system tissue is referred to as neural *induction*. In contrast, the dual processes called primary and secondary *neurulation* refer to the further differentiation of this neural tissue into, respectively, the brain and the spinal cord (for recent review of neural induction and neurulation, see Lumsden & Kintner, 2003).

The thin layer of undifferentiated tissue that lines the ectoderm is gradually transformed into an increasingly thick layer of tissue that will become the *neural plate*. A class of chemical agents referred to as transforming growth factors is responsible for the subsequent transformation of this undifferentiated tissue into nervous system tissue (Murloz-Sanjuan & Brivanfou, 2002). What one observes morphologically is the shift from neural plate to neural tube. Specifically, the neural plate buckles, forming a crease down its longitudinal axis. The tissue then folds inward, the edges rise up, and a tube is formed. This process begins on approximately Day 22 of gestation (Keith, 1948), fusing first at the midsection and progressing outward in either direc-

tion until approximately Day 26 (Sidman & Rakic, 1982). The rostral portion of the tube eventually forms the brain, and the caudal portion develops into the spinal cord.

Cells trapped inside the tube typically go on to comprise the central nervous system (CNS); however, there is a cluster of cells trapped between the outside of the neural tube and the dorsal portion of the ectodermal wall that is referred to as the *neural crest*. Neural crest cells typically develop into the autonomic nervous system (ANS).

A fair amount is now known about the genes that regulate many aspects of brain development, including neurulation. Much of this knowledge is based on studies of invertebrates and vertebrates, in which alterations in morphogenesis are observed after genes are selectively deleted ("knock-out") or in a more recently developed method, added ("knock-in"). Although at first glance, one might be suspicious about the generalizability of such work to the human, reassurance can be found in the observation that humans share more than 61% of their genes with fruit flies and 81% with mice. Of course, not everything we know is based on animal models: Increasingly our knowledge of the molecular biology of brain development is based on careful genetic analysis of nervous system tissue that has failed to develop correctly.

The patterning of the neuroaxis (i.e., head to tail) is for the most part completed by about the 5th prenatal week. Based on mouse studies, many of the transcription factors[1] responsible for this process are well known. As reviewed by Levitt (2003), some of the genes involved

---

[1] Transcription factors refer to the regulation of the proteins involved in the transcription of other genes.

**TABLE 1.1   Neurodevelopmental Timeline from Conception through Adolescence**

| Developmental Event | Timeline | Overview of Developmental Event |
| --- | --- | --- |
| Neurulation | 18–24 prenatal days | Cells differentiate into one of three layers: endoderm, mesoderm, and ectoderm, which then form the various organs in the body. |
| | | The neural tube (from which the central nervous system is derived) develops from the ectoderm cells; the neural crest (from which the autonomic nervous system is derived) lies between the ectodermal wall and the neural tube. |
| Neuronal migration | 6–24 prenatal weeks | Neurons migrate at the ventricular zone along radial glial cells to the cerebral cortex. |
| | | The neurons migrate in an inside-out manner, with later generations of cells migrating through previously developed cells. |
| | | The cortex develops into six layers. |
| Synaptogenesis | 3rd trimester–adolescence | Neurons migrate into the cortical plate and extend apical and basilar dendrites. |
| | | Chemical signals guide the developing dendrites toward their final location, where synapses are formed with projections from subcortical structures. |
| | | These connections are strengthened through neuronal activity, and connections with very little activity are pruned. |
| Postnatal neurogenesis | Birth–adulthood | The development of new cells in several brain regions, including: |
| | | –Dentate gyrus of the hippocampus |
| | | –Olfactory bulb |
| | | –Possibly cingulate gyrus; regions of parietal cortex |
| Myelination | 3rd trimester–middle age | Neurons are enclosed in a myelin sheath, resulting in an increased speed of action potentials. |
| Gyrification | 3rd trimester–adulthood | The smooth tissue of the brain folds to form gyri and sulci. |
| Structural development of the prefrontal cortex | Birth–late adulthood | The prefrontal cortex is the last structure to undergo gyrification during uterine life. |
| | | The synaptic density reaches its peak at 12 months; however, myelination of this structure continues into adulthood. |
| Neurochemical development of the prefrontal cortex | Uterine life–adolescence | All major neurotransmitter systems undergo initial development during uterine life and are present at birth. |
| | | Although it is not well studied in humans, it is thought that most neurotransmitter systems do not reach full maturity until adulthood. |

in dorsal patterning include members of the emx, Pax, and ihx families of genes, whereas nkx and dlx gene families may play a role in ventral patterning.

*Atypical Development*

Unfortunately, errors do occur in neural induction and neurulation. *Neural tube defects* are disorders of primary neurulation and include *craniorachischisis totalis* (in which there is a total failure of neural induction), *anencephaly* (where the anterior portion of the neural tube fails to close completely), *holoprosencephaly* (where there is one undifferentiated forebrain, rather than a forebrain that has two halves), and most commonly, *myelomeningocele* (where the posterior portion of the neural tube fails to close normally). Holoprosencephay appears to be due to mutations in the sonic hedgehog transcription factor (ZIC2 genes; e.g., S. A. Brown et al., 1998), whereas myelomeningocele (also referred

to as *spina bifida*) may be due to mutations in the Pax1 gene (Hof et al., 1996). Importantly, neural tube defects generally have been associated with a deficiency of folic acid, and supplementing the diet of pregnant women with this nutrient appears to have reduced the incidence of these disorders in the general population.

*Proliferation*

Once the neural tube has closed, cell division leads to a massive proliferation of new neurons (neurogenesis), generally beginning in the 5th prenatal week, and peaking between the 3rd and 4th prenatal months (Volpe, 2000; for review, see Bronner-Fraser & Hatten, 2003). The term *massive* barely captures this process. It has been estimated, for example, that at its peak, several hundred thousand new nerve cells are generated *each minute* (M. Brown, Keynes, & Lumsden, 2001). Proliferation begins in the innermost portion of the neural tube, referred to as the ventricular zone (Chenn & McConnell, 1995), a region that is derived from the subependeymal location that lines the neural tube. In a process called *interkinetic nuclear migration,* new neural cells travel back and forth between the inner and outer portions of the ventricular zone. The new cell first travels toward the outer portion of the ventricular zone—the so-called S phase of mitosis—where DNA is synthesized, creating a duplicate copy of the cell. Once the S phase has been completed, the cell migrates downward toward the innermost portion of the ventricular zone where it divides into two cells (for a generally accessible description of these phases, see Takahashi, Nowakowski, & Caviness, 2001). Each of these new cells then begins the process again. As cells divide, a new zone is created, the marginal zone, which contains processes (axons and dendrites) from the cells of the ventricular zone. During the second phase of proliferation, neurons actually begin to form. However, for each dividing cell, only one daughter cell will continue to divide; the nondividing cell goes on to migrate to its final destination (Rakic, 1988).

Before turning to disorders of proliferation, three points should be noted. First, with the exception of cells that comprise the olfactory bulb, the dentate region of the hippocampus, and possibly regions of the neocortex, virtually every one of the estimated 100 billion neurons we possess (Naegele & Lombroso, 2001) are of prenatal origin (see section on postnatal neurogenesis); glia follow this same general pattern, although the development of glia (with the exception of radial glial cells; see section on migration that follows) lags somewhat behind neuronal development. What needs to be underscored about this observation is its importance in the context of plasticity: Unlike all other cells, the brain *generally* does not make new neurons after birth, which means that the brain does not repair itself in response to injury or disease by making new neurons.

Second, as cells continue to proliferate, the general shape of the neural tube undergoes a dramatic transformation—specifically, three distinct vesicles are formed: the *proencephalon* (forebrain), *mesencephalon* (midbrain), and *rhombencephalon* (hindbrain). Further proliferation leads to the proencephalon splitting into the *telencephalon,* which will give rise to the cerebral hemispheres, and the *diencephalon,* which gives rise to the thalamus and hypothalamus. The rhombencephalon will in turn give rise to the metencephalon (from which the pons and cerebellum are derived) and the myelen-

cephalon (which will give rise to the medulla). The mesencephalon gives rise to the midbrain.

Finally, our knowledge of the molecular biology of cell proliferation is gradually advancing. The Foxg1 gene has been implicated in this process (Hanashima, Li, Shen, Lai, & Fishell, 2004), but undoubtedly many other genes are involved as well.

### Disorders of Neurogenesis

There are a numner of examples of errors of cell proliferation, although most fall into two categories: microencephaly (small brain) and macroencephaly (large brain; see Volpe, 2000). Microencephaly is generally thought to occur during the asymmetric period of cell division, generally the 6th through 18th weeks of gestation. The cause of the microencephalies can be either genetic or environmental; examples of the latter include rubella, irradiation, maternal alcoholism, excessive vitamin A, and human immunodeficiency virus (e.g., Kozlowski et al., 1997; Warkany, Lemire, & Cohen, 1981). Macroencephaly is generally thought to be due to an underlying genetic disorder; for example, if genes that regulate normal cellular proliferation do not turn off, this failure could lead to an overproduction of new cells. Assuming survival, both micro- and macrocencephaly generally lead to varying degrees of mental and physical retardation/impairment.

### Postnatal Neurogenesis

With the exception of cells in the olfactory bulb, it was assumed until recently that the nervous system at birth had virtually all the neurons it would ever have, and that no new neurons were added. Like many aspects of neuroscience, we have now had to revise this view, due in part to the advent of new methods—specifically, the use of new staining methods for looking at DNA turnover (e.g., 5′-Bromo-2-deoxyuridine [BrdU]). Based on work with both human (e.g., Gage, 2000) and nonhuman primates (e.g., Bernier, Bédard, Vinet, Lévesque, & Parent, 2002; Gould, Beylin, Tanapat, Reeves, & Shors, 1999; Kornack & Rakic, 1999) and rodents (Gould et al., 1999), there is now widespread agreement that in certain regions of the brain, new cells are added for many years after birth. Where this agreement breaks down is in determining precisely which regions experience this postnatal birth of new neurons. There is little controversy that the dentate gyrus of the hippocampus experiences this process; controversy exists, however, concerning regions of the neocortex, such as the cingulate gyrus and segments of the parietal cortex (for review and discussion, see Gould & Gross, 2002). There is also a recent report of postnatal neurogenesis in the amygdala, piriform cortex, and inferior temporal cortex in nonhuman primates (Bernier et al., 2002), although to date these findings have not been replicated (for a highly readable review of postnatal neurogenesis generally, see Barinaga, 2003).

Particularly relevant to this chapter is the observation that the addition of such cells can be influenced by experience (e.g., Gould et al., 1999; Mirescu, Peters, & Gould, 2004). For example, the number of cells produced in the rodent dentate gyrus is increased when rats are placed in contexts in which demands are placed on learning and memory. Similarly, the presence of the hormone prolactin in pregnant rats appears to increase the number of new cells in the forebrain subventricular zone. Because this zone gives rise to olfactory neurons, it has been assumed that this adaptive response may facilitate olfactory recognition of offspring (see Shingo et al., 2003). In contrast, stress in adulthood (e.g., the presence of novel odors such as the smell of a fox) appears to down-regulate neurogenesis in the rat dentate gyrus. Moreover, when rodents are housed together, dominance hierarchies develop, and the dominant animals produce more new neurons than the nondominant animals (Gould, 2003). Interestingly, if these same animals are then housed in complex environments (see subsequent section on plasticity), there is an up-regulation of neurogenesis in the dentate, although the dominant animals continue to fare better than the nondominant animals. Finally, inflammation (which commonly occurs following brain injury) can lead to a down-regulation of dentate hippocampal cells (Ekdahl, Claasen, Bonde, Kokaia, & Lindvall, 2003). Collectively, experience appears to have a profound influence on postnatal neurogenesis.

Postnatally derived cells may differ in several respects from prenatally derived cells. For example, the former differentiate and appear to be normal in all respects, although these cells may have a relatively short half-life (Gould, Vail, Wagers, & Gross, 2001). Furthermore, it is not yet clear how such cells might work their way into existing synaptic circuits (although Song, Stevens, & Gage, 2002, have demonstrated that postnatally derived cells both express neurotransmitter and form synaptic connections, which is a requirement for cell functioning). Finally, this revised view of neurogenesis is not without its critics (e.g., Rakic, 2002a,

2002b). (For an enlightened discussion of this topic, the reader is encouraged to see a special issue of the *Journal of Neuroscience,* 2002, vol. 22, issue 3.) Resolution of this matter will prove vitally important to our understanding of plasticity and to the development of interventions and therapeutics; regarding the latter, for example, there is strong evidence that exercise (in rodents) leads to an up-regulation of neurogenesis in the dentate gyrus of the hippocampus (for a general discussion of the possible link between postnatal neurogenesis and therapeutics, see Lie, Song, Colamarino, Ming, & Gage, 2004).

### Cell Migration

The cortex proper (arguably the seat of cognition) is formed by a process whereby newly formed cells migrate out beyond their birthplace to ultimately give rise to a six-layered cortex. As discussed by M. Brown et al. (2001), the ventricular zone (the epithelium that lines the lateral ventricular cavities) gives rise to cells that undergo cell division, with the postmitotic cell migrating through the intermediate zone to its final point of destination. The cells born earliest take up residence in the preplate (the first layer of cortical neurons), which subsequently divides into the subplate and the marginal zone, both of which are derived from the cortical plate.

The postmitotic cells move in an inside-out (ventricular-to-pial) direction, such that the earliest migrating cells occupy the deepest layer of the cortex (and play an important role in the establishment of cortical connections), with subsequent migrations passing through the previously formed layer(s) (note that this rule applies only to the cortex; the dentate gyrus and the cerebellum are formed in an outside-in pattern). At approximately 20 weeks gestation, the cortical plate consists of three layers, and by the 7th prenatal month the final contingent of six layers can be seen (Marin-Padilla, 1978).

There are two types of migratory patterns—radial and nonradial (generally tangential). Radial migration generally refers to the propagation of cells from the ventricular zone outward, or from the deepest to most superficial layers of the cortex. Approximately 70% to 80% of migrating neurons use this radial pathway. In contrast, cells adopting a tangential migratory pattern (generally interneurons for the cortex and nuclei of the brain stem) move along a tangential ("across") path. Pyramidal neurons, the major projection neurons in the brain, along with oligodendrocytes and astrocytes, enlist radial glial cells to migrate through the layers of cortex (Kriegstein & Götz, 2003), whereas cortical interneurons (for local connections) migrate via tangential migration within a cortical layer (Nadarajah & Parnavelas, 2002). Radial migration is particularly noteworthy for several reasons. First, there are different types of radial migration. *Locomotion* is characterized by migration along a radial glial fiber. In *somal translocation* the cell body (soma) of a cell advances toward the pial surface by way of a leading process. Finally, cells that move from the intermediate zone (IZ) to the subventricular zone (SVZ) appear to migrate using *multipolar* migration (Tabata & Nakajima, 2003). A number of genes are involved in the regulation of migratory movement (see Hatten, 2002, and Ridley et al., 2003 for recent reviews).

### Disorders of Cell Migration

There are many examples of disorders of cell migration (for review, see Naegele & Lombroso, 2001; Tanaka & Gleeson, 2000; Volpe, 2000). *Subcortical band heterotopia* (also known as X-linked *lissencephaly*), in which neural tissue is misplaced (e.g., cell bodies where only axons should exist) has been associated with mental retardation and epilepsy, and with the DCX gene. *Schizencephaly* is a case in which there is a cleft in the frontal cortex, whereas in *holoprosencephaly* the telencephalon fails to cleave, resulting in one undifferentiated hemisphere. Perhaps the best known disorder of migration is agenesis of the corpus callosum, in which the corpus callosum (the major bundle of fibers that connects the two hemispheres) is partially or entirely absent. As a class, disorders of cell migration generally result in varying degrees of behavioral or psychological disturbance; a case in point may be the psychiatric disorder schizophrenia, which has been hypothesized to result from a migrational disorder (see Elvevåg & Weinberger, 2001).

### The Growth and Development of Processes—
### Axons and Dendrites

Once a neuron has completed its migratory journey, it generally proceeds along one of two roads: The cell can differentiate and develop axons and dendrites (the topic of this section), or it can be retracted through the normative process of *apoptosis* (programmed cell death), a phenomenon that is widespread (e.g., 40% to 60% of all neurons may die; for review, see Oppenheim & Johnson, 2003).

### The Development of Axons

*Growth cones,* small structures that sit on top of axons, appear to play a key role both in developing the axon and in guiding it to its target (e.g., Raper & Tessier-Lavigne, 1999; for review, see Raper & Tessier-Lavigne, 2003). Using cues from the extracellular matrix surrounding the neuron (Jessell, 1988), and possibly local gene expression (Condron, 2002), the growth cone directs the axon toward some targets and away from others.

As Raper and Tessier-Lavigne (1999) discuss, *lamellipodia* and *filopodia* play primary roles in axon guidance. Lamellipodia are thin fan-shaped structures, whereas filopodia are long, thin spikes that radiate forward. In both cases, these structures provide the axon with the ability to move through parenchymal (brain) tissue micrometer by micrometer until the axon is within synapse range of a neighboring neuron. They do so by sampling the local environment for molecular cues (e.g., aminin, tenascin, collagen; see Bixby & Harris, 1991; de Castro, 2003; Erskine et al., 2000; Hynes & Lander, 1992; Schachner, Taylor, Bartsch, & Pesheva, 1994, for discussion).

Over and above these molecular cues, there are also molecules that sit on the surface of established axons and act as guides (Tessier-Lavigne & Goodman, 1996). An example is *cell adhesion molecules* (CAMs; Rutishauser, 1993; Takeichi, 1995). Whether the molecules reside in the extracelluar matrix or on the axon proper, axons are guided toward (attractant cues) or away from (repellant cues) neighboring neurons (Tessier-Lavigne & Goodman, 1996).

### The Development of Dendrites

Recent work has indicated that the gene calcium-regulated transcriptional activator *(CREST)* plays an important role in the development of dendrites (Aizawa et al., 2004). The earliest dendrites make their appearance as thick processes with few spines (small protuberances) extending from the cell body. As dendrites mature, spine number and density increase, thereby increasing the chance of making contact with a neighboring axon. Not surprisingly, dendrites grow and develop in conjunction with axons. Dendritic sprouting begins to occur at approximately 15 weeks, about the same time that axons reach the cortical plate. Between the 25th and 27th weeks of gestation, dendritic spines begin appearing on both pyramidal and nonpyramidal neurons. This sprouting continues to expand through the 24th postnatal month in some cortical regions (Mrzljak, Uylings, Kostovic, & VanEden, 1990). Additionally, there appears to be an overproduction of both axons and dendrites during development with the final number achieved through competitive elimination.

### Disorders of Axon and Dendrite Development

There are a number of environmental agents that lead to disorders associated with errors in axonal and dendritic development, including oxygen deprivation, toxins, malnutrition, or genetic anomalies (Webb, Monk, & Nelson, 2001). In addition, genetic disorders such as Angelman syndrome, fragile X syndrome, autism, and Duchenne muscular dystrophy show possible errors in dendritic development (Volpe, 1995).

### Synaptogenesis

**Background.**   Synapses generally refer to the point of contact between two neurons. Depending on the receiving neuron, the resulting action can be excitatory (promoting an action potential) or inhibitory (reducing the likelihood of an action potential).

**Development.**   The first synapses are generally observed by about the 23rd week of gestation (Molliver, Kostovic, & Van der Loos, 1973), although the peak of production does not occur until sometime in the 1st year of life (for review, see Webb et al., 2001). It is now well known that there is a massive overproduction of synapses distributed across broad regions of the brain, followed by a gradual reduction in synapses; it has been estimated that 40% more synapses are produced than exist in the final (adult) complement of synapses (see Levitt, 2003). The peak of the overproduction varies by brain area. For example, in the visual cortex, a synaptic peak is reached between roughly the 4th and 8th postnatal months (Huttenlocher & de Courten, 1987), whereas in the middle frontal gyrus (in the prefrontal cortex) the peak synaptic density is not obtained until after 15 postnatal months (Huttenlocher & Dabholkar, 1997).

There is evidence that the overproduction of synapses is largely under genetic control, although little is known about the genes that regulate synaptogenesis. For example, Bourgeois and colleagues (Bourgeois, Reboff, & Rakic, 1989) have reported that being born prematurely or even removing the eyes of monkeys prior to birth has little effect on the overproduction of synapses in the monkey visual cortex. Thus, in both cases the absolute number of synapses is the same as if the monkey experi-

enced a typical, full-term birth. This suggests a highly regularized process with little influence by experience. As we demonstrate, however, the same cannot be said for synaptic pruning and the cultivating of synaptic circuits, both of which are strongly influenced by the environment.

**Synaptic Pruning.**   The process of retracting synapses until some final (and presumably optimal) number has been reached is dependent in part on the communication among neurons. Pruning appears to follow the Hebbian principle of use/disuse: Thus, more active synapses tend to be strengthened and less active synapses tend to be weakened or even eliminated (Chechik, Meilijson, & Ruppin, 1999). Neurons organize and support synaptic contact through neurotransmitter receptors (both excitatory and inhibitory) on the presynaptic cell (the cell attempting to make contact) and through neurotrophins expressed by the postsynaptic cell (the cell on which contact is made). Synapses are modulated and stabilized by the distribution of excitatory and inhibitory inputs (Kostovic, 1990). The adjustments that are made in the pruning of synapses can either be quantitative (reducing the overall number of synapses) or qualitative (refining connections such that incorrect or abnormal connections are eliminated; for review, see Wong & Lichtman, 2003).

As has been thoroughly reported in both the lay and scientific press, the pruning of synapses appears to vary by area. As seen in Figure 1.2, synapse numbers in the human occipital cortex peak between 4 and 8 months of age and are reduced to adult numbers by 4 to 6 years of age. In contrast, synapses in the middle frontal gyrus of the human prefrontal cortex reach their peak closer to

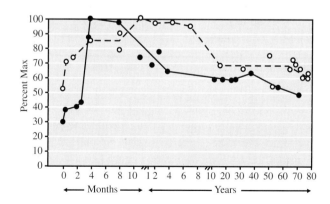

**Figure 1.2**   Synapse overproduction and elimination in the occipital and frontal cortices.

one to $1\frac{1}{2}$ years of age, but are not reduced to adult numbers until mid to late adolescence. Unfortunately, these data are based on relatively few brains (thus leaving open the question of the range of individual differences) and relatively old methods (i.e., density of synapses per unit area, which increases the risk that nonsynaptic and even nonneuronal elements may be counted, such as glial cells). We should expect improved figures in the years to come with advances in new methods, a point that applies to much of the literature reviewed thus far.

**Synaptic Plasticity.** The initial development of synapses is generally quite tenuous. Thus, it is only after a synapse has been activated repeatedly that it becomes stabilized; frequently, synapses that do not receive confirmation are eliminated or reabsorbed (Changeux & Danchin, 1976). Moreover, synapse stabilization also depends on chemical communication, such as the local release of neurotrophins by postsynaptic cells (Huang & Reichardt, 2001) or through the activation of receptors such as glutamate that in turn mediate postsynaptic activation of cortical cells. Finally, even in the mature brain, synaptic plasticity is driven by synaptic activity. For example, reducing activity in a given neuron *before* a synapse has been formed leads to a reduction in functional inputs to that neuron (from neighboring neurons); in contrast, reducing activity to a given neuron *after* a synapse has been established leads to an increase in synaptic input (Burrone, O'Byrne, & Murthy, 2002).

### Disorders of Synaptogenesis

There are several disorders of synaptogenesis, with fragile X syndrome being perhaps the best known. In fragile X, it appears that the disruption in the transcription of the FMR1 gene may be responsible for the abnormality in synapses (perhaps due in part to an exuberance in dendritic spines, e.g., Churchill, Beckel-Mitchener, Weiler, & Greenough, 2002).

### Myelination

Myelin is a lipid/protein substance that wraps itself around an axon as a form of insulation and, as a result, increases conduction velocity. *Oligodendroglia* produce myelin in the CNS, whereas *schwann* cells produce myelin in the ANS. Myelination occurs in waves beginning prenatally and ending in young adulthood (and in some regions, as late as middle age; see Benes, Turtle, Khan, & Farol, 1994). Historically, myelin was examined in postmortem tissue using staining methods. From

such work, it was revealed that myelination begins prenatally with the peripheral nervous system, motor roots, sensory roots, somesthetic cortex, and the primary visual and auditory cortices (in this chronological order). During the first postnatal year, regions of the brain stem myelinate, as does the cerebellum and splenium of corpus callosum; by 1 year, myelination of all regions of the corpus callosum is underway.

Although staining for myelin is undoubtedly the most sensitive metric for examining the course of myelination, an obvious disadvantage to this procedure is that it can only be done on a relatively small number of postmortem brains; in addition, as is the case with human synaptogenesis, it is also of concern how representative these brains are of the general population. Fortunately, advances in magnetic resonance imaging (MRI) have now made it possible to acquire detailed information about myelination in living children; importantly, several longitudinal studies have examined the course of myelination from early childhood through early adulthood (Giedd, Snell, et al., 1996; Giedd, Vatuzis, et al., 1996; Jernigan, Trauner, Hesselink, & Tallal, 1991; Paus et al., 1999; Sowell et al., 1999; Sowell, Thompson, Holmes, Jernigan, & Toga, 2000). The results of this work paint the following picture: The pre- through postadolescent period witnesses an increase in gray matter volume, followed by a decrease, whereas white matter shows first a decrease and then an increase.[2] During this same age period (pre-post adolescence), particular changes of note occur in the dorsal, medial, and lateral regions of the frontal lobes, whereas relatively smaller changes are observed in the parietal, temporal, and occipital lobes. This suggests, not surprisingly, that the most dramatic changes in myelination occur in the frontal lobes through the adolescent period (for a general overview, see Durston et al., 2001).

### Summary

Overall, brain development begins within weeks of conception and continues through the adolescent period.

---

[2] Gray matter is composed primarily of cell bodies and neuropil, whereas white matter consists mostly of axons. An increase in gray matter, therefore, suggests that there is an increase in new neurons, whereas a decrease in gray matter would likely be due to an increase in apoptosis (and corresponding *loss* of neurons). An increase in white matter refers to an increase in the number of myelinated axons or simply the amount of myelin present on such axons.

This general statement does not do justice to the age-specific changes that occur during the first 2 decades of life. Thus, the assembly of the basic architecture of the brain occurs during the first two trimesters of fetal life, with the last trimester and the first few postnatal years reserved for changes in connectivity and function. The most prolonged changes occur in the wiring of the brain (synaptogenesis) and in making the brain work more efficiently (myelination), both of which show dramatic, nonlinear changes from the preschool period through the end of adolescence.

## NEURAL PLASTICITY

Having established how the anatomical and physiological properties of the brain are laid down over the first 2 decades of life, we may have inadvertently created the impression that these events simply unfold of their own accord—that is, they are largely maturational in nature. Although that is true to a great extent prenatally, it vastly underrepresents the powerful role of experience in sculpting the fine architecture of the brain. Before providing specific examples of experience-induced changes in brain development and brain function, we must first provide some background.

It is important to understand at the outset that experiences don't just happen to the brain; rather, experience is the product of an ongoing, reciprocal interaction between the environment and the brain. Second, experience has typically been defined by the properties of the environment in which an individual lives. Here it must be stressed that experience is not simply a function of the environment per se, but is the result of a complex, bidirectional interaction between that environment and the developing brain. Third, experience interacts importantly with genetics. Two examples suffice, one from the rodent literature, one from the human literature. Regarding the former, Francis, Szegda, Campbell, Martin, and Insel (2003) cross-fostered two strains of mice with one another, either prenatally (in which hours-old embryos from one strain were implanted in the mothers of the other strain) and postnatally (in which newborn pups from one strain were placed with the mothers of the other strain). The offspring of the two original (noncross-fostered) strains served as controls. All animals were tested at 3 months of age. As expected, the control animals differed reliably from one another on four dimensions: (1) differences in explo-

ration of an open field; (2) relative time on the open arms of a plus maze; (3) latency to find a hidden platform in the Morris water maze; and (4) acoustic startle prepulse inhibition. Animals that had been cross-fostered prenatally *or* postnatally did not exert any effects on the expected phenotype. However, mice that had been prenatally *and* postnatally cross-fostered exhibited the same behavioral phenotype as the adopted strain, despite differing genetically from the adopted strain. The fact that the mice that had been cross-fostered prenatally did not show this effect supported the authors' contention that the effects of the combined cross-fostering must be due to nongenetic factors, and the powerful role of experience on gene expression.

Moving to the human, Turkheimer, Haley, Waldron, D'Onofrio, and Gottesman (2003) examined IQ in 7-year-old twins, a substantial number of whom were drawn from families living at or below the poverty level. The authors reported that the heritability of IQ varied nonlinearly as a function of socioeconomic standard (SES). Thus, among twins living in impoverished environments, a substantial portion of the variance was accounted for by environmental factors, with relatively little variance accounted for by genetics; in contrast, this effect was nearly completely reversed among twins living in affluent families.

Collectively, these two studies demonstrate the powerful role of the environment in moderating and mediating effects of genes on behavior. Animal studies, adopting both knockout and knock-in molecular tools, coupled with careful rearing studies will undoubtedly shed light on the pattern of gene expression and nongenetic inheritance patterns.

Within this context, any given experience can vary enormously under identical environmental conditions, depending on the history, maturation, and state of the individual's brain. Even the experience that results from a simple physical manipulation, for example, may vary widely depending on the background and state of the individual involved.

The relative maturity of the brain also has an enormous impact on experience. Different areas of the central nervous system mature at different rates. A young child who is exposed to information before his or her brain is capable of processing that information will not have the same experience as an older child who has more advanced capability. A less mature brain is affected largely by more fundamental features of the environment, such as patterned light or the speech train. As the brain matures and changes with experience, more detailed aspects of the environment influence it. Thus, as an individual's brain changes, particularly during the early developmental periods, the same physical environment can result in very different experiences.

Certain properties of the brain differ dramatically across individuals and within individuals over time. Therefore, because experience is defined as the interaction of the brain with the environment, a scientific description of an experience must include a description of the background, developmental stage, and state of the brain as well as a description of the specific experience to which the individual is exposed. By the same token, an analysis of the effect of an experience also must take into account variability in those same factors.

The impact of experience on the brain is not constant throughout life. As the brain passes through its different developmental stages, its sensitivity to experience varies accordingly—hence the concept of *sensitive periods* (see Knudsen, 2003a). Early experience often exerts a particularly strong influence in shaping the functional properties of the immature brain. Many neural connections pass through a period during development when the capacity for experience-driven modification is greater than it is in adulthood. Thus, individual capabilities reflect the combined influences of both evolutionary learning and personal experience.

In the following sections, we will deconstruct plasticity into two types: developmental and adult. By this, we simply mean plastic processes that operate during the time of brain *development* (presumably the first 2 decades of life) versus the postdevelopmental period (when the brain is certainly capable of *changing* but not in the same fashion as the child's brain). We revisit this simplistic view at the end of this section by discussing whether the plastic processes that operate during development are the same as or different from those that operate during adulthood.

We, and others, have recently provided overviews to the myriad ways experience influences the developing and developed brain (Black, Jones, Nelson, & Greenough, 1998; Cline, 2003; de Haan & Johnnson, 2003a; Grossman, Churchill, Bates, Kleim, & Greenough, 2002; Huttenlocher, 2002; Knudsen, 2003b, in press; Nelson, 1999, 2000a, 2002; Nelson & Bloom, 1997). Our purpose is simply to provide a brief overview to this topic, beginning with a discussion of developmental plasticity and proceeding to a discussion of adult plasticity. Within each of these sections, we draw on a range of

species, although we focus mainly on rodents, monkeys, and humans. Finally, we limit our discussion to perceptual and cognitive functions, and do not discuss aspects of plasticity from social and emotional development.

## Developmental Plasticity

### Auditory Function

Sur and Leamey (2001) published a rather amazing example of plasticity in the auditory system. Normal retinal inputs pass through the lateral geniculate nucleus (LGN) of the thalamus on their way to the visual cortex, whereas normal auditory inputs pass through the medial geniculate nucleus (MGN) on their way to the auditory cortex. In this study, retinal projections in the young ferret were routed through the MGN. When electrophysiological recordings were made from the auditory cortex, normal *visual* responses were observed; for example, these auditory cells showed orientation selectivity to visual stimuli.

Recently, Cheng and Merzenich (2003) reported that infant rats reared in an environment of continuous, moderate-level noise were delayed in the organization of the auditory cortex; specifically, the auditory receptive fields differed from what would be expected under normal auditory rearing conditions. When these rats reached young adulthood, the auditory cortex appeared to be very similar to infants—that is, the auditory receptive fields had not yet crystallized into the adult pattern and had retained their juvenile appearance. To test the hypothesis that rearing the rats in continuous noise from birth delayed the closing of the critical period for organizing the auditory cortex, the authors exposed some of the same rats to a 7 kHz tone train for 2 weeks. This led to a reorganization of the auditory cortex, supporting the hypothesis that degraded acoustic inputs early in life delayed the organizational maturation of the auditory cortex. This led the authors to speculate that early exposure to abnormal auditory inputs (e.g., loud noise) could contribute to some auditory and/or linguistic delays in human children.

It has been known for some time that human adults have great difficulty in discriminating speech contrasts from various nonnative languages. This differs dramatically from the ceiling-level ability to discriminate speech contrasts from their own (English) language. Importantly, between 6 and 12 months of life, the infants' ability to discriminate phonemes from languages to which they are not exposed declines dramatically (for review, see Saffran, Werker, & Werner, Chapter 2, this *Handbook,* this volume; Werker & Vouloumanos, 2001). It appears however, that the door does not shut completely on retaining the ability to discriminate nonnative contrasts; for example, Kuhl and colleagues (Kuhl, Tsao, & Liu, 2003) have reported that if before 12 months of age infants are given additional experience with speech sounds in a nonnative language, this ability is retained. Collectively, these speech data have been interpreted to suggest that the speech system remains open to experience for a certain period, but if experience in a particular domain (such as hearing speech contrasts in different languages) is not forthcoming, the window begins to close within the 1st year of life.

### Linguistic Function

There has long been great controversy over the sensitive period for acquiring a second (or third or fourth) language. Dehaene et al. (1997) have reported that the neural representation of a second language is identical to that of a first language in truly bilingual individuals. However, if linguistic competence of the second language is not as strong as the first, then the functional neuroanatomy (based on PET data) is different. Since the bilinguals studied in this work had acquired their second language early in life, the initial conclusion was that the second language needed to be acquired early to be represented in the brain in the same location as the first language. This conclusion has recently been challenged, however. Perani et al. (1998) asked whether it was the *age* at which the second language was acquired that was the critical variable, or the *proficiency* with which this language was spoken. In this study, the age at which the second language had been mastered covaried with how well this language was spoken. The authors reported that it was the latter dimension that was most critical. Thus, regardless of when the second language was acquired, speaking this language with equal proficiency as the first language led to shared neural representation for both languages. Importantly, similar findings have been obtained with congenitally deaf individuals who are proficient in sign language; thus, the areas of the brain involved in sign are identical to those of hearing speakers using spoken language (Petitto et al., 2000).

Is there a critical period for acquiring American sign language (ASL)? Mayberry, Lock, and Kazmi (2002) have reported that proficiency in sign language among deaf individuals was far greater among subjects who had been exposed to either sign language early in life (among those born congenitally deaf) or individuals exposed to spoken language early in life but who subsequently lost their hearing than among congenitally deaf individuals *not* exposed to either signed or spoken language early in life. Furthermore, Newman, Bavelier, Corina, Jezzard, and Neville (2002) have reported that ASL is represented in the same location as spoken language only among individuals who acquired ASL before puberty. Thus, although there does not appear to be a sensitive period for acquiring ASL in general, there does appear to be a sensitive period for representing ASL in the same regions of the brain as spoken language, and for signing with a high level of proficiency.

### Visual Function

The development of stereoscopic depth perception is made possible by the development of ocular dominance columns, which represent the connections between each eye and layer IV of the visual cortex. If the two eyes are not aligned properly, or can't move together (vergence movements), then the ocular dominance columns that support normal stereoscopic depth perception fail to develop normally. If this situation is not corrected by 4 to 5 years of age—when the number of synapses begins to reach adult values—the child will not develop normal stereoscopic vision. Thus, normal visual input to an intact visual system during a sensitive period is necessary for the development of binocular vision.

Another example of sensitive periods for visual development can be found in an elegant series of studies by Maurer and colleagues (Maurer, Lewis, Brent, & Levin, 1999). These authors have reported on a longitudinal study of children with cataracts. A particularly attractive feature of this work is that some infants are born with cataracts, and others acquire them a few years after birth; moreover, some have their cataracts removed in the first months of life, and others undergo this procedure a few years later. The authors have reported that among infants born with cataracts that are removed and new lenses placed within months of birth, even just a few *minutes* of visual experience leads to a dramatic change in visual acuity. The longer the cataracts are left untreated, reducing the amount of visual experience, the less favorable the outcome. Note, however, that although most visual functions undergo dramatic improvements following early cataract removal, some aspects of *face* processing remain impaired for years (Le Grand, Mondloch, Maurer, & Brent,

2001). From this observation comes the idea of a differential sensitive period: specifically, the sensitive period for visual acuity may differ from that of face processing.

### Learning and Memory Function

Hormones have long been associated with mediating cognitive differences between males and females due to their organizing effect on the brain. This association can even be observed prenatally. For example, Shors and Miesegaes (2002) capitalized on previous findings in which exposure to stressful and traumatic events enhances new learning in adult male rats, but impairs new learning in adult female rats. In the present study, the authors performed two experiments. In the first, male rats were castrated at birth, whereas female rats were injected with testosterone; both groups were then tested on a hippocampal-dependent learning task (trace eye-blink conditioning). The castrated male rats still exhibited enhanced learning, *as did the testosterone-injected females* (opposite the normal pattern of response, in which reduced learning is typically observed for females). In the second experiment, pregnant female rats were injected with a testosterone antagonist, thereby depriving the offspring of testosterone. The male and female offspring were subsequently tested as adults on the same learning task following exposure to a stressor (loud noise bursts). Male *and* female rats now both exhibited reduced learning, pointing to the powerful role of early experience with testosterone.

## Adult Plasticity

For many years, it was commonly believed that once the brain was fully developed (thought to be the end of adolescence), its ability to be molded by experience and to recover from injury was greatly limited. This view has been turned on its head in recent years; indeed, research on so-called adult plasticity is currently receiving tremendous attention in the field of neuroscience. In this section, we provide an overview to several domains in which the adult brain is now known to be plastic.

### Motor Learning

Countless examples could be offered about the plasticity of motor functions, many of which have been reviewed elsewhere (e.g., Nelson, 1999, 2000a; Nelson & Bloom, 1997). Three will suffice. First, Elbert and colleagues (Elbert, Pantev, Wienbruch, Rockstroh, & Taub, 1995)

have reported (using MEG) that the somatosensory cortex representing the fingers of the left hand (used for fine finger board movements) in highly proficient stringed instrument players is larger than (a) the analogous area in the opposite hemisphere representing the right hand (used to bow) and (b) the analogous area in nonmusicians. Similarly, Stewart et al. (2003) reported a study in which musically naive subjects were scanned using functional magnetic resonance imaging (fMRI) before and after they had been taught to read music and play keyboard. When subjects played melodies from musical notation after training, activation was seen in a cluster of voxels within the right superior parietal cortex consistent with the view that music reading involves spatial sensorimotor mapping. Third, Draganski et al. (2004) have recently reported that individuals who had been given 3 months to learn to juggle showed increased neural activation (as revealed by fMRI) bilaterally in the midtemporal area and in the left posterior intraparietal sulcus; importantly, 3 months after this group of jugglers stopped juggling, there was a decrease in activation. There was a dose/response effect between juggling performance and gray matter changes. Finally, nonjugglers over the 6-month period showed no changes in brain activation.

### Visual and Auditory Function

As was the case for motor functions, just a few examples will be provided for adult visual plasticity. First, it has been well established that congenitally blind individuals show activation of the visual cortex when reading Braille or performing other tactile discrimination functions (Lanzenberger et al., 2001; Sadato et al., 1998; Uhl, Franzen, Lindinger, Lang, & Deecke, 1991). Interestingly, a Braille-reading woman blind since birth who subsequently suffered a bilateral stroke of the visual cortex in adulthood lost the ability to read Braille although other somatosensory functions remained intact (Hamilton, Keenan, Catala, & Pascual-Leone, 2000). And, Sadato, Okada, Honda, and Yonekura (2002) have now reported that among Braille-reading individuals who lost their sight *after* age 16, activation of the V1 cortex was absent, whereas such activation was present among those who lost their sight *before* age 16. Such findings are consistent with a sensitive period for visual function. Finally, Finney, Fine, and Dobkins (2001) have reported that deaf individuals show activation of the auditory cortex to visual stimuli.

Collectively, it appears that the somatosensory, visual, and auditory cortices are capable of reorganizing well into adulthood, although there is some hint that there may still be a sensitive period for such reorganization.

### Learning and Memory Function

No area of plasticity has received more attention in the neuroscience literature than that of learning and memory. It has been known for over 30 years, for example, that rats raised in complex laboratory environments (those containing lots of toys and social contacts) perform certain cognitive tasks better than rats reared in isolation (e.g., Greenough, Madden, & Fleischmann, 1972). Looking closely at the brain reveals that (a) several regions of the dorsal neocortex are heavier and thicker and have more synapses per neuron; (b) dendritic spines and branching patterns increase in number and length; and (c) there is increased capillary branching, thereby increasing blood and oxygen volume (for examples of both original findings and overviews, see Black, Jones, Nelson, & Greenough, 1998; Greenough & Black, 1992; Greenough et al., 1972; Greenough, Juraska, & Volkmar, 1979; Kolb & Whishaw, 1998).

Moving up to the systems level of the nervous system, Erickson, Jagadeesh, and Desimone (2000) have reported a study in which multicolored complex stimuli (some familiar, some novel) were presented to monkeys. Neuronal activity was recorded from the perirhinal cortex, an area known to be strongly involved in episodic memory (see later section on memory). After only 1 day of experience viewing the stimuli, performance of neighboring neurons became highly correlated, whereas viewing novel stimuli revealed little correlated neuronal activity. These findings suggest that visual experience leads to functional changes in an area of the brain known to be involved in memory.

Perhaps the most dramatic example of experience-induced changes in the neural architecture underlying memory is the now well-known "London cabdriver study." Here structural MRI scans were obtained from London cabdrivers, all highly expert at navigating the streets of London. The authors (Maguire et al., 2000) reported that the posterior hippocampus (hypothesized to serve as the storage location for spatial representations) of these drivers was larger than in a comparison group. Not surprisingly, there was also a positive correlation between hippocampal volume and the amount of experience the driver had.

Overall, there are now ample data to suggest that learning and memory are correlated with changes in the brain at multiple levels, from changes in pre- and postsynaptic functioning mediated by glutomate receptors to the molar changes at the level of anatomy. There is no sense that there is a sensitive period for learning and memory to occur (for a tutorial on the *development* of learning and memory, see Nelson, 1995, 2000b). Indeed, there is some sense that activities that engage the learning and memory system may confer some protection on lifelong learning and memory function (see Nelson, 2000b, and later for discussion).

### What Are the Effects of Enriched Environments on Brain Development and Function?

Although a great deal is known about the effects of deprivation on brain development and function, very little is known about enrichment. Indeed, in the work on complex environments discussed earlier, such environments, while enriched relative to typical laboratory conditions, are still impoverished relative to real-world environments. Over and above the challenge of defining what is meant by enrichment (e.g., what may be considered enriched in one context may be impoverished in another), there is also the challenge of employing measures that possess the sensitivity to detect such effects. One example of enrichment effects on human brain function can be found in a recent study by Colcombe et al. (2004). These authors have reported that highly aerobically fit older adults or providing aerobic training to older adults who were previously unfit was associated with improved performance on a test of executive function, and with increases in task-related activity in the superior and middle frontal gyrus, the superior parietal lobule, and reduced activity in the anterior cingulate cortex, regions all associated with attentional control. This not only speaks to the plasticity of these cortical regions well into the life span, but also demonstrates that enrichment confers benefits on brain function over and above typical living conditions (in which many older Americans lack cardiovascular fitness).

### What Is the Difference between Development and Plasticity?

At a deep neurobiological level, one might argue that the molecular processes that underlie plasticity (e.g., changes in the neurochemical profile of a synapse, anatomical changes such as growth of an axon or sprouting new dendritic spines) are no different in the developing brain than they are in the mature brain. Once the cellular machinery is in place, it generally operates the same regardless of the age of its container. Similarly, the sprouting of new dendritic spines in response to complex environments may be the same regardless of the age of the brain involved—and the molecular events that underlie changes in dendritic function are also likely the same or vastly similar. However, there are still a number of fundamental differences in the way plastic processes might work in the developing brain and in the developed brain.

First, the local cellular, anatomical, and metabolic environment in which plastic processes operate are vastly different early in the life span versus later in the life span. Thus, the newborn brain has countless more neurons and synapses than an adult brain, and many of these are not yet committed to particular functions. Thus, an axon that is growing toward its target has a very different terrain to negotiate in the newborn brain than in the adult brain. Similarly, modifying already-committed synapses (i.e., rewiring the brain) is quite different from committing synapses to a particular circuit for the first time (i.e., wiring the brain).

An example of this point can be found in a paper by Carleton, Petreanu, Lansford, Alvarez-Buylla, and Lledo (2003). These authors report that the development of the electrophysiological properties of neurons born in adulthood differ from those born pre- or perinatally. For example, spiking activity (the excitability of the cell) was delayed in late-born versus early-born cells; that is, this was not observed until the cell was nearly fully mature. The authors argue that this could be due to the need to make sure the late-born new cell does not interrupt the existing circuit until it is ready to be part of that circuit. Suffice to say, this illustrates a fundamental difference between neurogenesis in the developing brain versus the developed brain.

A second example of this point can be found in the work on postnatal neurogenesis. For example, Gould (2003) has reported that the number of prenatally derived cells tends to be fairly stable across development, with only a slight reduction with aging. In contrast, cells derived in adulthood (see earlier section on postnatal neurogenesis) tend to be massively produced but relatively short-lived (e.g., the adult rodent dentate

gyrus may contain a total of 1.5 million cells, with 250,000 of these being generated anew each month).

Another way to illustrate the difference between developmental versus adult plasticity can be found at a more systems or behavioral level. The goal of infancy is to develop neural circuits in the service of some behavior. In the adult, however, these systems are already in place and must simply be reconfigured for a different, albeit related, purpose such as acquiring a second or third language. Thus, second language learning may in fact be fundamentally different from first language learning because, in the former case, there is already a scaffold on which to build, whereas in the latter case there is not. This example builds on our first point, as second language learning may involve either *re*wiring or extending existing neural circuits to a new, albeit related, domain, whereas learning a first language surely involves new wiring.

There is a third point that illustrates the possible difference between developmental versus adult plasticity: specifically, whether there is a difference between development versus plasticity. Developmental psychologists are familiar with the principles that underlie behavioral change across age. Yet neuroscientists are also aware that the molecular, anatomic, physiologic, and neurochemical changes that underlie changes in behavior generally are likely operating in the background. Thus, if the processes that mediate changes in behavior in general at the cellular/atomical level are the same as those that mediate changes across age, then what is the difference between development and plasticity? We would contend that these terms are fundamentally the same; the difference, however, is that we view plasticity as lifelong, whereas we view development as something that happens over the first 2 (or so) decades of life. If this is true, it then raises the possibility that the plastic processes that exist throughout life may be different from those operating to direct development during the first 2 decades of life (and surely there are differences within this developmental plastic process within this timeframe).

Admittedly, our answer to the question of whether developmental and adult plasticity are different is not fully satisfying; we remain somewhat on the fence, although leaning toward arguing for a difference. It is our hope that a more satisfying answer to this question will be found in the coming years as research in neural plasticity increases. But, it is important to ponder this question as developmental theory gradually becomes more neurobiological in its orientation.

## THE NEURAL BASES OF COGNITIVE DEVELOPMENT

Having laid the foundation for how the human brain develops, we now turn our attention to the neural bases of specific cognitive functions. As is the case with many of the topics targeted for review in this chapter, the reader is encouraged to consult more comprehensive treatises (e.g., de Haan & Johnson, 2003b; Johnson, 2001; Nelson & Luciana, 2001). Also note that because the focus of our discussion is on the *neural bases* of cognitive development, we restrict our discussion to the literature that directly relates a specific cognitive ability to brain development; the basic cognitive developmental behavioral literature is thoroughly reviewed in other chapters contained in this and previous volumes.

### Memory

#### *Why Is Memory Important?*

We begin our discussion of brain and cognitive functions with a discourse about memory and lead with the question of why memory is important.

Memory is a cornerstone ability on which many general cognitive functions are assembled. Our knowledge of the world is predicated on a store of information that is acquired through acts of memory. Thus, it would seem important to delineate the developmental trajectory of this ability, particularly since our understanding of the cognitive and neural processes that underlie intelligence is not well established.

The abilities to encode and subsequently recall information are likely ones that have been conserved across species and have proved reproductively adaptive. Three examples suffice. First, in migratory birds, it is imperative that a bird return to its breeding ground to give birth to and provide care for the next generation. How does a bird remember the location of the breeding ground after many months? Mettke-Hofmann and Gwinner (2003) demonstrated that migrant birds can recall the location of a particular feeding site for 12 months, whereas nonmigrant birds can do so for only 2 weeks. More importantly, among migrant birds, the hippocam-

pus increases in size from the first to the 2nd year of life as the bird reaches sexual maturity, whereas no such increase is observed among nonmigrants. Thus, the ability of the hippocampus to adapt to the bird's environmental niche represents an example of the evolutionary significance of memory.

A similar and equally impressive example of memory can be found in a report by Tomizawa et al. (2003). These authors note that the hormone oxytocin, which has typically been associated with inducing labor and facilitating caregiving behavior, has also been associated with two cognitive functions: social recognition (Ferguson, Aldag, Insel, & Young, 2001; Ferguson et al., 2000) and improved spatial memory (Kinsley et al., 1999). Tomizawa et al. (2003) demonstrated that in hippocampal slices perfused with oxytocin, long-term potentiation (LTP)[3] was facilitated, and among hippocampal slices taken from mice that had previously given birth (and in which no exogenous oxytocin was administered), CREB phosphorylation (the gene expression cascade believed to contribute to memory formation) was increased. Moreover, spatial memory could be improved in mice that had never given birth but were treated with oxytocin. In contrast, an oxytocin antagonist administered to mice who *had* given birth impaired spatial memory.

A final example of the adaptive significance of memory may be found in the observation that the young of many species appear to have a proclivity to attend disproportionately to novelty; indeed, Nelson (2000b) has speculated that (a) this proclivity may be obligatory and ensures that infants continually add to their knowledge base, and (b) this preference for novelty early in life may set the stage for the lifelong facility for memory formation.

In light of the ontogenetic and evolutionary importance of memory, let us turn to what is known about the neural bases of memory. Before addressing this question, a brief tutorial on what we mean by memory is in order.

#### *Memory Systems*

Tulving (1972) opened the door to questioning the prevailing dogma that memory was a unitary trait by proposing that there are two memory systems, which he termed *semantic* and *episodic*. Tulving's argument was

---

[3] Based on Hebbian principles, LTP is thought to reflect one of the molecular mechanisms underlying memory formation.

based on behavioral dissociations, although over the next 30 years this was augmented by experimental work with nonhuman animals and neuroimaging data from human adults. However, perhaps the turning point was the data derived from patient H. M. As Eichenbaum and colleagues discuss, H. M. (who underwent a bilateral resection of the temporal lobes for relief of intractable epilepsy; see Scoville & Milner, 1957, for original report, or Corkin, 2002, for recent report) provided crucially important data to the argument in favor of multiple memory systems (Eichenbaum, 2002; Eichenbaum et al., 1999). For example, although H. M. suffers from a severe deficit in encoding new facts, he can learn new motor skills, although he has no conscious recollection of having done so.

Since Tulving's seminal paper in 1972, countless studies of rodents, monkeys, and humans have collectively pointed to a major dissociation of two types of memory: Explicit or declarative memory, on one hand, and implicit or nondeclarative memory (also sometimes referred to as procedural memory) on the other. The standard definition of the former generally refers to memory for facts and events that can be brought to conscious awareness and that can be expressed explicitly. In contrast, implicit or nondeclarative memory generally refers to the acquisition of skills or procedures that are expressed nonconsciously through motor activity or changes in processing speed. Not surprisingly, there are different types of memory within each of these systems; thus, traditional recognition and recall memory fall under the rubric of explicit memory, whereas both priming and procedural learning fall under the rubric of implicit memory.

Additional evidence for the segregation of these two memory systems can be found in the neuroscience literature. For example, at least in the adult, the explicit memory system appears to involve select neocortical areas (e.g., visual cortex for visual explicit memory), the cortical areas that surround the hippocampus (e.g., entorhinal cortex, parahippocampal gyrus), and the hippocampus proper. In contrast, nondeclarative memory involves circuits specific to the particular type of memory (although the medial temporal lobe tends not to be involved). The acquisition of habits and skills appears to depend on the neostriatal system, whereas sensory-to-motor adaptations and the adjustment of reflexes appear to depend disproportionately on the cerebellum (for recent reviews, see Eichenbaum, 2003).

Like many dichotomies, this distinction between memory systems is not wholly satisfying, as there are many gray areas that fall between and within systems. As Cycowicz (2000) discusses, the distinction between recognition memory (a type of explicit memory) and repetition priming (a type of implicit memory) has more to do with the instructions issued to the subject than anything inherent in memory itself. Thus, in tests of recognition memory, subjects are explicitly asked to identify previously experienced stimuli or events (e.g., by verbal response, pressing a button), whereas in tests of repetition priming, subjects are typically asked to perform an incidental task (e.g., "press button A if the stimulus is oriented normally and button B if the stimulus is inverted"), and priming is inferred by speeded reaction times to previously experienced (albeit often unconsciously) stimuli. In addition, there can be overlap in the neural circuits that underlie each system (e.g., the visual cortex is required in both visual recognition memory and repetition priming for visual stimuli). Still, the field of memory has by and large accepted this distinction, various pitfalls notwithstanding.

### The Development of Memory Systems— Some Background

Drawing on data from both juvenile and mature nonhuman primates, neuropsychological and neuroimaging data with adult humans, and the limited neuroimaging literature with developing humans, Nelson (1995) proposed that explicit qua explicit memory begins to develop some time after the first half year of life, as inferred from tasks such as deferred imitation, cross-modal recognition memory, delayed nonmatch-to-sample (DNMS), modified "oddball" designs in which event-related potentials (ERPs) are recorded, and preferential looking and habituation procedures that impose delays between familiarization (or habituation) and test. As is the case with the adult, this system depends on a distributed circuit that includes neocortical areas (such as the inferior temporal cortical area TE), the tissue surrounding the hippocampus (particularly the entorhinal cortex), and the hippocampus proper. However, Nelson also proposed that the development of explicit memory is preceded by an earlier form of memory referred to as *preexplicit* memory. What most distinguishes preexplicit from explicit memory is that the former (a) appears at or shortly after birth, (b) is most evident in simple novelty preferences (often reflected in the visual paired compar-

**TABLE 1.2   Neural Bases of Memory Development**

| General System | Subsystems | Tasks | Neural Systems Related to Tasks |
| --- | --- | --- | --- |
| Implicit memory (nondeclarative memory) | Procedural learning | Serial reaction time task | Striatum, supplementary motor association, motor cortex, frontal cortex |
| Implicit memory (nondeclarative memory) | Procedural learning | Visual expectation paradigm | Frontal cortex, motor areas |
| Implicit memory (nondeclarative memory) | Conditioning | Conditioning | Cerebellum, basal ganglia |
| Implicit memory (nondeclarative memory) | Perceptual representation system | Perceptual priming paradigms | Modality dependent: parietal cortex, occipital cortex, inferior temporal cortex, auditory cortex |
| Explicit memory system | Preexplicit memory | Novelty detection in habituation and paired comparison tasks | Hippocampus, possibly entorhinal cortex |
| Explicit memory system | Semantic (generic knowledge) | Semantic retrieval, word priming, and associative priming | Left prefrontal cortex, anterior cingulate |
| Explicit memory system | Semantic (generic knowledge) | Semantic retrieval, word priming, and associative priming | Hippocampal cortex |
| Explicit memory system | Episodic (autobiographical) | Episodic encoding | Left prefrontal cortex, left orbitoprefrontal cortex |
| Explicit memory system | Episodic (autobiographical) | Recall and recognition | Right prefrontal, anterior cingulate, parahippocampal gyrus, entorhinal cortex |

ison procedure), and (c) is largely dependent on the hippocampus proper.

These proposals (subsequently updated and elaborated by Nelson & Webb, 2003) were built less on direct visualization of brain-behavior relations than on the integration of data from many sources. This renders the model a useful heuristic, albeit one that would benefit from more data and less speculation. The challenge is that relatively little is known about the development of the circuitry purported to be involved in different memory systems and different types of memory; similarly, there are relatively few investigators using neuroimaging tools of any sort to examine brain-memory relations. Nevertheless, advances over the past decade in the testing of developing nonhuman and human primates have provided much needed additional information.

Table 1.2 summarizes our current thinking about the neural bases of memory development. We focus first on the development of explicit memory, and then turn our attention to implicit memory.

### Current Findings—Explicit Memory in the Mature Brain

Although there is no consensus in the adult literature on the neural circuitry involved in explicit memory, Eichen-

baum's model (2003) is nicely representative of the field, and of our own thinking about development.[4] According to Eichenbaum, the parahippocampal region (composed of the entorhinal, perirhinal, and parahippocampal cortices) is disproportionately involved in mediating the representation of isolated items, and is capable of holding these items in memory for short periods (e.g., several minutes). In contrast, the hippocampus proper appears to play a more prominent role in mediating the relational and representational properties of the stimuli: For example, during the time the parahippocampal region is holding individual items in memory, the hippocampus would be comparing these items to others already in memory; similarly, the hippocampus will be involved in extracting similar information across multiple exemplars or across multiple contexts. Data from studies of human adults and

---

[4] Extending adult models of memory function to infants or children is problematic for many reasons, not the least of which is that we are uncertain about whether the structure-function relations that hold in the adult will hold in the developing child. Nevertheless, it is more useful to begin with the adult configuration and then modify and expand accordingly than to start from the ground up. As attractive as the latter is, there are currently too few studies on brain-memory relations to permit adequate model building.

developing and adult monkeys with select hippocampal lesions indicate that the hippocampus also mediates novelty preferences (e.g., Manns, Stark, & Squire, 2000; McKee & Squire, 1999). Finally, the neocortex is likely the storage site for long-term information, and in the case of the frontal cortex, the site that facilitates storage through mnemonic strategies (e.g., chunking, and so on; for review of the neuroimaging literature on declarative memory, see Yancey & Phelps, 2001).

### Current Findings—Explicit Memory in the Developing Brain

As is the case with studies of the mature organism, it is critical to consider the task being used to evaluate memory in deriving an understanding of what structure or circuit is involved. As discussed by Nelson (1995), Nelson and Webb (2003), and most recently, Hayne (2004), the very same task, used in different ways, could impose different task demands on the subject and recruit different underlying circuitry (see discussion of the DNMS task later in this chapter).

There is now very good evidence from the monkey literature that lesions of the hippocampus lead to disruptions in visual recognition memory, at least under certain circumstances, and at least as inferred from novelty preferences. Pascalis and Bachevalier (1999) have reported that in monkeys, neonatal lesions of the hippocampus (but not amygdala; see Alvarado, Wright, & Bachevalier, 2002) impair visual recognition memory as tested in the Visual Paired Comparison (VPC) procedure, at least when the delay between familiarization and test is more than 10 seconds. Nemanic, Alvarado, and Bachevalier (2004) have reported similar effects in adult monkeys. Specifically, lesions of the hippocampus, perirhinal cortex, and the parahippocampal cortex all impair performance on the VPC, although differentially so. Thus, lesions of the perirhinal cortex, parahippocampal cortex, and hippocampus proper lead to impairments when the delay between familiarization and test exceeds 20 seconds, 30 seconds, and 60 seconds, respectively. These findings are consistent with those from the human adult, where, for example, individuals with known damage to the hippocampus also show deficits in novelty preferences under short delay conditions (McKee & Squire, 1993). Importantly, in the human adult work, the same individuals who hours later fail to show novelty preferences *do* show intact recognition memory (Manns et al., 2000). Moreover, patient Y.R. with selective hip-

pocampal damage shows impairments on the VPC task but relatively intact recognition memory (Pascalis, Hunkin, Holdstock, Isaac, & Mayes, 2004). Together, these results suggest that recognition memory per se may be mediated by *extra-hippocampal* tissue (a point to which we will return), whereas novelty preferences are likely mediated by the hippocampus proper. The monkey data are only partially consistent with this view, as they suggest that the hippocampus *and* surrounding cortex all play a role in novelty preferences, although differentially so, at least in the adult.

Further evidence for the role of the hippocampus in encoding the relations among stimuli (versus encoding individual stimuli, which may be the domain of the parahippocampal region) can be found in a recent paper by A. J. Robinson and Pascalis (2004). These authors tested groups of 6-, 12-, 18-, and 24-month-old infants using the VPC. Rather than evaluate memory for individually represented stimuli, the authors required infants to encode the properties of stimuli in context. During familiarization, stimuli were presented against one background, and during testing the same stimulus, paired with a novel stimulus, was presented against the same or a different background. The authors report that although all age groups showed strong novelty preferences when the background was the same, only the 18- and 24-month-olds showed novelty preferences when the backgrounds were changed. This would suggest that this particular function of the hippocampus—studying the relations among stimuli or encoding stimuli in context— is somewhat slower to develop than recognizing stimuli in which the context is the same.[5] Support for this claim can be found in the developmental neuroanatomy literature. Specifically, although the hippocampus proper, the entorhinal cortex, and the connections between them are known to mature early in life (e.g., Serres, 2001), it is also known that the development of dentate gyrus of the hippocampus matures more slowly (see Serres, 2001), as does the perirhinal cortex (see Alvarado & Bachevalier, 2000). Thus, if Pascalis and colleagues are correct that their context-dependent task is dependent on the hippocampus, then in theory the delayed maturation observed on this task reflects the delayed maturation of

---

[5] In theory, an alternative interpretation of these data is that the backgrounds were more salient to older versus younger infants, and thus, the novelty preferences have more to do with stimulus salience generally than with relational memory qua memory.

some specific region of the hippocampus, such as the dentate gyrus.

This last observation underscores an important point, which is that although explicit memory *emerges* sometime between 6 and 12 months of life, it is far from fully developed by this age. The fact that even very young infants (i.e., a few months of age) do quite well on standard preferential looking paradigms suggests that there is either enough hippocampal function to subserve task performance (as would be inferred from the monkey work performed by Bachevalier and colleagues) *or* that perhaps the parahippocampal region (about which virtually nothing is known developmentally) is mediating task performance. Thus, consistent with the neuroscience literature, the full, adultlike expression of explicit memory awaits the subsequent development of subregions of the hippocampus along with the connections to and from associated neocortical areas.

### Novelty Preferences

Because of the prominent role novelty preferences have played in evaluating memory in infants and young children, it is worth discussing at some length the putative neural bases of such preferences. As stated, we have concluded from monkey data that the hippocampus plays a prominent role in novelty preferences, primarily based on the perturbations observed in such preferences when the hippocampus is lesioned. However, we need not restrict ourselves to data from monkeys. Neuroimaging studies with human adults have also reported that the hippocampus is involved in novelty preferences (see Dolan & Fletcher, 1997; Strange, Fletcher, Hennson, Friston, & Dolan, 1999; Tulving, Markowitsch, Craik, Habib, & Houle, 1996). In contrast, Zola et al. (2000) reported that hippocampal lesions in mature monkeys did not affect novelty preferences at 1-second delays, and thus, that impairment (i.e., decline in performance) at subsequent delays was due to problems in memory, not novelty detection. Similarly, Manns et al. (2000) have shown that among intact human adults, novelty preferences and recognition memory are both intact shortly after familiarization, although with increasing delay novelty preferences disappear, and recognition memory remains intact. This work, coupled with that from Zola et al. (2000), argues for a dissociation between novelty preferences and recognition memory and raises two questions. First, are novelty preferences truly mediated by the hippocampus or perhaps by extra-hippocampal tissue, and second, what does this dissociation say about

the infancy literature in which recognition memory is typically inferred from novelty preferences?

First, it may be unwise to assume that all tasks that tap novelty preferences by default place the same demands on memory. For example, our view is that in tasks that require the subject to generalize discrimination across multiple exemplars of the same category of stimuli (e.g., to distinguish male faces from female faces), novelty preferences may depend on the ability to examine the relations among stimuli, and thus, depend disproportionately on the hippocampus. In contrast, if the task simply requires one to discriminate two individual exemplars (e.g., one female face from another), then perhaps the parahippocampal region is involved. Second, novelty preferences and recognition memory may not represent the same or different processes as much as related ones. Thus, in the VPC procedure, perceptual support is provided by presenting the familiar and novel stimuli simultaneously. In so doing, recognition may be facilitated at very short delays, perhaps due to some iconic store rather than the need to compare the novel stimulus to one stored in memory. This may occur in short-term memory and be supported by the parahippocampal region.

Whereas it is easy to dissociate novelty preferences from recognition memory in children or adults (in whom instructions can be given), the same is not true for infants, particularly when behavioral measures are employed. However, using ERPs, Nelson and Collins (1991, 1992) appeared to dissociate these processes to some degree. Four- through 8-month-old infants were initially familiarized to two stimuli; during the test trials, one of these stimuli was presented on a random 60% of the trials (frequent-familiar), the other on a random 20% of the trials (infrequent-familiar), and on each of the remaining 20% of the trials, a different novel stimulus (infrequent-novel) was presented. In theory, if recognition memory is independent of how often a stimulus is seen (i.e., its probability of occurrence), then all infants should treat the two familiar stimuli as equivalent, regardless of how often they are presented during the test trials. The authors reported that it was not until 8 months that infants responded equivalently to the two classes of familiar events and differently to the novel events. In contrast, at 6 months infants responded differently to the two classes of familiar events and differently yet again to the novel events. These findings were interpreted to reflect an improvement in memory from 6 to 8 months, specifically, the ability to ignore how often a stimulus is seen (inherent in novelty responses) from whether the stimulus is familiar (inherent in recognition memory).

At this point in time, it is difficult to say with certainty whether, in human children, it is the hippocampus or parahippocampal region that subserves novelty preferences and whether novelty preferences reflect a subroutine involved in recognition memory or reflect a proxy for recognition memory per se. These are questions that await further study.

### Delayed Non-Match-to-Sample

What about other tasks that have been thought to reflect explicit memory, such as the DNMS task? Here a subject is presented with a sample stimulus, and following some delay (during which the stimulus cannot be observed), the sample and a novel stimulus are presented side by side. In the case of monkeys, the animal is rewarded for retrieving the novel stimulus; in the case of humans, some investigators implement a similar reward system and essentially adopt the animal-testing model (e.g., see Overman, Bachevalier, Sewell, & Drew, 1993), whereas others have modified the task such that no reward is administered and looking at the novel stimulus rather than reaching for it serves as the dependent measure (see A. Diamond, 1995).[6] In the classic DNMS task, it is generally reported that monkeys do not perform at adult levels until they approach 1 year of age, and performance among children does not begin to resemble adults until they are approximately 4 years of age (assuming the standard 1:4 ratio of monkey to human years, these data are remarkably consistent). Interestingly, Pascalis and Bachevalier (1999) have reported that neonatal lesions of the hippocampus do *not* impair performance on the DNMS task, suggesting that the DNMS likely depends on extra-hippocampal structures and does *not* depend on just novelty preferences (i.e., unlike the VPC task, the DNMS task requires the subject to coordinate action schemes with what is represented in memory, and as well, inhibit a response to the familiar stimulus). Support for this can be found in studies reported by Málková, Bachevalier, Mishkin, and Saunders (2001) and Nemanic et al. (2004), in which lesions of the perirhinal cortex in adult monkeys led to impairments in

visual recognition memory as inferred from the DNMS; importantly, data from the Nemanic et al. (2004) study suggests that lesions of the hippocampus and parahippocampal regions have little effect on DNMS performance. Of note is the observation that these data contradict those reported by other groups (e.g., Zola et al., 2000), where hippocampal lesions in adult monkeys *do* lead to impairments on DNMS performance. Our group has reported hippocampal activation in human adults tested with the DNMS task (Monk et al., 2002). What is to account for these differences? First, it could be that there is a fundamental difference in structure function relations in young versus mature subjects (see footnote 4); thus, the same function could be subserved by a different structure in the developing versus the developed individual. Second, it could mean that the demands of the DNMS task differ (or are interpreted differently) depending on developmental age (e.g., the reward value of reinforcing stimuli could differ; how the child/juvenile monkey interprets the task demands could be different from how the adult/mature monkey interprets the task demands). Third, earlier studies of hippocampal lesions in adult monkeys could have included lesions of the surrounding cortex, thus making it difficult to distinguish between impairments due to the hippocampus or perirhinal cortex.[7] Finally, in the Monk et al. (2002) neuroimaging work, it was difficult to distinguish the hippocampus from adjacent cortex, and therefore, it is possible that the surrounding cortex was most involved in performance on the DNMS task.

### Elicited Imitation

Deferred or elicited imitation is a task that has now received considerable attention by memory researchers. In the case of humans, a sequence of events is modeled, and following some delay, and without benefit of practice, the subject is then presented with the props used in

---

[6] It must be acknowledged that by modifying the task in this way, the task requirements change dramatically, and thus, it is difficult to argue that the two tasks are the same. This makes it difficult to compare across species.

[7] Until approximately the late 1990s, most surgical approaches to lesioning the hippocampus involved going through the surrounding cortex, thereby damaging this region (e.g., entorhinal cortex) and fibers of passage. As a result, it was often difficult to ascertain whether it was lesions of the hippocampus proper that led to perturbations in performance, lesions of the surrounding cortex, or the severing of connections between the hippocampus and surrounding cortex. Recent methodological advances now employ the administration of neurotoxins directly to the targeted structure, destroying cell bodies but leaving fibers of passage intact.

the original sequence. Correct scores are given for the number of steps in the sequence that are correctly "recalled." Used extensively by Bauer and colleagues (see Bauer, Chapter 9, this *Handbook,* this volume), Hayne and colleagues (e.g., Collie & Hayne, 1999; Hayne, Boniface, & Barr, 2000), and Meltzoff and colleagues (e.g., Meltzoff, 1985, 1988, 1995), among others, the prevailing evidence is that there is dramatic improvement in this ability starting at 6 months and continuing through at least 24 months. In this case, improvement is defined as the ability to reproduce longer sequences of objects over increasing delays. Indeed, as infants traverse their first birthday, under certain circumstances memory for temporal order is retained over months.

Of particular relevance to this chapter is a trio of related observations. First, McDonough, Mandler, McKee, and Squire (1995) have reported that human adults with bilateral damage to the medial temporal lobe (including the hippocampus) perform poorly on this task. Similarly, individuals who sustained bilateral hippocampal damage during childhood show impairments on the same task, although interestingly, the impairments are not so severe as those observed in adults by McDonough et al. (1995; Adlam, Vargha-Khadem, Mishkin, & de Haan, 2004). Second, Eichenbaum and colleagues (e.g., Agster, Fortin, & Eichenbaum, 2002; Fortin, Agster, & Eichenbaum, 2002) have reported that rodents trained to remember a sequence of odors show impairments in distinguishing one sequence from another when the hippocampus proper is lesioned. Finally, our group (e.g., DeBoer, Georgieff, & Nelson, in press; de Haan, Bauer, Georgieff, & Nelson, 2000) has demonstrated impairments in elicited imitation in populations of infants presumed to have experienced pre- or perinatal damage to the hippocampus (e.g., those born very prematurely or experiencing hypoxia-ischemia prenatally). Consistent with conclusions drawn by Bauer and colleagues (e.g., Bauer, Wenner, Dropik, & Wewerka, 2000; Bauer, Wiebe, Carver, Waters, & Nelson, 2003; Carver, Bauer, & Nelson, 2000), Nelson (1995) and Hayne (2004), these data would appear to support the view that performance on elicited or deferred imitation tasks depend on the integrity of the hippocampus. However, as recently discussed by Nelson and Webb (2003), like the DNMS task, the elicited imitation task is complex and comprises a collection of subtasks. Infants must encode not just the properties of the objects but as well, the order in which these objects are presented.

Historically, it has long been known that lesions of the frontal cortex perturb the ability to reproduce a sequence of events in the correct order (for review, see Lepage & Richer, 1996). In addition to recalling the sequence in which objects are presented, the participants must also encode the physical actions performed on the objects. Here again, the frontal cortex may be involved; Nishitani and Hari (2000) found that observing and imitating manual actions activated the left inferior prefrontal cortex as well as the premotor cortex and the occipital cortex. The supplementary motor area has also been implicated in motor sequencing and may encode the numerical order of components (Clower & Alexander, 1998). Collectively, although the hippocampus may underlie elements of the elicited imitation task (perhaps the recognition or recall memory of specific components, such as recognizing a familiar object or recalling a familiar sequence; see Carver et al., 2000), other components of the task may be under control of the prefrontal cortex (and presumably the basal ganglia for the coordination of the reaching and memory components). As with much of the developmental literature on memory, further insight into the neural correlates of elicited imitation will have to await our ability to image the brain in action.

### What of the Role of Frontal Cortex in Explicit Memory?

In the context of development, virtually nothing is known about the role of the prefrontal cortex in explicit memory. It is well known in the adult, however, that damage to frontal cortex impairs performance on tasks that require strategies or organizational manipulation (for discussion, see Yancey & Phelps, 2001). The ability to transform, manipulate, or evaluate memories appears to be a distinctly frontal lobe function (see Milner, 1995). In this context, it should not be surprising to learn that frontal lobe damage has little if any effect on recognition memory but can have a dramatic impact on recall memory, presumably because recall involves manipulating and evaluating information. Memory tasks particularly affected by damage to the frontal lobes include *source memory* (e.g., knowing who presented the information or where the information was presented; see Janowsky, Shimamura, & Squire, 1989), *frequency memory* (e.g., which item is presented most or least often; see M. L. Smith & Milner, 1988), and consistent with our discussion of elicited imitation, *memory for temporal order* (e.g., which item was presented most recently; see Butters, Kaszniak, Glisky, Eslinger, & Schacter, 1994). What are the implications of these observations for memory development? In brief, the ability to use strategies to encode and retrieve information and the ability to perform mental operations on the contents of one's memory are skills that develop beginning in the preschool period and continue through the immediate preadolescent period (for review of the development of prefrontal cortical functions, see Luciana, 2003). Not surprisingly, this is a period of rapid development of the prefrontal cortex, including synapse elimination and myelination. Thus, the changes that have been observed in memory across the preschool and elementary school years (for review, see Flavell, Miller, & Miller, 1993; Siegler, 1991) are likely not due to further maturation of medial temporal lobe structures, but rather to maturation of frontal lobe structures and importantly, to increased connectivity between the medial temporal lobe and the prefrontal cortex. With the ability to employ fMRI across this age range, it would be our hope that this tool will one day be applied to test this connectivity hypothesis.

### Summary

Piecing together heterogeneous sources of information, it appears that an early form of explicit memory emerges shortly after birth (assuming a full-term delivery). This *preexplicit* memory is dependent predominantly on the hippocampus. As infants enter the second half of their 1st year of life, hippocampal maturation, coupled with development of the surrounding cortex, makes possible the emergence of *explicit* memory. A variety of tasks have been used to evaluate explicit memory, some unique to the human infant, others adopted from the monkey. Based on such tasks, one observes a gradual improvement in memory across the first few years of life, most likely due to changes in the hippocampus proper (e.g., dentate gyrus), to the surrounding cortex (e.g., parahippocampal cortex), and to increased connectivity between these areas. The changes one observes in memory from the preschool through elementary school years are likely due to changes in prefrontal cortex, and connections between the prefrontal cortex and the medial temporal lobe. Such changes make possible the ability to perform mental operations on the contents of memory, such as the ability to use strategies to encode and retrieve information. Finally, changes in long-term memory are likely due to the development of the

neocortical areas that are thought to store such memories, and the improved communication between the neocortex and the medial temporal lobe (MTL). It is most likely these changes that usher in the end of infantile amnesia (for elaboration, see Nelson, 1998; Nelson & Carver, 1998).

### Disorders of Memory

Recent evidence suggests that bilateral hippocampal damage sustained during childhood can lead to specific impairments in memory, a condition labeled developmental amnesia (Gadian et al., 2000; Temple & Richardson, 2004; Vargha-Khadem et al., 1997).[8] Interestingly, the neuropsychological profile of these cases appears to differ somewhat from the amnesia observed in adults following medial temporal lobe damage. One difference is that, unlike adult amnesiacs who show impairments in both recognition and recall, in at least one intensively studied case of developmental amnesia, delayed recognition memory was relatively preserved, whereas delayed recall was severely impaired (Baddeley, Vargha-Khadem, Mishkin, 2001). A second difference is that, unlike adult amnesiacs who tend to show impairments in both episodic and semantic memory, patients with developmental amnesia tend to show severe impairments in episodic memory with semantic memory remaining fairly intact (Vargha-Khadem et al., 1997).

The reason for this difference in profile between developmental and adult-onset cases remains a matter of debate. One possibility is that the patients with developmental amnesia generally show a milder memory impairment than adult amnesiacs because their damage is more selective. Many of the adult cases reported in the literature have widespread damage including additional areas within the temporal lobe and also extra-temporal brain regions. By contrast, at least within the medial temporal lobe, the perirhinal, entorhinal, and parahippocampal cortices of patients with developmental amnesia appear intact as measured by volumetric analysis (Schoppik et al., 2001). It is possible that these regions normally subserve recognition memory and semantic recall, and their preservation in developmental amnesia allows for a relative preservation of these skills (Vargha-Khadem,

---

[8] Here it must be stressed that in such cases the brain damage is not generally confined to the hippocampus, but rather, is somewhat more diffuse, involving a number of medial temporal lobe structures (such as the rhinal cortex).

Gadian, & Mishkin, 2001). Consistent with this view are reports that adult patients with more selective hippocampal lesions also show some preserved semantic learning (e.g., Verfaellie, Koseff, & Alexander, 2000). However, others have reported that adult patients with lesions reportedly restricted to the hippocampus show a more general memory deficit (e.g., Manns & Squire, 1999) and that a patient with more widespread damage sustained at 6 years of age also showed relatively preserved semantic learning (Brizzolara, Casalini, Montanaro, & Posteraro, 2003). These findings would suggest that age of injury, rather than extent, may be critical. Understanding the separate and combined contribution of the selectivity of damage within the MTL, the degree of extra-hippocampal damage (e.g., abnormalities in the putamen, posterior thalamus, and right retrosplenial cortex are reported in developmental amnesia; Vargha-Khadem et al., 2003) and age of injury will be important questions for future studies.

Interestingly, for early onset injuries the degree of hippocampal damage appears to affect the pattern of memory impairment (Isaacs et al., 2003). Compared with controls, patients with developmental amnesia (average bilateral hippocampal volume reduction of 40%, ranging from 27% to 56%) were impaired on tests of delayed recall, whereas preterm children (average reduction of 8% to 9%, ranging to 23%) showed no deficit in delayed recall (but did show a deficit in prospective memory and route following). These differences cannot be accounted for by general differences in ability level as the groups were matched on IQ. However, the possibility of differences in extra-hippocampal damage, which may vary as a function of degree of hippocampal damage, is not known.

Another possible explanation for the differing profiles between child- and adult-onset cases is that early-onset cases show milder impairments because the plasticity of the developing brain allows for compensation of function. In children with neonatal damage, memory impairments are not typically noted until children are of school age (Gadian et al., 2000). This would appear surprising given that the hippocampus is believed to play a critical role in memory from birth, as discussed earlier. A possible explanation is that there is a degree of compensation that allows relatively good initial memory skills but that ultimately leads to a mild form of memory impairment. A neuroimaging case study has shown that the remaining hippocampal tissue in developmental amnesia appears to be functional during memory tasks (Maguire, Vargha-Khadem, &

Mishkin, 2001). However, while intact individuals showed primarily left hippocampal activation, the patient showed bilateral activation, as well as a different pattern of connectivity of the hippocampus with other brain areas compared to controls (Maguire et al., 2001). It is thus possible that the remaining areas of functioning hippocampus organize with other brain regions to mediate the preserved memory abilities. If this is true, then one might expect that age of injury would affect the ultimate outcome, with early injury leading to better outcome than later injury due to greater plasticity. A recent report does not support this prediction, showing that delayed memory does not differ for children who sustained their injury before 1 year of age and those who sustained injury after 6 years of age (Vargha-Khadem et al., 2003). However, those with earlier lesions performed better than those with later lesions on some tests of immediate memory, suggesting that some plasticity may be operating.

## Nondeclarative Memory

Nondeclarative or implicit forms of learning and memory functions represent an essential aspect of human cognition by which information and skills can be learned through mere exposure or practice, without requiring conscious intention or attention and eventually becoming automatic. Although controversy exists regarding the definition of nondeclarative memory or learning, performance on most nondeclarative tasks does not appear to depend on medial temporal lobe structures. Patients like H. M., mentioned earlier, demonstrate severe deficits in explicit memory consistent with known insults to or disruption of medial temporal lobe memory systems (see Figure 1.3). However, these patients are not impaired on classic tests of implicit memory and learning, such as perceptual priming or serial reaction time (SRT) learning (Milner, Corkin, & Teuber, 1968; Shimamura, 1986; Squire, 1986; Squire & Frambach, 1990; Squire, Knowlton, & Musen, 1993; Squire & McKee, 1993).

A multitude of tasks have emerged in the cognitive literature to assess nondeclarative cognitive functions (see Seger, 1994; Reber, 1993). Reber (1993) proposes making a distinction between two broad categories of nondeclarative function: implicit memory (the end-state representation of knowledge available to an individual, of which he or she is unaware) and implicit learning (the unintentional and unconscious acquisition of

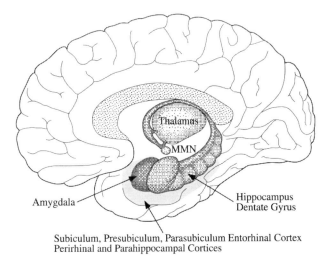

**Figure 1.3**   Diagram of the medial temporal lobe memory system.

knowledge). Implicit learning involves learning of underlying rules and structure in the absence of any conscious awareness of those regularities. Such learning is slow and requires repeated exposure to the information to be retained. In contrast, implicit memory may occur with a single exposure to a stimulus and results in an increased processing efficiency for subsequent presentations of that stimulus or closely related stimuli. Not only do these categories differ in their basic cognitive nature (representation versus acquisition of knowledge), but they seem to differ in their underlying neural substrates as well. In a now well-known classification of memory systems, Squire (1994) identified three primary forms of implicit learning and memory: priming, procedural learning (skills and habits), and classical conditioning (associative learning), each relying on separable neural systems.

### Visual Priming

Evidence for this taxonomy comes from animal and human lesion studies as well as neuroimaging methods. For example, priming, or improvements in detecting or processing a stimulus based on a recent exposure to that stimulus, appears to rely on neocortical brain regions relevant to the stimulus of interest. That is, when healthy adults are presented with a visual stimulus repeatedly, areas of extrastriate visual cortex show decreased activity, presumably reflecting diminished processing requirements when reactivating the sensory circuit (Schacter & Buckner, 1998; Squire et al., 1992).

Similarly, priming in the context of an object classification task is associated with decreased activity in inferior temporal cortex and ventral prefrontal cortex (Buckner et al., 1998), regions previously linked to explicit object identification.

Although a number of studies have examined visual priming performance in infancy and early childhood (Drummey & Newcombe, 1995; Hayes & Hennessy, 1996; Parkin & Streete, 1988; Russo, Nichelli, Gibertoni, & Cornia, 1995; Webb & Nelson, 2001), few have applied brain-imaging methods to examine the brain bases of this function. In general, behavioral evidence overwhelmingly suggests that young children and even infants show priming effects that are very similar to those of adults, supporting the idea that implicit learning and memory functions may show very little developmental change while explicit learning and memory demonstrate protracted development. Webb and Nelson (2001) used ERP measures to assess visual perceptual priming in 6-month-old infants compared with adults. Although developmental differences were observed in ERP components between adults and infants, these differences were similar to differences observed during explicit memory function. However, ERP evidence of memory (an activity difference between new and repeated stimuli) was observed only at an early ERP component typically associated with attention, and not at the late component typically associated with explicit memory (Nelson, 1994; Nelson & Monk, 2001; see DeBoer, Scott, & Nelson, 2004 for review of infant ERP components).

### Implicit Sequence Learning

In contrast to priming, implicit learning—also termed habit learning, skill learning, or procedural learning—involves the slow acquisition of a knowledge base or behavioral skill set over time. In everyday life, learning to ride a bicycle involves the gradual acquisition of a skill that is very difficult or impossible to describe verbally. Although intentionally trying to learn the skill, the learner is typically unaware of what exactly is being learned. Implicit learning has most frequently been tested using sequence learning (e.g., Nissen & Bullemer, 1987) or artificial grammar learning paradigms (Reber, 1993). In the SRT task, individuals are asked to map a set of spatial or object stimuli onto an equal number of response buttons. Reaction times to match the stimulus and the button are recorded. Unknown to the participant, whereas stimuli often appear in random order, at other times, the order of stimulus presentation follows a predictable and repeating sequence. Implicit learning is assumed when participants show reaction time improvements during the sequential trials compared with random trials, despite no conscious awareness of the underlying regularity.

Patients with temporal lobe amnesia perform normally on sequence learning tasks. However, patients with basal ganglia damage, such as those with Parkinson's or Huntington's diseases, have been shown to be impaired on the serial reaction time task (Ferraro, Balota, & Connor, 1993; Heindel, Salmon, Shults, Walicke, & Butters, 1989; Knopman & Nissen, 1991; Pascual-Leone et al., 1993). Importantly, these patients perform normally on measures of explicit memory as well as on measures of perceptual and conceptual priming (Schwartz & Hastroudi, 1991), providing support for the separability of implicit learning and implicit memory at the neural systems level. Neuroimaging data provide supporting evidence for the role of subcortical structures in serial reaction time learning. Common findings across a number of laboratories (Bischoff-Grethe, Martin, Mao, & Berns, 2001; Grafton, Hazeltine, & Ivry, 1995; Hazeltine, Grafton, & Ivry, 1997; Schendan, Searl, Melrose, & Ce, 2003) demonstrate differential activity in frontal—basal ganglia—thalamic circuits for sequential trials compared with random trials. Further evidence suggests that connections among these fronto-striatal loops and fronto-cerebellar loops may be an important aspect of implicit learning. Pascual-Leone et al. (1993) observed that, although adults with basal ganglia insults demonstrated significant reductions in implicit sequence learning, adults with cerebellar degeneration showed no evidence of learning on the SRT task.

Significant controversy exists regarding the developmental trajectory of implicit learning. In a study of SRT learning in 6- to 10-year-old children and adults, Meulemans, van der Linden, and Perruchet (1998) observed equivalent learning of a ten-step spatial sequence across age groups, despite overall reaction time differences with age. These data support the notion that implicit cognition may mature very early in infancy and show little variation or improvement with age (Reber, 1992). However, other measures of implicit pattern learning or contingency learning, as well as SRT data from an alternate group, are less clear. Maybery, Taylor, and O'Brien-

Malone (1995) report age-related improvements in covariation learning, with older children showing larger learning effects than younger children. However, Lewicki (1986) found no evidence of age-related learning effects on the original version of the same task. Similarly, Thomas and Nelson (2001) found that, although the size of the implicit learning effect was similar between 4-, 7-, and 10-year-olds who showed evidence of sequence learning on an SRT task, older children were more likely to show learning. In fact, the probability of significant learning was inversely related to age, with fully one-third of the youngest age group showing no evidence of learning (whereas all 10-year-olds showed a learning effect). Evidence for age-related improvements in implicit sequence learning come from an infant analogue of the SRT task: visual expectancy formation. In this task, infants are shown a repeating pattern of visual stimuli, and eye movements are recorded to determine whether the infant learns to anticipate the location of the upcoming stimuli over time. Although we cannot rule out the possibility that this behavior is explicitly learned, the task has many similarities to the adult SRT paradigm. Interestingly, although infants as young as 2 and 3 months of age can show reliable visual expectancy formation (Canfield, Smith, Brezsnyak, & Snow, 1997; Haith, Hazan, & Goodman, 1988), older infants are able to learn more complicated sequential relationships than younger children (Clohessy, Posner, & Rothbart, 2002; P. Smith, Loboschefski, Davidson, & Dixon, 1997).

In a recent pediatric imaging study of the SRT task, Thomas et al. (in press) compared the neural systems subserving implicit sequence learning in 7- to 11-year-old children and adults. Overall, results from adults were consistent with previous neuroimaging studies implicating fronto-striatal circuitry in visuomotor sequence learning. In particular, activity in the basal ganglia was positively correlated with the size of the implicit learning effect (greater learning was associated with increased activity in the caudate nucleus). Although children and adults showed many of the same regions of activity, relative group differences were observed overall, with children showing greater subcortical activity and adults showing greater cortical activity. Consistent with recent findings from adult SRT studies (Schendan et al., 2003), both adults and children showed activity in the hippocampus despite no explicit awareness of the sequence. This activity is unlikely to be either necessary or sufficient for implicit sequence learning given the adult literature indicating spared performance following lesions to the hippocampus. Instead, this activity may reflect a sensitivity to stimulus novelty, a function of the hippocampus discussed earlier in this chapter. Children showed an inverse pattern of hippocampal activity as compared to adults (random trials elicited greater hippocampal activity than sequence trials for child participants). Interestingly, the SRT task used here produced significant developmental differences in the magnitude of the learning effect, with children demonstrating significantly less learning than adults. Unlike prior behavioral studies, this effect was not driven by a difference in the percentage of nonlearners in the two age groups. Rather, despite significant individual learning in both groups, adults learned to a greater extent with the same degree of exposure.

Finally, some evidence exists to address the effects of basal ganglia insults early in development. Although early insults may lead to lasting impairments in functions subserved by the affected systems, the plastic nature of the developing brain may also allow for redistribution of function to other regions which are unaffected. Structural neuroimaging studies have identified childhood attention-deficit/hyperactivity disorder (ADHD), as well as perinatal complications such as intraventricular hemorrhage as risk factors for disrupted basal ganglia circuitry. Castellanos et al. (2001, 2002) have reported decreases in caudate volume in children with ADHD compared with nonaffected controls. Similarly, functional imaging studies of attentional control (see Executive Functions, later in this chapter) suggest a lack of typical basal ganglia activity in children with ADHD (Vaidya et al., 1999). A recent paper addressing reading disabilities suggests a possible link between reduced motor sequence learning and symptoms of ADHD (Waber et al., 2003). Thomas and colleagues reported evidence of significant decrements in sequence learning for 6- to 9-year-old children diagnosed with ADHD (Thomas, Vizueta, Teylan, Eccard, & Casey, 2003). These authors also examined implicit sequence learning in children with perinatal histories of intraventricular hemorrhage (IVH), or bleeding into the lateral ventricles at birth. Children whose IVH was moderate (bilateral grade II or more severe) evidenced significant decrements in the magnitude of the implicit learning effect. In contrast, children whose perinatal IVH had been relatively mild (unilateral grade II or less severe) showed no difference in learning from a full-term, age- and gender-matched control group. Together, these studies suggest a potential long-term deficit in implicit learning resulting from early insults to basal ganglia circuitry.

### Conditioning or Associative Learning

In contrast to priming and implicit sequence learning, the existing knowledge regarding the brain bases of conditioning derives largely from animal studies. In conditioning paradigms, the subject learns the contingency between two previously unrelated stimuli through either association with a cue or signal (classical conditioning) or an outcome or reward (instrumental conditioning). Studies of classical eyeblink conditioning in rabbits have implicated the cerebellum and its connections to brain stem nuclei (particularly the interpositus nucleus) as key regions necessary for normal conditioning to occur (Woodruff-Pak, Logan, & Thompson, 1990). Lesions of either of these structures can completely prevent acquisition of the conditioned response, while lesions of the cerebrum have no effect on either acquisition of the response or its maintenance (Mauk & Thompson, 1987). The hippocampus also is not required for classical delay eyeblink conditioning. Patients with temporal lobe amnesia show normal performance on delay conditioning paradigms (Woodruff-Pak, 1993) whereas those with lesions of the lateral cerebellum are severely impaired in acquiring the conditioned eye-blink response (Woodruff-Pak, Papka, & Ivry, 1996). In contrast, emotional fear conditioning (pairing a neutral stimulus with a shock) appears to rely heavily on the amygdala (LaBar, Gatenby, Gore, LeDoux, & Phelps, 1998; Pine et al., 2001).

Developmentally, newborn infants (10 days old) are able to acquire a conditioned eyeblink response. Therefore, like implicit sequence learning, the basic mechanism supporting conditioned responding must be present and functional at birth, although this in no way implies that its function is fully mature. Developmental improvements are observed in conditioning paradigms. For example, with age, children can handle longer and longer delays between the neutral signal and the unconditioned stimulus (Orlich & Ross, 1968). Such developmental effects might be expected given the very protracted maturational trajectory of the cerebellum (Keller et al., 2003). Much less is known regarding the development of the amygdala response in fear conditioning. Similarly, although significant behavioral research has been conducted addressing instrumental conditioning in infancy (Rovee-Collier, 1997a), relatively little is known regarding the brain systems underlying this form of learning.

Rovee-Collier (1997b) and colleagues have observed increases in the retention duration for conditioning with age. That is, older children remember the contingencies for longer periods than younger children do (Hartshorn et al., 1998). Few, if any, studies have examined the brain bases of this form of learning in childhood.

## SPATIAL COGNITION

Spatial cognition refers to a range of abilities involved in perceiving, remembering, and mentally manipulating spatial relations and orientation at several scales including features of a single object, objects and their context, and oneself in space.

### Mental Rotation

Mental rotation is a form of visual imagery involving ". . . the imagined circular movement of a given object about an imagined pole in either 2 or 3 dimensional space" (Ark, 2002, p. 1). In adults, the superior parietal lobe appears to be involved in the actual act of imaginary rotation, as it is not only active during mental rotation tasks but its extent of activation is related to reaction time (Richter et al., 2000; Richter, Ugurbil, Georgopoulos, & Kim, 1997). Activations in visual area MT (M. S. Cohen et al., 1996) and motor and premotor areas in the frontal cortex (Johnston, Leek, Atherton, Thacker, & Jackson, 2004; Richter et al., 2000; Windischberger, Lamm, Bauer, & Moser, 2003) have also been observed in some, but not all, studies. These activations suggest that some of the processes involved in mental rotation overlap with processes involved in actual physical rotation of a stimulus: MT activation occurs when subjects observe objects moving, and premotor and motor areas are activated when subjects physically move objects. In support of this idea, one study demonstrated bilateral premotor activation during mental rotation of pairs of hands but only left premotor activation during mental rotation of tools (Vingerhoets, de Lange, Vandemaele, Delbaere, & Achten, 2002). This pattern suggests that participants were using motor imagery and imagined moving both hands in the hand condition and imagined using and/or moving the tools with their preferred (right) hand in the tool condition (Vingerhoets et al., 2002).

Between 8 and 12 years of age, children's mental rotation abilities become adultlike in several respects (e.g., nature of errors, relation of reaction time to degree of rotation; see Dean, Duhe, & Green, 1983; Waber,

Carlson, & Mann, 1982). This is consistent with evidence that the parietal lobe begins to obtain adultlike status at about 10 to 12 years of age (Giedd et al., 1999). Neuroimaging studies comparing activation in children and adults confirm that parietal areas are activated in 8- to 12-year-old children as in adults (Booth et al., 1999, 2000; Chang, Adleman, Dienes, Menon, & Reiss, 2002; Shelton, Christoff, Burrows, Pelisari, & Gabrieli, 2001). Parietal areas are activated during mental rotation tasks regardless of individual differences in ability level (Shelton et al., 2001). However, differences between children and adults in the overall pattern of activation have been noted. For example, in one study, adults and 9- to 12-year-olds were asked to mentally rotate a letter or number from one of four different rotations to its upright position and then to determine whether it was forward or backward (Booth et al., 2000). Both age groups showed similar overall levels of performance and showed the typical pattern of increasing reaction time and errors with increasing degree of rotation. Despite the similarities in behavioral performance, adults showed more activation in the superior parietal and middle frontal areas, whereas children showed more activation in the supramarginal gyrus. The authors suggest that this may reflect strategy differences, with adults engaging in more mental rotation and children engaging in more processing of the noncanonical orientations of the letters and numbers. The idea that the neural processes underlying mental rotation may differ even when performance is equated is echoed in results of electroencephalogram (EEG) studies, in which greater parietal activation was reported in 8-year-old boys than girls during 2-D mental rotation despite similar levels of behavioral performance (Roberts & Bell, 2002).

It is possible that some of the differences observed between children and adults are related not to developmental change in mental rotation abilities per se, but to failure to match on gender. In adults, differences in brain areas activated during mental rotation have been noted between men and women (Roberts & Bell, 2002). Even when performance is equated, women tend to show more bilateral activation and men more right-lateralized activation in parietal regions (Jordan, Wustenberg, Heinze, Peters, Jäncke, 2003); women also tend to show greater activation in frontal regions (Thomsen et al., 2000; Weiss et al., 2003).

Consistent with neuroimaging results in children, which have reported bilateral parietal activation, both right and left hemisphere lesions in children appear to impair performance on mental rotation tasks (Booth et al., 2000). Adults tested in those neuroimaging studies also showed bilateral activation, although other studies have reported evidence for either left or right lateralization (Harris & Miniussi, 2003; Roberts & Bell, 2002, 2003; Zacks, Gilliam, & Ojemann, 2003). Children with unilateral lesions showed activations in similar regions as healthy children and adults, but only in the intact hemisphere (Booth et al., 2000).

## Spatial Pattern Processing

Spatial analysis involves the ability both to segment a pattern into a set of constituent parts and to integrate these parts into a coherent whole (Stiles, Moses, Passarotti, Dick, & Buxton, 2003). In adults, the left inferior temporal gyrus and parts of the left fusiform gyrus are more active than the homologous right hemisphere during pattern segmentation (local processing), while the homologous areas in the right are more active than those in the left during pattern integration (global processing; Martinez et al., 1997). In addition, occipito-parietal regions in the area of the intraparietal sulcus, particularly on the right, are active during both types of task, with larger areas activated during pattern integration than segmentation (Martinez et al., 1997; Sasaki et al., 2001). This latter finding is consistent with the zoom lens analogy of selective attention: Attention to local features activates cortical foveal representations, whereas attention to global aspects activates peripheral areas (Sasaki et al., 2001). Studies of adult patients with brain damage have revealed parallel results, with pattern integration being linked to right hemisphere damage and pattern segmentation to left hemisphere damage (Delis, Roberston, & Efron, 1986).

Behavioral studies indicate that processing of global information develops more quickly than processing of local information, with both types reaching adult levels by 14 years of age. Roe, Moses, and Stiles (1999) tested children aged 7 to 14 years using hierarchical stimuli and found that, while the left visual field advantage for global levels appeared sooner than the right visual field advantage for local levels, both are present in adultlike form by age 14 (but see Mondloch, Geldart, Maurer, & de Schonen, 2003). There appears to be a gradual emergence of the left hemisphere bias for local levels of forms between 7 and 14 years of age.

In children, neuroimaging studies have shown that areas similar to those activated in adults are activated in typically developing 12- to 14-year-olds performing spatial processing tasks (Moses et al., 2002). Specifically, children, like adults, showed faster reaction time to global than to local stimuli in the left visual field/right hemisphere but the reverse pattern of reaction time to stimuli in the right visual field/left hemisphere; they also showed the adultlike pattern of lateralized occipito-temporal activation for the two tasks. However, not all children displayed this mature pattern. A subgroup of children failed to show the expected lateral differences in the split-visual field task and also showed no task-related lateral differences during the fMRI study, only a generally greater right-hemisphere activation during both types of task (Moses et al., 2002). The authors suggest that this pattern indicates that a greater degree of brain lateralization is linked to a greater degree of skill or more mature abilities.

With respect to brain lesions, several studies of pediatric patients with right or left hemisphere damage confirm the importance of these areas for global and local processing respectively. When children are shown hierarchical forms and asked to reproduce them, children with left hemisphere injury have difficulty reproducing local elements, whereas children with right hemisphere lesions have difficulty reproducing the global structure (adults: Delis et al., 1986; children: Stiles, Bates, Thal, Trauner, & Reilly, 1998); these impairments persist to school age. By contrast, children as young as 4 can reproduce both levels accurately (Dukette & Stiles, 1996). On other tasks such as block construction and copying and memory for complex figures, children with either type of lesion show delays. And, even when children eventually produce relatively accurate constructions, the strategies they use to produce them are often simplified and more representative of those seen in typically developing children at a younger age.

While damage to the developing brain can produce a pattern of deficit similar to that seen in adults, these effects may be less pronounced and show more improvement with time than in adults. While performance on block construction and complex pattern memory are clearly delayed, children eventually can produce accurate responses. To investigate the brain bases of this plasticity, Stiles, Moses, Roe, et al. (2003) investigated two children with frank parietal lesions and white matter loss more posteriorly, one with right hemisphere involvement and one with left hemisphere involvement. During tasks requiring pattern segmentation and integration, patients showed lateralization of activity to the contralesional hemisphere, suggesting that the intact hemisphere can take on some abilities normally subserved by the damaged one.

Children initially seem to show bilateral activation during both global and local processing, and pediatric patients with unilateral lesions appear to be able to use a single hemisphere to process both types of pattern; these facts seem at odds with other findings suggesting that hemispheric biases in spatial processing are already apparent very early in life. For example, 8-month-olds tend to process configural aspects more than featural aspects of faces (e.g., Schwarzer & Zauner, 2003), and by a similar age they show a right-hemisphere bias in the processing of faces (de Haan & Nelson, 1997, 1999; de Schonen & Mathivet, 1990) but not objects (de Haan & Nelson, 1999). More direct evidence comes from studies in which the sensitivity of the right versus the left hemisphere to featural/local changes compared with configural changes has been assessed by split visual field presentation with infants. These studies also suggest that the left visual field/right hemisphere is more sensitive to global changes while the right visual field/left hemisphere is more sensitive to local changes (Deruelle & de Schonen, 1991, 1995).

The bilateral activation seen in some young children during both local and global processing may reflect less a lack of hemisphere bias and more an immature pattern in which task difficulty demands recruiting all available resources for the task at hand. Similarly, when patients with unilateral lesions are presented with these tasks, they devote all their limited resources to complete them. With development, in this view there is increasing specialization such that improved performance is related to recruitment of a smaller set of brain areas that are able to perform a particular task most efficiently (Johnson, 2001; Stiles, Moses, Roe, et al., 2003). In other words, there is a selective recruitment of resources rather than a recruitment of all available resources. Experience with processing the different types of stimuli is thought in part to drive this process. In support of this view, neuroimaging studies with adults have shown that perceptual learning is associated with an increased efficiency in the brain areas activated as expertise is acquired (Gauthier, Tarr, Anderson, Skudlarski, & Gore, 1999).

**Visuospatial Working Memory**

Working memory is the "moment to moment monitoring, processing and maintenance of information" (Baddeley

& Logie, 1999, p. 28). It "allows humans . . . to maintain a limited amount of information in an active state for a brief period of time and to manipulate that information" (E. E. Smith & Jonides, 1998, p. 12061). For adults, the number of items is estimated at 1 to10 over a time span of 0 to 60 seconds (E. E. Smith & Jonides, 1998).

Working memory is often divided into three components: the central executive that controls and regulates the working memory system, and two domain-specific slave systems responsible for processing information in the phonological (phonological loop) or visuospatial (visuospatial sketchpad) forms (Baddeley, 1986; Baddeley & Hitch, 1974).

Visuospatial working memory improves with age into adolescence (e.g., Luciana & Nelson, 1998). What drives these changes? One factor that is known to be related to improvements in visuospatial working memory is phonological encoding. From about 8 years of age, children increasingly use verbal strategies during visual memory tasks (e.g., object memory); improvements in phonological encoding facilitate use of this strategy (Pickering, 2001a). However, this cannot completely account for developmental changes in visuospatial working memory as there are also developmental changes on tasks that are more purely visuospatial (e.g., Isaacs & Vargha-Khadem, 1989). These changes may be due to (a) changes in knowledge base, (b) changes in strategy, (c) changes in processing speed, and (d) changes in attentional focus (reviewed in Pickering, 2001a).

With respect to neural substrates, studies with adults show that a frontoparietal network (especially on the right) plays an important role in visuospatial working memory. There may also be a dorsal-ventral distinction in frontal areas for visual versus spatial processing (Ruchkin, Johnson, Grafman, Canoune, & Ritter, 1997; Sala, Rama, & Courtney, 2003). This has been studied mainly for visuospatial working memory, but there is some evidence for activation of similar pathways during audiospatial working memory tasks (Martinkauppi, Rama, Aronen, Korvenoja, & Carlson, 2000; though single-cell studies suggest different but parallel populations of neurons are involved, Kikuchi-Yorioka & Sawaguchi, 2000). The visual superior posterior parietal and premotor areas may be involved in rehearsal (that can reactivate rapidly decaying contents of the storage component), while inferior posterior parietal and anterior occipital regions may mediate storage (whose contents decay rapidly). A frontoparietal network also appears to be involved in children, and in this gross anatomical sense, there are similarities between children and adults (Casey et al., 1995; Kwon, Reiss, & Menon, 2002; Nelson, Lin, et al., 2000; Thomas et al., 1999; Zago & Tzourio-Mazoyer, 2002). However, there are also changes that occur with development. Older children show higher activation in the superior frontal and intraparietal cortex than younger children. Working memory capacity is significantly correlated with brain activity in these same regions (Klingberg, Forssberg, & Westerberg, 2002; Kwon et al., 2002), suggesting that increases in working memory with age are related to increases in activation in these regions. Regions thought to underlie the phonological loop are activated during spatial tasks (Kwon et al., 2002).

These studies collectively suggest that increases in working memory are associated with increases in activation in the frontoparietal network. One question that arises is whether this represents mainly the maturation or coming online of the frontoparietal network. In support of this view, diffusion tensor imaging studies in children suggest that developmental increases in gray matter activation in frontal and parietal cortices could be due to maturation of white matter connections (Olesen, Nagy, Westerberg, & Klingberg, 2003). However, studies with adults also show increased activity in these areas with improvements in working memory following training (Olesen, Westerberg, & Klingberg, 2004). These results show that increased activity in these areas can also occur as a result of experience and practice. The extent to which the increases in activation in the working memory network seen in adults following training and during normal development reflect similar or different mechanisms requires further investigation. In children, diffusion tensor imaging studies suggest that developmental increases in gray matter activation in frontal and parietal cortices could be due to maturation of white matter connections (Olesen et al., 2003). Thus, there is evidence of increased activation of the working memory network with increases in age and working memory abilities.

The developmental increases in working memory performance coincide with the timing of several neurodevelopmental processes, including a decrease in synaptic density (Bourgeois & Rakic, 1993), axonal elimination (LaMantia & Rakic, 1990), changes in global cerebral metabolism (Chugani & Phelps, 1986), myelination (Paus et al., 1999), and changes in catecholamine receptor structure and density. The inferior parietal cortex is one of the last areas to myelinate, a change that would

increase transmission locally within parietal cortex and also its communication with frontal cortex. This could result in more stable frontoparietal activity during working memory delays and cue periods, and thus less resistance to interference (Klinberg et al., 2002). Synaptic pruning and axonal pruning could also result in less competition with input from other areas, leaving the frontoparietal network more stable.

Several developmental disorders also implicate a frontoparietal network in visuospatial working memory. With respect to lesions, right frontal cortex damage at 7 years has been related to impairments in visuospatial working memory (Eslinger & Biddle, 2000). Turner's syndrome (a sex chromosome disorder affecting girls, in which one of the two X chromosomes is missing) is associated with deficits in visuospatial working memory (Cornoldi, Marconi, & Vecchi, 2001; Haberecht et al., 2001). In Turner's syndrome, imaging studies show decreased activation in the supramarginal gyrus, dorsolateral prefrontal cortex, and the caudate nucleus, with a suggestion that these abnormalities in frontoparietal and frontostriatal circuits are related to poor working memory performance (Haberecht et al., 2001). Individuals with fragile X syndrome are also known to have impairments in visuospatial working memory and appear to be unable to modulate activation in the prefrontal and parietal cortex in response to an increasing working memory load. These deficits may be related to a lower level of FMRP expression in individuals with fragile X syndrome compared with typical subjects (Kwon et al., 2001).

**Visuospatial Recognition and Recall Memory**

In addition to the frontoparietal network implicated in spatial processing and working memory, medial temporal lobe structures, particularly in the right hemisphere, have been implicated in visuospatial memory in adults. The question of whether a similar hemispheric bias exists in children has been investigated in neuropsychological studies of children with unilateral temporal lobe epilepsy. In one study, children who had either early (0 to 5 years) or later (5 to 10 years) onset of seizures were tested with visual and verbal tasks; children with early-onset epilepsy performed generally poorly, whereas children with later onset showed a material-specific pattern of deficit (Lespinet, Bresson, N'Kaoua, Rougier, & Claverie, 2002). Two other studies investigating children following temporal lobectomy noted that visuospatial deficits were both pronounced and persistent (Hepworth

& Smith, 2002; Mabbott & Smith, 2003). These results suggest that hemispheric biases (left verbal, right visuospatial) develop at some point after 5 years of age.

## Spatial Navigation

The ability to remember locations and routes in the visual environment relies on both body-centered (e.g., ocentric) and environment-centered (allocentric) spatial information. In adults, the hippocampus appears to be involved in spatial memory (Astur, Taylor, Mamelak, Philpott, & Sutherland, 2002; Nunn, Polkey, & Morris, 1998), particularly with respect to allocentric spatial memory (Abrahams, Pickering, Polkey, & Morris, 1997; Holdstock et al., 2000; Incisa della Rocchetta et al., 2004). It has been suggested that the hippocampus is involved in the consolidation of allocentric information into long-term memory, rather than the initial encoding of allocentric spatial information (Holdstock et al., 2000).

A case study of a patient with perinatal selective hippocampal damage also shows deficits in allocentric spatial processing. This patient was tested in a virtual reality town and showed a massive additional impairment when tested from a shifted viewpoint compared with a mild, list length-dependent impairment when tested from the original viewpoint (King, Burgess, Hartley, Vargha-Khadem, & O'Keefe, 2002). The same patient was impaired on all topographical tasks on a second virtual reality study and on his recall of the context-dependent questions. In contrast, he showed normal recognition of objects from the virtual town, and of topographical scenes (Spiers, Burgess, Hartley, Vargha-Khadem, & O'Keefe, 2001). These results suggest a relative lack of developmental plasticity following hippocampal lesions, at least with respect to allocentric spatial encoding.

## OBJECT RECOGNITION

### Face/Object Recognition

Among the numerous visual inputs that we receive each moment, the human face is perhaps one of the most salient. The importance of the many signals it conveys (e.g., emotion, identity, direction of eye gaze), together with the speed and ease with which adults typically process this information, are compelling reasons to suppose that there may exist brain circuits specialized for pro-

cessing faces. Neuropsychological studies provided the first evidence to support this view, with reports of double dissociation of face and object processing. That is, there are patients who show impaired face processing but relatively intact general vision and object processing (with the occasional exception of color vision; reviewed in Barton, 2003), and other patients who show the opposite pattern of deficit (e.g., Moscovitch, Winocur, & Behrmann, 1997). These studies also hinted that damage to the right hemisphere might be necessary for the face-processing impairments to be observed. More recently, ERP, MEG, and fMRI methods have been used to identify the pathways involved in face processing in the intact brain. These studies have confirmed and extended findings from brain-injured patients, indicating that a distributed network of regions in the brain mediate face processing: occipito-temporal regions are important for the early perceptual stages of face processing, with more anterior regions, including areas of the temporal and frontal cortices and the amygdala, involved in processing aspects such as identity and emotional expression (Adolphs, 2002; Haxby, Hoffman, & Gobbini, 2002). In this section, we focus mainly on the involvement of occipito-temporal cortex and the amygdala, as these are the areas for which the most developmental data are available.

### Occipito-Temporal Cortex

In adults, a network including the inferior occipital gyrus, the fusiform gyrus, and the superior temporal sulcus is important for the early stages of face processing (Haxby et al., 2002). In this view, the inferior occipital gyrus is primarily responsible for early perception of facial features, while the fusiform gyrus and the superior temporal sulcus are involved in more specialized processing (Haxby et al., 2002). In particular, the fusiform gyrus is thought to be involved in the processing of invariant aspects of faces (such as the perception of unique identity), whereas the superior temporal sulcus is involved in the processing of changeable aspects (such as perception of eye gaze, expression, and lip movement; Haxby et al., 2002; Hoffman & Haxby, 2000).

Perhaps the most intensively studied of these regions is an area of fusiform gyrus labeled the fusiform *face area* (Kanwisher, McDermott, & Chun, 1997; Puce, Allison, Asgari, Gore, & McCarthy, 1996). This region is more activated to faces compared with other objects or body parts (Kanwisher et al., 1997; Puce et al., 1996).

Although some investigators have argued against the view of face-specific patches of cortex and have instead emphasized the distributed nature of the representation of object feature information over the ventral posterior cortex (Haxby et al., 2001), even these authors acknowledge that the response to faces appears unique in certain ways (e.g., extent of activation, modulation by attention; Ishai, Ungerleider, Martin, & Haxby, 2000).

Although these studies appear to suggest that particular regions of cortex are devoted specifically to face processing, this interpretation has been questioned. In particular, it has been argued that the supposed face-specific cortical areas are not specific to faces per se, but instead are recruited for expert-level discrimination of complex visual patterns, whether faces or other classes of objects (R. Diamond & Carey, 1986; Gauthier et al., 1999). In this view, the mechanisms active during development of face processing could be the same as those observed in adults learning an equally challenging visual perceptual task. In support of this view, studies have shown that the fusiform face area is also activated by nonface objects (e.g., cars) if the subjects are experts with that category (Gauthier, Skudlarski, Gore, & Anderson, 2000), and activation in the fusiform face areas increases following training of expertise with a category of visual forms (Gauthier et al., 1999).

Developmental studies can provide important information to constrain the claims of the different sides of this debate. For example, by studying when and how face-specific brain responses emerge, developmental studies can provide some hints as to whether and how much experience might be needed for these responses to emerge. Behavioral studies provide a suggestion that face-processing pathways may be functional from very early in life: newborn babies move their eyes, and sometimes their heads, longer to keep a moving facelike pattern in view than several other comparison patterns (Johnson, Dzuirawiec, Ellis, & Morton, 1991). While there is a debate as to whether this reflects a specific response to facelike configurations or a lower-level visual preference (e.g., for patterns with higher density of elements in the upper visual field, see Turati, Simion, Milani, & Umilta, 2002; see also Banks & Ginsburg, 1985; Banks & Salapatek, 1981), there is some agreement among the divergent views that the ultimate result is that facelike patterns are preferred to other arrangements from the first hours to days of life.

While this might seem to support the notion that face-specific cortical areas are active from birth, the prevailing view is that this early preferential orienting to faces is likely mediated by subcortical mechanisms (e.g., superior colliculus; for a review of the evidence, see Johnson & Morton, 1991), and that cortical mechanisms do not begin to emerge until 2 to 3 months of age. At this early age, cortical areas are thought to be relatively unspecialized (Johnson & Morton, 1991; Nelson, 2001). One possible role of the earlier-developing subcortical system is to provide a "face-biased" input to the slower-developing occipito-temporal cortical system, and to provide one mechanism whereby an initially more broadly tuned processing system becomes increasingly specialized to respond to faces during development (Johnson & Morton, 1991; Nelson, 2001).

The only functional neuroimaging study to investigate face processing in human infants confirms that occipito-temporal cortical pathways are involved by 2 to 3 months of age. In this study, 2-month-olds' positron emission tomography (PET) activation in the inferior occipital gyrus and the fusiform gyrus, but not the superior temporal sulcus, was greater in response to a human face than to a set of three light diodes (Tzourio-Mazoyer et al., 2002). These results demonstrate that areas involved in face processing in adults can also be activated in infants by 2 months of age, although they do not address the question of whether these areas are specifically activated by faces rather than by other visual stimuli. It is interesting that the superior temporal sulcus, suggested to be involved in the processing of information relevant to social communication, was not activated in this study. One possible explanation is that the stimuli (static and neutral) were not optimal for activating processing in the superior temporal sulcus. However, the observation that activation in the superior temporal sulcus has been found in adults even in response to static, neutral faces (e.g., Kesler-West et al., 2001) argues against this interpretation. It is possible that the superior temporal sulcus plays a different role in the face-processing network in infants than in adults, since in primates its connectivity with other visual areas is known to differ in infants compared with adult monkeys (Kennedy, Bullier, & Dehay, 1989).

Event-related potential studies support the idea that cortical mechanisms are involved in face processing from at least 3 months of age. However, these studies also suggest that when cortical mechanisms become involved in infants' processing of faces, they are less "tuned in" to faces than is the mature system. Two studies have shown that face-responsive ERP components are more specific to human faces in adults than in infants (de Haan, Pascalis, & Johnson, 2002; Halit, de

Haan & Johnson, 2003). In adults, the N170, a negative deflection over occipito-temporal electrodes that peaks approximately 170 ms after stimulus onset, is thought to reflect the initial stage of the structural encoding of the face. Although the location in the brain of the generator(s) of the N170 remains a matter of debate, it is generally believed that regions of the fusiform gyrus (Shibata et al., 2002), the posterior inferior temporal gyrus (Bentin et al., 1996; Shibata et al., 2002), lateral occipito-temporal cortex (Schweinberger, Pickering, Jentzsch, Burton, & Kaufman, 2002), and the superior temporal sulcus (Henson et al., 2003) are involved. The N170 is typically of larger amplitude and/or has a longer latency for inverted than upright faces (Bentin et al., 1996; de Haan et al., 2002; Eimer, 2000; Itier & Taylor, 2002; Rossion et al., 2000), a pattern that parallels behavioral studies showing that adults are slower at recognizing inverted than upright faces (Carey & Diamond, 1994). In adults, the effect of inversion on the N170 is specific for human faces and does not occur for inverted compared with upright exemplars of nonface object categories (Bentin et al., 1996; Rebai, Poiroux, Bernard, & Lalonde, 2001; Rossion et al., 2000), even animal (monkey) faces (de Haan et al., 2002).

Developmental studies have identified two components, the N290 and the P400, believed to be precursors of the N170. Both components are maximal over posterior cortex, with the N290 peaking at about 290 ms after stimulus onset and the P400 about 100 ms later. The N290 shows an adultlike modulation of amplitude by stimulus inversion by 12 months of age: inversion increases the amplitude of the N290 for human but not monkey faces (Halit et al., 2003). The P400 has a quicker latency for faces compared with objects by 6 months of age (de Haan & Nelson, 1999) and shows an adultlike effect of stimulus inversion on peak latency by 12 months of age: It is of longer latency for inverted than upright human faces but does not differ for inverted compared with upright monkey faces (Halit et al., 2003). At 3 and 6 months, the N290 is unaffected by inversion; and the P400, while modulated by inversion, does not show effects specific to human faces (de Haan et al., 2002; Halit et al., 2003). Overall, these findings suggest that there is a gradual emergence of face-selective response over the first year of life (and beyond). This finding is consistent with results of a behavioral study showing a decrease in discrimination abilities for nonhuman faces with age; 6-month-olds can discriminate between individual humans and monkeys, whereas 9-month-olds and adults tested with the *same*

procedure discriminate only between individual human faces (Pascalis, de Haan, & Nelson, 2002). The results also suggest that the structural encoding of faces may be dispersed over a longer time in infants than in adults. It is possible that, as the processes become more automated, they are carried out more quickly and/or in parallel rather than in serial fashion.

Interestingly, the spatial distribution of the N170 and P400 both change from 3 to 12 months, with maxima shifting laterally for both components (de Haan et al., 2002; Halit et al., 2003). In addition, the maxima of these components appear more superior than in adults, a result consistent with studies in children finding a shift from superior to inferior maximum of the N170 with age (Taylor, Edmonds, McCarthy, & Allison, 2001). This might reflect a change in the configuration of generators underlying these components with age.

Investigations with older children also support the view of a gradual specialization of face processing. ERP studies suggest that there are gradual, quantitative improvements in face processing from 4 to 15 years of age rather than stagelike shifts (Taylor, McCarthy, Saliba, & Degiovanni, 1999). The ERP studies also provide evidence that there is a slower maturation of configural than featural processing: Responses to eyes presented alone matured more slowly than responses to eyes presented in the configuration of the face (Taylor et al., 2001). There have not been many functional imaging studies of face processing during childhood, but one study examining facial identity processing suggests that changes in the network are activated in 10- to 12-year-olds compared with adults (Passarotti et al., 2003). Children showed a more distributed pattern of activation compared with adults. Within the fusiform gyrus, children tended to show more activation in lateral areas of the right hemisphere than did adults: In the left hemisphere, children showed greater lateral than medial activation, whereas adults showed no difference for the two areas. In addition, children showed twice as much activation of the middle temporal gyrus as adults. The authors interpret these results as suggesting that increased skill is associated with a more focal pattern of activation.

Studies of children with autistic spectrum disorders support the view that atypical activation of occipito-temporal cortex is related to impairments in face processing. Autistic spectrum disorders are characterized by impairments in processing of social information, including faces. Functional imaging studies indicate that when individuals with autism or Asperger syndrome view faces, they show a diminished response in the fusiform gyrus compared with controls (Hubl et al., 2003; Pierce, Muller, Ambrose, Allen, & Courchesne, 2001; Schultz et al., 2000) and show an increased activation of object-processing areas in the inferior temporal cortex (Hubl et al., 2003; Schultz et al., 2000). It is possible that this reflects a different processing strategy in which individuals with autism focus more on featural rather than configural information in the face. In other words, individuals with autism may rely more on general purpose object-processing pathways rather than specialized face-processing pathways when viewing faces.

## Amygdala

The amygdala is a heterogeneous collection of nuclei located in the anterior temporal lobe. Several studies in adults have shown that lesions to the amygdala impair emotion recognition, even when they leave other aspects of face processing intact (e.g., identity recognition; Adolphs, Tranel, Damasio, & Damasio, 1994). Lesion studies also indicate that recognition of fearful expressions is particularly vulnerable to such damage (Adolphs et al., 1994, 1999; Broks et al., 1998; Calder et al., 1996). Functional imaging studies in healthy adults and school-age children complement these findings, with some studies showing that the amygdala responds to a variety of positive, negative, or neutral expressions (Thomas et al., 2001; Yang et al., 2002), and other studies suggesting that the amygdala is particularly responsive to fearful expressions (Morris et al., 1996; Whalen et al., 2001).

There is indirect evidence that the amygdala plays a role in processing facial expressions in infants. Balaban (1995) used the eye-blink startle response (a reflex blink initiated involuntarily by sudden bursts of loud noise) to examine the psychophysiology of infants' responses to facial expressions. In adults, these reflex blinks are augmented by viewing slides of unpleasant pictures and scenes, and they are inhibited by viewing slides of pleasant or arousing pictures and scenes (Lang, Bradley, & Cuthbert, 1990, 1992). Consistent with the adult findings, Balaban found that 5-month-old infants' blinks were augmented when they viewed angry expressions and were reduced when they viewed happy expressions, relative to when they viewed neutral expressions. As animal studies indicate that the fear potentiation of the startle response is mediated by the amygdala (Davis,

1989; Holstege, van Ham, & Tan, 1986), these results suggest that by 5 months of age, portions of the amygdala circuitry underlying the response to facial expressions may be functional.

Interestingly, there is evidence that early damage to the amygdala may have a more pronounced effect on recognition of facial expression than damage sustained later in life. For example, in one study of emotion recognition in patients who had undergone temporal lobectomy as treatment for intractable epilepsy, emotion recognition in patients with early, right mesial temporal sclerosis, but not those with left-sided damage or extratemporal damage, showed impairments on tests of recognition of facial expressions of emotion but not on comparison tasks of face processing (Meletti et al., 2003). This deficit was most pronounced for fearful expressions, and the degree of deficit was related to the age of first seizure and epilepsy onset.

## Role of Experience

The preceding studies suggest that the cortical system involved in face processing becomes increasingly specialized for faces throughout the course of development. Several developmental theories propose that experience is necessary for this process of specialization to occur (e.g., Nelson, 2001). Only a few studies have directly examined the role of experience in development of face processing. In one series of studies, the face-processing abilities of patients with congenital cataracts who were deprived of patterned visual input for the first months of life were tested years after this period of deprivation. These patients show normal processing of featural information (e.g., subtle differences in the shape of the eyes and mouth), but show impairments in processing configural information (i.e., the spacing of features within the face; Le Grand et al., 2001; Geldart, Mondloch, Maurer, de Schonen, & Brent, 2002). This pattern was specific to faces in that both featural and configural aspects of geometric patterns were processed normally (Le Grand et al., 2001). Moreover, when patients were examined whose visual input had been restricted mainly to one hemisphere during infancy, it was found that visual input to the right hemisphere, but not the left hemisphere, was critical for an expert level of face processing to develop (Le Grand, Mondloch, Maurer, & Brent, 2003). These studies suggest that visual input during early infancy is necessary for the normal development of at least some aspects of face processing.

Another way in which the role of experience has been investigated is by studying children who experience atypical early emotional environments. For example, Pollak and colleagues have found that perception of the facial expression of anger, but not other expressions, is altered in children who are abused by their parents. Specifically, they report that, compared with nonabused children, abused children show a response bias for anger (Pollak, Cicchetti, Hornung, & Reed, 2000), identify anger based on less perceptual input (Pollak & Sinha, 2002), and show altered category boundaries for anger (Pollak & Kistler, 2002). These results suggest that atypical frequency and content of their emotional interactions with their caregivers result in a change in the basic perception of emotional expressions in abused children.

### Is There a Visuospatial Module?

There are different perspectives regarding whether visuospatial processing is mediated by a specific module in the brain. According to the innate modularity view, the cognitive modules observed in adults are genetically specified and are already present from the beginnings of development. This view predicts that, even early in development, one or more modules can be impaired without affecting other modules. Williams syndrome, together with another developmental disorder called Specific Language Impairment (SLI), provides support for this view. In Williams syndrome, language is a strength despite lowered intellect; in SLI, language is impaired despite normal intellect. The double dissociation of language and general intellect across the two developmental disorders is taken by some to support the view that there is a language module that can be selectively spared or impaired. Also consistent with this view is the finding that LIMK1 hemizygosity in Williams syndrome is related to impaired visuospatial constructive cognition (Frangiskakis et al., 1996).

An opposing view is that the brain is not initially organized into distinct modules and only becomes so during development as an emergent property of both biological maturation and experience in the environment. One piece of evidence in support of this view is that the cognitive profile of Williams syndrome is not constant over development. Whereas adults and older children with Williams syndrome show a strength in verbal skills and weakness in number skills, infants show the opposite pattern (Paterson, Brown, Gsodl, Johnson, & Karmiloff-Smith, 1999). This finding is incompatible

with the innate modularity view that certain modules are impaired or intact from the start, since it shows that early abilities do not necessarily predict later ones.

Advocates of the innate modularity view might argue that there could still be innate modules, because face processing has been noted as a strength even from early in life in Williams syndrome. Moreover, adults with Williams syndrome can achieve near normal performance on standardized tests of face recognition. Could this be an intact innate module? Proponents of the interactive specialization view suggest that, if so, face recognition should be accomplished by the same cognitive mechanisms as in typically developing individuals. However, several studies show this is not the case. Individuals with Williams syndrome appear to rely less than typically developing children on cues from the configuration of features in the face to recognize identity (Deruelle, Mancini, Livet, Casse-Perrot, & de Schonen, 1999). In addition, their ERPs show atypical patterns within the first several hundred milliseconds of processing (Grice et al., 2001.). Together, these results argue against the view that the cognitive strengths in Williams syndrome reflect the operation of intact, specific modules.

## EXECUTIVE FUNCTIONS

Most high-level cognitive functions involve executive processes, or cognitive control functions, such as attention, planning, problem solving, and decision making. These processes are largely voluntary (as opposed to automatic) and are highly effortful. Such functions, including selective and executive attention, inhibition, and working memory, are hypothesized to improve with age and practice, and to vary with individual differences in motivation or intelligence. These cognitive control processes have been described as providing a "supervisory attention system" (Shallice, 1988)—a system for inhibiting or overriding routine or reflexive behaviors in favor of more controlled or situationally appropriate or adaptive behaviors. Desimone and Duncan (1995) describe this system as an attentional bias that provides a mechanism for attending to relevant information by simultaneously inhibiting irrelevant information (Casey, Durston, & Fossella, 2001). The ability to override a dominant response or ignore irrelevant information is critical in everyday life, as evidenced by the functional impairments associated with chronic inattention, behavioral impulsivity, or poor planning and decision making.

Classic lesion cases, such as the famous case of Phineas Gage, indicate that injury to the prefrontal cortex can result in difficulties in behavioral regulation, such as impulsivity and socially inappropriate behavior (Fuster, 1997), as well as disruptions in planning, working memory, and focused attention. Cognitive developmentalists will recognize these same functions as showing relatively protracted behavioral maturation, often not reaching adult levels of performance until late adolescence (Anderson, Anderson, Northam, Jacobs, & Catroppa, 2001). It is therefore not surprising that prefrontal cortex shows one of the longest periods of development of any brain region (A. Diamond, 2002; Luciana, 2003, for reviews). In fact, the relations between prefrontal cortex development and the development of executive functions is probably one of the clearest relations in the developmental cognitive neuroscience literature. However, this does not imply that we fully understand the instantiation of attention, working memory, or inhibition in the brain. Instead, we have significant evidence from lesion and neuroimaging methods to relate subregions of prefrontal cortex to specific aspects of cognitive control in adulthood, as well as a growing body of literature addressing the normative and atypical function of these regions, and their connected networks of structures, in the development of cognitive control. For reasons of space, only illustrative examples from normative behavioral development, animal models, adult and pediatric neuroimaging studies, and atypical developmental populations are provided here (Casey, Durston, et al., 2001; A. Diamond, 2002; Luciana, 2003).

## Domains of Executive Function

Many researchers have identified working memory and behavioral inhibition as the primary functions of prefrontal cortex, and by extension, the basic components of executive function (e.g., A. Diamond, 2001). Working memory has typically been associated with dorsolateral prefrontal cortex (DLPFC; J. Cohen et al., 1994; Fuster, 1997; Levy & Goldman-Rakic, 2000), while more ventral regions have been implicated in inhibition of a prepotent behavioral response (Casey, Trainor, Orendi, et al., 1997; Kawashima et al., 1996; Konishi et al., 1999). Other investigators have parsed their definition of executive functions somewhat differently in an effort to include the voluntary and effortful aspects of atten-

tional control as well as response inhibition. Whatever scheme is used, it is apparent that the classic executive function tasks involve more than one of the preceding aspects of voluntary control or regulation. In the following sections, we provide examples of behavioral tasks thought to tap various aspects of executive function across development, as well as provide select examples that evidence the role of specific regions of prefrontal cortex in supporting cognitive control. Of course, prefrontal cortex does not act in isolation. Other brain regions are assumed to be integral to the executive function system, providing input and feedback, as well as receiving inputs from prefrontal cortex. Developmental improvements in executive function may arise as much from the development of such functional integration as from the architectural and physiological development of prefrontal cortex (Anderson et al., 2001; Anderson, Levin, & Jacobs, 2002).

## Working Memory Revisited

Perhaps the task most clearly associated with both child development and prefrontal cortex is the classic A-not-B task. In this paradigm (or its close cousin, the delayed response task), an infant or animal watches an object being hidden at one of two identical locations, and after some delay is rewarded for retrieving the object. This task requires both holding information in mind across a delay and, on subsequent trials when the hiding location changes, inhibiting a prepotent tendency to return to a previously correct response location (A. Diamond, 1985). Animal lesion studies support the importance of DLPFC in successful performance on the A-not-B and delayed response tasks (A. Diamond & Goldman-Rakic, 1989; Fuster & Alexander, 1970; Goldman & Rosvold, 1970). In addition, electrophysiological studies indicate that cells in this region actively respond during the delay interval, suggesting that DLPFC is involved in the maintenance of information in working memory (Funahashi, Bruce, & Goldman-Rakic, 1989; Fuster & Alexander, 1971). Further investigation demonstrates that lesions to this region impair performance only under delay conditions and not during immediate object retrieval (A. Diamond & Goldman-Rakic, 1989). Functional imaging studies suggest that developmental differences in working memory function, at least in middle childhood, may be reflected in less efficient or less focal activation of DLPFC. That is, pediatric fMRI studies have demonstrated that children activate similar regions of DLPFC compared with adults during both verbal and spatial working memory tasks, but also may activate additional areas of prefrontal cortex, including ventral lateral regions (VLPFC; Casey et al., 1995; Nelson, Lin, et al., 2000; Thomas et al., 1999).

## Inhibitory Control

Although working memory has been associated with dorsolateral regions of the prefrontal cortex, the ability to inhibit inappropriate behaviors has typically been associated with ventral medial or orbital frontal cortex (Casey, Trainor, Orendi, et al., 1997; Konishi et al., 1999). In adults, lesions to ventral prefrontal cortex lead to impulsive and socially inappropriate behavior (Barrash, Tranel, & Anderson, 1994; Damasio, Grabowski, Frank, Galaburda, & Damasio, 1994). One common developmental measure of response inhibition is the go/no-go paradigm. In this task, children are asked to respond to every stimulus *except* one (e.g., all letters except X). The task is designed such that the majority of trials are "go" trials, building up a compelling behavioral response tendency. The child's ability to refrain from making the response at the occurrence of the "no-go" stimulus is used as an index of inhibitory control. Performance on such tasks has been shown to improve across the preschool and school-age years (Casey, Durston, et al., 2001; Ridderinkhof, van der Molen, Band, & Bashore, 1997). Neuroimaging studies using the go/no-go paradigm have demonstrated signal increases in ventral PFC during periods high in inhibitory demand (Casey, Forman, et al., 2001; Casey, Trainor, Orendi, et al., 1997), with correspondingly lower levels of activity during periods of low inhibitory demand. Konishi et al. (1999) observed increased ventral PFC activation during no-go trials in an event-related fMRI paradigm. Recent pediatric neuroimaging studies have demonstrated both developmental differences in activation of ventral prefrontal cortex (Bunge, Dudukovic, Thomason, Vaidya, & Gabrieli, 2002), with children showing reduced signal compared with adults, and increasing activation of ventral lateral PFC with increasing inhibitory load (Durston, Thomas, & Yang, 2002). Durston and colleagues (2002) showed that behavioral performance on the go/no-go task was significantly correlated with activity in inferior frontal cortex, as well as other prefrontal regions, including the anterior cingulate gyrus (ACC).

Importantly, these same studies highlight the importance of regions beyond the prefrontal cortex. In particular, basal ganglia structures have also been shown to be involved in response inhibition (e.g., Luna et al., 2001), perhaps particularly so for children (Bunge et al., 2002; Casey, Trainor, Orendi, et al., 1997; Durston et al., 2002). Children with ADHD show significantly lower activity in basal ganglia regions during performance of a go/no-go task than typically developing children (Durston et al., 2003; Vaidya et al., 1998) and show high rates of false alarms on the task. In a recent study, children with ADHD showed additional recruitment of dorsolateral PFC not observed for the control group who performed at a high rate of accuracy (Durston et al., 2003). Interestingly, when taking medication to treat their inattention and impulsivity, children with ADHD show basal ganglia activity equivalent to the typically developing group along with parallel improvements in behavioral performance (Vaidya et al., 1998). Other developmental disorders, such as Tourette syndrome, obsessive-compulsive disorder, and childhood-onset schizophrenia also have been associated with disruption of frontal-striatal circuitry (connections between basal ganglia and frontal cortex) and impaired performance on tasks involving attentional control.

## Attentional Control

Beyond the general processes of working memory or inhibition, many real-world and experimental tasks require selectively focusing attention on relevant task information while simultaneously suppressing interference from salient but irrelevant or misleading information (Casey, Durston, et al., 2001). Perhaps the most studied adult task of this type is the color-word Stroop paradigm, in which participants are asked to identity the color of ink in which a word is written but, in the case of a color word, have to inhibit a natural tendency to read the word instead (e.g., the word "BLUE" presented in red ink). Neuroimaging data from the Stroop paradigm identify medial prefrontal cortex, specifically the anterior cingulate cortex, as particularly important in detecting (e.g., Botvinick, Braver, Barch, Carter, & Cohen, 2001; Bush et al., 1999; Bush, Luu, & Posner, 2000; Duncan & Owen, 2000; Fan, Flombaum, McCandliss, Thomas, & Posner, 2003; MacDonald, Cohen, Stenger, & Carter, 2000; Posner & Petersen, 1990) and perhaps even resolving this type of attentional conflict.

DLPFC and other regions of prefrontal cortex may also be activated during cognitive conflict depending on demands of the specific task. In the Simon task, a spatial conflict is created between the location of a stimulus (left or right side of the screen) and the required response (left or right button; Gerardi-Caulton, 2000). In a study by Fan et al. (2003), this conflict was associated with activation of superior frontal gyrus as well as anterior cingulate cortex, while conflict in the Stroop task was associated with activity in ventral lateral prefrontal cortex. When the same adult participants performed the Eriksen flanker task, which requires focusing attention on a central stimulus and actively ignoring competing flanking stimuli, these authors observed attention-related activity in premotor cortex. Despite these task-related differences in MR signal, further analyses demonstrated overlapping regions of activity in the anterior cingulate gyrus and the left prefrontal cortex across all three tasks, suggesting some common activity related to cognitive control or management of cognitive conflict (Fan et al., 2003). Other neuroimaging studies of the Eriksen flanker task have indicated that prefrontal cortex is differentially activated based on the degree of cognitive conflict within the same task (Casey et al., 2000; Durston et al., 2003). Recently, Durston and colleagues (2003) found that parametric manipulations of conflict on the flanker task were associated with monotonic increases in both DLPFC and ACC. Of course, additional brain regions are activated beyond the prefrontal cortex, such as the superior parietal cortex, perhaps related to the spatial nature of the task. Applying the concept of a "spotlight of attention" (Posner & Raichle, 1997), the flanker task requires narrowing the spatial distribution of attentional focus to reduce interference or conflict from the irrelevant flanking stimuli. Activation of superior parietal cortex may be related to this spatial feature of the task (also see Orienting, later in this chapter).

Behaviorally, the cognitive control tasks previously described show significant developmental changes across early and middle childhood, and in some cases, even into adolescence. Casey, Durston, and Fossella (2001) provide developmental data demonstrating that, for tasks such as the Eriksen flanker and Stroop, adultlike performance is not achieved until early adolescence. A. Diamond (2002) has shown similar trajectories for Stroop-like tasks including the Simon task, with evidence of protracted development. Rueda and colleagues (2004) showed evidence of increased cognitive conflict in 6- and 7-year-olds com-

pared with 8- to 10-year-olds and adults. Despite a significant literature demonstrating developmental improvements in cognitive control across early and middle childhood, fewer studies have addressed the brain bases of this development. A. Diamond (2001) has shown that children with presumed functional disruptions of prefrontal cortex (children treated for phenylketonuria or PKU) are impaired on their performance of Stroop-like and inhibitory control tasks like the go/no-go task, suggesting that typical developmental function is relying on this brain region that is continuing to develop across childhood. Similar effects on other executive function tasks have also been observed in this population (Luciana, Sullivan, & Nelson, 2001). Likewise Casey, Tottenham, and Fossella (2002) have demonstrated that children with psychiatric disorders associated with frontal-striatal circuitry show specific impairments on tests of cognitive conflict. Children with obsessive-compulsive symptomatology showed deficits when required to inhibit a well-learned response set, but no impairment in a Stroop-like task. In contrast, children with diagnoses of childhood onset schizophrenia were impaired on the Stroop-like task but not on the response selection task or on a go/no-go inhibition task, suggesting potential differences within prefrontal cortex.

A related aspect of cognitive control arises when the individual is required not only to ignore irrelevant information, but also to shift among multiple rules for responding. The classic adult task of this type is the Wisconsin Card Sorting Task (WCST), in which participants must discover the sorting rule simply on the basis of binary feedback received during card-sorting performance. Healthy adults show rapid acquisition of the initial sorting rule and quickly alter their behavior if and when the rule is changed. Lesions to the left DLPFC but not other regions of prefrontal cortex impair performance on switching tasks, resulting in perseverative errors (Keele & Rafal, 2000; Owen et al., 1993; Shallice & Burgess, 1991). Neuroimaging studies provide convergent evidence for the role of DLPFC and basal ganglia circuits in task switching and reversal learning (Cools, Clark, & Robbins, 2004; Cools, Clark, Owen, & Robbins, 2004).

Perhaps not surprisingly, typically developing 3-year-old children perform very similarly to adults with frontal lobe lesions. Zelazo et al. (1996) have described a dramatic developmental shift in set-switching performance in the preschool years using the dimensional card sorting task. This task requires the child to first sort cards by one criterion (e.g., shape), and then to shift and sort the cards by another criterion (e.g., color). While 3-year-olds have no trouble sorting by the first criterion, whether it is shape or color, they frequently fail to shift their sorting behavior when the criterion changes despite being able to verbalize the rule, reminiscent of some patients with prefrontal cortex damage (REF). However, 5-year-olds generally have no difficulty with this task. Kirkham and colleagues have suggested that this developmental shift is predominantly the result of improved inhibitory control (A. Diamond, Kirkham, & Amso, 2002).

The developmental neuroimaging data in this domain are still sparse, although a number of groups are working in this direction. Additional work will be needed to assess developmental changes in the recruitment and efficiency of prefrontal cortex in such cognitive conflict or cognitive control tasks. It remains to be seen whether the normal developmental pattern of functional brain activity engages the same circuits known to be disrupted in adult lesion populations with executive dysfunctions.

## NONEXECUTIVE ASPECTS OF ATTENTION

The previously discussed concepts of attentional control and cognitive conflict, while well-studied in adult populations, are more difficult to apply to the earliest periods of development. Although tasks such as the A-not-B or delayed response fall under the broad rubric of executive functions, the majority of research on infants' attention involves more basic processes, such as maintaining an alert state, and orienting to stimuli in the environment. While these functions can involve voluntary or controlled processes (Posner & Raichle, 1997), often they reflect automatic or obligatory responses. Not unlike the memory literature discussed previously, the various forms of attention have been associated with somewhat separable brain systems (Posner & Raichle, 1997).

### Alerting, Vigilance, or Arousal

One major function of the attentional system is to maintain alertness or vigilance (also called arousal). Vigilance processes allow the brain to prepare for upcoming stimuli that may require decision making and/or a behavioral response. Alertness or arousal is associated with improved behavioral performance in a nonspecific or unfocused way (Posner & Raichle, 1997). Although researchers have proposed various neural mechanisms

subserving arousal, one common view of arousal is Posner's alerting model, identifying regions of right frontal and parietal cortices and the norepinephrine system as critical players in vigilance (Lewin et al., 1996). In this model, alertness leads to quieting of other activity in the brain through the release of norepinephrine (NE) from the locus coeruleus. The presence of NE is hypothesized to bring on the state of alertness by enhancing the signal-to-noise ratio in regions where it is acting. As alerting-related activity in right frontal cortex increases, activity in the anterior cingulate cortex, a region associated with target detection decreases. Posner suggests that this decrease in activity is important for the brain to reduce potential sources of interference during the waiting period prior to the appearance of a target stimulus (Posner & Raichle, 1997). Arousal or sustained attention is associated with decreases in heart rate, both in adults and in infants, reflecting activity of cardioinhibitory centers in the brain, particularly in orbitofrontal cortex (Richards, 2001). Using heart rate measures as an index of the brain's arousal system, Richards and colleagues have demonstrated developmental improvements in sustained attention over the first 6 months of life (Casey & Richards, 1988; Richards, 1994). Likewise, certain components of the ERP in infancy are thought to reflect automatic alerting responses, particularly in response to novel stimuli (Courchesne, 1978). ERP studies of the response to familiar and novel events in 6-month-olds show that the early negative component (Nc) typically elicited by stimulus novelty is enhanced during periods of sustained attention (as indexed by heart rate deceleration), compared with periods of attention termination (Richards, 1998). However, Richards found that, during sustained attention, the Nc component did not differentiate among familiar and novel stimuli. Instead, a later component, the positive slow wave (PSW), was enhanced to familiar but infrequently occurring stimuli (Richards, 1998), suggesting that this basic alerting function may modulate the brain response to stimulus novelty, as might be expected behaviorally.

### Orienting

The third arm of the Posner model of attentional networks is the orienting network. Posner describes both overt and covert forms of orienting, or attentional shifting in adults (Posner & Raichle, 1997; Posner, Walker, Friedrich, & Rafal, 1984). When a cue stimulus flashes in the periphery, adults tend to automatically shift eye gaze to the periphery (overt attention shift). In contrast, a centrally presented stimulus can cue the individual to either overtly orient (by shifting eye gaze to fixate) or covertly orient (by shifting attention without shifting eye gaze). Therefore, in adults, centrally presented cues allow the individual to choose to orient in a controlled manner, whereas peripheral cues tend to elicit automatic orienting responses. An extensive neuropsychological literature implicates parietal cortex in the ability to orient attention (e.g., Posner et al., 1984). Adults with parietal lesions show a deficit in the ability to disengage attention from one stimulus in order to shift attention elsewhere. Single cell recordings in animals suggest that cells in the thalamus and parietal cortex show increased activity during covert shifts of attention (D. Robinson, Bowman, & Kertzman, 1995). Lesions in other brain regions can mimic the unilateral behavioral neglect observed with parietal lesions, but do not appear to disrupt covert orienting (Posner et al., 1984). Functional imaging studies of covert orienting in adults show activity in superior parietal cortices, particularly contralateral to the direction of attention (Corbetta, Kincade, Ollinger, McAvoy, & Shulman, 2000). However, in contrast to the inability to disengage observed with parietal lesions, damage to the midbrain visual system (superior colliculus) involved in saccadic eye movements leads to difficulty in moving between stimuli, a separate step in visual orienting (Rafal, Posner, Friedman, Inhoff, & Bernstein, 1988). Finally, damage to the pulvinar (part of the thalamus) yields difficulties in reengaging attention or amplifying the target location once a movement has been made (Danziger, Ward, Owen, & Rafal, 2001).

Several major developments occur in visual orienting behavior that are assumed to reflect development of the brain systems supporting orienting in adults. Around 1 month of age, once infants are able to voluntarily fixate on a stimulus, infants experience a period of obligatory looking, during which they stare fixedly at objects and may have difficulty disengaging their fixation. This obligatory looking can be distressing when a baby becomes fixated on strong visual stimuli, such as high-contrast checkerboard patterns, but is very adaptive for forming social bonds when the baby is fixated on the caregiver's face. Obligatory looking disappears around 4 months of age when infants develop more voluntary control of their orienting (Posner & Raichle, 1997), presumably reflecting development of the orienting network of brain regions. The developmental trajectory of orienting behavior has been examined most often using the inhibition of return paradigm. Inhibition of return refers to the tendency to avoid returning attention to a location just previously attended. Adult studies by Rafal, Calabresi, Brennan, and Scioloto (1989) indicate that inhibition of return occurs only in situations in which an eye movement is prepared, even if the actual movement is never made. Studies of infants 3, 4, 6, 12, and 18 months of age showed that, although 6- to 18-month-olds showed inhibition of return equivalent to adults, 3- and 4-month-olds showed no evidence of inhibition of return (Clohessy, Posner, Rothbart, & Vecera, 1991; Johnson, Posner, & Rothbart, 1994). This age coincides with behavioral evidence of the development of saccadic eye movements, as well as PET evidence of the age at which parietal metabolism reaches adult levels (Chugani, Phelps, & Mazziotta, 1987). Hood et al. (1998) have demonstrated that 4-month-olds can show evidence of covert orienting, however. When a cue is too short in duration to elicit an eye movement, 4-month-olds show improved performance for targets presented at the cued location (Hood, Atkinson, & Braddick, 1998). The importance of the development of the abilities to disengage, shift, and reengage attention is probably obvious to developmental psychologists. These abilities are critical for learning new information from our environments—perceptual, cognitive, social, and emotional—and impairments in this system result in significant problems in everyday life.

## THE FUTURE OF DEVELOPMENTAL COGNITIVE NEUROSCIENCE

Based on our extensive review of the literature, the field of developmental cognitive neuroscience has clearly advanced since the fifth edition of the *Handbook* was published. We know a considerable amount about the neural bases of a variety of cognitive abilities, although our knowledge base is uneven both between and within developmental periods. We know more about the neural bases of memory in infancy than we do in childhood, and we know more about some executive functions than others (e.g., working memory versus planning).

What does the future hold for those interested in this area? For starters, as our knowledge of brain development improves, our ability to ground behavior in the brain should similarly improve. This, in turn, should permit establishing more biologically plausible models of behavioral development (connectionist models, in particular, should benefit from this advance). Second, as our knowledge of neural plasticity and molecular biology increases, we will do a better job of designing studies that shed light on which behaviors are derived from experience-dependent versus experience-independent processes. This, in turn, should lead us away from strongly held nativist beliefs, at least in the context of higher-level cognitive functions. Third, we anticipate a judicious increase in the study of clinical populations, as such study has the potential to provide converging information on typical development. Fourth, given increased interest in using neuroimaging tools to study affective development, we anticipate increased interest in linking cognitive and emotional development in the context of brain development. Fifth, increased attention will be paid to the coregistration of imaging modalities, particularly ERPs with fMRI and optical imaging. Sixth, as investigators gain more experience in conducting fMRI studies with children, and as physicists and engineers improve MR scanning parameters, the field should experience a downward shift in the age at which such studies can be performed. Scanning infants will always prove difficult, but scanning preschool-age children may prove less challenging.

These are just a few of the areas of growth we anticipate in the coming decade—others will surface as the field evolves. But, we remain optimistic that interest in linking brain with behavior in the context of development is now firmly entrenched in developmental psychology.

# REFERENCES

Abrahams, S., Pickering, A., Polkey, C. E., & Morris, R. G. (1997). Spatial memory deficits in patients with unilateral damage to the right hippocampal formation. *Neuropsychologia, 35,* 11–24.

Adlam, A., Vargha-Khadem, F., Mishkin, M., & de Haan, M. (2004). *Deferred imitation in developmental amnesia.* Manuscript submitted for publication.

Adolphs, R. (2002). Recognizing emotion from facial expressions: Psychological and neurological mechanisms. *Behavioural and Cognitive Neuroscience Reviews, 1,* 21–61.

Adolphs, R., Tranel, D., Damasio, H., & Damasio, A. (1994). Impaired recognition of emotion in facial expressions following bilateral damage to the human amygdala. *Nature, 372,* 669–672.

Adolphs, R., Tranel, D., Hamann, S., Young, A. W., Calder, A. J., Phelps, E. A., et al. (1999). Recognition of facial emotion in nine individuals with bilateral amygdala damage. *Neuropsychologia, 37,* 1111–1117.

Agster, K. L., Fortin, N. J., & Eichenbaum, H. (2002). The hippocampus and disambiguation of overlapping sequences. *Journal of Neuroscience, 22,* 5760–5768.

Aizawa, H., Hu, S.-C., Bobb, K., Balakrishnan, K., Ince, G., Gurevich, I., et al. (2004). Dendrite development regulated by CREST, a calcium-regulated transcriptional activator. *Science, 303,* 197–202.

Alvarado, M. C., & Bachevalier, J. (2000). Revisiting the maturation of medial temporal lobe memory functions in primates. *Learning and Memory, 7*(5), 244–256.

Alvarado, M. C., Wright, A. A., & Bachevalier, J. (2002). Object and spatial relational memory in adult rhesus monkeys is impaired by neonatal lesions of the hippocampal formation but not the amygdaloid complex. *Hippocampus, 12,* 421–433.

Anderson, V., Anderson, P., Northam, E., Jacobs, R., & Catroppa, C. (2001). Development of executive functions through late childhood and adolescence in an Australian sample. *Developmental Neuropsychology, 20*(1), 385–406.

Anderson, V., Levin, H., & Jacobs, R. (2002). Executive functions after frontal lobe injury: A developmental perspective. In D. Stuss & R. Knight (Eds.), *Principles of frontal lobe function* (pp. 504–527). New York: Oxford University Press.

Ark, W. S. (2002, January). Neuroimaging studies give new insight to mental rotation. *Proceedings of the 35th Hawaii International Conference on System Sciences, 5,* 136, Hawaii.

Astur, R. S., Taylor, L. B., Mamelak, A. N., Philpott, L., & Sutherland, R. J. (2002). Humans with hippocampus damage display severe spatial memory impairments in a virtual Morris water task. *Behavioural Brain Research, 132,* 77–84.

Baddeley, A. (1986). *Working memory.* Oxford, England: Clarendon Press.

Baddeley, A., & Hitch, G. J. (1974). Working memory. In G. A. Bower (Ed.), *Recent advances in learning and motivation* (Vol. 7, pp. 47–90). New York: Academic Press.

Baddeley, A., & Logie, R. H. (1999). Working memory: The multiple-component model. In A. Miyake & P. Shah (Eds.), *Models of working memory* (pp. 28–61). New York: Cambridge University Press.

Baddeley, A., Vargha-Khadem, F., Mishkin, M. (2001). Preserved recognition in a case of developmental amnesia: Implications for the acquisition of semantic memory? *Journal of Cognitive Neuroscience, 13*(3), 357–369.

Baillargeon, R. (1987). Object permanence in $3\frac{1}{2}$- and $4\frac{1}{2}$-month-old infants. *Developmental Psychology, 23,* 655–664.

Baillargeon, R., Spelke, E., & Wasserman, S. (1985). Object permanence in 5-month-old infants. *Cognition, 20,* 191–208.

Balaban, M. T. (1995). Affective influences on startle in 5-month-old infants: Reactions to facial expressions of emotion. *Child Development, 66,* 28–36.

Banks, M. S., & Ginsburg, A. P. (1985). Infant visual preferences: A review and new theoretical treatment. *Advances in Child Development and Behavior, 19,* 207–246.

Banks, M. S., & Salapatek, P. (1981). Infant pattern vision: A new approach based on the contrast sensitivity function. *Journal of Experimental Psychology, 31,* 1–45.

Barinaga, M. (2003). Newborn neurons search for meaning. *Science, 299,* 32–34.

Barrash, J., Tranel, D., & Anderson, S. (1994). Assessment of dramatic personality changes after ventromedial frontal lesions. *Journal of Clinical and Experimental Neuropsychology, 18,* 355–381.

Barton, J. J. (2003). Disorders of face perception and recognition. *Neurologic Clinics, 21*(2), 521–548.

Bauer, P. J., Wenner, J. A., Dropik, P. L., & Wewerka, S. S. (2000). Parameters of remembering and forgetting in the transition from infancy to early childhood. *Monographs of the Society for Research in Child Development, 65,* 1–204.

Bauer, P. J., Wiebe, S. A., Carver, L. J., Waters, J. M., & Nelson, C. A. (2003). Electrophysiological indices of long-term recognition predict infants' long-term recall. *Psychological Science, 14,* 629–635.

Benes, F., Turtle, M., Khan, Y., & Farol, P. (1994). Myelination of a key relay zone in the hippocampal formation occurs in the human brain during childhood, adolescence, and adulthood. *Archives of General Psychiatry, 51,* 477–484.

Bernier, P. J., Bédard, A., Vinet, J., Lévesque, M., & Parent, A. (2002). Newly generated neurons in the amygdala and adjoining cortex of adult primates. *Proceedings of the National Academy of Sciences, 99,* 11464–11469.

Bischoff-Grethe, A., Martin, M., Mao, H., & Berns, G. (2001). The context of uncertainty modulates the subcortical response to predictability. *Journal of Cognitive Neuroscience, 13*(7), 986–993.

Bixby, J. L., & Harris, W. A. (1991). Molecular mechanisms of axon growth and guidance. *Annual Review of Cell Biology, 7,* 117–159.

Black, J. E., Jones, T. A., Nelson, C. A., & Greenough, W. T. (1998). Neuronal plasticity and the developing brain. In N. E. Alessi, J. T. Coyle, S. I. Harrison, & S. Eth (Eds.), *Handbook of child and adolescent psychiatry: Vol. 6. Basic psychiatric science and treatment* (pp. 31–53). New York: Wiley.

Booth, J. R., MacWhinney, B., Thulborn, K. R., Sacco, K., Voyvodic, J., & Feldman, H. M. (1999). Functional organization of activation patterns in children: Whole brain fMRI imaging during thee different cognitive tasks. *Progress in Neuro-Psychopharmacology and Biological Psychiatry, 23,* 669–682.

Booth, J. R., MacWhinney, B., Thulborn, K. R., Sacco, K., Voyvodic, J., & Feldman, H. M. (2000). Developmental and lesion effects in brain activation during sentence comprehension and mental rotation. *Developmental Neuropsychology, 18,* 139–169.

Botvinick, M., Braver, T., Barch, D., Carter, C., & Cohen, J. (2001). Conflict monitoring and cognitive control. *Psychological Review, 108*(3), 624–652.

Bourgeois, J. P., & Rakic P. (1993). Changes of synaptic density in the primary visual cortex of the macaque monkey from fetal to adult stage. *Journal of Neuroscience, 13,* 2801–2820.

Bourgeois, J.-P., Reboff, P. J., & Rakic, P. (1989). Synaptogenesis in visual cortex of normal and preterm monkeys: Evidence from intrinsic regulation of synaptic overproduction. *Proceedings of the National Academy of Sciences, 86,* 4297–4301.

Brizzolara, D., Casalini, C., Montanaro, D., & Posteraro F. (2003). A case of amnesia at an early age. *Cortex, 39*(4/5), 605–625.

Broks, P., Young, A. W., Maratos, E. J., Coffey, P. J., Calder, A. J., Isaac, C. L., et al. (1998). Face processing impairments after encephalitis: Amygdala damage and recognition of fear. *Neuropsychologia, 36*(1), 59–70.

Bronner-Fraser, M., & Hatten, M. B. (2003). Neurogenesis and migration. In L. R. Squire, F. E. Bloom, S. K. McConnell, J. L. Roberts, N. C. Spitzer, & M. J. Zigmond (Eds.), *Fundamental neuroscience* (2nd ed., pp. 391–416). New York: Academic Press.

Brown, M., Keynes, R., & Lumsden, A. (2001). *The developing brain.* Oxford, England: Oxford University Press.

Brown, S. A., Warburton, D., Brown, L. Y., Yu, C. Y., Roeder, E. R., Shengel-Rutkowski, S., et al. (1998). Hologrosencephaly due to mutations in ZIC2, a homologue of Drosophila odd-paired. *Nature Genetics, 20,* 180–193.

Buckner, R., Goodman, J., Burock, M., Rotte, M., Koutstaal, W., Schacter, D., et al. (1998). Functional-anatomic correlates of object priming in humans revealed by rapid event-related fMRI. *Neuron, 20,* 285–296.

Bunge, S., Dudukovic, N., Thomason, M., Vaidya, C., & Gabrieli, J. (2002). Immature frontal lobe contributions to cognitive control in children: Evidence from fMRI. *Neuron, 33*(2), 301–311.

Burrone, J., O'Byrne, M., & Murthy, V. N. (2002). Multiple forms of synaptic plasticity triggered by selective suppression of activity in individual neurons. *Nature, 420,* 414–418.

Bush, G., Frazier, J., Rauch, S., Seidman, L., Whalen, P., Jenike, M., et al. (1999). Anterior cingulate cortex dysfunction in attention-deficit/hyperactivity disorder revealed by fMRI and the counting stroop. *Biological Psychiatry, 45*(12), 1542–1552.

Bush, G., Luu, P., & Posner, M. (2000). Cognitive and emotional influences in anterior cingulate cortex. *Trends in Cognitive Sciences, 4,* 215–222.

Butters, M. A., Kaszniak, A. W., Glisky, E. L., Eslinger, P. J., & Schacter, D. L. (1994). Recency discrimination deficits in frontal lobe patients. *Neuropsychologia, 8,* 343–353.

Calder, A. J., Young, A. W., Rowland, D., Perett, D. I., Hodges, J. R., & Etcoff, N. L. (1996). Facial emotion recognition after bilateral amygdala damage: Differentially severe impairment of fear. *Cognitive Neuropsychology, 13,* 699–745.

Canfield, R., Smith, E., Brezsnyak, M., & Snow, K. (1997). Information processing through the first year of life: A longitudinal study using the visual expectancy paradigm. *Monographs of the Society for Research in Child Development, 62*(2).

Carey, S., & Diamond, R. (1994). Are faces perceived as configurations more by adults than children? *Visual Cognition, 1,* 253–274.

Carleton, A., Petreanu, L. T., Lansford, R., Alvarez-Buylla, A., & Lledo, P.-M. (2003). Become a new neuron in the adult olfactory bulb. *Nature Neuroscience, 6,* 507–518.

Carver, L. J., Bauer, P. J., & Nelson, C. A. (2000). Associations between infant brain activity and recall memory. *Developmental Science, 3,* 234–246.

Casey, B., Cohen, J., Jezzard, P., Turner, R., Noll, D., Trainor, R., et al. (1995). Activation of prefrontal cortex in children during a nonspatial working memory task with functional MRI. *Neuroimage, 2,* 221–229.

Casey, B., Durston, S., & Fossella, J. (2001). Evidence for a mechanistic model of cognitive control. *Clinical Neuroscience Research, 1,* 267–282.

Casey, B., Forman, S., Franzen, P., Berkowitz, A., Braver, T., Nystrom, L., et al. (2001). Sensitivity of prefrontal cortex to changes in target probability: A functional MRI study. *Human Brain Mapping, 13,* 26–33.

Casey, B., & Richards, J. (1988). Sustained visual attention in young infants measured by with an adapted version of the visual preference paradigm. *Child Development, 59,* 1515–1521.

Casey, B., Thomas, K., Welsh, T., Badgaiyan, R., Eccard, C., Jennings, J., et al. (2000). Dissociation of response conflict, attentional control, and expectancy with functional magnetic resonance imaging (fMRI). *Proceedings of the National Academy of Sciences, USA, 97*(15), 8728–8733.

Casey, B. J., Tottenham, N., & Fossella, J. (2002). Clinical, imaging, lesion, and genetic approaches toward a model of cognitive control. *Developmental Psychobiology, 40*(3), 237–254.

Casey, B., Trainor, R., Orendi, J., Schubert, A., Nystrom, L., Cohen, J., et al. (1997). A pediatric functional MRI study of prefrontal activation during performance of a go-no-go task. *Journal of Cognitive Neuroscience, 9,* 835–847.

Castellanos, F., Giedd, J., Berquin, P., Walter, J., Sharp, W., Tran, T., et al. (2001). Quantitative brain magnetic resonance imaging in girls with attention-deficit/hyperactivity disorder. *Archives of General Psychiatry, 58,* 289–295.

Castellanos, F., Lee, P., Sharp, W., Jeffries, N., Greenstein, D., Clasen, L., et al. (2002). Developmental trajectories of brain volume abnormalities in children and adolescents with attention-deficit/hyperactivity disorder. *Journal of the American Medical Association, 288,* 1740–1748.

Chang, K. D., Adleman, N., Dienes, K., Menon, V., & Reiss, A. (2002, October). *FMRI of visuospatial working memory in boys with bipolar disorder.* Poster session presented at the 49th annual meeting of the American Academy of Child and Adolescent Psychiatry, San Francisco, CA.

Changeux, J.-P., & Danchin, A. (1976). Selective stabilization of developing synapses as a mechanism for the specification of neuronal networks. *Nature, 64*(5588), 705–712.

Chechik, G., Meilijson, I., & Ruppin, E. (1999). Neuronal regulation: A mechanism for synaptic pruning during brain maturation. *Neural Computation, 11*(8), 2061–2080.

Chenn, A., & McConnell, S. K. (1995). Cleavage orientation and the asymmetric inheritance of Notch1 immunoreactivity in mammalian neurogenesis. *Cell, 82,* 631–641.

Cheng, E. F., & Merzenich, M. M. (2003). Environmental noise retards auditory cortical development. *Science, 300,* 498–502.

Chugani, H. T., & Phelps, M. E. (1986). Maturational changes in cerebral function in infants determined by 18FDG positron emission tomography. *Science, 231,* 840–843.

Chugani, H. T., Phelps, M., & Mazziotta, J. (1987). Positron emission tomography study of human brain functional development. *Annals of Neurology, 22*(4), 487–497.

Churchill, J. D., Beckel-Mitchener, A., Weiler, I. J., & Greenough, W. T. (2002). Effects of fragile X syndrome and an FMR1 knock-out mouse model on forebrain neuronal cell biology. *Microscopy Research and Techniques, 57,* 156–158.

Churchill, J. D., Grossman, A. W., Irwin, S. A., Galvez, R., Klintsova, A. Y., Weiler, I. J., et al. (2002). A converging-methods approach to fragile X syndrome. *Developmental Psychobiology, 40,* 323–328.

Cline, H. (2003). Sperry and Hebb: Oil and vinegar? *Trends in Neuroscience, 26,* 655–661.

Clohessy, A., Posner, M., & Rothbart, M. (2002). Development of the functional visual field. *Acta Psychologia, 106*(1/2), 51–68.

Clohessy, A., Posner, M., Rothbart, M., & Vecera, S. (1991). The development of inhibition of return in early infancy. *Journal of Cognitive Neuroscience, 3*(4), 345–350.

Clower, W. T., & Alexander, G. E. (1998). Movement sequence-related activity reflecting numerical order of components in supplementary and presupplementary motor areas. *Journal of Neurophysiology, 80,* 1562–1566.

Cohen, J., Forman, S., Braver, T., Casey, B., Servan-Schreiber, D., & Noll, D. (1994). Activation of prefrontal cortex in a non-spatial working memory task with functional MRI. *Human Brain Mapping, 1,* 293–304.

Cohen, M. S., Kosslyn, S. M., Breiter, H. C., DiGirolamo, G. J., Thompson, W. L., Anderson, A. K., et al. (1996). Changes in cortical activity during mental rotation. A mapping study using functional MRI. *Brain, 119,* 89–100.

Colcombe, S. J., Kramer, A. F., Erikson, K. I., Scalf, P., McAuley, E., Cohen, N. J., et al. (2004). Cardiovascular fitness, cortical plasticity, and aging. *Proceedings of the National Academy of Science, 101,* 3316–3321.

Collie, R., Ettayne, H. (1999). Deferred imitation by 6- and 9-month-old infants: More evidence for declarative memory. *Developmental Psychobiology, 35,* 83–90.

Condron, B. (2002). Gene expression is required for correct axon guidance. *Current Biology, 12*(19), 1665–1669.

Cools, R., Clark, L., Owen, A., & Robbins, T. (2002). Defining the neural mechanisms of probabilistic reversal learning using event-related functional magnetic resonance imaging. *Journal of Neuroscience, 22*(11), 4563–4567.

Cools, R., Clark, L., & Robbins, T. (2004). Differential responses in human striatum and prefrontal cortex to changes in object and rule relevance. *Journal of Neuroscience, 24*(5), 1129–1135.

Corbetta, M., Kincade, J., Ollinger, J., McAvoy, M., & Shulman, G. (2000). Voluntary orienting is dissociated from target detection in human posterior parietal cortex. *Nature Neuroscience, 3*(3), 292–297.

Corkin, S. (2002). What's new with amnesic patient H. M.? *Nature Reviews Neuroscience, 3,* 153–160.

Cornoldi, C., Marconi, F., & Vecchi. T. (2001). Visuospatial working memory in Turner's syndrome. *Brain and Cognition, 46,* 90–94.

Courchesne, E. (1978). Neurophysiological correlates of cognitive development: Changes in long-latency event-related potentials from childhood to adulthood. *Electroencephalography and Clinical Neurophysiology, 45,* 468–482.

Cycowicz, Y. M. (2000). Memory development and event-related brain potentials in children. *Biological Psychology, 54,* 145–174.

Damasio, H., Grabowski, T., Frank, R., Galaburda, A., & Damasio, A. (1994). The return of Phineas Gage: Clues about the brain from the skull of a famous patient. *Science, 264,* 1102–1105.

Danziger, S., Ward, R., Owen, V., & Rafal, R. (2001). The effects of unilateral pulvinar damage in humans on reflexive orienting and filtering of irrelevant information. *Behavioral Neurology, 13*(3/4), 95–104.

Davis, M. (1989). The role of the amygdala and its efferent projections in fear and anxiety. In P. Tyrer (Ed.), *Psychopharmacology of anxiety* (pp. 52–79). Oxford, England: Oxford University Press.

Dean, A. L., Duhe, D. A., & Green, D. A. (1983). The development of children's mental tracking strategies on a rotation task. *Journal of Experimental Child Psychology, 36,* 226–240.

DeBoer, T., Georgieff, M. K., & Nelson, C. A. (in press). Elicited imitation: A tool to investigate the impact of abnormal prenatal environments on memory development. In P. Bauer (Ed.), *Varieties of early experience: Influences on declarative memory development.* Hillsdale, NJ: Erlbaum.

DeBoer, T., Scott, L., & Nelson, C. (2004). Event-related potentials in developmental populations. In T. Handy (Ed.), *Event-related potentials: A methods handbook* (pp. 263–297). Cambridge, MA: MIT Press.

de Castro F. (2003). Chemotropic molecules: Guides for axonal pathfinding and cell migration during CNS development. *News Physiological Sciences, 18,* 130–136.

de Haan, M., Bauer, P. J., Georgieff, M. K., & Nelson, C. A. (2000). Explicit memory in low-risk infants aged 19 months born between 27 and 42 weeks of gestation. *Developmental Medicine and Child Neurology, 42,* 304–312.

de Haan, M., & Johnson, M. H. (2003a). *The cognitive neuroscience of development.* London: Psychology Press.

de Haan, M., & Johnson, M. H. (2003b). Mechanisms and theories of brain development. In M. de Haan & M. H. Johnson (Eds.), *The cognitive neuroscience of development* (pp. 1–18). London: Psychology Press.

de Haan, M., & Nelson, C. A. (1997). Recognition of the mother's face by 6-month-old infants: A neurobehavioral study. *Child Development, 68,* 187–210.

de Haan, M., & Nelson, C. A. (1999). Brain activity differentiates face and object processing in 6-month-old infants. *Developmental Psychology, 35,* 1113–1121.

de Haan, M., Pascalis, O., & Johnson, M. H. (2002). Specialization of neural mechanisms underlying face recognition in human infants. *Journal of Cognitive Neuroscience, 14*(2), 199–209.

DeHaene, S., Dupoux, E., Mehler, J., Cohen, L., Paulesu, E., Perani, D., et al. (1997). Anatomical variability in the cortical representation of first and second language. *NeuroReport, 8,* 3809–3815.

Delis, D. C., Roberston, L. C., & Efron, R. (1986). Hemispheric specialization of memory for visual hierarchical stimuli. *Neuropsychologia, 24,* 205–214.

DeRegnier, R.-A., Nelson, C. A., Thomas, K., Wewerka, S., & Georgieff, M. K. (2000). Neurophysiologic evaluation of auditory recognition memory in healthy newborn infants and infants of diabetic mothers. *Journal of Pediatrics, 137,* 777–784.

Deruelle, C., & de Schonen, S. (1991). Hemispheric asymmetries in visual pattern processing in infancy. *Brain and Cognition, 16,* 151–179.

Deruelle, C., & de Schonen, S. (1995). Pattern processing in infancy: Hemispheric differences in the processing of shape and location visual components. *Infant Behavior and Development, 18,* 123–132.

Deruelle, C., Mancini, J., Livet, M. O., Casse-Perrot, C., & de Schonen, S. (1999). Configural and local processing of faces in children with Williams syndrome. *Brain and Cognition, 41,* 276–298.

de Schonen, S., & Mathivet, E. (1990). Hemispheric asymmetry in a face discrimination task in infants. *Child Development, 61,* 1192–1205.

Desimone, R., & Duncan, J. (1995). Neural mechanisms of selective visual attention. *Annual Review of Neuroscience, 18,* 193–222.

Diamond, A. (1985). Development of the ability to use recall to guide action, as indicated by infants' performance on A-not-B. *Child Development, 56,* 868–883.

Diamond, A. (1995). Evidence of robust recognition memory early in life even when assessed by reaching behavior. *Journal of Experimental Child Psychology, 59,* 419–456.

Diamond, A. (2001). A model system for studying the role of dopamine in the prefrontal cortex during early development in humans: Early and continuously treated phenylketonuria. In C. Nelson & M. Luciana (Eds.), *Handbook of developmental cognitive neuroscience* (pp. 433–472). Cambridge, MA: MIT Press.

Diamond, A. (2002). Normal development of prefrontal cortex from birth to young adulthood: Cognitive functions, anatomy, and biochemistry. In D. Stuss & R. Knight (Eds.), *Principles of frontal lobe function* (pp. 466–503). New York: Oxford University Press.

Diamond, A., & Goldman-Rakic, P. (1989). Comparison of human infants and rhesus monkeys on Piaget's A-not-B task: Evidence for

dependence on dorsolateral prefrontal cortex. *Experimental Brain Research, 74,* 24–40.

Diamond, A., Kirkham, N., & Amso, D. (2002). Conditions under which young children can hold two rules in mind and inhibit a prepotent response. *Developmental Psychology, 38,* 352–363.

Diamond, R., & Carey, S. (1986). Why faces are and are not special: An effect of expertise. *Journal of Experimental Psychology: General, 115,* 107–117.

Dolan, R. J., & Fletcher, P. C. (1997). Dissociating prefrontal and hippocampal function in episodic memory encoding. *Nature, 388*(6642), 582–585.

Draganski, B., Gaser, C., Busch, V., Schuierer, G., Bogdahn, U., & May, A. (2004). Changes in grey matter induced by training. *Nature, 427,* 311–312.

Drummey, A., & Newcombe, N. (1995). Remembering versus knowing the past: Children's explicit and implicit memories for pictures. *Journal of Experimental Child Psychology, 59,* 549–565.

Duncan, J., & Owen, A. (2000). Common regions of the human frontal lobe recruited by diverse cognitive demands. *Trends in Neurosciences, 23,* 475–483.

Durston, S., Hulshoff Pol, H. E., Casey, B. J., Giedd, J. N., Buitelaar, J. K., & van Engeland, H. (2001). Anatomical MRI of the developing human brain: What have we learned? *Journal of the American Academy of Child and Adolescent Psychiatry, 40,* 1012–1020.

Durston, S., Thomas, K., & Yang, Y. (2002). The development of neural systems involved in overriding behavioral responses: An event-related fMRI study. *Developmental Science, 5,* 9–16.

Durston, S., Tottenham, N., Thomas, K., Davidson, M., Eigsti, I., Yang, Y., et al. (2003). Differential patterns of striatal activation in young children with and without ADHD. *Biological Psychiatry, 53*(10), 871–878.

Eichenbaum, H. (2002). *The cognitive neuroscience of memory.* London: Oxford University Press.

Eichenbaum, H. (2003). Learning and memory: Brain systems. In L. R. Squire, F. E. Bloom, S. K. McConnell, J. L. Roberts, N. C. Spitzer, & M. J. Zigmond (Eds.), *Fundamental neuroscience* (2nd ed., pp. 1299–1327). New York: Academic Press.

Eichenbaum, H. B., Cahill, L. F., Gluck, M. A., Hasselmo, M. E., Keil, F. C., Martin, A. J., et al. (1999). Learning and memory: Systems analysis. In M. J. Zigmond, F. E. Bloom, S. C. Landis, J. L. Roberts, & L. R. Squire (Eds.), *Fundamental neuroscience* (pp. 1455–1486). New York: Academic Press.

Eimer, M. (2000). The face-specific N170 component reflects late stages in the structural encoding of faces. *NeuroReport, 11,* 2319–2324.

Ekdahl, C. T., Claasen, J.-H., Bonde, S., Kokaia, Z., & Lindvall, O. (2003). Inflamation is detrimental for neurogenesis in adult brain. *Proceedings of the National Academy of Sciences, 100,* 13622–13637.

Elbert, T., Pantev, C., Wienbruch, C., Rockstroh, B., & Taub, E. (1995). Increased cortical representation of the fingers of the left hand in string players. *Science, 270,* 305–307.

Elvevåg, B., & Weinberger, D. R. (2001). The neuropsychology of schizophrenia and its relationship to the neurodevelopmental model. In C. A. Nelson & M. Luciana (Eds.), *Handbook of developmental cognitive neuroscience* (pp. 577–594). Cambridge, MA: MIT Press.

Erickson, C. A., Jagadeesh, B., & Desimone, R. (2000). Clustering of perirhinal neurons with similar properties following visual experience in adult monkeys. *Nature Neuroscience, 3*(11), 1143–1148.

Erskine, L., Williams, S. E., Brose, K., Kidd, T., Rachel, R. A., Goodman, C. S., et al. (2000). Retinal ganglion cell axon guidance in the mouse optic chiasm: Expression and function of robos and slits. *Journal of Neuroscience, 20*(13), 4975–4978.

Eslinger, P. J., & Biddle, K. R. (2000). Adolescent neuropsychological development after early right prefrontal cortex damage. *Developmental Neuropsychology, 18,* 297–329.

Fan, J., Flombaum, J., McCandliss, B., Thomas, K., & Posner, M. (2003). Cognitive and brain consequences of conflict. *NeuroImage, 18*(1), 42–57.

Farah, M. J., Rabinowitz, C., Quinn, G. E., & Liu, G. T. (2000). Early commitment of neural substrates for face recognition. *Cognitive Neuropsychology, 17,* 117–124.

Ferguson, J. N., Aldag, J. M., Insel, T. R., & Young, L. J. (2001). Oxytocin in the medial amygdala is essential for social recognition in the mouse. *Journal of Neuroscience, 21,* 8278–8285.

Ferguson, J. N., Young, L. J., Hearn, E. F., Matzuk, M. M., Insel, T. R., Ervinslow, J. T. (2000). Social amnesia in mice lacking the oxytocin gene. *Nature Genetics, 25,* 284–288.

Ferraro, F., Balota, D., & Connor, L. (1993). Implicit memory and the formation of new associations in nondemented Parkinson's disease individuals and individuals with senile dementia of the Alzheimer type: A serial reaction time (SRT) investigation. *Brain and Cognition, 21,* 163–180.

Finney, E. M., Fine, I., & Dobkins, K. R. (2001). Visual stimuli activate auditory cortex in the deaf. *Nature Neuroscience, 4,* 1171–1173.

Flavell, J. H., Miller, P. H., & Miller, S. A. (1993). *Cognitive development* (3rd ed.). Englewood Cliffs, NJ: Prentice-Hall.

Fortin, N. J., Agster, K. L., & Eichenbaum, H. B. (2002). Critical role of the hippocampus in memory for sequences of events. *Nature Neuroscience, 5,* 458–462.

Francis, D. D., Szegda, K., Campbell, G., Martin, W. D., & Insel, T. R. (2003). Epigenetic sources of behavioral differences in mice. *Nature Neuroscience, 6,* 445–448.

Frangiskakis, J. M., Ewart, A. K., Morris, C. A., Mervis, C. B., Bertrand, J., Robinson, B. F., et al. (1996). LIM-kinase1 hemizygosity implicated in impaired visuospatial constructive cognition. *Cell, 86,* 59–69.

Funahashi, S., Bruce, C., & Goldman-Rakic, P. (1989). Mnemonic coding of visual space in the monkey's dorsolateral prefrontal cortex. *Journal of Neurophysiology, 61,* 1–19.

Fuster, J. (1997). *The prefrontal cortex: Anatomy, physiology, and neuropsychology of the frontal lobe* (3rd ed.). Philadelphia: Lippencott-Raven Press.

Fuster, J., & Alexander, G. (1970). Delayed response deficit by cryogenic depression of frontal cortex. *Brain Research, 61,* 79–91.

Fuster, J., & Alexander, G. (1971). Neuron activity related to short-term memory. *Science, 173,* 652–654.

Gadian, D. G., Aicardi, J., Watkins, K. E., Porter, D. A., Mishkin, M., & Vargha-Khadem, F. (2000). Developmental amnesia associated with early hypoxic-ischaemic injury. *Brain, 123,* 499–507.

Gage, F. H. (2000). Mammalian neural stem cells. *Science, 287*(5457), 1433–1438.

Gauthier, I., Skudlarski, P., Gore, J. C., & Anderson, A. W. (2000). Expertise for cars and birds recruits brain areas involved in face recognition. *Nature Neuroscience, 3,* 191–197.

Gauthier, I., Tarr, M. J., Anderson, A. W., Skudlarski, P., & Gore, J. C. (1999). Activation of the middle fusiform "face area" increases with expertise in recognizing novel objects. *Nature Neuroscience, 2,* 568–573.

Geldart, S., Mondloch, C. J., Maurer, D., de Schonen, S., & Brent, H. P. (2002). The effect of early visual deprivation on the development of face processing. *Developmental Science, 5*(4), 490–501.

Geraldi-Caulton, G. (2000). Sensitivity to spatial conflict and the development of self-regulation in children 24 to 30 months of age. *Developmental Science, 3,* 397–404.

Giedd, J. N., Blumenthal, J., Jeffries, N. O., Castellanos, F. X., Liu, H., Zijdenbos, A., et al. (1999). Brain development during childhood and adolescence: A longitudinal MRI study. *Nature Neuroscience, 2,* 861–863.

Giedd, J. N., Snell, J., Lange, N., Rajapakse, J., Casey, B., Kozuch, P., et al. (1996). Quantitative magnetic resonance imaging of human brain development: Ages 4 to 18. *Cerebral Cortex, 6,* 551–560.

Giedd, J. N., Vatuzis, A. C., Hamburger, S. D., Lange, N., Rajapakse, J. C., Matsen, D., et al. (1996). Quantitative MRI of the temporal lobe, amygdala, and hippocampus in normal human development: Ages 4 to 18 years. *Journal of Comparative Neurology, 366,* 223–230.

Goldman, P., & Rosvold, H. (1970). Localization of function within the dorsolateral prefrontal cortex of the rhesus monkey. *Experimental Neurology, 29,* 291–304.

Goldman-Rakic, P. S. (1987). Development of cortical circuitry and cognitive function. *Child Development, 58*(3), 601–622.

Gould, E. (2003, July). *Neurogenesis in the adult brain.* Paper presented at the Merck Summer Institute on Developmental Disabilities, Princeton University, Princeton, NJ.

Gould, E., Beylin, A., Tanapat, P., Reeves, A., & Shors, T. J. (1999). Learning enhances adult neurogenesis in the hippocampal formation. *Nature Neuroscience, 2,* 260–265.

Gould, E., & Gross, C. G. (2002). Neurogenesis in adult mammals: Some progress and problems. *Journal of Neuroscience, 22,* 619–623.

Gould, E., Vail, N., Wagers, M., & Gross, C. G. (2001). Adult-generated hippocampal and neocortical neurons in macaques have a transient existence. *Proceedings of the National Academy of Sciences, USA, 98,* 10910–10917.

Grafton, S., Hazeltine, E., & Ivry, R. (1995). Functional mapping of sequence learning in normal humans. *Journal of Cognitive Neuroscience, 7*(4), 497–510.

Greenough, W. T., & Black, J. E. (1992). Induction of brain structure by experience: Substrates for cognitive development. In M. R. Gunnar & C. A. Nelson (Eds.), *Minnesota Symposia on Child Psychology: Vol. 24. Developmental behavioral neuroscience* (pp. 155–200). Hillsdale, NJ: Erlbaum.

Greenough, W. T., Juraska, J. M., & Volkmar, F. R. (1979). Maze training effects on dendritic branching in occipital cortex of adult rats. *Behavioral and Neural Biology, 26,* 287–297.

Greenough, W. T., Madden, T. C., & Fleischmann, T. B. (1972). Effects of isolation, handling, and enriched rearing on maze learning. *Psychonomic Science, 27,* 279–280.

Grice, S. J., Spratling, M. W., Karmiloff-Smith, A., Halit, H., Csibra, G., de Haan, M., et al. (2001). Disordered visual processing and oscillatory brain activity in autism and Williams syndrome. *NeuroReport, 12,* 2697–2700.

Grossman, A. W., Churchill, J. D., Bates, K. E., Kleim, J., & Greenough, W. T. (2002). A brain adaptation view of plasticity: Is synaptic plasticity an overly limited concept? In M. A. Hofman, G. J. Boer, A. J. G. D. Holtmaat, E. J. W. Van Someren, J. Verhaagen, &

D. F. Swaab (Eds.), *Progress in brain research* (Vol. 138, pp. 91–108). New York: Elsevier Science.

Haberecht, M. F., Menon, V., Warsofsky, I. S., White, C. D., Dyer-Friedman, J., Glover, G. H., et al. (2001). Functional neuroanatomy of visuo-spatial working memory in Turner syndrome. *Human Brain Mapping, 14,* 96–107.

Haith, M., Hazan, C., & Goodman, G. (1988). Expectation and anticipation of dynamic visual events by 3$^1$/$_2$-month-old babies. *Child Development, 59,* 467–479.

Halit, H., de Haan, M., & Johnson, M. H. (2003). Cortical specialisation for face processing: Face sensitive-event related potential components in 3- and 12-month-old infants. *Neuroimage, 19,* 1180–1193.

Hamilton, R., Keenan, J. P., Catala, M., & Pascual-Leone, A. (2000). Alexia for Braille following a bilateral occipital stroke in an early blind woman. *NeuroReport, 11,* 237–240.

Hanashima, C., Li, S. C., Shen, L., Lai, E., & Fishell, G. (2004). *Foxg1* suppresses early cortical cell fate. *Science, 303,* 56–59.

Harris, I. M., & Miniussi, C. (2003). Parietal lobe contribution to mental rotation demonstrated with rTMS. *Journal of Cognitive Neuroscience, 15,* 315–323.

Hartshorn, K., Rovee-Collier, C., Gerhardstein, P., Bhatt, R., Klein, P., & Aaron, F. (1998). Developmental changes in the specificity of memory over the first year of life. *Developmental Psychobiology, 33,* 61–78.

Hatten, M. E. (2002). New directions in neuronal migration. *Science, 297,* 1660–1663.

Haxby, J. V., Gobbini, M. I., Furey, M. L., Ishai, A., Schouten, J. L., & Pietrini, P. (2001). Distributed and overlapping representations of faces and objects in ventral temporal cortex. *Science, 293,* 2425–2430.

Haxby, J. V., Hoffman, E. A., & Gobbini, M. I. (2002). Human neural systems for face recognition and social communication. *Biological Psychiatry, 51,* 59–67.

Hayes, B., & Hennessy, R. (1996). The nature and development of nonverbal implicit memory. *Journal of Experimental Child Psychology, 63,* 22–43.

Hayne, H. (2004). Infant memory development: Implications for childhood amnesia. *Developmental Review, 24,* 33–73.

Hayne, H., Boniface, J., & Barr, R. (2000). The development of declarative memory in human infants: Age-related changes in deferred imitation. *Behavioral Neuroscience, 114*(1), 77–83.

Hazeltine, E., Grafton, S., & Ivry, R. (1997). Attention and stimulus characteristics determined the locus of motor sequence encoding: A PET study. *Brain, 120,* 123–140.

Heindel, W., Salmon, D., Shults, C., Walicke, P., & Butters, N. (1989). Neuropsychological evidence for multiple implicit memory systems: A comparison of Alzheimer's, Huntington's, and Parkinson's disease patients. *Journal of Neuroscience, 9*(2), 582–587.

Henson, R. N., Goshen-Gottstein, Y., Ganel, T., Otten, L. J., Quayle, A., & Rugg, M. D. (2003). Electrophysiological and haemodynamic correlates of face perception, recognition and priming. *Cerebral Cortex, 13,* 795–805.

Hepworth, S., & Smith, M. (2002). Learning and recall of story content and spatial location after unilateral temporal-lobe excision in children and adolescents. *Neuropsychology, Development, and Cognition. Section C. Child Neuropsychology, 8,* 16–26.

Hof, F. A., Geurds, M. P., Chatkupt, S., Shugart, Y. Y., Balling, R., Schrander-Stumpel, C. T., et al. (1996). PAX genes and human neural tube defects: An amino acide substitution in PAS1 in a patient with spina bifida. *Journal of Medical Genetics, 33,* 655–660.

Hoffman, E., & Haxby, J. V. (2000). Distinct representations of eye gaze and identity in the distributed human neural system for face perception. *Nature Neuroscience, 3,* 80–84.

Holdstock, J. S., Mayes, A. R., Cezayirli, E., Isaac, C. L., Aggleton, J. P., & Roberts, N. (2000). A comparison of egocentric and allocentric spatial memory in a patient with selective hippocampal damage. *Neuropsychologia, 38,* 410–425.

Holstege, G., van Ham, J. J., & Tan, J. (1986). Afferent projections to the orbicularis oculi motoneural cell group: An autoradiographical tracing study in the cat. *Brain Research, 374,* 306–320.

Hood, B., Atkinson, J., & Braddick, O. (1998). Selection-for-action and the development of orienting and visual attention. In J. Richards (Ed.), *Cognitive neuroscience of attention: A developmental perspective* (pp. 219–250). Mahwah, NJ: Erlbaum.

Huang, E. J., & Reichardt, L. F. (2001). Neurotrophins: Roles in neuronal development and function. *Annual Review of Neuroscience, 24,* 677–736.

Hubl, D., Bolte, S., Feineis-Matthews, S., Lanfermann, H., Federspiel, A., Strik, W., et al. (2003). Functional imbalance of visual pathways indicates alternative face processing strategies in autism. *Neurology, 61,* 1232–1237.

Huttenlocher, P. R. (2002). *Neural plasticity: The effects of environment on the development of the cerebral cortex.* Cambridge, MA: Harvard University Press.

Huttenlocher, P. R., & Dabholkar, A. S. (1997). Regional differences in synaptogenesis in human cerebral cortex. *Journal of Comparative Neurology, 387*(2), 167–178.

Huttenlocher, P. R., & de Courten, C. (1987). The development of synapses in striat cortex of man. *Human Neurobiology, 6,* 1–9.

Hynes, R. O., & Lander, A. D. (1992). Contact and adhesive specificities in the associations, migrations, and targeting of cells and axons. *Cell, 68*(2), 303–322.

Incisa della Rocchetta, A., Samson, S., Ehrle, N., Denos, M., Hasboun, D., & Baulac M. (2004). Memory for visuospatial location following selective hippocampal sclerosis: The use of different coordinate systems. *Neuropsychology, 18,* 15–28.

Isaacs, E. B., & Vargha-Khadem, F. (1989). Differential course of development of spatial and verbal memory span: A normative study. *British Journal of Developmental Psychology, 7,* 377–380.

Isaacs, E. B., Vargha-Khadem, F., Watkins, K. E., Lucas, A., Mishkin, M., & Gadian, D. G. (2003). Developmental amnesia and its relationship to degree of hippocampal atrophy. *Proceedings of the National Academy of Sciences, USA, 100*(22), 13060–13063.

Ishai, A., Ungerleider, L. G., Martin, A., & Haxby, J. V. (2000). The representation of objects in the human occipital and temporal cortex. *Journal of Cognitive Neuroscience, 12*(Suppl. 2), 35–51.

Itier, R. J., & Taylor, M. J. (2002). Inversion and contrast polarity reversal affect both encoding and recognition processes of unfamiliar faces: A repetition study using ERPs. *NeuroImage, 15*(2), 353–372.

Janowsky, J. S., Shimamura, A. P., & Squire, L. R. (1989). Source memory impairment in patients with frontal lobe lesions. *Neuropsychologia, 8,* 1043–1056.

Jernigan, T. L., Trauner, D. A., Hesselink, J. R., & Tallal, P. A. (1991). Maturation of human cerebrum observed in vivo during adolescence. *Brain, 114,* 2037–2049.

Jessell, T. M. (1988). Adhesion molecules and the hierarchy of neural development. *Neuron, 1*(1), 3–13.

Johnson, M. H. (1998). The neural basis of cognitive development. In W. Damon, D. Kuhn, & R. S. Siegler (Editor-in-Chief) & D. Kuhn & R. S. Siegler (Vol. Eds.), *Handbook of child psychology: Vol. 2.*

*Cognition, perception and language* (5th ed., pp. 1–49). New York: WileyPress.

Johnson, M. H. (2001). Functional brain development in humans. *Nature Reviews Neuroscience, 2,* 475–483.

Johnson, M. H., Dziurawiec, S., Ellis, H., & Morton, J. (1991). Newborns' preferential tracking of face-like stimuli and its subsequent decline. *Cognition, 40,* 1–19.

Johnson, M. H., & Morton, J. (1991). *Biology and cognitive development: The case of face recognition.* Oxford, England: Blackwell.

Johnson, M. H., Posner, M., & Rothbart, M. (1994). Facilitation of saccades toward a covertly attended location in early infancy. *Psychological Science, 5*(2), 90–93.

Johnston, S., Leek, E. C., Atherton, C., Thacker, N., & Jackson, A. (2004). Functional contribution of medial premotor cortex to visuo-spatial transformation in humans. *Neuroscience Letters, 355,* 209–212.

Jordan, K., Wustenberg, T., Heinze, H. J., Peteres, M., & Jäncke, L. (2003). Women and men exhibit different cortical activation patterns during mental rotation tasks. *Neuropsychologia, 40,* 2397–2408.

Kanwisher, N., McDermott, J., & Chun, M. M. (1997). The fusiform face area: A module in human extrastriate cortex specialized for face perception. *Journal of Neuroscience, 17,* 4302–4311.

Kawashima, R., Satoh, K., Itoh, H., Ono, S., Furumoto, S., Grotoh, R., et al. (1996). Functional anatomy of go/no-go discrimination and response selection: A PET study in man. *Brain Research, 728,* 79–89.

Keele, S., & Rafal, R. (2000). Deficits of task set in patients with left prefrontal cortex lesions. In S. Monsell & J. Driver (Eds.), *Control of cognitive processes, attention and performance* (Vol. 18). Cambridge, MA: MIT Press.

Keith, A. (1948). *Human embryology and morphology.* London: Edward Arnold & Company.

Keller, A., Castellanos, F. X., Vaituzis, A. C., Jeffries, N. O., Giedd, J. N., & Rapoport, J. L. (2003). Progressive loss of cerebellar volume in childhood-onset schizophrenia. *American Journal of Psychiatry, 160*(1), 128–133.

Kennedy, H., Bullier, J., & Dehay, C. (1989). Transient projection from the superior temporal sulcus to area 17 in the newborn macaque monkey. *Proceedings of the National Academy of Sciences, USA, 86,* 8093–8097.

Kesler-West, M. L., Andersen, A. H., Smith, C. D., Avison, M. J., Davis, C. E., Kryscio, R. J., et al. (2001). Neural substrates of facial emotion processing using fMRI. *Brain Research: Cognitive Brain Research, 11,* 213–226.

Kikuchi-Yorioka, Y., & Sawaguchi, T. (2000). Parallel visuospatial and audiospatial working memory processes in the monkey dorsolateral prefrontal cortex. *Nature Neuroscience, 3,* 1075–1076.

Kinsley, C. H., Madonia, L., Gifford, G. W., Tureski, K., Griffin, G. R., Lowry, C., et al. (1999). Motherhood improves learning and memory. *Nature, 402,* 137–138.

Klingberg, T., Forssberg, H., & Westerberg, H. (2002). Increased brain activity in frontal and parietal cortex underlies the development of visuospatial working memory capacity during childhood. *Journal of Cognitive Neuroscience, 14*(1), 1–10.

Knopman, D., & Nissen, M. (1991). Procedural learning is impaired in Huntington's disease: Evidence from the serial reaction time task. *Neuropsychologia, 29*(3), 245–254.

Knudsen, E. I. (2003a). Early experience and critical periods. In L. R. Squire, F. E. Bloom, S. K. McConnell, J. L. Roberts, N. C. Spitzer, & M. J. Zigmond (Eds.), *Fundamental neuroscience* (2nd ed., pp. 555–573). New York: Academic Press.

Knudsen, E. (2003b). MacArthur Foundation research network on. *Early Experience and Brain Development.* Annual report.

Knudsen, E. (in press). Sensitive periods in the development of the brain and behavior. *Journal of Cognitive Neuroscience.*

Kolb, B., & Whishaw, I. Q. (1998). Brain plasticity and behavior. *Annual Review of Psychology, 49,* 43–64.

Konishi, S., Nakajima, K., Uchida, I., Kikyo, H., Kameyama, M., & Miyashita, Y. (1999). Common inhibitory mechanism in human inferior prefrontal cortex revealed by event-related functional MRI. *Brain, 122,* 981–999.

Kornack, D. R., & Rakic, P. (1999). Continuation of neurogenesis in the hippocampus of the adult macaque monkey. *Proceedings of the National Academy of Sciences, USA, 98,* 5768–5773.

Kostovic, I. (1990). Structural and histochemical reorganization of the human prefrontal cortex during perinatal and postnatal life. *Progress in Brain Research, 85,* 223–239.

Kozlowski, P. B., Brudkowska, J., Kraszpulski, M., Sersen, E. A., Wrzolek, M. A., Anzil, A. P., et al. (1997). Microencephaly in children congenitally infected with human immunodeficiency virus: A gross-anatomical morphometric study. *Acta Neuropathologica, 93*(2), 136–145.

Kriegstein, A. R., & Götz, M. (2003). Radial glia diversity: A matter of cell fate. *Glia, 43,* 37–43.

Kuhl, P. K., Tsao, F. M., & Liu, H. M. (2003). Foreign-language experience in infancy: Effects of short-term exposure and social interaction on phonetic learning. *Proceedings of the National Academy of Sciences, 100,* 9096–9101.

Kwon, H., Menon, V., Eliez, S., Warsofsky, I. S., White, C. D., Dyer-Friedman, J., et al. (2001). Functional neuroanatomy of visuospatial working memory in fragile X syndrome: Relation to behavioral and molecular measures. *American Journal of Psychiatry, 158,* 1040–1051.

Kwon, H., Reiss, A. L., & Menon, V. (2002). Neural basis of protracted developmental changes in visuo-spatial working memory. *Proceedings of the National Academy of Science, USA, 99,* 13336–13341.

LaBar, K., Gatenby, J., Gore, J., LeDoux, J., & Phelps, E. (1998). Human amygdala activation during conditioned fear acquisition and extinction: A Mixed-Trial fMRI Study. *Neuron, 20,* 937–945.

LaMantia, A. S., & Rakic, P. (1990). Axon overproduction and elimination in the corpus callosum of the developing rhesus monkey. *Journal of Neuroscience, 10,* 2156–2175.

Lang, P. J., Bradley, M. M., & Cuthbert, B. N. (1990). Emotion, attention, and the startle reflex. *Psychological Review, 97,* 377–395.

Lang, P. J., Bradley, M. M., & Cuthbert, B. N. (1992). A motivational analysis of emotion: Reflex-cortex connections. *Psychological Science, 3,* 44–49.

Lanzenberger, R., Uhl, F., Windischberger, C., Gartus, A., Streibl, B., Edward, V., et al. (2001). Cross-modal plasticity in congenitally blind subjects. *International Society for Magnetic Resonance Medicine, 9.*

Le Grand, R., Mondloch, C. J., Maurer, D., & Brent, H. P. (2001). Early visual experience and face processing. *Nature, 410,* 890.

Le Grand, R., Mondloch, C. J., Maurer, D., & Brent, H. P. (2003). Expert face processing requires input to the right hemisphere during infancy. *Nature Neuroscience, 6,* 1108–1112.

Lepage, M., & Richer, F. (1996). Inter-response interference contributes to the sequencing deficit in frontal lobe lesions. *Brain, 119,* 1289–1295.

Lespinet, V., Bresson, C., N'Kaoua, B., Rougier, A., & Claverie, B. (2002). Effect of age of onset of temporal lobe epilepsy on the severity and the nature of preoperative memory deficits. *Neuropsychologia, 40,* 1591–1600.

Levitt, P. (2003). Structural and functional maturation of the developing primate brain. *Journal of Pediatrics, 143*(Suppl. 4), S35–S45.

Levy, R., & Goldman-Rakic, P. (2000). Segregation of working memory functions within the dorsolateral prefrontal cortex. *Experimental Brain Research, 133*(1), 23–32.

Lewicki, P. (1986). Processing information about covariations that cannot be articulated. *Journal of Experimental Psychology: Learning, Memory, and Cognition, 12,* 135–146.

Lewin, J., Friedman, L., Wu, D., Miller, D., Thompson, L., Klein, S., et al. (1996). Cortical localization of human sustained attention: Detection with functional MR using a vigilance paradigm. *Journal of Computer Assisted Tomography, 20*(5), 695–701.

Lie, D. C., Song, H., Colamarino, S. A., Ming, G.-I., & Gage, F. H. (2004). Neurogenesis in the adult brain: New strategies for central nervous system diseases. *Annual Review of Pharmacology and Toxicology, 44,* 399–421.

Luciana, M. (2003). The neural and functional development of human prefrontal cortex. In M. de Haan & M. H. Johnson (Eds.), *The cognitive neuroscience of development* (pp. 157–179). London: Psychology Press.

Luciana, M., & Nelson, C. A. (1998). The functional emergence of prefrontally-guided working memory systems in 4- to 8-year-old children. *Neuropsychologia, 36,* 272–293.

Luciana, M., Sullivan, J., & Nelson, C. A. (2001). Individual differences in phenylalanine levels moderate performance on tests of executive function in adolescents treated early and continuously for PKU. *Child Development, 72,* 1637–1652.

Lumsden, A., & Kintner, C. (2003). Neural induction and pattern formation. In L. R. Squire, F. E. Bloom, S. K. McConnell, J. L. Roberts, N. C. Spitzer, & M. J. Zigmond (Eds.), *Fundamental neuroscience* (2nd ed., pp. 363–390). New York: Academic Press.

Luna, B., Thulborn, K., Munoz, D., Merriam, E., Garver, K., Minshew, N., et al. (2001). Maturation of widely distributed brain function subserves cognitive development. *NeuroImage, 13,* 786–793.

Mabbott, D. J., & Smith, M. L. (2003). Memory in children with temporal or extra-temporal excisions. *Neuropsychologia, 41,* 995–1007.

MacDonald, A., Cohen, J., Stenger, V., & Carter, C. (2000). Dissociating the role of the dorsolateral prefrontal and anterior cingulate cortex in cognitive control. *Science, 288*(5472), 1835–1838.

Maguire, E. A., Gadian, D. G., Johnsrude, I. S., Good, C. D., Ashburner, J., Frackowiak, R. S. J., et al. (2000). Navigation-related structural change in the hippocampi of taxi drivers. *Proceedings of the National Academy of Sciences, 97,* 4398–4403.

Maguire, E. A., Vargha-Khadem, F., & Mishkin, M. (2001). The effects of bilateral hippocampal damage on fMRI regional activations and interactions during memory retrieval. *Brain, 124,* 1156–1170.

Málková, L., Bachevalier, J., Mishkin, M., & Saunders, C. (2001). Neurotoxic lesions of perirhinal cortex impair visual recognition memory in rhesus monkeys. *NeuroReport, 12,* 1913–1917.

Manns, J. R., & Squire, L. R. (1999). Impaired recognition memory on the Doors and People Test after damage limited to the hippocampal region. *Hippocampus, 9*(5), 495–499.

Manns, J. R., Stark, C. E., & Squire, L. R. (2000). The visual paired-comparison task as a measure of declarative memory. *Proceedings of the National Academy of Sciences, 97*(22), 12375–12379.

Marin-Padilla, M. (1978). Dual origin of the mammalian neocortex and evolution of the cortical plate. *Anatomical Embryology, 152,* 109–126.

Martinez, A., Moses, P., Frank, L., Buxton, R., Wong, E., & Stiles, J. (1997). Hemispheric asymmetries in global and local processing: Evidence from fMRI. *NeuroReport, 8,* 1685–1689.

Martinkauppi, S., Rama, P., Aronen, H. J., Korvenoja, A., & Carlson, S. (2000). Working memory of auditory localization. *Cerebral Cortex, 10,* 889–898.

Mauk, M., & Thompson, R. (1987). Retention of classically conditioned eyelid responses following acute decerebration. *Brain Research, 403,* 89–95.

Maurer, D., Lewis, T. L., Brent, H. P., & Levin, A. V. (1999). Rapid improvement in the acuity of infants after visual input. *Science, 286,* 108–110.

Mayberry, R. I., Lock, E., & Kazmi, H. (2002). Linguistic ability and early language exposure. *Nature, 417,* 38.

Maybery, M., Taylor, M., & O'Brien-Malone, A. (1995). Implicit learning: Sensitive to age but not to IQ. *Australian Journal of Psychology, 47,* 8–17.

McDonough, L., Mandler, J. M., McKee, R. D., & Squire, L. R. (1995). The deferred imitation task as a nonverbal measure of declarative memory. *Proceedings of the National Academy of Sciences, 92,* 7580–7584.

McKee, R. D., & Squire, L. R. (1993). On the development of declarative memory. *Journal of Experimental Psychology: Learning, Memory, and Cognition, 19,* 397–404.

Meletti, S., Benuzzi, F., Rubboli, G., Cantalupo, G., Stanzani Maserati, M., Nichelli, P., et al. (2003). Impaired facial emotion recognition in early-onset right mesial temporal epilepsy. *Neurology, 60,* 426–431.

Meltzoff, A. N. (1985). Immediate and deferred imitation in 14- and 24-month-old infants. *Child Development, 56,* 62–72.

Meltzoff, A. N. (1988). Infant imitation and memory: Nine-month-olds in immediate and deferred tests. *Child Development, 59,* 217–225.

Meltzoff, A. N. (1995). What infant memory tells us about infantile amnesia: Long-term recall and deferred imitation. *Journal of Experimental Child Psychology, 59,* 497–515.

Mettke-Hofmann, C., & Gwinner, E. (2003). Long-term memory for a life on the move. *Proceedings of the National Academy of Sciences, USA, 100,* 5863–5866.

Meulemans, T., van der Linden, M., & Perruchet, P. (1998). Implicit sequence learning in children. *Journal of Experimental Child Psychology, 69,* 199–221.

Milner, B. (1995). Aspects of human frontal lobe function. In H. H. Jasper, S. Riggio, & P. S. Goldman-Rakic (Eds.), *Epilepsy and the functional anatomy of the frontal lobe.* New York: Raven Press.

Milner, B., Corkin, S., & Teuber, H. (1968). Further analysis of the hippocampal amnesic syndrome: 14-year follow-up study of HM. *Neuropsychologia, 6,* 215–234.

Mirescu, C., Peters, J. D., & Gould, E. (2004). Early life experience alters response of adult Neurogenesis to stress. *Nature Neuroscience, 7,* 841–846.

Molliver, M., Kostovic, I., & Van der Loos, H. (1973). The development of synapses in the human fetus. *Brain Research, 50,* 403–407.

Mondloch, C., Geldart, S., Maurer, D., & de Schonen, S. (2003). Developmental changes in the processing of hierarchical shapes continue into adolescence. *Journal of Experimental Child Psychology, 84,* 20–40.

Monk, C. S., Zhuang, J., Curtis, W. J., Ofenloch, I. T., Tottenham, N., Nelson, C. A., et al. (2002). Human hippocampal activation in the delayed matching- and nonmatching-to-sample memory tasks: An event-related functional MRI approach. *Behavioral Neuroscience, 116*, 716–721.

Morris, J. S., Frith, C. D., Perrett, K. I., Rowland, D., Young, A. W., Calder, A. J., et al. (1996). A differential neural response in the human amygdala to fearful and happy facial expressions. *Nature, 383*, 812–815.

Moscovitch, M., Winocur, G., & Behrmann, M. (1997). What is special about face recognition? Nineteen experiments on a person with visual object agnosia but normal face recognition. *Journal of Cognitive Neuroscience, 9*, 555–604.

Moses, P., Roe, K., Buxton, R. B., Wong, E. C., Frank, L. R., & Stiles, J. (2002). Functional MRI of global and local processing in children. *Neuroimage, 16*, 415–424.

Mrzljak, L., Uylings, H. B. M., Kostovic, I., & VanEden, C. (1990). Prenatal development of neurons in the human prefrontal cortex: Vol. I. A qualitative golgi study. *Journal of Comparative Neurology, 271*, 355–386.

Murloz-Sanjuan, I., & Brivanfou, A. H. (2002). Neural induction: The default model and embryonic stem cells. *Nature Reviews Neuroscience, 3*(4), 271–280.

Nadarajah, B., & Parvavelas, J. G. (2002). Models of neuronal migration in the developing cerebral cortex. *Nature Reviews Neuroscience, 3*, 423–432.

Naegele, J. R., & Lombroso, P. J. (2001). Genetics of central nervous system developmental disorders. *Child and Adolescent Psychiatric Clinics of North America, 10*, 225–239.

Nelson, C. (1994). Neural correlates of recognition memory in the first postnatal year of life. In G. Dawson & K. Fischer (Eds.), *Human behavior and the developing brain* (pp. 269–313). New York: Guilford Press.

Nelson, C. A. (1995). The ontogeny of human memory: A cognitive neuroscience perspective. *Developmental Psychology, 31*, 723–738.

Nelson, C. A. (1998). The nature of early memory. *Preventive Medicine, 27*, 172–179.

Nelson, C. A. (1999). Neural plasticity and human development. *Current Directions in Psychological Science, 8*, 42–45.

Nelson, C. A. (2000a). Change and continuity in neurobehavioral development. *Infant Behavior and Development, 22*, 415–429.

Nelson, C. A. (2000b). Neural plasticity and human development: The role of early experience in sculpting memory systems. *Developmental Science, 3*, 115–130.

Nelson, C. A. (2001). The development and neural bases of face recognition. *Infant and Child Development, 10*, 3–18.

Nelson, C. A. (2002). Neural development and life-long plasticity. In R. M. Lerner, F. Jacobs, & D. Wetlieb (Eds.), *Promoting positive child, adolescent, and family development: Handbook of program and policy interventions* (pp. 31–60). Thousand Oaks, CA: Sage.

Nelson, C. A., & Bloom, F. E. (1997). Child development and neuroscience. *Child Development, 68*, 970–987.

Nelson, C. A., & Carver, L. J. (1998). The effects of stress on brain and memory: A view from developmental cognitive neuroscience. *Development and Psychopathology, 10*, 793–809.

Nelson, C. A., & Collins, P. F. (1991). Event-related potential and looking time analysis of infants' responses to familiar and novel events: Implications for visual recognition memory. *Developmental Psychology, 27*, 50–58.

Nelson, C. A., & Collins, P. F. (1992). Neural and behavioral correlates of recognition memory in 4- and 8-month-old infants. *Brain and Cognition, 19*, 105–121.

Nelson, C. A., Lin, J., Carver, L. J., Monk, C. S., Thomas, K. M., & Truwit, C. L. (2000). Functional neuroanatomy of spatial working memory in children. *Developmental Psychology, 36*(1), 109–116.

Nelson, C. A., & Luciana, M. (Eds.). (2001). *Handbook of developmental cognitive neuroscience.* Cambridge, MA: MIT Press.

Nelson, C. A., & Monk, C. S. (2001). The use of event-related potentials in the study of cognitive development. In C. Nelson & M. Luciana (Eds.), *Handbook of developmental cognitive neuroscience* (pp. 125–136). Cambridge, MA: MIT Press.

Nelson, C. A., & Webb, S. J. (2003). A cognitive neuroscience perspective on early memory development. In M. de Haan & M. H. Johnson (Eds.), *The cognitive neuroscience of development* (pp. 99–125). London: Psychology Press.

Nemanic, S., Alvarado, M. C., & Bachevalier, J. (2004). The hippocampal/parahippocampal regions and recognition memory: Insights from visual paired comparison versus object-delayed nonmatching in monkeys. *Journal of Neuroscience, 24*, 2013–2026.

Newman, A. J., Bavelier, D., Corina, D., Jezzard, P., & Neville, H. J. (2002). A critical period for right hemisphere recruitment in American sign language processing. *Nature Neuroscience, 5*, 76–80.

Nishitani, N., & Hari, R. (2000). Temporal dynamics of cortical representation for action. *Proceedings of the National Academy of Sciences, USA, 97*, 913–918.

Nissen, M., & Bullemer, P. (1987). Attentional requirements of learning: Evidence from performance measures. *Cognitive Psychology, 19*, 1–32.

Nunn, J. A., Polkey, C. E., & Morris, R. G. (1998). Selective spatial memory impairment after right unilateral temporal lobectomy. *Neuropsychologia, 36*, 837–848.

Olesen, P. J., Nagy, Z., Westerberg, H., & Klingberg, T. (2003). Combined analysis of DTI and fMRI data reveals a joint maturation of white and grey matter in a fronto-parietal network. *Brain Research: Cognitive Brain Research, 18*, 48–57.

Olesen, P. J., Westerberg, H., & Klingberg, T. (2004). Increased prefrontal and parietal activity after training of working memory. *Nature Neuroscience, 7*, 75–79.

Oppenheim, R. W., & Johnson, J. E. (2003). Programmed cell death and neurotrophic factors. In L. R. Squire, F. E. Bloom, S. K. McConnell, J. L. Roberts, N. C. Spitzer, & M. J. Zigmond (Eds.), *Fundamental neuroscience* (2nd ed., pp. 499–532). New York: Academic Press.

Orlich, E., & Ross, L. (1968). Acquisition and differential conditioning of the eyelid response in normal and retarded children. *Journal of Experimental Child Psychology, 6*, 181–193.

Overman, W. H., Bachevalier, J., Sewell, F., & Drew, J. (1993). A comparison of children's performance on two recognition memory tasks: Delayed nonmatch-to-sample-versus-visual-paired-comparison. *Developmental Psychobiology, 26*, 345–357.

Owen, A., Roberts, A., Hodges, J., Summers, B., Polkey, C., & Robbins, T. (1993). Contrasting mechanisms of impaired attentional set shifting in patients with frontal lobe damage or Parkinson's disease. *Brain, 119*, 1597–1615.

Parkin, A., & Streete, S. (1988). Implicit and explicit memory in young children and adults. *British Journal of Psychology, 79*, 361–369.

Pascalis, O., & Bachevalier, J. (1999). Neonatal aspiration lesions of the hippocampal formation impair visual recognition memory when assessed by paired-comparison task but not by delayed non-matching-to-sample task. *Hippocampus, 9,* 609–616.

Pascalis, O., de Haan, M., & Nelson, C. A. (2002). Is face processing species specific during the first year of life? *Science, 296,* 1321–1323.

Pascalis, O., Hunkin, N. M., Holdstock, J. S., Isaac, C. L., & Mayes, A. R. (2004). Visual paired comparison performance is impaired in a patient with selective hippocampal lesions and relatively intact item recognition. *Neuropsychologia, 42,* 1230–1293.

Pascual-Leone, A., Grafman, J., Clark, K., Stewart, M., Massaquoi, S., Lou, J.-S., et al. (1993). Procedural learning in Parkinson's disease and cerebellar degeneration. *Annals of Neurology, 34,* 594–602.

Passarotti, A. M., Paul, B. M., Bussiere, J. R., Buxton, R. B., Wong, E. C., & Stiles, J. (2003). The development of face and location processing: An fMRI study. *Developmental Science, 6,* 100–117.

Paterson, S. J., Brown, J. H., Gsodl, M. K., Johnson, M. H., & Karmiloff-Smith, A. (1999). Cognitive modularity and genetic disorders. *Science, 28,* 2355–2358.

Paus, T., Zijdenbos, A., Worsley, K., Collins, D. L., Blumenthal, J., Giedd, J. N., et al. (1999). Structural maturation of neural pathways in children and adolescents: In vivo study. *Science, 283,* 1908–1911.

Perani, D., Paulesu, E., Galles, N. S., Dupoux, E., Dehaene, S., Bettinardi, V., et al. (1998). The bilingual brain: Proficiency and age of acquisition of the second language. *Brain, 121,* 1841–1852.

Petitto, L. A., Zatorre, R. J., Gauna, K., Nikeiski, E. J., Dostie, D., & Evans, A. C. (2000). Speech-like cerebral activity in profoundly deaf people processing signed languages: Implications for the neural basis of human language. *Proceedings of the National Academy of Sciences, 97,* 13961–13966.

Pickering, S. J. (2001a). Cognitive approaches to the fractionation of visuo-spatial working memory. *Cortex, 37,* 457–473.

Pickering, S. J. (2001b). The development of visuo-spatial working memory. *Memory, 9,* 423–432.

Pierce, K., Muller, R. A., Ambrose, J., Allen, G., & Courchesne, E. (2001). Face processing occurs outside the fusiform "face area" in autism: Evidence from functional MRI. *Brain, 124,* 2059–2073.

Pine, D., Fyer, A., Grun, J., Phelps, E., Szesko, P., Koda, V., et al. (2001). Methods for developmental studies of fear conditioning circuitry. *Biological Psychiatry, 50,* 225–228.

Pollak, S. D., Cicchetti, D., Hornung, K., & Reed, A. (2000). Recognizing emotion in faces: Developmental effects of child abuse and neglect. *Developmental Psychology, 36*(5), 679–688.

Pollak, S. D., & Kistler, D. J. (2002). Early experience is associated with the development of categorical representations for facial expressions of emotion. *Proceedings of the National Academy of Sciences, USA, 99*(13), 9072–9076.

Pollak, S. D., & Sinha, P. (2002). Effects of early experience on children's recognition and facial displays of emotion. *Developmental Psychology, 38*(5), 784–791.

Posner, M., & Petersen, S. (1990). The attention system of the human brain. *Annual Review of Neuroscience, 13,* 25–42.

Posner, M., & Raichle, M. (1997). *Images of mind.* New York: Scientific American Library.

Posner, M., Walker, J., Friedrich, F., & Rafal, R. (1984). Effects of parietal injury on covert orienting of attention. *Journal of Neuroscience, 4*(7), 1863–1874.

Puce, A., Allison, T., Asgari, M., Gore, J. C., & McCarthy, G. (1996). Differential sensitivity of human visual cortex to faces, letter-strings, and textures: A functional magnetic resonance imaging study. *Journal of Neuroscience, 16,* 5205–5215.

Rafal, D., Calabresi, P., Brennan, C., & Scioloto, T. (1989). Saccade preparation inhibits reorienting to recently attended locations. *Journal of Experimental Psychology: Human Perception and Performance, 15,* 673–685.

Rafal, R., Posner, M., Friedman, J., Inhoff, A., & Bernstein, E. (1988). Orienting of visual attention in progressive supranuclear palsy. *Brain, 111*(2), 267–280.

Rakic, P. (1988). Specification of cerebral cortical areas. *Science, 241,* 170–176.

Rakic, P. (2002a). Adult neurogenesis in mammals: An identity crisis. *Journal of Neuroscience, 22,* 614–618.

Rakic, P. (2002b). Neurogenesis in adult primate neocortex: An evaluation of the evidence. *Nature Reviews Neuroscience, 3,* 65–71.

Raper, J. A., & Tessier-Lavigne, M. (1999). Growth cones and axon pathfinding. In M. J. Zigmond, F. E. Bloom, S. C. Landis, J. L. Roberts, & L. R. Squire (Eds.), *Fundamental neuroscience* (pp. 579–596). New York: Academic Press.

Raper, J., & Tessier-Lavigne, M. (2003). Growth cones and axon pathfinding. In L. R. Squire, F. E. Bloom, S. K. McConnell, J. L. Roberts, N. C. Spitzer, & M. J. Zigmond (Eds.), *Fundamental neuroscience* (2nd ed., pp. 449–467). New York: Academic Press.

Rebai, M., Poiroux, S., Bernard, C., & Lalonde, R. (2001). Event-related potentials for category-specific information during passive viewing of faces and objects. *Internal Journal of Neuroscience, 106*(3/4), 209–226.

Reber, A. (1992). The cognitive unconscious: An evolutionary perspective. *Consciousness and Cognition, 1,* 93–133.

Reber, A. (1993). *Implicit learning and tacit knowledge: An essay on the cognitive unconscious* (Vol. 19). New York: Oxford University Press.

Richards, J. (1994). Baseline respiratory sinus arrhythmia and heart rate responses during sustained visual attention in preterm infants from 3 to 6 months of age. *Psychophysiology, 31,* 235–243.

Richards, J. (1998). Development of selective attention in young infants. *Developmental Science, 1,* 45–51.

Richards, J. (2001). Attention in young infants: A developmental psychophysiological perspective. In C. Nelson & M. Luciana (Eds.), *Handbook of cognitive neuroscience* (pp. 321–338). Cambridge, MA: MIT Press.

Richter, W., Somorjai, R., Summers, R., Jaramasz, M., Menon, R. S., Gati, J. S., et al. (2000). Motor area activity during mental rotation studied by time-resolved single-trial fMRI. *Journal of Cognitive Neuroscience, 12,* 310–320.

Richter, W., Ugurbil, K., Georgopoulos, A., & Kim, S.-G. (1997). Time-resolved fMRI of mental rotation. *NeuroReport, 8,* 3697–3702.

Ridderinkhof, K., van der Molen, M., Band, G., & Bashore, T. (1997). Sources of interference from irrelevant information: A developmental study. *Journal of Experimental Child Psychology, 65,* 315–341.

Ridley, A. J., Schwartz, M. A., Burridge, K., Firtel, R. A., Ginsberg, M. H., Borisy, G., et al. (2003). Cell migration: Integrating signals from front to back. *Science, 302,* 1704–1709.

Roberts, J. E., & Bell, M. A. (2002). The effects of age and sex on mental rotation performance, verbal performance, and brain electrical activity. *Developmental Psychobiology, 40,* 391–407.

Roberts, J. E., & Bell, M. A. (2003). Two- and three-dimensional mental rotation tasks lead to different parietal laterality for men and women. *International Journal of Psychophysiology, 50,* 235–246.

Robinson, A. J., & Pascalis, O. (2004). Development of flexible visual recognition memory in human infants. *Developmental Science, 7,* 527–533.

Robinson, D., Bowman, E., & Kertzman, C. (1995). Covert orienting of attention in macques: Vol. 2. Contributions of parietal cortex. *Journal of Neurophysiology, 74*(2), 698–712.

Roe, K., Moses, P., & Stiles, J. (1999). Lateralization of spatial processes in school aged children [Abstracts]. *Cognitive Neuroscience Society, 41.*

Rossion, B., Gauthier, I., Tarr, M. J., Despland, P., Bruyer, R., Linotte, S., et al. (2000). The N170 occipito-temporal component is delayed and enhanced to inverted faces but not inverted objects: An electrophysiological account of face-specific processes in the human brain. *NeuroReport, 11,* 69–74.

Rovee-Collier, C. (1997a). Development of memory in infancy. In N. Cowan (Ed.), *The development of memory in childhood* (pp. 5–39). London: University College London Press.

Rovee-Collier, C. (1997b). Dissociations in infant memory: Rethinking the development of implicit and explicit memory. *Psychological Review, 104,* 467–498.

Ruchkin, D. S., Johnson, R., Jr., Grafman, J., Canoune, H., & Ritter, W. (1997). Multiple visuospatial working memory buffers: Evidence from spatiotemporal patterns of brain activity. *Neuropsychologia, 35*(2), 195–209.

Rueda, M. R., Fan, J., McCandliss, B. D., Halparin, J. D., Gruber, D. B., Lercari, L. P., et al. (2004). Development of attentional networks in childhood. *Neuropsychologia, 42*(8), 1029–1040.

Russo, R., Nichelli, P., Gibertoni, M., & Cornia, C. (1995). Developmental trends in implicit and explicit memory: A picture completion study. *Journal of Experimental Child Psychology, 59,* 566–578.

Rutishauser, U. (1993). Adhesion molecules of the nervous system. *Current Opinion in Neurobiology, 3,* 709–715.

Sadato, N., Okada, T., Honda, M., & Yonekura, Y. (2002). Critical period for cross-modal plasticity in blind humans: A functional MRI study. *Neuroimage, 16,* 389–400.

Sadato, N., Pascual-Leone, A., Grafman, J., Deiber, M. P., Ibanez, V., & Hallett, M. (1998). Neural networks for Braille reading by the blind. *Brain, 121,* 1213–1229.

Sala, J. B., Rama, P., & Courtney, S. M. (2003). Functional topography of a distributed neural system for spatial and nonspatial information maintenance in working memory. *Neuropsychologia, 41*(3), 341–356.

Sasaki, Y., Hadijkhani, M., Fischl, B., Liu, A. K., Marrett, S., Dale, A. M., et al. (2001). Local and global attention are mapped retinotopically in human occipital cortex. *Proceedings of the National Academy of Sciences, USA, 98,* 2077–2082.

Schachner, M., Taylor, J., Bartsch, U., & Pesheva P. (1994). The perplexing multifunctionality of janusin, a tenascin-related molecule. *Perspectives in Developmental Neurobiology, 2*(1), 33–41.

Schacter, D., & Buckner, R. (1998). On the relations among priming, conscious recollection, and intentional retrieval: Evidence from neuroimaging research. *Neurobiology of Learning and Memory, 70,* 284–303.

Schendan, H., Searl, M., Melrose, R., & Ce, S. (2003). An FMRI study of the role of the medial temporal lobe in implicit and explicit sequence learning. *Neuron, 37*(6), 1013–1025.

Schoppik, D., Gadian, D. G., Connelly, A., Mishkin, M., Vargha-Khadem, F., & Saunders, R. C. (2001). Volumetric measurement of the subhippocampal cortices in patients with developmental amnesia. *Society for Neuroscience, 27,* 1400.

Schultz, R. T., Gauthier, I., Klin, A., Fulbright, K. A., Anderson, A. W., Volkmar, F., et al. (2000). Abnormal ventral temporal cortical activity during face discrimination among individuals with autism and Asperger syndrome. *Archives of General Psychiatry, 57,* 331–340.

Schwartz, B., & Hashtroudi, S. (1991). Priming is independent of skill learning. *Journal of Experimental Psychology: Learning, Memory and Cognition, 17*(6), 1177–1187.

Schwarzer, G., & Zauner, N. (2003). Face processing in 8-month-old infants: Evidence for configural and analytical processing. *Vision Research, 43,* 2783–2793.

Schweinberger, S. R., Pickering, E. C., Jentzsch, I., Burton, A. M., & Kaufmann, J. M. (2002). Event-related brain potential evidence for a response of inferior temporal cortex to familiar face repetitions. *Brain Research: Cognitive Brain Research, 14,* 398–409.

Scoville, W. B., & Milner, B. (1957). Loss of recent memory after bilateral hippocampal lesions. *Journal of Neurology, Neurosurgery, and Psychiatry, 20,* 11–21.

Seger, C. (1994). Implicit learning. *Psychological Bulletin, 115*(2), 163–196.

Serres, L. (2001). Morphological changes of the human hippocampal formation from midgestation to early childhood. In C. A. Nelson & M. Luciana (Eds.), *Handbook of developmental cognitive neuroscience* (pp. 45–58). Cambridge, MA: MIT Press.

Shallice, T. (1988). *From neuropsychology to mental structure.* New York: Cambridge University Press.

Shallice, T., & Burgess, P. (1991). Higher-order cognitive impairments and frontal lobe lesions in man. In H. Levin, H. Eisenberg, & A. Benton (Eds.), *Frontal lobe function and dysfunction* (pp. 125–138). Oxford, England: Oxford University Press.

Shelton, A. L., Christoff, K., Burrows, J. J., Pelisari, K. B., & Gabrieli, J. D. E. (2001). Brain activation during mental rotation: Individual differences. *Society for Neuroscience Abstracts, 27,* 456.

Shibata, T., Nishijo, H., Tamura, R., Miyamoto, K., Eifuku, S., Endo, S., et al. (2002). Generators of visual evoked potentials for faces and eyes in the human brain as determined by dipole localization. *Brain Topography, 15,* 51–63.

Shimamura, A. (1986). Priming effects in amnesia: Evidence for a dissociable memory function. *Quarterly Journal of Experimental Psychology, 38A,* 619–644.

Shingo, T., Gregg, C., Enwere, E., Fujikawa, H., Hassam, R., Geary, C., et al. (2003). Pregnancy-stimulated neurogenesis in the adult female forebrain mediated by prolactin. *Science, 299,* 117–120.

Shors, T. J., & Miesegaes, G. (2002). Testosterone in utero and at birth dictates how stressful experience will affect learning in adulthood. *Proceedings of the National Academy of Sciences, 99,* 13955–13960.

Sidman, R., & Rakic, P. (1982). Development of the human central nervous system. In W. Haymaker & R. D. Adams (Eds.), *Histology and histopathology of the nervous system.* Springfield, IL: Charles C Thomas.

Siegler, R. S. (1991). *Children's Thinking* (2nd ed.). Englewood Cliffs, NJ: Prentice-Hall.

Smith, E. E., & Jonides J. (1998). Neuroimaging analyses of human working memory. *Proceedings of the National Academy of Sciences, USA, 95,* 12061–12068.

Smith, M. L., & Milner, B. (1988). Estimation of frequency of occurrence of abstract designs after frontal or temporal lobectomy. *Neuropsychologia, 26,* 297–306.

Smith, P., Loboschefski, T., Davidson, B., & Dixon, W. (1997). Scripts and checkerboards: The influence of ordered visual information on remembering locations in infancy. *Infant Behavior and Development, 13,* 129–146.

Song, H., Stevens, C. E., & Gage, F. H. (2002). Neural stem cells from adult hippocampus develop essential properties of functional CNS neurons. *Nature Neuroscience, 5,* 438–445.

Sowell, E. R., Thompson, P. M., Holmes, C. J., Batth, R., Jernigan, T. L., & Toga, A. W. (1999). Localizing age-related changes in brain structure between childhood and adolescence using statistical parametric mapping. *Neuroimage, 9,* 587–597.

Sowell, E. R., Thompson, P. M., Holmes, C. J., Jernigan, T. L., & Toga, A. W. (2000). In vivo evidence for post-adolescent brain maturation in frontal and striatal regions. *Nature Neuroscience, 2,* 859–961.

Spelke, E. S. (2000). Core knowledge. *American Psychologist, 55,* 1233–1243.

Spiers, H. J., Burgess, N., Hartley, T., Vargha-Khadem, F., & O'Keefe, J. (2001). Bilateral hippocampal pathology impairs topographical and episodic memory but not visual pattern matching. *Hippocampus, 11,* 715–725.

Squire, L. (1986). Mechanisms of memory. *Science, 232,* 1612–1619.

Squire, L. (1994). Declarative and nondeclarative memory: Multiple brain systems supporting learning and memory. In D. L. Schacter & E. Tulving (Eds.), *Memory systems* (pp. 203–231). Cambridge, MA: MIT Press.

Squire, L., & Frambach, M. (1990). Cognitive skill learning in amnesia. *Psychobiology, 18,* 109–117.

Squire, L., Knowlton, B., & Musen, G. (1993). The structure and organization of memory. *Annual Review of Psychology, 44,* 453–495.

Squire, L., & McKee, R. (1993). Declarative and nondeclarative memory in opposition: When prior events influence amnesic patients more than normal subjects. *Memory and Cognition, 21*(4), 424–430.

Squire, L., Ojemann, J., Miezin, F., Petersen, S., Videen, T., & Raichle, M. (1992). Activation of the hippocampus in normal humans: A functional anatomical study of memory. *Proceedings of the National Academy of Sciences, USA, 89,* 1837–1841.

Stewart, L., Henson, R., Kampe, K., Walsh, V., Turner, R., & Frith, U. (2003). Becoming a pianist: An fMRI study of musical literacy acquisition. *Annals of the New York Academy of Sciences, 999,* 204–208.

Stiles, J., Moses, P., Passarotti, A., Dick, F. K., & Buxton, R. B. (2003). Exploring developmental change in the neural bases of higher cognitive functions: The promise of magnetic resonance imaging. *Developmental Neuropsychology, 24,* 641–668.

Stiles, J., Moses, P., Roe, K., Akshoomoff, N. A., Trauner, D. J., Wong, E. L. R., et al. (2003). Alternative brain organization after prenatal cerebral injury: Convergent fMRI and cognitive data. *Journal of the International Neuropsychological Society, 9,* 604–622.

Strange, B. A., Fletcher, P. C., Hennson, R. N. A., Friston, K. J., & Dolan, R. J. (1999). Segregating the functions of the human hippocampus. *Proceedings of the National Academy of Sciences, 96,* 4034–4039.

Sur, M., & Leamey, C. A. (2001). Development and plasticity of cortical areas and networks. *Nature Reviews Neuroscience, 2*(4), 251–262.

Tabata, H., & Nakajima, K. (2003). Multipolar migration: The third mode of radial neuronal migration in the developing cerebral cortex. *Journal of Neuroscience, 23*(31), 9996–10001.

Takahashi, T., Nowakowski, R. S., & Caviness, V. S. (2001). Neocortical neurogeneisis: Regulation, control points, and a strategy of structural variation. In C. A. Nelson & M. Luciana (Eds.), *Handbook of developmental cognitive neuroscience* (pp. 3–22). Cambridge, MA: MIT Press.

Takeichi, M. (1995). Morphogenetic roles of classic caherins. *Current Opinion in Cell Biology, 7,* 619–627.

Tanaka, T., & Gleeson, J. G. (2000). Genetics of brain development and malformation syndromes [Related articles]. *Current Opinions in Pediatrics, 12*(6), 523–528.

Taylor, M. J., Edmonds, G. E., McCarthy, G., & Allison, T. (2001). Eyes first! Eye processing develops before face processing in children. *NeuroReport, 12,* 1671–1676.

Taylor, M. J., McCarthy, G., Saliba, E., & Degiovanni, E. (1999). ERP evidence of developmental changes in processing of faces. *Clinical Neurophysiololgy, 110,* 910–915.

Temple, C. M., & Richardson, P. (2004). Developmental amnesia: A new pattern of dissociation with intact episodic memory. *Neuropsychologia, 42,* 764–781.

Tessier-Lavigne, M., & Goodman, C. S. (1996). The molecular biology of axon guidance. *Science, 274,* 1123–1133.

Thomas, K. M., Drevets, W. C., Whalen, P. J., Eccard, C. H., Dahl, R. E., Ryan, N. D., et al. (2001). Amygdala response to facial expressions in children and adults. *Biological Psychiatry, 49,* 309–316.

Thomas, K. M., Hunt, R., Vizueta, N., Sommer, T., Durston, S., Yang, Y., et al. (in press). Evidence of developmental differences in implicit sequence learning: An fMRI study of children and adults. *Journal of Cognitive Neuroscience.*

Thomas, K. M., King, S. W., Franzen, P. L., Welsh, T. F., Berkowitz, A. L., Noll, D. C., et al. (1999). A developmental functional MRI study of spatial working memory. *Neuroimage, 10,* 327–338.

Thomas, K. M., & Nelson, C. (2001). Serial reaction time learning in preschool- and school-age children. *Journal of Experimental Child Psychology, 79,* 364–387.

Thomas, K. M., Vizueta, N., Teylan, M., Eccard, C., & Casey, B. (2003, April). *Impaired learning in children with presumed basal ganglia insults: Evidence from a serial reaction time task.* Paper presented at the annual meeting of the Cognitive Neuroscience Society, New York, NY.

Thomsen, T., Hugdahl, K., Ersland, L., Barndon, R., Lundervold, A., Smievoll, A. I., et al. (2000). Functional magnetic resonance imaging (fMRI) study of sex differences in a mental rotation task. *Medical Science Monitor, 6,* 1186–1196.

Tomizawa, K., Iga, N., Lu, Y., Moriwaki, A., Matushita, M., Li, S., et al. (2003). Oxytocin improves long-lasting spatial memory during motherhood through MAP kinase cascade. *Nature neuroscience, 6,* 384–390.

Tulving, E. (1972). Episodic and semantic memory. In E. Tulving & W. Donaldson (Eds.), *Organization of memory* (pp. 381–403). New York: Academic Press.

Tulving, E., Markowitsch, H. J., Craik, F. E., Habib, R., & Houle, S. (1996). Novelty and familiarity activations in PET studies of memory encoding and retrieval. *Cerebral Cortex, 6,* 71–79.

Turati, C., Simion, F., Milani, I., & Umilta, C. (2002). Newborns' preferences for faces: What is crucial. *Developmental Psychology, 38,* 875–882.

Turkheimer, E., Haley, A., Waldron, M., D'Onofrio, B., & Gottesman, I. I. (2003). Socioeconomic status modifies heritability of IQ in young children. *Current Directions in Psychological Science, 14,* 623–628.

Tzourio-Mazoyer, N., de Schonen, S., Crivello, F., Reutter, B., Aujard, Y., & Mazoyer, B. (2002). Neural correlates of woman face processing by 2-month-old infants. *NeuroImage, 15,* 454–461.

Uhl, F., Franzen, P., Lindinger, G., Lang, W., & Deecke, L. (1991). On the functionality of the visually deprived occipital cortex in early blind person. *Neuroscience Letters, 124,* 256–259.

Vaidya, C., Austin, G., Kirkorian, G., Ridlehuber, H., Desmond, J., Glover, G., et al. (1998). Selective effects of methylphenidate in attention deficit hyperactivity disorder: A functional magnetic resonance study. *Proceedings of the National Academy of Sciences, USA, 95*(24), 14494–14499.

Vargha-Khadem, F., Gadian, D. G., & Mishkin, M. (2001). Dissociations in cognitive memory: The syndrome of developmental amnesia. *Philosophical Transactions of the Royal Society of London, Biological Sciences, 356*(1413), 1435–1440.

Vargha-Khadem, F., Gadian, D. G., Watkins, K. E., Connelly, A., Van Paesschen, W., & Mishkin, M. (1997). Differential effects of early hippocampal pathology on episodic and semantic memory. *Science, 277*(5324), 376–380.

Vargha-Khadem, F., Salmond, C. H., Watkins, K. E., Friston, K. J., Gadian, D. G., & Mishkin, M. (2003). Developmental amnesia: Effect of age at injury. *Proceedings of the National Academy of Sciences, USA, 100*(17), 10055–10060.

Verfaellie, M., Koseff, P., & Alexander, M. P. (2000). Acquisition of novel semantic information in amnesia: Effects of lesion location. *Neuropsychologia, 38*(4), 484–492.

Vingerhoets, G., de Lange, F. P., Vandemaele, P., Deblaere, K., & Achten, E. (2002). Motor imagery in mental rotation: An fMRI study. *Neuroimage, 17,* 1623–1633.

Volpe, J. J. (1995). *Neurology of the newborn* (3rd ed.). Philadelphia: Saunders.

Volpe, J. J. (2000). Overview: Normal and abnormal human brain development. *Mental Retardation and Developmental Disabilities Research Reviews, 6,* 1–5.

Waber, D. P., Carlson, D., & Mann, M. (1982). Developmental and differential aspects of mental rotation in early adolescence. *Child Development, 53,* 1614–1621.

Waber, D., Marcus, D., Forbes, P., Bellinger, D., Weiler, M., Sorensen, L., et al. (2003). Motor sequence learning and reading ability: Is poor reading associated with sequencing deficits? *Journal of Experimental Child Psychology, 84*(4), 338–354.

Warkany, J., Lemire, R. J., & Cohen, M. M. (1981). *Mental retardation and congenital malformations of the central nervous system.* Chicago: Year Book Medical.

Webb, S. J., Monk, C. S., & Nelson, C. A. (2001). Mechanisms of postnatal neurobiological development in the prefrontal cortex and the hippocampal region: Implications for human development. *Developmental Neuropsychology, 19,* 147–171.

Webb, S. J., & Nelson, C. A. (2001). Perceptual priming for upright and inverted faces in infants and adults. *Journal of Experimental Child Psychology, 79,* 1–22.

Weiss, E., Siedentopf, C. M., Hofer, A., Deisenhammer, E. A., Hoptman, M. J., Kremser, C., et al. (2003). Sex differences in brain activation pattern during a visuospatial cognitive task: A functional magnetic resonance imaging study in healthy volunteers. *Neuroscience Letters, 344,* 169–172.

Werker, J. F., & Vouloumanos, A. (2001). Speech and language processing in infancy: A neurocognitive approach. In C. A. Nelson & M. Luciana (Eds.), *Handbook of developmental cognitive neuroscience.* Cambridge, MA: MIT Press.

Whalen, P. J., Shin, L. M., McInerney, S. C., Fisher, H., Wright, C. I., & Rauch, S. L. (2001). A functional MRI study of human amygdala responses to facial expressions of fear versus anger. *Emotion, 1,* 70–83.

Windischberger, C., Lamm, C., Bauer, H., & Moser, E. (2003). Human motor cortex activity during mental rotation. *Neuroimage, 20,* 225–232.

Wong, R. O., & Lichtman, J. W. (2003). Synapse elimination. In L. R. Squire, F. E. Bloom, S. K. McConnell, J. L. Roberts, N. C. Spitzer, & M. J. Zigmond (Eds.), *Fundamental neuroscience* (2nd ed., pp. 533–554). New York: Academic Press.

Woodruff-Pak, D. (1993). Eyeblink classical conditioning in HM: Delay and trace paradigms. *Behavioral Neuroscience, 107,* 911–925.

Woodruff-Pak, D., Logan, C., & Thompson, R. (1990). Neurobiological substrates of classical conditioning across the lifespan. In A. Diamond (Ed.), *The development and neural bases of higher cognitive functions* (Vol. 608, pp. 150–173). New York: New York Academy of Sciences.

Woodruff-Pak, D., Papka, M., & Ivry, R. (1996). Cerebellar involvement in eyeblink classical conditioning in humans. *Neuropsychology, 10,* 443–458.

Wynn, K. (1992). Addition and subtraction by human infants. *Nature, 358,* 749–750.

Wynn, K., Bloom, P., & Chiang, W.-C. (2002). Enumeration of collective entities by 5-month-old infants. *Cognition, 83*(3), B55–B62.

Yancey, S. W., & Phelps, E. A. (2001). Functional neuroimaging and episodic memory: A perspective. *Journal of Clinical and Experimental Neuropsychology, 23,* 32–48.

Yang, T. T., Menon, V., Eliez, S., Blasey, C., White, C. D., Reid, A. J., et al. (2002). Amygdalar activation associated with positive and negative facial expressions. *NeuroReport, 13*(14), 1737–1741.

Zacks, J. M., Gilliam, F., & Ojemann, J. G. (2003). Selective disturbance of mental rotation by cortical stimulation. *Neuropsychologia, 41,* 1659–1667.

Zago, L., & Tzourio-Mazoyer, N. (2002). Distinguishing visuospatial working memory and complex mental calculation areas within the parietal lobes. *Neuroscience Letters, 331,* 45–49.

Zelazo, P. D., Frye, D., & Rapus, T. (1996). An age-related dissociation between knowing rules and using them. *Cognitive Development, 11,* 37–63.

Zola, S. M., Squire, L. R., Teng, E., Stefanacci, L., Buffalo, E. A., & Clark, R. E. (2000). Impaired recognition memory in monkeys after damage limited to the hippocampal region. *Journal of Neuroscience, 20,* 451–463.

# CHAPTER 2

## The Infant's Auditory World: Hearing, Speech, and the Beginnings of Language

JENNY R. SAFFRAN, JANET F. WERKER, and LYNNE A. WERNER

INFANT AUDITION   59
Development of the Auditory Apparatus:
   Setting the Stage   59
Measuring Auditory Development   60
Frequency Coding   61
Intensity Coding   63
Temporal Coding   67
Spatial Resolution   69
Development of Auditory Scene Analysis   70
Implications for the Development of
   Speech Perception   71
INFANT SPEECH PERCEPTION AND WORD
   LEARNING: BEGINNINGS OF LANGUAGE   72
Emergence of the Field: Phonetic Perception   72
A Preference for Speech   75
Perception of the Visible Information in Speech   76
Perception of Prosodic Attributes of the
   Speech Signal   77
Perception of Other Aspects of the Speech Signal   78
IMPLICIT DISCOVERY OF CUES IN THE
   INPUT: A DRIVE TO MAKE SENSE OF
   THE ENVIRONMENT   80

Stress and Phonotactic Cues   80
Higher-Level Units   81
LEARNING MECHANISMS   81
Units for Computations   83
BUILDING FROM THE INPUT DURING THE
   1ST YEAR   83
Learning Phonology and Phonotactics   84
Word Segmentation   84
Beginnings of Word Recognition   88
Listening for Meaning   89
Beginnings of Grammar   91
CONCLUSIONS AND FUTURE DIRECTIONS   92
Relationship between Auditory Processing and
   Speech Perception   92
Constraints on Learning   93
Domain Specificity and Species Specificity   93
The Infant's Auditory World   94
REFERENCES   95

The auditory world provides a rich source of information to be acquired by the developing infant. We are born with well-developed auditory systems, capable of gathering a wealth of knowledge even prior to birth. Audi-

We thank Dick Aslin, Suzanne Curtin, LouAnn Gerken, Lincoln Gray, Jim Morgan, and Erik Thiessen for their helpful comments on a previous draft. Support for the preparation of this chapter was provided by grants from NIH (R01 HD37466) and NSF (BCS-9983630) to J. R. S., from the Natural Science and Engineering Research Council of Canada, Social Sciences and Humanities Research Council of Canada, The Canada Research Chair Program, and the Human Frontiers Science Program to J. F. W., and from NIH (R01 DC00396, P30 DC04661) to L. A. W.

This chapter is dedicated to the memory of Peter Jusczyk.

tion provides a channel for many important sources of inputs, including a variety of critical environmental sounds such as music and spoken language. For these reasons alone, it has long been of great interest to characterize the nature of this system as it develops.

But studying how infants use their auditory environments can tell us more than just how these developmental processes unfold. In the past decade, studies of infant audition, speech, and the beginnings of language have increasingly begun to bear on central debates in developmental cognitive science and cognitive neuroscience. We are moving beyond such classic questions such as whether speech is special (i.e., subserved by a dedicated neural system that is not shared by other aspects of perception) to begin to study the actual learning mechanisms underlying infants' precocious acquisition of the speech sounds of their native language. Similarly, studies of the origins of infants' linguistic knowledge have moved beyond descriptions of *when* infants know about various features of their native language to studies that ask *how* that learning occurred. Increasingly, such behavioral studies are paired with research using psychophysiological methods to study the neural underpinnings of the behavior, experiments using nonhuman animals to probe the species-specificity of the behavior, and studies using materials drawn from other domains to assess the domain-specificity of the behavior.

In this chapter, we review the state of the art in our field, using the ever-increasing interdisciplinarity of research on infant audition, speech perception, and early language acquisition to highlight several themes. One broad theme is the cause of developmental change. Are changes due to maturation of central and/or peripheral neural structures? Or are they due to learning mechanisms, which are continually discovering complex structure in the environment? A related broad theme concerns the nature of these perceptual and learning processes, and the extent to which they are specifically tailored for a single task (e.g., learning about speech) as opposed to available more generally for learning across domains. We will also consider constraints on perception and learning—arising from our perceptual systems, neural structures, species-specific limitations on learning, and domain-specific limitations on learning—that will help to inform our theories of how these processes are related to other aspects of infant development. Finally, we will point to many of the open questions that continue to drive research in this field, and which we hope to see answered in the subsequent edition of this *Handbook*.

## INFANT AUDITION

Most infant auditory research has focused on infants' perception of speech. In subsequent sections of this chapter, we review many of these studies that demonstrate that even newborns are capable of making many phonetic and other speech distinctions. Clearly infants have the auditory capacity to represent some of the critical acoustic features of speech. Little is known, however, about the acoustic information that infants use to make these fine-grained distinctions. Immature

auditory processing will result in imprecise representations of speech as well as other sounds, and hence limit the information that is available to the infant. In this section, we consider whether limitations of auditory processing may serve to constrain early speech perception.

The auditory system is designed to locate and identify sound sources in the environment. Sounds entering the ear are shaped by the structures of the outer ear to optimize detection of relevant sounds and to allow determination of a sound's location in space. The sound is then analyzed into frequency bands by the inner ear. Periodicity, intensity and temporal fluctuations are represented within each band. This code provides the basis of all auditory perception, but the auditory system must calculate some sound characteristics from the basic code. For example, the shape of a sound's spectrum is extracted and differences between the ears are calculated in the auditory brainstem. Once all of this coding and calculation, referred to as primary processing, is completed, however, the system must still determine which frequency bands emanate from a common source, on the basis of commonalities in frequency, periodicity, intensity, temporal fluctuations, location, and spectral shape. The latter stage of processing is known as sound source segregation or auditory scene analysis (Bregman, 1990). Failure to segregate a sound source from the background makes a listener less sensitive to that sound; factors that promote sound source segregation tend to make listeners more sensitive to a sound. These processes are likely to undergo important developmental change during infancy. Finally, it is important to recognize that attention, motivation, memory and other cognitive processes influence auditory scene analysis, and in a very real way, hearing. These effects are described collectively as "processing efficiency," and they also contribute to auditory development.

### Development of the Auditory Apparatus: Setting the Stage

In humans, the inner ear begins to function during the second trimester of gestation. If humans are like other mammals, neural responses to sound are possible as soon as the inner ear begins to transduce sound. The consensus is that scalp-recorded auditory evoked potentials and behavioral responses can be observed in fetuses and in preterm infants as young as 28 weeks gestational age. The possibility of prenatal hearing has important implications for understanding the effects of early experience on neural development. Fetuses' experience with sound is severely limited by the sound transmission properties of maternal tissue and amniotic fluid, by the conduction of sound to the fetal inner ear, and by immaturities of the inner ear and auditory nervous system (Smith, Gerhardt, Griffiths, & Huang, 2003). Nonetheless, several studies have documented differential fetal responsiveness to sounds of different intensities and frequencies (e.g., Lecanuet, Gramer-Deferre, & Busnel, 1988; Shahidullah & Hepper, 1994). Further, several studies have demonstrated that prenatal experience with sound can influence later auditory responses, at least in the immediate postnatal period. This is most dramatically shown in the preference for mother's voice shown at birth (DeCasper & Fifer, 1980) and in the preference for a story and/or song heard prenatally (DeCasper & Spence, 1986). At the same time, little is known about the importance of prenatal experience with sound for auditory or other aspects of development.

At term, the neonate is believed to have a mature inner ear (but see Abdala, 2001; for example, Bargones & Burns, 1988; Bredberg, 1968). However, the conduction of sound through the external and middle ear to the inner ear is less efficient in neonates than in adults (Keefe, Bulen, Arehart, & Burns, 1993; Keefe, Burns, Bulen, & Campbell, 1994; Keefe et al., 2000). The transmission of information through the auditory neural pathway is slow and inefficient (e.g., Gorga, Kaminski, Beauchaine, Jesteadt, & Neely, 1989; Gorga, Reiland, Beauchaine, Worthington, & Jesteadt, 1987; Ponton, Moore, & Eggermont, 1996). The implications of this pattern of immaturities for postnatal auditory development are discussed in the sections that follow.

Approximately 2 to 3 in 1,000 infants are born with a hearing loss, 1 in 1,000 with a severe to profound hearing loss. However, 20% to 30% of hearing-impaired children develop hearing loss postnatally. These children can be identified, even as neonates, with appropriate hearing screening (Norton et al., 2000), although in the recent past, the average age of identification of hearing-impaired children was 2½ years. Disruption of nearly all aspects of development, but particularly of language development, is typical in hearing-impaired children. Recent evidence suggests, however, that early identification of hearing loss—with intervention beginning prior to 6 months of age—facilitates the development of language skills (signed and/or spoken) within the normal range in childhood (Yoshinaga-Itano, Sedey, Coulter, & Mehl, 1998).

## Measuring Auditory Development

Sounds differ in three basic dimensions—frequency, intensity, and changes in frequency and intensity over time. The auditory system encodes the frequency and intensity of sound and extracts information about temporal variation. In addition, the auditory system calculates additional information about differences between sounds arriving at the two ears, or interaural differences. In psychoacoustics, auditory capacities are approached from two directions. One is to describe the accuracy with which a dimension is coded, or resolution. The other is to describe the function relating the acoustic dimension to its perception. Both approaches have been taken in characterizing hearing during infancy, although the former is more straightforward in a nonverbal subject.

Except as noted, the studies described in this section used one of three varieties of discrimination learning procedures to estimate infants' thresholds for detecting or discriminating between sounds. Each depends upon teaching the infant that when a sound occurs or when a sound changes in some way, a response will be reinforced by the presentation of an interesting audiovisual event. The common reinforcers are mechanical toys and video displays. Two of the procedures teach infants to make a head turn when the appropriate sound occurs. In one variant, infants learn to turn toward the reinforcer (e.g., Berg & Smith, 1983; Nozza & Wilson, 1984). In the other variant, sounds are presented from one of two loudspeakers on a random schedule. The infant learns to turn toward the speaker producing the sound (e.g., Trehub, Schneider, & Edman, 1980). Infants older than about 6 months of age can be successfully tested using either of these procedures. However, younger infants do not make the crisp directional head turns that older infants do. To get around this difficulty, observer-based conditioning procedures capitalize on whatever response the infant makes to the sound (e.g., Tharpe & Ashmead, 2001; Werner, 1995). In this method, which was originally developed to study infants' visual acuity (Teller, 1979), an observer watching the infant knows when a sound may be presented but not whether it was in fact presented. On the basis of the infant's response, the observer must judge whether or not the sound was presented. The infant is reinforced for producing a response that leads to a correct observer judgment. Infants as young as 1 month of age have been successfully tested using this technique.

Once children are 3 or 4 years old, they can be tested using a variant of adult psychophysical procedures (e.g., Wightman, Allen, Dolan, Kistler, & Jamieson, 1989). Commonly, three intervals are presented to the child, only one of which randomly contains the signal to be processed. The child is asked to choose the interval containing the different sound. The intervals can be presented with cartoon indicators, making the whole procedure more like a video game.

## Frequency Coding

Frequency is coded in the auditory system by two mechanisms. The basilar membrane in the inner ear vibrates in response to incoming sound, and because the stiffness of the membrane varies along its length, each position along the membrane responds maximally to a particular frequency. Hair cells are positioned along the length of the basilar membrane. Outer hair cells provide mechanical feedback that results in higher amplitude and more restricted, or sharper, basilar membrane responses to a given frequency. Each inner hair cell transduces basilar membrane motion into a neural response in the auditory nerve fibers that exclusively contact it. Thus activity in a particular auditory nerve fiber indicates the presence of frequencies within a band about a third of an octave wide. The frequency content of any sound, then, is represented in the pattern of activity across auditory nerve fibers innervating different positions along the basilar membrane. This neural representation of sound is referred to as the place code. Because the basilar membrane vibrates at the frequency of stimulation, the action potentials in auditory nerve fibers tend to occur at the frequency of stimulation. Thus, for frequencies below 5,000 Hz, the intervals between action potentials provide another code for frequency.[1] This phenomenon is known as phase locking, and it provides the basis for the temporal code for frequency. The bulk of evidence from adults indicates that both frequency codes are involved

in determining pitch, the perceptual dimension correlated with sound frequency. Further, in adults, it is the processing of sound in the inner ear that limits the representation of complex sounds.

### Frequency Resolution

The most common way to assess the resolution of the place code of frequency is to determine the frequencies of competing sounds that interfere with a listener's ability to detect a frequency-specific sound. The phenomenon of one sound's increasing the difficulty of detecting another is called masking. The interfering sound is the masker; the sound to be detected is called the signal or probe. When masking occurs, the threshold ratio of probe to masker intensity required to detect the probe is higher. It has long been known that one sound will only mask another if their frequencies are separated by less than about a third of an octave (there are exceptions to this rule which are discussed below). It is fairly easy to understand, then, that masking occurs when the masker evokes activity in the same auditory nerve fibers that respond to the probe, and that masking provides a method for assessing the quality of the place code for frequency.

Both behavioral and electrophysiological measures indicate that frequency resolution measured using masking is immature at birth, but is mature by about 6 months of age. For example, Spetner and Olsho (1990) showed that a 4,000 or 8,000 Hz tone was masked by a broader range of frequencies for 3-month-olds than for 6-month-olds and adults. Three-month-olds' frequency resolution was mature only at 1,000 Hz, and 6-month-olds demonstrated mature frequency resolution at all frequencies. Studies by Schneider, Morrongiello, and Trehub (1990) and Olsho (1985) confirmed that frequency resolution was mature at 6 months of age. Although a few studies purported to show immature frequency resolution at 4 years of age (Allen, Wightman, Kistler, & Dolan, 1989; Irwin, Stillman, & Schade, 1986), Hall and Grose (1991) subsequently showed that children of this age had mature frequency resolution when thresholds were appropriately measured. Thus, frequency resolution at low frequencies appears to be mature by birth. At high frequencies, frequency resolution becomes adultlike some time between 3 and 6 months.

Lack of development of the auditory nervous system appears to be responsible for early immaturity of frequency resolution. The consensus is that the inner ear mechanisms responsible for frequency resolution are mature at birth (but see Abdala, 2001; for example, Bargones & Burns, 1988; Bredberg, 1968). However, the

---

[1] Single auditory nerve fibers do not fire on every cycle of a continuing periodic sound; at frequencies above about 1,000 Hz, single nerve fibers cannot fire fast enough to provide a temporal code for frequency. However, each nerve fiber responds at the same phase of the sound and different nerve fibers randomly respond on different cycles. By combining the responses of many auditory nerve fibers responding to the same frequency, a code for frequency can be derived up to 5,000 Hz.

mature frequency resolution established in the inner ear is not faithfully transmitted through the auditory nervous system. Like the studies based on behavioral measures, several studies based on brainstem evoked-potential measures of frequency resolution report maturity at low frequencies, but not at high frequencies for 3-month-old infants (Abdala & Folsom, 1995a, 1995b; Folsom & Wynne, 1987). By 6 months, these measures indicate mature resolution across the frequency range. The parallels between behavioral and neural evoked potentials results suggest a neural basis for the immaturities observed early in infancy.

### Frequency Discrimination

Frequency resolution is a measure of the precision of the place code for frequency. Discrimination between sounds on the basis of frequency, however, is accomplished via both the place code and the temporal code for frequency. Despite the fact that 6-month-olds have mature frequency resolution, frequency discrimination remains immature, at least at low frequencies. Olsho (1984) first reported that 6-month-olds needed about twice the frequency change that adults did to detect a change in frequencies below 2,000 Hz. At 1,000 Hz, several studies have estimated that 6-month-old infants can detect a 1.5% to 3% change in frequency, while adults can detect a change of 1% or less (Aslin, 1989; Olsho, 1984; Olsho, Koch, & Halpin, 1987; Olsho, Schoon, Sakai, Turpin, & Sperduto, 1982; Sinnott & Aslin, 1985). At higher frequencies, Olsho (1984) reported that 6-month-olds detected frequency changes as well as adults did. Sinnott and Aslin (1985) and Olsho et al. (1987) reported results generally consistent with that pattern. Olsho et al. also tested 3-month-old infants and found that they performed similarly to 6-month-olds at low frequencies, but that they had higher frequency discrimination thresholds at high frequencies.

Several studies of preschool and school-age children show that pure-tone frequency discrimination is not adultlike until 10 years of age (Jensen & Neff, 1993; Maxon & Hochberg, 1982; Thompson, Cranford, & Hoyer, 1999). Maxon and Hochberg reported that the discrimination of low frequencies was more immature than that of high frequencies at 4 years, consistent with the results of the infant studies. However, these investigators did report some improvement in discrimination of high frequencies between 4 and 12 years. Nonetheless, the greatest changes in high-frequency discrimination appear to occur during the first 6 months of life, while the greatest changes in low-frequency discrimination appear to occur between 4 and 6 years of age.

The change in high-frequency discrimination between 3 and 6 months is consistent with the improvement in frequency resolution observed at this age. The nature of the prolonged developmental course for low frequency discrimination is less obvious. It has been suggested that adults use the temporal code to represent low frequency tones and the place code to represent high frequency tones (B. C. J. Moore, 1973). One possible explanation for poor low-frequency discrimination by infants and children is that they do not use the temporal code in pure-tone frequency discrimination or that they use the temporal code inefficiently. However, Allen, Jones, and Slaney (1998) reported that, compared to adults, 4-year-olds' detection is more dependent on the periodicity, or "pitchiness" of a tone. The temporal code is the basis of that sound quality (B. C. J. Moore, 1996). In addition 7-year-olds' pure tone frequency discrimination is more affected by decreases in tone duration than is that of adults', which would suggest that children are more dependent on the temporal code (Thompson et al., 1999). However, by 7 years of age, children are also good at low-frequency discrimination (Maxon & Hochberg, 1982). The other possible explanation for poor low-frequency discrimination is that it takes longer to learn to discriminate between low frequencies than high (Demany, 1985; Olsho, Koch, & Carter, 1988). If infants and young children generally take longer to learn a task than adults do, then they might be at a particular disadvantage in learning to discriminate between low frequencies. An analysis of infant frequency discrimination by Olsho, Koch, and Carter (1988) suggests that training effects might account for some, but not all, of the difference between infants and adults in low-frequency discrimination

### Perception of Pitch

The relative importance of the temporal and place codes has been debated extensively in the literature on complex pitch perception. A complex tone consists of multiple frequency components, a fundamental frequency and harmonics. The perception of complex pitch is said to be unitary. That is, although the pitch of a complex tone generally matches the pitch of its fundamental, the complex is perceived as having a single pitch, and the higher harmonics contribute to that percept (B. C. J. Moore, 1996). Clarkson and her colleagues have carried out an impressive series of studies of infants' perception of complex pitch. In many respects, complex pitch perception in 7- to 8-month-olds appears to be adultlike: Infants are able to categorize complexes on the basis of fundamental frequency, even when the fundamental frequency component is missing from the complex (Clarkson & Clifton, 1985; Montgomery & Clarkson, 1997). Infants have difficulty categorizing inharmonic complexes on the basis of pitch, as do adults (Clarkson & Clifton, 1995). However, when only high-frequency harmonics are present, adults are still able to hear the pitch of the missing fundamental, while infants are not (Clarkson & Rogers, 1995). Because periodicity in the waveform of combined high-frequency harmonics provides the basis of this percept in adults, Clarkson and Rogers' result suggests, again, that infants have difficulty using the temporal code in pitch perception.

## Intensity Coding

The primary code for intensity in the auditory system is the firing rate of auditory nerve fibers. There are several studies of developing nonhumans that suggest that immature neurons cannot sustain a response over time and that the maximum firing rate achieved by auditory nerve fibers increases with development (Sanes & Walsh, 1998). In humans, evoked potential amplitude increases more slowly with increasing intensity in infants than in adults (Durieux-Smith, Edwards, Picton, & McMurray, 1985; Jiang, Wu, & Zhang, 1990). Further, because the external and middle ear grow during infancy and childhood, the conduction of sound to the inner would be expected to improve with age. Thus, there is reason to believe that intensity processing would undergo postnatal developmental change in humans.

### Intensity Resolution

Some sensory processes can be measured by comparing thresholds across masking conditions. In the studies of infant frequency resolution described earlier (Olsho, 1985; Schneider et al., 1990; Spetner & Olsho, 1990), 6-month-olds' thresholds for detecting a tone were always higher than those of adults, but their thresholds changed as the frequency or bandwidth of the masker changed exactly as adults' thresholds did. It is the pattern of change in threshold that indicates resolution. Making it difficult to judge intensity resolution to be immature is the fact that measures of intensity resolution tend to be absolute measures; they do not depend on a comparison of performance across conditions, but on the absolute

level of performance. It is difficult to distinguish intensity coding effects from processing efficiency effects on an absolute measure. Few experiments have been carried out that allow for this distinction, and a major question in this area is the relative contributions of auditory capacities and processing efficiency to age-related changes in thresholds.

Intensity resolution is typically measured psychophysically by finding the smallest intensity change that a listener can detect. When the change detected is from "no sound" to "sound," we say we are measuring absolute sensitivity. When change is detected in an audible sound, we say we are measuring intensity discrimination, increment detection or masking. In the classic intensity discrimination paradigm, a listener hears two or more sounds, and responds to the more intense. In increment detection, the background sound is continuous; the listener responds when the intensity of the background increases. Simultaneous masking is a special case of intensity discrimination or increment detection in that the addition of a signal to the masker is detected as an increase in the intensity of the stimulus. All of these measures largely depend on the same underlying processes, so the expectation is that they will develop along a similar course, with one exception: The "noise" that limits absolute sensitivity is neural and physiological noise. It is not conducted through the external and middle ear. Immaturity of the conductive apparatus will affect the level of a signal played into the ear, but not the level of the background when absolute threshold is measured. In masking, intensity discrimination and increment detection, the conductive apparatus affects both the signal and the background, leaving the signal-to-noise ratio unchanged. Thus, conductive immaturity will be reflected in absolute thresholds, but not the other measures of intensity resolution.

The most commonly measured aspect of intensity processing is the absolute threshold, the intensity of sound that is just detectable in a quiet environment. Some studies have measured absolute thresholds in infants 3 months and younger. Weir (1976, 1979) estimated the behavioral threshold of neonates, based on their spontaneous responses to tones. The thresholds she measured ranged from 68 dB SPL at 250 Hz to 82 dB SPL at 2,000 Hz, approximately 30 and 70 dB higher than adult thresholds at these frequencies, respectively. Ruth, Horner, McCoy, and Chandler (1983) and Kaga and Tanaka (1980) reported behavioral observation audiometry thresholds for 1-month-olds that are similar to those reported by Weir for neonates. However, thresholds measured at 1 to 2 months of age using observer-based procedures are quite a bit lower, about 40 to 55 dB SPL, 35 to 45 dB higher than adults' thresholds (Tharpe & Ashmead, 2001; Trehub, Schneider, Thorpe, & Judge, 1991; Werner & Gillenwater, 1990; Werner & Mancl, 1993). The difference between 1-month-olds' and adults' threshold is about 10 dB greater at 500 Hz than at 4,000 Hz (Werner & Gillenwater, 1990). Whether infants' sensitivity actually improves by 25 dB between birth and 1 month is not clear, given the differences in the procedures used to assess threshold.

By 3 months, thresholds appear to improve by about 10 dB at 500 Hz and by nearly 20 dB at 4,000 Hz (Olsho, Koch, Carter, Halpin, & Spetner, 1988). Compared to adults, 3-month-olds are still about 5 dB less sensitive at the higher frequency. A longitudinal, observer-based study of infants' detection thresholds for a broad noise band confirmed an improvement of about 15 dB between 1 and 3 months (Tharpe & Ashmead, 2001). Between 3 and 6 months, very little improvement is observed in the 500-Hz threshold, but a further 15 dB improvement is seen in the 4,000-Hz threshold (Olsho, Koch, Carter, et al., 1988). Tharpe and Ashmead observed about a 15 dB improvement in threshold for a noise band between 3 and 6 months. In the Olsho et al. study, the performance difference between 6-month-olds and adults at 4,000 Hz is about 15 dB, while at 500 Hz it is about 20 dB. There is general consensus that in the vicinity of 1,000 Hz, 6-month-olds are about 15 dB less sensitive than adults (Berg & Smith, 1983; Nozza & Wilson, 1984; Olsho, Koch, Carter, et al., 1988; Ruth et al., 1983; Sinnott, Pisoni, & Aslin, 1983; Tharpe & Ashmead, 2001; Trehub et al., 1980).

More extensive work has documented absolute sensitivity from 6 months to adulthood. Trehub, Schneider, Morrengiello, and Thorpe (1988) measured thresholds for noise bands centered at different frequencies for listeners ranging from 6 months of age through the school years to adulthood. They report that threshold improves by about 25 dB at 400 Hz, about 20 dB at 1,000 Hz, but only 10 dB at 10,000 Hz. Further, the higher the frequency, the earlier adult levels are achieved: 10 years or later at 1,000 Hz, but before 5 years of age at 4,000 and 10,000 Hz.

The ability to detect a change in the intensity of an audible sound is frequently measured by intensity discrimination, that is, by asking the listener to respond to an intensity difference between sounds. Several studies of infants indicate that they are poorer at intensity dis-

crimination than are adults. Few data are available for infants younger than 6 months of age, but there is evidence that newborns respond to an intensity change in a speech sound as small as 6 dB (Tarquinio, Zelazo, & Weiss, 1990). By 7 to 9 months, Sinnott and Aslin (1985) found that infants detected intensity differences of 6 dB between 1,000 Hz tones, while adults could detect differences of about 2 dB. Kopyar (1997) reported that infants of this age detected differences of 9 dB between tones or between broadband noises. Adults detected differences of about 4 dB between tones, but about 3 dB between noises.

Intensity discrimination has not been examined in children between 9 months and 4 years of age. Maxon and Hochberg (1982) tested intensity discrimination of tones in children older than 4 years. They found a steady improvement in the discrimination threshold from about 2 dB at age 4 years to about 1 dB at 12 years, when the level of tones was near 60 dB above the child's absolute threshold. Thus, by 4 years, intensity discrimination appears to be quite good. Only minor improvements occur thereafter, at least for tones well above absolute threshold.

Increment detection matures somewhat earlier than does discrimination between discrete sounds. Several studies have shown that 7- to 9-month-olds can detect 3 to 5 dB increments in a broad noise band (Berg & Boswell, 1998; Kopyar, 1997; Werner & Boike, 2001), under conditions in which adults detect increments of 1 to 2 dB. Schneider, Bull, and Trehub (1988) reported that 12-month-olds could detect 3 dB increments in a continuous broadband noise, while adults could detect increments less than 1 dB. Berg and Boswell (2000) measured increment detection thresholds in 1- and 3-year-old children, for a 2-octave wide noise band centered at 4,000 Hz. Their results for 1-year-olds are similar to those reported by Schneider et al.; 3-year-olds appeared to be adultlike in this task.

The only thresholds for detection of an increment in a tone were reported by Kopyar (1997). Infants do relatively worse in detecting tone increments than noise increments, requiring increments of 8 dB, compared to 2 dB for adults. A number of studies have examined the development of detection of a tone or narrow noise band masked by a noise, essentially the detection of an increment in an ongoing sound. Schneider, Trehub, Morrongiello, and Thorpe (1989) estimated masked thresholds for a 1-octave band noise, centered at frequencies ranging from 400 to 10,000 Hz, masked by a broadband noise, in children ranging from 6 months to

10 years of age and adults. At 6 months, the infants' detection threshold was equivalent to a 7 dB increment; adults detected a 1 dB increment.[2] The age difference was about the same across the frequency range. Relatively large improvements in performance were reported between 6 and 18 months and between 4 years and 8 years. There was little difference between 10-year-olds and adults. Other studies have examined infants' and children's detection of tones in noise (Allen & Wightman, 1994; Bargones, Werner, & Marean, 1995; Berg & Boswell, 1999; Nozza & Wilson, 1984). They report similar results, although it is clear that there is considerable variability across children in this task (e.g., Allen & Wightman, 1994).

### Perception of Timbre

Timbre, or sound quality, is determined by the relative amplitudes of the components of a complex sound, and thus involves the comparison of intensities across frequency. The physical dimension associated with timbre is referred to as spectral shape. Vowel perception and sound localization depend on spectral shape processing. A few studies have examined the development of timbre perception. Seven-month-olds can discriminate between sounds of different timbres, complex tones with the same pitch that contain different harmonics (Clarkson, Clifton, & Perris, 1988). Trehub, Endman, and Thorpe (1990) also showed that infants could categorize tonal complexes on the basis of "spectral shape." The sharpness of infants' representation of spectral shape has not been assessed. Allen and Wightman (1992) used a complex sound with a sinusoidal spectral shape to measure children's threshold for detecting changes in spectral shape. They were unable to elicit discrimination between such complexes in 4-year-olds. Five and 7-year-olds performed the task, but only 9-year-olds performed as well as adults. These results suggest that spectral shape, or timbre, discrimination follows a long developmental course. It is not clear that performance on this task generalizes to vowel perception.

### Perception of Loudness

A final measure of intensity processing is loudness. In adults, loudness is measured by having listeners match sounds in loudness or by having them rate loudness by

some means. Children as young as 5 years of age are able to rate the loudness of tones numerically and with line length. Moreover, loudness appears to grow with increasing intensity in the same way for children and adults (Bond & Stevens, 1969; Collins & Gescheider, 1989). The evidence on loudness growth in infants is sparse. Leibold and Werner (2002) examined the relationship between intensity and reaction time in 7- to 9-month-olds and adults. Reaction time decreased with increasing sound intensity in both age groups, but the rate of decrease was greater for infants than for adults. This finding suggests that loudness grows more rapidly with increasing intensity in infants, but again, the implications of this finding for early audition are not clear.

In summary, absolute threshold, intensity discrimination, detection of tones masked by noise and spectral shape discrimination all undergo relatively large age-related improvements during infancy and the preschool years. However, adult levels of performance are not reached until 8 or 10 years of age. Interestingly, increment detection in broadband sounds appears to mature earlier, around 3 years of age. Nozza (1995; Nozza & Hensen, 1999) showed that the level at which a noise would just start to mask a tone was 8 dB more intense for infants than for adults. This clever experiment demonstrates that immature thresholds of 8- to 11-month-olds are due largely to changes in sensitivity, rather than performance factors. Several factors are known to contribute to age-related improvements in intensity processing. For example, the frequency response of the infant ear canal changes during infancy. While the adult ear canal conducts sounds best in the range between 2,000 and 5,000 Hz, the infant ear canal conducts higher frequency sounds better (Keefe et al., 1994). Further, the efficiency with which the middle ear conducts sound into the inner ear has been shown to increase over a long age period, from birth to perhaps 10 years of age (Keefe et al., 1993, 2000; Keefe & Levi, 1996; Okabe, Tanaka, Hamada, Miura, & Funai, 1988). The largest improvements occur during the 1st year of life, especially for frequencies over about 1,000 Hz. It has been estimated that the efficiency of the conductive apparatus improves by as much as 20 dB at 3,000 Hz between birth and adulthood, with about half of that improvement occurring during infancy. Age-related improvement in conductive efficiency is smaller at lower frequencies, with about a 5 dB improvement between birth and adulthood (Keefe et al., 1993). Thus, one factor in the development of absolute sensitivity is the development of the conductive apparatus. It is likely that

---

[2] If the threshold is expressed as the sound pressure level of the signal added to the masker, 6-month-olds' threshold for detecting a noise band or a tone in noise is 8 to 10 dB higher than adults'.

recover from adaptation, the response at the offset of the gap will be reduced. A psychophysical paradigm for measuring adaptation is forward masking: a relatively intense sound, the masker, is presented, quickly followed by a probe sound. If the interval between the initial and following sound is less than about 100 ms, the audibility of the probe is reduced relative to the unmasked condition. The development of forward masked thresholds has been examined in infants and in children. Werner (1999) measured forward masked thresholds for a 1-kHz tone in 3- and 6-month-old infants at masker-probe intervals ranging from 5 to 100 ms. Her results showed that the amount of forward masking decreased as the interval increased, and in the same way, for each age group. The audibility of the probe tone was affected more for the 3-month-olds than it was for older listeners. However, 6-month-olds were more or less adultlike in the amount of forward masking demonstrated at all intervals. Thus, by this measure of temporal resolution, 3-month-olds are immature, but 6-month-olds are not. This conclusion argues against the idea that adaptation effects are responsible for variation in gap detection thresholds of 6-month-olds. Buss, Hall, Grose, and Dev (1999) also report that the amount of forward masking demonstrated by 5- to 11-year-old children is adultlike.

A measure of temporal resolution that has received considerable attention from developmentalists in recent years is backward masking, in which a probe tone is masked by a relatively intense masker that follows it by a short interval (0 to 50 ms). Tallal and her colleagues (Tallal, Miller, Jenkins, & Merzenich, 1997; Tallal & Piercy, 1973, 1974) have long argued that a deficit in auditory temporal resolution is the underlying cause of specific language impairment. Wright et al. (1997) collected psychophysical data from children with language impairment and typically developing children. They found that children with language impairment did not differ from typically developing children in simultaneous masked thresholds. Their thresholds were a little higher in forward masking, but their thresholds were considerable higher in backward masking. This finding was taken to support Tallal's position and has spurred research in this area. It has also spurred an interest in the development of backward masking, which had heretofore not been examined. For example, Hartley, Wright, Hogan, and Moore (2000) reported 6-year-olds' backward masked threshold for a 1,000-Hz tone to be 34 dB higher than adults'. At 10 years, backward masked thresholds were nearly 20 dB higher than those of adults. Even if the absolute threshold of 6-year-olds are

5 dB or so higher than those of adults, that still means that they are exhibiting 30 dB more masking than adults. Other studies confirm that children at this age are more susceptible to backward masking than adults (Buss et al., 1999; Rosen, van der Lely, Adlard, & Manganari, 2000). Werner (2003) has also reported that 7- and 11-month-olds have higher backward masked thresholds than adults, although the age difference in amount of masking is not clear. A recent study, however, suggests that at least among children, the apparent susceptibility to backward masking may not reflect immaturity of temporal resolution. Hartley and Moore (2002) showed that a listener with normal temporal resolution, but poor processing efficiency, will be relatively more susceptible to backward masking than to forward or simultaneous masking. It should be noted that a similar conclusion could be drawn about the nature of the perceptual deficit associated with language impairment.

The gold standard of temporal resolution measures is the temporal modulation transfer function (TMTF, Viemeister, 1979). Listeners are asked to detect amplitude modulation (AM) in a sound. The depth, or amount, of modulation is manipulated to define the threshold for AM detection. AM detection threshold is estimated over a range of modulation frequencies. For adults, the result is a function, the TMTF, with a "low-pass characteristic": AM detection threshold is fairly constant from a 4-Hz modulation rate to about 50 Hz. Beyond 50 Hz modulation rate, the AM detection threshold grows poorer at rate of about 3 dB per doubling of modulation frequency. The modulation frequency at which AM detection begins to deteriorate is taken as the measure of temporal resolution. Hall and Grose (1994) described the TMTF of 4- to 10-year-old children. The AM detection threshold of 4- to 7-year-olds was poorer than that of adults across the range of modulation rates; 9- to 10-year-olds were adultlike in this respect. However, the shape of the TMTF was the same for all ages; AM detection began to deteriorate at about 50 to 60 Hz in all age groups. When the TMTF becomes mature is uncertain. Levi and Werner (1996) reported AM detection thresholds of 3-month-olds, 6-month-olds and adults at two modulation rates, 4 and 64 Hz. The difference between thresholds at the two modulation rates for 3- and 6-month-olds was 3 dB. This difference suggests that infants have an adultlike TMTF and mature temporal resolution.

The development of temporal integration has also been of recent interest. In adults, increasing the duration of a sound by a factor of 10 leads to a little less than 10-

dB decrease in the absolute threshold for that sound. This means that adults are integrating information about the sound over time nearly perfectly. Sound energy cannot be integrated, however, over intervals longer than 200 to 300 ms. Several studies of infants have reported that the maximum interval over which infants integrate sound energy in detection is similar to the adult value (e.g., Berg & Boswell, 1995; Thorpe & Schneider, 1987). However, it was also reported that increasing the duration of sound had a much greater than expected effect on infants' absolute threshold. For example, Thorpe and Schneider found that increasing the duration of a noise band by a factor of 6.3 leads to a 20-dB decrease in 6- to 7-month-olds' absolute threshold. Berg and Boswell argued that infants' temporal integration was mature, but that infants had difficulty detecting short duration sounds (see also Bargones et al., 1995). Maxon and Hochberg (1982) reported temporal integration data for 4- to 10-year-olds. For durations of 50 ms and longer, thresholds decreased with increasing duration at an adultlike rate, and thresholds leveled off between 200 and 400 ms duration. The only difference between children and adults was at quite short durations: increasing the duration from 25 to 50 ms leads to a 7-dB decrease in threshold at 4 years. By 12 years, the decrease is only 5 dB, but still greater than expected in adults. Thus, as children get older they appear to be able to deal with progressively shorter sounds. The nature of the immaturity is not clear; Berg and Boswell suggest that it actually could result from immaturity in the growth of neural response with intensity (Fay & Coombs, 1983) or that the immature auditory system is less able to process onset responses and hence, transient stimuli.

## Spatial Resolution

Locating sound sources in space involves several processes including evaluation of spectral shape and intensity, as well as binaural comparisons. Under normal circumstances, spectral shape is the primary cue to position in elevation, while binaural time and intensity differences are the primary cues to position in azimuth (the plane that runs through your ears parallel to the ground).

Development of the ability to use these cues has been well studied in infants via measurements of the minimum audible angle (MAA), the threshold for detecting a change in the position of a sound source. The MAA in azimuth has been shown to decrease from about 27° at 1 month to less than 5° at 18 months (Ashmead, Clifton, & Perris, 1987; Clifton, Morrongiello, Kulig, & Dowd,

1981; Morrongiello, 1988; Morrongiello, Fenwick, & Chance, 1990; Morrongiello, Fenwick, Hillier, & Chance, 1994; Morrongiello & Rocca, 1987a, 1990). The MAA is adultlike, 1° to 2°, in 5-year-olds. The MAA in elevation decreases from a value greater than 16° at 6 to 8 months to about 4° at 18 months, which is comparable to the adult MAA in elevation (Morrongiello & Rocca, 1987b, 1987c). In adults, the MAA in azimuth is generally smaller than that in elevation, because additional, binaural, cues can be used to localize sounds in azimuth. Interestingly, during infancy the MAA in azimuth is similar to that in elevation (Morrongiello & Rocca, 1987b, 1987c). That the MAA is similar in the two dimensions suggests that infants may rely more heavily on spectral shape in sound localization than on binaural differences. Finally, several studies have suggested that infants are sensitive to the changes in sound intensity that signal a change in sound source distance (Clifton, Perris, & Bullinger, 1991; Morrongiello, Hewitt, & Gotowiec, 1991). The accuracy with which infants can judge sound source distance has not been examined.

Humans and other mammals base their judgments of a sound source's location on information that first reaches their ears; they are able to suppress information carried in echoes of the original sound. This effect is known as the precedence effect. It is known that infants also demonstrate this effect (Clifton, Morrongiello, & Dowd, 1984). Interestingly, Litovsky (1997) found that while sound localization is influenced to some degree by the presence of echoes in adults, 5-year-olds are more affected. This difference suggests that while the traditional MAA is mature by 5 years, sound localization in real environments may continue to be refined beyond that age.

The mechanisms underlying the development of sound localization are not completely understood. One obvious change that will influence this ability is the growth of the head and external ear. As the head grows, the size of interaural differences increases (Clifton, Gwiazda, Bauer, Clarkson, & Held, 1988), and discrimination of interaural time differences has been shown to improve during infancy (Ashmead, Davis, Whalen, & Odom, 1991). Ashmead et al. (1991), however, showed that immaturity of interaural discrimination does not appear to be great enough to account for early immaturity of sound localization. One possible explanation for early sound localization immaturity is that infants are more dependent on spectral shape than interaural differences in determining a sound source location. Infants' ability to use spectral shape cues will also improve as the external ear grows. Another explanation is that infants can process the cues to sound location adequately, but that they have not yet developed the ability to translate a set of acoustic cues into a precise location in space (Gray, 1992). In other animals, it has been shown that multimodal experience is required to grow such a map of sensory space (e.g., Binns, Withington, & Keating, 1995; King, Hutchings, Moore, & Blakemore, 1988). Further, humans who have only monaural hearing early in life may be able to discriminate interaural differences normally when hearing is restored to the previously deprived ear, but still be unable to locate sounds in space (Wilmington, Gray, & Jahrsdorfer, 1994).

Besides allowing us to localize sounds with precision, interaural differences improve our sensitivity to sound. In the laboratory this improvement in sensitivity is called the masking level difference (MLD): Threshold for a tone presented to both ears is lower if there are interaural differences in the masker presented to the two ears. It appears that infants derive less benefit from interaural differences than adults do, and that by 5 years of age the MLD is adultlike (Hall & Grose, 1990; Nozza, 1987). However, 5-year-olds may still derive less benefit from listening with two ears when the listening situation is complex (Hall & Grose, 1990).

## Development of Auditory Scene Analysis

Once the auditory system has analyzed incoming sound and extracted information about its spectral shape, temporal fluctuations and location, it remains to resynthesize the auditory scene. Information in different frequency bands must be grouped according to source on the basis of the initial analysis. Moreover, once the scene has been reconstructed, the listener may choose to attend to one sound source, while ignoring others. The development of these processes has not been studied extensively. A few studies suggest that the process of grouping components on the basis of source, called sound source segregation, is functional in infancy, but it is not clear how accurately or efficiently it operates.

Demany (1982), for example, used repeating tone sequences to study source segregation. In one sequence, three of four tones were close in frequency while the fourth was somewhat higher in frequency. Adult listeners perceived this sequence as coming from two sources, one producing three different low frequencies, the other producing the single higher frequency tone. If the order

of the tones in this sequence was reversed, adults had no trouble reporting the change. In another sequence, two pairs of near-frequency tones were repeated. Adults heard this sequence as coming from two sources, each of which produced two alternating tones. When the order of this sequence was reversed, adults had difficulty hearing the change. Demany tested 2- to 4-month-olds' ability to discriminate an order change in these two sequences, using a habituation/dishabituation task wherein looking time was the dependent variable. Infants appeared to discriminate the order change in the first sequence, but not in the other sequence, paralleling adults' perception. This result suggests that infants can organize sounds on the basis of frequency.

Demany's (1982) study has been criticized on methodological grounds. It is possible to discriminate some of the sequences he used from their reversed version on the basis of the frequency contour, even if the sequence is not perceived as two parallel streams. Fassbender (1993) corrected this problem and tested 2- to 5-month-olds on sequences that adults organized on the basis of frequency, amplitude or timbre. Infants discriminated order changes in the sequences as adults did, supporting the idea that infants group sounds at least qualitatively like adults. In addition, McAdams and Bertoncini (1997) tested 3- to 4-day-old infants on sequences that adults segregated on the basis of both location and timbre. Again, infants discriminated order reversals as adults did, although it is not clear whether the sequences were organized by location, by timbre, or by both location and timbre. In this test paradigm, note, listeners are never asked to segregate simultaneously occurring sounds, as most frequently occurs in natural environments. Thus, the conclusions that can be drawn about infants' sound source segregation are currently limited.

Only one study has been conducted bearing on the issue of sound source segregation in children. Sound in different frequency bands that fluctuate over time in the same way tend to be grouped together by adults. In fact, an adult will detect a signal at a lower level if the masker consists of multiple frequency bands with common amplitude modulation than when the masker is a single frequency band centered on the signal or if the masker noise bands have different amplitude fluctuations. This effect is known as comodulation masking release (CMR). Grose, Hall, and Gibbs (1993) first showed that 4-year-old children derived the same benefit from adding off-frequency, comodulated frequency bands as do adults. Hall, Grose, and Dev (1997) subsequently confirmed this finding in slightly older children. However, Hall et al. also reported that when the masker band centered on the signal frequency and the off-frequency comodulated bands were slightly asynchronous, adults' CMR was reduced, but children's CMR was eliminated or became negative. Thus, it would appear that the basic process of grouping frequency bands on the basis of common temporal fluctuations is functional early in life, but the process is more easily disrupted in children than it is in adults. These findings may have considerable relevance to children's listening in modern, complex sound environments.

Finally, to process sound emanating from one among several sources, listeners must be able to ignore irrelevant sounds. Consider that under normal circumstances, the irrelevant sounds in the environment may vary from moment to moment in unpredictable ways. One of the most intriguing findings in psychoacoustics is that uncertainty about the sounds to be ignored makes it much more difficult for listeners to detect a known sound (e.g., Kidd, Mason, & Arbogast, 2002; Neff & Callaghan, 1988; Neff & Green, 1987; Oh & Lutfi, 1999), even when the sounds to be ignored are distant in frequency from the sound to be detected. Reduction in the audibility of one sound due to the introduction of a second sound that does not interfere with the peripheral processing of the signal sound is called informational masking (Pollack, 1975).

In some respects, infants act as if they are uncertain about an irrelevant sound, even when the irrelevant sound does not change over time. Werner and Bargones (1991) showed that 7- to 9-month-olds' thresholds for detecting a tone increased when a noise band distant in frequency was presented simultaneously. Adults did not demonstrate masking under the same condition. If competing distant-frequency tones of varying frequency are presented with the tone to be detected, infants exhibit the same increase in threshold as adults do relative to the condition in which the competing tones are constant in frequency (Leibold & Werner, 2003). Thus, infants may be equally affected by increased uncertainty, even though they are more uncertain than adults under nonvariable conditions.

By contrast, additional uncertainty appears to have more dramatic effects on older children than it does on adults. Allen and Wightman (1995), for example, found that half of 4- to 8-year-olds could not detect a tone at all when two competing tones varying in frequency were presented. The average threshold of the children who could perform the task was much higher than that of adults. Oh, Wightman, and Lutfi (2001) reported that preschool children demonstrated about 50 dB more masking than adults on average when a varying distant-frequency, two-tone masker was presented with the tone to be detected. Moreover, Wightman, Callahan, Lutfi, Kistler, and Oh (2003) found that while presenting the varying masker tones to the ear contralateral to the signal ear eliminated such informational masking in adults, this manipulation did little to reduce informational masking in preschool children. Since acoustic factors that increase the listener's ability to perceptually segregate the signal and masker typically reduce informational masking in adults, this finding suggests that children's ability to segregate sound sources is not as robust as that of adults. Stellmack, Willihnganz, Wightman, and Lutfi (1997) quantified the extent to which irrelevant information entered into children's perceptual decisions about intensity, finding that preschool children tended to weight information at different frequencies equally, even when they were asked to attend to a single frequency.

## Implications for the Development of Speech Perception

The preceding review of infant audition has several implications for their perception of the complex sounds of human language. In the first 6 months of postnatal life, it is likely that the neural representation of sounds is not as sharp or detailed as it is in adulthood. This representational limitation may in turn limit infants' ability to extract information from those sounds. By 6 months of age, infants probably have adultlike representations of speech and other complex sounds. However, this is not to say that their *perception* of complex sounds is adultlike. It is clear that infants do not attend to the information within complex sounds in the same way that adults do. They do not appear to focus on the spectral or temporal details that are most informative. They identify the spatial location of a sound source rather grossly, and they may also have difficulty segregating speech from competing sounds. Adult caregivers may compensate for these immature processing abilities by exaggerating important details and by speaking to infants in a way that makes their speech stand out from background sounds, as indicated at various points in the following sections. We return to the possible links between early auditory processing and resulting effects on speech and language learning at the end of this chapter.

## INFANT SPEECH PERCEPTION AND WORD LEARNING: BEGINNINGS OF LANGUAGE

### Emergence of the Field: Phonetic Perception

When the first studies of infant speech perception were launched in 1971, a number of studies had been published revealing that adults show categorical perception of speech, but not nonspeech sounds. For example, adults presented with an equal step-size continuum of stimuli spanning two phonetic categories (e.g., a voicing difference between /b/ and /p/ or a place of articulation difference between /b/ and /d/) categorically labeled the first several steps along the continuum as one phoneme (e.g., /b/), and the next several steps as the other (e.g., /p/), with a very sharp boundary in between. Moreover, their labeling performance predicted discrimination. When presented with pairs of stimuli of equal sized differences, adults reliably discriminated only those differences to which they were able to assign different phonetic category labels. This perceptual skill is very important to language processing. There are tremendous variations in the way each individual phoneme is pronounced as a function of the other phonemes around it (/b/ is somewhat different in "bat" than in "boot" due to the coarticulation from the following vowel), as a function of speaking rate, and as a function of the voice quality of the individual speaking. Categorical perception allows listeners to treat these differences as equivalent, and thus to recover the word (and hence the meaning) rapidly when listening to others speak. On the basis of the studies published until 1970, it was believed that categorical perception, and perceptual normalization for speaking rate, vowel context, and so on, was unique to humans and unique to speech versus other types of acoustic signals (see Liberman, Cooper, & Shankweiler, 1967; Repp, 1984).

To explore the ontogeny of this capacity, Eimas and his colleagues (Eimas, Siqueland, Jusczyk, & Vigorito, 1971) published a classic study using the high amplitude sucking method, in which infant habituation and dishabituation are measured via rate of sucking on a nonnutritve pacifier (see also Moffit, 1971). Their results demonstrated that 1- and 4-month-old infants, like English-speaking adults, are better able to discriminate stimuli from the /ba/-/pa/ continuum that constitute between, rather than within, category differences (according to adult perceptual performance). Given the difficulty of obtaining labeling data from infants, these findings showing better between than within category discrimination, were taken as evidence that infants also show categorical perception. A year later, Morse (1972) extended this work to show that 2-month-old infants can categorically discriminate /ba/ versus /ga/, but fail on nonspeech counterparts to these syllabic forms. Similarly, Eimas (1974) showed that infants, like adults, only discriminate between stimuli that adults label as instances of different categories, holding acoustical distinctiveness constant. A number of additional studies extended this work to other consonant types (e.g., Eimas, 1975a; Hillenbrand, 1984), to consonants in medial as well as initial position (Jusczyk, Copan, & Thompson, 1978), and even to newborn infants (Bertoncini, Bijeljac-Babic, Blumstein, & Mehler, 1987). Subsequent studies demonstrated that phonetic categories in young infants show many other properties observed in adults. The boundaries between categories are not absolute values, as would be indicated by auditory models. Instead, they are influenced by other articulatory variables, such as speaking rate (Miller, 1987). Infants (Eimas & Miller, 1992), like adults (Whalen & Liberman, 1987) show a phenomenon called "duplex perception" wherein the exact same stimulus can be simultaneously heard as both speech and nonspeech with categorical perception of the speech percept and continuous (no sharp category boundaries) perception of the nonspeech percept.

Similar results were found with vowels. Infants, like adults, show categorical perception of brief (Swoboda, Morse, & Leavitt, 1976; Trehub, 1973) but not more extended, isolated vowels (Swoboda, Kass, Morris, & Leavitt, 1978), and categorize vowels as equivalent even across variations in speaker and gender (Kuhl, 1979). In more recent work, Kuhl and colleagues provided data suggesting that vowel categories are organized around prototypes, with "best" central instances (see Grieser & Kuhl, 1989). These central instances have been described as "magnets" which warp the vowel space (Kuhl, 1991; though see Lotto, Kluender, & Holt, 1998, for an alternative account). A comprehensive review of this sizeable early work on consonants and vowels can be found in Eimas, Miller, and Jusczyk (1987). Taken together, these studies led to the claim that speech perception is special in infants just as it is in adults, and must therefore reflect the operation of a domain-specific ability.

A number of studies examining cross-language speech perception complement the above studies of native-language speech perception. Languages differ in many properties, including their phoneme inventories. English, for example, contains a contrast between /r/ and /l/ which is lacking in Japanese, but English lacks the retroflex /D/ versus dental /d/ distinction that is used in Hindi and other South Asian languages. A series of cross-language speech perception studies in the 1970s revealed that adults have difficulty perceiving acoustically similar nonnative contrasts, and are constrained to distinguishing only those differences that are used phonemically in the native language (e.g., Lisker & Abramson, 1971; Strange & Jenkins, 1978) whereas young infants discriminate phonetic contrasts whether or not they are used in the language they are learning (Aslin, Pisoni, Hennessy, & Percy, 1981; Lasky, Syrdal-Lasky, & Klein, 1975; Streeter, 1976; Trehub, 1976). To capture this pattern of results, Eimas (1975b) proposed that babies are born with broad-based, universal sensitivities and that lack of listening experience leads to loss of unused initial sensitivities. Aslin and Pisoni (1980) formalized this view in their "universal theory" of speech perception, drawing on the notion of "maintenance" as the perceptual mechanism accounting for cross-linguistic differences (Gottlieb, 1976; Tees, 1976).

However, these comparisons of infants and adults relied on different testing procedures for the two populations, and in most cases, tests in different labs on different contrasts. Werker, Gilbert, Humphrey, and Tees (1981) addressed this problem by comparing English infants aged 6 to 8 months, English adults, and Hindi adults on their ability to discriminate both an English and two (non-English) Hindi consonant contrasts, using precisely the same methodology—the conditioned head-turn procedure—with the three groups. Their results confirmed the developmental change. All three groups discriminated the English /ba/-/da/ contrast, but only the Hindi adults and the English infants discriminated the two Hindi distinctions.

Werker and her colleagues subsequently completed a series of studies designed to identify the age at which the change from "universal" to language-specific phonetic perception might occur (Werker & Tees, 1983), and found important changes occurring across the 1st year of life. At 6 to 8 months of age, English-learning infants

successfully discriminate the Hindi retroflex-dental distinction and another non-English (Interior Salish, Nthlakampx glottalized velar versus uvular) distinction, but by 10 to 12 months of age English infants were no longer discriminating non-English distinctions (Werker & Tees, 1984). Confirming that the change was one of maintenance via language-specific listening exposure, and not simply a general decline at 10 to 12 months for all difficult phonetic contrasts, Werker and Tees (1984) showed that infants of the same age (10 to 12 months) raised with Hindi or Nthlakampx did successfully discriminate the contrasts from their native languages.

In the years since this initial work, there have been a number of replications and extensions of this finding. Several studies have confirmed an effect of listening experience on the phonetic differences infants can discriminate by the end of the 1st year of life. A decline in performance on nonnative contrasts was the common pattern in the first wave of studies (Best, McRoberts, Lafleur, & Silver-Isenstadt, 1995; Pegg & Werker, 1997; Tsushima et al., 1994; Werker & Lalonde, 1988; Werker & Tees, 1984). Moreover, the basic pattern of findings from these behavioral studies has been replicated by recording event-related potentials (Cheour et al., 1998; Rivera-Gaxiola, Silva-Pereyra, & Kuhl, 2005). Werker showed in her earliest work that this decline likely involves a reorganization of attention rather than a loss of basic discriminatory capacity (Werker & Logan, 1985).

In the past several years, some revealing exceptions to this pattern of findings have appeared. It is now known that vowel perception likely reorganizes at a somewhat younger age than consonant perception (Kuhl, Williams, Lacerda, Stevens, & Lindblom, 1992; Polka & Werker, 1994), and that acoustically quite distinct contrasts that lie outside the phonological space of the native language (e.g., click contrasts) may remain discriminable even without listening experience (Best, McRoberts, & Sithole, 1988). Indeed, there are differences across nonnative contrasts, with some showing the pattern of decline noted above, and others remaining discriminable (e.g., Best & McRoberts, 2003; Polka & Bohn, 1996), with one influential model suggesting that the assimilability to the native language phonology is the best predictor of maintenance versus decline (Best, 1994). Moreover, experience not only maintains native distinctions, but also seems to improve the sharpness of the native categories (Kuhl, Tsao, Liu, Zhang, & de Boer, 2001; Polka, Colantonio, & Sundara, 2001). This observation has led to a reanalysis of the original Eimas (1974) claim of universal phonetic sensitivities from birth, with experience playing primarily a maintenance role. Now it appears that although substantial organization may be evident from birth, learning also plays a role (Kuhl, 2000; Werker & Curtin, 2005). As we will later address further, an exciting new development is attempting to ascertain just how powerful learning might be.

In addition to the empirical evidence suggesting innate biases in phonetic perception, considerable research supported the notion that speech might be special. Early studies suggested that while speech is perceived categorically, listeners typically perceive nonspeech analogues in a more continuous fashion (e.g., Mattingly, Liberman, Syrdal, & Halwes, 1971) and utilize specialized areas or structures in the left hemisphere when engaged in phonetic discrimination tasks (Phillips, Pellathy, & Marantz, 1999; Studdert-Kennedy & Shankweiler, 1970). Similar types of findings were revealed in infant studies (e.g., Eimas et al., 1971). Dichotic tasks with infants showed a significant right ear (LH) advantage in phonetic discrimination tasks by 3 months of age (Glanville, Levenson, & Best, 1977) and possibly earlier (Bertoncini et al., 1989). Even in these initial reports, however, some results did not support the notion of a right-ear/left-hemisphere advantage for phonetic discrimination in young infants (see Best, Hoffman, & Glanville, 1982; Vargha-Khadem & Corballis, 1979, for contradictory studies).

The use of electrophysiology, with the event related potential (ERP) as the dependent variable, has helped clarify the early neuropsychological work. For example, Dehaene-Lambertz and Baillet (1998), using ERP, found brain areas that show activation to a change in phonetic category, but not to an equal sized change within a phonetic category in 3-month-old infants. More recently, they have shown the same pattern of findings when multiple voices are used, showing that the infant brain can extract phonetic categories across variations in speakers (Dehaene-Lambertz & Peña, 2001). ERP studies also consistently reveal asymmetries in phonetic discrimination tasks, but the pattern of asymmetries appears to vary with stimulus type and infant age. Some studies reveal a left hemisphere (LH) advantage for stop consonant discrimination (Dehaene-Lambertz & Baillet, 1998; Dehaene-Lambertz & Dehaene, 1994; Molfese & Molfese, 1979, 1980, 1985) whereas others indicate bilateral responses at birth, with the emergence of right hemisphere (RH) dominance at 3 months of age

(e.g., Novak, Kurtzberg, Kreuzer, & Vaughan, 1989). Molfese consistently found the LH advantage for place-of-articulation differences reported above, but a stronger RH ERP response to a change in voicing (Molfese, Burger-Judish, & Hans, 1991; Molfese & Molfese, 1979). The pattern seen with vowels also suggests asymmetrical processing, in this case favoring the RH (Cheour-Luhtanen et al., 1995). The findings of early sensitivity to potential phonetic distinctions and the possibility of specialized neural systems subserving this discrimination strengthened the notion that "speech is special" and computed by dedicated neural systems.

As is the case with any complex research endeavor, not all the data fit the pattern so nicely. Shortly after the first studies were published revealing categorical-like perception for speech sounds, similar studies were published showing that both adults (Pisoni, 1977) and infants (Jusczyk, Pisoni, Walley, & Murray, 1980) perceive some nonspeech sounds categorically. Moreover, nonhuman animals seem to show similar category boundaries to human infants. Chinchillas (Kuhl & Miller, 1978; Kuhl & Paden, 1983) show categorical perception for both voicing (e.g., /pa/-/ba/) and place (e.g., /ba/-/da/) continua, and several other animal species can also discriminate between consonants (Morse & Snowdon, 1975; Waters & Wilson, 1976). Japanese quail show perceptual constancy of consonant categories across variations in vowels (Kluender, Diehl, & Kileen, 1987), and budgies similarly discriminate consonants (Dooling, Best, & Brown, 1995). Similar findings have been reported for vowels. Monkeys and even cats discriminate /i/ from /u/ (Dewson, 1964), and studies with Old World monkeys suggest the same pattern of vowel perception as seen in humans, with excellent discrimination of distinct vowels and more confusion of close vowels such as /E/ (as in bet) and /ae/ (as in bat; Sinnott, 1989). It was initially thought that only humans (adults and infants) show the prototype magnet effect (see Kuhl, 1991), but even rats and birds show a warping of their perceptual space to reveal a prototype organization following brief exposures to vowel categories (Kluender, Lotto, Holt, & Bloedel, 1998; Pons, in press). The animal work raises the strong possibility that speech perception is not necessarily a specialized human capacity, but perhaps instead reflects perceptual biases that are common at least across primates, and perhaps beyond.

To summarize, the first generation of infant speech perception work took as its starting point the work on phonetic perception in adults, and was designed to assess whether infants showed the same types of responses to phonetic differences as do adults, and if so, whether they used the same underlying neural mechanisms. This research led to increasingly sophisticated methods and techniques, and to studies with both human and nonhuman animals. The findings greatly enriched our understanding of the development of speech perception, and the explanations offered to explain these findings provided rich theoretical fodder for subsequent work. However, one of the insights guiding research for the past several years has been the realization that there is much more to speech than just phonetic categories, and that infants may be sensitive to many other characteristics of the speech around them.

## A Preference for Speech

One of the first questions one might ask is whether infants' perceptual systems help them to separate speech from other types of acoustic signals in the environment. An early appearing preference for speech would help infants orient to just those signals in the environment which are essential for language acquisition. Although it is widely believed that infants prefer to listen to speech over other sounds from the first moments of life, there are actually very few data that specifically address this question. Indeed, until very recently the studies upon which this widely held belief was founded were not actually designed to test infants' preference for speech over nonspeech. For example, one study that is widely cited as showing a neonatal preference for speech over nonspeech showed that 4- to 5-month-old infants look longer to a target when it is paired with continuous female speech than when it is paired with white noise (Colombo & Bundy, 1981). Today no one would accept the aversive sound of white noise as an appropriate control for human speech, but in fact Colombo and Bundy had not designed the experiment to test for a preference for speech. Rather, they were attempting to develop a method for assessing infants' responsiveness to different types of speech sounds. Moreover, what is not noted is that 2-month-old infants in Columbo and Bundy's (1981) study, in contrast to older infants, did not respond differently to speech and white noise. The only other early study directly assessing a listening preference for speech was one by Glenn, Cunningham, and Joyce (1981) in which 9-month-old infants pulled a lever more frequently to listen to a female singing a song in comparison with three solo musical instruments playing the same tune.

More recently, a set of studies has examined infants' preference for acoustic stimuli that have the structural properties of isolated syllables of human speech in comparison to carefully matched nonspeech tokens. Vouloumanos, Kiehl, Werker, and Liddle (2001) used complex nonspeech analogues modeled on sine-wave analogues of speech (Remez, Rubin, Pisoni, & Carrell, 1981). The speech stimuli consisted of the syllable "lif" repeated several times in the high pitch, highly modulated speech that parents use when speaking to their infants. The nonspeech counterparts replaced the fundamental frequency and three most intense higher order frequency components (formants) with a sine wave that tracked their changes across time. Thus, in contrast to the earlier studies investigating preference for speech over nonspeech, these stimuli were carefully matched for duration, timing, fundamental frequency, and area in the spectrum in which information was presented. However, human vocal tracts cannot produce the sine wave nonspeech stimuli.

In the first set of studies, Vouloumanos and Werker (2004) used a sequential preferential looking procedure (e.g., Cooper & Aslin, 1990) to test the listening preferences of 2- to 6-month-old infants. The infants preferred the speech over the complex nonspeech analogues, listening longer on the alternating trials during which speech versus nonspeech was presented. In the second set of studies, newborn infants were tested with these same stimuli, with HAS (high amplitude sucking) as the dependent variable. Like their older counterparts, the newborn infants chose to deliver more HA sucks on the alternating minutes in which speech versus complex nonspeech was presented (Vouloumanos & Werker, 2002). To attempt to rule out a role of experience in eliciting this preference, Vouloumanos created stimuli that would sound like those available to the fetus by filtering them using the filtering characteristics of the uterine wall. Neonates treated the filtered speech and nonspeech as equivalent, even though they discriminate the nonfiltered counterparts. This strengthens the possibility that the preference seen in the newborn is not a direct result of prenatal listening experience with human speech, and argues instead for an evolutionarily given perceptual predisposition for sounds that have the structural characteristics of those which could be produced by a human vocal tract. Moreover, the preference for communicative signals extends beyond spoken language.

In a recent study, Krentz and Corrina (2005) have shown that hearing infants show a preference for watching sign language over carefully matched nonlinguistic gestures. Taken together, these studies suggest a broad-based perceptual bias for communicative signals.

These results are corroborated by studies using neuroimaging techniques. In an event-related fMRI study completed with adults, Vouloumanos et al. (2001) found that the typical speech areas in the left hemisphere of the temporal cortex are more activated by a change to the speech than a change to the complex nonspeech stimuli described above. This finding complements many other studies with adults showing greater activation of specialized brain areas in the left hemisphere in response to speech than to other types of sounds (e.g., Benson et al., 2001; Binder et al., 1997; Fiez et al., 1995; Price et al., 1996; Zatorre, Evans, Meyer, & Gjedde, 1992; but see also Binder et al., 2000; Zatorre, Meyer, Gjedde, & Evans, 1996).

To date, only two studies have used imaging techniques to determine if the infant brain responds differently to speech versus nonspeech. Both of these studies have contrasted the perception of forward versus backwards speech (for related adult studies, see, Dehaene et al., 1997; Wong, Mihamoti, Pisoni, Sehgal, & Hutchins, 1999). Using both optical topography (Peña et al., 2003), and fMRI (Dehaene-Lambertz, Dehaene, & Hertz-Panier, 2002), speech stimuli elicited greater activation in the infants' LH than the RH. In the Peña et al. (2003) study neonates were tested, and the increased activation was in the classic language areas over the temporal lobe. The Dehaene, Dehaene, and Hertz-Pannier (2002) study tested 3-month-olds, eliciting bilateral activation to both the forwards and backwards speech over the temporal lobes, with greater LH activation more posteriorly. Further experimentation with nonhuman primates is necessary to determine whether these early perceptual and neural markers of human speech perception are specific to humans or are instead part of our shared evolutionary history.

## Perception of the Visible Information in Speech

Speech perception involves not only the acoustic signal, but also visible articulatory information. The best known example of this is the McGurk effect (McGurk & MacDonald, 1976). When watching a speaker produce the syllable /ga/ while listening to /ba/, adults typically report perceiving an unambiguous /da/ or /tha/, a syllable that combines features of both the heard and seen stimuli. This effect is robust across many testing conditions and languages (see Green, 1998 for a review) and has been interpreted as part of our endowment for phonetic perception. Yet, there is also evidence of learning. The McGurk effect is stronger in adults than in children (Hockley & Polka, 1994; MacDonald & McGurk, 1978; Massaro, Thompson, Barron, & Laren, 1986), is reduced further in children who have difficulty articulating (Desjardins, Rogers, & Werker, 1997), and shows the same kind of language-specific influences as is seen in the perception of audible speech with nonnative "visemes" assimilated to those used in the native language (Massaro, Cohen, & Smeele, 1995; Werker, Frost, & McGurk, 1992).

Two kinds of studies have explored whether the visible information in speech is available prior to learning. In one, infants are presented with side-by-side displays of two faces articulating two different syllables. An acoustic syllable that matches the syllable being articulated by one of the faces is then presented at mid-line, and the amount of time the infant looks at each face is recorded. Using this method, Kuhl and Meltzoff (1982) showed that infants of 4.5 months look preferentially at the face articulating the heard vowel sound (/a/ versus /i/). This finding has since been replicated with other vowels (Kuhl & Meltzoff, 1988), with male as well as female faces and voices (Patterson & Werker, 1999), with disyllables (e.g., *"mama," "lulu"*; MacKain, Studdert-Kennedy, Speiker, & Stern, 1983), and with a high amplitude sucking method (Walton & Bower, 1993). Moreover, these young infants often display mouth movements themselves that correspond to the concordant bimodal display (Kuhl & Meltzoff, 1988; Patterson & Werker, 1999; 2002), suggesting connections including not only the visual and auditory perceptual modalities, but also articulatory processes. More recently it has been shown that the matching effect is equally robust in 2-month-old infants (Patterson & Werker, 2003). The precocity of this matching ability is particularly striking when compared to other types of biologically important information. Infants do not match gender in the face and voice until 7 to 9 months of age (Walker-Andrews, Bahrick, Raglioni, & Diaz, 1991) even when they are tested using precisely the same stimuli for which they show vowel matching (Patterson & Werker, 2002).

Evidence for the McGurk effect itself is less convincing in the infancy period. Although there are reports of infants' percepts showing the same kind of "fusion" or "visual capture" as seen by adults when mismatched auditory and visual stimuli are presented (Burnham & Dodd, 2004; Desjardins & Werker, 2004; Rosenblum, Schmuckler, & Johnson, 1997), the effect is not nearly as strong or as consistent as that seen in adults. Taken together, these studies suggest that the infant may be endowed from an early age with a perceptual system which is sensitive to both heard and seen features of phonetic segments, but that this system is perfected and tuned through experience listening to and articulating speech. A recent study suggests that we are not the only primate species to use both heard and seen information in perceiving communicative stimuli (Ghazanfar & Logothetis, 2003), suggesting that the intermodality of speech might be deeply ingrained in our evolutionary heritage.

## Perception of Prosodic Attributes of the Speech Signal

One of the fundamental characteristics of human languages is their prosody—the musical aspects of speech, including their rhythm and intonation. Languages have classically been categorized according to their predominant rhythmic properties into three major types: stress-timed, syllable-timed, and mora-timed (Abercrombie, 1967; Pike, 1945). Stress-timed languages, like English and Dutch, tend to alternate between strong and weak syllables, and the strong syllables are roughly equally spaced in time, thus the term *stress-timed*. Languages like Spanish and Italian, however, use the syllable as the basic unit of timing; syllables are similarly stressed and roughly equally spaced in time. Finally, languages like Japanese are timed-based on the mora, a rhythmic unit roughly corresponding (in English) to a consonant followed by a short vowel ("the" contains one mora, while "thee" contains two). This nomenclature has been refined and quantified by two key properties: percent vowel per syllable and the variability in the consonants (Ramus, Nespor, & Mehler, 1999). These rhythmical properties of the language influence adults' processing of speech; speakers of different languages employ different units as their primary unit of segmentation. Speakers of syllable-timed languages (e.g., French, Spanish, Catalan, & Portuguese) show a processing advantage for the syllable (e.g., Mehler, Dommergues, Frauenfelder, & Segui, 1981; Morais, Content, Cary, Mehler, & Segui, 1989; Sebastián-Gallés, Dupoux, Segui, & Mehler, 1992), speakers of stress-timed languages such as En-

glish and Dutch show greater access to the phoneme (Cutler, Mehler, Norris, & Segui, 1986; Cutler & Norris, 1988; Vroomen, van Zon, & de Gelder, 1996), and Japanese adults use the mora as the primary unit of segmentation (Otake, Hatano, Cutler, & Mehler, 1993). These differences not only describe the surface properties of languages, but may also provide cues to the underlying syntactic structure, that is, the head direction, of the language (Nespor, Guasti, & Christophe, 1996).

Human infants are sensitive to rhythmical differences from birth. Since the classic study by Demany, McKenzie, and Vurpilot (1977) showing that 2- to 3-month-old infants can discriminate tones based on their rhythmical sequences, there is growing evidence that young infants can use rhythm to detect the timing characteristics of speech (Fowler, Smith, & Tassinary, 1986). Indeed, there is now considerable evidence that infants utilize rhythmical characteristics to discriminate one language from another at birth. In a seminal experiment, Mehler et al. (1988) demonstrated that newborns can discriminate French from Russian produced by a single bilingual speaker—as long as one of these languages is the infant's native language. Interestingly, at least part of this discrimination is based on prosodic characteristics of speech. The same results were obtained using low-pass filtered speech, in which the phonetic characteristics were removed while retaining the prosodic rhythm of the speech samples. Given that these are the same speech characteristics maintained in the uterine environment, an initial interpretation of these data was that newborn speech capacities are influenced by prenatal maternal exposure. A subsequent reanalysis of the initial data, however, revealed that discrimination was not limited to the native versus an unfamiliar language, but instead was evident as well when the French infants listened to English versus Italian, two unfamiliar languages (Mehler & Christophe, 1995). This weakened the interpretation that it is prenatal experience that leads to language discrimination.

Indeed, there is now abundant evidence that infants use such rhythmical differences to discriminate among a wide variety of languages, suggesting that rhythm may be prioritized in infants' early speech representations. Consistent with this hypothesis, infants' discriminations are predictable based on languages' membership in rhythmic classes. For example, newborns and 2-month-olds can discriminate between two languages from two different classes, but not two languages from the same class (Mehler et al., 1988; Moon, Cooper, & Fifer, 1993;

Nazzi, Bertoncini, & Mehler, 1998). This discrimination ability is present for forward speech but not backwards speech, which disrupts rhythmic cues. Nonhuman primates show this same pattern of performance, suggesting that processing of the rhythmic characteristics of speech is not specific to humans (Ramus, Hauser, Miller, Morris, & Mehler, 2000). Only by 5 months of age does experience with one's native language allow infants to discriminate it from other languages in the same class (e.g., Nazzi, Jusczyk, & Johnson, 2000). There is thus an interplay between an inherent bias to attend to rhythmic distinctions in languages and the learning processes required to distinguish one's own language from others. Even by 5 months of age, infants can't distinguish between two unfamiliar languages from the same rhythmic class.

Languages from different rhythmical classes differ not only in their timing characteristics, but also in their intonation contours. And, in some cases, this information is also adequate to discriminate two languages that have been low-pass filtered at 400 Hz (which removes phonetic content while preserving intonation cues), including English versus Japanese (Ramus & Mehler, 1999). As indicated earlier, young infants are highly sensitive to differences in pitch. Moreover, they are able to use intonation to discriminate vowels (Bull, Eilers, & Oller, 1984; Karzon & Nicholas, 1989), and even to distinguish lists of words differing in pitch contour (Nazzi, Floccia, & Bertoncini, 1998). The preference for infant directed speech (Cooper & Aslin, 1990; Fernald, 1984; Werker & McLeod, 1989) may be explained, at least in part, by this exquisite sensitivity to fundamental frequency (see Colombo & Horowitz, 1986).

It is thus of interest to determine whether infants' ability to discriminate languages is a function of their perception of rhythm, intonation, or both cues in tandem. To do so, Ramus and Mehler (1999) resynthesized natural speech, preserving the rhythm while holding intonation constant. With these stimuli, French newborns were still able to discriminate languages from two different rhythmic classes (Ramus, 2002; Ramus et al., 2000), although levels of discrimination were somewhat attenuated. These results confirm that while infants may be using intonation to boost performance, rhythm alone is sufficient to distinguish one family of languages from another.

These early language discrimination abilities may be particularly useful in bilingual environments. Infants exposed to multiple languages may use these rhythmic distinctions to segregate the input into the different lan-

guages they hear. Such a process would likely facilitate successful bilingual language acquisition by alerting infants to the fact that their input is drawn not from one but two language systems. In the absence of this information, infants may not have a way to determine that they are hearing multiple languages, leading to potential confusions during the learning process.

To begin to address these issues, Bosch and Sebastián-Gallés (2001) assessed the language recognition abilities of 4-month-olds learning both Spanish and Catalan. Importantly, these two Romance languages belong to the same rhythmic category, which should make them quite difficult to discriminate. Nevertheless, these bilingual-to-be infants were able to discriminate between the two languages present in their home environments. These results suggest the availability of an early capacity to distinguish languages given simultaneous bilingual exposure, potentially based on the presence of vowel reduction (since rhythmic cues do not distinguish the two languages). More recently, it has been shown that bilingual-exposed infants process languages differently even from birth (see Werker, Weikum, & Yoshida, in press). When tested on their preference for English over a rhythmically distinct language, Tagalog, English-exposed newborns showed a robust preference for filtered English speech over filtered Tagalog speech. However, newborns exposed to both English and Tagalog prenatally did not show this preference, and indeed, chose to listen equally to filtered English and Tagalog. Contrary to hypotheses suggesting that lexical knowledge is needed to engage in language differentiation (e.g., Genesee, 1989), the basic capacities for language differentiation may be in place well prior to the onset of spoken language. However, these results leave open the question of whether infants actually represent the two languages as separate systems, as opposed to discriminable components of a single system.

## Perception of Other Aspects of the Speech Signal

In addition to their sensitivity to speech itself, to phonetic segments, to visual speech, and to rhythm and intonation, even the youngest infants also show impressive sensitivities to many other types of information carried by the speech signal. They are sensitive to some kinds of within phonetic category variation. At 3 to 4 months, infants show graded perception of VOT (Miller & Eimas, 1996), and at 6 months can discriminate within-category differences from along the VOT continuum if tested in sufficiently sensitive tasks (McMurray &

Aslin, 2005). Moreover, infants of 6 to 8 months (but not 10 to 12 months) can even treat multiple instances of the voiced, unaspirated [d] versus voiceless, unaspirated [t] (created by removing the "s" from /sta/) as two separate categories, even though adult English speakers treat both of these syllables as equivalently acceptable instances of the phoneme /d/ (Pegg & Werker, 1997).

Sensitivity to within category phonetic variation is necessary in some language processing tasks (see Werker & Curtin, 2005). One illustration comes from the work on allophone discrimination. Allophones are different phonetic realizations of the same phoneme with precise phonetic characteristics that vary depending on their position in words. By 2 months of age, infants can detect the allophonic difference between the unaspirated, unreleased /t/ in "*night rate*" from the aspirated, released, partially retroflex /t/ in "*nitrate*" (Hohne & Jusczyk, 1994), a sensitivity which will ultimately be useful in word segmentation, as discussed next.

Infants are also sensitive to syllable form. Newborn French infants can "count" syllables, discriminating lists of bi- versus trisyllabic words even when the words are modified to have the same overall duration (Bijeljac-Babic, Bertoncini, & Mehler, 1993). They show better discrimination of stimuli that correspond to "good" syllable forms—those with a vocalic nucleus (/tap/ versus /pat/), in comparison to /tsp/ versus /pst/ (Bertoncini & Mehler, 1981). Sensitivity to rhyme (Hayes, Slater, & Brown, 2000), alliteration (Jusczyk, Goodman, & Baumann, 1999), and full syllable repetition (Jusczyk, Goodman, et al., 1999) have all also been demonstrated in infants from 7 to 9 months of age.

One such auditory sensitivity may be of use in the acquisition of grammatically relevant knowledge. Infants are astonishingly sensitive to the acoustic and phonological cues that distinguish grammatical classes. Just as languages differ in their phoneme inventories and in their rhythmical characteristics, they also differ in the number and kinds of grammatical categories words might belong to. For example, while English has prepositions, Chinese has postpositions. The languages of the world seem to all share a fundamental distinction between open-class (lexical words, such as nouns, verbs, adjectives, etc.) and closed-class (grammatical words, such as determiners, prepositions, etc.) categories. These classes of words can be distinguished on the basis of acoustic and phonological cues such as syllable complexity, syllable number, duration, loudness, and presence of reduced vowels (see Kelly, 1992). These differences are magnified in the speech directed to infants,

and are evident in maternal speech across typologically distinct languages (Morgan, Shi, & Allopenna, 1996; Shi, Morgan, & Allopenna, 1998).

In a recent series of studies, Shi and colleagues showed that infants become increasingly able to use these cues across development. Newborn infants categorically discriminate content from function words, even when the words are equated for volume and number of syllables (Shi, Werker, & Morgan, 1999). Specific prenatal listening experience cannot account for this discrimination capacity; the same pattern of results emerges when the items are drawn from an unfamiliar language. By 6 months of age, infants prefer to listen to the content words (Shi & Werker, 2001). This preference cannot be accounted for by specific knowledge of highly familiar items because, again, it is seen even when infants are tested on words from an unfamiliar language (Shi & Werker, 2003). Thus the phenomenon must be based on a developing preference for items with the acoustic and phonological patterns seen in content words. These findings do not necessarily suggest that infants are born with knowledge of important grammatical categories. They do, however, show that infants' perceptual biases facilitate dividing words into two fundamental categories. Subsequently, as infants approach the age of learning word meanings, they selectively focus on the louder and generally more salient content word category.

When they first begin to speak, infants typically omit function morphemes (e.g., *the, -ed, -s*), raising the question of whether infants simply do not perceive them or whether there are other reasons for the omissions, such as constraints on speech production (e.g., Gerken & McIntosh, 1993). Several lines of evidence suggest that infants do in fact perceive these weak items. For example, 11-month-olds, but not 10-month-olds, show a different pattern of scalp-recorded ERPs to stories that contained either correct or modified English function morphemes (Shafer, Shucard, Shucard, & Gerken, 1998). Similar results using the head-turn preference procedure with German infants suggest that 7- to 9-month-olds, but not 6-month-olds, can recognize previously familiarized closed class items (Höhle & Weissenborn, 2003). By 11 months of age, infants prefer nonsense words preceded by a familiar high frequency function word over that same nonsense word preceded by a mispronunciation of the function word (e.g., English infants listen longer to "the brink" over "ke brink"), and do so even for low frequency function words such as "its" or "her" by 13 months of age (Shi, Werker, & Cutler, 2003). Indeed, by 11 months of age it appears that familiar high frequency function words such as "the" facilitate segmentation and learning of new words. Infants show better recognition of nonce word forms if they are first presented in a phrase with a familiar closed class item such as "the" (Shi, Werker, Cutler, & Cruickshank, 2004).

The importance of familiar function words becomes more pronounced when children are at the peak of learning new words, and then shows an apparent decline. In a preferential looking task (side by side pictures) infants of 18 months were most accurate when the labels for the objects were preceded by a correctly pronounced function word and least accurate when the function word was mispronounced. Their performance was intermediate for labels with missing function words. Infants of 24 months showed a similar, but less pronounced pattern, and by 36 months of age children were able to ignore the function word information (Zangl & Fernald, 2003). The role of function words extends beyond segmentation and identification. By 2 years of age infants are able to use function words as cues to new versus old information in a sentence context (Shady & Gerken, 1999).

Speech also carries paralinguistic (sometimes called "indexical") information—cues that convey emotion, speaker identity, and emphasis—to which infants are sensitive. They show a preference for infant-directed over adult-directed speech (Cooper & Aslin, 1994; Fernald, 1984). They discriminate individual voices (De-Casper & Prescott, 1984; Floccia, Nazzi, & Bertoncini, 2000) and show a robust preference for their mother's voice (DeCasper & Fifer, 1980) from birth, indicating prenatal learning. Indexical cues may also aid in the perception of specifically linguistic information. Phonetic discrimination, for example, is facilitated when the contrasting syllable is produced at the pitch peak in motherese, as shown by Karzon (1985) in infants' discrimination of /marana/ versus /malana/. This may be in part because the distinctiveness of segments may be clarified in motherese, as shown in the acoustic exaggeration of voicing (Ratner & Luberoff, 1984) and of the vowel space (Kuhl et al., 1997; Ratner, 1984) in infant-directed speech. Indeed, research shows that maternal clarification of the vowel space is correlated with superior speech discrimination in 6- to 12-month-old infants (Liu, Kuhl, & Tsao, 2003). Of interest, although speech directed to pets has many of the characteristics of infant-directed speech, the exaggeration of acoustic cues distinguishing vowels is evident only in speech directed to human infants (Burnham, Kitamura, &

Vollmer-Conna, 2003). This fact raises the possibility that the interplay between paralinguistic and linguistic factors may be part of, and exclusive to, within-species communication.

## IMPLICIT DISCOVERY OF CUES IN THE INPUT: A DRIVE TO MAKE SENSE OF THE ENVIRONMENT

During the second half of the first year, an explosion occurs in infants' knowledge of detailed aspects of the sound structure of their native language(s), as noted in the earlier discussion of age related changes in phonetic perception. In this section, we document developmental changes in perception of other properties of language. The following section addresses the mechanisms that may be responsible for these learning trajectories.

### Stress and Phonotactic Cues

Languages differ greatly in their internal prosodic regularities. By adulthood, speakers use these regularities to generate predictions about possible word structures. For example, English-speaking adults expect words to be trochaic—to begin with stressed syllables—mirroring the distribution of stress in their native language (e.g., Cutler & Carter, 1987; Cutler & Norris, 1998). This "trochaic bias" emerges early in the process of language acquisition, well before infants are producing words. For example, 9-month-olds prefer to listen to words that exemplify their native language's stress pattern (Jusczyk, Cutler, & Redanz, 1993), and are even sensitive to heavy versus light syllables (e.g., syllables with a long vowel and/or final consonant versus syllables with only a short vowel and no final consonant; Turk, Jusczyk, & Gerken, 1995). These results cannot be explained by recourse to inherent preferences for particular stress patterns, because 6-month-olds fail to show native-language stress preferences. This is an example of a potent learning process; somehow, English-learning infants must have discovered a probabilistic prosodic regularity in the input.

Infants' sensitivities are not confined to syllable-level patterns. By 9 months of age, infants have learned a great deal about the probabilistic phonotactic patterns of their native language: the rates with which certain phoneme sequences occur in particular orders in particular positions in syllables and words. For example, the sequence /ds/ can end, but cannot begin, syllables in English. Phonotactics are not a simple function of pronounceability; sequences that are legal in some languages are illegal in others. Effects of phonotactic structure are observed in studies of adult word recognition (e.g., Vitevitch & Luce, 1999; Vitevitch, Luce, Charles-Luce, & Kemmerer, 1997). Similarly, children are affected by phonotactic probabilities when learning novel object names (e.g., Storkel, 2001) and nonword repetition tasks (Coady & Aslin, in press). By 9 months of age, infants prefer to listen to phonotactically legal sequences, whereas 6-month-olds do not (Friederici & Wessels, 1993; Jusczyk, Friederici, Wessels, Svenkerud, & Jusczyk, 1993), with frequent phonotactic structures preferred over infrequent structures (Jusczyk, Luce, & Charles-Luce, 1994). Interestingly, infants in bilingual environments exhibit similar knowledge of phonotactic structure (Sebastián-Gallés & Bosch, 2002). Differences were obtained as a function of language dominance: infants were most sensitive to phonotactic patterns in their to-be-dominant language, suggesting that infants may be limited in the number of phonotactic systems they can acquire in parallel.

Some types of subsyllabic regularities appear to be more salient to infants than others. For example, Jusczyk, Goodman, et al. (1999) demonstrated that 9-month-olds were sensitive to sound patterns that recurred at the beginnings of words, but not the ends of words (for related findings, see Vihman, Nakai, dePaolis, & Hallé, 2004). These results suggest that certain parts of words may be privileged relative to others in infants' early speech representations, such that onsets may contain more detail than codas. Such findings are particularly interesting in light of the conventional wisdom that infants are highly attuned to rhyming, as well as data suggesting that the ends of words may be privileged in young children's lexical representations (Echols & Newport, 1992; Slobin, 1973).

### Higher-Level Units

Infants' representations of the sound structure of their language also encompass larger prosodic patterns, spanning multiple words. Beginning in the 1980s, researchers have been interested in how such prosodic patterns might provide cues to infants to allow them to break into the syntax of their native language. Such prosodic bootstrapping accounts, beginning with Gleitman and Wanner's (1982) proposal for the use of weak

syllable function words as cues to grammar, have generally supported the claim that infants are attuned to the kinds of prosodic variables that are correlated with syntactic structure (for review, see Morgan & Demuth, 1996). One such prosodic cue is changes in pitch and duration at the ends of clauses in infant-directed speech (Fisher & Tokura, 1996; Jusczyk et al., 1992). In a classic study, Hirsh-Pasek et al. (1987) found that 7-month-olds listened longer to speech samples with pauses inserted at clause boundaries than sentences with pauses inserted clause-medially, suggesting that infants detected the disruptions in the latter case. Similar results emerge for musical stimuli as well, suggesting that detection of prosodic markers serving as unit boundaries is not limited to language learners (Jusczyk & Krumhansl, 1993; Krumhansl & Jusczyk, 1990). More recent evidence suggests a similar process for phrase units, at least under some circumstances (Soderstrom, Seidl, Kemler Nelson, & Jusczyk, 2003), despite less clear prosodic markers of phrases (Fisher & Tokura, 1996). Indeed, even newborns have been shown to be sensitive to cues correlated with prosodic boundaries (Christophe, Mehler, & Sebastián-Gallés, 2001).

Of course, this evidence doesn't demonstrate that infants "know" that these prosodic cues point to syntactic boundaries. And the prosodic phrases to which infants are sensitive correlate only imperfectly with syntactic boundaries (Gerken, Juscyk, & Mandel, 1994). Nonetheless, this sensitivity is a prerequisite for the use of prosodic cues to discover syntactic structure. There is evidence from adult studies using artificial languages that such grouping cues do assist learners in breaking into syntax (e.g., Morgan, Meier, & Newport, 1987; Morgan & Newport, 1981). Other evidence suggests that prosodic structure helps infants as young as 2 months of age to organize and group word sequences in memory (e.g., Mandel, Jusczyk, & Kemler Nelson, 1994). However, the degree to which prosodic structure facilitates infants' discovery of syntactic structure remains unknown.

## LEARNING MECHANISMS

It is of paramount importance to understand *how* the myriad information in the linguistic environment becomes part of the infant's native language knowledge base. Until the advent of new testing techniques, this question was only addressable via analyses of production from older children, or via logical arguments regarding the structure of the problems facing the child and the possible solutions that might be part and parcel of the child's linguistic endowment (e.g., Pinker, 1984, 1989). Research with computational models also suggested possible ways to structure a learning system that might be compatible with some of the facts of language acquisition (Elman, 1990; Rumelhart & McClelland, 1986).

In the past decade, researchers have developed experimental methods that help to identify potential learning processes. Saffran, Aslin, and Newport (1996) used one such task to determine whether infants could track statistical properties of speech. Eight-month-old infants listened to a 2 minute continuous sequence of syllables containing multisyllabic words: for example, *golabu-pabikututibubabupugolabu....* They subsequently tested infants' ability to discriminate the words of this "language" from syllable sequences spanning word boundaries. Infants' success at this task, as evidenced by different listening times to the two types of sequences, indicated that they were able to detect and use the statistical properties of the speech stream.

Similar methods can be used to test specific hypotheses about the types of learning mechanisms used by infants. For example, infants could have succeeded in the preceding task using two quite different types of statistics: the probabilities of co-occurrence of syllables (e.g., the transitional probability of "la" given "go"), or a simpler computation, frequencies of occurrence (test words occurred more often in the input than the other test sequences). Aslin, Saffran, and Newport (1998) teased apart these two possibilities, demonstrating that infants succeeded at this task even when the test items were matched for frequency of occurrence in the input. A recent computational analysis of infant directed speech confirms that probabilities of syllable co-occurrence predict word boundaries better than frequencies of syllable co-occurrences (Swingley, 2005).

We must still track frequencies to discover probabilities. And these frequencies are quite salient to infants in some linguistic domains. For example, infants represent the frequencies of phonotactic patterns in their native language (Jusczyk et al., 1994; Mattys, Jusczyk, Luce, & Morgan, 1999). Moreover, infants learn about frequent properties of the input before they learn about infrequent ones. Anderson, Morgan, and White (2003) showed that English infants show a decline at a younger age in their perception of the non-English retroflex-dental /da/-/Da/ distinction than the non-English velar-

uvular /k/-/q/ distinction, presumably because "d's" are more frequent in the input than are "k's," giving infants a better opportunity to learn the native language category structure. Similarly, Shi et al. (2004) found that infants recognize and utilize high frequency function words earlier than infrequent ones.

Infant learning mechanisms are also sensitive to the statistical *distribution* of elements in the input. Maye, Werker, and Gerken (2002) presented 6- and 8-month-old infants with stimuli that simulated one of two types of languages. Materials in the unimodal condition collapsed a continuum of phonemes into a single category, such as English does with the two Hindi /d/ sounds, by presenting more instances of stimuli from the center of the continuum. Materials in the bimodal condition divided the continuum into two categories, such as Hindi does with the dental versus retroflex /d/, by including more instances of stimuli drawn from closer to the two ends of the continuum. The results suggested that infants were extremely sensitive to the distributions of the exemplars presented during exposure, with different test discrimination exhibited as a function of presentation of the unimodal versus bimodal materials. Distributional statistics can affect category structure, raising the possibility that sensitivity to the distributional information in the native language may contribute to the establishment of native language phonetic categories in the 1st year of life.

Infants also appear to be sensitive to nonstatistical regularities in the input. Marcus, Vijayan, Rao, and Vishton (1999) exposed infants to 3-syllable sentences following a particular pattern (e.g., *ga ti ga, li fa li*). Infants were then tested on novel sentences that either exemplified or violated the exposure pattern (e.g., *wo fe wo* versus *wo fe fe*). Successful discrimination suggested that the infants acquired abstract information, reflecting knowledge beyond just the specific syllable patterns observed in the input. Marcus et al. (1999) interpreted their results as evidence for a rule-based learning mechanism that detected algebraic rules (operating over variables). This claim has been controversial, as others have suggested that infants could have performed this task without rule-like representations (e.g., Altmann & Dienes, 1999; Christiansen & Curtin, 1999; Seidenberg & Elman, 1999). Investigators studying adults have similarly argued that the evidence supports a distinction between rule-based and statistical knowledge (Peña et al., 2003). However, it remains difficult to clearly distinguish between the two types of learning systems empirically (for discussion, see Seidenberg, MacDonald, & Saffran, 2003).

## Units for Computations

In order to specify the processes that go into the operation of any learning mechanism, it is necessary not just to note the structure of the learning mechanism (e.g., what computations are performed?) but also to determine the primitives over which those computations are performed. Consider the simplest possible mechanism, a frequency counter that tracks how often some event occurs. Depending on the event in question, the output of the learning mechanism could be vastly different. For example, if the mechanism is applied to a flock of birds, does it compute the total number of birds, or the number of birds' feet, or the number of swallows versus doves? Each of these primitives, serving as input to the learning process, renders a different answer.

The issue of primitives has been prominent in the study of speech representations. Artificial speech recognition systems intended to simulate early language development have largely focused on the phoneme as the relevant unit for modeling (e.g., Brent & Cartwright, 1996; Christiansen, Allen, & Seidenberg, 1998; Jusczyk, 1997). Although some research supports this unit as important in infant speech perception, other work suggests that this idealization may be a mismatch to infants' capabilities.

Shortly after the field of infant speech perception emerged, researchers began to focus on what the unit of representation might be. One long-standing controversy concerns whether syllables or phonemes (or both) are psychologically real to infants. Studies using discrimination tasks in which either the syllable changes, or a phonetic feature in the segment changes, provided convincing evidence that both syllable-level and segment (phoneme) level features are accessed and used by 2- to 4-month-old infants (Eimas & Miller, 1981; Miller & Eimas, 1979). However, studies using similarity assessments (Bertoncini, Bijeljac-Babic, Jusczyk, Kennedy, & Mehler, 1988; Jusczyk & Derrah, 1987) yielded a different pattern of results, suggesting that young infants are sensitive to changes in the number of syllables in a word, but not the number of phonemes (Bijeljac-Babic et al., 1993). Despite the contradictions in the studies with younger infants, older infants include some subsyllabic structures in their representations (Jusczyk, Goodman, et al., 1999). Moreover, with

development and/or literacy, adults represent both syllables and phonemes (Nygaard & Pisoni, 1995), and recent adult studies suggest that segmental representations may serve as the primitives for at least some kinds of language learning tasks (Newport & Aslin, 2004). Of additional interest, there may be differences across languages in which unit adults use for word segmentation, with French adults showing a pronounced syllable bias and English adults showing sensitivity to segmental information as well (Cutler, Mehler, Norris, & Segui, 1983, 1986).

One interpretation of this body of work is that the syllable is privileged as a unit of representation (Bertoncini & Mehler, 1981), and may be used as the unit in computations across linguistic input. Another interpretation is that both syllables and phonemes are privileged, but for different types of tasks: the syllable is the primary unit for counting, but segmental detail plays a role in segmentation, at least in stress-timed languages (see Werker & Curtin, 2005). Further research will help distinguish between these possibilities.

## BUILDING FROM THE INPUT DURING THE 1ST YEAR

The foregoing review provides some clues regarding the types of linguistic information infants acquire during the 1st year, as well as potential learning mechanisms that subserve this acquisition process. We can now turn to the burgeoning literature that puts these two pieces together: studies concerning the acquisition of particular linguistic structures. Some of these studies teach infants new information during a laboratory exposure session. Other studies ask how infants use what they've previously learned about their native language to discover structure in novel input.

Many of these studies use artificial nonsense languages, a methodology taken from the adult literature, in which specific cues can be isolated in a way that is impossible in natural speech (e.g., Gómez & Gerken, 2000; Morgan et al., 1987). Such languages are particularly useful in infant studies because they permit the development of brief exposure materials, fitting the task demands of infants with limited attention spans. On the other hand, artificial materials sacrifice ecological validity. An issue currently confronting researchers is the need to demonstrate that the learning abilities uncovered using artificial methods are the same as those infants use when acquiring their native language. While ecological validity is always an issue in laboratory learning studies, it is particularly salient given exposure regimens that are so clearly unlike natural language input.

## Learning Phonology and Phonotactics

Phonotactic knowledge is a prime candidate for learning studies, because it is so clearly tied to the structure of particular languages. Moreover, phonotactics is somewhat different from many of the other features of language that infants acquire. Phonotactic patterns are both general (they apply across the whole language, and are not specific to known words) and specific (they consist of segmental patterns, unlike the syllabic and prosodic patterns that often appear to be the focus of infants' attention). Studies of phonotactics in adults suggest a learning process in which mere exposure to phonotactic regularities influences expectations about possible word form regularities (Dell, Reed, Adams, & Meyer, 2000; Onishi, Chambers, & Fisher, 2002).

Chambers, Onishi, and Fisher (2003) extended their adult studies to include 16.5-month-old infants. The materials consisted of nonsense word sequences in which consonant positions were restricted; for example, /b/ could occur word-initially but not word-finally. Following exposure, infants listened longer to syllables that were phonotactically legal than those that violated the exposure patterns. Impressively, infants were also able to learn 2nd order phonotactic regularities, in which the presence of one element was conditioned on the presence of the other (e.g., that /k/ begins syllables if and only if the subsequent vowel is /ae/).

To determine whether certain phonotactic regularities are harder to learn than others, Saffran and Thiessen (2003) exposed infants to two different types of phonotactic patterns. One was consistent with the types of patterns found cross-linguistically, while the other was unlike natural language structure. Infants rapidly learned regularities of the first type, which involved generalizations across sets of acoustic/linguistic features (such as voicing, the feature that clumps /p/, /t/, and /k/ into a separate category from /b/, /d/, and /g/). However, infants failed to learn regularities that disregard such linguistic features (such as the grouping of /p/, /d/, and /k/ versus the grouping of /b/, /t/, and /g/), which are unlike natural language patterns. These results suggest a possible explanation for *why* languages show the types of patterning that they do. Sound structures that are hard for infants to learn may be less likely to recur cross-linguistically. More generally, studies that uncover infants' failures may turn out to be as illuminating as those that display infants' considerable strengths at learning, by highlighting constraints on infant learning mechanisms.

The acquisition of phonological knowledge is also of great interest, given the rapidity with which infants acquire such knowledge in their native language. This learning process requires infants to integrate different types of information, an ability that likely emerges between 6 and 9 months of age (e.g., Morgan & Saffran, 1995). For example, consider the trochaic bias—the expectation that (at least for English-learning infants) words begin with stressed syllables. To learn this pattern, you must know something about the relationship between stressed syllables and their positions within words. If you have yet to discover any word boundaries, it would be impossible to know that stressed syllables fall in predictable places in words. Thus, to acquire a trochaic bias, infants must learn correspondences between stress and word position. This is only possible if infants first know some trochaic words, which may explain the lack of such a bias in 6-month-old infants. Indeed, $6\frac{1}{2}$-month-old infants can be taught a rhythmic bias by briefly exposing them to word lists exemplifying the bias, and 9-month-olds' biases can be similarly altered (Thiessen & Saffran, 2004).

Other studies investigate how infants acquire more abstract phonological knowledge concerning the stress assignment patterns of their native language. Gerken (2004) presented infants with artificial language stimuli designed to exhibit particular patterns of metrical phonology—the structural principles for stress assignment in multisyllabic words. Following a brief exposure to a word list in which certain stress assignments were exemplified, infants were tested to determine whether they had inferred stress pattern structures that had not actually occurred in the input. The results suggest that 9-month-olds generalize to new words using abstract knowledge of possible stress patterns, opening the door to additional studies probing the extent to which infants are able to learn the types of abstract phonological structures that typify human languages.

## Word Segmentation

The problem of how infants discover words in fluent speech, which lacks consistent physical cues to word boundaries (Cole & Jakimik, 1980) has played a prominent role in studies of early language learning. While interest in this problem is a relatively recent development in the field of language acquisition, there are some notable exceptions. Roger Brown began his classic 1973 volume on language acquisition by describing his own problems with word segmentation while taking a Berlitz course in Japanese; later he described an early model of distributional learning in word segmentation by Olivier (1968). Gleitman and Wanner (1982) also treated the problem seriously, hypothesizing that stressed syllables may mark words for young learners. These two early discussions of the segmentation problem, invoking distributional and prosodic cues, were prescient, as these two sources of information are currently at the forefront of theories regarding infant word segmentation.

In a seminal study, Jusczyk and Aslin (1995) used the head-turn preference procedure to determine when infants begin to segment words. They first presented 7½-month-old infants with a word segmentation problem: sentences in fluent speech containing a particular target word (e.g., *"Mommy's* cup *is on the table. Do you see the* cup *over there?"*). Following this familiarization period, infants were tested on the target words (e.g., *"cup"*) versus novel words (e.g., *"bike"*). Each item was played for as long as the infant maintained a head-turn in the direction of a speaker from which the word was played. Jusczyk and Aslin (1995) found a significant difference in listening times between the familiar and novel words, suggesting that the 7½-month-olds discovered the target words in fluent speech. Six-month-olds, however, failed to show any significant differences between the familiar and novel test items, suggesting either that the ability to segment word from fluent speech develops sometime between 6 and 7½ months of age, or that younger infants require additional exposure and/or cues to successfully perform the task. Support for the latter view comes from a study by Thiessen and Saffran (2003), in which 6½- to 7-month-olds successfully performed a word segmentation task in which they received more familiarization with the target words, and a study by Bortfeld, Morgan, Golinkoff, and Rathbun (2005) demonstrating word segmentation by 6-month-olds using additional cues.

How do infants solve such a complicated task? A growing body of evidence suggests that infants are attuned to a number of cues correlated with word boundaries. One such source of information was initially suggested in the linguistics literature in the mid-twentieth century (e.g., Harris, 1955), reflecting the observation that words consist of predictable sequences of

sounds. To see this statistical structure, consider the following example: because the syllable *pre* precedes a small set of syllables in English, the probability that *pre* is followed by *ty* is quite high. However, because the syllable *ty* occurs word-finally, it can be followed by any syllable that can begin an English word. Thus, the probability that *ty* is followed by *ba,* as in *pretty baby,* is extremely low. Indeed, infants are sensitive to such probabilistic cues, and use them for word segmentation (e.g., Aslin, Saffran, & Newport, 1998; Goodsitt, Morgan, & Kuhl, 1993; Saffran et al., 1996).

Several lines of research have converged to suggest that particular languages contain prosodic cues that facilitate word segmentation. For example, English-learning 7½-month-olds can make use of their knowledge that bisyllabic words tend to be trochaic to successfully segment strong-weak words (those stressed on their first syllable) such as "KINGdom" from fluent speech, while failing to segment weak-strong words (those stressed on their second syllable) like "guiTAR" (Jusczyk, Houston, & Newsome, 1999). In the latter case, infants treat the stressed syllable "TAR" as a word. Interestingly, they will combine TAR with a subsequent weak syllable if they are paired consistently, suggesting the integration of stress-based and statistically based strategies. Thus, infants use their expectations about word structure to assist in segmentation (for related results, see also Curtin, Mintz, & Christiansen, 2005; Houston, Jusczyk, Kuijpers, Coolen, & Cutler 2000; Houston, Santelmann, & Jusczyk, 2004; Nazzi, Dilley, Jusczyk, Shattuck-Hufnagel, & Jusczyk, in press).

Younger infants are unable to take advantage of stress-based segmentation cues, demonstrating that this knowledge must be learned (e.g., Echols, Crowhurst, & Childers, 1997; Jusczyk, Houston, et al., 1999; Thiessen & Saffran, 2003). Further evidence for a learning account comes from research on languages that incorporate different stress patterns, such as French (Polka, Sundara, & Blue, 2002). Artificial language studies also indicate that stress-based segmentation strategies are learnable (Thiessen & Saffran, 2004). Moreover, infants must learn not to overly focus on stress, which, like all individual cues to word boundaries, is fallible; only by 10½ months do infants successfully segment weak-strong words (Jusczyk, Houston, et al., 1999).

The fact that infants can use the distribution of stress cues as a cue to word boundaries raises a "chicken-and-egg" problem. If stress is a critical cue to word boundaries, how can infants have discovered the utility of this cue prior to knowing words? One must know something about the words of one's native language to discover the correlation between stress position and word boundaries. One possibility is that infants learn the predominant stress pattern of words in their native language by hearing words spoken in isolation (e.g., Jusczyk, Houston, et al., 1999). This seems intuitively plausible, particularly given analyses of infant-directed speech suggesting that a nontrivial proportion of utterances consist of single words (e.g., Brent & Siskind, 2001). On this view, infants might learn words like "kitty" and "mommy" by hearing them spoken in isolation, and then use that nascent corpus to discover the stress patterns characteristic of their native language. However, a recent analysis suggests that this explanation is unlikely to be correct (Swingley, 2005). Only 14% of the bisyllabic utterances in English spoken to infants are trochaic; most bisyllables conform to a strong-strong pattern. Thus, infants must have some other means of discovering the predominant lexical stress pattern of their native language.

One possibility is that early access to sequential statistical segmentation cues provides infants with the beginnings of the corpus they need to subsequently discover prosodic regularities. Swingley's (2005) computational analysis suggests that words that are discoverable via statistical cues render the correct prosodic template, unlike words heard in isolation. A study by Thiessen and Saffran (2003) suggests a trajectory of cue usage over development consistent with this view. When 9-month-olds are confronted with continuous speech in which stress and statistical cues conflict, they follow the stress cues, as previously demonstrated by Johnson and Jusczyk (2001). However, 6- to 7-month-olds exhibit the opposite strategy, relying on statistical cues rather than stress cues, presumably because they do not yet know their native language's stress pattern. The stress strategy, then, is presumably bootstrapped from the regularities in the initial corpus acquired via sequential statistical cues (Thiessen & Saffran, 2004).

Other important cues to word boundaries become available to infants beginning around 9 or 10 months of age. For example, infants are able to use the distributions of allophones—the subtle differences in phonemes that are a function of the context in which the phoneme occurs—as word boundary cues. Certain sounds only occur in certain positions in words; the /t/ that begins English words differs from the /t/ that occurs word-medially or word-finally (Church, 1987). Young infants are sensitive to allophonic cues which might signal word boundaries, shown, for example, by their ability to dis-

criminate the bisyllable /mati/ when the /ma/ and the /ti/ are pulled from either a single word or from the final syllable in one word versus the first syllable in the next (Christophe, Dupoux, Bertoncini, & Mehler, 1994). By 9 months of age, infants can detect word boundaries in contrasts such as *nitrates* versus *night rates,* which consist of the same sequence of phonemes but different allophones, suggesting the availability of allophonic cues for segmentation (Jusczyk, Hohne, & Baumann, 1999; Mattys & Jusczyk, 2001). Moreover, at this same age infants' phonetic categories reflect sensitivity to position-specific allophonic variants (Pegg & Werker, 1997). These findings raise the same sort of "chicken and egg" problem as the stress findings—one must first know something about words to discover cues correlated with internal word structures. It is thus likely not an accident that this ability emerges at roughly the same time for different types of cues. By 9 months of age, infants have likely segmented enough words using statistical cues and other types of information to have developed a sufficiently large corpus to discover these word-internal cues.

Phonotactic cues are also correlated with word boundaries (e.g., Brent & Cartwright, 1996; Cairns, Shillcock, Chater, & Levy, 1997; Vitevitch & Luce, 1998). For example, Mattys et al. (1999) demonstrated that infants use the likelihood that particular consonant clusters occur within or between words in their native language as a segmentation cue. Infants' ability to segment sequences such as *nongkuth* versus *nomkuth* was examined. Critically, while the consonant clusters in the middle of each sequence are equally likely in English, the former is more likely to occur within words (/ngk/) while the latter is more likely to span a word boundary (/mk/). Nine-month-olds used this subtle distinction as a segmentation cue, inferring word boundaries in the middle of *nomkuth* but not *nongkuth.* A segmentation strategy based on phonotactics requires the infant to already know enough words for these regularities to become apparent. Related segmentation cues may require no prior lexical experience. For example, 12-month-old infants follow the "Possible Word Constraint": they generate segmentations that only create possible words, while avoiding stranding sequences that are not possible words, such as sequences consisting of a single consonant (Johnson, Jusczyk, Cutler, & Norris, 2003). This constraint may help infants to segment speech appropriately and to avoid errors without requiring a lexicon from which to induce the constraint.

It should be clear at this point in the discussion that no single cue underlies word segmentation. This conclusion is evident both from the empirical literature demonstrating that infants are sensitive to myriad cues and from the fact that each cue, in isolation, only solves part of the problem for infants. Studies using multiple cues have largely asked how infants weight conflicting cues. For example, 6- to 7-month-olds prioritize statistics over stress, while 9-month-olds prioritize stress over statistics (Johnson & Jusczyk, 2001; Thiessen & Saffran, 2003). Interestingly, Mattys et al. (1999) found that 9-month-olds also prioritize stress over phonotactic cues, supporting the hypothesis that, while imperfect, stress cues are relatively easy to detect and use (Thiessen & Saffran, 2003); Mattys et al. (1999) suggest that "prosody is an initial cue yielding a coarse first pass at word boundaries that is subsequently supplemented with additional cues such as phonotactic and allophonic constraints" (p. 482). However, it remains unknown how such cues are combined in infants' emerging segmentation strategies (see Morgan & Saffran, 1995, for an example of a study looking at additive effects of cue combinations).

One avenue of research that has effectively explored the use of cue combinations for the discovery of word boundaries is the computational literature (for an extensive review, see Batchelder, 1997). For example, Christiansen et al. (1998), building on the work of Aslin, Woodward, LaMendola, and Bever (1996), examined the efficacy of phonotactic cues that predict ends of utterances as a cue to word boundaries in a corpus of child-directed speech. While this cue worked only moderately well in isolation, inclusion of lexical stress cues markedly improved the performance of the network. A different approach to this problem was pursued by Curtin et al. (2005), who found that including stress information in a corpus enhanced performance by allowing the network to represent stressed and unstressed variants of the same syllable as distinct. One of the messages provided by the computational literature is that more cues are probably better than fewer cues, despite the paradoxical fact that this makes the input more complex. Awaiting future research is the determination of exactly which cues infants attend to, and whether these cues are weighted in the manner predicted by the computational models.

Throughout this section, we have been discussing word segmentation as though it is clear that infants are discovering words in the input, and subsequently representing these sound sequences as units, available for later mapping to meaning. However, it is certainly possible that infants are engaged in a simpler process. Return-

ing to the original Jusczyk and Aslin (1995) study, we earlier described the results as evidence that infants had segmented the word "cup" from the fluent speech. It is equally possible, though, that infants' test performance—discriminating "cup" from "bike"—rests on simply recognizing that the former set of sounds is more familiar than the latter. Doing so would not necessitate segmentation per se; instead, infants would be responding based on the familiarity of the sounds, without having represented "cup" as a distinct lexical representation. Indeed, one early study suggested that in segmentation tasks, infants pull out metrical feet (a rhythmical unit) rather than actual words (Myers et al., 1996). It is thus of great interest to ask what the output of word segmentation actually is. Saffran (2001) addressed this issue with respect to the statistical learning results. When infants respond to *golabu* during testing, after exposure to *golabupabikututipugolabu* . . . , are they treating *golabu* as a word, or as a familiar sound sequence? Based on results from a task in which infants are tested on words like *golabu* embedded in English sentences after exposure, Saffran (2001) suggested that infants treat these nonsensical patterns as primitive English words (i.e., whatever a word is to an 8-month-old, in the absence of mapping to meaning).

Recent studies by Curtin et al. (2005) with 7-month-old infants further suggest that stress cues are represented in these newly segmented proto-lexical representations. Curtin et al. used analyses of child-directed speech to argue that infant learners would be more successful if they represent stressed and unstressed syllables differently during word segmentation. In particular, the analyses suggest that incorporation of stress into infants' representational landscape would result in better distribution-based word segmentation, as well as an advantage for stress-initial syllable sequences. Results of a behavioral study corroborated these analyses. In particular, if items in the test phase were placed in a sentence context and the target was an exact match (*BEdoka*) as opposed to a sequence with the same segments but a different stress pattern (*beDOka*) or another type of nonmatching control sequences, infants demonstrated an overwhelming preference for the exact match. These results suggest that stress information in the ambient language not only shapes how statistics are calculated over the speech input, but that it is also encoded in the representations of parsed speech sequences.

Once some sequences have been segmented from the speech stream to become new lexical entries, can these words assist in segmentation of subsequent fluent speech, helping infants to discover other adjacent words (e.g., Brent & Cartwright, 1996; Dahan & Brent, 1999)? A recent study by Bortfeld et al. (2005) provides evidence that 6-month-old infants can use known words to segment new words from fluent speech. Infants heard continuous speech in which the word to be segmented appeared adjacent to the infant's own name, which infants recognize early in the 1st year (Mandel, Jusczyk, & Pisoni, 1995). The familiar name served as a strong segmentation cue, providing the first positive evidence for word segmentation in infants as young as 6 months. By demonstrating that infants' prior knowledge alters the manner in which they process new input, the Bortfeld et al. (2005) results suggest a promising new tact for studies of word segmentation and infant learning more generally.

## Beginnings of Word Recognition

Once infants have segmented words into discrete units, they are ready to begin recognizing familiar words, matching internal representations of words to their instantiation in subsequent input. This is no simple matter, because words are not static invariant patterns. The sounds of any given word are shaped by properties of the speaker (such as speaker's voice, sex, speaking rate, and affect) and by the context in which the words are produced (such as coarticulation effects).

What words might one expect infants to first recognize? Mandel et al. (1995) hypothesized that infants' names might be particularly salient. They occur frequently, are often presented in isolation, and likely carry affective prosody that attracts infants' attention. Using the preferential listening procedure, $4\frac{1}{2}$-month-olds heard either their own name or an unfamiliar name. Infants preferred to listen to their own names, suggesting that they matched internal representations of these familiar sounds to the input played during the experiment. This does not mean that these infants knew the meanings of these sounds. However, by 6 months of age, infants can recognize highly familiar words based on their meanings. When presented with side-by-side video displays of their mother and father, infants look longer to the display that matches auditory presentations of "*mommy*" versus "*daddy*" (Tincoff & Jusczyk, 1999).

These results suggest that infants' developing lexical representations are not fleeting, but are built up incrementally and maintained over time, despite the variabil-

ity in the input. To explicitly investigate the time course of memory for new lexical representations, Jusczyk and Hohne (1997) exposed 8-month-olds to stories containing particular vocabulary items. After 10 days of exposure to the stories, a 2-week retention interval was introduced, during which infants did not hear the stories. Infants were then tested on their recognition of words from the stories versus similar words that had not occurred in the stories. Despite the 2-week retention interval, during which infants heard a vast array of potentially interfering speech, the infants listened longer to the words from the previously familiarized stories, suggesting that auditory representations that were garnered weeks before were sufficiently robust to support later word recognition.

How detailed are these early representations? Infants appear not to confuse similar sounding words, at least under certain circumstances. Infants in Jusczyk and Aslin's (1995) experiments did not incorrectly treat "zeet" as familiar after being exposed to "feet," suggesting that these early representations are fairly specific. Similarly, after repeated exposures to a word and object, 8-month-old infants show robust evidence of detecting a change to a new word that differs in only a single phonetic feature (Stager & Werker, 1997).

Early word representations also appear to include a level of acoustic detail that corresponds to the positions of syllables relative to structural boundaries in sentences, such as phonological phrases. Acoustic cues corresponding to phonological phrase boundaries are detected even by newborn infants (e.g., Christophe et al., 1994, 2001). By 13 months of age, infants can use this distinction in word recognition (Christophe, Gout, Peperkamp, & Morgan, 2003). For example, infants trained on the word "paper" were tested on sentences in which paper was either a word ("The college with the biggest *paper* forms is best") or in which paper spanned a phonological phrase boundary ("The butler with the highest *pay per*forms the best"). Despite the fact that the syllable sequence was the same in both cases, with equivalent statistical and stress cues, the results suggested that the infants' representations included the subtle acoustic differences between "paper" and "pay per."

One source of information that may aid infants in speech processing is coarticulation. In order to produce speech as rapidly as we do, whenever we produce a segment, syllable, or word, we move the lips, tongue, and jaw in a way that maintains the positions required for that segment as well as for both the preceding and following consonants and vowels. For example, because of coarticulation, the phoneme /b/ is different in the word "beet" than in the word "boot." Adults are sensitive to this coarticulatory information, but only under some listening conditions. For example, when words in a string are presegmented by the insertion of pauses, adult listeners show better recognition of those familiar syllables that maintain the same coarticulatory information as used during familiarization. However, when the pauses are omitted and adults must rely on only transitional information, their access to coarticulatory information is no longer evident (Curtin, Werker, & Ladhar, 2002). Seven-month-old infants are also sensitive to coarticulatory information, but under the opposite conditions as adults. When the syllables are presegmented by the insertion of pauses, infants' recognition of familiar words is not enhanced by matching coarticulatory cues. However, in tasks that require the infant to segment syllables from a continuous stream of speech, matching coarticulatory information significantly improves performance (Curtin et al., 2002).

Infants also appear to represent indexical information that affects word recognition. For example, 7½-month-old infants readily recognize words previously heard produced by a speaker of the same sex, but show no evidence of word recognition when the target is produced by a speaker of the opposite sex (Houston & Jusczyk, 2000). It seems likely that infants' representations include perceptual features of the speaker, such as components of pitch, that make cross-sex matching challenging. Similarly, 7½-month-olds represent the affective state of the speaker, showing word recognition only when the affective state of the familiarized words matched the targets (Singh, Morgan, & White, 2004). Related arguments are emerging in the field of infant music perception, where researchers are actively investigating the "grain" at which infants represent musical experiences in memory for subsequent recognition (e.g., Ilari & Polka, 2002; Palmer, Jungers, & Jusczyk, 2001; Saffran, Loman, & Robertson, 2001; Trainor, Wu, & Tsang, 2004).

## Listening for Meaning

In contrast to the detailed, multiple levels of information available to prelinguistic infants in word recognition and segmentation tasks, infants who have begun to assemble a more sizeable lexicon seem to be more selective and more limited in which detail they use to recog-

nize words. For example, although 14-month-olds can learn to associate two different nonsense words with two different objects (Schafer & Plunkett, 1998; Werker, Cohen, Lloyd, Casasola, & Stager, 1998; Woodward, Markman, & Fitzsimmons, 1994), they fail at this same age if the two nonsense words are phonetically similar such as "bih" and "dih" (Stager & Werker, 1997) or "pin" and "din" (Pater, Stager, & Werker, 2004). Importantly, 14-month-old infants succeed in a virtually identical task when the word is paired with a visual display that is unlikely to evoke labeling (Stager & Werker, 1997). Moreover, when an easier variant of the task was used in which a single object was paired with a single word, the 14-month-olds still failed to notice the change to a phonetically similar word, whereas 8-month-olds succeeded in this same task. The failure to learn minimally contrastive words was shown to be short-lived. When tested in exactly the same task, 17- and 20-month-old infants succeeded at learning phonetically similar words (Werker, Fennell, Corcoran, & Stager, 2002), as did even infants of 14 months who had particularly sizeable vocabularies (Werker et al., 2002; see also Beckman & Edwards, 2000 for a discussion of the potential role of vocabulary size). An identical pattern of results was obtained using an ERP paradigm in which a higher amplitude deflection is seen to known versus unknown words (Mills et al., 2004).

Why might 14-month-old infants fail to distinguish phonetically similar words in a word-learning task when they could still discriminate these two words, and when both younger and slightly older (or even more advanced same-aged infants) succeed? Stager and Werker (1997) speculated that for the novice word learners, the computational demands of linking a word with an object are so great that attentional resources are not available to utilize all the word-level detail that is perceived (see Kahneman, 1973, for the original postulation of attention as a limited resource). However, other interpretations of these findings were that they revealed evidence of a discontinuity between the representations used in phonetic versus phonological (or lexical) representations. Indeed, there is a long-standing tradition in child phonology that posits such a representational discontinuity (see Brown & Matthews, 1997; Rice & Avery, 1995; Shvachkin, 1948). Empirical work by Hallé and de Boysson-Bardies (1994) provided potential support for this discontinuity hypothesis. They used a word recognition task requiring infants to listen to lists of highly familiar versus unknown words, and found that although infants of 7 and 11 months both showed a preference when the unknown words were phonetically dissimilar from the known words (Hallé & de Boysson-Bardies, 1994), if phonetically similar foils were used, only the 7-month-old infants succeeded.

A number of subsequent studies have now disconfirmed the discontinuity hypothesis. When tested in a simpler word recognition procedure wherein infants are shown two pictures and presented with a single word that either matches one of the objects or is a mispronunciation of the same name for that object (e.g., "baby" versus "vaby"), infants from 20 (Swingley & Aslin, 2000) down to 14 months (Swingley & Aslin, 2002) can detect the mispronunciation. Sometimes this detection is shown in longer looking to the correct object when the word is pronounced correctly (Swingley & Aslin, 2002), and sometimes it is evident in a shorter latency to look away from the mismatch (Swingley & Aslin, 2000), but it is consistently evident. This success is seen for well-known words in the associative task used by Stager and Werker (1997). If habituated to the word "ball" paired with the moving object "ball," and the word "doll" paired with a visual display of a "doll," 14-month-old infants detect a switch in the word object pairing in the test phase (Fennell & Werker, 2003). Thus, as suggested by both Stager and Werker (1997) and Swingley and Aslin (2000), it appears that an attentional resource limitation rather than a representational discontinuity accounts for the failure of 14-month-old infants under some circumstances.

An attentional resource limitation may not fully explain the preceding findings. It is still necessary to know why it is that phonetic detail is dropped. Is this the only detail that infants drop at 14 months, or is other detail also ignored? The word segmentation and recognition studies revealed that 7- to 9-month-old infants utilize many different kinds of information in the signal. This is evident, for example, in their failure to recognize words if there is a change in speaker gender (Houston & Jusczyk, 2000), or affect (Singh, Bortfeld, & Morgan, 2002). However, by $10\frac{1}{2}$ months of age, infants successfully recognize words spoken by opposite-sex speakers (Houston & Jusczyk, 2000), and are able to ignore changes in affect and still show evidence of recognizing familiar words (Singh et al., 2002). One increasingly popular account, which is somewhat different from the traditional view in which indexical information is not part of lexical representations, is that a rich tapestry of

information—phonetic, indexical, coarticulatory—is included in the lexicon (e.g., Goldinger, 1992), but that not all of this information is used in every task situation (Werker & Curtin, 2005).

Evidence in support of this possibility is provided in recent work with 2.5- and 3-year-olds by Fisher, Church, and Chambers (2004). They demonstrated that children represent both abstract and detailed linguistic information pertaining to the specifics of pronunciation of familiar words. For example, their participants represented the distinction between a medial /t/ and a more /d/-like flap pronunciation of the same phoneme, despite the fact that both pronunciations are legal. Interestingly, the same pattern of results emerged in a related study using nonwords, suggesting that even new lexical representations—formed after just a few exposures to a word—are flexible, in that they are both abstract and specific (Fisher, Hunt, Chambers, & Church, 2001). These findings suggest that perceptual learning mechanisms used flexibly throughout life to adapt to new linguistic input may operate from the beginning of the word learning process (Fisher et al., 2004).

It may be that in the earliest stages of word learning, infants are less able to flexibly select which information to attend to. With the attentional resource demands of attaching meaning to words, infants at the cusp of word learning may be captured by that information which is most salient. To test this hypothesis, Curtin and Werker (cited in Werker & Curtin, 2005) recently tested the ability of 12-month-old infants to learn words that are similar in all respects except stress pattern. They found that these infants, a full 2 months younger than the infants who failed to learn phonetically similar words, could successfully learn to map words such as DObita versus doBIta (where capitals indicate stress) onto two different objects.

With these studies, the links between infant speech perception, word segmentation, word recognition, and word learning are being much more fully described. Moreover, the infant literature is beginning to interface much more richly with the large literature on adult lexical access. Infancy researchers are no longer restricted to asking questions like "what is the unit of representation"? Instead, the field is now poised to allow the asking of much more nuanced questions such as "what information is utilized, when, and why?"

The advent of new methodologies has allowed researchers to go beyond asking which words infants recognize to assess the time course of word recognition. Eye-tracking has become an important tool in assessing adults' lexical representations (e.g., Allopenna, Magnuson, & Tanenhaus, 1998; Tanenhaus, Spivey-Knowlton, Eberhard, & Sedivy, 1995). Adapting these methods to study infants, Fernald, Pinto, Swingley, Weinberg, and McRoberts (1998) assessed infants' speed and accuracy at word recognition over the course of the 2nd year. To do so, the experimenters measured infants' eye movements as they viewed computer-displayed pictures of familiar objects while listening to the names of these objects. Speed and reliability were correlated with age, suggesting that infants' lexical representations likely become more robust and the cognitive machinery underlying word recognition becomes more fluent during the 2nd year. Like adults, 24-month-olds do not need to hear an entire word to recognize it; instead, word recognition is incremental (Swingley, Pinto, & Fernald, 1999). For example, these infants rapidly distinguished *doggie* from *tree,* correctly fixating on the matching picture, but took 300 ms longer to distinguish *doggie* from *doll,* reflecting the increased phonetic overlap of the latter pair. Interestingly, infants recognize parts of words just as rapidly as whole words, supporting the view that infants, like adults, process words incrementally (Fernald, Swingley, & Pinto, 2001). This ability appears to be associated with infants' productive vocabularies, suggesting a link between lexical growth and the efficiency with which infants recognize words. These facts about how infants process words are consistent with corpus analyses suggesting that the words in infants' early vocabularies are sufficiently overlapping in phonological space to necessitate detailed lexical representations (e.g., Coady & Aslin, 2003).

Experience with particular words appears to enhance these nascent lexical representations. Church and Fisher (1998) observed long-term auditory priming in 2- to 3-year-olds very similar to that of adults, showing effects of experience with specific words on subsequent word identification and repetition. Similar effects emerged in a study with 18-month-olds using a preferential looking task, suggesting that just two repetitions of a word assisted infants in subsequently identifying the target word (Fisher et al., 2004). Similarly, neuroimaging tasks are broadening the range of questions that can be explored. For example, infants may fail to discriminate a nonnative contrast given the task demands of a behavioral task, yet still show evidence of a neurophysiological response to the change, indicating that at some level in the brain the information is available (Rivera-Gaxiola et al., 2005).

## Beginnings of Grammar

Since most infants do not begin combining words grammatically until the ripe old age of 18 to 24 months or beyond, is there any reason to suspect that the capacity to acquire grammatical structure is present earlier in life? Indeed, researchers have demonstrated early evidence for grammatical knowledge of the native language during infancy, as well as precocious abilities to learn new, simple, grammatical structures using artificial language methodologies (see Tomasello, Chapter 6, this *Handbook,* this volume, for a review of the literature on subsequent aspects of grammar learning). Comprehension studies suggest that infants have a sophisticated grasp of certain syntactic structures by the end of the 2nd year. For example, Naigles (1990) tested young 2-year-olds in a cross-modal matching task that required them to induce the meaning of a new verb. The infants heard either transitive structures, such as "The duck is kradding the bunny," or intransitive structures, such as "The duck and bunny are kradding." Infants looked longer at a video that matched the syntactic structure of the sentence they heard. These results suggest that infants can engage in what is known as "syntactic bootstrapping": using their prior knowledge of syntactic syntax (here, transitivity) to determine the meaning of *kradding.*

Infants' morphological knowledge is similarly advanced. For example, Santelmann and Jusczyk (1998) exposed infants to passages that contained either a grammatical English dependency between the auxiliary verb *is* and a main verb ending with *-ing,* or an ungrammatical combination of the modal auxiliary *can* and a main verb ending with *-ing.* Eighteen-month-olds, but not 15-month-olds, discriminated between the two types of passages. These results suggest that by the middle of the 2nd year, infants have learned how certain types of discontinuous grammatical dependencies operate in their native language.

A number of recent studies have employed artificial grammar methodologies to uncover the learning mechanisms underlying this process. When exposed to word sequences ordered by simple rules (e.g., Marcus et al., 1999) or finite state grammars (Gómez & Gerken, 1999), infants treat test items that violate those patterns as novel, even if they are instantiated in new vocabulary. For example, Gómez and Gerken (1999) used the head-turn preference procedure to assess whether 12-month-olds could acquire a miniature artificial grammar. Infants discriminated new grammatical strings from ungrammatical strings after less than 2 minutes of training, with evidence that they acquired both specific information (e.g., legal beginnings and ends of sentences, and internal pair-wise combinations) and abstract information (e.g., grammatical structures produced using a new set of vocabulary). Ongoing research is probing the circumstances under which infants are more or less likely to generalize beyond the input given (e.g., Gómez, 2002; Gómez & Maye, 2005).

Saffran and Wilson (2003) extended this line of research to ask how infants might approach learning tasks consisting of multiple levels of information. Twelve-month-olds listened to a continuous speech stream in which the words were ordered via a finite-state grammar. The infants were thus presented concurrently with a word segmentation task and a syntax learning task. The results suggest that infants can first segment novel words and then discover syntactic regularities relating the new words—all within the same set of input. Studies of this type indicate that artificial learning situations can be scaled up to begin to represent some of the problems confronting learners faced with natural language input. For example, Gerken, Wilson, and Lewis (2005) performed a hybrid artificial/natural language learning study in which infants heard a small subset of Russian words marked with correct gender morphology. The results demonstrate that certain types of patterns that occur in natural language input (here, redundant cues) play an important role in learning, as indicated by performance in this lab-based learning task.

## CONCLUSIONS AND FUTURE DIRECTIONS

As we hope has been reflected throughout this chapter, infants' accomplishments in the auditory domain are nothing short of extraordinary. In the absence of external guidance or reinforcement, our perceptual systems hone in on the dimensions of the auditory environment that are most relevant for the development of our communicative capacity, and we learn extremely complex and detailed information about how our auditory environment is structured, all during our 1st postnatal year. While much remains to be learned about how these

processes unfold, it is evident that they are heavily multidetermined, influenced by factors from the development of the peripheral auditory system to the nature of our learning mechanisms. We close by considering some limitations on these processes, which may be very important for future work aimed toward illuminating the nature of infants' accomplishments.

## Relationship between Auditory Processing and Speech Perception

That even newborns can discriminate between speech sounds and recognize voices has led many to believe that hearing does not constrain speech perception or learning during infancy. It is clear, however, that several aspects of hearing remain immature early in infancy, and it is likely that these immaturities do constrain speech perception to some extent. There are suggestions in the literature that 2-month-olds, for example, represent speech with less detail than older infants do (Bertoncini et al., 1988; Bijeljac-Babic et al., 1993). It is likely that some aspects of speech perception and language learning are delayed until 6 months, when representations of the acoustic characteristics of sound are adultlike. In any case, it should be possible to make predictions about young infants' speech discrimination abilities based on what is known about their hearing, and to test specifically to determine whether hearing immaturity has any bearing on early speech perception.

A related question is whether infants use the same information in speech as adults do when they are discriminating between speech sounds. Because there are multiple cues to phonetic identity, it is possible that infants use cues that they hear better, or that they attend to more salient cues and ignore others, or that they weight all cues equally. That infants do not attend to the components of a complex sound as adults do in a simple psychophysical task (Bargones et al., 1995; Bargones & Werner, 1994; Leibold & Werner, 2003; Werner & Boike, 2001) suggests that their approach to speech may differ from that of adults. Nittrouer's studies of speech discrimination in children suggest that preschool children do not, in fact, weight cues to phonetic identity as adults do (e.g., Nittrouer, Crowther, & Miller, 1998; Nittrouer & Miller, 1997; Nittrouer & Studdert-Kennedy, 1987). It would be surprising to find, then, that infants weight cues in an adultlike way. There are now correlational techniques that can be used to assess the weights that listeners place on various components of a complex sound in making discriminations and these techniques have been successfully applied to young children (e.g., Stellmack et al., 1997). An interesting problem in the future will be to apply these techniques to infants, particularly in the realm of speech perception.

## Constraints on Learning

Much of the previous discussion has focused on infants' remarkable capacity to glean structure from complex input. However, it is important to note that demonstrations of powerful learning mechanisms alone do not represent a satisfying solution to the problems facing young language learners. How do learners hone in on the right patterns and structures given the massive amount of data in the input? The "richness of the stimulus problem" is that there are an infinite number of patterns that an unbiased learner might detect. Clearly, human infants are not such learners, and it is incumbent upon researchers to show not just all the things that infants can learn, but also what infants find more difficult to learn, to elucidate the limits on learning. It is also possible to ask how the structure of the task itself affects the types of learning that occur, as some types of input may elicit different learning mechanisms than others (e.g., Peña et al., 2003; Saffran, Reeck, Niehbur, & Wilson, 2005).

Thus far, this research strategy has primarily been carried out with adult learners, with implications to be drawn for infant learners. For example, Newport and Aslin (2004) demonstrated that while adults readily track the dependencies between adjacent syllables (e.g., the probability that *pa* is followed by *bu*), they do not do so when the relevant dependency skips an intervening syllable. Such nonadjacent dependencies are apparently not automatically tracked by learners. Interestingly, however, adults do detect nonadjacent dependencies when the intervening material is different in kind. For example, adults can detect dependencies between two consonants with intervening vowels, or two vowels with intervening consonants (Newport & Aslin, 2004). Because these latter types of structures recur in human languages (in Semitic languages, and in languages like Turkish that use vowel harmony), while the former do not, Newport and Aslin (2004) suggest that languages may be constrained by the limits on human learning. That is, only those structures that are learnable by humans persist in our languages. Saffran (2002) makes a similar argument based on adult grammatical studies.

The extent to which similar findings emerge with young learners is the object of active research

## Domain Specificity and Species Specificity

Much of the foregoing discussion has focused on learning from the input, and the types of information captured by infant learning mechanisms. A critical open question is the degree to which this learning is subserved by mechanisms tailored for speech and language. One possibility is that, perhaps due to the adaptive significance of human communication systems, we have evolved sophisticated learning machinery specifically tailored for language. Alternatively, these early learning processes may tap mechanisms that are available for more general tasks.

A growing body of results suggests that at least one of the learning mechanisms we have discussed, sequential statistical learning, is quite general. For example, infants can track sequences of musical tones, discovering "tone-word" boundaries via statistical cues (e.g., Saffran, 2003a; Saffran & Griepentrog, 2001; Saffran, Johnson, Aslin, & Newport, 1999), and can learn statistically defined visual patterns (e.g., Fiser & Aslin, 2002; Kirkham, Slemmer, & Johnson, 2002). These findings and others suggest that at least these basic learning processes are not tailored solely for language acquisition (e.g., Saffran, 2002, 2003b).

Another source of evidence bearing on this issue comes from studies of nonhuman primates. Hauser and his colleagues (Hauser, Newport, & Aslin, 2001; Hauser, Weiss, & Marcus, 2002) have tested cotton-top tamarins, a new world monkey species, on the linguistic tasks used by Saffran et al. (1996) and Marcus et al. (1999). Intriguingly, the monkeys showed the same pattern of performance as human infants, despite their presumed lack of evolved abilities to acquire human language (Hauser et al., 2001, 2002). Even rats detect some language-relevant patterns (Toro & Trobalan, 2004)! These findings reinforce the view that at least some of the learning mechanisms that subserve the beginnings of language learning are not evolutionary adaptations specialized for the linguistic domain.

Results like these lead immediately to the question of why, if monkeys share our learning machinery, language is uniquely human. That is, if monkeys learn like us, shouldn't they be as linguistically sophisticated as we are? Several avenues of explanation are currently being explored. One, of course, is the traditional view that humans possess innate linguistic knowledge that other species lack (e.g., Pinker, 1984). Other investigators are focusing on the degree to which human learning mechanisms may in fact diverge from those possessed by other species. For example, tamarins and human adults do not show the same pattern of learning of nonadjacencies discussed in the previous section, suggesting that the constraints on human learning mechanisms may diverge from those seen in other species (Newport, Hauser, Spaepen, & Aslin, 2004). Similarly, Hauser, Chomsky, and Fitch (2002) have suggested that while humans and nonhumans may share much of their learning machinery, humans are differentiated by their ability to perform recursion operations—the capacity to generate an infinite range of expressions from a finite set of elements (see also Fitch & Hauser, 2004). On this view, humans and nonhumans should show similar performance when learning about such things as speech contrasts and word segmentation, and diverge as grammatical complexity increases (e.g., Saffran, Hauser, Seibel, Kapfhamer, Tsao, & Cushman, 2005). While these central questions remain to be resolved, their answers are likely to have broad impact on such issues as the modularity of mind and the ontogenesis of specific domains of knowledge.

There is another component to early language learning that may be relevant to species differences—social interaction between the speaker and the learner. While such issues as joint attention have played a prominent role in the literature on how young children map sound to meaning (e.g., Harris, Chapter 19; Tomasello, Chapter 6, this *Handbook,* this volume), the role of social interaction has not received significant attention in the literature on how infants acquire sound structure itself. Certainly, there is ample evidence that caregivers manipulate the input so it is well tailored to infants' perceptual predilections (e.g., Kuhl et al., 1997; see Trehub, 2003, for related evidence in the domain of music perception). The higher pitches and enhanced pitch contours of infant directed speech are well-established attention-getters and affect communicators (e.g., Cooper & Aslin, 1990; Fernald, 1992). Intriguing new results suggest, however, that the role of social interaction extends beyond the sound structure of the input. Kuhl, Tsao, and Liu (2003) manipulated infants' perception of nonnative speech contrasts such that English-learning infants maintained a Mandarin speech contrast well beyond the age at which their ability to discriminate the contrast would typically have declined. Critically, however, human social interaction was required in the presentation of the Mandarin input. When infants received the same input via high-quality DVD recordings, no impact on their speech perception was observed. These results suggest that, like some species of birds, the learning system requires a certain type of interactive input to affect perception. If this is the case, then differences in social interaction may also help to explain some cross-species differences in who learns what.

## The Infant's Auditory World

In this review, we have considered recent developments in our understanding of how infants begin to make sense of their auditory environments. A great deal of progress has been made in elucidating the basic sensory and perceptual mechanisms that provide auditory input to infant learners, as well as the learning mechanisms that track this input and integrate it with infants' existing knowledge.

In future studies, we expect that the relationship between infants' auditory abilities and the rest of language acquisition (see Tomasello, Chapter 6; Waxman & Lidz, Chapter 7, this *Handbook,* this volume) will become clearer. Audition is the gateway to spoken language, and infants' early accomplishments in acquiring the sound structure of their native language(s) lay critical groundwork for subsequent learning. Recent studies linking the acquisition of sound structure to later accomplishments in word learning provide important suggestions about how infants' early abilities are likely to influence later language learning (e.g., Hollich, Jusczyk, & Luce, 2002; Saffran & Graf Estes, 2004; Swingley & Aslin, 2002; Thiessen, 2004; Werker et al., 2002). For example, early speech perception abilities may predict some aspects of word learning many months later (Tsao, Liu, & Kuhl, 2004). Similarly, researchers are beginning to investigate the effects of the amelioration of early sensory deprivation via cochlear implants on subsequent auditory perception and language learning abilities (Houston, Pisoni, Kirk, Ying, & Miyamoto, in press). Such integrative research enterprises will serve to illuminate the links between the talents of infant listeners in the auditory realm and the many linguistic (and nonlinguistic) tasks that lie ahead of them. Similarly, much remains to be learned about the neural underpinnings of the abilities described throughout our review, and knowledge about these neural substrates will help us to better understand the behaviors that they subserve. Many fascinating open questions thus remain, and in the next edition of the *Handbook*, we hope to read the answers—including the answers to the many questions that we do not yet know to ask.

# REFERENCES

Abdala, C. (1998). A developmental study of distortion product otoacoustic emission (2f1-f2) suppression in humans. *Hearing Research, 121,* 125–138.

Abdala, C. (2001). Maturation of the human cochlear amplifier: Distortion product otoacoustic emission suppression tuning curves recorded at low and high primary tone levels. *Journal of the Acoustical Society of America, 110,* 1465–1476.

Abdala, C., & Chatterjee, M. (2003). Maturation of cochlear nonlinearity as measured by distortion product otoacoustic emission suppression growth in humans. *Journal of the Acoustical Society of America, 114,* 932–943.

Abdala, C., & Folsom, R. C. (1995a). The development of frequency resolution in humans as revealed by the auditory brain-stem response recorded with notched-noise masking. *Journal of the Acoustical Society of America, 98,* 921–930.

Abdala, C., & Folsom, R. C. (1995b). Frequency contribution to the click-evoked auditory brain stem response in human adults and infants. *Journal of the Acoustical Society of America, 97,* 2394–2404.

Abercrombie, D. (1967). *Elements of general phonetics.* Edinburgh, Scotland: Edinburgh University Press.

Allen, P., Jones, R., & Slaney, P. (1998). The role of level, spectral, and temporal cues in children's detection of masked signals. *Journal of the Acoustical Society of America, 104,* 2997–3005.

Allen, P., & Wightman, F. (1992). Spectral pattern discrimination by children. *Journal of Speech and Hearing Research, 35,* 222–233.

Allen, P., & Wightman, F. (1994). Psychometric functions for children's detection of tones in noise. *Journal of Speech and Hearing Research, 37,* 205–215.

Allen, P., & Wightman, F. (1995). Effects of signal and masker uncertainty on children's detection. *Journal of Speech and Hearing Research, 38,* 503–511.

Allen, P., Wightman, F., Kistler, D., & Dolan, T. (1989). Frequency resolution in children. *Journal of Speech and Hearing Research, 32,* 317–322.

Allopenna, P. D., Magnuson, J. S., & Tanenhaus, M. K. (1998). Tracking the time course of spoken word recognition: Evidence for continuous mapping models. *Journal of Memory and Language, 38,* 419–439.

Altmann, G. T. M., & Dienes, Z. (1999). Rule learning by 7-month-old infants and neural networks. *Science, 284,* 875.

Anderson, J. L., Morgan, J. L., & White, K. S. (2003). A statistical basis for speech sound discrimination. *Language and Speech, 46*(2/3), 155–182.

Ashmead, D. H., Clifton, R. K., & Perris, E. E. (1987). Precision of auditory localization in human infants. *Developmental Psychology, 23,* 641–647.

Ashmead, D. H., Davis, D., Whalen, T., & Odom, R. (1991). Sound localization and sensitivity to interaural time differences in human infants. *Child Development, 62,* 1211–1226.

Aslin, R. N. (1989). Discrimination of frequency transitions by human infants. *Journal of the Acoustical Society of America, 86,* 582–590.

Aslin, R. N., & Pisoni, D. B. (1980). Some developmental processes in speech perception. In G. H. Yeni-Komshian, J. F. Kavanagh, & C. A. Ferguson (Eds.), *Child phonology: Vol. 2. Perception* (pp. 67–96). New York: Academic Press.

Aslin, R. N., Pisoni, D. B., Hennessy, B. L., & Percy, A. J. (1981). Discrimination of voice onset time by human infants: New findings and implications for the effects of early experience. *Child Development, 52*(4), 1135–1145.

Aslin, R. N., Saffran, J. R., & Newport, E. L. (1998). Computation of conditional probability statistics by 8-month-old infants. *Psychological Science, 9*(4), 321–324.

Aslin, R. N., Woodward, J. Z., LaMendola, N. P., & Bever, T. G. (1996). Models of word segmentation in fluent maternal speech to infants. In J. L. Morgan & K. Demuth (Eds.), *Signal to syntax: Bootstrapping from speech to grammar in early acquisition* (pp. 117–134). Hillsdale, NJ: Erlbaum.

Bargones, J. Y., & Burns, E. M. (1988). Suppression tuning curves for spontaneous otoacoustic emissions in infants and adults. *Journal of the Acoustical Society of America, 83,* 1809–1816.

Bargones, J. Y., & Werner, L. A. (1994). Adults listen selectively: Infants do not. *Psychological Science, 5,* 170–174.

Bargones, J. Y., Werner, L. A., & Marean, G. C. (1995). Infant psychometric functions for detection: Mechanisms of immature sensitivity. *Journal of the Acoustical Society of America, 98,* 99–111.

Batchelder, E. O. (1997) *Computational evidence for the use of frequency information in discovery of the infant's first lexicon.* Unpublished doctoral dissertation, New York, City University.

Beckman, M. E., & Edwards, J. (2000). The ontogeny of phonological categories and the primacy of lexical learning in linguistic development. *Child Development, 71*(1), 240–249.

Benson, R. R., Whalen, D. H., Richardson, M., Swainson, B., Clark, V. P., Lai, S., et al. (2001). Parametrically dissociating speech and nonspeech perception in the brain using fMRI. *Brain and Language, 78,* 364–396.

Berg, K. M., & Boswell, A. E. (1995). Temporal summation of 500-Hz tones and octave-band noise bursts in infants and adults. *Perception and Psychophysics, 57,* 183–190.

Berg, K. M., & Boswell, A. E. (1998). Infants' detection of increments in low- and high-frequency noise. *Perception and Psychophysics, 60,* 1044–1051.

Berg, K. M., & Boswell, A. E. (1999). Effect of masker level on infants' detection of tones in noise. *Perception and Psychophysics, 61,* 80–86.

Berg, K. M., & Boswell, A. E. (2000). Noise increment detection in children 1 to 3 years of age. *Perception and Psychophysics, 62,* 868–873.

Berg, K. M., & Smith, M. C. (1983). Behavioral thresholds for tones during infancy. *Journal of Experimental Child Psychology, 35,* 409–425.

Bertoncini, J., Bijeljac-Babic, R., Blumstein, S., & Mehler, J. (1987). Discrimination of very short CV syllables by neonates. *Journal of the Acoustical Society of America, 82,* 31–37.

Bertoncini, J., Bijeljac-Babic, R., Jusczyk, P. W., Kennedy, L. J., & Mehler, J. (1988). An investigation of young infants' perceptual representations of speech sounds. *Journal of Experimental Psychology: General, 117*(1), 21–33.

Bertoncini, J., & Mehler, J. (1981). Syllables as units in infant speech perception. *Infant Behavior and Development, 4*(3), 247–260.

Bertoncini, J., Morais, J., Bijeljac-Babic, R., McAdams, S., Peretz, I., & Mehler, J. (1989). Dichotic perception and laterality in neonates. *Brain and Language, 37*(4), 591–605.

Best, C. T. (1994). The emergence of native-language phonological influences in infants: A perceptual assimilation model. In J. C. Goodman & H. C. Nusbaum (Eds.), *The development of speech perception: The transition from speech sounds to spoken words* (pp. 167–224). Cambridge, MA: MIT Press.

Best, C. T., Hoffman, H., & Glanville, B. B. (1982). Development of infant ear asymmetries for speech and music. *Perception and Psychophysics, 31*(1), 75–85.

Best, C. T., & McRoberts, G. W. (2003). Infant perception of nonnative contrasts that adults assimilate in different ways. *Language and Speech, 46*(2/3), 183–216.

Best, C. T., McRoberts, G. W., LaFleur, R., & Silver Isenstadt, J. (1995). Divergent developmental patterns for infants' perception of two nonnative consonant contrasts. *Infant Behavior and Development, 18*(3), 339–350.

Best, C. T., McRoberts, G. W., & Sithole, N. M. (1988). Examination of perceptual reorganization for nonnative speech contrasts: Zulu click discrimination by English-speaking adults and infants. *Journal of Experimental Psychology: Human Perception and Performance, 14*(3), 345–360.

Bijeljac-Babic, R., Bertoncini, J., & Mehler, J. (1993). How do 4-day-old infants categorize multisyllabic utterances? *Developmental Psychology, 29*(4), 711–721.

Binder, J. R., Frost, J. A., Hammeke, T. A., Bellgowan, P. S. F., Springer, J. A., Kaufman, J. N., et al. (2000). Human temporal lobe activation by speech and nonspeech sounds. *Cerebral Cortex, 10*(5), 512–528.

Binder, J. R., Frost, J. A., Hammeke, T. A., Cox, R. W., Rao, S. M., & Prieto, T. (1997). Human brain language areas identified by functional magnetic resonance imaging. *Journal of Neuroscience, 17*(1), 353–362.

Binns, K. E., Withington, D. J., & Keating, M. J. (1995). The developmental emergence of the representation of auditory azimuth in the external nucleus of the inferior colliculus of the guinea-pig: The effects of visual and auditory deprivation. *Developmental Brain Research, 85,* 14–24.

Bond, B., & Stevens, S. S. (1969). Cross-modality matching of brightness to loudness by 5-year-olds. *Perception and Psychophysics, 6,* 337–339.

Bonfils, P., Avan, P., Francois, M., Trotoux, J., & Narcy, P. (1992). Distortion-product otoacoustic emissions in neonates: Normative data. *Acta Otolaryngologica, 112,* 739–744.

Bonfils, P., Francois, M., Avan, P., Londero, A., Trotoux, J., & Narcy, P. (1992). Spontaneous and evoked otoacoustic emissions in preterm neonates. *Laryngoscope, 102,* 182–186.

Bortfeld, H., Morgan, J., Golinkoff, R., & Rathbun, K. (2005). *Mommy and me: Familiar names help launch babies into speech stream segmentation.* Manuscript in preparation.

Bosch, L., & Sebastián-Gallés, N. (2001). Early language differentiation in bilingual infants. In J. Cenoz & F. Genesee (Eds.), *Trends in bilingual acquisition* (pp. 71–93). Amsterdam: Benjamins.

Bredberg, G. (1968). Cellular pattern and nerve supply of the human organ of Corti. *Acta Otolaryngologica* (Suppl.), 236.

Bregman, A. S. (1990). *Auditory scene analysis: The perceptual organization of sound.* Cambridge, MA: MIT Press.

Brent, M. R., & Cartwright, T. A. (1996). Distributional regularity and phonotactic constraints are useful for segmentation. *Cognition, 61*(1/2), 93–125.

Brent, M. R., & Siskind, J. M. (2001). The role of exposure to isolated words in early vocabulary development. *Cognition, 81*(2), B33–B44.

Brown, A. M., Sheppard, S. L., & Russell, P. (1994). Acoustic Distortion Products (ADP) from the ears of term infants and young adults using low stimulus levels. *British Journal of Audiology, 28,* 273–280.

Brown, C., & Matthews, J. (1997). The role of feature geometry in the development of phonemic contrasts. In S. J. Hannahs & M. Young-Scholten (Eds.), *Focus on phonological acquisition: Vol. 16. Language acquisition and language disorders* (pp. 67–112). Amsterdam: Benjamins.

Brown, R. (1973). *A first language: The early stages.* Cambridge, MA: Harvard University Press.

Bull, D., Eilers, R. J., & Oller, D. K. (1984). Infants' discrimination of intensity variation in multisyllabic stimuli. *Journal of the Acoustic Society of America, 76*(1), 13–17.

Burnham, D., & Dodd, B. (2004). Audiovisual speech perception by prelinguistic infants: Perception of an emergent consonant in the McGurk effect. *Developmental Psychobiology, 45*(4), 202–220.

Burnham, D., Kitamura, C., & Vollmer-Conna, U. (2002). What's new, pussycat? On talking to babies and animals. *Science, 296*(5572), 1435.

Burns, E. M., Campbell, S. L., & Arehart, K. H. (1994). Longitudinal measurements of spontaneous otoacoustic emissions in infants. *Journal of the Acoustical Society of America, 95,* 384–394.

Buss, E., Hall, J. W., Grose, J. H., & Dev, M. B. (1999). Development of adult-like performance in backward, simultaneous, and forward masking. *Journal of Speech Language and Hearing Research, 42,* 844–849.

Cairns, P., Shillcock, R., Chater, N., & Levy, J. (1997). Bootstrapping word boundaries: A bottom-up corpus-based approach to speech segmentation. *Cognitive Psychology, 33*(2), 111–153.

Chambers, K. E., Onishi, K. H., & Fisher, C. (2003). Infants learn phonotactic regularities from brief auditory experiences. *Cognition, 87*(2), B69–B77.

Cheour, M., Ceponiene, R., Lehtokoski, A., Luuk, A., Allik, J., Alho, K., et al. (1998). Development of language-specific phoneme representations in the infant brain. *Nature Neuroscience, 1*(5), 351–353.

Cheour-Luhtanen, M., Alho, K. l., Kuijala, T., Sainio, K., Reinikainen, K., et al. (1995). Mismatch negativity indicates vowel discrimination in newborns. *Hearing Research, 82*(1), 53–58.

Christiansen, M. H., Allen, J., & Seidenberg, M. S. (1998). Learning to segment speech using multiple cues: A connectionist model. *Language and Cognitive Processes, 13,* 2–3.

Christiansen, M. H., & Curtin, S. L. (1999). Transfer of learning: Rule acquisition or statistical learning? *Trends in Cognitive Sciences, 3,* 289–290.

Christophe, A., Dupoux, E., Bertoncini, J., & Mehler, J. (1994). Do infants perceive word boundaries? An empirical study of the bootstrapping of lexical acquisition. *Journal of the Acoustical Society of America, 95*(3), 1570–1580.

Christophe, A., Gout, A., Peperkamp, S., & Morgan, J. (2003). *Discovering words in the continuous speech stream: The role of prosody.* Manuscript in preparation.

Christophe, A., Mehler, J., & Sebastián-Gallés, N. (2001). Perception of prosodic boundary correlates by newborn infants. *Infancy, 2,* 358–394.

Church, B. A., & Fisher, C. (1998). Long-term auditory word priming in preschoolers: Implicit memory support for language acquisition. *Journal of Memory and Language, 39,* 523–542.

Church, K. W. (1987). Phonological parsing and lexical retrieval. *Cognition, 25,* 53–69.

Clarkson, M. G., & Clifton, R. K. (1985). Infant pitch perception: Evidence for responding to pitch categories and the missing fundamental. *Journal of the Acoustical Society of America, 77,* 1521–1528.

Clarkson, M. G., & Clifton, R. K. (1995). Infants' pitch perception: Inharmonic tonal complexes. *Journal of the Acoustical Society of America, 98*(3), 1372–1379.

Clarkson, M. G., Clifton, R. K., & Perris, E. E. (1988). Infant timbre perception: Discrimination of spectral envelopes. *Perception and Psychophysics, 43,* 15–20.

Clarkson, M. G., & Rogers, E. C. (1995). Infants require low-frequency energy to hear the pitch of the missing fundamental. *Journal of the Acoustical Society of America, 98,* 148–154.

Clifton, R. K., Gwiazda, J., Bauer, J., Clarkson, M., & Held, R. (1988). Growth in head size during infancy: Implications for sound localization. *Developmental Psychology, 24,* 477–483.

Clifton, R. K., Morrongiello, B. A., & Dowd, J. M. (1984). A developmental look at an auditory illusion: The precedence effect. *Developmental Psychobiology, 17,* 519–536.

Clifton, R. K., Morrongiello, B. A., Kulig, J. W., & Dowd, J. M. (1981). Developmental changes in auditory localization in infancy. In R. Aslin, J. Alberts, & M. R. Petersen (Eds.), *Development of perception* (Vol. 2, pp. 141–160). New York: Academic Press.

Clifton, R. K., Perris, E. E., & Bullinger, A. (1991). Infants' perception of auditory space. *Developmental Psychology, 27,* 187–197.

Coady, J. A., & Aslin, R. N. (2003). Phonlogical neighbourhoods in the developing lexicon. *Journal of Child Language, 30,* 441–469.

Coady, J. A., & Aslin, R. N. (in press). Young children's sensitivity to probabilistic phonotactics in the developing lexicon. *Journal of Experimental Child Psychology.*

Cole, R., & Jakimik, J. (1980). *A model of speech perception.* Hillsdale, NJ: Erlbaum.

Collins, A. A., & Gescheider, G. A. (1989). The measurement of loudness in individual children and adults by absolute magnitude estimation and cross-modality matching. *Journal of the Acoustical Society of America, 85,* 2012–2021.

Colombo, J. A., & Bundy, R. S. (1981). A method for the measurement of infant auditory selectivity. *Infant Behavior and Development, 4*(2), 219–223.

Colombo, J., & Horowitz, F. D. (1986). Infants' attentional responses to frequency modulated sweeps. *Child Development, 57*(2), 287–291.

Cooper, R. P., & Aslin, R. N. (1990). Preference for infant-directed speech in the first month after birth. *Child Development, 61*(5), 1584–1595.

Cooper, R. P., & Aslin, R. N. (1994). Developmental differences in infant attention to the spectral properties of infant-directed speech. *Child Development, 65*(6), 1663–1677.

Curtin, S., Mintz, T. H., & Christiansen, M. H. (2005). Stress changes the representational landscape: Evidence from word segmentation. *Cognition, 96,* 233–262.

Curtin, S., Werker, J. F., & Ladhar, N. (2002). Accessing coarticulatory information. *Journal of the Acoustical Society of America, 112,* 2359.

Cutler, A., & Carter, D. M. (1987). The predominance of strong initial syllables in the English vocabulary. *Computer Speech and Language, 2,* 3–4.

Cutler, A., Mehler, J., Norris, D., & Segui, J. (1983). A language-specific comprehension strategy. *Nature, 304*(5922), 159–160.

Cutler, A., Mehler, J., Norris, D., & Segui, J. (1986). The syllable's differing role in the segmentation of French and English. *Journal of Memory and Language, 25*(4), 385–400.

Cutler, A., & Norris, D. (1988). The role of strong syllables in segmentation for lexical access. *Journal of Experimental Psychology: Human Perception and Performance, 14*(1), 113–121.

Dahan, D., & Brent, M. R. (1999). On the discovery of novel wordlike units from utterances: An artificial-language study with implications for native-language acquisition. *Journal of Experimental Psychology: General, 128*(2), 165–185.

Dai, H., Scharf, B., & Buus, S. (1991). Effective attenuation of signals in noise under focused attention. *Journal of the Acoustical Society of America, 89,* 2837–2842.

DeCasper, A. J., & Fifer, W. P. (1980). Of human bonding: Newborns prefer their mothers' voices. *Science, 208*(4448), 1174–1176.

DeCasper, A. J., & Prescott, P. (1984). Human newborns' perception of male voices: Preference, discrimination and reinforcing value. *Developmental Psychobiology, 17,* 481–491.

DeCasper, A. J., & Spence, M. J. (1986). Prenatal maternal speech influences newborns' perception of speech sounds. *Infant Behavior and Development, 9,* 133–150.

Dehaene, S., Dupoux, E., Mehler, J., Cohen, L., Paulesu, D., Perani, D., et al. (1997). Anatomical variability in the cortical representation of first and second languages. *Neuroreport: For Rapid Communication of NeuroScience Research, 8,* 3809–3815.

Dehaene-Lambertz, G., & Baillet, S. (1998). A phonological representation in the infant brain. *NeuroReport, 9*(8), 1885–1888.

Dehaene-Lambertz, G., & Dehaene, S. (1994). Speed and cerebral correlates of syllable discrimination in infants. *Nature, 370*(6487), 292–295.

Dehaene-Lambertz, G., Dehaene, S., & Hertz-Pannier, L. (2002). Functional neuroimaging of speech perception in infants. *Science, 298*(5600), 2013–2015.

Dehaene-Lambertz, G., & Peña, M. (2001). Electrophysiological evidence for automatic phonetic processing in neonates. *NeuroReport, 12*(14), 3155–3158.

Dell, G. S., Reed, K. D., Adams, D. R., & Meyer, A. S. (2000). Speech errors, phonotactic constraints, and implicit learning: A study of the role of experience in language production. *Journal of Experimental Psychology: Learning, Memory, and Cognition, 26*(6), 1355–1367.

Demany, L. (1982). Auditory stream segregation in infancy. *Infant Behavior and Development, 5,* 261–276.

Demany, L. (1985). Perceptual learning in frequency discrimination. *Journal of the Acoustical Society of America, 78,* 1118–1120.

Demany, L., McKenzie, B., & Vurpillot, E. (1977). Rhythm perception in early infancy. *Science, 266,* 718–719.

Desjardins, R. N., Rogers, J., & Werker, J. F. (1997). An exploration of why preschoolers perform differently than do adults in audiovisual speech perception tasks. *Journal of Experimental Child Psychology, 66*(1), 85–110.

Desjardins, R., & Werker, J. F. (2004). Is the integration of heard and seen speech mandatory for infants? *Developmental Psychobiology, 45*(4), 187–203.

Dewson, J. H. (1964). Speech sound discrimination by cats. *Science, 141,* 555–556.

Dooling, R. J., Best, C. T., & Brown, S. D. (1995). Discrimination of synthetic full-formant and sinewave/rala/continua by budgerigars (Melopsittacus undulatus) and zebra finches (Taeniopygia guttata). *Journal of the Acoustical Society of America, 97*(3), 1839–1846.

Durieux-Smith, A., Edwards, C. G., Picton, T. W., & McMurray, B. (1985). Auditory brainstem responses to clicks in neonates. *Journal of Otolaryngology, 14,* 12–18.

Echols, C. H., Crowhurst, M. J., & Childers, J. B. (1997). The perception of rhythmic units in speech by infants and adults. *Journal of Memory and Language, 36,* 202–225.

Echols, C. H., & Newport, E. L. (1992). The role of stress and position in determining first words. *Language Acquisition, 2*(3), 189–220.

Eddins, D. A., & Green, D. M. (1995). Temporal integration and temporal resolution. In B. C. J. Moore (Ed.), *Hearing* (pp. 207–242). San Diego, CA: Academic Press.

Eimas, P. D. (1974). Auditory and linguistic processing of cues for place of articulation by infants. *Perceptual Psychophysiology, 16,* 513–521.

Eimas, P. D. (1975a). Auditory and phonetic coding of the cues for speech: Discrimination of the {r-l} distinction by young infants. *Perception and Psychophysics, 18*(5), 341–347.

Eimas, P. D. (1975b). Speech perception in early infancy. In L. B. Cohen & P. Salapatek (Eds.), *Infant perception: From sensation to cognition* (pp. 193–231). New York: Academic Press.

Eimas, P. D., & Miller, J. L. (1981). Organization in the perception of segmental and suprasegmental information by infants. *Infant Behavior and Development, 4,* 395–399.

Eimas, P. D., & Miller, J. L. (1992). Organization in the perception of speech by young infants. *Psychological Science, 3,* 340–345.

Eimas, P. D., Miller, J. L., & Jusczyk, P. W. (1987). On infant speech perception and the acquisition of language. In S. Harnad (Ed.), *Categorical perception: The groundwork of cognition* (pp. 161–195). New York: Cambridge University Press.

Eimas, P. D., Siqueland, E. R., Jusczyk, P., & Vigorito, J. (1971). Speech perception in infants. *Science, 171*(968), 303–306.

Elfenbein, J. L., Small, A. M., & Davis, M. (1993). Developmental patterns of duration discrimination. *Journal of Speech and Hearing Research, 36,* 842–849.

Elman, J. L. (1990). Finding structure in time. *Cognitive Science, 14,* 179–211.

Fassbender, C. (1993). *Auditory grouping and segregation processes in infancy.* Norderstedt, Germany: Kaste Verlag.

Fay, R. R., & Coombs, S. (1983). Neural mechanisms in sound detection and temporal summation. *Hearing Research, 10,* 69–92.

Fennell, C. T., & Werker, J. F. (2003). Early word learners' ability to access phonetic detail in well-known words. *Language and Speech, 46*(2/3), 245–264.

Fernald, A. (Ed.). (1984). *The perceptual and affective salience of mothers' speech to infants.* Norwood, NJ: Ablex.

Fernald, A. (1992). Prosody in speech to children: Prelinguistic and linguistic functions. *Annals of Child Development, 8.*

Fernald, A., Pinto, J. P., Swingley, D., Weinberg, A., & McRoberts, G. W. (1998). Rapid gains in speed of verbal processing by infants in the 2nd year. *Psychological Science, 9*(3), 228–231.

Fernald, A., Swingley, D., & Pinto, J. P. (2001). When half a word is enough: Infants can recognize spoken words using partial phonetic information. *Child Development, 72*(4), 1003–1015.

Fiez, J. A., Tallal, P. A., Raichle, M. E., Miezin, F. M., Katz, W., Dobmeyer, S., et al. (1995). PET studies of auditory and phonological processing: Effects of stimulus type and task condition. *Journal of Cognitive Neuroscience, 7,* 357–375.

Fiser, J., & Aslin, R. N. (2002). Statistical learning of new visual feature combinations by infants. *Proceedings of the National Academy of Sciences, 99,* 15822–15826.

Fisher, C., Church, B., & Chambers, K. E. (2004). Learning to identify spoken words. In D. G. Hall & S. R. Waxman (Eds.), *Weaving a lexicon* (pp. 3–40). Cambridge, MA: MIT Press.

Fisher, C., & Tokura, H. (1996). Acoustic cues to grammatical structure in infant-directed speech: Cross-linguistic evidence. *Child Development, 67*(6), 3192–3218.

Fisher, C. H., Hunt, C. M., Chambers, C. K., & Church, B. (2001). Abstraction and specificity in preschoolers' representations of novel spoken words. *Journal of Memory and Language, 45*(4), 665–687.

Fitch, W. T., & Hauser, M. D. (2004). Computational constraints on syntactic processing in a nonhuman primate. *Science, 303,* 377–380.

Floccia, C., Nazzi, T., & Bertoncini, J. (2000). Unfamiliar voice discrimination for short stimuli in newborns. *Developmental Science, 3*(3), 333–343.

Folsom, R. C., & Wynne, M. K. (1987). Auditory brain stem responses from human adults and infants: Wave 5—Tuning curves. *Journal of the Acoustical Society of America, 81,* 412–417.

Fowler, C. A., Smith, M. R., & Tassinary, L. G. (1986). Perception of syllable timing by prebabbling infants. *Journal of the Acoustical Society of America, 79,* 814–825.

Friederici, A. D., & Wessels, J. M. I. (1993). Phonotactic knowledge of word boundaries and its use in infant speech perception. *Perception and Psychophysics, 54*(3), 287–295.

Fujikawa, S. M., & Weber, B. A. (1977). Effects of increased stimulus rate on brainstem electric response (BER) audiometry as a function of age. *Journal of the American Audiology Society, 3,* 147–150.

Fujimoto, S., Yamamoto, K., Hayabuchi, I., & Yoshizuka, M. (1981). Scanning and transmission electron microscope studies on the organ of corti and stria vascularis in human fetal cochlear ducts. *Archives of Histology Japan, 44,* 223–235.

Fujita, A., Hyde, M. L., & Alberti, P. W. (1991). ABR latency in infants: Properties and applications of various measures. *Acta Otolaryngologica, 111,* 53–60.

Genesee, F. (1989). Early bilingual development: One language or two? *Journal of Child Language, 16,* 161–179.

Gerken, L. A. (2004). Nine-month-olds extract structural principles required for natural language. *Cognition, 93,* B89–B96.

Gerken, L., Jusczyk, P. W., & Mandel, D. R. (1994). When prosody fails to cue syntactic structure: 9-month-olds' sensitivity to phonological versus syntactic phrases. *Cognition, 51*(3), 237–265.

Gerken, L. A., & McIntosh, B. J. (1993). The interplay of function morphemes and prosody in early language. *Developmental Psychology, 29,* 448–457.

Gerken, L. A., Wilson, R., & Lewis, W. (2005). 17-month-olds can use distributional cues to form syntactic categories. *Journal of Child Language, 32,* 249–268.

Ghazanfar, A. A., & Logothetis, N. K. (2003). Facial expressions linked to monkey calls. *Nature, 423,* 937–938.

Glanville, B. B., Levenson, R., & Best, C. T. (1977). A cardiac measure of cerebral asymmetries in infant auditory perception. *Developmental Psychology, 13*(1), 54–49.

Gleitman, L. R., & Wanner, E. (1982). Language acquisition: The state of the state of the art. In E. Wanner & L. R. Wanner (Eds.), *Language acquisition: The state of the art* (pp. 3–48). Cambridge, England: Cambridge University Press.

Glenn, S. M., Cunningham, C. C., & Joyce, P. F. (1981). A study of auditory preferences on nonhandicapped infants with Down's syndrome. *Child Development, 52,* 1303–1307.

Goldinger, S. D. (1992). Words and voices: Implicit and explicit memory for spoken words. *Dissertation Abstracts International, 53*(6), 3189.

Gómez, R. L. (2002). Variability and detection of invariant structure. *Psychological Science, 13*(5), 431–436.

Gómez, R. L., & Gerken, L. (1999). Artificial grammar learning by 1-year-olds leads to specific and abstract knowledge. *Cognition, 70*(2), 109–135.

Gómez, R. L., & Gerken, L. A. (2000). Infant artificial language learning and language acquisition. *Trends in Cognitive Sciences, 4,* 178–186.

Gómez, R. L., & Maye, J. (2005). The developmental trajectory of non-adjacent dependency learning. *Infancy, 7,* 183–206.

Goodsitt, J. V., Morgan, J. L., & Kuhl, P. K. (1993). Perceptual strategies in prelingual speech segmentation. *Journal of Child Language, 20,* 229–252.

Gorga, M. P., Kaminski, J. R., Beauchaine, K. L., Jesteadt, W., & Neely, S. T. (1989). Auditory brainstem responses from children 3 months to 3 years of age: Vol. 2. Normal patterns of response. *Journal of Speech and Hearing Research, 32,* 281–288.

Gorga, M. P., Reiland, J. K., Beauchaine, K. A., Worthington, D. W., & Jesteadt, W. (1987). Auditory brainstem responses from graduates of an intensive care nursery: Normal patterns of response. *Journal of Speech and Hearing Research, 30,* 311–318.

Gottlieb, G. (1976). The roles of experience in the development of behavior and the nervous system. In G. Gottlieb (Ed.), *Neural and behavioral specificity* (pp. 25–53). New York: Academic Press.

Gray, L. (1992). Interactions between sensory and nonsensory factors in the responses of newborn birds to sound. In L. A. Werner & E. W. Rubel (Eds.), *Developmental psychoacoustics* (pp. 89–112). Washington, DC: American Psychological Association.

Green, K. P. (1998). The use of auditory and visual information during phonetic processing: Implications for theories of speech perception. In R. Campbell, B. Dodd, & D. Burnham (Eds.), *Hearing by eye: Vol. 2. Advances in the psychology of speechreading and auditory-visual speech* (pp. 3–25). Hove, England: Psychology Press.

Greenberg, G. Z., Bray, N. W., & Beasley, D. S. (1970). Children's frequency-selective detection of signals in noise. *Perception and Psychophysics, 8,* 173–175.

Grieser, D., & Kuhl, P. K. (1989). Categorization of speech by infants: Support for speech-sound prototypes. *Developmental Psychology, 25*(4), 577–588.

Grose, J. H., Hall, J. W. I., & Gibbs, C. (1993). Temporal analysis in children. *Journal of Speech and Hearing Research, 36,* 351–356.

Hall, J. W., & Grose, J. H. (1990). The masking level difference in children. *Journal of the American Academy of Audiology, 1,* 81–88.

Hall, J. W., & Grose, J. H. (1991). Notched-noise measures of frequency selectivity in adults and children using fixed-masker-level and fixed-signal-level presentation. *Journal of Speech and Hearing Research, 34,* 651–660.

Hall, J. W., & Grose, J. H. (1994). Development of temporal resolution in children as measured by the temporal modulation transfer function. *Journal of the Acoustical Society of America, 96,* 150–154.

Hall, J. W., Grose, J. H., & Dev, M. B. (1997). Auditory development in complex tasks of comodulation masking release. *Journal of Speech Language and Hearing Research, 40,* 946–954.

Hallé, P. A., & de Boysson-Bardies, B. (1994). Emergence of an early receptive lexicon: Infants' recognition of words. *Infant Behavior and Development, 17,* 119–129.

Harris, Z. (1955). From phoneme to morpheme. *Language, 31,* 190–222.

Hartley, D. E. H., & Moore, D. R. (2002). Auditory processing efficiency deficits in children with developmental language impairments. *Journal of the Acoustical Society of America, 112,* 2962–2966.

Hartley, D. E. H., Wright, B. A., Hogan, S. C., & Moore, D. R. (2000). Age-related improvements in auditory backward and simultaneous masking in 6- to 10-year-old children. *Journal of Speech Language and Hearing Research, 43,* 1402–1415.

Hauser, M. D., Chomsky, N., & Fitch, W. T. (2002). The faculty of language: What is it, who has it, and how did it evolve? *Science, 298*(5598), 1569–1579.

Hauser, M. D., Newport, E. L., & Aslin, R. N. (2001). Segmentation of the speech stream in a nonhuman primate: Statistical learning in cotton-top tamarins. *Cognition, 78,* B53–B64.

Hauser, M. D., Weiss, D., & Marcus, G. (2002). Rule learning by cotton-top tamarins. *Cognition, 86,* B15–B22.

Hayes, R. A., Slater, A., & Brown, E. (2000). Infants' ability to categorise on the basis of rhyme. *Cognitive Development, 15*(4), 405–419.

Hillenbrand, J. A. (1984). Speech perception by infants: Categorization based on nasal consonant place of articulation. *Journal of the Acoustical Society of America, 75*(950), 1613–1622.

Hirsh-Pasek, K., Kemler Nelson, D. G., Jusczyk, P. W., Wright Cassidy, K., Druss, B., & Kennedy, L. (1987). Clauses are perceptual units for young infants. *Cognition, 26,* 269–286.

Hockley, N. S., & Polka, L. (1994). *A developmental study of Audiovisual Speech Perception Using the McGurk Paradigm.* Unpublished masters thesis, McGill University, Montreal, Canada.

Höhle B., & Weissenborn J. (2003). German-learning infants' ability to detect unstressed closed-class elements in continuous speech. *Developmental Science, 6*(2), 122–127.

Hohne, E. A., & Jusczyk, P. W. (1994). Two-month-old infants' sensitivity to allophonic differences. *Perception and Psychophysics, 56,* 613–623.

Hollich, G., Jusczyk, P., & Luce, P. (2002). Lexical neighborhood effects in 17-month-old word learning. *Proceedings of the 26th Annual Boston University Conference on Language Development* (pp. 314–323). Boston: Cascadilla Press.

Hoshino, T. (1990). Scanning electron microscopy of nerve fibers in human fetal cochlea. *Journal of Electron Microscopy Technique, 15,* 104–114.

Houston, D. M., & Jusczyk, P. W. (2000). The role of talker-specific information in word segmentation by infants. *Journal of Experimental Psychology: Human Perception and Performance, 26*(5), 1570–1582.

Houston, D. M., Jusczyk, P. W., Kuijpers, C., Coolen, R., & Cutler, A. (2000). Cross-language word segmentation by 9-month-olds. *Psychonomic Bulletin and Review, 7*(3), 504–509.

Houston, D. M., Pisoni, D. B., Kirk, K. I., Ying, E. A., & Miyamoto, R. T. (in press). Speech perception skills of deaf infants following cochlear implantation: A first report. *International Journal of Pediatric Otorhinolaryngology.*

Houston, D. M., Santelmann, L., & Jusczyk, P. W. (2004). English-learning infants' segmentation of trisyllabic words from fluent speech. *Language and Cognitive Processes, 19,* 97–136.

Igarashi, Y., & Ishii, T. (1979). Development of the cochlear and the blood-vessel-network in the fetus: A transmission electrographic observation. *Audiology, Japan, 22,* 459–460.

Igarashi, Y., & Ishii, T. (1980). Embryonic development of the human organ of Corti: Electron microscopic study. *International Journal of Pediatric Otorhinolaryngology, 2,* 51–62.

Igarashi, Y., Yamazaki, H., & Mitsui, T. (1978). An electronographic study of inner/outer haircells of human fetuses. *Audiology, Japan, 21,* 375–377.

Ilari, B., & Polka, L. (2002). *Memory for music in infancy: The role of style and complexity.* Paper presented at the International Conference on Infant Studies, Toronto, Ontario, Canada.

Irwin, R. J., Stillman, J. A., & Schade, A. (1986). The width of the auditory filter in children. *Journal of Experimental Child Psychology, 41*, 429–442.

Jensen, J. K., & Neff, D. L. (1993). Development of basic auditory discrimination in preschool children. *Psychological Science, 4*, 104–107.

Jiang, Z. D., Wu, Y. Y., & Zhang, L. (1990). Amplitude change with click rate in human brainstem auditory-evoked responses. *Audiology, 30*, 173–182.

Jiang, Z. D., Wu, Y. Y., Zheng, W. S., Sun, D. K., Feng, L. Y., & Liu, X. Y. (1991). The effect of click rate on latency and interpeak interval of the brain-stem auditory evoked potentials in children from birth to 6 years. *Electroencephalography and Clinical Neurophysiology, 80*, 60–64.

Johnson, E. K., & Jusczyk, P. W. (2001). Word segmentation by 8-month-olds: When speech cues count more than statistics. *Journal of Memory and Language, 44*(4), 548–567.

Johnson, E. K., Jusczyk, P. W., Cutler, A., & Norris, D. (2003). Lexical viability constraints on speech segmentation by infants. *Cognitive Psychology, 46*(1), 65–97.

Jusczyk, P. W. (1997). Finding and remembering words: Some beginnings by English-learning infants. *Current Directions in Psychological Science, 6*(6), 170–174.

Jusczyk, P. W., & Aslin, R. N. (1995). Infants' detection of the sound patterns of words in fluent speech. *Cognitive Psychology, 29*, 1–23.

Jusczyk, P. W., Copan, H., & Thompson, E. (1978). Perception by 2-month-old infants of glide contrasts in multisyllabic utterances. *Perception and Psychophysics, 24*(6), 515–520.

Jusczyk, P. W., Cutler, A., & Redanz, N. J. (1993). Infants' preference for the predominant stress patterns of English words. *Child Development, 64*, 675–687.

Jusczyk, P. W., & Derrah, C. (1987). Representation of speech sounds by young infants. *Developmental Psychology, 23*, 648–654.

Jusczyk, P. W., Friederici, A. D., Wessels, J. M., Svenkerud, V. Y., & Jusczyk, A. M. (1993). Infants' sensitivity to the sound patterns of native language words. *Journal of Memory and Language, 32*, 402–420.

Jusczyk, P. W., Goodman, M. B., & Baumann, A. (1999). Nine-month-olds' attention to sound similarities in syllables. *Journal of Memory and Language, 40*(1), 62–82.

Jusczyk, P. W., Hirsh-Pasek, K., Nelson, D. G. K., Kennedy, L. J., Woodward, A., & Piwoz, J. (1992). Perception of acoustic correlates of major phrasal units by young infants. *Cognitive Psychology, 24*, 252–293.

Jusczyk, P. W., & Hohne, E. A. (1997). Infants' memory for spoken words. *Science, 277*, 1984–1986.

Jusczyk, P. W., Hohne, E. A., & Baumann, A. (1999). Infants' sensitivity to allophonic cues to word segmentation. *Perception and Psychophysics, 61*, 1465–1476.

Jusczyk, P. W., Houston, D. M., & Newsome, M. (1999). The beginnings of word segmentation in English-learning infants. *Cognitive Psychology, 39*(3/4), 159–207.

Jusczyk, P. W., & Krumhansl, C. L. (1993). Pitch and rhythmic patterns affecting infants' sensitivity to musical phrase structure. *Journal of Experimental Psychology: Human Perception and Performance, 19*(3), 627–640.

Jusczyk, P. W., Luce, P. A., & Charles-Luce, J. (1994). Infants' sensitivity to phonotactic patterns in the native language. *Journal of Memory and Language, 33*(5), 630–645.

Jusczyk, P. W., Pisoni, D. B., Reed, M. A., Fernald, A., & Myers, M. (1983). Infants' discrimination of the duration of a rapid spectrum change in nonspeech signals. *Science, 222*, 175–177.

Jusczyk, P. W., Pisoni, D. B., Walley, A., & Murray, J. (1980). Discrimination of relative onset time of two-component tones by infants. *Journal of the Acoustical Society Of America, 67*(1), 262–270.

Kaga, K., & Tanaka, Y. (1980). Auditory brainstem response and behavioral audiometry: Developmental correlates. *Archives of Otolaryngology, 106*, 564–566.

Kahneman, D. (1973). *Attention and effort.* Englewood Cliffs, NJ: Prentice-Hall.

Karzon, R. G. (1985). Discrimination of polysyllabic sequences by 1- to 4-month-old infants. *Journal of Experimental Child Psychology, 39*, 326–342.

Karzon, R. G., & Nicholas, J. G. (1989). Syllabic pitch perception in 2- to 3-month-old infants. *Perception and Psychophysics, 45*(1), 10–14.

Keefe, D. H., Bulen, J. C., Arehart, K. H., & Burns, E. M. (1993). Ear-canal impedance and reflection coefficient in human infants and adults. *Journal of the Acoustical Society of America, 94*, 2617–2638.

Keefe, D. H., Burns, E. M., Bulen, J. C., & Campbell, S. L. (1994). Pressure transfer function from the diffuse field to the human infant ear canal. *Journal of the Acoustical Society of America, 95*, 355–371.

Keefe, D. H., Folsom, R. C., Gorga, M. P., Vohr, B. R., Bulen, J. C., & Norton, S. J. (2000). Identification of neonatal hearing impairment: Ear-canal measurements of acoustic admittance and reflectance in neonates. *Ear and Hearing, 21*, 443–461.

Keefe, D. H., & Levi, E. C. (1996). Maturation of the middle and external ears: Acoustic power-based responses and reflectance typmanometry. *Ear and Hearing, 17*, 1–13.

Kelly, M. H. (1992). Using sound to solve syntactic problems: The role of phonology in grammatical category assignments. *Psychological Review, 99*(2), 349–364.

Kidd, G., Jr., Mason, C. R., & Arbogast, T. L. (2002). Similarity, uncertainty, and masking in the identification of nonspeech auditory patterns. *Journal of the Acoustical Society of America, 111*, 1367–1376.

King, A. J., Hutchings, M. E., Moore, D. R., & Blakemore, C. (1988). Developmental plasticity in the visual and auditory representations in the mammalian superior colliculus. *Nature, 332*, 73–76.

Kirkham, N. Z., Slemmer, J. A., & Johnson, S. P. (2002). Visual statistical learning in infancy: Evidence for a domain general learning mechanism. *Cognition, 83*(2), B35–B42.

Klein, A. J., Alvarez, E. D., & Cowburn, C. A. (1992). The effects of stimulus rate on detectability of the auditory brain stem response in infants. *Ear and Hearing, 13*, 401–405.

Kluender, K. R., Diehl, R. L., & Killeen, P. R. (1987, September 4). Japanese quail can learn phonetic categories. *Science, 237*, 1195–1197.

Kluender, K. R., Lotto, A. J., Holt, L. L., & Bloedel, S. L. (1998). Role of experience for language-specific functional mappings of vowel sounds. *Journal of the Acoustical Society of America, 104*, 3568–3582.

Kopyar, B. A. (1997). *Intensity discrimination abilities of infants and adults: Implications for underlying processes.* Unpublished doctoral dissertation, University of Washington, Seattle.

Krentz, U. C., & Corina, D. C. (2005). *Preference for language in early infancy: The human language bias is not speech specific.* Manuscript submitted for publication.

Krumhansl, C. L., & Jusczyk, P. W. (1990). Infants' perception of phrase structure in music. *Psychological Science, 1*(1), 70–73.

Kuhl, P. K. (1979). Speech perception in early infancy: Perceptual constancy for spectrally dissimilar vowel categories. *Journal of the Acoustical Society of America, 66*(6), 1668–1679.

Kuhl, P. K. (1991). Human adults and human infants show a "perceptual magnet effect" for the prototypes of speech categories, monkeys do not. *Perception and Psychophysics, 50*(2), 93–107.

Kuhl, P. K. (2000). Language, mind, and brain: Experience alters perception. In M. S. Gazzaniga (Ed.), *The new cognitive neurosciences* (2nd ed., pp. 99–115). Cambridge, MA: MIT Press.

Kuhl, P. K., Andruski, J. E., Chistovich, I. A., Chistovich, L. A., Kozhevnikova, E. V., Ryskina, V. L., et al. (1997). Cross-language analysis of phonetic units in language addressed to infants, *Science, 277,* 684–686.

Kuhl, P. K., & Meltzoff, A. N. (1982). The bimodal perception of speech in infancy. *Science, 218*(4577), 1138–1141.

Kuhl, P. K., & Meltzoff, A. N. (1988). Speech as an intermodal object of perception. In A. Yonas (Ed.), *Minnesota Symposia on Child Psychology: Perceptual development in infancy* (pp. 235–266). Hillsdale, NJ: Erlbaum.

Kuhl, P. K., & Miller, J. D. (1978). Speech perception by the chinchilla: Identification function for synthetic VOT stimuli. *Journal of the Acoustical Society of America, 63,* 905–917.

Kuhl, P. K., & Padden, D. M. (1983). Enhanced discriminability at the phonetic boundaries for the place feature in macaques. *Journal of the Acoustical Society of America, 73,* 1003–1010.

Kuhl, P. K., Tsao, F.-M., & Liu, H.-M. (2003). Foreign-language experience in infancy: Effects of short-term exposure and social interaction on phonetic learning. *Proceedings of the National Academy of Sciences, USA, 100,* 9096–9101.

Kuhl, P. K., Tsao, F.-M., Liu, H.-M., Zhang, Y., & de Boer, B. (2001). Language/Culture/Mind/Brain: Progress at the margins between disciplines. In A. Domasio et al. (Eds.), *Unity of knowledge: The convergence of natural and human science* (pp. 136–174). New York: New York Academy of Sciences.

Kuhl, P. K., Williams, K. A., Lacerda, F., Stevens, K. N., & Lindblom, B. (1992). Linguistic experience alters phonetic perception in infants by 6 months of age. *Science, 255,* 606–608.

Lary, S., Briassoulis, G., de Vries, L., Dubowitz, L. M. S., & Dubowitz, V. (1985). Hearing threshold in preterm and term infants by auditory brainstem response. *Journal of Pediatrics, 107,* 593–599.

Lasky, R. E. (1984). A developmental study on the effect of stimulus rate on the auditory evoked brain-stem response. *Electroencephalography and Clinical Neurophysiology, 59,* 411–419.

Lasky, R. E. (1991). The effects of rate and forward masking on human adult and newborn auditory evoked response thresholds. *Developmental Psychobiology, 24,* 21–64.

Lasky, R. E. (1993). The effect of forward masker duration, rise/fall time, and integrated pressure on auditory brain stem evoked responses in human newborns and adults. *Ear and Hearing, 14,* 95–103.

Lasky, R. E. (1997). Rate and adaptation effects on the auditory evoked brainstem response in human newborns and adults. *Hearing Research, 111,* 165–176.

Lasky, R. E., & Rupert, A. (1982). Temporal masking of auditory evoked brainstem responses in human newborns and adults. *Hearing Research, 6,* 315–334.

Lasky, R. E., Syrdal-Lasky, A., & Klein, R. E. (1975). Vot discrimination by 4- to 6-month-old infants from Spanish environments. *Journal of Experimental Child Psychology, 20,* 215–225.

Lavigne-Rebillard, M., & Bagger-Sjoback, D. (1992). Development of the human stria vascularis. *Hearing Research, 64,* 39–51.

Lavigne-Rebillard, M., & Pujol, R. (1987). Surface aspects of the developing human organ of corti. *Acta Otolaryngologica, 436,* 43–50.

Lavigne-Rebillard, M., & Pujol, R. (1988). Hair cell innervation in the fetal human cochlea. *Acta Otolaryngologica, Stockholm, 105,* 398–402.

Lavigne-Rebillard, M., & Pujol, R. (1990). Auditory hair cells in human fetuses: Synaptogenesis and ciliogenesis. *Journal of Electron Microscopy Technique, 15,* 115–122.

Lecanuet, J.-P., Granier-Deferre, C., & Busnel, M.-C. (1988). Fetal cardiac and motor responses to octave-band noises as a function of central frequency, intensity and heart rate variability. *Early Human Development, 18,* 81–93.

Leibold, L., & Werner, L. A. (2002). Relationship between intensity and reaction time in normal hearing infants and adults. *Ear and Hearing, 23,* 92–97.

Leibold, L., & Werner, L. A. (2003). Infants' detection in the presence of masker uncertainty. *Journal of the Acoustical Society of America, 113,* 2208.

Levi, E. C., & Werner, L. A. (1996). Amplitude modulation detection in infancy: Update on 3-month-olds. *Abstracts of the Association for Research in Otolaryngology, 19,* 142.

Liberman, A. M., Cooper, F. S., Shankweiler, D. P., & Studdert-Kennedy, M. (1967). Perception of the speech code. *Psychological Review, 74,* 431–461.

Lisker, L., & Abramson, A. S. (1971). Distinctive features and laryngeal control. *Language, 47,* 767–785.

Litovsky, R. Y. (1997). Developmental changes in the precedence effect: Estimates of minimum audible angle. *Journal of the Acoustical Society of America, 102*(3), 1739–1745.

Liu, H.-M., Kuhl, P. K., & Tsao, F.-M. (2003). An association between mothers' speech clarity and infants' speech discrimination skills. *Developmental Science, 6*(3), F1–F10.

Lotto, A. J., Kluender, K. R., & Holt, L. L. (1998). Depolarizing the perceptual magnet effect. *Journal of the Acoustical Society of America, 103,* 3648–3655.

MacDonald, J., & McGurk, H. (1978). Visual influences on speech perception process. *Perception and Psychophysics, 24,* 253–257.

MacKain, K., Studdert-Kennedy, M., Spieker, S., & Stern, D. (1983, March 18). Infant intermodal speech perception is a left-hemisphere function. *Science, 219,* 1347–1349.

Mandel, D. R., Jusczyk, P. W., & Kemler Nelson, D. G. (1994). Does sentential prosody help infants organize and remember speech information? *Cognition, 53,* 155–180.

Mandel, D. R., Jusczyk, P. W., & Pisoni, D. B. (1995). Infants' recognition of the sound patterns of their own names. *Psychological Science, 6*(5), 315–318.

Marcus, G. F., Vijayan, S., Rao, S. B., & Vishton, P. M. (1999). Rule learning by 7-month-old infants. *Science, 283*(5398), 77–80.

Massaro, D. W., Cohen, M. M., & Smeele, P. M. T. (1995). Cross-linguistic comparisons in the integration of visual and auditory speech. *Memory and Cognition, 23*(1), 113–131.

Massaro, D. W., Thompson, L. A., Barron, B., & Laren, E. (1986). Developmental changes in visual and auditory contributions to speech perception. *Journal of Experimental Child Psychology, 41,* 93–113.

Mattingly, I. G., Liberman, A. M., Syrdal, A. K., & Halwes, T. (1971). Discrimination in speech and non-speech modes. *Cognitive Psychology, 2,* 131–157.

Mattys, S. L., & Jusczyk, P. W. (2001). Phonotactic cues for segmentation of fluent speech by infants. *Cognition, 78*(2), 91–121.

Mattys, S. L., Jusczyk, P. W., Luce, P. A., & Morgan, J. L. (1999). Phonotactic and prosodic effects on word segmentation in infants. *Cognitive Psychology, 38*(4), 465–494.

Maxon, A. B., & Hochberg, I. (1982). Development of psychoacoustic behavior: Sensitivity and discrimination. *Ear and Hearing, 3,* 301–308.

Maye, J., Werker, J. F., & Gerken, L. (2002). Infant sensitivity to distributional information can affect phonetic discrimination. *Cognition, 82*(3), B101–B111.

McAdams, S., & Bertoncini, J. (1997). Organization and discrimination of repeating sound sequences by newborn infants. *Journal of the Acoustical Society of America, 102*(5, Pt. 1), 2945–2953.

McGurk, H., & MacDonald, J. (1976). Hearing lips and seeing voices. *Nature, 264*(5588), 746–748.

McMurray, B., & Aslin, R. N. (2005). Infants are sensitive to within-category variation in speech perception. *Cognition, 95*(2), B15–B26.

Mehler, J., & Christophe, A. (1995). Maturation and learning of language in the first year of life. In M. S. Gazzaniga (Ed.), *The cognitive neurosciences* (pp. 943–954). Cambridge, MA: MIT Press.

Mehler, J., Dommergues, J., Frauenfelder, U., & Segui, J. (1981). The syllable's role in speech segmentation. *Cognitive Psychology, 18,* 1–86.

Mehler, J., Jusczyk, P. W., Lambertz, G., Halsted, N., Bertoncini, J., & Amiel-Tison, C. (1988). A precursor of language acquisition in young infants. *Cognition, 29,* 143–178.

Miller, J. L. (1987). Rate-dependent processing in speech perception. In A. Ellis (Ed.), *Progress in the psychology of language* (Vol. 3, pp. 119–157). Hillsdale, NJ: Erlbaum.

Miller, J. L., & Eimas, P. D. (1979). Organization in infant speech perception. *Canadian Journal of Psychology, 33,* 353–367.

Miller, J. L., & Eimas, P. D. (1996). Internal structure of voicing categories in early infancy. *Perception and Psychophysics, 58*(8), 1157–1167.

Mills, D. L., Prat, C., Zangl, R., Stager, C. L., Neville, H. J., & Werker, J. F. (2004). Language experience and the organization of brain activity to phonetically similar words: ERP evidence from 14- and 20-month-olds. *Journal of Cognitive Neuroscience, 16*(8), 1–13.

Moffit, A. R. (1971). Consonant cue perception by 20- to 24-week-old infants. *Child Development, 42,* 505–511.

Molfese, D. L., Burger-Judisch, L. M., & Hans, L. L. (1991). Consonant discrimination by newborn infants: Electrophysiological differences. *Developmental Neuropsychology, 7*(2), 177–195.

Molfese, D. L., & Molfese, V. (1979). Hemisphere and stimulus differences as reflected in the cortical responses of newborn infants. *Developmental Psychology, 15,* 505–511.

Molfese, D. L., & Molfese, V. (1980). Cortical responses of preterm infants to phonetic and nonphonetic speech stimuli. *Developmental Psychology, 16,* 574–581.

Molfese, D. L., & Molfese, V. (1985). Electrophysiological indices of auditory discrimination in newborn infants: The bases for predicting later language development? *Infant Behavior and Development, 8,* 197–211.

Montgomery, C. R., & Clarkson, M. G. (1997). Infants' pitch perception: Masking by low- and high-frequency noises. *Journal of the Acoustical Society of America, 102,* 3665–3672.

Moon, C., Cooper, R. P., & Fifer, W. P. (1993). Two-day-olds prefer their native language. *Infant Behavior and Development, 16*(4), 495–500.

Moore, B. C. J. (1973). Frequency difference limens for short-duration tones. *Journal of the Acoustical Society of America, 54,* 610–619.

Moore, B. C. J. (1996). *Introduction to the psychology of hearing* (5th ed.). New York: Academic Press.

Moore, B. C. J., Glasberg, B. R., Plack, C. J., & Biswas, A. K. (1988). The shape of the ear's temporal window. *Journal of the Acoustical Society of America, 83,* 1102–1116.

Moore, J. K. (2002). Maturation of human auditory cortex: Implications for speech perception. *Annals of Otology Rhinology and Laryngology, 111,* 7–10.

Moore, J. K., & Guan, Y. L. (2001). Cytoarchitectural and axonal maturation in human auditory cortex. *Journal of the Association for Research in Otolaryngology, 2,* 297–311.

Moore, J. K., Guan, Y. L., & Shi, S. R. (1997). Axogenesis in the human fetal auditory system, demonstrated by neurofilament immunohistochemistry. *Anatomy and Embryology, Berlin, 195,* 15–30.

Moore, J. K., Perazzo, L. M., & Braun, A. (1995). Time course of axonal myelination in human brainstem auditory pathway. *Hearing Research, 87,* 21–31.

Moore, J. K., Ponton, C. W., Eggermont, J. J., Wu, B. J., & Huang, J. Q. (1996). Perinatal maturation of the auditory brain stem response: Changes in path length and conduction velocity. *Ear and Hearing, 17,* 411–418.

Mora, J. A., Exposito, M., Solis, C., & Barajas, J. J. (1990). Filter effects and low stimulation rate on the middle-latency response in newborns. *Audiology, 29,* 329–335.

Morais, J., Content, A., Cary, L., Mehler, J., & Segui, J. (1989). Syllabic segmentation and literacy. *Language and Cognitive Processes, 4*(1), 57–67.

Morgan, J. L., & Demuth, K. (1996). *Signal to syntax: Bootstrapping from speech to grammar in early acquisition.* Hillsdale, NJ: Erlbaum.

Morgan, J. L., Meier, R. P., & Newport, E. L. (1987). Structural packaging in the input to language learning: Contributions of intonational and morphological marking of phrases to the acquisition of language. *Cognitive Psychology, 19,* 498–550.

Morgan, J. L., & Newport, E. L. (1981). The role of constituent structure in the induction of an artificial language. *Journal of Verbal Learning and Verbal Behavior, 20,* 67–85.

Morgan, J. L., & Saffran, J. R. (1995). Emerging integration of sequential and suprasegmental information in preverbal speech segmentation. *Child Development, 66,* 911–936.

Morgan, J. L., Shi, R., & Allopenna, P. (1996). Perceptual bases of rudimentary grammatical categories: Toward a broader conceptualization of bootstrapping. In J. L. M. K. Demuth (Ed.), *Signal to syntax* (pp. 263–283). Hillsdale, NJ: Erlbaum.

Morrongiello, B. A. (1988). Infants' localization of sounds in the horizontal plane: Estimates of minimum audible angle. *Developmental Psychology, 24,* 8–13.

Morrongiello, B. A., Fenwick, K., & Chance, G. (1990). Sound localization acuity in very young infants: An observer-based testing procedure. *Developmental Psychology, 26,* 75–84.

Morrongiello, B. A., Fenwick, K. D., Hillier, L., & Chance, G. (1994). Sound localization in newborn human infants. *Developmental Psychobiology, 27,* 519–538.

Morrongiello, B. A., Hewitt, K. L., & Gotowiec, A. (1991). Infants' discrimination of relative distance in the auditory modality: Approaching versus receding sound sources. *Infant Behavior and Development, 14,* 187–208.

Morrongiello, B. A., & Rocca, P. T. (1987a). Infants' localization of sounds in the horizontal plane: Effects of auditory and visual cues. *Child Development, 58,* 918–927.

Morrongiello, B. A., & Rocca, P. T. (1987b). Infants' localization of sounds in the median sagittal plane: Effects of signal frequency. *Journal of the Acoustical Society of America, 82,* 900–905.

Morrongiello, B. A., & Rocca, P. T. (1987c). Infants' localization of sounds in the median vertical plane: Estimates of minimal audible angle. *Journal of Experimental Child Psychology, 43,* 181–193.

Morrongiello, B. A., & Rocca, P. T. (1990). Infants' localization of sounds within hemifields: Estimates of minimum audible angle. *Child Development, 61,* 1258–1270.

Morrongiello, B. A., & Trehub, S. E. (1987). Age-related changes in auditory temporal perception. *Journal of Experimental Child Psychology, 44,* 413–426.

Morse, P. A. (1972). The discrimination of speech and non-speech stimuli in early infancy. *Journal of Experimental Child Psychology, 14*(3), 477–492.

Morse, P. A., & Snowdon, C. T. (1975). An investigation of categorical speech discrimination by rhesus monkeys. *Perception and Psychophysics, 17*(1), 9–16.

Myers, J., Jusczyk, P. W., Kemler Nelson, D. G., Charles-Luce, J., Woodward, A. L., & Hirsh-Pasek, K. (1996). Infants' sensitivity to word boundaries in fluent speech. *Journal of Child Language, 23*(1), 1–30.

Naigles, L. (1990). Children use syntax to learn verb meaning. *Journal of Child Language, 17,* 357–374.

Nakai, Y. (1970). An electron microscopic study of the human fetus cochlea. *Practica of Otology, Rhinology and Laryngology, 32,* 257–267.

Nazzi, T., Bertoncini, J., & Mehler, J. (1998). Language discrimination by newborns: Toward an understanding of the role of rhythm. *Journal of Experimental Psychology: Human Perception and Performance, 24*(3), 756–766.

Nazzi, T., Dilley, L., Jusczyk, A. M., Shattuck-Hufnagel, S., & Jusczyk, P. (in press). English-learning infants' segmentation of verbs from fluent speech. *Language and Speech.*

Nazzi, T., Floccia, C., & Bertoncini, J. (1998). Discrimination of pitch contours by neonates. *Infant Behavior and Development, 21,* 779–784.

Nazzi, T., Jusczyk, P. W., & Johnson, E. K. (2000). Language discrimination by English-learning 5-month-olds: Effects of rhythm and familiarity. *Journal of Memory and Language, 43*(1), 1–19.

Neff, D. L., & Callaghan, B. P. (1988). Effective properties of multicomponent simultaneous maskers under conditions of uncertainty. *Journal of the Acoustical Society of America, 83,* 1833–1838.

Neff, D. L., & Green, D. M. (1987). Masking produced by spectral uncertainty with multicomponent maskers. *Perception and Psychophysics, 41,* 409–415.

Nespor, M., Guasti, M. T., & Christophe, A. (1996). Selecting word order: The rhythmic activation principle. In U. Kleinhenz (Ed.), *Interfaces in phonology* (pp. 1–26). Berlin, Germany: Akademie Verlag.

Newport, E. L., & Aslin, R. N. (2004). Learning at a distance: I. Statistical learning of non-adjacent dependencies. *Cognitive Psychology, 48*(2), 127–162.

Newport, E. L., Hauser, M. D., Spaepen, G., & Aslin, R. N. (2004). Learning at a distance: II. Statistical learning of non-adjacent dependencies in a non-human primate. *Cognitive Psychology, 49,* 85–117.

Nittrouer, S., Crowther, C. S., & Miller, M. E. (1998). The relative weighting of acoustic properties in the perception of s+stop clusters by children and adults. *Perception and Psychophysics, 60,* 51–64.

Nittrouer, S., & Miller, M. E. (1997). Predicting developmental shifts in perceptual weighting schemes. *Journal of the Acoustical Society of America, 101,* 3353–3366.

Nittrouer, S., & Studdert-Kennedy, M. (1987). The role of coarticulatory effects in the perception of fricatives by children and adults. *Journal of Speech and Hearing Research, 30,* 319–329.

Norton, S. J., Gorga, M. P., Widen, J. E., Folsom, R. C., Sininger, Y., Cone-Wesson, B., et al. (2000). Identification of neonatal hearing impairment: Summary and recommendations. *Ear and Hearing, 21,* 529–535.

Novak, G. P., Kurtzberg, D., Kreuzer, J. A., & Vaughan, H. G. (1989). Cortical responses to speech sounds and their formants in normal infants: Maturational sequence and spatiotemporal analysis. *Electroencephalography and Clinical Neurophysiology, 73*(4), 295–305.

Nozza, R. J. (1987). The binaural masking level difference in infants and adults: Developmental change in binaural hearing. *Infant Behavior and Development, 10,* 105–110.

Nozza, R. J. (1995). Estimating the contribution of non-sensory factors to infant-adult differences in behavioral thresholds. *Hearing Research, 91,* 72–78.

Nozza, R. J., & Henson, A. M. (1999). Unmasked thresholds and minimum masking in infants and adults: Separating sensory from nonsensory contributions to infant-adult differences in behavioral thresholds. *Ear and Hearing, 20,* 483–496.

Nozza, R. J., & Wilson, W. R. (1984). Masked and unmasked pure-tone thresholds of infants and adults: Development of auditory frequency selectivity and sensitivity. *Journal of Speech and Hearing Research, 27,* 613–622.

Nygaard, L. C., & Pisoni, D. B. (1995). Speech perception: New directions in research and theory. In J. L. Miller & P. D. Eimas (Eds.), *Handbook of perception and cognition: Vol. 11. Speech, language, and communication* (2nd ed., pp. 63–96). San Diego, CA: Academic Press.

Oh, E. L., & Lutfi, R. A. (1999). Informational masking by everyday sounds. *Journal of the Acoustical Society of America, 106,* 3521–3528.

Oh, E. L., Wightman, F., & Lutfi, R. A. (2001). Children's detection of pure-tone signals with random multitone maskers. *Journal of the Acoustical Society of America, 109,* 2888–2895.

Okabe, K. S., Tanaka, S., Hamada, H., Miura, T., & Funai, H. (1988). Acoustic impedance measured on normal ears of children. *Journal of the Acoustical Society of Japan, 9,* 287–294.

Olivier, D. C. (1968). *Stochastic grammars and language acquisition mechanisms.* Unpublished doctoral dissertation, Harvard University, Cambridge, MA.

Olsho, L. W. (1984). Infant frequency discrimination. *Infant Behavior and Development, 7,* 27–35.

Olsho, L. W. (1985). Infant auditory perception: Tonal masking. *Infant Behavior and Development, 7,* 27–35.

Olsho, L. W., Koch, E. G., & Carter, E. A. (1988). Nonsensory factors in infant frequency discrimination. *Infant Behavior and Development, 11,* 205–222.

Olsho, L. W., Koch, E. G., Carter, E. A., Halpin, C. F., & Spetner, N. B. (1988). Pure-tone sensitivity of human infants. *Journal of the Acoustical Society of America, 84,* 1316–1324.

Olsho, L. W., Koch, E. G., & Halpin, C. F. (1987). Level and age effects in infant frequency discrimination. *Journal of the Acoustical Society of America, 82,* 454–464.

Olsho, L. W., Schoon, C., Sakai, R., Turpin, R., & Sperduto, V. (1982). Auditory frequency discrimination in infancy. *Developmental Psychology, 18,* 721–726.

Onishi, K. H., Chambers, K. E., & Fisher, C. (2002). Learning phonotactic constraints from brief auditory experience. *Cognition, 83*(1), B13–B23.

Otake, T., Hatano, G., Cutler, A., & Mehler, J. (1993). Mora or syllable? Speech segmentation in Japanese. *Journal of Memory and Language, 32*(2), 258–278.

Palmer, C., Jungers, M. K., & Jusczyk, P. W. (2001). Episodic memory for musical prosody. *Journal of Memory and Language, 45*(4), 526–545.

Pater, J., Stager, C. L., & Werker, J. F. (2004). The lexical acquisition of phonological contrasts. *Language, 80*(3), 361–379.

Patterson, M. L., & Werker, J. F. (1999). Matching phonetic information in lips and voice is robust in 4$^1/_2$-month-old infants. *Infant Behavior and Development, 22*(2), 237–247.

Patterson, M. L., & Werker, J. F. (2002). Infants' ability to match dynamic phonetic and gender information in the face and voice. *Journal of Experimental Child Psychology, 81*(1), 93–115.

Patterson, M. L., & Werker, J. F. (2003). Two-month-olds match vowel information in the face and voice. *Developmental Science, 6*(2), 191–196.

Pegg, J. E., & Werker, J. F. (1997). Adult and infant perception of two English phones. *Journal of the Acoustical Society of America, 102*(6), 3742–3753.

Peña, M., Maki, A., Kovacic, D., Dehaene-Lambertz, G., Koizumi, H., Bouquet, F., et al. (2003). Sounds and silence: An optical topography study of language recognition at birth. *Proceedings of the National Academy of Sciences, 100*(20), 11702–11705.

Phillips, C., Pellathy, T., & Marantz, A. (1999, October). *Magnetic mismatch field elicited by phonological feature contrast.* Paper presented at the Cognitive Neuroscience Society Meeting, Washington, DC.

Pike, K. L. (1945). Step-by-step procedure for marking limited intonation with its related features of pause, stress and rhythm. In C. C. Fries (Ed.), *Teaching and learning English as a foreign language* (pp. 62–74). Ann Arbor, MI: Publication of the English Language Institute.

Pinker, S. (1984). *Language learnability and language development.* Cambridge, MA: Harvard University Press.

Pinker, S. (1989) *Learnability and cognition: The acquisition of argument structure.* Cambridge, MA: MIT Press.

Pinker, S. (1994). *The language instinct.* New York: HarperCollins.

Pisoni, D. B. (1977). Identification and discrimination of the relative onset of two component tones: Implications for voicing perception in stops. *Journal of the Acoustical Society of America, 61,* 1352–1361.

Plessinger, M. A., & Woods, J. R. (1987). Fetal auditory brain stem response: Effect of increasing stimulus rate during functional auditory development. *American Journal of Obstetrics and Gynecology, 157,* 1382.

Polka, L., & Bohn, O. S. (1996). A cross-language comparison of vowel perception in English-learning and German-learning infants. *Journal of the Acoustical Society of America, 100*(1), 577–592.

Polka, L., Colantonio, C., & Sundara, M. (2001). A cross-language comparison of /d/-/th/ perception: Evidence for a new developmental pattern. *Journal of the Acoustical Society of America, 109*(Suppl. 5, Pt. 1), 2190–2201.

Polka, L., Sundara, M., & Blue, S. (2002, June 3–7). *The role of language experience in word segmentation: A comparison of English, French, and bilingual infants.* Paper presented at the the 143rd Meeting of the Acoustical Society of America: Special Session in Memory of Peter Jusczyk, Pittsburgh, PA.

Polka, L., & Werker, J. F. (1994). Developmental changes in perception of nonnative vowel contrasts. *Journal of Experimental Psychology: Human Perception and Performance, 20*(2), 421–435.

Pollack, I. (1975). Auditory informational masking. *Journal of the Acoustical Society of America, 57*(Suppl. 1), 5.

Pons, F. (in press). The effects of distributional learning on rats' sensitivity to phonetic information. *Journal of Experimental Psychology: Animal Behavior Processes.*

Ponton, C. W., Eggermont, J. J., Coupland, S. G., & Winkelaar, R. (1992). Frequency-specific maturation of the eighth-nerve and brain-stem auditory pathway: Evidence from derived Auditory Brain-Stem Responses (ABRs). *Journal of the Acoustical Society of America, 91,* 1576–1587.

Ponton, C. W., Eggermont, J. J., Don, M., Waring, M. D., Kwong, B., Cunningham, J., et al. (2000). Maturation of the mismatch negativity: Effects of profound deafness and cochlear implant use. *Audiology and Neuro Otology, 5,* 167–185.

Ponton, C. W., Moore, J. K., & Eggermont, J. J. (1996). Auditory brain stem response generation by parallel pathways: Differential maturation of axonal conduction time and synaptic transmission. *Ear and Hearing, 17,* 402–410.

Price, C., Wise, R., Warburton, E., Moore, C., Howard, D., Patterson, K., et al. (1996). Hearing and saying: The functional neuroanatomy of auditory word processing. *Brain, 119*(3), 919–931.

Pujol, R., & Lavigne-Rebillard, M. (1992). Development of neurosensory structures in the human cochlea. *Acta Otolaryngologica, 112,* 259–264.

Ramus, F. (2002). Language discrimination by newborns: Teasing apart phonotactic, rhythmic, and intonational cues. *Annual Review of Language Acquisition, 2,* 85–115.

Ramus, F., Hauser, M. D., Miller, C., Morris, D., & Mehler, J. (2000). Language discrimination by human newborns and by cotton-top tamarin monkeys. *Science, 288*(5464), 349–351.

Ramus, F., & Mehler, J. (1999). Language identification with suprasegmental cues: A study based on speech resynthesis. *Journal of the Acoustical Society of America, 105*(1), 512–521.

Ramus, F., Nespor, M., & Mehler, J. (1999). Correlates of linguistic rhythm in the speech signal. *Cognition, 73*(3), 265–292.

Ratner, N. B. (1984). Patterns of vowel modification in mother-child speech. *Journal of Child Language, 11,* 557–578.

Ratner, N. B., & Luberoff, A. (1984). Cues to post-vocalic voicing in mother-child speech. *Journal of Phonetics, 12,* 285–289.

Remez, R. E., Rubin, P. E., Pisoni, D. B., & Carrell, T. D. (1981). Speech perception without traditional speech cues. *Science, 212*(4497), 947–949.

Repp, B. H. (1984). Against a role of "chirp" identification in duplex perception. *Perception and Psychophysics, 35*(1), 89–93.

Rice, K., & Avery, P. (1995). Variability in a deterministic model of language acquisition: A theory of segmental acquisition. In J. Archibald (Ed.), *Phonological acquisition and phonological theory* (pp. 23–42). Hillsdale, NJ: Erlbaum.

Rivera-Gaxiola, M., Silva-Pereyra, J., & Kuhl, P. K. (2005). Brain potentials to native and non-native speech contrasts in 7- and 11-month-old American infants. *Developmental Science, 8,* 162–172.

Rosen, S., van der Lely, H., Adlard, A., & Manganari, E. (2000). Backward masking in children with and without language disorders [Abstract]. *British Journal of Audiology, 34,* 124.

Rosenblum, L. D., Schmuckler, M. A., & Johnson, J. A. (1997). The McGurk effect in infants. *Perception and Psychophysics, 59*(3), 347–357.

Rumelhart, D. E., & McClelland, J. L. (1986). *Parallel distributed processing*. Cambridge, MA: MIT Press.

Ruth, R. A., Horner, J. S., McCoy, G. S., & Chandler, C. R. (1983). Comparison of auditory brainstem response and behavioral audiometry in infants. *Audiology, Scandinavian, 17,* 94–98.

Saffran, J. R. (2001). The use of predictive dependencies in language learning. *Journal of Memory and Language, 44*(4), 493–515.

Saffran, J. R. (2002). Constraints on statistical language learning. *Journal of Memory and Language, 47*(1), 172–196.

Saffran, J. R. (2003a). Absolute pitch in infancy and adulthood: The role of tonal structure. *Developmental Science, 6*(1), 35–43.

Saffran, J. R. (2003b). Statistical language learning: Mechanisms and constraints. *Current Directions in Psychological Science, 12*(4), 110–114.

Saffran, J. R., Aslin, R. N., & Newport, E. L. (1996). Statistical learning by 8-month-old infants. *Science, 274*(5294), 1926–1928.

Saffran, J. R., & Graf Estes, K. M. (2004, May). *What are statistics for? Linking statistical learning to language acquisition in the wild*. Paper presented at the International Conference on Infant Studies, Chicago, IL.

Saffran, J. R., & Griepentrog, G. (2001). Absolute pitch in infant auditory learning: Evidence for developmental reorganization. *Developmental Psychology, 37*(1), 74–85.

Saffran, J. R., Hauser, M., Seibel, R., Kapfhamer, J., Tsao, F., & Cushman, F. (2005). *Cross-species differences in the capacity to acquire language: Grammatical pattern learning by human infants and monkeys*. Manuscript submitted for publication.

Saffran, J. R., Johnson, E. K., Aslin, R. N., & Newport, E. L. (1999). Statistical learning of tone sequences by human infants and adults. *Cognition, 70*(1), 27–52.

Saffran, J. R., Loman, M. M., & Robertson, R. R. W. (2000). Infant memory for musical experiences. *Cognition, 77,* 15–23.

Saffran, J. R., Reeck, K., Niehbur, A., & Wilson, D. P. (in press). Changing the tune: Absolute and relative pitch processing by adults and infants. *Developmental Science, 7*(7), 53–71.

Saffran, J. R., & Thiessen, E. D. (2003). Pattern induction by infant language learners. *Developmental Psychology, 39*(3), 484–494.

Saffran, J. R., & Wilson, D. P. (2003). From syllables to syntax: Multilevel statistical learning by 12-month-old infants. *Infancy, 4*(2), 273–284.

Sanes, D. H., & Walsh, E. J. (1998). The development of central auditory function. In E. W. Rubel, R. R. Fay, & A. N. Popper (Eds.), *Development of the auditory system* (pp. 271–314). New York: Springer Verlag.

Santelmann, L. M., & Jusczyk, P. W. (1998). Sensitivity to discontinuous dependencies in language learners: Evidence for limitations in processing space. *Cognition, 69*(2), 105–134.

Schafer, G., & Plunkett, K. (1998). Rapid word learning by 15-month-olds under tightly controlled conditions. *Child Development, 69*(2), 309–320.

Schneider, B. A., Bull, D., & Trehub, S. E. (1988). Binaural unmasking in infants. *Journal of the Acoustical Society of America, 83,* 1124–1132.

Schneider, B. A., Morrongiello, B. A., & Trehub, S. E. (1990). The size of the critical band in infants, children, and adults. *Journal of Experimental Psychology: Human Perception and Performance, 16,* 642–652.

Schneider, B. A., Trehub, S. E., Morrongiello, B. A., & Thorpe, L. A. (1989). Developmental changes in masked thresholds. *Journal of the Acoustical Society of America, 86,* 1733–1742.

Sebastián-Gallés, N., & Bosch, L. (2002). Building phonotactic knowledge in bilinguals: Role of early exposure. *Journal of Experimental Psychology: Human Perception and Performance, 28*(4), 974–989.

Sebastián-Gallés, N., Dupoux, E., Segui, J., & Mehler, J. (1992). Contrasting syllabic effects in Catalan and Spanish. *Journal of Memory and Language, 31,* 18–32.

Seidenberg, M., & Elman, J. L. (1999). Do infants learn grammar with algebra or statistics? *Science, 284,* 433.

Seidenberg, M. S., MacDonald, M. C., & Saffran, J. R. (2003). Are there limits to statistical learning? *Science, 300,* 53–54.

Shady, M. E., & Gerken, L. A. (1999). Grammatical and caregiver cues in early sentence comprehension. *Journal of Child Language, 26,* 1–13.

Shafer, V. L., Shucard, D. W., Shucard, J. L., & Gerken, L. (1998). An electrophysiological study of infants' sensitivity to the sound patterns of English speech. *Journal of Speech, Language, and Hearing Research, 41*(4), 874–886.

Shahidullah, S., & Hepper, P. G. (1994). Frequency discrimination by the fetus. *Early Human Development, 36*(1), 13–26.

Shi, R., Morgan, J. L., & Allopenna, P. (1998). Phonological and acoustic bases for earliest grammatical category assignment: A cross-linguistic perspective. *Journal of Child Language, 25*(1), 169–201.

Shi, R., & Werker, J. F. (2001). Six-month-old infants' preference for lexical words. *Psychological Science, 12*(1), 71–76.

Shi, R., & Werker, J. F. (2003). The basis of preference for lexical words in 6-month-old infants. *Developmental Science, 6*(5), 484–488.

Shi, R., Werker, J. F., & Cutler, A. (2003). Function words in early speech perception. In *Proceedings of the 15th International Conference of Phonetic Sciences* (pp. 3009–3012). Adelaide, Australia: Causal Productions.

Shi, R., Werker, J. F., Cutler, A., & Cruickshank, M. (2004, April). *Facilitation effects of function words for word segmentation in infants*. Poster presented at the International Conference of Infant Studies, Chicago.

Shi, R., Werker, J. F., & Morgan, J. L. (1999). Newborn infants' sensitivity to perceptual cues to lexical and grammatical words. *Cognition, 72*(2), B11–B21.

Shvachkin, N. K. (1948). The development of phonemic speech perception in early childhood. In C. A. Ferguson & D. I. Slobin (Eds.), *Studies of child language development* (pp. 91–127). New York: Holt, Rinehart and Winston.

Singh, L., Bortfeld, H., & Morgan, J. (2002). Effects of variability on infant word recognition. In A. H. J. Do, L. Domínguez, & A. Johansen (Eds.), *Proceedings of the 26th Annual Boston University Conference on Language Development* (pp. 608–619). Somerville, MA: Cascadilla Press.

Singh, L., Morgan, J., & White, K. (2004). Preference and processing: The role of speech affect in early spoken word recognition. *Journal of Memory and Language, 51,* 173–189.

Sininger, Y., & Abdala, C. (1996). Auditory brainstem response thresholds of newborns based on ear canal levels. *Ear and Hearing, 17,* 395–401.

Sininger, Y. S., Abdala, C., & Cone-Wesson, B. (1997). Auditory threshold sensitivity of the human neonate as measured by the auditory brainstem response. *Hearing Research, 104,* 1–22.

Sinnott, J. M. (1989). Detection and discrimination of synthetic English vowels by Old World monkeys (Cercopithecus, Macaca) and humans. *Journal of the Acoustical Society of America, 86,* 557–565.

Sinnott, J. M., & Aslin, R. N. (1985). Frequency and intensity discrimination in human infants and adults. *Journal of the Acoustical Society of America, 78,* 1986–1992.

Sinnott, J. M., Pisoni, D. B., & Aslin, R. M. (1983). A comparison of pure tone auditory thresholds in human infants and adults. *Infant Behavior and Development, 6,* 3–17.

Slobin, D. I. (1973). Cognitive prerequisites for the development of grammar. In C. A. Ferguson & D. I. Slobin (Eds.), *Studies of child language development* (pp. 175–208). New York: Holt, Rinehart and Winston.

Smith, S. L., Gerhardt, K. J., Griffiths, S. K., & Huang, X. (2003). Intelligibility of sentences recorded from the uterus of a pregnant ewe and from the fetal inner ear. *Audiology and Neuro Otology, 8,* 347–353.

Soderstrom, M., Seidl, A., Kemler Nelson, D. G., & Jusczyk, P. W. (2003). The prosodic bootstrapping of phrases: Evidence from prelinguistic infants. *Journal of Memory and Language, 49*(2), 249–267.

Spetner, N. B., & Olsho, L. W. (1990). Auditory frequency resolution in human infancy. *Child Development, 61,* 632–652.

Stager, C. L., & Werker, J. F. (1997). Infants listen for more phonetic detail in speech perception than in word-learning tasks. *Nature, 388*(6640), 381–382.

Stellmack, M. A., Willihnganz, M. S., Wightman, F. L., & Lutfi, R. A. (1997). Spectral weights in level discrimination by preschool children: Analytic listening conditions. *Journal of the Acoustical Society of America, 101,* 2811–2821.

Storkel, H. L. (2001). Learning new words: Phonotactic probability in language development. *Journal of Speech, Language, and Hearing Research, 44*(6), 1321–1337.

Strange, W., & Jenkins, J. J. (1978). Role of linguistic experience in the perception of speech. In R. D. Walk & H. L. Pick (Eds.), *Perception and experience* (pp. 125–169). New York: Plenum Press.

Streeter, L. A. (1976). Language perception of 2-month-old infants shows effects of both innate mechanisms and experience. *Nature, 259,* 39–41.

Studdert-Kennedy, M., & Shankweiler, D. P. (1970). Hemispheric specialization for speech perception. *Journal of the Acoustical Society of America, 48*(2, Pt. 2), 579–595.

Swingley, D. (2005). Statistical clustering and the contents of the infant vocabulary. *Cognitive Psychology, 50,* 86–132.

Swingley, D., & Aslin, R. N. (2000). Spoken word recognition and lexical representation in very young children. *Cognition, 76*(2), 147–166.

Swingley, D., & Aslin, R. N. (2002). Lexical neighborhoods and the word-form representations of 14-month-olds. *Psychological Science, 13*(5), 480–484.

Swingley, D., Pinto, J. P., & Fernald, A. (1999). Continuous processing in word recognition at 24 months. *Cognition, 71*(2), 73–108.

Swoboda, P., Kass, J., Morse, P. A., & Leavitt, L. A. (1978). Memory factors in infant vowel discrimination of normal and at-risk infants. *Child Development, 49,* 332–339.

Swoboda, P. J., Morse, P. A., & Leavitt, L. A. (1976). Continuous vowel discrimination in normal and at risk infants. *Child Development, 47*(2), 459–465.

Tallal, P., Miller, S. L., Jenkins, W. M., & Merzenich, M. M. (1997). The role of temporal processing in the developmental language-based learning disorders: Research and clinical implications. In B. Blachman (Ed.), *Foundations of reading acquisition and dyslexia* (pp. 49–66). Mahwah, NJ: Erlbaum.

Tallal, P., & Piercy, M. (1973). Defects of non-verbal auditory perception in children with developmental aphasia. *Nature, 241,* 468–469.

Tallal, P., & Piercy, M. (1974). Developmental aphasia: Rate of auditory processing and selective impairment of consonant perception. *Neuropsychologia, 12,* 83–93.

Tanenhaus, M. K., Spivey-Knowlton, M. J., Eberhard, K. M., & Sedivy, J. E. (1995). Integration of visual and linguistic information in spoken language comprehension. *Science, 268,* 1632–1634.

Tarquinio, N., Zelazo, P. R., & Weiss, M. J. (1990). Recovery of neonatal head turning to decreased sound pressure level. *Developmental Psychology, 26,* 752–758.

Tees, R. C. (1976). Perceptual development in mammals. In G. Gottlieb (Ed.),*Studies on development of behavior and the nervous system* (pp. 281–326). New York: Academic Press.

Teller, D. Y. (1979). The forced-choice preferential looking procedure: A psychophysical technique for use with human infants. *Infant Behavior and Development, 2,* 135–153.

Tharpe, A. M., & Ashmead, D. H. (2001). A longitudinal investigation of infant auditory sensitivity. *American Journal of Audiology, 10,* 104–112.

Thiessen, E. D. (2004). *The role of distributional information in infants' use of phonemic contrast.* Unpublished doctoral dissertation, University of Wisconsin, Madison.

Thiessen, E. D., & Saffran, J. R. (2003). When cues collide: Use of stress and statistical cues to word boundaries by 7- to 9-month-old infants. *Developmental Psychology, 39*(4), 706–716.

Thiessen, E. D., & Saffran, J. R. (2004). Infants' acquisition of stress-based word segmentation strategies. In A. Brugos, L. Micciulla, C. Smith (Eds.), *Proceedings of the 28th annual Boston University Conference on Language Development, 2,* 608–619.

Thompson, N. C., Cranford, J. L., & Hoyer, E. (1999). Brief-tone frequency discrimination by children. *Journal of Speech Language and Hearing Research, 42,* 1061–1068.

Thorpe, L. A., & Schneider, B. A. (1987, April). *Temporal integration in infant audition.* Paper presented at the Society for Research in Child Development, Baltimore, MD.

Tincoff, R., & Jusczyk, P. W. (1999). Some beginnings of word comprehension in 6-month-olds. *Psychological Science, 10,* 172–175.

Toro, J. M., & Trobalón, J. B. (2004). *Statistical computations over a speech stream in a rodent.* Manuscript submitted for publication.

Trainor, L. J., Wu, L., & Tsang, C. D. (2004). Long-term memory for music: Infants remember tempo and timbre. *Developmental Science, 7,* 289–296.

Trehub, S. E. (1973). Infants' sensitivity to vowel and tonal contrasts. *Developmental Psychology, 9*(1), 91–96.

Trehub, S. E. (1976). The discrimination of foreign speech contrasts by infants and adults. *Child Development, 47,* 466–472.

Trehub, S. E. (2003). Musical predispositions in infancy: An update. In I. Peretz & R. J. Zatorre (Eds.), *The cognitive neuroscience of music* (pp. 3–20). Oxford, England: Oxford University Press.

Trehub, S. E., Endman, M. W., & Thorpe, L. A. (1990). Infants' perception of timbre: Classification of complex tones by spectral structure. *Journal of Experimental Child Psychology, 49,* 300–313.

Trehub, S. E., Schneider, B. A., & Edman, M. (1980). Developmental changes in infants' sensitivity to octave-band noises. *Journal of Experimental Child Psychology, 29,* 282–293.

Trehub, S. E., Schneider, B. A., & Henderson, J. (1995). Gap detection in infants, children, and adults. *Journal of the Acoustical Society of America, 98,* 2532–2541.

Trehub, S. E., Schneider, B. A., Morrengiello, B. A., & Thorpe, L. A. (1988). Auditory sensitivity in school-age children. *Journal of Experimental Child Psychology, 46,* 273–285.

Trehub, S. E., Schneider, B. A., Thorpe, L. A., & Judge, P. (1991). Observational measures of auditory sensitivity in early infancy. *Developmental Psychology, 27,* 40–49.

Tsao, F.-M., Liu, H.-M., & Kuhl, P. K. (2004). Speech Perception in Infancy Predicts Language Development in the Second Year of Life: A longitudinal study. *Child Development, 75,* 1067–1084.

Tsushima, T. T. O., Sasaki, M., Shiraki, S., Nishi, K., Kohno, M., Menyuk, P., et al. (1994). Discrimination of English /r-l/ and /w-y/ by Japanese infants at 6–12 months: Language-specific developmental changes in speech perception abilities. *Proceedings of International Conference of Spoken Language Processing, Yokohama, 94,* 1695–1698.

Turk, A. E., Jusczyk, P. W., & Gerken, L. (1995). Do English-learning infants use syllable weight to determine stress? *Language and Speech, 38*(2), 143–158.

Vargha-Khadem, F., & Corballis, M. C. (1979). Cerebral asymmetry in infants. *Brain and Language, 8*(1), 1–9.

Viemeister, N. F. (1979). Temporal modulation transfer functions based upon modulation thresholds. *Journal of the Acoustical Society of America, 66,* 1380–1564.

Viemeister, N. F. (1996). Auditory temporal integration: What is being accumulated? *Current Directions in Psychological Science, 5,* 28–32.

Viemeister, N. F., & Plack, C. J. (1993). Time analysis. In W. A. Yost, A. N. Popper, & R. R. Fay (Eds.), *Human psychophysics* (Vol. 3, pp. 116–154). New York: Springer-Verlag.

Viemeister, N. F., & Schlauch, R. S. (1992). Issues in infant psychoacoustics. In L. A. Werner & E. W. Rubel (Eds.), *Developmental psychoacoustics* (pp. 191–210). Washington, DC: American Psychological Association.

Viemeister, N. F., & Wakefield, G. H. (1991). Temporal integration and multiple looks. *Journal of the Acoustical Society of America, 90,* 858–865.

Vihman, M., Nakai, S., dePaolis, R., & Hallé, P. (2004). The role of accentual pattern in early lexical representation. *Journal of Memory and Language, 50*(3), 336–353.

Vitevitch, M. S., & Luce, P. A. (1998). Probabilistic phonotactics and neighborhood activation in spoken word recognition. *Journal of Memory and Language, 40,* 374–408.

Vitevitch, M. S., Luce, P. A., Charles-Luce, J., & Kemmerer, D. (1997). Phonotactics and syllable stress: Implications for the processing of spoken nonsense words. *Language and Speech, 40,* 47–62.

Vouloumanos, A., Kiehl, K. A., Werker, J. F., & Liddle, P. F. (2001). Detection of sounds in the auditory stream: Event-related fMRI evidence for differential activation to speech and nonspeech. *Journal of Cognitive Neuroscience, 13*(7), 994–1005.

Vouloumanos, A., & Werker, J. F. (2002, April). *Infants' preference for speech: When does it emerge?* Poster presented at the 13th biennial International Conference of Infant Studies, Toronto, Ontario, Canada.

Vouloumanos, A., & Werker, J. F. (2004). Tuned to the signal: The privileged status of speech for young infants. *Developmental Science, 7*(3), 270–276.

Vroomen, J., van Zon, M., & de Gelder, B. (1996). Cues to speech segmentation: Evidence from juncture misperceptions and word spotting. *Memory and Cognition, 24*(6), 744–755.

Walker-Andrews, A. S., Bahrick, L. E., Raglioni, S. S., & Diaz, I. (1991). Infants' bimodal perception of gender. *Ecological Psychology, 3*(2), 55–75.

Walton, G. E., & Bower, T. G. R. (1993). Amodal representation of speech in infants. *Infant Behavior and Development, 16,* 233–243.

Waters, R. A., & Wilson, W. A., Jr. (1976). Speech perception by rhesus monkeys: The voicing distinction in synthesized labial and velar stop consonants. *Perception and Psychophysics, 19,* 285–289.

Weir, C. (1976). Auditory frequency sensitivity in the neonate: A signal detection analysis. *Journal of Experimental Child Psychology, 21,* 219–225.

Weir, C. (1979). Auditory frequency sensitivity of human newborns: Some data with improved acoustic and behavioral controls. *Perception and Psychophysics, 26,* 287–294.

Werker, J. F., Burns, T., & Moon, E. (in press). *Bilingual exposed newborns prefer to listen to both of their languages.* Manuscript in preparation.

Werker, J. F., Cohen, L. B., Lloyd, V. L., Casasola, M., & Stager, C. L. (1998). Acquisition of word-object associations by 14-month-old infants. *Developmental Psychology, 34*(6), 1289–1309.

Werker, J. F., & Curtin, S. (2005). PRIMIR: A developmental framework of infant speech processing. *Language Learning and Development, 1*(2), 197–234.

Werker, J. F., Fennell, C. T., Corcoran, K. M., & Stager, C. L. (2002). Infants' ability to learn phonetically similar words: Effects of age and vocabulary size. *Infancy, 3*(1), 1–30.

Werker, J. F., Frost, P. E., & McGurk, H. (1992). La langue et les levres: Cross-language influences on bimodal speech perception. *Canadian Journal of Psychology, 46*(4), 551–568.

Werker, J. F., Gilbert, J. H., Humphrey, K., & Tees, R. C. (1981). Developmental aspects of cross-language speech perception. *Child Development, 52*(1), 349–355.

Werker, J. F., & Lalonde, C. E. (1988). Cross-language speech perception: Initial capabilities and developmental change. *Developmental Psychology, 24*(5), 672–683.

Werker, J. F., & Logan, J. S. (1985). Cross-language evidence for three factors in speech perception. *Perception and Psychophysics, 37*(1), 35–44.

Werker, J. F., & McLeod, P. J. (1989). Infant preference for both male and female infant-directed talk: A developmental study of attentional and affective responsiveness. *Canadian Journal of Psychology, 43*(2), 230–246.

Werker, J. F., & Tees, R. C. (1983). Developmental changes across childhood in the perception of non-native speech sounds. *Canadian Journal of Psychology, 37*(2), 278–286.

Werker, J. F., & Tees, R. C. (1984). Cross-language speech perception: Evidence for perceptual reorganization during the first year of life. *Infant Behavior and Development, 7*(1), 49–63.

Werker, J. F., Weikum, W. M., & Yoshida, K. A. (in press). Bilingual speech processing. In W. Li (Series Ed.) & E. Hoff & P. McCardle (Vol. Eds.), *Multilingual Matters.*

Werner, L. A. (1992). Interpreting developmental psychoacoustics. In L. A. Werner & E. W. Rubel (Eds.), *Developmental psychoacoustics* (pp. 47–88). Washington, DC: American Psychological Association.

Werner, L. A. (1995). Observer-based approaches to human infant psychoacoustics. In G. M. Klump, R. J. Dooling, R. R. Fay, &

W. C. Stebbins (Eds.), *Methods in comparative psychoacoustics* (pp. 135–146). Boston: Birkhauser Verlag.

Werner, L. A. (1999). Forward masking among infant and adult listeners. *Journal of the Acoustical Society of America, 105,* 2445–2453.

Werner, L. A. (2003, March). *Development of backward masking in infants.* Paper presented at the American Auditory Society, Scottsdale, AZ.

Werner, L. A., & Bargones, J. Y. (1991). Sources of auditory masking in infants: Distraction effects. *Perception and Psychophysics, 50,* 405–412.

Werner, L. A., & Boike, K. (2001). Infants' sensitivity to broadband noise. *Journal of the Acoustical Society of America, 109,* 2101–2111.

Werner, L. A., Folsom, R. C., & Mancl, L. R. (1993). The relationship between auditory brainstem response and behavioral thresholds in normal hearing infants and adults. *Hearing Research, 68,* 131–141.

Werner, L. A., Folsom, R. C., & Mancl, L. R. (1994). The relationship between auditory brainstem response latencies and behavioral thresholds in normal hearing infants and adults. *Hearing Research, 77,* 88–98.

Werner, L. A., & Gillenwater, J. M. (1990). Pure-tone sensitivity of 2- to 5-week-old infants. *Infant Behavior and Development, 13,* 355–375.

Werner, L. A., & Mancl, L. R. (1993). Pure-tone thresholds of 1-month-old human infants. *Journal of the Acoustical Society of America, 93,* 2367.

Werner, L. A., Marean, G. C., Halpin, C. F., Spetner, N. B., & Gillenwater, J. M. (1992). Infant auditory temporal acuity: Gap detection. *Child Development, 63,* 260–272.

Whalen, D. H., & Liberman, A. M. (1987). Speech perception takes precedence over nonspeech perception. *Science, 237,* 169–171.

Wightman, F., & Allen, P. (1992). Individual differences in auditory capability among preschool children. In L. A. Werner & E. W. Rubel (Eds.), *Developmental psychoacoustics* (pp. 113–133). Washington, DC: American Psychological Association.

Wightman, F., Allen, P., Dolan, T., Kistler, D., & Jamieson, D. (1989). Temporal resolution in children. *Child Development, 60,* 611–624.

Wightman, F., Callahan, M. R., Lutfi, R. A., Kistler, D. J., & Oh, E. (2003). Children's detection of pure-tone signals: Informational masking with contralateral maskers. *Journal of the Acoustical Society of America, 113,* 3297–3305.

Wilmington, D., Gray, L., & Jahrsdorfer, R. (1994). Binaural processing after corrected congenital unilateral conductive hearing loss. *Hearing Research, 74,* 99–114.

Wong, D., Miyamoto, R. T., Pisoni, D. B., Sehgal, M., & Hutchins, G. (1999). PET imaging of cochlear-implant and normal-hearing subjects listening to speech and nonspeech stimuli. *Hearing Research, 132,* 34–42.

Woodward, A. L., Markman, E. M., & Fitzsimmons, C. M. (1994). Rapid word learning in 13- and 18-month-olds. *Developmental Psychology, 30,* 553–566.

Wright, B. A., Lombardino, L. J., King, W. M., Puranik, C. S., Leonard, C. M., & Merzenich, M. M. (1997). Deficits in auditory temporal and spectral resolution in language-impaired children. *Nature, 387,* 129–130.

Yoshinaga-Itano, C., Sedey, A. L., Coulter, D. K., & Mehl, A. L. (1998). Language of early- and later-identified children with hearing loss. *Pediatrics, 102,* 1161–1171.

Zangl, R., & Fernald, A. (2003, October). *Sensitivity to function morphemes in on-line sentence processing: Developmental changes from 18 to 36 months.* Paper presented at the biennial meeting of the Boston University Conference on Child Language Development, Boston, MA.

Zatorre, R. J., Evans, A. C., Meyer, E., & Gjedde, A. (1992). Lateralization of phonetic and pitch discrimination in speech processing. *Science, 256*(5058), 846–849.

Zatorre, R. J., Meyer, E., Gjedde, A., & Evans, A. (1996). PET studies of phonetic processing of speech: Review, replication, and reanalysis. *Cerebral Cortex, 6*(1), 21–30.

# CHAPTER 3

# *Infant Visual Perception*

PHILIP J. KELLMAN and MARTHA E. ARTERBERRY

THEORIES OF PERCEPTUAL DEVELOPMENT 110
The Constructivist View 110
The Ecological View 112
The Contemporary Situation in Perceptual Theory 113
BASIC VISUAL SENSITIVITIES IN INFANCY 114
Visual Acuity 114
Contrast Sensitivity 116
Orientation Sensitivity 119
Pattern Discrimination 119
Color Vision 120
Motion Perception 124
SPACE PERCEPTION 126
Kinematic Information 127
Stereoscopic Depth Perception 129
Pictorial Depth Perception 131
OBJECT PERCEPTION 134
Multiple Tasks in Object Perception 134

Edge Detection and Edge Classification 135
Detection and Classification of Contour Junctions 136
Boundary Assignment 137
Perception of Object Unity 137
Perception of Three-Dimensional Form 142
Perception of Size 145
FACE PERCEPTION 146
Preference for Facelike Stimuli 146
Perceiving Information about People through Faces 148
Mechanisms of Face Perception 149
CONCLUSION 150
Levels of Analysis 150
Hardwiring versus Construction in
    Visual Development 151
Future Directions 152
REFERENCES 152

How visual perception develops has long been a central question in understanding psychological development generally. During its emergence as a separate discipline in the late 1800s, psychology was focused primarily on how human knowledge originates (e.g., Titchener, 1910; Wundt, 1862), an emphasis inherited from concerns in philosophy. Much of the focus was on the relation between sensation and perception, especially in vision. The prevailing view, inherited from generations of empiricist philosophers (e.g., Berkeley, 1709/1963; Hobbes, 1651/1974; Hume, 1758/1999; Locke, 1690/1971), was that at birth, a human being experiences only meaning-

less sensations. Coherent, meaningful, visual reality emerges only through a protracted learning process in which visual sensations become associated with each other and with touch and action (Berkeley, 1709/1963).

Through most of the twentieth century, even as psychology increasingly emphasized findings of empirical research, this primarily philosophical view cast a long shadow. Its influence was so great as to be essentially a consensus view of development. William James (1890) echoed its assumptions in his memorable pronouncement that the world of the newborn is a "blooming, buzzing, confusion." Modern developmental psychology, shaped greatly by Piaget, incorporated the same ideas. Although Piaget combined contributions of both maturation and learning in his theories, his view of the starting points of perception was standard empiricist (e.g., Piaget, 1952, 1954). He did place greater emphasis on *action*, rather

Preparation of this chapter was supported in part by research grants R01 EY13518-01 from the National Eye Institute and REC 0231826 from the National Science Foundation to PJK. We thank Heidi Vanyo for helpful assistance.

than mere sensory associations, as the means by which meaningful reality emerges from initially meaningless sensations.

This basic story about early perception and knowledge persisted, in part, because researchers lacked methods for investigating these topics scientifically. The arguments of Berkeley and others were primarily logical ones. Claims about the origins of knowledge in the association of sensations initially came from theory and thought experiments. Later, a few experiments with adults were used to make inferences about aspects of perception that might be based on learning (e.g., Wallach, 1976) or not so based (e.g., Gottschaldt, 1926). Finding a more direct window into perception and knowledge of a young infant seemed unlikely. As Riesen (1947, p. 107) put it: "The study of innate visual organization in man is not open to direct observation in early infancy, since a young baby is too helpless to respond differentially to visual excitation."

In the time since Riesen's (1947) observation, the scientific landscape in this area has changed entirely. Although the development of visual perception is among the most long-standing and fundamental concerns in the field, it is also an area that is conspicuous in terms of recent and rapid progress. Beginning in the late 1950s, the door to progress has been the development of methods for studying sensation, perception, and knowledge in human infants. The results of scientific efforts, continuing to the present, have changed our conceptions of how perception begins and develops. These changes, in turn, have generated important implications about the early foundations of cognitive, linguistic, and social development.

In this chapter, we consider current knowledge of early visual perception and its development. Besides describing the origins and development of these perceptual capabilities, we use them to illustrate general themes: the several levels of explanation required to understand perception; the roles of hardwired abilities, maturation, and learning in perception; and some of the methods that allow assessment of early perception. These themes all have broader relevance for cognitive and social development.

## THEORIES OF PERCEPTUAL DEVELOPMENT

As a backdrop for considering research in early vision, we describe two general theories of perceptual develop-

ment. These serve as valuable reference points in understanding how recent research has changed our conceptions of how perception begins.

### The Constructivist View

The term *constructivism* here refers to the view that perceptual reality must be constructed through extended learning. Choosing one term to label this idea is efficient, but also unfortunate, as this set of ideas has many names. In philosophy, this kind of account is most often called *empiricism,* emphasizing the role of input from experience in forming perception. If, as is usually the case, associations among sensations are held to dominate perceptual development, the position may also be aptly labeled *associationism.* In the earliest days of psychology as an independent discipline, the merging of current and remembered sensations to achieve objects in the world was called *structuralism* (Titchener, 1910). Helmholtz (1885/1925) is often credited with applying the label *constructivism* to the idea that sensations are combined with previously learned information using unconscious inference to achieve perceptual reality. This pedigree, along with Piaget's later emphasis on inputs from the learner's actions in constructing reality, make constructivism perhaps the best term to characterize modern versions of this view. Unfortunately, the term has been used elsewhere with different shades of meaning. In considering issues in learning, developmental and educational psychologists often contrast constructivism with associationism, where constructivism emphasizes the active contributions of the learner. Although a common thread extends through the uses of constructivism, its use here will be confined to the notion that perception is constructed from sensations and actions through learning. Our primary concern in addressing perception is to consider, not particular modes of learning, but whether basic perceptual abilities are learned at all. For this reason, and others, the verdict on constructivism in this domain may differ from the fates of constructivisms in other studies of development.

The constructivist account of how perception develops is familiar to many. The key assumption is that at birth, sensory systems function to produce only their characteristic sensations. Stimulation of the visual system yields sensations of brightness and color, along with some quality (a "local sign") correlating with a position on the retina. Stimulation of the auditory system produces loudnesses and pitches, and so on. Of course, perceptual reality consists not of disembodied colors and loudnesses, but of objects arranged in space, relations among them, and events, characterized by motion and change within that space. On the constructivist view of perceptual development, all these commonplace occupants of adult perceptual reality—*any* tangible, material object existing in the external world and, indeed, the external spatial framework itself—are hard-won constructions achieved by *learning*. What allows construction of external reality is associative processes. Experiences of visual sensations coupled with touch, according to Berkeley (1709/1963), allow creation of the idea that seen objects have substance. Connecting the muscular sensations of reaching with visual sensations allows the creation of depth and space. Sensations obtained from one view of an object at a given time are associated by contiguity in space and time, and by similarity. Sensations obtained a moment later from another view may become associated with the previous ones. An object becomes a structure of associated sensations stored in memory. In John Stuart Mill's memorable formulation, for the mind, an object consists of all the sensations it might give us under various circumstances: An object is "the permanent possibilities of sensation" (Mill, 1865). For Piaget (1952, 1954), the account is similar, except that voluntary *actions,* not just tactile and muscular sensations, become associated, making objects consist initially of "sensorimotor" regularities.

How did this basic story of perceptual development attain such preeminent status in philosophy and psychology? The question is puzzling because the account was not based on scientific study in any meaningful way. Just to anticipate a different possibility, we might consider the life of a mountain goat. Unlike a human baby, a mountain goat is able to locomote soon after birth. Remarkably, the newborn mountain goat appears to perceive solid surfaces on which to walk and precipices to avoid. When tested on a classic test apparatus for the study of depth perception—the "visual cliff"—newborn mountain goats unfailingly avoid the side with the apparent drop-off (Walk & Gibson, 1961).

This example puts a fine point on the issue. Although mountain goats appear innately able to perceive solidity and depth, generations of philosophers and psychologists have argued that, as a matter of logic, humans must be born helpless and must construct space, substance, and objects through a long associative process. The humble mountain goat, as well as many other species, provides a stark contradiction to any logical argument

that perception must be learned. From an evolutionary perspective, it might also be considered curious that humans have been so disadvantaged, beset with a frail and complicated scheme for attaining what mountain goats possess from birth.

The preceding questions are not meant to be critical of generations of serious thinkers who have held the constructivist position. Asking these questions helps to highlight what the issues were and how things have now changed. The key fact is that the constructivist position was embraced nearly universally because the arguments for it were logical. If valid, these arguments admitted few alternatives. We can better understand current views if we briefly review these logical arguments, sometimes described as the *ambiguity* argument and the *capability* argument (Kellman & Arterberry, 1998).

The ambiguity argument traces to Berkeley and his 1709/1963 book *Essay toward a New Theory of Vision.* Analyzing the projection of light onto the retina of a single eye, Berkeley pointed out that while the projection onto different retinal locations might carry information into the image about the left-right and up-down relations of objects in the world, there was no direct information to indicate the distance to an object. A given retinal image could be the product of an infinitely large set of possible objects (or, more generally, scenes) in the world. Because of this ambiguity, vision cannot provide knowledge of the solid objects in the world or their three-dimensional (3D) positions and relations. Since vision is ambiguous, the seeming ability of adult perceivers to see objects and space must derive from associating visual sensations with extravisual sensations (such as those involved in eye-muscle adjustments, and with touch and locomotion).

The capability argument drew more on physiology than philosophy. The history of progress in understanding the nervous system reflects a progression from the outside in. Long before much was known about the visual cortex of the brain, parts of the eye were somewhat understood. Even in the nineteenth century, it was clear that the retina contained numerous tiny receptors and that information left the eye for the brain in a bundle of fibers (the optic nerve). It is not surprising that reasoning about the capabilities of the visual system centered on these known elements. Consider the world of a single visual receptor, at some location on the retina. If it absorbs light, this receptor can signal its activation at that point. Receiving only tiny points of light, the receptor can know nothing of objects and spatial layout and, as

Berkeley contended, certainly nothing about the third dimension (depth). To understand the system in aggregate, one need only think of many receptors in many locations, each capable of signaling locally activations that the visual system encodes as brightness and color. Clusters of brightnesses and colors are not objects or scenes; thus, perceiving objects and scenes requires something beyond sensations generated by activity in these receptors.

To make matters worse, it was understood as a logical matter that such sensations existed not in the world but in the mind. As Johannes Muller (1838/1965) had emphasized in his famous doctrine of *specific nerve energies,* whether one presses on the eyeball or whether retinal receptors absorb light, the mind experiences brightness and color. Similarly, pressure or shock to the auditory system produces experiences of sound. It seems that sensory qualities are specific to the separate senses, regardless of the energy used to evoke them. If the visual system can produce only its own characteristic sensations, how can it be said to obtain knowledge of the world? This is the capability argument: The visual system, as a system that generates its own characteristic sensations, usually on stimulation by light, is not capable of directly revealing the objects, layout, and events of the external world.

These powerful logical arguments have two consequences. One is that the apparent direct contact that we have through vision with a structured, meaningful, external world must be a developmental achievement, accomplished through learning to infer the meanings of our sensations. The other consequence is that perceptual knowledge in general must be an inference. Different versions of this theoretical foundation have characterized perception as inference, hypothesis, results of past experience, and imagination. In Helmholtz's classic statement: "Those objects are imagined to be in the field of view that have frequently given rise to similar sensations in the past" (Helmholtz, 1885/1925). Lest one think that this section has only historical significance, it is not uncommon to encounter precisely these same arguments today (e.g., Purves & Lotto, 2003).

**The Ecological View**

Until recently, students of development have been less familiar with an alternative to constructivist views of perceptual development. The view is important, not only

as a viable possibility, but as we will see, a perspective compatible with much of the scientific evidence about how perception develops.

We call this view *ecological* because it connects perceptual capabilities to information available in the world of the perceiver. Crucial among this information are regularities and constraints deeply connected to the basic structure and operation of the physical world. These regularities have existed across evolutionary time, and have shaped the operation of perceptual mechanisms.

The emergence of ecological views of perception and perceptual development owes most to the work of James J. and Eleanor J. Gibson (E. Gibson, 1969; J. Gibson, 1966, 1979). Earlier influences included the work of the physiologist Hering (1861–1864), who described the operation of the two eyes in binocular depth perception as an integrated, and likely innate, system, and the Gestalt psychologists (e.g., Koffka, 1935; Wertheimer, 1923/1958) who emphasized the importance of abstract form and pattern, rather than concrete sensory elements, in perception. Important strands of J. Gibson's theories of perception have since been advanced in computational approaches to perception, especially that of Marr (1982).

Numerous facts lead naturally to a consideration of ecological ideas in perceptual development. Perhaps the simplest is the observation that some species exhibit effectively functioning perceptual systems from birth, as in the case of the mountain goat. Historically, however, the issue that raised the curtain for contemporary views is the nature of *information* in perception (J. Gibson, 1966, 1979).

In a certain sense, this is the logical starting point. If the constructivist view was deemed correct because of logical limits on information received by the senses, then any alternative view would need to address the ambiguity and capability arguments head-on. This is one way of summarizing a several-decades-long effort led by J. Gibson, foreshadowed in his 1950 book, *The Perception of the Visual World,* and emerging fully in *The Senses Considered as Perceptual Systems* (1966) and *The Ecological Approach to Visual Perception* (1979). According to Gibson, both the ambiguity and capability arguments rest on misunderstandings of the information available for perception.

*Ecology and Ambiguity*

Ambiguity claims about vision centered on analysis of static retinal images given to a single eye. If these constraints are admitted, the analyses by Berkeley and others are correct: For any given retinal image, there are infinitely many possible configurations in the world that could give rise to it. The problem with the analysis, however, is that the inputs to human vision are not restricted to single, static retinal images. As Hering (1861–1864) had already noted, the two eyes sample the world from two distinct vantage points. This arrangement makes possible direct information about the third dimension (which lay at the heart of Berkeley's ambiguity concerns). J. Gibson argued that another primary fact had been missed: Sophisticated visual systems are the property of *mobile* organisms. Motion and change provide important information for perception. Although a single retinal image is ambiguous, the transformations over time of the optic array as the perceiver *moves* are highly specific to the arrangement of objects, space, and events. If one can assume that the world is not deforming contingent on the perceiver's motion, this kind of information *specifies* the layout. Evolution may well have picked up on such sources of information, allowing perceptual systems to deliver meaningful information not derived from learning. Whereas the mountain goat provides an existence proof of functional perception without learning, the analysis given by J. Gibson explained how this might be possible.

### Ecology and Capability

Ambiguity issues focus on the information in the world. Corresponding to the arguments about information are revised ideas about the capabilities of a perceptual system (J. Gibson, 1966). The description of inputs to vision in terms of brightness and color responses at individual locations is inadequate. Further along in the system are mechanisms sensitive to higher order relationships in stimulation. There were precedents to this view. Corresponding to Hering's point about triangulation (sampling from two positions) was his assessment that the brain handled inputs to the two eyes as a system, detecting disparities between the two eyes' views to perceive depth. Likewise, the Gestalt psychologists emphasized the contribution of brain mechanisms in processing relations in the input. J. Gibson pointed out the importance of higher order information and suggested that perceptual systems are naturally attuned to pick up such information. He did not deal much with neurophysiological or computational details, and he confused some by saying that perceptual systems "resonate" to information. Gibson's views still evoke controversy, yet

researchers in perception and perceptual development have been busy ever since exploring the computations and mechanisms that extract higher order information.

### The Contemporary Situation in Perceptual Theory

Philosophers, most cognitive scientists, and psychologists embrace the notion that, in a formal sense, perception has the character of an inference (specifically, an *ampliative* inference, in which the conclusion is not guaranteed by the premises or data, Swoyer, 2003). As virtual reality systems show us (and as dreams and hallucinations impressed Descartes and others), the perceptual experience of 3D space and certain objects and events does not guarantee their objective existence.

Such arguments have been elaborated in detail (Fodor & Pylyshyn, 1981; Ullman, 1980; but see Turvey, Shaw, & Reed, 1981) to attack J. Gibson's assertion that perception is "direct" (it does not require inference). If perception is formally inferential, perhaps Berkeley and his intellectual descendants were correct after all about how perception must develop. Is there a paradox in holding an ecological view while admitting that perception has a formally inferential character?

Resolving this apparent paradox by separating the two issues is important to understanding perceptual development. Perception has the formal character of an inference, but that does not imply that perception in humans must be learned, or that vision must be supplemented by touch or action. Perceptual inferences may be exactly the kinds of things that have been built into perceptual systems by evolution. Rock (e.g., 1984), a perceptual theorist who stressed the inferential nature of perception, and Marr (1982), who put computational approaches to perception on a clear footing, were among the earliest to articulate that perception could be both inferential *and* innate.

The analyses by the Gibsons and later investigators influenced the debate about perceptual development by altering conceptions of the information available for perception. For a moving, two-eyed observer with mechanisms sensitive to stimulus relations, the ambiguities envisioned by Berkeley—many different ordinary scenes leading to the same retinal image—do not exist. For Berkeley, visual ambiguity is so expansive that vision requires lots of outside help. For J. Gibson (1979), visual information specific to arrangements of scenes and events is available, and humans possess perceptual mechanisms attuned to such information. In Marr

(1982) may be found a synthesis of the two extremes: Visual ambiguity is intrinsic but can be handled by relatively few, general constraints. The interpretation of optic flow patterns in terms of 3D spatial layout requires the assumption that the scene (or whatever provides images to the two eyes) is not changing contingent on the observer's movements. This assumption is rarely, if ever, violated in ordinary perception, although it is exactly the assumption that is violated when an observer dons the viewing goggles or helmet in a virtual reality system. Many researchers have suggested that certain assumptions (e.g., the lack of observer-contingent scene changes or the movement of objects on continuous space-time paths) have come to be reflected in perceptual machinery through evolution (J. Gibson, 1966; Johansson, 1970; Kellman, 1993; Kellman & Arterberry, 1998; Shepard, 1984).

This possibility has far-reaching consequences with the potential to overturn a persistent and dominant view of perception based on learning. Yet it is important to recognize that the mere *possibility* of innate perceptual mechanisms (incorporating assumptions about the world) does not decide their reality. Unlike mountain goats, human infants are not mobile at birth, and until recently, their perceptual abilities were mostly unknown. Our discussion of constructivist and ecological views of perceptual development culminates in the observation that the answer is a matter for empirical science. Moreover, different perceptual abilities may have different contributions from native endowments, maturation, and learning. Researchers must write the story of each perceptual capacity based on experimental evidence.

This conclusion sets our agenda for the remainder of this chapter. We consider the emerging scientific picture of development for the crucial components of visual perception. This picture indicates decisively that, although learning may be involved in calibration and fine-tuning, visual perception depends heavily on inborn and early maturing mechanisms. This picture has begun to strongly influence views in other areas of development, as well as conceptions of the nature of perception. More unsettling is the failure to attend to the evidence on infant perception in some recent trends in cognitive science and neuroscience. After considering the evidence, we return to these issues at chapter's end.

Our review of the field is necessarily selective. A goal of the present chapter is to place what has been learned about infant vision in a more general historical and philosophical context, so that it may be easily appre-

ciated and used by those in related fields. The particular topics reflect our areas of expertise and our views of areas that are rapidly advancing and in which important knowledge has been gained. Some parts of this chapter are modestly updated from the previous edition of the *Handbook of Child Psychology* (Kellman & Banks, 1998), whereas others are new. In what follows, we first consider basic visual sensitivities in the infant, including acuity and contrast sensitivity, sensitivity to color, pattern, and motion. We then consider spatial perception, object perception, and face perception.

## BASIC VISUAL SENSITIVITIES IN INFANCY

The function of visual perception is to provide the perceiver with information about the objects, events, and spatial layout in which he or she must think and act. Starting from this concern, the study of basic visual sensitivity and the psychophysical methods used to study infants' visual perception may seem arcane to the nonspecialist. Yet, all higher-level abilities to see the forms, sizes, textures, and positions of objects, as well as to apprehend spatial relations of objects at rest and in motion, depend on basic visual capabilities to resolve information about spatial position. For this reason, the development of spatial vision has been a topic of great concern to those interested in infant perception.

We begin an examination of spatial vision by considering sensitivities to variation across changing locations in the optic array. Two of the most basic dimensions of sensitivity in describing spatial vision are visual acuity and contrast sensitivity. Our discussion of these basic capacities leads naturally into an assessment of basic pattern discrimination abilities. We then consider color vision and motion perception.

### Visual Acuity

*Acuity* is a vague term, meaning something like "precision." A particular variety of acuity is so often used to describe visual performance that the phrase "visual acuity" has become its common label. This type of acuity is more technically known as *minimum separable acuity* or *grating acuity*. Object recognition and identification depend on the ability to encode differences across positions in the retinal image in luminance or spectral composition. *Visual acuity* thus refers to the resolving capacity of the visual system—its ability to distinguish fine details or differences in adjacent positions.

Measuring this type of visual acuity by various means is by far the most common way of assessing ocular health and suitability for specific visual tasks, such as operating cars or aircraft.

To assess acuity, high-contrast, black-and-white patterns of various sizes are presented at a fixed distance. The smallest pattern or smallest critical pattern element that can be reliably detected or identified is taken as the threshold value and is usually expressed in angular units. Many different acuity measures have been used with adults, but only two have been widely used in developmental studies, grating acuity and vernier acuity.

*Grating acuity* tasks require resolving the stripes in a repetitive pattern of stripes. The finest resolvable grating is taken as the measure of acuity and it is generally expressed in terms of spatial frequency, which is the number of stripes per degree of visual angle. Adult grating acuity under optimal conditions is 45 to 60 cycles/degree, which corresponds to a stripe width of $\frac{1}{2}$ to $\frac{2}{3}$ minutes of arc (Olzak & Thomas, 1986). By optimal conditions, we mean that the stimulus is brightly illuminated, high in contrast, presented for at least $\frac{1}{2}$ second, and viewed foveally with a well-focused eye. Change in any of these viewing parameters causes a reduction in grating acuity.

*Vernier acuity* is tested in tasks requiring discrimination of positional displacement of one small target relative to another. The most common variety involves distinguishing whether a vertical line segment is displaced to the left or right relative to a line segment just below it. In adults, the just-noticeable offset under optimal conditions is 2 to 5 seconds of arc (Westheimer, 1979). Because this distance is smaller than the diameter of a single photoreceptor in the human eye, this kind of performance has been called *hyperacuity* (Westheimer, 1979). As with grating acuity, the lowest vernier acuity thresholds are obtained when the stimulus is brightly illuminated, high in contrast, presented for at least $\frac{1}{2}$ second, and viewed foveally with a well-focused eye.

There have been numerous measurements of grating acuity (the highest detectable spatial frequency at high contrast) in human infants. Figure 3.1 plots grating acuity as a function of age for some representative studies. The displayed results were obtained using three response measurement techniques: Forced-choice preferential looking (FPL), optokinetic nystagmus (OKN), and the visual evoked potential (VEP). This figure illus-

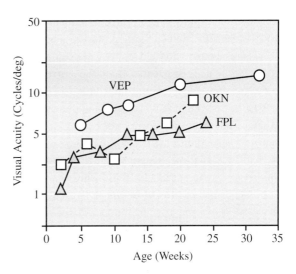

**Figure 3.1** Visual acuity estimates at different ages. The highest detectable spatial frequency of a high-contrast grating stimulus is plotted as a function of age. Circles: Visual evoked potential estimates. Squares: Optokinetic nystagmus (OKN) estimates. Triangles: Forced-choice preferential looking estimates. *Sources:* "Measurement of Visual Acuity from Pattern Reversal Evoked Potentials," by S. Sokol, 1978, *Vision Research, 18,* pp. 33–40. Reprinted with permission; "Maturation of Pattern Vision in Infants during the First 6 Months," by R. L. Fantz, J. M. Ordy, and M. S. Udelf, 1962, *Journal of Comparative and Physiological Psychology, 55,* pp. 907–917. Reprinted with permission; "Visual Acuity Development in Human Infants up to 6 Months of Age," by J. Allen, 1978, unpublished master's thesis, University of Washington, Seattle, WA. Reprinted with permission.

trates two points. First, acuity is low at birth and develops steadily during the 1st year. Grating acuity during the neonatal period is so low that these infants could be classified as legally blind. Second, the acuity estimates obtained with behavioral techniques such as FPL and OKN are generally lower than those obtained using electrophysiological techniques such as VEP. Grating acuity develops beyond the 1st year and reaches adult levels around 6 years of age (e.g., Skoczenski & Norcia, 2002). We discuss the optical, receptoral, and neural factors that determine grating acuity as a function of age in the section on contrast sensitivity.

There have been fewer measurements of vernier acuity; nonetheless, some intriguing observations have been reported. Shimojo and colleagues (Shimojo, Birch, Gwiazda, & Held, 1984; Shimojo & Held, 1987) and Manny and Klein (1984, 1985) used FPL to measure the smallest offset infants could respond to at different ages. They found that vernier acuity was much poorer in 8- to 20-week-old infants than in adults. The ratio of adult vernier acuity divided by 8-week olds' vernier acuity is significantly greater than the corresponding ratio for grating acuity. A similar finding has emerged from VEP measurements of vernier and grating acuity; adult levels of hyperacuity were not reached until 10 to 14 years of age (Skoczenski & Norcia, 2002). This suggests that the visual mechanisms that limit vernier acuity undergo greater change with age than do the mechanisms limiting grating acuity. Different hypotheses have been offered concerning the differing growth rates (Banks & Bennett, 1988; Shimojo & Held, 1987; Skoczenski & Norcia, 2002); however, direct empirical tests are needed.

## Contrast Sensitivity

Contrast sensitivity refers to the ability to detect variations in luminance. Most acuity testing is done at high contrast (e.g., black characters on a white background or gratings varying from white to black). Testing for contrast sensitivity involves finding the least difference between luminances that allows detection of structure. The contrast sensitivity function (CSF) represents the visual system's sensitivity to sinusoidal gratings of various spatial frequencies. The CSF has generality as an index of visual sensitivity because any two-dimensional pattern can be represented by its spatial frequency content and, consequently, one can use the CSF along with linear systems analysis to predict visual sensitivity to a wide range of spatial patterns (Banks & Salapatek, 1983; Cornsweet, 1970). Thus, measurements of contrast sensitivity as a function of age should allow the prediction of sensitivity to and even preference for many visual stimuli (Banks & Ginsburg, 1985; Gayl, Roberts, & Werner, 1983).

The adult CSF has a peak sensitivity at 3 to 5 cycles/degree, so the lowest detectable contrasts occur for gratings of medium spatial frequency. At those spatial frequencies, the just-detectable grating has light stripes that are only 0.5% brighter than the dark stripes. At progressively higher spatial frequencies, sensitivity falls monotonically to the so-called high-frequency cutoff at about 50 cycles/degree. This is the finest grating an adult can detect when the contrast is 100% and it corresponds to the person's grating acuity. At low spatial frequencies, sensitivity falls as well, although the steepness of this falloff is highly dependent on the conditions of measurements.

Adult contrast sensitivity and grating acuity are limited by optical, receptoral, and neural factors. Sensitivity is best with good lighting, foveal fixation, sufficiently long stimulus duration, and a well-focused eye. Decreased illumination reduces both contrast sensitivity and the high-frequency cutoff (van Nes & Bouman, 1967). Similar changes in contrast sensitivity occur when the stimulus is imaged on the peripheral retina (Banks, Sekuler, & Anderson, 1991) or the eye is not well focused (Green & Campbell, 1965). Understanding limitations on adult vision has been aided by modeling the early stages of vision as a series of filtering stages. Visual stimuli pass sequentially through the eye's optics, which are responsible for forming the retinal image; the photoreceptors, which sample and transduce the image into neural signals; and two to four retinal neurons, which transform and transmit those signals into the optic nerve and eventually to the central visual pathways. In these early stages of visual processing, considerable information is lost. The high-frequency falloff observed in the adult CSF is determined, by and large, by the filtering properties of the eye's optics and the photoreceptors (Banks, Geisler, & Bennett, 1987; Pelli, 1990; Sekiguchi, Williams, & Brainard, 1993). The loss of high-frequency sensitivity with peripheral viewing has been modeled successfully by examination of the optics, receptors, and retinal circuits of the peripheral retina (Banks et al., 1991). The sensitivity loss that accompanies a reduction in illumination has also been modeled reasonably successfully, at least at high spatial frequencies (Banks et al., 1987; Pelli, 1990) as has the loss that accompanies errors in the eye's focus (Green & Campbell, 1965). From the emerging understanding of the optical, receptoral, and neural mechanisms that determine contrast sensitivity in adults, attempts have been made to use similar techniques to understand the development of contrast sensitivity in human infants.

Figure 3.2 displays an adult CSF measured using a psychophysical procedure, along with infant CSFs measured using forced-choice preferential looking (Atkinson, Braddick, & Moar, 1977; Banks & Salapatek, 1978) and the visual evoked potential (Norcia, Tyler, & Allen, 1986; Pirchio, Spinelli, Fiorentini, & Maffei, 1978). These data illustrate two common observations. First, contrast sensitivity (and grating acuity) in young infants is substantially lower than that of adults, with the difference diminishing rapidly during the 1st year. Second, as we saw earlier in Figure 3.1, measurements with the visual evoked potential typically yield higher sensitivity

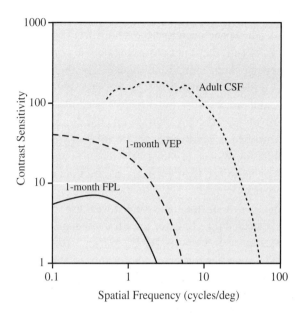

**Figure 3.2** Adult and 1-month-old infant contrast sensitivity functions (CSFs). Contrast sensitivity is plotted as a function of spatial frequency (the numbers of grating cycles per degree of visual angle). The upper dotted curve is an adult CSF that was measured psychophysically. The lower solid curve is the average of 1-month CSFs, measured using forced-choice preferential looking. The middle dash curve is the average of 1-month CSFs, measured using visual-evoked potential. *Sources:* "Acuity and Contrast Sensitivity in 1-, 2-, and 3-Month-Old Human Infants," by M. S. Banks and P. Salapatek, 1978, *Investigative Ophthalmology and Visual Science, 17,* pp. 361–365. Reprinted with permission and "Development of Contrast Sensitivity in the Human Infant," by A. M. Norcia, C. W. Tyler, and R. D. Hammer, 1990, *Vision Research, 30,* pp. 1475–1486.

(and acuity) estimates than do behavioral techniques (see Mayer & Adrendt, 2001 for a review). The time course differs depending on whether a behavioral or electrophysiological technique is used. With evoked potential measurements, peak sensitivity approaches adult values by 6 months of age, whereas behavioral measurements exhibit a slower developmental time course. Not illustrated is the systematic variability in the CSF across infants (Peterzell, Werner, & Kaplan, 1995). Although group functions are smooth in shape, individual functions are not.

What accounts for the development of acuity and contrast sensitivity? Infants who experience visual deprivation early in life due to monocular or binocular cataracts show newborn levels of acuity once the cataract(s) are removed (Maurer & Lewis, 1999), despite being 1 to 9 months of age. Longitudinal follow-up, however, shows

rapid increases in acuity suggesting that visual input is necessary for visual functioning. Beyond knowing that visual input is necessary, the specific causes, anatomical and physiological, of the striking functional deficits observed during the first few months of life are still being debated. Some investigators have proposed that one can explain the low contrast sensitivity and grating acuity of neonates as due to information losses caused by optical and retinal immaturities (Jacobs & Blakemore, 1988; Wilson, 1988, 1993); others have argued that those immaturities are not the whole story (Banks & Bennett, 1988; Banks & Crowell, 1993; Brown, Dobson, & Maier, 1987).

Development of the eye and retina are important factors. Large ocular and retinal changes occur in development and they have profound effects on the ability to see spatial patterns. The eye grows significantly from birth to adolescence, with most growth occurring in the 1st year. The distance from the cornea at the front of the eye to the retina at the back is 16 to 17 mm at birth, 20 to 21 mm at 1 year, and 23 to 25 mm in adolescence and adulthood (Hirano, Yamamoto, Takayama, Sugata, & Matsuo, 1979; Larsen, 1971). Shorter eyes have smaller retinal images. So, for example, a 1-degree target subtends about 200 microns on the newborn's retina and 300 microns on the adult's (Banks & Bennett, 1988; Brown et al., 1987; Wilson, 1988). Thus, if newborns had the retinae and visual brains of adults, one would expect their visual acuity to be about two-thirds that of adults simply because they have smaller retinal images to work with.

Another ocular factor relevant to visual sensitivity is the relative transparency of the ocular media. Two aspects of ocular media transmittance are known to change with age: the optical density of the crystalline lens pigment and that of the macular pigment. In both cases, transmittance is slightly higher in the young eye, particularly at short wavelengths (Bone, Landrum, Fernandez, & Martinez, 1988; Werner, 1982). Thus, for a given amount of incident light, the newborn's eye actually transmits slightly more to the photoreceptors than does the mature eye. This developmental difference ought to favor the newborn compared with the adult, but only slightly.

The ability of the eye to form a sharp retinal image is yet another relevant ocular factor. This ability is typically quantified by the optical transfer function. There have been no measurements of the human neonate's optical transfer function, but the quality of the retinal image almost certainly surpasses the resolution performance of the young visual system (Banks & Bennett,

1988). Thus, it is commonly assumed that the optical transfer function of the young eye is adultlike (Banks & Crowell, 1993; Wilson, 1988, 1993). Refractive errors or accommodation errors diminish the sharpness of the retinal image and thereby decrease sensitivity to high spatial frequencies (Green & Campbell, 1965). Hyperopic and astigmatic refractive errors are common in infants (Banks, 1980a; Howland, 1982); they tend not to accommodate accurately until 12 weeks (Banks, 1980b; Braddick, Atkinson, French, & Howland, 1979; Haynes, White, & Held, 1965). Nonetheless, it is widely believed that infants' refractive and accommodative errors do not constrain sensitivity or visual acuity significantly (Banks, 1980a, 1980b; Braddick et al., 1979; Howland, 1982).

If optical imperfections do not contribute significantly to the visual deficits observed in young infants, receptoral and postreceptoral processes must do so. The retina and central visual system all exhibit immaturities at birth (Banks & Salapatek, 1983; Hendrickson, 1993; Hickey & Peduzzi, 1987; Yuodelis & Hendrickson, 1986), but morphological immaturities are evident in the fovea, particularly among the photoreceptors.

The development of the fovea is dramatic in the 1st year of life, but subtle morphological changes continue until at least 4 years of age (Yuodelis & Hendrickson, 1986). The fovea, defined as the part of the retina that contains no rods, is much larger at birth than in adulthood: Its diameter decreases from roughly 5.4 degrees at birth to 2.3 degrees at maturity. Moreover, the individual cells and their arrangements are very different at birth than they will be later on. The newborn's fovea possesses three discernible layers of neurons—the photoreceptors, the neurons of the outer nuclear layer, and the retinal ganglion cells—whereas the mature fovea contains only one layer, which is composed of photoreceptors. The most dramatic histological differences, however, are the sizes and shapes of foveal cones. Neonatal cones have inner segments that are much broader and shorter. The outer segments are distinctly immature, too, being much shorter than their adult counterparts. These shape and size differences render the newborn's foveal cones less sensitive than those of the adult (Banks & Bennett, 1988; Brown et al., 1987).

To estimate the efficiency of the neonate's lattice of foveal cones, Banks and colleagues calculated the ability of the newborn's cones to capture light in the inner segment, funnel it to the outer segment, and produce a visual signal (Banks & Bennett, 1988; Banks & Crowell, 1993). They concluded that the adult foveal cone lattice is dramatically better at absorbing photons of light and converting them into visual signals. By their calculations, if identical patches of light were presented to newborn and adult eyes, roughly 350 photons would be effectively absorbed in adult foveal cones for every photon absorbed in newborn cones. Similar estimates were obtained by Wilson (1988, 1993). The newborn's fovea is less able to use light entering the eye than is the mature fovea.

The cones of the immature fovea are also more widely spaced than those of the adult (Banks & Bennett, 1988; Banks & Crowell, 1993; Wilson, 1988, 1993). Cone-to-cone separation in the center of the fovea is about 2.3, 1.7, and 0.58 minutes of arc in neonates, 15-month-olds, and adults, respectively. These dimensions impose a physical limit (the so-called Nyquist limit) on the highest spatial frequency that can be resolved without distortion or aliasing (Williams, 1985). From the current estimates of cone spacing, the foveas of newborns, 15-month-olds, and adults should theoretically be unable to resolve gratings with spatial frequencies above 15, 27, and 60 cycles/degree, respectively.

Investigators have calculated the contrast sensitivity and visual acuity losses that ought to be observed if the only difference between the spatial vision of newborns and adults were the eye's optics and the properties of the foveal cones (Banks & Bennett, 1988; Banks & Crowell, 1993; Wilson, 1988, 1993). The expected losses are substantial: Contrast sensitivity to medium and high spatial frequencies is predicted to be as much as 20-fold lower in neonates than in adults. Nonetheless, the observed contrast sensitivity and grating acuity deficits in human newborns are even larger than predicted (e.g., Skoczenski & Aslin, 1995), so this analysis of information losses in the optics and receptors implies that there are other immaturities, presumably among retinal neurons and central visual circuits, that contribute to the observed loss of contrast sensitivity and grating acuity.

Another hypothesis concerning the contrast sensitivity and visual acuity of young infants has been offered. Because of the obvious immaturity of the fovea, perhaps infants use another part of the retina to process points of interest in the visual scene. Cones in the parafoveal and peripheral retina are relatively more mature at birth than their foveal counterparts, but they, too, undergo postnatal development (Hendrickson, 1993). The data, however, do not support this hypothesis: Young infants' best acuity and contrast sensitivity is obtained with foveal stimulation. Lewis, Maurer, and Kay (1978) found that newborns could best detect a narrow light bar against a dark background when it was presented in central vision, and D. Allen, Tyler, and Norcia (1996) showed that visual evoked potential (VEP) acuity and contrast sensitivity is higher in central than in peripheral vision in 8- to 39-week-olds, by an average factor of 2.3.

An important question that will be pursued vigorously in future research is what factors not considered in the preceding analyses account for the unexplained portion of the contrast sensitivity and grating acuity losses. There are numerous candidates including internal neural noise (such as random addition of action potentials at central sites; Skoczenski & Norcia, 1998), inefficient neural sampling, and poor motivation to respond.

## Orientation Sensitivity

Sensitivity to orientation is an important foundation of much of higher level vision, such as perception of edges, patterns, and objects. In monkeys, it is well established that orientation sensitivity is innately present (Wiesel & Hubel, 1974), and in cats orientation sensitivity also appears soon after birth, with or without visual experience (Hubel & Wiesel, 1963). Paradoxically, development of orientation sensitivity has been the topic of numerous learning simulations in recent years (Linsker, 1989; Olshausen & Field, 1996; von der Malsburg, 1973). These results suggest interesting relations between orientation-sensitive cortical units and the statistics of images of natural scenes. Such studies are often interpreted as showing how the visual brain gets "wired up by experience" after birth (e.g., Elman, Bates, Johnson, Karmiloff-Smith, Parisi, & Plunkett, 1996).

Yet the evidence suggests that basic orientation sensitivity in humans, as in monkeys and cats, is present at birth. Some maturation of orientation processing was suggested by visual evoked potential (VEP) studies by Braddick, Atkinson, and Wattam-Bell (1986). Their results showed responses emerging at 2 to 3 weeks for slowly modulated orientation changes (3 reversals/ second) and responses at 5 to 6 weeks for more rapid orientation changes. In an elegant analysis, these investigators showed that the pace of these developments was maturational, in that preterm infants of the same gestational age showed patterns of development similar to full-term infants. In other words, gestational age, not weeks of visual experience was crucial.

Direct behavioral tests of orientation sensitivity have revealed evidence that it is innate. Slater, Morison, and Somers (1988) used habituation measures with high-contrast striped patterns. They found dishabituation to changed orientation in situations where other stimulus variables (such as whether a particular screen position was black or white) could be ruled out. Their results were confirmed by Atkinson, Hood, and Wattam-Bell (1988). Orientation sensitivity appears to be innate in humans, although it improves in the early weeks of life.

## Pattern Discrimination

Assessing acuity and contrast sensitivity largely involve comparing responses to something versus nothing. The exquisite spatial resolution of vision, however, serves functions beyond mere detection. Encoding and discriminating patterns, surfaces, and objects are key tasks of visual processing. Thus, describing pattern-processing capabilities in infant vision is important. But how can pattern-perception capabilities be assessed in a comprehensive way? As in studies of adult vision, linear systems theory from mathematics and signal processing is useful. Any distribution of luminance (light and dark) in an image can be described, using a 2D Fourier transform, as a set of sinusoidally varying luminance components having particular frequencies and amplitudes, in particular orientations. Because any image can be analyzed in this way, the frequency components form an important characterization of the pattern. If the spatial phase of each component is also encoded, the pattern is completely described. Researchers have made progress characterizing infant pattern discrimination using linear systems concepts. This work has used tests of infants' abilities to distinguish simple, suprathreshold patterns that vary in contrast or in phase.

Sensitivity to contrast differences is typically measured by presenting two sine-wave gratings of the same spatial frequency and orientation but differing contrasts. In experiments with adults, a participant is asked to indicate the grating of higher contrast. The increment in contrast required to make the discrimination varies depending on the common contrasts of the two stimuli; as the common contrast is increased, a successively larger increment is required (Legge & Foley, 1980). Six- to 12-week-old infants require much larger contrast increments than adults when the common contrast is near detection threshold. At high common contrasts, however, infants' discrimination thresholds resemble those of adults (Brown, 1993; Stephens & Banks, 1987). These findings suggest that infants' ability to distinguish spatial patterns on the basis of contrast differences is poor at low contrast and reasonably good at high contrast. Different explanations for infants' performance in this task have been offered, but none has been confirmed by empirical observation (Brown, 1993; Stephens & Banks, 1987).

Studies have also addressed discrimination based on spatial phase differences. Spatial phase refers to the relative position of the spatial frequency components (the sine-wave gratings) of which the pattern is composed (Piotrowski & Campbell, 1982). Phase information is crucial for the features and relations that are involved in object perception, such as edges, junctions, and shape. Altering phase information in a spatial pattern greatly affects its appearance and perceived identity to adults (Oppenheim & Lim, 1981). In phase discrimination tasks, the subject is asked to distinguish between two patterns—usually gratings—that differ only in the phase relationships among their spatial frequency components. Adults are able to distinguish patterns that differ only slightly in the phases of their components when the stimulus is presented to the fovea (Badcock, 1984). The ability to discriminate phase can fall dramatically, however, when the stimulus is presented in the peripheral visual field (Bennett & Banks, 1987; Rentschler & Treutwein, 1985).

Relatively little work has directly addressed infants' ability to use phase differences to discriminate spatial patterns. Braddick et al. (1986) presented periodic patterns composed of different spatial frequency components. When the components were added in one phase relationship, the resultant was a square-wave grating (a repeating pattern of sharp-edged light and dark stripes); when the components were added in another phase, the resultant appeared to adults to be a very different, more complex pattern. Eight-week-olds were able to discriminate these patterns. Remarkably, however, 4-week-olds seemed unable to make the discrimination.

In a similar vein, Kleiner (1987) and Kleiner and Banks (1987) examined visual preferences for patterns in which the phases of the constituent components were altered. Kleiner and colleagues found that newborns and 8-week-olds exhibit reliable fixation preferences for a schematic face over a rectangle lattice (Fantz & Nevis, 1967). To examine the influence of spatial phase on fixation preference, Kleiner used an image-processing technique in which the contrasts of the constituent spatial frequencies from one pattern were combined with the phases of the constituent frequencies from the other pattern. The perceptual appearance of these hybrid patterns is most closely associated with the pattern from which the phases rather than the contrasts came (Oppenheim & Lim, 1981; Piotrowski & Campbell, 1982); stated another way, the hybrid pattern that appears most facelike is the one that contains the phases from the original schematic face. Not surprisingly, 8-week-olds preferred to fixate the hybrid that contained the phases of the face and the contrasts of the lattice. Newborns' preferences, however, were for the hybrid that contained the phases of the lattice and the contrasts of the face. One interpretation of this finding is that newborns are relatively insensitive to spatial phase, but other interpretations have been suggested (e.g., Badcock, 1990).

The observation that young infants seem relatively insensitive to variations in spatial phase is extremely important. If valid, it suggests that young infants' ability to discriminate spatial patterns has a significant deficiency that is at least qualitatively similar to the deficiency observed in the peripheral visual field of normal adults (Bennett & Banks, 1987; Rentschler & Treutwein, 1985) and in the central visual field of amblyopic adults (Levi, Klein, & Aitsebaomo, 1985). In functional terms, infants' processing of basic perceptual properties of objects, such as unity, size, shape, texture, and so on depend implicitly on processing of phase information. To the extent that it is poor in the earliest weeks of life, these abilities will be limited. Conversely, tests of certain of these perceptual abilities, to be discussed, indicate striking newborn perceptual competencies (e.g., for seeing object size and faces). One of the challenges of infant vision research is reconciling certain poor sensitivity to basic sensory properties, such as phase, with evidence of higher order abilities, such as face perception. The most likely resolution of the apparent paradox is that infant sensory capacities for properties such as phase and orientation are worse than adults' but not completely lacking, even at birth (for further discussion, see Kellman & Arterberry, 1998).

## Color Vision

The term *color* refers to the component of visual experience characterized by the psychological attributes of *brightness, hue,* and *saturation.* Two of these—hue and saturation—are chromatic attributes, and the other—brightness—is actually an achromatic attribute. Hue is primarily correlated with the dominant wavelength of the stimulus whereas brightness is primarily correlated, but not isomorphic, with stimulus intensity. Saturation is correlated with the distribution of wavelengths in a stimulus; stimuli with more broad band light mixed in are seen as less saturated. We refer to visual discriminations on the basis of differences in hue or saturation as *chromatic discriminations* and discriminations on the basis of differences in brightness as *achromatic discriminations.*

The functional importance of perceiving color has been a matter of debate. Humans readily perceive objects and events from nonchromatic displays, such as those in black-and-white movies or television. Why, then, have we evolved elaborate color vision mechanisms? In ordinary seeing, chromatic information probably aids object segmentation and recognition. In cases in which an object and its background are equal or nearly equal in luminance, the object's shape can be perceived from chromatic differences. Chromatic information can also help distinguish one version of an object (a red apple) from another (a green apple). Less well understood, but important, are the obvious contributions of color to our aesthetic experiences.

The human visual system has four types of photoreceptors, one type of rod and three types of cones. The cones are active under daylight viewing conditions and subserve color vision; rods are active under quite dim illumination. We consider only cones in our discussion of color vision.

The three cone types are sensitive to different, but overlapping, bands of wavelength. The cone types are generally called *short-wavelength-sensitive (S), medium-wavelength-sensitive (M),* and *long-wavelength-sensitive (L)* cones. (We prefer this terminology to the terms *blue, green,* and *red* cones because those terms imply that each cone type is responsible for the perception of a particular hue, and this is not the case.) Each type of photoreceptor responds in an untagged fashion; that is, only response quantity, and nothing else, varies with changes in the incident light. The consequences of untagged responding are profound. The output of any single photoreceptor type can be driven to a given level by virtually any wavelength of light simply by adjusting the light's intensity. Thus, information about the wavelength of a stimulus cannot be extracted from the output of a single photoreceptor type. Instead the visual system must use the relative activities of the three photoreceptor types to distinguish different colors.

The subsequent stages of the visual process must utilize the outputs of the different receptor types in a complex way to produce the conscious experience of color. Psychophysical evidence from adult humans and physiological evidence from adult monkeys indicate that the signals of the three cone types undergo a major transformation in the retina. Signals from two or three kinds of cones are combined additively to form achromatic channels (coding brightness primarily) and are combined subtractively to form two kinds of chromatic channels (coding hue primarily). The subtractive, chromatic channels (red/green and blue/yellow) have been called *opponent processes* because different wavelength bands evoke different directions of neural response.

Many of the characteristics of photoreceptors and subsequent neural stages were originally inferred from adult behavioral studies. Our discussion of color vision centers on two questions:

1. What hues are infants sensitive to and when?
2. What mechanisms account for the development of color vision?

### Origins of Hue Discrimination

When can infants discriminate stimuli on the basis of hue alone? Before 1975, a large number of behavioral studies attempted to answer this question, but they all failed to eliminate the possibility that infants were basing their discriminations on brightness cues rather than hue (or saturation) cues (Kessen, Haith, & Salapatek, 1970). To demonstrate convincingly that infants can discriminate on the basis of hue alone, researchers have used two strategies to rule out brightness artifacts. (Elsewhere, we describe in detail the importance and difficulty of separating hue from brightness responses; Kellman & Arterberry, 1998; Kellman & Banks, 1997.)

The methods involve presenting two stimuli differing in hue (e.g., red and green) and looking for a systematic response (e.g., directional eye movement, VEP, or FPL) to one as evidence for hue discrimination. One strategy for eliminating brightness artifacts involves using the spectral sensitivity function to match the brightnesses of two stimuli to a first approximation and then by varying the luminances (a measure of stimulus intensity) of the stimuli unsystematically from trial to trial over a wide-enough range to ensure that one is not always brighter than the other. Systematic responding by the infant to one of the two chromatic stimuli, across luminances, can therefore not be attributed to discrimination on the basis of brightness. Using this strategy, Oster (1975), and Schaller (1975) demonstrated hue discrimination in 8- and 12-week-old infants, respectively.

The second strategy for eliminating brightness cues was developed by Peeples and Teller (1975); subsequently, many others have used this strategy, so we explain it in some detail. They also used spectral sensitivity data to match approximately the brightnesses of their stimuli. They then varied luminance systematically around the estimate of the brightness match. Several luminances were presented, bridging a 0.8 log unit range in small steps. Consequently, at least one of the luminance pairings must have been equivalent in brightness for each of the infants. Peeples and Teller showed that 8-week-olds could discriminate red from white for all luminance pairings. They concluded that 8-week-olds make true hue discriminations.

Thus, three reports in 1975, using different techniques, provided the first convincing evidence that 8- to 16-week-olds can make chromatic discriminations. Today, the story has been further refined: M and L cones appear to function by 8 weeks of age and possibly as early as 4 weeks (e.g., Bieber, Knoblauch, & Werner, 1998; Kelly, Borchert, & Teller, 1997); however, S cone functionality does not appear to emerge until at least 3 to 4 months of age (e.g., Crognale, Kelly, Weiss, & Teller, 1998; Suttle, Banks, & Graf, 2002). At birth, infants may have very limited color experience, and during the first 4 months of life their world becomes increasingly filled with color. And by 4 months, infants have color preferences that mirror adults: Saturated colors (such as royal blue) are preferred over less saturated colors (such as pale blue; Bornstein, 1975).

### Assessing Color Vision

Three sorts of hue discriminations—Rayleigh, tritan, and neutral-point—are particularly interesting theoretically, and research on infants' ability to make these discriminations fills out the picture of early competencies and deficits.

The *neutral-point test* is based on the observation that color-normal adults are able to distinguish all spectral (single wavelength) lights from white; that is, they do not exhibit a neutral point in such a comparison. Peeples and Teller (1975) and Teller, Peeples, and Sekel (1978)

used a neutral-point test to examine 8-week-olds' color vision. They examined both white-on-white luminance discrimination and discrimination of chromatic targets from white. The colors of the test targets and background are represented in Figure 3.3, which is a chromaticity diagram. Eight-week-olds discriminated many colors from white: red, orange, some greens, blue, and some purples; these colors are represented by the filled

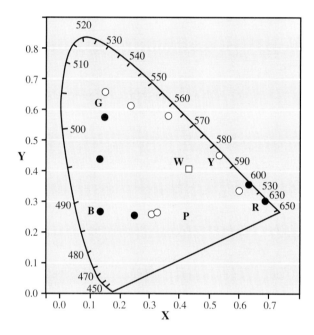

**Figure 3.3**  The stimuli used in neutral-point experiments. Participants in both experiments were 8-week-old infants. The format of the figure is the CIE Chromaticity diagram, which allows one to plot chromatic stimuli differing in hue and saturation. Saturated colors are represented at the exterior of the diagram, and unsaturated colors toward the middle. The right corner of the diagram (around 650) represents a hue of red, the top of the diagram represents a hue of bluish-green (labeled 520) and the lower left corner represents a hue of violet (near 400). Each circular symbol represents a color that was presented to infants in these two experiments. Open symbols represent hues that all infants failed to discriminate from white (W). Half-filled symbols represent hues that some, but not all, infants discriminated from white. Filled symbols represent hues that all infants reliably discriminated from white. *Sources:* "Color Vision and Brightness Discrimination in Human Infants," by D. R. Peeples and D. Y. Teller, 1975, *Science, 189,* pp. 1102–1103. Reprinted with permission and "Discrimination of Chromatic from White Light by 2-Month-Old Human Infants," by D. Y. Teller, D. R. Peeples, and M. Sekel, 1978, *Vision Research, 18,* pp. 41–48. Reprinted with permission.

symbols in the figure. Eight-week-olds did not discriminate yellow, yellow-green, one green, and some purples from white; these are represented by the open symbols in the figure. Thus, 8-week-old infants seemed to exhibit a neutral zone running from short wavelengths to yellow and green, resulting from deficient S cones (in color parlance, they have tritanopia or tritanomalous trichromacy; Teller et al., 1978). Later, Adams, Courage, and Mercer (1994) reported that the majority of newborns were able to discriminate broadband red from white and the majority were unable to discriminate blue, green, and yellow from white. These results are quite similar to the 8-week results reported by Teller et al. (1978).

A *tritan test* is designed to assess the function of S cones. By presenting two lights that activate M and L cones equally, the test isolates the S cones. Varner, Cook, Schneck, McDonald, and Teller (1985) asked whether 4- to 8-week infants could distinguish two such lights. Specifically, they presented violet targets in a green background. Eight-week-olds distinguished the two lights at all luminances, so they do not appear to have an S-cone deficiency. Four-week olds, on the other hand, did not discriminate the two lights reliably, suggesting that they have an S-cone defect. D. Allen, Banks, and Schefrin (1988) and Clavadetscher, Brown, Ankrum, and Teller (1988) confirmed this finding: In their experiment, 3- to 4-week-olds could not distinguish a violet target on a green background, but 7- to 8-week-olds could. More recently, Teller, Brooks, and Palmer (1997) found that tritan stimuli did not drive directionally appropriate eye movements even at 16 weeks of age.

*Rayleigh discrimination tests* involve distinguishing brightness-matched, long-wavelength lights such as red and green. They are diagnostically important because adults with the most common color defects—deuteranopia (lacking M cones) and protanopia (lacking L cones)—are unable to make such discriminations. Hamer, Alexander, Teller (1982) and Packer, Hartmann, and Teller (1984) examined the ability of 4-, 8-, and 12-week-olds to make Rayleigh discriminations. Either a green or red target was presented at one of a variety of luminances on a yellow background. Most 8-week-olds and essentially all 12-week-olds made these discriminations reliably, providing clear evidence that most infants do not exhibit deutan or protan defects by 8 weeks of age. In contrast, the majority of 4-week-olds did not exhibit the ability to make either discrimination. Packer et al. (1984) also found a significant effect of target size.

Twelve-week-olds were able to make Rayleigh discriminations with 4- and 8-degree targets, but not 1- and 2-degree targets. D. Allen et al. (1988) and Clavadetscher et al. (1988) confirmed the Rayleigh discrimination finding. They reported that 3- to 4-week-olds could not distinguish a red target on a green background; 7- to 8-week-olds could make this discrimination reliably.

In sum, there is little evidence that the majority of infants 4 weeks of age or younger make hue discriminations with the exception of discriminating red from white. The paucity of positive evidence is consistent with the hypothesis that human neonates are generally color deficient. By 4 months of age, infant color vision abilities approximate adult abilities, although there continue to be differences between infants' and adults' chromatic profiles throughout the 1st year of life (Crognale et al., 1998). We now turn to the question of what mechanism(s) underlie this development.

### How Does Early Color Vision Develop?

Two explanations have been proposed to account for young infants' hue discrimination failures. One possibility is the absence or immaturity of different cone types or immaturities among postreceptoral chromatic channels. Banks and Bennett (1988) have called this the *chromatic deficiency hypothesis.* There is, however, another possibility, raised initially by Banks and Bennett (1988) and elaborated by Brown (1990), Banks and Shannon (1993), Teller and Lindsey (1993), and D, Allen, Banks, and Norcia (1993). Perhaps neonates have a full complement of functional cone types and the requisite neural machinery to preserve and compare their signals, but overall visual sensitivity is so poor that it does not allow them to demonstrate their chromatic capabilities. On this account, older infants may exhibit reliable chromatic discrimination because of increased visual sensitivity. In this context, visual sensitivity might include discrimination performance of a visual system limited by optical and photoreceptor properties plus a general postreceptoral loss. This hypothesis has been called the *visual efficiency hypothesis* (D. Allen et al., 1993) and the *uniform loss hypothesis* (Teller & Lindsey, 1993).

There is an interesting way to compare the chromatic efficiency and visual efficiency explanations experimentally. Consider measurements of hue discrimination threshold (e.g., the chromatic contrast required to mediate the discrimination of two lights of equal brightness but different wavelength compositions—the "chromatic threshold") and a brightness discrimination threshold (e.g., the luminance contrast required to mediate the discrimination of two lights of the same wavelength composition but different luminances—the "luminance threshold"). The chromatic deficiency hypothesis predicts that the ratio of luminance threshold divided by chromatic threshold will decrease with increasing age. That is, luminance and chromatic thresholds may both improve with age, but chromatic thresholds change more. The visual efficiency or uniform loss hypothesis predicts that the ratio of luminance threshold divided by chromatic threshold is constant with age. That is, luminance and chromatic thresholds decrease at the same rates with increasing age because they are both limited by a common factor such as overall visual sensitivity. Banks and Bennett (1988) and Banks and Shannon (1993) showed that this hypothesis can in fact account for the poor Rayleigh and neutral-point discriminations of neonates.

Other investigators have tested the chromatic deficiency and visual efficiency hypotheses empirically, but no clear consensus has yet emerged. The challenge has been to develop paradigms in which infants' sensitivity can be made high enough to distinguish the predictions of the two hypotheses. In particular, recent work has focused on determining which hypothesis provides a better account of young infants' ability to use M and L cones to make Rayleigh discriminations (e.g., Adams & Courage, 2002; D. Allen et al., 1993, 1988; Clavadetscher et al., 1988; Morrone, Burr, & Fiorentini, 1993; Teller & Lindsey, 1993; Teller & Palmer, 1996; Varner et al., 1985). On balance, the discrimination failures observed with the youngest children and, for small targets, with older children do not necessarily imply deficiencies among chromatic mechanisms per se. Rather the ratio of chromatic divided by luminance sensitivity may well remain constant across age, suggesting that neonates' apparent inability to make Rayleigh and neutral-point discriminations is caused by an overall loss in visual efficiency. The predictions of the visual efficiency hypothesis, however, are inconsistent with the tritan discriminations. Therefore, young infants may in fact possess some form of color anomaly involving a deficiency among S cones.

Future work will be needed to illuminate infants' loss of visual efficiency and/or deficiency in S cones. Researchers are also taking an interest in the difference between processing moving versus static chromatic stimuli, which has implications for the relative involvement and development of the magnocelluar and parvocelluar pathways, which are responsible for spatial and temporal locations of chromatic changes and color identity, respectively (e.g., Dobkins & Anderson, 2002; Dobkins, Anderson, & Kelly, 2001; Dobkins, Lia, & Teller, 1997; Teller, 1998; Thomasson & Teller, 2000).

## Motion Perception

Moving and perceiving are deeply linked. Many of the most significant features of an environment to be perceived are moving objects and the events in which they participate. Motion of the observer is also crucial, in two ways. To locomote safely through space requires that our visual system be structured to deal with continuously changing views of the environment. Moreover, information given by transforming views of the world turn out to be a rich indicator not only of events but of persisting properties of the world, such as spatial layout (J. Gibson, 1966, 1979; Johansson, 1970). Later, in discussing space perception, we consider ways in which motions of objects and observers offer high-fidelity information about spatial layout and object form.

Early research on infant visual motion perception showed that motion strongly attracts infant attention (Fantz & Nevis, 1967; Haith, 1983; Kremenitzer, Vaughan, Kurtzberg, & Dowling, 1979; White, Castle, & Held, 1964). Progress has been made in analyzing the limits and probable mechanisms of motion sensitivity, including directional sensitivity, velocity sensitivity, and perception of motion and stability.

### Directional Selectivity

The ability to detect motion direction is one of the most basic and important perceptual capacities, but its development has been poorly understood until the last decade or so. Using both behavioral and visual evoked potential (VEP) measures, Wattam-Bell (1991, 1992) tested directional sensitivity in longitudinal studies. In the VEP studies, it was expected that if infants detected direction reversals in an oscillating checkerboard pattern, a measurable electrical response should be found at the frequency of the stimulus reversals. Reliable VEPs were first found at a median age of 74 days for 5 degrees/second patterns and 90 days for 20 degree/second patterns. Behavioral studies (Wattam-Bell, 1992) employed a different type of display. In one condition, an array of randomly changing dots was shown in which appeared a vertical strip of coherently (vertically) moving dots. In another condition, the vertical motion was shown against a background having opposite direction motion. A visual preference paradigm was used in which the target display appeared adjacent to a control display having random or uniform motion. If an infant detected the vertical target strip having unique, coherent motion, the infant was expected to look longer at this display. The element displacement per frame was manipulated to find the greatest displacement that supported motion detection ($d_{max}$). This measure was found to increase markedly from 8 to15 weeks of age. The younger infants (8 to 11 weeks) could tolerate only about a .25 degree of visual angle displacement (frame duration was 20 millisecond), whereas 14 to 15-week-olds showed a $d_{max}$ of about .65. (The value for adults is about 2 degrees in this task.)

Poor performance in the earliest weeks may be due to a lack of motion detectors sensitive to high velocities, that is, large displacements in short time intervals. This interpretation is supported by additional data that showed an increase in $d_{max}$ when the temporal interval between frames was lengthened (Wattam-Bell, 1992).

### Velocity Sensitivity

Human adults perceive motion over a great range of velocities. Under optimal conditions, a motion as slow as 1 to 2 minutes of visual angle per second may be detected as motion, as may faster motions up to 15 to 30 degrees/second, at which blurring or streaking occurs (Kaufman, 1974). Estimates of the slowest velocity to which infants respond have varied. Volkmann and Dobson (1976) used checkerboard patterns (check size = 5.5 degrees) and found a moving display was clearly preferred to a stationary one by 2- and 3-month-olds for a velocity as slow as 2 degrees/second. One-month-olds showed a weaker preference. Using rotary motion displays, Kaufmann, Stucki, and Kaufmann-Hayoz (1985) estimated thresholds at about 1.4 degrees/second at 1 month and 0.93 degrees/second at 3 months, also using a visual preference technique.

Later studies designed to distinguish various possible mechanisms by which moving patterns might be detected have yielded higher threshold estimates. Dannemiller and Freedland (1989), using unidirectional linear motion of a single bar, found no reliable motion preferences at 8 weeks. They estimated thresholds at about 5 degrees/second for 16-week-olds and about 2.3 degrees/second for 20-week-olds. For vertically moving gratings, Aslin and Shea (1990) found velocity thresholds of about 9 degrees/second at 6 weeks dropping to 4 degrees/second at 12 weeks. Thresholds for detecting a difference between two velocities were studied by Dannemiller and Freedland (1991) using paired displays with horizontal bars oscillating at different rates; their 20-month-old subjects distinguished bars moving at 3.3 degrees/second from 2.0 degrees/second, but not from 2.5 degrees/second.

Much lower thresholds for motion detection were obtained by von Hofsten, Kellman, and Putaansuu (1992). In habituation studies of observer-contingent motion with 14-week-olds, von Hofsten et al. found sensitivity to a differential velocity of .32 degrees/second but not .16 degrees/second. Infants were also found to be sensitive to the relation of the motion direction to their own motion. Higher sensitivity in this paradigm might have two explanations. It is possible that visual preference paradigms understate infant capacities. As is true in general with preference measures, infants might detect a difference (e.g., between moving and stationary patterns) but have no differential interest or attention to the two displays. A second possibility is that the key difference relates to observer motion contingency in the von Hofsten et al. study. It is plausible that small, observer-contingent motions are processed by the motion perspective system as specifiers of object depth, rather than as moving objects. Thus, a depth-from-motion system may have greater sensitivity than a motion detection system, and the former might be engaged only by observer movement (von Hofsten et al., 1992).

### Mechanisms for Processing Moving Patterns: Velocity, Flicker, and Position

A moving stimulus may be characterized in different ways. Similarly, a response to a moving stimulus may be based on more than one kind of mechanism. Consider a vertical sine-wave grating drifting horizontally. Each edge moves at a certain velocity. At a given point, alternating dark and light areas will pass at a certain rate, presenting a temporal frequency of modulation or flicker rate. This flicker rate depends both on the velocity of the pattern and on its spatial frequency (cycles per degree). Now consider preferential attention to such a stimulus over a nonmoving grating or a blank field. The preference could be based on a direction-sensitive mechanism, a velocity-sensitive mechanism, or a flicker-sensitive mechanism. Sustained flicker could be avoided by use of a single object in motion as opposed to a repetitive pattern, but then the possibility arises that the motion could be detected by noting the change in position of some unique object feature, that is, a position-sensitive mechanism may operate. Some research on motion sensitivity has aimed to separate these possibilities experimentally.

Perhaps the first effort to disentangle velocity-sensitive, position-sensitive, and flicker-sensitive mechanisms was carried out by Freedland and Dannemiller (1987). Several combinations of temporal frequency and spatial displacement were presented with random black and white checkerboard displays. Infants' preferences were affected by both of these factors and were not a simple function of velocity. The role of flicker could not be directly assessed in these experiments. Sensitivity to flicker versus velocity was examined by Aslin and Shea (1990) with vertically moving, square-wave gratings. Various combinations of spatial frequency and velocity were used to vary flicker independent of velocity. For example, the flicker rate (temporal frequency) at any point in the display remains constant if spatial frequency is doubled and velocity is cut in half. Aslin and Shea (1990) found that velocity, not flicker, determines preferences in infants 6 and 12 weeks of age. Converging evidence for velocity-sensitive mechanisms was reported by Dannemiller and Freedland (1991). By using a display with motion of a single bar flanked by stationary reference bars, they excluded ongoing flicker in any spatial position. Moreover, manipulating extent of displacement allowed them to test the possibility that infants' responses were determined by the extent of positional displacement. Results were consistent with velocity-sensitive mechanisms.

### Perceiving Motion and Stability

Perceiving moving objects is inextricably tied to its converse: perceiving nonmoving objects and surfaces as stationary. The latter ability is less straightforward than it might at first appear. Neural models of motion detectors suggest that these should respond to image features, such as edges, that change position on the retina over time. Yet such retinal displacement occurs in perfectly stationary environments whenever perceivers make eye, head, or body movements. Perception of objects remaining at rest during observer motion, called *position constancy,* requires use of information beyond that available to individual motion-sensing units. Such information might involve comparison of retinal changes with those expected from self-produced movements (von Holst, 1954; Wallach, 1987) or more global relationships among optical changes occurring at a given time (Duncker, 1929; J. Gibson, 1966).

In the case of passive (non-self-produced) observer motion, relations in optic flow or some contribution from the vestibular system must be used in perceiving a stable world. There is some indication that young infants show position constancy under such conditions. Later, we mention work in object perception (Kellman, Gleitman, & Spelke, 1987) suggesting that moving infants discriminate moving from stationary objects and perceive object unity only from real object motion. More direct studies of position constancy and motion perception by moving observers have also been carried out (Kellman & von Hofsten, 1992). In these studies, infants were moved laterally while viewing an array of objects. On each trial, one object in the array, either on the left or right, moved while others remained stationary. The object motion was parallel to the observer's motion. Whether the optical change given to the observer in this situation comes from a moving or stationary object depends on the object's distance. Thus, a stationary object placed on the opposite side of the array at a different distance matched the optical displacement of the moving object. Infants were expected to look more at the moving object if its motion was detected. Both 8- and 16-week-olds showed this pattern when the object and observer motions were opposite in phase, but only 16-week-olds appeared to detect the motion when object and observer moved in phase (Kellman & von Hofsten, 1992). It is not clear why the younger infants showed detection of the moving object only in the opposite phase condition. Further study indicated that motion detection was eliminated in monocular viewing. It appears that some ability to distinguish moving and stationary objects during observer motion is in place as early as 8 weeks of age and that binocular convergence may provide the distance information needed in this task (Kellman & von Hofsten, 1992).

## SPACE PERCEPTION

In considering how we obtain knowledge through perception, the philosopher Kant (1781/1902) concluded that the mind must contain built-in (*a priori*) categories of space and time into which experience is organized. Psychologically, understanding the origins and development of spatial perception has more nuances. Whether we approach perception from the perspective of the philosopher, cognitive scientist, psychologist, or engineer, however, we will rediscover Kant's insight that space is fundamental. Our earlier treatment of basic spatial vision set out the sensory limitations—in acuity, contrast sensitivity, and sensitivity to pattern variation—that constrain the pickup of information. As we explore space perception here, our main concern is the acquisition of knowledge of positions and arrangements of objects and surfaces in the three-dimensional environment.

Theoretical controversy about the development of visual space perception has centered on depth perception. When we examine the human visual apparatus, it is relatively easy to see how we acquire information about two of three spatial dimensions. The optics of the eye ensure, to a high degree, that light originating from points in different directions from the observer will be mapped onto distinct points on the retina. The result is a map that preserves information about adjacency in two spatial dimensions (up-down and left-right). The apparent problem lies in the third (depth) dimension. Nothing in this map immediately indicates how far a ray of light has traveled to get from an object to the eye.

Traditionally, it has most often been claimed that perception of three-dimensional (3D) space is a product of learning (Berkeley, 1709/1963; Helmholtz, 1885/1925). Before the invention of methods to study infants' perception, the basis for this view was the logical problem of recovering three dimensions from a projection of the world onto a surface of two dimensions (the retina). Learning might overcome the limitation through the associating and storing of sensations of vision and touch, allowing relevant information about tactile correlates of visual sensations; these in turn could be retrieved when familiar visual input recurred (Berkeley, 1709/1963; Helmholtz, 1885/1925; Titchener, 1910). Piaget went a step further in arguing that self-initiated action and its consequences provide the necessary learning.

Modern analyses of the information available for vision have raised a radically different possibility for the origins of spatial perception. Transforming optical input given to a moving organism carries information specific to the particular 3D layout (J. Gibson, 1966, 1979; Johansson, 1970), and humans and animals may well have evolved mechanisms to extract such information. On this *ecological* view of development (E. Gibson, 1979; Shepard, 1984), the rudiments of 3D perception might be present even in the newborn, and their refinement might depend on sensory maturation and attentional skill, rather than on associative learning.

Research on spatial perception has gone a considerable distance toward answering this question of the constructivist versus ecological origins of the third dimension. Moreover, the emerging picture of early abilities provides important insights about functionally distinct classes of information and their neurophysiological underpinnings. Anticipating some of these distinctions, we divide spatial perception abilities into four categories: kinematic, oculomotor, stereoscopic, and pictorial. The classification reflects both differences in the nature of information and in the perceptual mechanisms at work in extracting information (Kellman, 1995; Kellman & Arterberry, 1998; Yonas & Owsley, 1987).

## Kinematic Information

For guiding action and furnishing information about the 3D environment, kinematic or motion-carried information may be the most important class of visual information for adult humans. One reason for its centrality is that it overcomes the ambiguity problems present with some other kinds of information, such as pictorial cues to depth. A stationary image given to one eye may be a cuddly kitten or a gigantic tiger further off, as Berkeley noted, or even a flat, 2D cutout of a cat or tiger. To the moving observer, the transforming optic array reveals whether the object is planar or 3D and furnishes information about relative distance and size. The mapping between the optical transformations and the 3D scene is governed by projective geometry, and under reasonable constraints, it allows recovery of many properties of the layout (Koenderink, 1986; Lee, 1974; Ullman, 1979). Among the residual ambiguities is a problem analogous to the one Berkeley raised about a single image. If objects and surfaces in the scene *deform* (alter their shapes) contingent on the observer's motion, a unique 3D scene is not recoverable. Now the problem is recovering four dimensions (spatial layout plus change over time) from three (two spatial dimensions of the input plus time). In ordinary perception, simulation of the exact projective changes consistent with a particular, but not present, layout, would almost never occur by chance.

It does, however, make possible the realistic depiction of 3D space in television, motion pictures, and in virtual reality setups. Because kinematic information about space depends on geometry, not on knowledge of what particular spatial layouts exist in the world, it is imaginable that perceptual mechanisms have evolved to make use of it. An additional reason to suspect that sensitivity to this kind of information might appear early is that early learning about the environment may be optimized by relying on sources of information that are most accurate (Kellman, 1993; Kellman & Arterberry, 1998). On the other hand, adults acquire much kinematic information from their own movements through the environment. The human infant does not self-locomote until the second half-year of life although kinematic information could still be made available from moving objects, from the infant being carried through the environment, or from self-produced head movements.

Motion-carried or kinematic information is often divided into subcategories, of which we consider three. Relative depths of surfaces can be specified by *accretion/deletion of texture*. Relative motion between an object and observer may be given by *optical expansion/contraction*. Relative depth, and under some conditions perhaps metric information about distance, can be provided by *motion parallax* or *motion perspective*. Another important kinematically based spatial ability, recovery of object shape from transforming optical projections (*structure-from-motion*), is discussed in connection with object perception.

### Accretion/Deletion of Texture

In the late 1960s, Kaplan, Gibson, and their colleagues discovered a new kind of depth information, a striking achievement given that depth perception had at that point been systematically studied for over 200 years (J. Gibson, Kaplan, Reynolds, & Wheeler, 1969; Kaplan, 1969). Most surfaces have visible texture—variations of luminance and color across their surfaces. The new type of depth information involves what happens to visible points of texture (texture elements) when an observer or object moves. When the observer moves while viewing a nearer and more distant object, the elements on the nearer surface remain visible whereas those on the more distant surface gradually pass out of sight along one side (deletion) of the nearer object and come into view along the other side (accretion). The same kind of transformation occurs when the motion is given by a moving object instead of a moving observer. This kind of information

has been shown to be used in adult visual perception, to establish both depth order and shape, even when no other sources of information are available (Andersen & Cortese, 1989; Kaplan, 1969; Shipley & Kellman, 1994).

Infants' shape perception from accretion/deletion of texture was studied by Kaufmann-Hayoz, Kaufman, and Stucki (1986). They habituated 3-month-olds to one shape specified by accretion/deletion and tested recovery from habituation to the same and a novel shape. Infants dishabituated more to the novel shape. Although this result suggests that accretion/deletion specifies edges and shape at 3 months, we cannot tell much about perceived depth order from this study. That accretion/deletion specifies depth order at 5 to 7 months is suggested by a different study (Granrud, Yonas, et al., 1985). These investigators assumed that infants would reach preferentially to a surface perceived as nearer than another. Computer generated, random dot, kinematic displays were shown in which a vertical boundary was specified by only accretion/deletion information. Infants of 5 and 7 months of age were tested, and both groups showed modestly greater reaching to areas specified as nearer by accretion/deletion than to areas specified as farther. More recently Johnson and Mason (2002) provided evidence that 2-month-olds are able to use accretion/deletion of texture for perceiving depth relations.

Craton and Yonas (1990) suggested that ordinary accretion/deletion displays actually contain two kinds of information. In addition to the disappearance and appearance of texture elements, there are relationships of individual elements to the location of the boundary between surfaces. A visible element on one side of a boundary remains in a fixed relation to it, whereas an element on the other side (the more distant surface) changes its separation from the boundary over time. This separate information, termed *boundary flow,* appears to be usable by adults in the absence of element accretion/deletion (Craton & Yonas, 1990) and possibly by 5-month-old infants (Craton & Yonas, 1988).

### Optical Expansion/Contraction

When an object approaches an observer on a collision course, its optical projection expands symmetrically. It can be shown mathematically that a ratio of an object point's retinal eccentricity and its retinal velocity gives its *time to contact,* that is, the time until it will hit the observer. Newborns of other species show defensive responses to this kind of information (Schiff, 1965).

When presented with optical expansion patterns, human infants of 1 to 2 months of age were reported to retract their heads, raise their arms, and blink (Ball & Tronick, 1971; Bower, Broughton, & Moore, 1970). Not all of these responses, however, may indicate perception of an approaching object (Yonas et al., 1977). Head movement may result from infants tracking visually the top contour of the pattern, and relatively undifferentiated motor behavior may cause the arms to rise in concert. Yonas et al. tested this hypothesis using a display in which only the top contour moved. This optical change is not consistent with approach of an object. Infants from 1 to 4 months displayed similar head and arm movements to this new display as to an optical expansion display. The result supports the hypothesis that tracking the top contour, rather than defensive responding, accounts for the behavior infants show to expansion displays.

It turns out, however, that both the tracking hypothesis and the hypothesis of defensive responding appear to be correct. When eye blink was used as the dependent measure, reliably more responding was observed to the approach display than to the moving top contour display. It appears that blinking may best access infant perception of object approach and does so reliably from about 1 month of age (Nanez, 1988; Nanez & Yonas, 1994; Yonas, 1981; Yonas, Pettersen, & Lockman, 1979).

### Motion Perspective

Motion perspective is an important source of spatial layout information. When an observer moves and looks perpendicular to the movement direction, the visual direction of a nearer object changes at a faster velocity than that of a more distant object. Comparing two such objects or points defines the classical depth cue of motion parallax. J. Gibson (1950, 1966) argued that perceptual systems might use relative velocities of many points, that is, gradients of relative motion provide more information than a pair of points. To express this concept, he coined the term *motion perspective*. Some experimental evidence indicates that gradients are in fact used by human perceivers (e.g., E. Gibson, Gibson, Smith, & Flock, 1959).

Motion perspective is virtually always available to a moving observer in a lighted environment, and it ordinarily provides unambiguous indication of depth order. Given these considerations, one might expect that neural mechanisms have evolved to exploit this kind of information, and that accordingly, it might appear early in development. Several investigators have suggested that it

functions quite early, but these suggestions have been based on indirect evidence (Walk & Gibson, 1961; Yonas & Owsley, 1987). Walk and Gibson (1961) studied newborns of various species on the visual cliff and noted that some species made lateral head movements before choosing the "shallow" side of the cliff over the "deep" side. It is difficult to make a similar inference about human infants, because they do not self-locomote until around 6 months of age.

Some results relevant to the development of motion perspective in 4-month-old infants were reported by von Hofsten et al. (1992). Infants moved back and forth while viewing an array of three vertical bars. The middle bar was moved in concert with the infant's chair, giving it an optical displacement that would have been consistent with a stationary rod placed somewhat further away. If motion perspective operates, the observer contingent motion should indicate that the middle rod is furthest from the subject (see Figure 3.4). After habituation to such an array, moving infants looked more at a stationary array consisting of three aligned, stationary rods than to another stationary array with the middle rod 15 cm further away than the others. (The latter display produced identical motion perspective as the habituation display.) Two other experiments showed that the effect disappeared if the contingent motion was reduced from the original .32 degrees/second to .16 degrees/second and that infants were sensitive to the contingency between the optical changes and their own movement. These results are consistent with infants' early use of motion perspective. They might also be explained, however, by infants responding to particular optical changes and the contingency of these optical changes on the observer's movement. The results do not include any test to verify that the optical changes were taken to indicate depth. An interesting possibility is that the perceptual process that uses motion perspective to assign depth is far more sensitive to optical displacement than processes used to see moving objects.

## Stereoscopic Depth Perception

Stereoscopic depth perception refers to the use of differences in the optical projections at the two retinas to determine depth. This ability is among the most precise in adult visual perception. Under optimal conditions, an adult observer may detect depth when the angular difference in a viewed point's location at the two eyes

Habituate

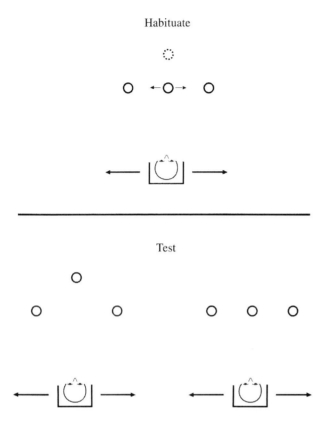

**Figure 3.4** Top views of displays used in motion parallax experiment. *Top:* Moving observers were habituated to a linear array of rods in which the center rod moved in phase with the observer. The dotted line indicates the virtual object specified by motion parallax. *Bottom:* The two test arrays pictured were shown after habituation. *Source:* "Young Infants' Sensitivity to Motion Parallax," by C. von Hofsten, P. Kellman, and J. Putaansuu, 1992, *Infant Behavior and Development, 15*(2), pp. 245–264. Reprinted with permission.

(binocular disparity) is only 5 to 15 seconds of arc (Westheimer & McKee, 1980). A 5-second disparity would translate into detection of a 1.4 mm depth difference between two objects at a distance of one meter. We can distinguish two types of binocular disparity, *crossed* and *uncrossed*. A prerequisite for precise computation of disparity between the two eyes is fixation by the two eyes on a common environmental point. We can measure the disparities of other imaged points by comparison to this zero disparity fixation point. Other points at roughly the same distance from the observer as the fixated point will project to corresponding retinal locations, that is, having the same angular separation and direction from the fovea on each of the two eyes. Points

more distant than the fixation point will have *uncrossed disparity.* The visual direction of such a point will be more to the left in the visual field of the left eye than in the right eye. *Crossed disparity* characterizes points nearer than the fixated point. The visual direction of these points will be more leftward in the right eye than in the left.

Observations from other species suggest the existence of innate brain mechanisms subserving stereoscopic depth perception, specifically, cortical cells tuned to particular disparities at birth or soon after (Hubel & Wiesel, 1970; Pettigrew, 1974; Ramachandran, Clarke, & Whitteridge, 1977). Such single-cell recording studies are not possible in human infants; moreover, they do not directly address functional operation of stereoscopic depth perception. Evidence about human infants comes mostly from behavioral studies and suggests that stereoscopic depth perception arises around 4 months of age as a result of maturational processes.

A number of studies have used stationary displays and preferential looking as the dependent variable. One of two adjacently presented displays contains binocular disparities that might specify depth differences within the pattern. Infants are expected to look longer at a display containing detectable depth differences than at a similar one having no depth variation (Atkinson & Braddick, 1976; Held, Birch, & Gwiazda, 1980). A different method eliminates any possible monocular cues. Using random dot kinematograms, Fox, Aslin, Shea, and Dumais (1980) presented disparity information that would, if detected, specify a moving square. Using the forced-choice preferential looking method, adult observers judged the direction of motion on each trial solely by watching the infant's responses.

Estimates of the age of onset of disparity sensitivity from these methods show reasonable agreement. In longitudinal studies by Held and his colleagues (Birch, Gwiazda, & Held, 1982; Held et al., 1980), reliable preferences for a vertical grating pattern with disparity variation appeared at 12 weeks for crossed disparities and 17 weeks for uncrossed. Fox et al. (1980) found that 3- to 5-month-olds reliably oriented to a moving square specified by disparity, but infants younger than 3 months did not. Petrig, Julesz, Kropfl, and Baumgartner (1981) found a similar onset of sensitivity using recordings of visual evoked potentials.

A thorny issue in the interpretation of these studies is whether the observed behavioral responses index depth perception from binocular disparity or merely sensitivity to disparity itself. It is hard to settle this issue with certainty; however, some observations suggest that depth is perceived. Held et al. (1980), for example, found that infants who showed clear preferences for vertical line displays containing horizontal disparity showed no such preferences when the displays were rotated 90 degrees to give 34 minutes of vertical disparity (a condition that produces rivalry for adults). Fox et al. (1980) observed that infants did not track a moving object specified by very large disparities that do not signal depth to adults. They found instead that infants reliably looked away from such displays. This result is double-edged: Although it shows different reactions by infants to different magnitudes of disparity as might be expected if only some disparities produce perceived depth, it also shows that disparities per se can affect infants' fixation. From these studies, it is plausible but not certain that infants' responses in these studies indicate functional stereoscopic depth perception. Other studies have shown that disparity-sensitive infants outperform disparity-insensitive infants on tasks involving depth and three-dimensional shape perception (Granrud, 1986; Yonas, Arterberry, & Granrud, 1987a).

What mechanisms are responsible for the onset of stereoscopic sensitivity after several months of life? An argument for maturational causes is that sensitivity very quickly attains adultlike precision. Held et al. (1980) reported that thresholds change over 3 to 4 weeks from greater than 60 minutes to less than 1 minute of disparity, with the latter measured value limited by the apparatus; even so, this value is comparable to adult sensitivity under some conditions.

What mechanisms might be maturing at this time? One possibility is that disparity-sensitive cortical cells are coming online. Another is that improvements in the mechanisms of convergence or visual acuity that are prerequisites to fine stereopsis might explain the observed onset of disparity sensitivity. Some evidence suggests that the onset of stereopsis is not dependent on improvements in visual acuity (grating acuity). When both acuity and disparity sensitivity are measured longitudinally in the same infants, little or no change in grating acuity is found during the period in which stereopsis appears (Held, 1993). A different method pointing toward the same conclusion comes from a study by Westheimer and McKee (1980). Adults were given artificially reduced acuity and contrast sensitivity designed to approximate those present at 2 months of age. Under these conditions, stereoacuity was reduced substantially, but not sufficiently to explain infants' inability to respond to large disparities before 3 to 4 months of age. Developmental changes in convergence also appear unlikely to explain the onset of stereoacuity. Evidence on the development of convergence (Hainline, Riddell, Grose-Fifer & Abramov, 1992) indicates that it may be nearly adultlike at 1 to 2 months of age. Also, convergence changes would not explain differences in the onset of crossed and uncrossed disparity (Held et al., 1980).

Given these considerations, most investigators believe the explanation for the onset of stereoscopic vision is some maturational change in cortical disparity-sensitive units. Such a mechanism underlies improvement of stereoscopic discrimination performance in kittens (Pettigrew, 1974; Timney, 1981). In humans, it has been suggested that the particular change in disparity-sensitive cells may be segregation of *ocular dominance columns* in layer 4 of the visual cortex (Held, 1985, 1988). At birth, cells in layer 4 generally receive projections from both eyes. Between birth and 6 months, inputs from the two eyes separate into alternating columns receiving input from the right and left eyes (Hickey & Peduzzi, 1987). Eye-of-origin information is needed to extract disparity information, so this neurological development is a plausible candidate for the onset of stereoscopic function.

## Pictorial Depth Perception

The *pictorial cues* are so named because they allow depth to be portrayed in a flat, two-dimensional picture. Sometimes these are called the classical depth cues, because they have been discussed and used by artists and students of perception for centuries. Theoretically, they have been central to classical arguments about the need for learning in spatial perception. The fact that the same information can be displayed in a flat picture or a real 3D scene immediately points to their ambiguity as signifiers of reality. It is a short step to the classical perspective on the acquisition of such cues: If these cues are not unequivocally tied to particular spatial arrangements, our perception of depth from these cues must derive from learning about what tends to be the case in our particular environment. (The environment, until recently, had many more 3D scenes offering information than 2D representations.)

Ecologically, the pictorial cues to depth are diverse, but many of them rest on similar foundations. The laws of projection ensure that a given physical magnitude projects an image of decreasing extent at the retina with increasing distance from the observer. Applying this geometry in reverse, if two physical extents are known or assumed to have the same physical (real) size, then differences in their projected size can be used to establish their depth order. This information comprises the depth cue of *relative size*. Very similar is *linear perspective*. If two lines in the world are known or assumed to be parallel, then their convergence in the optical projection may be taken to indicate their extending away from the observer in depth. Generalizing this notion to whole fields of visible elements comprises the rich source of information in natural scenes known as *texture gradients* (J. Gibson, 1950). If a surface is assumed to be made up of physically uniform or stochastically regular tokens (pebbles, plants, floor tiles, etc.), then the decreasing projective size of texture elements indicates increasing depth. A different kind of assumed equality is illustrated by the depth cue of *shading*. If the light source comes from above, a dent in a wall will have a lower luminance at the top because the surface is oriented away from the light, whereas the bottom part, oriented toward the light, will have higher luminance. Perception of depth from these luminance variations implicitly assumes that the surface has a homogeneous reflectance; variations in luminance are then taken to indicate variations in surface orientation.

Pictorial cues are not as ecologically valid as kinematic or stereoscopic information because the assumptions behind them, such as the assumption of physical equality, may be false. In a picture, it is easy to make two similar objects of different sizes or two parts of a connected surface with different reflectances. Misleading cases of pictorial depth information are not difficult to find in ordinary environments. Sometimes apparently converging lines really are converging lines, and sometimes the average size of texture elements changes with distance, as do the sizes of particles at the seashore (smaller particles get washed further up the beach).

Studies of the development of pictorial depth perception reveal a consistent pattern. Sensitivity to these cues appears to be absent until about 7 months of age. Around 7 months of age, infants seem to be sensitive to virtually all pictorial depth cues that have been tested. Much of this emerging picture of the origins of pictorial depth has come from systematic studies by Yonas and his colleagues (see Yonas, Arterberry, & Granrud, 1987b; Yonas & Owsley, 1987 for reviews). For brevity, we consider only two examples: interposition and familiar size. The development of other pictorial cues that have been studied, such as linear perspective and shading, appears to be similar.

## Interposition

The depth cue of *interposition*, sometimes called overlap, specifies relative depth of surfaces based on contour junction information. When surface edges form a "T" junction in the optical projection, the edge that comes to an end at the intersection point (the vertical edge in the letter T; see Figure 3.5A) belongs to a surface passing behind the surface bounded by the other edge (the horizontal edge in the letter T). Interposition is a powerful depth cue in human vision (Kellman & Shipley, 1991). Infant use of interposition information was tested by Granrud and Yonas (1984). They used three similar displays made of three parts each but differing in the presence of interposition information. In the interposition display, the left panel overlapped the middle, which overlapped the right. In a second display, all contours changed direction at intersection points, giving indeterminate depth order. In a third display, the three surface sections were displayed slightly separated, so that no contour junctions were relating them. Infants at 5 and 7 months of age viewed these displays monocularly (to eliminate conflicting binocular depth information), and reaching was measured. All parts of the displays were coplanar and located the same distance from the subjects. Infants' reaches to different parts of the displays were recorded. In one ex-

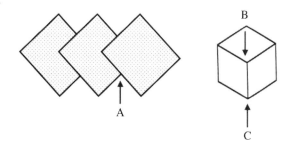

**Figure 3.5**  Examples of line junctions giving information for three-dimensional structure. A shows a T junction specifying ordering in depth. B and C show Y and arrow junctions, respectively, that contribute to the perception of three-dimensional structure.

periment, the interposition display was compared with the indeterminate control display and in a second experiment, the interposition display was compared with the control display having separated areas. In both experiments, 7-month-old infants reached reliably more often to the "nearest" part of the interposition display than to the same region in the control displays. Five-month-olds showed some tendency to reach more to the nearest part of the interposition display than one of the control displays, but not the other. These results provide evidence that interposition is usable by 7 months, but the results are equivocal or negative about its availability at 5 months of age.

*Familiar Size*

Perhaps the clearest case of learning in space perception involves the cue of familiar size. If an object has a known physical size (and this size is represented in memory) and the object produces a particular projective size in a given viewing situation, the distance to the object can in principle be calculated (Ittleson, 1951). Using a preferential reaching method, Yonas, Pettersen, and Granrud (1982) tested infants' perception of depth from familiar size. As with interposition, 7-month-olds showed evidence of using familiar size, whereas 5-month-olds did not. In a later experiment, Granrud, Haake, and Yonas (1985) tested familiar size using two pairs of objects unfamiliar to the subjects before the experiment. Each pair consisted of a large and small version of an object having identical shape and color. Infants were encouraged to play with the small object from one pair and the large object from the other pair for 6 to 10 minutes. After this familiarization period, infants viewed a simultaneous presentation of both large objects. It was expected that infants would reach more often to the object whose small version had been handled during familiarization if the cue of familiar size influenced perceived distance. (Memory for the physical sizes in the earlier exposure, combined with equal projective sizes in the test, would lead to interpretation of the previously smaller object as being much closer.) Infants at 7 months of age who viewed the test displays binocularly reached equally to the two objects, but infants of the same age who viewed the test displays monocularly reached more to the previously smaller object. Five-month-olds showed no variations in reaching related to the size of objects in the familiarization period. These results suggest that by 7 but not 5 months infants may obtain depth information

from familiar size, but this information is overridden when conflicting stereoscopic information is available.

*Conclusions Regarding Pictorial Depth*

Two decades ago little was known about the development of pictorial depth. Today, largely due to programmatic research by Yonas, Granrud, and their colleagues, we have a fairly clear picture about the timing of the appearance of pictorial cues. The picture is strikingly consistent across members of the category. Pictorial cues to depth arise sometime between the 5th and 7th month of age, and tests of individual infants across time reveal variability in the age of onset across this 2-month period (Yonas, Elieff, & Arterberry, 2002). It is possible that younger infants are sensitive to some of the informational properties of pictorial depth cues, such as different line junctions or textural arrangements, which may provide a foundation for perceiving the third dimension (Bhatt & Bertin, 2001; Bhatt & Waters, 1998; Kavsek, 1999).

The appearance of various pictorial cues around the same time has been interpreted as suggesting that maturation of some higher visual processing area in the nervous system is the mechanism (Granrud & Yonas, 1984). Research with macaque monkeys lends additional support to a maturational explanation. Pictorial cues appear as a group around 7 to 8 weeks of life (Gunderson, Yonas, Sargent, & Grant-Webster, 1993). As Gunderson et al. put it, this result is compatible with the idea that "pictorial depth perception may have ancient phylogenetic origins" (p. 96). A key to this interpretation is that the timing fits the rough ratio of 1:4 in terms of time after birth in nonhuman primates and humans, a relation that fits the maturation of numerous other abilities (a function that matures at 4 weeks in nonhuman primates appears at about 16 weeks in human infants).

Alternatively, the similarity of onset of these sources of information might be explained by learning. It is suggestive that the depth cue of familiar size, which necessarily involves learning, becomes operative in the same period as other pictorial depth cues. Their appearance at this time could reflect enhanced possibilities for learning brought about by some other developmental advances, such as the appearance of crawling abilities around 6 months of age. One study that correlated individual sensitivity to linear perspective and texture gradients with crawling ability (Arterberry, Yonas, & Bensen, 1989) found no predictive relationship, however. Seven-month-olds seemed to utilize pictorial depth in their reaching regardless of whether they had learned to crawl.

Further research is needed to discover the mechanisms underlying the onset of pictorial depth perception. Longitudinal studies of multiple pictorial depth cues would be helpful, as would be formulation and tests of more specific neurophysiological candidates for maturation and, alternatively, potential processes of learning.

## OBJECT PERCEPTION

One of the most important functions of visual perception is to deliver representations of the environment in terms of discrete physical entities or *objects*. There are many ways to describe and encode the streams of light that hit the retinas of the eyes. In ordinary perceiving, we receive, not descriptions of light, but descriptions of the physical objects that last reflected the light. These descriptions of the locations, boundaries, shapes, sizes, and substances of objects are indispensable for action and thought. Normally, the separate objects in our perceptual world correspond to units in the physical world. This knowledge allows us to predict the results of action: how the world divides, which things will detach from adjacent things, and which will remain coherent if moved, thrown, or sat on. All this we can know visually from a distance, without actually contacting the objects.

Beyond these most basic kinds of knowledge, perception of shapes and sizes, object rigidity, and so on, gives us a wealth of information about objects' possible affordances for action. For the experienced observer, storing in memory the shapes and surface qualities of many perceived objects makes possible rapid and automatic recognition of familiar objects, even from partial information. The adaptive value of object perception and recognition systems can hardly be overestimated. Matching this importance is the complexity of understanding the processes and mechanisms of object perception. The challenges become apparent when we see how little of human object perception can currently be emulated by artificial vision systems. For the ordinary observer in a familiar environment, however, the task seems not complex, but easy.

The lack of a complete scientific understanding of adult object perception abilities might seem to handicap efforts to trace their development. Examining object perception in infancy has at least one advantage. The minimal experience of infants makes it easier to examine object perception *per se* as opposed to recognition from partial information, reasonable inferences based on prior knowledge, and other valuable cognitive talents that adults use to ruin otherwise sound perceptual experiments. Studies of early object perception reveal the developmental course of these abilities and shed light on the complexities of object perception in general.

### Multiple Tasks in Object Perception

As the study of object perception has advanced, it has become clear that it is computationally complex, involving multiple tasks. (For recent discussions of the information processing tasks in object perception, see Kellman, 2003). One component is *edge detection*—locating significant contours that may indicate where one object ends and another object or surface begins. Edge detection alone is ambiguous, because visible contours can result from object boundaries but also from other sources, such as shadows or markings on a surface. A second requirement, then, is *edge classification*—sorting visible contours into object boundaries as opposed to other sources. Next is *boundary assignment.* When an edge corresponding to an object boundary is located, it most commonly bounds one object, while the surface or object seen on the other side of the boundary passes behind the first object. Determining which way each boundary bounds is crucial for knowing, for example, whether we are viewing objects or holes. Along with edge processes, detection and classification of junctions of edges is important in the segmentation and grouping processes that lead to perceived objects.

Early processes involving edges and junctions do not by themselves yield perceived objects. Several other problems need to be solved to accomplish object formation. For one thing, because of occlusion a single object in the world may project to multiple, spatially separated locations on the retinas of the eyes. Also, at each occlusion boundary, some surface continues behind; recovering the structure of objects in the world requires solutions to how visible parts connect. These are the questions of *segmentation* and *unit formation*. A single static image raises these issues; more complex versions occur when observers move, causing the visible fragments of objects to change continuously. To form units, the visual system assigns shape descriptions. Thus perceiving *form*—the three-dimensional arrangement of the object—is another important component. Finally, there are perceptible properties relating to *object sub-*

*stance:* its rigidity or flexibility, surface texture, and so on. We consider what is known about each of these aspects of object perception early in development.

## Edge Detection and Edge Classification

What information makes edge detection possible? In general, the answer is discontinuities across space in some perceptible properties. These differences can be in the luminance or spectral composition of light coming from adjacent areas. These differences may mark object boundaries because objects tend to be relatively homogeneous in their material composition. Parts of a homogeneous object will absorb and reflect light in similar fashion, whereas an adjacent object, made of some different material, may differ. Thus, discontinuities of luminance and spectral composition in the optic array may mark object boundaries. When average luminance and spectral characteristics are similar for adjacent objects, higher order patterns of optical variation—texture—may distinguish them. Another source of information comes from depth gradients. Depth values of visible points of a continuous object will change smoothly, but at an object boundary discontinuities will often occur. In similar fashion, optic flow provides information about edges. When the observer moves, the optical displacements for visible points will tend to vary more smoothly within objects than between objects.

None of these sources of information for detecting objects' edges is unequivocal. Discontinuities in luminance and/or spectral values may arise from reflectance differences of cast shadows along the surface of a continuous object. They may also come from surface orientation differences in a complex object, due to different geometric relations between a light source, surface patches, and the observer. The same may be true for depth or motion discontinuities: They will often but not always mark object boundaries. A second requirement for object perception, then, is edge classification. Which luminance variations are probably object edges and which arise from illumination changes, such as shadows or patterns on a continuous surface?

We have primarily indirect evidence about infant edge detection and edge classification abilities. The literatures on visual acuity and pattern discrimination both offer useful clues. One implication of newborns' poor acuity relative to adults is that their ability to process object edges must be much reduced, especially for distant objects.

If the shape of a 2D pattern is detected, one might argue, the contour comprising that edge must certainly be detected and perhaps classified as an object boundary. Since the pioneering studies of Fantz and colleagues (e.g., Fantz, Fagan, & Miranda, 1975), many studies have shown that infants discriminate patterns from the earliest weeks of life. Discrimination, however, can be based on any registered difference between patterns; contour perception may not necessarily be implied. A visual pattern may be analyzed into sinusoidal luminance components. An object's edge may trigger responses in a population of cortical neurons but not be represented as a single pattern feature. In short, different patterns may evoke different neural activity but not perception of edges or forms per se. This possibility is consistent with the evidence noted earlier that infants are somewhat insensitive to spatial phase information before about 8 weeks of age.

Other lines of research, however, imply that edges and forms may be perceived by newborns under at least some circumstances. Slater and colleagues (Slater, Matock, & Brown, 1990) reported evidence for some degree of size and shape constancy in the first few days of life. Size constancy is the ability to perceive the physical size of an object despite changes in the object's projected size for an observer at different distances. Shape constancy in this context refers to the perceiver's ability to detect a constant planar (2D) shape despite variations in its 3D slant (e.g., perceiving a rectangle although its slant in depth produces a trapezoidal retinal projection). Size and planar shape constancy are discussed later in this chapter. Here we merely note that both seem to require some boundary perception abilities. It is hard to imagine any way to achieve constancy if the newborn's visual representation consists of an unintegrated collection of activations in independent frequency channels. More likely, higher stages of processing function to some degree to localize edges of objects.

Several observations suggest that early edge classification and boundary assignment capacities may depend selectively on a subset of information sources available to adults. For adults, surface quality differences such as luminance and spectral differences can specify object boundaries. As noted by Rubin (1915) in his classic studies of figure-ground organization, an area whose surround differs in luminance or spectral characteristics ordinarily appears as a bounded figure in front of a background surface. There is reason to believe that infants do *not* segregate objects using this information before about 9 months of age. Piaget (1954) noted that his son Laurent at 7 months reached for a box of matches when it was placed on the floor but not when it was placed on a book; instead he reached for the edges of the book. If the box slid on the book, Laurent reached for the box. This sort of observation led to three tentative conclusions:

1. A stationary object on a large extended surface (a floor or table) may be segregated from the background.
2. A stationary object adjacent to another stationary object will not be segregated by surface quality differences.
3. Two objects can be segregated by relative motion.

Subsequent experimental work has supported Piaget's interpretations. Spelke, Breinlinger, Jacobson, and Phillips (1993) tested infants' responses to adjacent object displays. *Homogeneous* displays had parts with identical luminance, color, and texture, and the parts' boundaries were continuous at their intersection points. *Heterogenous* displays had two adjacent parts differing in luminance and color, and also had discontinuities (T junctions) at the intersection points. After familiarization with a display, infants viewed two test events. In one, both parts moved together, whereas in the other only the top part moved, detaching from the other part. If the original display had been perceived as two separate objects, infants were expected to look longer at the event in which the whole display moved as a unit. If the two parts had been perceived as connected, infants were expected to look longer at the detachment event. Three-month-old infants showed this latter result, suggesting they had perceived both the homogeneous and heterogeneous displays as connected. Ambiguous results were found with 5- and 9-month-olds; infants looked longer at the detachment event for the homogeneous display, but when the heterogeneous display moved as one piece, they did not show a novelty effect. Similarly, Needham (1999) showed that 4-month-olds did not respond to differences in surface features for segregating static objects.

These conclusions are consistent with earlier research. Von Hofsten and Spelke (1985) used infants' reaching behavior to address perceived unity. Displays were designed to approximate closely the situations considered by Piaget. Spatial and motion relationships were varied among a small, near object, a larger, further object, and an extended background surface. It was as-

sumed that reaches would be directed to perceived boundaries of graspable objects. When the whole array was stationary and the objects were adjacent, greater reaching was observed to the edges of the larger, further object. Separation of the two objects in depth led infants to reach more for the nearer, smaller object. When the larger object moved while the smaller object did not, reaching was directed more toward the smaller object. This result suggested that motion segregated the objects rather than merely attracted reaching, because infants reached more to the stationary object. From these results, it appears that discontinuities in motion or depth segregate objects, whereas luminance discontinuities and overall shape variables do not. These results make sense in that motion and depth indicate object boundaries with greater ecological validity than luminance or spectral variations alone (Kellman, 1995; von Hofsten & Spelke, 1985). That is, ambiguous or misleading cases are less likely to arise with motion or depth discontinuities.

### Detection and Classification of Contour Junctions

Detecting and classifying contour junctions is important for many aspects of object perception. Many models of object perception and recognition, as well as other aspects of perceptual organization, include contour junctions as important sources of information (e.g., Heitger, Rosenthaler, von der Heydt, Peterhans, & Kubler, 1992; Hummel & Biederman, 1992; Kellman & Shipley, 1991). Junctions are important in unit formation, both in segmenting objects from their backgrounds and in triggering contour interpolation processes (e.g., Heitger et al., 1992; Kellman & Shipley, 1991) and in encoding object representations for recognition (Barrow & Tenenbaum, 1986; Hummel & Biederman, 1992; Waltz, 1975). Beyond mere detection, classification of junction type is important (see Figure 3.5). As mentioned, a T junction in an interposition display indicates where one contour intersects another contour, thus allowing for the separation of the two surfaces in depth (Waltz, 1975; Winston, 1992). Line junctions can also play a role in specifying the three-dimensional shape of an object. For example, "Y" and "arrow" junctions specify the three-dimensional structure and orientation of objects.

Until recently, not much was known about the development of sensitivity to contour junctions. Studies on interposition suggest that by 7 months of age, infants are responsive to T junctions. In addition, Yonas and Arter-berry (1994) showed that 7.5-month-olds distinguish be-tween lines in two-dimensional drawings that represent edge contours (arrow and Y junctions) and lines that represent surface markings, an important first step in using line junction information for perceiving spatial structure. More recently, Bhatt and Bertin (2001) found evidence that 3-month-olds are sensitive to line junction cues that signal three-dimensional structure and orienta-tion information to adults. Whether infants perceive the three-dimensional structure has not been directly tested but would be a good question for future investigation.

## Boundary Assignment

The question of boundary assignment applies to per-haps the most important subcategory of edges—oc-cluding edges. These are contours that mark the end of an object or surface. As has been known for a long time (Koffka, 1935), most such edges are "one-sided," in that the contour marks the edge of an object on one side but on the other, some surface continues behind. Boundary assignment involves the question of which way such edges bound. Some of the same considera-tions we raised regarding edge classification apply to boundary assignment. Evidence that infants distinguish shapes, or figures from grounds, might indicate that boundary assignment is occurring. It is problematic, however, to prove that infants perceive shape rather than a hole. These two possibilities differ in terms of the direction of boundary assignment.

We noted that early shape constancy seems to presup-pose boundary assignment. If this inference is correct, the relevant information probably comes from disconti-nuities in depth at object edges. Boundary assignment from depth discontinuities follows the straightforward rule that the nearer surface owns the boundary. Another source of boundary assignment information is accre-tion/deletion of texture. When one surface moves rela-tive to a more distant surface, texture elements on the latter surface go out of sight at the leading edge of the nearer object and come into sight at the trailing edge. This information constitutes a powerful source of boundary information, depth order, and shape in adult perception (Andersen & Cortese, 1988; J. Gibson et al., 1969; Shipley & Kellman, 1994). Infants as young as 3 and 5 months of age respond to accretion and deletion of texture to perceive object shape and depth, respectively,

suggesting perception of both depth order and boundary ownership (Granrud, Yonas, et al., 1985; Kaufmann-Hayoz, Kaufmann, & Stucki, 1986).

Other behavior suggests appropriate detection of ob-ject boundaries in younger infants. When an object ap-proaches an infant, certain defensive responses often occur, including withdrawal of the head and blinking, as discussed earlier. The importance of boundary assign-ment for this ability was tested by Carroll and Gibson (1981). They presented 3-month-old-infants with arrays in which all surfaces were covered with random dot texture. Using accretion/deletion of texture, an ap-proaching object was specified in one condition and an approaching aperture (opening in the surface) was spec-ified by the information in the other condition. Infants appeared to use the information: They responded defen-sively more often to approaching objects than to ap-proaching apertures.

## Perception of Object Unity

Processes of edge detection, classification, and bound-ary assignment parse the optic array into significant pieces and reveal some of the boundaries of objects, but they do not yield representations corresponding to phys-ical objects. Together, they may feed into a representa-tion of distinct visible areas along with the labeling of which way contours dividing these areas bound (Kellman, 2003; Palmer & Rock, 1994). As mentioned earlier, the difference between such representations and perceived objects is that objects may unify multiple vis-ible areas. How can the visual system move from visible pieces to complete objects when some parts of objects are partly hidden? This is the question of per-ceiving object unity, or unit formation. It involves prob-lems of spatial occlusion as a 3D world is projected onto 2D receptive surfaces and also changes in the optic pro-jections over time as the observer or objects move.

### Multiple Processes in Unity Perception

Research suggests several kinds of information lead to perceived unity. One is the common motion process ("common fate") first described by Wertheimer (1923/1958): Things that move together are seen as con-nected. Some more rigorous definition of "move to-gether" is needed, of course. The class of rigid motions as defined in projective geometry, as well as some non-rigid motion correspondences, can evoke perception of unity in human adults (Johansson, 1970, 1975). The common motion process does not depend on relationships between oriented edges and for that reason has been called the *edge-insensitive process* (Kellman & Shipley, 1991).

The other process depends on continuity in edge relationships. Related to the Gestalt principle of good continuation (Wertheimer, 1923/1958), it has been termed the *edge-sensitive process*. Whereas good continuation applies to the breakup of fully visible arrays into parts, perception of unity across gaps in the input depends on particular relationships of oriented edges. Specifically, they appear to be governed by a mathematical criterion of *relatability* (Kellman, Garrigan, & Shipley, 2005; Kellman & Shipley, 1991). Informally, relatability characterizes boundary completions as smooth (differentiable at least once) and monotonic (singly inflected). Figure 3.6 gives some examples of relatable and nonrelatable edges. These are illustrated both in occlusion cases and in illusory figure cases (in which completed surfaces appear in front of other surfaces, rather than behind). Research suggests that interpolation of contours in occluded and illusory contexts depend on common mechanisms (Kellman et al., 2005; Kellman, Yin, & Shipley, 1998; Ringach & Shapley, 1996). Complementing the contour interpolation process is a surface interpolation process. Correspondences in surface quality (e.g., lightness and color) can also unify visible areas (Grossberg & Mingolla, 1985; Kellman & Shipley, 1991; Yin, Kellman, & Shipley, 1997, 2000).

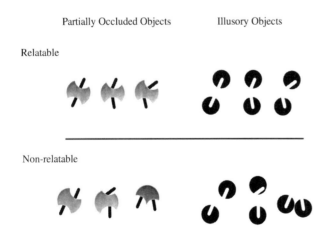

**Figure 3.6** Relatable and nonrelatable edges. Connections (occluded surfaces or illusory surfaces between the two visible bars) are seen in the relatable displays, but not in the nonrelatable ones.

How does unit formation develop? We consider these several information sources in attempting to answer that question.

### The Edge-Insensitive Process: Common Motion

Evidence suggests that the edge-insensitive (common motion) process appears earliest in development. Infants' perception of partly occluded objects can be assessed using generalization of habituation (Kellman & Spelke, 1983). If two visible parts whose possible connection is occluded are perceived as connected, then after habituation of visual attention to such a display, infants should look less to an unoccluded complete object (because it is familiar) and more to an unoccluded display containing unoccluded, separate pieces (because it is novel).

In a series of studies of 16-week-old infants, Kellman and Spelke (1983) found evidence that common motion of two object parts, visible above and below an occluding object, led to infants' perception of unity. After habituation to such a display, infants attend more to a moving "broken" display—two parts separated by a visible gap—than to a moving complete display. This outcome occurs no matter whether the two visible parts are similar in orientation, color, and texture. Initial studies used a common lateral translation (horizontal motion, perpendicular to the line of sight), but later research indicated that vertical translation and translation in depth also specify object unity at 16 weeks (Kellman, Spelke, & Short, 1986). Translation in depth is especially informative about the underlying perceptual process, because its stimulus correlates are much different from the other translations. Whereas translation in the plane (a plane perpendicular to the line of sight) is given in terms of image displacements at the retina or pursuit eye movements to cancel such displacements, translation in depth is specified by optical expansion or contraction in the object's projection or by changes in convergent eye movements as the object moves. The use of stimuli that specify object translation in space suggests that infants' unity perception depends on registered object motion, not on a particular stimulus variable.

The class of motion relationships effective early in life does not appear to encompass the full range of rigid motions as defined mathematically. Rigid motions include all object displacements in 3D space that preserve 3D distances among object points. After habituation to a rotation display in which two visible parts rotate around the line of sight, 16-week-olds generalized habituation equally to rotating complete and broken displays (Eizenman & Bertenthal, 1998; Kellman & Short, 1987b). Eizenman and Bertenthal (1998) found that 6-month-olds perceived a rotating rod as complete only if it underwent a complete rotation (360 degrees) as opposed to merely oscillated (90-degree rotation with reversal of direction). It appears that infants' unity perception is governed by a subset of rigid motions.

Further research revealed that perception of object unity is dependent on perceived object motion, not merely retinal motion (Kellman, Gleitman, & Spelke, 1987). Most experiments on motion relationships in unity perception have used stationary observers and moving objects. Many theorists have observed that certain optical consequences of motion may be duplicated when a moving observer looks at a stationary object (Helmholtz, 1885/1925; James, 1890). The retinal displacement of a laterally moving object, for example, may be duplicated by an observer's head or body movement while a stationary object is in the observer's visual field. This similarity raises a crucial question about the role of motion in object unity: Does perceived unity depend on actual object motion or on certain optical events, such as image displacement, that may be caused by either observer motion or object motion?

Embedded in this question is another one, at least as fundamental. Can infants tell the difference between optical changes caused by their own motion and those caused by the motions of objects? Recall this ability is called position constancy: perceiving the unchanging positions of objects in the world despite one's own motion. Kellman et al. (1987) took up these questions in a study of 16-week-olds. In each of two conditions, the infant's chair moved in a wide arc around a point between the observer and occlusion displays in front. In one condition (conjoint motion), the moving chair and a partly occluded object were rigidly connected underneath the display table, so that they both rotated around a point in between. In this condition, the object's motion was real; however, there was no subject-relative displacement. Thus, no eye or head movements were required to maintain fixation on the object. If perceiving the unity of this partly occluded display depends on real object motion, infants were expected to perceive unity in this condition. In the other condition (observer movement) the observer's chair moved in the same way, but the partly occluded object remained stationary. If optical displacement caused by observer motion can specify unity, infants were expected to perceive a complete object in this

condition. As in earlier research, dishabituation patterns to unoccluded complete and broken displays after habituation were used to assess perception of unity, and the test displays in each condition had the same motion characteristics as in habituation.

Results indicated that only the infants in the conjoint-motion condition perceived the unity of the partly occluded object. Analyses based on looking-time differences suggested that infants in the conjoint-motion condition perceived object motion during their own motion, whereas observer-movement infants responded as if they perceived the occlusion display as stationary. These results suggest that the common motion or edge-insensitive process depends on perceived object motion. The outcome makes sense ecologically, in that rigid relationships in truly moving visible parts are highly unlikely to occur unless the parts are actually connected. For optical displacements caused by movement of the observer, areas at similar distances from the observer will share similar displacements, yet it is hardly the case that all objects near each other are connected.

What are the origins of the edge-insensitive process? From findings that the motion relationships specify object unity to infants before they actively manipulate objects or crawl through the environment, Kellman and Spelke (1983) hypothesized that perceiving unity from motion is accomplished by innate mechanisms. The hypothesis also reflects the ecological importance of common motion information. Coherent motion is closely tied to the very notion of an object (Spelke, 1985), and common motion of visible areas has very high ecological validity as a signifier of object unity (Kellman, 1993).

The basis of unity perception in innate or early maturing mechanisms is consistent with more recent studies showing perception of unity by 2-month-old infants under conditions in which the block occluded less of the rod than in traditional displays (Johnson & Aslin, 1995, 1996; Johnson & Nanez, 1995). Also, it has been found that the ability to perceive unity of partly occluded objects from common motion is innate in chicks (Lea, Slater, & Ryan, 1996).

Studies of human newborns, however, have not found evidence for perceived unity from common motion. Slater and his colleagues have shown a consistent preference for the complete rod following habituation to moving rod-block displays (Slater, Johnson, Brown, & Badenoch, 1996; Slater, Johnson, Kellman, & Spelke, 1994; Slater, Morison, Somers, Mattock, Brown, & Taylor, 1990). This finding suggests that newborn infants perceived the rod as broken during the habituation phase, even though the size of the rod and depth separation of the rod and block was increased compared with that used with 4-month-olds (Slater, Johnson, Kellman, & Spelke, 1994) and when the block height was reduced and texture was added to the background to increase the available information specifying the depth relations (Slater, Johnson, Brown, & Badenoch, 1996). The implication of these findings is that newborns make their perceptual judgments based on the visible parts of the displays, and they cannot make judgments about the parts of the visual array that are occluded.

Using a somewhat different stimulus, Kawabata, Gyoba, Inoue, and Ohtsubo (1999) have found at least one condition in which 3-week-old infants perceive a partly occluded region as complete. Instead of using the traditional rod-block display, they presented infants with drifting sine-wave gratings that were occluded by either a narrow or broad (wide) central occluder. When the spatial frequency of the grating was low (.04 cycles per degree [cpd] of visual angle; that is, the black and white bars were thick) and the occluder was narrow (1.33 degrees, LN in Figure 3.7) infants looked significantly longer at the broken test display (SG). This finding suggests that they perceived the low frequency

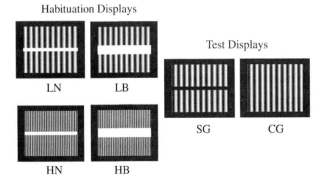

**Habituation Displays**

LN  LB

**Test Displays**

SG  CG

HN  HB

**Figure 3.7**  Habituation and test displays to test 3-week-old infants' perception of unity. LN refers to the low-spatial frequency display behind a narrow occluder. LB refers to low-spatial frequency display behind a broad occluder. HN refers to a high-spatial frequency display behind a narrow occluder. HB refers to high-spatial frequency display behind a broad occluder. SG refers to "separate grating" (analogous to a broken rod). CG refers to "complete grating" (analogous to a complete rod). *Source:* "Visual Completion of Partly Occluded Grating in Young Infants under 1 Month of Age," by H. Kawabata, J. Gyoba, H. Inoue, and H. Ohtsubo, 1999, *Vision Research, 39*, pp. 3586–3591. Reprinted with permission.

grating as continuing behind the narrow occluder. In contrast, when the spatial frequency was high (1.2 cpd; the black and white bars were narrow) and the occluder was broad (4.17 degrees; HB in Figure 3.7), 3-week-olds looked significantly longer at a complete grating (CG) as opposed to a broken grating (SG). This finding suggests that they perceived the high spatial frequency grating as two separate regions. Further manipulations revealed that there is an interaction between spatial frequency and occluder width. Infants looked equally to the two test gratings when they viewed a high spatial frequency grating behind a narrow occluder (HN in Figure 3.7) and when they viewed a low spatial frequency grating with a broad occluder (LB in Figure 3.7). In both of these conditions, infants provided ambiguous results regarding whether they perceived the gratings as complete or broken.

These several findings permit at least two explanations. One is that the use of common motion to specify object unity arises by learning between 3 and 8 weeks of life. This account would fit with classical empiricist notions about the starting point of perceptual development: Infants may see visible patches but may have to construct whole objects. One problem with this account is the learning mechanism. Both the findings of Kawabata et al. (1999) at 3 weeks and several researchers at 8 weeks are inconsistent with any of the traditionally proposed means by which infants might learn about objects, namely association of visual impressions with touch (e.g., Berkeley, 1709/1963) or with self-initiated action (e.g., Piaget, 1954). Infants at these early ages do not walk, crawl, or even perform directed reaching. One can imagine, however, purely visual forms of learning. Two parts of an object seen at one time may emerge from behind an occluder, allowing learning of the rule about common motion. This account, while imaginable, would have as its primary virtue minimizing what must be attributed to innate or rapidly maturing capacities. Paradoxically, as Kellman and Arterberry (1998) noted, this account places a heavy burden on innate concepts of physics. To unlearn an incorrect perceptual rule (two moving visible pieces are not connected) through later images, the child must be constrained by an assumption that it is impossible (or unlikely) for two pieces to have been separate and subsequently to have merged.

A more plausible account of these findings is that infant unity perception from common motion depends on sensory capacities that are maturing in the first 8 weeks of life. Common motion may well be an unlearned principle of object perception, but using it requires accurate mapping of the direction and velocities of separated, moving regions of the visual field. The preference for a complete rod after habituation in newborns may arise from their ability to see motion (allowing segmentation of visible regions) but with poor direction and/or velocity sensitivity. Recall our earlier consideration of the emergence of directional sensitivity in infant motion perception. Programmatic work by Wattam-Bell (1991, 1992, 1996a, 1996b) addressed the emergence of directional sensitivity and velocity perception in infants. Using both behavioral and electrophysiological techniques, Wattam-Bell found no reliable visual evoked potential (VEP) to reversals of motion direction until about 74 days of age. Behavioral discriminations of coherent from random motion in random dot displays showed no evidence of this discrimination in 1-month-olds with either visual preference or habituation methods (Wattam-Bell, 1996a, 1996b). This discrimination was found to be robust at 15 weeks and weakly present at 8 weeks of age.

Connecting these two lines of research, it appears that perception of unity from common motion in humans is found at the same age that reliable discrimination of motion direction is first observed. This account fits with the variation found with stimulus variables (e.g., Kawabata et al., 1999), as directional selectivity is improving steadily through the period studied. It may not be a coincidence that the earliest use of common motion was found in studies using multiple, moving, oriented edges. Developing abilities to detect motion direction may have been better engaged by such displays.

In the absence of accurate encoding of motion direction, it is not surprising that unity based on common motion is not found in the human newborn. The evidence of how motion sensitivity develops is hard to reconcile with a learning account of common motion as a determinant of perceived unity. Based on available evidence, directional sensitivity and perceived unity appear at about the same time. Whereas unit formation from common motion with the standard kinds of stimuli appears around 8 weeks, the first discernible VEP to motion direction was reported at 74 days of age (Wattam-Bell, 1992). In short, in addition to the question of what kind of learning process could generate unity perception at this age, there is no discernible interval during which learning might occur. Available evidence is consistent

with the idea that perception of unity from common motion is unlearned, awaiting only the development of mechanisms of direction sensitivity in the infant's visual system.

### The Edge-Sensitive Process: Unity Based on Edge Orientations and Relations

Whereas the edge-insensitive process is dependent only on motion relationships, the edge-sensitive process involves completion based on spatial orientations and relations of edges. These relations can be revealed in a static display or dynamically, over time, as when an observer views a scene through shrubbery (Palmer, Kellman, & Shipley, 2004). Thus the edge-sensitive process includes object completion in stationary arrays as well as in dynamic ones where edge relationships are crucial, such as kinetic occlusion and kinetic illusory contours (Kellman & Cohen, 1984).

Most work with infants on the edge-sensitive process has involved static displays. In contrast to the perception of unity from common motion, unity from edge relationships in static displays does not appear during the first half year of life (Kellman & Spelke, 1983; Slater, Morison, et al., 1990). The typical result is that after habituation to a stationary, partly occluded display, infants show equal looking to the complete and broken test displays. Based on evidence that infants do encode the visible areas and are sensitive to occlusion (Kellman & Spelke, 1983), this pattern has been interpreted as indicating the perceiver's neutrality about what happens behind the occluder.

By 6.5 months, infants perceive partly occluded objects as complete in the absence of kinematic information, thus relying on static information. Craton (1996) found that 6.5-month-olds perceived a static rectangle as unified when a bar occluded its center. However, infants at this age provided no evidence of perceiving the shape of the occluded region. When the removal of the occluder revealed a cross instead of a rectangle (the horizontal piece of the cross had been completely hidden behind the occluder), infants younger than 8 months did not show looking patterns indicative of surprise. At 8 months of age, infants looked longer at the "cross event" than at the "complete object event," suggesting that before 8 months infants expected the partially occluded rectangle to be a single unit but were agnostic regarding its specific form. Even when motion is present, such as the case of a rectangle appearing out from either side of a central occluder, infants' perception of unity appears to precede their perception of form (van de Walle & Spelke, 1996). In this case, 5-month-olds perceived the rectangle as unified but showed no evidence of knowing the shape of the occluded parts. Converging evidence comes from studies of illusory contours, which appear to depend on the same underlying process (Kellman et al., 1998). Infants of 7 months, but not 5 months, appear to be sensitive to static and kinetic illusory contour displays (Bertenthal, Campos, & Haith, 1980; Kaufmann-Hayoz, Kaufmann, & Walther, 1988).

How does perceived unity from edge-sensitive process emerge? Maturation, learning, or some combination are possible explanations. Granrud and Yonas (1984) suggested that pictorial depth cues appearing around 7 months of age might depend on maturation of a perceptual module, a finding bolstered by evidence from macaque monkeys (Gunderson et al., 1993). It is possible that edge-sensitive unity perception might be connected to this emergence. It has been noted that the depth cue of interposition is closely related to boundary completion under occlusion (Kellman & Shipley, 1991). Another argument for maturational origins comes from work on the neurophysiology of the edge-sensitive process (von der Heydt, Peterhans, & Baumgartner, 1984). It appears that some edge-sensitive interpolation processes are carried out at very early stages of visual processing, certainly as early as V2 and possibly V1, the first visual cortical area (von der Heydt et al., 1984). Models of early visual filtering at these levels typically postulate operations carried out by dedicated neural machinery in parallel across much of the visual field. Although learning explanations for such circuitry can be imagined, the existence of early parallel operations that carry out interpolation is congenial to maturational accounts. Other considerations suggest that learning may play a role (e.g., Needham, 2001; see Cohen & Cashon, 2001b; Kellman, 2001; Quinn & Bhatt, 2001; Yonas, 2001 for related discussions). Of interest to potential learning accounts is recent work by Geisler and colleagues (Geisler, Perry, Super, & Gallogly, 2001). Their work in analyzing natural scenes suggests that the edge relationships described by contour relatability are highly diagnostic of visible edges that belong to unitary objects. Such ecological facts, of course, might be relevant to both evolutionary and learning accounts of the edge-sensitive process, but the relatively late onset of this ability at least makes it possible that experience

with an object's views under occlusion contributes to this ability.

## Perception of Three-Dimensional Form

Form is among the most important properties of an object because it is closely tied to its functional possibilities. Representations of form are also primary in triggering object recognition processes. Even when some other property of an object may be of greatest concern to us, we often locate and recognize the object by its form. There are many levels of form—local surface topography, the two-dimensional projection of an object seen from a stationary vantage point, and three-dimensional (3D) form, to name a few. Arguably, it is the 3D forms of objects that are most important in human cognition and behavior. Whereas the particular 2D projection from an object varies with the observer's position, the object's arrangement in 3D space does not. Perceiving the unchanging object given changing optical information constitutes the important ability of *shape constancy*. In addition to being of greatest significance among form concepts, 3D form also constitutes the greatest battleground in perceptual theory. Adults are versatile in their 3D form perception abilities, and each mode of perceiving naturally suggests a different account of the development of 3D form perception (Kellman, 1984). Adults can usually detect the overall form of an object from a single, stationary view. If the object is a familiar one, this ability is compatible with the idea that an object's 3D form is a collection of 2D views obtained from different vantage points, and any single view recalls the whole collection to mind (e.g., Mill, 1865). On this account, 3D form develops from associating experiences of different views, perhaps guided by activity in manipulating objects (Piaget, 1954).

Another way to get whole form from a single view is to apply general rules that extrapolate 3D form. Use of rules would explain how we might see 3D forms of unfamiliar objects from a single viewpoint. Gestalt psychologists argued for unlearned, organizational processes in the brain that serve this purpose. An alternative account of rules of organization was suggested by Helmholtz (1885/1925) and elaborated by Brunswik (1956). Perceptual rules might be abstracted from experiences with objects. These two accounts of perceptual rules that map 2D views into 3D objects make diametrically opposed developmental predictions. On the Helmholtz/Brunswik account, these rules must be learned laboriously through experiences in seeing objects from different viewpoints and manipulating them. On the Gestalt view, organizational processes should operate as soon as the underlying brain mechanisms are mature.

Several decades ago, a new and different analysis of 3D form perception emerged. Based on initial discoveries such as the *kinetic depth effect* (Wallach & O'Connell, 1953) and later programmatic research on *structure-from-motion* (e.g., Ullman, 1979), the idea is that perceived 3D form results from mechanisms specifically sensitive to optical transformations. Transformations in an object's optical projection over time, given by object or observer movement, are governed by projective geometry. These transformations provide information that can specify the 3D structure of an object. Several theorists have proposed that human perceivers extract this kind of information using neural mechanisms specially evolved for this purpose (J. Gibson, 1966; Johansson, 1970; Shepard, 1984). Such an arrangement makes sense for mobile organisms: The complexity and speed of human adult perception of structure from motion makes it seem unlikely that these abilities derive from general purpose mechanisms that encode motion properties and general purpose inference mechanisms that might have allowed relevant regularities to be discovered.

### Optical Transformations in Infant Form Perception

Research with human infants indicates that the most basic ability to perceive 3D form involves optical transformations. This dynamic information indicates 3D form as early as it has been tested, whereas other sources of information about form appear unusable by infants until well past the first half year.

A method to separate responses to 3D form from responses to particular 2D views was developed by Kellman (1984). When an object is rotated, its projection contains optical transformations over time, but it also might be registered as several discrete 2D snapshots. A way to separate 3D form from 2D views is to habituate infants to an object rotating around one axis and test for recognition of the object (by generalization of habituation) in a new axis of rotation. For a suitably asymmetrical object, each new axis of rotation provides a different set of 2D views, but providing there is some rotation in depth, each conveys information about the same 3D structure. A remaining problem is that dishabituation by

infants may occur for either a novel form or a novel rotation. To combat this problem, infants were habituated to two alternating axes of rotation on habituation trials and tested afterward with familiar and novel 3D objects in a third, new axis of rotation. This manipulation reduced novelty responding for a changed rotation axis in the test trials. Sixteen-week-old infants tested with videotaped displays showed the effects expected if 3D form was extracted from optical transformations. When habituated to one of two 3D objects, they generalized habituation to the same object in a new rotation and dishabituated to a novel object in the same new rotation axis. Two control groups tested whether dynamic information was the basis of response or whether generalization patterns might have come from 3D form perception based on single or multiple 2D views. In the two control groups, infants were shown sequential static views of the objects taken from the rotation sequences. Two numbers (6 and 24) of views were used along with two different durations (2 seconds and 1 second per view); in neither static view case, however, were continuous transformations available as in the dynamic condition. Results showed no hint of recognition of 3D form based on the static views, indicating that 3D form perception in the dynamic case was based on optical transformations.

Later research showed that this result occurs at 16 weeks with moving wire frame objects having no surface shading information, a finding that implicates the importance of projective transformations of edges. Moreover, 3D form perception occurs when infants are moved around stationary objects (Kellman & Short, 1987a), indicating that projective transformations, not object motions per se, provide the relevant information. By 8 weeks, infants perceive 3D form in kinetic random dot displays in which the relative motions of the dots create surfaces and the edges between them (Arterberry & Yonas, 2000). Yonas et al. (1987a) showed that 3D form obtained from optical transformations could be recognized when form information was subsequently given stereoscopically. Paradoxically, transfer does not seem to occur in the other direction; that is, initial representations of 3D form do not seem to be obtained by infants from stereoscopic depth information in stationary viewing.

### Static Form Perception

Form perception from optical transformation appears to be a basic foundation of human perception. It appears early and depends on information of great complexity, suggesting the existence of neural mechanisms evolved to map changing 2D projections onto 3D object representations. Another reason for regarding dynamic information as fundamental is that other sources of form information do not seem to be usable in the early months of life. This picture of early form perception turns on its head the classical empiricist notion that psychologically an object's 3D form is a construction from stored collections of static views.

Earlier, we described two conditions in which sequences of static views evoked no representation of 3D form in 16-week-olds. This finding—inability to perceive 3D form from single or multiple static views—has appeared consistently in research using real objects or photographic slides, up to an age of 9 months (Kellman, 1984; Kellman & Short, 1987a; Ruff, 1978). The inability to extract 3D form from static views is perplexing given that adults ubiquitously develop 3D form representations from single or multiple static views of objects. The one situation in which infants show some 3D form perception from static viewing involves recognition of 3D forms that had previously been given kinematically (Owsley, 1983; Yonas et al., 1987a). Perhaps this task of detecting similarity to a previously obtained representation is simpler than developing a full 3D object representation initially by means of static, binocular views. Alternatively, it could be a more general limitation of developing representations based on static information. In studies of categorization, infants transfer information about object category from kinetic to static conditions but not vice versa (Arterberry & Bornstein, 2002).

### Nonrigid Unity and Form

Both the concept and process of 3D form perception are easiest to understand in the case of rigid objects whose forms do not change. Perception of rigid structure from motion is well understood computationally in terms of the projective geometry relating 3D structure, relative motion of object and observer, and transforming 2D optical projections at the eye. Many objects of ordinary experience, however, do not have rigid shape. In a moving person, a point on the wrist and one on the waist do not maintain a constant separation in 3D space. Nonrigidities may be given by joints, as in animals or people, but also by flexible substances, as in a pillow whose shape readily deforms. The possibility of perceiving or representing any useful information about shape for an object whose shape varies depends on the existence of constraints on the variation. A human body can assume many, but not unlimited, variations in shape; the class of possibilities is constrained by factors such as joints and musculature. A jellyfish may be even less constrained, but even it has a shape, defined as a constrained class of possibilities, and characteristic deformations that depend on its structure and composition. Some progress has been made in the analysis of nonrigid motion and processes that might allow us to perceive it (Bertenthal, 1993; Cutting, 1981; Hoffman & Flinchbaugh, 1982; Johansson, 1975; Webb & Aggarwal, 1982), but the problems are difficult.

Whereas scientists have not succeeded in discovering the rules for determining nonrigid unity and form, such rules appear to exist in the young infant's visual processing. In work with adult perceivers, Johansson (1950, 1975) pioneered methods for testing form and event perception from motion relationships alone. His use of moving points of light in a dark surround, in the absence of any visible surfaces, has become the method of choice in structure from motion research. When such lights are attached to the major joints of a walking person, adult observers viewing the motion sequence immediately and effortlessly perceive the lights as forming a connected walking person. Turning such a display upside down eliminates recognition of a human form (Sumi, 1984).

Studies of the development of perception of nonrigid unity and form have been carried out by Bertenthal, Proffitt and their colleagues (Bertenthal, 1993; Bertenthal, Proffitt, & Cutting, 1984; Bertenthal, Proffitt, & Kramer, 1987; Bertenthal, Proffitt, Kramer, & Spetner, 1987). A basic finding is that when infants of 3 to 5 months are habituated to films of an upright walking person, specified by light points, they subsequently dishabituate to an inverted display. This result suggests some level of perceptual organization, rather than apprehension of the displays as containing meaningless, individual points. The younger infants (at 3 months) may not perceive a person walking, however. Some later experiments used phase shifting of the lights to disrupt the impression of a walking person. Three-month-olds discriminated phase-shifted from normal walker displays whether the displays were presented in an upright or inverted orientation (Bertenthal & Davis, 1988), and they appear to process the absolute and relative motions within a single limb (Booth, Pinto, & Bertenthal, 2002). Both 5- and 7-month-olds, in contrast, showed poorer discrimination with inverted than with upright displays, and 5-month-olds perceive relations among limbs in walkers and runners (Booth et al., 2002). One interpretation of these findings is that older infants, like adults, perceive only the upright, normal phase displays as a walking person, so that disruption of the phase relations is salient for these displays. Because inverted displays are not perceived as people, phase disruption is not so noticeable. On this line of reasoning, 3-month-olds show perceptual organization of the displays but not classification of the upright displays as a walking person (*biomechanical motion*). The younger infants are thus sensitive to differences in upright or inverted displays.

Although a more direct measure of perception of a walking person has been difficult to devise, the findings suggest the attunement of the infant's visual system to certain nonrigid motion relationships. The basic sensitivity that allows detection and encoding of motion relations may begin much earlier than the point at which recognition performance is measurable. Preferences for motion patterns generated by a walking person or a hand opening and closing have been demonstrated in 2-month-olds (Fox & McDaniel, 1982).

### Conclusions Regarding Form Perception

Earliest competence to perceive 3D form depends on mechanisms that recover object structure from optical transformations. These abilities are present before abilities to extrapolate 3D structure from single views of objects and also before the maturation of self-locomotion and directed reaching. Both rigid and nonrigid motion relationships provide structural information to young perceivers. What we know about early 3D form perception fits the conjecture of ecological views that perception of structure from motion depends on dedicated perceptual machinery developed over evolutionary time (J. Gibson, 1966, 1979; Johansson, 1970; Shepard, 1984).

## Perception of Size

An object of constant real size projects a larger image on the retina when it is close to the observer than when it is farther away. Perception of constant physical size can be achieved by running this geometry in reverse: From the projective size at the eye and information about distance, the physical size of the object can be perceived (Holway & Boring, 1941). In some situations, relational variables may allow more direct perception of size, such as the amount of ground surface covered by an object in

a situation where the surface has regular or stochastically regular texture (J. Gibson, 1950).

Among the most exciting developments in infant perception research has been the emerging conclusion that some degree of size constancy—the ability to perceive the correct physical size of an object despite changes in viewing distance (and resulting changes in projective size)—is an innate ability of human perceivers. Early research suggested that infants of about 4 months of age perceive an object's constant physical size at different distances and show a novelty response to a different-sized object, even when the novel object has a projective size similar to the previously seen object (Day & McKenzie, 1981). Studies of newborns have provided evidence that size constancy may be present from birth. Slater, Mattock, et al. (1990) tested visual preferences for pairs of identically shaped cubes of two real sizes (5.1 cm or 10.2 cm) at different distances (23 to 69 cm). Infants preferred the object of larger retinal (projective) size whenever it differed between the two displays. In a second experiment, infants were familiarized with either a large or small cube of constant physical size that appeared at different distances (and varying projective sizes) across trials in the familiarization period. After familiarization, infants were given a paired-preference test between the large and small cube on each of two test trials. For the test trials, the large and small cubes were placed at distances giving them equal projective sizes. This projective size was novel, that is, the cube that had been presented in familiarization was placed at a distance at which it had not appeared earlier (61 cm away for the 10.2 cm cube and 30.5 cm away for the 5.1 cm cube). Figure 3.8 illustrates the arrangements in familiarization and test conditions. Every infant ($n = 12$) looked longer at the object of novel physical size in the test trials, and the percentage of test trial looking allocated to the novel object was about 84%. Other evidence tends to support the conclusion that size constancy is observable in neonates (Granrud, 1987; Slater & Morison, 1985).

Research on newborn size perception has not addressed directly the possible mechanism(s) underlying constancy. This topic would seem to be an important one for future research. There are not many possibilities, however. The objects in both the Slater et al. (1985) and Granrud (1987) experiments hung in front of homogeneous backgrounds, precluding use of relational information potentially available when an object rests on a textured ground surface. In the situations used, it would faces as older infants do (Rubenstein, Kalakanis, & Langlois, 1999; Slater, Quinn, Hayes, & Brown, 2000; Slater et al., 1998). Newborns' recognition of their mothers may be based on external features such as hairline (Pascalis et al., 1995), but perception of attractiveness appears to rely on internal features and possibly their configuration (Bartrip, Morton, & de Schonen, 2001; Slater et al., 2000). The data on attractiveness suggest that infants must process the internal features of faces to a fine level of detail. At this time, we do not know how they do it, either in terms of specific face perception mechanisms or general capacities of the neonate visual system.

### Perceiving Information about People through Faces

Beyond the newborn period, infants are sensitive to facial information that may be useful for recognizing specific people, perceiving characteristics of people, and for engaging in nonverbal communication. The ability to recognize a person across different views, or person constancy, is an important skill because faces (and people in general) are dynamic objects. Faces show differing expressions, and infants have the opportunity to view them from different perspectives. To recognize key people in their environment, infants must be able to perceive the constancy of a person despite proximal stimulus differences. One of the earliest studies of infants' perception of people across different views was conducted by Cohen and Strauss (1979). In this study, infants were habituated to views of the same female and then tested with an *enface* view. Infants did not recognize the *enface* view as the same person until 7 months of age. More recent studies have shown that babies may be able to recognize familiar faces (their mother but not a stranger) in different views, *enface*, but not in profile, as early as 1 month of age (Sai & Bushnell, 1988); and babies recognize faces across differing intensities of an emotional expression, namely smiling, at least by 5 months of age (Bornstein & Arterberry, 2003).

Infants have the opportunity to view faces in many perspectives, and certainly from angles different from those adults typically experience. Supine infants may often see faces oriented at 90 degrees or even completely upside down. For adults and older children, inversion of a face significantly disrupts recognition. This has been attributed to a processing strategy based on the relation between facial features ("configural" processing) as opposed to processing the facial features independent of each other ("featural" processing; e.g., Carey & Diamond, 1977, 1994; Sergent, 1984). If and when infants are susceptible to this inversion effect (reduced recognition of inverted faces) has generated interest because of its implications for how infants may be processing faces. Presenting stimuli upside down to infants has been a procedure used by some researchers as a control for responding to specific features within a face (e.g., Bahrick, Netto, & Hernandez-Reif, 1998; Kestenbaum & Nelson, 1990; Slater et al., 2000); however, few direct tests of the inversion effect have been conducted. Cashon and Cohen (Cashon & Cohen, 2004; Cohen & Cashon, 2001a) habituated infants to two female faces. They were tested with a familiar face (one of the two viewed in the habituation phase), a novel face, and a combination face that consisted of the internal features of one of the habituation faces and the external features of the other habituation face. For half of the infants, the faces were presented upright and for the other half the faces were inverted. Across 3 to 7 months of age, infants showed movement toward configural processing of upright faces, and this type of processing was clearly evident by 7 months of age (see Cohen & Cashon, Chapter 5, this *Handbook*, this volume, for a representation of these data). For inverted faces, at most of the ages tested, infants showed no evidence of configural processing. An unexpected result was the lack of a monotonic change between 3 and 7 months in configural processing, a finding Cashon and Cohen (2004) attribute to general information-processing strategies that are not necessarily specific to face perception (see Cohen & Cashon, Chapter 5, this *Handbook*, this volume).

In addition to recognizing particular faces, infants may use information contained in faces to categorize people into classes, such as male and female. Perception of gender by adults can be based on superficial cues, such as hair length, facial hair, and makeup or on structural cues, such as the distance between the eye and brow (e.g., Bruce et al., 1993; Campbell, Benson, Wallace, Doesbergh, & Coleman, 1999). Infants' perception of gender has been assessed in the context of categorization tasks; infants are shown either male or female faces and are tested with a novel face of the same gender and a novel face of the opposite gender. Using this procedure, Leinbach and Fagot (1993) showed that infants categorize gender by 9 months of age with the aid of superficial features (stereotyped hair length and clothing). However, their findings were asymmetrical. Infants habituated to male faces looked significantly longer to

Allen, D., Banks, M. S., & Schefrin, B. (1988). Chromatic discrimination in human infants. *Investigate Ophthalmology and Visual Science, 29*(Suppl.), 25.

Allen, D., Tyler, C. W., & Norcia, A. M. (1996). Development of grating acuity and contrast sensitivity in the central and peripheral visual field of the human infant. *Vision Research, 36,* 1945–1953.

Allen, J. (1978). *Visual acuity development in human infants up to 6 months of age.* Unpublished master's thesis, University of Washington, Seattle, WA.

Andersen, G. J., & Cortese, J. M. (1989). 2-D contour perception resulting from kinetic occlusion. *Perception and Psychophysics, 46*(1), 49–55.

Arterberry, M. E., & Bornstein, M. H. (2002). Infant perceptual and conceptual categorization: The roles of static and dynamic attributes. *Cognition, 86,* 1–24.

Arterberry, M. E., & Yonas, A. (2000). Perception of structure from motion by 8-week-old infants. *Perception and Psychophysics, 62,* 550–556.

Arterberry, M. E., Yonas, A., & Bensen, A. S. (1989). Self-produced locomotion and the development of responsiveness to linear perspective and texture gradients. *Developmental Psychology, 25*(6), 976–982.

Aslin, R. N. (1977). Development of binocular fixation in human infants. *Journal of Experimental Child Psychology, 23*(1), 133–150.

Aslin, R. N., & Shea, S. L. (1990). Velocity thresholds in human infants: Implications for the perception of motion. *Developmental Psychology, 26*(4), 589–598.

Atkinson, J., & Braddick, O. (1976). Stereoscopic discrimination in infants. *Perception, 5*(1), 29–38.

Atkinson, J., Braddick, O., & Moar, K. (1977). Development of contrast sensitivity over the first 3 months of life in the human infant. *Vision Research, 17,* 1037–1044.

Atkinson, J., Hood, B., & Wattam-Bell, J. (1988). Development of orientation discrimination in infancy. *Perception, 17,* 587–595.

Badcock, D. R. (1984). Spatial phase or luminance profile discrimination? *Visual Research, 24,* 613–623.

Badcock, D. R. (1990). Phase- or energy-based face discrimination: Some problems. *Journal of Experimental Psychology: Human Perception and Performance, 16*(1), 217–220.

Bahrick, L. E., Netto, D., & Hernandez-Reif, M. (1998). Intermodal perception of adult and child faces and voices by infants. *Child Development, 69,* 1263–1275.

Ball, W., & Tronick, E. (1971). Infant responses to impending collision: Optical and real. *Science, 171*(3973), 818–820.

Banks, M. S. (1980a). The development of visual accommodation during early infancy. *Child Development, 51,* 646–666.

Banks, M. S. (1980b). Infant refraction and accommodation: Their use in ophthalmic diagnosis. *International Ophthalmology Clinics, Electrophysiology and Psychophysics, 20,* 205–232.

Banks, M. S., & Bennett, P. J. (1988). Optical and photoreceptor immaturities limit the spatial and chromatic vision of human neonates. *Journal of the Optical Society of America, A5,* 2059–2079.

Banks, M. S., & Crowell, J. A. (Eds.). (1993). A re-examination of two analyses of front-end limitations to infant vision. In K. Simons (Ed.), *Early visual development: Normal and abnormal* (pp. 91–116). New York: Oxford University Press.

Banks, M. S., Geisler, W. S., & Bennett, P. J. (1987). The physical limits of grating visibility. *Visual Research, 27,* 1915–1924.

Banks, M. S., & Ginsburg, A. P. (1985). Early visual preferences: A review and a new theoretical treatment. In H. W. Reese (Ed.), *Advances in child development and behavior* (pp. 207–246). New York: Academic Press.

Banks, M. S., & Salapatek, P. (1978). Acuity and contrast sensitivity in 1-, 2-, and 3-month-old human infants. *Investigative Ophthalmology and Visual Science, 17,* 361–365.

Banks, M. S., & Salapatek, P. (1983). Infant visual perception. In M. M. Haith. & J. Campos (Eds.), *Handbook of child psychology: Biology and infancy* (pp. 435–572). New York: Wiley.

Banks, M. S., Sekuler, A. B., & Anderson, S. J. (1991). Peripheral spatial vision: Limits imposed by optics, photoreceptor properties, and receptor pooling. *Journal of the Optical Society of America, A8,* 1775–1787.

Banks, M. S., & Shannon, E. S. (1993). Spatial and chromatic vision efficiency in human neonates. In C. Granrud (Ed.), *Carnegie Mellon Symposium on Cognition* (Vol. 21, pp. 1–46). Hillsdale, NJ: Erlbaum.

Barrow, H. G., & Tenenbaum, J. M. (1986). Computational approaches to vision. In K. R. Boff & L. Kaufman (Eds.), *Handbook of perception and human performance: Vol. 2. Cognitive processes and performance* (pp. 1–70). Oxford, England: Wiley.

Bartrip, J., Morton, J., & de Schonen, S. (2001). Responses to mother's face in 3-week to 5-month-old infants. *British Journal of Developmental Psychology, 19,* 219–232.

Bednar, J. A., & Miikkulainen, R. (2003). Learning innate face preferences. *Neural Computation, 15,* 1525–1557.

Bennett, P. J., & Banks, M. S. (1987). Sensitivity loss among odd-symmetric mechanisms underlies phase anomalies in peripheral vision. *Nature, 326,* 873–876.

Berkeley, G. (1963). An essay towards a new theory of vision. In C. M. Turbayne (Ed.), *Works on vision.* Indianapolis, IN: Bobs-Merrill. (Original work published 1709)

Bertenthal, B. I. (1993). Infants' perception of biomechanical motions: Intrinsic image and knowledge-based constraints. In G. Carl (Ed.), *Carnegie Mellon Symposium on Cognition: Visual perception and cognition in infancy* (Vol. 21, pp. 175–214): Hillsdale, NJ: Erlbaum.

Bertenthal, B. I., Campos, J. J., & Haith, M. M. (1980). Development of visual organization: The perception of subjective contours. *Child Development, 51*(4), 1072–1080.

Bertenthal, B. I., & Davis, P. (1988, November). *Dynamic pattern analysis predicts recognition and discrimination of biomechanical motions.* Paper presented at the annual meeting of the Psychonomic Society, Chicago, IL.

Bertenthal, B. I., Proffitt, D. R., & Cutting, J. E. (1984). Infant sensitivity to figural coherence in biomechanical motions. *Journal of Experimental Child Psychology, 37*(2), 213–230.

Bertenthal, B. I., Proffitt, D. R., & Kramer, S. J. (1987). Perception of biomechanical motions by infants: Implementation of various processing constraints. The ontogenesis of perception [Special issue]. *Journal of Experimental Psychology: Human Perception and Performance, 13*(4), 577–585.

Bertenthal, B. I., Proffitt, D. R., Kramer, S. J., & Spetner, N. B. (1987). Infants' encoding of kinetic displays varying in relative coherence. *Developmental Psychology, 23*(2), 171–178.

Bhatt, R. S., & Bertin, E. (2001). Pictorial cues and three-dimensional information processing in early infancy. *Journal of Experimental Child Psychology, 80,* 315–332.

Bhatt, R. S., & Waters, S. E. (1998). Perception of three-dimensional cues in early infancy. *Journal of Experimental Child Psychology, 70,* 207–224.

Bieber, M. L., Knoblauch, K., & Werner, J. S. (1998). M- and l-cones in early infancy: Vol. 2. Action spectra at 8 weeks of age. *Vision Research, 38,* 1765–1773.

Birch, E. E., Gwiazda, J., & Held, R. (1982). Stereoacuity development for crossed and uncrossed disparities in human infants. *Vision Research, 22*(5), 507–513.

Bone, R. A., Landrum, J. T., Fernandez, L., & Martinez, S. L. (1988). Analysis of macular pigment by HPLC: Retinal distribution and age study. *Investigative Ophthalmology and Visual Science, 29,* 843–849.

Booth, A. E., Pinto, J., & Bertenthal, B. I. (2002). Perception of the symmetrical patterning of human gait by infants. *Developmental Psychology, 38,* 554–563.

Bornstein, M. H. (1975). Qualities of color vision in infancy. *Journal of Experimental Child Psychology, 19,* 401–409.

Bornstein, M. H., & Arterberry, M. E. (2003). Recognition, categorization, and apperception of the facial expression of smiling by 5-month-old infants. *Developmental Science, 6,* 585–599.

Bower, T. G., Broughton, J. M., & Moore, M. K. (1970). The coordination of visual and tactual input in infants. *Perception and Psychophysics, 8*(1), 51–53.

Braddick, O., Atkinson, J., French, J., & Howland, H. C. (1979). A photorefractive study of infant accommodation. *Vision Research, 19,* 1319–1330.

Braddick, O., Atkinson, J., & Wattam-Bell, J. R. (1986). Development of the discrimination of spatial phase in infancy. *Vision Research, 26*(8), 1223–1239.

Brown, A. M. (1990). Development of visual sensitivity to light and color vision in human infants: A critical review. *Vision Research, 30,* 1159–1188.

Brown, A. M. (1993). Intrinsic noise and infant visual performance. In K. Simons (Ed.), *Early visual development: Normal and abnormal* (pp. 178–196). New York: Oxford University Press.

Brown, A. M., Dobson, V., & Maier, J. (1987). Visual acuity of human infants at scotopic, mesopic, and photopic luminances. *Visual Research, 27,* 1845–1858.

Bruce, V., Burton, A. M., Hanna, E., Healey, P., Mason, O., Coombes, A., et al. (1993). Sex discrimination: How do we tell the difference between male and female faces? *Perception, 22,* 131–152.

Brunswik, E. (1956). *Perception and the representative design of psychological experiments.* Berkeley: University of California Press.

Bushnell, I. W. R. (2001). Mother's face recognition in newborn infants: Learning and memory. *Infant and Child Development, 10,* 67–74.

Bushnell, I. W. R., Sai, F., & Mullin, J. T. (1989). Neonatal recognition of the mother's face. *British Journal of Developmental Psychology, 7,* 3–15.

Campbell, R., Benson, P. J., Wallace, S. B., Doesbergh, S., & Coleman, M. (1999). More about brows: How poses that change brow position affect perceptions of gender. *Perception, 28,* 489–504.

Carey, S., & Diamond, R. (1977). From piecemeal to configurational representation of faces. *Science, 195,* 312–314.

Carey, S., & Diamond, R. (1994). Are faces perceived as configurations more by adults than by children? *Visual Cognition, 1,* 253–274.

Carroll, J. J., & Gibson, E. J. (1981, April). *Infants' differentiation of an aperature and an obstacle.* Paper presented at the meeting of the Society for Research in Child Development, Boston, MA.

Cashon, C. H., & Cohen, L. B. (2004). Beyond U-shaped development in infants' processing of faces: An information-processing account. *Journal of Cognition and Development, 5,* 59–80.

Chomsky, N. (1965). *Aspects of the theory of syntax.* Cambridge, MA: MIT Press.

Chomsky, N. (1980). *Rules and representations.* New York: Columbia University Press.

Chong, S. C. F., Werker, J. F., Russell, J. A., & Carroll, J. M. (2003). Three facial expressions mothers direct to their infants. *Infant and Child Development, 12,* 211–232.

Clavadetscher, J. E., Brown, A. M., Ankrum, C., & Teller, D. Y. (1998). Spectral sensitivity and chromatic discrimination in 3- and 7-week-old-infants. *Journal of the Optical Society of America, 5,* 2093–2105.

Cohen, L. B., & Cashon, C. H. (2001a). Do 7-month-old infants process independent features or facial configurations? *Infant and Child Development, 10,* 83–92.

Cohen, L. B., & Cashon, C. H. (2001b). Infant object segregation implies information integration. *Journal of Experimental Child Psychology, 78,* 75–83.

Cohen, L. B., & Strauss, M. S. (1979). Concept acquisition in the human infant. *Child Development, 50,* 419–424.

Cornsweet, T. (1970). *Visual perception.* New York: Academic Press.

Craton, L. G. (1996). The development of perceptual completion abilities: Infants' perception of stationary, partially occluded objects. *Child Development, 67,* 890–904.

Craton, L. G., & Yonas, A. (1988). Infants' sensitivity to boundary flow information for depth at an edge. *Child Development, 59*(6), 1522–1529.

Craton, L. G., & Yonas, A. (1990). The role of motion in infants' perception of occlusion. In T. E. James (Ed.), *The development of attention: Research and theory* (pp. 21–46). Amsterdam: North Holland.

Crognale, M. A., Kelly, J. P., Weiss, A. H., & Teller, D. Y. (1998). Development of spatio-chromatic Visual Evoked Potential (VEP): A longitudinal study. *Vision Research, 38,* 3283–3292.

Cutting, J. E. (1981). Coding theory adapted to gait perception. *Journal of Experimental Psychology: Human Perception and Performance, 7*(1), 71–87.

Dannemiller, J. L., & Freedland, R. L. (1989). The detection of slow stimulus movement in 2- to 5-month-olds. *Journal of Experimental Child Psychology, 47*(3), 337–355.

Dannemiller, J. L., & Freedland, R. L. (1991). Speed discrimination in 20-week-old infants. *Infant Behavior and Development, 14,* 163–173.

Danemiller, J. L., & Stephens, B. R. (1988). A critical test of infant pattern preference models. *Child Development, 59,* 210–216.

Darwin, C. (1965). *The expression of emotions in man and animals.* Chicago: University of Chicago Press. (Original work published 1872)

Day, R. H., & McKenzie, B. E. (1981). Infant perception of the invariant size of approaching and receding objects. *Developmental Psychology, 17*(5), 670–677.

de Haan, M., Pascalis, O., & Johnson, M. H. (2002). Specialization of neural mechanisms underlying face recognition in human infants. *Journal of Cognitive Neuroscience, 14,* 199–209.

Deruelle, C., & de Schonen, S. (1991). Hemispheric asymmetries in visual pattern processing in infancy. *Brain and Cognition, 16,* 151–179.

Dobkins, K. R., & Anderson, C. M. (2002). Color-based motion processing is stronger in infants than in adults. *Psychological Science, 13,* 76–80.

Dobkins, K. R., Anderson, C. M., & Kelly, J. (2001). Development of psychophysically-derived detection contours in L- and M-cone contrast space. *Vision Research, 41,* 1791–1807.

Dobkins, K. R., Lia, B., & Teller, D. Y. (1997). Infant color vision: Temporal contrast sensitivity functions for chromatic (red/green) stimuli in 3-month-olds. *Vision Research, 37,* 2699–2716.

Dobson, V. (1976). Spectral sensitivity of the 2-month-old infant as measured by the visual evoked cortical potential. *Vision Research, 16,* 367–374.

Duncker, K. (1929). Ueber induzierte bewegung. *Psychologische Forschung, 22,*180–259.

Easterbrook, M. A., Kisilevsky, B. S., Muir, D. W., & Laplante, D. P. (1999). Newborns discriminate schematic faces from scrambled faces. *Canadian Journal of Experimental Psychology, 53,* 231–241.

Eizenman, D. R., & Bertenthal, B. I. (1998). Infants' perception of object unity in translating and rotating displays. *Developmental Psychology, 34,* 426–434.

Elman, J. L., Bates, E. A., Johnson, M. H., Karmiloff-Smith, A., Parisi, D., & Plunkett, K. (1996). *Rethinking innateness.* Cambridge, MA: MIT Press.

Fantz, R. L. (1961). The origin of form perception. *Scientific American, 204,* 66–72.

Fantz, R. L., Fagan, J. F., & Miranda, S. B. (1975). Early visual selectivity. In L. B. Cohen & P. Salapatek (Eds.), *Infant perception: From sensation to cognition* (pp. 249–345). New York: Academic Press.

Fantz, R. L., & Nevis, S. (1967). Pattern preferences and perceptual-cognitive development in early infancy. *Merrill-Palmer Quarterly, 13*(1), 77–108.

Fantz, R. L., Ordy, J. M., & Udelf, M. S. (1962). Maturation of pattern vision in infants during the first 6 months. *Journal of Comparative and Physiological Psychology, 55,* 907–917.

Fodor, J. A., & Pylyshyn, Z. W. (1981). How direct is visual perception? Some reflections on Gibson's "ecological approach." *Cognition, 9,* 139–196.

Fox, R., Aslin, R. N., Shea, S. L., & Dumais, S. T. (1980). Stereopsis in human infants. *Science, 207*(4428), 323–324.

Fox, R., & McDaniel, C. (1982). The perception of biological motion by human infants. *Science, 218*(4571), 486–487.

Freedland, R. L., & Dannemiller, J. L. (1987). Detection of stimulus motion in 5-month-old infants. The ontogenesis of perception [Special issue]. *Journal of Experimental Psychology: Human Perception and Performance, 13*(4), 566–576.

Gayl, I. E., Roberts, J. O., & Werner, J. S. (1983). Linear systems analysis of infant visual pattern preferences. *Journal of Experimental Child Psychology, 35,* 30–45.

Gauthier, I., & Nelson, C. A. (2001). The development of face expertise. *Current Opinion in Neurobiology, 11,* 219–224.

Geisler, W. S., Perry, J. S., Super, B. J., & Gallogly, D. P. (2001). Edge co-occurrence in natural images predicts contour grouping performance. *Vision Research, 41,* 711–724.

Geldart, S., Mondloch, C. J., Maurer, D., de Schonen, S., & Brent, H. (2002). The effect of early visual deprivation on the development of face processing. *Developmental Science, 5,* 490–501.

Gibson, E. J. (1969). *Principles of perceptual learning and development.* New York: Appleton-Century-Crofts.

Gibson, E. J. (1979). Perceptual development from the ecological approach. In M. Lamb, A. Brown, & B. Rogoff (Eds.), *Advances in developmental psychology* (Vol. 3, pp. 243–285). Hillsdale, NJ: Erlbaum.

Gibson, E. J., Gibson, J. J., Smith, O. W., & Flock, H. R. (1959). Motion parallax as a determinant of perceived depth. *Journal of Experimental Psychology, 58,* 40–51.

Gibson, J. (1950). *The perception of the visual world.* New York: Appleton-Century-Crofts.

Gibson, J. J. (1966). *The senses considered as perceptual systems.* Boston: Houghton Mifflin.

Gibson, J. J. (1979). *The ecological approach to visual perception.* Boston: Houghton Mifflin.

Gibson, J. J., Kaplan, G. A., Reynolds, H. N., Jr., & Wheeler, K. (1969). The change from visible to invisible: A study of optical transitions. *Perception and Psychophysics, 5*(2), 113–116.

Goren, C., Sarty, M., & Wu, P. (1975). Visual following and pattern discrimination of face-like stimuli by newborn infants. *Pediatrics, 56,* 544–549.

Gottschaldt, K. (1938). Gestalt factors and repetition. In W. D. Ellis (Ed.), *A sourcebook of Gestalt psychology.* London: Kegan Paul, Trech, Tubner. (Original work published 1926)

Granrud, C. E. (1986). Binocular vision and spatial perception in 4- and 5-month-old infants. *Journal of Experimental Psychology: Human Perception and Performance, 12,* 36–49.

Granrud, C. E. (1987). Size constancy in newborn human infants. *Investigative Ophthalmology and Visual Science, 28*(Suppl.), 5.

Granrud, C. E., Haake, R. J., & Yonas, A. (1985). Infants' sensitivity to familiar size: The effect of memory on spatial perception. *Perception and Psychophysics, 37*(5), 459–466.

Granrud, C. E., & Yonas, A. (1984). Infants' perception of pictorially specified interposition. *Journal of Experimental Child Psychology, 37*(3), 500–511.

Granrud, C. E., Yonas, A., Smith, I. M., Arterberry, M. E., Glicksman, M. L., & Sorknes, A. (1985). Infants' sensitivity to accretion and deletion of texture as information for depth at an edge. *Child Development, 55,* 1630–1636.

Green, D. G., & Campbell, F. W. (1965). Effect of focus on the visual response to a sinusoidally modulated spatial stimulus. *Journal of the Optical Society of America, 55,* 1154–1157.

Grossberg, S., & Mingolla, E. (1985). Neural dynamics of form perception: Boundary completion, illusory figures, and neon color spreading. *Psychological Review, 92,* 173–211.

Gunderson, V. M., Yonas, A., Sargent, P. L., & Grant-Webster, K. S. (1993). Infant macaque monkeys respond to pictorial depth. *Psychological Science, 4*(2), 93–98.

Hainline, L., Riddell, P., Grose-Fifer, J., & Abramov, I. (1992). Development of accommodation and convergence in infancy. Normal and abnormal visual development in infants and children [Special issue]. *Behavioural Brain Research, 49*(1), 33–50.

Haith, M. (1983). Spatially determined visual activity in early infancy. In A. Hein & M. Jeannerod (Eds.), *Spatially oriented behavior* (pp. 175–214). New York: Springer.

Hamer, D. R., Alexander, K. R., & Teller, D. Y. (1982). Rayleigh discriminations in young infants. *Vision Research, 22,* 575–587.

Haynes, H., White, B. L., & Held, R. (1965). Visual accommodation in human infants. *Science, 148,* 528–530.

Heitger, F., Rosenthaler, L., von der Heydt, R., Peterhans, E., & Kübler, O. (1992). Simulation of neural contour mechanisms: From simple to end-stopped cells. *Vision Research, 32,* 963–981.

Held, R. (1985). Binocular vision: Behavioral and neural development. In J. Mehler & R. Fox (Eds.), *Neonate cognition: Beyond the blooming buzzing confusion* (pp. 37–44). Hillsdale, NJ: Erlbaum.

Held, R. (1988). Normal visual development and its deviations. In G. Lennerstrand, G. K. von Noorden & E. C. Campos (Eds.), *Strabismus and ambyopia* (pp. 247–257). New York: Plenum Press.

Held, R. (1993). What can rates of development tell us about underlying mechanisms. In C. Granrud (Ed.), *Carnegie Mellon Symposium on Cognition: Visual perception and cognition in infancy* (Vol. 21, pp. 75–89). Hillsdale, NJ: Erlbaum.

Held, R., Birch, E. E., & Gwiazda, J. (1980). Stereoacuity of human infants. *Proceedings of the National Academy of Sciences, USA, 77,* 5572–5574.

Helmholtz, H. von (1925). *Treatise on physiological optics* (Vol. 3). New York: Optical Society of America. (Original work published 1885 in German)

Hendrickson, A. E. (1993). Morphological development of the primate retina. In K. Simons (Ed.), *Early visual development: Normal and abnormal* (pp. 287–295). New York: Oxford University Press.

Hering, E. (1861–1864). *Beitrage zur physiologie.* Leipzig, Germany: Engelmann.

Hickey, T. L., & Peduzzi, J. D. (1987). Structure and development of the visual system. In P. Salapatek & L. B. Cohen (Eds.), *Handbook of infant perception: From sensation to perception* (pp. 1–42). New York: Academic Press.

Hirano, S., Yamamoto, Y., Takayama, H., Sugata, Y., & Matsuo, K. (1979). Ultrasonic observations of eyes in premature babies: Pt. 6. Growth curves of ocular axial length and its components. *Acta Societais Ophthalmologicae Japonicae, 83,* 1679–1693.

Hobbes, T. (1974). *Leviathan.* Baltimore: Penguin. (Original work published 1651)

Hoffman, D. D., & Flinchbaugh, B. E. (1982). The interpretation of biological motion. *Biological Cybernetics, 42*(3).

Holway, A. H., & Boring, E. G. (1941). Determinants of apparent visual size with distance variant. *American Journal of Psychology, 54,* 21–37.

Howland, H. C. (1982). Infant eye: Optics and accommodation. *Current Eye Research, 2,* 217–224.

Hubel, D. H., & Wiesel, T. N. (1962). Receptive fields, binocular interaction, and functional architecture in the cat's visual cortex. *Journal of Physiology, London, 160,* 106–154.

Hubel, D. H., & Wiesel, T. N. (1970). Stereoscopic vision in macaque monkey: Cells sensitive to binocular depth in area 18 of the macaque monkey cortex. *Nature, 225,* 41–42.

Hume, D. (1999). *An enquiry concerning human understanding* (T. L. Beauchamp, Ed.). Oxford, England: Oxford University Press. (Original work published 1758)

Hummel, J. E., & Biederman, I. (1992). Dynamic binding in a neural network for shape recognition. *Psychological Review, 99,* 480–517.

Ittleson, W. H. (1951). Size as a cue to distance: Static localization. *American Journal of Psychology, 64,* 54–67.

Jacobs, D. S., & Blakemore, C. (1988). Factors limiting the postnatal development of visual acuity in the monkey. *Vision Research, 28,* 947–958.

James, W. (1890). *The principles of psychology.* New York: Henry Holt.

Johansson, G. (1950). *Configurations in event perception.* Uppsala, Sweden: Almqvist & Wiksells.

Johansson, G. (1970). On theories for visual space perception: A letter to Gibson. *Scandinavian Journal of Psychology, 11*(2), 67–74.

Johansson, G. (1975). Visual motion perception. *Scientific American, 232*(6), 76–88.

Johnson, M. H. (1997). *Developmental cognitive neuroscience.* Cambridge, MA: Blackwell Press.

Johnson, M. H., Dziurawiec, S., Ellis, H., & Morton, J. (1991). Newborn's preferential tracking of face-like stimuli and its subsequent decline. *Cognition, 40,* 1–19.

Johnson, S. P., & Aslin, R. N. (1995). Perception of object unity in 2-month-old infants. *Developmental Psychology, 31*(5), 739–745.

Johnson, S. P., & Aslin, R. N. (1996). Perception of object unity in young infants: The roles of motion, depth, and orientation. *Cognitive Development, 11,* 161–180.

Johnson, S. P., & Mason, U. (2002). Perception of kinetic illusory contours by 2-month-old infants. *Child Development, 73,* 22–34.

Johnson, S. P., & Nanez, J. E. (1995). Young infants' perception of object unity in two-dimensional displays. *Infant Behavior and Development, 18,* 133–143.

Kanwisher, N., McDermott, J., & Chun, M. M. (1997). The fusiform area: A module in human extrastriate cortex specialized for face perception. *Journal of Neuroscience, 17,* 4302–4311.

Kant, I. (1902). *Critique of pure reason* (2nd ed., F. M. Muller, Trans.). New York: Macmillan. (Original work published 1781)

Kaplan, G. A. (1969). Kinetic disruption of optical texture: The perception of depth at an edge. *Perception and Psychophysics, 6*(4), 193–198.

Kaufman, L. (1974). *Sight and mind.* New York: Oxford University Press.

Kaufmann, F., Stucki, M., & Kaufmann-Hayoz, R. (1985). Development of infants' sensitivity for slow and rapid motions. *Infant Behavior and Development, 8*(1), 89–98.

Kaufmann-Hayoz, R., Kaufmann, F., & Stucki, M. (1986). Kinetic contours in infants' visual perception. *Child Development, 57*(2), 292–299.

Kaufmann-Hayoz, R., Kaufmann, F., & Walther, D. (1988, April). *Perception of kinetic subjective contours at 5 and 8 months.* Paper presented at the Sixth International Conference on Infant Studies, Washington, DC.

Kavsek, M. J. (1999). Infants' responsiveness to line junctions in curved objects. *Journal of Experimental Child Psychology, 72,* 177–192.

Kawabata, H., Gyoba, J., Inoue, H., & Ohtsubo, H. (1999). Visual completion of partly occluded grating in young infants under 1 month of age. *Vision Research, 39,* 3586–3591.

Kellman, P. J. (1984). Perception of three-dimensional form by human infants. *Perception and Psychophysics, 36*(4), 353–358.

Kellman, P. J. (1993). Kinematic foundations of infant visual perception. In G. Carl (Ed.), *Carnegie Mellon Symposium on Cognition: Visual perception and cognition in infancy* (Vol. 21, pp. 121–173). Hillsdale, NJ: Erlbaum.

Kellman, P. J. (1995). Ontogenesis of space and motion perception. In R. Gelman & T. K. Au (Eds.), *Perceptual and cognitive development* (2nd ed., pp. 3–48). New York: Academic Press.

Kellman, P. J. (2001). Separating processes in object perception. *Journal of Experimental Child Psychology, 78,* 84–97.

Kellman, P. J. (2002). Perceptual learning. In R. Gallistel (Ed.), *Stevens' handbook of experimental psychology: Learning, motivation, and emotion* (3rd ed., Vol. 3). Wiley.

Kellman, P. J. (2003). Segmentation and grouping in object perception: A 4-dimensional approach. In R. Kimchi, M. Behrmann, &

C. R. Olson (Eds.), *Carnegie Mellon Symposium on Cognition: Vol. 31. Perceptual organization in vision—Behavioral and neural perspectives* (pp. 155–201). Hillsdale, NJ: Erlbaum.

Kellman, P. J., & Arterberry, M. E. (1998). *The cradle of knowledge: Development of perception in infancy.* Cambridge, MA: MIT Press.

Kellman, P. J., & Banks, M. S. (1997). Infant visual perception. In R. Siegler & D. Kuhn (Eds.), *Handbook of child psychology: Vol. 2. Cognition, perception, and language* (5th ed., pp. 103–146). New York: Wiley.

Kellman, P. J., & Cohen, M. H. (1984). Kinetic subjective contours. *Perception and Psychophysics, 35*(3), 237–244.

Kellman, P. J., Garrigan, P., & Shipley, T. F. (2005). Object interpolation in three dimensions. *Psychological Review, 112*(3), 586–609.

Kellman, P. J., Gleitman, H., & Spelke, E. S. (1987). Object and observer motion in the perception of objects by infants. The ontogenesis of perception [Special issue]. *Journal of Experimental Psychology: Human Perception and Performance, 13*(4), 586–593.

Kellman, P. J., & Shipley, T. F. (1991). A theory of visual interpolation in object perception. *Cognitive Psychology, 23*(2), 141–221.

Kellman, P. J., & Short, K. R. (1987a). Development of three-dimensional form perception. *Journal of Experimental Psychology: Human Perception and Performance, 13*(4), 545–557.

Kellman, P. J., & Short, K. R. (1987b). *Infant perception of partly occluded objects: The problem of rotation.* Paper presented at the Third International Conference on Event Perception and Action, Uppsala, Sweden.

Kellman, P. J., & Spelke, E. S. (1983). Perception of partly occluded objects in infancy. *Cognitive Psychology, 15*(4), 483–524.

Kellman, P. J., Spelke, E. S., & Short, K. R. (1986). Infant perception of object unity from translatory motion in depth and vertical translation. *Child Development, 57*(1), 72–86.

Kellman, P. J., & von Hofsten, C. (1992). The world of the moving infant: Perception of motion, stability, and space. *Advances in Infancy Research, 7,* 147–184.

Kellman, P. J., Yin, C., & Shipley, T. F. (1998). A common mechanism for illusory and occluded object completion. *Journal of Experimental Psychology: Human Perception and Performance, 24,* 859–869.

Kelly, J. P., Borchert, J., & Teller, D. Y. (1997). The development of chromatic and achromatic contrast sensitivity in infancy as tested with the sweep VEP. *Vision Research, 37,* 2057–2072.

Kessen, W., Haith, M. M., & Salapatek, P. H. (1970). Human infancy: A bibliography and guide. In P. H. Mussen (Ed.), *Carmichael's manual of child psychology* (pp. 287–445). New York: Wiley.

Kestenbaum, R., & Nelson, C. A. (1990). The recognition and categorization of upright and inverted emotional expressions by 7-month-old infants. *Infant Behavior and Development, 13,* 497–511.

Kleiner, K. A. (1987). Amplitude and phase spectra as indices of infants' pattern preferences. *Infant Behavior and Development, 10,* 45–55.

Kliener, K. A., & Banks, M. S. (1987). Stimulus energy does not account for 2-month-olds' face preferences. *Journal of Experimental Psychology: Human Perception and Performance, 13,* 594–600.

Koenderink, J. J. (1986). Optic flow. *Vision Research, 26,* 161–180.

Koffka, K. (1935). *Principles of Gestalt psychology.* New York: Harcourt, Brace & World.

Kremenitzer, J. P., Vaughan, H. G., Kurtzberg, D., & Dowling, K. (1979). Smooth-pursuit eye movements in the newborn infant. *Child Development, 50*(2), 442–448.

Kuchuk, A., Vibbert, M., & Bornstein, M. H. (1986). The perception of smiling and its experiential correlates in 3-month-old infants. *Child Development, 57,* 1054–1061.

Larsen, J. S. (1971). The sagittal growth of the eye: Vol. 4. Ultrasonic measurement of the axial length of the eye from birth to puberty. *Acta Ophthalmologica, 49,* 873–886.

Lea, S. E. G., Slater, A. M., & Ryan, C. M. E. (1996). Perception of object unity in chicks: A comparison with the human infant. *Infant Behavior and Development, 19,* 501–504.

Lee, D. (1974). Visual information during locomotion. In R. B. MacLeod & H. L. Pick (Eds.), *Perception: Essays in honor of J. J. Gibson* (pp. 250–267). Ithaca, NY: Cornell University Press.

Legge, G. E., & Foley, J. M. (1980). Contrast masking in human vision. *Journal of the Optical Society of America, 70,* 1458–1471.

Leinbach, M. D., & Fagot, B. I. (1993). Categorical habituation to male and female faces: Gender schematic processing in infancy. *Infant Behavior and Development, 16,* 317–332.

Levi, D. M., Klein, S. A., & Aitsebaomo, A. P. (1985). Vernier acuity, crowding, and cortical magnification. *Vision Research, 25,* 963–977.

Lewis, T. L., Maurer, D., & Kay, D. (1978). Newborns' central vision: Whole or hole? *Journal of Experimental Child Psychology, 26,* 193–203.

Linsker, R. (1989). How to generate ordered maps By maximizing the mutual information between input and output signals. *Neural Computation, 1,* 402–411.

Locke, J. (1971). *Essay concerning the human understanding.* New York: World Publishing. (Original work published 1690)

Ludemann, P. M., & Nelson, C. A. (1988). Categorical representation of facial expressions by 7-month-old infants. *Developmental Psychology, 24,* 492–501.

Manny, R. E., & Klein, S. A. (1984). The development of vernier acuity in infants. *Current Eye Research, 3,* 453–462.

Manny, R. E., & Klein., S. A. (1985). A three alternative tracking paradigm to measure vernier acuity of older infants. *Vision Research, 25,* 1245–1252.

Marr, D. (1982). *Vision.* San Francisco: Freeman.

Maurer, D. (1985). Infants' perception of facedness. In T. M. Field & N. A. Fox (Eds.), *Social perception in infants* (pp. 73–100). Norwood, NJ: Ablex.

Mayer, D., & Arendt, R. E. (2001). Visual acuity assessment in infancy. In L. T. Singer & P. S. Zeskind (Eds.), *Biobehavioral assessment of the infant* (pp. 81–94). New York: Guilford Press.

Maurer, D., & Lewis, T. (1999). Rapid improvement in the acuity of infants after visual input. *Science, 286,* 108–110.

Mill, J. S. (1865). Examination of Sir William Hamilton's philosophy. In R. Herrnstein & E. G. Boring (Eds.), *A source book in the history of psychology* (pp. 182–188). Cambridge, MA: Harvard University Press.

Mondloch, C. J., Lewis, T. L., Budreau, D. R., Maurer, D., Dannemiller, J. D., Stephens, B. R., et al. (1999). Face perception during early infancy. *Psychological Science, 10,* 419–422.

Montague, D. P. F., & Walker-Andrews, A. S. (2002). Mothers, fathers, and infants: The role of person familiarity and parental involvement in infants' perception of emotional expressions. *Child Development, 73,* 1339–1353.

Morrone, M. C., Burr, D. C., & Fiorentini, A. (1993). Development of infant contrast sensitivity to chromatic stimuli. *Vision Research, 33,* 2535–2552.

Morton, J., & Johnson, M. H. (1991). Conspec and conlern: A two-process theory of infant face recognition. *Psychological Review, 2,* 164–181.

Muller, J. (1965). Handbuch der physiologie des menschen: bk. V. Coblenz (W. Baly, Trans.) [Elements of physiology: Vol. 2 (1842,

London)]. In R. Herrnstein & E. G. Boring (Eds.), *A sourcebook in the history of psychology* (pp. 26–33). Cambridge, MA: Harvard University Press. (Original work published 1838)

Nanez, J. E. (1988). Perception of impending collision in 3- to 6-week-old infants. *Infant Behavior and Development, 11,* 447–463.

Nanez, J. E., & Yonas, A. (1994). Effects of luminance and texture motion on infant defensive reactions to optical collision. *Infant Behavior and Development, 17,* 165–174.

Needham, A. (1999). The role of shape in 4-month-old infants' object segregation. *Infant Behavior and Development, 22,* 161–178.

Needham, A. (2001). Object recognition and object segregation in 4½-month-old infants. *Journal of Experimental Child Psychology, 78,* 3–24.

Nelson, C. A. (2001). The development and neural bases of face recognition. *Infant and Child Development, 10,* 3–18.

Norcia, A. M., Tyler, C. W., & Allen, D. (1986). Electrophysiological assessment of contrast sensitivity in human infants. *American Journal of Optometry and Physiological Optics, 63,* 12–15.

Norcia, A. M., Tyler, C. W., & Hammer, R. D. (1990). Development of contrast sensitivity in the human infant. *Vision Research, 30,* 1475–1486.

Olshausen, B. A., & Field, D. J. (1996). Emergence of simple-cell receptive field properties by learning a sparse code for natural images. *Nature, 381,* 607–609.

Olzak, L. A., & Thomas, J. P. (1986). Seeing spatial patterns. In K. R. Boff, L. Kaufman, & J. P. Thomas (Eds.), *Handbook of perception and human performance: Sensory processes and perception* (pp. 7.1–7.56). New York: Wiley.

Oppenheim, A. V., & Lim, J. S. (1981). The importance of phase in signals. *Proceedings of the IEEE, 69,* 529–541.

Oster, H. E. (1975). *Color perception in human infants.* Unpublished masters thesis, University of California, Berkeley.

O'Toole, A. J., Deffenbacher, K. A., Valentin, D., & Abdi, H. (1994). Structural aspects of face recognition and the other-race effect. *Memory and Cognition, 22,* 208–224.

Owsley, C. (1983). The role of motion in infants' perception of solid shape. *Perception, 12*(6), 707–717.

Packer, O., Hartmann, E. E., & Teller, D. Y. (1984). Infant colour vision, the effect of test field size on Rayleigh discrimination. *Vision Research, 24,* 1247–1260.

Palmer, E. M., Kellman, P. J., & Shipley, T. F. (2004). *A theory of contour interpolation in the perception of dynamically occluded objects.* Manuscript in preparation.

Palmer, S., & Rock, I. (1994). Rethinking perceptual organization: The role of uniform connectedness. *Psychonomic Bulletin and Review, 1*(1), 29–55.

Pascalis, O., de Haan, M., & Nelson, C. A. (2002). Is face processing species-specific during the first year of life? *Science, 296,* 1321–1323.

Pascalis, O., de Schonen, S., Morton, J., Deruelle, C., & Fabre-Grenet, M. (1995). Mother's face recognition in neonates: A replication and extension. *Infant Behavior and Development, 18,* 79–85.

Peeples, D. R., & Teller, D. Y. (1975). Color vision and brightness discrimination in human infants. *Science, 189,* 1102–1103.

Pelli, D. (Ed.). (1990). *Quantum efficiency of vision.* Cambridge, England: Cambridge University Press.

Peterzell, D. H., Werner, J. S., & Kaplan, P. S. (1995). Individual differences in contrast sensitivity functions: Longitudinal study of 4-, 6-, and 8-month-old human infants. *Vision Research, 35,* 961–979.

Petrig, B., Julesz, B., Kropfl, W., & Baumgartner, G. (1981). Development of stereopsis and cortical binocularity in human infants: Electrophysiological evidence. *Science, 213*(4514), 1402–1405.

Pettigrew, J. D. (1974). The effect of visual experience on the development of stimulus specificity by kitten cortical neurones. *Journal of Physiology, 237,* 49–74.

Piaget, J. (1952). *The origins of intelligence in children.* New York: International Universities Press.

Piaget, J. (1954). *The construction of reality in the child.* New York: Basic Books.

Piotrowski, L. N., & Campbell, F. W. (1982). A demonstration of visual importance and flexibility of spatial-frequency amplitude and phase. *Perception, 11,* 337–346.

Pirchio, M., Spinelli, D., Fiorentini, A., & Maffei, L. (1978). Infant contrast sensitivity evaluated by evoked potentials. *Brain Research, 141,* 179–184.

Purves, D., & Lotto, R. B. (2003). *Why we see what we do: An empirical theory of vision.* Sunderland, MA: Sinauer Associates.

Quinn, P. C., & Bhatt, R. S. (2001). Object recognition and object segregation in infancy: Historical perspective, theoretical significance, "kinds" of knowledge and relation to object categorization. *Journal of Experimental Child Psychology, 78,* 25–34.

Quinn, P. C., Yahr, J., Kuhn, A., Slater, A. M., & Pascalis, O. (2002). Representation of the gender of human faces by infants: A preference for female. *Perception, 31,* 1109–1121.

Ramachandran, V. S., Clarke, P. G., & Whitteridge, D. (1977). Cells selective to binocular disparity in the cortex of newborn lambs. *Nature, 268*(5618), 333–335.

Rentschler, I., & Treutwein, B. (1985). Loss of spatial phase relationships in extrafoveal vision. *Nature, 313,* 308–310.

Riesen, A. H. (1947). The development of visual perception in man and chimpanzee. *Science, 106,* 107–108.

Ringach, D. L., & Shapley, R. (1996). Spatial and temporal properties of illusory contours and amodal boundary completion. *Visual Research, 36,* 3037–3050.

Rochat, P. (1999). *Early social cognition: Understanding others in the first months of life.* Mahwah, NJ: Erlbaum.

Rock, I. (1984). *Perception.* New York: Scientific American Books.

Rolls, E. T., & Baylis, G. C. (1986). Size and contrast have only small effects on the responses to faces of neurons in the cortex of the superior temporal sulcus of the monkey. *Experimental Brain Research, 65,* 38–48.

Rubenstein, A. J., Kalakanis, L., & Langois, J. H. (1999). Infant preferences for attractive faces: A cognitive explanation. *Developmental Psychology, 35,* 848–855.

Rubin, E. (1915). *Synoplevede figurer.* Copenhagen, Denmark: Gyldendalske.

Ruff, H. A. (1978). Infant recognition of the invariant form of objects. *Child Development, 49*(2), 293–306.

Russell, J. A., & Fernandez-Dols, J. M. (1997). *The psychology of facial expression.* New York: Cambridge University Press.

Sai, F., & Bushnell, I. W. R. (1988). The perception of faces in different poses by 1-month-olds. *British Journal of Developmental Psychology, 6,* 35–41.

Schaller, M. J. (1975). Chromatic vision in human infants: Conditioned operant fixation to "hues" of varying intensity. *Bulletin of the Psychonomic Society, 6,* 39–42.

Schiff, W. (1965). Perception of impending collision: A study of visually directed avoidant behavior. *Psychological Monographs, 79*(Whole No. 604).

Sekiguchi, N., Williams, D. R., & Brainard, D. H. (1993). Aberration-free measurements of the visibility of isoluminant gratings. *Journal of the Optical Society of America, 10,* 2105–2117.

Sergent, J. (1984). An investigation into component and configural processes underlying face perception. *British Journal of Psychology, 75,* 221–242.

Serrano, J. M., Iglesias, J., & Loeches, A. (1992). Visual discrimination and recognition of facial expressions of anger, fear, and surprise in 4- to 6-month-old infants. *Developmental Psychobiology, 25,* 411–425.

Shepard, R. N. (1984). Ecological constraints on internal representation: Resonant kinematics of perceiving, imagining, thinking, and dreaming. *Psychological Review, 91*(4), 417–447.

Shimojo, S., Birch, E. E., Gwiazda, J., & Held, R. (1984). Development of vernier acuity in human infants. *Vision Research, 24,* 721–728.

Shimojo, S., & Held, R. (1987). Vernier acuity is less than grating acuity in 2- and 3-month-olds. *Vision Research, 27,* 77–86.

Shipley, T. F., & Kellman, P. J. (1994). Spatiotemporal boundary formation: Boundary, form, and motion perception from transformations of surface elements. *Journal of Experimental Psychology: General, 123*(1), 3–20.

Simion, F., Cassia, V. M., Turati, C., & Valenza, E. (2001). The origins of face perception: Specific versus non-specific mechanisms. *Infant and Child Development, 10,* 59–65.

Skoczenski, A. M., & Aslin, R. N. (1995). Assessment of vernier acuity development using the "equivalent instrinsic blur" paradigm. *Vision Research, 35,* 1879–1887.

Skoczenski, A. M., & Norcia, A. M. (1998). Neural noise limitations on infant visual sensitivity. *Nature, 391,* 697–700.

Skoczenski, A. M., & Norcia, A. M. (2002). Late maturation of visual hyperacuity. *Psychological Science, 13,* 537–541.

Slater, A., & Findlay, J. M. (1975). Binocular fixation in the newborn baby. *Journal of Experimental Child Psychology, 20*(2), 248–273.

Slater, A., Johnson, S. P., Brown, E., & Badenoch, M. (1996). Newborn infant's perception of partly occluded objects. *Infant Behavior and Development, 19,* 145–148.

Slater, A., Johnson, S., Kellman, P. J., & Spelke, E. (1994). The role of three-dimensional depth cues in infants' perception of partly occluded objects. *Journal of Early Development and Parenting, 3*(3), 187–191.

Slater, A., Mattock, A., & Brown, E. (1990). Size constancy at birth: Newborn infants' responses to retinal and real size. *Journal of Experimental Child Psychology, 49*(2), 314–322.

Slater, A., & Morison, V. (1985). Shape constancy and slant perception at birth. *Perception, 14*(3), 337–344.

Slater, A., Morrison, V., & Somers, M. (1988). Orientation discrimination and cortical function in the human newborn. *Perception, 17,* 597–602.

Slater, A., Morison, V., Somers, M., Mattock, A., Brown, E., & Taylor, D. (1990). Newborn and older infants' perception of partly occluded objects. *Infant Behavior and Development, 13,* 33–49.

Slater, A., Quinn, P. C., Hayes, R., & Brown, E. (2000). The role of facial orientation in newborn infants' preference for attractive faces. *Developmental Science, 3,* 181–185.

Slater, A., Von der Schulenburg, C., Brown, E., Badenoch, M., Butterworth, G., Parsons, S., et al. (1998). Newborn infants prefer attractive faces. *Infant Behavior and Development, 21,* 345–354.

Sokol, S. (1978). Measurement of visual acuity from pattern reversal evoked potentials. *Vision Research, 18,* 33–40.

Spelke, E. S. (1985). Perception of unity, persistence and identity: Thoughts on infants' conceptions of objects. In J. Mehler & R. Fox (Eds.), *Neonate cognition* (pp. 89–113). Hillsdale, NJ: Erlbaum.

Spelke, E. S., Breinlinger, K., Jacobson, K., & Phillips, A. (1993). Gestalt relations and object perception: A developmental study. *Perception, 22*(12), 1483–1501.

Stephens, B. R., & Banks, M. S. (1987). Contrast discrimination in human infants. *Journal of Experimental Psychology: Human Perception and Performance, 13,* 558–565.

Striano, T., Brennan, P. A., & Vanmann, E. J. (2002). Maternal depressive symptoms and 6-month-old infants' sensitivity to facial expressions. *Infancy, 3,* 115–126.

Sumi, S. (1984). Upside-down presentation of the Johansson moving light-spot pattern. *Perception, 13*(3), 283–286.

Suttle, C. M., Banks, M. S., & Graf, E. W. (2002). FPL and sweep VEP to tritan stimuli in young human infants. *Vision Research, 42,* 2879–2891.

Swoyer, C. (2003, Spring). Relativism. In E. N. Zalta (Ed.), *The Stanford Encyclopedia of Philosophy.* Retrieved May 2005 from http://plato.stanford.edu/archives/spr2003/entries/relativism.

Teller, D. Y. (1998). Spatial and temporal aspects of infant color vision. *Vision Research, 38,* 3275–3282.

Teller, D. Y., Brooks, T. E. W., & Palmer, J. (1997). Infant color vision: Moving tritan stimuli do not elicit directionally appropriate eye movements in 2- and 4-month-olds. *Vision Research, 37,* 899–911.

Teller, D. Y., & Lindsey, D. T. (1993). Infant color vision: OKN techniques and null plane analysis. In K. Simons (Ed.), *Early visual development: Normal and abnormal* (pp. 143–162). New York: Oxford University Press.

Teller, D. Y., & Palmer, J. (1996). Infant color vision-motion nulls for red-green versus luminance-modulated stimuli in infants and adults. *Vision Research, 36,* 955–974.

Teller, D. Y., Peeples, D. R., & Sekel, M. (1978). Discrimination of chromatic from white light by 2-month-old human infants. *Vision Research, 18,* 41–48.

Thomasson, M. A., & Teller, D. Y. (2000). Infant color vision: Sharp chromatic edges are not required for chromatic discrimination in 4-month-olds. *Vision Research, 40,* 1051–1057.

Timney, B. (1981). Development of binocular depth perception in kittens. *Investigative Ophthalmology and Visual Science, 21,* 493–496.

Titchener, E. B. (1910). *A textbook of psychology.* New York: Macmillan.

Turvey, M. T., Shaw, R. E., & Reed, E. S. (1981). Ecological laws of perceiving and acting: In reply to Fodor and Pylyshyn. *Cognition, 9,* 237–304.

Ullman, S. (1979). *The interpretation of visual motion.* Cambridge, MA: MIT Press.

Ullman, S. (1980). Against direct perception. *Behavioral and Brain Sciences, 3,* 373–415.

Van de Walle, G. A., & Spelke, E. S. (1996). Spatiotemporal integration and object perception in infancy: Perceiving unity versus form. *Child Development, 67,* 2621–2640.

van Nes, F. L., & Bouman, M. A. (1967). Spatial modulation transfer in the human eye. *Journal of the Optical Society of America, 57,* 401.

Varner, D., Cook, J. E., Schneck, M. E., McDonald, M. A., & Teller, D. Y. (1985). Tritan discrimination by 1- and 2-month-old human infants. *Vision Research, 25,* 821–831.

Volkmann, F. C., & Dobson, M. V. (1976). Infant responses of ocular fixation to moving visual stimuli. *Journal of Experimental Child Psychology, 22*(1), 86–99.

von der Heydt, R., Peterhans, E., & Baumgartner, G. (1984). Illusory contours and cortical neuron responses. *Science, 224*(4654), 1260–1262.

von der Malsburg, C. (1973). Self-organisation of orientation sensitive cells in the striate cortex. *Kybernetik, 14,* 85–100.

von Hofsten, C., Kellman, P., & Putaansuu, J. (1992). Young infants' sensitivity to motion parallax. *Infant Behavior and Development, 15*(2), 245–264.

von Hofsten, C., & Spelke, E. S. (1985). Object perception and object-directed reaching in infancy. *Journal of Experimental Psychology: General, 114*(2), 198–212.

von Holst, E. (1954). Relations between the central nervous system and the peripheral organs. *British Journal of Animal Behavior, 2,* 89–94.

Walk, R. D., & Gibson, E. J. (1961). A comparative and analytical study of visual depth perception. *Psychological Monographs, 75.*

Wallach, H. (1976). *On perception.* Oxford, England: Quadrangle.

Wallach, H. (1987). Perceiving a stable environment when one moves. *Annual Review of Psychology, 38,* 1–27.

Wallach, H., & O'Connell, D. N. (1953). The kinetic depth effect. *Journal of Experimental Psychology, 45,* 205–217.

Waltz, D. (1975). Understanding line drawings in scenes with shadows. In P. H. Winston (Ed.), *The psychology of computer vision* (pp. 19–91). New York: McGraw-Hill.

Wattam-Bell, J. (1991). Development of motion-specific cortical responses in infancy. *Vision Research, 31*(2), 287–297.

Wattam-Bell, J. (1992). The development of maximum displacement limits for discrimination of motion direction in infancy. *Vision Research, 32*(4), 621–630.

Wattam-Bell, J. (1996a). Visual motion processing in 1-month-old infants: Habituation experiments. *Vision Research, 36,* 1679–1685.

Wattam-Bell, J. (1996b). Visual motion processing in 1-month-old infants: Preferential looking experiments. *Vision Research, 36,* 1671–1677.

Webb, J. A., & Aggarwal, J. K. (1982). Structure from motion of rigid and jointed objects. *Artificial Intelligence, 19,* 107–130.

Werker, J. F. (1994). Cross-language speech perception: Developmental change does not involve loss. In H. Nusbaum & J. Goodman (Eds.), *The transition from speech sounds to spoken words: The development of speech perception* (pp. 95–120). Cambridge, MA: MIT Press.

Werner, J. S. (1982). Development of scotopic sensitivity and the absorption spectrum of the human ocular media. *Journal of the Optical Society of America, 72,* 247–258.

Wertheimer, M. (1958). Principles of perceptual organization. In D. C. Beardslee & M. Wertheimer (Eds.), *Readings in perception* (pp. 115–135). Princeton, NJ: Van Nostrand. (Original work published 1923)

Westheimer, G. (1979). The spatial sense of the eye. *Investigative Ophthalmology and Visual Science, 18,* 893–912.

Westheimer, G., & McKee, S. P. (1980). Stereoscopic acuity with defocused and spatially filtered retinal images. *Journal of the Optical Society of America, 70*(7), 772–778.

Whalen, P. J., Rauch, S. L., Etcoff, N. L., McInerney, S. C., Lee, M. B., & Jenike, M. A. (1998). Masked presentations of emotional facial expressions modulate amygdale activity without explicit knowledge. *Journal of Neuroscience, 18,* 411–418.

White, B., Castle, R., & Held, R. (1964). Observations on the development of visually directed reaching. *Child Development, 35,* 349–364.

Wiesel, T. N., & Hubel, D. H. (1974). Ordered arrangement of orientation columns in monkeys lacking visual experience. *Journal of Comparative Neurology, 158,* 307–318.

Williams, D. R. (1985). Visibility of interference fringes near the resolution limit. *Journal of the Optical Society of America, A2,* 1087–1093.

Wilson, H. R. (1988). Development of spatiotemporal mechanisms in infant vision. *Vision Research, 28,* 611–628.

Wilson, H. R. (1993). Theories of infant visual development. In K. Simons (Ed.), *Early visual development: Normal and abnormal* (pp. 560–572). New York: Oxford University Press.

Winston, P. H. (1992). *Artificial intelligence.* Reading, MA: Addison-Wesley.

Wundt, W. (1862). *Beitrage zur theorie der sinneswahrnehmung.* Leipzig, Germany: C. F. Winter.

Yin, C., Kellman, P. J., & Shipley, T. F. (1997). Surface completion complements boundary interpolation in the visual integration of partly occluded objects. *Perception, 26,* 1459–1479.

Yin, C., Kellman, P. J., & Shipley, T. F. (2000). Surface integration influences depth discrimination. *Vision Research, 40*(15), 1969–1978.

Yonas, A. (1981). Infants' responses to optical information for collision. In R. N. Aslin, J. Alberts, & M. Petersen (Eds.), *Development of perception: Psychobiological perspectives—The visual system* (Vol. 2, pp. 313–334). New York: Academic Press.

Yonas, A. (2001). Reflections on the study of infant perception and cognition: What does Morgan's canon really tell us to do? *Journal of Experimental Child Psychology, 78,* 50–54.

Yonas, A., & Arterberry, M. E. (1994). Infants' perceive spatial structure specified by line junctions. *Perception, 23,* 1427–1435.

Yonas, A., Arterberry, M. E., & Granrud, C. E. (1987a). Four-month-old infants' sensitivity to binocular and kinetic information for three-dimensional object shape. *Child Development, 58,* 910–917.

Yonas, A., Arterberry, M. E., & Granrud, C. E. (1987b). Space perception in infancy. *Annals of Child Development, 4,* 1–34.

Yonas, A., Bechtold, A., Frankel, D., Gordon, F., McRoberts, G., Norcia, A., et al. (1977). Development of sensitivity to information for impending collision. *Perception and Psychophysics, 21*(2), 97–104.

Yonas, A., Elieff, C. A., & Arterberry, M. E. (2002). Emergence of sensitivity to pictorial depth cues: Charting development in individual infants. *Infant Behavior and Development, 25,* 495–514.

Yonas, A., & Owsley, C. (1987). Development of visual space perception. In P. Salapetek & L. B. Cohen (Eds.), *Handbook of infant perception: From perception to cognition* (pp. 80–122). New York: Academic Press.

Yonas, A., Pettersen, L., & Granrud, C. E. (1982). Infants' sensitivity to familiar size as information for distance. *Child Development, 53*(5), 1285–1290.

Yonas, A., Pettersen, L., & Lockman, J. J. (1979). Young infants' sensitivity to optical information for collision. *Canadian Journal of Psychology, 33*(4), 268–276.

Yuodelis, C., & Hendrickson, A. (1986). A qualitative and quantitative analysis of the human fovea during development. *Vision Research, 26,* 847–855.

CHAPTER 4

# Motor Development

KAREN E. ADOLPH and SARAH E. BERGER

**RECLAIMING MOTOR DEVELOPMENT** 161
**The Formal Structure of Movements** 161
**Perceptual Control of Motor Actions** 163
**Chapter Overview** 164
**MOTOR DEVELOPMENT AS A MODEL SYSTEM** 165
**Qualitative Changes** 165
**Emergent Developments** 166
**Developmental Trajectories** 172
**Variability** 176
**Time, Age, and Experience** 177
**Movement Is Ubiquitous** 181
**Summary: Models of Change** 183

**MOTOR DEVELOPMENT AS A PERCEPTION-
   ACTION SYSTEM** 184
**Prospective Control** 184
**Centrality of Posture** 187
**Perceiving Affordances** 189
**The Perception-Action Loop** 196
**Creating New Affordances for Action** 200
**Summary: Getting into the Act** 201
**REFERENCES** 202

## RECLAIMING MOTOR DEVELOPMENT

For many years, motor development has been the area of developmental psychology that dare not speak its name. In lieu of *motor development,* researchers have preferred terms like *perceptual-motor development, perception and action,* and *motor skill acquisition.* Perhaps the eponym "motor development" does not sound sufficiently psychological, whereas names like perceptual-motor development remind readers that the adaptive control of motor actions involves proper psychological processes such as perception, planning, decision making, memory, motivation, intentions, and goals.

The field of motor development has lost two of its great leaders, Esther Thelen (1941–2004) and Eleanor Gibson (1910–2002). We dedicate this chapter to them. We thank Robert Siegler, Beatrix Vereijken, Peter Gordon, Scott Robinson, Rick Gilmore, Blandine Bril, Rachel Keen, Neil Berthier, Claes von Hofsten, Catherine Tamis-LeMonda, Dick Aslin, Amy Joh, Jesse Young, Simone Gill-Alvarez, Jessie Garciaguirre, and Katherine Dimitropoulou for their helpful comments. We thank Jessie Garciaguirre, Sharon Lobo, and Felix Gill-Alvarez for their tireless assistance and Judy Kwak and Lana Karasik for their gracious help. Work on this chapter was supported by National Institutes of Health grants HD-33486 and HD-42697 to Karen Adolph.

Sure, every introductory textbook contains a chapter called "Motor Development," usually paired with physical growth. But, the textbook inventories of infantile reflexes, motor milestones, and growth charts do not reflect the kind of work that currently characterizes the field. Most of us do, in fact, study perception-action coupling with the aim of understanding developmental changes in the perceptual, cognitive, social, and emotional processes that contribute to the adaptive control of motor actions. However, many developmental psychologists also study the formal structure of movements with the aim of using motor development as a model system for understanding more general developmental processes and principles. In recognition that motor development involves two kinds of research—using the formal structure of infants' movements to elucidate general principles of development as well as a focus on developmental changes in the perceptual control of motor actions—we have, without apology, entitled this chapter, "Motor Development."

### The Formal Structure of Movements

A remarkable thing about motor skills is that movements are directly observable. Most domains of psychological development are the hidden denizens of mental activity. The content of children's thoughts, percepts, emotions, intentions, concepts, memories, and linguistic representations must be inferred from overt motor behaviors such as speech, gestures, facial expressions, and eye movements, or in more technically sophisticated labs, from images of brain activity. Likewise, the moment-to-moment time course of mental activities must be inferred from children's vocalizations, patterns of looking behavior, manual and facial expressions, or from the traces of brain activity on an electroencephalogram. Descriptions of developmental changes in mental activity can be even more removed from direct observation because researchers frequently must rely on different tasks and procedures to study children at different ages, typically looking behaviors at younger ages and manual or vocal behaviors at older ages (Hofstadter & Reznick, 1996; Keen, 2003).

In contrast to the covert nature of mental events, motor behaviors are out in the open. As Gesell (1946) wrote in an earlier chapter in this *Handbook,* motor behaviors "have shape" (p. 297). Every wiggle and step occurs over measurable time and space. The traces of motor activity on a video monitor or three-dimensional motion-recording device are a direct readout of the movement itself. No inferential leap separates a motor skill from a description of its form. What you see is what you get.

Moreover, researchers can observe the changing form of children's movements over multiple, nested time scales. The time-space trajectory of infants' first awkward arm extensions can be compared with changes in the speed and straightness of the reaching trajectory over the trials in a single session, and across multiple sessions conducted over days, weeks, and months of practice. Milliseconds and millimeters are nested within larger time-space units. Changes in real time can be tracked directly over learning and development.

A benefit of being so conspicuously available to observation is that motor development makes a unique model system for studying general developmental processes—the origins of new behavioral forms; the extent to which development is patterned, orderly, and directional; the role of variability in facilitating or impeding development; whether developmental trajectories are continuous or stagelike; whether changes are universal across individuals and cultures; and so on. Such general issues of form and timing can be fruitfully addressed with a model system in which form and timing are transparent.

Inspired by Coghill's (1929) example of linking developmental changes in the swimming patterns of salamander embryos with general principles of embryological development, the great pioneers in motor development—McGraw, Gesell, and Shirley—used changes in the form and temporal structure of infants' movements as illustrations and existence proofs of general developmental processes. The focus on formal structure is beautifully exemplified in the line drawings that figured prominently in the work of the early pioneers (see Figure 4.1). Infants (like salamanders) are drawn abstracted from the surrounding context to highlight the changing morphology of the movements. Gesell (1946) described changes in the temporal structure and spatial configuration of infants' crawling movements to demonstrate the existence of qualitative changes in human development. Likewise, contemporary researchers, led by Thelen and her colleagues (e.g., Thelen & Ulrich, 1991), have used the changing shape of infants' reaching, grasping, kicking, stepping, crawling, walking, and jumping movements to illustrate developmental trajectories, propose general principles of developmental change, and speculate about biologically plausible developmental mechanisms.

Whereas most model systems are scaled-down versions of the target phenomenon, the beauty of using the changing shape of infants' movements to understand development stems solely from the fact that we can see infants' movements, not from their simplicity or

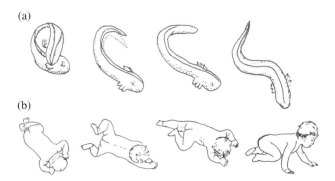

(a)

(b)

**Figure 4.1**  Examples of line drawings used by early pioneers in motor development to illustrate the changing morphology of movements. (a) Coghill's drawings of 4 positions from a real-time sequence of swimming movements in the salamander embryo. *Source:* From *Anatomy and the Problem of Behavior,* by G. E. Coghill, 1929, New York: Hafner. Reprinted with permission. (b) Drawings of Gesell's 6th, 7th, 9th, and 18th stages of infant crawling. *Source:* From "The Ontogenetic Organization of Prone Behavior in Human Infancy," by A. Gesell and L. B. Ames, 1940, *Journal of Genetic Psychology, 56,* pp. 247–263. Reprinted with permission.

tractability. Coghill (1929) expressly selected salamanders for a model system of embryological development because salamanders' primitive C- and S-shaped swimming movements and simple nervous systems are scaled-down versions of locomotion and its correlated activity in the central nervous system (CNS) of higher vertebrates. In contrast, infants' movements are not scaled-down versions of adults' movements, nor are infants' movements easy to elicit or record. Rather, babies' clumsy walking steps, reaches, and head and eye movements are notoriously variable and complex compared with those of adults. Even newborn reflexes and infants' spontaneous writhing and flailing have a variable and complex spatial and temporal structure.

In fact, to describe developmental changes in the time-space trajectories of infants' movements, researchers in motor development have led the field of developmental psychology in devising techniques to elicit, catalog, record, and analyze time-based behavioral data. In the 1930s, Gesell and Thompson (1934, 1938) designed a "behavioral interview" to systematically elicit developmental changes in various motor skills over infants' first 2 years of life. Gesell's tasks and detailed catalog of age-based changes are the basis for the famous Bayley Scales of Infant Development (1993) and other modern developmental screening tests (e.g., Frankenburg & Dodds, 1967).

Decades before behavioral coding from video recordings was a mainstay of every developmental laboratory, McGraw (1935, 1945) and Gesell and Thompson (1934, 1938) had devised sophisticated techniques for capturing infants' movements on high-speed film. Long before researchers in other areas of development had compiled databases of children's behaviors such as the CHILDES database of children's language, McGraw (1935), Gesell and Thompson (1938), Shirley (1931), and their contemporaries had constructed archival libraries of infants' movements. A century before the recent advent of time-based eye-tracking and brain-imaging techniques with infants, researchers in motor development struggled with the problem of representing and analyzing time-based data.

## Perceptual Control of Motor Actions

Being out in the open has implications beyond visibility: The functional outcome of motor actions is inextricably bound to the biomechanical facts of children's bodies and the physical properties of their environments. In A. Clark's (1997) words, motor actions are always "embodied" and "embedded," always performed by a creature with certain bodily capabilities and deficiencies and always performed in an environment with certain supports and hindrances. James and Eleanor Gibson's concept of "affordances" captures the functional significance of embodiment and embeddedness: Possibilities for action depend on the fit between actors' bodies and the surrounding environmental properties (E. J. Gibson, 1982; E. J. Gibson & Pick, 2000; J. J. Gibson, 1979). Whereas mental activity can be modeled profitably with a mathematical equation or a computer program at some remove from the limits and propensities of a physical body in a real world, a formal model of motor action is probably best simulated in a physically instantiated, free-wheeling robot (Brooks, 1991; Kuniyoshi et al., 2005). Like us, but unlike equations or computer software, robots are subject to physical forces.

Possibilities for action depend on all the myriad facts of embodiment. The size, shape, mass, compliance, strength, flexibility, and coordination of the various body parts can all affect the biomechanical constraints on action. The same functional outcome can require very different motor actions depending on the body's status. For example, to bring their hands to their mouths at 7 weeks after conception, fetuses must raise their arms at the shoulder because their arm buds are so short (Moore & Persaud, 1993). To produce the same hand-to-mouth action several weeks later, fetuses must deeply bend their arms at the shoulder and elbow because their arms are much longer (Robinson & Kleven, in press).

Reciprocally, affordances for action depend on the mundane constraints of the environment in which infants' bodies are embedded—the surfaces and media that support the body, the objects toward which movements are directed, and the effects of gravity acting on the various body parts. Again, fetal development provides a simple but compelling example. At 7 weeks post-conception, vigorous leg kicks can somersault the fetus through the amniotic fluid (deVries, Visser, & Prechtl, 1982). At 38 weeks, when the growing fetus is pressed against the walls of the uterus, the same muscle actions will fail even to extend the legs. After birth, when infants have ample room to move freely but have lost the buoyancy of a watery environment, the same muscle actions are subject to the pull of gravity. Now a vigorous kick merely flexes and extends the leg.

Our examples from fetal development illustrate a central and inescapable feature of motor action: The constraints of the body and the environment are continually changing. The facts of embodiment vary due to developmental changes in the body (such as the length-ening and differentiation of the fetal arm) and the flux of everyday activities (Adolph, 2002; Reed, 1989). Car-rying a toy under one arm, lifting a leg, or even drawing a deep breath create moment-to-moment changes in functional body dimensions and in the location of the body's center of mass. Similarly, the environmental con-text is a shifting landscape, not a still life. Developmen-tal changes in infants' bodies and skills continually introduce them to new objects and surfaces and invite new possibilities for interaction. Observing children at a playground, for example, is a revelation in attention to new affordances (E. J. Gibson, 1992). The slide might serve as tent, downhill track, or uphill path; the monkey bars as canopy or ground surface; the swing set leg as barrier, maypole, or fire pole, depending on children's changing propensities. The perfect robot simulation of infant motor development would require a machine whose body and environment develop.

Novelty in local conditions is the rule, not the excep-tion. Behavioral flexibility is imperative, not optional. Contemporary researchers in motor development have focused so much of their attention on perception-action coupling because it is only through perceptual informa-tion that infants can guide their movements prospec-tively and adaptively (e.g., von Hofsten, 2003, 2004). Changes in the biomechanical constraints on action alter the forces required to produce the desired functional outcome. Perception specifies the current status of the body and the environment in which it is embedded, thereby giving infants access to the current constraints on action (J. J. Gibson, 1979). Perception allows actions to be planned prospectively and gears action to the envi-ronment. Motor actions complete the perception-action loop by generating information for perceptual systems and bringing the appropriate sensory apparatus to the available information. In Gibson's (1979) words, "We must perceive in order to move, but we must also move in order to perceive" (p. 223). The interreliance between perception and action is so important for the adaptive control of motor actions that the chapter on motor devel-opment in the fifth edition of this *Handbook* (Bertenthal & Clifton, 1998) was entitled "Perception and Action."

## Chapter Overview

In addition to the chapter in the previous edition of the *Handbook* (Bertenthal & Clifton, 1998), the literature has amassed several detailed and comprehensive reviews of research on motor development, including chronolo-gies of normative changes in motor skill acquisition and in-depth treatments of particular action systems such as looking, reaching, object manipulation, posture, and lo-comotion (e.g., Adolph, 1997; Adolph & Berger, 2005; Bushnell & Boudreau, 1993; Campos et al., 2000; E. J. Gibson & Schmuckler, 1989; Vereijken, 2005; von Hof-sten, 1989; Woollacott & Jensen, 1996). Moreover, nu-merous articles and books present the two dominant theoretical perspectives in research on motor develop-ment, the dynamic systems and ecological approaches (e.g., Adolph, Eppler, & Gibson, 1993b; E. J. Gibson, 1988; E. J. Gibson & Pick, 2000; Goldfield, 1995; Smith & Thelen, 1993; Spencer & Schöner, 2003; Thelen, 1995; Thelen, Schöner, Scheier, & Smith, 2001; Thelen & Smith, 1994, 1998; von Hofsten, 2003, 2004; Zanone, Kelso, & Jeka, 1993). Proponents of dynamic systems views tend to stress the formal structure of movements with the aim of building a unified theory of develop-ment. Proponents of the ecological approach emphasize the functional links between perception and motor ac-tions in an effort to understand the psychological under-pinnings of motor development. However, most researchers agree that the ideas and methods of each ap-proach are highly compatible and complementary (e.g., Bertenthal & Clifton, 1998).

Our aims are somewhat different from the previous efforts. Instead of presenting a comprehensive chronol-ogy of motor behaviors, updating earlier reviews of the various body parts and action systems, or evaluating the relative merits of the dynamic systems and ecological approaches, we focus on the concepts, questions, issues, and principles that excite researchers in motor develop-ment and that are likely to be of interest to readers in other areas of developmental psychology. Thus, our re-view is organized around ideas.

The chapter is divided into two large sections repre-senting the two kinds of research programs that charac-terize current work in motor development. The first section treats motor development as a model system. We focus on the formal structure of movements and de-scribe how researchers have used the changing shape of infants' movements as a model system to address gen-eral issues of developmental processes and to propose general principles of change. The second section treats motor development as a perception-action system. We focus on the functional links between perceptual infor-mation and motor actions and describe how develop-mental changes in the interplay between perception and action make infants' motor actions increasingly flexible and adapted to features of the environment. In principle, findings generated by the perception-action approach could be used to draw general lessons about development. In practice, however, researchers have focused on the particular perception-action system that they are studying. In both sections, we present case studies that are especially useful illustrations of conceptual insights, fruitful arguments, and new ways of thinking about motor development. The case studies highlight motor development during the first 2 years of life to reflect the period where most research has focused.

## MOTOR DEVELOPMENT AS A MODEL SYSTEM

Motor development in infancy is truly remarkable. Developmental changes in the form and structure of infants' movements are tremendous in scope. At birth, babies can barely lift their heads. Eighteen months later, infants run across the room and navigate a tiny bit of food from plate to mouth with a pincer grip. Even to an untrained eye, many of infants' dramatic accomplishments involve a clear mapping of babies' clumsy head/eye, arm/hand, torso/leg movements onto adultlike looking, reaching, sitting, and walking movements. Conversely, some of the most dramatic developmental changes involve apparent disjunctions between behavioral forms—the disappearance, for example, of "newborn reflexes" and infants' abandonment of transient forms such as "tripod sitting" (propped on the arms between the outstretched legs), crawling on belly and hands and knees, and sideways "cruising" while hanging onto furniture for support.

The case studies in this section highlight many of the dramatic accomplishments and disjunctions in motor development to illustrate general issues of developmental process. In addition, we focus on an equally remarkable aspect of infants' movements: the ubiquity of movement across real time and development. Mundane eye scans, startles, wiggles, and flails of every body part from toes to tongue constitute a pervasive background of movement against which the more dramatic motor milestones appear in spotlight. Normally, background movements are so ubiquitous and seamless that they go unnoticed. However, when infants' development goes awry due to prematurity or impairment, abnormalities in muscle tone, coordination, and motor control bring background

movements to the fore. Simply breathing can become a struggle. Thus, we conclude this section by describing the background chorus of movements that are so typically overlooked by researchers and parents.

### Qualitative Changes

Motor development has always been a testing ground for addressing the nature of developmental change. Is development continuous, marked solely by changes in the relative quantities of behaviors? Or, are changes discontinuous, such that development also entails qualitative, stagelike transformations?

#### *Developmental Stages*

The most widely recognized legacy of the early pioneers in motor development is their normative descriptions of stagelike changes in reaching, grasping, crawling, and walking and their focus on maturation as the driving force of development (Ames, 1937; Burnside, 1927; Gesell & Ames, 1940; Gesell & Thompson, 1934; Halverson, 1931; McGraw, 1945; Shirley, 1931). McGraw (1945) described visually guided reaching as a six-stage progression beginning with neonates who cannot unequivocally fixate a target object and ending with children in Stage 6 who retrieve objects casually and successfully, taking the target's location and size into account without outward signs of "undue attention" (p. 99). Halverson (1931) described 10 milestones in the development of grasping, beginning with the "primitive squeeze" and culminating in the "superior-forefinger grasp." Shirley (1931) described four stages in the development of walking: newborn stepping movements, standing with support, walking when led, and finally walking alone toward the end of the 1st year. Gesell, the consummate list-maker, described detailed series of stages for 40 different motor behaviors—58 stages of grasping a pellet, from newborns' visual regard to toddlers' "plucks pellet with precise pincer prehension" at the finale; 23 stages of crawling, from "passive kneeling" in Stage 1 to crawling on hands and knees in Stage 19; and so on (Ames, 1937; Gesell, 1933, 1946; Gesell & Thompson, 1938).

To modern researchers in motor development, the reifying of behaviors into stagelike lists seems old-fashioned, and attributing maturation as the driving force for infants' progress through the various stages seems simplistic (Bertenthal & Clifton, 1998; Thelen & Adolph, 1992). Ironically, Gesell (1946), McGraw

(1935), and Shirley (1931) explicitly noted that most children straddled adjacent stages, skipped stages, reverted to earlier stages, exhibited behaviors that did not fit the structural descriptions of stages, and displayed vast individual differences. The enterprise of distilling real-time structure from variable motions and essentializing invariant sequences from developmental variability was instigated by a direct and conscious opposition to prevailing theories of conditioning and habit formation (Adolph & Berger, 2005; Thelen & Adolph, 1992). Likewise, the intense focus on maturation as the causal agent for development was a response to the extreme versions of behaviorism that were so popular at the time (Senn, 1975).

### What's New?

What then, might we take from the early pioneers? The so-called stages of infants' motor skills highlight a central question in developmental psychology: Is there ever anything truly new? On the one hand, the qualitative changes in formal structure between earlier and later appearing stages of motor skills provide *prima facie* evidence that new behavioral forms can appear in development. Visual prehension, crude raking motions, and precise pincer prehension do not merely reflect changes in the speed, accuracy, and variability of a grasp. These behaviors are qualitatively different forms. Passive kneeling, belly crawling, hands-knees crawling, and Gesell's 20 other stages of crawling share the common feature of prone body position, but these behaviors are qualitatively different in terms of the relevant body parts used for balance and propulsion and the temporal-spatial coordination of the various limbs. Such qualitative changes in the directly observable domain of motor skills provide a model system for evaluating arguments that development can entail qualitative change. One of the most influential ideas in research on cognitive development is that children's mental structures can reorganize into qualitatively different, incommensurable ways of thinking (Carey, 1985; Piaget, 1954).

On the other hand, the reasonableness of each behavioral series points to core commonalities between stages in motor skill acquisition. Armed with modern, high resolution recording technologies that allow exquisitely detailed descriptions of infants' movements, muscle actions, and force profiles, current research findings have tended to blur the distinction between stages by highlighting more continuous changes in the subtle elabora-tion and increasing precision of reaching and walking movements (Berthier, Rosenstein, & Barto, 2005; Bril & Breniere, 1992). Moreover, the notion that earlier appearing behaviors may be preformations of later appearing behaviors is a well-accepted concept in developmental psychology (Thelen & Adolph, 1992), as witnessed in von Hofsten's (1984) prereaching, Meltzoff and Moore's (1983) neonatal imitation, and Trevarthen's (1993) protocommunication. In cognitive development, Spelke and others (Spelke, Breinlinger, Macomber, & Jacobson, 1992; Spelke & Newport, 1998) argue that core concepts presage mature thinking in domains of physical, biological, and psychological reasoning. On these views, the adultlike endpoint is an elaboration of the initial concept, rather than a metamorphosis or true transformation.

## Emergent Developments

The most prevalent view of development among both academics and laypersons is that developmental changes are driven by some factor or set of factors, located in the environment, the brain, or the genes. These factors, either acting alone or in combination, are the drivers—the causal agents—of developmental change. An alternative *systems* view of development was spearheaded largely by Thelen and colleagues' work on infants' leg and arm movements (e.g., Thelen & Smith, 1994). On this account, motor development, like developmental changes in any domain, may result from the spontaneous self-organization of the various components in the system. The emergent product of the mix is different from and greater than the sum of its component parts.

### Brain-Based Explanations

Although most modern researchers scoff at Gesell's idea that neural maturation drives motor skill acquisition lockstep through a series of stages, many modern researchers assume that neural maturation plays a pivotal role in motor development. Researchers presume that differences in pre- and postnatal neural maturation contribute to differences in locomotor abilities between precocial animals such as chicks and altricial animals such as rats (Muir, 2000). Maturation of postural mechanisms in the central nervous system (CNS) underlie age-related changes in children's response to balance disruptions (Forssberg & Nashner, 1982; Riach & Hayes, 1987; Shumway-Cooke & Woollacott, 1985).

Maturational changes in the speed of information processing facilitate walking onset toward the end of infants' 1st year (P. R. Zelazo, 1998; P. R. Zelazo, Weiss, & Leonard, 1989). Alternatives to maturation tend to emphasize experience-driven changes in the CNS. For example, some of the differences in motor precocity between chicks and rats may result from the longer period of time that chick embryos spend moving their legs compared with rat fetuses prior to hatching or birth (Muir & Chu, 2002). Experience maintaining balance in a variety of upright postures and tasks may reorganize how the CNS controls the various body parts when balance is disrupted (Ledebt & Bril, 1999; Roncesvalles, Woollacott, & Jensen, 2001).

Modern brain-based explanations for motor development are in good company. Theoretical debates about the sources of cognitive and perceptual development also center around maturation versus experience-driven changes in the CNS (e.g., M. H. Johnson, Munakata, & Gilmore, 2002; Spelke & Newport, 1998). Researchers' shared partiality for the brain over other body parts makes sense: The brain is of psychological interest, whereas the elbow and the knee are not. Using the developmental trajectory of infants' leg movements as an extended case study, we describe the alternative possibility that no factor, including the brain, is logically responsible for development. In this alternative account, changes in more homely factors normally outside the purview of psychologists' interest, may be the critical facilitators of development. Undoubtedly, important changes in the brain and nervous system occur throughout development. At issue is whether these changes must enjoy a privileged status in explaining developmental progress.

### Alternating Leg Movements

We begin with the observations and puzzles that originally fascinated researchers. The observations are these: Newborn infants perform alternating leg movements if an experimenter holds them upright with their feet against a solid surface (see Figure 4.2a). The "steps" are painfully slow and exaggerated (Forssberg & Wallberg, 1980; Shirley, 1931), but, like mature walking, first one leg moves and then the other. At approximately 8 weeks of age, upright stepping movements disappear. Infants either stand rooted to the ground (McGraw, 1935) or perform bouncing movements by simultaneously flexing both legs and then extending them

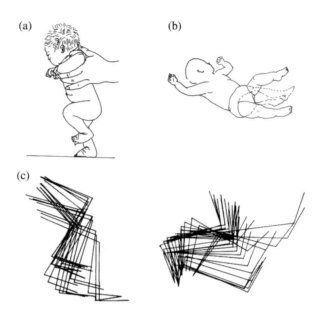

**Figure 4.2** Alternating leg movements in newborn infants. (a) Upright stepping. Courtesy of Karen E. Adolph, New York University. (b) Supine kicking. *Source:* From "Rhythmical Stereotypies in Normal Human Infants," by E. Thelen, 1979, *Animal Behavior, 27,* pp. 699–715. Reprinted with permission. (c) Stick diagrams of leg movements in upright stepping and supine kicking in a representative 2-week-old infant. The lines chart the movements of one of the infant's legs at toe, ankle, knee, and hip every 33 milliseconds. *Source:* From "Newborn Stepping: An Explanation for a 'Disappearing Reflex,'" by E. Thelen and D. M. Fisher, 1982, *Developmen-*

(J. E. Clark, Whitall, & Phillips, 1988; McGraw, 1932). Upright stepping returns toward the end of the 1st year when infants begin to walk with support and eventually to take independent walking steps. This U-shaped developmental progression raises three intriguing puzzles:

1. What makes newborns step?
2. Why do infants exhibit the alternating pattern rather than some other pattern of leg movements?
3. What makes upright stepping disappear and then reappear months later to cause the U-shaped trajectory?

### Reflexes

Puzzle 1—why newborns step—is a question about proximal cause. The most commonly held answer is that the movements are a spinal reflex elicited by the upright position and the feeling of the floor beneath infants' feet (McGraw, 1945; P. R. Zelazo, 1976, 1983). In fact, stepping is prominently featured in most developmental textbooks as an example of a newborn reflex (e.g., Berk,

2003; Siegler, DeLoache, & Eisenberg, 2003). However, newborn stepping does not fit well with a traditional notion of a reflex. In contrast to an eye blink response to a puff of air or a withdrawal response from a pinprick, stepping is inconsistent across infants and instances (Saint-Anne Dargassies, 1986) and particular eliciting stimuli are not necessary. Infants exhibit stepping movements on walls and ceilings in sideways and upside-down positions (Andre-Thomas & Autgaerden, 1966; Peiper, 1963). They step spontaneously without any stimulation to the bottoms of their feet while in the uterus (Prechtl, 1986) and while held with their legs dangling in the air (Thelen & Fisher, 1982; Touwen, 1976; B. D. Ulrich, 1989). Moreover, as illustrated in Figure 4.2b, infants frequently kick their legs in the same alternating pattern while lying on their backs (Thelen, 1979; Thelen, Bradshaw, & Ward, 1981; Thelen & Fisher, 1982, 1983b). Stepping and kicking appear so similar in form that stick diagrams of stepping look like kicking if you turn the figure sideways (see Figure 4.2c).

Stepping and kicking movements are most frequent when infants are aroused and fussy but not crying and tonically rigid (e.g., Thelen, 1981a; Thelen, Fisher, Ridley-Johnson, & Griffin, 1982). Similarly, when late gestation rat fetuses and newborn rat pups are aroused by sensory stimulation or drug injections, they also increase the frequency of alternating stepping movements in their fore and hind limbs while held in various positions (Robinson & Smotherman, 1992). Thus, some researchers view newborns' alternating leg movements as a spontaneous by-product of arousal, rather than a reflex (Thelen et al., 1982). The upright posture, pressure of the experimenter's hands around the chest, feeling of the floor under the feet, and so on may increase infants' arousal. As infants become aroused, energy flows through their muscles and powers up their legs (Thelen & Smith, 1994).

### Pattern Generators

Puzzle 2—why the alternating pattern instead of some other pattern—concerns the real-time, moment-to-moment control of movements. In principle, newborns might move one leg at a time or both legs simultaneously (and they occasionally do), so why might the alternating pattern predominate? Neither a spinal reflex nor an arousal account specifically addresses the alternation between the legs. The similarity in form between newborn stepping and later walking has led many researchers to view newborn stepping as an example of a

core competence that is later co-opted and adapted for functional purposes in mature walking (Spelke & Newport, 1998). The core propensity to move the legs in alternation might reside in animals' neural anatomy in a so-called central pattern generator (e.g., Forssberg, 1985; Muir, 2000; Yang, Stephens, & Vishram, 1998)—a neuronal network in the spinal cord that produces locomotor movements of the legs through rhythmic alternations in flexor and extensor muscles (Grillner, 1975; Grillner & Wallen, 1985; Kiehn & Butt, 2003). Indeed, anencephalic infants step (Monnier, 1973), indicating that higher brain regions are not necessary for performing the movements. Similarly, insects and spinal preparations of rats, cats, lampreys, and chicks produce alternating bursts of neural activity in the flexor and extensor muscles responsible for locomotion (e.g., Orlovsky, Deliagina, & Grillner, 1999).

Intact animals, however, may display the alternating pattern without the benefit of (or despite the availability of) a neural pattern generator. Although researchers cannot study the neural activity in the isolated spinal cords of human infants, muscle activations revealed by electromyography are not strictly consistent with the notion of a central pattern generator. In some studies, infants' alternating leg movements do not appear to result from rhythmic bursts of flexor and then extensor muscles. Instead, infants bend their legs to kick or to step by co-contracting flexor and extensor muscles in their hips and ankles simultaneously (Forssberg, 1985; Thelen & Cooke, 1987; Thelen & Fisher, 1982, 1983b). Because the flexor muscles are stronger, the leg bends. Infants straighten their legs without the need for muscle activation. Instead, the springiness of the leg reverses the direction of motion from flexion to extension and the force of gravity pulls the leg straight (Thelen, 1996).

In fact, co-contraction of the muscles that power up a movement and the muscles that oppose the movement may be the norm rather than the exception in infants' movements (e.g., Forssberg, 1985; Forssberg & Wallberg, 1980). Co-contraction makes movements slower and stiffer and can even freeze a movement (as when crying infants become tonically rigid or when we "make a muscle" by co-contracting biceps and triceps). Although undifferentiated muscle actions are emblematic of early periods in skill acquisition and produce clumsy-looking, energetically costly movements (Damiano, 1993), co-contraction may serve a useful function by "chunking" individual muscles into larger groups and thereby simplifying the control problem (Spencer, Vereijken, Diedrich, & Thelen, 2000; Thelen & Spencer, 1998).

Co-contractions and springy muscles highlight a central maxim in current views of real-time motor control: Central pattern generators, like any other neural mechanism in the CNS, can only control muscle forces (Pearson, 1987; Winter & Eng, 1995). Movements, however, are composed of multiple forces (Bernstein, 1967; Woollacott & Jensen, 1996; Zernicke & Schneider, 1993). The net force responsible for a movement can be decomposed into the active forces produced by the muscles and the passive forces produced by the springiness and stickiness of the muscles and joints, gravity, inertia, and the motion-dependent torques created by moving other body parts (the hip bone is connected to the thigh bone, etc.). If you lift your arm from a stationary position at your side, muscle force contributes significantly to the total force required for the movement. However, if you drop your arm downward from overhead, the movement is nearly entirely controlled by gravity and inertia. If you wave your upper arm while allowing your wrist to go limp, the movement of your hand results from motion-dependent torques. Thus, movements with the same outward appearance can be caused by very different patterns of muscle activation (reciprocal enervation, co-contraction, etc.). The CNS acts more like a team player than a star soloist in determining real-time movement outcomes.

### Behavioral Flexibility

A final piece to Puzzle 2 concerns the flexibility of the alternating pattern. A central pattern generator that can flexibly modulate, alter, and discard its pattern to suit the task is just a fancy name for the CNS (Thelen & Spencer, 1998). Although leg alternation normally predominates, it is not obligatory, and although leg alternation is displayed by anencephalic infants, the movement pattern is not impervious to perceptual feedback and supraspinal influences. One reason for alternation may be movement economics. Lifting both their legs off the floor simultaneously while an experimenter holds infants upright under their arms and bending and straightening both legs together while infants lie on their backs might require infants to exert more work in their abdominal and torso muscles than lifting their legs in alternation (Thelen & Smith, 1994). Under task constraints that alter the balance of effort, infants switch from alternating to simultaneous leg movements. An elastic yoke between the legs of 4-month-olds caused infants to

switch from predominately alternating and single leg movements to simultaneous movements that did not require them to pull against the yoke (Thelen, 1994). Similarly, in several studies, a pliable yoke between the hind limbs of fetal rats and newborn rat pups elicited a switch from alternating and single leg kicks to simultaneous leg movements (Robinson & Kleven, in press). A yoke between the fore and hind limbs on one side elicited increased synchrony between that pair of limbs. In other words, human infants and baby rats might simply perform the easiest pattern of movements given the current circumstances.

Like simultaneous leg movements, single-leg movements can also predominate when researchers arrange the appropriate contingencies. With the new biomechanical constraints introduced by a weight around one ankle, 6-week-old infants maintained their overall kick rate relative to baseline, but they broke up the alternating pattern by kicking more frequently with their unweighted leg (Thelen, Skala, & Kelso, 1987). With a tiny weight attached to one leg, 1- and 2-day-old rat fetuses produced more kicks on their unweighted leg and they scaled their kick frequency to the size of the weights (Brumley & Robinson, 2002, in press).

With the introduction of motivational factors, infants kick a single leg quite purposefully. In the most popular paradigm, researchers link an infant's leg movements with a desirable goal by attaching one end of a soft ribbon to the infant's foot and the other end to an overhead mobile. Dozens of experiments by Rovee-Collier and her colleagues showed that infants increased the frequency and size of leg kicks when their movements caused the mobile elements to jiggle (e.g., Rovee & Rovee, 1969; Rovee-Collier & Gekoski, 1979; Rovee-Collier, Sullivan, Enright, Lucas, & Fagen, 1980). In terms of intralimb kinematics and electromyogram (EMG) patterns, the spontaneous baseline kicks were continuous with the exploratory kicks during acquisition and the intentional kicks during extinction, meaning that infants harnessed the available movements for functional action (Thelen & Fisher, 1983a). After learning the contingency with one leg, 3-month-olds quickly learned to kick the formerly noncontingent leg when the ribbon was switched (Rovee-Collier, Morrongiello, Aron, & Kupersmidt, 1978). Perhaps most impressive in terms of flexibility, 3-month-olds learned to flex and extend their contingent leg to particular criterion angles under a strict conditioning arrangement that required these specific joint angles to activate the mobile (Angulo-Kinzler, 2001;

Angulo-Kinzler & Horn, 2001; Angulo-Kinzler, Ulrich, & Thelen, 2002).

## Regressions

Puzzle 3—why upright stepping disappears and subsequently reappears—concerns regressions and continuity over development. A long-held explanation credits neural maturation as the primary factor in driving the U-shaped developmental trajectory (e.g., Forssberg, 1985, 1989; Forssberg & Wallberg, 1980; McGraw, 1940, 1945). On this account, cortical maturation suppresses newborns' spinally generated stepping movements at 8 weeks. With increasing myelinization of the cortical-spinal tract, stepping movements reappear under volitional, cortical control at 8 months. Finally, maturation of neural structures and circuitry increases information-processing speed and efficiency so that infants walk independently at approximately 12 months (P. R. Zelazo, 1998; P. R. Zelazo et al., 1989).

Several lines of evidence indicate that continuity may underlie the apparent regression. That is, alternating leg movements are only masked in an upright position; they do not disappear. One line of evidence is that infants continue to display spontaneous kicking movements during the same 2- to 8-month time period when they do not display upright stepping (Thelen, 1979; Thelen & Fisher, 1982). Given the structural similarities between kicking and stepping in their real-time trajectories, the difference in developmental trajectories appears due to posture rather than propensity.

A second argument for continuity is that normally nonstepping 2- to 7-month-old infants exhibit alternating steps when they are supported over a motorized treadmill (Thelen & Ulrich, 1991). Like stepping in newborns, stepping in older treadmill walkers appears to be nonvolitional; infants rarely look down or show interest in the movement of their lower limbs (Thelen, 1986). However, as in kicking, the legs are responsive to the biomechanical context. In several studies, infants altered the speed of their steps in accordance with treadmill speed (Thelen, 1986; Vereijken & Thelen, 1997; Yang et al., 1998). With one leg on a faster moving treadmill belt and the other leg on a slower moving belt, infants maintained alternating movements. But, to do so, they relinquished the normal 50% phasing relationship between the legs and treadmill walking looked like limping (Thelen, Ulrich, & Niles, 1987). When the movements of one leg were disrupted by manually holding the leg in place or by pulling the leg back at a speed faster than the moving treadmill belt, infants typically adapted by keeping only one leg in the air at a time (Pang & Yang, 2001). In the event that infants momentarily lost the alternating pattern, they quickly regained it in the step immediately following the disturbance.

A third line of evidence concerns the effects of practice. When parents give their infants daily practice moving their legs in an upright position as part of an experimental training regimen or as part of a cultural belief in infant exercise, infants retain the alternating movements for longer periods (N. A. Zelazo, Zelazo, Cohen, & Zelazo, 1993; P. R. Zelazo, Zelazo, & Kolb, 1972) or display the movements continuously over the 1st year of life (Konner, 1973). Similarly, regular practice stepping on a motorized treadmill results in a higher frequency of alternating steps and more adult-like muscle actions (Vereijken & Thelen, 1997; Yang et al., 1998). A related argument for continuity is that typically developing infants who receive regular practice with stepping movements begin to walk at younger ages compared with infants in control groups who did not receive daily practice and infants in cultures that do not emphasize the exercise of upright postures (Hopkins & Westra, 1990; Keller, 2003; Super, 1976; P. R. Zelazo et al., 1972, 1989). Similarly, children with Down syndrome who receive daily practice walking on a treadmill begin walking independently at younger ages than matched controls (D. A. Ulrich, Ulrich, Angulo-Barroso, & Yun, 2001).

## Contextual Factors

The remaining piece to Puzzle 3 concerns why upright steps might normally be masked. Just as nonneural, biomechanical factors may constrain and facilitate movements in real time, the culprit in the developmental course of infants' leg movements may be the decidedly nonneural factor of leg fat. Over the first few months of life, normal gains in leg fat typically outstrip gains in muscle strength (Thelen, 1984b). On this leg-fat account, supine kicking may continue during the same period when upright stepping disappears because supine kicking requires less muscle strength than upright stepping (think of performing bicycling movements with your legs in a supine position compared with marching movements while standing upright). Gravity assists hip flexion while infants are lying down by pulling infants' thighs toward their chests, but gravity works against lifting the legs while infants are standing up by pulling the leg downward (Thelen, Fisher, & Ridley-Johnson,

1984). Accordingly, naturally slimmer infants produce more upright steps than chubbier ones (Thelen et al., 1982). When infants' legs were loaded with small weights to simulate normal gains in leg fat, previously stepping infants stopped stepping (Thelen et al., 1984). Conversely, when infants' legs were submerged in a tank of water to alleviate the effects of gravity, nonstepping infants stepped once again.

Consistent with the leg-fat explanation, nonstepping infants might exhibit steps on a motorized treadmill because the treadmill belt provides the necessary energy to lift the leg against gravity. The treadmill stretches the leg backward and allows it to pop forward like a spring (Thelen, 1986). Alternating steps may predominate over simultaneous leg movements because lifting both legs together requires more work in the abdominal muscles. Regular practice moving the legs in an upright posture may prolong stepping movements beyond the 8-week cutoff and accelerate walking onset before the end of the 1st year by building up the requisite strength for infants to lift one leg through the air and to support their body weight on the other leg. Specificity of training effects provides further evidence that practice builds strength. Training regimens for newborn stepping do not facilitate newborn sitting and vice versa (N. A. Zelazo et al., 1993).

### Facial Wiping

Our choice of newborn stepping as an extended case study was not accidental. For nearly a century, infants' alternating leg movements have served as a favored model system for illustrating general principles in maturationist (e.g., McGraw, 1940), learning (e.g., P. R. Zelazo, 1998), core competence (e.g., Forssberg, 1985; Spelke & Newport, 1998), and dynamic systems (e.g., Thelen & Smith, 1994) views of development. The favored status of infants' leg movements stems both from the centrality of walking for human functioning and from the fascinating puzzle of developmental regressions. Our aim here is to illustrate the plausibility of the argument that, at least in principle, factors outside the province of the CNS may sometimes be the critical facilitators of development. Toward that end, we describe a lesser known, but equally fascinating example.

Just as alternating leg movements are a highly patterned response in the behavioral repertoire of human infants, facial wiping is a highly stereotyped response for rats. The animals bring one or both forepaws to their ears and stroke downward toward their nose in bouts of

single or simultaneous limb movements (Berridge, 1990). Under normal circumstances, adult rats exhibit facial wiping during grooming. In an experimental arrangement, a noxious stimulus such as an infusion of quinine or lemon into the mouth elicits facial wiping (Grill & Norgren, 1978). Like the U-shaped trajectory of infants' leg movements, facial wiping also exhibits a developmental regression. Facial wiping to a lemon infusion appears in completely exteriorized fetal rats at 20 to 21 days of gestation (rats have a 21-day gestation). After birth, facial wiping to lemon disappears. The classic limb movements to a noxious lemon infusion reappear 11 days later when rats stand up on their hind legs and wipe their face with their front legs (Smotherman & Robinson, 1989).

Like stepping in human infants, the propensity for facial wiping in rat pups is merely masked; the movements have not actually disappeared. At 19 days of gestation, the age when completely exteriorized fetuses fail to facial wipe to a lemon infusion, partially exteriorized fetuses exhibit wiping movements inside the amnion (Robinson & Smotherman, 1991). What factor might underlie the dramatic difference in behavior caused by the subtle difference in context? Between 19 and 20 days of gestation, fetuses acquire the ability to stabilize their head. For 19-day-olds, the amnion provides an important stabilizing function. The amniotic membranes hold the head steady and help the paws to contact the face.

Why, then, do the movements disappear after birth? In newborn pups, the facial wiping behavior competes for expression with a strong tendency to maintain contact against a surface with their belly and all four feet (Pellis, Pellis, & Teitelbaum, 1991). With forelimbs freed from contact with the ground by neck-deep immersion in water, 1- to 3-day-old rat pups exhibited facial wiping to lemon (Smotherman & Robinson, 1989). Although the urge to keep the body pressed against a contact surface dissipates after a few days, full-blown facial wiping awaits sufficient postural control for rats to stand up on their hind legs at 11 days postbirth. In the meantime, 7- to 9-day-old rat pups compensate for inadequate balance by improvising the necessary support (Robinson & Smotherman, 1992). For example, they support their bodies on their elbows and lower their head for simultaneous wiping between the two forepaws.

### Rate-Limiting Factors

The factors involved in unmasking facial wiping in rat pups are reminiscent of the role played by the treadmill, the tank of water, and the supine position in unmasking alternating leg movements in human infants. The amnion, water tanks, and so on served as external scaffolds that temporarily replaced missing elements and thus promoted the expression of the target behaviors (Smotherman & Robinson, 1996). In a sense, the ability to lift the forelimbs to the face or to move the legs in an alternating pattern resides as much in the scaffolds as in the infants.

Both case studies—alternating leg movements and facial wiping—highlight the epigenetic nature of development (Oyama, 1985). That is, current behavior emerges from the changing interplay between the various components in the organism and the various components in the local environment (Smotherman & Robinson, 1996). New developments might be more than the sum of the component parts and new behavioral forms might arise as the product of spontaneous self-organization.

Given a particular environment, each organismic component must be above some threshold level of developmental readiness to produce the target behavior. Many writers refer to the set of component abilities, processes, propensities, and bodily features as a "confluence of factors" (Bertenthal & Clifton, 1998, p. 87; Freedland & Bertenthal, 1994, p. 26; Spencer & Schöner, 2003, p. 397; Thelen, 1995, p. 83) to emphasize the fluid and changeable nature of the entire behavioral system. Like a developmental chemistry experiment, over time, factors may enter and disappear from the mix and the various combinations and interactions of components may result in new behaviors. At any given point in development, the critical, rate-limiting factor that triggers the system to reorganize into a new configuration might be a psychological function governed by the CNS (e.g., motivation, balance control), or it might be a more peripheral factor such as gravity or leg fat.

## Developmental Trajectories

Developmental regressions underscore the importance of describing developmental trajectories, especially in individuals. Motor development and physical development are uniquely suited for such a task because the dependent variables—movements and body growth—can be observed and mapped directly. Historically, research in motor development has always recognized the value of careful, detailed descriptions of individual developmental trajectories. McGraw's (1935) daily observations of identical twins Jimmy and Johnny are the most famous example. However, other examples abound. Re-

searchers have tracked the course of fetal motility (de-Vries et al., 1982; Robertson, 1990), infants' eye movements (von Hofsten, 2004), rhythmical stereotypies (Thelen, 1979, 1981a), treadmill-elicited stepping (Thelen & Ulrich, 1991; Vereijken & Thelen, 1997), reaching (Clifton, Muir, Ashmead, & Clarkson, 1993; Corbetta & Bojczyk, 2002; Halverson, 1931; Spencer et al., 2000; Thelen et al., 1993; von Hofsten, 1991), crawling (Adolph, Vereijken, & Denny, 1998; Freedland & Bertenthal, 1994), walking (Bril & Breniere, 1989, 1992, 1993; Shirley, 1931), crawling and walking over slopes (Adolph, 1997), everyday crawling and walking experience (Adolph, 2002; Garciaguirre & Adolph, 2005b), and stair-climbing (Gesell & Thompson, 1929).

What can be gained from so much complex, individualized description? What new understandings might warrant the additional work and expense of microgenetic analyses? Although cross-sectional studies can identify interesting developmental milestones, microgenetic descriptions of individual children may yield a more accurate picture of developmental progress (see Siegler, Chapter 11, this *Handbook,* this volume). The rate and amplitude of change vary across children and sometimes critical features in the shape of the trajectory vary across children (Corbetta & Thelen, 1996). Thus, one argument for microgenetic analyses is that averaging across children and time-based observations can lead to erroneous assumptions about the underlying trajectory (Lampl, Johnson, & Frongillo, 2001). Such errors can, in turn, misinform theories about the mechanisms of developmental change and distort the design of subsequent studies to test the putative mechanisms.

A second argument for microgenetic analyses is that based on individual trajectories, researchers can identify possible causes of change (Ledebt, 2000; Thelen & Corbetta, 2002). For example, reaching for small objects shows a zigzag trajectory over the 1st year of life. First, infants reach with two hands for small objects, then one hand, then they revert to the less efficient bimanual reach, then back to one hand (Fagard, 2000). The timing of the zigzag, however, varies across infants. Microgenetic observations of individual children suggested that the reversion to bimanual reaching might stem from an increased coupling between the arms in walking. In the same few weeks when infants reverted to bimanual reaching, they began to walk using the typical "high-guard" position of the arms to help themselves keep balance (Corbetta & Bojczyk, 2002). In subsequent weeks, as the arms gradually lowered and differentiated into a reciprocal swinging pattern in walking, the arms also redifferentiated into one-handed reaching.

### One Step Backward, Two Steps Forward

The path of development is often tortuous and uneven. Sometimes when skill performance reaches asymptote, the only route to forward progress involves a detour. Infants may need to relinquish the accuracy, efficiency, and stability that they have fought so hard to attain with an earlier developing skill in order to make progress with a later developing skill that will eventually enable a higher level of functioning. In terms of both form and function, development can be a process of moving one step backward for every two steps forward (P. H. Miller, 1990; P. H. Miller & Seier, 1994).

The transition from crawling to walking provides a wonderful illustration of uneven developmental progress. After weeks of steady improvement, infants achieve high levels of performance in crawling on hands and knees (Adolph et al., 1998; Freedland & Bertenthal, 1994). Their quadruped gait is fast, beautifully modulated, and highly functional. Ironically, the switch from the earlier developing skill of crawling to the more mature skill of walking requires expert crawlers to cope with an initial decrement in performance. At first, upright walking is slow, variable, and so teeming with errors that infants may fall after every few steps (Shirley, 1931). On some level, infants may be aware that their new upright skill comes with a cost. Newly walking infants sometimes revert from walking to crawling if they want to get somewhere quickly (McGraw, 1935; Zanone et al., 1993). Nonetheless, many researchers have noted that children appear pulled, perhaps by the sheer novelty of the new skill or the motivation for advancement, toward relinquishing the old in favor of the new (e.g., Rosander & von Hofsten, 2000; Shrager & Siegler, 1998; von Hofsten, 2004). New walkers prefer to face locomotor obstacles in their less efficient upright posture than in their more functional and familiar crawling posture (Adolph, 1997). When placed in their old familiar crawling posture at the top of an impossibly steep slope, new walkers sometimes stand themselves up, walk haplessly over the brink, and fall.

Like the developmental change from crawling to walking, the acquisition of locomotion involves an initial decrement in performance. Infants must relinquish the hard-won stability of a stationary posture for a new, more precarious dynamic posture in which they are likely to fall. After infants finally acquire sufficient arm strength to push up and keep balance on all fours, they may spend weeks practicing their new balancing act, sometimes rocking back and forth rhythmically (Adolph et al., 1998; Gesell & Ames, 1940; Goldfield, 1989; Thelen, 1979), as if aroused and eager to go, but stuck with both hands on the ground. The developmental transition from expert, controlled quadruped to novice, falling-down walker requires infants to give up developmental stability for variability and poor performance. Similarly, after infants finally acquire sufficient strength and control to maintain balance in an upright standing position, they experience an initial decrement in performance when they take their first walking steps a few weeks later.

The real-time process of gait initiation—taking the first step in a walking sequence—literally invites falling, but in this case, falling is deliberate and controlled. Walkers must deliberately induce disequilibrium to shift the body weight onto one foot and to produce the propulsive forces necessary to move the body forward (Breniere & Do, 1991; Breniere, Do, & Bouisset, 1987; Ledebt, Bril, & Breniere, 1998). In adults, gait initiation begins before the swinging foot ever leaves the ground. First, in a preparatory phase that disrupts the equilibrium of the standing posture, the center of foot pressure moves backward toward the heels and sideways, first, slightly away then rapidly toward the standing foot (Breniere & Do, 1986; Breniere et al., 1987; Jian, Winter, Ishac, & Gilchrist, 1993). The change in foot pressure causes the center of mass to accelerate in the opposite direction: forward and toward the swinging foot. Next, in a takeoff phase, the swinging foot lifts from the ground and the total weight of the body is carried by the stance leg. Now, the body is falling forward and the velocity of the center of mass increases exponentially.

By the time that the swinging foot recontacts the ground, the center of gravity is moving at peak progression velocity (Breniere & Do, 1986; Breniere et al., 1987; Jian et al., 1993). At the end of the first step, the velocity is nearly at the steady state velocity of the entire walking sequence. How do walkers manage this? For faster intended walking speeds, adults lean their bodies farther forward by shifting their center of foot pressure farther backward (Breniere et al., 1987). As in sprinting, these actions build up more propulsive forces during the preparatory phase before the walker's foot has left the ground. For slower intended speeds, adults exhibit less forward lean, and foot pressure exhibits a smaller backward excursion. These findings are remarkable because they indicate an exquisite anticipation of the forces needed for the intended walking speed. Thus, for adults, the real-time process of gait initiation is loosely analogous to the developmental process of moving backward initially to facilitate forward progress eventually. In this case, the initial back step is beautifully coordinated with the size of the forward step.

For infants, the problem of gait initiation is somewhat different: Babies must cope with the two competing necessities of minimizing the disequilibrium inherent in their new upright posture and creating the disequilibrium required to move (Ledebt et al., 1998). In contrast to adults, infants do not initiate gait with a consistent backward and sideways displacement of their center of foot pressure prior to liftoff, and they do not show anticipation of their intended walking speed by building up the appropriate propulsive forces before the end of their first step (Breniere, Bril, & Fontaine, 1989). Instead, in the earliest days after walking onset, infants' strategies for inducing disequilibrium and catching the body appear to be variable and idiosyncratic (Adolph, Vereijken, & Shrout, 2003; McCollum, Holroyd, & Castelfranco, 1995; McGraw, 1945). With a "falling" strategy, infants raise up on tiptoe and allow themselves to fall forward. With a "twisting" strategy, they wind their trunk like a spring and then let fly bringing their swinging leg around using the torque and angular momentum of the trunk. With a "stepping" strategy, they lift the swinging leg by bending the knee and minimize the fall by taking very small forward steps.

Adultlike anticipatory control of gait initiation takes years to acquire (Ledebt et al., 1998). After the first few months of walking, in the preparatory phase of gait initiation, infants apply vertical force with the swinging leg to load the standing leg and unload the swinging leg. They move the swinging leg forward by tilting the stance leg and pelvis sideways (Assaiante, Woollacott, & Amblard, 2000). As infants' bodies begin to accelerate forward during the takeoff phase, the swinging foot reaches out to catch the body and infants simply control the fall as best they can. Even as the foot lifts, the pelvis drops on the side of the swinging leg as if infants' bodies are collapsing downward into the fall (Bril & Breniere, 1993). Both before and after liftoff, infants' legs, pelvis, trunk, and head oscillate more in sideways and front-back directions compared with preschool-age children and adults (Assaiante et al., 2000). At 4 years of age, children finally show a backward shift in the center of

foot pressure and they achieve steady state velocity by the end of their first step, but the size of the backward shift is not yet correlated with walking velocity (Ledebt et al., 1998). At 6 years, the size of the preparatory backward displacement in foot pressure is correlated with walking velocity but is still not at adult levels.

### Fits and Starts

In contrast to motor development where research has enjoyed a long history of tracking trajectories in individual children, microgenetic descriptions of physical growth are rare. The typical approach to studying body growth is to collect measurements from large cross-sectional samples or to measure children's bodies longitudinally at quarterly or yearly intervals. Given the high variability between children at the same age and the relative paucity of data points for individual children at different ages, the typical analytic strategy is to average over children and interpolate between observations, mathematically smoothing out any jitter in the growth curve. Thus, as illustrated by the curve shown in Figure 4.3a, body growth is depicted as a smooth continuous function. From birth to adulthood, the standard growth curve has three bends caused by a rapidly decelerating rate of growth over infancy, a relatively slow but constant rate of growth during middle childhood, and the pubertal growth spurt prior to reaching final adult size (e.g., Tanner, 1990).

Microgenetic descriptions of physical growth in individual children provide a very different picture of development. As illustrated in Figure 4.3b, actual growth spurts bear no resemblance to the mathematically smoothed bump on the standard growth curve that represents researchers' traditional view of the adolescent growth spurt. Children's growth is episodic, not continuous (M. L. Johnson, Veldhuis, & Lampl, 1996; Lampl, 1993; Lampl et al., 2001; Lampl & Johnson, 1993; Lampl, Veldhuis, & Johnson, 1992). Brief periods (24 hours) of extremely rapid growth are interspersed with long periods of stasis during which no growth occurs for days or weeks on end. Episodic development is characteristic of changes in height, weight, head circumference, and leg bone growth and of every period of development—fetal (Lampl & Jeanty, 2003), infancy (Lampl, 1993; Lampl & Emde, 1983), middle childhood (Lampl, Ashizawa, Kawabata, & Johnson, 1998; Togo & Togo, 1982), and adolescence (Lampl & Johnson, 1993; Togo & Togo, 1982). When measured daily, infants' height increased by 0.5 to 1.65 cm punctuated by 2- to

(a)

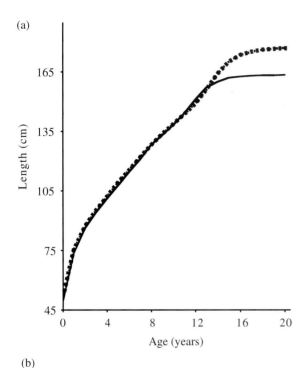

(b)

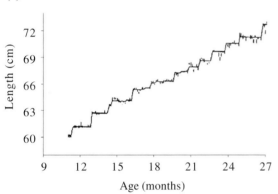

**Figure 4.3**  Growth curves for height. (a) Standard growth curves from birth to 18 years. Data are mathematically smoothed and averaged over children. Dashed line represents boys. Solid line represents girls. *Source:* From growth charts developed by the National Center for Health Statistics in collaboration with the National Center for Chronic Disease Prevention and Health Promotion (2000). (b) Microgenetic episodic growth curve for one exemplar infant. Each vertical line represents daily replicate observations. *Source:* From "Saltation and Stasis: A Model of Human Growth," by M. Lampl, J. D. Veldhuis, and M. L. Johnson, 1992, *Science, 258,* pp. 801–803. Reprinted with permission.

28-day periods of no growth (Lampl et al., 1992). Sampling at weekly intervals preserved the episodic nature of children's growth but had the effect of reducing the number of growth spurts, increasing the amplitude of the spurts, and increasing the periods of stasis (e.g., for

infants observed at weekly intervals, height increased by 0.5 to 2.5 cm interspersed by 7- to 63-day periods of no growth). Although episodic growth characterized every child measured, the timing of spurts, the size of the growth increments, and the length of the plateaus showed large intra- and intersubject variability.

Even within a 24-hour period, growth is not continuous. Children appear to grow more at night while lying down than during the day while standing and walking, especially in their weight-bearing extremities (Lampl, 1992; Noonan et al., 2004). For years, pediatricians assumed a link between nighttime growth and nighttime lower leg pains, but there were no data to corroborate speculations about the source of children's "growing pains." In a recent tour de force of micromeasurement, researchers collected direct measures of lower leg bone growth at 3-minute intervals over a 3-week period via microtransducers implanted into the tibia bones of 3 free-ranging lambs (Noonan et al., 2004). Video recordings synchronized with the activity of the microtransducers specified the lambs' activities during periods of growth and stasis. Approximately 90% of all growth occurred while the lambs were lying down. Weight bearing while standing or walking resulted in biomechanical compression of the growth plate cartilage.

### Evidence for Developmental Stages

The dramatic example of body growth shows how inadequate sampling intervals can lead researchers to mischaracterize the underlying developmental trajectory. If the sampling interval is too large, findings will be insensitive to important fluctuations in the data. Skills that are indexed with interval data (such as height and weight) will appear continuous regardless of whether the underlying trajectory is episodic or U-shaped. Skills that are indexed with binary data (such as object permanence and conservation of quantities) will look stage-like regardless of whether the actual trajectory is variable. The risk is that erroneous descriptions of development can compromise theorizing about underlying mechanisms. Given the expense of collecting increasingly microscopic observations, researchers need to know how small is small enough to capture the essential shape of change.

To answer this question, Adolph and colleagues (Adolph, Robinson, Young, & Gill-Alvarez, 2005; Young, Webster, Robinson, Adolph, & Kanani, 2003) sampled 32 infant motor skills (rolling, sitting, crawling, cruising, walking, etc.) from 11 infants on a daily basis using a checklist diary with parents as the informants. The period of observation averaged 13 months per child. Due to missing data and skills, 261 time series were available. Of these, only 42 time series (16%) showed single stage-like developmental transitions. In these cases, infants never demonstrated the skill prior to the onset day and always demonstrated the skill after the onset day. In the other 84% of the time series, trajectories were variable. Skills sputtered in and out of infants' repertoires, with 3 to 72 transitions between skill absence and presence. In these cases, the selection of an onset day is arbitrary because an infant might walk on Monday, but not again until Thursday, and then not again until the following week, and so on. The data argue against the widely held practice of using punctate estimates of onset dates in normative screening tests (e.g., Frankenburg & Dodds, 1967) and in estimates of infants' motor experience (e.g., Adolph et al., 2003; Bril & Ledebt, 1998; Campos et al., 2000).

Most important, the consequence of sampling at intervals larger than a single day was a dramatic loss of sensitivity to detect the variability in the data (Adolph, Robinson, et al., 2005; Young et al., 2003). Sampling at 2- to 30-day intervals was simulated by systematically removing observations, then reconstructing the developmental trajectories based on the reduced number of observations. The resulting data set included the original data (1-day interval) and the sum of the 2- to 30-day simulated intervals by phase multiplied by the original 261 available time series for a total of 129,456 time series. Of these, 109,120 were variable.

Loss of sensitivity followed an inverse power function (visualize a curve with a sharp initial drop-off that slowly tapers toward 0 over an extended tail). For each day that widened the sampling interval, the loss of sensitivity increased at a greater rate. At the simulated sampling frequency of once per week (considered heroic in microgenetic studies of motor skill acquisition), 51% of the variable time series erroneously appeared stagelike. At the simulated rate of once per month, 91% of the variable time series appeared stagelike. In other words, stagelike developmental trajectories may be an artifact of inadequate sampling rather than a true description of the underlying course of development.

## Variability

Traditionally, researchers in cognitive and perceptual development viewed variability as error variance to be minimized or stochastic noise to be ignored. Currently, however, variability is enjoying a sort of renaissance in these areas, where researchers have begun to recognize change in variability as an important marker of learning and development (e.g., Siegler, 1994, 1996; Siegler & Munakata, 1993). For example, while learning new strategies to solve math, matrix completion, and conservation of quantity problems, children show a spike in variability between erroneous and correct ways of thinking (Alibali, 1999; Goldin-Meadow, Alibali, & Church, 1993).

In contrast to the long disregard of variability in cognitive and perceptual development, researchers in motor development and motor learning have a tradition of using measures of real-time variability (e.g., the standard deviation, coefficient of variation, or category counts) as dependent variables to index learning and development in motor skill acquisition (e.g., Adolph et al., 2003; J. E. Clark et al., 1988; Vereijken, van Emmerick, Whiting, & Newell, 1993). The movements of infants and novices are notoriously variable and unreliable, whereas movements of adults and experts are typically smooth and consistent.

### Crawling

Prior to crawling on hands and knees, many infants belly crawl with their abdomen resting on the floor for at least part of each cycle. Even excluding solutions wherein infants hitch along sitting, crab on their backs, and log roll, belly crawling may be the most variable, idiosyncratic, and creative of all infants' motor skills (McGraw, 1945). Infants use their arms, legs, chests, bellies, and heads in various combinations, sometimes pushing with only one limb in a girdle and dragging the lame limb behind, sometimes ignoring both arms and scraping along with the cheek on the floor or dragging both legs like a marine, sometimes pushing with first the knee then the foot on one leg, sometimes launching themselves from knees or feet onto the belly, and so on (Adolph et al., 1998; Gesell, 1946; Gesell & Ames, 1940). Even when all four limbs move, patterns of interlimb timing are variable (Adolph et al., 1998; Freedland & Bertenthal, 1994). Infants move ipsilateral limbs together like goose-stepping, move arms and legs on alternate sides of the body together like a trot, lift front then back limbs like a bunny hop, and lift all four limbs into the air at once like a swim. Belly crawling is so variable that infants change the configuration of limbs used for support and propulsion and the timing between limbs from cycle to cycle (Adolph et al., 1998). Variability in belly crawling is all the more striking because infants show a dramatic decrease in the variability of interlimb timing within a week or two of crawling on hands and knees (Adolph et al., 1998; Freedland & Bertenthal, 1994).

### Reasons for Variability

What can we make of such variability? With the new renaissance of variability in developmental psychology, researchers in motor development have begun to herald variability as a causal agent of change rather than merely a marker or correlate (e.g., Bertenthal, 1999; Goldfield, 1995; Goldfield, Kay, & Warren, 1993). Indeed, Freedland and Bertenthal (1994, p. 31) wrote with regard to belly and hands-knees crawling, "Variability in performance is one of the driving forces for the emergence of new behaviors." Changes in variability around real-time transitions illustrate researchers' shift from describing changes in variability to treating variability as a causal mechanism. In Kelso's (1995) classic task, adults point both index fingers first to the right then to the left. At slow speeds, variability in the coordination between the two fingers is low. As participants try to wiggle their fingers back and forth at faster and faster speeds, variability increases until the fingers shift to an in-out pattern, at which point variability sharply decreases. On some accounts, the loss of stability is the chief mechanism that causes such changes in behavioral patterns (Bertenthal, 1999; Spencer & Schöner, 2003; Zanone et al., 1993). That is, variability is a prerequisite for any change between stable states, whether in real time, over the course of learning, or over development.

A second current conceptualization of behavioral variability concerns its exploratory function. On analogy to the evolutionary process of variability and selection and the neural process of overproduction and pruning, some researchers view variability as providing the fodder for subsequent selection and sculpting based on feedback from ongoing movements (e.g., Bertenthal & Clifton, 1998; Berthier et al., 2005; E. J. Gibson & Pick, 2000; Thelen & Smith, 1994). On this view, variable belly crawling steps (Bertenthal, 1999; Freedland & Bertenthal, 1994), arm flaps (Thelen et al., 1993), leg kicks (Thelen & Fisher, 1983a), and so on could create the raw materials for more efficient movements by generating an information-rich array of possibilities.

Of course, important exploratory functions could arise as a developmental by-product of variability (Adolph, 1997), just as many important physiological and behavioral forms can be evolutionary exaptations—characters that evolved for other uses or no function at all that were co-opted later for their current role (Gould

& Vrba, 1982). However, many researchers portray variability in infants' movements as intentional exploration motivated by a search for information (e.g., Bertenthal & Clifton, 1998; Goldfield, 1995; von Hofsten, 1997). Furthermore, in some cases, variability is viewed as both an active search for alternatives and as an impetus for exploration: Inconsistency in performance impels infants to explore alternative behaviors until they settle on a more efficient solution (Freedland & Bertenthal, 1994; Goldfield, 1995).

Although new views of variability have stimulated thinking and research, some of the proposals are problematic. The problem with imbuing variability in skills like crawling and reaching with intent is that the evidence for intentional exploration and active searching is simply the finding of variability itself. The problem with treating variability as an independent variable, moderator, or mediator—a causal prerequisite for learning and development—is that variability can also serve as a dependent variable for explaining the same phenomena. Natural selection may not be a useful metaphor in every case of behavioral development (just as evolution may include multiple mechanisms such as exaptation and spontaneous mutation) and generalizations from simple laboratory tasks such as finger-wiggling may not always hold true.

Belly crawlers show no evidence of selection or pruning and no evidence of a sudden spike in variability around the transition to crawling on hands and knees (Adolph et al., 1998). Rather, infants showed improvements in speed and proficiency despite unabated variability over weeks of belly crawling, and nearly every infant used an alternating gait pattern to crawl on hands and knees regardless of whether they had previously crawled on their bellies. Without a salient cost to performance, variability may continue unabated (Vereijken & Adolph, 1999). Perhaps the safest conclusion is that development is a many-splendored thing and variability may play multiple roles in the developmental process (see Siegler, Chapter 11, this *Handbook*, this volume). Frequently, changes in variability inform on that process, but sometimes variability may simply reflect noise.

## Time, Age, and Experience

Development is about change over time. Thus, a central question for developmental psychologists is how best to conceptualize the passing of time and the factors that accompany it (e.g., Wohlwill, 1970). How should we order repeated observations and assign participants into groups? The most common solution is to put children's chronological age at the time of testing on the x-axis. Indeed, many researchers do not consider a study to be developmental without comparisons between age groups. The most common alternative is to retain the regularity of days, weeks, months, and so on, but to normalize observations and subject groupings by children's experience, calculated with reference to an estimated day of skill onset (e.g., Adolph et al., 1998; Bertenthal, Campos, & Kermoian, 1994; Bril & Breniere, 1992; Corbetta & Bojczyk, 2002). Thus, instead of comparing individuals at 3 and 6 months of age or comparing groups of 3- and 6-month-olds, researchers might compare children over the first few months of reaching or the first few years of walking. Similar research strategies include retaining the serial order of milestone events (e.g., standers, new walkers, experienced walkers, runners) without retaining the interval spacing (e.g., Sundermier, Woollacott, Roncesvalles, & Jensen, 2001; Witherington et al., 2002) and holding age constant while varying experience with particular motor skills (e.g., Adolph, 2000; Campos et al., 2000). Here, we focus on the development of walking to illustrate some of the issues involved in representing, describing, and explaining change over time.

### Improvements in Walking Skill

After 75 years or so of research on the development of walking, researchers have compiled a consistent constellation of related parameters that change with age and experience. Between 10 and 16 months of age, most infants take their first independent walking steps (Adolph et al., 2003; Frankenburg & Dodds, 1967). Initially, infants have such difficulty surmounting the dual problems of balance and propulsion that their walking gait resembles that of Charlie Chaplin. They take small forward steps with their legs splayed wide from side to side (e.g., Adolph et al., 2003; Bril & Breniere, 1992; Burnett & Johnson, 1971; McGraw, 1945; Shirley, 1931). Their hips are externally rotated and their toes point out to the sides to further increase the base of support (e.g., Adolph, 1995; Ledebt, van Wieringen, & Savelsbergh, 2004). They co-contract extensor and flexor muscles in their legs (Okamoto & Goto, 1985) and their excessively bent knees fail to cushion the downward fall at foot contact and fail to extend the leg fully at toe-off (Sutherland, Olshen, Cooper, & Woo, 1980). They spend a relatively long time with both feet on the ground and a relatively short time with one foot swinging through the air (e.g., Bril & Breniere, 1989, 1991, 1993); as a consequence, overall progression velocity is slow, step frequency is high, and infants land flat-footed or on their toes because there is no time for them to dorsiflex their ankles (McGraw, 1940; Thelen, Bril, & Breniere, 1992). The time and distance of each step is variable and asymmetrical, suggesting that infants are recovering balance from step to step (Adolph et al., 2003; J. E. Clark et al., 1988; J. E. Clark & Phillips, 1987; Ledebt et al., 2004; McGraw & Breeze, 1941). New walkers hold their arms stationary in a high-guard position, with elbows bent, palms turned up, and hands raised above waist level (Ledebt, 2000; McGraw, 1940). Their heads and trunks wobble up and down and from side to side (Bril & Ledebt, 1998; Ledebt, Bril, & Wiener-Vacher, 1995). Most telling, the vertical acceleration of infants' center of gravity is negative at foot contact, meaning that babies are falling downward rather than propelling forward during periods of single leg support (Bril & Breniere, 1993).

Figure 4.4 shows the characteristic time course and direction of improvements in walking skill over infancy and early childhood. The base of support narrows as infants take longer steps with their legs closer together laterally and their toes pointed more straight ahead (e.g., Adolph et al., 2003; Bril & Breniere, 1992). Muscle actions become more reciprocal (Okamoto & Goto, 1985) and steps appear less jarring and variable (e.g., J. E. Clark et al., 1988; Ledebt et al., 2004). As the relative duration of double support decreases and single support increases, walking speed increases and infants land on their heel at foot contact (Bril & Breniere, 1989, 1991, 1993; Thelen et al., 1992). Arms lower toward infants' sides and begin to swing in alternation with leg movements (Ledebt, 2000). Infants stabilize the pitch and roll of their head and trunk (Ledebt et al., 1995) by rigidly locking their upper body parts together "en bloc" (Assaiante, 1998). Eventually, children unlock the rigid coupling between the head and trunk and begin to coordinate the pitch and roll of the head with the reactive up/down and sideways movements of the body caused by each walking step (Assaiante, Thomachot, Aurenty, & Amblard, 1998; Bril & Ledebt, 1998). The size of the negative value of the vertical acceleration of the center of gravity at foot contact slowly decreases until the sign of the function finally becomes positive as in adult walkers (Bril & Breniere, 1993). At this point, when children can "push off" during single leg support,

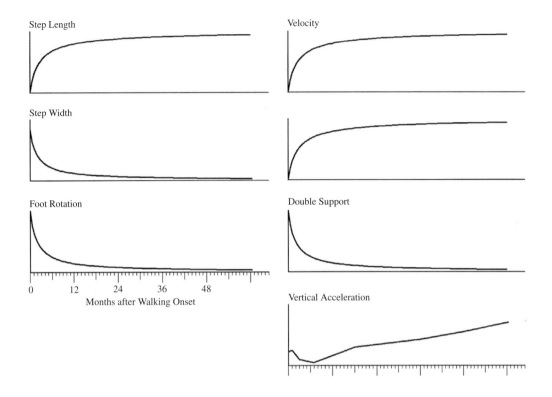

**Figure 4.4** The characteristic time course of improvement in several measures of children's walking gait over the first 60 months of independent walking. Step length = Distance between consecutive steps; Step width = Lateral distance between steps; Foot rotation = Absolute value of in/out-toeing from path of progression; Velocity = Overall distance/time; Swing time = Amount of time with one foot moving through the air; Double support = Amount of time that both feet are on the floor; Vertical acceleration of the center of gravity = Rate of change in velocity of the center of gravity along the vertical axis. *Source:* Figure adapted from "Head Coordination as a Means to Assist Sensory Integration in Learning to Walk," by B. Bril and A. Ledebt, 1998, *Neuroscience and Biobehavioral Reviews, 22,* pp. 555–563. Curves for step length, step width, and foot rotation drawn from data presented in "What Changes in Infant Walking and Why," by K. E. Adolph, B. Vereijken, and P. E. Shrout, 2003, *Child Development, 74,* pp. 474–497; curves for velocity, swing time, and double support derived from *Baby Carriage: Infants Walking with Loads,* by J. S. Garciaguirre and K. E. Adolph, 2005a, manuscript submitted for publication; *Step by Step: Tracking Infants' Walking and Falling Experience,* by J. S. Garciaguirre and K. E. Adolph, 2005b, manuscript submitted for publication; Curve for vertical acceleration drawn from data presented in "Posture and Independent Locomotion in Early Childhood: Learning to Walk or Learning Dynamic Postural Control," by B. Bril and Y. Breniere, 1993, *The Development of Coordination in Infancy,* pp. 337–358. Reprinted with permission.

they have finally mastered control over both balance and disequilibrium.

Since the 1930s, researchers have shared widespread agreement about the proximal cause of the characteristic improvements in walking skill: Infants must acquire sufficient muscle strength to propel their bodies forward while supporting their body weight on one leg and sufficient postural control to maintain balance, especially during periods of single limb support (e.g., Bril & Breniere, 1993; Bril & Ledebt, 1998; McGraw, 1945; Thelen, 1984a). Where most modern and early researchers diverge concerns their assumptions about the

distal source of improvement in the development of walking—the factors that drive increases in muscle strength and balance control. The early pioneers plotted developmental changes in walking skill with infants' age on the x-axis to emphasize the role of neural maturation and body growth in facilitating improvements. In contrast, most modern researchers plot similar graphs with infants' walking experience on the x-axis to emphasize the role of learning and practice.

Given the 6-month range in infants' age at walking onset, normalizing the data to children's walking onset age rather than their birth date facilitates graphical and statistical comparisons between children (e.g., Bril & Breniere, 1993; Bril & Ledebt, 1998; J. E. Clark et al., 1988; Corbetta & Bojczyk, 2002). Note, for representing and describing change in individual infants, age and experience are equivalent measures. In addition, formal statistical models comparing the respective roles of infants' walking experience, chronological age, and body dimensions show that only walking experience explains unique variance in skill improvement over the first 2 years of life (Adolph et al., 2003; cf., Kingsnorth & Schmuckler, 2000). Over the next several years, developmental milestones are a more sensitive measure of improvements than age (Sundermier et al., 2001).

Moreover, as illustrated in Figure 4.4, for many measures, the development of walking skill resembles the negatively accelerated performance curves found in most motor learning tasks (Schmidt & Lee, 1999): Initial improvements are rapid and dramatic while subsequent improvements are more gradual and subtle. Most researchers identify the elbow in the rate of change at 3 to 6 months after walking onset (e.g., Adolph et al., 2003; Bril & Breniere, 1992, 1993; Bril & Ledebt, 1998; McGraw, 1945). Analogous to motor-learning tasks, the initial phase where the performance curve is steepest may reflect infants' struggle to discover the relevant parameters that allow forward progression and balance. The subsequent period of more gradual change may reflect a process of honing and fine-tuning the values of the gait parameters to maximize the biomechanical efficiency of walking.

### Empty Time

Regardless of the relative predictive power of children's chronological age versus their walking experience, neither factor alone or in combination provides an explanation for the improvements in children's walking skill. The widespread use of age and experience as predictor variables in analysis of variance and regression analyses imbues these factors with the causal quality of independent variables (Wohlwill, 1970). However, they are not. Children are not randomly assigned to age or experience groups and each child is (or will be) a member of every group (e.g., in contrast to ethnic and sex groups). Cohort effects and cultural differences are well documented in the development of walking (e.g., Hopkins & Westra, 1990; Super, 1976). In addition, time could just as easily be the dependent measure, as typified by the common use of trials to criterion and time on task as

dependent variables in motor-learning studies (Schmidt & Lee, 1999). Most problematic, the passing of time since infants' birth date or date of walking onset is merely a convenient proxy for age- or experience-related factors that are currently unspecified or difficult to measure. In Wohlwill's (1970) harsh assessment, time itself is conceptually empty. It serves as a "cloak for ignorance" (p. 50).

Rather than relying on age as a crude stand-in for developmental changes in infants' brains and body dimensions, a more optimal research strategy would be to measure the putative causal factors and correlates more directly. For example, the frontal lobes show a temporary surge of electroencephalogram (EEG) activity in the first few weeks of crawling (Bell & Fox, 1996), consistent with an initial overproduction and subsequent pruning in neural connections. The otolith channel of the vestibular-ocular reflex shows a sharp increase in sensitivity to linear accelerations at the time of walking onset (Wiener-Vacher, Ledebt, & Bril, 1996), linking the ability to stabilize gaze while the head moves with the onset of an activity that accelerates the head through space. The natural slimming-down of infants' body proportions is correlated with improvements in walking skill (e.g., Adolph, 1997; Shirley, 1931) and more babyish top-heavy proportions (experimentally induced with lead-weighted shoulder packs or platform shoes) result in decrements to walking skill (Adolph & Avolio, 2000; Garciaguirre & Adolph, 2005a; Schmuckler, 1993; Vereijken, Pedersen, & Storksen, 2005; Yanez, Domakonda, Gill-Alvarez, Adolph, & Vereijken, 2004), suggesting that biomechanical constraints affect strength and balance.

### What Infants Experience

Just as age is only a crude stand-in for unspecified developmental changes, the number of days since walking onset is only a proxy for practice and exposure. Researchers rely on locomotor experience as a causal factor in development for a range of psychological domains (e.g., Bertenthal et al., 1994; Campos et al., 2000). However, the construct of locomotor experience is largely unexamined. Ironically, the abundance of laboratory data collected over the past 100 years with infants walking short straight paths on flat ground under conditions of steady state velocity cannot speak to the quantity or content of infants' everyday experiences with balance and locomotion. In everyday life, infants travel along circuitous paths for large distances over variable ground surfaces with variable walking speeds.

In particular, daily checklist diaries, "step-counters" in infants' shoes, and video recordings of infants walking in everyday environments reveal large individual differences in the amount of practice that infants acquire with walking and large fluctuations for individuals across situations and days (Adolph, 2002, 2005; Adolph, Robinson, et al., 2005; Chan, Biancaniello, Adolph, & Marin, 2000; Chan, Lu, Marin, & Adolph, 1999; Garciaguirre & Adolph, 2005b). Many infants walk intermittently in the first several weeks after onset, vacillating between days when they walk and days when they do not (Adolph, Robinson, et al., 2005). Within days, walking experience is distributed in bouts of activity interspersed with periods of quiet stance when infants stop to play, manipulate objects, or interact with a caregiver (Garciaguirre & Adolph, 2005b). During trips toward a distant destination (on a city sidewalk with a caregiver), bouts tend to be longer in duration ($M = 18$ s) and contain more consecutive steps ($M = 45$ steps) than during free play where destinations are more transient and caregivers are less likely to encourage infants to walk ($M$ bout length = 5 s, $M$ steps = 11).

Accumulated over the course of a normal waking day, the quantity and variety of infants' experience is truly massive (e.g., Adolph, 2002, 2005; Adolph et al., 2003). Each day, infants take more than 9,000 steps and travel the distance of more than 29 football fields. They travel over nearly a dozen different indoor and outdoor surfaces varying in friction, rigidity, and texture. They visit nearly every room in their homes and they engage in balance and locomotion in the context of varied activities. Minor inconsequential falls are common, averaging 15 times per hour, but serious falls that cause infants to engage in sustained crying or that result in minor injuries occur less than once per month (Garciaguirre & Adolph, 2005b).

In sum, infants' everyday walking experiences resemble a type of practice regimen that would be highly conducive to motor learning: massive amounts of variable and distributed practice largely free from aversive consequences for errors (Gentile, 2000; Schmidt & Lee, 1999). However, practice is not doled out evenly across infants and days and researchers have not yet linked the various features of infants' practice regimen with improvements in walking skill. Thus, to infuse the construct of locomotor experience with conceptually mean-

ingful content, researchers might quantify practice or exposure by putting the number of walking steps, number of walking bouts, distance traveled, duration of time engaged in balance and locomotion, number of surfaces traversed, number of falls, or the like on the x-axis instead of simply counting the number of elapsed days since walking onset.

## Movement Is Ubiquitous

Movement is perhaps the most ubiquitous, pervasive, and fundamental of all psychological activity. It is the hallmark of animacy and the essence of agency. Across development, self-initiated movements of the eyes, head, limbs, and body provide the largest source of infants' perceptual experiences.

### Epochs of Movement

As illustrated in the case of walking, the sheer quantity of infants' experiences with movement is staggering. By the time that infants begin to show visual expectancies in laboratory tasks at 3.5 months of age, they may have performed 3 to 6 million eye movements outside the laboratory and viewed countless examples of occlusion and other visual events (Haith, Hazan, & Goodman, 1988; S. P. Johnson, Slemmer, & Amso, 2004). By the time that children succeed at spatial search tasks at 10 months of age, they have likely accumulated enough crawling steps to travel more than half the length of Manhattan (Adolph, 2005). By the time that infants are 12 months old, they have likely experienced over 110,000 bouts of wiggles, waves, kicks, and flaps of 47 different types of spontaneous rhythmical stereotypies in their legs, arms, heads, and trunks (Thelen, 1979, 1981b). The connectionist notion of "epochs" of experience (Munakata, McClelland, Johnson, & Siegler, 1997) is the appropriate metric for measuring the quantity of infants' movement.

The vast quantity of experience, however, does not imply an unremitting march. The bursts and bouts of infants' movements wax and wane with daily sleep/wake cycles and the acquisition of new motor skills. Although newborns are asleep most of the day, they are still moving (e.g., Erkinjuntti, 1988; Fukura & Ishihara, 1997). Sleeping movements include gross movements of the limbs and trunk together, localized movements of one limb, and fast twitches (Fukumoto, Mochizuki, Takeshi, Nomura, & Segawa, 1981). Waking movements are more frequent and of higher amplitude, shifting from slow, writhing movements due to excessive co-contractions in the first weeks of life to smaller, more graceful, and purling fidgety movements between 8 and 12 weeks of life (Cioni, Ferrari, & Prechtl, 1989; Hadders-Algra & Prechtl, 1992; Hadders-Algra, van Eykern, Klip-Van den Nieuwendijk, & Prechtl, 1992; Prechtl & Hopkins, 1986). Rhythmical stereotypies are apparent from the 1st month of life and are most common when infants are awake and aroused but not crying (Thelen, 1979, 1981b). Peak frequencies of particular stereotypies coincide with the acquisition of new motor skills (e.g., kicking and rocking appear prior to crawling, waving the arms appears prior to reaching, and swaying appears prior to independent standing; Gesell & Thompson, 1934; Mc-Graw, 1945; Spencer et al., 2000; Thelen, 1996).

### Movement Is Pervasive in Development

From the very beginning of life, movement is a pervasive feature of development. Fetuses' first spontaneous self-produced movements appear somewhere between 5 and 6 weeks after conception, within a few days after fetuses develop body parts to move (Moore & Persaud, 1993). The earliest movements are tiny, barely discernible head bends and back arches (e.g., deVries et al., 1982; Nilsson & Hamberger, 1990; Prechtl, 1985). At 6 to 7 weeks postconception, fetuses slowly wave their limbs (de-Vries et al., 1982; Sparling & Wilhelm, 1993) and display quick, general startle movements, beginning in the limbs and radiating to the neck and trunk (deVries et al., 1982). Between 7 and 10 weeks postconception, limb waves and body bends become larger and more rapid and forceful (deVries et al., 1982). In addition, fetuses begin moving their arms and legs separately from the rest of their bodies, bend their heads up and down, turn their heads from side to side, open their mouths, hiccup, and bring their hands to their faces (deVries et al., 1982; Sparling, van Tol, & Chescheir, 1999). They begin to execute their first "breathing" movements, moving their diaphragm and abdomen in and out to draw small amounts of amniotic fluid in and out of the lungs (James, Pillai, & Smoleniec, 1995; Pillai & James, 1990).

Starting at 12 weeks after conception, two thirds of fetuses' arm movements are directed toward objects in the uterus—their own faces and bodies, the wall of the uterus, and the umbilical cord (Sparling et al., 1999). Many hand-to-body and hand-to-object movements occur in brief bouts of activity (Sparling et al., 1999),

like fetal versions of Piaget's (1952) primary and secondary circular reactions. By 13 weeks after conception, the fetal movement repertoire has expanded to more than 16 different types of movements including whole body stretching, alternating leg movements, somersaults, yawns, sucking, and swallowing of the amniotic fluid through the nose and mouth (Cosmi, Anceschi, Cosmi, Piazze, & La Torre, 2003; deVries et al., 1982; Dogtrop, Ubels, & Nijhuis, 1990; James et al., 1995; Kuno et al., 2001; Nilsson & Hamberger, 1990; Pillai & James, 1990). By 16 weeks, fetuses' hands can find their mouths so that they can suck their thumbs (Hepper, Shahidullah, & White, 1991). Fetuses begin moving their eyes even before the lids unfuse at 26 weeks (Dogtrop et al., 1990; Moore & Persaud, 1993; Prechtl & Nijhuis, 1983).

Fetal activities follow a daily rhythm, increasing during the evening and decreasing in early morning (Arduini, Rizzo, & Romanini, 1995). Across weeks of gestation, whole body movements and large movements of the arms and legs peak at 14 to 16 weeks postconception, averaging nearly 60% of each observation, then begin to decrease as fetuses' growing bodies occupy increasingly more space in the uterus (D'Elia, Pighetti, Moccia, & Santangelo, 2001; Kuno et al., 2001). By 37 weeks or so, fetuses are so cramped that their hands are often molded to the shape of their heads with the back of their hands pressed against the uterine wall (Sparling et al., 1999).

### Movement Is Fundamental

Movements are not only omnipresent in development, they are literally as basic to life as breathing. Drawing air into the lungs requires movement of the diaphragm and intercostal muscles to expand the chest cavity (Goss, 1973; Marieb, 1995). After infants' first dramatic breaths at birth, breathing movements typically fade into the background of most researchers' awareness. Breathing, however, must be actively controlled when it occurs in conjunction with other movements, as when adults control their breathing movements during meditation, swimming, late stages of labor, and so on.

Like breathing, the seemingly simple acts of swallowing and sucking are often taken for granted. Although fetuses have ample practice exercising the muscles and body parts used for breathing and swallowing, fetuses do not breathe air and the two types of movements do not need to be coordinated (J. L. Miller,

Sonies, & Macedonia, 2003). In contrast, after birth, the anatomy of the body requires that breathing and swallowing movements be staggered in time so that infants do not get gas pains from ingesting air or choke from aspirating milk. Initially, milk and air share the same passage as they enter the body through the pharynx, but milk must divert to the esophagus and air to the trachea.

Sucking also begins prenatally (Humphrey, 1970). After birth, infants suck to feed and they display nonnutritive sucking movements while sleeping or sucking a finger or pacifier (Wolff, 1987). Although sucking is possible while breathing, healthy term infants most frequently stagger non-nutritive sucking and breathing movements with a complex 3:2 ratio of sucks to breaths (Goldfield, Wolff, & Schmidt, 1999a, 1999b).

The sophisticated temporal coordination between breathing, swallowing, and sucking movements is highlighted when infants have problems feeding (Craig & Lee, 1999). When coordination breaks down, breathing is typically the bottleneck (van der Meer, Holden, & van der Weel, in press). The need to breathe competes with the need to swallow (Goldfield, 2005). Premature infants are especially at risk for feeding problems, in part because it is difficult for them to regulate their breathing. Thus, they cannot coordinate the sucking, breathing, and swallowing movements required for feeding (Goldfield, 2005). For example, at 32 weeks postconception, preterm infants stop breathing for a few moments before and after each swallow (Mizuno & Ueda, 2003). The pauses allow infants to feed without choking on the milk, but they also result in insufficient amounts of oxygen while feeding. Like full term infants, by 35 weeks postconception, preterm infants can intersperse their swallows between the parts of a breath, swallowing between breathing out and breathing in (Mizuno & Ueda, 2003; van der Meer et al., in press).

During nursing, as milk flow increases, so too do sucking and swallowing. Milk accumulates in the mouth after several bursts of sucking, then it is swallowed. Additional swallows clear any residual milk left in the mouth (Newman, Keckley, et al., 2001). In addition to coordinating these movements during nursing, infants also change the ratios of sucking and swallowing to breathing over the course of a feeding session as they become satiated and the intensity of their sucking decreases (Goldfield, Richardson, Saltzman, Lee, & Margetts, 2005). When milk delivery is accommodated to premature infants' irregular breathing patterns (with a cleverly instrumented bottle system), premature infants can better coordinate breathing, sucking, and swallowing to feed more effectively (Goldfield, 2005).

## Summary: Models of Change

How might the details of infant sucking, wiggling, crawling, walking, kicking, and so on pertain to psychological research outside the domain of motor development? At a time when so much of the work in developmental journals consists of developmentally atheoretical descriptions or narrow developmental theories about highly specialized phenomena, an effort to extract general principles of development seems an important and refreshing enterprise (E. J. Gibson, 1994; Siegler & Munakata, 1993; Thelen & Smith, 1994). Indeed, Gesell's most important and enduring legacy may be his example of using the formal structure of infants' movements as a model system for understanding general principles of developmental change. With the case studies in this section, we provided the flavor of a model system approach to motor development by describing how researchers have used changes in the temporal structure and spatial configuration of infants' movements to address some of the big issues that all developmental psychologists must face: Can development create qualitatively new forms? What causes development to emerge? What is the role of variability in performance? How can we determine the shape of a developmental trajectory? How should we understand the passage of time? And, how ubiquitous is the stuff of development?

Thelen and Bates (2003) affirmed in a recent special issue on dynamic systems and connectionism their belief "that there are general principles of development: mechanisms and processes that hold true whatever the content domain" (p. 378). In motor development, Thelen's influential work stands as a testament to the effort to discover such general principles and to construct a unified dynamic systems approach to development (Thelen, 1995; Thelen et al., 2001; Thelen & Smith, 1994, 1998; Thelen & Ulrich, 1991). Dynamic systems may prove to be a grand unifying theory of development or it may not. Our guess is that any single approach may prove to be too limiting or too specious to do justice to the many guises that development takes and to the many issues that are raised by developmental research. However, without the effort to transcend the particulars of a phenomenon or a content domain, researchers will never establish a science of development. Our aim in this section was to illustrate how a small, clear, specialized model system can be used to investigate large, complex, general issues in development. Moreover, the transparent nature of infants' movements nested over multiple time scales provides a uniquely tractable and generative model system for undertaking the enterprise of developmental science.

## MOTOR DEVELOPMENT AS A PERCEPTION-ACTION SYSTEM

In contrast to movements, actions, by definition, imply intentionality and a goal (Pick, 1989; Reed, 1982). Whereas infants' rhythmical leg kicks and arm flaps may be a by-product of arousal or random neural activity, infants' actions on objects and surfaces are intentional and purposeful. Whereas spontaneous movements may serendipitously create functional outcomes, actions are goal-directed from the outset and are expressly performed to serve an immediate function. The speed at which 10-month-olds reach for a ball, for example, depends on whether their goal is to fit the ball into a tube or to toss it into a tub (Claxton, Keen, & McCarty, 2003). Each part of the action anticipates the next part and is geared toward the final destination.

Satisfying goals through action requires animals to detect affordances, select among them, and sometimes create new possibilities for action. Behavior must be flexibly adapted to the local conditions. Povinelli and Cant's (1995) description of primate locomotion through the jungle canopy provides a wonderful example. Long-tailed macaques are so lightweight that they can safely ignore the strength and compliance of the arboreal support surface. They travel along the tops of branches and vines on all fours like squirrels, stepping over small gaps between supports and leaping over large ones. Siamangs are a bit heavier. They circumvent falling by suspending themselves below the canopy and swinging along from arm to arm. They judge the distance between branches and vines in terms of their arm length and the boost provided by a springy branch and the inertia of their swing. Orangutans are so heavy—the size of a large man—that the strength and the compliance of each branch are of crucial importance. They solve the problem of locomotion through the canopy by distributing their body weight over multiple supports, testing each branch and vine before shifting their weight, and bridging the gaps between neighboring supports by bending a tapering tree trunk under their weight until grasping a branch on the far side.

Like primate locomotion, the case studies in this section exemplify the issues involved in realizing affordances for action. The starting assumption is that adaptive actions are always goal directed and always embodied and contextually embedded. As described in the previous section, infants walking over a straight, flat path at steady state velocity provide a wonderfully rich paradigm for analyzing the formal structure of gait patterns. However, as frustrated researchers quickly learn when they try to elicit steady state velocity from toddlers over repeated trials, infants usually have different goals in mind: Infants alter their own functional body dimensions by holding their arms out and carrying toys; they stop and start to investigate a detail of the testing walkway; they accelerate to run into their parents' open arms. Thus, researchers who study motor development as a perception-action system focus on infants' ability to achieve their goals by detecting and adapting to changes in their physical propensities and surrounding environments. Researchers vary the available perceptual information by experimentally manipulating infants' functional body dimensions and level of balance control, altering the properties of target objects and surfaces, and providing infants with various types of social support for action.

We begin this section with the prospective, future-oriented nature of goal-directed looking and reaching and describe how even the simplest movements of the eyes, head, trunk, and extremities require infants to anticipate disruptions to a stable postural base. We use infants' responses to challenging ground surfaces to illustrate both flexibility and specificity in learning to detect affordances for action and we describe how exploratory movements provide the perceptual basis for guiding actions. We conclude this section with examples of how tools create new possibilities for action.

### Prospective Control

The development of action is basically a matter of increasing prospective control: preparing and guiding actions into the future (von Hofsten, 1993, 1997, 2003, 2004). Time only runs in one direction. Thus, the only part of an action that can be controlled is the part that has not yet happened (von Hofsten, 2003). Reactive responding is only a method of last resort. In the worst case scenario, actions are irreversible and reactive responses result in dire consequences (trips, slips, collisions, falling from the jungle canopy). In the best case scenario, reactive post hoc corrections cause actions to be jerky and inefficient because of the neural time lag in transmitting information through the body and the mechanical time lag in getting the various body parts to move. Perceptual information links time past with time future by using feedback from just prior movements to anticipate the consequences of future actions and by using updates from recent perceptual events to predict what will happen next. Perception provides a time bubble to continually extend action into the future, like a protective cushion between the body and its surrounds.

### Early Action Systems

Infants' looking behaviors are so frequently used to make inferences about perceptual and cognitive processes that developmental psychologists sometimes forget that the visual system is an action system, designed to scan the world and to track objects and events. Without the ability to control eye movements, to keep the fovea on a target, the visual system is functionally useless (von Hofsten, 2003). Like looking, a function of prehension is to bring a highly sensitive information-gathering device—the hands—to external objects. Prehension also functions to bring objects to the eyes for close-up visual inspection. Reciprocally, keeping the hands in view allows vision to aid in steering infants' reaches and grasps.

Indeed, eye and arm movements may be sufficiently coordinated in newborns to jump-start visual-manual exploration and goal-directed reaching. For example, newborns will actively work to keep their hands in the field of view. While lying supine with small weights tied to both wrists, newborns allowed the weight to pull their arm down on the side toward the back of their heads but resisted the weight on the arm toward which their face was turned (van der Meer, van der Weel, & Lee, 1996). Their hand-to-face action did not merely reflect the fencing posture of the asymmetric tonic neck reflex because when view of the hands was occluded, both arms sank. When view of the hand toward the back of infants' head was provided on a video monitor rather than directly, infants resisted the weight on the side opposite to the fencing posture (van der Meer, van der Weel, & Lee, 1995). Similarly, in a dim room, newborns kept their hand positioned in a narrow beam of light (van der Meer, 1997a). Viewing the hand appeared to be inten-

tional and prospective because infants moved their hand when the light beam moved and they slowed down their arm movements before the hand arrived in the light, rather than after they noticed that they could see it.

Moreover, months before infants can reach or grasp, newborns orient toward objects with eyes and arms as if pointing their available "feelers" toward it (von Hofsten, 1982). When strapped securely around the chest into a slightly reclined seat or held by the head to prevent collapsing under the pull of gravity, newborns' flailing arm movements became more directed toward a target object when the target was visually fixated than when they were looking elsewhere (Amiel-Tison & Grenier, 1986; von Hofsten, 1982).

### Common Paths to Prospectivity

On a generous interpretation, infants' earliest actions show the inklings of prospectivity. For example, by 1 month of age, infants can smoothly pursue a moving target with their eyes (Aslin, 1981; Rosander & von Hofsten, 2000; von Hofsten & Rosander, 1996), indicating an intent to follow the target and the ability to match target velocity with eye velocity. Smooth pursuit anticipates the target's motion by extrapolating from the just seen motions to predict what will happen next (von Hofsten, 1997, 2003). However, neonates' smooth pursuit occurs only in short bursts. As their eyes begin to trail behind the target, they are forced to use jerky, reactive, saccades to catch up (Phillips, Finoccio, Ong, & Fuchs, 1997). The initial saccade may so dramatically undershoot the target that a series of small steps may be required to move the eye to the goal (Aslin & Salapatek, 1975). Moreover, prospective control is fragile in neonates and easily disrupted by demanding tasks and unsupportive contexts (von Hofsten & Rosander, 1997). The target must be quite large and move slowly in predictable sinusoidal motions from side to side for neonates to keep it in sight (von Hofsten & Rosander, 1997). With larger objects infants perform fewer catch-up saccades because less precision is required to keep the target on the fovea (Rosander & von Hofsten, 2002).

As shown in Figure 4.5a, over the ensuing weeks, smooth pursuit comprises an increasing portion of infants' visual tracking and corrective saccades comprise a decreasing portion, with the most rapid improvements between 6 and 14 weeks of age (Richards & Holley, 1999; Rosander & von Hofsten, 2002; von Hofsten & Rosander, 1997). Infants succeed at tracking smaller objects moving at faster speeds (Phillips et al., 1997;

(a)

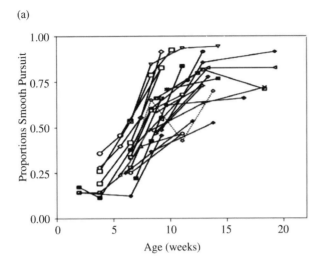

(b)

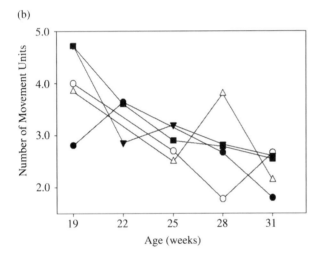

**Figure 4.5** Developmental trajectories derived from longitudinal observations of eye and arm movements. (a) Smooth pursuit eye movements. *Source:* From "An Action Perspective on Motor Development," by C. von Hofsten, 2004, *Trends in Cognitive Sciences, 8,* pp. 266–272. Reprinted with permission. (b) Movement units in reaching. *Source:* From "Structuring of Early Reaching Movements: A Longitudinal Study," by C. von Hofsten, 1991, *Journal of Motor Behavior, 23,* pp. 280–292. For both looking and reaching, each curve represents a different infant. Note the large individual differences in the rate and amplitude of developmental change.

Richards & Holley, 1999; Rosander & von Hofsten, 2002). By 4 to 5 months, looking is sufficiently predictive for infants to track targets moving behind an occluder (e.g., Rosander & von Hofsten, 2004). Brief exposure to an unoccluded trajectory makes infants' looking more anticipatory to occluded trajectories so that their eyes wait on the far side of the occluder to

catch the target when it reappears (S. P. Johnson, Amso, & Slemmer, 2003). By 3 months of age, infants can use rules instead of local extrapolation to predict the shifting location of a target (Adler & Haith, 2003; Wentworth, Haith, & Hood, 2002). By 5 months, they successfully track objects that abruptly reverse their direction of motion (von Hofsten & Rosander, 1997). By 6 months, they can use an arbitrary shape cue to anticipate the shifting location of a target (Gilmore & Johnson, 1995).

Infants' prehensile actions show a similar developmental trajectory to looking. Reaching for stationary objects appears between 12 and 18 weeks (e.g., Berthier & Keen, in press; Clifton et al., 1993) and catching moving objects appears at approximately 18 weeks (von Hofsten, 1979, 1980). Just as infants' first eye movements are saccadic and lagging rather than smooth and on-target, their first goal-directed reaches and catches are typically jerky and crooked. Initial reaches contain several "movement units," where infants' arms speed up and slow down and change directions before the hand finally contacts the toy (e.g., Berthier, Clifton, McCall, & Robin, 1999; Berthier & Keen, in press; Thelen et al., 1993; von Hofsten, 1980, 1983, 1991; von Hofsten & Lindhagen, 1979; Wentworth, Benson, & Haith, 2000). Corrections are more pronounced during faster reaches (Thelen, Corbetta, & Spencer, 1996).

Movement units and direction changes decrease after a few months until infants' reaches and catches are made up of only two movement units, the first to bring the hand near the target and the second to grasp it (Figure 4.5b). Prospective extrapolations of target motion become increasingly resilient to loss of visual information. By 9 months, infants reach for moving objects on an unobstructed path but inhibit reaching when a barrier blocks the path (Keen, Carrico, Sylvia, & Berthier, 2003). By 11 months, infants catch moving objects as they appear from behind an occluder (van der Meer, van der Weel, & Lee, 1994).

What makes infants' initial reaches so jerky and crooked? An initial suggestion was that movement units reflect visual corrections for a misaligned arm path (e.g., Bushnell, 1985). However, infants successfully reach for objects in the dark within a week or two of reaching in the light (Clifton et al., 1993), suggesting that they can use proprioceptive information to guide the reach. Indeed, by 5 to 7 months, infants can catch moving objects without sight of their hand by gauging the speed of the glowing object in the dark (Robin,

Berthier, & Clifton, 1996) and by 9 months, they preorient their hands to grasp in the dark (McCarty, Clifton, Ashmead, Lee, & Goubet, 2001). Several alternatives have been proposed. Possibly, the increased precision required to position the hand for grasping may prompt new reachers to plan the action as a series of small steps (Berthier, 1996, 1997; Berthier et al., 2005). Alternatively, some of the movement units might simply reflect unanticipated reactive forces (Berthier et al., 2005; Thelen et al., 1996; von Hofsten, 1997). Or, infants may have little motivation for efficient reaching (Witherington, 2005)—the functional penalty for extra movement units is low—and might even use variable arm paths to explore the capabilities of their new action system (Berthier, 1996, 1997; Berthier et al., 2005).

### Divergent Developments in Prospective Looking and Prehension

Looking and prehension involve more than the eyes and the arms. Visual tracking requires fine-grained coordination between eye movements and head movements to keep the eyes on the target while the head and body move, especially during locomotion or while being carried (Daniel & Lee, 1990; von Hofsten, 2003). Prehension involves decisions about whether to use one or two arms, which arm to move, and coordinating reaching with grasping—all in relation to the features of the target object.

Prospective control over the components of looking and prehension develop asynchronously. Predictive eye movements do not transfer automatically to predictive head movements and predictive one-armed reaches do not transfer automatically to prospective control of grasping or decisions about whether to use one or two arms. For example, weeks after infants can smoothly track moving objects with their eyes, they begin to make large tracking movements with their heads (von Hofsten, 2004; von Hofsten & Rosander, 1997). However, infants have difficulty suppressing the vestibular-ocular reaction and initially their heads lag so far behind the target that they must put their eyes ahead of the target to keep it in view. The functional consequence of discord between eyes and head is a decrease in tracking precision.

Similarly, the components of prehension develop asynchronously. For many weeks after infants can smoothly transport their hand to an object, they misalign their hand position vis-à-vis the object's orientation (Wentworth et al., 2000; Witherington, 2005) and fail to adjust their hand opening to the object's size (Fagard,

2000; von Hofsten & Ronnqvist, 1988). Infants reach with their feet a full month before they reach with their hands (Galloway & Thelen, 2004). At the same age when infants show skilled reaches when one object is presented at midline, they respond haphazardly with one- and two-armed reaches to variations in object size (Corbetta, Thelen, & Johnson 2000; Fagard, 2000). Although infants may cross the midline of their bodies for two-armed reaches to large objects (van Hof, van der Kamp, & Savelsbergh, 2002), they fail to reach across midline when two objects are presented simultaneously (McCarty & Keen, 2005).

Like the developmental dissociations between the components of looking and prehension, prospective tracking and reaching for moving objects behind occluders appear at different ages. In general, infants demonstrate prospective control of looking before reaching. Their heads and eyes are on the target object when it reappears from behind the occluder while their hands seem lost or lag behind (Jonsson & von Hofsten, 2003; Spelke & von Hofsten, 2001; von Hofsten, Vishton, Spelke, Feng, & Rosander, 1998). By 11 months of age, infants can also intercept the occluded object with their hands (van der Meer et al., 1994).

## Centrality of Posture

Maintaining balance is not optional. Actions require a stable postural base. Moreover, simply maintaining balance is usually not an end in itself (Riley, Stoffregen, Grocki, & Turvey, 1999). Rather, infants and adults maintain various postures to set up the necessary conditions for looking around, handling objects, holding conversations, or going somewhere (Stoffregen, Smart, Bardy, & Pagulayan, 1999).

### Nested Actions

One reason for discrepant developments in the various components of looking and prehension is that actions are nested within other actions. Visual tracking with the eyes is nested within visual tracking with the head. Grasping with the hands and fingers is nested within reaching with the arms. Both looking and prehension—like all other actions—are embedded, in turn, within the most basic action of all: posture (Bernstein, 1967; E. J. Gibson & Pick, 2000; Reed, 1982, 1989).

Accordingly, one reason that newborns could demonstrate the inklings of prospective looking and reaching is that researchers eliminated the need for infants to maintain the stable postural base required for action: Experimenters strapped infants around the chest into reclined seats or cradle-boards, supported their heads with side cushions, or held infants' heads in their hands. Without the supporting scaffolds provided by the experimenters, young infants would not have been able to turn their heads to track or extend their arms to reach (Spencer et al., 2000; von Hofsten, 2003). By 4 to 6 months of age, infants exploit the features of a normal high chair to create a stable base for reaching by using the back of the chair and the edge of the tray to help support their trunks (van der Fits, Otten, Klip, van Eykern, & Hadders-Algra, 1999). Even with the benefit of supports, posture exerts effects on reaching through gravity. At 3 to 4 months, infants reach more frequently while strapped sitting into a special seat than while lying supine, where the entire body is supported by the cot, because less muscle torque in the arms is required to fight gravity in an upright posture (Savelsbergh & van der Kamp, 1994).

Unsupported reaching awaits infants' ability to provide a stable postural base for themselves (Bertenthal & von Hofsten, 1998; Spencer et al., 2000). Reaching freely from a prone posture appears at approximately 5 months when infants can prop up their chest with one arm and reach with the other without tipping (Bly, 1994; Mc-Graw, 1945). Reaching freely from a sitting posture appears between 6 and 8 months when infants can keep their heads balanced between their shoulders and maintain equilibrium in the trunk with their legs outstretched along the floor in a "V" (van der Fits et al., 1999). When infants first achieve propped sitting in a tripod position (propped on the arms between the outstretched legs), postural requirements compete with action goals. For example, new sitters reach with only one hand and avoid leaning forward because if they lift the supporting arm or disrupt the fragile equilibrium of the posture, they are likely to fall (Rochat, 1992; Rochat & Goubet, 1995).

### Anticipatory Postural Adjustments

Establishing a stable postural base for actions requires infants to control balance prospectively (von Hofsten, 1993, 1997, 2003, 2004). Moving one part of the body to look, reach, or locomote creates disequilibrium by displacing the location of the entire body's center of gravity. Moreover, movements of the head or limbs create reactive forces on body parts far removed because all of the body is mechanically linked (Gahery & Massion, 1981). Lifting an arm requires forces to be directed forward and upward. As a consequence, destabilizing forces of equal magnitude act in the opposite direction on the trunk. To prevent movement-induced disequilibrium from reverberating through the body, infants must anticipate postural disruptions and deal with them prospectively. In anticipation of the arms moving upward, adults activate neck and trunk muscles to stabilize the torso prior to activating arm and shoulder muscles to lift the arm. Or, adults shift the center of gravity backward prior to its being displaced forward. Without such prospective corrections to posture, the entire action can be disrupted and induce loss of balance and a fall.

Before 15 to 18 months of age, infants in a sitting posture rarely show anticipatory muscle activations of the trunk and neck to prepare for a reach (van der Fits & Hadders-Algra, 1998; van der Fits et al., 1999; von Hofsten, 1993). Instead, infants tend to activate arm, neck, and trunk muscles simultaneously. However, infants show other evidence of prospective control of balance during reaching. While strapped loosely around the waist in an infant seat, some 5-month-olds increased their reaching space by leaning forward (Yonas & Hartman, 1993). Attempts to reach decreased with increasing object distance, but infants who leaned attempted reaches at farther distances than the infants who did not lean. When balance constraints were altered with small wrist weights, 6-month-olds were less likely to stretch forward to reach than when they were not weighted (Rochat, Goubet, & Senders, 1999). Between 8 and 10 months of age, infants leaned forward in anticipation of raising their arm to reach for distant objects, suggesting that they perceived the additional stretch provided by their trunks and used the leaning posture to set up the framework for action (McKenzie, Skouteris, Day, Hartman, & Yonas, 1993).

As in a sitting posture, consistent anticipatory muscle activations in a standing posture appear between 15 and 17 months of age (Witherington et al., 2002). Lifting an object or pulling a weight with the arms causes a forward displacement of the center of mass. Adults' calf muscles anticipate the disruption by firing just prior to activation of the arm muscles. In a clever adaptation of the adult paradigm, infants were encouraged to pull open a small weighted drawer (Witherington et al., 2002). Anticipatory postural adjustments became more frequent, consistent, and finely timed between 10 and 17 months. After 3 months of walking experience, 80% of the trials involved anticipatory activation of the leg muscles.

Some researchers have argued for age-related, developmental stages in the acquisition of a stable postural base for action (Assaiante & Amblard, 1995), with increasing levels of control through sitting, standing, and walking stages. However, other researchers argue that the changes are likely to be related to expertise, regardless of the period of development (B. Bril, personal communication, December 15, 2004). Novice adults sitting on a unicycle or standing while wearing Rollerblades are in the same precarious position as novice infants trying to sit and reach or stay upright and walk.

## Perceiving Affordances

Affordances are possibilities for action. As described below, infants must learn to discriminate actions that are possible from those that are not. In some cases, infants' learning is impressively flexible and transfers to novel situations. But, in other cases, learning is surprisingly specific and fails to transfer beyond the particulars of the training context. Together, flexibility and specificity of learning provide important insights into what it is that infants learn in the development of adaptive motor action.

### The Actor-Environment Fit

Affordances reflect the objective state of affairs regarding infants' physical capabilities and the behaviorally relevant features of the environment (J. J. Gibson, 1979; Warren, 1984). Actions are possible or not, regardless of whether infants perceive, misperceive, or take advantage of the possibilities. Because affordances are relational, the facts of embodiment must be taken with reference to the properties of the environment and vice versa. For example, walking is possible only when infants have sufficient strength, postural control, and endurance relative to the length of the path, obstacles along the way, and the slant, rigidity, and texture of the ground surface.

In fact, bodily propensities and environmental properties are so intimately connected for supporting motor actions that changes in a single factor on either side of the affordance relationship alter the probability of successful performance. Researchers have experimentally manipulated possibilities for locomotion by loading infants with weights, extending their leg length with platform shoes, and dressing them in roller skates or rubber- and Teflon-soled shoes to alter their body dimensions and level of postural control. (An alternative

approach is to treat naturally occurring changes in infants' bodies and skills as predictors.) To alter possibilities for locomotion by manipulating environmental properties, researchers have varied the slant, friction, and rigidity of the ground surface, created gaps in the path, terminated the path in a cliff, blocked the path with overhead or underfoot barriers, varied the height of stair risers and pedestals, varied the width of bridges spanning a precipice, and varied the substance and extent of handrails used for manual support (for reviews, see Adolph, 1997, 2002, 2005; Adolph & Berger, 2005; Adolph et al., 1993b).

Following Warren, Mark, and colleagues' (Mark & Vogele, 1987; Warren & Whang, 1987) elegant psychophysical approach to describing affordances in adults, researchers have used a psychophysical staircase procedure to describe the probability of successful motor performance in infants (e.g., Adolph, 1995, 1997, 2000; Adolph & Avolio, 2000; Corbetta, Thelen, & Johnson, 2000; Mondschein, Adolph, & Tamis-LeMonda, 2000; Schmuckler, 1996; Tamis-LeMonda & Adolph, 2005). The staircase procedure is a classic method in psychophysics for estimating a perceptual threshold using a minimal number of trials (Cornsweet, 1962). When estimating a perceptual threshold, researchers plot the function spanning the increments where the observer's accuracy is 1.0 to those where the observer guesses at 0.50 chance levels. To describe an affordance, researchers estimate a "motor threshold" along a function spanning the increments where success rates are 1.0 to those where success rates drop to 0. (The success rate is the number of successful attempts to perform the target action divided by the sum of successful plus failed attempts. Trials where infants refuse to attempt the action do not enter the calculations.) Coarser estimates require approximately 15 to 20 well-placed trials per infant; more precise estimates require upward of 40 trials per infant.

Like many psychophysical functions, the curves that characterize the transition from possible to impossible actions are generally steep S-shaped functions with long extended tails. As a consequence, most actions are either possible or impossible for a wide range of situations and have a shifting probability of success under a narrow range of increments. To illustrate, for a typical 14-month-old on a sloping walkway covered in rubber, the probability of walking successfully may be close to 1.0 on slopes from 0° to 18°, close to 0 on slopes from 28° to 90°, and show a sharply decreasing function on slopes from 18° to 28° that encompasses the motor threshold (Adolph, 1995; Adolph & Avolio, 2000); see dashed curve in Figure 4.6a. For the same infant on a walkway covered in slippery vinyl, the entire function shifts leftward along the x-axis; see solid curve in Figure 4.6a. The probability of walking successfully may be close to 1.0 on slopes from 0° to 6°, close to 0 on slopes from 16° to 90°, and show a sharply decreasing function on slopes from 6° to 16° (Adolph, Eppler, Joh, Shrout, & Lo, 2005; Lo, Avolio, Massop, & Adolph, 1999).

Typically, infants show a wide range in motor thresholds even when tested at the same age. For example, the range for 14-month-olds walking down carpeted slopes is 4° to 28° (Adolph, 1995; Adolph & Avolio, 2000). The size of infants' motor thresholds reflects their level of locomotor skill, duration of locomotor experience, age, body dimensions, and the specifics of the task (e.g., Adolph, 2002; Kingsnorth & Schmuckler, 2000; van der Meer, 1997b). In contrast to older children and adults where body dimensions are frequently the critical determinant of affordances for locomotion (Konczak, Meeuwson, & Cress, 1992; van der Meer, 1997b; Warren, 1984; Warren & Whang, 1987), with infants, skill and experience are generally the strongest predictors because between-subject variability is due more to differences in infants' strength and balance than to the geometry of their bodies.

### Learning to Perceive Affordances

The critical question for understanding the adaptive control of action is whether affordances are perceived—whether infants can select appropriate actions to meet their goals by detecting affordances (or lack of them) prospectively (see Adolph et al., 1993b for a review; E. J. Gibson, 1982; E. J. Gibson & Pick, 2000; E. J. Gibson & Schmuckler, 1989). In essence, the perceptual problem is to determine whether a potential future action lies on one of the tails of the affordance function or along the inflection of the curve. Because the location of the affordance function along the x-axis varies with changes in local conditions (e.g., whether the slope is covered in carpet or slippery vinyl, whether the infant is carrying a load), to solve the perceptual problem, infants would need to continually update information about the current status of their own action systems relative to environmental conditions.

For human infants and other altricial animals, determining the current state of affairs is no easy feat. The problem of perceiving affordances is complicated by

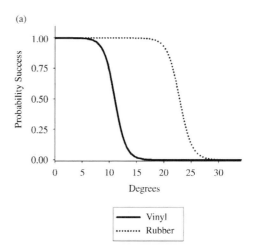

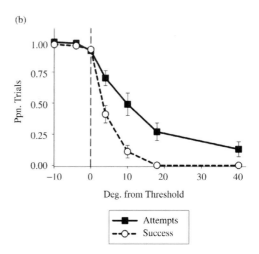

**Figure 4.6** (a) Fitted curves showing the probability of walking successfully down high-friction rubber (dashed curve) and slippery vinyl (solid curve) covered slopes for a typical 14-month-old infant. *Source:* From *Walking Down Slippery Slopes: How Infants Use Slant and Friction Information,* by K. E. Adolph, M. A. Eppler, A. S. Joh, P. E. Shrout, and T. Lo, 2005, manuscript submitted for publication. (b) Actual (dashed curve) and perceived (solid curve) possibilities for walking down carpet covered slopes for a sample of 14-month-old infants. Success rate = (Successes)/(Successes + Failures). Attempt rate = (Successes + Failures)/(Successes + Failures + Refusals). Error bars represent standard errors. Data are normalized to each infant's motor threshold (represented by 0 on the x-axis). Positive numbers on the x-axis denote slopes steeper than infants' motor thresholds; negative numbers denote slopes shallower than infants' motor thresholds. Perfect perceptual judgments would be evidenced if the curves were superimposed. Parallel curves show that infants scaled their responses to their own skill levels. *Source:* From "Walking Infants Adapt Locomotion to Changing Body Dimensions" by K. E. Adolph and A. M. Avolio, 2000, *Journal of Experimental Psychology: Human Perception and Performance, 26,* pp. 1148–1166. Reprinted with permission.

rapid, large-scale developmental changes in infants' bodies, skills, and environments. As described earlier in this chapter, infants' bodies grow in sudden overnight spurts; reaching, sitting, crawling, and walking skills improve most dramatically over the first few months after onset; and the environments to which infants are exposed are continually expanding. Moreover, in contrast to many other altricial animals, human infants spend prolonged periods—months—coping with objects and navigating surfaces after achieving each postural milestone in development. Typically, infants sit independently at approximately 6 months of age, crawl at 8 months, cruise (move sideways in an upright posture) at 10 months, and walk at 12 months (Frankenburg & Dodds, 1967). Given the changeable nature of the actor-environment fit, several authors have proposed that infants must learn to detect possibilities for action (e.g., Adolph, 2005; Campos et al., 2000; E. J. Gibson & Pick, 2000).

The classic paradigm for studying infants' perception of affordances is the "visual cliff" (E. J. Gibson & Walk, 1960; Walk, 1966; Walk & Gibson, 1961). As illustrated in Figure 4.7a, crawling infants or other animals are placed on a narrow, 30-cm center board dividing a large glass-covered table. The glass is carefully lighted from beneath so that it is invisible from infants' vantage point. On one side of the table, a patterned ground surface lies 0.6 cm beneath the glass. On the other side, the ground surface is 102 cm below the safety glass. Although locomotion is possible in either direction over the sturdy safety glass, visually, the "shallow" side specifies safe passage and the "deep" side specifies an impossibly large drop-off. With babies, caregivers beckon to their infants from first one side and then the other, with 1 or 2 trials per side. With other animals, the experimenters place them on the center board to descend to the shallow or deep side on their own.

Dozens of experiments have yielded fascinating but conflicting findings regarding the roles of locomotor experience and fear in infants' avoidance of the apparent drop-off. The earliest studies showed that precocial animals such as chicks, kids, lambs, and piglets avoid the deep side of the visual cliff from their first days of life (E. J. Gibson & Walk, 1960; Walk & Gibson, 1961). If forcibly placed onto the safety glass, the animals brace their legs, bleat, tremble, and back up as if afraid of being unsupported in mid-air. Some altricial animals, such as kittens, rabbits, puppies, and monkeys, venture off the centerboard onto the deep side when they are newly locomotor or if they are prevented from acquiring

visual feedback from their own locomotor activities by rearing them in the dark or in a "kitty carousel" (Held & Hein, 1963; Walk & Gibson, 1961). However, rats, also an altricial species, do not require visual experience with locomotion to avoid the drop-off (Walk, Gibson, & Tighe, 1957).

With human infants, a frequently cited cross-sectional study found that crawling experience predicted avoidance responses (Bertenthal & Campos, 1984; Bertenthal, Campos, & Barrett, 1984). At the very same age at testing—7.5 to 8.5 months of age—only 35% of inexperienced crawlers ($M = 11$ days of crawling experience) avoided the apparent drop-off compared with 65% of more experienced infants ($M = 41$ days of crawling experience). However, other cross-sectional experiments controlling for crawling experience or test age found opposite results, where experience predicted crossing onto the deep side rather than avoidance (Richards & Rader, 1981, 1983). Longitudinal data are inconclusive because infants learn from repeated testing that the safety glass provides support for locomotion (Titzer, 1995). Avoidance attenuated in some experienced crawlers, and other infants used a compromise strategy of detouring along the wooden wall at the edge of the table (Campos, Hiatt, Ramsay, Henderson, & Svejda, 1978; Eppler, Satterwhite, Wendt, & Bruce, 1997).

In some cases, locomotor experience appears to be posture-specific: The same crawlers who avoided the drop-off when tested on their hands and knees crossed over the cliff when tested moments later in an upright posture in a wheeled baby-walker (Rader, Bausano, & Richards, 1980). In other cases, locomotor experience appears to generalize across postures: 12-month-old walkers avoided the apparent drop-off after only 2 weeks of walking experience appended to their several weeks of crawling experience (Witherington, Campos, Anderson, Lejeune, & Seah, 2005).

Findings are equally discrepant with regard to the role of fear. Seven-month-olds showed accelerated heart rate—a measure associated with wariness or fear—when they were lowered toward the deep side of the visual cliff after only 1 week of crawling experience or 40 hours of upright locomotor experience wheeling around in a mechanical baby-walker (Bertenthal et al., 1984; Campos, Bertenthal, & Kermoian, 1992). However, crawling experience was not related to heart rate in 9- and 12-month-olds and the 9-month-olds showed cardiac deceleration—a measure associated with interest—to placement on the deep side (Richards & Rader, 1983).

**Figure 4.7** Illustrations of several paradigms for testing infants' perception of affordances for locomotion: (a) crawling infant approaching an apparent drop-off on a visual cliff. *Source:* From "A Comparative and Analytical Study of Visual Depth Perception," by R. D. Walk and E. J. Gibson, 1961, *Psychological Monographs, 75*(15, Whole No. 519). Reprinted with permission; (b) crawling infant at the top of an adjustable slope. *Source:* From "Learning in the Development of Infant Locomotion," by K. E. Adolph, 1997, *Monographs of the Society for Research in Child Development, 62*(3, Serial No. 251). Reprinted with permission; (c) sitting infant leaning forward over an adjustable gap in the surface of support; (d) crawling infant approaching an adjustable gap in the surface of support. *Source:* From "Specificity of Learning: Why Infants Fall over a Veritable Cliff," by K. E. Adolph, 2000, *Psychological Science, 11,* pp. 290–295. Reprinted with permission; (e) walking infant exploring a bridge over a precipice; (f) walking infant using a handrail to augment balance on a narrow bridge. *Source:* From "Infants Use Handrails as Tools in a Locomotor Task," by S. E. Berger and K. E. Adolph, 2003, *Developmental Psychology, 39,* pp. 594–605. Reprinted with permission. Caregivers (shown in a, not shown in b–f) stand at the far side of each apparatus and encourage infants to cross. Plexiglas ensures infants' safety on the visual cliff. An experimenter (shown in b-f) ensures infants' safety on the other obstacles.

Infants fussed slightly while lowered toward both the shallow and deep sides of the table but they also displayed positive vocalizations during placement on the deep side (Richards & Rader, 1983). Mothers' fearful facial expressions produced higher rates of avoidance in 12-month-old crawlers on a 30-cm drop-off than did mothers' joyful expressions, but the infants' own facial expressions were positive or neutral—not negative or fearful—on the trials when they avoided the drop-off (Sorce, Emde, Campos, & Klinnert, 1985).

Albeit the most famous test paradigm, the visual cliff is not optimal. The discrepant findings may result from methodological problems stemming from the use of the safety glass, the procedure of starting infants on the center board, the fixed dimensions of the cliff, and the practice of testing each infant in only 1 or 2 trials. Due to the safety glass, visual and haptic information are in conflict. The drop-off looks risky but feels safe and is, in fact, perfectly safe as infants discover over repeated trials. Similarly, when the visual cliff was modified by replacing the drop-off with a deformable waterbed (agitated from below to create ripples), 14- to 15-month-old walkers refused to walk when they could feel the rippling surface, but walked over the waterbed when it was covered with safety glass (E. J. Gibson et al., 1987).

Moreover, placing infants on the narrow center board gives them little room to maneuver; sometimes avoidant infants accidentally move onto the deep side or start onto the glass and then retreat (Campos et al., 1978; E. J. Gibson & Walk, 1960). The fixed dimensions on the visual cliff preclude researchers from assessing whether perception is scaled to action and from testing the accuracy of infants' perceptual judgments. The heights of the shallow and deep sides in the standard arrangement lie far on the tails of the affordance function, rather than along the inflection of the curve. Finally, data from a single trial per infant per condition are less stable than data from a single forced-choice trial (E. J. Gibson et al., 1987), and both procedures are more vulnerable to errant responses than methods that involve multiple trials per infant at each increment.

### Specificity of Learning

Perception of affordances, like any perceptual judgment, involves observers' sensitivity to the signal and observers' response criterion. Both factors are highly influenced by the vicissitudes of single trials, especially with infant and animal subjects. To circumvent the methodological problems on the visual cliff, researchers have devised testing arrangements involving slopes, gaps, and barriers where perceptual information was concordant with the actual affordance, errors in judgment had actual consequences, mobile infants began on a runway several steps prior to the obstacle, and the dimensions of the test apparatus were adjustable. Most important, each infant contributed multiple trials at each stimulus increment (e.g., Adolph, 1995, 1997, 2000; Adolph & Avolio, 2000; Schmuckler, 1996; for examples with older children, see Plumert, 1995, 1997; Plumert, Kearney, & Cremer, 2004; Pufall & Dunbar, 1992; van der Meer, 1997b).

Following Warren, Mark, and others' work with adults (e.g., Mark, 1987; Warren, 1984; Warren & Whang, 1987), researchers assessed the correspondence between infants' perceptual judgments and the actual possibilities for action. Because infants are preverbal, perceptual judgments were determined based on an attempt rate: The number of successful plus failed attempts to perform the target action divided by the sum of successful attempts, failed attempts, and refusals to attempt the action. (The inverse avoidance rate yields the same information.) As shown in Figure 4.6b, decreasing attempt rates relative to the motor threshold provide evidence that perception is scaled to action. A close correspondence between attempt rates and the actual probability of success indicates that perceptual judgments are accurate.

Several experiments used the psychophysical procedure to examine infants' perception of affordances for crawling and walking over slopes (for reviews, see Adolph, 2002, 2005; Adolph & Eppler, 2002). For each infant, researchers compared the correspondence between infants' perceptual judgments and the actual probability of success. As illustrated in Figure 4.7b, flat starting and landing platforms flanked an adjustable slope (0° to 90°). Rather than safety glass, an experimenter followed alongside infants to ensure their safety. Infants received easy baseline trials after each failure or refusal to renew their motivation to crawl or walk; parents stood at the end of the landing platform, encouraging infants to descend and applauding their efforts after each trial. The procedure biased infants toward using a liberal response criterion (meaning a higher false alarm rate) and thus provided a conservative test of infants' ability to detect affordances and respond adaptively.

Both cross-sectional (Figure 4.8a) and longitudinal data (Figure 4.8b) suggest that infants learn to perceive affordances for locomotion through everyday crawling

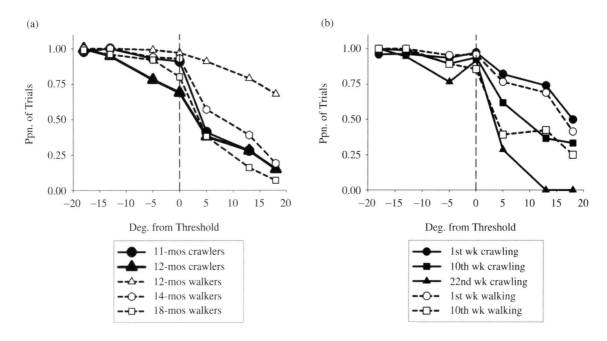

**Figure 4.8** Perceptual judgments indexed by infants' attempts to crawl (solid curves) and walk (dashed curves) down slopes. (a) Cross-sectional data. *Source:* From "A Psychophysical Assessment of Toddlers' Ability to Cope with Slopes," by K. E. Adolph, 1995, *Journal of Experimental Psychology: Human Perception and Performance, 21,* pp. 734–750; "Walking Infants Adapt Locomotion to Changing Body Dimensions," by K. E. Adolph and A. M. Avolio, 2000, *Journal of Experimental Psychology: Human Perception and Performance, 26,* pp. 1148–1166; *Specificity of Infants' Knowledge for Action,* by K. E. Adolph, A. S. Joh, S. Ishak, S. A. Lobo, and S. E. Berger, October 2005, paper presented to the Cognitive Development Society, San Diego, CA; Gender Bias in Mothers' Expectations about Infant Crawling," by E. R. Mondschein, K. E. Adolph, and C. S. Tamis-LeMonda, 2000, *Journal of Experimental Child Psychology, 77,* pp. 304–316. (b) Longitudinal data. *Source:* From "Learning in the Development of Infant Locomotion," by K. E. Adolph, 1997, *Monographs of the Society for Research in Child Development, 62*(3, Serial No. 251). Attempt rate = (Successes + Failures)/(Successes + Failures + Refusals). Data are normalized to each infant's motor threshold (represented by 0 on the x-axis). Negative numbers on the x-axis represent safe slopes shallower than infants' motor thresholds. Positive numbers represent risky slopes steeper than infants' motor thresholds. Note that perceptual errors (attempts on risky slopes) depend on infants' motor experience within a posture, not on their age or the locomotor posture per se.

and walking experience. Moreover, learning appears to be specific to crawling and walking postures. In their first weeks of both crawling and walking, infants attempted slopes far beyond their ability and required rescue by the experimenter. Over weeks of crawling and walking, false alarms steadily decreased. Perceptual judgments gradually honed in to infants' actual ability until attempts to descend closely matched the probability of success. The decrease in errors reflects remarkable behavioral flexibility because infants' motor thresholds changed from week to week.

There was no evidence of transfer between crawling and walking postures. Infants tested repeatedly over weeks of crawling and walking showed no sign of savings in the transition from quadruped to upright postures, and infants in control groups matched for age and experience behaved similarly to infants tested repeatedly. Learning

was so posture-specific that new walkers avoided descent of an impossibly steep 36° slope in their experienced crawling posture but plunged down the same hill moments later when tested in their inexperienced walking posture (Adolph, 1997). Twelve-month-old crawlers avoided a 50° slope; 12-month-old walkers stepped blithely over the brink (Adolph, Joh, Ishak, Lobo, Berger, 2005). As Campos and colleagues (2000) wrote, "The mapping between vision and posture that results from crawling experience will need to be remapped as the infant acquires new motor skills such as standing and walking. . . . In fact, remapping is likely to occur with the acquisition of every new motor skill in a continuously coevolving perception-action cycle" (p. 174).

Posture-specific learning is not limited to crawling and walking postures or to locomotion over slopes. In a modern twist on the classic visual cliff, Adolph (2000) used the psychophysical procedure to test 9.5-month-old infants' perception of affordances at the edge of a real 76-cm drop-off in sitting and crawling postures (Figure 4.7c to 4.7d). The apparatus was adjustable; the precipice lay below a 0- to 90-cm gap in the surface of support. The largest 90-cm gap was the size of the visual cliff. Caregivers encouraged their infants to lean forward over the gap to retrieve a toy. When tested in their experienced sitting posture ($M = 104$ days), infants perceived precisely how far forward they could lean without falling into the precipice; they matched the probability of attempting with the probability of success. However, when facing the gaps in their inexperienced crawling posture ($M = 45$ days), the same infants fell into impossibly large gaps. Nearly half of the sample in each of two experiments crawled over the brink of a 90-cm gap on multiple trials.

Similarly, infants showed specificity of learning between sitting and crawling postures when tested with barriers in their path. Over longitudinal observations, sitting infants reached around a barrier to retrieve a target object several weeks before they demonstrated the ability to crawl around the barrier (Lockman, 1984). When tested cross-sectionally, 10- and 12-month-olds were more successful at retrieving objects from behind a barrier when they were tested in a sitting position than when they had to execute the detour by crawling (Lockman & Adams, 2001). When the task was to learn a location based on repeated trips to mothers' hiding place, experienced crawlers fared better than younger novice crawlers and better than older novice walkers (Clearfield, 2004). Younger crawlers attempted locomotion over a rippling waterbed on hands and knees but older walkers refused to step onto the waterbed or switched from their typical upright posture to quadruped (E. J. Gibson et al., 1987).

Infants may even show posture-specific learning between two upright postures: cruising and walking (Adolph, 2005; Adolph & Berger, 2005; Leo, Chiu, & Adolph, 2000). Like walking, cruising involves an upright posture. However, in contrast to walking, cruising infants move sideways and cling to a handrail or furniture for support. Using the psychophysical procedure, 11-month-old cruising infants were tested in two conditions. The handrail condition was relevant for maintaining balance with the arms in cruising: a solid floor with an adjustable gap (0 to 90 cm) in a handrail. The floor condition was relevant for maintaining balance with the legs in walking: a solid handrail with an adjustable gap

(0 to 90 cm) in the floor. Infants correctly gauged how far they could stretch their arms to cruise over the gap in the handrail but the same infants erred when judging how far they could stretch their legs to cruise over the gap in the floor beneath their feet. New walkers erred in both conditions, failing to judge how far they could travel between manual supports in the handrail and stepping into impossibly large gaps in the floor.

### What Infants Learn

What might infants learn that would lead to posture-specific perception of affordances? Several possibilities can be eliminated. In the slopes and gaps experiments where perceptual errors caused infants to fall, babies were not learning that the experimenter would catch them. Although the experimenter did rescue them as they fell, infants in longitudinal studies became more cautious over sessions, not more reckless; and in cross-sectional studies, the same infants who were caught dozens of times in their inexperienced posture avoided the obstacle when tested in their experienced posture.

Learning fear of heights is a frequently cited explanation (e.g., Campos et al., 2000). However, external manifestations of fear are not required for mediating an adaptive avoidance response, and it is unlikely that fear would wax and wane with changes in body postures. As on the visual cliff, crawling and walking infants in both cross-sectional and longitudinal studies showed primarily positive and neutral facial expressions and vocalizations, not fearful expressions or crying, as they avoided impossibly steep slopes (Adolph & Avolio, 1999; Fraisse, Couet, Bellanca, & Adolph, 2001; Stergiou, Adolph, Alibali, Avolio, & Cenedella, 1997). When infants' mothers provided them with encouraging and discouraging social messages, 18-month-olds only deferred to their mothers' unsolicited advice when the probability of success was uncertain (0.50 as determined by the psychophysical procedure). Moreover, they displayed primarily positive facial expressions and vocalizations at every increment regardless of whether they walked or avoided (Karasik et al., 2004; Tamis-LeMonda, Adolph, Lobo, Karasik, & Dimitropoulou, 2005).

Perhaps the most commonsense explanation is that infants learn that drop-offs, steep slopes, and the like are dangerous. However, the finding of posture-specific learning belies the notion that infants might learn to use particular facts about the environment to guide their actions, even when those facts hold true. Infants always require a sturdy floor to support their bodies. A 50° slope and 90-cm gap are risky for every infant in every pos- ture. The location of a hidden object is the same whether infants are sitting, crawling, or walking.

Similarly, the finding of flexibility within postures belies the notion that infants learn static facts about their physical propensities. In the longitudinal slopes study, experienced infants updated their perceptual judgments to reflect naturally occurring improvements in their crawling or walking skill (Adolph, 1997). In a cross-sectional experiment, when infants' bodies were made more top-heavy and their balance more precarious by loading them with lead-weighted shoulder packs, in- fants recalibrated their perception of affordances from trial to trial (Adolph & Avolio, 2000). They correctly treated the same degree of slant as risky while wearing lead-weighted shoulder packs and as safe while wearing feather-weighted packs.

Along the same lines, infants do not learn simple stimulus-response (S-R) associations or fixed patterns of responding to particular environmental conditions. Rather, variety of responding is a common feature in studies where infants encounter obstacles to locomotion (e.g., Berger, 2004; Berger & Adolph, 2003). Experi- enced walkers displayed alternative locomotor strate- gies for coping with risky slopes: crawling down on hands and knees, sliding headfirst prone in a Superman position, backing down feet first, sliding in a sitting po- sition, holding onto the experimenter for support, and avoiding traversal entirely by remaining on the starting platform (e.g., Adolph, 1995, 1997). Individual infants used multiple strategies at the same increment of slope within the same test session.

What, then, do infants learn that promotes flexible transfer across changes in bodies and skills but not across postural milestones? Since Thorndike's (1906; Thorndike & Woodworth, 1901) classic theory of identi- cal elements, researchers in motor skill acquisition have assumed that transfer depends on the extent to which el- ements of the training context are similar to elements of the performance context (Adams, 1987; J. R. Anderson & Singley, 1993). In our view, given the novelty and variability of motor actions, the notion of identical ele- ments in simple association learning is far too static and narrow to account for learning to perceive affordances (Adolph & Eppler, 2002).

Harlow's (1949, 1959; Harlow & Kuenne, 1949) no- tion of "learning sets" represented a try at something broader than simple association learning. His idea was that learners might acquire a set of exploratory proce- dures and strategies for figuring out solutions to novel problems within a circumscribed problem space (Stevenson, 1972). This set of information-gathering be- haviors and heuristic strategies allows learners to solve novel problems of a certain type. The scope of transfer should be limited only to the boundary of the problem space. Rather than learning particular solutions, facts, or cue-consequence associations, learners are, in Har- low's words, "learning to learn."

In Harlow's classic learning set paradigm, monkeys acquired a "win-stay/lose-shift" rule that would allow them to solve new instances of discrimination problems. But, solving novel problems in the circumscribed space of discrimination problems is a far cry from solving novel problems in the world of everyday motor actions. A fixed rule cannot provide the necessary flexibility to cope with a varying body, a varying environment, and moment-to- moment variations in biomechanical constraints.

Learning to learn in the context of controlling every- day motor actions requires something even bigger, some- thing akin to the information-gathering procedures and strategies of Harlow's learning sets, but more flexible than a rule. As suggested in the next section, infants as- semble a repertoire of exploratory behaviors to generate the requisite perceptual information to specify affor- dances (Adolph & Eppler, 2002). Once infants can both generate and detect information about their physical capabilities and environmental properties, they are equipped to perceive possibilities for action. To the ex- tent that each postural control system functions as a sep- arate perception-action system (i.e., a distinct problem space), perceptual information will fail to transfer be- tween postural milestones in development (Adolph, 2002, 2005).

## The Perception-Action Loop

Perception and action are linked together in a continu- ously evolving loop (J. J. Gibson, 1979; von Hofsten, 2003). The textbook image of a motionless eyeball wait- ing to receive perceptual information is overly simplis- tic. In real life, eye, head, limb, and body movements bring the perceptual systems to the available informa- tion; "We don't simply see, we look" (E. J. Gibson, 1988, p. 5). The traditional distinction between percep- tion and motor control is largely artificial. Every move- ment is accompanied by perceptual feedback, and many types of visual, haptic, vestibular, and proprioceptive in- formation do not exist without movement (J. J. Gibson, 1979). Reciprocally, prospective control of action relies on perceptual information. Perceptual feedback from ongoing movements creates the potential for feed-forward control. Thus, the perception-action loop can guide future actions rather than merely elicit them.

Over time, the loop comes to reflect developmental changes in infants' perception-action systems, and experience refines infants' actions toward more optimal function (E. J. Gibson, 1988; von Hofsten, 2003). Improvements in eye/head, manual, and postural control help infants glean visual information about external events and spurs their attention to the properties of objects and surfaces (Eppler, 1995; Needham, Barrett, & Peterman, 2002). Reciprocally, interesting visual displays motivate infants to seek information through looking. Feedback from interactions with objects and experiences with stance and locomotion facilitates improvements in prehension and locomotion.

For example, even the quiet touch of an infant's hand resting on a stable surface provides information (and support) for postural stability. Infants in the early stages of upright balance used a manual support reactively to control their postural sway; they altered downward forces on the supporting handrail after their bodies began to sway (Barela, Jeka, & Clark, 1999; Metcalfe & Clark, 2000). More experienced walkers stabilized posture prospectively by changing the amount of downward force prior to body sway. Over the 4-month period between pulling themselves upright and acquiring 1.5 months of walking experience, the amount of vertical force applied to the handrail decreased by 50%.

### Sensitivity to Perceptual Information

What is required to detect affordances? Perceptual information is a necessary but not a sufficient condition for perceiving possibilities for action. Without the appropriate information, infants have no basis for selecting or modifying actions and prospective control is doomed to fail: Walkers will trip over an obstacle in their path if they do not see it. Even with information available, infants must know where to direct their attention and be able to distinguish the relevant information structures. To illustrate with a classic (and hilarious) example of perceptual learning, both naive and expert adults looked at the same pairs of chick genitals, but only the experts could reliably differentiate their sex (Biederman & Shiffrar, 1987; E. J. Gibson, 1969). In short, prospective control will fail without both the appropriate exploratory behaviors to generate the crucial information and the perceptual expertise to tell the difference.

In the laboratory, experimenters can simply make information available to infants and measure their reac-

tions. Differential responding would provide evidence for perceptual sensitivity. In the case of locomotion, insensitivity to visual information for depth, rigidity, slant, and self-motion is surely not responsible for perceptual errors at the edge of a cliff, waterbed, and steep slope. Infants show sensitivity to visual information about properties of surfaces and about the equilibrium of their own bodies long before they are independently mobile and even before they can sit up, reach, or fully control their heads. Newborns respond differentially to visual information for a drop-off versus solid ground, deformable versus rigid surfaces, and to surfaces slanting to different degrees in depth (e.g., Campos, Langer, & Krowitz, 1970; E. J. Gibson & Walker, 1984; Slater & Morison, 1985).

Prelocomotor infants also are sensitive to visual information for self-motion. Newborns pushed their heads backward in response to optic flow displayed on monitors along the sides of their heads (Jouen, 1988; Jouen, Lepecq, Gapenne, & Bertenthal, 2000). Remarkably, the speed and amplitude of their head movements were related to the velocity of the optic flow. Infants 3 to 4 months old distinguished a looming obstacle from an approaching aperture, indicating sensitivity to visual information about collision and safe passage (Gibson, 1982; Schmuckler & Li, 1998). Infants 3 to 6 months old even showed crude sensitivity to visual information for the direction of heading (> 22°) based solely on patterns of optic flow (Gilmore, Baker, & Grobman, 2004; Gilmore & Rettke, 2003).

The standard apparatus for testing sensitivity to visual information for self-motion is a "moving room" (e.g., Lee & Lishman, 1975; Lishman & Lee, 1973). Infants sit or stand on the stationary floor while the walls and ceiling in a mini-room around them swing forward and backward. Movement of the room in one direction simulates the optic flow that would result from a body sway in the opposite direction. Although the moving room puts visual and muscle-joint information into conflict (infants see that they are moving but feel that they are stationary), the sensation of induced sway is very compelling. To compensate for perceived disequilibrium, sitting infants sway their heads and torsos and standing or walking infants sway, step, stagger, and fall in the direction of the room movement (e.g., Bertenthal & Bai, 1989; Butterworth & Hicks, 1977; Lee & Aronson, 1974). Adults differentiate two kinds of flow structure, primarily using lamellar flow from movement of the side walls (optic texture elements stream in parallel along the sides of the path) to control their posture while reserving radial flow from the front wall (optic texture elements stream outward from a central point of expansion) to guide their direction of heading (e.g., Stoffregen, 1985, 1986; Warren, Kay, & Yilmaz, 1996). Moreover, adults functionally differentiate the velocity of the flow, primarily using sway frequencies less than 0.5 Hz to control balance (Stoffregen, 1986; van Asten, Gielen, & van der Gon, 1988).

With age and experience, infants show more modulated behavioral responses to induced self-motion, increased functional differentiation of optic flow structures, and a tighter coupling between their sway responses and the timing and amplitude of room movements. In an upright position, younger children (< 24 months) were literally bowled over in the moving room, but older children (2 to 6 years) and adults responded with smaller, more modulated postural sways (e.g., Schmuckler, 1997; Stoffregen, Schmuckler, & Gibson, 1987; Wann, Mon-Williams, & Rushton, 1998). Seated 9-month-olds showed functional differentiation of optic flow structure by producing directionally appropriate sways in response to whole room and side wall movement; 7-month-olds responded appropriately to whole room movement; but 5-month-olds responded indiscriminately (Bertenthal & Bai, 1989). Greater attention to the functional significance of optic flow structures in the older infants may have been facilitated by experience with locomotion; 8-month-olds with locomotor experience showed more postural responses to side wall movements than did precrawling infants of the same age (Campos et al., 2000; Higgins, Campos, & Kermoian, 1996). Similarly, standing and walking infants (12 to 24 months of age) displayed more staggers and falls to whole room and side wall movements than to front wall movements (Stoffregen et al., 1987). The dual task of steering while maintaining balance in a "moving hallway" caused more postural disruptions than walking along an open path (1- to 5-year-olds), and younger, less experienced walkers were more aversely affected (Schmuckler & Gibson, 1989).

Continuously oscillating movements of the whole room entrained sitting and standing infants' postural responses so that they swayed back and forth like puppets in accordance with the room movements (Barela, Godoi, Freitas, & Polastri, 2000; Delorme, Frigon, & Lagace, 1989). The timing and amplitude of sway responses in older, more experienced sitters (9- and 13-month-olds) were more tightly linked to the frequency and amplitude of the continuously oscillating visual flow than the sways of younger, less experienced sitters (5- and 7-month-olds; Bertenthal, Rose, & Bai, 1997). Unlike adults, sitting 9-month-olds and standing 3- to 6-year-olds swayed in response to continuous room oscillations from 0.2 to 0.8 Hz (Bertenthal, Boker, & Xu, 2000; Schmuckler, 1997). However, like adults, sitting infants showed a linear decrease in the correlation between the swaying movements of their heads and the driving frequency of the room.

### Information-Generating Behaviors

Outside the laboratory, disruptions to posture are generally self-induced by infants' prior movements, not externally imposed by moving the surrounding room. There is no experimenter to distill perceptual information and present it to infants for their reactions. Instead, infants must do much of the information gathering for themselves. Even then, the availability of perceptual information does not guarantee that it will be detected.

To examine information gathering, researchers observe the exploratory behaviors of freely moving infants as they approach various obstacles in their path. Walking infants hesitated longer and engaged in more visual scanning and touching at the edge of a rippling waterbed (agitated from beneath) compared with the brink of a rigid surface (E. J. Gibson et al., 1987). Both crawling and walking infants—at all levels of age and experience—exhibited longer latencies and more looking and touching as they approached risky slopes compared with safe ones (Adolph, 1995, 1997; Adolph & Avolio, 2000; Adolph, Eppler, & Gibson, 1993a). Walkers generated visual and mechanical information by standing with their feet straddling the brink and rocking back and forth over their ankles. Crawlers leaned forward with both hands on the slope and rocked over their wrists (drawn in Figure 4.7b).

Sitting, crawling, and cruising infants generated information about the size of a gap in the floor by stretching their arm (or leg in the case of cruisers) out over the precipice and then retracting it (Adolph, 2000; Leo et al., 2000). Figure 4.7c to 4.7d illustrates examples. Cruisers explored the size of a gap in the handrail by stretching and retracting their arms over the gap. Similarly, walkers explored possibilities for crossing a deep precipice via a narrow bridge by peering into the gap, dipping their foot into the gap, touching the bridge with their feet, and holding onto a support pole while stretching out a foot to see how far they could walk onto the bridge before having to let go (see Figure 4.7e; Berger &

Adolph, 2003; Berger, Adolph, & Lobo, 2005). Across studies, latency, looking, and touching were elevated on risky increments compared with safe ones.

On waterbeds, slopes, gaps, bridges, and the visual cliff, infants of all ages produced another kind of information-generating behavior: social expressions (e.g., Fraisse et al., 2001; Karasik et al., 2004; Richards & Rader, 1983; Sorce et al., 1985; Stergiou et al., 1997; Tamis-LeMonda & Adolph, 2005). Most infants vocalized (primarily babbles, open vowels, calls, and grunts rather than whimpers and cries; few words) and older infants also used manual gestures (e.g., arms outstretched toward their parents, pointing). Like perceptual exploration, infants' social expressions were most frequent at risky increments. Researchers instructed caregivers about how to respond so as to manipulate or control for their social messages. However, under more natural conditions, presumably caregivers would respond with sensible and individually tailored social information in the form of encouragement or prohibition.

### The Real-Time Loop

Largely absent from the infant and adult literatures on perceptually guided locomotion is a mechanistic account of the real-time, perception-action loop. What prompts infants in the ongoing course of locomotion to shift their attention to an obstacle, engage in concerted looking and touching, vocalize, look toward a caregiver, and so on? Given that infants' exploratory behaviors are not random or indiscriminate, one thing must lead to another. The loop must spiral along from moment to moment until infants select a different action and begin again.

We offer two suggestions. First, not all information gathering need be deliberate (Adolph, 1997). Some types of information can arise serendipitously as a consequence of ongoing movements. Optic flow, for example, arises as a by-product of locomotion. With the eyes parked in front of the walker's face, both radial flow for steering and lamellar flow for balance become instantly available (Patla, 1998). New walkers, however, have a problem. Tipping their heads downward to look at the ground near their feet throws their bodies off-balance (hence, toddlers' "Frankenstein" gait). Thus, visual scanning of the near ground is likely to be deliberate.

In contrast, newly crawling infants tend to point their faces downward, perhaps because lifting the head requires more balance and neck strength. For them, visual information about the ground near their hands is cheaply available. Moreover, new crawlers frequently move in

bursts punctuated by bouts of rocking. Such movements create torque around infants' wrists and shoulders and shear force between their hands and the ground—all useful types of mechanical information (especially if they occur at the edge of a slope, waterbed, foam pit, or slippery surface) arising as a happy by-product of poor crawling skill.

Like looking and touching, social information gathering need not be deliberate. Individual animals (or entire species) can co-opt happenstance forms in adaptive ways. Young infants might vocalize without the intent to communicate and thereby serendipitously elicit useful social information from their caregivers. A similar notion of communicative exaptations is well documented in the animal literature. For example, rat pups emit ultrasonic vocalizations when they are separated from the nest. Although the squeaks serve a communicative function by prompting dams to return pups to the nest, pups are not deliberately calling to their mothers for help. The cause is simply a physiological response to rapid body cooling (Blumberg & Sokoloff, 2001, 2003). In the course of locomotion, rodents emit ultrasonic squeaks, horses wheeze, and dogs bark due to the compression of the thorax as their forelimbs hit the ground (Blumberg, 1992). Human infants 9 to 13 months old emitted grunts as a consequence of physical effort while crawling, moving from standing to squatting positions, and trying to lift the lid on a bottle (McCune, Vhiman, Roug-Hellichius, Delery, & Gogate, 1996). In the case of perceptually guided locomotion, infants' vocalizations might arise as a by-product of arousal caused by the first sight of a large drop-off or steep slope; or, infants' noises might stem from the physical exertion of mustering a crawling burst. Either way, an acoustic by-product of an underlying physiological maneuver does not preclude the listener from hearing a useful communicative signal. Regardless of infants' initial intent, caregivers respond and are likely to precipitate a sort of "conversation" about the wisdom of attempting traversal.

A second suggestion for the precipitating events in a real-time perception-action loop concerns the role of visual information from a distance. Variations in the geometric layout of the terrain—cliffs, slopes, gaps, barriers, passageways, elevations, and so on—are specified by a host of visual depth cues. In addition to optical expansion and contraction, infants are sensitive to motion parallax, accretion and deletion of texture, stereoscopic information, convergence, and several pictorial depth cues (for review, see Kellman & Arterberry,

2000). Thus, the real-time sequence of information gathering is likely to begin with visual information about the surface layout (Adolph, Eppler, Marin, Weise, & Clearfield, 2000). When the ground surface appears relatively flat and continuous (as in the baseline trials or control condition in most experiments), infants crawl or walk without hesitation or breaking stride. When infants detect depth information for a change in the layout, like adults, they may be prompted to modify their gait (Mohagheghi, Moraes, & Patla, 2004; Patla, 1991; Patla, Prentice, Robinson, & Neufeld, 1991) and to engage in more concerted looking and touching.

In most cases, reliance on visual depth cues is highly efficient. However, when the ground is deformable or slippery, visual information from a distance may fail to elicit the appropriate exploratory behaviors (Adolph, Eppler, et al., 2005; Joh & Adolph, in press; Lo et al., 1999; Marigold & Patla, 2002). Adults may rely on erroneous intuitions about the predictive relationship between deformable surfaces and rounded contours and between slippery surfaces and shine (Joh, Adolph, Campbell, & Eppler, in press). For example, more than 300 participants (15- to 39-month-old children and adults) walked straight into a large foam pit and fell. Apparently, the rounded edges and irregular surface of the foam blocks were not adequate to specify deformability. (Note, in the Gibson et al., 1987, waterbed experiments, event information for deformability was created by a researcher agitating the surface from underneath.)

## Creating New Affordances for Action

Possibilities for action are not always constrained by infants' immature bodies and limited skills. Happily, infants live in a world that is populated by caregivers who are willing to lend a helping hand, a world that abounds with objects and surfaces that can be incorporated as tools into an action plan. Although researchers typically do not consider social interaction and cognition to be central to the perception-action approach, social supports and tools can expand affordances for action and even create new possibilities for action.

### Parents' Role in Promoting Action

The development of action is not a lonely enterprise. Infants typically acquire new motor skills in a supportive social context (Tamis-LeMonda & Adolph, 2005). Before infants can exploit affordances for action on their own, caregivers create affordances for them. Caregivers scaffold prewalkers into walking infants simply by offering them a finger to hold onto for support. Similarly, in recent clever experimental manipulations, researchers have promoted new actions at earlier ages than if infants had to discover them on their own. For example, 3-month-olds who normally lack the motor skill to handle objects manually wore "sticky mittens" with Velcro-covered palms as they played with Velcro-edged toys (Needham et al., 2002). After the training, infants could pick up the toys and explore them as well as 5-month-olds who acquired their manual skills naturally. Seven-month-old prelocomotor infants learned to move around the room using a powered-mobility-device—a joystick controlled, battery operated buggy (D. I. Anderson et al., 2001; Campos et al., 2000).

Differences in child-rearing practices highlight parents' role in providing opportunities for action. Parents promote action by organizing and constraining the circumstances surrounding infants' developing skills (Reed & Bril, 1996). Caregivers decide whether infants are on the floor (Adolph, 2002; Campos et al., 2000), whether they have access to stairs (Berger, Theuring, & Adolph, 2005), and whether they sleep on their stomachs or on their backs (Davis, Moon, Sachs, & Ottolini, 1998; Dewey, Fleming, Golding, & Team, 1998). In some cultures, caregivers carry newborns as if they were a fragile carton of eggs and protect them from intense stimulation. In others, they throw newborns into the air and catch them, and stretch and massage their limbs (Bril & Sabatier, 1986; Hopkins & Westra, 1988, 1989, 1990; Super, 1976). Some cultures encourage new skills verbally. Others "train" infants, for example, by propping 3- to 4-month-olds in a special hole in the ground to promote sitting (Hopkins & Westra, 1988, 1989, 1990; Super, 1976) and jumping infants up and down to promote walking (Keller, 2003). As a consequence of the variation in child-rearing practices, infants acquire their sitting, crawling, walking, and stair-climbing at different rates—at later ages for children with fewer opportunities and less practice.

### Tools Expand Possibilities for Action

Implementing a tool allows infants to create new affordances for action by themselves. When infants' current physical abilities are inadequate for achieving a goal, tools can improve the actor-environment fit (Bongers, Smitsman, & Michaels, 2003). Tool use requires infants to (1) perceive a gap between their own motor abilities and a desired goal, (2) realize that an object or environmental support can serve as an alternative means to bridge the gap, and (3) implement the tool successfully (Berger & Adolph, 2003). Although most researchers focus on the cognitive skills required by the second step (Chen & Siegler, 2000; Piaget, 1954), perceptual-motor skills are central to all three steps (Lockman, 2000). The first step to successful tool use involves perceiving (lack of) affordances for action—understanding that a desired object is too far out of reach or that the intended action is blocked by an obstacle (Berger et al., 2005). Developmentally, perceiving impediments to action appears before a concerted search for alternative means and both may appear prior to a search that incorporates an external object or environmental support (McCarty, Clifton, & Collard, 2001; Piaget, 1952; Willatts, 1984).

The means-ends problem solving that is so critical for the second step to tool use may have its roots in the perceptual-motor activity of relating objects to surfaces through actions (Lockman, 2000). For example, 8-month-olds relate objects to surfaces according to their respective material properties (Lockman, 2005). They perform banging actions with solid objects on solid tabletops but not when the object or surface is soft. Eventually, physical limitations cease to prevent infants from achieving their goals. By 10 months, infants show evidence of the second step to successful tool use. They extend their reaching abilities using sticks, hooks, rakes, and rings to drag over distant objects and show evidence of means/ends analysis by choosing an appropriate tool for a job (Bates, Carlson-Luden, & Bretherton, 1980; Brown, 1990; Chen & Siegler, 2000; Leeuwen, Smitsman, & Leeuwen, 1994). Similarly, in Köhler's (1925) famous work on tool use in chimps, the animals pieced sticks together to retrieve an object beyond their reach.

The third step involves the biomechanics of tool use (Berger & Adolph, 2003; Berger et al., 2005). Beyond knowing that a tool is necessary for task completion and that certain items make appropriate tools, successful implementation of a tool requires knowing how to use it. Infants' early action patterns may serve as the rudimentary foundations for later tool implementation (Lockman, 2000). Sliding objects back and forth over a surface may be an early precursor for writing and scribbling, and banging a hard object on a solid surface may prefigure hammering (Greer & Lockman, 1998).

Before 12 months of age, infants have difficulty planning an implementation strategy. Instead, they must correct their actions after they have already begun to use the tool. For example, 9- to 12-month-olds grab a spoon by the bowl- instead of the handle-end or hold it with the bowl-end pointing away from their mouth (McCarty, Clifton, & Collard, 1999, 2001). To correct, they must awkwardly rotate their hands or switch hands to get the bowl in their mouth. When experimenters highlighted the orientation of a spoon's handle by repeatedly presenting it pointing in the same direction, 12-month-olds used the most effective radial grasp (McCarty & Keen, 2005). By 18 months of age, infants know which end of a spoon to grasp, how to grasp it, and how to plan the implementation so that they reach for the tool with the appropriate hand orientation instead of resorting to post hoc corrections (McCarty et al., 1999, 2001). Eighteen-month-olds can even adjust their typical tool-use strategies to cope with novel situations. Infants modified their grasp orientation, the location of their grip along the handle of the spoon, and the angle at which they held the spoon when they had to retrieve food through a narrow opening in a lid or when they had to use a spoon with a bent handle to scoop food from a bowl (Achard & von Hofsten, 2002; Steenbergen, van der Kamp, Smitsman, & Carson, 1997).

Tools are not limited to hand-held objects. Tool use can involve the whole body in action (Berger & Adolph, 2003). Köhler's (1925) chimpanzees used poles to vault themselves into the air to retrieve bananas that were hanging from the ceiling. McGraw's (1935) twins, Jimmy and Johnny, stacked boxes on top of each other to climb to a toy suspended high out of reach. Similarly, in a series of experiments involving whole-body tool use (Figure 4.7e to 4.7f), 16-month-old walking infants recognized that handrails could augment their balance for crossing narrow bridges (Berger & Adolph, 2003; Berger et al., 2005). When no handrail was available, infants refused to cross narrow bridges altogether. On wide bridges, infants ran straight across regardless of whether a handrail was available. Moreover, infants used wooden but not wobbly handrails for crossing narrow bridges, suggesting that they took the material composition of the handrail into account for determining its effectiveness as a tool (Berger et al., 2005).

## Summary: Getting into the Act

Historically, developmental psychology has acquired a sort of split personality: Are we movement scientists, perception psychologists, cognitive psychologists, social psychologists, and language acquisition researchers? Or, are we developmental psychologists? And if so, development of what? The fractionation of psychology into separate content domains has created a field of developmental psychologists who do not study common phenomena or even speak a common language. Research on motor development holds some promise for helping to forge a shared developmental science.

Perhaps the most far-ranging consequence of a perception-action approach to motor development is that motor skills have become relevant to developmental psychologists who would not normally worry about motor control. Rather than a simple response measure for making inferences about the workings of the mind, motor actions are now viewed as both a facilitator and beneficiary of psychological functions. On one side of the perception-action loop, researchers—like Piaget before them—study the effects of developing motor actions on perception, cognition, language, and social interaction (e.g., Biringen, Emde, Campos, & Applebaum, 1995; Campos et al., 2000; Needham et al., 2002; Sommerville & Woodward, 2005; Sommerville, Woodward, & Needham, in press). On the other side of the loop, researchers study the mental representations viewed as integral to motor actions (e.g., Gilmore & Johnson, 1995; S. P. Johnson et al., 2003, 2004; Munakata et al., 1997; Shinskey & Munakata, 2003; Spelke & von Hofsten, 2001; Spencer & Schöner, 2003). In short, researchers from a range of backgrounds are "getting into the act."

In looking back over a career spanning 70 years, E. J. Gibson (1994) said in a keynote address to the American Psychological Society that nothing is so exciting as the search for encompassing principles. She offered ideas such as prospectivity and flexibility as a starting place for a grand unified theory of psychology, and she urged younger researchers to continue to search. In that spirit, we close with a final suggestion: The perception-action approach can serve as a model system for the study of developmental psychology. Research from the perception-action approach illustrates the utility and feasibility of studying infants, with all their many body parts and psychological functions, everything continually changing, embedded in a rich and varied physical environment populated by other people. Bridging the traditional divisions between content areas is certainly possible and may be the best bet for understanding how movements, learning, development—any kind of psychological change—occurs in the real-time processes of a moving and perceiving animal.

## REFERENCES

Achard, B., & von Hofsten, C. (2002). Development of the infants' ability to retrieve food through a slit. *Infant and Child Development, 11,* 43–56.

Adams, J. A. (1987). Historical review and appraisal of research on the learning, retention, and transfer of human motor skills. *Psychological Bulletin, 101,* 41–74.

Adler, S. A., & Haith, M. M. (2003). The nature of infants' visual expectations for event content. *Infancy, 4,* 389–421.

Adolph, K. E. (1995). A psychophysical assessment of toddlers' ability to cope with slopes. *Journal of Experimental Psychology: Human Perception and Performance, 21,* 734–750.

Adolph, K. E. (1997). Learning in the development of infant locomotion. *Monographs of the Society for Research in Child Development, 62*(3, Serial No. 251).

Adolph, K. E. (2000). Specificity of learning: Why infants fall over a veritable cliff. *Psychological Science, 11,* 290–295.

Adolph, K. E. (2002). Learning to keep balance. In R. Kail (Ed.), *Advances in child development and behavior* (Vol. 30, pp. 1–30). Amsterdam: Elsevier Science.

Adolph, K. E. (2005). Learning to learn in the development of action. In J. Lockman & J. Reiser (Eds.), *Minnesota Symposia on Child Development: Vol. 32. Action as an organizer of learning and development* (pp. 91–122). Hillsdale, NJ: Erlbaum.

Adolph, K. E., & Avolio, A. M. (1999, April). *Infants' social and affective responses to risk.* Poster presented at the meeting of the Society for Research in Child Development, Albuquerque, NM.

Adolph, K. E., & Avolio, A. M. (2000). Walking infants adapt locomotion to changing body dimensions. *Journal of Experimental Psychology: Human Perception and Performance, 26,* 1148–1166.

Adolph, K. E., & Berger, S. E. (2005). Physical and motor development. In M. H. Bornstein & M. E. Lamb (Eds.), *Developmental science: An advanced textbook* (5th ed., pp. 223–281). Mahwah, NJ: Erlbaum.

Adolph, K. E., & Eppler, M. A. (2002). Flexibility and specificity in infant motor skill acquisition. In J. W. Fagen & H. Hayne (Eds.), *Progress in infancy research* (Vol. 2, pp. 121–167). Mahwah, NJ: Erlbaum.

Adolph, K. E., Eppler, M. A., & Gibson, E. J. (1993a). Crawling versus walking infants' perception of affordances for locomotion over sloping surfaces. *Child Development, 64,* 1158–1174.

Adolph, K. E., Eppler, M. A., & Gibson, E. J. (1993b). Development of perception of affordances. In C. K. Rovee-Collier & L. P. Lipsitt (Eds.), *Advances in infancy research* (Vol. 8, pp. 51–98). Norwood, NJ: Ablex.

Adolph, K. E., Eppler, M. A., Joh, A. S., Shrout, P. E., & Lo, T. (2005). *Walking down slippery slopes: How infants use slant and friction information.* Manuscript submitted for publication.

Adolph, K. E., Eppler, M. A., Marin, L., Weise, I. B., & Clearfield, M. W. (2000). Exploration in the service of prospective control. *Infant Behavior and Development, 23,* 441–460.

Adolph, K. E., Joh, A. S., Ishak, S., Lobo, S. A., & Berger, S. E. (2005, October). *Specificity of infants' knowledge for action.* Paper presented to the Cognitive Development Society, San Diego, CA.

Adolph, K. E., Robinson, S. R., Young, J. W., & Gill-Alvarez, F. (2005). *Is there evidence for developmental stages?* Manuscript submitted for publication.

Adolph, K. E., Vereijken, B., & Denny, M. A. (1998). Learning to crawl. *Child Development, 69,* 1299–1312.

Adolph, K. E., Vereijken, B., & Shrout, P. E. (2003). What changes in infant walking and why. *Child Development, 74,* 474–497.

Alibali, M. W. (1999). How children change their minds: Strategy change can be gradual or abrupt. *Developmental Psychology, 35,* 127–145.

Ames, L. B. (1937). The sequential patterning of prone progression in the human infant. *Genetic Psychology Monographs, 19,* 409–460.

Amiel-Tison, C., & Grenier, A. (1986). *Neurological assessment during the first year of life.* New York: Oxford University Press.

Anderson, D. I., Campos, J. J., Anderson, D. E., Thomas, T. D., Witherington, D. C., Uchiyama, I., et al. (2001). The flip side of perception-action coupling: Locomotor experience and the ontogeny of visual-postural coupling. *Human Movement Science, 20,* 461–487.

Anderson, J. R., & Singley, M. K. (1993). The identical elements theory of transfer. In J. R. Anderson (Ed.), *Rules of the mind* (pp. 183–204). Hillsdale, NJ: Erlbaum.

Andre-Thomas, & Autgaerden, S. (1966). *Locomotion from pre- to post-natal life.* Lavenham, Suffolk, England: Spastics Society Medical Education and Information Unit and William Heinemann Medical Books.

Angulo-Kinzler, R. M. (2001). Exploration and selection of intralimb coordination patterns in 3-month-old infants. *Journal of Motor Behavior, 33*(4), 363–376.

Angulo-Kinzler, R. M., & Horn, C. L. (2001). Selection and memory of a lower limb motor-perceptual task in 3-month-old infants. *Infant Behavior and Development, 24,* 239–257.

Angulo-Kinzler, R. M., Ulrich, B., & Thelen, E. (2002). Three-month-old infants can select specific motor solutions. *Motor Control, 6,* 52–68.

Arduini, D., Rizzo, G., & Romanini, C. (1995). Fetal behavioral states and behavioral transitions in normal and compromised fetuses. In J.-P. Lecanuet, & W. P. Fifer (Eds.), *Fetal development: A psychobiological perspective* (pp. 83–99). Hillsdale, NJ: Erlbaum.

Aslin, R. N. (1981). Development of smooth pursuit in human infants. In D. F. Fischer, R. A. Monty, & E. J. Senders (Eds.), *Eye movements: Cognition and visual development* (pp. 31–51). Hillsdale, NJ: Erlbaum.

Aslin, R. N., & Salapatek, P. (1975). Saccadic localization of peripheral targets by the very young human infant. *Perception and Psychophysics, 17,* 293–302.

Assaiante, C. (1998). Development of locomotor balance control in healthy children. *Neuroscience and Biobehavioral Reviews, 22,* 527–532.

Assaiante, C., & Amblard, B. (1995). An ontogenetic model for the sensorimotor organization of balance control in humans. *Human Movement Science, 14,* 13–43.

Assaiante, C., Thomachot, B., Aurenty, R., & Amblard, B. (1998). Organization of lateral balance control in toddlers during the first year of independent walking. *Journal of Motor Behavior, 30*(2), 114–129.

Assaiante, C., Woollacott, M. H., & Amblard, B. (2000). Development of postural adjustment during gait initiation: Kinematic and EMG analysis. *Journal of Motor Behavior, 32,* 211–226.

Barela, J. A., Godoi, D., Freitas, P. B., & Polastri, P. F. (2000). Visual information and body sway coupling in infants during sitting acquisition. *Infant Behavior and Development, 23,* 285–297.

Barela, J. A., Jeka, J. J., & Clark, J. E. (1999). The use of somatosensory information during the acquisition of independent upright stance. *Infant Behavior and Development, 22*(1), 87–102.

Bates, E., Carlson-Luden, V., & Bretherton, I. (1980). Perceptual aspects of tool using in infancy. *Infant Behavior and Development, 3,* 127–140.

Bayley, N. (1993). *Bayley scales of infant development* (2nd ed.). New York: Psychological Corporation.

Bell, M. A., & Fox, N. A. (1996). Crawling experience is related to changes in cortical organization during infancy: Evidence from EEG coherence. *Developmental Psychobiology, 29,* 551–561.

Berger, S. E. (2004). Demands on finite cognitive capacity cause infants' perseverative errors. *Infancy, 5*(2), 217–238.

Berger, S. E., & Adolph, K. E. (2003). Infants use handrails as tools in a locomotor task. *Developmental Psychology, 39,* 594–605.

Berger, S. E., Adolph, K. E., & Lobo, S. A. (2005). Out of the toolbox: Toddlers differentiate wobbly and wooden handrails. *Child Development.*

Berger, S. E., Theuring, C. F., & Adolph, K. E. (2005). *Social, cognitive, and environmental factors influence how infants learn to climb stairs.* Manuscript submitted for publication.

Berk, L. E. (2003). *Child development.* Boston: Allyn & Bacon.

Bernstein, N. (1967). *The coordination and regulation of movements.* Oxford, England: Pergamon Press.

Berridge, K. C. (1990). Comparative fine structure of action rules of form and sequence in the grooming patterns of six rodent species. *Behaviour, 113,* 21–56.

Bertenthal, B. I. (1999). Variation and selection in the development of perception and action. In G. J. P. Savelsbergh (Ed.), *Nonlinear analyses of developmental processes* (pp. 105–120). Amsterdam: Elsevier Science.

Bertenthal, B. I., & Bai, D. L. (1989). Infants' sensitivity to optical flow for controlling posture. *Developmental Psychology, 25,* 936–945.

Bertenthal, B. I., Boker, S. M., & Xu, M. (2000). Analysis of the perception-action cycle for visually induced postural sway in 9-month-old sitting infants. *Infant Behavior and Development, 23,* 299–315.

Bertenthal, B. I., & Campos, J. J. (1984). A reexamination of fear and its determinants on the visual cliff. *Psychophysiology, 21,* 413–417.

Bertenthal, B. I., Campos, J. J., & Barrett, K. C. (1984). Self-produced locomotion: An organizer of emotional, cognitive, and social development in infancy. In R. N. Emde & R. J. Harmon (Eds.), *Continuities and discontinuities in development* (pp. 175–210). New York: Plenum Press.

Bertenthal, B. I., Campos, J. J., & Kermoian, R. (1994). An epigenetic perspective on the development of self-produced locomotion and its consequences. *Current Directions in Psychological Science, 3,* 140–145.

Bertenthal, B. I., & Clifton, R. K. (1998). Perception and action. In W. Damon (Editor-in-Chief) & D. Kuhn & R. S. Siegler (Vol. Eds.), *Handbook of child psychology: Vol. 2. Cognition, perception, and language* (5th ed., pp. 51–102). New York: Wiley.

Bertenthal, B. I., Rose, J. L., & Bai, D. L. (1997). Perception-action coupling in the development of visual control of posture. *Journal of Experimental Psychology: Human Perception and Performance, 23*(6), 1631–1643.

Bertenthal, B. I., & von Hofsten, C. (1998). Eye, head and trunk control: The foundation for manual development. *Neuroscience and Biobehavioral Review, 22*(4), 515–520.

Berthier, N. E. (1996). Learning to reach: A mathematical model. *Developmental Psychology, 32,* 811–823.

Berthier, N. E. (1997). Analysis of reaching for stationary and moving objects in the human infant. In J. W. Donahoe & V. P. Dorsel

(Eds.), *Neural-network models of cognition: Biobehavioral foundations* (pp. 283–301). Amsterdam: North-Holland/Elsevier Science.

Berthier, N. E., Clifton, R. K., McCall, D. D., & Robin, D. J. (1999). Proximodistal structure of early reaching in human infants. *Experimental Brain Research, 127*, 259–269.

Berthier, N. E., & Keen, R. E. (in press). Development of reaching in infancy. *Experimental Brain Research.*

Berthier, N. E., Rosenstein, M. T., & Barto, A. G. (2005). Approximate optimal control as model for motor learning. *Psychological Review, 122*, 329–346.

Biederman, I., & Shiffrar, M. M. (1987). Sexing day-old chicks: A case study and expert systems analysis of a difficult perceptual learning task. *Journal of Experimental Psychology: Learning, Memory, and Cognition, 13*, 640–645.

Biringen, Z., Emde, R. N., Campos, J. J., & Applebaum, M. I. (1995). Affective reorganization in the infant, the mother, and the dyad: The role of upright locomotion and its timing. *Child Development, 66*, 499–514.

Blumberg, M. S. (1992). Rodent ultrasonic short calls: Locomotion, biomechanics, and communication. *Journal of Comparative Psychology, 106*, 360–365.

Blumberg, M. S., & Sokoloff, G. (2001). Do infant rats cry? *Psychological Review, 108*, 83–95.

Blumberg, M. S., & Sokoloff, G. (2003). Hard heads and open minds: A reply to Panksepp. *Psychological Review, 110*, 389–394.

Bly, L. (1994). *Motor skills acquisition in the first year.* San Antonio, TX: Therapy Skill Builders.

Bongers, R. M., Smitsman, A. W., & Michaels, C. F. (2003). Geometrics and dynamics of a rod determine how it is used for reaching. *Journal of Motor Behavior, 35*, 4–22.

Breniere, Y., Bril, B., & Fontaine, R. (1989). Analysis of the transition from upright stance to steady state locomotion in children with under 200 days of autonomous walking. *Journal of Motor Behavior, 21*, 20–37.

Breniere, Y., & Do, M. C. (1986). When and how does steady state gait movement induced from upright posture begin? *Journal of Biomechanics, 19*, 1035–1040.

Breniere, Y., & Do, M. C. (1991). Control of gait initiation. *Journal of Motor Behavior, 23*, 235–240.

Breniere, Y., Do, M. C., & Bouisset, S. (1987). Are dynamic phenomena prior to stepping essential to walking? *Journal of Motor Behavior, 19*, 62–76.

Bril, B., & Breniere, Y. (1989). Steady-state velocity and temporal structure of gait during the first 6 months of autonomous walking. *Human Movement Science, 8*, 99–122.

Bril, B., & Breniere, Y. (1991). Timing invariances in toddlers' gait. In J. Fagard & P. H. Wolff (Eds.), *The development of timing control and temporal organization in coordinated action: Invariant relative timing, rhythms and coordination* (Advances in Psychology Series, Vol. 81, pp. 231–244). Amsterdam: North-Holland.

Bril, B., & Breniere, Y. (1992). Postural requirements and progression velocity in young walkers. *Journal of Motor Behavior, 24*, 105–116.

Bril, B., & Breniere, Y. (1993). Posture and independent locomotion in early childhood: Learning to walk or learning dynamic postural control. In G. J. P. Savelsbergh (Ed.), *The development of coordination in infancy* (pp. 337–358). Amsterdam: North-Holland/Elsevier Science.

Bril, B., & Ledebt, A. (1998). Head coordination as a means to assist sensory integration in learning to walk. *Neuroscience and Biobehavioral Reviews, 22*, 555–563.

Bril, B., & Sabatier, C. (1986). The cultural context of motor development: Postural manipulations in the daily life of Bambara babies (Mali). *International Journal of Behavioral Development, 9*, 439–453.

Brooks, R. A. (1991). New approaches to robotics. *Science, 253*, 1227–1232.

Brown, A. (1990). Domain specific principles affect learning and transfer in children. *Cognitive Science, 14*, 107–133.

Brumley, M. R., & Robinson, S. R. (2002, November). *Unilateral forelimb weighting alters spontaneous motor activity in newborn rats* (Program No. 633.21.2002 Abstract Viewer/Intinerary Planner). Paper presented at the Society for Neuroscience, Orlando, FL.

Brumley, M. R., & Robinson, S. R. (2005). Effects of unilateral limb weighting on spontaneous limb movements and tight interlimb coupling in the neonatal rat. *Behavioral Brain Research.*

Burnett, C. N., & Johnson, E. W. (1971). Development of gait in childhood: Pt 2. *Developmental Medicine and Child Neurology, 13*, 207–215.

Burnside, L. H. (1927). Coordination in the locomotion of infants. *Genetic Psychology Monographs, 2*, 279–372.

Bushnell, E. W. (1985). The decline of visually guided reaching during infancy. *Infant Behavior and Development, 8*, 139–155.

Bushnell, E. W., & Boudreau, J. P. (1993). Motor development and the mind: The potential role of motor abilities as a determinant of aspects of perceptual development. *Child Development, 64*, 1005–1021.

Butterworth, G., & Hicks, L. (1977). Visual proprioception and postural stability in infancy: A developmental study. *Perception, 6*, 255–262.

Campos, J. J., Anderson, D. I., Barbu-Roth, M. A., Hubbard, E. M., Hertenstein, M. J., & Witherington, D. C. (2000). Travel broadens the mind. *Infancy, 1*(2), 149–219.

Campos, J. J., Bertenthal, B. I., & Kermoian, R. (1992). Early experience and emotional development: The emergence of wariness of heights. *Psychological Science, 3*, 61–64.

Campos, J. J., Hiatt, S., Ramsay, D., Henderson, C., & Svejda, M. (1978). The emergence of fear on the visual cliff. In M. Lewis & L. Rosenblum (Eds.), *The development of affect* (pp. 149–182). New York: Plenum Press.

Campos, J. J., Langer, A., & Krowitz, A. (1970). Cardiac responses on the visual cliff. *Science, 170*, 196–197.

Carey, S. (1985). *Conceptual change in childhood.* Cambridge, MA: MIT Press.

Chan, M. Y., Biancaniello, R., Adolph, K. E., & Marin, L. (2000, July). *Tracking infants' locomotor experience: The telephone diary.* Poster presented at the meeting of the International Conference on Infant Studies, Brighton, England.

Chan, M. Y., Lu, Y., Marin, L., & Adolph, K. E. (1999). A baby's day: Capturing crawling experience. In M. A. Grealy & J. A. Thompson (Eds.), *Studies in perception and action V* (pp. 245–249). Mahwah, NJ: Erlbaum.

Chen, Z., & Siegler, R. S. (2000). Across the great divide: Bridging the gap between understanding of toddlers' and older children's thinking. *Monographs of the Society for Research in Child Development, 65*(2, Serial No. 261).

Cioni, G., Ferrari, F., & Prechtl, H. F. R. (1989). Posture and spontaneous motility in fullterm infants. *Early Human Development, 18*, 247–262.

Clark, A. (1997). *Being there: Putting brain, body, and world together again.* Cambridge, MA: MIT Press.

Clark, J. E., & Phillips, S. J. (1987). The step cycle organization of infant walkers. *Journal of Motor Behavior, 19*, 412–433.

Clark, J. E., Whitall, J., & Phillips, S. J. (1988). Human interlimb coordination: The first 6 months of independent walking. *Developmental Psychobiology, 21,* 445–456.

Claxton, L. J., Keen, R., & McCarty, M. E. (2003). Evidence of motor planning in infant reaching behavior. *Psychological Science, 14*(4), 354–356.

Clearfield, M. W. (2004). The role of crawling and walking experience in infant spatial memory. *Journal of Experimental Child Psychology, 89,* 214–241.

Clifton, R. K., Muir, D. W., Ashmead, D. H., & Clarkson, M. G. (1993). Is visually guided reaching in early infancy a myth? *Child Development, 64*(4), 1099–1110.

Coghill, G. E. (1929). *Anatomy and the problem of behavior.* New York: Hafner.

Corbetta, D., & Bojczyk, K. E. (2002). Infants return to two-handed reaching when they are learning to walk. *Journal of Motor Behavior, 34*(1), 83–95.

Corbetta, D., & Thelen, E. (1996). The developmental origins of bimanual coordination: A dynamic perspective. *Journal of Experimental Psychology: Human Perception and Performance, 22,* 502–522.

Corbetta, D., Thelen, E., & Johnson, K. (2000). Motor constraints on the development of perception-action matching in infant reaching. *Infant Behavior and Development, 23,* 351–374.

Cornsweet, T. N. (1962). The staircase-method in psychophysics. *American Journal of Psychology, 75,* 485–491.

Cosmi, E. V., Anceschi, M. M., Cosmi, E., Piazze, J. J., & La Torre, R. (2003). Ultrasonographic patterns of fetal breathing movements in normal pregnancy. *International Journal of Gynecology and Obstetrics, 80,* 285–290.

Craig, C. M., & Lee, D. N. (1999). Neonatal control of sucking pressure: Evidence for an intrinsic tau-guide. *Experimental Brain Research, 124,* 371–382.

Damiano, D. L. (1993). Reviewing muscle contraction: Is it a developmental, pathological, or motor control issue? *Physical and Occupational Therapy in Pediatrics, 12,* 3–21.

Daniel, B. M., & Lee, D. N. (1990). Development of looking with head and eyes. *Journal of Experimental Child Psychology, 50,* 200–216.

Davis, B. E., Moon, R. Y., Sachs, H. C., & Ottolini, M. C. (1998). Effects of sleep position on infant motor development. *Pediatrics, 102*(5), 1135–1140.

D'Elia, A., Pighetti, M., Moccia, G., & Santangelo, N. (2001). Spontaneous motor activity in normal fetuses. *Early Human Development, 65,* 139–147.

Delorme, A., Frigon, J. Y., & Lagace, C. (1989). Infants' reactions to visual movement of the environment. *Perception, 18,* 667–673.

deVries, J. I. P., Visser, G. H. A., Prechtl, H. F. R. (1982). The emergence of fetal behavior: Vol. 1. Qualitative aspects. *Early Human Development, 7,* 301–322.

Dewey, C., Fleming, P., Golding, J., & Team, A. S. (1998). Does the supine sleeping position have any adverse effects on the child? II. Development in the first 18 months. *Pediatrics, 101*(1), e5.

Dogtrop, A. P., Ubels, R., & Nijhuis, J. G. (1990). The association between fetal body movements, eye movement and heart rate patterns in pregnancies between 25 and 30 weeks of gestation. *Early Human Development, 23,* 67–73.

Eppler, M. A. (1995). Development of manipulatory skills and the deployment of attention. *Infant Behavior and Development, 18,* 391–405.

Eppler, M. A., Satterwhite, T., Wendt, J., & Bruce, K. (1997). Infants' responses to a visual cliff and other ground surfaces. In

M. A. Schmuckler & J. M. Kennedy (Eds.), *Studies in perception and action IV* (pp. 219–222). Mahwah, NJ: Erlbaum.

Erkinjuntti, M. (1988). Body movements during sleep in healthy and neurologically damaged infants. *Early Human Development, 16,* 283–292.

Fagard, J. (2000). Linked proximal and distal changes in the reaching behavior of 5- to 12-month-old human infants grasping objects of different sizes. *Infant Behavior and Development, 23,* 317–329.

Forssberg, H. (1985). Ontogeny of human locomotor control: Vol. 1. Infant stepping, supported locomotion, and transition to independent locomotion. *Experimental Brain Research, 57,* 480–493.

Forssberg, H. (1989). Infant stepping and development of plantigrade gait. In C. V. Euler, H. Forssberg, & H. Lagercrantz (Eds.), *Neurobiology of early infant behavior* (pp. 119–128). Stockholm: Stockton Press.

Forssberg, H., & Nashner, L. M. (1982). Ontogenetic development of postural control in man: Adaptation to altered support and visual conditions during stance. *Journal of Neuroscience, 2,* 545–552.

Forssberg, H., & Wallberg, H. (1980). Infant locomotion: A preliminary movement and electromyographic study. In K. Berg & B. Eriksson (Eds.), *Children and exercise IX* (pp. 32–40). Baltimore: University Park Press.

Fraisse, F. E., Couet, A. M., Bellanca, K. J., & Adolph, K. E. (2001). Infants' response to potential risk: Social interaction and perceptual exploration. In G. A. Burton & R. C. Schmidt (Eds.), *Studies in perception and action VI* (pp. 97–100). Mahwah, NJ: Erlbaum.

Frankenburg, W. K., & Dodds, J. B. (1967). The Denver developmental screening test. *Journal of Pediatrics, 71,* 181–191.

Freedland, R. L., & Bertenthal, B. I. (1994). Developmental changes in interlimb coordination: Transition to hands-and-knees crawling. *Psychological Science, 5*(1), 26–32.

Fukumoto, K., Mochizuki, N., Takeshi, M., Nomura, Y., & Segawa, M. (1981). Studies of body movements during night sleep in infancy. *Brain Development, 3,* 37–43.

Fukura, K., & Ishihara, K. (1997). Development of human sleep and wakefulness rhythm during the first 6 months of life: Discontinuous changes at the 7th and 12th week after birth. *Biological Rhythm Research, 28,* 94–103.

Gahery, Y., & Massion, J. (1981). Co-ordination between posture and movement. *Trends in Neurosciences, 4,* 199–202.

Galloway, J. C., & Thelen, E. (2004). Feet first: Object exploration in young infants. *Infant Behavior and Development, 27,* 107–112.

Garciaguirre, J. S., & Adolph, K. E. (2005a). *Baby carriage: Infants walking with loads.* Manuscript submitted for publication.

Garciaguirre, J. S., & Adolph, K. E. (2005b). *Step-by-step: Tracking infants' walking and falling experience.* Manuscript in preparation.

Gentile, A. M. (2000). Skill acquisition: Action, movement, and neuromotor processes. In J. Carr & R. Shepard (Eds.), *Movement science: Foundations for physical therapy in rehabilitation* (2nd ed., pp. 111–187). New York: Aspen Press.

Gesell, A. (1933). Maturation and the patterning of behavior. In C. Murchison (Ed.), *A handbook of child psychology* (2nd ed., pp. 209–235). Worcester, MA: Clark University Press.

Gesell, A. (1946). The ontogenesis of infant behavior. In L. Carmichael (Ed.), *Manual of child psychology* (pp. 295–331). New York: Wiley.

Gesell, A., & Ames, L. B. (1940). The ontogenetic organization of prone behavior in human infancy. *Journal of Genetic Psychology, 56,* 247–263.

Robinson, S. R., & Smotherman, W. P. (1992). Fundamental motor patterns of the mammalian fetus. *Journal of Neurobiology, 23,* 1574–1600.

Rochat, P. (1992). Self-sitting and reaching in 5- to 8-month-old infants: The impact of posture and its development on early eye-hand coordination. *Journal of Motor Behavior, 24*(2), 210–220.

Rochat, P., & Goubet, N. (1995). Development of sitting and reaching in 5- to 6-month-old infants. *Infant Behavior and Development, 18,* 53–68.

Rochat, P., Goubet, N., & Senders, S. J. (1999). To reach or not to reach? Perception of body effectivities by young infants. *Infant and Child Development, 8,* 129–148.

Roncesvalles, M. N. C., Woollacott, M. H., & Jensen, J. L. (2001). Development of lower extremity kinetics for balance control in infants and young children. *Journal of Motor Behavior, 33,* 180–192.

Rosander, K., & von Hofsten, C. (2000). Visual-vestibular interaction in early infancy. *Experimental Brain Research, 133,* 321–333.

Rosander, K., & von Hofsten, C. (2002). Development of gaze tracking of small and large objects. *Experimental Brain Research, 146,* 257–264.

Rosander, K., & von Hofsten, C. (2004). Infants' emerging ability to represent occluded object motion. *Cognition, 91,* 1–22.

Rovee, C. K., & Rovee, D. T. (1969). Conjugate reinforcement of infant exploratory behavior. *Journal of Experimental Child Psychology, 8,* 33–39.

Rovee-Collier, C. K., & Gekoski, M. (1979). The economics of infancy: A review of conjugate reinforcement. In H. W. Reese & L. P. Lipsitt (Eds.), *Advances in child development and behavior* (Vol. 13, pp. 195–255). New York: Academic Press.

Rovee-Collier, C. K., Morrongiello, B. A., Aron, M., & Kupersmidt, J. (1978). Topographical response differentiation and reversal in 3-month-old infants. *Infant Behavior and Development, 1,* 323–333.

Rovee-Collier, C. K., Sullivan, M., Enright, M. K., Lucas, D., & Fagen, J. W. (1980). Reactivation of infant memory. *Science, 208,* 1159–1161.

Saint-Anne Dargassies, S. (1986). *The neuro-motor and psycho-affective development of the infant.* New York: Elsevier.

Savelsbergh, G. J. P., & van der Kamp, J. (1994). The effect of body orientation to gravity on early infant reaching. *Journal of Experimental Child Psychology, 58,* 510–528.

Schmidt, R. A., & Lee, T. D. (1999). *Motor control and learning: A behavioral emphasis* (3rd ed.). Champaign, IL: Human Kinetics.

Schmuckler, M. A. (1993). Perception-action coupling in infancy. In G. J. P. Savelsbergh (Ed.), *The development of coordination in infancy* (pp. 137–173). Amsterdam: Elsevier Science.

Schmuckler, M. A. (1996). Development of visually guided locomotion: Barrier crossing by toddlers. *Ecological Psychology, 8*(3), 209–236.

Schmuckler, M. A. (1997). Children's postural sway in response to low- and high-frequency visual information for oscillation. *Journal of Experimental Psychology: Human Perception and Performance, 23,* 528–545.

Schmuckler, M. A., & Gibson, E. J. (1989). The effect of imposed optical flow on guided locomotion in young walkers. *British Journal of Developmental Psychology, 7,* 193–206.

Schmuckler, M. A., & Li, N. S. (1998). Looming responses to obstacles and apertures: The role of accretion and deletion of background texture. *Psychological Science, 9,* 49–52.

Senn, M. J. E. (1975). Insights on the child development movement in the United States. *Monographs of the Society for Research in Child Development, 40*(3/4, Serial No. 161).

Shinskey, J. L., & Munakata, Y. (2003). Are infants in the dark about hidden objects? *Developmental Science, 6,* 273–282.

Shirley, M. M. (1931). *The first 2 years: A study of twenty-five babies.* Minneapolis: University of Minnesota Press.

Shrager, J., & Siegler, R. S. (1998). SCADS: A model of children's strategy choices and strategy discoveries. *Psychological Science, 9,* 405–410.

Shumway-Cooke, A., & Woollacott, M. H. (1985). The growth of stability: Postural control from a developmental perspective. *Journal of Motor Behavior, 17,* 131–147.

Siegler, R. S. (1994). Cognitive variability: A key to understanding cognitive development. *Current Directions in Psychology, 3,* 1–5.

Siegler, R. S. (1996). *Emerging minds: The process of change in children's thinking.* New York: Oxford University Press.

Siegler, R. S., DeLoache, J., & Eisenberg, N. (2003). *How children develop.* New York: Worth.

Siegler, R. S., & Munakata, Y. (1993, Winter). Beyond the immaculate transition: Advances in the understanding of change. *SRCD Newsletter 3,* 10–11, 13.

Slater, A., & Morison, V. (1985). Shape constancy and slant perception at birth. *Perception, 14,* 337–344.

Smith, L. B., & Thelen, E. (Eds.). (1993). *A dynamic systems approach to development: Applications.* Cambridge, MA: MIT Press.

Smotherman, W. P., & Robinson, S. R. (1989). Cryptopsychobiology: The appearance, disappearance, and reappearance of a species-typical action pattern during early development. *Behavioral Neuroscience, 103,* 246–253.

Smotherman, W. P., & Robinson, S. R. (1996). The development of behavior before birth. *Developmental Psychology, 32*(3), 425–434.

Sommerville, J. A., & Woodward, A. L. (2005). Pulling out the intentional structure of action: The relation between action processing and action production in infancy. *Cognition, 95,* 1–30.

Sommerville, J. A., Woodward, A. L., & Needham, A. (in press). Action experience alters 3-month-old infants' perception of others' actions. *Cognition.*

Sorce, J. F., Emde, R. N., Campos, J. J., & Klinnert, M. D. (1985). Maternal emotional signaling: Its effects on the visual cliff behavior of 1-year-olds. *Developmental Psychology, 21,* 195–200.

Sparling, J. W., van Tol, J., & Chescheir, N. C. (1999). Fetal and neonatal hand movement. *Physical Therapy, 79*(1), 24–39.

Sparling, J. W., & Wilhelm, I. J. (1993). Quantitative measurement of fetal movement: Fetal-Posture and Movement Assessment (F-PAM). *Physical and Occupational Therapy in Pediatrics, 12,* 97–114.

Spelke, E. S., Breinlinger, K., Macomber, J., & Jacobson, K. (1992). Origins of knowledge. *Psychological Review.*

Spelke, E. S., & Newport, E. L. (1998). Nativism, empiricism, and the development of knowledge. In W. Damon (Editor-in-Chief) & Richard M. Lerner (Vol. Ed.), *Handbook of child psychology: Vol. 1. Theoretical models of human development* (5th ed., pp. 275–340). New York: Wiley.

Spelke, E. S., & von Hofsten, C. (2001). Predictive reaching for occluded objects by 6-month-old infants. *Journal of Cognition and Development, 2,* 261–281.

Spencer, J. P., & Schöner, G. (2003). Bridging the representational gap in the dynamic systems approach to development. *Developmental Science, 6*(4), 392–412.

Spencer, J. P., Vereijken, B., Diedrich, F. J., & Thelen, E. (2000). Posture and the emergence of manual skills. *Developmental Science, 3*(2), 216–233.

Steenbergen, B., van der Kamp, J., Smitsman, A. W., & Carson, R. G. (1997). Spoon handling in 2- to 4-year-old children. *Ecological Psychology, 9*(2), 113–129.

Stergiou, C. S., Adolph, K. E., Alibali, M. W., Avolio, A. M., & Cenedella, C. (1997). Social expressions in infant locomotion: Vocalizations and gestures on slopes. In M. A. Schmuckler & J. M. Kennedy (Eds.), *Studies in perception and action IV* (pp. 215–219). Mahwah, NJ: Erlbaum.

Stoffregen, T. A. (1985). Flow structure versus retinal location in the optical control of stance. *Journal of Experimental Psychology: Human Perception and performance, 11*, 554–565.

Stoffregen, T. A. (1986). The role of optical velocity in the control of stance. *Perception and Psychophysics, 39*, 355–360.

Stoffregen, T. A., Schmuckler, M. A., & Gibson, E. J. (1987). Use of central and peripheral optical flow in stance and locomotion in young walkers. *Perception, 16*, 113–119.

Stoffregen, T. A., Smart, L. J., Bardy, B. G., & Pagulayan, R. J. (1999). Postural stabilization of looking. *Journal of Experimental Psychology: Human Perception and Performance, 25*, 1641–1658.

Sundermier, L., Woollacott, M. H., Roncesvalles, M. N. C., & Jensen, J. L. (2001). The development of balance control in children: Comparisons of EMG and kinetic variables and chronological and developmental groupings. *Experimental Brain Research, 136*, 340–350.

Super, C. M. (1976). Environmental effects on motor development: The case of African infant precocity. *Developmental Medicine and Child Neurology, 8*(5), 561–567.

Sutherland, D. H., Olshen, R., Cooper, L., & Woo, S. (1980). The development of mature gait. *Journal of Bone and Joint Surgery, 62*, 336–353.

Tamis-LeMonda, C. S., & Adolph, K. E. (2005). Social cognition in infant motor action. In B. Homer & C. S. Tamis-LeMonda (Eds.), *The development of social cognition and communication* (pp. 145–164). Mahwah, NJ: Erlbaum.

Tamis-LeMonda, C. S., Adolph, K. E., Lobo, S. A., Karasik, L. B., & Dimitropoulou, K. A. (2005). *When infants take mothers' advice.* Manuscript submitted for publication.

Tanner, J. M. (1990). *Fetus into man.* Cambridge, MA: Harvard University Press.

Thelen, E. (1979). Rhythmical stereotypies in normal human infants. *Animal Behavior, 27*, 699–715.

Thelen, E. (1981a). Kicking, rocking, and waving: Contextual analysis of rhythmical stereotypies in normal human infants. *Animal Behavior, 29*, 3–11.

Thelen, E. (1981b). Rhythmical behavior in infancy: An ethological perspective. *Developmental Psychology, 17*, 237–257.

Thelen, E. (1984a). Learning to walk: Ecological demands and phylogenetic constraints. *Advances in Infancy Research, 3*, 213–260.

Thelen, E. (1984b). Walking, thinking, and evolving: Further comments toward an economical explanation. *Advances in Infancy Research, 3*, 257–260.

Thelen, E. (1986). Treadmill-elicited stepping in 7-month-old infants. *Child Development, 57*, 1498–1506.

Thelen, E. (1994). Three-month-old infants can learn task-specific patterns of interlimb coordination. *Psychological Science, 5*, 280–285.

Thelen, E. (1995). Motor development: A new synthesis. *American Psychologist, 50*, 79–95.

Thelen, E. (1996). Normal infant stereotypies: A dynamic systems approach. In R. L. Sprague & K. M. Newell (Eds.), *Stereotyped*

*movements: Brain and behavior relationships* (pp. 139–165). Washington, DC: American Psychological Association.

Thelen, E., & Adolph, K. E. (1992). Arnold L. Gesell: The paradox of nature and nurture. *Developmental Psychology, 28*, 368–380.

Thelen, E., & Bates, E. (2003). Connectionism and dynamic systems: Are they really different? *Developmental Science, 6*, 378–391.

Thelen, E., Bradshaw, G., & Ward, J. A. (1981). Spontaneous kicking in month old infants: Manifestations of a human central locomotor program. *Behavioral and Neural Biology, 32*, 45–53.

Thelen, E., Bril, B., & Breniere, Y. (1992). The emergence of heel strike in newly walking infants: A dynamic interpretation. In M. H. Woollacott & F. Horak (Eds.), *Posture and gait: Control mechanisms* (Vol. 2, pp. 334–337). Eugene: University of Oregon Books.

Thelen, E., & Cooke, D. W. (1987). Relationship between newborn stepping and later walking: A new interpretation. *Developmental Medicine and Child Neurology, 29*, 380–393.

Thelen, E., & Corbetta, D. (2002). Microdevelopment and dynamic systems: Applications to infant motor development. In N. Granott & J. Parziale (Eds.), *Microdevelopment: Transition processes in development and learning—Cambridge studies in cognitive perceptual development* (pp. 59–79). New York: Cambridge University Press.

Thelen, E., Corbetta, D., Kamm, K., Spencer, J. P., Schneider, K., & Zernicke, R. F. (1993). The transition to reaching: Mapping intention and intrinsic dynamics. *Child Development, 64*, 1058–1098.

Thelen, E., Corbetta, D., & Spencer, J. P. (1996). Development of reaching during the first year: Role of movement speed. *Journal of Experimental Psychology: Human Perception and Performance, 22*, 1059–1076.

Thelen, E., & Fisher, D. M. (1982). Newborn stepping: An explanation for a "disappearing reflex." *Developmental Psychology, 18*, 760–775.

Thelen, E., & Fisher, D. M. (1983a). From spontaneous to instrumental behavior: Kinematic analysis of movement changes during very early learning. *Child Development, 54*, 129–140.

Thelen, E., & Fisher, D. M. (1983b). The organization of spontaneous leg movements in newborn infants. *Journal of Motor Behavior, 15*, 353–377.

Thelen, E., Fisher, D. M., & Ridley-Johnson, R. (1984). The relationship between physical growth and a newborn reflex. *Infant Behavior and Development, 7*, 479–493.

Thelen, E., Fisher, D. M., Ridley-Johnson, R., & Griffin, N. J. (1982). The effects of body build and arousal on newborn infant stepping. *Developmental Psychobiology, 15*, 447–453.

Thelen, E., Schöner, G., Scheier, C., & Smith, L. B. (2001). The dynamics of embodiment: A field theory of infant perseverative reaching. *Behavioral and Brain Sciences, 24*(1), 1–34.

Thelen, E., Skala, K., & Kelso, J. A. S. (1987). The dynamic nature of early coordination: Evidence from bilateral leg movements in young infants. *Developmental Psychology, 23*, 179–186.

Thelen, E., & Smith, L. B. (1994). *A dynamic systems approach to the development of cognition and action.* Cambridge, MA: MIT Press.

Thelen, E., & Smith, L. B. (1998). Dynamic systems theories. In W. Damon (Editor-in-Chief) & Richard M. Lerner (Vol. Ed.), *Handbook of child psychology: Vol. 1. Theoretical models of human development* (5th ed., pp. 563–634). New York: Wiley.

Thelen, E., & Spencer, J. P. (1998). Postural control during reaching in young infants: A dynamic systems approach. *Neuroscience and Biobehavioral Review, 22*, 507–514.

Thelen, E., & Ulrich, B. D. (1991). Hidden skills: A dynamic systems analysis of treadmill stepping during the first year. *Monographs of the Society for Research in Child Development, 56*(1, Serial No. 223).

Thelen, E., Ulrich, B. D., & Niles, D. (1987). Bilateral coordination in human infants: Stepping on a split-belt treadmill. *Journal of Experimental Psychology: Human Perception and Performance, 13,* 405–410.

Thorndike, E. L. (1906). *Principles of teaching.* New York: A. G. Seiler.

Thorndike, E. L., & Woodworth, R. S. (1901). The influence of improvement in one mental function upon the efficiency of other functions. *Psychological Review, 8,* 247–261.

Titzer, R. (1995, March). *The developmental dynamics of understanding transparency.* Paper presented at the meeting of the Society for Research in Child Development, Indianapolis, IN.

Togo, M., & Togo, T. (1982). Time-series analysis of stature and body weight in five siblings. *Annals of Human Biology, 9*(5), 425–440.

Touwen, B. C. (1976). *Neurological development in infancy.* London: Heinemann.

Trevarthen, C. (1993). The self born in intersubjectivity: The psychology of an infant communicating. In U. Neisser (Ed.), *The perceived self: Ecological and interpersonal sources of self-knowledge* (pp. 121–173). New York: Cambridge University Press.

Ulrich, B. D. (1989). Development of stepping patterns in human infants: A dynamical systems perspective. *Journal of Motor Behavior, 21,* 392–408.

Ulrich, D. A., Ulrich, B. D., Angulo-Barroso, R., & Yun, J. K. (2001). Treadmill training of infants with Down syndrome: Evidence-based developmental outcomes. *Pediatrics, 108*(5), 1–7.

van Asten, W. N. J. C., Gielen, C. C. A. M., & van der Gon, J. J. D. (1988). Postural movements induced by rotations of visual scenes. *Journal of the Optical Society of America, 5,* 1781–1789.

van der Fits, I. B. M., & Hadders-Algra, M. (1998). The development of postural response patterns during reaching in healthy infants. *Neuroscience and Biobehavioral Review, 22,* 521–526.

van der Fits, I. B. M., Otten, E., Klip, A. W. J., van Eykern, L. A., & Hadders-Algra, M. (1999). The development of postural adjustments during reaching in 6- to 18-month-old infants. *Experimental Brain Research, 126,* 517–528.

van der Meer, A. L. H. (1997a). Keeping the arm in the limelight: Advanced visual control of arm movements in neonates. *European Journal of Paediatric Neurology, 4,* 103–108.

van der Meer, A. L. H. (1997b). Visual guidance of passing under a barrier. *Early Development and Parenting, 6,* 149–157.

van der Meer, A. L. H., Holden, G., & van der Weel, F. R. (in press). Coordination of sucking, swallowing, and breathing in healthy newborns. *Journal of Pediatric Neonatology.*

van der Meer, A. L. H., van der Weel, F. R., & Lee, D. (1994). Prospective control in catching by infants. *Perception, 23,* 287–302.

van der Meer, A. L. H., van der Weel, F. R., & Lee, D. N. (1995). The functional significance of arm movements in neonates. *Science, 267,* 693–695.

van der Meer, A. L. H., van der Weel, F. R., & Lee, D. N. (1996). Lifting weights in neonates: Developing visual control of reaching. *Scandinavian Journal of Psychology, 37,* 424–436.

van Hof, P., van der Kamp, J., & Savelsbergh, G. J. P. (2002). The relation of unimanual and bimanual reaching to crossing the midline. *Child Development, 73,* 1353–1362.

Vereijken, B. (2005). Motor development. In B. Hopkins (Ed.), *Cambridge encyclopedia in child development.* Cambridge, MA: Cambridge University Press.

Vereijken, B., & Adolph, K. E. (1999). Transitions in the development of locomotion. In G. J. P. Savelsbergh, H. L. J. van der Maas & P. C. L. van Geert (Eds.), *Non-linear analyses of developmental processes* (pp. 137–149). Amsterdam: Elsevier.

Vereijken, B., Pedersen, A. V., & Storksen, J. H. (2005). *The effect of manipulating postural control and muscular strength requirements on early independent walking.* Manuscript in preparation.

Vereijken, B., & Thelen, E. (1997). Training infant treadmill stepping: The role of individual pattern stability. *Developmental Psychobiology, 30,* 89–102.

Vereijken, B., van Emmerick, R. E. A., Whiting, H. T. A., & Newell, K. M. (1993). Free(z)ing degrees of freedom in skill acquisition. *Journal of Motor Behavior, 24,* 133–142.

von Hofsten, C. (1979). Development of visually directed reaching: The approach phase. *Journal of Human Movement Studies, 30,* 369–382.

von Hofsten, C. (1980). Predictive reaching for moving objects by human infants. *Journal of Experimental Child Psychology, 30,* 369–382.

von Hofsten, C. (1982). Foundations for perceptual development. *Advances in Infancy Research, 2,* 239–262.

von Hofsten, C. (1983). Catching skills in infancy. *Journal of Experimental Psychology: Human Perception and Performance, 9*(1), 75–85.

von Hofsten, C. (1984). Developmental changes in the organization of prereaching movements. *Developmental Psychology, 20,* 378–388.

von Hofsten, C. (1989). Mastering reaching and grasping: The development of manual skills in infancy. In S. A. Wallace (Ed.), *Perspectives on the coordination of movement* (pp. 223–258). Amsterdam: North Holland.

von Hofsten, C. (1991). Structuring of early reaching movements: A longitudinal study. *Journal of Motor Behavior, 23*(4), 280–292.

von Hofsten, C. (1993). Prospective control: A basic aspect of action development. *Human Development, 36,* 253–270.

von Hofsten, C. (1997). On the early development of predictive abilities. In C. Dent-Read & P. Zukow-Goldring (Eds.), *Evolving explanations of development: Ecological approaches to organism-environment systems* (pp. 163–194). Washington, DC: American Psychological Association.

von Hofsten, C. (2003). On the development of perception and action. In K. J. Connolly & J. Valsiner (Eds.), *Handbook of developmental psychology* (pp. 114–140). London: Sage.

von Hofsten, C. (2004). An action perspective on motor development. *Trends in Cognitive Sciences, 8*(6), 266–272.

von Hofsten, C., & Lindhagen, K. (1979). Observations on the development of reaching for moving objects. *Journal of Experimental Child Psychology, 28,* 158–173.

von Hofsten, C., & Ronnqvist, L. (1988). Preparation for grasping an object: A developmental study. *Journal of Experimental Psychology: Human Perception and Performance, 14,* 610–621.

von Hofsten, C., & Rosander, K. (1996). The development of gaze control and predictive tracking in young infants. *Vision Research, 36*(1), 81–96.

von Hofsten, C., & Rosander, K. (1997). Development of smooth pursuit tracking in young infants. *Vision Research, 37,* 1799–1810.

von Hofsten, C., Vishton, P. M., Spelke, E. S., Feng, Q., & Rosander, K. (1998). Predictive action in infancy: Tracking and reaching for moving objects. *Cognition, 67,* 255–285.

Walk, R. D. (1966). The development of depth perception in animals and human infants. *Monographs of the Society for Research in Child Development, 31*(5, Serial No. 107), 82–108.

Walk, R. D., & Gibson, E. J. (1961). A comparative and analytical study of visual depth perception. *Psychological Monographs, 75*(15, Whole No. 519).

Walk, R. D., Gibson, E. J., & Tighe, T. J. (1957). Behavior of light- and dark-reared rats on a visual cliff. *Science, 126,* 80–81.

Wann, J. P., Mon-Williams, M., & Rushton, K. (1998). Postural control and co-ordination disorder: The swinging room revisited. *Human Movement Science, 17,* 491–513.

Warren, W. H. (1984). Perceiving affordances: Visual guidance of stair climbing. *Journal of Experimental Psychology: Human Perception and Performance, 10*(5), 683–703.

Warren, W. H., Kay, B. A., & Yilmaz, E. H. (1996). Visual control of posture during walking: Functional specificity. *Journal of Experimental Psychology: Human Perception and Performance, 22,* 818–838.

Warren, W. H., & Whang, S. (1987). Visual guidance of walking through apertures: Body-scaled information for affordances. *Journal of Experimental Psychology: Human Perception and Performance, 13,* 371–383.

Wentworth, N., Benson, J. B., & Haith, M. M. (2000). The development of infants' reaches for stationary and moving objects. *Child Development, 71,* 576–601.

Wentworth, N., Haith, M. M., & Hood, R. (2002). Spatiotemporal regularity and inter-event contingencies as information for infants' visual expectations. *Infancy, 3,* 303–321.

Wiener-Vacher, S., Ledebt, A., & Bril, B. (1996). Changes in otolith VOR to off vertical axis rotation in infants learning to walk. *Annals of the New York Academy of Sciences, 781,* 709–712.

Willatts, P. (1984). The stage IV infants' solution of problems requiring the use of supports. *Infant Behavior and Development, 7,* 125–134.

Winter, D. A., & Eng, P. (1995). Kinetics: Our window into the goals and strategies of the central nervous system. *Behavioral Brain Research, 67,* 111–120.

Witherington, D. C. (2005). The development of prospective grasping control between 5 and 7 months: A longitudinal study. *Infancy, 7*(2), 143–161.

Witherington, D. C., Campos, J. J., Anderson, D. I., Lejeune, L., & Seah, E. (2005). Avoidance of heights on the visual cliff in newly walking infants. *Infancy, 7*(3), 285–298.

Witherington, D. C., von Hofsten, C., Rosander, K., Robinette, A., Woollacott, M. H., & Bertenthal, B. I. (2002). The development of anticipatory postural adjustments in infancy. *Infancy, 3*(4), 495–517.

Wohlwill, J. P. (1970). The age variable in psychological research. *Psychological Review, 77,* 49–64.

Wolff, P. H. (1987). *The development of behavioral states and the expression of emotions in early infancy.* Chicago: University of Chicago Press.

Woollacott, M. H., & Jensen, J. L. (1996). Posture and locomotion. In H. Heuer & S. W. Keele (Eds.), *Handbook of perception and action: Vol. 2. Motor skills* (pp. 333–403). San Diego, CA: Academic Press.

Yanez, B. R., Domakonda, K. V., Gill-Alvarez, S. V., Adolph, K. E., & Vereijken, B. (2004, May). *Automaticity and plasticity in infant and adult walking.* Poster presented at the meeting of the International Conference on Infant Studies, Chicago, IL.

Yang, J. F., Stephens, M. J., & Vishram, R. (1998). Infant stepping: A method to study the sensory control of human walking. *Journal of Physiology, 507,* 927–937.

Yonas, A., & Hartman, B. (1993). Perceiving the affordance of contact in 4- and 5-month-old infants. *Child Development, 64,* 298–308.

Young, J. W., Webster, T. W., Robinson, S. R., Adolph, K. E., & Kanani, P. H. (2003, November). *Effects of sampling interval on developmental trajectories.* Poster presented at the meeting of the International Society for Developmental Psychobiology, New Orleans, LA.

Zanone, P. G., Kelso, J. A. S., & Jeka, J. J. (1993). Concepts and methods for a dynamical approach to behavioral coordination and change. In G. J. P. Savelsbergh (Ed.), *The development of coordination in infancy* (pp. 89–134). Amsterdam: North-Holland/Elsevier.

Zelazo, N. A., Zelazo, P. R., Cohen, K. M., & Zelazo, P. D. (1993). Specificity of practice effects on elementary neuromotor patterns. *Developmental Psychology, 29,* 686–691.

Zelazo, P. R. (1976). From reflexive to instrumental behavior. In L. P. Lipsitt (Ed.), *Developmental psychobiology: The significance of infancy* (pp. 87–108). Hillsdale, NJ: Erlbaum.

Zelazo, P. R. (1983). The development of walking: New findings on old assumptions. *Journal of Motor Behavior, 2,* 99–137.

Zelazo, P. R. (1998). McGraw and the development of unaided walking. *Developmental Review, 18,* 449–471.

Zelazo, P. R., Weiss, M. J., & Leonard, E. (1989). The development of unaided walking: The acquisition of higher order control. In P. R. Zelazo & R. G. Barr (Eds.), *Challenges to developmental paradigms* (pp. 139–165). Hillsdale, NJ: Erlbaum.

Zelazo, P. R., Zelazo, N. A., & Kolb, S. (1972). "Walking" in the newborn. *Science, 176,* 314–315.

Zernicke, R. F., & Schneider, K. (1993). Biomechanics and developmental neuromotor control. *Child Development, 64,* 982–1004.

CHAPTER 5

# *Infant Cognition*

LESLIE B. COHEN and CARA H. CASHON

WHAT IS INFANT COGNITION?  214
Our Perspective: A Constructivist Information-
    Processing Approach  216
The Relation of This Chapter to Previous *Handbook*
    Chapters on Infant Cognition  217
METHODOLOGICAL ISSUES  218
Habituation and Related Paradigms  218
Object Exploration and Sequential Touching  220
Deferred Imitation  220
INFANTS' UNDERSTANDING OF OBJECTS  221
Object Permanence  221
Other Areas Related to Object Permanence  225
INFANTS' UNDERSTANDING OF EVENTS  228
Simple Causal Events  228
Complex Causal Chains  231

Complex Event Sequences  233
INFANT CATEGORIZATION  234
Categorization Paradigms  235
Feature Correlations and Categorization  235
Connectionist Models of Infant Categorization  237
Perceptual versus Conceptual Categories  239
INFANT FACE PROCESSING  240
Newborns' Preferences for Faces  241
Development of Face Processing  242
A Constructivist Information-Processing Account of
    Infant Face Processing  242
THE ANIMATE-INANIMATE DISTINCTION  244
SUMMARY AND CONCLUSIONS  245
REFERENCES  246

Since the chapter on infant cognition in the fifth edition of this *Handbook* was published (Haith & Benson, 1998), infant cognition has continued to grow, develop, and become a more complex field of study. In this chapter, we discuss some of these changes, and throughout, we expand on and extend Haith and Benson's treatment of the topic. We begin by defining *infant cognition* and then present our perspective—a constructivist, domain-general, information-processing approach—on the development of cognition during infancy. Subsequently, we discuss some of the newer and more popular research methods used in the field, considering both their advantages and disadvantages. Finally, we present recent findings across various topic areas. To present a comprehensive picture of the current state of our field, we limit most of our discussion to recent research and theory.

## WHAT IS INFANT COGNITION?

It is appropriate to begin this chapter with the difficult task of defining infant cognition. Deciding which areas of study to include and exclude is an obstacle in arriving at a clear definition. Consider the continuum in Figure 5.1. It represents roughly a continuum from implicit to explicit processes, or from lower level to higher level brain structures. Depending, in all likelihood, on one's research perspective, there are several ways to partition the continuum. Most researchers working on infant sensory processes would assume their work has close ties to infant perception, but much looser ties to infant cognition and language (see Version A). On the other hand, most researchers on infant language acquisition would see close ties to aspects of infant cognition (e.g., categorization), but much looser ties to infant sensation and perception

Preparation of this manuscript was facilitated by NIH Grant, HD-23397, awarded to L. B. Cohen and by NIH grant #P20 RR017702 from the COBRE Program of the National Center for Research Resource to Cara H. Cashon.

    We wish to thank Miye N. Cohen and Jennifer Balkan for their careful reading of this manuscript and their many helpful editorial suggestions.

Version A

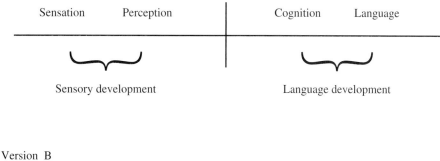

Version B

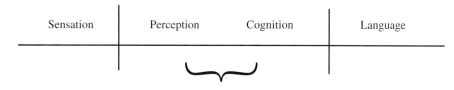

**Figure 5.1**   Possible ways of categorizing traditional areas with infant development. Adapted from "An Information-Processing Approach to Infant Perception and Cognition" (pp. 277–300), by L. B. Cohen, in *The Development of Sensory, Motor, and Cognitive Capacities in Early Infancy,* F. Simion and G. Butterworth (Eds.), 1998, East Sussex, England: Psychology Press. Reprinted with permission.

(also shown in Version A). In contrast, many of those who study infant perception or cognition find it difficult to distinguish perception from cognition, yet find the ties to infant sensation or infant language to be more distant (see Version B).

Our constructivist information-processing view (Cohen, Chaput, & Cashon, 2002) places us closer to Version B. We believe inserting an artificial boundary between infant perception and infant cognition can be detrimental when attempting to understand the underlying processes of developmental change. Consider object individuation, the ability to understand that one object is independent of another object even when their surfaces may be touching (Needham & Baillargeon, 1997). This ability depends on both the infant's differentiating the objects' surface characteristics, such as color, shape, and pattern, and the infant's perceiving object unity in understanding that the visible parts of a partially occluded moving object are really part of the same object (Cohen & Cashon, 2001b). Differentiating surface characteristics and recognizing object unity are assumed to involve perceptual processes, but understanding of object individuation is generally assumed to be cognitive. Thus, it is our position that imposing an artificial dividing line between cognition and perception may mask the true nature of infant development.

Whether a sharp distinction exists between infant perception and infant cognition is a contentious issue. Not all researchers agree that one should consider these topics as falling on a continuum from perception to cognition. Some who take a more nativist "core knowledge" approach (Baillargeon, 1994; Carey, 2000; Spelke, 1998) emphasize the infant's supposed thoughtful cognitive decision making over more passive automatic perceptual processes. Others (e.g., Gibson, 2000) suppose infant perception and cognition can be subsumed under "direct perception" without resorting to mental representations (cognition). Consider the multiple interpretations of how infants perceive a simple launching event. Object A moves across a screen until it contacts Object B. Object B then moves the remaining distance across the screen. At one age, infants respond to this scene as a causal event with Object A being the agent and Object B being the patient. To some, this response indicates the infant's "core knowledge" (Carey, 2000; Leslie, 1982) or a basic conceptual unit (Mandler, 1992). Yet, at an earlier age infants respond to Objects A and B as two independently moving objects. They respond to perceptual changes in the movement and lo-cation of each object. Furthermore, the age at which in-fants first respond to the event as causal depends, in part, on surface characteristics of the objects. So where does one draw the line between infant perception and cognition and at what age?

Answering this question becomes more difficult when we consider the various research methods used to study infant cognition. In the previous *Handbook* chapter on infant cognition, Haith and Benson (1998) raise the same issue about the indistinct definitional bound-ary between perception and cognition. They believe that certain cases represent perceptual processing, such as when an infant reacts to a static property of an object such as its color, shape, or form. However, they also be-lieve there are cases of cognitive processing, such as when infants react to a functional property of an object or two interacting objects in a dynamic event. They note that the problem may be exacerbated by the use of per-ceptual paradigms, such as visual habituation, to ad-dress cognitive issues. Mandler (1992, 2000b) makes a similar point about research on infant categorization. She argues that habituation or other visual attention paradigms tap into perceptual categories, whereas man-ual exploration or imitation paradigms tap into concep-tual categories.

We take a more neutral stance in defining paradigms as either perceptual or conceptual. We believe that the paradigm used does not necessarily elicit one type of processing over another. Findings by several re-searchers provide support for this view. Oakes, Cop-page, and Dingel (1997), Oakes, Madole, and Cohen (1991), and Younger and Fearing (1998) all showed that the results from a manual exploration task with three-dimensional objects were similar to those from visual habituation tasks involving two-dimensional pictures. Furthermore, there is some evidence that infants can at-tend to more conceptual information that goes beyond surface perceptual features in visual paradigms as well as object manipulation paradigms. Madole, Oakes, and Cohen (1993) were able to use visual habituation to ex-amine infants' understanding of functional as well as visual properties of objects. Thus, the type of paradigm does not limit the mode of processing used by the in-fant, and there is evidence that a variety of tasks can elicit both perceptual and cognitive processes.

We prefer to use the more neutral term of *infant in-formation processing* instead of drawing a sharp distinc-tion between infant perception and cognition. Thus, we define infant cognition loosely as the set of processes by which infants organize and interpret information pro-vided by their environment. These processes may be im-plicit and automatic or explicit and intentional. The information may be unimodal or multimodal and may be static (e.g., a two-dimensional visual pattern) or dy-namic (e.g., a causal event whose items interact and change over space and time). Such a broad definition ob-viously overlaps other areas of study such as early per-ceptual development and early language acquisition. We view this overlap as a strength rather than a weakness in that it allows investigating commonalities in processing across seemingly disparate areas using various para-digms or methods.

To be both comprehensive and up to date, this chapter presents different points of view about infant cognition and its development. However, we are not com-pletely neutral with respect to these views. It is impor-tant to emphasize both infants' competencies and their inadequacies. We also emphasize developmental change and try to show how such changes are consistent with the information-processing principles outlined here.

## Our Perspective: A Constructivist Information-Processing Approach

Perception and cognition entail infants processing and reacting to different types of information in their envi-ronment. Furthermore, this information may be uni-modal or multimodal; it may or may not involve overt motor activity; but it is always relational. Infants are not simply processing raw sensory inputs; they are process-ing one or more relationships among those inputs, and those relationships determine our tendency to label the processing as perceptual or cognitive. An information-processing approach attempts to identify those relations and show how they change and become more complex and abstract with development.

Our examination of developmental changes in varied areas, from simple angle perception to the understanding of causal events, has led us to propose a set of six infor-mation-processing principles that are domain general. We describe them briefly here (for a more complete ex-planation plus a computational model applying these principles, see Cohen, Chaput, and Cashon, 2002):

1. Infants are endowed with an innate information-processing system that allows them to access low-level featural information, such as color, form,

sound, movement, texture, and so on, with a propensity to process the relations among these features in the environment.

2. Infants form higher units of information from the relationships (e.g., correlational and causal) among lower level units.

3. Higher units serve as components for yet higher units. In other words, the learning system is both constructive and hierarchical.

4. Infants have a bias to process information using the highest formed units, usually the most adaptive strategy. However, the lower-level units are still potentially available and may be accessed if the context requires it.

5. If the system becomes overloaded, infants will regress to a lower level of processing and attempt to incorporate the additional information.

6. This learning system is domain general and may be the mechanism by which we all acquire proficiency or expertise in some domain. It just happens that the most relevant domain for developing infants is the immediate physical and social world impinging on them.

### The Relation of This Chapter to Previous *Handbook* Chapters on Infant Cognition

Approximately 15 years elapsed between the *Handbook* chapters written by Harris (1983) and by Haith and Benson (1998). Whereas the Harris chapter reflected the importance and influence of grand theories, such as those of Piaget and Gibson, Haith and Benson provided a comprehensive report of the major empirical and theoretical changes that had occurred subsequently in the field. Their focus was on the growth of "mini theories" (used to explain a single, relatively constrained ability rather than all of cognitive development), the emergence of nativist explanations (or the assumed precocity of infants), the use of perceptual paradigms to assess cognitive abilities, and the de-emphasis of developmental change.

Since the 1998 *Handbook* chapter, the field of infant cognition has seen some things change and some stay the same. The trend toward minitheories continues. The grand theories described so well by Harris are still mentioned in current research literature but they tend to be cited more as historical views or as foils than as specific predictors of particular types of infant behavior.

The tendency to report an infant's precocity also continues; however that view is beginning to be challenged.

For some, the emphasis remains on when an ability emerges, rather than on how the ability is acquired or on how it becomes more refined with development. As Haith and Benson (1998) note (see also Horowitz, 1995), in many studies of infant cognition, age may not even be a factor in the design. If it is reported, the purpose is just to demonstrate that at one age infants can do something they cannot do at an earlier age. This approach can lead to some strange contradictions when comparing results from different laboratories that presumably are studying the same topic. We see an example in the section on object individuation, in which age of acquisition appears to range from 4 months to 12 months.

A problem with these studies is the assumption that an infant's ability is dichotomous: Either the infant has it or does not have it. When examining developmental changes in most cognitive abilities more closely, one often finds that (a) developmental change occurs gradually over time; (b) change is often situation or task specific; (c) change does not always produce improvement—in some cases infants' development may, at least superficially, appear to regress to a simpler way of processing; and (d) change may appear stagelike but the underlying process may be gradual and continuous. A reemphasis on developmental change and progressions can lead to valuable information regarding issues such as the viability of innate modules or core abilities. At the very least, such information raises questions about what may be changing over age and how central those changes are to understanding an infant's cognitive ability. A similar point was made by Fischer and Bidell (1991).

Once the importance of developmental change is acknowledged, the most critical question becomes the mechanisms of change. We know from plotting such changes by age that the answer is not always simple or obvious. As noted, in some cases older infants actually appear to do more poorly than younger infants (e.g., Madole & Cohen, 1995). We also know these changes are not tightly tied to particular ages but tend to be domain and task specific. Not only are today's researchers interested in describing age differences, but also in uncovering how those changes occur and how one might design models that simulate those changes. A recent trend in the field has been to investigate actual mechanisms of change. Researchers study these underlying mechanisms by using a convergence of methods including connectionist modeling and neurophysiological techniques, as well as more sophisticated and creative behavioral measures and experimental designs.

## METHODOLOGICAL ISSUES

An obvious challenge for any investigator of infant cognition is to use a method that will indicate what infants are perceiving or understanding about objects and events in their environment. The most obvious and direct technique, of course, would be to ask the infant, but in most cases it is highly unlikely one would receive a meaningful response. As a result, researchers have turned to more indirect methods. These methods have evolved considerably over the past 40 years, and the most popular ones have usually involved some assessment of infant visual attention.

### Habituation and Related Paradigms

For over 30 years, two related paradigms, visual habituation and novelty preference, have been the most popular methods for assessing infant cognitive ability. Their popularity stems from their ease of administration, the availability of the necessary equipment and software, and the apparent simplicity of their underlying assumptions. Both paradigms are based on the assumption that infants will tend to prefer (look longer at) something novel over something familiar. In a typical habituation experiment, infants are repeatedly shown the same stimulus until their looking time drops to some predetermined criterion (usually 50% of the initial looking time). In a subsequent test phase, novel and familiar stimuli are presented on successive trials and an infant who can discriminate the difference should look longer at the novel stimulus. In the related novelty preference paradigm, infants are familiarized with one stimulus for some preset amount of time and then are tested with simultaneous presentations of a novel and familiar stimulus. If infants can discriminate between the two, they should look a greater proportion of the time at the novel stimulus.

Both paradigms were originally used in the 1960s and 1970s to examine infant attention and perceptual discrimination (e.g., Fantz, 1964). The paradigms have been modified several times since then to investigate cognitive processes. The first adaptation occurred in the 1970s to examine infant visual memory. Delays were inserted between the end of habituation (or familiarization) and the test phase. These studies showed (a) the two paradigms produced similar results; (b) 5-month-old infants could retain briefly presented visual information for at least 2 weeks, and (c) this memory (probably most akin to a type of recognition memory) was relatively immune to the effects of interference (Cohen & Gelber, 1975).

A second popular adaptation was introduced in the late 1970s and early 1980s to study infant categorization. Instead of habituating or familiarizing infants to a single stimulus, infants were presented with a sequence of stimuli, all of which were members of the same category (e.g., stuffed animals, dogs, faces). In the test phase, one of these familiar stimuli was presented along with a new exemplar from the old category and a novel noncategory item. Categorization was inferred when the infants responded to the new category exemplar in the same way as to the familiar test stimulus.

A third adaptation that also first appeared in the 1980s has been called the *switch* design (Cohen, 1988). It allows investigators to examine how and when infants come to associate or bind together different pieces of information. In the habituation phase, infants are presented with two stimuli, each of which has two attributes or aspects (e.g., Object A performing Function 1 and Object B performing Function 2). In the test phase, infants are shown three test stimuli. One of these is familiar, so that researchers can acquire a baseline for looking time to a familiar stimulus, and another is a novel stimulus. These novel and familiar markers are important—as Hunter and Ames (1988) showed and as others have subsequently confirmed (Roder, Bushnell, & Sasseville, 2000; Shilling, 2000). Incomplete familiarization (particularly when relatively young infants receive complex stimuli) can actually lead to longer looking time to the familiar than to the novel test stimulus. Thus, having a familiar test trial is particularly important in providing evidence that infants have in fact habituated and do not have a familiarity preference. In addition to a familiar and a novel stimulus, infants are also shown a switched stimulus. The switched stimulus is constructed from two familiar components, but in a novel combination (e.g., Object A performing Function 2). The question is whether the infants respond to the switched stimulus as novel or as familiar. Because the individual aspects of this stimulus are familiar, if infants respond to the new combination as novel, it is inferred that they are sensitive to the association between, or binding of, the components. Since the 1980s, the switched design has become an invaluable tool in furthering our understanding of infants' featural versus relational processing, allowing researchers to look beyond discrimination abilities and preference tests to how infants actually process the input.

Another adaptation of a traditional habituation experiment is called the *violation-of-expectation* paradigm. In these studies, the perceptual novelty of an event is pitted against the impossibility of the event. Instead of the experimenter knowing a priori which test stimulus will be more novel or unexpected for the infant, the infant must indicate to the experimenter which stimulus is more novel or unexpected. In an early use of this paradigm, infants were first habituated to a screen that rotated up and then down 180 degrees, at the front of an empty stage. In the test, an object was placed on the stage behind the screen so that it would block the screen's rotation. Then the screen either rotated 112 degrees (a physically possible event) or 180 degrees, a physically impossible event (Baillargeon, Spelke, & Wasserman, 1985). According to the investigators, the 112-degree rotation should be more novel, but the 180-degree rotation should be more unexpected. Infants tended to look longer at the 180-degree screen rotation, and it was inferred that infants had the knowledge or understanding necessary to view the event as unexpected or surprising. A frequently overlooked potential problem with this type of design is that the surprising or unexpected test event is also the more familiar one. If infants had a familiarity preference at the time of the test phase, longer looking at the unexpected test event would become uninterpretable since a familiarity preference would produce the same result as looking longer at the unexpected, impossible event. Thus, results can be difficult to interpret if careful steps are not taken to ensure that infants have a preference for novelty over familiarity during the test phase (a basic assumption in habituation studies).

Furthermore, as is the case in many violation-of-expectation experiments, relatively young infants are shown long, complex events that often include one or more real moving objects as well as noise and are presented over a large visual field. According to Hunter and Ames (1988), these are optimal conditions for producing a familiarity preference rather than a novelty preference. Familiarity preferences can arise if infants are not fully habituated; for example, a situation where infants never meet a habituation criterion or a stimulus is shown for a fixed number of trials rather than to criterion. Thus, problems in interpreting

the data can arise when nonhabituators, who would be most likely to show a familiarity preference, are included with habituators in an analysis. Some researchers do not attempt to habituate infants but give infants only a brief warm-up trial or two before presenting the test trials. This practice further increases the chances of a familiarity preference. We are not claiming that all violation-of-expectation results can be explained by familiarity preferences, but care and proper controls must be included to ensure that results are not due to familiarity preferences.

Although measures of infant visual attention continue to provide a viable and popular means for assessing infant cognitive ability, they have drawbacks. A valid criticism, expressed by Haith and Benson (1998), is that even though looking time is a continuous variable, an infant's response to novelty (or to a violation of their expectation for that matter) leads to a dichotomous conclusion. Infants either do or do not respond differently to a novel stimulus, or they do or do not notice the impossibility of an event. In fact, there is usually no good evidence that an individual infant will actually respond in a graded fashion to different degrees of novelty. Furthermore, not all measures of infant visual attention are equal. A number of investigators have reported that only a portion of an infant's look actually involves focused rather than casual attention to the stimulus (Ruff, 1986; Ruff & Rothbart, 1996). Focused attention seems to be the measure most closely associated with information processing. Numerous investigators have reported that infants are more resistant to a distracter stimulus when engaged in sustained attention. Sustained attention and resistance to distraction also seem to be associated with a decrease in heart rate (Hunter & Richards, 2003; Oakes, Tellinghuisen, & Tjebkes, 2000).

Whether one uses total fixation time or focused fixation time, infant looking is still passive and is usually interpreted in an all-or-none manner. A difference in looking indicates that infants prefer novelty or can discriminate between two stimuli. Haith and Benson (1998) note that a more direct tie exists between these attentional measures and novelty, familiarity, and salience than between these measures and more cognitive processes such as belief, reasoning, and inference. Some would argue that inference is being tapped in many looking-time studies, particularly those that involve objects that disappear and then reappear from behind an occluder. But Mandler (1992, 1993, 2000a) who claims a major distinction between infant perception and infant cognition argues that visual attention and habituation measures assess primarily perceptual, not cognitive processing. She believes an accurate assessment of early cognitive processing requires tasks such as object exploration, sequential touching, and imitation that involve more active manipulation and interaction on the part of the infant.

## Object Exploration and Sequential Touching

Ruff (1986) was among the first in studying infants' active exploration of objects to examine infant attention and its development. In these studies, infants were given objects one at a time and then allowed to manipulate and examine them. "Examining" was defined as focused looking in the presence or absence of manipulation. Ruff found that examining could be used as an indicator of active information processing as early as 6 or 7 months of age. Subsequent research has shown active examining to be a function of the complexity of the objects being examined as well as distracting stimuli (Oakes et al., 2000). It also seems to be an effective way to investigate infant categorization (Mandler & McDonough, 1993; Oakes et al., 1991).

Another more active technique for investigating infant categorization is the sequential touching paradigm (e.g., Rakison & Butterworth, 1998b). In this paradigm, objects from two categories (e.g., animals and vehicles) are randomly placed on a table in front of the infant. The sequential order by which the infant examines the objects is recorded. Any deviation from randomness (usually greater than chance runs of touching objects from the same category) is taken as evidence that the infant is responding on the basis of a category. Although both object exploration and sequential touching are measures requiring more active participation by the infant, it is not clear that their use brings us closer to examining cognitive processes such as belief, reasoning, or inference. Recent studies of infant imitation do seem to be a move in that direction, however.

## Deferred Imitation

The development of young infant's imitation was a cornerstone of Piaget's theory of sensorimotor development (Harris, 1983). Early imitation also has been a signifi-

cant area of research and debate (Anisfeld et al., 2001) since Meltzoff and Moore's (1977) classic report that neonates will imitate an adult's tongue protrusion as well as other facial gestures. Imitation is a more active response than simply looking, and in cases such as those reported by Meltzoff and Moore, the infants appear to be doing more than just attempting to reproduce the stimulation they received from the model. There must be some translation of the visual stimulation they received into a particular motor output, labeled by Meltzoff and Moore as *active intermodal matching*. Furthermore, it must involve more than recognition memory given that infants as young as 6 weeks of age demonstrate imitation even after a 24-hour delay and may even be using their imitative response for identifying and communicating with the model (Meltzoff & Moore, 1994).

Although the mechanism underlying newborn imitation continues to be debated, in this chapter we emphasize how imitation is now being used as a tool to examine other cognitive phenomena. Mandler and McDonough (1996) used what they called *generalized imitation* to examine infant's concept knowledge. A model produced an action, such as pretending to feed a toy dog out of a cup, and they examined whether infants' imitation would generalize to animals other than the dog, but not to nonanimals such as vehicles. By 11 to 14 months of age, infants' imitation did generalize to other animals, and one interpretation would be that the infants were making an inference based on common concept or category membership.

Deferred imitation (imitation after a delay) is an excellent paradigm for investigating infant long-term recall memory. To imitate after a delay, the infant must do more than just recognize that a particular event is novel or familiar; the infant has to recall a past event and attempt to reproduce it. Numerous experimenters (e.g., Bauer, Wiebe, Carver, Waters, & Nelson, 2003) have used a deferred imitation paradigm (or a modified version called *elicited imitation*) to investigate an infant's ability to recall sequences of past events and the developmental changes in that ability. They found that in some cases infants as young as 9 months of age can remember and reproduce a sequence of 2 or 3 complex events for as long as 1 month (Bauer et al., 2003; Carver, Bauer, & Nelson, 2000; see also Barr and Hayne, 2000; or Bauer, Chapter 9, this *Handbook,* this volume).

## INFANTS' UNDERSTANDING OF OBJECTS

Considerable research on infant cognition has examined and continues to examine what infants understand about the existence and nature of physical objects. In this section, we review three of the most studied topics in this area. We begin with a hallmark of infant cognitive achievement, at least from a Piagetian point of view, an infant's understanding of an object's permanence. We then turn to the issue of object unity. How and when does an infant perceive two visible parts of a partially occluded object as a single unified object? Finally, we consider the related question of object individuation. How and when does an infant understand that a particular object is a unique entity, independent of and different from another object?

### Object Permanence

For more than half a century, developmental researchers have been examining object permanence. In 1954, Piaget described a constructive developmental process by which infants progress through 6 distinct stages during the first 2 years of life, the sensorimotor period. This progression begins in Stage 1 with newborns simply looking reflexively at an object placed in their visual field and ends at Stage 6 with 18- to 24-month-old infants solving invisible displacement problems in which one object serves as a symbol for a second object that is hidden from view (Harris, 1983, 1987). Few would dispute that more research time and effort have been devoted to investigating some aspect of infants' developing understanding of objects and their permanence than any other topic falling within the rubric of infant cognition. The previous *Handbook* chapters by Harris (1983) and Haith and Benson (1998) provide thorough reviews of the object permanence literature through the mid-1990s. Therefore, in the present section we concentrate on research and theory of the past 10 years. Since the types of research questions and studies have changed over the years, we first provide a brief summary of the object permanence literature as a whole, divided into discrete phases.

### *Phase 1: Demonstration and Modification*

When one examines this immense body of research from the broad perspective of 40 to 50 years, a certain evolu-

tionary change appears in the topics being examined and the methods used to examine them. During the first phase, from the 1960s through the mid 1980s, both large-scale and small-scale studies attempted to standardize, but remain true to, the original tasks described by Piaget. A 14-item standardized test was developed of Piaget type object permanence tasks to tap individual differences in infant performance across all 6 stages (Uzgiris & Hunt, 1975). More typically, restricted studies were concentrated on infants' performance during a single stage. Usually a small toy or other attractive object was hidden under an opaque box or cloth in front of an infant, and the infant was given an opportunity to reach for and retrieve the object. Many variations in this task were used to assess performance at different stages. If the object were only partially hidden, it would be a test of Stage 3 performance. If it were totally hidden, it would be a test of Stage 4 performance, and if it were hidden several times in one location before being hidden in a second location, it would be a test of the A, not B, error with success indicative of performance at Stage 5.

Other variations were used, such as replacement of the opaque box with a transparent one (Diamond, 1981), changing the spatial location of the toy after it was hidden (Sophian, 1984; Wishart & Bower, 1982), delaying the time interval between hiding and retrieval, or the use of three rather than two hiding places (Sophian & Wellman, 1983). These variations were employed to examine possible mechanisms underlying both correct and incorrect behavior. In general, these studies tended to support the basic developmental sequence proposed by Piaget even though researchers disagreed to some extent over the exact ages the transitions from one stage to another occurred and the mechanisms responsible for these changes. Harris (1983) discusses many of these Phase 1 research findings, as well as the theoretical issues generated by them. Readers are encouraged to examine his chapter in the fourth edition of the *Handbook* for a more thorough review.

### *Phase 2: Refutation and Rejection*

The second phase of research on object permanence can be traced back at least to Bower (1974, 1977, 1979), but it became most prevalent in the 1980s and 1990s. Researchers of this era have argued that infants are much more precocious than Piaget believed. They proposed that infants have certain core or innate knowledge about objects that is present early in life, if not at birth. They introduced new simplified tasks that relied more on an infant looking at an object than having to reach for the object. A new variation of the habituation procedure, called the *violation-of-expectation* paradigm, was developed and used to uncover this precocious ability. In this procedure, an object often would be made to completely disappear behind an occluder and then reappear in either a predictable or unpredictable (often impossible) manner. Longer looking at the unpredictable event was considered an indication first, that the infant had inferred that the object continued to exist behind the occluder and, second, that whatever happened behind the occluder in an unpredictable event was impossible and unexpected. These cleverly designed studies also often pitted a response to novelty against a response to impossibility.

We have already noted an example of this type of study (Baillargeon, 1987; Baillargeon et al., 1985). Researchers first habituated infants to a screen that rotated 180 degrees, up and then down from a horizontal surface. In a subsequent test, an object was placed behind the screen and its view was obstructed as the screen rotated upward. Infants were then shown a possible event in which the screen rotated 112 degrees before stopping (when it presumably hit the object) versus an impossible event in which the screen continued to rotate the full 180 degrees (as in habituation) despite the apparent presence of the object. Infants as young as 3.5 months of age looked longer at the impossible 180-degree test event than at the possible 112-degree event. Baillargeon concluded that these results indicate infants much younger than those predicted by Piaget have mastered the equivalent of Stage 4 object permanence since they must have inferred the presence of the block even though it was totally occluded by the moving screen.

Many researchers using a version of this violation-of-expectation paradigm have reached similar conclusions. In one version, a car rolled down a ramp behind an occluder and reappeared at the other side even though it should have been stopped by an obstacle in its path behind the occluder (Baillargeon, 1986), or a ball was dropped behind an occluder presumably onto a solid table only to reappear under the table when the occluder was removed (Spelke, Breinlinger, Macomber, & Jacobson, 1992), or a rabbit was moved from left to right behind an occluder and either appeared (as it should) or failed to appear in a window in the center of the occluder (Baillargeon & Graber, 1987). In each case, infants much younger than 8 months of age looked longer at the surprising or impossible event, which according to

the authors supported their nativist view that infants at birth or shortly thereafter are equipped with certain core principles about physical objects, such as continuity of motion and solidity, which produce a much more sophisticated understanding of object permanence than had previously been believed. Both Haith and Benson (1998) and Fischer and Bidell (1991) review this research along with some contentious issues, such as how important it is, according to some views, for infants to demonstrate their understanding of object permanence through some physical action. As was the case for Phase 1 research on object permanence, we encourage readers to review either of these chapters for a synopsis of this Phase 2 research, which purports to refute the developmental views of Piaget (1954).

### Phase 3: Rebuttal and Recent Evidence

The material covered in Phase 3 falls into two broad categories. The first is an empirical counterattack to some of the nativist studies presented in Phase 2. The second is a new set of theoretical proposals designed to bridge the gap between the evidence in Phase 1 and Phase 2.

**Recent Empirical Evidence.**    Some of the studies demonstrating infant precocity have been questioned on methodological grounds. For the rotating screen example, Rivera, Wakeley, and Langer (1999) noted that infants should have a preference for 180-degree events since these events contain more movement. They also argued that if infants were actually looking longer because of the impossibility of the event, no prior habituation should be necessary. They tested 5.5-month-old infants on Baillargeon's tasks but without the habituation phase and found that infants looked longer at a 180-degree rotation than at a 112-degree rotation, no matter whether the event included a block. As both Bogartz (Bogartz & Shinskey, 1998; Bogartz, Shinskey, & Speaker, 1997) and we noted earlier, the violation-of-expectation paradigm may, on occasion, be subject to a certain artifact. Whenever responses based on novelty are contrasted with responses based on impossibility, an infant's preference for familiarity will be confounded with the infant's preference for impossibility.

Recently, the journal *Infancy* published a collection of studies all providing evidence that infants' responses in studies similar to the original rotation studies by Baillargeon et al. (1985), and Baillargeon (1987) could be accounted for by a preference for familiarity rather than impossibility. A potential problem with the original studies is that even though Baillargeon had used a version of a habituation paradigm, she grouped together both habituators and nonhabituators in her tests. If the habituators had shown no effect, but the nonhabituators had shown a familiarity effect, she would have obtained the results she reported.

This collection of studies was followed by a series of invited commentaries as well as a rebuttal by the authors of the three original articles. (We encourage readers having an interest in this topic to read the entire set of articles and commentaries.) In her commentary, Baillargeon (2000) presented a rebuttal that included the point that these three studies did not accurately replicate all aspects of her procedure. But, perhaps her most significant argument was the listing of 30 other reports, all of which supported her conclusion that infants between 2.5 and 7.5 months of age can represent fully hidden objects (in other words, have the equivalent of Stage 4 object permanence). Furthermore, not all these studies used her version of the violation-of-expectation design, and most, but not all, were conducted in her laboratory. One of them (Baillargeon and Graber's 1987 rabbit-in-the-window experiment) has already been criticized by Bogartz and Shinsky (1998) on grounds similar to those discussed in relation to the rotating-screen experiment.

But let us consider in detail another example mentioned by Baillargeon in her list of 30. This study by Wynn (1992) presented a series of experiments not conducted in Baillargeon's laboratory. Wynn did not habituate infants; she only gave them a series of test trials. She did not even report a direct test of object permanence, but claimed to show that 5-month-old infants can add and subtract. She also must have assumed that infants at this age are able to represent hidden objects, since the objects they were supposed to count were placed on a stage behind an occluding screen. She also used a version of the violation-of-expectation paradigm since, on some trials, the screen was lowered to reveal the wrong number of objects and infants looked longer on these trials than on trials with the correct number of objects.

Recently Cohen and Marks (2002) examined Wynn's procedure and discovered that even though no habituation trials were used, in both addition and subtraction conditions a possible violation-of-expectation was confounded with familiarity. When it was assumed that infants expected to see one object but instead saw two objects, the presence of two objects was also more familiar than the presence of one object. Likewise, when it

was assumed that infants expected to see two objects but instead saw one object, it was now more familiar than two objects. Cohen and Marks conducted a series of experiments confirming this familiarity effect. In one of these experiments, infants responded in the same way as in the Wynn study even when no objects were added or subtracted. Let us examine that experiment from the point of view of object permanence. In a sense, this study can be viewed as a straightforward example of an object permanence study, using a violation-of-expectation paradigm. Five-month-old infants were shown a series of trials in which either one or two objects were placed on a stage, a screen was then raised occluding the object or objects, and then lowered again after a two-second pause to reveal either the same number of objects or a different number of objects. In some cases, the screen was lowered to reveal no objects on the stage. In other cases, it revealed one, two, or three objects on the stage. If infants at 5 months of age have achieved object permanence, they should unquestionably look longer when the screen reveals the incorrect number. Instead, the infants looked longer when they saw the correct number because, given the paradigm that was used, that number was more familiar. As Hunter and Ames noted, familiarity preferences tend to occur most when the stimuli are complex and the infants are young and have had limited exposure to the stimuli, all conditions that fit both Cohen and Marks' (2002) and Wynn's (1992) experiments.

Another issue raised by the violation-of-expectation studies is why investigators find such advanced levels of object permanence in young infants compared with the findings from standard Piagetian types of tasks. An important difference between these two paradigms is that the violation-of-expectation studies require only looking, whereas standard object permanence studies require both manual search and often removal of an obstacle to obtain the desired object. Haith and Benson (1998) have argued that manual search is a necessary condition to access information infants have about their own effect on objects or the spatial location of objects with respect to themselves, both of which are characteristics of object permanence according to Piaget (1954). Others (Baillargeon, Graber, DeVos, & Black, 1990; Diamond, 1991), however, argue that young infants actually know that an object continues to exist when it cannot be seen, but they have a motor or a means-end deficit that prevents them from actually reaching for the object or removing the occluder. Support for this means-end deficit position comes from studies by Clifton, Rochat, Litovsky, and Perris (1991) and Hood and Willatts (1986), who found that young infants will reach for objects in the dark even when they do not reach for objects occluded by some barrier in the light. Bertier et al. (2001) also conducted a series of studies that attempted to disassociate visual tracking from reaching. They used a task similar to the violation-of-expectation study reported earlier by Spelke et al. (1992), in which she claimed infants as young as 2.5 months were surprised when a ball rolled behind an occluder and apparently went through one barrier (a wall) to stop at a second barrier (but see Cohen, 1995, for contrary evidence). Bertier et al. recorded 6.5- to 9.5-month-old infants' tracking and reaching for a ball that rolled behind an occluder. On some trials, the experimenter placed a barrier behind the occluder and found that the presence of the barrier tended to disrupt tracking more than reaching. However, this disruption only occurred when the infants could see the top of the barrier above the occluder. Bertier et al. concluded that their tracking results supported Spelke et al. but that reaching was quite difficult for these infants and may have interfered with their integration of visual information and spatiotemporal reasoning.

Several studies have compared results with transparent versus opaque barriers and found infants retrieved visible toys more often than ones that cannot be seen (Munakata, 1997; Shinskey, 2002; Shinskey, Bogartz, & Poirier, 2000; Shinskey & Munakata, 2001, 2003). In one study (Shinskey, 2002), 6-month-old infants were more likely to retrieve an object visible in water than hidden in milk. Since retrieval of the object in either liquid requires the same motor behavior, the only difference between the water task and the milk task was that in the latter, the object could not be seen. If the infants truly had achieved Stage 4 object permanence, the failure to see the object should have not been a problem.

What conclusions should be reached regarding the argument about young infants' understanding of object permanence? The evidence obviously is mixed and has been used to justify both a nativist position that infants as young as 2 or 3 months of age can represent fully hidden objects as well as the more traditional view that they must be 8 or 9 months of age before they can do so. The argument between these two positions is misguided for three reasons. First, the dichotomy is usually cast in either-or terms, when in all likelihood the process of ac-

quiring a representation of completely hidden objects is a gradual process that develops over age. This point has also been made by Fischer and Bidell (1991). Second, each argument is based on selective use of only the portion of evidence that supports a particular position rather than making an attempt to integrate all the relevant evidence into a more comprehensive explanation. Spelke (1998) has argued eloquently for a nativist position. Her paper along with Haith's (1998) counterargument should be required readings in developmental psychology. Although we agree more with Haith than with Spelke, we endorse Spelke's guideline that "all theories of early cognitive development must encompass all the relevant data" (p. 192). Third, the dichotomy distracts us from understanding the mechanisms underlying the representation of an object and its development. We may or may not believe, along with Piaget, or Fischer and Bidell (1991), that the motor action of reaching for the object is an essential aspect of that representation. But our theoretical goal should be to discover the nature of that representation, how it is acquired, and how it changes over the first 2 years of life.

**Recent Theoretical Proposals.**    Recently two theoretical papers have appeared that should receive special attention because they attempt to explain the discrepancy between performance on looking tasks and reaching tasks, and both attribute the discrepancy to changes in the underlying representation. Melzoff and Moore (1998) assume that from birth infants have the ability to form representations of objects and events that persist over time and can be accessed even when the objects are absent. These representations (or memories) include both spatiotemporal information (locations and trajectories) and specific item information (perceptual features and functions) that combine to determine an object's identity. Object identity, however, is very different from object permanence. It allows an infant to predict where and when an object can be seen, and to identify the object when it reappears, but not to assume that the object continues to exist when unseen. Melzoff and Moore believe this representation of object identity is sufficient to explain most of the violation-of-expectation results, but that an additional type of representation, one of the object's existence and changes in movement while behind an occluder, is necessary for true object permanence. They assume this latter type of representation develops later than object identity.

Munakata and Stedron (2002) propose a similar solution. They assume that different types of memory or different strengths of memory may be responsible for the difference in performance on violation-of-expectation versus manual search tasks. They acknowledge Meltzoff and Moore's distinction between identity and permanence but suggest that active versus latent memory may also be a factor with active memories of hidden objects required for search tasks and latent memories sufficient for violation-of-expectation tasks. They also assume that infants gradually acquire the ability to remember hidden objects, and different strengths of memory may also be necessary for different types of task. Munakata and Stedron showed that connectionist models that included these memory systems were able to successfully simulate performance on a variety of tasks from violation-of-expectation, to simple reaching for objects behind occluders, to Stage 4 error problems in which an infant will return to a previous hiding place even though the object has been clearly hidden in a new location.

Our constructivist information-processing perspective is compatible with the theoretical positions of either Meltzoff and Moore (1998) or Munakata and Stedron (2002), who both advocate developmental changes in infant representation or memory. Melzoff and Moore, in particular, were explicit about the tasks that should require only object identity and the one that requires object permanence. These tasks are reproduced schematically in Figure 5.2.

They reported a series of experiments by Moore, Borton, and Darby (1978), who found based on these tasks that 5-month-olds were responsive to both an object's features and its trajectory (the object's identity), but only 9-month-olds were successful on the object permanence task.

Our approach would make a similar distinction but go a step further. We would argue that an understanding of object identity requires an integration of featural information with movement and trajectory information. By 5 months of age, as Moore et al. (1978) found, infants should have little trouble with this integration. But, younger infants could well respond to feature and trajectory information independently. We would predict that infants' understanding of objects should be a constructive process that undergoes a number of hierarchical integrations. According to this view, object permanence should develop later than 5 months of age since it represents a higher form of processing involving the integration of identity information from two objects (the object of interest and the occluder) as well as spatial relationship information between these two objects.

## Other Areas Related to Object Permanence

Two additional areas of infant research, the perception of object unity and the understanding of object individuation, received their original impetus from the study of object permanence. Although at one time, they could have been categorized as subtopics within the area of object permanence, each of them has generated enough recent research (and controversy) to have become a significant topic for consideration in its own right.

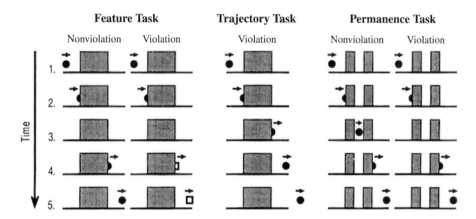

**Figure 5.2**  Schematic diagram of Feature, Trajectory, and Object Permanence tasks. *Source:* From "Object Representation, Identity, and the Paradox of Early Permanence: Steps toward a New Framework," by A. N. Meltzoff and M. K. Moore, 1998, *Infant Behavior and Development, 21,* p. 208. Reprinted with permission.

*Object Unity*

The object permanence events we have considered so far include only those in which an object is totally occluded for a period of time by a cover or some other object. The ability to represent that object when fully occluded is characteristic of Stage 4 in Piaget's 6-stage sequence. Infants at Stage 3, by contrast, should be able to represent partially occluded objects. The research on object unity represents the most systematic effort to discover the nature of that representation.

The classic studies in this area were reported by Kellman and Spelke (1983) and, in fact, were among the first to use a version of the violation-of-expectation.

In their initial study, 4-month-old infants were habituated to a rod moving back and forth behind a box that occluded the middle portion of the rod. In the tests, the occluder was removed and the infants saw for the first time either the entire rod including the invisible center portion or just the upper and lower portions of the rod that had been visible during habituation. If the infants had just processed the visible portions of the rod during habituation, they should look longer at the complete rod since it would be novel, but if they had perceived or inferred the existence of the entire rod, they should look longer at the two separate rod pieces. Kellman and Spelke (1983) found their infants did in fact look longer at the separate pieces. Several control studies have also been reported that indicate the common motion of the upper and lower portions of the rod played a major role in specifying object unity (see Kellman, 1993, 1996). A factor of particular interest is that the perceptual similarity between the shape, color, texture, and so on of the upper and lower portions did not seem to be significant until the infants were 7 months of age. Yet, infants at 4 months certainly can distinguish between shapes, colors, and textures. Thus this finding is consistent with our notion that infants will process featural and motion properties of an object independently before they are able to integrate the two.

Many aspects of the original Kellman and Spelke (1983) events have been examined including whether the event was three-dimensional or two-dimensional (Johnson & Nanez, 1995), whether the top and bottom portions were relatable (P. J. Kellman & Shipley, 1991), whether as the rod moved there was accretion and deletion of background texture (Johnson & Aslin, 1996), or even the effect of rotation of an object about its vertical axis rather than its translation (its movement from left

to right; Johnson, Cohen, Marks, & Johnson, 2003). The present chapter cannot cover all this evidence, but for the interested reader, more comprehensive reviews can be found in Johnson (2000) and in Kellman and Arterberry (Chapter 3, this *Handbook,* this volume).

The issue we would like to address more fully is the presence or absence of age differences. Kellman and Spelke (1983) suggested that the perception of unity is innate. They claimed infants are born with a tendency to experience objects as coherent and unified. Thus from their view, one would predict that infants younger than 4 months of age should respond in these tasks much like the 4-month-olds.

That does not appear to be the case. Two-month-old infants will respond in terms of object unity, but only under restricted conditions such as when a greater portion of the rod is visible (Johnson & Aslin, 1998). Even more significant are the results reported with neonates. In a series of studies, Slater and colleagues (Slater, Johnson, Brown, & Badenoch, 1996; Slater, Johnson, Kellman, & Spelke, 1994; Slater et al., 1990) found that newborns look longer at the complete rod, not the broken rod. If one uses the same logic as in the Kellman and Spelke (1983) study with 4-month-olds, newborns must be processing the visible portion of the rod as separate pieces, not as a whole. Thus there appears to be a developmental trend from processing independent parts to integrating those parts into a unified whole, just as predicted by our constructivist information-processing view.

Finally, Eizenman and Bertenthal (1998) reported a developmental change between 4 and 6 months of age. They used a translating rod and found that 4-month-olds, as in previous studies, looked longer at the pieces than at the complete rod. When the rod rotated (around the z axis, as a propeller), however, 4-month-olds looked longer at the complete rod (like the behavior of younger infants), but 6-month-olds looked longer at the pieces. Furthermore, when the event was made more complex by having the rod oscillate rather than just rotate, the 6-month-olds looked longer at the complete rod. If one assumes that a rotating rod (with its changing orientations and angles with respect to the occluder) contains more complex information than a translating rod, and that an oscillating rod contains more complex information than a rotating rod, then these data also fit the constructivist information-processing view quite well. Recall that information-processing principle 5 stated that if the system becomes overloaded, infants will tend to fall back to a lower level of processing. That is exactly what seems to have happened to the 4-month-olds with the rotating rod and to the 6-month-olds with the oscillating rod.

### Object Individuation

Even when an object is completely visible, it does not follow that the infant regards it as a distinct three-dimensional entity that moves as a whole. Perception of the number and nature of distinct objects present in an event is termed *object individuation.* For example, how does an infant know that an object that moves from one location to another location is the same object? Does it matter if the object in the second location is the same color, shape, size, and texture as the object in the first location? Most investigators agree that an understanding of object individuation requires, at a minimum, certain spatiotemporal criteria, including that an object cannot be in two places at the same time, two objects cannot occupy the same space, and objects travel on spatiotemporally connected paths (Xu, 2003). Some investigators (e.g., Leslie & Kaldy, 2001; Leslie, Xu, Tremoulet, & Scholl, 1998) also make a distinction between object individuation, which allows infants to determine the number of distinct objects, and object identification, which allows them to distinguish between objects based on their featural differences.

The most important question is how one should assess infants for object individuation. Many of those who investigate this topic tend to make certain additional assumptions. They likely assume that by 5 months of age, if not earlier, infants have the equivalent of Stage 4 object permanence and that the most appropriate way to assess object individuation is to use some version of the violation-of-expectation paradigm. As noted, both of these assumptions remain open to debate. To make matters a bit more complicated, most violation-of-expectation studies no longer begin with a complete habituation phase, so familiarity preferences are more likely to occur.

Putting those matters aside, the most contentious issue seems to be the earliest age at which infants demonstrate their understanding of object individuation. That issue, in turn, hinges on whether use of featural information is considered to be a necessary condition. As with object unity, this area has taken on a life of its own, and so many studies have now been reported that it is impossible to summarize them all. For readers interested in obtaining more information, we recommend two recent chapters with moderately different points of view (Wilcox, Schweinle, & Chapa, 2003; Xu, 2003).

The types of events used to demonstrate object individuation are variations of those shown in Figure 5.2. Spelke et al. (1995) habituated infants to an event similar to the permanence task shown in the right side of the figure. Two screens were presented, and in one condition (like the violation condition in Figure 5.2) infants saw one object repeatedly appear and disappear behind the first screen. An identical looking object appeared and disappeared behind the second screen, but no object was seen between the two screens. In the test phase, the screens were removed to reveal either one or two objects. The investigators assumed that if the infants could individuate objects, this event would specify two different objects since they never saw an object move between the two screens; therefore the infants should look longer at one object than at two objects. In a second condition, like the nonviolation condition shown in Figure 5.2, infants saw the object travel between the two screens and therefore if they could individuate objects, they should look longer at two objects in the test than at one object. Some evidence for individuation was obtained at 4 months of age. Infants did look longer at one object than at two objects in the violation condition, but they did not look longer at two objects than at one object in the nonviolation condition. Xu and Carey (1996) found that 10-month-old infants looked longer at two objects in the nonviolation condition. It is thus a bit unclear whether there was evidence for individuation at 4 months of age or only at 10 months of age. Whatever conclusion one reaches, infants did not have to use featural information because the two objects shown were identical.

Other studies have been reported that more closely resemble the Feature Task shown on the left side of Figure 5.2. In one type of experiment conducted by Xu and Carey (1996), infants were shown a single screen with one object (a ball) appearing and disappearing from the left side of the screen and a different object (a toy duck) appearing and disappearing from the right side of the screen. In the test, the screen was removed to reveal the two different objects, the expected outcome, or a single object, an unexpected outcome. Twelve-month-old infants, but not younger ones, looked longer at the unexpected outcome. Wilcox and Baillargeon (1998) obtained similar results. They presented infants with either the nonviolation or the violation version of the Feature Task and then removed the screen to reveal a single object. Infants at 11.5 months of age, but not younger, looked longer at the single object in the violation condition, presumably because they expected to see both objects.

From these and other results, Xu (2003) concluded that infants younger than 12 months of age base object individuation almost entirely on spatiotemporal information. At 12 months of age and older, infants incorporate perceptual property (featural) information and respond to objects at a "kind," that is, category level. Wilcox et al. (2003) take issue with this conclusion and argue that the age at which evidence for individuation can be found depends on the type and complexity of the task. They point to evidence using simpler tasks (event monitoring rather than event matching) that indicates infants as young as 4.5 months of age are sensitive to at least some featural information. Xu (2003) counters by arguing that these tasks show that the infants are sensitive to featural information but not necessarily object individuation.

On the surface, the debate between these two groups seems to be over the earliest age that infants display object individuation. But it actually appears to be centered more on what the minimal necessary conditions are to label infants' behavior as indicative of object individuation. Regardless of which position is taken, the evidence seems to be clear that infants can process spatiotemporal information about an object's movement and featural information such as the object's size, shape, color, and texture independently, prior to their being able to integrate those two types of information (see Cohen & Cashon, 2001b, for a more complete presentation of this point). The evidence provided by Wilcox et al. (2003) that more complex events delay the appearance of object individuation is consistent with the view that an overload of information can cause infants to regress to an earlier mode of processing.

## INFANTS' UNDERSTANDING OF EVENTS

An event can be defined as a dynamic change in one or more objects over space and time. Technically, most of the objects shown to infants in the studies described in the previous section on object knowledge have been presented in the context of an event. In those studies, the emphasis is on the location, unity, or continued existence of a single object. In this section, we consider events that involve multiple objects and the relation between them. The type of event receiving the most extensive investigation over the past 20 years is a simple

causal event in which two objects collide. The question most often investigated is whether infants perceive or understand that the second object's movement was caused by the first object (Cohen, Amsel, Redford, & Casasola, 1998). We examine research on infants' understanding of these simple causal events first and then consider their understanding of more complex events.

## Simple Causal Events

Philosophical debate over the origin of our understanding of causality dates back, at least, to Hume (1777/1993) and Kant (1794/1982). Hume assumed the notion of causality was acquired through experience, whereas Kant assumed it was innate. For Piaget (1954), an understanding of causality is also a function of experience but develops through several stages and is tied intimately to the infant's actions. According to Piaget, infants at first have no notion of causality. It emerges gradually through their learning that they can have an effect on the people and objects around them, strengthening a sense of power over their environment. Later, as infants gain object permanence and come to distinguish themselves from external physical objects, they learn to differentiate between psychological causality, in which they act as the agent, and physical causality, which is based on the interaction of external objects with one another independent of the infants' own actions.

Research on infants' perception of causality has been described in review articles (Cohen et al., 1998; Oakes & Cohen, 1994), including the chapter by Haith and Benson in the fifth edition of the *Handbook* (1998). As we have done with other topics, we do not dwell on studies that have already been summarized in previous reviews. Instead we note the most important points of these early studies and give greater emphasis to recent research.

A few researchers, beginning with Ball (1973) used an occluding screen to examine infants' perception of causality. In Ball's study, and in later ones (Lucksinger, Cohen, & Madole, 1992; Oakes, 1994; Van de Walle, Woodward, & Phillips, 1994), the actual contact (or lack of contact) between two simple objects was hidden and infants had to infer from the timing of the moving objects whether a causal collision had taken place. As Cohen et al. (1998) note in their review, the evidence for infants less than 10 months of age inferring causality when the collision takes place behind an occluder is equivocal.

The evidence is more definitive for visible collisions. Based on Michotte's (1963) seminal research on adults' perception of simple causal events, Leslie (1982, 1984, 1986, 1988; Leslie & Kaldy, 2001; Leslie & Keeble, 1987) reported findings from several experiments on 6-month-old infants' reactions to simple launching events such as those shown in Figure 5.3. These studies and subsequent ones from other laboratories (Cohen & Amsel, 1998; Cohen & Oakes, 1993; Desrochers, 1999; Lecuyer & Bourcier, 1994; Oakes & Cohen, 1990) suggest that by around 6 months of age, infants have at least a basic understanding of a simple, causal launching event.

The logic behind most of these studies is fairly simple. Infants are habituated to one type of event and then tested on one or more modifications of that event. If in-

fants are processing an event in terms of its perceptual characteristics, that is, the spatial and temporal information composing the event, the difference between a delayed launching and a no-collision event should be greater than the difference between a direct launching event and *either* a delayed launching or no-collision event. This is so because the delayed launching and no-collision events differ from one another on both spatial and temporal dimensions. In contrast, the direct launching event differs from the delayed and no-collision events on only one dimension, temporal and spatial respectively. On the other hand, if infants are processing the events on some causality dimension, then the delayed and no-collision events are both noncausal and should be

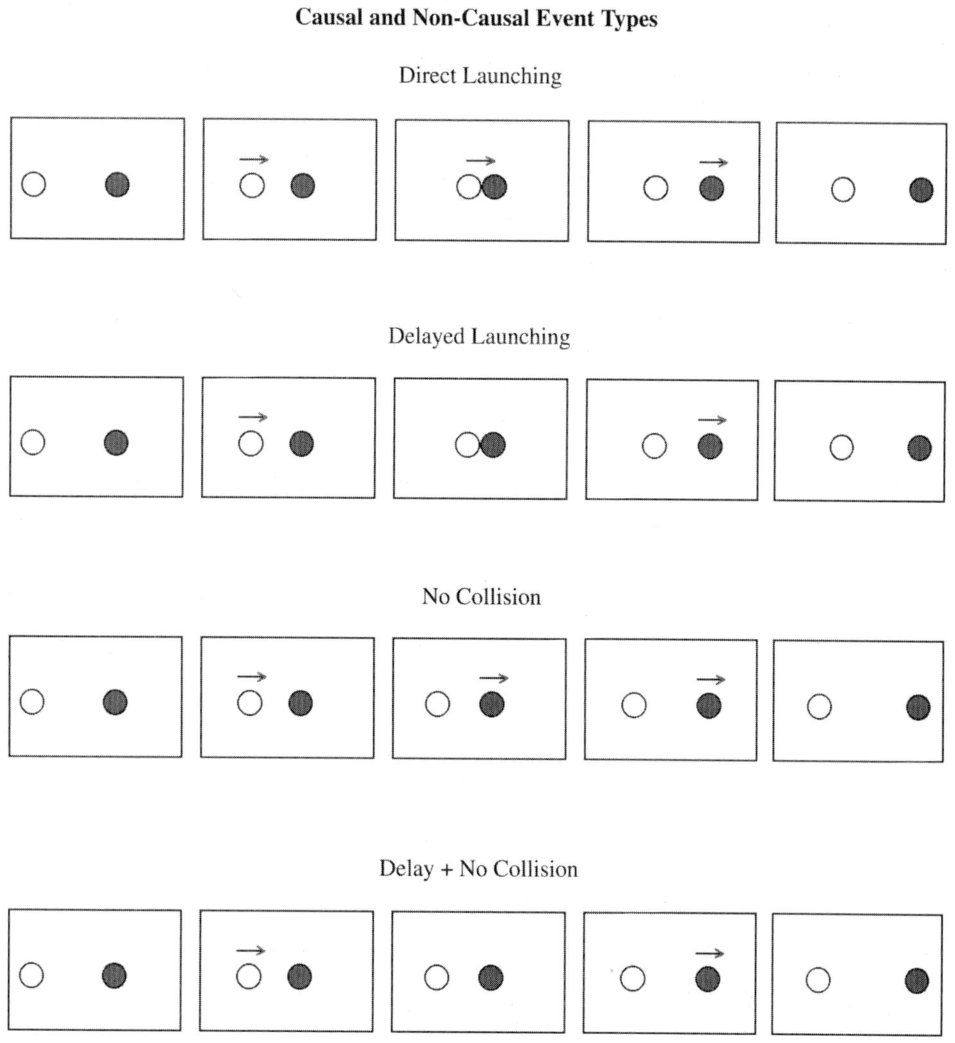

## Causal and Non-Causal Event Types

### Direct Launching

### Delayed Launching

### No Collision

### Delay + No Collision

**Figure 5.3**   Four types of launching events used in studies of infant causal perception. Adapted from "A Constructivist Model of Infant Cognition," by L. B. Cohen, H. H. Chaput, and C. H. Cashon, 2002, *Cognitive Development, 17,* p. 1332. Reprinted with permission.

treated similarly, but both should be quite different from the direct launching since it is a causal event.

In one set of studies, Leslie (1984) habituated 6.5-month-old infants to one of the events shown in Figure 5.3 and then tested them with one of the other events. Infants dishabituated more to a change from a causal to a noncausal event than to a change from one noncausal to another noncausal event. As noted, this pattern is indicative of responding in terms of causality. In another study (Leslie & Keeble, 1987), infants were habituated either to a direct launching or a delayed launching event and then tested on the same event in the reverse direction. Infants dishabituated more to the reversal of the direct launching than to the delayed launching, presumably because the former was also a reversal of the agent and patient. Leslie (1986) assumed from these data that infants were responding on the basis of an innate causal module that can serve as the basis of future development but is not the product of previous development.

Named a *spatiotemporal continuity gradient* by Leslie (1986), the product of this innate causal module is sensitive to the spatial and temporal information in a launching event and produces a gradient of causality, with a direct launching event at one end, no-collision and delay events in the middle, and the no-collision plus delay event at the other end. Some researchers, such as Carey (2000), accept Leslie's assumption of an innate causal module and believe it represents a type of core knowledge present early in life. Others, such as Mandler (2000a), accept the idea of an abstract causal module. She considers it to be an "image schema," but believes it develops early in infancy as a function of the infant's "perceptual analysis" of environmental events. In either case, this module is activated automatically by the spatiotemporal characteristics of the event and should be insensitive to other factors, such as the type of objects engaging in the event.

In contrast, our constructive information-processing approach assumes that an infant's understanding of causal events will be a slow constructive process characterized by an integration of information at several different levels and temporary regression periods when the system becomes overloaded. We believe this approach represents a more accurate developmental picture than either the one proposed by Leslie or the one proposed by Mandler.

Consider first the issue of innateness. Leslie (1984) demonstrated some degree of causal perception or understanding by 6.5 months of age. Cohen and Amsel (1998) replicated Leslie's result with 6.25-month-old infants but also tested infants at 4 and at 5.5 months of age. Four-month-olds responded only to the continuous movement in an event and 5.5-month-olds responded to the spatial and temporal differences between these moving objects, but not the causality. The failure of younger infants to perceive the causality of such events has been reported recently by others as well. Belanger and Desrochers (2001) replicated Leslie's positive results for causal perception at 6 months. However, Desrochers (1999) did not find infants responding to causality at 3.5 months. Belanger and Desrochers reported also that in an entrainment version of a causal event (in which the first object continues to push the second object after the collision), even the 6-month-olds did not respond in terms of causality.

This developmental evidence seems to be more consistent with the constructive information-processing account than with the presence of an innate module. However, a person who claims existence of an innate module might answer that innateness does not imply presence at birth. Perhaps the module somehow becomes activated at 6 months of age. Partially in response to this criticism, Cohen, Chaput, and Cashon (2002) developed a connectionist model, called "CLA" (Constructive Learning Architecture), that follows the six information-processing principles mentioned earlier. CLA is a hierarchical neural network model that is unsupervised and self-organized. It uses Hebbian learning to organize the highest level in the model from the correlational information provided by lower levels. When processing simple launching events, it works with only two sets of inputs, the spatial distance between the two objects at any point in time and the movement or nonmovement of each object integrated over a very short period. These two inputs form separate Layer 1 maps, one for the spatial changes that take place during the course of an entire event and the other for the changes in movements of the two objects during the course of that event.

With training (learning), correlational information between these two Layer 1 maps project to a single Layer 2 map, whose overall activation becomes related to the degree of causality of each event. In fact, once the network has learned, it evaluates simple events in terms of a causality continuum similar to Leslie's spatiotemporal continuity gradient. Thus, the CLA connectionist network actually learns causality from the simple perceptual features, spatial distance and movement, both of which should be readily available to a young infant. Learning takes place from the bottom up, with Layer 1 maps organizing before the Layer 2 map forms, consistent with the hierarchical information-processing view described earlier. Once the model "learned," we simulated an information overload by introducing some random variation in the events the model had succeeded in classifying as causal or noncausal. The result was that the model regressed to processing the events at the lower Layer 1 levels in an attempt to reorganize itself, just as the information-processing principles would predict. In other words, CLA learned causality simply from being exposed to causal and noncausal events. So, at the very least, the success of CLA provides an example that the notion of causality need not be innate, but instead can be learned through experience with simple causal and noncausal events and the ability to detect correlations among simple features in those events.

Another prediction generated by an innate module approach relates to the type of objects involved in these causal and noncausal events. According to either the modular or image schema viewpoint, the type of object should not matter; it is the spatiotemporal relations that determine whether the event is causal or noncausal. However, some research indicates that the type of object does matter. Oakes and Cohen (1990) replicated Leslie (1984) by showing the same launching type events using complex, realistic moving toys, rather than moving squares or circles. They found that rather than responding in terms of causality, 6-month-olds now focused on the individual objects. Ten-month-olds, in contrast, did respond in terms of causality. Apparently the complexity of the realistic toys overloaded the 6-month-olds, forcing them back to a simpler way of processing, but did not have this effect on the 10-month-olds.

Cohen and Oakes (1993) also used realistic toys when presenting launching events to 10-month-olds, but in this case the actual toys changed from trial to trial. Because the objects changed but the type of event did not, the task was essentially an event category task. Again, from modular or image schema points of view, changing the specific objects used from trial to trial should be irrelevant and causal perception should not be affected. From our constructive information-processing point of view, however, the task demands of the category task should definitely produce complications in perceiving causality. In support of our viewpoint, Cohen and Oakes found that the 10-month-olds no longer processed the events as causal. Instead, they regressed to process-ing the events in terms of the independent spatial and temporal differences between them.

## Complex Causal Chains

The constructive information-processing approach makes another prediction. According to its principles, not only can higher units of information be formed from the relationships among lower units, but these higher units can also serve as components in yet higher units. Apprehending the causal relation between two moving toys in a launching event certainly represents the formation of a higher unit produced from two lower units. The question to be addressed next is whether that simple causal event can serve as a single element in an even higher unit.

Cohen, Rundell, Spellman, and Cashon (1999) showed 10- and 15-month-old infants complex event sequences called "causal chains." In these events (see Figure 5.4), one moving toy hit a second toy that moved to a house. When the second toy made contact with the house, a dog's head abruptly emerged from under the roof of the house (similar to a jack-in-the-box) coinciding with a "boing" sound. Each collision was also accompanied by an appropriate noise. Although this causal chain event is obviously much more complex than the simple launching events mentioned earlier, the first half of the event is exactly the same type of simple causal event, with realistic toys, used earlier by Oakes and Cohen (1990) and by Cohen and Oakes (1993).

In this causal chain study, one half of the infants at each age were habituated to an event in which the first two toys were involved in a direct launching. That event is illustrated in Figure 5.4. For the other half of the infants, the first two toys were involved in a delayed launching. A 2-second delay occurred between contact of the first toy and movement of the second toy. All infants continued to see the same type of event in the test that they had seen during habituation (beginning with either a direct or delayed launching), but on one test trial the first toy was replaced by a novel toy, and on another test trial the second toy was replaced by a novel toy. The authors reasoned that if the causal agent in the event sequence was the most important object to the infant, then replacing that object should produce more dishabituation than replacing the other object. In the direct launching event, the first object should be the most important since it is the agent; it causes the second object to hit the house and the dog's head to pop up. In

Causal Chain – Habituation                Causal Chain – Test 1                Causal Chain – Test 2

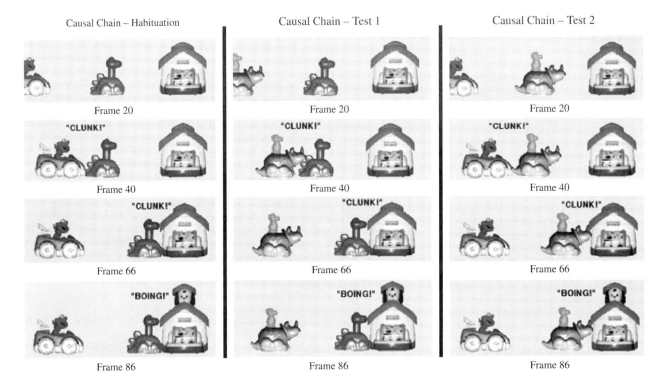

**Figure 5.4**   Selected frames from events in infant causal chain experiments. *Source:* From "Infants' Perception of Causal Chains," by L. B. Cohen, L. J. Rundell, B. A. Spellman, and C. H. Cashon, 1999, *Psychological Science, 10,* p. 414.

contrast, the second object is the most important in the delayed launching event. Its self-initiated movement makes it the agent that collides with the house causing the dog's head to pop up.

If infants were processing the entire event sequence as a unified causal event, they should have dishabituated more when the first object was replaced if it was involved in a direct launching, but should have dishabituated more when the second object was replaced if it was involved in a delayed launching.

That is exactly the pattern of results obtained with 15-month-old infants. Ten-month-olds, however, responded most to a change in the first object regardless of its relationship (direct launching versus delayed launching) with the second object. The 10-month-olds were apparently overloaded by this complex event sequence involving numerous objects and actions. It is interesting to note though that they did not respond randomly to the change in first and second object. They responded systematically to a change in the first object regardless of whether it was involved in a direct or delayed launching. That type of responding suggests that these 10-month-old infants had indeed regressed to a simpler way of processing (e.g., attending only to the

first object that moved), as would be predicted by an overload explanation.

In a final set of causal chain studies, Cohen, Cashon, and Rundell (2004) presented 15- and 18-month-old infants with the same causal chain events, but in the context of a category task. During habituation, each infant saw two sequences, one that began with a direct launching and one that began with a delayed launching. For both sequences, the same toy was used as the causal agent of the final outcome. During habituation, infants were presented with a direct event in which Toy A launches Toy B, which immediately moves to the dog house making the dog appear. These same infants were also presented with a delay event in which Toy B hits Toy A, and after a 2-second pause, Toy A then moves to the dog house to make the dog appear. Thus, in both of these events, Toy A can be considered the causal agent of the dog's appearance. In the test, the roles of the two toys were switched, such that Toy B rather than Toy A was now the agent for the first time. The 18-month-olds, but not the 15-month-olds, noticed the switch in agent, as indexed by longer looking at the test event with the switched agent. To do so, they had to coordinate information about the order of movement of the toys along with the type of event in which the toys were involved (direct versus delayed launching). The 15-month-olds apparently could not respond to these complex events in terms of agency. A subsequent control study indicated that they were sensitive to the order of movement of the toys and to the type of event in which the toys appeared, but could not correlate these two types of information to respond in terms of agency.

## Complex Event Sequences

The events described so far have progressed from simple launching episodes in which two squares or circles collide with one another, to the same type of event with more realistic toys, and then to causal chains that involve two separate collisions. More complex causal events are possible, as are other types of event sequences or scenarios in which multiple events occur sequentially. Our constructive information-processing framework, like most other approaches, predicts that infants should be able to process two sequential events before they can process three or four such events. It also predicts that pairs of events that have some logical or necessary tie between them should have greater potential of being grouped together into a single higher-order unit than two arbitrarily grouped, independent events.

Some violation-of-expectation studies qualify as showing infants multiple event sequences. Earlier, we noted one of the more spectacular by Wynn (1992), who claimed that 5-month-old infants can add and subtract. In her addition condition, infants first saw one toy object on a stage; next a screen came up to occlude the object and a hand carrying a second identical object moved behind the screen and reappeared without the object; finally the screen was lowered to reveal either two objects on the stage (a possible event) or only one object on the stage (an impossible event). The infants looked longer at one object, the impossible event. A similar procedure was used in the subtraction condition except that first the infants initially saw two objects on the stage; then the hand went behind the screen and removed one object; and finally, the screen was lowered to reveal one or two objects. In this condition the infants looked longer at two objects, once again the impossible event.

For 5-month-old infants to have actually added and subtracted in these situations, they had to know more than that $1 + 1 = 2$ and $2 - 1 = 1$. They also had to process and integrate information from three separate events—the initial opening of a curtain to reveal either one or two

objects on a stage; the raising of an occluder along with the action of the hand first going behind it either with or without an object, and then reappearing either without or with an object; and finally the lowering of the occluder again to reveal one or two objects. The infants would not only have to integrate these three separate events but would also have to make an inference about what action was taking place behind the occluder.

From our information-processing point of view, this should be an impossibly complex task for 5-month-old infants. As noted in our discussion of the object concept, evidence suggests a simpler explanation of the infants' performance (Cohen, 2002; Cohen & Marks, 2002). An analysis of the actual sequence of events shown to infants indicated that in the addition task, each infant actually saw one item on the stage nine times and two items only three times. Similarly in the subtraction event, each infant saw two items nine times and one item three times. If the infants had a preference for familiarity, which is likely given their relatively young age and the complexity of the events, they should look longer at what appears to be impossible events, that is one item in the addition task and two items in the subtraction task.

As already mentioned, in an experiment designed to test this familiarity hypothesis, Cohen and Marks (2002) replicated the Wynn procedure but without the hand coming in to add or subtract anything. Infants looked longer when the more familiar number of items was on the stage. That is, they looked longer at what would have been an impossible event, but since the hand did not add or subtract any items, no addition or subtraction of items occurred. Thus, one can interpret the behavior of the 5-month-olds in the Wynn (1992) task as a consequence of repetitions of a single event along with a familiarity preference, not a consequence of the integration of three events plus knowledge of addition and subtraction.

Paradigms that use either habituation or violation-of-expectation procedures, and measure only looking-times to understand how infants process complex event sequences, have several inherent limitations in addition to those mentioned in our discussion of methodological issues. One is that a sequence of events often lasts more than a minute and infants must look continuously the entire time to obtain the necessary information, which is difficult, if not impossible for many of them to do. A second is that looking-time paradigms tap only recognition memory, but if infants have to reconstruct events that are not currently being experienced, a measure of recall memory may be more appropriate. A third is that visual-looking paradigms tap only all-or-none discriminations, whereas paradigms that require more active motor behavior by infants tap their understanding of more graded cognitive and functional information. Mandler (2003) makes a similar point in her distinction between infants' acquisition of perceptual categories versus cognitive concepts.

For these and other reasons related to explicit versus implicit memory (Bauer, Burch, & Kleinknecht, 2002; Meltzoff, 1990, 1995), investigators have turned to a different paradigm, elicited-imitation (Bauer & Mandler, 1992), to study how infants process and remember multiple event sequences.

In a typical experiment, infants see a model perform a sequence of two or three events and the infants' imitation of those events is assessed both immediately and after a delay that might range from a week to several months (Bauer, Chapter 9, this *Handbook,* this volume; Bauer, Hertsgaard, & Wewerka, 1995). In some sequences, the events are considered to be enabling (contingent on one another). The events must necessarily occur in a specific order, such as in the following sequence involved in making a gong: (a) putting a stick horizontally on a frame, (b) hanging a metal plate on the stick, and (c) hitting the plate with a hammer. In other sequences, the order of events is arbitrary, such as in the following making-a-hat sequence: (a) putting a balloon on top of a cone, (b) placing a band around the cone, and (c) placing a sticker on the face of the cone. Investigators tend to measure both the number and order of infants' imitative responses. In general, the older the infants, the more likely they will imitate multiple events. They also tend to model enabling sequences at an earlier age than arbitrary ones. Recent studies on elicited imitation have provided valuable insights into both the development of infant long-term declarative memory and regions of the brain that are involved in such memory (Bauer, Chapter 9, this *Handbook,* this volume).

One of the more interesting findings is the increase with age in number of events remembered and modeled (Barr, Dowden, & Hayne, 1996). Six-month-old infants seem limited to one event. Approximately 50% of 9-month-old infants imitate more than one event (Carver & Bauer, 1999), and by 14 or 15 months, infants have little difficulty recalling temporally ordered sequences. These age differences are similar to those reported earlier for remembering single causal events versus causal chains.

The developmental progression in performance on these imitation tasks from processing one sequence to processing multiple sequences would be predicted by the constructive information-processing principles presented earlier. However, a stronger prediction would pertain to how infants at different ages organize the multiple events they experience. Very little research has been reported on infants' organization of event sequences. In one creative approach to the topic, Baldwin, Baird, Saylor, and Clark (2001) familiarized 10- to 11-month-old infants to a videotape of a woman performing more than one action. Infants might see a woman noticing a towel on the kitchen floor, reaching for and grasping it, and then placing it on a towel rack. Two types of tests were presented in which a 1.5 s pause was inserted in the action. In the "Interrupting" test, the pause was inserted during the middle of an action, whereas in the "Completing" test the pause was inserted between two actions. The infants looked longer at the "Interrupting" test suggesting that the infants had parsed the video movie into discrete actions. The authors also note, however, that it is unclear from this study at what level of description the infants are organizing the video. For example, they could be responding to separate independent events such as picking up the towel and placing a towel in the rack. Or they could be responding to events at a more global level, such as putting the towel away or cleaning up the kitchen. By manipulating the order of the specific events as well as the location of pauses, it should be possible to gain a better understanding of how such event sequences are processed by infants at different ages. We would predict that at an early age infants should be sensitive to the disruption of a specific event, but not necessarily to the event order. At a later age, infants should be sensitive to a disruption in the order of events, particularly when the events are enabling, or when the order suggests a unified goal or intension.

## INFANT CATEGORIZATION

Over the past 25 years, one of the most prolific areas of research in infant cognition has been infant categorization. The popularity of this area results in part from an understanding of categorization's fundamental importance for learning and development and in part from the evolution of research paradigms to examine categorization in infants. The importance of the ability to categorize is obvious. Imagine if infants, children, or even adults, for that matter, could not group objects or events into categories and make inferences about new objects or events based on their presumed membership in those categories. Given that no two experiences are identical, we could not learn from past experience or generalize what we have learned to new experiences. Oakes and Madole (2003) make the case for infant categorization a bit more conservatively: "the ability to categorize may be especially important in infancy, when an enormous amount of new information is encountered every day. By forming groups of similar objects, infants can effectively reduce the amount of information they must process, learn and remember" (p. 132).

## Categorization Paradigms

Realizing the necessity of early categorization is not the same as understanding its origins in infancy. Several paradigms have been used to examine infant categorization. These include (a) a version of habituation and the switch design (Younger, 2003; Younger & Cohen, 1986); (b) an object-examination task that is similar to the habituation one except that infants get to inspect real three-dimensional toys (Oakes et al., 1991); (c) a sequential touching task, in which toys from two categories are placed on a table and infants' touching of the toys is examined to see if the sequence of touches occurs in a systematic order (Rakison & Butterworth, 1998a, 1998b); and (d) deferred imitation, in which infants see a model do something with one toy category member (such as helping it to drink from a cup) and then imitation of the model's action is assessed with either a new member from the same category or a member from a different category (Mandler & McDonough, 1996, 1998). These paradigms vary in the ages for which they are appropriate and in how active the infants must be to demonstrate categorization. According to some theorists, the paradigms also differ in whether they are assumed to apply to perceptual categorization, to more abstract concept formation, or to both perceptual categorization and concept formation (Mandler, 2000a, 2003). But all the paradigms are based on the minimal assumption that the demonstration of infant categorization requires infants to treat discriminably different stimuli in an equivalent manner (Cohen & Younger, 1983; Quinn, 2003).

As with previous portions of this chapter, we treat the current section on infant categorization as an extension and update of the material presented by Haith and Benson (1998). We do not reproduce their excellent review of the infant categorization literature and recommend it to interested readers. Although we mention some of the most relevant older literature, we concentrate on more recent empirical work on infant categorization and its theoretical implications.

## Feature Correlations and Categorization

An important distinction is the one between *demonstration* studies that simply describe categories to which an infant attends and *process* studies that attempt to explain the mechanism by which infants acquire categories (Oakes & Madole, 2003; Younger & Cohen, 1985). Most models of infant categorization assume that each category exemplar can be described in terms of a set of features. These features may be perceptual (e.g., form, color, texture), functional (e.g., what they can do or be used for), and also linguistic (e.g., what labels are associated with them) (Oakes & Madole, 2003). The feature values of a particular exemplar help determine whether it is a member of a category as well as any inferences that can be drawn from its category membership. An important aspect of category items is the correlational structure of their feature values, that is, whether groups of feature values tend to co-occur. Considerable research by Younger (Younger & Cohen, 1983, 1985, 1986; Younger & Fearing, 1999) has also shown that whether an infant groups all items into a single category or segregates items into two separate categories depends on the infant's age, the distinctiveness of the feature values, and most importantly the pattern of correlation among features.

The importance of correlational structure for infant categorization was first reported by Younger and Cohen (1983, 1986). In one study, they habituated 4-, 7-, and 10-month-olds to a series of line drawings of imaginary animals. The animals differed from one another in feature values (e.g., the type of body, tail, and legs) but for any one animal a subset of the values were correlated with one another. So, for example the type of feet might have been free to vary but a bear body always co-occurred with a horse's tail, and a giraffe body always co-occurred with a rabbit's tail. In the test, infants were given a familiar habituation animal, a new animal that violated the correlation, but was constructed from familiar parts (e.g., a bear body with a rabbit tail) and a totally novel animal.

Within the infant literature at least, this was the first use of the switch design (see Gentner, 1978, for an earlier use of the design with children). If infants were sensitive to the correlation among feature values, the uncorrelated test animal should be treated as novel. If infants were not sensitive to the correlation, all the feature values would be independent, and since they were equally familiar, the uncorrelated test animal should be treated like one of the familiar animals seen during habituation.

Younger and Cohen (1986) reported a developmental progression. At 4 months of age, infants responded only in terms of independent features. At 10 months, they responded to a violation of the correlation. The performance of 7-month-olds was particularly interesting. When all the features were correlated, the 7-month-olds had no trouble detecting that correlation. However, when only two of the three features were correlated, they had great difficulty with the task and did not even habituate. When they were given more habituation trials and essentially forced to habituate, the 7-month-olds dropped to the level of 4-month-olds and responded only to independent features.

Even though these correlation studies were conducted a number of years ago, they are relevant to at least three different contemporary issues. First, they provide early evidence for the constructivist information-processing principles we have presented throughout this chapter. The 4-month-old infants were processing only the lower-level independent parts of the animals, but by 10 months, they were at a more advanced level and processing the relation among the parts (the correlation among features). Seven-month-olds could process this relation when all features were correlated. When only a subset of features was correlated, however, the categorical nature of the task evidently overloaded them and they regressed to the level of the 4-month-olds.

Second, the importance of correlational information goes well beyond the integration of body parts in line drawings of animals. The developmental progression from first processing independent lower-order units to later relating those units to some higher-order whole has been observed repeatedly in infants, often using some version of the switch design. We have found it with respect to 3- to 7-month-olds' face perception (Cashon & Cohen, 2003) and 6- to 18-month-olds' understanding of

causal events (Cohen, 2004a). It has also been found in infants learning to relate an object's form to its function (Madole & Cohen, 1995; Madole et al., 1993) and their learning to associate verbal labels with objects (Werker, Cohen, Lloyd, Casasola, & Stager, 1998). The switch design has even been used to demonstrate possible precursors to early racial (Levy, 2003) and gender (Levy & Haaf, 1994) stereotyping.

Third, processing correlational information plays a prominent role in several contemporary accounts of developmental change in infant categorization. Younger (2003), for example, assumes that the age at which infants can process feature correlations depends on the nature of the features. Correlations between a subset of simple features such as color and form can be noticed as early as 3 months of age (Bhatt & Rovee-Collier, 1994; Bhatt & Rovee-Collier, 1996), but infants must be 7 to 10 months of age to notice the correlation between two features in a more complex animal categorization task (Younger & Cohen, 1986). Younger (2003) also assumes sensitivity to correlational information allows 10-month-old infants to process more than one category at a time and to move from a form of implicit categorization to a form of explicit categorization.

Oakes and Madole (2003) summarize early category development in terms of three principles related to infants' increasing access to information:

1. The pool of available features increases due to increases in motor, information processing, and linguistic ability.
2. The ability to take advantage of information in different contexts widens.
3. An increase in background knowledge constrains the pool of relevant features.

So not all correlations remain equal. Those that we learn are appropriate, such as the correlation between an object and its function, are maintained. But those that are arbitrary or inappropriate, such as the correlation between an object and some other object's function, come to be ignored (Madole & Cohen, 1995). Each of these principles incorporates a change in use of correlational information with development.

Correlations also play a central role in Rakison's (2003) account of infant category acquisition. He argues that, to understand early category and concept development, one should focus on processes related to informa-

changes, are essential aspects of the research on infants' processing of faces. Moreover, many developmental changes that occur in infant face processing fit in nicely with the domain-general, information-processing principles to which we have frequently referred.

A better understanding of the early development of face processing also may play an important role in resolving issues, both in the adult and infant literature, that have been debated for decades. For example, by studying the development of face processing in infants, particularly newborns, researchers can shed light on whether we come into the world with a specialized innate module in the cortex for processing faces or whether areas in the cortex become specialized to process faces through experience (Kanwisher, 2000; Tarr & Gauthier, 2000). Furthermore, research with newborns might also help researchers resolve the issue of whether infants come into the world with a preference to attend to faces and facelike stimuli over other stimuli and, if so, why this is the case (de Haan, Humphreys, & Johnson, 2002; Turati, 2004).

We discuss here some of the current research that may provide answers to these questions. First, we examine recent research on newborns' apparent preference for faces (or facelike stimuli) and how that preference might enlighten our understanding of the innate module assumption. Second, we consider how infants' processing of faces changes over age, in particular becoming more specialized to process upright, human faces. Third, we discuss how these changes are related to featural versus holistic processing of upright and inverted faces as well as to infants' discrimination of same- and different-species' faces. We recognize that we are covering only a subset of the issues and research associated with early face perception (for additional information on this topic, see Kellman and Arterberry, Chapter 3, this *Handbook,* this volume).

## Newborns' Preferences for Faces

Several studies have indicated that newborns orient farther with their eyes, and sometimes with their heads, to moving schematic drawings of faces than to nonface patterns (Goren, Sarty, & Wu, 1975; Johnson, Dziurawiec, Ellis, & Morton, 1991; Maurer & Young, 1983). Johnson et al. (1991) also reported, however, that this preference disappears around 1 month of age, only to reappear around 2 months of age. Based on these findings, Johnson and Morton (Johnson & Morton, 1991; Morton &

Johnson, 1991) put forth a highly cited account of newborns' apparent preference for faces, and the U-shaped developmental pattern that occurs over age, by positing two mechanisms to account for infants' face preference at birth and around 2 months of age. One mechanism, thought to be present at birth, is a *subcortical* device, referred to as CONSPEC. It provides crude information about the structure of faces and leads newborns to attend to faces. The second mechanism, believed to have its influence a month or two later, is a separate *cortical* mechanism, called CONLERN. It allows infants to learn about the individual identities of faces. According to this theory, the reason the preference for facelike stimuli disappears about 1 month of age is that at around this age CONSPEC has become inhibited and the second mechanism, CONLERN, has not yet become fully engaged. In response to one line of thinking in the adult literature suggesting that we are born with prespecified cortical circuitry intended to process faces, Johnson and de Haan (2001) have tried to make it clear that the CONLERN mechanism is not an innate module prespecified to process faces, but rather is a cortical system that develops out of experience with faces, an idea much in line with those posited by Elman et al. (1996).

More recent research in this area has focused on the nature of CONSPEC. A connectionist model by Bednar and Miikkulainen (2000), is designed to uncover possible origins of the structural information about faces used by CONSPEC. Bednar and Miikkulainan's model shows that, prenatally, the primary visual cortex can self-organize to attend to a three-dot pattern, which essentially looks like a face, by abstracting this pattern from the spontaneous firing of retinal waves thought to be produced during REM sleep. Thus, their model provides a possible mechanism by which innate structural information about faces and even visual preferences for faces might appear, without requiring any specific information in the genes other than a simple learning mechanism that builds on a three-dot pattern.

Whereas Bednar and Miikkulainan's (2000) model provides a possible explanation for how a newborn's system might develop a preference for a facelike configuration, it is unclear from much of the behavioral research whether infants actually are attracted to a three-dot pattern when they show this preference. Recent research suggests that newborns actually may not be attending to the entire region of the face that includes the two eyes and the mouth. Instead, infants may be attracted to a facial configuration because there is more information in the upper half than in the bottom half of the stimulus. By comparing infants' looking times to nonface patterns that varied in the number and arrangement of elements in the top and bottom halves of the stimuli, Simion, Valenza, Cassia, Turati, and Umilta (2002) found that newborns preferred those items with more complexity in the top half of a rectangular contour. Turati, Simion, Milani, and Umilta (2004) found this to be true when the elements appeared inside a facelike contour. The authors referred to this as *up-down symmetry*. These findings suggest that newborns' immature sensory capabilities may lead them to prefer stimuli with up-down symmetry and thus, may play a role in their apparent preference for facelike stimuli (for a discussion, see also Simion, Cassia, Turati, & Valenza, 2001; Turati, 2004).

To be fair, it should be mentioned that Johnson and colleagues do not regard these findings as contradictory to their original, two-mechanism theory. They maintain that newborns come into the world with subcortical information about the structure of faces, but they are flexible about exactly what that structural information might be. Furthermore, the more important point from their perspective is the following:

> Whatever the exact description of the basis of the newborn's orienting tendencies, none contradict our proposal that these reflect more primitive biases that could provide input to developing cortical areas rather than the existence of an innate cortical "face module." (de Haan, Humphreys, & Johnson, 2002, p. 204)

## Development of Face Processing

Building on this idea that infants' processing of faces develops and takes time to become adultlike, recent research suggests that as we get older, we develop a specialization for upright, human faces. A recent study published in *Science* traces some of the developmental changes in infants' processing of same versus other species' faces. Using a visual discrimination task, Pascalis, de Haan, and Nelson (2002) found that whereas 6-month-olds showed evidence of discriminating between two human faces or two faces of Macaque monkeys, 9-month-olds and adults were found to discriminate only between the two human faces. This apparent deterioration in performance over age suggests that during the 1st year of life, infants become tuned to process faces of their own species and to disregard differences among other species. With respect to both the deterioration and

the ages involved, this apparent loss of discrimination ability is reminiscent of a similar loss in early speech perception of the ability to discriminate nonnative phonetic contrasts (Werker & Tees, 1984).

## A Constructivist Information-Processing Account of Infant Face Processing

It is commonly believed that adults process faces in a holistic or configural manner when the face is in an upright orientation, but featurally when the face is in an inverted position (e.g., Farah, Tanaka, & Drain, 1995). Recent results indicate that by 7 months of age, infants show a similar pattern (Cohen & Cashon, 2001a); still other reports show that prior to this age, there is no difference in mode of processing between upright and inverted faces (Cashon & Cohen, 2003, 2004).

To assess the question of developmental changes in infants' featural versus holistic processing of faces, Cashon and Cohen used a version of the switch habituation design described earlier. Infants were habituated to two female faces and after meeting the habituation criterion, they were tested on a familiar test face (one of the two habituation faces), a novel test face (one they had only seen once during the pretest), and a switch test face (composed of the internal features—the eyes, nose, and mouth—from one of the habituation faces and the external features—the remaining features, such as the eyebrows, forehead, chin, ears, hair—from the other habituation face). Because all the facial features of the switch test face were seen during habituation, it was assumed that these elements were familiar to the infants. Thus, it was reasoned that if infants looked longer to the switch than to the familiar test face, it would be because it presented a new *relationship* between the internal and external parts of the faces. (Many researchers use different operational definitions of holistic and configural processing, and Cashon and Cohen are no exception. As can be seen from the description of their task, their definition of holistic processing is based on infants' sensitivity to the relationship between the internal and external features of a face.)

In testing infants between 3 and 10 months of age, Cashon and Cohen found many changes in processing taking place during these months (Cashon & Cohen, 2003, 2004). As illustrated in Figure 5.6, the oldest two groups, the 7- and 10-month-olds, behaved in a manner consistent with adult performance; that is, they processed upright faces holistically and inverted faces featurally. Results

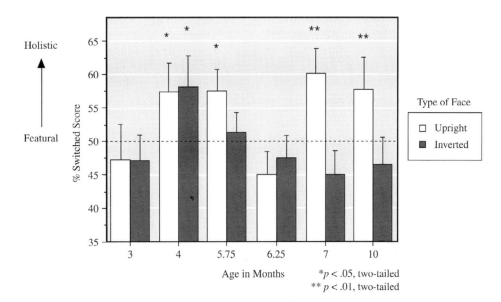

Holistic

Featural

**Figure 5.6** Data showing the developmental changes in infants' featural versus holistic processing of upright (white bar) and inverted (grey bar) faces between 3 and 10 months of age. The "% switched score" is equal to infants' looking time to the switched test face divided by the total looking to the switched plus familiar test faces. The authors inferred that if the % switched score was significantly higher than 50%, infants were engaging in holistic processing. Adapted from "The Construction, Deconstruction, and Reconstruction of Infant Face Perception" (p. 61), by C. H. Cashon and L. B. Cohen, in *The Development of Face Processing in Infancy and Early Childhood.* A. Slater and O. Pascalis (Eds.), 2003, New York: NOVA Science. Reprinted with permission.

with younger infants indicated that this differential processing of upright and inverted faces does not develop until 7 months of age. Three-month-olds were found to process both upright and inverted faces featurally. At 4 months, a developmental shift to holistic processing was found for both upright and inverted faces. Six-month-olds also showed no difference between upright and inverted faces, but surprisingly, they returned to processing the faces featurally. A possible reason that infants show this peculiar, curvilinear developmental pattern is discussed shortly. For now, however, the message is that although there is evidence that at some point we become specialized to upright human faces, these findings provide further support for the notion that such specialization develops and most likely results from extensive and meaningful experience with faces (see also Le Grand, Modloch, Maurer, & Henry, 2001; Nelson, 2001; Nelson & Monk, 2001).

The behavioral findings just mentioned fit nicely with ERP results (de Haan, Pascalis, & Johnson, 2002) demonstrating that the neural correlates of infants' sensitivity to the orientation of faces changes between 6 months of age and adulthood. The de Haan, Pascalis, et al. results also indicate that around 6 months of age,

infants are not as specialized in their processing of faces as adults. Together, the results of the ERP study and our behavioral research suggest that what differs during the first half of the 1st year of life compared with the second half is not that infants do not attend to the orientation of faces prior to 7 months of age, but rather that they are not completely attuned to the special status of upright faces until that time.

Returning to why infants might show the curvilinear developmental pattern found between 3 and 7 to 10 months of age, the answer can be found in the constructivist information-processing approach. The change found between 3 and 4 months, from processing a face featurally to holistically, is consistent with the constructive development proposed by the information-processing principles presented earlier. Subsequent regression to processing a face featurally again around 6 months of age also fits with these principles, if it results from an information overload. As discussed, results from de Haan, Pascalis, et al. (2002) indicate that infants are sensitive to facial orientation at this age and that upright faces have some sort of special status for adults. One possibility is that 6 months is about the age at which infants become sensitive to the meaningfulness of upright faces. If so, the social meaning of the face may overload the system temporarily while infants reorganize their understanding of faces. The subsequent finding—that by 7 months of age, infants, for the first time, engage in different modes of processing for upright and inverted faces—supports this idea that a type of reorganization has occurred.

## THE ANIMATE-INANIMATE DISTINCTION

We have proposed that, in at least a few respects, infants consider faces to be special. Infants have an early bias to attend to facelike stimuli over other stimuli; they develop a specialized response to human upright faces during the 1st year of life; and the developmental changes that occur prior to this specialization transpire much earlier with faces than with other complex stimuli. A question that arises from these findings is whether infants extend this special status just to faces or to all animate entities. Another way of asking the question is, do infants make an animate-inanimate distinction?

Research on the animate-inanimate distinction, for the most part, has focused on preschoolers (Gelman, Spelke, & Meck, 1983) and to some extent toddlers (Poulin-Dubois & Forbes, 2002). Although relatively fewer studies involve infants (e.g., Woodward, 1998), researchers have shown an interest in this area for several reasons. First, investigations of infant categorization have begun to emphasize more complex, deeper category structure, moving beyond perceptually based category research (Rakison, 2003). Second, understanding the distinction between animates and inanimates may influence infants' language acquisition. According to Slobin (1981), the prototypical agent is animate and the patient is inanimate. Thus, it could be argued that the animate-inanimate distinction might be helpful in learning semantic categories (Childers & Echols, 2004). Third, one of the differences between animate and inanimate beings is that animate entities act according to goals, desires, and intentions (Premack, 1990). Thus, infants' distinction between animates and inanimates may shed light on precursors to a later understanding of intentionality and theory of mind (Poulin-Dubois, Lepage, & Ferland, 1996; Woodward, 1998).

Rakison and Poulin-Dubois (2001) provide a summary of research on infants' animate-inanimate distinction. Here, we emphasize the most recent research in the area and discuss how these findings relate to our con-

structivist information-processing approach. A primary issue relates to the nature of the distinction between an animate entity and inanimate entity. Although several proposals have been made about what makes animates and inanimates distinct (Rakison & Poulin-Dubois, 2001), most include at least one aspect that centers on different types of motion. Mandler (1992, 2000a) has argued that during the 1st year of life infants have "image schemas" for various object movements, including self-motion versus caused motion, irregular trajectories versus straight trajectories, and movement caused at a distance versus movement caused by direct physical contact. According to Mandler, some of these schemas combine to produce a concept of animacy.

There is evidence that infants are sensitive to these different types of motion. Seminal work by Bertenthal (1993) showed that infants in the first 6 months of life are sensitive to how humans move; they discriminate upright versus inverted point-light displays of a human walking as well as dots depicting a human walking versus randomly varying dots. Furthermore, Bertenthal reported a developmental change in this respect between 3 and 5 months of age. The detection of differences in point-light displays becomes orientation specific by 5 months. Bertenthal interprets this difference as indicating that the older infants are responding at a higher level, based on meaning, rather than just perceptual structure. We agree, and would argue that meaning emerges from infants' developing sensitivity to the relation between the overall configuration of moving dots and their experience with animate objects in the world. Rakison and Poulin-Dubois (2001) note that although these findings show that infants can detect a difference between normal human movement and random movement, it remains to be seen whether this distinction extends to the entire class of animate versus inanimate entities or only to human versus nonhuman movement.

More recent evidence with point-light displays suggests that young infants make a distinction between animate and inanimate entities that goes beyond humans as the subject matter. Using a categorization-habituation task, Arterberry and Bornstein (2001) reported that 3-month-olds categorized moving point-light displays of animals separately from those of vehicles, and vice versa. This finding suggests that young infants' sensitivity to the kinds of movements objects make may extend beyond human versus nonhuman movement. They also reported that infants categorized animals and vehicles separately using static picture stimuli. Thus, it is not entirely clear that infants in Arterberry and Bornstein's studies categorized animals and vehicles based on movement alone, given that the same results were found with static pictures. It is also not known whether the results of this set of studies, or Bertenthal's for that matter, extend to the broader notion of animate versus inanimate.

The studies by Bertenthal (1993) and by Arterberry and Bornstein (2001) indicate that infants can associate a type of movement with a particular object by 5 to 6 months of age. We would predict that infants' next step should be learning the relation between two moving objects in an event. As discussed with respect to causal perception, it is not until the second half of the 1st year of life that infants become sensitive to the relation between two objects in a causal event. In addition to those studies discussed, in which inanimate objects were involved in the events, Schlottmann and Surian (1999) reported that infants around 9 months of age are sensitive to causality when animate objects are involved. Their study was based on Leslie and Keeble's (1987) causal reversal paradigm but involved squares that traveled in an animate manner like a caterpillar. They were specifically interested in the notion of causality-at-a-distance whereby an object moves in response to another object approaching it, before they actually touch. Schlottmann and Surian reported that in the case of such an event, 9-month-old infants perceived the movement of the second object to be an intentional response caused by the approaching first object, even though the two objects never touched. To the authors, this finding suggested that by 9 months of age infants associate animate objects with certain nonphysical causation. What is unclear from their report is on what basis the infants perceived the objects to be animate. It is possible that the infants attended primarily to the irregular, caterpillar-like motion, or to the fact that the objects' initiation of movement was self-propelled, or perhaps to both cues. By testing infants in other conditions that involve manipulations of the type of object (animate versus inanimate), the object's position, and its starting motion, the cues to which infants attend can be determined. In any case, we predict that whereas associating animacy with a particular object might be possible at 6 months of age, detecting the relation between two animate objects may not happen until later in the 1st year, as reported by Schlottmann and Surian.

A study by Rakison and Poulin-Dubois (2002) explored in more detail how infants come to associate certain kinds of movement with particular objects. Using the switch design to test infants' associations between an object's motion and its parts versus the whole object, Rakison and Poulin-Dubois found developmental changes across three age groups, 10-, 14-, and 18-month-olds. The 10-month-olds attended to the object characteristics, that is, to the parts of each object as well as to each object as a whole, but not to the movement of the objects. The 14-month-olds attended to the association between the part of an object and the object's movement, while the 18-month-olds also attended to the association between the whole object and its movement. These developmental differences are consistent with our version of an information-processing perspective in that they involve a parts-to-whole progression as well as an integration of more and more complex information.

## SUMMARY AND CONCLUSIONS

Research on infant cognition is going on at an active, even accelerating pace. In some respects, this activity represents a continuation of research on major topics such as object permanence and causality that have been examined since Piaget's (1954) early work and have been summarized in earlier *Handbook* chapters. In other respects, this activity represents a return to certain central Piagetian issues notably developmental change and constructive processes of development, which were deemphasized by researchers in the 1980s and 1990s in their search for core knowledge and innate modules. In yet other respects, recent activity indicates a breakthrough into exciting new approaches, such as connectionist modeling, that have the potential for specifying actual mechanisms of early learning and development.

Over the past decade, we also have seen changes in the significance of certain topics, such as perception of object unity and individuation, processing of human faces, and understanding of causality, animacy, and intentionality. These topics, which may initially have been thought of as aspects of traditional areas such as object permanence, have now become relatively independent areas worthy of research and theory in their own right.

We have also seen the reemergence of theorizing at a broader, more domain-general level, rather than at a local, domain-specific level. This trend certainly is apparent in attempts to explain infant categorization and its development, whether one advocates a single evolving system that progresses from processing mainly perceptual information to processing functional and linguistic information as well (Oakes & Madole, 2003; Rakison, 2003), or a dual system that includes separate perceptual and conceptual components (Mandler, 2003).

In this chapter, we have argued that the dividing line between infant perception and infant cognition is arbitrary, and attempting to draw a sharp line is generally nonproductive when seeking to explain early cognitive development. Instead, we have proposed a set of information-processing principles that are domain general and are relevant across multiple areas of infant perception and cognition (Cohen, 1988). We have shown how our approach makes specific predictions about constructive developmental progressions as well as fallbacks to simpler ways of processing when the system becomes overloaded. In some respects, it represents a return to Piagetian principles, although it does not advocate the incorporation of motor actions to the same extent Piaget did. This approach is also concrete enough to lead to a formal connectionist model that so far has made accurate predictions regarding infants' developing understanding of simple causal events and has the potential to predict many other aspects of cognitive development (Cohen et al., 2002).

Whether one endorses our approach or some other one, the area of infant cognition is evolving on both empirical and theoretical grounds. Traditionally independent areas are merging with one another to generate new answers to difficult questions. We have emphasized the integration of cognitive and computational approaches in the development of new connectionist models. Another important merger that we only touched on is the combination of cognitive and neuroscience approaches. Bauer's chapter on infant memory (Chapter 9, this *Handbook*, this volume) provides an example of how fruitful such a merger can be.

Finally, we have been unable to include all the significant topics currently being investigated in the field of infant perception and cognition. It is not that we consider these areas to be unimportant. We simply did not have the space to include all of them. Some of these topics, such as the relation between infant perception and action or infant deferred memory and imitation, are covered in other chapters.

Nevertheless, the present chapter reflects the breadth and depth of current research on infant cognitive development. The field is changing. It no longer can be studied in isolation, but must become part of an interdisciplinary approach that includes both cognitive science and neuroscience. Developmental psychology as a whole is evolv-

ing, and recent research on infant cognition represents an important part of that evolution.

## REFERENCES

Anisfeld, M., Turkewitz, G., Rose, S. A., Rosenberg, F. R., Sheiber, F. J., Couturier-Fagan, D. A., et al. (2001). No compelling evidence that newborns imitate oral gestures. *Infancy, 2,* 111–123.

Arterberry, M. E., & Bornstein, M. H. (2001). Three-month-old infants' categorization of animals and vehicles based on static and dynamic attributes. *Journal of Experimental Child Psychology, 80,* 333–346.

Baillargeon, R. (1986). Representing the existence and the location of hidden objects: Object permanence in 6- and 8-month-old infants. *Cognition, 23,* 21–41.

Baillargeon, R. (1987). Object permanence in $3\frac{1}{2}$- to $4\frac{1}{2}$-month-old infants. *Developmental Psychology, 23,* 655–664.

Baillargeon, R. (1994). How do infants learn about the physical world. *Current Directions in Psychological Science, 3,* 133–140.

Baillargeon, R. (2000). Reply to Bogartz, Shinskey, and Schilling; Schilling; and Cashon and Cohen. *Infancy, 1,* 447–463.

Baillargeon, R., & Graber, M. (1987). Where's the rabbit? $5\frac{1}{2}$-month-old infants' representation of the height of a hidden object. *Cognitive Development, 2,* 375–392.

Baillargeon, R., Graber, M., DeVos, J., & Black, J. (1990). Why do young infants fail to search for hidden objects? *Cognition, 36,* 255–284.

Baillargeon, R., Spelke, E. S., & Wasserman, S. (1985). Object permanence in 5-month-old infants. *Cognition, 20,* 191–208.

Baldwin, D. A., Baird, J. A., Saylor, M. M., & Clark, M. (2001). Infants parse dynamic action. *Child Development, 72,* 708–717.

Ball, W. A. (1973). *The perception of causality in the infant* (Rep. No. 37). Ann Arbor, MI: University of Michigan, Department of Psychology, Developmental Program.

Barr, R., Dowden, A., & Hayne, H. (1996). Developmental changes in deferred imitation by 6- to 24-month-old infants. *Infant Behavior and Development, 19,* 159–170.

Barr, R., & Hayne, H. (2000). Age-related changes in imitation: Implications for memory development. In C. Rovee-Collier, L. P. Lipsitt, & H. Hayne (Eds.), *Progress in infancy research* (Vol. 1, pp. 21–68). Mahwah, NJ: Erlbaum.

Bauer, P. J., Burch, M. M., & Kleinknecht, E. E. (2002). Developments in early recall memory: Normative trends and individual differences. In R. V. Kail (Ed.), *Advances in Child Development and Behavior, 30,* 103–152.

Bauer, P. J., Hertsgaard, L. A., & Wewerka, S. S. (1995). Effects of experience and reminding on long-term recall in infancy: Remembering not to forget. *Journal of Experimental Child Psychology, 59*(2), 260–298.

Bauer, P. J., & Mandler, J. M. (1992). Putting the horse before the cart: The use of temporal order in recall of events by 1-year-old children. *Developmental Psychobiology, 28,* 441–452.

Bauer, P. J., Wiebe, S. A., Carver, L. J., Waters, J. M., & Nelson, C. A. (2003). Developments in long-term explicit memory late in the first year of life: Behavioral and electrophysiological indices. *Psychological Science, 14*(6), 629–635.

Bednar, J. A., & Miikkulainen, R. (2000). Self-organization of innate face preferences: Could genetics be expressed through learning. In *Proceedings of the Seventeenth National Conference on Artificial Intelligence* (pp. 117–122). Cambridge, MA: MIT Press.

Belanger, N. D., & Desrochers, S. (2001). Can 6-month-old infants process causality in different types of causal events? *British Journal of Developmental Psychology, 19,* 11–21.

Bertenthal, B. I. (1993). Infants' perception of biomechanical motions: Intrinsic image and knowledge based constraints. In C. Granrud (Ed.), *Visual perception and cognition in infancy* (pp. 175–214). Hillsdale, NJ: Erlbaum.

Berthier, N. E., Bertenthal, B. I., Seaks, J. D., Sylvia, M. R., Johnson, R. L., & Clifton, R. K. (2001). Using object knowledge in visual tracking and reaching. *Infancy, 2,* 257–284.

Bhatt, R. S., & Rovee-Collier, C. (1994). Perception and 24-hour retention of feature relations in infancy. *Developmental Psychology, 30,* 142–150.

Bhatt, R. S., & Rovee-Collier, C. (1996). Infants' forgetting of correlated attributes and object recognition. *Child Development, 67*(1), 172–187.

Bogartz, R. S., & Shinskey, J. L. (1998). On perception of a partially occluded object in 6-month-olds. *Cognitive Development, 13*(2), 141–163.

Bogartz, R. S., Shinskey, J. L., & Speaker, C. J. (1997). Interpreting infant looking: The event set x event set design. *Developmental Psychology, 33,* 408–422.

Bower, T. G. R. (1974). *Development in infancy.* San Francisco: Freeman.

Bower, T. G. R. (1977). *A primer of infant development.* San Francisco: Freeman.

Bower, T. G. R. (1979). *Human development.* San Francisco: Freeman.

Carey, S. (2000). The origins of concepts. *Journal of Cognition and Development, 1*(1), 37–41.

Carver, L. J., & Bauer, P. J. (1999). When the event is more than the sum of its parts: Nine-month-olds' long-term ordered recall. *Memory, 7,* 147–174.

Casasola, M., & Cohen, L. B. (2002). Infant categorization of containment, support and tight-fit spatial relationships. *Developmental Science, 5,* 247–264.

Casasola, M., Cohen, L. B., & Chiarello, E. (2003). Six-month-old infants' categorization of containment spatial relations. *Child Development, 74,* 679–693.

Cashon, C. H., & Cohen, L. B. (2003). The construction, deconstruction, and reconstruction of infant face perception. In A. Slater & O. Pascalis (Eds.), *The development of face processing in infancy and early childhood* (pp. 55–68). New York: NOVA Science.

Cashon, C. H., & Cohen, L. B. (2004). Beyond u-shaped development in infants' processing of faces [Special issue]. *Journal of Cognition and Development, 5,* 59–80.

Childers, J. B., & Echols, C. H. (2004). Two$^1/_2$-year-old children use animacy and syntax to learn a new noun. *Infancy, 5,* 109–125.

Clifton, R. K., Rochat, P., Litovsky, R. Y., & Perris, E. E. (1991). Object representation guides infants' reaching in the dark. *Journal of Experimental Psychology: Human Perception and Performance, 17,* 319–323.

Cohen, L. B. (1973). A two-process model of infant visual attention. *Merrill-Palmer Quarterly, 19,* 157–180.

Cohen, L. B. (1988). An information processing approach to infant cognitive development. In L. Weiskrantz (Ed.), *Thought without language* (pp. 211–228). Oxford, England: Oxford University Press.

Cohen, L. B. (1995, March). *How solid is infants' understanding of solidity.* Paper presented at the Society for Research in Child Development, Indianapolis, IN.

Cohen, L. B. (1998). An information-processing approach to infant perception and cognition. In F. Simion & G. Butterworth (Eds.), *The development of sensory, motor, and cognitive capacities in early infancy* (pp. 277–300). East Sussex, England: Psychology Press.

Cohen, L. B. (2002, April). *Can infants really add and subtract?* Paper presented at the International Conference on Infant Studies, Toronto, Ontario, Canada.

Cohen, L. B. (2004a, May). *The development of infants' perception of causal events.* Paper presented at the International conference on infant studies, Chicago, IL.

Cohen, L. B. (2004b). Modeling the development of infant categorization. *Infancy, 5,* 127–130.

Cohen, L. B., & Amsel, G. (1998). Precursors to infants' perception of the causality of a simple event. *Infant Behavior and Development, 21*(4), 713–731.

Cohen, L. B., Amsel, G., Redford, M. A., & Casasola, M. (1998). The development of infant causal perception. In A. Slater (Ed.), *Perceptual development: Visual, auditory and speech perception in infancy* (pp. 167–209). East Sussex, England: Psychology Press.

Cohen, L. B., & Cashon, C. H. (2001a). Do 7-month-old infants process independent features or facial configurations? *Infant and Child Development, 10,* 83–92.

Cohen, L. B., & Cashon, C. H. (2001b). Infant object segregation implies information integration. *Journal of Experimental Child Psychology, 78*(1), 75–83.

Cohen, L. B., Cashon, C. H., & Rundell, L. J. (2004, May). *Infants' developing knowledge of a causal agent.* Paper presented at the International conference on infant studies, Chicago, IL.

Cohen, L. B., & Chaput, H. H. (2002). Connectionist models of infant perceptual and cognitive development. *Developmental Science, 5,* 173.

Cohen, L. B., Chaput, H. H., & Cashon, C. H. (2002). A constructivist model of infant cognition. *Cognitive Development, 17*(3/4), 1323–1343.

Cohen, L. B., & Gelber, E. R. (1975). Infant visual memory. In L. B. Cohen & P. Salapatek (Eds.), *Infant perception: From sensation to cognition* (Vol. 1, pp. 347–403). New York: Academic Press.

Cohen, L. B., & Marks, K. S. (2002). How infants process addition and subtraction events. *Developmental Science, 5,* 186–201.

Cohen, L. B., & Oakes, L. M. (1993). How infants perceive simple causality. *Developmental Psychology, 29,* 421–433.

Cohen, L. B., Rundell, L. J., Spellman, B. A., & Cashon, C. H. (1999). Infants' perception of causal chains. *Psychological Science, 10,* 412–418.

Cohen, L. B., & Younger, B. A. (1983). Perceptual categorization in the infant. In E. Scholnick (Ed.), *New trends in conceptual representation* (pp. 197–220). Hillsdale, NJ: Erlbaum.

de Haan, M., Humphreys, K., & Johnson, M. H. (2002). Developing a brain specialized for face perception: A converging methods approach. *Developmental Psychobiology, 40,* 200–212.

de Haan, M., Pascalis, O., & Johnson, M. H. (2002). Specialization of neural mechanisms underlying face recognition in human infants. *Journal of Cognitive Neuroscience, 14,* 199–209.

Desrochers, S. (1999). The infant processing of causal and noncausal events at 3$^1/_2$ months of age. *Journal of Genetic Psychology, 160*(3), 294–302.

Diamond, A. (1981, April). *Retrieval of an object from an open box: The development of visual-tactile control of reaching in the first year of life.* Paper presented at the Society for Research in Child Development, Boston, MA.

Diamond, A. (1991). Neuropsychological insights into the meaning of object concept development. In S. Carey & R. Gelman (Eds.), *The epigenesis of mind* (pp. 67–110). Hillsdale, NJ: Erlbaum.

Eizenman, D. R., & Bertenthal, B. I. (1998). Infants' perception of object unity in translating and rotating displays. *Developmental Psychology, 34*(3), 426–434.

Elman, J., Bates, E., Johnson, M. H., Karmiloff-Smith, A., Parisi, D., & Plunkett, K. (1996). *Rethinking innateness: A connectionist perspective on development.* Cambridge, MA: MIT Press.

Fantz, R. L. (1964). Visual experience in infants: Decreased attention familar patterns relative to novel ones. *Science, 146,* 668–670.

Farah, M. J., Tanaka, J. W., & Drain, H. M. (1995). What causes the face inversion effect? *Journal of Experimental Psychology: Human Perception and Performance, 21,* 628–634.

Fischer, K. W., & Bidell, T. T. (1991). Constraining nativist inferences about cognitive capacities. In S. Carey & R. Gelman (Eds.), *The epigenesis of mind* (pp. 199–236). Hillsdale, NJ: Erlbaum.

Gelman, R., Spelke, E. S., & Meck, E. (1983). What preschoolers know about animate and inanimate objects. In D. Rogers & J. A. Sloboda (Eds.), *The acquisition of symbolic skills* (pp. 297–326). New York: Plenum Press.

Gentner, D. (1978). What looks like a jiggy but acts like a zimbo: A study of early word meaning using artificial objects. *Papers and Reports on Language Development, 15,* 1–6.

Gibson, E. J. (2000). Commentary on perceptual and conceptual processes in infancy. *Journal of Cognition and Development, 1*(1), 43–48.

Gopnik, A., & Nazzi, T. (2003). Words, kinds, and causal powers: A theory perspective on early naming and categorization. In D. H. Rakison & L. M. Oakes (Eds.), *Early category and concept development* (pp. 303–329). New York: Oxford University Press.

Goren, C. C., Sarty, M., & Wu, P. Y. K. (1975). Visual following and pattern discrimination of face-like stimuli by newborn infants. *Pediatrics, 56,* 544–549.

Gureckis, T. M., & Love, B. C. (2004). Common mechanisms in infant and adult category learning. *Infancy, 5,* 173–198.

Haith, M. M. (1998). Who put the cog in infant cognition? Is rich interpretation too costly? *Infant Behavior and Development, 21*(2), 167–179.

Haith, M. M., & Benson, J. B. (1998). Infant cognition. In W. Damon (Editor-in-Chief) & D. Kuhn & R. S. Siegler (Vol. Eds.), *Handbook of child psychology: Vol. 2. Cognition, perception, and language* (5th ed., pp. 199–254). New York: Wiley.

Harris, P. L. (1983). Infant cognition. In M. M. Haith & J. J. Campos (Eds.), *Handbook of child psychology: Vol. 2. Infancy and developmental psychobiology* (4th ed., pp. 689–782). New York: Wiley.

Harris, P. L. (1987). The development of search. In P. Salapatek & L. B. Cohen (Eds.), *Handbook of infant perception: Vol. 2. From perception to cognition* (pp. 155–207). Orlando, FL: Academic Press.

Hood, B., & Willatts, P. (1986). Reaching in the dark to see an object's remembered position: Evidence for object permanence in 5-month-old infants. *British Journal of Developmental Psychology, 4,* 57–65.

Horowitz, F. D. (1995). The challenge facing infant research in the next decade. In G. J. Suci & S. S. Robertson (Eds.), *Future directions in infant development research.* New York: Springer-Verlag.

Hume, D. (1993). *An enquiry concerning human understanding.* Indianapolis, IN: Hackett. (Original work published 1777)

Hunter, M. A., & Ames, E. W. (1988). A multifactor model of infant preferences for novel and familiar stimuli. In C. Rovee-Collier & L. P. Lipsitt (Eds.), *Advances in infancy research* (Vol. 5, pp. 69–95). Norwood, NJ: Ablex.

Hunter, S. K., & Richards, J. E. (2003). Peripheral stimulus localization by 5- to 14-week-old infants during phases of attention. *Infancy, 4,* 1–25.

Johnson, M. H., & de Haan, M. (2001). Developing cortical specialization for visual-cognitive function: The case of face recognition. In J. L. McClelland & R. S. Siegler (Eds.), *Mechanisms of cognitive development: Behavioral and neural perspectives* (pp. 253–270). Mahwah, NJ: Erlbaum.

Johnson, M. H., Dziurawiec, S., Ellis, H. D., & Morton, J. (1991). Newborns preferential tracking of facelike stimuli and its subsequent decline. *Cognition, 40,* 1–21.

Johnson, M. H., & Morton, J. (1991). *Biology and cognitive development: The case of face recognition.* Oxford, England: Blackwell.

Johnson, S. P. (2000). The development of visual surface perception: Insights into the ontogeny of knowledge. In C. Rovee-Collier, L. P. Lipsitt, & H. Hayne (Eds.), *Progress in infancy research* (Vol. 1, pp. 113–154). Mahwah, NJ: Erlbaum.

Johnson, S. P., & Aslin, R. N. (1996). Perception of object unity in young infants: The roles of motion, depth, and orientation. *Cognitive Development, 11,* 161–180.

Johnson, S. P., & Aslin, R. N. (1998). Young infants' perception of illusory contours in dynamic displays. *Perception, 27,* 341–353.

Johnson, S. P., Cohen, L. B., Marks, K. S., & Johnson, K. L. (2003). Young infants' perception of object unit in rotation displays. *Infancy, 4,* 285–296.

Johnson, S. P., & Nanez, J. E. (1995). Young infants' perception of object unity in two-dimensional displays. *Infant Behavior and Development, 18*(2), 133–143.

Kant, I. (1982). *Critique of pure reason* (W. Schwarz, Trans.). Aalen, Germany: Scientia. (Original work published 1794)

Kanwisher, N. (2000). Domain specificity in face perception. *Nature Neuroscience, 3,* 759–763.

Kellman, P. (1993). Kinematic foundations of infant visual perception. In C. E. Granrud (Ed.), *Visual perception and cognition in infancy* (pp. 121–173). Hillsdale, NJ: Erlbaum.

Kellman, P. (1996). The origins of object perception. In R. Gelman & T. Au (Eds.), *Handbook of perception and cognition: Perceptual and cognitive development* (pp. 3–48). San Diego, CA: Academic Press.

Kellman, P. J., & Shipley, T. F. (1991). A theory of visual interpolation in object perception. *Cognitive Psychology, 23,* 141–221.

Kellman, P., & Spelke, E. S. (1983). Perception of partly occluded objects in infancy. *Cognitive Psychology, 15,* 483–524.

Lecuyer, R., & Bourcier, A. (1994). Causal and noncausal relations between collision events and their detection by 3-month-olds. *Infant Behavior and Development, 17,* 218.

Le Grand, R., Modloch, C. J., Maurer, D., & Henry, B. (2001). Early visual experience and face processing. *Nature, 410,* 890.

Leslie, A. M. (1982). The perception of causality in infants. *Perception, 11,* 15–30.

Leslie, A. M. (1984). Spatiotemporal continuity and the perception of causality in infants. *Perception, 13,* 287–305.

Leslie, A. M. (1986). Getting development off the ground: Modularity and the infant's perception of causality. In P. van Geert (Ed.), *Theory building in developmental psychology* (pp. 406–437). Amsterdam: North Holland.

Leslie, A. M. (1988). The necessity of illusion: Perception and thought in infancy. In L. Weiskrantz (Ed.), *Thought without language* (pp. 406–437). Oxford, England: Oxford Science Publications.

Leslie, A. M., & Kaldy, Z. (2001). Indexing individual objects in infant working memory. *Journal of Experimental Child Psychology, 78*(1), 61–74.

Leslie, A. M., & Keeble, S. (1987). Do 6-month-olds perceive causality? *Cognition, 25,* 265–288.

Leslie, A. M., Xu, F., Tremoulet, P. D., & Scholl, B. (1998). Indexing and the object concept: Developing "what" and "where" systems. *Trends in Cognitive Sciences, 2,* 10–18.

Levy, G. D. (2003). Perception of correlated attributes involving African-American and White females' faces by 10-month-old infants. *Infant and Child Development, 12,* 197–203.

Levy, G. D., & Haaf, R. A. (1994). Detection of gender-related categories by 10-month-old infants. *Infant Behavior and Development, 17,* 457–459.

Lucksinger, K. L., Cohen, L. B., & Madole, K. L. (1992, May). *What infants infer about hidden objects and events.* Paper presented at the International Conference on Infant Studies, Miami, FL.

Madole, K. L., & Cohen, L. B. (1995). The role of object parts in infants' attention to form-function correlations. *Developmental Psychology, 31*(4), 637–648.

Madole, K. L., & Oakes, L. M. (1999). Making sense of infant categorization: Stable processes and changing representations. *Developmental Review, 19,* 263–296.

Madole, K. L., Oakes, L. M., & Cohen, L. B. (1993). Developmental changes in infants' attention to function and form-function correlations. *Cognitive Development, 8,* 189–209.

Mandler, J. M. (1992). How to build a baby: Vol. 2. Conceptual primitives. *Psychological Review, 99,* 587–604.

Mandler, J. M. (1993). On concepts. *Cognitive Development, 8,* 141–148.

Mandler, J. M. (2000a). Perceptual and conceptual processes in infancy. *Journal of Cognition and Development, 1*(1), 3–36.

Mandler, J. M. (2000b). Reply to the commentaries on perceptual and conceptual processes in infancy. *Journal of Cognition and Development, 1*(1), 67–79.

Mandler, J. M. (2003). Conceptual categorization. In D. H. Rakison & L. M. Oakes (Eds.), *Early category and concept development* (pp. 103–131). New York: Oxford University Press.

Mandler, J. M. (2004). *The foundations of mind: Origins of conceptual thought.* New York: Oxford University Press.

Mandler, J. M., & Bauer, P. J. (1988). The cradle of categorization: Is the basic level basic? *Cognitive Development, 3,* 247–264.

Mandler, J. M., Bauer, P. J., & McDonough, L. (1991). Separating the sheep from the goats: Differentiating global categories. *Cognitive Psychology, 23,* 263–298.

Mandler, J. M., & McDonough, L. (1993). Concept formation in infancy. *Cognitive Development, 8,* 291–318.

Mandler, J. M., & McDonough, L. (1996). Drinking and driving don't mix: Inductive generalization in infancy. *Cognition, 59*(3), 307–335.

Mandler, J. M., & McDonough, L. (1998). Studies in inductive inference in infancy. *Cognitive Psychology, 37,* 60–96.

Marcus, G. F. (2002). The modules behind the learning. *Developmental Science, 5,* 175.

Mareschal, D. (2000). Connectionist modelling and infant development. In D. Muir & A. Slater (Eds.), *Essential readings in psychology: Infant development* (pp. 55–65). Oxford, England: Blackwell.

Mareschal, D. (2003). The acquisition and use of implicit categories. In D. H. Rakison & L. M. Oakes (Eds.), *Early category and concept development* (pp. 360–383). New York: Oxford University Press.

Mareschal, D., & French, R. (1997). A connectionist account of interference effects in early infant memory and categorization. In M. G. Shafto & P. Langley (Eds.), *Proceedings of the 19th annual conference of the cognitive science society* (pp. 484–489). Mahwah, NJ: Erlbaum.

Mareschal, D., & French, R. (2000). Mechanisms of categorization in infancy. *Infancy, 1*(1), 59–76.

Mareschal, D., French, R., & Quinn, P. C. (2000). A connectionist account of asymmetric category learning in infancy. *Developmental Psychobiology, 36,* 635–645.

Mareschal, D., & Johnson, S. P. (2002). Learning to perceive object unity: A connectionist account. *Developmental Science, 5,* 151–172.

Mareschal, D., Quinn, P. C., & French, R. M. (2002). Asymmetric interference in 3- to 4-month-olds' sequential category learning. *Cognitive Science, 26*(3), 377–389.

Maurer, D., & Young, R. (1983). Newborns' following of natural and distorted arrangements of facial features. *Infant Behavior and Development, 6,* 127–131.

Meltzoff, A. N. (1990). The implications of cross-modal matching and imitation for the development of representation and memory in infants. In A. Diamond (Ed.), *The development and neural bases of higher cognitive functions* (pp. 1–37). New York: New York Academy of Science.

Meltzoff, A. N. (1995). What infant memory tells us about infantile amnesia: Long-term recall and deferred imitation. *Journal of Experimental Child Psychology, 59,* 497–515.

Meltzoff, A. N., & Moore, M. K. (1977). Imitation of facial and manual gestures by human neonates. *Science, 198,* 75–78.

Meltzoff, A. N., & Moore, M. K. (1994). Imitation, memory, and the representation of persons. *Infant Behavior and Development, 17*(1), 83–99.

Meltzoff, A. N., & Moore, M. (1998). Object representation, identity, and the paradox of early permanence: Steps toward a new framework. *Infant Behavior and Development, 21*(2), 201–235.

Mervis, C. B., Pani, J. R., & Pani, A. M. (2003). Transation of child cognitive-linguistic abilities. In D. H. Rakison & L. M. Oakes (Eds.), *Early category and concept development* (pp. 242–274). New York: Oxford University Press.

Michotte, A. (1963). *The perception of causality.* New York: Basic Books.

Moore, M. K., Borton, R., & Darby, B. L. (1978). Visual tracking in young infants: Evidence for object identity or object permanence? *Journal of Experimental Child Psychology, 25,* 183–198.

Morton, J., & Johnson, M. H. (1991). CONSPEC and CONLERN: A two-process theory of infant face recognition. *Psychological Review, 98,* 164–181.

Munakata, Y. (1997). Perseverative reaching in infancy: The roles of hidden toys and motor history in the AB task. *Infant Behavior and Development, 20*(3), 405–416.

Munakata, Y., McClelland, J. L., Johnson, M. H., & Siegler, R. S. (1997). Rethinking infant knowledge: Toward an adaptive process account of successes and failures in object permanence tasks. *Psychological Review, 104,* 686–713.

Munakata, Y., & Stedron, J. M. (2002). Modeling infants' perception of object unity: What have we learned? *Developmental Science, 5,* 176.

Needham, A., & Baillargeon, R. (1997). Object segregation in 8-month-old infants. *Cognition, 62*(2), 121–149.

Nelson, C. A. (2001). The development and neural bases of face recognition. *Infant and Child Development, 10,* 3–18.

Nelson, C. A., & Monk, C. S. (2001). The use of event-related potentials in the study of cognitive development. In C. A. Nelson & M. Luciana (Eds.), *Handbook of developmental cognitive neuroscience* (pp. 125–136). Cambridge, MA: MIT Press.

Oakes, L. M. (1994). Development of infants' use of continuity cues in their perception of causality. *Developmental Psychology, 30,* 869–879.

Oakes, L. M., & Cohen, L. B. (1990). Infant perception of a causal event. *Cognitive Development, 5,* 193–207.

Oakes, L. M., & Cohen, L. B. (1994). Infant causal perception. In C. Rovee-Collier & L. P. Lipsitt (Eds.), *Advances in infancy research* (Vol. 9, pp. 1–54). Norwood, NJ: Ablex.

Oakes, L. M., Coppage, D., & Dingel, A. (1997). By land or by sea: The role of perceptual similarity in infants' categorization of animals. *Developmental psychology, 33,* 396–407.

Oakes, L. M., & Madole, K. L. (2003). Principles of developmental change in infants' category formation. In D. H. Rakison & L. M. Oakes (Eds.), *Early category and concept learning* (pp. 132–158). New York: Oxford University Press.

Oakes, L. M., Madole, K. L., & Cohen, L. B. (1991). Object examining: Habituation and categorization. *Cognitive Development, 6,* 377–392.

Oakes, L. M., Tellinghuisen, D. J., & Tjebkes, T. L. (2000). Competition for infants' attention: The interactive influence of attentional state and stimulus characteristics. *Infancy, 1*(3), 347–361.

Pascalis, O., de Haan, M., & Nelson, C. A. (2002). Is face processing species-specific during the first year of life? *Science, 296,* 1321–1323.

Piaget, J. (1954). *The child's construction of reality.* New York: Basic Books.

Poulin-Dubois, D., & Forbes, J. N. (2002). Toddlers' attention to intentions-in-action in learning novel action words. *Developmental Psychology, 38*(1), 104–114.

Poulin-Dubois, D., Lepage, A., & Ferland, D. (1996). Infants' concept of animacy. *Cognitive Development, 11*(1), 19–36.

Premack, D. (1990). The infants' theory of self-propelled objects. *Cognition, 35,* 1–16.

Quinn, P. C. (2003). Concepts are not just for objects: Categorization of spatial relation information by infants. In D. H. Rakison & L. M. Oakes (Eds.), *Early category and concept development: Making sense of the blooming, buzzing confusion* (pp. 50–76). Oxford, England: Oxford University Press.

Quinn, P. C., Adams, A., Kennedy, E., Shettler, L., & Wasnik, A. (2003). Development of an abstract category representation for the spatial relation between 6- to 10-month-old infants. *Developmental Psychology, 39*(1), 151–163.

Quinn, P. C., & Eimas, P. D. (1997). A reexamination of the perceptual-to-conceptual shift in mental representations. *Review of General Psychology, 1,* 271–287.

Quinn, P. C., & Eimas, P. D. (2000). The emergence of category representations during infancy: Are separate perceptual and conceptual processes required? *Journal of Cognition and Development, 1,* 55–61.

Quinn, P. C., Eimas, P. D., & Rosenkrantz, S. L. (1993). Evidence for representations of perceptually similar natural categories by 3-month-old and 4-month-old infants. *Perception, 22,* 463–475.

Quinn, P. C., & Johnson, M. H. (2000). Global-before-basic object categorization in connectionist networks and 2-month-old infants. *Infancy, 1*(1), 31–46.

Rakison, D. H. (2003). Parts, motion and the development of the animate-inanimate distinction in infancy. In D. H. Rakison & L. M. Oakes (Eds.), *Early categorization and concept development* (pp. 159–192). New York: Oxford University Press.

Rakison, D. H., & Butterworth, G. E. (1998a). Infants' attention to object structure in early categorization. *Developmental Psychology, 34*(6), 1310–1325.

Rakison, D. H., & Butterworth, G. E. (1998b). Infants' use of object parts in early categorization. *Developmental Psychology, 34*(1), 49–62.

Rakison, D. H., & Poulin-Dubois, D. (2001). Developmental origin of the animate-inanimate distinction. *Psychological Bulletin, 127,* 209–228.

Rakison, D. H., & Poulin-Dubois, D. (2002). You go this way and I'll go that way: Developmental changes in infants attention to correlations among dynamic features in motion events. *Child Development, 73,* 682–699.

Rivera, S., Wakeley, A., & Langer, J. (1999). The drawbridge phenomenon: Representational reasoning or perceptual preference? *Developmental Psychology, 35,* 427–435.

Roder, B. J., Bushnell, E. W., & Sasseville, A. M. (2000). Infants' preferences for familiarity and novelty during the course of visual processing. *Infancy, 1*(4), 491–507.

Ruff, H. A. (1986). Components of attention during infants' manipulative exploration. *Child Development, 5,* 105–114.

Ruff, H. A., & Rothbart, M. K. (1996). *Attention in early development: Themes and variations.* New York: Oxford University Press.

Schlottmann, A., & Surian, L. (1999). Do 9-month-olds perceive causation-at-a-distance? *Perception, 28,* 1105–1113.

Shilling, T. H. (2000). Infants' looking at possible and impossible screen rotations: The role of familiarization. *Infancy, 1,* 389–402.

Shinskey, J. L. (2002). Infants' object search: Effects of variable object visibility under constant means-end demands. *Journal of Cognition and Development, 3*(2), 119–142.

Shinskey, J. L., Bogartz, R. S., & Poirier, C. R. (2000). The effects of graded occlusion on manual search and visual attention in 5- to 8-month-old infants. *Infancy, 1*(3), 323–346.

Shinskey, J. L., & Munakata, Y. (2001). Detecting transparent barriers: Clear evidence against the means-end deficit account of search failures. *Infancy, 2*(3), 395–404.

Shinskey, J. L., & Munakata, Y. (2003). Are infants in the dark about hidden objects? *Developmental Science, 6,* 273–282.

Shultz, T. R. (2003). *Computational developmental psychology.* Cambridge, MA: MIT Press.

Shultz, T. R., & Bale, A. C. (2001). Neural network simulation of infant familiarization to artificial sentences: Rule-like behavior without explicit rules and variables. *Infancy, 2*(4), 501–536.

Shultz, T. R., & Cohen, L. B. (2004). Modeling age differences in infant category learning. *Infancy, 5,* 153–171.

Simion, F., Cassia, V. M., Turati, C., & Valenza, E. (2001). The origins of face perception: Specific versus non-specific mechanisms. *Infant and Child Development, 10,* 59–65.

Simion, F., Valenza, E., Cassia, V. M., Turati, C., & Umilta, C. (2002). Newborns' preference for up-down asymmetrical configurations. *Developmental Science, 5,* 427–434.

Slater, A., Johnson, S. P., Brown, E., & Badenoch, M. (1996). Newborn infants' perception of partly occluded objects. *Infant Behavior and Development, 19*, 145–148.

Slater, A., Johnson, S. P., Kellman, P. J., & Spelke, E. S. (1994). The role of three-dimensional depth cues in infants' perception of partly occluded objects. *Early Development and Parenting, 3*, 187–191.

Slater, A., Morison, V., Somers, M., Mattock, A., Brown, E., & Taylor, D. (1990). Newborn and older infants' perception of partly occluded objects. *Infant Behavior and Development, 13*, 33–49.

Slobin, D. I. (1981). The origins of grammatical encoding of events. In W. Deutsch (Ed.), *The child's construction of language* (pp. 185–199). New York: Academic Press.

Smith, L. B. (2002). Teleology in connectionism. *Developmental Science, 5*, 178.

Sokolov, E. N. (1963). *Perception and the conditioned reflex.* Hillsdale, NJ: Erlbaum.

Sophian, C. (1984). Spatial transpositions and the early development of search. *Developmental Psychology, 35*, 369–390.

Sophian, C., & Wellman, H. M. (1983). Selective information use and perseveration in the search behavior of infants and young children. *Journal of Experimental Child Psychology, 35*, 369–390.

Spelke, E. S. (1998). Nativism, empiricism, and the origins of knowledge. *Infant Behavior and Development, 21*, 181–200.

Spelke, E. S., Breinlinger, K., Macomber, J., & Jacobson, K. (1992). Origins of knowledge. *Psychological Review, 99*, 605–632.

Spelke, E. S., Kestenbaum, R., Simons, D. J., & Wein, D. (1995). Spatiotemporal continuity, smoothness of motion and object identity in infancy. *British Journal of Developmental Psychology, 13*(2), 113–142.

Tarr, M. J., & Gauthier, I. (2000). FFA: A flexible fusiform area for subordinate-level visual processing automatized by expertise. *Nature Neuroscience, 3*, 764–769.

Turati, C. (2004). Why faces are not special to newborns: An alternative account of the face preference. *Current Directions in Psychological Science, 13*, 5–8.

Uzgiris, I., & Hunt, J. M. (1975). *Assessment in infancy: Ordinal scales of psychological development.* Urbana: University of Illinois Press.

Van de Walle, G. A., Woodward, A. L., & Phillips, A. (1994, June). *Infants' inferences about contact relations in a causal event.* Paper presented at the International Conference on Infant Studies, Paris, France.

Waxman, S. R. (2003). Links between object categorization and naming: Origins and emergence in human infants. In D. H. Rakison & L. M. Oakes (Eds.), *Early category and concept development* (pp. 213–241). New York: Oxford University Press.

Werker, J. F., Cohen, L. B., Lloyd, V. L., Casasola, M., & Stager, C. L. (1998). Acquisition of word-object associations by 14-month-old infants. *Developmental Psychology, 34*(6), 1289–1309.

Werker, J. F., & Tees, R. C. (1984). Cross-language speech perception: Evidence for perceptual reorganization during the first year of life. *Infant Behavior and Development, 7*, 49–63.

Westermann, G., & Mareschal, D. (2004). From parts to wholes: Mechanisms of development in infant visual object processing. *Infancy, 5*, 131–151.

Wilcox, T., & Baillargeon, R. (1998). Object individuation in infancy: The use of featural information in reasoning about occlusion events. *Cognitive Psychology, 37*(2), 97–155.

Wilcox, T., Schweinle, A., & Chapa, C. (2003). Object individuation in infancy. In H. Hayne & J. W. Fagen (Eds.), *Progress in infancy research* (Vol. 3, pp. 193–243). Mahwah, NJ: Erlbaum.

Wishart, J. G., & Bower, T. G. R. (1982). The development of spatial understanding in infancy. *Journal of Experimental Child Psychology, 33*, 363–385.

Woodward, A. L. (1998). Infants selectively encode the goal object of an actor's reach. *Cognition, 69*(1), 1–34.

Wynn, K. (1992). Addition and subtraction by human infants. *Nature, 358*, 749–750.

Xu, F. (2003). The development of object individuation in infancy. In H. Hayne & J. W. Fagen (Eds.), *Progress in infancy research* (Vol. 3, pp. 159–192). Mahwah, NJ: Erlbaum.

Xu, F., & Carey, S. (1996). Infants' metaphysics: The case of numerical identity. *Cognitive Psychology, 30*, 111–153.

Younger, B. A. (1985). The segregation of items into categories by 10-month-old infants. *Child Development, 56*, 1574–1583.

Younger, B. A. (2003). Parsing objects into categories: Infants' perception and use of correlated attributes. In D. H. Rakison & L. M. Oakes (Eds.), *Early category and concept development* (pp. 77–102). New York: Oxford University Press.

Younger, B. A., & Cohen, L. B. (1983). Infant perception of correlations among attributes. *Child Development, 54*, 858–867.

Younger, B. A., & Cohen, L. B. (1985). How infants form categories. In G. Bower (Ed.), *The psychology of learning and motivation: Vol. 19. Advances in research and theory* (pp. 211–247). New York: Academic Press.

Younger, B. A., & Cohen, L. B. (1986). Developmental change in infants' perception of correlations among attributes. *Child Development, 57*, 803–815.

Younger, B. A., & Fearing, D. D. (1998). Detecting correlations among form attributes: An object-examining test with infants. *Infant Behavior and Development, 21*(2), 289–297.

Younger, B. A., & Fearing, D. D. (1999). Parsing items into separate categories: Developmental change in infant categorization. *Child Development, 70*, 291–303.

Younger, B. A., Johnson, K. E., & Furrer, S. D. (2004, May). *Generalized imitation following multi-exemplar modeling: Already down to basic?* Paper presented at the International Conference on Infant Studies, Chicago, IL.

# Cognition and Communication

CHAPTER 6

# Acquiring Linguistic Constructions

MICHAEL TOMASELLO

HISTORY AND THEORY   256
The Role of Linguistics   256
Two Theories   257
Constructions   258
EARLY ONTOGENY   259
The Language Children Hear   260
Earliest Language   261
Item-Based Constructions   262
Marking Syntactic Roles   265
Constructing Lexical Categories   269
LATER ONTOGENY   271
Abstract Constructions   271

Constraining Generalizations   276
Nominal and Verbal Constructions:
    Learning Morphology   278
Complex Constructions   283
PROCESSES OF LANGUAGE ACQUISITION   285
The Growing Abstractness of Constructions   285
Psycholinguistic Processes of Development   286
Individual Differences   289
Atypical Development   291
CONCLUSIONS   292
REFERENCES   293

Human linguistic communication differs from the communication of other animal species in three main ways. First, and most importantly, human linguistic communication is symbolic. Linguistic symbols are social conventions by means of which one individual attempts to share attention with other individuals by directing their attentional or mental states to something in the outside world. Other animal species do not communicate with one another using linguistic symbols, most likely because they do not understand that conspecifics have attentional or mental states that they could attempt to direct or share (Tomasello, 1998c, 1999). This mental dimension of linguistic symbols gives them unparalleled communicative power, enabling their users to refer to and to predicate all kinds of diverse perspectives on objects, events, and situations in the world.

The second main difference is that human linguistic communication is grammatical. Human beings use their linguistic symbols together in patterned ways, and these patterns, known as linguistic constructions, come to take on meanings themselves—deriving partly from the meanings of the individual symbols but, over time, at least partly from the pattern itself. The process by which this occurs over historical time is called *gram-*

*maticalization,* and grammatical constructions add still another dimension of communicative power to human languages by enabling all kinds of unique symbol combinations. Grammatical constructions are also uniquely human, of course, because if a species does not use symbols, the question of grammar is moot.

Third, unlike all other animal species, human beings do not have a single system of communication used by all members of the species. Rather, different groups of humans have conventionalized over historical time different, mutually unintelligible systems of communication (there are more than 6,000 natural languages in the world). This means that children, unlike other animal species, must learn the communicative conventions used by those around them—indeed they take several years to acquire the many tens of thousands, perhaps even hundreds of thousands, of linguistic symbols and constructions of their natal group(s). This is much more learning in this domain—by many orders of magnitude—than is characteristic of any other species.

This chapter is about the way children master a language, the way they learn to communicate using the linguistic conventions used by those around them in both their symbolic and grammatical dimensions. We begin with some background history and theory of the field, proceed in the next two sections to outline the major ontogenetic steps of language acquisition, and conclude the chapter with a focus on the cognitive and social processes involved in becoming a competent user of a natural language.

## HISTORY AND THEORY

To investigate how children acquire a language, we must first know what a language is. This is not as straightforward as it might seem, since the specialists involved—linguists—do not agree among themselves.

### The Role of Linguistics

Large-scale theories and approaches to child language acquisition are mainly characterized by the theory of linguistics that they assume as their foundation. Thus, using the linguistics of the 1950s (viz., American Structural Linguistics), the first modern researchers of child language acquisition in the 1960s attempted to identify the items and structures in children's language using exclusively the method of distributional analysis. Making basically no assumptions about possible correspondences between child and adult linguistic competence, the main finding was that many of children's earliest word combinations consisted of one constant word that could be freely combined with one of many variable words. Many of these lexically based patterns also seemed to show some consistencies among one another, however, especially with respect to ordering, and so Braine (1963) formalized these patterns into a three-rule Pivot Grammar that was supposed to be what children used to generate their language:

1. $P^1$ + O (*More* juice, *More* milk, *There* Daddy, *There* Joe, etc.).
2. O + $P^2$ (Juice *gone,* Mommy *gone,* Flowers *pretty,* Janie *pretty,* etc.).
3. O + O (Ball table, Mommy sock, and so on—that is, utterances without a pivot).

The main problem with Pivot Grammar was that, while it did capture something of the spirit of children's early language, in its formalized form it was empirically inadequate since: (a) children did not always use the same pivot in a consistent sequential position, (b) children

sometimes combined two pivots with one another, and (c) the O + O rule was essentially a wastebasket for noncanonical utterances (Bloom, 1971). It was also unclear in this account how young children could ever get from these purely childlike syntactic categories to the more adultlike syntactic categories that were being described by the linguists of the time.

The natural next attempt, therefore, was to apply the new adult linguistic models of the 1960s and 1970s to the data of child language acquisition. These attempts—which included several versions of Transformational Generative Grammar, Case Grammar, Generative Semantics, and others—were reviewed and evaluated by Brown (1973). Brown's basic conclusion was that, while children's linguistic productions could be forced into any one of the models, none of the models was totally satisfactory in accounting for all the data. But the more fundamental problem was that there was really no evidence that children employed, or even needed, the adultlike linguistic categories and rules that were being attributed to them in these models. For example, Schlesinger (1971) and Bowerman (1976) surveyed the utterances produced by several children learning several languages and found that—on internal grounds—there was no reason to assume that they were underlain by abstract syntactic categories such as "subject," "direct object," and "verb phrase." There was also a suspicion among many people who looked broadly at languages across different cultures that no single formal grammar would be adequate to account for the acquisition process in all of the world's many thousands of languages (Slobin, 1973).

Several theorists—including Brown (1973), Slobin (1970), Schlesinger (1971), Bloom (1973), and others—then suggested a semantic-cognitive basis for children's early language: the so-called Semantic Relations approach. The basic observation was that most of the semantic-syntactic relations apparent in children's early language correspond rather closely to some of the categories of sensory-motor cognition as outlined by Piaget (1952). For example, infants know nonlinguistically some things about the causal relations among agents, actions, and objects, and this might form the basis for a linguistic schema of the type: Agent-Action-Object (and similarly for Possessor-Possessed, Object-Location, Object-Attribute, etc.). While again this approach seemed to be capturing something of the spirit of early language—children mostly talk about a fairly delimited set of events, relations, and objects that correspond in some ways to Piagetian sensory-motor categories—it was also empirically inadequate as many child utterances fit into none of the categories while others fit into several (Howe, 1976). Moreover, echoing the theoretical problems of Pivot Grammar, there were basically no serious theoretical proposals about how young children got from these semantically based syntactic categories to the more abstract syntactic categories of adults.

Swinging the pendulum back in the adult direction once again, in the 1980s a new group of theorists began to advocate a return to adult grammars, but in this case using some new formal models such as Government and Binding theory, Lexical Functional Grammar, and the like (e.g., Baker & McCarthy, 1981; Hornstein & Lightfoot, 1981; Pinker, 1984). The general consensus was that proposing a discontinuity from child to adult language—as seemed to be the case in such things as Pivot Grammar and the Semantic Relations approach—created insurmountable logical problems, that is to say, problems of learnability. These logical problems were thought by learnability theorists to be sufficient justification to make the continuity assumption, namely, that children operate with the same basic linguistic categories and rules as adults (Pinker, 1984). This general point of view was strongly associated with linguistic nativism, in which all human beings possess the same basic linguistic competence, in the form of a universal grammar, throughout their lives (Chomsky, 1968, 1980). The inadequacies of this approach soon became apparent as well, most fundamentally its inability to deal with the problems of cross-linguistic variation and developmental change—how children could "link" an abstract and unchanging universal grammar to the structures of a particular language, and why, if this was the process, children's language looked so different from adults'. And again, there was no evidence that children actually use abstract adultlike categories—continuity was only an assumption.

**Two Theories**

It is easy to see in this historical sketch two distinct strands. One derives from researchers who take a formal approach to language and its acquisition—a more adult-centered approach emanating from Chomsky's theory of generative grammar—and the other derives from researchers who take a more functional, usage-based approach to language and its acquisition—a potentially more child-centered approach with room for serious de-

velopmental change. It is these two basic orientations that still structure the current theoretical debate in the study of child language acquisition.

Chomskian generative grammar is a *formal* theory, meaning that it is based on the supposition that natural languages are like formal languages (e.g., algebra, predicate logic). Natural languages are thus characterized in terms of: (a) a unified set of abstract algebraic rules that are both meaningless themselves and also insensitive to the meanings of the elements they algorithmically combine, and (b) a lexicon containing meaningful linguistic elements that serve as variables in the rules. Principles governing the way the underlying algebra works constitute a universal grammar, the core of linguistic competence. The linguistic periphery involves such things as the lexicon, the conceptual system, irregular constructions and idioms, and pragmatics.

With regard to language acquisition, Chomskian generative grammar begins with the assumption that children innately possess a universal grammar abstract enough to structure any language of the world. Acquisition then consists of two processes:

1. Acquiring all the words, idioms, and quirky constructions of the particular language being learned (by "normal" processes of learning).
2. Linking the particular language being learned, that is, its core structures, to the abstract universal grammar.

This is the so-called *dual process* approach—also sometimes called the *words and rules* approach (Pinker, 1999)—since the "periphery" of linguistic competence is learned but the "core" is innately given in universal grammar. Because it is innate, universal grammar does not develop ontogenetically but is the same throughout the life span: This is the so-called continuity assumption (Pinker, 1984). This assumption allows generativists to use adultlike formal grammars to describe children's language and so to assume that the first time a child utters, for example, "I wanna play" that she has an adultlike understanding of infinitival complement sentences and so can generate similar infinitival complement sentences *ad infinitum*.

In sharp contrast is the group of theories most often called *Cognitive-Functional Linguistics,* but which are sometimes also called *Usage-Based Linguistics* to emphasize their central processing tenet that language structure emerges from language use (e.g., Bybee, 1985, 1995; Croft, 1991, 2001; Givón, 1995; Goldberg, 1995;

Langacker, 1987a, 1991; see Tomasello, 1998a, 2003, for other similar approaches). Usage-based theories hold that the essence of language is its symbolic dimension, with grammar being derivative. The ability to communicate with conspecifics symbolically (conventionally, intersubjectively) is a species-specific biological adaptation. The grammatical dimension of language derives from historical processes of grammaticalization, which create various grammatical constructions (e.g., the English passive construction, noun phrase construction, or -*ed* past tense construction). As opposed to linguistic rules conceived as algebraic procedures for combining words and morphemes that do not contribute to meaning, linguistic constructions are meaningful linguistic symbols. They are nothing other than the patterns in which meaningful linguistic symbols are used in communication (e.g., the passive construction is used to communicate about an entity to which something happens). In this approach, mature linguistic competence is conceived as a structured inventory of meaningful linguistic constructions—including both the more regular and the more idiomatic structures in a given language (and all structures in between).

According to the usage-based theory, there is no such thing as universal grammar and so the theoretical problem of how a child links it to a particular language does not exist. It is a single-process theory of language acquisition, in the sense that children are thought to acquire the more regular and rule-based constructions of a language in the same way they acquire the more arbitrary and idiosyncratic constructions: They learn them. And, as in the learning of all complex cognitive activities, they then construct abstract categories and schemas out of the concrete things they have learned. Thus, in this view, children's earliest acquisitions are concrete pieces of language—words (e.g., *cat*), complex expressions (e.g., *I-wanna-do-it*), or mixed constructions (e.g., *Where's-the* _____, which is partially concrete and partially abstract)—because early in development they do not possess the fully abstract categories and schemas of adult grammar. Children construct these abstractions only gradually and in piecemeal fashion, with some categories and constructions appearing much before others that are of a similar type from an adult perspective—due quite often to differences in the language that individual children hear ("input"). Children construct their language using general cognitive processes falling into two broad categories: (1) intention-reading (joint attention, under-

standing communicative intentions, cultural learning), by which they attempt to understand the communicative significance of an utterance; and (2) pattern-finding (categorization, schema formation, statistical learning, analogy), by which they create the more abstract dimensions of linguistic competence.

## Constructions

In this chapter, we adopt a usage-based theoretical perspective on the process of language acquisition. We thus assume that what children are learning initially is concrete pieces of language, of many different shapes and sizes, across which they then generalize to construct more abstract linguistic constructions—which underlies their ability to generate creative new utterances. The central theoretical construct is therefore the construction.

A linguistic construction is prototypically a unit of language that comprises multiple linguistic elements used together for a relatively coherent communicative function, with subfunctions being performed by the elements as well. Consequently, constructions may vary in their complexity depending on the number of elements involved and their interrelations. For example, the English regular plural construction (N+*s*) is relatively simple, whereas the passive construction (X *was* VERB*ed by* Y) is relatively complex. Independent of complexity, however, constructions may also vary in their abstractness. For example, the relatively simple English regular plural construction and the more complex English passive construction are both highly (though not totally) abstract. To repeat, even these most abstract constructions are still symbolic, as they possess a coherent, if abstract, meaning in relative independence of the lexical items involved (Goldberg, 1995). Thus, in the utterance *Mary sneezed John the football,* our construal of the action is influenced more by the transfer of possession meaning of the ditransitive construction than it is by the verb *sneeze* (since sneezing is not normally construed as transferring possession). Similarly, we know that the nonce noun *gazzers* very likely indicates a plurality without even knowing what a gazzer is.

Importantly, however, some complex linguistic structures are not based on abstract categories, but rather on particular linguistic items (Fillmore, 1988, 1989; Fillmore, Kaye, & O'Conner, 1988). The limiting case is totally fixed expressions such as the idiom *How do you do?*

which is a structure of English with an idiosyncratic meaning that dissolves if any of the particular words is changed. (One does not normally, with the same intended meaning, ask *How does she do?*) Other clear examples are such well-known idioms as *kick the bucket* and *spill the beans,* which have a little more flexibility and abstractness as different people may kick the bucket and they may do so in past, present, or future tense—but we cannot, with the same meaning, kick the pail or spill the peas. It turns out that, on inspection, a major part of human linguistic competence—much more than previously believed—involves the mastery of all kinds of routine formulas, fixed and semi-fixed expressions, idioms, and frozen collocations. Indeed one of the distinguishing characteristics of native speakers of a language is their control of these semi-fixed expressions as fluent units with somewhat unpredictable meanings (e.g., I wouldn't *put it past* him; He's *getting to me* these days; *Hang in there*; That won't *go down well* with the boss; She *put me up to* it; and so on; Pawley & Syder, 1983).

The theoretical problem for algebraic approaches such as generative grammar is what to do with these fixed and semi-fixed complex structures. They are complex and somewhat regular, and so they would seem to be a part of the core grammar to be generated by rules. But as fixed expressions, they would seem to be a part of the periphery to be memorized like words. For example, consider the "-er" construction:

The bigger they are, the nicer they are.

The more you try, the worse it gets.

The faster I run, the behinder I get.

This construction is clearly noncanonical, as both of the two clauses are difficult to classify using classical grammatical techniques. But there are obvious canonical elements as well. Also, consider such things as:

This hair dryer needs fixing.

My house needs painting.

Note in this case that although *hairdryer* and *house* are the subjects of the sentences they are the logical objects of the predicates *fixing* and *painting* (they are the objects to be acted on), which are expressed as participles. It turns out that virtually no other verbs besides *need* work in this construction of the English language (some people will accept the semantically similar verbs *re-*

*quire* and *want*). It would thus seem that this construction, while basically canonical, is at the same time best described in lexically specific terms.

The impossibility of making a clear distinction between the core and the periphery of linguistic structure suggests that language structure emerges from language use, and that a community of speakers may conventionalize from their language use all kinds of linguistic structures—from the more concrete to the more abstract, from the more regular to the more idiomatic, with all kinds of mixed constructions as well. If we take these points seriously, an important question for acquisition researchers becomes: if many, perhaps most, of the structures of a language (as embodied in various kinds of semifixed expressions, irregular formations, schematic idioms, and the like) may be acquired through normal processes of learning and abstraction—as they are in all theoretical accounts—then why cannot the more regular and canonical aspects of a language be acquired in this same straightforward way? Indeed, in the current approach, we will assume that all linguistic structures are acquired in the same basic way.

## EARLY ONTOGENY

It is widely believed that young children begin their linguistic careers by learning words, which they then combine together by means of rules. But this is not exactly accurate. Children hear and attempt to learn whole adult utterances, instantiating various types of constructions used for various communicative purposes. Sometimes children only learn parts of these complex wholes, and so their first productions may correspond to adult words. But these are always packaged in conventional intonational patterns indicating such things as requests, comments, or questions—which correspond to the general communicative functions for which adults use more complex constructions. From the beginning, children are attempting to learn not isolated words, but rather communicatively effective speech forms corresponding to whole adult constructions. Learning words—which will not be a topic of this chapter (see Waxman & Lidz, Chapter 7, this *Handbook,* this volume)—is essentially a process of extracting elements (including their function) from these larger wholes.

In this section, our account of the early ontogeny of language focuses first, on the language children hear;

then on their early holophrases (single words or phrases that have a larger, holistic meaning); then on their early word combinations, pivot schemas, and item-based constructions; and finally on the linguistic devices they use early in development for marking basic syntactic roles such as agent and patient.

## The Language Children Hear

To understand how children acquire a language, we must know something about the language they hear—both in terms of specific utterances and in terms of the constructions these instantiate. Surprisingly, very few studies have attempted to document the full range of linguistic expressions and constructions that children hear in their daily lives. The majority of studies of child-directed-speech (CDS) have focused on specific aspects (for classic studies, see the papers in Galloway & Richards, 1994; Snow & Ferguson, 1977).

Cameron-Faulkner, Lieven, and Tomasello (2003) examined all the CDS of 12 English-speaking mothers during samples of their linguistic interactions with their 2- to 3-year-old children. They first categorized each of the mothers' utterances in terms of very general constructional categories, resulting in the percentages displayed in Table 6.1 (which also includes a comparable analysis of the data of Wells, 1983, whose children were

**TABLE 6.1   Most General Construction Types Mothers Use in Talking to Their 2-Year-Old Children**

| | Cameron-Faulkner et al. (2003) | Wells (1983) |
|---|---|---|
| **Fragments** | **.20** | **.27** |
| One word | .07 | .08 |
| Multiword | .14 | .19 |
| **Questions** | **.32** | **.22** |
| Wh- | .16 | .08 |
| Yes/no | .15 | .13 |
| **Imperatives** | **.09** | **.14** |
| **Copulas** | **.15** | **.15** |
| **Subject-Predicate** | **.18** | **.18** |
| Transitives | .10 | .09 |
| Intransitives | .03 | .02 |
| Other | .05 | .07 |
| **Complex** | **.06** | **.05** |

*Sources:* From "A Construction Based Analysis of Child Directed Speech," by T. Cameron-Faulkner, E. Lieven, and M. Tomasello, 2003, *Cognitive Science, 27,* pp. 843–873. Reprinted with permission. *Learning through Interaction: The Study of Language Development,* by G. Wells, 1983, Cambridge, England: Cambridge University Press. Reprinted with permission.

sampled in a wider variety of activities). The overall findings were that:

- Children heard an estimated 5,000 to 7,000 utterances per day.
- Between one-quarter and one-third of these were questions.
- More than 20% of these were not full adult sentences, but instead were some kind of fragment (most often a noun phrase or prepositional phrase).
- About one-quarter of these were imperatives and utterances structured by the copula.
- Only about 15% of these had the canonical English SVO form (i.e., transitive utterances of various kinds) supposedly characteristic of the English language; and over 80% of the SVOs had a pronoun subject.

In a second analysis, these investigators looked at the specific words and phrases with which mothers initiated utterances in each of these general construction types, including such item-based frames as *Are you . . . , I'll . . . , It's . . . , Can you . . . , Here's . . . , Let's . . . , Look at . . . , What did . . . ,* and so on. It was found that more than half of all maternal utterances began with one of 52 highly frequent item-based frames (i.e., frames used more than an estimated 40 times per day for more than half the children), mostly consisting of 2 words or morphemes. Further, using the same kind of analysis, more than 65% of all of the mothers' utterances began with one of just 156 item-based frames. And perhaps most surprising, approximately 45% of all maternal utterances began with one of just 17 lexemes: *What* (8.6%), *That* (5.3%), *It* (4.2%), *You* (3.1%), *Are/Aren't* (3.0%), *Do/Does/Did/Don't* (2.9%), *I* (2.9%), *Is* (2.3%), *Shall* (2.1%), *A* (1.7%), *Can/Can't* (1.7%), *Where* (1.6%), *There* (1.5%), *Who* (1.4%), *Come* (1.0%), *Look* (1.0%), and *Let's* (1.0%). Interestingly, the children used many of these same item-based frames in their speech, in some cases at a rate that correlated highly with their own mother's frequency of use.

The language-learning child is thus faced with a prodigious task: acquiring simultaneously many dozens and dozens (perhaps hundreds) of constructions based on input in which all of the many different construction types are semi-randomly strewn. On the other hand, the task is made a bit easier by the fact that many of, indeed the majority of, the utterances children hear are grounded in highly repetitive item-based frames that they experience dozens, in some cases hundreds, of times every day. Indeed, many of the more complex utterances children hear have as a major constituent some well-practiced item-based frame. This means that the more linguistically creative utterances that children hear every day constitute only a small minority of their linguistic experience, and even these quite often rest on the foundation of many highly frequent and relatively simple item-based utterance frames.

## Earliest Language

Most Western, middle-class children begin producing conventional linguistic symbols in utterances in the months following their first birthdays. By the time they begin doing this, they typically have been communicating with other people gesturally and vocally for some months. Children's first linguistic expressions are learned and used in the context of these prior forms of nonlinguistic communication and for the same basic motives—declarative (statements) and imperative (requests)—and children soon learn to ask things interrogatively (questions) as well. There is typically a distinctive intonational pattern for each of these three speech act types. Children's first declarative utterances are sometimes about shared, topical referents and sometimes aimed at focusing the listener's attention on something new (typically assessed only from their own egocentric point of view; Greenfield & Smith, 1976).

At this early age, the communicative functions of children's early single-word utterances are an integral aspect of their reality for the child, and initially these functions (e.g., imperative or interrogative) may not be well differentiated from the more referential aspects of the utterance (Ninio, 1992, 1993). That is to say, children's early one-word utterances may be thought of as *holophrases* that convey a holistic, undifferentiated communicative intention, most often the same communicative intention as that of the adult expression from which it was learned (Barrett, 1982; Ninio, 1992). Many of children's early holophrases are relatively idiosyncratic and their uses can change and evolve over time in a somewhat unstable manner. Some holophrases, however, are a bit more conventional and stable. Children speaking all the languages of the world use their holophrases to do such things as:

- Request or indicate the existence of objects (e.g., by naming them with a requestive or neutral intonation).

- Request or describe the recurrence of objects or events (e.g., *More, Again, Another*).
- Request or describe dynamic events involving objects (e.g., as described by *Up, Down, On, Off, In, Out, Open, Close*).
- Request or describe the actions of people (e.g., *Eat, Kick, Ride, Draw*).
- Comment on the location of objects and people (e.g., *Here, Outside*).
- Ask some basic questions (e.g., *Whats-that?* or *Where-go?*).
- Attribute a property to an object (e.g., *Pretty* or *Wet*).
- Use performatives to mark specific social events and situations (e.g., *Hi, Bye, Thank you,* and *No*).

An important issue for later language development is what parts of adult expressions children choose for their initial holophrases. The answer lies in the specific language they are learning and the kinds of discourse in which they participate with adults, including the perceptual salience of particular words and phrases in adults' speech (Slobin, 1985). Thus, in English, most beginning language learners acquire so-called relational words such as *more, gone, up, down, on,* and *off,* presumably because adults use these words in salient ways to talk about salient events (Bloom, Tinker, & Margolis, 1993; McCune, 1992). Many of these words are verb particles in adult English, and so the child at some point must learn to talk about the same events with phrasal verbs such as *pick up, get down, put on, take off,* and so forth. In Korean and Mandarin Chinese, on the other hand, children learn fully adult verbs from the onset of language development because this is what is most salient in adult speech to them (Gopnik & Choi, 1995; Tardif, 1996). When they begin with an adult verb as a holophrase, children must then at some point learn, at least for some discourse purposes, to fill in linguistically the nominal participants involved in the scene (e.g., "Take-off *shirt!*"). Children in all languages also learn object labels for some events, for example, "Bike!" as a request to ride a bicycle or "Birdie" as a comment on a passing flight, which means that they still need to learn to linguistically express the activity involved (e.g., "*Ride* bike!" or "*See* birdie").

In addition, most children begin language acquisition by learning some unparsed adult expressions as holophrases—such things as "I-wanna-do-it," "Lemmesee," and "Where-the-bottle." The prevalence of this pattern in the early combinatorial speech of English-speaking children has been documented by Pine and Lieven (1993), who found that almost all children have at least some of these so-called frozen phrases in their early speech. This is especially true of some children (especially later-born children who observe siblings; Barton & Tomasello, 1994; Bates, Bretherton, & Snyder, 1988). In these cases, there is different syntactic work to do if the child is to extract productive linguistic elements that can be used appropriately in other utterances, in other linguistic contexts, in the future. For this, the child must engage in a process of segmentation, with regard not only to the speech stream but also to the communicative intentions involved—so as to determine which components of the speech stream go with which components of the underlying communicative intention. Functionally speaking, then, children's early one-unit utterances are entire semantic-pragmatic packages—holophrastic expressions—that express a single relatively coherent, yet undifferentiated, communicative intention. Why children begin with only one-unit expressions—either individual words or holistic expressions—is not known at this time. But it is presumably the case that in many instances they initially only attend to limited parts of adult utterances, or can only process one linguistic unit at a time.

## Item-Based Constructions

Children produce their earliest multiword utterances to talk about many of the same kinds of things they talked about previously with their holophrases—since indeed many, though not all, early multiword constructions may be traced back to earlier holophrases. From the point of view of linguistic form, the utterance-level constructions underlying these multiword utterances come in three types: word combinations, pivot schemas, and item-based constructions.

### Word Combinations

Beginning at around 18 months of age, many children combine two words or holophrases in situations in which they both are relevant—with both words having roughly equivalent status. For example, a child has learned to name a ball and a table and then spies a ball on a table and says, "Ball table." Utterances of this type include both "successive single-word utterances" (with a pause between them; Bloom, 1973) and "word combinations"

or "expressions" (under a single intonational contour). The defining feature of word combinations or expressions is that they partition the experiential scene into multiple symbolizable units—in a way that holophrases obviously (by definition) do not—and they are totally concrete in the sense that they are comprised only of concrete pieces of language, not categories.

### Pivot Schemas

Beginning at around this same age, however, many of children's multiword productions show a more systematic pattern. Often there is one word or phrase that seems to structure the utterance in the sense that it determines the speech act function of the utterance as a whole (often with help from an intonational contour), with the other linguistic item(s) simply filling in variable slot(s)—the first type of linguistic abstraction. Thus, in many of these early utterances, one event-word is used with a wide variety of object labels (e.g., "More milk," "More grapes," "More juice") or, more rarely, something like a pronoun or other general expression is the constant element (e.g., *I* _____ or _____ *it* or even *It's* _____ or *Where's* _____). Following Braine (1963), we may call these pivot schemas.

Braine (1976) established that this is a widespread and productive strategy for children acquiring many of the world's languages. And Tomasello, Akhtar, Dodson, and Rekau (1997) found that 22-month-old children who were taught a novel name for an object knew immediately how to combine this novel name with other pivot-type words already in their vocabulary. That is, when taught a novel object label as a single word utterance (e.g., "Look! A wug!"), children were able to use that new object label in combination with their existing pivot-type words in utterances such as "Wug gone" or "More wug." This productivity suggests that young children can create linguistic categories at this young age, specifically categories corresponding to the types of linguistic items that can play particular roles in specific pivot schemas (e.g., "things that are gone," "things I want more of"). However, these same children do not make generalizations across the various pivot schemas. Thus, Tomasello et al. (1997) also found that when taught a novel verb as a single-word utterance for a novel scene (e.g., "Look! Meeking!" or "Look what she's doing to it. That's called meeking."), these same 22-month-old children were not then able to say creative things like "Ernie meeking!"—because they had never heard how *meeking* structured a pivot schema with an actor. Each pivot schema is thus at this point a constructional island, and so at this stage of development, children do not have an overarching grammar of their language.

### Item-Based Constructions

Not only are pivot schemas organized locally, but even within themselves they do not have syntax; that is, "Gone juice" does not mean something different from "Juice gone" (and there is no other marking to indicate syntactic role for elements in pivot schemas). The consistent ordering patterns in many pivot schemas are very likely direct reproductions of the ordering patterns children have heard most often in adult speech, with no communicative significance. This means that although young children are using their early pivot schemas to partition scenes conceptually with different words, they are not using syntactic symbols—such as word order or case marking—to indicate the different roles being played by different participants in that scene.

On the other hand, item-based constructions go beyond pivot schemas in having syntactic marking as an integral part of the construction. The evidence that children have, from fairly early in development, such syntactically marked item-based constructions is solid. Most important are a number of comprehension experiments in which children barely 2 years of age respond appropriately to requests that they "Make the bunny push the horse" (reversible transitives) that depend crucially and exclusively on a knowledge of canonical English word order (e.g., Bates et al., 1984; DeVilliers & DeVilliers, 1973; Roberts, 1983). Successful comprehension of word order with familiar verbs is found at even younger ages if preferential looking techniques are used (Hirsh-Pasek & Golinkoff, 1991, 1996). In production as well, many children around their second birthdays are able to produce transitive utterances with familiar verbs that respect canonical English word order marking (Tomasello, 2000).

However, there is abundant evidence from many studies of both comprehension and production that the syntactic marking in these item-based constructions is still verb specific, depending on how a child has heard a particular verb being used. For example, Tomasello (1992) found that almost all of his daughter's early multiword utterances during her second year of life revolved around the specific verbs or predicative terms involved. The lexically specific pattern of this phase of combinatorial speech was evident in the patterns of participant roles with which individual verbs were used. Thus, during exactly the same developmental period, some verbs were used in only one type of construction and that construction was quite simple (e.g., *Cut _____* ), whereas other verbs were used in more complex frames of several different types (e.g., *Draw _____* , *Draw _____ on _____* , *Draw _____ for _____* , *_____ draw on _____* ). Interestingly and importantly, within any given verb's development, there was great continuity such that new uses of a given verb almost always replicated previous uses and then made one small addition or modification (e.g., the marking of tense or the adding of a new argument). In general, by far the best predictor of this child's use of a given verb on a given day was not her use of other verbs on that same day, but rather her use of that same verb on immediately preceding days. (See Lieven, Pine, & Baldwin, 1997; Pine & Lieven, 1993; Pine, Lieven, & Rowland, 1998, for some very similar results in a sample of 12 English-speaking children from 1 to 3 years of age. For additional findings of this same type in other languages, see Allen, 1996, for Inuktitut; Behrens, 1998, for Dutch; Berman, 1982, for Hebrew; Gathercole, Sebastián, & Soto, 1999, for Spanish; Pizutto & Caselli, 1992, for Italian; Rubino & Pine, 1998, for Portugese; Serrat, 1997, for Catalan; and Stoll, 1998, for Russian.)

Similarly, in experimental studies, when children who are themselves producing many transitive utterances are taught a new verb in any one of many different constructions, they mostly cannot transfer their knowledge of word order from their existing item-based constructions to this new item until after their third birthdays—and this finding holds for comprehension as well (Tomasello, 2000). These findings would seem to indicate that young children's early syntactic marking—at least with English word order—is only local, learned for different verbs on a one-by-one basis (see next section for a review of these studies). What little experimental evidence we have from nonce verb studies of case-marking languages (e.g., Berman, 1993; Wittek & Tomasello, 2005) is in general accord with this developmental pattern.

The main point is that unlike in pivot schemas, in item-based constructions children use syntactic symbols such as morphology, adpositions, and word order to syntactically mark the roles participants are playing in these events, including generalized slots that include whole categories of entities as participants. But all of this is done on an item-specific basis; that is, the child does not generalize across scenes to syntactically mark similar participant roles in similar ways without having heard those participants used and marked in adult discourse for each verb specifically. This limited generality is presumably due to the difficulty of categorizing or schematizing entire utterances, including reference to both the event and the participant roles involved, into more abstract constructions—especially given the many different kinds of utterances children hear and must sort through. Early syntactic competence is therefore best characterized as a semi-structured inventory of relatively independent verb island constructions that pair a scene of experience and an item-based construction, with very few structural relationships among these constructional islands.

### Processes of Schematization

From a usage-based perspective, word combinations, pivot schemas, and item-based constructions are things that children construct out of the language they hear around them using general cognitive and social-cognitive skills. It is thus important to establish that, at the necessary points in development, children have the skills they need to comprehend, learn, and produce each of these three types of early constructions.

First, to produce a word combination under a single intonation contour, children must be able to create a multiple-step procedure toward a single goal, assembled conceptually ahead of time (what Piaget, 1952, called "mental combinations"). They are able to do this in nonlinguistic behavior quite readily, from about 14 to 18 months of age in their own problem solving, and, moreover, they are also able to copy such sequences from the behavior of other persons at around this same age. Thus, Bauer (1996) found that 14-month-old infants were quite skillful at imitatively learning both 2- and 3-step action sequences from adults—mostly involving the constructing of complex toy objects (e.g., a toy bell) that they saw adults assembling. Children were sensitive to the order of the steps involved as well. These would seem to be the right skills at the right time for constructing word combinations.

Second, the process by which pivot schemas are formed—as abstractions across individual word combinations—is presumably very similar to the way 1-year-olds form other kinds of sensory-motor schemas, including those learned through observation of others' behavior: what may be called schematization. Thus, Piaget (1952) reports that when infants repeatedly enact the same action on different objects, they form a sensory-motor schema consisting of (a) what is general in all of the various actions and (b) a kind of slot for the variable component. As one example, Brown and Kane (1988) taught 2-year-old children to use a certain kind of action with a particular object (e.g., pull a stick) and then gave them transfer problems in which it was possible for them to use the same action but with a different object creatively (e.g., they learned to pull stick, pull rope, pull towel). Their skill at doing this demonstrates exactly the kind of cognitive ability needed to create a pivot schema across different utterances so as to yield something like *Pull X*. Ultimately, if the child forms a generalized action or event schema with a variable slot for some class of items (e.g., *Throw X*), that slot and class of items are defined by their role in the schema, which is why Nelson (1985) calls them slot-filler categories. This means that in the case of pivot schemas such as *Throw X, X gone,* and *Want X,* the slot could be thought of as something like "throwable things," "things that are gone," "things I want more of," and so forth. This primacy of the schema in defining the slot leads to the kinds of coercion evidenced in creative uses of language in which an item is used in a schema that requires us to interpret it in an unusual way. For example, under communicative pressure, a child might say "I'm juicing it" as she pours juice onto something, or "Where's-the swimming?" as she looks for a picture of a swimming activity in a book. This process of "functional coercion" is perhaps the major source of syntactic creativity in the language of 1- and 2-year-old children.

Third and finally, it is not clear how young children learn about syntactically marking their utterance-level constructions, so creating item-based constructions. Essentially what they need to learn is that whereas some linguistic symbols are used for referring and predicating things about the world, others (including word order) are used for more grammatical functions. These functions are many and various but they all share the property that they are parasitic on the symbols that actually carry the load of referring and predicating. Thus, with special reference to utterance-level constructions, an accusative case marker (or an immediate postverbal position) can only function symbolically if there is some referential expression to indicate the entity that is the object of some action; we may thus call syntactic markers second-order symbols (Tomasello, 1992). Although children do engage in nonlinguistic activities that have clear and generalized roles, there is really nothing in nonlinguistic activities that corresponds to such second-order symbols. (The closest might be the designation of participant roles in some forms of pretend play—but that is typically a much later developmental achievement.)

Children presumably learn to deal with such symbols when they hear such things as, in English, *X is pushing Y* and then on another occasion *Y is pushing X,* each paired with its own real world counterpart. From this, they begin to see that the verb island construction involving *push* is structured so that the "pusher" is in the preverbal position and "pushee" is in the postverbal position regardless of the specific identity of that participant.

## Marking Syntactic Roles

From a psycholinguistic point of view, linguistic constructions are comprised of four and only four types of symbolic elements: words, morphological markers on words, word order, and intonation/prosody (Bates & MacWhinney, 1982). Of special importance for utterance-level constructions are the syntactic devices used for marking the participant roles (typically expressed as noun phrases, NPs) to indicate the basic "who-did-what-to-whom" of the utterance, what are sometimes called agent-patient relations. The two major devices that languages use for this purpose are (1) word order (mainly of NPs) and (2) morphological marking (casemarking on NPs and agreement marking between NPs and verb).

### Word Order

In their spontaneous speech, young English-speaking children use canonical word order for most of their verbs, including transitive verbs, from very early in development (Bloom, 1992; Braine, 1971; Brown, 1973). And as reported, in comprehension tasks, children as young as 2 years of age respond appropriately to requests that they "Make the doggie bite the cat" (reversible transitives) that depend crucially and exclusively on a knowledge of canonical English word order (e.g., DeVilliers & DeVilliers, 1973). But to really discover the nature of children's underlying linguistic representations, we need to examine utterances we know children are producing creatively; this means overgeneralization errors (which they could not have heard from adults) and the use of novel words introduced in experiments.

First, children's overgeneralization errors—indicating a more abstract understanding of word order and constructional patterns—include such things as *She falled me down* or *Don't giggle me* in which the child uses intransitive verbs in the SVO transitive frame productively. Pinker (1989) compiled examples from many sources and found that children produce a number of such overgeneralizations, but few before about 3 years of age.

Second, production experiments focused on the marking of agent-patient relations by word order in English typically introduce young children to a novel verb in a syntactic construction such as an intransitive or passive and then see if they can later use that verb in the canonical SVO transitive construction. Cues to syntactic roles other than word order (e.g., animacy of the S and O participants, use of case-marked pronouns) are carefully controlled and/or monitored. Experiments of this type have clearly demonstrated that by $3\frac{1}{2}$ or 4 years of age most English-speaking children can readily assimilate novel verbs to an abstract SVO schema that they bring to the experiment. For example, Maratsos, Gudeman, Gerard-Ngo, and DeHart (1987) taught children from $4\frac{1}{2}$ to $5\frac{1}{2}$ years of age the novel verb *fud* for a novel transitive action (human operating a machine that transformed the shape of Play-Doh). Children were introduced to the novel verb in a series of intransitive sentence frames such as "The dough finally fudded," "It won't fud," and "The dough's fudding in the machine." Children were then prompted with questions such as "What are you doing?" (which encourages a transitive response such as "I'm fudding the dough"). The general finding was that the vast majority of children from $4\frac{1}{2}$ to $5\frac{1}{2}$ years of age could produce a canonical transitive SVO utterance with the novel verb, even though they had never heard it used in that construction.

But the same is not true for younger children. Over a dozen studies similar to that of Maratsos et al. (1987) have been done with 2- and 3-year-olds, and they are generally not productive (see Tomasello 2000, for a review). When findings across all ages are compiled and quantitatively compared, we see a continuous developmental progression in which children gradually become more productive with novel verbs in the transitive SVO construction during their third and fourth years of life and beyond, evidencing a growing understanding of the working of canonical English word order (see Figure 6.1).

Akhtar (1999) used a different novel verb methodology to investigate young children's knowledge of English word-order conventions. An adult modeled novel verbs for novel transitive events for young children at 2;8, 3;6, and 4;4 years of age. One verb was modeled in canonical English SVO order, as in *Ernie meeking the car,* whereas two others were in noncanonical orders, either SOV (*Ernie the cow tamming*) or VSO (*Gopping Ernie the cow*). Children were then encouraged to use the novel verbs with neutral questions such as *What's happening?* Almost all of the children at all three ages produced exclusively SVO utterances with the novel

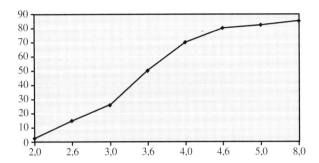

**Figure 6.1** Percentage of children who produce transitive utterances using novel verbs in different studies. Adapted from "Do Young Children Have Adult Syntactic Competence?" by M. Tomasello, 2000, *Cognition, 74,* pp. 209–253. Reprinted with permission.

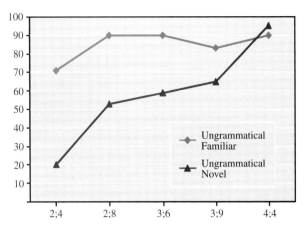

**Figure 6.2** Percentage of utterances in which children "corrected" weird word order to canonical English SVO with familiar and unfamiliar verbs in two studies. *Source:* From "Acquiring Basic Word Order: Evidence for Data-Driven Learning of Syntactic Structure," by N. Akhtar, 1999, *Journal of Child Language, 26,* pp. 339–356. Reprinted with permission; "What Children Do and Do Not Do with Ungrammatical Word Orders," by K. Abbot-Smith, E. Lieven, and M. Tomasello, 2001, *Cognitive Development, 16,* pp. 1–14. Reprinted with permission.

verb when that is what they heard. However, when they heard one of the noncanonical SOV or VSO forms, children behaved differently at different ages. In general, the older children used their verb-general knowledge of English transitivity to correct the noncanonical uses of the novel verbs to canonical SVO form. The younger children, in contrast, much more often matched the ordering patterns they had heard with the novel verb, no matter how bizarre that pattern sounded to adult ears. Abbot-Smith, Lieven, and Tomasello (2001) have recently extended this methodology to younger ages (children at 2;4, using intransitives) and found that even fewer children (less than half as many as Akhtar's youngest children) corrected the adult's strange word order utterances. The results of these two studies combined are depicted in Figure 6.2.

Perhaps surprisingly, young children also fail to show a verb-general understanding of canonical English word order in comprehension studies using novel verbs in which they must act out (with toys) a scene indicated by an SVO utterance. Thus, Akhtar and Tomasello (1997) exposed young children to many models of *This is called dacking* used to describe a canonical transitive action. They then, using novel characters, asked the children to *Make Cookie Monster dack Big Bird.* All 10 of the children 3;8 were excellent in this task, whereas only 3 of the 10 children at 2;9 were above chance in this task—even though most did well on a control task using familiar verbs. In a second type of comprehension test, children just under 3 years of age first learned to act out a novel action on a novel apparatus with two toy characters, and only then (their first introduction to the novel verb) did the adult hand them two new characters and request *Can you make X meek Y* (while pushing the ap-

paratus in front of them)? In this case, children's only exposure to the novel verb was in a very natural transitive sentence frame used for an action they already knew how to perform. Since every child knew the names of the novel characters and on every trial attempted to make one of them act on the other in the appropriate way, the only question was which character should play which role. These under-3-year-old children were, as a group, at chance in this task, with only 3 of the 12 children performing above chance as individuals. Similar results, using a different comprehension methodology (a token placement task), were found by Bridges (1984). Using a comprehension methodology in which children had to point to the agent of an utterance—the main clue to which was word order, Fisher (1996) found positive results for children averaging 3;6 years of age (and Fisher, 2002, found somewhat weaker evidence for the same effect in children at 2;6).

Another technique used to assess children's comprehension of various linguistic items and structures is so-called preferential looking. In this technique, a child is shown two displays (often on two television screens) and hears a single utterance (through a centrally located loudspeaker) that describes only one of the pictures felicitously. The question is which picture she will look at longer. The relevant studies are those using novel or very low frequency verbs, so we know that children have had no previous experience with them. In almost all of these studies, the comparison is between transitives and intransitives. Thus, Naigles (1990) found that when they hear canonical SVO utterances English-speaking children from 2;1 prefer to look at one participant doing something to another (causative meaning) rather than two participants carrying out synchronous independent activities. This study shows that in the preferential looking paradigm young 2-year-old children know enough about the simple transitive construction to know that it goes with asymmetrical activities (one participant acting on another) rather than symmetrical activities (two participants engaging in the same activity simultaneously). What it does *not* show, as is sometimes claimed, is an understanding of word order. That is, it does not show that young children can connect the preverbal position with the agent (or subject) and the postverbal position with the patient (or object) in a transitive utterance—which would be required for a full-blown representation of the transitive construction, and which is indeed required of children in both act-out comprehension tasks and novel verb production tasks.[1]

The overall conclusion is thus that in both production and comprehension the majority of English-speaking children do not fully understand word order as a verb-general, productive syntactic device for marking agents and patients (subjects and objects) until after 3 years of age (although some minority of children may understand it before). In some cases, even the presence of animacy cues (agents were animate, patients inanimate) does not help. But, of course, most English-speaking children are hearing SVO utterances with one or more case-marked pronouns (*I-me, he-him, they-them, we-us,* etc.), and so we now turn to an investigation of their understanding of case marking—which is much more important in some other languages than it is in English.

### Case and Agreement

In the 1960s and 1970s, a number of investigators speculated that word order should be easier than case and

---

[1] The only preferential looking study that attempted to examine this knowledge is by Fisher (2000). However, the sentences she gave children (ages 1;9 and 2;2) had prepositional phrases that provided additional information (e.g., *The duck is gorping the bunny up and down*). Thus, the child merely had to interpret *bunny up and down* to prefer the picture in which the bunny was indeed moving up and down.

agreement for children to learn as a syntactic device because canonical ordering is so fundamental to so many sensory-motor and cognitive activities (Braine, 1976; Bruner, 1975; McNeill, 1966; Pinker, 1981). However, cross-linguistic research has since exploded this word order myth (Weist, 1983). That is, cross-linguistic research has demonstrated that in their spontaneous speech, children learning many different languages—regardless of whether their language relies mainly on word order, case marking, or some combination of both—generally conform to adult usage and appear to mark agent-patient relations equally early and appropriately. Indeed, on the basis of his review, Slobin (1982) concluded that children learning languages that mark agent-patient relations clearly and simply with morphological (case) markers, such as Turkish, comprehend agent-patient syntax earlier than children learning word order languages such as English. In support of his argument, Slobin cited the fact that some children learning case marking languages overgeneralize case markers in ways indicating productive control while they are still only 2 years old (Slobin, 1982, 1985).

In comprehension experiments, children learning morphologically rich languages, in which word order plays only a minor role in indicating agent-patient relations, comprehend the syntactic marking of agent-patient relations as early or earlier than children learning word order languages such as English. Representative studies are reported by Slobin and Bever (1982) for Turkish, Hakuta (1982) for Japanese, and Weist (1983) for Polish (see Slobin, 1982, and Bates & MacWhinney, 1989, for reviews). But it should be noted that in neither comprehension nor production do we have the kind of nonce word studies that could provide the most definitive evidence of children's productive knowledge of case marking. The few nonce verb studies we have of case-marking languages (e.g., Berman, 1993; Wittek & Tomasello, 2005) show a very slow and gradual developmental pattern of increasing productivity, just as with word order marking in English and similar languages.

For English, most of the discussion of case marking has centered around pronoun case errors, such as *me do it* and *him going.* About 50% of English-speaking children make such errors, most typically in the 2- to 4-year age range, with much variability across children. The most robust phenomenon is that children often substitute accusative forms for nominative forms ("Me going") but very seldom do the reverse ("Billy hit I"). Rispoli (1994, 1998) notes that the particular pronouns that

English-speaking children overgeneralize proportionally most often are the objective forms *me* and *her* (and not the subjective forms *I* and *she*). Rispoli attributes these facts to the morphophonetic structure of the English personal pronoun paradigm:

| I  | she | he  | they  |
|----|-----|-----|-------|
| me | her | him | them  |
| my | her | his | their |

It is easily seen that *he-him-his* and *they-them-their* each has a common phonetic core (*h-* and *th-*, respectively) whereas *I-me-my* and *she-her-her* do not. And indeed, the errors that are made most often are ones in which children in these latter two cases use the forms that have a common initial phoneme (*me-my* and *her-her*) to substitute for the odd-man-out (*I* and *she*), with the *her*-for-*she* error having the overall highest rate (because of the fact, according to Rispoli, that *her* occurs as both the objective and genetive form; the so-called double-cell effect). The overall idea is thus that children are making retrieval errors based on both semantic and phonological factors.

Currently, there is no widely accepted explanation of children's pronoun case errors in English, and it is likely that several different factors play a role. Of most importance to resolve the issue in a theoretically interesting way is cross-linguistic research enabling the examination of pronoun paradigms with different morphophonemic and syntactic properties.

### Cue Coalition and Competition

In all languages, there are multiple potential cues indicating agent-patient relations. For example, in many languages, both word order and case marking are at least potentially available, even though one of them might most typically be used for other functions (e.g., in many morphologically rich languages, word order is used primarily for pragmatic functions such as topicalization). In addition, in attempting to comprehend adult utterances, children might also attend to information that is not directly encoded in the language; for example, they may use animacy to infer that in an utterance containing the lexical items *man, ball,* and *kick,* the most likely interpretation is that the man kicked the ball, regardless of how those items are syntactically combined.

In an extensive investigation of language acquisition in a number of different languages, Slobin (reviewed in 1982) identified some of the different comprehension strategies that children use to establish agent-patient relations, depending on the types of problems their particular language presents to them. A central discovery of this research, as noted, was that children can more easily master grammatical forms expressed in "local cues" such as bound morphology as opposed to more distributed cues such as word order and some forms of agreement. This accounts for the fact that Turkish-speaking children master the expression of agent-patient relations at a significantly earlier age than do English-speaking children. In addition, Turkish is especially "child friendly," even among languages that rely heavily on local morphological cues. Slobin (1982) outlines 12 reasons why Turkish agent-patient relations are relatively easy to learn. An adaptation of that list (focusing on nominal morphology) follows. Turkish nominal grammatical morphemes are:

- Postposed, syllabic, and stressed, which makes them perceptually more *salient.*
- Obligatory and employ almost perfect one-to-one mapping of form to function (no fusional morphemes or homophones), which makes them more *predictable.*
- Bound to the noun, rather than freestanding, which makes them more *local.*
- Invariably regular across different nominals and pronominals, which makes them readily *generalizable.*

All of these factors coalesce to make Turkish agent-patient relations especially easy to learn, and their identification is a major step in discovering the basic processes of language acquisition that are employed by children in general.

A central methodological problem, however, is that in natural languages many of these cues go together naturally, and so it is difficult to evaluate their contributions separately. Therefore, Bates and MacWhinney (summarized in 1989) conducted an extensive set of experimental investigations of the cues children use to comprehend agent-patient relations in a number of different languages. The basic paradigm is to ask children to act out utterances using toy animals, with agent-patient relations indicated in different ways—sometimes in semi-grammatical utterances with conflicting cues. For example, an English-speaking child might be presented with the utterance "The spoon kicked the horse." In this case, the cue of word order is put in competition with the most likely real-world scenario in which animate beings more often kick inanimate things than the reverse. From an early age, young English-speaking children make the spoon "kick" the horse, which simply shows the power of word order in English. Interestingly, when presented with an equivalent utterance, Italian-speaking children ignore word order and make the horse kick the spoon. This is because word order is quite variable in Italian, and so, since there is no case marking (and in this example agreement is no help because both the horse and the spoon are third-person singular), semantic plausibility is the most reliable cue available. German-speaking children gradually learn to ignore both word order and semantic plausibility (animacy) and simply look for nominative and accusative marking on the horse and the spoon (Lindner, 2003).

## Constructing Lexical Categories

Syntactic roles such as agent and patient, or subject and object, represent syntagmatic categories defined by the role of the element in the larger constructional whole. As utterance-level constructions gradually become more abstract, therefore, these categories become more abstract with them. Another important part of the process of grammatical development is the construction of paradigmatic categories such as noun and verb. Unlike syntactic roles, paradigmatic categories are not explicitly marked in language. That is, whereas such things as agent/subject are symbolically indicated by word order or grammatical morphology in the construction, nouns and verbs have no explicit marking (despite the fact that they often have some morphology serving other functions, e.g., plural markers on nouns, that can be used to identify them). Consequently, the category cannot be organized around any specific linguistic symbol, but can only be based on commonalities in the way the members of the category function (i.e., on distribution). Thus, *pencil* and *pen* occur in many of the same linguistic contexts in utterances—that is, do many of the same kinds of things in combining with articles to make reference to an object, in indicating subjects and objects as syntactic roles, and so on—and so a language user will come to form a category containing these and similarly behaving words in it.

The prototypical paradigmatic linguistic categories, and the only ones that are even candidates for universal status, are nouns and verbs. The classic notional definitions—nouns indicate person, place, or thing, and verbs indicate actions—clearly do not hold, as many nouns indicate actions or events (e.g., *party, discussion*) and many verbs indicate nonactional state's affairs that are sometime very difficult to distinguish from things indi-

cated by adjectives (e.g., *be noisy, feel good,* which in different languages may be indicated by either a verb or an adjective). On the other hand, Maratsos (1982) points out that both nouns and verbs have characteristic small-scale combinatorial properties; for example, nouns occur with determiners and plural markers and verbs occur with tense and aspect markers. Although these can be used to recognize instances of the categories once they are formed, obviously the core notions underlying nouns and verbs are cognitively and communicatively much deeper. Evidence for this is the simple fact that some of the most prototypical nominals do not have the same small-scale combinatorial properties as others; that is, pronouns and proper names do not occur with determiners or plural markers.

Langacker (1987b) provides a functionally based account of nouns and verbs that goes much deeper than both simplistic notional definitions and purely formal properties. Langacker stresses that nouns and verbs are used not to refer to specific kinds of things but rather to invite the listener to construe something in a particular way in a particular communicative context. Thus, we may refer to the very same experience as either "exploding" or "an explosion," depending on our communicative purposes. In general, nouns are used to construe experiences as bounded entities (like an explosion), whereas verbs are used to construe experiences as processes (like exploding). Hopper and Thompson (1984) contend further that the discourse functions of reference and predication provide the communicative reason for construing something as either a bounded entity, to which one may refer with a noun, or a process that one may predicate with a verb. Importantly, it is these communicative functions that explain why nouns are associated with such things as determiners, whose primary function is to help the listener locate a referent in actual or conceptual space; and verbs are associated with such things as tense markers, whose primary function is to help the listener locate a process in actual or conceptual time (Langacker, 1991). After an individual understands the functional basis of nouns and verbs, formal features such as determiners and tense markers may be used to identify further instances.

From a functional point of view, Bates and MacWhinney (1979, 1982) propose that early nouns are anchored in the concept of a concrete object and early verbs are anchored in the concept of concrete action—and these are generalized to other referents only later. The problem is that young children use adult nouns from quite early in development to refer to all kinds of nonobject entities such as *breakfast, kitchen, kiss, lunch, light, park, doctor, night,* and *party,* and they use many of their verbs to predicate nonactional states of affairs (e.g., *like, feel, want, stay, be;* Nelson, Hampson, & Shaw, 1993). Also problematic for accounts such as these, grounded in the reference of terms, is that early in development young children also learn many words that are used as both nouns and verbs (e.g., *bite, kiss, drink, brush, walk, hug, help,* and *call;* Nelson, 1995). It is unclear how any theory that does not consider communicative function primary, in the sense of the communicative role a word plays in whole utterances, can account for the acquisition of these dual category words.

Instead, the developmental data support the view that children initially understand paradigmatic categories very locally and mosaically, in terms of the particular kinds of things particular words can and cannot do communicatively. Thus, with respect to nouns, Tomasello et al. (1997) found that when 22-month-old children were taught a novel name for a novel object in a syntactically neutral context ("Look! A wuggie.") they immediately combined this new word with many predicative terms ("Hug wuggie," "Wuggie gone," etc.), indicating that they saw something in common between wuggies and the kinds of things one can hug or that can be gone (perhaps aided by the article *a*). Children of this same tender age also were able to indicate when they saw two "Wuggie*s*," even though they had never heard this word used as a plural. However, a very interesting fact helping to specify the processes involved is that these two productive achievements, in syntax and morphology, were very poorly correlated. The children who could productively combine *wuggie* with other words syntactically were not the same ones who could create a productive plural with this same word. This suggests that children are forming their paradigmatic categories for very local communicative purposes, in mosaic and piecemeal fashion, not for all of the many more abstract and interrelated functions that underlie these categories in adults. Exactly how these processes might apply to words that fit the adult category of noun less well (nonobject common nouns, proper nouns, mass nouns) is not known at this time.

With respect to verbs, Akhtar and Tomasello (1997) did a similar study with slightly older 2- and 3-year-old children and found that, as in the analogous case with nouns, children became productive with novel verbs syntactically and morphologically in an uncorrelated fash-

ion—again suggesting local, functionally specific, mosaically acquired, paradigmatic categories. Evidence from other languages also suggests that young children's paradigmatic categories develop in a gradual and piecemeal way as they attempt to assimilate to their more locally based categories the wider array of more abstract functions that underlie the adult version of the category (see Rispoli, 1991, for various types of evidence).

Overall, children's early paradigmatic categories are best explained in the same theoretical terms as their other cognitive categories. As noted in the discussion of slot-filler categories in early pivot schemas, Nelson (1985, 1996) and Mandler (2000) have both argued that the essence of concepts lies in function; human beings group together things that behave in similar ways in events and activities. In the case of linguistic categories such as noun and verb, however, it is important to be clear that these are categories not of entities in the world (i.e., not referents) but of pieces of language (words and phrases). When words and phrases are grouped together according to similarities in what they do communicatively—grounded in such functions as reference and predication—cognitively and linguistically coherent categories are the result.

The main cognitive skill necessary to form such categories is statistical or distribution learning. Importantly, it has recently been discovered that even prelinguistic infants are able to find patterns in sequentially presented auditory stimuli. Thus, Saffran, Aslin, and Newport (1996) exposed 8-month-old infants to 2 minutes of synthesized speech consisting of four trisyllabic nonsense words such as bidakupadotigolabubidakutupiropadoti. . . . They were then exposed to two new streams of synthesized speech simultaneously (one presented to the left and one presented to the right) to see which they preferred to listen to (as indicated by the direction they turned their head). One of these streams contained "words" from the original (e.g., tupiro and golabu), whereas the other contained the same syllables but in a different order (i.e., there were no words from the original). Infants preferred to look toward the speech stream containing the words to which they had originally been exposed.

Subsequent studies have shown that infants can also find patterns even when the syllables from the original speech stream and the test speech stream are not the same. Thus, Marcus, Vijayan, Bandi Rao, & Vishton (1999) found that 7-month-old infants exposed repeatedly over a three-minute period to tri-syllabic nonsense words with the pattern ABB (e.g., wididi, delili) preferred in subsequent testing to look toward the speech stream containing other words having this same ABB pattern even though the specific syllables involved were totally new (e.g., bapopo). Gómez and Gerken (1999) found a very similar results with 12-month-old infants. Interestingly, infants can also find patterns of this same type in both nonlinguistic tone sequences and even in visually presented sequences (Kirkham, Slemmer, & Johnson, in press; Saffran, Johnson, Aslin, & Newport, 1999). These pattern-finding skills are thus not specific to language learning. Also, when tamarin monkeys are tested in these same procedures, they show these same abilities (Hauser, Weiss, & Marcus, 2002; Newport, Aslin, & Hauser, 2001; Ramus, Hauser, Miller, Morris, & Mehler, 2000). These pattern-finding skills are thus not uniquely human.

## LATER ONTOGENY

During the preschool years, English-speaking children begin to be productive with a variety of abstract utterance-level constructions, including such things as: transitives, intransitives, ditransitives, attributives, passives, imperatives, reflexives, locatives, resultatives, causatives, and various kinds of question constructions. Many of these are so-called argument-structure constructions, and they are used to refer to experiential scenes of the most abstract kind, including such things as: people acting on objects, objects changing state or location, people giving people things, people experiencing psychological states, objects or people being in a state, things being acted on, and so forth (Goldberg, 1995). It is presumably the case that these abstract constructions represent children's generalizations across many dozen (or more) item-based constructions, especially verb island constructions.

Children also construct smaller constructions that serve as the major internal constituents of utterance-level constructions. Most especially, they construct nominal constructions (NPs) in order to make reference to things in various ways (*Bill, my father, the man who fell down*) and verbal constructions (VPs) in order predicate for something about those things (*is nice, sleeps, hit the ball*). Children also create, a bit later in development, larger and more complex constructions containing multiple predicates such as infinitival complements (*I want him to go*), sentential complements (*I think it will fall over*), and relative clauses (*That's the doggy I bought*). These smaller and larger constructions

also are important components in children's later linguistic competence.

Theoretically, we are concerned here again with the nature of the cognitive processes that enable young children to generalize from their linguistic experience and so build up these highly abstract constructions. In addition, in this section, we also address the difficult question of why children make just the generalizations they do, and not some others that might be reasonable from an adult point of view.

### Abstract Constructions

The most abstract constructions that English-speaking children use early in development have mostly been studied from an adult perspective—using constructions defined from an adult model. We follow suit here, but the truth is that many of the constructions listed here probably should be differentiated in a more fine-grained way (as families of subconstructions) once the necessary empirical work is done.

#### Identificationals, Attributives, and Possessives

Among the earliest utterance-level constructions used by many English-speaking children are those that serve to identify an object or to attribute to it some property, including a possessor or simple location (Lieven, Pine, & Dresner-Barnes, 1992). In adult language, these would almost invariably require some form of the coplua, *to be,* although children do not always supply it. Quite often, these constructions revolve around one or a few specific words. Most common for the identification function are such things as *It's a/the X; That's a/the X; or This's a/the X.* Most common for the attributive function are such things as: *Here's a/the X; There's a/the X.* Most common for the possessive function are such things as: *(It's) X's _____ ; That's X's/my _____ ; This is X's/your _____ .* Clancy (2000) reports some very similar constructions for Korean-speaking children, and a perusal of the studies in Slobin's cross-linguistic volumes reveals many other languages in which these are frequently used child constructions for focusing attention on, or attributing a property to, an external entity.

#### Simple Transitives, Simple Intransitives, and Imperatives

The simple transitive construction in English is used for depicting a variety of scenes that differ greatly from one another. The prototype is a scene in which there are two participants and one somehow acts on the other. English-speaking children typically produce utterances of this type in their spontaneous speech early in language development for various physical and psychological activities that people perform on objects—everything from pushing to having to dropping to knowing. The main verbs young children use in the transitive construction are such things as *get, have, want, take, find, put, bring, drop, make, open, break, cut, do, eat, play, read, draw, ride, throw, push, help, see, say,* and *hurt.*

The simple intransitive construction in English is also used for a wide variety of scenes. In this case, the only commonality is that they involve a single participant and activity. The two main types of intransitives are the so-called unergatives, in which an actor does something (e.g., *John smiled*) and the so-called unaccusatives, in which something happens to something (e.g., *The vase broke*). English-speaking children typically produce utterances of both of these types early in language development, with unergatives such as *sleep* and *swim* predominating (unaccusatives occurring most often with the specific verbs *break* and *hurt*). The main verbs young children use in the intransitive construction—including imperative uses—are such things as *go, come, stop, break, fall, open, play, jump, sit, sing, sleep, cry, swim, run, laugh, hurt,* and *see.*

### Ditransitives, Datives, and Benefactives

All languages of the world have utterance-level constructions for talking about the transfer of objects (and other things) between people (Newman, 1996). In English, there is a constellation of three related constructions for doing this: the *to*-dative, the *for*-dative (or benefactive), and the double-object dative (or ditransitive). Many verbs occur in both the *to*-dative and the double-object dative constructions (e.g., *give, bring, offer*), with the choice of which construction to use jointly affected by the semantic and discourse status of the participants (Erteschik-Shir, 1979). Most clearly, the prepositional form is most appropriate when the recipient is new information and what is being transferred is known (compare the natural "Jody sent it to Julie" with the unnatural "Jody sent Julie it"). However, the selection of a construction is only partially determined by discourse because a great many English verbs occur only in the prepositional form (e.g., *donate*) and a few occur only in the ditransitive (e.g., *cost, deny, fine*). The main verbs young children use in the ditransitive construction are such things as *get, give, show, make, read,* *being, buy, take, tell, find,* and *send* (see Campbell & Tomasello, 2001).

### Locatives, Resultatives, and Causatives

Beginning with their first words and pivot schemas, English-speaking children use a variety of locative words to express spatial relationships in utterance-level constructions. These include prepositions such as *X up, X down, X in, X out, on X, off X, over X,* and *under X,* and verb + particle constructions such as *pick X up, wipe X off,* and *get X down.* Once children start producing more complex structures designating events with two or more participants, two-argument locative constructions are common. For Tomasello's (1992) daughter, these included such utterances as "Draw star on me" and "Peoples on there boat" which were produced at 20 months of age. By 3 years of age, most children have sufficient flexibility with item-based constructions to talk explicitly about locative events with three participants, most often an agent causing a theme to move to some object-as-location (e.g., "He put the pen on the desk").

The resultative construction (as in "He wiped the table clean") is used, most typically, to indicate both an action and the result of that action. Although no experimental studies of the resultative construction have yet been conducted with novel verbs, the occurrence of novel resultatives in spontaneous speech attests to the productivity of the construction from sometime after the third birthday. In Bowerman's (1982) study of her two daughters, the following developmental progression was observed. At around 2 years of age, the two children learned various combinations of "causing verb + resulting effect" such as *pull+up* and *eat+all gone.* For the next year or so, each child accumulated an assortment of these forms that were used in an apparently adultlike manner. Subsequently, each child, at some point after her third birthday, seemed to reorganize her knowledge of the independently learned patterns and extract a more abstract schema. Evidence for this reorganization came from each child's production of a number of novel resultative utterances such as "And the monster would eat you in pieces" and "I'll capture his whole head off."

Causative notions may be expressed in English utterance-level constructions either lexically or phrasally. Lexical causatives are simply verbs with a causative meaning used in the transitive construction (e.g., "He killed the deer"). Phrasal causatives are important because they supply an alternative for causativizing an intransitive verb that cannot be used transitively. Thus, if Bowerman's daughter had been skillful with phrasal causatives, she could have said, instead of "Don't giggle me," "Don't make me giggle"; and instead of "Stay this open" she could have said "Make this stay open." *Make* is thus the direct causation matrix verb in English, but an important related verb—that is in fact the most frequent such verb for young English learners—is *let,* as in "Let her do it," or "Let me help you." Another common matrix verb that follows this same pattern is *help,* as in "Help her get in there" or "Help him put on his shoes." It is unknown whether young children see any common pattern among the utterances in which these three different matrix verbs are used.

### Passives, Middles, and Reflexives

The English passive construction consists of a family of related constructions that change the perspective from the agent of a transitive action (relative to active voice constructions) to the patient and what happened to it. Thus, "Bill was shot by John" takes the perspective of Bill and what happened to him, rather than focusing on John's act of shooting (with the truncated passive "Bill was shot" serving to strengthen this perspective further). In addition to this general function of the passive, Budwig (1990) has shown that the "get" and "be" forms of the passive are themselves associated with distinct discourse perspectives. Thus, the prototypical "get" passive in "Spot got hit by a car" or "Jim got sick from the water" tends to be used when there is a negative consequence which occurs when an animate patient is adversely affected by an inanimate entity or a nonagent source. In contrast, the "be" passive construction in "The soup was heated on the stove" is used when there is a neutral outcome of an inanimate entity undergoing a change of state where the agent causing the change of state is unknown or irrelevant. In general, actional transitive verbs can be used in passive constructions quite readily, whereas many stative verbs seem to fit less well (e.g., *She was loved by him*). This was demonstrated experimentally by Sudhalter and Braine (1985), who found that preschoolers were much better at comprehending passive utterances containing actional verbs (e.g., *kick, cut, dress*) than they were at comprehending passive utterances containing experiential verbs (e.g., *love, see, forget*).

English-speaking children typically do not produce full passives in their spontaneous speech until 4 or 5 years of age, although they produce truncated passives (often with *get*) and adjectival passives much earlier (e.g., "He got dunked" or "He got hurt"). Israel, Johnson, and Brooks (2000) analyzed the development of chil-

dren's use of the passive participle. They found that children tended to begin with stative participles (e.g., *Pumpkin stuck),* then use some participles ambiguously between stative and active readings (e.g., *Do you want yours cut?*—do you want it to undergo a cutting action or, alternatively, do you want to receive it already in a cut state), then finally use the active participles characteristic of the full passive (e.g., *The spinach was cooked by Mommy*). Although passive utterances are infrequent in English-speaking children's spontaneous speech, a number of researchers have observed that older preschoolers occasionally create truncated passives with verbs that in adult English do not passivize, for example, "It was bandaided," "He will be died and I won't have a brother anymore," indicating some productivity with the construction (Bowerman, 1982, 1988; Clark, 1982).

It is important to note that children acquiring certain non-Indo-European languages typically produce passive sentences quite early in development. This result has been obtained for children learning Inuktitut (Allen & Crago, 1996), K'iche' Mayan (Pye & Quixtan Poz, 1988), Sesotho (Demuth, 1989, 1990), and Zulu (Suzman, 1985). Allen and Crago (1996) report that a child at age 2.0–2.9 (as well as two slightly older children) produced both truncated and full passives quite regularly. Although a majority of these were with familiar actional verbs, they also observed passives with experiential predicates and several clearly innovative forms with verbs that do not passivize in adult Inuktitut. The reasons for this precocity relative to English-speaking children are hypothesized to include the facts that: (a) Inuktitut passives are very common in child-directed speech; and (b) passive utterances are actually simpler than active voice constructions in Inuktitut because the passivized verb has to agree only with the subject, whereas the transitive verb has to agree with both subject and object.

There is very little research on English-speaking children's use of so-called middle voice constructions (medio-passives) such as "This bread cuts easily" or "This piano plays like a dream" (see Kemmer, 1993). The prototype of this construction involves an inanimate entity as subject, which is held responsible for the predicate (i.e., why the adverb is typically needed; "This bread cuts" or "This piano plays" by themselves are scarcely grammatical). Budwig, Stein, and O'Brien (2001) looked at a number of utterances of young children involving inanimate subjects and found that the most frequent constructions of this type in young English-speaking children's speech were such things as "This doesn't pour good." Reflexives are also not common in English-speaking children's early language (or in adult English), although they do produce a few things such as "I hurt myself." However, reflexives are quite common in the speech of young children learning languages in which these constructions are frequent in child-directed speech. For example, most Spanish-speaking youngsters hear and use quite early such things as *Se cayó* (It fell down), *Me siento* (I sit down), *Levántate* (Stand up!), and *Me lavo las manos* (I wash my hands).

## Questions

Questions are used primarily to seek information from an interlocutor. In many languages, this is done quite simply through a characteristic intonation ("He bought a *house*?") or by the replacement of a content word with a question word ("He bought a *what*?"). Although both of these are possible in English, two other forms are more common: wh- questions and yes/no questions. In the classic structural linguistic analysis, English questions are formed by subject-auxiliary inversion (sometimes with do-support) and wh- movement. These rules assume that the speaker has available a simple declarative linguistic representation, which she then transforms into a question by moving, rearranging, or inserting grammatical items. Thus, "John kicked the ball" becomes either "Did John kick the ball?" or "What did John kick?"

But this rule-based analysis is highly unlikely initially in development for two main reasons. First, some English-speaking children learn some wh- question constructions before they learn any other word combinations. For instance, Tomasello's (1992) daughter learned to ask where-questions (e.g., "Where's-the bottle?") and what-questions (e.g., "What's that"?) as her first multiword constructions. Second, everyone who has studied children's early questions has found that their earliest constructions are tied quite tightly to a small number of formulae. For example, in their classic analysis, Klima and Bellugi (1966) suggested that almost all the wh-questions of Adam, Eve, and Sarah emanated from two formulae: *What NP (doing)?* and *Where NP (going)?* Fletcher's (1985) subject produced almost all of her early questions with one of three formulae: *How do . . . , What are . . . ,* and *Where is . . .* More recently, Dabrowska (2001) looked in detail at one child's earliest uses of wh-questions in English and found that 83% of her questions during her third year of life came from one of just 20 formulas such as *Where's THING? Where THING go? Can I ACT? Is it PROPERTY?*

One phenomenon that bears on this issue is so-called inversion errors. English-speaking children sometimes invert the subject and auxiliary in wh- questions and sometimes not—leading to errors such as *Why they're not going?* A number of fairly complex and abstract rule-based accounts have been proposed to account for these errors, and, as usual, some researchers have claimed that children know the rules but apply them only optionally or inconsistently (e.g., Ingram & Tyack, 1979). However, in a more detailed analysis, Rowland and Pine (2000) discovered the surprising fact that the child they studied from age 2 to age 4 consistently inverted or failed to invert particular wh-word–auxiliary combinations on an item-specific basis. He thus consistently said such incorrect things as *Why I can . . . ? What she will . . . ? What you can . . . ?* but at the same time, he also said such correct things as *How did . . . ? How do . . . ? What do . . . ?* In all, of the 46 particular wh-word auxiliary pairs this child produced, 43 of them were produced either 100% correctly or 100% incorrectly (see also Erreich, 1984, who finds equal number of inversion errors in wh- and yes/no questions). Again, the picture is that children learn questions as a collection of item-based constructions, moving only gradually to more abstract representations.

## Analogy

Children begin to form abstract utterance-level constructions by creating analogies among utterances emanating from different item-based constructions. The process of analogy is very like the process of the schematization for item-based schemas/constructions; it is just that analogies are more abstract. Thus, whereas all instances of a particular item-based schema have at least one linguistic item in common (e.g., the verb in a verb island schema), in totally abstract constructions (such as the English ditransitive construction) the instances need have no items in common. So the question is: On what basis does the learner make the alignments among constituents necessary for an analogy among complex structures?

The answer is that the learner must have some understanding of the functional interrelationship that makes up the two structures being aligned. In the most systematic research program on the topic, Gentner and colleagues (Gentner & Markman, 1995; Gentner & Medina, 1998) stress that the essence of analogy is the focus on relations. When an analogy is made, the objects involved are effaced; the only identity they retain is their role in the relational structure. Gentner and colleagues have much evidence that young children focus on relations quite naturally and so are able to make analogies quite readily. An example is as follows. Children are shown two pictures: one of a car towing a boat (hitched to its rear) and one of a truck towing a car (hitched to its rear), and this car is identical in appearance to the car in the other picture. After some training in making analogies, the experimenter then points to the car in the first picture and asks the child to find the one doing the same thing in the second picture. Children have no trouble ignoring the literal match of cars across the two pictures and choosing the truck. In essence, they identify in both pictures the "tow-er," or the agent, based on the role it is playing in the entire action depicted.

Gentner and colleagues also stress what they call the systematicity principle: In making analogies structures are aligned as wholes, as "interconnected systems of relations." In the current context, this simply means that learners align whole utterances or constructions, or significant parts thereof, and attempt to align all the elements and relations in one comparison. In doing this, learners search for "one-to-one correspondence" among the elements involved and "parallel connectivity" in the relations involved. In the current context, this means that the learner makes an analogy between utterances (or constructions) by aligning the arguments one to one, and in making this alignment, she is guided by the functional roles these elements play in the larger structure. For example, in aligning *the car is towing the boat* and *the truck is towing the car,* the learner does not begin to match elements on the basis of the literal similarity between the two *cars,* but aligns *the car* and *the truck* because they are doing the same job from the perspective of the functional interrelations involved. This analysis implies that an important part of making analogies across linguistic constructions is the meaning of the relational words, especially the verbs, involved—particularly in terms of such things as the spatial, temporal, and causal relations they encode. But there is basically no systematic research relevant to the question of how children might align verb meanings in making linguistic analogies across constructions.

Gentner and colleagues also have some specific proposals relevant to learning. For example, they propose that even though in some sense neutralized, the object elements that children experience in the slots of a structure can facilitate analogical processes. In particular, they propose that in addition to type variability in the slots, also important is consistency of the items in the slots (i.e., a given item occurs only in one slot and not in others). When all kinds of items occur promiscuously in all of the slots in two potentially analogous relational structures, structure mapping is made more difficult (Gentner & Medina, 1998). For example, children find it even easier to make the analogy cited earlier if in the two pictures a car is towing a boat and a car is towing a trailer, so that the tow-er is identical in the two cases. This principle explains why children begin with item-based constructions. They find it easier to do structural alignments when more of the elements and relations are not just similar functionally but also similar, or even identical, perceptually—the process of schematization as it works in, for example, verb island constructions. Children then work their way up to the totally abstract analogies gradually. There are also some proposals from the morphological domain, that a certain number of exemplars is needed—a "critical mass"—before totally abstract analogies can be made (Marchman & Bates, 1994). But if this is true, the nature of this critical mass (e.g., verb types versus verb tokens) is not known at this time; there is no research.

It is thus possible that abstract linguistic constructions are created by a structural alignment across different item-based constructions, or the utterances emanating from them. For example, some verb island constructions that children have with the verbs *give, tell, show, send,* and so forth, share a "transfer" meaning, and appear in the form: NP1 + V + NP2 + NP3. In the indicated transfer, NP1 is the giver, NP2 is the receiver, and NP3 is the gift. So the aligning must be done on the basis of *both* form and function: Two utterances or constructions are analogous if a "good" structure mapping is found both on the level of linguistic form (even if these are only categorically indicated) and on the level of communicative function. This consideration is not really applicable in nonlinguistic domains. It may also be that in many cases particular patterns of grammatical morphology in constructions (e.g., X *was* VERB*ed*)—which typically designate abstract relations of one sort or another—facilitate, or even enable, recognition of an utterance as instantiating a particular abstract construction.

The only experimental study of children's construction of an abstract linguistic construction (as tested by their ability to assimilate a nonce verb to it) was conducted by Childers and Tomasello (2001). In this training study, 2½-year-old English-speaking children heard several hundred transitive utterances, such as *He's kicking it,* involving 16 different verbs across three separate sessions. Half the children learned new English verbs (and so increased their transitive verb vocabularies during training—toward a critical mass) whereas the other half heard only verbs they already knew. Within these groups, some children heard all the utterances with full nouns as agent and patient, whereas others heard utterances with both pronouns (i.e., *He's VERB-ing it*) and also full nouns as agent and patient. They were then tested to see if they could creatively produce a transitive utterance with a nonce verb. The main finding was that children were best at generalizing the transitive construction to the nonce verb if they had been trained with pronouns and nouns, regardless of the familiarity of the trained verbs (and few children in a control condition generalized to the novel verb at all). That is, the consistent pronoun frame *He's VERB-ing it* (in combination with type variation in the form of nouns as well) seemed to facilitate children's formation of a verb-general transitive construction to a greater degree than the learning of additional transitive verbs with nouns alone, in the absence of such a stabilizing pronominal frame.

The results of this study are consistent with Gentner's more general analysis of the process of analogy in several ways. First, they show that children can make generalizations, perhaps based on analogy, across different item-based constructions. Second and more specifically, they also show that the material that goes in the slots, in this case NP slots, plays an important role (see also Dodson & Tomasello, 1998). In English, the pronoun *he* only goes in the preverbal position, and, although the pronoun *it* may occur in either position in spontaneous speech, it occurs most frequently in postverbal position in child-directed speech, and that is the only position in which the children heard it during training. These correspondences between processes in the creation of nonlinguistic analogies and in the creation of abstract linguistic constructions constitute impressive evidence that the process is basically the same in the two cases.

## Constraining Generalizations

Importantly, there must be some constraints on children's linguistic abstractions, and this is a problem for both of the major theories of child language acquisition. Classically, a major problem for generative theories is that as the rules and principles are made more elegant and powerful through theoretical analyses, they become so abstract that they generate too large a set of grammatical utterances; and so constraints (e.g., the subjacency

constraint) must be posited to restore empirical accuracy. In usage-based theories, children are abstracting as they learn, but they cannot do this indiscriminately; they must make just those generalizations that are conventional in the language they are learning and not others. It is thus clear that any serious theory of syntactic development, whatever its basic assumptions, must address the question of why children make just the generalizations they do and not others.

We may illustrate the basic problem with so-called dative alternation constructions. The situation is this: Some verbs can felicitously appear in both ditransitive and prepositional dative constructions, but others cannot; for example:

He gave/sent/bequeathed/donated his books to the library.
He gave/sent/bequeathed/*donated the library his books.

Why should the other three verbs be felicitous in both constructions, but *donate* be felicitous only in the prepositional dative? The four verbs have very similar meanings, and so it would seem likely that they should all behave the same. Another example is:

She said/told something to her mother.
She *said/told her mother something.

Again, the meanings of the verbs are very close, and so the difference of behavior seems unprincipled and unpredictable (Bowerman, 1988, 1996). Other similar alternations are the causative alternation (*I rolled the ball; The ball rolled*) and the locative alternation (*I sprayed paint on the wall; I sprayed the wall with paint*)—both of which also apply only to limited sets of verbs.

One solution is quite simple. Perhaps children only learn verbs for the constructions in which they have heard them. Based on all of the evidence reviewed here, this is very likely the case at the earliest stages of development. But it is not true later in development, especially in the 3- to 5-year age period. Children at this age overgeneralize with some regularity, as documented most systematically by Bowerman (1982, 1988; see Pinker, 1989, for a summary of evidence). As reported earlier, her two children produced things like: "Don't giggle me" (at age 3.0) and "I said her no" (at age 3.1). It is thus not the case that children are totally conservative throughout development, and so this cannot be the whole answer.

A second solution is also simple. When children make overgeneralization errors, adults may correct them, and so children's overgeneralization tendencies are constrained by the linguistic environment. But this is not true in the sense that adults do not explicitly correct child utterances for their grammatical correctness (Brown & Hanlon, 1970). Adults, at least Western middle-class adults, do respond differently to well-formed and ill-formed child utterances, however. For example, they continue conversing to well-formed utterances, but they revise or recast ill-formed utterances (e.g., Bohannon & Stanowicz, 1988; Farrar, 1992). But this kind of indirect feedback is generally not considered by most theorists sufficient to constrain children's overgeneralization tendencies because it is far from consistent. It is also not clear that this type of feedback is available to all children learning all languages. Nevertheless, it is still possible that linguistic feedback from adults may play some role—although neither a necessary nor a sufficient role—in constraining children's overgeneralization tendencies.

Given the inadequacy of these simple solutions, three factors have been most widely discussed. First, Pinker (1989) proposed that there are certain very specific and (mostly) semantic constraints that apply to particular English constructions and to the verbs that may or may not be conventionally used in them. For example, a verb can be used felicitously with the English transitive construction if it denotes "manner of locomotion" (e.g., *walk* and *drive* as in *I walked the dog at midnight* or *I drove my car to New York*), but not if it denotes a "motion in a lexically specified direction" (e.g., *come* and *fall* as in *He came her to school* or *She falled him down*). How children learn these verb classes—and they must learn them since they differ across languages—is unknown at this time. Second, it has also been proposed that the more frequently children hear a verb used in a particular construction (the more firmly its usage is entrenched), the less likely they will be to extend that verb to any novel construction with which they have not heard it used (Bates & MacWhinney, 1989; Braine & Brooks, 1995; Clark, 1987; Goldberg, 1995). And third, if children hear a verb used in a linguistic construction that serves the same communicative function as some possible generalization, they may infer that the generalization is not conventional—the heard construction preempts the generalization. For example, if a child hears *He made the rabbit disappear,* when she might have expected *He disappeared the rabbit,* she may infer that *dis-*

*appear* does not occur in a simple transitive construction—since the adult seems to be going to some lengths to avoid using it in this way (the periphrastic causative being a more marked construction).

Two experimental studies provide evidence that indeed all three of these constraining processes—entrenchment, preemption, and knowledge of semantic subclasses of verbs—are at work. First, Brooks, Tomasello, Lewis, and Dodson (1999) modeled the use of a number of fixed-transitivity English verbs for children from 3;5 to 8;0 years—verbs such as *disappear* that are exclusively intransitive and verbs such as *hit* that are exclusively transitive. There were four pairs of verbs, one member of each pair typically learned early by children and typically used often by adults (and so presumably more entrenched) and one member of each pair typically learned later by children and typically used less frequently by adults (less entrenched). The four pairs were: *come-arrive, take-remove, hit-strike, disappear-vanish* (the first member of each pair being more entrenched). The finding was that, in the face of adult questions attempting to induce them to overgeneralize, children of all ages were less likely to overgeneralize the strongly entrenched verbs than the weakly entrenched verbs; that is, they were more likely to produce *I arrived it* than *I comed it.*

Second, Brooks and Tomasello (1999b) taught novel verbs to children 2.5, 4.5, and 7.0 years of age. They then attempted to induce children to generalize these novel verbs to new constructions. Some of these verbs conformed to Pinker's (1989) semantic criteria, and some did not. Additionally, in some cases, experimenters attempted to preempt generalizations by providing children with alternative ways of using the new verb (thus providing them with the possibility of answering *What's the boy doing?* with *He's making the ball tam*—which allows the verb to stay intransitive). In brief, the study found that both of these constraining factors worked, but only from age 4.5. Children from 4.5 years showed a tendency to generalize or not generalize a verb in line with its membership in one of the key semantic subclasses, and they were less likely to generalize a verb to a novel construction if the adult provided them with a preempting alternative construction. But the younger children showed no such tendency.

Overall, entrenchment seems to work early, from 3;0 or before, as particular verb island constructions become either more or less entrenched depending on usage. Preemption and semantic subclasses begin to work sometime later, perhaps not until 4 years of age or later, as children learn more about the conventional uses of verbs and about all of the alternative linguistic constructions at their disposal in different communicative circumstances. Thus, just as verb-argument constructions become more abstract only gradually, so also are they constrained only gradually.

## Nominal and Verbal Constructions: Learning Morphology

Across the languages of the world, utterance-level constructions are constituted by two major types of subconstructions: nominal and verbal constructions. Actually, in real discourse, nominal and verbal constructions are often used alone as full utterances, which is one strong piece of evidence for their reality as functionally coherent and independent constructions. Thus, when someone is asked "Who is that over there?" a reasonable utterance in response is the nominal "Bill" or "My father," and when someone is asked further "What is he doing?" a reasonable utterance in response is the verb or verb phrase "Sleeping" or "Playing tennis." Of course many utterances are constituted by some combination of nominals and verbals: "My father is playing tennis."

### Nominal Constructions

Nominals are used by people to make reference to "things." In many theories, the prototype is concrete objects (people, places, and things). But it is well known that nominals may be used to refer to basically any kind of entity at all, real or imagined. Thus, when the need arises, there are ways of construing actions, properties, and relationships as if they were things, on analogy with concrete objects. For example, we may say such things as "Skiing promotes good health," "That blue looks awful in my painting," and "Bigger is better." Indeed, there are some languages that do not really have a clear-cut class of concrete nouns specialized for the single function of reference, such as *dog* and *tree;* but rather they have a single class composed of words that can be used as either nouns or verbs depending on whether they are used as nouns or verbs—similar to English words such as *cut* (*I cut the bread, There's a cut on my finger*) or *hammer* (*I'm hammering in this nail with my hammer*). Langacker (1987b) notes that the discourse function of identifying the participants in events and states of affairs requires language users to construe whatever

they wish to talk about as a thing, so that it can be referred to, no matter its true ontological status.

In making reference to a thing, speakers must choose among various nominal constructions—for example, proper name, noun + article, pronoun—based on the exigencies of the communicative situation at hand. Of most importance for this choice is the speaker's assessment of the knowledge and expectations of the listener at any given moment based on their currently shared perceptual situation and on their previously shared experience, especially in the immediately preceding discourse context. In the terminology of Langacker (1991), speakers must "ground" their conventional act of reference in the current speech situation involving particular persons in a particular usage event. In the terminology of pragmatic theorists, speakers must assess the cognitive availability (accessibility, topicality, givenness) of the referent for the listener (Ariel, 1988; Givón, 1993; Gundel, Hedberg, & Zacharski, 1993).

Typically, speakers choose to use a pronoun (*he*) or a proper name (*Jennie*) to refer to an entity that is either in the current attentional focus of speaker and listener or else can easily be recovered from memory (e.g., because it is shared knowledge who Jennie is). The most studied referential strategy of young children is one used when recoverability is harder, specifically, the use of a full noun phrase containing some kind of common noun and some kind of determiner(s). Such full noun phrases do not assume, at least not to the same degree as pronouns and proper names, shared knowledge between speaker and listener. In addition, they also employ a more analytic technique of reference than proper names and pronouns, typically using multiple words or morphemes to indicate the intended referent. Thus, full noun phrases typically comprise two separately indicated subfunctions: A common noun (*boy, yard, party*) is used to indicate a category of things, and a determiner (*a, the, my*) is used to help the listener to specify an individual member of that category.

Children produce full noun phrases in their very earliest multiword speech, sometimes as whole utterances (e.g., saying "A clown" when asked "What is that?" or "My blanket" when asked "What do you want?"). The determiners used in these early utterances fall mainly into three categories. The first is demonstratives, as in *this ball* or *that cookie*. These are often used deictically with pointing, but their perspectival aspect (physical or psychological distance from speaker) is not mastered for several years. The second category is possessives, as in *my shoes* or *Maria's bike*. These are also used quite early in language development and they are of special importance because they seem to be used quite accurately from the beginning (see, e.g., Tomasello, 1998b). This early mastery of possessive noun phrases means that all of the trouble that children have with other kinds of noun phrases involving such things as definite and indefinite articles, are not due to general difficulties with forming a phrase consisting of a common noun plus a determiner. Their difficulties must come from somewhere else, presumably the additional perspectival and/or pragmatic dimensions that must be mastered for appropriate use of these other types of determiners in noun phrases.

The determiners that have been studied most extensively in English acquisition are the definite and indefinite articles, *the* and *a*. Appropriate usage of these is notoriously difficult for second-language learners of English, especially for those coming from languages that do not have articles at all (e.g., Japanese or Russian). Although textbook accounts quite often present these words as contrasting alternatives, the fact is that each of them has a wide range of uses, some of which are quite unrelated to one another. Indeed, the historical situation is that across many languages the definite determiner derives from a demonstrative—a mainly deictic function—whereas the indefinite determiner derives from the number word for *one*—a very different function. In English, the definite determiner was grammaticized from a demonstrative many generations before the indefinite determiner was grammaticized from the number word for *one* (Trask, 1996).

There are two main difficulties that children have to overcome to use English articles appropriately. The first difficulty is that these words encode two different, but highly correlated, dimensions of the referential situation: specificity and givenness. On the one hand, the definite article *the* serves to pick out a specific entity, as in "I want the cookie" (that's in your hand), whereas the indefinite article *a* serves to pick out a nonspecific entity, as in "I want a cookie" (any cookie). On the other hand, the definite article *the* is used when the speaker can assume that the referent is to some degree given (or available) for the listener (e.g., "I have the kite"—the one we just talked about), whereas the indefinite article *a* is used to introduce a new referent into the discourse situation even if that entity is definite (e.g., "I have a kite"—you'll find it upstairs). These two aspects, specificity and givenness, most often occur in a totally confounded manner, and indeed it is only in somewhat

special uses that they are unconfounded. The second difficulty is that this second dimension of article use—taking into account listener perspective (givenness)—may be especially difficult cognitively for 2- and 3-year-old children. Much research in developmental psychology has demonstrated that the requisite perspective-taking skills are much better developed in 4-year-olds (see Flavell, 1997, for a review).

Brown's (1973) naturalistic observations have documented that by 3 years of age English-speaking children use the definite and indefinite articles quite flexibly and appropriately with respect to the specificity of the referent intended. However, Brown also notes that this spontaneous usage provides little evidence one way or the other for children's skills with the perspectival component, especially in the most demanding case in which the intended referent is known by the speaker but unknown to the listener (i.e., where givenness is different for speaker and listener). This especially difficult case has been the target of a number of experimental investigations, and not surprisingly, the general finding is that when young children have a referent they wish to introduce to someone for whom it is totally new in the discourse context, they tend to overuse the definite article (the egocentric error). For example, with no introductory comments whatsoever, they might tell a friend, "Tomorrow we'll buy the toy" (Maratsos, 1976).

Emslie and Stevenson (1981) had children tell a story from a set of pictures to another child sitting on the other side of a partition. They found that 3-year-olds used the articles consistently and appropriately with regard to specificity. With regard to perspective, the key task was one in which children were asked to narrate a story from a series of pictures to another child, and in the middle of the series a picture of a completely new and irrelevant object or person appeared—definitely requiring an indefinite article for its introduction (e.g., "And then a snake appeared in the grass . . ."). They found that only the 4-year-olds (not the 3-year-olds) consistently used the indefinite article to introduce the novel referent for their unsuspecting listener. In a similar experimental task, Garton (1983) found that children before their fourth birthdays did not use the definite and indefinite articles differentially for adults either wearing or not wearing a blindfold.

### Verbal Constructions

Just as nominals are grounded in space, in the sense that they help the listener to locate the intended referent, clauses are grounded in time to help the listener identify which particular event is being indicated (Langacker, 1991). This is typically done in two ways that work together. The internal temporal contour of a clause is designated by some marking of its grammatical aspect (e.g., progressive aspect marks ongoingness, as in *X is/was smiling*), while the external placement of the event along a time line, grounded in the speech moment, is designated by some marker of its tense (e.g., past tense; Comrie, 1976). These work together in narrative discourse to enable such temporal juggling as *While I was Xing, she Yed*. In addition, and importantly, many clauses also contain some indication of the speaker's attitude toward the event or state of affairs. For example, in English, people frequently mark their attitude through the use of modal auxiliaries such as *may, can, can't, won't, should, might, must, could, would,* and so on—and with a number of different kinds of things in other languages (e.g., marking how the speaker came to know what she is saying, so-called evidentiality). All of this works together—with some grammatical morphemes in some languages being plurifunctional in the extreme—in what is called tense-aspect-modality (TAM) marking. TAM marking may be done either with freestanding words or with grammatical morphology, depending on exactly which of these things in a given language has been grammaticized, and to what degree.

To ground their clauses in the current speech event, speakers must locate the symbolized state or event in time. Weist (1986), building on Smith (1980), proposes four stages in children's ability to linguistically indicate the temporal ordering of events using tense marking in an adultlike manner:

1. *Age 1;6:* talk about events in the here and now only.
2. *Age 1;6 to 3;0:* talk about the past and future.
3. *Age 3;0 to 4;6:* begin to talk about past and future relative to a reference time other than now (typically indexed with adverbs such as *when*).
4. *Age 4;6 and older:* talk about past and future relative to a reference time other than now using adultlike tensing system (typically verb morphology).

The problem with this neat account is that the linguistic indication of tense interacts in complex ways with the linguistic indication of aspect, and it does this differently in different languages. As one example, the best-known hypothesis about children's early ability to indicate temporal relations in their early language is the Aspect Before

Tense hypothesis. Beginning with Antinucci and Miller (1976), it has been noted that children tend to use past tense most often with change of state (telic) verbs and present tense (or present progressive) most often with activity (atelic) verbs. In the strongest version of the Aspect Before Tense hypothesis, Antinucci and Miller hypothesized that until about 2;6 children use past tense only for changes of state in which at the end state is still perceptually present, and indeed children at this age think that the past tense marker actually indicates that an event is bounded (telic) and completed (perfective), rather than one that occurred in the past (independent of its telicity and perfectiveness). Thus, the first past tense verbs are prototypically things like *dropped, spilled,* and *broke* in which all of these things are confounded.

Antinucci and Miller (1976) attributed this pattern of use to children's immature conception of time. However, this strictly cognitive explanation is no longer held by anyone. This is because, first of all, even before their second birthdays many children do on some occasions clearly refer to past situations with activity verbs that have no current perceptual manifestations (Gerhardt, 1988). Second, in a number of comprehension experiments in which children must choose the picture that best depicts a present tense, past tense, or future tense utterance regardless of aspect, they perform well from a relatively early age (e.g., see Weist, Wysocka, Witkowska-Stadnik, Buczowska, & Konieczna, 1984; Weist, Lyytinen, Wysocka, & Atanassova, 1997, for Polish-speaking children; and McShane & Whittaker, 1988, and Wagner, 2001, for English-speaking children). And third, a number of studies on second language acquisition have shown that second language learning children and adults also use tense-aspect marking in the same biased way as young children, and they presumably are not cognitively immature (Li & Shirai, 2000).

Nevertheless, it is a fact that in basically all languages that have been studied, children much prefer to use the past tense for events construed as telic and perfective, such as *broke* and *made,* and they much prefer to use present tense (or progressive) for events construed as atelic and imperfective, such as *playing* and *riding.* Thus, it is relatively rare to hear a 1-year-old or young 2-year-old saying things like *breaking* or *making, played* or *rode.* The languages for which this has been documented include English, Italian, French, Polish, Portuguese, German, Japanese, Mandarin Chinese, Hebrew, and Turkish (see Li & Shirai, 2000, for a review). Quantitatively, in a diary study Clark (1996) found that, between the ages of 1;7 and 3;0, her son used the progressive -ing with activity verbs about 90% of the time, and he used the past tense -ed with the accomplishment subclass of change-of-state verbs about 60% of the time. Tomasello (1992) found that an even higher percentage of -ed use occurred with change-of-state verbs.

It turns out that one major reason children show this pattern is quite straightforward: This is the pattern they hear in the language around them. Shirai and Andersen (1995) call this the *distributional bias* hypothesis, namely, that the distribution of tense and aspect markers with particular classes of verbs in children's speech follows the distribution the children hear in the language around them. And so, once again, what we see is an adult pattern in the use of grammatical words and morphemes that most often conflates and/or confounds distinctions that the child will need to segregate if she is to attain adultlike competence with these grammatical words and morphemes. Presumably, to make all the appropriate distinctions in the current case, the child needs to hear and comprehend enough instances of activity verbs construed imperfectively in the past tense, change-of-state verbs construed in the progressive aspect, and all other possible combinations. Only wide and varied experience with many different such patterns provides the raw material necessary for the child to segment and sort out which components of a given clausal construction are being used to indicate which components of the temporal profile the speaker intends to indicate. As in the case of a nominal constructions with determiners—in which the child must sort out such things as referent specificity and listener perspective, which are often confounded—it is no surprise that it takes children many years to do this, and that it is easier to do in languages in which historical grammaticalization patterns have led to fewer conflations and confoundings of these types (Slobin, 1985, 1997).

### Learning Morphology

The need to ground nominal and verbal constructions in the ongoing speech event is present constantly. Although there are major differences among languages, these constant communicative pressures have led in many cases to the grammaticalization of forms for effecting these functions, and recurrent functions other than grounding may also lead to the creation of grammatical morphology (e.g., plurals and case marking). From the point of view of learning and generalization, grammatical morphology displays a number of interesting properties. Among these is the fact that children sometimes overregularize grammatical morphemes, which has put them in the center of some major theoretical debates about the

nature of cognitive representation in general. In addition, because they are often not very salient in the speech stream—and perhaps for other reasons such as their plurifunctionality in many cases—second language learners and children with the specific language impairment often have special problems with grammatical morphemes.

One of the most intriguing phenomena of child language acquisition is U-shaped developmental growth. That is, in some cases children seem to learn the conventional adult way of saying things early in development, but then become worse as they get older, for instance, saying such things as *mans, feets, comed, sticked, putted* and so forth—returning only later to the conventional adult forms. The traditional interpretation of this developmental pattern is that early on children learn, for example, the past tense form *came* by rote as an individual lexical item; later they learn to use the regular past tense morpheme -*ed* and apply it whenever they want to refer to the past (sometimes inappropriately, as in *comed*). Finally, before school-age, they learn that there are exceptions to the general rule and display adultlike competence (Bowerman, 1982; Kuczaj, 1977). U-shaped developmental growth is thus intriguing because it seems to signal changes in underlying linguistic representations and processes.

Perhaps ironically, given that English is a morphologically impoverished language, the grammatical morpheme that has been studied most intensively in this regard is the English past tense -*ed*. The largest and most systematic study of children's acquisition of the English past tense was conducted by Marcus et al. (1992). They examined written transcripts of 83 English-speaking preschool-age children and found that overgeneralization errors were relatively rare proportionally (2.5% of irregular tokens produced had, inappropriately, the -*ed*), and they occurred at this same low rate throughout the preschool period. Typically, for a given verb children produced the correct past tense form before they produced the overgeneralized form, and they made the overgeneralization error least often with the irregular verbs they heard most often in parental speech. For a particular child's use of a specific verb, there was sometimes a relatively extended period (weeks to months) in which both the correct form and the overgeneralized form coexisted.

Marcus et al. (1992) explain these results with one form of a dual process model. Children acquire the irregular forms by rote learning, but they acquire the regular forms by establishing a rule. Rote learning is subject to all the parameters of "normal" learning, such as the effects of frequency and similarity among exemplars; rule learning is impervious to these effects. (The existence of these different processes is supposed to be of great theoretical significance because they confirm the existence of rule-based cognitive representations that are not subject to the normal laws of learning; Pinker, 1991, 1999). But the specifics of English past tense acquisition clearly do not fit this neat picture; children sometimes misapply the rule (overgeneralize), even in some cases using both correct and incorrect forms during the same developmental period. Marcus et al. explain these anomalies by invoking in addition the principle of preemption (what they call the uniqueness principle or blocking) and some factors that affect its application. The basic idea is that the regular rule applies whenever it is not blocked (i.e., it is a default rule). This means that when children have an irregular form (e.g., *sang*) it blocks application of the regular *-ed* rule, but when they do not have such a form, they might reasonably produce *singed*. The problem with this account, of course, is the finding that children often use both the correct and overgeneralized forms at the same time. Marcus et al. deal with this empirical problem by hypothesizing that blocking sometimes does not work as it is supposed to, basically due to "performance errors." Lexical retrieval is probabilistic and frequency dependent; children sometimes have trouble retrieving infrequent irregular forms and so the rule gets applied simply because it is not properly blocked.

However, some aspects of this account have been called into question. Maratsos (2000) points out that the error rate reported by Marcus et al. (1992) was computed by pooling all verbs together, and thus very high frequency verbs statistically swamped out low frequency verbs. Indeed, verbs that appeared infrequently for a given child (less than 10 times) were excluded from some analyses altogether. Thus, for example, one child produced 285 past tenses for the verb *say,* with a very low error rate of 1%. This same child, however, produced 40 different verbs less than 10 times each (155 tokens altogether). The overgeneralization error rate for these individual verbs was 58%. But because of their low token frequency, all of these verbs together contributed less to the computation of the overall error rate than the verbs *say* by itself. In addition, Maratsos also points out that many individual verbs used by individual children are used in both correct and overgeneralized forms for a period of many months (in a few cases, years), which

could only happen in the rule + blocking account if the child experienced persistent and long-lived retrieval problems of a type Marcus et al. do not discuss.

Maratsos' alternative account is based on the notion of competition—a weaker, frequency-based kind of preemption. In this account, children can produce past tense forms either by rote or by rule, and there may be a period in which they produce both for a given verb. The winner of the competition will be determined eventually by the form the child hears most often in the speech around her (and perhaps by other factors); that is, the most frequent form comes gradually to block the less frequent form, regardless of which is regular or irregular. In contrast, in the Marcus et al. (1992) account, there is an asymmetry between regulars and irregulars; the regular does not even need to be heard a single time to win, since it is a default. The only role for frequency is as a performance factor that interferes with the normal mechanism.

In general, the acquisition of productive systems of grammatical morphology in natural languages is extremely difficult. According to Klein and Perdue (1997), most adult second-language learners, especially those learning in more natural settings outside the classroom, develop what they call the *basic variety* of a language. This consists of lexical items combined in syntactic constructions, but typically with only one morphological form of each word. Similarly, McWhorter (1998) argues and presents evidence that one of the distinguishing characteristics of pidgin and Creole languages (typically relatively new languages created under unusual situations of language contact) is their relatively impoverished systems of grammatical morphology. It is also well known that one of the major diagnostic features of children with specific language impairment is their relatively poor mastery of the grammatical morphemes in their language (Bishop, 1997; Leonard, 1998). Finally, when perfectly competent adult speakers of a language are put under various kinds of processing pressure as they listen to a story (e.g., the spoken language describing the story is distorted by white noise or subjects must perform a distracting task while listening), what falls apart most readily in subsequent tests of retention is the grammatical morphology (Dick et al., 2001).

There are three basic reasons that grammatical morphology is an especially weak link in language learning. First, it is typically expressed in phonologically reduced, unstressed, monosyllabic bits in the interstices of utterances and constructions. Second, in some though by no means all cases, it also carries very little concrete semantic weight; for example, the English third person -s agreement marker is in most cases almost totally semantically redundant. Research with children with specific language impairment has shown that greater semantic weight facilitates children's acquisition of a grammatical morpheme (Bishop, 1997; Leonard, 1998). Third, many grammatical morphemes are plurifunctional (e.g., English articles encoding specificity and definiteness) in ways that make acquisition of the full range of uses in appropriate contexts extremely difficult. Perhaps for all these reasons, Farrar (1990, 1992) found that children's acquisition of some particular grammatical morphemes in English (e.g., past tense -ed, plural -s, progressive -ing) was facilitated when mothers used these morphemes as immediate recasts of the child's utterances that were missing them. Recasts are well-known to help children identify elements with low salience since they provide the child with an immediate comparison of her own immature utterance and the corresponding full adult morphology (Nelson, 1986).

## Complex Constructions

All natural languages have ways for talking about multiple events and states of affairs related to one another in complex ways. In the most straightforward cases, a speaker simply strings together different clauses across time, linking them with various kinds of appropriate connectors (or not). In other cases, however, the different clauses are more tightly interrelated and thus appear as constituents in a single complex construction under a single intonation contour, which in most cases is a historical grammaticalization of discourse sequences in which specific types of clauses have recurred together repeatedly in the speech community. The linking of clauses, whether more loosely or more tightly, serves various discourse functions. These include expressing speaker attitudes about things (as in infinitival and sentential complements), specifying referents in more detail (as in relative clauses), and indicating the spatial-temporal-causal interrelations among events (as in adverbial clauses—not dealt with here).

### *Infinitival Complement Constructions*

Between 2 and 3 years of age, English-speaking children begin to acquire complex constructions indicating speaker attitudes about such things as intention, volition, or compulsion. The most common are *wanna V, hafta V, gotta V, needta V* (and perhaps *gonna V*), and

they typically structure the earliest complex sentences that English-speaking children learn and use—typically emerging at around the second birthday. Gerhardt (1991) analyzes children's use of *wanna* as indicating "internal volition" or desire, their use of *hafta* (and *gotta*) as indicating "external compulsion" (often due to a social norm such as a rule), and *needta* as indicating "internal compulsion" (almost no choice due to an internal state).

Following the classic studies of Limber (1973) and Bloom, Tackeff, and Lahey (1984), Diessel (2004) reported the largest study to date of nonfinite complement clauses. He studied a wider range of constructions, including participial and *wh* infinitive constructions; and he investigated four children up to 5 years of age in quantitative detail. The first finding is that over 95% of children's utterances with nonfinite complement clauses contained to-infinitives, and these were the first to emerge as well. (The other 5% were such things as the participials *Start V-ing* and *Stop V-ing* and a very few wh infinitives such as "I know what to do.") Like Bloom et al. (1989), Diessel found that the first matrix verbs to appear were *wanna, hafta,* and *gotta,* which emerged at about 23 and accounted for over 90% of all the to-infinitives over the course of the entire study. Initially children used these in very formulaic ways. That is, almost all of the first to-infinitives produced by these children had as subjects the first-person pronoun *I,* they were in present tense (assuming *gotta* as present tense), and they were not negated; thus the prototype was things like *I wanna play ball, I hafta do that,* and *I gotta go.*

From age 2 to age 5, these children's growing linguistic sophistication with this class of constructions was manifest in three main ways. First, their use of the semimodals became less formulaic and more diverse, so that they now included third-person subjects (e.g., "Dolly wanna drink that") and negatives (e.g., "I don't like to do all this work"). Second, they learned a wider range of matrix verbs, including such things as *forget* (e.g., "I forgot to buy some soup") and *say* (e.g., "The doctor said to stay in bed all day"). Third, the children learned more complex constructions with an NP between the two verbs. As in Bloom et al.'s study, these first emerged at around 2;6 to 3;0, and were dominated by four matrix verbs that accounted for 88% of all the utterances of this type:

| | |
|---|---|
| *See* X VERB-*ing* | *Want X to* VERB |
| Watch *X VERB*-ing | Make X *VERB* |

After 3 years of age, other matrix verbs representing a more diverse set of constructions emerged. In general, Diessel found a developmental progression from constructions in which the matrix verb and main verb were more tightly integrated—utterances with the semi-modals *wanna, hafta,* and *gotta*—to those in which the two verbs were more distinct, as in the constructions with an intervening NP, and two full propositions were expressed.

### Sentential Complement Constructions

Whereas many of the most common matrix verbs with infinitival complements are generally similar to deontic modals (*should, must*) in their concern with purpose/intention/compulsion, many of the most common matrix verbs with sentential complements are similar to epistemic modals (*may, might*) in their concern with certainty/perception/knowledge. But again, the matrix verbs in sentential complements—such things as *think, know, believe, see, say*—are not modal auxiliaries but tensed verbs. In addition, and in contrast to infinitival complements, the second clause in sentential complement constructions is also a fully tensed clause with an overt subject (i.e., it is a fully independent clause). The prototype, then, is utterances like "I know she hit him" and "I think I can do it." Once again, the classic studies are by Limber (1973) and Bloom and colleagues (Bloom, Rispoli, Gartner, & Hafitz, 1989), who found that sentential complement constructions emerged later than infinitival complement constructions, typically between 2;6 and 3;0. They also found that the earliest verbs used in these constructions were a very delimited set, mainly *think, know, look,* and *see.*

Diessel and Tomasello (2001) looked at young English-speaking children's earliest utterances with sentential complements from 2 to 5 years of age. They found that virtually all of them were composed of a simple sentence schema that the child had already mastered combined with one of a delimited set of complement-taking matrix verbs (see also Bloom, 1992). These matrix verbs were of two types. First were epistemic verbs such as *think* and *know.* As one example, in almost all cases, children used *I think* to indicate their own uncertainty about something, and they basically never used the verb *think* in anything but this first-person, present tense form; that is, there were virtually no examples of *He thinks . . . , She thinks . . . ,* and so on, virtually no examples of *I don't think . . . , I can't think . . . ,* and so on, and virtually no examples of *I thought . . . , I didn't think . . . ,* and so on. And there were almost no uses with a complementizer (virtually no examples of *I think that . . .*). It thus appears that for many young children, *I think* is a relatively fixed phrase meaning something like *Maybe.* The child then pieces together this fixed phrase (or one of the other similar phrases like *I hope . . . , I bet . . . ,* etc.) with a full proposition, with its function being as a sort of evidential marker (not as a matrix clause that embeds another as in traditional analyses). The second kind of matrix verbs were attention-getting verbs like *look* and *see,* used in conjunction with full finite clauses. In this case, children used these matrix verbs almost exclusively in imperative form (again almost no negations, no nonpresent tenses, no complementizers), suggesting again an item-based approach not involving syntactic embedding. Thus, when examined closely, children's earliest complex sentences look much less like adult sentential complements (which are used most often in written discourse) and much more like various kinds of pastiches of established item-based constructions.

### Relative Clause Constructions

Relative clauses are not like complement clauses because they do not involve coordination with a main clause at all. Rather, relative clauses serve the very different function of specifying noun phrases in detail. Textbook descriptions focus on so-called restrictive relative clauses; for example, "The dog that barked all night dies this morning," in which the relative clause serves to identify a noun by using presupposed information (both speaker and listener already know that there was barking all night; that's why it can be used as identifying information). Because relative clauses are a part of a noun phrase argument, they are classically characterized as embedded clauses, and so they have attracted much research attention in both linguistics and developmental psycholinguistics.

The largest study of children's acquisition of relative clauses is by Diessel and Tomasello (2000), who studied four English-speaking children between ages 1;9 and 5;2 in quantitative detail. In this study, they made a surprising discovery: virtually all of these children's earliest relative clauses were of the same general form, and this form was not the form typically described in textbooks. Examples would be:

Here's the toy that spins around.

That's the sugar that goes in there.

What is noteworthy here is (a) the main clause is a presentational construction (predicate nominal or closely related), basically introducing a new topic using a pro-form (*here, that*) and the copula (-'*s*); and (b) the information in the relative clause is not presupposed, as in textbook (restrictive) relative clauses, but rather is new information about the just-introduced referent. The main point is that even this very complex construction is firmly based in a set of simpler constructions (copular presentationals) that children have mastered as item-based constructions some time before relative clauses are first acquired and produced.

## PROCESSES OF LANGUAGE ACQUISITION

From a cognitive science point of view, the central issue in the study of language development is the nature of children's underlying linguistic representations and how these change during ontogeny. Summarizing all that has gone before in this chapter, we now address directly these two issues.

### The Growing Abstractness of Constructions

Based on all the available evidence, it would appear that children's early linguistic representation are highly concrete, based in concrete and specific pieces of language not in abstract categories (although they have some open slot-filler categories as well). We have cited: (a) analyses of children's spontaneous productions showing very restricted ranges of application of many early linguistic items and structures, asynchronous development of item-based constructions that from an adult point of view should have similar structures, and gradual and continuous development within specific item-based structures; (b) production experiments in which young children use nonce verbs in the way adults have used them, failing to generalize them to other of their existing constructions—suggesting that these existing constructions are item-based and not verb-general; and (c) comprehension experiments in which young children, who know the activity they are supposed to act out in response to a nonce verb, fail to assign the correct agent-patient roles to the characters involved based on canonical word order cues (in English)—again suggesting that their constructions at this point are item-based and not totally general.

There is one other recent finding that supports this same conclusion further. Savage, Lieven, Theakston, and Tomasello (2003) primed English-speaking children with either active or passive sentences, in some cases with high lexical overlap between the priming sentence and the sentence the child was likely to produce (i.e., the prime used some pronouns and grammatical morphemes that the child could use in her target utterance even though different objects and actions were involved) and in some cases with very low lexical overlap (i.e., the prime used only nouns, which the child could not use in her target utterance since different objects were involved). In some ways, this method could be considered the most direct test yet of children's early syntactic representations because successful priming in the high lexical overlap condition would suggest that their linguistic knowledge is represented more in terms of specific lexical items, whereas priming in the low lexical overlap condition would suggest that their linguistic knowledge is represented more abstractly. The answer is that the older children, around 6 years of age, could be structurally primed to produce a particular construction such as the passive. The younger children, who had just turned 3 years old, could not be primed structurally; but they were primed by the more lexically specific primes. Four-year-old children fell somewhere in between these two extremes. So once more—in this case using a very different method, widely accepted in the adult psycholinguistic community—we find that children's early linguistic representations are very likely based in specific item-based constructions (with some abstract slots), and it is only in the late preschool period that their utterance-level constructions take on adultlike abstractness.

But rather than thinking of children's utterance-level constructions as either concrete or abstract, it is probably better to think of them as growing gradually in abstractness over time as more and more relevant exemplars are encountered and assimilated to the construction. One reasonable interpretation of all of the studies directly aimed at children's underlying linguistic representation—as reviewed here—is thus as follows. From about 2 or 2½ years of age children have only very weak verb-general representations of their utterance-level constructions, and so these show up only in preferential looking tasks that require weak representations. But over the next months and years, their linguistic representations grow in strength and abstractness, based on both the type and token frequency with which they hear certain linguistic structures. These now begin to show themselves in tasks requiring more active behavioral decision making or even language production requiring require stronger representations. This hypothesis is in the general spirit of a number of proposals suggesting that, if cognitive representations retain information about the variety of individual instances, they may be felicitously described as being either weaker or stronger based mainly on their type and token frequency (e.g., Munakata et al., 1997). It is also consonant with the view that linguistic knowledge and linguistic processing are really just different aspects of the same thing. Thus, things like frequency and the probabilistic distribution of lexical items in the input not only play a crucial role in how children build up their linguistic representations, but also form an integral part of those representations in the end state (see the papers in Barlow & Kemmer, 2000; Elman et al., 1996).

## Psycholinguistic Processes of Development

In accounting for how children learn linguistic constructions and make generalizations across them, we have argued and presented evidence for the operation of certain general cognitive processes. Tomasello (2003) argues that we may segregate these into the two overall headings: intention-reading, comprising the species-unique social cognitive skills responsible for symbol acquisition and the functional dimensions of language; and pattern-finding, the primate-wide cognitive skills involved in the abstraction process. More specifically, these two kinds of general cognitive abilities interact in specific acquisition tasks to yield the processes we have outlined in various places previously. Thus, we have previously made reference to four specific sets of processes:

1. Intention-Reading and Cultural Learning, which account for how children learn linguistic symbols in the first place (discussed here very little).
2. Schematization and Analogy, which account for how children create abstract syntactic constructions (and syntactic roles such as subject and direct object) out of the concrete pieces of language they have heard.
3. Entrenchment and Competition, which account for how children constrain their abstractions to those that are conventional in their linguistic community.
4. Functionally Based Distributional Analysis, which accounts for how children form paradigmatic categories of various kinds of linguistic constituents (e.g., nouns and verbs).

These are the processes by which children construct a language, that is, a structured inventory of linguistic constructions. For a full account, we also need to look briefly at the processes by which children actually produce utterances. By way of summary, we look at each of these processes in turn.

### Intention-Reading and Cultural Learning

Because natural languages are conventional, the most fundamental process of language acquisition is the ability to do things the way that other people do them, that is, social learning broadly defined. The acquisition of most cultural skills, including skills of linguistic communication, depend on a special type of social learning involving intention-reading that is most often called cultural learning, one form of which is imitative learning (Tomasello, Kruger, & Ratner, 1993). This can be seen most clearly in experimentals in which young children reproduce an adult's intended action even when she does not actually perform it (Meltzoff, 1995) and in which they selectively reproduce only an adult's intentional, but not accidental, actions (Carpenter, Akhtar, & Tomasello, 1998a). To make matters more complicated, the acquisition of language involves the imitative learning of adult behaviors expressing not just simple intentions but communicative intentions (roughly, intentions toward my intentions). Children's ability to read and learn the expression of communicative intentions can be seen most clearly in word-learning studies in which young children have to identify the adult's intended referent in a wide variety of situations in which word and referent are not both present simultaneously (Tomasello, 2001).

In human linguistic communication, the most fundamental unit of intentional action is the utterance as a relatively complete and coherent expression of a communicative intention, and so the most fundamental unit of language learning is stored exemplars of utterances. This is what children do in learning holophrases and other concrete and relatively fixed linguistic expressions (e.g., *Thank you, Don't mention it*). But as they are attempting to comprehend the communicative intention underlying an utterance, children are also attempting to comprehend the functional roles being played by its various components. This is a kind of "blame assignment" procedure in which the attempt is to determine the functional role of a constituent in the communicative intention as a whole—what we have called segmenting communicative intentions. Identifying the functional roles of the components of utterances is only possible if the child has some (perhaps imperfect) understanding of the adult's overall communicative intention—because understanding the functional role of X means understanding how X contributes to some larger communicative structure. This is the basic process by means of which children learn the communicative functions of particular words, phrases, and other utterance constituents and, with help from pattern-finding skills, categories of these terms.

### Schematization and Analogy

Young children hear and use, on a numbingly regular basis, the same utterances repeated over and over but with systematic variation, for example, as instantiated in item-based schemas such as *Where's-the X?, I wanna X, Let's X, Can you X?, Gimme X, I'm Xing it.* Forming schemas of this type means imitatively learning the recurrent concrete pieces of language for concrete functions, as well as forming a relatively abstract slot designating a relatively abstract function. This process is called schematization, and its roots may be observed in various primates who schematize everything from food-processing skills (Whiten, 1998) to arbitrary sequences in the laboratory (Conway & Christiansen, 2001).

The variable elements or slots in linguistic schemas correspond to the variable item of experience in the referential event for which that schema is used. Thus, in *Where's-the X,* the speaker's seeking is constant across instances but the thing being sought changes across situations; in *I'm Xing it,* the acting on an object is constant but the particular action varies. The communicative function of the item in a slot is thus constrained by the overall communicative function of the schema, but it is still somewhat open; it is a slot-filler category in the sense of Nelson (1985). This primacy of the schema leads to the kinds of functional coercion evidenced in creative uses of language in which an item is used in a schema that requires the listener to interpret that item in an unusual way; for example, under communicative pressure a child might say something like "Allgone sticky," as she watches Mom wiping candy off her hands.

One special form of schematization is analogy, or alternatively, we might say that one special form of analogy is schematization. Both exemplify the process by which children try to categorize, in the general sense of this term, whole utterances and/or significant other linguistic constructions (e.g., nominals). In general, we may say that an analogy can be made only if there is some understanding of the functional interrelations of

the component parts of the two entities to be analogized across. In the case of syntactic constructions, analogies are made not on the basis of surface form but on the basis of the functional interrelations among components in the two constructions being analogized. Thus, the *X is Y-ing the Z* and the *A is B-ing the C* are analogous because the same basic relational situation is being referred to in each case; and X and A play the role of actor, Y and B the activity, and Z and C the undergoer. In this way, different constructions develop their own syntactic roles, first locally in item-based constructions (e.g., "thrower" and "thing thrown"), and then more globally in abstract constructions (e.g., transitive-subject, ditransitive-recipient). There may even emerge late in development, in some languages, a super-abstract subject-predicate construction containing an abstract syntactic role such as "subject" more generally, based on abstractions across various abstract constructions. Perceptual similarity (or even identity) of the objects involved in analogies, while not strictly necessary, does in many cases facilitate human beings in their attempts to make analogies (the study of Childers & Tomasello, 2001, provides support for this hypothesis). If so, this explains why children begin by schematizing across utterances with common linguistic material. Thus they create item-based constructions before they attempt to make totally abstract analogies based on a structure-mapping that involves little or no common linguistic material across utterances.

An important part of item-based and abstract constructions is various kinds of syntactic marking, specifically indicating the syntactic roles that participants are playing in the scene or event as a whole. Special symbols such as case markers and word order are the most common devices that languages use in general to mark the basic "who's doing what to whom" of an utterance. This kind of marking of roles may be thought of as the use of second-order symbols, since the function of the markers is to indicate how the linguistic items they mark should be construed in the meaning of the utterance as a whole.

### Entrenchment and Preemption

There must be constraints to schematization and analogy, and these are provided by entrenchment and preemption. Entrenchment simply refers to the fact that when an organism does something in the same way successfully enough times, that way of doing it becomes habitual and it is very difficult for another way of doing that same thing to enter into the picture. Preemption, or contrast, is a communicative principle of roughly the form: If someone communicates to me using Form X, rather than Form Y, there was a reason for that choice related to the speaker's specific communicative intention. This motivates the listener to search for that reason and so to distinguish the two forms and their appropriate communicative contexts. Together, entrenchment and preemption may be thought of as a single process of competition in which the different possible forms for effecting different classes of communicative functions compete with one another based on a number of principles, including frequency/entrenchment.

It is nevertheless true that we know very little about the specifics of how all this works. Thus, we know very little about the nature and frequency of the syntactic overgeneralization errors that children make at different developmental periods. Further, there is only one empirical study evaluating the effectiveness of entrenchment in preventing syntactic overgeneralizations (Brooks et al., 1999), and that study has no direct measures of the exact frequency of the verbs involved. Similarly, there is only one study of preemption and of semantic classes of verbs as constraining factors (Brooks & Tomasello, 1999a), and this study worked with only a narrow range of structures and verbs. And so, until we actually do some of the empirical work necessary to see how these general principles are applied to specific linguistic items and structures in specific languages, we will still be doing a fair amount of hand waving about how children make exactly the generalizations they do and not others. But of course it must be added that generative approaches engage in a fair amount hand waving themselves in appealing to abstract principles of universal grammar to constrain children's generalizations as well.

### Functionally Based Distrbutional Analysis

Paradigmatic categories such as noun and verb provide language learners with many creative possibilities because they enable learners to use newly learned items in the way that other similar items have been used in the past—with no direct experience. These categories are formed through a process of functionally based distributional analysis in which concrete linguistic items (e.g., words or phrases) that serve the same communicative function in utterances and constructions over time are grouped together into a category. Thus, noun is a paradigmatic category based on the functions that different words of this type serve within nominal constructions—with related categories being such things as pronouns and common nouns, based on the related but different

functions these perform. Paradigmatic categories are thus defined in functional terms by their distributional-combinatorial properties: Nouns are what nouns do in larger linguistic structures. This provides the functional basis by means of which these paradigmatic linguistic categories cohere.

It is important to emphasize that this same process of functionally based distributional analysis also operates on units of language larger than words. For example, what is typically called a noun phrase may be constituted by anything from a proper name to a pronoun to a common noun with a determiner and a relative clause hanging off it. But for many syntactic purposes, these may all be treated as the same kind of unit. How can this be, given their very different surface forms? The only reasonable answer is that they are treated as units of the same type because they all do the same job in utterances: They identify a referent playing some role in the scene being depicted. Because of the varying form of the nominals involved, it is difficult to even think of an alternative to this functionally based account.

Categorization is one of the most heavily researched areas in the cognitive sciences, including developmental psychology. But how children form categories in natural languages—a process of grouping together, not items of perceptual or conceptual experience, but rather items used in linguistic communication—has been very little investigated. The arguments made here suggest that future research on children's skills of linguistic categorization should focus on communicative function as an essential element analogous to the focus on function in the work of Nelson and Mandler on event categories and slot-filler categories in nonlinguistic domains. It is only by investigating how children identify and equate the functional roles linguistic items play in the different constructions of which they are a part that we will discover how children build the abstract categories responsible for so much of linguistic creativity.

### Production

If children are not putting together creative utterances with meaningful words and meaningless rules, then how exactly do they do it? In the current view, what they are doing is constructing utterances out of various already mastered pieces of language of various shapes, sizes, and degrees of internal structure and abstraction—in ways appropriate to the exigencies of the current usage event. To engage in this process of symbolic integration, in which the child fits together into a coherent whole such things as an item-based construction and a novel item to go in the slot, the child must be focused on both form and function. The growth of working memory is an integral part of this process (Adams & Gathercole, 2000).

Lieven, Behrens, Speares, and Tomasello (2003) recorded a 2-year-old child learning English using extremely dense taping intervals: 5 hours per week for 6 weeks. To investigate this child's constructional creativity, all her utterances produced during the last one-hour taping session at the end of the 6-week period were designated as target utterances. Then, for each target utterance, there was a search for similar utterances produced by the child (not the mother) in the previous 6 weeks of taping. The main goal was thus to determine for each utterance recorded on the final day of the study what kinds of syntactic operations were necessary for its production, that is to say, in what ways did the child have to modify things she had previously said (her stored linguistic experience) to produce the thing she was now saying. We may call these operations *usage-based syntactic operations* since they explicitly indicate that the child does not put together each of her utterances from scratch, morpheme by morpheme, but rather, she puts together her utterances from a motley assortment of different kinds of preexisting psycholinguistic units.

What was found by this procedure was that (a) about two-thirds of the multiword utterances produced on the target day were exact verbatim repetitions of utterances the child had said before (only about one-third were novel utterances); (b) of the novel multiword utterances, about three-quarters consisted of repetition of some part of a previously used utterance with only one small change, for example, some new word was filled into a slot or added on to the beginning or end. For example, the child had said many hundreds of times previously *Where's the _____?* and on the target tape she produced the novel utterance *Where's the butter?* The majority of the item-based, utterance-level constructions that the child used on the last day of the study had been used by the child many times during the previous 6 weeks; (3) only about one-quarter of the novel multiword utterances on the last tape (a total of 5% of all utterances during the hour) differed from things this child had said before in more than one way. These mostly involved the combination of filling in and adding onto an established utterance-level construction, but there were several utterances that seemed to be novel in more complex ways.

It is important to note that there was also very high functional consistency across different uses of this child's utterance-level constructions, that is, the child filled a given slot with basically the same kind or kinds

of linguistic items or phrases across the entire 6-week period of the study. Based on these findings, we might say that children have three basic options for producing an utterance on a particular occasion of use (1) they might retrieve a functionally appropriate concrete expression and just say it as they have heard it said; (2) they might retrieve an utterance-level construction and simultaneously "tweak" it to fit the current communicative situation by filling a new constituent into a slot in the item-based construction, adding a new constituent onto the beginning or end of an utterance-level construction or expression, or inserting a new constituent into the middle of an utterance-level construction or expression; or (3) they might produce an utterance by combining constituent schemas without using an utterance-level construction on the basis of various kinds of pragmatic principles governing the ordering of old and new information.

These processes of utterance production may be called usage-based syntactic operations because the child does not begin with words and morphemes and glue them together with contentless rules; rather, she starts with already constructed pieces of language of various shapes, sizes, and degrees of abstraction (and whose internal complexities she may control to varying degrees), and then "cuts and pastes" these together in a way appropriate to the current communicative situation. It is important to note in this metaphor that to cut and paste effectively, a speaker is always making sure that the functions of the various pieces fit together functionally in the intended manner—one does not cut and paste indiscriminately in a word-processing document but in ways that fit. These processes may also work at the level of utterance constituents and their internal structure.

## Individual Differences

Most of the work on individual differences in language development has focused on vocabulary. Individual differences in grammar, the learning of constructions, is much less well-documented. But there is at least some interesting work on individual differences in both the rate and the style of early grammatical development (see Bates et al., 1988, and Lieven, 1997, for overviews).

### Rate

There are several widely used standardized instruments for measuring the rate of children's grammatical development (often in clinical settings), but they are fairly labor intensive and require linguistically sophisticated researchers. Consequently, there is only one that has been used to conduct large-scale norming studies and that is the MacArthur Communicative Development Inventory (MCDI; Fenson et al., 1994), which is basically a standardized parent interview. The section of the instrument that deals with grammar asks parents to mark on a computerized form which of two alternatives "sounds most like the way your child talks right now." For example, parents are asked to choose between *Baby crying* and *Baby is crying* or between *I like read stories* and *I like to read stories* or between *I want that* and *I want the one you got* or between *I no do it* and *I can't do it.*

Fenson et al. (1994) conducted a large-scale norming study with the MCDI with over 1,000 English-speaking children from 16 to 30 months of age. Giving a score of 1 for the more sophisticated alternative of each pair (and 0 for the less sophisticated), they found that at 24 months of age 25% of English-speaking children obtain a score of 2 or less, whereas another 25% obtain a score of 25 or more (out of a total possible 37). At 30 months of age, the lowest 25% of the children scored 15 or below, whereas the highest 25% were basically at ceiling with a score of 36 or greater. To the extent that this "quick and dirty" assessment is accurate (and the score children obtain correlates well with their grammatical sophistication as scored by more complex methods in the laboratory), we can see that children's grammatical skills are extremely highly variable for the first $2\frac{1}{2}$ years of life at the very least.

Explanations for this variability basically fall into two categories. On the one hand, it may be that some children are more efficient learners than others. For example, girls consistently score slightly higher than boys on the MCDI as a whole, and this may be because they are better language learners. There also some very interesting data showing that children with larger working memories seem to learn and process language more efficiently (Adams & Gathercole, 2000). But in general, we have very little information on specific child variables that may be responsible for individual differences in typically developing children in the domain of grammar.

On the other hand, we have very large amounts of data demonstrating that the language learning environment in which children grow up is responsible for at least some of the individual differences in rate of development. Nelson (1977) found that providing young children with extra exemplars of some complex syntactic constructions facilitated their acquisition of those con-

structions. Similarly, the training study of Childer's and Tomasello (2001), described earlier, also demonstrated that a large number of exemplars of a syntactic construction given to children over a short period can facilitate their acquisition of that construction quite dramatically. And Huttenlocher, Vasilyeva, Cymerman, and Levine (2003) have found that children's mastery of complex constructions (multiclause sentences) are strongly related not only to the frequency with which their parents use these constructions, but also to the frequency with which their teachers at school use these constructions (thus diminishing the plausibility of shared genetics between parent and child as an explanation for the parent-child correlations).

But it is not only the quantity of language that children hear that affects their language development, in some cases, it is also the quality of that language. For example, Farrar (1990, 1992) found that children's acquisition of some particular grammatical morphemes in English (e.g., past tense *-ed,* plural *-s,* and progressive *-ing*) was facilitated when mothers used these morphemes as immediate recasts of the child's utterances that were missing them; for example, the child might say "I kick it" and the mother might reply "Yes, you kicked it." Adult conversational replies that maintain the child's topic and to some extent her meaning, while at the same time recasting it into a more adultlike form, are thought to be especially important in helping children to identify grammatical elements with low salience since they provide them with an immediate comparison of their own immature utterance and the corresponding full adult form with full morphology and grammar (Nelson, 1986).

### Style

Nelson (1973) proposed that some children acquire linguistic competence by focusing mostly on words, whereas others acquire their language by focusing more on larger phrases and fixed expressions such as *Gimmedat.* She called the first type of learner "referential" and the second type "expressive" (Bates et al., 1988, called the first type of learner "analytic" and the second type "holistic"). As a dichotomous classification, this typology has not fared well empirically, as most children acquire both words and larger phrases/expressions simultaneously. However, there does seem to be a continuum such that some children seemed to acquire large vocabularies before they produce longer sentences, whereas other children produce seemingly longer expressions (whose internal structure they may or may not understand) from early in development (Lieven, 1997).

The factors responsible for such individual differences in language acquisition style are not known. Noting that there are also individual differences that may be characterized as analytic-holistic in human visual information processing, Bates et al. (1988) speculated that perhaps some children may be more inclined toward analytic or holistic processing strategies naturally. Also interesting is the possibility that some children are naturally greater risk takers than others, and so attempt longer utterances with less well-developed skills than others (Dale & Crain-Thoreson, 1993, report that it is more advanced children that tend to make *I-you* reversal errors, perhaps because they are greater risk takers). On the other hand, there is some evidence that later-born children tend to adopt more holistic strategies; it is therefore possible that being exposed to more third-party, child-directed speech (i.e., as parents talk to the sibling) plays some role (Barton & Tomasello, 1994). It is also possible that experiencing language mostly in imperative utterances also tends to make children more holistic learners (Barton & Tomasello, 1994).

## Atypical Development

Because language is such a complicated phenomenon, it can go wrong in many different ways. The scientific study of atypical language development has for the most part focused on four developmental disorders that have serious consequences for language acquisition: Down syndrome, Williams syndrome, autism, and specific language impairment. Although there is much clinical literature focused on issues of language diagnosis and assessment for all of these groups, there is actually surprisingly little basic research on the process of grammatical development in any of them.

### Down Syndrome

Children with Down syndrome are significantly delayed in their grammatical development. And it is not just an overall delay; they produce simpler and shorter sentences than typically developing children and Williams syndrome children who have the same vocabulary size (Singer et al., 1994, as cited in Tager-Flusberg, 1999). Most Down syndrome children never master truly complex syntactic constructions involving sentence embedding and the like (Fowler, 1990), even though significant

gains in language development continue to occur in many of these children well into adolescence (Chapman, Schwartz, & Kay-Raining Bird, 1991).

Although not enough research has been done to be sure, it would seem that the main problem of children with Down syndrome is a cognitive one. They have a number of cognitive weaknesses—many but not all of which show up on standard IQ tests—that might plausibly be linked to their delayed language development. In particular, although no experiments have been done, there is some suggestive correlational evidence that the specific problem, or at least one specific problem, may be with working memory in the auditory domain (Jarrold, Baddeley, & Phillips, 2002; Laws & Gunn, 2004).

### Williams Syndrome

Children with Williams syndrome also have a number of cognitive deficits—some but not all of which show up on standard IQ tests—especially in the domain of spatial perception and cognition (Mervis, Morris, Bertrand, & Robinson, 1999). Although initial reports suggested that these children might nevertheless have relatively normal language development (e.g., Bellugi, Marks, Bihrle, & Sabo, 1988), more recent research demonstrates that they do indeed have significantly delayed syntactic development in general, with the majority of Williams children never able to correctly understand complex syntax such as sentence embedding (Karmiloff-Smith et al., 1998; Mervis et al., 1999).

One reason why Williams syndrome children were originally thought to have such amazing syntactic skills is because in the original studies they were compared to children with Down syndrome, and as noted, these children have syntactic development that is poorer than would be expected from their vocabulary sizes. Williams syndrome children, on the other hand, have syntactic development that is accurately predicted both by their vocabulary size and by their mental age as assessed by IQ tests (see Tager-Flusberg, 1999, for a review). In addition, just as for children with Down syndrome, there is correlational evidence for children with Williams syndrome that a specific cognitive problem contributing to their language delay is auditory working memory (Mervis et al., 1999).

### Children with Autism

Autism is a disorder less of general cognition than of social cognition and social relations. It is thus not surprising that about half of all children with autism do not have the social-cognitive and communication skills necessary to acquire any serviceable language, and those who do almost invariably have abnormal pragmatic skills. In a study looking at standardized language scores for young adults with autism who used some language, Howlin, Goode, Hutton, and Rutter (2004) found that 44% had a language age below 6 years; 35% scored within the 6- to 15-year range; and only 16% scored above the 15-year level.

The grammatical development of those children with autism who do speak has been very little studied, but it is clear that it is significantly delayed (Tager-Flusberg et al., 1990). When sentences of equal length are compared between children with autism and typically developing children, the sentences of children with autism are significantly less complex syntactically (Scarborough et al., 1991). The most plausible explanation for this finding is that children with autism are highly echolalic/imitative/repetitive. They have quite a bit of formulaic speech, which makes them appear more syntactically competent than they really are (Tager-Flusberg & Calkins, 1990), although these researchers did not find that sentences which were immediate repetitions of adult utterances were syntactically more complex than spontaneously produced sentences). In general, there are very few studies of grammatical development in children with autism, and no studies of older children involving complex syntax.

### Specific Language Impairment

The diagnosis specific language impairment (SLI) is intended to identify children who have language problems but no other obvious cognitive or social-cognitive deficits (including no problems with hearing). This means that children with this diagnosis actually form a fairly heterogeneous group, whose only commonality is that their language development gets off to a fairly slow start and continues to be an area of weakness. There are no widely accepted subgroupings of children with SLI, but some researchers refer to a minority of these children as having pragmatic language impairment (PLI), which resembles autism in some ways (Bishop, 1997). More commonly, researchers refer to expressive SLI and expressive-receptive SLI, with the most severe problems associated with the latter diagnosis which involves problems of language comprehension.

Although not typically detectable on IQ tests, it turns out that SLI children, or at least some of these children, quite often have relatively subtle perceptual or cognitive

deficits of one kind or another (Leonard, 1998, chaps. 5 and 6). Thus, a possible problem for some SLI children is in processing speech, that is, in dealing with the rapid vocal-auditory sequences that make up complex sentences (Tallal, 2000). This can often result in problems specifically with grammatical morphology, which is often of low perceptual salience in the speech stream (Leonard et al., 2003). Also, there is very good recent evidence that, like many children with atypical language development, some of SLI children's problems with language may derive from problems with auditory working memory (Bishop, North, & Donlan, 1996; Conti-Ramsden, 2003; Gathercole & Baddeley, 1990).

## CONCLUSIONS

Acquiring a language is one of the most complicated tasks facing developing children. To become competent users of natural language, children must, at the very least, be able to comprehend communicative intentions as expressed in utterances; segment communicative intentions and ongoing speech and so extract individual words from these utterances; create linguistic schemas with slots; mark syntactic roles in item-based constructions; form abstract constructions across these schemas via analogy; perform distributional analyses to form paradigmatic categories; learn to take their current listener's perspective into account in both forming and choosing appropriately among conventional nominal and clausal constructions; learn to comprehend and express different modalities and negation (speaker attitude); acquire competence with complex constructions containing two or more predicates; learn to manage conversations and narratives, keeping track of referents over long stretches of discourse; cut and paste together stored linguistic units to produce particular utterances appropriate to the current communicative context; and on and on.

There are no fully adequate theoretical accounts of how young children do all of this. One problem has been that quite often the study of language acquisition has been cut off from the study of children's other cognitive and social skills with linguistic theories that barely make reference to these other skills. But in the current view, our best hope for unraveling some of the mysteries of language acquisition rests with approaches that incorporate multiple factors, that is, with approaches that incorporate not only some explicit linguistic model, but also the full range of biological, cultural, and psycholinguistic processes involved. Specifically, it has been argued here that children need to be able (a) to read the intentions of others to acquire the productive use of meaningful linguistic symbols and constructions and (b) to find patterns in the way people use symbols and thereby to construct the grammatical dimensions of language. The outstanding theoretical question in the field is whether, in addition, children's language learning also incorporates an innate universal grammar and, if so, what functions this additional element might serve.

In the meantime, there is much to be done empirically. We know very little about how children segment the communicative intentions behind utterances into their subcomponents. We know very little about how children form analogies across complex linguistic constructions. Perhaps the weakest part of all theories of language acquisition is how children come to constrain the generalizations that they make to just those generalizations that are conventional in their linguistic community. And how children use their mind-reading skills to take into account listener perspective is only now being seriously studied. The utterance production process is also one that requires much more intensive investigation. In
general, the way forward in the study of language acquisition involves both more intensive empirical investigations of particular phenomena and more breadth in the range of theoretical and methodological tools utilized.

# REFERENCES

Abbot-Smith, K., Lieven, E., & Tomasello, M. (2001). What children do and do not do with ungrammatical word orders. *Cognitive Development, 16,* 1–14.

Adams, A. M., & Gathercole, S. E. (2000). Limitations in working memory: Implications for language development. *International Journal of Language and Communication Disorders, 35,* 95–116.

Akhtar, N. (1999). Acquiring basic word order: Evidence for data-driven learning of syntactic structure. *Journal of Child Language, 26,* 339–356.

Akhtar, N., & Tomasello, M. (1997). Young children's productivity with word order and verb morphology. *Developmental Psychology, 33,* 952–965.

Allen, S. (1996). *Aspects of argument structure acquisition in Inuktitut.* Amsterdam: John Benjamins.

Allen, S. E. M., & Crago, M. B. (1996). Early passive acquisition in Inuktitut. *Journal of Child Language, 23,* 129–156.

Antinucci, F., & Miller, R. (1976). How children talk about what happened. *Journal of Child Language, 3,* 167–189.

Ariel, M. (1988). Referring and accessibility. *Journal of Linguistics, 24,* 65–87.

Baker, C. L., & McCarthy, J. J. (1981). *The logical problem of language acquisition.* Cambridge, MA: Massachusetts Institute of Technology Press.

Barlow, M., & Kemmer, S. (2000). (Eds.). *Usage based models of language acquisition.* Stanford: CSLI Publications.

Barrett, M. (1982). The holophrastic hypothesis: Conceptual and empirical issues. *Cognition, 11,* 47–76.

Barton, M., & Tomasello, M. (1994). The rest of the family: The role of fathers and siblings in early language development. In C. Gallaway & B. Richards (Eds.), *Input and interaction in language acquisition* (pp. 109–134). Cambridge, England: Cambridge University Press.

Bates, E., Bretherton, I., & Snyder, L. (1988). *From first words to grammar: Individual differences and dissociable mechanisms.* Cambridge, England: Cambridge University Press.

Bates, E., & MacWhinney, B. (1979). The functionalist approach to the acquisition of grammar. In E. Ochs & B. Schieffelin (Eds.), *Developmental pragmatics.* New York: Academic Press.

Bates, E., & MacWhinney, B. (1982). A functionalist approach to grammatical development. In E. Wanner & L. Gleitman (Eds.), *Language acquisition: The state of the art.* Cambridge, England: Cambridge University Press.

Bates, E., & MacWhinney, B. (1989). Functionalism and the competition model. In B. MacWhinney & E. Bates (Eds.), *The cross-linguistic study of sentence processing.* Cambridge, England: Cambridge University Press.

Bates, E., MacWhinney, B., Caselli, C., Devoscovi, A., Natale, F., & Venza, V. (1984). A cross-linguistic study of the development of sentence comprehension strategies. *Child Development, 55,* 341–354.

Bauer, P. (1996). What do infants recall of their lives? Memory for specific events by 1- to 2-year-olds. *American Psychological Association, 51,* 29–41.

Behrens, H. (1998). *Where does the information go?* Paper presented at Max-Planck-Institute Workshop on Argument Structure. Nijmegen, The Netherlands.

Bellugi, U., Marks, S., Bihrle, A., & Sabo, H. (1988). Dissociations between language and cognitive functions in children with Williams syndrome. In D. Bishop & K. Mogford (Eds.), *Language development in exceptional circumstances* (pp. 177–189). London: Churchill Livingston.

Berman, R. (1982). Verb-pattern alternation: The interface of morphology, syntax, and semantics in Hebrew child language. *Journal of Child Language, 9,* 169–191.

Berman, R. (1993). Marking verb transitivity in Hebrew-speaking children. *Journal of Child Language, 20,* 641–670.

Bishop, D. V. M. (1997). *Uncommon understanding: Development and disorders of language comprehension in children.* Hove, England: Psychology Press.

Bishop, D., North, T., & Donlan, C. (1996). Nonword repetition as a behavioural marker for inherited language impairment: Evidence from a twin study. *Journal of Child Psychology and Psychiatry, 37,* 391–403.

Bloom, L. (1971). Why not pivot grammar? *Journal of Speech and Hearing Disorders, 36,* 40–50.

Bloom, L. (1973). *One word at a time.* The Hague, The Netherlands: Mouton.

Bloom, L. (1992). *Language development from 2 to 3.* Cambridge, England: Cambridge University Press.

Bloom, L., Rispoli, M., Gartner, B., & Hafitz, J. (1989). Acquisition of complementation. *Journal of Child Language, 16,* 101–120.

Bloom, L., Tackeff, J., & Lahey, M. (1984). Learning to speak in complement constructions. *Journal of Child Language, 11,* 391–406.

Bloom, L., Tinker, E., & Margulis, C. (1993). The words children learn: Evidence for a verb bias in early vocabularies. *Cognitive Development, 8,* 431–450.

Bohannon, N., & Stanowicz, L. (1988). The issue of negative evidence: Adult responses to children's language errors. *Developmental Psychology, 24,* 684–689.

Bowerman, M. (1976). Semantic factors in the acquisition of rules for word use and sentence construction. In D. Morehead & A. Morehead (Eds.), *Directions in normal and deficient child language.* Baltimore: University Park Press.

Bowerman, M. (1982). Reorganizational processes in lexical and syntactic development. In L. Gleitman & E. Wanner (Eds.), *Language acquisition: The state of the art.* Cambridge, England: Cambridge University Press.

Bowerman, M. (1988). The "no negative evidence" problem: How do children avoid constructing an overgeneral grammar? In J. A. Hawkins (Ed.), *Explaining language universals.* Oxford: Basil Blackwell.

Bowerman, M. (1996). Learning how to structure space for language: A cross-linguistic perspective. In P. Bloom, M. Peterson, L. Nadel & M. Garret (Eds.), *Language and space.* Cambridge, MA: MIT Press.

Braine, M. (1963). The ontogeny of English phrase structure. *Language, 39,* 1–14.

Braine, M. (1971). On two types of models of the internalization of grammars. In D. I. Slobin (Ed.), *The ontogenesis of grammar.* New York: Academic Press.

Braine, M. (1976). Children's first word combinations. *Monographs of the Society for Research in Child Development, 41*(1).

Braine, M., & Brooks, P. (1995). Verb-argument structure and the problem of avoiding an overgeneral grammar. In M. Tomasello & W. Merriman (Eds.), *Beyond names for things: Young children's acquisition of verbs.* Hillsdale, NJ: Erlbaum.

Bridges, A. (1984). Preschool children's comprehension of agency. *Journal of Child Language, 11,* 593–610.

Brooks, P., & Tomasello, M. (1999a). Young children learn to produce passives with nonce verbs. *Developmental Psychology, 35,* 29–44.

Brooks, P., & Tomasello, M. (1999b). How young children constrain their argument structure constructions. *Language, 75,* 720–738.

Brooks, P., Tomasello, M., Lewis, L., & Dodson, K. (1999). Children's overgeneralization of fixed transitivity verbs: The entrenchment hypothesis. *Child Development, 70,* 1325–1337.

Brown, A., & Kane, M. (1988). Preschool children can learn to transfer: Learning to learn and learning from example. *Cognitive Psychology, 20,* 493–523.

Brown, R. (1973). *A first language: The early stages.* Cambridge, MA: Harvard University Press.

Brown, R., & Hanlon, C. (1970). Derivational complexity and order of acquisition in child speech. In J. R. Hayes (Ed.), *Cognition and the development of language.* New York: John Wiley & Sons.

Bruner, J. (1975). The ontogenesis of speech acts. *Journal of Child Language, 2,* 1–20.

Budwig, N. (1990). The linguistic marking of nonprototypical agency: An exploration into children's use of passives. *Linguistics, 28,* 1221–1252.

Budwig, N., Stein, S., & O'Brien, C. (2001). Non-agent subjects in early child language: A crosslinguistic comparison. In K. Nelson, A. Aksu-Ko, & C. Johnson (Eds.), *Children's language, Volume 11: Interactional contributions to language development.* Mahwah, NJ: Lawrence Erlbaum.

Bybee, J. (1985). *Morphology: A study of the relation between meaning and form.* Amsterdam: John Benjamins.

Bybee, J. (1995). Regular morphology and the lexicon. *Language and Cognitive Processes, 10,* 425–455.

Cameron-Faulkner, T., Lieven, E., & Tomasello, M. (2003). A construction based analysis of child directed speech. *Cognitive Science, 27,* 843–873.

Carpenter, M., Akhtar, N., & Tomasello, M. (1998). Sixteen-month-old infants differentially imitate intentional and accidental actions. *Infant Behavior and Development, 21,* 315–330.

Chapman, R. S., Schwartz, S. E., & Kay-Raining Bird, E. (1991). Language skills of children and adolescents with Down syndrome: I. Comprehension. *Journal of Speech and Hearing Research, 34,* 1106–1120.

Childers, J., & Tomasello, M. (2001). The role of pronouns in young children's acquisition of the English transitive construction. *Developmental Psychology, 37,* 739–748.

Chomsky, N. (1968). *Language and mind.* New York: Harcourt Brace Jovanovich.

Chomsky, N. (1980). Rules and representations. *Behavioral and Brain Sciences, 3,* 1–61.

Clancy, P. (2000). The lexicon in interaction: Developmental origins of preferred argument structure in Korean. In J. DuBois (Ed.), *Preferred argument structure: Grammar as architecture for function.* John Benjamins.

Clark, E. V. (1982). The young word maker: A case study of innovation in the child's lexicon. In E. Wanner & L. R. Gleitman (Eds.), *Language acquisition: The state of the art.* New York: Cambridge University Press.

Clark, E. (1987). The principle of contrast: A constraint on language acquisition. In B. MacWhinney (Ed.), *Mechanisms of language acquisition.* Hillsdale, NJ: Erlbaum.

Clark, H. (1996). *Uses of language.* Cambridge, England: Cambridge University Press.

Comrie, B. (1976). *Aspect: An introduction to the study of verbal aspect and related problems.* Cambridge, England: Cambridge University Press.

Conti-Ramsden, G. (2003). Processing and linguistic markers in young children with specific language impairment (SLI). *Journal of Speech, Language and Hearing Research, 46,* 1029–1037.

Conway, C. M., & Christiansen, M. H. (2001). Sequential learning in nonhuman primates. *Trends in Cognitive Sciences, 5,* 529–546.

Croft, W. (1991). *Syntactic categories and grammatical relations: The cognitive organization of information.* Chicago: University of Chicago Press.

Croft, W. (2001). *Radical construction grammar.* Oxford, England: Oxford University Press.

Dabrowska, E. (2001). Learning a morphological system without a default: The Polish genitive. *Journal of Child Language, 28,* 545–574.

Dale, P. S., & Crain-Thoreson, C. (1993). Pronoun reversals: Who, when, and why? *Journal of Child Language, 20,* 573–589.

Demuth, K. (1989). Maturation and the acquisition of the Sesotho passive. *Language, 65,* 56–80.

Demuth, K. (1990). Subject, topic, and Sesotho passive. *Journal of Child Language, 17,* 67–84.

DeVilliers, J., & DeVilliers, P. (1973). Development of the use of word order in comprehension. *Journal of Psycholinguistic Research, 2,* 331–341.

Dick, F., Bates, E., Wulfeck, B., Utman, J., Dronkers, N., & Gernsbacher, M. A. (2001). Language deficits, localization, and grammar: Evidence for a distributive model of language breakdown in aphasics and normals. *Psychological Review, 108*(4), 759–788.

Diessel, H. (2004) The acquisition of complex sentences. *Cambridge Studies in Linguistics 105.* Cambridge, England: Cambridge University Press.

Diessel, H., & Tomasello, M. (2000). The development of relative constructions in early child speech. *Cognitive Linguistics, 11,* 131–152.

Diessel, H., & Tomasello, M. (2001). The acquisition of finite complement clauses in English: A usage based approach to the development of grammatical constructions. *Cognitive Linguistics, 12,* 97–141.

Dodson, K., & Tomasello, M. (1998). Acquiring the transitive construction in English: The role of animacy and pronouns. *Journal of Child Language, 25,* 555–574.

Elman, J. L., Bates, E., Johnson, M., Karmiloff-Smith, A., Parisi, D., & Plunkett, K. (1996). *Rethinking innateness: A connectionist perspective on development.* Cambridge, MA: Massachusetts Institute of Technology Press.

Emslie, H., & Stevenson, R. (1981). Pre-school children's use of the articles in definite and indefinite referring expressions. *Journal of Child Language, 8,* 313–328.

Erteschik-Shir, N. (1979). Discourse constraints on dative movements. In T. Giv'on (Ed.), *Syntax and semantic 12: Discourse and syntax.* New York: Academic Press.

Erreich, A. (1984). Learning how to ask: Patterns of inversion in yes-no and wh-questions. *Journal of Child Language, 11,* 579–592.

Farrar, J. (1990). Discourse and the acquisition of grammatical morphemes. *Journal of Child Language, 17,* 607–624.

Farrar, J. (1992). Negative evidence and grammatical morpheme acquisition. *Developmental Psychology, 28,* 90–98.

Fenson, L., Dale, P., Reznick, J. S., Bates, E., Thal, D., & Pethick, S. (1994). Variability in early communicative development. *Monographs of the Society for Research in Child, 59*(5, Serial No. 242).

Fillmore, C. (1988). The mechanisms of construction grammar. *Berkeley Linguistics Society, 14,* 35–55.

Fillmore, C. (1989). Grammatical construction theory and the familiar dichotomies. In R. Dietrich & C. F. Graumann (Eds.), *Language processing in social context.* Amsterdam: North-Holland/Elsevier.

Fillmore, C., Kaye, P., & O'Conner, M. (1988). Regularity and idiomaticity in grammatical constructions: The case of let alone. *Language, 64,* 501–538.

Fisher, C. (1996). Structural limits on verb mapping: The role of analogy in children's interpretations of sentences. *Cognitive Psychology, 31,* 41–81.

Fisher, C. (2000). *Who's blicking whom? Word order in early verb learning.* Poster presented at the 11th International Conference on Infant Studies, Brighton, England.

Fisher, C. (2002). Structural limits on verb mapping: The role of abstract structure in $2\frac{1}{2}$-year-old's interpretations of novel verbs. *Developmental Science, 5*(1), 55–64.

Flavell, J. (1997). *Cognitive development.* Englewood Cliffs, NJ: Prentice Hall.

Fletcher, P. (1985). *A child's learning of English.* Oxford: Basil Blackwell Press.

Fowler, A. E. (1990). Language abilities in children with Down syndrome: Evidence for a specific syntactic delay. In D. Cicchetti & M. Beeghly (Eds.), *Children with Down syndrome: A developmental perspective.* Cambridge, England: Cambridge University Press.

Galloway, C., & Richards, B. J. (1994). *Input and interaction in language acquisition.* Cambridge, England: Cambridge University Press.

Garton, A. (1983). An approach to the study of determiners in early language development. *Journal of Psycholinguistic Research, 12,* 513–525.

Gathercole, S., & Baddeley, A. (1990). Phonological memory deficits in language disordered children: Is there a causal connection? *Journal of Memory and Language, 29,* 336–360.

Gathercole, V., Sebastián, E., & Soto, P. (1999). The early acquisition of Spanish verbal morphology: Across-the-board or piecemeal knowledge? *International Journal of Bilingualism, 3,* 133–182.

Gentner, D., & Markman, A. (1995). Similarity is like analogy: Structural alignment in comparison. In C. Cacciari (Ed.), *Similarity in language, thought and perception.* Brussels: BREPOLS.

Gentner, D., & Medina, J. (1998). Similarity and the development of rules. *Cognition, 65,* 263–297.

Gerhardt, J. (1988). From discourse to semantics: The development of verb morphology and forms of self-reference in the speech of a two-year-old. *Journal of Child Language, 15*(2), 337–393.

Gerhardt, J. (1991). The meaning and use of the modals hafta, needta and wanna in children's speech. *Journal of Pragmatics, 16*(6), 531–590.

Givón, T. (1993). *English grammar: A function-based introduction.* Amsterdam: John Benjamins.

Givón, T. (1995). *Functionalism and grammar.* Amsterdam: John Benjamins.

Goldberg, A. (1995). *Constructions: A construction grammar approach to argument structure.* Chicago: University of Chicago Press.

Gómez, R., & Gerken, L. (1999). Artificial grammar learn by 1-year-olds leads to specific and abstract knowledge. *Cognition, 70,* 109–135.

Gopnik, A., & Choi, S. (1995). Names, relational words, and cognitive development in English and Korean speakers: Nouns are not always learned before verbs. In M. Tomasello & W. E. Merriman (Eds.), *Beyond names for things: Young children's acquisition of verbs.* Hillsdale, NJ: Erlbaum.

Greenfield, P. M., & Smith, J. H. (1976). *The structure of communication in early language development.* New York: Academic Press.

Gundel, J., Hedberg, N., & Zacharski, R. (1993). Cognitive status and the form of referring expressions. *Language, 69*(2), 274–307.

Hakuta, K. (1982). Interaction between particles and word order in the comprehension and production of simple sentences in Japanese children. *Developmental Psychology, 18,* 62–76.

Hauser, M. D., Weiss, D., & Marcus, G. F. (2002). Rule learning by cotton-top tamarins. *Cognition, 86*(1), B15–B22.

Hirsh-Pasek, K., & Golinkoff, R. M. (1991). Language comprehension: A new look at some old themes. In N. Krasnegor, D. Rumbaugh, M. Studdert-Kennedy, & R. Schiefelbusch (Eds.), *Biological and behavioral aspects of language acquisition.* Hillsdale, NJ: Erlbaum.

Hirsh-Pasek, K., & Golinkoff, R. M. (1996). *The origins of grammar: Evidence from early language comprehension.* Cambridge, MA: Massachusetts Institute of Technology Press.

Hopper, P., & Thompson, S. (1984). The discourse basis for lexical categories in universal grammar. *Language, 60,* 703–752.

Hornstein, D., & Lightfoot, N. (1981). *Explanation in linguistics.* London: Longman, Brown, Green, and Longmans.

Howe, C. (1976). The meaning of two-word utterances in the speech of young children. *Journal of Child Language, 3,* 29–48.

Howlin, P., Goode, S., Hutton, J., & Rutter, M. (2004). Adult outcome for children with autism. *Journal of Child Psychology and Psychiatry, 45,* 212–229.

Huttenlocher, J., Vasilyeva, M, Cymerman, E., & Levine, S. (2003). Language input and child syntax. *Cognitive Psychology, 45*(3), 337–374.

Ingram, D., & Tyack, D. (1979). The inversion of subject NP and aux in children's questions. *Journal of Psycholinguistic Research, 4,* 333–341.

Israel, M., Johnson, C., & Brooks, P. J. (2000). From states to events: The acquisition of English passive participles. *Cognitive Linguistics, 11*(1–2), 103–129.

Jarrold, C., Baddeley, A. D., & Phillips, C. E. (2002). Verbal short-term memory in Down syndrome: A problems of memory, audition or speech? *Journal of Speech, Language and Hearing Research, 45,* 531–544.

Karmiloff-Smith, A., Tyler, L. K., Voice, K., Sims, K., Udwin, O., Davies, M., et al. (1998). Linguistic dissociations in Williams syndrome: Evaluating receptive syntax in on-line and off-line tasks. *Neuropsychologia, 36*(4), 342–351.

Kemmer, S. (1993). *The middle voice.* Amsterdam/Philadelphia: John Benjamins.

Kirkham, N., Slemmer, J., & Johnson, S. (in press). Visual statistical learning in infancy: Evidence for a domain general learning mechanism. *Cognition.*

Klein, W., & Perdue, C. (1997). The Basic Variety (or: Couldn't natural languages be much simpler?). *Second Language Research, 13*(4), 301–347.

Klima, E., & Bellugi, U. (1966). Syntactic regularities in the speech of children. In J. Lyons & R. J. Wales (Eds.), *Psycholinguistic papers.* Edinburgh, Scotland: Edinburgh University Press.

Kuczaj, S. (1977). The acquisition of regular and irregular past tense forms. *Journal of Verbal Learning and Verbal Behavior, 16,* 589–600.

Langacker, R. (1987a). *Foundations of cognitive grammar* (Vol. 1). Stanford, CA: Stanford University Press.

Langacker, R. (1987b). Nouns and verbs. *Language, 63,* 53–94.

Langacker, R. (1991). *Foundations of cognitive grammar* (Vol. 2). Stanford, CA: Stanford University Press.

Laws, G., & Gunn, D. (2004). Phonological memory as a predictor of language comprehension in Down syndrome: A 5-year follow up study. *Journal of Child Psychology and Psychiatry, 45,* 326–337.

Leonard, L. B. (1998). *Children with specific language impairment.* Cambridge, MA: Massachusetts Institute of Technology Press.

Leonard, L., Deevy, P., Miller, C., Rauf, L., Charest, M., & Kurtz, R. (2003). Surface forms and grammatical functions: Past tense and passive participle use by children with specific language impairment. *Journal of Speech, Language and Hearing Research, 46,* 43–55.

Li, P., & Shirai, Y. (2000). *The acquisition of lexical and grammatical aspect.* Berlin/New York: Mouton de Gruyter.

Lieven, E. (1997). Variation in a crosslinguistic context. In D. I. Slobin (Ed.), *The Crosslinguistic Study of Language Acquisition* (Vol. 5). Hillsdale, NJ: Lawrence Erlbaum.

Lieven, E., Behrens, H., Speares, J., & Tomasello, M. (2003). Early syntactic creativity: A usage based approach. *Journal of Child Language, 30,* 333–370.

Lieven, E., Pine, J., & Baldwin, G. (1997). Lexically-based learning and early grammatical development. *Journal of Child Language, 24,* 187–220.

Lieven, E., Pine, J., & Dresner-Barnes, H. (1992). Individual differences in early vocabulary development. *Journal of Child Language, 19,* 287–310.

Limber, J. (1973). The genesis of complex sentences. In T. Moore (Eds.), *Cognitive development and the acquisition of language.* New York: Academic Press.

Lindner, K. (2003). The development of sentence interpretation strategies in monolingual German-learning children with and without specific language impairment. *Linguistics, 41*(2), 213–254.

Mandler, J. M. (2000). Perceptual and conceptual processes in infancy. *Journal of Cognition and Development, 1,* 3–36.

Maratsos, M. (1976). *The use of definite and indefinite reference in young children.* Cambridge, England: Cambridge University Press.

Maratsos, M. (1982). The child's construction of grammatical categories. In E. Wanner & L. Gleitman (Eds.), *Language acquisition: State of the art.* Cambridge, England: Cambridge University Press.

Maratsos, M. (2000). More overregularizations after all. *Journal of Child Language, 28,* 32–54.

Maratsos, M., Gudeman, R., Gerard-Ngo, P., & DeHart, G. (1987). A study in novel word learning: The productivity of the causative. In B. MacWhinney (Ed.), *Mechanisms of language acquisition.* Hillsdale, NJ: Erlbaum.

Marchman, V., & Bates, E. (1994). Continuity in lexical and morphological development: A test of the critical mass hypothesis. *Journal of Child Language, 21,* 339–366.

Marcus, G. F., Pinker, S., Ullman, M., Hollander, M., Rosen, T. J., & Xu, F. (1992). Overregularization in language acquisition. *Monographs of the Society for Research in Child Development, 57,* 34–69.

Marcus, G. F., Vijayan, S., Bandi Rao, S., & Vishton, P. M. (1999). Rule learning by 7-month-old-infants. *Science, 283,* 77–80.

McCune, L. (1992). First words: A dynamic systems view. In C. Ferguson, L. Menn, & C. Stoel-Gammon (Eds.), *Phonological development: Models, research, and implications.* Parkton, MD: York Press.

McNeill, D. (1966). The creation of language by children. In J. Lyons & R. J. Wales (Eds.), *Psycholinguistic papers: Proceedings of the 1966 Edinburgh Conference.* Edinburgh, Scotland: Edinburgh University Press.

McShane, J., & Whittaker, S. (1988). The encoding of tense and aspect by 3- to 5-year-old children. *Journal of Experimental Child Psychology, 45,* 52–70.

McWhorter, J. H. (1998). Identifying the Creole prototype: Vindicating a typological class. *Language, 74,* 788–818.

Meltzoff, A. (1995). Understanding the intentions of others: Reenactment of intended acts by 18-month-old children. *Developmental Psychology, 31,* 838–850.

Mervis, C., Morris, C., Bertrand, J., & Robinson, B. (1999). Williams syndrome: Findings from an integrated program of research. In (H. Tager-Flusberg, Ed.), *Neurodevelopmental disorders.* Cambridge, MA: Massachusetts Institute of Technology Press.

Munakata, Y., McClelland, J. L., Johnson, M. H., & Siegler, R. S. (1997). Rethinking infant knowledge: Toward an adaptive process account of successes and failures in object permanence tasks. *Psychological Review, 104,* 686–713.

Naigles, L. (1990). Children use syntax to learn verb meanings. *Journal of Child Language, 17,* 357–374.

Nelson, K. (1973). Structure and strategy in learning to talk. *Monographs of the Society for Research in Child Development, 38*(149).

Nelson, K. (1977). Facilitating children's syntax acquisition. *Developmental Psychology, 13,* 101–107.

Nelson, K. (1985). *Making sense: The acquisition of shared meaning.* New York: Academic Press.

Nelson, K. (1986). *Event knowledge: Structure and function in development.* Hillsdale, NJ: Erlbaum.

Nelson, K. (1995). The dual category problem in the acquisition of action words. In M. Tomasello & W. Merriman (Eds.), *Beyond names for things: Young children's acquisition of verbs.* Hillsdale, NJ: Erlbaum.

Nelson, K. (1996). *Language in cognitive development.* New York: Cambridge University Press.

Nelson, K., Hampson, J., & Shaw, L. K. (1993). Nouns in early lexicons: Evidence, explanations and implications. *Journal of Child Language, 20,* 61–84.

Newport, E. L., Aslin, R. N., & Hauser, M. D. (2001, November). *Learning at a distance: Statistical learning of non-adjacent regularities in humans and tamarin monkeys.* Presented at the Conference on Language Development, Boston University, Boston, MD. Ninio, A. (1992). The relation of children's single word utterances to single word utterances in the input. *Journal of Child Language, 19,* 87–110.

Ninio, A. (1993). On the fringes of the system: Children's acquisition of syntactically isolated forms at the onset of speech. *First Language, 13,* 291–314.

Pawley, A., & Syder, F. (1983). Two puzzles for linguistic theory. In J. Richards & R. Smith (Eds.), *Language and communication.* New York: Longmans.

Piaget, J. (1952). *The origins of intelligence in children.* New York: Norton. (Original work published 1935)

Pine, J., & Lieven, E. (1993). Reanalysing rote-learned phrases: Individual differences in the transition to multi word speech. *Journal of Child Language, 20,* 551–571.

Pine, J., Lieven, E., & Rowland, G. (1998). Comparing different models of the development of the English verb category. *Linguistics, 36,* 4–40.

Pinker, S. (1981). A theory of graph comprehension. In R. Freedle (Ed.), *Artificial intelligence and the future of testing.* Hillsdale, NJ: Erlbaum.

Pinker, S. (1984). *Language learnability and language development.* Cambridge, MA: Harvard University Press.

Pinker, S. (1989). *Learnability and cognition: The acquisition of verb-argument structure.* Cambridge, MA: Harvard University Press.

Pinker, S. (1991). Rules of language. *Science, 253,* 530–535.

Pinker, S. (1999). *Words and rules.* New York: Morrow Press.

Pizzuto E., & Caselli, M. C. (1992). The acquisition of Italian morphology: Implications for models of language development. *Journal of Child Language, 19,* 491–557.

Pye, C., & Quixtan Poz, P. (1988). Precocious passives and antipassives in Quiche Mayan. *Papers and Reports on Child Language Development, 27,* 71–80.

Ramus, F., Hauser, M. D., Miller, C., Morris, D., & Mehler, J. (2000). Language discrimination by human newborns and by cotton-top tamarin monkeys. *Science, 288,* 349–351.

Rispoli, M. (1991). The mosaic acquisition of grammatical relations. *Journal of Child Language, 18,* 517–551.

Rispoli, M. (1994). Structural dependency and the acquisition of grammatical relations. In Y. Levy (Ed.), *Other children, other languages: Issues in the theory of language acquisition.* Hillsdale, NJ: Erlbaum.

Rispoli, M. (1998). Patterns of pronoun case error. *Journal of Child Language, 25,* 533–544.

Roberts, K. (1983). Comprehension and production of word order in stage 1. *Child Development, 54,* 443–449.

Rowland, C., & Pine, J. M. (2000). Subject-auxiliary inversion errors and wh-question acquisition: "What children do know?" *Journal of Child Language, 27,* 157–181.

Rubino, R., & Pine, J. (1998). Subject-verb agreement in Brazilian Portugese: What low error rates hide. *Journal of Child Language, 25,* 35–60.

Saffran, J., Aslin, R., & Newport E. (1996). Statistical learning by 8-month old infants. *Science, 274,* 1926.

Saffran, J. R., Johnson, E. K., Aslin, R. N., & Newport, E. L. (1999). Statistical learning of tone sequences by human infants and adults. *Cognition, 70*(1), 27–52.

Savage, C., Lieven, E., Theakston, A., & Tomasello, M. (2003). Testing the abstractness of young childrens linguistic representations: Lexical and structural priming of syntactic constructions? *Developmental Science, 6,* 557–567.

Scarborough, H. S., Rescorla, L. R., Tager-Flusberg, H., Fowler, A. E., & Sudhalter, V. (1991). The relation of utterance length to grammatical complexity in normal and language-disordered samples. *Applied Psycholinguistics, 12,* 23–45.

Schlesinger, I. (1971). Learning of grammar from pivot to realization rules. In R. Huxley & E. Ingram (Eds.), *Language acquisition: Models and methods.* New York: Academic Press.

Serrat, E. (1997). *Acquisition of verb category in Catalan.* Unpublished doctoral dissertation.

Shirai, Y., & Andersen, R. W. (1995). The acquisition of tense/aspect morphology: A prototype account. *Language, 71,* 743–762.

Slobin, D. (1970). Universals of grammatical development in children. In G. Flores D'Arcais & W. Levelt (Eds.), *Advances in psycholinguistics.* Amsterdam: North Holland.

Slobin, D. (1973). Cognitive prerequisites for the development of grammar. In C. Ferguson & D. Slobin (Eds.), *Studies of child language development.* New York: Holt, Rinehart, Winston.

Slobin, D. (1982). Universal and particular in the acquisition of language. In L. Gleitman & E. Wanner (Eds.), *Language acquisition: The state of the art.* Cambridge, England: Cambridge University Press.

Slobin, D. (1985). Crosslinguistic evidence for the language-making capacity. In D. I. Slobin (Ed.), *The crosslinguistic study of language acquisition: Vol. 2. Theoretical issues.* Hillsdale, NJ: Erlbaum.

Slobin, D. I. (1997). *The crosslinguistic study of language acquisition: Vol. 4 and Vol. 5. Expanding the contexts.* Mahwah, NJ: Lawrence Erlbaum Associates.

Slobin, D., & Bever, T. (1982). Children use canonical sentence schemas: A crosslinguistic study of word order and inflections. *Cognition, 12,* 229–265.

Smith, C. S. (1980). The acquisition of time talk: Relations between child and adult grammars. *Journal of Child Language, 7,* 263–278.

Snow, C. E., & Ferguson, C. A. (1977). *Talking to children.* Cambridge, England: Cambridge University Press.

Stoll, S. (1998). The acquisition of Russian aspect. *First Language, 18,* 351–378.

Sudhalter, V., & Braine, M. (1985). How does comprehension of passives develop? A comparison of actional and experiential verbs. *Journal of Child Language, 12,* 455–470.

Suzman, S. M. (1985). Learning the passive in Zulu. *Papers and Reports on Child Language Development, 24,* 131–137.

Tager-Flusberg, H. (1999). Language development in atypical children. In M. Barrett (Ed.), *The development of language.* Hove: Psychology Press.

Tager-Flusberg, H., & Calkins, S. (1990). Does imitation facilitate the acquisition of grammar? Evidence from a study of autistic, Down's syndrome and normal children. *Journal of Child Language, 17,* 591–606.

Tager-Flusberg, H., Calkins S., Nolin, Z., Baumberger, T., Anderson, M., & Chadwick-Dias, A. (1990). A longitudinal study of language acquisition in autistic and Downs syndrome children. *Journal of Autism & Developmental Disorders, 20,* 1–21.

Tallal, P. (2000). Experimental studies of language learning impairments: From research to remediation. In D. Bishop & L. Leonard (Eds.), *Speech and language impairments in children* (pp. 131–156). Hove, England: Psychology Press.

Tardif, T. (1996). Nouns are not always learned before verbs: Evidence from Mandarin speakers' early vocabularies. *Developmental Psychology, 32*(3), 492–504.

Tomasello, M. (1992). *First verbs: A case study of early grammatical development.* Cambridge, England: Cambridge University Press.

Tomasello, M. (1998a). *The new psychology of language: Vol. 1. Cognitive and functional approaches to language structure.* Mahwah, NJ: Erlbaum.

Tomasello, M. (1998b). One child's early talk about possession. In J. Newman (Ed.), *The linguistics of giving* (pp. 349–373). Amsterdam: John Benjamins.

Tomasello, M. (1998c). Reference: Intending that others jointly attend. *Pragmatics and Cognition, 6,* 229–244.

Tomasello, M. (1999). *The cultural origins of human cognition.* Cambridge, MA: Harvard University Press.

Tomasello, M. (2000). Do young children have adult syntactic competence? *Cognition, 74,* 209–253.

Tomasello, M. (2001). Perceiving intentions and learning words in the second year of life. In M. Bowerman & S. Levinson (Eds.), *Language Acquisition and Conceptual Development.* Cambridge, England: Cambridge University Press.

Tomasello, M. (2003). *Constructing a language: A usage-based theory of language acquisition.* Cambridge, MA: Harvard University Press.

Tomasello, M., Akhtar, N., Dodson, K., & Rekau, L. (1997). Differential productivity in young children's use of nouns and verbs. *Journal of Child Language, 24,* 373–387.

Tomasello, M., Kruger, A., & Ratner, H. (1993). Cultural learning. *Behavioral and Brain Sciences, 16,* 495–552.

Trask, L. (1996). *Historical linguistics: An introduction.* New York: St. Martin's Press.

Wagner, L. (2001). Aspectual influences on early tense comprehension. *Journal of Child Language, 28,* 661–682.

Weist, R. (1983). Prefix versus suffix information processing in the comprehension of tense and aspect. *Journal of Child Language, 10,* 85–96.

Weist, R. (1986). Tense and aspect. In P. Fletcher & M. Garman (Eds.), *Language acquisition* (2nd. ed.). Cambridge, England: Cambridge University Press.

Weist, R., Lyytinen, P., Wysocka, J., & Atanassova, M. (1997). The interaction of language and thought in children's language acquisition: A crosslinguistic study. *Journal of Child Language, 24,* 81–121.

Weist, R., Wysocka, H., Witkowska-Stadnik, K., Buczowska, E., & Konieczna, E. (1984). The defective tense hypothesis: On the emergence of tense and aspect in child Polish. *Journal of Child Language, 11,* 347–374.

Wells, G. (1983). *Learning through interaction: The study of language development.* Cambridge, England: Cambridge University Press.

Whiten, A. (1998). Imitation of the sequential structure of actions by chimpanzees (Pan troglodytes). *Journal of Comparative Psychology, 112,* 270–281.

Wittek, A., & Tomasello, M. (2005). German-speaking children's productivity with syntactic constructions and case morphology: Local cues help locally. *First Language, 25,* 103–125.

CHAPTER 7

# Early Word Learning

SANDRA R. WAXMAN and JEFFREY L. LIDZ

*That living word awakened my soul, gave it light, hope, joy, and set it free!*
—HELEN KELLER, 1904

EARLY WORD LEARNING: THE GATEWAY
BETWEEN LINGUISTIC AND
CONCEPTUAL ORGANIZATION   299
**The Puzzle of Word Learning**   300
**Early Solutions to the Puzzle of Word Learning**   301
PLAN OF THE CHAPTER   302
**Cross-Linguistic Evidence**   303
**The Privileged Position of Nouns**   303
**Structure: In the Input or in the Mind**   303
SETTING THE STAGE FOR WORD LEARNING:
FOUNDATIONAL CAPACITIES   304
**Identifying the Words**   304
**Identifying the Relevant Concepts**   305
**Interpreting the Intentions of Others**   306

Conclusions about Initial Acquisitions   306
FIRST STEPS INTO WORD LEARNING: A BROAD
INITIAL LINK BETWEEN WORDS AND
CONCEPTS   306
**Specificity of the Initial Link**   307
LATER STEPS INTO WORD LEARNING: MORE
SPECIFIC LINKS BETWEEN KINDS OF WORDS
AND KINDS OF CONCEPTS   309
**The Acquisition of Nouns**   309
**The Acquisition of Adjectives**   315
**The Acquisition of Verbs**   320
THE FUTURE OF WORD-LEARNING RESEARCH   326
REFERENCES   327

## EARLY WORD LEARNING: THE GATEWAY BETWEEN LINGUISTIC AND CONCEPTUAL ORGANIZATION

Word learning, perhaps more than any other developmental achievement, stands at the very crossroad of human conceptual and linguistic organization (P. Bloom, 2000; S. A. Gelman, Coley, Rosengren, Hartman, & Pappas, 1998; Hollich, Hirsh-Pasek, & Golinkoff, 2000; Waxman, 2002; Woodward & Markman, 1998). Like Janus, the two-headed Roman god of beginnings, word learners must set their sights in two distinct directions. Facing the conceptual domain, infants form core *concepts*[1] to capture the relations among the objects and

events that they encounter. Facing the linguistic domain, infants cull *words* and *phrases* from the melody of the human language in which they are immersed. Even before they take their first steps, infants make important advances in each of these domains. And perhaps even more remarkably, recent evidence reveals that from the onset of word learning, infants' advances in the conceptual and linguistic domains are powerfully linked.

Janus was known to the Romans not only as the god of beginnings, but also as the guardian of gateways and transitions. Like Janus, young word learners stand at an important gateway. Across the world's communities, infants' first words are greeted with a special joy because they mark infants' entrance into a truly symbolic system

---

The National Institutes of Health (HD-28730 and DC-006829 to the first and second authors, respectively), the National Science Foundation (BCS-0418309 to the second author), and the CNRS (Paris) provided support for this chapter. We are grateful to A. Booth, D. G. Hall, T. Lavin, E. Leddon, and the editors of this volume for comments on earlier versions.

[1] We use the term *concept* to refer to a symbolic mental representation. For the concepts considered in this chapter (e.g., DOG or FURRY), the extension of that representation include

individual instances that the infant has encountered (e.g., her own pet dog; its furry tail). The representation must also be sufficiently abstract to include in its extension (at least some) instances that she has not encountered (e.g., my dog; her furry ears). Used in this way, the term *concept* refers to an abstract mental representation that may be built up from infants' direct experiences and whose semantics may be organized around various kinds of relations, including category-based, property-based, or action-based commonalities.

of social commerce. In acquiring their first words, infants acquire much more than a symbolic means of reference. Word learning serves as a gateway into the fundamental social, conceptual, and linguistic abilities that are the hallmark of the human mind. From a social perspective, word learning permits infants to apprehend and to influence the contents of other minds. From a conceptual perspective, word learning supports the evolution of the increasingly abstract and flexible mental representations that are the signature of the human conceptual system. There is no doubt that other species of animals also have sophisticated social and conceptual abilities (see Cole, Chapter 15, this *Handbook,* this volume). But in the human, these systems stand out for their flexibility, force, and inductive strength; and each of these is supported strongly by language. As will become apparent as the chapter unfolds, word learning both contributes to and is supported by infants' discovery of the fundamental syntactic and semantic properties of human language, and the interactions among these.

Just as young word learners are faced with the task of pulling together their knowledge with the linguistic and conceptual domains, our goal in this chapter is to bring together two distinct intellectual traditions—generative linguistics and cognitive psychology—within a distinctly developmental framework. In wedding these two disciplines, our primary aim is to highlight synergies between them and to forge a path for new investigations that take advantage of the contributions of each. We therefore focus on those facets of word learning where the two intellectual traditions come together most richly, which leads us to focus primarily on how the links between the conceptual and linguistic systems evolve. More specifically, we consider the developmental trajectory of several kinds of words (e.g., nouns, adjectives, verbs) and how they become linked to meaning. We acknowledge that one grammatical form—*noun*—has held a privileged position, dominating both the infants' early lexicon and the developmental research agenda. But we also point out that nouns are not, in fact, the paradigm case for word learning. After underscoring the central role played by nouns in acquisition, we move on to highlight the very different conceptual entailments and linguistic requirements underlying the acquisition of other grammatical forms, including adjectives and verbs.

**The Puzzle of Word Learning**

In the course of their daily lives, human infants naturally find themselves in situations in which an individual (perhaps a parent or an older sibling) gazes at an ongoing stream of activity (perhaps a puppy playing in a park) and utters a string of words (perhaps "Look at that adorable puppy! He's running away! Let's go find its mommy"). To successfully learn a word (e.g., *puppy*) from this (indeed from any) context, infants must (a) identify the relevant entity from the ongoing stream of activity (focusing in this case on the puppy and not the act of running, etc.), (b) parse the relevant piece of sound (pup´ē) from the ongoing stream of continuous speech, and (c) establish a mapping between that entity and that sound.

At first glance, this appears to be straightforward. After all, don't we essentially solve the puzzle for infants when we focus their attention on the object of interest while introducing its name? Certainly, adults may strive to teach words in this way, and they apparently do so more in some cultural communities than in others (cf. Hoff, 2002; Ochs & Schieffelin, 1984). However, a closer look reveals that word-learning tutorials like these are the exception instead of the rule. To begin, many words, even in infant-directed speech, do not refer to an object or to anything else that we can point to (e.g., "He's *running* away!" or "*No!*"). And even for words that do refer, the referent is often absent at the time of the naming episode (e.g., "Time to go get your *sister,*" "Where'd your *mom* put your *shoes*?" or "You really need a *nap*").

Even in the most straightforward tutorials, when the word has a referent and the referent is present throughout the naming episode, matters are not so simple. Successful word learning requires that the learner map a word (e.g., *puppy*) to a concept (PUPPY),[2] and this means extending that word systematically beyond the individual(s) with which the word was initially introduced.[3] In our example, this means extending the word *puppy* to certain other objects (other puppies), but excluding all the rest (kitties, adult dogs, bunnies, and televisions).

---

[2] Throughout this chapter, we use the following typographical conventions: italics = refer to a word, small capitals = refer to a concept.

[3] There is one special class of word—the proper noun (e.g., *Lassie*)—whose function is to pick out a distinct individual (e.g., the dog Lassie). However, two points bear mentioning. First, these words do refer to concepts (that happen to include only one unique member; see Hall, 1999; Hall & Lavin, 2004; Macnamara, 1994; Markman & Jaswal, 2004; Xu, Carey, & Welch, 1999). Second, the vast majority of words, and indeed most of the words first acquired by infants, do not refer to a distinct individual but to a range of individuals.

Notice, then, that the names for concrete objects depend on a pairing between a word and an abstract concept. To establish such mappings, infants must hold some principled expectations about the range of possible extensions for a given word, and these may come from the conceptual, perceptual, or linguistic system (Bates & Goodman, 1997; Chomsky, 1975; Murphy, 2002; Quine, 1960; Quinn & Eimas, 2000).

Finding the linguistic units also requires the learner to engage in a certain degree of abstraction. Just as knowledge of a concept like PUPPY requires that one be able to inspect anything in the world and decide whether it is a puppy (whether it is in the extension of the concept), knowledge of the phonological form of a word requires that one be able to pull out varying instances of that word in the flow of the speech stream. Just as the concept PUPPY requires us to abstract over instances of short puppies, black puppies, and furry puppies, knowledge of the phonological word / pup´ē/ requires us to abstract over different utterances of the word that show wide variation in acoustic features due either to differences between speakers, to effects of coarticulation with surrounding words, or to phonological rules that alter the form of the word (e.g., *electric/electricity;* see Saffran, Werker, & Werner, Chapter 2, this *Handbook,* this volume for an excellent review; also Aslin, Saffran, & Newport, 1998; Fisher, Church, & Chambers, 2004; Fisher & Tokura, 1996; Jusczyk, 1997; Mehler et al., 1988; Morgan & Demuth, 1996).

The third piece of the word-learning puzzle—establishing a mapping between the conceptual and linguistic units—is also much richer than it appears at first glance. It is a universal feature of human language that many kinds of words (e.g., nouns, adjectives, verbs) can be applied correctly in the very same naming episode, and that each kind of word highlights a unique aspect of that episode and supports a unique pattern of extension. Consider again the vision of puppies playing in the park. Count nouns (e.g., "Look, it's a *puppy*") not only refer to an individual puppy, but extend broadly to other members of the same object category (to other puppies, but not to bunnies). In contrast, proper nouns (e.g., "Look, it's *Lassie*"), which refer specifically to the named individual, cannot be extended further. And if we provide an adjective ("Look, it's *fluffy*"), the meaning is again quite different. Here, we refer to a property of the named individual, but not the individual itself, and we can extend that word to other instances of that property, independent of the particular entity embodying it (e.g., to any other fluffy thing, including [some, but not all] puppies,

bunnies, and bedroom slippers). Finally, verbs ("Look, it's *running*") refer to a relation or an activity involving that individual at that moment in time, and are extended to similar activities, involving very different actors (e.g., horses, children) at different times and places.[4]

To summarize, to be successful word learners, infants must (a) identify the relevant conceptual units (e.g., an individual, a category of individuals, an event), (b) identify the relevant linguistic units (e.g., words), and (c) establish a mapping between them. We have argued that at its core, word learning requires a certain degree of abstraction in each of these domains. Any given utterance of a word must be related to an abstract phonological representation, and any given individual must be related to an abstract concept.

## Early Solutions to the Puzzle of Word Learning

Despite these apparent logical difficulties, infants learn words with impressive ease and alacrity. By roughly 12 months, infants reliably recognize words in fluent speech and are beginning to produce words on their own; by roughly 24 months, they produce hundreds of words and begin to combine them systematically to form phrases. Perhaps more remarkable still is the fact that by 2 to 3 years of age, they discover that there are distinct kinds of words (distinct grammatical forms) and that these are linked to distinct kinds of meaning (Brown, 1957, 1958; Gentner, 1982; Macnamara, 1979; Waxman, 1990; Waxman & Gelman, 1986). In fact, the evidence reveals that they mine these links, taking the grammatical form of a novel word as a cue to establishing its meaning (for thorough reviews of recent literature, see Hall & Lavin, 2004; Markman & Jaswal, 2004; Woodward & Markman, 1998).

Toddlers acquiring English systematically restrict the extension of a proper noun to the named individual (Hall, 1991, 1999; Hall & Lavin, 2004; Jaswal & Markman, 2001), but extend count nouns more broadly, to the named individual and to other members of the same object category (Waxman, 1999; Waxman & Markow, 1995). They systematically extend adjectives to properties of objects (Klibanoff & Waxman, 2000; Mintz & Gleitman, 2002; Prasada, 1997; Waxman & Klibanoff, 2000; Waxman &

---

[4] And, don't forget that the speaker is under no obligation to talk about what is happening in the world at that moment. A speaker is about as likely to say, "remember our camping trip last summer" as "what a cute puppy" in the context of a puppy (Chomsky, 1959).

Markow, 1998) and verbs to categories of events (Fisher & Tokura, 1996; Hollich, Hirsh-Pasek, et al., 2000; Naigles, 1990; Tomasello, 2003; Tomasello & Merriman, 1995).

But how do infants discover the mappings between grammatical form and meaning? The full repertoire of such mappings cannot be innately specified because languages differ in the grammatical forms that they represent, in the way they mark these grammatical forms on the surface, and in the ways they recruit these forms to convey fundamental bits of meaning (Baker, 2001; Croft, 1991; Frawley, 1992; Hopper & Thompson, 1980). In the face of these differences, there appear to be some universals. In particular, in all human languages, object concepts are lexicalized as nouns and event concepts as verbs (Brown, 1957, 1958; Dixon, 1982). But at the same time, there is considerable cross-linguistic variation. Within the class of nouns, some languages (like English) make a grammatical distinction between mass and count nouns, whereas others (like Japanese) may not (Imai & Haryu, 2004). Even more dramatic evidence for this kind of flexibility comes from cross-linguistic comparisons of the grammatical form *adjective*. Some languages (including English, Spanish, and the African language Dyirbal) have richly developed, open-class systems of adjectives, but others (e.g., the Bantu languages) have sparse adjective systems, including as few as 10 terms (Dixon, 1982; Lakoff, 1987). Moreover, in many languages (e.g., Mohawk, Mandarin) it is extremely difficult to determine whether there is a grammatical category *adjective* that is distinct from the category *verb*. In Mohawk, for example, most morphological and syntactic tests put the class of concepts that are labeled by adjectives in English into the class of verbs (Baker, 2001).[5]

---

[5] In some languages, it is even difficult to determine whether any words can be assigned to specific grammatical categories at all, leading some to argue that in these languages, the grammatical categories are perhaps better characterized as phrase-size units rather than as words (Davis & Matthewson, 1999; Demirdache & Matthewson, 1996; Wojdak, 2001). The putative category-neutrality in these languages makes it clear that we should separate the lexical category of a word from its syntactic usage. That is, a word may be lexically specified as, say, being a noun, but in certain uses, it will be performing the function of a verb (or vice versa). This point can be seen clearly even in English when we examine gerunds (e.g., The *sinking* of the boat was ordered by the admiral), where a verbal concept (SINK) is used as the head of a noun phrase. In cases like this, a word that is lexically a verb behaves syntactically like a noun. (see Abney, 1987; Frank & Kroch, 1995; Harley & Noyer, 1998 for discussion and analysis).

Even within a given language, the boundaries around the grammatical forms are permeable. Although a core semantic function of nouns is to refer to object concepts (e.g., PUPPY, TABLE), nouns can also be used to refer to properties (e.g., HEIGHT, BELIEF), events (e.g., EARTHQUAKE, DESTRUCTION), and abstract notions (e.g., FREEDOM, IDEA). And although a core semantic function of verbs is to refer to events (DECIDE, JUMP), verbs can also refer to properties (APPEAR, KNOW) or states (LIKE, STAND). Indeed, the very same underlying concept can sometimes be expressed by both a noun and a verb:

(1)  The results of the election were a *surprise* to me (N).

The results of the election *surprised* me (V).

It therefore follows that the links between grammatical categories (noun, verb) and semantic categories (thing, event) are not rigidly fixed, even within a given language, but are correlational (P. Bloom, 1994; Macnamara, 1986; Pinker, 1989).

How do infants discover these links? It would be unreasonable to assume that from the start, infants' expectations mirror those of the mature speakers of their language, because as we have seen, infants must discover which grammatical forms are represented in their language and how they are recruited to convey meaning. It is reasonable, however, to ask whether infants might approach the task of acquisition with some language-general expectations in place to guide acquisition from the start and which could then be fine-tuned as the infant gained experience with the details of their native language (see Saffran et al., Chapter 2, this *Handbook*, this volume, for a similar developmental view).

## PLAN OF THE CHAPTER

To address these issues, we open with a section on initial acquisitions, focusing briefly on the linguistic, conceptual, and social underpinnings that precede the advent of infants' first words. We then consider infants' initial forays into mapping their first words to meaning. To foreshadow, recent evidence reveals that infants cross the threshold into word learning equipped with a powerful and initially general expectation linking the linguistic and conceptual units. This general initial link gets bona fide word learning off the ground and sets the stage for subsequent lexical, grammatical, and conceptual developments. In the next section, we ask how young word learners move beyond this initially broad link. The evidence suggests that infants first tease out the grammatical category *noun* from among the other grammatical forms, and map them specifically to individual objects and categories of objects. This early establishment of a noun-to-category link serves as the foundation that enables infants to discover the other essential grammatical forms (e.g., adjectives, verbs) and map them to their respective meanings. After considering several consequences of the early acquisition of nouns, we focus on the acquisition of adjectives and verbs. In both cases, the patterns of acquisition differ importantly from the acquisition of nouns, and appear to depend on the prior acquisition of (at least some) nouns. We suggest that this follows directly from the distinct informational requirements and conceptual entailments of each of these distinct predicate forms.

Several overarching themes appear throughout the chapter. Each has figured largely in the history of research on word learning and each continues to exert considerable force in contemporary theoretical and empirical work.

### Cross-Linguistic Evidence

One theme is related to the place of cross-linguistic evidence in theories of acquisition. As noted, the mappings between grammatical and conceptual categories vary across languages. This variability illustrates two related points. First, the precise mappings between particular grammatical and conceptual categories must involve learning. Second, cross-linguistic comparisons can be a powerful tool for discovering which aspects of word learning (if any) might derive from principles of grammatical architecture and which might be more malleable across development and across languages (Bornstein et al., 2004; Bowerman & Levinson, 2001; Gentner, 1982; Imai & Gentner, 1997; Maratsos, 1998; Sera, Bales, & del Castillo Pintado, 1997; Sera et al., 2002; Snyder, Senghas, & Inman, 2001; Uchida & Imai, 1999).

### The Privileged Position of Nouns

This chapter also calls attention to the developmental priority of one grammatical form—*noun*—in early acquisition. We consider the evidence for and the sources underlying the dominance of nouns over other grammatical forms in the early lexicon. But we also point out that the very fact that nouns are acquired so early serves as a strong signal that this grammatical category may differ importantly from the others. From this observation, it

follows that noun learning may not be the paradigmatic case for word learning more generally. As a result, the vast majority of research and theory on word learning, which has focused predominantly on the acquisition of nouns (primarily those nouns referring to individual objects and categories of objects), can only take us so far. Language is filled with words referring to properties (*blue*), events (*jump*), and relations (*meet*) and with words that quantify over objects (*the, every, some*) and events (*always, never, sometimes*). The language learner must ultimately come to understand the mapping between a wide range of linguistic devices and the meanings they convey. A fully representative theory of word learning requires that we adopt a broad perspective, encompassing the acquisition of the full range of word-types learned by children. In essence, then, we are suggesting that the very real developmental priority for nouns in early acquisition should not be equated with a research priority to focus on nouns to the exclusion of other kinds of words.

### Structure: In the Input or in the Mind

The cognitive sciences have been shaped by the fundamental tension between nature and nurture, and the field of word learning is no exception. Although this tension has traditionally been viewed as oppositional, it is now clear that these are best seen as complementary, working hand-in-glove to support acquisition. Researchers must study the input to detect what structure, if any, is available to help infants discover words and assign them to meanings (L. Bloom, 2000; Bornstein et al., 2004; Hoff, 2002; Hoff & Naigles, 2002; Huttenlocher, Haight, Bryk, Seltzer, & Lyons, 1991; Huttenlocher & Smiley, 1987; Huttenlocher, Vasilyeva, Cymerman, & Levine, 2002; MacWhinney, 2002; Naigles & Hoff-Ginsberg, 1995, 1998; Samuelson, 2002; Tomasello, 2003). It is also important to bear in mind that what *counts* as the input may be a function of development. At different developmental points, the learner may be able to apprehend different aspects of the very same piece of input, due either to maturation of their perceptual and conceptual systems or to their knowledge about the particular language they are learning.

In addition to examining the input, researchers must examine the representational capacities of the learner to detect what structure, if any, is inherent in the mind to make acquisition possible (R. Gelman & Williams, 1998). In these ventures, one must be mindful that structure may derive from the perceptual system (Jusczyk, 1997; Quinn & Eimas, 2000; Smith, 1999), the conceptual system (Baillargeon, 2000; Spelke, 2003), the linguistic system (Crain, 1991; Lidz, Waxman, & Freedman, 2003), or might be the product of interactions among these systems (Hirsh-Pasek, Golinkoff, Hennon, & Maguire, 2004). Moreover, because word learning is a cascading developmental phenomenon, different representational structures or constraints on acquisition may become available at different points in development.

Recent research has made great strides in integrating these formerly oppositional sources of acquisition, documenting that learners are exquisitely sensitive to the input and at the same time, that there is structure within the learner that guides acquisition. The current mandate is to be as precise as possible about the balance between these sources and the interplay between them as development unfolds.

In word learning, this interplay between expectations inherent in the learner and the shaping role of the environment is essential (P. Bloom, 2000; Chomsky, 1980; Gleitman, 1990; Gleitman, Cassidy, Nappa, Papafragou, & Trueswell, in press; N. Goodman, 1955; Jusczyk, 1997; Quine, 1960). Certainly, infants cull information from the environment, for they learn precisely the words and the grammatical forms of the language that surrounds them, and precisely the concepts to which they are exposed (e.g., CD PLAYERS and SQUIRRELS in the United States; SCYTHES and PECCARIES in rural Mexico). But just as certainly, infants are guided by powerful internal expectations that guide the process and are themselves shaped in the course of acquisition.

This observation is especially important because, as pointed out, human languages differ not only in their cadences and their individual words, but also in the ways in which kinds of words (e.g., nouns, adjectives, verbs) are recruited to express fundamental aspects of meaning. Any theory of word learning must be sufficiently constrained to account for what appear to be universal patterns of acquisition in the face of this cross-linguistic variation. At the same time, it must be sufficiently flexible to accommodate the systematic variations that occur across languages and across developmental time.

In view of these overarching themes, our goal is to consider word learning from an integrative, dynamic, and distinctly developmental perspective, treating seriously the relative contributions of expectations held by the learner and the shaping role of the environment, as they unfold over time. In our view, infants' initial expectations, and their initial perceptual, conceptual, social, and linguistic sensitivities are not rigidly fixed. At each

step along the way, their abilities and sensitivities unfold, calibrated on the basis of the knowledge and structure that they have culled from the ambient language. Word learning, then, is a cascading process, in which information becomes available incrementally, as learners work their way toward solving pieces of the acquisition puzzle. Each accomplishment makes apparent a new problem and a new set of potential solutions.

## SETTING THE STAGE FOR WORD LEARNING: FOUNDATIONAL CAPACITIES

In this section, we consider the linguistic, conceptual, and social underpinnings to word learning and their evolution over the 1st year of life.

### Identifying the Words

Before word-learning can begin in earnest, infants must be able to parse a word from the continuous speech stream, and recognize that word across a range of utterances and from a range of different speakers. This task is difficult because there are few overt breaks in the speech stream and because the acoustic signature of a word varies dramatically as a function of the surrounding words and the speaker. Infants' solution to this piece of the word-learning puzzle emerges gradually over the 1st year of life. During this very active period, their sensitivities become increasingly tailored by the structural features of the native language in which they are immersed. Because this very active area of research is covered ably and in elegant detail in Saffran et al. (Chapter 2, this *Handbook,* this volume), we touch only briefly on two issues that are intimately tied to word learning (for other excellent reviews, see Aslin et al., 1998; Echols & Marti, 2004; Fisher et al., 2004; Guasti, 2002; Jusczyk, 1997; Werker & Fennell, 2004).

### *Discovering the Words and Word-Sized Units*

Decades of research have revealed that there is considerable structure in the linguistic input, to which infants gradually and systematically become sensitive. But it is also clear that infants approach the task equipped with some perceptual preferences or biases that enable them to take advantage of the structure in the input and, in this way, to discover the potential words of their language (Christophe, Mehler, & Sebastián-Gallés, 2001;

Fernald & McRoberts, 1996; Johnson, Jusczyk, Cutler, & Norris, 2003; Jusczyk, 1997; Liu, Kuhl, & Tsao, 2003; Morgan & Demuth, 1996).

Even at birth, infants prefer human speech (and particularly infant-directed speech, with its exaggerated rhythmic and pitch contours) over other sources of auditory stimulation (Jusczyk & Luce, 2002; Mehler et al., 1988; Singh, Morgan, & White, 2004; Vouloumanos & Werker, 2004). However, infants' attentional preferences for particular features undergo dramatic developmental change. During roughly the first 5 to 6 months, the melodies of infant-directed speech serve a primarily affective and attentional function, engaging and modulating infants' attention. By approximately 6 months of age, "words begin to emerge from the melody" (Fernald, 1992, p. 403) as infants become increasingly sensitive to cues in the speech stream that permit them to segment the continuous speech signal into word-sized units (Echols & Marti, 2004; Guasti, 2002; Jusczyk & Aslin, 1995; Saffran, Aslin, & Newport, 1996). Some cues (e.g., distributional, prosodic, and coarticulatory cues) appear to be universal and to be available early enough to get the process of word segmentation and identification off the ground. Other cues (e.g., phonetic, phonotactic, and morphologic cues) appear to be language-specific and to become available later, as infants discover which features carry the most weight in the language they are acquiring (Bosch & Sebastián-Gallés, 1997; Friederici & Wessels, 1993; Kuhl, Williams, Lacerda, Stevens, & Lindblom, 1992; Nazzi, Jusczyk, & Johnson, 2000; Werker & Tees, 1984).

But whatever their origin, infants' evolving attention to these cues supports their discovery of the word and phrase boundaries of their native language. By 5 to 6 months of age, infants recognize their own names (Mandel, Jusczyk, & Pisoni, 1995), and by 6 to 7 months, they have begun to establish the meaning of other highly salient words (Tincoff & Jusczyk, 1999). These segmentation skills, in turn, make it possible for infants to track the relations (statistical and algebraic) among linguistically relevant units (Brent & Cartwright, 1996; Chambers, Onishi, & Fisher, 2003; Gomez & Gerken, 1999; Marcus, Vijayan, Rao, & Vishton, 1999; Mintz & Gleitman, 2002; Pena et al., 2003; Saffran et al., 1996; Shi & Werker, 2001; Shi, Werker, & Morgan, 1999). This is key, because successful word learning depends not only on the individual elements (sounds, syllables, words) but also on the relations among them.

### Discovering the Distinction between Open- and Closed-Class Words

Infants' sensitivity to the relations among words permits them to distinguish between two very broad classes of words: open class (content words, including nouns, adjectives, verbs) and closed class words (function words, including determiners, quantifiers, and prepositions; Gómez, 2002; Morgan, Shi, & Allopenna, 1996; Shady, 1996; Shady & Gerken, 1999; Shi et al., 1999; Shi & Werker, 2003). By 9 to 10 months of age, infants prefer to listen to open class words, possibly because they receive greater stress and enjoy more interesting melodic contours than do closed class words.

This preference for open class words represents an important step on the way to word learning, for it ensures that by the close of their 1st year, infants not only parse words successfully, but also devote special attention to just those words (the open class, content words) that have rich conceptual content and that will appear first in their productive lexicon. Moreover, infants' rather exquisite sensitivity to the relative position of open and closed class words provides an entry point into the discovery of other distinct grammatical form categories (Brent & Cartwright, 1996; Gómez, 2002; Redington, Chater, & Finch, 1998; Shi & Werker, 2003).

### Identifying the Relevant Concepts

The solution to this second piece of the puzzle rests on the infants' ability to identify objects and events in the environment, and to notice relations among them. Once again, the evidence suggests that this ability is supported both by structure that is available in the input (perceptual similarities among members of a given concept) and structure in the infant. In particular, there is evidence that even before they begin to learn words, infants have an impressive repertoire of core concepts involving objects, events, and relations (Baillargeon, 2000; Spelke, 2003). Some of their prelinguistic concepts are focused primarily on perceptual or sensory properties (e.g., RED, FAST, HAS EYES; see Quinn & Eimas, 2000); other prelinguistic concepts are more conceptual in nature. By 6 or 7 months, infants can identify distinct objects (e.g., a particular puppy) and can also categorize individuals into several different richly structured object categories at various levels of abstraction (e.g., basic-level categories like *dog,* and more abstract domain-level categories, like *animate*; Behl-Chadha, 1995; Mandler & McDonough,

1998; Quinn & Johnson, 2000; see S. A. Gelman & Kalish, Chapter 16, this *Handbook,* this volume, for a discussion of animacy; and Booth & Waxman, 2002b; Keil, 1994; Prasada, 2003; Spelke & Newport, 1998, for evidence pertaining to the early emergence of the concept ANIMATE). Infants also appear to represent individual actions within a host of richly structured event-based relations, including CAUSE, CONTAINMENT, and SUPPORT (Baillargeon, 2000; Leslie & Keeble, 1987; Michotte, Thines, & Crabbe, 1991; Oakes & Cohen, 1994; Wagner & Carey, 2003).

The richness and depth of the infants' early conceptual repertoire is impressive in and of itself. But it also raises a thorny problem for the infant as she breaks into a system of word learning: For if infants appreciate such a rich range of concepts and relations, and if each is a viable candidate for a word's meaning, then how do infants discover which of these candidates is to be mapped to the word that they have parsed (Quine, 1960)? In the next section, we consider the ways in which infants' sensitivity to the intentions of others helps them to solve this piece of the learning puzzle.

## Interpreting the Intentions of Others

Neither the ability to identify a novel word nor the ability to represent individuals or concepts guarantees that the infant will successfully weave these linguistic and conceptual units together. To successfully map words onto their intended referents, the infant must also be able to infer something about the goals and intentions of the speakers around them. Research into this issue has flourished in the past decade, fueled in large part by an ingenious program of research aimed at uncovering what infants understand about the intentions of others and how they recruit their emerging social and pragmatic acumen to infer the intention of speakers in the task of word learning (see Woodward & Markman, 1998, for an excellent overview; also Baldwin & Moses, 2001; L. Bloom & Tinker, 2001; Jaswal & Markman, 2003; Meltzoff, 2002; Tomasello & Olguin, 1993; Woodward, 2004; Woodward & Guajardo, 2002). By 9 to 10 months of age, infants successfully and spontaneously follow speakers' eye-gaze and gestures (especially pointing), and they use these to home in on the intended focus in a naming episode: Infants are more likely to map a novel word to an object if the speaker is attending to that object than if her attention is directed elsewhere (Brooks & Meltzoff, 2002; Carpenter, Akhtar, & Tomasello, 1998; Hollich, Hirsh-Pasek, et al., 2000;

Meltzoff, Gopnik, & Repacholi, 1999; Moore, Angelopoulos, & Bennett, 1999; Woodward, 2003).

## Conclusions about Initial Acquisitions

By the close of their 1st year, the foundations for word learning are in place. Infants have made significant headway in identifying the phonological units that will become their first words and in representing the conceptual units that will underlie their first meanings; and they are sensitive to the social and pragmatic cues that help them to weave these linguistic and conceptual units together (Baldwin & Baird, 1999; Baldwin & Markman, 1989; L. Bloom, 1998, 2000; Diesendruck, Markson, Akhtar, & Reudor, 2004; Echols & Marti, 2004; Fulkerson & Haaf, 2003; Gogate, Walker-Andrews, & Bahrick, 2001; Guajardo & Woodward, 2000; Tomasello & Olguin, 1993). In the next section, we consider how infants, armed with these foundational capacities, make their first forays into word learning.

## FIRST STEPS INTO WORD LEARNING: A BROAD INITIAL LINK BETWEEN WORDS AND CONCEPTS

How can we best characterize infants' initial steps over the threshold into word learning? This issue has been a virtual magnet for attention on both the theoretical and empirical fronts. Some have argued forcefully that infants cross this threshold as *tabulae rasae,* with no links between their linguistic and conceptual units to serve as guides. In one especially influential version of this argument, Smith and her colleagues have claimed that early word learning is no different from any other kind of learning (Smith, 1999; Smith, Colunga, & Yoshida, in press). In this view, infants' first words are acquired in the absence of any guiding expectations, and it is only after infants have acquired a sizable productive lexicon that they begin to detect any links between linguistic and conceptual units (Smith, 1999). Moreover, in this view, words are tied tightly to perceptual experience, with little or no influence of conceptual relations. Others have argued with equal force for a very different view, asserting that infants harbor powerful, albeit general, expectations linking linguistic, perceptual, and conceptual units from the start (Balaban & Waxman, 1997; Booth & Waxman, 2003; Gopnik & Nazzi, 2003; Graham, Baker, & Poulin-Dubois, 1998; Poulin-Dubois,

Graham, & Sippola, 1995; Waxman & Booth, 2003; Waxman & Markow, 1995; Xu, 2002).

To adjudicate between these positions, we must start at the beginning, asking whether we can discern any links, however rudimentary, between the linguistic and conceptual systems of infants at the very onset of word learning. As noted, if such links exist, they will likely be less precise than those of mature speakers, because languages vary in the grammatical forms they represent and the way they recruit these forms to convey meaning. But it is certainly possible that infants begin with a broad language-general link that supports infants' first steps in lexical acquisition and that can then be more finely tuned as infants gain experience with the particular language being acquired.

Waxman and Markow (1995) used a novelty-preference design to discover whether infants ranging from 12 to 14 months of age harbor any links between linguistic and conceptual organization. During a *familiarization phase,* an experimenter offered the infant four different toys from a given object category (e.g., four animals), one at a time, in random order. This phase was immediately followed by a *test phase,* in which the experimenter simultaneously presented both (a) a new member of the now-familiar category (e.g., another animal) and (b) an object from a novel category (e.g., a fruit). Infants manipulated the toys freely throughout the task. Their total accumulated manipulation time served as the dependent measure. Each infant completed this task with four different sets of objects, two involving basic level categories (e.g., horses versus cats) and two involving superordinate level categories (e.g., animals versus fruit).

To identify any influence of novel words, infants were randomly assigned to one of three conditions that differed only during the familiarization phase of the experiment. Infants in the noun condition heard, for example, "See the *fauna?*" Those in the adjective condition heard "See the *faun-ish* one?" Those in a no-word control condition heard "See here?" At test, infants in all conditions heard precisely the same phrase ("See what I have?"). The experimenters presented novel words, rather than familiar ones, because their goal was to discover what links, if any, infants hold when it comes to mapping a new word to its meaning. If they had used familiar words (e.g., *dog*), performance could have been influenced by their understanding of those particular words, and could not speak to the more fundamental issue of the links between words and meaning.

The predictions were as follows: If infants noticed the category-based commonality among the four familiar-ization objects, then they should reveal a preference for the novel object at test. If infants detected the presence of the novel words, and if these words directed their attention toward the commonalities among the objects presented during familiarization, then infants hearing novel words should be more likely than those in the no word control condition to reveal a novelty preference. Finally, if the initial link between words and concepts is general at the start, then infants in both the noun and adjective conditions should be more likely than those in the no word condition to form categories.

These predictions were borne out. Infants in the no-word control condition revealed no novelty preference, suggesting that they had not detected the category-based commonalities among the familiarization objects. In contrast, infants in both the noun and adjective conditions revealed reliable novelty preferences, indicating that they had successfully formed object categories.

This result provides clear evidence for an early, foundational link between word learning and conceptual organization. Infants in these experiments reliably detected the novel words, and these words held consequences for their conceptual organization. In essence, the words served as *invitations* to form categories (Brown, 1958). Providing infants with a common name (at this developmental point, either a noun or an adjective) for a set of distinct objects highlighted the commonalities among them and promoted the formation of object categories. More recent work has revealed that this invitation does more than simply highlight concepts that infants may already represent; it also supports the discovery of entirely novel concepts, comprised of entirely novel objects (P. Bloom, 2001; Booth & Waxman, 2002a; Fulkerson & Haaf, 2003; Gopnik, Sobel, Schulz, & Glymour, 2001; Maratsos, 2001; Nazzi & Gopnik, 2001). Moreover, this invitation has considerable conceptual force: Although novel words were presented only during the familiarization phase, their influence extended beyond the named objects, directing infants' attention to the new—and unnamed—objects present at test.

## Specificity of the Initial Link

This demonstration of a broad initial link between words and concepts attracted considerable attention and raised several further questions, especially concerning the specificity of this phenomenon. On the linguistic side, researchers have asked whether infants' early expectation is specific to words, or whether it is apparent with sounds more generally. This question bears on issues of domain specificity. On the conceptual side, researchers have explored whether the invitation is specific to the kinds of commonalities that underlie object categories or whether it also applies to a broader range of candidate meanings (e.g., property-based, event-related commonalities).

### Words or Sounds?

A key question is whether the facilitative effect of novel words on infants' categorization stems specifically from the presentation of novel words or whether this might be the consequence of a more general, attention-engaging function associated with any auditory stimuli. To address this issue, several research programs have compared the effects of novel words to the effects of nonlinguistic stimuli (e.g., tones, melodies, mechanical noises produced by simple toys). The results are somewhat mixed. On the one hand, at 9 to 12 months of age, when infants have just begun to reliably parse words from the speech stream, novel words promote categorization, but novel tones (matched precisely to the naming phrase in amplitude, duration, and pause length) and other, more complex nonlinguistic stimuli (e.g., repetitive, nonlinguistic mouth sounds; a brief melodic phrase) fail to do so (Balaban & Waxman, 1997). This suggests that there is indeed something special about words at this early developmental moment (but see Gogate et al., 2001; Sloutsky & Lo, 1999).

This is not to say that nonlinguistic stimuli have no effect on object categorization. Under certain circumstances, nonlinguistic sounds (e.g., whistles, melodic phrases), gestures, and even pictograms appear to promote object categorization in infants and toddlers. But the key finding is that they do so only in certain restricted experimental contexts, and in particular when an experimenter makes it clear that her intention is to treat these nonlinguistic stimuli as object names. For example, if nonlinguistic stimuli are presented within familiar naming routines or if they are produced intentionally by an experimenter who is interacting directly with the infant and a salient object, then these nonlinguistic stimuli can promote object categorization (Fulkerson, 1997; Fulkerson & Haaf, 2003; Namy & Waxman, 1998, 2000, 2002; Woodward & Hoyne, 1999). In contrast, when these social and pragmatic cues are stripped away, nonlinguistic elements fail to support object categorization (Balaban & Waxman, 1997; Campbell & Namy, 2003; Fulkerson & Haaf, 2003).

This pattern of results is consistent with the position that infants take advantage of several kinds of cues to dis-

cover word meaning (Hall & Waxman, 2004; Hollich, Hirsh-Pasek, et al., 2000). When the cues converge with sufficient strength, nonlinguistic elements can be interpreted as "names for things." Absent these cues, nonlinguistic elements fail in this regard. Moreover, infants' willingness to accept nonlinguistic elements as names decreases over the course of the 2nd year of life, as they become aware that although nonlinguistic stimuli (including gestures) certainly augment spoken language, they do not typically function as category names (for a review of gesture, see Goldin-Meadow, Chapter 8, this *Handbook*, this volume; Namy, Campbell, & Tomasello, 2004). Thus, from the earliest stages of word learning, there appears to be something special about words. Infants interpret words, but not other sounds or gestures, as inherently connected to meaning.

### Object Categories or a Broader Range of Concepts?

In addition to gaining clarity on what counts as a word at this early juncture, researchers have also explored more broadly the evidence on the conceptual side, asking whether infants initially link novel words exclusively to category-based commonalities (e.g., rabbits, animals), or whether this early link might encompass a wider range of commonalities, including property-based commonalities (e.g., color: pink things; texture: soft things) and event-based commonalities (e.g., flying; rolling).

Notice, however, that in all the experiments reviewed thus far, the only candidates for word meaning were individual objects or categories of objects. Yet, object categories represent only a small portion of the concepts that infants entertain and that words can denote. Therefore, to better characterize the scope of infants' initial expectation, it is necessary to examine a broader range of candidate meanings in word-learning experiments. With this goal in mind, Waxman and Booth (2001) went one step further, asking whether novel words highlight property-based commonalities (e.g., color, texture) as well as category-based commonalities among objects. The design of this series of experiments is described fully in the Acquisition of Nouns section later in this chapter. For the moment, we simply highlight one result from that series indicating that infants begin word learning with a broad expectation for candidate meanings. At 11 months of age, novel words (presented as either nouns or adjectives) directed infants' attention broadly to both category- and property-based commonalities.

This is an important finding because, thus far, only a handful of experimental studies have documented successful word learning in infants at this age (Balaban & Waxman, 1997; Fulkerson & Haaf, 2003; Welder & Graham, 2001; Woodward, Markman, & Fitzsimmons, 1994). But even more important, the results revealed that infants begin the task of bona fide word learning equipped with a broad expectation that links content words (including both nouns and adjectives) to a broad range of candidate meanings (allowing for either category- or property-based commonalities).

### Advantages of a Broad Initial Link

From the perspective of the learner, this general expectation offers an important developmental advantage. Because different languages make use of different sets of grammatical categories and because they use these to carve up semantic space in slightly different ways, it is to the learner's advantage to begin with only the most general expectations that highlight a range of commonalities and enable the learner to break into the system of word learning in the first place.

This broad initial link serves (at least) three essential functions. First, because words initially direct attention to a broad range of commonalities, they facilitate the formation of an expanding repertoire of concepts, and help to focus infants' attention on concepts that may otherwise have gone undetected. Second, this broad initial link between words and concepts provides infants with a means to establish a stable rudimentary lexicon. Finally, this initially broad expectation sets the stage for the evolution of the more precise expectations found in their native language.

## LATER STEPS INTO WORD LEARNING: MORE SPECIFIC LINKS BETWEEN KINDS OF WORDS AND KINDS OF CONCEPTS

Our goal in this section is to ask how infants advance beyond an initially general expectation for words, how they establish a more precise set of expectations, and how they tease apart the distinct grammatical forms and discover their links to meaning.

Facing the linguistic domain, the question is when (and under what circumstances) infants begin to distinguish among the major grammatical forms (e.g., noun, adjective, verb) that are represented in their language. Facing the conceptual domain, the question is when they begin to map these grammatical forms to distinct kinds of meaning (e.g., category, property, actions, relations).

### The Acquisition of Nouns

The evidence indicates that infants first tease out the nouns from among the other grammatical forms and map them specifically to category-based commonalities. We consider the conceptual consequences of this noun-to-category link, as well as the linguistic and conceptual forces supporting its emergence.

### The Evolution of a Link between Nouns and Object Categories

The first evidence for the evolution of a more precise link between kinds of words and kinds of meaning comes from infants at roughly 13 to 14 months of age. Retaining the logic of the novelty-preference task described earlier, Waxman and Booth (2001, 2003) shifted the focus to include objects (e.g., purple animals) that shared both category-based commonalities (e.g., animal) and property-based commonalities (e.g., color: purple things). This design feature permitted them to examine infants' conceptual flexibility as well as the influence of novel words on conceptual organization. More specifically, they asked (a) whether infants could construe the very *same* set of objects (e.g., four purple animals) flexibly, either as members of an *object category* (e.g., animals) or as embodying an *object property* (e.g., color: purple), and (b) whether infants' construals were influenced systematically by novel words. For a discussion of the psychological distinction between category- versus property-based commonalities, see Waxman, 1999; Waxman & Booth, 2001; S. A. Gelman & Kalish, Chapter 16, this *Handbook,* this volume.[6]

---

[6] This approach is predicated on the assumption that there is, indeed, a principled psychological distinction between categories versus properties of objects. Most current theorists distinguish object categories (also known as *kinds* or *sortals*) from other types of groupings (e.g., *purple things, things to pull from a burning house*) on at least three (related) grounds: Object categories (1) are richly structured, (2) capture many commonalities, including deep, nonobvious relations among properties (as opposed to isolated properties), and (3) serve as the basis for induction (Barsalou, 1983; Bhatt & Rovee-Collier, 1997; S. A. Gelman & Medin, 1993; Kalish & Gelman, 1992; Macnamara, 1994; Medin & Heit, 1999; Murphy & Medin, 1985; Younger & Cohen, 1986). Although infants and children have less detailed knowledge about many object categories than do adults, they clearly expect named object categories to serve these functions (S. A. Gelman, 1996; Keil, 1994; Waxman, 1999; Welder & Graham, 2001).

This experiment consisted of three phases. Each infant completed the entire procedure four times, using four different sets of objects. In the *familiarization phase,* infants in all conditions viewed four distinct objects (e.g., four different purple animals), all drawn from the *same object category* (e.g., animal) and embodying the *same object property* (e.g., purple). These objects were presented two at a time, and the experimenter's comments when she presented them varied as a function of the infant's condition assignment. In the noun condition, she presented the two objects saying, for example, "These are *blickets.* This one is a *blicket* and this one is a *blicket.*" In the adjective condition, she said, "These are *blickish.* This one is *blickish* and this one is *blickish.*" In the no-word control condition, she said, "Look at these. Look at this one and look at this one."

In the *test phase,* they saw a category match (e.g., a blue horse; same category as familiarization objects, but new property) pitted directly against a property match (e.g., a purple spatula; same property as familiarization objects, but a new category). To assess *novelty-preference,* the experimenter placed the test pair easily within the infant's reach, saying, "Look at these." No labels were provided, and infant's attention to the objects was recorded. Next, to assess *word-extension,* the experimenter presented a target object (one of the original familiarization objects, e.g., a purple elephant), and pointed to it saying, "This one is a *blicket*" (noun condition), "This one is *blickish*" (adjective condition) or "Look at this one" (no-word condition). She then presented the two test objects, placing them easily within the infant's reach, saying, "Can you give me the *blicket?*" (noun condition), "Can you give me the *blickish* one?" (adjective condition) or "Can you give me one?" (no-word condition). By assessing both novelty-preference and word-extension, these researchers were able to ask whether infants' early expectations, previously evident in novelty-preference tasks only, are sufficiently robust to influence performance in the more active word-extension task.

Infants at 11 months revealed evidence for a broad initial expectation: They mapped novel words (either nouns or adjectives) to commonalities among objects (either category- or property-based commonalities; Waxman & Booth, 2003). In contrast, by 14 months, infants distinguished novel nouns from adjectives. They mapped novel nouns specifically to category-based (but not to property-based) commonalities among objects. Yet, at this same developmental moment, their mapping

for novel adjectives remained more general. As was the case at 11 months, 14-month-old infants typically tended to map novel adjectives broadly, either to category- or property-based commonalities. Although in some tasks, infants showed a more advanced pattern, mapping novel adjectives specifically to property-based (and not category-based) commonalities, this was a fragile effect, evident only under certain circumstances (Waxman & Booth, 2001).

In an independent line of research using the preferential-looking procedure, Echols has documented a similar developmental pattern (Echols & Marti, 2004). Focusing on infants' expectations for nouns and verbs, these researchers provide converging evidence that the link between nouns and object categories is first to emerge from a more general expectation. Infants in this task faced two video monitors. In the *familiarization phase,* infants watched as a novel object (e.g., an anteater) produced a novel action (e.g., opening/closing a cup). The infants saw this event first on one screen, then on the other, and then finally on both screens simultaneously. In the *test phase,* the scenes that were depicted changed, with one screen depicting the now-familiar object engaged in a novel action (e.g., the anteater spinning the cup) and the other depicting a novel object engaged in the now-familiar action (e.g., a manatee opening/closing the cup).

To identify whether the grammatical form of the novel word influenced infants' construal of these scenes, infants were randomly assigned to either a novel noun, novel verb, or no-word control condition. In the novel noun condition, infants heard, for example, "That's a *gep;* it's a *gep.*" Those in the novel verb condition heard "It is *gepping;* it *geps.*" At test, infants heard either "Look at the *gep!*" or "Look at it *gepping*" in the novel noun and novel verb conditions, respectively. If infants can distinguish novel nouns from verbs, and if they use grammatical form to infer novel words meanings, then infants hearing nouns should prefer the scene with the familiar object, and those hearing verbs should prefer the scene with the familiar action. And if infants' expectations regarding nouns emerges first, then infants hearing nouns should prefer the scene with the novel action, but infants hearing verbs should show no preference. This result would run parallel to those described earlier for nouns and adjectives (Waxman & Booth, 2001, 2003).

The results were consistent with the hypothesis that the link between nouns and object categories is the first to emerge in acquisition. At 13 months, infants in the novel noun condition revealed a reliable preference for the familiar object, but those in the novel verb condition revealed no preference, looking equally to the two test screens. By 18 months, infants had acquired a more specific expectation for verbs. At this point, they mapped the novel nouns specifically to the familiar objects *and* the novel verbs specifically to the familiar actions (for related evidence, see Casasola & Cohen, 2000; Forbes & Poulin-Dubois, 1997).

Taken together, this research suggests that by 13 to 14 months, infants are sensitive to (at least some of) the relevant cues that distinguish among the grammatical forms, and they recruit these distinctions actively. At this developmental moment, they map nouns rather specifically to object categories, but their expectations for adjectives and verbs remain somewhat broad. Infants' sensitivity to the more specific expectations mapping these latter grammatical forms to their associated range of meanings represents a subsequent developmental achievement.

Summarizing to this point, we have argued that infants' broad initial expectations in word learning serve as a foundation for two discoveries: that there are distinct kinds of words (grammatical categories) in their language, and that there are correlations between these grammatical categories and the types of meaning that they convey. We suspect that these two discoveries go hand-in-hand, each adjusting gradually to the other, in a process akin to Quine's now-classic example of the child scrambling "up an intellectual chimney, supporting himself against each side by pressure against the others." (Quine, 1960, p. 93). We suspect that infants discover that there are distinct grammatical forms when they begin to notice the distinct patterns or grammatical frames in which distinct (kinds of) words occur (e.g., that some tend to be inflected or stressed, that some tend to be preceded consistently by (unstressed) closed class words, that some tend to occupy particular positions within phrases; Brent & Cartwright, 1996; Maratsos, 1998; Mintz, 2003; Mintz, Newport, & Bever, 2002).

Moreover, we have argued that as infants begin to scramble up the chimney of lexical acquisition, they first identify the nouns (from among the other grammatical forms) and map these specifically to object categories (from among the other types of commonalities, including property-based or action-based commonalities). Subsequent links (e.g., those for adjectives and verbs) will build on this fundamental base and will be fine-tuned as a function of experience with the specific correlations

between particular grammatical categories and their associated meanings in the language being acquired.

### *Further Evidence Concerning Nouns*

The evidence for the early emergence of a link between nouns and object categories makes contact with an impressive array of literature focusing on the acquisition of nouns and their relation to object categories (see Woodward & Markman, 1998 for an excellent review; also see P. Bloom, 2000; Golinkoff et al., 2000; Hirsh-Pasek et al., 2004). Decades of devoted research on this topic have led to several important insights. Several research programs have focused on how children map *particular* nouns to their *particular* meaning. In this arena, researchers have discovered in infants and young children a strong tendency to interpret a novel noun (e.g., *dog*), applied to an individual object, as referring to a category of objects at the basic level within a conceptual hierarchy (Hall & Waxman, 1993; Markman & Hutchinson, 1984; Markman & Jaswal, 2004; Mervis, 1987; Rosch, Mervis, Gray, Johnson, & Boyes-Braem, 1976; Schafer & Plunkett, 1998; Waxman, 1990). Only after having established a name for the basic level category do children go on to interpret novel nouns as referring to categories at other hierarchical levels of abstraction (e.g., terrier, mammal, animal), or to individuals (e.g., Rover). This priority for naming objects at the basic level, which appears to be evident broadly across languages and cultures (Berlin, 1992; Berlin, Breedlove, & Raven, 1973), likely facilitates the process of word learning: This conceptual priority to name at the basic level effectively narrows the range of candidate meanings. Having established a basic level name, infants and children then go on to add names for categories at other hierarchical levels and to coordinate those names within semantic space (Diesendruck, Gelman, & Lebowitz, 1998; Diesendruck & Shatz, 2001; Imai & Haryu, 2004; Waxman & Senghas, 1992).

Other research has focused on how children discover the various *types* of nouns that are represented in their language (e.g., count nouns, mass nouns, proper nouns, generic nouns) and how these types map to meaning (Hall & Lavin, 2004; Markman & Jaswal, 2004; Prasada, 2000). Central to this endeavor has been an examination of cross-linguistic evidence, since languages differ in whether and how these distinctions are made within the nominal system (Bowerman & Levinson, 2001; Gathercole & Min, 1997; Gathercole, Thomas, & Evans, 2000; Imai, 1999; Imai & Gentner, 1997; Imai &

Haryu, 2004; Lucy & Gaskins, 2001; Wierzbicka, 1984). Current evidence with English-acquiring infants suggests that these distinctions among types of nouns may emerge toward the end of the 2nd year (Belanger & Hall, in press), at roughly the same time as the expectations for adjectives and verbs (Echols & Marti, 2004; Waxman & Booth, 2003).

Because the very rich research documenting an early talent for mapping nouns to meaning has been reviewed ably and elegantly elsewhere (P. Bloom, 2000; Gentner & Boroditsky, 2001; Golinkoff et al., 2000; Hall & Waxman, 2004; Woodward & Markman, 1998), we leave these issues aside to focus on newer advances.

### The Noun Advantage

The evidence previously reviewed, documenting the early emergence of a link between nouns and categories of objects, resonates with the long-held observation that early word learning is characterized by an abundance of nouns relative to words from other grammatical categories (Caselli et al., 1995; Gentner & Boroditsky, 2001; Huttenlocher, 1974; Woodward & Markman, 1998; and see Bornstein et al., 2004 for an excellent cross-linguistic review). This observation has been the subject of some controversy. A number of researchers have claimed that this noun advantage is not universal, and have focused on the relative frequency of nouns versus verbs in the speech of children learning languages like Korean (Choi, 1998, 2000; Choi & Gopnik, 1995; Gopnik & Choi, 1995; Gopnik, Choi, & Baumberger, 1996) and Mandarin (Tardif, 1996; Tardif, Gelman, & Xu, 1999; Tardif, Shatz, & Naigles, 1997) in which verbs may be more salient in the input (Slobin, 1985; see also Sandhofer, Smith, & Luo, 2000). Others, however, have focused primarily on the relative frequency of nouns and verbs in mothers' reports of their children's speech, and have argued that children acquiring a wide variety of languages, including Dutch, French, Hebrew, Italian, Japanese, Kaluli, Korean, Mandarin, Navajo, Spanish, and Turkish, show an advantage for nouns over verbs, mirroring that reported for English-learning children (Au, Dapretto, & Song, 1994; Bassano, 2000; L. Bloom, Tinker, & Margulis, 1993; Camaioni & Longobardi, 2001; Fernald & Morikawa, 1993; Gentner, 1982; Goldfield, 2000; Kim, McGregor, & Thompson, 2000).

Despite these controversies, one conclusion is clear: Although the strength of the noun advantage may vary across languages and across vocabulary measures, there are no reported cases in which verb learning outstrips

noun learning. This early noun advantage calls for an explanation, and three have been put forth, each of which may account for some portion of the data.

The natural partitions/relational relativity hypothesis (Gentner, 1982; Gentner & Boroditsky, 2001; Gentner & Namy, 2004) argues that the noun advantage is a consequence of a conceptual or perceptual advantage in identifying objects in the world over relations among them. On this view, because objects come in tidy preindividuated packages, they are easy to identify and therefore serve as good candidates for word meaning. Because relational concepts (even for concrete, observable actions) are more nebulous, they are harder to identify. As a consequence, terms that refer to these relational meanings are learned later and are more variable across languages (Papafragou, Massey, & Gleitman, 2002). The natural partitions/relational relativity position, which focuses heavily on the conceptual and perceptual requirements of word learning, has been influential. However, it does not take into account that most nouns, even those concrete nouns that predominate in the early lexicon, do not refer to individual objects, but are instead extended quite spontaneously beyond the individuals on which they were learned. This observation is very important, because it means that infants' early words point to rather abstract concepts and not to tidy preindividuated packages (Waxman & Markow, 1995). This being the case, the question is whether *object concepts* are in some sense simpler than *relational concepts,* an issue that has yet to be resolved (Chierchia & McConnell-Ginet, 2000; Heim & Kratzer, 1998; Moltmann, 1997).

A second explanation for the noun advantage focuses more directly on cultural and linguistic factors. In brief, the claim is that the noun advantage may be related to cultural factors that make objects more salient than relations among them. On this view, cultural factors work in concert with other acoustic, prosodic, or syntactic factors that make nouns more salient than other grammatical forms in speech to children (S. A. Gelman & Tardif, 1998; Lavin, Hall, & Waxman, in press).

A third explanation for the noun advantage, to which we have already alluded, highlights the differences in the linguistic requirements underlying the acquisition of nouns compared with other grammatical categories (Fisher, Hall, Rakowitz, & Gleitman, 1994; Fisher & Tokura, 1996; Gillette, Gleitman, Gleitman, & Lederer, 1999; Gleitman, 1990; Mintz & Gleitman, 2002). Because adjectives and verbs are predicates that require arguments for their meaning, and because it is the nouns that serve as these arguments, the acquisition of these grammatical forms and their links to meaning must be grounded in the prior acquisition of at least some nouns. Because nouns typically have fewer linguistic prerequisites, they can be learned first, and can then be used as a foothold for the subsequent acquisition of words from other grammatical categories.

### More Than "Names for Things": Consequences of Early Noun Learning

In recent years, researchers have begun to explore more broadly the *consequences* of acquiring nouns on infants' conceptual and linguistic representations. A growing body of evidence, based on several experimental paradigms, has converged to suggest that when infants acquire their first words, they acquire more than names for things. Noun learning engages and supports some of the most fundamental logical and conceptual capacities of the human mind, including the processes of object individuation, object categorization, and inductive inference. Infants' efficiency in identifying and processing nouns in the input also increases rapidly in infancy.

**Conceptual Consequences: Individuation** Object individuation, or the ability to track the identity of distinct individuals over time and place (Macnamara, 1982), is a fundamental conceptual and logical capacity. It permits us to know whether, for example, the dog we see now is the same dog we saw previously, or whether these are two different individuals. Under certain circumstances, infants have difficulty tracking the identity of two distinct objects (e.g., a ball and a duck; Van de Walle, Carey, & Prevor, 2000; Wilcox & Baillargeon, 1998; Xu, 1999; Xu & Carey, 1996). This was demonstrated in a series of experiments in which infants, seated before a stage with a small screen, watched as one object (e.g., a ball) emerged from one side of the screen and then returned. Next a different object (e.g., a duck) emerged from the other side of the screen and returned. After several such appearances and disappearances, the screen was lowered to reveal either one or two objects. If infants were able to track the identity of the two distinct objects, they should look longer on test trials revealing one object (the unexpected outcome) than on those revealing two (the expected outcome). Although 12-month-olds succeeded, 10-month-olds had difficulty tracking identity in this complex task (but see Wilcox, 1999; Wilcox & Baillargeon, 1998, for evidence that they succeed in simpler tasks).

However, Xu (1999) went on to examine the effect of naming each object as it appeared, and in so doing, documented a powerful role for naming in object individuation. Ten-month-old infants who were introduced to the same name for the two appearing and disappearing objects (e.g., "It's a toy!") continued to have difficulty in this object individuation task. In contrast, those who heard distinct names for each object (e.g., "It's a ball. . . . It's a duck!") succeeded. Apparently, then, providing distinct names for distinct objects highlights their uniqueness (rather than their commonalities) and supports very young infants' ability to trace their identity over time.

Converging evidence for this view comes from infants' performance in object categorization tasks. When objects (e.g., four different animals) are introduced with *distinct* (rather than common) names, infants fail to form categories (Graham, Kilbreath, & Welder, 2004; Waxman & Braun, 2005). It therefore appears that even for infants as young as 10 to 12 months of age, the conceptual consequences of word learning is nuanced. Providing the same name for a set of distinct individual objects highlights their commonalities and supports the formation of object categories, but does not support individuation. In contrast, providing *distinct* names for each individual highlights distinctions among them and promotes the process of object individuation (Van de Walle et al., 2000; Wilcox, 1999; Wilcox & Baillargeon, 1998; Xu, 1999). Thus, naming not only supports the establishment of a stable repertoire of object categories, but also provides infants with a means of tracing the identity of individuals within these categories.

**Conceptual Consequences: Induction.** One of the reasons that object categories have figured so largely in cognitive psychology, cognitive development, and cognitive science is that they have considerable inductive force. If we discover a property (e.g., bites if you pull its tail) that is true of one individual (e.g., Fido), we can infer that this property is also true of other members of the same object category (e.g., dogs). This is important because it permits us to extend our knowledge powerfully and systematically, taking us beyond our firsthand experience with distinct individuals and supporting category-based inferences. This inductive capacity is especially powerful when it comes to acquiring knowledge about nonobvious properties of objects.

There is now considerable evidence that, for adults and preschool-age children, naming strongly supports category-based induction. Naming permits us to go beyond the perceptible commonalities that we can observe firsthand, and points us toward the deeper, perhaps hidden commonalities that characterize some of our most fundamental concepts (see Diesendruck, 2003; S. A. Gelman & Kalish, Chapter 16, this *Handbook,* this volume). More recent research reveals that naming may also support inductive inference in infants.

In an ingenious line of experimental work, Graham and her colleagues (Graham et al., 2004; Welder & Graham, 2001) have documented the role of naming in infants' inductive inference. In their tasks, an experimenter introduced 13-month-old infants to a target object. For half the infants, the experimenter named the target object with a novel noun; for the remaining infants, no names were provided. All infants then witnessed the experimenter perform an action with the object. Crucially, this action revealed a property of the object that was not available by visual inspection alone (e.g., that it made a particular noise when shaken). Infants were then provided with an opportunity to explore a series of other objects; no names were provided for these objects. The results were striking. In the absence of naming, infants generalized the hidden property narrowly, trying to elicit it only with test objects that strongly resembled the target object. In the novel noun condition, however, infants revealed a very different pattern. They now generalized the "hidden" property of the target object more broadly to other members of the object category, even if they did not bear as strong a perceptual resemblance to the target object (Booth & Waxman, 2002a; Gopnik & Sobel, 2000; Graham et al., 2004; Nazzi & Gopnik, 2001; Welder & Graham, 2001).

Thus, for infants as young as 13 months of age, nouns do more than merely support the establishment of object categories; they also lend inductive force and advance the acquisition of category-based knowledge.

**Processing Consequences.**   In another exciting line of new research, investigators have begun to examine with precision the time-course underlying infants' processing of spoken words in real time. Although infants as young as 9 to 12 months of age can learn the meanings of (some) words, the efficiency with which they are able to process the words that they hear improves dramatically over the 2nd year of life (Fernald, McRoberts, & Swingley, 2001a; Fernald, Pinto, Swingley, Weinberg, & McRoberts, 1998; Swingley & Aslin, 2000; Swingley, Pinto, & Fernald, 1999). Swingley and Fernald (2002)

demonstrated this phenomenon in a series of innovative experiments. Infants in their experimental paradigm are presented with visual images of two familiar objects (e.g., a ball and a shoe). These are presented simultaneously, on two sides of a screen, while an experimenter directs the infant's attention to one of the objects by naming it (e.g., "Where is the ball?"). The likelihood that an infant will happen to be looking at the appropriate object at the moment that the experimenter mentions the noun is 50%. But the focus in this technique is on those infants who happen to be looking at the unnamed object when the naming event occurs (e.g., the shoe, in our example). Swingley and Fernald reasoned that if these infants understand the meaning of the noun, then they should switch their attention from the unnamed to the named object. They further reasoned that the latency of infants' switches could serve as an index of the infants' processing time for these familiar nouns. Analyses of infants' latency to switch revealed that their processing of familiar nouns increased markedly in the 2nd year of life. Moreover, they documented that infants begin to process words even as the words are being uttered. That is, they use partial information (e.g., the first half of a word) to begin to map that word to meaning (Fernald, Swingley, & Pinto, 2001b).

We suggest that infants' rapid gains in processing efficiency for familiar nouns is likely to facilitate several additional aspects of word learning as well. In particular, their increasing facility in recognizing familiar nouns should also help them to detect those circumstances in which a novel word has been uttered. This in turn will permit them to devote their resources (both conceptual and linguistic) toward identifying the meaning of that word. Infants' gains in processing efficiency for familiar nouns should also support their ability to notice the relations among words within an utterance, and to use these relations to establish the meaning of a novel word. In a clever demonstration, Goodman and her colleagues (J. C. Goodman, McDonough, & Brown, 1998) presented infants with sentences that contained a novel noun (e.g., "Mommy feeds the ferret"). Their results revealed that 2-year-olds successfully discovered the meaning of the novel nouns (e.g., ferret) based on their semantic and syntactic relations to the familiar words in the sentence.

Infants' increasing efficiency in processing spoken words may be related to other changes in word learning during the 2nd year of life. Recent evidence reveals that during this period, as infants become more proficient word learners, their patterns of neural activation in response to familiar words shifts from a bilateral to a left-lateralized response (Mills, Coffey-Corina, & Neville, 1997). This suggests that they become more efficient in processing words. This increased efficiency facilitates word learning in general, and may be especially helpful in their efforts to assign distinct meanings to words that are close phonological neighbors (Hollich, Jusczyk, & Luce, 2000; Schafer, Plunkett, & Harris, 1999; Werker, Cohen, Lloyd, Casasola, & Stager, 1998; Werker & Fennell, 2004; Saffran et al., Chapter 2, this *Handbook,* this volume) and to words whose referents are absent.

### Conclusions about Nouns

Infants as young as 13 months of age have already begun to discover some precise links between kinds of words and kinds of meaning. As they move from the broad initial link, they first tease apart the nouns from among the various other grammatical forms (e.g., adjectives, verbs) and map them specifically to objects and object categories (and not to object properties, including color, texture). This conclusion raises two (related) points.

First, the developmental advantage for acquiring nouns converges well with the view that learners must first identify the nouns and map them to entities in the world if they are to discover the other grammatical forms and their links to meaning (Fisher & Gleitman, 2002; Maratsos, 1998; Snedeker & Gleitman, 2004; Talmy, 1985; Wierzbicka, 1984). In addition to the conceptual and processing advantages conferred by the acquisition of nouns, there are important linguistic consequences of noun learning. In particular, the acquisition of nouns provides a gateway into the discovery of other grammatical categories and their mappings to meaning. More specifically, acquiring nouns enables the learner to build a rudimentary syntactic structure that contributes to the identification of other grammatical categories.

Second, it is now apparent that nouns are not the paradigm case for word learning. Their developmental trajectory and informational requirements differ markedly from those of the other major grammatical categories. Therefore, it is important to consider carefully the developmental trajectories of these other grammatical forms. Accordingly, we turn our focus to two such forms: adjectives and verbs.

### The Acquisition of Adjectives

Although theoretical and empirical interest in the acquisition of the grammatical form *adjective* has lagged far behind that of nouns (and even verbs), recent years have witnessed an increase in interest. The evidence thus far makes it clear that at least some of the processes underlying the acquisition of adjectives differ substantially from those underlying the acquisition of nouns. As discussed, substantially more developmental and cross-linguistic variation is associated with adjectives than with nouns (see the first section for cross-linguistic evidence pertaining to adjectives). Adjectives tend to appear later than nouns in the early lexicon, and the specific link between adjectives and properties of objects emerges later than the link between nouns and categories. In essence, then, the link between adjectives and properties of objects is elusive.

This developmental picture is somewhat surprising. After all, adjectives are prevalent in infant-directed speech and even from the first months of life, infants are exquisitely sensitive to the concepts marked by adjectives (e.g., sensory and perceptual properties, including color, size, texture, temperature). This being the case, the mappings from adjectives to properties of objects should be straightforward. This was the conclusion expressed by John Locke, who claimed, "Thus the same colour being observed to-day in chalk or snow, which the mind yesterday received from milk, it considers that appearance alone, makes it a representative of all of that kind; and having given it the name *whiteness,* it by that sound signifies the same quality wheresoever to be imagined or met with." (Locke, 1690/1975, Bk. II, chaps. xi, p. 9).

Yet, Locke's account fails to capture the developmental process. Although infants certainly detect many properties that are named by adjectives, and although they rely on these properties when reasoning about objects and events (Needham & Baillargeon, 1998; Wilcox, 1999), they somehow do not consider such properties to be primary candidates for word meaning. In fact, when presented with a novel adjective (*white*) in the context of a novel object (a white llama), infants and toddlers tend to interpret that adjective as a name for the object category (e.g., llama) rather than to a property (e.g., its color). This robust finding has been documented in children up to 3 years of age (Hall & Lavin, 2004; Markman & Jaswal, 2004). This interpretive error is telling, because children at this age certainly distinguish nouns from adjectives. Moreover, we know that they already have established a link between adjectives and object properties because when they are presented with familiar objects (objects for which they have already acquired noun labels), they readily map novel adjectives to object properties rather than to categories. It is when they are presented with objects for which they have not yet acquired a noun label that they persist in mapping adjectives to categories, instead of to properties. Thus, children's interpretation of a novel adjective varies with the familiarity of the noun that it modifies. Further, their interpretive error (mapping a novel adjective to a category- rather than property-based commonality when the noun label for the category is unknown) suggests that there is a conceptual or linguistic priority for lexicalizing an object's category (and in particular, its basic level category) before any of its properties or parts (Hall & Waxman, 1993; Hall, Waxman, & Hurwitz, 1993; Imai & Haryu, 2004; Markman, 1989; Markman & Hutchinson, 1984).

To complicate developmental matters still further, even when they succeed in mapping an adjective to a property of an object, infants do not follow Locke's optimistic program. Instead of extending novel adjectives freely and liberally (e.g., extending *white* from cats to milk, snow, and mittens), their initial tendency is to extend adjectives very narrowly, only to other members of the same basic level category that share that property (e.g., extending *white* from one cat to another; Klibanoff & Waxman, 2000; Mintz & Gleitman, 2002; Waxman & Markow, 1998).

Why is the mapping from adjectives to object properties so elusive? In the following section, we address this question. We focus primarily on the early acquisition of adjectives referring to color and texture, because most of the recent developmental work has been centered here. However, not all adjectives are created equal. Some adjectives (e.g., *big* versus *small*) refer primarily to the poles of an entire dimension (e.g., size), whereas others pick out a range of values (e.g., *red, orange, yellow*) along the entire dimension (e.g., color; Landau & Gleitman, 1985). Although we will not treat this issue directly here, we point out that factors like these will probably have consequences for patterns of acquisition for most property terms.

### Developmental Work

Several different approaches have been adopted to capture the developmental processes underlying infants' and young children's acquisition of adjectives (Gasser & Smith, 1998; Hall & Belanger, in press; Hall, Quantz, & Persoage, 2000; Mintz & Gleitman, 2002; Prasada, 1997; Waxman & Markow, 1998). These approaches

share some key design elements. To maximize the likelihood that infants will map the novel word to an object property, most experiments (a) introduce objects for which infants have already acquired a basic level noun label, (b) use properties that infants find salient (e.g., color; texture),[7] and (c) present the novel adjectives within short syntactic frames, using the intonational contours of infant-directed speech. Yet despite these design features, infants and toddlers reveal an intriguing difficulty establishing the mappings for adjectives, and when they do succeed, their interpretations appear to depend on the nouns that they modify.

**Linking Adjectives to Object Properties.** Although there are slight hints suggesting that infants as young as 14 months have begun to map adjectives to object properties, the earliest systematic evidence comes from infants at 21 months. This is also the point at which infants begin to produce adjectives on their own (Fenson et al., 1994; Waxman & Markow, 1998). In a forced-choice task, infants were introduced to a single target (e.g., a yellow object) and asked to choose between two test objects. The matching test object shared a property-based commonality with the target (e.g., it was yellow). The contrasting test object embodied a contrasting value along that dimension (e.g., it was red). For half of the infants, the target (e.g., a yellow snake) and test objects (e.g., another yellow snake; a red snake) were members of the same basic level category. For the others, the target (e.g., a yellow dog) and test objects (e.g., a yellow snake, a red snake) were from different basic level categories. If infants map adjectives specifically to object properties, then infants hearing the target labeled with a novel adjective ("This is a(n) *X* one") should reveal a

---

[7] Most investigations include texture (e.g., soft versus hard) because these property terms emerge fairly early in the lexicon (Fenson et al., 1994) and color (e.g., yellow versus green). Color represents an interesting case. Although color terms are almost universally marked as adjectives (Dixon, 1982; Wetzer, 1992), and although infants' color perception is remarkably similar to that of adults (Bornstein, Kessen, & Weiskopf, 1976), young children nonetheless appear to have a curious difficulty mapping specific color terms to their meaning (Bornstein, 1985a; Landau & Gleitman, 1985; Rice, 1980; Sandhofer & Smith, 1999, 2001; Soja, 1994). Most of the evidence has suggested that color terms emerge late, relative to other property terms, and that the initial mappings for color terms tend to be inconsistent (Bornstein, 1985b; but see Macario, 1991; Shatz, Behrend, Gelman, & Ebeling, 1996).

preference for the matching test object. If this effect is specific to adjectives, then infants hearing the target labeled with a novel noun (e.g., "This is an X") or with no novel word (e.g., "Look at this one") should reveal no such preference.

The results revealed clear competences as well as limitations. At 21 months, when the target and test objects were all drawn from the same familiar basic level category (e.g., all snakes), infants successfully extended novel adjectives (but not nouns) specifically to the test object sharing the same property. This indicates that they had distinguished adjectives from nouns and mapped them specifically to property-based commonalities. In sharp contrast, when the target (e.g., a dog) and test objects (e.g., snakes) were drawn from different basic level categories, infants were unable to accomplish this mapping.

**Basic Level Categories as an Entry Point.**   This reliance on basic level object categories is not a fleeting phenomenon, evident only in very young word learners, or only with a small set of adjectives. It has also been documented in 3-year-olds performing word-extension tasks (Hall & Lavin, 2004; Klibanoff & Waxman, 2000; Markman & Jaswal, 2004), in adults performing online processing tasks (Allopenna, Magnuson, & Tanenhaus, 1998; Halff, Ortony, & Anderson, 1976; Medin & Shoben, 1988; Pechmann & Deutsch, 1982) and in connectionist models (Gasser & Smith, 1998). These findings are consistent with the observation that the precise meaning of a given adjective is influenced by the noun it modifies.

To see why this might be the case, consider a property term like *soft* or *red*. *Soft* slippers and *soft* ice-cream do not have the same texture; *red* hair and *red* Corvettes are not really the same color. This reflects that most adjectives must be related to a standard of comparison, and this standard is typically determined by the noun that the adjective modifies (Graff, 2000; Kennedy, 1997; Kennedy & McNally, in press; Rotstein & Winter, in press).[8]

Moreover, cross-linguistic evidence suggests that the semantic, syntactic, morphological, and lexical dependencies of adjectives on nouns may be universal. In languages that mark grammatical gender or number, ad-

jectives must agree with the nouns they modify. This linguistic fact, coupled with the conceptual primacy of basic level categories, suggests that basic-level *nouns* may serve as an entry point for the acquisition of adjectives.

**Moving beyond the Basic Level.**   Although novel adjectives may initially be interpreted within the context of familiar basic level categories, they are eventually extended more broadly. Children learn to extend *wet* to diapers, grass, finger-paintings; and *red,* to balloons, apples, shoes. What factors motivate this advance? The evidence suggests that to accomplish this task, infants integrate information from a wide range of sources, including cognitive, pragmatic, and linguistic cues. The importance of these additional cues is especially clear for infants acquiring languages (e.g., Japanese, Mandarin) where there are scant grammatical cues to distinguish nouns (count, mass, and proper nouns) from adjectives (Imai & Haryu, 2004). In such languages, where the grammatical cues are relatively weak, learners must depend more heavily on these additional sources of evidence if they are to assign words to grammatical categories and map them to meaning.

Current evidence suggests that several general cognitive processes are instrumental in discovering these mappings. The process of comparison operates in conjunction with naming to support children's ability to extend adjectives across diverse basic level categories (Waxman & Klibanoff, 2000). Three-year-old children succeed in mapping novel adjectives beyond the basic level if they are first provided with an opportunity for comparison. For example, if they are permitted to compare two members of the same basic level category that differ only in the property of interest (e.g., a red versus a blue car), and if they are told that one is *blickish* and the other is not, children readily home in on the inference that *blickish* refers to the property and they go on to extend it broadly to other red objects, from a range of different basic level categories (Au, 1990; Heibeck & Markman, 1987; Waxman & Booth, 2001; Waxman & Klibanoff, 2000). Similarly, if they are permitted to compare two members of different basic level categories that share a particular property (e.g., a red car and a red cup), and if they are told that each is blickish, they infer that blickish refers to the property and extend it broadly to objects bearing that property from various basic level kinds (Mintz & Gleitman, 2002; Waxman & Klibanoff, 2000). In fact, it turns out that mothers provide just this kind of information when they are instructed to teach

---

[8] The standard of comparison for adjectives can also be set by context. For example, "my Fiat is a big car" may be true in the context of a discussion of Italian cars, but false in the context of a discussion of American cars.

their infants and toddlers the meaning of a novel adjective (Hall, Burns, & Pawluski, 2003; Manders & Hall, 2002). General cognitive processes may also help infants and children discover how reference to a particular dimension, like color or texture, is reflected in the lexicon (Sandhofer & Smith, 1999).

Pragmatic cues also facilitate adjectival mappings. Consider a scenario in which a novel animate object is introduced, saying, "This is *daxy*." This phrase is ambiguous, because *daxy* could be a proper noun, mass noun, or an adjective (Hall & Belanger, 2001; Hall & Lavin, 2004; Haryu & Imai, 2002; Imai & Haryu, 2004). Hall and his colleagues (Hall & Belanger, in press) demonstrated that 3-year-old children acquiring English resolve the ambiguity by attending to the number of individuals to which the word is applied. If it is applied only to a single novel animal (e.g., a llama), they restrict the word to that individual, suggesting that they interpreted it as a proper noun. However, if the word is applied to two different animals, then children extend it to other animals that share that property, suggesting that they interpreted it as an adjective. Imai and Haryu (2001, 2004) demonstrated that children acquiring Japanese show an overwhelming preference to interpret a novel word in an ambiguous phrase as referring to the basic level category. Once a basic level category term has been acquired, they go on to interpret a novel word in that same phrase as referring to a property of the object.

Finally, linguistic factors also contribute to the use of basic level categories as an entry point for adjectival acquisition. Mintz and Gleitman (2002) noted that in constructions like "This is a *blickish* one," the term *one* refers to an (unspecified) object category. Because in experimental tasks, this term is typically applied to a single individual (e.g., a dog), and because basic level object categories are so salient, such constructions are likely to support the extension of the novel adjective within, but not across, that (unspecified) basic level category. If this is the case, then replacing the unspecified pronoun *one* with a lexically specific head noun (e.g., "This is a *blickish* dog. Can you give me a *blickish* car?") should support a broader range of adjectival extension. The results revealed that in such cases, 2-year-olds successfully extended novel adjectives beyond the limits of basic level categories (Klibanoff & Waxman, 2000; Mintz & Gleitman, 2002). Providing the lexically specific head noun essentially blocked a basic level interpretation of the adjective because this noun provides explicit information indicating that a broader range of

extension (one that includes both a dog and a car) for the novel adjective is required.

Summarizing to this point, we have shown that in the absence of explicit (linguistic, pragmatic, or conceptual) evidence to the contrary, basic level kinds serve as the entry point for assigning meaning to a novel adjective (see Goldvarg-Steingold, 2003 for evidence that higher level categories may also serve this function). By enriching the conceptual, pragmatic, or linguistic information available, infants and children move beyond this entry point to extend adjectives broadly and appropriately across basic level kinds.

### Cross-Linguistic Work

We have argued that cross-linguistic and developmental observations suggest (a) that the link between nouns and object categories, which emerges early in infants, may be a universal phenomenon, and (b) that the specific link between adjectives and their associated meaning, which emerge later in development, vary systematically as a function of the structure of the language under acquisition.

Empirical support for this position comes from recent research comparing monolingual children acquiring English, French, Italian, or Spanish (Hall, Waxman, Bredart, & Nicolay, 2003; Waxman, Senghas, & Benveniste, 1997). Although these languages are closely related, they provided an interesting set of cross-linguistic comparisons, primarily because of differences in the syntactic contexts and semantic functions associated with the grammatical form *adjective*. These differences permit us to examine how expectations for *adjectives* are shaped by the language being acquired.

To get a flavor for these differences, consider a cupboard holding several different coffee cups. Speakers of English and French distinguish the cups linguistically using a determiner, an adjective, and an overt noun (e.g., "a *blue* cup" or "the *blue* one"). In Italian and Spanish, although such constructions are sometimes apt, whenever the referent of the noun (cup) is recoverable from the context, it is omitted obligatorily from the surface of the sentence, leaving the determiner and adjective alone (e.g., "uno *azul*" or "a *blue*"). That is, in contexts where English speakers would say "the blue one," Spanish and Italian speakers allow the noun to be elided.

These constructions, known to linguists as *det*-A constructions, are ubiquitous in Italian and Spanish. Although *det*-A constructions also appear in English and French, they do so under highly restricted circumstances. Moreover, although *det*-A constructions are permissible in a slightly broader range of circumstances in French than in English, in both languages, this construction is relatively rare, and appears to be learned on a case-by-case basis rather than emerging as the product of a productive grammatical rule, as in Italian and Spanish (see Gathercole & Min, 1997, for other semantic/syntactic factors in Spanish and English, and their relation to acquisition; and Waxman et al., 1997, for a more detailed treatment of the *det*-A construction in these languages). Snyder et al. (2001) documented that Spanish-speaking children as young as 2 years of age produce *det*-A constructions broadly and spontaneously (see also, MacWhinney & Snow, 1990).

There are two important features to notice about the adjectives in *det*-A constructions. First, the adjectives in these constructions appear in syntactic contexts that appear to be identical to those where count nouns typically occur.[9] Second, adjectives in these constructions appear to adopt a semantic function that is customarily associated with count nouns. *Det*-A constructions can refer to the named object *qua* object and can be extended to include other members of its object category, if these members also share the named property. Importantly, then, in Italian and Spanish there is considerable overlap in both the surface syntactic contexts and the semantic extensions for nouns and adjectives.

Does experience with these different languages lead to different outcomes in the expectations concernin the grammatical form *adjective*? As a first step in examining this hypothesis, Waxman and her colleagues (Waxman et al., 1997) conducted a cross-linguistic investigation involving preschool-age monolingual children acquiring either English, French, Italian, or Spanish. Each child "read" through a picture book with an experimenter (a native speaker of the child's language). On each page, there were five pictures: a target (e.g., a cow), two category-based alternatives (e.g., a fox and a zebra), and two thematically related alternatives (e.g., a barn and milk). Children were assigned to one of three conditions. In the no-word condition, the experimenter pointed to the target and said, "See this? Can you find another one?" In the novel noun condition, she said, for example, "See this *fopin*? Can you find another *fopin*?"

In the novel adjective condition, she said, "See this *fopish* one? Can you show me another one that is *fopish*?"

The predictions were straightforward. (a) If a link between nouns and object categories is universal, then all children should extend the novel nouns to the category-based test objects; (b) If cross-linguistic differences regarding the grammatical form *adjective* have consequences on acquisition, then children's extensions of the novel adjectives should vary as a function of native language. In Italian and Spanish, where adjectives are permitted to adopt some of the syntactic and semantic features associated with nouns, children may extend novel adjectives (like nouns) to other members of the same category. In contrast, in English and in French, where this nominal interpretation of novel adjectives is not available, children should fail to extend novel adjectives to category members and should perform at chance levels.

The results were consistent with these predictions. Children from each language community consistently extended the novel nouns to the category-based alternatives. But performance in the *novel adjective* condition varied systematically as a function of language. As predicted, children acquiring French and English performed at the chance level, while those acquiring Italian and Spanish extended novel adjectives (like novel nouns) to the category-based alternatives. Although this taxonomic inclination was less pronounced for adjectives than for nouns, it was quite robust, holding up in children ranging from 3 to 7 years of age. Perhaps most striking, these children extended novel adjectives to the category-based alternatives not only when they were presented in *det*-A phrases (and therefore could have been either nouns or adjectives), but also when they were presented in phrases incorporating an overt noun (e.g., *cosa*). Thus, even when the syntactic contexts were unambiguously adjectival and fully comparable to those in English and French, Italian- and Spanish-speaking children extended the novel adjectives on the basis of category membership.

These results suggest that children's expectations for adjectives are tailored by features of the particular language being acquired. For children acquiring English or French, languages in which nouns (but not adjectives) can refer to objects and can be extended to other category members, children build an expectation that nouns (but not adjectives) can take on this semantic function. For children acquiring Italian and Spanish, experience steers the acquisition process along a slightly different

---

[9] The adjectives in these *det*-A phrases retain their syntactic status as adjectives (see Kester, 1994; Snyder, 1995; and Waxman et al., 1997, for the relevant diagnostics).

developmental course, permitting children to build an expectation that both nouns and adjectives can be extended on the basis of category membership.

This suggests one way in which language-specific experience shapes the acquisition of the predicate forms. In future work, it will be important to examine these effects in a wider range of languages and to explore the developmental implications of this distributional overlap for infants' ability to distinguish nouns from adjectives.

### Conclusions about Adjectives

We have conveyed several insights into the acquisition of adjectives. Although adjectives are plentiful in the input that children hear, and although even infants are sensitive to the properties that are typically encoded by early adjectives (e.g., color, texture, size, temperature, temperament), mapping adjectives to their associated meaning is surprisingly elusive. The mapping for adjectives emerges later than that for nouns and varies as a function of the structure of the ambient language. Moreover, there is a linguistic or conceptual priority to name an object's kind (and especially its basic level category) before marking its properties, however salient those properties may be.

The acquisition of the grammatical form *adjective* appears to rest on the prior acquisition of (at least some) nouns and to require a richer set of linguistic and conceptual cues than nouns (Mintz & Gleitman, 2002; Waxman & Klibanoff, 2000). Moreover, the interpretation of any particular adjective appears to depend (at least in the initial stages of acquisition) on the particular noun that it modifies. These observations have led to the conclusion that early noun learning serves as a gateway for the acquisition of adjectives. We also suggest that noun learning serves as a gateway for the acquisition of verb meaning.

### The Acquisition of Verbs

Because not all words share the same grammatical and conceptual requirements, we expect to find differences in the information that learners use to acquire different kinds of words. Most nouns are not argument taking but most verbs are; it may therefore be the case that identifying a verb requires prior identification of the phrases that serve as its arguments. Noun phrases serve this function by helping the learner identify the event denoted by the verb from the extralinguistic context. From

this perspective, early noun learning sets the stage for the subsequent acquisition of other grammatical categories like verbs (Gleitman, 1990). Learning the nouns enables the learner to project noun phrases in the syntax. These noun phrases represent the scaffolding on which infants assemble a rudimentary representation of the structure of the native language (Fisher et al., 1994; Fisher & Tokura, 1996; Naigles, 2002) and this, in turn, provides a foundation for the acquisition of the other essential grammatical forms. The critical idea is that a learner who can identify the nouns in a sentence can build noun phrases, which then serve as the arguments of the verb. Identifying the arguments of the verb leads to a rudimentary syntactic structure which, in turn, is informative of the meaning of the verb. On this view, verb learning is dependent on syntactic structure, which can be partially identified through the identification of the nouns in the sentence.

### Informational Differences between Nouns and Verbs

One of the strongest pieces of evidence that the informational requirements for learning verbs are steeper than those for nouns comes from experiments with adult participants in a simulated word-learning environment (Gillette et al., 1999; Snedeker & Gleitman, 2004). Adults were presented a series of videotaped scenes depicting the visual context of a parent uttering a word to their child, but with the sound removed. The participants' task was to identify the word that was uttered by the parent. Participants were divided into several conditions that differed by how much information they received about the linguistic context of the utterance. Participants experienced either (a) just the visual scene, (b) the scene plus the nouns that co-occurred with the novel word, (c) the syntactic frame with nonsense words replacing all the content words, (d) the syntactic frame with co-occurring nouns, or (e) all this information together. Crucially, the proportion of words that were correctly identified and the type of words that were identifiable changed significantly as a function of information type. When presented with no information beyond the visual scene, participants correctly identified nouns more often than they correctly identified verbs. Although participants were least successful at identifying verbs when only the visual scene was presented, they improved as the amount of syntactic information increased. Syntactic information was more effective than the co-occurring nouns in leading participants to the right answer, and the combination of these cues was more effective than either of these alone. These results lend support to the idea that successful verb learning requires information beyond the observation of extralinguistic context. In particular, syntactic argument structure and the co-occurrence of known nouns serving as syntactic arguments were crucial to adults' success in identifying the missing verbs.

### Children's Use of Syntax to Learn Verb Meanings

In addition to these simulations with adult learners, there is by now a wealth of evidence identifying the crucial role of syntax in helping children identify the meanings of novel verbs. Naigles (1990) used the preferential looking paradigm to investigate this issue. Two-year-olds saw a videotaped scene depicting the following two actions simultaneously: A duck forces a rabbit to squat by pushing on its head, while the duck and rabbit each wheel their free arm in a circle. Notice that there is a causal interpretation of the observed event ("to force to squat") and a noncausal interpretation ("to rotate one's arm"). While both interpretations involve two participants, only under one of these interpretations are the two in a causer-to-caused relation. While watching this scene, half the infants heard a disembodied voice say "The duck is biffing the bunny" while the other half heard "The duck and the bunny are biffing." Each utterance thus mentions two entities, but only in the first one do the two entities show up in two different argument positions ("the duck and the bunny" is a single complex noun phrase occupying one argument position; namely, the subject position). This video was then removed and the voice said, "Find biffing now!" Two new videos now appeared, one displayed to the left of the watching child, the other to the right. In one, the duck was shown forcing the rabbit to squat but without arm-wheeling. In the other, the duck and rabbit were shown standing side by side wheeling their arms. Infants attended longest to the scene that matched the syntax. When the novel verb was presented as a transitive verb ("the duck is biffing the bunny"), infants took that verb to refer to the causative event in which the duck causes the bunny to squat. When the novel verb was presented as an intransitive ("the duck and the bunny are biffing"), they looked longest at the noncausal action in which the characters were wheling their arms. Evidently the syntactic structure was decisive in cueing which aspect of the complex initial scene was relevant to the interpretation of *biffing* (Naigles, 1990; see also Fisher et al., 1994; Naigles,

1996; Naigles & Kako, 1993). This work demonstrates that 2-year-olds can use the syntax to assign a meaning to a novel verb.

Bunger and Lidz (2004) used the preferential looking paradigm to show that syntax can be useful not only in distinguishing which of two simultaneously occurring events is labeled by a novel verb, as in Naigles' studies, but also in distinguishing which aspect of a single internally complex event is so labeled. The relevant case also involved causative events that, although typically expressed as one lexical unit (e.g., *kill, roll*), can be decomposed into two subevents (Dowty, 1979; Hale & Keyser, 1993; Jackendoff, 1990; Levin & Rappaport-Hovav, 1995; McCawley, 1968). The conceptual structure of a causative event can be represented as in (2), with open argument positions to be filled by the causer of the event and the affected entity:

(2) [[X DO SOMETHING] CAUSE [Y BECOME STATE]].

The first subpart of this structure [X DO SOMETHING] specifies the causing subevent, or the means, and the second subpart [Y BECOME STATE] specifies the resulting change of state. For example, a verb like *bounce* (a) can be represented as in (b):

(3) a. The girl bounced the ball.
   b. [[The girl HITS THE BALL] CAUSE [the ball BECOME BOUNCING]]

Bunger and Lidz (2004) asked three questions. First, do young children have internally complex representations like (2) for the concepts labeled by causative verbs? Second, can different syntactic structures differentially direct children's attention to these subevents (thereby influencing their interpretation of a novel verb used to describe the event). Third, are children limited to using syntax to distinguish between multiple distinct events in the world as in Naigles (1990), or can they also use it to parse single events that are internally complex.

To answer these questions, they conducted a preferential looking study in which 2-year-old children saw internally complex causative events labeled by a novel verb occurring in distinct syntactic structures. Children were first familiarized to an event of direct causation (e.g., a girl bouncing a ball) described by a novel verb. The syntactic frame in which the novel verb was presented varied across children in four ways: control ("Look at that"), transitive ("The girl is pimming the ball"), unaccusative[10] ("The ball is pimming"), or multiple frame (transitive + unaccusative: "The girl is pimming the ball." "Do you see the ball pimming?"). This training phase was followed by a test phase, identical for all conditions, in which children heard the novel verb ("Where's pimming now?") while they saw, on opposite sides of the screen, the separate subevents depicting the means (the girl patting a ball, but no bouncing) and the result (the ball bouncing with the girl standing idly by) of the complex causative presented during training.

Because the unaccusative variant of a causative verb labels the result subevent without making reference to the means, Bunger and Lidz (2004) predicted that children in the unaccusative and multiple-frame conditions would be more likely than children in the transitive and control conditions to interpret the novel verb as referring to the result subevent. This prediction was borne out. At test, children in the control and transitive conditions showed no significant preference for either subevent. Crucially, however, children in the unaccusative and multiple-frame conditions demonstrated a significant preference for the result subevent. Thus, the syntactic context in which novel verbs were presented guided children's interpretations of those verbs, even when the verbs referred to subparts of internally complex events.

In an interesting refinement, Fisher and her colleagues (Fisher et al., 2004; Fisher & Tokura, 1996) asked whether these kinds of syntactic bootstrapping effects result from the syntax per se, or whether they might result from children's knowledge of the meanings of the co-occurring nouns. Her method was to provide children with structural cues without providing contentful noun phrases. Two- and three-year-old children saw two same-gender individuals participating in a single event. For example, a woman was being twirled in a swivel chair by another woman, by the stratagem of pulling on a long ribbon attached to the former woman's waist. The children were asked to "Show me the one who's pilking around" or "Show me the one who's pilking her around" by pointing to one of the depicted women. These children used the number and position of noun phrases in the sentence to determine which of the two women was being referred to, even though these

noun phrases were just pronouns. When they heard the transitive sentence, they picked the woman doing the twirling; that is, they interpreted the two-noun phrase sentence as describing the causal aspect of the observed event; symmetrically, when they heard the intransitive sentence, they picked the woman being twirled. Thus, we see that although the identification of nouns can help to build a syntactic structure, it is this structure, and not only the semantic information contained in the nouns, that guides children's acquisition of novel verbs. This conclusion does not mean that verb learning is independent of noun learning. Rather, to the extent that learning nouns leads to learning verbs, this support is mediated through the projection of syntactic structure.

An additional kind of evidence for children's use of syntax to guide verb learning comes from their interpretations of known verbs in novel syntactic contexts (Lidz, 1998; Naigles, Fowler, & Helm, 1992; Naigles & Kako, 1993). In these experiments 2-, 3-, and 4-year-old children used objects from a Noah's ark playset to act out sentences presented to them by an experimenter. Some of the sentences were grammatical, whereas others were ungrammatical in English, but represented structures that are possible in some language. Some sentences added an argument to an intransitive verb, as in "the zebra comes the giraffe to the ark," while others subtracted a required argument from a transitive verb, as in "the zebra brings to the ark." While children uniformly provided accurate enactments of the grammatical sentences, their behavior in response to the ungrammatical sentences was crucial in providing a window into the learning process. For these sentences, children essentially had two choices. They could ignore the additional or missing argument, relying on their knowledge of the verb. Alternatively, they could integrate the novel structure into their interpretation, modifying their interpretations of these known verbs. These children adopted the latter strategy. When presented with a sentence like "The zebra comes the giraffe to the ark," children acted out a scene in which the zebra brings the giraffe to the ark, showing that the extra argument is interpreted as a causal agent. By the same token, "The giraffe brings to the ark" was acted out with the giraffe coming to the ark, with no causal agent.

These studies show that children use the number of noun phrase arguments to broaden the scope of the events that they think a known verb refers to. Although *come* expresses only motion toward a location in the adult language, if this verb is presented with an additional syntactic argument, children who have not yet set-

---

[10] The term "unaccusative" refers to an intransitive verb whose subject behaves in some ways like an object, as in pairs like "the navy sank the boat" versus "the boat sank" (see Burzio, 1986; Levin & Rappaport-Hovav, 1995; Perlmutter & Postal, 1984, for discussion).

tled on a fixed representation of the verb's meaning will take that additional syntactic argument as evidence that the verb can also express caused motion. These studies provide clear evidence for the power of syntax in licensing inferences about verb meaning. Moreover, they enable us to ask whether children are constrained in how they extend known verbs into novel contexts. We now turn to this question.

### Cross-Linguistic Evidence and Constraints on Verb Learning

The fact that children can use syntax as one source of information in learning novel verbs allows us to ask questions not only about how children learn verbs but also about the existence of constraints on verb learning. We can ask whether children are limited in their verb learning by the kinds of constraints that appear to hold across diverse languages. The research strategy is to look for cross-linguistically stable generalizations and then ask whether children's learning reflects those generalizations. The idea behind this strategy is that linguistic universals derive from principled constraints on what a possible human language is. Thus, to the extent that these constraints can be found in verb learners, we add to the evidence in support of them. From another perspective, cross-linguistically stable generalizations provide us with hypotheses about constraints on verb learning that can then be tested on children who are developing a lexicon. Moreover, to the extent that a property of verb meaning or linking can vary cross-linguistically, we expect to find that property to be highly sensitive to aspects of the linguistic environment, since it will depend not on principled constraints from the learner, but on the observation of the particular language being learned (the linguistic input).

**Syntactic and Semantic Types of Arguments.** The method of testing children's extensions of known verbs to novel contexts has been used to investigate children's knowledge of the connection between syntactic and semantic types of arguments and the range of possible verb meanings (Lidz, Gleitman, & Gleitman, 2004). The rationale for this manipulation is based on the observation that some aspects of the mapping from event participants to syntactic categories are universal, while other aspects are more variable both within and across languages. A propositional argument can be realized as a tensed clause (*John thinks that Mary will win*) or an infinitival clause (*John expects Mary to win*) but not as a noun phrase referring to an individual (*\*John thinks the winner*).[11] The choice of tensed or untensed clause, however, is subject to lexical variability and must be learned on a verb-by-verb basis. Similarly, some change-of-state verbs that can occur with one argument (*the vase dropped*) can also occur with two (*I dropped the vase*), while others do not allow this alternation (*the vase fell; \*I fell the vase*). But, verbs in this class never have their arguments realized as sentential complements (*\*John falls that it is Bill; \*John drops Bill to be here*).

Given the existence of principled constraints on the syntax-semantics mapping (e.g., that verbs denoting relations between individuals and propositions can take clausal arguments), as well as lexically specific constraints (e.g., that *think* takes a tensed sentence complement but not an infinitival complement), we can ask whether children are limited in the ways that they are willing to extend known verbs in accordance with these constraints. To do this, Lidz et al. (2004) examined 3-year-old children's understanding of known verbs in syntactic contexts that are permitted by language, but not by the language they happen to be learning (*the zebra falls the giraffe; the zebra thinks the giraffe to go to the ark*) and compared this with their understanding of known verbs in syntactic contexts that are not permitted by any language (*\*the zebra falls that the giraffe goes to the ark; \*the zebra thinks the giraffe*). The reasoning behind this manipulation was the following: If children are constrained to allow only those mappings that are allowed by language in general, then they should distinguish these two types of extensions. Children should be willing to extend verbs in ways that are possible in principle, but happen not to occur for those particular verbs in their language. They should be unwilling to extend verbs in ways that are in conflict with the principles of syntax-semantics mapping that are found across all languages.

This expectation was met. Lidz et al. (2004) found that children relied on the syntactic structure to guide their enactments only when the novel verb-sentence pairing was a possible pairing in principle (although not in English). In the cases in which the novel syntactic structure would violate principles of syntax to semantic mapping (like *\*the zebra falls that the giraffe goes to the ark*), children performed actions that relied more heavily on what they already knew about the verb. In other words, children accepted extensions of known verbs into

---

[11] The asterisk (*) is used to indicate that a sentence is grammatically anomalous.

new syntactic frames only when the verb-frame pairing was one that might have been possible. This finding suggests that children's knowledge of the syntax-semantics mapping guides their acquisition of novel verbs even when their lexical representations for certain verbs have not yet solidified. Some aspects of the syntax to semantics mapping do not have to be learned but rather guide learners' hypotheses from the start.

**Universals in the Expression of Causativity.**    The domain of causation, because it has some universal components and some cross-linguistically variable components, has provided another opportunity to isolate the relative contributions of linguistic constraints and linguistic experience. As noted, many change-of-state verbs (e.g., *break*) have both a transitive and intransitive use that differ with respect to causativity. The transitive version (4a) includes an argument to play the role of causer, whereas the intransitive version (4b) does not:

(4)  a.  Kim broke the vase.
     b.  The vase broke.

This relation between transitivity and causativity is found in all languages (Comrie, 1985; Haspelmath, 1993, among others). One thing that does vary cross-linguistically is whether the alternation is morphologically marked. In many languages, the intransitive variants are basic, and an additional causative morpheme is used to indicate causation. In other languages, the transitive variants are basic and an additional anti-causative morpheme indicates the lack of causation. In still other languages, both strategies exist for different verbs. Thus, the addition and subtraction of arguments is used universally to mark causative status, whereas the use of verbal affixes to mark causative status varies both cross-linguistically and within a language.

This state of affairs presents an interesting research question—whether children use argument number as a cue to causativity because this cue is reliably present in their language or because they are predisposed to do so. Lidz, Gleitman, and Gleitman (2003) pitted the universal property of argument number against the cross-linguistically variable property of morphology in Kannada, a language with causative morphology, to distinguish the effect of inherent constraints on the learner from the effect of the language environment. Do children use argument number as a cue to causal verb meaning as a result of observing this relationship in the input? Or is this

relationship in the input because all language learners expect their language to express it?

Kannada is an appropriate probe language because of its abundant use of the morphological cue to causativity. In Kannada, any verb can be made causative through the addition of a causative morpheme. Moreover, whenever this morpheme is present, the causal interpretation is entailed. Finally, in Kannada, as in all languages, many verbs with two arguments are not interpreted causally. Given this pattern of facts, the causative morpheme is a more reliable cue for causation than is the number of arguments.

Because the presence of the causative morpheme guarantees a causal interpretation but the presence of two arguments is only probabilistically associated with causal interpretation, Kannada can offer some insight into the origins of the connection between argument number and causal interpretation.

Lidz et al. (2003) used the Noah's ark methodology described earlier with 3-year-old children learning Kannada as their first language. Children were presented with known verbs with either one or two noun phrase arguments and either with or without the causative morpheme. The predictions were as follows. If children use the most reliable cues in their language input to determine the syntax to semantics mapping, we would expect children learning Kannada to rely more heavily on the causative morpheme as an expression of causativity than on the number of arguments. On the other hand, if children are guided by expectations about the syntax-semantics mapping that are based on the universal grammatical principles, they should rely more heavily on argument number than causative morphology. In the latter case, children would be expected to override the most reliable cue in the input in favor of the less reliable cue determined by inherent grammatical constraints.

The data were clear. Three-year-old Kannada-learning children treated argument number but not morphology as an indication of causativity, despite the fact that the latter is the more reliable cue in their language. In sum, children acted out two-noun-phrase sentences as causative and one-noun-phrase sentences as noncausative, independent of the presence or absence of the causative morpheme.

In effect, these children ignored the more reliable morphological cue to verb meaning and instead relied on the syntactic cue (noun phrase number). This result provides evidence for the priority of the principle aligning noun phrases with semantic participants. The observation that learners discarded the best cue in favor of a weaker one reveals the active role that learners play in acquiring verb meanings. Learners use argument number as a cue to verb meaning not because it is there in the input, but because they expect to find it there.[12]

**Universals and Constraints on Locative Verbs.** Yet another source of evidence for inherent constraints on syntax semantics mapping comes from studies of locative verbs—verbs expressing the movement of some object (the figure) to a location (the ground). Verbs that describe the manner of motion (*pour, spill, shake*) require the figure to occur as the direct object, whereas verbs that describe a change of state (*fill, cover, decorate*) require the ground to occur as the direct object (Rappaport & Levin, 1988):

(5) a. Edward poured water into the glass.
    (figure frame)
   b. *Edward poured the glass with water.
    (ground frame)
   c. *Edward filled water into the glass.
    (figure frame)
   d. Edward filled the glass with water.
    (ground frame)

Studies of the acquisition of these verbs find that children use this syntax-semantics mapping to guide their interpretations and productions (Gropen, Pinker, Hollander, & Goldberg, 1991a, 1991b; Pinker, 1989). However, it has also been observed that children make some errors in production in this domain. Bowerman (1982) found evidence of children using the figure frame inappropriately with change of state verbs in their spontaneous productions. This effect was replicated by Gropen et al. (1991a) and Kim, Landau, and Phillips (1999) in elicited production studies.

Importantly, however, in none of these studies were children reported to have made errors in which they used manner of motion verbs with the ground frame. This asymmetry is important because it mirrors the cross-linguistic variation in this domain. Kim et al. (1999) exam-

ined a wide range of unrelated languages and found that locative change of state verbs vary cross-linguistically in whether they can occur in the figure frame. However, no language was found in which manner of motion verbs can occur in the ground frame. Thus, children's errors are limited to the places where languages can vary. In cases where there are universal constraints on linking patterns, children obey those constraints throughout acquisition. In cases where there are no such constraints, children must rely on their input to guide acquisition.

### The Role of Input in Verb Learning

We have seen (a) that children use syntax to guide their acquisition of novel verbs, and (b) that inherent constraints guide children's use of syntax in this regard. However, we also expect to find children showing a sensitivity to the input exactly when inherent constraints from the learner do not exist. In determining a division of labor between the child's internally generated constraints and the child's experience with the language environment, we expect to find sensitivity to the input just in those cases in which the child has no internally generated expectations about verb meaning and verb syntax. This is what we find.

One study showing children's sensitivity to the input in verb learning involved the verb extension methodology discussed earlier. Naigles et al. (1992) examined 2- to 5-year-old children's extensions of motion verbs like *come, go, bring,* and *take* into syntactic frames where these verbs do not occur. As in the studies previously discussed, these authors found that children, but not adults, adjusted their meanings of these verbs to fit the syntactic context. Thus, when *come* was presented transitively (*the zebra comes the giraffe to the ark*), children treated it as expressing the causal event in which the zebra brings (= cause to come) the giraffe to the ark. Adults on the other hand seemed to interpret the sentence as an error and repaired the syntax, acting out a noncausal scenario (e.g., the zebra and the giraffe come to the ark). Interestingly, the transition to adult behavior varied as a function of age and, most importantly, as a function of verb frequency. In particular, intransitive *bring* and *take* were repaired earlier than transitive *come* and *go*. This finding is important because the intransitive (ungrammatical) variants of *bring* and *take* express the same meanings as the intransitive (but grammatical) variants for *come* and *go*. Likewise, the transitive (ungrammatical) variants of *come* and *go* express the same meanings as the transitive (grammatical) variants of

---

[12] Kannada-speaking adults eventually do acquire this special ("language specific") feature of their language. To say that they did not would mean that the Kannada language had changed. So it is reassuring to find, as we did, that Kannada adults show sensitivity both to argument number and to the causative morpheme when they participate in the Noah's ark experiment.

*bring* and *take*. Thus, the learner at some point should recognize that these verbs represent suppletive pairs (e.g., *come = bring*; and *go = take,* modulo the difference in causation) and stop allowing the intransitives to be used transitively and vice versa. But, importantly, what Naigles et al. found was that the repairs did not all begin at the same time. Instead, the more frequent verbs (*come* and *go*) were repaired later than the less frequent verbs (*bring* and *take*). This can be understood as the effect of frequency on suppletion. The higher frequency items allow children to build stable lexical representations earlier. Thus, these representations block the use of other words to express those same meanings. *Bring* is disallowed as an intransitive because the child has learned that *come* expresses that meaning. Experience with a given verb determines the learner's willingness to accept other verbs as expressing that same meaning. Most importantly, from the present perspective, the effect of experience appears here because there are no expectations or constraints from children to tell them whether a verb like *come* can or cannot be used transitively. This must come from experience.

Other studies also highlight the importance of children's sensitivity to the input in verb learning (e.g., Childers & Tomasello, 2002; Naigles & Hoff-Ginsberg, 1998; Snedeker & Trueswell, in press; Tomasello, 1992, among others). These studies tell us that for properties of verb representation that can vary within a language, children are extremely sensitive to the frequency of occurrence of those representations. As expected, when there are no constraints from the child on what the verb's representation should be like, the linguistic environment exerts a strong influence.

### *Conclusions about Verbs*

We have conveyed several messages about the state of the art in verb learning. First, because verbs have complex representations that depend on the prior acquisition of certain other linguistic properties (minimally, the recognition of syntactic arguments), they are acquired later than nouns. Second, by paying attention to the details of how verbs are represented in the minds of adult speakers and whether these details can and cannot vary across languages, we can develop very clear predictions about the kinds of constraints on verb learning that we should find in children. In cases where cross-linguistic evidence suggests that a linking may be universal, we suspect that inherent constraints may be at play and therefore that we should be able to see these constraints

in experimental manipulations with young learners. Where properties of representation can vary, however, we expect to find little evidence of inherent constraints. Instead, we expect to see a strong influence of the linguistic environment. As we have argued throughout this chapter, the important question in language acquisition and in word learning is not whether there are inherent constraints on learners. Rather, the crucial questions are where we expect to see the effects of constraints, where we expect to see the effects of experience, and how constraints interact with experience to guide acquisition.

## THE FUTURE OF WORD-LEARNING RESEARCH

The study of word learning must take into account the variety of word types found in natural languages. In this chapter, we have focused on the acquisition of the major grammatical categories—noun, adjective, and verb—highlighting that nouns tend to emerge first in language acquisition and serve as the foundation for the discovery of the other grammatical forms and their meanings.

The kinds of words that we have examined, however, only scratch the surface of those found in natural languages. Languages include words that quantify over individuals (*a, the, every, two*), words that compare sets of individuals (*most, more, less*), words that refer back to previously mentioned entities (*he, she, one, herself*), words that quantify over events (*always, sometimes*), words that describe the manner of an event (*quickly, repeatedly*), and so on. As we have suggested, each kind of word points to a restricted range of concepts. Moreover, the relation between linguistic and conceptual structure is bidirectional. Distinct grammatical forms highlight distinct kinds of meaning; but at the same time, linguistic structure is in many ways derived from the meaning of the words involved. Differences in meaning therefore lead to differences in syntax. Consequently, examining the role of syntax in word learning is crucial, as the syntax provides a surface cue that the learner can use to infer the meaning of the word and that the developmental researcher can use to infer what might count as knowledge of the word.

We have also underscored the argument that the field of word learning must be sensitive to cross-linguistically stable and cross-linguistically variable properties of words and grammatical categories. Cross-linguistic research can be instrumental in developing hypotheses both about the kinds of structures within the learner that guide acquisition and about the kinds of linguistic input that shape word learning. A maximally general theory of word learning must still be constrained enough to explain the speed with which children grow a lexicon and flexible enough to allow this growth to occur in a wide range of linguistic environments. By placing word learning firmly within the context of development and of comparative linguistics, we have provided a foundation for future research in which we consider the full range of words represented in human language and the full range of concepts to which these apply. Current word-learning research reveals that learners exhibit some general sensitivities and expectations at the onset of acquisition that later become tuned to the child's particular language environment.

We began this chapter with a reference to Janus, the god of gateways and transitions. We have argued throughout this chapter that word learning resides on the boundary between conceptual and linguistic knowledge and that word learning represents a doorway through which constraints from the learner interact with the vagaries of linguistic environment. We end with a final reference to Janus. Word-learning research now stands at an important threshold, having reached a point where a focus on noun learning can be replaced with a broader, more inclusive, conception of the range of concepts and grammatical knowledge involved in word learning. Crossing this threshold will require the field to continue to integrate ideas, methods, and generalizations from developmental psychology, cognitive psychology, and comparative linguistics.

## REFERENCES

Abney, S. (1987). *The English noun phrase in its sentenial aspect.* Unpublished doctoral dissertation, Massachusetts Institute of Technology, Cambridge, MA.

Allopenna, P. D., Magnuson, J. S., & Tanenhaus, M. K. (1998). Tracking the time course of spoken word recognition using eye movements: Evidence for continuous mapping models. *Journal of Memory and Language, 38*(4), 419–439.

Aslin, R. N., Saffran, J. R., & Newport, E. L. (1998). Computation of conditional probability statistics by 8-month-old infants. *Psychological Science, 9,* 321–324.

Au, T. K. (1990). Children's use of information in word learning. *Journal of Child Language, 17*(2), 393–416.

Au, T. K., Dapretto, M., & Song, Y. K. (1994). Input versus constraints: Early word acquisition in Korean and English. *Journal of Memory and Language, 33*(5), 567–582.

Baillargeon, R. (2000). How do infants learn about the physical world. In D. Muir & A. Slater (Eds.), *Infant development: Essential readings in development psychology* (pp. 195–212). Malden, MA: Blackwell.

Baker, M. (2001). *The atoms of language: The mind's hidden rules of grammar.* New York: Basic Books.

Balaban, M. T., & Waxman, S. R. (1997). Do words facilitate object categorization in 9-month-old infants? *Journal of Experimental Child Psychology, 64*(1), 3–26.

Baldwin, D. A., & Baird, J. A. (1999). Action analysis: A gateway to intentional inference. In P. Rochat (Ed.), *Early social cognition: Understanding others in the first months of life* (pp. 215–240). Mahwah, NJ: Erlbaum.

Baldwin, D. A., & Markman, E. M. (1989). Establishing word-object relations: A first step. *Child Development, 60*(2), 381–398.

Baldwin, D. A., & Moses, L. J. (2001). Links between social understanding and early word learning: Challenges to current accounts. *Social Development, 10,* 309–329.

Barsalou, L. W. (1983). Ad hoc categories. *Memory and Cognition, 11*(3), 211–227.

Bassano, D. (2000). Early development of nouns and verbs in French: Exploring the interface between lexicon and grammar. *Journal of Child Language, 27,* 521–559.

Bates, E., & Goodman, J. C. (1997). On the inseparability of grammar and the lexicon: Evidence from acquisition, aphasia and real-time processing. *Language and Cognitive Processes, 12*(5/6), 507–584.

Behl-Chadha, G. (1995). Perceptually-driven superordinate-like categorical representations in early infancy. *Dissertation Abstracts International: Section B: Sciences and Engineering, 55*(7-B), 3033.

Belanger, J., & Hall, D. G. (in press). Learning proper names and count nouns: Evidence from 16- and 20-month-olds. *Journal of Cognition and Development.*

Berlin, B. (1992). *Ethnobiological classification.* Princeton, NJ: Princeton University Press.

Berlin, B., Breedlove, D. E., & Raven, P. H. (1973). General principles of classification and nomenclature in folk biology. *American Anthropologist, 75,* 214–242.

Bhatt, R. S., & Rovee-Collier, C. (1997). Dissociation between features and feature relations in infant memory: Effects of memory load. *Journal of Experimental Child Psychology, 67*(1), 69–89.

Bloom, L. (1998). Language acquisition in its developmental context. In W. Damon (Editor-in-Chief) & D. Kuhn & R. Siegler (Vol. Eds.), *Handbook of child psychology: Vol. 2. Cognition, perception, and language* (5th ed., pp. 309–370). New York: Wiley.

Bloom, L. (2000). The intentionality model of word learning: How to learn a word, any word. In R. M. Golinkoff, K. Hirsh-Pasek, N. Akhtar, L. Bloom, G. Hollich, L. Smith, et al. (Eds.), *Becoming a word learner: A debate on lexical acquisition* (pp. 19–50). New York: Oxford University Press.

Bloom, L., & Tinker, E. (2001). The intentionality model of language acquisition. *Monographs of the Society for Research in Child Development, 66*(4).

Bloom, L., Tinker, E., & Margulis, C. (1993). The words children learn: Evidence against a noun bias in early vocabularies. *Cognitive Psychology, 8,* 431–450.

Bloom, P. (1994). *Language acquisition: Core readings.* Cambridge, MA: MIT Press.

Bloom, P. (2000). *How children learn the meanings of words.* Cambridge, MA: MIT Press.

Bloom, P. (2001). Precis of how children learn the meanings of words. *Behavioral and Brain Sciences, 24,* 1095–1103.

Booth, A. E., & Waxman, S. R. (2002a). Object names and object functions serve as cues to categories for infants. *Developmental Psychology, 38*(6), 948–957.

Booth, A. E., & Waxman, S. R. (2002b). Word learning is "smart": Evidence that conceptual information affects preschoolers' extension of novel words. *Cognition, 84*(1), B11–B22.

Booth, A. E., & Waxman, S. R. (2003). Mapping words to the world in infancy: On the evolution of expectations for count nouns and adjectives. *Journal of Cognition and Development, 4*(3), 357–381.

Bornstein, M. H. (1985a). Human infant color vision and color perception. *Infant Behavior and Development, 8*(1), 109–113.

Bornstein, M. H. (1985b). On the development of color naming in young children: Data and theory. *Brain and Language, 26*(1), 72–93.

Bornstein, M. H., Cote, L. R., Maital, S., Painter, K., Park, S.-Y., Pascual, L., et al. (2004). Cross-linguistic analysis of vocabulary in young children: Spanish, Dutch, French, Hebrew, Italian, Korean, and American English. *Child Development, 75*(4), 1115–1139.

Bornstein, M. H., Kessen, W., & Weiskopf, S. (1976). The categories of hue in infancy. *Science, 191*(4223), 201–202.

Bosch, L., & Sebastián-Gallés, N. (1997). Native-language recognition abilities in 4-month-old infants from monolingual and bilingual environments. *Cognition, 65,* 33–69.

Bowerman, M. (1982). Reorganizational processes in lexical and syntactic development. In E. Wanner & L. Gleitman (Eds.), *Language acquisition: The state of the art* (pp. 319–346). Cambridge, England: Cambridge University Press.

Bowerman, M., & Levinson, S. C. (Eds.). (2001). *Language acquisition and conceptual development.* Cambridge, England: Cambridge University Press.

Brent, M. R., & Cartwright, T. A. (1996). Distributional regularity and phonotactic constraints are useful for segmentation. *Cognition, 61*(1/2), 93–125.

Brooks, R., & Meltzoff, A. N. (2002). The importance of eyes: How infants interpret adult looking behavior. *Developmental Psychology, 38,* 958–966.

Brown, R. (1957). Linguistic determinism and the part of speech. *Journal of Abnormal and Social Psychology, 55,* 1–5.

Brown, R. (1958). *Words and things.* Glencoe, IL: Free Press.

Bunger, A., & Lidz, J. (2004, November). *Syntactic bootstrapping and the internal structure of causative events.* Paper presented at the Boston University Conference on Language Development, Boston, MA.

Burzio, L. (1986). *Italian syntax: A government-binding approach.* Dordrecht, The Netherlands: Reidel.

Camaioni, L., & Longobardi, E. (2001). Nouns versus verb emphasis in Italian mother-to-child speech. *Journal of Child Language, 28,* 773–785.

Campbell, A. L., & Namy, L. L. (2003). The role of social-referential context in verbal and nonverbal symbol learning. *Child Development, 74*(2), 549–563.

Carpenter, M., Akhtar, N., & Tomasello, M. (1998). Fourteen- through 18-month-old infants differentially imitate intentional and accidental actions. *Infant Behavior and Development, 21*(2), 315–330.

Casasola, M., & Cohen, L. B. (2000). Infants' association of linguistic labels with causal actions. *Developmental Psychology, 36*(2), 155–168.

Caselli, M. C., Bates, E., Casadio, P., Fenson, L., Sanderl, L., & Weir, J. (1995). A cross-linguistic study of early lexical development. *Cognitive Development, 10,* 159–199.

Chambers, K. E., Onishi, K. H., & Fisher, C. L. (2003). Infants learn phonotactic regularities from brief auditory experience. *Cognition, 87,* B69–B77.

Chierchia, G., & Mc-Connell-Ginet, S. (2000). *Meaning and grammar: An introduction to semantics* (2nd ed.). Cambridge, MA: MIT Press.

Childers, J. B., & Tomasello, M. (2002). Two-year-olds learn novel nouns, verbs, and conventional actions from massed or distributed exposures. *Developmental Psychology, 38*(6), 967–978.

Choi, S. (1998). Verbs in early lexical and syntactic development in Korean. *Linguistics, 36*(4), 755–780.

Choi, S. (2000). Caregiver input in English and Korean: Use of nouns and verbs in book-reading and toy-play contexts. *Journal of Child Language, 27,* 69–96.

Choi, S., & Gopnik, A. (1995). Early acquisition of verbs in Korean: A cross-linguistic study. *Journal of Child Language, 22*(3), 497–529.

Chomsky, N. (1959). A review of B. F. Skinner's verbal behavior. *Language, 35*(1), 26–58.

Chomsky, N. (1975). *Reflections on language.* New York: Pantheon.

Chomsky, N. (1980). *Rules and representations.* London: Basil Blackwell.

Christophe, A., Mehler, J., & Sebastián-Gallés, N. (2001). Perception of prosodic boundary correlates by newborn infants. *Infancy, 2*(3), 385–394.

Comrie, B. (1985). *Tense.* Cambridge, England: Cambridge University Press.

Crain, S. (1991). Language acquisition in the absence of experience. *Journal of Behavioral and Brain Sciences, 4,* 597–650.

Croft, W. (1991). *Syntactic categories and grammatical relations: The cognitive organization of information.* Chicago: University of Chicago Press.

Davis, H., & Matthewson, L. (1999). On the functional determination of lexical categories. *Revue Quebecoise de Linguistique, 27*(2), 27–67.

Demirdache, H., & Matthewson, L. (1996, October). *On the universality of syntactic categories.* Paper presented at the North East Linguistic Society 25, University of Pennsylvania, Philadelphia.

Diesendruck, G. (2003). Categories for names or names for categories: The interplay between domain-specific conceptual structure and the language. *Language and Cognitive Processes, 18*(5/6), 759–787.

Diesendruck, G., Gelman, S. A., & Lebowitz, K. (1998). Conceptual and linguistic biases in children's word learning. *Developmental Psychology, 34,* 823–839.

Diesendruck, G., Markson, L., Akhtar, N., & Reudor, A. (2004). Two-year-olds' sensitivity to speakers' intent: An alternative account of Samuelson and Smith. *Developmental Science, 7,* 33–41.

Diesendruck, G., & Shatz, M. (2001). Two-year-olds' recognition of hierarchies: Evidence from their interpretation of the semantic relation between object labels. *Cognitive Development, 16,* 577–594.

Dixon, R. M. W. (1982). *Where have all the adjectives gone?* Berlin, Germany: Mouton.

Dowty, D. (1979). *Word meaning and montague grammar: The semantics of verbs and times in generative semantics and Mon-*

*tague's PTQ (Proper Treatment of Quantification).* Dordrecht, The Netherlands: Reidel.

Echols, C., & Marti, C. N. (2004). The identification of words and their meaning: From perceptual biases to language-specific cues. In D. G. Hall & S. R. Waxman (Eds.), *Weaving a lexicon* (pp. 41–78). Cambridge, MA: MIT Press.

Fenson, L., Dale, P. S., Reznick, J. S., Bates, E., Thal, D. J., & Pethick, S. J. (1994). Variability in early communicative development. *Monographs of the Society for Research in Child Development, 59*(5), v–173.

Fernald, A. (1992). Human maternal vocalizations to infants as biologically relevant signals: An evolutionary perspective. In J. H. Barkow, L. Cosmides, & J. Tooby (Eds.), *The adapted mind: Evolutionary psychology and the generation of culture* (pp. 391–428). New York: Oxford University Press.

Fernald, A., & McRoberts, G. (1996). Prosodic bootstrapping: A critical analysis of the argument and the evidence. In J. L. Morgan & K. Demuth (Eds.), *Signal to syntax: Bootstrapping from speech to grammar in early acquisition* (pp. 365–388). Mahwah, NJ: Erlbaum.

Fernald, A., McRoberts, G. W., & Swingley, D. (2001a). Infants' developing competence in recognizing and understanding words in fluent speech. In J. Weissenborn & B. Hoehle (Eds.), *Approaches to bootstrapping: Phonological, lexical, syntactic, and neurophysiological aspects of early language acquisition* (pp. 97–123). Amsterdam: Benjamins.

Fernald, A., & Morikawa, H. (1993). Common themes and cultural variations in Japanese and American mothers' speech to infants. *Child Development, 64,* 637–656.

Fernald, A., Pinto, J. P., Swingley, D., Weinberg, A., & McRoberts, G. (1998). Rapid gains in speed of verbal processing by infants in the second year. *Psychological Science, 9,* 228–231.

Fernald, A., Swingley, D., & Pinto, J. P. (2001b). When half a word is enough: Infants can recognize spoken words using partial phonetic information. *Child Development, 72,* 1003–1015.

Fisher, C., Church, B. A., & Chambers, K. E. (2004). Learning to identify spoken words. In D. G. Hall & S. R. Waxman (Eds.), *Weaving a lexicon.* Cambridge, MA: MIT Press.

Fisher, C., & Gleitman, L. R. (2002). Language acquisition. In H. Pashler & R. Gallistel (Eds.), *Steven's handbook of experimental psychology: Vol. 3. Learning, motivation, and emotion* (3rd ed., pp. 445–496). New York: Wiley.

Fisher, C., Hall, G., Rakowitz, S., & Gleitman, L. (1994). When it is better to receive than to give: Syntactic and conceptual constraints on vocabulary growth. *Lingua, 92,* 333–376.

Fisher, C., & Tokura, H. (1996). Acoustic cues to grammatical structure in infant-directed speech: Cross-linguistic evidence. *Child Development, 67,* 3192–3218.

Forbes, J. N., & Poulin-Dubois, D. (1997). Representational change in young children's understanding of familiar verb meaning. *Journal of Child Language, 24,* 389–406.

Frank, R., & Kroch, A. (1995). Generalized transformations and the theory of grammar. *Studia Linguistica, 49,* 103–151.

Frawley, W. (1992). *Linguistic semantics.* Hillsdale, NJ: Erlbaum.

Friederici, A., & Wessels, J. (1993). Phonotactic knowledge of word boundaries and its use in infant speech perception. *Perception and Psychophysics, 54,* 287–295.

Fulkerson, A. L. (1997). *New words for new things: The relationship between novel labels and 12-month-olds' categorization of novel objects.* Unpublished manuscript.

Fulkerson, A. L., & Haaf, R. A. (2003). The influence of labels, non-labeling sounds, and source of auditory input on 9- and 15-month-olds' object categorization. *Infancy, 4,* 349–369.

Gasser, M., & Smith, L. B. (1998). Learning nouns and adjectives: A connectionist account. *Language and Cognitive Processes, 13,* 269–306.

Gathercole, V. C. M., & Min, H. (1997). Word meaning biases or language-specific effects? Evidence from English, Spanish, and Korean. *First Language, 17*(49), 31–56.

Gathercole, V. C. M., Thomas, E. M., & Evans, D. (2000). What's in a noun? Welsh-, English-, and Spanish-speaking children see it differently. *First Language, 20,* 55–90.

Gelman, R., & Williams, E. M. (1998). Enabling constraints for cognitive development and learning: A domain-specific epigenetic theory. In D. Kuhn & R. Siegler (Eds.), *Cognition, perception, and language* (5th ed., Vol. 2, pp. 575–630). New York: Wiley.

Gelman, S. A. (1996). Concepts and theories. In R. Gelman & T. Kit-Fong (Eds.), *Handbook of perception and cognition: Perceptual and cognitive development* (2nd ed., pp. 117–150). San Diego, CA: Academic Press.

Gelman, S. A., Coley, J. D., Rosengren, K. S., Hartman, E., & Pappas, A. (1998). Beyond labeling: The role of maternal input in the acquisition of richly structured categories. *Monographs of the Society for Research in Child Development, 63*(1), v–148.

Gelman, S. A., & Medin, D. L. (1993). What's so essential about essentialism? A different perspective on the interaction of perception, language, and conceptual knowledge. *Cognitive Development, 8*(2), 157–167.

Gelman, S. A., & Tardif, T. (1998). A cross-linguistic comparison of generic noun phrases in English and Mandarin. *Cognition, 66,* 215–248.

Gentner, D. (1982). Why nouns are learned before verbs: Linguistic relativity versus natural partitioning. In S. Kuczaj (Ed.), *Language development: Vol. 2. Language, thought, and culture* (pp. 301–334). Hillsdale, NJ: Erlbaum.

Gentner, D., & Boroditsky, L. (2001). Individuation, relativity, and early word learning. In M. Bowerman & S. Levinson (Eds.), *Language acquisition and conceptual development* (pp. 215–256). New York: Cambridge University Press.

Gentner, D., & Namy, L. L. (2004). The role of comparison in children's early word learning. In D. G. Hall & S. R. Waxman (Eds.), *Weaving a lexicon* (pp. 533–568). Cambridge, MA: MIT Press.

Gillette, J., Gleitman, H., Gleitman, L., & Lederer, A. (1999). Human simulations of vocabulary learning. *Cognition, 73*(2), 135–176.

Gleitman, L. (1990). The structural sources of verb meanings. *Language Acquisition: A Journal of Developmental Linguistics, 1*(1), 3–55.

Gleitman, L. R., Cassidy, K., Nappa, R., Papafragou, A., & Trueswell, J. C. (in press). Hard words. *Language Learning and Development, 1.*

Gogate, L., Walker-Andrews, A. S., & Bahrick, L. E. (2001). Intersensory origins of word comprehension: An ecological-dynamic systems view. *Developmental Science, 4,* 1–37.

Goldfield, B. A. (2000). Nouns before verbs in comprehension versus production: The view from pragmatics. *Journal of Child Language, 27,* 501–520.

Goldvarg-Steingold, E. G. (2003, April). *Global domains may be guiding acquisition of adjectives.* Paper presented at the Society for Research in Child Development Biennial Meeting, Tampa, FL.

Golinkoff, R. M., Hirsh-Pasek, K., Bloom, L., Smith, L. B., Woodward, A. L., Akhtar, N., et al. (2000). *Becoming a word learner: A debate on lexical acquisition.* New York: Oxford University Press.

Gómez, R. (2002). Variability and detection of invariant structure. *Psychological Science, 13,* 431–436.

Gómez, R. L., & Gerken, L. A. (1999). Artificial grammar learning by 1-year-olds leads to specific and abstract knowledge. *Cognition, 70,* 109–135.

Goodman, J. C., McDonough, L., & Brown, N. (1998). The role of semantic context and memory in the acquisition of novel nouns. *Child Development, 69,* 1330–1344.

Goodman, N. (1955). *Fact, fiction, and forecast.* Cambridge, MA: Harvard University Press.

Gopnik, A., & Choi, S. (1995). Names, relational words and cognitive development in English and Korean speakers: Nouns are not always learned before verbs. In M. Tomasello & W. Merriman (Eds.), *Beyond names for things: Young children's acquisition of verbs* (pp. 63–80). Hillsdale, NJ: Erlbaum.

Gopnik, A., Choi, S., & Baumberger, T. (1996). Cross-linguistic differences in early semantic and cognitive development. *Cognitive Development, 11*(2), 197–227.

Gopnik, A., & Nazzi, T. (2003). Word, kinds and causal powers: A theory perspective on early naming and categorization. In D. H. Rakison & L. M. Oakes (Eds.), *Early category and concept development: Making sense of the blooming, buzzing confusion* (pp. 303–329). New York: Oxford University Press.

Gopnik, A., & Sobel, D. M. (2000). Detecting blickets: How young children use information about novel causal powers in categorization and induction. *Child Development, 71*(5), 1205–1222.

Gopnik, A., Sobel, D. M., Schulz, L. E., & Glymour, C. (2001). Causal learning mechanisms in very young children: 2-, 3-, and 4-year-olds infer causal relations from patterns of variation and covariation. *Developmental Psychology, 37*(5), 620–629.

Graff, D. (2000). Shifting sands: An interest-relative theory of vagueness. *Philosophical Topics, 28*(1), 45–81.

Graham, S. A., Baker, R. K., & Poulin-Dubois, D. (1998). Infants' expectations about object label reference. *Canadian Journal of Experimental Psychology, 52*(3), 103–113.

Graham, S. A., Kilbreath, C. S., & Welder, A. N. (2004). 13-month-olds rely on shared labels and shape similarity for inductive inferences. *Child Development, 75,* 409–427.

Gropen, J., Pinker, S., Hollander, M., & Goldberg, R. (1991a). Affectedness and direct objects: The role of lexical semantics in the acquisition of verb argument structure. *Cognition, 41,* 153–195.

Gropen, J., Pinker, S., Hollander, M., & Goldberg, R. (1991b). Syntax and semantics in the acquisition of locative verbs. *Journal of Child Language, 18,* 115–151.

Guajardo, J. J., & Woodward, A. L. (2000, July). *Using habituation to index infants' understanding of pointing.* Paper presented at the 12th Biennial Meeting of the International Society for Infant Studies, Brighton, England.

Guasti, M. T. (2002). *Language acquisition: The growth of grammar.* Cambridge, MA: MIT Press.

Hale, K., & Keyser, S. J. (1993). On argument structure and the lexical expression of syntactic relations. In K. Hale & S. J. Keyser (Eds.), *The view from building 20: Essays in honor of Sylvain Bromberger* (pp. 53–108). Cambridge, MA: MIT Press.

Halff, H. M., Ortony, A., & Anderson, R. C. (1976). A context-sensitive representation of word meanings. *Memory and Cognition, 4,* 378–383.

Hall, D. G. (1991). Acquiring proper nouns for familiar and unfamiliar animate objects: 2-year-olds' word-learning biases. *Child Development, 62*(5), 1142–1154.

Hall, D. G. (1999). Semantics and the acquisition of proper names. In R. Jackendoff, P. Bloom, & K. Wynn (Eds.), *Language, logic, and concepts: Essays in memory of John Macnamara* (pp. 337–372). Cambridge, MA: MIT Press.

Hall, D. G., & Belanger, J. (2001). Young children's use of syntactic cues to learn proper names and count nouns. *Developmental Psychology, 37,* 298–307.

Hall, D. G., & Belanger, J. (in press). Young children's use of range of reference information in word learning. *Developmental Science.*

Hall, D. G., Burns, T., & Pawluski, J. (2003). Input and word learning: Caregivers' sensitivity to lexical category distinctions. *Journal of Child Language, 30,* 711–729.

Hall, D. G., & Lavin, T. A. (2004). The use and misuse of part-of-speech information in word learning: Implications for lexical development. In D. G. Hall & S. R. Waxman (Eds.), *Weaving a lexicon* (pp. 339–370). Cambridge, MA: MIT Press.

Hall, D. G., Quantz, D., & Persoage, K. (2000). Preschoolers' use of form class cues in word learning. *Developmental Psychology, 36,* 449–462.

Hall, D. G., & Waxman, S. R. (1993). Assumptions about word meaning: Individuation and basic-level kinds. *Child Development, 64*(5), 1550–1570.

Hall, D. G., & Waxman, S. R. (Eds.). (2004). *Weaving a lexicon.* Cambridge, MA: MIT Press.

Hall, D. G., Waxman, S. R., Bredart, S., & Nicolay, A.-C. (2003).Preschooler's use of form class cues to learn descriptive proper names. *Child Development, 74*(5), 1547–1560.

Hall, D. G., Waxman, S. R., & Hurwitz, W. M. (1993). How 2- and 4-year-old children interpret adjectives and count nouns. *Child Development, 64*(6), 1651–1664.

Harley, H., & Noyer, R. (1998, October). *Mixed nominalizations, short verb movement, and object shift in English.* Paper presented at the North East Linguistic Society 28. University of Toronto, Ontario, Canada.

Haryu, E., & Imai, M. (2002). Reorganizing the lexicon by learning a new word: Japanese children's inference of the meaning of a new word for a familiar artifact. *Child Development, 73,* 1378–1391.

Haspelmath, M. (1993). More on the typology of inchoative/causative verb alternations. In B. Comrie & M. Polinsky (Eds.), *Causatives and transitivity* (pp. 87–120). Amsterdam: Benjamins.

Heibeck, T. H., & Markman, E. M. (1987). Word learning in children: An examination of fast mapping. *Child Development, 58*(4), 1021–1034.

Heim, I., & Kratzer, A. (1998). *Semantics in generative grammar.* Malden, MA: Blackwell.

Hirsh-Pasek, K., Golinkoff, R. M., Hennon, E. A., & Maguire, M. J. (2004). Hybrid theories at the frontier of developmental psychology: The emergentist coalition model of word learning as a case in point. In D. G. Hall & S. R. Waxman (Eds.), *Weaving a lexicon* (pp. 173–204). Cambridge, MA: MIT Press.

Hoff, E. (2002). Causes and consequences of SES-related differences in parent-to-child speech. In M. Bornstein & R. Bradley

(Eds.), *Socioeconomic status, parenting, and child development* (pp. 147–160). Mahwah, NJ: Erlbaum.

Hoff, E., & Naigles, L. (2002). How children use input to acquire a lexicon. *Child Development, 73*(2), 418–433.

Hollich, G. J., Hirsh-Pasek, K., & Golinkoff, R. M. (Eds.). (2000). *Breaking the language barrier: Vol. 65. An emergentist coalition model for the origins of word learning.* Malden, MA: Blackwell.

Hollich, G., Jusczyk, P. W., & Luce, P. (2000, December). *Infant sensitivity to lexical neighborhoods during word learning.* Paper presented at the Meeting of the Acoustical Society of America, Newport Beach, CA.

Hopper, P., & Thompson, S. A. (1980). Transitivity in grammar and discourse. *Language, 56,* 251–299.

Huttenlocher, J. (1974). The origins of language comprehension. In R. L. Solso (Ed.), *Loyola Symposium: Theories in cognitive psychology* (pp. 331–368). Potomac, MD: Erlbaum.

Huttenlocher, J., Haight, W., Bryk, A., Seltzer, M., & Lyons, T. (1991). Early vocabulary growth: Relation to language input and gender. *Developmental Psychology, 27,* 236–248.

Huttenlocher, J., & Smiley, P. (1987). Early word meanings: The case of object names. *Cognitive Psychology, 19*(1), 63–89.

Huttenlocher, J., Vasilyeva, M., Cymerman, E., & Levine, S. (2002). Language input and child syntax. *Cognitive Psychology, 45*(3), 337–374.

Imai, M. (1999). Constraint on word learning constraints. *Japanese Psychological Research, 41,* 5–20.

Imai, M., & Gentner, D. (1997). A cross-linguistic study of early word meaning: Universal ontology and linguistic influence. *Cognition, 62*(2), 169–200.

Imai, M., & Haryu, E. (2001). Learning proper nouns and common nouns without clues from syntax. *Child Development, 72*(3), 787–802.

Imai, M., & Haryu, E. (2004). The nature of word-learning biases and their roles for lexical development: From a cross-linguistic perspective. In D. G. Hall & S. R. Waxman (Eds.), *Weaving a lexicon* (pp. 411–444). Cambridge, MA: MIT Press.

Jackendoff, R. (1990). *Semantic structures.* Cambridge, MA: MIT Press.

Jaswal, V. K., & Markman, E. M. (2001). Learning proper and common names in inferential versus obstensive contexts. *Child Development, 72*(3), 768–786.

Jaswal, V. K., & Markman, E. M. (2003). The relative strengths of indirect and direct word learning. *Developmental Psychology, 39,* 745–760.

Johnson, E. K., Jusczyk, P. W., Cutler, A., & Norris, D. (2003). Lexical viability constraints on speech segmentation by infants. *Cognitive Psychology, 46,* 31–63.

Jusczyk, P. (1997). *The discovery of spoken language.* Cambridge, MA: MIT Press.

Jusczyk, P., & Aslin, R. N. (1995). Infants' detection of the sound patterns of words in fluent speech. *Cognitive Psychology, 29*(1), 1–23.

Jusczyk, P. W., & Luce, P. A. (2002). Speech perception. In H. Pashler & S. Yantis (Eds.), *Steven's handbook of experimental psychology: Vol. 1. Sensation and perception* (3rd ed., pp. 493–536). New York: Wiley.

Kalish, C. W., & Gelman, S. A. (1992). On wooden pillows: Multiple classification and children's category-based inductions. *Child Development, 63*(6), 1536–1557.

Keil, F. C. (1994). The birth and nurturance of concepts by domains: The origins of concepts of living things. In L. A. Hirschfeld & S. A. Gelman (Eds.), *Mapping the mind: Domain specificity in cognition and culture* (pp. 234–254). New York: Cambridge University Press.

Keller, H. (1904). *The story of my life.* New York: Doubleday.

Kennedy, C. (1999). *Projecting the adjective: The syntax and semantics of gradability and comparison.* New York: Garland Press.

Kennedy, C., & McNally, L. (in press). Scale structure and the semantic typology of gradable predicates. *Language.*

Kester, E. (1994). Adjectival inflection and the licensing of "pro". *University of Maryland Working Papers in Linguistics, 2,* 91–109.

Kim, M., Landau, B., & Phillips, C. (1999, November). *Cross-linguistic differences in children's syntax for locative verbs.* Paper presented at the Boston University Conference on Language Acquisition, Boston.

Kim, M., McGregor, K. K., & Thompson, C. K. (2000). Early lexical development in English- and Korean-speaking children: Language-general and language-specific patterns. *Journal of Child Language, 27*(2), 225–254.

Klibanoff, R. S., & Waxman, S. R. (2000). Basic level object categories support the acquisition of novel adjectives: Evidence from preschool-aged children. *Child Development, 71*(3), 649–659.

Kuhl, P. K., Williams, K. A., Lacerda, F., Stevens, K. N., & Lindblom, B. (1992). Linguistic experience alters phonetic perception in infants by 6 months of age. *Science, 255,* 606–608.

Lakoff, G. (1987). *Women, fire, and dangerous things: What categories reveal about the mind.* Chicago: Chicago University Press.

Landau, B., & Gleitman, L. (1985). *Language and experience: Evidence from the blind child.* Cambridge, MA: Harvard University Press.

Lavin, T. A., Hall, D. G., & Waxman, S. R. (in press). East and west: A role for culture in the acquisition of nouns and verbs. In K. Hirsh-Pasek & R. M. Golinkoff (Eds.), *Action meets word: How children learn verbs.* New York: Oxford University Press.

Leslie, A. M., & Keeble, S. (1987). Do 6-month-old infants perceive causality? *Cognition, 25*(3), 265–288.

Levin, B., & Rappaport-Hovav, M. (1995). *Unaccusativity: At the syntax-lexical semantics interface* (Vol. 26). Cambridge, MA: MIT Press.

Lidz, J. (1998, November). *Constraints on the syntactic bootstrapping procedure for verb learning.* Paper presented at the Boston University Conference on Language Development, Boston.

Lidz, J., Gleitman, H., & Gleitman, L. (2003). Understanding how input matters: The footprint of universal grammar on verb learning. *Cognition, 87,* 151–178.

Lidz, J., Gleitman, H., & Gleitman, L. (2004). Kidz in the 'hood: Syntactic bootstrapping and the mental lexicon. In D. G. Hall & S. R. Waxman (Eds.), *Weaving a lexicon* (pp. 603–636). Cambridge, MA: MIT Press.

Lidz, J., Waxman, S., & Freedman, J. (2003). What infants know about syntax but couldn't have learned: Experimental evidence for syntactic structure at 18 months. *Cognition, 89,* B65–B73.

Liu, H. M., Kuhl, P. K., & Tsao, F. M. (2003). An association between mothers' speech clarity and infants' speech discrimination skills. *Developmental Science, 6,* F1–F10.

Locke, J. (1975). *An essay concerning human understanding.* Oxford, England: Clarendon Press. (Original work published 1690)

Lucy, J. A., & Gaskins, S. (2001). Grammatical categories and the development of classification preferences: A comparative approach. In M. Bowerman & S. C. Levinson (Eds.), *Language acquisition and conceptual development* (pp. 257–283). Cambridge, England: Cambridge University Press.

Macario, J. F. (1991). Young children's use of color and classification: Foods and canonically colored objects. *Cognitive Development, 6,* 17–46.

Macnamara, J. (1979). How do babies learn grammatical categories. In D. Sankoff (Ed.), *Linguistic variation: Models and methods* (pp. 257–283). New York: Academic Press.

Macnamara, J. (1982). *Names for things: A study of human learning.* Cambridge, MA: MIT Press.

Macnamara, J. (1986). Principles and parameters: A response to Chomsky. *New Ideas in Psychology, 4*(2), 215–222.

Macnamara, J. (1994). Logic and cognition. In J. Macnamara & G. E. Reyes (Eds.), *The logical foundations of cognition: Vol. 4. Vancouver studies in cognitive science* (pp. 11–34). New York: Oxford University Press.

MacWhinney, B. (2002). Language emergence. In P. Burmeister, T. Piske, & A. Rohde (Eds.), *An integrated view of language development: Papers in honor of Henning Wode* (pp. 17–42). Trier, Germany: Wissenshaftliche Verlag.

MacWhinney, B., & Snow, C. (1990). The child language data exchange system: An update. *Journal of Child Language, 17,* 457–472.

Mandel, D., Jusczyk, P. W., & Pisoni, D. (1995). Infants' recognition of the sound pattern of their own names. *Psychological Science, 6,* 314–317.

Manders, K., & Hall, D. G. (2002). Comparison, basic-level categories, and the teaching of adjectives. *Journal of Child Language, 29,* 923–937.

Mandler, J. M., & McDonough, L. (1998). Inductive inference in infancy. *Cognitive Psychology, 37,* 60–96.

Maratsos, M. (1998). The acquisition of grammar. In D. Kuhn & R. S. Siegler (Eds.), *Cognition, perception, and language* (5th ed., Vol. 2, pp. 421–466). New York: Wiley.

Maratsos, M. (2001). How fast does a child learn a word? *Behavioral and Brain Sciences, 24,* 1111–1112.

Marcus, G. F., Vijayan, S., Rao, S. B., & Vishton, P. M. (1999). Rule learning by 7-month-old infants. *Science, 283*(5398), 77–80.

Markman, E. M. (1989). *Categorization and naming in children: Problems of induction.* Cambridge, MA: MIT Press.

Markman, E. M., & Hutchinson, J. E. (1984). Children's sensitivity to constraints on word meaning: Taxonomic versus thematic relations. *Cognitive Psychology, 16*(1), 1–27.

Markman, E. M., & Jaswal, V. K. (2004). Acquiring and using a grammatical form class: Lessons from the proper-count distinction. In D. G. Hall & S. R. Waxman (Eds.), *Weaving a lexicon* (pp. 371–409). Cambridge, MA: MIT Press.

McCawley, J. (1968, April). *Lexical insertion in a transformational grammar without deep structure.* Paper presented at the Fourth Regional Meeting of the Chicago Linguistics Society, Chicago.

Medin, D. L., & Heit, E. (1999). Categorization. In D. E. Rumelhart & B. O. Martin (Eds.), *Handbook of cognition and perception* (pp. p. 99–143). San Diego, CA: Academic Press.

Medin, D. L., & Shoben, E. J. (1988). Context and structure in conceptual combination. *Cognitive Psychology, 20*(2), 158–190.

Mehler, J., Jusczyk, P. W., Lambertz, G., Halsted, N., Bertoncini, J., & Amiel-Tison, C. (1988). A precursor of language acquisition in young infants. *Cognition, 29,* 143–178.

Meltzoff, A. N. (2002). Elements of a developmental theory of imitation. In A. N. Meltzoff & W. Prinz (Eds.), *The imitative mind: Development, evolution, and brain bases* (pp. 19–41). Cambridge, England: Cambridge University Press.

Meltzoff, A. N., Gopnik, A., & Repacholi, B. M. (1999). Toddlers' understanding of intentions, desires and emotions: Explorations of the dark ages. In P. D. A. J. W. Zelazo (Ed.), *Developing theories of intention: Social understanding and self-control* (pp. 17–41). Mahwah, NJ: Erlbaum.

Mervis, C. B. (1987). Child-basic object categories and early lexical development. In U. Neisser (Ed.), *Emory Symposia in Cognition: Concepts and conceptual development: Vol. 1. Ecological and intellectual factors in categorization* (pp. 201–233). New York: Cambridge University Press.

Michotte, A., Thines, G., & Crabbe, G. (1991). Amodal completion of perceptual structures. In G. Thines, A. Costall, & G. Butterworth (Eds.), *Michotte's experimental phenomenology of perception* (pp. 140–167). Hillsdale, NJ: Erlbaum.

Mills, D. L., Coffey-Corina, S. A., & Neville, H. J. (1997). Language comprehension and cerebral specialization from 13–20 months. In D. Thal & J. Reilly (Eds.), *Developmental Neuropsychology, 13*(3), 397–446.

Mintz, T. H. (2003). Frequent frames as a cue for grammatical categories in child directed speech. *Cognition, 90*(1), 91–117.

Mintz, T. H., & Gleitman, L. R. (2002). Adjectives really do modify nouns: The incremental and restricted nature of early adjective acquisition. *Cognition, 84*(3), 267–293.

Mintz, T. H., Newport, E. L., & Bever, T. G. (2002). The distributional structure of grammatical categories in speech to young children. *Cognitive Science, 26*(4), 393–424.

Moltmann, F. (1997). *Parts and wholes in semantics.* New York: Oxford University Press.

Moore, C., Angelopoulos, M., & Bennett, P. (1999). Word learning in the context of referential and salience cues. *Developmental Psychology, 35*(1), 60–68.

Morgan, J. L., & Demuth, K. (Eds.). (1996). *Signal to syntax: Bootstrapping from speech to grammar in early acquisition.* Mahwah, NJ: Erlbaum.

Morgan, J. L., Shi, R., & Allopenna, P. (1996). Perceptual bases of rudimentary grammatical categories: Toward a broader conceptualization of bootstrapping. In J. L. Morgan & K. Demuth (Eds.), *Signal to syntax: Bootstrapping from speech to grammar in early acquisition* (pp. 263–283). Mahwah, NJ: Erlbaum.

Murphy, G. L. (2002). *The big book of concepts.* Cambridge, MA: MIT Press.

Murphy, G. L., & Medin, D. L. (1985). The role of theories in conceptual coherence. *Psychological Review, 92*(3), 289–316.

Naigles, L. (1990). Children use syntax to learn verb meanings. *Journal of Child Language, 17,* 357–374.

Naigles, L. (1996). The use of multiple frames in verb learning via syntactic bootstrapping. *Cognition, 58,* 221–251.

Naigles, L. (2002). Form is easy, meaning is hard: Resolving a paradox in early child language. *Cognition, 86*(2), 157–199.

Naigles, L., Fowler, A., & Helm, A. (1992). Developmental changes in the construction of verb meanings. *Cognitive Development, 7,* 403–427.

Naigles, L. R., & Hoff-Ginsberg, E. (1995). Input to verb learning: Evidence for the plausibility of syntactic bootstrapping. *Developmental Psychology, 31,* 827–837.

Naigles, L. R., & Hoff-Ginsberg, E. (1998). Why are some verbs learned before other verbs? Effects of input frequency and structure on children's early verb use. *Journal of Child Language, 25,* 95–120.

Naigles, L., & Kako, E. (1993). First contact in verb acquisition: Defining a role for syntax. *Child Development, 64,* 1665–1687.

Namy, L., Campbell, A., & Tomasello, M. (2004). Developmental change in the role of iconicity in symbol learning. *Journal of Cognition and Development, 5,* 37–56.

Namy, L. L., & Waxman, S. R. (1998). Words and gestures: Infants' interpretations of different forms of symbolic reference. *Child Development, 69*(2), 295–308.

Namy, L. L., & Waxman, S. R. (2000). Naming and exclaiming: Infants' sensitivity to naming contexts. *Journal of Cognition and Development, 1*(4), 405–428.

Namy, L. L., & Waxman, S. R. (2002). Patterns of spontaneous production of novel words and gestures within an experimental setting in children ages 1;6 and 2;2. *Journal of Child Language, 29*(4), 911–921.

Nazzi, T., & Gopnik, A. (2001). Linguistic and cognitive abilities in infancy: When does language become a tool for categorization? *Cognition, 80*(3), B11–B20.

Nazzi, T., Jusczyk, P. W., & Johnson, E. K. (2000). Language discrimination by English learning 5-month-olds: Effects of rhythm and familiarity. *Journal of Memory and Language, 43,* 1–19.

Needham, A., & Baillargeon, R. (1998). Effects of prior experience on 4$\frac{1}{2}$-month-old infants' object segregation.

Oakes, L. M., & Cohen, L. B. (1994). Infant causal perception. *Advances in Infancy Research, 9,* 1–57.

Ochs, E., & Schieffelin, B. (1984). Language acquisition and socialization. In R. Shweder & R. LeVine (Eds.), *Culture theory* (pp. 276–320). Cambridge, England: Cambridge University Press.

Papafragou, A., Massey, C., & Gleitman, L. (2002). Shake, rattle, 'n' roll: The representation of motion in language and cognition. *Cognition, 84,* 189–219.

Pechmann, T., & Deutsch, W. (1982). The development of verbal and nonverbal devices for reference. *Journal of Experimental Child Psychology, 34,* 330–341.

Pena, M., Maki, A., Kovacic, D., Dehaene-Lambertz, G., Koizumi, H., Bouquet, F., et al. (2003). Sounds and silence: An optical topography study of language recognition at birth. *Proceedings of the National Academy of Sciences, 100*(20), 11702–11705.

Perlmutter, D., & Postal, P. (1984). The 1-advancement exclusiveness law. In D. Perlmutter & C. Rosen (Eds.), *Studies in relational grammar* (Vol. 2, pp. 81–125).

Pinker, S. (1989). *Learnability and cognition.* Cambridge, MA: MIT Press.

Poulin-Dubois, D., Graham, S., & Sippola, L. (1995). Early lexical development: The contribution of parental labelling and infants' categorization abilities. *Journal of Child Language, 22*(2), 325–343.

Prasada, S. (1997, April). *Sentential and non-sentential cues to adjective meaning.* Paper presented at the Meeting of the Society for Research in Child Development, Washington, DC.

Prasada, S. (2000). Acquiring generic knowledge. *Trends in Cognitive Sciences, 4,* 66–72.

Prasada, S. (2003). Conceptual representation of animacy and its perceptual and linguistic reflections. *Developmental Science, 6,* 18–19.

Quine, W. V. O. (1960). *Word and object: An inquiry into the linguistic mechanisms of objective reference.* New York: Wiley.

Quinn, P. C., & Eimas, P. D. (2000). The emergence of category representations during infancy: Are separate perceptual and conceptual processes required? *Journal of Cognition and Development, 1,* 55–62.

Quinn, P. C., & Johnson, M. H. (2000). Global before basic category representations in connectionist networks and 2-month-old infants. *Infancy, 1,* 31–46.

Rappaport, M., & Levin, B. (1988). What to do with theta-roles. In W. Wilkins (Ed.), *Syntax and semantics 21: Thematic relations* (pp. 7–36). New York: Academic Press.

Redington, M., Chater, N., & Finch, S. (1998). Distributional information: A powerful cue for acquiring syntactic categories. *Cognitive Science, 22,* 425–469.

Rice, M. (1980). *Cognition to language: Categories, word meanings, and training.* Baltimore: University Park Press.

Rosch, E., Mervis, C., Gray, W., Johnson, D, & Boyes-Braem, P. (1976). Basic objects in natural categories. *Cognitive Psychology, 8*(3), 382–439.

Rotstein, C., & Winter, Y. (in press). Total adjectives versus partial adjectives: Scale structure and higher-order modifiers. *Natural Language Semantics.*

Saffran, J. R., Aslin, R. N., & Newport, E. L. (1996). Statistical learning by 8-month-old infants. *Science, 274*(5294), 1926–1928.

Samuelson, L. K. (2002). Statistical regularities in vocabulary guide language acquisition in connectionist models and 15- to 20-month-olds. *Developmental Psychology, 38*(6), 1016–1037.

Sandhofer, C., & Smith, L. B. (1999). Learning color words involves learning a system of mappings. *Developmental Psychology, 35,* 668–679.

Sandhofer, C., & Smith, L. B. (2001). Why children learn color and size words so differently: Evidence from adults' learning of artificial terms. *Journal of Experimental Psychology: General, 130*(4), 600–620.

Sandhofer, C. M., Smith, L. B., & Luo, J. (2000). Counting nouns and verbs in the input: Differential frequencies, different kinds of learning? *Journal of Child Language, 27*(3).

Schafer, G., & Plunkett, K. (1998). Rapid word learning by 15-month-olds under tightly controlled conditions. *Child Development, 69*(2), 309–320.

Schafer, G., Plunkett, K., & Harris, P. L. (1999). What's in a name? Lexical knowledge drives infants' visual preferences in the absence of referential input. *Developmental Science, 2*(2), 187–194.

Sera, M. D., Bales, D., & del Castillo Pintado, J. (1997). "Ser" helps speakers of Spanish identify real properties. *Child Development, 68,* 820–831.

Sera, M., Elieff, C., Forbes, J., Burch, M. C., Rodriguez, W., & Poulin-Dubois, D. (2002). When language affects cognition and when it does not: An analysis of grammatical gender and classification. *Journal of Experimental Psychology, 131*(3), 377–397.

Shady, M. (1996). *Infants' sensitivity to function morphemes.* New York: State University of New York at Buffalo.

Shady, M., & Gerken, L. (1999). Grammatical and caregiver cues in early sentence comprehension. *Journal of Child Language, 26*(1), 163–175.

Shatz, M., Behrend, D., Gelman, S. A., & Ebeling, K. S. (1996). Colour term knowledge in 2-year-olds: Evidence for early competence. *Journal of Child Language, 23,* 177–199.

Shi, R., & Werker, J. F. (2001). Six-month-old infants' preference for lexical over grammatical words. *Psychological Science, 12*(1), 70–75.

Shi, R., & Werker, J. F. (2003). The basis of preference for lexical words in 6-month-old infants. *Developmental Science, 6*(5), 484–488.

Shi, R., Werker, J. F., & Morgan, J. L. (1999). Newborn infants' sensitivity to perceptual cues to lexical and grammatical words. *Cognition, 72*(2), B11–B21.

Singh, L., Morgan, J., & White, K. (2004). Preference and processing: The role of speech affect in early spoken word recognition. *Journal of Memory and Language, 51*(2), 173–189.

Slobin, D. I. (1985). Cross-linguistic evidence for the language-making capacity. In D. I. Slobin (Ed.), *The cross-linguistic study of language acquisition: Vol. 2. Theoretical issues* (pp. 1157–1256). Hillsdale, NJ: Erlbaum.

Sloutsky, V. M., & Lo, Y.-F. (1999). How much does a shared name make things similar? Pt. 1. Linguistic labels and the development of similarity judgment. *Developmental Psychology, 35*(6), 1478–1492.

Smith, L. B. (1999). Children's noun learning: How general learning processes make specialized learning mechanisms. In B. MacWhinney (Ed.), *The emergence of language* (pp. 277–303). Mahwah, NJ: Erlbaum.

Smith, L. B., Colunga, E., & Yoshida, H. (in press). Making an ontology: Cross-linguistic evidence. In D. H. Rakison & L. M. Oakes (Eds.), *Early category and concept development: Making sense of the blooming, buzzing confusion*. New York: Oxford University Press.

Snedeker, J., & Gleitman, L. (2004). Why it is hard to label our concepts. In D. G. Hall & S. R. Waxman (Eds.), *Weaving a lexicon* (pp. 257–294). Cambridge, MA: MIT Press.

Snedeker, J., & Trueswell, J. (in press). The developing constraints on parsing decisions: The role of lexical-biases and referential scenes in child and adult sentence processing. *Cognitive Psychology*.

Snyder, W. (1995). *Language acquisition and language variation: The role of morphology.* Unpublished doctoral dissertation, Massachusetts Institute of Technology, MIT Working Papers in Linguistics, Cambridge, MA.

Snyder, W., Senghas, A., & Inman, K. (2001). Agreement morphology and the acquisition of noun-drop in Spanish. *Language Acquisition: A Journal of Developmental Linguistics, 9*(2), 157–173.

Soja, N. N. (1994). Young children's concept of color and its relation to the acquisition of color words. *Child Development, 65*, 918–937.

Spelke, E. S. (2003). Core knowledge. In N. Kanwisher & J. Duncan (Eds.), *Attention and performance: Vol. 20. Functional neuroimaging of visual cognition* (pp. 1233–1243). New York: Oxford University Press.

Spelke, E. S., & Newport, E. (1998). Nativism, empiricism, and the development of knowledge. In W. Damon (Editor-in-Chief) & R. Lerner (Ed.), *Handbook of child psychology: Vol. 1. Theoretical models of human development* (5th ed., pp. 275–285). New York: Wiley.

Swingley, D., & Aslin, R. N. (2000). Spoken word recognition and lexical representation in very young children. *Cognition, 76*, 147–166.

Swingley, D., & Fernald, A. (2002). Recognition of words referring to present and absent objects by 24-month-olds. *Journal of Memory and Language, 46*, 39–56.

Swingley, D., Pinto, J. P., & Fernald, A. (1999). Continuous processing in word recognition at 24 months. *Cognition, 71*(2), 73–108.

Talmy, L. (1985). Lexicalization patterns: Semantic structure in lexical forms. In T. Shopen (Ed.), *Language typology and syntactic description* (Vol. 3, pp. 249–291). San Diego, CA: Academic Press.

Tardif, T. (1996). Nouns are not always learned before verbs: Evidence from Mandarin speakers' early vocabularies. *Developmental Psychology, 32*(3), 492–504.

Tardif, T., Gelman, S. A., & Xu, F. (1999). Putting the "noun bias" in context: A comparison of Mandarin and English. *Child Development, 70*, 620–635.

Tardif, T., Shatz, M., & Naigles, L. (1997). Caregiver speech and children's use of nouns versus verbs: A comparison of English, Italian, and Mandarin. *Journal of Child Language, 24*(3), 535–565.

Tincoff, R., & Jusczyk, P. W. (1999). Some beginnings of word comprehension in 6-month-olds. *Psychological Science, 10*, 172–175.

Tomasello, M. (1992). *First verbs: A case study of early grammatical development*. Cambridge, England: Cambridge University Press.

Tomasello, M. (2003). *Constructing a language: A usage-based theory of language acquisition*. Cambridge, MA: Harvard University Press.

Tomasello, M., & Merriman, W. E. (Eds.). (1995). *Beyond names for things: Young children's acquisition of verbs*. Hillsdale, NJ: Erlbaum.

Tomasello, M., & Olguin, R. (1993). Twenty-three-month-old children have a grammatical category of noun. *Cognitive Development, 8*(4), 451–464.

Uchida, N., & Imai, M. (1999). Heuristics in learning classifiers: The acquisition of the classifier system and its implications for the nature of lexical acquisition. *Japanese Psychological Research, 4*(1), 50–69.

Van de Walle, G., Carey, S., & Prevor, M. (2000). Bases for object individuation in infancy: Evidence from manual search. *Journal of Cognition and Development, 1*, 249–280.

Vouloumanos, A., & Werker, J. F. (2004). Tuned to the signal: The privileged status of speech for young infants. *Developmental Science, 7*(3), 270–276.

Wagner, L., & Carey, S. (2003). Individuation of objects and events: A developmental study. *Cognition, 90*(2), 163–191.

Waxman, S. R. (1990). Linguistic biases and the establishment of conceptual hierarchies: Evidence from preschool children. *Cognitive Development, 5*(2), 123–150.

Waxman, S. R. (1999). Specifying the scope of 13-month-olds' expectations for novel words. *Cognition, 70*(3), B35–B50.

Waxman, S. R. (2002). Early word learning and conceptual development: Everything had a name, and each name gave birth to a new thought. In U. Goswami (Ed.), *Blackwell handbook of childhood cognitive development* (pp. 102–126). Oxford, England: Blackwell.

Waxman, S. R., & Booth, A. E. (2001). Seeing pink elephants: Fourteen-month-olds' interpretations of novel nouns and adjectives. *Cognitive Psychology, 43*, 217–242.

Waxman, S. R., & Booth, A. E. (2003). The origins and evolution of links between word learning and conceptual organization: New evidence from 11-month-olds. *Developmental Science, 6*(2), 130–137.

Waxman, S. R., & Braun, I. E. (2005). Consistent (but not variable) names as invitations to form object categories: New evidence from 12-month-old infants. *Cognition, 95*, B59-B68.

Waxman, S. R., & Gelman, R. (1986). Preschoolers' use of superordinate relations in classification and language. *Cognitive Development, 1*(2), 139–156.

Waxman, S. R., & Klibanoff, R. S. (2000). The role of comparison in the extension of novel adjectives. *Developmental Psychology, 36*(5), 571–581.

Waxman, S. R., & Markow, D. B. (1995). Words as invitations to form categories: Evidence from 12- to 13-month-old infants. *Cognitive Psychology, 29*(3), 257–302.

Waxman, S. R., & Markow, D. B. (1998). Object properties and object kind: Twenty-one-month-old infants' extension of novel adjectives. *Child Development, 69*(5), 1313–1329.

Waxman, S. R., & Senghas, A. (1992). Relations among word meanings in early lexical development. *Developmental Psychology, 28*(5), 862–873.

Waxman, S. R., Senghas, A., & Benveniste, S. (1997). A cross-linguistic examination of the noun-category bias: Its existence and specificity in French- and Spanish-speaking preschool-aged children. *Cognitive Psychology, 32*(3), 183–218.

Welder, A. N., & Graham, S. A. (2001). The influence of shape similarity and shared labels on infants' inductive inferences about nonobvious object properties. *Child Development, 72,* 1653–1673.

Werker, J. F., Cohen, L. B., Lloyd, V. L., Casasola, M., & Stager, C. L. (1998). Acquisition of word-object associations by 14-month-old infants. *Developmental Psychology, 34*(6), 1289–1309.

Werker, J. F., & Fennell, C. (2004). Listening to sounds versus listening to words: Early steps in word learning. In D. G. Hall & S. R. Waxman (Eds.), *Weaving a lexicon* (pp. 79–110). Cambridge, MA: MIT Press.

Werker, J. F., & Tees, R. C. (1984). Cross-language speech perception: Evidence for perceptual reorganization during the first year of life. *Infant Behavior and Development, 7,* 49–63.

Wetzer, H. (1992). "Nouny" and "verby" adjectivals: A typology of predicate adjectival constructions. In M. Kefer & J. van der Auwera (Eds.), *Meaning and grammar: Cross-linguistic perspectives* (pp. 223–262). Berlin, Germany: Mouton.

Wierzbicka, A. (1984). Apples are not a "kind of fruit": The semantics of human categorization. *American Ethnologist, 11,* 313–328.

Wilcox, T. (1999). Object individuation: Infants' use of shape, size, pattern, and color. *Cognition, 72*(2), 125–166.

Wilcox, T., & Baillargeon, R. (1998). Object individuation in infancy: The use of featural information in reasoning about occlusion events. *Cognitive Psychology, 37,* 97–155.

Wojdak, R. (2001, February). *An argument for category neutrality?* Paper presented at the West Coast Conference on Formal Linguistics 20, University of Southern California, Los Angeles.

Woodward, A. L. (2003). Infants' developing understanding of the link between looker and object. *Developmental Science, 6*(3), 297–311.

Woodward, A. L. (2004). Infants' use of action knowledge to get a grasp on words. In D. G. Hall & S. R. Waxman (Eds.), *Weaving a lexicon* (pp. 149–172). Cambridge, MA: MIT Press.

Woodward, A. L., & Guajardo, J. J. (2002). Infants' understanding of the point gesture as an object-directed action. *Cognitive Development, 17*(1), 1061–1084.

Woodward, A. L., & Hoyne, K. L. (1999). Infants' learning about words and sounds in relation to objects. *Child Development, 70,* 65–77.

Woodward, A. L., & Markman, E. M. (1998). Early word learning. In W. Damon (Editor-in-Chief) & D. Kuhn & R. Siegler (Vol. Eds.), *Handbook of child psychology: Vol. 2. Cognition, perception and language* (pp. 371–420). New York: Wiley.

Woodward, A. L., Markman, E. M., & Fitzsimmons, C. M. (1994). Rapid word learning in 13- and 18-month-olds. *Developmental Psychology, 30*(4), 553–566.

Xu, F. (1999). Object individuation and object identity in infancy: The role of spatiotemporal information, object property information, and language. *Acta Psychologica, 102,* 113–136.

Xu, F. (2002). The role of language in acquiring object kind concepts in infancy. *Cognition, 85,* 223–250.

Xu, F., & Carey, S. (1996). Infants' metaphysics: The case of numerical identity. *Cognitive Psychology, 30*(2), 111–153.

Xu, F., Carey, S., & Welch, J. (1999). Infants' ability to use object kind information for object individuation. *Cognition, 70*(2), 137–166.

Younger, B. A., & Cohen, L. B. (1986). Developmental change in infants' perception of correlations among attributes. *Child Development, 57*(3), 803–815.

# CHAPTER 8

# Nonverbal Communication: The Hand's Role in Talking and Thinking

SUSAN GOLDIN-MEADOW

SITUATING GESTURE WITHIN THE REALM OF
  NONVERBAL BEHAVIOR   337
THE DEVELOPMENT OF GESTURE IN
  LANGUAGE-LEARNING CHILDREN   338
Becoming a Gesture Producer   338
Becoming a Gesture Comprehender   342
The Gestural Input Children Receive   344
GESTURE WHEN LANGUAGE-LEARNING
  GOES AWRY   345
When Children *Cannot* Learn Language   345
When Children *Do Not* Learn Language   346
GESTURE IS A WINDOW ON THE MIND   349
Gesture Can Reveal Thoughts Not Found in Speech   349
Gesture Offers Unique Insight into a
  Child's Knowledge   350

WHAT MAKES PEOPLE GESTURE?   352
Does Having a Conversation Partner Make
  Us Gesture?   352
Does Thinking Hard Make Us Gesture?   354
WHAT FUNCTIONS DOES GESTURE SERVE?   355
Gesture's Role in Communication: Does Gesture Convey
  Information to the Listener?   355
Gesture's Role in Communication: Does Gesturing
  Influence How Listeners React to the Speaker?   358
Gesture's Role in Thinking: Does Gesturing Influence
  the Speaker's Cognition?   361
CONCLUSION   365
REFERENCES   365

A student waves her arm wildly when the teacher asks a question. Another shrinks into her seat while trying hard not to make eye contact. Both are letting the teacher know whether they want to answer the question. Such acts are part of what is called *nonverbal communication*. A wide-ranging array of behaviors count as nonverbal communication—the home and work environments we create; the distance we establish between ourselves and our listeners; whether we move our bodies, make eye contact, or raise our voices—all collaborate to send messages about us (Knapp, 1978). But these messages, while important in framing a conversation, are not the conversation itself. The student's extended arm or averted gaze does not constitute the answer to the teacher's question but simply reflects the student's attitude toward answering that question.

According to Argyle (1975), nonverbal behavior expresses emotion, conveys interpersonal attitudes, presents one's personality, and helps manage turn-taking, feedback, and attention (see also Wundt, 1900/1973). Argyle's characterization fits with most people's intuitions about the role nonverbal behavior plays in communication. But people do not instinctively realize that nonverbal behavior can reveal thoughts as well as feelings. The striking omission from Argyle's list is that it gives absolutely no role to nonverbal behavior in conveying a message—only a role in conveying the speaker's attitude toward the message or in regulating the interaction between speaker and listener.

This is the traditional view. Communication is divided into content-filled verbal and affect-filled nonverbal components. Kendon (1980) was among the first to challenge this view, arguing that at least one form of nonverbal behavior—gesture—cannot be separated from the content of the conversation. As McNeill (1992) has shown in his groundbreaking studies of gesture and

Preparation of this chapter was supported in part by grant R01 DC00491 from NIDCD and grants R01 HD47450 and P01 HD40605 from NICHD.

speech, the hand movements we produce as we talk are tightly intertwined with that talk in timing, meaning, and function. To ignore the information conveyed in these hand movements, these gestures, is to ignore part of the conversation.

This chapter is about children's use of gesture—how they produce gestures of their own and understand the gestures that others produce. I focus on gesture as opposed to other forms of nonverbal behavior precisely because gesture has the potential to reveal information about how speakers think, information that is not always evident in their words. I begin by situating gesture within behaviors traditionally identified as nonverbal. Because gesture is intimately tied to speech, I next chart its development not only in children whose language-learning follows a typical course but also in children for whom language-learning has gone awry. We will see that gesture is remarkably versatile and assumes a new form when circumstances require it to assume a new function. Gesture is shaped by the functions it serves, not by the modality in which it is produced, and thus has the potential to tell us about those functions. I then show that gesture fulfills its potential, providing insight into a child's thoughts and, at times, offering a unique picture of those thoughts. In the remainder of the chapter, I explore the mechanisms and functions of gesture: What makes us gesture, and what purpose does gesture serve? I focus, in particular, on whether gesture plays a role in communication and thinking and, as a result, has an impact on cognitive change—whether gesture goes beyond reflecting a child's thoughts to having a hand in shaping those thoughts.

## SITUATING GESTURE WITHIN THE REALM OF NONVERBAL BEHAVIOR

In 1969, Ekman and Friesen proposed a scheme for classifying nonverbal behavior and identified five types:

1. *Affect displays,* whose primary site is the face, convey the speaker's emotions, or at least those emotions that the speaker does not wish to mask (Ekman, Friesen, & Ellsworth, 1972).

2. *Regulators,* which typically involve head movements or slight changes in body position, maintain the give-and-take between speaker and listener and help pace the exchange.

3. *Adaptors* are fragments or reductions of previously learned adaptive hand movements that are maintained by habit; for example, smoothing the hair, pushing glasses up the nose even when they are perfectly positioned, holding or rubbing the chin. Adaptors are performed with little awareness and no intent to communicate.

4. *Emblems* are hand movements that can be produced with speech or without it. They have conventional forms and meanings; for example, the "thumbs up," the "okay," the "shush." Speakers are always aware of having produced an emblem and produce them to communicate with others, often to control their behavior.

5. *Illustrators* are hand movements that are directly tied to speech and often illustrate that speech; for example, a child says that the way to get to her classroom is to go upstairs and, at the same time, bounces her hand upward.

The focus in this chapter is on the last category—illustrators—called *gesticulation* by Kendon (1980) and plain old *gesture* by McNeill (1992), the term I use here. Gestures can mark the tempo of speech (beat gestures), point out referents of speech (deictic gestures), or exploit imagery to elaborate the contents of speech (iconic or metaphoric gestures). Gestures sit somewhere between adaptors and regulators at one end and emblems at the other end of the awareness spectrum. People are almost never aware of having produced an adaptor or regulator and are almost always aware of having produced an emblem. Because gestures are produced along with speech, they take on the intentionality of speech. Gestures are produced in the service of communication and, in this sense, are deliberate, but they rarely come under conscious control.

Gestures differ from emblems in other ways (McNeill, 1992). Gestures depend on speech; emblems do not. Indeed, emblems convey their meanings perfectly well when produced without any speech at all. In contrast, the meaning of a gesture is constructed in an ad hoc fashion in the context of the speech it accompanies. In the earlier example, the bouncing-upward gesture referred to taking the stairs. If that same movement were produced in the context of the sentence "production increases every year," it would refer instead to yearly incremental increases. In contrast, emblems have a constant form-meaning relation that does not depend on the vagaries of the conversation. The thumbs-up emblem means "things are good" independent of the particular sentence it accompanies and even if not accompanied by any sentence whatsoever. Emblems are also held to standards of form. Imagine making the thumbs-up sign with the pinky, instead of the thumb—it just doesn't work. But producing the bouncing-upward gesture with either a pointing hand, an open palm, or even an O-shaped hand seems perfectly acceptable. In this sense, emblems (but not gestures) are like words, with established forms that members of the community can understand and critique in the absence of context or explanation.

It is precisely because gestures are produced as part of an intentional communicative act (unlike adaptors) and are constructed at the moment of speaking (unlike emblems) that they are of interest to us. They participate in communication, yet they are not part of a codified system. As such, they are free to take on forms that speech cannot assume or, for a child who has not yet mastered a task, forms that the child cannot yet articulate in speech.

## THE DEVELOPMENT OF GESTURE IN LANGUAGE-LEARNING CHILDREN

Children typically use gesture before they are able to speak and become gesture producers early in development.

### Becoming a Gesture Producer

At a time in their development when children are limited in what they can say, gesture offers an additional avenue of expression, one that can extend the range of ideas that a child can express. And young children take advantage of this offer (Bates, 1976; Bates, Benigni, Bretherton, Camaioni, & Volterra, 1979; Petitto, 1988). In a group of 23 children learning Italian, all 23 used gestures at 12 months (only 21 used words; Camaioni, Caselli, Longobardi, & Volterra, 1991). Moreover, the children's gestural vocabularies, on average, were twice the size of their speech vocabularies (11 gestures versus 5.5 words). Strikingly, even deaf children acquiring sign language produce gestures, and at the earliest stages of language-learning, they produce more gestures than signs (Capirci, Montanari, & Volterra, 1998).

### *Gesture Is an Early Form of Communication*

Children typically begin to gesture between 8 and 12 months (Bates, 1976; Bates et al., 1979). They first use deictics, pointing or hold-up gestures, whose meaning is given entirely by the context and not by their form. For example, a child of 8 months may hold up an object to draw an adult's attention to it and then, several months later, point at the object. In addition to deictic gestures, children produce the conventional gestures common in their cultures such as nods and side-to-side headshakes. Finally, at about a year, children begin to produce iconic gestures, although the number tends to be small and variable across children (L. P. Acredolo & Goodwyn, 1988). A child might open and close her mouth to represent a fish or flap her hands to represent a bird (Iverson, Capirci, & Caselli, 1994). Children do not begin to produce beat or metaphoric gestures until much later in development (McNeill, 1992).

Deictic gestures and iconic gestures offer children a relatively accessible route into language. Pointing gestures precede spoken words by several months for some children. These early gestures are unlike nouns in that an adult must follow the pointing gesture's trajectory to its target to figure out which object the child means to indicate. In this sense, they more closely resemble the context-sensitive pronouns "this" or "that." Despite their reliance on the here-and-now, pointing gestures constitute an important early step in symbolic development and pave the way for learning spoken language. Iverson, Tencer, Lany, and Goldin-Meadow (2000; see also Iverson & Goldin-Meadow, 2005) observed five children at the earliest stages of language-learning, and calculated how many objects a child referred to using speech only ("ball"), gesture only (point at ball), or both ("ball" and point at ball, produced either at the same time or at separate moments). The children referred to a surprisingly small percentage of objects in speech only, and an even smaller percentage in both speech and gesture. Over half of the objects the children mentioned were referred to *only* in gesture. This pattern is consistent with the view that gesture serves a bootstrapping function in lexical development—it provides a way for the child to refer to objects in the environment without having to produce the appropriate verbal label.

Unlike a pointing gesture, the form of an iconic gesture captures aspects of its intended referent. Its meaning is consequently less dependent on context. These gestures therefore have the potential to function like words, and according to Goodwyn and Acredolo (1998, p. 70), they do just that. Children use their iconic gestures to label a wide range of objects (tractors, trees, rabbits, rain). They use them to describe how an object looks (big), how it feels (hot), and even whether it is there (all gone). They use them to request objects (bottle) and actions (out). However, there are differences across children in how often they use iconic gestures, and also in whether they use these gestures when they cannot yet use words. Goodwyn and Acredolo (1993) compared the ages at which children first used words and iconic gestures symbolically. They found that the onset of words occurred at the same time as the onset of gestures for only 13 of their 22 children. The other 9 began producing gestural symbols at least 1 month before they began producing verbal symbols; some began as much as 3 months before. Importantly, none of the children produced verbal symbols before they produced gestural symbols. In other words, none of the children found words easier than gestures, but some did find gestures easier than words.

Not surprisingly, children stop using symbolic gestures as words as they develop. They use fewer gestural symbols once they begin to combine words with other words, whether the language they are learning is English (L. P. Acredolo & Goodwyn, 1985, 1988) or Italian (Iverson et al., 1994). There appears to be a shift over developmental time: At the beginning, children seem to be willing to accept either gestural or verbal symbols, but as they develop, children begin to rely more heavily on verbal symbols. Namy and Waxman (1998) have found experimental support for this developmental shift. They tried to teach 18- and 26-month-old English-learning children novel words and novel gestures. Children at both ages learned the words, but only the *younger* children learned the gestures. The older children had already figured out that words, not gestures, carry the communicative burden in their worlds.

Children thus exploit the manual modality at the very earliest stages of language-learning. Perhaps they do so because the manual modality presents fewer burdens. It certainly seems easier to produce a pointing gesture to indicate a bird than to articulate the word *bird*. It may even be easier to generate a wing-flap motion than to say "bird." Children may need more motor control to make their mouths produce words than to make their hands produce gestures. Whatever the reason, gesture seems to provide an early route to first words, at least for some children.

Even though they treat gestures like words in some respects, children rarely combine their gestures with other gestures, and if they do, the phase tends to be short-lived (Goldin-Meadow & Morford, 1985). But children frequently combine their gestures with words, and they produce these word-plus-gesture combinations well before they combine words with words. Children's earliest gesture-speech combinations contain gestures that convey information redundant with the information conveyed in speech; for example, pointing at an object while naming it (de Laguna, 1927; Greenfield & Smith, 1976; Guillaume, 1927; Leopold, 1949). The onset of these gesture-speech combinations marks the beginning of gesture-speech integration in the young child's communications.

### Gesture Becomes Integrated with Speech during the One-Word Period

The proportion of a child's communications that contains gesture seems to remain relatively constant throughout the single-word period. What changes over this time period is the relationship gesture holds to speech. At the beginning of the one-word period, three properties characterize children's gestures:

1. Gesture is frequently produced alone; that is, without any vocalizations at all, either meaningless sounds or meaningful words.
2. On the rare occasions when gesture is produced with a vocalization, it is combined only with meaningless sounds and not with words; this omission is striking given that the child is able to produce meaningful words without gesture during this period.
3. The few gesture-plus-meaningless sound combinations that the child produces are not timed in an adult fashion; the sound does not occur on the stroke or the peak of the gesture (cf. Kendon, 1980; McNeill, 1992).

During the one-word period, two notable changes take place in the relationship between gesture and speech (Butcher & Goldin-Meadow, 2000). First, gesture-alone communications decrease, and in their place, the child begins to produce gesture-plus-meaningful-word combinations for the first time. Gesture and speech thus begin to have a *coherent semantic* relationship. Second, gesture becomes synchronized with speech, not only with the meaningful words that compose the novel combinations but also, importantly, with the old combinations that contain meaningless sounds (in other words, temporal synchronization applies to both meaningful and meaningless units and is therefore a separate phenomenon from semantic coherence). Thus, gesture and speech begin to have a *synchronous temporal* relationship. These two properties—semantic coherence and temporal synchrony—characterize the integrated gesture-speech system found in adults (McNeill, 1992) and appear to have their origins during the one-word period.

This moment of integration is the culmination of the increasingly tight relation that has been evolving between hand and mouth (Iverson & Thelen, 1999). Infants produce rhythmic manual behaviors prior to the onset of babbling. These manual behaviors entrain vocal activity so that the child's vocalizations begin to adopt the hand's rhythmical organization, thus assuming a pattern characteristic of reduplicated babble (Ejiri & Masataka, 2001). These rhythmic vocalizations become more frequent with manual behaviors and less frequent with nonmanual behaviors. Thus, by 9 to 12 months, when children produce their first words and gestures, the link between hand and mouth is strong, specific, and stable, and ready to be used for communication (Iverson & Fagan, 2004).

Moreover, the onset of gesture-speech integration sets the stage for a new type of gesture-speech combination—combinations in which gesture conveys different information from that conveyed in speech. For example, a child can gesture at an object while describing the action to be done on that object in speech (pointing to an apple and saying "give") or gesture at an object while describing the owner of that object in speech (pointing at a toy and saying "mine"; Goldin-Meadow & Morford, 1985; Greenfield & Smith, 1976; Masur, 1982, 1983; Morford & Goldin-Meadow, 1992; Zinober & Martlew, 1985). This type of gesture-speech combination allows a child to express two elements of a proposition (one in gesture and one in speech) at a time when the child is not yet able to express those elements in a single spoken utterance. Children begin to produce combinations in which gesture conveys different information from speech (point at box + "open") at the same time as, or later than—but *not* before—combinations in which gesture and speech convey the same information (point at box + "box"; Goldin-Meadow & Butcher, 2003; see also Iverson & Goldin-Meadow, 2005). Thus, combinations in which gesture and speech convey different information are not produced until *after* gesture and speech become synchronized, and thus appear to be a product of an integrated gesture-speech system (rather than a product of two systems functioning independently of one another).

In turn, combinations in which gesture and speech convey different information predict the onset of two-word combinations. Goldin-Meadow and Butcher (2003) found in six English-learning children that the correlation between the age of onset of this type of gesture-speech combination and the age of onset of two-

word combinations was high ($r_s = .90$) and reliable. The children who were first to produce combinations in which gesture and speech conveyed different information were also first to produce two-word combinations. Importantly, the correlation between gesture-speech combinations and two-word speech was specific to combinations in which gesture and speech conveyed *different* information. The correlation between the age of onset of combinations in which gesture and speech conveyed the *same* information and the age of onset of two-word combinations was low and unreliable. It is the *relation* that gesture holds to speech that matters, not merely gesture's presence (see also Ozcaliskan & Goldin-Meadow, 2005b).

In sum, once gesture and speech become integrated into a single system (as indexed by the onset of semantically coherent and temporally synchronized gesture-speech combinations), the stage is set for the child to use the two modalities to convey two distinct pieces of a single proposition within the same communicative act. Moreover, the ability to use gesture and speech to convey different semantic elements of a proposition is a harbinger of the child's next step—producing two elements within a single spoken utterance, that is, producing a simple sentence (see also Capirci et al., 1998; Goodwyn & Acredolo, 1998; Iverson & Goldin-Meadow, 2005).

### Gesture Continues to Play a Role in Communication over the Course of Development

The findings described thus far suggest that gesture and speech become part of a unified system sometime during the one-word period of language development. Over time, children become proficient users of their spoken language. At the same time, rather than dropping out of children's communicative repertoires, gesture continues to develop and play an important role in communication. Older children frequently use hand gestures as they speak (Jancovic, Devoe, & Wiener, 1975), gesturing when asked to narrate a story (e.g., McNeill, 1992), give directions (e.g., Iverson, 1999), or explain their reasoning on a series of problems (e.g., Church & Goldin-Meadow, 1986).

As in earlier stages, older children often use their hands to convey information that overlaps with the information conveyed in speech. Take, for example, a child participating in a Piagetian conservation task. The child is asked whether the amount of water changed when it was poured from a tall, skinny container into a short, wide container. The child says that the amount of water did change "cause that's down lower than that one," while first pointing at the relatively low water level in the short, wide container and then at the higher water level in the tall, skinny container (Figure 8.1a). The child is focusing on the height of the water in both speech and gesture and, in this sense, has produced a *gesture-speech match.*

However, children also use their gestures to introduce information that is not found in their speech. Consider another child who gave the same response in speech, "cause this one's lower than this one," but indicated the *widths* (not the heights) of the containers with her hands

(two C-shaped hands held around the relatively wide diameter of the short, wide container, followed by a left C-hand held around the narrower diameter of the tall, skinny container; Figure 8.1b). In this case, the child is focusing on the height of the water in speech, but on its width in gesture, and has produced a *gesture-speech mismatch* (Church & Goldin-Meadow, 1986).

As in the early stages of language development (see Goldin-Meadow & Butcher, 2003; Iverson & Goldin-Meadow, 2005), gesture and speech adhere to the principles of gesture-speech integration described by McNeill (1992), even when the two modalities convey different information. Consider the child in Figure 8.1b. She says

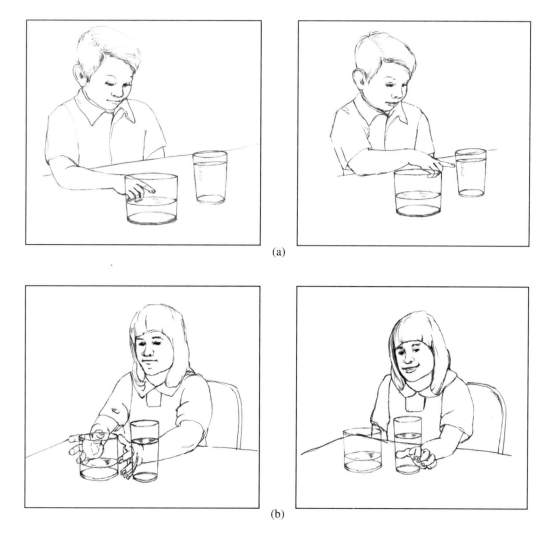

(a)

(b)

**Figure 8.1**   Examples of children explaining why they think the amount of water in the two containers is different. Both children say that the amount is different because the water level is lower in one container than the other. The child in the top two pictures (a) conveys the *same* information in gesture (he indicates the height of the water in each container)—he has produced a gesture-speech match. The child in the bottom two pictures (b) conveys *different* information in gesture (she indicates the width of each container)—she has produced a gesture-speech mismatch.

the amount is different because the water in the short wide container is "lower" while indicating the width of the container in her gestures. Although this child is expressing two different pieces of information in gesture and speech, she is nevertheless describing the same object in the two modalities. Moreover, the timing of the gesture-speech mismatch also reflects an integrated system. The child produces the width gesture as she says "this one's lower," thus synchronously expressing her two perspectives on the container.

Further evidence that gesture-speech mismatches reflect an integrated system comes from the fact that, as in the transition from one- to two-word speech, the relationship between gesture and speech is a harbinger of the child's next step. Children who produce many gesture-speech mismatches when explaining their solutions to a task appear to be in a transitional state with respect to that task—they are more likely to profit from instruction and make progress in the task than children who produce few mismatches. Thus, the child in Figure 8.1b is more likely to profit from instruction in conservation than the child in Figure 8.1a (Church & Goldin-Meadow, 1986). Gesture can serve as an index of readiness-to-learn not only for conservation but for other tasks as well: mathematical equivalence as it applies to addition (Perry, Church, & Goldin-Meadow, 1988), balancing a beam on a fulcrum (Pine, Lufkin, & Messer, 2004) and, as described, making the transition from one- to two-word speech (Goldin-Meadow & Butcher, 2003; Iverson & Goldin-Meadow, 2005). If gesture and speech were independent of one another, their mismatch would be a random event and, as a result, should have no cognitive consequence whatsoever. The fact that gesture-speech mismatch is a reliable index of a child's transitional status suggests that the two modalities are, in fact, *not* independent of one another (Goldin-Meadow, Alibali, & Church, 1993).

Importantly, gesture-speech mismatch is not limited to a particular age, nor to a particular task. Communications in which gesture conveys different information from speech have been found in a variety of tasks and over a large age range:

- Eighteen-month-old infants going through their vocabulary spurt (Gershkoff-Stowe & Smith, 1997).
- Preschoolers reasoning about a board game (M. A. Evans & Rubin, 1979) and learning to count (T. A. Graham, 1999).

- Elementary school-age children reasoning about conservation (Church & Goldin-Meadow, 1986) and mathematics (Perry et al., 1988) problems.
- Middle-schoolers reasoning about seasonal change (Crowder & Newman, 1993).
- Children and adults reasoning about moral dilemmas (Church, Schonert-Reichl, Goodman, Kelly, & Ayman-Nolley, 1995) and explaining how they solved Tower of Hanoi puzzles (Garber & Goldin-Meadow, 2002).
- Adolescents predicting when rods of different materials and thicknesses will bend (Stone et al., 1992).
- Adults reasoning about gears (Perry & Elder, 1997) and problems involving constant change (Alibali, Bassok, Olseth, Syc, & Goldin-Meadow, 1999).
- Adults describing pictures of landscapes, abstract art, buildings, people, machines, and so on (Morrel-Samuels & Krauss, 1992) and narrating cartoon stories (Beattie & Shovelton, 1999a; McNeill, 1992; Rauscher, Krauss, & Chen, 1996).

Moreover, communications in which gesture and speech convey different information can be frequent within an individual. At certain points in their acquisition of a task, children have been found to produce gesture-speech mismatches in over half of their explanations of that task (Church & Goldin-Meadow, 1986; Perry et al., 1988; Pine et al., 2004).

Thus, gesture continues to accompany speech throughout childhood (and adulthood), forming a complementary system across the two modalities. At all ages, gesture provides a medium for conveying ideas that is analog in nature. It is also a medium that is not codified and therefore not constrained by rules and standards of form, as is speech.

## Becoming a Gesture Comprehender

Not only do children produce gestures, they also receive them. There is good evidence that by 12 months, infants can understand the gestures that others produce (e.g., at 12 to 15 months, children look at a target to which an adult is pointing; Butterworth & Grover, 1988; Leung & Rheingold, 1981; Murphy & Messer, 1977). But do young children integrate the information they get from the pointing gesture with the message they are getting from speech?

Allen and Shatz (1983) asked 18-month-olds a series of questions with and without gesture, for example, "what says meow?" uttered while holding up a toy cat or cow. The children were more likely to provide some sort of response when the question was accompanied by a gesture. However, they were no more likely to give the *right* response, even when the gesture provided the correct hint (holding up the cat versus the cow). From these observations, we might guess that, for children of this age, gesture serves merely as an attention-getter, not as a source of information.

Macnamara (1977) presented children of roughly the same age with two gestures—the pointing gesture or the hold-out gesture (extending an object out to a child, as though offering it)—and varied the speech that went with each gesture. In this study, the children responded to the gesture, although nonverbally; they looked at the objects that were pointed at and reached for the objects that were held out. Moreover, when there was a conflict between the information conveyed in gesture and speech, the children went with gesture (e.g., if the pointed-at object was not the object named in the speech, the child looked at the object indicated by the gesture).

From these studies, we know that very young children notice gesture and can even respond appropriately to it. However, we do not know whether very young children can integrate information across gesture and speech. To find out, we need to present them with information that has the possibility of being integrated. Morford and Goldin-Meadow (1992) did just that in a study of children in the one-word stage. The children were given "sentences" composed of a word and a gesture, for example, "push" said while pointing at a ball; or "clock" said while producing a *give* gesture (flat hand, palm facing up, held at chest level). If the children could integrate information across gesture and speech, they ought to respond to the first sentence by pushing the ball and to the second by giving the clock. If not, they might throw the ball or push some other object in response to the first sentence, and shake the clock or give a different object in response to the second sentence. The children responded by pushing the ball and giving the clock; that is, their responses indicated that they were able to integrate information across gesture and speech. Moreover, they responded more accurately to the "push" + point at ball sentence than to the same information presented entirely in speech—"push ball." For these one-word children, gesture + word combinations were *easier*

to interpret than word + word combinations conveying the same information.

One more point deserves mention—the gesture + word combinations were more than the sum of their parts. Morford and Goldin-Meadow (1992) summed the number of times the children pushed the ball when presented with the word "push" alone (0.7) with the number of times the children pushed the ball when presented with the point at ball gesture on its own (1.0). That sum was significantly smaller than the number of times the children pushed the ball when presented with the "push" + point at ball combination (4.9). The children needed to experience *both* parts of the gesture + word combination to produce the correct response. Gesture and speech together evoked a different response from the child than either gesture alone or speech alone.

Kelly (2001) found the same effect in slightly older children responding to more sophisticated messages. The situation was as natural as possible. A child was brought into a room and the door was left ajar. In the speech only condition, the adult said, "it's going to get loud in here" and did nothing else. In the gesture only condition, the adult said nothing and pointed at the open door. In the gesture + speech condition, the adult said, "it's going to get loud in here" while pointing at the door. The adult wanted the child to get up and close the door, but he didn't indicate his wishes directly in either gesture or speech. The child had to make a pragmatic inference to respond to the adult's intended message.

Even 3-year-olds were able to make this inference, and were much more likely to do so when presented with gesture + speech than with either part alone. Kelly (2001) summed the proportion of times the 3-year-olds responded correctly (they closed the door) when presented with speech alone (.12) and when presented with gesture alone (.22). That sum (.34) was significantly smaller than the proportion of times the children responded correctly when presented with gesture + speech (.73). Interestingly, 4-year-olds did not show this emergent effect. Unlike younger children who needed both gesture and speech to infer the adult's intended meaning, 4-year-olds could make pragmatic inferences from either speech or gesture on its own. Thus, for 3-year-olds (but not 4-year-olds), gesture and speech must work together to codetermine meaning in sentences of this type. Gesture on its own is ambiguous in this context, and needs speech (or a knowing listener) to constrain its meaning. However, *speech* on its own is ambiguous in the same way, and needs gesture to constrain its meaning. It appears to be a two-way street.

Not surprisingly, older children are also able to get meaning from gesture. Moreover, they look like adults in their ability to do so (to be discussed later in this chapter). Kelly and Church (1997) asked 7- and 8-year-old children to watch the videotapes of other children participating in conservation tasks. In half of the examples, the children on the videotape produced gestures that conveyed the same information as their speech (gesture-speech matches; see Figure 8.1a); in the other half, they produced gestures that conveyed different information from their speech (gesture-speech mismatches; Figure 8.1b). The children in the study simply described to the experimenter how they thought the child in the videotape explained his or her answer. The child observers were able to glean substantive information from gesture, often picking up information that the child in the videotape had produced *only* in gesture. If asked to assess the child in Figure 8.1b, children would attribute knowledge of the widths of the containers to the child although she had expressed width only in her gestures.

Children thus get meaning from the gestures that accompany speech. Moreover, those meanings affect how much information is gleaned from the speech. Goldin-Meadow, Kim, and Singer (1999; see also Goldin-Meadow & Singer, 2003) found that teachers' gestures can affect the way their students interpret their *speech* in a math tutorial—at times gesture helps comprehension; at other times, gesture hurts it. Children were *more* likely to repeat a problem-solving strategy the teacher produced in speech when that speech was accompanied by a matching gesture than when it was accompanied by no gesture at all. Consequently, when gesture conveys the same message as speech, perhaps not surprisingly, it helps the child arrive at that message. Conversely, children were *less* likely to repeat a strategy the teacher produced in speech when that speech was accompanied by a mismatching gesture than when it was accompanied by no gesture at all. When gesture conveys a different message from speech, it may detract from the child's ability to arrive at the message presented in speech.

### The Gestural Input Children Receive

Very little is known about the gestures that children receive as input during development. Bekken (1989) observed mothers interacting with their 18-month-old daughters in an everyday play situation and examined the gestures that those mothers produced when talking to their children. She found that mothers gestured less frequently overall talking to a child compared with talking to an adult, but produced proportionately more simple pointing gestures. Shatz (1982) similarly found that, when talking to young language-learning children, adults produce a small number of relatively simple gestures (pointing gestures rather than metaphoric and beat gestures).

Iverson, Capirci, Longobardi, and Caselli (1999) observed Italian mothers interacting with their 16- to 20-month-old children, and found that the mothers gestured less than their children did. However, when the mothers did gesture, their gestures co-occurred with speech, were conceptually simple (pointing or conventional gestures), referred to the immediate context, and were used to reinforce the message conveyed in speech. In other words, the mothers' gestures took on a simplified form reminiscent of the simplified "motherese" they used in speech. In addition, the mothers varied widely in their overall production of gesture and speech, some talking and gesturing quite a bit and others less so. And those differences were relatively stable over time despite changes in the children's use of gesture and speech (see Ozcaliskan & Goldin-Meadow, 2005a).

Namy, Acredolo and Goodwyn (2000) found that the number of gestures parents produced during a book-reading task with their 15-month-old children was highly correlated with the number of gestures the children themselves produced. L. P. Acredolo and Goodwyn (1985, 1988; Goodwyn & Acredolo, 1993) found that the majority of gestures acquired by infants are derived from gestural or motor routines that parents engage in with them, either deliberately (e.g., the itsy-bitsy spider song which is routinely accompanied by a finger gesture depicting a spider crawling motion) or unwittingly (e.g., sniffing a flower). In a cross-cultural analysis, Goldin-Meadow and Saltzman (2000) found that Chinese mothers gestured significantly more when talking to their orally trained deaf children (and to their hearing children) than did American mothers. In turn, the Chinese deaf children produced more gestures than the American deaf children (Wang, Mylander, & Goldin-Meadow, 1993).

Moreover, evidence from experimental situations suggests that the gestures adults produce are not just correlated with child gesture but can have an impact on child language-learning. Children are significantly more likely to learn a novel word if it is presented with gesture than without it (Ellis Weismer, & Hesketh, 1993). When parents are asked to teach their children in the one-word stage gestures for objects and actions, children not only learn the gestures, but increase their verbal vocabularies as well (L. P. Acredolo, Goodwyn, Horrobin, & Emmons, 1999; Goodwyn, Acredolo, & Brown, 2000), suggesting that, at least at this stage, appropriately used gesture can facilitate word learning.

The gestures that parents produce seem to have an impact on how often children gesture and may even influence the ease with which children learn new words. However, parental gesture cannot be essential for either development. Children who are blind from birth not only are capable language-learners (Andersen, Dunlea, & Kekelis, 1984, 1993; Dunlea, 1989; Dunlea & Andersen, 1992; Landau & Gleitman, 1985; Iverson et al., 2000), but also gesture when they talk even though they have never seen anyone gesture. On certain tasks, congenitally blind children produce gestures at the same rate and in the same distribution as sighted children (Iverson & Goldin-Meadow, 1997, 1998). Children do not have to see gesture in order to use it.

## GESTURE WHEN LANGUAGE-LEARNING GOES AWRY

Some children cannot easily learn the spoken language that surrounds them and end up being language-delayed. Other children, although potentially able to learn language, are deprived of a usable model for language; for example, deaf children who cannot learn to speak and are not exposed to sign. The question we address in this section is whether children who cannot and children who do not learn language turn to gesture.

### When Children *Cannot* Learn Language

Thal, Tobias, and Morrison (1991) observed a group of children in the one-word stage of language acquisition who were in the lowest 10% for their age group in terms of size of productive vocabulary. They characterized the children's verbal and gestural skills at the initial observation session when the children ranged in age from 18 to 29 months, and then observed each child again, 1 year later. They found that some of the children were no longer delayed at the 1-year follow-up; they had caught

up to their peers. The interesting point about these so-called late bloomers is that they had actually shown signs of promise a year earlier, and they showed this promise in gesture. The late bloomers had performed significantly better on a series of gesture tests taken during the initial observation session than did the children who, a year later, were still delayed. Indeed, the late bloomers' gesture performance was no different from normally developing peers. Thus, children whose language development was delayed but whose gestural development was not had a better prognosis than children who were delayed in both language and gesture. At the least, gesture seems to reflect skills that can help children recover from language delay—it may even serve as one of those skills.

However, gesture may not be at the forefront for all moments of language development and for all learners. Iverson, Longobardi, and Caselli (2003) observed five children with Down syndrome (mean age 48 months) and matched them on language level, essentially vocabulary size, with five typically developing children (mean age 18 months). The typically developing children showed the pattern found by Goldin-Meadow and Butcher (2003): a large number of combinations in which gesture conveys information that is different from the information conveyed in speech, the gesture + speech combination that heralds the onset of two-word speech. However, the children with Down syndrome did not show this pattern. Thus, at this particular stage of development, the Down syndrome children did not display a gestural advantage, suggesting that they were not yet ready to produce two-word utterances.

What happens to children whose language continues to be delayed at later stages of development? Some children fail to acquire age-appropriate language skills, yet they seem to have no other identifiable problems (no emotional, neurological, visual, hearing, or intellectual impairments). Children who meet these criteria are diagnosed as having Specific Language Impairment (SLI). J. L. Evans, Alibali, and McNeil (2001) studied a group of SLI children ranging in age from 7 to 9.5 years. They asked each child to participate in a series of Piagetian conservation tasks, and compared their performance with a group of normally developing children who were matched to the SLI children on number of correct judgments on the tasks. The task-matched normally developing children turned out to be somewhat younger (7 to 8) than the children with SLI (7 to 9.5).

The question that J. L. Evans and her colleagues (2001) asked was whether the children with SLI would turn to gesture to alleviate the difficulties they had with spoken language. They found that the SLI children did *not* use gesture more often than the task-matched children without SLI. However, the children with SLI were far more likely than the task-matched children to express information in their explanations that could *only* be found in gesture. Thus, when given a water conservation task, an SLI child might behave like the child in Figure 8.1b, indicating the height of the container in words but its width in gesture. If we consider information encoded in *both* gesture and speech, the child in Figure 8.1b has expressed the essential components of a conserving explanation—the tall container is not only taller than the short container but it is also thinner (the two dimensions can compensate for each other). When J. L. Evans and colleagues coded gesture and speech together, the children with SLI ended up producing significantly more conserving explanations than the task-matched children without SLI. It may not be surprising that the children with SLI knew more about conservation than their task-matched peers—they were older. However, all the extra knowledge that the SLI children had was in gesture. The children seemed to be using gesture as a way around their difficulties with speech.

Throughout development, speakers seem to be able to use gesture to detour around whatever roadblocks prevent them from expressing their ideas in words. These detours may not always be obvious to the ordinary listener, to the researcher, or even to the clinician. They may reside, not in how much a speaker gestures, but in the type of information the speaker conveys in those gestures. The gestures the SLI children produced did not form a substitute system replacing speech. Rather, the children's gestures seemed no different from the gestures that any speaker produces along with talk. The children with SLI appear to be exploiting the gesture-speech system that all speakers employ, and using it to work around their language difficulties.

## When Children *Do Not* Learn Language

We turn next to a situation in which children do not learn a spoken language, not because they are unable to acquire language, but because they unable to hear. It turns out to be extremely difficult for deaf children with profound hearing losses to acquire spoken language. But if these children are exposed to sign language, they learn that language as naturally and effortlessly as hearing children learn spoken language (Lillo-Martin, 1999; Newport & Meier, 1985). However, most deaf children are not born to deaf parents who could provide them with input from a sign language from birth. Rather, 90% of deaf children are born to hearing parents (Hoffmeister & Wilbur, 1980). These parents typically do not know sign language and would prefer that their deaf children learn the spoken language that they and their relatives speak. As a result, many profoundly deaf children of hearing parents are sent to oral schools for the deaf—schools that focus on developing a deaf child's oral potential, using visual and kinesthetic cues and eschewing sign language to do so. Most profoundly deaf children do not achieve the proficiency in spoken language that hearing children do. Even with intensive instruction, deaf children's acquisition of speech is markedly delayed when compared either with the acquisition of speech by hearing children of hearing parents, or with the acquisition of sign by deaf children of deaf parents. By age 5 or 6, and despite intensive early training programs, the average profoundly deaf child has only a very reduced oral linguistic capacity (Conrad, 1979; Mayberry, 1992; K. Meadow, 1968).

The question we address is whether deaf children who are unable to learn spoken language and have not yet been exposed to sign language turn to gesture to communicate. If so, do the children use gestures in the same way that the hearing speakers who surround them do (as though they were accompanying speech), or do they refashion their gestures into a linguistic system reminiscent of the sign languages of deaf communities?

It turns out that deaf children who are orally trained often communicate using their hands (Fant, 1972; Lenneberg, 1964; Mohay, 1982; Moores, 1974; Tervoort, 1961). These hand movements even have a name—"home signs." It may not be all that surprising that deaf children exploit the manual modality for communication—after all, it is the only modality that is accessible to them, and they are likely to see gesture used in communicative contexts when their hearing parents talk to them. What is surprising, however, is that the deaf children's gestures are structured in language-like ways (Goldin-Meadow, 2003b). Like hearing children at the earliest stages of language-learning, deaf children who have not yet been exposed to sign language use both pointing gestures and iconic gestures to communicate. The difference between deaf and hearing children is that, as they get older, the deaf children's gestures blossom—they begin to take on the *functions* and the *forms* that are typically assumed by conventional language, spoken or signed.

## Home Signs Resemble Language in Function and Form

Like hearing children learning spoken languages, the deaf children of hearing parents request objects and actions from others, but they do so using gesture. For example, one child pointed at a nail and gestured "hammer" to ask his mother to hammer the nail. Moreover, and again like hearing children, these deaf children comment on the actions and attributes of objects and people in the room. A deaf child gestured "march" and then pointed at a wind-up toy soldier to comment on the fact that the soldier was, at that very moment, marching.

Among language's most important functions is making reference to objects and events that are not perceptible to either the speaker or the listener—displaced reference (cf. Hockett, 1960). Displacement allows us to describe a lost hat, to complain about a friend's slight, and to ask advice on college applications. Just like hearing children learning spoken languages, the deaf children communicate about nonpresent objects and events (Butcher, Mylander, & Goldin-Meadow, 1991; Morford & Goldin-Meadow, 1997). One deaf child produced the following string of gesture sentences to indicate that the family was going to move a chair downstairs in preparation for setting up a cardboard Christmas chimney: He pointed at the chair and then gestured "move-away." He pointed at the chair again and pointed downstairs where the chair was going to be moved. He gestured "chimney," "move-away" (produced in the direction of the chair) "move-here" (produced in the direction of the cardboard chimney). The deaf children also use their gestures to tell stories (Phillips, Goldin-Meadow, & Miller, 2001) and can even use them to serve some of language's more exotic functions—to talk to themselves (Goldin-Meadow, 1993) or to comment on their own and others' gestures (Singleton, Morford, & Goldin-Meadow, 1993).

In addition to assuming the functions of language, the deaf children's gestures assume its forms. One of the biggest differences between the deaf children's gestures and those used by hearing children is that the deaf children often combine their gestures into strings that have many of the properties of sentences. The deaf children even combine their gestures into sentences that convey more than one proposition; they produce complex gesture sentences. A child produced the following gesture

sentence to indicate that he would clap the bubble (proposition 1) after his mother twisted open the bubble jar (proposition 2) and blew it (proposition 3): He gestured "clap," pointed at himself, gestured "twist" then "blow," and pointed at his mother.

Moreover, the deaf children's gesture combinations are structured at underlying levels just like hearing children's early sentences (Goldin-Meadow, 1985). For example, the framework underlying a gesture sentence about giving, in addition to the predicate *give*, contains three arguments—the *giver* (actor), the *given* (patient), and the *givee* (recipient). In contrast, the framework underlying a sentence about eating, in addition to the predicate *eat*, contains two arguments—the *eater* (actor) and the *eaten* (patient). These underlying frameworks influence how likely it is that a deaf child will produce a gesture for a particular argument (in fact, the likelihood with which gestures are produced provides evidence for the underlying frameworks, Goldin-Meadow, 1985).

The deaf children's gesture combinations are also structured at surface levels, containing many of the devices to mark "who does what to whom" that are found in the early sentences of hearing children (Goldin-Meadow, Butcher, Mylander, & Dodge, 1994; Goldin-Meadow & Mylander, 1984, 1998). The deaf children indicate objects that play different thematic roles using three devices:

1. Preferentially producing (as opposed to omitting) gestures for objects playing particular roles (e.g., pointing at the drum, the patient, as opposed to the drummer, the actor).
2. Placing gestures for objects playing particular roles in set positions in a gesture sentence (e.g., producing the gesture for the patient, "drum," before the gesture for the act, "beat").
3. Displacing verb gestures toward objects playing particular roles (e.g., producing the "beat" gesture near the patient, drum).

The deaf children's gesture combinations therefore adhere to rules of syntax, albeit simple ones. On this basis, the children's gesture combinations warrant the label "sentence"—they thus resemble hearing children's *words*, not their gestures.

The deaf children's gestures are distinct from hearing children's gestures in having a set of elements (gestures) that combine systematically to form novel larger units (sentences). What further distinguishes the deaf children's gestures is that this combinatorial feature is found at yet another level—the gestures that combine to form sentences are themselves composed of parts (morphemes). Each gesture in a deaf child's repertoire is composed of a handshape component (e.g., an O-handshape representing the roundness of a penny) and a motion component (e.g., a short arc motion representing a putting-down action). The meaning of the gesture as a whole is a combination of the meanings of its parts ("round-put-down"; Goldin-Meadow, Mylander, & Butcher, 1995). In contrast, the gestures produced by hearing speakers (including hearing children and the children's own hearing parents) are composed of sloppy handshapes that do not map neatly onto categories of meanings, combined with motions that also do not map neatly onto categories of meanings (Goldin-Meadow et al., 1995; Goldin-Meadow, Mylander, & Franklin, 2005; Singleton, Goldin-Meadow, & Morford, 1993).

A final characteristic of the deaf children's gestures distinguishes them from hearing children's gestures— gestures serving nounlike functions are different in form from gestures serving verblike functions (Goldin-Meadow et al., 1994). For example, when a deaf child uses a "twist" gesture as a verb in a sentence meaning "twist-open the jar," he is likely to produce the gesture (a) without abbreviation (with several rotations rather than one), (b) with inflection (the gesture is directed toward a relevant object, in this case, the jar), and (c) *after* a point at the jar. In contrast, when the child uses the twist gesture as a noun in a sentence meaning "that's a twistable object, a jar," he is likely to produce it (a) with abbreviation (with one rotation rather than several), (b) without inflection (in neutral space rather than directed at an object), and (c) *before* the point at the jar.

The deaf children's gestures thus resemble conventional languages, both signed and spoken, in having combinatorial regularities at both the sentence and word levels, and having a noun-verb distinction. The children have invented gesture systems that contain many of the basic properties found in all natural languages. The deaf children's gesture systems, however, are not full-blown languages, and for good reason. The children are inventing their gesture systems on their own without a community of communication partners. When home-sign children are brought together into a community (as they were in Nicaragua after the first school for the deaf was opened in the late 1970s), their sign systems begin to co-

here into a recognized and shared language. That language becomes increasingly complex, particularly after a new generation of deaf children learns the system as a native language (Kegl, Senghas, & Coppola, 1999; Senghas, 1995, 2000; Senghas, Coppola, Newport, & Supalla, 1997). The manual modality can take on linguistic properties, even in the hands of a young child not yet exposed to a conventional language model. But it grows into a full-blown language only with the support of a community that can transmit the system to the next generation.

### The Deaf Children's Gestures Do Not Look Like Their Hearing Parents' Gestures

The deaf children described in the preceding section had not been exposed to a conventional sign language and thus could not have fashioned their gesture systems after such a model. They were, however, exposed to the gestures that their hearing parents used when they talked to them. These parents were committed to teaching their children English and therefore talked to them as often as they could. And when they talked, they gestured. The parents' gestures might have displayed the language-like properties found in their children's gestures. It turns out, however, that they did not (Goldin-Meadow et al., 1994, 1995, 2005; Goldin-Meadow & Mylander, 1983, 1984): The parents' gestures looked just like any hearing speaker's gestures.

Why didn't the hearing parents display language-like properties in their gestures? In a sense, the deaf children's hearing parents did not have the option of displaying these properties in their gestures simply because they produced all their gestures with talk. Their gestures formed a single system with the speech they accompanied and had to fit, both temporally and semantically, with that speech—they were not free to take on language-like properties. In contrast, the deaf children had no such constraints on their gestures. They had essentially no productive speech and thus always produced gesture on its own, without talk. Moreover, because gesture was the only means of communication open to these children, it had to take on the full burden of communication. The result was language-like structure. The deaf children may (or may not) have used their hearing parents' gestures as a starting point. However, it is very clear that the children went well beyond that point. They transformed the speech-accompanying gestures they saw into a system that looks very much like language.

We are now in a position to appreciate just how versatile the manual modality is. It can take on linguistic properties when called on to do so, as in the deaf children (and, of course in conventional sign languages). But it can also assume a nonsegmented global form when it accompanies speech, as in the deaf children's hearing parents (and all other hearing speakers). This versatility is important because it tells us that the form gesture assumes is *not* entirely determined by the manual modality. Quite the contrary, it seems to be determined by the functions gesture serves, and thus has the potential to inform us about those functions. As described in the following section, speech-accompanying gestures can provide insight into how the mind works.

## GESTURE IS A WINDOW ON THE MIND

The gestures that speakers produce along with their talk are symbolic acts that convey meaning. It is easy to overlook the symbolic nature of gesture simply because its encoding is iconic. A gesture often looks like what it represents (e.g., a twisting motion in the air resembles the action used to open a jar), but the gesture is no more the actual act of twisting than is the word "open." Because gesture can convey substantive information, it can provide insight into a speaker's mental representation (Kendon, 1980; McNeill, 1985, 1987, 1992).

### Gesture Can Reveal Thoughts Not Found in Speech

Gesture encodes meaning differently from speech. Gesture conveys meaning globally, relying on visual and mimetic imagery. Speech conveys meaning discretely, relying on codified words and grammatical devices. Because gesture and speech employ such different forms of representation, it is difficult for the two modalities to contribute identical information to a message. Indeed, even deictic pointing gestures are not completely redundant with speech. When a child utters "chair" while pointing at the chair, the word labels and thus classifies (but doesn't locate) the object. The point, in contrast, indicates where the object is but not what it is. Word and gesture do not convey identical information, but they work together to more richly specify the same object. But, as described, there are times when word and gesture convey information that overlaps very little, if at all. A point can indicate an object that is not referred to

in speech—the child says "daddy" while pointing at the chair. Word and gesture together convey a simple proposition—"the chair is daddy's" or "daddy sat on the chair"—that neither modality conveys on its own.

Consider the children participating in the Piagetian conservation task described earlier. The child in Figure 8.1a said that the amount of water changed "'cause that's down lower than that one," while pointing at the water levels in the two containers. Here, too, word and gesture do not convey identical information; speech tells us that the water level is low, gesture tells us how low. Yet, the two modalities work together to more richly convey the child's understanding. In contrast, the child in Figure 8.1b used her gestures to introduce completely new information not found in her speech. She said the amount of water changed "'cause this one's lower than this one," but indicated the widths of the containers with her hands. In this case, word and gesture together allow the child to convey a contrast of dimensions—this one's lower but wide, that one's higher but skinny—that neither modality conveys on its own.

We can posit a continuum based on the overlap of information conveyed in gesture and speech (Goldin-Meadow, 2003a). At one end of the continuum, gesture elaborates on a topic that has already been introduced in speech. At the other end, gesture introduces new information that is not mentioned at all in speech. Although at times, it is not clear where to draw a line to divide the continuum into two categories, the ends of the continuum are obvious and relatively easy to identify. As mentioned, we have called cases in which gesture and speech convey overlapping information *gesture-speech matches* and those in which gesture and speech convey nonoverlapping information *gesture-speech mismatches*.

The term *mismatch* adequately conveys the notion that gesture and speech express different information. However, mismatch also brings with it an unintended notion of conflict. The pieces of information conveyed in gesture and in speech in a mismatch need not conflict and, in fact, rarely do. There is almost always some framework within which the information conveyed in gesture can be fitted with the information conveyed in speech. In Figure 8.1b, it may seem as though there is a conflict between the height information conveyed in the child's words ("lower") and the width information conveyed in her gestures. However, in the context of the water conservation problem, the two dimensions actually compensate for one another. Indeed, it is essential to understand this compensation—that the water may be lower than it was in the original container, but it is also wider—to master conservation of liquid quantity.

As observers, we are often able to envision a framework that would resolve a potential conflict between the information encoded in children's talk and the information encoded in their gestures. However, the children may not be able to envision such a framework, particularly if left to their own devices. But children can profit from a framework if someone else provides it. Take the training study in conservation described earlier. When given instruction that provides a framework for understanding conservation, children who produce gesture-speech mismatches in their conservation explanations profit from that instruction and improve on the task. Children who do not yet produce mismatches and thus do not have the ingredients of a conserving explanation in their repertoires, do not profit from the instructions (Church & Goldin-Meadow, 1986; see also Perry et al., 1988; Pine et al., 2004). In sum, gesture can reflect thoughts that are quite different from the thoughts a child conveys in speech. Moreover, if such a child is offered instruction that provides a framework for those thoughts, the child is likely to learn.

## Gesture Offers Unique Insight into a Child's Knowledge

The information conveyed by gesture in a gesture-speech match is obviously accessible to speech. But what about the information conveyed by gesture in a gesture-speech mismatch? The child does not express the information in speech *in that response*—otherwise we would not call it a mismatch. But perhaps the child does not express that information *anywhere* in his or her explanations of the task. Perhaps the information conveyed in the gestural component of a mismatch is truly unique to gesture.

Goldin-Meadow, Alibali, et al. (1993) examined the problem-solving strategies that a group of 9- to 10-year-old children produced in speech and gesture when solving and explaining six mathematical equivalence problems. They found that if a child produced a problem-solving strategy in the gestural component of a mismatch, that child rarely produced that strategy *anywhere* in his or her speech. Interestingly, this was not true of the problem-solving strategies found in the spoken component of the children's mismatches—these

spoken strategies could almost always be found in gesture on some other response. What this means is that whatever information the children were able to express in speech they were also able to express in gesture, not necessarily on the same problem, but at some point during the task. Thus, at least on this task, when children can articulate a notion in speech, they are also able to express that notion in gesture. But the converse is not true—when children express a notion in gesture, sometimes they are also able to express that notion in speech and sometimes they are not.

Even in judgments of others' explanations, there seems to be an asymmetrical relation between gesture and speech; when children notice a speaker's words, they also notice that speaker's gesture, but not vice versa. T. A. Graham (1999) asked very young children to "help" a puppet learn to count. Half the time, the puppet counted correctly, but the other half of the time, the puppet added an extra number (e.g., the puppet would say "one, two, three" while counting two objects). In addition, when the puppet made these counting errors, he either produced the same number of pointing gestures as number of words (three in this example), a larger or smaller number of pointing gestures (four or two pointing gestures), or no pointing gestures at all. The child's job was to tell the puppet whether his counting was correct and, if incorrect, to explain why the puppet was wrong. The interesting result from the point of view of this discussion concerns whether children made reference to the puppet's number words (speech only) or points (gesture only) or both (gesture + speech) in their explanations. The 2-year-olds did not refer to either gesture or speech; 3-year-olds referred to gesture but not speech (gesture only); and 4-year-olds referred to both gesture and speech (gesture + speech). Very few children across all three ages referred to the puppet's speech without also referring to the puppet's gesture. In other words, when they noticed the puppet's speech, they also noticed his gesture, but not necessarily vice versa.

We now know that children can express knowledge in gesture that they do not express in speech. But is there some other means by which children can tell us that they "have" this knowledge? Knowledge that is accessible to gesture but not to speech, by definition, cannot be articulated. But perhaps this knowledge can be accessed in some other less explicit way, for example, by a rating task (cf. C. Acredolo & O'Connor, 1991; Horobin & Acredolo, 1989; Siegler & Crowley, 1994). In a rating task, all the raters need do is make a judgment about information provided by the experimenter. They do not need to express the information themselves.

Garber, Alibali, and Goldin-Meadow (1998) addressed this issue with respect to mathematical equivalence. If a child produces a problem-solving strategy uniquely in gesture, will the child later accept the answer generated by that strategy on a rating task? In Figure 8.2, for the problem $7 + 6 + 5 = \underline{\phantom{xxx}} + 5$, the child puts 18 in the blank and says "7 plus 6 is 13 plus 5 more is 18 and that's all I did"—in other words, she gives an "add-numbers-to-equal-sign" strategy in speech. In gesture, however, she points at all four numbers (the 7, the 6, the left 5, and the right 5), thus giving an "add-all-numbers" strategy in gesture. She does not produce the add-all-numbers strategy in speech in any of her explanations. When later asked to rate the acceptability of possible answers to this problem, the child, of course, accepts 18 (the number you get when you add up

the numbers to the equal sign). However, the child is also willing to accept 23, the number you get when you add all of the numbers in the problem—that is, the answer you get when you use the problem-solving strategy that this child produced *uniquely* in gesture.

Children thus can express knowledge with their hands that they do not express *anywhere* in their speech. This knowledge is not fully explicit (it cannot be stated in words). However, it is not fully implicit either (it is evident not only in gesture but also in a rating task). Knowledge expressed uniquely in gesture thus appears to represent a middle point along a continuum of knowledge states, bounded at one end by fully implicit knowledge that is embedded in action, and at the other by fully explicit knowledge that is accessible to verbal report (cf. Dienes & Perner, 1999; Goldin-Meadow & Alibali, 1994, 1999; Karmiloff-Smith, 1986, 1992).

A growing group of researchers have come to believe that linguistic meaning is grounded in bodily action

**Figure 8.2** Example of a child producing a gesture-speech mismatch on a mathematical equivalence problem. The child says that she added the numbers on the left side of the equation (an add-numbers-to-equal-sign strategy). In gesture, however, she points at the last number on the right side of the equation as well as the three on the left (add-all-numbers strategy).

(Barsalou, 1999; Glenberg & Kaschak, 2002; Glenberg & Robertson, 1999)—that meaning derives from the biomechanical nature of bodies and perceptual systems and, in this sense, is embodied (Glenberg, 1997). Under this view, it is hardly surprising that gesture reflects thought. Gesture may be an overt depiction of the action meaning embodied in speech. However, gesture has the potential to do more—it could play a role in shaping those meanings. There are (at least) two ways in which gesture could play a role in creating, rather than merely reflecting, thought:

**1.** Gesture could play a role in shaping thought by displaying, for all to see, the learner's newest, and perhaps undigested, thoughts. Parents, teachers, and peers would then have the opportunity to react to those unspoken thoughts and provide the learner with the input necessary for future steps. Gesture, by influencing the input learners receive from others, would then be part of the process of change itself. In other words, gesture's participation in *communication* could contribute to cognitive change.

**2.** Gesture could play a role in shaping thought more directly by influencing the learners themselves. Gesture externalizes ideas differently and therefore may draw on different resources from speech. Conveying an idea across modalities may, in the end, require less effort than conveying the idea within speech alone. In other words, gesture may serve as a "cognitive prop," freeing up cognitive effort that can be used on other tasks. If so, using gesture may actually ease the learner's processing burden and, in this way, function as part of the mechanism of change. In other words, gesture's participation in the process of *thinking* could contribute to cognitive change.

Gesture thus has the potential to contribute to cognitive change indirectly by influencing the learning environment (through communication) or more directly by influencing the learner (through thinking). Before considering the possible *functions* that gesture might serve, we take a moment to consider the factors or *mechanisms* responsible for gesturing.

## WHAT MAKES PEOPLE GESTURE?

We begin our exploration of the mechanism underlying gesture production by focusing on communicative fac-

tors that might encourage us to gesture. We then consider cognitive factors that could lead to gesture.

## Does Having a Conversation Partner Make Us Gesture?

To explore whether communicative factors play a role in the mechanism responsible for creating gesture, we need to manipulate factors relevant to communication and determine whether those factors influence gesturing. In this section, we ask whether one factor essential to communication—having a conversation partner—affects whether speakers gesture.

### We Gesture More When Listeners Are Present

Our goal in this section is not to figure out whether listeners get meaning from gesture (we address this question in a later section), but to figure out whether the need to communicate information to others is the force that drives us to gesture. The easiest way to explore this question is to ask people to talk when they can see their listener and when they can't. If the need to convey information to conversation partners is what motivates us to gesture, we ought to gesture more when others can see those gestures.

A number of studies have manipulated the presence of a listener and observed the effect on gesture. In most studies, the speaker has a face-to-face conversation with a listener in one condition, and a conversation in which a barrier prevents the speaker and listener from seeing one another in the second condition. In some studies, the second condition is conducted over an intercom, and in some the first condition is conducted over a videophone. In some studies, the camera is hidden so that the speakers have no sense that they are being watched. It doesn't really seem to matter. In most studies (although not all), people gesture more when they can see their listener than when they cannot (Alibali, Heath, & Myers, 2001; Bavelas, Chovil, Lawrie, & Wade, 1992; Cohen & Harrison, 1973; Krauss, Dushay, Chen, & Rauscher, 1995; the exceptions were Lickiss & Wellens, 1978; Rimé, 1982). For example, Alibali, Heath, and Myers (2001) asked speakers to watch an animated cartoon and narrate the story to a visible versus nonvisible listener. Speakers produced more representational gestures (gestures that depict semantic content) when they could see their listener than when they could not, but not more beat gestures (simple, rhythmic gestures that do not convey semantic content). Thus, speakers increase their production of at least some gestures when someone is watching.

But do speakers really intend to produce gestures for their listeners? There is no doubt that speakers change their *talk* in response to listeners. Perhaps the changes in gesture come about as a by-product of these changes in speech. Speakers could alter the form and content of their talk and those changes could automatically bring with them changes in gesture. To address this possibility, we need to examine not only changes that occur in gesture as a function of who the listener is, but also changes that occur in the accompanying speech. Alibali, Heath, et al. (2001) did just that but found no differences anywhere—speakers used the same number of words, made the same number of speech errors, and said essentially the same things no matter whether a listener was present. Thus, when the speakers in this study produced more gestures with visible than nonvisible listeners, it was not because they had changed their talk; at some level, albeit not consciously, they meant to change their gestures.

### Congenitally Blind Speakers Gesture Even When Addressing Blind Listeners

Speakers gesture more when they address visible listeners than nonvisible listeners, suggesting that there is a communicative aspect to gesturing. In another sense, however, the more striking finding in each of these studies is that speakers continue to gesture even when no listener is there at all. Although statistically less likely, gesture was produced in all the experimental conditions in which there was no possibility of a communicative motive. As an example that everyone can relate to, people gesture when talking on the telephone although there is no one around to see those gestures. Why? If the need to communicate with the listener is the only force behind gesturing, why do we continue to move our hands when listeners can no longer see us?

One possibility is that we gesture out of habit. We are used to moving our hands around when we speak to others and old habits die hard. This hypothesis predicts that if someone were to spend a great deal of time talking only to unseen people, eventually that person's gestures would fade away. Another possibility is that, even when no one is around, we imagine a listener and we gesture for that listener. The only way to test these hypotheses is to observe speakers who have never spoken to a visible listener. Individuals who are blind from birth offer an excellent test case. Congenitally blind individuals have

never seen their listeners and thus cannot be in the habit of gesturing for them. Moreover, congenitally blind individuals never see speakers moving their hands as they talk and thus have no model for gesturing. Do they gesture despite their lack of a visual model?

Iverson and Goldin-Meadow (1998, 2001) asked children and adolescents blind from birth to participate in a series of conservation tasks, and compared their speech and gesture on these tasks to age- and gender-matched sighted individuals. All the blind speakers gestured as they spoke, even though they had never seen gestures or their listeners. The blind group gestured at the same rate as the sighted group, and conveyed the same information using the same range of gesture forms. Blind speakers apparently do not require experience receiving gestures before spontaneously producing gestures of their own. Congenitally blind children produce gestures at the earliest stages of language-learning just as sighted children do (Iverson et al., 2000). They even produce pointing gestures at distal objects, although those gestures are not as frequent as in sighted children and are produced with a palm hand rather than a pointing hand. Moreover, blind children produce spontaneous gestures along with their speech even when they know that their listener is blind and therefore unable to profit from whatever information gesture offers (Iverson & Goldin-Meadow, 1998, 2001).

To sum up thus far, gesture seems to be an inevitable part of speaking. We do not need others around in order to gesture (although having others around increases our gesture rate). We do not need to have ever seen anyone gesture to produce gestures of our own. Gesture thus appears to be integral to the speaking process, and the mechanism by which gesture is produced must be tied in some way to this process. Gesture frequently accompanies speech in reasoning tasks where the speaker must think through a problem. In conservation tasks, for example, participants must consider and manipulate relationships between several different spatial dimensions of the task objects simultaneously (e.g., in the liquid quantity task, the relationship between container height and width and water level). It may be easier to express aspects of these dimensions and their relationships in the imagistic medium offered by gesture than in the linear, segmented medium provided by speech (cf. McNeill, 1992). Gesture may thus provide children with a channel for expressing thoughts that are difficult to articulate in speech. As a result, children—even blind children—may produce gestures when explaining their reasoning in a conservation task because some of their thoughts about the task lend themselves more readily to gesture than to speech. Gesture, in other words, might simply reflect a child's thoughts in a medium that happens to be relatively transparent to most listeners. We next explore whether cognitive factors play a role in the mechanism underlying gesturing.

## Does Thinking Hard Make Us Gesture?

When do we gesture? One possibility is that we gesture when we think hard. If so, we would expect gesture to increase when the task is made more difficult.

### Gesturing When Speaking Is Difficult

Consider first what happens when speaking is made more difficult. When we talk, we hear ourselves, and this feedback is an important part of the speaking process. If the feedback we get from our own voice is delayed, speaking becomes much more difficult. McNeill (1992) carried out a series of experiments observing what happens to gesture under delayed auditory feedback—the experience of hearing your own voice continuously echoed back. Delayed auditory feedback slowed speech down and stuttering and stammering became frequent. But it also had an effect on gesture, which increased in all speakers. (Interestingly, gesture did not lose its synchrony with speech, an outcome we might have expected given that gesture and speech form a unified system.) The most striking case was a speaker who produced absolutely no gestures at all under conditions of normal feedback, and began gesturing only during the second half of the narration, when feedback was delayed. When the act of speaking becomes difficult, speakers seem to respond by increasing their gestures.

We see a similar increase in gesturing in individuals suffering from aphasia. These individuals, typically as a result of stroke, trauma, or tumor, have greatly impaired language abilities relative to individuals without brain injury—speaking is difficult for aphasic individuals. When Feyereisen (1983) asked aphasic individuals to describe how they passed an ordinary day, they produced many more gestures than nonaphasic speakers. Again, increased gesturing seems to be associated with difficulty in speaking.

Finally, bilinguals who are not equally fluent in their two languages have more difficulty speaking their nondominant language than their dominant language. Marcos (1979) asked Spanish-English bilinguals, some dominant in English and others dominant in Spanish, to talk about love or friendship in their nondominant language. The less proficient a speaker was in his or her nondominant language, the more gestures that speaker produced when speaking that language (see also, Gulberg, 1998). The assumption is that speaking the nondominant language is more difficult for these individuals, and they respond by increasing their rate of gesturing.

### Gesturing When the Number of Items in a Task Increases

Gesturing also increases when the focal task is itself made more difficult. For example, T. A. Graham (1999) asked 2-, 3-, and 4-year-old children to count sets of 2, 4, and 6 object arrays. Children learn to count small numbers before learning to count large numbers (Gelman & Gallistel, 1978; Wynn, 1990). If children gesture only when the counting problem is hard, we might expect them to gesture more on arrays with 4 and 6 objects than on arrays with only 2 objects. The 4-year-olds did just that (apparently, the 2- and 3-year-olds were challenged by all three arrays and gestured as much as possible on each one). When the counting task is hard, children rely on gesture (see also Saxe & Kaplan, 1981).

Gesturing has also been found to increase when speakers have options to choose among. Melinger and Kita (in press) asked native speakers of Dutch to describe map-like pictures, each depicting a path with several destinations (marked by colored dots). The speaker's task was to describe from memory the path that leads past all the destinations. Importantly, some of the maps had routes that branched in two directions, which meant that the speaker had a choice of paths (more than one item to choose among). The question is whether speakers would produce more gestures when describing the branching points on the maps than when describing points where no choices needed to be made. They did. Controlling for the amount of directional talk the speakers produced, Melinger and Kita (in press) calculated the percentage of directional terms that were accompanied by gesture at branching points versus nonbranching points and found that the speakers gestured more at branching points. The presumption is that the branching points elicited more gestures because they offered the speaker more than one item to choose among and, in this sense, were conceptually challenging.

### Gesturing When Describing from Memory

Describing a scene from memory ought to be more difficult than describing a scene within view. We might therefore expect speakers to produce more gestures when asked to retrieve information from memory. De Ruiter (1998) asked Dutch-speakers to describe pictures on a computer screen so that the listener could draw them. Half of the pictures were described while they were visible on the computer screen, and half were described from memory. The speakers produced more gestures when describing the pictures from memory than when describing them in full view.

Wesp, Hesse, Keutmann, and Wheaton (2001) found the same effect in English-speakers. They asked speakers to describe still-life watercolor paintings so that the listener could later pick the painting out of a set of paintings. Half of the speakers were asked to look at the painting, form an image of it, and then describe it from memory. The other half were asked to describe the painting as it sat in front of them. Speakers who described the paintings from memory produced more gestures than those who described the paintings in full view. When the description task becomes difficult, speakers react by increasing their gesture rates.

### Gesturing When Reasoning Rather Than Describing

Reasoning about a set of objects ought to be more difficult than merely describing those same objects, and thus ought to elicit more gestures. Alibali, Kita, and Young (2000) asked a group of kindergartners to participate in both a reasoning and a description task. In the reasoning task, the children were given six Piagetian conservation problems tapping their understanding of continuous quantity and mass. In the description task, they were presented with precisely the same objects, but this time they were asked to describe how the objects looked rather than to reason about their quantities. The children produced more iconic gestures (but not more deictic gestures) when *reasoning* about the objects than when *describing* the objects. In other words, they produced more gestures that conveyed substantive information when doing the harder task.

An increase in task difficulty does not always bring with it an increase in gesture (Cohen & Harrison, 1973; De Ruiter, 1998). For example, De Ruiter (1998) found no differences in the rate of gesturing for pictures that were easy versus hard to describe. Null effects are difficult to interpret. Perhaps the task was not hard enough to inspire gesture. But then, we need to specify what we mean by "hard enough." If gesture and speech are interlinked in a specific way, then we might expect only certain types of tasks and verbal difficulties to lead to an increase in gesture. Ideally, theories

of how gesture and speech relate to one another ought to be sufficiently specified to predict the kinds of difficulties that will lead to more gesture, but we haven't achieved the ideal yet. None of the current theories can explain these null results.

## WHAT FUNCTIONS DOES GESTURE SERVE?

Thus far, we have examined studies that manipulate communicative and cognitive factors and then chart the effects of those manipulations on gesture. And we have found that the manipulations have an impact on gesturing, suggesting that both communicative and cognitive factors play a causal role in gesture production. The studies thus provide convincing evidence with respect to the *mechanisms* that underlie gesturing, the process by which gesture comes about.

The studies, however, are not conclusive with respect to the *functions* that gesture serves. Just because gesturing increases in situations where a listener is present doesn't mean that the listener gleans information from gesture. To determine whether gesture functions to communicate information to listeners, we need to manipulate *gesture* and explore the effects of that manipulation on *listener comprehension*. Similarly, just because gesturing increases on tasks that require more thought does not mean that gesturing plays a causal role in thinking. Gesture may be reflecting the speaker's thought processes, rather than causing them. To explore whether gesture functions to help us think, we need to manipulate *gesture* and observe the effect of the manipulation on *thinking*. We turn to studies of this sort in the next sections, focusing on the functions gestures might serve first in communication and then in thinking.

### Gesture's Role in Communication: Does Gesture Convey Information to the Listener?

A child's gestures can signal to parents and teachers that a particular notion is already in that child's repertoire but is not quite accessible. These listeners can then alter their behavior accordingly, perhaps giving explicit instruction in just these areas. In response to the child's utterance, "dada" + point hat, an adult might say "yes, that's dada's hat," thus translating the information the child conveyed across two modalities into the spoken modality and providing just the right target for a learner who had this notion in mind (Goldin-Meadow, Goodrich, Sauer, & Iverson, 2005). This process can only work if adults are able to glean substantive information from a child's gesture. Although there is little disagreement in the field about whether information is displayed in gesture, there is great disagreement about whether ordinary listeners take advantage of that information. Does someone who has not taken a course in gesture-coding understand gesture? Do gestures communicate? Some researchers are completely convinced that the answer is "yes" (e.g., Kendon, 1994). Others are equally convinced that the answer is "no" (e.g., Krauss, Morrel-Samuels, & Colasante, 1991). Several approaches have been taken to this question, some more successful than others.

### Looking at Gesture in the Context of Speech

We glean very little information from gesture when it is presented on its own (Feyereisen, van de Wiele, & Dubois, 1988; Krauss et al., 1991). However, we may still benefit from gesture when it is viewed as it was meant to be viewed—in the context of speech. There are hints that we get information from gesture when it accompanies speech in observations of how listeners behave in conversation. Heath (1992, cited in Kendon, 1994) describes several interchanges in which the recipient seems to grasp the meaning of an utterance before its completion, and to do so on the basis of gesture. A doctor is explaining that a particular medicine will "damp down" a symptom and makes several downward movements of his hand as he does so. The timing, however, is important. He says "they help sort of you know to dampen down the inflammation," and has already completed three downward strokes of his gesture by the time he says "you know"—he gestures before he actually produces the word "dampen." It is at this point, after the gesture but before the word dampen, that the listener looks at the doctor and begins to nod. The listener appears to have gotten the gist of the sentence well before its end, and to have gotten that gist from gesture.

Examples of this sort are suggestive but not at all definitive. We really have no idea what the listener is actually understanding when he nods his head. The listener may *think* he's gotten the point of the sentence, but he may be completely mistaken. He may even be pretending to understand. We need to know exactly what recipients are taking from gesture to be sure that they have truly grasped its meaning. To do that, we need a more experimental approach.

J. A. Graham and Argyle (1975) asked people not to gesture on half of their descriptions of drawings and then examined how accurate listeners were in recreating those drawings when they were described with and without gesture. The listeners were significantly more accurate with gesture than without it. However, when speakers are forced not to use their hands, they may change the way they speak. In other words, the speech in the two conditions (messages with gesture versus without it) may differ, and this difference could be responsible for the accuracy effect. J. A. Graham and Heywood (1975) addressed this concern by reanalyzing the data with this issue in mind. But a more convincing approach to the problem would be to hold speech constant while exploring the beneficial effects of gesture. This manipulation can easily be accomplished with videotape.

Krauss et al. (1995) asked speakers to describe abstract graphic designs, novel synthesized sounds, or samples of tea. Listeners then saw and heard the videotape of the speakers or heard only the sound track, and were asked to select the object being described from a set of similar objects. Accuracy was straightforwardly measured by the number of times the correct object was selected. In none of the experiments was accuracy enhanced by allowing the listener to see the speaker's gestures. Thus, in certain situations, gesture can add *nothing* to the information conveyed by speech.

Other researchers have found that gesture enhances the message listeners take from a communication (e.g., Berger & Popelka, 1971; Riseborough, 1981; Thompson & Massaro, 1986). For example, Riseborough (1981) gave listeners extracts from videotapes of a speaker describing an object (e.g., a fishing rod) to another person. The extracts were presented with both video and sound or with sound alone. Listeners guessed the correct object more rapidly when they could see the iconic gestures that accompanied the description than when they could not. In a subsequent experiment, Riseborough made sure that it wasn't just the hand waving that mattered. She compared responses (this time accuracy scores) to speech accompanied by vague movements versus well-defined iconic gestures, and found that accuracy was much better with the real gestures.

It is possible that listeners are not gleaning *specific* information from gesture. Gesture could be doing nothing more than heightening the listener's attention to speech which, in turn, results in more accurate and faster responses. Beattie and Shovelton (1999b) avoided this concern by examining in detail the types of information that listeners took from a message when they heard it with and without gesture. Each listener saw clips drawn from a narration of a cartoon in the audio + video condition (sound track and picture), the audio condition (just the sound track), and the video condition (just the picture). After each clip, the listener answered a series of planned questions about the objects and actions in the clip (e.g., "What object(s) are identified here?" "What are the object(s) doing?" "What shapes are the object(s)?").

The results were quite clear. When the listeners could see the iconic gestures as well as hear the speech, they answered the questions more accurately than when they just heard the speech. All 10 listeners showed the effect. However, gesture was more beneficial with respect to certain semantic categories than others, for example, the relative position and the size of objects. In one videoclip, the speaker said "by squeezing his nose" while opening and closing his left hand. All the listeners in both the audio + video and the audio condition accurately reported the squeezing action. However, listeners in the audio + video condition were much more likely than those in the audio condition to accurately report the size and shape of the nose, its position with respect to the squeezing hand, and whether it was moving. It is not surprising that the listeners in the audio condition did not report these pieces of information—they didn't hear them *anywhere* in the sound track they were given. But it may be surprising (depending on your point of view) that the listeners in the audio + video condition not only noticed the extra information conveyed in gesture, but were able to integrate that information into the mental image they were developing on the basis of speech. Listeners really can glean specific information from gesture.

### Looking at Gesture with Mismatching Speech

When gesture conveys precisely the same information as speech, we can never really be sure that the listener has gotten specific information from gesture. Even if a listener responds more accurately to speech accompanied by gesture than to speech alone, it could be because gesture is heightening the listener's attention to the speech; gesture could be serving as an energizer or focuser, rather than as a supplier of information. The data from the Beattie and Shovelton (1999b) study are not plagued by this problem. We are convinced that the listeners in this study are gleaning specific information from gesture simply because that information does not appear *anywhere* in speech. It must be coming from gesture—it has no place else to come from. In general, the best place

to look for effects of gesture on listeners is in gesture-speech mismatches—instances where gesture conveys information that is not found in speech.

McNeill, Cassell, and McCullough (1994) asked listeners to watch and listen to a videotape of someone recounting a "Tweety Bird" cartoon. The listener never sees the cartoon, only the narration. Unbeknownst to the listener, the narrator is performing a carefully choreographed program of mismatching gestures along with a number of normally matching gestures. The listener's task is to retell the story to yet another person, and that narration is videotaped. The question is whether we will see in the listener's own narration traces of the information conveyed by gesture in the mismatched combinations planted in the video narrative. And we do. Consider an example. The narrator on the videotape says, "he comes out the bottom of the pipe," while bouncing his hand up and down—a verbal statement that contains no mention of how the act was done (no verbal mention of the bouncing manner), accompanied by a gesture that does convey bouncing. The listener resolves the mismatch by inventing a staircase. In her retelling, the listener talks about going "downstairs," thus incorporating the bouncing information found *only* in the narrator's gestures into her own speech. The listener must have stored the bouncing manner in some form general enough to serve as the basis for her *linguistic* invention ("stairs"). The information conveyed in gesture is often noticed by listeners, but it is not necessarily tagged as having come from gesture (see also Bavelas, 1994).

We find the same effects when adult listeners are asked to react to gesture-speech mismatches that children spontaneously produce on either a mathematical equivalence task (Alibali, Flevares, & Goldin-Meadow, 1997) or a conservation task (Goldin-Meadow, Wein, & Chang, 1992). Half of the videotapes that the adults saw were gesture-speech matches (e.g., Figure 8.1a) and half were gesture-speech mismatches (e.g., Figure 8.1b and Figure 8.2). The adults, half of whom were teachers and half undergraduate students, were simply asked to describe the child's reasoning. Recall that a mismatch contains two messages, one in speech and one in gesture. A match contains only one. If adults are gleaning information from child gesture, we might therefore expect them to say more when they assess a child who produces a mismatch than when they assess a child who produces a match. And they did. In both studies, the adults produced many more "additions"—that is, they mentioned information that could not be found anywhere in the speech of the child they were assessing—when evaluating children who produced mismatches than when evaluating children who produced matches. Moreover, over half of these additions could be traced back to the gestures that the children produced in their mismatches. Consider this example. In the conservation task, one child said that the rows contained different numbers of checkers after the top row had been spread out "because you moved 'em." However, in his accompanying gesture, the child indicated that the checkers in one row could be matched in a one-to-one fashion with the checkers in the other row (he pointed to a checker in one row and then to the corresponding checker in the other row, and repeated this gesture with another pair of checkers). An adult described this child as saying " 'you moved 'em' but then he pointed . . . he was matching them even though he wasn't verbalizing it," while producing a one-to-one correspondence gesture of her own. Thus, the adult had attributed to the child reasoning that was explicitly mentioned in the child's speech (reasoning based on the fact that the checkers had been moved), along with reasoning that appeared only in the child's gesture (reasoning based on one-to-one correspondence).

In this example, the adult explicitly referred to the child's gestures. Some of the adults were very aware of the children's gestures and remarked on them in their assessments. However, these adults were no better at gleaning substantive information from the children's gestures than were the adults who failed to mention gesture. Thus, being explicitly aware of gesture (at least enough to talk about it) is not a prerequisite for decoding gesture. Moreover, teachers were no better at gleaning information from the children's gestures than were the undergraduates. At first glance, this finding seems surprising given that teachers have both more experience with children and more knowledge about learning processes than undergraduates. However, from another perspective, the lack of difference suggests that integrating knowledge from both modalities is, in fact, a basic feature of the human communication system, as McNeill (1992) would predict. Everyone can read gesture, with or without training.

### Looking at Adult Reactions to Children Gesturing "Live"

When the best examples of gesture-speech mismatches are pulled out and shown to adults twice on a videotape so they can hardly help but notice the gesture, untrained adults are able to glean substantive meaning from ges-

ture. But this experimental gesture-reading situation is a bit removed from the real world. At the least, it would be nice to study adults reacting to real-live children producing whatever gestures they please.

Goldin-Meadow and Sandhofer (1999) asked adults to watch children responding to Piagetian conservation tasks "live." After each task, the adult's job was to check off on a list all the explanations that the child expressed on that task. After all the data had been collected, the explanations that the children produced were coded and analyzed. The children produced gesture-speech mismatches in a third of their explanations; that is, they conveyed information found *only* in gesture a third of the time. And the adults were able to decode these gestures. They checked explanations that children expressed in the gesture half of a gesture-speech mismatch, and did so significantly more often than they checked those explanations when they were not produced in either gesture or speech. The adults were thus able to glean substantive information from a child's gestures, information that did not appear anywhere in that child's speech, and could do so in a relatively naturalistic context. Listeners can get meaning from gesture even when it is unedited and fleeting.

However, this situation hardly approaches conditions in the real world. The listeners were not really listeners at all; they were "overhearers," observing gesturers but not participating in a conversation with them. Goldin-Meadow and Singer (2003) videotaped eight teachers who had been asked to individually instruct a series of children in mathematical equivalence. They found that all the teachers were able to glean substantive information from the children's gestures. The teachers paraphrased or reiterated explanations that the children produced in the gestural component of a mismatch. Moreover, when they reiterated these explanations, the teachers often translated the information conveyed uniquely in child gesture into their own speech, making it clear that they had truly understood the information conveyed in the child's gestures.

### Gesture's Role in Communication: Does Gesturing Influence How Listeners React to a Speaker?

One of gesture's most salient features is that it is "out there," a concrete manifestation of ideas for all the world to see. Gesture could be a signal to parents and teachers that a particular notion is already in a child's repertoire, although not quite accessible. These listeners could then alter their behavior accordingly, perhaps offering instruction in just these areas. If so, children would be able to shape their own learning environments just by moving their hands.

### Children's Gestures Shape Their Learning Environment

Several facts need to be established to support the hypothesis that gesturing shapes learning through its communicative effects.

- Ordinary listeners must be able to process the gestures children produce and glean substantive information from them, not just in laboratory situations but in real live interactions with children.
- Those listeners must change their behavior in response to the children's gestures, treating children differently simply because of the gestures the children produce.
- Those changed behaviors must have an effect on the child, preferably a beneficial effect.

We have reviewed evidence for the first of these points. Adults (teachers and nonteachers alike) can read the gestures that children produce in naturalistic situations. Moreover, there is good evidence for the second point. When asked to instruct children, teachers provide different instruction as a function of the children's gestures. Before instructing each child, the teachers in the Goldin-Meadow and Singer (2003) study watched that child explain how he or she solved six math problems to the experimenter. Some children produced mismatches during this pretest. The teachers seemed to notice and adjust their instruction accordingly; they gave more variable instruction to the children who produced mismatches than to those who did not produce mismatches: (a) They exposed the mismatchers to more types of problem-solving strategies; (b) they gave the mismatchers more explanations in which the strategy that they expressed in gesture did not match the strategy that they expressed in speech; in other words, the teachers produced more of their own mismatches. Thus, the gestures that children produce can influence the instruction they get from their teachers.

The final point to address in terms of gesture's role in bringing about cognitive change is whether the instruction that teachers spontaneously offer children in response to their gestures is helpful for learning (the

third point). But first we consider why teachers might produce gesture-speech mismatches of their own.

### Why Do Teachers Produce Gesture-Speech Mismatches?

It is easy to understand why a teacher might produce a variety of different problem-solving strategies when instructing a child. But why would a teacher present one strategy in one modality and a different strategy in the other modality? In other words, why would a *teacher* produce a gesture-speech mismatch?

Children who produce mismatches are in a state of cognitive uncertainty, possessing knowledge about the task that they cannot quite organize into a coherent whole. Teachers generally are not uncertain about how to solve the math problems they teach. However, they may be uncertain about how best to *teach* children to solve the problems, particularly mismatching children who are producing many inconsistent strategies. It is this uncertainty that may then be reflected in a teacher's mismatches. In general, a mismatch reflects the fact that the speaker is holding two ideas in mind—two ideas that the speaker has not yet integrated into a single unit (see Garber & Goldin-Meadow, 2002; Goldin-Meadow, Nusbaum, Garber, & Church, 1993)—in the teacher's case, a single instructional unit. This way of describing mismatch is, at least plausibly, as applicable to adults when teaching as it is to children when explaining.

However, teachers' mismatches do differ from the children's (Goldin-Meadow & Singer, 2003), and these differences may be important. Not surprisingly, teacher's mismatches for the most part contain correct problem-solving strategies, often two correct strategies that complement one another. For example, on the problem 7 + 6 + 5 = _____ + 5, one teacher expressed an equalizer strategy in speech ("we need to make this side equal to this side") while expressing a grouping strategy in gesture (point at the 7 and the 6, the two numbers which, if added, give the answer that goes in the blank). Both strategies lead to correct solutions yet do so via different routes. In contrast, children's mismatches contain as many incorrect strategies as correct ones.

Even more important, teachers' mismatches do not contain unique information, but children's mismatches do. Recall that children often convey information in the gestural component of their mismatches that cannot be found *anywhere* else in their repertoires. The children's mismatches thus convey their newest ideas. Although these ideas are not always correct, the experimentation displayed in these mismatches may be essential in promoting cognitive change. The children's mismatches thus display the kind of variability that could be good for learning (cf. Siegler, 1994; Thelen, 1989). In contrast, teachers do not convey unique information in their mismatches (Goldin-Meadow & Singer, 2003). All the strategies that the teachers express in the gestural component of a mismatch can be found, on some other problem, in their speech. The teachers' mismatches do not contain new and undigested thoughts and, consequently, do not reflect the kind of variability that leads to cognitive change. Indeed, teachers' mismatches can best be characterized in terms of the kind of variability that comes with expertise—the back-and-forth around a set point that typifies expert (as opposed to novice) performance on a task (cf. Bertenthal, 1999). Both experts and novices exhibit variability. However, the variability that experts display is in the service of adjusting to small (and perhaps unexpected) variations in the task. In contrast, the variability that novices display reflects experimentation with new ways of solving the task and, in this way, has the potential to lead to cognitive change.

It is important to point out that mismatch *can* reflect experimentation in adults. When adults are uncertain about how to solve a problem, they too produce mismatches (e.g., Perry & Elder, 1997), and it is likely that those mismatches will exhibit the properties found in child mismatches rather than those found in teacher mismatches, that is, information that cannot be found anywhere else in the speaker's repertoire. In other words, when adults are learning a task, their mismatches are likely to exhibit the kind of variability that can lead to cognitive change.

### Do Teachers Spontaneously Give Children What They Need?

Teachers instinctively expose children who produce mismatches to instruction containing a variety of problem-solving strategies and many mismatches (Goldin-Meadow & Singer, 2003). Is this instruction good for learning? Mismatching children do indeed profit from the instruction, but they, of course, are ready to learn this task. To find out whether this particular type of instruction promotes learning, we need to move to a more experimental procedure.

Singer and Goldin-Meadow (2005) gave 9- and 10-year-old children instruction that contained either one or two problem-solving strategies in speech. In addition,

they varied the relation between that speech and gesture. Some children received no gesture at all, some received gesture that matched its accompanying speech, and some received gesture that mismatched its accompanying speech. The results were clear and surprising. One strategy in speech was much more effective than two strategies in speech. Thus, it does not seem to be such a good idea for teachers to offer their students a variety of spoken strategies. However, regardless of whether children received one or two strategies in speech, mismatching gesture was more effective than either matching gesture or no gesture at all. Offering children gesture-speech mismatches appears to be an effective instructional strategy.

Why might mismatching gestures be so effective in promoting learning? The children in Singer and Goldin-Meadow's (2005) study were able to profit from a second strategy in instruction, but only when that second strategy was presented in gesture in a mismatch. Mismatching gesture provides the learner with additional information, and presents that information in a format that may be particularly accessible to a child on the cusp of learning. The visuospatial format found in gesture not only captures global images easily, but also allows a second (gestured) strategy to be presented *at the same time as* the spoken strategy. By placing two different strategies side by side within a single utterance (one in speech and one in gesture), mismatches can highlight the contrast between the two strategies. This contrast may, in turn, highlight the fact that different approaches to the problem are possible—an important concept for children grappling with a new idea.

### Can Gesture Be Put to Better Use?

Teachers spontaneously use gesture to promote learning. But they don't always use it as effectively as possible. Can gesture be put to better use? There are at least two ways in which gesture can be harnessed to promote cognitive change. We can teach adults to be better gesture-readers, and we can teach adults to be better gesture-producers.

Kelly, Singer, Hicks, and Goldin-Meadow (2002) taught adults to read the gestures that children produce on either conservation or mathematical equivalence tasks. Adults were given a pretest, instruction in gesture-reading, and then a posttest. Instruction varied from just giving a hint ("pay close attention not only to what the children on the videotape say with their words, but also to what they express with their hands"), to giving general instruction in the parameters that experts use when describing gesture (handshape, motion, placement), to giving specific instruction in the kinds of gestures children produce on that particular task. The adults improved with instruction, more so when given explicit instruction but even when given a hint. Moreover, the adults were able to generalize the instruction they received to new gestures they had not seen during training. Importantly, improvement in reading gesture did *not* affect the adults' ability to glean information from the children's speech on the conservation task; they identified the child's spoken explanations perfectly before and after instruction. There was, however, a slight decrement in the number of spoken explanations the adults reported after instruction on the math task, although this decrement was offset by an increase in the number of gestured explanations the adults reported after instruction. The challenge for us in the future is to figure out ways to encourage teachers and other adults to glean information from children's gestures while at the same time not losing their words.

Children are more likely to profit from instruction when it is accompanied by gesture than when that same instruction is not accompanied by gesture (Church, Ayman-Nolley, & Mahootian, 2004; Perry, Berch, & Singleton, 1995; Valenzeno, Alibali, & Klatzky, 2003). But the gestures that teachers spontaneously use with their children are not *always* helpful. The following interchange occurred when a teacher was asked to teach a child mathematical equivalence. The teacher had asked the child to solve the problem $7 + 6 + 5 = \underline{\hspace{1cm}} + 5$ and the child put 18 in the blank, using an incorrect "add-numbers-to-equal-sign" strategy to solve the problem. In her speech, the teacher made it clear to the child that he had used this strategy: She said, "so you got this answer by adding these three numbers." In her gestures, however, she produced an "add-all-numbers" strategy: She pointed at the 7, the 6, the 5 on the left side of the equation *and* the 5 on the right side of the equation (see Figure 8.3 and compare it with Figure 8.2). After these gestures, the teacher went on to try to explain how to solve the problem correctly but, before she could finish, the child offered a new solution—23, precisely the number you get if you add up all of the numbers in this problem. The teacher was genuinely surprised at her student's answer and was completely unaware that she herself might have given him the idea to add up all the numbers in the problem. A teacher's gestures can lead the child astray. The larger point, however, is that the gestures teachers produce have an impact on what children take from their lessons and therefore may affect learning. If so, teachers (and other adults) need to be encouraged to pay more attention to the gestures that they themselves produce.

Gesture may require our attention not only in teaching situations but also in legal interviews that involve children. Given the prevalence of gesture, it is not hard to imagine that children will gesture when responding to questions in a forensic interview and that those gestures will, at times, convey information that is not found in their speech. If so, the interesting question—both theoretically and practically—is whether adult interviewers pick up on the information that children convey uniquely in gesture and, if not, whether they can be trained to do so. The flip side of the question is also of great importance: Do adult interviewers convey information in their gestures that they do not consciously intend to convey, and if so, does that information influence how children respond to their queries? In other words, is a sub rosa conversation taking place in gesture that does not make it onto the transcripts that become the legal documents for forensic interviews (see Broaders, 2003; Broaders & Goldin-Meadow, 2005, for evidence that gesture can play this type of role in an interview situation)? Because the details children recall of an event can often be influenced by the way in which the interviewer poses the question (e.g., Ceci, 1995), this issue becomes a timely one and one in which attention to gesture might make a difference.

### Gesture's Role in Thinking: Does Gesturing Influence the Speaker's Cognition?

We have seen that gesture can convey information to listeners. The question we address in this section is whether gesture serves a function for speakers as well as listeners. The fact that we persist in gesturing even when there are no obvious communicative gains (e.g., when talking on the phone) propels us to seek a within-speaker function.

#### *Gesturing Can Lighten the Speaker's Cognitive Load*

There is indeed evidence that gesturing is a boon to the gesturer. In some circumstances, speakers find speaking

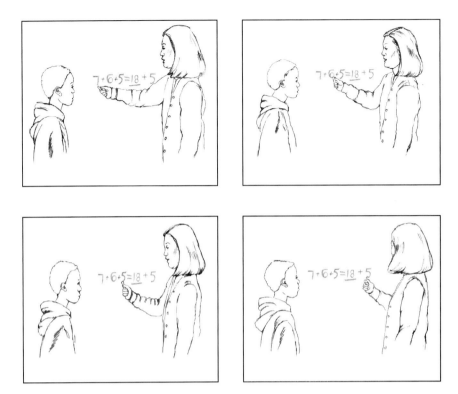

**Figure 8.3**  The gestures teachers produce can have an impact on the student. In her speech, the teacher points out to the child that he added the first three numbers to get his incorrect answer of 18. However, in her gesture, she points at all the numbers in the problem, including the last number on the right side of the equation (an add-all-numbers strategy; see Figure 8.2 for an example of a child-produced add-all-numbers strategy). The child's response was to add up all the numbers in the problem and give 23 as his answer. He had paid attention to his teacher's gestures.

cognitively less effortful when they gesture than when they do not gesture. Goldin-Meadow, Nusbaum, Kelly, and Wagner (2001) asked children and adults to solve math problems (addition problems for the children, factoring problems for the adults). Immediately after solving a problem, the child or adult was given a list of items to remember (words for the children, letters for the adults). The participants were then asked to explain how they solved the math problem and, after their explanation, to recall the list of items. Note that the participants produced their explanations while keeping the list in memory; the two tasks thus made demands on the same cognitive resources. On half of the problems, the participants were given no instructions about their hands. On the other half, they were told to keep their hands still during their explanations of the problems. The participants gave the same types of explanations for the math problems when they gestured and when they did not gesture. However, the number of items they remembered was not the same. Both children and adults remembered significantly more items when they gestured than when

they did not gesture, suggesting that a spoken explanation accompanied by gesture takes less cognitive effort than a spoken explanation without gesture.

There is one potential problem with these findings. Perhaps asking people not to move their hands may add a cognitive load to the task. If so, the recall pattern might not reflect the beneficial effects of gesturing but rather the demands of this extra cognitive load. Data from a subset of the participants address this concern. These participants gestured on only some of the problems on which they were allowed to move their hands; as a result, on some problems they did not gesture *by choice*. The number of items that these participants remembered when they gestured was significantly higher than the number they remembered when they did not gesture either *by choice* or *by instruction*. Indeed, the number of items remembered did not differ when the participants did not gesture by choice or by instruction. Thus, the instructions not to gesture did not add to cognitive load and the beneficial effects on recall appear to be attributable to gesture.

Why might gesture lighten a speaker's cognitive load? Perhaps gesture lightens cognitive load by raising the overall activation level of the system so that words reach a firing level more quickly (Butterworth & Hadar, 1989). If so, the act of moving one's hands ought to affect recall, not what those hand movements mean. However, the meaning of the gestures does have an impact on recall (Wagner, Nusbaum, & Goldin-Meadow, 2004): Speakers remember fewer words when their gestures convey a different message from their speech, that is, when they convey two messages (one in speech and one in gesture), rather than one (the same message in speech and gesture).

Instead of merely adding activation to the system, gesture might help speakers retrieve just the right word in their explanations (which would, in turn, save them cognitive effort so that they could perform better on the memory task). Gesture, particularly iconic gestures, might assist word finding by exploiting another route to the phonological lexicon, a route mediated by visual coding (Butterworth & Hadar, 1989). Some evidence, in fact, suggests that gesture can facilitate lexical recall (Rauscher et al., 1996; but see Alibali et al., 2000; Beattie & Coughlan, 1998, 1999).

Lexical access does not account for all the beneficial effects of gesture. Gesture may also help link or "index" words and phrases to real-world objects. Glenberg and Robertson (1999) argue that indexing is essential for comprehension; once a word is indexed to an object, the listener's knowledge of that particular object can guide his or her interpretation of the language. Making these links might be important, not only for listeners but also for speakers. Alibali and DiRusso (1999) explored the benefits of gestural indexing for preschoolers performing a counting task. Sometimes the children were allowed to gesture, in particular, to tick off the items, while they counted and sometimes they were not. The children counted more accurately when they gestured than when they did not gesture. Thus, using gesture to hook word to world can improve performance on a task.

Finally, gesturing could help speakers organize information for the act of speaking and in this way ease the speaker's cognitive burden. Kita (2000) has argued that gesture helps speakers "package" spatial information into units appropriate for verbalization. If this hypothesis is correct, speakers should find it easier to convey spatial information when they gesture than when they do not gesture. Rimé, Schiaratura, Hupet, and Ghysselinckx (1984) prevented speakers from gesturing and

found that these speakers produced less visual imagery in their talk when they did not gesture than when they did. Alibali, Kita, Bigelow, Wolfman, and Klein (2001) performed the same manipulation and found that their child speakers produced fewer perceptual-based explanations when they did not gesture than when they did.

So what have we learned about gesture's effect on the gesturer? We know that speakers tend to gesture more when the task becomes difficult. They appear to do so, not merely as a reflection of the cognitive effort they are expending, but as a way to *reduce* that effort. Giving an explanation while gesturing actually takes *less* cognitive effort than giving an explanation without gesturing. However, we do not yet understand the mechanism by which gesturing lightens the speaker's load.

### Gesture's Direct Impact on the Learner: Can Gesturing Create Ideas?

We have seen that gesturing can aid thinking by reducing cognitive effort. That effort can then be used on some other task, one which would have been performed less well had the speaker not gestured on the first task. Gesturing thus allows speakers to do more with what they have and, in this way, can promote cognitive change. But gesturing has the potential to contribute to cognitive change in other ways as well—it could affect the *direction* that the change takes.

Gesture offers a route, and a unique one, through which new information can be brought into the system. Because the representational formats underlying gesture are mimetic and analog rather than discrete, gesture permits speakers to represent ideas that lend themselves to formats (e.g., shapes, sizes, spatial relationships)— ideas that, for whatever reason, may not be easily encoded in speech. Take, for example, a child who expresses one-to-one correspondence in gesture but not in speech. This child may find it relatively easy to focus on aligning the two rows of checkers in the visuospatial format that gesture offers—and at a time when he does not have sufficient grasp of the idea to express it in words. Gesture provides a format that makes it easy for the child to discover one-to-one correspondence and thus allows this novel idea to be brought into his repertoire earlier than it would have been without gesture. Once brought in, the new idea can then serve as a catalyst for change.

The suggestion here is that gesture does not just *reflect* the incipient ideas that a learner has, but it actually helps the learner formulate and therefore *develop* these new ideas. One implication of this hypothesis is that thought would have been different had the speaker not gestured. To test the hypothesis, we need a technique for assessing thought that is independent of gesture and speech; we need a way to figure out whether thought has been altered that does *not* involve looking at either gesture or speech. At the moment, no studies have been designed with this particular goal in mind. We do, however, have examples of studies that explore gesture's effect on *talk,* studies in which gesture is manipulated (either discouraged or encouraged) and the effect of the manipulation on talk is then examined.

Alibali, Kita, and colleagues (2001) *discouraged* children from gesturing by asking them to explain their answers to a series of conservation tasks when they could move their hands freely and when their hands were placed in a muff and therefore restrained. As expected under the view that gesture helps speakers organize spatial information, the children produced more perceptual-based explanations when they were allowed to move their hands freely than when they were not. The idea is that the act of gesturing promotes thinking, in particular, spatial thinking—and not gesturing inhibits it (see also Rimé et al., 1984).

But note that we can also *encourage* speakers to move their hands while they talk. If children are asked to move their hands when they explain their solutions to a math problem, they begin to produce problem-solving strategies that they have never produced before, some correct and some incorrect (Broaders & Goldin-Meadow, 2002). For the most part, these new strategies can be found only in the children's gestures. The interesting question is what would happen if these children were given instruction in mathematical equivalence. Having enlarged their store of implicit problem-solving strategies after being encouraged to gesture, would the children now be particularly likely to profit from instruction? If so, children may be able to improve their ability to learn just by moving their hands.

Wolff and Gutstein (1972) not only asked speakers to gesture but they dictated which movements the speakers produced. The experimenters could therefore make specific predictions about the kinds of ideas that ought to infiltrate the stories accompanied by gesture. They taught speakers either a circular or linear movement. Some of the speakers were asked to generate short stories while performing the assigned gesture with their eyes closed. Others generated their stories while watching an experimenter perform the assigned gesture.

Raters were asked to judge whether the stories had linear or circular content. Speakers who produced linear gestures created stories that were judged more linear than the stories created by speakers who produced circular gestures. And speakers who watched linear gestures also created stories that were judged more linear than the stories created by speakers who watched circular gestures. A third control group was taught either the linear or circular gesture but did not use or see the gesture when producing stories. There were no differences in the ratings of the stories generated by these speakers. These results suggest that waving your hands about in prescribed ways can affect what you are going to say. Moreover, the impact of gesture is not restricted to producing gesture. Its impact was felt even by those speakers who merely witnessed others' hand movements, a finding that confirms the conclusion we came to earlier—gesture does have an impact on listeners.

An elegant aspect of the Wolff and Gutstein (1972) study is that the speakers who produced gestures did so with their eyes closed. Thus, they felt their gestures but did not see them. It is consequently very clear that there can be separable effects on the content of talk of *seeing* and *feeling* hand movements. The effects could be additive—had the speakers been allowed to both see and feel their own gestures (which is, after all, what typically happens when speakers talk), the content of their stories might have been that much more skewed. Alternatively, feeling one's own gestures may be such a powerful stimulus that little is added by watching them. Moreover, the perspective we have on our own gestures is distinctly different from the perspective we have on others' gestures. We may get something out of watching other speakers' gestures, but little out of watching our own. This is an area where many questions remain.

The Wolff and Gutstein (1972) findings are striking because the gestures were completely unrelated to the storytelling task. However, from an educational (or even a conversational) point of view, it would be worth exploring the effects on thinking of movements that are more directly related to the task. For example, what would happen if we asked a child who did not know how to solve the problem $4 + 5 + 3 = \_\_\_ + 3$ to produce a V-hand under the 4 and the 5 and a point at the blank while explaining the problem? This gesture represents the "grouping" strategy—group 4 and 5 together, add them, and put the sum in the blank. If the actions that the children are forced to produce do, in fact, influence their thinking, we might expect them to produce more correct solutions on these problems than children who are not required to make these movements—or even more telling, more correct solutions than children who are required to make other less targeted movements. In this way, gesturing could shape thinking.

## CONCLUSION

Why do we gesture? Perhaps gesturing is a vestige of the evolutionary process that gave us speech. It could be a hanger-on that accompanies the act of speaking but plays no active role in how we speak or think. If so, gesture would be of interest for what it can reveal to us about the process of speaking or thinking, but it would have no influence on the process itself. This is the least we can say about gesture. But evidence is mounting in favor of the view that gesture does more than just reflect thought—it shapes it as well. If we find that gesture is causally involved in change, its effect is likely to be widespread. Gesture is pervasive, appearing in all sorts of situations and over all ages and cultures. Gesture is ever-present, and we notice it even though we typically do not know we are noticing it. The time seems ripe to include gesture as a full-fledged part of the conversation.

## REFERENCES

Acredolo, C., & O'Connor, J. (1991). On the difficulty of detecting cognitive uncertainty. *Human Development, 34,* 204–223.

Acredolo, L. P., & Goodwyn, S. W. (1985). Symbolic gesture in language development: A case study. *Human Development, 28,* 40–49.

Acredolo, L. P., & Goodwyn, S. W. (1988). Symbolic gesturing in normal infants. *Child Development, 59,* 450–466.

Acredolo, L. P., Goodwyn, S. W., Horrobin, K. D., & Emmons, Y. D. (1999). The signs and sounds of early language development. In C. Tamis-LeMonda & L. Balter (Eds.), Child psychology: A handbook of contemporary issues. *Psychology Press,* 116–139.

Alibali, M. W., Bassok, M., Olseth, K. L., Syc, S. E., & Goldin-Meadow, S. (1999). Illuminating mental representations through speech and gesture. *Psychological Sciences, 10,* 327–333.

Alibali, M. W., & DiRusso, A. A. (1999). The function of gesture in learning to count: More than keeping track. *Cognitive Development, 14,* 37–56.

Alibali, M. W., Flevares, L., & Goldin-Meadow, S. (1997). Assessing knowledge conveyed in gesture: Do teachers have the upper hand? *Journal of Educational Psychology, 89,* 183–193.

Alibali, M. W., Heath, D. C., & Myers, H. J. (2001). Effects of visibility between speaker and listener on gesture production: Some gestures are meant to be seen. *Journal of Memory and Language, 44,* 1–20.

Alibali, M. W., Kita, S., Bigelow, L. J., Wolfman, C. M., & Klein, S. M. (2001). Gesture plays a role in thinking for speaking. In C.

Cave, I. Guaitella, & S. Santi (Eds.), *Oralite et gestualite: Interactions et comportements multimodaux dans la communication* (pp. 407–410). Paris: L'Harmattan.

Alibali, M. W., Kita, S., & Young, A. J. (2000). Gesture and the process of speech production: We think, therefore we gesture. *Language and Cognitive Processes, 15,* 593–613.

Allen, R., & Shatz, M. (1983). "What says meow?" The role of context and linguistic experience in very young children's responses to *what*-questions. *Journal of Child Language, 10,* 14–23.

Andersen, E. S., Dunlea, A., & Kekelis, L. S. (1984). Blind children's language: Resolving some differences. *Journal of Child Language, 11,* 645–664.

Andersen, E. S., Dunlea, A., & Kekelis, L. S. (1993). The impact of input: Language acquisition in the visually impaired. *First Language, 13,* 23–49.

Argyle, M. (1975). *Bodily communiction.* New York: International Universities Press.

Barsalou, L. W. (1999). Perceptual symbols systems. *Behavioral and Brain Sciences, 22,* 577–660.

Bates, E. (1976). *Language and context: The acquisition of pragmatics.* New York: Academic Press.

Bates, E., Benigni, L., Bretherton, I., Camaioni, L., & Volterra, V. (1979). *The emergence of symbols: Cognition and communication in infancy.* New York: Academic Press.

Bavelas, J. B. (1994). Gestures as part of speech: Methodological implications. *Research on Language and Social Interaction, 27,* 201–221.

Bavelas, J. B., Chovil, N., Lawrie, D. A., & Wade, A. (1992). Interactive gestures. *Discourse Processes, 15,* 469–489.

Beattie, G., & Coughlan, J. (1998). Do iconic gestures have a functional role in lexical access? An experimental study of the effects of repeating a verbal message on gesture production. *Semiotica, 119,* 221–249.

Beattie, G., & Coughlan, J. (1999). An experimental investigation of the role of iconic gestures in lexical access using the tip-of-the-tongue phenomenon. *British Journal of Psychology, 90,* 35–56.

Beattie, G., & Shovelton, H. (1999a). Do iconic hand gestures really contribute anything to the semantic information conveyed by speech? An experimental investigation. *Semiotica, 123,* 1–30.

Beattie, G., & Shovelton, H. (1999b). Mapping the range of information contained in the iconic hand gestures that accompany spontaneous speech. *Journal of Language and Social Psychology, 18,* 438–462.

Bekken, K. (1989). *Is there "Motherese" in gesture?* Unpublished doctoral dissertation, University of Chicago, IL.

Berger, K. W., & Popelka, G. R. (1971). Extra-facial gestures in relation to speech-reading. *Journal of Communication Disorders, 3,* 302–308.

Bertenthal, B. I. (1999). Variation and selection in the development of perception and action. In G. Savelsbergh (Ed.), *Non-linear developmental processes* (pp. 105–121). Amsterdam: Elsevier Science.

Broaders, S. (2003). *Children's susceptibility to suggestion conveyed by the gesture of the interviewer.* Unpublished doctoral dissertation, University of Chicago, IL.

Broaders, S., & Goldin-Meadow, S. (2002, June). *Making children gesture: What role does it play in thinking?* Paper presented at the annual meeting of the Piaget Society, Philadelphia, PA.

Broaders, S., & Goldin-Meadow, S. (2004). *Leading children by the hand: The impact of gesture on eyewitness testimony.* Manuscript submitted for publication.

Butcher, C., & Goldin-Meadow, S. (2000). Gesture and the transition from one- to two-word speech: When hand and mouth come together. In D. McNeill (Ed.), *Language and gesture* (pp. 235–257). New York: Cambridge University Press.

Butcher, C., Mylander, C., & Goldin-Meadow, S. (1991). Displaced communication in a self-styled gesture system: Pointing at the non-present. *Cognitive Development, 6,* 315–342.

Butterworth, G., & Grover, L. (1988). The origins of referential communication in human infancy. In L. Weiskrantz (Ed.), *Thought without language* (pp. 5–24). Oxford, England: Carendon.

Butterworth, B., & Hadar, U. (1989). Gesture, speech, and computational stages: A reply to McNeill. *Psychological Review, 96,* 168–174.

Camaioni, L., Caselli, M. C., Longobardi, E., & Volterra, V. (1991). A parent report instrument for early language assessment. *First Language, 11,* 345–359.

Capirci, O., Montanari, S., & Volterra, V. (1998). Gestures, signs, and words in early language development. In J. M. Iverson & S. Goldin-Meadow (Eds.), *New directions for child development series: The nature and functions of gesture in children's communications* (No 79, pp. 45–60). San Francisco: Jossey-Bass.

Ceci, S. J. (1995). False beliefs: Some developmental and clinical considerations. In D. L. Schacter (Ed.), *Memory distortion: How minds, brains, and societies reconstruct the past* (pp. 91–125). Cambridge, MA: Harvard University Press.

Church, R. B., Ayman-Nolley, S., & Mahootian, S. (2004). The role of gesture in bilingual instruction. *International Journal of Bilingual Education and Bilingualism, 7,* 303–319.

Church, R. B., & Goldin-Meadow, S. (1986). The mismatch between gesture and speech as an index of transitional knowledge. *International Journal of Bilingual Education and Bilingualism, 7,* 303–319.

Church, R. B., Schonert-Reichl, K., Goodman, N., Kelly, S. D., & Ayman-Nolley, S. (1995). The role of gesture and speech communication as reflections of cognitive understanding. *Journal of Contemporary Legal Issues, 6,* 123–154.

Cohen, A. A., & Harrison, R. P. (1973). Intentionality in the use of hand illustrators in face-to-face communication situations. *Journal of Personality and Social Psychology, 28,* 276–279.

Conrad, R. (1979). *The deaf child.* London: Harper & Row.

Crowder, E. M., & Newman, D. (1993). Telling what they know: The role of gesture and language in children's science explanations. *Pragmatics and Cognition, 1,* 341–376.

de Laguna, G. (1927). *Speech: Its function and development.* Bloomington: Indiana University Press.

De Ruiter, J.-P. (1998). Gesture and speech production. *MPI Series in Psycholinguistics, 6.* Max Planck Institute for Psycholinguistics.

Dienes, Z., & Perner, J. (1999). A theory of implicit and explicit knowledge. *Brain and Behavioral Science, 22,* 735–780.

Dunlea, A. (1989). *Vision and the emergence of meaning.* New York: Cambridge University Press.

Dunlea, A., & Andersen, E. S. (1992). The emergence process: Conceptual and linguistic influences on morphological development. *First Language, 12,* 95–115.

Ejiri, K., & Masataka, N. (2001). Co-occurrence of preverbal vocal behavior and motor action in early infancy. *Developmental Science, 4,* 40–48.

Ekman, P., & Friesen, W. (1969). The repertoire of nonverbal behavioral categories. *Semiotica, 1,* 49–98.

Ekman, P., Friesen, W. V., & Ellsworth, P. (1972). *Emotion in the human face.* New York: Pergamon Press.

Ellis Weismer, S., & Hesketh, L. J. (1993). The influence of prosodic and gestural cues on novel word acquisition by children with specific language impairment. *Journal of Speech and Hearing Research, 36,* 1013–1025.

Evans, J. L., Alibali, M. W., & McNeil, N. M. (2001). Divergence of embodied knowledge and verbal expression: Evidence from gesture and speech in children with specific language impairment. *Language and Cognitive Processes, 16,* 309–331.

Evans, M. A., & Rubin, K. H. (1979). Hand gestures as a communicative mode in school-aged children. *Journal of Genetic Psychology, 135,* 189–196.

Fant, L. J. (1972). *Ameslan: An introduction to American sign language.* Silver Springs, MD: National Association of the Deaf.

Feyereisen, P. (1983). Manual activity during speaking in aphasic subjects. *International Journal of Psychology, 18,* 545–556.

Feyereisen, P., van de Wiele, M., & Dubois, F. (1988). The meaning of gestures: What can be understood without speech. *Cahiers de Psychologie Cognitive, 8,* 3–25.

Garber, P., Alibali, M. W., & Goldin-Meadow, S. (1998). Knowledge conveyed in gesture is not tied to the hands. *Child Development, 69,* 75–84.

Garber, P., & Goldin-Meadow, S. (2002). Gesture offers insight into problem-solving in children and adults. *Cognitive Science, 26,* 817–831.

Gelman, R., & Gallistel, C. R. (1978). *The child's understanding of number.* Cambridge, MA: Harvard University Press.

Gershkoff-Stowe, L., & Smith, L. B. (1997). A curvilinear trend in naming errors as a function of early vocabulary growth. *Cognitive Psychology, 34,* 37–71.

Glenberg, A. M. (1997). What memory is for. *Behavioral and Brain Sciences, 20,* 1–55.

Glenberg, A. M., & Kaschak, M. (2002). Grounding language in action. *Psychonomic Bulletin and Review, 9,* 558–565.

Glenberg, A. M., & Robertson, D. A. (1999). Indexical understanding of instructions. *Discourse Processes, 28,* 1–26.

Goldin-Meadow, S. (1985). Language development under atypical learning conditions: Replication and implications of a study of deaf children of hearing parents. In K. Nelson (Ed.), *Children's language* (Vol. 5, pp. 197–245). Hillsdale, NJ: Erlbaum.

Goldin-Meadow, S. (1993). When does gesture become language? A study of gesture used as a primary communication system by deaf children of hearing parents. In K. R. Gibson & T. Ingold (Eds.), *Tools, language and cognition in human evolution* (pp. 63–85). New York: Cambridge University Press.

Goldin-Meadow, S. (2003a). *Hearing gesture: How our hands help us think.* Cambridge, MA: Harvard University Press.

Goldin-Meadow, S. (2003b). *The resilience of language: What gesture creation in deaf children can tell us about how all children learning language.* New York: Psychology Press.

Goldin-Meadow, S., & Alibali, M. W. (1994). Do you have to be right to redescribe? *Behavioral and Brain Sciences, 17,* 718–719.

Goldin-Meadow, S., & Alibali, M. W. (1999). Does the hand reflect implicit knowledge? Yes and no. *Behavioral and Brain Sciences, 22,* 766–767.

Goldin-Meadow, S., Alibali, M. W., & Church, R. B. (1993). Transitions in concept acquisition: Using the hand to read the mind. *Psychological Review,* 279–297.

Goldin-Meadow, S., & Butcher, C. (2003). Pointing toward two-word speech in young children. In S. Kita (Ed.), *Pointing: Where language, culture, and cognition meet* (pp. 85–107). Hillsdale, NJ: Erlbaum.

Goldin-Meadow, S., Butcher, C., Mylander, C., & Dodge, M. (1994). Nouns and verbs in a self-styled gesture system: What's in a name? *Cognitive Psychology, 27,* 259–319.

Goldin-Meadow, S., Goodrich, W., Sauer, E., & Iverson, J. M. (2005). *Children use their hands to tell their mothers what to say.* Manuscript submitted for publication.

Goldin-Meadow, S., Kim, S., & Singer, M. (1999). What the teacher's hands tell the student's mind about math. *Journal of Educational Psychology, 91,* 720–730.

Goldin-Meadow, S., & Morford, M. (1985). Gesture in early child language: Studies of deaf and hearing children. *Merrill-Palmer Quarterly, 31,* 145–176.

Goldin-Meadow, S., & Mylander, C. (1983). Gestural communication in deaf children: The non-effects of parental input on language development. *Science, 221,* 372–374.

Goldin-Meadow, S., & Mylander, C. (1984). Gestural communication in deaf children: The effects and non-effects of parental input on early language development. *Monographs of the Society for Research in Child Development, 49,* 1–121.

Goldin-Meadow, S., & Mylander, C. (1998). Spontaneous sign systems created by deaf children in two cultures. *Nature, 91,* 279–281.

Goldin-Meadow, S., Mylander, C., & Butcher, C. (1995). The resilience of combinatorial structure at the word level: Morphology in self-styled gesture systems. *Cognition, 56,* 195–262.

Goldin-Meadow, S., Mylander, C., & Franklin, A. (2005). *How children make language out of gesture: Morphological structure in gesture systems developed by American and Chinese deaf children.* Manuscript submitted for publication.

Goldin-Meadow, S., Nusbaum, H., Garber, P., & Church, R. B. (1993). Transitions in learning: Evidence for simultaneously activated strategies. *Journal of Experimental Psychology: Human Perception and Performance, 19,* 92–107.

Goldin-Meadow, S., Nusbaum, H., Kelly, S. D., & Wagner, S. (2001). Explaining math: Gesturing lightens the load. *Psychological Sciences, 12,* 516–522.

Goldin-Meadow, S., & Saltzman, J. (2000). The cultural bounds of maternal accommodation: How Chinese and American mothers communicate with deaf and hearing children. *Psychological Science, 11,* 311–318.

Goldin-Meadow, S., & Sandhofer, C. M. (1999). Gesture conveys substantive information about a child's thoughts to ordinary listeners. *Developmental Science, 2,* 67–74.

Goldin-Meadow, S., & Singer, M. A. (2003). From children's hands to adults' ears: Gesture's role in teaching and learning. *Developmental Psychology, 39*(3), 509–520.

Goldin-Meadow, S., Wein, D., & Chang, C. (1992). Assessing knowledge through gesture: Using children's hands to read their minds. *Cognition and Instruction, 9,* 201–219.

Goodwyn, S. W., & Acredolo, L. P. (1993). Symbolic gesture versus word: Is there a modality advantage for onset of symbol use? *Child Development, 64,* 688–701.

Goodwyn, S. W., & Acredolo, L. P. (1998). Encouraging symbolic gestures: A new perspective on the relationship between gesture and speech. In J. M. Iverson & S. Goldin-Meadow (Eds.), *New directions for child development series: The nature and functions of gesture in children's communication* (No. 79, pp. 61–73). San Francisco: Jossey-Bass.

Goodwyn, S., Acredolo, L., & Brown, C. A. (2000). Impact of symbolic gesturing on early language development. *Journal of Nonverbal Behavior, 24,* 81–104.

Graham, J. A., & Argyle, M. (1975). A cross-cultural study of the communication of extra-verbal meaning by gestures. *International Journal of Psychology, 10,* 57–67.

Graham, J. A., & Heywood, S. (1975). The effects of elimination of hand gestures and of verbal codability on speech performance. *European Journal of Social Psychology, 2,* 189–195.

Graham, T. A. (1999). The role of gesture in children's learning to count. *Journal of Experimental Child Psychology, 74,* 333–355.

Greenfield, P., & Smith, J. (1976). *The structure of communication in early language development.* New York: Academic Press.

Guillaume, P. (1927). Les debuts de la phrase dans le langage de l'enfant. *Journal de Psychologie, 24,* 1–25.

Gulberg, M. (1998). *Gesture as a communication strategy in second language discourse: A study of learners of French and Swedish.* Lund, Sweden: Lund University Press.

Hockett, C. F. (1960). The origin of speech. *Scientific American, 203*(3), 88–96.

Hoffmeister, R., & Wilbur, R. (1980). Developmental: The acquisition of sign language. In H. Lane & F. Grosjean (Eds.), *Recent perspectives on American sign language* (pp. 61–78). Hillsdale, NJ: Erlbaum.

Horobin, K., & Acredolo, C. (1989). The impact of probability judgments on reasoning about multiple possibilities. *Child Development, 60,* 183–200.

Iverson, J. M. (1999). How to get to the cafeteria: Gesture and speech in blind and sighted children's spatial descriptions. *Developmental Psychology, 35,* 1132–1142.

Iverson, J. M., Capirci, O., & Caselli, M. S. (1994). From communication to language in two modalities. *Cognitive Development, 9,* 23–43.

Iverson, J. M., Capirci, O., Longobardi, E., & Caselli, M. C. (1999). Gesturing in mother-child interaction. *Cognitive Development, 14,* 57–75.

Iverson, J. M., & Fagan, M. K. (2004). Infant vocal-motor coordination: Precursor to the gesture-speech system? *Child Development, 75,* 1053–1066.

Iverson, J. M., & Goldin-Meadow, S. (1997). What's communication got to do with it: Gesture in blind children. *Developmental Psychology, 33,* 453–467.

Iverson, J. M., & Goldin-Meadow, S. (1998). Why people gesture as they speak. *Nature, 396,* 228.

Iverson, J. M., & Goldin-Meadow, S. (2001). The resilience of gesture in talk: Gesture in blind speakers and listeners. *Developmental Science, 4,* 416–422.

Iverson, J. M., & Goldin-Meadow, S. (2005). Gesture paves the way for language development. *Psychological Science, 16,* 368–371.

Iverson, J. M., Longobardi, E., & Caselli, M. C. (2003). Relationship between gestures and words in children with Down's syndrome and typically developing children in the early stages of communicative development. *International Journal of Language and Communication Disorders, 38,* 179–197.

Iverson, J. M., Tencer, H. L., Lany, J., & Goldin-Meadow, S. (2000). The relation between gesture and speech in congenitally blind and sighted language-learners. *Journal of Nonverbal Behavior, 24,* 105–130.

Iverson, J. M., & Thelen, E. (1999). Hand, mouth, and brain: The dynamic emergence of speech and gesture. *Journal of Consciousness Studies, 6,* 19–40.

Jancovic, M. A., Devoe, S., & Wiener, M. (1975). Age-related changes in hand and arm movements as nonverbal communication: Some conceptualizations and an empirical exploration. *Child Development, 46,* 922–928.

Karmiloff-Smith, A. (1986). From meta-processes to conscious access: Evidence from children's metalinguistic and repair data. *Cognition, 23*(2), 95–147.

Karmiloff-Smith, A. (1992). *Beyond modularity: A developmental perspective on cognitive science.* Cambridge, MA: MIT Press.

Kegl, J., Senghas, A., & Coppola, M. (1999). Creation through contact: Sign language emergence and sign language change in Nicaragua. In M. DeGraff (Ed.), *Language creation and language change: Creolization, diachrony, and development* (pp. 179–237). Cambridge, MA: MIT Press.

Kelly, S. D. (2001). Broadening the units of analysis in communication: Speech and nonverbal behaviours in pragmatic comprehension. *Journal of Child Language, 28,* 325–349.

Kelly, S. D., & Church, R. B. (1997). Can children detect conceptual information conveyed through other children's nonverbal behaviors? *Cognition and Instruction, 15,* 107–134.

Kelly, S. D., Singer, M. A., Hicks, J., & Goldin-Meadow, S. (2002). A helping hand in assessing children's knowledge: Instructing adults to attend to gesture. *Cognition and Instruction, 20,* 1–26.

Kendon, A. (1980). Gesticulation and speech: Two aspects of the process of utterance. In M. R. Key (Ed.), *Relationship of verbal and nonverbal communication* (pp. 207–228). The Hague, The Netherlands: Mouton.

Kendon, A. (1994). Do gestures communicate? A review. *Research on Language and Social Interaction, 27,* 175–200.

Kita, S. (2000). How representational gestures help speaking. In D. McNeill (Ed.), *Language and gesture* (pp. 162–185). New York: Cambridge University Press.

Knapp, M. L. (1978). *Nonverbal communication in human interaction* (2nd ed.). New York: Holt, Rinehart and Winston.

Krauss, R. M., Dushay, R. A., Chen, Y., & Rauscher, F. (1995). The communicative value of conversational hand gestures. *Journal of Experimental Social Psychology, 31,* 533–553.

Krauss, R. M., Morrel-Samuels, P., & Colasante, C. (1991). Do conversational hand gestures communicate? *Journal of Personality and Social Psychology, 61,* 743–754.

Landau, B., & Gleitman, L. R. (1985). *Language and experience: Evidence from the blind child.* Cambridge, MA: Harvard University Press.

Lenneberg, E. H. (1964). Capacity for language acquisition. In J. A. Fodor & J. J. Katz (Eds.), *The structure of language: Readings in the philosophy of language* (pp. 579–603). Englewood Cliffs, NJ: Prentice-Hall.

Leopold, W. (1949). *Speech development of a bilingual child: Vol. 3. A linguist's record.* Evanston, IL: Northwestern University Press.

Leung, E., & Rheingold, H. (1981). Development of pointing as a social gesture. *Developmental Psychology, 17,* 215–220.

Lickiss, K. P., & Wellens, A. R. (1978). Effects of visual accessibility and hand restraint on fluency of gesticulator and effectiveness of message. *Perceptual and Motor Skills, 46,* 925–926.

Lillo-Martin, D. (1999). Modality effects and modularity in language acquisition: The acquisition of American sign language. In W. C. Ritchie & T. K. Bhatia (Eds.), *Handbook of child language acquisition* (pp. 531–567). New York: Academic Press.

Macnamara, J. (1977). From sign to language. In J. Macnamara (Ed.), *Language learning and thought* (pp. 11–36). New York: Academic Press.

Marcos, L. R. (1979). Hand movements and nondominant fluency in bilinguals. *Percpetual and Motor Skills, 48,* 207–214.

Masur, E. F. (1982). Mothers' responses to infants' object-related gestures: Influences on lexical development. *Journal of Child Language, 9,* 23–30.

Masur, E. F. (1983). Gestural development, dual-directional signaling, and the transition to words. *Journal of Psycholinguistic Research, 12,* 93–109.

Mayberry, R. I. (1992). The cognitive development of deaf children: Recent insights. In F. Boller & J. Graffman (Series Eds.) & S. Segalowitz & I. Rapin (Vol. Eds.), *Handbook of neuropsychology: Vol. 7. Child neuropsychology* (pp. 51–68). Amsterdam: Elsevier.

McNeill, D. (1985). So you think gestures are nonverbal? *Psychological Review, 92,* 350–371.

McNeill, D. (1987). *Psycholinguistics: A new approach.* New York: Harper & Row.

McNeill, D. (1992). *Hand and Mind.* Chicago: University of Chicago Press.

McNeill, D., Cassell, J., & McCullough, K.-E. (1994). Communicative effects of speech-mismatched gestures. *Research on Language and Social Interaction, 27,* 223–237.

Meadow, K. (1968). Early manual communication in relation to the deaf child's intellectual, social, and communicative functioning. *American Annals of the Deaf, 113,* 29–41.

Melinger, A., & Kita, S. (in press). Does gesture help processes of speech production? Evidence for conceptual level facilitation. *Proceedings of the Berkeley Linguistic Society.*

Mohay, H. (1982). A preliminary description of the communication systems evolved by two deaf children in the absence of a sign language model. *Sign Language Studies, 34,* 73–90.

Moores, D. F. (1974). Nonvocal systems of verbal behavior. In R. L. Schiefelbusch & L. L. Lloyd (Eds.), *Language perspectives: Acquisition, retardation, and intervention* (pp. 377–417). Baltimore: University Park Press.

Morford, M., & Goldin-Meadow, S. (1992). Comprehension and production of gesture in combination with speech in one-word speakers. *Journal of Child Language, 19,* 559–580.

Morford, J. P., & Goldin-Meadow, S. (1997). From here to there and now to then: The development of displaced reference in homesign and English. *Child Development, 68,* 420–435.

Morrel-Samuels, P., & Krauss, R. M. (1992). Word familiarity predicts temporal asynchrony of hand gestures and speech. *Journal of Experimental Psychology: Learning, Memory, and Cognition, 18,* 615–622.

Murphy, C. M., & Messer, D. J. (1977). Mothers, infants and pointing: A study of Gesture. In H. R. Schaffer (Ed.), *Studies in mother-infant interaction* (pp. 325–354). New York: Academic Press.

Namy, L. L., Acredolo, L., & Goodwyn, S. (2000). Verbal labels and gestural routines in parental communication with young children. *Journal of Nonverbal Behavior, 24,* 63–80.

Namy, L. L., & Waxman, S. R. (1998). Words and gestures: Infants' interpretations of different forms of symbolic reference. *Child Development, 69,* 295–308.

Newport, E. L., & Meier, R. P. (1985). The acquisition of American sign language. In D. I. Slobin (Ed.), *The cross-linguistic study of language acquisition: Vol. 1. The data* (pp. 881–938). Hillsdale, NJ: Erlbaum.

Ozcaliskan, S., & Goldin-Meadow, S. (2005a). Do parents lead their children by the hand? *Journal of Child Language, 32,* 481–505.

Ozcaliskan, S., & Goldin-Meadow, S. (2005). Gesture is at the cutting edge of early language development. *Cognition, 96,* B101–B113.

Perry, M., Berch, D., & Singleton, J. (1995). Constructing shared understanding: The role of nonverbal input in learning contexts. *Journal of Contemporary Legal Issues, 6,* 213–235.

Perry, M., Church, R. B., & Goldin-Meadow, S. (1988). Transitional knowledge in the acquisition of concepts. *Cognitive Development, 3,* 359–400.

Perry, M., & Elder, A. D. (1997). Knowledge in transition: Adults' developing understanding of a principle of physical causality. *Cognitive Development, 12,* 131–157.

Petitto, L. A. (1988). "Language" in the pre-linguistic child. In F. Kessel (Ed.), *The development of language and language researchers: Essays in honor of Roger Brown* (pp. 187–221). Hillsdale, NJ: Erlbaum.

Phillips, S. B., Goldin-Meadow, S., & Miller, P. J. (2001). Enacting stories, seeing worlds: Similarities and differences in the cross-cultural narrative development of linguistically isolated deaf children. *Human Development, 44,* 311–336.

Pine, K. J., Lufkin, N., & Messer, D. (2004). More gestures than answers: Children learning about balance. *Developmental Psychology, 40,* 1059–1067.

Rauscher, F. H., Krauss, R. M., & Chen, Y. (1996). Gesture, speech, and lexical access: The role of lexical movements in speech production. *Psychological Science, 7,* 226–231.

Rimé, B. (1982). The elimination of visible behaviour from social interactions: Effects on verbal, nonverbal and interpersonal variables. *European Journal of Social Psychology, 12,* 113–129.

Rimé, B., Schiaratura, L., Hupet, M., & Ghysselinckx, A. (1984). Effects of relative immobilization on the speaker's nonverbal behavior and on the dialogue imagery level. *Motivation and Emotion, 8,* 311–325.

Riseborough, M. G. (1981). Physiographic gestures as decoding facilitators: Three experiments exploring a neglected facet of communication. *Journal of Nonverbal Behavior, 5,* 172–183.

Saxe, G. B., & Kaplan, R. (1981). Gesture in early counting: A developmental analysis. *Perceptual and Motor Skills, 53,* 851–854.

Senghas, A. (1995). The development of Nicaraguan sign language via the language acquisition process. *Proceedings of Boston University Child Language Development, 19,* 543–552.

Senghas, A. (2000). The development of early spatial morphology in Nicaraguan sign language. *Proceedings of Boston University Child Language Development, 24,* 696–707.

Senghas, A., Coppola, M., Newport, E. L., & Supalla, T. (1997). Argument structure in Nicaraguan sign language: The emergence of grammatical devices. *Proceedings of Boston University Child Language Development, 21,* 550–561.

Shatz, M. (1982). On mechanisms of language acquisition: Can features of the communicative environment account for development. In E. Wanner & L. R. Gleitman (Eds.), *Language acquisition: The state of the art* (pp. 102–127). New York: Cambridge University Press.

Siegler, R. S. (1994). Cognitive variability: A key to understanding cognitive development. *Current Directions in Psychological Science, 3,* 1–5.

Siegler, R. S., & Crowley, K. (1991). The microgenetic method: A direct means for studying cognitive development. *American Psychologist, 46*(6), 606–620.

Singer, M. A., & Goldin-Meadow, S. (2005). Children learn when their teachers' gestures and speech differ. *Psychological Science, 16,* 85–89.

Singleton, J. L., Morford, J. P., & Goldin-Meadow, S. (1993). Once is not enough: Standards of well-formedness in manual communication created over three different timespans. *Language, 69,* 683–715.

Stone, A., Webb, R., & Mahootian, S. (1992). The generality of gesture-speech mismatch as an index of transitional knowledge: Evidence from a control-of-variables task. *Cognitive Development, 6,* 301–313.

Tervoort, B. T. (1961). Esoteric symbolism in the communication behavior of young deaf children. *American Annals of the Deaf, 106,* 436–480.

Thal, D., Tobias, S., & Morrison, D. (1991). Language and gesture in late talkers: A one year followup. *Journal of Speech and Hearing Research, 34,* 604–612.

Thelen, E. (1989). Self-organization in developmental processes: Can systems approaches work. In M. Gunnar & E. Thelen (Eds.), *Minnesota Symposia on Child Psychology: Systems and development* (pp. 77–117). Hillsdale, NJ: Erlbaum.

Thompson, L., & Massaro, D. (1986). Evaluation and integration of speech and pointing gestures during referential understanding. *Journal of Experimental Child Psychology, 57,* 327–354.

Valenzeno, L., Alibali, M. W., & Klatzky, R. (2003). Teachers' gestures facilitate students' learning: A lesson in symmetry. *Contemporary Educational Psychology, 28,* 187–204.

Wagner, S., Nusbaum, H., & Goldin-Meadow, S. (2004). Probing the mental representation of gesture: Is handwaving spatial? *Journal of Memory and Language, 50,* 395–407.

Wang, X.-L., Mylander, C., & Goldin-Meadow, S. (1993). Language and environment: A cross-cultural study of the gestural communication systems of Chinese and American deaf children. *Belgian Journal of Linguistics, 8,* 167–185.

Wesp, R., Hesse, J., Keutmann, D., & Wheaton, K. (2001). Gestures maintain spatial imagery. *American Journal of Psychology, 114,* 591–600.

Wolff, P., & Gutstein, J. (1972). Effects of induced motor gestures on vocal output. *Journal of Communication, 22,* 277–288.

Wundt, W. (1973). *The language of gestures.* The Hague, The Netherlands: Mouton. (Original work published 1900)

Wynn, K. (1990). Children's understanding of counting. *Cognition, 36,* 155–193.

Zinober, B., & Martlew, M. (1985). Developmental changes in four types of gesture in relation to acts and vocalizations from 10 to 21 months. *British Journal of Developmental Psychology, 3,* 293–306.

# Cognitive Processes

CHAPTER 9

# Event Memory

PATRICIA J. BAUER

WHAT IS EVENT MEMORY AND WHY IS
    IT IMPORTANT?   374
THE SCOPE OF THIS CHAPTER   374
TRADITIONAL ACCOUNTS OF THE
    DEVELOPMENT OF EVENT MEMORY   376
Changing the Course of Research on Developments
    in Event Memory   377
Event Memory in Infancy and Early Childhood   380
EVENT MEMORY IN THE FIRST 2 YEARS
    OF LIFE   380
Assessing Event Memory Using Elicited and
    Deferred Imitation   381
Developmental Trends   382
What Accounts for Developmental Changes over the
    First 2 Years of Life?   385
Group and Individual Differences in Event
    Memory in Infancy   390
DEVELOPMENTS IN AND AFTER THE
    PRESCHOOL YEARS   392
Children's Memories for Routine Events   393
Children's Memories for Unique Events   393
Age-Related Changes in Preschoolers' Recall
    of Past Events   394
Emergence of Autobiographical or
    Personal Memory   397

What Develops in Preschoolers' Recall of
    Past Events?   398
Developmental Changes in Basic
    Mnemonic Processes   398
Conceptual Developments   401
Developmental Changes in and the Socialization of
    Narrative Production   402
Summary and Conclusions   405
Group and Individual Differences in Event and
    Autobiographical Memory in the
    Preschool Years   405
CONTINUITIES AND DISCONTINUITIES IN THE
    DEVELOPMENT OF EVENT MEMORY   411
Explicit Memory in the First 6 Months of Life   411
The Transition from Infancy to Early Childhood   412
Summary and Evaluation   413
IS MEMORY FOR STRESSFUL OR TRAUMATIC
    EVENTS "SPECIAL"?   414
Memories of Stressful or Traumatic Events   414
Summary   416
CONCLUSION AND DIRECTIONS FOR
    FUTURE RESEARCH   416
REFERENCES   418

It may come as a surprise that the current volume of the venerable *Handbook of Child Psychology* is the first to contain a chapter on "event memory." With some notable exceptions (e.g., Bartlett, 1932), it was not until the mid-1970s that research on entities termed "events" became

I gratefully acknowledge the support of the NICHD for the work from my laboratory cited in this review (HD-28425, HD-42483). I also extend my heartfelt appreciation to my colleagues Robyn Fivush, Jean Mandler, and Katherine Nelson, for their comments on a draft version of this review; for their foundational and ongoing contributions to the field I have had the privilege to represent; and for the many spirited conversations in which we have engaged that have served to sharpen and otherwise further my perspective on developmental changes in event memory. Thank you.

common in the adult cognitive literature, with research on stories (e.g., Rumelhart, 1975), scripts (e.g., Schank & Abelson, 1977), and schemas (e.g., Kintsch, 1974). Whereas developmental scientists were not far behind in the effort (Mandler & Johnson, 1977; K. Nelson, 1978; Stein & Glenn, 1979), at the time of preparation of the 1983 (fourth) edition of the *Handbook,* a review of the data on children's memories for the events of their lives nevertheless consumed only 4 pages of Jean Mandler's (1983) 57-page (excluding References) chapter, "Representation" (with additional space devoted to representation of stories). By the time the fifth edition was published in 1998, there was a wealth of new information about children's memories for events, but the body of data was not yet recognized as constituting a coherent domain. Instead, the themes that are brought together in this chapter were distributed across several chapters, most prominently "Infant Cognition" (Haith & Benson, 1998), "Representation" (once again by Mandler, 1998), and "Memory" (Schneider & Bjorklund, 1998).

## WHAT IS EVENT MEMORY AND WHY IS IT IMPORTANT?

What kind of memory is event memory? At its most basic, an event can be almost anything: a leaf fluttering in the breeze, ice forming on a pond, or ink running on a piece of paper. For a coherent body of work to be summarized under the heading "Event Memory," the term *event* needs to be defined in a meaningful way. Borrowing from Katherine Nelson (1986), for purposes of this chapter, I define events as "involv(ing) people in purposeful activities, and acting on objects and interacting with each other to achieve some result" (p. 11). Purposeful activity unfolds over time: It has a beginning, a middle, and an end. Moreover, because the actions in events are oriented toward a goal or result (even if not all the participants in or observers of the event are privy to it), there frequently are constraints on the order in which they unfold: Actions preparatory to an outcome must occur before it in time. This definition eliminates from consideration simple physical transformations such as fluttering, freezing, and smearing, which do not involve actors engaged in purposeful activity. In contrast, the definition effectively includes the activities in which individuals engage as they move through a typical day (such as eating breakfast, going to school, and having dinner at a restaurant) as well as the unique experiences that ultimately define us as individuals. It is memory for these episodes with which this chapter is concerned. The definition also specifies what there is to be remembered about events—actors, actions, objects, and the orders in which the elements combine to achieve specific goals.

Defining events as purposeful activities in which individuals engage highlights why the ability to remember events is important and, thus, why the study of the development of event memory is important. First, memories of past events guide present behavior and are a basis on which we plan future behavior. Although we think about memory as being about the past, most of the uses to which we put memory concern the present and the fu-

ture. For example, we use our experience of prior trips to the grocery store to guide our behavior on the current trip (e.g., we look for our favorite cookies in Aisle 1, based on our memory of finding them there in the past), as well as to plan for future trips (e.g., we reorder next week's shopping list because we remember that the store moved the cookies from Aisle 1 to Aisle 6).

Second, events and stories about them are major instructional tools, both informally and formally. It is through participating in events that we learn that cookies and fruit both make good snacks; that it feels better to win the game than to lose it; and that when you are running late, the bus leaves on time (without you!). In formal academic settings, it is through listening to and reading stories and enacting events from the past that we learn about the forces that shaped history and the political lessons that could, were we to heed them, prevent us from repeating it. The episodes of our own and others' lives are major sources of semantic content and knowledge.

Third, memories of the events in which we participated are self-defining: Who we are is who we were and what we did. Memories of personally relevant experiences and events (termed *autobiographical memories*) are the ones that we share when we are getting to know new people or reconnecting with old acquaintances. We use our past experiences to explain our present behavior and to motivate choices for the future. For these reasons and more, the ability to remember past events is important to the mature as well as the developing human.

## THE SCOPE OF THIS CHAPTER

From the partial list of the functions of event memory just presented, it is possible to discern at least some of the topics of this chapter. It includes reviews of the literature on children's developing ability to remember the experiences of their lives—both routine and unique. Focus is on children's abilities to recall the actors, actions, and objects of events, the order in which the activities unfold, and the goals of activities. There are discussions of age-related changes in the basic processes of memory (encoding, consolidation, storage, and retrieval) that permit children to remember more, more accurately, over longer periods. There also are discussions of some factors that affect event memory, as well as the factors that shape narrative skills for its expression. Both normative developmental trends and individual variability are featured. Possible sources of individual differences and mechanisms responsible for developmental trends are suggested.

There also are some topics that are not covered in this chapter even though they are relevant to how past events are remembered. First, as already noted, events have temporal extent: They unfold over time. Events also have spatial extent: They occur in a particular place. Whereas being able to locate an event in space is important to memory for it, memory for spatial location is covered in another chapter of the *Handbook* (Newcombe & Huttenlocher, Chapter 17, this *Handbook,* this volume), and thus is not a focus of specific discussion here. Second, there are times when individuals are called on to report on specific episodes in legal contexts. Most typically, the events on which they are required to report are at least unpleasant and possibly traumatic. Some of the literature on children's recall of negative, stressful, or traumatic events is reviewed in the course of comparison with their memories for positive or neutral experiences (see section "Is Memory for Stressful . . . ," later in this chapter). The forensic and social policy issues surrounding children as eyewitnesses are not, however, a focus here.

Third, much of what is remembered about events was not intentionally or deliberately encoded for later retrieval. With the obvious exceptions of major transitional events such as weddings and births, we do not go about our daily activities deliberately attempting to remember them. As such, we do not necessarily engage in specific activities designed to preserve the events in memory, such as rehearsal. This is not to say that we do not make deliberate efforts to learn from our experiences. Everyday and unique events are full of "life lessons" that we may intentionally attempt to extract. For example, we may deliberately make a note to remember that a new red sweater should not be included in a laundry load of whites. The object of our intention is the lesson, though, not the event or episode that gave rise to the lesson: We hope to remember to separate by color, not the time and place that we learned the necessity of doing so. Because we do not typically make deliberate or strategic attempts to remember most of the episodes of our lives, whether and how children employ deliberate strategies for remembering events has not been a major focus in the event memory literature. Developments in strategic memory are reviewed elsewhere in the

*Handbook* (Pressley & Hilden, Chapter 12, this *Handbook,* this volume).

Finally, to say that much of what we remember about everyday and unique events is not deliberately encoded into memory is not to say that our memories for events are unconscious or outside awareness. There is a major distinction in the broader domain of memory between conscious, declarative, or explicit memory and unconscious, nondeclarative, procedural, or implicit memory. Although it is not universally accepted (see, e.g., Roediger, Rajaram, & Srinivas, 1990; Rovee-Collier, 1997), by both developmental and adult cognitive scientists, it is widely recognized that the different types of memory constitute different systems or processes that serve distinct functions and are characterized by fundamentally different rules of operation (e.g., Schacter, Wagner, & Buckner, 2000; Squire, Knowlton, & Musen, 1993). *Explicit* memory involves the capacity for conscious recognition or recall of the *who, what, where, when, why,* and *how* of experience. It is devoted to recollection of such things as names, dates, places, facts, and events, as well as descriptive details about them. These are entities that we think of as being encoded symbolically and that thus can be described with language. Explicit memory is characterized as fast (e.g., supporting one-trial learning), fallible (e.g., memory traces degrade, retrieval failures occur), and flexible (not tied to a specific modality or context). In contrast, the type of memory termed *implicit* represents nonconscious abilities, including the capacity for learning skills and procedures, priming, and some forms of conditioning. The knowledge tied up in skills and procedures is not of names, dates, facts, and events, but of finely tuned motor patterns and perceptual skills. It is not encoded symbolically and thus is not accessible to language. Implicit memory is characterized as slow (with the exception of priming, it results from gradual or incremental learning), reliable, and inflexible.

Under ordinary circumstances, explicit and implicit memory operate in parallel. That is, in most cases, one derives both explicit and implicit knowledge from the same experience. Learning to drive is a good example. Student drivers consciously learn components of the skill. From their instructors and instruction manuals they learn that to stop the car they should depress the brake; if the car is moving fast, they should allow more time for braking. Drivers can verbally express these elements of their knowledge: They are quite explicit. Yet few drivers—even highly skilled ones—can state the amount of time or the number of pounds of pressure on the brake pedal required to bring to a stop a slow-moving versus a fast-moving vehicle. This knowledge is not conveyed to the novice driver through spoken or written language. Nor is it acquired by observation of other drivers' actions. Rather, it is acquired through practice, practice, and more practice executing the motor movements of braking. The resulting knowledge is tied up in the driver's muscles and joints (the new driver "gets the feel for it") and is not accessible to conscious reflection. How do we know when something is accessible to conscious reflection? Köhler and Moscovitch (1997) suggest that "one is conscious or aware of [a memory] when a verbal or nonverbal description can be provided of [it] or a voluntary response can be made that comments on it" (p. 306).

Another important point is that, in most cases, explicit knowledge and implicit knowledge not only are acquired in parallel but continue to coexist, even after execution of the behavior no longer seems to require conscious awareness. Whereas the skill of driving starts out very demanding of attentional resources, it eventually can be performed almost automatically (without conscious attention paid to it). Such changes tempt the conclusion that once these skills no longer require conscious attention to execute, they have become implicit (or procedural). A moment's reflection reveals the flaw in this logic: If explicit knowledge were to become implicit, it would mean that it was no longer explicit. The fact that I can tell you that to stop the car you apply pressure to the brake proves that my knowledge remains accessible to consciousness. I still have the explicit knowledge, even though I do not depend on that knowledge to execute the behavior. Although the explicit and implicit memory systems operate in parallel, in the domain of event memory, research has been concerned almost exclusively with the explicit aspects of experience. In keeping with this tradition, the literature reviewed in this chapter is on explicit memory. Moreover, the primary focus is developments in recall as opposed to recognition.

## TRADITIONAL ACCOUNTS OF THE DEVELOPMENT OF EVENT MEMORY

As in so many areas of cognitive developmental science, the study of memory development got "off the ground"

with Piaget (1952). Before his writings were translated into English and made widely available to an English-speaking audience, the study of child development focused primarily on motor and physical development and on children's affective development (see Hartup, Johnson, & Weinberg, 2001, for a review). Much of the early work on cognition concerned the development of general intellectual ability and reasoning and problem-solving skills as opposed to specific cognitive developments such as memory (a notable exception was Foster, 1928, who conducted one of the earliest studies of memory for prose material by preschool-age children). In contrast, Piaget made clear and strong predictions about many specific cognitive capacities, including memory. He suggested that for the first 18 to 24 months of life infants lacked symbolic capacity, and thus, the ability to mentally represent objects and events. Instead, they were thought to live in a "here-and-now" world that included physically present entities with no past and no future. In other words, infants were described as living an "out-of-sight, out-of-mind" existence.

Compelling illustrations of the out-of-sight, out-of-mind attitude were provided in Piaget's (1952, 1962) extensive observations of his own children. An example from his daughter, Lucienne, makes the point. At 8 months of age, Lucienne was playing with a toy stork. Piaget took the toy and in full view of Lucienne, hid it under a cover. As long as Piaget hid only a portion of the stork, Lucienne removed the cover and retrieved it. However, when Piaget hid the entire stork under the cover, Lucienne simply stared at Piaget, or began playing with another toy. The change in attitude toward the stork was not for lack of interest in it, for if Piaget then revealed the stork, Lucienne smiled and tried to grasp it. Nor was the problem the need to remove the cover: As long as a portion of the stork was visible, Lucienne easily moved the cover out of the way to get the toy. Piaget interpreted this collection of behaviors as evidence that when the toy was out of sight, it no longer existed for the child. He suggested that the reason for this rather bizarre behavior was that infants lacked the symbolic means to represent information not available to the senses (to mentally *re-present* it).

Piaget hypothesized that by 18 to 24 months of age, children had constructed the capacity for mental representation. Even then, they were thought to be without the necessary cognitive structures to organize events along coherent dimensions that would make the events memorable. Consistent with this suggestion, in retelling fairy tales, children as old as 7 years made errors in temporal sequencing (Piaget, 1926, 1969). Piaget attributed their poor performance to the lack of reversible thought. Without it, children could not organize information temporally and thus could not tell a story from beginning, to middle, to end.

With the rise of information-processing theories in the 1960s and 1970s, researchers began to think about changes in memory as due not to developments in reversible thought, but to hypothesized changes in the efficiency of encoding, storage, and retrieval processes. The major interest was in how properties of the to-be-remembered materials, study conditions, activities during the retention interval, and so forth, influenced memory. A prototypical memory experiment from the 1960s and 1970s was to give children of different ages lists of words or pictures to study and remember. In a classic study, John Flavell and his colleagues gave picture lists to children 5, 7, and 10 years of age. They found that whereas the youngest children did little to help themselves remember (they did not employ memory strategies) and in fact remembered few pictures, the oldest children verbally rehearsed the materials and presumably as a consequence, remembered more (Flavell, Beach, & Chinsky, 1966; see Pressley & Hilden, Chapter 12, this *Handbook,* this volume, for a review of the literature on deliberate and strategic remembering). Indeed, the way to ensure that your experiment "worked" was to include younger and older children, thereby assuring a nice pattern of developmental change.

## Changing the Course of Research on Developments in Event Memory

Three "events" happened in the late 1970s and early 1980s that changed the direction of research on children's memory. One of the events was recognition of the importance to memory of the organization or structure within to-be-remembered materials. A second, and related, event was recognition of the importance to memory of familiarity with the event or domain of the to-be-remembered material. The third event was development of a means of assessing event memory in pre- and early verbal children.

### *The Importance of Organization or Structure*

Recognition that not all to-be-remembered material is created equal contributed to change in the landscape of developmental research on memory. As just noted, re-

search on children's memory undertaken in the 1960s and 1970s frequently used lists of words or pictures for stimuli. In some cases, the lists included related items (e.g., several pictures of animals interspersed with several pictures of clothing items), but in many experiments, following the tradition established in the adult literature (as early as Ebbinghaus, 1885/1913), the materials were virtually devoid of meaning or structure. This allowed researchers to examine the properties of memory (e.g., speed of acquisition, decay rate) without the potentially confounding factor of familiarity (and in the developmental literature, potentially *differential* familiarity, as a function of age and experience). Yet, many of the things that individuals experience and remember are highly structured. The stories that we hear and read are not made up of randomly ordered bits but of antecedent actions followed by consequences. Early work by Piaget (1926, 1969) implied that appreciation of this structure was a relatively late developmental achievement. Contrary to this expectation, in an influential series of studies, Jean Mandler and her colleagues (e.g., Mandler & DeForest, 1979; Mandler & Johnson, 1977) demonstrated not only that children are sensitive to the structure inherent in story materials, but that their memory for them is qualitatively similar to that of adults.

The work was based on the recognition that stories and other types of narratives follow a common hierarchical organization. They begin with an introduction of the protagonist of the story and establishment of the time and place of the events ("Once upon a time, in a land far away, there lived a beautiful princess..."). This setting information is followed by an episode in which the protagonist carries out some action or sequence of actions designed to fulfill a goal. After one or more attempts to achieve the goal, the story wraps up with an outcome of the actions (the goal is either achieved or thwarted) and an ending ("And they lived happily ever after"). The work of Mandler and her colleagues (e.g., Mandler & DeForest, 1979; Mandler & Johnson, 1977; see also Stein & Glenn, 1979) indicated that even young children are sensitive to this structure. For example, children have higher levels of recall of stories that follow the canonical form, relative to stories that violate it. In addition, children tend to "correct" poorly organized stories, to conform to the hierarchical structure (see Mandler, 1984, for a review). Findings such as these made two things abundantly clear: First, event memory is affected by the organization or structure of to-be-remembered events; and second, when to-be-remembered events are well organized, even young children can be expected to recall them.

## The Importance of Familiarity

A second formative experience for the study of developments in event memory was recognition of the importance of familiarity with a domain or event for memory performance. An illustrative example is Michelene Chi's (1978) research on expertise in the domain of chess. Chi asked children and adults to participate in two tests: one in which participants had to remember chess positions and another in which they had to remember random strings of digits. What made the study unique was that the children in the study (who had a mean age of 10 years), were more knowledgeable about chess relative to the adults. Chi found that in the domain of strings of digits, as was expected, the adults outperformed the children. However, in the domain of chess, the children outperformed the adults. Based on these and similar results from other studies, Chi concluded that knowledge of a domain was an important determinant of memory performance.

The importance of knowledge of a domain also was apparent in research on event memory. Indeed, by asking children for reports in domains that they knew well, Katherine Nelson and her colleagues discovered mnemonic competence in children as young as 3 years of age. Rather than asking children to recall lists of words or pictures, or even stories of a protagonist's experiences, they asked, "What happens when you make cookies?" and "What happens when you go to McDonald's" (K. Nelson, 1978; K. Nelson & Gruendel, 1981; see also Todd & Perlmutter, 1980). In this work, Nelson and her colleagues were guided by the script model advanced by Schank and Abelson (1977). Schank and Abelson posited cognitive structures termed *scripts* that guide adults' actions in familiar situations. For example, most adults have a script for "what happens" at a fast-food restaurant. When we enter a restaurant and find a counter, behind which is mounted a menu board, we know that we should approach the counter to order. We "know" that we should behave in this way, even if we have never visited the particular restaurant location before, and even if we have never frequented that particular restaurant chain before. We know not only the elements of the activity, but the order in which the actions should be carried out (e.g., we will be asked to pay for our order before we receive it). Scripts also tell us what *not* to expect: It is our fast-

food restaurant script that would cause us to be surprised if, on driving up to a fast-food restaurant, a tuxedo-clad valet offered to park our car.

To determine whether young children also seem to be guided by scripts for what to do Nelson and her colleagues adopted a straightforward research design:

> Our research design was simple: We asked 3- and 4-year-old children to tell us what happened when they engaged in some everyday routines. Following Abelson and Schank's lead that adults have prototypical restaurant scripts, one of our first script questions was "what happens when you go to MacDonald's." . . . Even the 3-year-olds turned out to be extraordinarily good at this, and produced the first systematic evidence that 3- and 4-year-olds could reliably order an extended sequence of actions according to its temporal and causal relations. (K. Nelson, 1997, p. 3)

On average, the children mentioned 11 different acts in the McDonald's event, and they agreed on 82% of them. K. Nelson and Gruendel (1986) interpreted the fact that all the children mentioned the act of eating as evidence that they appreciated the central goal of the event. In addition, the children's temporal ordering of the acts was virtually flawless. Moreover, children did not require multiple experiences of events to evidence formation of scriptlike representations. Fivush interviewed kindergarten children after only a single day of school. Although the children had experienced the school-day routine just once, they nevertheless appeared to have general representations of it, as evidenced by this response from one of the participants to the question, "What happens when you go to school?":

> Play. Say hello to the teacher and then you do reading or something. You can do anything you want to . . . clean up and then you play some more and then clean up and then play some more and then clean up. And then you go to the gym or playground. And then you go home. Have your lunch and go home. You go out the school and you ride on the bus or train and go home. (Fivush & Slackman, 1986, p. 78)

## Assessing Event Memory Nonverbally

The third major "event" that changed the direction of research on young children's memory was development of an experimental means of testing assumptions about limitations on explicit memory in infants younger than 18 to 24 months. In the first of a series of papers, Andrew Meltzoff (1985) reported that 24-month-old infants were able to defer imitation for 24 hours. Piaget (1952) had identified deferred imitation as one of the hallmarks of the development of symbolic thought: He used his daughter Jacqueline's deferred imitation of a cousin's temper tantrum as an illustration of her developing representational capacity. What Meltzoff did was to bring deferred imitation under experimental control by presenting to infants, not temper tantrums, but another novel action, namely, pulling apart a dumbbell-shaped toy. He found that 80% of the 24-month-olds imitated the action immediately after seeing it modeled. Among the children required to defer imitation for 24 hours, 70% produced the behavior. In contrast, 20% of children who had seen the toy but had not seen the specific action performed on it (naive control children) produced the behavior immediately and 25% produced it after the delay.

Whereas the finding that 24-month-olds were able to defer imitation was in keeping with the estimates set forth by Piaget, another of Meltzoff's findings (1985) was not. Specifically, he reported that 14-month-olds also were able to defer imitation over 24 hours: 45% of the infants who had seen the action modeled performed it 24 hours later (compared with 7.5% of naive controls). Shortly thereafter, Bauer and Shore (1987) published findings that over a 6-week delay, infants 17 to 23 months of age remembered not only individual actions but temporally ordered sequences of action. Even after 6 weeks, they were able to reproduce in the correct temporal order the steps of putting a ball into a cup, covering it with another cup, and shaking the cups to make a rattle. Most striking of all was the finding that 9-month-olds were able to defer imitation of single actions over 24 hours (Meltzoff, 1988c). Indeed, the capacity for deferred imitation appeared quite robust: The same levels of performance were observed when 9-month-olds were required to defer imitation as when they were permitted to imitate immediately. These findings initiated concerted efforts to map the development of explicit memory in the first years of life.

It is important to note that evidence of imitation after a delay was not the first indication of memory in children younger than 18 to 24 months of age. As early as 1956, Fantz had introduced the visual paired comparison task as a measure of infant memory. In visual paired comparison, two identical stimuli are placed side by side for a period of time after which one of the stimuli is replaced by a novel stimulus. Longer looking at the novel stimulus is taken as evidence of memory for the familiarization stimulus. In addition, in the 1960s, Rovee-Collier began publishing results from her conjugate reinforcement paradigm (see Rovee-Collier, 1997, for a review). In this task, a mobile is suspended above an infant's crib or sling seat. After a brief baseline period during which researchers measure the rate at which infants kick, they tether the infant's leg to the mobile with a ribbon such that, as the infant kicks, the mobile moves. Infants readily learn the contingency between their own kicking and the movement of the mobile. Once the conditioned response is acquired, a delay is imposed, after which the mobile again is suspended above the infant. This time, however, the infant's leg is not attached to the mobile. If the posttraining rate of kicking is greater than the rate of kicking in the procedurally identical baseline (before the infant experienced the contingency), then memory is inferred (e.g., Rovee-Collier & Gerhardstein, 1997).

What was different about the imitation procedures used by Meltzoff (1985, 1988c) and Bauer and Shore (1987; see also Bauer & Mandler, 1989) relative to the other infant memory paradigms was that the imitation procedures provided tests of a capacity that Piaget himself had identified as indicative of representational ability. In contrast, the behaviors evidenced in the visual paired comparison and mobile conjugate reinforcement paradigms appeared sensorimotor in nature. Visual paired comparison (and other attentional preference techniques) provided experimental demonstrations of the sorts of recognition behaviors that Piaget had described in his own infants (and for which he saw no need to invoke representational ability). The patterns of generalization, extinction, and reinstatement exhibited by infants in the conjugate reinforcement paradigm were typical of those in operant conditioning paradigms used with a range of animal species (e.g., Campbell, 1984). As a consequence, although these other techniques had been used for many years, they did not serve as an impetus for research on explicit memory in the first years of life to the same extent as the findings from imitation-based tasks.

Whereas originally the argument that imitation-based paradigms provide a means of testing explicit memory was based in Piaget's (1952) observations, some characteristics support the claim. Because the argument has been developed in detail elsewhere (e.g., Bauer, 2005b, 2006; Carver & Bauer, 2001), I present only two components of it. First, as reviewed in the section "Continuities and Discontinuities . . . ," later in this chapter, once children acquire the requisite language, they talk about events that they experienced as preverbal infants, in the context of imitation tasks (e.g., Bauer, Wenner, & Kroupina, 2002). This is strong evidence that the format in which the memories are encoded is explicit, as opposed to implicit or procedural (formats inaccessible to language). Second, the paradigm passes the "amnesia test." Whereas intact adults accurately imitate sequences after a delay, patients with amnesia due to hippocampal lesions perform no better than naive controls (McDonough, Mandler, McKee, & Squire, 1995). Adolescents and young adults who sustained hippocampal damage early in life also exhibit deficits in performance on the task (Adlam, Vargha-Khadem, Mishkin, & de Haan, 2005). This suggests that the paradigm taps the type of memory that gives rise to recall. For these reasons, the task has come to be widely accepted as a nonverbal analogue to verbal report (e.g., Bauer, 2002; Mandler, 1990b; Meltzoff, 1990; K. Nelson & Fivush, 2000; Rovee-Collier & Hayne, 2000; Schneider & Bjorklund, 1998; Squire et al., 1993).

### Event Memory in Infancy and Early Childhood

The events just described (research on children's recall of stories, preschoolers' scripts, and development of a nonverbal means of assessing explicit memory in infancy) proved that even young children have substantial mnemonic competence. These events did more than that though. In a very real sense, they gave birth to the domain of this chapter—research on the development of children's event memory for ordinary experiences in their everyday lives, as well as novel, one-time experiences that they encounter either in the laboratory or in the world outside it. The developments also motivated research on event memory in infancy and very early childhood. If by 3 years of age, children already have well-organized event representations, then the capacity to form them must have developed earlier. Imitation-based tasks provided the means to test this critical assumption.

In the following sections, I outline what we have learned about event memory over roughly 2 decades of research. Although it has the unfortunate by-product of perpetuating the traditional sense of discontinuity between infancy and childhood, the literatures on these major developmental periods are discussed separately.

Separate treatment is almost demanded by the dramatic differences in the research methodologies. Whereas in infancy, nonverbal, imitation-based tasks are used to assess event memory, the literature on childhood is based almost exclusively on verbal reports.

### EVENT MEMORY IN THE FIRST 2 YEARS OF LIFE

Contrary to the traditional conceptualization of the first 2 years of life as a period devoid of the capacity to recall the past, event memory develops rapidly and substantially during this time. For a number of reasons, the literature reviewed to substantiate this conclusion is restricted to the nonverbal imitation-based paradigms of elicited and deferred imitation. First, why the task must be nonverbal is obvious—infants (from the Latin *infantia* meaning "inability to speak") cannot talk. Second, as noted, whereas there are a number of nonverbal paradigms for assessing memory in infancy (e.g., visual paired comparison, mobile conjugate reinforcement), imitation-based tasks are the most widely accepted analogue to the prototypical measure of recall memory, verbal report. Third, imitation-based tasks permit tests of infants using materials that are similar to the events commonly tested with older children. That is, infants are presented with actions or sequences of actions performed by actors on objects in order to reach a clear goal (though it is not discussed, there is evidence that infants perceive the actions and event sequences as goal based: e.g., Carpenter, Akhtar, & Tomasello, 1998; Meltzoff, 1995a; Travis, 1997). This feature of the paradigm affords a point of contact with the literature from older children. In addition, reproduction of sequences in the correct temporal order provides especially compelling evidence that infants' and children's behavior is guided by recall: Once the model is complete, there is no perceptual support for the order in which the actions should be produced. Fourth, the other nonverbal paradigms are used almost exclusively with infants in the 1st year of life (although see Hartshorn et al., 1998, for an exception). In contrast, imitation-based tasks have been used with infants as young as 6 months and as old as 36 months, thereby, again, permitting assessment of continuity. Finally, since the other nonverbal paradigms are used almost exclusively in the 1st year of life, results from them are reviewed elsewhere in the *Handbook* (see Cohen & Cashon, Chapter 5, this *Handbook,* this volume).

## Assessing Event Memory Using Elicited and Deferred Imitation

In imitation-based tasks of event memory, an adult uses props to produce an action or sequence of actions that the infant or child then is permitted to imitate. An example sequence is "making a rattle" by putting a ball or block into a nesting cup, covering it with a second cup, and shaking the cups to make a rattling sound. In *deferred imitation* the opportunity to imitate comes only after a delay of minutes to months. By contrast, *elicited imitation* is a more generic term describing techniques in which imitation may be permitted prior to imposition of a delay. Imitation-based tasks are well suited for use with human infants because they do not require either verbal instructions or a verbal response. Instead, they capitalize on the natural tendency to copy interesting actions. Although the task does not depend on verbalization, in some laboratories, testers narrate their actions as they produce them ("Let's make a rattle. Put the ball in the cup. Cover it up. Shake it") and may even provide verbal "reminders" of the sequences at the time of test ("You can use this stuff to make a rattle"; Bauer, Hertsgaard, & Wewerka, 1995). In other cases, testers present the target actions in silence and response periods are signaled only by presentation of the props to the infant (e.g., Meltzoff, 1988c).

There are other procedural variants on the task. For example, in some cases, single object-specific actions (e.g., pulling apart a dumbbell-shaped object) are demonstrated as many as three times, followed by a time-limited response period (e.g., Meltzoff, 1988a). In other cases, sequences varying in length from 2 to 9 steps are demonstrated two times, followed by a child-controlled response period (e.g., Bauer et al., 1995). This is not the place for a review of the implications of task differences, many of which are unknown. However, one task difference, whether infants are permitted to imitate prior to imposition of a delay, merits discussion. Some researchers have pointed out the desirability of permitting imitation prior to imposition of a delay, in order to obtain a measure of initial learning (e.g., Bauer, 2005a; Howe & Courage, 1997b). However, because Piaget's (1952) original argument regarding the signifi-

cance of imitation of a novel behavior concerned deferred imitation, it has been suggested that valid use of imitation-based tasks as tests of recall requires that imitation be deferred (e.g., Hayne, Barr, & Herbert, 2003; Meltzoff, 1990). The concern is that if infants are permitted to imitate prior to final test they might form an implicit or procedural memory of the action(s) or sequence, thereby complicating interpretation of later imitation as an index of explicit memory. The concern has proven to be unfounded. First, as noted, implicit or procedural memory is characterized by gradual acquisition. Even in healthy adults, implicit learning of sequences of motor movements, such as acquired in serial reaction time tasks, requires multiple interactive trials to establish (e.g., Knopman & Nissen, 1987). There is little cause for concern then that a single behavioral reproduction would be a sufficient basis for implicit learning in an infant.

Second, it is not clear that prior opportunity to imitate affects later performance. Whereas some studies have indicated that the opportunity for immediate imitation enhances memory (e.g., Bauer et al., 1995; Meltzoff, 1990), other studies have found no effects (e.g., Barr & Hayne, 1996; Bauer, Wenner, Dropik, & Wewerka, 2000). Moreover, when enhancing effects are found, they are consistent with those associated with more elaborative encoding, as opposed to qualitatively different memory representations. For example, whereas electrophysiological (event-related potentials, ERPs—discussed in a later section) responses to photographs of previously experienced events are faster and more robust for infants permitted the opportunity to imitate, relative to infants who only watched events modeled, the scalp distribution and morphology of the responses are the same in the two groups (Lukowski et al., 2005). Quantitative differences in the face of qualitative similarities in electrophysiological responses to events enacted and observed also are apparent in adult participants (e.g., Senkfor, Van Petten, & Kutas, 2002).

Third, the suggestion that the opportunity for prior imitation results in an implicit memory is contraindicated by the finding that, once they develop the language skills necessary to do so, children talk about events they experienced as preverbal infants in the context of imitation-based tasks. Importantly, they talk about events for which imitation was deferred and also about events that they were permitted to imitate (e.g., Bauer, Wenner, et al., 2002). In fact, for children who were younger at the time of the original experience of events, later verbal memory is more robust for events previously imitated relative to events for which imitation was deferred (Bauer, Kroupina, Schwade, Dropik, & Wewerka, 1998). If prior imitation resulted in an implicit memory, it would not be accessible to language, once acquired. In summary, both logical argument and the weight of empirical evidence suggest that the opportunity for prior imitation does not render a memory implicit, as opposed to explicit. For this reason, the results from elicited and deferred paradigms are discussed together.

## Developmental Trends

Over the first 2 years of life, there are developmental changes in event memory along many dimensions. Six-month-olds, the youngest infants tested with imitation-based paradigms,[1] have fragile memories of short events that they retain for a limited period. By 24 months of age, children have robust memories for long, temporally complex sequences that they retain over extended periods. The changes indicate substantial and significant development. After outlining the normative trends of these developmental changes, I discuss what is known about the mechanisms of developmental change, and then review the literature on individual and group differences in development.

### Changes in the Length of Time
### That Infants Remember

Perhaps the most salient change in memory over the first 2 years of life is in the length of time over which it is apparent. Because, like any complex behavior, the length of time an event is remembered is multiply determined, there is no "growth chart" function that specifies children of X age should remember for Y long. Nonetheless, evidence has emerged across numerous studies that with increasing age, infants tolerate

---

[1] Neonates have been found to imitate facial and hand gestures (e.g., Meltzoff & Moore, 1977). However, because of questions concerning the robustness of the effect (e.g., Kaitz, Meschulach-Sarfaty, Auerbach, & Eidelman, 1988), and debates as to whether the mechanisms that support imitation by neonates and older infants are one and the same (e.g., Jacobson, 1979), the results of this line of research are not included in this review.

lengthier retention intervals. In the first published study of deferred imitation by 6-month-olds, Barr, Dowden, and Hayne (1996) found that the infants remembered an average of one action of a 3-step sequence (taking a mitten off a puppet's hand, shaking the mitten which, at the time of demonstration, held a bell that rang, and replacing the mitten) for 24 hours. Collie and Hayne (1999) found that 6-month-olds remembered an average of one out of five possible actions over a 24-hour delay. That such young infants have recall after 24 hours is remarkable in the context of traditional conceptualizations of developments in re-presentational ability. On the other hand, such low levels of performance after 24 hours have not inspired researchers to examine retention over longer intervals.

By 9 to 11 months of age, the length of time over which memory for laboratory events is apparent has increased substantially. Nine-month-olds remember individual actions over delays from 24 hours (Meltzoff, 1988c) to 5 weeks (Carver & Bauer, 1999, 2001). By 10 to 11 months of age, infants remember over delays as long as 3 months (Carver & Bauer, 2001; Mandler & McDonough, 1995). Thirteen- to 14-month-olds remember actions over delays of 4 to 6 months (Bauer et al., 2000; Meltzoff, 1995b). By 20 months of age, children remember the actions of event sequences over as many as 12 months (Bauer et al., 2000).

Infants also recall the temporal order of actions in multistep sequences, though retaining order information presents a cognitive challenge to young infants, in particular, as evidenced by low levels of ordered recall and substantial within-age-group variability in the 1st year. Although 67% of Barr et al.'s (1996) 6-month-olds remembered some of the actions associated with the puppet sequence over 24 hours, only 25% of them remembered actions in the correct temporal order. Collie and Hayne (1999, Experiment 1) reported no ordered recall after 24 hours by 6-month-olds (the infants were exposed to three target events, two of which required two steps to complete). Among 9-month-olds, approximately 50% of infants exhibit ordered reproduction of sequences after a 5-week delay (Bauer, Wiebe, Carver, Waters, & Nelson, 2003; Bauer, Wiebe, Waters, & Bangston, 2001; Carver & Bauer, 1999). By 13 months of age, the substantial individual variability in ordered recall has resolved: 78% of 13-month-olds exhibit ordered recall after 1 month. Nevertheless, throughout the 2nd year of life, there are age-related differences in children's recall of the order in which actions of multistep sequences unfolded. The differences are especially apparent under conditions of greater cognitive demand, such as when less support for recall is provided, and after longer delays (Bauer et al., 2000).

### Changes in Robustness of Memory

Over the first 2 years, there also are changes in the robustness of memory. For instance, there are changes in the number of experiences that seem to be required for infants to remember. In Barr et al. (1996), at 6 months, infants required six exposures to remember events 24 hours later. If instead, they saw the actions demonstrated only three times, they showed no memory after 24 hours (performance of infants who had experienced the puppet sequence did not differ from that of naive control infants). By 9 months of age, the number of times actions need to be demonstrated to support recall after 24 hours has reduced to three (e.g., Meltzoff, 1988c). Indeed, 9-month-olds who see sequences modeled as few as two times within a single session recall individual actions of them 1 week later (Bauer et al., 2001). Over the same delay, however, ordered recall was observed only among infants who had seen the sequences modeled a total of six times, distributed over three exposure sessions. Three exposure sessions also supports ordered recall over the longer delay of 1 month. By the time infants are 14 months of age, a single exposure session is all that is necessary to support recall of multiple different single actions over 4 months (Meltzoff, 1995b). Ordered recall of multistep sequences is apparent after as many as 6 months for infants who received a single exposure to the events at the age of 20 months (Bauer, 2004).

Another index of the robustness of memory is the extent to which it is disrupted by interference in the form of exposure to new, potentially distracting material during the retention interval, or in the form of changes in the context between encoding and retrieval. The extent to which young infants are susceptible to interference from potentially distracting material is not known. In most studies (Barr et al., 1996, being an exception), infants are exposed to multiple single actions (e.g., Meltzoff, 1988c) or to multiple multistep sequences (e.g., Carver & Bauer, 1999, 2001) within a single session. Whether levels of recall would be higher were infants exposed to fewer stimuli (or would have been lower had infants in Barr et al. been exposed to multiple stimuli) has not been examined systematically. One direct comparison suggests that exposure to potentially interfering

stimuli during a brief retention interval is not disruptive to infants by 20 months of age. In Bauer, Van Abbema, and de Haan (1999), 10-minute deferred imitation was tested under two conditions. In one, 20-month-olds were exposed to two multistep sequences and experienced an unfilled delay period prior to test: During the delay, infants were given a snack; or they engaged in play with blocks, stacking rings, or a ball. In the other condition, infants experienced a filled delay: In the 10 minutes between exposure to the sequences and test for recall of them, the infants were exposed to and received immediate recall tests on four other multistep sequences. Performance after the delay did not differ as a function of the filler activity. Nor did it differ from performance when no delay between demonstration and test was imposed. Whether distracting experiences would be more disruptive if imitation were deferred for a longer period or would produce interference in younger infants has not been examined systematically.

There are mixed reports of the extent to which infants and very young children are sensitive to contextual changes between the time of encoding and the time of test for event memory. There are some suggestions that recall is disrupted if the appearance of the test materials is changed between exposure and test. In research by Hayne, MacDonald, and Barr (1997), when 18-month-olds experienced the puppet sequence demonstrated on a cow puppet and then were tested with the same puppet, they showed robust retention over 24 hours. However, when they experienced the sequence modeled on a cow puppet and then were tested with a duck puppet, they did not show evidence of memory. At the age of 21 months, infants remembered the sequence whether tested with the same or a different puppet (see also Hayne, Boniface, & Barr, 2000; Herbert & Hayne, 2000).

There also are reports of robust generalization from encoding to test by infants across a wide age range. Infants have been shown to generalize imitative responses across changes in (a) the size, shape, color, and material composition of the objects used in demonstration versus test (e.g., Bauer & Dow, 1994; Bauer & Fivush, 1992; Lechuga, Marcos-Ruiz, & Bauer, 2001); (b) the appearance of the room at the time of demonstration of modeled actions and at the time of memory test (e.g., Barnat, Klein, & Meltzoff, 1996; Klein & Meltzoff, 1999); (c) the setting for demonstration of the modeled actions and the test of memory for them (e.g., Hanna & Meltzoff, 1993;

Klein & Meltzoff, 1999); and (d) the individual who demonstrated the actions and the individual who tested for memory of the actions (e.g., Hanna & Meltzoff, 1993). Infants are even able to use three-dimensional objects to produce events that they have only seen modeled on a television screen (Meltzoff, 1988a; although see Barr & Hayne, 1999). Evidence of flexible extension of event knowledge is seen in infants as young as 9 to 11 months of age (e.g., Baldwin, Markman, & Melartin, 1993; McDonough & Mandler, 1998). In summary, whereas there is evidence that with age, infants' memories as tested in imitation-based paradigms become more generalizable (e.g., Herbert & Hayne, 2000), there is substantial evidence that from an early age, infants' memories survive changes in context and stimuli.

### Changes in Sensitivity to the Temporal Structure of Events

A robust finding is that ordered recall is facilitated by enabling relations in events. Enabling relations are said to exist when, for a given end-state or goal, one action is temporally prior to and necessary for a subsequent action. For example, to enjoy a meal of pasta with sauce, one must first cook the pasta. Because alternative temporal orders of the steps of events constrained by enabling relations either are physically impossible, logically unlikely, or both, they occur in an invariant temporal order. In contrast, actions in an event are arbitrarily ordered when there are no inherent constraints on their temporal position in the sequence. To continue the example, whether one consumes a salad before or after the pasta course is a matter of personal preference or cultural convention; there is no logical or necessary reason one course must come before the other.

Young children's ordered recall of multistep event sequences with enabling relations consistently is greater than that of arbitrarily ordered sequences. The advantage is apparent whether children are tested immediately (e.g., Bauer, 1992; Bauer & Mandler, 1992; Bauer & Thal, 1990) or after a delay (e.g., Barr & Hayne, 1996; Bauer & Dow, 1994; Bauer et al., 1995; Bauer & Hertsgaard, 1993; Bauer & Mandler, 1989; Mandler & McDonough, 1995). It also is apparent even after several experiences of arbitrarily ordered events in an invariant temporal order (Bauer & Travis, 1993; see Bauer, 1992, 1995; Bauer & Travis, 1993, for discussions of the means by which enabling relations in events may influ-

ence ordered recall). Moreover, the advantage is obvious early in development: At least by 11 months of age, children show superior ordered recall of events with enabling relations relative to events that are arbitrarily ordered (Mandler & McDonough, 1995). The advantage in ordered recall is observed even though the number of individual actions of sequences with and without enabling relations that infants recall does not differ.

Whereas from a young age, infants evidence sensitivity to enabling relations in events, development of the ability to reliably reproduce arbitrarily ordered sequences is protracted (Bauer, Hertsgaard, Dropik, & Daly, 1998; Wenner & Bauer, 1999). It is not until children are 20 months or older that they accurately reproduce arbitrarily ordered events. At that age, performance is affected by the length of the sequence. Children are reliable on shorter event sequences (3 steps in length) but not on longer ones (5 steps in length). In addition, children accurately reproduce arbitrarily ordered sequences immediately but not after a 2-week delay. In contrast, by 28 months, children recall arbitrarily ordered events even after a delay (Bauer, Hertsgaard, et al., 1998).

### Changes in the Efficacy of Different Types of Reminders

In older children, cues or reminders of previously experienced events facilitate memory after a delay (e.g., Fivush, 1997; Fivush, Hudson, & Nelson, 1984; Hudson & Fivush, 1991). Verbal reminding also aids retrieval in children as young as 13 months of age (Bauer et al., 1995, 2000). Indeed, verbal reminding has the effect of reducing age-related differences in the amount of information that young children recall after a delay. In Bauer et al. (2000) for example, age-related differences in the amount remembered after various delay intervals were larger when recall was supported by event-related props alone, relative to when it was supported by event-related props and verbal reminders of to-be-remembered events. The finding that memories can be triggered by verbal reminders is particularly important to recall after long periods of time: Over significant delays, regardless of age, little that is not reminded is retrieved (e.g., Hudson & Fivush, 1991). Other reminders also are effective in aiding retrieval during the 2nd year of life. At 18 months, exposure to a videotape of another child performing activities facilitates memory for them. Still photographs of previously experienced events do not, however, serve as effective reminders. By 24 months, even still photographs facilitate memory after a delay (Hudson, 1991, 1993; Hudson & Sheffield, 1998).

## What Accounts for Developmental Changes over the First 2 Years of Life?

The last 2 decades of the twentieth century yielded a wealth of descriptive data on event memory. As is common when research is in its infancy, there was little focus on the mechanisms of age-related change. Ultimately, several sources of variance will be implicated in the explanation of developments in memory. They will range from changes in the neural processes and systems and basic mnemonic processes that permit memories to be formed, retained, and later retrieved, to the social forces that shape what children ultimately come to view as important to remember about events and even how they express their memories. In the first 2 years of life, to the extent that there has been focus on mechanisms of change, it has been primarily at the "lower" level of neural systems and basic mnemonic processes. As preparation for review of the literature, I provide a brief discussion of the neural network thought to subserve explicit event memory in the adult and the course of its development. I then examine each of the basic mnemonic processes in turn, to evaluate its contribution to age-related changes in explicit event memory.

### The Neural Substrate of Explicit Event Memory and Its Development

Although a thorough review of the neural substrate of explicit event memory and its development is beyond the scope of this chapter (see Bauer, 2006; C. A. Nelson, Thomas, & de Haan, Chapter 1, this *Handbook,* this volume), a brief review of it is essential to the goal of identifying possible mechanisms of developmental change in explicit memory in the first years of life. In adults, the formation, maintenance, and retrieval of explicit memories over the long term is thought to depend on a multicomponent neural network involving temporal and cortical structures (e.g., Eichenbaum & Cohen, 2001; Markowitsch, 2000; Zola & Squire, 2000). Briefly, on experience of an event, sensory and motor inputs from multiple brain regions distributed throughout the cortex converge on parahippocampal structures within the temporal lobes (e.g., entorhinal cortex). The work of binding the elements together to create a durable, integrated

memory trace is carried out by another temporal lobe structure, the hippocampus. Cortical structures are the long-term storage sites for memories. Prefrontal structures are implicated in their retrieval after a delay. Thus, long-term recall requires multiple cortical regions, including prefrontal cortex; temporal structures; and intact connections between them.

At a general level, the time course of changes in behavior is consistent with what is known about developments in the temporal-cortical network that supports explicit memory (Bauer, 2002, 2004, 2006; C. A. Nelson, 2000; C. A. Nelson et al., Chapter 1, this *Handbook,* this volume). There are indicators that in the human, many of the medial temporal lobe components of the explicit memory system develop early. As reviewed by Seress (2001), the cells that make up most of the hippocampus are formed in the first half of gestation and virtually all are in their adult locations by the end of the prenatal period. The neurons in most of the hippocampus also begin to connect early in development—synapses are present as early as 15 weeks gestational age. The number and density of synapses both increase rapidly after birth and reach adult levels by approximately 6 postnatal months. Perhaps as a consequence, glucose utilization in the temporal cortex reaches adult levels at the same time (by about 6 months: Chugani, 1994; Chugani & Phelps, 1986). Thus, there are numerous indices of early maturity of major portions of the medial temporal components of the network.

In contrast to early maturation of most of the hippocampus, development of the dentate gyrus of the hippocampus is protracted (Seress, 2001). At birth, the dentate gyrus includes only about 70% of the adult number of cells. Thus, roughly 30% of the cells are produced postnatally. It is not until 12 to 15 postnatal months that the morphology of the structure appears adultlike. Maximum density of synaptic connections in the dentate gyrus also is delayed, relative to that in the other regions of the hippocampus. In humans, synaptic density increases dramatically (to well above adult levels) beginning at 8 to 12 postnatal months and reaches its peak at 16 to 20 months. After a period of relative stability, excess synapses are pruned until adult levels are reached at about 4 to 5 years of age (Eckenhoff & Rakic, 1991).

Although the functional significance of later development of the dentate gyrus is not clear, there is reason to speculate that it impacts behavior. As noted, on experience of an event, information from distributed regions of cortex converges on the entorhinal cortex. From there, it makes its way into the hippocampus via either a "long route" or a "short route." The long route involves projections from the entorhinal cortex into the hippocampus, by way of the dentate gyrus; the short route bypasses the dentate gyrus. Whereas the short route may support some forms of memory (C. A. Nelson, 1995, 1997), based on data from rodents, it seems that adult-like memory behavior depends on passage of information through the dentate gyrus (Czurkó, Czéh, Seress, Nadel, & Bures, 1997; Nadel & Willner, 1989). This implies that maturation of the dentate gyrus of the hippocampus may be a rate-limiting variable in the development of explicit memory early in life (Bauer, 2002, 2004, 2006; Bauer, Wiebe, et al., 2003; C. A. Nelson, 1995, 1997, 2000).

Like the dentate gyrus of the hippocampus, the association areas develop slowly (Bachevalier, 2001). It is not until the 7th prenatal month that all six cortical layers are apparent. The density of synapses in prefrontal cortex increases dramatically at 8 postnatal months and peaks between 15 and 24 months. Pruning to adult levels is delayed until puberty (Huttenlocher, 1979; Huttenlocher & Dabholkar, 1997; see Bourgeois, 2001, for discussion). Although the maximum density of synapses may be reached as early as 15 postnatal months, it is not until 24 months that synapses develop adult morphology (Huttenlocher, 1979). There also are changes in glucose utilization and blood flow over the second half of the 1st year and into the 2nd year; blood flow and glucose utilization increase above adult levels by 8 to 12 and 13 to 14 months of age, respectively (Chugani, Phelps, & Mazziotta, 1987). Other maturational changes in prefrontal cortex, such as myelination, continue into adolescence, and adult levels of some neurotransmitters are not seen until the 2nd and 3rd decades of life (Benes, 2001).

Because the full network that supports explicit memory in the human involves medial temporal and cortical components, it can be expected to function as an integrated whole only when each of its components, as well as the connections between them, is functionally mature. This state is reached as the number of synapses peaks; full maturity is achieved as the number of synapses is pruned to adult levels (Goldman-Rakic, 1987). Adoption of this metric leads to the prediction of emergence of explicit memory by late in the 1st year of life, with significant development over the course of the

2nd year, and continued development for years thereafter. With the exception of the dentate gyrus of the hippocampus, the medial temporal components of the network would be expected to reach maturity between the 2nd and 6th postnatal months. The cortical components, and the connections both within the medial temporal lobe (i.e., those involved in the "long route" into the hippocampus, via the dentate gyrus) and between the cortex and the medial temporal lobe, would be expected to reach functional maturity late in the 1st year and over the course of the 2nd year. The network would continue to develop, albeit less dramatically, for years thereafter. The time frame is based on increases in synaptogenesis from 8 to 20 months in the dentate gyrus (Eckenhoff & Rakic, 1991), and from 8 to 24 months in the prefrontal cortex (Huttenlocher, 1979; Huttenlocher & Dabholkar, 1997). The expectation of developmental changes for months and years thereafter stems from the schedule of protracted pruning both in the dentate gyrus (until 4 to 5 years; e.g., Eckenhoff & Rakic, 1991) and in the prefrontal cortex (throughout adolescence; e.g., Huttenlocher & Dabholkar, 1997).

What are the consequences for behavior of the slow course of development of the neural network that supports explicit event memory? At a general level, we may expect concomitant behavioral development: As the neural substrate develops, so does behavior (and vice versa). But precisely how do changes in the medial temporal and cortical structures, and their interconnections, produce changes in behavior? How do they affect memory representations? To address this question, we must consider how the brain builds a memory, and thus, how the "recipe" for a memory might be affected by changes in the underlying neural substrate. In other words, we must consider how developmental changes in the substrate for memory relate to changes in the efficacy and efficiency with which information is encoded and stabilized for long-term storage, in the reliability with which it is stored, and in the ease with which it is retrieved.

### Changes in Basic Mnemonic Processes

**Encoding.** Association cortices are involved in the initial registration and temporary maintenance of experience. Because prefrontal cortex in particular undergoes considerable postnatal development, it is likely that neurodevelopmental changes in it are at least partially responsible for changes over the 1st year of life in the time required to encode stimuli. For example, the number of seconds required to encode a stimulus (as evidenced by the familiarization required to produce a novelty preference) decreases from roughly 30 seconds at 3 months of age to 15 seconds at 6 months (Rose, Gottfried, Melloy-Carminar, & Bridger, 1982).

In the 1st year of life, age-related differences in encoding are related to age-related differences in event memory. We have found that relative to 9-month-olds, 10-month-olds evidence more robust encoding (as indexed by event-related potentials—ERPs—to familiar and novel events immediately after exposure) and more robust recall (as indexed by deferred imitation). ERPs are scalp recorded electrical oscillations associated with excitatory and inhibitory postsynaptic potentials. Because they are time locked to a stimulus, differences in the latency and amplitude of the response to different classes of stimuli—familiar and novel, for example—can be interpreted as evidence of differential neural processing. To test recognition, we recorded infants' ERPs as they looked at photographs of props used in events to which they had been exposed interspersed with photographs of props from novel events. The amplitudes of responses to old stimuli at 10 months were larger than those of the same infants at 9 months (the study was longitudinal); there were no differences in responses to new stimuli. The differences at encoding were related to differences at recall. One month after the ERP, we tested long-term recall of the events. The infants had higher rates of recall of the events to which they had been exposed at 10 months, relative to the events to which they had been exposed at 9 months (Bauer, Wiebe, Carver, Lukowski, Haight, Waters, et al., 2006).

Age-related differences in encoding do not end at 1 year of age. Relative to 15-month-olds, 12-month-olds require more trials to learn multistep events to a criterion (learning to a criterion indicates that the material was fully encoded). In turn, 15-month-olds are slower to achieve criterion, relative to 18-month-olds (Howe & Courage, 1997b). Indeed, across development, older children learn more rapidly than younger children (Howe & Brainerd, 1989).

Whereas age-related differences in encoding (as indexed by differences in the number of learning trials required to reach a criterion) are apparent throughout the first 2 years of life, they alone do not account for the age trends in long-term explicit event memory. Even with levels of encoding controlled, older children remember more relative to younger children. In Bauer

et al. (2000), with the variance in levels of initial encoding controlled statistically, across delays ranging from 1 to 12 months, there were reliable age differences in recall of both the actions and temporal order of multistep events: Older children performed at higher levels than younger children. In samples matched for levels of encoding, younger children lost more information from memory, relative to older children (Bauer, 2005a). Similarly, Howe and Courage (1997b) found that with level of encoding controlled through a criterion learning design, after 3 months, 15-month-olds remembered more than 12-month-olds, and 18-month-olds remembered more than 15-month-olds. Findings such as these strongly suggest that changes in postencoding processes also contribute to developmental changes in event memory.

**Consolidation and Storage.** Although these phases are separable in the life of a memory trace, at the level of analysis available in the existing developmental data, consolidation and storage cannot be effectively separated; for this reason, I discuss them in tandem. As reviewed briefly earlier, medial temporal structures are implicated in the processes by which new memories become "fixed" for long-term storage; cortical association areas are the presumed repositories for long-term memories. In a fully mature, intact adult, the changes in synaptic connectivity associated with memory trace consolidation continue for hours, weeks, and even months, after an event. Memory traces are vulnerable throughout this time: Lesions inflicted during the period of consolidation result in deficits in memory, whereas lesions inflicted after a trace has been consolidated do not (e.g., Kim & Fanselow, 1992; Takehara, Kawahara, & Kirino, 2003). For the developing organism, the road to a consolidated memory trace may be a bumpier one than that traveled by the adult. Not only are some of the implicated neural structures relatively undeveloped (the dentate gyrus and prefrontal cortex), but the connections between them are still being sculpted and thus are less than fully effective and efficient. As a consequence, even once children have successfully encoded an event, as evidenced by achievement of a criterion level of learning, for example, they remain vulnerable to forgetting. Younger children may be more vulnerable to forgetting, relative to older children (Bauer, 2004).

To examine the role of consolidation and storage processes in long-term explicit event memory in

9-month-old infants, Bauer, Wiebe, et al. (2003) combined ERP measures of immediate recognition (as an index of encoding), ERP measures of 1-week delayed recognition (as an index of consolidation and storage), and deferred imitation measures of recall after 1 month. After the 1-month delay, 46% of the infants evidenced ordered recall of the sequences, and 54% did not. At the immediate ERP test, regardless of whether they subsequently recalled the events, the infants evidenced recognition: Their ERP responses were different to the old and new stimuli. This strongly implies that the infants had encoded the events. Nevertheless, 1 week later, at the delayed recognition test, the infants who would go on to recall the events recognized the props, whereas infants who would not evidence ordered recall did not. Thus, despite having encoded the events, a subset of 9-month-olds failed to recognize them after 1 week and subsequently failed to recall them after 1 month. Moreover, the size of the difference in delayed-recognition response predicted recall performance 1 month later. Thus, infants who had stronger memory representations after a 1-week delay exhibited higher levels of recall 1 month later. The pattern is a replication of Carver, Bauer, and Nelson (2000). These data strongly imply that at 9 months of age, consolidation and storage processes are a source of individual differences in mnemonic performance.

In the 2nd year of life, there are behavioral suggestions of between-age group differences in consolidation and storage processes, as well as a replication of the finding among 9-month-olds that intermediate-term consolidation and storage failure relate to recall over the long term. In Bauer, Cheatham, Cary, and Van Abbema (2002), 16- and 20-month-olds were exposed to multistep events and tested for recall immediately (as a measure of encoding) and after 24 hours. Over the delay, the younger children forgot a substantial amount of the information they had encoded: they produced only 65% of the target actions and only 57% of the ordered pairs of actions that they had learned just 24 hours earlier. For the older children, the amount of forgetting over the delay was not statistically reliable. It is not until 48 hours have elapsed that children 20 months of age exhibit significant forgetting (Bauer et al., 1999). These observations suggest age-related differences in the vulnerability of memory traces during the initial period of consolidation.

The vulnerability of memory traces during the initial period of consolidation is related to the robustness of recall after 1 month. This is apparent from another of the experiments in Bauer, Cheatham, et al. (2002), this one involving 20-month-olds only. The children were exposed to multistep events and then tested for memory for some of the events immediately, some of the events after 48 hours (a delay after which, based on Bauer et al., 1999, some forgetting was expected), and some of the events after 1 month. Although the children exhibited high levels of initial encoding (as measured by immediate recall), they nevertheless exhibited significant forgetting after both 48 hours and 1 month. The robustness of memory after 48 hours predicted 25% of the variance in recall 1 month later; variability in level of encoding did not predict significant variance. This effect is a conceptual replication of that observed with 9-month-olds in Bauer, Wiebe, et al. (2003). In both cases, the amount of information lost to memory during the period of consolidation predicted the robustness of recall 1 month later.

The data just reviewed suggest that even once children have successfully encoded an event, they remain vulnerable to forgetting. *Within an age group,* differences in vulnerability to intermediate-term forgetting (over 48 hours and 1 week in Bauer, Cheatham, et al., 2002; and Bauer, Wiebe, et al., 2003; respectively) account for significant variance in long-term recall. *Between age groups,* younger children are more vulnerable to intermediate-term forgetting relative to older children. In the case of the ERP data, the source of intermediate-term forgetting can with relative confidence be attributed to consolidation or storage failure: (a) The immediate recognition data indicated that the events had been encoded; and (b) the suggestion of consolidation or storage failure after 1 week was apparent on a recognition measure, a task that makes low demands on retrieval processes, effectively eliminating them as a potential source of variance. The behavioral data are more ambiguous. It is possible that age-related differences in performance should be attributed to retrieval processes instead of to differences in consolidation or storage processes. Older children may appear to remember more because the available retrieval cues are more effective for them, relative to the younger children. This issue is considered next.

**Retrieval.** Retrieval of memories from long-term storage sites is thought to depend on the prefrontal cortex. The prefrontal cortex undergoes a long period of postnatal development, making it a likely candidate source of age-related differences in long-term recall.

Liston and Kagan (2002) implicated changes in retrieval processes associated with developments in the prefrontal cortex as the explanation for their finding that infants exposed to laboratory events at the ages of 17 and 24 months recalled them 4 months later, whereas infants 9 months at the time they experienced the events did not.

Although retrieval processes are a compelling candidate source of developmental differences in long-term recall, there are few data with which to evaluate their contribution. A major reason is that most studies do not allow for assignment of relative roles of encoding, consolidation and storage, and retrieval processes. As discussed in the section on encoding, older children learn more rapidly than younger children. Yet age-related differences in encoding effectiveness rarely are taken into account. (Liston & Kagan, 2002, provided no information on encoding.) In studies that rely exclusively on deferred imitation (e.g., Hayne et al., 2000), it is impossible to evaluate the potential role of encoding differences because no measures of encoding are obtained. In addition, with standard testing procedures, it is difficult to know whether a memory representation has lost its integrity and become unavailable (consolidation or storage failure) or whether the memory trace remains intact but has become inaccessible with the cues provided (retrieval failure). Implication of retrieval processes as a source of developmental change requires that encoding be controlled and that memory be tested under conditions of high support for retrieval. One study in which these conditions were met was Bauer, Wiebe, et al. (2003; that is, ERPs indicated that the events had been encoded; the suggestion of consolidation or storage failure was apparent on a recognition memory task). The results, described in the preceding section, clearly implicated consolidation and storage, as opposed to retrieval.

Another study that permits assessment of the contributions of consolidation and storage relative to retrieval processes is Bauer et al. (2000). In addition to providing data on children of multiple ages (13, 16, and 20 months) tested over a range of delays (1 to 12 months), the study has three other features that makes it an attractive source of data relevant to the question of interest. First, because immediate recall of half of the events was tested, measures of encoding are available. Second, the children were given what amounted to multiple test trials, without intervening study trials, thereby providing multiple opportunities for retrieval. As discussed by Howe and his colleagues (e.g., Howe & Brainerd, 1989; Howe & O'Sullivan, 1997), the first test trial could be expected to initi-

ate a retrieval attempt. If a memory trace remained and was at a reasonably high level of accessibility, the event would be recalled. If, on the other hand, a memory trace remained but was relatively inaccessible, the retrieval would strengthen the trace and route to retrieval of it, increasing accessibility on the second test trial. Conversely, lack of improvement across test trials would imply that the trace was no longer available (although see Howe & O'Sullivan, 1997, for multiple nuances of this argument). Third, immediately after the recall tests, relearning was tested. After the second test trial, the experimenter demonstrated each event once, and allowed the children to imitate. Since Ebbinghaus (1885/1913), relearning has been used to distinguish between an intact but inaccessible memory trace and a trace that has disintegrated. If the number of trials required to relearn a stimulus was smaller than the number required to learn it initially, savings in relearning were said to have occurred. Savings presumably accrue because the products of relearning are integrated with an existing (though not necessarily accessible) memory trace. Conversely, the absence of savings is attributed to storage failure: There is no residual trace on which to build. In developmental studies, age-related differences in relearning would suggest that the residual memory traces available to children of different ages are differentially intact.

To eliminate encoding processes as a potential source of developmental differences in long-term recall, in a reanalysis of the data from Bauer et al. (2000) subsets of 13- and 16-month-olds and subsets of 16- and 20-month-olds were matched for levels of encoding (as measured by immediate recall; Bauer, 2005a). The amount of information the children forgot over the delays was then examined. For both comparisons, even though they were matched for levels of encoding, younger children exhibited more forgetting relative to older children. The age effect was apparent on both test trials. Moreover, in both cases, for older children, levels of performance after the single relearning trial were as high as those at initial learning. In contrast, for younger children, performance after the relearning trial was lower than at initial learning (Bauer, 2005a). Together, the findings of age-related differential loss of information over time and of age effects in relearning strongly implicate storage processes, as opposed to retrieval processes, as the major source of age-related differences in delayed recall.

**Summary.** Ultimately, a number of factors will be found to explain age-related variance in event memory in the first years of life. At present, one of the few sources of change to be evaluated is that associated with developments in the basic mnemonic processes of encoding, consolidation and storage, and retrieval. Evaluation of their relative contributions implicates consolidation and storage as a major source of developmental change. That is, age-related differences in long-term recall remain even when differences in encoding are eliminated. Moreover, age-related differences in long-term recall are apparent even after multiple retrieval attempts; even after relearning, younger children do not perform as well as older children. This conclusion is consistent with the loci of developments in the neural substrate of explicit memory. Late in the 1st year and throughout the 2nd year of life, there are pronounced changes in the temporal lobe structures implicated in integration and consolidation of memory traces. A likely consequence is changes in the efficiency and efficacy with which information is stabilized for storage, with resulting significant behavioral changes in resistance to forgetting.

## Group and Individual Differences in Event Memory in Infancy

Whereas there are regular developments in event memory in the first years of life, there is not a growth-chart-type function for the length of time over which we expect infants and children of specific ages to remember. A limitation on such a function is that many task differences influence performance. Infants and children who receive multiple exposures to events, the orders of which are constrained by enabling relations, and who are provided with effective reminders at the time of retrieval, will, on average, recall them over weeks and even months. In contrast, infants and children who receive a single exposure to events that lack enabling relations, and who at the time of retrieval, have little support for recall, will, on average, recall little of their experiences. Even with task parameters controlled, there are individual differences in children's performance throughout the period of transition from infancy to early childhood. For example, whereas some 20-month-old children recall all possible actions of multistep events, others recall as few as one action (Bauer et al., 2000).

Consideration of the mechanisms of age-related change in event memory suggests some likely candidate sources of group and individual variability. One possible source is differences in the rate of maturation that may affect brain development and thus, the efficacy and efficiency with which memories are encoded, consolidated and stored, and later retrieved. At a group level, this suggestion has been explored by examining possible gender differences in early event memory. Differences in event memory also may result from individual variability in factors that could be expected to affect the operation of the basic mnemonic processes, including the speed with which information is processed (e.g., Rose, Feldman, & Jankowski, 2003) and the success with which attentional resources are regulated (e.g., Colombo, Richman, Shaddy, Greenhoot, & Maikranz, 2001). Whereas these specific sources of variance have not as yet been examined for their effects on event memory as measured in imitation-based tasks, another potential source of variance—language—has received attention. Individual differences in language comprehension, language production, or both, could be expected to facilitate encoding and to enhance the efficacy of verbal retrieval cues in particular. Conversely, systematic variability in event memory could be expected to result from early experiences that may negatively impact the development of neural structures implicated in consolidation and storage, for example. Each of these possibilities is explored.

### Children's Gender

Attention to children's gender as a possible source of group differences in early event memory has been prompted by suggestions that girls mature more rapidly than boys (e.g., Hutt, 1978; although see Reinisch, Rosenblum, Rubin, & Schulsinger, 1991). Consistent with this possibility, some studies have reported gender-related differences in performance at what might be viewed as "transitional" points in the development of event memory. First, at 9 months of age—an age marked by substantial variability in long-term ordered recall—gender differences have been detected in three experiments. In one case, the effect of gender favored girls (Carver & Bauer, 1999). However, in the other two cases, the effect favored boys (Bauer et al., 2001; Experiments 1 and 2). Second, at 28 months of age—an age at which children make great strides in recall of arbitrarily ordered events—girls have been found to perform at higher levels, relative to boys (Bauer, Hertsgaard, et al., 1998). With these exceptions, tests for possible gender effects either have not been carried out or have been found to be nonsignificant.

As discussed in Bauer, Burch, and Kleinknecht (2002), a possible reason for the lack of significant gender effects is that most studies of early event memory feature small samples (ranging from 8 to 32 participants per cell of a research design with a modal sample size of 12 participants). This was not the case in Bauer, et al. (2000), in which 360 13- to 20-month-olds (185 of whom were girls) were tested. On the first test trial, when the children were prompted only by the event-related props, some isolated gender differences emerged. For example, 16- and 20-month-old girls tested for recall after 9 months had lower levels of performance than same-age boys. There were no reliable gender effects in any of the other four delay conditions (1, 3, 6, and 12 months). Notably, on the second test trial (which featured verbal reminders in addition to event-related props), even the isolated gender-related effects disappeared (Bauer, Burch, et al., 2002). Although we cannot prove the null hypothesis, the lack of meaningful effects in a large-scale study, coupled with isolated and sometimes contradictory findings in smaller-scale studies, implies that gender is not a major source of systematic variability in early event memory.

### Children's Language

Although imitation-based tasks are nonverbal, individual variability in language comprehension, language production, or both, could contribute variance in event memory. In many studies, demonstration of to-be-remembered events is accompanied by verbal narration (e.g., Bauer et al., 2000). Better comprehension of the narration would support more elaborative encoding. Children who comprehend more of the language associated with an event also would be expected to derive greater benefit from language-based retrieval cues. Even when narration is not provided (e.g., Meltzoff, 1985, 1988a, 1988b, 1995b), language development is a possible source of variability because children with greater language skills potentially could verbally encode the events that they observe, thus providing themselves with additional retrieval cues. As discussed later in the section "Continuities and Discontinuities . . .," the ability to "augment" nonverbal representations with language plays a role in the later verbal accessibility of memories likely encoded without the benefit of language (Bauer, Kroupina, et al., 1998; Bauer, Wenner, et al., 2002; Bauer & Wewerka, 1995, 1997; Cheatham & Bauer, 2005).

Although language skills are a potential source of systematic variability in early event memory, their effects have rarely been examined. One such test was undertaken by Bauer, Burch, et al. (2002), based on the sample of 360 13- to 20-month-olds tested in Bauer et al. (2000). In the sample, MacArthur-Bates Communicative Development Inventories for Toddlers (20-month-olds) and for Infants (13- and 16-month-olds; Fenson et al., 1994) were available on 336 of the 360 children. The MacArthur-Bates Communicative Development Inventories are well normed, valid, parent-report instruments for assessing children's early communicative development. Based on the inventories, children's reported productive vocabulary scores ranged from 0 to 651 words (across the 13- to 20-month age range); their reported receptive vocabulary scores ranged from 11 to 393 words (across the 13- to 16-month age range). The sample thus featured ample power and variability to permit detection of systematic relations between children's language and children's recall memory performance. Nevertheless, none of the correlations was statistically significant. Thus, as measured in this large sample of children, neither reported productive nor receptive vocabulary was reliably related to event memory (Bauer, Burch, et al., 2002).

### Children from Special Populations

Between the time an event is encoded and the time the resulting representation of it is stored and retrieved, memory traces undergo consolidation processes subserved by hippocampal structures. As discussed, the protracted development of portions of the hippocampal formation is a source of age-related variability in event memory. Individual differences also are apparent. Many potential sources of individual variability—such as the speed with which information is processed—have not as yet been investigated. In contrast, possible effects of pre- and postnatal insults to the hippocampus and surrounding structures have been examined in three special populations: infants raised for the first months of life in international orphanages and then adopted into homes in the United States, infants born to mothers with diabetes, and infants born prior to term but otherwise healthy. The results suggest that consolidation processes are subject to perturbation. They might be taken to suggest that similar yet less extreme circumstances may account for variability in the general population.

For each of the target special populations, there were *a priori* reasons to expect variability in event memory.

In the case of infants adopted from international orphanages, the stress and deprivation (both social and cognitive) associated with institutional care would be expected to negatively impact brain development in general and the hippocampus in particular (the hippocampus is especially vulnerable to effects of stress and deprivation; see Gunnar, 2001, for a review). Work with animal models has shown that infants of mothers with diabetes are exposed prenatally to chronic metabolic insults, including iron deficiency. For reasons that are not clear at this time, the hippocampus is a region of the brain that is at particular risk for reductions in iron uptake (Erikson, Pinero, Connor, & Beard, 1997). Finally, there is an extensive literature documenting poor cognitive outcomes for preterm infants with medical risk factors (e.g., infants who had very low birth weight or experienced intraventricular hemorrhages). Relatively less is known about the later developmental status of infants who survive prematurity sustaining no measurable neurological damage and with few to no social risk factors. In light of mounting evidence that experience plays a crucial role in shaping normative brain development, it is reasonable to expect that later- and more slowly developing memory systems may be vulnerable to variations in postnatal experience.

The data from each of the three special populations were collected in different studies. Nevertheless, in each study, using imitation-based techniques, the infants were tested for immediate and 10-minute delayed recall of multistep events. The measure of immediate recall afforded a means of controlling for possible differences in encoding. The measure of 10-minute deferred imitation was expected to be diagnostic of memory function: (a) adults suffering from medial temporal lobe amnesia exhibit deficits in performance on tasks with delays as brief as 5 to 10 minutes (e.g., Reed & Squire, 1998); (b) medial temporal lesions inflicted on nonhuman primates produce deficits after delays of 10 minutes (e.g., Zola-Morgan, Squire, Rempel, Clower, & Amaral, 1992); and (c) in normally developing human infants, recall after a 10-minute delay is correlated with recall after a 48-hour delay (Bauer et al., 1999). These observations suggest that performance after a 10-minute delay provides information as to the integrity of medial temporal function.

In Kroupina, Bauer, Gunnar, and Johnson (2004), children who as infants had been adopted from international orphanages showed deficits on the 10-minute deferred imitation task, relative to matched home-reared infants. The deficits were apparent even after controlling for differences in encoding. Consistent with suggestions that prenatal iron deficiency may compromise hippocampal function, at 12 months of age, infants born to mothers with diabetes showed deficits in memory after a 10-minute delay (DeBoer, Wewerka, Bauer, Georgieff, & Nelson, in press). The groups did not differ on immediate imitation. Finally, among infants who were otherwise healthy at the time of their preterm birth, performance after a 10-minute delay was correlated with gestational age at birth (infants born prematurely performed poorly on the task, relative to full-term infants; de Haan, Bauer, Georgieff, & Nelson, 2000). Preterm birth was associated with higher levels of immediate imitation, relative to term birth. In each of these cases, 10-minute deferred imitation proved to be especially sensitive to subtle differences in cognitive function associated with atypical prenatal environments, postnatal environments, or both. Whereas these effects were observed in targeted special populations, they suggest possible sources of individual variability in the larger population. That is, chronic stress and relative cognitive and perhaps social deprivation are associated with poverty; many maternal health conditions could be expected to have a negative impact on fetal nutritional status; and even in developed nations, there are high rates of preterm birth.

## DEVELOPMENTS IN AND AFTER THE PRESCHOOL YEARS

To study event memory in the first 2 years of life, researchers rely on nonverbal measures. Beginning in the 3rd year, verbal means of assessment become a viable alternative. This opens up new possibilities: Children can be tested for memory not only of controlled laboratory events but of events from their lives outside the laboratory as well. This combination of approaches has yielded a wealth of data about children's memories for the routine events that make up their everyday lives, such as making cookies, going to school, and going to the grocery store, and about their memories for unique events, such as the time the stove caught on fire while making cookies, the 1st day of school, and the flat tire on the way to the store. Some of the events are personally significant and contribute to an emerging autobiography or personal past. Major findings from each of these categories are reviewed.

## Children's Memories for Routine Events

As noted in the section "Traditional Accounts . . . ," earlier in this chapter, early studies of young children's memories for the events of their own lives focused on their scriptlike representations of everyday, routine events. The research revealed "minimalist," yet nevertheless accurate, reports of "what happens" in the context of everyday activities by children as young as 3 years of age. The children's reports included actions common to the activities and almost invariably, the actions were mentioned in the temporal order in which they typically occurred. Representative of the findings was the answer provided by a 3-year-old child to the question "What happens when you have a birthday party?": "You cook a cake and eat it" (K. Nelson & Gruendel, 1986, p. 27).

The early studies of young children's memories for everyday events and routines contained other important findings (summarized in K. Nelson, 1986, 1997). For example, they showed that children were both veridical and consistent in their sequencing of the actions in events. These qualities were especially apparent for events that tend to unfold in the same order time and again, such as those characterized by causal and enabling relations (discussed earlier in this chapter). In addition, the studies revealed a great deal of both interchild commonality and intrachild consistency in the elements of events that children apparently found worthy of mention in their reports. Almost invariably, the actions were those most central or important to the event (e.g., a cake at a birthday party), suggesting that children appreciated the goals of many of the events of their everyday lives. The studies also hinted at the power of scriptlike representations for young children. Because the memory representations were general rather than specific (they described what *usually* or *generally* happens, as opposed to *what happened* at a particular time), they served as a basis from which to predict what would happen in the future. They also provided a basis for generating possible alternative actions or outcomes. That is, because the form was general (e.g., "you eat"), many alternatives could be conceived to fill any given role in the event, thereby providing a foundation from which to construct not only knowledge about how

events unfold, but the parts that different actors and objects play in them as well.

The early research on children's event memories revealed evidence of significant mnemonic competence. It also indicated developmental differences. First, older children's reports of everyday events included more information, relative to younger children. Whereas a 3-year-old told of cooking a cake and then eating it, 6- and 8-year-old children told of putting up balloons, receiving and then opening presents from party guests, eating birthday cake, and playing games. Second, relative to younger children, older children more frequently mentioned alternative actions: "and then you have lunch *or whatever you have.*" Third, with age, children include in their reports more optional activities, such as "*Sometimes* then they have three games . . . then *sometimes* they open up the other presents." Finally, with increasing age, children mentioned more conditional activities, such as "*If* you're like at Foote Park or something, *then* it's time to go home." (K. Nelson & Gruendel, 1986, p. 27).

Some of the differences in younger and older children's reports might reflect the greater number of experiences of events such as birthday parties that older children have, relative to younger children. It would only be with experience that one would come to learn that the number of games played at a party or the precise timing of opening of presents varies from party to party, for example. Indeed, many of the age-related changes noted in this research also were seen to take place as children accrued experience with events (Fivush & Slackman, 1986). Yet, experience alone does not account for the developmental differences. In laboratory research in which children of different ages are given the same amount of experience with a novel event, older children produce more elaborate reports relative to younger children (e.g., Fivush, Kuebli, & Clubb, 1992; Price & Goodman, 1990).

## Children's Memories for Unique Events

Research on children's memories for the routine events of their lives literally changed the way that researchers viewed young mnemonists: Rather than as a "floor effect" comparison group for children who were older and more competent, children as young as 3 were viewed as reliable informants about past events. The research had another impact as well: it opened the door for the study of children's memories for unique events. Researchers noted that whereas young children seem to form general-ized memories of the events of their lives, they also distinguish between "what happens" (in general) and "what happened" (in particular). When children were asked a general question such as "What happens when you have snack at camp?" they responded in the timeless present tense (e.g., "We *have* cookies"). In contrast, when they were asked a specific question such as "What happened when you had snack at camp yesterday?" children responded in the past tense (e.g., "We *had* grape juice"; K. Nelson & Gruendel, 1986). Children's specific responses to questions about unique episodes strongly suggested that memory for unique events coexisted with generalized event memories. This suggestion was timely, given that within the adult literature on autobiographical or personal memory, the phenomenon of infantile or childhood amnesia was being "re-discovered" (Pillemer & White, 1989; White & Pillemer, 1979). Labeled by Sigmund Freud (1905/1953), the "remarkable amnesia of childhood," infantile or childhood amnesia is the relative paucity among adults of memories for unique events from the first 3 to 4 years of life. Adults report a steadily increasing number of memories of events that took place from the age of 3 years to 7 years, yet the number of memories from this period is smaller than the number expected based on adult rates of forgetting alone. Virtually universally, theories to explain the amnesia suggested that adults had few memories from early in life because as children they had not formed them (for a review, see Bauer, 2006). Research on children's recall of unique events promised to provide an empirical test of this tenacious assumption.

An early and influential study of young children's recall of specific past events was conducted by Fivush, Gray, and Fromhoff (1987). They interviewed 2- to 3-year-old children about events that had occurred within the past 3 months and about events that had occurred more than 3 months ago. A striking finding was that all 10 children in the sample recalled at least one event that had happened 6 or more months in the past. Indeed, the children reported the same amount of information about events that had taken place more than 3 months ago as they did about events that had taken place within 3 months. This study thus convincingly demonstrated that children quite young at the time of experience of specific, unique events are able to remember them over long periods. This conclusion was further supported by a study of 3- and 4-year-old children's recall of a trip to DisneyWorld (Hamond & Fivush, 1991). Whether the

children had experienced the event 6 months previously or 18 months previously, the amount recalled did not differ. Moreover, the older and younger children did not differ in the number of information units they provided. The number of elements of the experience reported by children who were only 3 years of age when they visited DisneyWorld was not different from the number reported by children who were a full year older. The age groups did differ, however, in how elaborate their reports were. Whereas the younger children tended to provide the minimum required response to a question, the older children tended to provide more elaborate responses. For example, when asked "What did you see at DisneyWorld," younger children tended to reply "Dumbos," whereas older children tended to embellish their response by reporting, for example, the size of the Dumbos: "big Dumbos."

## Age-Related Changes in Preschoolers' Recall of Past Events

Studies such as those conducted by Fivush et al. (1987) and Hamond and Fivush (1991) made clear that even over long delays, 2- to 3-year-old children remember specific events. Although the ability is in evidence at an early age, it nevertheless undergoes changes with development. The changes could be expected to affect both the sheer number of events remembered from the preschool years, and the robustness of the memories formed. After outlining the developmental changes, I discuss an important consequence of the changes—development of a autobiographical or personal past. I then discuss possible mechanisms of the changes, followed by patterns of individual and group differences in the normative trends.

### Age-Related Changes in How Long Children Remember

Taking our cues from the literature on memory development in the first 2 years of life, we might expect to see increases in the length of time over which preschool-age children remember. In actuality, the available data are mixed. On the one hand, there are studies such as Hamond and Fivush (1991) suggesting no difference after an 18-month delay in the number of units of information reported by children who had been 3 versus 4 years of age at the time of the event of a trip to DisneyWorld. Similarly, Sheingold and Tenney (1982) reported the results of a study in which they asked older children and adults specific questions about the birth of a younger sibling. For births that occurred when the participant was older than age 3 years (range 3 to 17 years), high levels of recall were observed. For adult participants who had been at least 3 years of age at the time of their siblings' births, it did not matter whether the birth had taken place when the participant was 3 years of age or 17 years of age: The number of questions that they were able to answer about the birth did not differ.

Whereas some studies suggest that the amount of time over which children remember is relatively unaffected by their age at the time of the experience, others suggest that the memories of older children are more robust, relative to those of younger children. For example, Quas and her colleagues assessed children 3 to 13 years of age for their memories for a painful medical procedure that they had experienced between the age of 2 and 6 years (Quas et al., 1999). Children who were older at the time of the procedure provided clearer evidence of recall of it. In contrast to the older children's detailed reports, the reports of the younger children were vague or the children evidenced no recall of the event. In fact, none of the children who had been 2 years of age at the time of the procedure demonstrated clear memory for it later, whereas most of the children who had been at least 4 years old at the time of the procedure remembered it (Quas et al., 1999). Similar patterns were observed by Peterson and Whalen (2001), who interviewed children 7 to 18 years of age about injuries incurred 5 years previously, when they were 2 to 13 years of age, and Pillemer, Picariello, and Pruett (1994), who interviewed 9- and 10-year-old children about an unexpected fire alarm that they had experienced 6 years previously, when they were 3 or 4 years of age. In both cases, the older the child at the time of the experience the more robust the memory years later.

It is worthy to note that the studies that suggest no effect of age are of positive events: a trip to DisneyWorld and birth of a sibling. In contrast, the studies that suggest effects of age are of negative events: medical procedures that were painful, stressful, or both, and an unexpected fire alarm. The reasons for this apparent difference are unclear. It is possible that positive events may be better remembered because they more readily lend themselves to discussion and interpretation after the fact, resulting in a stronger memory representation. Alternatively, the difference may be due to children's differential comprehension of events of different types.

The positive events that have been studied may have been better understood by younger children, relative to the negative events that have been studied. The importance of children's understanding of the causal and temporal structure of events for later recall is suggested by the work of Pillemer, Picariello, and Pruett. When they were interviewed 2 weeks after the unexpected fire alarm, most of the 3- and 4-year-old children were able to provide at least some information about the event. The younger children made more errors in their reports though; the larger number of errors may have been related to their poorer understanding of the event. For instance, only 33% of the younger children, in contrast to 75% of the older children, described a sense of urgency in leaving the building. In addition, 44% of the older children, but only 8% of the younger children, mentioned the cause of the alarm spontaneously. When the children were interviewed 6 years later, when they were 9 and 10 years of age, there were striking age differences in recall. Of the children who had been 4 at the time of the experience, 57% were able to provide either a full or at least a fragmentary narrative about the event, whereas only 18% of the children who had been 3 at the time of the experience were able to do so (Pillemer et al., 1994). The authors concluded that for the children who showed higher levels of recall after the long delay "causal reasoning at time 1 may have served as an organizing principle for thinking about the event, for imposing temporal order on the sequence of events, and for constructing a story-like narrative memory" (p. 103). Although the suggestion is compelling, additional research is necessary to determine whether the forgetting functions for more and less positive events differ from one another (see additional discussion later in this chapter).

### Age-Related Changes in the Productivity of External Cues to Recall

Whereas even young children remember events over the long term, there are suggestions that their recall is more dependent on external cues and reminders, relative to that of older children. For example, in Hamond and Fivush's (1991) study of children's reports of trips to DisneyWorld, only 22% of the children's recall was spontaneous. The balance of the information was elicited in response to direct questions. Although the effect was not substantial, the younger children produced less information spontaneously (19%) relative to the older children (25%). Thus, whereas an older child's response to a question like "What did you do at DisneyWorld?" might be

"We rode fun rides," a younger child might simply respond "rides." If the interviewer wanted more information about the rides, such as whether they were fun, she would need to ask: "Was it fun?" in response to which the younger child likely would respond "Yes." The net effect was that younger children required more cues to retrieve the same amount of information.

A potential consequence of younger children's greater reliance on external prompts and cues, relative to older children, is a lower level of consistency in the information retrieved about an event. As discussed by Fivush and Hamond (1990), if each time a child is asked to retrieve an event memory the same cues are provided, then the same elements will be retrieved each time. If the cues are different on each retrieval attempt, then different elements will be retrieved on each trial. The result would be a low level of consistency in recall from trial to trial. Fivush and Hamond provided data consistent with this suggestion. They asked mothers of 2-year-olds to talk with their children about novel events from the past (e.g., the first airplane trip, going to the beach). Six weeks later, a different interviewer asked the children about the same events. A striking finding was that 76% of the information that the children reported at the second interview was new and different relative to that provided at the first interview. Nevertheless, the information was judged by the children's mothers' to be accurate. The inconsistency in young children's recall contrasts with consistency in adults (e.g., McCloskey, Wible, & Cohen, 1988). Critically, over time, it may contribute to instability of the memory trace: Children may preserve a small core of features that is called up each time they talk about an event; the less stable "fringe" around the core may eventually become inaccessible. Younger children may be more susceptible to this source of instability, relative to older children.

### Age-Related Changes in What Children Report

With age, children report different types of information. Older children and adults focus on what is unique or distinctive about an experience, whereas younger children seem to comment on what is common across experiences or what is routine. Indications of this tendency were apparent in some of the earliest work on young children's recall of past events. For example, Todd and Perlmutter (1980) reported that roughly 50% of the past events mentioned in the context of conversations between adult experimenters and children were initiated by the children. Of the child-nominated events, 66% concerned routine, as opposed to novel, experiences (see also K. Nelson, 1989).

The tendency to focus on routine or common features continues into the early preschool years. Fivush and Hamond (1990) report that, in response to the interviewer's invitation to talk about going camping, a 2-year-old child, after providing the interviewer with the distinctive information that the family had slept in a tent, went on to mention the more typical features of the camping experience:

**Interviewer:** You slept in a tent? Wow, that sounds like a lot of fun.
**Child:** And then we waked up and eat dinner. First we eat dinner, then go to bed, and then wake up and eat breakfast.
**Interviewer:** What else did you do when you went camping? What did you do when you got up, after you ate breakfast?
**Child:** Umm, in the night, and went to sleep. (p. 231)

In the study from which this excerpt was taken, 48% of the information that the children reported was judged to be distinctive, implying that 52% of it was not. Given that many of the events that young children experience are "firsts" (e.g., first camping trip, first airplane ride, first visit to the dentist), in order to understand them, children may focus on what the novel experience has in common with previous experiences. This pattern changes over time. By 4 years of age, children report about three times more distinctive information than typical information (Fivush & Hamond, 1990).

What are the potential consequences of focus on the features that different events have in common, as opposed to what makes them unique? A suggestion comes from research on children's memories for repeated experiences of the same or a highly similar event. The work has revealed that with repeated experience, event memories become generalized and schematized. For instance, in research in which kindergartners were asked to tell "what happens" at school multiple times over the first weeks of experience, the children omitted details of their experiences and substituted generic information (Fivush, 1984; Fivush & Slackman, 1986). On the 2nd day of kindergarten, a child noted that on arrival at school: "We play with blocks over there, and the puppet thing over there, and we could paint." By the 10th week of school, the same prompt yielded a response such as "We can play." As the typical features of the event are abstracted, the episodic quality of the memory for each individual experience is lost. The end result is a highly stable, but generic, representation of what typically happens, as opposed to "what happened one time" (Hudson, 1986). By extension, an expected consequence of focus on what is common across experience is that a unique event such as camping gets "fused" into the daily routine of eating and sleeping. In the process, the features that distinguish events from one another may fade into the background and be lost. The result would be fewer memories of episodes that are truly unique. Conversely, with increasing age, children seem to focus on the more distinctive features of events, with a resulting increase in the number of memories that are truly unique.

### Age-Related Changes in How Much Children Report

With age, not only do children include different types of information in their narratives, but they include more information, both spontaneously and in response to prompts and cues. In research by Fivush and Haden (1997), children during the period from 3 to 6 years of age increased the number of prepositions in their average narrative more than twofold, from 10 to 23. Young children's narratives include basic information about what actions occurred in the event; they feature intensifiers, qualifiers, and internal evaluations; and the actions in the narrative are joined by simple temporal and causal connections (e.g., *then, before, after;* and *because, so, in order to,* respectively). What accounts for the increase in narrative length over this age period are age-related increases in orienting devices, conditional actions, and descriptive details. With age, as children recount events, they provide (a) more information about who was involved and when and where the event occurred, (b) more information about optional or variable actions (e.g., "*When it turned red light,* we stopped"; Fivush & Haden, 1997, p. 186), and (c) more elaborations (Fivush & Haden, 1997). As a result, relative to younger children's, older children's stories are more complete, easier to follow, and more engaging.

The dramatic increases with age in the amount of information that children *report* tempts the conclusion that there also are age-related increases in the amount of information that children *remember* about events. This is not a safe conclusion, however. It is relatively clear that perhaps especially for younger children, verbal reports underestimate the richness of memories. First, as noted, children often report new and different information each time they are interviewed about an event. This strongly implies that in any given interview, children are providing only a portion of what they remember. Second, as children get older, they have been shown to provide *more* information about an event, relative to the amount provided when they were younger. Children interviewed at the age of 9 to 10 years provided twice as much information about Hurricane Andrew (a Class IV hurricane that hit southern Florida in 1992) than they had shortly after the storm, which occurred when they were 3 to 4 years of age (117 and 57 propositions, respectively: Fivush, Sales, Goldberg, Bahrick, & Parker, 2004). This trend is precisely the opposite of the typical decline in recall over time. The trend could not be attributed to acquisition of more general knowledge about hurricanes or other storms in the time between interviews; overwhelmingly, the new information provided specific details about the experiences of the children's families, as opposed to general information about storms. Because we have no reason to believe that the children's actual memories improved with time, the pattern implies that the younger children remembered more than they reported. Children report more with age, but because of the inevitable confounding between increases in age and increases in narrative skills, it is not clear whether they also remember more.

## Emergence of Autobiographical or Personal Memory

Changes in how long unique experiences or events are remembered, in the productivity of external cues to recall, in the uniqueness of events remembered, and in how much is reported about past events are critical ingredients in the development of a particular type of memory for specific events that emerges during the preschool years—*autobiographical* or *personal* memory. Autobiographical or personal memories are the memories of events and experiences that make up one's life story or personal past. They are the stories that we tell about ourselves that reveal who we are and how our experiences have shaped our characters. As implied by this description, autobiographical memories differ from "run-of-the-mill" event memories in that autobiographical memories are infused with a sense of personal involvement or ownership in the event. They are memories of events that happened to one's self; in which one participated; and about which one had emotions, thoughts, reactions, and reflections. It is this feature that puts the "auto" in *auto*biographical.

In addition to the defining feature that autobiographical memories are about one's self, there are characteristic features that mark memories as autobiographical, one of which is that autobiographical memories tend to be of unique events that happened at a specific place, at a specific time. In other words, they are memories of particular episodes or experiences. Autobiographical memories also entail a sense of conscious awareness that one is reexperiencing an event that happened at some point in one's own past. This specific type of awareness, termed *autonoetic* or self-knowing (Tulving, 1983), has been associated with memory from the time of William James (1890). Indeed, for James, "Memory requires more than the mere dating of a fact in the past. It must be dated in *my* past. . . . I must think that I directly experienced its occurrence" (p. 612).

Evidence that, over the course of the preschool years, event memories take on more and more autobiographical features is readily apparent in children's narratives. From a very young age, children include references to themselves in their narratives: "*I* fell down." With age, they increasingly pepper their narratives with the subjective perspective that indicates the significance of the event for the child (Fivush, 2001). For example, they go beyond comment on the objective reality of "falling down" to convey how they felt about the fall: "I fell down and *was so embarrassed* because everybody was watching!" It is this subjective perspective that provides the explanation for why events are funny, or sad, for instance, and thus of significance to one's self.

There also are changes in the marking of events as having taken place at a specific place and time. Children increasingly include specific references to time, such as "on my birthday," "at Halloween," or "last winter" (K. Nelson & Fivush, 2004). Markings such as these not only establish that an event happened at a time different from the present, but they begin to establish a time line along which an organized historical record of when events occurred can be constructed. Children also include in their narratives more orienting information, including where events took place and who participated in them (e.g., Fivush & Haden, 1997). These changes serve to distinguish events from one another, thereby making them more distinctive.

Finally, with age, children include in their narratives an increasing number of elements that suggest rich detail that would contribute to the sense of reliving the experience. They include more intensifiers ("Cause she was *very* naughty"), qualifiers ("I *didn't like* her videotape"), elements of suspense ("And *you know what?*"; examples from Fivush & Haden, 1997), and even repetition of the dialogue spoken in the event ("I said, 'I hope my Nintendo my Super Nintendo is still here'"; from Ackil, Van Abbema, & Bauer, 2003). The amount of descriptive detail that children provide in their narratives increases dramatically over the preschool years. In Fivush and Haden (1997), for example, children went from using approximately 4 descriptive terms per event at age 3 years to using 12 such terms per event at 6 years. The result is a much more elaborate narrative that brings both the storyteller and the listener to the brink of reliving the experience. It is tempting to conclude that these changes account for the finding among adults of a steadily increasing number of memories of events that took place from the age of 3 years to 7 years (Bauer, 2006).

## What Develops in Preschoolers' Recall of Past Events?

Over the preschool years, there are changes in children's recall of specific past events, including events considered autobiographical. A likely source of the developmental changes is improvement in the efficiency of the basic mnemonic processes of encoding, consolidation, storage, and retrieval. These changes affect the strength and integrity of the memory representation, as well as accessibility of it. Extramnemonic factors are implicated as well. For instance, increases in memories that are personally relevant and located in a particular place and time likely are associated with developments in self-concept and temporal concepts, respectively. Changes in children's abilities to report what they remember also are likely contributors to observed developmental changes. Each of these sources of age-related change is discussed in turn.

## Developmental Changes in Basic Mnemonic Processes

A prominent source of age-related changes in basic mnemonic processes is brain development. Whereas the temporal-cortical network that supports explicit memory develops late in the 1st year and throughout the 2nd year of life, neural events continue for years beyond infancy. Neurogenesis in the dentate gyrus of the hippocampus continues throughout childhood and adulthood (Tanapat, Hastings, & Gould, 2001). Whereas maximum synaptic density in the dentate gyrus is reached by 16 to 20 postnatal months, pruning to adult levels continues until at least 4 to 5 years of age (Eckenhoff & Rakic, 1991). It is only then that we would expect mature levels of function to be achieved (Goldman-Rakic, 1987). In the prefrontal cortex, synaptic density peaks between 15 and 24 months and pruning of synapses to adult levels begins near puberty (Bourgeois, 2001). In the years between, in some cortical layers there are changes in the sizes of cells and the lengths and branching of dendrites (Benes, 2001). Throughout the prefrontal cortex, myelination continues during this time, and neurotransmitters such as acetylcholine increase to adult levels (Benes, 2001). In short, well beyond infancy there is continued development in the neural substrate supporting long-term explicit memory. Whereas these later neurodevelopmental changes may not be associated with functional changes as dramatic as those in the first 2 years of life, they nevertheless can be expected to have consequences throughout the preschool years.

### Encoding

Developmental changes in prefrontal cortex in particular can be expected to contribute to age-related changes in the efficiency with which preschool-age children encode information. For example, there are changes in short-term memory span, as measured by tests such as memory for digits or words. Whereas children 2 years of age are able to hold only about 2 units of information in mind, by the ages of 5 and 7, they can remember 4 and 5 units, respectively. Over the preschool years, children become more effective at keeping task-irrelevant thoughts out of short-term memory, thereby reducing the potentially interfering material that otherwise would limit capacity. Although the most pronounced changes in memory strategies are apparent in the school years, even in the preschool years there are developmental increases in the use of rehearsal to maintain the accessibility of to-be-remembered material over time (see Pressley & Hilden, Chapter 12, this *Handbook,* this volume). The net result of these changes is that children become increasingly adept not only at maintaining information in temporary registration, but in initiating the type of organizational processing that promotes consolidation of it.

Although there is sound rationale for expecting that developmental changes in encoding over the preschool years might contribute to age-related changes in event memory over the same period, few studies can be brought to bear to evaluate the hypothesized relation. One reason for the paucity of relevant data is that researchers interested in long-term memory frequently either have not measured initial encoding (memory is tested only well after the event), or levels of encoding have not been controlled (immediate memory may be tested, but the impact of age-related differences in initial learning is not controlled).

Whereas there are not studies in which the variance associated with differential encoding has been evaluated for its potential impact on recall over spans of months to years, there are some experimental studies in which encoding has been controlled by bringing children of different ages to a criterion level of learning. Most such studies have been conducted with school-age children (7- to 11-year-olds; e.g., Brainerd & Reyna, 1995), or with very young children (12- to 18-month-olds; Howe & Courage, 1997b, reviewed earlier), as opposed to preschoolers. As outlined earlier, with levels of learning controlled in this way, age-related differences in infants' and very young children's long-term memory still obtain (Howe & Courage, 1997b; see also Bauer, 2005a; Bauer et al., 2000, for the same result when children are matched for levels of encoding and when variance is controlled statistically, respectively). The same result is obtained with school-age children and, using a much smaller database, with preschool-age children as well (Howe & O'Sullivan, 1997). These studies suggest that developmental differences in encoding alone do not account for age-related variance in long-term memory.

### Consolidation and Storage

Changes in the processes by which memory representations are consolidated and stored can be expected throughout the preschool years, in association with neurodevelopmental changes within the medial temporal and prefrontal structures, as well as in the connections between them. Neuroimaging techniques such as ERPs could be brought to bear on the question, as they are in the infancy period (Bauer et al., 2006; Bauer, Wiebe, et al., 2003; Carver et al., 2000). However, such studies have not been conducted with preschool-age children. Neither is there a plethora of behavioral studies to address the question. Interpretation of most existing behavioral data is complicated by an inability to separate the contributions of the basic mnemonic processes. On the basis of a single test, it is difficult, if not impossible, to know whether a memory representation remains intact but is inaccessible given the cues provided (retrieval failure) or whether the trace has lost its integrity (consolidation/storage failure; Tulving, 1983). Moreover, as noted, an additional complication in developmental research is the likelihood of uncontrolled and even unmeasured age-related differences in encoding. The result is that few research traditions yield data that can productively be applied to the question of whether hypothesized age-related differences in consolidation and storage processes contribute to age-related differences in the robustness of long-term recall.

Researchers working in the context of the trace-integrity framework (Brainerd, Reyna, Howe, & Kingma, 1990) and conceptually related fuzzy-trace theory (Brainerd & Reyna 1990) have produced a series of studies designed to evaluate the relative contributions of storage versus retrieval processes. To eliminate encoding differences as a source of age-related effects, participants are brought to a criterion level of learning prior to imposition of a delay. In addition, to permit evaluation of the contributions of storage processes versus retrieval processes, participants are provided multiple test trials, without intervening study trials (see earlier discussion of the logic of this experimental approach). In one such study, 4- and 6-year-old children learned and then recalled 8-item picture lists (Howe, 1995). In this study, as in virtually every other study conducted within this tradition (reviewed in Howe & O'Sullivan, 1997), the largest proportion of age-related variance in children's recall was accounted for by memory failure at the level of consolidation and storage, as opposed to retrieval. The observation that consolidation and storage failure rates decline throughout childhood implies that these processes are a source of developmental change.

### Retrieval

Retrieval of memories from long-term storage is thought to depend on prefrontal cortex, a neural structure that undergoes an extremely protracted course of postnatal development. Because they would be expected to change slowly as a consequence, retrieval processes seem to provide a ready answer to the question: "What develops in memory during the preschool years." The results of research from the trace-integrity framework and fuzzy-trace theory traditions stand in apparent contradiction of this expectation, however: Whereas consolidation and storage failure rates decline throughout childhood, retrieval failure rates remain at relatively constant levels (Howe & O'Sullivan, 1997). The apparent lack of change in retrieval failure rates

throughout childhood undermines the suggestion that retrieval processes are a major source of developmental change during this period.

If changes in retrieval processes are not a major source of age-related changes in long-term recall in childhood, then why do younger children seem to be more dependent on external retrieval cues, relative to older children? The answer to this question may lie in recognition that the presence or absence of retrieval cues makes an enormous difference *regardless of age*. Even at our peak of mnemonic competence, we are dependent on cues to retrieval. Indeed, all recall is cued, be it by an external prompt or an internal association (Spear, 1978). Thus, the developmental phenomenon is not that, with increasing age, children gain independence from cueing—but that, with increasing age, children provide more information per cue. The change in rate of return from external prompts and probes may imply that cues "spread" further for older children relative to younger children. That is, it is possible that in older children, a given cue activates more associated elements, relative to the number activated in a younger child. An alternative possibility is that the "spread per cue" does not change with age, but that older children simply report more of the coactivated elements, relative to younger children.

Another possibility is that with age, children are able to benefit from a wider and wider array of cues. Such changes are apparent in the infancy literature. At 18 months of age, exposure to a videotape of another child performing laboratory events facilitates children's memories, but exposure to still photographs of the same activity does not. At 24 months, exposure to still photographs of activities facilitates memory, but simply hearing the activity described does not. By the age of 3 years, a verbal description is sufficient to activate event memory (Hudson, 1991, 1993; Hudson & Sheffield, 1998). In a similar vein, whether they encountered them in the laboratory in which they had been used or at home, the props used to produce event sequences facilitate 3-year-old children's verbal memories for events experienced at the age of 20 months. In contrast, still photographs of the props do not (Bauer et al., 2004). These specific examples are of apparent changes in the sensitivity to different types of external representations (props, videotapes, and still photographs) as cues by children during the transition from infancy to early childhood. Across the preschool period, analogous changes may occur in children's responses to different verbal cues to recall. If this is the case (no research has explicitly tested the possibility), then more cues may be necessary to obtain the same amount of information from younger relative to older children because for the younger children, some of the cues simply were not effective aids to retrieval.

Does the fact that regardless of age recall is dependent on cueing imply that developmental changes in prefrontal cortex have nothing to do with memory development in childhood? Although possible, it is highly unlikely. It is more likely that the role played by developmental changes in prefrontal cortex differs from that previously assumed (Bauer, 2006). Rather than on retrieval processes, a major effect of developments in prefrontal structures may be on consolidation and storage processes. Consolidation is an interactive process between medial temporal and cortical structures. As such, changes in cortical structures may be as important to developments in consolidation processes as are changes in medial temporal structures. Moreover, the ultimate storage sites for long-term memories are the association cortices. Prefrontal cortex is thought to play an especially significant role in storage of information about the *where* and *when* of events and experiences, the very features that distinguish experiences from one another and contribute to their autobiographical quality. Thus, developmental changes in prefrontal cortex may play their primary role in supporting more efficient consolidation and more effective storage; their role in improving retrieval processes may be secondary.

## Conceptual Developments

Changes in basic mnemonic processes associated with brain development are not the only source of developmental change in the preschool years. There is reason to expect that developments in conceptual domains also contribute to age-related changes in memories of specific past events in general and autobiographical memories in particular. Because they are features that define and characterize autobiographical memories, developments in three conceptual domains are especially relevant: self-concept, spatial and temporal concepts, and autonoetic awareness.

### Self-Concept

Throughout the preschool years, there are changes in the self-concept that could be expected to contribute to an increasingly autobiographical perspective in children's

reports of past events. There are two senses of self that comprise one's self-concept: a subjective sense of "I" as an entity with thoughts and feelings, and an objective sense of "me" as an entity with features and characteristics that make one different and separate from others. Some scholars suggest that by the second half of the 2nd year of life the "I" and the "me" have coalesced into a self system sufficient to serve as an organizer for experiences that are relevant to the self (e.g., Howe & Courage, 1993, 1997a). This development is signaled by children's abilities to identify themselves in pictures and to recognize themselves in mirrors. One suggestion that achievement of this very basic sense of self is related to autobiographical memory development comes from a longitudinal study conducted by Harley and Reese (1999). They found that children who were earlier to recognize themselves in a mirror (assessed at 19 months) made faster progress in independent autobiographical memory reports (assessed at 25 and 32 months), relative to children who were later to evidence mirror self-recognition.

There are additional developments in the self-concept that take place over the preschool years, each of which could be expected to contribute to increased "personalization" of memories for specific past events. Between 2 and 4 years of age, children seem to develop a sense of the *self in time* (K. Nelson, 1989) or *temporally extended self* (Povinelli, 1995)—a self that extends backward and forward in time. Recognition of continuity of self over time makes possible establishment of a history of experience of significance to the self. It makes experiences from the past relevant to the present in a way that an ahistorical self-concept simply cannot. Consistent with the suggestion that development in this aspect of the self-concept may have relevance for developments in autobiographical memory is the finding that 3-year-old children who are able to identify themselves in a time-delayed video make more contributions to autobiographical memory conversations with their mothers, relative to 3-year-olds who do not show evidence of appreciation of themselves as existing over time (Welch-Ross, 2001).

Another aspect of the self that is later to develop (relative to recognition of one's physical features) is an *evaluative* or *subjective perspective* that specifies how an event made the experiencer think or feel. Throughout the preschool years, there are steady increases in children's references to emotional and cognitive states in reports about past events (e.g., Kuebli, Butler, & Fivush,

1995). Variability in the evaluative or subjective stance is predictive of 36-month-old children's contributions to autobiographical memory conversations with their mothers (Welch-Ross, 2001). The finding is consistent with the suggestion that an increasingly subjective perspective on experience facilitates inclusion of events in an autobiographical record: Experiences are not just objective events that played out, but are events that influenced the self in one way or another.

### Placing Events in a Specific Time and Place

Autobiographical memories are of events that took place at a particular place and time. Logically then, developments in the ability to locate events in time and place should be related to age-related changes in autobiographical memory (K. Nelson & Fivush, 2004). By 9 months of age, a large subset of infants remember the temporal order in which event sequences unfold. By 20 months of age, this ability is both reliable and robust. These findings make clear that infants know that *within an event,* Action 1 happened before Action 2. They do not, however, provide evidence that such young children have an appreciation of *when the entire event occurred,* relative to when another entire event occurred.

The ability to place events on a time line develops over the preschool years. For example, Friedman (1990, 1993) has shown developmental changes in preschool-age children's understanding of the order of familiar, daily activities, as well as their understanding of the sequence, duration, and distance of events, relative to one another. In addition, there are developmental changes in children's use of linguistic markers that place events in relation to one another on a time line (e.g., "my birthday" comes after "Halloween"), consistent use of which is not apparent until children are 4 to 5 years of age. Although children's understanding of temporal relations develops over the preschool years, and there is a logical argument that such developments might relate to age-related changes in autobiographical memory (K. Nelson & Fivush, 2004), there is not a body of data relating the two domains. Also missing from the literature are studies examining children's ability to locate memories in a particular place as well as how this ability relates to autobiographical memory. The literature on children's memories for the source of information (e.g., whether they learned a fact from a puppet or an experimenter) is relevant in this regard (Drummey & Newcombe, 2002). However, how memory for source relates to autobio-

graphical memory development has not been explored systematically.

### Developments in Autonoetic Awareness

A characteristic feature of autobiographical memories is that retrieval of them is accompanied by autonoetic awareness: a sense that the event recollected is one that happened in the past (Tulving, 1983). This type of awareness depends on the more general ability to identify the source or origin of one's knowledge. There are age-related changes in this ability throughout the preschool years. For instance, it is not until 4 to 6 years of age that children (a) seem to know what sense organ to use to find out the properties of an object (e.g., that one uses one's eyes, not one's hands, to determine color: O'Neill, Astington, & Flavell, 1992); (b) accurately identify the source of learning of newly acquired words versus words that they have known for a long time (e.g., Taylor, Esbensen, & Bennett, 1994); and (c) distinguish true knowledge from a lucky guess (Sodian & Wimmer, 1987). Consistent with the suggestion that development of these abilities is related to improvements in recall is the finding that 3- and 5-year-old children who successfully distinguished a lucky guess from true knowledge showed higher levels of free recall of items on a list, relative to same-age peers who failed to make the distinction (Perner & Ruffman, 1995). In addition, children who understand what senses can be used to gain what types of information show an advantage in recall for pictures directly experienced relative to pictures seen only on video, whereas children who fail to evidence such knowledge do not (Perner, 2001). It remains to be seen whether relations between these concepts and reports of autobiographical memories also would obtain.

### Developmental Changes in and the Socialization of Narrative Production

One of the most salient sources of developmental change during the preschool years is in the expression of memory: Older children report more about events from the past, relative to younger children. As noted, whether that means that older children also remember more, relative to younger children, is an open question. Yet, it is a basic fact of mnemonic life that more elaborated memory representations are better remembered, relative to less elaborated ones. Thus, even if the differences in narrative competence do not *originate* from differences in memory, per se, they may *contribute* to them, over time. Sources of change in narrative competence include the medium of expression—the basic elements of language—and socialization of the narrative form of storytelling.

### Basic Elements of Language

Because developments in the basic elements of language are discussed elsewhere in the *Handbook* (see Tomasello, Chapter 6; Waxman & Lidz, Chapter 7, this *Handbook,* this volume), my treatment of them is brief. Over the first 4 years of life, most normally developing children go from being strictly nonverbal to using most of the adult forms of grammar. Although there are individual differences, children typically utter their first words sometime between 9 and 15 months of age. By roughly 18 months, on average, they have 50 words in their vocabularies. From this age until first grade, children are estimated to learn 5.5 words per day; by the fifth grade, they understand approximately 40,000 words (Anglin, 1993). Often coincident with the milestone of 50 words, children begin producing simple multiword forms, such as "more juice." The first elements of grammar (e.g., morphological markings) are apparent by 30 months of age. By age 4 years, all but the more intricate grammatical forms (e.g., passive constructions) are apparent (in English, that is; there is considerable cross-linguistic variability in grammatical development). Acquiring the structures of complex sentences and forms continues well into the school years. With developments in the basic elements of language, children are able to convey the contents of their memories more effectively and efficiently.

### Socialization of Narrative Production

As soon as children begin acquiring the basic elements of language, they recruit them in their efforts to communicate. Much (though certainly not all) of early language use is instrumental: Children are trying to accomplish something when they utter "more juice." Whereas children refer to events in the *here-and-now* as soon as they have words, there is a longer course of development for using language to refer to the *there-and-then.* There is strong evidence that children's competence in reporting on past events is influenced by the narrative environment in which they are raised. The evidence comes primarily from investigations of children's developing autobiographical memory abilities.

Children first begin using language to talk about the past by the middle of the 2nd year. At this young age, past-tense forms typically are used to refer to events from the very recent past or for everyday events (see K. Nelson & Fivush, 2000, 2004, for reviews). Children participate in conversations about past events primarily by answering questions posed by adult partners. The adult might say, "We had ice cream, didn't we?" and the child participates by responding, "Yes!" By the age of 2 years, children begin to provide mnemonic content. At this age, when parents ask their children, "What did we have?" they can expect an answer: "Ice cream!" Children do not, however, go on to elaborate their responses. Around 3 years of age, children become fuller participants in memory conversations. Whereas at this age, most memory conversations still are initiated by the parents, children bring up past events as potential topics of conversations. Some children are able to tell complete, albeit brief, stories about past events. More commonly, they participate by providing content-filled responses to inquiries from their parents, as well as some elaborations. As noted, over the preschool years, children assume more of the conversational burden by producing longer, more detailed narratives and by providing more information in response to questions from their conversational partners.

Children do not construct event memory narratives in a vacuum. It is in the context of dialogues, often with parents, that they learn both the skills for narrative construction and the social purposes of narrative. Since the middle 1980s, it has been apparent that parents differ in the way they support or scaffold their children's developing narrative skills. Moreover, it is increasingly obvious that variability among parents is systematically related to individual differences in children's developing autobiographical narrative skills.

**Parental Styles of Conversation.** Although several labels have been used to capture the differences, there is consensus that parents exhibit two styles that vary in terms of the parents' contributions to conversations (K. Nelson, 1993; K. Nelson & Fivush, 2000, 2004). Parents who frequently engage in conversations about the past, provide rich descriptive information about previous experiences, and invite their children to "join in" on the construction of stories about the past, are said to use a *high elaborative* style. In contrast, parents who provide fewer details about past experiences and instead pose specific questions to their children, are said to use a *low elaborative* or *repetitive* style. Two examples from conversations recorded in my laboratory help illustrate the difference, as well as why the low elaborative style also is described as "repetitive." In both cases, the conversations are between mothers and their 3-year-old children.

*High Elaborative Style*

> **Mother:** Say, J . . . , what was at Lauren's house a long time ago at her birthday party?
> **Child:** (no response)
> **Mother:** What did you hold—they were so tiny—at Lauren's house? Remember?
> **Child:** A baby.
> **Mother:** A baby kitty.
> **Child:** Yeah, a baby kitty.
> **Mother:** That's right. Oh and it was so soft. How many kitties did she have?
> **Child:** Um, five.
> **Mother:** Uh-huh. That's right.
> **Child:** And they got away.
> **Mother:** And they got away from you. Yeah.

*Low Elaborative or Repetitive Style*

> **Mother:** E . . ., do you remember going to Sandy's house and playing at her house?
> **Child:** (nods in agreement)
> **Mother:** Did they have some kids at her house?
> **Child:** Yeah.
> **Mother:** What kinds of kids were at her house?
> **Child:** David.
> **Mother:** David. Was he the only child that was at her house?
> **Child:** (nods in agreement)
> **Mother:** What other kids were at her house?

Stylistic differences are robust and extend beyond the context of mother-child conversations about past events. For example, although much of the research on stylistic differences in early autobiographic contexts has been with mothers, the limited research done with fathers indicates that they, too, exhibit stylistic differences (Haden, Haine, & Fivush, 1997). Whereas both mothers and fathers become more elaborative as their children get older and more skilled in autobiography, levels of elaboration nevertheless are correlated over time (Reese, Haden, & Fivush, 1993). In addition, mothers, at least, show similar patterns with multiple chil-

dren in the family (Haden, 1998; K. D. Lewis, 1999; the relevant studies with fathers have not yet been done). Finally, stylistic differences are apparent not only when parents are eliciting memory reports from their children, but also as events are being experienced and thus, encoded (Bauer & Burch, 2004; Haden, Ornstein, Eckerman, & Didow, 2001; Tessler & Nelson, 1994).

**Relations between Parental Style and Children's Event Memory Narratives.** Parental stylistic differences have implications for children's autobiographical memory reports. Specifically, both concurrently and over time, children of parents using a more elaborative style report more about past events than children of parents using a less elaborative style (e.g., Bauer & Burch, 2004; Fivush, 1991; Fivush & Fromhoff, 1988; Peterson & McCabe, 1994). Both of these patterns are nicely illustrated in a longitudinal study conducted by Reese et al. (1993). The researchers examined conversations between 19 mother-child pairs, over four time points: 40, 46, 58, and 70 months. Concurrent correlations between maternal elaborations and children's memory responses were observed at all four time points. The correlations ranged in strength from .59 to .85. Thus, at each session, the more elaborations mothers provided, the more memory contributions their children made. Concurrent correlations between maternal elaborations and children's participation in memory interviews have been observed in samples of children as young as 19 months (Farrant & Reese, 2000) and 24 to 30 months (Hudson, 1990) of age. There also are concurrent correlations between maternal verbal elaborations and 24-month-old children's performance in an imitation-based task (Bauer & Burch, 2004). Thus, relations with maternal elaboration extend beyond verbal paradigms to nonverbal measures of children's memory performance in a controlled laboratory task.

Also apparent in the data from Reese et al. (1993) are cross-lagged relations between maternal verbal behavior and children's memory contributions. Mothers who used more elaborations when their children were 40 months of age had children who at 58 and 70 months made more memory contributions. Maternal elaborations at the 58-month time point were related to children's memory contributions at the 70-month time point. Largely absent were relations within children, across time (e.g., children's memory responses at 40 months were not related to their memory responses at 46 months); and between children's behavior at earlier time points and mothers' behavior at later time points (e.g., children's memory responses at 40 months were not related to mother elaborations at 46 months). In both cases, the only such relations were observed between 58 and 70 months. The entire pattern is consistent with suggestions that the process of event memory narrative development is one of social construction, with more experienced partners scaffolding the performance of their younger collaborators. Harley and Reese (1999) extended the pattern of findings to mother-child dyads enrolled at 19 months of age and followed longitudinally until 32 months of age. These results imply that scaffolding begins well before children are making independent contributions to memory conversations.

If, through conversations about past events, children internalize the canonical narrative form for organizing and expressing their memories, we should see evidence that their skills extend beyond the context of mother-child conversations. Several studies have demonstrated that children whose mothers use a more elaborative style exhibit greater narrative competence not only in conversations with their mothers, but in independent narratives as well (e.g., Bauer & Burch, 2004; Boland, Haden, & Ornstein, 2003; Fivush, 1991; Peterson & McCabe, 1992; although see Harley & Reese, 1999, for negative evidence in younger children).

### Summary and Conclusions

As is the case for event memory in the first 2 years of life, changes in basic mnemonic processes are a source of developmental change in event memory in the preschool years. The changes presumably are related to developments in the neural substrate that supports explicit event memory. Much additional work is necessary both to examine the relative contributions of each of the basic mnemonic processes and to test the relations. For autobiographical memory in particular, there is reason to believe that developments in self-concept, in understanding of temporal and spatial concepts, and of the origins of the contents of mind, are additional sources of developmental change. The relatively small number of empirical tests of relations between autobiographical memory and these concepts that have been conducted are largely consistent with these suggestions.

A larger body of work has addressed a third source of developmental change in the preschool years, socialization of event memory narratives. There is strong evidence that variability in the narrative environment in which children craft their narrative skills is related to

the proficiency that children gain. Working in collaboration with a parent who uses a more elaborative style, over time, children come to produce longer memory reports, to include more sophisticated narrative devices, and to include more evaluative comments. Each of these features contributes to a more "colorful" narrative. However, a more detailed narrative account is not the same as a more detailed memory representation (e.g., Bauer, 1993; Mandler, 1990a). Individuals who produce shorter, less dramatic accounts of their experiences may have memory representations every bit as detailed, integrated, and coherent as individuals who produce more dramatic ones: The difference may be in the public story, rather than in the private memory representation. This consideration does not make the study of social influences on narrative development any less important. But it is desirable to keep this possibility in mind as we consider the mechanisms of event memory development.

### Group and Individual Differences in Event and Autobiographical Memory in the Preschool Years

Given the sources of developmental change identified, what would we expect to see in terms of group and individual differences in event and autobiographical memory in the preschool years? As was the case in infancy, we might expect to see group differences in basic mnemonic processes as a function of maturation, and individual differences as a function of language and information-processing variables such as speed of processing and attention. Moreover, as children are called on to report on events from their everyday lives, we might expect to see variability as a function of background knowledge or expertise. We might also expect to see differences in mastery of theoretically relevant concepts as a function of children's experience with the domains. Consideration of possible sources of variance in narrative socialization suggests that we might expect to see effects of variables that affect parent-child interaction and thus socialization, including children's temperament and the dyadic variable of attachment status. Finally, there is the possibility of culture group differences. Each is discussed in turn.

#### Group and Individual Differences in Basic Mnemonic Processes

In keeping with the cognitive tradition of focus on group trends, relatively little attention has been paid to how group differences or individual characteristics of the child might relate to variability in basic mnemonic processes. They have received the most attention in the context of research on the factors affecting children's eyewitness testimony and suggestibility. Even within this literature, however, the corpus of research is relatively meager.

**Gender.** In infancy, the expectation of possible gender differences stems from consideration of overall maturational changes favoring girls. In the preschool years, it stems from the observation that most often memory is tested verbally, and in general, girls are more verbal than boys (Maccoby & Jacklin, 1974). The possibility of better performance on verbal memory tasks by girls relative to boys has been examined in the literature on deliberate remembering and strategy use (with mixed results: see Pressley & Hilden, Chapter 12, this *Handbook*, this volume). Gender-related differences also have been a focus in the literature on narrative socialization (and are discussed in a subsequent section). They have not, however, been a focus in examinations of the basic processes of encoding, consolidation, storage, and retrieval.

**Language.** As discussed, there is potential for language to influence basic mnemonic processes. In the preschool years, there is additional reason to expect effects of language on memory, given that in most studies, memory is measured verbally. Yet, as in the early years of life, in the preschool period, language variables have not been found to be a reliable or robust source of individual differences in event memory. Whereas there are some reports of relations between children's language development and their mnemonic performance (e.g., Bauer & Wewerka, 1995; Walkenfeld, 2000; Welch-Ross, 1997), there also are reports of failure to find relations within the same age periods (Greenhoot, Ornstein, Gordon, & Baker-Ward, 1999; Reese & Brown, 2000; Reese & Fivush, 1993). At this point, the relations between language and basic mnemonic processes of event memory in the preschool years are unclear.

**Information Processing Variables.** There is a tradition of research on information-processing variables as a source of individual differences in children's memory. Most of this research has focused on deliberate or strategic remembering, as opposed to event memory. In addition, rather than information-processing variables per se, the predictor variable usually is intelligence or aptitude. The general finding is that more gifted children (children with higher IQ and aptitude scores) perform at higher levels on tests of memory, relative to less gifted children (e.g., Schneider & Bjorklund, 1998). Given that, as measured by elementary cognitive tasks, gifted children are faster processors, it is likely that faster information processing and more attentional control results in more effective and more efficient encoding and consolidation, as well as deployment and use of strategies.

**Background Knowledge.** As noted, one of the forces that led to research on children's event memory was the finding that background knowledge or expertise affected children's memory (e.g., Chi, 1978). The relation between memory performance and background knowledge is firmly established in the event memory literature. For example, Goodman, Quas, Batterman-Faunce, Riddlesberer, and Kuhn (1994) found relations between children's knowledge of a painful medical procedure and their subsequent reports of it. Children who knew more about the procedure in advance of it subsequently reported less inaccurate information and were more resistant to suggestive questions than children who were less knowledgeable. Knowledge also can have deleterious effects on performance. In situations in which aspects of a single experience deviate from knowledge of "what usually happens," general knowledge may actually interfere with recall of the specific features of an episode (e.g., Ornstein, Merritt, Baker-Ward, Furtado, Gordon, & Principe, 1998). Even this example makes clear that background knowledge is a source of individual difference in event memory. In most cases, it has a facilitating effect on memory performance.

### Group and Individual Differences in Conceptual Developments

Consideration of possible group and individual differences in conceptual domains that theoretically bear relations with event memory in general and autobiographical memory in particular originated from a somewhat unlikely source: the search for universals in cognitive development. To help determine whether basic cognitive achievements, such as a sense of self, are universally acquired, environmental influences, such as those associated with different family constellations and different socialization practices, were assessed. The relevant literature is small; possible variability in children's understanding of temporal and spatial marking of specific events has not been systematically explored, and for this reason, the concept is not discussed.

**Family Constellation Variables.**   Although there is variability in early self-recognition, it is not related to demographic variables such as maternal education, socioeconomic status, birth order, and number of siblings (M. Lewis & Brooks-Gunn, 1979). Whether such variables affect the later-developing aspects of the self-concept has not been systematically explored. Perhaps most relevant to the question of whether there are group or individual differences in children's understanding of the sources of knowledge is research by Dunn and her colleagues. They found that the quality of sibling interactions before age 3 years predicted false-belief task performance at age 4 years (Dunn, Brown, Slomkiwski, Tesla, & Youngblade, 1991). Research by Lewis and his colleagues suggested that it is not simply a sibling effect but an *older* sibling effect. The number of older siblings 3- to 5-year-old children have is related to their success on false-belief tasks: Firstborn children, who thus have no older siblings, have the lowest rate of success (C. Lewis, Freeman, Kyriakidou, Maridaki-Kassotaki, & Berridge, 1996).

**Different Socialization Practices.**   Another possible source of variability in young children's conceptual development is socialization practices. Consistent with this suggestion, there is evidence that parental narrative style relates to the development of an evaluative or subjective self. Children whose mothers used a number of evaluative terms in autobiographical memory conversations when the children were 3 years of age used a number of such terms when they were 6 years of age (Fivush, 2001). Moreover, there are culture group differences for this practice. When Chinese mothers and their children talk about the past, they make fewer mentions of the child, relative to mothers from the United States. Perhaps not coincidentally, in conversations about the past, children from Asian cultures refer to themselves less frequently and provide fewer personal evaluations (Han, Leichtman, & Wang, 1998; Wang, Leichtman, & Davies, 2000). Finally, there is some evidence that parental narrative style relates to children's understanding of the sources of knowledge. Welch-Ross (1997) found that maternal elaborations were positively related to and ma-

ternal repetitions were negatively related to 3- to 4-year-old children's scores on tasks designed to assess their understanding of mind.

### Group and Individual Differences in Narrative Socialization

In contrast to the limited literature on group and individual differences in basic mnemonic processes and on conceptual developments, research on group and individual differences in narrative socialization has been especially active and productive. Several sources of systematic variability have been identified.

**Gender.**   In the context of the literature on the socialization of event and autobiographical memory narratives, gender was considered a potential source of variance in part because of gender differences in adult women's and adult men's autobiographical narratives and the possibility that they are a consequence of early socialization. Relative to men, when women talk about past events, they tend to produce narratives that are longer, more detailed, and more vivid. One of the most salient differences in the narratives of women and men is the way they represent emotion. Women report talking about emotions more frequently than do men (Allen & Hamsher, 1974); their memory narratives are more saturated with emotion language, relative to those of men (Bauer, Stennes, & Haight, 2003); and memories about emotional experiences seem to be more readily accessible to women than to men (Davis, 1999).

There is evidence that girls and boys are differentially socialized in the context of conversations about past events. First, there is a consistent finding that parents are more elaborative in conversations about past events with their daughters than with their sons (e.g., Fivush, Berlin, Sales, Mennuti-Washburn, & Cassidy, 2003; see Fivush, 1998, for a review). Parents also more frequently confirm the participation of their daughters in conversations, relative to their sons. These findings suggest that relative to boys, girls receive more reinforcement for participating in conversations about past events and participate in more detailed and elaborate narratives.

Second, differences associated with the gender of the child also are apparent in the emotional content of conversations about past events. Adams, Kuebli, Boyle, and Fivush (1995) reported that across the 40- to 70-month time period, parents used both a greater number and a greater variety of emotion words with daughters than with sons. In a separate sample of 32- to 35-month-olds and their mothers, however, this trend was not apparent and, in fact, was even reversed (Fivush & Kuebli, 1997). Whether the different patterns are the result of the different ages considered or differences in the samples themselves cannot be determined from the existing data. Mothers also tend to talk about different emotions with their 3-year-old daughters and sons. Mothers have more frequent and longer conversations about sadness with daughters than with sons; mothers have more frequent and longer conversations about anger with sons than with daughters (e.g., Fivush & Kuebli, 1997; although see Fivush, Berlin, et al., 2003 for an exception). The findings about sadness persist over time and are still apparent at 6 years. Mothers do not differ in the amount of time they spend talking with their daughters and sons about events in which their children were scared or happy. Together, these findings suggest that both mothers and fathers discuss emotional aspects of past events differently with daughters and with sons.

The "lessons" about narrative in general and emotion language in particular offered by their parents are not lost on preschool-age children. Buckner and Fivush (1998) found that 7-year-old girls tend to produce longer, more coherent, and more detailed narratives than same-age boys. In addition, relative to boys', more girls' narratives are social in their theme. Girls and boys also differ in use of emotion language in their narratives. As discussed by Kuebli et al. (1995), in the longitudinal sample that was the source of much of the data described in this section (Reese et al., 1993), across the 40-, 58-, and 70-month time points, both the number and variety of emotion words used by girls increased. For boys, neither metric increased. As a consequence, whereas girls and boys did not differ in the number or variety of emotion words used at 3 years of age, by the time the children were 6 years of age, girls were producing both a greater number and a larger variety of emotion words, relative to boys. Over the preschool years then, girls come to pepper their event memory narratives with emotion, whereas boys do not increase their emotional expressiveness. This pattern is reflected in adults' autobiographical narratives about events from their childhoods (Bauer, Stennes, et al., 2003).

**Language.**    There has been relatively little work on the question of whether differences in children's language abilities affect socialization of event memory nar-

rative production. Farrant and Reese (2000) found that both children's expressive language abilities and their receptive language abilities were correlated with maternal reminiscing style concurrently as well as over 19 to 40 months. Bauer and Burch (2004) reported that in the context of an elicited-imitation task in which mothers demonstrated multistep sequences and tested their 24-month-old children's memories for them, mothers who reported that their children had larger productive vocabularies produced more elaborations as they modeled shorter (but not longer) sequences. These two studies of relations between young children's language abilities and maternal verbal behavior are suggestive. They should serve to motivate additional research with children early in the socialization process, as well as with children throughout the preschool years.

**Temperament.**    Temperament or behavioral style refers to patterns of responding to environmental stimuli (e.g., Rothbart & Bates, 1998). It has emerged as a potential source of individual differences in children's event memory and narrative socialization because of speculation that variability in emotionality and its regulation might relate to children's responses to parental socialization attempts, to their abilities to talk about emotional states, or both. For example, K. D. Lewis (1999) argued that highly sociable children may elicit more social interaction from their parents and thus might also encourage a more elaborative style of conversation. In contrast, children who have difficulty regulating their attention or level of activity might elicit a higher level of regulatory speech, perhaps manifested in more repetitions.

Consistent with these suggestions, in samples of 3- and 5-year-old children and their parents, with children's ages and memory talk controlled statistically, children rated by their parents as more sociable and active received fewer repetitions and evaluations, and proportionally more elaborations (K. D. Lewis, 1999). Lewis interpreted these effects to suggest that mothers who perceive their children to be less active may feel the need to engage them in the task, by using evaluations and repetitions of their utterances. Conversely, children perceived to be more sociable may be viewed as good conversational partners. In the preschool years, readiness to participate in conversation likely is a major component of what gets termed "sociability." Precisely this relation has been found between 24-month-old children and their mothers. Mothers who rated their children high on the Interest and Persistence subscale of the Toddler Behavior Assessment Questionnaire (TBAQ) were especially verbally engaged with their children, as measured by higher rates of production of elaborations, repetitions, affirmations, and total category tokens (Bauer & Burch, 2004). Thus, children who were perceived as typically showing interest and persistence received more verbal scaffolding in the elicited-imitation context. In contrast to K. D. Lewis's (1999) observations with older children, maternal verbal behavior was unrelated to scores on the Activity Level subscale of the TBAQ. Again, although far from definitive, these two studies of relations between children's temperament characteristics and maternal behavior in conversations about past events are suggestive and should motivate additional research.

**The Attachment History of the Dyad.** Rather than being a characteristic of the child, attachment history is a feature of the parent-child dyad. Fivush and Vasudeva (2002) developed the argument that given the social purpose of reminiscing, aspects of the socioemotional relationship between the adult and child might be related to their style of coconstruction of the events of their lives. This expectation is derived in part from the observation that mothers seem to have different goals as they reminisce with their children. Mothers who are less elaborative appear to have a pragmatic purpose: to get their children to remember specific pieces of information. Mothers who are more elaborative appear to engage their children in conversation for the sake of sharing. The goals of engagement and sharing of experience not only are facilitated by a strong interpersonal relationship, but actually emerge from it. That is, it is the strong socioemotional connection that motivates one to share to begin with.

The concept of mother-child attachment has a long and distinguished history that I do not undertake to review in this chapter. For present purposes, it is sufficient to note that parents and their children differ in the "quality" of their attachment relationship. Most mothers are sensitive to their children's needs and respond to their infants' signals in a timely and appropriate manner. Their infants are likely to develop a secure attachment that keeps them in proximity to the mother yet permits them to move beyond her to explore the world and gain a measure of independence from the caregiver, apparently confident in the knowledge that on return, mother not only will be there, but will be welcoming.

Other mothers exhibit less sensitivity to their infants' signals and needs. They might respond less contingently, or not at all, presumably engendering in their infants a sense that the caregiver cannot be counted on. Their infants are likely to develop an insecure attachment that is less successful in promoting developmentally appropriate levels of dependence and independence. The fruits of early attachment relationships are preserved well beyond infancy, as evidenced by relations with adult romantic relationships (Roisman, Madsen, Henninghausen, Sroufe, & Collins, 2001; although see M. Lewis, Feiring, & Rosenthal, 2000).

A body of research within the attachment tradition suggests that the mother-child attachment relationship might be related to the style of reminiscing in the dyad. Dyads with a secure attachment relationship have been described as engaging in more open communication, relative to dyads with less secure relationships (e.g., Bretherton, 1990). In addition, children who are classified as securely attached evidence more sophisticated narrative skills in tasks in which they are asked to complete a story with a socioemotional theme (e.g., Waters, Rodriguez, & Ridgeway, 1998). Discussions of emotional and evaluative aspects of events may be especially affected by the attachment relationship, given that they involve a measure of interpretation of the internal states of others.

Although there is compelling motivation and rationale for investigating possible relations between the attachment relationship and maternal style of reminiscing, there have been few empirical studies. Fivush and Vasudeva (2002) examined the possibility of a relation in a sample of mothers and their 4-year-old children. There was a significant relation between maternal rating of attachment and maternal elaboration: Mothers who indicated a more secure attachment relationship with their children were more elaborative in the memory conversation context. The relation was apparent for both mother-daughter and mother-son dyads. In addition, mothers who used a high proportion of emotion terms had girls who produced a large number of memory elaborations; the relation was not observed among mother-son dyads. As argued by the authors, the pattern as a whole suggests that children in securely attached dyads are more likely to engage in elaborative parent-child reminiscing that, in turn, promotes development of skills for autobiographical narrative production.

Newcombe and Reese (2003) conducted a longitudinal investigation of possible relations between maternal reminiscing style and children's narrative development as a function of the security of the attachment relationship. The families were enrolled in the study when the children were 19 months of age and followed longitudinally with observations at 25, 32, 40, and 51 months. Attachment status was assessed at the last session. Mothers in dyads that were assessed as securely attached increased their use of evaluations over the course of the study, whereas mothers in dyads that were insecurely attached did not. Across time points, children in securely attached dyads produced more evaluations than did children in insecurely attached dyads. In addition, for securely attached dyads, beginning when children were 25 months of age, there were both concurrent and cross-lagged correlations between mothers' and children's use of evaluations in the context of conversations about past events. These results suggest that the development of aspects of a child's narrative competence are influenced by the quality of the socioemotional relationship between the mother and her child. Together with the findings of Fivush and Vasudeva (2002), they compel additional research.

**Culture Group Differences.** The final source of variability in narrative socialization to be considered is that associated with cultural group. In the adult literature, there are striking differences in the age of earliest reportable autobiographical memory for European Americans compared with Asian Americans and Koreans living in America (e.g., MacDonald, Uesiliana, & Hayne, 2000; Mullen, 1994; Wang, 2001). The age of earliest memory for European Americans is several months earlier than that of Asian Americans or Koreans. The difference may be associated with variability in cultural perspectives on the value and goals of reminiscing (K. Nelson, 1988). As described by Mullen (1994):

> The difference between Asians and Caucasians may reflect two very different sets of socialization goals: one in which conformity to norms of social behavior is highly valued and dwelling on one's own subjective experiences is maladaptive, and one in which adults actively encourage children to elaboratively narrativize their personal experiences as part of a process of developing a sense of individuality and self-expression that is valued in the culture. (pp. 76–77)

If it is the case that differences in adults' autobiographical memories from early childhood are influenced by differences in socialization, then those differences ought to be apparent in early parent-child interaction. To

begin to test this hypothesis, Mullen and Yi (1995) analyzed naturally occurring conversations between American and Korean mothers and their 40-month-old children. They found that Korean dyads engaged in talk about the past less frequently than American dyads. In addition, the conversations of the Korean dyads included fewer details than those of American dyads (see also Choi, 1992, for comparison of Korean and Canadian mothers). These differences in the base rate of talk about the past are reminiscent of differences in mothers who exhibit an elaborative compared with a low-elaborative style: Dyads in which the mother exhibits an elaborative style tend to have longer conversations that include more narrative content.

To determine whether mother-child conversations about the past also differ in other features that distinguish the elaborative from the low-elaborative maternal style, Wang et al. (2000) collected memory narratives from American mothers and their 3- to 4-year-old children and from Chinese mothers and their 3- to 4-year-old children. The samples included comparable numbers of girls and boys, and the children were well matched for their levels of language development, as measured by mean length of utterance. The dyads were observed in their homes in the United States and China, respectively, by an experimenter from the same native country as the dyad. American mothers produced fewer repetitions and more evaluations when talking with their children, relative to Chinese mothers, and American children produced more elaborations than Chinese children. Analyses of the contingencies of the conversations between mothers and their children revealed that the tendency to follow an elaboration with an elaboration was higher among American than among Chinese dyads. Thus, American mothers tended to elaborate their children's contributions and American children tended to elaborate their mothers' contributions in a truly coconstructive manner. This tendency was less prominent among the Chinese dyads.

To conclude that cross-cultural differences in narrative socialization are a major source of variance in adults' recollections of their childhoods, it would be necessary to find that relations with maternal style variables extend to children's independent memory narratives. Han et al. (1998) asked samples of Korean, Chinese, and American 4- and 6-year-old children to talk with an experimenter about recent, personally experienced events. American children had longer and more detailed narratives, relative to Korean children. Their narratives also included more details that distinguished the specific episode under discussion from other, potentially similar, events. Chinese children's narratives were more comparable to those of American children, yet they were less detailed and less specific. American children also included in their narratives more information about their own and others' internal states (e.g., cognition terms, statements of preference, evaluations, emotion terms), relative to Chinese and Korean children. In addition, whereas children in all three culture groups frequently mentioned themselves in their narratives, American children had the highest proportion of mention of themselves relative to others. Finally, gender differences were observed in the American sample only: American girls produced more words, more words per proposition, more temporal markers, more descriptive terms, and more internal states terms than American boys.

Together, the results of Han et al. (1998) paint a picture of American children (and especially American girls) producing autobiographical narratives that are longer, more detailed, more specific, and more "personal" (both in terms of mention of self, and mention of internal states), than narratives by children from China and Korea. The pattern is consistent with expectations derived from the finding that in their conversations about past events, American mothers and their children are more elaborative and more focused on autonomous themes, relative to Chinese mothers and their children (Wang et al., 2000); and that Korean mothers and their children have less frequent and less detailed conversations about the past, relative to American dyads (Mullen & Yi, 1995). It is tempting to relate these findings to those observed in studies of adults' recollections of their childhoods (e.g., Mullen, 1994; Wang, 2001). As discussed by Han and her colleagues, "It is distinctly possible that the more elaborated content of American children's narratives, as compared with those of Asian children, contributes to the earlier first memories found in American adult populations" (Han et al., 1998, p. 710). Only prospective research will tell, however.

## CONTINUITIES AND DISCONTINUITIES IN THE DEVELOPMENT OF EVENT MEMORY

As noted early in this chapter, historically, there were expectations of profound discontinuities in children's memories. Piagetian theory suggested that for the first 18 to 24 months of life, infants were incapable of what today is recognized as explicit memory (conscious recognition or recall). Across the preschool years, be-

cause they lacked operational structures, children were thought incapable of forming organized memory representations. Instead, the memory of the preschool-age child was described as "a medley of made-up stories and exact but chaotic reconstructions, organized memory developing only with the progress of intelligence as a whole" (Piaget, 1962, p. 187). In other words, Piaget suggested that even when children had constructed the capacity to represent past events, they still were without the cognitive structures needed to organize events along coherent dimensions for making the events memorable. He suggested that it was not until children approached the concrete operational period (at approximately 5 to 7 years of age) that they developed the ability to sequence events temporally.

The last 2 decades of the twentieth century produced theory and research that forced a radical revision of this perspective. It now is clear that at least by the second half of the 1st year of life, infants form relatively enduring explicit event memories; preschool-age children organize memories of both routine and one-time only events along coherent temporal dimensions. There remain, however, at least two points at which continuity in event memory development can be questioned: the first 6 months and the period of transition from infancy to early childhood.

### Explicit Memory in the First 6 Months of Life

One of the most salient continuities in event memory is that the ability to remember events is apparent from very early in development. At least by 6 months of age, infants are able to retain explicit event memories over 24 hours. Whether the ability is present even earlier in development is unclear. Certainly there are data on memory earlier than 6 months of age. Infants perform well on tasks such as visual paired comparison and mobile conjugate-reinforcement. As noted, however, it is not clear that these tasks measure explicit memory. There also is evidence that infants only a few days old engage in imitation (of tongue protrusion and mouth opening; e.g., Meltzoff & Moore, 1977). Yet, whether neonatal imitation is supported by the same mechanisms as imitation in infants 6 months of age and older is a matter of debate. Whereas Meltzoff and Moore argue that the ability is continuous, others have suggested alternative mechanisms and explanations (e.g., fixed action patterns; Jacobson, 1979) and thus, discontinuity.

Given that there is no empirical resolution to the question, we are left with theoretical and conceptual arguments as to whether the continuity in explicit event memory extends to the first months of life. Consideration of the timing and course of brain development introduces doubt that the continuity extends so far. As noted, aspects of the multicomponent network that supports explicit memory are late to develop. Development of the components implicated in consolidation of memories for long-term storage is especially protracted. As a result, recall over the long term may not be apparent until the second half of the 1st year of life. Critically, this argument does not imply that long-term explicit event memory suddenly "bursts forth" on the scene at 6 months of age. On the contrary, the prediction is of gradual emergence of the ability to retain more and more information over longer and longer delays. This is the pattern that is apparent beginning at 6 months. There is every reason to expect a similar pattern prior to 6 months of age, as the neural structures that support explicit memory begin their long course of maturation and development. This argument is consistent with that set forth by C. A. Nelson (1995, 1997, 2000) of "preexplicit" memory that depends on portions of the explicit memory network. It also is consistent with Mandler's (1988, 1992, 1998) argument that although the tools necessary to form accessible representations of events and experiences are available shortly after birth, the products of their operation may not be apparent because the representations that are formed are so very fragile.

### The Transition from Infancy to Early Childhood

The suggestion of discontinuity between infancy and early childhood is deeply ingrained theoretically. For a long time, the field was dominated by a perspective that suggested a shift in representational format at roughly 18 to 24 months of age. A modern version of the perspective is invoked as an explanation for the observation that even after language is available, children do not seem to talk about events from early in life. The apparent lack of later verbal accessibility of early memories has led to skepticism about the actual status of early, preverbal memories. For example, in Pillemer and White's 1989 review of the literature on autobiographical memory and the phenomenon of childhood amnesia, they suggested that if early and later memories were qualitatively similar, then early memories "should become verbally expressible when the child has the ability to reconstrue preverbal events in narrative form" (p. 321; see also Nelson & Ross 1980; Pillemer, 1998a, 1998b). In the absence of such evidence, early memories are described as indicative of

the function of a "behavioral memory system" that in some cases, supports "early memory images (that) are persistent enough to influence feelings and behaviors after months or years" (Pillemer, 1998a, p. 115), but which are implicit, rather than explicit. This argument is, in effect, a modern version of the suggestion that older children's (and adults') inability to recall the events of their lives (verbally), is evidence that the capacity for explicit memory is late to develop.

The results of some studies suggest that even when children have gained the linguistic ability to describe events from the past, they do not do so. Peterson and Rideout (1998) interviewed children about trips to the emergency room necessitated by accidents that resulted in broken bones, burns, and cuts that required suturing. The accidents occurred when the children were 13 to 34 months of age; the interviews were conducted in the children's homes shortly thereafter, and again 6 months, 12 months, and 18 or 24 months later. Children who were 26 months or older at the time of the experience provided verbal reports at all interviews. Although the children who were injured between 20 and 25 months were not able to describe their experiences at the time, they were able to provide verbal reports 6 months later. In contrast, among the children who were 13 to 18 months at the time of their injuries, none was able to provide a complete verbal account of the experience, even though, at the later interviews, they had the requisite language ability to do so. Peterson and Rideout attributed the youngest children's difficulty verbally describing their experiences to unavailability of a verbal means of encoding at the time of the events (see also Myers, Perris, & Speaker, 1994; Simcock & Hayne, 2002). Studies such as these suggest that if events were not encoded with language, then language cannot be used to describe them.

The results of other studies suggest that the critical ingredient in later verbal accessibility is not the availability of language at the time of encoding of events, but the opportunity to augment nonverbal memory representations with language. This conclusion is drawn from a series of studies in which pre- and early verbal children exposed to multistep sequences in the context of elicited and deferred imitation were tested for verbal recall of them months later (Bauer, Kroupina, et al., 1998; Bauer, Wenner, et al., 2002). Children who were enrolled in Bauer et al. (2000) at the ages of 13, 16, and 20 months, and who participated in nonverbal tests of memory 1 to 12 months later, took part in a follow-up study at the age of 3 years. Because 3-year-olds can be expected to participate in verbal interviews (e.g., Fivush et al., 1987), during the 3-year visit, the children were explicitly asked to describe the events they had experienced. The strongest predictor of verbal expression of memory at age 3 years was children's spontaneous verbal expression of memory at the earlier, nonverbal test: It explained 30% of the variance in children's elicited verbal recall at age 3 years (Cheatham & Bauer, 2005). Critically, variables from the time of initial experience of the events (age and verbal ability) failed to predict children's later verbal recall. These studies imply that the important ingredient in later verbal accessibility of early memories is not language at the time of encoding, but an opportunity to augment a nonverbal memory representation with language. In the case of the studies just described, that opportunity was presented by the earlier nonverbal recall test.

If early memories later can be described verbally, why then are there so few examples of verbal access to early, preverbal memories? The answer may lie in the conditions under which later verbal recall typically is tested. In Peterson and Rideout (1998), children were interviewed in their homes about events that had occurred in the emergency room; the interviews were conducted without the aid of any but verbal prompts and cues. Similarly, in Simcock and Hayne (2002), children's verbal recall was supported only by the experimenter's verbal prompts and photographs. As discussed earlier, there is a developmental progression in children's sensitivity to verbal and pictorial reminders of past events (Hudson, 1991, 1993). This raises the possibility that the failure to observe verbally accessible memories under these conditions may have been due not to the lack of availability of language at the time of encoding, but to failure to effectively reinstate the event memory, given the cues provided. In Bauer, Wenner, et al. (2002), children's recall was supported by the props that had been used to produce the multistep events. Props have proven to be effective cues for reinstatement even when they are presented in a context different from that in which they were encountered (originally encountered in the laboratory and used as cues in the children's homes: Bauer et al., 2004). Given effective reinstatement, newly acquired words can be mapped onto their past-event referents. In this way, preverbal memories may be "infused" with language, thereby permitting later verbal as well as nonverbal access to them.

The suggestion that, at least under some circumstances, early memories can be augmented by language and then verbally described raises the question of whether, given the right cues, older children and even adults could be treated to a flood of memories from the first years of life. This is a highly unlikely scenario for at least three important reasons. First, as noted, the ability to retain and later retrieve explicit event memories likely does not reach "critical mass" until the second half of the 1st year of life. Thus, from the first 6 months, precious few—if any—memories survive.

Second, even once explicit memory becomes reliable and robust (near the end of the 2nd year of life), forgetting occurs. Because of changes in the basic mnemonic processes of consolidation and storage, in particular, that occur throughout the preschool years, the rate of forgetting is accelerated, relative to that in later childhood and early adulthood. As a result, although memories are formed, many are forgotten.

Third, as I have argued elsewhere (Bauer, 2006), the periods of later infancy and early childhood are marked by gradually increasing representation of the features that make event memories autobiographical and thus, long lasting. As described earlier in this chapter, there are conceptual developments that allow for formation of memories referenced to self that are distinctive and clearly of past events. There also are critical developments in language and in the socialization of narrative forms that facilitate not only the retelling of events and experiences but their very organization and, thus, maintenance and subsequent retrieval. The net effect is that it is only gradually, over the course of the preschool years, that children's autobiographical memories become prototypical of their class. Eventually, the rate of formation of prototypical autobiographical memories outstrips the rate at which events are forgotten. The result is the distribution of memories found in virtually every study of adults' retrospective reports of events from early in life: a relative paucity of memories from the first 3 to 4 years, followed by a steadily increasing number of memories of events that took place between ages 3 and 7 years (see Bauer, 2006, for further discussion).

## Summary and Evaluation

Until the late 1970s, memory development was viewed as largely discontinuous. Infants were thought incapable of forming accessible memories and preschoolers' memories were thought to be disorganized. With the development of nonverbal means of assessing infants' event memories and the observation that preschoolers accurately remembered the events of their own lives, these perspectives changed dramatically. It now is clear that at least by the second half of the 1st year of life, infants form enduring explicit event memories. Whether the ability extends to the first months of life as well is an unanswered question. However, consideration of the timing and course of brain development suggests that early in postnatal life, there may be narrow restrictions on the formation of lasting explicit event memories. Beyond the first months of life, continuities in event memory abound. Nonverbal and verbal tests of memory indicate that children form organized representations of events that they recall at later points in time. Under certain circumstances, early preverbal memories later are accessible to verbal report. Nevertheless, throughout the preschool years, the rate of forgetting is relatively high. In addition, it is only gradually that children's memories of events take on the features of prototypical autobiographical memories. Evidence of the adultlike distribution of autobiographical memories becomes apparent as the number of prototypical autobiographical memories formed begins to outpace the number of event memories forgotten (Bauer, 2006).

## IS MEMORY FOR STRESSFUL OR TRAUMATIC EVENTS "SPECIAL"?

In discussions thus far, all events have been treated as essentially equal. The focus has been on developmental changes and characteristics of children that might affect their event memories. There has been no explicit discussion of whether some events are inherently more memorable than others, however. Within the literature on event memory, there is a fair amount of speculation that memories of events that were particularly stressful or traumatic are either quantitatively or qualitatively different from memories of nonstressful or nontraumatic events. There is not a definitive answer to this question, but several suggestions bear on it.

### Memories of Stressful or Traumatic Events

The expectation that memories of stressful or traumatic experiences might be different from memories of nontraumatic experiences is deeply rooted. A classic basis for the expectation is the Yerkes-Dodson law of optimal arousal (Yerkes & Dodson, 1908). Briefly, a relation between level of arousal and performance is predicted, such that when arousal is either too low or too high, performance will be impaired, relative to when arousal level is optimal. Stressful or traumatic experiences are expected to increase arousal, relative to benign events. Assuming that the level of arousal associated with a traumatic experience is high, but not too high, then application of the Yerkes-Dodson law leads to the prediction that the experience will be well remembered. If the level of arousal associated with the traumatic event exceeds the optimal level, then memory for the experience will be impaired (Easterbrook, 1959). In addition to the number of details remembered, there are suggestions that memories for traumatic and nontraumatic experiences differ qualitatively (see Goodman & Quas, 1997, for discussion). Some have indicated that memories of traumatic experiences have a vivid "flashbulb" quality (e.g., R. Brown & Kulik, 1977; Winograd & Neisser, 1992). Others have suggested that in traumatic circumstances, attention is focused on the central features of the event, with correspondingly poorer memory for peripheral features (e.g., Christianson, 1992).

For obvious practical and ethical reasons, researchers cannot intentionally subject children to highly stressful or traumatic events to study their memories for them. They can, however, examine children's memories for emergency medical treatments and prescribed medical procedures for insights on how stress and trauma affect event memory. Though socially sanctioned and performed for children's benefit, such measures nonetheless are perceived by children as unpleasant, painful, and frightening. Despite the associated stress and trauma, even young children remember these events. Peterson and Rideout (1998) reported that children who were as young as 26 months at the time of injuries that necessitated visits to the emergency room were able to provide accounts of the experiences 2 years later. Children's memories for natural disasters also have been a focus of research. Bahrick, Parker, Merritt, and Fivush (1998) found that 3- to 4-year-old children who experienced Hurricane Andrew provided lengthy accounts of it when they were interviewed within 6 months of the storm. Six years later, when the children were 9 and 10 years of age, they not only remembered the experience, but their accounts of it were more than twice as long as the accounts they had provided 6 years earlier (Fivush et al., 2004).

Whereas it is clear that young children remember traumatic experiences, the question of whether there are quantitative and qualitative differences between memories of traumatic and nontraumatic events remains open. One reason is that it is difficult to study relations between trauma and memory experimentally. An effective alternative to an experimental approach is the medical-procedures model, in which researchers compare, for example, the memory performance of children who endured a stressful medical procedure (e.g., voiding cystourethrogram flouroscopy—VCUG) with that of children who experienced a substantially less stressful medical procedure (e.g., a pediatric examination; D. Brown, Salmon, Pipe, Rutter, Craw, & Taylor, 1999). A variant on the approach is to compare the memory performance of children who were more and less stressed while experiencing a painful medical procedure such as inoculation or the VCUG (e.g., Goodman, Hirschman, Hepps, & Rudy, 1991). Overall, researchers have found that stressful procedures are recalled at least as well, and in some cases, better than more benign procedures (e.g., Ornstein, 1995; see Fivush, 1998, 2002, for reviews). In some studies, however, children who experienced high levels of stress have been found to produce more memory errors, relative to children who were less stressed (e.g., Goodman & Quas, 1997).

The medical-procedures model has been very productive and informative. However, because it necessitates a between-subjects analysis, it does not permit direct comparison of memories of stressful or traumatic experiences and memories of more positive experiences from the same participant. Fivush, Hazzard, Sales, Sarfati, and Brown (2002) provided just such a comparison. The researchers interviewed 5- to 12-year-old children about nontraumatic events, such as family outings, vacations, and parties; and stressful or traumatic events, such as serious illness or death, minor illness or injury, property damage, violent and minor interpersonal altercations, and parental separation. Overall, children's narratives about the stressful or traumatic and nontraumatic events were comparable in length. However, the children included more descriptions (adjectives, adverbs, possessives, and modifiers), and mentioned more objects and persons when recounting nontraumatic experiences than when recounting stressful or traumatic experiences. Conversely, the children provided more information about internal states (emotional, cognitive, and volitional states of self or other) when recounting traumatic relative to nontraumatic experiences. In addition, narratives about traumatic experiences were rated by the researchers as more narratively coherent, compared with narratives about nontraumatic experiences.

The results of this study suggest that the memory narratives about traumatic and nontraumatic experiences differ qualitatively, with narratives about traumatic events being more complete and better integrated, and more internally focused, relative to narratives about nontraumatic events.

Sales, Fivush, and Peterson (2003) examined conversations between parents (primarily mothers) and their 3- to 5-year-old children about two types of events: a positive event chosen by the parent (e.g., family vacation) and the stressful or traumatic experience of a medical emergency for the child, sufficient to necessitate a trip to the emergency room (e.g., cuts requiring stitches, broken bones). Both parents and their children spent proportionally more time discussing the causes of behavior (e.g., "What did you do to get hurt?" p. 192) in their conversations about traumatic events, relative to positive events. Conversely, both parents and children spent proportionally more time talking about emotions in their conversations about positive events, relative to traumatic events. In addition, when talking about the positive events, parents included a higher proportion of positively valenced, relative to negatively valenced, emotion; when talking about the traumatic medical emergencies, they included a higher proportion of negatively valenced relative to positively valenced emotion. Children's use of emotion language was too infrequent to support a parallel analysis.

The third investigation featuring a direct comparison of reports of traumatic and nontraumatic events is one in which mothers and their 3- to 11-year-old children were interviewed about a devastating tornado that hit the small, rural town of St. Peter, Minnesota (population 9,500), on March 29, 1998 (Ackil et al., 2003; Bauer, Stark, et al., 2005). Approximately 4 months after the tornado, mothers and their children were asked to talk about the storm and about two non-tornado-related events: one that had taken place within 3 months prior to the tornado, and one that had taken place since the storm, but that was not related to the tornado. Six months after the first interview (10 months after the storm), the dyads were interviewed again about the same three events, thereby permitting assessment of changes in event narratives over time. At both time points, narratives about the tornado were twice as long as narratives about the two nontraumatic events, which did not differ from one another. The lengths of the narratives did not differ between Session 1 and Session 2 for any of the events. Critically, even with conversational length controlled, conversations about the traumatic event were more narratively complete and coherent, relative to conversations about the nontraumatic events. Moreover, the differences largely endured over the 6-month interval between sessions. Although the range in ages of the children in the study was large, age-related differences were not especially pronounced and there were no interactions with age at Session 1 and few at Session 2.

## Summary

In the relatively young literature on event memory in children, there has been a lot of attention on and controversy surrounding whether stressful and traumatic events are remembered better than, not as well as, or the same as nonstressful and nontraumatic events. There have been surprisingly few direct comparisons of the question. It is clear that children remember stressful and traumatic events. There also are suggestions in the literature that the narratives that children provide about traumatic events are more coherent and perhaps more internally focused, relative to narratives about nontraumatic events. This characteristic could be expected to result in better memory for traumatic relative to nontraumatic events over time. These findings indicate that although children's memories for events of a highly emotional nature likely follow a developmental course similar to that for more benign events, they likely differ in important ways as well.

## CONCLUSION AND DIRECTIONS FOR FUTURE RESEARCH

Though still in its "adolescence" at the time of the writing of this chapter, the field of study of developments in event memory is already quite mature. In the 1970s and early 1980s, researchers began to challenge the traditional assumption, derived from laboratory studies of memory for lists of words or pictures, that preschoolers were rather mnemonically inept. By asking young children to recall stories and to report on the events of their everyday lives, they learned that virtually as soon as they were able to participate in verbal tests of event memory, they "passed" these tests by providing temporally ordered reports of their experiences that included most if not all of the components of a complete narrative (the *who, what, where, when, why,* and *how* of events).

Findings of mnemonic competence in preschoolers, coupled with development of nonverbal means of assessing event memory in infants, led to challenges of another traditional assumption, that the period of infancy is devoid of the capacity to form, retain, and later retrieve explicit memories of past events. Studies using imitation-based tasks have revealed that at least by the middle of the 1st year, infants recall past events. By the end of the 2nd year, event memories are relatively robust and long lasting. Under some circumstances, memories likely encoded without the benefit of language survive the transition from infancy to early childhood and can be described verbally. Thus, in sharp contrast to expectations of developmental discontinuities in event memory, there is ample evidence that the capacity to remember past events develops early and continuously.

To say that the capacity to form, retain, and later retrieve event memories is early in developing is not to say that it does not change with age. On the contrary, throughout infancy and the preschool period there are changes along several dimensions, including the length of time over which children remember, the robustness of their memories, and the efficacy and productivity of different types of reminders. In addition, children's memories are affected by background knowledge that, in many cases, is related to age. As children gain verbal fluency and narrative competence, there also are changes in how much they report about events and in the quality of the stories that they tell about past experiences. Although research on the mechanisms of age-related change lags behind that designed to describe its trajectories, there are strong reasons to believe that the developments are linked with changes in the neural substrate that supports explicit memory, which in turn affects the efficiency with which memories are encoded, consolidated, stored, and subsequently retrieved. In addition, there is increasing evidence that changes in children's verbal reports of past events and perhaps their nonverbal "reports" as well are affected by aspects of their social worlds, including the narrative cultures that surround them.

The strides made in understanding developments in event memory have been significant. However, substantial and significant work remains to be done. To begin, we still need a great deal of descriptive work. Three areas stand out. First, research is needed to determine how the early memory abilities tapped by paradigms such as elicited and deferred imitation relate to the deliberate memory skills tested in educational settings and the autobiographical or personal memory skills that are so essential and prominent in social settings. Reliable and robust encoding, storage, and retrieval of memories is necessary, but not sufficient, for these later-developing capacities. Preliminary findings from ongoing studies in my own and other laboratories (Catherine Haden, Loyola University, and Peter Ornstein, University of North Carolina, Chapel Hill) suggest continuity between early developing recall memory skills and later strategic remembering. There already is strongly suggestive evidence that through conversations with more accomplished partners (e.g., parents), children capitalize on basic memory abilities to construct personalized narratives that form the basis for autobiography (K. Nelson & Fivush, 2000, 2004). Between now and the next *Handbook,* we may look forward to an expansion of these research efforts.

Second, as a result of the starting point, the largest proportion of work on event memory has been done with infants and preschool-age children. The event memory abilities of school-age and older children—and developmental changes therein—have been largely ignored. This needs to be remedied. Whereas changes in the school years may not be as dramatic as those in the periods of infancy and the preschool years, they are a significant part of the puzzle of how a fundamental cognitive capacity changes over the course of development.

Third, more attention needs to be paid to individual differences, which has never been the strong suit of research in cognitive development. The "usual suspects" of children's gender and their levels of receptive and expressive language have not proven especially predictive of event memory performance. In contrast, important insights have been gained by giving attention to effects of variability associated with parental style and culture group differences, as well as to how children's temperaments and the attachment history of dyads relate to developments in narrative abilities. Additional attention to individual differences is important not only to a full description of developmental change, but also can shed light on the mechanisms thereof. For example, the results of research with special populations of infants suggest that consolidation and storage processes are a major source of vulnerability in early event memory. Pursuing the "leads" suggested by these findings promises to inform theories of normative development.

Descriptive goals do not exhaust the menu for future research. We also can hope for advances in our knowl-

edge of explanatory mechanisms. Three areas in particular seem promising. First, it is desirable to expand the focus on links between brain and behavior. Relative to the adult literature—in which there has been significant progress establishing relations between structure and function—the developmental literature is far behind. Some neuroimaging techniques, such as positron emission tomography (PET) never will develop into workhorse paradigms for developmental research because they require ionizing radiation, the use of which is contraindicated in healthy children. Others, including event-related potentials and functional magnetic resonance imaging (fMRI), already are yielding insight into the neural generators of cognitive events. High-density arrays of electrodes permit identification of the origins of electrical signals recorded on the scalp (C. A. Nelson & Monk, 2001), and fMRI scans of the brain engaged in cognitive processing can be obtained from children as young as 7 years of age (Casey, Thomas, & McCandliss, 2001). Further expanding the arsenal with neural network models (Munakata & Stedron, 2001) and comparisons with performance by developing nonhuman animals (Overman & Bachevalier, 2001), will permit substantial progress in identification of the neural sources of specific behavioral change.

A second avenue to pursue in the quest to explain developmental changes in event memory is to explicitly recognize that it has multiple determinants. A reasonably complete yet still not exhaustive list of likely determinants of event memory includes those discussed in this chapter: language, self-concept, comprehension of temporal concepts for locating events in time, the ability to locate events in space, an understanding of the sources of knowledge, and the skills for conveying memories to others (Bauer, 2006; K. Nelson & Fivush, 2004). Because multiple factors contribute to developments in event memory, single causal models always will fall short of a full explanation of the timing and course of developmental changes. Models that explicitly recognize the multiple cognitive as well as multiple social influences on memory development will have more predictive utility.

Finally, and related to the point just made, progress in understanding the mechanisms of developmental change in event memory will be made when the full range of potential causes is examined in each major developmental period. At present, in infancy, most of the attention on the mechanisms of development is on neural changes and their implications for the basic mnemonic processes of encoding, consolidation, storage, and retrieval. With a few noteworthy exceptions (e.g., Farrant & Reese, 2000), less attention is paid to the likely social determinants, such as patterns of interaction between caregivers and children. Conversely, in the preschool years, most of the attention on mechanisms of developmental change is on social determinants. Again, with a few notable exceptions (e.g., Brainerd et al., 1990), less attention is paid to potential changes in basic mnemonic processes. A complete account of age-related changes in event memory will require that the contributions of multiple different factors be evaluated across development. Movement in these directions will ensure that there is significant progress to be reported as the next edition of the *Handbook* goes to print.

## REFERENCES

Ackil, J. K., Van Abbema, D. L., & Bauer, P. J. (2003). After the storm: Enduring differences in mother-child recollections of traumatic and nontraumatic events. *Journal of Experimental Child Psychology, 84,* 286–309.

Adams, S., Kuebli, J., Boyle, P. A., & Fivush, R. (1995). Gender differences in parent-child conversations about past emotions: A longitudinal investigation. *Sex Roles, 33,* 309–323.

Adlam, A.-L. R., Vargha-Khadem, F., Mishkin, M., & de Haan, M. (2005). Deferred imitation of action sequences in developmental amnesia. *Journal of Cognitive Neuroscience, 17,* 240–248.

Allen, J. G., & Hamsher, J. H. (1974). The development and validation of a test of emotional styles. *Journal of Counseling and Clinical Psychology, 42,* 663–668.

Anglin, J. (1993). Vocabulary development: A morphological analysis. *Monographs of the Society for Research in Child Development, 58*(10, Serial No. 238).

Bachevalier, J. (2001). Neural bases of memory development: Insights from neuropsychological studies in primates. In C. A. Nelson & M. Luciana (Eds.), *Handbook of developmental cognitive neuroscience* (pp. 365–379). Cambridge, MA: MIT Press.

Bahrick, L., Parker, J., Merritt, K., & Fivush, R. (1998). Children's memory for Hurricane Andrew. *Journal of Experimental Psychology: Applied, 4,* 308–331.

Baldwin, D. A., Markman, E. M., & Melartin, R. L. (1993). Infants' ability to draw inferences about nonobvious properties: Evidence from exploratory play. *Child Development, 64,* 711–728.

Barnat, S. B., Klein, P. J., & Meltzoff, A. N. (1996). Deferred imitation across changes in context and object: Memory and generalization in 14-month-old children. *Infant Behavior and Development, 19,* 241–251.

Barr, R., Dowden, A., & Hayne, H. (1996). Developmental change in deferred imitation by 6- to 24-month-old infants. *Infant Behavior and Development, 19,* 159–170.

Barr, R., & Hayne, H. (1996). The effect of event structure on imitation in infancy: Practice makes perfect? *Infant Behavior and Development, 19,* 253–257.

Barr, R., & Hayne, H. (1999). Developmental changes in imitation from television during infancy. *Child Development, 70,* 1067–1081.

Bartlett, F. C. (1932). *Remembering: A study in experimental and social psychology.* Cambridge, UK: Cambridge University Press.

Bauer, P. J. (1992). Holding it all together: How enabling relations facilitate young children's event recall. *Cognitive Development, 7,* 1–28.

Bauer, P. J. (1993). Identifying subsystems of autobiographical memory: Commentary on Nelson. In C. A. Nelson (Ed.), *Minnesota Symposium on Child Psychology: Vol. 26. Memory and affect in development* (pp. 25–37). Hillsdale, NJ: Erlbaum.

Bauer, P. J. (1995). Recalling the past: From infancy to early childhood. *Annals of Child Development, 11,* 25–71.

Bauer, P. J. (2002). Long-term recall memory: Behavioral and neurodevelopmental changes in the first 2 years of life. *Current Directions in Psychological Science, 11,* 137–141.

Bauer, P. J. (2004). Getting explicit memory off the ground: Steps toward construction of a neurodevelopmental account of changes in the first two years of life. *Developmental Review, 24,* 347–373.

Bauer, P. J. (2005a). Developments in explicit memory: Decreasing susceptibility to storage failure over the second year of life. *Psychological Science, 16,* 41–47.

Bauer, P. J. (2005b). New developments in the study of infant memory. In D. M. Teti (Ed.), *Blackwell handbook of research methods in developmental science* (pp. 467–488). Oxford, England: Blackwell.

Bauer, P. J. (2006). *Remembering the times of our lives: Memory in infancy and beyond.* Mahwah, NJ: Erlbaum.

Bauer, P. J., & Burch, M. M. (2004). Developments in early memory: Multiple mediators of foundational processes. In J. Lucariello, J. A. Hudson, R. Fivush, & P. J. Bauer (Eds.), *Development of the mediated mind: Culture and cognitive development—Essays in honor of Katherine Nelson* (pp. 101–125). Mahwah, NJ: Erlbaum.

Bauer, P. J., Burch, M. M., & Kleinknecht, E. E. (2002). Developments in early recall memory: Normative trends and individual differences. In R. Kail (Ed.), *Advances in child development and behavior* (pp. 103–152). San Diego, CA: Academic Press.

Bauer, P. J., Cheatham, C. L., Cary, M. S., & Van Abbema, D. L. (2002). Short-term forgetting: Charting its course and its implications for log-term remembering. In S. P. Shohov (Ed.), *Advances in psychology research* (Vol. 9, pp. 53–74). Huntington, NY: Nova Science.

Bauer, P. J., & Dow, G. A. A. (1994). Episodic memory in 16- and 20-month-old children: Specifics are generalized, but not forgotten. *Developmental Psychology, 30,* 403–417.

Bauer, P. J., & Fivush, R. (1992). Constructing event representations: Building on a foundation of variation and enabling relations. *Cognitive Development, 7,* 381–401.

Bauer, P. J., & Hertsgaard, L. A. (1993). Increasing steps in recall of events: Factors facilitating immediate and long-term memory in 13½- and 16½-month-old children. *Child Development, 64,* 1204–1223.

Bauer, P. J., Hertsgaard, L. A., Dropik, P., & Daly, B. P. (1998). When even arbitrary order becomes important: Developments in reliable temporal sequencing of arbitrarily ordered events. *Memory, 6,* 165–198.

Bauer, P. J., Hertsgaard, L. A., & Wewerka, S. S. (1995). Effects of experience and reminding on long-term recall in infancy: Remembering not to forget. *Journal of Experimental Child Psychology, 59,* 260–298.

Bauer, P. J., Kroupina, M. G., Schwade, J. A., Dropik, P. L., & Wewerka, S. S. (1998). If memory serves, will language? Later verbal accessibility of early memories. *Development and Psychopathology, 10,* 655–679.

Bauer, P. J., & Mandler, J. M. (1989). One thing follows another: Effects of temporal structure on 1- to 2-year-olds' recall of events. *Developmental Psychology, 25,* 197–206.

Bauer, P. J., & Mandler, J. M. (1992). Putting the horse before the cart: The use of temporal order in recall of events by 1-year-old children. *Developmental Psychology, 28,* 441–452.

Bauer, P. J., & Shore, C. M. (1987). Making a memorable event: Effects of familiarity and organization on young children's recall of action sequences. *Cognitive Development, 2,* 327–338.

Bauer, P. J., Stark, E. N., Lukowski, A. F., Rademacher, J., Van Abbema, D. L., & Ackil, J. K. (2005). Working together to make sense of the past: Mothers' and children's use of internal states language in conversations about traumatic and non-traumatic events. *Journal of Cognition and Development, 6,* 463–488.

Bauer, P. J., Stennes, L., & Haight, J. C. (2003). Representation of the inner self in autobiography: Women's and men's use of internal states language in personal narratives. *Memory, 11,* 27–42.

Bauer, P. J., & Thal, D. J. (1990). Scripts or scraps: Reconsidering the development of sequential understanding. *Journal of Experimental Child Psychology, 50,* 287–304.

Bauer, P. J., & Travis, L. L. (1993). The fabric of an event: Different sources of temporal invariance differentially affect 24-month-olds' recall. *Cognitive Development, 8,* 319–341.

Bauer, P. J., Van Abbema, D. L., & de Haan, M. (1999). In for the short haul: Immediate and short-term remembering and forgetting by 20-month-old children. *Infant Behavior and Development, 22,* 321–343.

Bauer, P. J., Van Abbema, D. L., Wiebe, S. A., Cary, M. S., Phill, C., & Burch, M. M. (2004). Props, not pictures, are worth a thousand words: Verbal accessibility of early memories under different conditions of contextual support. *Applied Cognitive Psychology, 18,* 373–392.

Bauer, P. J., Wenner, J. A., Dropik, P. L., & Wewerka, S. S. (2000). Parameters of remembering and forgetting in the transition from infancy to early childhood. *Monographs of the Society for Research in Child Development, 65*(4, Serial No. 263).

Bauer, P. J., Wenner, J. A., & Kroupina, M. G. (2002). Making the past present: Later verbal accessibility of early memories. *Journal of Cognition and Development, 3,* 21–47.

Bauer, P. J., & Wewerka, S. S. (1995). One- to two-year-olds' recall of past events: The more expressed, the more impressed. *Journal of Experimental Child Psychology, 59,* 475–496.

Bauer, P. J., & Wewerka, S. S. (1997). Saying is revealing: Verbal expression of event memory in the transition from infancy to early childhood. In P. van denBroek, P. J. Bauer, & T. Bourg (Eds.), *Developmental spans in event representation and comprehension: Bridging fictional and actual events* (pp. 139–168). Mahwah, NJ: Erlbaum.

Bauer, P. J., Wiebe, S. A., Carver, L. J., Lukowski, A. F., Haight, J. C., Waters, J. M., et al. (2006). Electrophysiological indices of encoding and behavioral indices of recall: Examining relations and developmental change late in the first year of life. *Developmental Neuropsychology, 29*(2), 293–320.

Bauer, P. J., Wiebe, S. A., Carver, L. J., Waters, J. M., & Nelson, C. A. (2003). Developments in long-term explicit memory late in the first year of life: Behavioral and electrophysiological indices. *Psychological Science, 14,* 629–635.

Bauer, P. J., Wiebe, S. A., Waters, J. M., & Bangston, S. K. (2001). Reexposure breeds recall: Effects of experience on 9-month-olds' ordered recall. *Journal of Experimental Child Psychology, 80,* 174–200.

Benes, F. M. (2001). The development of prefrontal cortex: The maturation of neurotransmitter systems and their interaction. In C. A. Nelson & M. Luciana (Eds.), *Handbook of developmental cognitive neuroscience* (pp. 79–92). Cambridge, MA: MIT Press.

Boland, A. M., Haden, C. A., & Ornstein, P. A. (2003). Boosting children's memory by training mothers in the use of an elaborative conversational style as an event unfolds. *Journal of Cognition and Development, 4,* 39–65.

Bourgeois, J.-P. (2001). Synaptogenesis in the neocortex of the newborn: The ultimate frontier for individuation. In C. A. Nelson & M. Luciana (Eds.), *Handbook of developmental cognitive neuroscience* (pp. 23–34). Cambridge, MA: MIT Press.

Brainerd, C. J., & Reyna, V. F. (1990). Gist is the grist: Fuzzy-trace theory and the new intuitionism. *Developmental Review, 10,* 3–47.

Brainerd, C. J., & Renya, V. F. (1995). Learning rate, learning opportunities, and the development of forgetting. *Developmental Psychology, 31,* 251–262.

Brainerd, C. J., Reyna, V. F., Howe, M. L., & Kingma, J. (1990). The development of forgetting and reminiscence. *Monographs of the Society for Research in Child Development, 55*(3/4, Serial No. 222).

Bretherton, I. (1990). Open communication and internal working models: Their role in the development of attachment relationships. In R. A. Thompson (Ed.), *Nebraska Symposium on Motivation: Vol. 36. Socioemotional development* (pp. 59–113). Lincoln: University of Nebraska Press.

Brown, D. A., Salmon, K., Pipe, M.-E., Rutter, M., Craw, S., & Taylor, B. (1999). Children's recall of medical experiences and the impact of stress. *Child Abuse and Neglect, 23,* 209–216.

Brown, R., & Kulik, J. (1977). Flashbulb memories. *Cognition, 5,* 73–99.

Buckner, J. P., & Fivush, R. (1998). Gender and self in children's autobiographical narratives. *Applied Cognitive Psychology, 12,* 407–429.

Campbell, B. A. (1984). Reflections on the ontogeny of learning and memory. In R. Kail & N. E. Spear (Eds.), *Comparative perspectives on the development of memory* (pp. 129–157). Hillsdale, NJ: Erlbaum.

Carpenter, M., Akhtar, N., & Tomasello, M. (1998). Fourteen- through 18-month-old infants differentially imitate intentional and accidental actions. *Infant Behavior and Development, 21,* 315–330.

Carver, L. J., & Bauer, P. J. (1999). When the event is more than the sum of its parts: 9-month-olds' long-term ordered recall. *Memory, 7,* 147–174.

Carver, L. J., & Bauer, P. J. (2001). The dawning of a past: The emergence of long-term explicit memory in infancy. *Journal of Experimental Psychology: General, 130,* 726–745.

Carver, L. J., Bauer, P. J., & Nelson, C. A. (2000). Associations between infant brain activity and recall memory. *Developmental Science, 3,* 234–246.

Casey, B. J., Thomas, K. M., & McCandliss, B. (2001). Applications of magnetic resonance imaging to the study of development. In C. A. Nelson & M. Luciana (Eds.), *Handbook of developmental cognitive neuroscience* (pp. 137–147). Cambridge, MA: MIT Press.

Cheatham, C. L., & Bauer, P. J. (2005). Construction of a more coherent story: Prior verbal recall predicts later verbal accessibility of early memories. *Memory, 13,* 516–532.

Chi, M. T. H. (1978). Knowledge structures and memory development. In R. S. Siegler (Ed.), *Children's thinking: What develops?* (pp. 73–95). Hillsdale, NJ: Erlbaum.

Christianson, S.-A. (1992). Emotional stress and eyewitness memory: A critical review. *Psychological Bulletin, 112,* 284–309.

Choi, S. H. (1992). Communicative socialization processes: Korea and Canada. In S. Iwasaki, Y. Kashima, & L. Leung (Eds.), *Innovations in cross-cultural psychology* (pp. 103–122). Amsterdam: Swets & Zeitlinger.

Chugani, H. T. (1994). Development of regional blood glucose metabolism in relation to behavior and plasticity. In G. Dawson & K. Fischer (Eds.), *Human behavior and the developing brain* (pp. 153–175). New York: Guilford Press.

Chugani, H. T., & Phelps, M. E. (1986). Maturational changes in cerebral function determined by 18FDG positron emission tomography. *Science, 231,* 840–843.

Chugani, H. T., Phelps, M., & Mazziotta, J. (1987). Positron emission tomography study of human brain functional development. *Annals of Neurology, 22,* 487–497.

Collie, R., & Hayne, H. (1999). Deferred imitation by 6- and 9-month-old infants: More evidence of declarative memory. *Developmental Psychobiology, 35,* 83–90.

Colombo, J., Richman, W. A., Shaddy, D. J., Greenhoot, A. F., & Maikranz, J. M. (2001). Heart rate-defined phases of attention, look duration, and infant performance in the paired-comparison paradigm. *Child Development, 72,* 1605–1616.

Czurkó, A., Czéh, B., Seress, L., Nadel, L., & Bures, J. (1997). Severe spatial navigation deficit in the Morris water maze after single high dose of neonatal X-ray irradiation in the rat. *Proceedings of the National Academy of Science, 94,* 2766–2771.

Davis, P. J. (1999). Gender differences in autobiographical memory for childhood emotional experiences. *Journal of Personality and Social Psychology, 76,* 498–510.

DeBoer, T., Wewerka, S., Bauer, P. J., Georgieff, M. K., & Nelson, C. A. (in press). Explicit memory performance in infants of diabetic mothers at 1 year of age. *Developmental Medicine and Child Neurology.*

de Haan, M., Bauer, P. J., Georgieff, M. K., & Nelson, C. A. (2000). Explicit memory in low-risk infants aged 19 months born between 27 and 42 weeks of gestation. *Developmental Medicine and Child Neurology, 42,* 304–312.

Drummey, A. B., & Newcombe, N. S. (2002). Developmental changes in source memory. *Developmental Science, 5,* 502–513.

Dunn, J., Brown, J., Slomkowski, C., Tesla, C., & Youngblade, L. (1991). Young children's understanding of other people's feelings and beliefs: Individual differences and their antecedents. *Child Development, 62,* 1352–1366.

Easterbrook, J. A. (1959). The effect of emotion on cue utilization and the organization of behavior. *Psychological Review, 66,* 183–201.

Ebbinghaus, H. (1913). *On memory* (H. A. Ruger & C. E. Bussenius, Trans.). New York: Teachers' College. (Original work published 1885)

Eckenhoff, M., & Rakic, P. (1991). A quantitative analysis of synaptogenesis in the molecular layer of the dentate gyrus in the rhesus monkey. *Developmental Brain Research, 64,* 129–135.

Eichenbaum, H., & Cohen, N. J. (2001). *From conditioning to conscious recollection: Memory systems of the brain.* New York: Oxford University Press.

Erikson, K. M., Pinero, D. J., Connor, J. R., & Beard, J. L. (1997). Regional brain iron, ferritin, and transferrin concentrations during iron deficiency and iron repletion in developing rats. *Journal of Nutrition, 127,* 2030–2038.

Fantz, R. L. (1956). A method for studying early visual development. *Perceptual and Motor Skills, 6,* 13–15.

Farrant, K., & Reese, E. (2000). Maternal style and children's participation in reminiscing: Stepping stones in children's autobiographical memory development. *Journal of Cognition and Development, 1,* 193–225.

Fenson, L., Dale, P. S., Reznick, J. S., Bates, E., Thal, D. J., & Pethick, S. J. (1994). Variability in early communicative development. *Monographs of the Society for Research in Child Development, 59*(5).

Fivush, R. (1984). Learning about school: The development of kindergarteners' school scripts. *Child Development, 55,* 1697–1709.

Fivush, R. (1991). The social construction of personal narratives. *Merrill-Palmer Quarterly, 37,* 59–82.

Fivush, R. (1997). Event memory in early childhood. In N. Cowan (Ed.), *The development of memory in childhood* (pp. 139–161). Hove, England: Psychology Press.

Fivush, R. (1998). Gendered narratives: Eleboration, structure, and emotion in parent-child reminiscing across the preschool years. In C. P. Thompson, D. J. Herrmann, D. Bruce, J. D. Read, D. G. Payne & M. P. Toglia (Eds.), *Autobiographical memory: Theoretical and applied perspectives* (pp. 79–103). Mahwah, NJ: Erlbaum.

Fivush, R. (2001). Owning experience: Developing subjective perspective in autobiographical narratives. In C. Moore & K. Lemmon (Eds.), *The self in time: Developmental perspectives* (pp. 35–52). Mahwah, NJ: Erlbaum.

Fivush, R. (2002). Scripts, schemas, and memory of trauma. In N. L. Stein, P. J. Bauer, & M. Rabinowitz (Eds.), *Representation, memory, and development: Essays in honor of Jean Mandler* (pp. 53–74). Mahwah, NJ: Erlbaum.

Fivush, R., Berlin, L. J., Sales, J., Mennuti-Washburn, J., & Cassidy, J. (2003). Functions of parent-child eminiscing about emotionally negative events. *Memory, 11,* 179–192.

Fivush, R., & Fromhoff, F. (1988). Style and structure in mother-child conversations about the past. *Discourse Processes, 11,* 337–355.

Fivush, R., Gray, J. T., & Fromhoff, F. A. (1987). Two-year-olds talk about the past. *Cognitive Development, 2,* 393–409.

Fivush, R., & Haden, C. A. (1997). Narrating and representing experience: Preschoolers' developing autobiographical accounts. In P. van den Broek, P. J. Bauer, & T. Bourg (Eds.), *Developmental spans in event representation and comprehension: Bridging fictional and actual events* (pp. 169–198). Mahwah, NJ: Erlbaum.

Fivush, R., & Hamond, N. R. (1990). Autobiographical memory across the preschool years: Toward reconceptualizing childhood amnesia. In R. Fivush & J. A. Hudson (Eds.), *Knowing and remembering in young children* (pp. 223–248). New York: Cambridge University Press.

Fivush, R., Hazzard, A., Sales, J. M., Sarfati, D., & Brown, T. (2003). Creating coherence out of chaos? Children's narratives of emotionally positive and negative events. *Applied Cognitive Psychology, 17,* 1–19.

Fivush, R., Hudson, J. A., & Nelson, K. (1984). Children's long-term memory for a novel event: An exploratory study. *Merrill-Palmer Quarterly, 30,* 303–316.

Fivush, R., & Kuebli, J. (1997). Making everyday events emotional: The construal of emotion in parent-child conversations about the past. In N. L. Stein, P. A. Ornstein, B. Tversky, & C. Brainerd (Eds.), *Memory for everyday and emotional events* (pp. 239–266). Mahwah, NJ: Erlbaum.

Fivush, R., Keubli, J., & Clubb, P. A. (1992). The structure of events and event representations: Developmental analysis. *Child Development, 63,* 188–201.

Fivush, R., Sales, J. M., Goldberg, A., Bahrick, L., & Parker, J. F. (2004). Weathering the storm: Children's long-term recall of Hurricane Andrew. *Memory, 12,* 104–118.

Fivush, R., & Slackman, E. (1986). The acquisition and development of scripts. In K. Nelson (Ed.), *Event knowledge: Structure and function in development* (pp. 71–96). Hillsdale, NJ: Erlbaum.

Fivush, R., & Vasudeva, A. (2002). Remembering to relate: Socioemotional correlates of mother-child reminiscing. *Journal of Cognition and Development, 3,* 73–90.

Flavell, J. H., Beach, D. R., & Chinsky, J. H. (1966). Spontaneous verbal rehearsal in a memory task as a function of age. *Child Development, 37,* 283–299.

Foster, J. C. (1928). Verbal memory in the preschool child. *Journal of Genetic Psychology, 35,* 26–44.

Freud, S. (1953). Three essays on the theory of sexuality. In J. Strachey (Ed.), *The standard edition of the complete psychological works of Sigmund Freud* (Vol. 7, pp. 135–243). London: Hogarth Press. (Original work published 1905)

Friedman, W. J. (1990). Children's representations of the pattern of daily activities. *Child Development, 61,* 1399–1412.

Friedman, W. J. (1993). Memory for the time of past events. *Psychological Bulletin, 11,* 44–66.

Goldman-Rakic, P. S. (1987). Circuitry of primate prefrontal cortex and regulation of behavior by representational memory. In F. Plum (Ed.), *Handbook of physiology, the nervous system, higher functions of the brain* (Vol. 5, pp. 373–417). Bethesda, MD: American Physiological Society.

Goodman, G. S., Hirschman, J. E., Hepps, D., & Rudy, L. (1991). Children's memory for stressful events. *Merrill-Palmer Quarterly, 37,* 109–158.

Goodman, G. S., & Quas, J. A. (1997). Trauma and memory: Individual differences in children's recounting of a stressful experience. In N. L. Stein, P. A. Ornstein, B. Tversky, & C. Brainerd (Eds.), *Memory for everyday and emotional events* (pp. 267–294). Hillsdale, NJ: Erlbaum.

Goodman, G. S., Quas, J. A., Batterman-Faunce, J. M., Riddlesberger, M., & Kuhn, J. (1994). Predictors of accurate and inaccurate memories of traumatic events experienced in childhood. *Consciousness and Cognition, 3,* 269–294.

Greenhoot, A. F., Ornstein, P. A., Gordon, B. N., & Baker-Ward, L. (1999). Acting out details of a pediatric check-up: The impact of interview condition and behavioral style on children's memory reports. *Child Development, 70,* 363–380.

Gunnar, M. R. (2001). Effects of early deprivation: Findings from orphanage-reared infants and children. In C. A. Nelson & M. Luciana (Eds.), *Handbook of developmental cognitive neuroscience* (pp. 617–629). Cambridge, MA: MIT Press.

Haden, C. A. (1998). Reminiscing with different children: Relating maternal stylistic consistency and sibling similarity in talk about the past. *Developmental Psychology, 34,* 99–114.

Haden, C. A., Haine, R., & Fivush, R. (1997). Development narrative structure in parent-child conversations about the past. *Developmental Psychology, 33,* 295–307.

Haden, C. A., Ornstein, P. A., Eckerman, C. O., & Dodow, S. M. (2001). Mother-child conversational interactions as events un-

fold: Linkages to subsequent remembering. *Child Development, 72,* 1016–1031.

Haith, M. M., & Benson, J. B. (1998). Infant cognition. In W. Damon (Editor-in-Chief) & D. Kuhn & R. S. Siegler (Vol. Eds.), *Handbook of child psychology: Vol. 2. Cognition, perception, and language* (5th ed., pp. 199–254). New York: Wiley.

Hamond, N. R., & Fivush, R. (1991). Memories of Mickey Mouse: Young children recount their trip to DisneyWorld. *Cognitive Development, 6,* 433–448.

Han, J. J., Leichtman, M. D., & Wang, Q. (1998). Autobiographical memory in Korean, Chinese, and American children. *Developmental Psychology, 34,* 701–713.

Hanna, E., & Meltzoff, A. N. (1993). Peer imitation by toddlers in laboratory, home, and day-care contexts: Implications for social learning and memory. *Developmental Psychology, 29,* 702–710.

Harley, K., & Reese, E. (1999). Origins of autobiographical memory. *Developmental Psychology, 35,* 1338–1348.

Hartshorn, K., Rovee-Collier, C., Gerhardstein, P., Bhatt, R. S., Wondoloski, T. L., Klein, P., et al. (1998). The ontogeny of long-term memory over the first year-and-a-half of life. *Developmental Psychobiology, 32,* 69–89.

Hartup, W. W., Johnson, A., & Weinberg, R. A. (2001). *The institute of child development: Pioneering in science and application 1925–2000.* Minneapolis: University of Minnesota Printing Services.

Hayne, H., Barr, R., & Herbert, J. (2003). The effect of prior practice on memory reactivation and generalization. *Child Development, 74,* 1615–1627.

Hayne, H., Boniface, J., & Barr, R. (2000). The development of declarative memory in human infants: Age-related changes in deferred imitation. *Behavioral Neuroscience, 114,* 77–83.

Hayne, H., MacDonald, S., & Barr, R. (1997). Developmental changes in the specificity of memory over the second year of life. *Infant Behavior and Development, 20,* 233–245.

Herbert, J., & Hayne, H. (2000). Memory retrieval by 18- to 30-month-olds: Age-related changes in representational flexibility. *Developmental Psychology, 36,* 473–484.

Howe, M. L. (1995). Interference effects in young children's long-term retention. *Developmental Psychology, 31,* 579–596.

Howe, M. L., & Brainerd, C. J. (1989). Development of children's long-term retention. *Developmental Review, 9,* 301–340.

Howe, M. L., & Courage, M. L. (1993). On resolving the enigma of infantile amnesia. *Psychological Bulletin, 113,* 305–326.

Howe, M. L., & Courage, M. L. (1997a). The emergence and early development of autobiographical memory. *Psychological Review, 104,* 499–523.

Howe, M. L., & Courage, M. L. (1997b). Independent paths in the development of infant learning and forgetting. *Journal of Experimental Child Psychology, 67,* 131–163.

Howe, M. L., & O'Sullivan, J. T. (1997). What children's memories tell us about recalling our childhoods: A review of storage and retrieval processes in the development of long-term retention. *Developmental Review, 17,* 148–204.

Hudson, J. A. (1986). Memories are made of this: General event knowledge and the development of autobiographical memory. In K. Nelson (Ed.), *Event knowledge: Structure and function in development* (pp. 97–118). Hillsdale, NJ: Erlbaum.

Hudson, J. A. (1990). The emergence of autobiographical memory in mother-child conversation. In R. Fivush & J. A. Hudson (Eds.), *Knowing and remembering in young children* (pp. 166–196). Cambridge, MA: Cambridge University Press.

Hudson, J. A. (1991). Learning to reminisce: A case study. *Journal of Narrative and Life History, 1,* 295–324.

Hudson, J. A. (1993). Reminiscing with mothers and others: Autobiographical memory in young 2-year-olds. *Journal of Narrative and Life History, 3,* 1–32.

Hudson, J. A., & Fivush, R. (1991). As time goes by: Sixth graders remember a kindergarten experience. *Applied Cognitive Psychology, 5,* 347–360.

Hudson, J. A., & Sheffield, E. G. (1998). Déjà vu all over again: Effects of reenactment on toddlers' event memory. *Child Development, 69,* 51–67.

Hutt, C. (1978). Biological bases of psychological sex differences. *American Journal of Diseases in Children, 132,* 170–177.

Huttenlocher, P. R. (1979). Synaptic density in human frontal cortex: Developmental changes and effects of aging. *Brain Research, 163,* 195–205.

Huttenlocher, P. R., & Dabholkar, A. S. (1997). Regional differences in synaptogenesis in human cerebral cortex. *Journal of Comparative Neurology, 387,* 167–178.

Jacobson, S. W. (1979). Matching behavior in the young infant. *Child Development, 50,* 425–430.

James, W. (1890). *Principles of psychology.* Cambridge, MA: Harvard University Press.

Kaitz, M., Meschulach-Sarfaty, O., Auerbach, J., & Eidelman, A. (1988). A reexamination of newborns' ability to imitate facial expressions. *Developmental Psychology, 24,* 3–7.

Kim, J. J., & Fanselow, M. S. (1992). Modality-specific retrograde amnesia of fear. *Science, 256,* 675–677.

Kintsch, W. (1974). *The representation of meaning in memory.* Hillsdale, NJ: Erlbaum.

Klein, P. J., & Meltzoff, A. N. (1999). Long-term memory, forgetting, and deferred imitation in 12-month-old infants. *Developmental Science, 2,* 102–113.

Knopman, D. S., & Nissen, M. J. (1987). Implicit learning in patients with probably Alzheimer's disease. *Neurology, 5,* 784–788.

Köhler, S., & Moscovitch, M. (1997). Unconscious visual processing in neuropsychological syndromes: A survey of the literature and evaluation of models of consciousness. In M. D. Rugg (Ed.), *Cognitive neuroscience* (pp. 305–373). London: United College of London Press.

Kroupina, M. G., Bauer, P. J., Gunnar, M., & Johnson, D. (2004). *Explicit memory skills in post-institutionalized toddlers.* Unpublished manuscript.

Kuebli, J., Butler, S., & Fivush, R. (1995). Mother-child talk about past emotions: Relations of maternal language and child gender over time. *Cognition and Emotion, 9,* 265–283.

Lechuga, M. T., Marcos-Ruiz, R., & Bauer, P. J. (2001). Episodic recall of specifics and generalization coexist in 25-month-old children. *Memory, 9,* 117–132.

Lewis, C., Freeman, N. H., Kyriakidou, C., Maridaki-Kassotaki, K., & Berridge, D. M. (1996). Social influences on false belief assess: Specific sibling influences or general apprenticeship? *Child Development, 67,* 2930–2947.

Lewis, K. D. (1999). Maternal style in reminiscing: Relations to child individual differences. *Cognitive Development, 14,* 381–399.

Lewis, M., & Brooks-Gunn, J. (1979). *Social cognition and the acquisition of self.* New York: Plenum Press.

Lewis, M., Feiring, C., & Rosenthal, S. (2000). Attachment over time. *Child Development, 71,* 707–720.

Liston, C., & Kagan, J. (2002). Memory enhancement in early childhood. *Nature, 419,* 896.

Lukowski, A. F., Wiebe, S. A., Haight, J. C., DeBoer, T., Nelson, C. A., & Bauer, P. J. (in press). Forming a stable memory representation in the first year of life: Why imitation is more than child's play. *Developmental Science.*

Maccoby, E. E., & Jacklin, C. N. (1974). *The psychology of sex differences.* Stanford, CA: Stanford University Press.

MacDonald, S., Uesiliana, K., & Hayne, H. (2000). Cross-cultural and gender differences in childhood amnesia. *Memory, 8,* 365–376.

Mandler, J. M. (1983). Representation. In P. Mussen (Series Ed.) & J. H. Flavell & E. M. Markman (Vol. Eds.), *Handbook of child psychology: Vol. 3. Cognitive development* (4th ed., pp. 420–494). New York: Wiley.

Mandler, J. M. (1984). *Stories, scripts and scenes: Aspects of schema theory.* Hillsdale, NJ: Erlbaum.

Mandler, J. M. (1988). How to build a baby: On the development of an accessible representational system. *Cognitive Development, 3,* 113–136.

Mandler, J. M. (1990a). Recall and its verbal expression. In R. Fivush & J. A. Hudson (Eds.), *Knowing and remembering in young children* (pp. 317–330). New York: Cambridge University Press.

Mandler, J. M. (1990b). Recall of events by preverbal children. In A. Diamond (Ed.), *The development and neural bases of higher cognitive functions* (pp. 485–516). New York: New York Academy of Science.

Mandler, J. M. (1992). How to build a baby: Pt. 2. Conceptual primitives. *Psychological Review, 99,* 587–604.

Mandler, J. M. (1998). Representation. In W. Damon (Editor-in-Chief) & D. Kuhn & R. S. Siegler (Vol. Eds.) *Handbook of child psychology: Vol. 2. Cognition, perception, and language* (5th ed., pp. 255–308). New York: Wiley.

Mandler, J. M., & DeForest, M. (1979). Is there more than one way to recall a story? *Child Development, 50,* 886–889.

Mandler, J. M., & Johnson, N. S. (1977). Remembrance of things parsed: Story structure and recall. *Cognitive Psychology, 9,* 111–151.

Mandler, J. M., & McDonough, L. (1995). Long-term recall of event sequences in infancy. *Journal of Experimental Child Psychology, 59,* 457–474.

Markowitsch, H. J. (2000). Neuroanatomy of memory. In E. Tulving & F. I. M. Craik (Eds.), *Oxford handbook of memory* (pp. 465–484). New York: Oxford University Press.

McCloskey, M., Wible, C. G., & Cohen, N. J. (1988). Is there a special flashbulb memory mechanism? *Journal of Experimental Psychology: General, 117,* 171–181.

McDonough, L., & Mandler, J. M. (1998). Inductive generalization in 9- and 11-month-olds. *Developmental Science, 1,* 227–232.

McDonough, L., Mandler, J. M., McKee, R. D., & Squire, L. R. (1995). The deferred imitation task as a nonverbal measure of declarative memory. *Proceedings of the National Academy of Sciences, 92,* 7580–7584.

Meltzoff, A. N. (1985). Immediate and deferred imitation in 14- and 24-month-old infants. *Child Development, 56,* 62–72.

Meltzoff, A. N. (1988a). Imitation of televised models by infants. *Child Development, 59,* 1221–1229.

Meltzoff, A. N. (1988b). Infant imitation after a 1-week delay: Long-term memory for novel acts and multiple stimuli. *Developmental Psychology, 24,* 470–476.

Meltzoff, A. N. (1988c). Infant imitation and memory: 9-month-olds in immediate and deferred tests. *Child Development, 59,* 217–225.

Meltzoff, A. N. (1990). The implications of cross-modal matching and imitation for the development of representation and memory in infants. In A. Diamond (Ed.), *The development and neural bases of higher cognitive functions* (pp. 1–31). New York: New York Academy of Science.

Meltzoff, A. N. (1995a). Understanding the intentions of others: Re-enactment of intended acts by 18-month-old children. *Developmental Psychology, 31,* 838–850.

Meltzoff, A. N. (1995b). What infant memory tells us about infantile amnesia: Long-term recall and deferred imitation. *Journal of Experimental Child Psychology, 59,* 497–515.

Meltzoff, A. N., & Moore, M. K. (1977). Imitation of facial and manual gestures by human neonates. *Science, 198,* 75–78.

Mullen, M. K. (1994). Earliest recollections of childhood: A demographic analysis. *Cognition, 52,* 55–79.

Mullen, M. K., & Yi, S. (1995). The cultural context of talk about the past: Implications for the development of autobiographical memory. *Cognitive Development, 10,* 407–419.

Munakata, Y., & Stedron, J. M. (2001). Neural network models of cognitive development. In C. A. Nelson & M. Luciana (Eds.), *Handbook of developmental cognitive neuroscience* (pp. 159–171). Cambridge, MA: MIT Press.

Myers, N. A., Perris, E. E., & Speaker, C. J. (1994). Fifty months of memory: A longitudinal study in early childhood. *Memory, 2,* 383–415.

Nadel, L., & Willner, J. (1989). Some implications of postnatal maturation of the hippocampus. In V. Chan-Palay & C. Köhler (Eds.), *The hippocampus—New vistas* (pp. 17–31). New York: Alan R. Liss.

Nelson, C. A. (1995). The ontogeny of human memory: A cognitive neuroscience perspective. *Developmental Psychology, 31,* 723–738.

Nelson, C. A. (1997). The neurobiological basis of early memory development. In N. Cowan (Ed.), *The development of memory in childhood* (pp. 41–82). Hove, England: Psychology Press.

Nelson, C. A. (2000). Neural plasticity and human development: The role of early experience in sculpting memory systems. *Developmental Science, 3,* 115–136.

Nelson, C. A., & Monk, C. S. (2001). The use of event-related potentials in the study of cognitive development. In C. A. Nelson & M. Luciana (Eds.), *Handbook of developmental cognitive neuroscience* (pp. 125–136). Cambridge, MA: MIT Press.

Nelson, K. (1978). How young children represent knowledge of their world in and out of language. In R. S. Siegler (Ed.), *Children's thinking: What develops?* (pp. 255–273). Hillsdale, NJ: Erlbaum.

Nelson, K. (1986). *Event knowledge: Structure and function in development.* Hillsdale, NJ: Erlbaum.

Nelson, K. (1988). The ontogeny of memory for real events. In U. Neisser & E. Winograd (Eds.), *Remembering reconsidered: Ecological and traditional approaches to the study of memory* (pp. 244–276). New York: Cambridge University Press.

Nelson, K. (1989). *Narratives from the crib.* Cambridge, MA: Harvard University Press.

Nelson, K. (1993). The psychological and social origins of autobiographical memory. *Psychological Science, 4,* 7–14.

Nelson, K. (1997). Event representations then, now, and next. In P. van den Broek, P. J. Bauer, & T. Bourg (Eds.), *Developmental*

*spans in event representation and comprehension: Bridging fictional and actual events* (pp. 1–26). Mahwah, NJ: Erlbaum.

Nelson, K., & Fivush, R. (2000). Socialization of memory. In E. Tulving & F. I. M. Craik (Eds.), *Oxford handbook of memory* (pp. 283–295). New York: Oxford University Press.

Nelson, K., & Fivush, R. (2004). The emergence of autobiographical memory: A social cultural developmental theory. *Psychological Review, 111,* 486–511.

Nelson, K., & Gruendel, J. (1981). Generalized event representations: Basic building blocks of cognitive development. In M. E. Lamb & A. L. Brown (Eds.), *Advances in developmental psychology* (Vol. 1, pp. 131–158). Hillsdale, NJ: Erlbaum.

Nelson, K., & Gruendel, J. (1986). Children's scripts. In K. Nelson (Ed.), *Event knowledge: Structure and function in development* (pp. 21–46). Hillsdale, NJ: Erlbaum.

Nelson, K., & Ross, G. (1980). The generalities and specifics of long-term memory in infants and young children. In M. Perlmutter (Ed.), *New directions for child development—Children's memory* (pp. 87–101). San Francisco: Jossey-Bass.

Newcombe, R., & Reese, E. (2003, April). *Reflections on a shared past: Attachment security and mother-child reminiscing.* Paper presented at the 70th Biennial Meeting of the Society for Research in Child Development, Tampa, FL.

O'Neill, D. K., Astington, J. W., & Flavell, J. H. (1992). Young children's understanding of the role that sensory experiences play in knowledge acquisition. *Child Development, 63,* 474–490.

Ornstein, P. A. (1995). Children's long-term retention of salient personal experiences. *Journal of Traumatic Stress, 8,* 581–605.

Ornstein, P. A., Merritt, K. A., Baker-Ward, L., Furtado, E., Gordon, B. N., & Principe, G. (1998). Children's knowledge, expectation, and long-term retention. *Applied Cognitive Psychology, 12,* 387–405.

Overman, W. H., & Bachevalier, J. (2001). Inferences about the functional development of neural systems in children via the application of animal tests of cognition. In C. A. Nelson & M. Luciana (Eds.), *Handbook of developmental cognitive neuroscience* (pp. 109–124). Cambridge, MA: MIT Press.

Perner, J. (2001). Episodic memory: Essential distinctions and developmental implications. In C. Moore & K. Lemmon (Eds.), *The self in time: Developmental perspectives* (pp. 181–202). Mahwah, NJ: Erlbaum.

Perner, J., & Ruffman, T. (1995). Episodic memory and autonoetic consciousness: Developmental evidence and a theory of childhood amnesia. *Journal of Experimental Child Psychology, 59,* 516–548.

Peterson, C., & McCabe, A. (1992). Parental styles of narrative elicitation: Effect on children's narrative structure and content. *First Language, 12,* 299–321.

Peterson, C., & McCabe, A. (1994). A social interactionist account of developing decontextualized narrative skill. *Developmental Psychology, 30,* 937–948.

Peterson, C., & Rideout, R. (1998). Memory for medical emergencies experienced by 1- and 2-year-olds. *Developmental Psychology, 34,* 1059–1072.

Peterson, C., & Whalen, N. (2001). Five years later: Children's memory for medical emergencies. *Applied Cognitive Psychology, 15,* S7–S24.

Piaget, J. (1926). *The language and thought of the child.* New York: Harcourt, Brace.

Piaget, J. (1952). *The origins of intelligence in children.* New York: International Universities Press.

Piaget, J. (1962). *Play, dreams and imitation in childhood.* New York: Norton.

Piaget, J. (1969). *The child's conception of time.* London: Routledge & Kegan Paul.

Pillemer, D. B. (1998a). *Momentous events, vivid memories: How unforgettable moments help us understand the meaning of our lives.* Cambridge, MA: Harvard University Press.

Pillemer, D. B. (1998b). What is remembered about early childhood events? *Clinical Psychology Review, 18,* 895–913.

Pillemer, D. B., Picariello, M. L., & Pruett, J. C. (1994). Very long-term memories of a salient preschool event. *Applied Cognitive Psychology, 8,* 95–106.

Pillemer, D. B., & White, S. H. (1989). Childhood events recalled by children and adults. In H. W. Reese (Ed.), *Advances in child development and behavior* (Vol. 21, pp. 297–340). Orlando, FL: Academic Press.

Povinelli, D. J. (1995). The unduplicated self. In P. Rochat (Ed.), *The self in early infancy* (pp. 161–192). Amsterdam: Elsevier.

Price, D. W. W., & Goodman, G. S. (1990). Visiting the wizard: Children's memory for a recurring event. *Child Development, 61,* 664–680.

Quas, J. A., Goodman, G. S., Bibrose, S., Pipe, M.-E., Craw, S., & Ablin, D. S. (1999). Emotion and memory: Children's long-term remembering, forgetting, and suggestibility. *Journal of Experimental Child Psychology, 72,* 235–270.

Reed, J. M., & Squire, L. R. (1998). Retrograde amnesia for facts and events: Findings from four new cases. *Journal of Neuroscience, 18,* 3943–3954.

Reese, E., & Brown, N. (2000). Reminiscing and recounting in the preschool years. *Applied Cognitive Psychology, 14,* 1–17.

Reese, E., & Fivush, R. (1993). Parental styles of talking about the past. *Developmental Psychology, 29,* 596–606.

Reese, E., Haden, C. A., & Fivush, R. (1993). Mother-child conversations about the past: Relationships of style and memory over time. *Cognitive Development, 8,* 403–430.

Reinisch, J. M., Rosenblum, L. A., Rubin, D. B., & Schulsinger, M. F. (1991). Sex differences in developmental milestones during the first year of life. *Journal of Psychology and Human Sexuality, 4,* 19.

Roediger, H. L., Rajaram, S., & Srinivas, K. (1990). Specifying criteria for postulating memory systems. *Annals of the New York Academy of Sciences, 608,* 572–589.

Roisman, G. I., Madsen, S. D., Henninghausen, K. H., Sroufe, L. A., & Collins, W. A. (2001). The coherence of dyadic behavior across parent-child and romantic relationships as mediated by the internalized representation of experience. *Attachment and Human Development, 3,* 156–172.

Rose, S. A., Feldman, J. F., & Jankowski, J. J. (2003). Infant visual recognition memory: Independent contributions of speed and attention. *Developmental Psychology, 39,* 563–571.

Rose, S. A., Gottfried, A. W., Melloy-Carminar, P., & Bridger, W. H. (1982). Familiarity and novelty preferences in infant recognition memory: Implications for information processing. *Developmental Psychology, 18,* 704–713.

Rothbart, M. K., & Bates, J. E. (1998). Temperament. In W. Damon (Editor-in-Chief) & N. Eisenberg (Vol. Ed.), *Handbook of child psychology: Vol. 3. Social, emotional and personality development* (5th ed., pp. 105–176). New York: Wiley.

Rovee-Collier, C. (1997). Dissociations in infant memory: Rethinking the development of implicit and explicit memory. *Psychological Review, 104,* 467–498.

Rovee-Collier, C., & Gerhardstein, P. (1997). The development of infant memory. In N. Cowan (Ed.), *The development of memory in childhood* (pp. 5–39). Hove, England: Psychology Press.

Rovee-Collier, C., & Hayne, H. (2000). Memory in infancy and early childhood. In E. Tulving & F. I. M. Craik (Eds.), *The Oxford handbook of memory* (pp. 267–282). New York: Oxford University Press.

Rumelhart, D. E. (1975). Notes on a schema for stories. In D. LaBerge & J. Samuels (Eds.), *Representation and understanding: Studies in cognitive science* (pp. 211–236). New York: Academic Press.

Sales, J. M., Fivush, R., & Peterson, C. (2003). Parental reminiscing about positive and negative events. *Journal of Cognition and Development, 4,* 185–209.

Schacter, D. L., Wagner, A. D., & Buckner, R. L. (2000). Memory systems of 1999. In E. Tulving & F. I. M. Craik (Eds.), *Oxford handbook of memory* (pp. 627–643). New York: Oxford University Press.

Schank, R. C., & Abelson, R. P. (1977). *Scripts, plans, goals and understanding.* Hillsdale, NJ: Erlbaum.

Schneider, W., & Bjorklund, D. F. (1998). Memory. In W. Damon (Editor-in-Chief) & D. Kuhn & R. S. Siegler (Vol. Eds.) *Handbook of child psychology: Vol. 2. Cognition, perception, and language* (5th ed., pp. 467–521). New York: Wiley.

Senkfor, A. J., Van Pettern C., & Kutas, M. (2002). Episodic action memory for real objects: An ERP investigation with perform, watch, and imagine action encoding tasks versus a non-action encoding task. *Journal of Cognitive Neuroscience, 14,* 402–419.

Seress, L. (2001). Morphological changes of the human hippocampal formation from midgestation to early childhood. In C. A. Nelson & M. Luciana (Eds.), *Handbook of developmental cognitive neuroscience* (pp. 45–58). Cambridge, MA: MIT Press.

Sheingold, K., & Tenney, Y. J. (1982). Memory for a salient childhood event. In U. Neisser (Ed.), *Memory observed: Remembering in natural contexts* (pp. 201–212). New York: Freeman.

Simcock, G., & Hayne, H. (2002). Breaking the barrier? Children fail to translate their preverbal memories into language. *Psychological Science, 13,* 225–231.

Sodian, B., & Wimmer, H. (1987). Children's understanding of inference as a source of knowledge. *Child Development, 58,* 424–433.

Spear, N. E. (1978). *The processing of memories: Forgetting and retention.* Hillsdale, NJ: Erlbaum.

Squire, L. R., Knowlton, B., & Musen, G. (1993). The structure and organization of memory. *Annual Review of Psychology, 44,* 453–495.

Stein, N. L., & Glenn, C. G. (1979). An analysis of story comprehension in elementary school children. In R. O. Freedle (Ed.), *New directions in discourse processing* (Vol. 5, pp. 53–120). Hillsdale, NJ: Erlbaum.

Takehara, K., Kawahara, S., & Kirino, Y. (2003). Time-dependent reorganization of the brain components underlying memory retention in trace eyeblink conditioning. *Journal of Neuroscience, 23,* 9897–9905.

Tanapat, P., Hastings, N. B., & Gould, E. (2001). Adult neurogenesis in the hippocampal formation. In C. A. Nelson & M. Luciana (Eds.), *Handbook of developmental cognitive neuroscience* (pp. 93–105). Cambridge, MA: MIT Press.

Taylor, M., Esbensen, B., & Bennett, R. T. (1994). Children's understanding of knowledge acquisition: The tendency for children to report they have always known what they have just learned. *Child Development, 65,* 1581–1604.

Tessler, M., & Nelson, K. (1994). Making memories: The influence of joint encoding on later recall by young children. *Consciousness and Cognition, 3,* 307–326.

Todd, C. M., & Perlmutter, M. (1980). Reality recalled by preschool children. In M. Perlmutter (Ed.), *New directions for child development: Children's memory* (pp. 69–85). San Francisco: Jossey-Bass.

Travis, L. L. (1997). Goal-based organization of event memory in toddlers. In P. van den Broek, P. J. Bauer, & T. Bourg (Eds.), *Developmental spans in event comprehension and representation: Bridging fictional and actual events* (pp. 111–138). Hillsdale, NJ: Erlbaum.

Tulving, E. (1983). *Elements of episodic memory.* Oxford, England: Oxford University Press.

Walkenfeld, F. F. (2000). *Reminder and language effects on preschoolers' memory reports: Do words speak louder than actions?* Unpublished doctoral dissertation, City University of New York Graduate Center, New York, NY.

Wang, Q. (2001). Culture effects on adults' earliest childhood recollection and self-description: Implications for the relation between memory and the self. *Journal of Personality and Social Psychology, 81,* 220–233.

Wang, Q., Leichtman, M. D., & Davies, K. I. (2000). Sharing memories and telling stories: American and Chinese mothers and their 3-year-olds. *Memory, 8,* 159–177.

Waters, H. S., Rodriguez, L. M., & Ridgeway, D. (1998). Cognitive underpinnings of narrative attachment assessment. *Journal of Experimental Child Psychology, 71,* 211–234.

Welch-Ross, M. K. (1997). Mother-child participation in conversation about the past: Relationships to preschoolers' theory of mind. *Developmental Psychology, 33,* 618–629.

Welch-Ross, M. (2001). Personalizing the temporally extended self: Evaluative self-awareness and the development of autobiographical memory. In C. Moore & K. Lemmon (Eds.), *The self in time: Developmental perspectives* (pp. 97–120). Mahwah, NJ: Erlbaum.

Wenner, J. A., & Bauer, P. J. (1999). Bringing order to the arbitrary: 1- to 2-year-olds' recall of event sequences. *Infant Behavior and Development, 22,* 585–590.

White, S. H., & Pillemer, D. B. (1979). Childhood amnesia and the development of a socially accessible memory system. In J. F. Kihlstrom & F. J. Evans (Eds.), *Functional disorders of memory* (pp. 29–73). Hillsdale, NJ: Erlbaum.

Winograd, E., & Neisser, U. (1992). *Affect and accuracy in recall.* New York: Cambridge University Press.

Yerkes, R. M., & Dodson, J. D. (1908). The relation of strength of stimulation to rapidity of habit formation. *Journal of Comparative Neurology of Psychology, 18,* 459–482.

Zola, S. M., & Squire, L. R. (2000). The medial temporal lobe and the hippocampus. In E. Tulving & F. I. M. Craik (Eds.), *Oxford handbook of memory* (pp. 485–500). New York: Oxford University Press.

Zola-Morgan, S., Squire, L. R., Rempel, N. L., Clower, R. P., & Amaral, D. G. (1992). Enduring memory impairment in monkeys after ischemic damage to the hippocampus. *Journal of Neuroscience, 9,* 4355–4370.

# CHAPTER 10

# *Information Processing Approaches to Development*

YUKO MUNAKATA

WHY MODEL?  427
HISTORICAL CONTEXT  429
OVERVIEW AND EXAMPLE OF EACH KIND  430
Production Systems  430
Neural Networks  432
Dynamic Systems  435
Ad Hoc Models  436
General Comparisons across Frameworks  437
DETAILED COMPARISONS: DIFFERENT MODELS
    OF THE SAME PHENOMENA  438

Problem Solving: The Balance Scale Task  438
Language: The Past Tense  444
Memory: The A-not-B Task  448
GENERAL ISSUES  454
Why Model? (Revisited)  454
Future Directions  456
CONCLUSION  458
REFERENCES  458

Why do children think the way they do? What leads to the remarkable changes in thinking that they show with development? What accounts for the variation in thinking observed across children? These questions are challenging, but not intractable. Developmental researchers have made great progress in addressing such questions using a vast array of methods. These include behavioral, neuroimaging, and genetic studies, with both typically and atypically developing populations.

This chapter describes a set of *information processing* approaches that have also supported significant contributions to the study of fundamental development questions. Broadly speaking, these approaches treat thinking as the processing of information. When applied to development, these approaches thus focus on what information children represent, how they represent and process this information, how these representations guide their

behaviors, and what mechanisms lead to changes in these processes across development. Developmental change is often explained within information processing approaches in terms of self-modification processes, in which children's thinking and behaviors shape the way that they subsequently process information.

Information processing approaches have been associated with the use of formalisms that allow researchers to specify or simulate in detail the processes contributing to thinking and behavior. These formalisms may be viewed as varying along a soft-core to hard-core continuum (Klahr, 1989, 1992). *Soft-core* versions might include flowcharts and diagrams to describe models of children's thinking (e.g., Aguiar & Baillargeon, 2000; Case, 1986; Siegler, 1976), whereas *hard-core* versions are actually implemented in computational models. Computational models take the form of codes (e.g., mathematical equations and commands) that specify how a system transforms and responds to inputs; these codes can be run on a computer to observe the processing and behavior of the system under many different circumstances. As in earlier reviews (Klahr & MacWhinney, 1998), this chapter focuses on hard-core

The writing of this chapter was supported by NICHD Grant HD037163. I thank Robert Siegler, Randy O'Reilly, and members of the Cognitive Development Center at the University of Colorado, Boulder, for useful comments and discussion, and Karen Adolph for inspiration.

information processing approaches. For a review of other variants of information processing approaches, see Siegler and Alibali (2005).

This chapter first addresses the question: Why should anyone care about computational models of development? The discussion explains how such models have served as a complement to other approaches of studying development, to support many advances in understanding how change occurs. The chapter then describes some of the historical context that set the stage for computational modeling endeavors. An overview and example are provided for each of four types of information processing approaches to development: production systems, neural networks, dynamic systems, and ad hoc models. Some aspects of children's development (problem solving, language, and memory) have been investigated through more than one type of information processing model, allowing direct comparisons to be made about how such models have informed the study of development. Next, the chapter focuses on such comparisons. The chapter closes with a discussion of general issues in the information processing endeavor and promising directions for future work.

## WHY MODEL?

At first blush, computational approaches seem to require more motivation and justification than perhaps all other prevalent approaches to the study of development, despite each approach having its unique strengths and limitations. Behavioral studies with children and adults are of obvious importance when the questions of interest concern how we behave and why, even though behavioral observations alone cannot specify the mechanisms underlying the behaviors. Neuroimaging approaches generate great excitement about the prospects of watching the brain as it thinks, despite providing only indirect measures of neural activity. Studies with special populations and patients with brain damage may shed light on not only atypical but also typical functioning, despite the many complexities involved in trying to make inferences about exactly what mechanisms have been impaired, preserved, and compensated for in such cases. And animal studies can support invasive measures and controlled environments not possible in human studies, even if the lessons learned may not always generalize to other species. All these methods are generally appreciated in the context of their strengths and their limitations.

Computational models of development, and of cognition and behavior more generally, similarly have their strengths and limitations, but their potential may be less apparent. After all, watching an artificial system on a computer as it develops and behaves does not have quite the impact of observing the behaviors of real children or nonhuman animals, or their corresponding brain images. So why model? Many compelling arguments and examples have been put forth to answer this question (e.g., Elman et al., 1996; Klahr, 1995; O'Reilly & Munakata, 2000; Simon & Halford, 1995a). A common theme to these answers is that it is challenging to understand how change occurs, an issue at the heart of developmental study (Siegler, 1989). Flavell (1984) noted, "[S]erious theorizing about basic mechanisms of cognitive growth has actually never been a popular pasttime. . . . The reason is not hard to find: good theorizing about mechanisms is very, very hard to do" (p. 189). Computational models may provide a particularly useful tool for this challenging task.

One benefit of computational models may be most evident when considering other fields of study, such as meteorology and physics, where the need for models as a complementary approach is highly appreciated. Understanding the weather and the physical world requires comprehending complex interactions among many elements. Various phenomena emerge from such interactions, so that the whole is impossible to understand by considering the elements in isolation. As a simple example, consider two gears of different sizes that can interlock. To understand how they behave, it is insufficient to consider each in isolation. Instead, behavior emerges from the interaction of the two gears, with the smaller gear driving the larger gear to yield a decrease in rotational speed and an increase in torque. As the interactions among elements become more intricate, as in the weather and physics, computational models become increasingly important. Such models allow the observation and manipulation of interactions among elements and associated emergent phenomena. Similarly, models can be essential in helping us comprehend the intricacies of all the interacting elements that produce our thoughts and behaviors. And, understanding this complexity may be even more challenging during intense periods of change in thinking and behaving, as observed during childhood. Thus, one reason to use models in the study of development is the extraordinary *complexity* of the issues under question; development is far too complicated to be defined solely in terms of simple processes that can be captured through purely verbal description. As other methods become increasingly sophisticated, providing large amounts of detailed information about our behaviors and their neural bases, computational models will only become more important in helping to make sense of this complexity.

A second answer to the question of "Why model?" focuses on the need to be explicit about assumptions and constructs in theory development and evaluation. Purely verbal theories may rely on constructs that are not specified well enough to be rigorously tested or understood. The Piagetian notions of assimilation and accommodation were criticized in this regard:

> For 40 years now we have had assimilation and accommodation, the mysterious and shadowy forces of equilibration, the Batman and Robin of the developmental processes. What are they? How do they do their thing? Why is it after all this time, we know no more about them than when they first sprang on the scene? What we need is a way to get beyond vague verbal statements of the nature of the developmental process. (Klahr, 1982, p. 80)

Klahr (1995) also said of one of Piaget's descriptions of assimilation and accommodation, "Although it has a certain poetic beauty, as a scientist, I do not understand it, I do not know how to test it, and I doubt that any two readers will interpret it in the same way." Creating a working computational model of such processes forces one to address these issues explicitly and to confront aspects of the problem that might have otherwise been ignored. The resulting model can also be run to generate novel predictions. Thus, creating models can help make *explicit* theoretical assumptions, constructs, and predictions—an essential step in evaluating and advancing theory. Again, as other methods provide increasingly detailed information about brain and behavior, and various theories are formulated to make sense of such data, computational models will only become more important in assessing the viability of such theories.

A third reason to model is that computational models arguably allow the greatest levels of *control* for testing theories. A single variable, such as the firing rate of artificial neurons or exposure to particular words in the environment, can be manipulated in isolation to see the effects on the functioning and development of a simulated system. Multiple variables can be manipulated in a coordinated way to observe their interactions. This kind of control is essential for making headway on some of the thorniest questions in development. Debates about the roles of nature versus nurture, domain-general and domain-specific learning mechanisms, and so on, often hinge on what could (or could not) be learned from general learning mechanisms and exposure to the typical environment. Could infants come to understand the physical world through general learning mechanisms and exposure to objects in the world? Do children require innate, language-specific learning mechanisms to make sense of the language surrounding them? The remarkable degree of control afforded by models allows researchers to test the role of factors in such debates in ways that would otherwise be impossible. As other methods reveal more and more potential factors affecting thought and behavior, models will become increasingly important for allowing a controlled and systematic investigation of the possible effects of such factors.

Finally, models can also be helpful for providing a *unified framework* for understanding behavior (e.g., Anderson et al., 2004; Newell, 1990; Rumelhart & McClelland, 1986b). Such unified frameworks can support more stringent testing because they can be evaluated across a range of behaviors instead of a single phenomenon. Unified frameworks can also encourage more parsimonious explanations, rather than what sometimes seems like a hodgepodge of explanations proposed across development. Infants show a gradual progression in their understanding of object permanence, the continued existence of objects after they are no longer perceptible (Piaget, 1954). Infants first show a sensitivity to object permanence in their looking times to unexpected events with hidden objects (Baillargeon, 1999; Spelke, Breinlinger, Macomber, & Jacobson, 1992), then by reaching for objects hidden in the dark (Goubet & Clifton, 1998; Hood & Willatts, 1986; Shinskey & Munakata, 2003), followed by reaching for objects hidden in the light (Piaget, 1952b). Later still, infants succeed in reaching for an object hidden in a new location after it was repeatedly retrieved from a different hiding location (Diamond, 1985; Piaget, 1954). Some accounts attribute each of these task-dependent developments to a different factor, with motor developments supporting successful reaching in the dark; problem-solving developments supporting search in the light; and working memory and inhibitory developments supporting successful searching with multiple hiding locations (e.g., Baillargeon, Graber, DeVos, & Black, 1990; Diamond, 1985; Willatts, 1990). Although each of these independent factors may contribute to the observed developmental progression, more unified developmental processes may also play a role. Models provide a natural framework for exploring such possibilities.

For all these reasons, models provide an important tool for understanding the complexity of development. Models are an essential complement to other methods, and vice versa. And, the need for models should only increase as we learn more about behavior and the brain, and must then formulate and evaluate increasingly complex theories of development.

## HISTORICAL CONTEXT

In many ways, the history of information processing approaches to development parallels the history of information processing approaches more generally. These approaches developed as part of the cognitive psychology movement that served as a contrast to behaviorism, they began with relatively rigid notions of cognitive structures and processing, and they became increasingly dynamic and emergent as the field progressed. The behaviorism movement, which focused on explaining behavior without reference to mental processes, dominated psychological work during much of the first half of the twentieth century (Skinner, 1953; Watson, 1912). In sharp contrast, cognitive psychologists in the 1950s began embracing questions about the nature of inner thought processes (Bruner, Goodnow, & Austin, 1956; Chomsky, 1957). Within the field of cognitive psychology, some early information processing theorists focused on the computational bases for thought processes.

A critical step in the development of information processing approaches was the idea that cognitive theories could be stated (and run) as computer programs (Newell & Simon, 1972). Many cognitive theories (e.g., Anderson & Lebiere, 1998; Newell & Simon, 1972) were developed around the computer metaphor, with human cognition viewed as similar to processing in a standard serial computer (e.g., with cognitive processing separated from knowledge, in the same way that the processing machinery of a computer's central processing unit [CPU] is separated from knowledge structures in random-access memory [RAM]). However, the idea of stating cognitive theories as computer programs does *not* actually require that human cognition resemble processing on a computer. In the same way, computer models of the weather do not require that weather forces resemble computer processing. Instead, models can be completely distinct from the computers on which they are implemented and tested.

In fact, other information processing frameworks, such as neural networks and dynamic systems, increased in prominence in part as challenges to some of the more rigid notions of cognitive processing associated with the computer metaphor. In neural network and dynamic system frameworks, the lines between knowledge and processing are relatively blurred. Much of cognitive processing occurs in parallel, rather than serially. And thinking unfolds in an emergent, dynamic way, through the interactions of many low-level processes. Over time, production systems have also incorporated some of these characteristics (e.g., Anderson, 1983).

Information processing approaches to development followed a similar chronology. With Piaget's (1952b, 1954) extensive observations and theorizing about children's thinking, the field of cognitive development was born. The relevance of information processing approaches for the study of development was noted early in their history:

> If we can construct an information-processing system with rules of behavior that lead it to behave like the dynamic system we are trying to describe, then this system is a theory of the child at one stage of the development. Having described a particular stage by a program, we would then face the task of discovering what additional information-processing mechanisms are needed to simulate developmental change—the transition from one stage to the next. That is, we would need to discover how the system could modify its own structure. Thus, the theory would have two parts—a program to describe performance at a particular stage and a learning program governing the transitions from stage to stage. (Simon, 1962, pp. 154–155)

According to this view, developmental processes can be described in terms of programs that transform earlier stages into later ones, and the stages themselves can also be described in terms of a different set of programs. Many early production systems of development fit this view, in which programs for performance in a given stage were distinct from programs for transitions between stages (Baylor & Gascon, 1974; Klahr & Wallace, 1976; Young, 1976). Just as some rigid distinctions in cognitive processing were blurred over time within information processing approaches more generally, this distinction between performance and transition mechanisms in development has become more blurred as the field has progressed (Klahr & MacWhinney, 1998). In many recent information processing approaches, transition mechanisms operate throughout a model's development, and common processes contribute to a model's stable performance and transitions between stable periods.

The point about distinguishing between models and computers has not always been appreciated in the context of information processing models of development. Such approaches have been criticized because "A system that cannot grow, or show adaptive modification to a changing environment, is a strange metaphor for human thought processes which are constantly changing over the life span of an individual." (Brown, 1982). Because models and the computers they run on are distinct, this criticism can apply to computers without applying to the computational models running on them (Klahr & MacWhinney, 1998). This point should become clear in the context of the numerous adaptively modifying models described in this chapter.

Because the information processing umbrella is so broad, including a wide range of cognitive theories, many other historical developments were fairly specific to particular variants of information processing approaches. Advances in neurobiology and neurally inspired models and theories (Hebb, 1949; McCulloch & Pitts, 1943; Rosenblatt, 1958; Shepherd, 1992) were particularly informative for the development of neural network approaches. Advances in the understanding of complex systems at the biological, mathematical, and psychological levels (Kuo, 1967; Lehrman, 1953; Lewin, 1936; von Bertalanffy, 1968; Waddington, 1957) laid the foundation for dynamic systems approaches.

Building on such foundations, and on the key idea that cognitive theories can be stated as computer programs, other major contributions in the history of information processing approaches took the form of introductory texts, which often included computational models for the reader to explore. Such introductory texts played a large role in widely disseminating ideas behind production systems (Anderson, 1976; Newell & Simon, 1972), neural network models (McClelland & Rumelhart, 1986; Rumelhart & McClelland, 1986b), and dynamic systems approaches (Kelso, 1995). Similarly, introductory texts arguably generated a great deal of interest and activity in investigating developmental questions through information processing approaches, with neural networks (Elman et al., 1996; Plunkett & Elman, 1997), dynamic systems (Thelen & Smith, 1994), and production systems (Klahr & Wallace, 1976).

## OVERVIEW AND EXAMPLE OF EACH KIND

This section focuses on four major types of information processing approaches: production systems, neural networks, dynamic systems, and ad hoc models. Each type is first considered in isolation, in terms of the basic assumptions and components of the approach, and the kinds of applications to development that have been investigated, with one example considered in detail. At the end of this section, broad comparisons are drawn across some of these types of information processing approaches. The next section provides more detailed comparisons, by evaluating different models of the same developmental phenomena.

## Production Systems

There are many variations of production systems, such as SOAR (Newell, 1990), ACT-R (Anderson & Lebiere, 1998), and 3CAPS (Just & Carpenter, 1992).

### Basics

As described in many sources (e.g., Anderson, 1993; Klahr, Langley, & Neches, 1987; Klahr & MacWhinney, 1998; Newell & Simon, 1972), production systems focus on cognitive skills that take the form of production rules. Production systems consist of two interacting structures:

1. *Production memory:* This is the system's enduring knowledge, and consists of a large number of condition-action (or IF-THEN) rules called *productions.* The conditions specify the circumstances under which the production applies. In the case of number conservation (Piaget, 1952a), the condition for one production might be: "If you have a goal of stating the numerical relation between two collections, and the collections had the same number of objects before a transformation and the transformation did not involve adding or subtracting objects" (Klahr & Wallace, 1976). The actions specify the actions to be taken under those circumstances. The corresponding action for the number conservation example might be: "then the rows still have the same number of objects." The conditions and actions for productions can apply to either the external world or to mental states.

2. *Working memory:* This is the system's representation of the current situation and consists of a collection of symbol structures called working memory *elements.* Information in working memory may come from both the external world and through the actions associated with productions.

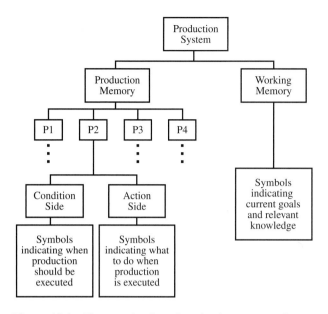

**Figure 10.1**  The organization of production systems. *Source:* From *Children's Thinking,* fourth edition, by R. S. Siegler and M. W. Alibali, 2005, Upper Saddle River, NJ: Prentice-Hall. Reprinted with permission.

The organization of these structures is shown in Figure 10.1.

Distinct processes relate production memory and working memory as follows:

1. *Recognition* or *matching* process: This process finds productions with conditions that match information in working memory. This process can lead to conflict, because several productions may have conditions that match the current state of working memory, and a single production may match the current state of working memory in different ways.
2. *Conflict resolution* process: This process selects which of the matching productions will be applied.
3. *Act* process: This process applies the actions of the selected productions.

This process works iteratively, with each action leading to new information in working memory, so that the three-step cycle begins again. This processing has both parallel and serial components. The search for productions with conditions that match the contents of working memory occurs in parallel. The execution of actions occurs in serial.

Learning in these production systems takes the form of the creation and modification of productions as a result of experience. For example, redundant steps may be

dropped from productions, and two productions may be combined into one, as a result of experience.

### Applications to Development

Production systems have been used for understanding many different aspects of cognitive development, including higher level cognitive processes such as problem solving across different domains (e.g., Klahr & Siegler, 1978; Klahr & Wallace, 1976; Simon & Halford, 1995a; van Rijn, van Someren, & van der Maas, 2003). This kind of tradition is evident in some more recent production systems models. Jones, Ritter, and Wood (2000) used production systems to investigate different theories of what leads to developmental improvements on a problem-solving task that requires constructing a pyramid from 21 wooden blocks. Production systems may provide the most natural fit for modeling such processes, given the way in which higher level information can be represented in production memory. However, as discussed in subsequent sections, other models can be applied to the study of such higher level processes as well. And as discussed next, production systems can be applied to the study of arguably more basic forms of processing.

One example concerns infants' understanding of number. Can infants add and subtract? Do they "innately possess the capacity to perform simple arithmetical calculations" (Wynn, 1992)? Some researchers have argued that the answer is yes, based on infants' looking times to events that lead to expected or unexpected outcomes. In one event, infants see one toy sitting on a puppet stage. A screen is then raised, occluding the toy. Infants then see another toy being placed behind the screen. The screen is then dropped, revealing either two toys (an expected event) or one toy (an unexpected event). Five-month-old infants look longer at the unexpected event (Wynn, 1992). Control conditions demonstrate that infants do not simply prefer to look at outcomes with one toy over outcomes with two toys. Thus, one interpretation is that infants look longer at the unexpected outcome based on their computation of 1 + 1 = 2; after computing that two toys should be on the stage, they look longer at outcomes that violate this expectation.

However, this interpretation is controversial. Many alternative explanations have been proposed for infants' longer looking times to unexpected outcomes. Infants might respond based not on the number of objects on the stage, but on some other factor that varies along with number, such as surface area (Feigenson, Carey, &

Spelke, 2002) or contour length (Clearfield & Mix, 1999; Mix, Huttenlocher, & Levine, 2002). Alternatively, infants might accurately track the objects without performing arithmetic computations (Simon, 1997). Or, infants might look longer at unexpected outcomes due to artifacts of the habituation procedures used in such studies, with infants responding on the basis of which displays are more familiar (L. B. Cohen & Marks, 2002).

Information processing approaches and computational models may be particularly useful in such cases of controversy. Models can help to clarify the assumptions of each theory, and exactly how they explain observed behaviors. Models of alternative accounts can serve as existence proofs that observed behaviors can arise through means other than those proposed. Such models can also be probed and manipulated to assess whether competing accounts represent true alternatives, or whether at core they are relying on common processes.

A production system model was put forth as an implementation of a "nonnumerical" account of infant behavior in violation-of-expectation studies (Simon, 1998). This model simulated infants' longer looking to unexpected outcomes, based on domain-general processes: memory, individuation, object permanence, and spatiotemporal representations. Thus, the model was put forth as an existence proof of how infants' responses can be understood without attributing numerical representations to them.

The model relied on creating indexes for each object encountered: physical object indexes for visible objects, and memory object indexes for objects that become hidden. The memory object indexes copied the spatiotemporal characteristics of the physical object indexes, and supported the formation of predictions. When such predictions were violated, longer looking times resulted due to searches for other possible matches in the display. The productions supporting this process are described in Table 10.1.

This production system model simulated infants' looking times to standard "addition" $(1 + 1 = 2)$ and "subtraction" $(2 - 1 = 1)$ events. The workings of the model, which can be closely inspected, thus suggest the following possibility (Simon, 1997). Infants can encode spatiotemporal information about objects, use such information to individuate different objects, represent the continued existence of objects when hidden, and compare what they remember to what they see. These processes can support the recognition of an unexpected

**TABLE 10.1   Productions**

Longer looking to unexpected events is driven by the final production, which requires extra actions of checking additional locations for information when expectations are violated:

P1: **If** you have newly created physical object indexes and preexisting memory objects, **then** set a goal of comparing the predicted and actual states of the world.

P2: **If** your goal is to compare the predicted and actual states of the world, **then** set a goal of carrying out a one-to-one match process for each prediction.

P3: **If** your goal is to compare the predicted and actual states of the world, **and** you know the result of that comparison, then terminate looking.

P4: **If** your goal is to carry out a one-to-one match process for a prediction, **then** set a goal of seeing if a preexisting memory object matches a physical object.

P5: **If** your goal is to see if a preexisting memory object matches a physical object, **and** a match occurs, then verify the prediction for that preexisting memory object and move on to predictions for other preexisting memory objects.

P6: **If** your goal is to see if a preexisting memory object matches a physical object, **and** a match does not occur, **then** search other locations for other possible physical object matches.

Adapted from Simon's (1998) nonnumerical production system model of infant behavior in violation-of-expectation studies.

event, without requiring numerical representations or calculations. Thus, a "$1 + 1 = 1$" event can be recognized as unexpected simply because an object and another object are expected, but the display reveals only an object. In the same way, the sudden disappearance of an object can be recognized as unexpected, simply because an object was expected, and not because $1 - 0 = 1$.

The working production system model allows various questions to be asked of this nonnumerical account. Is a nonnumerical account sufficient to explain the range of behaviors observed in infants, and could these be simulated within a single model? Would Simon's (1997) model be able to simulate infants' sensitivity to the ordinal relations of numbers (Brannon, 2002)? These kinds of questions highlight strengths of information processing approaches and computational models; the explicitness of assumptions can lead to a honing of theoretical claims (e.g., what it means for processes to be numerical or nonnumerical) and testing of behavioral predictions.

## Neural Networks

Neural network models are also known as connectionist or parallel distributed processing models. Each of these names captures aspects of how processing occurs in these models, in parallel across a network of interconnected nodes.

## Basics

There are many variations of neural network models (e.g., Arbib, 2002), but all models share the common features of units and weights (McClelland & Rumelhart, 1986; O'Reilly & Munakata, 2000; Rumelhart & McClelland, 1986b):

- *Units* are neuronlike entities that represent information through their activity, which can be communicated to other units.
- *Weights,* or connections, link units to one another. The strength of connections changes through learning, in a manner akin to changes in the efficacy of synapses with learning.

Information is represented in neural network models in terms of patterns of activation across units. Units are typically organized into layers, such as an input layer that represents information available in the environment, an output layer that represents the network's actions or decisions, and hidden layers in between that allow patterns of activity to be transformed between the input and output layers. The activity of any given unit is a function of the activity of other units and the strength of the connections between units.

Representations of information in neural networks are often distributed, graded, and interactive. For example, a network's representation of the concept of number might be distributed across multiple units in the network, which also participate in the representation of related concepts (e.g., quantity and counting). These units can vary in their levels of activation, supporting gradedness in the strength of the associated concepts. And, because of the connections that send activity from one unit to another, networks of units can be highly interconnected, leading to interactive representations that can have large effects on one another.

Learning occurs through changes to connections between units. A number of learning algorithms have been investigated through neural network models. Two broad classes can be delineated (O'Reilly & Munakata, 2000): error-driven and self-organizing learning. Error-driven learning is guided by the goal of reducing errors, mea-

sured as a function of the difference between target activations and a network's actual activations. Such targets can come from various sources, such as a teacher explicitly correcting a student's behavior, the environment providing a target signal for one's expectations about what will happen next, and a person's goal for a motor action providing a target signal for the attempted motor action. Backpropagation (Rumelhart, Hinton, & Williams, 1986a) is one of the most common variants of error-driven learning algorithms.

Self-organizing learning entails forming representations that capture important aspects of the environmental structure, based on patterns of simultaneous activation among processing units. Hebbian learning algorithms (e.g., Oja, 1982), whereby "units that fire together, wire together," are one of the most common forms of self-organizing learning algorithms. Algorithms have also been developed that combine error-driven and self-organizing learning, and demonstrate how each benefits from the other (O'Reilly & Munakata, 2000).

## Applications to Development

Neural network models have been applied to a broad range of domains in the study of cognitive development (see reviews in Elman et al., 1996; Munakata & McClelland, 2003; Quinlan, 2003; Shultz, 2003), including language (Elman, 1993; Plunkett & Marchman, 1993; Seidenberg & McClelland, 1989), categorization (Mareschal & French, 2000; Rogers & McClelland, 2004), and object knowledge (Mareschal, Plunkett, & Harris, 1999; Munakata, McClelland, Johnson, & Siegler, 1997). Many of these models have been focused on understanding the kinds of learning processes and representational changes that support the changes observed in infants and children during development. Most of these models have focused on typical development. However, as discussed next, neural network models can also be informative in the study of atypical development, given their abilities to capture nonlinear dynamics and emergent properties of complex developing systems (Morton & Munakata, 2005).

In the study of developmental disorders, the nature-nurture debate takes a familiar form. Early arguments pitted genetic contributions against environmental ones, whereas now researchers generally agree that both contribute in important ways. Nonetheless, two contrasting perspectives can still be identified (Karmiloff-Smith,

2005). A *modular* approach assumes (implicitly or explicitly) a static view of brain function, in which neural systems or modules are innately specified for particular functions. From this perspective, developmental disorders arise due to genetic alterations that target particular associated cognitive functions. As a result, a developmental disorder may lead to specific cognitive impairments, similar to those observed in cases of adult brain damage. In contrast, within the neural network framework, it is more natural to consider particular functions emerging in particular brain areas through a highly interactive process of development. Rather than different brain regions simply having their functions prespecified, they develop as they do in part because of how other regions are developing and through small differences in start state. From this perspective, developmental disorders emerge through genetic alterations leading to small changes in low level properties of a system's start state that interact with processes of development (Karmiloff-Smith, 1998).

Information processing approaches and computational models may be particularly useful for investigating the complexity of such emergent processes. A number of neural network models have demonstrated how small, quantitative differences in the starting state of systems can lead through a process of development to qualitative differences in outcome (Harm & Seidenberg, 1999; Joanisse & Seidenberg, 2003; Oliver, Johnson, Karmiloff-Smith, & Pennington, 2000; O'Reilly & Mc-Clelland, 1992; Thomas & Karmiloff-Smith, 2002, 2003). Because of the complexity of the developmental process, damage to a system early in development can lead to very different behaviors than damage to the same system late in development (Thomas & Karmiloff-Smith, 2002, 2003).

One model demonstrated how deficits in syntactic processing, observed in individuals with specific language impairment (SLI), can arise through development from small disturbances in phonological representations (Joanisse & Seidenberg, 2003). The model simulated the sentence comprehension profile of individuals with SLI across sentences of varying complexity. Thus, the model demonstrated how apparently specific deficits can arise through low-level variations, rather than the genetic specification of cognitive modules.

The model's task was to map sequences of words onto their meanings. The model consisted of four layers: a phonological input layer, two hidden layers, and a se-

mantic output layer. The hidden layers sent and received activity from one another, which allowed information to be maintained across several time steps. These layers thus supported the network's working memory, which could aid in the mapping of a word onto its meaning. To explore the effects of small differences in start state, two versions of this model were trained: an intact version, and a version in which the phonological inputs to the network were distorted through the addition of a small amount of noise.

These networks were trained on a corpus of 40,000 sentences that varied in syntactic complexity. Sentences were presented one word at a time, and the networks had to identify the meaning of and syntactic dependencies between each word to activate an appropriate set of units in the semantic output layer. For example, the sentence "John says Bill likes himself" was presented to the network as "John" "says" "Bill" "likes" and "himself." After the presentation of the final word "himself," the network was trained to activate the meaning of this word in this context: the [MALE], [REFLEXIVE-PRONOUN], [HUMAN], and [BILL] units of the semantic output layer. After training, syntactic processing was tested using novel sentences that were not part of the training corpus. The test set included sentences with reflexives that could only be resolved syntactically (e.g., "Harry says Bob likes himself"), and similar sentences but with nouns or reflexives modified so that the reflexive could be resolved with the help of gender information (e.g., "Sally says Bob likes himself").

The intact network performed near ceiling on both sets of sentences, simulating the performance of typical individuals. In contrast, the network with phonological deficits showed a selective deficit in resolving reflexives based on syntactic information alone, simulating the performance of individuals with SLI. Thus, a low-level deficit in phonological processing led to selective grammatical deficits. Specifically, the deficit in phonological processing made it more difficult for the network to form and maintain consistent representations in working memory. For sentences such as "Harry says Bob likes himself," in which the meaning of "himself" could only be resolved on the basis of syntactic information, the network's working memory representations were insufficient to resolve the sentences. In contrast, for sentences such as "Sally says Bob likes himself," which could be resolved on the basis of syntactic and semantic information, the network's working memory representations were more robust to noise, so that these sentences could still be resolved.

## Dynamic Systems

Dynamic systems approaches focus on understanding complex, nonlinear changes in systems over time, through both verbal description and formal simulation.

### Basics

There are many variations in this approach (e.g., von Bertalanffy, 1968; Fischer & Bidell, 1998; Kelso, 1995; Smith & Thelen, 1993; van der Maas & Molenaar, 1992), but most include some form of the following ideas:

- Behavior is multiply determined, influenced by processes at multiple levels, within the organism and between the organism and the environment.
- Systems are softly assembled (Kugler & Turvey, 1987), flexibly adapted in a self-organizing manner, rather than being hard/wired or programmed.
- Some resulting states are more stable than others, and constitute "attractors."

In the case of walking, movements are viewed as softly assembled based on factors such as the environment, level of arousal, leg mass, and so on (Thelen & Ulrich, 1991). Certain patterns are more stable than others (e.g., walking, trotting, and galloping in the case of quadrupeds). This kind of dynamic systems approach contrasts with the notion of a central pattern generator that endogenously generates the neural activation patterns that drive locomotion. Within the dynamic systems framework, one goal is to understand the processes at multiple levels that contribute to behavior, and how different parameter values of those processes lead to different attractors and behaviors.

### Applications to Development

Dynamic systems approaches have been adopted to investigate aspects of development (Lewis, 2000; Thelen & Smith, 1994, 1998) from early work on personality development (Lewin, 1935, 1936), to seminal work on motor development (Thelen, Kelso, & Fogel, 1987), to more recent work in domains that might be considered more cognitive (Thelen, Schöner, Scheier, & Smith, 2001; van Geert, 1998). Much of the work in this tradition has taken the form of verbal theories, using dynamic systems constructs as a metaphor for reconceptualizing

development (Spencer & Schöner, 2003). This is a useful and important step, but implemented models should aid in the assessment of this approach and comparison to alternatives.

One set of implemented simulations focused on cognitive growth (van Geert, 1991, 1993, 1998). The overall approach with these models was to identify a set of relevant variables in the domain of interest, express the relations between these variables in mathematical equations, assign parameter values in the equations, and then run the equations to test the fit of the model's developmental trajectory to the observed behavioral data. When good fits were observed, the models served as a demonstration that development might proceed as hypothesized, in terms of the posited variables, relations, and parameter values.

A specific model focused on lexical and syntactic growth in children (van Geert, 1993). In this case, the relevant variables might include things like the number of words and different syntactic rules acquired at a given point in time. Various parameters to be set in the equations included growth rate (the amount of growth over a specific time interval), and feedback delay (which affected how quickly a given state of the system affected subsequent states). One curve to be fit characterized the number of words in a child's lexicon week by week (Dromi, 1986). Poor fits to the empirical data were obtained with no feedback delay; better fits were obtained with a feedback delay of 2 weeks and growth rate of .71 for the early part of the empirical curve, and with a feedback delay of 1 week and growth rate of .35 for the later part of the empirical curve. Models of this sort have also been applied to fitting curves of various general aspects of development, including discontinuous change (van Geert, 1998).

Clear strengths and weaknesses have been identified with this type of dynamic systems model (Aslin, 1993; Thelen & Smith, 1998). One strength is forcing experimenters to think about their systems in precise ways, by collecting detailed data that are amenable to dynamic models and carefully considering potential contributing components, their relations, and relevant parameter values. Like all models, these models can also lead to empirical predictions that can be tested. However, some examples of this kind of modeling approach have been criticized for being "theory-rich and data-poor" (Thelen & Smith, 1998), with much of the models' components, interactions, and parameters being largely hypothetical.

As a result, the process of curve-fitting may be too unconstrained to be informative (Aslin, 1993).

## Ad Hoc Models

*Ad hoc models* refer to models focused on the information processing demands of the domain under consideration, without being constrained by all the assumptions and claims of global frameworks, such as production system, neural network, and dynamic systems approaches (Klahr & MacWhinney, 1998). Ad hoc models can employ a wide variety of architectures and learning algorithms. For this reason, they cannot readily be compared as a group against other frameworks, and so will not be focused on beyond this section.

Ad hoc models have proven useful in the investigation of strategic development (e.g., Shrager & Siegler, 1998; Siegler & Shipley, 1995; Siegler & Shrager, 1984). Such models have demonstrated how relatively simple processes can support the discovery of new strategies and the making of adaptive choices among strategies—two abilities that children show very early (e.g., Adolph, 1997) and reliably (Siegler, 1996).

A unified model focused on choosing among strategies *and* developing new strategies; these processes had previously only been simulated in isolation across separate models (R. Jones & VanLehn, 1991; Neches, 1987; Siegler & Shipley, 1995; Siegler & Shrager, 1984). The unified model was called SCADS, for Strategy Choice and Discover Simulation (Shrager & Siegler, 1998). This model focused on the development of simple addition strategies and captured many aspects of children's behavior on addition problems, including choosing adaptively among diverse strategies and discovering the same strategies in the same sequence and manner as children do.

The model comprised three broad components:

1. An associative learning strategy choice component that represented strategies as sets of operators (e.g., "choose addend, say addend, clear echoic buffer, count out fingers to represent addend") and recorded statistics about the speed and accuracy of strategies.

2. A working memory system that maintained traces of each strategy's execution and results, so that they were available for analysis.

3. A metacognitive system that analyzed strategies, identified potential improvements, and generated new strategies by recombining operators from exist-

ing strategies. This metacognitive system had three components: an attentional spotlight that increased resources allocated to new strategies, strategy-change heuristics that eliminated redundancy and recognized the importance of order of operations in strategies, and goal-sketch filters that prevented the execution of invalid strategies.

The model began each run with only two strategies: retrieval (providing an answer based on memory) and the sum strategy (put up the number of fingers corresponding to one addend, count, put up the number of fingers corresponding to the other addend, count, and finally count all the fingers up). The sum strategy was chosen often initially, because the system did not have strong enough associations between problems and answers to use retrieval. Attentional resources were needed in this early use of the sum strategy. With continued practice, attentional resources were freed so that the system could discover new strategies. If the strategies passed the goal sketch filters (which required both addends to be represented and used in reporting a result), the strategies were kept. If the strategies were efficient and accurate, they were used more and more. New strategies were also discovered through the elimination of redundant steps in existing strategies. The shortcut sum strategy (put up fingers for both addends and count them once) was formed from the sum strategy, by dropping the redundant steps of first counting the fingers for each addend. Next, the redundancy of counting the first addend could be dropped to simply state the value of that addend and count from there. This strategy was more efficient when starting with the larger addend, leading to the min strategy (counting up from the larger addend).

From these basic processes, the model chose adaptively among diverse strategies and discovered the same strategies in the same sequence and manner as children. The adaptive choice reflected the model's associative learning of the strengths of various strategies, based on their associated speeds and accuracies. The model's strategy discovery process was based on fairly simple constraints: satisfying the basic goal sketch, eliminating redundancy, and attending to the importance of order of operations. These constraints were sufficient to yield the same strategies that children use. Moreover, because these processes could occur whenever attentional resources were available, the model discovered new strategies in a manner paralleling that of children; for example, following correct as well as incorrect performance, and without requiring trial-and-error learning. The model discovered new strategies in the same order as children, in part through dropping redundant steps from one strategy to create a new strategy.

In this way, the SCADS model provided insight into the possible processes underlying children's strategy discovery and choice. What might otherwise seem like mysterious processes may be driven by relatively basic processes of associative learning and heuristic knowledge use.

## General Comparisons across Frameworks

Comparisons among information processing approaches are most straightforward in the context of different models of the same phenomenon, which is the focus of the next section. This section first briefly considers some general comparisons that may be drawn across production systems, neural network, and dynamic systems approaches. This is a difficult exercise, given the many varieties of each type of information processing approach. It is no coincidence that others who have attempted such comparisons have introduced them as "open to extensive criticism" (Thelen & Bates, 2003) or noted that others are likely to question and argue with the comparisons (Anderson & Lebiere, 2003). The same applies to the current comparison, summarized in Table 10.2. Dynamic systems approaches could be viewed as an overarching theory that includes dynamic models of all kinds, including neural network models as one particular case. And, for each characterization listed for each approach, exceptions can probably be found. But these characterizations capture some general differences between these approaches as they have typically been investigated.

### Representations

Historically, these three approaches have been quite different in their treatment of mental representations.

Production systems focused on a symbolic level of representations, with working memory consisting of symbol structures and production memory taking the form of If-Then propositions. Neural network models focused on a subsymbolic level of representations, the "microstructure of cognition" (Rumelhart & McClelland, 1986b) with representations distributed across connections and patterns of activation. Dynamic systems researchers largely eschewed the "R-word," because of its possible connotation of a static entity sitting in the head (see discussion in Spencer & Schöner, 2003; Thelen & Bates, 2003).

Again, none of these characterizations are absolute. Production systems have incorporated continuous and noisy activation values (e.g., Anderson & Lebiere, 1998; Just & Carpenter, 1992), and neural network models have been used to address the development of symbol-like rules (Rougier, Noelle, Braver, Cohen, & O'Reilly, 2005). And some recent dynamic systems models have investigated representations, at a subsymbolic level, in terms of particular states of a system at particular times (Spencer & Schoner, 2003).

### Relative Strengths and Weaknesses

Each approach has its relative strengths and weaknesses, which in some cases may be viewed as trade-offs, where one feature is emphasized at the expense of another. Production systems may have a relative strength in simulating flexible behavior because complex behaviors can be handled through sequences of productions (e.g., Taatgen, 2002), and symbolic representations can be used flexibly across variations in perceptual input. However, the flexibility of these models might come at the cost of being less suited to capture emergent effects in cognition. Small changes in perceptual processing can lead to large changes at the cognitive level, as explored in the study of developmental

**TABLE 10.2  Comparison of Three Major Information Processing Frameworks**

|  | Production Systems | Neural Networks | Dynamic Systems |
|---|---|---|---|
| Representations | Symbolic | Subsymbolic | Initially unaddressed, now subsymbolic |
| Relative strength | Flexible behavior | Biological plausibility | Embodiment |
| Relative weakness | Emergent effects | Abstraction | Learning |
| Strongest track record | Higher level cognition (e.g., problem-solving) | Language (e.g., reading) | Motor (e.g., locomotion) |

Note: These characterizations are not absolute, and exceptions exist, as described in the text.

disorders. These emergent effects may be better captured by nonproduction systems models, in which knowledge is represented in ways that are less flexible and more tied to specific lower level processes. Neural networks may have a relative strength in biological plausibility, in terms of the mapping between the computational elements of units and weights and biological elements of neurons and synapses, and in the development of biologically plausible learning algorithms and architectures (e.g., O'Reilly & Rudy, 2001). However, because of the way that these models learn based on particular experiences, with units becoming committed to representing specific information, the knowledge in such models has been criticized for not being sufficiently abstract (Marcus, 1998). Dynamic systems models may have a relative strength in their focus on embodiment, and the effects on cognition and development of being situated in a physical body. However, development in these models is often simulated through changes to external control variables, without explanation of how such changes come about. As a result, such models have not addressed learning processes that might underlie such changes.

Again, these characterizations are relative. Production systems have yielded predictions about neural function that have been tested through neuroimaging studies (Fincham, VanVeen, Carter, Stenger, & Anderson, 2002). Neural network models have been used to address questions about processes of abstraction and generalization (Christiansen & Curtin, 1999; Munakata & O'Reilly, 2003; Rougier et al., 2005; Seidenberg & Elman, 1999). And learning has been incorporated into some dynamic systems models (van Geert, 1993).

### Strongest Track Record

Finally, these three approaches have differed in their domains of application. Production systems approaches arguably have their strongest track record in simulating aspects of higher-level cognition, such as problem solving. Neural network models have addressed many aspects of language, whereas dynamic systems approaches have probably had their greatest impact in the study of motor processing. Such distinctions may be based in part on how readily different modeling approaches can fit the empirical phenomena. However, these approaches also have some overlap in their domains of application, or the next section of this chapter would not be possible.

## DETAILED COMPARISONS: DIFFERENT MODELS OF THE SAME PHENOMENA

This section compares different types of models that have been applied to understanding the same developmental phenomena, across the domains of problem-solving, language, and memory. In the problem-solving domain, children's development on the Piagetian balance scale task (Inhelder & Piaget, 1958) has been investigated through production systems and neural network approaches. In the domain of language, children's developing abilities to conjugate the past tense of verbs has been investigated through neural network and production systems approaches. Finally, in the domain of memory, infants' memory for hidden objects as assessed through the Piagetian A-not-B task (Piaget, 1954) has been investigated through neural network and dynamic systems approaches. In each case, the insights afforded by each modeling approach are compared and contrasted.

### Problem Solving: The Balance Scale Task

Children appear to pass through qualitatively different stages in solving certain tasks (Case, 1985; Piaget, 1952b). In the balance scale task (Inhelder & Piaget, 1958), children view a scale with weights on each side at particular distances from the fulcrum, and they must decide which arm of the scale will fall when supports underneath the scale are released. Children initially answer problems randomly, using no apparent rule about the physical properties of weight and distance to guide their decisions. They then employ different information to help them solve the task, progressing through four rules (Figure 10.2, Siegler, 1976, 1981). With Rule I, children attend to only the amount of weight on each side of the fulcrum. With Rule II, children also attend to the distance of weights from the fulcrum, if weights are equal on each side of the fulcrum. With Rule III, children consider both weight and distance information in all cases, but when this information conflicts, children make a random prediction. Finally, Rule IV represents mature knowledge of the task, which requires the computation of torque (sum of weights times distances).

Models of many different flavors have been applied to understanding children's performance on the balance scale task (Newell, 1990; Sage & Langley, 1983; Schmidt & Ling, 1996; Shultz, Schmidt, Buckingham, & Mareschal, 1995). For purposes of comparison,

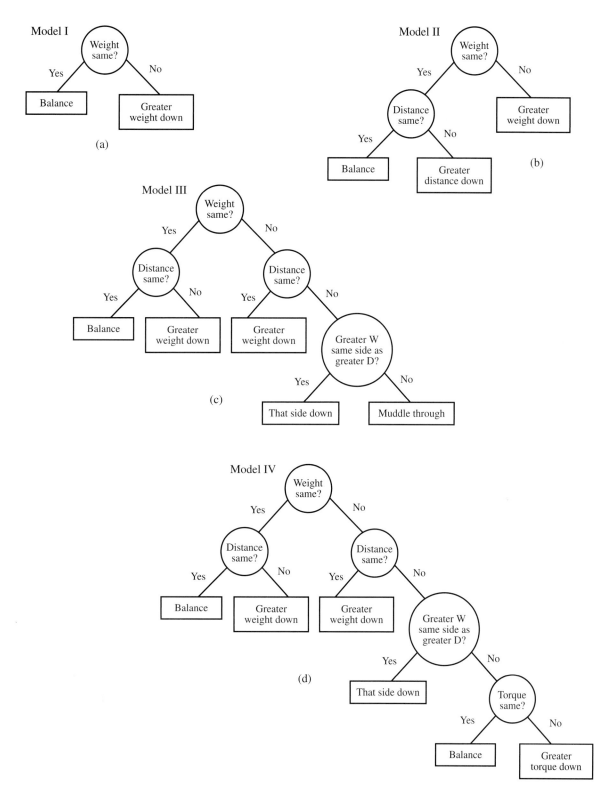

**Figure 10.2** Decision tree representation of children's rules on the balance scale task. *Source:* "The Representation of Children's Knowledge" (pp. 61–116), by D. Klahr and R. S. Siegler, in *Advances in Child Development and Behavior,* volume 12, H. W. Reese and L. P. Lipsitt (Eds.), 1978, New York: Academic Press. Reprinted with permission.

the current discussion focuses on an early production system model (Klahr & Siegler, 1978), a subsequent neural network model (McClelland, 1989, 1995), and a recent production system model (van Rijn et al., 2003).

### Early Production System Model

The early production system model of balance scale performance (Klahr & Siegler, 1978) focused on the productions and operators required to carry out the four rules used by children on the balance scale task. Thus, this model provided a more precise characterization of the dynamics of processing underlying the decision tree representation shown in Figure 10.2.

The productions for models employing each of the four rules are listed in Figure 10.3. For each production, the conditions are shown on the left and the actions are

Model I

   P1: ((Same W) → (Say "balance"))
   P2: ((Side X more W) → (Say "X down"))

Model II

   P1: ((Same W) → (Say "balance"))
   P2: ((Side X more W) → (Say "X down"))
   P3: ((Same W) (Side X more D) → (Say "X down"))

Model III

   P1: ((Same W) → (Say "balance"))
   P2: ((Side X more W) → (Say "X down"))
   P3: ((Same W) (Side X more D) → (Say "X down"))
   P4: ((Side X more W) (Side X less D) → muddle
        through)
   P5: ((Side X more W) (Side X more D) → (Say "X
        down"))

Model IV

   P1: ((Same W) → (Say "balance"))
   P2: ((Side X more W) → (Say "X down"))
   P3: ((Same W) (Side X more D) → (Say "X down"))
   P4: ((Side X more W) (Side X less D) → (get Torque))
   P5: ((Side X more W) (Side X more D) → (Say "X
        down"))
   P6: ((Same Torque) → (Say "balance"))
   P7: ((Side X more Torque) → (Say "X down"))

Transitional requirements

|  | Productions | Operators |
|---|---|---|
| I → II | add P3 | add distance encoding and comparison |
| II → III | add P4, P5 | |
| III → IV | modify P4; add P6, P7 | add torque computation and comparison |

**Figure 10.3**  Production system representations of children's rules on the balance scale task (Klahr & Siegler, 1978). W = Weight and D = Distance. *Source:* From "Information Processing" (pp. 631–678), by D. Klahr and B. MacWhinney, in *Handbook of Child Psychology,* volume 2, fifth edition, W. Damon (Editor-in-Chief), and D. Kuhn and R. S. Siegler (Eds.), 1998, New York: Wiley. Reprinted with permission.

shown on the right. The conditions all check for sameness or difference, in weight, distance, or torque. When the conditions for a production match the information in working memory, the associated action (saying which side will go down) is produced. In the simplest model (employing Rule I), if the information in working memory indicates that the two sides have the same weight, P1 will fire and the response will be to say that the two sides balance. If the information in working memory indicates that one side has more weight than the other, P2 will fire and the response will be to say that side will go down.

The models become more elaborated to capture more advanced rule use (Figure 10.3). The model employing Rule II has an additional production, whereby if the two sides have the same amount of weight but one side has more distance, the response will be to say that side will go down. Based on this specification of what is required to use each rule, it is straightforward to see what modifications are required to progress from one model to the next (bottom of Figure 10.3). Transitioning from Rule I to Rule II requires adding the production that responds based on unequal distance when the weights are equal, and adding operators that encode and compare distances. This model did not actually simulate such transitions however.

### Neural Network Model

Subsequent models have focused more attention on the transitions between rules. A neural network model of the balance scale task (McClelland, 1989, 1995) demonstrated how stage-like progressions from one rule to the next can result from small, successive adjustments to connection weights.

The model (Figure 10.4a) consisted of an input layer representing weights and distances on the left and right sides of a balance scale, a hidden layer with separate units for representing weight and distance information, and an output layer representing the choices for which side should go down: left, right, or balance (if the activations of the two output units were similar). The input layer represented weight and distance information in terms of localist patterns of activation for each side of the balance scale, with each unit corresponding to a certain number of weights or a certain distance from the fulcrum. In the problem shown in Figure 10.4, there are four weights located two pegs from the fulcrum on the right side. These are represented through activation of the corresponding units in the input layer (the 4th weight unit and the 2nd distance unit for the right side).

This model was presented with many balance scale problems of this sort. It received greater exposure to

(a)

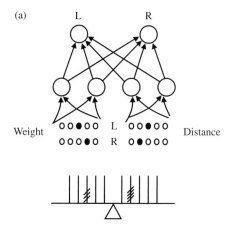

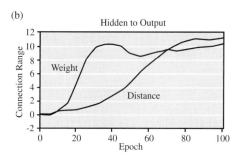

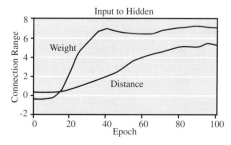

according to the backpropagation learning algorithm: The model activated responses to each problem that was presented to it (which could be viewed as predictions about balance scale outcomes), and its connections were adjusted to reduce errors—the discrepancy between the model's output and the actual outcome. Based on this experience, the model progressed from random responding to Rule I behavior, from Rule I to Rule II behavior, and from Rule II to Rule III behavior. This progression was stage-like, in that the model showed relatively stable performance on each rule, punctuated by relatively rapid transitions between rules.

Why did the model display stage-like transitions? The network's initially random weights were slowly modified with each experience to reduce the discrepancies between the network's predictions about balance scale problems and the actual outcomes. The network first began to develop representations of weight in its hidden layer, given the greater predictive power of this factor in the problems presented. Early in this process, the network's output still reflected random answers because the connections from between the input, hidden, and output layers were not yet sufficiently meaningful. As these connections became more fully formed, units became more distinct in their activation patterns, such that changes to connections could proceed rapidly to stage-like improvements in the network's performance. Figure 10.4b shows these accelerations in the connection weight changes for the connections from the input to the hidden layer (bottom) and from the hidden layer to the output layer (top). The accelerations in the connections for the weight information correspond to the transition to the Rule I stage, and the accelerations in the onset of the distance information correspond to the transitions to Rules II and III. In this way, incremental weight adjustments in neural networks can result in small representational changes that then support relatively fast learning, producing stage-like behavior.

Although the model simulated children's stage-like progression from no-rule behavior to Rule I, Rule II, and Rule III behaviors, it did not capture a clear transition to the most sophisticated Rule IV; instead, at the end of training, the model vacillated between Rules III and IV. This might reflect that a different kind of learning (e.g., based on explicit teaching) may underlie the transition to Rule IV use (McClelland, 1995).

### Recent Production System Model

A recent production system model of the balance scale task (van Rijn et al., 2003) was aimed at addressing

**Figure 10.4**  A neural network model of the balance scale problem: (a) architecture and inputs corresponding to the balance scale problem shown, (b) connection-based knowledge about weight and distance on the balance scale, as a function of learning through exposure to training examples. Incremental changes in connections from the input to the hidden layer (bottom) and from the hidden to output layer (top) support stage-like transitions between rules. *Source:* From "Parallel Distributed Processing: Implications for Cognition and Development" (pp. 8–45), by J. L. McClelland, in *Parallel Distributed Processing: Implications for Psychology and Neurobiology,* R. G. M. Morris (Ed.), 1989, Oxford, England: Oxford University Press. Reprinted with permission.

problems where weight predicted the outcome than to problems where distance predicted the outcome, reflecting the possibility that children have more experience with the effects of variations in weight than with the effects of variation in distance. The model learned several possible limitations with earlier models. Although McClelland's neural network model relied on learning from errors to drive developmental transitions, children can show transitions in their balance scale performance in the absence of feedback. A small percentage of children switched from Rule I to Rule II after being presented with problems that highlighted distance information, without any feedback (Jansen & van der Maas, 2001). These problems involved gradually and systematically increasing the distance between weights and the fulcrum across problems, and then decreasing this distance. In this sequence, 4% of the children switched from Rule I to Rule II and back again at the same point in the sequence (as distance increased and as it decreased); 3% switched from Rule I to Rule II and back again at different points in the sequence; and 9% switched from Rule I to Rule II as the distance difference increased and did not switch back to Rule I. To capture such effects, a model would need to learn not only in response to error feedback.

In addition, the production system model was aimed at capturing qualitative transitions between rules. Although McClelland's model was characterized as capturing stage-like progressions based on quantitative underlying changes, it has been criticized for not being truly stage-like. This model has been criticized for not showing qualitative transitions between rules (Raijmakers, van Koten, & Molenaar, 1996) and for not following a distinct set of rules as analyzed through a statistical technique of latent class analysis (Jansen & van der Maas, 1997).

Van Rijn et al.'s (2003) production system model was aimed at capturing these kinds of phenomena, as well as the basic developmental progression observed from Rule I to Rule IV. The model was composed of IF-THEN productions and knowledge in the form of declarative memory chunks. There were three main factors underlying the model's behavior and development:

1. *Mechanisms:* These included processes such as the composition of new production rules, and the updating of the values associated with such productions (their utility), as well as with declarative memory chunks (their activation levels). Another mechanism was the general strategy of solving balance scale problems by searching for differences between the left and right sides of the balance scale.

2. *Task-specific concepts (weight, distance, addition, and multiplication):* These were represented as chunks in

declarative memory, with their availability mediated by the activation of these chunks.

3. *Capacity constraints:* These limited the number of differences the model could search for in trying to solve balance scale problems.

The concepts and capacity constraints were manipulated in the model to simulate differences across development (Figure 10.5). The task-specific concepts (weight, distance, etc.) were made available to the model at different points in its development, through changes to the activation of the declarative chunks representing those concepts. The capacity limitations were manipulated so that early in development models could search for only one difference between the two sides of the balance scale, whereas later in development, they could search for more than one difference. The concepts and capacity manipulations were motivated by empirical observations about children's encoding (Siegler, 1976; Siegler & Chen, 1998) and developmental theories about capacity (Case, 1985).

The model simulated the progression from Rule I to Rule IV and showed stable performance with each rule. Before any of the task-specific concepts were sufficiently activated, the model could only generate answers by guessing, which led to poor performance and low utility associated with this strategy. As soon as the

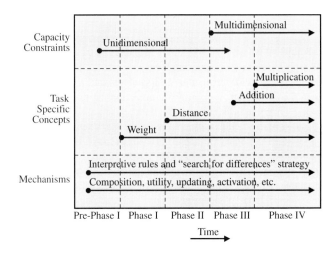

**Figure 10.5**   Availability of components in the van Rijn et al. (2003) production system model of the balance scale task. *Source:* From "Modeling Developmental Transitions on the Balance Scale Task," by H. van Rijn, M. van Someren, and H., van der Maas, 2003, *Cognitive Science, 27,* pp. 227–257. Reprinted with permission.

weight concept became available, the model thus began to use this concept (Rule I). When the distance concept became available, the capacity constraints limited the model to attending to only one dimension at a time. This led to the model attending to distance only if the weights were equal (Rule II). When the model's capacity increased to include more than one dimension, the model then considered weight and distance (Rule III). Finally, when the concept of multiplication became available, the model could then progress to computing torque (Rule IV). Behaviors associated with each of the rules were stable, based on the availability (or lack) of task-specific concepts and capacity, and the utility associated with production rules.

The model also simulated the finding that transitions from Rule I to Rule II may occur in the absence of feedback, and it showed the three types of transition patterns observed behaviorally (Jansen & van der Maas, 2002). As in the behavioral studies, the model was presented with sequences of problems with increasing and then decreasing distance differences, without feedback. The activation formula was revised to include a saliency term, computed as a function of the distance difference. As a result, problems with bigger distance differences were more salient, and led to increased activation of the distance concept. As soon as the distance concept became sufficiently activated, the distance values were used in solving the problem. That is, the model transitioned from Rule I to Rule II. If this occurred while the distance difference was increasing across problems, distance would continue to be used because the concept's activation would be greater from both the previous problem and the increased salience of distance information on the current problem. When the distance differences began to decrease across problems, the distance concept's total activation also began to decrease. Differences between models (e.g., in activation updating) contributed to whether or when this distance concept activation became so low that the model reverted back to Rule I.

### Comparison of Models

A distinct difference among the models of the balance scale previously discussed is whether they attempted to account for the transitions between rules. The earliest model (Klahr & Siegler, 1978) did not, while subsequent models (McClelland, 1989, 1995; van Rijn et al., 2003) did. The fact that both of the subsequent models attempted to account for transitions demonstrates that this is not a distinction between neural network and produc-

tion system models. However, these models attempted to address transitions in notably different ways. The neural network model explained transitions in terms of the same kinds of learning mechanisms applied in a consistent way across experience, with stages arising through changes in representations and how they could be used. In contrast, the production system model explained transitions through the introduction of new knowledge and capacity. On the one hand, these could be viewed as conflicting explanations; the production system model posited changes that are viewed as unnecessary within the neural network. On the other hand, these could be viewed as explanations at different levels; perhaps changes in the production system model could be implemented through changes at the neural network level. For example, apparent changes in capacity can emerge from learning about specific tasks (MacDonald & Christiansen, 2002). Specific models should prove useful in investigating such potential points of contact and contrast between approaches.

Another difference between these models concerns the behaviors that were viewed as central for the models to explain. Although capturing stage-like transitions was central to both McClelland's (1989, 1995) and van Rijn et al.'s (2003) models, these approaches may differ in exactly how stage-like the target behavior was viewed to be. As mentioned, the stage-like progression of McClelland's model was criticized for not being sufficiently stage-like (Jansen & van der Maas, 1997; Raijmakers et al., 1996). This criticism was based in part on the statistical technique of latent class analysis, which was used to try to assess the number and kind of rules leading to observed behaviors on balance scale problems. However, this statistical technique and associated conclusions have been criticized on multiple grounds (Siegler & Chen, 2002). The rules identified through the latent class analysis technique can be very unstable, even within a short test session in which problems are presented in a consistent way. Thus, it is not clear that such analyses truly reveal stable rules being used by children. Furthermore, these techniques have been used to make claims about the abruptness of transitions between rules; however, they would need to be applied to longitudinal data to make such claims, which has not been done.

Other differences between the models might be reconciled in a relatively straightforward way. The van Rijn et al. (2003) model is presented as unique in accounting for transitions between rules in the absence of feedback. This represents an important advance, given that other models had not simulated this effect. However, other models might be able to accommodate such findings in much the same way that van Rijn et al.'s model did. Van Rijn et al.'s model increased activation of the distance concept with increasing distance differences; in the same way, if McClelland's model were to increase activation of distance processing units, it might lead to similar results. Such a finding would be consistent with the manipulation and conclusions from the van Rijn et al. model. Another possibility is that different models might provide different explanations, or different levels of explanation, for the finding that children can transition between rules in the absence of feedback. For example, neural networks might account for such findings through self-organizing learning algorithms (e.g., Hebbian learning algorithms) that do not rely on feedback.

### Language: The Past Tense

In addition to progressing through different stages as described in the balance scale case, children sometimes show U-shaped curves in their developmental trajectories. As these children learn, they first get worse at a task, moving from a higher level of performance to a lower level, and then ultimately progressing back up to a higher level. This kind of behavior should provide important constraints on theories of development, and has been the subject of much discussion (e.g., Zelazo, 2004).

In the case of language learning, children can show a U-shaped learning curve in their production of the past tense inflection for irregular verbs, such as "go." They may initially produce the correct inflection ("went"), but then go through a period where they make overregularizations (saying "goed"), and finally produce correct inflections again. Why children show such U-shaped curves in the learning of the past tense has been the source of considerable debate (e.g., Marcus et al., 1992; McClelland & Patterson, 2002b; Pinker & Prince, 1988; Pinker & Ullman, 2002; Plunkett & Marchman, 1993). In what follows, we consider answers provided through investigations with neural network (e.g., Rumelhart & McClelland, 1986a) and production system models (Taatgen & Anderson, 2002).

#### Neural Network Models

Neural network models of past tense learning have been used to investigate how U-shaped learning curves might arise through a single representational system, which handles both regular and irregular verbs (Daugherty &

Seidenberg, 1992; Hare & Elman, 1992; MacWhinney & Leinbach, 1991; Plunkett & Juola, 1999; Plunkett & Marchman, 1991, 1993, 1996; Rumelhart & McClelland, 1986a). Such models have been presented with the task of mapping word stems (such as "go") onto their past tense forms ("went"), and have learned through error-driven algorithms. Thus, they learned from changes to connection weights that reduced the discrepancies between their outputs and target outputs. Although children do not often receive explicit error feedback on their syntactic errors (Pinker, 1984), they might receive implicit feedback by comparing their guesses about what inflected form they would hear with what they actually heard.

Rumelhart and McClelland (1986a) presented the first attempt to explain the U-shaped overregularization curve in a single representational system. This model consisted primarily of two layers that mapped a phonological input representation of a word stem to a phonological output representation of the past tense of that stem. With repeated exposures to words, connections in this network were adjusted until the model was able to produce the past tense forms of both regular verbs and exceptions. The network also included a fixed encoding network on the input side that converted representations from a string of individual phonemes to conjunctive representations of phonemes, and a fixed decoding network on the output side that performed the reverse conversion. In this single system, the same units and connections were used for processing regulars and exceptions. As a result, the model naturally handled a key aspect of exception words: They tend to show similarities with regular words, and thus have been termed "quasi-regular" (McClelland & Patterson, 2002b; Plaut, McClelland, Seidenberg, & Patterson, 1996). The majority of exception past tenses in English end in /d/ or /t/ (e.g., had, told, cut, slid, taught), as do regular past tenses. Of the exception past tenses that do not show this pattern, most are quasi-regular in other ways, such as in preserving the consonants from the stem in the past tense form (e.g., sing-sang, rise-rose). Given this structure to the language, the model could leverage the same units and connections developed for mapping the regular past tense in forming past tenses of exception words.

The model also simulated the U-shaped overregularization curve (Figure 10.6); however, it was heavily criticized for relying on questionable manipulations in the training set for this effect (Pinker & Prince, 1988). The model was initially trained on a corpus of 10 verbs (8 ir-

(a)

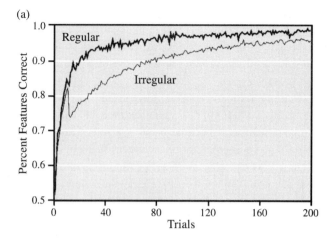

(b)

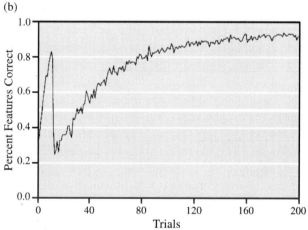

**Figure 10.6**    Performance of a neural network model of past tense learning broken down by (a) proportion of correct responses and (b) overregularization (computed as irregular correct/irregular correct + irregular regularized). *Source:* From "On Learning the Past Tenses of English Verbs" (pp. 216–271), by D. E. Rumelhart and J. L. McClelland, in *Parallel Distributed Processing: Vol. 2. Psychological and Biological Models,* J. L. McClelland, D. E. Rumelhart, and PDP Research Group (Eds.), 1986, Cambridge, MA: MIT Press. Reprinted with permission from MIT Press.

regular and 2 regular); then 410 verbs (most of which were regulars) were suddenly added to the corpus. This sudden addition of regular words drove the onset of overregularization, as connection weights were adjusted to reduce errors on regular words. These changes led to an increased tendency of the model to regularize in forming the past tense, even with exception words. However, there is no evidence of such a shift in the input to children.

As reviewed elsewhere (e.g., O'Reilly & Munakata, 2000; Taatgen & Anderson, 2002), subsequent neural

network models have aimed to demonstrate how U-shaped overregularization curves can result without questionable manipulations of the training corpus. These models have provided various advances, such as incorporating semantic constraints (e.g., Joanisse & Seidenberg, 1999) and investigating interactions in the acquisition of verb and noun morphology (Plunkett & Juola, 1999). However, these models have not been completely successful in capturing the U-shaped pattern of learning. Models using a static training corpus failed to show an early correct period before overregularization (MacWhinney & Leinbach, 1991; Plunkett & Marchman, 1991). Other models that did show the full U-shaped overregularization curve included manipulations of the training environment (Plunkett & Juola, 1999; Plunkett & Marchman, 1993). Some of these manipulations were not necessary for models to show U-shaped learning (Plunkett & Marchman, 1996). And, attempts were made to justify some manipulations by drawing a distinction between what children perceive and produce and a subset of this information (which served as input to the networks) that drives children's learning (Plunkett & Marchman, 1993). However, a more complete account would show how a model internally focuses on such a subset of information, rather than relying on external manipulations of the training environment.

### Production System Model

A production system model of learning the past tense (Taatgen & Anderson, 2002) was used to investigate how U-shaped learning curves might arise through a dual representational system—one system that memorizes specific examples, and a second system that learns the rule to produce regular past tenses (Marcus et al., 1992; Pinker & Prince, 1988). The production systems approach focused on the costs and benefits of regular and irregular verbs. Regular verbs have an advantage in memory demands since only one rule needs to be remembered, whereas irregular past tense words have an advantage in usually being slightly shorter than regular past tense words. Thus, each type of verb has associated costs and benefits. The particular strategy used for forming the past tense at any given time depends on the balance between such costs and benefits, which is a function of the frequency of the words and the previous success of different strategies.

The model began with three strategies for producing a past tense from the stem of a verb:

1. *Retrieval:* The model retrieved the past tense from declarative memory, if it was sufficiently active.

2. *Analogy:* The model retrieved a past tense from memory and used it as a template. This strategy was implemented through two rules, the first focusing on the suffix (e.g., "ed"), the second focusing on the stem (e.g., "walk"). The first rule retrieved a past tense from memory; if the past tense had a suffix, it was copied into the suffix for the current word's past tense. If the goal was to produce the past tense of "walk" and the model retrieved the past tense "followed" from memory, the "ed" suffix from "followed" would be copied into the suffix for the past tense of "walk." The second rule retrieved a past tense from memory; if the stem was identical in the past and present tense forms of that word, the stem for the current word's past tense was copied in an analogous way. That is the stem for the past tense was set to be identical to the stem for the present tense. If the goal was to produce the past tense of "walk" and the model retrieved the past tense "followed" from memory, the model would set the stem for the past tense of "walk" to be the same as the stem for the present tense ("walk"), because the stem was identical in "followed" and "follow". This rule was relatively costly.

3. *Zero strategy:* The models simply used the stem as the past tense.

New production rules were learned by combining two rules into one rule after they had been used consecutively. And, the number of retrievals from declarative memory was restricted to one per rule, so that when rules were combined, what was retrieved through one rule was substituted into the new rule. The regular rule was produced under the following circumstances: The first analogy rule (which set the suffix) retrieved a regular past tense from memory, and then the second analogy rule (which copied the stem) was used. The new combined rule that resulted set the suffix to "ed" and copied the stem from the current word.

The model was presented with the 478 verbs (89 irregular, 389 regular) that children or their parents use (Marcus et al., 1992), according to their frequency (Francis & Kucera, 1982). For each word, the model's goal was to produce the past tense. The model learned by adding past tenses it perceived and produced to its declarative memory, by producing new production rules, and by updating its production rules based on their execution times. None of the three initial rules (zero, re-

trieve, and analogy) was particularly effective at the start. Before the model knew how to inflect any verbs, retrieval and analogy failed, so the model could only use the zero rule, producing the stem of a word as the past tense.

Changes in the model's production rules across learning are shown in Figure 10.7. As the model learned more examples, retrieval became a more viable strategy, for words that were sufficiently active in memory. Higher frequency words were more active, and thus more likely to be retrieved. When words were not sufficiently active to be retrieved, analogy was a viable strategy, since other words could be retrieved as templates.

The model required a certain amount of experience before new rules such as the regular rule appeared, for two reasons. First, the model could form new rules only after it had sufficient experience with the component rules. Second, to learn the regular rule, the model needed to select a regular verb in applying the analogy rule. The chances of this happening were relatively low because the regular verbs were relatively low frequency, and the analogy rule was not used that often because it was costly. Once the regular rule was learned, however, its efficiency made it a viable approach as learning progressed. Retrieval remained the dominant rule, but if the words were not sufficiently active in memory, the regular rule would be applied. With continued learning, most words had sufficient activation in declarative memory for their past tenses to be retrieved, and the

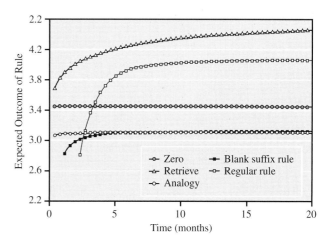

**Figure 10.7** Expected outcomes of rules for the production systems model of past tense learning. *Source:* From "Why Do Children Learn to Say 'Broke'? A Model of Learning the Past Tense without Feedback," by N. A. Taatgen and J. R. Anderson, 2002, *Cognition, 86,* pp. 123–155. Reprinted with permission.

regular rule was used only for low-frequency regulars and novel words.

The model's performance is shown in Figure 10.8. The model improved its performance on regular verbs (shown in both graphs), through both retrieval and regular rule use. Coincident with learning of the regular rule, the model showed a dip in its performance on irregular verbs, shown in the top graph as a decrease in "Irregular correct" and an increase in "Irregular regularized," and in the bottom graph through a standard measure of overregularization: irregular correct (irregular correct + irregular regularized). This model was also able to simulate individual differences in children's overregularization in terms of differences in environmental input; the greater the ratio of inputs from the environment relative to inputs

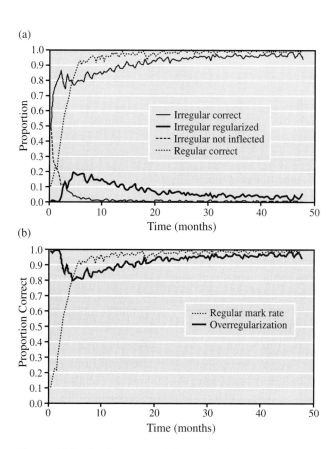

**Figure 10.8**   Performance of the production systems model of past tense learning broken down by (a) proportion of responses and (b) overregularization (computed as irregular correct/irregular correct + irregular regularized) and regular mark rate (computed as regular correct/regular correct + regular incorrect). *Source:* From "Why Do Children Learn to Say 'Broke'? A Model of Learning the Past Tense without Feedback," by N. A. Taatgen and J. R. Anderson, 2002, *Cognition, 86,* pp. 123–155. Reprinted with permission.

from the child's own production, the less overregularization models showed.

### Comparison of Models

The production systems and neural network models both approach past tense learning in terms of producing past tenses from stems. However, these approaches differ in multiple ways and are based on different assumptions about the basis for learning. First, the neural network models learned through error signals, which may be based on discrepancies between a child's understanding of past tense words and what is actually heard in the environment. In contrast, the production system model learned to adjust its rule use based on internal feedback about what it had done. It also stored the past tenses that it had produced and perceived. Second, the neural network models learned through a single representational system that handled both regulars and exceptions; in each case, past tenses were produced through activation of shared units, and were learned through changes to shared connection weights. In contrast, the production system model relied on a dual representation system, one that memorized specific examples and another that learned the regular rule.

Each model may be viewed in terms of its relative strengths and weaknesses. Taatgen and Anderson's (2002) model better captured what is known about the frequencies of different words in the environment, whereas most neural network models relied on changes in the statistics of the training corpus to yield U-shaped developmental curves (Plunkett & Juola, 1999; Plunkett & Marchman, 1993; Rumelhart & McClelland, 1986a). This criticism can also be applied to some symbolic past tense models (Ling & Marinov, 1993), so that it is not specific to neural network models. However, neural network models using backpropagation or other error-driven algorithms may be uniquely dependent on such changes in the environmental input to produce U-shaped learning curves of the past tense (O'Reilly & Hoeffner, submitted). Without such environmental changes, error-driven models might be expected to show no early correct period with exception words or no worsening in performance (overregularizations) across time. If the environmental input led to regulars dominating learning, the weights would favor the regular form of the past tense, so models should overregularize early in learning without showing an early correct period. If, instead, the environmental input provided enough experience with exceptions to support an early correct period, the exceptions should thus be sufficiently dominant to not be overwhelmed by the regulars. In this case, there might be no worsening in performance (overregularizations) with time and learning of the regular past tense. In other domains, error-driven learning models with fixed training environments have shown U-shaped developmental curves (Rogers & McClelland, 2004). However, it remains to be seen whether the environmental structure that leads to such curves is relevant to domains such as learning of the past tense.

A relative strength of the neural network models is their ability to capture important commonalities across regular and exception words, such as the tendency to end in /d/ or /t/ as discussed earlier. Again, such commonalities were handled very naturally in neural network models because connections that supported such endings to past tense forms were shared across regular and exception words. In contrast, the production systems model generated past tenses through the use of one production at a time, which prevented it from leveraging any learning of the regular past tense that would be applicable to learning of exceptions (McClelland, Plaut, Gotts, & Maia, 2003). For any given word, the past tense would be formed either by a production that used the regular rule or by a production that was specific to that word as an exception. There could be no benefit on exception words that shared properties with regulars. This is problematic, given that exceptions tend to be quasi-regular, but might be remediable in such production system models if processing were distributed across multiple, shared productions (McClelland et al., 2003).

Taatgen and Anderson (2002) discuss another difference between models: The production system model could learn its incorrect productions, which may explain why children sometimes do not respond to corrections to their production. Taatgen and Anderson (2002) point out that existing neural network models of past tense production would have difficulty simulating this effect, because no learning occurs based on productions per se, and experience with the correct information should lead to rapid learning of the correct past tense. However, error-driven learning is not always rapid, as evidenced by stage-like stable periods of performance in the balance scale case. In addition, self-organizing neural network models have been shown to learn from their incorrect productions (e.g., McClelland, 2005), and such mechanisms have been incorporated into neural network models of past tense learning (O'Reilly & Hoeffner, submitted; discussion in O'Reilly & Munakata, 2000).

Thus, this difference may not be an inherent one between neural network and production systems approaches.

Finally, the models differ in their levels of analysis, although in some ways they are closer to one another than earlier competing accounts. Graded learning in production rules (Taatgen & Anderson, 2002) is more in line with graded activations of representations (Rumelhart & McClelland, 1986a) and contrasts with earlier, sharper distinctions (e.g., graded versus discrete) between competing accounts (McClelland & Patterson, 2002a). Much of the earlier debates focused on comparing dual representation accounts that were unimplemented (Marcus et al., 1992; Pinker, 1991)—and thus less well specified and less amenable to testing—with single representation accounts that had a fairly extensive history of implementation (Daugherty & Seidenberg, 1992; Hare & Elman, 1992; MacWhinney & Leinbach, 1991; Plunkett & Juola, 1999; Plunkett & Marchman, 1991, 1993, 1996; Rumelhart & McClelland, 1986a). The availability of implemented models of competing accounts should help advance the debate about the mechanisms underlying children's U-shaped past tense learning curves, and inform the study of language learning and cognitive development more generally.

## Memory: The A-not-B Task

The final domain in which comparable models are considered in this chapter is infants' memory for objects that are presented and then hidden. As described, infants show a gradual task-dependent progression in their sensitivity to the continued existence of such objects. Infants appear sensitive to object permanence in violation-of-expectation studies with hidden objects within the first few months of life (Baillargeon, 1999; Spelke et al., 1992), but they fail to search for hidden objects for several more months (Goubet & Clifton, 1998; Piaget, 1954), even after developing the requisite motor and problem-solving skills for retrieving the objects (Munakata et al., 1997; Shinskey & Munakata, 2001; Spelke, Vishton, & von Hofsten, 1995).

Even after infants successfully search for objects hidden in a single location, they fail the Piagetian A-not-B task (Piaget, 1954; Marcovitch & Zelazo, 1999; Wellman, Cross, & Bartsch, 1986). In this task, infants watch as an object is hidden in one location (the A location). Typically, infants are allowed to search for the object, and these A trials are repeated several times. Then, infants watch as the object is hidden in a new location (the B location). Infants often perseverate, reaching back to the previous hiding location instead of the correct one, making the A-not-B error. Infants make such errors from as soon as they begin reaching for hidden objects. And, they continue to make them as they develop, with only a longer delay period needed after the object is hidden before infants are allowed to reach to produce the error in older infants (Diamond, 1985).

Even as infants reach perseveratively to a previous hiding location for a toy, they occasionally gaze at the correct hiding location (Piaget, 1954; Diamond, 1985; Hofstadter & Reznick, 1996). Further, in violation-of-expectation variants of the A-not-B task, infants look longer when a toy hidden at B is revealed at A than when it is revealed at B, following delays at which they would nonetheless search perseveratively at A (Ahmed & Ruffman, 1998).

We next describe and compare neural network and dynamic systems models of the A-not-B error.

### Neural Network Model

A neural network model of the A-not-B error (Munakata, 1998; see also Morton & Munakata, 2002; Stedron, Sahni, & Munakata, 2005) was built on a distinction between active and latent memory traces in the neural network framework (see also J. D. Cohen, Dunbar, & McClelland, 1990; J. D. Cohen & Servan-Schreiber, 1992). Active traces take the form of sustained activations of network processing units (roughly corresponding to the firing rates of neurons), and latent traces take the form of changes to connection weights between units (roughly corresponding to the efficacy of synapses). According to the active-latent account:

- Latent memory traces, subserved primarily by posterior cortical regions, form when organisms change their biases toward a stimulus after processing it, so that they may respond differently to the stimulus on subsequent presentations. For example, after infants repeatedly attend to a hiding location and reach there, they lay down latent traces biasing them toward that location, making them more likely to reach there in the future. These latent traces are not accessible to other brain areas, because synaptic changes in one part of the brain cannot be communicated to other areas. Rather, latent traces can only influence processing elsewhere in the system in terms of how they affect the processing of subsequent stimuli, and resulting patterns of activation.

- Active memory traces, subserved primarily by prefrontal cortical regions, result when organisms actively maintain representations of a stimulus. For example, infants in the A-not-B task might maintain active memory traces for the most recent hiding location of an object. Unlike latent traces, such active representations may be accessible to other brain areas in the absence of subsequent presentations of the stimulus, because neuronal firing in one region can be communicated to other areas.

- Perseveration and flexible behavior can be understood in terms of the relative strengths of latent and active memory traces. The increasing ability to maintain active traces of current information, dependent on developments in prefrontal cortex, leads to improvements in performance on tasks such as A-not-B.

As described in detail elsewhere (Munakata, Morton, & Stedron, 2003), this active-latent account is motivated by behavioral and neuroscience data supporting the existence, localization, and development of these distinct types of representation (e.g., Casey, Durston, & Fossella, 2001; J. D. Cohen et al., 1997; Fuster, 1989; Miller & Desimone, 1994; Miller, Erickson, & Desimone, 1996). This account also shares several features with and builds on existing accounts of perseveration (e.g., Dehaene & Changeux, 1991; Diamond, 1985; Roberts, Hager, & Heron, 1994; Wellman et al., 1986).

The network consisted of two input layers that encoded information about the location and identity of objects, an internal representation layer, and two output layers for gaze/expectation and reach (Figure 10.9a). The gaze/expectation layer could respond (update the activity of its units) throughout the A-not-B task, whereas the reaching layer could respond only when the hiding apparatus was made available for a choice. This constraint was meant to capture that infants are allowed to reach at only one point during each A-not-B trial, when the apparatus is moved to within their reach, whereas they may gaze and form expectations (which may underlie longer looking to impossible events) throughout each trial.

The network's feedforward connectivity included an initial bias to respond appropriately to location information, so that the network would look to location A if something were presented there. The network also developed further biases based on its experience during the A-not-B task. Learning occurred according to a Hebbian learning rule, such that connections between units

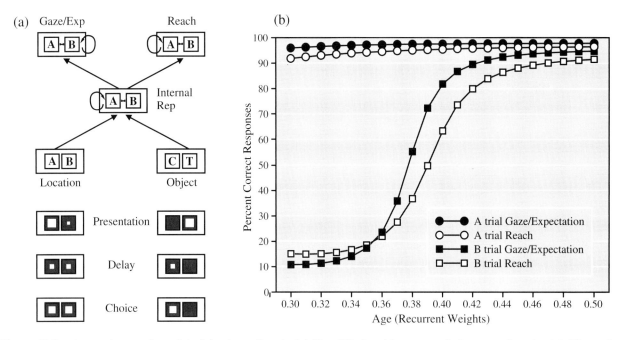

**Figure 10.9**  A neural network model of the A-not-B task: (a) Simplified architecture and elements of an A trial: The activation level of the input units for the three segments of the trial is shown by the size of the white boxes. The "Object" input indicated whether a cover ("C") or toy ("T") was visible. (b) Performance as a function of age: On A trials, the network is accurate across all levels of recurrence shown. On B trials, the network responds non-perseveratively only as the recurrent weights get stronger. The network responds correctly through gaze/expectation earlier in development than through reaching. *Source:* From "Infant Perseveration and Implications for Object Permanence Theories: A PDP Model of the Task," by Y. Munakata, 1998, *Developmental Science, 1,* pp. 161–184. Reprinted with permission.

that were simultaneously active tended to be relatively strong. The network's latent memory thus took the form of these feedforward weights, which reflected the network's prior experiences and influenced its subsequent processing.

Each unit in the hidden and output layers had a self-recurrent excitatory connection back to itself. These recurrent connections were largely responsible for the network's ability to maintain representations of a recent hiding location. The network's active memory thus took the form of maintained representations on the network's hidden and output layers, as supported by its recurrent connections. To simulate gradual improvements with age in the network's active memory, the strength of the network's recurrent connections was increased. This manipulation might be viewed as a proxy for experience-based weight changes that have been explored elsewhere (e.g., Munakata et al., 1997).

The simulated A-not-B task consisted of four pretrials (corresponding to the practice trials typically provided at the start of an experiment to induce infants to

reach to A), two A trials, and one B trial. Each trial consisted primarily of three segments: the *presentation* of a toy at the A or B location, a *delay* period, and a *choice* period (Figure 10.9a). During each segment, patterns of activity were presented to the input units corresponding to the visible aspects of the stimulus event. The levels of input activity represented the salience of aspects of the stimulus, with more salient aspects producing more activity. For example, the levels of input activity for the A and B locations were higher during *choice* than during *delay,* to reflect the increased salience of the stimulus when it was presented for a response.

Like infants, the model made the A-not-B error (successful reaching on A trials with perseverative reaching on B trials), improved with age, and showed earlier sensitivity on trials in its gaze/expectation than in its reach (Figure 10.9b). The network performed well on trials at all ages because latent changes to the feedforward weights, built up over previous trials in which the network represented and responded to A, favored A over B. These latent memories thus supported enough activity at

A that the network's ability to maintain activity at A had little effect on performance. In contrast, the network's ability to maintain activity for the most recent hiding location was critical to its performance on trials, because the network had to maintain a representation of B in the face of the latent bias to respond to A. In particular, the network's connection weights had learned to favor activity at A over B, based on repeatedly attending and responding to the location. With weak recurrent connections, the active memory for B faded during the *delay,* and the network perseverated to A. Stronger recurrent weights allowed older networks to maintain an active memory of B during the delay. These networks were thus better able to hold information about a recent hiding location in mind, rather than simply falling back to biases for previous locations.

The network's greater sensitivity in its gaze/expectation than in its reach can be understood in terms of the different rates of responding in these systems and their interaction with graded strengths of active memories of the correct location. As the network became increasingly able to maintain active representations of a recent hiding location, the gaze/expectation system was able to take advantage of this information with its constant updating, showing correct responding during *presentation* and *delay,* which carried over to *choice.* In contrast, the reaching system was only able to respond at *choice.* Because the network's active memory for the most recent location faded with time, by the *choice* point, the network's internal representation reflected more of the network's latent memory of A. The gaze/expectation system was thus able to make better use of relatively weak active representations of the recent hiding location. In the same way, infants may show earlier success in gaze/expectation variants of the A-not-B task because they can constantly update their gazing and their expectations. As a result, they can counter perseverative tendencies on B trials by gazing at and forming expectations about B during the *presentation, delay,* and *choice* trial periods. In contrast, infants can only reach at the *choice* point, by which time their memories have become more susceptible to perseverative biases.

### Dynamic Systems Model

The dynamic systems approach to understanding the A-not-B error reflects many of the hallmarks of dynamic systems approaches more generally, as discussed earlier. Infants' knowledge of hidden objects is viewed as softly assembled within the particular task context, rather than taking the form of enduring concepts that infants have or do not have. Whether infants err is multiply determined, influenced by factors such as age and delay as already mentioned, but also by many others including number of A trials (Marcovitch & Zelazo, 1999; Smith, Thelen, Titzer, & McLin, 1999) and distinctiveness of hiding locations (Bremner, 1978; Wellman et al., 1986).

A dynamic systems model of the A-not-B error (Thelen et al., 2001) focused on motor planning fields, where visual input and motor memory are integrated, and decisions to reach (e.g., to location A or B) are generated. According to this account:

- Three types of inputs are provided to the motor planning field: Task input (e.g., the location, distinctiveness, and attractiveness of targets at the A and B locations), specific input (e.g., the transient drawing of attention to the B location), and memory input (the history of all previous reaches).

- Motor planning fields evolve over time, based on their prior states and the inputs to the system. Different sites in the field interact, with close sites exciting one another, and more distant sites inhibiting one another. Activations are thresholded, such that only sites with certain levels of activation participate in these interactions.

- Perseveration and correct reaching arise as a function of these interactions in the motor planning fields. In the equations specifying these interactions, small quantitative changes in parameters can lead to qualitative differences in reaching (e.g., to the previous A location or to the correct B location).

As described in detail elsewhere (Thelen et al., 2001), this dynamic systems account was motivated by behavioral and neuroscientific studies supporting the notion of graded, continuously evolving motor plans (Fisk & Goodale, 1995; Georgopoulos, 1995; Hening, Favilla, & Ghez, 1988).

The model dynamics are specified mathematically, with separate equations for computing the task input, specific input, and memory input to the motor planning field. These inputs are then summed. The state of the motor planning field at any given time is a function of those summed inputs and the previous state of the motor planning field.

A key parameter in these equations sets a resting level to the motor planning field. This resting level has important effects on the degree to which the system is driven by inputs to it. With a small value, strong input is required for sites to have sufficient activity to reach threshold and contribute to the motor planning field dynamics. With larger values, additional sites can reach threshold and contribute to these dynamics. Self-sustained excitation in the absence of continual input may be possible under such circumstances.

Two runs of this system with different values are shown in Figure 10.10, with a younger model (with lower value) shown in the upper panel and an older model (with higher value) shown in the lower panel. The task, specific, and memory inputs are shown in the left columns of each panel, and are identical across the two runs. The task input reflects the existence of two identical lids at locations A and B, present across the trial. The specific input reflects attention being drawn to location B transiently, only at the start of the trial. The memory input reflects the longer-term memory of previous trials at A.

The corresponding motor planning fields at the two different ages show different patterns. Although both show greater activation at B than at A at the start of the trial (while there is specific input at B as attention is drawn to the B location), this activation is weaker in the younger model. This activation decays across the delay in the younger model, so that by the end of the delay, activation is greater at A, leading to an incorrect reach. In contrast, the greater activation at B in the older model is maintained during the delay, leading to a correct reach.

These differences in performance were driven solely by changes to the resting level of the motor planning field. With lower resting levels, fewer sites can reach threshold and contribute to the motor planning field dynamics. As a result, the system relies relatively strongly on the input coming into it for sites to have sufficient activity. As the trial unfolds, the system thus shows greater activation at A, because it has greater input from the memory input. In contrast, with higher resting levels, more sites can reach threshold and contribute to the motor planning field dynamics. As a result, the system relies less on the input coming into it for sites to have sufficient activity. Instead, neighboring sites in the system have sufficient activity to stably excite one another. As a result, as the trial unfolds, the system is less sensitive to the greater memory input for A, and can maintain activation for B.

This model did not specifically simulate the differences observed in the measures of the A-not-B task (e.g., reaching versus gazing versus expectation). How-

ever, such differences might be captured naturally within such models, in terms of different equations to capture the distinct dynamics of different behaviors (Thelen et al., 2001), which would lead to differences in motor planning fields and memory input.

### *Comparison of Models*

These neural network and dynamic systems models of the A-not-B task have important similarities and differences (Munakata & McClelland, 2003; Munakata, Sahni, & Yerys, 2001; Smith & Samuelson, 2003; Thelen et al., 2001). In terms of similarities, first, both models focus on the importance of stability in activation dynamics, particularly the stability of currently relevant information. In both models, development was simulated through changes to a single parameter affecting this stability (strength of recurrent connections in the neural network model, and resting level in the dynamic systems model). Small changes to the single parameter in each model led the models to progress from reaching perseveratively to an old location to reaching successfully to a new location. Second, both models could account for a wide range of A-not-B findings beyond those covered here. In both cases, the models could naturally capture why so many factors affect performance, through the influence of such factors on the basic components guiding behavior in the models (e.g., activity levels). Third, both models have been extended to explain cases of perseveration in older children (Morton & Munakata, 2002; Schutte & Spencer, 2002). Fourth, both models have led to novel predictions that have since been supported (e.g., Munakata & Yerys, 2001; Spencer, Smith, & Thelen, 2001). In some cases, the models have led to the same prediction. Both models led to the prediction that infants should show a U-shaped pattern of development on the A-not-B task if younger infants could be tested. That is, infants should first show worse performance with increasing age, and then better performance. This prediction has been confirmed (Clearfield & Thelen, 2000). The models are thus compatible in many ways.

The main substantive differences concern the focus of the models. An important difference is in the focus on learning in the neural network model versus embodiment in the dynamic systems model (see Elman, 2003; Spencer & Schöner, 2003, for discussion of this general issue). Neural network models tend to stress learning as the engine of change in development, whereas in many dynamic systems models, developmental differences

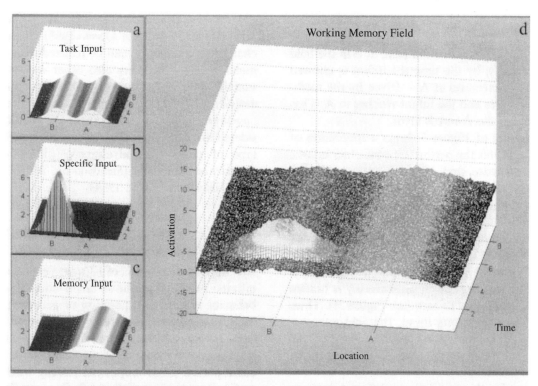

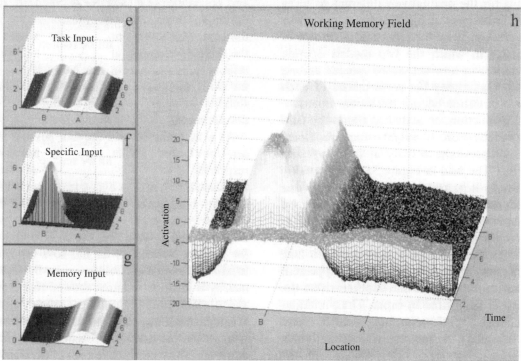

**Figure 10.10** Dynamic systems account of the A-not-B error. The two panels correspond to the model at two ages (two different levels of the resting activity level). Each panel shows the three inputs to the model in the left column, and the resulting motor planning field on the right. In each graph, the x-axis represents location, the y-axis represents time, and the z-axis represents activation. Motor planning fields are referred to as "working memory fields." *Source:* From "The Dynamics of Embodiment: A Field Theory of Infant Perseverative Reaching," by E. Thelen, G. Schöner, C. Scheier, and L. B. Smith, 2001, *Behavioral and Brain Sciences, 24,* 1–86; Adapted from "Bridging the Representational Gap in the Dynamic Systems Approach to Development," by J. P. Spencer and G. Schöner, 2003, *Developmental Science, 6,* pp. 392–412. Reprinted with permission.

are attributed to differences in a control variable whose change as a function of age is assumed but not explained. In the neural network model of the A-not-B task, recurrent connections supporting active representations are posited to increase over the course of experience; the details of how experience may shape such changes have been investigated in various neural network models of object knowledge (e.g., Mareschal et al., 1999; Munakata et al., 1997). In contrast, in the dynamic systems model of the A-not-B task, an external control variable changes as a proxy for development, without an explanation of what leads to such changes. On the other hand, dynamic systems approaches have tended to emphasize the importance of embodiment, with factors such as reaching kinematics, body posture, and so on affecting behavior, whereas such factors have not typically been incorporated into neural network models. The dynamic systems model of the A-not-B task uses specific equations to try to capture some of the dynamics specific to reaching. Although looking behaviors are not simulated, these might require different equations to capture the unique dynamics of the oculomotor system. In contrast, in the neural network model of the A-not-B task, the looking and reaching components of the system are identical aside from how often they update.

Another important difference between the two models concerns the focus on motor planning dynamics in the dynamic systems model versus distinct types of representations in the neural network model. In the dynamic systems model, all inputs are summed to yield their contribution to the motor planning field. The resulting unified field is viewed as an essential aspect of embodiment. In contrast, in the neural network framework, information may be represented in qualitatively different ways (e.g., in synaptic changes versus in the firing of populations of neurons). These distinct kinds of representation may interact in complex ways that are not captured in a single planning field representation.

Additional differences between the models exist, but seem less inherent to the two modeling approaches and so could likely be reconciled. The dynamic systems model includes noise (e.g., the model occasionally reaches to B on A trials), whereas the neural network model does not. The neural network model represents input in terms of a unified representation of the visible environment, whereas the dynamic systems model separates the input into task (static) and specific (transient) inputs.

## GENERAL ISSUES

As reviewed in this chapter, information processing approaches have helped to inform the study of development in many ways. However, the contributions from such approaches have perhaps not always been appreciated to their fullest extent. This final section covers potential criticisms of models that may contribute to this underappreciation, responses to such criticisms, and directions for future modeling work that may have significant impact on our understanding of development.

### Why Model? (Revisited)

Criticisms have been raised to discount the possible contributions of models. In evaluating any specific model, these criticisms are important to keep in mind; however, it is misguided to use them to discount the entire modeling endeavor and what can be learned from models. This argument may become clearest when comparing the process of constructing models with the process of constructing theories. The importance of constructing theories to understand data has long been appreciated across diverse fields. In the study of behavior and cognition, Newell (1973) argued, "You can't play 20 questions with nature and win," in a chapter by the same name. He reasoned that you cannot hope to fully understand the complexity of the human mind by simply posing yes/no questions and collecting data ad infinitum to try to determine the answer. A richer and more complete theoretical model is needed.

Potential criticisms of models could also be applied to theories. In the case of theories, the natural reaction is likely to be one of trying to determine how to address the criticisms and develop better theories, rather than abandoning the entire endeavor of formulating and testing theories. The same reaction is arguably warranted in the case of models.

### *The Indeterminacy Problem*

A common criticism of computational models is that they are powerful enough to simulate anything, so their ability to simulate human behavior is uninteresting (Roberts & Pashler, 2000). Relatedly, multiple different models can be constructed to simulate the same behavior, the indeterminacy problem. They all work and they can't all be right, so the models are too powerful. As a result, simply getting a model to work does not tell us anything about the processes underlying behavior and development. Although these are important considerations, they should help shape the evaluation of models, instead of challenging the modeling endeavor altogether.

First, criticisms about too much power and indeterminacy are relevant for any attempts at scientific theorizing and are not unique to computational models. There are multiple competing verbal theories—of language development, memory development, and so on—that can explain the same data. These theories may be powerful enough to explain such data (as well as new data as it is provided), in part because of the flexibility of positing new constraints on the theories as new data become available.

However, this does not mean that the process of developing theories tells us nothing, in the same way that issues of power and indeterminacy do not mean that developing models tells us nothing. Instead, competing theories and models can be evaluated according to many more criteria than simply accounting for a set of data. For example, which theories or models provide the most coherent, principled account of the data, as opposed to requiring post hoc adjustments to account for each finding? Which provide unique predictions that have been tested and confirmed? Which generalize best to findings outside of those targeted for the theory/model? When multiple models are constructed to address the same phenomena (as in the cases of the balance scale task, past tense learning, and the A-not-B task considered here), this process may be particularly useful in highlighting the relative strengths and weaknesses of different approaches, even if all the models can simulate the main behaviors of interest.

Second, although computational models are very powerful, the contributions from some models have come from instances where they fail. The effects of brain damage in adults can be studied by lesioning corresponding areas or processes in working models (e.g., J. D. Cohen, Romero, Farah, & Servan-Schreiber, 1994; Farah et al., 1993; Farah & McClelland, 1991; Haarmann et al., 1997; Kimberg & Farah, 1993; Plaut, 1995). In these cases, the models were trained to perform correctly, but were informative in how and why they performed incorrectly after damage. Similarly, atypical functioning can be incorporated into models during their development, to observe the effects on the overall system and to compare developmental disorders to cases of adult brain damage (Thomas & Karmiloff-Smith, 2002, 2003). Again, the

original models were trained to perform correctly, but the models were informative in their failures with alterations during different stages of development. Finally, in other cases, failures of models have provided insight into the need for multiple, specialized information processing systems to satisfy computational trade-offs (McClelland, McNaughton, & O'Reilly, 1995; O'Reilly & Munakata, 2000).

### Models Are Too Complex

A related criticism is that models are too complex; given how difficult it is to understand why they behave the way they do, how could they possibly help us to understand child development?

Again, scientific theories in general may be subject to the same criticism. Purely verbal theories might have so many factors, caveats, interactions, and so on that they seem to yield little in the way of understanding what is happening in the child. In fact, when theories seem less complex than models, this may only reflect vagueness about the details of how the theory actually works—exactly the kind of details that must be confronted when constructing models.

However, criticisms of unwieldy complexity do not mean the processes of scientific theorizing or computational modeling should be abandoned. Rather, specific theories and models can be evaluated according to whether they provide coherent and principled accounts. If a complex model or theory simply accounts for existing data, without contributing to a greater understanding of behavior, then the complexity is not worth the cost. However, if a complex model or theory not only accounts for existing data, but provides a satisfying account of the principles guiding behavior, then the cost of the complexity may be worth the benefits to understanding. Again, models may be particularly useful in this trade-off, because complex phenomena can be captured and understood in such models.

### Models Are Too Simple

Another common criticism of models is that they are too simple, so they are unrealistic and cannot inform the study of child development. This criticism might be aimed at various aspects of models, such as the way that they represent the child's environment, the task of interest, the child's thought processes, the underlying biology, and so on.

Such criticisms are relevant for any attempts at scientific theorizing and are not unique to computational models. One verbal theory might not pay sufficient attention to the role of social interactions in a child's development, while another theory might fail to make contact with underlying biological mechanisms or even seem to directly contradict what is known about the underlying biology. However, such limitations are typically viewed as challenges to particular theories, rather than to the whole process of scientific theorizing. In the same way, limitations to particular models should not be viewed as challenges to the whole modeling endeavor.

Models (and theories) are by definition simplifications. Factors that are thought to be relevant are incorporated so that they can be manipulated and tested, while other factors are not incorporated. Thus, simply pointing to a way in which a model is simplified does not constitute a clear challenge to the model. Instead, the more important question is whether the simplifications miss factors that are critical to the behavior of interest, and if so, what are those factors and what role do they play? Models can be particularly useful tools for informing such questions in scientific theorizing, because models help to make explicit which factors are thought to be relevant and which not, and to then support the testing of the roles played by both the factors of interest and other factors.

### Models Are Reductionistic

Finally, another common concern is that models are reductionistic, focusing on low-level mechanisms that cannot possibly capture or inform the study of the richness of human cognition and development. This point also is relevant to scientific theorizing more generally. There is a tendency for sciences to become more reductionistic as they progress. Early in the biological sciences, ephemeral, vitalistic theories were common, where components were posited without physical evidence for them. With the advent of modern molecular biology, the underlying physical components (proteins, nucleic acids, etc.) could be measured and localized, and theories updated accordingly. Reductionism of this sort—reducing complex phenomena into their simpler underlying components—is an inherent part of the scientific process. Verbal theories may reduce the richness of human behaviors down to low-level mechanisms in just the same way as models; models may simply be more explicit about this reduction.

In both cases, the essential consideration may be the complementary process of understanding the complexity that emerges from the interaction of simpler underlying components. Understanding the component pieces alone may not be sufficient for understanding the whole. A complementary process has been emphasized across different theoretical frameworks. Predecessors to dynamic systems theory (von Bertalanffy, 1968) emphasized the importance of relationships among biological elements and the resulting system that required a level of description distinct from that for the individual elements. Physiological psychologists (Teitelbaum, 1967) advocated complementary processes of analysis (dissecting and simplifying to understand basic elements of a system) and synthesis (combining elements to understand their interactions). And, some neural network approaches (O'Reilly & Munakata, 2000) have emphasized that reductionism requires a complementary process of *reconstructionism*. Understanding neurons is not sufficient for understanding human cognition; human cognition emerges from the complex interaction of such components. Thus, the larger phenomenon must be reconstructed from an understanding of the pieces.

## Future Directions

How can information processing approaches and computational models continue to inform our understanding of development? Constructivist models, all-purpose models, multiple models, and accessible models represent directions for future work that seem particularly promising.

### Constructivist Models

Piaget emphasized constructive processes in development, whereby children play an active role in their own development rather than simply being passive recipients of their environments. Children can shape their environments and the kinds of stimuli that are available to learn from, through their actions. Infants who reach for objects receive different sensory information about the objects than infants who simply gaze at the objects. The language children produce affects the language directed at them, the problem-solving skills children demonstrate might affect the kinds of activities they are presented with, and so on.

In contrast, much work within the information processing approach to development has focused on how children react to and learn from a fixed set of stimuli, with less attention given to the complementary process of children affecting their environments. Most models are fed their inputs, stimulus after stimulus, regardless of what they output. Language learning models see sentence after sentence, no matter how poorly the models do in their comprehension. Similarly, models see the same objects in their environments regardless of how they behave toward the objects.

A promising direction for future work thus focuses on models that shape their environments (Schlesinger & Parisi, 2001). How these models behave influences their subsequent inputs, rather than receiving a fixed stream of inputs.

### All-Purpose Models

Most models are designed for and tested on a single task within a single domain, such as the balance scale task, learning the past tense, or searching for hidden objects. Typically, a single model sees only this single task during the course of its development. Again, in contrast, children face a multitude of tasks across a range of domains each day. Capturing this important aspect of processing requires models that take in a variety of types of information and determine how to appropriately process them to perform successfully across numerous tasks (discussion in, e.g., Karmiloff-Smith, 1992; Newell, 1973).

One model representing a step in this direction focused on the effects of engaging in one task versus multiple tasks across development (Rougier et al., 2005). The tasks in this simulation included naming objects, matching objects, and making different kinds of comparisons among objects. Although these are only a small subset of the numerous tasks children face, they represent more variety than models are typically presented with, and they allowed an exploration of the developmental effects of multitasking. The primary finding was that training on multiple tasks led to the formation of more abstract, flexible knowledge representations, which could be generalized to new situations. Thus, such models may yield insight into the developmental progressions leading up to the unique flexibility of human knowledge.

### Multiple Models

Another important step in future work will be the continued comparison of models. Given the indeterminacy problem, it is not enough to have models that simulate data (or theories that account for data). Models must be compared along many other dimensions to support an assessment of how they inform an understanding of behavior and development. This comparison process will be relevant for competing models of the same type (e.g., two production system models of the balance scale task) and for models of different types, which may or may not

be compatible. This chapter focused on contrasts between production systems and neural network models, and between dynamic systems and neural network models, with both important similarities and differences noted. Future work should include additional types of comparisons among the four information processing approaches discussed here and more abstract Bayesian models (Anderson, 1990; Gopnik, 2005; Oaksford & Chater, 1994), more detailed neurobiological models (Medina & Mauk, 2000), and hybrid models that incorporate both production systems and neural network components (Hummel & Holyoak, 1997).

Such comparative work can be very difficult, just as it can be difficult to systematically compare the strengths and limitations of verbal theories. Nonetheless, in both cases such comparisons are critical for advancing the field. Three factors may aid in the ability to make such comparisons in the case of information processing models. The first is the training of researchers who are well versed in multiple modeling paradigms. This will be supported by attempts to compare modeling paradigms explicitly (Anderson & Lebiere, 2003; Spencer & Thelen, 2003). A second step that may make comparing models more feasible is adversarial collaboration (Mellers, Hertwig, & Kahneman, 2001), whereby researchers with different theoretical perspectives agree on criteria and methods for testing their perspectives, and then collaborate on conducting such tests. Finally, the process of comparing models should become easier as research models are made available for others to investigate.

### Accessible Models

Finally, making information processing and computational modeling work more accessible is another important step for yielding the biggest impact on the understanding of development. Although this kind of work has yielded many insights, as demonstrated through the examples reviewed in this chapter, this work has not always been easily accessible to researchers in the field. Part of this problem may be inherent to these approaches, and to any other formal approaches that require the understanding of an overall framework to provide the context of any individual account or simulation. In a commentary chapter in Simon and Halford's (1995b) edited volume of information processing chapters, Klahr (1995) described the collection as:

> not always easy reading. Compared to the standard fare of developmental theory, these chapters introduce a bewildering variety of technical terms, concepts, notation, and

representations. Understanding them requires a familiarity with a technical language that is unlikely to have been a major part of the graduate training of most developmentalists. Both production systems and connectionist models [and he could add dynamic systems to the list!] involve new concepts, new terminology, even new reading styles (when following an account of how a model is organized, how it runs, and how it is matched to the data). p. 368

Although he concluded that these chapters were "worth the struggle" (and hopefully the same applies to this chapter), it will be important to address the accessibility problem where possible in future work. Better methods of analyzing and presenting information processing approaches and computational models may help to clarify their contributions. Clearer graphical representations have been and will continue to be an essential component in this process for conveying the dynamic processes of changes to productions in production systems, to neural network connections and what they come to represent, and to dynamic systems variables and how they interact. And, the more explicit the links can be between processes in information processing models and processes in the child, the better. Explanations of models' behaviors can sometimes be steeped in modeling or information processing terms, without the additional step of explicitly specifying what these processes correspond to in the child. Finally, information processing and computational modeling approaches may become more accessible as the simulations become more readily available, in terms of both basic models that help to illustrate key components of the overall framework, and research models that investigate particular questions of scientific interest. The greater availability of such models will allow more people to manipulate them on their own and observe the effects, so that their contributions can be more accessible.

## CONCLUSION

To return to the questions this chapter opened with: Why do children think the way they do? What leads to the changes they show across development, and to the variations observed across children? This chapter has reviewed insights into such questions from information processing approaches and computational models. These contributions span a range of domains (e.g., problem solving, language, and memory) and patterns of developmental change (e.g., stage-like progressions, U-shaped

learning curves, and task-dependent progressions). Different information processing approaches and models provide different answers to fundamental developmental questions. However, they share a common focus on what information children represent (whether symbolic or subsymbolic), how they represent and process this information (whether through productions or distributed patterns of activity), how these representations guide their behaviors (whether in an abstract, flexible way or in a task-dependent, softly assembled way), and what mechanisms lead to changes in these processes across development (e.g., the combination of productions, the introduction of new knowledge and capacity, or learning mechanisms applied in a consistent way across experience). Many interesting challenges and questions remain in the attempt to understand the behaviors simulated in these models, as well as many behaviors that have yet to be addressed through models. Each information processing account and each computational model raises new questions about children's thinking and development, but these are likely productive questions. Addressing them should be an essential step toward understanding the processes contributing to development. The rigorous test bed of information processing explorations should continue to be instrumental in this endeavor.

## REFERENCES

Adolph, K. E. (1997). Learning in the development of infant locomotion. *Monographs of the Society for Research in Child Development, 62*(3, Serial No. 251).

Aguiar, A., & Baillargeon, R. (2000). Perseveration and problem solving in infancy. In H. Reese (Ed.), *Advances in child development and behavior* (Vol. 27, pp. 135–180). New York: Academic Press.

Ahmed, A., & Ruffman, T. (1998). Why do infants make A not B errors in a search task, yet show memory for the location of hidden objects in a non-search task? *Developmental Psychology, 34,* 441–453.

Anderson, J. R. (1976). *Language, memory, and thought.* Hillsdale, NJ: Erlbaum.

Anderson, J. R. (1983). *The architecture of cognition.* Cambridge, MA: Harvard University Press.

Anderson, J. R. (1990). *The adaptive character of thought.* Hillsdale, NJ: Erlbaum.

Anderson, J. R. (1993). *Rules of the mind.* Hillsdale, NJ: Erlbaum.

Anderson, J. R., Bothell, D., Byrne, M. D., Douglass, S., Lebiere, C., & Qin, Y. (2004). An integrated theory of mind. *Psychological Review, 111,* 1036–1060.

Anderson, J. R., & Lebiere, C. (1998). *The atomic components of thought.* Mahwah, NJ: Erlbaum.

Anderson, J. R., & Lebiere, C. (2003). The Newell test for a theory of mind. *Behavioral and Brain Sciences, 26*(5), 587–639.

Arbib, M. A. (Ed.). (2002). *The handbook of brain theory and neural networks* (2nd ed.). Cambridge, MA: MIT Press.

Aslin, R. (1993). Commmentary: The strange attractiveness of dynamic systems to development. In L. B. Smith & E. Thelen (Eds.), *A dynamic systems approach to development: Applications* (pp. 385–399). Cambridge, MA: MIT Press.

Baillargeon, R. (1999). Young infants' expectations about hidden objects: A reply to three challenges. *Developmental Science, 2*(2), 115–132.

Baillargeon, R., Graber, M., DeVos, J., & Black, J. (1990). Why do young infants fail to search for hidden objects? *Cognition, 36,* 255–284.

Baylor, G. W., & Gascon, J. (1974). An information processing theory of aspects of the development of weight seriation in children. *Cognitive Psychology, 6,* 1–40.

Brannon, E. M. (2002). The development of ordinal numerical knowledge in infancy. *Cognition, 83,* 223–240.

Bremner, J. G. (1978). Spatial errors made by infants: Inadequate spatial cues or evidence of egocentrism? *British Journal of Psychology, 69,* 77–84.

Brown, A. L. (1982). Learning and development: The problem of compatibility, access and induction. *Human Development, 25,* 89–115.

Bruner, J. S., Goodnow, J. J., & Austin, G. A. (1956). *A study of thinking.* New York: Wiley.

Case, R. (1985). *Intellectual development: A systematic reinterpretation.* New York: Academic Press.

Case, R. (1986). The new stage theories in intellectual development: Why we need them, what they assert. In M. Perlmutter (Ed.), *Perspectives for intellectual development* (pp. 57–91). Hillsdale, NJ: Erlbaum.

Casey, B. J., Durston, S., & Fossella, J. A. (2001). Evidence for a mechanistic model of cognitive control. *Clinical Neuroscience Research, 1,* 267–282.

Chomsky, N. (Ed.). (1957). *Syntactic structures.* The Hague, The Netherlands: Mouton.

Christiansen, M. H., & Curtin, S. (1999). Transfer of learning: Rule acquisition or statistical learning? *Trends in Cognitive Sciences, 3,* 289–290.

Clearfield, M. W., & Mix, K. S. (1999). Number versus contour length in infants' discrimination of small visual sets. *Psychological Science, 10,* 408.

Clearfield, M. W., & Thelen, E. (2000, July). *Reaching really matters: The development of infants' perseverative reaching.* Paper presented at the meeting of the International Conference on Infant Studies, Brighton, England.

Cohen, J. D., Dunbar, K., & McClelland, J. L. (1990). On the control of automatic processes: A parallel distributed processing model of the stroop effect. *Psychological Review, 97*(3), 332–361.

Cohen, J. D., Perlstein, W. M., Braver, T. S., Nystrom, L. E., Noll, D. C., Jonides, J., et al. (1997). Temporal dynamics of brain activation during a working memory task. *Nature, 386,* 604–608.

Cohen, J. D., Romero, R. D., Farah, M. J., & Servan-Schreiber, D. (1994). Mechanisms of spatial attention: The relation of macrostructure to microstructure in parietal neglect. *Journal of Cognitive Neuroscience, 6,* 377.

Cohen, J. D., & Servan-Schreiber, D. (1992). Context, cortex, and dopamine: A connectionist approach to behavior and biology in schizophrenia. *Psychological Review, 99,* 45–77.

Cohen, L. B., & Marks, K. S. (2002). How infants process addition and subtraction events. *Developmental Science, 5,* 186–201.

Daugherty, K., & Seidenberg, M. S. (1992). Rules or connections? The past tense revisited. In *Proceedings of the 14th annual conference of the Cognitive Science Society* (pp. 259–264). Hillsdale, NJ: Erlbaum.

Dehaene, S., & Changeux, J.-P. (1991). The Wisconsin Card Sorting Test: Theoretical analysis and modeling in a neuronal network. *Cerebral Cortex, 1,* 62–79.

Diamond, A. (1985). Development of the ability to use recall to guide action, as indicated by infants' performance on A. *Child Development, 56,* 868–883.

Dromi, E. (1986). The one-word period as a stage in language development: Quantitative and qualitative accounts. In I. Levin (Ed.), *Stage and structure: Reopening the debate.* Norwood, NJ: Ablex.

Elman, J. L. (1993). Learning and development in neural networks: The importance of starting small. *Cognition, 48*(1), 71–99.

Elman, J. L. (2003). Development: It's about time. *Developmental Science, 6,* 430–433.

Elman, J. L., Bates, E. A., Johnson, M. H., Karmiloff-Smith, A., Parisi, D., & Plunkett, K. (1996). *Rethinking innateness: A connectionist perspective on development.* Cambridge, MA: MIT Press.

Farah, M. J., & McClelland, J. L. (1991). A computational model of semantic memory impairment: Modality specificity and emergent category specificity. *Journal of Experimental Psychology: General, 120,* 339–357.

Farah, M. J., O'Reilly, R. C., & Vecera, S. P. (1993). Dissociated overt and covert recognition as an emergent property of a lesioned neural network. *Psychological Review, 100,* 571–588.

Feigenson, L., Carey, S., & Spelke, E. (2002). Infants' discrimination of number versus continuous extent. *Cognitive Psychology, 44,* 33–66.

Fincham, J. M., VanVeen, V., Carter, C. S., Stenger, V. A., & Anderson, J. R. (2002). Integrating computational cognitive modeling and neuroimaging: An event-related fMRI study of the Tower of Hanoi task. *Proceedings of National Academy of Science, 99,* 3346–3351.

Fischer, K. W., & Bidell, T. R. (1998). Dynamic development of psychological structures in action and thought. In W. Damon (Editor-in-Chief) & R. M. Lerner (Vol. Ed.), *Handbook of child psychology: Vol. 1. Theoretical models of human development* (5th ed., pp. 467–561). New York: Wiley.

Fisk, J. D., & Goodale, M. A. (1995). The organization of eye and limb movements during unrestricted reaching in targets in contralateral and ipsilateral visual space. *Experimental Brain Research, 60,* 159–178.

Flavell, J. H. (1984). Discussion. In R. J. Sternberg (Ed.), *Mechanisms of cognitive development* (pp. 187–209). New York: Freeman.

Francis, W. N., & Kucera, H. (1982). *Frequency analysis of English usage.* Boston: Houghton Mifflin.

Fuster, J. (1989). *The prefrontal cortex* (2nd ed.). New York: Raven Press.

Georgopoulos, A. P. (1995). Motor cortex and cognitive processing. In M. S. Gazzaniga (Ed.), *The cognitive neurosciences* (pp. 507–517). Cambridge, MA: MIT Press.

Gopnik, A. (2005). Changing causal representations: Causal bayes nets and theory-formation in children. In Y. Munakata & M. H. Johnson (Eds.), *Processes of change in brain and cognitive development: Attention and performance XXI* (pp. 349–372). Oxford, England: Oxford University Press.

Goubet, N., & Clifton, R. (1998). Object and event representation in $6\frac{1}{2}$-month-old infants. *Developmental Psychology, 34,* 63–76.

Haarmann, H. J., Just, M. A., & Carpenter, P. A. (1997). Aphasic sentence comprehension as a resource deficit: A computational approach. *Brain and Language, 59*(1), 76–120.

Hare, M., & Elman, J. L. (1992). A connectionist account of English inflectional morphology: Evidence from language change. In *Proceedings of the 14th annual conference of the Cognitive Science Society* (pp. 265–270). Hillsdale, NJ: Erlbaum.

Harm, M. W., & Seidenberg, M. S. (1999). Phonology, reading acquisition, and dyslexia: Insights from connectionist models. *Psychological Review, 106*(3), 491–528.

Hebb, D. O. (1949). *The organization of behavior.* New York: Wiley.

Hening, W., Favilla, M., & Ghez, C. (1988). Trajectory control in targeted force impulses: Gradual specification of response amplitude. *Experimental Brain Research, 71,* 116–128.

Hofstadter, M. C., & Reznick, J. S. (1996). Response modality affects human infant delayed-response performance. *Child Development, 67,* 646–658.

Hood, B., & Willatts, P. (1986). Reaching in the dark to an object's remembered position: Evidence for object permanence in 5-month-old infants. *British Journal of Developmental Psychology, 4,* 57–65.

Hummel, J. E., & Holyoak, K. J. (1997). Distributed representations of structure: A theory of analogical access and mapping. *Psychological Review, 104*(3), 427–466.

Inhelder, B., & Piaget, J. (1958). *The growth of logical thinking from childhood to adolescence.* New York: Basic Books.

Jansen, B. R. J., & van der Maas, H. L. J. (1997). Statistical test of the rule assessment methodology by latent class analysis. *Developmental Review, 17,* 321–357.

Jansen, B. R. J., & van der Maas, H. L. J. (2001). Evidence for the phase transition from Rule I to Rule II on the Balance Scale Task. *Developmental Review, 21,* 450–494.

Jansen, B. R. J., & van der Maas, H. L. J. (2002). The development of children's rule use on the Balance Scale Task. *Journal of Experimental Child Psychology, 81,* 383–416.

Joanisse, M. F., & Seidenberg, M. S. (1999). Impairments in verb morphology after brain injury: A connectionist model. *Proceedings of the National Academy of Sciences, 96,* 7592.

Joanisse, M. F., & Seidenberg, M. S. (2003). Phonology and syntax in specific language impairment: Evidence from a connectionist model. *Brain and Language, 86,* 40–56.

Jones, G., Ritter, F. E., & Wood, D. J. (2000). Using a cognitive architecture to examine what develops. *Psychological Science, 11,* 93–100.

Jones, R. M., & VanLehn, K. (1991). Strategy shifts without impasses: A computational model for the sum-to-min transition. In K. J. Hammond & D. Gentner (Eds.), *Proceedings of the Thirteenth annual conference of the Cognitive Science Society* (pp. 358–363). Hillsdale, NJ: Erlbaum.

Just, M., & Carpenter, P. (1992). A capacity theory of comprehension: Individual differences in working memory. *Psychological Review, 99,* 122–149.

Karmiloff-Smith, A. (1992). *Beyond modularity: A developmental perspective on cognitive science.* Cambridge, MA: MIT Press.

Karmiloff-Smith, A. (1998). Development itself is the key to understanding developmental disorders. *Trends in Cognitive Sciences, 2,* 389–398.

Karmiloff-Smith, A. (2005). Modules, genes, and evolution: What have we learned from atypical development. In Y. Munakata & M. H. Johnson (Eds.), *Processes of change in brain and cognitive development: Attention and performance XXI.* Oxford, England: Oxford University Press.

Kelso, J. A. S. (1995). *Dynamic patterns: The self-organization of brain and behavior.* Cambridge, MA: MIT Press.

Kimberg, D. Y., & Farah, M. J. (1993). A unified account of cognitive impairments following frontal lobe damage: The role of working memory in complex, organized behavior. *Journal of Experimental Psychology: General, 122,* 411–428.

Klahr, D. (1982). Nonmonotone assessment of monotone development: An information processing approach. In S. Strauss (Ed.), *U-shaped behavioral growth* (pp. 63–86). New York: Academic Press.

Klahr, D. (1989). Information processing approaches. In R. Vasta (Ed.), *Annals of child development* (pp. 131–185). Greenwich, CT: JAI Press.

Klahr, D. (1992). Information processing approaches to cognitive development. In M. H. Bornstein & M. E. Lamb (Eds.), *Developmental psychology: An advanced textbook* (3rd ed., pp. 273–335). Hillsdale, NJ: Erlbaum.

Klahr, D. (1995). Computational models of cognitive change: The state of the art. In T. J. Simon & G. S. Halford (Eds.), *Developing cognitive competence: New approaches to process modeling* (pp. 355–375). Hillsdale, NJ: Erlbaum.

Klahr, D., Langley, P., & Neches, R. (Eds.). (1987). *Production system models of learning and development.* Cambridge, MA: MIT Press.

Klahr, D., & MacWhinney, B. (1998). Information processing. In W. Damon (Editor-in-Chief) & D. Kuhn & R. S. Siegler (Eds.), *Handbook of child psychology* (5th ed., Vol. 2, pp. 631–678). New York: Wiley.

Klahr, D., & Siegler, R. S. (1978). The representation of children's knowledge. In H. W. Reese & L. P. Lipsitt (Eds.), *Advances in child development and behavior* (Vol. 12, pp. 61–116). New York: Academic Press.

Klahr, D., & Wallace, J. G. (1976). *Cognitive development: An information-processing view.* Hillsdale, NJ: Erlbaum.

Kugler, P. N., & Turvey, M. T. (1987). *Information, natural law, and the self-assembly of rhythmic movement.* Hillsdale, NJ: Erlbaum.

Kuo, Z. (1967). *The dynamics of behavior development: An epigenetic view.* New York: Random House.

Lehrman, D. S. (1953). A critique of Konrad Lorenz's theory of instinctive behavior. *Quarterly Review of Biology, 28,* 337–363.

Lewin, K. (1935). *A dynamic theory of personality.* New York: McGraw-Hill.

Lewin, K. (1936). *Principles of topological psychology.* New York: McGraw-Hill.

Lewis, M. D. (2000). The promise of dynamic systems approaches for an integrated account of human development. *Child Development, 71,* 36–43.

Ling, C. X., & Marinov, M. (1993). Answering the connectionist challenge: A symbolic model of learning the past tense of English verbs. *Cognition, 49,* 235–290.

MacDonald, M. C., & Christiansen, M. H. (2002). Reassessing working memory: Comment on Just and Carpenter (1992) and Waters and Caplan (1996). *Psychological Review, 109,* 35–54.

MacWhinney, B., & Leinbach, J. (1991). Implementations are not conceptualizations: Revising the verb learning model. *Cognition, 40,* 121–153.

Marcovitch, S., & Zelazo, P. D. (1999). The A-not-B error: Results from a logistic meta-analysis. *Child Development, 70,* 1297–1313.

Marcus, G. F. (1998). Rethinking eliminative connectionism. *Cognitive Psychology, 37,* 243.

Marcus, G. F., Pinker, S., Ullman, M., Hollander, M., Rosen, J. T., & Xu, F. (1992). Overregularization in language acquisition.

*Monographs of the Society for Research in Child Development, 57*(4), 1–165.

Mareschal, D., & French, R. (2000). Mechanisms of categorization in infancy. *Infancy, 1,* 59–76.

Mareschal, D., Plunkett, K., & Harris, P. (1999). A computational and neuropsychological account of object-oriented behaviors in infancy. *Developmental Science, 2,* 306–317.

McClelland, J. L. (1989). Parallel distributed processing: Implications for cognition and development. In R. G. M. Morris (Ed.), *Parallel distributed processing: Implications for psychology and neurobiology* (pp. 8–45). Oxford, England: Oxford University Press.

McClelland, J. L. (1995). A connectionist perspective on knowledge and development. In T. J. Simon & G. S. Halford (Eds.), *Developing cognitive competence: New approaches to process modeling* (pp. 157–204). Hillsdale, NJ: Erlbaum.

McClelland, J. L. (2005). How far can you go with Hebbian learning, and when does it lead you astray. In Y. Munakata & M. H. Johnson (Eds.), *Processes of change in brain and cognitive development: Attention and performance XXI* (pp. 33–59). Oxford, England: Oxford University Press.

McClelland, J. L., McNaughton, B. L., & O'Reilly, R. C. (1995). Why there are complementary learning systems in the hippocampus and neocortex: Insights from the successes and failures of connectionist models of learning and memory. *Psychological Review, 102,* 419–457.

McClelland, J. L., & Patterson, K. (2002a). Rules or connections in past tense inflections: What does the evidence rule out? *Trends in Cognitive Sciences, 6,* 465–472.

McClelland, J. L., & Patterson, K. (2002b). 'Words *or* rules' cannot exploit the regularity in exceptions. *Trends in Cognitive Sciences, 6,* 464–465.

McClelland, J. L., Plaut, D. C., Gotts, S. J., & Maia, T. V. (2003). Developing a domain-general framework for cognition: What is the best approach? *Behavioral and Brain Sciences, 26*(5), 611–613.

McClelland, J. L., & Rumelhart, D. E. (Eds.). (1986). *Parallel distributed processing: Vol. 2. Psychological and biological models.* Cambridge, MA: MIT Press.

McCulloch, W. S., & Pitts, W. (1943). A logical calculus of the ideas immanent in nervous activity. *Bulletin of Mathematical Biophysics, 5,* 115–133.

Medina, J. F., & Mauk, M. D. (2000). Computer simulation of cerebellar information processing. *Nature Neuroscience, 3,* 1205–1211.

Mellers, B., Hertwig, R., & Kahneman, D. (2001). Do frequency representations eliminate conjunction effects? an exercise in adversarial collaboration. *Psychological Science, 12,* 269–275.

Miller, E. K., & Desimone, R. (1994). Parallel neuronal mechanisms for short-term memory. *Science, 263,* 520–522.

Miller, E. K., Erickson, C. A., & Desimone, R. (1996). Neural mechanisms of visual working memory in prefontal cortex of the macaque. *Journal of Neuroscience, 16,* 5154–5167.

Mix, K. S., Huttenlocher, J., & Levine, S. C. (2002). Multiple cues for quantification in infancy: Is number one of them? *Psychological Bulletin, 128.*

Morton, J. B., & Munakata, Y. (2002). Active versus latent representations: A neural network model of perseveration and dissociation in early childhood. *Developmental Psychobiology, 40,* 255–265.

Morton, J. B., & Munakata, Y. (2005). What's the difference? Contrasting modular and neural network approaches to understanding developmental variability. *Journal of Developmental-Behavioral Pediatrics.*

Munakata, Y. (1998). Infant perseveration and implications for object permanence theories: A PDP model of the task. *Developmental Science, 1,* 161–184.

Munakata, Y., & McClelland, J. L. (2003). Connectionist models of development. *Developmental Science, 6,* 413–429.

Munakata, Y., McClelland, J. L., Johnson, M. H., & Siegler, R. (1997). Rethinking infant knowledge: Toward an adaptive process account of successes and failures in object permanence tasks. *Psychological Review, 104,* 686–713.

Munakata, Y., Morton, J. B., & Stedron, J. M. (2003). The role of prefrontal cortex in perseveration: Developmental and computational explorations. In P. Quinlan (Ed.), *Connectionist models of development* (pp. 83–114). East Sussex, England: Psychology Press.

Munakata, Y., & O'Reilly, R. C. (2003). Developmental and computational neuroscience approaches to cognition: The case of generalization. *Cognitive Studies: Bulletin of the Japanese Cognitive Science Society, 10,* 76–92.

Munakata, Y., Sahni, S. D., & Yerys, B. E. (2001). An embodied theory in search of a body: Challenges for a dynamic systems model of infant perseveration. *Behavioral and Brain Sciences, 24,* 56–57.

Munakata, Y., & Yerys, B. E. (2001). All together now: When dissociations between knowledge and action disappear. *Psychological Science, 12*(4), 335–337.

Neches, R. (1987). Learning through incremental refinement procedures. In D. Klahr, P. Langley, & R. Neches (Eds.), *Production system models of learning and development* (pp. 163–219). Cambridge, MA: MIT Press.

Newell, A. (1973). You can't play 20 questions with nature and win: Projective comments on the papers of this symposium. In W. G. Chase (Ed.), *Visual information processing* (pp. 283–308). New York: Academic Press.

Newell, A. (1990). *Unified theories of cognition.* Cambridge, MA: Harvard University Press.

Newell, A., & Simon, H. (1972). *Human problem solving.* Englewood Cliffs, NJ: Prentice-Hall.

Oaksford, M., & Chater, N. (1994). A rational analysis of the selection task as optimal data selection. *Psychological Review, 101,* 608–631.

Oja, E. (1982). A simplified neuron model as a principal component analyzer. *Journal of Mathematical Biology, 15,* 267–273.

Oliver, A., Johnson, M. H., Karmiloff-Smith, A., & Pennington, B. (2000). Deviations in the emergence of representations: A neuroconstructivist framework for analysing developmental disorders. *Developmental Science.*

O'Reilly, R. C., & Hoeffner, J. H. (2005). *Competition, priming, and the past tense U-shaped developmental curve.* Manuscript submitted for publication.

O'Reilly, R. C., & McClelland, J. L. (1992). *The self-organization of spatially invariant representations* (Parallel Distributed Processing and Cognitive Neuroscience, 92, 5). Pittsburgh, PA: Carnegie Mellon University, Department of Psychology.

O'Reilly, R. C., & Munakata, Y. (2000). *Computational explorations in cognitive neuroscience: Understanding the mind by simulating the brain.* Cambridge, MA: MIT Press.

O'Reilly, R. C., & Rudy, J. W. (2001). Conjunctive representations in learning and memory: Principles of cortical and hippocampal function. *Psychological Review, 108,* 311–345.

Piaget, J. (1952a). *The child's conception of number.* New York: Norton.

Piaget, J. (1952b). *The origins of intelligence in childhood.* New York: International Universities Press.

Piaget, J. (1954). *The construction of reality in the child.* New York: Basic Books.

Pinker, S. (1984). *Language learnability and language development.* Cambridge, MA: Harvard University Press.

Pinker, S. (1991). Rules of language. *Science, 253,* 530–535.

Pinker, S., & Prince, A. (1988). On language and connectionism: Analysis of a parallel distributed processing model of language acquisition. *Cognition, 28,* 73–193.

Pinker, S., & Ullman, M. T. (2002). The past and future of the past tense. *Trends in Cognitive Sciences, 6,* 456–463.

Plaut, D. C. (1995). Double dissociation without modularity: Evidence from connectionist neuropsychology. *Journal of Clinical and Experimental Neuropsychology, 17*(2), 291–321.

Plaut, D. C., McClelland, J. L., Seidenberg, M. S., & Patterson, K. E. (1996). Understanding normal and impaired word reading: Computational principles in quasi-regular domains. *Psychological Review, 103,* 56–115.

Plunkett, K., & Elman, J. L. (1997). *Exercises in rethinking innateness: A handbook for connectionist simulations.* Cambridge, MA: MIT Press.

Plunkett, K., & Juola, P. (1999). A connectionist model of English past tense and plural morphology. *Cognitive Science, 23,* 463.

Plunkett, K., & Marchman, V. A. (1991). U-shaped learning and frequency effects in a multi-layered perceptron: Implications for child language acquisition. *Cognition, 38,* 43–102.

Plunkett, K., & Marchman, V. A. (1993). From role learning to system building: Acquiring verb morphology in children and connectionist nets. *Cognition, 48*(1), 21–69.

Plunkett, K., & Marchman, V. A. (1996). Learning from a connectionist model of the acquisition of the English past tense. *Cognition, 61,* 299.

Quinlan, P. (Ed.). (2003). *Connectionist models of development.* Hove, England: Psychology Press.

Raijmakers, M. E. J., van Koten, S., & Molenaar, P. C. M. (1996). On the validity of simulating stagewise development by means of PDP networks: Application of catastrophe analysis and an experimental test of rule-like network performance. *Cognitive Science, 20,* 101–136.

Roberts, R., Hager, L., & Heron, C. (1994). Prefrontal cognitive processes: Working memory and inhibition in the antisaccade task. *Journal of Experimental Psychology: General, 123*(4), 374–393.

Roberts, S., & Pashler, H. (2000). How persuasive is a good fit? A comment on theory testing. *Psychological Review, 107,* 358–367.

Rogers, T. T., & McClelland, J. L. (2004). *Semantic cognition: A parallel distributed processing approach.* Cambridge, MA: MIT Press.

Rosenblatt, F. (1958). The perceptron: A probabilistic model for information storage and organization in the brain. *Psychological Review, 65,* 386–408.

Rougier, N. P., Noelle, D., Braver, T. S., Cohen, J. D., & O'Reilly, R. C. (2005). Prefrontal cortex and the flexibility of cognitive control: Rules without symbols. *Proceedings of the National Academy of Sciences, 102,* 7338–7343.

Rumelhart, D. E., Hinton, G. E., & Williams, R. J. (1986). Learning representations by back-propagating errors. *Nature, 323,* 533–536.

Rumelhart, D. E., & McClelland, J. L. (1986a). On learning the past tenses of English verbs. In J. L. McClelland, D. E. Rumelhart, & PDP Research Group (Eds.), *Parallel distributed processing: Vol. 2. Psychological and biological models* (pp. 216–271). Cambridge, MA: MIT Press.

Rumelhart, D. E., & McClelland, J. L. (Eds.). (1986b). *Parallel distributed processing: Vol. 1. Foundations.* Cambridge, MA: MIT Press.

Sage, S., & Langley, P. (1983). Modeling cognitive development on the balance scale task. In A. Bundy (Ed.), *Proceedings of the Eighth International Joint Conference on Artificial Intelligence* (Vol. 1, pp. 94–96). Karlsruhe, West Germany: Morgan Kaufmann.

Schlesinger, M., & Parisi, D. (2001). The agent-based approach: A new direction for computational models of development. *Developmental Review, 21,* 121–146.

Schmidt, W. C., & Ling, C. X. (1996). A Decision-Tree Model of Balance Scale Development. *Machine Learning, 24,* 203–230.

Schutte, A., & Spencer, J. (2002). Generalizing the dynamic field theory of the A-not-B error beyond infancy: Three-year-olds' delay- and experience-dependent location memory biases. *Child Development, 73,* 377–404.

Seidenberg, M. S., & Elman, J. L. (with reply by Marcus, G.). (1999). Networks are not "hidden rules." *Trends in Cognitive Science, 3*(8), 288–289.

Seidenberg, M. S., & McClelland, J. L. (1989). A distributed, developmental model of word recognition and naming. *Psychological Review, 96,* 523–568.

Shepherd, G. M. (1992). *Foundations of the neuron doctrine.* New York: Oxford University Press.

Shinskey, J., & Munakata, Y. (2001). Detecting transparent barriers: Clear evidence against the means-end deficit account of search failures. *Infancy, 2,* 395–404.

Shinskey, J., & Munakata, Y. (2003). Are infants in the dark about hidden objects? *Developmental Science, 6,* 273–282.

Shrager, J., & Siegler, R. S. (1998). A model of children's strategy choices and strategy discoveries. *Psychological Science, 9*(5), 405–410.

Shultz, T. R. (2003). *Computational developmental psychology.* Cambridge, MA: MIT Press.

Shultz, T., Schmidt, W., Buckingham, D., & Mareschal, D. (1995). Modeling cognitive development with a generative connectionist algorithm. In T. J. Simon & G. S. Halford (Eds.), *Developing cognitive competence: New approaches to process modeling* (pp. 157–204). Hillsdale, NJ: Erlbaum.

Siegler, R. (1976). Three aspects of cognitive development. *Cognitive Psychology, 8,* 481–520.

Siegler, R. (1981). Developmental sequences within and between concepts. *Monographs of the Society for Research in Child Development, 46*(2, Serial No. 189).

Siegler, R. (1989). Mechanisms of cognitive development. *Annual Review of Psychology, 40,* 353–379.

Siegler, R. (1996). *Emerging minds: The process of change in children's thinking.* New York: Oxford University Press.

Siegler, R. S., & Alibali, M. W. (2005). *Children's thinking* (4th ed.). Upper Saddle River, NJ: Prentice-Hall.

Siegler, R. S., & Chen, Z. (1998). Developmental differences in rule learning: A microgenetic analysis. *Cognitive Psychology, 36,* 273–310.

Siegler, R. S., & Chen, Z. (2002). Development of rules and strategies: Balancing the old and the new. *Journal of Experimental Child Psychology, 81,* 446–457.

Siegler, R. S., & Shipley, C. (1995). Variation, selection, and cognitive change. In T. Simon & G. Halford (Eds.), *Developing cognitive competence: New approaches to process modeling* (pp. 31–76). Hillsdale, NJ: Erlbaum.

Siegler, R. S., & Shrager, J. (1984). Strategy choices in addition and subtraction: How do children know what to do. In C. Sophian (Ed.), *The origins of cognitive skills* (pp. 229–293). Hillsdale, NJ: Erlbaum.

Simon, H. A. (1962). An information processing theory of intellectual development. *Monographs of the Society for Research in Child Development, 27.*

Simon, T. J. (1997). Reconceptualizing the origins of number knowledge: A 'non-numerical' account. *Cognitive Development, 12,* 349–372.

Simon, T. J. (1998). Computational evidence for the foundations of numerical competence. *Developmental Science, 1,* 71–78.

Simon, T. J., & Halford, G. S. (1995a). *Computational models and cognitive change* (pp. 1–30). Hillsdale, NJ: Erlbaum.

Simon, T. J., & Halford, G. S. (Eds.). (1995b). *Developing cognitive competence: New approaches to process modeling.* Hillsdale, NJ: Erlbaum.

Skinner, B. F. (1953). *Science and human behavior.* New York: Macmillan.

Smith, L. B., & Samuelson, L. K. (2003). Different is good: Connectionism and dynamic systems theory are complementary emergentist approaches to development. *Developmental Science, 6,* 434–439.

Smith, L. B., & Thelen, E. (Eds.). (1993). *A dynamic systems approach to development: Applications.* Cambridge, MA: MIT Press.

Smith, L. B., Thelen, E., Titzer, B., & McLin, D. (1999). Knowing in the context of acting: The task dynamics of the A-not-B error. *Psychological Review, 106,* 235–260.

Spelke, E., Breinlinger, K., Macomber, J., & Jacobson, K. (1992). Origins of knowledge. *Psychological Review, 99,* 605–632.

Spelke, E., Vishton, P., & von Hofsten, C. (1995). Object perception, object-directed action, and physical knowledge in infancy. In M. S. Gazzaniga (Ed.), *The cognitive neurosciences* (pp. 165–179). Cambridge, MA: MIT Press.

Spencer, J. P., & Schöner, G. (2003). Bridging the representational gap in the dynamic systems approach to development. *Developmental Science, 6,* 392–412.

Spencer, J. P., Smith, L. B., & Thelen, E. (2001). Tests of a dynamic systems account of the A-not-B error: The influence of prior experience on the spatial memory abilities of 2-year-olds. *Child Development, 72,* 1327–1346.

Spencer, J. P., & Thelen, E. (2003). Connectionist and dynamic systems approaches to development [Special issue]. *Developmental Science, 6.*

Stedron, J., Sahni, S. D., & Munakata, Y. (2005). Common mechanisms for working memory and attention: The case of perseveration with visible solutions. *Journal of Cognitive Neuroscience.*

Taatgen, N. A. (2002). A model of individual differences in skill acquisition in the Kanfer-Ackerman air traffic control task. *Cognitive Systems Research, 3,* 103–112.

Taatgen, N. A., & Anderson, J. R. (2002). Why do children learn to say "broke"? A model of learning the past tense without feedback. *Cognition, 86,* 123–155.

Teitelbaum, P. (1967). *Physiological psychology.* Englewood Cliffs, NJ: Prentice-Hall.

Thelen, E., & Bates, E. (2003). Connectionism and dynamic systems: Are they really different? *Developmental Science, 6,* 378–391.

Thelen, E., Kelso, J. A. S., & Fogel, A. (1987). Self-organizing systems and infant motor development. *Developmental Review, 7,* 39–65.

Thelen, E., Schöner, G., Scheier, C., & Smith, L. B. (2001). The dynamics of embodiment: A field theory of infant perseverative reaching. *Behavioral and Brain Sciences, 24,* 1–86.

Thelen, E., & Smith, L. B. (1994). *A dynamic systems approach to the development of cognition and action.* Cambridge, MA: MIT Press.

Thelen, E., & Smith, L. B. (1998). Dynamic systems theories. In W. Damon (Editor-in-Chief) & R. M. Lerner (Vol. Ed.), *Handbook of child psychology: Vol. 1. Theoretical models of human development* (5th ed., pp. 563–634). New York: Wiley.

Thelen, E., & Ulrich, B. D. (1991). Hidden skills: A dynamic systems analysis of treadmill stepping during the first year. *Monographs of the Society for Research in Child Development, 56*(Serial No. 223).

Thomas, M., & Karmiloff-Smith, A. (2002). Are developmental disorders like cases of adult brain damage? Implications from connectionist modelling. *Behavioral and Brain Sciences, 25,* 727–788.

Thomas, M., & Karmiloff-Smith, A. (2003). Modelling language acquisition in atypical phenotypes. *Psychological Review, 110,* 647–682.

van der Maas, H. L. J., & Molenaar, P. C. M. (1992). Stagewise cognitive development: An application of catastrophe theory. *Psychological Review, 99,* 395–417.

van Geert, P. (1991). A dynamic systems model of cognitive and language growth. *Psychological Review, 98,* 3–53.

van Geert, P. (1993). A dynamic systems model of cognitive growth: Competition and support under limited resource conditions. In L. B. Smith & E. Thelen (Eds.), *A dynamic systems approach to development* (pp. 265–331). Cambridge, MA: MIT Press.

van Geert, P. (1998). A dynamic systems model of basic developmental mechanisms: Piaget, Vygotsky and beyond. *Psychological Review, 105,* 634–677.

van Rijn, H., van Someren, M., & van der Maas, H. (2003). Modeling developmental transitions on the balance scale task. *Cognitive Science, 27,* 227–257.

von Bertalanffy, L. (1968). *General system theory.* New York: George Braziller.

Waddington, C. H. (1957). *The strategy of the genes: A discussion of some aspects of theoretical biology.* London: Allen & Unwin.

Watson, J. B. (1912). Psychology as the behaviorist views it. *Psychological Review, 20,* 158–177.

Wellman, H. M., Cross, D., & Bartsch, K. (1986). Infant search and object permanence: A meta-analysis of the A-not-B error. *Monographs of the Society for Research in Child Development, 51*(3, Serial No. 214).

Willatts, P. (1990). Development of problem-solving strategies in infancy. In D. F. Bjorklund (Ed.), *Children's strategies: Contemporary views of cognitive development* (pp. 23–66). Hillsdale, NJ: Erlbaum.

Wynn, K. (1992). Addition and subtraction by human infants. *Nature, 358,* 749–750.

Young, R. M. (1976). *Seriation by children: An artificial intelligence analysis of a Piagetian task.* Basel, Switzerland: Birkhauser.

Zelazo, P. D. (2004). U-shaped changes in behavior and their implications for cognitive development [Special issue]. *Journal of Cognition and Development, 5.*

# CHAPTER 11

# Microgenetic Analyses of Learning

ROBERT S. SIEGLER

THE CENTRALITY OF LEARNING TO
    CHILDREN'S DEVELOPMENT   464
History   465
MICROGENETIC METHODS FOR
    STUDYING LEARNING   469
Essential Properties   469
Applicability   469
History   471
Methodological Issues   472
OVERLAPPING WAVES THEORY   477
THE NEW FIELD OF CHILDREN'S LEARNING   480
Variability   480
Basic Empirical Phenomena   480

Influences of Child and Environment   484
Theoretical Implications and Questions   486
Path of Change   487
Rate of Change   490
Breadth of Change   494
Sources of Change   496
RELATIONS BETWEEN LEARNING
    AND DEVELOPMENT   499
CHANGE MECHANISMS   501
CONCLUSION   503
REFERENCES   504

This chapter is based on three propositions: (1) Learning is central to child development, (2) microgenetic analyses yield unique information about learning, and (3) the information yielded by microgenetic analysis is helping to create a vibrant new field of children's learning. The remainder of the chapter provides arguments and evidence for these three propositions, as well as describing the new field of children's learning.

Preparation of this chapter was supported in part by grant HD19011 from the National Institutes of Child Health and Human Development and grant R305H020060 from the U.S. Department of Education. Thanks also go to the following individuals for helpful comments about an earlier draft of this chapter: Jennifer Amsterlaw, Zhe Chen, Thomas Coyle, James Dixon, Kathryn Fletcher, Emma Flynn, David Geary, Annette Karmiloff-Smith, David Klahr, Deanna Kuhn, Kang Lee, Anne McKeough, Patrick Lemaire, Patricia Miller, Bethany Rittle-Johnson, Wolfgang Schneider, Jeff Shrager, Patricia Stokes, Matija Svetina, Erika Tunteler, and Han van der Maas. I would also like to thank my dedicated and hard-working research team who put many hours into this project: Theresa Treasure, Mary Wolfson, and Jenna Zonneveld.

## THE CENTRALITY OF LEARNING TO CHILDREN'S DEVELOPMENT

Learning is basic to human existence in all periods of life, but it is especially so in childhood. Its centrality is now recognized even for changes that were once attributed entirely to maturation, such as the beginning of reaching, kicking, and stepping (Thelen & Corbetta, 2002). The very concept of childhood can be defined in terms of learning: Childhood is the period of life in which learning is the primary goal.

The reasoning underlying this perspective can be appreciated by contrasting the relative importance of performance and learning in adulthood to their relative importance in childhood. Adulthood is the period during which performance is primary: Adults' success in doing their jobs, in choosing a mate, in child rearing, in deciding where to live, and even in mundane tasks such as driving has profound implications for themselves and their families. Considerable learning also takes place during adulthood, of course, but adults' performance in the here and now is foremost. A farmer who makes unwise planting and harvesting decisions and whose crops fail is not a successful farmer even if he learned from his less successful decisions the year before, nor is a driver successful who learned enough to improve from six traffic accidents to three from one year to the next. In contrast, a farmer who makes wise planting and harvesting decisions is successful even if he learns nothing, as is a driver who avoids all accidents but whose skill remains unchanged.

The balance between learning and performance is very different in childhood. Children have more to learn than do adults, and the capabilities they need to acquire include many that are fundamental to their future: comprehension and production of language; acquisition of fundamental concepts such as time, space, number, and mind; academic competencies such as reading, writing, and mathematics; emotional control; social interaction skills; and so on. Thus, the adage "the work of childhood is learning" embodies an important truth. In contrast, children's absolute level of performance rarely matters in and of itself. It is unfortunate if a kindergartner lags behind in knowledge of numbers and letters, or does not work and play well with others, but the problem is serious only if it continues. A kindergartner who has made substantial progress toward catching up with her classmates in knowledge of letters and numbers or in getting along with other children, but who still does less well than most of them, has had a good year—unlike the driver who reduced his traffic accidents from six to three.

Although the process of learning always has been central within children's development, the study of learning only sometimes has been central within the field of child development. From the 1930s through the 1960s, children's learning was a booming area of developmental psychology. Then the area went into eclipse. A sense of the magnitude and rapidity of the shift is conveyed by the chapters on children's learning in two successive editions of the *Handbook of Child Psychology,* both written by the same authority, Harold Stevenson. First consider Stevenson's evaluation of the state of the field in the 1970 *Handbook,* near the end of the boom in the study of children's learning:

> The number and quality of studies on children's learning published each year have continued to increase. . . . By now there have been so many studies of children's learning that it is impossible to review them adequately in one chapter. . . . Because of the vast number of publications, no attempt is made to include all possibly relevant studies. (pp. 849, 851, 852)

Now consider Stevenson's (1983) evaluation 13 years later, after the boom ended:

> By the mid-1970s, articles on children's learning dwindled to a fraction of the number that had been published in the previous decade, and by 1980, it was necessary to search with diligence to uncover any articles at all. (p. 213)

Indicative of this change, the length of Stevenson's review of the literature on children's learning decreased from 90 pages in 1970 to 23 pages in 1983. This change did not just reflect one man's opinion. In the 1970 *Handbook* volume that focused on cognitive development, 10 of the 19 chapters included learning as an index entry; in the corresponding volume of the 1983 *Handbook,* only 2 of the 13 chapters included such an entry.

Since the publication of the 1983 *Handbook,* the pendulum has swung back—somewhat. On one hand, the prominence of learning within the field of developmental psychology remains far less than its prominence within children's lives. On the other hand, the amount of research on children's learning has increased, and the quality of this research has been high enough to create an exciting new field of children's learning. The present chapter first provides a brief overview of the history of research on children's learning, then examines how microgenetic methods have helped reinvigorate the area, and then examines the new field of children's learning that is emerging.

## History

### Early Flowering

The rise of learning theories within developmental psychology came later than in experimental psychology and the learning theory approach never became as dominant (White, 1970). Nonetheless, learning theories were a major force in developmental psychology for many years, shaping what was studied, how it was studied, and how the results were interpreted. Many early studies of children were direct extensions of previous learning theory studies of rats, pigeons, or human adults. For example, in the 1946 edition of the *Handbook,* Munn's chapter on children's learning included the observation:

> Investigations of learning in children, rather than introducing new problems and essentially novel techniques, have followed the leads of animal and adult human

psychology. . . . In many investigations of learning inclusion of children has been merely incidental. (pp. 370, 371)

Consistent with this perspective, Munn's chapter focused in large part on topics emphasized within the adult and animal experimental psychology of the day: conditioning, paired associate learning, motor learning, and so on.

The emphasis within the field of children's learning on theories and methods imported from experimental psychology continued for many years. Consider the similarity between the evaluation just quoted and that of Stevenson (1970), a quarter century later:

Research on children's learning is for the most part a derivative of psychological studies of learning in animals and human adults. Although the impetus for studying children's learning is related to practical concerns in the educating and rearing of children, the field characteristically has been dominated by the methods and problems of the experimental psychologist. . . . The close alliance with experimental psychology has been productive. (p. 849)

It is easy to recognize these influences of learning theory on a wide variety of prominent developmental research of the 1950s and 1960s. For example, Hull's (1943) and Spence's (1952) approaches to discrimination learning led to the developmental research on the same topic of Kendler and Kendler (1962) and Zeaman and House (1967); the social learning approach of N. E. Miller and Dollard (1941) led to the developmental research of Bandura and Walters (1963) and Rosenblith (1959); the operant conditioning approach of Skinner (1938) led to the developmental research of Bijou and Baer (1961) and Siqueland and Lipsitt (1966); and so on. Thus, although Stevenson's (1970) characterizations of the field of children's learning as both derivative and productive might seem contradictory, both descriptors seem justified.

### Dormancy

The withering of the field of children's learning after 1970 reflected both its own limitations and the emergence of attractive alternatives. Learning theory emphasized simple nonverbal tasks that bore only an abstract resemblance to problems that children encounter in the world outside the laboratory. The intent was to measure basic learning processes that occur in a wide range of situations, but the tasks and experimental paradigms

differed so greatly from everyday ones that it was uncertain if the learning processes used in and out of the lab shared more than a label. For example, numerous learning theory studies of concept formation required children (or adults or nonhuman animals) to choose between pairs of objects that varied in size, shape, color, and the side on which they appeared (e.g., Levine, 1966; Restle, 1962). The correct answer was whatever the experimenter said it was; the rule could be as simple as "Choose the larger one" or as complex as "Choose either a large T on the left or a small X on the right or a large X on the left or a small T on the right." The degree of similarity between the processes used to acquire such arbitrary concepts and those used to acquire natural concepts such as "animal" or "mountain" is far from clear. In addition, the lack of ecological validity of these tasks was so extreme that it created increasing dissatisfaction with the whole learning theory enterprise among a wide range of psychologists.

Developmental psychologists also were dissatisfied for several other reasons. One was the portrayal of children as passive, inactive organisms whose learning lacked distinctive characteristics. Brown, Bransford, Ferrara, and Campione noted in their 1983 *Handbook* chapter that learning theories assumed that the same basic principles could be applied universally across all kinds of learning, all kinds of species, and all ages. Not surprisingly, investigators who did not believe in developmental or species differences in learning did not discover much about them. This issue was evident quite early. Munn (1946) noted, "So far as discovering anything fundamentally new concerning the learning process is concerned, the investigations on learning in children have failed" (p. 441). Although Munn recognized that this might be attributable to the tasks and procedures that were used, he concluded that "A more likely reason, however, is that the phenomenon of learning is fundamentally the same, whether studied in the animal, child, or adult" (p. 441). Some later learning theory approaches did attempt to explain developmental differences in learning (e.g., Kendler & Kendler, 1962), and their efforts attracted considerable interest for a time, but increasing numbers of developmentalists had become disillusioned with learning theory and were looking in other directions.

The marginalization of the field of children's learning reflected not only the deficiencies of learning theories but also the emergence of attractive alternative approaches that did not emphasize learning. The most influential alternative was Piaget's theory, particularly as distilled in Flavell's (1963) book "The Developmental Psychology of Jean Piaget." Piaget's theory was not new, of course, but Flavell's clear and compelling presentation greatly expanded its appeal. Unfortunately, for the study of learning, Piaget (1964) drew a sharp distinction between learning and development, a distinction that relegated learning to a subordinate position. For example,

> I would like to make clear the difference between two problems, the problem of development in general and the problem of learning. I think these problems are very different, although some people do not make the distinction. The development of knowledge is a spontaneous process, tied to the whole process of embryogenesis. Learning presents the opposite case. In general, learning is provoked by situations—provoked by a psychological experimenter; or by a teacher, with respect to some didactic point; or by an external situation. It is provoked, in general, as opposed to spontaneous. In addition, it is a limited process—limited to a single problem, or to a single structure. (p. 20)

It is worth noting that not all classic theorists shared Piaget's rather dismissive attitude toward learning. Theorists such as Werner (1948, 1957) and Vygotsky (1934/1962) viewed short-term change as a miniature version of long-term change, generated by similar underlying processes and characterized by identical sequences of qualitatively distinct stages. This view is basically similar to the present perspective. However, Piaget's theory was so dominant at the time, and his observations of age-related changes so interesting, that they shifted attention toward children's thinking and away from their learning. This shift affected not only adherents of Piaget's theory but critics as well. Thus, approaches that originated as alternatives to Piaget's theory, such as core knowledge approaches (Spelke & Newport, 1998), differed in many ways from the Piagetian perspective but maintained the focus on knowledge rather than learning.

A second major influence on the field of cognitive development, information processing theories, also shifted attention away from children's learning, though for a different reason. Information processing approaches recognized learning as a central problem and as crucial for understanding how development occurs.

However, their agenda was first to describe children's knowledge states at different ages and only then to focus on how transitions occur. This perspective is aptly captured in Simon's (1962) suggestion,

> If we can construct an information processing system with rules of behavior that lead it to behave like the dynamic system we are trying to describe, then this system is a theory of the child at one stage of development. Having described a particular stage by a program, we would then face the task of discovering what additional information-processing mechanisms are needed to simulate developmental change—the transition from one stage to the next. (p. 632)

As with Piaget's theory, this approach led to many fascinating discoveries regarding how children think at different ages. In addition, some researchers who adopted an information-processing perspective did advance intriguing hypotheses about transition processes in cognitive development (e.g., Klahr & Wallace, 1976). In general, however, the information processing theory of the 1960s and 1970s, like Piagetian theory, shifted attention away from how children learn.

Scientific approaches create their own momentum. The intriguing findings on children's existing knowledge generated by Piagetian, information processing, and core knowledge approaches led to many controversies. These controversies, in turn, generated new intriguing findings and new controversies regarding what children do and do not understand at particular ages, especially in infancy and the preschool period (e.g., Haith & Benson, 1998; Spelke & Newport, 1998). The development of innovative methods for studying infant cognition added to this trend, because it allowed examination of fundamental issues that could not be studied previously.

These trends produced a large body of excellent research that greatly broadened understanding of development. However, they also entailed a serious cost: an imbalanced portrayal of children that focused on static states rather than change. This tendency was evident in Piagetian, information processing, and core knowledge approaches alike; all focused primarily on skills and knowledge at particular ages rather than on the processes through which children acquired the skills and knowledge. The imbalance is understandable—knowledge states are easier to describe than change processes, and describing them is crucial for establishing the changes that need to be explained. However, the prolonged emphasis on documenting static states resulted in a distorted description of development, one in which children appeared to spend far more time being than becoming.

## Germination

After a period in which children's learning received little attention, some far-sighted investigators began to envision a new field of children's learning. For example, Brown, Bransford, Ferrara, and Campione (1983) noted the same trend toward reduced focus on learning as Stevenson (1983), but they also predicted that the metaphor of children as active organisms who devise strategies to pursue their goals would form the foundation of a new field of children's learning. They foresaw that the study of memory for rich and varied real world content would provide a useful model for this new field, and they anticipated the emergence of several specific issues that have become central in the area. How do the characteristics of the learner, the nature of the material, and the criterion task combine to determine learning? Why do children fail to transfer useful strategies to new content? What develops to allow older children to learn many types of material more effectively than younger children?

A further insight of Brown et al. (1983) was anticipating the role that microgenetic studies would play in the resurgence of the field of children's learning. They suggested that after documenting age-related changes in thinking, researchers would go on:

> to attack the problem of development head-on . . . by observing learning actually taking place within a subject over time. This is essentially the microgenetic approach advocated by Vygotsky (1978) and Werner (1961). . . . The revived interest in microgenetic analysis of both adult (Anzai & Simon, 1979) and children's (Karmiloff-Smith, 1979a, 1979b) learning enables psychologists to concentrate not only on qualitative descriptions of stages of expertise but also to consider transition phenomena that accompany the progression from novice to expert status. (p. 84)

The history of the past 20 years indicates the prescience of Brown et al.'s (1983) predictions. Again, changes within the *Handbook* document this trend. Learning assumed a considerably larger role in the 1998 *Handbook* than in its 1983 predecessor. M. H. Johnson (1998) noted that rather than neural development being largely prespecified, as once was assumed, the develop-

ing brain changes according to the input that it encounters; that is, the developing brain changes with learning. Aslin, Jusczyk, and Pisoni (1998) focused on how children learn to segment speech into words, and also how learning leads them to lose their early ability to discriminate some phonemic contrasts that are absent from their native language. Gelman and Williams (1998) focused on how conceptual constraints influence learning in core domains. Maratsos (1998) argued that contrary to the view that people are born with a universal grammar that only requires a small amount of tuning, the remarkably idiosyncratic and variable nature of natural grammars demands a great deal of highly specific learning. Rogoff (1998) examined how children learn through participation in socially important activities, and Klahr and MacWhinney (1998) reviewed computational models of children's learning.

Several developments contributed to this change in *Handbook* coverage and to the more general resurgence of the field of children's learning. One was the increasing influence of theories that see development as rising in large part out of learning. These include dynamic systems, sociocultural, and information processing theories. Such theories have motivated increasing amounts of empirical research on learning. For example, dynamic systems theory motivated researchers to examine whether acquisitions that traditionally had been viewed as a function of the child's developmental stage, such as object permanence, could be explained by learning within the specific experimental situation, such as learning of particular arm movements and activation of particular representations. Smith, Thelen, Titzer, and McLin's (1999) and Spencer and Schutte's (2004) empirical demonstrations that such explanations were viable created a new way of conceptualizing object permanence.

Another important contributor to the resurgence of the field of children's learning has been methods capable of tracing the process of learning while it occurs. Microgenetic methods in particular have made possible increasingly nuanced understanding of children's learning. The availability of such methods, together with videocassette recorders and other useful technologies, allow theorists to raise questions about the dynamics of development that otherwise would be impossible to answer, such as what happens immediately before a child makes a discovery and whether periods of transition are accompanied by especially high variability.

Other methods are also being used to study learning. They include operant conditioning (Saffran, Aslin, &

Newport, 1996; Stokes & Harrison, 2002), elicited imitation (Bauer, Chapter 9, this *Handbook,* this volume), formal modeling (Munakata, Chapter 10, this *Handbook,* this volume), and brain imaging (Nelson, Chapter 1, this *Handbook,* this volume). In addition, microgenetic methods are being used to study adults' learning (Anzai & Simon, 1979; Staszewski, 1988), as well as that of children. Limitations of space, together with the presence in this volume of the chapters by Nelson, Bauer, and Munakata, contributed to the decision to focus the present chapter on contributions of microgenetic studies to understanding of children's learning.

## MICROGENETIC METHODS FOR STUDYING LEARNING

Scientific methods and theories exert reciprocal influences. Typical cross-sectional and longitudinal methods, which sample the thinking of children at different ages, reinforce and are reinforced by theories that emphasize such questions as "By what age do children understand _____?" and "Does X develop before, after, or concurrently with Y?" In contrast, the cross sectional and longitudinal methods are less useful in testing theories that emphasize such questions as, "Through what processes do children learn _____?" and "Is Strategy X transitional to Strategy Y?" The problem is that observations of emerging competence in cross-sectional and longitudinal studies are too widely spaced to yield detailed information about the learning process. For example, a longitudinal design might involve observing children's performance on the false belief task at 3, 4, and 5 years. The year between observations would severely limit the information that could emerge regarding the processes through which children's understanding of false belief improves.

### Essential Properties

This is where microgenetic methods are essential: for answering questions about *how* learning occurs. Microgenetic methods have three main properties:

1. Observations span the period of rapidly changing competence.
2. Within this period, the density of observations is high, relative to the rate of change.

3. Observations are analyzed intensively, with the goal of inferring the representations and processes that gave rise to them.

The second property is especially important. Densely sampling changing competence during the period of rapid change provides the temporal resolution needed to understand the learning process. If children's learning usually proceeded in a beeline toward advanced competence, such dense sampling of ongoing changes would be unnecessary. We could examine thinking before and after changes occurred, identify the shortest path between the two states, and infer that children moved directly from the less advanced one to the more advanced one. Detailed observations of ongoing changes, however, indicate that such beelines are the exception rather than the rule (Siegler, 2000). Cognitive changes involve regressions as well as progressions, odd transitional states that are present only briefly but that are crucial for the changes to occur, generalization along some dimensions from the beginning of learning but lack of generalization along other dimensions for years thereafter, and many other surprising features. Simply put, the only way to find out how children learn is to study them closely while they are learning.

The logic of densely sampling changes as they occur is not unique to the microgenetic approach; the same logic underlies a number of other methods. One example is neural imaging methods such as fMRI. The dense temporal sampling of brain activity allowed by increasingly powerful magnets and software has led to many insights into the neural substrate of performance (e.g., Casey, 2001). Other neural techniques such as single cell recording are based on the same logic, as are behavioral techniques such as eye movement analysis (Just & Carpenter, 1987). In all cases, the dense sampling of performance over time allows insights into cognitive processes.

### Applicability

Microgenetic designs are broadly applicable along multiple dimensions:

- *Ages of participants:* Microgenetic methods have proven useful for studying people of all ages: infants (Adolph, 1997), toddlers (Chen & Siegler, 2000), preschoolers (P. H. Miller & Aloise-Young, 1995), elementary school children (Schauble, 1996), college students (Metz, 1998) and older adults (Kruse, Lindenberger, & Baltes, 1993).

- *Domain:* Microgenetic analyses have proven useful for studying development in highly diverse domains: problem solving (Fireman, 1996), attention (P. H. Miller & Aloise-Young, 1995), memory (Schlagmüller & Schneider, 2002), theory of mind (Flynn, O'Malley, & Wood, 2004), scientific reasoning (Kuhn, Garcia-Mila, Zohar, & Anderson, 1995), mathematical reasoning (Alibali, 1999), spoken language (Robinson & Mervis, 1998), written language (Jones, 1998), motor activity (Spencer, Vereijken, Diedrich, & Thelen, 2000), and perception (Shimojo, Bauer, O'Connell, & Held, 1986). In addition to these applications to the study of cognitive development, investigators have begun to apply microgenetic analyses to social development (e.g., Lavelli & Fogel, 2002; Lewis, 2002).

- *Setting:* Microgenetic methods are applicable not only in laboratory settings but also in naturally occurring contexts and classrooms. For example, they have been used to study infants' kicking and reaching in their cribs (Thelen & Corbetta, 2002), young children's learning of narrative skills in preschool and first-grade classes (McKeough, Davis, Forgeron, Marini, & Fung, 2005; McKeough & Sanderson, 1996), and fourth graders learning math skills in a collaborative learning context (Taylor & Cox, 1997). (For a review of applications of microgenetic methods to classroom research, see Chinn, in press.)

- *Theoretical underpinning:* Microgenetic studies have proven useful for testing predictions of all of the major theories of cognitive development: Piagetian (Karmiloff-Smith & Inhelder, 1974; Saada-Robert, 1992), neo-Piagetian (Fischer & Yan, 2002; McKeough & Sanderson, 1996), dynamic systems (Lewis, 2002; Thelen & Corbetta, 2002), theory (Amsterlaw & Wellman, 2004; Flynn et al., 2004), sociocultural (Duncan & Pratt, 1997; Wertsch & Hickmann, 1987), and information processing (Schlagmüller & Schneider, 2002; Siegler & Svetina, 2002). This is not coincidence. Part of the reason that these approaches are viewed as major developmental theories is that they make important predictions about how change occurs. Such predictions often can be tested most precisely through microgenetic studies, in which changes are observed in detail.

Despite these large variations in age groups, content areas, settings, and investigators' theoretical orientation, microgenetic studies of children's learning have yielded surprisingly consistent findings. As Kuhn (2002) observed:

> Although the empirical findings that microgenetic research has produced are both interesting and consequential, the single most striking thing about them is their consistency. This consistency has been maintained despite variations in methodology and despite the wide range of content areas to which the method has been applied. Consistency of this sort is unusual in developmental psychology. (p. 109)

Other reviewers of the microgenetic literature (P. H. Miller & Coyle, 1999; Siegler, 2000) have been struck by this same consistency of research findings. Ironically, it may reflect the correctness of one of the core beliefs of the earlier generation of learning theorists: More regularity may be present in how people learn than in what they know at a given age. Prominent developmental theories, such as the Piagetian, neo-Piagetian, and theory-theory approaches, have been based on the assumption that substantial regularities in thinking are present at particular ages, either across all areas of thinking or within broad domains, such as psychology or biology (Case & Okamoto, 1996; Piaget, 1952; Wellman & Gelman, 1998). The evidence for such regularities in thinking at particular ages is mixed at best (Siegler, 1996).

In contrast, the consistent findings yielded by microgenetic studies suggest that considerable regularity may be present in how children learn. This regularity in findings regarding children's learning has been noted in reviews of studies that have not used microgenetic methods as well as in ones that have. For example, R. Gelman and Williams (1998) highlighted the importance of constraints for facilitating learning in all types of domains, both biologically privileged and nonprivileged. Similarly, Keil (1998) and Wellman and S. Gelman (1998) emphasized formation of causal connections as crucial to children's learning in a broad range of domains. The greater regularity in studies of learning is likely due to their eliminating a number of sources of variability that limit investigators' ability to demonstrate commonalities in thinking across different problems: differences in wording of questions, task difficulty, amount of direct experience with each task, similarity to better-understood tasks, motivational properties, and so on. Thus, yet another reason for focusing on children's learning is that doing so promises to help overcome the fractionation of the field of developmental psychology and to identify common underlying principles.

Table 11.1 lists a number of the most consistent and important phenomena that have emerged within micro-

**TABLE 11.1    Twenty Major Findings about Children's Learning**

1. Substantial within-child variability is present during all phases of learning and at every level of analysis: associations, concepts, rules, strategies, and so on.
2. Within-child variability tends to be greatest during periods of rapid learning, though substantial variability is present in relatively stable periods as well.
3. Within-child variability tends to be cyclical, with periods of lesser and greater variability alternating over the course of learning.
4. Within-child variability is substantial at all ages from infancy to older adulthood.
5. Initial within-child variability tends to be positively related to subsequent learning.
6. Learning reflects addition of new strategies, greater reliance on relatively advanced strategies that are already being used, improved choices among strategies, and improved execution of strategies.
7. Learning tends to progress through a regular sequence of knowledge states that parallel those that characterize untutored development.
8. The path of learning is usually similar for learners of different ages and different intellectual levels.
9. Learning often includes short-lived transitional approaches that play important roles in the acquisition of more enduring approaches.
10. New approaches are generated following success as well as failure of existing approaches.
11. For most types of learning, older and more knowledgeable children learn more quickly, and show greater appropriate generalization, than younger children.
12. The rate of change is of human scale: faster than connectionist models imply, but slower than most symbolic models imply.
13. New approaches usually are used inconsistently; discovery of new approaches tends to be the beginning of learning rather than the end.
14. Once new approaches have been generated, their rate of uptake is positively related to the degree to which their accuracy is superior to that of existing approaches.
15. The breadth of change also is of human scale, including everything from instantaneous to extremely gradual generalization.
16. The likelihood of choosing any given approach can be increased either by increasing the strength of that approach or by weakening the strength of competing approaches.
17. Causal understanding plays a crucial role in learning.
18. Requests to explain observations often promote learning above and beyond the effects of feedback and practice.
19. The mechanisms underlying the effects of explanatory activity include increased likelihood of learners generating any explanation, increased persistence of explanatory efforts, and diagnosis and repair of flaws in mental models.
20. Learning often proceeds with little or no trial and error; conceptual understanding often allowing children to reject inappropriate strategies without ever trying them.

genetic studies of children's learning. Each of the phenomena is discussed in some depth later in the chapter.

## History

Both the name *microgenetic* and the idea of microgenetic designs appear to have originated with Heinz Werner (Catan, 1986). Werner (1948) hypothesized that cognitive changes over diverse time spans, ranging from milliseconds to years, include important commonalities. Therefore, in the mid-1920s, he began to perform what he labeled "genetic experiments," that is, experiments aimed at describing the sequence of states within psychological events (this use of the term *genetic,* like Piaget's description of himself as a "genetic epistemologist," is based on the original definition of genetic as "pertaining to genesis or origins.") For example, Werner (1940) described how repeated presentation of a sequence of 12 ascending, initially indiscriminable tones eventually allowed people to form a representation in which the tones could be discriminated. Because the very rapid sequence of such mental states was believed to parallel the much slower sequence of states in development with age, the experiments were also labeled "mi-

crogenetic." Soviet contemporaries, including Vygotsky (1930/1978), cited with approval Werner's genetic experiments and argued for studying concepts and skills that were "in the process of change" (p. 65) rather than ones that were "fossilized" (p. 68).

Despite this promising beginning, the microgenetic method was rarely used in the ensuing years. The first spate of modern microgenetic articles appeared in the 1970s and early 1980s. Among the early adopters were Karmiloff-Smith and Inhelder (1974), Wertsch and Hickmann (1987), Karmiloff-Smith (1979b), and Kuhn and Phelps (1982). This last study was particularly important because it was the first microgenetic experiment that included all three defining features listed earlier.

Although classifications of studies as microgenetic inevitably are somewhat subjective, the prevalence of microgenetic studies clearly has increased greatly in recent years. Of the 105 studies classified as microgenetic for purposes of this review, only 10 were published before 1985. The growing frequency of microgenetic studies has several likely sources. One is the increasing emphasis on learning within prominent theories of cognitive development. Another is the increasing availability and sophistication of video recording technology and software and hardware tools that allow faster extraction of information than was possible until recently. A third is the increasingly broad range of tasks for which precise age norms have been established, thus setting the stage for microgenetic studies.

Probably the most important reason for the increased prevalence of microgenetic methods, however, is that it has become apparent that the value of the precise data on cognitive change that microgenetic designs yield more than offsets the time and effort required to obtain the data. Consider how the data obtained in microgenetic studies have allowed investigators to address one fundamental issue: how children discover new strategies. Microgenetic methods, unlike other developmental designs, allow identification of the exact trial on which each participant first used the new approach. Identifying the trial on which a new approach was first used allows examination of the nature of the discovery: whether a child was excited about the innovation, whether the child was even aware of having used a new approach, and whether he or she could explain why the new approach was advantageous. Knowing exactly when the new approach was first used also allows examination of performance just before the discovery: what types of problems preceded the discovery, whether the child failed to solve the immediately preceding problems, whether the child was taking an unusually long time to solve those problems, and so on. Moreover, knowing when the discovery was made allows examination of performance just after the discovery: how consistently the child used the new strategy on the same type of problem, how broadly the child generalized the new strategy to other types of problems, how efficiently the child executed the new strategy, and how all of these dimensions of performance changed as the child gained experience with the new approach. These are the benefits that are leading increasing numbers of investigators to use the microgenetic approach to study children's learning.

## Methodological Issues

Microgenetic studies raise a variety of methodological issues, including ones of experimental design, strategy assessment, and data analysis.

### Issues of Experimental Design

Because microgenetic studies generally require coding strategy use or other units of behavior on a great many trials, the distribution of experimental designs used in such studies differs from the overall distribution of experimental designs in the field. Quite a few microgenetic studies employ single subject designs, either with or without instruction (e.g., Agre & Shrager, 1990; K. E. Johnson & Mervis, 1994; Schoenfeld, Smith, & Arcavi, 1993). In one such case, Lawler (1985) described his daughter's learning of how to debug simple computer programs, solve simple arithmetic problems, and play tic tack toe over 90 sessions during a 4-month period. In another such study, Robinson and Mervis (1998) analyzed Mervis' son's acquisition of grammatical and lexical forms over almost 400 sessions over 13 months.

Another common type of microgenetic design involves focusing on the learning of a relatively small number of participants over a substantial period without any experimental intervention (e.g., Saada-Robert, 1992; Thelen & Ulrich, 1991). For example, Spencer et al. (2000) observed four infants' reaching in a free-play situation twice per week between 3 and 30 weeks of age and every other week between 32 and 52 weeks of age. Shimojo et al. (1986) study of 16 infants' acquisition of binocular depth perception over 31 weekly sessions between 1 and 8 months is another example. Thus, microgenetic methods can be applied to studying change over relatively long as well as relatively short time periods, and to study changes that might be described as "developmental," because they do not involve explicit experimental interventions, as well as changes that do involve such interventions and thus are more prototypic of "learning studies."

A third common microgenetic design involves presenting children with an unusually high density of an experience, with the goal of speeding up the typical developmental process, thus allowing more detailed analysis of change than would otherwise be possible (e.g., Siegler & Jenkins, 1989). This type of design, like the first two, does not include a control group, because the focus is on the way in which the change occurs rather than on establishing the effectiveness of the experience relative to changes that might have happened anyway. Examples of this design include Karmiloff-Smith's (1979b) study of changes within a single session in children's drawing of route maps, Kuhn, Schauble, and Garcia-Mila's (1992) study of changes in 10-year-olds' learning of scientific experimentation skills over 18 sessions in a 9-week period, and Schlagmüller and Schneider's (2002) study of changes in 9- and 11-year-olds' organization of pictures of objects on a sort-recall task in nine experimental sessions over an 11-week period.

Pressley (1992) criticized these three types of microgenetic designs by arguing that without a control group, they were subject to a variety of sources of experimental invalidity. However, it often is unclear what an appropriate control group would be in such studies, given that the focus is on describing how changes occur under the particular experimental condition, rather than on contrasting how different experimental conditions influence behavior. In addition, the studies have yielded fine-grain data about acquisition of complex skills, concepts, and domains, data that would have been unlikely to have been obtained in any other way and that have contributed a great deal to understanding of learning.

Moreover, despite Pressley's concern that the demands of microgenetic methods inherently preclude use of true experimental designs, increasing numbers of microgenetic studies have employed them (e.g., Chen & Siegler, 2000; Church, 1999; Siegler & Stern, 1998). For example, Alibali (1999) randomly assigned third and fourth graders to one of five experimental groups to compare learning about mathematical equality under varying conditions, and Klahr and Chen (2003) randomly assigned 4- and 5-year-olds to one of two groups to contrast learning about indeterminacy under the alternative conditions.

Although his claim that microgenetic methods preclude true experimental designs proved incorrect, Pressley (1992) did identify a number of tradeoffs that shape microgenetic research—tradeoffs among number of participants, number of sessions, sampling density, and type of task. Some of these tradeoffs are fairly obvious, but others are quite subtle.

One obvious tradeoff is that between number of participants and number of sessions. Microgenetic studies have included from 1 to more than 300 sessions and from 1 to more than 150 participants. In general, the greater the number of sessions, the smaller the number of participants. To cite the extremes, Robinson and Mervis (1998) observed one child for more than 300 sessions, whereas Alibali (1999) observed 178 participants for a single session.

Both number of participants and number of sessions trade off with density of observations. Microgenetic studies have involved within-trial analyses (e.g., Coyle & Bjorklund, 1997; Graham & Perry, 1993), trial-by-trial analyses (e.g., Blöte, Resing, Mazer, & Van Noort, 1999; Siegler & Jenkins, 1989), and session-by-session analyses (Jones, 1998; Shimojo et al., 1986). As a general rule, the higher the rate of change of the phenomenon

under the experimental conditions, the higher the density of observations needs to be. The demands of high-density observation militate toward either a small number of participants, a small number of sessions, or both.

All of these variables also trade off in a rather nonintuitive way with the prevalence of the task in the everyday environment. Some microgenetic studies present everyday tasks that children have encountered but not mastered; other studies present novel tasks. Similarly, some studies present tasks under more typical circumstances than other studies. Although it may seem surprising, changes on familiar tasks presented under quite natural circumstances tend to occur more slowly than changes on novel tasks presented under conditions that are by definition novel. For example, studies of everyday tasks, such as reaching (Thelen & Corbetta, 2002) and arithmetic (Siegler & Jenkins, 1989) have generally reported quite slow rates of change, whereas studies of novel tasks such as Tower of Hanoi (McNamara, Berg, Byrd, & McDonald, 2003) and number conservation (Church & Goldin-Meadow, 1986) have generally reported more rapid changes. Presumably, on familiar tasks most children have already made the easiest discoveries, so that the remaining ones tend to require more time or more facilitative conditions. Thus, although ecologically valid tasks and conditions might be expected to elicit more rapid change than novel tasks and circumstances, the opposite tends to be true.

One way of minimizing these trade-offs is by applying multiple methods, with different sets of advantages and disadvantages, to the same task. This approach has been used to good advantage in the study of semantic organization strategies. By combining cross sectional and longitudinal studies with microgenetic studies, Schneider and his colleagues were able to establish that changes occurred considerably more rapidly than suggested by the cross-sectional data (Schlagmüller & Schneider, 2002; Schneider, Kron, Hünnerkopf, & Krajewski, 2004).

### Issues of Strategy Assessment

A second class of methodological issues raised by microgenetic studies involves the reliability and validity of trial-by-trial strategy assessments. Although neither limited to microgenetic studies nor invariably used in them, trial-by-trial assessments are fundamental to many microgenetic studies. Precise analyses of strategy discoveries, of generalization of new strategies beyond their initial context, and of the precursors of discoveries require identification of when the strategy first emerges. This emergence can be specified most precisely through trial-by-trial assessments.

Before discussing issues of trial-by-trial assessment of strategies, however, it is necessary to define the term *strategy*. The present definition of strategy is one that was first advanced by Siegler and Jenkins (1989, p. 11): a "procedure that is nonobligatory and goal directed." This definition distinguishes strategy from procedure, in that some procedures are obligatory (they are the only way to achieve the goal). The definition also distinguishes strategy from behavior, in that behaviors do not imply any particular goal. Finally, the definition does not imply a rational generation process, conscious choice, or reportability. Including such criteria would exclude many activities that can profitably be conceptualized and analyzed within the present framework, as well as raising truly thorny issues, such as deciding what constitutes a rational generation process.

Returning to issues of assessment, the desirability of assessing strategy use on a trial-by-trial basis has shaped microgenetic research in several ways. Perhaps the most striking influence is that it has led researchers to rely on tasks that involve substantial overt behavior: crawling, walking, reaching, and stepping (e.g., Adolph, 1997; Thelen & Corbetta, 2002); writing and telling stories (Jones, 1998; Jones & Pellegrini, 1996; McKeough & Sanderson, 1996); manipulating physical apparatuses, such as gear systems, bridges, and robots (Dixon & Bangert, 2002; Granott, 1998; Parziale, 2002; Perry & Lewis, 1999; Thornton, 1999); doing mathematics (Blöte et al., 2004; Fletcher, Huffman, Bray, & Grupe, 1998; Goldin-Meadow & Alibali, 2002; Grupe, 1998); organizing to-be-remembered pictures or objects (Blöte et al., 1999; Coyle & Bjorklund, 1997; Schlagmüller & Schneider, 2002); and solving problems collaboratively (Ellis, 1995; Granott, Fischer, & Pariziale, 2002; Wertsch & Hickmann, 1987) among them. The possibilities created by trial-by-trial analysis also have influenced choices of dependent measures. Instead of relying solely on accuracy or solution times, researchers who conduct microgenetic studies also tend to assess the strategy used on each trial through use of videotapes of ongoing behavior, immediately retrospective verbal reports, notebooks that document scientific observations and conclusions, and other external indicators of thinking. This reliance on audible and visible behavior to infer thought processes is atypical of cognitive developmental research (though the reasons for other types of research

not making greater use of these external manifestations of thinking are unclear).

Microgenetic studies of children 4 years and younger have usually relied entirely on overt behavior to assess strategies. This approach has been followed, for example, in studying infant motor development (Adolph, 1997; Vereijken & Thelen, 1997), toddlers' problem solving (Chen & Siegler, 2000), and 3- and 4-year-olds' counting, memory, and attentional strategies (Bjorklund, Coyle, & Gaultney, 1992; Blöte et al., 2004; P. H. Miller & Aloise-Young, 1995).

Some studies of older children also have relied entirely on overt behavior to assess strategies (e.g., Bray, Huffman, & Fletcher, 1999; Lemaire & Siegler, 1995). However, in most recent studies of children 5 years and older, researchers have based strategy assessments on a combination of overt behavior and verbal reports provided during performance or (typically) immediately after. In most studies, the overt behavior is the basis of classification on trials on which it provides unambiguous evidence of which strategy was used; the verbal reports are used on trials on which overt behavior is absent or ambiguous. The combination of overt behavior and verbal reports has proved applicable for assessing strategy use on a wide range of tasks and among diverse populations, for example children with learning disabilities (Ostad, 1997).

Although use of verbal reports to infer strategy use has been widespread, the practice also has been questioned. Concerns have been raised about the veridicality and reactivity of such reports, with some investigators arguing that the need to generate verbal reports affects strategy use and other aspects of performance (Cooney & Ladd, 1992; Russo, Johnson, & Stephens, 1989). The data on which these criticisms were based, however, came from studies that lacked criteria of strategy use independent of the verbal reports (Bray et al., 1999). Results from studies that have included measures of strategy use independent of verbal reports (e.g., solution times, observations of overt behavior) have led to much more optimistic conclusions regarding the value of using verbal reports along with overt behavior.

**Veridicality.**   The most basic issue regarding verbal reports is whether the assessments yielded by using them are accurate. Ericsson and Simon (1984) reviewed the literature on this issue and concluded that retrospective reports generally are veridical when (a) the verbal report is obtained while the trace of processing activity remains in short-term memory, (b) the processes being described are of sufficient duration (roughly 1 second) that they produce a symbol in working memory, and (c) the processes are relatively easy to describe.

Since the publication of Ericsson's and Simon's seminal book, a great deal of evidence has supported their conclusion (Crutcher, 1994; K. M. Robinson, 2001; Siegler, 1987, 1989). In particular, among 5-year-olds and older individuals, classifying strategy use for each participant on each trial on the basis of both overt behavior and immediately retrospective self-reports has been found to increase the accuracy of classifications relative to that possible through classifying each participant's strategy use solely on the basis of overt behavior (Siegler, 1996).

To illustrate the type of data on which this conclusion is based, consider one study that tested whether examining immediately retrospective verbal reports as well as ongoing overt behavior results in more accurate strategy assessments than relying on the overt behavior alone (McGilly & Siegler, 1990). This study investigated 5- to 9-year-olds' serial recall strategies under verbal-report and no-verbal-report conditions. Children in the verbal-report condition were asked on each trial to describe what, if anything, they had done to help them remember; children in the no-verbal-report condition were not asked about their strategy use but were otherwise treated identically. A variety of measures indicated that the verbal reports added to the validity of the strategy assessments. In particular, the verbal reports revealed considerably more use of repeated rehearsal than was evident without them (74% versus 47% of trials), and did not bias the children's behavior (as indicated by the amount and types of visible strategy use being highly similar in verbal-report and no-verbal-report conditions). Bray et al. (1999), obtained similar findings with mentally retarded children on a different memory task. Thus, for children 5 years and older on tasks that meet the criteria described by Ericsson and Simon (1984), examining verbal reports as well as overt behavior on each trial increases the accuracy of strategy assessments over that possible from examining overt behavior alone.

**Reactivity of Self-Reports.** The above-cited finding of McGilly and Siegler (1990) that overt strategy use was essentially identical regardless of whether verbal reports were requested provided some evidence that requests for self-reports of strategy use do not alter the strategies that children use. Results of other studies and

from other measures also indicate that immediately retrospective verbal reports are usually nonreactive. For example, Bray et al. (1999) and Robinson (2001) found that requests for such verbal reports had no effect on accuracy and also did not affect the frequency of use of overt strategies on organizational memory and arithmetic tasks.

To minimize the possibility of reactivity, it is essential to avoid instructions that bias participants in favor of one strategy or another; such biased instructions can have large effects on strategy use (Kirk & Ashcraft, 1997). With that caveat, however, it appears that trial-by-trial strategy assessments, based on both observations of ongoing behavior and immediately retrospective verbal reports, can provide veridical and nonreactive strategy assessments for 5-year-olds and older individuals.

### Issues of Data Analysis

Investigating change introduces a variety of complex issues regarding data analysis, issues sufficiently difficult that a number of methodologists have argued that no good inferential statistical solution exists for many problems at present (Willett, 1997). These analytic complexities have led to a greater reliance on graphical techniques than is typical in developmental research as a whole and also the use of several inferential statistical techniques that are specialized for analysis of change. Two techniques that have proven particularly useful in microgenetic research are presented here; for more comprehensive discussions see Allison (1984), Singer and Willett (2003), Collins and Sayer (2001), and Moskowitz and Hershberger (2002).

**Graphical Techniques.** Microgenetic studies often rely heavily on graphical presentation of data. Such graphical analyses have been particularly common in portrayals of discrete aspects of change, for example discovery of new strategies. One graphical technique that has proven especially revealing for examining discrete aspects of change is backward trial graphing. This is a technique in which the event of interest for each participant is aligned with the zero point on the X-axis, regardless of when it occurred in the sequence of trials. In almost all cases, the event of interest occurs for different participants on different trials. Thus, one participant's zero point might occur on the 10th trial of the experiment, another on the 20th, and another on the 30th. All other points on the X-axis are defined relative to the zero point. The −1 trial or trial block is defined as the one immediately before the event of interest, the −2 trial or trial block is defined as the one immediately before that, the +1 trial or trial block is defined as the one immediately after the event of interest, and so on. Thus, backward trial graphs reveal what led up to the event of interest and what happened immediately after it.

The way in which this graphical technique has been used to illuminate change processes within microgenetic studies can be illustrated by describing its use in a study that examined whether unconscious discoveries sometimes precede conscious ones (Siegler & Stern, 1998). Second graders were presented problems of the form, $A + B − B = \underline{\hspace{1cm}}$ (e.g., $18 + 5 − 5 = \underline{\hspace{1cm}}$). These problems were of special interest for investigating unconscious discovery because they could be solved by different strategies that implied very different solution times. The computation strategy, which involved adding the first two numbers and then subtracting the third, implied long solution times, because the computations take young children considerable time. In contrast, the shortcut strategy, which involved reasoning that because $B − B = 0$, the answer must be A, could be executed much more quickly, because no computation was required.

This logic was borne out by the data; the mean reaction time (RT) when children used the computation strategy (as indicated by overt behavior and verbal report) was 16 seconds, whereas the mean RT when they used the shortcut strategy was 3 seconds. Especially important, there was virtually no overlap in solution times; almost all times were either 8 seconds or more, indicating use of computation, or 4 seconds or less, indicating use of the shortcut strategy. This fact, together with the fact that the second graders who participated invariably started out using computation, allowed unusually direct examination of unconscious strategy discovery. In particular, if children's solution times suddenly declined from the computation range to the shortcut range, but the children continued to report using the computation strategy, then it could be inferred that they had discovered the shortcut at an unconscious level (an approach labeled the "unconscious shortcut strategy").

The predicted data pattern was observed. Children's solution times dropped from an average of 12 seconds on the three trials just before their first use of the unconscious shortcut to an average of less than 3 seconds on the first trial on which they used the unconscious shortcut. This finding motivated use of backward trial graphs to examine children's discoveries in more detail.

Figure 11.1 includes two backward trial graphs, which show the patterns of strategy use leading up to the first use of the unconscious shortcut (left) and the first use of the conscious shortcut (right). As shown in the graph on the left, before children's first use of the unconscious shortcut, they consistently used the computation strategy. After the initial use of the unconscious shortcut, most children continued to use the unconscious shortcut over the next three trials. By the fourth trial after the initial use of the unconscious shortcut, half of the children were conscious of using the shortcut (as indicated by their verbal reports).

The graph on the right shows a parallel backward trial graph centered on children's first conscious use of the shortcut. On each of the three trials immediately preceding the first conscious use of the shortcut, roughly 80% of children used the unconscious shortcut (as opposed to less than 10% use of this strategy for the study as a whole). Once children began to report using the shortcut, they continued to use it quite consistently for the rest of that session (though most forgot and needed to rediscover it in the next session a week later). As this example illustrates, backward trial graphing procedures can reveal in considerably detail the events surrounding strategy discovery and other events of interest.

**Inferential Statistical Techniques.** Inferential statistical techniques for analyzing the type of categorical, repeated measures, nonlinear patterns of data typically yielded by microgenetic studies are not as well developed as techniques based on the general linear model, such as regression and ANOVA. However, some inferential statistical techniques are specifically useful for analyzing microgenetic data. One such class of statistical approaches is collectively labeled "event history analysis" (Allison, 1984; Singer & Willett, 2003). This class of techniques has been used most widely to analyze the type of one-time events that interest epidemiologists (e.g., death). However, the techniques are equally applicable to one-time events of interest to psychologists, such as discovery of a new strategy or walking unaided for the first time. Moreover, event history analysis can also be applied to events that occur multiple times. The technique is particularly useful because it allows examination of time-dependent predictor variables, such as mean solution time on the previous N trials, and because it handles in a nonarbitrary way cases in which the event of interest fails to occur during the study (right censored

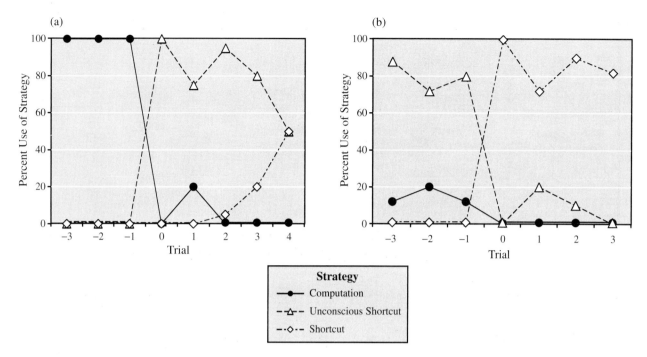

**Figure 11.1**    (a) Strategy use on trials immediately before and after each child's first use of the unconscious shortcut strategy on A + B − B problems. (b) Strategy use on trials immediately before and after each child's first use of the shortcut strategy on A + B − B problems. *Source:* From "A Microgenetic Analysis of Conscious and Unconscious Strategy Discoveries," by R. S. Siegler and E. Stern, 1998, *Journal of Experimental Psychology: General, 127,* pp. 377–397. Reprinted with permission.

data). Moreover, it yields results that can be interpreted like the results of standard regression techniques.

In explaining the applicability of event history analysis to microgenetic data, Dixon and Bangert (2002) noted the centrality of two concepts: the risk set and the hazard rate. The risk set includes all participants who have not yet experienced the event of interest, for example those who have not yet generated a strategy. This set decreases over the course of the experiment, as more participants experience the event of interest. The hazard rate is the probability of an event occurring on a given trial; calculation of this probability must reflect the risk set on that trial. For dichotomous variables such as strategy discovery, logistic regression can be used to determine which variables influence the hazard rate.

Dixon and Bangert (2002) used event history analysis to examine discovery of strategies for solving gear movement problems. To determine the relation of prior performance to the likelihood of discovery, they examined speed and accuracy of solutions both on all preceding trials and on a moving window of the immediately preceding five trials. Solution times on the five previous trials, though not on all trials, predicted discovery; the longer the solution times on those recent trials, the more

likely that children would discover a new strategy. This predictive relation held true for two different advanced strategies. The event history analysis also revealed that other aspects of recent past performance, including inaccuracy and low rate of guessing, were positively related to the likelihood of discovery. Thus, techniques such as event history analysis and backward trial graphing are useful for analyzing microgenetic data.

## OVERLAPPING WAVES THEORY

Microgenetic studies have consistently indicated that children's thinking is more variable than recognized within most theories of cognitive development. Different children use different strategies; individual children use different strategies on different problems within a single session; individual children often use different strategies to solve the same problem on two occasions close in time; and so on (Siegler, 1996).

To capture these and other findings, Siegler (1996) proposed overlapping waves theory. Perhaps because this theory co-evolved with microgenetic methods, it has

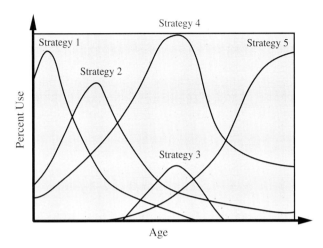

**Figure 11.2**   The overlapping waves model.

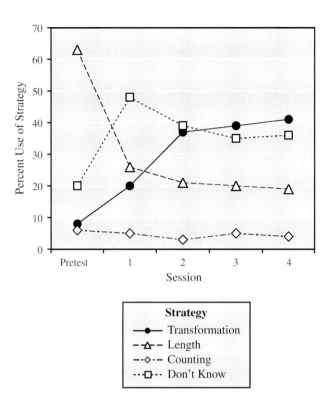

**Figure 11.3**   Strategy use on number conservation problems. *Source:* From "How Does Change Occur: A Microgenetic Study of Number Conservation," by R. S. Siegler, 1995, *Cognitive Psychology, 25,* pp. 225–273. Reprinted with permission.

proven particularly useful for integrating findings from such research.

The basic assumption of overlapping waves theory is that development is a process of variability, choice, and change. As illustrated in Figure 11.2, the theory posits that children typically know and use varied strategies for solving a given problem at any one time. With age and experience, the relative frequency of each strategy changes, with some strategies becoming less frequent (Strategy 1), some becoming more frequent (Strategy 5), some becoming more frequent and then less frequent (Strategy 2), and some never becoming very frequent (Strategy 3). In addition to changes in relative use of existing strategies, new strategies are discovered (Strategies 3 and 5), and some older strategies abandoned (Strategy 1).

In many cases, several of these patterns are evident within a single study. Consider a study of number conservation (Siegler, 1995) in which 5-year-olds were given a pretest and four learning sessions. During the learning sessions, children needed to explain the logic underlying the experimenter's answer on each trial. As shown in Figure 11.3, over the course of the experiment, reliance on the relative lengths of the two rows of objects decreased, reliance on the type of transformation that had been performed increased, reliance on counting stayed at a constant low level, and answering "I don't know," first increased and then decreased. Interestingly, roughly half of the 5-year-olds first used the most advanced type of reasoning, reliance on the type of transformation, on a pretest trial. For these children, learning involved increased reliance on transformational reasoning; for the others, it involved discovery of the new approach as well as increasing reliance on it.

As this example illustrates, an important feature of overlapping waves theory is that it provides a means of integrating qualitative and quantitative aspects of learning within a single framework. The approach recognizes that children discover qualitatively novel strategies and concepts; it also recognizes that much of development is due to quantitative shifts in the frequency and efficiency of execution of strategies, and in the adaptiveness of choices among them. Learning clearly involves both qualitative and quantitative changes; there is no reason for developmental theories to focus on one to the exclusion of the other.

Overlapping waves theory also makes several assumptions that are not evident in Figure 11.2. One such assumption is that from early in learning, children usually choose adaptively among strategies; that is, they choose strategies that fit the demands of problems and circumstances, and that yield desirable combinations of speed and accuracy, given the strategies and available knowledge that children possess. A related assumption is that such choices among alternative approaches generally become even more adaptive with experience in the content area. For example, from the beginning of their experience with ramps, toddlers adjust their descent strategies to the steepness of the ramp (Adolph, 1997). They use quicker but riskier strategies on the shallower ramps and slower but surer strategies on the steeper ones. With age and locomotor experience, their descent strategies become even more finely calibrated to the ramp's slope. A further assumption is that improvements in performance during childhood reflect a combination of generation of superior new approaches; greater reliance on relatively advanced approaches that are already known; increasingly adaptive choices among approaches; and improved execution of all approaches.

Of particular importance for the present discussion, overlapping waves theory suggests that cognitive change can be analyzed along five dimensions: source, path, rate, breadth, and variability. The *source of change* refers to the causes that set the change in motion. The *path of change* is the sequence of knowledge states, representations, or predominant behaviors that children use while gaining competence. The *rate of change* concerns how much time or experience separates initial use of a new approach from consistent use of it. The *breadth of change* involves how widely the new approach is generalized to other problems and contexts. The *variability of change* refers to differences among children in the other dimensions of change, as well as to the changing set of strategies used by individual children.

To see how change can be analyzed in terms of these dimensions, again consider the Siegler (1995) study of number conservation. The source of the most dramatic change in this study was a combination of feedback on the correctness of answers and requests that the 5-year-olds explain why the correct answer (which had been indicated by the experimenter) was correct. This combination led to greater learning than feedback alone. The path of change involved children who were asked to explain the experimenter's reasoning initially relying most often on the relative length of the rows, then going through a period in which they abandoned this approach but did not adopt any consistent alternative, and then usually adopting the correct approach of relying on the type of transformation that the experimenter had performed. The rate of change was moderate; most children required several sessions to progress from initial use to consistent use of the transformational strategy. The breadth of change was relatively narrow; even some of the best learners in the study continued in the final session to often advance length explanations (rather than transformational ones) of the experimenter's reasoning on problems on which the longer row also had more ob-

jects. Finally, there was substantial variability both within and between children. At the level of within-child variability, only 2% of children relied on a single strategy throughout the study; 70% of children used three or more approaches. At the level of between-child variability, individual differences in learning could be predicted by two pretest measures: total number of strategies used by the child and whether the child ever used two different strategies on the same problem. Thus, distinguishing among the source, path, rate, breadth, and variability of change provided a useful framework for analyzing children's learning.

The remainder of this chapter uses the five dimensions of change specified by overlapping waves theory to examine the new field of children's learning and how microgenetic studies have contributed to it. The conclusions are based on 105 studies that met at least one of three criteria for being microgenetic. One criterion was self-description; I attempted to include all studies whose authors used the term microgenetic in the title or abstract (as indicated by a PsychLit search undertaken when I started to write the review) and that focused on children's learning. A second criterion was identification in prior reviews: I attempted to include studies that were described as microgenetic in one of three previous reviews of the literature: Siegler and Crowley (1991), Kuhn (1995), and P. H. Miller and Coyle (1999). A third criterion was meeting the three definitional standards for microgenetic designs, regardless of whether the authors or previous reviewers labeled them "microgenetic."

A few caveats are in order. The boundaries of the category "microgenetic studies" are inherently somewhat subjective, and either narrower or broader criteria could have been adopted. For example, studies that examined pretest-posttest changes, but not the intervening change process, were excluded on the logic that they did not allow detailed, data-based specification of the representations and processes that led to learning. For the same reason, studies that did not present quantitative analyses of changing competence, or that only examined changes in percentage of correct answers rather than also examining changes in strategy use, were excluded. Good arguments certainly could be made for other inclusion criteria that would have resulted in broader, narrower, or overlapping coverage with that in the present review. Even within the present criteria, studies that fit have almost certainly been inadvertently omitted. However, the studies that were examined provide a good sampling of results that have emerged from microgenetic studies of children's learning.

## THE NEW FIELD OF CHILDREN'S LEARNING

The findings yielded by microgenetic studies are organized in terms of their implications for the five dimensions of learning described: variability, path, rate, breadth, and source. The discussion of each dimension begins with a summary of basic findings, then examines influences of child and environment on that dimension, and concludes with a discussion of implications and unresolved questions.

### Variability

Perhaps the single central phenomenon that has been revealed by microgenetic studies is the great variability of learning (Granott, 2002; Kuhn, 1995; Lee & Karmiloff-Smith, 2002; P. H. Miller & Coyle, 1999; Siegler & Crowley, 1991). Such variability is especially evident in microgenetic studies, because the trial-by-trial assessments characteristic of the approach reveal different processing approaches within as well as between individuals. The variability is evident at every level of analysis. It is present in all domains, not just motor activities and memory where it has long been recognized, but in higher cognitive processes, such as problem solving, reasoning, and conceptual understanding, as well. It is present not only during delimited transitional periods, where it has long been recognized, but in periods where change is less rapid. It is present, moreover, not just at the neural and associative levels, where it has long been recognized, but also at the level of rules, strategies, theories, and other units of higher-level cognition. Finally, the variability is present not only between different people, but also within a single person solving the same problem at two points close in time and even within an individual's actions on a single trial. This section presents evidence for this pervasive variability and for how the variability is related to learning.

### Basic Empirical Phenomena

#### Within-Child Variability

Massive variability of thought and action characterizes people of all ages. It is characteristic of infants; for example, Adolph (1997) found that in descending down ramps, 5- to 15-month-olds sometimes crawled, sometimes slid on their belly, sometimes slid on their behind, sometimes slid head first, sometimes slid feet first, sometimes descended in a sitting position, and some-

times refused to go down at all. It was not the case that one baby used one approach and a different baby another; on relatively shallow slopes, each baby used an average of five distinct strategies, and on relatively steep slopes, each baby used an average of six (Adolph, 1997; Wechsler & Adolph, 1995).

Toddlers' thoughts and actions are similarly variable. Chen and Siegler (2000) found that 18- to 35-month-olds who needed to select an appropriate tool to pull in a desirable toy sometimes used a tool, sometimes reached with their hands, sometimes requested their mother's help, and sometimes just sat and stared at the toy, perhaps hoping that someone would help them. Among the toddlers, 74% used at least three of these strategies during the 13 trials of the experiment, and only 3% used a single strategy throughout.

Comparable variability has been found in microgenetic studies of preschoolers. Most 3- and 4-year-olds use multiple selective attention strategies (P. H. Miller & Aloise-Young, 1995); most 4-year-olds use multiple strategies to solve analogy problems (Tunteler & Resing, 2002); most 4- and 5-year-olds use multiple arithmetic strategies (Siegler & Jenkins, 1989); and so on.

Older children's and adults' strategies are similarly variable. For example, Alibali (1999) found that third and fourth graders used six incorrect strategies and four correct strategies in both speech and gesture while solving mathematical equality problems. Kuhn, Schauble, and Garcia-Mila (1992) found that fifth graders changed their minds about the causal status of features in a scientific reasoning context an average of 10 times; in another study that used a similar task, fifth graders and adults changed their mind about the causal status of features an average of 14 times (Schauble, 1996). Variability of spelling strategies is similarly variable; in Kwong and Varnhagen (2005), each of four strategies was used by a majority of first graders, and each of seven strategies was used by a majority of adults. Thus, thought and action are highly variable within individual infants, toddlers, children, and adults.

This trial-to-trial variability in strategy use is not attributable to people moving in an orderly progression from less adequate strategies to somewhat more adequate strategies to yet more adequate strategies over the course of an experiment. Children often use more-advanced approaches on one trial and then regress to less-advanced ones on the next (Blöte, Van Otterloo, Stevenson, & Veenman, 2004; Coyle & Bjorklund, 1997; Kuhn & Phelps, 1982; Tunteler & Resing, 2002). Illustratively, P. H. Miller and Aloise-Young (1995) found that 41% of changes in information gathering strategies from one trial to the next were regressions from more advanced to less advanced approaches. These regressions are temporary—the longer trajectory of change was upward in all of these studies—but the progress reflects a back and forth competition rather than a steady march forward.

The trial-to-trial variability cannot be explained in terms of children using different strategies on different problems. The variability is present even when the same problem is presented twice, relatively close in time. These changes, like those on successive trials, often reflect surprisingly even balances between improvements and regressions in situations in which children are not given instruction. Siegler and Shrager (1984) found that 45% of changes of level of basic addition strategies were in a negative direction, and Siegler and McGilly (1989) found that 43% of changes of level of time telling strategies were in a negative direction. In these cases and others, progressions outnumber regressions, but the difference is smaller than might have been expected.

The trial-to-trial variability also is not limited to tasks on which the two strategies differ in efficiency but not in their logical quality. Children have been found to show regressions from logically superior strategies to logically inferior ones surprisingly often. Such regressions have been found on numerous tasks that allow logically superior and inferior strategies, including mathematical equality (Alibali, 1999), matrix completion (Siegler & Svetina, 2002), number conservation (Church & Goldin-Meadow, 1986), control of variables (Schauble, 1990), and logical inference (Kuhn et al., 1992). Adults in the same studies have been found to regress from more advanced to less advanced logic on the last three of these tasks as well. For example, adults as well as children often generate valid inference forms in reasoning about causality and then regress to invalid forms of reasoning (Kuhn et al., 1995). Even Charles Darwin frequently regressed from more to less advanced thinking about evolution, as reflected in the reasoning in his notebooks (Fischer & Yan, 2002).

Cognitive variability also has been demonstrated within a single trial. The most extensive demonstrations of this phenomenon have come from research on gesture-speech mismatches (Alibali & Goldin-Meadow, 1993; Church & Goldin-Meadow, 1986; Graham & Perry, 1993; Perry & Lewis, 1999). On a variety of tasks, including number conservation, mathematical equality, and gear motion, children frequently express one strategy in speech but a different strategy in gesture. For ex-

ample, in Church's (1999) conservation study, 53% of children generated gesture-speech mismatches on at least three of the six problems. When such mismatches occur, children typically express more advanced understanding in gesture than in speech; for example, they might simply cite the height of the liquid columns in explaining their reasoning about liquid quantity conservation, but their hand gestures might include both vertical motions comparing the heights of the two liquid columns and horizontal motions comparing their cross sectional areas.

A variety of other types of within-trial variability have also been documented. On sort/recall memory tasks, children often use multiple strategies on a single trial, such as first organizing the objects into groups and then rehearsing either the names of the groups or the names of the items within each group (Coyle & Bjorklund, 1997; Schlagmüller & Schneider, 2002). On number conservation problems, children sometimes explain their reasoning in terms of both the length of the rows and the type of transformation on items where the two lead to the same answer (Siegler, 1995). On gear problems, children fairly often advance an explanation and follow it with second thoughts, such as, "Wait a minute, I made a mistake" (Perry & Lewis, 1999).

### Significance of Within-Child Variability

The fact that substantial within-child variability exists does not necessarily mean that such variability is important. Traditional approaches have recognized the existence of within-subject variability but have treated it as a nuisance to be minimized—error variance (van Geert, 2002). Microgenetic studies, however, have revealed that within-child variability is important—for predicting change, for analyzing change, and for understanding change mechanisms.

**Significance for Predicting Change.** High initial variability of strategy use often predicts substantial later learning. This relation has been documented with numerous types of variability in numerous content areas. Number of strategies used by each child on a pretest has been found to correlate positively with the child's subsequent learning on number conservation and sort-recall tasks (Coyle & Bjorklund, 1997; Siegler, 1995). Number of strategies used by each adult on a pretest has been found similarly predictive of the adult's subsequent learning on gear problems (Perry & Elder, 1997). In addition, children's use of multiple strategies on a single trial (as opposed to over the entire set of problems) has been found predictive of their learning on mathematical representation problems (Fujimura, 2001), on taxonomic memory problems (Schlagmüller & Schneider, 2002), and on number conservation problems (Siegler, 1995). The number of different explanations and the number of arguments that a child advances in support of a given explanation on conservation problems also has been found to predict the child's learning (Church, 1999). In addition, progressing through a variable state, in which gestures and speech express different understandings, has been found predictive of generalization to a novel task (Goldin-Meadow & Alibali, 2002).

Positive relations between initial variability and subsequent learning have emerged not only regarding the variability of what children say but also the variability of how they say it. Pauses, vagueness, false starts, talking to oneself, tapping the table, and verbal disfluencies all have been demonstrated to be positive predictors of learning (Bidell & Fischer, 1994; Caron & Caron-Pargue, 1976; Hosenfeld, van der Maas, & van den Boom, 1997; Siegler & Engle, 1994; Siegler & Jenkins, 1989). For example, in Graham and Perry (1993), 64% of children who produced vague pretest explanations for answers to mathematical equality problems succeeded on posttest and transfer problems, versus 23% of children who produced more specific explanations.

To specify the influence of different types of verbal variability, Perry and Lewis (1999) presented fifth graders with gear movement problems and obtained independent measures of four types of variability during children's verbal protocols: long pauses, false starts, omissions of nouns or verbs (a form of vagueness), and metacognitive comments about the problem solving process (e.g., "I'm confused here"). They found that children who subsequently mastered the task were higher on all four measures of pretest variability than were other children, that the measures of pretest variability were only modestly related to each other, and that a composite measure of variability predicted learning more effectively than did age, instructional condition, or number of correct pretest answers. Long pauses and frequent metacognitive comments were the types of variability most strongly related to learning. In addition, all measures of variability decreased as children mastered the task.

The decrease in variability with increasing task mastery suggests that the positive relation between initial variability and learning is due to children whose initial behavior is highly variable being in a state in which they are especially likely to learn, rather than to the high variability being a stable characteristic of good learners. Whether there are in fact consistent individual differences in variability is unknown. A number of investigators have hypothesized that gifted and creative people are especially high in variability (Gardner, 1993; Janos & Robinson, 1985; Stokes, 2001), but some data argue against the hypothesis (Coyle, Read, Gaultney, & Bjorklund, 1998).

Not all types of variability are positively related to learning. Coyle (2001) examined five measures of variability on sort-recall tasks, a type of problem on which multiple strategies can be used within a given trial: number of strategies used at least once during the experiment, mean number of strategies used on each trial, number of pairs of consecutive trials on which different strategies were used, mean number of strategies added and deleted on consecutive trials, and number of strategy combinations used on different trials. A factor analysis of the data on these measures from eight sort-recall experiments indicated two main factors: strategy diversity and strategy change. The first two measures loaded most heavily on the strategy diversity factor, the last three on the strategy change factor. Consistent with past findings, the strategy diversity factor, which corresponded to the kinds of variability described previously in this section, correlated positively with recall. In contrast, strategy changes, the factor on which the last three measures loaded most heavily, correlated negatively with recall. It seems likely that this negative relation was generated by recall failures leading children to shift strategies from one trial to the next or to try new combinations of strategies. More generally, distinguishing among types of variability and determining their relation to learning seems a crucial task for future research.

**Significance for Analyzing Change.** Accurately assessing within-child variability allows more precise theoretical analyses of how learning occurs than would otherwise be possible. In particular, trial-by-trial assessments allow researchers to analyze the contributions to learning of four component processes: acquisition of new approaches, increasing use of the most advanced existing approaches, increasingly efficient execution of approaches, and improved choices among approaches.

To illustrate how this taxonomy can be used to analyze learning, consider Lemaire and Siegler's (1995) study of the growth of proficiency in single-digit multiplication among French second graders. The children's strategy use, accuracy, and speed was observed three times during the year: 1 week, 3 months, and 5 months after the beginning of multiplication instruction. Multiplication skill greatly increased over this period. Contrary to what might have been expected, however, the learning did not reflect addition of new strategies: from the first assessment, which was conducted within a week of the beginning of multiplication instruction, children used the same strategies—retrieval, repeated addition, and guessing—as they did 5 months later. Instead, increased multiplication proficiency reflected the operation of the other three processes. There were large changes in the relative frequency with which the three approaches were used; use of retrieval increased, whereas use of the other two strategies decreased. The adaptiveness of choices among strategies improved; children increasingly focused their use of retrieval on the problems on which retrieval was most likely to yield the correct answer. Finally, efficiency of execution showed large improvements; children executed repeated addition and retrieval far more quickly and accurately at the end of the year than at the beginning.

The finding that improved execution of strategies was a major contributor to learning is not limited to second graders' multiplication. Although contemporary analyses of higher-level cognition have tended to emphasize the contributions of qualitative changes, such as acquisition of new strategies and representations, microgenetic analyses have consistently indicated that quantitative improvements in execution of strategies also play a large role. For example, Schauble (1990, 1996), Kuhn et al. (1995), and Kuhn and Phelps (1982) found that even when children and adults performed ideal experiments for identifying the effects of a given variable, the adults were more likely to learn the effect of the variable, because they more accurately remembered what they did and what happened in the experiment. Chen and Siegler's (2000) examination of toddlers' tool use, P. H. Miller and Aloise-Young's (1995) analysis of preschoolers' selective attention strategies, and Shrager and Callanan's (1991) observations of mothers and preschoolers cooking together are three other cases in which improved execution of strategies contributed substantially to learning.

Another way in which assessment of within-child variability can enhance analyses of learning is through providing sufficiently detailed data to allow investigators to focus on the most informative children and

strategies. Trial-by-trial analyses often indicate that all of the learning shown by a group of children derives from a subgroup of the children; focusing analyses on this subgroup can provide a much sharper focus on how learning occurred than mixing their data with data from children who learned little or nothing (Schlagmüller & Schneider, 2002; Siegler & Svetina, 2002). For example, identifying a subgroup of children who showed substantial learning allowed Gelman, Romo, and Francis (2002) to make more precise statements about changes in ESL students' science notebooks than would otherwise have been possible. Similarly, examining within-child variability allows identification of strategies that do and do not produce learning, which again allows more focused analyses of learning processes than would otherwise be possible. Blöte, Resing, Mazer, and Van Noort (1999), for example, found that on a selective attention task, all of the learning of the 4-year-old participants derived from improved ability to execute one of the three strategies that they used, and Siegler (1995) found that 5-year-olds' learning of number conservation was entirely attributable to increased reliance on one of the five strategies that they used.

**Significance for Identifying Change Mechanisms.** Examination of within-child variability also has promoted formulation of mechanisms that specify how such variability leads to cognitive growth. Among these mechanisms are ones for bridging between less and more advanced strategies (Granott et al., 2002), for coordinating multiple types of knowledge and procedures through metacognitive understanding (Kuhn, 2002; Lee & Karmiloff-Smith, 2002), for progressively shifting strategy choices toward the more effective approaches (Siegler & Shipley, 1995), and for indicating how gesture-speech mismatch contributes to cognitive growth (Goldin-Meadow & Alibali, 2002).

Findings from microgenetic studies also convey general lessons relevant to a variety of mechanisms. One such lesson involves the existence of conceptual constraints on learning. Contrary to the emphasis of earlier learning theories on blind trial-and-error, microgenetic analyses indicate that children's learning in meaningful domains shows remarkably little trial and error (Bidell & Fischer, 1994; Siegler & Jenkins, 1989). Thus, even untutored 1- and 2-year-olds do not choose randomly among tools when they start to use them; they prefer tools that have the right type of head for pulling in the desired object and that are long enough to reach it (Chen

& Siegler, 2000). As discussed in more detail in the section on learning mechanisms, such findings suggest the existence of mechanisms that constrain children's strategies to those that are conceptually plausible.

Another general lesson of findings regarding within-child variability is that seemingly insignificant variations in children's initial behavior can exert large influences on subsequent strategy discoveries. For example, Thornton (1999) found that 5-year-olds who played the game "20 Questions" typically began by asking whether the answer was a particular object. However, the exact phrasing that they used proved surprisingly predictive of their learning beyond this point. In a game that included several cars as potential answers, only 10% of children who initially asked questions that clearly specified the object of interest (e.g., "Is it the red car?") or who did not name any object characteristics (e.g., "Is it this one?") progressed to asking questions that were informative about multiple objects (e.g., "Is it one of the cars?"). In contrast, 90% of children who initially used a slightly different, ambiguous phrasing (e.g., "Is it the car?") later asked these more informative questions. Thornton hypothesized that the very ambiguity of asking questions such as "Is it the car?" when multiple cars were present made it easier to advance to more informative questions such as "Is it *a* car?" or "Is it *one of the cars?*" Similarly, Childers and Tomasello (2001) found that 2.5-year-olds who were presented verbs with pronoun frames (e.g., "He kicked it"; "She pushed it") were more likely than peers who heard the same verbs with more specific noun frames (e.g., "Sam kicked the ball"; "Jane pushed the car") to generalize the past tense form to novel verbs (e.g., "She tunned it"; "Jane tunned the car"). The authors hypothesized that the greater consistency of the pronoun frames facilitated learning and generalization of the past tense verbs by making it easier for the children to focus on the verb ending. Thus, subtle differences in the conditions of learning can lead to substantial variation in the learning that occurs.

## Influences of Child and Environment

### Within-Child Variability

Amount of within-child variability often changes over the course of development, but the changes do not conform to any single pattern. With age and experience, variability can increase (Coyle & Bjorklund, 1997; Dowker, 2003), decrease (Braswell & Rosengren, 2000; Spencer et al., 2000), increase and then decrease (Gershkoff-Stowe & Smith, 1997; Verijken & Thelen, 1997), stay constant (Flynn et al., 2004; Siegler, 1987), and so on.

Microgenetic studies of children's learning suggest that these disparate patterns may have a common source. Over the course of development, performance often oscillates between less and more variable periods. Therefore, the changes with age and expertise that are observed in any particular study depend on the part of the cycle that is observed. The basic idea that periods of stability (i.e., low variability) alternate with periods of transition (i.e., high variability) was proposed by Piaget (e.g., 1975), and similar ideas have since been suggested by Siegler and Taraban (1986), Goldin-Meadow, Alibali, and Church (1993), Thelen (1994), and van Geert (1997), among others. Microgenetic studies provide considerable support for the idea.

One source of support for the view that variability tends to wax and wane in a cyclical fashion comes from studies of Piagetian problem-solving tasks. On such problems, children often begin with a systematically wrong approach, then move to a variable state in which they oscillate among a variety of strategies, and then move to relatively consistent use of a more advanced approach. This pattern has emerged among children learning about balance scales (Siegler & Chen, 1998), matrix completion (Siegler & Svetina, 2002), and conservation (van der Maas & Molenaar, 1996). The pattern has emerged in microgenetic studies of other reasoning problems as well. For example, Hosenfeld et al. (1997) found that on an analogical reasoning task, children who began the study with a consistently incorrect approach moved over eight sessions toward almost equal use of three different approaches. In contrast, children who began in a more variable state, in which they fairly often used all three approaches, moved toward consistent use of the single most advantageous approach.

Another source of support for the conclusion that variability is cyclical comes from studies of motor development. Many infants, after an early period of bias toward reaching with the right hand, oscillate among varied reaching approaches (e.g., sometimes reaching with both hands, sometimes reaching with one hand, and sometimes reaching with the other) for a prolonged period before eventually returning to consistent right-handed reaching (Corbetta & Thelen, 1999). Similarly, infants' spontaneous kicking oscillates between periods of stability, in which a single form dominates (e.g., kicking one leg only), and periods of instability, in which several forms are used (e.g., kicking one leg repeatedly, kicking both legs simultaneously, and alternating between right and left leg kicks) (Thelen & Corbetta, 2002).

The oscillation between periods of lesser and greater variability is also evident in within-trial analyses. When given relevant experience on mathematical equality problems, children who initially produced the same type of incorrect strategy in speech and gesture tended to progress to a more variable state, in which their gestures reflected a correct strategy and their speech did not. In contrast, children who were given the same relevant experience but who began in a variable state, in which their gestures but not their speech expressed a correct strategy, usually progressed to a less variable state, in which gesture and speech expressed the same correct strategy (Alibali & Goldin-Meadow, 1993).

Performance of children in the same experiment who did not receive relevant experience provides a different type of support for the cyclical interpretation. Children who were initially in a variable state, in which their gesture expressed a correct strategy and their speech did not, often regressed to a consistent state, in which both were incorrect. In contrast, as noted in the previous paragraph, children who were initially in the variable state were especially likely to progress to a more advanced stable state if they did receive relevant experience. This finding suggests that high gesture-speech variability may signal "teachable moments" that need to be seized or otherwise be lost. To summarize, findings from microgenetic studies suggest that the disparate observations of age trends in variability are due to the observations tapping different phases of cyclical increases and decreases in variability.

One question raised by this perspective is whether there is a typical pattern of change in within-child variability with increasing age and knowledge. Siegler and Taraban (1986) addressed this question by suggesting the moderate experience hypothesis: that children usually progress from low variability when they have little relevant experience with the task to high variability when they have a moderate amount of experience, to low variability when they have substantial experience with it. The logic is that children often begin with only one or a few ways of solving a problem, then generate a larger variety of ways, and then settle on the best way or ways. Certainly, many examples fit this model: arithmetic, matrix completion, false belief, mathematical equality, and number conservation, to cite five (Alibali & Goldin-Meadow, 1993; Church & Goldin-Meadow, 1986; Flynn et al., 2004; Geary, 1994; Siegler &

Svetina, 2002). Determining whether it is the most common progression, however, is complex. Some questions are definitional: are we talking about variability on a single, narrowly defined type of problem or variability across a whole domain of problems? To illustrate with an everyday example, professional basketball players possess a far greater range of shooting motions than do high school players, but for any single type of shot (e.g., free throws), their motions are far less variable (Gilovich, Vallone, & Tversky, 1985). A second issue is whether we are talking about adaptive or nonadaptive variability. Returning to the basketball example, nonadaptive variability (e.g., variation in the motion of free throws) may decrease with experience, but adaptive variability (e.g., the variety of effective adjustments that can be made when a taller defender unexpectedly comes to block a lay up) may increase. A third issue is whether we are talking about competence or performance. A professional basketball player may know more ways of shooting free throws than a high school player, but may be less variable in her performance in games. Resolving this question is well beyond the limits of this paper, but it certainly is an important and interesting challenge for future research.

### Between-Child Variability and Learning

Learning is influenced by between-child as well as within-child variation. Not surprisingly, age is a particularly pervasive influence. Older toddlers learn to use tools more rapidly and consistently than do younger toddlers (Chen & Siegler, 2000). Older preschoolers learn how to bake a cake from watching and interacting with their mothers more effectively than do younger preschoolers (Shrager & Callanan, 1991). Older elementary school students learn more rapidly from experience with Tower of Hanoi problems than do younger students (Bidell & Fischer, 1994). Adults learn more rapidly than 10-year-olds about the effects of variables on unfamiliar scientific reasoning problems and about how to perform controlled experiments (Kuhn et al., 1995; Schauble, 1996).

Between-child variation in initial knowledge also exercises a pervasive influence on learning. Children who use defined rules, as opposed to guessing or not using any systematic rule, show greater learning regarding balance scales (Siegler & Chen, 1998), biological concepts (Opfer & Siegler, 2004), gear problems (Dixon & Bangert, 2002), and scientific experimentation (Kuhn & Phelps, 1982). Similarly, children who can verbalize rules as well as generate responses consistent with them show greater learning than peers who cannot verbalize the rules but generate similar nonverbal responses (Pine & Messer, 2000). Among children who use systematic rules, those who use more advanced pretest rules learn more about balance scales (Chletsos & De Lisi, 1991). Children with more advanced conceptual knowledge of a domain are superior in learning procedures for solving problems in the domain (Rittle-Johnson & Alibali, 1999; Rittle-Johnson, Siegler, & Alibali, 2001). Knowledge of which features of problems to encode is also positively related to subsequent learning, as indicated by findings on balance scale and mathematical equality tasks (Alibali & Perret, 1996; Siegler & Chen, 1998).

Numerous sources of between-child variability other than age and initial knowledge also influence learning. Children with higher IQs tend to learn more than peers with lower IQs (K. E. Johnson & Mervis, 1994; Siegler & Svetina, 2002). Children who place a greater value on organization are more likely to learn organizational memory strategies than are ones who do not place as great a value on organization (Schlagmüller & Schneider, 2002). Quality of social relationships also influences learning; children learn more about writing when they collaborate with friends than with other classmates (Jones, 1998; Jones & Pellegrini, 1996).

## Theoretical Implications and Questions

One implication of research on within-child variability is that typical cross sectional and long-term longitudinal studies systematically exaggerate the changes that occur with age. Sampling at wide intervals makes change appear more abrupt than when sampling is more frequent, because it often eliminates periods of high variability and short-term regressions. In a clever recent demonstration of this point, Robinson, Adolph, and Young (2004) simulated varying sampling intervals by systematically removing observations from a high-density (daily) sampling of infant motor activities. They found that the wider the sampling interval, the more stage-like that development appeared.

A related problem is that classifying children as possessing an ability when they reach some arbitrary criterion (e.g., 75% correct) leads to ignoring the partial understanding manifested earlier. Children who use an advanced strategy on 25% of trials, for example, often are classified as if they had no understanding, when in fact they clearly do have some understanding. Conversely, failures to apply the desired reasoning at the

older age are ignored as long as the child meets the criterion, again leading to the amount and abruptness of change appearing to be greater than they are. Such exaggerated depictions of change may have contributed to the field's traditional weakness in explaining change, by seeming to demand mechanisms that produce larger and more rapid changes than the changes that actually occur.

Another intriguing theoretical issue concerns why within-child variability tends to be positively related to subsequent learning. Several explanations have been advanced. Dynamic systems theory postulates that for a system to change, it must first become unstable (Hosenfeld et al., 1997; Thelen & Corbetta, 2002). Variability in the behavior of interest is one sign of such instability. Another hypothesis is that variability reflects simultaneous activation of conflicting representations, which facilitates the extension of the more advanced representation from one modality to the other (Goldin-Meadow & Alibali, 2002). A third interpretation is that new strategies are often constructed from subroutines of existing approaches, and that assembling subroutines from different strategies is easier if the relevant strategies have been used recently and thus are relatively active (Siegler, 2002).

Although different in their particulars, all of these interpretations have a common core: Learning is most likely when previously dominant approaches weaken. This weakening can come about in varied ways: through the dominant approach failing, as when it results in negative feedback; through the learner being asked to explain why dominant incorrect approaches are incorrect; or through changes in other aspects of the system, as when improved postural control changes infants reaching. The general lesson is that change reflects not only the emergence and strengthening of new variants, but also the weakening of previous approaches.

With regard to differences between children, one issue that has only begun to be addressed concerns the determinants of individual differences in variability. One factor that appears to be important is the conditions under which children first acquire knowledge in the domain. Stokes (1995) demonstrated that if initial learning occurs under conditions that require highly variable responding, the high variability persists, even when the conditions change and high variability is no longer required or advantageous. In contrast, introducing the requirement of high variability later in learning does not produce a similar effect; participants produce high variability while it is rewarded, but return to lower levels of variability once the requirement is no longer in effect. Personality and cognitive style differences also may contribute to such individual differences (Stokes, 2001).

## Path of Change

One of the appealing aspects of the new field of children's learning is that it integrates quantitative and qualitative aspects of change. This is perhaps best exemplified by the new field's depiction of the path of change.

### Basic Phenomena

In many tasks and domains, children (and adults) display qualitatively discrete understandings, such as rules, strategies, theories, mental models, and schema. Piagetian, theory-theory, and many information-processing approaches suggest that children progress through a regular developmental sequence of such understandings. Young children show a single, simple understanding; older children a different, more advanced understanding; yet older children a yet more advanced understanding; and so on.

The pervasive within-child variability described in the previous section indicates that such depictions of developmental sequences are too simple. Children cannot progress from one approach to another if at all times they know and use multiple understandings. However, this does not mean that the basic idea of the developmental sequence needs to be abandoned. Instead, the implication is that accurate depictions of the path of change must incorporate not only acquisition of new, qualitatively distinct approaches, but also quantitative changes in the frequency of use of both new and previous approaches.

Even infants progress through regular, age-related sequences of multiple, qualitatively distinct approaches. As noted earlier, infants use a variety of approaches to descend down relatively steep ramps: crawling; walking; sliding head first, sliding feet first, or in a sitting position; or refusing to go down in any way (Adolph, 1997). These approaches emerge in a quite consistent order. Refusing to go down at all is the first response, other than crawling, during the period in which crawling is infants' dominant mode of locomotion. Sliding down head first is typically the next strategy to emerge, followed by sliding down in a sitting position for some infants and sliding down feet first for others. On average, the infants used between three and four distinct descent strategies per session, with the relative frequency of these approaches changing greatly with age and experience. For example, in infants' first weeks of crawling, they refused to go down the ramp altogether on 100% of trials on which they did not attempt to crawl down. By the time that crawling was about to give way to walking as the main locomotor strategy, infants refused to go down on only 1% of trials on which they did not attempt to crawl down.

The path of change of the 1- and 2-year-olds in Chen and Siegler (2000) showed a similar mix of qualitative and quantitative changes. When the tool use task was introduced, two approaches predominated and were equally frequent: reaching for the goal object and just sitting and looking at it. Next, reaching became the dominant approach, being used on about 65% of trials, though looking, using a tool, and asking for help also continued to be used. With experience on the task and exposure to modeling or a verbal hint, tool use increased in frequency to the point where it was employed on the majority of trials. However, all three other approaches remained as well.

Preschoolers generate similar paths of change in single-digit addition, false belief, selective attention, and other tasks (Amsterlaw & Wellman, 2004; Flynn et al., 2004; P. H. Miller & Aloise-Young, 1995; Siegler & Jenkins, 1989). For example, Siegler and Jenkins (1989) presented 4- and 5-year-olds who knew how to add but did not know the *min strategy* (counting from the larger addend) with 20 to 30 sessions of addition problems. At the outset of the study, the preschoolers counted from one on about 40% of trials, retrieved the answer from memory on about 25%, and used a variety of other approaches (but not the min strategy) on the remaining 35%. By the end of the study, most children had discovered two new strategies (one of which was the min approach), as well as changing their frequency of previous approaches so that retrieval became the single most common strategy. Similarly, the large majority of 3-year-olds studied by Amsterlaw and Wellman (2004) progressed over 12 sessions from never correctly answering false belief problems, to sometimes generating correct false belief reasoning, to consistently answering correctly. None of the 3-year-olds progressed directly from incorrect to consistently correct responding; instead, children required a median of three sessions from the time they first showed correct false belief reasoning to the time when they first generated consistently correct answers. In addition, all children regressed to chance level performance in at least one session after having responded consistently correctly in a session. Thus, the path of change included a qualitative shift (the first use of correct false belief reasoning) and also a quantitative change (the gradual increase in use of such reasoning).

The broad outlines of the paths of change revealed by microgenetic studies generally have paralleled those observed in cross-sectional and long-term longitudinal studies (Kuhn, 1995; P. H. Miller & Coyle, 1999; Siegler, 2000). Microgenetic studies, however, yield fine-grain as well as broad depictions of paths of change, and thus add invaluable information about them. Some of these types of information about paths of change have already been described: the longer solution times and heightened verbal and nonverbal variability that often immediately precede discovery, for example. However, understanding of paths of change has also been enhanced by numerous other findings from microgenetic studies.

One such contribution is information about short-lived transitional approaches. Certain phenomena that are seen only briefly, and sometimes not very often even then, are nonetheless crucial to understanding the learning process. One example involves naming errors during vocabulary acquisition. When toddlers start to speak, their word learning is extremely slow; it often takes them 6 months to learn their first 50 words. After children use 50 to 100 words, however, vocabulary acquisition greatly accelerates, with children often learning numerous words per day (Dromi, 1987). Gershkoff-Stowe's and Smith's (1997) microgenetic study of word acquisition revealed a surprising feature of this path of change; the acceleration in word learning was accompanied by a short-lived increase in naming errors. Both before and after this time, children rarely chose an incorrect word to name objects, but they frequently did so during the transition period. This transition period was brief and emerged at different ages for different children, probably because it was more a function of vocabulary size than of age; thus, the phenomenon would have been unlikely to be discovered without dense sampling of changing competence.

Numerous other paths of change also have been illuminated by detailed observation of transition periods. One example emerged in Karmiloff-Smith's (1979b) microgenetic study of map drawing. She found that after generating maps that were entirely sufficient for purposes of the task, 6- to 11-year-olds sometimes began to generate redundant markings that were unnecessary for purposes of solving the problem but that reflected the children's increasing metaprocedural understanding of their own strategies. Chiu, Kessel, Moschkovich, and Munoz-Nunez's (2001) examination of a seventh graders' learning how to graph linear functions provides another example. In response to instruction, the child neither adopted the instructed strategy nor persisted with his original approach. Instead, he merged the two in an unanticipated way, using the instruction to create a refined version of his original approach.

In addition to revealing unsuspected transitional strategies, microgenetic analyses also sometimes reveal that hypothesized transition states do not occur or are not part of the transition. In Siegler's (1995) study of number conservation, no child was observed vacillating between reliance on the length of a row and reliance on its density, the transitional strategy hypothesized by Piaget (1952). In a study of single-digit addition, Siegler and Jenkins (1989) found that a transition state between the sum and min strategies that had been hypothesized by Neches (1987)—counting-on from the first addend—was not used by any child. In a study of categorizations of life status, Opfer and Siegler (2004) observed all three states that had been hypothesized previously (Hatano et al., 1993): the E-Rule (everything is alive), the A-Rule (only animals are alive), and the L-Rule (only plants and animals are alive). However, none of the children followed the hypothesized progression from the E-Rule to the A-Rule to the L-Rule. Instead, all children who used the E-Rule on the pretest progressed directly to the L-Rule.

The trial-by-trial analyses of microgenetic studies yield sufficient data about individual children's learning to examine the consistency of the path of change across individuals. Often, the path has proven to be quite consistent. For example, in Siegler and Stern's (1998) study of discovery of an arithmetic insight strategy, 13 of the 16 children in one group progressed through the same sequence of four strategies (in terms of the order in which they first used each strategy), and 2 of the other 3 children used the same four strategies but reversed the order of the first two approaches.

Deviations from the usual path can also be informative. On mathematical equality problems, for example, some children progress directly from a state in which both gesture and speech express the same incorrect understanding to a state in which both gesture and speech express the same correct understanding, thus skipping the usual intermediate state of gesture-speech mismatch (Perry, Church, & Goldin-Meadow, 1988). Deviating from the typical path in this way is associated with narrower generalization than following it. Most children who follow the usual sequence generalize their understanding of the equal sign, which they learned in the context of addition, to multiplication, whereas most children who deviate from the usual sequence do not generalize to multiplication (Alibali & Goldin-Meadow, 1993).

By allowing identification of the trial of discovery (the trial on which a child first used a new strategy), microgenetic methods have also made it possible to examine the experience of discovery. Such examinations indicate that even for a single task, experimental procedure, and discovery, the experience varies a great deal among individuals. Of the 4- and 5-year-olds in Siegler and Jenkins' (1989) study of discovery of the min strategy, for example, some children were highly aware of using a novel strategy and commented on it, whereas others showed no awareness of having done anything unusual. Even among those who were aware of using a new approach, some were excited and others not. The experiential aspects of discovery seem to have longer-term consequences; those children who were aware of using a new strategy subsequently generalized it more extensively than those who did not. Excitement at making a discovery seems to have similarly positive effects on adults' generalization of new approaches (Siegler & Engle, 1994).

### Influences of Child and Environment

As noted earlier, the path of change tends to be similar among different children of the same age exposed to the same experimental procedure. The commonality in paths of change extends further as well. Children who show similar initial knowledge of a task but who are of different ages tend to progress along the same path. On tool use problems, both 1- and 2-year-olds first either just looked at the goal toy or reached for it; then, reaching became the main strategy with the tool strategy also becoming fairly frequent; then, use of tools became dominant, with increasing focus on the optimal tool (Chen & Siegler, 2000). Similarly, 4- and 5-year-olds progressed through the same set of balance scale rules when both were presented feedback on their answers and asked to explain the reasoning that led to the experimenter's answers (Siegler & Chen, 1998).

Even when both age and initial knowledge differ, the path tends to be similar. For example, Kuhn et al. (1995) found that although adults' scientific reasoning started at a more advanced level than that of 10-year-olds, the children and adults progressed along a common path of theory-evidence coordination. The path involved first noting that evidence from experiments is relevant to beliefs about the causal status of variables; then supporting prior beliefs that a variable matters by citing a result from a single experiment that is consistent with the prior belief; and then supporting prior beliefs that a variable does not matter by citing single instances consistent with that belief. Next comes citation of multiple observations to justify prior beliefs, followed by the development of controlled experimentation and a gradual increase in the frequency of valid inferences on the basis of the experimental evidence. Adults tended to start further along this path and to progress further along it than the 10-year-olds, but the progression was the same.

The path of change also tends to be similar for children with and without mental retardation. For a task on which external memory aids could be used to help remember the location of objects, children with and without mental retardation who were matched for mental age showed the same path of change. Both groups initially did not use the external memory aids, then manipulated individual tokens but did not place them in ways that would help in recalling the target locations, and then arranged the objects so that they provided straightforward cues to the locations that needed to be remembered (Fletcher & Bray, 1995). Similarly, Fletcher et al. (1998) reported that 8-year-olds with mild mental retardation showed a path of change in basic arithmetic similar to that of the typical preschoolers in Siegler and Jenkins (1989).

This consistency of the path of change across individuals is not perfect. In most studies, people vary somewhat in their paths of change. This is true even in the studies cited above as illustrations of the consistency of change across individuals. For example, in Siegler and Jenkins (1989), discovery of the shortcut sum strategy usually was followed quickly by discovery of the min strategy, but one child in the study discovered the min strategy without ever using the shortcut sum, and another child used the shortcut sum many times over a protracted period before discovering the min approach. Sometimes there are two common paths of change. In one such case, Lavelli and Fogel (2002) examined amount of infant-mother communication on a weekly basis over the infants' first 14 weeks. They found that for roughly half of infant-mother dyads, face-to-face communication increased steadily over the period, whereas for the other half, the amount of communication increased until about 8 weeks and then steadily decreased. Another example of inter-child variability in the path of change comes from the area of motor development. Spencer et al. (2000) observed babies' reaching each week between 3 and 30 weeks and every other week between 30 and 52 weeks. The components involved in development of stable reaching were similar across infants—improved control of the head and upper torso, independent sitting, ability to extend the hand to a distant target, and ability to touch and grasp nearby objects—but different infants mastered the components in different orders.

### Theoretical Questions and Implications

These results indicate that the traditional view of developmental sequences is outdated; children rarely progress directly from one consistent understanding to a different consistent understanding to a third consistent understanding. Both the amount of within-child variability—children using multiple approaches over protracted time periods—and the amount of between-child variability—different children showing different paths of change—indicate that the traditional conception is too simple.

These findings raise the issue of whether it makes sense to talk at all about developmental sequences in a post-Piagetian world. I think that it does, because it calls attention to a central developmental phenomenon: that children generate increasingly adequate, qualitatively distinct, strategies and understandings prior to mastering concepts and problem solving skills. These partially correct strategies and understandings frequently reflect broadly applicable ways of thinking that children apply when they lack superior alternatives, for example 5-year-olds focusing exclusively on the single most salient dimension on liquid quantity conservation, balance scale, shadow projection, and other problems.

The challenge, then, is to refine the concept of developmental sequences so that it is consistent with current data on paths of change yet also as parsimonious as possible given those data. One promising approach would be to recognize that developmental sequences are multifaceted and therefore need to be characterized in multiple ways. For example, the path of change might be charac-

terized in terms of the order in which strategies are first used, also in terms of the order in which different strategies become the single most common approach, and also in terms of the mixture of strategies used at various points. In some cases, the first and second of these characterizations will coincide, as they did in Siegler and Stern (1998). In other cases, each approach will yield a unique perspective, as when some early developing strategies never become common (as in Siegler & Jenkins, 1989). Together, these multiple depictions of paths of change may contribute to an accurate and nuanced understanding of developmental sequences.

### Rate of Change

Both scientific and everyday theories about strategy discovery vary greatly in the rate of change they envision. Theories that emphasize trial and error suggest that discovery of new approaches will be a slow process; theories that depict discoveries as arising from flashes of insight, as in the tale of Archimedes in the bathtub, suggest a rapid if not instantaneous rate of change.

The concept *rate of change* can be usefully divided into two components: amount of time/experience before the first use of a new approach (here labeled the *rate of discovery,* and amount of time/experience before frequency of the new approach reaches its asymptotic level here labeled the *rate of uptake*). Distinguishing between the two types of information is essential, because the relation between them varies considerably. Sometimes, discovery is quite rapid but uptake takes a long time. For example, second graders in Siegler and Stern (1998) took an average of only seven trials to discover an arithmetic insight strategy, but did not use the strategy on the majority of trials in any session until five sessions (100 trials) later. In contrast, kindergartners in Siegler and Svetina (2002) required an average of about 50 trials before they discovered a correct strategy for solving matrix completion problems, but required only about 12 trials beyond that point to use it consistently.

Experimental conditions also affect the two rates of change differently. For example, in Opfer and Siegler's (2004) study of categorization of life status, the teleology condition led to slower discoveries than did the two other experimental conditions, but once the discovery was made, its uptake was much faster in the teleology condition. In Blöte et al. (2004), discoveries occurred most often on easy problems, but uptake of the new strategy was comparable on easy and difficult problems.

In Siegler and Jenkins (1989), introducing challenge problems did not influence the rate of discovering the min strategy, but it greatly increased the uptake of the strategy among children who already had discovered it. Thus, a comprehensive description of the rate of change requires information regarding both the rate of discovery and the rate of uptake.

### Basic Phenomena

Perhaps the most basic question regarding the rate of discovery is whether discoveries tend to be made quickly or slowly. Phrased in terms of models of discovery, a good answer might be "Faster than connectionist models imply, slower than symbolic models imply." Connectionist models tend to discover new approaches extremely slowly (to the extent they discover them at all). For example, McClelland's (1995) model of balance scale learning requires thousands of trials to learn each new rule. Clearly, children discover new rules much faster than that. On the other hand, children rarely discover new rules in a single trial, as symbolic approaches such as Newell's (1990) model of balance scale learning do. Instead, results from microgenetic studies suggest that when feedback is given (as presupposed in both connectionist and symbolic models), discoveries usually take anywhere from a handful of trials to a few hundred trials. We might label this *human-scale learning*.

The difference between human scale learning and that of connectionist and symbolic models is evident in the difference between Siegler and Chen's (1998) empirical data on 5-year-olds' discovery of balance scale rules and the discovery of the same rules by McClelland's (1995) and Newell's (1990) simulation models. Over the course of 16 problems, two-thirds of the 5-year-olds in Siegler and Chen (1998) who initially used no identifiable rule discovered Rule I. Over the same number of problems, one-third of 5-year-olds who initially used Rule I discovered Rule II. Sixteen trials is reasonably representative of human scale strategy discovery, but it is far different from either a single trial or thousands of trials. Rates of strategy discovery vary considerably across studies, depending on characteristics of the children, experimental situation, and relation between old and new strategies. However, as the Siegler and Chen results indicate, discovery is rarely as fast as symbolic models suggest or as slow as connectionist models imply.

Children's learning tends to differ from that of the simulation models not only in the rate of discovery but also in the rate of uptake. Both symbolic and connectionist models tend to use a superior new strategy consistently on a given problem once the strategy has been discovered and used on that problem. Children, however, often extend newly discovered strategies surprisingly slowly. The relatively slow extension of advanced thinking extends even to problems that are viewed as reflecting fundamental developmental advances that have broad ramifications for a wide range of thought. For example, 43% of children who were just beginning to use transformational reasoning on number conservation problems used that reasoning again when the same problem was presented two sessions (24 trials) later, and 76% used it when the same problem was presented four sessions (48 trials) later (Siegler, 1995). The same relatively slow uptake is usually evident when new problems are structurally identical but differ in their particulars from earlier ones. Thus, in three microgenetic studies of acquisition of understanding of false belief (Amsterlaw & Wellman, 2004; Flynn, 2005; Flynn et al., 2004), uptake was quite gradual. Only 4 of 13 3-year-olds who acquired understanding of false belief in Flynn et al. (2004) consistently displayed such understanding thereafter. Similarly, all children in Amsterlaw and Wellman (2004) who improved their false belief understanding regressed from one session to the next at least once during the study, though the overall trend was toward improved performance.

Slow uptake of new ways of thinking has been documented with a wide variety of other tasks and age groups as well. For example, 4-year-olds who spontaneously used rather sophisticated analogical reasoning strategies in one session often regressed to less sophisticated strategies for several sessions thereafter (Tunteler & Resing, 2002). Regressions have also been found to be common in the quality of 4-year-olds' storytelling (McKeough & Sanderson, 1996), in 8-year-olds' use of organizational memory strategies (Coyle & Bjorklund, 1997), in 11-year-olds' solving of gear problems (Perry & Lewis, 1999), and in adults' use of scientific reasoning strategies (Kuhn et al., 1995).

Uptake of new strategies tends to be slow even when children can explain why the new approach is superior to the old. For example, in Siegler and Jenkins (1989), one child, on her trial of discovery of the min strategy, explained why she didn't count from one by saying, "Cause then you have to count all those numbers" (p. 66). Another child in the same study commented on her first use of the min strategy by saying, "Yeah—smart answer"

(p. 80). Yet, both of these children, like others in the study, generalized use of the new strategy quite slowly (though faster than children whose visible behavior indicated that they had used the min strategy but who claimed that they had counted from one).

Although uptake of newly discovered strategies is generally quite slow, this is not always the case. For example, Schlagmüller and Schneider (2002) found that 8- to 12-year-olds adopted an organizational strategy for remembering groups of objects quite rapidly once they began to use it, and Thornton (1999) observed similarly rapid uptake of an efficient strategy for playing "20 Questions" in a 5-year-old. A number of factors that have been found to influence the rate of discovery and uptake of new strategies are considered in the next section.

### Influences of Child and Environment

Rates of both discovery and uptake increase with age. Toddlers between 27- and 35-months discover effective tool use strategies more rapidly than 18- to 26-month-olds and their uptake of the strategy is also quicker (Chen & Siegler, 2000). Among preschoolers, 5-year-olds are faster than 4-year-olds to learn that certain relations are indeterminate (Klahr & Chen, 2003). The trend continues with older children; 13-year-olds are quicker than 10-year-olds to discover and generalize an organizational strategy to enhance memory (Bjorklund, 1988), and adults are more likely than 10-year-olds to discover and generalize effective scientific experimentation and inference strategies (Kuhn et al., 1995; Schauble, 1996). To illustrate the magnitude of the differences among age groups that sometimes emerges, in Thornton (1999)'s study of how children build toy bridges, 5-year-olds required more than three times as many trials as 7-year-olds to discover an insightful strategy. In addition, younger children sometimes fail to maintain learning under circumstances in which older peers do so. For example, 4-year-olds who received training in understanding indeterminate relations frequently regressed when their understanding was assessed 7 months later, though all 5-year-olds maintained their original learning (Klahr & Chen, 2003).

Other characteristics with which children enter studies also influence their rate of learning. Rates of discovery and uptake of new approaches tend to be greater for children with higher IQs (K. E. Johnson & Mervis, 1994; Siegler & Svetina, 2002). Similarly, children who start with more advanced rules tend to progress to yet more advanced approaches more rapidly than children whose initial rules are less advanced (Fujimura, 2001;

Siegler & Chen, 1998). Relatively advanced encoding and conceptual understanding are also associated with rapid discovery and uptake of new approaches (Rittle-Johnson et al., 2001; Siegler & Chen, 1998).

In addition to these influences of child variables, a variety of experiential variables also influence rates of discovery and uptake. Direct instruction in problem solving produces faster discovery and uptake of new approaches, through narrower generalization, than does instruction in underlying principles (Alibali, 1999; Opfer & Siegler, 2004). Exposure to a model who both selects the most appropriate tool and demonstrates how to use it to obtain the goal leads to faster discovery and uptake of the new approach than does a verbal hint that identifies which tool to use but does not demonstrate its use (Chen & Siegler, 2000). Encountering problems that are moderately beyond current understanding produces faster discovery than encountering ones that are far beyond it (Siegler & Chen, 1998).

Relations between new and existing approaches also exert a large influence on the rate of uptake of new approaches. Strategies that offer large advantages in accuracy and speed on the problems being presented have a faster rate of uptake than strategies that offer smaller advantages. Evidence for this point can be found in Siegler and Jenkins' (1989) 11-week study of discovery of the min strategy. The first 7 weeks of this period were spent on problems with addends 1 to 5. Exposure to such problems led most children to discover the min strategy, but only to very gradual uptake of it. Therefore, in Week 8, Siegler and Jenkins presented children with challenge problems, problems such as 22 + 3, on which counting from 1 would work badly but on which the min strategy would work well. Encountering the challenge problems led children who had already discovered the min strategy to greatly increase their use of it, not only on those problems but on subsequent small addend problems as well.

Between-experiment evidence is consistent with this conclusion that uptake (but not necessarily discovery) is faster when the new strategy has large advantages over previously discovered alternatives for solving the types of problems being presented. Problems on which the new strategy leads to consistently correct performance, and on which older strategies lead to systematically incorrect or chance performance, evoke the fastest uptake of new strategies. Thus, uptake of new strategies has been relatively rapid on mathematical equality, number conservation, matrix completion, Tower of Hanoi, and balance scale tasks (Alibali & Goldin-Meadow, 1993; Bidell &

Fischer, 1994; Church & Goldin-Meadow, 1986; Siegler & Chen, 1998; Siegler & Svetina, 2002). Uptake is slower when the new strategy produces smaller improvement in accuracy and when its main advantage is speed. Examples include use of the arithmetic shortcut strategy rather than addition and subtraction to solve $A + B - B$ problems (Siegler & Stern, 1998), use of systematic experimental design strategies rather than unsystematic comparisons to learn about the causal influence of variables (Kuhn & Phelps, 1982; Kuhn et al., 1995; Schauble, 1996), use of organizational strategies for remembering objects that can be organized into a few categories (Coyle & Bjorklund, 1997; Fletcher et al., 1998), and use of bridging, a strategy of envisioning a rough outline of a strategy prior to formulation of the strategy, in construction of robots and bridges (Granott, 1998; Parziale, 2002).

Even strategies that bring large benefits sometimes have relatively slow uptakes. One reason is that newly discovered strategies are subject to forgetting (i.e., to their strength diminishing below the point at which they would be chosen) and therefore sometimes need to be rediscovered. One type of evidence for the role of forgetting is that extension of new strategies tends to be more gradual in multisession microgenetic studies than in single session ones. Children fairly often continue to use a newly discovered strategy quite consistently in the session in which it is discovered (e.g., Alibali, 1999; Siegler & Chen, 1998). However, when children return a few days or a week later, they often have forgotten the strategy, thus necessitating rediscovery. This phenomenon was particularly dramatic in Siegler and Stern's (1998) study of discovery of the shortcut strategy for solving problems of the form $A + B - B = \underline{\hspace{1cm}}$. After discovering the shortcut strategy, children used it on between 70% and 90% of the remaining trials in the session. However, 0 of the 15 children who discovered the shortcut approach used it on the first trial of the next session, a week later; not until the sixth trial of the new session did a majority of children again use it. By the end of that session, all 15 children were again using the shortcut strategy. However, the "off again, on again" pattern continued; even five sessions after the initial discovery, most children began the session by using the standard computation strategy (adding A and B and then subtracting C), though the rediscoveries of the shortcut strategy were made increasingly quickly in later sessions.

Forgetting plagues not only everyday discoveries but also profound ones. Wegener (1915/1966), the father of plate tectonic theory, claimed that he generated the basic idea in 1910 or 1911, shortly before his classic 1915 publication describing it. A friend, however, recalled Wegener describing the idea to him in 1903 when they were both graduate students (Giere, 1988). Thus, the cycle of discovering, forgetting, and rediscovering characterize even the most profound insights.

### Theoretical Implications and Questions

Probably the most intriguing question raised by findings regarding the rate of change is why the uptake of effective new strategies is so often slow. After discovering a strategy that is both more accurate and logically superior to prior approaches, why not use it all the time? Several contributing factors have already been cited: forgetting of newly discovered approaches; the omnipresence and generally adaptive value of within-child variability; and associations between frequently used strategies and the types of problems on which they have been used, which must be weakened for the new approach to be chosen consistently. However, other factors almost certainly contribute as well.

One likely contributing factor is the benefits and costs of using newly discovered strategies. When children first use a strategy, they often execute it less effectively, and at a greater cost in mental resources, than will be the case after greater use (Guttentag, 1984). Such utilization deficiencies have frequently been observed in microgenetic research; indeed, because microgenetic studies allow examination of newly discovered strategies, they provide the ideal situation for observing utilization deficiencies. In one example of a utilization deficiency arising within a microgenetic study, 3- and 4-year-olds' discovery of a potentially effective selective attention strategy did not initially improve their accuracy (P. H. Miller & Aloise-Young, 1995). In another example, 4- and 5-year-olds' initial uses of the min strategy did not improve their accuracy or solution times relative to counting from one on small number problems (Siegler & Jenkins, 1989). In a third example, 9-year-olds' initial use of an organizational strategy did not improve their memory of the objects that had been organized (Bjorklund et al., 1992). And in a fourth particularly striking case, the first two uses of an organizational strategy led to below chance accuracy, whereas the last few uses of the same strategy produced almost perfect accuracy (Blöte et al., 1999). Thus, part of the reason for the slow uptake of seemingly useful new strategies is that the strategies at first are less useful than they later will be.

A second question regarding the rate of change (and also its path and variability) concerns the sources of within-condition variability that cannot be traced to children's demographic characteristics or initial knowledge. Even when age and knowledge are comparable, children within any given experimental condition vary greatly in the rate of discovery and uptake of new strategies. Consider the extent of such variation in Siegler and Jenkins (1989). Among the seven children who discovered the min strategy, the first discovery occurred in the 2nd session, the last in the 22nd. Despite this substantial variation, neither age nor prior knowledge of addition nor other relevant types of numerical knowledge predicted the rate of discovery.

Similar within-condition variations due to unknown causes in rate of discovery and uptake of new approaches have arisen among other age groups and on other tasks. For example, 33% of 3- and 4-year-olds in Flynn et al. (2004) showed abrupt change over seven sessions of presentation of a seven-task theory of mind test. Abrupt change was defined as children at least once during the study passing at least three more tasks than in the previous session. The other 67% of children showed gradual change. Similarly, 24% of the third and fourth graders in Alibali (1999) showed abrupt change (as defined by use of a nonoverlapping set of strategies on the pretest and posttest), whereas the other 76% did not. In P. H. Miller and Aloise-Young's (1995) similar analysis of 3- and 4-year-olds' acquisition of a selective attention strategy, the corresponding percentage of abrupt and gradual changes was 37% and 63%. Kuhn and Phelps (1982) and Siegler (1995) also found that although the majority of children showed gradual change, a minority showed abrupt change. Thus, although a variety of child and environmental variables have been found to influence the rate of discovery and generalization, much variance remains to be explained.

## Breadth of Change

In general, learning is neither as narrow nor as broad as could be imagined. It almost always generalizes beyond the item on which a new approach was generated, and it rarely is instantly extended to all items and tasks on which the discovery is relevant. Thus, just as there seems to be a human-scale *rate* of learning, there also seems to be a human-scale *breadth* of learning.

This similarity between findings regarding the breadth and the rate of change is not coincidental. Except in cases in which the same item is presented re-

peatedly, the uptake of new strategies always involves problems that differ in some way from the item on which the discovery occurred. In all such instances, whether the uptake of new strategies is viewed as an issue of the rate of change or the breadth of change is to some degree a matter of definition. For purposes of this chapter, extensions of new approaches to different problems on the same task were discussed under the rate of change heading; the discussion of breadth of change in this section is limited to cases in which new approaches are extended to a different task (though even that distinction winds up being somewhat subjective, as will become evident later).

### *Basic Phenomena*

Many volumes have been written lamenting children's lack of transfer and the narrowness of their learning (e.g., Bransford, Brown, & Cocking, 1999; Cognition and Technology Group at Vanderbilt, 1997; Lave, 1988). Much less has been written about the fact that learning also tends to be far from literal. Indeed, there may be a tendency to define "transfer problems" as problems on which useful known strategies tend not to be spontaneously applied, and to define problems on which children spontaneously extend appropriate strategies as not requiring transfer.

Another reason why learning often seems narrower than our intuitions suggest it ought to be is that new strategies and capabilities can transform a familiar task into a novel one. The transition from crawling to walking provides a revealing example. As infants who could crawl but not walk gained experience with crawling, they adjusted their descent strategies increasingly precisely to their physical limits. In particular, they increasingly used descent strategies safer than crawling (e.g., sliding in a prone position) when the slope was too steep for them to crawl down safely (Adolph, 1997). When the same children began walking, however, their descent strategies became less well calibrated to their capabilities; they often tried to walk down steep slopes and fell. Thus, the new capability of walking converted a familiar task, on which children chose appropriate strategies, into a novel task that initially elicited riskier choices.

This example also illustrates another reason why learning is often narrower than seems ideal. New learners invariably face two challenges: extending their learning to the cases in which it is useful, and not extending it to the cases in which it is not useful. Accomplishing these goals requires knowing when the strategy will be useful and also often requires knowing how to adapt the strategy to a novel context. Each of these difficulties is evident in children's learning about mathematical equality. When third and fourth graders learn how to solve addition problems of the form $A + B + C =$ ___ $+ C$, many fail to transfer their learning to multiplication problems of the form $A \times B \times C =$ _____ $\times C$ (Alibali, 1999; Alibali & Goldin-Meadow, 1993). However, learners often overextend new mathematical equality strategies to superficially similar problems on which the new strategy is not applicable. For example, after correctly solving several problems of the form $A + B + C =$ ___ $+ C$ by adding A and B, third and fourth graders often add A and B to answer similar looking problems on which that strategy produces incorrect answers, such as $A + B + C =$ _____ $+ D$ (Siegler, 2002). In this regard, older learners are no different than 2-year-olds, who sometimes both overextend and underextend the same newly learned word (Bowerman, 1982).

Despite the difficulty posed by these twin pitfalls, learners within microgenetic studies sometimes do show impressive transfer. One context in which this has been found repeatedly is acquisition of the control of variables strategy for scientific experimentation. Second, third, and fourth graders who were provided explicit instruction in the control of variables scheme on one problem (e.g., factors influencing extension of springs) showed almost complete transfer of the scheme to superficially unrelated but structurally parallel problems (e.g., factors influencing speed of objects sinking in water). Even more impressive, the children maintained the gains over a 7-month period with no further experimental intervention (Chen & Klahr, 1999).

In this study, the transfer was to different physical reasoning tasks. Broad transfer of the control of variables scheme also has been demonstrated between physical and social reasoning. When fifth graders and adults were first presented reasoning problems in one domain (physical or social), and then presented problems from the other domain, their proportion of valid experiments and inferences in the new domain did not even temporarily diminish relative to the highest level reached in the initial domain (Kuhn et al., 1995).

An intriguing feature of this relatively broad learning of the control of variables scheme is that it can emerge as a by-product of trying to learn specific content. The children and adults in Kuhn's and Schauble's studies of this scheme (Kuhn, Amsel, & O'Laughlin, 1988; Kuhn & Phelps, 1982; Kuhn et al., 1992, 1995; Schauble, 1990, 1996) were not instructed in the control of variables scheme, nor did the instructions they re-

ceived call attention to it. They were simply asked to find out which variables mattered on the particular tasks that they were presented. The learners made considerable progress in inferring which variables were, in fact, influential, but along the way, they also learned how to conduct experiments. Thus, relatively broad learning at times arises out of problem-solving activity aimed at meeting other goals.

### Influence of Child and Environment

Consistent with findings regarding the other components of change, the breadth of learning increases with age. Older preschoolers show broader learning than younger toddlers (Chen & Siegler, 2000), older school age children show broader learning than younger ones (Bjorklund, 1988; Dixon & Bangert, 2002), and adults show broader learning than do school age children (Schauble, 1996). When initial learning is equated, however, this relation fairly often disappears; younger preschoolers who learned an initial problem to the same extent as older ones showed comparable transfer (Brown, Kane, & Echols, 1986), as did younger elementary school and middle school children who learned balance scale and tic tac toe problems as well as older peers (Chletsos & De Lisi, 1991; Crowley & Siegler, 1999).

A variety of other variables also have been found to influence the breadth of learning. Recognizing the value of new strategies influences extension of them to new problems (Paris, Newman, & McVey, 1982). Learning a strategy on problems on which the strategy is always applicable leads both to more correct extensions and to more overextensions than does learning the strategy on problems on which it sometimes applies and sometimes does not (Siegler & Stern, 1998). To the extent that the influence of variables violates learners' expectations, they tend to perform fewer experiments about the effects of the variables and to learn less about them (Schauble, 1996).

### Theoretical Implications and Questions

One implication of these findings from microgenetic studies is that what is often taken as lack of transfer actually reflects a lack of stability in the initial learning. Particularly direct evidence for this view came from Opfer and Siegler's (2004) study of 5-year-olds learning about biological categories. On the posttest of this study, children were asked to categorize the life status of the specific plants, animals, and inanimate objects about which they earlier received feedback and also to categorize novel plants, animals, and inanimate objects.

The posttest classifications were far from perfect, but they were equally imperfect on familiar and novel items; the percent correct categorization was almost identical on the two. Given the diversity of objects within the experiment (the plants included flowers, trees, grass, beans, and clover; the animals included cats, crocodiles, bees, worms, and octopi), the breadth of learning was more impressive than would have been evident without data on use of the new categorization scheme on repetitions of the original entities. Similar evidence came from Siegler's (1995) number conservation study, in which use of transformational reasoning on repetitions of the same problem was no higher than generalization of the reasoning to problems on which the reasoning was not used earlier. Thus, the general high variability of use of new strategies may underlie many apparent failures to transfer learning to different types of problems; distinguishing between the two interpretations requires presenting examples identical to those originally learned as well as novel examples.

A second theoretical implication concerns the crucial role of encoding of categories in determining the breadth of learning. The heterogeneity of members of each superordinate category in Opfer and Siegler (2004) provided little reason to expect broad transfer. However, children appeared to encode "living" as a property that applies to all objects or to no object within each superordinate category. Thus, they thought that either all plants or no plants are alive. Children did not show similar consistent categorization for two other biological properties—capacity for growth and need for water—when asked whether the same objects possessed those properties. Why properties are encoded as applying more or less broadly to classes of objects is an important question for future studies on the breadth of children's learning.

## Sources of Change

Microgenetic studies have demonstrated that a wide variety of experiences can evoke change: practice, feedback, direct instruction, social collaboration, requests to explain observations, and so on. In this respect, they are like training studies. Where microgenetic studies go beyond training studies is in the depth of their portrayal of how the particular sources of change produce learning.

### Basic Phenomena

Physical maturation and general experience produce substantial changes in many capabilities, even without any specifically relevant experience with the experimental situation (e.g., Shimojo et al., 1986; Spencer et al., 2000; Thelen & Ulrich, 1991). At times, these general changes are as sizeable as those that occur over the same age range among children given directly relevant experience. Thus, in Adolph (1997), control group infants who never had descended down ramps generated strategies and strategy choices equivalent to those of age peers who had encountered the ramps on a weekly basis for several months. Amount of experience at home going up and down stairs and climbing on to and off of furniture (as measured by parental report) appeared to be a crucial factor. Such experience at home was related, above and beyond the effect of age, to individual differences in the infants' ability to discriminate safe from risky ramps.

Although the practice and feedback obtained by the infants in Adolph (1997) did not enhance their ramp descent skills, problem-solving experience often does produce learning. This is unsurprising when children receive feedback or instruction that guides them toward improved solutions. More surprising, problem-solving experience in the absence of feedback or instruction also often helps children learn. Even when children receive feedback, learning frequently occurs following success rather than failure of existing strategies, a phenomenon first noted by Karmiloff-Smith (1979b) in the context of map drawing and language learning and replicated in many other contexts since then. Learning without negative feedback has been shown for theory of mind inferences (Flynn, 2005), scientific reasoning (Kuhn et al., 1992, 1995; Schauble, 1996), analogical reasoning (Hosenfeld, van den Boom, & van der Maas, 1997; Tunteler & Resing, 2002), memory strategies (Bjorklund, 1988; Coyle & Bjorklund, 1997), and other problem-solving skills. Learning without feedback or instruction often involves generation of new strategies, as well as improved execution of existing strategies. Regardless of whether the activity is a game of 20 questions (Thornton, 1999), a set of mathematical equality problems (Alibali, 1999), a map-drawing task (Karmiloff-Smith, 1979b), or rediscovery of the decimal system following brain injury (Siegler & Engle, 1994), people generate new approaches even without specially designed instruction or failure of existing approaches. Thus, problem solving per se can be a source of change.

Another source of change that has received considerable attention in microgenetic research is social collaborative problem solving. Microgenetic analyses of collaboration have been applied to mother-infant interaction (Wertsch & Hickmann, 1987), pairs of 5- to 9-year-olds learning about balance scales (Tudge, 1992; Tudge, Winterhoff, & Hogan, 1996), pairs of first graders learning to write narratives (Jones, 1998; Jones & Pellegrini, 1996), small groups of fourth graders solving mathematical word problems via reciprocal instruction (Taylor & Cox, 1997), pairs of fifth graders learning about decimal fractions (Ellis, Klahr, & Siegler, 1993), pairs of fifth and seventh graders building bridges (Parziale, 2002), pairs of sixth, seventh, and eighth graders solving science reasoning problems (Kuhn & Pearsall, 2000), a classroom of ninth-grade ESL students learning a science curriculum (Gelman et al., 2002), and small groups of adults designing robotic devices (Granott, 1998; Granott et al., 2002). The large amount of overt behavior, both conversations and actions, generated by collaborative problem solving makes such situations ideal for microgenetic analysis.

A particularly interesting finding that has emerged from these studies is that the degree of engagement of the partners is crucial to the effectiveness of learning (Ellis et al., 1993; Forman & MacPhail, 1993; Glachen & Light, 1982; Perret-Clermont, Perret, & Bell, 1991; Tudge, 1992; Tudge et al., 1996). Listening intently to partners' explanations, requesting clarification of them, and reaching shared understanding strongly influence how much learning occurs.

A number of factors probably contribute to the effects of engagement on learning. Engagement seems likely to reflect interest in the subject matter, general motivation to learn, and the quality of the relationship between or among collaborators.

Engagement also seems likely to be related to a learning process that is powerful—in both collaborative and noncollaborative situations—extracting causal relations. Listening intently, requesting clarifications, and reaching shared understandings may help learners probe deeply enough to understand underlying causal relations within the problems, and such understanding of causal relations may be crucial to learning.

Evidence from studies of individual as well as collaborative learning attests to the crucial role of causal understanding in all kinds of understanding.

Ability to form causal connections among events starts in the 1st year of life (e.g., Kotovsky & Baillargeon, 1994). Even 1-year-olds find it easier to learn to reproduce causally coherent sequences of actions than arbitrary sequences (Bauer, Chapter 9, this *Handbook,* this volume). Thus, ability to explain the causes of events seems to be a basic property of human beings.

Despite this early development, even older children and adults fail to grasp causal relations in many situations in which doing so would be useful. This poses an especially large problem for understanding mathematics and science. Even among adults at elite universities, causal understanding of physical and biological phenomena tends to be extremely shallow (Rozenblit & Keil, 2002).

Somewhat surprisingly, given this poor understanding of causality underlying physical and biological phenomena, microgenetic studies have revealed that people are highly motivated to learn about causal relations. When children expect some physical or biological variables to be causal and others not to be, they generate more experiments regarding the effects of the variables that they expect to be causal (Kuhn et al., 1988, 1992). Both 10-year-olds and adults more effectively learn that particular physical variables are causally related than that they are not related (Schauble, 1996). Children also are reluctant to abandon a belief that a variable exerts a causal influence in favor of the conclusion that the variable is not causal (Kuhn & Pearsall, 1998).

Understanding causal relations is also crucial to learning. Children learn more when actively testing causal hypotheses through self-generated experiments than they do from watching the same experiments generated by other children, where they do not know the hypothesized cause being tested (Kuhn & Ho, 1980). Understanding why a given memory strategy exerts a positive effect is closely related to whether children choose to use the strategy when not required to do so (Paris et al., 1982). In addition, among older children and adults, individual differences in efforts to explain the causal hows and whys in science and math textbooks are closely related to the amount learned (Chi, Bassok, Lewis, Reimann, & Glaser, 1989; Chi, de Leeuw, Chiu, & LaVancher, 1994; Nathan, Mertz, & Ryan, 1994).

How does causal understanding enhance learning? One path is through avoiding trial and error and limiting searches for new approaches to plausible alternatives. For example, understanding how counterbalancing produces stable physical structures allows school age children to construct superior new bridges if their initial attempts collapse (Thornton, 1999). Similarly, understanding the goals that successful addition strategies must meet allows preschoolers to discover effective addition strategies without any trial-and-error (Siegler & Crowley, 1994). Conversely, misunderstanding causal relations often produces distorted recollections of experiments and results, which impedes learning (Kuhn et al., 1995). And as noted earlier, causal relations, once learned, are more memorable than arbitrary relations (Bauer, Chapter 9, this *Handbook,* this volume). Thus, causal understanding motivates, guides, and maintains learning.

### Influences of Child and Environment

Although infants and toddlers sometimes identify causal relations, and although adults fairly often fail to identify such relations, the frequency with which people identify causal connections on any given task generally increases with age. In scientific reasoning contexts, adults consistently are superior to older children, and older children are superior to younger ones, in learning which variables exert a causal influence (Chen & Klahr, 1999; Kuhn et al., 1992, 1995; Schauble, 1996). The same age trends are apparent on other types of problem-solving tasks; for example, on the previously mentioned bridge building task that required understanding of the causal role of counterbalancing, 10% of 5-year-olds, 40% of 7-year-olds, and 70% of 9-year-olds succeeded (Thornton, 1999).

The pervasive positive effect of understanding causal relations raises the issue of whether encouraging children to seek causal understanding improves their learning. Numerous experiments indicate that the answer is "yes." Asking 5-year-olds to explain why an experimenter advanced the number conservation answer that she did leads to greater learning than does asking peers to explain their own answers or simply providing feedback (Siegler, 1995). Asking 7-year-olds to explain why some representations are better than others leads to their subsequently generating better representations themselves (Triano, 2004). Asking 5- to 9-year-olds to explain why a balance scale rotated as it did leads to greater learning than just having them observe the movements (Pine & Messer, 2000). Asking 12-year-olds to explain statements within eighth-grade biology textbooks enhances their learning, even relative to having them read the textbook twice (Chi et al., 1994). Asking first through fourth graders to explain both why correct answers are correct and why incorrect answers are incorrect leads to greater learning of mathematical equality and sinking objects problems than does asking peers to explain the correct answer alone or to explain their own reasoning (Siegler, 2002; Siegler & Chen, in preparation). The same has been found in classroom settings; asking children to explain why wrong answers are wrong as well as why right answers are right is more ef-

fective instructionally than just modeling the correct answer. The difference is particularly large on problems fairly far removed from the original problem (Taylor & Cox, 1997). This tendency for understanding of causal relations to be especially important on transfer problems has also appeared in laboratory studies of other tasks (Alibali, 1999; Crowley & Siegler, 1999; Rittle-Johnson & Alibali, 1999; Siegler, 2002).

### Theoretical Implications and Questions

Why does being asked to explain observations enhance learning, and why does being asked to also explain why wrong answers are wrong enhance learning further? The phenomena are not attributable to time on task; encouragement to explain observations heightens learning even when time on task is controlled (Aleven & Koedinger, 2002; Chi et al., 1994; Renkl, 1997).

At a general level, self-explanation seems to work by increasing learners' depth of processing. One way in which it does this is to increase the likelihood of learners generating any explanation. People often accept observations without asking "why." However, when people are explicitly asked, "Why do you think that happened?" they are more likely to think about the observation deeply enough to generate an explanation or, in Chi's (2000) formulation, to repair their mental model. Constructing such an explanation is often harder than it might appear; learners who generate incorrect answers and who then are asked to explain the correct answer often initially respond by saying, "I don't know" (Flynn, submitted; Siegler, 1995). However, in these same studies, increasing numbers of children eventually did generate the correct explanation, and it became the most frequent approach.

A related process through which encouragement to explain may enhance learning is by increasing the persistence of explanatory efforts. In Siegler's (2002) study of mathematical equality, the third- and fourth-grade participants took around 11 seconds on Trial 1 to generate an answer to the $A + B + C = \underline{\hspace{1cm}} + C$ problem that they were presented. After being asked to explain both why the right answer was right and why the wrong answer was wrong, children in that condition took much longer to generate answers to the same type of problems on the next few trials; the mean solution time rose to 22 seconds on Trial 2 and 25 seconds on Trial 3. This extra time was not attributable to the correct strategy that they eventually learned inherently taking longer; after two more trials, their times returned to the original level of around 11 seconds. Peers who received feedback on the same problems but who were not asked to generate explanations did not show this pattern of increasing and then decreasing solution times; their mean times remained around 11 seconds on all trials. Instead, the extra time taken by children who were asked to explain correct and incorrect answers seemed to reflect a deeper search for a strategy that could generate correct answers.

Consistent with this explanation, although children in both feedback and self-explanation groups of Siegler (2002) generated ways of solving the problems correctly by the end of the training session, the discoveries differed in quality. Most children in the feedback group generated a strategy that yielded correct answers on the problems that were presented (A + B + C = _____ + C problems); they simply added A + B. This strategy worked on these problems, but it did not generalize beyond them. In contrast, most children who were asked to explain both correct and incorrect answers relied on one of two more advanced and general approaches: these children either computed what they needed to add to C to equalize the values on the two sides of the equal sign or subtracted C from both sides. The result was that on the posttest, the percent correct on problems of the type presented during training did not differ for the two groups, but there were substantial differences on transfer problems such as A + B + C = _____ + D, on which the more sophisticated strategies would work and the less sophisticated one would not. Thus, the effectiveness of encouragement to explain observations also is probably due in part to such encouragement producing deeper searches of existing knowledge.

A third mechanism through which self-explanation may exercise its effects is by decreasing the strength of existing, incorrect ways of thinking. Evidence for such a weakening process again was found in Siegler (2002). The frequency of children's predominant incorrect strategy, adding A + B + C, fell much more rapidly in the group asked to explain both why wrong answers were wrong and why right answers were right than in a group asked only to explain why right answers were right. On the initial trial, before feedback or requests for explanations, 80% of children in both groups used the A + B + C approach. On the next trial, 50% of children in the feedback group continued to use this approach, but only 25% of children in the self-explanation group did. As emphasized throughout this chapter, incorrect approaches often persist for substantial periods of time, even after

superior approaches are also known; instructional approaches that undermine the incorrect approaches, in this case by having children explain why they are incorrect, can speed learning by undermining the logic that supports them and thus decreasing their appeal.

## RELATIONS BETWEEN LEARNING AND DEVELOPMENT

The relation between short-term and long-term change (aka learning and development; microdevelopment and macrodevelopment; change at short and long time scales) is among the enduring issues in developmental psychology. Classical theorists have taken sharply conflicting stances regarding the issue. Werner (1948, 1957) and Vygotsky (1934/1962) viewed short-term change as a miniature version of long-term change, generated by similar underlying processes and characterized by identical sequences of qualitatively distinct stages. Learning theorists such as Kendler and Kendler (1962) also viewed the two as fundamentally similar, but unlike Werner and Vygotsky, they viewed both short-term and long-term change as proceeding through gradual incremental processes with no qualitatively distinct stages. Piaget (e.g., 1964, 1970) expressed a third perspective; he viewed the two types of change, which he referred to as learning and development, as fundamentally dissimilar. In his view, development created new cognitive structures; learning merely filled-in specific content.

The relation of short-term to long-term change continues to be discussed by contemporary theorists: dynamic systems (e.g., van Geert, 1998), neo-Piagetian (e.g., Case, 1998), and information processing (e.g., Elman et al., 1996). There appears to be a broad consensus that changes over short and long time periods resemble each other, but much less agreement as to the level of detail at which the resemblance holds. Some investigators have concluded that the similarity is a deep one; for example, Thelen and Corbetta (2002) wrote:

> We study microdevelopment because we believe that the processes that cause change in a matter of minutes or hours are the same as those working over months or years. In other words, the principles underlying behavioral change work at multiple time scales. (p. 60)

Other investigators (e.g., P. H. Miller & Coyle, 1999; Pressley, 1992) have concluded that the degree of similarity between microgenetic and age-related change is uncertain, both at the level of the descriptive course of change and at the level of underlying mechanisms. They also have noted that the conditions used to elicit change in microgenetic studies often differ from those that elicit it in the everyday environment. Even when the eliciting events are basically similar, the higher density of relevant experiences and the more consistent feedback in the laboratory setting could result in the changes being quite different in their specifics. These issues led P. H. Miller and Coyle (1999) to conclude: "Although the microgenetic method reveals how behavior *can* change, it is less clear whether behavior typically *does* change in this way in natural settings" (p. 212).

After noting this uncertainty regarding the precision of the resemblance between microgenetic and age-related change, Fischer and Granott (1995) and Kuhn (1995) suggested a solution: Set up direct comparisons with identical populations, methods, and measures of the changes observed in microgenetic studies and those observed in cross-sectional and long-term longitudinal studies. To provide such a direct comparison, Siegler and Svetina (2002) combined cross-sectional and microgenetic designs within a single experiment. In the cross-sectional part, they presented 6-, 7-, and 8-year-olds with standard matrix completion and conservation problems of the type used by Inhelder and Piaget (1964) and Piaget (1952). Then, a randomly chosen half of 6-year-olds were presented four sessions of feedback and self-explanation prompts on matrix completion problems, followed 2 months later by a posttest on matrix completion and conservation. The other half of the 6-year-olds did not receive the four feedback-and-self-explanation sessions, and thus served as a control group.

The overall magnitude of change among children in the microgenetic condition, as indicated by the percent correct answers, proved comparable to the magnitude of the change between ages 6-years and 7-years among children in the cross-sectional part of the study. This comparability of overall change allowed a reasonable comparison to be made of the detailed patterning of changes on 11 measures of performance.

Microgenetic and age-related changes were similar on 10 of the 11 measures. On five of these measures, both groups showed significant changes, and on another five, neither group did. The specificity of many of the matches was quite striking. For example, there were changes over both sessions and years in number of answers correct on the size dimension, but no changes over sessions or years in the number of explanations that

mentioned size. Qualitative aspects of change were also similar. For example, children in both groups produced the same predominant error; in both cases, it accounted for about 70% of total errors. The learning of children in the microgenetic condition also was highly stable over time and generalized to the conservation tasks, qualities that Piaget identified as defining characteristics of developmental change. Thus, at least in this case, microgenetic change proved extremely similar to age-related changes that occurred without any experimental manipulation.

Similar broad parallels in the path of microgenetic and age-related change have been found on balance scale, sort-recall, mathematical equality, addition, language development, map drawing, false belief, and many other problems (Alibali & Goldin-Meadow, 1993; Chletsos & De Lisi, 1991; Flynn et al., 2004; Grupe, 1998; Karmiloff-Smith, 1979a; Schlagmüller & Schneider, 2002). To cite one example, experience performing a selective attention task produced the same inverted U-shaped function in amount of private speech as emerged between ages 3 and 5 years without such experience (Winsler, Diaz, & Montero, 1997). To cite another example, the same type of balance scale rule progressions that emerged in cross-sectional studies between ages 5 and 8 years emerged over trials within a single session when 5-year-olds were given feedback and asked to explain their observations (Siegler & Chen, 1998).

Clearly, microgenetic and age-related change will not always be so similar. When direct instruction is provided, people may often follow paths different than the ones they would otherwise have followed. To illustrate, children who produce gesture-speech mismatches while solving mathematical equality problems usually progress toward correct gesture and speech if given direct instruction; however, they usually regress toward incorrect gesture and speech in the absence of instruction (Goldin-Meadow & Alibali, 2002). Highly directive instruction also can alter the path of change in another way; it at times produces immediate consistent use of the correct approach and thus eliminates intermediate approaches that would otherwise have appeared (Opfer & Siegler, 2004). Nonetheless, when microgenetic studies do not involve directive instruction, microgenetic and age-related changes tend to be highly similar. As Kuhn (2002) noted:

> Microgenetic analysis achieves a reintegration of learning and development as processes that have fewer differences

than they do commonalities. . . . Rather than standing in opposition to the study of development, fine-grained studies of learning illuminate, indeed are essential to understanding, the more macro-level phenomena of development. (p. 111)

## CHANGE MECHANISMS

Deeply understanding how change occurs is the holy grail of developmental psychology: a profound goal, never fully attained, probably not attainable, but worth pursuing nonetheless. One reason for the impossibility of fully succeeding is that change processes are inherently unobservable; they can only be inferred from behavioral observations at different points in time. Another reason is that such mechanisms can be described at multiple levels that vary in specificity (maturation, improved working memory, automatization), time gain (years, seconds, milliseconds), and system (behavioral, computational, neural). Progress in understanding mechanisms at each level of specificity, time gain, and system inevitably raises questions about the other levels.

Despite these inherent limits on understanding change processes, the detailed descriptions of change yielded by microgenetic analyses can move us toward the goal, both by suggesting candidate mechanisms that are consistent with the wide range of data yielded by such studies and by ruling out alternatives that are inconsistent with them. One good example comes from studies of gesture-speech mismatches. Alibali and Goldin-Meadow (1993) hypothesized on the basis of microgenetic data that gesture-speech mismatches reflected competition between representations, and that simultaneous activation of competing representations would require more cognitive resources than would activating a single idea. To test this hypothesis, Goldin-Meadow, Nusbaum, Garber, and Church (1993) asked children to remember a set of unrelated words while they solved mathematical equality problems. All of the children generated incorrect mathematical equality strategies in speech, but some generated correct strategies in gesture. Strikingly, the children who generated correct strategies in gesture, and who thus were more knowledgeable about mathematical equality, did less well on the concurrent task of remembering words. This evidence strongly suggested that simultaneous activation of competing representations is one mechanism underlying gesture-speech mismatches.

Microgenetic studies also can illuminate neural mechanisms that underlie learning. For example, Haier et al. (1992) found that as college students learned to play the video game Tetris, they reduced their overall glucose metabolism, with the decrease being greatest in brain areas that did not seem essential for playing the game. The largest changes in glucose metabolism were seen among the participants who showed the largest improvements in game playing skill.

The detailed data yielded by microgenetic studies also constrain mechanistic accounts and raise process-level issues that otherwise would not arise. One such case involves learning in the face of success. Microgenetic studies of map drawing, counting, balance scales, arithmetic, sort-recall, and selective attention tasks have shown that strategy discoveries follow success as well as failure (Blöte et al., 1999, 2004; Karmiloff-Smith, 1979b; P. H. Miller & Aloise-Young, 1995; Siegler & Jenkins, 1989). The observation has created a need for models that, unlike connectionist and many symbolic models, generate new approaches without error detection.

Another way in which microgenetic data can help specify mechanisms is by revealing relations among multiple changes. In one illustrative study, Robinson and Mervis (1998) sampled a single child's language development on a daily basis between the ages of 11 and 25 months. Of particular interest were their findings concerning the relation between vocabulary size and grammatical development. They found that the precursor mechanism proposed by van Geert (1991) fit their data. This mechanism links two asynchronously developing capabilities: a predecessor (earlier developing) capability and a successor (later developing) capability. The predecessor (in this case, vocabulary) needs to reach a critical value before the successor (in this case, use of plurals) begins to emerge. The emergence of the successor capability initially increases the rate of development of the predecessor. Over time, however, the successor becomes a competitor for resources with the predecessor, and development of the predecessor slows. Finally, the successor reaches an asymptotic level and stops competing for resources, and the rate of development of the predecessor again increases. As in the other examples in this section, the microgenetic data were critical for linking this mechanism to the change being explained.

Microgenetic studies can be particularly useful for enhancing understanding of change mechanisms when they are part of a back-and-forth process involving them, formal modeling, and traditional cross-sectional and longitudinal empirical studies. Research on the development of basic arithmetic illustrates this process.

A number of early cross-sectional studies indicated that preschoolers and young elementary school children use varied strategies to solve simple addition problems (e.g., Fuson, 1982). As noted earlier, preschoolers' most common approach is the sum strategy, which involves putting up fingers on one hand to represent the first addend, putting up fingers on the other hand to represent the second addend, and then counting all of the fingers. First and second graders' most common approach is the min strategy, which involves counting up from the larger addend.

This information provided the basis for Siegler and Jenkins' (1989) microgenetic study of discovery of the min strategy. Children of the age just prior to when the discovery would usually be made (4- and 5-year-olds) were presented 20 to 30 brief sessions of experience with addition. The study yielded eight main findings, which also could be viewed as eight main constraints that a satisfactory model of discovery of the min strategy would need to meet: (1) Almost all children discovered the min strategy; (2) all children used varied strategies both before and after the discovery; (3) the shortcut sum strategy, which incorporated some aspects of the sum strategy and some aspects of the min strategy, usually was generated shortly before discovery of the min strategy; (4) discoveries often occurred in the context of success rather than failure; (5) generalization of the min strategy was slow; (6) presenting challenge problems on which the min strategy was particularly advantageous hastened generalization; (7) strategy choices were at all times responsive to problem characteristics; and (8) children discovered the min strategy without any trial and error.

This last finding was particularly intriguing. Despite solving between 140 and 210 problems and generating a number of novel addition strategies, none of the children ever generated an illegal strategy. It was not that no illegal strategies were possible; for example, children could have added the first addend twice and ignored the second one, or added the first addend to the second one and then added the second one again. This raised the question of how children were able to invent legal strategies without any trial and error with illegal strategies.

To address the question, Siegler and Jenkins hypothesized that even before children discover the min strategy,

they possess a goal sketch, a conceptual structure that indicates the goals that a legal strategy must meet. The goal sketch for addition indicates that legal strategies must include procedures for quantifying each addend and combining the two addends into a single answer.

This hypothesis motivated Siegler and Crowley (1994) to perform a new empirical study to test whether children possess such a goal sketch even before they discover the min strategy. They asked 5-year-olds, some who already used the min strategy and some who did not, to judge the smartness of three addition procedures that a puppet executed: the sum strategy, which all of the children already used in their own problem solving; the min strategy, which some children used and some did not; and counting the first addend twice, which none of the children used. The question was whether children who did not yet use the min strategy would view it as smarter than counting the first addend twice, which they also did not use. It turned out that they viewed the min strategy as much smarter than counting the first addend twice; in fact, they viewed the min strategy as being slightly smarter than the strategy they used most often, the sum strategy. This finding led to the conclusion that children possess conceptual understanding of addition akin to the goal sketch before they discover the min strategy and that this understanding helps them avoid trial and error in the discovery process.

These data from Siegler and Crowley (1994), together with the prior cross-sectional and microgenetic findings, provided crucial constraints on a computer simulation of discovery of the min strategy (Shrager & Siegler, 1998). The model began with two strategies—retrieval and the sum strategy—and was presented addition problems like those in Siegler and Jenkins (1989). Through solving these problems, the model learned which types of strategies work best in general and on particular types of problems. The mechanisms that produced learning and discovery within this model are illustrated schematically in Figure 11.4.

As shown at the top of Figure 11.4, within this model when strategies are used to solve problems, the process yields information about the answers to the problems, as well as the speeds and accuracies characteristic of the strategies and the problems. The model learns which strategies are most effective in general and which work best on problems with specific features, as well as which work best on particular problems. Each problem-solving effort also yields a trace of the processing per-

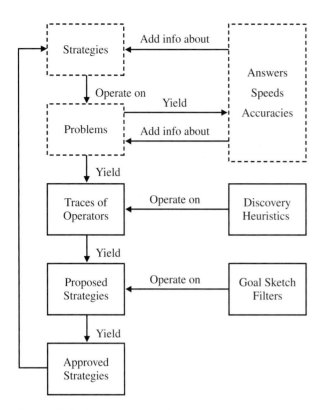

**Figure 11.4** SCADS model of strategy choice and strategy discovery. The way in which children choose among strategies and learn about the characteristics of problems, strategies, and their interaction is schematically represented at the top of the diagram; the way in which they generate appropriate new strategies and avoid generating inappropriate ones is schematically represented in the bottom part. *Source:* From "SCADS: A Model of Children's Strategy Choices and Strategy Discoveries," by J. Shrager and R. S. Siegler, 1998, *Psychological Science, 9,* pp. 405–410. Reprinted with permission.

formed on that trial. As problem solving became increasingly automatized, working memory resources are freed, which allows discovery heuristics to examine these traces to see if more efficient processing is possible. If so, the model proposes a new, potentially more efficient strategy, and compares it to goal sketch filters, which test whether the proposed strategy satisfies the basic goals of addition. This mechanism eliminates potential illegal strategies before they lead to behavior, and at the same time allows legal strategies to be tried. The overall result was that the simulation generated behavior that matched all eight key characteristics of children in the microgenetic study and that generated numerous other phenomena that had been observed in prior cross-sectional studies.

Siegler and Araya (2005) recently expanded the model to simulate Siegler and Stern's (1998) findings regarding how children generate an arithmetic insight. That model produces variations in performance under different experimental conditions, regressions between sessions, learning within sessions, patterns of overgeneralization and undergeneralization, and both conscious and unconscious strategy discoveries. Of particular interest, the model indicates that what looked at a behavioral level to be five distinct strategies is at a mechanistic level only two strategies combined in different ways and with different levels of activation. As these examples suggest, combining microgenetic data, data on changes with age, and formal modeling techniques offers considerable promise for enhancing understanding of how children learn.

## CONCLUSION

The research summarized in this chapter supports the view that children's learning is inherently a process of variability, choice, and change. This characterization is not unique to children's learning; indeed, mechanisms that generate variability, choice, and change are essential to all adaptive systems, from plants and animals to cultures and corporations. The specific mechanisms that produce these characteristics vary greatly, but the characteristics themselves are invariant.

Microgenetic studies have revealed numerous aspects of how variability, choice, and change operate in the context of children's learning. Such studies have revealed that children are constantly generating new variants, not just during delimited transition periods and not just when existing approaches fail, but at all times. They also have revealed that the varying approaches that children generate are constrained by conceptual understanding, rather than being a process of trial and error. They also have revealed that choices among variants are surprisingly adaptive from the beginning of learning, that this is true even in infancy, and that the choices become yet more adaptive with experience in the specific domain. And the research also has revealed that the uptake of even the best new approaches often is slow and halting, and that this is true even when children can explain why the new approach is superior to alternatives.

All of these characteristics seem to be true of what has traditionally been called "development" as well as what has traditionally been called "learning." Indeed, the distinction between development and learning seems increasingly artificial, given that both are processes of variability, choice, and change, and that studies of age-related changes and learning reveal so many empirical commonalities. However, this may only be how things appear at present. Detailed analysis of the mechanisms that operate over shorter and longer time periods may reveal more substantial differences than are currently evident. Mechanistic models of short-term change, guided by and constrained by microgenetic data, are being created in increasing number. Testing whether the mechanisms that produce changes within these models can also account for long-term changes—and determining how, if at all, they need to be changed to do so—promises to be a particularly exciting frontier for the new field of children's learning.

## REFERENCES

Adolph, K. E. (1997). Learning in the development of infant locomotion. *Monographs of the Society for Research in Child Development, 62*(3, Serial No. 251).

Agre, P., & Shrager, J. (1990). Routine evolution as the microgenetic basis of skill acquisition. *Proceedings of annual conference of the Cognitive Science Society.* Hillsdale, NJ: Erlbaum.

Aleven, V. A. W. M. M., & Koedinger, K. R. (2002). An effective metacognitive strategy: Learning by doing and explaining with a computer-based Cognitive Tutor. *Cognitive Science, 26,* 147–179.

Alibali, M. W. (1999). How children change their minds: Strategy change can be gradual or abrupt. *Developmental Psychology, 35,* 127–145.

Alibali, M. W., & Goldin-Meadow, S. (1993). Gesture-speech mismatch and mechanisms of learning: What the hands reveal about a child's state of mind. *Cognitive Psychology, 25,* 468–523.

Alibali, M. W., & Perret, M. A. (1996, June). *The structure of children's verbal explanations reveals the stability of their knowledge.* Paper presented at the 26th annual meeting of the Jean Piaget Society, Philadelphia, PA.

Allison, P. D. (1984). *Event history analysis: Regression for longitudinal event data.* Beverly Hills, CA: Sage.

Amsterlaw, J., & Wellman, H. M. (2004). *Theories of mind in transition: A microgenetic study of the development of false belief understanding.* Manuscript submitted for publication.

Anzai, Y., & Simon, H. A. (1979). The theory of learning by doing. *Psychological Review, 86,* 24–140.

Aslin, R. N., Jusczyk, P. W., & Pisoni, D. P. (1998). Speech and auditory processing during infancy: Constraints on and precursors to language. In W. Damon (Editor-in-Chief) & D. Kuhn & R. S. Siegler (Vol. Eds.), *Handbook of child psychology: Vol. 2. Cognition, perception and language* (5th ed., pp. 147–198). New York: Wiley.

Bandura, A., & Walters, R. (1963). *Social learning and personality development.* New York: Holt, Rinehart and Winston.

Bidell, T. R., & Fischer, K. W. (1994). Developmental transitions in children's early on-line planning. In M. Haith, B. Pennington, &

J. Benson (Eds.), *The development of future-oriented processes* (pp. 141–176). Chicago: University of Chicago Press.

Bijou, S., & Baer, D. M. (1961). *Child development: Vol. 1. A systematic and empirical theory.* New York: Appleton-Century-Crofts.

Bjorklund, D. F. (1988). Acquiring a mnemonic: Age and category knowledge effects. *Journal of Experimental Child Psychology, 45,* 71–87.

Bjorklund, D. F., Coyle, T. R., & Gaultney, J. F. (1992). Developmental differences in the acquisition and maintenance of an organizational strategy: Evidence for the utilization deficiency hypothesis. *Journal of Experimental Child Psychology, 54,* 434–438.

Blöte, A. W., Resing, W. C. M., Mazer, P., & Van Noort, D. A. (1999). Young children's organizational strategies on a same-different task: A microgenetic study and a training study. *Journal of Experimental Child Psychology, 74,* 21–43.

Blöte, A. W., Van Otterloo, S. G., Stevenson, C. E., & Veenman, M. V. J. (2004). Discovery and maintenance of the many-to-one county strategy in 4-year-olds: A microgenetic study. *British Journal of Developmental Psychology, 22,* 83–102.

Bowerman, M. (1982). Starting to talk worse: Clues to language acquisition from children's late speech errors. In S. Strauss (Ed.), *U-shaped behavioral growth* (pp. 101–145). New York: Academic Press.

Bransford, J. D., Brown, A. L., & Cocking, R. R. (Eds.). (1999). *How people learn: Brain, mind, experience, and school.* Washington, DC: National Academy Press.

Braswell, G. S., & Rosengren, K. K. (2000). Decreasing variability in the development of graphic production. *International Journal of Behavioral Development, 24,* 153–166.

Bray, N. W., Huffman, L. F., & Fletcher, K. L. (1999). Developmental and intellectual differences in self-report and strategy use. *Developmental Psychology, 35,* 1223–1236.

Brown, A. L., Bransford, J. D., Ferrara, R. A., & Campione, J. C. (1983). Learning, remembering, and understanding. In P. H. Mussen (Series Ed.) & J. H. Flavell & E. M. Markman (Vol. Eds.), *Handbook of child psychology: Vol. 3. Cognitive development* (4th ed., pp. 77–166). New York: Wiley.

Brown, A. L., Kane, M. J., & Echols, K. (1986). Young children's mental models determine analogical transfer across problems with a common goal structure. *Cognitive Development, 1,* 103–122.

Caron, J., & Caron-Pargue, J. (1976). Analysis of verbalization during problem solving. *Bulletin de Psychologie, 30,* 551–562.

Case, R. (1998). The development of conceptual structures. In W. Damon (Editor-in-Chief) & D. Kuhn & R. S. Siegler (Vol. Eds.), *Handbook of child psychology: Vol. 2. Cognition, perception and language* (5th ed., pp. 745–800). New York: Wiley.

Case, R., & Okamoto, Y. (1996). The role of central conceptual structures in the development of children's thought. *Monographs of the Society for Research in Child Development, 61*(1/2).

Casey, B. J. (2001). Disruption of inhibitory control in developmental disorders: A mechanistic model of implicated frontostriatal circuitry. In J. L. McClelland & R. S. Siegler (Eds.), *Mechanisms of cognitive development: Behavioral and neural perspectives* (pp. 327–349). Mahwah, NJ: Erlbaum.

Catan, L. (1986). The dynamic display of process: Historical development and contemporary uses of the microgenetic method. *Human Development, 29,* 252–263.

Chen, Z., & Klahr, D. (1999). All other things being equal: Children's acquisition of the Control of Variables Strategy. *Child Development, 70,* 1098–1120.

Chen, Z., & Siegler, R. S. (2000). Across the great divide: Bridging the gap between understanding of toddlers' and older children's thinking. *Monographs of the Society for Research in Child Development, 65*(2, Whole No. 261).

Chi, M. T. H. (2000). Self-explaining expository texts: The dual process of generating inferences and repairing mental models. In R. Glaser (Ed.), *Advances in Instructional Psychology* (pp. 161–238). Hillsdale, NJ: Erlbaum.

Chi, M. T. H., Bassok, M., Lewis, M., Reimann, P., & Glaser, R. (1989). Self-explanations: How students study and use examples in learning to solve problems. *Cognitive Science, 13,* 145–182.

Chi, M. T. H., de Leeuw, N., Chiu, M.-H., & LaVancher, C. (1994). Eliciting self-explanations improves understanding. *Cognitive Science, 18,* 439–477.

Childers, J. B., & Tomasello, M. (2001). The role of pronouns in young children's acquisition of the English transitive construction. *Developmental Psychology, 37,* 739–748.

Chinn, C. A. (in press). The microgenetic method: Current work and extensions to classroom research. In J. L. Green, G. Camilli, & P. B. Elmore (Eds.), *Complementary methods for research in education* (3rd ed.). Washington, DC: American Educational Research Association.

Chiu, M. M., Kessel, C., Moschovich, J., & Munoz-Nunez, A. (2001). Learning to graph linear functions: A case study of conceptual change. *Cognition and Instruction, 19,* 215–252.

Chletsos, P. N., & De Lisi, R. (1991). A microgenetic study of proportional reasoning using balance scale problems. *Journal of Applied Developmental Psychology, 12,* 307–330.

Church, R. B. (1999). Using gesture and speech to capture transitions in learning. *Cognitive Development, 14,* 313–342.

Church, R. B., & Goldin-Meadow, S. (1986). The mismatch between gesture and speech as an index of transitional knowledge. *Cognition, 23,* 43–71.

Cognition and Technology Group at Vanderbilt. (1997). *The Jasper project: Lessons in curriculum, instruction, assessment, and professional development.* Mahwah, NJ: Erlbaum.

Collins, L. M., & Sayer, A. G. (Eds.). (2001). *New methods for the analysis of change.* Washington, DC: American Psychological Association.

Cooney, J. B., & Ladd, S. F. (1992). The influence of verbal protocol methods on children's mental computation. *Learning and Individual Differences, 4,* 237–257.

Corbetta, D., & Thelen, E. (1999). Lateral biases and fluctuations in infants' spontaneous arm movements and reaching. *Developmental Psychology, 34,* 237–255.

Coyle, T. R. (2001). Factor analysis of variability measures in eight independent samples of children and adults. *Journal of Experimental Child Psychology, 78,* 330–358.

Coyle, T. R., & Bjorklund, D. F. (1997). Age differences in, and consequences of, multiple- and variable-strategy use on a multiple sort-recall task. *Developmental Psychology, 33,* 372–380.

Coyle, T. R., Read, L. E., Gaultney, J. F., & Bjorklund, D. F. (1998). Giftedness and variability in strategic processing on a multitrial memory task: Evidence for stability in gifted cognition. *Learning and Individual Differences, 10,* 273–290.

Crowley, K., & Siegler, R. S. (1999). Explanation and generalization in young children's strategy learning. *Child Development, 70,* 304–317.

Crutcher, R. J. (1994). Telling what we know: The use of verbal report methodologies in psychological research. *Psychological Science, 5,* 241–244.

Dixon, J. A., & Bangert, A. S. (2002). The prehistory of discovery: Precursors of representational change in solving gear system problems. *Developmental Psychology, 38,* 918–933.

Dowker, A. (2003). Young children's estimates for addition: The zone of partial knowledge and understanding. In A. J. Baroody & A. Dowker (Eds.), *The development of arithmetic concepts and skills: Constructing adaptive expertise* (pp. 243–265). Mahwah, NJ: Erlbaum.

Dromi, E. (1987). *Early lexical development.* Cambridge, England: Cambridge University Press.

Duncan, R. M., & Pratt, M. W. (1997). Microgenetic change in the quantity and quality of preschoolers' private speech. *International Journal of Behavioral Development, 20,* 367–383.

Ellis, S. (1995, April). *Social influences on strategy choice.* Paper presented at the meetings of the Society for Research in Child Development, Indianapolis, IN.

Ellis, S., Klahr, D., & Siegler, R. S. (1993, April). *The birth, life, and sometimes death of good ideas in collaborative problem solving.* Paper presented at the annual meeting of the American Educational Research Association, New Orleans, LA.

Elman, J. L., Bates, E. A., Johnson, M. H., Karmiloff-Smith, A., Parisi, D., & Plunkett, K. (1996). *Rethinking innateness: A connectionist perspective on development.* Cambridge, MA: MIT Press.

Ericsson, K. A., & Simon, H. A. (1984). *Protocol analysis.* Cambridge, MA: MIT Press.

Fireman, G. (1996). Developing a plan for solving a problem: A representational shift. *Cognitive Development, 11,* 107–122.

Fischer, K. W., & Granott, N. (1995). Beyond one-dimensional change: Multiple, concurrent, socially distributed processes in learning and development. *Human Development, 38,* 302–314.

Fischer, K. W., & Yan, Z. (2002). Darwin's construction of the theory of evolution: Microdevelopment of explanations of variation and change in species. In N. Granott & J. Parziale (Eds.), *Microdevelopment: Transition processes in development and learning* (pp. 294–318). Cambridge, England: Cambridge University Press.

Flavell, J. (1963). *The developmental psychology of Jean Piaget.* Princeton, NJ: Van Nostrand.

Fletcher, K. L., & Bray, N. W. (1995). External and verbal strategies in children with and without mental retardation. *American Journal on Mental Retardation, 99,* 363–375.

Fletcher, K. L., Huffman, L. F., Bray, N. W., & Grupe, L. A. (1998). The use of the microgenetic method with children with disabilities: Discovering competence. *Early Education and Development, 9,* 358–373.

Flynn, E. (2005). *A microgenetic investigation of stability and continuity in theory of mind development.* Manuscript submitted for publication.

Flynn, E., O'Malley, C., & Wood, D. (2004). A longitudinal, microgenetic study of the emergence of false belief understanding and inhibition skills. *Developmental Science, 7,* 103–115.

Forman, E. A., & MacPhail, J. (1993). Vygotskian perspective in children's collaborative problem solving activity. In E. A. Forman, N. Minick, & C. A. Stone (Eds.), *Contexts for learning: Sociocultural dynamics in children's development* (pp. 213–229). Oxford, England: Oxford University Press.

Fujimura, N. (2001). Facilitating children's proportional reasoning: A model of reasoning processes and effects of intervention on strategy change. *Journal of Educational Psychology, 93,* 589–603.

Fuson, K. C. (1982). An analysis of the counting-on solution procedure in addition. In T. P. Carpenter, J. M. Moser, & T. A. Romberg (Eds.), *Addition and subtraction: A cognitive perspective* (pp. 67–82). Hillsdale, NJ: Erlbaum.

Gardner, H. (1993). *Creating minds.* New York: Basic Books.

Geary, D. C. (1994). *Children's mathematical development: Research and practical implications.* Washington, DC: American Psychological Association.

Gelman, R., Romo, L., & Francis, W. S. (2002). Notebooks as windows on learning: The case of a science-into-ESL program. In N. Granott & J. Parziale (Eds.), *Microdevelopment: Transition processes in development and learning* (pp. 269–293). Cambridge, England: Cambridge University Press.

Gelman, R., & Williams, E. (1998). Enabling constraints for cognitive development and learning: Domain specificity and epigenesis. In W. Damon (Editor-in-Chief) & D. Kuhn & R. S. Siegler (Vol. Eds.), *Handbook of child psychology: Vol. 2. Cognition, perception and language* (5th ed., pp. 575–630). New York: Wiley.

Gershkoff-Stowe, L., & Smith, L. B. (1997). A curvilinear trend in naming errors as a function of early vocabulary growth. *Cognitive Psychology, 34,* 37–71.

Giere, R. N. (1988). *Explaining science: A cognitive approach.* Chicago: University of Chicago Press.

Gilovich, T., Vallone, R., & Tversky, A. (1985). The hot hand in basketball: On the misperception of random sequences. *Cognitive Psychology, 17,* 295–314.

Glachen, M., & Light, P. (1982). Peer interaction and learning: Can two wrongs make a right. In G. Butterworth & P. Light (Eds.), *Social cognition: Studies of the development of understanding* (pp. 238–262). Brighton, England: Harvester Press.

Goldin-Meadow, S., & Alibali, M. W. (2002). Looking at the hands through time: A microgenetic perspective on learning and instruction. In N. Granott & J. Parziale (Eds.), *Microdevelopment: Transition processes in development and learning* (pp. 80–105). Cambridge, England: Cambridge University Press.

Goldin-Meadow, S., Alibali, M. W., & Church, R. B. (1993). Transitions in concept acquisition: Using the hand to read the mind. *Psychological Review, 100,* 279–297.

Goldin-Meadow, S., Nusbaum, H. C., Garber, P., & Church, R. B. (1993). Transitions in learning: Evidence for simultaneously activated strategies. *Journal of Experimental Psychology: Human Perception and Performance, 19,* 92–107.

Graham, T., & Perry, M. (1993). Indexing transitional knowledge. *Developmental Psychology, 29,* 779–788.

Granott, N. (1998). We learn, therefore we develop: Learning versus development: Or developing learning. In C. Smith & T. Pourchot (Eds.), *Adult learning and development: Perspectives from educational psychology* (pp. 15–35). Mahwah, NJ: Erlbaum.

Granott, N. (2002). How microdevelopment creates macrodevelopment: Reiterated sequences, backward transitions, and the Zone of Current Development. In N. Granott & J. Parziale (Eds.), *Microdevelopment: Transition processes in development and learning* (pp. 213–242). Cambridge, England: Cambridge University Press.

Granott, N., Fischer, K. W., & Parziale, J. (2002). Bridging to the unknown: A transition mechanism in learning and development. In N. Granott & J. Parziale (Eds.), *Microdevelopment: Transition processes in development and learning* (pp. 131–156). Cambridge, England: Cambridge University Press.

Grupe, L. (1998). *A microgenetic study of strategy discovery in young children's addition problem solving: A thesis.* Unpublished master's thesis, University of Alabama at Birmingham.

Guttentag, R. E. (1984). The mental effort requirement of cumulative rehearsal: A developmental study. *Journal of Experimental Child Psychology, 37,* 92–106.

Haier, R. J., Siegel, B. V., Jr., MacLachlan, A., Soderling, E., Lottenberg, S., & Buchsbaum, M. S. (1992). Regional glucose metabolic changes after learning a complex visuospatial/motor task: A positron emission tomographic study. *Brain Research, 570,* 134–143.

Haith, M., & Benson, J. (1998). Infant cognition. In W. Damon (Editor-in-Chief) & D. Kuhn & R. S. Siegler (Vol. Eds.), *Handbook of child psychology: Vol. 2. Cognition, perception and language* (5th ed., pp. 199–254). New York: Wiley.

Hatano, G., Siegler, R. S., Richards, D. D., Inagaki, K., Stavy, R., & Wax, N. (1993). The development of biological knowledge: A multi-national study. *Cognitive Development, 8,* 47–62.

Hosenfeld, B., van der Maas, H. L. J., & van den Boom, D. C. (1997). Indicators of discontinuous change in the development of analogical reasoning. *Journal of Experimental Child Psychology, 64,* 367–395.

Hull, C. L. (1943). *Principles of behavior.* New York: Appleton-Century-Crofts.

Inhelder, B., & Piaget, J. (1964). *The early growth of logic in the child: Classification and seriation.* London: Routledge.

Janos, P. M., & Robinson, N. M. (1985). Psychosocial development in intellectually gifted children. In F. D. Horowitz & M. O'Brien (Eds.), *The gifted and talented: Developmental perspectives* (pp. 149–195). Washington, DC: American Psychological Association.

Johnson, K. E., & Mervis, C. B. (1994). Microgenetic analysis of first steps in children's acquisition of expertise on shorebirds. *Developmental Psychology, 30,* 418–435.

Johnson, M. H. (1998). The neural basis of cognitive development. In W. Damon (Editor-in-Chief) & D. Kuhn & R. S. Siegler (Vol. Eds.), *Handbook of child psychology: Vol. 2. Cognition, Perception and Language* (5th ed.). New York: Wiley.

Jones, I. (1998). Peer relationships and writing development: A microgenetic analysis. *British Journal of Educational Psychology, 68,* 229–241.

Jones, I., & Pellegrini, A. D. (1996). The effects of social relationships, writing media, and microgenetic development on first-grade students' written narratives. *American Educational Research Journal, 33,* 691–718.

Just, M. A., & Carpenter, P. A. (1987). *The psychology of reading and language comprehension.* Needham Heights, MA: Allyn & Bacon.

Karmiloff-Smith, A. (1979a). *A functional approach to child language: A study of determiners and reference.* New York: Cambridge University Press.

Karmiloff-Smith, A. (1979b). Micro- and macro-developmental changes in language acquisition and other representational systems. *Cognitive Science, 3,* 91–118.

Karmiloff-Smith, A., & Inhelder, B. (1974). If you want to get ahead, get a theory. *Cognition, 3,* 195–212.

Keil, F. C. (1998). Cognitive science and the origins of thought and knowledge. In W. Damon (Editor-in-Chief) & R. M. Lerner (Vol.

Ed.), *Handbook of child psychology: Vol. 1. Theoretical models of human development* (5th ed., pp. 341–414). New York: Wiley.

Kendler, H. H., & Kendler, T. S. (1962). Vertical and horizontal processes in problem solving. *Psychological Review, 69,* 1–16.

Kirk, E. P., & Ashcraft, M. H. (1997). Telling stories: The perils and promise of using verbal reports to study math strategies. *Journal of Experimental Psychology: Learning, Memory, and Cognition, 27,* 157–175.

Klahr, D., & Chen, Z. (2003). Overcoming the positive-capture strategy in young children: Learning about indeterminacy. *Child Development, 74,* 1275–1296.

Klahr, D., & MacWhinney, B. (1998). Information processing. In W. Damon (Editor-in-Chief) & D. Kuhn & R. S. Siegler (Vol. Eds.), *Handbook of child psychology: Vol. 2. Cognition, perception and language* (5th ed., pp. 631–678). New York: Wiley.

Klahr, D., & Wallace, J. G. (1976). *Cognitive development: An information processing view.* Hillsdale, NJ: Erlbaum.

Kotovsky, L., & Baillargeon, R. (1994). Calibration-based reasoning about collision events in 11-month-old infants. *Cognition, 51,* 107–129.

Kruse, A., Lindenberger, U., & Baltes, P. B. (1993). Longitudinal research on human aging: The power of combining real-time, microgenetic, and simulation approaches. In D. Magnusson & P. J. M. Casaer (Eds.), *Longitudinal research on individual development: Present status and future perspectives* (pp. 153–193). New York: Cambridge University Press.

Kuhn, D. (1995). Microgenetic study of change: What has it told us? *Psychological Science, 6,* 133–139.

Kuhn, D. (2002). A multi-component system that constructs knowledge: Insights from microgenetic study. In N. Granott & J. Parziale (Eds.), *Microdevelopment: Transition processes in development and learning* (pp. 109–130). Cambridge, England: Cambridge University Press.

Kuhn, D., Amsel, E., & O'Laughlin, M. (1988). *The development of scientific thinking skills.* San Diego, CA: Academic Press.

Kuhn, D., Garcia-Mila, M., Zohar, A., & Anderson, C. (1995). Strategies of knowledge acquisition. *Monographs of the Society for Research in Child Development, 60*(4, Serial No. 245).

Kuhn, D., & Ho, V. (1980). Self-directed activity and cognitive development. *Journal of Applied Developmental Psychology, 1,* 119–133.

Kuhn, D., & Pearsall, S. (1998). Relations between metastrategic knowledge and strategic performance. *Cognitive Development, 13,* 227–247.

Kuhn, D., & Pearsall, S. (2000). Developmental origins of scientific thinking. *Journal of cognition and Development, 1,* 113–129.

Kuhn, D., & Phelps, E. (1982). The development of problem-solving strategies. In H. Reese (Ed.), *Advances in child development and behavior* (Vol. 17, pp. 1–44). New York: Academic Press.

Kuhn, D., Schauble, L., & Garcia-Mila, M. (1992). Cross-domain development of scientific reasoning. *Cognition and Instruction, 9,* 285–327.

Kwong, T. E., & Varnhagen, C. K. (2005). Strategy development and learning to spell new words: Generalization of a process. *Developmental Psychology, 41,* 148–159.

Lave, J. (1988). *Cognition in practice: Mind, mathematics, and culture in everyday life.* Cambridge, MA: Cambridge University Press.

Lavelli, M., & Fogel, A. (2002). Developmental changes in mother: Infant face-to-face communication: Birth to 3 months. *Developmental Psychology, 38,* 288–305.

Lawler, R. W. (1985). *Computer experience and cognitive development: A child's learning in a computer culture.* New York: Wiley.

Lee, K., & Karmiloff-Smith, A. (2002). Macro- and microdevelopmental research: Assumptions, research strategies, constraints, and utilities. In N. Granott & J. Parziale (Eds.), *Microdevelopment: Transition processes in development and learning* (pp. 243–265). Cambridge, England: Cambridge University Press.

Lemaire, P., & Siegler, R. S. (1995). Four aspects of strategic change: Contributions to children's learning of multiplication. *Journal of Experimental Psychology: General,* 83–97.

Levine, M. (1966). Hypothesis behavior by humans during discrimination learning. *Journal of Experimental Psychology, 71,* 331–336.

Lewis, M. D. (2002). Interacting time scales in personality (and cognitive) development: Intentions, emotions, and emergent forms. In N. Granott & J. Parziale (Eds.), *Microdevelopment: Transition processes in development and learning* (pp. 183–212). Cambridge, England: Cambridge University Press.

Maratsos, M. (1998). Some problems in grammatical acquisition. In W. Damon (Editor-in-Chief) & D. Kuhn & R. S. Siegler (Vol. Eds.), *Handbook of child psychology: Vol. 2. Cognition, perception and language* (5th ed., pp. 421–466). New York: Wiley.

McClelland, J. L. (1995). A connectionist perspective on knowledge and development. In T. J. Simon & G. S. Halford (Eds.), *Developing cognitive competence: New approaches to process modeling* (pp. 157–204). Hillsdale, NJ: Erlbaum.

McGilly, K., & Siegler, R. S. (1990). The influence of encoding and strategic knowledge on children's choices among serial recall strategies. *Developmental Psychology, 26,* 931–941.

McKeough, A., Davis, L., Forgeron, N., Marini, A., & Fung, T. (2005). Improving story complexity and cohesion: A developmental approach to teaching story composition. *Narrative Inquiry, 15,* 241–266.

McKeough, A., & Sanderson, A. (1996). Teaching storytelling: A microgenetic analysis of developing narrative competency. *Journal of Narrative and Life History, 6,* 157–192.

McNamara, J. P. H., Berg, W. K., Byrd, D. L., & McDonald, C. A. (2003, March). *Preschoolers' strategy use on the Tower of London task.* Poster presented at the biennial meeting for the Society for Research in Child Development, Tampa, FL.

Metz, K. E. (1998). Emergent understanding and attribution of randomness: Comparative analysis of the reasoning of primary grade children and undergraduates. *Cognition and Instruction, 16,* 285–365.

Miller, N. E., & Dollard, J. (1941). *Social learning and imitation.* New Haven, CT: Yale University Press.

Miller, P. H., & Aloise-Young, P. A. (1995). Preschoolers' strategic behavior and performance on a same-different task. *Journal of Experimental Child Psychology, 60,* 284–303.

Miller, P. H., & Coyle, T. R. (1999). Developmental change: Lessons from microgenesis. In E. K. Scholnick, K. Nelson, S. A. Gelman, & P. H. Miller (Eds.), *Conceptual development: Piaget's legacy* (pp. 209–239). Mahwah, NJ: Erlbaum.

Moskowitz, D. S., & Hershberger, S. L. (Eds.). (2002). *Modeling intraindividual variability with repeated measures data: Methods and application.* Mahwah, NJ: Erlbaum.

Munn, N. L. (1946). Learning in children. In L. Carmichael (Ed.), *Manual of child psychology.* New York: Wiley.

Nathan, M. J., Mertz, K., & Ryan, B. (1994, April). *Learning through self-explanation of mathematics examples: Effects of cognitive load.* Poster presented at the 1994 annual meeting of the American Educational Research Association, Chicago, IL.

Neches, R. (1987). Learning through incremental refinement procedures. In D. Klahr, P. Langley, & R. Neches (Eds.), *Production system models of learning and development.* Cambridge, MA: MIT Press.

Newell, A. (1990). *Unified theories of cognition.* Cambridge, MA: Harvard University Press.

Opfer, J. E., & Siegler, R. S. (2004). Revisiting preschoolers' living things concept: A microgenetic analysis of conceptual change in basic biology. *Cognitive Psychology, 49,* 301–332.

Ostad, S. A. (1997). Developmental differences in addition strategies: A comparison of mathematically disabled and mathematically normal children. *British Journal of Educational Psychology, 67,* 345–357.

Paris, S. G., Newman, R. S., & McVey, K. A. (1982). Learning the functional significance of mnemonic actions: A microgenetic study of strategy acquisition. *Journal of Experimental Child Psychology, 34,* 490–509.

Parziale, J. (2002). Observing the dynamics of construction: Children building bridges and new ideas. In N. Granott & J. Parziale (Eds.), *Microdevelopment: Transition processes in development and learning* (pp. 157–180). Cambridge, England: Cambridge University Press.

Perret-Clermont, A.-N., Perret, J.-F., & Bell, N. (1991). The social construction of meaning and cognitive activity in elementary school children. In L. B. Resnick, J. M. Levine, & S. D. Teasley (Eds.), *Perspectives on socially shared cognition* (pp. 41–62). Washington, DC: American Psychological Association.

Perry, M., Church, R. B., & Goldin-Meadow, S. (1988). Transitional knowledge in the acquisition of concepts. *Cognitive Development, 3,* 359–400.

Perry, M., & Elder, A. D. (1997). Knowledge in transition: Adults' developing understanding of a principle of physical causality. *Cognitive Development, 12,* 131–157.

Perry, M., & Lewis, J. L. (1999). Verbal imprecision as an index of knowledge in transition. *Developmental Psychology, 35,* 749–759.

Piaget, J. (1952). *The child's concept of number.* New York: Norton.

Piaget, J. (1964). Development and learning. In T. Ripple & V. Rockcastle (Eds.), *Piaget rediscovered* (pp. 7–20). Ithaca, NY: Cornell University Press.

Piaget, J. (1970). *Psychology and epistemology.* New York: Norton.

Piaget, J. (1975). Phenocopy in biology and the psychological development of knowledge. In H. E. Gruber & J. J. Voneche (Eds.), *The essential Piaget: An interpretive reference and guide* (pp. 803–813). New York: Basic Books.

Pine, K. J., & Messer, D. J. (2000). The effect of explaining another's actions on children's implicit theories of balance. *Cognition and Instruction, 18,* 35–51.

Pressley, M. (1992). How *not* to study strategy discovery. *American Psychologist, 47,* 1240–1241.

Renkl, A. (1997). Learning from worked-out examples: A study on individual differences. *Cognitive Science, 21,* 1–29.

Restle, R. (1962). The selection of strategies in cue learning. *Psychological Review, 69,* 329–343.

Rittle-Johnson, B., & Alibali, M. W. (1999). Conceptual and procedural knowledge of mathematics: Does one lead to the other? *Journal of Educational Psychology, 91,* 175–189.

Rittle-Johnson, B., Siegler, R. S., & Alibali, M. W. (2001). Developing conceptual understanding and procedural skill in mathematics: An iterative process. *Journal of Educational Psychology, 93,* 346–362.

Robinson, B. F., & Mervis, C. B. (1998). Disentangling early language development: Modeling lexical and grammatical acquisition using an extension of case-study methodology. *Developmental Psychology, 34,* 363–375.

Robinson, K. M. (2001). The validity of verbal reports in children's subtraction. *Journal of Educational Psychology, 93,* 211–222.

Robinson, S. R., Adolph, K. E., & Young, J. W. (2004, May). *Continuity versus discontinuity: How different time scales of behavioral measurement affect the pattern of developmental change.* Poster presented at the International Conference on Infancy Studies, Chicago, IL.

Rogoff, B. (1998). Cognition as a collaborative process. In W. Damon (Editor-in-Chief) & D. Kuhn & R. S. Siegler (Vol. Eds.), *Handbook of child psychology: Vol. 2. Cognition, perception and language* (5th ed., pp. 679–744). New York: Wiley.

Rosenblith, J. F. (1959). Learning by imitation in kindergarten children. *Child Development, 33,* 103–110.

Rozenblit, L., & Keil, F. (2002). The misunderstood limits of folk science: An illusion of explanatory depth. *Cognitive Science, 26,* 521–562.

Russo, J. E., Johnson, E. J., & Stephens, D. L. (1989). The validity of verbal protocols. *Memory and Cognition, 17,* 759–769.

Saada-Robert, M. (1992). Understanding the microgenesis of number: Sequence analyses. In J. Bideaud, C. Meljac, & J.-P. Fischer (Eds.), *Pathways to number: Children's developing numerical abilities* (pp. 265–282). Hillsdale, NJ: Erlbaum.

Saffran, J. R., Aslin, R. N., & Newport, E. L. (1996). Statistical learning by 8-month-old infants. *Science, 274,* 1926–1928.

Schauble, L. (1990). Belief revision in children: The role of prior knowledge and strategies for generating evidence. *Journal of Experimental Child Psychology, 49,* 31–57.

Schauble, L. (1996). The development of scientific reasoning in knowledge-rich contexts. *Developmental Psychology, 32,* 102–119.

Schlagmüller, M., & Schneider, W. (2002). The development of organizational strategies in children: Evidence from a microgenetic longitudinal study. *Journal of Experimental Child Psychology, 81,* 298–319.

Schneider, W., Kron, V., Hünnerkopf, M., & Krajewski, K. (2004). The development of young children's memory strategies: First findings from the Würzburg Longitudinal Memory Study. *Journal of Experimental Child Psychology, 88,* 193–209.

Schoenfeld, A. H., Smith, J. P., III, & Arcavi, A. (1993). Learning: The microgenetic analysis of one student's evolving understanding of a complex subject matter domain. In R. Glaser (Ed.), *Advances in instructional psychology* (Vol. 4, pp. 55–175). Hillsdale, NJ: Erlbaum.

Shimojo, S., Bauer, J., O'Connell, K. M., & Held, R. (1986). Pre-stereoptic binocular vision in infants. *Vision Research, 26,* 501–510.

Shrager, J., & Callanan, M. (1991, August). *Active language in the collaborative development of cooking skill.* Paper presented at the annual meeting of the Cognitive Science Society, Chicago, IL.

Shrager, J., & Siegler, R. S. (1998). SCADS: A model of children's strategy choices and strategy discoveries. *Psychological Science, 9,* 405–410.

Siegler, R. S. (1987). The perils of averaging data over strategies: An example from children's addition. *Journal of Experimental Psychology: General, 116,* 250–264.

Siegler, R. S. (1989). Hazards of mental chronometry: An example from children's subtraction. *Journal of Educational Psychology, 81,* 497–506.

Siegler, R. S. (1995). How does change occur: A microgenetic study of number conservation. *Cognitive Psychology, 25,* 225–273.

Siegler, R. S. (1996). *Emerging minds: The process of change in children's thinking.* New York: Oxford University Press.

Siegler, R. S. (2000). The rebirth of children's learning. *Child Development, 71,* 26–35.

Siegler, R. S. (2002). Microgenetic studies of self-explanation. In N. Granott & J. Parziale (Eds.), *Microdevelopment: Transition processes in development and learning* (pp. 31–58). Cambridge, England: Cambridge University Press.

Siegler, R. S., & Araya, R. (2005). A computational model of conscious and unconscious strategy discovery. In R. Kail (Ed.), *Advances in child development and behavior* (Vol. 33, pp. 1–42). Oxford, England: Elsevier.

Siegler, R. S., & Chen, Z. (1998). Developmental differences in rule learning: A microgenetic analysis. *Cognitive Psychology, 36,* 273–310.

Siegler, R. S., & Chen, Z. (2005). *Understanding water-displacement laws: A microgenetic study of children's learning.* Manuscript in preparation.

Siegler, R. S., & Crowley, K. (1991). The microgenetic method: A direct means for studying cognitive development. *American Psychologist, 46,* 606–620.

Siegler, R. S., & Crowley, K. (1994). Constraints on learning in nonprivileged domains. *Cognitive Psychology, 27,* 194–227.

Siegler, R. S., & Engle, R. A. (1994). Studying change in developmental and neuropsychological contexts. *Current Psychology of Cognition, 13,* 321–350.

Siegler, R. S., & Jenkins, E. A. (1989). *How children discover new strategies.* Hillsdale, NJ: Erlbaum.

Siegler, R. S., & McGilly, K. (1989). Strategy choices in children's time-telling. In I. Levin & D. Zakay (Eds.), *Time and human cognition: A life span perspective* (pp. 185–218). Amsterdam: Elsevier.

Siegler, R. S., & Shipley, C. (1995). Variation, selection, and cognitive change. In T. Simon & G. Halford (Eds.), *Developing cognitive competence: New approaches to process modeling* (pp. 31–76). Hillsdale, NJ: Erlbaum.

Siegler, R. S., & Shrager, J. (1984). Strategy choices in addition and subtraction: How do children know what to do. In C. Sophian (Ed.), *The origins of cognitive skills* (pp. 229–293), Hillsdale, NJ: Erlbaum.

Siegler, R. S., & Stern, E. (1998). A microgenetic analysis of conscious and unconscious strategy discoveries. *Journal of Experimental Psychology: General, 127,* 377–397.

Siegler, R. S., & Svetina, M. (2002). A microgenetic/cross-sectional study of matrix completion: Comparing short-term and long-term change. *Child Development, 73,* 793–809.

Siegler, R. S., & Taraban, R. (1986). Conditions of applicability of a strategy choice model. *Cognitive Development, 1,* 31–51.

Simon, H. A. (1962). An information processing theory of intellectual development. *Monographs of the Society for Research in Child Development, 27*(2, Serial No. 82).

Singer, J. D., & Willett, J. B. (2003). *Applied longitudinal data analysis.* New York: Oxford University Press.

Siqueland, E. R., & Lipsitt, L. P. (1966). Conditioned head turning in human newborns. *Journal of Experimental Child Psychology, 3,* 356–376.

Skinner, B. F. (1938). *The behavior of organisms: An experimental analysis.* New York: Appleton-Century.

Smith, L. B., Thelen, E., Titzer, R., & McLin, D. (1999). Knowing in the context of acting: The task dynamics of the A-not-B error. *Psychological Review, 106,* 235–260.

Spelke, E. S., & Newport, E. L. (1998). Nativism, empiricism, and the development of knowledge. In W. Damon (Editor-in-Chief) & R. M. Lerner (Vol. Ed.), *Handbook of child psychology: Vol. 1. Theoretical models of human development* (5th ed., pp. 275–340). New York: Wiley.

Spence, K. W. (1952). The nature of the response in discrimination learning. *Psychological Review, 59,* 89–93.

Spencer, J. P., & Schutte, A. R. (2004). Unifying representations and responses: Perseverative biases arise from a single behavioral system. *Psychological Science, 15,* 187–193.

Spencer, J. P., Vereijken, B., Diedrich, F. J., & Thelen, E. (2000). Posture and the emergence of manual skills. *Developmental Science, 3,* 216–233.

Staszewski, J. J. (1988). Skilled memory and expert mental calculation. In M. T. H. Chi, R. Glaser, & M. J. Farr (Eds.), *The nature of expertise* (pp. 71–128). Hillsdale, NJ: Erlbaum.

Stevenson, H. W. (1970). Learning in children. In P. H. Mussen (Ed.), *Carmichael's manual of child psychology* (Vol. 1, 3rd ed., pp. 849–938). New York: Wiley.

Stevenson, H. W. (1983). How children learn: The quest for a theory. In P. H. Mussen (Series Ed.) & W. Kessen (Vol. Ed.), *Handbook of child psychology: Vol. 1. History, theory, and methods* (4th ed., pp. 213–236). New York: Wiley.

Stokes, P. D. (1995). Learned variability. *Animal Learning and Behavior, 23,* 164–176.

Stokes, P. D. (2001). Variability, constraints, and creativity: Shedding light on Claude Monet. *American Psychologist, 36,* 355–359.

Stokes, P. D., & Harrison, H. M. (2002). Constraints have different concurrent effects and aftereffects on variability. *Journal of Experimental Psychology: General, 131,* 553–566.

Taylor, J., & Cox, B. D. (1997). Microgenetic analysis of group-based solution of complex two-step mathematical word problems by fourth graders. *Journal of the Learning Sciences, 6,* 183–226.

Thelen, E. (1994). Three-month-old infants can learn task-specific patterns of interlimb coordination. *Psychological Science, 5,* 280–285.

Thelen, E., & Corbetta, D. (2002). Microdevelopment and dynamic systems: Applications to infant motor development. In N. Granott & J. Parziale (Eds.), *Microdevelopment: Transition processes in development and learning* (pp. 59–79). Cambridge, England: Cambridge University Press.

Thelen, E., & Ulrich, B. D. (1991). Hidden skills. *Monographs of the Society for Research in Child Development, 56*(1, Serial No. 223).

Thornton, S. (1999). Creating the conditions for cognitive change: The interaction between task structures and specific strategies. *Child Development, 70,* 588–603.

Triano, L. (2004). *Putting pencil to paper: Learning what and how to include information in inscriptions.* Unpublished doctoral dissertation, Carnegie Mellon University, Pittsburgh, PA.

Tudge, J. (1992). Processes and consequences of peer collaboration: A Vygotskian analysis. *Child Development, 63,* 1364–1379.

Tudge, J. R. H., Winterhoff, P. A., & Hogan, D. M. (1996). The cognitive consequences of collaborative problem solving with and without feedback. *Child Development, 67,* 2892–2909.

Tunteler, E., & Resing, W. C. M. (2002). Spontaneous analogical transfer in 4-year-olds: A microgenetic study. *Journal of Experimental Child Psychology, 83,* 149–166.

van der Maas, H. L. J., & Molenaar, P. C. M. (1996). Catastrophe analysis of discontinuous development. In A. A. van Eye & C. C. Clogg (Eds.), *Categorical variables in developmental research: Methods of analysis* (pp. 77–105). San Diego, CA: Academic Press.

van Geert, P. (1991). A dynamic systems model of cognitive and language growth. *Psychological Review, 98,* 3–53.

van Geert, P. (1997). Variability and fluctuations: A dynamic view. In E. Amsel & K. A. Renninger (Eds.), *Change and development: Issues of theory, method, and application* (pp. 193–212). Mahwah, NJ: Erlbaum.

van Geert, P. (1998). A dynamic systems model of basic developmental mechanisms: Piaget, Vygotsky, and beyond. *Psychological Review, 105,* 634–677.

van Geert, P. (2002). Developmental dynamics, intentional action, and fuzzy sets. In N. Granott & J. Parziale (Eds.), *Microdevelopment: Transition processes in development and learning* (pp. 319–343). Cambridge, England: Cambridge University Press.

Vereijken, B., & Thelen, E. (1997). Training infant treadmill stepping: The role of individual pattern stability. *Developmental Psychology, 30,* 89–102.

Vygotsky, L. S. (1962). *Thought and language.* New York: Wiley. (Original work published 1934)

Vygotsky, L. S. (1978). *Mind in society: The development of higher mental processes.* Cambridge, MA: Harvard University Press. (Original work published 1930)

Wechsler, M. A., & Adolph, K. E. (1995, April). *Learning new ways of moving: Variability in infants' discovery and selection of motor strategies.* Poster presented at the meeting of the Society for Research in Child Development, Indianapolis, IN.

Wegener, A. (1966). *The origin of continents and oceans* (J. Biram, Trans.). New York: Dover. (Original work published 1915)

Wellman, H. M., & Gelman, S. A. (1998). Knowledge acquisition in foundational domains. In W. Damon (Editor-in-Chief) & D. Kuhn & R. S. Siegler (Vol. Eds.), *Handbook of child psychology: Vol. 2. Cognition, perception and language* (5th ed., pp. 523–574). New York: Wiley.

Werner, H. (1940). Musical microscales and micromelodies. *Journal of Psychology, 10,* 149–156.

Werner, H. (1948). *Comparative psychology of mental development.* New York: International Universities Press.

Werner, H. (1957). The concept of development from a comparative and organismic point of view. In D. B. Harris (Ed.), *The concept of development: An issue in the study of human behavior* (pp. 125–148). Minneapolis: University of Minnesota Press.

Wertsch, J. V., & Hickmann, M. (1987). Problem solving in social interaction: A microgenetic analysis. In M. Hickmann (Ed.), *Social and functional approaches to language and thought* (pp. 251–266). San Diego, CA: Academic Press.

White, S. (1970). The learning theory approach. In P. Mussen (Ed.), *Carmichael's manual of child psychology* (Vol. 1, pp. 657–702). New York: Wiley.

Willett, J. B. (1997). Measuring change: What individual growth modeling buys you. In E. Amsel & K. A. Renninger (Eds.), *Change and development: Issues of theory, method, and application.* Mahwah, NJ: Erlbaum.

Winsler, A., Diaz, R. M., & Montero, I. (1997). The role of private speech in the transition from collaborative to independent task performance in young children. *Early Childhood Research Quarterly, 12,* 59–79.

Zeaman, D., & House, B. J. (1967). The relation of IQ and learning. In R. M. Gagne (Ed.), *Learning and individual differences* (pp. 192–212). Columbus, OH: Merrill.

CHAPTER 12

# Cognitive Strategies

MICHAEL PRESSLEY and KATHERINE HILDEN

**DEFINITION OF STRATEGY**  512
**CLASSICAL RESEARCH ON DEVELOPMENT OF MEMORY STRATEGIES**  513
**INFORMATION-PROCESSING THEORY IN THE 1960S AND STUDIES OF THE DEVELOPMENT OF CHILDREN'S VERBAL LIST LEARNING STRATEGIES**  515
**Rehearsal Strategies**  515
**Organizational Strategies**  516
**Elaboration**  517
**Conclusions**  517
**THE STRATEGIES PRODUCTIVE PRESCHOOLER (AT LEAST SOME OF THE TIME)**  518
**Retrieving Hidden Objects**  518
**Remembering Instructions**  519
**Summary**  519
**AN INFORMATION-PROCESSING MODEL OF INTENTIONAL, STRATEGIC MEMORY: ESSENTIAL COMPONENTS TO UNDERSTAND STRATEGY USE AND STRATEGY INSTRUCTION**  519
**Working/Short-Term Memory**  519
**Strategy Knowledge as Procedural Knowledge**  521
**Metacognition**  521
**World Knowledge**  523
**Conclusions**  525
**STRATEGY USE AS THE COORDINATION OF INFORMATION-PROCESSING COMPONENTS**  526

**BASIC RESEARCH ANALYSES OF EXCEPTIONAL CHILDREN WHO BENEFIT FROM STRATEGIES INSTRUCTION**  527
**Meichenbaum's Analyses of Attention Deficit Hyperactivity**  528
**Strategy Instruction with Students with Mental Retardation**  528
**Strategy Instruction with Students with Learning Disabilities**  529
**Strategies Use by Gifted Students**  530
**Conclusions**  530
**APPLIED STRATEGIES INSTRUCTIONAL RESEARCH**  531
**Word Recognition**  531
**Comprehension Strategies Instruction**  532
**Writing Strategies Instruction**  537
**Mathematical Problem Solving**  538
**Scientific Reasoning, Argument Skills, and Strategies**  540
**Conclusions**  542
**CONCLUDING REFLECTIONS ON STRATEGIES DEVELOPMENT**  543
**What Is Known about the Development of Strategic Competence**  543
**Much Remains to Be Learned about Strategies Instruction**  545
**REFERENCES**  547

This chapter is about intentional and strategic processes that children can use to perform cognitive tasks. Five overarching conclusions follow from this wide-ranging review:

1. Often children do not use strategies to perform cognitive tasks, ones they are capable of using, with such nonuse traditionally labeled a production deficiency (Flavell, 1970; Waters, 2000). Production deficiency can be due to a number of causes: (a) not knowing a strategy that could be used in the present situation, (b) not knowing that it is appropriate to use a known strategy or strategies in this situation, (c) not understanding how to adapt known strategies to the present situation, (d) using an approach that is not overtly strategic (e.g., relying on the first idea that comes to mind to solve a problem presented rather than carefully reflecting and trying alternatives), or (e) simply

not being motivated to exert the effort to carry out known strategies (e.g., Pressley, Borkowski, & Schneider, 1987, 1989). Production deficiencies are common in children, with many situations where adults also are production deficient.

2. Sometimes even very young children are strategic, most prominently, when asked to carry out familiar tasks in familiar situations.

3. Children sometimes use strategies that are less efficient and/or effective than ones they could use (Kuhn, 2002a, 2002b; Siegler, 1996).

4. Children who do not use strategies (or the most effective strategies) on their own often can be taught to use effective strategies with clear benefits in performance that can motivate future use of the strategies (Borkowski, Carr, Rellinger, & Pressley, 1990). This conclusion has been substantiated in many investigations.

5. In the absence of strategies instruction, children often discover strategies just from performing a task repeatedly, although leaving strategic competence to discovery does not always result in children acquiring strategies quickly or acquiring the most effective strategies.

## DEFINITION OF STRATEGY

What is a strategy as research psychologists understand it? On the positive side, strategy means about the same to psychologists as it does to laymen. Thus, one definition of strategy is: "A *strategy* is a general plan or set of plans intended to achieve something" (Sinclair, 2001, p. 1540). All of the elements of strategy considered important by psychologists are in that simple definition. A strategic learner plans in advance, with the plan motivated by some goal, a desire to achieve some end. So, a savvy adult confronting the task of memorizing the driver's license test book has a goal—passing the written driving exam. To do so requires some preparation, which can be tedious, for example, if the reader decides simply to read the booklet over and over until it is memorized. Alternatively, the strategic reader will identify the sections she or he does not know and focus on those. Perhaps for especially detailed points that might be on the written driving test, the reader will use a classic mnemonic (e.g., remembering to park at least 10 feet from a fire plug by forming an image of a basketball player shooting a basketball at the fire plug as if it were the basket, recognizing that the basketball rim is 10 feet high).

There is one tricky aspect to the notion of strategy, however (see Schneider & Pressley, 1997, chap. 5 for a review of this issue). When people are first learning to use strategies, their employment of them seems more deliberate, conscious, and intentional than is the case when they have had experience with the task and used the strategy many times. That is, with increasing experience, strategy use becomes more automated and effortless. To be considered a strategy, however, the process has to be controllable. That is, the user can interrupt the automatic cognition and take charge of the cognitive processes, performing them consciously and intentionally. Thus, Pressley, Forrest-Pressley, Elliot-Faust, and Miller (1985) offered the following definition of strategy, "A strategy is composed of cognitive operations over and above the processes that are natural consequences of carrying out the task, ranging from one such operation to a sequence of interdependent operations. Strategies achieve cognitive purposes (e.g., comprehending, memorizing) and are potentially conscious and controllable activities" (p. 4). In this definition they captured that the strategy user does not always have to be conscious of and in control of strategic processes, but there must be potential for this to occur in order to be considered strategic.

Some of the most historically prominent research on strategies was carried out with respect to children's memory and memorizing, and, thus, there will be substantial attention in this chapter to memory strategy development. Strategies can be classified as either memory encoding or memory retrieval strategies. For example, a task may require a learner to remember pairs of words or pictures presented to them. An encoding strategy is to construct a mental image that includes the paired items when the pairs are presented (e.g., if given the pair, *cow* and *rock,* perhaps imagining a *cow* eating the grass around a *rock* that is in the pasture). The ability to use such imagery encoding strategies increases with age between 5 and 11 years of age (see Pressley, 1977). Later, on the test, when the item *cow* is presented, if the learner thinks back to the image of the *cow* nibbling grass around a *rock,* that would be using a retrieval strategy (i.e., remembering the interactive image to remember the pair-mate). The use of such a retrieval strategy develops during the early elementary years (Pressley & MacFadyen, 1983). Because there has been much more research on encoding than retrieval strategies, most of the memory strategic work considered in this chapter focuses on encoding strategies.

Because consciousness is at least always possible when strategies are functioning, researchers in memory strategy development have typically studied explicit memory. Explicit memory contrasts with implicit memory, in that the latter does not depend on conscious mediation (Graf & Schacter, 1985; Jacoby, 1991). In general, explicit memory improves with development, largely because of strategy use and the development of metacognitive understandings (i.e., cognitive regulative understandings, such as knowing when, where, and how to apply particular strategies), which also will be considered in this chapter. Increasing such metacognitive understandings increases the likelihood that children will use the strategies they know appropriately (Murphy, McKone, & Slee, 2003).

One advantage of the definition offered by Pressley and colleagues (Pressley, Forest-Pressley, et al., 1985) is that it includes potential consciousness rather than fully conscious use as necessary for cognitive processes to be considered strategic. Alternative definitions that require the thinker being in conscious control would not be consistent with some of the strategies reviewed in this chapter. When a reader automatically relates what is being read to prior knowledge, that strategy is covered by the Pressley, Forest-Pressley, et al. (1985) definition, but would not be included if conscious planfulness was part of the definition.

## CLASSICAL RESEARCH ON DEVELOPMENT OF MEMORY STRATEGIES

Much of the early work on strategic processes in children was conducted with reference to children's memory and memory development. Thus, both the fourth and fifth editions of the *Handbook of Child Psychology* included long chapters devoted to the topic of memory development (Brown, Bransford, Ferrara, & Campione, 1983; Schneider & Bjorkland, 1998), with both of these chapters including substantial information about children's memory strategies and active attempts to remember. This reflected substantial research activity during the concluding third of the twentieth century to determine what strategies children use to remember and how their memory strategies develop.

Since the last edition of the *Handbook of Child Development,* however, the cognitive developmental literature has included very little work on the development of memory strategies in children. The last major wave of memory strategies work was with preschoolers. A cadre of researchers, in fact, succeeded in identifying situations where even 2- and 3-year-old children are strate-

gic, quite intentionally engaging in cognitive acts intended to improve memory and other performances. Such work, which was conducted in the late 1970s and 1980s, will be covered in this chapter as well.

Due to a lack of recent research on memory strategies, at least one observer asked in print whether memory development belongs on the endangered topic list in developmental psychology (Kuhn, 2000a). This question makes a lot of sense with respect to study of memory strategies, but probably not children's memory more generally, for at least some of the memory developmentalists have turned their attention in recent years to other problems of memory development. Eyewitness memory is one such area that has received much recent attention (for a review, see Gordon, Baker-Ward, & Ornstein, 2001). For the most part, researchers interested in children's eyewitness memory have focused on situations where children were not trying to memorize (i.e., people rarely were trying to memorize when they see an activity that is the focus of court testimony). Thus, more attention has been paid to studying how factors out of children's control that can distort their memories rather than studying what children might do intentionally to remember events (Ceci, Fitneva, & Gilstrap, 2003). This movement toward understanding children's eyewitness memory was fueled, in part, by many important findings in the 1970s and 1980s about adult eyewitness memory (see Thompson et al., 1998).

Basic theory and research on strategies development and instruction, especially in the area of memory, proceeded in an orderly way for several decades, however, the history of strategies development has been a history of attempting to explain individual differences in development that went beyond mere developmental differences indexed by age. Thus, the early memory development researchers became aware that there were large differences in memory within developmental levels, differences that often could be explained by the strategies used by children as they tackled memory tasks. The insights from this work now inspire researchers who are trying to close the gap between normally achieving students and those who fail to learn to read, write, and problem solve in school. Although there has rarely been a complete closing of such gaps, there has often been vast improvement in the functioning of struggling learners who have been taught strategies. That there has been a progression from basic to applied work over the years requires that this chapter be organized both historically, beginning with the work of the 1960s and 1970s, with simultaneous movement toward contemporary work and more applied research.

One researcher did more than anyone else to inspire the body of research on strategies. Work on cognitive strategies was launched when Flavell and his colleagues (Flavell, Beach, & Chinsky, 1966) asked children to remember a list of pictures so that they could recall them after they were removed from sight. The researchers especially watched the lips of the children after the items had been presented but before recall occurred. Among 5-year-olds, only 2 of 20 children rehearsed the labels for the pictures that were to be remembered. In contrast, 17 of the 20 10-year-olds in the study did so. In addition, they found a strong relationship between whether a child verbally rehearsed and performance on the memory recall test. Children who rehearsed more recalled more. This was the beginning of a program of research and writing for Flavell on children's use of rehearsal strategies. Many followed Flavell's lead to memory strategy development as a topic deserving of scientific study.

Many also followed his lead when he and another group of student colleagues (Kreutzer, Leonard, & Flavell, 1975) began to study children's metamemory, or what they knew about their memories. This first investigation was an interview study in which children were asked questions to determine if they understood factors effecting memory, including strategic factors. Thus, one question asked children to think of ways that they could remember to take a pair of ice skates to a party they would be attending. Six- and 7-year-olds did not think of as many ways to remember the skates, as did the 9- and 11-year-old children. Flavell and his colleagues hypothesized that before children would use a strategy, they needed to know about it, that such metamemory was critical for strategies to be used. This first study of metamemory would become one of the most cited studies in the cognitive development literature. The field of metacognition, which includes metamemory and many other metas (e.g., meta-attention, meta-communication, meta-perception), requires volumes to summarize (e.g., Metcalfe & Shimamura, 1996).

For almost 30 years, studies about the development of memory strategies were prominent in the field. Then, suddenly in the early to middle 1990s, the work on memory strategy development stopped. In fact, Pressley recalls vividly a Society for the Research of Child Development meeting in the mid-1990s where some of those who had been players in the work on memory strategies assembled for dinner. The topic of conversation was, "What happened?"

We think that what happened was the following: Much had been discovered by those studying intentional memory and memory strategies, so much that the subfield had entered a period of incrementalism, where new studies did not add much. The very visible scientists who had carried out most of the work on memory strategy development followed Flavell's lead in another way. He liked to do work that defined new fields. He moved on to other work once the research on memory strategies and metacognition was launched. Most of those sitting at that dinner, and others who would have been like-minded company, were now off studying other problems, defining new areas, doing what Flavell had done. Many went on to study use of strategies in other task situations, including reading and writing (e.g., the present authors are immersed in the study of children's use of comprehension strategies during reading; see Pressley, 2000). In particular, there has been considerable interest in studying meaningful strategies instruction in content areas such as reading and writing directed at children with learning difficulties, who often benefit substantially from such instruction (Swanson, 1999, 2000). Such studies lead us to believe that research on strategies instruction has great relevance to education (Pressley, 1995).

Even so, it is simply undeniable that the work on intentional memory strategies development that was conducted in the 1960s, 1970s, 1980s, and 1990s was a monumental contribution to cognitive development and developmental psychology more generally. Much of what is known about how mind functions and how mental functioning shifts with development is known because of this body of research. Thus, this chapter is a summary of what was found by those studying intentional, strategic memory, about the model of cognitive development that resulted from their efforts.

The early work in basic cognitive development that advanced the idea that strategy production deficiencies can be overcome through instruction has inspired contemporary applied developmental psychologists. Such researchers have shown that strategies matter in academic cognition and children can be taught strategies that improve their academic cognition. Before discussing those contributions, however, we open the chapter with a summary of the general information-processing perspective on memory, and begin with the basics that framed many of the questions posed by memory development researchers in the 1960s and 1970s. We conclude this discussion with a much more complete model of information processing that includes constructivist, sociocognitive, and motivational perspectives. We emphasize elaborations and shifts from the original model. Then, we turn our attention to how the information-processing model has informed understanding of individual differences in children's cognitive competencies, including gifted children, children with mental retardation, and children with learning disabilities. We stress the point that some of the researchers who were interested in memory development simultaneously contributed to understanding cognition in special populations. Then we turn the discussion to how scientists interested in improving children's reading, writing, and mathematical problem solving are teaching strategies in ways that are very well informed by the basic research and theory of the 1960s through 1990s. By the conclusion of the chapter, we hope that readers will come away with the understanding that while memory development is not as active an area of research as it was in the last portion of the twentieth century, the understandings of children's information processing produced by memory developmental researchers remain exceptionally important in the new century, and, if anything, their impact is expanding.

## INFORMATION-PROCESSING THEORY IN THE 1960S AND STUDIES OF THE DEVELOPMENT OF CHILDREN'S VERBAL LIST LEARNING STRATEGIES

At the time Flavell and associates (1966) conducted their study, there was much discussion in the emerging cognitive psychology literature about two-store models of memory (Atkinson & Shiffrin, 1968; Broadbent, 1958; Waugh & Norman, 1965). A small amount of information (i.e., seven or so items) could be held in short-term memory for a short period of time, remaining there only so long as it was actively processed (e.g., rehearsed if it was a list of picture labels; Miller, 1956). If the participant rehearsed the labels sufficiently, the labels would transfer into long-term memory and could be recalled later. Thus, someone going to the store to buy "eggs, milk, butter, and mayonnaise" can remember the list by repeating the list over and over, but after awhile can stop, for the list will have been stored in long-term memory.

The new two-store models were replacing associative learning models, which had predominated in memory research in the 1950s. Even so, the associationists still influenced Flavell's thinking about memory as he began his work. W. A. Bousfield (1953) observed that when adults studied lists with words that belonged to several mutually exclusive categories, they tended to cluster categorically related items together in their recall, even if the items had been presented randomly during study. This finding prompted much work on how learners organize and reorganize material to be learned based on their associative knowledge base.

The framework of the 1960s on memory inspired developmentalists to conduct studies on memory similar in style to those conducted by researchers studying adults, only with children as the participants. Thus, many studies were carried out in which children were asked to learn verbal materials in classic or close to classic verbal learning paradigms (i.e., the classic approaches used to study the memories of students enrolled in introductory psychology courses in the 1950s and 1960s), which involved learning lists of various sorts. These studies proved to be very informative about children's rehearsal, organizational, and elaborative strategies. The work of William Rohwer (1973), serves as one such example. He studied paired-associate learning in children and adolescents. Rohwer demonstrated that when children embedded to-be-learned paired-associates into meaningful sentences (e.g., when asked to learn the pair *bear-blanket,* constructing a phrase such as, "The *bear* grabbed the *blanket* with its paw"), recall of the pairings increased dramatically (e.g., when given *bear* on a text, recall that *blanket* went with it). Rohwer also established that adolescents were more likely to use this strategy on their own than were children, although children could construct such sentences with great benefits for memory when they were instructed to do so.

### Rehearsal Strategies

Given this intellectual backdrop, the time seemed right for studies of children's rehearsal strategies during list learning. What was established over a number of studies was that children did rehearse. If an item was presented early in a list, it was especially likely to be remembered because there were more opportunities to rehearse it (i.e., the strategic child would say the word when presented, then say it again along with the second word presented, and then with the second and third word). The finding that items presented first were recalled better later became known as the primacy effect, with the primacy effect increasing during childhood. Although 5- to 6-year-olds did not evidence much primacy, older children did, reflecting that the younger children did not rehearse as actively or completely as the older children (e.g., the younger children would say the names of the items one time, when they were presented, with the older children continuing to say the name as long as they could and then cumulatively rehearsing all of the items previously presented as each new item was presented). There were consistent and strong correlations between observations of cumulative rehearsal in children and memory of the early items in a list (e.g., Belmont & Butterfield, 1977; Cuvo, 1975; Hagen & Stanovich, 1977; Kellas, Ashcraft, & Johnson, 1973; Naus, Ornstein, & Aivano, 1977; Ornstein, Naus, & Liberty, 1975). Additional support for the conclusion that use of the cumulative rehearsal produced primacy effects was produced in experiments in which primacy varied depending on whether the operations in the experiment encouraged rehearsal (i.e., participants were instructed to rehearse; for example, Gruenenfelder & Borkowski, 1975; Hagen, Hargrave, & Ross, 1973; Hagen & Kingsley, 1968; Keeney, Cannizzo, & Flavell, 1967; Kingsley & Hagen, 1969) or prevented it (e.g., did not permit enough time for rehearsal to occur; Allik & Siegel, 1976; Hagen & Kail, 1973).

The finding that instruction positively affected young children's abilities to rehearse, and thereby remember more, was especially influential. The researchers who conducted these studies established that the children's memory problem was that they were not using the rehearsal strategy. If the children used the rehearsal strategy, their memory improved. All that was required for them to use the strategy was for someone to instruct them to do so. Flavell (1970) referred to the young children's problem as a production deficiency; they failed to produce a strategy that permitted them to accomplish the intellectual task they were to accomplish. That children could benefit from instruction in strategy use was a hugely important finding that resulted in the flood of research on strategies instruction. This is an area of basic research that would link directly to real world instructional applications, some of which is discussed later in this chapter.

Those studying rehearsal also established that use of less than maximally efficient strategies was not just a childhood phenomenon. The best way to learn a list of

items is to rehearse the items cumulatively as they are presented up to the presentation of the last few items. As those are presented, speed up the cumulative rehearsal and finish the list quickly. Then, on the recall test, recall the last few items first. This improves recall because the last few items on the list will still be in short-term memory at the time of the test. Once those are recalled, the person can then retrieve from long-term memory the items from the beginning of the list that received so many cumulative rehearsals (Barclay, 1979). This cumulative rehearsal, fast finish strategy is used by college students, but not by children. The development of efficient list-learning strategies extends into early adulthood.

## Organizational Strategies

Memory development researchers also asked children to study and remember lists consisting of items that can be semantically related to one another (e.g., a list containing some fruit items, names of several pieces of furniture, and various types of vehicles). In general, when children in the primary grades recall such lists, the order of recall is fairly random. By 10 to 11 years of age, children tend to recall the related items together, with the interpretation of this recall pattern being that the students made use of the categorical relationships in the list to study and learn items (e.g., Cole, Frankel, & Sharp, 1971; Moely, Olson, Halwes, & Flavell, 1969; Neimark, Slotnick, & Ulrich, 1971). Even so, if the lists are composed of saliently associated items, even preschool children produce recall organized around the categories in the to-be-learned list (e.g., Myers & Perlmutter, 1978; Rossi & Wittrock, 1971; Sodian, Schneider, & Perlmutter, 1986). It also helps if participants are instructed to notice the inter-relationships within to-be-learned lists, for example, by being asked to place like-category items in piles during study. Such strategy instruction can increase recall, even in young elementary grade children (Black & Rollins, 1982; Kee & Bell, 1981; Lange & Griffith, 1977; Moely et al., 1969; Schneider, Borkowski, Kurtz, & Kerwin, 1986).

In general, with increasing age during the elementary school years, children's recall of categorizable lists increases, with increased organization of the output (i.e., items from the same category are more likely to be recalled together by older than younger children). A variety of analyses were carried out to determine whether this increased organization at recall reflected increasing deliberate and strategic use of the categorical information in the lists. In other words, the learner mindfully noted that the items were categorizable and he or she deliberately thought about the list items in categories. The alternative was that, because the learner's knowledge of categories was expanding with development, the categorical nature of the list was noticed and used automatically as the learner read the list (i.e., with advancing age, the learner automatically notices there are animals on the list and associates the animals without thinking about it, with the same happening for pieces of furniture or types of vehicles). Because the learner does not exert intentional effort to use the categories, this is considered a knowledge base effect (i.e., the learner's prior knowledge enables automatic recognition and use of the categorical structure of the list, resulting in improved memory and organization at recall). In fact, both strategic and knowledge base effects probably mediate the increasing recall (e.g., Bjorklund, Muir-Broaddus, & Schneider, 1990; Ornstein, Baker-Ward, & Naus, 1988; Ornstein & Naus, 1985; Rabinowitz & Chi, 1987; Schneider, 1993), with the particular mix of conscious strategy use of automatic knowledge-base mediation depending somewhat on the child (e.g., a child with a great deal of knowledge of a category is more likely to use categorical information automatically, without thinking; Gaultney, Bjorklund, & Schneider, 1992; Schneider & Bjorklund, 1992; Schneider, Bjorklund, & Maier-Brückner, 1996).

## Elaboration

For the most part, researchers studied elaboration strategies with paired-associate learning. Typically, investigators presented participants with pairs of items (e.g., shoe and balloon, car and candy, dog and sandwich), with the task of remembering the pairs. At testing, the participant was presented one of the paired items and had to recall the pair mate. This is a very challenging task, unless participants use an elaboration strategy. Verbal elaboration involves creating a meaningful verbal context that includes the paired items. "The *balloon* popped when the *shoe* stepped on it," "The *candy* melted in the hot *car*," and "The *dog* ate the *sandwich*" would be verbal elaborations that could mediate (improve) recall of the sample pairs. Alternatively, participants could be asked to construct mental images embedding the items (e.g., the participant sees a shoe kicking a balloon in his or her mind). Rohwer, Levin,

Kee, and Pressley, in particular, did much work on the development of elaboration strategies abilities in children. Basically, children rarely used such strategies on their own. However, even preschool children benefit from instructions to use verbal elaborations, instructions to use imagery strategies proved increasingly helpful as children advanced through the elementary school years (see Pressley, 1982, for a review).

## Conclusions

The verbal learning and information-processing traditions of the 1950s and 1960s set the stage for the field of memory development, which emerged in the 1960s. A great deal was discovered by conducting studies with children, using traditional paradigms used with adults such as free recall of lists of items, serial recall of lists of items (i.e., recall of the items in order), and associative recall of lists of items. As a general rule, there were many production deficiencies discovered. Often children did not use strategies on their own.

Even so, children often proved to be able to carry out strategies if instructed in their operations. This was observed with respect to rehearsal, organizational, and verbal elaborative strategies. This work was foundational with respect to what would become the field of cognitive strategies instruction, providing demonstration that often children could be taught to do what they would not do on their own. That said, once taught, children did not always continue to use the instructed strategies. They did not maintain use of strategies learned or transfer them to other situations where they could be useful. (This is a topic that we discuss in more detail as the chapter unfolds.)

We close this section noting that other deficiencies besides production deficiencies were proposed over the decades of study of basic memory development. For example, Reese (1970) coined the term "mediational deficiency." Mediational deficiencies occur when a child produces a strategy but the strategy fails to improve memory. There has been little evidence of such deficiency in the memory development literature, however (Waters, 2000). A slight variant of this is a *utilization deficiency,* when a younger child would carry out a strategic procedure as completely as an older child but not receive the same amount of benefit from use of the strategy (Bjorklund, Miller, Coyle, & Slawinski, 1997; Miller & Seier, 1994), or a learning disabled student would carry out a strategic procedures as completely as a normally achieving student and fail to obtain as much benefit (Gaultney, 1998). Again, there is little evidence of such a deficiency (Waters, 2000), with evidence for utilization deficiency even less compelling when longitudinal analyses are employed rather than cross-sectional analyses (Schneider & Sodian, 1997). That said, there will be enough mentions of utilization deficiency in what follows to conclude that there are situations where children seem to carry out strategies but do not benefit from them. However, why this is the case is not understood at present. The possibility that a child might construct a cognitive mediator during study by using a strategy and fail to use the strategy when testing also has received support (i.e., there is support for the construct of retrieval deficiency; Kobasigawa, 1977; Pressley & Levin, 1980; Pressley & MacFadyen, 1983). Despite some attention to mediation, utilization, and retrieval deficiencies, work on these problems is not nearly as extensive as on production deficiencies. Throughout this chapter, we will provide massive evidence that children often do not produce strategies that they could execute profitably.

What may be surprising to many readers is that so little mention of preschoolers has been made until this point. One reason is that preschool was definitely not a focus of research on strategies for a very long time. The conclusion that was implicit in the early studies was that children were strategies production deficient until elementary school, with little strategic behavior inferred from the performances of kindergarten or first-grade students in the early studies of rehearsal, organization, and elaboration. Brown and her colleagues (Brown & DeLoache, 1978; DeLoache, 1980), however, alerted us to one reason that 5- and 6-year-olds might have seemed so nonstrategic in memory studies. Verbal recall and associative memory tasks probably seemed pretty strange and unfamiliar to them. While these activities bear some resemblance to school tasks encountered during the primary years, they do not resemble demands put on kindergarten children before they enter school. In fact, when preschoolers were studied in familiar situations, they often proved to be quite strategic.

## THE STRATEGIES PRODUCTIVE PRESCHOOLER (AT LEAST SOME OF THE TIME)

Because early childhood does include memory demands, conceptually it made sense to study memory from ages 0 to 5 as a complement to the work conducted with older children and reviewed thus far in the chapter. A great deal of memory research was conducted with infants in the 1970s and 1980s (e.g., Rovee-Collier & Gerhardstein, 1997). As a result, researchers interested in the development of strategic memory in the preschool years (i.e., ages 2 to 5) began to modify tasks that had been used in infancy studies (Daehler & Greco, 1985). In fact, preschoolers proved to be strategic when given memory tasks that were similar to ones encountered in the real world of early childhood.

### Retrieving Hidden Objects

Studying how preschoolers respond to hiding and finding games proved to be a good way to learn about strategic behaviors in preschoolers, revealing that, at least some of the time, preschoolers can be strategic (although strategic retrieval is anything but certain in other situations). Ritter (1978) carried out the first study to assess whether preschoolers would use a retrieval cue strategy when they were in a situation where using retrieval cues was essential for adequate performance. Participants were placed in front of a turntable with six covered cups. Their task was to find a piece of candy that would be hidden in one of the cups, with the turntable then spun quickly enough that it would not be possible to visually track the cup with the piece of candy. There were paper clips and gold stars readily available that could be used to mark the cup with the piece of candy, if the participants thought to do so when the experimenter used a nondirective question, "Is there something you can do to help you find the candy right away?" If the child did not do so with this question, increasingly explicit prompts were given to the child, from pointing to the clips and stars and saying, "Can these help you find the candy right away?" to "Do you want to leave the marker there or put it some other place?"

All of the third-grade participants in the study used the markers with the most nondirective prompt. None of the preschoolers responded to this least directive prompt, although most of preschoolers did respond to more directive prompts. In general, the younger the preschooler, the more directive the prompt that was required for the children to use the markers. More than one-third of children between 3 and 4.5 years of age, however, did not use the retrieval cues even with the most explicit prompting, however. Other investigators using similar setups obtained results very much consistent with Ritter's (1978) outcomes. They confirmed that strategic use of retrieval cues must be prompted during the preschool years, when use of such cues is observed at all (Beal & Fleisig, 1987; Whittaker, McShane, & Dunn, 1985).

DeLoache, Cassidy, and Brown (1985) studied a retrieval situation that was even more familiar to young children than Ritter's (1978) hiding game. The study took place in a living room setting, with the experimenter hiding a Big Bird doll right in front of the child (the child saw the experimenter put the doll under a pillow on a couch in the living room). When the 18- to 24-month-old participants knew that they would later have to find the doll, they literally kept their eyes on it! Even though the experimenter provided attractive toys to occupy the participants as they waited to retrieve the object, the children kept looking back at the pillow. The researchers controlled the study enough to infer that the children used a memory strategy. Thus, when the doll was placed on the couch in full view with the child knowing they would have to retrieve it later, the child did not keep looking back. There was no need to do so, since there was no memory requirement (i.e., the doll was in full view). The DeLoache et al. (1985) study provided clear evidence that, at least some of the time, even 2-year-olds can be highly strategic: They can be strategic when given a familiar task in a familiar setting. Anyone who has raised a preschooler knows that finding toys around the house is a daily routine for 2-year-olds. In fact, during the 1980s, researchers produced a number of demonstrations that children 3-years-old and older can be very strategic when it comes to remembering where objects have been hidden (Haake, Somerville, & Wellman, 1980; Wellman & Somerville, 1982; Wellman, Somerville, & Haake, 1979).

### Remembering Instructions

If a child does something different when told to remember material currently being presented versus when material is presented without memory instruction, one can make the inference that the child is doing something intentionally strategic. Baker-Ward, Ornstein, and Holden (1984) provided a compelling demonstration that preschoolers are more likely to use memory strategies when asked to remember. Specifically, Baker and colleagues (1984) presented toys to 4-, 5-, and 6-year-olds, with them instructed to play with the toys. In the memorization condition of the study, however, participants were also asked to remember a subset of the toys forever. The participants in the remember condition played less

with the toys and more frequently verbalized the names of the to-be-remembered toys. That is, the researchers observed memory strategy use by preschoolers in this study. Actual memory of items was better in the memorization condition only for 6-year-olds, suggesting a utilization deficiency in the preschoolers. Even though they used a memory strategy, it did not benefit their memory (Miller & Seier, 1994). Subsequent studies would constructively replicate the Baker-Ward et al. (1984) results, providing support for the position that preschool-age children can be strategic when learning lists of objects but that the strategies they carry out are not always effective in improving memory (e.g., Lange, MacKinnon, & Nida, 1989; Newman, 1990).

### Summary

Memory development researchers established that preschoolers do evidence some strategies use when involved with familiar tasks such as playing with toys. As is the case for research on memory strategies use in the elementary years, there has been relatively little research on preschoolers' use of memory strategies. That does not mean there has not been study of memory. In fact, there has been an impressive amount of study of preschoolers' memory development, as will be evident in the next section documenting the developmental study of the many components of memory. Once these components are reviewed, a more complete and contextualized model of strategy use and development is possible.

## AN INFORMATION-PROCESSING MODEL OF INTENTIONAL, STRATEGIC MEMORY: ESSENTIAL COMPONENTS TO UNDERSTAND STRATEGY USE AND STRATEGY INSTRUCTION

As a result, of the research that investigated the development of memory strategies with age, much was learned about the factors affecting use and utility of intentional memory strategies. This work was foundational in understanding children's information processing more generally but also how strategies instruction can stimulate the complex information processing required for real academic achievement.

### Working/Short-Term Memory

A fundamental question in human cognition is how much information the mind can manage at once. This is a critical question because human thinking skill very much depends on being able to manipulate information in consciousness. Although all theories of human information processing include a short-term capacity construct, the functioning of the construct is construed differently in the various models. Some view short-term capacity as a passive container (e.g., Atkinson & Shiffrin, 1968), others portray short-term capacity as attentional capacity, which hints at greater activity than storage (e.g., Cowan, 1995; Kahneman, 1973), while still others emphasize mental activity even more, referring to the short-term capacity as working memory (e.g., Baddeley, 1987). In the more complex of models, working memory can be subdivided into subcomponents. For instance, working memory may consist of separate components, verbal and visuospatial working memory, which permit juggling of both verbal and nonverbal chunks of information (e.g., Logie, 1995).

Researchers often test short-term capacity by asking participants to remember pieces of information presented as a list at a rate of one item per second. Researchers present participants with lists until they can no longer recall all of the items. Usually, adults can recall between five and nine items on such tasks, with seven items as the average (Miller, 1956). While even young preschoolers can remember an item or two, the capacity to remember increases with development during childhood (Dempster, 1981). Developmental psychologists have expended considerable effort to understand why short-term memory capacity increases with age, and whether the observed performance increase represents a fundamental increase in underlying mental capacity or something else. For example, one viable possibility is that performance on short-term capacity tasks depends on an individual's speed of information processing, with slower processing individuals less able to attend to (operate on, mentally juggle) as many pieces of information as individuals who process information more rapidly (Cowan, 2002). From this perspective, the fact that processing speed increases with age, explains the developmental increase in observed performances on tasks that measure short-term memory capacity (e.g., Kail, 1995, 1997a, 2000; Kail & Hall, 2001). However, to date, there is no resolution about what exactly accounts for developmental increases in short-term memory tasks (see Schneider & Pressley, 1997, chap. 3, for a review of the possibilities).

Although performance on short-term capacity demanding tasks increases with age during childhood, individual differences exist at any given age in the ability

to do these tasks, with some children seeming to be able to deal with more information than other children. Given these individual differences and developmental shifts in short-term capacity, children with greater short-term capacity relative to age-mates and older children, when compared to younger children, can more effectively implement memory strategies that require considerable mental effort (Guttentag, 1989; Kee, 1994). That is, at least some developmental differences in ability to use memory strategies might be explained by short-term capacity differences in children. This possibility has been assessed with respect to imagery strategies.

For instance, children in the upper-elementary grades benefit more from instructions to use imagery strategies to learn verbal materials than do children in the primary grades (for a review, see Pressley, 1977). Pressley, Cariglia-Bull, Deane, and Schneider (1987) evaluated whether this developmental shift could be explained by short-term capacity differences among elementary-age children. They asked 6- to 13-year-old children to learn sentences that depicted vivid, easily imagined actions. For example, the participants studied sentences like, "The angry bird shouted at the white dog," and "The fat boy ran with the grey balloon." Participants in the imagery condition were instructed to construct vivid images representing the meanings of the sentences in order to remember them. Control participants were simply urged to try hard to remember the sentences. Consistent with previous research, the imagery instruction was effective with older children in the study but not with younger children. They found that memory of the sentences was better in the imagery compared to the control condition for the older participants in the investigation but not for the younger participants. More importantly, short-term capacity differences explained performance in the imagery condition but not in the control condition. In the imagery condition, participants with greater short-term capacity outperformed participants who had relatively less short-term capacity. In the control condition, there was no relationship between short-term capacity and performance. Cariglia-Bull and Pressley (1990) replicated this finding, thereby increased confidence in the earlier finding that at least some of the developmental differences in improved performance under imagery instructions can be explained by short-term capacity differences in children.

Kail (1997b) provided an analysis linking information-processing speed, children's imagery skills, and performance on short-term memory tasks requiring imagery. This analysis bolstered the case that short-term capacity matters in children's memory when mediated by capacity-demanding processes, such as imagery generation. Similarly, Woody-Dorning and Miller (2001) constructed an analysis of selective study procedures with kindergarten and grade-1 students. Thus, they demonstrated that a short-term memory capacity deficiency could explain the utilization deficiency observed in some children. (Some students produced the selective strategy but did not seem to benefit from it.)

## Strategy Knowledge as Procedural Knowledge

When strategies are first learned, they are executed very mindfully. Anyone who has watched a child in the primary grades participate in a memory strategy instruction experiment knows that for many children, it takes all the mental capacity they can muster to be able to complete tasks such as rehearsing long lists of words, using an organizational strategy to put to-be-learned content into memorable piles, or constructing meaningful semantic relationships between pairs of items that are not obviously related. Of course, this is no different than learning any skill. Experimental psychologists over more than a century of research have repeatedly demonstrated that practice makes faster, and easier. And as a result, less working memory is required to carry out the procedure (Johnson, 2003).

Those who teach children strategies have to keep in mind that their acquisition is going to be like any other skill acquisition. At first, the strategy will only be carried out very consciously, requiring a great deal of attention on the part of the child. With practice, the child will automatize execution of the strategy, and will require much less effort to carry out the strategy (J. R. Anderson, 1980, 1983). In fact, as this chapter proceeds, we provide many examples of cognitive strategies instruction which includes a great deal of practice of the strategies being taught. This reflects the work of contemporary applied researchers who have found that efficient execution of strategies that are taught takes practice.

## Metacognition

Metacognition is knowledge and awareness of one's thinking and thinking processes (e.g., Flavell, 1981). This awareness is important in self-regulation of thinking (McCormick, 2003). Therefore, one type of metacognition is knowing when and how to use the various strategies and how to apply them to newly encountered

situations (Flavell, 1979; Paris & Winograd, 1990; Pressley et al., 1987, 1989). With respect to memory strategies, metacognitively competent individuals might know to apply organizational strategies whenever they are presented information to learn that can be divided into categories (Pressley et al., 1987, 1989). That is, transfer very much depends on a learner knowing when and where a strategy can be used, as well as how the strategy can be adapted to new tasks, points that can be made during strategy instruction (e.g., O'Sullivan & Pressley, 1984; Pressley et al., 1987, 1989). A learner is more likely to understand and successfully apply a strategy to a new situation if he or she has been encouraged to think about why the strategy works and has received instruction about why it works (Crowley & Siegler, 1999). With increasing age, there is greater transfer of strategies taught, although transfer is rarely as complete as it could be (for an illustration about how to determine the difference between actual transfer and potential transfer, see Pressley & Dennis-Rounds, 1979). Again, good strategies instruction results in learners who can and will transfer the strategies they are learning. It typically includes information about the effects produced by a strategy, as well as information about when and where to use the strategy being acquired (Pressley, Borkowski, & O'Sullivan, 1984, 1985).

Another important form of metacognition that is critical to effective strategies use is awareness of how one is doing on a task (e.g., recognizing that one has not studied enough to do well on an upcoming test or recognizing that the text being read is not understood). We refer to such awareness as monitoring. Being aware that learning or comprehension is not complete can serve as a cue for using strategies (e.g., deciding to study some more, deciding to reread a text). Thus, monitoring is a key to self-regulated use of cognitive strategies (e. g., Markman, 1985). A very consistent finding is that people often mis-monitor. This phenomenon that has been found again and again across a variety of populations, using a number of procedures (e.g., Dunning, Johnson, Ehrlinger, & Kruger, 2003). For example, children in the primary grades often believe they are more ready for a test than they really are (Kelly, Scholnick, Travers, & Johnston, 1976; Levin, Yussen, DeRose, & Pressley, 1977; Monroe & Lange, 1977; Worden & Sladewski-Awig, 1982). Sometimes children think they understand a text when they do not (Markman, 1985). When children mis-monitor they should be encouraged to pay attention to cues that alert them to the fact that they do not understand. Furthermore, children need to interpret these cues as signals for applying more effort rather than signals to give up, believing the task is too difficult (e.g., Meichenbaum, 1977; Weiner, 1979).

Some strategies have a built-in monitoring component. If a child is using a cumulative rehearsal strategy and cannot remember the items on the list to rehearse them, that is a clear signal the material has not been learned. Also, if a child cannot retell a story just read, that provides powerful cuing that the story was not understood well enough (e.g., Thiede & Anderson, 2003; Thiede, Anderson, & Therriault, 2003). A very important finding in the monitoring literature was that practice tests provide tremendously powerful information about whether one is ready. Often, in advance of a practice test, people will believe they are going to succeed. If they experience difficulties on the practice test, they realize that their preferred strategies are not working, which motivates them to use other strategies (Pressley & Ghatala, 1990; Pressley, Levin, & Ghatala, 1984). Students should be encouraged to test themselves as they are trying to learn or understand content, given that their monitoring is often very poor, and that practice tests can inform them when their learning and understanding are incomplete.

A learner who can transfer the cognitive strategies they know broadly and appropriately is sometimes thought of as meta-strategic (Kuhn, 1999, 2000a, 2000b). Kuhn (e.g., 2001, 2002) currently leads the way in theorizing about how generalized use of strategies occurs. First of all, unlike the conception of memory strategy instruction in the 1960s and 1970s, Kuhn recognizes that a child often has several different strategies she or he could employ in a task situation. This is consistent with Siegler's view that learners typically have several strategies that they can apply to a task, with some more likely than others to be used at particular points in development (Siegler, 1996, 2000). Thus, for simple free recall list learning, the child could simply listen, say the name of the just revealed object one time, say it multiple times, could cumulatively rehearse the items on the list (i.e., saying over and over the names of all the objects revealed so far), or could create a mental image or invent a story incorporating all the list items. At any point in development, some of the strategies are more likely to be used than others.

For example, 5-year-olds often verbally name objects one time, right after the object is presented. On some trials, however, they might use rudimentary cumulative rehearsal, perhaps naming the most recently presented object and the object that preceded it. After the researcher presents all the objects on a list, the child's recall is tested. The occurrence of the test might increase awareness (i.e., metacognition), making clearer to the participant child that the goal of this exercise is to remember the items on the list. As the child recalls the list, she or he may notice that some items are remembered better than others, for example, the cumulatively rehearsed items are remembered better. With some reflection on that task, the child's understanding of the utility and potency of the various strategies available to him or her changes in ways that can effect subsequent strategy use. Thus, if given a similar list learning task a day later, the child might be more likely to use cumulative rehearsal, recognizing its benefits from the previous experience. Eventually, as successful recall attempts occur and the child recognizes that cumulative rehearsal helped, the child's understanding that cumulative rehearsal is potent in list learning increases. The result is that cumulative rehearsal becomes the most likely strategy used during such list learning for the child. In short, a child has theories about how to do well in list learning, theories about strategies that work for these tasks. These theories drive strategy use, but as a strategy is used and list learning tested, the child has opportunities to reflect on the strategies used and change his or her understanding about what works in list learning. These new understandings affect subsequent strategy use. Thus, this growing awareness leads to greater use of little implemented, but effective strategies and reduces use of previously deployed but less effective strategic procedures.

Kuhn's (2001, 2002a, 2002b) emphasis on meta-strategic understandings as driving forces in strategy choice is consistent with classical conceptions of the role of metacognition in mediating strategy choice (e.g., Borkowski et al., 1990). Kuhn has reported some investigations where she has mapped strategy shifts as a function of experience with strategies and tasks, consequent development of understanding of tasks, and understanding of the strategies that can be used to accomplish tasks (for a review see Kuhn, 2001, 2002a). Understanding of this process can be accomplished using a microgenetic approach (Siegler, Chapter 11, this *Handbook*, this volume). This methodology involves observing how participants use and change strategies over many attempts to accomplish similar tasks, as well as documenting their shifts in understanding of the strategies being used (i.e., changes in metacognition that drive future application of the strategies the learner knows that can be applied to the task).

Some of the most important information a learner can acquire about strategies is that they improve performance in certain situations. Such metacognitive understanding increases the motivation to transfer effective strategies from previously encountered tasks to new, similar tasks. (This is a point we elaborate on in the next subsection). In fact, one of the most reliable findings in the strategies instruction literature is that providing information about a strategy's benefits greatly increases the likelihood that the learner will continue to use a strategy being taught (see Pressley et al., 1984, 1985; Schunk & Zimmerman, 2003). Also, learners are more likely to continue to use a strategy if they can successfully carry out the strategy well enough that it works (i.e., does produce benefit). That is, they must possess self-efficacy with respect to use of the strategies being learned (Schunk & Zimmerman, 2003).

## World Knowledge

Many strategies cannot be carried out by a learner unless she or he has substantial world knowledge. Consider an elaborative strategy for learning facts. Suppose a person is asked to learn the following facts about Canada: Baseball was first played in the province of Ontario. There are more teamsters in British Columbia than any other province. The first museum was in Ontario. As it turns out, when many facts are presented, this is a difficult task, even for students from Canada. However, a Canadian can make it an easier task by asking her- or himself a question as each fact is processed, such as why does it make sense that this happened in this particular province? This strategy dramatically increases learning only for people with a lot of background knowledge about Canada. When Germans are asked to use this strategy to learn content about Canada, there is no improvement in their learning (Woloshyn, Pressley, & Schneider, 1992). Likewise, if Germans are asked to learn facts about German states, they benefit from the strategy, whereas Canadians do not (Woloshyn et al., 1992). Martin and Pressley (1991) evaluated a number of possible explanations of the effects of such why-questioning. Why-questioning works by encouraging learners to relate what they are learning to relevant prior knowledge. This does not seem to occur automatically in the absence of why questions. Thus, encouraging students to ask why facts they are learning make sense produces a

large increase in learning. However, that is only possible if learners possess prior knowledge that permits them to answer the why questions they are asking.

Many strategies depend on prior knowledge. Organizational strategies cannot be applied to list learning if learners do not know the categorical information required to organize the material in the list. A common reading strategy, which we will discuss later in the chapter, is to make predictions about what is going to be covered in a text based on the title and pictures. Such predictions are possible only if the learner possesses prior knowledge about the text topic. Similarly, readers are often taught to associate ideas encountered in text to what they know already. Again, this strategy can only be carried out if learners possess relevant prior knowledge.

In addition to enabling strategy use, development of knowledge can replace strategy use, with the work of Siegler and his colleagues especially informative on this point (see Siegler, 1996, for a review). Consider the specific case of spelling. Suppose that you ask children in first and second grade to spell some first-grade words (e.g., moon, fish, bug). There are two ways that this task can be done. One way is to sound out each word. The other way is simply to retrieve the proper spelling from long-term memory. The latter is only possible if the child knows the word. Rittle-Johnson and Siegler (1999), found that first graders rely more on the sounding out strategy, whereas second graders are more likely simply to retrieve such words from their prior knowledge. Retrieving is easier and faster than sounding out! Apparent in the Rittle-Johnson and Siegler (1999) data as well as in Siegler's other investigations of strategy use is the fact that children do not consistently use just one strategy in any task situation. Thus, for spelling, sometimes they sound out and sometimes they retrieve the spelling from memory. Similarly, when asked answers to arithmetic fact problems (e.g., $5 + 4 + ?$, $7 - 3 = ?$), children sometimes will use a counting strategy and sometimes they will just know the answer based on prior knowledge (e.g., Steel & Funnell, 2001). Barrouillet and Fayol (1998) confirmed that an increase in retrieval of answers from memory, when combined with advancing age, occurred when there has been increasing experience with an arithmetic task. In basic memory situations, even some children who use a very efficient strategy some of the time (e.g., some form of elaboration to learn paired associates) will use a less efficient and less certain strategy (e.g., repeating paired associates over and over) some of the time (Pressley & Levin,

1977). Mixed strategy use is very much the norm, a point made clearly in the next subsection. However, occasions certainly exist when trial-to-trial variability in strategy use involves moving from a less effective to a more effective strategy. For example, Schlagmueller and Schneider (2002) showed that 8- to 12-year-olds who first attempted to learn categorizable lists without using a categorizing, clustering strategy, would suddenly shift to employing such a strategy, and then sticking with it from that point on. Also, there are some data consistent with the conclusion that high ability learners are more likely to use effective strategies consistently to the exclusion of less effective strategies (e.g., Coyle, Read, Gaultney, & Bjorklund, 1998).

In general, however, an important lesson from this body of work is that as the prior knowledge base expands, learners rely more and more on what they know rather than working it out using strategies, although they may occasionally revert to strategy use just to make sure (e.g., Steel & Funnell, 2001). Even mature thinkers shift their thinking as they learn more. Thus, early in a course of study (e.g., a law school course), students are more likely to use strategies as they read that do not depend much on prior knowledge. As a course progresses, however, they are increasingly likely to relate what they are encountering in text to other knowledge of the law, more likely to elaborate new information by thinking about other information they have acquired (Stromso, Braten, & Samuelstuen, 2003).

We emphasize that world knowledge develops early in life. We do so, because, for the first half of the twentieth century, the assumption was that very young children (i.e., during the first 1.5 to 2 years of life) did not form memories, or, if they did, their memories were quickly forgotten. Piaget (e.g., 1952, 1962) conceived of infancy as a buzz of perceptual confusion, a period of time when children had not yet developed symbolic competencies essential for memory. Freud (e.g., 1963) claimed that anything that was encoded during childhood was eventually repressed.

At mid-century, Fantz (1956) demonstrated that infants prefer novel visual stimuli. That could only occur if babies remembered something about stimulation they had experienced previously. As the century proceeded, the finding that infants had visual pattern memory had received substantial research support (Fantz, 1956). DeCasper and Spence (1986), when studying attentional preferences, found that children remembered sounds

they heard while in the womb. Thus, infants seem to have some memory even before they are born.

By the end of the 1st year of life, babies begin to be able to recall sequences of events such as a sequence of events required to make a simple toy operate (Carver & Bauer, 1999, 2001). This rapidly improves during early childhood. Bauer, Wenner, Dropik, and Wewerka (2000) observed that about 67% of their 32-month-old participants could recall a sequence they had experienced a year earlier. There are many contextual factors that effect recall of sequences (see Bauer, 2003, Chapter 9, this *Handbook,* this volume, for a review). Children are more likely to recall logically ordered sequences than arbitrary sequences. Also, memory is better if exposure to sequences is repeated. Active participation in the event sequence also improves memory of the sequence. Finally, memory is better if the child is provided some hints at testing.

By 2 years of age, children remember much about the events in their life. Ask a 2.5-year-old about a visit to the emergency room that occurred 6 months earlier and the child can recall quite a bit (Peterson & Rideout, 1998). In fact, 3-year-olds can recall many types of events that they have participated in, from making cookies to visiting Disney World. Moreover, they have very detailed knowledge about frequently repeated events, such as birthday parties and going to McDonalds (see Fivush, 1997, for a review). Children can remember events that happened in kindergarten years later (Hudson & Fivush, 1991). Such data make clear that the experiences a preschooler has go far in determining what the child knows. Children largely know what they experience.

Beyond the experiences, however, opportunities to talk about what has been experienced also effect young children's memories, or at the very least, their abilities to access and talk about their memories of the past. Children who have mothers who talk with them a great deal about their experiences, who ask their children questions and elaborate on their children's answers, have children who are much better able to talk about their past experiences than mothers who do not so completely engage their children in conversations about life events (P. J. Bauer, 2003; Fivush, 1994, 1997; Nelson, 1993a, 1993b). Children remember what they talk about with others. Interpersonal communications are tremendously important in building a knowledge base.

One indication of extensive knowledge of the world is vocabulary. A child's vocabulary knowledge provides a good indication of their ability to comprehend new events that occur in their world, for example, understanding of new texts that are encountered (e.g., Venezky, 1984). An analysis by Hart and Risley (1995) concerning the development of vocabulary during the preschool years, powerfully suggested that experience determines the development of preschoolers' world knowledge. Hart and Risley observed preschoolers and their families in their homes over a 2.5-year period, beginning when children uttered their first words. The most striking difference over 1,300 hours of observations in 42 homes was that children living in professional families (i.e., mom and dad were educated) heard more than 2,000 words an hour, with many of the words occurring in conversations involving the child. In contrast, in working class families, children heard about 1,200 words per hour, with less parent-child conversation in general. In families receiving welfare, children heard about 600 words per hour, with much less parent-child conversation. With respect to the quality of the verbal interactions, professional families were more likely to respond to what their children said than did working class families, who were more responsive than the families receiving public assistance. The latter disproportionately talked to their children about what they should not do compared to more socioeconomically advantaged families.

By 3 years of age, there were clear differences in the amount of vocabulary possessed by the children in Hart and Risley's study. For example, the child in the professional family with the least vocabulary development knew more words than the child in a family on welfare with the most extensive vocabulary. The authors studied the children again when they were 9 and 10 years old, and observed a strong relationship between vocabulary development during the preschool years and success in reading. These data have received a great deal of attention in recent years as evidence that interactive language experiences during the preschool years go far in determining knowledge development that effects later intellectual competence. These data are complemented by an extensive experimental literature establishing that when parents of preschoolers are taught how to interact with their children over books (i.e., how to ask questions of their children during a reading and respond to children's remarks and questions) the children's language development improves, especially as indexed by increased vocabulary (e.g., Whitehurst et al., 1988, 1994). In short,

there is converging evidence that world knowledge is a critical component in children's memory and intellectual performance in general, and depends, in part, on linguistic interactions during early childhood.

## Conclusions

In the decade following the first research on children's use of strategies to mediate and improve memory, researchers conducted studies to determine whether preschoolers are strategic in memory situations. They are, at least when given simple memory tasks in familiar settings. However, when given the types of verbal learning tasks that proved revealing about memory strategy use by school-age children, there was little to no evidence of preschoolers using strategies to impact their memory performance. A conclusion about preschoolers' memory that emerged from the work on strategies was that memory during this period of time was fragile, and that children were only successful in using strategies in specific contexts.

The problem with this conclusion is apparent to anyone who has ever raised a child. Preschoolers seem to remember quite a bit. Bauer (Chapter 9, this *Handbook*, this volume) and her colleagues have demonstrated that before children can speak, they are learning about complex sequences they experience in their worlds. Indeed, when Bauer's analyses are combined with work in perceptual recognition, it is clear that the knowledge base of children is developing even before they are born.

Researchers such as Nelson (1993) and Fivush (1994, 1997) have analyzed in detail just how complete such memories are, and have completed detailed analyses about how interactions between parents and their children at home serve to consolidate and refine memories of important experiences. Hart and Risley (1995) also carefully observed preschoolers in their home settings. They established clear linkages between the richness of children's verbal interactions with their parents and the development of world knowledge as indexed by vocabulary knowledge.

Whitehurst and associates (1988, 1994) complemented this work with experimental studies in which there was a causal relationship between verbal interactions with parents and language and knowledge development. Whitehurst's work provides a different way of thinking about strategy instruction and children's development. He taught parents strategies for interacting with their preschoolers over picturebooks. This instruction led to changes in parent-child interactions that translated into differences in children's vocabulary knowledge. An examination of exemplary preschool environments that have improved children's intellectual functioning (for a review, see Eckenrode, Izzo, & Campa-Muller, 2003), such as the Perry Preschool Project (Hohmann & Weikart, 2002) and the Carolina Abecedarian approach (Martin-Johnson, Attermeier, & Hacker, 1996), reveals that a centerpiece in their interventions is teaching adults to interact with children in ways that will enrich adult-child interactions and encourage children to engage in mind expanding activities intended to increase children's knowledge of the world.

It is important to distinguish between intentional memory and incidental memory (Bauer, Chapter 9, this *Handbook,* this volume). Although preschoolers are sometimes very intentional in forming memories (e.g., making certain they remember where Big Bird is hidden), more often whatever memories are formed are incidental to their real goal at the moment. Thus, as children converse, their goal is to communicate, but in doing so, they incidentally remember some of the verbal labels that parents supply about the objects being discussed (e.g., Bloom, 2000). There is no doubt at this point that preschoolers acquire massive amounts of information incidentally.

In summary, a major discovery about children's memory during the last third of the twentieth century was that preschoolers can develop extensive world knowledge if they experience a conceptually rich world. These analyses make clear that extensive and meaningful interactions with others make a huge difference in the preparedness of children to cope with the demands made on them later, for example, in school. The child who arrives at the kindergarten classroom door with extensive vocabulary is more likely to thrive in school than the child who does not. Such a child is better prepared for school. This includes being better prepared to use the strategies taught in school in a self-regulated way.

## STRATEGY USE AS THE COORDINATION OF INFORMATION-PROCESSING COMPONENTS

Self-regulated use of all types of strategies, including memory strategies (e.g., J. Alexander & Schwanenflugel, 1994; DeMarie & Ferron, 2003), depends on coordination of the information-processing components

reviewed in this section such as strategies, metacognition, motivation, and prior (i.e., world) knowledge. Although interest in basic memory in children waned in the past decade, interest in strategy use in other problem areas soared. We will discuss several important directions in the second half of this chapter. Among these directions will be text processing, or how people attempt to understand and remember what they read. Skilled, adult readers are unambiguously strategic as they process text. Much of the convincing evidence for this conclusion has emerged from verbal protocols of reading. Researchers employing verbal protocol methodology ask readers to think aloud as they read, and report whatever they are thinking as they read (Pressley & Afflerbach, 1995). Good readers coordinate their use of a variety of strategies in order to make sense of challenging texts. In other words, competent readers are very meta-strategic. The interaction between the reader's prior knowledge and strategies use is also apparent.

Thus, what do skilled readers do to comprehend a text? Often, they have a goal for reading (e.g., to learn information to prepare for a talk on the subject of the text). They may skim the text, perhaps identifying parts that deserve to be read quickly versus more carefully. They might activate prior knowledge (e.g., if it is an article about the comforts of a new type of jet airliner, perhaps remembering how uncomfortable she or he has been on airliners in the past). By the end of the skim, many readers will have made predictions about what will be in the text on the basis of reading the title, looking at headings and pictures, and prior knowledge about the topic of the text.

Then comes the reading itself, which is often done selectively (i.e., skimming some parts, skipping others, reading what are perceived as the most novel or most important points with special care). As reading proceeds, the reader might make notes or try to summarize large sections of the text, pausing to reflect upon parts of the text that are particularly relevant to the reading goal. The prereading predictions might be reconsidered in light of the reading, with new predictions made about what might be next. As reading proceeds, the reader increasingly refines understanding of the messages in the text. He or she might jump back and forth while doing this, to understand the facts in the text, with the intent of specifically remembering the parts that are most novel. Flipping back and forth through a text may also aid a skilled reader's attempt to integrate the ideas in the text.

There often is a great deal of conscious inference making. This means going beyond the information given in the text, based both on attention to ideas that are in the text and relevant prior knowledge. Thus, the meanings of unfamiliar words sometimes are inferred. Sometimes the reader relates the information in text to their personal experiences (e.g., when reading that the new plane has only aisle and window seats, the reader recalls how uncomfortable it had been to be in a middle seat on other airliners). The reader might make inferences about the author (e.g., this writer must work for the plane manufacturer, given how positive and uncritical he is about the new plane). Also, the reader often comes up with questions (e.g., How can flying such a small airliner be profitable?) and is especially attentive to subsequent sections of text that answer the questions that surface.

Much of the meaning is in the text, but much of it also emanates from the reader's prior knowledge. That is, readers interpret what they read, with any given text permitting a large number of interpretations. After reading, the reader might reflect additionally on the text, making certain she or he knows the most important points of the text, perhaps reflecting on whether these ideas are consistent with the reader's own perspectives, and perhaps considering updating or changing one's views depending on whether the text was persuasive or not.

While reading, skilled readers monitor their understanding of text and pay attention to points that are confusing or inconsistent within text. They are aware of whether the ideas in the text were known to them previously as well as whether they agree with the ideas in the text. When confused, capable readers often will go back and re-read and, or reduce their reading speed in an effort to understand better. Good readers monitor whether they are paying enough attention or being distracted. They especially monitor whether their efforts are paying off. That is, if they perceive that the text is not informing their reading goal, they might decide to speed up reading, or skim, or stop reading a text altogether. If the text is full of ideas advancing their thought, they may increase their strategy use by reading more slowly, deliberately reflecting on the text, and taking notes.

Excellent readers pay attention to individual words in the text that they do not know. If they sense that understanding a particular word is critical to understanding the text, they may analyze the text for cues to its meaning or even look up the word. If they decide that they do not need to know the word in order to understand the text, the reader often will just continue reading.

All of the skilled reading behaviors that we have just summarized take place in working memory. Although knowledge about strategies is stored in long-term memory, when strategies are activated, they operate in working memory. Likewise, prior knowledge is stored in long-term memory, when knowledge is activated and consciously thought about, the activation occurs in working memory. Similarly, motivational thought (e.g., I can do this task if I exert effort.) also occurs in working memory. In order for all of the information-processing components to function, strategy execution and knowledge access must be fairly automatic, so as not to exceed the capacity limits of working memory.

In summary, skilled reading is massively strategic, involving metacognitive processes (i.e., knowing when to use which strategies), and relating ideas in a current text to prior knowledge. The complicated information processing that is the skilled reading just described is decidedly more complicated than children's approaches to understanding a text, which often boils down to little more than straightforward reading of the words in the text from beginning to end (e.g., Kucan, 1993; Lytle, 1982; Meyers, Lytle, Palladino, Devenpeck, & Green, 1990; Phillips, 1988). That is, children readers are generally production deficient with respect to the reading strategies and processes used by skilled, adult readers. Consistent with the second overarching conclusion of this chapter, however, later we review the evidence that children can be taught the comprehension strategies that are at the heart of skilled, adult reading. Such instruction can result in children who are active, metacognitive, and motivated enough to continue using the strategies when reading in a self-regulated fashion. Before doing that, however, we take up discussion of strategies instruction with exceptional child populations.

## BASIC RESEARCH ANALYSES OF EXCEPTIONAL CHILDREN WHO BENEFIT FROM STRATEGIES INSTRUCTION

As research on strategies use by normal students proceeded, basic researchers also turned their attention to atypical students, including children with mental retardation, students with learning disabilities, and children suffering from attention deficit and hyperactivity. This work informed and inspired many who were searching for ways to improve the intellectual lives of disadvantaged children. In this section, we review the basic work with atypical populations that convinced many that struggling students should be taught strategies.

## Meichenbaum's Analyses of Attention Deficit Hyperactivity

Donald Meichenbaum's (1977) text, *Cognitive Behavior Modification,* summarized a body of work that stimulated others to follow suit. Meichenbaum and Goodman (1969) involved second graders with attention deficit and hyperactivity, who were asked to do a matching task that required careful comparison of several similar geometric figures. The researchers asked the students to select from a set of similar figures one that matched the test figure exactly. This is a very difficult task for young students with attention deficit-hyperactivity because they characteristically fail to consider task details carefully, and respond to a task before reflecting on it.

Meichenbaum and Goodman (1969) taught the participants in the experimental condition a strategy for accomplishing such a difficult task. Basically, they taught the students to tell themselves to slow down when doing such a task and to reflect before responding, and look carefully at each feature on the test stimulus and the choices (i.e., to self-instruct themselves to be careful and reflective). At first, a teacher modeled and explained the strategy, then provided support as students tried the approach on their own. Performance on this difficult task improved because of this strategy training. There were many follow-up studies by a number of researchers (see Meichenbaum, 1977; Pressley, 1979), who concluded that teaching the self-instruction strategy to hyperactive learners improved their ability to do tasks that required slow and careful processing.

Over the years, Meichenbaum and his colleagues have spent much time with educators to encourage them to teach their students to use the self-instruction strategy. They paid attention to how instruction can be delivered in a way that facilitates students' continued strategies use. The conclusions (e.g., Meichenbaum & Biemiller, 1998, chap. 10) that follow from their clinical-classroom work (and that of others) are very consonant with some of the conclusions from the basic memory development literature. Their recommendations include the following:

- Students should be taught to transfer, with teachers letting them know from the beginning that transfer is the goal.

- When students are in a situation where they might apply a strategy they know (but seem not to be doing so), teachers should give them a hint to reflect on the situation and use a strategy they know.

- Teachers should discuss with students different contexts that are appropriate for a particular strategy.

- Students should have practice opportunities with diverse situations where strategies they are learning could be applied. Such practice should occur as part of long-term instruction that permits students to become more proficient in strategy use as they become more aware of when strategy use is helpful.

- Students should practice using a strategy with diverse tasks and diverse settings because this increases awareness of when to use a strategy.

- Students should think aloud as they do tasks. This provides a window for the instructor documenting whether the student is attempting to transfer the strategies being taught.

In short, the main message from Meichenbaum's work and the clinical practice inspired by his work is that students can be taught to use strategies. A broad application of strategies is most likely to occur if the teaching is long term, varied, and complete, and continues until there is evidence that students are transferring what they are learning. This perspective is reflected in much of the strategy instruction that will be considered subsequently.

## Strategy Instruction with Students with Mental Retardation

Many of the researchers who were concerned with memory development in children with normal intelligence also studied memory development in children with mental retardation, especially children who are considered to be educable (i.e., they can learn, although typically more slowly than normal students, achieving less, and are not as capable of taking on tasks as difficult as normal age mates). One major finding was that children with mental retardation are much less likely to develop memory strategies than are normally achieving children (Ellis, 1979). More positively, when children with retardation are instructed to use memory strategies, often they can do so with improved performance. They can rehearse list items, use categories to organize clusterable lists, and construct verbal elaborations of paired associates. However, their performances rarely approach the levels of normal children using these strategies (Blackman & Lin, 1984; Brown, 1978; Taylor & Turnure, 1979). Even so, like normal children, after being taught memory strategies, children with mental retardation rarely continued to use the strategies, even in situations almost identical to the training situation (Borkowski & Cavanaugh, 1979; Brown, 1974; Brown & Campione, 1978; Campione & Brown, 1977). To use Flavell's (1970) term, these children were production deficient with respect to memory strategies with simple instruction of strategies not resulting in long-term use of them.

Belmont, Butterfield, and Ferretti (1982) offered a critical analysis that illuminated conditions when memory strategies instruction is more effective for children with mental retardation. They evaluated more than 100 studies of strategy instruction directed at children with mental retardation. They found little evidence of continued use of strategies, especially in situations that differed even a small amount from the training situation (i.e., failure to transfer the strategies taught). A few studies did produce longer-term use of the strategies taught. Of the seven studies that resulted in some evidence of transfer, six of them shared a common characteristic. Instruction was especially complete with respect to the components that Meichenbaum (1977, chap. 7) has identified as important in promoting self-regulated use of strategies in children with attention deficit and hyperactivity. In the studies in which students produced some evidence of transfer, students were taught to formulate a goal (e.g., remember the list items), make a plan to attain the goal, and monitor whether the plan was working as it was being carried out (e.g., asking themselves, "Did the plan work?"). If the children did not successfully learn the material they were taught to cope, by deciding whether they used their plan, trying to use the plan again, or trying to come up with a new plan.

Why might this teaching work? An important problem for students with mental retardation is that they do not self-regulate. The type of instruction advocated by Meichenbaum (1977) is intended to increase self-regulation, especially using language, which is something that students with mental retardation fail to do (Whitman, 1990). In addition, such instruction encourages students to monitor, to appraise whether they are making progress on the task, and to be aware that there is a connection between the strategies they are learning and their performance outcomes (see Borkowski & Kurtz, 1987).

The demonstrations of improved performance for students with mental retardation as a result of self-regulated strategy instruction greatly impacted educators of special populations. Additionally, these studies greatly motivated much of the work covered in the remainder of this chapter, and contributed to the hypothesis that children's performance will improve if they are taught to use strategies that are well matched to task demands. And while students with mental retardation may not persist in their strategy use as long as other students, there was reason to believe that instruction emphasizing self-regulated use of strategies might produce enduring strategy instructional effects (Belmont et al., 1982; Campione, Brown, Ferrara, Jones, & Steinberg, 1985; Meichenbaum, 1977).

## Strategy Instruction with Students with Learning Disabilities

The defining characteristics of students with learning disabilities is that they have difficulty learning some type of academic content, despite being otherwise normally intelligent. Because failure to learn to read has such negative consequences tied to it, learning disabilities in reading have received much attention (e.g., Siegel, 2003; Vellutino, 1979). Math learning disabilities have also captured the attention of a number of researchers, again, because failing to learn math is obviously problematic, for learning arithmetic and more advanced mathematical skills are foundational in western education (Geary, 2003).

While a plethora of theories of learning disability exist, the potential biological bases of learning disabilities have received the most attention in recent years. Thus, behavioral genetics studies of the heritability of learning disabilities have provided substantial evidence that difficulties in learning particular skills often pass from parents to children following patterns most consistent with genetic mediation (for a brief review, see Thomson & Raskind, 2003). The most visible biologically oriented work in learning disabilities, however, is concerned with determining whether there are neurobiological differences between students with learning disabilities and normally achieving students (Shaywitz & Shaywitz, 2003). Researchers generating neuro-images as students perform academic tasks (e.g., basic reading tasks) have identified some differences in the neuro-imagery patterns between students with learning disabilities and normal students.

a long time that synthetic phonics had more impact than other forms of phonics instruction.

Lovett and her associates at the Hospital for Sick Children in Toronto have led the way in evaluating the benefits of asking students to learn and use a repertoire of phonics strategies, rather than just one (Lovett et al., 2000). The participants in this study were 6- to 13-year-olds with severe reading difficulties. Everyone received 70 hours of intervention. Some received both instruction in sounding out of words and a form of decoding by analogy instruction, which had them learn keywords, each representing one of the 120 key spelling patterns in English (e.g., *cat* as a keyword for the pattern *–at*). Other participants were taught only to sound out words, while others only received decoding by analogy instruction. Control participants experienced math tutoring with some classroom survival skills training. At the end of instruction, participants receiving the combined sounding-out and decoding by analogy training demonstrated significantly better word recognition.

Much more work needs to be done on the effects produced by teaching struggling readers both to use sounding-out strategies and analogy approaches. Such flexibility in decoding instruction may be especially important for students who experience difficulties either with analyzing and blending or with decoding analogically using word chunks. For students experiencing the former problem, instruction should focus more on the word chunks and use of analogies to decode words. For students experiencing the latter problem, downplaying word families and word chunks in favor of analyzing and blending would make sense. In short, what is needed might be decoding instruction that accommodates individual differences in students rather than being one-size-fits-all instruction. Working out the specifics of such instruction is going to be challenging, however.

Again, Lovett, Barron, and Benson (2003) are currently evaluating an intervention that involves teaching struggling beginning readers to use five strategies as a repertoire: (1) sounding out words, (2) decoding by analogy to known words (i.e., a rhyming strategy), (3) peeling off prefixes and suffixes and isolating a smaller root word, (4) trying each of the sounds a word's vowels could make, and (5) looking for smaller, known words in a longer unknown word. They seem to have been influenced by Meichenbaum's (1977) thinking, since their intervention includes instructing students to self-instruct their use of strategies. For example, if trying to decode the word *unstacking*, a student would self-regulate strategy use through four steps (Lovett et al., 2003, p. 285, table 17.1): (1) They would choose a strategy, saying to themselves something like the following: "My game plan is first to use peeling off. Then I am going to use the rhyming strategy and look for the spelling patterns I know." (2) The students would use these strategies, self-verbalizing as they do so: "I am peeling off *un* and *ing*. My next game plan is rhyming. I see the spelling pattern *–ack*. The key word is *pack*. If I know *pack*, then I know *stack*." (3) The reader would then check: "I have to stop and think about whether I am using the strategies properly. Is it working? Yes, I'll keep on going. I will put all the parts together—*un-stack-ing*." (4) The student self-reinforces by declaring she or he "scored," if the word seems correct. If not, the student would start the sequence again, choosing, using, and checking strategy use: "The word is *unstacking*. I scored. I used peeling off and rhyming to help me figure out this word and they worked." Evaluations of this self-instruction approach are underway as this chapter is being written, consistent with a great deal of ongoing research on a variety of word recognition strategies.

## Comprehension Strategies Instruction

Although instructing students to use a repertoire of word recognition strategies in a self-regulated fashion is a recent trend, researchers have been teaching students to use comprehension strategies in a self-regulated fashion for more than a quarter of a century. The first such study was carried out by Meichenbaum and Bommarito (reported in Meichenbaum & Asarnow, 1979). Those investigators taught comprehension strategies to middle-school students who could decode but were experiencing difficulties understanding what they read. Instruction began with an adult modeling self-verbalized regulation of comprehension strategies such as, looking for the main idea, attending to the sequence of important events in a story, and attending to how characters in a story feel and why they feel the way they do, as well as some other strategies helpful during reading.

The students saw the adult read as they heard the following verbalizations by the adult:

Well, I've learned three big things to keep in mind before I read a story and while I read it. One is to ask myself what the main idea of the story is. What is the story about? A second is to learn important details of the story as I go along. The order of the main events or their sequence is an especially important detail. A third is to know how the characters feel and why. So, get the main idea. Watch sequences. And learn how the characters feel and why.

While I'm reading I should pause now and then. I should think of what I'm doing. And I should listen to what I'm saying to myself. Am I saying the right things?

Remember, don't worry about mistakes. Just try again. Keep cool, calm, and relaxed. Be proud of yourself when you succeed. Have a blast. (pp. 17–18)

By the end of six training sessions, the students were self-verbalizing covertly, with control gradually transferred to the students over the course of six sessions. There was greater pretest-to-posttest gain on a standardized comprehension test for students receiving instruction than for control condition participants. This was the first demonstration that teaching students to use a small repertoire of comprehension strategies in a self-regulated fashion makes a difference in the understanding of text.

During the 1970s and 1980s, however, most research on comprehension strategies was not about teaching their self-regulated use or even teaching students to use several strategies in combination. Rather, researchers typically employed true experiments to demonstrate that many individual comprehension strategies (e.g., creating mental images representing the meanings in text, asking questions about text content, summarization) improved elementary students' comprehension and memory of text (for reviews, see National Reading Panel, 2000; Pressley, Johnson, Symons, McGoldrick, & Kurita, 1989). This work made clear that elementary students were production deficient with respect to these strategies, but they could execute them, if instructed to do so, and thereby improve their comprehension and memory of text.

A major problem with respect to the experiments on individual strategies was that good readers never employ a single strategic process. Rather they flexibly articulate a variety of strategies as they attempt to make sense of text (Pressley & Afflerbach, 1995). Moreover, professional educators who taught study skills to students had recognized for years that tasks such as reading and learning from text required integrated use of a variety of strategies (e.g., the SQ3R approach encouraged students to survey a text before reading, ask questions about the text based on headers and pictures, read the text, recall

and review it; Robinson, 1961). Thus, reading research had plenty of inspiration to explore the possibility of teaching students to use repertoires of individual comprehension strategies that had been validated in the experiments of the 1970s and 1980s.

### Reciprocal Teaching

Palincsar and Brown (1984) developed a comprehension strategies technique that amalgamated tactics emphasized in the study skills literature and strategies studied by comprehension researchers in the late 1960s. Stauffer's (1969) Directed Reading-Thinking Activity focused on prediction, including reader revision of predictions as information is encountered in text. Another influence on reciprocal teaching was Manzo's (1968) ReQuest, which involved students and teacher reading part of text and then taking turns asking each other questions about it (i.e., engaging in reciprocal questioning). Through generating questions, the teacher modeled questioning for the student. The teacher also provided feedback to students about the questions they generated. Markman (1985) also influenced reciprocal teaching. She emphasized the finding that capable readers monitor whether they understand when they read and respond with repair strategies when they detect less than complete comprehension (e.g., seeking further clarification). Finally, many demonstrations existed where teaching students to summarize their understanding as they read improved comprehension and memory of text (Armbruster, Anderson, & Ostertag, 1987; Berkowitz, 1986; Brown & Day, 1983; Rinehart, Stahl, & Erickson, 1986; B.M. Taylor, 1982; B. M. Taylor & Beach, 1984). Thus, Palincsar and Brown (1984) taught students to make predictions before reading, question as they read, seek clarification when confused, and summarize after reading a section of text. They did so first in the context of a study that became the most visible comprehension strategies instructional study ever conducted.

Palincsar and Brown's first study (1984) included seventh-grade readers, who were adequate decoders but poor comprehenders. In the reciprocal teaching condition, the participants were taught the four comprehension strategies. Each intervention day began with the adult teacher discussing the topic of the day's text, calling for predictions about the content of the passage based on the title, if the passage was completely new, or calling for a review of main points covered thus far for passages that had been begun the previous day. The adult teacher then assigned one of the two students to be the "teacher." Adult teacher and students then read the first paragraph of the day's reading silently, with the student teacher then posing a question about the paragraph, summarizing it, and either predicting upcoming content or seeking clarification if there was some confusion about the ideas in the paragraph. If the student teacher faltered, the adult teacher prompted these activities (e.g., "What question do you think a teacher might ask?" "Remember, a summary is a shortened version," or, "If you're having a hard time thinking of a question, why don't you summarize first?"). Students were praised for their teaching and given feedback about the quality of it (e.g., "You asked that question well, a question I would have asked would have been . . ."). Students took turns as the student teacher, with a session lasting about 30 minutes. Throughout the intervention the students were explicitly informed that questioning, summarization, prediction, and seeking clarification were strategies that were to help them to understand better and that they should try to use the strategies when they read on their own. The students were also informed that being able to summarize passages and being able to predict the questions on upcoming tests were good ways to assess whether what was read was understood. There were approximately 20 days of intervention for the students in the reciprocal teaching condition, followed by 5 days of posttesting immediately after the intervention period. Eight weeks later, Palincsar and Brown conducted 3 days of long-term follow-up testing. Students in a control condition received the same pretests and posttests as strategies-instructed students but received no instruction and did not experience daily assessments.

Relative to the control condition, reciprocal teaching positively affected all measures of text comprehension and memory that were collected. The results of Study 1 provided plenty of reason for enthusiasm about reciprocal teaching. Nonetheless, with only 2 students per teacher in Study 1 and an experimenter as the teacher, it was difficult to make a case for the classroom validity of the intervention. Then in their second study, Palincsar and Brown (1984) evaluated the usefulness of reciprocal teaching in a realistic classroom situation. Four small groups of middle-school students who could decode adequately but who experienced comprehension problems participated in reciprocal teaching reading groups. Their reading was compared to students who did not receive reciprocal teaching. In general, the positive effects observed in Study 1 were replicated in Study 2, although no

standardized test data were collected in the second study.

The reciprocal teaching research had a wide-ranging impact on practice. For instance, reciprocal teaching stimulated textbook publishers to include strategies instruction, focusing on summarization, questioning, prediction, and seeking clarification in their elementary-level reading series in the late 1980s and early 1990s. Palincsar and Brown (1984) also inspired additional study of the method. Ten years later Rosenshine and Meister (1994) conducted a meta-analysis of the impact of reciprocal teaching. They concluded that the approach produced consistent, striking effects on cognitive process measures, such as those tapping summarization and self-questioning skills. However, with respect to standardized comprehension, the effects were less striking, with an average effect size of 0.3 standard deviations. A very important finding in Rosenshine and Meister's (1994) meta-analysis was that reciprocal teaching was more successful when there was more direct teaching of the four comprehension strategies. This finding is important in light of conclusions we offer later in favor of greater direct explanation as part of strategies instruction.

### Other 1980s-Era Studies of Comprehension Strategies Instruction

News of Palincsar and Brown's (1984) work inspired a flurry of interest in teaching repertoires of comprehension strategies. Much was learned during this period about how to do such work successfully as well as how not to teach comprehension strategies.

For example, Paris and his colleagues devised and evaluated a 30-hour approach to teaching a variety of comprehension strategies in classrooms (Paris, Cross, & Lipson, 1984; Paris & Jacobs, 1984; Paris & Oka, 1986). The approach emphasized student understanding of the strategic processes. However, there was only limited application of the processes, and such teaching took place in whole classroom groups. Thus, it lacked the intensity of the teaching in Palincsar and Brown (1984). More positively, there was a lot of teacher explanation and modeling of the processes, as well as teacher-directed discussion of the strategies. The students who experienced this instruction learned about strategic processes as evidenced by being able to answer a few more questions about the strategies than students who did not experience the curriculum (e.g., Jacobs & Paris, 1987). Students experiencing the curriculum also did better on some comprehension measures than control participants, especially measures similar to ones experienced during strategies instruction lessons. Unfortunately, the approach made no impact on comprehension as measured by standardized achievement tests (Paris & Oka, 1986).

Bereiter and Bird (1985) taught seventh and eighth grade average-achieving students to use a set of comprehension strategies to engage text actively. These strategies included: restatement of the text content (i.e., summarization), backtracking when confused (i.e., clarifying), making connections between various parts of the text, and careful reflection on text (i.e., looking for inferences that should be made, close examination of portions of text that seem important, rejection of information in text after thinking about it). In the most complete condition, a teacher first modeled and extensively explained the strategies, with students then practicing them, including making judgments about when the strategies should be used. A second condition consisted of teacher modeling and student practice, but no explanation of the strategies. Bereiter and Bird also designed two control conditions. The students in the most complete condition reported greater strategy use when they read. And their standardized test performance greatly improved as compared to the participants in the other three conditions. Bereiter and Bird's (1985) finding that explanation of strategies was important as part of good comprehension instruction was complemented by the outcomes in another study conducted by Duffy and associates (1987).

Duffy and colleagues (1987) produced an extremely well designed investigation of the effects of direct explanation strategy instruction on third-grade reading. Ten of 20 groups of weak readers were assigned randomly to a direct explanation strategies instruction condition. The remaining 10 groups of students received their usual instruction and served as controls. They taught third-grade teachers to explain the strategies, skills, and processes directly that are part of skilled third-grade reading, including both word recognition and comprehension strategies. The study took place over the course of an entire academic year. The teachers were taught first to explain a strategy, skill, or process and then to model using it for students. Then came guided student practice, where the students initially carried out the processing overtly so that the teacher could monitor their use of the new strategy. Teacher assistance was reduced as students became more proficient. Teachers en-

couraged transfer of strategies by going over when and where the strategies being learned might be used. Teachers cued use of the new strategies when students encountered situations where the strategies might be applied profitably, regardless of when these occasions arose during the school day. Thus, teacher scaffolding, where teachers provide sufficient support to keep student learning on task continued throughout the school day (as conceptualized by Wood, Bruner, & Ross, 1976). Cuing and prompting was continued until students autonomously applied the strategies they were taught. By the end of the year, students in the direct explanation condition outperformed control students on standardized measures of reading, including one of two measures of comprehension included in the study. These results had a profound effect on the reading education community. Many educators began to incorporate direct explanation, as defined by Duffy and company (1987) as a part of their comprehension strategies instructions in their own schools. Direct explanation, modeling and teacher monitored practice of comprehension strategies applications would be the heart of comprehension instruction as practiced in many elementary schools across the country (Almasi, 2003; Block & Pressley, 2002; Harvey & Goudvis, 2000).

### Transactional Strategies Instruction

Teaching students to use repertoires of comprehension strategies that incorporated teacher explanation and modeling, and supported student practice of the strategies came to be known as transactional comprehension strategies instruction in the 1990s. The approach was so named because such instruction involved students responding to text (Rosenblatt, 1978), with predictions, questions, images, and summaries all reflecting student interpretations of what they were reading—interpretations effected both by the texts being read and readers' prior knowledge.

Three studies are usually cited as validation for transactional comprehension strategies instruction. In all three, the strategies instruction included extensive and long-term teacher modeling and explanation of strategies, as well as extensive and long-term student practice of the strategies.

Brown, Pressley, Van Meter, and Schuder (1996) conducted a school-year long quasi-experimental investigation of the effects of transactional strategies instruction on second graders' reading. Five second-grade classrooms receiving transactional strategies instruction were matched with second-grade classrooms taught by teachers who were well regarded as language arts teachers but who were not using a strategies-instruction approach. The target group of students consisted of readers who were low achieving at the beginning of second grade. In the fall, the strategies-instruction and control participants did not differ on standardized measures of reading comprehension and word attack skills. By the spring, there were clear differences on these measures favoring the students receiving transactional strategies instruction. In addition, there were differences favoring the strategies-instructed students on strategies use measures as well as interpretive measures. Strategies-instructed students made more diverse and richer interpretations of what they read than control students.

Collins (1991) produced improved comprehension in fifth- and sixth-grade students by providing a semester (3 days a week) of comprehension strategies lessons. With respect to standardized comprehension performance, the strategies-instructed students did not differ from control students before the intervention. On the posttest, however, there was a 3-standard deviation difference between treated and control conditions. This is a very large effect for the treatment.

Anderson (1992; see also Anderson & Roit, 1993) conducted a 3-month experimental investigation of the effects of transactional strategies instruction on reading disabled students in grades 6 through 11. Students were taught comprehension strategies in small groups. The investigators divided students into nine groups that experienced transactional strategies instruction and seven control groups. Although both strategies-instructed and control students made gains on standardized comprehension measures from before to after the study, the gains were greater in the transactional strategies groups than in the control condition. Anderson (1992) also collected a variety of qualitative data supporting the conclusions that reading for meaning improved in the strategies-instructed condition. Strategies instruction increased students' willingness to read difficult material, their attempts to understand it, their efforts to collaborate with classmates to discover meanings in text, and their reactions and elaborations of texts.

In summary, long-term transactional comprehension strategies instruction produces positive effects on comprehension for students from grade 2 through grade 11. Such teaching begins with teacher explanation and modeling of strategies followed by students practicing the strategies in small reading groups. As they do so, students discuss their predictions, reports of interpretive images, questions, summary comments, and reflections on how to deal with difficulties in understanding the text.

### Collaborative Strategic Reading

More recently, Vaughn and her colleagues have developed a multiple strategies instruction approach for reading expository text. They refer to it as collaborative strategic reading (CSR), since students read together in collaborative groups, using the strategies to understand the text. Consistent with transactional strategies instruction, a teacher models and explains strategies to small groups of students. The strategies include making predictions about the text, clarifying when readers sense some difficulty in understanding (i.e., rereading if the problem is not one of word recognition, some word-attack strategies if it is a word the reader does not recognize), a gist strategy (i.e., finding the main ideas), and a wrapping up strategy after the text is read (i.e., asking what should be understood after reading the text, determining whether the reader learned it, and reviewing the content).

Once the students are familiar with the strategies they use them in collaborative groups. As in reciprocal teaching (Palincsar & Brown, 1984), students take turns leading the group. Other roles are shifted from student to student. Thus, one member of the group reminds students how to make clarifications when necessary. Another member provides feedback to group members. Still another is responsible for the wrap up. The fifth member of the group watches the time, moving the group along in a reading if they spend too much time on one portion of text or carrying out a strategy. In an experimental validation involving fourth graders who learned and practiced collaborative strategic reading over an 11-day period, there was a small to moderate benefit for the trained students relative to controls on a standardized comprehension test (Klingner, Vaughn, & Schumm, 1998).

### Conclusions

There is no doubt that elementary-grade students can be taught comprehension strategies with benefit. Thus, when the National Reading Panel (2000) reviewed well-supported reading instruction, they concluded that students benefit from comprehension instruction. As a result, comprehension strategies instruction has been cited explicitly in the federal *No Child Left Behind Act of 2001* as an integral part of better reading education. In particular, there is great improvement in comprehension by teaching students a repertoire of strategies that are like the strategies used by very capable adult readers (Gersten, Fuchs, Williams, & Baker, 2001; Pressley & Afflerbach, 1995).

What is discouraging is that comprehension strategies, in fact, are not being taught much in schools (Pressley, Wharton-McDonald, Mistretta, & Echevarria, 1998; Taylor, Pearson, Clark, & Walpole, 2000), at least not as extensively as in the training studies cited here. One hypothesis is that teachers themselves are not very good comprehenders, in that they typically do not actively use the comprehension strategies (Keene & Zimmermann, 1997) that are employed by the most capable of adult readers (Pressley & Afflerbach, 1995). Keene and Zimmermann (1997) reason that if teachers do not use such strategies themselves, they cannot understand them well enough to teach them, and will not recognize how much comprehension strategies can improve reading. Anecdotally, teachers who learn to teach comprehension strategies report that their own reading becomes much more active, and that they are much better comprehenders than they were previously (e.g., Pressley et al., 1992). A study needs to be conducted in which teachers are first taught how to be better comprehenders by using comprehension strategies, with the hypothesis being that learning to use comprehension strategies will enable and motivate them to teach the strategies use to their students.

Another hypothesis is that teaching comprehension strategies well is very difficult (Pressley & El-Dinary, 1997). Even teaching the individual strategies is challenging, for each is conceptually complex, requiring multiple operations to execute. For example, Williams (2003) and her colleagues (Taylor & Williams, 1983; Williams, Taylor, & Granger, 1981) have demonstrated how difficult it is to teach elementary and middle school students variations on gleaning the main idea from texts. More positively, Williams (2003) found that even students with learning disabilities get better with practice at identifying the big ideas in text. However, students with reading difficulties are at very high risk of including information in summaries of text that is tangential to the main ideas (Williams, 1993). In Williams' most recent work on the topic, students with learning disabilities have been taught to reflect on the answers to a series of questions to identify the major themes of narrative texts they are reading (Wilder & Williams, 2001; Williams, Brown, Silverman, & de Cani, 1994; Williams et al., 2002). For example, while reading a story, these students respond to the following question prompts:

> Who is the main character? What was his or her problem? What did he or she do? What happened? Was this good or bad? Why was this good or bad? The main character should have (or should not have) _____. We should (or should not) _____. The theme of the story is _____. To whom would the theme of this story apply? When would it apply? In what situation will this help or not?

In general, teaching children, including those with learning disabilities, to reflect on these questions has increased their abilities to identify main ideas in stories. The point is that it takes a lot of practice and very explicit instruction to teach children to use even one strategy so they can apply it while reading texts.

We are optimistic that comprehension strategies instruction will become much more frequent in schools in the near future. First, it is being promoted by the *No Child Left Behind* programs. Second, there are many more educational materials and associated professional development opportunities being presented to educators to increase their awareness and understanding of comprehension strategies instruction (e.g., Blachowicz & Ogle, 2001; Harvey & Goudvis, 2000). In addition, there is a cadre of researchers who are working very hard to increase both understanding of comprehension instruction (Block & Pressley, 2002) as well as how to translate new research ideas into instructional practice (Block, Gambrell, & Pressley, 2002).

## Writing Strategies Instruction

Hayes and Flowers's (1980) analysis of skilled composing completely shifted the way that researchers and educators think about writing instruction. They documented that writers engage in extensive planning of what they write before they draft, followed by actual writing and revision. This is an on-going process for skilled writers in that planning, drafting, and revising inform one another. The result of this analysis has been a great deal of research on the consequences of teaching students to plan, draft, and revise. The need to do so is especially great with children, because in the absence of such instruction, they write down the first ideas that come to their minds until they run out of ideas, which typically is shortly after starting to write (Graham, 1990; McCutchen, 1988; Scardamalia & Bereiter, 1986; Thomas, Englert, & Gregg, 1987). Therefore, children do very little planning and revising on their own.

In a more optimistic light, students respond well to writing strategies instruction. For example, Englert, Raphael, Anderson, Anthony, and Stevens (1991) taught fourth and fifth graders to plan their writing of expository text by thinking about and answering a set of questions: Who am I writing for? Why am I writing this? What do I know? (This question was a cue for brainstorming.) How can I group my ideas? How can I organize them (compare/contrast or problem/solution, explanatory or other text structure)?

As a second example, Graham's research group (De La Paz, Swanson, & Graham, 1998; Graham, 1997) successfully taught students with writing disabilities to revise. Students in grades 5 and 6 were taught to revise one sentence at a time, checking their own sentences against seven evaluative criteria: "This doesn't sound right," "This is not what I want to say," "This is not useful to my paper," "People may not understand this part," "People won't be interested in this part," "People won't buy this part," and "This is good." Then, they select one of five revision tactics to apply to the sentence: "Leave it the same," "Say more," "Leave this part out," "Change the wording," or, "Cross out and say it a different way." Grade 8 students were taught a slightly more complicated approach, involving two phases. The first phase focused on global concerns (i.e., not enough ideas, parts of the essay are not in the right order). The second part of revision focused on the local problems captured by the evaluative criteria and revision tactics covered previously.

Graham and his associates (1997, 1998) have generated a number of investigations intended to get elementary and middle school students, especially those considered to have writing or learning disabilities, to use strategies that promote effective planning, drafting, and revising in a self-regulated fashion. In these studies, the students are taught strategies by teachers who then work interactively with the students as they attempt to use the strategies during writing. The teachers model the strategies and discuss them with the students. Students memorize the steps of the strategies. The students

set goals for their writing (e.g., with respect to length) and are taught to monitor whether they have met the goals. The instruction is very individualized, and continues with teacher re-explanations and student practice until the student can carry out the strategies effectively on their own.

With 26 studies completed, the evidence is overwhelming that such instruction dramatically improves the writing of elementary and middle school students, including those with writing disabilities, regardless of the criteria employed to evaluate the writing. There have been consistent, large effects for self-regulated writing strategies instruction (Gersten & Baker, 2001; Graham & Harris, 2003). The positive effects are maintained over time and generalize to writing genres other than the training genre. The writing of elementary and middle school students can be improved substantially through cognitive strategies instruction.

## Mathematical Problem Solving

There is no academic area with a longer history of cognitive strategies instruction than mathematical problem solving. Since the middle part of the twentieth century, mathematics students have implemented the principles of Polya's (1957) classic, *How to Solve It,* in which he recommends a four-part strategic approach to problem solving. These steps include understanding the problem, devising a plan to solve it, carrying out the plan, and looking back. In fact, there have been a number of successful demonstrations that teaching such an approach to elementary students improves their problem solving (see Burkell, Schneider, & Pressley, 1990). One of the best-known examples is Charles and Lester's (1984) true experimental evaluation of an instructional program based on these strategies that they conducted with fifth and seventh graders. Over the course of 23 weeks, they taught the students a variety of ways to carry out each of Polya's four steps. At the end of the experiment the students clearly benefited from the instruction. Montague and Bos (1986) devised an elaboration of Polya's approach that promoted problem solving in adolescent learners with mathematical learning disabilities. The students were taught the following steps: Read the problems, paraphrase, graphically display known and unknown information, state known and unknown information, hypothesize solution methods, estimate answers, calculate answers, and check answers. There was clear improvement in the students' problem solving as a function of learning and using the problem solving strategies. When all of the data are considered (and there are hundreds of studies evaluating the effects of teaching Polya-like strategies), teaching the strategies has greater impact on older students than elementary-age learners (Hembree, 1992), with the effect size increasing from a small benefit in the elementary and middle school years to a large effect in the high school years. The impact on the problem solving of college students is moderate.

A group at Vanderbilt University has been successful, however, in developing mathematical problem solving strategies instruction that seems to have greater impact on elementary students, including students who struggle to learn mathematics (for a review, see Fuchs & Fuchs, 2003). The goal in this work has been to teach third-grade students mathematical problem-solving strategies that transfer to situations other than the training context. That is, the goal is for students to be able to apply a learned strategy to problems encountered on standardized tests or other novel situations, even when the problem differs superficially in a number of ways from training problems. The Vanderbilt team has succeeded in obtaining such transfer in several well-designed true experiments.

First, the students in the Vanderbilt studies received substantial instruction and practice with the specific types of problems. For example, one type of problem they learned about has a "bag problem structure." Students were informed that each bag of something (e.g., candy) had so many pieces. They were required to figure out how many bags would be required to obtain $N$ pieces. The instruction was intended to develop a problem schema (Gick & Holyoak, 1983; Mayer, 1982), so that students recognized "bag problems" quickly and applied the correct problem solving approach (i.e., dividing $N$ by the number of pieces in a single bag and rounding up to a whole bag; for example, for 32 pieces of candy with 10 pieces to a bag, four bags are required). Students worked cooperatively to practice solving problems consistent with the schema.

In addition to learning problem schema and associated solutions, teachers taught students the concept of transfer, for example by pointing out that babies first learn to drink from a toddler cup and then transfer their drinking skills to a real cup and eventually to a soda pop bottle. Transfer instruction also included information about superficial ways that problems can change. Thus, the format of the problem can change (e. g., multiple choice rather than short answer, information can be presented in graphics rather than text). Key words can change (e.g., rather than "bag," the word "package" might be used). The problem can ask an additional question (e.g., "If each bag of candy cost $4, how much money will you spend?"). The problem can be put in a larger problem solving context, with additional details to consider (e.g., "You have $37 and your friend has $12. . . . You also buy a hat that costs $15").

This instruction positively affected students' problem solving, especially when the problems were more similar to training problems (Fuchs et al., 2003b). Nonetheless, there was a clear effect of learning the problem-solving strategies even on the far transfer problems that differed substantially in superficial appearance from training problems (i.e., they differed with respect to all four aspects of superficiality as well as some other novel features). In general, the complete problem-solving instruction (i.e., instruction which included lots of practice and the most explicit emphasis on transfer) produced benefits for third graders of all abilities, including students with mathematical learning disabilities.

Fuchs and colleagues (2003a) evaluated whether problem-solving instruction might be more potent with students in third grade if instruction emphasized using the strategies in a more self-regulated fashion. The enriched treatment included more instruction about general strategic tactics during problem solving such as making sure answers make sense, lining up numbers correctly to do math operations, and checking computations. To promote self-regulation, students were taught to score their problem-solution attempts using an answer key that credited both completeness of the problem-solving process and obtaining the correct answer. Then, students charted how well they did on the problem. Before the next session, students reviewed their charted scores and set a goal of doing better than previously. In addition, students scored homework with respect to process and outcome, and reported to the class how they were transferring the problem-solving strategies they were learning across the school day. Both homework performance and reports of transfer were charted by the class as a whole. In short, self-regulation was encouraged by lots of goal setting and reflection on whether goals (including transfer) were obtained.

In general, the most complete condition produced greater transfer than occurred in the other conditions. However, there was much room for additional far transfer by the students. It was still impressive that both average-achieving and low-achieving math students who received the transfer and self-regulation instruction solved more than twice as many far transfer problems than control participants who did not receive the problem-solving instruction. The fairest reading of the data across Fuch's group (2003a, 2003b) studies is that they are making clear progress in understanding how to teach mathematical problem-solving strategies to elementary students with the goal of students being able to broadly apply the strategies (i.e., to transfer problems, including those differing in many ways from problems experienced during instruction).

## Scientific Reasoning, Argument Skills, and Strategies

Inhelder and Piaget (1958) hypothesized that scientific thinking is not possible until adolescents reach formal operations. Thus, if adolescents are given a large basket of balls differing in size (i.e., large or small), color (i.e., dark or light), surface texture (i.e., smooth or rough), and ridging (i.e., ridged, not ridged) and are asked to figure out what features determine whether a ball can be served accurately (presumably when hit with a racket or paddle), it would be expected that they could do such an analysis, whereas, according to Piaget's theory children would not be able to successfully complete the task. The adolescents would know how to do controlled comparisons by testing balls differing in single characteristics to evaluate the effects of the characteristics on servability. For example, serving a large ball and a small ball, both of which were also dark, smooth, and ridged, would provide information about the effect of size. Such an approach is an example of a controlled comparison strategy.

Kuhn et al. (1988) did work that revealed much about children and young adults' use of the scientific strategy of making controlled comparisons. Specifically, they carried out studies where they presented students in third grade through college with sets of balls that either did or did not serve well. The researchers asked the participants questions as they considered the sets of balls and attempted to figure out which features mattered in determining servability. Kuhn and associates also carried out versions of the study where they asked students

to generate evidence to figure out what determined servability (e.g., for example, asked which of the sixteen possible balls might be compared to provide definitive evidence on whether size makes a difference in servability).

These researchers found that the participants had a great deal of difficulty addressing such problems. For example, they overemphasized evidence consistent with their pet theories of variables affecting servability and they underemphasized evidence inconsistent with their favored positions. Although there was improvement in working with the evidence and drawing conclusions with increasing grade level, even adults struggled with such problems. There was a great deal of support in the study for Piaget and Inhelder's insight that children do not use a control of variables strategy. More positively, consistent with Piagetian expectations, with increasing age, there was more use of the control of variables strategy. However, even the college students fell far short of the ideal of a completely rational experimenter who systematically makes all the paired comparisons that can be revealing about the variables under consideration.

Kuhn (1991) extended her work to the development of argument skills by asking teens to generate arguments about important social problems: What causes prisoners to return to crime when they are released? What causes children to fail in school? What causes unemployment? Rather than recognizing that there are no absolute right or wrong answers to these questions, most of the participants had strong opinions that they felt were correct. Although they recognized that there are contrary perspectives, they had difficulty creating counterarguments to their own beliefs, which is a classic argumentative strategy. The also had difficulty rebutting counters to their own positions, another important argument strategy. In short, the teens in Kuhn's (1991) study did not seem to argue well. They did not use the argument strategies used by those highly skilled in argument.

Kuhn's results (see Kuhn, 2002a, 2002b, for a more complete discussion of all of the evidence produced by her group) were consistent with results produced in the 1970s and 1980s suggesting that children and adults often do not think in a completely rational or scientific way (e.g., Baron & Sternberg, 1987; Perkins, Lochhead, & Bishop, 1987). They do not use important controlled comparison and argument skills, the kinds of skills presumably required to function well in the modern, scientific world. More positively, Kuhn's group (1988, Study 5; also, Kuhn & Phelps, 1982) provided evidence that at least some students in the upper elementary level can acquire such strategies, if, while they are attempting scientific problem solving, they receive some hints from scaffolding adults about aspects of problems they should notice and how they could interpret the evidence.

A variety of educators in addition to Kuhn devised instructional programs to support the development of control of variables, argumentation, and other scientific thinking skills and strategies in response to the finding that critical and scientific thinking strategies are underdeveloped in students. For the most part, the early work on teaching such skills produced few convincing outcomes. When there were positive effects at all, they seemed small relative to the efforts required to produce them, and often failed to generalize beyond the training situation (for detailed reviews, see Chipman, Segal, & Glaser, 1985; Segal, Chipman, & Glaser, 1985). Over time, however, this picture has changed as a number of investigators have reported success in fostering higher-order thinking strategies using a range of methods (see Kuhn & Franklin, Chapter 22, this *Handbook,* this volume, for further description).

In the 1980s and early 1990s researchers interested in strategies hypothesized that students might develop or discover such strategies (e.g., making controlled comparisons) as they attempted to solve problems as part of well structured, adult supported exploration. In a problem-driven classroom such as this, the teacher monitors student interactions and learning, and scaffolds instruction by providing the hints and supports required for students to make progress (Wood et al., 1976). Student collaborative efforts were also considered important as part of effective instruction, with such interactions requiring students to evaluate the problem solutions they devised, including constructing argumentative defenses of their solutions (Champagne & Bunce, 1991). Science educators were impressed by both Vygotskian (e.g., Rogoff, 1990, 1998; Vygotsky, 1978) and Piagetian (e.g., Damon, 1990; Enright, Lapsley, & Levy, 1983; Furth, 1992; Furth & Kane, 1992; Kruger, 1993; Youniss & Damon, 1992) theoretical and empirical analyses that peer discussions promoted cognitive growth and improving reasoning skills.

This conception of learning became prominent in science education following analyses of effective science instruction characterized by teacher-supported, collaborative student problem solving. Effective science teachers scaffolded their students as they worked on scientific problems cooperatively. Students in these classrooms discussed and argued about alternative ways of thinking about the problems and generated a variety of solutions to scientific problems (Garnett & Tobin, 1988; Tobin & Fraser, 1990; Treagust, 1991). Researchers have validated the finding through observational studies that collaborative problem solving in classrooms seemed to stimulate students to think more and better (i.e., making better arguments) than occurred during more conventional instruction (e.g., Amigues, 1988; Brown & Campione, 1990; Hatano & Inagaki, 1991; Newman, Griffin, & Cole, 1989; Pizzini & Shepardson, 1992). Also, research in this area supports the discovery that problem-solving skills (e.g., making controlled comparisons) develop more certainly in classrooms taught by teachers who are skilled in scaffolding student experimentation and collaborative problem solving (for a review of data and thinking from that era, see Glynn & Duit, 1995; Glynn, Yeany, & Britton, 1991).

There were also teachers who were not so skilled with such instruction but attempted to do it anyway. Unfortunately, but not surprisingly the outcomes were not as attractive in their settings. For example, it is very easy for individual students to dominate collaborative problem solving and discussions in such classrooms. As a result, other students do very little work or thinking (e.g., Gayford, 1989; Hogan, Nastasi, & Pressley, 2000; Hogan & Pressley, 1997). Worse yet, sometimes the students who dominate the interactions lead their fellow students astray, with fellow students following the lead since they do not know enough about the topic to recognize the inaccurate thinking being offered up by the student leader (Basili & Sanford, 1991).

Once again, Kuhn and her colleagues carried out revealing studies about this possibility. They demonstrated that peer discussions about complicated and controversial issues can promote cognitive growth. Kuhn, Shaw, and Felton (1997) had students in seventh and eighth grade and community college students engage in five dyadic conversations with peers about the merits of capital punishment. Each conversation occurred with a different partner, so that the points of view and subsequent conversations varied from occasion to occasion. Control participants experienced the same pretests and posttests as the dyadic-conversation condition participants but did not participate in conversations. Compared to the control participants, the dyadic-conversations participants improved their argument skills from pretest to posttest. Participating in the dyadic conversations increased the number of arguments a participant offered on the posttest, the variety of arguments (e.g., offering arguments on both sides of the issue), and the sophistication of the arguments.

Kuhn and Udell (2003) studied argument skills in inner-city students in seventh and eighth grades in another true experiment. Both students who favored and opposed capital punishment were led to believe that they needed to prepare for a showdown debate on the issue. The control participants in the study (with both positions represented) experienced some dyadic practice in arguing about capital punishment, and worked with peers in the context of adult scaffolding, to generate and refine arguments in favor of their position on capital punishment. Participants in the experimental condition, again including students who favored and students who opposed capital punishment, received the same dyadic practice as controls but also participated in scaffolded, dyadic practice generating counterarguments to criticisms of their position, where they focused on rebuttals of opposing positions. These dyadic experiences in the experimental condition also provided opportunities to think and reason about mixed evidence.

Kuhn and Udell's treatment participants evidenced growth in argument from pretest to posttest, more than control participants. Particularly, they improved in making counterarguments with respect to the position on capital punishment that they opposed. The treatment participants also increased their knowledge of the topic of capital punishment as a function of the dyadic experiences in generating counterarguments. For evidence from another research group that children's argument skills improve with opportunities to practice argument, see recent work by Richard C. Anderson and his colleagues in the area of reading (Clark et al., 2003). In conclusion, children can acquire scientific thinking and argument strategies by experiencing such problems, at least when a more knowledgeable adult monitors student thinking efforts and arguments, and offers hints and general support to keep thinking and arguments on track.

A primary methodology used in Kuhn's work has been the microgenetic method. This methodology involves careful monitoring and analyses of changes in problem solving and reasoning as a function of practice (see Siegler, Chapter 11, this *Handbook,* this volume, for more detailed description of this approach). Basically, while performance improves in scientific reasoning and argument skills with practice and reflection, there is also a great deal of variability from trial to trial. Students normally employ a mix of strategies, with the particular mix varying from trial to trial, depending somewhat on the problem and the success of first attempts to solve it (e.g., Kuhn, 1995; Kuhn, Garcia-Mila, Zohar, & Andersen, 1995). Instead of learning to problem solve and argue following a rigid strategic procedure, participants learn by practicing how to size up problems and flexibly make decisions to improve problem solving. For example, in the work on argument about capital punishment, the participants reasoned differently from trial to trial, responding to the particular issues raised by the partner in the dyadic interaction.

## Conclusions

Children often do not use the strategies required to accomplish important academic tasks, such as reading, writing, mathematical and scientific problem solving, and argumentation, unless they are taught (or learn through discovery) strategies for doing so. In the past quarter century when researchers have taught children strategies matched to the demands of academic tasks and have provided scaffolded practice, they have consistently improved children's academic thinking and performances. Frequently, the effects of academic strategies instruction have been large. Researchers have obtained the most striking effects when they teach students to use a repertoire of strategies in a self-regulated fashion. Although academic strategies researchers have focused more on academically at-risk students, a broad range of elementary, middle school, and high school students seem able to learn and use strategies.

In recent years, our work has involved many observations of primary grade classrooms (e.g., Pressley, Allington, Wharton-McDonald, Block, & Morrow, 2001; Pressley et al., 2003), although this past year was spent in middle schools and a high school environment (e.g., Pressley, Raphael, Gallagher, & DiBella, 2004). What strikes us as we reflect on those experiences is that when we have observed academic strategies instruction, or problem solving and argument practice in schools, it usually has been much less complete and intense than the instruction and practice situations considered in this section. Given the clear need to improve reading, writing, mathematical, scientific problem-solving and argument skills (see the *National Assessment of Educational Progress*), it seems to us that it is time for the educator community to take the interventions reviewed in this section more seriously. We suggest using this work as a guide for restructuring education so that students are given more opportunities to learn the strategies that are used by excellent readers, writers, problem solvers, and rhetoricians.

## CONCLUDING REFLECTIONS ON STRATEGIES DEVELOPMENT

There have been 4 decades of serious research by developmentally oriented scholars about children's use of strategies to accomplish intellectual tasks. As a consequence, much is now known about the development of strategic competence, with evidence produced in both basic and applied areas of research. The field was enhanced by studying the development of both normal children and children with exceptionalities. We review here the most important conclusions that emerge from this work, and then reflect on issues that deserve more study.

### What Is Known about the Development of Strategic Competence

Although preschoolers are production deficient when given tasks that are very unfamiliar to them, preschoolers definitely can be strategic in familiar situations. Even 2-year-olds can demonstrate the use of simple memory strategies! For example, the children in De-Loache and colleague's (1985) study were definitely intentional as they looked and talked about the Big Bird doll when the goal was to remember where Big Bird was hidden. We now know that by the later preschool years, children often have several strategies that they can use when doing familiar tasks. As an example, when Siegler and Robinson (1982) asked 4- and 5-year-olds to add small numbers (1 + 3, 3 + 2, 2 + 4), they observed that sometimes children relied on their memories (i.e., they knew the answer), sometimes they counted on their fingers, sometimes they used their fingers but did not count aloud, and sometimes they just counted aloud without using their fingers.

Although the classical memory development researchers tended to focus on single strategies such as rehearsal for recall of lists of nonrelated items, categorization for lists of related items, elaboration for paired associations, there are typically multiple strategies that

can be deployed in a task situation such as those studied in the classical memory development studies. For example, there are a number of strategies that children can implement to attempt to learn paired associates. These strategies include simply saying the pairings once, saying pairings over and over, constructing verbal elaborations (i.e., embedding paired words or objects in sentences or stories), and constructing interactive images (e.g., imagining the referents of paired words or objects in interactive images). In fact, children often use different strategies over the course of learning a number of pairings (Pressley & Levin, 1977). The general point is that there are now numerous demonstrations that diversity in strategy use is more the norm than the exception. Many children have and use diverse strategies for various types of problem solving, different aspects of reading, and both the lower-order (e.g., spelling) and higher-order (e.g., revising) components in writing. Some of the strategies that children use are less effective than others. Therefore, one source of inefficiency is that children will sometimes mix effective and ineffective strategies rather than simply using the most efficient and effective approach to a task.

The evidence is overwhelming that many strategies production deficiencies can be overcome if children are provided with strategies instruction. This is an important point since strategy production deficiencies are very common throughout childhood and into adulthood (e.g., even many adult readers are not nearly as strategically active as the best adult readers). Such production deficiencies are more prevalent in populations at risk for failing to achieve (e.g., very young children, children with mental retardation, students with learning disabilities). There have been many examples summarized in this chapter of strategies that can be taught to a wide range of children.

The early work on memory strategies instruction, going back to Flavell's pioneering efforts, involved little more than telling the child what process to execute and having them do it. Such an approach produced little enduring change since students did not continue to use the memory strategies taught, even in situations very similar to the teaching situation. Over the years, strategies instruction became more complex, as it has been informed by basic theoretical analyses of cognitive strategic functioning, especially in the area of memory strategies. Thus, contemporary instruction takes into account all of the cognitive components that interact with and determine strategic functioning. Such instruction has the following characteristics:

- Students are taught the strategies used by capable thinkers to accomplish tasks, often a repertoire of a few strategies that are used in coordination.

- Instruction begins with explanations and modeling of strategies. Teachers then provide supported practice of the strategies being learned. Practice continues until the students can carry out the procedures efficiently (i.e., using much less conscious capacity than when they first attempt the strategies). When a strategy can be carried out efficiently, it frees up conscious capacity that can be used to articulate the execution of the strategy with other components.

- Strategy practice often continues for a long time in order to get to the point that the strategy can be implemented with little effort. This permits opportunities for participants to apply the strategies being learned to a variety of materials and in a variety of situations. It also allows students opportunities to discover important metacognitive information, including where and when to use the strategies being learned and how to adapt the strategies to a variety of situations. Such metacognitive knowledge about strategies is essential if the learner is to continue using the strategies, both in situations where they were trained and new situations where the strategies are potentially applicable (Pressley, Borkowski, & O'Sullivan, 1984, 1985).

- Many strategies depend on the learner's world knowledge, with use of relevant prior knowledge encouraged as part of strategies execution. If students are able to get by without using a strategy because of a well-developed knowledge base, use of the knowledge base is encouraged. Thus, the child who knows a word by sight is not encouraged to sound out the word. A child who knows a math problem (e.g., 7 − 3 + ?) as a fact is not encouraged to compute the answer. Encouraging reliance on prior knowledge when it is available is important because strategies execution is short-term capacity demanding. The less cognitive capacity eaten up by unnecessary strategies execution, the more capacity left over for necessary strategies execution and coordination with other cognitive components.

- The most extensive contemporary cognitive strategies instruction is designed to promote long-term, self-regulated use of the strategies, by including metacognitive information in instruction. This includes information about when and where to use the strategies, as well as instruction to monitor the effectiveness of strategies. It also includes motivational information about the positive effects produced by the strategy, and reflections on performance before and after strategy use. There is clear expectation that students should attempt to transfer the strategies they are learning.

Although many children need instruction of at least some strategies, many children also discover many strategies on their own. Much has been learned about how they do so. A popular analytical strategy in this work has been the microgenetic design, where participants experience many trials doing a type of task with their strategies use and performances across trials analyzed (Siegler, Chapter 11, this *Handbook,* this volume). For example, the research of Kuhn and of Anderson, and their respective associates has focused on how argument strategies and skills improve as a function of arguing. Kuhn and her associates have also been studying how scientific reasoning strategies shift with practice. These studies make clear that while upper-elementary students shift their strategies use as they work and reflect on scientific problems requiring inductive reasoning (Kuhn & Pearsall, 1998, 2000; Pearsall, 1999), their initial use of strategies does not always produce great benefit. This finding is reminiscent of the utilization deficiencies reported sometimes in basic memory situations (e.g., Miller & Seier, 1994). Moreover, use of potentially efficient strategies is variable, with trial-to-trial changes in strategies deployment often observed in microgenetic studies.

It is not surprising that students' progress in using potentially potent strategies is often variable and not always beneficial. One of the most robust findings in the metamemory literature is that strategy use greatly depends on the understanding that the strategy produces performance advantage. This finding has been established in a number of very well-designed experiments carried out in the 1970s and early 1980s (Pressley, Borkowski, & O'Sullivan, 1984, 1985). When learners experience the advantages produced by a strategy, it can heighten their commitment to using the strategy in the future. This finding was also established in well-controlled experiments (Pressley, Levin, & Ghatala, 1984).

That is, when learners discover a strategy is effective, that discovery makes a difference in future use of strategies. Learner discoveries make a difference in strategy acquisition.

In short, there is growing evidence that effective strategies instruction requires development and articulation of a number of cognitive components. This contrasts with hypotheses of the past that focused on single factors in thinking and learning. Some of these hypotheses present significant challenges to the idea that teaching strategies should be emphasized at all. One version of this argument holds that thinking is much more about applying nonstrategic prior knowledge to tasks than using strategies (Anderson & Pearson, 1984; Chi, 1978). This emphasis on prior knowledge as the prime mover in thinking has given way to the understanding that world knowledge and strategies seem to work in concert in powerful thinking, whether the learner is faced with a memory task (Pressley, Borkowski, & Schneider, 1987) or the academic tasks common in school, from problem-solving (e.g., Schoenfeld, 1985, 1987, 1992), to reading (Pressley & Afflerbach, 1995) to writing (Flower, 1998).

Another long-held belief is that somehow discovery learning and discovery of strategies, in particular, result in better learning and more complete understanding than other approaches (e.g., Kohlberg & Mayer, 1972). This is so despite a very long history of discovery approaches producing less complete learning and understanding than more direct teaching (e.g., Mayer, 2004; Shulman & Keislar, 1966). That said, children can and probably do learn many important skills through discovery (e.g., Siegler, 1996). It is certainly possible to devise guided discovery situations where students are encouraged to reflect on their successes and failures as they work in a domain. This has occurred in some of the situations Kuhn (2002a, 2002b) and others have studied (Lehrer & Schauble, 2000). Good discovery learning occurs as children interact with each other, parents, and other cultural elements as they live and develop in the world (Rogoff, 2003).

The people in children's worlds may provide them with a great deal of metacognitive input by providing instruction about where and when to use skills, as well as how to adapt strategies and skills children have and are acquiring. Calls for direct instruction of strategies and skills with minimal metacognitive embellishment persist (Adams & Carnine, 2003) in spite of well-controlled demonstrations that metacognitive-promoting instruction increases the effectiveness of strategies instruction (e.g., Elliott-Faust & Pressley, 1986; O'Sullivan & Pressley, 1984). A positive outgrowth of this debate is strategies instruction, and teaching in general, that combines direct instruction with metacognitive embellishment through explanations and teacher-scaffolded opportunities for students to practice strategies during real problem-solving, reading, and writing (e.g., Duffy, 2003).

In short, there are some extreme positions about the role of strategies and prior knowledge in thinking, as well as extreme positions about how to do strategies instruction (i.e., focusing only on the strategies without concern for prior knowledge or metacognitive information about when and where to use strategies), complemented by extreme positions about leaving strategies to the child's discovery. In contrast, we emphasize that more balanced views have developed as research on strategies instruction has continued over the past 4 decades. We have made the case that the most effective strategies instruction includes direct explanation and modeling of strategies, provision of metacognitive information, opportunities to discover strategies during practice, efforts to motivate strategy use by assuring students experience benefits from strategy use, and emphasis on the mixing of strategies use and prior knowledge in solving problems, reading, and writing (see Alexander, Graham, & Harris, 1998).

## Much Remains to Be Learned about Strategies Instruction

The formal scientific evidence is growing that supports our claim that children can be taught cognitive strategies that serve important academic competencies in ways that result in self-regulated, long-term use, and transfer of the strategies. The effects of strategies instruction are often quite large. This provides plenty of motivation for additional work on cognitive strategies instruction in the K–12 curricula. Also, the work of Deshler and his colleagues (Deshler, Ellis, & Lenz, 1996), as well as others who have provided cognitive strategies instruction to disadvantaged learners, is inspiring. Their research and applications have affected hundreds of thousands of students with learning disabilities. These successful educational efforts have been developed through clinical efforts that greatly resemble the instruction developed by the meticulously careful research community. As we reflect on their implementation successes to date, we think that an important research direction is determining how to disseminate such instruction more broadly, as well as to identify parts of the curriculum that might still be addressed by strategies instruction that could be developed in the future.

A great strength of the strategies literature is that much of it has been very analytical, producing nontrivial, not-always-obvious understandings about how strategies function and develop. Still, as we read this literature, again and again, we found ourselves wanting more. For example, Kuhn's (2002a) conception of strategy growth through discovery and reflection prompted us to think hard about a number of issues. Kuhn posits that as a child works in a problem domain, she or he has initial theories about what might work to achieve the goal of solving the problem. The learner tries the strategy or strategies that are initially hypothesized to work, noting whether the problem was solved, perhaps experiencing peer or adult responses to the problem-solving attempt and outcome it produced. This experience with feedback increases understanding of the situation, perhaps resulting in a new understanding about the strategies tried, or even insights about new strategies that might be applied to the situation. These new understandings inform subsequent attempts to perform the task, with additional outcomes and feedback increasing understanding further. Over a number of trials gradual increases in strategic knowledge and understanding of the task situation take place.

As we contemplated Kuhn's work, we found ourselves wanting additional research detailing more of the strategies discovered, as well as the meta-cognitive understandings that are constructed by students. We also found ourselves wanting to know just how strategic and metacognitive components interact. We were intrigued that Kuhn is finding evidence for utilization deficiencies. We wonder why participants produce strategies that seem like they should work in the situation, but do not. As theorists and researchers interested in instruction, we also wondered what might happen if more teaching occurred as the children experimented. We assume their strategy and metacognitive growth would be accelerated, but is there a downside to such learning through teaching compared to discovery? In short, as we reflected on this contribution, we found ourselves wanting to know much more about strategies—more about strategy functioning, strategy development, develop-ment of metacognition about strategies, and strategies instruction through discovery. We add that we experienced this sense of only scratching the surface of strategies functioning and development at many points during the writing of this chapter. We hope this chapter will serve as an invitation to researchers to think about doing more work on strategies and their development. The research successes to date make clear that this is an area that can be illuminated by research. It takes little time with this literature to recognize there are many additional paths that could be followed that might lead to substantial theoretical and pragmatic understandings about how children can learn how to tackle many tasks in their world more efficiently and effectively through invention and use of strategies.

Given the importance of the academic tasks that have been studied by contemporary researchers interested in strategies instruction, we do not expect a massive exodus from study of problem solving, scientific reasoning, argument, reading, or writing in favor of a return to basic work on memory. That said, we are impressed that virtually all of these academic tasks include memory components. However, this research includes little to no study about how memory functions in these domains, or how learners might be taught so that they make the best use of their limited short-term capacity and seemingly unlimited long-term capacity (i.e., their world knowledge). For example, consider what happened when Graham (1990) prompted elementary students with writing disabilities to search their long-term memories for more information to include in essays they were writing. He found that the length and quality of the essays improved. We suspect there are many other ways in which an improved use of memory might contribute to students' academic achievements and development. Researchers who want to continue to study memory might find it exciting to conduct their work in the context of more authentic academic tasks than the memory tasks that predominated in the 1960s and 1970s. Such work has the potential for success to do much to improve the education of children, including many with intellectual disabilities. That memory strategies instruction all but disappeared in the past decade and a half does not mean it cannot reappear. It seems especially appropriate to develop a new generation of memory strategies development work as part of the development of strategies instruction that serves the needs of children as they tackle the academic demands that people ages three through adulthood face. If, as Kuhn suggested, memory development is on the endangered topics list, we think it time that researchers rise to the challenge of getting it off the list and back in the major journals (albeit in a form enriched by what we now know about cognitive development) and on the minds of everyone who is concerned with improving children's cognitive performances.

# REFERENCES

Adams, G., & Carnine, D. (2003). Direct instruction. In H. L. Swanson, K. R. Harris, & S. T. Graham (Eds.), *Handbook of learning disabilities* (pp. 403–416). New York: Guilford Press.

Alexander, J., & Schwanenflugel, P. J. (1994). Strategy regulation: The role of intelligence, metacognitive attribution, and knowledge base. *Developmental Psychology, 30,* 709–723.

Alexander, P. A., Graham, S., & Harris, K. R. (1998). A perspective on strategy research: Prospect and progress. *Educational Psychology Review, 10,* 129–154.

Allik, J. P., & Siegel, A. W. (1976). The use of the cumulative rehearsal strategy: A developmental study. *Journal of Experimental Child Psychology, 21,* 316–327.

Almasi, J. F. (2003). *Teaching strategic processes in reading.* New York: Guilford Press.

Amigues, R. (1988). Peer interaction in solving physics problems: Sociocognitive confrontation and metacognitive aspects. *Journal of Experimental Child Psychology, 45,* 141–158.

Anderson, J. R. (1980). *Cognitive psychology and its implications.* San Francisco: Freeman.

Anderson, J. R. (1983). *The architecture of cognition.* Cambridge, MA: Harvard University Press.

Anderson, R. C., & Pearson, P. D. (1984). A schema-theoretic view of basic processes in reading. In P. D. Pearson (Ed.), *Handbook of reading research* (pp. 255–291). New York: Longman.

Anderson, V. (1992). A teacher development project in transactional strategy instruction for teachers of severely reading-disabled adolescents. *Teaching and Teacher Education, 8,* 391–403.

Anderson, V., & Roit, M. (1993). Planning and implementing collaborative strategy instruction for delayed readers in grades 6–10. *Elementary School Journal, 94,* 121–137.

Armbruster, B. B., Anderson, T. H., & Ostertag, J. (1987). Does text structure/summarization instruction facilitate learning from expository text? *Reading Research Quarterly, 22,* 331–346.

Atkinson, R. C., & Shiffrin, R. M. (1968). Human memory: A proposed system and its control processes. In K. W. Spence & J. T. Spence (Eds.), *Advances in the psychology of learning and motivation research and theory* (Vol. 2, pp. 89–195). New York: Academic Press.

Baddeley, A. (1987). *Working memory.* Oxford, England: Clarendon Press.

Baker-Ward, L., Ornstein, P. A., & Holden, D. J. (1984). The expression of memorization in early childhood. *Journal of Experimental Child Psychology, 37,* 555–575.

Barclay, C. R. (1979). The executive control of mnemonic activity. *Journal of Experimental Child Psychology, 27,* 262–276.

Baron, J. B., & Sternberg, R. J. (1987). *Teaching thinking skills: Theory and practice.* New York: Henry Holt.

Barrouillet, P., & Fayol, M. (1998). From algorithmic computing to direct retrieval: Evidence from number and alphabetic arithmetic in children and adults. *Memory and Cognition, 26,* 355–368.

Basili, P. A., & Sanford, J. P. (1991). Conceptual change strategies and cooperative group work in chemistry. *Journal of Research in Science Teaching, 28,* 293–304.

Bauer, P. J. (2003). Early memory development. In U. Goswami (Ed.), *Blackwell handbook of childhood cognitive development* (pp. 127–146). Oxford, England: Blackwell.

Bauer, P. J., Wenner, J. A., Dropik, P. L., & Wewerka, S. (2000). Parameters of remembering and forgetting in the transition from infancy to early childhood. *Monographs of the Society for Research in Child Development, 65* (4, Serial No. 263).

Bauer, R. H. (1977a). Memory processes in children with learning disabilities. *Journal of Experimental Child Psychology, 24,* 415–430.

Bauer, R. H. (1977b). Short-term memory in learning disabled and nondisabled children. *Bulletin of the Psychonomic Society, 10,* 128–130.

Beal, C. R., & Fleisig, W. E. (1987, March). *Preschooler's preparation for retrieval in object relocation tasks.* Paper presented at the biennial meeting of the Society for Research in Child Development, Baltimore, MD.

Bebko, J. M., Bell, M. A., Metcalfe-Haggert, A., & McKinnon, E. (1998). Language proficiency and the production of spontaneous rehearsal in children who are deaf. *Journal of Experimental Child Psychology, 68,* 51–69.

Bebko, J. M., Lacasse, M. A., Turk, H., & Oyen, A. S. (1992). Recall performance on a central-incidental memory task by profoundly deaf children. *American Annals of the Deaf, 137,* 271–277.

Bebko, J. M., & McKinnon, E. E. (1990). The language experience of deaf children: Its relation to spontaneous rehearsal in a memory task. *Child Development, 61,* 1744–1752.

Bebko, J. M., & Metcalfe-Haggert, A. (1997). Deafness, language skills, and rehearsal: A model for the development of a memory strategy. *Journal of Deaf Studies and Deaf Education, 2,* 131–139.

Bebko, J. M., & Ricciuti, C. (2000). Executive functioning and memory strategy use in children with autism: The influence of task constraints on spontaneous rehearsal. *Autism, 4,* 299–320.

Belmont, J. C., & Butterfield, E. C. (1977). The instructional approach to developmental cognitive research. In R. V. Kail & J. W. Hagen (Eds.), *Perspectives on the development of memory and cognition* (pp. 437–481). Hillsdale, NJ: Erlbaum.

Belmont, J. M., Butterfield, E. C., & Ferretti, R. P. (1982). To secure transfer of training: Instruct self-management skills. In D. K. Detterman & R. J. Sternberg (Eds.), *How and how much can intelligence be increased?* (pp. 147–154). Norwood, NJ: Ablex.

Bereiter, C., & Bird, M. (1985). Use of thinking aloud in identification and teaching of reading comprehension strategies. *Cognition and Instruction, 2,* 131–156.

Berkowitz, S. J. (1986). Effects of instruction in text organization on sixth-grade students' memory for expository reading. *Reading Research Quarterly, 21,* 161–178.

Bjorklund, D. F., Miller, P. H., Coyle, T. R., & Slawinski, J. L. (1997). Instructing children to use memory strategies: Evidence of utilization deficiencies in memory training studies. *Developmental Review, 17,* 411–441.

Bjorklund, D. F., Muir-Broaddus, J. E., & Schneider, W. (1990). The role of knowledge in the development of strategies. In D. F. Bjorklund (Ed.), *Children's strategies: Contemporary views of cognitive development* (pp. 93–128). Hillsdale, NJ: Erlbaum.

Blachowicz, C., & Ogle, D. (2001). *Reading comprehension: Strategies for independent learners.* New York: Guilford Press.

Black, M. M., & Rollins, H. A. (1982). The effects of instructional variables on young children's organization and free recall. *Journal of Experimental Child Psychology, 33,* 1–19.

Blackman, L. S., & Lin, A. (1984). Generalization training in the educable mentally retarded: Intelligence and its educability revisited. In P. H. Brooks, R. Sperber, & C. McCauley (Eds.), *Learning and cognition in the mentally retarded* (pp. 237–263). Hillsdale, NJ: Erlbaum.

Block, C. C., Gambrell, L., & Pressley, M. (Eds.). (2002). *Improving comprehension instruction: Rethinking research, theory, and classroom practice.* San Francisco: Jossey-Bass.

Block, C. C., & Pressley, M. (Eds.). (2002). *Comprehension instruction.* New York: Guilford Press.

Bloom, P. (2000). *How children learn the meanings of words.* Cambridge, MA: MIT Press.

Borkowski, J. G., Carr, M., Rellinger, E. A., & Pressley, M. (1990). Self-regulated strategy use: Interdependence of metacognition, attributions, and self-esteem. In B. F. Jones (Ed.), *Dimensions of thinking: Review of research* (pp. 53–92). Hillsdale, NJ: Erlbaum.

Borkowski, J. G., & Cavanaugh, J. C. (1979). Maintenance and generalization of skills and strategies by the retarded. In N. R. Ellis (Ed.), *Handbook of mental deficiency* (2nd ed., pp. 569–618). Hillsdale, NJ: Erlbaum.

Borkowski, J. G., & Kurtz, B. E. (1987). Metacognition and executive control. In J. G. Borkowski & J. D. Day (Eds.), *Cognition in special children: Comparative approaches to retardation, learning disabilities, and giftedness* (pp. 123–152). Norwood, NJ: Ablex.

Bousfield, W. A. (1953). The occurrence of clustering in the recall of randomly arranged associates. *Journal of Genetic Psychology, 49,* 229–240.

Broadbent, D. E. (1958). *Perception and communication.* New York: Pergamon Press.

Brown, A. L. (1974). The role of strategic behavior in retardate memory. In N. R. Ellis (Ed.), *International review of research in mental retardation* (Vol. 7, pp. 55–104). New York: Academic Press.

Brown, A. L. (1978). Knowing when, where, and how to remember: A problem of metacognition. In R. Glaser (Ed.), *Advances in instructional psychology* (Vol. 4, pp. 77–165). Hillsdale, NJ: Erlbaum.

Brown, A. L., Bransford, J. D., Ferrara, R. A., & Campione, J. C. (1983). Learning, remembering, and understanding. In P. H. Mussen (Series Ed.) & J. H. Flavell, & E. M. Markman (Vol. Ed.), *Handbook of child psychology: Vol. 3. Cognitive development* (4th ed., pp. 77–166). New York: Wiley.

Brown, A. L., & Campione, J. C. (1978). Permissible inferences from cognitive training studies in developmental research. *Quarterly Newsletter of the Institute for Comparative Human Behavior, 2,* 46–53.

Brown, A. L., & Campione, J. C. (1990). Interactive learning environments and the teaching of science and mathematics. In M. Gardner, J. G. Greeno, F. Reif, A. H. Schoenfeld, A. DiSessa, & E. Stage (Eds.), *Toward a scientific practice of science education* (pp. 111–139). Hillsdale, NJ: Erlbaum.

Brown, A. L., & Day, J. D. (1983). Macrorules for summarizing texts: The development of expertise. *Journal of Verbal Learning and Verbal Behavior, 22,* 1–14.

Brown, A. L., & DeLoache, J. S. (1978). Skills, plans, and self-regulation. In R. S. Siegler (Ed.), *Children's thinking: What develops?* (pp. 3–36). Hillsdale, NJ: Erlbaum.

Brown, R., Pressley, M., Van Meter, P., & Schuder, T. (1996). A quasi-experimental validation of transactional strategies instruction with low-achieving second grade readers. *Journal of Educational Psychology, 88,* 18–37.

Burkell, J., Schneider, B., & Pressley, M. (1990). Mathematics. In M. Pressley & Associates. *Cognitive strategy instruction that really improves children's academic performance* (pp. 147–177). Cambridge, MA: Brookline Books.

Camilli, G., Vargas, S., & Yurecko, M. (2003). Teaching children to read: The fragile link between science and federal education policy. *Education Policy Analysis Archives, 11*(15). Retrieved January 29, 2004, from http://epaa.asu.edu/epaa/v11n15.

Campione, J. C., & Brown, A. L. (1977). Memory and metamemory development in educable retarded children. In R. V. Kail & J. W. Hagen (Eds.), *Perspectives on the development of memory and cognition* (pp. 367–406). Hillsdale, NJ: Erlbaum.

Campione, J. C., Brown, A. L., Ferrara, R. A., Jones, R. S., & Steinberg, E. (1985). Breakdowns in flexible use of information: Intelligence-related difference in transfer following equivalent learning performance. *Intelligence, 9,* 297–315.

Cariglia-Bull, T., & Pressley, M. (1990). Short-term memory differences between children predict imagery effects when sentences are read. *Journal of Experimental Child Psychology, 49,* 384–398.

Carver, L. J., & Bauer, P. J. (1999). When the event is more than the sum of its parts: Long-term recall of event sequences by 9-month-old infants. *Memory, 7,* 147–174.

Carver, L. J., & Bauer, P. J. (2001). The dawning of the past: The emergence of long-term explicit memory in infancy. *Journal of Experimental Psychology: General, 130,* 726–745.

Ceci, S. J., Fitneva, S. A., & Gilstrap, L. L. (2003). Memory development and eyewitness memory. In A. Slater & G. Bremner (Eds.), *An introduction to developmental psychology* (pp. 283–310). Malden, MA: Blackwell.

Chall, J. S. (1967). *Learning to read: The great debate.* New York: McGraw-Hill.

Champagne, A. B., & Bunce, D. M. (1991). Learning-theory-based science teaching. In S. M. Glynn, R. H. Yeany, & B. K. Britton (Eds.), *The psychology of learning science* (pp. 21–41). Hillsdale, NJ: Erlbaum.

Charles, R. I., & Lester, F. K., Jr. (1984). An evaluation of a process-oriented instructional program in mathematical problem solving in grades 5 and 7. *Journal for Research in Mathematics Education, 15,* 15–34.

Chi, M. T. H. (1978). Knowledge structure and memory development. In R. S. Siegler (Ed.), *Children's thinking: What develops?* (pp. 73–96). Hillsdale, NJ: Erlbaum.

Chipman, S. F., Segal, J. W., & Glaser, R. (1995). *Thinking and learning skills: Vol. 2. Research and open questions.* Hillsdale, NJ: Erlbaum.

Clark, A. M., Anderson, R. C., Kuo, L. J., Kim, I. H., Archodidou, A., & Nguyen-Jahiel, K. (2003). Collaborative reasoning: Expanding ways for children to talk and think in school. *Educational Psychology Review, 15,* 181–198.

Cole, M., Frankel, F., & Sharp, D. (1971). Development of free recall in children. *Developmental Psychology, 4,* 109–123.

Collins, C. (1991). Reading instruction that increases thinking abilities. *Journal of Reading, 34,* 510–516.

Cornoldi, C., Barbieri, A., Gaiani, C., & Zocchi, S. (1999). Strategic memory deficits in attention deficit disorder with hyperactivity participants: The role of executive processes. *Developmental Neuropsychology, 15,* 53–71.

Cowan, N. (1995). *Attention and memory: An integrated framework.* Oxford, England: University Press.

Cowan, N. (2002). Childhood development of working memory: An examination of two basic parameters. In P. Graf & N. Ohta (Eds.), *Lifespan development of human memory* (pp. 39–57). Cambridge, MA: MIT Press.

Coyle, T. R., Read, L. E., Gaultney, J. F., & Bjorklund, D. F. (1998). Giftedness and variability in strategic processing on a multitrial memory task: Evidence for stability in gifted cognition. *Learning and Individual Differences, 10,* 273–290.

Crowley, K., & Siegler, R. S. (1999). Explanation and generalization in children's strategy learning. *Child Development, 70,* 304–316.

Cunningham, A. E., & Stanovich, K. E. (1997). Early reading acquisition and its relation to reading experience and ability. *Developmental Psychology, 33,* 934–945.

Cuvo, A. J. (1975). Developmental differences in rehearsal and free recall. *Journal of Experimental Child Psychology, 19,* 265–278.

Daehler, M. W., & Greco, C. (1985). Memory in very young children. In M. Pressley & C. J. Brainerd (Eds.), *Cognitive learning and memory in children: Progress in cognitive developmental research* (pp. 49–79). New York: Springer-Verlag.

Dallago, M. L. L., & Moely, B. E. (1980). Free recall in boys of normal and poor reading levels as a function of task manipulations. *Journal of Experimental Child Psychology, 30,* 62–78.

Damon, W. (1990). Social relations and children's thinking skills. In D. Kuhn (Ed.), *Contributions to human development: Vol. 2. Developmental perspectives on teaching and learning thinking skills* (pp. 95–107). Basel, Switzerland: Karger.

DeCasper, A. J., & Spence, M. J. (1986). Prenatal maternal speech influences newborns' perceptions of speech sounds. *Infant Behavior and Development, 9,* 133–150.

De La Paz, S., Swanson, P., & Graham, S. (1998). The contribution of executive control to the revising of students with writing and learning difficulties. *Journal of Educational Psychology, 90,* 448–460.

DeLoache, J. S. (1980). Naturalistic studies of memory for object location in very young children. In M. Perlmutter (Ed.), *New directions for child development: Children's memory* (pp. 17–32). San Francisco: Jossey-Bass.

DeLoache, J. S., Cassidy, D. J., & Brown, A. L. (1985). Precursors of mnemonic strategies in very young children's memory. *Child Development, 56,* 125–137.

DeMarie, D., & Ferron, J. (2003). Capacity, strategies, and metamemory: Tests of a three-factor model of memory development. *Journal of Experimental Child Psychology, 84,* 167–193.

Dempster, F. N. (1981). Memory span: Sources of individual and developmental differences. *Psychological Bulletin, 89,* 63–100.

Deshler, D. D., Ellis, E. S., & Lenz, B. K. (1996). *Teaching adolescents with learning disabilities: Strategies and methods.* Denver, CO: Love.

Deshler, D. D., & Schumaker, J. B. (1988). An instructional model for teaching students how to learn. In J. L. Graden, J. E. Zins, & M. J. Curtis (Eds.), *Alternative educational delivery systems: Enhancing instructional options for all students* (pp. 391–411). Washington, DC: National Association of School Psychologists.

Deshler, D. D., & Schumaker, J. B. (1993). Strategy mastery by at-risk students: Not a simple matter. *Elementary School Journal, 94,* 153–167.

Duffy, G. G. (2003). *Explaining reading: A resource for teaching concepts, skills, and strategies.* New York: Guilford Press.

Duffy, G. G., Roehler, L. R., Sivan, E., Rackliffe, G., Book, C., Meloth, M., et al. (1987). Effects of explaining the reasoning associated with using reading strategies. *Reading Research Quarterly, 22,* 347–368.

Dunning, D., Johnson, K., Ehrlinger, J., & Kruger, J. (2003). Why people fail to recognize their own incompetence. *Current Directions in Psychological Science, 12,* 83–87.

Eckenrode, J., Izzo, C., & Campa-Muller, M. (2003). Early intervention and family support programs. In F. Jacobs, D. Wertlieb, & R. M. Lerner (Eds.), *Handbook of applied developmental science* (Vol. 2, pp. 161–195). Mahwah, NJ: Erlbaum.

Elliott-Faust, D. J., & Pressley, M. (1986). Self-controlled training of comparison strategies increase children's comprehension monitoring. *Journal of Educational Psychology, 78,* 27–32.

Ellis, N. R. (Ed.). (1979). *Handbook of mental deficiency: Psychological theory and research.* Hillsdale, NJ: Erlbaum.

Englert, C. S., Raphael, T. E., Anderson, L. M., Anthony, H. M., & Stevens, D. D. (1991). Making strategies and self-talk visible: Writing instruction in regular and special education classrooms. *American Educational Research Journal, 28,* 337–372.

Enright, R. D., Lapsley, D. K., & Levy, V. M. (1983). Moral education strategies. In M. Pressley & J. R. Levin (Eds.), *Cognitive strategy research: Educational applications* (pp. 43–83). New York: Springer-Verlag.

Fantz, R. L. (1956). A method for studying early visual development. *Perceptual and Motor Skills, 6,* 13–15.

Feldman, D. H. (1982). *Developmental approaches to giftedness and creativity.* San Francisco: Jossey-Bass.

Fivush, R. (1994). Constructing narrative, emotion, and self in parent-child conversations about the past. In U. Neisser & R. Fivush (Eds.), *The remembering self: Construction and accuracy in the self-narrative* (pp. 136–157). Cambridge, England: Cambridge University Press.

Fivush, R. (1997). Event memory in early childhood. In N. Cowan (Ed.), *The development of memory in childhood* (pp. 139–161). Hove, England: Psychology Press.

Flavell, J. H. (1970). Developmental studies of mediated memory. In H. W. Reese & L. P. Lipsitt (Eds.), *Advances in child development and behavior* (Vol. 5, pp. 181–211). New York: Academic Press.

Flavell, J. H. (1979). Metacognition and cognitive monitoring: A new area of cognitive-developmental inquiry. *American Psychologist, 34,* 906–911.

Flavell, J. H. (1981). Cognitive monitoring. In W. P. Dickson (Ed.), *Children's oral communication skills* (pp. 35–60). New York: Academic Press.

Flavell, J. H., Beach, D. H., & Chinsky, J. M. (1966). Spontaneous verbal rehearsal in a memory task as a function of age. *Child Development, 37,* 283–299.

Fletcher, K. L., Huffman, L. F., & Bray, N. W. (2003). Effects of verbal and physical prompts on external strategy use in children with and without mild mental retardation. *American Journal on Mental Retardation, 108,* 245–256.

Fletcher, K. L., Huffman, L. F., Bray, N. W., & Grupe, L. A. (1998). The use of the microgenetic method with children with disabilities: Discovering competence. *Early Education and Development, 9,* 357–373.

Flower, L. (1998). *Casebook: Writers at work.* Independence, KY: International Thomson.

French, B. F., Zentall, S. S., & Bennett, D. (2001). Short-term memory of children with and without characteristics of attention deficit hyperactivity disorder. *Learning and Individual Differences, 13,* 205–225.

Freud, S. (1963). Three essays on the theory of sexuality. In J. Strachey (Ed.), *The standard edition of the complete works of Freud* (Vol. 7, pp. 135–143). London: Hogarth Press.

Fuchs, L. S., & Fuchs, D. (2003). Enhancing the mathematical problem solving of students. In H. L. Swanson, K. R. Harris, & S. Graham (Eds.), *Handbook of learning disabilities* (pp. 306–322). New York: Guilford Press.

Fuchs, L. S., Fuchs, D., Prentice, K., Burch, M., Hamlett, C. L., Owen, R., et al. (2003a). Enhancing third-grade students' mathematical problem solving with self-regulated learning strategies. *Journal of Educational Psychology, 95,* 306–315.

Fuchs, L. S., Fuchs, D., Prentice, K., Burch, M., Hamlett, C. L., Owen, R., et al. (2003b). Explicitly teaching for transfer: Effects on third-grade students' mathematical problem solving. *Journal of Educational Psychology, 95,* 293–305.

Furth, H. (1992). The developmental origins of human societies. In H. Beilin & P. Pufall (Eds.), *Piaget's theory: Prospects and possibilities* (pp. 251–266). Hillsdale, NJ: Erlbaum.

Furth, H., & Kane, S. (1992). Children constructing society: A new perspective on children at play. In H. McGurk (Ed.), *Childhood social development* (pp. 149–173). Hove, England: Erlbaum.

Garnett, P. J., & Tobin, K. (1988). Teaching for understanding: Exemplary practice in high school chemistry. *Journal of Research in Science Teaching, 26,* 1–14.

Gayford, C. (1989). A contribution to a methodology for teaching and assessment of group problem-solving in biology among 15 year old pupils. *Journal of Biological Education, 23,* 193–198.

Gaultney, J. F. (1998). Utilization deficiencies among children with learning disabilities. *Learning and Individual Differences, 10,* 13–28.

Gaultney, J. F., Bjorklund, D. F., & Goldstein, D. (1996). To be young, gifted, and strategic: Advantages for memory performance. *Journal of Experimental Child Psychology, 61,* 43–66.

Gaultney, J. F., Bjorklund, D. F., & Schneider, W. (1992). The role of children's expertise in a strategic memory task. *Contemporary Educational Psychology, 17,* 244–257.

Geary, D. C. (2003). Learning disabilities in arithmetic: Problem-solving differences and cognitive deficits. In H. L. Swanson, K. R. Harris, & S. Graham (Eds.), *Handbook of learning disabilities* (pp. 199–212). New York: Guilford Press.

Geary, D. C., & Brown, S. C. (1991). Cognitive addition: Strategy choice and speed-of-processing differences in gifted, normal, and mathematically disabled children. *Developmental Psychology, 27,* 398–406.

Gersten, R., & Baker, S. (2001). Teaching expressive writing to students with learning disabilities: A meta-analysis. *Elementary School Journal, 101,* 251–272.

Gersten, R., Fuchs, L. S., Williams, J. P., & Baker, S. (2001). Teaching reading comprehension strategies to students with learning disabilities: A review of research. *Review of Educational Research, 71,* 279–320.

Gick, M. L., & Holyoak, K. J. (1983). Schema induction and analogical transfer. *Cognitive Psychology, 15,* 1–38.

Gill, C. B., Klecan-Aker, J., Roberts, T., & Fredenburg, K. A. (2003). Following directions: Rehearsal and visualization strategies for children with specific language impairment. *Child Language Teaching and Therapy, 19,* 85–101.

Glynn, S. M., & Duit, R. (Eds.). (1995). *Learning science in the schools: Research reforming practice.* Mahwah, NJ: Erlbaum.

Glynn, S. M., Yeany, R. H., & Britton, B. K. (1991). A constructive view of learning science. In S. M. Glynn, R. H. Yeany, & B. K. Britton (Eds.), *The psychology of learning science* (pp. 3–19). Hillsdale, NJ: Erlbaum.

Gordon, B. N., Baker-Ward, L., & Ornstein, P. A. (2001). Children's testimony: A review of research on memory for past experiences. *Clinical Child and Family Psychology Review, 4,* 157–181.

Graf, P., & Schacter, D. L. (1985). Implicit and explicit memory for new associations in normal and amnesic subjects. *Journal of Experimental Psychology: Learning, Memory and Cognition, 1,* 501–518.

Graham, S. (1990). The role of production factors in learning disabled students' compositions. *Journal of Educational Psychology, 82,* 781–791.

Graham, S. (1997). Executive control in the revising of students with learning and writing difficulties. *Journal of Educational Psychology, 89,* 223–234.

Graham, S., & Harris, K. R. (2003). Students with learning disabilities and the process of writing: A meta-analysis of SRSD studies. In H. L. Swanson, K. R. Harris, & S. Graham (Eds.), *Handbook of learning disabilities* (pp. 323–344). New York: Guilford Press.

Granott, N., & Parziale, J. (2002). *Microdevelopment: Transition processes in development and learning.* New York: Oxford University Press.

Gruenenfelder, T. M., & Borkowski, J. G. (1975). Transfer of cumulative-rehearsal strategies in children's short-term memory. *Child Development, 46,* 1019–1024.

Guttentag, R. E. (1989). Age differences in dual-task performance: Procedures, assumptions, and results. *Developmental Review, 9,* 146–170.

Haake, R. J., Somerville, S. C., & Wellman, H. M. (1980). Logical ability of young children in searching a large-scale environment. *Child Development, 51,* 1299–1302.

Hagen, J. W., Hargrave, S., & Ross, W. (1973). Prompting and rehearsal in short-term memory. *Child Development, 44,* 201–204.

Hagen, J. W., & Kail, R. V. (1973). Facilitation and distraction in short-term memory. *Child Development, 44,* 831–836.

Hagen, J. W., & Kingsley, P. R. (1968). Labeling effects in short-term memory. *Child Development, 39,* 113–121.

Hagen, J. W., & Stanovich, K. G. (1977). Memory: Strategies of acquisition. In R. V. Kail & J. W. Hagen (Eds.), *Perspectives on the development of memory and cognition* (pp. 89–111). Hillsdale, NJ: Erlbaum.

Hart, B., & Risley, T. R. (1995). *Meaningful differences in the everyday experience of young American children.* Baltimore: Paul H. Brookes.

Harvey, S., & Goudvis, A. (2000). *Strategies that work: Teaching comprehension to enhance understanding.* Portland, ME: Stenhouse.

Hatano, G., & Inagaki, K. (1991). Sharing cognition through collective comprehension activity. In L. Resnick, J. M. Levine, & S. D. Teasley (Eds.), *Perspectives on socially shared cognition* (pp. 331–348). Washington, DC: American Psychological Association.

Hayes, J., & Flower, L. (1980). Identifying the organization of writing processes. In L. Gregg & E. Steinberg (Eds.), *Cognitive processes in writing* (pp. 3–30). Hillsdale, NJ: Erlbaum.

Hembree, R. (1992). Experiments and relational studies in problem solving: A meta-analysis. *Journal for Research in Mathematics Education, 23,* 242–273.

Hogan, K., Nastasi, B. K., & Pressley, M. (2000). Discourse patterns and collaborative scientific reasoning in peer and teacher-guided discussions. *Cognition and Instruction, 17,* 379–432.

Hogan, K., & Pressley, M. (1997). Scaffolding scientific competencies within classroom communities of inquiry. In K. Hogan & M. Pressley (Eds.), *Scaffolding student instruction* (pp. 74–107). Cambridge, MA: Brookline Books.

Hohmann, M., & Weikart, D. P. (2002). *Educating young children: Active learning practices for preschool and child care programs* (2nd ed.). Ypsilanti, MI: High/Scope Press.

Hudson, J. A., & Fivush, R. (1991). As time goes by: Sixth graders remember a kindergarten experience. *Applied Cognitive Psychology, 5,* 346–360.

Inhelder, B., & Piaget, J. (1958). *The growth of logical thinking from childhood to adolescence.* New York: Basic Books.

Jackson, N. E., & Butterfield, E. C. (1986). A conception of giftedness designed to promote research. In R. J. Sternberg & J. E. Davidson (Eds.), *Conceptions of giftedness* (pp. 151–181). Cambridge, England: Cambridge University Press.

Jacobs, J. E., & Paris, S. G. (1987). Children's metacognition about reading: Issues in definition measurement, and instruction. *Educational Psychologist, 22,* 75–79.

Jacoby, L. L. (1991). A process dissociation framework: Separating automatic from intentional uses of memory. *Journal of Memory and Language, 30,* 513–541.

Johnson, A. (2003). Procedural memory and skill acquisition. In I. B. Weiner (Editor-in-Chief) & A. F. Healy & R. W. Proctor (Vol. Eds.), *Handbook of psychology: Vol. 4. Experimental psychology* (pp. 499–523). New York: Wiley.

Juel, C. (1988). Learning to read and write: A longitudinal study of 54 children from first through fourth grades. *Journal of Educational Psychology, 80,* 417–447.

Kahneman, D. (1973). *Attention and effort.* Englewood Cliffs, NJ: Prentice-Hall.

Kail, R. V. (1995). Processing speed, memory, and cognition. In F. E. Weinert & W. Schneider (Eds.), *Memory performance and competencies: Issues in growth and development* (pp. 71–88). Hillsdale, NJ: Erlbaum.

Kail, R. V. (1997a). Phonological skill and articulation time independently contribute to the development of memory span. *Journal of Experimental Child Psychology, 67,* 57–68.

Kail, R. V. (1997b). Processing time, imagery, and spatial memory. *Journal of Experimental Child Psychology, 64,* 67–78.

Kail, R. V. (2000). Speed of information processing: Developmental changes and links to intelligence. *Journal of School Psychology, 38,* 51–61.

Kail, R. V., & Hall, L. K. (2001). Distinguishing short-term memory from working memory. *Memory and Cognition, 29,* 1–9.

Kastner, S. B., & Rickards, C. (1974). Mediated memory with novel and familiar stimuli in good and poor readers. *Journal of Genetic Psychology, 124,* 105–113.

Kee, D. W. (1994). Developmental differences in associative memory: Strategy use, mental effort, and knowledge-access interactions. In H. W. Reese (Ed.), *Advances in child development and behavior* (Vol. 25, pp. 7–32). New York: Academic Press.

Kee, D. W., & Bell, T. S. (1981). The development of organizational strategies in the storage and retrieval of categorical items in free-recall learning. *Child Development, 52,* 1163–1171.

Keene, E. O., & Zimmermann, S. (1997). *Mosaic of thought: Teaching comprehension in a reader's workshop.* Portsmouth, NH: Heinemann.

Keeney, F. J., Cannizzo, S. R., & Flavell, J. H. (1967). Spontaneous and induced verbal rehearsal in a recall task. *Child Development, 38,* 953–966.

Kellas, G., Ashcraft, M. H., & Johnson, N. S. (1973). Rehearsal processes in the short-term memory performance of mildly retarded adolescents. *American Journal of Mental Deficiency, 77,* 670–679.

Kelly, M., Scholnick, E. K., Travers, S. H., & Johnson, J. W. (1976). Relations among memory, memory appraisal, and memory strategies. *Child Development, 47,* 648–659.

Kingsley, P. R., & Hagen, J. W. (1969). Induced versus spontaneous rehearsal in short-term memory in nursery school children. *Developmental Psychology, 1,* 4–46.

Klingner, J. K., Vaughn, S., & Schumm, J. S. (1998). Collaborative strategic reading during social studies in heterogeneous fourth-grade classrooms. *Elementary School Journal, 99,* 3–22.

Kobasigawa, A. (1977). Retrieval strategies in the development of memory. In R. V. Kail & J. W. Hagen (Eds.), *Perspectives on the development of memory and cognition* (pp. 177–201). Hillsdale, NJ: Erlbaum.

Kohlberg, L., & Mayer, R. (1972). Development as the aim of education: The Dewey view. *Harvard Educational Review, 42,* 449–496.

Kruetzer, M. A., Leonard, C., & Flavell, J. H. (1975). An interview study of children's knowledge about memory in fifth-grade children. *Monographs of the Society for Research in Child Development, 40*(Serial No. 159).

Kruger, A. (1993). Peer collaboration: Conflict, collaboration, or both? *Social Development, 2,*165–180.

Kucan, L. (1993, December). *Uncovering cognitive processes in reading.* Paper presented at the annual meeting of the National Reading Conference, Charleston, SC.

Kuhn, D. (1991). *The skills of argument.* Cambridge, England: Cambridge University Press.

Kuhn, D. (1995). Microgenetic study of change: What has it told us? *Psychological Science, 6,* 133–139.

Kuhn, D. (1999). A developmental model of critical thinking. *Educational Researcher, 28,* 16–26, 46.

Kuhn, D. (2000a). Does memory development belong on the endangered topic list? *Child Development, 71,* 21–25.

Kuhn, D. (2000b). Metacognitive development. *Current Directions in Cognitive Science, 9,* 178–181.

Kuhn, D. (2001). Why development does (and does not) occur: Evidence from the domain of inductive reasoning. In J. L. McClelland & R. S. Siegler (Eds.), *Mechanisms of cognitive development: Behavioral and neural perspectives* (pp. 221–249). Mahwah, NJ: Erlbaum.

Kuhn, D. (2002a). A multi-component system that constructs knowledge: Insights from microgenetic study. In N. Grannott & J. Parziale (Eds.), *Microdevelopment: Transition processes in development and learning: Cambridge studies in cognitive perceptual development* (pp. 109–130). New York: Cambridge University Press.

Kuhn, D. (2002b). What is scientific thinking and how does it develop. In U. Goswami (Ed.), *Blackwell handbook of childhood cognitive development* (pp. 371–393). Oxford, England: Blackwell.

Kuhn, D., Amsel, E., O'Loughlin, M., Schauble, L., Leadbeater, B., & Yotive, W. (1988). *The development of scientific thinking skills.* San Diego, CA: Academic Press.

Kuhn, D., Garcia-Mila, M., Zohar, A., & Andersen, C. (1995). Strategies of knowledge acquisition. *Monographs of the Society for Research in Child Development, 60*(4, Serial No. 245).

Kuhn, D., & Pearsall, S. (1998). Relations between metastrategic knowledge and strategic performance. *Cognitive Development, 13,* 227–247.

Kuhn, D., & Pearsall, S. (2000). Developmental origins of scientific thinking. *Journal of Cognition and Development, 1,* 113–129.

Kuhn, D., & Phelps, E. (1982). The development of problem-solving strategies. In H. Reese (Ed.), *Advances in child development and behavior* (Vol. 17, pp. 1–44). New York: Academic Press.

Kuhn, D., Shaw, V., & Felton, M. (1997). Effects of dyadic interaction on argumentive reasoning. *Cognition and Instruction, 15,* 287–315.

Kuhn, D., & Udell, W. (2003). The development of argument skills. *Child Development, 74,* 1245–1260.

Lange, G., & Griffith, S. B. (1977). The locus of organization failures in children's recall. *Child Development, 48,* 1498–1502.

Lange, G., MacKinnon, C. E., & Nida, R. E. (1989). Knowledge, strategy, and motivational contributions to preschool childrens' object recall. *Developmental Psychology, 25,* 772–779.

Lehrer, R., & Schauble, L. (2000). Developing model-based reasoning in mathematics and science. *Journal of Applied Developmental Psychology, 21,* 39–48.

Levin, J. R., Yussen, S. R., DeRose, T. M., & Pressley, M. (1977). Developmental changes in assessing recall and recognition memory. *Developmental Psychology, 13,* 608–615.

Logie, R. H. (1995). *Visuo-spatial working memory.* Hillsdale, NJ: Erlbaum.

Lovett, M. W., Barron, R. W., & Benson, N. J. (2003). Effective remediation of word identification and decoding difficulties in school-age children with reading disabilities. In H. L. Swanson, K. R. Harris, & S. Graham (Eds.), *Handbook of learning disabilities* (pp. 273–292). New York: Guilford Press.

Lovett, M. W., Lacerenza, L., Borden, S. L., Frijters, J. C., Steinbach, K. A., & De Palma, M. (2000). Components of effective remediation for developmental reading disabilities: Combining phonological and strategy-based instruction to improve outcomes. *Journal of Educational Psychology, 92,* 263–283.

Luciana, M., Lindeke, L., Georgieff, M., Mills, M., & Nelson, C. A. (1999). Neurobehavioral evidence for working-memory deficits in school-aged children with histories of prematurity. *Developmental Medicine and Child Neurology, 41,* 521–533.

Lytle, S. L. (1982). Exploring comprehension style: A study of twelfth-grade readers' transactions with texts. *Dissertation Abstracts International, 43*(7-A). (UMI No. 82-27292)

MacKinnon, D. W. (1978). *In search of human effectiveness.* Buffalo, NY: Creative Education Foundation.

Manzo, A. V. (1968). *Improving reading comprehension through reciprocal questioning.* Unpublished doctoral dissertation, Syracuse University, Syracuse, NY.

Markman, E. M. (1985). Comprehension monitoring: Developmental and educational issues. In S. F. Chapman, J. W. Segal, & R. Glaser (Eds.), *Thinking and learning skills: Research and open questions* (pp. 275–291). Mahwah, NJ: Erlbaum.

Martin, V. L., & Pressley, M. (1991). Elaborative interrogation effects depend on the nature of the question. *Journal of Educational Psychology, 83,* 113–119.

Martin-Johnson, N. M., Attermeier, S. M., & Hacker, B. (1996). *The Carolina curriculum for preschoolers with special needs.* Baltimore: Paul H. Brookes.

Mastropieri, M. A., Sweda, J., & Scruggs, T. E. (2000). Putting mnemonic strategies to work in an inclusive classroom. *Learning Disabilities Research and Practice, 15,* 69–74.

Mayer, R. E. (1982). Memory for algebra story problems. *Journal of Educational Psychology, 74,* 199–216.

Mayer, R. E. (2004). Should there be a three-strikes rule against pure discovery learning? *American Psychologist, 59,* 14–19.

McCormick, C. B. (2003). Metacognition and learning. In I. B. Weiner (Editor-in-Chief) & W. M. Reynolds & G. E. Miller (Vol. Eds.), *Handbook of psychology: Vol. 7. Educational psychology* (pp. 79–102). New York: Wiley.

McCutchen, D. (1988). "Functional automaticity" in children's writing: A problem of metacognitive control. *Written Communication, 5,* 306–324.

Meichenbaum, D. (1977). *Cognitive behavior modification.* New York: Plenum Press.

Meichenbaum, D., & Asarnow, J. (1979). Cognitive-behavioral modification and metacognitive development: Implications for the classroom. In P. C. Kendall & S. D. Hollon (Eds.), *Cognitive-behavioral interventions* (pp. 11–35). New York: Academic Press.

Meichenbaum, D., & Biemiller, A. (1998). *Nurturing independent learners: Helping students take charge of their learning.* Cambridge, MA: Brookline Books.

Meichenbaum, D., & Goodman, J. (1969). Reflection-impulsivity and verbal control of motor behavior. *Child Development, 40,* 785–797.

Metcalfe, J., & Shimamura, A. P. (1996). *Metacognition: Knowing about knowing.* Cambridge, MA: MIT Press.

Meyers, J., Lytle, S., Palladino, A., Devenpeck, G., & Green, M. (1990). Think-aloud protocol analysis: An investigation of reading comprehension strategies in fourth- and fifth-grade students. *Journal of Psychoeducational Assessment, 8,* 112–127.

Miller, C. J., Sanchez, J., & Hynd, G. W. (2003). Neurological correlates of reading disabilities. In H. L. Swanson & K. R. Harris (Eds.), *Handbook of learning disabilities* (pp. 242–255). New York: Guilford Press.

Miller, G. A. (1956). The magical number 7, plus-or-minus 2: Some limits on our capacity for processing information. *Psychological Review, 63,* 81–97.

Miller, P. H., & Seier, W. L. (1994). Strategy utilization deficiencies in children: When, where, and why. In H. W. Reese (Ed.), *Advances in child development and behavior* (Vol. 25, pp. 107–156). New York: Academic Press.

Moely, B. E., Olson, F. A., Halwes, T. G., & Flavell, J. H. (1969). Production deficiency in young children's clustered recall. *Developmental Psychology, 1,* 26–34.

Monroe, E. K., & Lange, G. (1977). The accuracy with which children judge the composition of their free recall. *Child Development, 48,* 381–387.

Montague, M., & Bos, C. S. (1986). The effect of cognitive strategy training on verbal math problem solving performance of learning disabled students. *Journal of Learning Disabilities, 19,* 26–33.

Murphy, K., McKone, E., & Slee, J. (2003). Dissociations between implicit and explicit memory in children: The role of strategic processing and the knowledge base. *Journal of Experimental Child Psychology, 84,* 123–165.

Myers, N. A., & Perlmutter, M. (1978). Memory in the years from 2 to 5. In P. A. Ornstein (Ed.), *Memory development in children* (pp. 191–218). Hillsdale, NJ: Erlbaum.

National Reading Panel. (2000). *Teaching children to read: An evidence-based assessment of the scientific research literature on reading and its implications for reading instruction.* Washington, DC: National Institute of Child Health and Development.

Naus, M. J., Ornstein, P. A., & Aivano, S. (1977). Developmental changes in memory: The effects of processing time and rehearsal instructions. *Journal of Experimental Child Psychology, 23,* 237–251.

Neimark, E., Slotnick, N. S., & Ulrich, T. (1971). Development of memorization strategies. *Developmental Psychology, 5,* 427–432.

Nelson, K. (1993a). Events, narrative, and memory: What develops. In C. A. Nelson (Ed.), *Minnesota Symposium on Child Psychology: Vol. 26. Memory and affect in development* (pp. 1–24). Hillsdale, NJ: Erlbaum.

Nelson, K. (1993b). Explaining the emergence of autobiographical memory in early childhood. In A. F. Collins, S. E. Gathercole, M. A. Conway, & P. E. Morris (Eds.), *Theories of memory* (pp. 365–385). Hillsdale, NJ: Erlbaum.

Newman, D., Griffin, P., & Cole, M. (1989). *The construction zone: Working for cognitive change in school.* Cambridge, England: Cambridge University Press.

Newman, L. S. (1990). Intentional and unintentional memory in young children. *Journal of Experimental Child Psychology, 50,* 243–258.

Ornstein, P. A., Baker-Ward, L., & Naus, M. J. (1988). The development of mnemonic skill. In F. E. Weinert & M. Perlmutter (Eds.), *Memory development: Universal changes and individual differences* (pp. 31–50). Hillsdale, NJ: Erlbaum.

Ornstein, P. A., & Naus, M. J. (1985). Effects of the knowledge base on children's strategies. In H. W. Reese (Ed.), *Advances in child development and behavior* (Vol. 19, pp. 113–148). Orlando, FL: Academic Press.

Ornstein, P. A., Naus, M. J., & Liberty, C. (1975). Rehearsal and organizational processes in children's memory. *Child Development, 46,* 818–830.

O'Sullivan, J. T., & Pressley, M. (1984). Completeness of instruction and strategy transfer. *Journal of Experimental Child Psychology, 38,* 275–288.

Palincsar, A. S., & Brown, A. L. (1984). Reciprocal teaching of comprehension-fostering and monitoring activities. *Cognition and Instruction, 1,* 117–175.

Paris, S. G., Cross, D. R., & Lipson, M. Y. (1984). Informed strategies for learning: A program to improve children's reading awareness and comprehension. *Journal of Educational Psychology, 76,* 1239–1252.

Paris, S. G., & Jacobs, J. E. (1984). The benefits of informed instruction for children's reading awareness and comprehension skills. *Child Development, 55,* 2083–2093.

Paris, S. G., & Oka, E. R. (1986). Children's reading strategies, metacognition, and motivation. *Developmental Review, 6,* 25–56.

Paris, S. G., & Winograd, P. (1990). How metacognition can promote academic learning and instruction. In B. F. Jones & L. Idol (Eds.), *Dimensions of thinking and cognitive instruction* (pp. 53–92). Hillsdale, NJ: Erlbaum.

Pearsall, S. H. (1999). Effects of metacognitive exercise on the development of scientific reasoning (fifth graders, sixth graders). (Doctoral dissertation, Columbia, 1990.) *Dissertation Abstracts International, 60,* 2389.

Perkins, D. N., Lochhead, J., & Bishop, J. (Eds.). (1987). *Thinking: The second international conference.* Hillsdale, NJ: Erlbaum.

Peterson, C. C., & Rideout, R. (1998). Memory for medical emergencies experienced by 1- and 2-year-olds. *Developmental Psychology, 34,* 1059–1072.

Phillips, L. M. (1988). Young readers' inference strategies in reading comprehension. *Cognition and Instruction, 5,* 193–222.

Piaget, J. (1952). *The origins of intelligence in children.* New York: International Universities Press. (Original work published 1936)

Piaget, J. (1962). *Play, dreams, and imitation in childhood.* New York: Norton.

Pizzini, E. L., & Shepardson, D. P. (1992). A comparison of the classroom dynamics of a problem-solving and traditional laboratory model of instruction using path analysis. *Journal of Research in Science Teaching, 29,* 243–258.

Polya, G. (1957). *How to solve it.* New York: Doubleday.

Pressley, M. (1977). Imagery and children's learning: Putting the picture in developmental perspective. *Review of Educational Research, 47,* 586–622.

Pressley, M. (1979). Increasing children's self-control through cognitive interventions. *Review of Education Research, 49,* 319–370.

Pressley, M. (1982). Elaboration and memory development. *Child Development, 53,* 296–309.

Pressley, M. (2000). What should comprehension instruction be the instruction of. In M. L. Kamil, P. B. Mosenthal, P. D. Pearson, & R. Barr (Eds.), *Handbook of reading research* (Vol. 3, pp. 545–561). Mahwah, NJ: Erlbaum.

Pressley, M. (2002). *Reading instruction that works: The case for balanced teaching* (2nd ed.). New York: Guilford Press.

Pressley, M. (with McCormick, C. B.) (1995). *Advanced educational psychology for educators, researchers, and policymakers.* New York: HarperCollins.

Pressley, M., & Afflerbach, P. (1995). *Verbal protocols of reading: The nature of constructively responsive reading.* Hillsdale, NJ: Erlbaum.

Pressley, M., Allington, R., Wharton-McDonald, R., Block, C. C., & Morrow, L. M. (2001). *Learning to read: Lessons from exemplary first grades.* New York: Guilford Press.

Pressley, M., Borkowski, J. G., & O'Sullivan, J. T. (1984). Memory strategy instruction is made of this: Metamemory and durable strategy use. *Educational Psychologist, 19,* 94–107.

Pressley, M., Borkowski, J. G., & O'Sullivan, J. T. (1985). Children's metamemory and the teaching of strategies. In D. L. Forrest-Pressley, G. E. MacKinnon, & T. G. Waller (Eds.), *Metacognition, cognition, and human performance* (pp. 111–153). Orlando, FL: Academic Press.

Pressley, M., Borkowski, J. G., & Schneider, W. (1987). Cognitive strategies: Good strategy users coordinate meta-cognition and knowledge. In R. Vasta & G. Whitehurst (Eds.), *Annals of child development* (Vol. 4, pp. 89–129). Greenwich, CT: JAI Press.

Pressley, M., Borkowski, J. G., & Schneider, W. (1989). Good information processing: What it is and what education can do to promote it. *International Journal of Educational Research, 13,* 866–878.

Pressley, M., Cariglia-Bull, T., Deane, S., & Schneider, W. (1987). Short-term memory, verbal competence, and age as predictors of imagery instructional effectiveness. *Journal of Experimental Child Psychology, 43,* 194–211.

Pressley, M., & Dennis-Rounds, J. (1980). Transfer of a mnemonic keyword strategy at two age levels. *Journal of Educational Psychology, 72,* 575–582.

Pressley, M., Dolezal, S. E., Raphael, L. M., Welsh, L. M., Bogner, K., & Roehrig, A. D. (2003). *Motivating primary-grades teachers.* New York: Guilford Press.

Pressley, M., & El-Dinary, P. B. (1997). What we know about translating comprehension strategies instruction research into practice. *Journal of Learning Disabilities, 30,* 486–488.

Pressley, M., El-Dinary, P. B., Gaskins, I., Schuder, T., Bergman, J. L., Almasi, J., et al. (1992). Beyond direct explanation: Transactional instruction of reading comprehension strategies. *Elementary School Journal, 92,* 511–554.

Pressley, M., Forrest-Pressley, D., Elliott-Faust, D. L., & Miller, G. E. (1985). Children's use of cognitive strategies, how to teach strategies, and what to do if they can't be taught. In M. Pressley & C. J. Brainerd (Eds.), *Cognitive learning and memory in children* (pp. 1–47). New York: Springer-Verlag.

Pressley, M., & Ghatala, E. S. (1990). Self-regulated learning: Monitoring learning from text. *Educational Psychologist, 25,* 19–34.

Pressley, M., Johnson, C. J., Symons, S., McGoldrick, J. A., & Kurita, J. A. (1989). Strategies that improve memory and comprehension of what is read. *Elementary School Journal, 90,* 3–32.

Pressley, M., & Levin, J. R. (1977). Developmental differences in subjects' associative learning strategies and performance: Assessing a hypothesis. *Journal of Experimental Child Psychology, 24,* 431–439.

Pressley, M., & Levin, J. R. (1980). The development of mental imagery retrieval. *Child Development, 51,* 558–560.

Pressley, M., Levin, J. R., & Ghatala, E. S. (1984). Memory strategy monitoring in adults and children. *Journal of Verbal Learning and Verbal Behavior, 23,* 270–288.

Pressley, M., & MacFadyen, J. (1983). Mnemonic mediator retrieval at testing by preschool and kindergarten children. *Child Development, 54,* 474–479.

Pressley, M., Raphael, L., Gallagher, D., & DiBella, J. (2004). Providence-St. Mel School: How a school that works for African-American Students works. *Journal of Educational Psychology, 96,* 216–235.

Pressley, M., Wharton-McDonald, R., Mistretta, J., & Echevarria, M. (1998). The nature of literacy instruction in ten grade-4 and -5 classrooms in upstate New York. *Scientific Studies of Reading, 2,* 159–191.

Pressley, M., Wood, E., Woloshyn, V. E., Martin, V., King, A., & Menke, D. (1992). Encouraging mindful use of prior knowledge: Attempting to construct explanatory answers facilitates learning. *Educational Psychologist, 27,* 91–110.

Rabinowitz, M., & Chi, M. T. H. (1987). An interactive model of strategic processing. In S. J. Ceci (Ed.), *Handbook of the cognitive, social, and physiological characteristics of learning disabilities* (Vol. 2, pp. 83–102). Hillsdale, NJ: Erlbaum.

Rayner, K., Foorman, B. R., Perfetti, C. A., Pesetsky, D., & Seidenberg, M. S. (2001). How psychological science informs the teaching of reading. *Psychology in the Public Interest, 2,* 31–74.

Reese, H. W. (1970). Imagery and contextual meaning. *Psychological Bulletin, 73,* 404–414.

Rinehart, S. D., Stahl, S. A., & Erickson, L. G. (1986). Some effects of summarization training on reading and studying. *Reading Research Quarterly, 21,* 422–438.

Ritter, K. G. (1978). The development of knowledge of an external retrieval cue strategy. *Child Development, 49,* 1227–1236.

Rittle-Johnson, B., & Siegler, R. S. (1999). Learning to spell: Variability, choice, and change in children's strategy use. *Child Development, 70,* 332–348.

Robinson, F. P. (1961). *Effective study* (Rev. ed.). New York: Harper & Row.

Robinson, J. A., & Kingsley, M. E. (1977). Memory and intelligence: Age and ability differences in strategies and organization of recall. *Intelligence, 1,* 318–330.

Rogoff, B. (1990). *Apprenticeship in thinking: Cognitive development in social context.* New York: Oxford University Press.

Rogoff, B. (1998). Cognition as a collaborative process. In W. Damon (Editor-in-Chief) & D. Kuhn & R. S. Siegler (Vol. Eds.), *Handbook of child psychology: Vol. 2. Cognition, perception, and language* (5th ed., pp. 679–744). New York: Wiley.

Rogoff, B. (2003). *The cultural nature of human development.* New York: Oxford University Press.

Rohwer, W. D., Jr. (1973). Elaboration and learning in childhood and adolescence. In H. W. Reese (Ed.), *Advances in child development and behavior* (Vol. 8, pp. 1–57). New York: Academic Press.

Rosenblatt, L. M. (1978). *The reader, the text, the poem: The transactional theory of the literary work.* Carbondale: Southern Illinois University Press.

Rosenshine, B., & Meister, C. (1994). Reciprocal teaching: A review of 19 experimental studies. *Review of Educational Research, 64,* 479–530.

Rossi, S., & Wittrock, M. C. (1971). Developmental shifts in verbal recall between mental ages 2 and 5. *Child Development, 42,* 333–338.

Rovee-Collier, C., & Gerhardstein, P. (1997). The development of infant memory. In N. Cowan (Ed.), *The development of memory in childhood: Studies in developmental psychology* (pp. 5–39). Hove, England: Psychology Press.

Saywitz, K. J., & Lyon, T. D. (2002). Coming to grips with children's suggestibility. In M. L. Eisen (Ed.), *Memory and suggestibility in the forensic interview* (pp. 85–113). Mahwah, NJ: Erlbaum.

Scardamalia, M., & Bereiter, C. (1986). Research on written composition. In M. C. Wittrock (Ed.), *Handbook of research on teaching* (3rd ed., pp. 778–803). New York: Macmillan.

Schlagmüller, M., & Schneider, W. (2002). The development of organizational strategies in children: Evidence from a microgenetic longitudinal study. *Journal of Experimental Child Psychology, 81,* 298–319.

Schneider, W. (1993). Domain-specific knowledge and memory performance in children. *Educational Psychology Review, 5,* 257–273.

Schneider, W., & Bjorklund, D. F. (1992). Expertise, aptitude, and strategic remembering. *Child Development, 63,* 461–473.

Schneider, W., & Bjorklund, D. F. (1998). Memory. In W. Damon (Editor-in-Chief) & D. Kuhn & R. S. Siegler (Vol. Eds.), *Handbook of child psychology: Vol. 2. Cognition, perception, and language* (5th ed., pp. 467–521). New York: Wiley.

Schneider, W., Bjorklund, D. F., & Maier-Brueckner, W. (1996). The effects of expertise and IQ on children's memory: When knowledge is, and when it is not enough. *International Journal of Behavioral Development, 19,* 773–796.

Schneider, W., Borkowski, J. G., Kurtz, B. E., & Kerwin, K. (1986). Metamemory and motivation: A comparison of strategy use and performance in German and American children. *Journal of Cross-Cultural Psychology, 17,* 315–336.

Schneider, W., & Pressley, M. (1997). *Memory development between 2 and 20* (2nd ed.). Hillsdale, NJ: Erlbaum.

Schneider, W., & Sodian, B. (1997). Memory strategy development: Lessons from longitudinal research. *Developmental Review, 17,* 442–461.

Schoenfeld, A. (1985). *Mathematical problem solving.* New York: Academic Press.

Schoenfeld, A. (1987). *Cognitive science and mathematics education.* Hillsdale, NJ: Erlbaum.

Schoenfeld, A. (1992). Learning to think mathematically: Problem solving, metacognition, and sense making in mathematics. In D. A. Grouws (Ed.), *Handbook of research on mathematics teaching and learning* (pp. 334–370). New York: Macmillan.

Schunk, D. H., & Zimmerman, B. J. (2003). Self-regulation and learning. In I. B. Weiner (Editor-in-Chief) & W. M. Reynolds & G. E. Miller (Vol. Eds.), *Handbook of psychology: Vol. 7. Educational psychology* (pp. 59–78), New York: Wiley.

Segal, J. W., Chipman, S. F., & Glaser, R. (1985). *Learning and thinking skills: Vol. 2. Relating instruction to research.* Hillsdale, NJ: Erlbaum.

Shallice, T., Marzocchi, G. M., Coser, S., Del Savio, M., Meuter, R. F., & Rumiati, R. I. (2002). Executive function profile of children with attention deficit hyperactivity disorder. *Developmental Neuropsychology, 21,* 43–71.

Shaywitz, S. E., & Shaywitz, B. A. (2003). Neurobiological indices of dyslexia. In H. L. Swanson, K. R. Harris, & S. Graham (Eds.), *Handbook of learning disabilities* (pp. 514–531). New York: Guilford Press.

Shulman, L. S., & Keislar, E. R. (Eds.). (1966). *Learning by discovery: Critical appraisal.* Chicago: Rand McNally.

Siegel, L. S. (2003). Basic cognitive processes and reading disabilities. In H. L. Swanson, K. R. Harris, & S. Graham (Eds.), *Handbook of learning disabilities* (pp. 158–181). New York: Guilford Press.

Siegler, R. S. (1996). *Emerging minds: The process of change in children's thinking.* New York: Oxford University Press.

Siegler, R. S. (2000). The rebirth of children's learning. *Child Development, 71,* 26–35.

Siegler, R. S., & Robinson, M. (1982). The development of numerical understandings. In H. W. Reese & L. P. Lipsitt (Eds.), *Advances in child development and behavior* (Vol. 16, pp. 242–312). New York: Academic Press.

Sinclair, J. (Editor-in-Chief). (2001). *Collins Cobuild English dictionary for advanced learners.* Glasgow, Scotland: HarperCollins.

Sodian, B., Schneider, W., & Perlmutter, M. (1986). Recall, clustering, and metamemory in young children. *Journal of Experimental Child Psychology, 41,* 395–410.

Stauffer, R. G. (1969). *Directing reading maturity as a cognitive process.* New York: Harper & Row.

Steel, S., & Funnell, E. (2001). Learning multiplication facts: A study of children taught by discovery methods in England. *Journal of Experimental Child Psychology, 108,* 245–256.

Stromso, H. I., Braten, I., & Samuelstuen, M. S. (2003). Students' use of multiple sources during expository text reading: A longitudinal think-aloud study. *Cognition and Instruction, 21,* 113–147.

Swanson, H. L. (1999). Instructional components that predict treatment outcomes for students with learning disabilities: Support for a combined strategy and direct instruction model. *Learning Disabilities Research and Practice, 14,* 129–140.

Swanson, H. L. (2000). Searching for the best cognitive model for instructing students with learning disabilities: A component and composite analysis. *Educational and Child Psychology, 17,* 101–121.

Swanson, H. L., & Sáez, L. (2003). Memory difficulties in children and adults with learning disabilities. In H. L. Swanson, K. R. Harris, & S. Graham (Eds.), *Handbook of learning disabilities* (pp. 182–198). New York: Guilford Press.

Tarver, S. G., Hallahan, D. P., Cohen, S. B., & Kauffman, J. M. (1977). The development of visual selective attention and verbal rehearsal in learning disabled boys. *Journal of Learning Disabilities, 10,* 26–52.

Tarver, S. G., Hallahan, D. P., Kauffman, J. M., & Ball, D. W. (1976). Verbal rehearsal and selective attention in children with learning disabilities: A developmental lag. *Journal of Experimental Child Psychology, 22,* 375–385.

Taylor, A. M., & Turnure, J. E. (1979). Imagery and verbal elaboration with retarded children: Effects on learning and memory. In N. R. Ellis (Ed.), *Handbook of mental deficiency: Psychological theory and research* (pp. 659–697). Hillsdale, NJ: Erlbaum.

Taylor, B. M. (1982). Text structure and children's comprehension and memory for expository material. *Journal of Educational Psychology, 74,* 323–340.

Taylor, B. M., & Beach, R. W. (1984). The effects of text structure instruction on middle-grade students' comprehension and production of expository text. *Reading Research Quarterly, 19,* 134–146.

Taylor, B. M., Pearson, P. D., Clark, K., & Walpole, S. (2000). Effective schools and accomplished teachers: Lessons about primary-grade reading instruction in low-income schools. *Elementary School Journal, 101,* 121–165.

Taylor, B. M., & Williams, J. P. (1983). Comprehension of LD readers: Task and text variations. *Journal of Educational Psychology, 75,* 743–751.

Thiede, K. W., & Anderson, M. C. M. (2003). Summarizing can improve metacomprehension accuracy. *Contemporary Educational Psychology, 28,* 129–160.

Thiede, K. W., Anderson, M. C. M., & Therriault, D. (2003). Accuracy of metacognitive monitoring affects learning of texts. *Journal of Educational Psychology, 95,* 66–73.

Thomas, C., Englert, C., & Gregg, S. (1987). An analysis of errors and strategies in the expository writing of learning disabled students. *Remedial and Special Education, 8,* 21–30.

Thompson, C. P., Herrmann, D. J., Read, J. D., Bruce, D., Payne, D. G., & Toglia, M. P. (Eds.). (1998). *Eyewitness memory: Theoretical and applied perspectives.* Mahwah, NJ: Erlbaum.

Thomson, J. B., & Raskind, W. H. (2003). Genetic influences on reading and writing disabilities. In H. L. Swanson, K. R. Harris, & S. Graham (Eds.), *Handbook of learning disabilities* (pp. 256–270). New York: Guilford Press.

Tobin, K., & Fraser, B. J. (1990). What does it mean to be an exemplary science teacher? *Journal of Research in Science Teaching, 27,* 3–25.

Torgesen, J. K. (1977). Memorization processes in reading-disabled children. *Journal of Educational Psychology, 69,* 571–578.

Torgesen, J. K., & Goldman, T. (1977). Verbal rehearsal and short-term memory in reading disabled children. *Child Development, 48,* 56–60.

Torgesen, J. K., Rashotte, C. A., & Alexander, A. W. (2001). Principles of fluency instruction in reading: Relationships with established empirical outcomes. In M. Wolf (Ed.), *Dyslexia, fluency, and the brain* (pp. 333–355). Timonium, MD: York Press.

Treagust, D. F. (1991). A case study of two exemplary biology teachers. *Journal of Research in Science Teaching, 28,* 329–342.

Vellutino, F. R. (1979). *Dyslexia: Theory and research.* Cambridge, MA: MIT Press.

Venezky, R. L. (1984). The history of reading research. In P. D. Pearson, R. Barr, M. L. Kamil, & P. Mosenthal (Eds.), *Handbook of reading research* (pp. 3–38). New York: Longman.

Vygotsky, L. S. (1978). *Mind in society: The development of higher psychological processes.* Cambridge, MA: Harvard University Press.

Waters, H. S. (2000). Memory strategy development: Do we need yet another deficiency? *Child Development, 71,* 1004–1012.

Waugh, N. C., & Norman, D. A. (1965). Primary memory. *Psychological Review, 72,* 89–104.

Weiner, B. (1979). A theory of motivation for some classroom experiences. *Journal of Educational Psychology, 71,* 3–25.

Wellman, H. M., & Somerville, S. C. (1982). The development of human search ability. In M. E. Lamb & A. L. Brown (Eds.), *Advances in developmental psychology* (Vol. 2, pp. 41–84). Hillsdale, NJ: Erlbaum.

Wellman, H. M., Somerville, S. C., & Haake, R. J. (1979). Development of search procedures in real-life spatial environment. *Developmental Psychology, 15,* 530–542.

White, D. A., Nortz, M. J., Mandernach, T., Huntington, K., & Steiner, R. D. (2001). Deficits in memory strategy use related to prefrontal dysfunction during early development: Evidence from children with phenylketonuria. *Neuropsychology, 15,* 221–229.

Whitehurst, G. J., Epstein, J. N., Angell, A. L., Payne, A. C., Crone, D. A., & Fischel, J. E. (1994). Outcomes of an emergent literacy intervention in Head Start. *Journal of Educational Psychology, 86,* 542–555.

Whitehurst, G. J., Falco, F. L., Lonigan, C. J., Fischel, J. E., DeBaryshe, B. D., Valdez-Menchaca, M. C., et al. (1988). Accelerating language development through picturebook reading. *Developmental Psychology, 24,* 252–259.

Whitman, T. L. (1990). Self-regulation and mental retardation. *American Journal on Mental Retardation, 94,* 347–362.

Whittaker, S., McShane, J., & Dunn, D. (1985). The development of cueing strategies in young children. *British Journal of Developmental Psychology, 3,* 153–161.

Wilder, A. A., & Williams, J. P. (2001). Students with severe learning disabilities can learn higher-order comprehension skills. *Journal of Educational Psychology, 93,* 268–278.

Williams, J. P. (1993). Comprehension of students with and without learning disabilities: Identification of narrative themes and idiosyncratic text representations. *Journal of Educational Psychology, 85,* 631–641.

Williams, J. P. (2003). Teaching text structure to improve reading comprehension. In H. L. Swanson, K. R. Harris, & S. Graham (Eds.), *Handbook of learning disabilities* (pp. 293–305). New York: Guilford Press.

Williams, J. P., Brown, L. G., Silverman, A. K., & de Cani, J. S. (1994). An instructional program for adolescents with learning disabilities in the comprehension of narrative themes. *Learning Disabilities Quarterly, 17,* 205–221.

Williams, J. P., Lauer, K. D., Hall, K. M., Lord, K. M., Gugga, S. S., Bak, S. J., et al. (2002). Teaching elementary school students to identify story themes. *Journal of Educational Psychology, 94,* 235–248.

Williams, J. P., Taylor, M. B., & Ganger, S. (1981). Text variations at the level of the individual sentence and the comprehension of simple expository paragraphs. *Journal of Educational Psychology, 73,* 851–865.

Woloshyn, V. E., Pressley, M., & Schneider, W. (1992). Elaborative interrogation and prior knowledge effects on learning of facts. *Journal of Educational Psychology, 84,* 115–124.

Wong, B. Y. L., Harris, K. R., Graham, S., & Butler, D. L. (2003). Cognitive strategies instruction research in learning disabilities. In H. L. Swanson, K. R. Harris, & S. Graham (Eds.), *Handbook of learning disabilities* (pp. 1383–1402). New York: Guilford Press.

Wood, S. S., Bruner, J. S., & Ross, G. (1976). The role of tutoring in problem solving. *Journal of Child Psychology and Psychiatry, 17,* 89–100.

Woody-Dorning, J., & Miller, P. (2001). Children's individual differences in capacity: Effects on strategy production and utilization. *British Journal of Developmental Psychology, 19,* 543–557.

Worden, P. E., & Sladewski-Awig, L. J. (1982). Children's awareness of memorability. *Journal of Educational Psychology, 74,* 341–350.

Youniss, J., & Damon, W. (1992). Social construction in Piaget's theory. In H. Beilin & P. Pufall (Eds.), *Piaget's theory: Prospects and possibilities* (pp. 267–286). Hillsdale, NJ: Erlbaum.

Zimmerman, B. J., & Martinez-Pons, M. (1990). Student differences in self-regulated learning: Relating grade, sex, and giftedness to self-efficacy and strategy use. *Journal of Educational Psychology, 82,* 51–59.

# CHAPTER 13

# *Reasoning and Problem Solving*

GRAEME S. HALFORD and GLENDA ANDREWS

CHARACTERISTICS OF REASONING AND
   PROBLEM SOLVING   557
Origins of Current Conceptions of Reasoning   558
Domain Specificity versus Generality   558
Methods of Analysis of Cognitive Processes   559
Strategies in Reasoning   559
Symbolic Processes in Reasoning   561
Changed Theories of Categorization   561
Complexity   563
Origins of Thinking in Infancy   567
CONCEPTS AND CATEGORIES
   IN CHILDHOOD   570
Prototype Categories   570
Theory-Based Categories   571
Essentialism   571
Class Inclusion and Hierarchical Classification   572
CONSERVATION AND QUANTIFICATION   577
Perceptual Factors, Compensation,
   and Conservation   578
Age of Attainment of Conservation   580

Number   582
RELATIONAL REASONING   585
Transitive Inference   585
Transitivity of Choice and Learning of Order   589
Relational Problems of Deduction   591
Relational Problem Solving   592
Fast Mapping and Exclusivity   592
Logical Deduction and Induction   592
Mental Models in Conditional Reasoning   592
Logical and Empirical Determinacy   594
SCIENTIFIC AND TECHNOLOGICAL
   THINKING   595
Basic Dimensions and Their Interrelations   595
Concept of the Earth   596
Balance Scale   597
CONCLUSION   599
REFERENCES   600

In this chapter, we first consider basic properties of reasoning and problem solving; then we briefly survey the way our conceptions of reasoning have developed over the past few decades. Next, we review the research on children's reasoning from the perspective of current knowledge of the domain. This will include analyses of the underlying cognitive processes. We will also look for coherence in the field, such as common processes that occur in tasks that otherwise appear to be different, or principles and theories that provide parsimonious explanations for relatively diverse phenomena. In pursuit of

these aims, we review some topics in historical depth to show the important underlying factors.

## CHARACTERISTICS OF REASONING AND PROBLEM SOLVING

To our knowledge, no generally accepted definition of reasoning or problem solving exists, and the distinction between them is also somewhat fuzzy. We will not attempt a formal definition; however, we note that reasoning entails operating on internal, cognitive representations of segments of the world, the goal being to yield decisions and actions that are adaptive in the person's environment. We discuss other properties as they become relevant to the research we review, but first we consider current conceptions of reasoning and see that

We would like to express our sincere thanks to Tracey Zielinski and Tarrant Cummins for their valuable help in preparing this chapter.

they have undergone major changes in the past few decades.

## Origins of Current Conceptions of Reasoning

Our present knowledge about children's thinking is partly the result of the way conceptions of human reasoning in general have evolved. Pioneering work in children's reasoning was dominated by Piaget and his collaborators (Inhelder & Piaget, 1958, 1964; Piaget, 1950, 1952, 1953, 1957, 1970) whose approach was based on psycho-logic. This approach has been heavily criticized (Bjorklund, 1997; Gopnik, 1996) although there have been some spirited defenses of the Piagetian tradition (Beilin, 1992; Lourenco & Machado, 1996), as well as a recent review of Piagetian research and logical reasoning (Smith, 2002), and there are signs that constructivism, one of Piaget's main tenets, is still alive and well (Bryant, 2002; Johnson, 2003; Quartz & Sejnowski, 1997). Nevertheless, our conception of human reasoning has undergone some fundamental changes that must be taken into account in any review of the topic.

Perhaps the most important change for our understanding of children's thinking is that it is no longer considered necessarily appropriate to use logic as a norm for correct reasoning or as a model of reasoning processes. When either children or adults make what appears to be a fallacious inference, it might be because their representation of the problem differs from the one assumed by the experimenter. The inference "if $p$ then $q$, $q$, therefore $p$" is a fallacy (affirmation of the consequent) in standard logic, but it might be a rational deduction if the conditional "if $p$ then $q$," were interpreted as the biconditional (if $p$ then $q$ and if $q$ then $p$). Studies of children's understanding of logical connectives "if then" and "or" show that they are interpreted in a way that is appropriate to everyday life and that there are systematic departures from standard logical definitions (Evans, Newstead, & Byrne, 1993; Halford, 1982). Consequently, we cannot conclude there is a lack of rationality solely because some answers do not match the norms of logical reasoning.

An alternative basis for assessing human reasoning is the rational analysis criterion (Anderson, 1990, 1991), which judges rationality by the way a particular behavior promotes the adaptation of the organism to its environment. A useful example is the way decisions are based on heuristics, such as availability in memory (Tversky & Kahneman, 1973). Such heuristics lead to

some well-known cognitive illusions, but do not imply lack of rationality (Cohen, 1981). Availability in memory is often a useful guide to the frequency with which items occur in the world, and only gives illusory frequencies in circumscribed conditions. Therefore, it is adaptive to use availability in predicting events.

There is sometimes a conflict between the logical interpretation of an expression and a pragmatic interpretation based on conversational implicatures (Grice, 1975). Thus *some* might be interpreted logically as "some or all," but in conversational pragmatics, it is more likely to mean "some but not all." In everyday life, it is frequently adaptive to apply conversational pragmatics instead of standard logic, and children's reasoning in test situations reflects these adaptive processes.

The reconceptualization of reasoning processes means that we no longer see reasoning as an application of the laws of logic, but as an emergent property of more fundamental processes. Production system models (Klahr & Wallace, 1976; Simon & Klahr, 1995) neural net models (Elman, 1991; Marcus, 2001; McClelland, 1995; Wilson, Halford, Gray, & Phillips, 2001) and dynamic systems models (Elman et al., 1996; Molenaar, Huizenga, & Nesselroade, 2003; van Geert, 1998) have all provided possible mechanisms that could underlie reasoning. These alternative approaches are reviewed by Halford (2005). We consider reasoning processes for each of the tasks we review.

## Domain Specificity versus Generality

Cognitive processes are frequently argued to be domain-specific rather than domain-general (Carey, 1985), or to be performed by specialized modules (Cosmides & Tooby, 1992; Fodor, 1983). There is also an intermediate position, according to which reasoning is based on pragmatic reasoning schemas of general validity induced from life experience (Cheng & Holyoak, 1985). Permission and obligation are pragmatic reasoning schemas, and their use in reasoning tasks such as the Wason selection task has yielded improved performance. Specialized reasoning processes are sometimes regarded as innate, supporting evidence being that understanding the distinction between artifacts and natural kinds (Keil, 1991), or understanding that animals move autonomously, have blood, and can die (Gelman, 1990; Keil, 1995), occur at a very early age. These findings are reflected in an increasing biological perspective in cognitive development (Kenrick, 2001) and imply a high degree of innate specialization in reasoning.

There are also strong defenses of domain-general processes (Hatano & Inagaki, 2000; Kuhn, 2001; Kuhn, Schauble, & Garcia-Mila, 1992). It can be argued that there must be central executive processes (Baddeley, 1996) that have a coordinating function, and processes such as analogical reasoning tend to create correspondences between thinking in different domains.

## Methods of Analysis of Cognitive Processes

A major change in research of both general cognition and cognitive development, beginning around 1960, was a greatly increased emphasis on detailed analysis of cognitive processes. This yielded new methodologies, and also much more detailed conceptualizations of reasoning processes. These will be two of the major themes in the review that follows.

One of the most important methods was rule assessment (Briars & Siegler, 1984; Siegler, 1981) which consisted of defining each cognitive process, or strategy, as represented by a unique pattern of responses. Doing so permitted precise and objective assessment of cognitive processes underlying each task, so we could determine not only *what* children did, but *how* they did it. This advance enabled cognitive development researchers to take the fundamentally important step from observing behavior to inferring the cognition that underlies the behavior.

An alternative method of analysis is information integration theory, which is designed to study the way an individual combines variables to estimate the value of a composite variable. It has been applied to children's understanding that Area = Length × Breadth (Anderson & Cuneo, 1978; Wilkening, 1980). Children are shown rectangular shapes that vary in both length and breadth and are asked to estimate their area. Each child's area estimates are subject to analysis of variance to determine which variables have influenced their judgments and how they are combined. If the main effects only are significant, this means they have combined length and breadth additively, but if the interaction is significant and of the appropriate (diverging) form, this means the dimensions have been combined multiplicatively. The methodology has been applied to a wide variety of concepts including the balance scale (Surber & Gzesh, 1984), and volume (Halford, Brown, & Thompson, 1986). Rule assessment and information integration theory have a further benefit in that they permit analysis of

strategies used by individual children, which avoids the artifacts that can be caused by aggregation of data over qualitatively distinct performances (Siegler, 1987).

Microgenetic methods (Kuhn, 1995; Kuhn & Phelps, 1982; Siegler, 1995; Siegler & Jenkins, 1989) have proved effective for studying cognitive change in a wide range of domains, providing detailed information about strategies, including the way they develop and the factors that influence the development, as well as individual differences. An important finding from microgenetic studies is that children's strategies progress in overlapping waves, so they may have more than one strategy available at any one time, and development consists of strengthening some strategies rather than others. A study by Chen and Siegler (2000) is particularly relevant to early development of thinking. They analyzed strategies used by 1- to 3-year-old children to reach for an object using an appropriate tool. The children progressed through a succession of strategies over three problems. Improvement occurred mainly in the modeling condition (in which an appropriate response was demonstrated) and the hint condition (where the experimenter suggested the right tool to use), and was more rapid for the older children. There was transfer of strategies to new problems, as shown by tool use on the first trial of new problems, even though the tool was different from those on which the child had been trained. This suggests that transfer was based on structural correspondence between tasks, rather than on similarity of elements of the tasks, and is therefore a form of analogy (Gentner, 1983; Halford, Bain, Maybery, & Andrews, 1998). Detailed individual differences in strategies were observed, and proficiency in the immediately preceding component of a strategy was the best predictor of progression to the succeeding component.

In this study, strategy development was observed in a remarkably direct manner as it occurred. This not only provides important information about the processes of strategy development, but it means that we no longer need to regard strategies as sufficient explanation for cognitive performances, but can refer to the factors that influence the development of strategies.

## Strategies in Reasoning

Advances in conceptions of how human reasoning functions have significantly changed the way we understand development of children's reasoning. Detailed models of strategies have been developed, drawing on the empirical analyses previously reviewed. There are also new conceptions of reasoning based on theories of analogy, mental models, categorization, cognitive complexity, and the origins of reasoning in infancy and early childhood. These will be major themes in the analyses that follow.

Strategies are now recognized as fundamental to reasoning, and growth in children's repertoire of strategies is one of the major components in the development of reasoning (see Pressley & Hilden, Chapter 12; Siegler, Chapter 11, this *Handbook,* this volume; Siegler, 1999; Siegler & Chen, 1998).

### *Verbal Strategies*

Vygotsky (1962) proposed that, while communication is the basic function of language, it later serves a representational function in problem solving, initially as private ("egocentric") speech, and later as inner speech. Winsler and Naglieri (2003) investigated use of overt or covert private speech in 5- to 17-year-olds during a Planned Connections Task, in which they drew lines between letters and numbers (similar to the Trail Making Task, Reitan, 1971). Use of verbal representation was relatively constant at about 60% over age, but there was a shift from overt to covert use of speech. The benefits obtained from speech also changed with age. Adolescents obtained no benefit, but the younger children of lower ability who used partially covert private speech performed better. It is possible that verbal representational strategies are beneficial where the task is difficult for the participants, and therefore a benefit might be observed for older participants with a more complex task. There have also been computational models of reasoning processes that we will consider in the context of the relevant domains.

*Analogy* appears to be fundamental to human reasoning (Hofstadter, 2001), which might be considered more analogical than logical (Halford, 1992). Mental models (Johnson-Laird & Byrne, 1991) and pragmatic reasoning schemas (Cheng & Holyoak, 1985) might be used as analogues of the premise information in a task (Halford, 1993). Analogies are also used in mathematics (Polya, 1954), in science (Dunbar, 2001) and in art, politics, and many other areas of life (Holyoak & Thagard, 1995). Analogy is also important in knowledge acquisition (Vosniadou, 1989). Concrete teaching aids, such as those used in school mathematics, are essentially ana-

logues (English & Halford, 1995). Analogy has been shown to be important even in early childhood (DeLoache, Miller, & Pierroutsakos, 1998; Goswami, 1991, 1992, 1996, 2001; Halford, 1993).

Analogy is a mapping from a base or source to a target (Gentner, 1983), where both source and target are defined as sets of relations. Typically, relations are mapped but attributes are not, and the mapping of relations is selective, based on systematicity, that is, those relations are mapped that enter into a coherent structure. The mapping is validated by structural correspondence between relations in source and relations in target. A number of contemporary models of analogical reasoning are presented by Gentner, Holyoak, and Kokinov (2001).

Much research has been devoted to simple proportional analogy of the form $A:B::C:D$ (e.g., horse:foal::cat:kitten). Performance on these analogies was found to improve when care was taken to ensure that children had the requisite knowledge of relations (Goswami & Brown, 1989). Thus 4-year-old children could understand the analogy between melting chocolate and melting snowmen (Goswami, 1991) because the relations between solid and melted chocolate, or between solid and melted snowmen, were familiar to them. Relational complexity theory (Halford, Wilson, & Phillips, 1998), to be reviewed later, predicts that if the requisite knowledge is available, 2-year-old children can perform proportional analogies, so even earlier success should be possible.

There is now a growing body of research into the uses of analogy in reasoning about content domains. Pauen and Wilkening (1997) found that 7- and 10-year-old children had some ability to understand the analogy between integration of weight and distance on the balance scale and integration of forces acting on two strings attached to an object. The use of graphs to represent functions also entails analogical mappings based on similarity of relations. This was investigated by Gattis (2002) with 6- to 7-year-olds. First they were taught to map single variables, such as quantity and time, to horizontal and vertical axes, then they were taught to integrate the mappings to provide a function line, the slope of which represented rate. Chen (2003) investigated how 3- to 5-year-olds used a picture analogy to solve a problem. Performance improved with age but even 3-year-olds succeeded if the difficulty of implementing the solution was reduced. If they conceptualized the information in the source picture, they could transfer it to an analogous problem. While many studies have emphasized the analogical abilities of very young children and even infants (Chen, Sanchez, & Campbell, 1997) developmental effects continue to be observed, and are being analyzed in detail. Hosenfeld, van der Maas, and van den Boom (1997) found evidence of discontinuity in the analogical reasoning of 6- to 8-year-olds.

### Mental Models and Analogy

It has been proposed that children's reasoning in tasks such as transitivity and class inclusion may be based, not on abstract principles of logic, but on mental models that are used as analogues (Halford, 1993). A transitive inference such as *John is taller than Mike; Peter is taller than John,* therefore *Peter is taller than Mike,* can be performed by mapping *Peter, John, Mike* into an ordering schema such as top-down or left-right. The ordering schema can be used as an analogue that represents the relations in the problem, and from which the inference can be easily read off. Similarly, a class inclusion problem can be performed by mapping into a familiar schema such as the family. A problem such as whether there are more apples or more fruit, can be performed by mapping the classes, fruit, apples, nonapples into family, parents, children, respectively. These processes are considered in more detail later.

### Implicit versus Explicit Process

Clark and Karmiloff-Smith (1993) distinguish implicit knowledge, which is representation *in* the system, from explicit knowledge, which is representation *to* the system. Explicit knowledge is more accessible to other cognitive processes, and includes ability to modify strategies and procedures, without retraining.

## Symbolic Processes in Reasoning

To serve the functions of thought, cognitive representations need to consist of symbols. Symbols are representations that have semantic referents. This is not true of all representations. Some of the representations in hidden units of neural net models do not have semantic referents (Smolensky, 1990). In addition, there must be some kind of system for operating on the symbols. Symbol systems need to have a structure that corresponds to the structure of some segment of the world or of the per-

son's environment (Halford & Wilson, 1980; Palmer, 1978; Suppes & Zinnes, 1963). Fodor and Pylyshyn (1988) defined two further properties needed by symbolic systems. They are compositionality and systematicity.

*Compositionality* means that, when elements are composed or combined, the components retain their identity and their meaning in the composition. So if we combine "happy" and "dog," we have "happy dog" but the components are still recoverable. We can ask: "What is the emotional state of that dog?" and the answer is "happy" or: "What is it that is happy?" and the answer is "dog." Furthermore, "happy" and "dog" mean the same (at least approximately) in the composition as when they are separate. This is not true of all representations. Some of the representations in certain types of neural net models have been criticized because they are not compositional, and the same is arguably true of categories based on prototypes.

*Systematicity* means that propositions can be generalized on the basis of form, independent of content. In its most absolute sense, it would mean generalization to all logically equivalent forms, but this is now recognized as psychologically unrealistic due to the well-established effects of content on human reasoning (Van Gelder & Niklasson, 1994). A more realistic interpretation of systematicity would be that if we understand a sentence with a particular form, we can understand novel sentences of a similar form. If we understand that John loves Mary, then in principle we can understand that Peter loves Jenny, Mary loves John, and so on. Systematicity is important to our ability to generate novel sentences, arguments, or inferences.

Some representations do not have the properties of symbols, but can be powerful for certain purposes. An example is prototypes, to be discussed under categorization. Such representations are said to be subsymbolic. This is only a brief account of the subtle but important distinction between symbolic and subsymbolic processes, which is relevant to aspects of infant cognition, to be considered later, as well as to other fields such as animal cognition and neural net models (Marcus, 1998a, 1998b; Phillips, 1994).

## Changed Theories of Categorization

Our theories of categorization have undergone considerable revision in recent decades, and this has influenced the way we conceptualize children's categorizations, which in turn influence their thinking.

### Prototypes and Family Resemblance

A major change to the theory of categorization occurred with the realization that natural categories are not based on defining attributes but on family resemblances (Wittgenstein, 1953). Natural categories tend to be built around prototypes, or most typical instances, and membership is not all-or-none, but a matter of degree (Rosch, 1978), so a robin is a more typical member of the bird category than an emu or a penguin. Prototypes also represent correlations between attributes, such as the correlation between having feathers, flying, and building a nest. It was also demonstrated that prototype formation tended to be automatic, with little or no conscious awareness of the basis of the category (Franks & Bransford, 1971; Posner & Keele, 1968). It was also shown that prototypes could be formed by relatively simple, pattern associators (McClelland & Rumelhart, 1986) or by three-layered neural nets (Quinn & Johnson, 1997). Prototypes tend to be based on perceptible attributes, so the bird prototype tends to be based on presence of wings, feathers, flying, and so on.

Prototypes have great information-processing power. They enable recognition of category membership, the central tendency of a category, the nature and extent of variations around the central tendency, and the correlations among attributes of instances in the category. However, they have limitations that make them unable to account for some aspects of categorization. Prototypes do not appear to be compositional (Fodor, 1994) which would imply that they are subsymbolic. The symbols for "dog" and "happy" can be composed to form "happy dog," but according to Fodor's argument, the prototypes for "happy" and "dog" cannot necessarily be composed to form the prototype of "happy dog." We can acquire the concept by experiencing happy dogs, but there is no assurance that the representation of happy in the prototype of happy dog is the same as the representation of happy in other contexts such as "happy girl." Furthermore, the representations of happy and dog cannot necessarily be recovered from a learned prototype of happy dog. Other problems have emerged with theories of categorization based on similarity, including both prototype and exemplar models (Medin, 1989). These have been addressed through the development of models of categorization based on theories.

### Theory-Based Categorization

Categories can be based on naive theories, such as that weapons can be used to kill people, or that animals have blood and can die (Gentner & Medina, 1998; Krascum & Andrews, 1998; Medin, 1989). One interpretation of theory-based categories is that they have an innate basis and are a precondition for learning. According to this view, learning depends on categorization, rather than the reverse, and all categorization is theory-based (see Gelman & Kalish, Chapter 16; Keil, Chapter 14; and Kuhn & Franklin, Chapter 22, this *Handbook,* this volume). However, this view has been challenged by Sloutsky (2003; Sloutsky & Fisher, 2004) who proposes learning mechanisms for category acquisition.

Another interpretation is that theory-based categories comprise propositions that are compositional and symbolic, and can be composed into higher-order propositions, such as causal relations that link lower-order propositions. According to this view, theory-based categories are compositional and are at a higher cognitive level than prototypes, which are not.

### Levels of Categorization

An alternative way to define levels of categorization was provided by Mandler (1999), who described three kinds of categories: categorical perception; perceptual categorization, and conceptual categorization. Categorical perception is used to group stimuli along a perceptual dimension and to distinguish phonemes such as /p/ and /b/. Perceptual categories are learned through exposure to multiple diverse instances. The process proceeds in an automatic and unselective fashion and there is limited central access to the information being used (Moscovitch, Goshen-Gottstein, & Vriezen, 1994). The perceptual system abstracts the principal components from a set of stimuli that bear some physical resemblance to one another to form a schema or prototype, as previously described.

Conceptual categorization depends on abstract forms of similarity, such as similarities of function or kind, rather than perceptual appearances. Unlike categorical perception and perceptual categorization, conceptual categorization is under voluntary control, is selective in its operation, and is accessible to conscious thought. Perceptual information is needed to identify objects as exemplars of a taxonomic or functional grouping. Simple categorical concepts can be based on characteristics such as kind of movements and interactions engaged in, which define the roles that animals and objects can take in events. Mandler (1999) stresses the importance of events to conceptual life, because of their focus on roles. Global conceptual categories develop before more specific, concrete conceptual categories. Conceptual categories provide a basis for inference. The emphasis on roles is similar to relational categories (Gray, 2003) which are defined by the role they serve in a relation. An example would be "orbiting body" (satellite, moon, planet) defined by being in orbit around a larger body. Alternatively, they can be defined by a relation such as "same" or "different" between elements (Oden, Thompson, & Premack, 1990; Zentall, Galizio, & Critchfield, 2002).

## Complexity

A growing body of evidence indicates that capacity to process information increases with age, due to factors such as synaptic growth, axonal arborization, and dendritic development (Quartz & Sejnowski, 1997). However, the theory that cognitive development depends mainly on knowledge acquisition and is analogous to, perhaps even synonymous with, acquisition of expertise (Carey & Gelman, 1991; Ceci & Howe, 1978; Keil, 1991) has tended to be seen as conflicting with conceptions based on complexity or capacity. There is no logical reason to regard knowledge and capacity explanations as mutually exclusive. A counterargument is that it is more parsimonious to rely on knowledge-based explanations. While no one doubts the fundamental importance of parsimony in science, it does not imply that simplistic theories should be favored. In science it is essential to find the dimensions that provide a conceptually powerful and consistent account of phenomena, without anomalies or contradictions. To illustrate by an analogous problem, consider what would have happened in physics if it had been considered more parsimonious to treat heat and temperature as one variable, as early physicists did (Carey, 1985). The result would have been intractable contradictions, and a consistent theory of thermodynamics would have been impossible. In this chapter, we present considerable evidence that complexity affects reasoning, and there is also evidence for capacity limitations (Cowan, 2001; Cowan et al., 2003; Halford, Baker, McCredden, & Bain, 2005; Luck & Vogel, 1997). It is appropriate, therefore, to consider knowledge and capacity as complementary factors, and not rule out either a priori.

The influence of complexity on cognitive development has been a major source of study for some decades, mainly by a group of researchers known as neo-Piagetians. McLaughlin (1963) provided the impetus for this development. It was then developed by Pascual-Leone (1970), Case and Okamoto (1996), Chapman (1987, 1990; Chapman & Lindenberger, 1989), Fischer (1980), and Halford (1982). These theories have been reviewed in detail by Halford (2002) and Demetriou, Christou, Spanoudis, and Platsidou (2002). There are many differences between the formulations, but their common purpose was to explain the development of children's cognition as observed by Piaget and others in terms of increasing information-processing ability.

More recent theories of cognitive complexity have a broader scope, and are applicable not only to Piagetian tasks but to a wide range of other tasks. Two current theories of cognitive complexity are the cognitive complexity and control (CCC) theory and relational complexity (RC) theory.

The cognitive complexity and control (CCC) theory (Frye, Zelazo, & Burack, 1998; Zelazo, 2004; Zelazo & Frye, 1998; Zelazo, Frye, & Rapus, 1996; Zelazo, Müller, Frye, & Marcovitch, 2003) proposes that preschoolers can adequately represent simple "if-then" rules, representing relations between antecedent and consequent conditions, but they cannot integrate these simple rules by embedding them under higher-order rules. Task complexity depends on the minimum number of levels of rule embedding required to solve the task successfully. Embedding involves a higher level of consciousness, which is brought about by a type of reflection that permits the rules to be considered in relation to each other (Zelazo, 2004). CCC theory has achieved considerable success in accounting for age-related changes during the preschool years.

CCC theory is well illustrated by the Dimensional Change Card Sort (DCCS) task, which requires children to switch between rules. Children sort colored shapes into two piles according to explicitly stated rule sets. Participants are shown two target cards (e.g., a red triangle and a blue square) and are given sort cards each of which differs from each target card on one dimension (e.g., a red square and a blue triangle). In the "color" game, the sort cards are placed beneath the target cards of corresponding *color*. After several trials of the color game, participants are told to switch to the "shape" game. In this, they place the sort cards beneath the target cards of corresponding *shape*. Preschoolers sort successfully under the first set of rules (shape or color) but tend to perseverate in postswitch trials despite being reminded of the relevant rules at commencement of each trial and despite knowing the second set of rules (Zelazo et al., 1996).

According to CCC theory, preschoolers can adequately represent simple "if-then" rules, allowing effective representation of relations between antecedent and consequent conditions. Therefore, they readily learn a color- or shape-sorting rule, but they cannot embed these rules into the hierarchy of rules. Formation of these embedded rules requires children to reflect on the rules that they have learned to use (Zelazo & Frye, 1998).

Recent research has shed more light on the reasons for the difficulty of the DCCS task. The difficulty is not in reversing the sorting because 3- to 4-year-olds can make simple reversals provided there is no variation in a second dimension (Brooks, Hanauer, Padowska, & Rosman, 2003; Perner & Lang, 2002). These and other findings (e.g., Bailystok & Martin, 2004) argue against an explanation in terms of inability to inhibit a prepotent response, and support explanations based on complexity. Nor is the hierarchical structure of rules an insurmountable source of difficulty because Perner and Lang found that 3- to 4-year-olds could perform variations in the task that had the same hierarchical structure as the DCCS. They tended to fail when there was a visual clash between target and sorting cards on the irrelevant dimension. Note that in the color game, the red square must be sorted below the red triangle target, but it matches the blue square in shape. Similarly, in the shape game, the blue triangle must be sorted below the red triangle target, but it matches the blue square in color. The visual clash hypothesis receives some support from the study by Towse, Redbond, Houston-Price, and Cook (2000), who found that 3- to 4-year-olds could switch from shape to sorting by color when there were no target cards. When target cards were present, performance was similar to that observed in the standard DCCS task. Performance can be improved if children identify cards in terms of the postswitch dimension before sorting (Kirkham, Cruess, & Diamond, 2003; Towse et al., 2000). The performance of 4-year-olds worsens when the sorted cards are left face-up (Kirkham et al., 2003). These results suggest that the salience of the preswitch attributes is a factor in the difficulty of the DCCS task.

The findings of Deák, Ray, and Pick (2004) might also be interpreted in these terms. They presented object triads in which the hybrid object (e.g., rectangular magnet) had the same shape as one target (e.g., rectangular eraser), but a different function. The hybrid object had the same function as the other target (e.g., round magnet), but a different shape. The 3-, 4-, and 5-year-olds in the switch group sorted the hybrid objects according to shape in block 1, then function in block 2 (or the reverse). Children in the control group sorted by either shape or function in both blocks. Although the function rule was more difficult than the shape rule, there was no difference between the switch and control groups in block 2. With the exception of the 3-year-olds, who experienced difficulty sorting by function, children performed relatively well on all preswitch and postswitch rules. One interpretation is that switching between sorting by a perceptual (shape) and a semantic (function) variable is easier than switching between two perceptual dimensions of approximately equal salience as required in the standard DCCS. If functions are less salient, then the visual clash that occurs in the standard DCCS might be avoided in this modified version.

Zelazo et al. (2003) argued against several explanations of children's difficulty. These were working memory limitations, representational redescription, and inhibition of particular stimulus configurations or the preswitch dimensions (but see Kirkham et al., 2003 for a different view). The findings of Zelazo et al.'s (2003) nine experiments using standard and modified versions of the DCCS were interpreted as showing that errors occur because rules (e.g., if blue then here, if red then there) are activated in the preswitch phase and this activation persists during the postswitch phase. However, there was also some evidence for the negative priming account, which attributes children's difficulty in the postswitch phase to their failure to disinhibit the previously irrelevant rule. Successful sorting by color in the preswitch phase entails selection and activation of color rules (if blue then here, if red then there). Focusing on the relevant (color) rules might result in automatic inhibition of the irrelevant (shape) rules (if rabbit then here, if boat then there). Sorting correctly by shape in the postswitch phase requires that the shape rules be activated (disinhibited). In the negative priming version used in Experiments 8 and 9, values on the dimensions that were relevant during the preswitch phase (blue and red in the example) were replaced (e.g., by yellow and green) in the postswitch phase. Persistent activation of the preswitch rules cannot explain children's failure in the postswitch phase on this version, yet children performed poorly. Experiment 9 established that negative priming occurs only when children must actively select one pair of rules against a competing alternative, that is, when there is a conflicting mismatch between target and test cards during the preswitch phase. When there is no conflict or visual clash between target and test cards in the preswitch phase, children are able to sort according to the postswitch rule. There seems to be some consistency between these studies, in that children experience difficulty only when they must shift between incompatible or conflicting rule-pairs. Halford and Bowman (2003) proposed, on the basis of relational complexity theory, to be considered next, that the visual clash and salience of the preswitch attributes prevented the DCCS from being segmented into two simple subtasks, and required participants to process a more complex rule in which game, color versus shape, constituted an additional variable that had to be processed. They also found that 3- to 4-year-olds could perform a hierarchically structured task when it could be segmented, but not when it was resistant to segmentation, as in the DCCS task.

### The Relational Complexity (RC) Metric

Halford, Wilson, et al. (1998) define complexity as a function of the number of variables that can be related in a single cognitive representation. This corresponds to the *arity,* or number of slots (arguments) of a relation, because each slot of a relation corresponds to a variable. One of the simplest relations is a binary relation, such as "an elephant is larger than a mouse." The larger-than relation has two slots or arguments, one for a larger and one for a smaller entity. Each slot can be instantiated in a number of ways: "elephant larger-than mouse," "mountain larger-than molehill," and so on. Consequently, each slot represents a variable or dimension. In general, an *n*-ary relation is a set of points in *n*-dimensional space. Quaternary relations (4 related variables) appear to be the most complex that can be processed in parallel by most adult humans, though a minority can process quinary relations under optimal conditions (Halford et al., 2005).

An example of a cognitive task involving a unary relation would be a binding between an instance and a category; "Rover is a dog" assigns Rover to the dog category, and can be represented in predicate calculus

terms as dog (Rover). The commonest relations in everyday life are binary relations, which include larger-than, faster-than, wiser-than, and so on, but also less obvious ones such as contained-in, or cuts (as in knife cuts apple).

An example of ternary relations would be arithmetic operations such as addition, defined as the set of ordered 3-tuples add { . . , (3,2,5), . . , (4,3,7). . }. Some important cognitive developmental reasoning tasks such as transitive inference, hierarchical classification, and appearance-reality, have been analyzed as requiring this level of complexity (Andrews, Halford, Bunch, Bowden, & Jones, 2003; Halford, 1993; Halford, Wilson, et al., 1998). A good example of a quaternary relation would be proportion, because it is a relation between four variables, $a/b = c/d$ (e.g., 2/4 = 5/10).

Normative data suggest that the median ages at which children acquire the capacity to process a given level of complexity are 1 year for unary relations, 1 to 2 years for binary relations, 5 years for ternary relations, and 11 years for quaternary relations (Andrews & Halford, 2002; Halford, 1993; Andrews, Halford, Bunch, Bowden, & Jones, 2003). Norms have been determined most precisely for ternary relations in the domains of transitivity, hierarchical classification, cardinality, comprehension of relative clause sentences, hypothesis testing, and class inclusion (Andrews & Halford, 2002). Acquisition is not sudden or stagelike, but gradual. The percentage of children estimated to be capable of processing ternary relations was 16 at ages 3 to 4, 48 at age 5, 70 at age 6, rising to 78 at ages 7 to 8 years. Correspondence was found across domains, and tasks at the same level constituted an equivalence class of equal structural complexity. Tasks in all domains loaded on a single factor, and factor scores were correlated with age ($r = .80$) and fluid intelligence ($r = .79$). Other studies have observed correspondence between property inferences for hierarchical categories, transitive inference, and class inclusion (Halford, Andrews, & Jensen, 2002), between processing sentences with embedded clauses, hierarchical classification, and transitivity (Andrews, Halford, & Prasad, 1998) and between concept of mind, transitivity, hierarchical classification, and cardinality (Halford, Wilson, et al., 1998). There is, therefore, substantial evidence of correspondence between ternary-relational tasks in a wide range of domains.

Complex tasks are *segmented* into components that do not overload capacity to process information in parallel. However, relations between variables in different segments become inaccessible (just as the 3-way interaction would be inaccessible if a 3-way experimental design were analyzed as 2-way analyses). Processing loads can also be reduced by *conceptual chunking,* which is equivalent to compressing variables (analogous to collapsing factors in a multivariate experimental design). For example, Velocity = Distance/Time, but can be recoded to a binding between a variable and a constant (e.g., Speed = 50 kph; Halford, Wilson, et al., 1998, Section 3.4.1). Conceptual chunking reduces processing load, but chunked relations become inaccessible (e.g., if we think of velocity as a single variable, we cannot determine what happens to velocity if we travel the same distance in half the time). The study by Halford and Bowman (2003), considered earlier, showed that when the DCCS task could not be segmented, it was performed at an age consistent with the norms for ternary-relational tasks; but when it could be segmented, it was mastered by younger children. The color and shape rules are binary-relational and can be represented as:

$$\text{Attribute}_{\text{color/shape}} \rightarrow \text{Sort}$$

whereas the combined rule is ternary-relational due to color/shape being an extra dimension, and can be represented as:

$$\text{Game, attribute}_{\text{color/shape}} \rightarrow \text{Sort}$$

Complexity analyses are based on principles that define when chunking and segmentation are possible. The core principle is *variables can be chunked or segmented only if relations between them do not need to be processed.* Two additional principles are:

1. Effective relational complexity for a cognitive process is the least complex relation required to represent the process. This can be determined algorithmically by a decomposition and recomposition technique (Halford, Wilson, et al., 1998, Section 3.4.3).

2. Where tasks entail more than one step, the processing complexity of the task is the relation that must be represented to perform the most complex process involved in the task, using the least demanding strategy available to humans for that task (Halford, Wilson, et al., 1998, Section 2.1).

According to relational complexity theory, children can perform analogies if they can represent the relevant relations. Consequently, analogies based on unary relations should be possible at 1 year, those based on binary relations should be possible from 1.5 to 2 years, and those based on ternary relations at 5 years. Current data appear to be broadly consistent with this prediction. The most contentious prediction is that analogies based on ternary relations will not be possible before 5 years. Goswami (1995) claims to have shown that 3- and 4-year-olds performed ternary-relational analogies, but Halford, Wilson, et al. (1998) argued that simpler strategies were not taken into account. It is also important that complexity analysis take account of decomposability of tasks. An analogy based on relations linking three variables will only be processed as ternary-relational if it is not possible to segment the representations into simpler subtasks.

In proportional analogy A:B C:D, the binary relation between A and B is mapped to a binary relation C and D. This mapping can be segmented into two binary relations, because relations between source and target pairs are not explicitly processed in analogical mapping. A proportional analogy such as 2:5::3:4000 is validated because the same relation, "less than," occurs in source and target (i.e., 2 < 5 and 3 < 4,000), but it is not a proportion because relations between 2 and 3, or between 5 and 4000, are not specified. This contrasts with a proportion, where relations are defined between all four variables (e.g., in 2/4 = 5/10, the same relation occurs not only between 2-4 and 5-10, but also between 2-5 and 4-10), and the concept consists of more than binary relations. Therefore, the so-called proportional analogy is not a proportion.

There is evidence for a developmental shift from mapping of attributes to mapping of relations (Gentner & Rattermann, 1998; Rattermann & Gentner, 1998). The relations in question are typically binary relations. Attributes can be conceptualized as propositions that are equivalent to unary relations and are less complex than binary relations, so the shift might in part be from simpler to more complex relations. This is not to suggest that relational knowledge acquisition is unimportant.

The interaction between complexity and strategies is neatly demonstrated in a study by Stiles and Stern (2001) of 2- to 5- year-old children's ability to make block constructions. They found that strategies varied with age and with the pattern to be constructed, but also that children used different strategies with more complex patterns. Complexity appeared to be influenced not only by the number of components that had to be integrated in any one step, but also by the strategy employed, some strategies being more demanding than others. Similarly, Cohen (2001; Cashon & Cohen, 2004; Cohen & Cashon, Chapter 5, this *Handbook,* this volume), found that an information overload forced infants to process information in a simpler, more primitive way.

### Summary of Complexity Research

Cognitive complexity and control (CCC) theory and relational complexity (RC) theory developed in parallel, but have some common ground, so some translation is possible between the hierarchical complexity analysis of CCC theory and the number of variables analysis of RC theory. Relational complexity theory applies to both hierarchically structured and nonhierarchical representations and has been applied to adult as well as child cognition. Cognitive complexity and control theory has been applied to the theory of executive functions (Zelazo et al., 2003). The theories complement each other; both have established important principles governing the way complexity affects performance, and the body of empirical evidence is growing.

A reservation that is sometimes expressed about complexity analyses is that they are "pessimistic" because they are seen as denying possibilities for improvement. Leaving aside the question of whether such value judgments have a place in science, complexity analyses can actually point the way to improvements. Better understanding of what makes tasks complex can assist in devising simpler tasks that can identify capacities of younger children. Proportion is inherently complex because it is defined by relations between 4 variables, and it is predicted that it will be difficult for children under 11 years to master completely. This does not preclude useful mastery of components of proportion, such as the concept of a fraction, which is a relation between two variables and should be understandable by 2 years of age, with suitable presentation (see Geary, Chapter 18, this *Handbook,* this volume). As described later, many precocious performances are due to simplification, and in some cases complexity analyses have yielded predictions of previously unobserved capabilities.

The assumed opposition between complexity and experience factors is further removed by evidence that experience is likely to increase capacity, due to neural plasticity (Quartz & Sejnowski, 1997). Thus, not only

does cognitive development depend on both capacity *and* knowledge, but experience may contribute to the development of both.

Complexity has long been recognized as a difficult concept, but there is increasing common ground about the conceptualization of complexity, the ground rules for analyzing tasks, and the basic parameters values, both in cognitive development and in general cognition. We also find complexity to be useful for interpreting task and developmental effects in the field, as subsequent sections show.

## Origins of Thinking in Infancy

Although infant cognition is considered elsewhere (Cohen & Cashon, Chapter 5, this *Handbook,* this volume), research has revealed some infant cognitive processes that are important precursors of later reasoning, and it is appropriate to consider them here. We need to consider what criteria should be used to determine whether infant cognition entails reasoning, as it is performed later in childhood and in adulthood.

*Image schemas* (Mandler, 1992) are seen as conceptual primitives in the 1st year of life that form building blocks of higher cognition. They include self-motion, animate motion, agency, path, support, and containment. Image schemas comprise linked elements, but the components of an image schema are fused and are inaccessible to other cognitive processes. They are not compositional or systematic in the senses discussed earlier and therefore are not symbolic.

### Recognition of Cause

Infants' perception of cause (Leslie & Keeble, 1987) seems similar to image schemas and configurations in that it is a modular representation and is computed automatically without being influenced by cognitive processes outside the module.

### Content-Independent Cognition

There is evidence from quite different sources that infants have some ability to process structure, independent of content. Tyrrell, Zingaro, and Minard (1993) selectively reinforced infants for looking at either a pair of identical toys or a pair of nonidentical toys by playing a short recording of a human voice when they fixated the positive pair. This appears to be a highly effective training procedure, and infants of 7 months not only learned the discrimination, but showed transfer to new pairs of toys that embodied the relation on which they had been trained. Marcus, Vijayan, Bandi Rao, and Vishton (1999) habituated 7-month-old infants to three-word sentences of the form ABA or ABB constructed from an artificial language, then tested them on three-word sentences composed of artificial words not used in habituation. Infants were familiarized with a 2-minute speech sample comprising three repetitions of each of 16 utterances (e.g., "ga ti ga," "li ti li"). In the test phase, 12 sentences that were either consistent (e.g., "wo fe wo") or inconsistent (e.g., "wo fe fe") with the habituation sequences, were presented. Infants looked longer toward the side where the sentences with the novel structure were presented. Thus they appeared to have represented the structure independent of content.

There has been a controversy as to whether the infants learned rules (Altmann & Dienes, 1999; Marcus, 1999; Seidenberg & Elman, 1999; Shastri, 1999) or whether the observed transfer could be based on processing of associations between patterns. It is possible that the pairs used by Tyrrell et al. (1993) and the triads used by Marcus et al. (1999) could be processed by representing degree of difference between stimuli, and this would provide a basis for transfer to sets of elements with a similar difference, but dissimilar materials. This is an important step toward symbolic processes, but it does not have all the properties of symbolic processes such as compositionality and systematicity.

### Infant Quantitative Reasoning

The evidence for infants' quantitative understanding comes primarily from studies using the habituation/dishabituation and violation of expectations paradigms, which capitalize on the fact that novel or surprising events capture attention. Research based on these methodologies has demonstrated three main findings. First, infants aged 6 to 12 months discriminate between displays with different numerosities (e.g., Starkey, Spelke, & Gelman, 1990). Most studies show success with small numerosities only; however, Xu and Spelke (2000) also demonstrated successful discrimination with set sizes of 8 versus 16, but not 8 versus 12. Second, from around 5 months, infants appear to have some understanding of addition and subtraction events involving small numbers because they look longer at arithmetically incorrect outcomes (Simon, Hespos, & Rochat, 1995; Wynn, 1992a. See, however, Cohen & Cashon, Chapter 5, this *Handbook,* this volume). Third, infants demonstrate sensitivity to the ordinal relations between

sets of different numerosities. Brannon (2002) habituated infants to either ascending or descending sequences of three numerical displays (e.g., 4, 8, 16 or 16, 8, 4), then tested them with both ascending and descending sequences with novel numerical values. In Experiments 1 and 2, 11-month-olds (but not 9-month-olds) dishabituated to the novel test sequences (cf. Tyrrell et al., 1993). Several models have been proposed to account for these and other empirical findings.

Meck and Church (1983) proposed an accumulator mechanism to characterize representation of nonverbal numerosity in human adults (Whalen, Gallistel, & Gelman, 1999) and infants (Xu & Spelke, 2000). According to this model, the nervous system has the equivalent of a pulse generator that generates activity at a constant rate. There is also a gate that opens to allow energy through to an accumulator that registers how much energy has been let through. In counting mode, the gate opens for a set amount of time for each item. The total energy accumulated is an analogue representation of number. For example "_ _" represents one, "_ _ _ _" represents two, and "_ _ _ _ _ _" represents three. The entire fullness of the accumulator, comprising all of the increments, represents the numerosity of the set of items counted. This single magnitude exhibits scalar variability. Successful discrimination of quantity is subject to Weber's law (discriminability of two magnitudes is a function of their ratio). Scalar variability means that numerosity is never represented exactly in the nonverbal or preverbal mind, with the possible exception of small (1 to 3 or 4) numerosities (Gallistel & Gelman, 2000).

Simon (1997) applied Kahneman and Treisman's (1984) object file mechanism, which is used in object recognition and tracking, to quantification in infancy. Infants are said to construct an imagistic representation of the experimental scene, creating one object-file for each object in the array. Infants represent numerosity implicitly, but there is no distinct symbol for the numerosity of the set and there is no counting process. Numerical equivalence is established by comparing two representations either by evaluating one-to-one correspondence or by comparing files on some continuous dimension. The absolute limit on number of individuals that can be represented in parallel and stored in short-term memory (STM) establishes an empirical set-size signature. This model accounts for quantification of sets of four or fewer objects, but it predicts high error rates and failure with larger numerosities.

Like the accumulator model, the amount model (Clearfield & Mix, 2001; Mix, Huttenlocher, & Levine, 2002) incorporates analogue representations of quantity; however, unlike the accumulator model, there is no counting mechanism. Early quantification of both discrete and continuous quantities is based on nonnumerical cues such as the combined surface area or contour length of the elements. Infants have a general sense of amount rather than discrete number. They can use spatiotemporal information to individuate objects from an early age, but do not apply this information in quantitative situations. Representations based on an undifferentiated sense of quantity are inherently inexact, but some success would be expected based on part-part or part-whole comparisons to reference quantities in the visual scene. Clearfield and Mix (2001, p. 256) argued that because number and amount tend to covary in the environment, such representations would be sufficient to discriminate between amounts in many situations.

Carey (1996) concluded that the object file model is sufficient to explain infants' addition and subtraction involving small numbers (e.g., Simon, 1997; Wynn, 1992a), but for operations involving larger numerosities, an analogue system of representation is required. Similarly, Xu (2003) interpreted infants' numerical discriminations as indicating the existence of two systems of representation. One is an object-tracking system with a set size limit of three or four items; the other is a number estimation system in which discrimination success accords with Weber's law.

These models provide important indications of the set quantification processes that might account for infant numerical performances. Like the models of content-independent transfer discussed earlier, they do not include symbols or symbol systems that are accessible to other cognitive processes and do not appear to have the properties of compositionality and systematicity. They have not, at least as yet, been shown to be symbolic, but they are important precursors of symbolic processes.

### Infant Category Formation

There is extensive evidence that infants can form prototypic categories (Cohen & Cashon, Chapter 5, this *Handbook,* this volume; Pauen, 2002; Quinn, 1994, 2002, 2003; Strauss, 1979; Younger, 1993; Younger & Fearing, 1999). The familiarization/novelty preference paradigm, in which preference or recognition of novelty is indicated by looking time, is commonly used in these studies. Infants are familiarized with different exemplars of the same category, then tested for preference of a novel stimulus from the same category and a novel stimulus from a different category. Preference for the novel stimulus from the different category is taken as evidence that infants categorized the other stimulus as belonging to the familiar category, and therefore as less novel. A typical study is that by Younger and Fearing (1999) in which 4-, 7-, and 10-month-old infants were familiarized for 15 seconds with five pairs of cats and five pairs of horses, then given six 10-second test trials, two with each of the following:

1. Novel cat paired with a dog.
2. Novel horse paired with a different dog (two basic level contrasts).
3. Novel cat or horse paired with a car (global level contrasts).

All age groups showed a preference for the car in (3) but only 10-month-olds showed a preference for the dog in (1) and (2). This tends to support the generalization that global category representations, such as animals, tend to be formed first and are later differentiated into more specific or basic categories such as dogs, cats, and horses. The perceptual nature of prototypes, the relative automatic way in which they are formed, the simplicity of the associative learning mechanisms required to learn them, and their lack of compositionality, as noted earlier, suggest that they are more primitive than later categorizations. Their presence in infants as young as 3 months may provide building blocks of later categorization.

Mandler (2000) proposes that infant categorization goes well beyond prototypes and comprises both perceptual and conceptual categories. Prototypes are basically perceptual, as noted, but conceptual categories are based more on function, goals, causes, and essences, which go beyond perceptual attributes. Function is observable to some extent, so a ball is identified by the fact that it rolls, but there is an aspect of function that goes beyond what is immediately observable, such as that a ball can be used to play a game. Cause also is unobservable because, as Carey (2000) points out, "attribution of causality goes beyond spatiotemporal analysis" (p. 38). Infants might categorize dogs, cats, and horses together because of their inner essences that cause them to be what they are.

To support her proposal, Mandler and McDonough (1996) tested the ability of 14-month-olds to make inductive inferences. First they saw a dog being given a drink, or sleeping in a bed. Alternately, they were shown a key being turned against a model car door. Then they were shown a different animal and a different vehicle. The children tended to model actions with objects from the same category, so they imitated giving a drink to another dog, not to a car, and key turning against another vehicle, not to an animal. Infants also tended to overgeneralize these properties, such as substituting a frying pan for a cup or a bath for a bed (Mandler & McDonough, 1998). Similar findings were reported for 12-month-olds by Waxman and Markow (1995).

Whereas perceptual categories and prototypes are useful for object recognition, conceptual categories permit inductive inferences that go beyond perceptual phenomena. Conceptual categories in infants certainly appear to be important precursors to the categorical inductions at which young children are so adept.

Mandler proposes that conceptual categories are acquired by perceptual analysis, "in which perceptual input is attentively analyzed and recoded into a new format" (Mandler, 2000, p. 18). However, Carey (2000), although generally supportive of Mandler's proposals, is skeptical that perceptual analysis constitutes an adequate explanation. She suggests that conceptual categories, like core knowledge, derive from innate learning mechanisms in intuitive mechanics and intuitive psychology. See also commentaries by Gibson (2000), Nelson (2000), Quinn and Eimas (2000), and Reznick (2000).

These findings of conceptual knowledge in infants are important, but there is a lack of information about both the cognitive processes involved and the mechanisms by which they develop. Like Carey (2000), we do not find perceptual analysis a convincing account of conceptual category acquisition without further demonstrations of its adequacy. However, Mandler makes another proposal that we find more plausible. This is that "it appears that infants observe the events in which animals and vehicles take part and use their interpretation of the events to conceptualize what sort of thing an animal or vehicle is" (Mandler, 2000, p. 26). This fits well with our own position that the transition to symbolic cognitive processes, which appears to begin around the end of the 1st year, depends on representation of relations. Events can be conceptualized as relations, so that, for example, unlocking a car with a key is a relation between the key and the car, or between a person, key, and car. If infants develop the ability to represent relations late in the 1st year, they would be able to gen-eralize on the basis of similarity between relations. As Halford and his collaborators have argued (Halford, 1997; Halford, Wilson, et al., 1998; Phillips, Halford, & Wilson, 1995), relations are more accessible than associations, and if conceptual categories are based on relations, they would be more accessible than perceptual categories that are based on associative mechanisms. While this explanation is insufficient in itself, it might suggest fruitful avenues for further research and theoretical modeling.

Our knowledge of infant cognition has been greatly enriched, but in subsequent sections, we consider how infants' capabilities compare with those of children. Keen (2003) has shown elegantly how infant capacities relative to those of toddlers can be exaggerated by different task demands. Infants' abilities are demonstrated solely by looking, whereas toddlers are often required to perform selection, which involves prediction and planning of a motor response. When these differences are removed, the apparent precocity of infants disappears. This is a salutary warning of how easy it is to overlook the effect that even apparently trivial procedural differences can have on the cognitive processes required in a task.

## CONCEPTS AND CATEGORIES IN CHILDHOOD

Concepts and categories are an important basis for many inferences. The categories children have, how they acquire them, and the way they use them to make inferences are an essential part of children's reasoning and problem solving.

### Prototype Categories

As discussed in the section on the origins of thinking in infancy, there is evidence that infants form prototypical categories, based on perceptible attributes, and they use conceptual categories based on function, goals, causes, and essences. Prototype categories remain important later in childhood, as they are for adults, but there is some evidence that specific exemplar information becomes more important by 11 years (Hayes & Taplin, 1993). In early childhood, there is a mushrooming of categorical development, resulting in many kinds of categories, and providing for powerful inferences.

Some categories are defined by function rather than by appearance (Keil, 1989). Kemler Nelson, Frankenfield, Morris, and Blair (2000) found that 4-year-olds more often extend the names of novel artifacts on the basis of demonstrated functions, as opposed to appearances, when the function helps to make sense of the artifact's structure, and when they respond slowly and deliberately.

## Theory-Based Categories

The observation that even young children make inductive inferences about categories that go beyond observable properties is consistent with categories based on theories. The property induction methodology has revealed that children have what appears to be sophisticated knowledge of categories (Carey, 1985; Deák & Bauer, 1996; Gelman & Markman, 1986, 1987; Gelman & Kalish, Chapter 16, this *Handbook,* this volume; Gelman & O'Reilly, 1988; Lopez, Gelman, Gutheil, & Smith, 1992).

While there is considerable variation, the basic logic of these studies is that participants are first shown a target picture of a familiar category, the category is named, and they are told an unfamiliar but plausible fact about the picture. They are tested for generalization of the fact to instances of the same or different categories that are similar or dissimilar to the target. They could be shown a picture of a dog and told it has a spleen inside (Carey, 1985), or shown a picture of a bluebird and told that it lives in a nest (Gelman & Coley, 1990). Then they are shown one or more of the following: a similar instance of the target category (another dog, another bluebird); a dissimilar instance of the target category (another animal); instances of a different category that is nevertheless similar to the target (e.g., pterodactyl that was similar to the bird). Typically, children are told the category to which the instance belongs. It has been consistently found that children, even those as young as 2 to 3 years of age, generalize to the same category, independent of appearances. Thus they have considerable ability to infer properties on the basis of category membership. This is remarkable, given that the properties are often unobservable to the child and that perceptible similarities may not provide a basis for categorization, though Sloutsky (2003) has proposed that similarity still has potential to account for children's categories. The categories are usually natural kinds, either living things such as plants and animals, or naturally occurring enti-

ties such as shells or lumps of mineral. However, generalizations based on material categories (e.g., wood) or object artifacts (e.g., chairs) have been observed (Kalish & Gelman, 1992). Furthermore, 3- to 4-year-old children selected a basis for categorization appropriate to the decision being made, so they categorized by object type (e.g., chair) when deciding in which room an object belonged, but by material type when deciding whether an object would be hard or soft. These findings seem to suggest that children's inferences are based on schemas that children have for various domains. However, the processes young children employ in making category-based inferences remain an important question in the field of children's reasoning.

## Essentialism

S. Gelman (2003, Gelman & Kalish, Chapter 16, this *Handbook,* this volume) has proposed that children's categories are based on *essences,* which are unobservable properties that cause things to be the way they are. She proposes further that essentialism is an ingrained cognitive predisposition that emerges early in childhood, that does not appear to depend on direct instruction, and that children's categories are based on early recognition of the causal basis of the properties of natural kinds.

The main kinds of empirical evidence for the essentialist position are the nonobvious property inferences that young children make on the basis of category membership, and their recognition that categories remain constant, despite changes in appearance or attempts at transformation. Young children tend to recognize that having blood and bones is linked to other properties, such as movement, gender, and certain traits, and this knowledge goes beyond the specific facts that children have learned (Gelman & Wellman, 1991; Simons & Keil, 1995). By about 8 years of age, children recognize that animals cannot be converted into a different species by changing their appearance or the way they behave, whereas artifacts can be transformed (Keil, 1989).

Language is an influence on development of essentialist categories, but not the sole driver, according to Gelman (2003). Names, or labels for categories, appear to play a role in development of essentialist categories. Names tell children which entities belong to a particular category, and the knowledge that a child has associated with a name indicates whether it refers to a kind. For example, "this animal is a cat" lets the child know that it has the properties the child has learned about cats, whereas "this animal is sleepy" indicates an ephemeral state rather than a kind.

Essentialism contrasts with many other domains we review in this chapter because there is little information as to how children's essentialist categories are formed, nor is it clear what kind of reasoning process might account for these performances. We cannot supply a ready-made model, but we would like to draw attention to an algorithm that corresponds to some properties of children's categories. This is the Relcon (Relational Concept) model developed in our laboratory by Brett Gray (2003). In essence it works like this. Suppose we consider what we know about some everyday object, such as a chair. We retrieve facts from semantic memory, such as "a chair can be sat on," "a chair can be made of wood," "a chair can be found in a living room." Now suppose we retrieve from semantic memory, other objects that have these same attributes; for example, "a table can be made of wood," "a table can be found in a living room," "a table can be found in a dining room," "a radio can be found in a living room." Now we continue our reflections by retrieving other attributes of the entities we have retrieved, such as "food can be placed on a table" or "you can listen to a radio."

Gray has shown that, with appropriate trimming of objects that share a subthreshold number of attributes with others, this process converges to a stable category representation. Furthermore, it captures some of the fundamental properties of theory-based categories, including the prototypicality—family resemblance correlation, and context sensitivity. The categories so formed are based on family resemblance, because no attribute belongs to every member of the category, and many attributes belong to very few members. Such an algorithm can account, at least in principle, for nonobservable attributes, because some attributes are attributed to the category when they have not been observed for some objects in the category. The propositions stored in semantic memory are not structurally complex in terms of relational complexity theory, being reducible to binary or ternary relations. Development of the category will depend more on knowledge accumulation than on processing complexity, which is consistent with Gelman's (2003) claims. The model is also consistent with Gelman's claim that essentialist concepts are not based on simple associative mechanisms, but are based on theories. The components of the knowledge are proposi-

tions, and theories are composed of propositions. Furthermore, the algorithm captures the dependence of essentialist categories on labels because labels are essential to the relational knowledge theory from which it was derived (Halford, Wilson, et al., 1998; Wilson et al., 2001). While this algorithm has not been developed specifically to account for children's essentialist categories, it might provide a simple and plausible mechanism that is relevant to this development. This proposal supports the suggestion of Sloutsky and Fisher (2004) that learning processes might account for some of the phenomena that are attributed to innate predispositions. One outcome of this research might be to show that some learning mechanisms, which in principle are relatively simple, can produce powerful cognitive processes through prolonged interaction with an enriched environment.

## Class Inclusion and Hierarchical Classification

According to Markman and Callanan (1984), the major intellectual achievement lies not in the formation of individual classes represented in isolation, but rather in the ability to relate these classes to one another. Relating classes hierarchically greatly enhances an individual's inferential capabilities. For example, knowing that a newly encountered entity is an animal allows us to infer properties that are characteristic of animals (e.g., it eats, breathes, moves around), and knowing it is also a fish enables us to infer attributes common to fish (has gills, lives only in water) and the likely absence of other properties (has feathers, flies, barks).

Blewitt (1994) explained the development of classification in terms of a developmental sequence of "knowing levels." Progress to higher levels is characterized as increasing explicitation of children's implicit knowledge of hierarchies, which occurs as the result of experience-related factors and the endogenous process of reflective abstraction. At Level I, no actual knowledge of hierarchies is granted. Children can form categories at different levels of generality, but they might fail to include the same objects in more than one category. For example, they might use words like *dog* and *animal* appropriately, except that *animal* would not be used to refer to a dog. At Level II, they include the same objects into categories at different levels of generality. As evidence for Level II knowledge, Blewitt (1994) cited Welch and Long's (1940) research in which children who identified dogs as *dogs,* also identified dogs and other animals as *animals.* In Blewitt's research, 2- and 3-year-olds accepted both basic level and superordinate level labels for the same objects suggesting that children could multiply categorize the same objects and hence that they had implicit knowledge of the hierarchical relation between categories. While Level I and II skills are present by the age of 2 years, working out the full implications of hierarchies may take many years. The stage of hierarchical categorization (Levels I and II) is followed by one or more stages of hierarchical inference. At Levels III and IV, children can draw inferences from hierarchies, but their inferential skills depend on their explicit understanding of the intercategory relations. Knowledge of these relations is incomplete at Level III; however, qualitative inferences about novel objects and categories are possible. They can deduce for example, that if dogs are animals, and "rumpies" are dogs, then "rumpies" are animals. Quantitative inferences, such as those required in Piagetian class inclusion tasks, involve an appreciation of interclass relations as asymmetrical and are not possible until Level IV. Thus the constraining factor is the ability to construct explicit representations of the hierarchical relations between classes. The complexity of such representations might be the reason for the late acquisition of Blewitt's Level IV skills.

Research by Diesendruck and Shatz (2001) also suggests that young children have some awareness of inclusion relations. They investigated 2-year-olds' sensitivity to the taxonomic relations between objects and to the hierarchical relation implied by different linguistic input. They presented sets of four objects, two target objects (A, B) and two distracters. Object A (e.g., shoe) was labeled using its familiar basic-level label (shoe). Object B (e.g., sandal) was given a novel label (fep). During presentation, either an inclusive or exclusive relation (Experiment 1) or no relation (Experiment 2) was specified between the targets. For example, *Here is a shoe. Here is a fep. A fep is a kind of shoe* (inclusive) or *A fep is not a shoe* (exclusive). After playing with the objects for a few minutes, the child was asked; *Can you show me a shoe?* then *Is there another shoe? Can you show me a fep? Is there another fep?* Children's responses were coded in terms of how they interpreted the semantic relation between the novel and familiar labels. *Mutually exclusive* responses were those where the child picked

only object A as the referent for the familiar label, and only object B as the referent for the novel label. *Subordinate* responses were those where the child chose A and B as referents of the familiar label and only B as a referent for the novel label. Subordinate responses are consistent with an inclusion relation between the labels, but might also reflect other overlapping relations. *Synonymy* responses were those where the child chose both objects as referents of both labels. *Familiar-only* responses were those where the child chose A and B as referents of the familiar label, but did not choose object B as referent of the novel label. Children's sensitivity to the taxonomic relations between objects and to the hierarchical relation implied by different linguistic input was inferred from their mutually exclusive and subordinate responses. Children were less likely to make mutually exclusive responses when an inclusive rather than an exclusive relation was provided. This suggests some sensitivity to inclusion relations. However, the frequency of subordinate responses was unaffected by this factor, suggesting that their understanding of hierarchical relations was incomplete.

One of the most paradoxical findings in cognitive development research is children's failure to answer the classical class inclusion question investigated by Inhelder and Piaget (1964). The task entails presenting children with an inclusion hierarchy such that a major subclass A and its complement A′ are included in a superordinate class B then asking them to compare the relative numerosities of B and A. For example, if shown seven apples and three bananas, then when asked if there are more apples or more fruit, children below about 7 to 8 years of age typically say there are more apples. When asked why, they often refer to the minor subclass A′: That is, they would say, "because there are only three bananas." There is no doubt that this phenomenon occurs as it has been replicated multiple times. See reviews by Brainerd and Reyna (1990), Halford (1982, 1989, 1993), and Winer (1980). The question is not whether it happens, but why.

Early explanations tended to be of two main kinds. Piaget and his collaborators (Inhelder & Piaget, 1964; Piaget, 1950) attribute young children's failures to deficiency in inclusion reasoning. However other explanations have focused on children's tendency to answer on the basis of subclass comparisons. That is, they compare A, not with B, but with A′, so in the preceding example, they would compare apples with bananas. This makes their explanation, "because there are only three bananas" understandable, even if the justification for it remains just as obscure.

The paradox is all the greater because it is common to observe that children who give the wrong answer nevertheless seem to know all about the inclusion hierarchy that is presented. In our preceding reference answer, the children would know that apples and bananas are both fruit, they could point to all the fruit in the display, as well as to all the apples and all the bananas, they know that if you take away the bananas you will still have fruit left, and so on.

Why do children reason this way? Numerous theories have been proposed to answer this question, and all tend to argue that children interpret class B to mean class B *but not* A. That is, "fruit" refers to nonapple fruit, bananas in our example. Part of the problem here is that the question form is unusual, as we do not normally ask about the relative quantities of superordinate classes and their subclasses. It is easy to construct a scenario in which even adults might give a seemingly illogical answer to such questions. Suppose you lived in a neighborhood with a large number of dogs, and someone asked whether there are more dogs or more animals in your neighborhood. You might well assume that the questioner wanted to know whether there are more dogs or more other kinds of animals, and as the animals in the neighborhood are mostly dogs, you might answer, "there are more dogs." This implies that the test is flawed because the question is easily misinterpreted, or reinterpreted in a way that may be rational in the adaptive sense discussed earlier, but is different from what the experimenter intended.

Methods have been developed to correct children's answers for the number of guesses and subclass comparisons (Hodkin, 1987; Thomas, 1995; Thomas & Horton, 1997). Furthermore, an entirely different way of implementing the inclusion relation by Halford and Leitch (1989) yielded similar findings. Children aged 3 to 6 years were asked to distinguish between sets that entail an inclusion hierarchy, such as a triangle and a square both of which are red, and noninclusive sets such as two red triangles (identical pair), or a red triangle and a blue square (pair different on both dimensions). Six-year-olds could do this, but 4-year-olds could not, even after extensive training, even though the procedure was child appropriate. Another innovation has been to assess class inclusion and hierarchical classification by property inference (Greene, 1994; Johnson, Scott, & Mervis, 1997)

rather than by the quantitative comparison method that has been used traditionally. Correct inferences require recognition of the asymmetrical relation between categories at different levels of the hierarchy. For example, properties of fruit apply to apples, but the reverse is not necessarily true, because apples have properties not shared with other fruit. Johnson et al. (1997) found that children aged 3 to 7 years showed some sensitivity to the hierarchical level of categories, but there was a marked increase with age. There was a discrepancy between ability to name objects at different hierarchical levels and understanding of hierarchical structure. Experiment 3 investigated understanding of basic-subordinate inclusion relations using quantified inclusion questions (e.g., *A banyan tree is a kind of tree. Are all banyan trees trees?*) and property judgment questions (e.g., *A banyan tree is a kind of tree. All trees have lignin all through them. Do all banyan trees have lignin all through them?*). The question type did not influence performance. However, performance improved with age, from 3% of the 3-year-olds performing above chance level to 32% of the 5-year-olds and 67% of the 7-year-olds. There was an effect of domain knowledge in that 5- and 7-year-olds made more correct judgments with familiar (fire truck: has siren) than unfamiliar (bike: has crank-set) properties.

Greene (1994) investigated 6-year-olds' understanding of the relations expressed in a four-level inclusion hierarchy, which related different classes of *imps,* imaginary creatures from outer space. Memory demands were minimized by using a tree diagram to depict the properties of imps at each hierarchical level. Results showed that 6-year-olds did not appreciate the asymmetrical nature of the inclusion relation.

There have been many claims that young children succeed on class inclusion if given age-appropriate tests (McGarrigle, Grieve, & Hughes, 1978; Siegel, McCabe, Brand, & Matthews, 1978). However, these studies have been criticized because performances were not shown to be better than chance or because they permitted a structurally simpler reasoning process (Halford, 1989, 1993). One of the most famous demonstrations was by McGarrigle et al. (1978) who presented an array of steps with a teddy bear at one end, a chair near step 4 and a table near step 6. The inclusion test entailed asking whether the teddy had more steps to the chair or more steps to the table, and 3- to 5-year-olds performed better than chance. The number of steps to the chair is included in the number of steps to the table in the display, but this does not necessarily mean that the children employed inclusion logic. It is entirely possible that the task was performed by comparing two lengths, and McGarrigle et al.'s own data suggest that this was the process used by the children (Halford, 1989, 1993).

Analysis of the study by McGarrigle et al. (1978) illustrates two points. First, comparison of two lengths is binary-relational and is therefore simpler than the inclusion task that is ternary-relational (to be discussed). There is value in finding structurally simpler tasks that younger children can perform, but we need to be aware that this is the case, so the findings are not misinterpreted. Second, it is easy to fall into the fallacy of assuming that cognitive processes that are in our minds when we devise a task are the processes the children actually use. Ingenious experimenters see an inclusion relation in the display of steps, but it does not follow that children generated their answers by processing this relation. Although this test was acclaimed as disconfirmation of Piagetian stage theory, more recent evidence makes it unlikely that it measured the class inclusion concept defined by Piaget. It would be reasonable to conclude that, although some ingenious methodological improvements have been made, the difficulty that young children have in understanding inclusion has not been removed.

More recent research has demonstrated that class inclusion entails a processing load. Rabinowitz, Howe, and Lawrence (1989) developed a formal model for diagnosing the subprocesses that are involved in class inclusion, thereby helping to obviate assessments based on guessed processes. They also added a color dimension to class inclusion, and found that this reduced performance even of older children and adults, suggesting that class inclusion reasoning is sensitive to processing load effects.

Two recent theories have proposed that the processing load imposed by class inclusion lies in mapping the inclusion principle into the problem. The first is Brainerd and Reyna's (1990, 1993; Reyna, 1991) fuzzy trace theory. They contend that children understand the cardinality principle—that if A is a proper subset of B, then there are more B than A. Apples are a proper subset of fruit (because there are also nonapple fruit) so there are more fruit than apples. To perform correctly, they have to apply the cardinality principle to the inclusion relations in the problem—that A and A′ are both subsets of B. However, children also encode the subset relations in the problem, and these are more salient because the relative sizes of A and A′ are represented physically in the display (we can see there are more apples than bananas in the reference display). By contrast, the inclusion rela-

tions are more subtle and conceptual. This tends to make it difficult to apply the cardinality principle to the inclusion relations, as it leads children into comparing the relative magnitudes of the subsets. Consequently 5- to 9-year-old children benefited from cues that prompted them to retrieve the cardinality principle.

The second contemporary theory is relational complexity theory (Halford, Wilson, et al., 1998) which was applied to class inclusion by Andrews and Halford (2002). There is common ground between fuzzy trace theory and relational complexity on this issue, insofar as both see the problem primarily in the mapping of the inclusion principle, or cardinality principle as Brainerd and Reyna call it, into the inclusion problem. However, Halford (1993) proposes that inclusion reasoning could be based on a schema, induced from experience with inclusive sets, which would serve as a mental model. A child's experience of a family, which includes parents and children, might provide a suitable mental model. This schema is mapped to an inclusion problem by analogical reasoning processes, discussed earlier, which means that the mapping is validated by structural correspondence. The difficulty of the task stems at least partly from the structural complexity of the relations. Andrews and Halford agree with Brainerd and Reyna that the structural complexity of the inclusion task is a factor in its difficulty.

Andrews and Halford (2002) interpret this difficulty in terms of the relational complexity metric. Inclusion entails relations among three classes, B, A, and A′. In terms of our reference example, apples and nonapple-fruit are included in fruit. This is a ternary relation between three classes; (fruit, apples, nonapple-fruit). There are also three binary relations; (fruit, apples); (fruit, nonapple-fruit); (apples, nonapple-fruit), but no single binary relation is sufficient for understanding inclusion. It is not enough to know that apples are related to fruit because, unless the relation between fruit-and nonapple-fruit is also considered, it is not possible to distinguish inclusion from complete overlap (Johnson et al., 1997). Therefore, the inclusion hierarchy cannot be decomposed into a set of binary relations without losing the essence of the concept. Therefore, the inclusion relation is inherently ternary. Furthermore, it cannot be simplified by conceptual chunking. We can chunk bananas, pears, and oranges into the single class nonapple-fruit, and we still have the inclusion hierarchy fruit, apples, nonapple-fruit. But if we chunk apples, bananas, pears, and oranges, we lose the inclusion hierarchy, because we would then have the class of fruit, and a class of (apples, bananas, pears and oranges), but we have no complementary subclass. Therefore, Andrews and Halford argue that the inclusion hierarchies cannot be reduced to less than a ternary relation.

The rest of the difficulty is because, as Halford (1993) has pointed out, it is only possible to determine that fruit is the superordinate by considering relations between all three classes. Fruit is not inherently a superordinate: It is the superordinate in the reference task because it includes at least two subclasses. Similarly, apples is not inherently a subordinate because if the hierarchy had been apples, Delicious apples, and Meuble apples, apples would have been a superordinate class. To assign fruit, apples, and nonapple fruit to the correct slots in the hierarchy requires that relations between all three classes be processed. Consequently, the difficulty of class inclusion is due to the requirement to map the inclusion principle or schema into the inclusion problem. The inclusion schema is inherently ternary-relational. If it is based on experience with (say) families, then it consists of a relation between family, children, and parents. Identification of the superordinate depends on the correct mapping of superordinate to superordinate and subordinates to subordinates (in our examples, fruit must be mapped to family). The difficulty of this mapping would explain why the task is so difficult for young children who also have difficulty with other ternary-relational tasks (Andrews & Halford, 2002). It also explains why it causes some difficulty for older children and adults, who show evidence of significant processing loads with other ternary-relational tasks such as transitive inference.

There is some degree of consensus that class inclusion performance depends on integration of the components into a valid solution strategy (Brainerd & Reyna, 1990; Rabinowitz et al., 1989). Relational complexity theory would explain this by proposing that recognition of the binary relations between B and A, B, and A′, and A and A′ imposes a lower processing load than integration into the inclusion relation, which is a ternary relation between B, A, and A′. It is easy to recognize that A is part of B, as also is A′ (apples are parts of the collection of fruit, as also are bananas), and that A′ is the complement of A (apples and bananas are different kinds of fruit). However, these binary relations do not constitute an inclusion relation, which depends on the ternary rela-

tion between B, A, and A′. The child who processes only binary relations is effectively looking at a three-dimensional structure through a series of two-dimensional windows. Such a child appears to know everything about the task, yet has never synthesized that knowledge into a coherent mental model. It is consistent with this view of class inclusion that any cues that indicate to children which is the superordinate class should help with the problem. This is because they tend to circumvent the considerable processing load required to map the problem and inclusion schema by matching the complex relations entailed in each.

Relational complexity theory has suggested why class inclusion and hierarchical classification are difficult before age 5, whereas category induction is attainable by 3-year-olds (Halford et al., 2002). Category induction involves a relation between a category and its complement. This is a binary relation, whereas class inclusion is a ternary relation. A property inference procedure based on that of Johnson et al. (1997) and carefully matched to that used with category induction, was developed to assess class inclusion. It was found that category induction was mastered by 3-year-olds, whereas class inclusion was mastered at a median age of 5 years, and the latter was predicted by other ternary-relational tasks. The study supports early competence in that the attainment of 3-year-olds is recognized as valid, but it also demonstrates an age effect because older children can master a more structurally complex concept. The study suggests that category induction and class inclusion are really one paradigm at two levels of complexity, which has potential to add some parsimony to the field.

Later developments in class reasoning include recognition of necessity (Barrouillet & Poirier, 1997), and understanding of double complementation, vicariant inclusion, and the law of duality (Müller, Sokol, & Overton, 1999). Müller et al. tested hypotheses derived from Piagetian theory about the relative order of difficulty of class reasoning tasks using a sample of children aged 7 to 13 years. Tasks required the coordination of increasingly complex affirmation and negation operations. Subclass comparisons were predicted to be the easiest because they involve only positive observable characteristics and no negation. Correct responses to class inclusion questions require that children conserve the including class (B) while making quantitative comparisons between it and the included class (A). This involves constructing the including class (an affirmative operation) and then reversing this operation (a negative operation) to decompose the including class. Children are said to construct each subclass through negation under the including class. Subclass comparison and class inclusion were assessed using sets of 15 picture cards depicting, for example, two kinds of fruit (9 apples, 6 bananas). There were three questions, subclass comparison, traditional inclusion questions, and inclusion questions with wider reference (e.g., *In the whole world are there more bananas or more fruit?*).

Vicariance operations are closely related to understanding of hierarchically related classes, but indicate that thinking has become more flexible and mobile. These operations allow children to understand that a class B can be partitioned in ways that leave the class B invariant (i.e., $A_1 + A_1' = A_2 + A_2' = B$). Thus flowers can be divided into roses and nonroses, or daisies and nondaisies. The different divisions are complementary substitutions of the same whole. Vicariance operations also allow understanding of vicariant inclusion, that each primary class ($A_1$) is included in the complement of the other primary class ($A_2'$). Thus the class roses is included in the class nondaisies; therefore nondaisies is the more numerous class (Müller et al., 1999).

Müller et al. (1999) assessed vicariant inclusion and double complementation using displays of clay balls arranged in color groups (6 red, 2 green, 3 yellow, 2 blue). After ensuring that children could identify the complement sets (e.g., not green), five questions were posed. Two questions required subclass comparisons (e.g., *Are there more red balls or more green balls?*); two required vicariant inclusion (e.g., *Are there more balls that are red or more balls that are not green?*); and one involved comparison of two complement sets (e.g., *Are there more balls that are not yellow or more balls that are not blue?*). Double complementation was hypothesized to be easier than vicariant inclusion but more difficult than class inclusion. A still later development involves the Law of Duality, which states that the complement A' of a subclass (A) is larger than the complement B' of its superordinate class (B). Thus the class nonroses is larger than the class nonflowers. This is said to involve nesting a class inclusion relation (A + A' = B) into a higher order class inclusion relation (B + B' = C). Law of Duality was assessed using the materials described for class inclusion with additional cards depicting cherry, lemon, tree, flower. One question referred to

this display (e.g., *Are there more things that are not bananas or more things that are not fruit?,* and another had wider reference *In the whole world are there more things that are not bananas or more things that are not fruit?*) Class reasoning problems and problems based on the four argument forms of logical implication were presented. Logical implication, like the law of duality, was hypothesized as a formal operational attainment.

Results of a Rasch analysis indicated the presence of a single underlying dimension and the following order of increasing difficulty: subclass comparison (least difficult); class inclusion; double complementation; vicariant inclusion and logical implication (equally difficult); Law of duality (most difficult). With the exception of logical implication, this ordering is consistent in most respects with predictions of Piagetian theory. Error analyses indicated that first graders had difficulty with class inclusion and double complementation tasks. Most third graders failed the vicariant inclusion task. Most fifth graders failed the Law of Duality task.

## CONSERVATION AND QUANTIFICATION

Conservation has declined in importance as a research topic in recent years, but it was a core domain for many years and the accumulated research on it is prodigious. This research has not so far yielded really clear answers to all the core questions. Nevertheless, we will consider how much coherence can be discerned in this large volume of data.

Conservation was a pivotal concept in Piaget's study of the child's conception of number (Piaget, 1952). He proposed, "conservation is a necessary condition for all rational activity" (p. 3) and every notion presupposes conservation, so inertia is conservation of rectilinear motion, a set is a collection that remains unchanged as relationships between its elements are unchanged, and so on. While there would be consensus about this rational analysis of conservation as a concept, there has been great controversy about the psychological measurement of conservation, and its attainment by children.

There have been many tests for conservation (Halford, 1982), but all entail recognizing that collections of material remain constant over certain transformations. Conservation of continuous quantity can be assessed by presenting two equal quantities in identical, transparent cylindrical vessels (e.g., two identical glasses of fruit juice). After establishing that the child recognizes the quantities are the same, one quantity is transformed by, for example, pouring it to a taller and narrower vessel. The child is then asked whether the quantities are the same or, if not, which one is more. Conservation of number or discontinuous quantity can be assessed by presenting two sets of objects in one-to-one correspondence, so the equality of the sets is apparent, then transforming one set by extending or compressing it. After the transformation, the child is tested for recognition that the quantities remain the same as before. The classical finding is that young children tend to say the quantities are now unequal because they no longer appear equal after the transformation. For example, pouring liquid into a taller and narrower vessel makes it appear more because the increase in height is greater than the decrease in width (because volume of a cylinder varies as a direct function of height and as the square of width), and making a row of objects longer makes the set appear more numerous. There is no reason to doubt that young children give nonconservation answers to these tests, because the findings have been replicated many times. There has been a great deal of doubt, however, what this shows about their understanding of conservation of quantity.

Some possible explanations for young children's apparent lack of understanding are quickly eliminated. For example, children who give nonconservation answers typically recognize that the quantity will be the same again if returned to its original configuration (e.g., if poured back to the original vessel, or if the row is returned to its original length). They also recognize that it is still the same material, that nothing has been added or subtracted and that there have been changes in two variables, for example, that the liquid quantity increased in height but decreased in breadth, or that the sets increased in length but decreased in density (due to increased space between elements). There has therefore been some mystification as to why they give nonconservation answers. Proponents of the Piagetian position held that nonconservation represents genuine lack of understanding of the invariance of quantity, but there have been many other explanations such as the following: The child was misled by the transformation, which made it appear that quantity or number had changed (Bruner, Olver, & Greenfield, 1966); the child misinterpreted the words used in the test believing, that "more" referred to height of the liquid or length of the row, rather than to

quantity (Donaldson & McGarrigle, 1974); or there was a conflict between knowledge of conservation and appearance of the display (Acredolo & Acredolo, 1979; Bryant, 1972).

## Perceptual Factors, Compensation, and Conservation

The proposal that children are misled by the appearance of the transformed quantity received some support from the finding that they tend to conserve more if the change in dimensions is screened from view (e.g., if the taller vessel is covered with a screen, and the liquid it contains after the transformation is visible only through a small hole in the screen, so the increase in height is not apparent). These experiments have been interpreted as showing that children could demonstrate their knowledge of conservation when they were not misled by appearances. Perhaps the most cogent evidence for this view was provided by Gelman (1969) who showed that children of approximately 5 years were more likely to conserve if they were taught by means of an oddity training procedure that quantity, rather than length, was the relevant dimension.

The emphasis on recognition of quantity is important, but a stable mental model of quantity would seem to require understanding how it relates to other dimensions. Length is not irrelevant to number of objects in a linear array but is highly correlated with it, as is height of a column of liquid with quantity. Suppose that someone has a glass of beer, and after being distracted, notices that the height of the column of liquid is reduced. The person knows, without having witnessed any transformation, that the quantity of beer is now less than before. And surely this knowledge is relevant to understanding of quantity. We would be reluctant to attribute conservation knowledge to a person who failed to recognize that a change in height of a column of liquid, with the diameter held constant, implied a change in quantity. Variables such as height of a column of liquid, or length of a row of objects, are correlated with continuous quantity or number respectively, and they provide useful cues. Thus understanding of conservation can hardly depend on simply learning to ignore dimensions like height, width, length, and so on. Rather it would seem to require a mental model that includes a stable representation of the relations between these dimensions and the more subtle one of quantity.

Piaget (1952) proposed that conservation depends in part on knowing the compensating nature of the changes in height and width, or length and density, in tasks such as those previously described. However many nonconserving children recognize compensation. Children may well recognize that width of a liquid decreased as its height increased, yet they still fail to conserve. A related hypothesis that compensation knowledge facilitated conservation acquisition in training studies (Curcio, Kattef, Levine, & Robbins, 1972) was found not to be supported when the correlation of both variables with pretest conservation was partialed out (Brainerd, 1976). This dissociation between conservation and compensation is paradoxical when we consider that compensation in some form is logically related to, perhaps even necessary for, conservation. For example, an increase in height of a liquid, with width maintained, is logically inconsistent with the quantity of liquid remaining unchanged. If we conclude that quantity remains constant while height increases, we *must* conclude that width decreases. A possible explanation is that compensation is much easier than conservation. Brainerd's (1976) data lend some support to this because nonconserving children performed at a much higher level on compensation than on conservation in a pretest. But the question remains why compensation should be easier than conservation, especially if there is a close logical connection between the two concepts.

Another approach to understanding conservation is to study the acquisition process, and this has yielded numerous training studies, which are reviewed by Field (1987) and Halford (1982). Many training procedures have achieved some success in improving conservation performance, yet no procedure appears to have been entirely successful. Children's performances are usually mixed, even after extensive training. It is difficult to establish the reason for this, but it is possible that acquisition depends jointly on suitable experience and on ability to construct a consistent mental representation of the phenomena. Thus conservation, more than a lot of concepts, might depend on appropriate reasoning processes being applied to input from the environment. It is also possible that there is no one path to conservation acquisition, but that a variety of strategies can be employed. In a microgenetic study, Siegler (1995) found that children often progressed from explanations of conservation based on length to explanations based on the transformation, but this was not a simple transition, and many different patterns were apparent. Furthermore, Siegler found that the number of explanations given was a good predictor of conservation acquisition. This is

consistent with the pluralist approach advocated by Caroff (2002) according to which cognitive development can progress by different pathways. It is entirely possible that recognition of height, or length, might not be distractions, and might not conflict with conservation acquisition. Conservation might depend, not on ignoring these variables, but on developing an integrated mental model that includes the transformation as well as the dimensions of height and width, or length and density.

Thus conflict between length (or height) and number (or quantity) may be just a step along the road to conservation acquisition. A person with a mature concept of conservation does not experience conflict between length and number, but recognizes that compensating changes in length and density are consistent with constant number. According to this argument, conservation acquisition would depend, not on finding a single relevant variable, but on integrating length and spacing with number, or height and width with continuous quantity, as Halford (1970) proposed. It should depend on knowing the relations between these three variables, such as how quantity increases if either height or width is increased without changing the other, or how an increase in one will be accompanied by a decrease in the other, whenever quantity remains unchanged. This provides an unexpected explanation for the failure of compensation to predict conservation. The reason is that compensation is a relation between two variables, length and density. In terms of the relational complexity metric, this is a binary relation. However, it is inadequate to predict conservation. The relation among all three variables, length, density, and number, provides a useful set of constraints. This is a ternary relation, and is more structurally complex than the relation between length and density, which would explain why the latter, binary relation develops earlier and does not predict conservation.

It is an important feature of conservation that the null, or no change transformation, is not obvious as such. If we pour liquid from a short-wide to a tall-narrow vessel, we would only know that the quantity was unchanged if we calculated the volumes of both columns of liquid and compared them, by the formula $V = \pi R^2 H$, where $V$ = Volume, $R$ = Radius, and $H$ = Height. However, this is a calculation that even adults would make rarely, if at all, and it is unlikely that it is ever made by children when they learn to conserve. Yet we are sure that pouring liquid from one vessel to another leaves quantity unchanged, even though the vessels are of different shape. Invariance of number is perhaps easier to assess, because when rows of objects are extended or compressed, the number of objects resulting can be determined more readily, especially when the sets are small. This does not explain how we know that counting provides an accurate indication of number. It is clear that we have learned to rely on counting to determine the numerosity of sets, but this begs the question of how we acquired that knowledge.

Similar problems arise if we rely on inversion as a criterion of number or quantity. Transformations such as pouring, extending, or compressing transformations can be inverted, so all dimensions will be the same as before, but to reason this way begs the question of how we know inversion indicates conservation. After all, there are many invertible transformations that do *not* leave the relevant quantity unchanged. A stretched rubber band can be returned to its original dimensions, but this does not imply that its length was unchanged when it was stretched. If we think about it, we may be surprised to realize that there is nothing inconsistent in saying that quantity can be increased by pouring to a taller-narrower vessel, and reduced by pouring back again. We only know this assertion is incorrect because of our understanding of quantity. Alternatively, we might say that it is because of our theories about quantity. However, a theory of conservation requires a specification of the theory, and an explanation of how a child arrives at the right theory, which brings us back to the same set of issues.

Part of the answer to this problem may be that conserving transformations are associated with compensating changes and are not directly observable. Conservation is a property that depends on relations between variables, in this case length, density, and number, or height, width, and quantity. It also depends on developing an understanding of quantity, or what might be called a *theory* of quantity. Children would need to understand that counting is a valid way to assess numerosity of sets, or they would need to learn to estimate quantities of liquid in different shaped vessels.

Estimation of quantity in different-shaped vessels might seem insuperably difficult, but this obstacle might be more apparent than real. Research on neural net models of cognition, as well as empirical studies of prototype formation, has shown that it is possible to develop representations of central tendency by relatively simple and automatic mechanisms. The neural net model of conservation by Shultz (1998) is relevant here. Using a cascade correlation architecture, in which hidden units were recruited as required, Shultz showed that conservation could develop by training the net to predict the equality of two sets on the basis of length, density, identity of transformed row, and the transformation performed (addition, subtraction, elongation, compression). The net was trained to predict whether the transformed row was more than, less than, or equal to, the nontransformed row. The only training input was information about error in the output of the net, that is, information about the discrepancy between output and the correct prediction of equality or inequality of the rows. This procedure was sufficient for the net to progress from an early focus on length and density to a focus on the transformation performed.

Once the transformation is fully understood, it might no longer be necessary to refer explicitly to dimensions. Thus if I see liquid poured from vessel to vessel, and I am sure that nothing has been added or subtracted, I know quantity remains the same without examining height or width. My knowledge of quantity has taught me that the transformation is sufficient to make a correct judgment of equality of quantity. However, I still know the links between the transformation and the dimensions, and I can refer to them if required. Thus, if I see a pouring transformation (without addition or subtraction) and I also know that height was increased, I can infer that breadth must have been decreased.

## Age of Attainment of Conservation

The traditional Piagetian finding was that conservation was not typically attained until the age of 7 to 8 years, which was also the age at which other concrete operational tasks were attained. This finding, however, like many of Piaget's age norms, has been the subject of many challenges (Bryant, 1972; Gelman, 1972; McGarrigle & Donaldson, 1975; Mehler & Bever, 1967).

A paradigm developed by Bryant (1972) was seen as crucial in demonstrating conservation ability in 3- to 4-year-old children. Children were shown two rows of objects in one-to-one correspondence, with an object in one row unmatched, so it was clear that there were more objects in that row. Then they were shown two equal-length rows with uneven spacing and in which the objects were not in correspondence. The number of objects in each row was the same as with the first display, so there was again one more object in one row than in the other. The first display produced above-chance judgments, and the second produced chance level judgments. The crucial result was that, when the above-chance display was transformed into the chance display, even 3- to 4-year-old children conserved; that is, having correctly judged that one row was more before transformation, they continued to maintain that the same row was more after the transformation. This judgment could not have been based on the posttransformation display because it yielded only chance judgments, so the children's performance reflects the influence of the pretransformation judgment on the posttransformation judgment. In this respect, it achieves something similar to the Piagetian conservation task, but without the interpretation difficulties caused by the conflict between number and length criteria.

Doubts have been raised about the validity of this assessment of conservation. One possibility is that because the posttransformation display provides no basis for judgment, children might default to their pretransformation judgment. Halford and Boyle (1985) presented displays of equal numbers of objects and of equal length, but with variable spacing and therefore no correspondence between objects in the rows. Children saw a succession of transformations from one display to another. Because neither display provided a criterion for judgment, a default judgment based on the first display was not an option. However, if children knew that number remained invariant across the transformations, they should show some consistency, judging the same row as more or (in Experiment 4 where "same" judgments were permitted) judging both as the same, both before and after the transformation. The 3- to 4-year-olds failed to show any consistency across transformations, whereas 6- to 7-year-olds did. When Bryant's (1972) procedure was repeated with "same" judgments being allowed as well as "more" and "less" judgments, findings of conservation by 3- to 4-year-olds were not replicated.

Sophian (1995) used a similar procedure to Bryant (1972) but assessed whether children's pretransformation judgments were based on length or number, and whether they showed indications of counting. The 3-, 5-, and 6-year-olds showed a strong association between observable counting, responding on the basis of number and conservation. There was very little evidence of conservation before age 6. Sophian's study provides important evidence of the link between conservation and knowledge of number.

Sophian also included a condition in which, instead of transforming a row, a different row was substituted.

Her argument was that the default hypothesis of Halford and Boyle (1985) implies that children should be as likely to maintain their pre- transformation judgment after substitution as after transformation. There was no tendency to maintain judgments after substitution, and conservation was much better after transformation, apparently in disconfirmation of the Halford and Boyle hypothesis. Note, however, that children would realize that the pre- and posttransformation rows were different objects in the substitution condition (otherwise their judgments would be the same as in the transformation condition, because substitution is the only way that condition differed from the transformation condition). Therefore, a modified default hypothesis would fit Sophian's findings. This would be that, if the children knew the pre- and posttransformation displays contained the same sets of objects, and if there was a basis for quantity judgment in the pre- but not in the posttransformation display, they would maintain their pretransformation judgment. However when the object sets were not the same, as in the substitution condition, the pretransformation display would provide no basis for judgment, and the children would guess, showing no evidence of conservation. Either way, the studies by Halford and Boyle (1985) and Sophian (1995) cast real doubt on claims that conservation has been demonstrated before age 5.

McGarrigle and Donaldson (1975) modified the conservation of number of task by employing an "accidental" transformation in which a "naughty teddy" accidentally transformed one of the rows, thereby avoiding any suggestion that the experimenter intended to change the number of objects in the row. A significant improvement in conservation was observed in children of 4;2 (4 years, 2 months) to 6;3. When the accidental transformation procedure was replicated by Halford and Boyle (1985) a significant improvement was observed in children aged 3;5 to 4;7, but performance did not exceed chance. Siegal, Waters, and Dinwiddy (1988) showed improvement in conservation but their findings are more consistent with Halford and Boyle (1985) than with Bryant (1972) in that they found an age effect over the age range 4 to 6 years, and they did not demonstrate above chance conservation under the age of 5 years.

Perhaps the most precocious claimed demonstration of conservation was that by Mehler and Bever (1967) with 2-year-olds. They showed children two equal rows of objects in one-to-one correspondence. In the crucial manipulation, one row was compressed and two objects added. Two-year-olds correctly chose the more numerous row, although it was shorter. This demonstrates that 2-year-olds can ignore length cues in some circumstances, but as Halford (1982) and Miller (1976) pointed out, it does not demonstrate that they recognized the transformation as number conserving, because simply observing that objects were added would enable making a correct choice.

Do training studies provide evidence of earlier conservation? In some ways, training outcomes provide a better estimate of capacity for conservation, because the estimate is less contaminated by knowledge deficiencies. However, training has not produced a major shift in the age of attainment, as most successes have been achieved with children at or above age 5 (Field, 1987; Halford, 1982).

There have not been many explicit theories of conservation, perhaps due to the difficulty in discerning a clear and consistent set of principles in the evidence. Simon and Klahr (1995) developed the Q-SOAR model, based on Newell's (1990) SOAR architecture, to account for Gelman's (1982) study of number conservation acquisition. Children are asked to say whether two equal rows are the same or different based on counting, then are asked to say whether they are still the same (or different) after transformation. Inability to answer this question is represented in Q-SOAR as an impasse. The model resolves this by quantifying the sets before and after the transformation, noting that they are the same, and develops the knowledge that the transformation did not change the numerosities, and therefore is conserving (Klahr & Wallace, 1976).

## Number

At some point, children must integrate their early quantitative knowledge into a coherent system that supports a mature understanding of number. This would include understanding of Gelman and Gallistel's (1978) five counting principles (one-to-one correspondence, stable order, cardinal word, abstraction, order irrelevance). It would also include acquisition of the number words of the language and their correct sequence, recognition of numerical equivalence of sets, the ordinal relationships between smaller and larger sets, the compositional relationships within sets, and the conservation of number. There are many different views regarding the age of acquisition of these skills and their order or emergence. We will examine this literature because of its relevance to the development of early quantitative concepts and to

some themes such as conceptual coherence. Geary (Chapter 18, this *Handbook,* this volume) provides a more comprehensive review of the development of mathematical understanding.

Huttenlocher, Jordan, and Levine (1994) examined young children's ability to match numerically equivalent sets and perform simple calculations with concrete materials using a procedure that did not require knowledge of number words. They found no reliable evidence of nonverbal calculation ability in children younger than 2.5 years, whose responses suggested reliance on an approximate quantification mechanism, as described earlier. Children aged 2.5 years and above performed better. Their responses were interpreted as evidence for use of a mental model in which imagined entities and transformations (adding or subtracting) are mapped analogically onto actual objects and their movements. The mental model incorporates several important principles. There is a one-to-one mapping between the elements in the mental model and the concrete objects. The mental model as a whole represents the cardinal value of the set of objects and numerosity increases (decreases) as objects are added (removed). Huttenlocher et al. described children's use of these mental models as a symbolic activity that emerges after the approximate skills of infancy, and prior to the conventional skills of school-age children. This ability to perform nonverbal calculation with small numbers is related to intellectual competence, suggesting that it is a manifestation of a general symbolic capacity rather than an innate modular capacity.

Acquisition of the conventional counting system is a protracted process that extends from about 2 to 4 years of age. Children know that number words refer to numbers, and can perform the count routine, well before they recognize that specific number words refer to the cardinal value of a set. Wynn (1992a) showed a picture of one blue fish and four yellow fish and asked, "Can you show me the four fish?" Even children aged 2;6 succeeded on this task. Success in choosing between four and five animals tended to occur at about 3;6 years. Later acquisitions include coordinating pointing with counting, realizing that counting yields the cardinal value of the set (cardinal word principle), and partitioning sets.

The cardinal word principle (Gelman & Gallistel, 1978) is assessed using various tasks. In the *How many* task, children count a set of stimuli, then they are asked, *How many (stimuli) were there?* Credit is given if children restate the final word of their count sequence without recounting the set. The age by which children succeed on this task varies between 3;6 (Wynn, 1990, 1992b) and

4;8 (Hodges & French, 1988). This variation might reflect differential rates of false positives and false negatives. False positives occur if children merely repeat the last word of the count without understanding that it indicates the numerosity of the set counted (Fuson & Mierkiewicz, 1980; Wynn, 1990). False negative assessments occur if children interpret the question as a request for a recount of the items, or if they mistakenly infer that their initial count was inaccurate (Wynn, 1990).

Wynn (1992b) suggested that the *Give-a-Number* task is a more reliable test. If children understand that numbers refer to sets of specific numerosities, they should show some success at forming or identifying such sets. In the task used by Wynn (1990, Experiment 2), children formed sets of one, two, three, five, and six toy dinosaurs from a pile of fifteen. Wynn's results suggest that success on *How Many* and *Give me X* tasks emerges at about the same age (3;6). Frye, Braisby, Lowe, Maroudas, and Nicholls (1989, Experiment 1, after condition) used a modified version of this task. Children counted sets of 4, 5, 12, and 14 counters; then they were asked, *Give me* X − *1 objects* on half the trials and on the remaining trials, *Give me* X *objects,* where X is the cardinal value. The children (mean age 4;6) found this task more difficult than the *How many* task. However, differences in set sizes, or the requirement to select a subset (X − 1) of the elements could account for the later age of mastery.

Understanding of the cardinal word principle appears to facilitate recognition of numerical equivalence. Mix (1999) investigated this using a matching task that required explicit comparison of sets. Target cards contained 1 to 5 black disks (high similarity condition), red pasta shells (low similarity, homogeneous sets), or collections of objects (low similarity, heterogeneous sets). The matching choice cards contained the same number of dots as the target cards, whereas the foil cards contained either n + 1 or n − 1 dots, where n = Number of elements on the target card. Choice cards were matched to each other on density or array length. Recognition of numerical equivalence emerged at around 3;6 for the high similarity condition, at around 4;6 for the low similarity, heterogeneous sets condition. Only those children with high scores on the *How Many* and *Give-a-number* tasks recognized equivalence in the low similarity objects-to-dots condition (see Mix, 1999, p. 279).

A minimal understanding of the cardinal word principle also facilitates ordinal comparisons. Brannon and Van de Walle (2001, Experiment 2) trained 2- and 3-year-olds to find a sticker under one of two trays. During training, the stickers were always hidden under the tray that held 2 boxes, and not under the tray that held one box. Approximately 72% of children met the learning criterion. The test phase consisted of six trials with novel numerosities. Successful transfer was evidenced by above-chance performance on all six comparisons. *How Many?* and *What's on this Card?* tasks were also administered. In the *What's on this Card* task, children described (using number words) cards that depicted varying numbers of objects. Children who performed poorly on this task performed at chance level in the test phase of ordinal comparison task, whereas those children who gave at least one correct cardinal response performed better. Similar patterns emerged when the participants were classified according to performance on the *How Many* task, suggesting that understanding of the cardinal word principle is necessary for ordinal comparison.

Rouselle, Palmers, and Noël (2004) used an explicit comparison task similar to Brannon and Van de Walle (2001) to investigate numerosity comparison. Three-year-old children were presented with pairs of cards. Each card depicted a set of sticks, and children indicated the more numerous set. Displays varied in terms of set size, ratio between the sets, and the type of perceptual support for the numerosity comparison. The probability of success on the comparison task was lower for pairs presented in the surface condition, which offered the least perceptual support, and higher for pairs with a ratio of 1:2 than for pairs with ratios of 2:3 or 3:4. Only those children who demonstrated some cardinal knowledge (assessed by *How Many* and *Give a Number* tasks) performed above chance level in all three perceptual conditions. Children without cardinal knowledge succeeded in conditions that provided more perceptual support. The results suggested that minimal cardinal knowledge was necessary, but perhaps not sufficient for successful numerical comparisons in the absence of strong perceptual support.

These studies provide evidence for some degree of coherence in children's understanding of number. They suggest that the ability to quantify the numerosity of sets is related to other aspects of their understanding including recognizing numerical equivalences and discriminating sets based on their ordinal value.

English and Halford (1995) and Andrews and Halford (2002) proposed three mental models of how the conventional count sequence might map onto children's conceptual understanding of number. The three models (successor, sets, and inclusion) are shown in parts a, b, and c respectively of Figure 13.1. The performance of children in the studies investigating the cardinal word principle, numerical equivalence (Mix, 1999), and ordinal comparisons (Brannon & Van de Walle, 2001; Rouselle et al., 2004) can be described in terms of these models.

In the successor model, numerals are assigned to individual objects, and there is a succession relation between objects. This model does not support the cardinal word principle because it implies that the final count

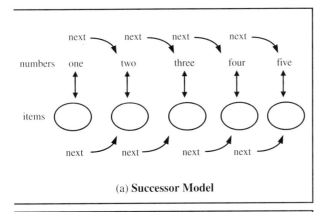

(a) **Successor Model**

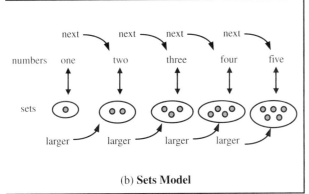

(b) **Sets Model**

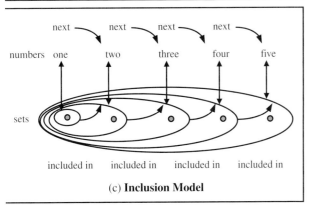

(c) **Inclusion Model**

**Figure 13.1**   Three mental models for counting: (a) Successor model, (b), Sets model, (c), Inclusion model.

word refers to the last object counted rather than to the entire set. Neither would it support numerical equivalence and ordinal comparison judgments because there is no representation of relative numerosity.

In the sets model, numerals are assigned to sets, and there is a magnitude relation between the sets. The sets model would enable children to recognize that a count word refers to the entire set of objects. It would yield success on *How Many, Give me, X* and *What's on this Card* tasks. It would also support success on numerical equivalence and numerical comparisons tasks, because judgments could be based on the magnitude relation. The sets model would not enable principled understanding of the order irrelevance principle, which specifies that cardinal value is unaffected by the order in which items are counted. It differs from the how-to-count principles (one-to-one correspondence, stable order, cardinal word) in that it specifies the absence, rather than presence, of a constraint on counting procedures. Order irrelevance depends on understanding that any object can be counted, provided that it has not been counted before. Thus previously counted objects must be distinguished from those not yet counted. This information is not incorporated in the sets model, because each number is assigned to a set, and previously counted objects are not distinguished from the currently counted object.

Unlike the sets model, the inclusion model (English & Halford, 1995, p. 82) can account for understanding the compositional relations between sets. In this model, each counting number is mapped to a set of sets of equal magnitude; the numbers occur in a fixed sequence; the sets to which the numbers are mapped increase in magnitude by one element with each successive number; each set is included in the next larger set; and counting continues until all objects are assigned to a counted set.

The inclusion model has some important consequences. The first is that the last number in the count routine represents the set of all objects counted and not just the final object counted. Thus the model embodies an understanding of the cardinal word principle. The inclusion model facilitates recognition of the compositional relationships among subsets and sets. For example, the set corresponding to the cardinal number five can be thought of as containing two subsets: one whose cardinal value is four and the other with a cardinal value of one. The subset of four in turn contains subsets with cardinal values of three and one and so on. Representation of the compositional relationships would seem to be necessary if children are to recognize that the set as a whole (cardinal value of five) is invariant under variant partitionings (e.g., 1 + 4; 3 + 2; Resnick, 1989). This model would support understanding of tasks that involve partitioning of sets. It would also support the order-irrelevance principle because it distinguishes between elements that have been previously counted and those that have not. Thus each set of $x$ elements consists of a subset of $x - 1$ previously counted elements, plus one element that is currently being counted.

Frye et al. (1989, Experiment 2) used an error detection technique to assess order-irrelevance and found that children (mean age 4;0) judged the cardinal values of nonstandard (valid) counts as incorrect, suggesting that these children did not understand order irrelevance. However, responses elicited using this technique are difficult to interpret. It is unclear whether children judge the validity of the counting procedure alone (that nonstandard counting orders are acceptable) or whether they also consider the impact on cardinal value (that nonstandard and standard counting orders yield the same cardinal value). Baroody (1984) referred to these as the *order irrelevance tagging schema* and the *order irrelevance principle* respectively. Baroody had children first count the array from one end and then predict what the cardinal value would be if they counted from the opposite end. His results showed that 45% of kindergarteners (mean age 5;6) and 87% of first graders (mean age 6;8) correctly predicted that the cardinal value would be unchanged. Andrews and Halford (2002) reported similar findings. Children under 5 years experienced difficulty understanding the order-irrelevance principle when assessed using Baroody's reverse count technique. A similar age of attainment was observed for a task that involved partitioning a set of seven bananas in different ways.

The research involving normally developing children indicates that the order-irrelevance principle and set partitioning are mastered later (5 to 7 years) than the cardinal word principle and ordinal judgments (3 to 4 years). Geary (2004) reported that children with mathematical learning disabilities have poor conceptual understanding of the order-irrelevance principle, although they understand the cardinal word and stable order principles. These findings can be explained in terms of relational complexity.

The mental models shown in Figure 13.1 differ in complexity. The successor model incorporates the succession relation, whereas the sets model incorporates the magnitude relation. The succession relation is binary, as it can be defined on a minimum of two entities,

for example, *next*(6, 5) or more generally, *next*($x$, $x - 1$), where $x$ is the number assigned to an object. The magnitude relation is also binary. It can be defined on a minimum of two entities, *larger than* ($x$, $< x$). The inclusion model is more complex because it depends on the relation among three entities: numerosity ($x$); numerosity ($x - 1$) and numerosity (1). The set of items previously counted ($x - 1$) and the currently counted item (1) are included in the set ($x$). This is a ternary relation. The later mastery of tasks that require the inclusion model is consistent with the greater complexity that it entails.

## RELATIONAL REASONING

Reasoning often entails processing relations. Analogy entails mapping between relations, as described earlier, but there are other domains that rely on relational processing, the most commonly investigated form being transitive inference, which we will consider next.

### Transitive Inference

A transitive inference is an argument of the form that, for any a, b, c, where R is a transitive relation, then given premises aRb, bRc, the conclusion aRc may be inferred: (aRb, bRc → aRc). For example, if a > b and b > c, then a > c, given that ">" ("more than") is a transitive relation. Examples of transitive relations are larger than, heavier than, faster than, and older than. A relation such as *next in line to* is intransitive because if *a* is next in line to *b* and *b* is next in line to *c*, it will never be the case that *a* is next in line to *c*. Relations such as *loves* are nontransitive (neither transitive nor intransitive) because if *a* loves *b* and *b* loves *c*, then it is not necessarily true that *a* loves c. However, it is possible that *a* loves *c* if, for example, *a* is mother of *b* and *c*.

Transitive inferences are important to the development of children's reasoning skills because they are essential to many forms of inference about quantities. Transitivity of an asymmetrical binary relation is a defining property of an ordered set. That is, if we order A, B, C, D, E for size, from smallest to largest, then A < B, B < C, C < D, D < E, but also A < C, A < D, A < E, B < D, B < E, C < E. Less than (<) is an asymmetrical relation because if A < B then B > A. An ordered set is essential to an ordinal scale, so transitivity in some form is essential to ordinal, interval, and ratio scales, that is, to any quantification beyond a nominal scale.

or second slot, but we need the premise *Peter is taller than John* to determine that John should be assigned to the second slot. Similarly, we need both premises to determine the correct assignment of the other elements. Premise integration is responsible for many errors in reasoning about ordinal position of elements in a series (Foos et al., 1976). It also produces load effects in adults as determined by probe reaction times (Maybery et al., 1986), and it is sensitive to frontal lobe functioning (Waltz et al., 1999).

Markovits, Dumas, and Malfait (1995) suggested a strategy that might make the Pears and Bryant task simpler than intended. If children first identified the relevant premises, B above C, and C above D by the presence of the common term C, they might recognize that B should be above D because of their relative position in these premises. They modified the premise presentation by including neutral white blocks so the premises were presented as White above A, A above B, and B above C, C above White, thereby neutralizing the effect of the relative positions of the critical elements A and C in the physical displays. With this presentation, success was not achieved until about 8 years. On the other hand, participants might have found it difficult to interpret the white blocks, given that they had no relation to the elements that had to be ordered. Markovits et al.'s hypothesis is reasonable, but it would imply that the task was reduced to processing a binary relation between B and D (or A and C) based on their ordinal positions in the display. However Andrews and Halford (1998) found a clear differentiation between tasks based on binary relations and those based on ternary relations, with all children 4 years and above succeeding on the former, but success on ternary relations occurred at a median age of 5 years.

In adults, the processing load of premise integration produces errors and increases decision times, but the task is performed with high accuracy. But what effect does this load have on reasoning of young children? Andrews and Halford (1998, 2002) presented premises in a similar manner to Pears and Bryant (1990) but controlled the amount of premise information required to perform the task. In the binary-relational condition, children were required to build a tower by placing pairs of blocks in accord with one premise at a time (e.g., place B above C in accordance with the premise, then add D, producing the top-down order B, C, D). As each premise represents one binary relation, this requires only one binary relation to be processed in each step. In

the ternary-relational task, children were required to place blocks B and D in the correct order. To recognize that B should be placed above D, two premises—*B above C* and *C above D*—have to be processed to determine that the top-down order is BCD, from which B above D can be deduced. This task entails assigning three blocks to ordinal positions in a single decision, and therefore is ternary-relational (Andrews & Halford, 1998; Halford, 1993). Whereas success rates were high for 4-year-olds on binary-relational problems, transitive inferences requiring ternary relations were made by 20% of 4-year-olds and 50% of 5-year-olds (Andrews & Halford, 1998). This is consistent with the findings of Pears and Bryant (1990).

A procedure that permits elements to be ordered by considering one binary relation at a time can produce very different processes from those that are required for ternary relations. This is especially true where premises are presented multiple times. If the pairs A < B, B < C, C < D, D < E are presented repeatedly, it is possible to detect that A is always *less* and that E is always *more,* so A and E can be detected as end elements. Having recognized (say) A as an end element, then B can be concatenated with it by processing the relation A < B, yielding the sequence AB. Now C can be concatenated with the set by processing B < C, yielding ABC, and so on. Thus the entire sequence can be constructed using only one binary relation at each step. By contrast, when BD must be ordered by reference to the premises, the relations B < C and C < D must be integrated in working memory to produce the ordered triple BCD, and this imposes a higher processing load. Thus these two procedures can induce very different processes and impose different processing loads.

The finding of Andrews and Halford (1998) implies that the structural complexity of transitive inference may be a factor in the difficulty that young children have with it. The requirement to process both premises in a single decision places a limit on segmentation, because neither premise can be processed fully without taking the other premise into account. This means that transitive inference is in the category of tasks that are difficult because they cannot be readily segmented into subtasks. An alternative explanation might be that children under 4 to 5 years lacked the requisite strategy for integrating the premises. There are factors that cast doubt on this explanation. First, processing load effects were found in university students by Maybery et al. (1986) even after hundreds of trials with the same procedure, which strongly suggests that load is a factor in the task, even if not the whole explanation. Second, Andrews and Halford (2002) found similar age norms for transitivity and ternary-relational tasks in other domains, and it would be very difficult to explain the difficulties of young children in this diverse set of tasks in terms of a strategy. It seems reasonable to conclude therefore that structural complexity, as measured by the relational complexity metric, is a factor in the difficulty that young children have with transitive inference. There is also the problem that strategy development itself needs to be explained, and it, too, may be a function of structural complexity.

Development of transitive inference strategies was modeled by Halford et al. (1995). Strategies were guided by a mental model of an ordered set, based on experience with ordered sets of at least three elements. The architecture of the model was based on a self-modifying production system. Early strategies processed only one relation at a time, but this led to error, resulting in weakening of the productions responsible and development of new ones that took account of two relations.

A significant change to our understanding of the transitive inference process was made by the fuzzy trace model of Reyna and Brainerd (Brainerd & Kingma, 1984; Reyna & Brainerd, 1990). The essential idea is that transitive inference ability is independent of ability to recall literal premise information. Children's performance on transitive inference and memory probe tasks was more consistent with a fuzzy, gistlike memory trace than with verbatim recall of premises (Brainerd & Kingma, 1984). This means that, instead of literally recalling ordered arrays such as A < B < C < D < E (< F), as suggested earlier, children stored global patterns such as "things get larger from left to right." Memory for literal premise information occurs only where the reasoning task requires it. Memory-reasoning independence seems surprising at first, but it is well established in reasoning domains (Brainerd & Reyna, 1993). An important implication of fuzzy trace theory is that different forms of the transitive inference problem will entail different types of memory trace.

An additional process has been inserted into transitive inference models by Wright (2001), who postulated a mechanism called the "transitive-switch" that determines whether a relation is transitive. This would avoid erroneous transitive inferences based on nontransitive relations, such as loves. This mechanism can be based on implicit knowledge about whether a relation is transitive. One type of cue as to whether a relation is transitive is whether it is represented by a verbal label that contains the suffix *er*, such as *taller*, or is preceded by a quantitive adjective such as *more* as in *more popular*. Wright also suggests that the creation of an ordered representation may entail either a low-level associative process, or a cue-based process that is somewhat reminiscent of Sternberg's (1980) model. For example, the premise *John is taller than Mike* might be coded as John is tall+; Mike is tall, then these linguistic deep structural base strings are integrated to form the ordered array.

## Transitivity of Choice and Learning of Order

The Bryant and Trabasso paradigm has been adapted for use with nonhuman animals. A seminal study was that of McGonigle and Chalmers (1977) who trained squirrel monkeys to choose one member of each pair in a series (A + B −, B + C −, C + D −, D + E −, where [+] indicates a rewarded choice and [−] indicates it is nonrewarded). To assess transitivity of choice, they were tested on untrained nonadjacent pairs, with most interest focusing on B and D, because B+ and B− had occurred equally often in training, as had D+ and D−, and because the animals had not been trained on that pair. Monkeys showed a 90% preference for B over D, and basically similar data have been found with species ranging from pigeons (von Fersen, Wynne, Delius, & Staddon, 1991) to chimpanzees (Boysen, Berntson, Shreyer, & Quigley, 1993) and human children (Chalmers & McGonigle, 1984).

There is evidence that at least some transitivity of choice tasks are performed by associative processes, without representation of structure. McGonigle and Chalmers (1977) found reduced performance on triads, so monkeys were much less efficient at choosing B in the presence of C and D than in the presence of D alone. This would not be expected if the task were performed by integrating representations of relations, as described for transitive inference tasks. If the task were performed by integrating relations such as AB, BC . . . DE to form an ordered array A, B, C, D, E, as proposed for transitive inference, then it would be predicted that if B is preferable to D it should be preferable to C and D together, because B occurs earlier in the series than both. Other investigations have also raised doubts as to whether transitivity of choice is comparable with the transitive inference paradigm. Wynne (1995) applied the Bush and Mosteller (1955) and Rescorla and Wagner (1972) models to data reported by von Fersen et al. (1991). These associative learning models predicted transitive choice (B versus D), plus serial position effects and the symbolic distance effect (better discrimination between elements further apart in the series). Other work corroborates this conclusion. Couvillon and Bitterman (1992) demonstrated that transitivity of choice data can be accounted for by simple associative learning models. The production system model of Harris and McGonigle (1994) is compatible with associative learning accounts. In their model, each production rule expresses a tendency to select or avoid a given stimulus. The surface form of the model appears different from associative learning accounts of transitivity of choice, but the model is consistent with associative models in that it attributes performance to the strength of the tendency, acquired as a function of experience, to respond to each stimulus. All these models are associative in the sense that they postulate response tendencies associated with stimuli, without transformation or composition into more complex structures.

There are other reasons to distinguish transitivity of choice from the transitive inference paradigm. Whereas transitive inference implies an ordinal scale of premise elements, in transitivity of choice there is no such scale underlying the relationship (Markovits & Dumas, 1992). Furthermore, the transitive inference task is performed dynamically in working memory, following a single presentation of premises, whereas transitivity of choice is based on representations created incrementally over many trials, and can be performed by associative processes.

The sensitivity of these paradigms to changes in procedure is demonstrated by a major difference in performance that can be produced by the seemingly trivial change of adding a pair to a series. If the pair F + X− is added to the series X + A−, A + B−, B + C−, C + D−, D + E−, E + F−, the structure becomes circular rather than linear, because the series implied by the pairs is closed. With pigeons, this causes reduced, but still above chance, discrimination of adjacent pairs, performance on the test pair BD is no longer better than chance, and serial position effects disappear (von Fersen et al., 1991). The task can no longer be learned by elemental association, but it can be learned by configural association. Both the Bush-Mosteller and Rescorla-Wagner models predict chance responding on all pairs (Wynne, 1995) because every element is

equally associated with reinforcement and nonreinforcement (in the preceding set of pairs, each of A, B, C, D, E, F, X occurs with [+] and [−]). However, the observed effects are predicted by a configural learning model in which a stimulus (say B) that acquires associative strength in the presence of C (B|BC) is different from the stimulus that loses associative strength in the presence of A (B|AB) (Wynne, 1995). Each pair is learned as a separate discrimination, and nothing is learned that corresponds to the circular structure of the series. This study illustrates how very similar procedures, in this case differing only in the presence or absence of the pair F + X−, can produce markedly different performances.

Terrace and McGonigle (1994) found evidence that children and monkeys form a linear representation of a list of stimuli, whereas pigeons did not. Participants were trained by the simultaneous chaining paradigm in which they were trained to respond first to A, then to A followed by B, then to A followed by B followed by C, and so on. The physical configuration was varied from trial to trial to ensure responding was based on a sequence of elements rather than to a spatial pattern. Having learned the sequence A, B, C, D, E, pigeons responded correctly to sequences of nonadjacent elements provided they included an end element, such as the sequences AB, AC, AD, AE, . . . , DE. This appears to be consistent with the associative processes demonstrated by Wynne (1995) in the transitivity of choice paradigm. However, when required to respond to a pair of items from a list, latencies of monkeys and children, but not pigeons, were a function of distance from the beginning of the list, suggesting that the representation of the list was searched to locate the ordinal position of each item.

Holcomb, Stromer, and Mackay (1997) trained 4-year-old children in overlapping two-stimulus sequences (A > B, B > C, C > D, D > E, E > F) using a procedure similar to that of Terrace and McGonigle (1994). They then tested them in two-stimulus sequences (e.g., B > D, B > E, . . . , A > C, . . . , A > E), and longer sequences (e.g., A > B > C, B > C > D, . . . , B > D > E). Transfer from training to test sequences tended to be high. The success of children in sequences of more than two stimuli (e.g., B > C > D) differentiates the findings from the performances of monkeys reported by McGonigle and Chalmers (1977). The results are consistent with an integrated representation of an ordered set, and associative processes do not appear to be sufficient to account for the performances. The study is important for the training techniques used, which appear to be a considerable advance on previous methods for teaching sequences. It is not entirely clear how the sequence representations were constructed, but concatenation would appear to be possible (e.g., represent AB, then ABC).

The transitivity of choice paradigm has the merit that it permits a wide range of species and procedures to be compared within the same paradigm, and it illustrates how some complex tasks can be performed by associative learning processes. However, the number and importance of the differences between the transitive inference paradigm and the transitivity of choice paradigm suggests that it is unwise to regard them as equivalent. Despite this, it is not uncommon to refer to both as measures of transitivity, as though they were equivalent measures of the same construct. On the surface, this appears to facilitate an optimistic account of animals' and young children's cognition, by making it appear that all are capable of the reasoning underlying transitivity. In the longer term, however, such assumptions are more likely to lead to conceptual confusion. What we know nowadays about cognitive processes should at least make us wary of assuming that such different procedures induce the same cognitive processes. As we have seen, there is extensive evidence that in fact they induce quite different processes that also make very different demands on processing resources. Performance of transitivity of choice by associative learning makes minimal demands on processing capacity; whereas integration of relational representations in working memory is difficult for children under 4 to 5 years of age and produces a measurable, and persisting, processing load even with university students. It is true that transitivity of choice can be performed by children, who are likely to use associative processes, but this reflects the demands of the paradigm. It does not show that animals and younger and older children all typically make transitive inferences by the same processes. As discussed, there is evidence that different processes may be used in at least some tasks by different species, and by children of different ages. Terrace and McGonigle (1994) proposed that young children were unable to seriate objects as required in the Piagetian seriation task because their unidirectional search strategies did not develop until after 7 years, as indicated by their lack of differentiation between monotonic and nonmonotonic sequences.

The concept of the middle element in a set of three is relevant to children's understanding of an ordered set because it is defined by relations to elements on either

side (e.g., smallest < middle < largest). Rabinowitz and Howe (1994) showed that there was an improvement in children's ability to identify the middle element over the age range 5 to 10 years, although there were variations due to which dimension was used (e.g., physical size, shade of blue, body parts). Children who were trained on two dimensions were better able to transfer to a new dimension than those who were trained on one dimension, consistent with a number of findings in the analogy literature (Gholson, Eymard, Morgan, & Kamhi, 1987; Gick & Holyoak, 1983).

## Relational Problems of Deduction

Research with transitivity and serial order tasks represents only a small fraction of the possibilities for inferences based on relations, but comparatively little research has been devoted to the wider topic. An encouraging start in this was made by English (1998) using problems such as the following:

> There are five houses along one side of a street. Use the clues to work out who lives in the middle house.
>
> - The Smiths live beside the Wilsons but not beside the McDonalds.
> - The Jones live in the second house on the left.
> - The Wilsons live somewhere between the Taylors and the McDonalds.
> - The Jones live beside the Taylors. (English, 1998, p. 250)

Four principles emerged from the problem solving of 264 children from Grades 4 through 7 (English, 1998, pp. 255–256):

*Principle 1:* Construct an initial model by selecting a premise that most readily yields an explicit problem-situation model.

*Principle 2:* Integrate premises where appropriate, and select premises that can be integrated most readily with an existing model/s.

*Principle 3:* During the course of model development and refinement, recognize when more than one new model, or tentative solution model, is possible.

*Principle 4:* Verify model construction, development, and refinement during the course of problem solution.

Mental model theory (Johnson-Laird & Byrne, 1991) and relational complexity theory, discussed earlier, were found to give a good account of the relative difficulties of different problem forms.

## Relational Problem Solving

Fireman (1996) conducted a microgenetic analysis of 6- to 8-year-old children's performance on a standard 3-disc Tower of Hanoi (TOH) problem. The TOH has three pegs and discs that vary in size. The goal is to shift all discs from peg A to peg C by shifting only one disc at a time, and without ever placing a larger disc above a smaller one. The task, together with the somewhat similar Tower of London task (Shallice, 1982), has been extensively used for research in problem solving with adults (VanLehn, 1991) and children (Klahr & Robinson, 1981). Fireman found that children's success depended largely on whether they made a transition from indeterminate actions (moves that were legal but inefficient or suboptimal) to an adequate solution plan. This transition required strategy development rather than strategy selection. Developing a successful plan entails processing embedded relations between discs and pegs in the task. For example, in order to move disc 3 (largest) from peg A to peg C, it is necessary to move discs 1 and 2 to peg B, and in order to move disc 2 to peg B it is first necessary to move disc 1 to peg C. Development of an efficient strategy requires that as much as possible of this structure be represented. The complexity of steps in a TOH problem can be quantified by relational complexity theory (Halford, Wilson, et al., 1998, Section 6.1.3).

Cohen (1996) studied strategy in 3- to 4-year-olds using a "play store" task in which the goal was to provide specific numbers of tomatoes, starting with different configurations. For example, if the order was for four tomatoes and there was a carton that already contained three tomatoes, the optimum strategy was to add one tomato, but if there was a carton with five tomatoes, subtraction of one tomato was the optimal strategy. Children's strategies quickly became more efficient, as indicated by reduced numbers of unnecessary moves.

## Fast Mapping and Exclusivity

Although fast mapping might not normally be interpreted as relational reasoning, it does appear to entail understanding of the relation of exclusivity. There is evidence that 2-year-old children understand this binary relation (Markman & Wachtel, 1988). A child who knows the meaning of "cup" and is shown a cup and a painter's palette, then asked, "Which one is the pilson?" tends to choose the palette. The child understands that if "pilson" and "cup" each refer to one of the objects (the "exclusivity" bias) and knows which object is the referent of "cup," it follows that the other object is the referent of "pilson." We could interpret this as indicating that children represent a binary relation of exclusivity that has two slots; exclusive (-,-), and the words are mapped into these slots, which is another case of analogy. If one object fills one slot, the other object fills the other slot. Furthermore, the representation is established dynamically, following a single presentation.

## Logical Deduction and Induction

Two of the topics that have been most extensively studied with children are conditional reasoning and causal reasoning. Both of these are examined in the chapter on adolescent reasoning by Kuhn and Franklin (Chapter 22, this *Handbook*, this volume). Because reasoning based on mental models is a major theme of this chapter, we will consider how it applies to conditional reasoning.

## Mental Models in Conditional Reasoning

A conditional is an expression of the form $p$ implies $q$, or if $p$ then $q$, written symbolically as $p \rightarrow q$. There are four possible argument forms, two of which are valid and two are fallacies. The valid forms are modus ponens ($p \rightarrow q$, $p$, therefore $q$) and modus tollens ($p \rightarrow q$, not $q$, therefore not $p$). The invalid forms are, denial of the antecedent ($p \rightarrow q$, not $p$ therefore not $q$), and affirmation of the consequent ($p \rightarrow q$, $q$ therefore $p$). Much research has been devoted to determining whether children distinguish valid from invalid argument forms, the influence of a number of variables, especially problem content, on their reasoning, and the processes they use to make their inferences.

Content affects syllogistic reasoning through the belief bias effect, in which prior knowledge and beliefs about the world tend to influence conclusions (Simoneau & Markovits, 2003). However, even young children show some ability to make inferences from contrary-to-fact premises. Richards and Sanderson (1999) showed that 2- to 4-year-olds were capable of counterfactual thinking if they were encouraged to use their imagination (e.g., to imagine that the counterfactual premises were true on another planet).

Mental model theory has enjoyed considerable success in accounting for reasoning processes in adults (Johnson-Laird & Byrne, 1991) and has been reformulated to account for most findings in development of conditional reasoning by Markovits and Barrouillet (2002). Mental models are iconic representations of the premises that have the status of analogues, as discussed in the introductory sections of this chapter. For conditional reasoning, the major premise $p \rightarrow q$ would be represented initially as follows:

$$p \qquad q$$
$$. . .$$

The first line represents a state of affairs in which $p$ and $q$ are both true, and there is a link between them. The dots on the next line represent implicit recognition that other possibilities exist. According to the model of Markovits and Barrouillet (2002) the representations will be fleshed out to give explicit representation of other possibilities as follows (where $\neg p$ represents "*not p*"):

$$p \qquad q$$
$$\neg p \qquad \neg q$$

This corresponds to a biconditional interpretation of the major premise, that is $p$ implies $q$ and $q$ implies $p$ ($p \leftrightarrow q$). Then the representation is further fleshed out as follows:

$$p \qquad q$$
$$\neg p \qquad \neg q$$
$$\neg p \qquad q$$

This corresponds to the canonical interpretation of a conditional (it is isomorphic to the truth table for a conditional). It does not correspond to a biconditional interpretation because it implies $p \rightarrow q$ but not $q \rightarrow p$.

The fleshing out is performed by retrieving information from semantic memory about relations that are appropriate for the content of the problem, using the minor premise as a supplementary retrieval cue. The fleshing out is governed by availability of examples in semantic memory and by the complexity of the resulting representation. Predictions are made by examining what inferences can be made by fleshing out the mental model in different ways.

Markovits and Barrouillet (2002) assume that children of 5 to 7 years will only be able to add one relation

to the simplest model, so they can flesh it out in one of two ways, depending on the minor premise. Modus tollens and denial of the antecedent entail minor premises that include negations, so they tend to activate the complementary class in semantic memory. The children can then retrieve a case of a — $\neg q$, where a is an element that is different from ("alternative to") p, and — represents some kind of relation or link between a and $\neg q$. Thus the model is expanded as follows:

$$p \qquad q$$
$$a \text{---} \neg q$$

This is equivalent to a biconditional interpretation. This would yield correct inferences in the form of modus ponens because when $p$ is true, $q$ is true, and modus tollens because when $\neg q$ is true, $\neg p$ (a) is true. However, it also yields inferences of the form affirmation of the consequent, because it does not represent cases where $q$ is true, but $\neg p$ is true.

If the minor premise is "$q$ is true," this will activate cases of elements that are linked to q, yielding the model:

$$p \qquad q$$
$$b \text{---} q$$

where $b$ is different from $p$. This will lead to the correct inference that if $q$ is true, it is uncertain whether $p$ is true or not true, so affirmation of the consequent will be rejected. Similarly, denial of the antecedent will be rejected because cases of $\neg p$ and $q$ are represented. Retrievability from memory will depend on the content of the premises, so if the major premise were "if an animal is a dog then it has legs," children can easily retrieve alternative cases such as "cats have legs," "horses have legs." Therefore, the theory predicts that resistance to denial of the antecedent and affirmation of the consequent will depend on the ease with which alternative cases can be retrieved. This is consistent with findings of content effects (Barrouillet & Lecas, 2002; Markovits et al., 1996). Manipulations that encouraged production of alternative conditions led to more rejection of affirmation of the consequent and denial of the antecedent inferences (Simoneau & Markovits, 2003). Disabling conditions (Cummins, 1995) can also be retrieved from semantic memory, possibly leading to rejection of modus ponens inferences. For example, if the major premise were "if it rains, the street will be wet" and the minor premise is "it is raining" then the correct inference is "the street is wet." A disabling condition might be "the street is covered (e.g., by an overpass)" in which case the inference will be rejected. The strength of association of disabling conditions has an effect on conditional reasoning (De Neys, Schaeken, & d'Ydewalle, 2003).

The theory of Markovits and Barrouillet has been applied to both class-based conditionals, where the major premise is in the form "All A are B" and causal conditionals, such as "If a rock is a thrown at a window, the window will break." Causal conditionals require more complex processing, according to the theory, because of the requirement for a naive theory to generate alternative and disabling conditions. It has also been applied to inferences based on premises that are contrary to world knowledge, such as: "If a car has lots of gas, then the car will not run." (Simoneau & Markovits, 2003, p. 971). If the minor premise is "The car has lots of gas," the correct (modus ponens) inference is that the car will not run. This requires that world knowledge must be inhibited. Simoneau and Markovits (2003) showed elegantly that there is an interaction between memory retrieval and inhibition. Older adolescents, who have more efficient retrieval, were more likely to reject modus ponens inferences, even though instructed to suppose that the major premise is true, because they are more likely to retrieve disabling conditions. Thus their reasoning is less logical than that of younger adolescents. When the adolescents were first given a contrary-to-fact problem, there was less tendency to reject the modus ponens inference. The contrary-to-fact problem helped participants to inhibit disabling conditions retrieved from memory.

The theory of Markovits and Barrouillet (2002) accounts for many findings of the effects of premise content on conditional reasoning. Even some studies that are not specifically interpreted by Markovits and Barrouillet appear to be consistent with it. For example, the effect of fantasy, as observed *inter alia* in the study by Richards and Sanderson (1999), or the effect of instruction as observed by Leevers and Harris (1999), could be interpreted as inhibiting retrieval of knowledge from semantic memory. It also makes many novel predictions, such as that belief bias interacts with other features of the task (see Markovits & Barrouillet, 2002, pp. 23–30).

The theory is also consistent with processes that have been found to have wide applicability in cognition and cognitive development, including analogy theory, mental model theory, retrieval from semantic memory, and cognitive complexity theory. Although the theory is limited to inferences made from premises and has not so far been applied to related tasks such as the Wason selection task, it takes an important step toward providing greater theoretical coherence in the field and generates many useful predictions. Such theories can do a lot to sharpen research issues.

Other issues go beyond the developmentally reformulated mental model theory. One of these concerns the important issue of conversational implicatures and their effect on inferences. Noveck (2001) showed that 7- to 9-year-olds are more likely than adults to adopt the logical interpretation of *might be x* as including *must be x* rather than the conversationally pragmatic interpretation *might but not must*. However mental model theory can presumably accommodate conversational implicatures in terms of their influence on the construction of mental models representing the premises. There appear to be possibilities for further theory and empirical research here.

## Logical and Empirical Determinacy

The ability to recognize determinacy of inferences is important in both scientific and everyday reasoning. An inference is *logically determinate* when the conclusion necessarily follows from the premises because of the logical form of the argument. Modus ponens, $p \rightarrow q$, $p$ therefore q, is a valid argument form and the conclusion, q, is necessarily true, given the premises $p \rightarrow q$ and p. Affirmation of the consequent, $p \rightarrow q$, q, therefore $p$, is not a valid argument form because the conclusion, p, is not necessarily true. There is considerable evidence that both children and adults find it difficult to determine when an argument is logically determinate. Johnson-Laird (1983) has shown that people tend not to check whether a mental model is the only one implied by the premises, so they sometimes fail to recognize that a conclusion that follows from the first mental model they construct is not necessarily true because it is not true in alternate models. There is considerable evidence that recognition of logical determinacy tends to develop later in children than ability to make inferences (Markovits, Schleifer, & Fortier, 1989; Moshman & Franks, 1986; Osherson & Markman, 1975). Ruffman (1999) showed that children under 6 years did not understand logical consistency, even though they could remember the premises, which were presented in a variety of formats, and could recognize factual inconsistency. An interesting finding was that understanding of logical consistency was positively related to number of older siblings in the family.

Reasoning is *empirically determinate* if a verbal description of a situation is consistent with only a single state of affairs. Again, however, there appear to be limitations to children's ability to recognize empirical determinacy. One reason for failure is a "positive capture" strategy in which one possibility is accepted without checking alternatives. Another is children's imperfect understanding of logical connectives *if,* and *or* (Braine & O'Brien, 1998). A third is that children do not recognize the need to distinguish between logical and conversational pragmatic interpretations of statements. An example is that "some" in conversation usually means "some but not all" because conversational implicatures (Grice, 1975) mean that if one meant "all," one would not say "some"; but logically "some" is interpreted as "some or all." These difficulties appear consistent with the limitations observed by Johnson-Laird in adult reasoning and are not unique to children.

Morris and Sloutsky (1998, 2002) showed that children below 11 to 12 years did not distinguish between logical and empirical problems because they did not fully represent the state of affairs implied by the propositions, but tended to base conclusions on only the first part of the evidence. Furthermore, some individuals showed this pattern consistently across a set of problems, suggesting that its occurrence was systematic rather than random. A possible benefit of the strategy is that it reduces processing load, but prolonged instruction led to improved performance. Fay and Klahr (1996) and Klahr and Chen (2003) have found that much younger children recognize empirical determinacy in some contexts, such as that a necklace of red beads must have been made by beads from a particular box if it was the only one containing red beads, but that the box used is indeterminate if more than one box contains red beads. However, 4- to 5-year-olds showed a pronounced positive capture strategy and training was more effective with 5- than with 4-year-olds. English (1997) showed that preadolescents improved their recognition of indeterminacy if they received training that induced both acceptance of lack of closure and construction of more complete models, but not if they received only one.

## SCIENTIFIC AND TECHNOLOGICAL THINKING

Scientific reasoning applies to some specialized domains, but it also offers insights into the nature of reasoning processes in general and the way they develop. We will consider some of the major domains in which the development of scientific concepts has been researched. Again, reference should be made to the chapter on adolescent reasoning by Kuhn and Franklin (Chapter 22, this *Handbook,* this volume).

### Basic Dimensions and Their Interrelations

The basic dimensions of the physical world include time, distance, speed, mass, specific gravity, and heat. There are interrelations between the basic dimensions: Speed = Distance/Time, area is length × breadth, volume is length × breadth × height, heat is temperature × specific heat × mass, and so on. Understanding these basic dimensions and their interrelations is important for understanding everyday and scientific phenomena. Early research into these concepts was influenced by Piaget and his collaborators, but other approaches have developed since. There are also classic treatments of the developmental psychology of time by Friedman (1978, 1982).

### *Time, Speed, and Distance*

Siegler and Richards (1979) applied the rule assessment technique to time, distance, and speed, and found a progression over three levels of rule in 5- to 11-year-olds. At the lowest level, Rule I, children based their judgments on a single factor such as stopping point; at Rule II, they considered a second factor if situations were equal on the first factor (stopping times if stopping points were the same); and at Rule III, they considered all variables. Wilkening (1981) and Wilkening, Levin and Druyan (1987) used information integration theory, using a turtle, guinea pig, or cat to represent different speeds. The animals were run for different distances or times, and children were asked to estimate the remaining variable. It was found that 5-year-olds combined time and speed multiplicatively in their estimates of distance, but they combined distance and speed additively to represent time, and used only distance to estimate speed, ignoring time. In a cross-sectional study, Matsuda (2001) had 4- to 11-year-old children judge relations between all three variables using toy trains traveling at varying speeds down tracks of varying lengths for varying durations. The younger children tended to process relations between pairs of variables, the positive relation between time and distance and speed and distance appearing first. The inverse relation between speed and time developed later, suggesting that younger children tended to base their judgments on a "more is more" relation, and only later differentiated this from the "more is less" relation between time and speed. Understanding of the system defined by all three variables developed around 10 to 11 years of age. The findings were confirmed in a longitudinal study. Whereas there is consensus that more complex concepts develop later, different methodologies have yielded somewhat different age norms suggesting that although methodologies are sophisticated and sensitive, there is scope for further refinement.

A neural net model that simulates the development of velocity, time, and distance concepts has been developed by Buckingham and Shultz (2000) based on the cascade correlation algorithm. Additional hidden units were recruited as the network progressed to more advanced rules, to capture the increased dimensionality of the task. This suggests that development of the concept may depend on increased representational capacity, consistent with the suggestion of Matsuda (2001). Friedman (2003) investigated whether young children understand the unidirectional nature of some changes over time, and found that even 3- to 4-year-olds could discriminate forward and reversed presentations of breaking a cookie or dropping a block.

### Area

Information integration theory has been used to study children's understanding of area. A classic finding is that young children tend to combine length and breadth additively, whereas after approximately 5 years of age they combine them multiplicatively (Anderson & Cuneo, 1978; Wilkening, 1979, 1980). A possible explanation is that additive effects can be segmented, so one can estimate the effect of a change in (say) length, then add the effect of breadth, but dimensions that are combined multiplicatively interact and cannot be segmented. To put this another way, with multiplicative combination, the effect of change in length is modified by any change in breadth, and vice versa. Therefore, in terms of relational complexity theory, additive combi-

nation amounts to two successive binary relations (length, area) and (breadth, area), whereas multiplicative combination precludes decomposition into separate relations and has the effective relational complexity of a ternary relation (length, breadth, area). Silverman, York, and Zuidema (1984) found evidence consistent with the hypothesis that additive composition of length and breadth might reflect decomposition into subtasks.

## Concept of the Earth

The concept of the earth is interesting because of its relevance to everyday thought, because it entails some complex relational concepts, and because it entails a conflict between observation and culturally transmitted information. The earth appears more flat than spherical when viewed from the perspective of a person living on the surface but we are taught, and photographs taken from space show us, that it is spherical. The resolution of this discrepancy is that the enormous diameter of the earth makes it looks flat to an observer on the surface. Another naive belief is that, perhaps by analogy with familiar objects, the earth must be supported, otherwise it would fall. Cultural information, however, is that because the earth orbits the sun, it does not need to be supported. To understand this requires some kind of intuitive mental model of orbital motion, which entails complex relations, including the balance between gravitational attraction between sun and earth, and the centrifugal effect of traveling in an orbit. Another conflict is due to common observation that unsupported objects fall, and cultural information that people can stand at any point on the spherical earth, including positions that appear to be "down under." The resolution of this depends on a more sophisticated mental model of gravity, as an attraction between two bodies. Objects fall because of attraction between the mass of the object and the mass of the earth.

Conceptual development cannot be based on simply substituting culturally transmitted information for common observation. We cannot forget or ignore that objects fall. To develop a mental model of gravity, we have to integrate observation with cultural information. This means understanding that the reason objects fall is that they are attracted toward the center of the earth. This means recognizing the correspondence between two relations: Attraction between object and earth corresponds to an object falling toward the ground. Four variables make this a complex concept.[1]

In general, understanding the earth involves some complex relations and higher-order relations, so complexity is inevitably a factor in understanding the concept of the earth.

Vosniadou and Brewer (1992) used a structured interview technique that included asking children to draw their conception of the earth, with first- to fifth-grade children. The children's conceptions seemed to reflect attempts to reconcile the conflicting notions previously mentioned. Children would draw a flattened sphere with people standing on top, or a hollow sphere with a horizontal platform inside for people to stand on, or even dual earths, one round and one flat. Some cultural influence has also been observed. Indian children tend to believe that the earth is supported by a body of water, a notion that is not observed in American or Australian children (Samarapungavan, Vosniadou, & Brewer, 1996). There are many similarities between conceptions in different cultures (Candela, 2001). This is possibly because there is a strong logic inherent in the nature of the earth and its relations to other cosmological bodies, as well as to such phenomena as the day-night cycle, seasons, and the effect of gravity.

Vosniadou and Brewer found evidence of mental models with some degree of coherence. If children thought that the earth was spherical, they were less likely to think it was possible to fall off the edge. However, the mental models interpretation has been challenged by Nobes et al. (2003), who found fragmented knowledge with 4- to 8-year-olds. Fragmentation may be typical of young children's conceptions, but on theoretical grounds it is hard to see how a concept of the earth could develop without some conceptual coherence. How

can we understand that the earth is spherical without recognizing that its flat appearance is due to its large diameter, or that gravitational attraction between the earth and objects explains why people can stand at any point on the surface. The finding by Hayes, Goodhew, Heit, and Gillan (2003) that children only progressed toward a spherical conception of the earth if they received instruction about both the size of the earth and gravity, seems to be consistent with the coherence theoretical view. Consistency of answers might be a function of the method of questioning. Vosniadou, Skopeliti, and Ikospentaki (2004) found that forced choice questioning increased the number of scientifically correct answers, but there was more internal consistency among answers elicited by an open method.

## Balance Scale

The balance scale comprises a beam balanced on a fulcrum with equally spaced pegs on each side on which weights can be placed. It was widely used in Piagetian investigations of cognitive development; but independent of specific theories, it is important theoretically and methodologically as a medium for studying children's understanding of proportion, and of the interaction between four variables. The past quarter century has seen considerable theoretical and methodological development, probably spearheaded by Siegler's (1976, 1981) rule assessment analysis. Siegler identified four rules: With Rule I, children consider only weights; with Rule II, they also consider distance, but only if weights on the two sides are equal. With Rule III, they consider weight first, then distance; but they have difficulty if the greater weight occurs on one side and greater distance on the other. With Rule IV, the torque principle is applied, according to which the side with the greater torque, defined as the product of weight and distance, went down. If torques on the two sides are equal, the beam balances. Children progressed from Rule I at age 5 to Rule III in adolescence. Rule IV tended to be rare, even in adults.

Surber and Gzesh (1984) conducted an information integration theory analysis. They found that 5-year-olds tended to use distance rather than weight, but in other respects children's progression was consistent with that found by Siegler. Information integration methodology can distinguish whether weight and distance are combined multiplicatively or additively, as noted earlier,

---

[1] There is a correspondence between falls-toward (object, ground) and attraction-between (object, earth). The first relation occurs because of the second, so *because* is a higher-order relation linking the two binary relations. According to relational complexity theory analyses, there are four variables corresponding to the two slots in each binary relation. Conceptual chunking or segmentation might reduce the processing load here, but this can only happen after the concept has developed. Consequently, development of a mental model of gravity is likely to prove difficult for young children, though it should be possible to devise teaching techniques that would give them a partial understanding.

and not even adults used the correct multiplicative combination consistently. Surber and Gzesh also found that children tended to use a compensation rule, according to which balance could be achieved by changing one dimension to compensate for a change in the other dimension, rather than Siegler's Rule III. The compensation rule is essentially an additive rule.

More recent research has resulted in some modifications of a rule-based conception. Jansen and van der Maas (2001) found that there is a discontinuity in the transition between Rule I and Rule II, as defined by the cusp model, a derivative of catastrophe theory. Rule II may require the ability to encode a second variable (Siegler & Chen, 1998), and this might entail a shift to a qualitatively different, or at least more complex, cognitive process. Latent class analyses by Jansen and van der Maas (2002) showed that children use rules, but not always consistently, and there was evidence of an additive rule in place of Siegler's Rule III. Their findings were consistent with Siegler's overlapping waves model of development, implying that rules are not used exclusively, but children of a given age might use more than one rule. They, too, found evidence that some transitions between rules were discontinuous.

Most studies have used response accuracy, or response patterns, as the dependent variable but van der Maas and Jansen (2003) used response times. Cluster analysis yielded six categories of performance, corresponding to Siegler's four rules, plus a compensation rule and a category that could not be interpreted as any rule. An apparently paradoxical finding was that young adults were slower to solve balance scale problems than children, due to using more complex rules. There were also some findings that modified the way the rules were originally defined. Children using Rule II considered distance on all items, not only when weights were equal, but they did not know how to combine it with weight. It was also found that whereas response patterns tended to be homogenous for items of a given type (as found in previous rule assessments), response times were not necessarily homogeneous.

Boom, Hoijtink, and Kunnen (2001) also used latent class analysis and found six classes of responses, two of which did not correspond to rules. They also suggested that development of the balance scale concept might entail both discrete and more gradual transitions. Rules might provide a somewhat idealized account of children's concept of the balance scale, but categorization into just four rules might reflect the restricted number of item types used in early studies and the restriction of the data to response patterns rather than decision times. More recent statistical assessments have indicated a more complex picture.

Children as young as 2 to 3 years have some understanding of the balance scale. Discriminations of weights with distance constant, or distances with weight constant, entail representing the binary relation between two weights, or two distances, according to relational complexity theory (Halford, Wilson, et al., 1998). These discriminations should be possible at the age when other binary-relational concepts are mastered (Halford, 1993). Items that entail integration of weight and distance require at least ternary-relational processing; this should be mastered by 5 years and should be predicted by other performances at the same level of complexity. These predictions were confirmed by Halford, Andrews, Dalton, Boag, and Zielinski (2002). Complexity theory was instrumental in the discovery of previously unrecognized abilities in young children, but the weight and distance discriminations, while better than chance, were not as systematic as the rule-governed behavior displayed by 5-year-olds, and are most appropriately interpreted as precursors. Note that making the apparatus and procedure more child friendly, while necessary to elicit optimum performance from young children, was not sufficient because the same procedure was used with ternary-relational tasks, and these were not mastered until 5 to 6 years.

McClelland (1995) developed a three-layered net model of children's understanding of the balance scale. The architecture comprises four sets of five input units, representing one to five weights on pegs one to five steps from the fulcrum, on both left and right sides. There are four hidden units, two of which compare weights and two compare distances, while the output units compute the balance state. The model captures crucial developmental results, and its progress through training has some correspondence to the course of development as defined by Siegler's (1981) rules. An interesting property is that training results in the units representing larger weights, or larger distances, having greater connection weights to the hidden units. Thus metrics for weight and distance emerge as a result of training and are not predefined in the net. This shows how structure can emerge from interaction with a learning environment.

This model computes the balance state as a function of weight and distance on left and right sides of the balance beam, but understanding the balance beam also entails other functions, such as determining weight or distance values that will make the beam balance (Surber & Gzesh, 1984). For example, if $W_l = 3$, $D_l = 2$ and $W_r = 2$, what value of $D_r$ will make the beam balance? (Answer = 3). Complete understanding of the balance scale would include being able to determine any variable given the others. The model has restricted generalization because if it is trained (say) on two or three weights on either side, it cannot generalize to problems with four or five weights (Marcus, 1998a), but it would be reasonable to expect that children would achieve this generalization. The model makes some important advances, but does not fully capture understanding of the concept as it is exhibited in middle childhood.

## CONCLUSION

Markovits and Barrouillet (2004) have noted a marked decrease in developmental work on children's reasoning recently. A possible reason is that the motivation to either support or rebut Piagetian theory has declined in importance, and has not been entirely replaced by a new paradigm for development of reasoning. Another factor might be research on infant cognitive abilities, which are sometimes seen as equivalent to the conceptual development that was once thought to occur in middle childhood. Thus Houdé (2000) interprets infants' performance as reflecting conservation of number, whereas Piagetian measures of the same concept are seen as also requiring inhibition of conflicting strategies. Similar arguments are made for class inclusion, where the difficulty of the Piagetian tests is attributed to the need to inhibit the subclass comparison strategy (Perret, Paour, & Blaye, 2003).

Claims that reasoning in infancy is equivalent to that in middle childhood cannot be based solely on rebuttal of Piagetian research. They must be reconciled with the large and diverse body of work that points to strong distinctions between cognitive abilities in infancy and middle childhood. The literature on the distinction between symbolic and subsymbolic processes spans many areas within psychology and several other disciplines. Children who are operating at a symbolic level can do many things that are not possible for infants operating at a subsymbolic level, as the literature we reviewed earlier in the chapter shows. It would be necessary to explain these differences, and it does not seem plausible that they are entirely attributable to growth of inhibitory control with age. In conservation, we saw how it was necessary to integrate length and number information, and it is not sufficient simply to inhibit attention to length. In class inclusion, avoidance of subclass comparison is not straightforward, but depends on representing the relations between superordinate and subclasses to determine which of the three possible comparisons is the appropriate one. And the concept of the earth cannot be developed by inhibiting knowledge that the earth appears flat when standing on its surface, but must be based on integration of this observation with knowledge of the great circumference of the earth.

Far from research on reasoning in childhood being rendered redundant by discovery of full-fledged infant reasoning capacities, the scope for research on development of reasoning is greater than ever. The fundamental changes that have occurred in our understanding of reasoning in recent decades create a wealth of opportunities for innovative investigations of children's thinking. A development that appears to have great potential is the mental models approach of Markovits and his collaborators. These researchers have shown the potential of a reasoning process based on fleshing out mental models by retrieving information from semantic memory. The model of Markovits and Barrouillet (2002) forms useful links between research on reasoning processes and the powerful influence of knowledge on children's reasoning.

There is also scope to reinterpret some demonstrations of precocious reasoning by applying more refined complexity analyses. We have seen many instances where younger children's reasoning reflects simpler tasks, but this can only be appreciated if we have a complexity metric for assessing the tasks. Such reassessments would in no way deny either the validity or the importance of reasoning capabilities that have been discovered. Rather, a number of benefits might flow from them. One is methodological, in that we should be more aware that when we change test procedures we also change the processes that children are likely to use. Much of the research on precocity has assumed that the same concept can be measured by a variety of assessments, with little attempt to verify that the observed performances do in fact reflect the same cognitive processes; but we have seen how often this strategy has led to fallacies. Another possible benefit is that complexity assessments might contribute to a more orderly and coherent interpretation of the database. As Frye and Zelazo (1998, p. 836) noted:

> Developmental psychology is commonly recognized as the study of change, but without a method for ordering the changes, the phenomena become as disorganized as those in the physical sciences would be without a periodic table.

Complexity analyses have also contributed to discovery of new abilities. Complexity need no longer be seen as a difficult concept to apply in experimental research because of the progress in techniques for analyzing and manipulating task complexity. Some of the major parameters of cognitive complexity have now been determined, as evidenced by the widespread consensus that adult cognition is limited to approximately four independent entities processed in parallel and that even quite different methodologies have converged on similar age-related capacities in children.

Having surveyed the literature on the development of reasoning, we can only remark on the awesome progress that has been made. However, we are equally impressed with the prospects for further discoveries.

## REFERENCES

Acredolo, C., & Acredolo, L. P. (1979). Identity, compensation, and conservation. *Child Development, 50,* 524–535.

Adams, M. J. (1978). Logical competence and transitive inference in young children. *Journal of Experimental Child Psychology, 25,* 477–489.

Altmann, G. T. M., & Dienes, Z. (1999). Rule learning by 7-month-old infants and neural networks. *Science, 284,* 875.

Anderson, J. R. (1990). *The adaptive character of thought.* Hillsdale, NJ: Erlbaum.

Anderson, J. R. (1991). Is human cognition adaptive? *Behavioral and Brain Science, 14,* 471–517.

Anderson, N. H., & Cuneo, D. O. (1978). The height + width rule in children's judgments of quantity. *Journal of Experimental Psychology: General, 107,* 335–378.

Andrews, G., & Halford, G. S. (1998). Children's ability to make transitive inferences: The importance of premise integration and structural complexity. *Cognitive Development, 13,* 479–513.

Andrews, G., & Halford, G. S. (2002). A cognitive complexity metric applied to cognitive development. *Cognitive Psychology, 45,* 153–219.

Andrews, G., Halford, G. S., Bunch, K. M., Bowden, D., & Jones, T. (2003). Theory of mind and relational complexity. *Child Development, 74,* 1476–1499.

Andrews, G., Halford, G. S., & Prasad, A. (1998, July). *Processing load and children's comprehension of relative clause sentences.* Paper presented at the XVth Bienniel conference of the International Society for the Study of Behavioral Development, Berne, Switzerland. (ERIC Document Reproduction Service No. ED420091.)

Baddeley, A. (1996). Exploring the central executive. *Quarterly Journal of Experimental Psychology: Human Experimental Psychology, 49A,* 5–28.

Bailystok, E., & Martin, M. M. (2004). Attention and inhibition in bilingual children: Evidence from the dimensional change card sort task. *Developmental Science, 7,* 325–339.

Baroody, A. J. (1984). More precisely defining and measuring the order-irrelevance principle. *Journal of Experimental Child Psychology, 38,* 33–41.

Barrouillet, P., & Lecas, J. (2002). Content and context effects in children's and adults' conditional reasoning. *Quarterly Journal of Experimental Psychology, 55A,* 839–854.

Barrouillet, P., & Poirier, L. (1997). Comparing and transforming: An application of Piaget's morphisms theory to the development of class inclusion and arithmetic problem solving. *Human Development, 40,* 216–234.

Beilin, H. (1992). Piaget's enduring contribution to developmental psychology. *Developmental Psychology, 28*(2), 191–204.

Bjorklund, D. F. (1997). In search of a metatheory for cognitive development (or Piaget is dead and I don't feel so good myself). *Child Development, 68,* 144–148.

Blewitt, P. (1994). Understanding categorical hierarchies: The earliest levels of skill. *Child Development, 65,* 1279–1298.

Boom, J., Hoijtink, H., & Kunnen, S. (2001). Rules in the balance: Classes, strategies, or rules for the balance scale task? *Cognitive Development, 16,* 717–735.

Boysen, S. T., Berntson, G. G., Shreyer, T. A., & Quigley, K. S. (1993). Processing of ordinality and transitivity by chimpanzees (pan troglodytes). *Journal of Comparative Psychology, 107,* 1–8.

Braine, M. D. S. (1959). The ontogeny of certain logical operations: Piaget's formulation examined by nonverbal methods. *Psychological Monographs, 73,* 1–43.

Braine, M. D. S., & O'Brien, D. P. (1998). The theory of mental-propositional logic: Description and illustration. In M. D. S. Braine & D. P. O'Brien (Eds.), *Mental logic* (pp. 79–89). Mahwah, NJ: Erlbaum.

Brainerd, C. J. (1976). Does prior knowledge of the compensation rule increase susceptibility to conservation training? *Developmental Psychology, 12,* 1–5.

Brainerd, C. J., & Kingma, J. (1984). Do children have to remember to reason: A fuzzy-trace theory of transitivity development. *Developmental Review, 4,* 311–377.

Brainerd, C. J., & Reyna, V. F. (1990). Gist is the grist: Fuzzy-trace theory and the new intuitionism. *Developmental Review, 10,* 3–47.

Brainerd, C. J., & Reyna, V. F. (1993). Memory independence and memory interference in cognitive development. *Psychological Review, 100,* 42–67.

Brannon, E. M. (2002). The development of ordinal numerical knowledge in infancy. *Cognition, 83,* 223–240.

Brannon, E. M., & Van de Walle, G. A. (2001). The development of ordinal numerical competence in young children. *Cognitive Psychology, 43,* 53–81.

Breslow, L. (1981). Reevaluation of the literature on the development of transitive inferences. *Psychological Bulletin, 89,* 325–351.

Briars, D., & Siegler, R. S. (1984). A featural analysis of preschoolers' counting knowledge. *Developmental Psychology, 20,* 607–618.

Brooks, P. J., Hanauer, J. B., Padowska, B., & Rosman, H. (2003). The role of selective attention in preschoolers' rule use in a novel dimensional card sort. *Cognitive Development, 18,* 195–215.

Bruner, J. S., Olver, R. R., & Greenfield, P. M. (1966). *Studies in cognitive growth.* New York: Wiley.

Bryant, P. (2002). Constructivism today. *Cognitive Development, 17,* 1283–1508.

Bryant, P. E. (1972). The understanding of invariance by very young children. *Canadian Journal of Psychology, 26,* 78–96.

Bryant, P. E., & Trabasso, T. (1971). Transitive inferences and memory in young children. *Nature, 232,* 456–458.

Buckingham, D., & Shultz, T. R. (2000). The developmental course of distance, time, and velocity concepts: A generative connectionist model. *Journal of Cognition and Development, 1,* 305–345.

Bush, R. R., & Mosteller, F. (1955). *Stochastic models for learning.* New York: Wiley.

Candela, A. (2001). Earthly talk. *Human Development, 44,* 119–125.

Carey, S. (1985). *Conceptual change in childhood.* Cambridge, MA: MIT Press.

Carey, S. (1996, May 30–June 1). *The representation of number by infants and nonhuman primates.* Paper presented at IIAS 3rd International Brain and Mind Symposium on Concept Formation: Thinking and Their Development, Kyoto, Japan.

Carey, S. (2000). The origin of concepts. *Journal of Cognition and Development, 1,* 37–41.

Carey, S., & Gelman, R. (1991). *The epigenesis of mind: Essays on biology and cognition.* Hillsdale, NJ: Erlbaum.

Caroff, X. (2002). What conservation anticipation reveals about cognitive change. *Cognitive Development, 17,* 1015–1035.

Case, R., & Okamoto, Y. (1996). The role of central conceptual structures in the development of children's thought. *Monographs of the Society for Research in Child Development, 61,* v–265.

Cashon, C. H., & Cohen, L. B. (2004). Beyond U-shaped development in infants' processing of faces: An information-processing account. *Journal of Cognition and Development, 5,* 59–80.

Ceci, S. J., & Howe, M. J. (1978). Age-related differences in free recall as a function of retrieval flexibility. *Journal of Experimental Child Psychology, 26,* 432–442.

Chalmers, M., & McGonigle, B. (1984). Are children any more logical than monkeys on the 5-term series problem? *Journal of Experimental Child Psychology, 37,* 355–377.

Chapman, M. (1987). Piaget, attentional capacity, and the functional limitations of formal structure. *Advances in Child Development and Behaviour, 20,* 289–334.

Chapman, M. (1990). Cognitive development and the growth of capacity: Issues in NeoPiagetian theory. In J. T. Enns (Ed.), *The development of attention: Research and theory* (pp. 263–287). Amsterdam: Elsevier.

Chapman, M., & Lindenberger, U. (1988). Functions, operations and decalage in the development of transitivity. *Developmental Psychology, 24,* 542–551.

Chapman, M., & Lindenberger, U. (1989). Concrete operations and attentional capacity. *Journal of Experimental Child Psychology, 47,* 236–258.

Chen, Z. (2003). Worth one thousand words: Children's use of pictures in analogical problem solving. *Journal of Cognition and Development, 4,* 415–434.

Chen, Z., Sanchez, R. P., & Campbell, T. (1997). From beyond to within their grasp: The rudiments of analogical problem solving in 10- and 13-month-olds. *Developmental Psychology, 33,* 790–801.

Chen, Z., & Siegler, R. S. (2000). Across the great divide: Bridging the gap between understanding of toddlers' and older children's thinking. *Monographs of the Society for Research in Child Development, 65,* v–96.

Cheng, P. W., & Holyoak, K. J. (1985). Pragmatic reasoning schemas. *Cognitive Psychology, 17,* 391–416.

Clark, A., & Karmiloff-Smith, A. (1993). The cognizer's innards: A psychological and philosophical perspective on the development of thought. *Mind and Language, 8,* 487–519.

Clearfield, M. W., & Mix, K. S. (2001). Amount versus number: Infants' use of area and contour length to discriminate small sets. *Journal of Cognition and Development, 2,* 243–260.

Cohen, L. B. (2001, October). *How complexity affects infant perception and cognition.* Paper presented at the Second Biennial Meeting of the Cognitive Development Society, Virginia Beach, VA.

Cohen, L. J. (1981). Can human irrationality be experimentally demonstrated? *Behavioral and Brain Sciences, 4,* 317–370.

Cohen, M. (1996). Preschoolers' practical thinking and problem solving: The acquisition of an optimal solution strategy. *Cognitive Development, 11,* 357–373.

Cosmides, L., & Tooby, J. (1992). Cognitive adaptations for social exchange. In J. H. Barkow, L. Cosmides, & J. Tooby (Eds.), *The adapted mind: Evolutionary psychology and the generation of culture* (pp. 163–228). New York: Oxford University Press.

Couvillon, P. A., & Bitterman, M. E. (1992). A conventional conditioning analysis of "transitive inference" in pigeons. *Journal of Experimental Psychology: Animal Behavior Processes, 18,* 308–310.

Cowan, N. (2001). The magical number 4 in short-term memory: A reconsideration of mental storage capacity. *Behavioral and Brain Sciences, 24,* 87–185.

Cowan, N., Towse, J. N., Hamilton, Z., Saults, J. S., Elliot, E. M., Lacey, J. F., et al. (2003). Children's working-memory processes: A response-timing analysis. *Journal of Experimental Psychology: General, 132,* 113–132.

Cummins, D. D. (1995). Naive theories and causal deduction. *Memory and Cognition, 23,* 646–658.

Curcio, F., Kattef, E., Levine, D., & Robbins, O. (1972). Compensation and susceptibility to conservation training. *Developmental Psychology, 7,* 259–265.

Deák, G. O., & Bauer, P. J. (1996). The dynamics of preschoolers' categorization choices. *Child Development, 67,* 740–767.

Deák, G. O., Ray, S. D., & Pick, A. D. (2004). Effects of age, reminders, and task difficulty on young children's rule-switching flexibility. *Cognitive Development, 19,* 385–400.

DeLoache, J. S., Miller, K. F., & Pierroutsakos, S. L. (1998). Reasoning and problem solving. In W. Damon (Editor-in-Chief) & D. Kuhn & R. S. Siegler (Vol. Eds.), *Handbook of child psychology: Vol. 2. Cognition, perception, and language* (pp. 801–850). New York: Wiley.

Demetriou, A., Christou, C., Spanoudis, G., & Platsidou, M. (2002). The development of mental processing: Efficiency, working memory, and thinking. *Monographs of the Society for Research in Child Development, 67*(Serial No. 268).

DeNeys, W., Schaeken, W., & d'Ydewalle, G. (2003). Causal conditional reasoning and strength of association: The disabling condition case. *European Journal of Cognitive Psychology, 15,* 161–176.

Diesendruck, G., & Shatz, M. (2001). Two-year-olds' recognition of hierarchies: Evidence from the interpretation of the semantic relation between object labels. *Cognitive Development, 16,* 577–594.

Donaldson, M., & McGarrigle, J. (1974). Some clues to the nature of semantic development. *Journal of Child Language, 1,* 185–194.

Dunbar, K. (2001). The analogical paradox: Why analogy is so easy in naturalistic settings, yet so difficult in the psychological laboratory. In D. Gentner, K. J. Holyoak, & B. K. Kokinov (Eds.), *The analogical mind: Perspectives from cognitive science* (pp. 313–334). Cambridge, MA: MIT Press.

Elman, J. L. (1991). Distributed representations, simple recurrent networks, and grammatical structure. *Machine Learning, 7,* 195–225.

Elman, J. L., Bates, E. A., Johnson, M. H., Karmiloff-Smith, A., Parisi, D., & Plunkett, K. (1996). *Rethinking innateness: A connectionist perspective on development.* London: MIT Press.

English, L. D. (1997). Interventions in children's deductive reasoning with indeterminate problems. *Contemporary Educational Psychology, 22,* 338–362.

English, L. D. (1998). Children's reasoning in solving relational problems of deduction. *Thinking and Reasoning, 4,* 249–281.

English, L. D., & Halford, G. S. (1995). *Mathematics education: Models and processes.* Hillsdale, NJ: Erlbaum.

Evans, J. S. B. T., Newstead, S. E., & Byrne, R. M. J. (1993). *Human reasoning: The psychology of deduction.* Hove, England: Erlbaum.

Fay, A. L., & Klahr, D. (1996). Knowing about guessing and guessing about knowing: Preschoolers' understanding of indeterminacy. *Child Development, 67,* 689–716.

Field, D. (1987). A review of preschool conservation training: An analysis of analyses. *Developmental Review, 7,* 210–251.

Fireman, G. (1996). Developing a plan for solving a problem: A representational shift. *Cognitive Development, 11,* 107–122.

Fischer, K. W. (1980). A theory of cognitive development: The control and construction of hierarchies of skills. *Psychological Review, 87,* 477–531.

Fodor, J. (1994). Concepts: A potboiler. *Cognition, 50,* 95–113.

Fodor, J. A. (1983). *Modularity of mind: An essay on faculty psychology.* Cambridge, MA: MIT Press.

Fodor, J. A., & Pylyshyn, Z. W. (1988). Connectionism and cognitive architecture: A critical analysis. *Cognition, 28,* 3–71.

Foos, P. W., Smith, K. H., Sabol, M. A., & Mynatt, B. T. (1976). Constructive processes in simple linear order problems. *Journal of Experimental Psychology: Human Learning and Memory, 2,* 759–766.

Franks, J. J., & Bransford, J. D. (1971). Abstraction of visual patterns. *Journal of Experimental Psychology, 90,* 65–74.

Friedman, W. J. (1978). *Development of time concepts in children.* New York: Academic Press.

Friedman, W. J. (1982). *The developmental psychology of time.* New York: Academic Press.

Friedman, W. J. (2003). Arrows of time in early childhood. *Child Development, 74,* 155–167.

Frye, D., Braisby, N., Lowe, J., Maroudas, C., & Nicholls, J. (1989). Young children's understanding of counting and cardinality. *Child Development, 60,* 1158–1171.

Frye, D., & Zelazo, P. D. (1998). Complexity: From formal analysis to final action. *Behavioral and Brain Sciences, 21,* 836–837.

Frye, D., Zelazo, P. D., & Burack, J. A. (1998). Cognitive complexity and control: Vol. 1. Theory of mind in typical and atypical development. *Current Directions in Psychological Science, 7,* 116–121.

Fuson, K. C., & Mierkiewicz, D. (1980, April). *A detailed analysis of the act of counting.* Paper presented at the annual meeting of the American Research Association, Boston, MA.

Gallistel, C. R., & Gelman, R. (2000). Non-verbal numerical cognition: From reals to integers. *Trends in Cognitive Science, 4,* 59–65.

Gattis, M. (2002). Structure mapping in spatial reasoning. *Cognitive Development, 17,* 1157–1183.

Geary, D. C. (2004). Mathematics and learning disabilities. *Journal of Learning Disabilities, 37,* 4–15.

Gelman, R. (1969). Conservation acquisition: A problem of learning to attend to relevant attributes. *Journal of Experimental Child Psychology, 7,* 167–187.

Gelman, R. (1972). Logical capacity of very young children: Number invariance rules. *Child Development, 43,* 75–90.

Gelman, R. (1982). Accessing one-to-one correspondence: Still another paper about conservation. *British Journal of Psychology, 73,* 209–220.

Gelman, R. (1990). First principles organize attention to and learning about relevant data: Number and the animate-inanimate distinction. *Cognitive Science, 14,* 79–106.

Gelman, R., & Gallistel, C. R. (1978). *The child's understanding of number.* Cambridge, MA: Harvard University Press.

Gelman, S. A. (2003). *The essential child.* New York: Oxford University Press.

Gelman, S. A., & Coley, J. D. (1990). The importance of knowing a dodo is a bird: Categories and inferences in 2-year-old children. *Developmental Psychology, 26,* 796–804.

Gelman, S. A., & Markman, E. M. (1986). Categories and induction in young children. *Cognition, 23,* 183–209.

Gelman, S. A., & Markman, E. M. (1987). Young children's inductions from natural kinds: The role of categories and appearances. *Child Development, 58,* 1532–1541.

Gelman, S. A., & O'Reilly, A. W. (1988). Children's inductive inferences within superordinate categories: The role of language and category structure. *Child Development, 59,* 876–887.

Gelman, S. A., & Wellman, H. M. (1991). Insides and essence: Early understandings of the non-obvious. *Cognition, 38,* 213–244.

Gentner, D. (1983). Structure-mapping: A theoretical framework for analogy. *Cognitive Science, 7,* 155–170.

Gentner, D., Holyoak, K. J., & Kokinov, B. (Eds.). (2001). *The analogical mind: Perspectives from cognitive science.* Cambridge, MA: MIT Press.

Gentner, D., & Medina, J. (1998). Similarity and the development of rules. *Cognition, 65,* 263–297.

Gentner, D., & Rattermann, M. J. (1998). Deep thinking in children: The case for knowledge change in analogical development. *Behavioral and Brain Sciences, 21,* 837–838.

Gholson, B., Eymard, L. A., Morgan, D., & Kamhi, A. G. (1987). Problem solving, recall, and isomorphic transfer among third-grade and sixth-grade children. *Journal of Experimental Child Psychology, 43,* 227–243.

Gibson, E. J. (2000). Commentary on perceptual and conceptual processes in infancy. *Journal of Cognition and Development, 1,* 43–48.

Gick, M. L., & Holyoak, K. J. (1983). Schema induction and analogical transfer. *Cognitive Psychology, 15,* 1–38.

Gopnik, A. (1996). The post-Piaget era. *Psychological Science, 7,* 221–225.

Goswami, U. (1991). Analogical reasoning: What develops? A review of research and theory. *Child Development, 62,* 1–22.

Goswami, U. (1992). *Analogical reasoning in children.* Hove, England: Erlbaum.

Goswami, U. (1995). Transitive relational mappings in 3- and 4-year-olds: The analogy of Goldilocks and the three bears. *Child Development, 66,* 877–892.

Goswami, U. (1996). Analogical reasoning and cognitive development. In H. Reese (Ed.), *Advances in child development and behaviour* (pp. 91–138). San Diego, CA: Academic Press.

Goswami, U. (2001). Analogical reasoning in children. In D. Gentner, K. J. Holyoak, & B. Kokinov (Eds.), *The analogical mind: Perspectives from cognitive science* (pp. 437–470). Cambridge, MA: MIT Press.

Goswami, U., & Brown, A. L. (1989). Melting chocolate and melting snowmen: Analogical reasoning and causal relations. *Cognition, 35,* 69–95.

Gray, B. (2003). *Relational models of feature based concept formation, theory-based concept formation and analogical retrieval/mapping.* Unpublished master's thesis, University of Queensland, Brisbane, Australia.

Greene, T. R. (1994). What kindergartners know about class inclusion hierarchies. *Journal of Experimental Child Psychology, 57,* 72–88.

Grice, H. P. (1975). *Logic and conversation.* New York: Academic Press.

Halford, G. S. (1970). A theory of the acquisition of conservation. *Psychological Review, 77,* 302–316.

Halford, G. S. (1982). *The development of thought.* Hillsdale, NJ: Erlbaum.

Halford, G. S. (1989). Reflections on 25 years of Piagetian cognitive developmental psychology, 1963–1988. *Human Development, 32,* 325–387.

Halford, G. S. (1992). Analogical reasoning and conceptual complexity in cognitive development. *Human Development, 35,* 193–217.

Halford, G. S. (1993). *Children's understanding: The development of mental models.* Hillsdale, NJ: Erlbaum.

Halford, G. S. (1997). Capacity limitations in processing relations: Implications and causes. In M. Ito (Ed.), *Proceedings of IIAS 3rd International Brain and Mind Symposium on Concept Formation: Thinking and Their Development* (pp. 49–58). Kyoto, Japan: International Institute for Advanced Studies.

Halford, G. S. (2002). Information processing models of cognitive development. In U. Goswami (Ed.), *Blackwell handbook of childhood cognitive development* (pp. 555–574). Oxford, England: Blackwell.

Halford, G. S. (2005). Development of thinking. In K. J. Holyoak & R. G. Morrison (Eds.), *Cambridge handbook of thinking and reasoning* (pp. 529–555). New York: Cambridge University Press.

Halford, G. S., Andrews, G., Dalton, C., Boag, C., & Zielinski, T. (2002). Young children's performance on the balance scale: The influence of relational complexity. *Journal of Experimental Child Psychology, 81,* 417–445.

Halford, G. S., Andrews, G., & Jensen, I. (2002). Integration of category induction and hierarchical classification: One paradigm at two levels of complexity. *Journal of Cognition and Development, 3,* 143–177.

Halford, G. S., Bain, J. D., Maybery, M., & Andrews, G. (1998). Induction of relational schemas: Common processes in reasoning and complex learning. *Cognitive Psychology, 35,* 201–245.

Halford, G. S., Baker, R., McCredden, J. E., & Bain, J. D. (2005). How many variables can humans process? *Psychological Science, 16*(1), 70–76.

Halford, G. S., & Bowman, S. (2003, July). *Cognitive task difficulty: Hierarchical structure or indecomposability.* Paper presented at the 13th Biennial Conference of the Australasian Human Development Association, Auckland, New Zealand.

Halford, G. S., & Boyle, F. M. (1985). Do young children understand conservation of number? *Child Development, 56,* 165–176.

Halford, G. S., Brown, C. A., & Thompson, R. M. (1986). Children's concepts of volume and flotation. *Developmental Psychology, 22,* 218–222.

Halford, G. S., & Kelly, M. E. (1984). On the basis of early transitivity judgments. *Journal of Experimental Child Psychology, 38,* 42–63.

Halford, G. S., & Leitch, E. (1989). Processing load constraints: A structure-mapping approach. In M. A. Luszcz & T. Nettelbeck (Eds.), *Psychological development: Perspectives across the lifespan* (pp. 151–159). Amsterdam: North-Holland.

Halford, G. S., Smith, S. B., Dickson, J. C., Maybery, M. T., Kelly, M. E., Bain, J. D., et al. (1995). Modeling the development of reasoning strategies: The roles of analogy, knowledge, and capacity. In T. Simon & G. S. Halford (Eds.), *Developing cognitive competence: New approaches to cognitive modeling* (pp. 77–156). Hillsdale, NJ: Erlbaum.

Halford, G. S., & Wilson, W. H. (1980). A category theory approach to cognitive development. *Cognitive Psychology, 12,* 356–411.

Halford, G. S., Wilson, W. H., & Phillips, S. (1998). Processing capacity defined by relational complexity: Implications for comparative, developmental, and cognitive psychology. *Behavioral and Brain Sciences, 21,* 803–831.

Harris, M. R., & McGonigle, B. O. (1994). A model of transitive choice. *Quarterly Journal of Experimental Psychology, 47B,* 319–348.

Hatano, G., & Inagaki, K. (2000). Domain-specific constraints of conceptual development. *International Journal of Behavioral Development, 24,* 267–275.

Hayes, B. K., Goodhew, A., Heit, E., & Gillan, J. (2003). The role of diverse instruction in conceptual change. *Journal of Experimental Child Psychology, 86,* 253–276.

Hayes, B. K., & Taplin, J. E. (1993). Developmental differences in the use of prototype and exemplar-specific information. *Journal of Experimental Child Psychology, 55,* 329–352.

Hodges, R. M., & French, L. A. (1988). The effect of class and collection labels on cardinality, class-inclusion, and number conservation tasks. *Child Development, 59,* 1387–1396.

Hodkin, B. (1987). Performance model analysis in class inclusion: An illustration with two language conditions. *Developmental Psychology, 23,* 683–689.

Hofstadter, D. R. (2001). Analogy as the core of cognition. In D. Gentner, K. J. Holyoak, & B. N. Kokinov (Eds.), *The analogical mind: Perspectives from cognitive science* (pp. 499–538). Cambridge: MIT Press.

Holcomb, W. L., Stromer, R., & Mackay, H. A. (1997). Transitivity and emergent sequence performances in young children. *Journal of Experimental Child Psychology, 65,* 96–124.

Holyoak, K. J., & Thagard, P. (1995). *Mental leaps.* Cambridge, MA: MIT Press.

Hosenfeld, B., van der Maas, H. L. J., & van den Boom, D. C. (1997). Indicators of discontinuous change in the development of analogical reasoning. *Journal of Experimental Child Psychology, 64,* 367–395.

Houdé, O. (2000). Inhibition and cognitive development: Object, number, categorization, and reasoning. *Cognitive Development, 15,* 63–73.

Huttenlocher, J., Jordan, N. C., & Levine, S. C. (1994). A mental model of early arithmetic. *Journal of Experimental Psychology: General, 123,* 284–296.

Inhelder, B., & Piaget, J. (1958). *The growth of logical thinking from childhood to adolescence* (A. Parsons, Trans.). London: Routledge & Kegan Paul. (Original work published 1955)

Inhelder, B., & Piaget, J. (1964). *The early growth of logic in the child.* London: Routledge & Kegan Paul.

Jansen, B. R. J., & van der Maas, H. L. J. (2001). Evidence for the phase transition from rule 1 to rule 2 on the balance scale task. *Developmental Review, 21,* 450–494.

Jansen, B. R. J., & van der Maas, H. L. J. (2002). The development of children's rule use on the balance scale task. *Journal of Experimental Child Psychology, 81,* 383–416.

Johnson, K. E., Scott, P., & Mervis, C. B. (1997). Development of children's understanding of basic-subordinate inclusion relations. *Developmental Psychology, 33,* 745–763.

Johnson, S. P. (2003). The nature of cognitive development. *Trends in Cognitive Science, 7,* 102–104.

Johnson-Laird, P. N. (1983). *Mental models.* Cambridge, England: Cambridge University Press.

Johnson-Laird, P. N., & Byrne, R. M. J. (1991). *Deduction.* Hillsdale, NJ: Erlbaum.

Kahneman, D., Slovic, P., & Tversky, A. (Eds.). (1982). *Judgment under uncertainty: Heuristics and biases.* New York: Cambridge University Press.

Kahneman, D., & Treisman, A. (1984). Changing views of attention and automaticity. In R. Parasuraman, D. R. Davies, & J. Beatty (Eds.), *Variants of attention* (pp. 29–61). New York: Academic Press.

Kalish, C. W., & Gelman, S. A. (1992). On wooden pillows: Multiple classification and children's category-based inductions. *Child Development, 63,* 1536–1557.

Kallio, K. D. (1982). Developmental change on a five-term transitive inference. *Journal of Experimental Child Psychology, 33,* 142–164.

Keen, R. (2003). Representation of objects and events: Why do infants look so smart and toddlers look so dumb? *Current Directions in Psychological Science, 12,* 79–83.

Keil, F. C. (1989). *Concepts, kinds, and cognitive development.* Cambridge, MA: MIT Press.

Keil, F. C. (1991). The emergence of theoretical beliefs as constraints on concepts. In S. Carey & R. Gelman (Eds.), *The epigenesis of mind: Essays on biology and cognition* (pp. 237–256). Hillsdale, NJ: Erlbaum.

Keil, F. C. (1995). An abstract to concrete shift in the development of biological thought: The insides story. *Cognition, 56,* 129–163.

Kemler Nelson, D. G., Frankenfield, A., Morris, C., & Blair, E. (2000). Young children's use of functional information to categorize artifacts: Three factors that matter. *Cognition, 77,* 133–168.

Kenrick, D. T. (2001). Evolutionary psychology, cognitive science, and dynamical systems: Building an integrative paradigm. *Current Directions in Psychological Science, 10,* 13–17.

Kirkham, N. Z., Cruess, L., & Diamond, A. (2003). Helping children apply their knowledge of their behavior on a dimension-switching task. *Developmental Science, 6,* 449–476.

Klahr, D., & Chen, Z. (2003). Overcoming the positive-capture strategy in young children: Learning about indeterminacy. *Child Development, 74,* 1275–1296.

Klahr, D., & Robinson, M. (1981). Formal assessment of problem-solving and planning processes in preschool children. *Cognitive Psychology, 13,* 113–148.

Klahr, D., & Wallace, J. G. (1976). *Cognitive development: An information processing view.* Hillsdale, NJ: Erlbaum.

Krascum, R. M., & Andrews, S. (1998). The effects of theories on children's acquisition of family-resemblance categories. *Child Development, 69,* 333–346.

Kuhn, D. (1995). Microgenetic study of change: What has it told us? *Psychological Science, 6,* 133–139.

Kuhn, D. (2001). Why development does (and does not) occur: Evidence from the domain of inductive reasoning. In J. D. McClelland & R. S. Seigler (Eds.), *Mechanisms of cognitive development: Behavioral and neural perspectives* (pp. 221–252). Hove, England: Erlbaum.

Kuhn, D., & Phelps, E. (1982). The development of problem-solving strategies. In H. Reese (Ed.), *Advances in child development and behavior* (Vol. 17, pp. 1–44). New York: Academic Press.

Kuhn, D., Schauble, L., & Garcia-Mila, M. (1992). Cross-domain development of scientific reasoning. *Cognition and Instruction, 9,* 285–327.

Leevers, H. J., & Harris, P. L. (1999). Persisting effects of instruction on young children's syllogistic reasoning with incongruent and abstract premises. *Thinking and Reasoning, 5,* 145–173.

Leslie, A., & Keeble, S. (1987). Do 6-month-old infants perceive causality? *Cognition, 25,* 265–288.

Lopez, A., Gelman, S. A., Gutheil, G., & Smith, E. E. (1992). The development of category-based induction. *Child Development, 63,* 1070–1090.

Lourenco, O., & Machado, A. (1996). In defense of Piaget's theory: A reply to 10 common criticisms. *Psychological Review, 103,* 143–164.

Luck, S. J., & Vogel, E. K. (1997). The capacity of visual working memory for features and conjunctions. *Nature, 390,* 279–281.

Mandler, J. M. (1992). How to build a baby: Vol. 2. Conceptual primitives. *Psychological Review, 99,* 587–604.

Mandler, J. M. (1999). Seeing is not the same as thinking: Commentary on "Making sense of infant categorization." *Developmental Review, 19,* 297–306.

Mandler, J. M. (2000). Perceptual and conceptual processes in infancy. *Journal of Cognition and Development, 1,* 3–36.

Mandler, J. M., & McDonough, L. (1996). Drinking and driving don't mix: Inductive generalization in infancy. *Cognition, 59,* 307–335.

Mandler, J. M., & McDonough, L. (1998). Studies in inductive inference in infancy. *Cognitive Psychology, 37,* 60–96.

Marcus, G. F. (1998a). Can connectionism save constructivism? *Cognition, 66,* 153–182.

Marcus, G. F. (1998b). Rethinking eliminative connectionism. *Cognitive Psychology, 37,* 243–282.

Marcus, G. F. (1999). Response to Altmann and Dienes: Rule learning by 7-month-old infants and neural networks. *Science, 284,* 875.

Marcus, G. F. (2001). *The algebraic mind: Integrating connectionism and cognitive science.* Cambridge, MA: MIT Press.

Marcus, G. F., Vijayan, S., Bandi Rao, S., & Vishton, P. M. (1999). Rule learning by 7-month-old infants. *Science, 283,* 77–80.

Markman, E. M., & Callanan, M. A. (1984). An analysis of hierarchical classification. In R. S. Sternberg (Ed.), *Advances in the psychology of human intelligence* (Vol. 2, pp. 325–365). Hillsdale, NJ: Erlbaum.

Markman, E. M., & Wachtel, G. F. (1988). Children's use of mutual exclusivity to constrain the meanings of words. *Cognitive Psychology, 20,* 121–157.

Markovits, H., & Barrouillet, P. (2002). The development of conditional reasoning: A mental model account. *Developmental Review, 22,* 5–36.

Markovits, H., & Barrouillet, P. (2004). Introduction: Why is understanding the development of reasoning important? *Thinking and Reasoning, 10,* 113–121.

Markovits, H., & Dumas, C. (1992). Can pigeons really make transitive inferences? *Journal of Experimental Psychology: Animal Behavior Processes, 18,* 311–312.

Markovits, H., Dumas, C., & Malfait, N. (1995). Understanding transitivity of a spatial relationship: A developmental analysis. *Journal of Experimental Child Psychology, 59,* 124–141.

Markovits, H., Schleifer, M., & Fortier, L. (1989). Development of elementary deductive reasoning in young children. *Developmental Psychology, 25,* 787–793.

Markovits, H., Venet, M., Janveau-Brenman, G., Malfait, N., Pion, N., & Vadeboncoeur, I. (1996). Reasoning in young children: Fantasy and information retrieval. *Child Development, 67,* 2857–2872.

Matsuda, F. (2001). Development of concepts of interrelationship among duration, distance, and speed. *International Journal of Behavioral Development, 25,* 466–480.

Maybery, M. T., Bain, J. D., & Halford, G. S. (1986). Information processing demands of transitive inference. *Journal of Experimental Psychology: Learning, Memory and Cognition, 12,* 600–613.

McClelland, J. L. (1995). A connectionist perspective on knowledge and development. In T. Simon & G. S. Halford (Eds.), *Developing cognitive competence: New approaches to cognitive modeling* (pp. 157–204). Hillsdale, NJ: Erlbaum.

McClelland, J. L., & Rumelhart, D. E. (Eds.). (1986). *Parallel distibuted processing—Explorations in the microstructure of cognition: Vol. 1. Foundations.* Cambridge, MA: MIT Press.

McGarrigle, J., & Donaldson, M. (1975). Conservation accidents. *Cognition, 3,* 341–350.

McGarrigle, J., Grieve, R., & Hughes, M. (1978). Interpreting inclusion: A contribution to the study of the child's cognitive and linguistic development. *Journal of Experimental Child Psychology, 26,* 528–550.

McGonigle, B. O., & Chalmers, M. (1977). Are monkeys logical? *Nature, 267,* 355–377.

McLaughlin, G. H. (1963). Psycho-logic: A possible alternative to Piaget's formulation. *British Journal of Educational Psychology, 33,* 61–67.

Meck, W. H., & Church, R. M. (1983). A mode control model of counting and timing processes. *Journal of Experimental Psychology: Animal Behavior Processes, 9,* 320–334.

Medin, D. L. (1989). Concepts and conceptual structure. *American Psychologist, 44,* 1469–1481.

Mehler, J., & Bever, T. G. (1967). Cognitive capacity of very young children. *Science, 158,* 141–142.

Miller, S. A. (1976). Nonverbal assessment of Piagetian concepts. *Psychological Bulletin, 83,* 405–430.

Mix, K. S. (1999). Similarity and numerical equivalence: Appearances count. *Cognitive Development, 14,* 269–297.

Mix, K. S., Huttenlocher, J., & Levine, S. C. (2002). Multiple cues for quantification in infancy: Is number one of them? *Psychological Bulletin, 128,* 278–294.

Molenaar, P. C. M., Huizenga, H. M., & Nesselroade, J. R. (2003). The relationship between the structure of interindividual and intraindividual variability: A theoretical and empirical vindication of developmental systems theory. In U. M. Staudinger & U. Lindenberger (Eds.), *Understanding human development: Dialogues with lifespan psychology* (pp. 339–360). New York: Kluwer Academic.

Morris, A. K., & Sloutsky, V. M. (1998). Understanding of logical necessity: Developmental antecedents and cognitive consequences. *Child Development, 69,* 721–741.

Morris, B. J., & Sloutsky, V. M. (2002). Children's solutions of logical versus empirical problems: What's missing and what develops? *Cognitive Development, 16,* 907–928.

Moscovitch, M., Goshen-Gottstein, Y., & Vriezen, E. (1994). Memory without conscious recollection: A tutorial review from a neuropsychological perspective. In C. Umilta & M. Moscovitch (Eds.), *Attention and performance XV: Conscious and nonconscious information processing* (pp. 619–660). Cambridge, MA: MIT Press.

Moshman, D., & Franks, B. A. (1986). Development of the concept of inferential validity. *Child Development, 57,* 153–165.

Müller, U., Sokol, B., & Overton, W. F. (1999). Developmental sequences in class reasoning and propositional reasoning. *Journal of Experimental Child Psychology, 74,* 69–106.

Nelson, K. (2000). Global and functional: Mandler's perceptual and conceptual processes in infancy. *Journal of Cognition and Development, 1,* 49–54.

Newell, A. (1990). *Unified theories of cognition.* Cambridge, MA: Harvard University Press.

Nobes, G., Moore, D. G., Martin, A. E., Clifford, B. R., Butterworth, G., Panagiotaki, G., et al. (2003). Children's understanding of the earth in a multicultural community: Mental models or fragments of knowledge? *Developmental Science, 6,* 72–85.

Noveck, I. A. (2001). When children are more logical than adults: Experimental investigations of scalar implicature. *Cognition, 78,* 165–188.

Oakhill, J. (1984). Why children have difficulty reasoning with three-term series problems. *British Journal of Developmental Psychology, 2,* 223–230.

Oden, D. L., Thompson, R. K. R., & Premack, D. (1990). Infant chimpanzees (pan troglodytes) spontaneously perceive both concrete and abstract same/different relations. *Child Development, 61,* 621–631.

Osherson, D. N., & Markman, E. (1975). Language and the ability to evaluate contradictions and tautologies. *Cognition, 3,* 213–216.

Palmer, S. E. (1978). *Fundamental aspects of cognitive representation.* Hillsdale, NJ: Erlbaum.

Pascual-Leone, J. A. (1970). A mathematical model for the transition rule in Piaget's developmental stages. *Acta Psychologica, 32,* 301–345.

Pauen, S. (2002). Evidence for knowledge-based category discrimination in infancy. *Child Development, 73,* 1016–1033.

Pauen, S., & Wilkening, F. (1997). Children's analogical reasoning about natural phenomenon. *Journal of Experimental Child Psychology, 67,* 90–113.

Pears, R., & Bryant, P. (1990). Transitive inferences by young children about spatial position. *British Journal of Psychology, 81,* 497–510.

Perner, J., & Lang, B. (2002). What causes 3-year-olds' difficulty on the dimensional change card sorting task? *Infant and Child Development, 11,* 93–105.

Perret, P., Paour, J., & Blaye, A. (2003). Respective contributions of inhibition and knowledge levels in class inclusion development: A negative priming study. *Developmental Science, 6,* 283–288.

Phillips, S. (1994). Connectionism and systematicity. In A. C. Tsoi & T. Downs (Eds.), *Proceedings of the Fifth Australian Conference on Neural Networks* (pp. 53–55). St. Lucia, Australia: University of Queensland, Electrical and Computer Engineering.

Phillips, S., Halford, G. S., & Wilson, W. H. (1995). The processing of associations versus the processing of relations and symbols: A systematic comparison. In J. D. Moore & J. F. Lehman (Eds.), *Proceedings of the Seventeenth annual conference of the Cognitive Science Society* (pp. 688–691). Pittsburgh, PA: Erlbaum.

Piaget, J. (1950). *The psychology of intelligence.* (M. Piercy & D. E. Berlyne, Trans.). London: Routledge & Kegan Paul. (Original work published 1947)

Piaget, J. (1952). *The child's conception of number.* (C. Gattengo & F. M. Hodgson, Trans.). London: Routledge & Kegan Paul. (Original work published 1941)

Piaget, J. (1953). *The origin of intelligence in the child.* London: Routledge & Kegan Paul.

Piaget, J. (1957). *Logic and psychology.* New York: Basic Books.

Piaget, J. (1970). *Structuralism.* (C. Maschler, Trans.). New York: Basic Books. (Original work published 1968)

Piaget, J., Inhelder, B., & Szeminska, A. (1960). *The child's conception of geometry.* London: Routledge & Kegan Paul.

Polya, G. (1954). *Mathematics and plausible reasoning: Vol. 1. Induction and analogy in mathematics.* Princeton, NJ: Princeton University Press.

Posner, M. I., & Keele, S. W. (1968). On the genesis of abstract ideas. *Journal of Experimental Psychology, 77,* 353–363.

Quartz, S. R., & Sejnowski, T. J. (1997). The neural basis of cognitive development: A constructivist manifesto. *Behavioral and Brain Sciences, 20,* 537–596.

Quinn, P. C. (1994). The categorization of above and below spatial relations by young infants. *Child Development, 65,* 58–69.

Quinn, P. C. (2002). Category representation in young infants. *Current Directions in Psychological Science, 11,* 66–70.

Quinn, P. C. (2003). Concepts are not just for objects: Categorization of spatial relation information by infants. In D. H. Rakison & L. M. Oakes (Eds.), *Early category and concept development: Making sense of the blooming, buzzing confusion* (pp. 50–76). London: Oxford University Press.

Quinn, P. C., & Eimas, P. D. (2000). The emergence of category representations during infancy: Are separate and conceptual processes required? *Journal of Cognition and Development, 1,* 55–61.

Quinn, P. C., & Johnson, M. H. (1997). The emergence of perceptual category representations in young infants: A connectionist analysis. *Journal of Experimental Child Psychology, 66,* 236–263.

Rabinowitz, F. M., & Howe, M. L. (1994). Development of the middle concept. *Journal of Experimental Child Psychology, 57,* 418–448.

Rabinowitz, F. M., Howe, M. L., & Lawrence, J. A. (1989). Class inclusion and working memory. *Journal of Experimental Child Psychology, 48,* 379–409.

Rattermann, M. J., & Gentner, D. (1998). More evidence for a relational shift in the development of analogy: Children's performance on a causal-mapping task. *Cognitive Development, 13,* 453–478.

Reitan, R. M. (1971). Trail making test results for normal and brain-damaged children. *Perceptual and Motor Skills, 33,* 575–581.

Rescorla, R. A., & Wagner, A. R. (1972). A theory of Pavlovian conditioning: Variations in the effectiveness of reinforcement and nonreinforcement. In A. H. Black & W. F. Prokasy (Eds.), *Classical conditioning: Vol. 2. Current theory and research* (pp. 64–99). New York: Appleton-Century-Crofts.

Resnick, L. B. (1989). Developing mathematical knowledge. *American Psychologist, 44,* 162–169.

Reyna, V. F. (1991). Class inclusion, the conjunction fallacy, and other cognitive illusions. *Developmental Review, 11,* 317–336.

Reyna, V. F., & Brainerd, C. J. (1990). Fuzzy processing in transitivity development. *Annals of Operations Research, 23,* 37–63.

Reznick, J. S. (2000). Interpreting infant conceptual categorization. *Journal of Cognition and Development,* 63–66.

Richards, C. A., & Sanderson, J. A. (1999). The role of imagination in facilitating deductive reasoning in 2-, 3- and 4-year-olds. *Cognition, 72,* B1–B9.

Riley, C. A. (1976). The representation of comparative relations and the transitive inference task. *Journal of Experimental Child Psychology, 22,* 1–22.

Riley, C. A., & Trabasso, T. (1974). Comparatives, logical structures and encoding in a transitive inference task. *Journal of Experimental Child Psychology, 17,* 187–203.

Rosch, E. (1978). *Principles of categorization.* Hillsdale, NJ: Erlbaum.

Rousselle, L., Palmers, E., & Noël, M.-P. (2004). Magnitude comparison in preschoolers: What counts? Influence of perceptual variables. *Journal of Experimental Child Psychology, 87,* 57–84.

Ruffman, T. (1999). Children's understanding of logical inconsistency. *Child Development, 70,* 872–886.

Samarapungavan, A., Vosniadou, S., & Brewer, W. F. (1996). Mental models of the earth, sun and moon: Indian children's cosmologies. *Cognitive Development, 11,* 491–521.

Seidenberg, M. S., & Elman, J. L. (1999). Do infants learn grammar with algebra or statistics. *Science, 284,* 433.

Shallice, T. (1982). Specific impairments of planning. *Philosophical Transactions of the Royal Society of London, B., 298,* 199–209.

Shastri, L. (1999). Infants learning algebraic rules. *Science, 285,* 1673.

Shultz, T. R. (1998). A computational analysis of conservation. *Developmental Science, 1,* 103–126.

Siegal, M., Waters, L. J., & Dinwiddy, L. S. (1988). Misleading children: Causal attributions for inconsistency under repeated questioning. *Journal of Experimental Child Psychology, 45,* 438–456.

Siegel, L. S., McCabe, A. E., Brand, J., & Matthews, J. (1978). Evidence for the understanding of class inclusion in preschool children: Linguistic factors and training effects. *Child Development, 49,* 688–693.

Siegler, R. S. (1976). Three aspects of cognitive development. *Cognitive Psychology, 8,* 481–520.

Siegler, R. S. (1981). Developmental sequences within and between concepts. *Monographs of the Society for Research in Child Development, 46,* 1–84.

Siegler, R. S. (1987). The perils of averaging data over strategies: An example from children's addition. *Journal of Experimental Psychology: General, 116,* 250–264.

Siegler, R. S. (1995). How does change occur: A microgenetic study of number conservation. *Cognitive Psychology, 28,* 225–273.

Siegler, R. S. (1999). Strategic development. *Trends in Cognitive Science, 3,* 430–435.

Siegler, R. S., & Chen, Z. (1998). Developmental differences in rule learning: A microgenetic analysis. *Cognitive Psychology, 36,* 273–310.

Siegler, R. S., & Jenkins, E. A. (1989). *How children discover new strategies.* Hillsdale, NJ: Erlbaum.

Siegler, R. S., & Richards, D. D. (1979). Development of time, speed, and distance concepts. *Developmental Psychology, 15,* 288–298.

Silverman, I. W., York, K., & Zuidema, N. (1984). Area-matching strategies used by young children. *Journal of Experimental Child Psychology, 38,* 464–474.

Simon, T., & Klahr, D. (1995). A computational theory of children's learning about number conservation. In T. Simon & G. S. Halford (Eds.), *Developing cognitive competence: New approaches to process modeling* (pp. 315–353). Hillsdale, NJ: Erlbaum.

Simon, T. J. (1997). Reconceptualizing the origins of number knowledge: A "non-numerical" account. *Cognitive Development, 12,* 349–372.

Simon, T. J., Hespos, S. J., & Rochat, P. (1995). Do infants understand simple arithmetic? A replication of Wynn (1992). *Cognitive Development, 10,* 253–269.

Simoneau, M., & Markovits, H. (2003). Reasoning with premises that are not empirically true: Evidence for the role of inhibition and retrieval. *Developmental Psychology, 39,* 964–975.

Simons, D. J., & Keil, F. C. (1995). An abstract to concrete shift in the development of biological thought: The insides story. *Cognition, 56,* 129–163.

Sloutsky, V. M. (2003). The role of similarity in the development of categorization. *Trends in Cognitive Science, 7,* 246–251.

Sloutsky, V. M., & Fisher, A. V. (2004). When development and learning decrease memory: Evidence against category-based induction in children. *Psychological Science, 15,* 553–558.

Smedslund, J. (1963). The development of concrete transitivity of length in children. *Child Development, 34,* 389–405.

Smith, L. (2002). Piaget's model. In U. Goswami (Ed.), *Blackwell handbook of childhood cognitive development* (pp. 515–537). Malden, MA: Blackwell.

Smolensky, P. (1990). Tensor product variable binding and the representation of symbolic structures in connectionist systems. *Artificial Intelligence, 46,* 159–216.

Sophian, C. (1995). Representation and reasoning in early numerical development: Counting, conservation and comparison between sets. *Child Development, 66,* 559–577.

Starkey, P., Spelke, E. S., & Gelman, R. (1990). Numerical abstraction by human infants. *Cognition, 36,* 97–128.

Sternberg, R. J. (1980). The development of linear syllogistic reasoning. *Journal of Experimental Child Psychology, 29,* 340–356.

Stiles, J., & Stern, C. (2001). Developmental change in spatial cognitive processing: Complexity effects and block construction performance in preschool children. *Journal of Cognition and Development, 2,* 157–187.

Strauss, M. S. (1979). Abstraction of prototypical information by adults and 10-month-old infants. *Journal of Experimental Psychology: Human Learning and Memory, 5,* 618–632.

Suppes, P., & Zinnes, J. L. (1963). Basic measurement theory. In R. D. Luce, R. R. Bush, & E. Galanter (Eds.), *Handbook of mathematical psychology* (pp. 1–76). New York: Wiley.

Surber, C. F., & Gzesh, S. M. (1984). Reversible operations in the balance scale task. *Journal of Experimental Child Psychology, 38,* 254–274.

Terrace, H. S., & McGonigle, B. (1994). Memory and representation of serial order by children, monkeys, and pigeons. *Current Directions in Psychological Science, 3,* 180–185.

Thayer, E. S., & Collyer, C. E. (1978). The development of transitive inference: A review of recent approaches. *Psychological Bulletin, 85,* 1327–1343.

Thomas, H. (1995). Modeling class inclusion strategies. *Developmental Psychology, 31,* 170–179.

Thomas, H., & Horton, J. J. (1997). Competency criteria and the class inclusion task: Modeling judgments and justifications. *Developmental Psychology, 33,* 1060–1073.

Towse, J. N., Redbond, J., Houston-Price, C. M. T., & Cook, S. (2000). Understanding the dimensional change card sort: Perspectives from task success and failure. *Cognitive Development, 15,* 347–365.

Trabasso, T. (1975). *Representation, memory, and reasoning: How do we make transitive inferences?* Minneapolis: University of Minnesota Press.

Trabasso, T. (1977). The role of memory as a system in making transitive inferences. In R. V. Kail & J. W. Hagen (Eds.), *Perspectives on the development of memory and cognition* (pp. 333–366). Hillsdale, NJ: Erlbaum.

Tversky, A., & Kahneman, D. (1973). Availability: A heuristic for judging frequency and probability. *Cognitive Psychology, 5,* 207–232.

Tyrrell, D. J., Zingaro, M. C., & Minard, K. L. (1993). Learning and transfer of identity-difference relationships by infants. *Infant Behavior and Development, 16,* 43–52.

van der Maas, H. L. J., & Jansen, B. R. J. (2003). What response times tell of children's behavior on the balance scale task. *Journal of Experimental Child Psychology, 85,* 141–177.

van Geert, P. (1998). A dynamic systems model of basic developmental mechanisms: Piaget, Vygotsky, and beyond. *Psychological Review, 105,* 634–677.

Van Gelder, T., & Niklasson, L. (1994). Classicalism and cognitive architecture. In A. Ram & K. Eiselt (Eds.), *Proceedings of the Sixteenth annual conference of the Cognitive Science Society* (pp. 905–909). Hillsdale, NJ: Erlbaum.

VanLehn, K. (1991). Rule acquisition events in the discovery of problem-solving strategies. *Cognitive Science, 15,* 1–47.

von Fersen, L., Wynne, C. D. L., Delius, J. D., & Staddon, J. E. R. (1991). Transitive inference formation in pigeons. *Journal of Experimental Psychology: Animal Behavior Processes, 17,* 334–341.

Vosniadou, S. (1989). Analogical reasoning as a mechanism in knowledge acquisition: A developmental perspective. In

S. Vosniadou & A. Ortony (Eds.), *Similarity and analogical reasoning* (pp. 413–437). New York: Cambridge University Press.

Vosniadou, S., & Brewer, W. F. (1992). Mental models of the earth: A study of conceptual change in childhood. *Cognitive Psychology, 24,* 535–585.

Vosniadou, S., Skopeliti, I., & Ikospentaki, K. (2004). Modes of knowing and ways of reasoning in elementary astronomy. *Cognitive Development, 19,* 203–222.

Vygotsky, L. S. (1962). *Thought and language.* Cambridge, MA: MIT Press. (Original work published 1934)

Waltz, J. A., Knowlton, B. J., Holyoak, K. J., Boone, K. B., Mishkin, F. S., de Menezes Santos, M., et al. (1999). A system for relational reasoning in human prefrontal cortex. *Psychological Science, 10,* 119–125.

Waxman, S. R., & Markow, D. B. (1995). Words as invitations to form categories: Evidence from 12- to 13-month-old infants. *Cognitive Psychology, 29,* 257–302.

Welch, L., & Long, L. (1940). The higher structural phases of concept formation in children. *Journal of Psychology, 9,* 59–95.

Whalen, J., Gallistel, C. R., & Gelman, R. (1999). Nonverbal counting in humans: The psychophysics of number representation. *Psychological Science, 10,* 130–137.

Wilkening, F. (1979). Combining of stimulus dimensions in children's and adult's judgment of area: An information integration analysis. *Developmental Psychology, 15,* 25–33.

Wilkening, F. (1980). Development of dimensional integration in children's perceptual judgment: Experiments with area, volume and velocity. In F. Wilkening, J. Becker, & T. Trabasso (Eds.), *Information integration in children* (pp. 47–69). Hillsdale, NJ: Erlbaum.

Wilkening, F. (1981). Integrating velocity, time and distance information: A developmental study. *Cognitive Psychology, 13,* 231–247.

Wilkening, F., Levin, I., & Druyan, S. (1987). Childrens' counting strategies for time quantification and integration. *Developmental Psychology, 23,* 823–831.

Wilson, W. H., Halford, G. S., Gray, B., & Phillips, S. (2001). The STAR-2 model for mapping hierarchically structured analogs. In D. Gentner, K. Holyoak, & B. Kokinov (Eds.), *The analogical mind: Perspectives from cognitive science* (pp. 125–159). Cambridge, MA: MIT Press.

Winer, G. A. (1980). Class-inclusion reasoning in children: A review of the empirical literature. *Child Development, 51,* 309–328.

Winsler, A., & Naglieri, J. (2003). Overt and covert verbal problem-solving strategies: Developmental trends in use, awareness, and relations with task performance in children aged 5 to 17. *Child Development, 74,* 659–678.

Wittgenstein, L. (1953). *Philosophical investigations.* New York: Macmillan.

Wright, B. C. (2001). Reconceptualizing the transitive inference ability: A framework for existing and future research. *Developmental Review, 21,* 375–422.

Wynn, K. (1990). Children's understanding of counting. *Cognition, 36,* 155–193.

Wynn, K. (1992a). Addition and subtraction by human infants. *Nature, 358,* 749–750.

Wynn, K. (1992b). Children's acquisition of the number words and the counting system. *Cognitive Psychology, 24,* 220–251.

Wynne, C. D. L. (1995). Reinforcement accounts for transitive inference performance. *Animal Learning and Behavior, 23,* 207–217.

Xu, F. (2003). Numerosity discrimination in infants: Evidence for two systems of representations. *Cognition, 89,* B15–B25.

Xu, F., & Spelke, E. S. (2000). Large number discrimination in 6-month-old infants. *Cognition, 74,* B1–B11.

Younger, B. A. (1993). Understanding category members as "the same sort of thing": Explicit categorization in 10-month infants. *Child Development, 64,* 309–320.

Younger, B. A., & Fearing, D. D. (1999). Parsing items into separate categories: Developmental change in infant categorization. *Child Development, 70,* 291–303.

Zelazo, P. D. (2004). The development of conscious control in childhood. *Trends in Cognitive Sciences, 8,* 12–17.

Zelazo, P. D., & Frye, D. (1998). Cognitive complexity and control: Vol. 2. The development of executive function in childhood. *Current Directions in Psychological Science, 7,* 121–126.

Zelazo, P. D., Frye, D., & Rapus, T. (1996). An age-related dissociation between knowing rules and using them. *Cognitive Development, 11,* 37–63.

Zelazo, P. D., Muller, U., Frye, D., & Marcovitch, S. (2003). The development of executive function in early childhood. *Monographs of the Society for Research in Child Development, 68*(3, Serial No. 274).

Zentall, T. R., Galizio, M., & Critchfield, T. S. (2002). Categorization, concept learning and behavior analysis: An introduction. *Journal of the Experimental Analysis of Behavior, 78,* 237–248.

# CHAPTER 14

# Cognitive Science and Cognitive Development

FRANK KEIL

BEGINNINGS   610
What Is the Initial State?   611
Is There an Adapted Mind?   614
PATTERNS OF CHANGE   617
Does Development Proceed from the Concrete
   to the Abstract?   617
What Is the Nature of Conceptual Change?   619
What Is the Difference between Learning
   and Development?   621
REPRESENTATIONAL FORMATS   622
What Representational Formats Underlie
   Developmental Change?   622

What Is the Role of Implicit and Explicit Thought in
   Cognitive Development?   624
What Is the Role of Association and Rules?   625
GENERALITY AND SPECIFICITY   626
Are There Developmental Universals?   626
What Constitutes a Cognitive Domain?   627
CONCLUSION   629
REFERENCES   629

The interdisciplinary field of cognitive science represents an important way to study cognitive development. It offers insights on the mind in development that are not always apparent when considering cognitive development more narrowly from the perspectives of one of the main constitutive domains of cognitive science: psychology, linguistics, computer science, neuroscience, anthropology, and philosophy. This chapter examines several ways in which a cognitive science approach has helped frame and address questions about cognitive development that either would not have been posed at all, or would have been posed in different ways when emerging from each of the disciplines. There are clear benefits to this approach, but there are also major challenges imposed by the need for researchers to master methods and theories across several disciplines. As the depth of knowledge in each local discipline increases rapidly, how can researchers who stay abreast of these new developments also take advantage of scholarship that is much farther afield from their usual area of work? This chapter illustrates ways to combine the necessary depth in any single field with the benefits of breadth as well.

The most powerful contribution of cognitive science lies in the ways in which convergences across disciplines offer insight not available from the perspective of just one. By building on insights, paradigms, methods, and models in other disciplines that are focused on the same or similar problems and questions, a cognitive science approach repeatedly offers new ways of understanding familiar phenomena. It also helps us see new phenomena through its unique lens. The idea of the benefits of research that incorporates diverse viewpoints is hardly new. At least since the time of Bacon, the value of converging forms of evidence was seen as important to induction (cf. Heit & Hahn, 2001). More than 150 years ago, just as the different sciences were starting to become recognized as distinct, the British polymath William Whewell discussed the insights offered by *the consiliences* that occur when widely divergent forms of evidence for a common pattern emerge (Whewell, 1840/1999). The recognition of cognitive science, however, as an arena in which important convergences could occur is far more recent, having gained serious attention roughly 30 years ago (Bechtel, Abrahamsen, & Graham, 1998; Keil, 1991, 2001). While relatively new, the benefits from this convergence have been among the most impressive of any interdisciplinary effort.

Developmental research has been the most prominent area of cognitive science in which theories and research have come together to yield powerful new insights. What is it about the study of the development of cognition that brings together theory and empirical research in psychology, linguistics, neuroscience, computer science, anthropology, and philosophy in ways that are rarely seen in studies of the mature form? This chapter focuses on how the study of the developing mind tends to bring together ideas in the cognitive science disciplines in especially fruitful ways. In particular, it illustrates how patterns of change over time in developing organisms are more likely to foster awareness of common problems across the disciplines.

The analogous chapter, "Cognitive Science and the Origins of Thought and Knowledge," which appeared in the previous edition of this *Handbook* (Keil, 1998), approached the topic by considering fundamental questions about the mind and how they are best informed by considering them from the vantage points of several distinct disciplines. Questions such as how to quantify entities, recognize individuals, or communicate successfully were considered. This way of understanding what cognitive science is and its impact on development has been highly effective and continues to be a prominent way of motivating and conducting research. One need only look at current research on the development of quantitative understanding (e.g., Deheane, 1998; Wynn, 1998), object tracking and individuation (e.g., Leslie, Xu, Tremoulet, & Scholl, 1998; Munakata, 2001; Scholl, 2004), and communication (e.g., Bloom, 2000; Gleitman & Bloom, 1998; Lightfoot, 1999; MacWhinney, 1998; Yang, 2004) to see the lively and productive benefits of a research strategy that poses questions in ways that draw on several disciplines at once.

This chapter could easily be an incremental review of those basically interdisciplinary questions and an update of the dramatic advances in research in each of these areas. The earlier chapter, however, provides a road map of sorts that would easily enable readers to make such extensions on their own. Instead, I have taken a different approach here. This chapter focuses on basic questions about cognitive development that have been posed in psychology for many decades, often for more than a century. It then explores how those questions have changed so as to be more inclusive of insights from other disciplines that make up the cognitive sciences. These changes occur both because of an emerging awareness of related questions in those other disciplines and because of a recognition of the limitations of posing them in their traditional narrow terms. The result has been a shift both in how the questions are posed and in the na-

ture of the likely answers. The strategy of the prior chapter was to start with developmental questions that were intrinsically interdisciplinary and show how different disciplines converged to answer them, whereas the strategy here is to focus on long-standing developmental questions that have traditionally been seen as centered in psychology and to show how their scope and breadth have changed. In the end, there is a convergence from both strategies on similar kinds of questions, but this account tends to reflect more closely the historical pattern from the perspective of psychologists. In addition, the questions addressed here are meant to be distinct from those of the earlier chapter so as to consider different perspectives. They are all posed in domain-general terms as opposed to the domain-specific format that governed the prior *Handbook* chapter. This shift does not mean that domain specificity is irrelevant to the answers to these questions; it merely uses a point of departure to organize this material. The final section of this chapter confronts domain specificity versus generality directly and, in doing so, links this chapter more closely with the prior one.

The questions addressed here are shown in the Chapter Contents. Ten questions are addressed here:

1. What is the initial state?
2. Is there an adapted mind?
3. Does development proceed from the concrete to the abstract?
4. What is the nature of conceptual change?
5. What is the difference between learning and development?
6. What are the representational formats underlying developmental change?
7. What is the role of implicit and explicit cognition in development?
8. What is the role of association and rules in development?
9. Are there developmental universals?
10. What constitutes a cognitive domain and how does domain structure influence development?

## BEGINNINGS

The earliest periods of cognitive development are of great interest to scholars from a wide range of disciplines. A focus on these periods leads naturally to questions about initial states and about the ways in which the mind might be adapted for learning.

## What Is the Initial State?

At least since the writings of Plato and Herodotus, scholars have asked about the "initial state" of the human child. What is the best way to characterize the newborn's cognitive architecture and capacities? In one sense, questions about the initial state at the moment of birth seem arbitrary and misleading. The particular moment of birth does not seem to be particularly important and can be influenced considerably by pharmacology and apparently random environmental triggers. Moreover, children are frequently born preterm, sometimes by more than 2 months, and as the viability of younger and younger preterm infants increases, the moment of birth becomes ever more blurred. With children surviving birth at times as early as 4 months prior to the typical due date, why talk about the normal birth date of 9.5 months postconception as the "initial state"?

There are several good reasons for continuing to focus on the question of the cognitive nature of the newborn delivered at the normal due date. First, despite clear evidence that learning can occur prenatally (De-Casper & Spence, 1986; Moon, Cooper, & Fifer, 1993; Nazzi, Bertoncini, & Mehler, 1998), there is little doubt that the opportunities to learn new information expand enormously after birth. Not only are all the sensory systems suddenly bombarded with dramatically new and much richer information, the event of birth, which places the newborn outside the womb, triggers a host of new interactions and inputs from caregivers and others around the infant (e.g., Fernald, 1992, 1993). Second, birth itself may coincide with new cognitive capacities, as is illustrated by comparisons of developmental capacities of full-term and preterm infants (Rose, Feldman, & Jankowski, 2001; Roy, Barsoum-Homsy, Orquin, & Benoit, 1995; Weinacht, Kind, Monting, & Gottlob, 1998). Birth may help accelerate or trigger cognitive capacities and abilities. Finally, even newborns are capable of a wide variety of actions on their environment that bring new experiences to them and that, in their own right, constitute important areas of learning.

From the perspective of developmental psychology, questions about the initial state were vague and largely ill formed until the past decade or two, when they have become sharpened by work in other disciplines. From

linguistics, the notion of learnability has been important. From computer science, learnability and massive parallel processing have become influential, as have ideas about architectural configurations of the initial state. From neuroscience, we now have precise neural accounts in other species of initial states and their modifications through experience as well as new paradigms for how endogenous experience, as well as exogenous experience, might structure the brain. From philosophy, there has been a considerable sharpening of ideas about initial states, and from anthropology, the notion of backward convergence with decreasing age toward a common mental structure has emerged. Each of these can be considered in more detail.

In one sense, the problem of learnability is straightforward. It asks what sorts of knowledge structures are learnable given a particular form of learning, a set of environmental inputs, and some notion of what it means to successfully achieve learning (Pinker, 1989, 1995). In many cases, it is impossible to learn a unique pattern given a limited set of data. A classic example involves trying to figure out what sort of function describes the curve that goes through a finite set of points. It is not possible to derive a unique function in most such cases, and even appeals to parsimony and simplicity are often not adequate to solve these riddles of induction (Goodman, 1965). This problem became especially evident in language acquisition where Chomsky's notion of the "poverty of the stimulus" was used to motivate the idea that many learning systems could not identify the grammar of a language given the normal "impoverished" inputs that those systems would encounter (Chomsky, 1975). Building on more formal demonstrations of the inability of some learning systems to identify a given language from a larger possible set (Gold, 1967; Wexler & Culicover, 1980), a number of scholars argued that the same formal approach could be applied to many other areas of learning and cognitive development (Jain, Osherson, Royer, & Sharma, 1999).

The learnability approach and the "poverty of the stimulus" argument, however, has not been accepted uncritically (e.g., Fodor & Crowther, 2002; Margolis & Laurence, 2002; Pullum & Scholz, 2002). It has been argued that the stimulus is far richer than previously thought and that much more convergent learning is therefore possible (Pullum & Scholz, 2002). The point here is not to evaluate what aspects of grammar in particular, and knowledge more generally, are learnable with a particular learning system. The critical message is that the learnability debate has helped sharpen questions concerning the initial state. Psychologists now are more likely to acknowledge that some forms of knowledge may only be learnable with certain kinds of architectures and that it is therefore important to develop precise ways of characterizing the knowledge representation, the learning strategy, the information provided, and the meaning of satisfactory levels of learning.

It would be a gross exaggeration to imply that formal learning procedures are foremost in the minds of most developmental psychologists, but there is a greater appreciation of the need to specify the relevant components of a learning system. At the same time, the challenge of using formal approaches to better delimit that initial state has become much larger than initially envisioned by many. Some workers, from a computer science perspective, have argued for dramatically different architectures to get around learnability issues, such as architectures that use massively parallel processing systems and radically different learning procedures. It has been argued that many aspects of category learning and conceptual change that seemed "unlearnable" in older, simpler associationist systems can be modeled nicely by these parallel architectures (Rogers & McClelland, 2004). Thus, computer science advances, both in more traditional learning architectures and in newer parallel ones, have refocused the study of the initial state.

Rapid advances in neuroscience have made it possible to look in detail at the initial state of some portion of a neural network and then examine how it changes as the organism learns. One of the most elegant and detailed analyses along these lines has been done with perceptual motor learning in the barn owl (Knudsen, 2002). It is possible to show how the barn owl learns to auditorily localize by tuning sets of neurons to inputs from both the eyes and the ears that appear to be gated in a complex manner related to timing of input (Gutfreund, Zheng, & Knudsen, 2002). In auditory localization learning in the barn owl, it is possible to describe, at the neural level, considerable prewiring that seems necessary to enable auditory learning but also considerable plasticity to allow for dramatic tuning and recalibration, which can be demonstrated experimentally by putting prisms on the owls' eyes or plugs in their ear holes. There is a still a long way to go from these neural models to formal learning models, but it is possible now to see potential benefits of the convergence of these different approaches. One can, for the first time, start to com-

putationally model initial states and their tuning functions based on neural data (Kardar & Zee, 2002). This a great leap forward from earlier claims that Parallel Distributed Processing (PDP) networks were modeled after the nervous system. These claims were largely based on loose analogies rather than on data-driven mappings from neural architecture to computer architecture.

Neuroscience has also helped shape questions about initial states through discoveries about how endogenous cycles of activation can create an internal experience that must be acknowledged as much as external experience. Thus, in addition to externally driven patterns of neural activity, there are endogenously driven ones that appear to be critical in guiding the tuning and sharpening of neural circuits (Zhang & Poo, 2001). For example, in both the retina and the thalamus, spontaneous cycles of endogenously generated electrical activity of neurons are thought to be causally involved in helping refine and sharpen orientation-specific circuits in the lateral geniculate nucleus and the visual cortex. These circuits then become further tuned after birth by visual experience. Apparently, molecular genetic specifications of structures must interact with these endogenous waves of activity, perhaps conserving an activity-dependent mechanism of tuning of neural architecture both pre and postnatally (Zhang & Poo, 2001). Discussions of initial states and poverty of the stimulus must now take into account the influences of internal cycles of this sort. More broadly, tremendous advances in the neurobiology of development are now helping constrain in much richer ways discussions of initial cognitive states (Marcus, 2004).

We have talked about computer science influences arising from the debates about architectures that are massively parallel versus serial. A different contrast concerns systems that are modeled by central cognitive control patterns as opposed to "behavior based" systems that are built up out of simple perception/action routines (Brooks, 2001). The idea was immortalized in an excerpt from the film *Fast, Cheap and Out of Control* (1997), in which the computer scientist Rodney Brooks waxes at length about the virtues of engaging in artificial intelligence research in a way that he sees as recapitulating phylogeny. By starting with relatively simply perception action circuits of the sort found in insects, it is possible to model behaviors in ways that seem to pay little attention to central cognitive control mechanisms (Brooks, 1997). Consider two ways of explaining the moth's behavior of flying toward flames. One might attempt to model that behavior by starting with a central cognitive system that recognizes bright light sources and then links that recognition routine to a motivational system that wants proximity to the light source and then, based on the interaction of these two systems outputs, a series of commands to a perceptual motor guidance system. Alternatively, one might ask about the crudest possible connection between the sensory inputs and actions. A simple version is shown in Figure 14.1. Imagine that the eye of the moth that is closer to, or more directly faces, a light source fires neural outputs more rapidly. Assume further that those outputs go to the wing on the opposite side of the moth from the eye, which will then flap more rapidly than the wing on the same side as the eye. As a result of this difference in wing flapping, the moth will turn toward the flame and fly toward it until both eyes receive equal stimulation; it then flies in a straight line toward the flame.

The actual story for most moths is probably considerably more complex (e.g., Hsiao, 1973); but this "toy" example illustrates the basic point: Complex goal-directed behavior may sometimes emerge from surprisingly simple noncentral perceptual motor mechanisms. The argument made by Brooks and his colleagues is that we should think of much of the complexity of human behavior as bottom-up concatenations of such insect-like routines. Analogously, one might think of learning in development as the concatenation of such routines (cf. Thelen, 2000). We may feel compelled to infer much more elaborate central control processes to certain behaviors but perhaps often inappropriately. An endearing robot known as Kismet provides an example. Kismet has several routines built into it for tracking eye gaze and body and head movement of humanoid faces and making automatic reactions back (Adams, Breazeal, Brooks, &

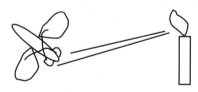

**Figure 14.1**  A noncognitive way to explain the moth's tendency to fly toward light sources is to hypothesize a cross-connection between the moth's eyes and wing muscles, such that the eye on the side of moth that is closer to a light source fires excitatory patterns to the contralateral wing, making it flap more rapidly and turn the moth toward the light source. In this manner, the moth will continually adjust its behavior until it is heading directly toward the light source.

Scassellati, 2000; Scassellati, 2001, 2002). The circuits that make up each of these face-responding routines are all seemingly simple and distinctly nonhuman like; and yet in real time, human observers see the behaving robot as having far more cognitive, motivational, and emotional structure than it really does.

Human infants may be nothing like Kismet, but research in that tradition has influenced thinking about possible initial states and has helped psychologists realize that highly interactive social behaviors might not on their own indicate rich internal cognitive processes or the rich initial states that those processes seem to entail. As demonstrations of ever more sophisticated social tracking and contingency responding routines occur in younger and younger infants (e.g., M. H. Johnson, 2000), debates in computer science about the appropriate architectures are ever more relevant.

In philosophy as well, recent discussions of initial states and the related issue of nativism have influenced more traditional views in developmental psychology. Philosophers have focused on classic ideas in psychology such as triggering and canalization (Ariew, 1999), domain specificity (Cowie, 1999; Samuels, 2002), and modules and their precursors (Carruthers, 2005), just as advances in developmental psychology have reinforced the relevance of these topics to philosophers interested in nativism. Philosophers have pointed out the challenges of adequately describing either representations, learning, or the available information in the environment. Philosophy has also often been the first vantage point from which interconnections are apparent between psychology, computer science, linguistics, and neuroscience.

The contributions of anthropology to characterizing the initial state are more tentative but there are exciting developments in this area as well (Sperber & Hirschfeld, 1999). As cognitive science techniques are used with more sophistication in cross-cultural research, patterns of interaction between cultural structures and cognitive structures become more accurately described. One pattern that can strongly inform questions about the initial state is seen in cases where adult diversity of cultures, when considered in younger and younger ages of a culture, tend to converge on a common format in the young child or infant. This convergence starts to make suggestions about initial states (Medin & Atran, 2004). A different tactic has been to argue that the ability of information to propagate through a culture depends on all members of that culture having a sufficiently shared cognitive common ground to act as a medium of transmission (Sperber & Hirschfeld, 2004). That common ground in turn leads to suggestions about initial states.

Given the complexities of characterizing the initial state, it is tempting to declare it irrelevant, just as others have declared the nativist/empiricist controversy as a nonissue. In neither case is this move correct. One of the major advances in recent years in cognitive science has been to flesh out in detail different facets of the problem of initial states across the disciplines, giving new insights to those engaged in developmental psychology research with the youngest of humans. Thus, questions about initial states have become considerably more refined as they have been considered across the disciplines.

## Is There an Adapted Mind?

In one sense, the answer to this question is obviously "yes." Human brains have a large number of adaptations that all would agree on. Glial sheaths are an adaptation that occurs more prominently in organisms with complex cortexes requiring transmission of larger packets of information over longer distances. Larger brains have ventricles filled with cerebrospinal fluid that help control and maintain the chemical environment of the brain. The convolutions of the cortex in primates are thought to be an adaptation to enable the packing of more cortical surface layer in a constrained volume. In all these functional and physiological senses, the brain is adapted. The more provocative question, however, is different and is at the core of evolutionary psychology (Tooby & Cosmides, 2005). To what extent are there adaptations for distinct cognitive faculties, and at what levels of processing? It is noncontroversial that there are adaptations of the sensory receptors such as the eyes and the ears, for different kinds of information. There is some disagreement, but mostly a consensus, about there being adaptations for modules that track objects (Mitroff, Scholl, & Wynn, in press), social agents (Leslie, 2000), depth (Sakata et al., 1997) and language (Hauser, Chomsky, & Fitch, 2002; Pinker & Bloom, 1990). But there is far more disagreement about whether humans or other species have evolved cognitive adaptations for detecting cheaters (Cosmides, 1989), picking attractive mates (Buss, 1994), or thinking about the living world (Atran, 1998; Bailenson et al., 2002). Although *evolutionary psychology* is a relatively new term, questions about an adapted mind were part of Darwin's thinking shortly after his proposal of the idea of evolution by nat-

ural selection. He discussed at length the adaptive function of the early emergence of emotions and their corresponding facial expressions (Darwin, 1872).

The debate about an adapted mind is making considerable advances as considerations across disciplines start to feed back on psychological questions. One of the most intriguing has occurred in computational biology, where scholars explore the adaptive value of modular versus general structures and ask under what sorts of environments and mechanisms of architectural change modules will appear (Calabretta, Di Ferdinando, Wagner, & Parisi, 2003; Wagner, Mezey, & Calabretta, 2004). Consider a line of work that asked about the optimal way to evolve a system that performs both "what" and "where" computations on objects in the visual array. Although earlier work had shown that it was possible for a single kind of architecture with one learning algorithm to "learn" to have two distinct modules (Jacobs, 1999), later research suggested that hybrid architectures using both a genetic algorithm and a variant of learning through back propagation, show a considerable advantage in the development of functionally specialized modules (Wagner et al., in press).

Networks were designed that could change their structures in two ways, either by production of variants of the initial network through random mutations (the genetic algorithm) or through a form of instructed learning in which weights were changed as function of task performance (back propagation). It was found that a hybrid network of this sort would rapidly create distinct functional modules for "what" and "where" tasks when the genetic algorithm preceded learning through back propagation. Moreover, the advantage occurred primarily in cases where the network first learned the simpler task (where) before the complex one (what). One way of interpreting these results is to argue that the genetic algorithm mimicked evolutionary change while the back propagation learning represented learning within a single organism's life span (Calabretta & Parisi, in press).

It is far too early to conclude that hybrid architectures modeling evolved modularity and learned modularity together have an advantage over those that only incorporate learned modularity. Indeed, many continue to argue that gradually learned modularity during infancy, through a competition process between networks subserving two distinct tasks, is the way to understand the emergence of distinct domains of cognition (Dailey & Cottrell, 1999; M. H. Johnson, 2000). By such accounts, there is no adapted mind in the sense of a priori domain-specific specializations for different kinds of information patterns corresponding to real-world categories such as social agents, living things, and faces. Instead, those specializations arise from channeling of information caused by much lower-level perceptual cues. The debate continues as other groups argue for strong evidence for evolutionarily adapted modules (Duchaine, Cosmides, & Tooby, 2001) and for a general progression in evolution of the replacement of general purpose learning systems with adaptively specialized ones (Gallistel, 2000). Either way, however, computational approaches now allow for the exploration of the relative advantages of domain-specific architectures that occur gradually and postnatally as a result of a single organism's learning experiences as opposed to those that occur through an evolutionary process across a species as whole.

There are profound problems in trying to model the richness of the environment and evolutionary processes. Researchers are forced to use highly idealized and necessarily oversimplified toy systems; but computational approaches of this sort are certainly starting to influence thought about the emergence of functional specializations and the extent to which we have adapted minds. In turn, that computational perspective has also led to new ideas about experimental research by psychologists with human infants (e.g., Munakata, McClelland, Johnson, & Siegler, 1997). As mentioned, in a broader sense, the mind is obviously adapted if one includes the structures of the sensory transducers, which do after all contain part of the nervous system. The debate revolves around whether principled boundaries limit the scope of such adaptations, such as applying only to the sensory transducers, only to lower-level perceptual input modules, or only to the highest levels of cognition. Thanks to computational perspectives, that debate is moving forward with more specificity and a greater effort to empirically support the different positions.

A related research strategy for examining the extent of the adapted mind is to use "reverse engineering." The idea is often used to describe forms of industrial espionage in which engineers take a competitor's product and, from its function, try to work backward to figure out how it works and why it was built the way it was. With respect to the mind, the idea is to consider the local functional value of a property or behavior (such as mating, child rearing, or cheating detection), frame that property as a goal, and then see what follows from such an assumption, as one tries to consider a system, its constraints, and the ways it might meet that goal. There is considerable debate about whether there are sufficient

constraints to be able to infer with some reliability the structure of the engineering solutions for the human mind (Lewens, 2002); but the strategy represents a new way of approaching questions about the adapted mind that draw on ideas in evolutionary biology.

Some have suggested that the reverse engineering strategy is empty, because it can be used to argue for the presence of anything, that is, if a pattern of thought is observed early in development and is seen in virtually all children in all cultures, it must have been selected for in evolution. Although such misleading inferences can occur, they can also occur in analyses of real engineered artifacts, which has not at all undermined use of reverse engineering as a strategy with devices (Lewens, 2002). It may well be that for more complex interconnected systems of both a biological and artificial nature, the reverse engineering strategy rarely misleads above a certain level of functional complexity. Moreover, cross-species comparisons often suggest common goals. Through broader evolutionary analyses of essential functions for social organisms, a small number of key functions may emerge, such as cooperation in groups, mating, child rearing, and self-protection (Pinker, 1997). Those functions, which are hardly controversial and have cross-species validity, can then be used to frame a wide range of questions about cognitive development.

A new look at individual differences has also arisen from questions about the role of an adapted mind in development. Traditionally, individual differences have been understood as a battleground over gene versus environment effects (e.g., Scarr, 1992); but that way of considering individual differences overlooks the ways in which patterns of variation can highlight foundational domains (Bjorklund & Pellegrini, 2000; Scarr, 1992; Segal & MacDonald, 1998). One precursor of this view comes from the work of Gardner (1983) on "multiple intelligences" that led to proposals of distinct domains of thought, such as logical, spatial, and interpersonal intelligence. Rather than ask whether the degree of manifestation of a trait, such as spatial reasoning skill, is largely a function of experience or genes, an evolutionary psychology approach to individual differences asks if, across patterns of variation among individuals, a common distinct functional architecture seems to emerge. In this way, the analysis converges with that of cross-cultural studies and developmental approaches, to ask if certain "mental organs" are highlighted by an individual-differences perspective. We are only beginning to see hints of this approach because of the large data sets involved. If, over a wide pattern of variation across individuals, certain aspects of cognition remain both invariant and domain specific, then the cognitive abilities involved should be considered as candidates for being adapted forms of thought.

More extreme forms of individual differences—patterns of pathology—have also been used to argue for an adapted mind. These more extreme forms are distinguished by being maladaptive and likely to threaten survival of those who would have such pathologies, especially if those individuals are living in traditional environments. Thus, one argument for a cognitive faculty being adapted is that, when it is severely damaged, it threatens survival. The domain of folk psychology has been studied more in this respect than any other in individuals with autism. While there remain extensive debates about the extent to which autism is solely the result of a cognitive deficit (Birlen, 1990; Cohen & Volkmar, 1997), in a large number of cases the primary deficit seems to be a specific cognitive problem in thinking about the mental states of others, such as how beliefs and desires can lead to actions, deception, and misunderstandings (Baron-Cohen, 1995, 2004; Leslie & Thaiss, 1992). Moreover, there appears to be a continuum along which individuals can be variably handicapped in their ability to have a "folk psychology," ranging from severely autistic individuals who have great difficulty understanding almost anything about how mental states lead to actions to more modest deficits such as Asperger's syndrome in which individuals are able to understand the mental lives of others, but only to a limited extent and with considerable difficulty (Klin, Volkmar, & Sparrow, 2000).

Patterns of neurological impairment and their resulting deficits in specific areas of thought do not automatically mean that those areas of thought are adapted domains. There have been many demonstrations of how a generalized learning system, such as one that learns through massively parallel processing, might nonetheless show domain-specific deficits with certain kinds of lesions. Thus, differential deficits in the abilities to think about tools or animals have been simulated in such systems (Farah & McClelland, 1991; Rogers & Plaut, 2002). Low-level differences in attention to perceptual and functional features have been argued as able to account for such differences (Borgo & Shallice, 2003). In other cases, however, specific impairments in thought are much more difficult to explain in terms of problems in domain-general learning (Humphreys & Forde, 2001;

Keil, Kim, & Greif, 2002; Vinson, Vigliocco, Cappa, & Siri, 2003).

Similar controversies exist about whether humans have specific areas of the brain adapted for perceiving faces (Duchaine, Dingle, Butterworth, & Nakayama, 2004; Duchaine & Nakayama, 2005; Gauthier, Curran, Curby, & Collins, 2003; Kanwisher, 2000; Kellman & Arterberry, Chapter 3, this *Handbook,* this volume). Those debates, in turn, have often brought in key developmental arguments about the possibility that specialized brain regions that are uniquely involved in one kind of task (e.g., face perception) might not have been initially "wired" to only process faces, but because of lower-level perceptual shunts, only received information about faces and thus, over time became organized preferentially for that kind of information (Johnson & Morton, 1991). Thus, development becomes critical to understanding whether cognitive specializations in the brain were selected for in the course of evolution or in the course of learning in a single lifetime, with both possibilities being proposed in several areas of cognition (Elman et al., 1996).

The potential insights of an evolutionary perspective, however, go far beyond arguments for specialized domains of thought and modularity. Questions about an adapted mind can also lead to insights about specific developmental trajectories and rates of development. Why, for example, do the three classes of cues for depth—three-dimensional dynamic cues (e.g., motion parallax), binocular cues (e.g., binocular disparity), and pictorial cues (e.g., linear perspective)—emerge in infancy in that order? (Kellman & Banks, 1998). One appealing explanation is that it makes adaptive sense for 3-D dynamic cues to emerge first because they are most robust under conditions of degradation common in young infants, such as low acuity and weak binocular coordination. Such dynamic cues might then form feedback for other sorts of cues that are used later. Similarly, earlier emergence of some cognitive skills relative to others can be understood in adaptive terms and then considered as a largely maturational pattern.

Arguments about adaptive developmental sequences in turn raise questions about whether a sequence of development is predesigned or is an inevitable unfolding of cognitive and perceptual systems in which some components must necessarily precede other ones. Thus, although one might argue that addition precedes multiplication in the development of mathematical thought because of a maturational program, it is much more plausible to argue that addition logically precedes multiplication and that the latter cannot be understood without a sense of the former (National Research Council, 2001). There is, therefore, a danger in being excessively promiscuous in adaptive explanations, a bias that is seen in much of biology (Gould & Lewontin, 1979). Nonetheless, although asking about developmental patterns in adaptive terms may sometimes be misleading, such a strategy often helps focus research on new sets of questions for empirical exploration.

Adaptive questions about developmental patterns can also be a fruitful way of asking about cross-species differences. Why are some organisms much more precocial with respect to some cognitive and perceptual skills than others that are more altricial with comparable or analogous skills? Why do young human infants, while clearly able to see objects in depth, show no fear or tendency to avoid the deep side of the visual cliff while other species show such a linkage at birth (Campos et al., 2000). One answer might focus on the mobility of newborns of other species and the need that mobility creates for a neonatal linkage of fear and avoidance with depth perception. That answer might further be supported by arguments for how, in the absence of mobility, it is advantageous for a fear-depth linkage to take time to develop.

More broadly, there are repeated trade-offs between the advantages of having precocious but inflexible cognitive perceptual systems as opposed to less precocious but more flexible systems. Again, adaptive explanations are not always going to inform questions about developmental sequences in the acquisition of knowledge in domains such as mathematical skills, folk psychology, folk biology, and folk physics; but they are likely to be part of the story in many of those domains and will often help frame questions that motivate more focused research. Other examples might include the use of object files and estimation skills in number knowledge before calculation-based methods (e.g., Wynn, 1998) or use of continuity, no action at distance, and solidity principles in object concepts before those of gravity and momentum/trajectory (Spelke, Breinlinger, Macomber, & Jacobson, 1992).

## PATTERNS OF CHANGE

Cognitive development intrinsically involves various notions of change. It has, however, been difficult to unambiguously characterize distinct patterns of change.

Debates occur both about the representational formats involved and about the degree and kind of change involved. Work across the cognitive sciences has greatly helped to sharpen some of these distinctions.

### Does Development Proceed from the Concrete to the Abstract?

Few things seem more commonsensical than the idea that development must proceed from the concrete to the abstract. This view has been discussed in different ways throughout much of the history of developmental psychology (e.g., Bruner, 1967; Inhelder & Piaget, 1958; Vygotsky, 1962; Werner, 1940). Yet, a cognitive science perspective on this question has started to raise serious questions about the ubiquity of this pattern. From the perspective of linguistic theory, a major shift in views of language acquisition was launched by Chomsky (1957, 1965, 1975). This shift was so major that it is now presupposed by most scholars in the area even as they might vigorously dispute many or all the details of how Chomsky describes the capacity for a natural language (e.g., Bresnan, 1982; Gazdar, Klein, Pullum, & Sag, 1985; Manning & Sag, 1995). The common presupposition is that there are abstract ways of characterizing language competence that are far above more concrete levels of analysis such as word tokens, simple word order patterns, or sentence size. At the concrete level, languages appear to be so dramatically different from each other as to suggest near infinite variation and little or no common structure. But with a more formal and abstract way of describing linguistic competence, as developed so powerfully by Chomsky, it was possible to see strong universals on structure that all languages share and that might be understood as guiding constraints on language acquisition (e.g., Anderson, 2004; Lightfoot, 1999; Pinker, 1994).

At an early age, children throughout the world seem to learn ordering relations based on abstract syntactic categories such as subject and object and not on number of words or word tokens. They appear to have abstract parameters that are "set" in ways that allow them to unpack the structure of a particular language (e.g., Lust, 1999; Yang, 2004). Again, this perspective can be debated (e.g., Seidenberg & Macdonald, 1999), but there is no doubt that a dominant model of language acquisition is that children start out with abstract skeletal expectations about a grammar of a language that they then fill in with more concrete language-specific details of tense marking, subject-verb agreement, and sentence embedding.

From a computer science perspective, there has been a surge of interest in whether concrete to abstract progressions are inevitable parts of systems that learn. While such a progression might seem to be necessary in simple systems that do little more than perform first-order tabulations of feature frequencies and correlations, it is striking how more contemporary models of learning often allow for, and even vigorously embrace, systems in which more abstract representations of the environment can have developmental precedence. Consider how advances in connectionist modeling can show this seemingly paradoxical result. Since many connectionist models work by tracking feature frequencies and correlations, they might seem especially good cases of concrete-to-abstract patterns of development. It is possible, however, to design architectures in which a system quickly abstracts away from lower-level feature frequencies and correlations in a manner that does not initially emphasize concrete categories but instead gives developmental priority to more abstract ones (e.g., Rogers & McClelland, 2004). Thus, there have been arguments for developmental patterns in which children first master abstract categories such as living thing, nonliving natural kind, and artifact and then gradually differentiate downward to knowledge of more specific categories (Keil, 1979); connectionist models have been designed to model such patterns (Rogers & McClleland, 2004). Or, very young children might show category clustering by categories such as vehicle and animal before clustering by categories such as car, boat, dog, and cat (Mandler, 2004). Again, there are now computational explorations of how to model such patterns (Rogers & McClelland, 2004). A related computational approach might construct a learning system that approximates the statistical process of factor analysis (Ghahramani & Hinton, 1998), a process in which abstract factors might emerge in a computational analysis long before more local patterns have any meaning.

Abstract performance might also precede concrete knowledge in a system in which a priori weights on an architecture embody some higher-order property in a domain. Thus, some connectionist approaches augment learning algorithms and node structures with predetermined weights on some links, or "clamps," on weight change. The aggregate structure of such clamps and weights might then embody an abstract cognitive principle such as a general principle of syntax (Yang, 2005).

There may still be profound limitations on many of these connectionist architectures (Marcus, 2001), but their evolution in recent years makes possible consideration of a wide range of patterns in which development proceeds from the abstract to the concrete. A rich array of psychological patterns that suggest abstract to concrete change (e.g., Ingaki & Hatano, 2002; Keil, Smith, Simons, & Levin, 1998; Mandler, 2004; Simons & Keil, 1995) have motivated newer computational models that now in turn feed back on and motivate further psychological questions (Goldstone & Son, in press).

In philosophy, the abstract versus concrete contrast has been a topic of active discussion in many forms. There are several levels of explanation of any system and there are complex discussions about which ones are most fruitful and how they should be characterized. As part of those discussions, it is commonly assumed the lowest level, most reductionist characterization of a process is often inappropriate and unfeasible (Fodor, 1974, 1975). Moreover, functional levels of analysis, far above levels of concrete mechanism are often embraced for their distinctive nature and importance in both science and daily thought (e.g., Block, 1980; Cummins, 1983; Lycan, 1996). Similarly, abstract notions of causal powers have been argued as more fundamental to natural science than mechanisms (Harre & Madden, 1975). All these discussions have served to provide different ways of instantiating what it means to be concrete versus abstract.

These philosophical discussions have powerful implications for developmental studies of the progression of thought. By illustrating the distinctive, and sometimes privileged, role of levels of explanation in modern science as well as in the history of science, philosophers help constrain discussion of how such structures might emerge in children.

Philosophical discourse also allows one to see more clearly not only why some patterns of abstract to concrete change might occur, but also why the opposite pattern often might seem to be more obvious. If one characterizes abstract thought in terms of the ability to explicitly describe an abstract relation in language, one is inclined to see thought as progressing from the concrete to the abstract. For reasons that may have little to do with underlying cognitive capacities (Bloom & Keil, 2001) it can be much more difficult to verbally describe a principle such as randomness than it is to label a concrete category such as dog or a concrete relation such as push. Yet, it is ever more evident that adults, children, and even infants can be sensitive to, and cognitively employ in everyday thought, highly abstract categories and relations that they cannot verbally describe (e.g., Csibra, Biro, Koos, & Gergely, 2003; Gelman, 2002, 2003; Gergely, Nadasdy, Csibra, & Biro, 1995; Keil, 2003b; Newman, Keil, Kuhlmeier, & Wynn, 2005). Young children may be hard pressed to articulate any version of essentialism directly but appear to show assumptions about essentialism extensively in their daily cognitions (Gelman, 2003; Medin & Ortony, 1989). Similarly, young children might see certain teleological modes of interpretation as especially resonant with living kinds (Greif, Kemler-Nelson, Keil, & Guitterez, in press) yet be unable to articulate that notion at all.

Philosophical discussions of language and thought and of the nature of language without thought bear closely on these issues (e.g., Fodor, 1975; Weiskrantz, 1988). They stand to help empirical researchers get a better handle on the ways in which the ability to articulate a concept in language might not be seen as the sole basis for making inferences about the presence of abstract versus concrete concepts.

Even neuroscience is relevant in such discussions. Certain patterns of brain damage resulting in difficulty in thought about categories, such as living things, might be best characterized as impairments at abstract levels of thought rather than more concrete ones (Keil, 2003c; Keil et al., 2002; Laiacona, Capitani, & Caramazza, 2003; Martin & Weisberg, 2003). A vigorous debate exists about the appropriate level of abstraction for describing the basis of a "living kinds deficit," including discussions of how a normal ability to encode living things might be represented at a genetic level. For example, in one analysis of an individual who had a congenital deficit in thinking about living things, it was concluded:

> [P]rior to any experience with living and nonliving things, we are destined to represent our knowledge of living and nonliving things with distinct neural substrates. This in turn implies that the distinction between living and nonliving things, and the anatomical localisation of knowledge of living things, are specified in the human genome. (Farah & Rabinowitz, 2003, p. 408)

Although this result contrasts with other claims in the literature, it illustrates how explorations of this controversy in neuroscience are offering new refined insights into how to understand the abstract versus concrete contrast in cognitive development.

Anthropological studies are brought to bear on this question because of frequently erroneous claims that members of a certain "primitive" (and usually non-Western) culture think in more concrete terms than those of another. Such claims have time and time again been debunked by careful analyses (e.g., Cole, Chapter 15, this *Handbook,* this volume; Cole & Means, 1981). More recently, cross-cultural studies have shown how quite dramatic patterns of variation in thought might reflect different but equally abstract characterizations of a domain, such as construing biology in ecological versus more taxonomic ways (Bailenson et al., 2002; Medin et al., in press).

In short, the notion of concrete and abstract forms of thought and the developmental relations between the two has been a frustrating and often ill-defined problem in developmental psychology. It has been greatly informed by discussions in several other disciplines of cognitive science that converge to make sense of them.

## What Is the Nature of Conceptual Change?

Psychologists have long been concerned with ways in which children's concepts change over the course of development (e.g., Baldwin, 1895; Piaget, 1954; Vygotsky, 1962). More commonly, anyone who engages in casual conversations with a 5- and 12-year-old about concepts as diverse as density, zero, or reproduction, soon becomes convinced that typical 5-year-olds often have very different concepts of certain things than 12-year-olds, with the obvious implication that powerful patterns of conceptual change occur during that period. This much seems straightforward. Much less straightforward, however, is the question of the type of conceptual change that is occurring. We have already seen how abstract to concrete progressions, and the reverse, are one way of talking about conceptual change, but another level of analysis is more structural in manner. It is at this level of analysis that work in other areas of cognitive science has been extremely influential, especially in more recent years.

In the philosophy and history of science, there have been extensive discussions of forms of conceptual change. One of the mostly widely discussed is Kuhn's original notion of scientific revolutions (Kuhn, 1962), a form of change in which a slowly building body of contrary evidence to a particular theory, or paradigm, ultimately reaches a critical mass that launches a dramatic shift to a new way of understanding some aspect of the world. That notion of revolutionary change powerfully influenced views of cognitive development. For example, young children have been regarded as initially understanding much of the biological world (especially animals) in psychological terms and not biological ones (Carey, 1985). Similar arguments have been made for children's shifting concepts of weight and mass (Smith, Carey, & Wiser, 1985) and force and motion (Tao & Gunstone, 1999). This is a particular view of conceptual change with intriguing predictions. For example, concepts in a prerevolutionary system of thought might be completely incommensurable with those in a later system such that individuals from the two systems would largely be talking past each other or mistakenly think they were referring to the same things when in fact they were not. This prediction in its strongest form seemed troubling in that communication with children often does not seem to create such impasses.

Later developments in philosophical discussions of conceptual change refined Kuhn's early ideas in ways that in turn informed models of what is happening with respect to conceptual change in children. Thus, notions of local incommensurability were introduced to deal with global incommensurability and thereby allow more effective communication as well as more gradual patterns of change (Kitcher, 1978, 1993). Others more directly challenged the entire notion of conceptual revolutions (e.g., Laudan, 1990), leading to more nuanced models of conceptual change in children (e.g., Carey & Spelke, 1994).

In computer science, attempts to model conceptual change in various systems motivated quite different models that naturally arose from certain architectures. Wholesale conceptual revolutions were often more difficult to model than gradual incremental differentiation of concepts that might ultimately drift to quite different patterns of thought but not have a revolutionary flavor (Moorman & Ram, 1998; Roschelle, 1995; Shultz, Mareschal, & Schmidt, 1994; Thagard, 1992).

In psychology, other models of conceptual change have existed for many years. These might include gradual differentiation of a set of conceptual distinctions or procedures. Here, too, computer science implementations were sources of inspiration. Thus, models of children's developing understanding of tasks such as balance beams as a differentiating set of rules were closely linked to work in artificial intelligence on production systems (Klahr, Langley, & Neches, 1987; Lan-

gley, 1987; Newell & Simon, 1972; Siegler, 1976, 1981). The development of the microgenetic method in psychology (Siegler, Chapter 11, this *Handbook*, this volume) was certainly influenced by incremental logs of scientific discovery in computational systems (Newell & Simon, 1972; Simon, 2000).

Beyond differentiation and conceptual revolutions however, recent work in psychology has drawn on several other models of conceptual change, and frequently through inspiration from other fields of cognitive science. The question of whether change is qualitative versus quantitative has been informed by formal discussions of such contrasts in both philosophy and linguistics (Briscoe, 2000; Christiansen & Chater, 1999).

More specifically, several different structural models have emerged through commerce with other disciplines in cognitive science. Consider two such examples that have emerged as alternatives to the ideas of conceptual revolutions and gradual incremental change: increasing access and shifting default biases (Inagaki & Hatano, 2002; Keil, 1999).

The notion of increasing access was initially proposed in the context of comparative considerations of how development varied across species (Rozin, 1976). A cognitive routine might be largely automatized and relatively encapsulated and then gradually become more and more available for use in other domains in some species, but not others. In development, Rozin suggested that increasing access to a phonological code might be the basis for major advances in learning to read (Rozin, 1976). In philosophy, notions of increasing access during the course of development figured prominently in accounts of modularity and conceptual change (Fodor, 1975, 1983; Karmiloff-Smith, 1992). In such accounts, a cognitive capacity might be present early on, in a narrow range of contexts, but then become available for deployment in a wider and wider range of situations. In anthropology, it is common to talk about how an innovation might initially be sequestered within a small group and then spread through a culture as access increases. The notion of increasing access to a cognitive skill or competency is an account of conceptual change that is starkly different from both gradual differentiation and revolutionary change. The mental structure or computational routine might be present and unchanged throughout the relevant developmental period but simply be unavailable for use in many tasks in younger children. A sharp increase in access can look like dramatic conceptual change even as the underlying conceptual structure changes little.

The notion of differing default biases suggests that children might have two quite different ways of understanding a system with the primary changes being which one first comes to mind or is seen as most relevant in particular tasks. Unlike increasing access, two different forms of thought may be fully accessible throughout a developmental period, but there may be a dramatic shift in which one is normally used first. Thus rather than seeing young children as only able to understand animals in psychological terms, this view might argue that, throughout much of development, children have both biological and psychological ways of understanding organisms but that younger children tend to default more to the psychological form (Gutheil, Vera, & Keil, 1998). In some tasks, slight reframings of contexts can get young children to use the lesser default (biology) in reasoning (Gutheil et al., 1998). This idea of shifting default biases was heavily influenced by cross-cultural work in anthropology showing that people in other cultures often did not simply have a radically different way of viewing the world, but rather had multiple ways of making sense of situations that might overlap closely with people in other cultures. What differed was which ways of thinking were first elicited in certain sets of contexts. Forms of reasoning about moral situations in terms of sacred violations, or interpersonal harm, or authority conformance, might all be available to people in all cultures, but have different default hierarchies as to which is elicited first in local contexts such as family, community, or peer interactions (Haidt, 2001; Shweder, Much, Mahapatra, & Park, 1997; Turiel & Perkins, 2004).

Shifting default biases are also informed by discussions in philosophy and linguistics of relevance and how it is determined in discourse (Sperber & Wilson, 1995). In those fields, a rich discussion has focused on principles guiding inferences about the relevance of various topics and propositions to situations and prior discourse. Those discussions in turn influence how psychologists think about how children might adopt one frame of reference versus another (Keil, 2003a).

Linguistic approaches to the study of language acquisition afforded unusually specific accounts of different patterns of conceptual change. Thus, debates about whether the very young child understood ordering relations in a language in radically different ways from older children, led to vigorous debates about how the nature of

natural grammar might change over time (Brown, 1973; Ingram, 1989; Lightfoot, 1999; Pinker, 1994). The precision of those different accounts and the ways in which evidence is brought to bear on them strongly influenced models of conceptual change in psychology.

In summary, as patterns of change are considered across a broader range of disciplines than just psychology, we start to see sharply contrasting ways in which change might occur. These patterns can then be used to motivate studies that directly explore which changes are actually occurring in cognitive development. Several studies now suggest that a much greater diversity of highly explicit models of conceptual change is needed to adequately model the changes we see in children. For example, as the microgenetic method offers more fine-grained images of developmental change, it also reveals how superficially similar patterns of change can have quite different underlying bases.

## What Is the Difference between Learning and Development?

It has long been a controversy in developmental psychology as to whether the patterns of learning seen in adults are of a different kind from those found in children (see chapters by Siegler, Chapter 11; Kuhn & Franklin, Chapter 22, this *Handbook,* this volume). Consider, for example, the patterns of qualitative change that occur as adults progress from novice to expert forms of knowledge and whether those patterns are essentially the same patterns as qualitative change in children (Brown, Bransford, Ferrara, & Campione, 1983; Chi, 1978). The debate has become considerably more sophisticated as a result of converging discussions in other disciplines that contribute to the cognitive sciences.

In computer science, there have been attempts to model increasing expertise in ways that have invoked both local and global aspects of cognition (Anderson, 2000; Ericsson, 1996; Gobet, 1997; Larkin, McDermott, Simon, & Simon, 1980; Schunn & Anderson, 2001). This contrast in turn informs the refined question as to whether children differ from adults primarily because they are universal novices rather than more local ones. Perhaps only those with local novice states can use analogies to grow knowledge in other domains because only they have expertise in another domain that they can use as a basis for an analogy. Adults might find it much easier to learn about computer programming by using analogies arising from domains where they are more expert, such as recipes in cooking, whereas children may not have such domains to use as launching pads for analogies. Computer scientists and psychologists in collaboration have, in turn, built simulations of how structure mapping might allow transfer of analogical relations to a new domain (Falkenhainer, Forbus, & Gentner, 1989; Gentner, in press). These simulations enable researchers to assess more precisely the benefits of expertise in one domain on a novice to expert transition in another.

At the level of neuroscience, changes in anatomy and functional status of brain regions postnatally start to place constraints on the learning versus development contrast. It is commonly assumed that considerable physical and functional maturation of the prefrontal cortex might influence development of cognition in domains as diverse as moral reasoning and intuitive physics (Zelazo, 2004; Zelazo, Muller, Frye, & Marcovitch, 2003). It is always risky to infer too much about psychological change from neurological change, but as techniques become ever more sophisticated in neuroscience, at the least, loose constraints emerge that might indicate how development would differ from learning. If there are global, brain-based limitations on executive processing that apply across all domains in young children, then no amount of learning in any of those domains in childhood will be the same as a novice-to-expert transition in one of those domains as an adult.

From anthropology, the influences may be more subtle but are still present. As one considers patterns of cognition across cultures, it is common to ask how a domain that has a long cultural tradition in one culture differs from cases in which it is relatively novel in another. People in one culture might well be considered experts in an area, because of their cultural heritage, while those in a different culture without that heritage might be considered novices. When scholars ask about how a culture came to a certain set of beliefs over time, they may ask about the extent to which that pattern of historical development was analogous to the pattern of development that might occur in individuals who are going from novice to expert states in one lifetime. There has been considerable discussion of how individuals in cultures such as China and Russia are learning, as adults, about capitalism, a kind of cultural novice-to-expert transition. It is natural, then, to contrast those patterns of change with those that gradually occurred as capital-

ism developed over many generations in other cultures (Asland, 2002; Cornia & Popov, 2001; Guthrie, 1999). Are the two end states the same, or are there intrinsic differences between how a practice develops over many generations in a culture and cases in which it emerges in less than one generation? These discussions may not have yet influenced issues of learning versus development in psychology, but they are likely to do so in future years as psychologists confront many of the same issues.

In linguistics, there has been a particularly focused approach to questions of learning versus development by exploring questions about first (L1) versus second (L2) language acquisition (Bialystok & Hakuta, 1994; Ellis, 1994; Gregg, 2001). The nature of L1 acquisition may be different from that of L2. Contrasts range from the influences of L1 on L2, thus drawing parallels to the universal versus local novice issue, to issues involving maturational and critical period effects (Johnson & Newport, 1989; Newport, 1990). Detailed structural comparisons about the precise nature of the two forms of acquisition shed considerable light on how to think more broadly about the learning versus development controversy. Thus, because formal linguistics enables language-acquisition researchers to carefully track structural change over time, it is possible to document differences in novice-expert shifts in adult L2 learning and child L1 learning. A key question is whether those differences will be unique to language because of special domain-specific properties or whether some aspects of those differences will shed broader light on the learning versus developmental controversy.

## REPRESENTATIONAL FORMATS

Questions about cognition often involve questions about the formats of mental representations. In considerations of the development of cognition, questions about representational formats become central, especially when considered in a cross-disciplinary manner.

### What Representational Formats Underlie Developmental Change?

In some ways, questions about representational formats underlying developmental change overlap with those just considered with respect to conceptual change. Thus abstract-to-concrete shifts are partially ones about format; but they also can be considered as more concerned with questions about the kind of information (e.g., high versus low category level) that is used at various points of development. Questions more directly focusing on format ask about how we might want to best represent knowledge at various points in development. Developmental psychology has long entertained claims about representational formats and how they might change, even during the times when behaviorists frowned on such discussions in many other areas of psychology. Consider the view of children progressing from enactive, or motor-based representations, to image-based ones, to more symbolic propositional ones (e.g., Bruner, 1967). This approach attracted considerable attention and was linked to a large set of empirical studies, but benefited greatly from philosophical considerations of the plausibility of particular representational formats and the mechanisms for making transitions between them. One analysis suggested that there was no feasible mechanism available in psychology for describing how a child could progress from understanding the world largely in terms of images to then understanding it in terms of language like propositions (Fodor, 1972, 1975). That question developed into a substantial philosophical literature (e.g., Davidson, 1999; Glock, 2000) that in turn led to reevaluations of such representational shifts in psychology.

In computer science, a vigorous debate has emerged concerning the intrinsic limitations on various forms of computational architectures. Many of these early debates centered around Turing machines, Markov machines, and perceptrons with some of the most detailed applications involving models of language learning and vision (Chomsky, 1957, 1965; Minsky & Papert, 1969). In some cases, these accounts were viewed as formal descriptions of learning procedures, but in others they were viewed as having representational implications. In both philosophy and linguistics, new ideas therefore emerged about links between representations and learning. Such questions became much more prominent, however, with the emergence of connectionism, which was frequently cast as a dramatic alternative to symbolic representational systems (Churchland & Sejnowski, 1994; Smolensky, 1988). The notion of a proposition-like language of thought that manipulated symbols in the manner of classic computer architectures was rejected in favor of "subsymbolic" forms of representation (Smolensky, 1988).

There remain vigorous debates about the merits of both approaches and about the nature of the formal computational limitations of each (Marcus, 2001); but there has also been intriguing feedback from such debates to models of the representational states of children and infants. There have been connectionist models of the object concept in infants that have led to novel predictions about performance on object search and retrieval tasks (Munakata, 2001; Munakata et al., 1997). Connectionist considerations of how past tense forms and word order might be learned have led to predictions as well (McClelland & Patterson, 2002). Similarly, as discussed earlier, attempts to model abstract patterns of conceptual change in terms of connectionist architectures (Rogers & McClelland, 2004) have led to new suggestions about how conceptual change might occur.

From a different computational perspective, there has been a surge of work on computational systems based on Bayesian approaches that are designed to track causal structure in the world (e.g., Gopnik et al., 2004; Sanjana & Tenenbaum, 2002; Tenenbaum & Griffiths, 2001). These approaches have afforded powerful new insights into how causal patterns might be apprehended and then elaborated on. In cases in which such simulations are successful, they can then be used as a basis for speculations about underlying representational formats. Thus, one key question is whether certain network graphs of probability relations can do away with any explicit use of the notion "cause" in a representational system.

Finally, from neuroscience, there has been impressive progress in describing neural circuits in ways that suggest how information might be represented and modified in the course of development (Gallistel, 2000). One of the best worked-out examples is seen in discussions of the neural structures underlying pattern recognition in various regions of the visual cortex. Some visual illusions, such as illusory contours, can be found to be computationally present in the first levels of processing of the visual cortex (e.g., Ramsden, Hung, & Roe, 2001). This finding in turn has led to computational models of development that include interactions between higher-order visual processes and more feature-based ones throughout all periods of development, rather than as a sequence from feature representations to those embodying illusions (Grossberg, 2003).

Questions about representational formats are at the very heart of much of cognitive science and have been the focus of intensive study in many different fields. Those lines of work are now intersecting more and more and, as a result, are refining views in developmental psychology of how to characterize the representational bases of developmental change.

## What Is the Role of Implicit and Explicit Thought in Cognitive Development?

In one form or another, developmental psychologists have long embraced the idea that some aspects of cognition develop outside awareness while others are very much part of our phenomenal experience. Freud's discussion of unconscious thought and its role in development (Freud, 1915) has been considered an early cognitive science theory of representations in development (Kitcher, 1992). Sensorimotor (Piaget, 1952) and enactive (Bruner, 1967) representations might be thought of as examples of implicit thought in early development. It is, in fact, common to think that a major part of infancy may be dominated by implicit thought, which yields to more explicit thought with the onset of language. But these older discussions in psychology were often quite vague in defining the two forms of thought. In more recent years, work in other areas of cognitive science has helped to refine the senses of these contrasts. In neuroscience, patterns of brain damage such as the classic case of HM, who had hippocampal regions removed to cure epilepsy (Corkin, 2002; Scoville & Milner, 1957), have illustrated how implicit learning can proceed while explicit learning seems blocked. Thus, amnesics like HM can show marked improvement on many tasks, such as the tower of Hanoi, while not explicitly remembering the task at all. Other work on visual processing streams, showed that the dorsal stream seems to be involved in implicit processing of visual information while the ventral stream is involved in more explicit processing (Goodale & Milner, 2002; Goodale, Milner, Jakobson, & Carey, 1991). That neuropsychological work has in turn been invoked to explain developmental changes in how infants regard the trajectories of objects (Mareschal, 2000; Von Hofsten, Vishton, Spelke, Feng, & Rosander, 1998).

In linguistic theory, there has long been a contrast between implicit linguistic knowledge in the form of a natural language grammar, and explicit understanding of the structure of a language, which may be largely absent in most normal users. Even though children and adults can show precise and powerful intuitions about grammaticality of sentences, they may have little or no explicit access to those grammatical rules. In some cases, perhaps the grammar of language, it is been argued that the implicit nature of the knowledge arises from it being a module that is informationally encapsulated and cognitively impenetrable (Fodor, 1983).

Philosophical work on modules (e.g., Fodor, 1983) in turn inspired newer psychological approaches asking if automatization of skills might be related to transitions from implicit to explicit and the opposite (Karmiloff-Smith, 1992). In particular, several of those psychological approaches attempted to explain how implicit domain-specific forms of representation and processing might emerge in an organism that had minimal innate biases for those forms of representations (Karmiloff-Smith, 1992). Thus, notions of implicit and explicit in developmental psychology have been considerably sharpened by philosophical proposals about how and why some aspects of cognition might work outside awareness.

Computational approaches that directly target the implicit/explicit contrast have been less prominent. Again, the rise of connectionism was accompanied by claims that processing at the subsymbolic level might also often be implicit (Churchland, 1990). It remains unclear, however, as to how explicit cognition can be best modeled as emerging from a connectionist architecture.

The emergence of research on metacognition in developmental psychology is also related to the implicit/explicit contrast. In that work, young children have complex cognitive systems involved in memory and attention yet often seem to be largely unaware of those systems (Flavell, 1979; Wellman, 1985). Many of the researchers studying metacognition turned their attention to "theory of mind" (Flavell, 1999; Wellman, 1992); they became more centrally interested in the question of how one gains an awareness of mental states in oneself and in others. That new focus brought in a rich philosophical literature on what it means to be aware of one's own mental states (Aydede & Güzeldere, in press).

More broadly, work on epistemology in philosophy has inspired psychological work asking about how children come to have an explicit awareness of their own knowledge states and of the processes of acquiring and evaluating knowledge (Kuhn, 1993, 1999; Kuhn & Franklin, Chapter 22, this *Handbook,* this volume). Naive epistemology connects to the implicit/explicit contrast because of the clear difference between having and using knowledge and being aware of that knowledge.

Developments in philosophy in the study of social epistemology, that is how knowledge is constructed in social groups (Goldman, 2002), have also influenced psychological work on how children seem to understand the division of cognitive labor in the world around them (Danovitch & Keil, 2004; Lutz & Keil, 2002).

The implicit/explicit contrast in many respects remains a puzzle. A simple noncircular account of explicit cognition continues to elude us, perhaps not surprisingly as it is closely related to the "hard problem" of consciousness—knowing what it is like phenomenally to have a conscious experience (Chalmers, 1996). At the same time, research is moving rapidly forward regarding many of the distinctive features correlated with cases of implicit cognition (instances more like the "easy problem" of consciousness; Chalmers, 1996). Moreover, work across the disciplines is helping inform our understanding of the relations between these two modes of thought in development. One important advance has occurred in work on the development of the self-concept, which might be considered a necessary part of explicit cognition. By breaking down the notion of self-knowledge into five distinct senses, ranging from a perceptual "ecological self" to a highly propositional "conceptual self," it is possible to see how some sense of self is present throughout development from the earliest moments of infancy (Neisser, 1988). That sort of analysis has helped foster views that no longer involve a shift from the cognitively implicit infant to a cognitive explicit child, but rather examine the ways in which a form of cognition may be manifested throughout the developmental period.

## What Is the Role of Association and Rules?

For almost a century, psychologists have been concerned with two very different ways of thinking about how humans might represent reality: in terms of rule-like representations or in terms of associative ones (Sloman, 1996). Associations were traditionally thought to be frequency-based tabulations of environmental contingencies and have a legacy at least as far back as the writings of the British empiricists in the eighteenth century (e.g., Hume, 1975). In developmental psychology, there has long been a suggestion that associative ways of representing information are more developmentally basic, or foundational, and are then later supplemented or replaced by rule-based forms (e.g., Inhelder & Piaget, 1958; Klaczynski, 2001; Kuhn

& Franklin, Chapter 22, this *Handbook,* this volume). Despite the intuitive sense that there is a powerful contrast at work, this notion has been difficult to explore further in developmental psychology until quite recently when developments in neuroscience, linguistics, and computer science began to suggest more detailed ways in which the contrast might, or might not, be implemented in a representational model.

From neuroscience, there emerged claims that rule-based and association-based knowledge of linguistic forms could be dissociated through patterns of brain damage as well as through different activation patterns as revealed by imaging studies. Some people have deficits that make them do poorly with irregular past tense forms, which may be learned in largely associative ways, while doing fine with regular tense forms. Others may show the opposite pattern (Marslen-Wilson & Tyler, 1997; Pinker, 2001; Tyler et al., 2002). This pattern of findings has in turn brought in computational modelers who vigorously debate whether two computational systems are needed (McClelland & Patterson, 2002; Pinker & Ullman, 2002). Those computational debates have subsequently inspired newer psychological approaches that attempt to model the rules versus association contrast in terms of a single system of representation, such as a largely associative one in which rules are single-dimension evaluations at one end of a continuum that invokes more normal multidimensional similarity at other parts of the continuum (Pothos, in press).

The rules versus association debate has also been prominent in other ways in linguistic and philosophical discussions of the existence and nature of rules that are nonetheless implicit (Davies, 1995). One facet of this debate has been the question of whether rule-like properties (such as syntactic compositionality and productivity), can emerge from implicit architectures. For example, techniques for modeling connectionist networks as sets of vectors have been argued as embodying, through those vectors, rule-like properties (Pacanaro & Hinton, 2002; Smolensky, 1990). These modeling projects in computer science have led psychologists to ask about a richer array of representational formats that might be able to underlie behaviors that appear to be based on both rules and associations. One approach has been to argue that symbols and rules are more perceptually grounded than they might appear at first and, as such, are based on analogue representations that might be more easily compatible with connectionist networks while still being able to account for rule-like patterns in how people acquire and use concepts (Barsalou, 1999; Prinz, 2002). This line of work has in turn been connected to theories about representations in infancy such as "image schemas" which appear to have at least some perceptual grounding (Mandler, 2004).

It is far too early to tell if abstractions, such as vectors or factors, over connectionist architectures, can fully model rule-like patterns without in the end simply becoming neural implementations of a symbolic system (Marcus, 2001). There is a major difference between views that one can model rule-like patterns without any need for rules or symbols, and whether they are very much a computational reality at the right level of description even in connectionist architectures (Chalmers, 1993; Marcus, 2001). Either way, the debate has been invaluable in sharpening the focus on the roles of rules and associations in development. A central developmental question concerns whether it is appropriate to see younger and younger children as more and more associative creatures, with rules only becoming important at later points (Klaczynski, 2001). Perhaps infants are best understood as largely associative creatures that only acquire rule-like representations after they have gained some mastery with language. Indeed, this account might be considered one facet of Vygotsky's theory (Vygotsky, 1962). Alternatively, it may be that human cognitions are necessary hybrids of association and more rule-like structures and that both must be present throughout development for learning to ever get off the ground and proceed successfully (Keil et al., 1998). Such hybrid architectures offer a fascinating way to think about the representational basis for development and in turn raise complex questions about how the two formats interact throughout the course of development. Rather than seeing one format in competition with another, it may be much more fruitful to think of them in mutually supporting roles (Farah & Rabinowitz, 2003; Keil et al., 1998; Sun, 2001).

## GENERALITY AND SPECIFICITY

Across the cognitive sciences there has been a convergence of interests on questions concerning the generality and specificity of cognitive structures and processes over the course of development. Many longstanding questions about the nature of cognitive development have been greatly informed by increased attention to the

kinds of universals and the kinds of domains that are needed to characterize the growth of the mind.

### Are There Developmental Universals?

Developmental psychologists over the years have proposed that inevitable patterns of development and knowledge structures might be built on each other in a sequence largely determined by the structure of that knowledge. Thus, Piaget's concept of epigenetic development included the idea that knowledge structures and cognitive skills developed to a point where their internal structure precipitated change to a new form. Similarly, models of conceptual change as revolutions are often described as the gradual accumulation of evidence that challenges the existing theory until that theory reaches a point when it undergoes a revolution in terms of how some aspect of the world is understood (Carey, 1985; Kuhn, 1962).

These views of development are compatible with an account involving universal patterns of cognitive growth, not because of innate universal constraints, but because there is only one way of developmentally assembling knowledge. As suggested, the knowledge itself, plus simple assumptions about learning in a normal range of environments, might be enough to account for universal patterns of developmental change. By way of analogy, with a certain set of building blocks, there may be only one sequence that enables building a structure above a certain height; with a set of functions, there may be only a certain sequence in which a computer program could be constructed. As noted, even in knowledge domains, such as mathematics, there are arguments for how certain forms of computation, such as addition, must be learned before others, such as multiplication (National Research Council, 2001).

In some cases, therefore, regardless of the instruction or the environment, a complex knowledge system or cognitive skill must be assembled in a fixed sequence. Thus, if development is to happen with respect to that system or skill, it must happen in the same way. The rate of developmental change may be heavily influenced by the environment and the child's capacities, but not the sequence. In principle, this is an easy point to make with many analogies available in building systems in biology, computer science, and mathematics. That said, it is much more difficult in more naturalistic situations to have a sufficiently detailed and complete description of the representational and computational aspects of a skill or kind of knowledge to know if it must follow a universal developmental sequence.

This area seems ripe for future investigation and is an area in which work in computer science, philosophy, and linguistics might be especially fruitful. Computer scientists for years have studied questions of optimality and necessity in the ordering of algorithms when designing large programs in traditional architectures. It is less clear whether the computational limitations of connectionist architectures are sufficiently constrained and shared across different versions as to suggest developmental universals, but this represents an interesting challenge for those working in such architectures. Similarly, in linguistic theory, formal models of acquisition often have a necessary order. One must have a set of parameters of different possible values before they can be set at each value. Similarly, certain abstract syntactic categories must be understood before ordering relations between them can be modeled. Philosophers, as well, frequently talk about necessary steps of an argument. It seems likely that, as work progresses in these fields on cognitive-science-related issues, it will greatly inform questions about universals in cognitive development.

In all discussions of developmental universals, anthropological and cross-cultural perspectives loom particularly large; for it is only in those more dramatic differences across kinds of environments that developmental universals can be explored. Thus, if it is claimed that a particular end-state knowledge structure must have arisen from a specific developmental sequence, the best test of such a claim is to consider the most radically different real-world environments possible and see if the same sequence repeatedly occurs.

In summary, questions about developmental universals are not as well studied as others in this chapter. However, they seem likely to be precisely the sort that will most benefit from a cognitive science perspective.

## What Constitutes a Cognitive Domain?

There has been a sea change in the study of cognitive development from talk about global patterns of change to talk about domain-specific ones (Gelman & Kalish, Chapter 16, this *Handbook,* this volume; Keil, 1981; Wellman & Gelman, 1997). In many cases, development in a particular domain has its own unique path quite different from that found in other domains. Yet, despite an embrace of domain specificity in many quarters, there remains a difficult and confused issue of

how to characterize a domain. That issue may well be better understood with the benefit of a cognitive science perspective. Depending on the different ways in which knowledge and cognitive skills are used, quite different senses of domains emerge with the contrasting senses becoming clearer when considered across the disciplines involved in cognitive science. Three different senses seem most common: domains as modules, domains as areas of expertise, and domains as modes of thought (cf. Wellman & Gelman, 1997).

In the sense of modules, we can think of distinct cognitive domains that fit the criteria laid down by Fodor (1983). Modules are relatively independent cognitive and perceptual systems that show properties of informational encapsulation and impenetrability. Thus, the information in a system is bounded and operated on in a manner distinct from other areas of thought and cannot be cognitively examined by more general thought processes. Modules are thought to be activated by particular informational patterns. They then automatically run through their processing routine with little or no control by other aspects of cognition. They are also assumed to have distinct and dedicated neural architectures that are innately predetermined.

The domains of thought corresponding to modules often have a quasi-perceptual nature and, indeed, some of the best worked-out examples involve perception. A common example is the perseverance of visual illusions even as higher-level cognition might state with certainty that they cannot exist. A viewer may know full well that two lines are of the same length or two circles are of the same size but be unable to overrule the phenomenal impression of differing sizes (Pylyshyn, 1999). Comparable properties were assumed to hold for more cognitive kinds of modules such as those that were involved in syntactic processing (Fodor, 1983) and theory of mind (Scholl & Leslie, 1999, 2001). The sense of domains that emerges is one in which there is often a strong perceptual grounding and the domains are often quite small in scope or are only part of a functioning cognitive system. Thus, if there is a theory of mind module, it may only apply to certain aspects of thinking about social beings and their mental states and not others. Similarly the modular component of natural language syntax may not account for all aspects of syntactic structure and certainly not all aspects of language structure.

There have been many discussions of Fodor's version of modularity, ranging from arguments for massive modularity in which the highest levels of cognition are modularized (Pinker, 1997; Sperber, 2002) to arguments that modularity should be strongly limited to a relatively small number of cases usually related to perceptual input systems (Fodor, 2000). A different line of criticism has been to suggest that modularity can also emerge through a process of modularization as a function of acquired expertise in a domain (Karmiloff-Smith, 1992). Domains organized around expertise, however, have a different grain and functionality from the original sense of modularity.

Expertise domains, the second possible sense of domain, can vary enormously in terms of the specificity of the domain. Quite young children can be an expert on characters in a particular video game, on dinosaurs (Chi, 1983), chess (Chi, 1978), and on any number of other topics and skills. Moreover, expertise confers cognitive advantages in terms of task performance. This sense of domain differs dramatically from that used in discussions of Fodorian modules. There is massive individual variation with respect to expertise domains, as opposed to relatively uniform performance levels for Fodorian domains. Expertise domains can, on at least some occasions, be cognitively penetrable and not automatic, although emerging automaticity can also occur with some forms of expertise such as reading, typing, and the like. Expertise domains can also be constantly evolving and changing and therefore may not have universal properties across cultures.

Finally, a third sense of domain specificity is based more on the idea of constrained frameworks of thought (Keil, 1981; Pinker, 1997). This sense of domain has sometimes been equated with having a theory (Gelman & Kalish, Chapter 16, this *Handbook*, this volume; Wellman & Gelman, 1997), but theories can vary considerably across individuals. It is useful therefore to contrast acquired theories (Gopnik & Wellman, 1994), such as those of cosmology, which can often be local and culturally specific and which are more likely to be part of a domain of expertise, with broader foundational ways of understanding the world that may be universal and often more implicit.

Advocates of radical conceptual change are more likely to embrace domains as theories that can vary considerably across individuals and cultures. By contrast, it may be that, even at the highest levels of thought, there are universal domain-specific constraints on the kinds of beliefs and conceptual systems that people develop. This last proposal is highly controversial, as some, such

as Fodor (1983), argue against any sort of domain-specific constraints on central cognitive structures. Consider how such constraints might work. There are, for example, different forms of argumentation, such as the teleological and mechanistic. If one associates the teleological with one domain and the mechanistic with another, it may be more difficult to frame arguments in the nonnatural form of argumentation. Thus, people may naturally be predisposed to make teleological arguments about living kinds (Atran, 1998; Keil, 1992) and in doing so may find it difficult to entertain arguments that are not teleological. Similarly, people may assume an essence for living kinds that they do not assume for artifacts (Gelman, 2003; Keil, 1989). That essentialist assumption powerfully constrains theory construction about living kinds versus artifacts.

Work in other areas of cognitive science has shed considerable light on domain specificity and its different senses. Thus, in philosophy and anthropology, there has been discussion of the extent to which there could be modularity at the highest levels of conceptual structure (Sperber, 2002). A particularly intriguing line of argument is that cultural transmission of knowledge may be greatly facilitated by having shared domain-specific constraints on conceptual systems, these constraints paradoxically allow for cultural diversity by providing a common ground that enables the spreading of ideas in an understandable manner (Boyer, 2001; Sperber, 1994). In computer science, a number of approaches have examined sequestering computational routines and data representations into distinct domains with their own unique principles. Thus, it is commonplace to have specialized chip architectures for processing video arrays as opposed to numeric computations. As mentioned, a fascinating series of studies has emerged in neuroscience, asking what senses of domains might be disrupted by damage to neural tissue with an interesting feedback from that work to computational modeling. That particular discussion is informative for the ways it has refined questions about what senses of domains are viable and how domains might get set up in development. In linguistics, there has been a major shift in perspectives regarding whether there are domain-specific constraints governing aspects of language learning as diverse as syntax and word meaning. In contrast to earlier work suggesting that word learning happened because of language-specific constraints on such meanings, it now appears that such constraints emerge from much broader facets of cognition (Bloom, 2000). In light of that more recent work, the relevant sense of domain shifts accordingly.

There remains a need to refine the different senses of domains and the claims that one wants to make about each in terms of patterns of cognitive development. Further refinements in developmental psychology will almost surely be heavily influenced from work on how different senses of domains are implemented in other areas of cognitive science.

## CONCLUSION

Why has the study of cognitive development become linked especially closely to the cognitive sciences in contrast to many areas of cognitive psychology that continue to function as freestanding enterprises largely unaffected by work in other disciplines? It may be because the study of change over time is such a powerful theme in so many areas of research. Whether it is the study of moral beliefs in a culture, a grammatical form in a Celtic language, the history of ideas about species, or the adaptation of a computer network to new inputs, there are interesting stories to tell about beginnings, patterns of change, representational formats, and the generality of the phenomena. These discussions have relevance for the study of cognitive development at levels far beyond those of analogy and metaphor. Repeatedly in this chapter, we have seen how highly explicit ideas in accounts of cognitive development have been inspired by work in other fields on the growth of a cognitive capacity. Developmental questions evoke converging threads from many disciplines in ways that few other questions do.

In this chapter, we have considered 10 questions that have a venerable history in developmental psychology: What is the initial state? Is there an adapted mind? Does development proceed from the concrete to the abstract? What is the nature of conceptual change? What is the difference between learning and development? What are the representational formats underlying developmental change? What is the role of implicit and explicit cognition in development? What is the role of association and rules in development? Are there developmental universals? What constitutes a cognitive domain and how does domain structure influence development? These 10 questions also have had long histories in the disciplines

of philosophy, linguistics, computer science, neuroscience, and anthropology. The striking new pattern is how researchers in psychology are starting to provide and receive benefits from work on similar versions of these questions in the other disciplines. A sense of the larger enterprise of cognitive science has fostered interactions between each of these fields in profound ways that were often unimaginable to those who originally posed these questions in their own disciplines in the past. As a result of these interactions, these questions have assumed a much greater precision and predictive value in each discipline, perhaps especially so in psychology. In many cases, the meanings of these questions are not only more precise, they have changed in ways that are different from their original form and, as a result have suggested new kinds of answers. By all indications, the decade ahead will only accelerate this trend.

## REFERENCES

Adams, B., Breazeal, C., Brooks, R. A., & Scassellati, B. (2000). Humanoid robots: A new kind of tool [Special issue]. *IEEE Intelligent Systems and Their Applications: Humanoid Robotics, 15*(4), 25–31.

Anderson, J. R. (2000). *Cognitive psychology and its implications* (5th ed.). New York: Worth Publishing.

Anderson, S. R. (2004). *Doctor Dolittle's delusion: Animals and the uniqueness of human language.* New Haven, CT: Yale University Press.

Ariew, A. (1999). Innateness is canalization: A defense of a developmental account of innateness. In V. Hardcastle (Ed.), *Biology meets psychology: Conjectures, connections, constraints* (pp. 117–138). Cambridge, MA: MIT Press.

Aslund, A. (2002). *Building capitalism: The transformation of the former soviet bloc.* New York: Cambridge University Press.

Atran, S. (1998). Folk biology and the anthropology of science: Cognitive universals and cultural particulars. *Behavioral and Brain Sciences, 21,* 547–611.

Aydede, M., & Güzeldere, G. (in press). Cognitive architecture, concepts, and introspection: An information-theoretic solution to the problem of phenomenal consciousness. *Noûs.*

Bailenson, J. N., Shum, M. S., Atran, S., Medin, D., & Coley, J. (2002). A bird's eye view: Biological categorization and reasoning within and across cultures. *Cognition, 84,* 1–53.

Baldwin, J. M. (1895). *Mental development in the child and the race: Methods and processes.* New York: Macmillan.

Barsalou, L. (1999). Perceptual symbol systems. *Behavioral and Brain Sciences, 22*(4), 577–609.

Baron-Cohen, S. (1995). *Mindblindness: An essay on autism and theory of mind.* Cambridge, MA: MIT Press.

Baron-Cohen, S. (2004). The extreme male brain theory of autism. *Trends in Cognitive Sciences, 6,* 248–254.

Bechtel, W., Abrahamsen, A., & Graham, G. (1998). The life of cognitive science. In W. Bechtel, G. Graham, & D. A. Balota (Eds.), *A companion to cognitive science* (pp. 2–104). Malden, MA: Blackwell.

Bialystok, E., & Hakuta, K. (1994). *In other words: The science and psychology of second language acquisition.* New York: Basic Books.

Birlen, D. (1990). Communication unbound: Autism and praxis. *Harvard Educational Review, 60,* 291–314.

Bjorklund, D. F., & Pellegrini, A. D. (2000). Child development and evolutionary psychology. *Child Development, 71*(6), 1687–1708.

Block, N. (1980). Introduction: What is functionalism. In N. Block (Ed.), *Readings in philosophy of psychology* (pp. 171–184). Cambridge, MA: Harvard University Press.

Bloom, P. (2000). *How children learn the meanings of words.* Cambridge, MA: MIT Press.

Bloom, P., & Keil, F. C. (2001). Thinking through language. *Mind and Language, 16,* 351–367.

Borgo, F., & Shallice, T. (2003). Category specificity and feature knowledge: Evidence from new sensory-quality categories. *Cognitive Neuropsychology, 20,* 327–353.

Boyer, P. (2001). *Religion explained: The evolutionary origins of religious thought.* London: Random House.

Bresnan, J. (Ed.). (1982). *The mental representation of grammatical relations.* Cambridge, MA: MIT Press.

Briscoe, E. (2000). Grammatical acquisition: Inductive bias and coevolution of language and the language acquisition device. *Language, 76*(2), 245–296.

Brooks, R. A. (2001). The relationship between matter and life. *Nature, 409,* 409–411.

Brooks, R. A. (1997). From earwigs to humans. *Robotics and Autonomous Systems, 20,* 291–304.

Brown, A., & DeLoache, J. (1978). Skills, plans and self regulation. In R. Siegler (Ed.), *Children's thinking: What develops?* (pp. 3–35). Hillsdale, NJ: Erlbaum.

Brown, A. L., Bransford, J. D., Ferrara, R. A., & Campione, J. C. (1983). Learning, remembering, and understanding. In P H. Mussen (Ed.), *Handbook of child psychology: Vol. 3. Cognitive development* (4th ed., pp. 76–166). New York: Wiley.

Brown, R. (1973). *A first language: The early stages.* London: Allen & Unwin.

Bruner, J. S. (1967). On cognitive growth. In J. S. Bruner, R. R. Olver, P. M. Greenfield, et al. (Eds.), *Studies in cognitive growth: A collaboration at the Center of Cognitive Studies* (Vols. 1–2, pp. 1–67). New York: Wiley.

Buss, D. M. (1994). *The evolution of desire: Strategies of human mating.* New York: Basic Books.

Calabretta, R., Di Ferdinando, A., Wagner, G. P., & Parisi, D. (2003). What does it take to evolve behaviorally complex organisms? *BioSystems, 69,* 254–262.

Calabretta, R., & Parisi, D. (in press). Evolutionary connectionism and mind/brain modularity. In W. Callabaut & D. Rasskin-Gutman (Eds.), *Modularity: Understanding the development and evolution of complex natural systems.* Cambridge, MA: MIT Press.

Campos, J. J., Anderson, D. I., Barbu-Roth, M. A., Hubbard, E. M., Hertenstein, M. J., & Witherington, D. (2000). Travel broadens the mind. *Infancy, 1*(2), 149–219.

Carey, S. (1985). *Conceptual change in childhood.* Cambridge, MA: Bradford Books, MIT Press.

Carey, S., & Spelke, E. S. (1994). Domain specific knowledge and conceptual change. In L. Hirschfeld & S. Gelman (Eds.), *Mapping the mind: Domain specificity in cognition and culture* (pp. 169–200). Cambridge, MA: Cambridge University Press.

Carruthers, P. (2005). Distinctively human thinking: Modular precursors and components. In P. Carruthers, S. Laurence, & S. Stich (Eds.), *The innate mind: Structure and content.* Oxford, England: Oxford University Press.

Chalmers, D. (1993). Why Fodor and Pylyshyn were wrong: The Simplest refutation. *Philosophical Psychology, 6,* 305–319.

Chalmers, D. J. (1996). *The conscious mind.* New York: Oxford University Press.

Chi, M. T. H. (1978). Knowledge structure and memory development. In R. Siegler (Ed.), *Children's thinking: What develops?* (pp. 73–96). Hillsdale, NJ: Erlbaum.

Chi, M. T. H., Hutchinson, J. E., & Robin, A. F. (1989). How inferences about novel domain-related concepts can be constrained by structured knowledge. *Merrill-Palmer Quarterly, 35,* 27–62.

Chomsky, N. (1957). *Syntactic structures.* The Hague, The Netherlands: Mouton.

Chomsky, N. (1965). *Aspects of the theory of syntax.* Cambridge, MA: MIT Press.

Chomsky, N. (1975). *Reflections on language.* New York: Pantheon.

Christiansen, M. H., & Chater, N. (1999). Connectionist natural language processing: The state of the art. *Cognitive Science, 23,* 417–437.

Churchland, P. M. (1990). *A neurocomputational perspective: The nature of mind and the structure of science.* Cambridge, MA: MIT Press.

Churchland, P. S., & Sejnowski, T. (1994). *The computational brain.* Cambridge, MA: MIT Press.

Cohen, D., & Volkmar, F. (Eds.). (1997). *Handbook of autism and pervasive developmental disorders* (2nd ed.). New York: Wiley.

Cole, M., & Means, B. (1981). *Comparative studies of how people think: An introduction.* Cambridge, MA: Harvard University Press.

Corkin, S. (2002). What's new with the amnesic patient H. M.? *Nature Reviews Neuroscience, 3*(2), 153–160.

Cornia, G., & Popov, V. (Eds.). (2001). *Transition and institutions: The experience of gradual and late reformers.* Oxford University Press.

Cosmides, L. (1989). The logic of social exchange: Has natural selection shaped how humans reason? Studies with the Wason selection task. *Cognition, 31,* 187–276.

Cowie, F. (1999). *Within? Nativism reconsidered.* New York: Oxford University Press.

Cummins, R. (1983). *The nature of psychological explanation.* Cambridge, MA: MIT Press.

Csibra, G., Biro, S., Koos, O., & Gergely, G. (2003). One-year-old infants use teleological representations of actions productively. *Cognitive Science, 27*(1), 111–133.

Dailey, M. N., & Cottrell, G. W. (1999). Organization of face and object recognition in modular neural network models. *Neural Networks, 12,* 1053–1073.

Danovitch, J. H., & Keil, F. C. (2004). Should you ask a fisherman or a biologist? Developmental shifts in ways of clustering knowledge. *Child Development, 5,* 918–931.

Darwin, C. (1872). *The expression of the emotions in man and animals.* London: John Murray.

Davidson, D. (1999). The emergence of thought. *Erkenntnis, 51,* 511–521.

Davies, M. (1995). Two notions of implicit rules. *Philosophical Perspectives, 9,* 153–183.

DeCasper, A. J., & Spence, M. J. (1986). Prenatal maternal speech influences newborns' perception of speech sounds. *Infant Behavior and Development, 9,* 133–150.

Dehaene, S. (1998). *The number sense: How the mind creates mathematics.* Oxford, England: Oxford University Press.

Duchaine, B., Cosmides, L., & Tooby, J. (2001). Evolutionary psychology and the brain. *Current Opinion in Neurobiology, 11*(2), 225–230.

Duchaine, B., Dingle, K., Butterworth, E., & Nakayama, K. (2004). Normal greeble learning in a severe case of developmental prosopagnosia. *Neuron, 43*(4), 469–473.

Duchaine, B., & Nakayama, K. (2005). Dissociations of face and object recognition in developmental prosopagnosia. *Journal of Cognitive Neuroscience, 17*(2), 249–261.

Ellis, R. (1994). *The Study of Second Language Acquisition.* Oxford, England: Oxford University Press.

Elman, J. L., Bates, E. A., Johnson, M. H., Karmiloff-Smith, A., Parisi, D., & Plunkett, K. (1996). *Rethinking innateness: A connectionist perspective on development.* Cambridge, MA: MIT Press.

Ericsson, K. A. (1996). The acquisition of expert performance: An introduction to some of the issues. In K. A. Ericsson (Ed.), *The road to excellence: The acquisition of expert performance in the arts and sciences, sports, and games* (pp. 1–50). Mahwah, NJ: Erlbaum.

Falkenhainer, B., Forbus, K. D., & Gentner, D. (1989). The structure-mapping engine: Algorithm and examples. *Artificial Intelligence, 41,* 1–63.

Farah, M. J., & McClelland, J. L. (1991). A computational model of semantic memory impairment: Modality specificity and emergent category specificity. *Journal of Experimental Psychology, 120*(4), 339–357.

Farah, M. J., & Rabinowitz, C. (2003). Genetic and environmental influences on the organisation of semantic memory in the brain: Is "living things" an innate category? *Cognitive Neuropsychology, 20*(3/6), 401–408.

Fernald, A. (1992). Human maternal vocalizations to infants as biologically relevant signals: An evolutionary perspective. In J. H. Barkow, L. Cosmides, & J. Tooby (Eds.), *The adapted mind: Evolutionary psychology and the generation of culture* (pp. 391–428). Oxford, England: Oxford University Press.

Fernald, A. (1993). Approval and disapproval: Infant responsiveness to vocal affect in familiar and unfamiliar languages. *Developmental Psychology, 64,* 657–674.

Flavell, J. H. (1979). Metacognition and cognitive monitoring: A new area of cognitive-developmental inquiry. *American Psychologist, 34,* 906–911.

Flavell, J. H. (1999). Cognitive development: Children's knowledge about the mind. *Annual Review of Psychology, 50,* 21–45.

Fodor, J. A. (1972). Some reflections on L. S. Vygotsky's thought and language. *Cognition, 1,* 83–95.

Fodor, J. A. (1974). Special Sciences. *Synthese, 28,* 97–115.

Fodor, J. A. (1975). *The language of thought.* Cambridge, MA: Harvard University Press.

Fodor, J. A. (1983). *The modularity of mind: An essay on faculty psychology.* Cambridge, MA: MIT Press.

Fodor, J. A. (2000). *The mind doesn't work that way: The scope and limits of computational psychology.* Cambridge, MA: MIT Press.

Fodor, J. A., & Pylyshyn, Z. W. (1988). Connectionism and cognitive architecture: A critical analysis. *Cognition, 28,* 3–71.

Fodor, J. D., & Crowther, C. (2002). Understanding stimulus poverty arguments. *The Linguistic Review, 19,* 105–145.

Freud, S. (1915). *The unconscious: The standard edition of the complete works of Sigmund Freud.* London: Hogarth Press.

Gallistel, C. R. (2000). The replacement of general-purpose learning models with adaptively specialized learning models. In M. Gazzaniga (Ed.), *The new cognitive neurosciences* (pp. 1179–1191). Cambridge, MA: MIT Press.

Gardner, H. (1983). *Frames of mind.* New York: Basic Books.

Gauthier, I., Curran, T., Curby, K. M., & Collins, D. (2003). Perceptual interference evidence for a non-modular account of face processing. *Nature Neuroscience, 6,* 428–432.

Gazdar, G., Klein, E., Pullum, G., & Sag, I. A. (1985). *Generalized phrase structure grammar.* Oxford, England: Basil Blackwell.

Gelman, R. (2002). Cognitive development. In H. Pashler & D. L. Medin (Eds.), *Stevens' handbook of experimental psychology* (3rd ed., Vol. 2, pp. 599–621). Wiley: New York.

Gelman, S. A. (2003). *The essential child: Origins of essentialism in everyday thought.* Oxford, England: Oxford University Press.

Gentner, D. (in press). The development of relational category knowledge. In L. Gershkoff-Stowe & D. H. Rakison (Eds.), *Building object categories in developmental time.* Hillsdale, NJ: Erlbaum.

Gergely, G., Nádasdy, Z., Csibra, G., & Biro, S. (1995). Taking the intentional stance at 12 months of age. *Cognition, 56*(2), 165–193.

Ghahramani, Z., & Hinton, G. E. (1998). Hierarchical nonlinear factor analysis and topographic maps. In M. I. Jordan, M. J. Kearns, & S. A. Solla (Eds.), *Advances in neural information processing systems* (Vol. 1, pp. 486–492). Cambridge, MA: MIT Press.

Gleitman, L., & Bloom, P. (1999). Language acquisition. In R. Wilson & F. Keil (Eds.), *MIT encyclopedia of cognitive science.* Cambridge, MA: MIT Press.

Glock, H. J. (2000). Animals, thoughts and concepts. *Synthese, 123*(1), 35–64.

Gobet, F. (1997). A pattern-recognition theory of search in expert problem solving. *Thinking and Reasoning, 3,* 291–313.

Gold, E. M. (1967). Language identification in the limit. *Information and Control, 10,* 447–474.

Goldman, A. (2002). *Pathways to knowledge: Private and public.* Oxford, England: Oxford University Press.

Goldstone, R. L., & Son, J. Y. (in press). The transfer of scientific principles using concrete and idealized simulations. *Journal of the Learning Sciences.*

Goodale, M. A., & Milner, A. D. (1992). Separate visual pathways for perception and action. *Trends in Neuroscience, 15,* 20–25.

Goodale, M. A., Milner, A. D., Jakobson, L. S., & Carey, D. P. (1991). A neurological dissociation between perceiving objects and grasping them. *Nature, 349,* 154–156.

Goodman, N. (1965). *Fact, fiction and forecast* (2nd ed.). Indianapolis, IN: Bobbs-Merrill.

Gopnik, A., Glymour, C., Sobel, D. M., Schulz, L. E., Kushnir, T., & Danks, D. (2004). A theory of causal learning in children: Causal maps and Bayes nets. *Psychological Review, 111,* 3–32.

Gopnik, A., & Wellman, H. M. (1994). The theory theory. In L. A. Hirschfeld & S. A. Gelman (Eds.), *Mapping the mind: Domain specificity in cognition and culture.* New York: Cambridge University Press.

Gould, S. J., & Lewontin, R. (1979). The spandrels of San Marco and the Panglossion paradigm: A critique of the adaptationist programme. *Proceedings of the Royal Society, London. Series B, Biological Sciences, 205,* 581–598.

Greif, M., Kemler Nelson, D., Keil, F. C., & Guitterez, F. (in press). What do children want to know about animals and artifacts? Domain-specific requests for information. *Psychological Science.*

Gregg, K. (2001). Learnability and second language acquisition theory. In P. Robinson (Ed.), *Cognition and second language instruction* (pp. 152–68). Cambridge, England: Cambridge University Press.

Grossberg, S. (2003). Linking visual cortical development to visual perception. In B. Hopkins & S. Johnson (Eds.), *Neurobiology of infant vision* (pp. 211–271). Newark, NJ: Ablex.

Gutfreund, Y., & Knudsen, E. I. (in press). Gated visual input to the auditory space map of the barn owl. *Science.*

Gutfreund, Y., Zheng, W., & Knudsen, E. I. (2002). Gated visual input to the central auditory system. *Science, 297,* 1562–1566.

Gutheil, G., Vera, A., & Keil, F. C. (1998). Do houseflies think? Patterns of induction and biological beliefs in development. *Cognition, 66,* 33–49.

Guthrie, D. (1999). *Dragon in a three-piece suit: The emergence of capitalism in China.* Princeton, NJ: Princeton University Press.

Haidt, J. (2001). The emotional dog and its rational tail. *Psychological Review, 108,* 814–834.

Harre, R., & Madden, E. (1975). *Causal Powers.* Oxford, England: Blackwell.

Hauser, M. D., Chomsky, N., & Fitch, W. T. (2002). The faculty of language: What is it, who has it, and how did it evolve? *Science, 298,* 1569–1579.

Heit, E., & Hahn, U. (2001). Diversity-based reasoning in children. *Cognitive Psychology, 43,* 243–273.

Hsiao, H. S. (1973). Flight paths of night-flying moths to light. *Journal of Insect Physiology, 19,* 1971–1976.

Hume, D. (1975). Enquiry concerning human understanding. In L. A. Selby-Bigge (Ed.), *Enquiries concerning human understanding and concerning the principles of morals* (3rd ed., pp. 1–242). Oxford, England: Clarendon Press.

Humphreys, G. W., & Forde, E. M. E. (2001). Hierarchies, similarity and interactivity in object recognition: On the multiplicity of "category specific" deficits in neuropsychological populations. *Behavioural and Brain Sciences, 24,* 453–509.

Inagaki, K., & Hatano, G. (2002). *Young children's naive thinking about the biological world.* New York: Psychological Press.

Inhelder, B., & Piaget, J. (1958). *The growth of logical thinking.* New York: Basic Books.

Ingram, D. (1989). *First language acquisition: Method, description, explanation.* Cambridge, England: Cambridge University Press.

Jacobs, R. A. (1999). Computational studies of the development of functionally specialized neural modules. *Trends in Cognitive Sciences, 3,* 31–38.

Jain, S., Osherson, D., Royer, J., & Sharma, A. (1999). *Systems that learn: An introduction to learning theory* (2nd ed.). Cambridge, MA: MIT Press.

Johnson, J. S., & Newport, E. L. (1989). Critical period effects in second-language learning: The influence of maturational state on the acquisition of English as a second language. *Cognitive Psychology, 21,* 60–90.

Johnson, M. H. (2000). Functional brain development in infants: Elements of an interactive specialization framework. *Child Development, 71,* 75–81.

Johnson, M. H., & Morton, J. (1991). *Biology and cognitive development: The case of face recognition.* Oxford, England: Blackwell.

Johnson, S. C. (2000). The recognition of mentalistic agents in infancy. *Trends in Cognitive Science, 4*(1), 22–28.

Kanwisher, N. (2000). Domain specificity in face perception. *Nature Neuroscience, 3,* 759–763.

Kardar, M., & Zee, A. (2002). Information optimization in coupled audio-visual cortical maps. *Proceedings of the National Academy of Sciences, 99*(25), 15894–15897.

Karmiloff-Smith, A. (1992). *Beyond modularity: A developmental perspective on cognitive science.* Cambridge, MA: MIT Press.

Keil, F. C. (1979). *Semantic and conceptual development: An ontological perspective.* Cambridge, MA: Harvard University Press.

Keil, F. C. (1981). Constraints on knowledge and cognitive development. *Psychological Review, 88*(3), 197–227.

Keil, F. (1989). *Concepts, kinds, and cognitive development.* Cambridge, MA: MIT Press.

Keil, F. C. (1991). On being more than the sum of the parts: The conceptual coherence of cognitive science. *Psychological Science, 2,* 283–293.

Keil, F. C. (1992). The Emergence of an Autonomous Biology. In M. Gunnar & M. Maratsos (Eds.), *Minnesota Symposia: Modularity and constraints in language and cognition* (pp. 103–138). Hilldale, NJ: Erlbaum.

Keil, F. C. (1998). Cognitive Science and the origins of thought and knowledge. In W. Damon (Editor-in-Chief) & R. M. Lerner (Ed.), *Handbook of child psychology: Vol. 1. Theoretical models of human development* (5th ed., pp. 341–413). New York: Wiley.

Keil, F. C. (1999). Conceptual Change. In R. Wilson & F. Keil (Eds.), *The MIT encyclopedia of cognitive sciences.* Cambridge: MIT Press.

Keil, F. C. (2001). The scope of the cognitive sciences. *Artificial Intelligence, 130,* 217–221.

Keil, F. C. (2003a). Categorization, causation and the limits of understanding. *Language and Cognitive Processes, 18,* 663–692.

Keil, F. C. (2003b). Folkscience: Coarse interpretations of a complex reality. *Trends in Cognitive Sciences, 7,* 368–373.

Keil, F. C. (2003c). That's life: Coming to understand biology. *Human Development, 46,* 369–377.

Keil, F. C., & Kelly, M. H. (1987). Developmental changes in category structure. In S. Harnad (Ed.), *Categorical perception* (pp. 491–510). Cambridge University Press.

Keil, F. C., Kim, N. S., & Greif, M. L. (2002). Categories and Levels of Information. In E. Forde & G. Humphreys (Eds.), *Category-specificity in brain and mind* (pp. 375–401). Hove, East Sussex, England: Psychology Press.

Keil, F. C., Smith, C., Simons, D. J., & Levin, D. T. (1998). Two dogmas of conceptual empiricism: Implications for hybrid models of the structure of knowledge. *Cognition, 65,* 103–135.

Kellman, P. J., & Banks, M. (1998). Infant visual perception. In W. Damon (Series Ed.) & D. Kuhn & R. S. Siegler (Vol. Eds.), *Handbook of child psychology: Vol. 2. Cognition, perception, and language* (5th ed., pp. 103–146). New York: Wiley.

Kitcher, P. (1978). Theories, theorists, and theoretical change. *Philosophical Review, 87,* 519–547.

Kitcher, P. (1992). *Freud's dream: A complete interdisciplinary science of mind.* Cambridge, MA: Bradford/MIT Press.

Kitcher, P. (1993). *The advancement of science.* Oxford, England: Oxford University Press.

Klaczynski, P. A. (2001). Analytic and heuristic processing influences on adolescent reasoning and decision-making. *Child Development, 72,* 844–861.

Klahr, D., Langley, P., & Neches, R. (Eds.). (1987). *Production system models of learning and development.* Cambridge, MA: MIT Press.

Klin, A., Volkmar, F., & Sparrow, S. (Eds.). (2000). *Asperger syndrome.* New York: Guilford Press.

Knudsen, E. I. (2002). Instructed learning in the auditory localization pathway of the barn owl. *Nature, 417,* 322–328.

Kuhn, D. (1993). Science as argument: Implications for teaching and learning scientific thinking. *Science Education, 77*(3), 319–337.

Kuhn, D. (1999). A developmental model of critical thinking. *Educational Researcher, 28,* 16–25.

Kuhn, T. (1962). *The structure of scientific revolutions.* Chicago: University of Chicago Press.

Laiacona, M., Capitani, E., & Caramazza, A. (2003). Category-specific semantic deficits do not reflect the sensory/functional organization of the brain: A test of the "sensory quality" hypothesis. *Neurocase, 9*(3), 221–231.

Langley, P. (1987). A general theory of discrimination learning. In D. Klahr, P. Langley, & R. Neches (Eds.), *Production system models of learning and development* (pp. 99–161). Cambridge, MA: MIT Press.

Larkin, J., McDermott, J., Simon, D. P., & Simon, H. A. (1980). Expert and novice performance in solving physics problems. *Science, 208,* 1335–1342.

Laudan, L. (1990). *Science and relativism: Some key controversies in the philosophy of science.* Chicago: University of Chicago Press.

Leslie, A. M. (2000). "Theory of mind" as a mechanism of selective attention. In M. Gazzaniga (Ed.), *The new cognitive neurosciences* (2nd ed., pp. 1235–1247). Cambridge, MA: MIT Press.

Leslie, A. M., Thaiss L. (1992). Domain specificity in conceptual development: Neuropsychological evidence from autism. *Cognition, 43,* 225–251.

Leslie, A. M., Xu, F., Tremoulet, P., & Scholl, B. (1998). Indexing and the object concept: Developing `what' and `where' systems. *Trends in Cognitive Sciences, 2,* 10–18.

Lewens, T. (2002). Adaptationism and engineering. *Biology and Philosophy, 17*(1), 1–31.

Lightfoot, D. (1999). *The development of language: Acquisition, change, and evolution.* Malden, MA: Blackwell.

Lust, B. (1999). Universal grammar: The strong continuity hypothesis in first language acquisition. In W. C. Ritchie & T. K. Bhatia (Eds.), *Handbook of child language acquisition* (pp. 111–155). San Diego, CA: Academic Press.

Lutz, D. R., & Keil, F. C. (2002). Early understanding of the division of cognitive labor. *Child Development, 73,* 1073–1084.

Lycan, W. (1996). *Consciousness and experience.* Cambridge, MA: MIT Press.

Magnani, L., & Nersessian, N. J. (Eds.). (2002). *Model-based reasoning: Science, technology, values.* New York: Kluwer Academic/Plenum Press.

Mandler, J. M. (2004). *The foundations of mind: Origins of conceptual thought.* New York: Oxford University Press.

Manning, C., & Sag, I. A. (1999). Dissociations between Argument Structure and Grammatical Relations. In A. Kathol, J.-P. Koenig, & G. Webelhuth (Eds.), *Lexical and constructional aspects of linguistic explanation* (pp. 63–77). Stanford, CA: CSLI Publications.

Marcus, G. F. (2001). *The algebraic mind.* MIT Press: Cambridge, MA.

Marcus, G. F. (2004). *The birth of the mind: How a tiny number of genes creates the complexities of human thought.* New York: Basic Books.

Mareschal, D. (2000). Object knowledge in infancy: Current controversies and approaches. *Trends in Cognitive Science, 4,* 408–416.

Margolis, E., & Laurence, S. (2001). The poverty of the stimulus argument. *British Journal for the Philosophy of Science, 52,* 217–276.

Marslen-Wilson, M., & Tyler, L. K. (1997). Dissociating types of mental computation. *Nature, 387,* 592–594.

Martin, A., & Weisberg, J. (2003). Neural foundations for understanding social and mechanical concepts. *Cognitive Neuropsychology, 20*(3/6), 575–587.

McClelland, J. L., & Patterson, K. (2002). Rules or connections in past-tense inflections: What does the evidence rule out? *Trends in Cognitive Science, 6,* 465–472.

MacWhinney, B. (1998). Models of the emergence of language. *Annual Review of Psychology, 49,* 199–227.

Medin, D. L., & Atran, S. (in press). The native mind: Biological categorization, reasoning and decision making in development across cultures. *Psychological Review.*

Medin, D. L., & Ortony, A. (1989). Psychological essentialism. In S. Vosniadou & A. Ortony (Eds.), *Similarity and analogical reasoning.* Cambridge, England: Cambridge University Press.

Medin, D. L., Ross, N., Atran, S., Cox, D., Wakaua, H. J., Coley, J. D., et al. (in press). The role of culture in the folkbiology of freshwater fish. *Cognitive Psychology.*

Minksy, M., & Papert, S. (1969). *Perceptrons: An introduction to computation geometry.* Cambridge, MA: MIT Press.

Mitroff, S. R., Scholl, B. J., & Wynn, K. (in press). The relationship between object files and conscious perception. *Cognition.*

Moon, C., Cooper, R. P., & Fifer, W. P. (1993). Two-day-olds prefer their native language. *Infant Behavior and Development, 16,* 495–500.

Moorman, K., & Ram, A. (1998). *Computional models of reading and understanding.* Cambridge, MA: MIT Press.

Munakata, Y. (2001). Graded representations in behavioral dissociations. *Trends in Cognitive Sciences, 5*(7), 309–315.

Munakata, Y., McClelland, J. L., Johnson, M. H., & Siegler, R. S. (1997). Rethinking infant knowledge: Toward an adaptive process account of successes and failures in object permanence tasks. *Psychological Review, 104,* 686–713.

National Research Council. (2001). *Adding it up: Helping children learn mathematics.* Washington, DC: Author.

Nazzi, T., Bertoncini, J., & Mehler, J. (1998). Language discrimination by newborns: Towards an understanding of the role of rhythm. *Journal of Experimental Psychology: Human Perception and Performance, 24*(3), 756–766.

Neisser, U. (1988). Five kinds of self-knowledge. *Philosophical Psychology, 1,* 35–59.

Newell, A., & Simon, H. A. (1972). *Human problem solving.* Englewood Cliffs, NJ: Prentice-Hall.

Newman, G. E., Keil, F. C., Kuhlmeier, V., & Wynn, K. (2005). *Infants understand that only intentional agents can create order.* Manuscript submitted for publication.

Newport, E. (1990). Maturational constraints on language learning. *Cognitive Science, 14,* 11–28.

Paccanaro, A., & Hinton, G. E. (2002). Learning hierarchical structures with linear relational embedding. In T. G. Dietterich, S. Becker, & Z. Ghahramani (Eds.), *Advances in neural information processing systems, 14* (pp. 857–864). Cambridge, MA: MIT Press.

Piaget, J. (1952). *The origins of intelligence in children.* New York: International University Press.

Piaget, J. (1954). *The construction of reality in the child.* New York: Basic Books. (Original work published 1937)

Pinker, S. (1989). *Learnability and cognition: The acquisition of argument structure.* Cambridge, MA: MIT Press.

Pinker, S. (1994). *The language instinct.* New York: Morrow.

Pinker, S. (1995). Language acquisition. In L. R. Gleitman, M. Liberman, & D. N. Osherson (Eds.), *An invitation to cognitive science: Vol. 1. Language* (2nd ed., pp. 135–182). Cambridge, MA: MIT Press.

Pinker, S. (1997). *How the mind works.* New York: Norto.

Pinker, S. (2001). Four decades of rules and associations, or whatever happened to the past tense debate. In E. Dupoux (Ed.), *Language, brain, and cognitive development: Essays in honor of Jacques Mehler* (pp. 157–179). Cambridge, MA: MIT Press.

Pinker, S., & Bloom, P. (1990). Natural language and natural selection. *Behavioral and Brain Sciences, 13,* 707–784.

Pinker, S., & Ullman, M. (2002). The past and future of the past tense. *Trends in Cognitive Science, 6,* 456–463.

Pothos, E. M. (in press). The rules versus similarity distinction. *Behavioral and Brain Sciences.*

Prinz, J. (2002). *Furnishing the mind: Concepts and their perceptual basis.* Cambridge, MA: MIT Press.

Pullum, G. K., & Scholz, B. C. (2002). Empirical assessment of stimulus poverty arguments. *Linguistic Review, 19*(1/2), 9–50.

Pylyshyn, Z. (1999). Is vision continuous with cognition? The case of impenetrability of visual perception. *Behavioral, 22,* 321–343.

Ramsden, B. M., Hung, C. P., & Roe, A. W. (2001). Real and illusory contour processing in Area V1 of the primate-A cortical balancing act. *Cerebral Cortex, 11,* 648–665.

Rogers, T. T., & McClelland, J. L. (2004). *Semantic cognition: A parallel distributed processing approach.* Cambridge, MA: MIT Press.

Rogers, T. T., & Plaut, D. C. (2002). Connectionist perspectives on category-specific deficits. In E. Forde & G. Humphreys (Eds.), *Category specificity in brain and mind* (pp. 251–284). Hove, East Sussex, England: Psychology Press.

Roschelle, J. (1995). Learning in interactive environments: Prior knowledge and new experience. In J. H. Falk & L. D. Dierking (Eds.), *Public institutions for personal learning: Establishing a research agenda* (pp. 37–51). Washington, DC: American Association of Museums.

Rose, S. A., Feldman, J. F., & Jankowski, J. J. (2001). Attention and recognition memory in the 1st year of life: A longitudinal study of preterm and full-term infants. *Developmental Psychology, 37*(1), 135–151.

Rozin, P. (1976). The evolution of intelligence and access to the cognitive unconscious. In J. N. Sprague & A. N. Epstein (Eds.), *Progress in psychology* (Vol. 6, pp. 245–280). New York: Academic Press.

Roy, M. S., Barsoum-Homsy, M., Orquin, J., & Benoit, J. (1995). Maturation of binocular pattern visual evoked potentials in normal full-term and preterm infants from 1 to 6 months of age. *Pediatric Research, 37*(2), 140–144.

Sakata, H., Taira, M., Kusunoki, M., Marata, A., & Tanaka, Y. (1997). The TINS lecture: The parietal association cortex in depth perception and visual control of hand action. *Trends in Neuroscience, 20,* 350–357.

Samuels, R. (2002). Nativism in cognitive science. *Mind and Language, 17*(3), 233–265.

Sanjana, N., & Tenenbaum, J. B. (2002). Bayesian models of inductive generalization. In S. Becker, S. Thrun, & K. Obermayer (Eds.), *Advances in neural information processing systems, 15* (pp. 51–58). Cambridge, MA: MIT Press.

Scarr, S. (1992). Developmental theories for the 1990s: Development and individual differences. *Child Development, 63,* 1–19.

Scassellati, B. (2001). Investigating models of social development using a humanoid robot. In B. Webb & T. Consi (Eds.), *Biorobotics* (pp. 145–168). Cambridge, MA: MIT Press.

Scassellati, B. (2002). Theory of mind for a humanoid robot. *Autonomous Robots, 12*(1), 13–24.

Scholl, B. J. (2004). Can infants' object concepts be trained? *Trends in Cognitive Sciences, 8*(2), 49–51.

Scholl, B. J., & Leslie, A. M. (1999). Modularity, development and "theory of mind." *Mind and Language, 14,* 131–153.

Scholl, B. J., & Leslie, A. M. (2001). Minds, modules, and meta-analysis. *Child Development, 72,* 696–701.

Schunn, C. D., & Anderson, J. R. (2001). Acquiring expertise in science: Explorations of what, when, and how. In K. Crowley, C. D. Schunn, & T. Okada (Eds.), *Designing for science: Implications from everyday, classroom, and professional settings* (pp. 83–114). Mahwah, NJ: Erlbaum.

Scoville, W. B., & Milner, B. (1957). Loss of recent memory after bilateral hippocampal lesions. *Journal of Neurology, Neurosurgery, and Psychiatry, 20,* 11–21.

Segal, N. L., & MacDonald, K. B. (1998). Behavioral genetics and evolutionary psychology: Unified perspective on personality research. *Human Biology, 70*(2), 159–184.

Seidenberg, M. S., & MacDonald, M. C. (1999). A probabilistic constraints approach to language acquisition and processing. *Cognitive Science, 23,* 569–588.

Shultz, T. R., Mareschal, D., & Schmidt, W. C. (1994). Modeling cognitive development on balance scale phenomena. *Machine Learning, 16*(1/2), 57–86.

Shweder, R. A., Much, N. C., Mahapatra, M., & Park, L. (1997). The big three of morality (autonomy, community, and divinity) and the big three explanations of suffering. In A. Brandt & P. Rozin (Eds.), *Morality and health* (pp. 119–169). New York: Routledge.

Siegler, R. S. (1976). Three aspects of cognitive development. *Cognitive Psychology, 8,* 481–520.

Siegler, R. S. (1981). Developmental sequences between and within concepts. *Monographs of the Society for Research in Child Development, 46*(Whole No. 189).

Simon, H. (2000). Discovering explanations. In F. Keil & R. Wilson (Eds.), *Explanation and cognition* (pp. 21–59). Cambridge, MA: MIT Press.

Simons, D., & Keil, F. C. (1995). An abstract to concrete shift in cognitive development: The inside story. *Cognition, 56,* 129–163.

Sloman, S. (1996). The empirical case for two systems of reasoning. *Psychological Bulletin, 11*, 3–22.

Smith, C., Carey, S., & Wiser, M. (1985). On differentiation: A case study of the development of size, weight, and density. *Cognition, 21*(3), 177–237.

Smith, E. E., & Sloman, S. A. (1994). Similarity-versus rule: Based categorization. *Memory and Cognition, 22*, 377–386.

Smolensky, P. (1988). On the proper treatment of connectionism. *Behavioural and Brain Sciences 11*, 1–74.

Smolensky, P. (1990). Tensor product variable binding and the representation of symbolic structures in connectionist systems [Special issue: Connectionist Symbol Processing]. *Artificial Intelligence, 46*(1/2).

Spelke, E. S., Breinlinger, K., Macomber, J., & Jacobson, K. (1992). Origins of knowledge. *Psychological Review, 99*, 605–632.

Sperber, D. (1994). The modularity of thought and the epidemiology of representations. In L. A. Hirschfeld & S. A. Gelman (Eds.), *Mapping the mind: Domain specificity in cognition and culture* (pp. 39–67). New York: Cambridge University Press.

Sperber, D. (2002). In defense of massive modularity. In E. Dupoux (Ed.), *Language, brain and cognitive development: Essays in honor of Jacques Mehler* (pp. 47–57). Cambridge, MA: MIT Press.

Sperber, D., & Hirschfeld, L. (1999). Culture, cognition, and evolution. In R. Wilson & F. Keil (Eds.), *MIT encyclopedia of the cognitive sciences* (pp. 61–82). Cambridge, MA: MIT Press.

Sperber, D., & Hirschfeld, L. (2004). The cognitive foundations of cultural stability and diversity. *Trends in Cognitive Sciences, 8*(1), 40–46.

Sperber, D., & Wilson, D. (1995). *Relevance: Communication and cognition* (2nd ed.). Oxford, England: Blackwell.

Sun, R. (2001). Hybrid systems and connectionist implementationalism. In L. Nadel (Ed.), *Encyclopedia of cognitive science* (pp. 727–732). New York: MacMillan.

Tao, P. K., & Gunstone, R. F. (1999). A process of conceptual change in force and motion during computer-supported physics instruction. *Journal of Research in Science Teaching, 37*, 859–882.

Tenenbaum, J. B., & Griffiths, T. L. (2001). Generalization, similarity, and Bayesian inference. *Behavioral and Brain Sciences, 24*, 629–664.

Thagard, P. (1992). *Conceptual revolutions*. Princeton, NJ: Princeton University Press.

Thelen, E. (2000). Grounded in the world: Developmental origins of the embodied mind. *Infancy, 1*, 3–28.

Tooby, J., & Cosmides, L. (2005). Conceptual foundations of evolutionary psychology. In D. M. Buss (Ed.), *The handbook of evolutionary psychology* (pp. 5–67). Hoboken, NJ: Wiley.

Turiel, E., & Perkins, S. A. (2004). Flexibilities of mind: Conflict and culture. *Human Development, 47*(3), 158–178.

Tyler, L. K., deMornay-Davies, P., Anokhina, R., Longworth, C., Randall, B., & Marslen-Wilson, W. D. (2002). Dissociations in processing past tense morphology: Neuropathology and behavioral studies. *Journal of Cognitive Neuroscience, 14*(1), 79–94.

Vinson, D. P., Vigliocco, G., Cappa, S., & Siri, S. (2003). The breakdown of semantic knowledge along semantic field boundaries: Insights from an empirically-driven statistical model of meaning representation. *Brain and Language, 86*, 347–365.

von Hofsten, C., Vishton, P. M., Spelke, E. S., Feng, Q., & Rosander, K. (1998). Predictive action in infancy: Tracking and reaching for moving objects. *Cognition, 67*, 255–285.

Vosniadou, S., & Brewer, W. F. (1992). Mental models of the earth: A study of conceptual change in childhood. *Cognitive Psychology, 24*, 535–585.

Vygotsky, L. S. (1962). *Thought and language*. Cambridge, MA: MIT Press.

Wagner, G. P., & Mezey, J. (in press). The role of genetic architecture constraints for the origin of variational modularity. In G. Schlosser & G. P. Wagner (Eds.), *Modularity in Development and Evolution*. Chicago: Chicago University Press.

Wagner, G. P., Mezey, J., & Calabretta, R. (2004). Natural selection and the origin of modules. In W. Callabaut & D. Rasskin-Gutman (Eds.), *Modularity: Understanding the development and evolution of complex natural systems* (pp. 114–153). Cambridge, MA: MIT Press .

Weinacht, S., Kind, C., Monting, J. S., & Gottlob, I. (1999). Visual development in preterm and full-term infants: A prospective masked study. *Investigative Ophthalmology and Vision Science., 40*(2), 346–353.

Weiskrantz, L. (Ed.). (1988). *Thought without language*. New York: Oxford University Press.

Wellman, H. M. (1985). The origins of metacognition. In D. L. Forrest-Pressley, G. E. MacKinnon, & T. G. Waller (Eds.), *Metacognition, cognition, and human performance* (Vol. 1, pp. 1–31). New York: Academic Press.

Wellman, H. M. (1992). *The child's theory of mind*. Cambridge: MIT Press.

Wellman, H. M., & Gelman, S. A. (1997). Knowledge acquisition in foundational domains. In D. Kuhn & R. S. Siegler (Eds.), *Handbook of child psychology* (Vol. 2, pp. 523–573). New York: Wiley.

Werner, H. (1940). *Comparative psychology of mental development*. New York: Harper.

Wexler, K., & Culicover, P. (1980). *Formal principles of language acquisition*. Cambridge, MA: MIT Press.

Whewell, W. (1999). *The philosophy of the inductive sciences, founded upon their history*. Bristol: Thoemmes Press. (Original work published 1840)

Wynn, K. (1998). Psychological foundations of number: Numerical competence in human infants. *Trends in Cognitive Sciences, 2*, 296–303.

Yang, C. (2004). Universal grammar, statistics, or both? *Trends in Cognitive Science, 8*, 451–456.

Zelazo, P. D. (2004). The development of conscious control in childhood. *Trends in Cognitive Sciences, 8*, 12–17.

Zelazo, P. D., Muller, U., Frye, D., & Marcovitch, S. (2003). The development of executive function in early childhood. *Monographs of the Society for Research in Child Development, 68*(3, Serial No. 2), 74.

Zhang, L. I., & Poo, M. M. (2001). Electrical activity and development of neural circuits. *Nature Neuroscience, 4*(Suppl.), 1207–1214.

# CHAPTER 15

# *Culture and Cognitive Development in Phylogenetic, Historical, and Ontogenetic Perspective*

MICHAEL COLE

DEFINITIONS: CULTURE, COGNITIVE
   DEVELOPMENT, AND ALLIED CONCEPTS  637
Culture  637
Development  639
Culture and Cognition: A Synthetic Framework  639
CULTURE AND PHYLOGENETIC
   DEVELOPMENT  640
Culture and Hominization  640
Living Primates  642
CULTURAL HISTORY  647
Cross-Sectional Cultural-Historical Comparisons  648
Longitudinal Studies of Cultural-
   Historical Change  650
The Cultural Evolution of Arithmetic
   in New Guinea  651

History, Social Differentiation, and Education  652
Cultural-Historical Change in IQ Scores  658
ONTOGENY  659
The Proximal Locus of Development: Activity Settings
   and Cultural Practices  660
The Intertwining of Biology and Cultural Practices in
   Conceptual Development  663
Beyond Core Domains  670
Culture and the Ontogeny of Autobiographical
   Memory  672
CONCLUSION  674
REFERENCES  678

This chapter is the third *Handbook* contribution devoted specifically to the topic of culture and cognitive development, although several chapters in prior editions, as well as those by Shweder and his colleagues, Chapter 11, this *Handbook,* Volume 1, and Greenfield and her colleagues, Chapter 17, this *Handbook,* Volume 4, include relevant material within the broader rubric of culture and development. In light of the increasing attention being given to culture's role in development, my goal is to complement these contributions by broadening the issue of culture and cognitive *ontogeny* (which has implicitly been the topic of all other *Handbook* chapters on culture and development) to place it in a broad evolutionary and historical framework.

This expanded analysis of culture in development seems an important task for several reasons. No one writing on this topic denies that human development is heavily constrained by our species' phylogenetic heritage. In

fact, Shweder and his colleagues (1998) explicitly state that human beings are creatures with a long, common phylogenetic past that provides constraints on development. They also invoke ideas about the influence of experience that come directly from work in developmental neuroscience. However, they do not explore how these phylogenetic factors are linked to culture and human ontogeny, restricting themselves to pointing out that whatever these primeval, shared, characteristics are, they "only gain character, substance, definition and motivational force . . . when . . . translated and transformed into, and through, the concrete actualities of some particular practice, activity setting, or way of life" (Shweder et al., 1998 p. 871). This perspective provides a good starting point, but if it is not elaborated on, it de facto places human phylogeny and cultural history so far into the background of their presentations that the ongoing relationships between these different spheres during ontogeny go unexamined. Rogoff (2003), who also presupposes but does not analyze species-specific phylogenetic foundations to cognitive development, focuses instead on shifting modes of participation within and between practices during ontogeny and historical changes in those practices.

The approach I adopt here reflects my long-term interest in the work of the Russian cultural-historical school of psychology, for whom human development was seen as the emergent outcome of phylogenetic, cultural-historical, ontogenetic, and microgenetic processes all acting simultaneously on the developing person (Vygotsky, 1997; Wertsch, 1985). This position makes contact with increasingly popular work in the field of evolutionary developmental psychology (e.g., Bjorklund & Pellegrini, 2002), which focuses on the relationship between phylogeny and ontogeny. The evolutionary developmental perspective, however, pays little attention to the role of cultural history, particularly with respect to the issue of *cognitive* development. Consequently, one of my goals is to bring cultural history into the study of human development without abandoning a commitment to an evolutionary perspective.

## DEFINITIONS: CULTURE, COGNITIVE DEVELOPMENT, AND ALLIED CONCEPTS

Since this chapter links the study of biological history cultural history and cognitive ontogeny, at least a brief discussion of the meanings of the terms *culture* and *cognition* as they appear in the different disciplines that I must draw on (e.g., anthropology, paleontology, primatology, and psychology) seems necessary.

### Culture

In its most general sense, the term culture ordinarily refers to the socially inherited body of past human accomplishments that serve as the resources for the current life of a social group ordinarily thought of as the inhabitants of a country or region (D'Andrade, 1996). Several issues perennially spur debate concerning the concept of culture vis-à-vis the study of cognitive development in ontogeny. These include whether culture is a unique property of human beings, the extent to which human cultures can be ranked in terms of level of development, the relationship between mental/ideal and material aspects of culture, and the extent to which culture can be assumed to be shared by members of a social group.

### Is Culture Unique to Humans?

In recent years, many primatologists have argued that the core notion of culture is "group-specific behavior that is acquired, at least in part, through social influences" (McGrew, 1998, p. 305) or "behavioral conformity spread or maintained by nongenetic means" through processes of social learning (Whitten, 2000, p. 284). By this minimalist definition, culture is not specific to human beings. Not only many primates, but members of other species display behavioral conformities that they have acquired by nongenetic means, although precisely what those means are is widely debated.

I return to this point when discussing phylogenetic contributions to the development of human cognition. For the present, it is sufficient to note that even those who argue for the presence of culture among nonhuman primates generally agree that there is more to human culture than nongenetically transmitted behavioral patterns, just as there is more to human cognition than is found in nonhuman primates. Disagreements about precisely what this "more" is and what the differences in the nature of culture among species tell us about the role of culture in human cognitive development have produced a massive and contentious literature (Byrne et al., 2004).

### Cultural History and Development

During the nineteenth century, culture was used more or less as a synonym for civilization, referring roughly to the progressive improvement of human creativity in areas such as the industrial arts, including the manufacturing techniques for metal tools and agricultural practices ; the extent of scientific knowledge; the complexity of social organization; the refinement of manners and various customs; and control over nature and oneself (Cole, 1996; Stocking, 1968).

During the twentieth century, owing to the work of Franz Boas and his colleagues, the notion of culture-as-progress was gradually replaced by the idea that all cultures are the products of local adaptations to the circumstances of the social group during its history up to the present. Consequently, anthropologists have generally resisted the idea that different cultures could be scaled with respect to overall value or virtue, since such judgments are historically and ecologically contingent.

However, there remain those who emphasize that cultures can be ranked in terms of lower and higher levels of complexity, if not virtue. The question then becomes how such cultural variations are associated with variations in psychological processes (e.g., Damerow, 1996; Feinman, 2000; Hallpike, 1979).

### Cultural Patterns: Shared or Distributed?

When early ethnographers such as Margaret Mead went to far-off, relatively isolated, nonliterate societies to study culture and development, their notions of culture were subsumable under the notion of "the socially inherited body of past human accomplishments that serves as the resources for current life of a social group in its historical and ecological circumstances." In Mead's case, parental attitudes toward adolescents and customs relating to young people's sexual activities, or the ways the people of Manus built their houses on stilts, watched over (or failed to watch over!) their children, or engaged in animistic explanations for events constituted the "inherited knowledge" and "current resources" of interest. She also made the additional assumptions that social inheritance is highly patterned, interconnected, homogeneously experienced, and pervasive. The heavy emphasis placed on cultures as monolithic, gestalt-like configurations gave way over subsequent decades to appreciation of internal heterogeneity at both the cultural and individual levels and to the consequent need for people actively to create and recreate their culture for it to exist at all (Schwartz, 1978).

The degree to which particular cultural elements are shared has become an important topic in anthropology in general and the study of culture and cognition in particular. Kim Romney and his colleagues have proposed what they refer to as a "cultural consensus model" to characterize the degree to which users of a culture share particular understandings (Romney & Moore, 2001; Romney, Weller, & Batchelder, 1986). Medin and Atran (2004) apply this model to characterize how different subgroups within a society think differently about particular domains (e.g., how they conceive of nature and, consequently, how they act with respect to it). Such a "distributed" notion of culture finds its natural counterpart in distributed theories of cognition (e.g., Hutchins, 1995).

### The Relation of the Ideal and Material in Culture

The proliferation of conceptions of culture by the middle of the twentieth century induced Alfred Kroeber and Clyde Kluckhohn (1952) to offer a famous omnibus definition that provided greater specification to the general "social learning" approach adopted by primatologists or the "social inheritance" approach noted by D'Andrade for the human case:

> Culture consists of patterns, explicit and implicit, of and for behavior acquired and transmitted by symbols, constituting the distinctive achievements of human groups, including their embodiment in artifacts; the essential core of culture consists of traditional (i.e., historically derived and selected) ideas and especially their attached values; cultural systems may on the one hand be considered as products of action, on the other as conditioning elements of further action. (Kroeber & Kluckhohn, 1952, p. 181)

Note that this definition contains a mixture of elements, some of which appear to be material things "out there in the world," whereas others appear to be mental entities (ideas and values) that are "in here," in the human mind. Here we see clearly the emergence of a division between the study of material culture and symbolic culture, which represents a major cleavage line in the field to this day. Moreover, Kroeber and Kluckhohn provide at least a crude evaluation of the relative importance of the ideal and material aspects of culture when they pick out ideas and values as the "essential core" of culture. This is not an innocent preference, but rather reflects the fact that in the middle of the twentieth century a steady movement began in anthropology away from definitions (theories) of culture that emphasize its behavioral/material aspects toward definitions (theories) that, following Kroeber and Kluckhohn, emphasize its ideational/mental aspects.

In recent years, it has become common to see efforts to combine the "culture is out there/material" and the "culture is in here/mental" views in definitions of culture.

For example, Shweder and his colleagues define human culture as *both* a symbolic *and* a behavioral inheritance:

> The symbolic inheritance of a cultural community consists of its received ideas and understandings . . . about persons, society, nature, and divinity. . . . The "behavioral inheritance" of a cultural community consists of its routine or institutionalized family life and social practices. (1998, p. 868)

Thomas Weisner and his colleagues have developed a similar perspective. Weisner (1996) argues that the locus for cultural influences on development is to be found in the activities and practices of daily routines that are central to family life. The relations between individuals and activities are not unidirectional, however, because participants take an active role in constructing the activities in which they participate. Consequently, "the subjective and objective are intertwined" in culturally organized activities and practices (Gallimore, Goldenberg, & Weisner, 1993, p. 541).

There are a great many suggestions about how culture operates as a constituent of human activity. In the early 1970s, Geertz cited with approval Max Weber's image of humankind as "an animal suspended in webs of significance he himself has spun," declaring that "I take culture to be those webs" (Geertz, 1973. p. 5). Owing to this metaphor, Geertz is often read as an anthropologist who adopts the conception of culture as exclusively inside-the-head-knowledge (e.g., Berry, 2000). It is significant, however, that Geertz (1973) explicitly rejected the strictly idealist notion of culture by suggesting that culture should be conceived by analogy with a recipe or a computer program, which he referred to as control mechanisms:

> The "control mechanism" view of culture begins with the assumption that human thought is basically both social and public—that its natural habitat is the house yard, the marketplace, and the town square. Thinking consists not of "happenings in the head" (though happenings there and elsewhere are necessary for it to occur) but of traffic in what have been called, by G. H. Mead and others, significant symbols—words for the most part but also gestures, drawings, musical sounds, mechanical devices like clocks. (p. 45)

In what follows, I adopt the view that symbols and meaning embodied in, and constitutive of, historically accumulated practices constitute human culture.

## Development

Because this chapter is intended for an audience dominated by developmental psychologists, the theory-laden nature of definitions of development requires far less exposition. If one thumbs through leading introductory texts on child development, it becomes clear that many of them simply don't define the term, but assume its meaning and focus on particular content domains, or methods of analysis. Other texts offer "least common

denominator" definitions that are filled in later through examinations of theory and data: "the sequence of changes that children undergo as they grow older—changes that begin with conception and continue throughout life" (Cole, Cole, & Lightfoot, 2005, p. 2). Still others provide definitions that are theory laden; for example, "development involves age-related, qualitative changes and behavioral reorganization that are orderly, cumulative, and directional" (Sroufe, Cooper, & DeHart, 1996, p. 6).

The same problem arises when we turn to the more specialized topic of culture and cognitive development. Rogoff (2003) for example, treats the terms "learning and development" as synonymous. Others, including myself, see learning and development as interleaved, but distinct, processes involved in the cognitive change as children grow older (see Keil, Chapter 14, Kuhn & Franklin, Chapter 22; and Siegler, Chapter 11, this *Handbook,* this volume, for varying perspectives on this issue). Learning implies accumulation of knowledge and skills, whereas development implies qualitative reorganization of different constituents of such knowledge and skills and a concomitant reorganization of the relationship between persons and their environments (Cole, 1996; R. Gelman & Lucariello, 2002; Vygotsky, 1978). Diagnosis of the notion of development implied in any given treatment of culture and cognitive development is often most readily inferred from the specific tasks that are used as indexes of cognition, drawn as they are from different theoretical traditions of developmental psychology.

## Culture and Cognition: A Synthetic Framework

As noted, the cultural-historical perspective from which I approach the question of culture and cognitive development requires that psychologists study not only ontogenetic change but also phylogenetic and historical change in relation to one another (Wertsch, 1985). According to the initiators of the cultural-historical perspective, each new "level of history" was associated with a new "critical turning point":

> Every critical turning point is viewed primarily from the standpoint of *something new* introduced by this stage into the process of development. Thus we treated each stage as a starting point for further processes of evolution. (Vygotsky & Luria, 1993, p. 37)

The turning point in phylogeny is the appearance of tool use in apes. The turning point in human history is the appearance of labor and symbolic mediation. The major turning point in ontogeny is the convergence of cultural history and phylogeny with the acquisition of language. The product of these fusions of different streams of history is the distinctly human, higher psychological function.

In bringing this perspective up to date, I first review current data and speculation about the human biological, cultural, and cognitive characteristics in phylogenetic perspective. Next, I turn to research on cultural-historical change, then age-related changes in children's thinking as mediated by culture and the microgenetic changes through which ontogenies are constructed. My discussion of phylogeny is divided into two sections—one on hominization in relation to cultural and cognitive development, and the other on comparative studies of human and nonhuman primates—since each area has been the subject of intense interest in recent decades and in combination they are used to make claims about culture and ontogenetic development.

## CULTURE AND PHYLOGENETIC DEVELOPMENT

I present the knot of phylogenetic issues in terms of two evolutionary lines. The first spans the several million years of human evolution beginning with the appearance of *Australopithecus* approximately 4 million years ago and ending with *Homo sapiens sapiens,* perhaps 60,000 years ago. The second focuses on the other branch of our phylogenetic tree, the great apes, especially contemporary chimpanzees and bonobos.

The logic uniting these two lines of investigation is the assumption that human beings and apes shared a common ancestor some 4 to 5 million years ago (Noble & Davidson, 1996). The successors to that common ancestor leading to *Homo sapiens* underwent massive changes not only in the brain and in physical morphology of the body (bipedalism, the structure of the arms, hands, and fingers, the vocal tract, etc.), but in physical ecology, cognitive capacities, and the accumulation of the products of the past in the form of human culture. By contrast, the anatomy, body size, physical morphology, behavior, cognitive abilities, and modes of life among nonhuman primates have not changed markedly over the past several million years. Hence, a three-way analysis of change, one that follows the homid line, one that follows the nonhuman primate line, and a third that compares the two should provide a "guestimate" of the initial capacities of archaic human predecessors, the processes of homid physical and mental evolution, and in particular, the role of culture in those processes. The results of this analysis then provide the essential context within which to consider human ontogeny and its relationship to human culture in evolutionary context.

### Culture and Hominization

According to the general view summarized in Figure 15.1 and Table 15.1, there are a few relatively uncontroversial facts that serve as anchors for more detailed accounts of hominid evolution prior to the advent of modern human beings.

First, there is the evident increase in size of the brain in the sequence of species leading to *Homo sapiens sapiens.* There are various ways of calculating this growth in brain size but since the work of Jerison (1973), brain size has in some way been treated in relation to overall body size, which he referred to as an encephalization quotient (EQ; Falk & Gibson, 2001). Jerison demonstrated that the EQs of species from the great apes through the hominid line increase markedly, so that the EQ of modern humans is almost three times that of the chimpanzee and other great apes. Bickerton (1990) created a graph that arrayed EQs as a percentage of that of *Homo sapiens sapiens* across the presumed sequence of major landmark species in the homid line that indicates an accelerating rate of change across time.

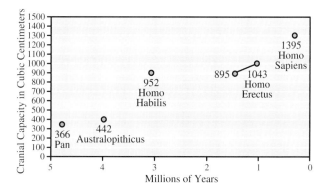

**Figure 15.1**   Evolutionary milestones for the hominid line, with divergence from chimpanzees at about 5 million years. Data represent cranial capacity in cubic centimeters associated with each new member of the hominid line. *Source:* From *The Human Primate* (p. 110), by R. Passingham, 1982, San Francisco: Freeman. Reprinted with permission.

**TABLE 15.1    The Chronology of Anatomical and Cultural Change**

Approximate time-line for the succession of hominids, in years before present.

5 million years: Hominid line and chimpanzee line split from a common ancestor:

4 million years: Oldest know australopithecines:
  –Erect posture
  –Shared food
  –Division of labor
  –Nuclear family structure
  –Larger number of children
  –Longer weaning period

2 million years: Oldest know habilines:
  –As above, with crude stone-cutting tools
  –Variable but larger brain size

1.5 million years: *Homo erectus:*
  –Much larger brain
  –More elaborate tools
  –Migration out of Africa
  –Seasonable base camps
  –Use of fire, shelters

0.3 million years: Archaic sapient humans:
  –Second major increase in brain size
  –Anatomy of vocal tract starts to assume modern form

0.05 million years: Fully modern humans

*Source:* From *Origins of the Modern Mind: Three Stages in the Evolution of Culture and Cognition,* by M. Donald, 1991, Cambridge, MA: Harvard University Press.

Although, as indicated in Table 15.1 and Figure 15.1, the overall and relative brain size of later hominids increased following the line from *Australopithecus* to *Homo sapiens sapiens,* this growth appears to have been especially pronounced in the frontal, prefrontal cortices, hippocampus, and cerebellum, all heavily implicated in cognitive changes both in phylogeny and ontogeny. Of special interest has been the appearance, derived from endocasts (moldings of the inside of skulls) for increased brain volume in Broca's area that appears with the advent of *Homo erectus* because of the relationship of Broca's area to language in normally developing modern humans.

There have also been many studies of morphological changes in other parts of the body associated with species changes following divergence from a common ancestor. These include bipedalism and various changes in anatomy with significance for hominization such as changes in the hand implicated in fine motor control (especially the opposable thumb), the pelvic region (which is crucial to the timing of birth and the length of infancy) and the vocal apparatus necessary for rapid and fluent speech (see Lewin & Foley, 2004, for a summary).

Data relevant to the cultural sphere, particularly the evidence of changes in material artifacts, are perhaps the second most reliable source of evidence concerning cognition-culture relations (Foley & Lahr, 2003). The first crude tools are often said to have appeared with *Homo habilis.* These tools were made of stone and, according to most interpreters, were probably made by shattering small rocks to make sharp-edged implements (choppers) and additional tools, such as knives, by chipping off flakes from the remaining stone core. With *Homo erectus,* there is generally believed to have been a quantum increase in size and the complexity of the tool kit. According to this line of interpreting the fossil record, tools now included hand axes with two cutting edges that required a much more complex manufacturing process. While initially change in the hominid tool kit was exceedingly slow, lasting perhaps a million years, the rate of change, the variety, and the complexity of tools increased in the course of human evolution, although the timing of changes is disputed (Foley & Lahr, 2003; Lewin & Foley, 2004).

With respect to behavior, which is inferred from the tools and the uses to which they were presumably put (e.g., cutting up large animals for meat, later for skins to be used as clothing) as well as evidence of group size and patterns of food consumption, *Homo erectus* appears to have been a critical turning point. For the first time there is evidence of creatures who lived in relatively permanent base camps, had stone tools that differed from any claimed for other species, and ventured out to hunt and gather; later in their 1.5 million years of existence, the use of fire makes its appearance. It is also *Homo erectus* that ventures out of Africa and migrates to Asia and Europe.

When we get to *Homo erectus,* the increased complexity of the tool kit (in particular, the symmetrical, crafted implements) provides evidence of greater cultural complexity and implies more complex cognitive abilities although it is uncertain what this increased cognitive complexity comprised. Some scholars argue that language was one such constituent (Bickerton, 1990; Deacon, 1997); special selective pressures for language development began early in evolution along the line to *Homo sapiens,* perhaps resulting from the need for increased cooperation in larger social groups, as with the appearance of *Homo sapiens* (Dunbar, 2004). Others argue that language came very late, with the advent of *Homo sapiens sapiens* owing to the development of a specialized vocal tract that could produce rapid speech (Lieberman, 1984). Whether early or late in hominization, symbolic language is agreed to be essential to the emergence of modern humans.

Suggestions for important cognitive changes that may or may not have accompanied language include increased ability to coordinate motor and spatial processing (Stout, Toth, Schick, Stout, & Hutchins, 2000; Wynn, 1989), increased ability to cooperate with others over extended periods to produce standardized products (Foley & Lahr, 2003), and an increased ability to imitate the behavior of others (Donald, 1991, 2001). (For discussion of Donald's views, pro and con, see Renfrew & Scarre, 1998.)

In some ways, the most well documented developmental change, from *Homo sapiens* to *Homo sapiens sapiens* is the most mysterious. Except for continued brain growth and some development in tools, there appears to be no clear reason for the sudden flowering of symbolic culture and the rapid expansion of human culture that is now clearly documentable, including sometimes elaborate burial with clear symbolic content, cave art, and ornamentation, not only of tools but for purposes that appear to have no direct utilitarian significance. The apparent discontinuity some 40 to 60 thousand years ago has led some to suggest a genetic mutation controlling the operation of a language module as *the* event leading to the appearance of modern humans (Berlim, Mattevi, Belmonte-de-Abreu & Crow, 2003). But this discontinuity position has been challenged by evidence of a great many species whose remains have been found in Africa that bespeak the presence of various elements of the "human revolution" (new technologies, long-distance trading, systematic use of pigment for art and decoration) tens of thousands of years earlier than previously thought but never fully developed in one place (McBrearty & Brooks, 2000). By this latter account, the human revolution was simply human evolution, in which many isolated changes in different species, combined with the changes in climate and population, brought disparate peoples together 40,000 years ago in Europe as it emerged from the latest Ice Age. The harsh climate had served to keep human groups apart, blocking the conditions of cultural and biological interaction among groups from which modern humans emerged.

If we seek to rise above the myriad disagreements among those who seek to synthesize processes at the phylogenetic level of analysis, the most important conclusion for our purposes is that the relations between biological, cultural, and cognitive change are reciprocal. The "virtuous circle" that the evidence most strongly supports is that changes in anatomy (increased relative brain volume) resulted from a change in diet, in particular greater intake of protein from the killing and ingestion of animals. The ability to kill and eat animals was the result of concomitant anatomical changes (the ability to run long distances that evolved following the evolution of the ability to walk upright, which also freed the hands and was accompanied by greater dexterity of the fingers)(Bramble & Lieberman, 2004). These biological changes were both cause and result of increased sophistication of the cultural tool kit, including the control of fire (clearly a cultural practice, but one whose origins are disputed across a million-year margin). This richer diet and the way of life associated with it enabled the growth of cognitive capacities that further enriched the cultural tool kit, which in turn further supported growth of the brain, and so on. In Henry Plotkin's (2001) felicitous phrasing, "biology and culture relate to each other as a two-way street of causation" (p. 93).

## Living Primates

Virtually all attempts to arrive at plausible speculations about cognitive change in phylogeny incorporate information from currently living species of nonhuman primates as an indirect way to make educated guesses about all the questions that arise when one is dealing solely with archeological evidence (see Joulian, 1996, for a discussion of this approach). Collectively, a number of remarkable events linking evolutionary biology, primatology, and developmental psychology in recent decades have revolutionized our ideas about the relationship between chimpanzees and bonobos (our closest primate kin) and modern humans (de Waal, 2001; Parker & McKinney, 1999).

In the middle of the twentieth century, those who considered culture a significant contributor to human development maintained that in many crucial respects, human beings are not just quantitatively, but qualitatively, different from other species in their cognitive abilities and in their use of culture as a medium of human life. At the time, DNA had not been decoded and the human genome project had not begun. Various hallmarks of human cognition and culture such as language, tool making, self-awareness, and intentional teaching were considered either nonexistent or extraordinarily underdeveloped in nonhuman primates. In short, there was something special about humans over and above their obvious morphological features associated with language and culture, which, in turn, were seen as co-

constituted. Human beings were considered exceptional not just because they have more brain cells, or differently organized brain cells, but an experiential way of life in which culture is both cause and effect of that experience.

The antiexceptionalism (continuity) side of this controversy, Darwinian saltation of cognitive capacity or cultural characteristics (producing a change in degree not kind), was revolutionized by DNA comparisons between humans and chimpanzees (Marks, 2002) and the ethnographic/ecological observations of communities of chimpanzees pioneered by Jane Goodall (1968). Together, the results of these landmark achievements make it more manageable to think of bonobos and chimpanzees as genetically very similar to humans. Matt Ridley (2003) sums up the shifting conceptions of chimpanzee mental, social, and cultural capacities when he refers to Goodall's descriptions of chimpanzee behavior in the wild over many years as "simian soap operas." Reading and then seeing videotapes of Goodall's chimpanzees, he wrote, their behavior seemed "like a soap opera written about the Wars of the Roses written by Jane Austin—all conflict and character." (p. 13). Goodall's chimps deceived each other, cheated on each other, and even killed each other. They also used leaves and sticks to fish for ants, and their children seemed to learn from seeing them do this.

I first examine current evidence concerning cognitive achievements and then the presence of culture among nonhuman primates before turning to the question of culture-cognition relations in these species and what issues those relations pose for scholars interested in culture-cognition relations in human ontogeny.

### Cognitive Achievements

Some of the primate literature supporting a continuity perspective grows out of, or is conducted in connection with, ontogenetic studies of such processes as imitation, numeration, self-awareness, attributions of intentionality, active teaching, and tool use, all of which have been implicated in the acquisition of cognitive capacities and the acquisition of human culture (Parker, Langer, & McKinney, 2000; Tomasello & Rackoczy, 2003; see also Boysen, & Hallberg, 2000).

### Language

The study of language in nonhuman primates has been one of the most visible lines of research pushing the envelope of continuity theory (Savage-Rumbaugh, Fields, & Taglialatela, 2001). Current enthusiasm for the idea that chimpanzees have the capacity to understand and produce language has been inspired by the work of Duane Rumbaugh & Sue Savage-Rumbaugh (Rumbaugh, Savage-Rumbaugh, & Sevcik, 1994). They provided their chimpanzees with a "lexical keyboard" whose keys bear symbols that stand for words, and they used standard reinforcement learning techniques to teach the chimpanzees the basic vocabulary symbols (e.g., "banana," "give"). In addition, the people who worked with the chimpanzees used natural language in everyday, routine activities such as feeding.

The Rumbaughs' most successful student has been Kanzi, a bonobo who initially learned to use the lexical keyboard by being present when his mother was being trained to use it. Kanzi is able to use the keyboard to ask for things and he can comprehend the meanings of lexical symbols created by others. He has also learned to understand some spoken English words and produce phrases of his own (Rumbaugh & Washburn, 2003).

Kanzi correctly acted out the spoken request to "feed your ball some tomato" (he picked up a tomato and placed it in the mouth of a soft sponge ball with a face embedded in it). He also responded correctly when asked to "give the shot [syringe] to Liz" and then to "give Liz a shot": in the first instance, he handed the syringe to the girl, and in the second, he touched the syringe to the girl's arm.

Kanzi's ability to produce language is not as impressive as his comprehension, however. Most of his utterances on the lexical keyboard are single words that are closely linked to his current actions. Most of them are requests. He uses two-word utterances in a wide variety of combinations, and occasionally makes observations. He produced the request "car trailer" on one occasion when he was in the car and wanted (or so his caretakers believed) to be taken to the trailer rather than to walk there. He has created such requests as "play yard Austin" when he wanted to visit a chimpanzee named Austin in the play yard. When a researcher put oil on him while he was eating a potato, he commented, "potato oil."

At present it appears that bonobos and chimpanzees can produce many aspects of language roughly at the level of a 2-year-old child using the lexical keyboard. In their productions, they form telegraphic utterances that encode the same semantic relations as young children (e.g., a two-symbol combination relating an agent to its action—"Kanzi eat"). These telegraphic utterances can either combine visual symbols or combine gesture with symbol (Savage-Rumbaugh, Murphy, Sevcik, & Brakke, 1993).

### Piagetian Developmental Milestones

An extensive line of work yielded evidence modeled on sensorimotor tasks favored by Piagetians to make the case for evolutionary continuity (e.g., Parker & McKinney, 1999). This research indicates that chimpanzees go through the same sequence of sensorimotor changes as human children, passing Piagetian sensorimotor tasks in various domains up to, and sometimes into, substage 6, the achievement of representational thought. Further evidence that substage 6 Piagetian understanding provides a meeting point of chimpanzee and human ontogenetic development comes from the work of Kuhlmeier and Boysen (2002) who have shown that that chimpanzees can recognize spatial and object correspondences between a scale model and its referent at a level of complexity roughly equivalent to that of 3-year-olds.

### Acquisition of Tools Use

At least from the time of Kohler's classic studies of problem solving, a great deal of attention has been focused on chimpanzee tool use and tool creation. McGrew's (1998) summary regarding tool use is worth quoting at length because it indicates current claims for chimpanzee tool use and tool-making capabilities:

> Each chimpanzee population has its own customary tool kit, made mostly of vegetation, that functions in subsistence, defense, self-maintenance, and social relations . . . many have tools sets, in which two or more different tools are used as composites to solve a problem. . . . The same raw material serves multiple functions: A leaf may be a drinking vessel, napkin, fishing probe, grooming stimulator, courtship signaler, or medication. . . . Conversely, a fishing probe may be made of bark, stem, twig, vine, or the midrib of a leaf. An archeologist would have no difficulty classifying the cross-cultural data in typological terms, based on artifacts alone; for example, only the far western subspecies . . . uses stone hammers and anvils to crack nuts. . . . Given this ethnographic record, it is difficult to differentiate, based on material culture, living chimpanzees from earliest *Homo* . . . or even from the simplest living human foragers. (pp. 317–318)

In line with McGrew's views, in at least one case it has been claimed that chimpanzees carry different tools with them to accomplish different goals (Boesch &

Boesch, 1984). The chimpanzees in question lived in the Ivory Coast. They encountered two kinds of nuts in their foraging, one with hard shells, the other with softer shells. For the hard nuts, they transported harder, heavier hammers (mostly stones) from their home base. They seemed to remember the location of stones and to choose the stones so as to keep the transport distance minimal.

Boesch and Boesch concluded that these chimpanzees possess a representation of Euclidian space that allows them to measure and remember distances; to compare several such distances so as to choose the stone with the shortest distance to a goal tree; to locate a new stone location with reference to different trees; and to change their reference point to measure the distance to each tree from any stone location. Overall, they appeared to combine the weight and the distance, leading Boesch and Boesch to infer these wild chimpanzees possess concrete operation abilities in the spatial domain. In a study with Kanzi, Savage-Rumbaugh and her colleagues obtained a similar result using lexigrams for location (Menzel, Savage-Rumbaugh, & Menzel, 2002).

### Theory of Mind

The domain of social cognition has received special attention because it appears to indicate that chimpanzees interpret correctly the state of mind of conspecifics. This work is thoroughly reviewed by Harris (Chapter 19, this *Handbook*, this volume) and does not bear detailed recapitulation here. Just a few points deserve highlighting to maintain continuity in the current context.

I find it significant that Boesch and Tomasello (1998), who used to be on different sides of the exceptionalism issue, have come to agree that chimpanzees acquire some parts of theory of mind, but not others (they understand some things about what others see or have seen in the recent past, and some aspects of others' goal-directed activities, but do not appear to distinguish gaze direction from attention or prior intentions that are no longer perceptually present). Most recently, Tomasello and his colleagues (Tomasello, Carpenter, Call, Behne, & Moll, 2005) have argued that the key cognitive difference is the adult human ability to engage in *shared* intentionality that permits engagement in complex collaborative activities and requires powerful skills of intention-reading as well as for a motivation to share psychological states with others. The intermingling of these abilities in human ontogeny, they argue, "produce[s] a unique development pathway for human cultural cognition, involving unique forms of social engagement, symbolic communication, and cognitive representation. Dialogic cognitive representations, as we have called them, enable older children to participate fully in the social-institutional-collective reality that is human cognition" (p. 16).

Additional examples of cognitive domains could be reviewed in which it has been claimed that chimpanzees exhibit at least the rudiments of cognitive abilities once believed to be the sole possession of human beings (myriad examples are provided by Bekoff, Allen, & Burghardt, 2002, and by de Waal, 2001). Extending such examples still leaves us with the question of how such cognitive similarities are related to the issue of central concern in this chapter—the relation of culture and cognition in development. To address this issue we need to look more closely at treatments of culture among the great apes and then return to examine the relation of culture to cognition in nonhuman species and humans.

### Culture among Apes

Belief in a narrow, quantitative gap between humans and nonhuman primate cognition is paralleled by belief in a narrow gap with respect to culture (Wrangham, McGrew, de Waal, & Heltne, 1994). Recall that in approaching the issue of primate culture, researchers define culture as behavioral traditions spread or maintained by nongenetic means through social learning. This kind of definition does not presuppose characteristics that are themselves arguably specifically human (e.g., religious beliefs, aesthetic values, social institutions). Hence, the analyst can remain agnostic with respect to culture-cognition relationships in different species (Byrne et al., 2004). At the same time, the definition allows examination of the extent to which cognitive characteristics claimed to be necessary for acquisition of human culture are present in displays of nonhuman primate behavioral traditions (cultures), such as deliberate teaching or tool making and use. I will focus here on chimpanzees, for which the most extensive evidence is available, but will include other well-researched examples as well (see McGrew, 1987, 1998).

The textbook example of a social tradition for which we know the origin and have data on its spread comes from sweet-potato-washing by Japanese macaque monkeys on Koshima Island (Matsuzawa, 2001). In 1953, a juvenile female monkey was observed washing a muddy sweet potato in a stream. This behavior first spread to

peers and then to older kin. Ten years later it was observed among more than 50% of the population and 30 years later by 71%. A few years later, the same monkey invented a form of "wheat-sluicing," in which wheat that had been mixed with sand was cast upon the sea so that the floating bits of wheat could be easily sorted from the sinking sand. Within 30 years, 93% of this group engaged in this behavior.

McGrew (1998) draws attention to other important characteristics of Japanese macaque cultural traditions. First, they do not remain entirely static. Koshima monkeys began by washing their potatoes in fresh water, but later adopted washing in seawater (presumably to add to the taste). A group of monkeys living in the far north adopted the tradition of bathing in warm springs in winter; initially the mothers left their offspring on the edge of the pools, but the young monkeys can now be seen swimming underwater. Second, cultural traditions develop with no discernible relation to subsistence activities; several groups of macaques routinely handle small stones in a variety of ways (rolling, rubbing, piling) that are not related to any identifiable adaptive function. These observations blunt attempts to find restrictions of the observed cultural behaviors to subsistence constraints.

The behavioral traditions involved have included the use of probes for termites and ants, nut cracking with sticks and stones, hunting strategies, nest building, and styles of grooming behavior (Matsuzawa, 2001; McGrew, 1998; Whitten, 2000; Wrangham et al., 1994). In light of their importance in discussions of both primate language and cognition, bonobos in the wild appear to display no evidence of tool use. This species difference should serve to block any simple equation between tool use and either cognitive development or the nature of social traditions.

### Culture, Cognition, and Nonhuman Primate Development

With respect to both cognition and culture considered separately, evidence appears to support the idea that members of the great ape family, particularly chimpanzees, attain levels of cognitive development that bring them to the threshold of the corresponding human domains. In the cultural realm, they form within-group social traditions through processes of social learning; these traditions include elementary kinds of tool use. In effect, nonhuman primates attain levels of cultural and cognitive development that terminate at approximately the transition from infancy to early childhood among human children. This brings us to the question of how cognition and culture are related among nonhuman primates.

Attempts to answer this question have focused on the cognitive mechanisms of social learning. The general answer given is that social learning requires some form of mimesis broadly interpreted as a process in which the behavior of one individual comes to be like another through some form of contact. But this broad understanding of mimesis is little more than restating what one means by a social tradition, since many different processes can lead to behavioral conformity. Consequently, the task of further specifying the processes of mimesis has garnered the bulk of scholarly attention (Byrne, 2002; Meltzoff & Prinz, 2002; Tomasello & Rakoczy, 2003; Whitten, 2000).

At the most elementary level, groups of the same species living in different locales may behave differently from each other, but in conformity with each other, because of differences in their local ecology. Each animal may be discovering the solution for itself, by this account.

In addition, situations may arise when members of a group are attracted to the location of conspecifics and, on their own, learn the behaviors that others have learned in the same circumstances. They may learn that grubs are located in the area, and learn to find the grubs and eat them, without any special orientation to the behavior of others. This source of social learning is termed *stimulus enhancement.*

A slightly more complex form of social influence is referred to as *emulation learning,* which occurs when, for example, an infant chimpanzee observes its mother turn over a log and sees that there are grubs under the log. Although the infant is not focused on the mother's goal-directed intentions (strategies), it learns something about objects in the environment and can then, on its own, learn about attaining such objects.

The most complex (and most controversial) claims about the source of acquiring social traditions in nonhuman primates are *imitation*—when the infant attempts to copy the goal-directed strategies of the mother. There is as yet no consensus on whether nonhuman primates raised in the wild engage in this form of mimesis (Byrne, 2002).

For those who believe that true imitation is present among the great apes, there is little to distinguish the re-

sulting forms of culture and their cognitive underpinnings among species (Parker & McKinney, 1999; Russon & Begun, 2002). We are again faced with a "threshold" phenomenon: Whether the threshold involves the presence of symbolic representation arising in substage 6 of Piaget's sensorimotor period or the extent to which chimpanzees are interpreting the intentions of conspecifics, the resulting culture may meet the minimal definition of culture as a socially acquired behavior pattern, but it does not involve either symbolic mediation of thought. It is also noteworthy that there are no claims for the ways in which chimpanzee culture influences chimpanzee cognition. The most that has been claimed is that chimpanzees raised by humans are likely to be poorly adapted to life in the wild, a perfectly reasonable conclusion that implicates learning of various kinds, but no cultural influences on the development of chimpanzee thought processes.

The only circumstances in which immersion in culture reveals clear consequences for the cognitive and linguistic development of nonhuman primates is where they are raised by human beings who seek to promote their cognitive development using all the (human) cultural means at their disposal. This point has been emphasized by Tomasello (1994), who has suggested that "a humanlike social-cognitive environment is essential to the development of human-like social-cognitive and imitative learning skills. . . . More specifically, for a learner to understand intentions of another individual requires that the learner be treated as an intentional agent" (pp. 310–311). As might be expected, those who attribute more mental capacities to nonhuman primates than does Tomasello dispute this idea and, to buttress their argument, point to observational evidence that primates raised by humans undergo hardships when introduced into their natural environment precisely because they have not been exposed to the appropriate culture (Parker & McKinney, 1999; Russon & Begun, 2002).

Unusual evidence concerning the influence of humans on primate culture/cognition comes from the work of Savage-Rumbaugh and her colleagues, who have worked for many years with a group of bonobos at their Language Research Center (Savage-Rumbaugh et al., 2001). For many years, these researchers have engaged in joint, mediated, activity with a group of bonobos and refer to the behavioral customs that have emerged in the process of these interactions as "*Pan/Homo*" culture. They readily admit that a variety of behaviors that appear in bonobos under these cultural conditions (e.g., tool use) would not evolve in the wild. But the message they take away from this state of affairs is, "These findings render moot old questions regarding limits of the ape brain. They raise instead more productive questions about the form and function of the perpetual dance that is constantly taking place between plastic neuronal systems and their external culturally devised ways of being" (p. 290).

Ironically, given the strong preference of these authors for a continuity perspective, the requirement that bonobos become enculturated into a unique, hybrid, ape/human culture in order to develop the more human-like forms of behavior at the upper range of their ability simultaneously provides support for the important cognitive differences between humans and apes and the role of human culture as both consequence and cause of that difference.

## CULTURAL HISTORY

Although there are innumerable differing explanations for the causes of the transition to *Homo sapiens sapiens* (a genetic change, a change in climate, a change in inter-activity among *Homo sapiens* creating a critical mass of cultural isolates, some combination of the above, etc.), there is reasonable agreement that something special emerged in the hominid line between 40,000 to 50,000 years ago, the "high Paleolithic" period of paleontology. The following set of changes are among those widely believed to have occurred (Cheyne, 2004):

- *Semeiosis—the act of creating signs that stand for objects.* The production of figurative and nonfigurative marks on stones, bones, plaques, cave walls and so on.
- *Production of second-order tools.* This refers to the production and use of tools to work bone, ivory, antler, and similar materials into a great variety of new tools such as points, awls, needles, pins, and spear-throwers.
- *Production and use of simple machines that exploited mechanical advantage (e.g., the spear-thrower and perhaps the so-called baton de commandment).*
- *An ability to visualize the complex action of tools or simple machines.* The production and use of fish hooks and harpoons appeared at this time. The me-

chanics of these devices required that the makers be able to visualize and understand or predict the sequence of remote events such as those of penetration, withdrawal, and secondary penetration of a barb.
- *Spatial structural organization of living sites.*
- *Long-distance transport of raw materials such as stones and shells over tens or even hundreds of kilometers.*

These psychological and cultural developments were associated with other changes of enduring significance. These included:

- A rapid expansion of human populations into all territories previously occupied by earlier developed forms of humans and the extremely rapid replacement of the indigenous populations
- Further expansion into territories not previously inhabited by humans
- An increase in population densities to levels comparable to those of hunting-and-gathering societies of historical times (Cheney, 2004)

Here, it appears, is the beginning of modern humans, the cavemen and hunter-gatherers of anthropological, paleontological, and historical lore.

I assume the following common story of change following the emergence of biologically modern humans to be roughly true (c.f. Diamond, 1997; Donald, 1991; Gellner, 1988). Some of the hunter-gatherers who inhabited many parts of the earth and lived in small bands went on to engage in sedentary agriculture. From that way of life there emerged in some places conglomerations of people larger than the small groups that preceded them; older ways of life disappeared or continued in very much the same way for millennia. In others there was a marked increase in sociocultural complexity (Feinman, 2000).

As a number of scholars interested in culture and cognitive development in prehistory have emphasized, a defining characteristic of the Paleolithic era was the appearance of external systems of symbolic, representational cave art, statuary, and perhaps elementary counting devices (Donald, 2001). While the symbolic nature of such artifacts and their probable incorporation in symbolically mediated rituals including burial practices is generally agreed to provide convincing proof of the evolution of symbolic activity among *Homo sapiens sapiens,* researchers have not yet agreed on the precise cognitive mechanisms involved. According to Damerow (1998), it seems most reasonable to consider the many millennia between the beginning of the Paleolithic period and the Neolithic period around 8000 B.C. (when people began to domesticate plants and animals and live in permanent villages) as a historical equivalent of the transition from sensorimotor to preoperational thinking. If, as McGrew (1987) argues, such societies approximate the level encountered in small face-to-face societies during the European age of exploration, it provides evidence in favor of the assumption that the cognitive processes of such peoples are best characterized as preoperational (Hallpike, 1979).

According to both Damerow (1998) and Donald (2001), it is with the urban revolution coinciding with the elaboration of tools, agricultural techniques, the smelting of copper and then bronze that one sees the transition from preoperational to operational thinking in human history. Two important lessons for the study of contemporary studies of culture and human ontogeny are emphasized by this literature. First, when concrete operational thinking begins to make an appearance, it is tightly bound to particular domains of culturally organized activity. Cuneiform writing, Damerow writes, represented mental models of the administrative activities that they mediated. Although they involved protonumerical systems, such systems did not embody principles of concrete operations and did not conclusively imply that their users could engage in reversible mental operations. Second, the causal relations between the development of culture and the development of cognition were reciprocal. Like Plotkin, quoted earlier, who was referring to a much earlier period of hominization, Donald (2001) is emphatic in his conclusion that the brain and culture "have evolved so closely that the form of each is greatly constrained by the other." Moreover, with the advent of literacy especially, "Culture actually configures the complex symbolic systems needed to support it by engineering the functional capture of the brain for epigenesis" (p. 23).

The difficulty with using prehistoric and even historical materials that have survived only in writing is that we have too little information about their contexts of use to make refined inferences about culture and cognitive development in ontogeny. For this reason, psychologists especially value studies enabled by rapid cultural-his-

torical change in most parts of the world over the past several decades. Conditions of rapid change make it easier to tease apart relations between cultural-historical and ontogenetic change because there are coexisting generations close to each other in age who engage in markedly different culturally organized activities.

## Cross-Sectional Cultural-Historical Comparisons

Perhaps the best known study on the relation of rapid cultural-historical change to cognitive change was carried out by Alexander Luria in the early 1930s, although the work was not fully published in Russian or any other language until the middle of the 1970s (Luria, 1976). Luria studied a cohort of people under conditions of rapid change in remotes parts of the Kirghizia and Uzbekistan.

The historical occasion was the collectivization of agricultural labor under state control, which brought with it changes such as formal schooling and exposure to bureaucratic state agencies, during what can fairly be described as a revolutionary period in that part of the world. Luria concluded that the new modes of life deeply affected the dominant modes of thought, such that the "premodern" group was restricted to a form of "graphical/functional" reasoning based on common experience, whereas modernization brought with it access to scientific concepts that subsumed and dominated the everyday modes of thought, replacing graphical/functional thinking.

Luria's research was not developmental in the sense of studying the impact of the historical changes on people of different ages. He relied primarily on psychological test data collected from adults with different degrees of exposure to Soviet collectivization. His conclusions are open to a series of criticisms, two of which are most important. First, data from tests and clinical interviews were generalized very broadly to activity-dependent experience, but there was no in-situ evaluation of such connections. The interview situation was an alien form of activity to the traditional pastoralists who served as subjects in Luria's experiments; their responses may have reflected as much the alien nature of the modes of discourse as the influence of their own cultural experience employed in indigenous activities. Second, this same abstraction from the theoretical site of change, the activities themselves, both made it difficult to grasp the processes at work in the course of change and made it appear that the changes from concrete-graphic to theoretical thinking were of a general nature. In this respect, Luria's research was typical of cross-cultural work. It is still valued, however, for its clever use of interview methods similar to those used by Piaget, rather than settling for simple, unchallenged test responses, and for Luria's use of a broad range of tests ranging from perception, through classification, logical reasoning, to reasoning about oneself.

Modern research by King Beach in an area of Nepal undergoing rapid historical change used methods that appear to overcome some of the shortcoming's of Luria's work (Beach, 1995). Beach studied changing forms of arithmetic calculations in a Nepalese village that underwent rapid socioeconomic and cultural change in the 1960s and 1970s. Roads from India moved closer to the village, schooling was introduced for the first time and continued to expand over ensuing decades, and shops that exchanged merchandise for money appeared during the same period and rapidly increased in number. At the time the research was initiated in the late 1980s, two coexisting generations of men experienced different relations between their experience of traditional farming, shopkeeping, and schooling. What all groups shared was some experience with subsistence agriculture and the need to buy and sell in the shops using traditional nonmetric units to measure a given length of cloth and then calculate price in terms of meters and centimeters, to which the monetary price was linked. The traditional system relied on using the length from the elbow to the tip of the middle finger while the newly introduced system involved use of a ruler and the metric system.

Senior high school students were apprenticed to shopkeepers in the village, and shopkeepers who had never had the opportunity to attend school were enrolled in an adult literacy/numeracy class. Farmers who had never attended school and had never worked in a shop also completed a shopkeeping apprenticeship or were enrolled in the adult education class. The transitions between education and work activities that were induced as a part of the study simulated larger scale changes taking place in rural Nepali society. Some of the problems posed by Beach to track changes in arithmetic during the shop apprenticeship involved purchases requiring translation and calculation between the two measurement systems. Problems presented to those enrolled in the adult education class were arithmetic problems of the kind typically encountered in school mathematics classes.

Traditionally, shopkeepers used arithmetic forms based on indigenous systems that bear little surface relationship either to metric measurement (arm lengths versus a metric measuring stick) or to the methods of calculating amounts and prices (the use of objects and other artifacts and decomposition strategies versus the use of paper and pencil to write equations and calculate with column algorithms). Those students becoming shopkeepers continued to use the written form they had learned in school after they entered the shops, even though reliable traditional methods long in use were prevalent there. Over time and with much pressure from the shopkeeper and customers, the students adapted the written form for use with the calculation strategies championed by the shopkeepers. Those who began as shopkeepers and were studying in the adult education class used their arms and traditional measurement objects to carry out their calculations, but eventually adopted a flexible approach of sometimes using traditional measurement units and calculation strategies and other times doing written calculations adapted to the problem at hand. Why?

From interviews with the participants, Beach was able to determine that students who were becoming shopkeepers viewed themselves as engaged in two activities, displays of school learning and shopkeeping that were initially in contradiction with each other. The status of schooling and of "being educated" made it difficult for them to give up the written form of calculation, though the speed and adaptability of the shopkeeper's calculations eventually induced them to adapt the written form to the shopkeeper's calculation strategies. In this way, their status as formally educated adults was retained, marked by their use of the written form, but they could use the written form to do the calculations as quickly and accurately as shopkeepers. The shopkeepers, however, even though they were in an evening school, always thought of themselves as engaged in their own shopkeeping activities and did not shift over to the school-based system except when they saw it as facilitating their ongoing work. Both by virtue of the tasks he presented and the way in which he presented them, Beach verified the linkage between cultural-historical and ontogenetic change that depended on both the history of relations between the activities and the individuals' developmental history at the point of participation in those activities. This leads to a process of ontogenesis that is much more variable and more content/artifact-specific than Luria's results would suggest.

## Longitudinal Studies of Cultural-Historical Change

Despite differences in methods, the research by Beach and Luria involved people with different amounts of exposure to new cultural practices.[1] A common feature of the two studies discussed in this section is that the same developmentalist returned after many years to the same place, using the same general methods, so that it is possible to document the cognitive development under changed sociocultural conditions for the same people at two disparate times.

Each of the studies reviewed here covers three generations: adults and children 30 to 40 years ago and grandparents, parents, and children recently. This relatively long time scale (in ontogenetic terms) meant that children in earlier studies could be studied as parents in the second, and the children-to-be in the first study replace the children-now-parents in the contemporary study.

### *Historical Change and Cognitive Change in Zinacantan*

In the late 1960s, Patricia Greenfield and her colleagues went to the Zinacantan, a Mayan group living in the state of Chiapas, Mexico, where they began to study the cognitive and social consequences of learning to weave (Greenfield & Childs, 1977). Their work included experimental tests of categorizing ability by both boys and girls, careful descriptions of the apprenticing of young girls into weaving and of the weaving process, and analysis of the products produced. In the 1990s, they returned to the same village and conducted parallel observations of parents (former child subjects) inducting their children into weaving and the products of this work (Greenfield, 1999; Greenfield, Maynard, & Childs, 2000).

In her recent writing comparing the relation between cultural change, modes of weaving, and modes of weaving instruction, Greenfield has emphasized the interconnectedness of historical change in economic activity,

exposure to new products and practices from contact with people from the modern sector of Mexican society, socialization practices (in particular, modes of socializing girls into weaving), and cognitive processes involving the mental representation of the patterns in woven cloth (Greenfield, 2002, 2004; Greenfield et al., 2000). These changes are viewed as interconnected.

### *Historical Changes*

The analysis begins with historical changes in general modes of living. In contrast to the late 1960s, in the mid-1990s this Mayan community shifted from an economy based primarily on subsistence agriculture and relative seclusion from the modern state to one based more heavily on involvement in the money economy, trade, and much more frequent interaction with people and trade from outside the village and the local region.

### *Socialization*

The instructional mode characterizing the mother-child weaving sessions in 1970 emphasized a long process of gradual apprenticeship involving many roles preparatory to weaving itself. When children first began to weave, mothers hovered close by and guided children with their own hands and bodies, using little verbal instruction. The entire system appeared to focus on maintenance of tradition and is characterized as "interdependent cultural learning."[2] In the 1990s, mothers who were more involved in the modern economy (e.g., by weaving products for sale) instructed their children verbally from a distance, sometimes using older siblings to take over instruction, and the children learned by a process that Greenfield and her colleagues characterize as "independent cultural learning" which involves a good deal more trial and error and self-correction of errors.

The variety of products changed. In the late 1960s, the products were limited, reflecting a very small set of "right ways to weave cloth." By the 1990s, there was no longer a small set of simple, "correct" patterns, but an efflorescence of patterns, indicating the increased

---

[1] Beach's students were in their early 20s, his shopkeepers in their 40s, but this age difference was not the object of his research and all were treated as adults.

[2] The importance of getting an early start on learning to weave reveals itself in the problems that American psychologists such as Greenfield and Rogoff experienced when attempting to master this skill. A major hurdle was the difficulty they had in maintaining the postural position required. This pervasively experienced fact is a reminder of how cultural practice shapes biological capacity during ontogeny.

respect paid to individual innovation that comes with a trial-and-error approach to learning. This proliferation in turn depended on, and contributed to, changes in weaving practices.

### Changing Modes of Mentally Representing Patterns

Accompanying the historical changes were changes in the way children represented weaving patterns in an experimental task that used sticks of varying width and color that could be inserted into a rack to reproduce model patterns from woven models. Instead of using, for example, three white sticks to represent a broad band of white cloth, a single broad white stick was more likely to be used in the later historical period and those who attended school were more likely to be able to create novel patterns. Importantly these historical changes were accompanied by an unchanging pattern of representational development related to age: older children in both historical periods were more able than younger children to represent more complex visual patterns, a fact that Greenfield et al. interpret as an indication of universal developmental processes accompanying culturally contingent ones. (I return to examine other results from this extensive research program in the section on ontogenetic developmental change.)

Based on her decades-long involvement with a Mayan community in the Yucatán, Suzanne Gaskins (1999, 2000, 2003) notes the same economic changes observed by Greenfield and her associates but provides a different, although compatible, explanation of the causal factors involved. Gaskins focuses on how the changing economic circumstances change maternal work patterns, suggesting that reduced time spent on traditional chores (e.g., not hauling water because there is running water, or having a longer day because of electricity) and time spent in the commercial sector outside the home, shift the division of labor inside the house in ways that reduce direct parental involvement with children's socialization in general, not just with respect to weaving. She also suggests that the efflorescence of weaving patterns may arise as much from copying models and parts of models imported by truck and the availability of money for foreign cultural goods as from any individual increase in creativity engendered by different modes of teaching.

Differences in interpretation of underlying process notwithstanding, the Greenfield et al. multigenerational study brings a whole new range of data to bear on mechanisms of cultural change and accumulation, suggesting a strong link between cultural change resulting from the interaction of cultures and the new means of teaching and learning that accompany the shift to more intensively commercially mediated forms of life.

## The Cultural Evolution of Arithmetic in New Guinea

A second "longitudinal cultural-historical" study was begun from 1978 to 1980 by Geoffrey Saxe and his colleagues, who conducted developmental studies among the Oksapmin in the remote highlands of central New Guinea (Saxe, 1982, 1994). His initial research followed the cross-cultural Piagetian tradition. He found that Oksapmin children acquired the ability to use counting strategies before they acquire conservation of number, which they acquire more slowly than their counterparts in New York (Saxe, 1981). But it was the number system that caught his attention. Traditionally, the Oksapmin use a 27-digit counting system that is based on body parts, beginning with the pinky of the right hand and ending at the pinky of the left hand, with stops in between for the elbow, biceps, eyes, nose, and so on.

When Saxe arrived, he found the traditional number system in wide use, but he also found that people who had traveled to earn money at nearby tea and copra plantations for 2 years at a time were likely to bring back a taste not only for some of the goods they encountered there, but also for money (a heretofore unknown phenomenon), which could be exchanged for those desirable consumer goods. Moreover, the outside world had penetrated Oksapmin life sufficiently to establish schools that taught in an English-related pidgin language in which children learned base 10 arithmetic and standard calculation procedures.

On the basis of ethnographic data, Saxe was convinced that traditionally the Oksapmin used their number system to count things such as pigs, identify the ordinal position of a house in a small hamlet, or to measure the length of an object. However, they did not habitually engage in arithmetic operations such as addition. Instead, for example, they would establish 1:1 or 1:N relations between objects being traded in economic exchanges.

So when Saxe asked people to use this system to engage in arithmetic operations, he expected performance to improve as a function of engagement in the use of money for everyday transactions. True to his supposition, the more people had been exposed to the use of money, the more complicated strategies for addition and subtraction they manifested and the more they were able to carry out such strategies when there were no coins present to serve as a tool for counting and adding (Saxe, 1985). He also found that Oksapmin children attending school both used their traditional system to help them solve problems (instead of counting on their fingers) and developed more of the same sort of complex strategies exhibited by the adults with the most exposure to transactions involving money.

More than 20 years later, Saxe and his colleagues returned to the Oksapmin. He had, in the meantime, carried out studies of the development of mathematical abilities among nonschooled children working in various occupations in Brazil that involved mathematical operations and put forth a general theory of how arithmetical forms and functions (means and ends) develop in ontogeny (Saxe, 1994). He had also studied the microgenesis of arithmetic knowledge in specially designed games involving arithmetic operations intended for use in school. This work helped him to focus on the microgenesis, the moment-to-moment changes, in the dance of form and function that produces developmental change (Saxe, 2002). During this same period, he was interacting with scholars interested in cultural practices as the proximal medium of cognitive development in any culture, and he began to take an interest in how cultural-historical development, or cultural evolution, comes about.

Consequently, the research he conducted when he returned to New Guinea was both more ambitious and more historically oriented than his prior work had been. He also had his prior work in the same villages to provide a benchmark for plotting the course of cultural change—in particular, changes in cultural practices (such as schooling that involves direct instruction in arithmetic using a foreign system and trade that involves the use of money).

As a means for studying population variations associated with varying experience of schooling or in the use of money (which was now much more prevalent in the area, associated with a high volume of trade in agricultural products and the introduction of mining in not-too-distant areas), Saxe and Esmonde (in press) traced the cultural history of a single lexical item, "fu," which they show underwent a number of changes during the period between 1978 and 2001. When Saxe first went to New Guinea, traditional Oksapmin, who had not yet learned pidgin, used fu to refer to the completion of counting a set of objects, as in, "1 . . . 27, done." During the ensuing 20 years, the English system of 20 shillings to the pound, which was relatively new to the Oksapmin when Saxe was first there, was replaced by a national Papua New Guinea (PNG) base-10 system in which 10 units that functioned like shillings summed to one PNG denomination called a kuan. People referred to a 2-kuan note by the same term they used to refer to a pound. In both cases, the number 20 is of exceptional importance. Saxe and his colleagues found that the number 20, which is at the left elbow, became a privileged site in the body-counting system, and at the same time, fu took on the new function of referring to completion of a count of shillings/2PNG kuan.

As a result of taking developmental change over a cultural-historical epoch as a focus of interest, Saxe and Esmonde were faced with the possibility that the changing meanings of fu were not the result of conscious human effort to create a more powerful arithmetic as a general cultural tool, but rather, arose as a by-product of the mixture of ways of using language and the body to represent number in conjunction with the ever-changing, and ever-more-commercialized, social and economic exchange practices that people engaged in.

## History, Social Differentiation, and Education

The historical development of formal schooling based on literacy and numeracy is an example of change at the cultural-historical level with implications for cognitive development (Cole, 2005; Rogoff, Correa-Chávez & Cotuc, 2005). Among academics, policymakers, and the general public, it is widely believed that education makes one more developed cognitively, either generally (United Nations Educational, Scientific, and Cultural Organization [UNESCO], 1951) or with respect to some more specific range of cognitive skills (Rogoff, 1981; Serpell & Hatano, 1997). Hence, historical changes in this form of culturally organized activity are an especially important example of the relationship between cultural change and cognitive development.

Although it is sometimes argued that the term, *education,* applies equally across all societies at all times because all human groups must prepare the next generation if the social group is to continue (Reagan, 2000), I find it more helpful to think of education as a particular form of schooling and schooling as a particular form of institutionalized enculturation. Tracing the process of education thus interpreted over historical time serves to concretize this ordering from enculturation (induction into the cultural order of the society), to schooling (deliberate instruction for specific skills), to education (an organized effort to "bring out" [educe] the full potential of the individual).

### Small, Face-to-Face Societies

Reminiscent of arguments that arise in the literature on culture formation in nonhuman primates, Jerome Bruner, in an influential monograph on culture and cognitive development, remarked that in watching "thousands of feet of film (about life among the Kung San Bushmen), one sees no explicit teaching in the sense of a 'session' out of the context of action to teach the child a particular thing. It is all implicit" (Bruner, 1966, p. 59). Elsewhere in the same essay, he comments that "the process by which implicit culture is 'acquired' by the individual . . . is such that awareness and verbal formulation are intrinsically difficult" (p. 58).

Similarly, Meyer Fortes, in his well-known monograph on education in Taleland emphasized that "the social sphere of the adult and child is unitary and undivided. . . . As between adults and children, in Tale society, the social sphere is differentiated only in terms of relative capacity. All participate in the same culture, the same round of life, but in varying degrees, corresponding to the stage of physical and mental development . . ." (Fortes, 1938, p. 8).

Reagan (2000) supports these descriptions of small, face-to-face societies in a recent review of ethnographic evidence from 76 societies in sub-Saharan Africa leading him to conclude that in the African setting, education "cannot (and indeed should not) be separated from life itself" (p. 29).

### Rudimentary Forms of Separation between Enculturation and Schooling

Even granting such a starting point, one encounters small societies where agriculture has displaced hunting and gathering as the mode of life, but they remain small in size and relatively isolated from each other. In such conditions, one witnesses the beginnings of differentiation of child and adult life involving forms of deliberate teaching that usually include a good deal of training. In many societies in rural Africa, what are referred to casually as *rites de passage* may be institutionalized activities that last for several years and teaching is certainly involved. For example, among the Kpelle and Vai peoples of Liberia, where I worked in the 1960s and 1970s, children were separated from their communities for 4 or 5 years in an institution referred to in Liberian pidgin as "bush school." There, children were instructed by selected elders in the essential skills of making a living as well as the foundational ideologies of the society, embodied in ritual and song. Some began there a years-long apprenticeship that would later qualify them to be specialists in bone setting, midwifery, and other valued arcane knowledge.

### Social Accumulation, Differentiation, and the Advent of Schooling

It appears that it is primarily, if not only, when a society's population grows numerous and it develops elaborate technologies enabling the accumulation of substantial material goods, that the form of enculturation to which we apply the term *schooling* emerges. As a part of the sea change in human life pattern associated with the transition from the Bronze Age to the Iron Age in what is now referred to as the Middle East, the organization of human life began a cascade of changes, which while unevenly distributed in time and space, appear to be widely, if not universally, associated with the advent of formal schooling. In the Euphrates valley, the smelting of bronze revolutionized economic and social life. With bronze, it became possible to till the earth in more productive ways, to build canals to control the flow of water, to equip armies with more effective weapons, and so on. Under these conditions, one part of the population could grow enough food to support large numbers beside themselves. This combination of factors made possible a substantial division of labor and development of the first city-states (Schmandt-Besserat, 1975).

Another essential technology that enabled this new mode of life was the elaboration of a previously existing, but highly restricted mode of representing objects by inscriptions on tokens and the elaboration of the first writing system, cuneiform, which evolved slowly over time. Initially, the system was used almost exclusively for record keeping, but it evolved to represent not only objects but the sounds of language, enabling letter writing and the recording of religious texts (Larsen 1986; Schmandt-Besserat, 1996).

The new system of cuneiform writing could only be mastered after long and systematic study, but record keeping was so essential to the coordination of activities in relatively large and complex societies, where crop sizes, taxes, troop provisioning, and multiple forms of exchange needed to be monitored for the society to exist, that these societies began to create a new institution and devote resources to support selected young men for the explicit purpose of making them scribes, people who could write. The places where young men were brought together for this purpose were the earliest formal schools.

Not only the interactional patterns of the activities that took place in these schools, but the architecture, the organization of activities, and the reigning ideologies within them were in many respects startlingly modern. The classrooms consisted of rows of desks, facing forward to a single location where a teacher stood, guiding students in repetitive practice of the means of writing and calculating as well as the operations that accompanied them. Instead of inkwells, the classrooms contained bowls where students could obtain wet clay to refresh clay tablets. In many such schools, the compiling of quantified lists of valued items (not unlike listing states of the United States or capitals of the world) was a major pastime, although some letter writing also occurred. These lists were often viewed as evidence of extraordinary cognitive achievements (Goody, 1977).[3]

Evidence concerning early schooling indicates that more than socially neutral, technical, literacy and numeracy skills were thought to be acquired there. Learning esoteric lists and the means for creating them were imbued with special powers such as are currently ascribed to those who are civilized, and it was recognized that socioeconomic value flowed from this knowledge.

In the Middle Ages, the focus of elementary schooling shifted to what LeVine and White (1986) refer to as "the acquisition of virtue" through familiarity with sacred texts, but a certain number of students were taught essential record-keeping skills commensurate with the forms of economic and political activity that needed to be coordinated through written records. Such is the state of schooling in many Muslim societies to this day, although there is great variation in Islamic schooling depending on whether the local population speaks Arabic and how formal schooling articulates with the state and religion in the country in question (see Serpell & Hatano, 1997, for a discussion of these variations and their implications).

As characterized by LeVine and White (1986), the shift from schools in large agrarian societies to the dominant forms found in most contemporary industrialized and industrializing societies manifests the following common features:

- Internal organization to include age grading, permanent buildings designed for this purpose, with sequentially organized curricula based on level of difficulty

- Incorporation of schools into larger bureaucratic institutions so that the teacher is effectively demoted from "master" to a low-level functionary in an explicitly standardized form of instruction

- Redefinition of schooling as an instrument of public policy and preparation for specific forms of economic activity—"manpower development"

- Extension of schooling to previously excluded populations, most notably women and the poor

Serpell and Hatano (1997) have dubbed this form of schooling "institutionalized public basic schooling" (IPBS). They point out that this European model evolved in the nineteenth century and followed conquering European armies into other parts of the world (LeVine, LeVine, & Schnell, 2001; LeVine & White, 1986; Serpell & Hatano, 1997). Local forms of enculturation, even of schooling, have by no means been obliterated, sometimes preceding (Wagner, 1993), sometimes coexisting with (LeVine & White, 1986) the more or less universal "culture of formal schooling" supported by, and supportive of, the nation-state. Often these more traditional forms emphasize local religious and ethical values (Serpell & Hatano, 1997). Nonetheless, these alternatives still retain many of the structural features already evident in the large agrarian societies of the Middle Ages.

As a consequence of these historical trends, the institutional form referred to as IPBS has become an ideal if not a reality in most of the world (the Islamic world providing an alternative in favor of adherence to religious/social laws, as written in the Q'uaran, a word which means "recitation" in Arabic). The IPBS approach operates in the service of the secular state, eco-

---

[3] Although some features differ, a similar story could be told for China, where bureaucratized schooling arose a thousand or so years later, and for Egypt, as well as for many of the civilizations that followed.

nomic development, and the bureaucratic structures through which rationalization of this process is attempted, and exists as a pervasive fact of contemporary life. According to a survey conducted by UNESCO in 2003, during the 1990s more than 80% of children in Latin America, Asia (excluding Japan), and Africa were enrolled in public school, although there are large disparities among regions and many children only complete a few years of schooling. Nonetheless, experience of IPBS has become a pervasive fact of growing up the world over (Serpell & Hatano, 1997).

With these considerations as background, I now turn to the consequences of this pervasive form of educational experience for the development of individual children, their communities, and humanity more generally, in the contemporary world. I pay special attention to the role of culture and cultural variations in shaping any such consequences.

### The Consequences of Formal Schooling in the IPBS Mode

The reader interested in a comprehensive survey or the intellectual and social consequences of school is referred to summaries by Rogoff (1981), Rogoff et al. (2005) and Serpell and Hatano (1997). For present purposes, I focus on three strategies for assessing the consequences of participation in the kind of formal schooling that has been dominant in the twentieth and twenty-first centuries. Each strategy has its advantages and its shortcomings.

### The School-Cutoff Strategy

In many countries, school boards require that children must be a certain age by a particular date to begin attending school. To enter Grade 1 in September of a given year, children in Edmonton, Alberta, Canada, for example, must have passed their sixth birthday by March 1 of that year. Six-year-olds born after that date must attend kindergarten instead, so their formal education is delayed for a year. Such policies allow researchers to assess the impact of early schooling while holding age virtually constant: They simply compare the intellectual performances of children who turn 6 in January or February with those who turn 6 in March or April, testing both groups at the beginning and at the end of the school year. This procedure is known as the school-cutoff strategy (Christian, Bachnan, & Morrison, 2001).

Researchers who have used the school-cutoff strategy find that the first year of schooling brings about a marked increase in the sophistication of some cognitive processes but not others. Frederick Morrison and his colleagues (Morrison, Smith, & Dow-Ehrensberger, 1995), for example, compared the ability of first graders and kindergartners to recall pictures of nine common objects. The first graders were, on average, only a month older than the kindergartners. The performances of the two groups were virtually identical at the start of the school year. At the end of the school year, however, the first graders could remember twice as many pictures as they did at the beginning of the year, whereas the kindergartners showed no improvement in memory at all. Significantly, the first graders engaged in active rehearsal during the testing, but the kindergartners did not. One year of schooling had brought about marked changes in the children's strategies and performance on this task.

The same pattern of results was obtained in recognition of the names of the letters of the alphabet, in standardized reading and mathematics tests, and in a variety of deliberate remembering tests. But *no effects* of attending a year of school were found when children were administered a standard Piagetian test of conservation or assessed for the coherence of their storytelling or for the number of vocabulary words they understood (Christian et al., 2001). Performance in these latter tasks improved largely as a consequence of children's more general experience. These findings both confirm the importance of schooling in promoting relatively specific cognitive abilities and support Piaget's belief that the ability to understand the conservation of quantity develops without any special instruction sometime between the ages of 5 and 7.

### Comparing Schooled and Nonschooled Children

Although the school-cutoff strategy provides an excellent way to assess the cognitive consequences of small amounts of schooling, it is, by definition, limited to only the 1st year. For a longer-range picture of the contribution of formal education to cognitive development, researchers have conducted studies in societies in which schooling is available to only a part of the population. We summarize evidence from three cognitive domains that have received a good deal of attention in studies of cognitive development: organization of word meaning, memory, and metacognitive skills.

**1.** *Organization of word meaning:* Donald Sharp and his coworkers studied the potential impact of schooling on the way Mayan Indians on the Yucatán peninsula of Mexico organize their mental lexicons (Sharp, Cole, & Lave, 1979). When adolescents who had attended high school one or more years were asked which words they associated with the word "duck," they responded with other words in the same taxonomic category, such as "fowl," "goose," "chicken," and "turkey." But when adolescents in the same area who had not attended school were presented with the same word, their responses were dominated by words that describe what ducks do ("swim," "fly") or what people do with ducks ("eat"). Such word associations are often used as a subscale on IQ tests, with duck-goose accorded a higher score than duck-fly. In addition, a good deal of developmental research shows that in the course of development, young children are more likely to produced duck-fly than duck-goose. The results of this study and findings from other parts of the world (Cole, Gay, Glick, & Sharp, 1971) suggest that schooling sensitizes children to the abstract, categorical meanings of words, in addition to building up their general knowledge.

**2.** *Spatio-temporal memory:* A meticulous study by Daniel Wagner suggested that children who attend school gain memory-enhancing skills (Wagner, 1974). His methods replicated those of Hagen, Meacham, and Mesibov (1970), who had demonstrated a marked increase in children's ability to remember the locations of cards after they reached middle childhood. But was this increase a result of universal maturational changes or participation in IPBS? To find out, Wagner also conducted his study among educated and uneducated Maya in the Yucatán, where the amount of schooling available to children varied from 0 to 16 years depending on whether the government had built a school with 3, 6, 9, 12, or 16 years of instruction available in the locale where they lived. Wagner asked a large number of people varying in age from 6 years to adulthood who had experienced different levels of schooling to recall the positions of picture cards laid out in a linear array. The items pictured on the cards were taken from a popular local version of bingo called *lotería,* which uses pictures instead of numbers, so Wagner could be certain that all the stimuli were familiar to all his subjects. On repeated trials, each of seven cards was displayed for two seconds and then turned face down. As soon as all seven cards had been presented, a duplicate of a picture on one of the cards was shown and people had to point to the position where they thought its twin was located. By selecting different duplicate pictures, Wagner in effect

manipulated the length of time between the first presentation of a picture and the moment it was to be recalled.

Wagner found that the performance of children who were attending school improved with age, just as in the earlier study by Hagen and his colleagues. However, older children and adults who did not attend school remembered no better than young children, leading Wagner to conclude that it was schooling that made the difference. Additional analyses of the data revealed that those who attended school systematically rehearsed the items as they were presented, leading to the improvement in their performance.

**3.** *Metacognitive skills:* Schooling appears to influence the ability to reflect on and talk about one's own thought processes (Rogoff, 2003; Tulviste, 1991). When children have been asked to explain how they arrived at the answer to a logical problem or what they did to make themselves remember something, those who have not attended school are likely to say something like "I did what my sense told me" or to offer no explanation at all. Schoolchildren, on the other hand, are likely to talk about the mental activities and logic that underlie their responses. The same results apply to metalinguistic knowledge. Scribner and Cole (1981) asked schooled and unschooled Vai people in Liberia to judge the grammatical correctness of several sentences spoken in Vai. Some of the sentences were grammatical, some not. Education had no effect on the interviewees' ability to identify the ungrammatical sentences; but schooled people could generally explain just what it was about a sentence that made it ungrammatical, whereas unschooled people could not.

### Questioning the Validity of the Evidence

Findings such as those cited previously, despite some residual concerns about selection artifacts, make it appear that at least with respect to some cognitive abilities, schooling helps children to develop a new, more sophisticated, cognitive repertoire to use in their everyday lives. In the case of word associations, a more mature, scientifically organized lexicon comes into being. In the study of memory, it appears that schooling promotes strategies for remembering. In the case of metacognitive awareness, schooling seems to enhance the ability to reflect on one's own reasoning processes (in this case, reasoning about language). Had this research been conducted in the United States, older children or adults who responded in the less sophisticated ways would have been suspected to have some form of developmental delay or retardation.

Yet there are serious reasons to doubt that differences obtained with standard psychological testing methods provide any logical evidence at all for *generalized* changes in classical categories of cognitive functioning. It is not plausible to believe that word meaning fails to develop among children who have not attended school. The nonliterate Mayan farmers studied by Sharp and his colleagues knew perfectly well that ducks are a kind of fowl. Although they did not refer to this fact in the artificial circumstances of the free-association task, they readily displayed awareness of it when they talked about the kinds of animals their families kept and the prices brought by different categories at the market. Similarly, when materials to be remembered were part of a locally meaningful setting, such as a folk story or the objects in a diorama of the subjects' town, the effects of schooling on memory performance disappear (Mandler, Scribner, Cole, & DeForest, 1980; Rogoff & Waddell, 1982). And the ability of nonschooled people to deploy language in strategic, self-conscious ways for their own advantage has long been documented in the anthropological literature (Bowen, 1964).

Consequently, such demonstrations using more-or-less standard cognitive tasks imported from Euro-American psychological traditions led some to conclude that when schooling appeared to induce new cognitive abilities, it might well be because the entire structure of standardized testing procedures served as covert models of schooling practices (Cole, 1996; Rogoff, 1981). Virtually all the experimental tasks used in such research, modified or not, bear a strong resemblance to the tasks children encounter in school, but bear little or no relation to the structure of the intellectual demands they face outside school.

The logic of this sort of comparative work appeared to demand the identification of tasks that schooled and unschooled children from the same town encounter with equal frequency, followed by demonstration that children who go to school solve such tasks in more sophisticated ways than their nonschooled peers and that these are tied specifically to their schooling. Failure to find tasks of equal familiarity, in effect, meant that we were treating psychological tasks as neutral with respect to their contexts of use, when this was patently false. But identifying cognitive tasks in everyday life circumstances not constructed by the research is a problematic undertaking (Cole, 1996).

At the same time, the finding of school/nonschool differences on more or less standard psychological tasks, if treated as specific forms of skill acquisition, does not mean that schooling exerts no significant impact on children. First, as many have noted, schools are places where children's activity is mediated through print, not only adding a new mode of representation to the child's repertoire, but also introducing a whole new mode of discourse (Olson, 1994) that has counterparts in everyday life. At a minimum, practice in representing language using writing symbols improves children and adults' ability to analyze the sound structure and grammar of their language (Morais & Kolinsky, 2001), a finding that Peter Bryant and his colleagues have made good use of in the design of programs for the teaching of reading (Bryant, 1995; Bryant & Nunes, 1998). But these effects, while not necessarily trivial, do not indicate that education produces any general influence on children's mental processes that can be considered superior to the kind of enculturation that has existed in all societies throughout human history.

Investigators have studied how children and adults who attend school versus those who engage in some other activity make various calculations using mathematically equivalent tasks (such as selling candy on the street, or measuring cloth, or calculating the area of a building site) (Nunes, Schliemann, & Carraher, 1993; Saxe, 1994). Such research has repeatedly shown that groups differing in their amount of school-based experience or everyday, work-related experience approach the same task (logically speaking) in different ways. The schooled subjects' reliance on written algorithms often led them to make egregious errors, whereas the mathematical activities arising in the course of selling candy or calculating the ratio of one board length to another were both quantitatively superior and free of nonsensical answers. Moreover, in many cases, the procedures acquired informally in the course of work were more adequately generalized, undermining the oft-repeated idea that such knowledge was somehow bound to particular contexts of use. Rather, it has turned out that it is knowledge acquired in school that is most vulnerable to becoming encapsulated.

### Intergenerational Studies of the Impact of Schooling

As noted, the difficulty with cross-sectional studies comparing schooled and nonschooled people is that the logic of comparison requires that we identify situations equally experienced by both groups, with the cognitive skills and modes of discourse (such as those learned in elementary school) finding application outside school. Although they did not pursue this issue in their monograph on the consequences of education in the Yucatán, Sharp and his colleagues suggested an answer that has been followed up subsequently:

> the information-processing skills which school attendance seems to foster could be useful in a variety of tasks demanded by modern states, including clerical and management skills in bureaucratic enterprises, or the lower-level skills of record keeping in an agricultural cooperative or a well-baby clinic. (Sharp, Cole, & Lave, 1979, p. 84)

In recent decades, Robert LeVine and his colleagues have pursued this path in a program of research that provides convincing evidence of the cognitive and social consequences of schooling. These researchers focused on the ways in which formal schooling changes the behavior of mothers toward their offspring and their interactions with people in modern, bureaucratic institutions, as well as the subsequent impacts on their children (LeVine & White, 1986; LeVine, LeVine & Schnell, 2001). These researchers propose a set of plausible habits, preferences, and skills that children acquire in school, retain into adulthood, and apply in raising their own children. Raising one's children can reasonably be considered a task with many cognitive elements that are common to schooled and nonschooled adults. These changes in parenting behavior include, in addition to use of rudimentary literacy and numeracy skills:

- Discourse skills using written texts for purposes of understanding and using oral communication that is directly relevant to negotiating interactions in health and educational settings involving their children
- Models of teaching and learning based on the scripted activities and authority structures of schooling, such that in subordinate positions schooled women adopt and employ behaviors appropriate to the student role, and in superordinate positions, adopt behaviors appropriate to the teacher role
- An ability and willingness to acquire and accept information from the mass media, such as following health prescriptions more obediently

As a consequence of these changes in the maternal behavior of young women who have attended school at least through elementary school, LeVine and his colleagues find that the children of women who have attended elementary school experience a lower level of infant mortality, better health during childhood, and greater academic achievement. Hence, while schooling may or may not have produced measurable cognitive effects at the time, such experience produces context-specific changes in behavior that have general consequences in child rearing, which in turn produce general consequences in the next generation.

The work of these researchers has been supported by direct observations of the teaching styles of Mayan mothers who have, or have not, been to school. Pablo Chavajay and Barbara Rogoff found that mothers who had experienced 12 years of schooling used school-like teaching styles when asked to teach their young children to complete a puzzle, while those with 0 to 2 years of schooling participated *with* their children in completing the puzzle and did not explicitly teach them (Chavajay & Rogoff, 2002). There is nothing inherently wrong with the unschooled mothers' teaching style, but it does not prepare their children well for schools, which rely heavily on the recitation script as the mode of instruction.

In sum, when the effects on health-related behaviors that affect the child's biological well-being are combined with changes in maternal ability to use modern social welfare institutions and to adopt new ways of interacting with their children, the effects of schooling appear to go well beyond cognitive effects to become general in the society.

## Cultural-Historical Change in IQ Scores

An interesting example of cultural-historical change in cognitive abilities that is probably related in various ways to the social complex of which universal formal school is a part has been referred to as the "Flynn effect." It is named after James Flynn (1987), a political scientist working in New Zealand, who observed that the standard intelligence test scores of adults from 14 different nations had consistently increased in recent decades. Since then, the "Flynn effect" has been confirmed by numerous studies (Daley, Whaley, Sigman, Espinosa, & Neumann, 2003; Nettlebeck & Wilson, 2004). An average increase of several IQ points per decade was found for several intelligence tests. At present, this pattern has been found in more than 20 countries including the United States, Canada, different European nations, and Kenya. One might expect that the Flynn effect would be clearest for tests that emphasize cultural knowledge or education. The opposite is true, however: the increase is most striking for tests measuring the ability to recognize abstract, nonverbal patterns (e.g., Raven Matrices), while tests emphasizing traditional school knowledge have generally shown less increase.

Since publication of Flynn's paper, there has been an ongoing debate about the meaning of the results (Daley et al., 2003; Neisser, 1998). In his initial paper, Flynn was unwilling to believe that his generation was significantly more intelligent than that of his parents. And when one extends the time span of the changes, the results are even more difficult to credit. Extrapolating Flynn's results would mean that that the average African American adult in 1990 had a higher IQ than the average European-American adult in 1940, and that the average English person in 1900 would score at the level currently considered to indicate mental retardation.

Noting that compared with the previous generation, the number of people who score high enough to be classified as "genius" has increased more than 20 times, Flynn argued that we should now be witnessing a cultural renaissance. Because he found this conclusion implausible, he suggested that what has risen is not intelligence but some kind of "abstract problem-solving ability."

Quite apart from raising again the issue of what IQ tests measure, the Flynn effect has given rise to explanations that include improvements in nutrition and health, increased environmental complexity (e.g., advanced technology, mechanical toys, video games, as well as ubiquitous exposure to television with its special conventions of interpretation and information-processing demands), decreased family size and concomitant changes in family structure (e.g., a higher percentage of children are firstborns), and increased parental education and literacy.

What is significant for present purposes is that all these factors, even if their proximal effect is biological (e.g., improved nutrition) are cultural in origin and speak to the importance of studying culture and cognitive development in relation to its cultural-historical context (for a similar argument, see Greenfield, Keller, Fuligni, & Maynard, 2003).

## ONTOGENY

When we come to the issue of the relationship of culture and cognitive development against the background of ev-

idence concerning hominization, primatology, and cultural history, several basic points stand out. First, the development of human beings at the beginning of the twenty-first century is but the most recent manifestation of life processes that at a minimum trace their origins back several million years (assuming that we begin with consideration of the common ancestor of *Homo sapiens sapiens* and the great apes).

Second, cultural resources and constraints have coevolved with the biological structure of *Homo sapiens* "from the beginning." Culture is, quite literally, a phylogenetic property of human beings.

Third, while biological changes may have been minimal in the "eyeblink" of phylogenetic time separating the Paleolithic period from the twenty-first century, cultural historical change, driven in significant measure by the invention and deployment of cultural artifacts, especially externalized symbol systems, has markedly increased the complexity and power of the human cultural tool kit, thereby changing the conditions of ontogenetic (and particularly) cognitive development in ways that reconfigure phylogeny-ontogeny relations.

Fourth, claims for marked discontinuities between human beings and near neighbors among the great apes must be tempered with respect to views that ascribe entirely unique cultural and cognitive processes to human beings. Rather, the achievements of our near-kin among other species offer important constraints on our theorizing about the process of culture and cognitive development that need to be exploited in development of a more powerful theory of human cognitive development. (At the same time, it would be an equally egregious error to assume that despite our close kinship to chimps and bonobos, modern human beings are merely highly talented apes, or that human culture, thought, and social organization are mere quantitative extensions of the behavioral and social patterns inferable among *Homo habilis* or observable in *Pan troglodytes*. Our phylogenetic and cultural history provide the fundament for contemporary human ontogeny, not an explanation of its emergent properties.)

Although these points are currently receiving wide acceptance, research that incorporates them into the study of human ontogeny is relatively sparse and concentrated within a few parts of the vast domain of culture and cognitive development. Overall, research on cognitive development in recent years has tended to focus on younger and younger age groups so that, for example, middle childhood, which received the lion's share of attention 20 years ago is sparsely represented in contemporary research, while the opposite situation holds for infancy (see also Kuhn & Franklin, Chapter 22, this *Handbook,* this volume). At the same time, research on infancy that considers cultural influences is more likely to be concentrated on socioemotional and physical than cognitive development, particularly research that uses cross-cultural methods. Even in cases where the same topic (e.g., the development of concept formation or memory) continues to yield new evidence, psychologists' theoretical preferences and the specific methods they use to gather evidence have changed, so that it is not possible to report the results of further research on topics formulated at an earlier period.

These circumstances make it difficult to maintain continuity with the previous chapters on culture and cognitive development. They also restrict the relevant data on which I can draw to summarize current knowledge (in the sense of research conducted in recent years).

I have adopted two strategies in response to these difficulties. First, at certain points I summarize culture-development relationships that spill beyond the cognitive domain, narrowly conceived, but that illustrate phylogeny-culture-ontogeny relationships with clear implications for cognitive development. Second, when dealing with cultural variations and cognitive development, I concentrate my attention on two areas of research where there has been relatively dense interest and hence a good deal of new data—conceptual development and autobiographical memory. Current research on conceptual development is particularly rich in implications for the intertwining of phylogenetic and cultural constraints in cognitive development. Autobiographical memory, by contrast, connects the study of cognitive development to presumed society-wide contrasts in broad cultural themes, thereby making contact with both earlier and contemporary research on culture and cognitive styles.

## The Proximal Locus of Development: Activity Settings and Cultural Practices

An important lesson from the primate literature on the process of acquiring culture is that to acquire cultural patterns during postnatal development, the young must be in close enough proximity to older members of the community who engage in those commonly patterned forms of behavior. Human beings are notable for the ex-

tremely immature state of their young at birth. They require many years of extraordinary support from their parents and community to survive into adulthood and acquire the cultural knowledge necessary for the social reproduction of the group (Bogin, 2001; Bruner, 1966).

As noted, developmentalists who study culture and development have highlighted the idea that the arrangements made in all societies to support the postnatal development of young children be conceived of as a "developmental niche" that merges practices to support physical care with parental beliefs about future requirements. This emergent sociocultural system, as Super (1987) commented, implies that "environments have their own structure and internal rules of operation, and thus, . . . what the environment contributes to development is not only isolated, unidimensional pushes and pulls but also structure" (p. 5).

Moreover, the nature of this niche within societies changes with the age of the child. Whiting and Edwards (1988), following Mead (1935), early on suggested periods of childhood that corresponded with the physical constraints on children's behavior. She referred to early infancy as the period of the "lap child," the period between 2 and 3 years as "knee children," who are kept close at hand but not continuously on the mother's lap or in a crib; 4- to 5-year-olds as "yard children" because they can leave their mothers' sides but are not allowed to wander far. In many modern, industrialized countries, children between 3 and 5 or 6 years of age spend part of the day in an environment designed to prepare them for school, which has led this time of life to be called the "preschool period," after which they become neighborhood children, free to roam, but not beyond the confines of the community.

In the early years of the study of culture and development, heavy emphasis was placed on the way in which the organization of this proximal developmental environment served as a locus within which the behavior of parents and older kin molded the child's behavior. Beatrice Whiting (1980, p. 97) extended this idea to suggest that the mother and father's greatest effect is in the assignment of the child to settings that have important socializing influences. Whiting's work was directed primarily at the development of social behavior and personality, but her insight has subsequently been influential in redirecting the focus of researchers' attention beyond the family and local community to the settings that children inhabit, the people to be found there, their changing forms of participation, and the part that activities within those settings play in the overall process of development—what Super and Harkness refer to as the child's developmental niche (Göncu, 1999; Rogoff, 2003; Super and Harkness, 1986, 1997).

Cultural differences in the organization of children's developmental niches are almost certainly more variable than the physical environments in which they live; there are many ways to achieve survival in a given ecological niche. Infants among the Aka foragers in the Central African Republic are held by their parents while the parents hunt, butcher, and share game (Hewlett, 1992). Quechua infants high in the Andes spend their early months wrapped in layers of woolen cloth strapped to their mothers' backs. The cloth forms a "manchua pouch" for the infants, who must survive the exceedingly cold, thin, dry air surrounding them, greatly restricting their vision and movement. Ache infants living in the rain forests of eastern Paraguay spend 80% to 100% of their time in physical contact with their parents and are almost never more than 3 feet away because these hunter-gatherers do not make permanent camps in the forest, but only clear an adequate space leaving stumps and roots that are hazardous for the children (Kaplan & Dove, 1987). Contrast these niches with those of American children with their own bedrooms and play areas, time spent in day care or preschool among many children the same age and one or two stranger-caretakers, while *Sesame Street* is playing on the television; or other American children living two families to a room in a crowded slum, reality TV playing on the television, and single unemployed mothers trying to keep order and their sanity. The range of developmental niches in contemporary human development is obvious.

As researchers have pointed out, these variations in developmental niches create experiential patterns making it difficult to reduce them to a single dimension, although clusters of attributes are discernible. According to Morelli and her colleagues, the Efe of the Democratic Republic of Congo (formerly Zaire) live in small groups of one or more extended families who forage with bow and arrow and work for members of nearby farm communities. Children are free to wander where they wish around their small camp to watch adults make tools and cook. Young children entertain themselves and may enter, uninvited, into most huts. From the age of at least 3 years, they accompany their parents to gather food, collect firewood, and work in gardens. Although they were only 2 to 4 years of age, Efe children were at least

present when adults were working in 74 of the observation periods and participated in specialized child-focused activities by adults only 5% of the time. A similar pattern was observed in San Pedro, an agricultural town in Guatemala, where people engage in agriculture and small business, family sizes are larger, the total number of the community members is far greater, and older children spend part of their time in school (Morelli, Rogoff, & Angelillo, 2003).

As different as they are from each other, in many ways these two traditional, rural communities exhibited relatively similar patterns of adult arrangement of 2- to 4-year-old children's activities. In contrast, children were present when adults were engaged in work only during 30% of the observations of two middle-class communities in the United States (one in Utah and one in Massachusetts, so they also differed in many ways). When Efe and San Pedro children were observed playing by themselves, their play almost always consisted of emulation of adult activities, but the play of the American children rarely emulated that of adult activities. In the two American samples, children were often engaged by adults in specialized child-focused activities including lessons or play that often mimicked schooling. The American adults also engaged their young children as conversational partners on child-focused topics in approximately 15% of the interactions observed, a category that was very rare in either of the other two communities.

These observations were complemented by Gaskins (1999, 2000, 2003) during her ethnographic work among rural Mayan children in the Yucatán. Her observations extended across a broad age range from a few months to 17 years. Gaskins, used a method of "spot observations" similar to that used by Morelli and her colleagues, supplemented by repeated discussions with Mayan adults. She identified four kinds of activities:

1. Maintenance activities (eating, bathing, grooming, dressing)
2. Social orientation (observing and keeping track of what others are doing or interacting with them directly)
3. Play
4. Work

Three cultural principles appear primary in interpreting Mayan children's behavior in these four basic kinds of activities:

1. *The primacy of adult work:* Mayan economic production occurs primarily in the family setting and adults believe that children should not be allowed to interfere with this priority. This means that they do not try to amuse children and allow them to enter into adult activities only in so far as they make a contribution. In their parental role of socializing agent, they believe they can have the most influence in teaching their children the particular skills and attitudes they need to be productive workers and members of their community. It is also expected that children will obey parental authority unquestioningly in these areas, and parents will use the threat (or the act) of force to ensure a child complies.

2. *The importance of parental beliefs:* First of all, parents have health concerns that they attend to in terms of local beliefs about the sources of threats to health, so they organize children to minimize perceived health risks. Second, they believe that development is internally programmed and it just "comes out by itself." Consequently, adults show little interest in promoting or even monitoring children's development, so long as they do not get in the way. As a result, parents do not take much initiative to influence the child's psychological characteristics nor responsibility for how the child turns out.

3. *The independence of children's motivation:* Children are expected to take care of themselves and interact with siblings, and adults do not spend time structuring when the children do what. This extends even to such issues as when to start school and how much to sleep or eat.

Gaskins reports that maintenance and social orientation activities are highest with 0- to 2-year-olds and diminish until the ages of 15 to 17, when interactions in work settings increase in frequency. Play peaks at 3 to 5 years old but decreases throughout childhood and is rarely seen after 12 years of age. Play almost always involves adult activities. Work is already a significant activity among 3- to 5-year-olds and grows steadily as children begin the passage from childhood to adulthood. No comparable research has been conducted in a highly industrialized society, but it is clear that the pattern of activities arranged for children at each age would be quite different, with pretend play replacing mimicking of adult activities and involvement in work with adults being replaced by schooling until a much later age.

Those engaged in the study of children's development in the activity settings they inhabit in nonindustrialized societies have accrued evidence to show that such children develop a special proclivity or ability for learning through keen observation, although it is not entirely clear if such skills involve higher order forms of imitation, motivation to emulate others, or some combination of such factors. Bloch (1989) reports that Senegalese children 2 to 6 years of age observed other people more than twice as much as European-American children in the same age range. Chavajay and Rogoff (1999) found that Guatemalan Mayan mothers and toddlers were more likely than middle-class European-American counterparts to attend simultaneously to several ongoing events, a practice that, they argue, supports learning by observing.

Rogoff and her colleagues (Rogoff, Paradise, Arauz, Correa-Chavez, & Angelillo, 2003) include observational learning in their notion of "intent participation," in which keen observation is motivated by the expectation that at a later time, the observer will be responsible for the action in question. Intent participation may involve more experienced participants facilitating a learner's participation and participating along with the learner, or it may involve direct verbal instruction (Maynard, 2002). But it places a heavy role on observation relative to verbal instruction of the sort characteristic of developmental processes that are prominent in formal schooling. Studies indicate that intent participation is a special form of learning by observation that has cultural roots and contributes to ongoing activities.

For example, Mejia-Arauz, Rogoff and Paradise (2005) arranged for Mexican-and European-heritage children whose parents had either a relatively high or low level of education to observe an "Origami lady" make two origami figures, after which they made figures of their own to keep. They found that all the children keenly observed the Origami lady's demonstration, but the children whose parents had little education completed their own origami figures without asking for further information while those whose parents had experienced more education were likely to ask for help.

I will not repeat here the material on the influences of schooling sketched out in the earlier section on cultural-historically organized forms of activity. Suffice it to say that, in study after study, mothers who have experienced higher levels of schooling are more likely to organize children's activities in ways that place less emphasis on intent participation and more emphasis on verbal explanation. Both the content of what children gain deep knowledge about and the way they attain that knowledge are influenced by the range of activities that adults arrange for them and the way that those activities are carried out. Further, these contents and ranges are strongly affected by the physical and social ecology of the groups in question.

## The Intertwining of Biology and Cultural Practices in Conceptual Development

For many years, the dominant line of cross-cultural research employed tasks in which children of different ages and backgrounds were presented sets of objects or drawings that could be classified along various dimensions (color, form, number, function, and taxonomic category were most frequently studied). This work was directly influenced by stimulus-response learning theories which assumed that concepts are built up from associations between specific attributes of stimuli brought about by some form of reinforcement (which, in the case of human beings, could be a simple designation of a response as correct or incorrect). It was further assumed that beyond the ability to perceive the stimuli, development or identification of the relevant categories was entirely a matter of experience; consequently, interest focused on what kinds of experiences different cultures provided. (See Cole and Scribner, 1974; Laboratory of Comparative Human Cognition, 1983 for reviews.)

During the past 2 decades, this line of work has withered away. In part, the evidence suggested that difficult-to-pin down factors are closely associated with the particular stimuli and experimental procedures that differentially influenced the performance of schooled and nonschooled populations in uncontrolled and uninterpretable ways; and in part, the general approach to concept development that it represented fell from favor. One of the new lines of research that arose to take its place focused on the categorization of natural kinds. Categorization of natural kinds was presumed to be constrained to a great extent by phylogenetically based cognitive predispositions. In addition, inductive judgments about new instances rather than sorting by similarity became the essential criterion of categorical knowledge (see S. A. Gelman and Kalish, Chapter 16, this *Handbook*, this volume; R. Gelman & Williams, 1998, for relevant reviews).

The concepts that have been featured in this recent work are often identified with cognitive domains, where domain is defined as "a body of knowledge that identifies and interprets a class of phenomena assumed to share certain properties and to be of a distinct and general type" (Hirschfeld & S. A. Gelman, 1994, p. 21).

Current disagreements focus on what these initial constraints are and how they limit or shape the role of experience (including culturally organized experience) in conceptual development. There is a rough scale that can be used to describe the particular theory of how phylogenetic constraints and culturally organized experience during ontogeny combine (see S. A. Gelman and Kalish, Chapter 16, this *Handbook*, this volume, for a more extensive account focused on ontogenetic change).

At one end of the scale is the view that gained popularity in connection with Chomsky's (1959, 1986) theory of language acquisition, which included the claim that while the specific surface forms of a language depend on cultural experience (e.g., French is different from Cantonese), the underlying deep structure is innately specified. Language is not acquired through environmental learning contingencies, as learning theorists had claimed (Skinner, 1957).

Chomsky's view was generalized to a broad range of intellectual domains by Fodor (1985), who coined the term *mental module* to refer to any "specialized, encapsulated mental organ that has evolved to handle specific information types of particular relevance to the species" (Elman et al., 1996, p. 36). In this view, knowledge acquisition in a modularized domain does not require extensive experience for its development; the role of the environment is merely to trigger the corresponding module. Particularly important for considerations of culture and development is the assertion that modular systems are "encapsulated," meaning that they rapidly produce mandatory outputs from given inputs. (An example would be the perceptual illusion that a stick half submerged in water is bent, even when the perceiver knows full well that it is straight.) Often, modularity theories are accompanied by the assumption of prespecified brain areas as the locus of the module in question (e.g., Broca's area is taken to be the brain locus of language).

Many developmentalists who have been convinced of the existence of domain-specific, biological constraints on conceptual development resist the notion of modularity, preferring instead to speak of "core" or "privileged" domains of knowledge, where biological constraints may provide "skeletal principles" that constrain how developing children attend to relevant features of the domain, but are not entirely encapsulated; rather, they require the infusion of cultural input and continued learning to develop past a rudimentary starting point (Baillargeon, 2004; Chen and Siegler, 2000; S. A. Gelman & Kalish, Chapter 16, this *Handbook*, this volume; R. Gelman & Lucariello, 2002; Hatano,

1997). Theorists in this camp differ from each other in precisely how to construe the role of environmental factors and the ways in which they operate.

Among those who argue that the role of experience in concept development goes beyond the triggering of modularized processes, some argue that environmental contingencies not dissimilar to those proposed by S-R (stimulus-response) theorists of earlier generations are essential (Elman et al., 1996), while others argue that domain-general cognitive mechanisms such as analogizing are key mechanisms in moving beyond initial states to more mature forms of conceptual thought (Springer, 1999).[4]

To further complicate matters, it appears plausible that the degree to which "highly specific innate constraints + minimal experience," versus "skeletal constraints + a good deal of culturally organized experience," are needed to account for development may differ with the domain in question. In the domain of physics, within months after birth children have some grasp of at least a few very basic physical principles, including expectations that two objects cannot occupy the same location at the same time or cannot pass through physical obstructions (Spelke, 1994). As a result of such findings, Spelke has argued that knowledge in the domain of physics is innate, domain-specific, encompasses constraints that apply to all entities in the domain, forms the core of mature knowledge, and is task specific. Similar claims have been made for the domains of number (Feigenson, Dehaene, & Spelke, 2000), agency (Gergeley, 2002; Gopnik & Meltzoff, 1997), biology (Atran, 1998), and theory of mind (Leslie, 1994), although in each case there are others who argue for hybrid positions that include domain-general reasoning abilities (Astuti, Solomon, & Carey, 2004; Springer, 1999).

Research on the influence of the environment, particularly cultural variations in environmental influence, have not been evenly distributed across the full range of conceptual domains that have preoccupied developmentalists. There is apparently no research on cultural differences in the development of naïve physics, although

even those who favor strong nativist claims have an interest in determining whether development beyond initial, core principles does in fact continue to adhere to the initial constraints they hypothesize on the basis of research with very young infants. There is, however, some cross-cultural research in the domain of number (the work of Saxe reviewed earlier with respect to cultural-historical change is relevant in this regard), and there is a good deal of research on the domains of psychology and biology. Consequently, my review focuses largely on these three domains.

### Number

In recent decades a good deal of evidence has been accumulated for elementary numerical abilities involving small quantities, including counting, addition, and subtraction, in both very young human infants and in primates, although there is controversy about the precise processes involved (Boysen & Hallberg, 2000; R. Gelman & Gallistel, 2004; Hauser & Carey, 1998). R. Gelman and Williams (1998) conclude that the pattern of errors evidenced by young infants asked to perform numerical operations on set sizes of three or less objects may indicate the presence of a "common preverbal counting mechanism similar to the one used in animals" (1998, p. 588). Hauser and Carey go somewhat further, concluding:

> Early primate evolution (and probably earlier), and early in the conceptual history of children, several of the building blocks for a representation of number are firmly in place. [These include] criteria for individuation and numerical identity (the sortal object, more specific sortals like cup and carrot, and quantifiers such as one and another). Furthermore, there are conceptual abilities . . . such as the capacity to construct one to one correspondence and the capacity to represent serial order relations . . . (p. 82)

Studies of numerical reasoning in early childhood indicate that it builds on these early starting conditions in an orderly fashion. Thus, Zur and R. Gelman (2004) report that when 3-year-olds who had not attended preschool viewed the addition or subtraction of $N$ objects from a known number and were asked to predict the answer and then check their prediction, they provided reasonable cardinal values as predictions and accurate counting procedures to test their predictions. Such rapid learning in the absence of explicit instruction, they argue, supports the idea that there are "skeletal mental

---

[4] As S.A. Gelman and Kalish (Chapter 16, this *Handbook,* this volume) point out, even those who deny the need to posit strong phylogenetic, domain-specific constraints assume that phylogenetic factors play a role in cognitive development, including concept formation. The disagreements center on how to characterize those phylogenetic constraints and the extent to which they are domain specific.

structures that expedite the assimilation and use of domain-relevant knowledge" (p. 135). Data such as these, despite uncertainties about mechanism, support the argument for number reasoning as a core domain, and hence a human universal.

Evidence from number development in other cultures appears, at least at first glance, to cast doubt on the universality of elementary number reasoning and leaves little doubt that Hatano and Inagaki (2002) are correct in arguing that, because innately specified knowledge is still skeletal, it is essential to study the ways in which cultural experience interacts with phylogenetic constraints to produce adult forms of numerical reasoning.

To begin with, a good many societies in the world appear to have at most a few count words on the order of "one, two, many" (Gordon, 2004; Pica, Lerner, Izard, & Dehaene, 2004). While no research has been conducted with infants in such societies using procedures comparable to those used by modularity and core-domain theorists, it is not clear how such impoverished systems could be considered evidence of a universal set of numerical knowledge. R. Gelman and Williams (1998) argue that this appearance may be deceiving. They cite evidence from a South African hunter-gatherer group which has only two numerical lexemes but report that this does not stop them, for example, from counting to ten by using the additional operation to generate successively larger cardinal numbers, so that the word corresponding to eight translates as $2 + 2 + 2 + 2$. However, Gordon (2004) has recently reported that while Pirahã adults living in a remote area of the Amazon jungle display elementary arithmetic abilities for very small arrays, their performance quickly deteriorates with larger numbers. But Pirahã children who learn Portuguese number words do not display the same limitations as their parents. Similar results are reported for another Amazonian group by Pica et al. (2004).

While number reasoning beyond the level achieved by some nonhuman primates and infants may be in doubt for some hunter-gatherer groups, this same evidence underscores how important cultural influences are for the elaboration of core numerical knowledge. A key factor appears to be the appearance of lexicalized arithmetic knowledge when economic activities begin to produce sufficient surplus to necessitate record keeping and trade. Recall that traditional Oksapmin number practices appear to have been at the very beginnings of such reasoning because, according to Saxe (1982), small amounts were traded and one-to-one correspondence often sufficed as a mechanism to mediate exchange.

Taking an example from two societies, both of which engaged in agricultural production, Jill Posner (1982) compared children from two neighboring groups in the Ivory Coast. The first she characterized as farmers using primitive agricultural methods to eke out a subsistence living; the second also farmed, but in addition engaged in trades such as tailoring and peddling that required frequent participation in the money economy. The children in both groups displayed knowledge of relative quantity, a skeletal principle, but the children from the subsistence farming group displayed far weaker counting skills and calculation skills than those from the group with more involvement in the money economy, a difference that was compensated for by schooling.

Research comparing the development of numerical knowledge and skills among middle-class and working-class children in the United States also supports the idea that culture elaborates core domain knowledge to different degrees, and perhaps in different ways but still within the framework of the core domain (Saxe, Guberman, & Gearhart, 1987). These researchers, observed children and their mothers in their homes, presented a variety of tasks to the children, and also observed mothers present prespecified problems to their children. They found that children from both social classes were regularly engaged with activities involving number, but by 4 years of age, children from middle-class homes displayed greater competence on more complex numerical tasks than did their working-class peers. During mother-child interactions, all mothers adjusted the goals of activities to reflect the child's ability, and children adjusted their goals to their mothers' efforts to organize the activity; but the working-class mothers were more likely to engage in greater simplification and to profess lower expectations for their children in conversation with the interviewer.

Overall, the research on development in the domain of number provides strong support for the "core domain plus cultural practice" perspective proposed by Hatano and Inagaki (2002). (See also the discussion of cognitive development in Chapter 11 by Shweder et al., this *Handbook,* Volume 1, and the position adopted by S. A. Gelman and Kalish in Chapter 16, this *Handbook,* this volume, although they do not speak of culture as the source of empirical input.)

Research in two other domains where there is greater disagreement about their status as core domains and the experiential factors that may affect development offer a more challenging picture in which phylogenetic and cultural contributions to development may not dovetail so neatly.

### *Naïve Psychology and Theory of Mind*

As applied to humans, the term *theory of mind* "refers to the tendency to construe people in terms of their mental states and traits" (Lillard & Skibbe, 2005). It is referred to as a theory because people use these inferences based on invisible entities (desire, beliefs, thoughts, emotion) to guide their action, and to predict the behaviors of others.

As indicated in the earlier section on chimpanzee cognition, Tomasello, Call, and Har's (2003) assertion that there is no evidence that chimpanzees or bonobos can think about the beliefs of others can stand as an agreed-on point of differentiation, because there is no doubt that human children growing up in industrialized countries where the requisite research has been done develop a "belief-desire" psychology of mind by about 4 years of age. The question then becomes one of whether this ability is universal in both its timing and nature. Again, because the role of culture on the ontogenetic course of theory of mind is extensively reviewed by Harris (Chapter 19, this *Handbook,* this volume), I simply summarize his thorough treatment to maintain continuity in the present discussion.

Research conducted in industrialized countries indicates that in the transition from infancy to early childhood, and all during early childhood, children gain a more comprehensive idea about how other peoples' desires and beliefs are related to how they act in the world. Even at the age of 2, children can distinguish between their own desires and those of others. From studies of American children's spontaneous speech in many settings, it has been established that by the age of 2 years, children are already capable of using terms such as *want* and *like* correctly (Wellman, Phillips, & Rodriguez, 2000; Wellman & Woolley, 1990). As discussed by Harris, the favorite experimental method for diagnosing the development of the ability to think about other people's beliefs and the relations of their beliefs to their actions is the "false belief" task which is presented in various ways.

By the time they are 3 years old, children can engage in deception in collaboration with an adult. As Lillard and Skibbe (2004) summarize the matter, "mentalizing abilities thus appear to begin during infancy." By the age of 5, children master the ability to reason about a false belief and mental representations in tasks that apply to others. Later, their theory grows to encompass secondary emotions such as surprise and pride.

This sequential, developmental progression of theory of mind capabilities led quickly to the suggestion that such a theory is a mental module (Leslie, 1994), which is part of the common inheritance of some nonhuman primates. Among humans, it appears to develop within a narrow age range, 3 to 5 years, and it appears to be a kind of rapid, unconscious, inference-generating device. Links between the asocial nature of autistic children and modularity are used as evidence favoring the nativist argument.

If theory of mind were modular, one would expect it to be impervious to cultural variation; it would develop on a universal time scale, much as does losing one's baby teeth. This expectation has not been tested for the full set of relevant age ranges, but there is reasonable consistency in how children deal with a key test of achieving a more adult-like form of thinking—the false-belief task.

The result has by no means yielded a foregone conclusion. There is ample evidence from cultures around the world that there is enormous variety in the extent and ways that mental states and actions are spoken about and presumably how they are conceived (Lillard, 1998a; Vinden, 1996, 1999). In terms of sheer number, English is at one extreme of the continuum, possessing more than 5,000 emotion words. By contrast, the Chewong people of Malaysia are reported to have only five terms to cover the entire range of mental processes, translated as *want, want very much, know, forget, miss* or *remember* (Howell, 1984). Anthropologists have also reported that, in many societies, there is a positive avoidance of talking about other people's minds (Paul, 1995).

At present, opinion about cultural variation using locally adapted versions of theory-of-mind tasks is divided (Harris, Chapter 19, this *Handbook,* this volume; Lillard & Skibbe, 2004). As Harris notes, ambiguities arise because people in some cultures are unlikely to talk in terms of psychological states in the head, and in some cases success on the theory-of-mind tasks was absent or partial (Vinden, 1999, 2002). But was performance poor because people lacked the vocabulary or inclination, or was it that they could not describe their intuitive understanding in words?

Callaghan et al. (n.d.) conducted a study that sought to avoid the issue of language by using a minimally verbal procedure where it was unnecessary to use difficult-to-translate words such as belief and emotion. With two experimenters present, they hid a toy under one of three bowls. Then one experimenter left and the other induced the child to put the toy under a different bowl before asking the child to point to which bowl the first experimenter would pick up when she returned. Notice that the procedure uses language at the level of behavior (picking up a bowl) with no reference to mental terms, so the prediction that the absent experimenter would look where the toy had been when she left would indicate ability to think about others' beliefs without using the term.

Under these conditions, a large number of children 3 to 6 years of age were tested in Canada, India, Samoa, and Peru. Performance improved with age, with 4 to 5 years of age being the point at which 50% of the children performed correctly, and 5 to 6 years of age the point at which all the children responded correctly. Here is a case where careful standardization of the precise, same procedure conducted in such a way that performance does not depend on the ability to communicate about mental language with people who do not use such terms produces universality (in line with a modularity view). This invariance taps into the most skeletal core of theory of mind behavior, devoid as it is of enrichment by the local vocabulary of any information about how the children would respond if they were asked to reason about beliefs. Thus, for example, Vinden (1999) found that while children from a variety of small scale, low technology groups in Cameroon and New Guinea were able to understand how belief affects behavior, they had difficulty predicting an emotion based on a false belief.

Using a different task, in which children were asked to explain the bad behavior of a story character, Lillard, Skibbe, Zeljo, and Harlan (2003) found culture, regional, and class differences in whether children attributed the behavior to an internal, psychological trait or external circumstances, a plausible element in any theory of mind a person uses to predict and interpret someone else's behavior. Lillard (2006) makes the important point that "cultural differences are usually a matter of degrees, of different patterns and frequencies of behaviors in different cultural contexts" (p. 73), a view put forward early on by Cole et al. (1971). Children in all groups gave both kinds of responses, internal and situational; it was the frequency and patterns of use that differed. They attribute the average results in this case to language socialization practices in different communities, noting that low socioeconomic status (SES) children or rural children are more likely to have parents who make situational attributions of behavior and model this form of interpretation for their children, whereas high SES or urban parents are more likely to use an internal model of interpretation that they embody in their interactions with their children. It has also been shown that children's theory of mind appears more rapidly if they have older siblings, who presumably provide them with extensive experience in mind-reading and mind-interpreting talk (Ruffman, Perner, Naito, Parkin, & Clements, 1998).

Both universality and cultural specificity appear to characterize the development of theories of minds. Given evidence that many (but not all) elements of a human theory of mind can be found, using suitable procedures, among chimpanzees (Tomasello et al., 2003), it should not come as a surprise that when a carefully stripped-down version of false-belief tasks is presented to people of widely different cultural backgrounds, they perform the same, while cultural variations appear when language and explanation are made part of the assessment. This pattern of results supports the idea of Hatano and Inagaki (2002) that both phylogeny and cultural history are necessary contributors to the development of an adult mode of thinking about the thoughts and situations of oneself and others.

### The Biological Domain

Among the domains considered here, the possibility of a core domain of biological knowledge has generated special controversy about the degree to which biology is a core domain and the extent to which the development of biological understanding is influenced by culturally organized experience. In an influential book, Carey (1985) argued that children's understanding of biological phenomena grows out of a naive psychology. Children interpret other living things by reference to, and by analogy with, human beings whose behavior is governed by their intentional beliefs and desires. They do not accept the idea that our bodily organs function independent of our intentions, and insofar as other entities are similar to humans, the same intentional causality should apply to them. Carey used a technique in which children are asked to judge whether a particular kind of entity shares a property with a target stimulus (e.g., if humans breathe do dogs breathe? do plants breathe? do rocks breathe?). According to her results, it is not until after the age of 7 that children begin to develop a theory that treats humans as one of many kinds of living things sharing many causal principles (in particular, a mechanistic causality of bodily organs). This change gives rise to a naive biology, which is a derivative domain.

In their work on the domain of biology, Hatano and Inagaki (2002) argued that biology is a core domain that does not arise from psychology but uses the human body as a cornerstone for interpreting other biological entities. According to their view, naive biology uses a mode of explanation (a naive theory) of living things in terms of their similarity to human beings (personification) and the idea that living phenomena are produced by a special form of causation—vital principle—as distinct from a purely chemical or physical force (vitalism). This form of domain-specific reasoning is based on a three-way relationship between food/water, activeness/liveliness (actively taking in vital power from food), and growth in size or number (the ingestion of vital power produces individual growth and production of offspring). This mode of reasoning is also assumed to be universal across cultures. Although the cross-cultural data are somewhat sparse, evidence in favor of this proposition has been found in Australia and North America, as well as Japan, where children exhibit such reasoning by 6 years of age (see Hatano & Inagaki, 2002, for more details).

However, Hatano and Inagaki also believe that participation in local cultural practices is important to development of biological thinking beyond the most skeletal knowledge. This kind of developmental process is illustrated by Inagaki (1990), who arranged for some 5-year-old Japanese children to raise goldfish at home while a comparison group had no such experience. The goldfish raisers soon displayed far richer knowledge about the development of fish than their counterparts who had not raised fish. They could even generalize what they had learned about fish to frogs. If asked, "Can you keep the frog in its bowl forever?" they answered, "No, we can't, because goldfish grow bigger. My goldfish were small before and now they are big" (quoted in Hatano & Inagaki, 2002, p. 272).

Additional evidence in favor of cultural involvement in the development of biological knowledge comes from the work of Atran and his colleagues on the growth of biological classifications. Atran (1998) once adopted the view with respect to biological categories that the taxonomy of living kinds is universal because it is a product of "an autonomous, natural classification scheme of the human mind" (p. 567). At present, however, he and his colleagues acknowledge that factors such as density of experience and local ecological significance contribute to the development of biological understanding beyond early childhood (Medin, Ross, Atran, Burnett, & Blok, 2002; Ross, Medin, Coley, & Atran, 2003). Moreover, they demonstrate that biological thinking does not universally begin by using one's own body as the foundation of reasoning.

In some of their studies, Atran, Medin, and their colleagues used a version of the procedure developed by Carey. For example, the child might be shown a picture of a wolf and asked "Now, there's this stuff called andro. Andro is found inside some kinds of things. One kind of thing that has andro inside is wolves. Now, I'm going to show you some pictures of other kinds of things, and I want you to tell me if you think they have andro inside like wolves do."

This questioning frame was then used with a number of "inferential bases" (in this case, human, wolf, bee, goldenrod, water) and a larger number of "target objects" from each of the taxonomic categories represented by the bases (e.g., raccoon, eagle, rock, bicycle) to see if the child believes that andro (or some other fictitious property) found in the base will also be found in the target object. Two questions were of primary interest: Does inference of the presence of a property (andro) decrease as the biological similarity of the target object decreases, and do children appear to use human beings as a unique base of inference when judging biological similarity (is personification a universal feature of the development of biological classification)?

This group of researchers conducted one such study with populations they term "urban majority culture children" and "rural majority children," and rural Native American (Menominee) children between the ages of 6 to 10 years. With respect to the first question, they found, like Carey, that the urban majority children generalized on the basis of the similarity of the comparison entity to human beings. But even the youngest rural children generalized in terms of biological affinity according to adult expert taxonomies (they did not use humans as a unique foundation of their reasoning). In addition, all ages of Native American children and the older rural majority culture children manifested ecological (systems) reasoning as well; they inferred the relations between the entities being compared on the basis of their relationships in an ecological system, such as a pond or forest.

With respect to the second question, they found that urban children displayed a bias toward using humans as a base of comparison, but the rural children, and particularly the rural Menominee children, did not, contradicting Carey's claim of anthropomorphism as a universal characteristic of folk theories of biology. Such results show that both culture and expertise (exposure to nature) play a role in the development of biological thought. Such evidence fits well with the views of Hatano and Inagaki, as well as Geertz (1973), that culturally organized experience is essential for completing the work of phylogeny.

The same experimental paradigm was used to study the development of biological induction among Yucatek Mayan children and adults (Atran et al., 2001). Adults decreased their inductions from humans to other living kinds and then to nonliving kinds, following the pattern predicted by standard biological taxonomies. But when bee was the base, they often made inferences of shared properties not only to other invertebrates, but to trees and humans. According to Atran et al., this pattern of inference is based on ecological reasoning: Bees build their nests in trees and bees are sought after by humans for their honey. Adults often explicitly used such ecological justifications in their responses.

Most important with respect to the issue of cultural influences on development, the Yukatek children's responses were similar to those of adults. Whatever the base concept, inductive inferences decrease as the target moves from mammals to trees. And, like Yukatek adults, the children showed no indication of personification: Inferences from humans did not differ from inferences beginning with animals or trees and they did not appear to favor humans as a basis of inference. If anything, the children preferred dogs as a basis of inference, perhaps based on their affection for and familiarity with this common household pet. Again, the evidence speaks to the importance of culturally organized experience in the development of inferences in the domain of biology.

A recent, extensive, and instructive study of phylogenetic and cultural influences on the development of biological understanding comes from a series of studies conducted in Madagascar by Rita Astuti and her colleagues (2004). Astuti and her colleagues assert that a core domain of biological knowledge should include concepts of birth, birth parent, biological inheritance, and innate potential. As these authors point out, claims for a core domain of biology are contentious. For example, evidence in favor of a core domain of biology comes from evidence obtained from preschool children, not infants. And cross-cultural evidence from North Ameri-

can and Nigerian children indicated that before the age of 7 to 9 years, children would not agree that if a raccoon (in the American case) gave birth to a certain animal and that this animal then gave birth to more raccoons, then the newborn animal was a raccoon, even if it looked like and acted like a skunk (Keil, 1989). Madagascar is a strategically interesting place to study biological understanding because it is one of the places in the world where people emphasize the importance of postnatal experience in determining kinship and similarity among people. When adults are asked why some babies appear or behave as they do, they give reasons such as "the mother spent a lot of time with a person who looks just like the baby" or that the baby was tampered with by a wandering spirit. Consequently, according to Astuti and her colleagues, it is difficult, from a Malagasy point of view, to differentiate between the baby as a biological organism and the baby as a social being.

These researchers carried out studies among three groups of people. The first two groups were the Vezo, who live on the coast and make their livelihood as fishermen, and the Masikoro who live inland, farm, and raise cattle. Both of these groups are ethnically Malagasy, having arrived on the island a thousand or more years ago. They share traditional religious beliefs, a form of ancestor worship, as well as a common language. The third group, the Karany, are descendents of Indo-Pakistani immigrants who are town dwellers; they are generally shopkeepers and moneylenders who are relatively wealthy and well educated. At birth, Vezo and Masikoro babies are indistinguishable, but Karany babies are easily distinguished by their lighter skin and straighter hair. The major questions were whether people of different ages would attribute similarities between a child and its parents to biological inheritance or social circumstances. Comparisons were made when the birth and adopted parents in the hypothetical problems were from the same group, or one of the other two groups. Three types of traits were queried: bodily traits (e.g., wide feet or narrow feet), beliefs (do cows have stronger teeth than horses), and skills (knows how to be a carpenter or a mechanic). The specific questions differed depending on whether the adoptive and birth parents were from the same or a different group to tease out conditions under which biological or social inference modes would display themselves.

When Vezo adults answered questions about the babies' bodily characteristics, they overwhelmingly chose biological inheritance as the crucial factor.

When asked about what social group the child would belong to, the children were judged to be members of the groups into which they were adopted, whether Masikoro or Karany—group identity depends on what people do, not on the biological identity of their parents. When asked about beliefs and skills, Vezo adults again selected the adoptive parents' group as the one that the child would acquire.

In two follow-up studies, Astuti and her colleagues presented the same task to groups of children (6 to 13 years old) and youths (17 to 20 years old). Contrary to the adults, the children were likely to say that the children's bodily characteristics, beliefs, and skills would all be determined primarily by their adoptive parents. The adolescents were most likely to follow the adult pattern, ascribing bodily characteristics to birth parents, while beliefs and skills were more like the adult pattern that ascribed bodily characteristics to biology while beliefs and skills were ascribed to cultural experience.

In a final study, children and adults were asked to make judgments about properties of baby birds that were adopted by a new mother bird. In this case, both adult and children ascribed the characteristics of the birds to their birth parents and gave biological inheritance reasons for doing so.

There are many other interesting findings in this set of studies, but for present purposes they raise two key issues. First, under some conditions (e.g., when reasoning about birds) young Malagasy children, like young children in Tokyo or Boston appear to understand basic biological principles of inheritance. Second, when reasoning about humans, Malagasy adults show that they understand these laws of inheritance, but in their everyday lives, they staunchly deny their significance.

Such results greatly complicate conclusions one can draw about biology as a core domain. While it seems reasonable to conclude that understanding of basic biological principles is universal when probed in an appropriate manner, it is difficult to understand how adults can elaborate a complex set of cultural beliefs which have great influence in people's everyday lives, yet contradict this same core biological knowledge. That Malagasy children should be slow to acquire the (universal) adult system of core biological understanding is easy enough to understand: They are constantly exposed to adults whose interpretations of their everyday experience deny principles of naive biology. But how does it come about that adults acquire that same knowledge while at the same time acquiring the cultural knowledge about kinship, ancestors, and sources of group similarity that contradict the skeletal principles of the core domain?

There is more to the organization of culturally organized belief and action than is captured by evidence of a core domain of biology. Astuti and her colleagues suggest that because the highest value of Malagasy society is to reach old age surrounded by a vast number of descendants, Malagasy systematically devalue and deemphasize biological ties in favor of social ties that make children the descendants of the entire village, not the birth parents alone. Whatever the case, the effect of this research is to emphasize the complex interweaving of biological constraints and cultural practices on the development of reasoning.

## Beyond Core Domains

As R. Gelman and Lucariello (2002) note, a great deal of knowledge that children must master does not fall within any recognized core domain. With respect to objects in the world, a major class of such objects is the class of artifacts defined earlier as aspects of the material world that have been transformed to carry out some goal-directed human action.

Ample evidence indicates that American children differentiate between artifacts and natural objects at an early age, although the conditions under which they differentiate these two categories of objects may vary (Kemler Nelson, Frankenfield, Morris, & Blair, 2000; Keil, 1989). When children were told that an item was a kind of food and taught a name for it and then shown a novel item and told it was a kind of food, they generalized the name they had learned on the basis of color. However, if they were told that the original object was a tool and the new object a tool, they generalized the name for it based on its shape. Another line of evidence for differentiation of artifacts and natural kinds comes from, among other places, studies in which the object in question undergoes a transformation of some kind and the child is asked whether it is the same or a different object, and why. If, for example, a young child is told about a goat that has had its horns removed and its hair curled and has been trained to say "baaahbaaaah" like a sheep, and is shown a picture of this transformed animal, very young children will maintain that it remains a goat because its insides haven't changed. Children assume there is something essential about it as goat that cannot be changed by changing its external appearance (S. A. Gelman & Opfer, 2002). This is the sort of response we would expect given the data on the development of knowledge in core domains, such as biology. Moreover, it is also well established that very early in life, children distinguish animate and inanimate objects, a central criterion distinguishing natural and artificial kinds.

When it comes to categorizing artificial objects, resort to essential, inner properties as indicators of an object's category membership no longer hold. A coin that is melted down and made into an ice pick no longer remains a coin. Faced with such transformations, young children are unlikely to say that the object retains its identity. Consequently, interest has focused on the criteria that children use to judge whether two artificial objects belong to the same category or not. Some believe that before the age of 3 to 4 years, most children categorize such objects according to a perceptual criterion: How similar do they look (in particular, are they the same shape or the same color)?

According to this view, at about 4 years of age the criterion changes to one of function, which is the criterion ordinarily used by adults, since by definition, an artifact is an object designed to achieve some goal. Under some conditions, American children as young as 2 years have been shown to generalize names learned for one artifact to another of the same function (e.g., two dissimilar looking objects that both functioned as a hinge) (Kemler Nelson et al., 2000); and reasoning based on categories of artifacts continues to develop over childhood and probably beyond (R. Gelman & Lucariello, 2002).

As Keil (2003, p. 369) comments, "most people seem to live in worlds of the artificial," which immediately poses a problem. While people may be able to make inferences about function from observing someone using an artifact and making inferences about their intentions, there appear to be no straightforward, domain-specific core principles that will help them draw proper inferences about the categories of artifacts involved and the functions they fulfill. R. Gelman and Lucariello make this same point using examples such as learning to play chess, "history, algebra, economics, and literature, and so on," that learning in the absence of support from core domains presents considerable challenges:

because there is no domain-relevant skeletal structure to start the learning ball rolling. The relevant mental structures must be acquired de novo, which means that learners acquire domain-relevant structures as well as a coherent knowledge base of domain-relevant knowledge about the content of the domain. . . . It is far from easy to assemble truly new conceptual structures and it usually takes a very long time. Something resembling formal instructions is often required and still this is not effective unless there is extended practice and effort on the part of the learner. (2000, p. 399)

Within the framework presented here, as indicated, formal instruction is a subset of the general category of historically evolved cultural practices. Consequently, the constraints that arise from the patterned forms of interaction that structure a great variety of cultural activities may enable concept formation in noncore domains. Unfortunately, to date, relatively little developmental research has been conducted with these issues in mind although some relevant research can be gleaned from what has come to be known as the study of "everyday cognition" (Rogoff & Lave, 1984; Schliemann, Carraher, & Ceci, 1997). The acquisition of concepts involved in learning to weave provide one example.

I have already presented some information about the acquisition of weaving in Zinacantan in considering research that integrates the study of cultural history and ontogenetic development. Here I return to a portion of that research project, headed by Patricia Greenfield, which focuses on contemporary cultural practices involved in weaving. These practices involve artifacts that include the production and dying of thread, the backstrap loom and its constituents (e.g., the warping frame), dowels that hold threads in place, and so on.

Whereas previously I highlighted changing interpersonal interactions in the organization of learning to weave over recent decades and changes in the products of weaving, here the focus changes to the closely related issue of the organization of the artifacts provided children at different ages and the way in which they reveal an implicit, indigenous theory of how to promote knowledge of the functions of the artifacts and skills in their use during ontogeny. What makes this story especially interesting is that the implicit ethnotheory embodied in the artifacts and their deployment is well aligned with a Piagetian stage theory of cognitive development.

Maynard and her colleagues (Maynard, 2002, 2003; Maynard, Greenfield, & Childs, 1999) report that before they begin to engage in the adult practice of weaving (perhaps at the age of 9 or 10), young girls are provided with simplified weaving tools of two levels of complexity. The simpler of the two is a tool for winding thread that maintains the orientation of the threads that will later be used in weaving the cloth; the more complex tool involves doubling the long (warp) threads around a dowel. This more complex approach requires the weaver to visualize the extended warp (undoubled) rather than simply seeing it. Threads on opposite sides of the dowel will end up at different ends of the loom, and the length of cloth produced is twice the length of the frame.

These researchers argue that the complex warping frame requires the ability to engage in mental transformations while the simplified winding frame does not ("the weaver simply winds the warp from top . . . to bottom of the loom . . . : What you see is what you get."). They note that parents and weaving teachers assign the simpler tool to 3- to 4-year-old children, and the more complex tool to 7- to 8-year-old children, corresponding to the canonical ages for Piagetian preoperational and concrete operational stages.

To test out this correspondence, the researchers compared performance on a task requiring children to match patterns on looms to patterns of cloth and in addition asked them to perform a perceptual matching task based on Piaget and Inhelder's (1956) research on the development of spatial thinking. The task involved six different colored beads strung as a necklace that were laid out as a necklace (requiring only a simple perceptual match), or as a figure eight, such that when the figure eight was unfolded as a circle, two pairs of beads in the middle of the figure were reversed, requiring a mental transformation to arrive at a match between a necklace laid out as a necklace or as a figure eight. These tests were presented to both boys and girls ranging in age from 4 to 13 years in both Zinacantan and Los Angeles.

Among the many interesting results of this study, most germane to this chapter are the following:

- Both Zinacantecan and North American children showed a developmental progression on both tasks that corresponded to expectations from Piagetian theory.
- While the progressions were the same in the two cultural groups, the American children had higher average scores on the bead matching/transformation tasks while the Zinacantecan children outperformed the

American children on weaving tasks. This is the pattern of results that one would expect on the basis of local familiarity.

- Correspondingly, Zinacantecan girls outperformed Zinacantecan boys on the weaving tasks and the Zinacantecan boys, who were at least familiar with the cloth patterns used and had seen weaving occur although they did not participate, outperformed the same-age children in Los Angeles.

Overall, these results fit well with Greenfield's theoretical claim that cultural practices build on species-wide patterns of maturation. They also provide evidence of the way in which cultural practices can provide the necessary constraints on learning in noncore domains.

## Culture and the Ontogeny of Autobiographical Memory

Although the topic of cultural influence on the development of remembering has a long history, the kinds of studies carried out at the time of prior reviews, like those on concept development, appear to have gone out of fashion (see Pressley & Hilden, Chapter 12, this *Handbook,* this volume). This earlier research was divided into studies for coherent stories and memory for arbitrary word lists which were then fashionable in experimental psychology.

Those approaches that focused on memory for coherent stories converged on the conclusion, consistent with theoretical claims made by Bartlett (1932) that people would remember parts of the story consistent with important local cultural themes, but inconsistent with Bartlett's idea that nonliterate people would be prone to remember events in a rote, serial order. In addition, cultural variations in overall amount of remembering for coherent stories were found to be minimal or absent. Studies that used lists of words or objects to be remembered often produced wide variations among populations, but when such differences appeared, they seemed to be associated with amount of schooling (for a review, see Cole, 1996, ch. 2). No substantial body of work has followed up on either of these traditions.

Coincident with the decline of interest in story recall and such questions as the influence of literacy on the way people remember arbitrary word lists has been a marked increase in studies that examine cultural influences on the development of autobiographical memory which is defined as an explicit memory of an event that occurred at a specific time and place in the person's past (Fivush & Haden, 2003; C. A. Nelson & Fivush, 2004).

In addition to there being a relatively substantial amount of research to make it worth reviewing in this venue, other reasons motivate discussion of culture and the development of autobiographical memory. First, people are asked to remember events in their own lives that are likely to be of significance to them rather than verbal or pictorial materials imported by researchers. Second, the topic of autobiographical memory makes theoretical links to the currently fashionable research on comparisons of societies characterized as independent or interdependent. I have chosen not to include this research here because little of it is developmental (see, however, Greenfield et al., Chapter 17, this *Handbook,* Volume 4, for a discussion of independence-interdependence in relation to schooling).

Three additional reasons motivate discussion of research on autobiographical memory in the context of this chapter. First, the onset as well as developmental increases in the quantity and quality of autobiographical memory have repeatedly been linked to ways that adults engage children in talk about the past, in particular past events experienced by the child (and usually, by the parent as well). Second, there have been several studies (unfortunately involving only a few distinctively different cultures) that indicate cultural variations in parental reminiscing practices and onset of autobiographical memories. Third, in contrast with earlier research on culture and memory linked up most distinctively with questions of literacy and schooling, the study of autobiographical memory links up most distinctively with questions of the development of the self and personality, providing a bridge to areas of research on culture and development that ordinarily fall outside the purview of cognitive development (see Shweder et al., Chapter 11 this *Handbook,* Volume 1, for a view of the landscape on the other side of this bridge).

In C. A. Nelson and Fivush's account of the development of autobiographical memory it is assumed that there is a species-general set of basic memory processes for events, people, and objects that are supported by species-general neurocognitive maturation. These basic processes enable the acquisition of understandings of intentionality and of others with regard to the self that

were discussed earlier in terms of core domains. Language is added to these early infantile processes along with the new forms of culturally mediated, social experiences that are required for its emergence and which in turn enable further cognitive development. Especially important in this regard is the emergence of genres of narrative, especially talk about personal episodes that come enmeshed in emotions and the entanglement of each child with those among whom the child develops. C. A. Nelson and Fivush summarize the centrality of narrative to autobiographical memory in these terms:

> Narrative adds layers of comprehensibility to events above and beyond what is available from direct experience by linking events together through causal, conditional, and temporal markers. Narratives are structured around meanings, emphasizing goals and plans, motivations and emotions, successful and failed outcomes, and their meaningful relation to the teller as well as to the other players. . . . Perhaps most important, through the use of evaluative devices, narratives provide for the expression of and reflection on personal meaning and significance that in turn allows for a more complex understanding of psychological motivation and causation. (p. 494)

In short, narratives constitute important general-purpose tools for thinking, acting, and feeling in the world.

For purposes of thinking about autobiographical memory and culture, the first central compelling line of evidence is that there are significant individual differences in the ways that U.S. parents organize conversations about the past with their young children and that these differences significantly influence the children's autobiographical memories. In their review of this literature, C. A. Nelson and Fivush differentiate maternal styles of reminiscing about past events in terms of "elaborativeness," by which they mean the frequency and degree of embellishment in their reminiscing conversations with their children. (It is important to note that elaborativeness is not the same as talkativeness: highly elaborative parents may not be talkative in other circumstances.) The major finding of their review, which includes longitudinal as well as cross-sectional evidence, is that greater parental elaborativeness produces better autobiographical remembering (measured by amount and coherence). This effect is found as much as 2 years after a particular reminiscing episode. Over time, the relationship between maternal and child remembering in these episodes shifts as children begin to contribute as much as what the parents recall in the conversations.

When we turn to research on cultural variation, a number of interesting findings have been reported. As summarized by Leichtman, Wang, and Pillemer (2003), a number of studies have reported cultural variations in the dominant forms of parent-child conversations about the past. These variations occur both in the degree to which parents engage in elaborative conversational patterns and the cultural values that they emphasize. Moreover, for Korean, Chinese, and Indian societies, where the bulk of the cross-cultural research has been carried out, these two aspects of parent-child discourse covary; compared with middle-class Americans, parents in these cultures, where low-elaborative styles dominate, are more likely to emphasize hierarchy, proper social relations, and good behavior. Also, consistent with results concerning the relation between conversational style and autobiographical memory, the earliest memories in the three non-U.S. societies were significantly later than those obtained in U.S. samples. This result was particularly striking in India, where only 12% of rural adults and 30% of urban adults reported *any* specific events about their childhoods and for a subset of those who did report events and the age at which they occurred, the range was between 6 and 11 years of age, far later than is characteristic in U.S. samples.

Researchers engaged in this work have linked such results to the distinction between cultures that privilege an interdependent versus an independent social orientation. The latter encourages a focus on oneself or others in construing one's self in relation to others (Markus & Kitayama, 1991; see also Shweder et al., Chapter 13, this *Handbook,* Volume 1). Without pretending to do justice to this line of theorizing, in the present context the distinction is captured by Mullen and Yi's (1995) idea that in interdependently oriented societies children are taught to see themselves as a collection of roles in a social network, whereas in independent societies children are taught to see themselves as a collection of individual attributes. The elaborative reminiscing style and relative lack of emphasis on social hierarchy with which it is associated thus promote the construction of coherent autobiographical narratives while the nonelaborative style blurs the distinction between self and group, in effect, diminishing the "auto" in the term autobiographical.

Research by Hayne and MacDonald (2003) reveals another cultural factor that influences autobiographical memory—the extent to which a society values narrative accounts of its own past. These researchers compared the autobiographical memories of Maori and European-descent New Zealanders, as well as the discourse styles of mothers from the two groups when talking with their children about the past.

The first interesting finding was that Maori adult women's earliest memories occurred at just under 3 years of age, while their European-descent counterparts' earliest memories occurred a year later, on average. This difference led the authors to the assumption, based on the work previously cited, that the Maori mothers would use a more elaborative style than European-descent mothers. But they found instead that the European-descent mothers were more likely to use an elaborative style that focused on the larger context of the event and salient details about people and objects present, while the Maori mothers were more likely to focus on a limited aspect of the event and repeatedly ask the same questions about it as if they were trying to elicit a particular response. It thus appears that early autobiographical memory can follow more than one path. These results provide strong support for K. Nelson's (2003b) "functional systems" approach to development "wherein memory is seen not as a singular structure but as a set of functions that employ similar processes to achieve different ends" (p. 14).

## CONCLUSION

I believe it is fair to say that never before have the chapters in the *Handbook of Child Psychology* reflected as great an interest in the role of culture and development as do the chapters in the present edition. Not only is the role of culturally organized experience examined in two other chapters that have the word *culture* in the title, but also in chapters that are focused on more or less traditional categories such as concept development and social cognition (and perhaps others to which I have not had advance access).

Most heartening from my perspective is that there seems to be a growing number of scholars who are genuinely rejecting the bedeviling nature-nurture controversy and beginning to treat culture as a phylogenetically evolved property of human beings. To be sure, programmatic statements of such a position have been discernible for many decades. To take two prominent examples from anthropology and psychology, consider the following:

> [M]an's nervous system does not merely enable him to acquire culture, it positively demands that he do so if it is going to function at all. Rather than culture acting only to supplement, develop, and extend organically based capacities logically and genetically prior to it, it would seem to be ingredient to those capacities themselves. A cultureless human being would probably turn out to be not an intrinsically talented, though unfulfilled ape, but a wholly mindless and consequently unworkable monstrosity. (Geertz, 1973, p. 68)

> Recall Sir Peter Medewar's *bon mot* about nature and nurture: Each contributes 100% to the variance of the phenotype. Man is not free of *either* his genome *or* his culture. (Bruner, 1986, p. 135)

What has changed since these lines were written is that they have begun to resonate far beyond anthropology. I have already quoted the psychobiologist, Henry Plotkin's remark that there is bidirectional causation between biology and culture. Even more pointed are the assertions of neuroscientists Steven Quartz and Terrence Sejnowski (2002), who write that culture "contains part of the developmental program that works with genes to build the brain that underlies who you are" (p. 58). They emphasize, especially, that the prefrontal cortex, which is the latest brain structure to develop in both phylogeny and ontogeny, and which is central to planning functions and complex social interaction, depends crucially on culture for its development. They refer to the emerging discipline required to bring these ideas to fruition as "cultural biology." As indicated earlier, I arrive at the same perspective from the broad theoretical framework referred to as cultural-historical activity theory, which traces its origins back to Lev Vygotsky and his students.

Whether approaching the task of developing a view of human ontogeny as the emergent process of development resulting from the intertwining of culture and phylogeny, from the perspective of cultural biology, or cultural-historical activity theory, one is driven to take seriously the need to conduct such an inquiry in light of the different "streams of history" or "genetic domains" that have organized this chapter.

To initiate this task, I note the conclusions suggested by my review of the literature on hominization, comparisons of human and nonhuman primates, and cultural

history. Against this backdrop, it should be possible to evaluate the new lines of research on conceptual and memory development reviewed earlier and to suggest other lines of research that appear to hold promise for theoretical progress.

## Overall Lessons from Phylogeny and Cultural History Relevant to Human Ontogeny

My reading of the literature on the paleological and primatological branches of human phylogenetic research suggests that each has a special contribution to make in thinking about culture and cognitive development in humans. In the literature on hominization, the features that stand out are the reciprocal relations between anatomical changes, changes in behavior that involve the creation and use of culture, and relations of individual organisms to each other and their environment. In particular, the influence of culture on biological change, seemingly so obscure in the case of modern humans, is particularly clear.

Several points stand out in the research on modern nonhuman primates. First, this work renders it plausible that who-or-whatever the common ancestor of contemporary humans and apes was, there was a small gap indeed between that progenitor and the earliest human beings. Nonetheless, that tiny difference was (to use Bateson's, 1972, phrase) "a difference that made a difference"—it started a complex dialectic of change in which biological, cultural, cognitive, and behavioral changes accumulated to produce *Homo sapiens sapiens* and made development through culture a defining characteristic of the species. Second, current research with nonhuman primates has contributed materially to deeper appreciation of such basic psychological mechanisms as imitation in the process of cognitive development of human beings.

In addition, research on culture understood as group-level social traditions turns attention to new questions about human culture. Now the question becomes: Why did culture appear to accumulate among early hominids and why has it become so central to humans, dominating their worlds, intertwining with their thinking, while it does not appear to do so at all in chimpanzees in the wild (Boesch & Tomasello, 1998)? It appears characteristic of human cultures that, except in unusual circumstances (Tasmania being cut off from Australia and isolated), there is a proclivity for cultural accumulation and increased complexity among human beings, both in the sphere of tool manufacture and design and the complexity of social practices and institutions. Tomasello (1999) has termed this tendency the "ratchet effect" and has argued that innovation, true imitation (e.g., imitation based on understanding others' intentions), and perhaps deliberate instruction are essential in this process. But the ratchet effect does not always work and it certainly does not always work rapidly. Boesch and Tomasello (1998) attribute this failure to slippage, but aside from the issue of specifying what makes a cultural ratchet durable or subject to slippage, there seems to be more to the issue of the conditions of (relatively pervasive) cultural evolution among *Homo sapiens sapiens.*

Two factors, often working together, appear essential. One is the use of external symbol-systems and the other is group interaction (both within groups and between groups). Each promotes vertical and horizontal cultural transmission. The case for the centrality of external symbol systems has been made persuasively by Donald (1991) and does not require review here. The Tasmanian case, as well as the flowering of modern *Homo sapiens sapiens,* point to intergroup interaction as an important factor in cumulative human cultural change because the frequent interaction of human groups provides rich opportunities for exogenously introduced innovation, a process that nineteenth- and early twentieth-century anthropologists referred to as diffusion. Such intergroup exchanges were infrequent during the Ice Age that preceded the appearance of modern humans and are infrequent among nonhuman primates.

Study of the phylogenetic and cultural-historical foundations of contemporary human cognitive abilities requires us to remember the cardinal importance of trying to keep in mind the *scale* of time involved in the processes of organic and cultural change. It is a difficult task. I can write *4 million years,* but I cannot, in any deep sense, comprehend it. Yet the evidence indicates that cultural changes along the hominid line over the past 4 million years have been staggering in their accelerating rate and their transformation of the environment, for better and for worse.

Even in the case of the study of cultural change among anatomically modern humans, the injunction to "study behaviors over time to see how they change" is easier said than done because culture among anatomically modern humans dates back at least 40,000 years and existing cultures characteristic of entire social

groups ordinarily exceed the lifetime of the researcher. These circumstances motivate research on those rare cases where it has proven possible to study changes in human cognition associated with rapid cultural changes occurring during specific historical circumstances.

The research by Beach, Greenfield, Luria, and Saxe provides a much closer look at the dynamics relating individual ontogenetic and microgenetic change to society-level collective cultural-historical change. So long as one studies such processes using tests of presumably general psychological functioning, or relies on the broad historical record, it is difficult if not impossible to gain access to the uneven, historically contingent interplay between microgenetic, ontogenetic, and cultural-historical levels of analysis that seem so central to the process of developmental change. But as soon as one focuses in on specific culturally organized activities and traces the changing location of these activities within the ways of life of which they are a part, processes of change appear to be linked proximally to specific forms of interaction involving people seeking to achieve their goals, or discovering new goals, under specifiable conditions using specifiable combinations of artifacts.

The cultural-historical line of research also highlights the importance of specialized institutions for the propagation of culture. These include modern schools and the specialized cognitive artifacts, written language and notation systems in particular, that mediate activities within those institutions and the society at large.

## Cultural Variation in Ontogeny

Serious consideration of culture-cognition relations in phylogeny and cultural history brings us to the study of cognitive development in ontogeny prepared to assume that maturational factors constrained heavily by phylogenetic history will be closely intertwined with cultural factors that are essential in the organization of social life in the society into which each child is born. However, given the relatively short duration of a single life (all the more so, a single childhood) relative to the long duration of a society's cultural history, let alone the unimaginably long time span of human evolution since the appearance of *Homo sapiens,* there is a strong, and almost irresistible, tendency of psychologists to treat phylogeny as invariant, and hence irrelevant, and to use cross-sectional studies (culturally speaking) of children growing up in different cultures as a means of under-standing culture-ontogeny relationships.

The historical obstacles that cross-cultural research has posed are well summarized in the Laboratory of Comparative Human Cognition (1983) *Handbook* chapter and elsewhere (e.g., Berry, Poortinga, & Pandey, 1997) and entered my earlier discussion of the difficulties of determining the impact of schooling on cognitive development in this chapter, so they need no review here. It is thus interesting that with some exceptions (to be noted), two lines of ontogenetic research reviewed in this chapter—concept development and memory—use methods that minimize those difficulties. With respect to the issue of the role of culture in conceptual developments, the key seems to be that instead of seeking directly to establish category membership or similarity relations by asking people to engage in sorting artificially constructed objects according to pre-set criteria, the experimenter gets at similarity relations by asking people to make inductions using question-asking discourse frames that are reasonable in local terms. Questions aimed at revealing conceptions about the causes of growth such as "Can you keep the frog in its bowl forever?" can pass as natural for young Japanese children who have been given frogs and other creatures to raise. To give another example from the concept formation work, children in all cultures are used to hearing words they do not understand, so when told that a wolf has andro inside and asked if a bird also has andro inside, the question can "pass as reasonable."

In an analogous manner, questions about memory for early events do not have the odd characteristic of being "known answer questions" that pervades so much of the research on memory development (and schooling). Researchers (and as a rule parents) have no idea what children will claim to be their earliest memories. While not totally immune to misinterpretation owing to features of the local language and culture, this verisimilitude that locates the crucial questions in a familiar cultural context helps establish their cultural-ecological validity. In like manner, the work of Greenfield and Saxe gains plausibility to the extent that they embed procedures in familiar cultural activities, modified only in sufficient degree to isolate crucial comparisons of theoretical interest.

Unsurprisingly, then, it is when experimental procedures have the "feel" of artificiality that controversies arise about the validity of cross-cultural comparisons.

With respect to the data on cultural variations in development of core domains, this is what occurs in efforts to use false-belief tasks where questions of language ordinarily play a large (and, many would argue, a key role) in children's performance. It is only when the procedure used is reduced to its behavioral core that cultural invariance appears but at the cost of being unable to explore important concomitants of children's theories of mind, such as the connections between false beliefs and emotions. It appears that decades of effort to satisfy the demands of cross-cultural comparison and ecological validity are beginning to yield some evidence of success.

Less progress has been made, however, in demonstrating the role of culture in forms of cognitive development that are assumed to have a strong biological foundation. The most promising arena for pursuing this kind of research may be with children who experience brain insults early in life and then undergo culturally organized environmental intervention by adults, operating on evidence of the activity-dependent nature of many forms of brain development. Antonio Battro (2000), took advantage of functional magnetic resonance imaging (f-MRI) technologies and computer programs to provide a child who had undergone a right hemispherectomy at the age of 3 years with dense, culturally organized, experience designed to build compensatory functional brain systems in the remaining cortex. He reports that the child attained a high level of cognitive accomplishment as a result of this "neuroeducation." In light of our current discussion, he also demonstrated the important role of culturally organized experience on brain development.

Other data combining variations in culturally organized activities that correspond to differences in the brain organization of behavior have been reported for adult abacus experts (Hanakawa et al., 2003; Tanaka, Michimata, Kaminaga, Honda, & Sadato, 2002). In tests of digit memory or mental arithmetic, f-MRI recordings of abacus experts show right hemisphere activation of the parietal area and other structures related to spatial processing. The f-MRI activity in nonexperts engaged in such tasks is in the left hemisphere, including Broca's area, indicating that they are solving the task by language-mediated, temporally sequential processing. When compared while engaged in verbal tasks, experts and nonexperts display the same forms of left-hemisphere-dominated f-MRI activity.

Although research that traces shifting brain localization of psychological processes is only beginning, existing cases nicely illustrate the ways in which cultural artifacts, incorporated into cultural practices, react back on the human brain so that nurture becomes nature.

In sum, a perspective on culture and cognitive development that takes seriously the simultaneous relevance of phylogenetic history, cultural history, and culturally organized activity during ontogeny promises to bring culture into the mainstream of developmental research without forcing us once again into the untenable bifurcation of nature and nurture. Our way of nurturing is our nature. The sooner we embrace this reality and begin to use it to organize our environments and ourselves, the brighter the future of human development.

# REFERENCES

Astuti, R., Solomon, G. E. A., & Carey, S. (2004). Constraints on conceptual development: A case study of the acquisition of folkbiological and folksociological knowledge in Madagascar. *Monographs of the Society for Research in Child Development, 69*(3, Serial No. 277).

Atran S. (1998). Folk biology and the anthropology of science: Cognitive universals and cultural particulars. *Behavioral and Brain Sciences, 21*(4), 547–609.

Atran, S., Medin, D., Lynch, E., Vapnarsky, V., Ek, E. U., & Soursa, P. (2001). Folkbiology does not come from folkpsychology: Evidence from Yukatek Maya in cross-cultural perspective. *Journal of Cognition and Culture, 1*(1), 3–41.

Baillargeon, R. (2004). Infants' physical world. *Current directions in psychological science, 13*(3), 89–94.

Bartlett, F. C. (1932). *Remembering.* Cambridge, England: Cambridge University Press.

Bateson, G. (1972). *Steps to an ecology of mind.* New York: Ballentine.

Battro, A. (2000). *Half a brain is enough: The story of Nico.* New York: Cambridge University Press.

Beach, K. (1995). Activity as a mediator of sociocultural change and individual development: The case of school-work transition in Nepal. *Mind, Culture and Activity, 2,* 285–302.

Bekoff, M., Allen, C., & Burghardt, G. M. (Eds.). (2002). *The cognitive animal: Empirical and theoretical perspectives on animal cognition.* Cambridge, MA: MIT Press.

Berlim, M. T., Mattevi, B. S., Belmonte-de-Abreu, P., & Crow, T. J. (2003). The etiology of schizophrenia and the origin of language: Overview of a theory. *Comprehensive Psychiatry, 44*(1), 7–14.

Berry, J. W. (2000). Cross-cultural psychology: A symbiosis of cultural and comparative approaches. *Asian Journal of Social Psychology, 3*(3), 197–205.

Berry, J. W., Poortinga, W. H., & Pandey, J. (Eds.). (1997). *Handbook of cross-cultural psychology: Vol. 1. Theory and method* (2nd ed.). Boston: Allyn & Bacon.

Bickerton, D. (1990). *Language and species.* Chicago: University of Chicago Press.

Bjorklund, D. F., & Pellegrini, A. D. (2002). *The origins of human nature: Evolutionary developmental psychology.* Washington, DC: American Psychological Association.

Bloch, M. N. (1989). Young boys' and girls' play at home and in the community. In M. N. Bloch & A. D. Pellegrini (Eds.), *The ecological context of children's play* (pp. 120–154). Norwood, NJ: Ablex.

Boesch, C., & Boesch, H. (1984). Mental map in wild chimpanzees: An analysis of hammer transports for nut cracking. *Primates, 25,* 160–170.

Boesch, C., & Tomasello, M. (1998). Chimpanzee and human cultures. *Current Anthropology, 39*(5), 591–614.

Bogin, B. (2001). *The growth of humanity.* New York: Wiley-Liss.

Bowen, E. (1964). *Return to laughter.* New York: Doubleday.

Boysen, S. T., & Hallberg, K. I. (2000). Primate numerical competence: Contributions toward understanding nonhuman cognition. *Cognitive Science, 24*(3), 423–443.

Bramble, D. M., & Lieberman, D. E. (2004). Endurance running and the evolution of Homo. *Nature, 432,* 345–352.

Bruner, J. S. (1966). On cognitive growth II. In J. S. Bruner, R. Olver, & P. M. Greenfield (Eds.), *Studies in cognitive growth* (pp. 30–67). New York: Wiley.

Bruner, J. S. (1986). *Actual minds, possible worlds.* Cambridge, MA: Harvard University Press.

Bryant, P. (1995). Phonological and grammatical skills in learning to read. In J. Morais (Ed.), *Speech and reading: A comparative approach* (pp. 249–256). Hove, England: Erlbaum.

Bryant, P., & Nunes, T. (1998). Learning about the orthography: A cross-linguistic approach. In H. M. Wellman (Ed.), *Global prospects for education: Development, culture, and schooling* (pp. 171–191). Washington, DC: American Psychological Association.

Byrne, R. (2002). Seeing actions as hierarchically organized structures: Great ape manual skills. In A. N. Meltzoff & W. Prinz (Eds.), *Cambridge Studies in Cognitive Perceptual Development: The imitative mind—Development, evolution, and brain bases* (pp. 122–140). New York: Cambridge University Press.

Byrne, R. W., Barnard, P. H., Davidson, I., Janik, V. M., McGrew, W. C., Miklósi, Á, et al. (2004). Understanding culture across species. *Trends in Cognitive Sciences, 8*(8), 341–346.

Callaghan, T., Rochat, P., Lillard, A., Claux, M. L., Odden, H., Itakura, S., et al. (n.d.). *Universal onset of mental state reasoning: Evidence from 5 cultures.* Unpublished manuscript, Xavier University of Louisiana at New Orleans.

Carey, S. (1985). *Conceptual change in childhood.* Cambridge, MA: MIT Press.

Chavajay, P., & Rogoff, B. (2002). Schooling and traditional collaborative social organization of problem solving by Mayan mothers and children. *Developmental Psychology, 38*(1), 55–66.

Chen, Z., & Siegler, R. S. (2000). Intellectual development in childhood. In R. Sternberg (Ed.), *Handbook of intelligence* (pp. 92–116). New York: Cambridge University Press.

Cheyne, J. A. (2004). Signs of consciousness: Speculations on the psychology of paleolithic graphics. Available from http://www.arts.uwaterloo.ca/~acheyne/signcon.html.

Chomsky, N. (1959). Review of B. F. Skinner's "Verbal Behavior." *Language, 35,* 16–58.

Chomsky, N. (1986). *Knowledge of language: It's nature, origin, and use.* London: Praeger.

Christian, K., Bachnan, H. J., & Morrison, F. J. (2001). Schooling and cognitive development. In R. J. Sternberg & E. L. Grigorenko (Eds.), *Environmental effects on cognitive abilities* (pp. 287–335). Mahwah, NJ: Erlbaum.

Cole, M. (1996). *Cultural psychology.* Cambridge, MA: Harvard University Press.

Cole, M. (2005). Cross-cultural and historical perspectives on the developmental consequences of education: Implications for the future. *Human Development, 48*(4), 195–216.

Cole, M., Cole, S., & Lightfoot, C. (2005). *The development of children* (5th ed.). New York: Scientific American.

Cole, M., Gay, J., Glick, J. A., & Sharp, D. W. (1971). *The cultural context of learning and thinking.* New York: Basic Books.

Cole, M., & Scribner, S. (Eds.). (1974). *Culture and thought: A psychological introduction.* New York: Wiley.

Daley, T. C., Whaley, S. E., Sigman, M. D., Espinosa, M. P., & Neumann, C. (2003). IQ on the rise: The Flynn effect in rural Kenyan children. *Psychological Science, 14*(3), 215–219.

Damerow, P. (1996). *Abstraction and representation: Essays on the cultural evolution of thinking.* Dordrecht, The Netherlands: Kluwer Academic.

Damerow, P. (1998). Prehistory and cognitive development. In J. Langer & M. Killen (Eds.), *Piaget, evolution and development* (pp. 247–270). Mahwah, NJ: Erlbaum.

D'Andrade, R. (1996). Culture. In J. Kuper (Ed.), *Social science encyclopedia* (pp. 161–163). London: Routledge.

Deacon, T. W. (1997). *The symbolic species: The co-evolution of language and the brain.* New York: Norton.

de Waal, F. (2001). *The ape and the sushi master.* New York: Basic Books.

Diamond, J. (1997). *Guns, germs, and steel: The fates of human societies.* New York: Norton.

Donald, M. (1991). *Origins of the modern mind: Three stages in the evolution of culture and cognition.* Cambridge, MA: Harvard University Press.

Donald, M. (2001). *A mind so rare: The evolution of human consciousness.* New York: Norton.

Dunbar, R. I. (2004). *The human story: A new history of mankind's evolution.* London: Faber & Faber.

Elman, J., Bates, E., Johnson, M. H., Karmiloff-Smith, A., Parisi, D., & Plunkett, K. (1996). *Rethinking innateness: A connectionist perspective on development.* Cambridge, MA: MIT Press.

Falk, D., & Gibson, K. (Eds.). (2001). *Evolutionary anatomy of the primate cerebral cortex.* New York: Cambridge University Press.

Feigenson, L., Dehaene, S., & Spelke, E. (2000). In G. M. Feinman & L. Manzanilla (Eds.), *Cultural evolution: Contemporary viewpoints.* New York: Kluwer Academic/Plenum Press.

Feinman, G. M. (2000). Cultural evolutionary approaches and archeology: Past, present, and future. In G. M. Feinman & L. Manzanilla (Eds.), *Cultural evolution: Contemporary viewpoints* (pp. 3–12). New York: Kluwer Academic/Plenum Press.

Fivush, R., & Haden, C. A. (Eds.). (2003). *Autobiographical memory and the construction of a narrative self.* Mahwah, NJ: Erlbaum.

Flynn, J. R. (1987). Massive IQ gains in 14 nations: What IQ tests really measure. *Psychological Bulletin, 101*(2), 171–191.

Fodor, J. A. (1985). Prècis of the modularity of mind. *Behavioral and Brain Sciences, 8*(1), 1–42.

Foley, R. A., & Lahr, M. M. (2003). On stony ground: Lithic technology, human evolution, and the emergence of culture. *Evolutionary anthropology, 12*(3), 109–122.

Fortes, M. (1938). Social and psychological aspects of education in Taleland (Published by Oxford University Press for the International Institute of African Languages and Culture). *Africa, 11*(4, Suppl.).

Gallimore, R., Goldenberg, C. N., & Weisner, T. S. (1993). The social construction and subjective reality of activity settings: Implications for community psychology. *American Journal of Community Psychology, 21*(4), 537–559.

Gaskins, S. (1999). Children's daily lives in a Mayan village: A Case Study of Culturally Constructed Roles and Activities. In A. Goncu (Ed.), *Children's engagement in the world: Sociocultural perspectives* (pp. 25–60). New York: Cambridge University Press.

Gaskins, S. (2000). Children's daily activities in a Mayan village: A culturally grounded description. *Cross-Cultural Research, 34*(4), 375–389.

Gaskins, S. (2003). From corn to cash: Change and continuity within Mayan families. *Ethos, 31*(2), 248–273.

Geertz, C. (1973). *The interpretation of culture.* New York: Basic Books.

Gellner, E. (1988). *Plough, sword, and book: The structure of human history.* London: Collins Harvill.

Gelman, R., & Gallistel, C. R. (2004). Language and the origin of numerical concepts. *Science, 306*(5695), 441–443.

Gelman, R., & Lucariello, J. (2002). The role of learning in cognitive development. In H. Pashler & R. Gallistel (Eds.), *Steven's handbook of experimental psychology: Vol. 3. Learning, motivation, and emotion* (3rd ed., pp. 395–443). Hoboken, NJ: Wiley.

Gelman, R., & Williams, E. M. (1998). Enabling constraints for cognitive development and learning: Domain specificity and epigenesis. In D. Kuhn & R. S. Siegler (Eds.), *Handbook of child psychology* (5th ed., Vol. 2, pp. 575–630). New York: Wiley.

Gelman, S. A., & Opfer, J. E. (2002). Development of the animate-inanimate distinction. In U. Goswami (Ed.), *Blackwell handbook of childhood cognitive development* (pp. 151–166). Malden, MA: Blackwell.

Gergely, G. (2002). The development of understanding self and agency. In U. Goswami (Ed.), *Blackwell handbook of childhood cognitive development* (pp. 26–46). Malden, MA: Blackwell.

Goodall, J. (1968). *The behaviour of free-living chimpanzees in the Gombe Stream Reserve.* London: Baillière, Tindall & Cassell.

Goody, J. (1977). *Domestication of the savage mind.* Cambridge, England: Cambridge University Press.

Göncü, A. (1999). *Children's engagement in the world: Sociocultural perspectives.* New York: Cambridge University Press.

Gopnik, A., & Meltzoff, A. (1997). *The scientist in the crib: Minds, brains, and how children learn.* New York: Morrow.

Gordon, P. (2004, October). Numerical cognition without words: Evidence from Amazonia. Science [Special Issue].*Cognition and Behavior, 306*(5695), 496–499.

Greenfield, P. M. (1999). Historical change and cognitive change: A 2-decade follow-up study in Zinacantan, a Maya community in Chiapas, Mexico. *Mind, Culture, and Activity, 6*(2), 92–108.

Greenfield, P. M. (2002). The mutual definition of culture and biology in development. In H. Keller, Y. H. Poortinga, & A. Schömerick (Eds.), *Between culture and biology: Perspectives on ontogenetic development* (pp. 57–76). New York: Cambridge University Press.

Greenfield, P. M. (2004). *Weaving generations together: Evolving creativity in the Maya of Chiapas.* Santa Fe, NM: School of American Research.

Greenfield, P. M., & Childs, C. P. (1977). Weaving, color terms and pattern representation: Cultural influences and cognitive development among the Zinacantecos of Southern Mexico. *Inter-American Journal of Psychology, 11,* 23–28.

Greenfield, P. M., Keller, H. H., Fuligni, A., & Maynard, A. E. (2003). Cultural pathways through universal development. *Annual Review of Psychology, 54,* 461–490.

Greenfield, P. M., Maynard, A. E., & Childs, C. P. (2000). History, culture, learning, and development. *Cross-Cultural Research: Journal of Comparative Social Science, 34*(4), 351–374.

Hagen, J. W., Meacham, J. A., & Mesibov, G. (1970). Verbal labeling, rehearsal, and short-term memory. *Cognitive Psychology, 1,* 47–58.

Hallpike, C. R. (1979). *The foundations of primitive thought.* Oxford, England: Clarendon Press.

Hanakawa, T., Immisch, I., Toma, K., Dimyan, M. A., van Gelderen, P., & Hallett, M. (2003). Neural correlates underlying mental calculations in abacus experts: A functional magnetic resonance imaging study. *NeuroImage, 19,* 296–307.

Hatano, G. (1997). Commentary: Core domains of thought, innate constraints, and sociocultural contexts. In H. M. Wellman & K. Inagaki (Eds.), *The emergence of core domains of thought: Children's reasoning about physical, psychological, and biological phenomena* (pp. 71–78). San Francisco: Jossey-Bass.

Hatano, G., & Inagaki, K. (2002). Domain-specific constraints of conceptual development. In W. W. Hartup & R. K. Silbereisen (Eds.), *Growing points in developmental science: An introduction* (pp. 123–142). New York: Psychology Press.

Hauser, M. D., & Carey, S. (1998). Building a cognitive creature from a set of primitives: Evolutionary and developmental insights. In D. Cummins Dellarosa & C. Allen (Eds.), *The evolution of mind* (pp. 51–106). London: Oxford University Press.

Hayne, H., & MacDonald, S. (2003). The socialization of autobiographical memory in children and adults: The roles of culture and gender. In R. Fivush & C. A. Haden (Eds.), *Autobiographical memory and the construction of a narrative self* (pp. 99–120). Mahwah, NJ: Erlbaum.

Hewlett, B. S. (1992). *Father-child relations: Cultural and biosocial contexts.* New York: Aldine De Gruyter.

Hirschfeld, L., & Gelman, S. A. (Eds.). (1994). *Mapping the mind: Domain specificity in cognition and culture.* New York: Cambridge University Press.

Howell, S. (1984). *Society and cosmos.* Oxford, England: Oxford University Press.

Hutchins, E. (1995). *Cognition in the wild.* Cambridge, MA: MIT Press.

Inagaki, K. (1990). Chilldren's use of knowledge in everyday biology. *British Journal of Developmental Psychology, 8*(3), 281–288.

Jerison, H. (1973). *Evolution of the brain and intelligence.* New York: Academic Press.

Joulian, F. (1996). Comparing chimpanzee and early hominid techniques: Some contributions to cultural and cognitive questions. In P. Mellars & K. Gibson (Eds.), *Modelling the early human mind* (pp. 173–189). Cambridge, England: McDonald Institute for Archaeological Research, University of Cambridge.

Kaplan, H., & Dove, H. (1987). Infant development among the Ache of eastern Paraguay. *Developmental Psychology, 23*(2), 190–198.

Keil, F. (1989). *Concepts, kinds, and cognitive development.* Cambridge, MA: MIT Press.

Keil, F. (2003). That's life: Coming to understand biology. *Human Development, 46*(6), 369–377.

Kemler Nelson, D. G., Frankenfield, A., Morris, C., & Blair, E. (2000). Young children's use of functional information to categorize artifacts: Three factors that matter. *Cognition, 77*(2), 133–168.

Kroeber, A. L., & Kluckhohn, C. (1952). Culture: A critical review of concepts and definitions. *Papers of the Peabody Museum, 47*(11), 1–223.

Kuhlmeier, V. A., & Boysen, S. T. (2002). Chimpanzees (Pan troglodytes) recognize spatial and object correspondences between a scale model and its referent. *Psychological Science, 13*(1), 60–63.

Laboratory of Comparative Human Cognition. (1983). Culture and development. In P. H. Mussen (Series Ed.) & W. Kessen (Vol. Ed.), *Handbook of child psychology: Vol. 1. History, theory, and methods* (4th ed., pp. 295–356). New York: Wiley.

Larsen, M. T. (1986). Writing on clay from pictograph to alphabet. *Newsletter of the Laboratory of Comparative Human Cognition, 8*(1), 3–7.

Leichtman, M. D., Wang, Q., & Pillemer, D. B. (2003). Cultural variations in interdependence and autobiographical memory: Lessons from Korea, China, India, and the United States. In R. Fivush & C. A. Haden (Eds.), *Autobiographical memory and the construction of a narrative self* (pp. 73–97). Mahwah, NJ: Erlbaum.

Leslie, A. M. (1994). ToMM, ToBy, and Agency: Core architecture and domain specificity. In L. Hirschfeld & S. A. Gelman (Eds.), *Mapping the mind: Domain specificity in cognition and culture* (pp. 119–148). New York: Cambridge University Press.

LeVine, R. A., LeVine, S. E., & Schnell, B. (2001). Improve the women: Mass schooling, female literacy, and worldwide social change. *Harvard Educational Review, 71*(1), 1–50.

LeVine, R. A., & White, M. I. (1986). *Human conditions: The cultural basis of educational development.* Boston: Routledge & Kegan Paul.

Lewin, R., & Foley, R. A. (2004). *Principles of human evolution.* Malden, MA: Blackwell.

Lieberman, P. (1984). *The biology and evolution of language.* Cambridge, MA: Harvard University Press.

Lillard, A. S. (1998a). Ethnopsychologies: Cultural variations in theories of mind. *Psychological Bulletin, 123*(1), 3–32.

Lillard, A. S. (2006). The socialization of theory of mind: Cultural and social class differences in behavior explanation. In A. Antonietti, O. Liverta-Sempio, & A. Marchetti (Eds.), *Theory of mind and language in developmental contexts* (pp. 65–76). New York: Springer.

Lillard, A. S., & Skibbe, L. (2004). Theory of mind: Conscious attribution and spontaneous trait inference. In R. Hassin, J. S. Uleman, & J. A. Bargh (Eds.), *The new unconscious* (pp. 277–305). Oxford, England: Oxford University Press.

Luria, A. R. (1976). *Cognitive development.* Cambridge, MA: Harvard University Press.

Mandler, J., Scribner, S., Cole, M., & DeForest, M. (1980). Cross-cultural invariance in story recall. *Child Development, 51,* 19–26.

Marks, J. (2002). *What it means to be 98% chimpanzee: Apes, people, and their genes.* Berkeley, CA: University of California Press.

Markus, H., & Kitayama, S. (1991). Culture and the self: Implications for cognition, emotion, and motivation. *Psychological Review, 98*(2), 224–253.

Matsuzawa, T. (Ed.). (2001). *Primate origins of human cognition and behavior.* Tokyo: Springer Verlag.

Maynard, A. E. (2002). Cultural teaching: The development of teaching skills in a Maya sibling interaction. *Child Development, 73*(3), 969–982.

Maynard, A. E. (2003). Implicit cognitive development in cultural tools and children: Lessons from Maya, Mexico. *Cognitive Development, 18*(4), 489–510.

Maynard, A. E., Greenfield, P. M., & Childs, C. P. (1999). Culture, history, biology, and body: Native and non-native acquisition of technological skill. *Ethos, 27*(3), 379–402.

McBrearty, S., & Brooks, A. S. (2000). The revolution that wasn't: A new interpretation of the origin of modern human behavior. *Journal of Human Evolution, 39*(5), 453–563.

McGrew, W. C. (1987). Tools to get food: The subsistants of Tasmanian aborigines and Tanzanian chimpanzees compared. *Journal of Anthropological Research, 43*(3), 247–258.

McGrew, W. C. (1998). Culture in nonhuman primates? *Annual Review of Anthropology, 27,* 301–328.

Mead, M. (1935). *Sex and temperament in three primitive societies.* New York: Morrow.

Medin, D. L., & Atran, S. (2004). The native mind: Biological categorization and reasoning in development and across cultures. *Psychological Review, 111*(4), 960–983.

Medin, D. L., Ross, N., Atran, S., Burnett, R. C., & Blok, S. V. (2002). Categorization and reasoning in relation to culture and expertise. In B. H. Ross (Ed.), *The psychology of learning and motivation: Advances in research and theory* (Vol. 41, pp. 1–41). San Diego, CA: Academic Press.

Mejia-Arauz, R., Rogoff, B., & Paradise, R. (2005). Cultural variation in children's observation during a demonstration. *International Journal of Behavioral Development, 29*(4), 282–291.

Meltzoff, A. N., & Prinz, W. (Eds.). (2002). *Cambridge Studies in Cognitive Perceptual Development: The imitative mind—Development, evolution, and brain bases.* New York: Cambridge University Press.

Menzel, R. C., Savage-Rumbaugh, S., & Menzel, E. W., Jr. (2002). Bonobo (pan paniscus) spatial memory in a 20-hectare forest. *International Journal of Primatology, 23,* 601–619.

Morais, J., & Kolinsky, R. (2001). The literate mind and the universal human mind. In E. Dupoux (Ed.), *Language, brain, and cognitive development: Essays in honor of Jacques Mehler* (pp. 463–480). Cambridge, MA: MIT Press.

Morelli, G. A., Rogoff, B., & Angellilo, C. (2003). Cultural variation in young children's access to work or involvement in specialised child-focused activities. *International Journal of Behavioral Development, 27*(3), 264–274.

Morrison, F. J., Smith, L., & Dow-Ehrensberger, M. (1995). Education and cognitive development: A natural experiment. *Developmental Psychology, 31*(5), 789–799.

Mullen, M. K., & Yi, S. (1995). The cultural context of talk about the past: Implications for the development of autobiographical memory. *Cognitive Development, 10*(3), 407–419.

Neisser, U. (1998). Introduction: Raising test scores and what they mean. In U. Neisser (Ed.), *The rising curve: Long-term gains in IQ and related measures* (pp. 3–22). Washington, DC: American Psychological Association.

Nelson, C. A., & Fivush, R. (2004). The emergence of autobiographical memory: A social cultural developmental theory. *Psychological Review, 111*(2), 486–511.

Nelson, K. (2003b). Narrative and self, myth and memory. In R. Fivush & C. A. Haden (Eds.), *Autobiographical memory and the construction of a narrative self* (pp. 3–28). Mahwah, NJ: Erlbaum.

Nettelbeck, T., & Wilson, C. (2004). The Flynn effect: Smarter not faster. *Intelligence, 32*(1), 85–93.

Noble, W., & Davidson, I. (1996). *Human evolution, language, and mind.* Cambridge, England: Cambridge University Press.

Nunes, Y., Schliemann, A. D., & Carraher, D. W. (1993). *Street mathematics and school mathematics.* Cambridge, England: Cambridge University Press.

Olson, D. (1994). *The world on paper.* New York: Cambridge University Press.

Parker, S., & McKinney, M. L. (1999). *Origins of intelligence: The evolution of cognitive development in monkeys, apes, and humans.* Baltimore: Johns Hopkins University Press.

Parker, S. T., Langer, J., & McKinney, M. L. (Eds.). (2000). *Biology, brains, and behavior: The evolution of human development.* Santa Fe, NM: School of American Research Press.

Paul, R. A. (1995). Act and intention in Sherpa culture and society. In L. Rosen (Ed.), *Other intentions: Cultural contexts and the attribution of inner states* (pp. 15–45). Santa Fe, NM: School of American Research Press.

Passingham, R. (1982). *The human primate.* San Francisco: Freeman.

Piaget, J., & Inhelder, B. (1956). *The child's conception of space.* New York: Humanities Press.

Pica, P., Lerner, C., Izard, V., & Dehaene, S. (2004). Exact and approximate arithmetic in an Amazonian indigenous group. *Science, 306*(5695), 499–503.

Plotkin, H. (2001). Some elements of a science of culture. In E. Whitehouse (Ed.), *The debated mind: Evolutionary psychology versus ethnography* (pp. 91–109). New York: Berg.

Posner, J. K. (1982). The development of mathematical knowledge in two West African societies. *Child Development, 53,* 200–208.

Quartz, S. R., & Sejnowski, T. J. (2002). *Liars, lovers, and heroes: What the new brain science reveals about how we become who we are.* New York: Morrow.

Reagan, T. (2000). *Non-western educational traditions: Alternative approaches to educational thought and practice.* Mahwah, NJ: Erlbaum.

Renfrew, C., & Scarre, C. (Eds.). (1998). *Cognition and material culture: The archeology of symbolic storage.* Oxford, England: Oxbow Books, University of Cambridge, McDonald Institute for Archeological Research.

Ridley, M. (2003). *Nature via nurture: Genes, experience and what makes us human.* New York: HarperCollins.

Rogoff, B. (1981). Schooling and the development of cognitive skills. In H. C. Triandis & A. Heron (Eds.), *Handbook of cross-cultural psychology* (Vol. 4, pp. 233–294). Boston: Allyn & Bacon.

Rogoff, B. (2003). *The cultural nature of human development.* New York, Oxford University Press.

Rogoff, B., Correa-Chávez, M., & Navichoc Cotuc, M. (2005). A cultural/historical view of schooling in human development. In

D. Pillemer & S. H. White (Eds.), *Developmental psychology and social change* (p. 225–263). New York: Cambridge University Press.

Rogoff, B., & Lave, J. C. (1984). *Everyday cognition: Its development in social context.* Cambridge, MA: Harvard University Press.

Rogoff, B., Paradise, R., Arauz, R., Correa-Chávez, M., & Angelillo, C. (2003). Firsthand learning through intent participation. *Annual Review of Psychology, 54,* 175–203.

Rogoff, B., & Waddell, K. (1982). Memory for information organized in a scene by children from two cultures. *Child Development, 53,* 1224–1228.

Romney, A. K., & Moore, C. C. (2001). Systemic culture patterns as basic units of cultural transmission and evolution. Cross-cultural research [Special issue]. *Journal of Comparative Social Science, 35*(2), 154–178.

Romney, A., Weller, S. C., & Batchelder, W. H. (1986). Culture as consensus: A theory of culture and informant accuracy. *American Anthropologist, 88*(2), 313–338.

Ross, N., Medin, D., Coley, J. D., & Atran, S. (2003). Cultural and Experimental Differences in the Development of Folkbiological Induction. *Cognitive Development, 18,* 25–47.

Ruffman, T., Perner, J., Naito, M., Parkin, L., & Clements, W. A. (1998). Older (but not younger) siblings facilitate false belief understanding. *Developmental Psychology, 34*(1), 161–174.

Rumbaugh, D. M., Savage-Rumbaugh, S., & Sevcik, R. (1994). Biobehavioral roots of language: A comparative perspective of chimpanzee, child, and culture. In R. W. Wrangham, W. C. McGrew, F. de Waal, & P. Heltne (Eds.), *Chimpanzee cultures* (pp. 319–334). Cambridge, MA: Harvard University Press.

Rumbaugh, D. M., & Washburn, D. A. (Eds.). (2003). *Intelligence of apes and other rational beings: Current perspectives in psychology.* New Haven, CT: Yale University Press.

Russon, A., & Begun, D. R. (2004). *The evolution of thought: Evolutionary origins of great ape intelligence.* Cambridge, England: Cambridge University Press.

Savage-Rumbaugh, S., Fields, W. M., & Taglialatela, J. P. (2001). Language, speech, tools and writing: A cultural imperative. *Journal of Consciousness Studies, 8*(5/7), 273–292.

Savage-Rumbaugh, S., Murphy, J., Sevcik, R. A., & Brakke, K. E. (1993). Language comprehension in ape and child. *Monographs of the Society for Research in Child Development, 58*(3/4), v–221.

Saxe, G. B. (1981). Body parts as numerals: A developmental analysis of numeration among the Oksapmin in Papua, New Guinea. *Child Development, 52*(1), 306–316.

Saxe, G. B. (1982). Developing form of arithmetical thought among the Osakpmin of Papua, New Guinea. *Developmental Psychology, 18,* 583–595.

Saxe, G. B. (1985). Effects of schooling on arithmetical understandings: Studies with Oksapmin children in Papua, New Guinea. *Journal of Educational Psychology, 77*(5), 503–513.

Saxe, G. B. (1994). Studying cognitive development in sociocultural contexts: The development of practice-based approaches. *Mind, Culture, and Activity, 1*(1), 135–157.

Saxe, G. B. (2002). Children's developing mathematics in collective practices: A framework for analysis. *Journal of the Learning Sciences.11*(2/3), 275–300.

Saxe, G. B., & Esmonde, I. (in press). Studying cognition in flux: A historical treatment of "fu" in the shifting structure of Oksapmin Mathematics. *Mind, Culture, and Activity.*

Saxe, G. B., Guberman, S. R., & Gearhart, M. (1987). Social processes in early number development. *Monographs of the Society for Research in Child Development, 52*(2), 1987, pp. 162.

Schliemann, A., Carraher, D., & Ceci, S. J. (1997). Everyday cognition. In J. W. Berry, P. R. Dasen, & T. S. Sarawathi (Eds.), *Handbook of cross-cultural psychology: Vol. 2. Basic processes and human development* (2nd ed., pp. 177–216). Needham Heights, MA: Allyn & Bacon.

Schmandt-Besserat, D. (1975). *First civilization: The legacy of Sumer* [Painting]. Austin: University of Texas Art Museum.

Schmandt-Besserat, D. (1996). *How writing came about.* Austin: University of Texas Press.

Schwartz, T. (1978). The size and shape of culture. In F. Barth (Ed.), *Scale and social organization* (pp. 215–252). New York: Columbia University Press.

Scribner, S., & Cole, M. (1981). *The psychology of literacy.* Cambridge, MA: Harvard University Press.

Serpell, R., & Hatano, G. (1997). Education, schooling, and literacy. In J. W. Berry, P. R. Dasen, & T.S. Saraswathi (Eds.), *Handbook of cross-cultural psychology: Vol. 2. Basic processes and human development* (2nd ed., pp. 339–376). Needham Heights, MA: Allyn & Bacon.

Sharp, D. W., Cole, M., & Lave, C. A. (1979). Education and cognitive development: The evidence from experimental research. *Monographs of the Society for Research in Child Development, 44*(1/2), 1–112.

Shweder, R., Goodnow, J., Hatano, G., LeVine, R., Markus, H., & Miller, P. (1998). The cultural psychology of development: One mind, many mentalities. In W. Damon (Editor-in-Chief) & R. M. Lerner (Vol. Ed.), *Handbook of child psychology: Vol. 1. Theoretical models of human development* (5th ed., pp. 865–938). New York: Wiley.

Skinner, B. F. (1957). *Verbal behavior.* New York: Appleton-Century-Crofts.

Spelke, E. (1994). Initial knowledge: Six suggestions. *Cognition, 50*(1/3), 431–445.

Springer, K. (1999). How a naïve theory of biology is acquired. In M. Siegal & C. Peterson (Eds.), *Children's understanding of biology and health* (pp. 45–70). Cambridge, England: Cambridge University Press.

Sroufe, L. A., Cooper, R. G., & DeHart, G. B. (1996). *Child development: Its nature and course.* New York: McGraw-Hill.

Stocking, G. (1968). *Race, culture, and evolution.* New York: Free Press.

Stout, D., Toth, N., Schick, K., Stout, J., & Hutchins, G. (2000). Stone tool-making and brain activation: Positron Tomogrpahy (PET) Studies. *Journal of Archeological Science, 27*(12), 1215–1233.

Super, C. M. (Ed.). (1987). *The role of culture in developmental disorder.* San Diego, CA: Academic Press.

Super, C. M., & Harkness, S. (1986). The developmental niche: A conceptualization at the interface of child and culture. *International Journal of Behavioral Development, 9,* 545–569.

Super, C. M., & Harkness, S. (1997). The cultural structuring of human development. In J. W. Berry, P. R. Dasen, & T.S. Saraswathi (Eds.), *Handbook of cross-cultural psychology: Vol. 2. Basic processes and human development* (2nd ed., pp. 1–39). Needham Heights, MA: Allyn & Bacon.

Tanaka, S., Michimata, C., Kaminaga, T., Honda, M., & Sadato, N. (2002). Superior digit memory of abacus experts: An event-related functional MRI study. *NeuroReport, 13*(17), 2187–2191.

Tomasello, M. (1994). The question of chimpanzee culture. In R. W. Wrangham, W. C. McGrew, F, B. N. de Waal, & P. G. Heltne (Eds.). *Chimpanzee cultures* (pp. 301–318). Cambridge, MA: Harvard University Press.

Tomasello, M. (1999). *The cultural origins of human cognition.* Cambridge, MA: Harvard University Press.

Tomasello, M., Call, J., & Hare, B. (2003). Chimpanzees understand psychological states—The question is which ones and to which extent. *Trends in Cognitive Sciences, 7,* 153–156.

Tomasello, M., Carpenter, M., Call, J., Behne, T., & Moll, H. (2005). Understanding and sharing intentions: The origins of cultural cognition. *Brain and Behavioral Sciences, 28*(5), 1–62.

Tomasello, M., & Rakoczy, H. (2003). What makes human cognition unique? From individual to shared to collective intentionality. *Mind and Language, 18,* 121–147.

Tulviste, P. (1991). *The cultural-historical development of verbal thinking.* Commack, NY: Nova Science.

United Nations Educational, Scientific, and Cultural Organization. (1951). *Learn and live: A way out of ignorance of 1,200,000,000 people.* Paris: Author.

United Nations Educational, Scientific, and Cultural Organization. (2003). *Gross net and gross enrollment ratios: Secondary education.* Montreal, Canada: Institute of Statistics.

Vinden, P. G. (1996). Junín Quechua children's understanding of mind. *Child Development, 67*(4), 1707–1716.

Vinden, P. G. (1999). Children's understanding of mind and emotion: A Multi-Culture Study. *Cognition and Emotion, 13*(1), 19–48.

Vinden, P. G. (2002). Understanding minds and evidence for belief: A Study of Mofu Children in Cameroon. *International Journal of Behavioral Development, 26*(5), 445–452.

Vygotsky, L. S. (1978). *Mind in society.* Cambridge, MA: Harvard University Press.

Vygotsky, L. S. (1997). *The collected works of L. S. Vygotsky: Problems of general psychology.* New York: Plenum Press.

Vygotsky, L. S., & Luria, A. R. (1993). *Studies on the History of Behavior: Ape, primitive, and child.* Mahwah, NJ: Erlbaum. (Original work published 1931)

Wagner, D. A. (1974). The development of short-term and incidental memory: A Cross-Cultural Study. *Child Development, 48*(2), 389–396.

Wagner, D. A. (1993). *Literacy, culture, and development: Becoming literate in Morocco.* New York: Cambridge University Press.

Weisner, T. S. (1996). The 5 to 7 transition as an ecocultural project. In A. J. Sameroff & M. M. Haith (Eds.), *The 5 to 7 year shift: The age of reason and responsibility* (pp. 295–326). Chicago: University of Chicago Press.

Wellman, H. M., Phillips, A. T., & Rodriguez, T. (2000). Young children's understanding of perception, desire, and emotion. *Child Development, 71*(4), 895–912.

Wellman, H. M., & Woolley, J. D. (1990). From simple desires to ordinary beliefs: The early development of everyday psychology. *Cognition, 35*(3), 245–275.

Wertsch, J. (1985). *Vygotsky and the social formation of mind.* Cambridge, MA: Harvard University Press.

Whiting, B. B. (1980). Culture and social behavior: A model for the development of social behavior. *Ethos, 8*(2), 95–116.

Whiting, B. B., & Edwards, C. P. (1988). *Children of different worlds: The formation of social behavior.* Cambridge, MA: Harvard University Press.

Whitten, A. (2000). Primate culture and social learning. *Cognitive Science, 24*(3), 477–508.

Wrangham, R. W., McGrew, W. C., de Waal, F. B. M., & Heltne, P. G. (Eds.). (1994). *Chimpanzee cultures.* Cambridge, MA: Harvard University Press.

Wynn, T. G. (1989). *The evolution of spatial competence.* Urbana: University of Illinois Press.

Zur, O., & Gelman, R. (2004, Spring). Young children can add and subtract by predicting and checking. *Early Childhood Research Quarterly, 19*(1), 121–137.

# Conceptual Understanding and Achievements

# CHAPTER 16

# *Conceptual Development*

SUSAN A. GELMAN and CHARLES W. KALISH

*There are more things in heaven and earth, Horatio,*
*Than are dreamt of in your philosophy.*
—HAMLET, ACT I, SCENE V

BACKGROUND AND OVERVIEW  688
Why Conceptual Development Is Important  688
Historical Background  689
Current Approaches to Children's Concepts  690
Organization of This Chapter  693
CONCEPTUAL DIVERSITY  693
Concepts Encoded in Language versus Those
    That Are Not  694
Levels of Categorization  696
Natural Kinds versus Arbitrary Groupings  698
Categories versus Individuals  700
Implications for Children's Concepts  701
CONCEPTS EMBEDDED IN THEORIES  702
Ontology  703
Causation  705
Nonobvious Properties  706
Summary  708

MECHANISMS OF CONCEPTUAL ACQUISITION
    AND CHANGE  709
Associative Mechanisms  710
Similarity  711
Limits of Similarity and Associations  712
Conceptual Placeholders  715
Causal Learning  717
Summary  718
EXPERIENCE AND INDIVIDUAL VARIATION  718
Individual Variation  719
Input  721
CONCLUSION  723
Interleaving Mechanisms  723
Beyond Initial Understandings  724
REFERENCES  724

Concepts organize experience. When an infant smiles at a human face, a 2-year-old points to the family pet and says "Doggie!", a 10-year-old plays a card game, or a scientist identifies a fossil, each is making use of concepts. One of the hallmarks of human cognition is that we organize experience flexibly, at many levels of abstraction, in many competing ways, identifying and reasoning about categories, individuals, properties, and relations. Therefore, the study of concepts is untidy, crosscutting many traditional subfields of psychology.

In this chapter, we take a broad view of concepts. Many theorists equate concepts and categories: Concepts are the mental representations that correspond to

categories of things in the world (Margolis, 1994; Oakes & Rakison, 2003; Smith, 1989). Examples include *dog, toy,* or *physical object.* We agree that categories are fundamental and one of the most important and well-studied conceptual structures. Nonetheless, they are not the only kind of concept available to adults or children. Concepts also include properties (*red, happy*), events or states (*running, being*), individuals (*Mama, Fido*), and abstract ideas (*time, fairness*). Concepts are generally understood to be the building blocks of ideas. To form the thought, "Fido is a happy dog," a child must possess the constituent concepts. At the same time, concepts are embedded in larger knowledge structures, and so cannot be understood wholly as isolated components. One of the goals of this chapter is to provide a framework for thinking about the full range of concepts available, what is currently known about their early emergence and development, and questions that remain for the future.

Preparation of this chapter was supported by NICHD grant RO1 HD36043 from NICHD to the first author. We thank Sandra Waxman for helpful discussions and Deanna Kuhn for detailed comments on an earlier draft.

## BACKGROUND AND OVERVIEW

Although human concepts deeply reflect our experiences of structure in the world, concepts do not reduce fully to world structure. Certainly there is structure to the world, and there are important perceptual clues that correlate with concepts. Rosch (1978) showed that object categories capture feature clusters; for example, the distinction between birds and mammals is over-determined: Birds (generally) have wings, feathers, claws, and beaks, whereas mammals (generally) have legs, fur, toes/hooves, and mouths. Studying how concepts relate to structure present in the world is a critically important topic. It would be a mistake, however, to equate concepts with experience. Instead, concepts are *interpretations* of experience. Piaget illustrated this vividly by showing us how different interpretations of even mundane experiences are possible: What we identify as the same object over time could instead be construed as a series of distinct objects; what we view as unthinking and inert (such as a stone) could instead be construed as living and feeling.

A related point is that concept learning includes a crucial inductive component. A concept extends beyond an instance presented at a given point in time and includes other instances (in the case of categories) or other manifestations over time (in the case of individuals). One of the inductive problems children face is how to extend a concept to novel instances (e.g., if I tell you that this is a hamster, how do you decide what other instances are also hamsters?). Another inductive problem that children face is figuring out when to use concepts. If a child sees her pet hamster eating a lettuce leaf, this observation becomes a conceptual problem: Is this an idiosyncratic event, or an event that can be applied to future instances? If the latter, has she learned something about her hamster, about hamsters in general, or about animals in general? Thus, another theme of the chapter will be that concepts entail active inductive processes and that human heuristics, predispositions, frameworks, and biases influence the form of concepts that children develop.

### Why Conceptual Development Is Important

Concepts play an important role in children's cognition. Children's memory, reasoning, problem solving, and word-learning all powerfully reflect their concepts (Bruner, Olver, & Greenfield, 1966; Rakison & Oakes,

2003). As numerous scholars have noted, concepts serve at least two critical functions: They are an efficient means of representing and storing experience (obviating the need to track each and every individual interaction or encounter), and they encourage people to extend knowledge and learn about the world by means of inductive inferences (e.g., Smith, 1989). By studying concepts, we learn about the representation of experience and about reasoning by induction.

Studies of conceptual development are also important for providing a detailed portrait of children's knowledge and beliefs about the world. Certain concepts are themselves basic and far-reaching in their consequences. Consider the concept of animacy (Gelman & Opfer, 2002). The distinction between animate and inanimate arises early in infancy (Rakison & Poulin-Dubois, 2001), appears to have neurophysiological correlates (Caramazza & Shelton, 1998), is cross-culturally uniform (Atran, 1999), and is central to a broad array of more complex understandings, including causal interpretations of action (Spelke, Phillips, & Woodward, 1995), attributions of mental states (Baron-Cohen, 1995), and attributions of biological processes (Carey, 1985). Indeed, a creature that was incapable of distinguishing animate from inanimate would be severely impaired. Oliver Sacks (1985) describes a real-life example of a man who could not identify things as animate or inanimate on the basis of visual perception, thus, for example, mistaking his wife for a hat (and attempting to place her head on his own).

Equally important, the study of concepts allows one to examine issues at the heart of the study of cognitive development: Are there innate concepts? Are cognitive systems modular? Can complex concepts emerge out of perceptually based associative learning mechanisms? How domain-general versus domain-specific is human cognition? Does children's thinking undergo qualitative reorganizations with age? These questions are not unique to the study of conceptual development, but studying conceptual development can provide unique insights into these questions.

Finally, understanding children's concepts has implications for many other developmental issues, both basic and applied. Three examples provide a flavor. First, children's stereotyping of social categories (such as caste, gender, or race) is rooted in children's concepts, and undergoes predictable developmental patterns as a function of developmental changes in children's concepts (Hirschfeld, 1996; Maccoby, 1998; Martin & Ruble,

2004). A second example, in the area of motivation and school achievement, concerns children's concepts of intelligence. Children who view intelligence as fixed and unchanging treat corrective feedback as evidence of failure, and lose motivation in the face of it. In contrast, children who view intelligence as flexible and changing treat feedback as information about where they can direct their efforts, and work harder in the face of it (Dweck, 1999). There appear to be cultural differences in the models of intelligence that are most endorsed, with more fixed, essentialist views in the United States, and more flexible, effort-based views in China and Japan (Stevenson & Stigler, 1992). As a third example, in the field of education, it is now generally recognized that providing children with appropriate instruction requires first understanding their conceptual errors, in order to revise misconceptions rather than superimpose new ways of understanding on these misconceptions (Carey, 1986). The need to do so becomes evident when trying to teach children (and adults!) evolutionary theory. Children first need to *unlearn* that categories are stable, unchanging, and fixed, before they can fully grasp that species can evolve (Evans, 2000; Mayr, 1991; Slotta, Chi, & Joram, 1995).

## Historical Background

As with so much of cognitive development, Piaget's work on concepts provides a useful initial framework (Inhelder & Piaget, 1964). In his view, concepts can be considered from two perspectives, either as logical structures or as components of a larger knowledge system. The first perspective focuses on form; the second focuses on content. In considering *logical structures,* Piaget assumed a strict and idealized characterization of what constitutes a true concept. In his view, defining features determine membership in a category. Thus, the intension of a concept (the rules or definition for inclusion) determines the extension of a concept (which things are classified into the category). When sorting geometric shapes, an adult may decide to put all the round shapes in one set, all the square shapes in another set, and so on. These "definitions" (round, square, etc.) determine the groupings. In contrast, a 3-year-old may switch rules repeatedly over time, first noting shape similarity, then noting color, then the holistic pattern obtained by spatial alignment of two shapes, and so on. Because young children do not successfully coordinate intension and extension, they are

said not to form true concepts. Piaget (1970) instead proposed a series of qualitative reorganizations that constituted progressive developmental stages. This characterization has been challenged (see, e.g., R. Gelman & Baillargeon, 1983), although the question of what form concepts take (their logical structure) is an enduring and fundamental one.

As *part of larger knowledge systems,* concepts reflect children's knowledge and understanding of the world (Piaget, 1929). Piaget's work in this area embodies a tension between focusing on general principles that govern the nature of children's concepts, and in-depth studies of children's knowledge and belief systems. For years, researchers avoided studying conceptual systems in detail; these were viewed as contingent, accumulations of facts, not revealing of deeper developmental principles. Why bother to learn what children know about any particular topic, if that knowledge is one tiny portion of the encyclopedic knowledge they are eventually to gain, and if gaining that knowledge is contingent on particular, idiosyncratic experiences? The answer, as we will see, is that knowledge about particular domains may turn out to be foundational, both in the sense of forming a basis for further knowledge, and in the sense of being robust across varying cultural contexts.

A tension between a focus on form versus content continues to the present day. The adult concept acquisition literature has long been an important source of theory and motivation for work with children, and has often focused on conceptual form. For example, prototypes, scripts, hierarchical classification, and exemplar models are all fruitful examples of how research with adults inspired and informed work with children (Eimas & Quinn, 1994; Johnson, Scott, & Mervis, 1997; Mandler & McDonough, 2000; Markman, 1989). Notably, this work tends to focus on form to the exclusion of content.

In the past, research on adult concepts often served as a contrast to developmental studies: Whatever it was that adults have, children were thought not to have. Thus, a whole host of developmental dichotomies were proposed: Children are perceptual, adults are conceptual; children are thematic, adults are taxonomic; children are concrete, adults are abstract (see Bruner et al., 1966; Inhelder & Piaget, 1964; Vygotsky, 1934/1962; Werner & Kaplan, 1963). These concepts acknowledged content in broad strokes only. As reviewed in detail later in this chapter, these contrasts are too simple, at least by the time children reach preschool age (i.e., by

2.5 years), if not earlier (Mandler, 2004). Preschool children consider an impressive range of cues, features, and conceptual structures. To characterize young children as perceptual would ignore their capacity to reason about intentions, number, and causation (R. Gelman & Williams, 1998). To characterize them as thematic would disregard the ease with which children extend novel words on the basis of shared features (Balaban & Waxman, 1997; Blanchet, Dunham, & Dunham, 2001; Waxman & Namy, 1997)—as well as the frequency with which adults rely on thematic relations (Lin & Murphy, 2001). To characterize children as concrete would overlook their capacity to talk and reason about abstract kinds of things (S. A. Gelman, 2003; Prasada, 2000; see also Uttal, Liu, & DeLoache, 1999, for evidence that concrete representations can at times limit—rather than scaffold—children's understanding of abstract concepts).

More recently, there has been a renewed focus on conceptual content in children and adults, with more reciprocal links between adult and child studies. There is much evidence that for both adults and children, concepts are influenced by knowledge-rich naive theories and explanatory models and cannot be characterized by form or structure alone (Keil, 1989; see Murphy, 2002, for review; Murphy & Medin, 1985; Rips & Collins, 1993). The past 30 years of research in developmental psychology have revealed surprisingly sophisticated domain-specific competencies in infancy and early childhood, in reasoning about physical objects, mental states, and biological processes (Wellman & S. A. Gelman, 1998). Young infants seem to have well-formed and fairly elaborate conceptual systems. In contrast to the blooming, buzzing confusion William James hypothesized in infancy, the world of the infant seems remarkably similar to that of adults.

Likewise, preschool children learn words with impressive speed. The oft-cited statistic, initially noted by Carey (1978), is that children between 18 months and 6 years of age learn on average one new word every waking hour. This accomplishment is particularly impressive given the well-known inductive problem children face: meanings are not simply sitting out there but rather need to be inferred from a complex set of cues (Quine, 1960; Waxman & Lidz, Chapter 7, this *Handbook,* this volume; Woodward & Markman, 1998). Bloom (2000) notes that this rate of word learning is not special to the preschool period, but is ever increasing (up to about

40,000 words by age 10), until at some point in adolescence, it reaches a plateau. This stunning achievement alone implies a wealth of corresponding concepts.

Conceptual development during childhood is profound. The course of concept acquisition is not random or piecemeal; the premise of conceptual development is that there are important regularities. Historically, researchers have focused on *formal* changes over development, such that children's concepts may differ from adults' in structural ways (e.g., from global to analytic, from thematic to taxonomic). Although this perspective continues to guide research, a considerable body of work now focuses on the *content* of children's concepts. One reason is that formal models of adult concepts have not fared as well as initially hoped (Carey, 1982; Murphy, 2002; Rosch, 1978). A second reason is that conceptual content appears to affect the acquisition of new concepts, so that what people know affects what they can learn. This perspective is most clearly articulated in theory-based accounts of concepts (Carey, 1985; Keil, 1989; Murphy & Medin, 1985). Much of conceptual development may be due not to structural changes in the nature of concepts but to the network of existing beliefs within which new concepts must fit (Carey, 1985).

## Current Approaches to Children's Concepts

There are three broad theoretical approaches to understanding concept acquisition, dating back to long-standing philosophical debates: nativist, empiricist, and naive theory approaches.

### *Nativist Approaches*

Nativist approaches come in all shapes and sizes. Indeed, there are as many nativist approaches as there are developmental approaches, for the simple reason that any theory of development assumes *some* innate capacities (Wanner & Gleitman, 1983). Even under the most domain-general and empiricist of approaches, children must have innate capacities (e.g., representational abilities, associational capacities). The questions that are under debate are how richly specified and detailed these innate capacities are, the variability of the resulting concepts across backgrounds and contexts, and the degree to which these capacities are open to modification from the environment. Accounts range from innate attentional biases due to perceptual limits in the infant (Mandler, 2004), to the possibility of innate concepts of *cause, animate,* and so on. (Spelke, 1994), to the extreme claim that all lexicalized concepts are innate (including *dog, cup, car;* Fodor, 1981). As Bates (1999) put it, with a focus on language development:

> The debate today . . . is not about nature versus nurture, but about the "nature of nature," that is, whether language is something that we do with an inborn language device, or whether it is the product of (innate) abilities that are not specific to language.

The same could be said of conceptual development: Are there innate concepts of a particular content or type (e.g., innate concepts of "animacy"), or rather more general innate capacities that can give rise to concepts?

Modular theories posit strong, innately specified, domain-specific constraints on conceptual acquisition and change. One of the most well-worked-out arguments for modularity comes from the domain of language, specifically, syntax:

> Evidence for the status of syntax as a module was its innate, biologically driven character—evident in all and only humans; its neurological localization and breakdown—the selective impairment of syntactic competence in some forms of brain damage; its rapid acquisition in the face of meager developmental data—syntactic categories of great abstraction, such as verb or subject, are easily acquired by small children faced with impoverished input; and the presence of critical periods and maturational timetables. (Pinker, 1994; Wellman & Gelman, 1998, p. 527)

Although it is widely accepted that human vision is modular (Marr, 1982), and often accepted that modularity aptly characterizes language (but see Tomasello, Chapter 6, this *Handbook,* this volume, for a critique of this view), more debatable is the suggestion that higher-level cognitive processes can be captured in this way (e.g., Elman et al., 1996). Evolutionary psychologists propose that an array of cognitive capacities is modularized, including reasoning about biological taxonomies, mate selection, and social exchange (Cosmides & Tooby, 2002; Pinker, 1994). They characterize cognitive modules as innately specified, and as impervious to revision. Thus, modules (in this view) are mandatory in their processing of environmental inputs: Experience provides inputs, and these inputs are represented in a mandatory, nonrevisable manner.

However, modularity is only one extreme in a continuum of innate structures. Innate conceptual structure may also be characterized as a set of skeletal principles (R. Gelman & Williams, 1998) or biases that provide initial conditions for conceptual development but may be modified, and even superseded, during development (Gopnik, Meltzoff, & Kuhl, 1999). Skeletal principles would be compatible with both associationist and theory-based accounts of conceptual development. R. Gelman (2002) proposes a "rationalist-constructivist" approach, in which innate skeletal principles get elaborated with experience and development.

### Empiricist Approaches

According to empiricism, knowledge derives from our senses. Concepts are therefore either direct representations of perceptual/sensory experience, or combinations of such experiences. The two-pronged argument against nativism is that conceptual structure may be derived from input via basic learning mechanisms and that experiential variation produces substantive conceptual variability. Theories of similarity provide formal accounts of concept representation and acquisition (see Hahn & Ramscar, 2001; Rakison & Oakes, 2003). The central focus of this work is on processes of comparison, association, and composition. How does the learner combine diverse experiences to arrive at a summary representation of a concept? The processes involved tend to be general ones; it is the structural relations that matter, not the content, domain, or specific features. Several researchers have argued that children's conceptual development is largely based on processes of similarity (Jones & L. B. Smith, 2002; Sloutsky, 2003). The challenge for empiricist accounts of development is to explain how the rich and complex set of adult concepts is produced by the operation of basic learning mechanisms over a reduced set of initial representations.

How might this work in development? L. B. Smith, Jones, and Landau (1996) suggest that a child could learn the distinction between count and mass nouns by noting that count nouns are uttered in the presence of consistent shapes (e.g., "This is *a book*" in the presence of rectangular solids; "This is *a banana*" in the presence of crescents), whereas mass nouns are uttered in the presence of consistent colors and textures (e.g., "This is *some rice*" in the presence of white, sticky stuff; "This is *some sand*" in the presence of tan, granular stuff). By tracking the empirical regularities of linguistic form and perceptual cues, children learn familiar words and build up expectations about novel words.

Empiricist approaches have had a resurgence in recent years, in part because it has been demonstrated that infants can track low-level statistical cues with much greater accuracy than had been thought (Baldwin, Baird, & Saylor, 2001; Saffran, Aslin, & Newport, 1996), and in part because new empiricist models provide a more detailed and realistic appreciation of children's concepts (Sloutsky & Fisher, 2004; Yoshida & Smith, 2003). Empiricism faces the following major issues: How much can it account for, and (relatedly) how great a challenge or contrast does it provide to other approaches, such as the naive theory approach? We return to empiricism later in the chapter, when we consider mechanisms of conceptual acquisition and change.

### Naive Theory Approaches

Naive theory approaches come in a wide variety, but all assume that children construct something like naive or commonsense theories in which concepts are embedded. The shared commitment is to some inferential processes of conceptual development. Roughly, concepts are acquired based on their meaningful relations with existing concepts and beliefs. In most cases, these inferential processes are seen as supplements to either nativist or associationist mechanisms, or both. Theory-based views are compatible with some amount of innate structure. The claim, however, is that innate structure is supplemented and revised in the face of evidence and attempts to explain and make predictions. Nature may provide initial conditions or general constraints, but there is room for substantial conceptual development and change (R. Gelman, 2002). Theory-based views also admit processes of association-based learning (S. A. Gelman & Medin, 1993; Keil, Smith, Simons, & Levin, 1998). Intuitive theories connect with data. People experience surprising outcomes, notice new connections, and realize failures of predictions. Associations are therefore important data for building theories.

Theory-based views are often taken as committed to the position that children are little scientists (or scientists are big children, Gopnik et al., 1999). Different strands of theory-based approaches take this connection more or less literally, though all acknowledge important differences between scientists and children in the *process* of constructing theories (see Gopnik & Wellman,

1994). The basic point may be that just as scientists have means of forming new concepts that go beyond maturation and association learning, so, too, do laypeople—including children. A way of posing the central research question for theory-based approaches is to ask whether the kinds of thinking demonstrated by scientists and other experts are unprecedented in everyday experience, or whether such "advanced" forms of thinking are somewhat continuous with basic processes of conceptual development. Research in the field often takes the form of demonstrating that associationist or maturational processes are not sufficient to account for some aspect of cognitive development, and thus theory-building must be admitted.

One way to characterize theory approaches is to review briefly relevant findings in the adult concept literature. How adults incorporate different features into their category judgments varies, depending on their theories about the domain (Wisniewski, 1995; Wisniewski & Medin, 1994). The probability of accepting novel instances as category members is also dependent on theoretical beliefs rather than statistical correlations alone (Medin & Shoben, 1988). Thus, in some cases a property equally true of two different concepts is more central to one than the other (e.g., the property *curved* is more central to boomerangs than to bananas, even though in all our prior experience, curved applies equally often to both concepts). There is also evidence that adults' ability to categorize successfully is intimately tied to the kinds of explanations they can generate. Murphy and his colleagues have designed experiments in which subjects form their own concepts of unfamiliar items (such as underwater dwelling or floating house) and have varied only whether the features of the items could be potentially linked by an explanatory scheme. In their results, categories that included features that were related and linked to a theme were learned much faster than those with unrelated features (Murphy & Allopenna, 1994). In general, people appear to benefit by their ability to form concepts in which features are linked in sensible causal frameworks.

A further crucial aspect of the theory approach is the assumption that conceptual change entails more-or-less radical reorganizations. The model for conceptual change is theory change in science (Smith, Carey, & Wiser, 1985). Just as science undergoes revolutions that introduce new concepts and mental organizations, so too, do children during normal development. The claim is that initial structures can be modified; they provide a starting point for conceptual development but not absolute limits.

The theory view does not *replace* approaches that argue people attend to online, at-hand statistical information: collation of features, salience, similarity, prototypes, exemplars, and the like; instead, it argues for their insufficiency. Prototypes are accurate descriptions of the information people use to identify category instances on many tasks (E. Smith & Medin, 1981). A wealth of evidence demonstrates that people classify robins (prototypical bird) more rapidly than penguins (atypical bird), which typicality influences the kinds of sentences people generate, and so on (Rosch, 1978). Importantly, however, prototype accounts do not provide the full story. Is a penguin any less a bird than a robin? Some researchers have argued it is not—that typicality and category membership are independent judgments that can be dissociated (Diesendruck & S. A. Gelman, 1999; Kalish, 1995; Rips & Collins, 1993). Later in this chapter, we will return to the theme that concepts are hybrids, incorporating both theory and similarity (Keil et al., 1998; Murphy, 2002).

### Approach in This Chapter

In this chapter, we assume a naive theory approach, as we find that it best accounts for the widest range of evidence. However, ideas from both nativist and empiricist traditions continue to have important influences. The mapping between approaches and mechanisms is neither simple nor clear-cut. The theory approach assumes some innate starting-points (Carey & Spelke, 1994) as well as the importance of associative mechanisms. Likewise, some (though not all) who espouse an empiricist or associationist approach recognize the need for innate constraints to get the system off the ground (Rakison, 2003a). And anyone who posits innate mechanisms also acknowledges the need for appropriate environmental input and support, as well as the mechanisms to enable environmental learning (Chomsky, 1975). We find most merit in a framework that assumes some role for each of these approaches. Specifically, the theory approach, which we endorse, assumes (a) some important innate frameworks to give children a conceptual grounding, (b) sophisticated associationist and statistical learning procedures to acquire new information and detect regularities in the environment, and (c) theory-building impulses and ca-

pacities, to enable fundamental reorganizations of the input over developmental time.

### Organization of This Chapter

The remainder of this chapter is organized around three central themes: *conceptual diversity, concepts embedded in theories,* and *mechanisms of conceptual acquisition and change.* First, we discuss the case for conceptual diversity, and its importance to understanding the vast literature on children's concepts. Concepts are not all alike, and concept learning is not a single, unitary process. Serious attention to conceptual variation promises to shed light on developmental regularities. Conversely, focusing on only one sort of concept can lead to a skewed portrait of what concept learning entails and what children bring to the task. Second, we make the case that at least by the time children are able to speak, a good portion of their concepts are embedded in theories. Third, we consider possible mechanisms of conceptual acquisition and change. Following consideration of these three major themes, we raise questions that to date have received rather less attention, though the questions are important and deserving of more focused research. In a section titled "Experience and Individual Variation," we consider variation due to individual differences and expertise, as well as the nature of the input children receive.

Any treatment of concepts must be selective. This chapter includes relatively little about concepts of mind, space, or number. These concepts are of fundamental importance in any consideration of children's thought, but they receive fuller treatment elsewhere in this *Handbook.* We also do not attempt to review the vast literature on concepts in infancy (see Cohen & Cashon, Chapter 5, this *Handbook,* this volume), although selected examples from the infancy literature are included, as relevant.

## CONCEPTUAL DIVERSITY

What is involved in learning a concept? This question is difficult to answer in part because not all concepts are alike. How college students acquire a concept of "red triangles" in a classic verbal learning experiment of the 1950s would appear to differ in important ways from how infants acquire a concept of animacy. Although there are innumerable ways to divide up concepts, many of them are doubtless irrelevant to processes of acquisition (e.g., the concepts "cat" and "dog" differ from each other but are learned in much the same way). In this section, we lay out some of the distinctions that are likely to have broad theoretical significance.

At minimum, the concepts children learn in the first few years of life include (but are not limited to):

- Concepts corresponding to words, including not just concrete nouns (dog, cookie, girl) but also mass nouns (water, sand), abstract nouns (furniture, toys), collective nouns (family, army), verbs (jump, think), adjectives (purple, good, little, happy, unfair, alive), and a range of other word types (three, in, because, all, mine)
- Concepts reflected in grammatical usage (e.g., singular versus plural; gender); "covert categories" (Whorf, 1956)
- Ontological distinctions that may or may not be encoded in language but lead to important predictions (e.g., animate versus inanimate entities)
- Concepts for individuals (including significant people or animals, as well as individual objects such as a favorite blanket or even a particular piece of candy)
- Systems for organizing concepts with respect to one another (e.g., hierarchies; scripts)

Concepts vary from one another in content (e.g., natural kinds versus artifacts; individuals versus kind), process (e.g., learned explicitly in school versus implicitly in ordinary interactions versus learned by overhearing), structure (e.g., basic versus superordinate level), and function (e.g., used for quick identification versus used for making inductive inferences). Strikingly, there are studies of each of these kinds of concepts in the cognitive development literature, often reaching different conclusions about children's skills and abilities.

We review this conceptual variety by considering several key contrasts among concepts. Our criteria for including a contrast are that it has far-reaching implications for how children reason and that there are relevant developmental data. Specifically, we consider concepts encoded in language versus those that are not encoded in language; object concepts versus relational concepts; concepts at different levels of abstraction; and natural kinds versus arbitrary groupings. In no case are we proposing developmental dichotomies (e.g., children can't do X but they can do Y). Rather, children have access to

multiple sorts of concepts, but the nature of the concept influences processing. There are many other important distinctions in the literature that we do not cover because of space limitations (e.g., scientific versus spontaneous concepts, Vygotsky, 1934/1962; object versus relational concepts, Bornstein et al., 2004, Gentner, 1982; Tardif, 1996; classes versus collections, Markman, 1989).

## Concepts Encoded in Language versus Those That Are Not

Many concepts correspond to a word in a language (e.g., *shoes*), whereas others do not (e.g., objects that begin with the letter *s*). The former are also called "lexicalized" concepts. Generally, we can assume that lexicalized concepts have some importance to speakers of the language: They are shared by a community, remembered over time, and passed down from one generation to the next. They are not simply a passing fancy in the mind of a specific individual. However, the converse is not true; important concepts are not necessarily lexicalized. For example, the concept *living thing* is rarely lexicalized across the world's languages (Waxman, in press).

There has been an upswing in research on the role of language in conceptual development (e.g., Bowerman & Levinson, 2001; Gentner & Goldin-Meadow, 2003). A classic question is how language changes or influences the nature of a concept. Piaget's proposal that language is simply a vehicle for thought is no longer tenable. Nor do concepts require a conventional language system: Witness the impressive conceptual abilities of preverbal infants, nonhuman primates, and deaf children with no language input (Cohen & Cashon, Chapter 5, this *Handbook,* this volume; Goldin-Meadow, 2003; Tomasello, 1999).

Rather, we must ask, What is the nature of the relation between words and concepts, and how are they coordinated in development? The question is particularly important from a developmental perspective, as language is an important means of expressing concepts.

The finding that speakers of different languages possess different concepts, particularly early in development, provides important evidence on this question. One example comes from the spatial domain. Whereas English distinguishes containment (*in*) versus support (*on*) relations, Korean distinguishes loose-fitting containment (*nehta*) versus tight-fitting containment (*kkita*). The relevant developmental evidence is that children, from their earliest word productions, use spatial language in a manner that conforms to the system presented by their language (Bowerman & Choi, 2003). Thus, English-speaking children and Korean-speaking children use spatial terms in cross-cutting ways, thereby apparently demonstrating contrasting conceptual frameworks.

A question raised by this work is whether the speakers of the two languages have acquired only the language-relevant system (i.e., support for language influencing initial concepts), or instead whether they have access to a wider range of spatial relations, including those of the other language, but choose to use only the conventional ones when talking because language is a conventional system. The latter is a weaker claim, according to which language influences "thinking for speaking" (Slobin, 1996). Recent work with adults provides more support for the first interpretation. When English-speaking adults are given a task that requires them to group spatial relations in the Korean way (i.e., loose- versus tight-fitting), they have great difficulty (McDonough, Choi, & Mandler, 2003). Interestingly, 5-month-old infants exposed to English were able to categorize both contrasts (Hespos & Spelke, 2004). It appears that children are initially open to a wider range of conceptual possibilities that become narrowed as a function of language experience (see Werker & Desjardins, 1995, for an analogous finding in speech perception).

In any case, these data suggest that concepts that were once thought to be innate (e.g., in, on) turn out to be language-specific, thereby arguing against there being a small set of universal primitives—at least in this domain. And children from their earliest word-learning acquire the spatial concepts provided by their language, not the spatial concepts provided by some universal conceptual set.

Relatedly, speakers of different languages seem to notice different aspects of experience, and to draw conceptual boundaries differently from one another. Lucy (1996; Lucy & Gaskins, 2003) studied speakers of Yucatec Mayan, who use a classifier system such that different-shaped things can receive the same name but with a different classifier attached. In Yucatec, the word for banana, banana leaf, and banana tree are all the same root word, varying only in the classifier. This pattern contrasts with the English system of naming, for which shape is a fairly good predictor of how a count noun is used (e.g., bananas are all crescent-shaped; trees are all roughly a certain shape). Correspondingly, when asked to group objects on the basis of either shape or substance in a nonlinguistic sorting task, English speakers are more likely to use shape, whereas Yucatec Mayan speakers are more likely to use substance. Surprisingly, however, this differentiation does not appear until somewhere between 7 and 9 years of age, suggesting that perhaps metalinguistic awareness of the language pattern is required for the effect.

Other examples of language influences on children's concepts can be found in the work of Imai and Gentner (1997) and Yoshida and Smith (2003), both of whom find that Japanese-speaking children draw the boundary between objects and substances differently than do English-speaking children. Whereas both English and Japanese speaking children agree that a complex object (such as a clock) is an individual and a continuous boundless mass (such as milk) is a substance, they differ when it comes to simple objects. A molded piece of plastic, for example, would be an object for the English speaker but a substance for the Japanese speaker. These findings do not suggest radically different ontologies for speakers of English and Japanese, but rather subtle effects at the margins.

A difficult question remains: Can language effect change or just direct attention? For example, can language create concepts that weren't there to begin with? Or does language serve to draw attention and highlight available concepts? Boroditsky (2001) shows that, for adults, time concepts in Chinese are conceptualized differently than time concepts in English, in ways that can be traced to differences in how English and Chinese speakers *talk* about time (either horizontally or vertically, respectively). However, she also finds that these differences can be readily reversed with a simple priming task, thus suggesting that the language effects are not deeply entrenched.

The difficulty in determining the effects of language can be seen by considering the effects of labeling on inductive inferences. Some have proposed that hearing the word *bird* for a wide variety of dissimilar birds (hummingbirds, eagles, ostriches) signals to the child that something other than surface similarity must bind these instances together (Hallett, 1991; Mayr, 1991). In this view, labels have a powerful causal force in directing children to look for underlying similarities that category members share. Consistent with this view, experimental work with children demonstrates that they draw more inferences to items that share a label than to instances that do not (S. A. Gelman & Markman, 1986; Welder &

Graham, 2001) and more generally respond differently to items that are labeled than to items that are not (Markman & Hutchinson, 1984; Waxman & Markow, 1995; Xu, 1999). Moreover, hearing a label for a concept provokes a more stable, immutable construal (e.g., a person who is "a carrot-eater" is assumed to eat carrots more consistently and persistently than someone who "eats carrots whenever she can"; S. A. Gelman & Heyman, 1999).

However, these findings do not unambiguously locate the source of the labeling effect. Is the relevant factor the label per se, or does the label work as a cue because it activates other assumptions, such as essentialism? We would argue the latter (see S. A. Gelman, 2003, for more extended discussion). A problem with assigning too central a role to language is that not all names promote inductive inferences. Children learn homonyms (Lily as a name versus lily as a flower), adjectives (sleepy), and nonkind nouns (passenger; pet), and these words do not seem to work in the same way as category labels such as bird or carrot-eater. When learning novel words, children do not automatically assume that the words promote inferences, if perceptual cues compete (Davidson & Gelman, 1990). A striking example of children's willingness to interpret a word for two dissimilar things as homonyms came from a 3-year-old who remarked: "Isn't it funny—'chicken' sounds just like 'chicken'"— not realizing that the bird and the food were indeed manifestations of the same kind. The point here is that sameness of label did not by itself command the inference that the instances shared deeper commonalities.

These examples suggest that language may provide important cues to children regarding their concepts, without necessarily being the mechanism by which concepts first emerge. If sameness of label is to convey underlying sameness, children must first have the capacity to understand that appearances can be deceiving. Armed with such an understanding, naming practices could provide important information to children about the structure of concepts. However, that initial understanding must already be in place for children to benefit from labeling.

Despite this caveat, there is reason to suspect that language may play a broader role in conceptual change. Spelke (2003) argues that language may provide a mechanism for acquiring concepts that go beyond those innately specified. She notes that innate concepts in humans are highly similar to and overlap with innate concepts in other species: object constancy, number

tracking, and so on. What seems to distinguish humans from nonhuman species is the ease with which we combine concepts across domains. In navigating space, we can combine geometric concepts (e.g., "to the left") with nongeometric concepts (e.g., "blue") to arrive at novel combinations ("to the left of the blue wall"). Strikingly, preverbal infants and nonhuman animals seem to lack the ability to construct such cross-domain concepts. When faced with a task that requires this sort of conceptual combination, only language-using humans can solve it. In further studies, Spelke has found that manipulating the use of language (either training children on a new linguistic expression or preventing internal or external use of language in adults) directly affects a person's capacity to use these combinations. She uses this same model to explain conceptual change in the realm of number. Language provides only a limited degree of flexibility, however, as the constituent concepts of a linguistically mediated combination must be initially established within an innate module.

## Levels of Categorization

Object concepts are universally organized into hierarchical systems of classification possessing 3 to 5 levels, in which an intermediate, "basic" level of abstraction is most commonly used by adults (Rosch, 1978). One of the most robust and well-studied findings regarding concepts in the 1970s and 1980s concerned the differences in processing and development of different levels of abstraction for concepts in a hierarchy. Concepts at a basic level of generality are learned first (Mervis & Crisafi, 1982). Children acquire the label *dog* before *collie* or *animal*. It is probably not coincidental that parents tend to label objects at the basic level (Shipley, Kuhn, & Madden, 1983). It is at the basic-level that children prefer to categorize and extend novel labels (Golinkoff, Shuff-Bailey, Olguin, & Ruan, 1995; Waxman, Lynch, Carsey, & Baer, 1997). Shown a picture of a collie and told it is a *dax,* children assume other dogs are daxes, rather than extending the label to all animals, or restricting it to only collies.

Children do acquire concepts at superordinate and subordinate levels, but such concepts may require special learning conditions (but see Callanan, 1989; Tenenbaum & Xu, 2000). Exposure to multiple distinct instances supports acquisition of superordinates (hearing a dog and a cat both called dax, Liu, Golinkoff, & Sak, 2001). Providing a novel label also encourages superordinate classification (Waxman & Gelman, 1986). Contrasts can support subordinate classification (Waxman & Namy, 1997). Domain knowledge also affects levels of categorization. Individuals with greater expertise are more likely to focus on subordinate level categories (Tanaka & Taylor, 1991); this includes child experts (Johnson & Eilers, 1998). When a single feature is recognized or important, young children will use that feature to make a subordinate level distinction (Waxman, Shipley, & Shepperson, 1991).

The finding of a basic-level advantage suggests a convergence among several distinct sources of evidence, including universal patterns of naming in language, processing patterns in adults, and developmental patterns of acquisition—implying the existence of common principles at work underlying all these diverse findings. The result is of interest because it demonstrates that children are not resolutely concrete in their first concepts. If they were, then children would start out with the most specific level of categorization (e.g., collie); instead, they seem to prefer categories at a moderately abstract level (e.g., dog).

However, despite the primacy of a basic level in language, there is controversy regarding whether children's first (nonlinguistic) concepts are also at this level. Mandler and McDonough (2000) find evidence that a global level of categorization emerges first. The global level is broader than the basic level. It might be something along the lines of *land animal,* including cats, dogs, horses, and pigs. The researchers use a generalized imitation technique, in which a researcher models a particular action with a given object (e.g., giving a toy dog a drink from a cup), then gives the child an opportunity to model that action on either or both of a pair of additional objects (e.g., a different dog and a cat, or a bird and an airplane). In an important series of studies with 14-month-olds, Mandler and McDonough found that infants treated members of different basic-level categories as equivalent, as long as they were within the same global category (either animals or vehicles). So, for example, 14-month-olds generalized drinking from a dog to a cat, a bird, and even an anteater (which was unfamiliar). They did not generalize across domains: They did not generalize drinking from a dog to a vehicle, either familiar, such as a car, or unfamiliar, such as a forklift. Mandler and McDonough (1998) obtained similar results with 9- and 11-month-olds. They concluded that 14-month-olds generally do not yet subdivide the domains of animals and vehicles into finer-grained categories (Mandler & McDonough, 1996, p. 331).

A potential problem for the global level argument is that much younger infants appear to have something like basic level concepts available to them. Quinn and his colleagues find that infants about 3 to 4 months of age demonstrate great facility in distinguishing different basic level categories, such as dogs versus cats (Eimas & Quinn, 1994). Babies make use of perceptual cues in the form of featural similarities to identify same-category instances (Quinn, Bhatt, Brush, Grimes, & Sharpnack, 2002). By 4 months of age, infants can form categorical representations of images of cats and dogs (Quinn, Eimas, & Tarr, 2001). However, Mandler (2004) argues that an important difference is that the basic-level categories shown by infants are represented at a perceptual level only, and not a conceptual level. These representations are based on perceptions of general contour information. For infants, head shape seems particularly salient. Infants are also highly sensitive to perceptual features and correlations among them (Bhatt, Wilk, & Hill, 2004; Younger, 1990). In contrast, Mandler and McDonough argue that the global-level advantage emerges on tasks that require children to process instances in a more active (arguably more conceptual) way: either sequential touching of objects, or induction of a novel property. Mandler and McDonough's results demonstrate several important findings: Even infants are not limited to basic-level categories but instead have access to broader categories; infants' inductive inferences need not conform to perceptual groupings; and inductive inferences yield different results from other classification tasks.

Where the jury is still out, however, is whether global categories are somehow privileged for young children, and conversely, whether basic-level categories are inaccessible to young children for induction. Several additional results would suggest that basic-level categories are also accessible even in infancy. By 9 to 12 months of age, infants draw novel inferences from one object to another of the same kind, when the property is distinctive to that sort of thing (e.g., turning a special kind of can upside-down to make a funny sound) (Baldwin, Markman, & Melartin, 1993). Twelve-month-olds also treat different basic-level categories (e.g., cup, duck, car, bottle) as distinct (Xu & Carey, 1996). Waxman and Markow (1995) found basic-level categorization in 12-month-olds, using the same task Mandler and McDonough (1993) had used. Finally, children's first words appear by about 13 months of age, and typically include names for basic-level categories (such as *dog, cracker,* or *ball*; K. Nelson, 1973). Also, children between 13 and 18 months are generally quite good at making at least one sort of category-based inference: reporting the distinctive sounds made by different animal kinds (e.g., cow says "moo"; dog says "woof-woof"). Perhaps the use of language on some of these tasks scaffolds children and permits use of a basic-level category earlier than on a nonlinguistic task.

A further possibility is that the global categories studied by Mandler et al. may in part reflect children's use of broader ontological categories (e.g., animate versus inanimate). Consider that one of the major pieces of evidence for global categories is that toddlers generalize from one animal to another, but not from an animal to a vehicle. If we focus on within-category similarity, this looks like a global category (the infant has formed a category that includes both dogs and cats). Yet if we focus on the between-category contrast, this looks like an ontological category (the infant has formed a contrast between animate and inanimate things). As noted years ago by Rosch (1978), both within-category similarity and between-category differences are relevant in considering the nature of a classification. As can be seen in Figure 16.1, depending on the contrast category selected, the same classification (e.g., Cats + Dogs) could

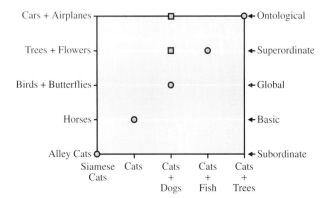

**Figure 16.1**  Levels of contrast as a function of within-category similarity and between-category difference. *Note:* Circles indicate contrasts in which within-category similarity occurs at the same level of abstraction as between-category similarity (e.g., cats and horses are basic-level categories, and the contrast between them represents a basic-level contrast). Squares indicate contrasts in which there is a mismatch between within-category similarity (for at least one category) and between-category similarity (e.g., cats + dogs and cars + airplanes are global categories, but the distinction between cats + dogs and cars + airplanes is an ontological distinction).

be evidence for either a global, superordinate, or ontological distinction. When Cats + Dogs is contrasted with Birds + Butterflies, a global-level category is revealed (land animals versus air animals). However, when Cats + Dogs is contrasted with Trees + Flowers, a superordinate-level category is revealed (animals versus plants). Moreover, when Cats + Dogs is contrasted with Cars + Airplanes, an ontological-level category is revealed (animate versus inanimate). Studies of categorization in young children must keep in mind both within- and between-category similarity.

## Natural Kinds versus Arbitrary Groupings

The designation *natural* has a long history in concept research. Kalish (2002) describes several senses in which concepts may be natural: They may refer to objects that are naturally occurring (versus construed by humans); they may possess clusters of co-occurring features (rather than single, arbitrary features); or they may have scientific content (rather than informal knowledge). One foundational sense of "natural" is the realist assumption that certain categories truly exist in the world—they are discovered (not invented); they carve up nature at its joints. Just as an individual tiger has a reality beyond our perception of it, so too does the *category* of tigers. Natural kinds contrast with artificial or nominal kinds. Nominal kinds are arbitrary collections having no basis outside the mind. The natural/nominal distinction is often traced back to Locke (Locke, 1671/1959) and is at the center of contemporary philosophy of language, particularly causal theories of reference (Kripke, 1972; Putnam, 1975).

John Stuart Mill (1843) similarly noted a distinction between natural and arbitrary concepts. The concept *green things* (green hat, green plant, green car, green frog) captures little beyond the property of being green. All other properties that green things share are linked to the fact that they are green. In contrast, other concepts seem to carve nature at its joints (pigs, maple trees, mammals). Mill refers to these "nature-carving" concepts as Kinds; other philosophers refer to them as "natural kinds" (e.g., Schwartz, 1977). In Mill's words:

> Our knowledge of the properties of a Kind is never complete. We are always discovering, and expecting to discover, new ones. (1843, p. 438)

Much of the older developmental work seemed to assume something more like the green-things model of concepts than a natural kind model of concepts. Inhelder and Piaget (1964) thought about categories as starting with a rule, and extending through logical application of that rule. A category might be something like "green triangles," and the challenge for children was to hold onto that rule and apply it with logical precision (a challenge that young children find difficult). In contrast, natural kinds do not seem to fit that model. Rather than starting with a defining rule, a natural kind category is a placeholder for properties that have not yet been learned.

A goal of more recent research is to explore when in development children begin to form natural kind concepts. One theory is that children's early concepts are simple tabulations of feature co-occurrences, and that only with the development of content knowledge and causal intuitions do children seek the explanations behind the experiential groupings (e.g., Quine, 1977). Keil (1989) describes this as the doctrine of "original sim" (where "sim" is short for "similarity"). He notes that although there is evidence for developmental shifts in conceptual representation (e.g., characteristic to defining; Keil, 1989), young children also have fundamental intuitions about conceptual kinds (Keil et al., 1998).

An alternative perspective is that children start out assuming that concepts represent natural kinds, and only over time come to appreciate the arbitrary or conventional nature of some categories. S. A. Gelman and Kalish (1993) describe this position as "categorical realism": labels and kinds pick out real objectively significant groups. Millikan (1998) proposes a similar developmental progression. In her terms, substance concepts are basic. Substances are entities that exist in the world and persist across experience. Individuals (*Mama*), masses (*milk*), and kinds (*mouse*) are all substances. The mental representation of a concept is not a definition, or even a probabilistic description, but is instead a set of heuristics for keeping track of a substance. A good way to tell if you are encountering a mouse is to check its insides, its parentage, and so on, but those properties do not define or characterize "mouseness."

Millikan's account is similar to other treatments of concepts current in the philosophical literature (Margolis, 1998). Millikan acknowledges that concepts can be used in a purely descriptive way. Thus "A home run is a fair ball hit out of the park" is not a heuristic for identi-

fying some preexisting category of things in the world—it is conventionally specified. Millikan suggests this perspective on concepts is a developmental achievement. Some evidence for this position comes from Kalish's (1998) finding that young children are more likely to treat category membership as an objective matter of fact. Whereas adults treat the distinction between a pot and a can as an arbitrary convention, children seem to feel there is a real difference that must be identified. Adults accept that the distinction is a matter of convention, so that people in other cultures could legitimately form different concepts. Young children seem to feel there is a fact to the matter; different categorization practices are errors.

Research on word learning (Markman, 1989), theory-based concepts (Keil, 1989; Murphy & Medin, 1985), and essentialism (S. A. Gelman, 2003) also involve the notion of conceptual naturalness. Natural kind concepts have several distinctive characteristics (Markman, 1989): they are inferentially rich, have a nonobvious basis, and have explanatory power.

Even quite young children treat concepts as natural. S. A. Gelman (2003) describes the inordinate power names have for children; to label something is to say something very deep about its nature (also Markman, 1989). Thus if one member of a natural kind is found to have a novel property, children assume that other members of the kind will share the property. This kind of category-based induction is characteristic even of toddlers (S. A. Gelman & Coley, 1990; Jaswal & Markman, 2002; Welder & Graham, 2001), and extends to reasoning about categories in the social domain (Heyman & Gelman, 1999, 2000b) and to children in varying cultural contexts (Diesendruck, 2001). An empirical orientation to concepts makes sense given children's positions as novice conceptualizers (see Kalish, 2002 for discussion). From a child's perspective, if adults in the community have identified a kind, it is prima facie evidence that the kind is important and meaningful.

Also central to the representation of a concept as natural is the idea that it characterizes things as they are, not just as they appear. Natural kinds may have a nonobvious basis; they reflect deep, not surface similarities (S. A. Gelman, 2003; Markman, 1989). Implicit here, too, is the importance of domain. Categories like *penguin, apple tree,* and *male* (all living things) imply inherent nonobvious properties and inductive potential in ways not found with categories like *window, crayon,* and *sidewalk* (all artifacts). Although artifacts, too, may have nonobvious properties (contrast an original Picasso painting with a reproduction; Bloom, 1996), for the most part simple artifacts cannot be natural in this sense.

### Categories versus Individuals

The study of concepts typically focuses on categories (e.g., dogs, chairs), but children also develop rich concepts of individuals. Among the most studied are the object concept (e.g., whether an infant realizes that an object continues to exist when out of sight) and the self-concept. Children are sensitive to linguistic differences that indicate whether an act of naming refers to a kind (e.g., dogs) or an individual (e.g., Fido) (Hall, Waxman, & Bredart, 2003; Macnamara, 1982). For example, "This is a fep" implies a kind, whereas "This is Fep" implies an individual—especially if the entity is animate. One of the central intuitions underlying concepts of individuals is persistence across time and transformations. Individual identity may persist despite changes in characteristic properties (Gutheil & Rosengren, 1996) and even material composition (Hall, 1998). For example, if a doll wearing a distinctive green cloth cape is named Daxy, and the doll is then moved to a new location and the distinctive cape is removed while a new doll is placed in the old location with the distinctive cape added, 3-year-olds report that the original doll—not the new doll—is Daxy (Sorrentino, 2001). Moreover, individual identity may persist across changes in category identity and labeling. Gutheil and Rosengren (1996) found that young children realized that a change in name did not necessarily signal a change in individual identity. Similarly, the same individual may change from a caterpillar to a butterfly (Rosengren, Gelman, Kalish, & McCormick, 1991). What is crucial to determining individual identity is historical path, not the location, appearance, or even name that was present at the original naming.

Anecdotal evidence suggests that, by about 2 years of age, children may be particularly sensitive to tracking identity of an individual through time and space—as seen by their fanatical attachments to transitional objects (Winnicott, 1969) and precocious sensitivity to ownership and possession. *My* and *mine* are among children's earliest words (Fenson, Dale, Reznick, & Bates, 1994).

Critically, individual identity is not independent of categories; for an individual to persist over time, it would typically retain at least some kinds of category identity

(fictional frogs turning into princes notwithstanding). Thus a table ground to dust and reconstituted at some later time in a similar form is a new table. One individual has been destroyed and another created. A table painted blue at one time and red at another persists as the same individual (Hirsch, 1982). Categories that function as conditions for individual persistence are called *sortals* and are typically encoded in common nouns such as dog or table (Hirsch, 1982). Macnamara (1986) notes that sortals are required for individuating entities. The question "How many?" makes no sense without supplying the sortal—how many *what* (e.g., dogs? legs? molecules?). Likewise, sortals are required for making judgments of identity. "Are these two things the same?" makes no sense without supplying the sortal—the same *what* (see also Carey & Xu, 1999, for discussion).

Sortal concepts have become significant in the developmental literature because of suggestions that the set of sortals may undergo fundamental developmental change; specifically, infants may appreciate only very global sortal concepts. Xu and Carey (1996) note that infants are often insensitive to radical changes in the appearance of individuals. If a cup moves behind a screen and a ball emerges from the other side, 10-month-old infants appear to construe this event as involving a single individual, whereas adults (and 12-month-olds) construe the event as involving two distinct individuals (but see Wilcox & Baillargeon, 1998, for an alternative interpretation of these data). Carey and Xu argue that the concept "object" functions as a sortal for young children (allows tracking of individuals), but more specific kinds do not.

There is a further way in which the distinction between categories and individuals is of great interest, and this concerns the uses to which concepts are put. Although most developmental studies of concepts focus on categories, they do not examine children's concepts of categories per se, but rather of individuals as instances of these categories. Consider the category *dog*. Most typically, a word-learning researcher might ask which things get called dog ("Is this a dog?" or "What is this?"). A categorization researcher might ask a child to sort instances ("Put the dogs in this box"), or make inferences ("Does this dog have an omentum inside?"). In all these cases, the category is considered with respect to the classification of individual instances (this dog, the dogs, a dog). However, a different type of use entails thinking about the category as a whole—so-called generic uses of the category. "Is this a dog?" or "Put the dogs in this box" are expressions that refer to individuals; "Dogs have four legs" or "I like dogs" refer to the larger category.

Traditional approaches to concepts often treated categories as reducible to individuals. The concept of bird was treated as a summary of individual birds. Yet this approach is flawed. Although the concept of bird is obviously related to its instances, a category is not just the sum of these instances. The issue here is the sense in which it is true to say "Birds fly" even though not every bird flies. This knowledge is represented in concepts of generics (S. A. Gelman, 2003; Prasada, 2000).

Generic knowledge is vital to human reasoning. Thinking about generic categories leads children to make rich inferences about the world (Shipley, 1993). As noted earlier, once a child learns that something is a member of a kind (e.g., that a dodo is a bird), he or she tends to infer that the entity shares properties with others of the same kind (S. A. Gelman & Markman, 1986). "Category-based" reasoning is predicated of kinds (Heit & Hahn, 2001; Lo, Sides, Rozelle, & Osherson, 2002; Osherson, Smith, Wilkie, Lopez, & Shafir, 1990). More generally, "semantic" (versus episodic) memory (e.g., Collins & Quillian, 1969) tends to be generic.

Despite the centrality of this form of reasoning, it poses a challenging learning problem for children (see Gelman, 2003). Generics are never directly instantiated in the world, but can only be theorized. One cannot show a child the generic class of dogs. One can never demonstrate, with actual exemplars, photos, or drawings, the distinction between a generic kind (dogs) versus a plurality of instances (some dogs). Furthermore, as noted, generic knowledge is not disconfirmed by counterexamples (e.g., birds lay eggs, even though a majority of birds—male birds and infant birds—do not; McCawley, 1981). Thus the puzzle, concisely framed by Prasada, is an extension of the classic riddle of induction: "How do we acquire knowledge about kinds of things if we have experience with only a limited number of examples of the kinds in question?" (2000, p. 66).

Sensitivity to generics in language seems to develop by about 2.5 to 3 years of age (S. A. Gelman & Raman, 2003; S. A. Gelman, Star, & Flukes, 2002). Young preschoolers interpret a generic noun phrase as referring to an abstract kind—even when it conflicts with the instances present during testing (e.g., when presented with a picture of two penguins, they report that "birds fly," but "the birds don't fly"). However, it is not until about 4 years of age that children show sensitivity to a distinction between generics ("birds") and quantified predications ("all birds," "some birds") (Hollander, Gelman, & Star, 2002). Although more research is needed in this area, it may be during the preschool years that children come to represent fully the notion of a kind as distinct from its instances.

## Implications for Children's Concepts

What are the implications of these distinctions for understanding children's concepts? The most direct implication to emerge from this review is that we cannot rely on a monolithic model of children's concepts (see also Siegler, 1996). Historically, it has often been assumed that there is a single, unitary process of categorization (Bruner, Goodnow, & Austin, 1956; Hull, 1920; see Smith, Patalano, & Jonides, 1998, for review). The work we have reviewed, however, makes clear that categorization cannot be said to be a single thing. The importance of naive theories can be overestimated when focusing exclusively on natural kind concepts and providing a task that requires children to make biological inferences. Likewise, children's reliance on outward appearances can be overrated when focused on nonlexicalized categories for which theories are barely possible—such as a U-shaped piece of plywood, for which children have little prior knowledge (Landau, Smith, & Jones, 1988). Some of the differences in theoretical positions may emerge in part from focusing on different parts of the elephant, so to speak (borrowing from the story of the blind men and the elephant). The information a child uses will be limited by the information supplied. If the only information children receive concerns shape, texture, and size, then frequent use of shape is unsurprising. In contrast, when children are reasoning about real-world living kinds, then dimensions related to biological classification (including parentage, ontology, essence, and kind) become important.

More controversially, Keil et al. (1998) proposes that *even when considering a single concept,* children consider multiple kinds of information: On the one hand, they focus on associations and feature tabulations; on the other hand, they consider propositions that interpret features and relations. Perceptual and conceptual are tightly linked—the salient perceptual features are those that give us conceptual purchase. Different conceptual structures also reflect task variability and conceptual variability. Rather than possessing a global or stable conceptual preference at any age, children and adults apparently have multiple kinds of categorization available to them (Lin & Murphy, 2001; Waxman & Namy, 1997).

A second implication to follow from considering conceptual diversity is the speculation that what is "concept-learning" for an adult is not what it is for a child. An adult who learns a concept in the laboratory already has a fully formed conceptual system in place. This adult already has a large stock of concepts to consult. He or she already has figured out which dimensions are relevant to a wide range of other concepts. "Concept-learning" for an adult is simply adding to a rich system of already available concepts. We cannot assume that children's concept learning is of the same sort (see also Jaswal & Markman, 2002; Rakison, 2003b for discussion of the distinction). This critical point needs to be kept in mind in any comparison of concept learning in children and adults.

In addition to conceptual differences, different tasks tap into different ways of thinking. We have already seen some of this when discussing the debate concerning whether the basic or global level develops first in children (see earlier subsection, "Levels of Categorization"). Categorization serves many different functions, and children recruit different sorts of information depending on the task at hand. Rapid identification calls for one kind of process; reasoning about genealogy calls for another. (However, as Keil et al., 1998 point out, even rapid processing could recruit theory-relevant information. One might identify a stick-insect as an animal after only a quick glance, if one happens to focus on its head and eyes, or if one happens to see it moving on its own.) Rips and Collins (1993) provides an elegant demonstration that task differences yield different categorization processes. For example, when adults are told to think about an object three inches in diameter (with no additional information), they judge it to be *more similar to* a quarter than a pizza, but *more likely to be* a pizza than a quarter.

Even when the task is restricted to object identification, people make use of different sorts of information depending on the task instructions (Yamauchi & Markman, 1998)—at times even in parallel on the same trial (Allen & Brooks, 1991). Smith, Patalano, and Jonides (1998) show that two separate categorization procedures—rule application and judging similarity to an exemplar—can readily apply to the same categories. These procedures seem qualitatively distinct, in that they activate different neural regions in the adult brain.

We suspect that some of the disagreements between theories of conceptual development stem from taking different kinds of concepts as paradigmatic. Children acquire a wealth of different kinds of concepts, and these likely develop in different ways. Certain concepts may have an innate basis; others may be readily acquired on the basis of perceptual learning; still others require causal reasoning and integration of facts within a growing commonsense theory. Furthermore, certain concepts are important in organizing others, and can be called *foundational* concepts. A concept such as *alive* is an example: Once one possesses the concept of alive, it has implications for how one thinks about a range of other concepts, such as plants (and how they are similar to animals) and clouds (and how they differ from animals, despite being apparently self-moving). In contrast, other concepts (e.g., *stapler, green triangles*) are unlikely to have implications for much other knowledge. Foundational concepts cannot be understood as distinct from a child's larger set of beliefs or theories. We turn to this issue next.

## CONCEPTS EMBEDDED IN THEORIES

There are two competing metaphors for thinking about concepts: the dictionary and the encyclopedia. The dictionary metaphor frames each concept as a self-contained unit that can be accessed and understood separately from all the others. In contrast, the encyclopedia frames a concept as interconnected with larger bodies of knowledge. Each metaphor has strengths and weaknesses: The dictionary metaphor provides a manageable enterprise (concepts can be studied in their own right) but artificially, in a way that ignores the ways in which concepts depend on assumptions and information outside the concept itself. The encyclopedia metaphor is more complete and realistic, but explodes the problem of understanding concepts into one that is far more complex and daunting.

Relatedly, Lin and Murphy (2001) make a distinction between the *internal structure* of a concept and its *external relations*. They point out that much research has focused on questions of internal structure: Do concepts have definitions? Are they characterized by prototypes? Are they based on perceptual or conceptual features? In contrast, concepts also have relations to entities outside themselves: larger bodies of knowledge, theories, functions, relations, goals, and so on. These external relations are, in a sense, the whole point of concepts: We construct them in order to use them in these larger knowledge systems. This section concerns these external relations—how concepts relate to larger bodies of knowledge.

We believe that the encyclopedia metaphor is more fruitful, and the external relations of concepts must be considered. An example from the history of science illustrates why. The concept *planet* has a long history in scientific thinking, stretching back in Western tradition to antiquity. We recognize the continuity of the concepts; in English the planets are still identified by their Roman names (derived from the Greek). Yet at the same time, the twenty-first century understanding of planets is radically different from that of ancient celestial observers. How has the concept changed? One could point to definitional changes: Modern planets must orbit stars, whereas ancient planets could include stars and moons (and exclude earth). Yet any such definitional differences would understate the conceptual differences. Modern and ancient concepts were located in radically incommensurate theories (T. Kuhn, 1962). The interrelated assumptions and beliefs that motivated the ancient concept of planet do not apply to the modern concept. It is only given the larger background of ancient belief systems that we can make sense of the old concepts. Similarly new astronomical facts change the larger context within which the concept planet is embedded. Given that concepts are enmeshed in larger knowledge structures, it becomes problematic to identify when two concepts are really the same, or when a concept has changed. The general point, however, is that internal (definitional) properties are not sufficient to characterize concepts.

As this example illustrates, concepts are domain-specific, embedded in larger explanatory structures, often described as theories (Wellman & Gelman, 1998). Thus a full account of foundational concepts such as *force, living thing,* and *belief*—or even a full account of more mundane concepts such as *drop, hamster,* or *afraid*—would require a discussion of the nature and development of children's thinking about physics, biology, and psychology (respectively). It is beyond the scope of this chapter to consider the domain-specific factors underlying development of the full range of children's concepts. To do so would be to provide an overview of cognitive development more generally (see other chapters in this volume). Rather, in this section we present evidence for the link between concepts and theories, drawing many of the examples from the specific domain of intuitive bi-

ology. We first review research evidence that children's categories are imbued with theories, by providing examples of how children attend to ontology, causation, function, and other nonobvious properties. For ease of exposition, we have organized the literature review into distinct sections that address each of these kinds of evidence separately; in reality, however, the different sections address overlapping issues.

## Ontology

Keil (1979, p. 1) defines ontological knowledge as "one's conception of the basic categories of existence, of what sorts of things there are." Ontologies form the foundation of intuitive framework theories. Physics deals with masses, velocities, and energy. Psychology deals with thoughts, desires, and beliefs. Biology deals with species, genes, and reproduction. The same entity can be construed in different theories: Thus, a person is at once a *physical* mass, possessing *psychological* states, and undergoing *biological* processes. The difference between an ontological distinction and other categorical distinctions is that, with ontologies, predicates assigned to the wrong ontological category are not false—they are nonsensical. For example, "The cow is green" is false but sensible; in contrast, "the cow is one hour long" is an ontological category error.

When do children begin to honor ontological distinctions, in their categories and in their language? There is a rich literature demonstrating that children honor at least two ontological distinctions quite early in life, that of mental versus physical (Wellman, 1990), and that of animate versus inanimate (Rakison & Poulin-Dubois, 2001). We focus primarily on the latter, as its relevance for categorization is especially clear.

Animacy is a central concern by the time children can talk. Cross-linguistically, animacy is marked through pronouns (as in English: he or she versus it), classifiers, selectional restrictions on which verbs can appear with which nouns (e.g., Silverstein, 1986), and so on. Although there is no single respect in which animacy influences syntactic development across the world's languages, animacy is a pervasive theme that informs and structures the way speakers communicate. For children learning English, subject nouns are typically animate, object nouns tend to be inanimate (Slobin, 1985), and children are aware of these regularities by preschool age if not earlier (Golinkoff, Harding, Carlson, & Sexton, 1984). For children learning English, animacy is an important factor in learning the passive construction (Lempert, 1989), in the types of implicit causal attributions children make when interpreting verbs (Corrigan & Stevenson, 1994), and in interpreting nouns such as "move" (S. A. Gelman & Koenig, 2001).

Thus, many studies show that even infants distinguish animate from inanimate on a variety of measures. An immediate question is whether this is correctly construed as a conceptual distinction, or instead can be reduced to other features that correlate with the ontological distinction. A child may distinguish mammals and vehicles in a manner that appears to reflect an ontological distinction between animate and inanimate. However, it is possible that lower-level perceptual analyses yield the categorical distinction. Cues such as spatial distribution of facial features (two eyes centered above a mouth, or, more schematically, three dots in an inverted triangle), irregular contour, dynamic patterns of movement (autonomous motion, contingent motion), and so forth, are all low-level correlates of animacy to which infants are sensitive (Bertenthal, Proffitt, Spetner, & Thomas, 1985; Bornstein & Arterberry, 2003; C. Nelson, 2001; Rakison, 2003b). An infant who distinguishes horses from airplanes (Mandler & McDonough, 1998) may not have an abstract concept of animacy, but instead a sensitivity to critical perceptual features.

One way to examine whether animacy is wholly a perceptually based distinction or one with ontological significance is to determine what meaning it has for the child (Legerstee, 1992). Some of the earliest evidence that infants distinguish people from inanimate objects comes from infants' socioemotional reactions including gazing, smiling, and cooing (Legerstee, Pomerleau, & Malcuit, 1987) as well as infants' novel inferences (Mandler & McDonough, 1998). Furthermore, several researchers have proposed that infants imbue animates (particularly people) with important psychological characteristics and distinguish surface behaviors from deeper psychological interpretations of those behaviors (Baron-Cohen, 1995; Legerstee, Barna, & DiAdamo, 2000; Meltzoff, 1995; Premack & Premack, 1997; Woodward, 1998).

A further piece of evidence is that, in children's classifications, ontology can trump other salient information, such as object shape. By 9 months of age, infants group together different basic-level animal categories (e.g., dogs and fish) and separate birds-with-outspread-wings from airplanes (Mandler & McDonough, 1993).

Ten-month-olds classify together containers differing in shape and distinguish between same-shaped objects that differ in their capacity to contain (Kolstad & Baillargeon, 1996). By age 2 years, children weight substance more heavily than shape on a match-to-sample task on which the items are nonsolid masses (Soja, Carey, & Spelke, 1991). Even children's overextension errors (e.g., referring to a cow as a "dog") are not based primarily on shape alone, but typically require similarity on both shape and taxonomic relatedness (S. A. Gelman, Croft, Fu, Clausner, & Gottfried, 1998).

By 3 and 4 years of age, children treat plants and animals as belonging to a single category (things that grow and self-heal), despite the extreme differences in shape between, say, a cow and a tree (Inagaki & Hatano, 2002). Conversely, children treat humans and apes as belonging to distinctly different categories, despite their greater similarity. Thus, when given triads consisting of a human, a nonhuman primate, and a nonprimate animal, elementary-school children are more likely than adults to group together the primate and the animal, isolating the human (Johnson, Mervis, & Boster, 1992). This pattern is also found among preschoolers, even when the primate and animal differ radically in shape (e.g., chimpanzee and centipede) (Coley, 1993).

A further argument is that the perceptual cues that correlate with animacy are insufficient. Prasada (2003) suggests that so-called animate motion, in fact, is not perceptually given, nor can it be represented as a correlation between properties, but rather requires "an appropriate relational structure" (p. 18) (see also R. Gelman & Williams, 1998). Self-motion (in the sense of self-generated movement) is not simply a matter of detecting whether an object moves without a visible causal agent because wind and magnets can be (and indeed sometimes are) imputed as causal agents in such cases (e.g., R. Gelman, Durgin, & Kaufman, 1995; S. A. Gelman & Gottfried, 1996; Subrahmanyam, R. Gelman, & Lafosse, in press). How to represent such relational structures on a perceptual-learning account is not clear (but see Yoshida & Smith, 2003, for suggestions).

Ontological concepts are significant because they provide a foundational structure for other concepts. Thus, learning that a sugar-glider is a kind of animal suggests one might be able to learn about the ways sugar-gliders reproduce and take in energy, but not about their truth-value or original inventor. There is no sharp dividing line between concepts that provide an organizing structure and those that do not. For example the distinction between plants and animals is conceptually important, but it is less clear whether plants and animals are different ontological kinds (Carey, 1985). Ontological status may best be understood as a kind of relative centrality. To the extent that a concept has vast implications for other concepts and knowledge, it can be considered ontological. Ontological status, then, is a consequence of laws and causal relations recognized within intuitive theories. This perspective highlights the role of causal relations in conceptual organization, to which we turn next.

## Causation

Some years ago, we proposed that, if children's categories are theory-based, then causes should be crucial to their category representations (S. A. Gelman & Kalish, 1993). Similarly, Ahn (1998) formulated the "causal status hypothesis," in which causal features are more central than effect features (see also Rehder, 2003). Thus, even given equal frequency, cause and effect features will be weighted differently. When the causal status of features is manipulated experimentally, adults weight the identical feature more heavily when it serves as a cause than when it serves as an effect (Ahn, 1998). Of particular interest to the present context, Ahn, Gelman, Amsterlaw, Hohenstein, and Kalish (2000) found evidence for the causal status effect in children 7 to 9 years of age. Children learned descriptions of novel animals, in which one feature caused two other features. When asked to determine which test item was more likely to be an example of the animal they had learned, children preferred an animal with a cause feature and an effect feature rather than an animal with two effect features.

Other studies add to the support for the importance of cause in children's concepts. Barrett, Abdi, Murphy, and Gallagher (1993) find that, when asked to categorize novel birds into one of two categories, children of elementary-school age noticed correlations that were supported by causal links, and used such correlations to categorize new members (e.g., correlation between brain size and memory). The children did not make use of features that correlated equally well but were unsupported by a theory (e.g., the correlation between structure of heart and shape of beak). Krascum and Andrew (1998) likewise found beneficial effects of causal infor-

mation on category learning in children as young as 4 and 5 years of age. As the authors note, "[T]he meaningfulness of individual features is not a significant factor in children's category learning, and instead, what is important is that attributes within a category can be linked in a theory-coherent manner" (p. 343).

Causal relations are central to concepts in theories because they involve explanatory as well as associative relations. Features in causal relations are linked by some sort of mechanism. Mechanisms provide a deeper explanatory structure to concepts and knit superficially disparate phenomena into a coherent theory. Preschool children recognize that baby animals tend to resemble their parents (Springer, 1996; Gelman & Wellman, 1991). They also recognize that there is a highly regular and constrained pattern of development across the lifetime of an individual animal (Rosengren et al., 1991). The two facts can be explained and integrated through the idea of some sort of intrinsic species essence. Similarly, young children recognize that many behaviors can lead to illness, including getting sneezed on, sharing a toothbrush, or eating a dirty piece of food. What links these apparently dissimilar events is a common underlying mechanism, transmission of germs (Kalish, 1996).

The detail with which children represent mechanisms remains an open question (Au & Romo, 1999; R. Gelman & Williams, 1998; Keil et al., 1998). For example, children might initially represent causal relations with an abstract mechanism placeholder. At the same time, the nature of the mechanism is where the critical theoretical connections lie. Consider the concept of "inheritance." Some researchers have argued that young children recognize a physical or biological mechanism mediating parent-offspring resemblance (Hirschfeld, 1996; Springer & Keil, 1991). This sort of representation links inheritance to a set of other beliefs and concepts, an intuitive theory of biology. Alternatively, if children assume that intentional or social mechanisms underlie inheritance (Solomon, Johnson, Zaitchik, & Carey, 1996; Weissman & Kalish, 1999), then the conceptually central links would be quite different. Use of a concept (e.g., "mother," "sick") involves, in part, coming to appreciate which mechanism is operative. The organization of concepts within intuitive theories entails imputing underlying, nonobvious properties and causal relations. Just which nonobvious properties children represent, and how that set changes, are the major questions driving research on the development of theory-based concepts. We turn next to consideration of some of these nonobvious properties.

## Nonobvious Properties

The importance of nonobvious properties can be seen in several respects. It is implicit in children's understanding of causation and ontology. It can also be seen more directly in children's formulation of domain-specific theories that posit nonvisible constructs: mental states in a naive theory of mind (Wellman, 2002), physical force and gravity in a naive theory of physics (Wellman & Inagaki, 1997), and a wealth of constructs in children's formulation of biological theories, including germs (Kalish, 1996; Siegal, 1988), vital powers (Gottfried & Gelman, in press; Inagaki & Hatano, 2002; Morris, Taplin, & Gelman, 2000), elements of reproduction (Springer, 1996), and cooties (Hirschfeld, 2002). That children appear to learn and accept such constructs readily would argue against the notion that their concepts depend on concrete, perceptually apparent properties.

Furthermore, studies that focus specifically on nonobvious properties, such as internal parts or substance, find that children rely on such properties for categorizing (see also R. Gelman & Williams, 1998). (Precisely when in development children do so is a matter of some dispute, however.) In a by-now classic series of studies, Keil (1989) asked children to consider animals and objects that had undergone transformations leading them to appear to be something else—for example, a raccoon that underwent an operation so that it looked and acted like a skunk. Second graders realized that animal identity was unaffected by superficial transformations (e.g., the animal was judged to be a raccoon despite its skunk-like properties).

Even younger children demonstrated a similar understanding when considering items that were transformed to resemble something from a different ontological category (e.g., preschoolers reported that a porcupine that was transformed to look like a cactus was still a porcupine), or that were transformed by means of a costume. Gelman and Wellman (1991) similarly found that preschool children appreciated that for some objects, insides are more important than outsides for judgments of identity and functioning (e.g., a dog without its insides cannot bark and is not a dog, whereas a dog without its outsides can bark and is a dog). Moreover, when asked what differentiates pairs of identical-looking animals that differ in kind (e.g., real dog versus toy dog; dog versus wolf), both 5-year-olds and adults are more likely to invoke internal parts/substance than the irrelevant property of age (S. A. Gelman, 2003; Lizotte & Gelman, 1999).

Interestingly, children appreciate that insides are important at an age when they do not yet know much about *what* insides objects have. For example, although 4-year-olds recognize that insides are crucial to object identity and expect that animal insides differ in consistent ways from machine insides, they cannot accurately identify which photo corresponds to the insides of an animal, or which photo corresponds to the insides of a machine (Simons & Keil, 1995). This result led Simons and Keil to suggest that children's grasp of insides is an abstract appreciation that precedes a concrete, detailed understanding. This is a surprising reversal of the usual developmental story (that concrete understandings precede abstractions), and implies that children may be predisposed to consider nonobvious properties important, even in the absence of direct evidence.

In the remainder of this section we briefly review two particular kinds of nonobvious properties: function and essence.

### *Function*

Kemler Nelson, Russell, Duke, and Jones (2000) explain the importance of function to a theory-based approach as follows:

> Attention to functional information can be understood as evidence for conceptual categories when it supplements or overrides the pull of superficial, functionally irrelevant aspects of appearance as the basis for using artifact names. The use of functional information implicates interpretive mechanisms beyond those of immediate perception and indicates a mode of categorization that is at least partly knowledge based, rather than strictly perceptually driven. (p. 1271)

However, the extent to which children are capable of using function for their classifications, particularly in word learning, is highly controversial. Smith, Jones, and Landau (1996) argued that 3-year-old children selectively ignore functional information when extending new labels. The basis of their argument is that word learning is guided by "dumb" (nonreflective, involuntary, automatic) attentional mechanisms. They conclude, on the basis of a series of experiments, that "children's naming was immune to influence from information about function" (p. 143). Their evidence included a series of four experiments in which 3-year-olds—unlike adults—failed to use function when extending novel labels to novel objects.

Landau, Smith, and Jones (1998) extended this line of work using a greater range of both novel and familiar objects. Across three studies of similar design, 2-, 3-, and 5-year-olds and adults were asked to extend labels (Naming task) or to infer novel functions (Function task; e.g., "Could you carry water with this one?"). In general, children selected based on function on the Function task, and selected based on shape on the Naming task, regardless of whether they were presented with explicit demonstrations of function. These results demonstrate the children are capable of reasoning about functional concepts. However, Landau et al. argue that when extending words, children are "pulled" by nonreflective attentional mechanisms that serve to spotlight the most salient (and unreflective) aspects of the situation.

If these provocative results are interpreted as the authors suggest, this would be damaging to the "concepts in theories" position. Nonetheless, the theory position could be saved in either of two ways: One possibility is that function is indeed used by children to categorize, but at a later point in development compared to the subjects in the Landau et al. experiments (Smith et al., 1996). This possibility, if true, would weaken the theory position, particularly the suggestion that theories contribute to concept development, rather than being the outcome of concept development (Murphy, 1993). It would argue for a developmental shift, from perceptually based to theory based categorization. A second possibility, and the argument we favor, is that children can and do use functional information while naming, but that certain items and tasks have limited children's capacity in prior studies. When care is taken to design tasks and items that reflect functions that are salient, sensible, and nonarbitrary, then young children incorporate function into their naming as early as 2 years of age. This latter argument has been pursued vigorously in the past few years, and we now turn to the evidence that supports it.

Kemler Nelson et al. (2000) point out that children cannot be expected to appreciate just any type of function they encounter, any more than would an adult. They suggest that, for a fair test, it is critical to examine function/structure relations that are "compelling and nonarbitrary in a way that young children can make sense of

(and may expect)" (p. 1272). Specifically, they posit that the functionally relevant aspects of an object's design should be easily perceptible, that structure/function relations should be based on principles of causality that are familiar to young children, and that function/structure relations should be "convincing." They introduced 3-, 4-, and 5-year-old children to a novel artifact that could function in two distinct and novel ways: to paint parallel lines (with brushes) and to make music (with wires that could be plucked). Thus, certain features were contingent on one function, whereas other features were contingent on the other function. Each child encountered only one of these functions, in either a Painter or Instrument condition, when the target artifact was named a *stennet*. When asked to extend the novel name to test objects that varied from the target in similarity and function, children tended to extend the name in accord with the function that they saw demonstrated (though similarity relations were also taken into account).

Similarly, Diesendruck and Markson (1999) argue that young children can appreciate function when it is a permanent, exclusive property of an object that is demonstrated and explained (e.g., "this was made for X"). In one study, 3-year-olds participated in a sorting task with triads of novel objects. Each target object was paired with an object similar in shape but which could not perform the function, and an object different in shape but that could perform the same function. When the function was explicitly stated, demonstrated, and shown to be exclusive to one of the test choices, children typically sorted based on function.

What is it that makes a function more compelling to children? Kemler Nelson, Frankenfield, Morris, and Blair (2000) found that 4-year-old children were more likely to generalize novel names for artifacts when functions "made sense" and were more reasonably related to structure and the designer's intent. A sensible (plausible) function for an object with a horizontal and vertical tube might be "when you put balls in here, it drops them one at a time," whereas an implausible function for the same object might be "a toy snake can wriggle in it." That is, although the object could readily carry out either of these functions, only the first is likely to be a function designed by the creator of the object.

Similarly, Bloom (2000) proposed that function is used to the extent that it is perceived as intended by the designer of the object under consideration. Children relied on function when it was highly specific and unlikely to be accidental (e.g., an object with a hinged part shaped to fit into its base like a puzzle-piece; Kemler Nelson, Frankenfield, et al., 2000) but did not rely on function when it was simple, general, and probably accidental (e.g., a square, U-shaped object that "a toy dog sits in"; Smith, Jones, & Landau, 1996). Indeed, when children view two objects of *identical* shape that have different intended functions (e.g., an object and its same-shaped container), they do not sort them together (Diesendruck, Markson, & Bloom, 2003; but see German & Johnson, 2002, for evidence that 5-year-olds attend to any intended goals for which an object is used, not just original intent).

### Essence

Another example of a nonobvious construct is that of an "essence" (S. A. Gelman, 2003). Essentialism is the view that categories have an underlying reality or true nature that one cannot observe directly but that gives an object its identity (S. A. Gelman, 2003; Locke, 1671/1959; Schwartz, 1977). According to essentialism, categories are real, in several senses: They are discovered (versus invented), they are natural (versus artificial), they predict other properties, and they point to natural discontinuities in the world. Essentialism requires no specialized knowledge, and people may possess an *essence placeholder* without knowing what the essence is (Medin, 1989). For example, a child might believe that girls have some inner, nonobvious quality that distinguishes them from boys and that is responsible for the many observable differences in appearance and behavior between boys and girls, before ever learning about chromosomes or human physiology.

Evidence for essentialism is indirect but extensive. It includes several expectations children hold about certain categories: that they permit rich underlying structure, have innate potential, and have sharp and immutable boundaries (S. A. Gelman, 2003). Essentialism is a powerful, fairly general structure for concepts. It specifies that underlying features are causally responsible for observable qualities but does not necessarily imply anything about the nature of the features or causal processes. Thus, essentialism may guide children's construction of social categories (Giles, 2003; Heyman & Gelman, 2000a; Hirschfeld, 1996; Rothbart & Taylor, 1990), of artifacts (Bloom, 2000), and of food (Hejmadi, Rozin, & Siegal, 2004). When children begin to acquire a novel concept, they assume that causal features will be the most central (Ahn et al., 2000; Gopnik & Sobel,

2000). Essentialist intuitions also lead to incorporation of new properties into the concept. The assumption of shared essence warrants the inference that properties possessed by one (or a few) instances will be true of the general kind. How children decide which categories to essentialize remains an unsolved puzzle.

Essentialism is a hypothesized construct based on indirect evidence, and so cannot be demonstrated definitively. Not surprisingly, then, there are debates as to whether this is the most apt characterization. One set of questions concerns whether there is a single essentialist stance (Keil, 1994), or instead an amalgamation of tendencies (S. A. Gelman, 2003). If the latter, then how coherent are essentialist beliefs? Do different strands (e.g., nativism, inductive potential, boundary intensification) all hang together, or do they develop piecemeal? Another set of issues was raised by Strevens (2000), who suggests that the data taken as evidence for psychological essentialism could instead be accounted for if people simply assume that there are causal laws connecting kind membership with observable properties. He terms such causal laws *K-laws* (kind laws), and his alternative formulation the Minimal Hypothesis. Strevens's account, though eschewing essentialism, overlaps with the current model in emphasizing that people treat surface features as caused and constrained by deeper features of concepts.

Other scholars have argued that the essentialist model cannot account for certain experimental findings with adults (Braisby, Franks, & Hampton, 1996; Malt, 1994; Sloman & Malt, 2003). For example, the extent to which different liquids are judged to be water is independent of the extent to which they share the purported essence of water, $H_2O$. At issue are questions such as, What is meant by *essentialism* (see S. A. Gelman & Hirschfeld, 1999, for several distinct senses that have been conflated in the literature)? Which concepts are essentialized? Can there be a mismatch between language and concepts (e.g., an essentialized concept of "pure water" that does not map neatly onto uses of the *word* "water")? Whether these findings undermine (or even conflict with) psychological essentialism is a matter of current debate (S. A. Gelman, 2003; Rips, 2001).

### Summary

Any developmental theory needs to account not only for the acquisition of simple concepts (both familiar, such as *cup,* and novel, such as *rif*) but also complex knowledge. By the time children are 2.5 to 3 years of age, many of their concepts incorporate properties that cannot be readily captured by perceptual description. We have reviewed several types of evidence to support this claim: the centrality of ontology, of causal features, and of nonobvious constructs (including function, intentionality, and internal parts). Children are not simply stringing together observed properties, but rather are searching for underlying causes and explanations. The resulting concepts are often called *theory-based.* In some cases, concepts are embedded in an identifiable, articulated theory (e.g., beliefs and desires in a theory of mind). In other cases, such a theory has not yet been identified, but the components of a theory (ontology, causation, nonobvious features) are present from an early age.

Theories are argued to contribute to concept development rather than to result from concept development (see Wellman & Gelman, 1998). Murphy (1993) argues that, without theoretical commitments of some sort, it may be difficult for children to acquire concepts at all. He posits that theories help concept learners in three respects:

1. Theories help identify those features that are relevant to a concept.
2. Theories constrain how (e.g., along which dimensions) similarity should be computed.
3. Theories can influence how concepts are stored in memory. The implication here is that concept acquisition may proceed more smoothly with the help of theories, even though the theories themselves are changing developmentally.

These data and arguments do not imply that perceptual features are unimportant to early concepts. Even within a "concepts-in-theories" framework, appearances provide crucial cues regarding category membership (Gelman & Medin, 1993). Similarity plays an important role in fostering comparisons of representations and hence discovery of new abstractions and regularities (Gentner & Medina, 1998). Rather than suggesting that perceptual cues are irrelevant, we suggest that many concepts have two distinct though interrelated levels: the level of observable reality and the level of explanation and cause.

It is this two-tier structure that may in fact serve to motivate further development, leading children to develop deeper, more thoughtful understandings (Wellman & Gelman, 1998). Most developmental accounts of cognitive change include something like this structure, such as equilibration (Inhelder & Piaget, 1958), competition (MacWhinney, 1987), theory change (Carey, 1985), analogy (Goswami, 1996), and cognitive variability (Siegler, 1996). In all these cases, children consider contrasting representations. Not surprisingly, children also look beyond observable features when forming concepts.

Theory-based approaches argue for the interdependence of categorization and other cognitive processes, such as causal reasoning or reading of intentionality. Certainly no one would argue that categorization is a wholly separate process unto itself (consider the well-appreciated links among categorization, perception, and memory). Theory-based approaches to concepts have powerfully made the point that categorization is intertwined with knowledge and belief systems (Murphy, 2002). However, the extent of this interdependence has not yet been sufficiently plumbed. It would be intriguing to know, for example, how categorization changes (if at all) for those people with impairments that affect other high-level reasoning processes. We need more fine-grained studies of categorization in autism (which devastates theory of mind) or Williams syndrome (which seems to undercut theory construction; see S. C. Johnson & Carey, 1998).

## MECHANISMS OF CONCEPTUAL ACQUISITION AND CHANGE

There is no doubt that by preschool age, children's concepts are rich, varied, context-sensitive, and not simply rooted in perceived similarities ("observables"). How to account for these early developments? Some similarity-based and associationist mechanisms have been proposed that suggest simple attentional mechanisms to account for concept learning—yet questions remain as to how well they capture the complexity of the phenomena. At the same time, more theory-based mechanisms for understanding conceptual change are beginning to receive attention—yet are currently less well understood. In this section, we briefly review some of the major arguments in favor of associative and similarity mechanisms, discuss some limitations that they face as a full account of concept learning, and consider other promising directions.

## Associative Mechanisms

Challenges to the concepts-in-theories position center around the idea that low-level associative mechanisms can account for children's seemingly sophisticated concepts, so that there is no need to appeal to higher-order processing. In this section we first review some of the evidence for the power of children's associative mechanisms, then arguments for why these are insufficient to account for children's concepts in full.

Human infants possess powerful mechanisms for detecting regularities in the environment and learning associations; they can respond to complex patterns of covariation. One kind of information infants use is frequency distributions. A basic principle of classical conditioning is that a learner who experiences that property A frequently co-occurs with property B but rarely with property C will learn to associate A and B over A and C. Infants are sensitive to associations between properties such as shape, movement, and texture (Madole & Oakes, 1999; Quinn & Eimas, 2000; Rakison & Poulin-Dubois, 2001). Saffran et al. (1996) showed that 8-month-old infants are impressively sensitive to distributional properties of sound patterns in speech. Such sensitivity allows babies to segment continuous speech into units; sounds with low frequencies of co-occurrence may mark word boundaries.

Associationist accounts have proposed that the basic mechanisms for conceptual change is bootstrapping. Bootstrapping is a process of multiple rounds or levels of statistical learning (Goldstone & Johansen, 2003). The basic principle of bootstrapping is that learners are initially sensitive to relatively low-level features that correlate with more abstract conceptual distinctions. In the field of language development, various bootstrapping models have emerged: Form can be a cue to meaning (syntactic bootstrapping), meaning can be a cue to form (semantic bootstrapping), intonation can be a cue to meaning or form, and so on (see Waxman & Lidz, Chapter 7, this *Handbook,* this volume). In the area of conceptual development more broadly, bootstrapping approaches include perceptual learning accounts (e.g., Goldstone, 1998) and form-function relations.

Language is one of the central inputs for conceptual bootstrapping. Language use provides patterns of associations between labels and objects. Infants initially respond to patterns of sound elements. Sound elements cluster into chunks (words). With these new clusters, infants can learn patterns of association between words or between words and other parts of experience (Werker, Cohen, Lloyd, Casasola, & Stager, 1998). Attention to the distributional properties of words gives the learner access to a greatly enriched set of distinctions and associations (Oakes & Madole, 2003; Samuelson, 2002). Smith and Yoshida (Smith, Colunga, & Yoshida, 2003; Yoshida & Smith, 2003) argue that foundational concepts (e.g., animacy) may be extracted from regularities in language. Syntactic structures are associated with conceptual distinctions between objects and substances (e.g., count nouns versus mass nouns in English) and between animates and inanimates (e.g., plural marking is more common for animates than inanimates, in Japanese). For the young child, animacy falls out of those perceptual and linguistic correlations that can be found in the input, thereby leading to different conceptualizations of animacy depending on the language being learned (English versus Japanese).

This is not to say that the higher-order concepts, computationally or phenomenologically, reduce to their constituent associations. As the conceptual system is built up, clusters of associations may be compiled into phenomenological primitives. Adults hear speech in their native language as a sequence of words (or even sequence of meanings). The patterns underlying those segments are not perceived and may not even be retrievable. Mill (1843) describes this process as mental chemistry. When various wavelengths of light are perceived together, the experience of the whole (white) is qualitatively different than the sum of the parts (colors). Critically, the whole may provide unique associations. The associations with white are not simply derivable from associations with constituent colors.

A case study examining the role of associative mechanisms comes from studies of children's reliance on shape to form concepts. Much research suggests that shape is a crucial component of children's semantic representations. Two-year-olds overextend familiar words to unrelated objects (e.g., calling the moon "a ball"; Clark, 1973), and preschoolers extend novel words on the basis of shape (see Woodward & Markman, 1998, for discussion).

On an associationist view, a shape bias builds up gradually over time, based on statistical regularities in the input (Smith, 2000). In favor of this view is evidence that the bias is not innate, but emerges at about age 2 years, after a cluster of initial words have been learned, and increases till about 36 months of age (Smith, 2000). Thus, attention to shape appears to undergo a characteristic developmental time course in which it grows more powerful as children acquire more experience with their own language—therefore suggesting that it may be the outcome rather than the source of word learning. The input children hear also seems to provide a rich source of data regarding such linkages between object shape and count nouns. The first count nouns that children learn in English tend to refer to categories for which shape is a salient dimension, suggesting that children may be hearing many shape-based count nouns. Exposure to different language inputs results in somewhat different word-learning biases, also implicating experience as an important influence on children's early assumptions about word meaning. Relatedly, experimental manipulation of the input by teaching shape-based nouns results in stronger noun-learning in early childhood (Gershkoff-Stowe & Smith, 2004).

One position we and others have argued is that the salience of shape derives largely from its value as an index or predictor of other information (S. A. Gelman & Ebeling, 1998; Medin, 1989; Soja, Carey, & Spelke, 1992; Woodward & Markman, 1998). When ontological knowledge and theoretical beliefs are available, and when they conflict with shape, children can and do sort and name on the basis of these other factors (see S. A. Gelman & Diesendruck, 1999, for review). If this interpretation is correct, then when children receive information about theoretical kind directly, this should influence which features are deemed relevant and used in children's judgments. Indeed, Booth and Waxman (2002) have demonstrated that conceptual information (in the form of verbal descriptions) affects children word extensions. In two experiments, 3-year-old children received a word-extension task with simple abstract objects, in which the objects were described as having either animal-relevant properties (e.g., "This dax has a mommy and daddy who love it very much . . . when this dax goes to sleep at night, they give it lots of hugs and kisses") or artifact-relevant properties (e.g., "This dax was made by an astronaut to do a very special job on her spaceship"). Children sorted the objects differently, depending on the conceptual information provided in the story. The data argue against the idea that children automatically activate purely percep-

tually based associations between the presence of eyes and the dimension of shape.

## Similarity

Many associationist theories present similarity as the strongest organizing principle for young children's concepts. Similarity is a summary of degree of overlap in features (Hahn & Ramscar, 2001). It is typically thought of as a relation between sets of perceptual properties, such as shape or visible parts, and thus particularly suited to associationist accounts of concepts. However, similarity is an abstract relation that may hold between any sets of features (including nonperceptual ones). Nonetheless, as a hypothesis about children's concepts, similarity typically implies that nonobservable, conceptual features are not represented (Mareschal, 2003; Sloutsky & Fisher, 2004).

Similarity is a global or holistic representation (as contrasted with a rule-based or analytic representation). There is a long tradition of describing children's thinking as moving from holistic to analytic (Kemler & Smith, 1978) or from a focus on sets of characteristic features to selective representations of defining features (Keil, 1989). Consider two people: your father's infant brother (A) and an adult friend of the family who always comes for holidays (B). Adult intuitions are that B is more similar to a typical uncle, but that only A actually is an uncle. A similarity-based account denies that children would make this differentiated judgment. The calculation of similarity is not context-dependent. It does not matter whether one is judging which person (A or B) is more likely to give you a present, or which person is more likely to share an inherited feature; rather, overall perceptual similarity drives predictions. In contrast, a more sophisticated sense of similarity would allow for differential judgments depending on context (Medin, Goldstone, & Gentner, 2000). For example, one would judge that the adult family friend would be more likely to give you a present, but that your father's brother would be more likely to share your father's blood type. Another capacity that extends beyond a similarity-based account involves weighting certain features absolutely, yielding rule-based categories. Thus for nominal kinds (such as "uncle"), kinship relations are necessary and sufficient (no other features matter). We can distinguish, then, the simple similarity model (global, noncontext-dependent) from two other sorts of models: one in which similarity is context-dependent, and one in which certain features are given absolute weights. A common developmental hypothesis is that the simple similarity model precedes both of these models.

Sloutsky (2003; Sloutsky & Fisher, 2004) has revived claims that young children's concepts are based on a relatively undifferentiated sense of overall similarity. Sloutsky has studied children's representations of animal kinds. Theory-based views describe young children's concepts as organized around biological essences and causal relations, with perceptual features providing evidence for underlying properties (S. A. Gelman, 2003). When judging which of two animals shares a novel property with a third, theory-based accounts suggest that children will base their judgment on biological relatedness, even when it conflicts with perceptual similarity. In contrast, Sloutsky proposes that young children fail to distinguish between perceptual and underlying features. One series of studies presented participants with a task in which they were asked to judge which of two objects shares an underlying biological property with a third (e.g., which of two items have blood; Sloutsky, Lo, & Fisher, 2001). Adults and older children use shared labels to the exclusion of perceptual features; the two entities with the same name share properties. Young children perform differently. Labels are accorded no special status, but just enter the similarity calculation as a kind of auditory-perceptual feature (Sloutsky & Fisher, 2004). Children judge two entities as more similar if they receive the same label (Sloutsky & Lo, 1999). Thus, children's inductive inferences from one animal to another are highly predicted by their judgments of how similar one animal is to another—at least as similarity is measured on this task.

## Limits of Similarity and Associations

To many, empiricism has the powerful allure of common sense (Keil et al., 1998; Pinker, 2002). It also seems to account for knowledge acquisition with a minimum of machinery. Processes of general induction, based on association learning and similarity assessment, are undoubtedly potent tools for acquiring categories. However, we suggest that such processes are insufficient to provide a complete account for concept acquisition and conceptual change.

### Context-Sensitivity

A major limitation of similarity-based models is accounting for context-sensitivity. Selective similarity is characteristic of young children's concepts. Preschool children realize that a person and a toy monkey look alike but are unlikely to share internal properties, whereas a worm and a person look different but are more likely to share insides (Carey, 1985). Simple attention to correlated attributes is not sufficient to account for even young children's knowledge. For example, 3- and 4-year-olds predict that a wooden pillow will be hard rather than soft, even though all the pillows children have previously encountered have been soft (Kalish & Gelman, 1992). Likewise, 2- to 4-year-old children are more likely to use perceptual similarity cues when similarity corresponds to function (McCarrell & Callanan, 1995). For example, after looking at pictures of two creatures that differed only in eye size and leg length, children were invited to make an inference concerning sight ("Which one sees really well in the dark?") or movement ("Which one can jump really high?"). Children attended selectively to different perceptual features depending on the particular function (eyes, when the question concerned sight; legs, when the question concerned movement). Giles and Heyman (2004) found that preschool children judged the same behavior differently depending on the category of the individual involved. If a girl (versus boy versus dog) spills a child's milk, the implications differ accordingly in how this is explained. These examples of selectivity would seem more readily explained as an instance of causal reasoning than as a reflection of attentional weights.

Unlike similarity accounts, associationist accounts have no difficulty in principle with context-sensitivity; indeed, they predict it (L. B. Smith, 2000). However, such accounts would assume that children have a prior database of associations that drive their judgments. In contrast, a theory-based model enables children to make novel inferences that are supported by theoretical assumptions (as in the wooden pillows study, where preschoolers correctly inferred that wooden pillows would be hard).

### Role of Labels

The similarity view is that words serve merely as an additional feature in an undifferentiated similarity judgment (Sloutsky, 2003). In contrast, an alternative proposal is that children treat different words as referring to different kinds of concepts (e.g., count nouns label taxonomic kinds; proper nouns label individuals), and these concepts mediate children's judgments. The best way to test between these hypotheses is to examine different kinds of words. The literature on children's sensitivity to different word types would suggest that a pure similarity model would have difficulty accounting for extant findings. S. A. Gelman and Markman (1986) found that children extended novel properties from one animal to another if their labels were synonymous (e.g., "puppy" and "baby dog"; identical labels were not required), and S. A. Gelman and Coley (1990) found that children did *not* extend novel properties from one animal to another if they received identical *adjectives* (e.g., labeling two birds as "sleepy"). Labels per se did not determine performance; rather, the concepts conveyed by the labels did.

Sloutsky and Fisher's (2004) results demonstrate that categorical (labeling) information is taken as more important for inductive inference than for judgments of similarity. S. A. Gelman and Markman (1986) offer an explanation: Shared properties are characteristic of members of the same category. Thus, when asked about shared properties, children look for cues about category membership. Shared labels are one such cue. When the task is to judge perceptual similarity, or shared perceptual properties (e.g., weight; S. A. Gelman & Markman, 1986), appearances are the better cues. Sloutsky and Fisher take issue with this account. First, they argue that Gelman and Markman are committed not just to labels being important to property projection, but to labels being criterial (they should override all other information). Second, they argue that labels function simply as auditory features rather than as cues to category identity. We examine both claims.

Sloutsky, Lo, and Fisher (2001) asked people to predict which of two animals would share a novel property. They manipulated information about common features: which animals looked alike, which shared labels, and which were biologically related. The finding was that children did not treat any single feature as criterial. However, it is not clear why criterial responding might be expected: Each feature is a reasonably good cue in this instance. The claim that category membership determines property projection is distinct from the claim that shared labels are criterial. Labels are only good

warrants for predicting shared membership; there may be other (competing) warrants. That two animals look alike is also generally fairly good justification for assuming that they share category identity (S. A. Gelman & Medin, 1993).

The second component of Sloutsky's similarity-based account is to deny any special status to labels. Instead, on this view, labels affect children's judgments because they are salient perceptual (auditory) features, and auditory features override visual features in children's processing. (This is a slippery claim to substantiate, as it is not clear how one could adequately calibrate the two dimensions to enable a head-to-head comparison.) This claim would seem incompatible with much of what is known about children's word learning. Not just any auditory association affects inferences. As reviewed by Bloom (2000), children make different judgments, depending on whether a label is a count noun, proper noun, mass noun, adjective, preposition, or verb (see also Waxman & Lidz, Chapter 7, this *Handbook,* this volume). If labels were simply attentional cues that are given heavy weight because of their auditory modality, then why should children differentiate between these different kinds of words? Even young children recognize that labels are intentions to refer (Tomasello & Barton, 1994). Jaswal (2004) found that children vary their attention to labels depending on the intentions of speakers: When a label was intended, then children relied on the label for drawing inferences, but when a label was accidental or un-informed, then it was not (see also Koenig & Echols, 2003; Sabbagh & Baldwin, 2001, for related results). This result is again consistent with the interpretation that children make use of labels to the extent that they indicate category membership, and not as a salient auditory cue. Young children use speaker intent to gauge value of the label: "[P]reschoolers do not treat labels as atheoretical features of objects; rather, they interpret them in light of their understanding of the labeler's communicative intent" (Jaswal, in press).

A related point is that the word-learning process itself relies heavily on impressively subtle social information. The manner in which children learn words would seem to belie simple associative learning mechanisms (though perhaps not more complex versions). Tomasello and Akhtar (2000, p. 181) list several ways that children as young as 24 months of age override spatiotemporal contiguity and perceptual salience when learning words:

- They assume that words refer to intentional actions, even if the target novel word is immediately followed by an accidental action and only later followed by an intentional action.
- They learn a word for an aspect of the context that is novel for the (adult) speaker, even though it is not novel for the child.
- They learn new action words for actions that they anticipate an adult will do, even when the adult has not actually performed the action.
- They use adult gaze direction rather than perceptual salience to determine reference.

Tomasello and Akhtar (2000) go on to point out that children are using well-known developmental mechanisms to acquire words (including speech processing, imitation, concept formation, and theory of mind)—but these mechanisms cannot reduce to associationism. See also Baldwin, 1993; Bloom, 2000; Diesendruck, Markson, Akhtar, and Reudor, 2004; Golinkoff and Hirsh-Pasek, 2000; and Woodward, 2000, for further arguments that associationism cannot be the sole mechanism of word learning.

### Constraints

The central challenge for associationist accounts is to describe constraints that are sufficient to produce just those concepts and developmental phenomena observed. How is it that children acquire the basic concepts in a fairly regular way, without gross deviations? The general answer, for an empiricist view, is that the structure of the input is responsible. A major focus of research has been to demonstrate that basic conceptual distinctions can be recovered from low-level features of input. This demonstration requires first showing that the relevant associations are present in children's experiences, and second, that children are sensitive to them. A challenge for this line of theorizing is to explain the associations that are *not* extracted (Keil, 1981). Of all the possible concepts that might be constructed given a child's experience, why is it that he or she comes up with just the standard set rather than some others?

Another way to put this is that developmental accounts also need to have something to say about when a concept *isn't* learned or *doesn't* change. All approaches try to characterize why children have the concepts they do. Yet why are children at times resistant to instruction or input? Innate constraints deal with this by saying that

the concepts aren't part of the innate tool kit children bring with them. The theory approach talks about a mismatch between competing conceptual systems—incommensurability between the child's preexisting concept and the instructional lesson. An empiricist approach would presumably say that past experience outweighs current input, but would also predict that eventually new input could override the old.

Associationist theories have begun to address this issue by looking at variations in experience to track just how alternative conceptions may be acquired. Cross-linguistic experience may be one of the key contexts. As mentioned, Japanese and English provide different cues regarding the animate-inanimate distinction, and young speakers of English versus Japanese seem to classify boundary cases differently (Imai & Gentner, 1997; Yoshida & Smith, 2003). These are important and provocative demonstrations. What is not yet known is how deep this mechanism is for development. Does this variation illustrate how infants *build* an ontology, or instead how children *tweak* an ontology? Strict associationist models may need to be supplemented with some innate dispositions, such as attentional biases (Rakison, 2003a).

### Conceptual Variation

A challenge for associationist accounts comes from claims that associations can account for all concept learning. Children are sensitive to patterns of covariation and basic similarity relations; yet mature examples of concept acquisition seem to extend beyond associations. Students in an advanced physics class are learning radically new ways of conceptualizing. Although physical intuitions, supported by long experience, continue to organize some aspects of thinking (diSessa, 1996), people also acquire abstract theoretical concepts that have no simple basis in associations given in experience. Is association the best way to characterize the processes of verbally and socially mediated learning? Most of us know the sun is a star (concept) and causes radio interference (causal relation) not because we have done the covariation analyses, but because other people have told us.

It is not clear whether associationists maintain that all thinking and learning is governed by the same basic principles—that cognition is associations "all the way down" (and up?). Rakison (2003b) seems to hold that communication (e.g., "the sun is a star") just provides associations, though perhaps between nonperceptual elements. Yet he also identifies "formal learning" in which people develop and apply explicit theories (Rakison, 2003b, p. 175). If both associationist and nonassociationist mechanisms of concept acquisition are possible, then the complex question becomes when is each active? Just because it is possible to acquire some concept through analysis of associations, is that the way that people typically do it? Associationist arguments for parsimony and simplicity also lose some force. If adolescents in school use various means of acquiring concepts, this would at least raise the possibility that these mechanisms are also available earlier in development (Gopnik et al., 1999).

## Conceptual Placeholders

There is a broad class of proposed mechanisms that we may call "placeholders." Conceptual acquisition does not occur all at once. Instead, the initial representation of a concept is a partial structure containing information about what more can be learned about the concept. Such partial representations underlie the "fast mapping" abilities to acquire concepts from brief and fragmentary presentations that make children such prolific word and concept learners (Carey, 1978). One area of current debate around conceptual placeholders is whether general principles of associative learning can produce such intuitions or whether their origins must be traced to innate structures or other learning mechanisms (Diesendruck & Bloom, 2003; Samuelson, 2002).

### *Words as Pointers*

Words seem to provide conceptual placeholders for children even at the dawn of word learning (Waxman & Markow, 1995). We have already seen that children assume that objects with the same label have common underlying properties (S. A. Gelman & Markman, 1986). Waxman and Markow (1995) refer to count nouns as "invitations" to form categories and look for relevant conceptual correlates: Common labels lead children to search for commonalities; distinct labels lead children to search for differences (see also Waxman & Lidz, Chapter 7, this *Handbook,* this volume). When hearing two items labeled with a word, even 9-month-olds are more likely to attend to relevant categorical similarities (Balaban & Waxman, 1997). Thus, children do not assume that labels are mere conveniences—ways of efficiently referring to perceptually encountered information in a shorthand way. Instead, children expect certain labels—and the categories to which they refer—to capture properties well beyond those they have already encountered.

The naming effect is particularly relevant in borderline or atypical cases, in which a nonlinguistic analysis might diverge from labeling. Children show these effects as early as 12 months of age—the very initial stages of word learning (Graham, Kilbreath, & Welder, 2004). In related work, Xu (2002) finds that hearing two identical labels for two objects encourages infants to treat them as the same kind of thing, whereas hearing two different labels for two objects encourages children to treat them as two different kinds of things.

Words can also serve as placeholders merely by linking to other words. Shatz and Backscheider (2001) have found that preschool children learn "word-word mappings" (e.g., that blue, green, and red are all kinds of "colors") before they have any conceptual content, that is, before they develop the appropriate "word-world mappings." The sketchy placeholder notion is that these words go together and form some sort of semantic domain. Only later does this minimal placeholder get linked to real-world referents. Shatz and Backscheider demonstrated evidence for these mappings in the domains of color words and number words. The phenomenon may be broader still. Consider that many concepts are acquired through language (oral or written; see Sternberg, 1987), and thus the only content for many words may be the surrounding linguistic context. At times, such context will supply rich conceptual information (e.g., if we hear "The tapir chased its prey," we will infer that a tapir is animate, from which a host of other inferences follow; Keil, 1979). But at other times, the context may supply only a word-word mapping of the sort that Shatz and Backscheider discuss.

The idea of words as conceptual placeholders leads to the question of whether concepts may be in part stored by others in the community rather than wholly stored in the individual child's mind. Several researchers have proposed that children may be sensitive to a division of labor—both linguistic and cognitive—such that some concepts are mere pointers to bodies of knowledge that only experts can access (Lutz & Keil, 2002; Markman & Jaswal, 2003; see also Coley, Medin, Proffitt, Lynch, & Atran, 1999, for an important distinction between knowledge and expectations). This idea follows from Putnam's famous example of elms and beeches: He knows they are different kinds of trees, but is unable to tell one type from the other.

After much more extensive argumentation, he concludes, "Concepts just ain't in the head!"

Experimental evidence suggests that adults defer to experts in matters of naming natural kinds (Malt, 1990; but see Kalish, 1995), and children do so even more strongly (Kalish, 1998). Children readily accept experimenter-provided labels, even when such labels are surprising and counterintuitive (S. A. Gelman & Coley, 1990; S. A. Gelman & Markman, 1986; Graham et al., 2004; Jaswal & Markman, 2002). In a detailed case study, Mervis, Pani, and Pani (2003) provide the example of a child who deferred to adults in the matter of naming, a process they refer to as the "authority principle," which seemed in place by about 20 months of age in the child under study (Ari). For example, when Ari's father said, "That birdie's a cardinal," Ari accepted that it was a subtype of bird, not a synonym for bird (p. 265). A 2-year-old in one study we conducted even articulated the authority principle explicitly: "I thought it was a stick, but the man [that is, the experimenter] said it was a snake."

It would be interesting to know the depths of children's deference to experts. Does it extend across the board in all knowledge domains, perhaps as a result of children's genuine ignorance about most things, or is it particularly strong in the case of naming? Do children defer to adult naming in all realms (including attribute terms and simple artifacts), or only for natural kinds? What is the developmental course of this willingness to incorporate others' knowledge? Are young children *most* open to expert knowledge because they are least knowledgeable and most in need of adult input? Or does deference to expert knowledge grow as children become more metacognitively aware of their own limitations?

More specific structures for concepts may be encoded by overhypotheses (Goodman, 1955; Shipley, 1993). Overhypotheses specify the kinds of features or dimensions that will be represented in a concept. Four-year-old children have a general expectation that, for animals, members of a kind tend to be alike with respect to habitat, diet, and movement. More plainly put, this means that when children encounter a novel kind (e.g., wallabies), they assume that members of this kind will all tend to live in the same kind of habitat, eat the same kinds of food, and move in the same manner—even before they learn the habitat, diet, or movement of a single instance. In this respect, children's category-based inferences partly reflect a specifically *biological* theory of animal kinds.

Superordinate concepts within a domain may be structured as sets of overhypotheses. Such a structure seems to characterize species of living things (Shipley, 1993) and kinds of illnesses (chicken pox, measles, and so on, Kalish, 2000). There are no necessary and sufficient conditions for something being an illness (Kalish, 1994). Rather, the superordinate concept of illness involves a representation of the kinds of properties that will characterize each kind of illness. Kinds of illnesses each specify values on the same dimensions (cause, cure, symptoms, time course, Lau & Hartman, 1983). Knowing that a concept is a kind of illness provides information about what can be learned about the concept; for example, it will have a characteristic cause and set of symptoms. In contrast, attributes not covered by overhypotheses may be treated as accidental. Like essentialist intuitions, overhypotheses provide means for elaborating on initial representations of concepts.

### Modes of Construal

How does domain-specific knowledge come about? Some suggest that many domain differences lie neither with the perceptual structure nor with the conceptual organization of the domain itself, but at the level of more abstract mechanisms or modes of understanding that come to be incorporated in different domains (Keil, 1994; Sperber, 1994). A relatively small number of modes of understanding (or modes of construal) have been proposed: an intentional mode, a mechanical mode, a teleological mode, an essentialist mode, perhaps a vitalistic mode (Inagaki & Hatano, 2002; Morris, Taplin, & Gelman, 2000), and a deontological mode (Atran, 1996).

Modes of construal involve recruiting fairly abstract representations of entities and interactions for explanatory purposes. Treating a phenomenon as involving goal-directed action provides a model or lens that directs explanations into certain forms. Positing an overarching goal suggests there might be subgoals, barriers to achieving goals, and adjustments to goal failures, and so on. Additional information about the system or phenomenon will serve to elaborate the general framework. What kinds of goals are pursued? What kinds of capacities for adjustment are present?

A good example of children's use of modes of construal can be found in Kelemen's work on teleology

(Kelemen, 1999, 2004). Young children seem prone to ascribe functions to objects in their experience. They adopt the functional stance of asking "What is this for?" From an adult perspective, young children apply this mode of construal too widely. They think of naturally occurring objects, such as rocks and rivers, as having functions (Kelemen, 1999). Young children do not at first make the distinctions that older children and adults do. For adults, artifacts have functions because people make them for specific reasons; living things have functional parts because of a history of selection; and nonliving objects may be used for purposes, but are not generally thought of as having functions. Such distinctions may be absent from young children's application of a teleological mode of construal.

Modes of construal are not uniquely assigned to particular domains. An essentialist mode would fit well with domains in which categories seem to capture clusters of information in the face of outward variation (such as living kinds), but would not be exclusively biological in any fixed sense. In several publications, Keil suggests that the linkage between mode of construal and domain occurs as children and adults search for resonances between modes of construal and the "real world structure" (1994, p. 252). Elsewhere he elaborates, proposing that "much of our adult intellectual adventures involve trying to see which mode of construal best fits a phenomenon, sometimes trying several different ones, such as thinking of a computer in anthropomorphic 'folk-psychology' terms, in fluid dynamic terms, or in physical-mechanical terms" (1995, p. 260).

The advantage of this approach is that it can accommodate phenomena such as essentialism that are broad in scope (e.g., applied to nonbiological categories, which is difficult for a biological modular position) but not promiscuous (e.g., not all categories are essentialized, thereby arguing against a wholly domain-general account).

## Causal Learning

Causal learning represents something of a bridge between associationist mechanisms and theory-based mechanisms. The inputs to causal learning are patterns of covariation. The outputs are representations of causal relations that would form the basis for theory building. Most accounts of causal induction within psychology focus on the problem of learning whether a causal connection exists between a set of given entities (Cheng & Novick, 1992; Shanks, Holyoak, & Medin, 1996). Such learning can be an important source for new concepts. Theory-based accounts hold that concepts form around networks of causal relations. As noted, features that are causally related are more central to a concept than those with merely spatial, temporal, or similarity associations.

Accounts of causal induction based on Bayesian networks have even more direct implications for conceptual change (Glymour, 2001; Pearl, 2000). Algorithms based on Bayesian networks also generate predictions about the existence of hidden variables. Given certain patterns of conditional dependence and independence between a set of entities, a learner might conclude that some additional, unknown entity is having a causal influence. Such a conclusion effectively provides the learner with a new (placeholder) concept: the kind of thing with such causal powers. The learner acquires not just new beliefs about relations between existing entities, but ideas about novel kinds of entities. These and other features of Bayesian networks seem to hold great promise as accounts of theory and conceptual development (Gopnik, Glymour, Sobel, et al., 2004).

Children as young as 2 years of age draw causal inferences from patterns of covariation (Gopnik, Sobel, Schulz, & Glymour, 2001). Gopnik and Sobel (2000) conducted studies in which 2-, 3-, and 4-year-olds learned that a novel object with a novel name (e.g., a "blicket") had a certain causal power (placing the object on a machine would, apparently, cause the machine to light up and play music). Results indicate that even 2-year-olds use causal information to guide both naming and induction. For example, objects that had the same causal effects were more likely to receive the same label than objects sharing perceptual appearance (but differing in causal powers). Importantly, merely being associated with machine activation (the experimenter activates the machine while holding the object nearby) does not product the same effects. Thus, correlational information alone did not determine children's naming. Instead, even 2-year-olds used causal information to guide both naming and induction.

One of the critical elements of Bayesian causal inference is the idea of conditional independence (Gopnik et al., 2004). Suppose one notices a relation between a set of objects and some causal power: Whenever a blue object and a red object are placed on a machine, the machine beeps. A way to identify which object is causing the beeps is to look for conditional independence. What happens given only the red or only the blue? If we observe an effect given only blue but none given only red, this pattern suggests that the blue object is the cause of beeping (beeping is independent of red given blue). Such patterns have the capacity to provide novel concepts. Critically, this kind of deconfounding seems distinct from mere inconsistent correlation. In this example, blue is associated with beeping 100% of the time, red only 50%. Producing the same rates of association without evidence of conditional independence (e.g., by showing two successful blue-only trials and one success and one failure with only red) does not produce the same effect. In cases of inconstant versus constant conjunction, children are at chance at selecting the causal object (Schulz & Gopnik, 2004). In contrast, the demonstration of conditional independence leads to reliable causal intuitions. Children even override existing domain-specific intuitions when patterns of conditional independence indicate novel causal relations (Schulz & Gopnik, 2004). As theories grow in complexity and scope, through causal learning and other mechanisms, so too will concepts.

Causal learning mechanisms raise a difficult question: If people seek causes, explanations, and nonobvious properties, then why is adults' knowledge in many domains so shallow, incomplete, and in error? If there is any doubt as to the truth of this last part of the paradox, we need look no further than the fundamental attribution error (Nisbett & Ross, 1980), error-laden reasoning heuristics (Kahneman, Slovic, & Tversky, 1982), and gaps and flaws in logical analyses (Johnson-Laird & Byrne, 1991). There are several relevant issues here. One issue is that gathering and evaluating evidence is difficult, even when children attempt to identify causes (D. Kuhn, 1989). The impulse to explain phenomena and discover causes is powerful even in childhood, but the scientific method poses difficulties throughout the life span. The question of when and how evaluation of evidence is relatively easier or more difficult is complicated and beyond the scope of this chapter. Kuhn and Franklin (Chapter 22, this *Handbook,* this volume) provide a more detailed discussion of the difficulties children face when attempting to coordinate prior expectations with new data (as contrasted with isolating causes in a multivariate context, which children do with greater ease). Another issue is that people tend to be satisfied with shallow explanations (Keil, 1998) and in fact have the illusion that their explanatory knowledge is deeper than it

actually is (Keil, 2003; Mills & Keil, 2004). When trying to figure out how a cell phone works, we do not seek, in an infinite regress, the electrical engineering principles that allow it to operate. Similarly, when reasoning about biological species (as well as social kinds), children appeal to underlying causes without constructing highly accurate biological models.

## Summary

Associationist and similarity accounts are powerful mechanisms in concept development, but appear to be insufficient in and of themselves without positing further conceptual and theory-building capacities. Such capacities include the two mechanisms reviewed here (conceptual placeholders and causal learning accounts), as well as other means of extending knowledge, such as structure mapping (see Larkey & Love, 2003, and A. Markman & Gentner, 2000, for review). Evidence *for* similarity cannot be taken as evidence *against* theories (and vice versa: evidence for theories does not argue against similarity). Rather, the two classes of accounts are likely to be mutually beneficial.

A relatively unexplored question is how information-processing demands are related to the development of intuitive theories. Researchers have explored the link between inhibitory control (IC) and conceptual development in the domain of theory of mind (Perner, Lang, & Kloo, 2002). One hypothesis is that tasks used to assess theory of mind have strong IC demands and thus may mask early conceptual competence. An alternative is that IC is a precondition for conceptual development in the domain of psychology and perhaps for other conceptual domains as well (Carlson & Moses, 2001; Flynn, O'Malley, & Wood, 2004). A third possibility is that, at least in this domain, conceptual development may drive improved information processing. As children acquire new concepts of mental function, they are better able to direct their thinking. Whether information-processing abilities have such a strong relation to conceptual development in other domains is an intriguing area for future research.

## EXPERIENCE AND INDIVIDUAL VARIATION

In the beginning of this chapter, we cautioned that concepts do not reduce to experience. Nonetheless, a full understanding of conceptual mechanisms requires an examination not just of concepts in the abstract, but also of the relation between experiences and conceptual structure. We examine the issue in this section, with a focus on individual variation and input.

## Individual Variation

One of the challenges for an account of concepts is addressing the tension between the shared and idiosyncratic natures of mental representations. On the one hand, shared concepts are a prerequisite for communication. On the other hand, each individual has some unique perspectives and associations. It is only because two people share the concept *dog* that they can talk about dogs, yet one representation of dog will differ somewhat from the next. Such conceptual variations are particularly salient when considering cultural differences. When do people have different concepts and when just different representations of the same concept? A similar question arises about conceptual development. In what sense do concepts change rather than undergo replacement? Is a 10-year-old's concept of dog a revised version of the concept she possessed at age 5, or a different concept altogether? In part, the issue of individual differences is the theoretical question of how concepts are identified and individuated. There are also important empirical questions about individual differences. Just how much variability is there across people in their concepts and what are the sources of these differences?

A central question for accounts of conceptual development is whether there is an in-principle distinction between different degrees of conceptual variation. Classical theories made a sharp distinction between differences in definition and differences in characteristic associations. Because *male* is one of the defining features of *bachelor*, people who disagree over whether there are female bachelors have different concepts. Because neatness is only a characteristic feature of bachelorhood, people may share the concept bachelor but disagree whether bachelors are slovenly. One of the consequences of a move from classical to similarity-based theories of concepts was abandonment of the distinction between characteristic and defining features. Similarity-based theories treat all conceptual distinctions as matters of degree. No two people ever have exactly the same concept, and no concepts remain the same across changes in experience.

Fodor (1998) sees this consequence of nonclassical theories as unacceptable and concludes that if mental representations provide no absolute basis for identity of concepts then concepts cannot be based on mental representations. Fodor argues, contra similarity theories, that virtually no differences in mental representation affect concept possession. One person's mental representation of dog may have nothing in common with another's, yet both have the same concept because both can think and talk about dogs. Such a view underlies the provocative claim cited earlier that meanings "just ain't in the head" (Putnam, 1975).

Foundational knowledge approaches attempt to reestablish the classical dichotomy between core and peripheral representations of concepts. Concepts are grounded within foundational theories. The core of the concept "heat," for example, is grounded in principles of physics. Smith, Carey, and Wiser (1985) describe different theories of physics that include different concepts of heat; a contemporary perspective that distinguishes heat from temperature and an older view that conflates the two senses. People holding different theories had incommensurable concepts; there was no direct way to represent one concept of heat within the conceptual framework of the other theory. Other conceptual differences are more like factual disagreements. Is light a particle or a wave? The concepts of light are different but the holder of one concept can represent the other. The disagreement is about which specific concept is represented. In the history of science, there are clear examples of incommensurable concepts. Carey (1985) argues there are examples across development. To what extent are individual and cultural differences characterized by incommensurability?

With these distinctions in mind, we now turn to variation due to expertise and variation due to cognitive style.

### *Expertise*

One of the most striking findings in the study of concepts is that young children can become highly expert in a domain, and that expertise has consequences for how concepts are organized (see Wellman & Gelman, 1998, for review). In a set of classic demonstrations, Chi and her colleagues found that young dinosaur experts not only had a larger set of facts at their disposal, but also organized this knowledge into a more cohesive hierarchical network of knowledge that permitted inductive inferences (Chi, Hutchinson, & Robin, 1989; Chi &

Koeske, 1983; Gobbo & Chi, 1986; see also Lavin, R. Gelman, & Galotti, 2001, for related findings with child Pokémon experts).

A particularly impressive example of the benefits of expertise can be found in Mervis, Pani, and Pani (2003), who report a detailed case study of a child bird expert between 10 to 23 months of age. This child had acquired 38 labels for types of birds, organized them into an appropriate hierarchical organization, and recognized the principle that baby animals must be the same species as their parents, even if they look like something else. Child experts also experience many other cognitive advantages in memory organization and problem solving (Chi et al., 1989; Gobbo & Chi, 1986). In the domain of theory of mind, children who have greater opportunity to engage in thinking about mental states develop more rapidly (Perner, Ruffman, & Leekam, 1994; Peterson & Slaughter, 2003).

Expertise affects conceptual organization even for adults (Medin, Lynch, Coley, & Atran, 1997; Shafto & Coley, 2003; Tanaka & Taylor, 1991). Medin and colleagues have found that expertise can lead to qualitatively distinct reasoning strategies. Whereas college undergraduates use diversity among premise exemplars as a basis for generalizing new facts about trees, tree experts do not. Further, experts develop unique conceptual schemes, such as quantum physics, population genetics, or dynamic systems models of psychology. It remains something of an open question whether such expert concepts actually replace foundational knowledge structures or whether expert knowledge remains a supplement alongside foundational knowledge (Carey & Spelke, 1994). Do physicists really experience objects as clouds of wavicles? Can mathematicians conceive of an N-dimensional object? Can biologists give up the decidedly nonbiological concept of tree?

Expertise is a phenomenon that leads to several key observations. First, it argues against qualitatively distinct, domain-general constraints on children's conceptual structures. At least some 2-year-olds *can* form taxonomic hierarchies and classify counter to outward similarity. Second, expertise demonstrates the importance of detailed experience. Third, expertise seems to increase conceptual interrelatedness (see also R. Gelman, 2002).

To some extent, the implications of expertise have not yet been fully tapped. Well-documented case studies of "naturally occurring" expertise tell us a great deal—but how far can expertise take the child? Can children acquire truly novel conceptual structures, with sufficient

expertise (and, importantly, sufficient motivation)? The broader, more difficult question that these findings raise is the following: Can different experiences result in different foundational concepts (see Slobin, 2001, for the suggestion that they can)?

### Cognitive Style

Cognitive style is a venerable idea that seems to be coming back in new form. Whereas prior work on cognitive style tended to focus on broad personality differences along dimensions such as creativity, field-dependence, and reflectivity-impulsivity (e.g., Kogan, 1983), current research suggests more local individual differences in conceptualization. At present, several unrelated findings are provocative for reminding us that conceptual development is not all of one piece. Here we discuss style differences in flexibility, essentializing, intense interests, and attention to thematic relations.

Deák (2003) has been pursuing the issue of conceptual flexibility. To measure conceptual flexibility, he constructed a word-meaning induction task, where children are given a linguistic cue to help them figure out the meaning of a new word. For example, a child might see a novel alien, hear a novel word in one of three predicate forms (e.g., "looks like a plexar," "is made of plexar," or "has a plexar"), and be asked to select another instance with the wording that was used during instructions (e.g., "Find another one that is made of plexar"). This task reveals marked developmental change between 3 and 6 years of age in children's ability to infer meaning *flexibly* (e.g., to switch from "looks like" to "has"). Deák notes that preschool children also vary considerably from one another in performance. Correlations between different versions of the task were fairly high, suggesting consistent individual differences among 3- and 4-year-olds.

Another kind of broad individual difference concerns children's preference for thematic versus taxonomic relations. Taxonomic relatedness is based on shared similarity—cows and horses are alike in that both are alive, have four legs, eyes, and so on. Thematic relatedness is based on interrelatedness in the world—cows and milk go together because cows give milk. The two kinds of relations are at times overlapping (cows and horses also share thematic relatedness, in that they both are found on farms). Although prior theorists had suggested a "thematic-to-taxonomic shift" (e.g., Smiley & Brown, 1979), more recent studies with young children have found no clear thematic preference even in young children (Blanchet, Dunham, & Dunham, 2001; Dunham & Dunham, 1995; Gelman, Coley, et al., 1998; Waxman & Namy, 1997). Some find a thematic bias across ages (Greenfield & Scott, 1986), some find a taxonomic bias overall (Dunham & Dunham, 1995), and others find highly mixed responses (Waxman & Namy, 1997). Moreover, adults are not averse to thematic relations, leading Murphy (2002, p. 838) to bluntly conclude: "[T]he idea of a thematic-to-taxonomic shift is wrong."

What is interesting in the present context is that individual differences in thematic versus taxonomic preferences at age 3 can be traced back to individual differences in behavior at 13 and 24 months of age (Dunham & Dunham, 1995). The authors propose that individual differences in perceptual-cognitive styles may be responsible. Likewise, Lin and Murphy (2001) find large individual differences in adult responses—some opting for thematic responses, others for taxonomic responses. Whether these adult patterns reflect anything stable, or instead momentary response strategies, cannot be known without further tracking the stability of these individual differences over time and contexts.

Individual differences in conceptual flexibility and thematic relatedness are (presumably) domain-general. In contrast, other kinds of individual differences in children's concepts seem to function at a more domain-specific level. An intriguing (though little-understood) example is that of intense interests (Simcock, Macari, & DeLoache, 2002). Certain children from a very young age become deeply fascinated with particular content areas, and develop highly specialized vocabularies and knowledge bases concerning those areas. This can be seen in cases of atypical development (e.g., Asperger syndrome), but also in normal development. These examples deserve further study. One question is whether there are stable differences in the intensity of specialized interests. Another concerns whether the concepts that develop in such cases are qualitatively distinct from those in nonintense domains. A further question is one of motivation: These children have highly developed motivation that leads them to attend to relevant inputs in a much more focused way; what are the effects of this motivational stance? If an "intensely interested" child and a "nonintensely interested" child were to get equal exposure to a novel concept in the relevant domain, would their representations vary significantly? In a sense, these children provide a special look at the expertise questions raised earlier.

A further content-specific example of individual differences concerns essentialism. Adults differ from one another in the degree to which they endorse essentialist views (Haslam, Rothschild, & Ernst, 2000). What about children? An example of individual variation in essentialist reasoning comes from children's beliefs about intelligence (Dweck, 1999). Dweck finds stable individual differences in this regard, with some children consistently endorsing an "entity" theory (that intelligence is fixed and immutable; in other words, an essentialist theory) and other children consistently endorsing an "incremental" theory (that intelligence is flexible and can be improved with practice and experience; in other words, a nonessentialist theory). These differences can be seen in children as young as first grade, and have powerful implications for children's persistence in the face of failure by fifth grade (Cain & Dweck, 1995). When entity theorists fail on a task, they more or less tell themselves, "I'm no good, so there's no point in my trying any more." When incremental theorists fail they tell themselves, in effect, "I need to improve, so I'd better try harder next time."

Even below first grade, children show individual differences in their beliefs about the stability of antisocial behavior (Giles & Heyman, 2003; Heyman, Dweck, & Cain, 1992). Among kindergartners, the belief that someone who misbehaves at the present time will always misbehave, is associated with "motivational vulnerability" (feeling as if one mistake means you are not smart, and difficulty generating strategies to solve academic difficulties; Heyman et al., 1992). And among 3- to 5-year-olds, the belief that antisocial behavior is stable is associated with the tendency to agree that hitting someone is an appropriate means to solve problems and with lower teacher ratings of children's social competence (Giles & Heyman, 2003). Although judgments of stability are not equivalent to essentialism, they are an important component.

The research literature on individual differences in conceptual development, though relatively sparse and scattered, is suggestive. Both domain-general and domain-specific differences have been suggested. Future research would do well to explore these in greater detail.

## Input

People learn from each other as well as by direct experience. Tomasello (1999) argues that such cultural learning is in fact an important contributor to what makes human conceptual systems human. This can be illustrated with examples both lofty (conceptual systems that are embedded in language and passed from one generation to the next, such as biological taxonomies) and mundane (individual facts, such as how to use a particular tool). Most of us did not acquire the belief that cigarette smoking causes cancer from direct experience of patterns of covariation; rather, this information was communicated to us from others (Ahn & Kalish, 2000).

Language can be an important source of information about novel causal and conceptual relations. Sperber (1996) provides the hypothetical example of the young child learning about plant reproduction who encounters the claim that there are male and female plants. The connection between the concepts of gender, plants, and reproduction may be largely incomprehensible at first. Such connections, though, provide a spur to theory development that ultimately generates enriched concepts. Similarly, children who are unable to receive detailed parental input perform much more poorly on false belief tasks, apparently reflecting their lack of opportunity for the conceptual enrichment provided by fully complex conversations (Peterson & Siegal, 2000).

We emphasize that more detailed characterizations of the input are needed. For many years, researchers have rightly focused on characterizing children's conceptual systems, with relatively little attention paid to the kinds of information children receive. Yet for a full understanding of what children bring to the task of conceptual learning, we also need to know much more about what they hear. Both matches and mismatches are informative. For some useful examples, see Jipson and Callanan (2003), Crowley, Callanan, Jipson, et al. (2001), S. A. Gelman, Coley, et al. (1998), and Sandhofer, Smith, and Luo (2000). Even in accounts that depend heavily (theoretically) on knowing what the input is, better characterizations are needed. For example, Smith (2000) makes assumptions about what children are exposed to based on what the *children* produce; it will be important to discover how tightly children's productions follow the input. Microgenetic methods also offer great potential for examining conceptual change as it occurs, with specific focus on the role of input (Opfer & Siegler, 2004; Siegler, Chapter 11, this *Handbook,* this volume; Siegler & Crowley, 1991).

Another point that arises from this work is the subtlety of the input that children are getting. In the case of psychological essentialism, parents provide no direct essentialist talk to their young children, but they do provide a wealth of *implicit* essentialism talk (e.g., talking about categories with generic noun phrases, "Bats live in caves," thereby implying that bats as a group are alike). See also S. A. Gelman, Taylor, and Nguyen (2004) for a detailed examination of the implicit ways that mothers emphasize gender categories to their preschool children, including referring to gender categories, providing gender labels, contrasting males and females, and giving approval to their children's stereotyped statements. Another example of implicit input comes from a study of parental talk to children during a visit to a science museum: Parents are more likely to explain science concepts to boys than to girls, despite talking equally often about the exhibits to girls and boys (Crowley, Callanan, Tenenbaum, & Allen, 2001). Subtlety in input can also extend to fine-grained conceptual distinctions. Sandhofer (2002) found that subtle aspects of parental input (e.g., either emphasizing the categorization of single objects, or emphasizing the comparison of multiple objects) seems to have implications for how children learn dimensional adjectives. Findings of subtle input cues and rich child concepts provide a pattern that is most consistent with interaction between the child's expectations and parental cues.

Considerations of input lead us to an important puzzle that is only now beginning to receive serious attention. Namely, what counts as knowledge or facts to a child's developing theories? Most strikingly, how do children screen off fiction, pretense, and metaphor from their factual knowledge base? How can a cartoon inform children that sponges are found in the sea without also convincing them that sponges walk, talk, and wear square pants? Or consider that an episode of *Sesame Street* might use singing Muppets to explain that animals but not rocks are alive. There are potentially numerous generalizations a child could form, including the biologically correct one (which things are alive) as well as biologically incorrect ones (that puppets talk and sing). Interestingly, 2-year-old children treat information differently depending on whether they believe it is coming from a TV screen versus being watched through a window directly (Troseth & DeLoache, 1998), suggesting that they may have some mechanisms for tagging certain kinds of input as not-real. Furthermore, 3- and 4-year-olds are skeptical of statements made by a speaker who previously said untrue things (Koenig, Clément, & Harris, in press). Presumably these assessments operate at a level other than the usual process of source-monitoring, which children (and adults) find difficult to track (Lindsay, Johnson, & Kwon, 1991).

Pretense is another interesting case. Does a child who sees her mother talking on a banana get confused about bananas and telephones? Lillard and Witherington (2004) make the interesting proposal that in the case of pretense, implicit cues in the input guide children to a nonliteral interpretation. When mothers pretend to have a snack with their 18-month-olds (versus really have a snack), they differ in behavioral variables, including talking about their behaviors, sound effects, increased smiling, and increased looking at the child. Importantly, children are sensitive to several of these behaviors.

Natural language, too, can be highly misleading regarding domain distinctions. Metaphors—including unintended metaphors—are rampant in everyday talk (Lakoff, 1987). We say that cars, batteries, and (alas) computers "die"; that deficits, crystals, and feelings "grow"; and the like. Are children ever misled by these cases? Are metaphorical uses somehow marked (by context or inflection) as nonliteral? Or do these observations imply that linguistic predicates have rather minimal consequences for children's developing theories?

The complexity of these issues suggests that existing concepts place constraints on new concepts. The nature of these constraints is currently largely unknown and will be fruitful to address in future research.

## CONCLUSION

The competing theoretical positions outlined in this chapter reflect a tension between two realities: children master so much so quickly, yet at the same time a young child still has so far to go before achieving adult competence. This tension can be seen in the competing metaphors of children (e.g., children as novices, as aliens, and as little adults; Wellman & Gelman, 1998).

### Interleaving Mechanisms

As we suggested earlier, there is no principled reason why different theoretical approaches could not be combined to account for conceptual learning even within a particular domain. R. Gelman (2002) reminds us that *innate* and *learning* can go hand-in-hand. This point is unquestionable in other species. For example, white-

crowned sparrows typically produce a characteristic song that has an innate template (acquired only by birds of this species) yet requires appropriate input between 10 and 50 days of age (Marler, 1991). In short, the song is both innate and learned.

An example that is closer to the current case can be seen in the domain of word learning, which overlaps considerably with concept learning (Waxman & Lidz, Chapter 7, this *Handbook,* this volume; but see Clark, 1983, for an important distinction between concepts and word meanings). Woodward (2000) proposes that different levels of explanation work together when children acquire word meanings, arguing strongly against monolithic accounts that try to explain word-learning wholly (or even primarily) in terms of just one kind of factor. Although theorists often argue for a particular position (e.g., social-constructivist, constraints-based, or associationist), she notes that each position explains different developmental phenomena. As she puts it, "There is no silver bullet for word learning" (p. 174).

We also have a sketch of how such coordination among levels might look, when considering the acquisition of intentions (the purposes that underlie actions). "Intention" is a concept informed by theory of mind. There are certainly many examples of intentions that are hidden, nonobvious, in conflict with surface cues, and that require understanding a web of motives, goals, and desires. Much of legal reasoning entails attempting to discern intentional from accidental action, on the basis of ambiguous behaviors for which multiple stories can be told. Nonetheless, despite the theoretical richness of the concept, Baldwin (2003) outlines how low-level patterns in the available percepts could form a basis for children's initial ability to detect intentions. She proposes that domain-general skills for covariation detection, sequence learning, and structure mapping may give rise to the detection of intentions (judging whether or not something was purposeful). For example, subtle cues regarding the acceleration of limbs toward goal objects might provide characteristic information about the beginning and end points of intentional sequences:

> predictable patterns emerge again and again in the sequencing and temporal dynamics of bodily motion that are probably unique to intentional action, and that correlate with the initiation and completion of intentional acts. For example, to act intentionally on an inanimate object, we first must locate that object with our sensors. . . . We then typically launch our bodies in the direction specified by

our sensors, extend our arms, shape our hands to grasp the relevant object, manipulate and ultimately release it. . . . All of this typically coincides with a characteristic kind of ballistic trajectory that provides a temporal contour or "envelope" demarcating one intentional act from the next. . . . This is all to say that on a purely structural level—the level of statistical regularities—there is considerable information correlated with intentions that is inherent in the flow of goal-directed action. Differing statistical patterns may even arise for intentional as opposed to unintentional action; for example, in intentional action we first locate with our sensors, and then display directed bodily motion. In unintentional actions, such as stubbing one's toe or slipping on a banana peel, motion comes first and location with sensors after the fact. (Baldwin & Baird, 2001, p. 174)

Initial evidence suggests that infants are sensitive to some of these low-level cues (Baldwin, Baird, & Saylor, 2001; Behne, Carpenter, Call, & Tomasello, in press). Importantly, the proposal is not that intention-detection reduces to low-level pattern detection, but rather that pattern detection jump-starts and facilitates intention detection. This integration of approaches seems to hold great promise for a full understanding of conceptual development.

## Beyond Initial Understandings

Much of the research on children's concepts that we have reviewed focuses on initial states and early frameworks—concepts in the first few years of life—in infants, toddlers, and preschool children. This is so for very good reason. Some researchers focus on this period to uncover developmental primitives; others do so to reveal developmental change. These initial states and early frameworks are critical to any understanding of concept acquisition. If nothing else, research on cognitive development over the past 30 years convinces us of the sophistication of conceptual processes in the ages 0 to 5 years. The process of acquiring concepts in young children cannot simply reduce to the models for adding on new concepts in adults (Markman & Jaswal, 2003; Rakison, 2003b). This central early period of concept development remains a highly fertile ground for future research.

Later developments are also critical—and perhaps even less well understood. Conceptual development is open-ended: We do not acquire all our concepts by age 5, or 10, or even 45. Issues of conceptual change can continue throughout a person's life. We have seen

glimpses of the complexities children face in trying to integrate bits of conceptual knowledge, adjudicate domain boundaries, and wrestle with incommensurate conceptual systems. Children also must consider larger cultural messages (Astuti, Solomon, & Carey, 2004; Coley, 2000; Lillard, 1999). Furthermore, later childhood raises important practical issues of the implications of basic research on conceptual development to issues of education and instruction (e.g., Au & Romo, 1999; Evans, 2000; Vosniadou, Skopeliti, & Ikospentaki, 2004). Schooling is only the most formal context in which conceptual change takes place. Any sort of communication (e.g., hearing a story, reading a newspaper) or informal learning (visiting a museum or zoo, tending a garden) depends on, and potentially modifies, existing concepts. To return to the metaphor that opened the chapter, if concepts are the building blocks of thought, manipulating these blocks is not mere child's play. The complexities of concepts and conceptual change are fundamental issues, and many puzzles remain.

## REFERENCES

Ahn, W. (1998). The role of causal status in determining feature centrality. *Cognition, 69,* 135–178.

Ahn, W., Gelman, S. A., Amsterlaw, J. A., Hohenstein, J., & Kalish, C. W. (2000). Causal status effect in children's categorization. *Cognition, 76,* B35–B43.

Ahn, W., & Kalish, C. W. (2000). The role of mechanism beliefs in causal reasoning. In F. C. Keil & R. A. Wilson (Eds.), *Explanation and cognition* (pp. 199–225). Cambridge, MA: MIT Press.

Allen, S. W., & Brooks, L. R. (1991). Specializing the operation of an explicit rule. *Journal of Experimental Psychology: General, 120,* 3–19.

Astuti, R., Solomon, G. E. A., & Carey, S. (2004). Constraints on conceptual development. *Monographs of the Society for Research in Child Development, 69*(3).

Atran, S. (1996). Modes of thinking about living kinds: Science, symbolism, and common sense. In D. Olson & N. Torrance (Eds.), *Modes of thought: Explorations in culture and cognition* (pp. 216–260). Cambridge: Cambridge University Press.

Atran, S. (1999). Itzaj Maya folk-biological taxonomy. In D. Medin & S. Atran (Eds.), *Folkbiology* (pp. 119–203). Cambridge, MA: MIT Press.

Au, T. K., & Romo, L. F. (1999). Mechanical causality in children's "folkbiology." In D. L. Medin & S. Atran (Eds.), *Folkbiology* (pp. 355–401). Cambridge, MA: MIT Press.

Balaban, M. T., & Waxman, S. R. (1997). Do words facilitate object categorization in 9-month-old infants? *Journal of Experimental Child Psychology, 64,* 3–26.

Baldwin, D. A. (1993). Early referential understanding: Infants' ability to recognize referential acts for what they are. *Developmental Psychology, 29,* 832–843.

Baldwin, D. (2003, October). *Socio-cognitive foundations for language acquisition and how they are acquired.* Paper presented at the Third Biennial Meeting of the Cognitive Development Society, Park City, UT.

Baldwin, D. A., & Baird, J. A. (2001). Discerning intentions in dynamic human action. *Trends in Cognitive Sciences, 5,* 171–178.

Baldwin, D. A., Baird, J. A., & Saylor, M. M. (2001). Infants parse dynamic action. *Child Development, 72,* 708–717.

Baldwin, D. A., Markman, E. M., & Melartin, R. L. (1993). Infants' ability to draw inferences about nonobvious object properties: Evidence from exploratory play. *Child Development, 64,* 711–728.

Baron-Cohen, S. (1995). *Mindblindness: An essay on autism and theory of mind.* Cambridge, MA: MIT Press.

Barrett, S. E., Abdi, H., Murphy, G. L., & Gallagher, J. M. (1993). Theory-based correlations and their role in children's concepts. *Child Development, 64,* 1595–1616.

Bates, E. (1999). On the nature and nurture of language. In R. Levi-Montalcini, D. Baltimore, R. Dulbecco, & F. Jacob (Series Eds.) & E. Bizzi, P. Calissano, & V. Volterra (Vol. Eds.), *Frontiere della biologia: The brain of homo sapiens* [Frontiers of biology]. Rome: Giovanni Trecanni.

Behne, T., Carpenter, M., Call, J., & Tomasello, M. (in press). Unwilling or unable? Infants' understanding of intentional action. *Developmental Psychology.*

Bertenthal, B. I., Proffitt, D. R., Spetner, N. B., & Thomas, M. A. (1985). The development of infant sensitivity to biomechanical motions. *Child Development, 56,* 531–543.

Bhatt, R. S., Wilk, A., & Hill, D. (2004). Correlated attributes and categorization in the first half-year of life. *Developmental Psychobiology, 44,* 103–115.

Blanchet, N., Dunham, P. J., & Dunham, F. (2001). Differences in preschool children's conceptual strategies when thinking about animate entities and artifacts. *Developmental Psychology, 37,* 791–800.

Bloom, P. (1996). Intention, history, and artifact concepts. *Cognition, 60,* 1–29.

Bloom, P. (2000). *How children learn the meanings of words.* Cambridge, MA: MIT Press.

Booth, A. E., & Waxman, S. R. (2002). Word learning is "smart": Evidence that conceptual information affects preschoolers' extension of novel words. *Cognition, 84,* B11–B22.

Bornstein, M. H., & Arterberry, M. (2003). Recognition, discrimination, and categorization of smiling by 5-month-old infants. *Developmental Science, 6,* 585–599.

Bornstein, M. H., Cote, L. R., Maital, S., Painter, K., Park, S., Pascual, L., et al. (2004). Cross-linguistic analysis of vocabulary in young children: Spanish, Dutch, French, Hebrew, Italian, Korean, and American English. *Child Development, 75,* 1115–1139.

Boroditsky, L. (2001). Does language shape thought? Mandarin and English speakers' conceptions of time. *Cognitive Psychology, 43,* 1–22.

Bowerman, M., & Choi, S. (2003). Space under construction: Language-specific spatial categorization in first language acquisition. In D. Gentner & S. Goldin-Meadow (Eds.), *Language in mind: Advances in the Study of Language and Thought* (pp. 389–427). Cambridge, MA: MIT Press.

Bowerman, M., & Levinson, S. C. (Eds.). (2001). *Language acquisition and conceptual development.* New York: Cambridge University Press.

Braisby, N. R., Franks, B., & Hampton, J. A. (1996). Essentialism, word use, and concepts. *Concepts, 59,* 247–274.

Bruner, J. S., Goodnow, J. J., & Austin, G. A. (Eds.). (1956). *A Study of Thinking.* New York: Wiley.

Bruner, J. S., Olver, R. R., & Greenfield, P. M. (1966). *Studies in Cognitive Growth.* New York: Wiley.

Cain, K. M., & Dweck, C. S. (1995). The relation between motivational patterns and achievement cognitions through the elementary school years. *Merrill-Palmer Quarterly, 41,* 25–52.

Callanan, M. A. (1989). Development of object categories and inclusion relations: Preschoolers' hypotheses about word meanings. *Developmental Psychology, 25,* 207–216.

Caramazza, A., & Shelton, J. R. (1998). Domain-specific knowledge systems in the brain: The animate-inanimate distinction. *Journal of Cognitive Neuroscience, 10,* 1–34.

Carey, S. (1978). The child as word learner. In M. Halle, J. Bresnan, & G. A. Miller (Eds.), *Linguistic theory and psychological reality* (pp. 264–293). Cambridge, MA: MIT Press.

Carey, S. (1982). Semantic development, state of the art. In L. Gleitman & E. Wanner (Eds.), *Language acquisition: State of the art* (pp. 347–389). New York: Cambridge University Press.

Carey, S. (1985). *Conceptual development in childhood.* Cambridge, MA: MIT Press.

Carey, S. (1986). Cognitive science and science education. *American Psychologist, 41,* 1123–1130.

Carey, S., & Spelke, E. (1994). Domain-specific knowledge and conceptual change. In L. A. Hirschfeld & S. A. Gelman (Eds.), *Mapping the mind: Domain specificity in cognition and culture* (pp. 169–200). New York: Cambridge University Press.

Carey, S., & Xu, F. (1999). Sortals and kinds: An appreciation of John Macnamara. In R. Jackendoff, P. Bloom, & K. Wynn (Eds.), *Language, logic, and concepts* (pp. 311–335). Cambridge, MA: MIT Press.

Carlson, S., & Moses, L. J. (2001). Individual differences in inhibitory control and children's theory of mind. *Child Development, 72,* 1032–1053.

Cheng, P. W., & Novick, L. R. (1992). Covariation in natural causal induction. *Psychological Review, 99,* 365–382.

Chi, M. T. H., Hutchinson, J. E., & Robin, A. F. (1989). How inferences about novel domain-related concepts can be constrained by structured knowledge. *Merrill-Palmer Quarterly, 35,* 27–62.

Chi, M. T. H., & Koeske, R. (1983). Network representation of a child's dinosaur knowledge. *Developmental Psychology, 19,* 29–39.

Chomsky, N. (1975). *Reflections on language.* New York: Random House.

Clark, E. V. (1973). What's in a word? On the child's acquisition of semantics in his first language. In T. E. Moore (Ed.), *Cognitive development and the acquisition of language.* New York: Academic Press.

Clark, E. V. (1983). Meanings and concepts. In P. H. Mussen (Series Ed.) & J. H. Flavell & E. M. Markman (Vol. Eds.), *Handbook of child psychology: Vol. 3. Cognitive development* (4th ed., pp. 787–840). New York: Wiley.

Coley, J. D. (1993). *Emerging differentiation of folkbiology and folkpsychology: Similarity judgments and property attributions.* Unpublished doctoral dissertation, University of Michigan, Ann Arbor.

Coley, J. D. (2000). On the importance of comparative research: The case of folkbiology. *Child Development, 71,* 82–90.

Coley, J. D., Medin, D. L., Proffitt, J. B., Lynch, E., & Atran, S. (1999). Inductive reasoning in folkbiological thought. In D. L. Medin & S. Atran (Eds.), *Folkbiology* (pp. 205–232). Cambridge, MA: MIT Press.

Collins, A. M., & Quillian, M. R. (1969). Retrieval time from semantic memory. *Journal of Verbal Learning and Verbal Behavior, 8,* 240–247.

Corrigan, R., & Stevenson, C. (1994). Children's causal attributions to states and events described by different classes of verbs. *Cognitive Development, 9,* 235–256.

Cosmides, L., & Tooby, J. (2002). Unraveling the enigma of human intelligence: Evolutionary psychology and the multimodular mind. In R. J. Sternberg & J. C. Kaufman (Eds.), *Evolution of intelligence* (pp. 145–198). Mahwah, NJ: Erlbaum.

Crowley, K., Callanan, M. A., Jipson, J. L., Galco, J., Topping, K., & Shrager, J. (2001). Shared scientific thinking in everyday parent-child activity. *Science Education, 85,* 712–732.

Crowley, K., Callanan, M. A., Tenenbaum, H. R., & Allen, E. (2001). Parents explain more often to boys than to girls during shared scientific thinking. *Psychological Science, 12,* 258–261.

Davidson, N. S., & Gelman, S. A. (1990). Inductions from novel categories: The role of language and conceptual structure. *Cognitive Development, 5,* 151–176.

Deák, G. O. (2003). The development of cognitive flexibility and language abilities. In R. Kail (Ed.), *Advances in Child Development and Behavior* (Vol. 31, pp. 271–327). San Diego, CA: Academic Press.

Diesendruck, G. (2001). Essentialism in Brazilian children's extensions of animal names. *Developmental Psychology, 37,* 49–60.

Diesendruck, G., & Bloom, P. (2003). How specific is the shape bias? *Child Development, 74,* 168–178.

Diesendruck, G., & Gelman, S. A. (1999). Domain differences in absolute judgments of category membership: Evidence for an essentialist account of categorization. *Psychonomic Bulletin and Review, 6,* 338–346.

Diesendruck, G., & Markson, L. (1999, April). *Function as a criterion in children's object naming.* Poster presented at the Biennial Meeting of the Society for Research in Child Development, Albuquerque, NM.

Diesendruck, G., Markson, L., Akhtar, N., & Reudor, A. (2004). Two-year-olds' sensitivity to speakers' intent: An alternative account of Samuelson and Smith. *Developmental Science, 7,* 33–41.

Diesendruck, G., Markson, L., & Bloom, P. (2003). Children's reliance on creator's intent in extending names for artifacts. *Psychological Science, 14,* 164–168.

diSessa, A. A. (1996). What do "just plain folk" know about physics. In D. R. Olson & N. Torrance (Eds.), *Handbook of education and human development: New models of learning, teaching and schooling* (pp. 709–730). Malden, MA: Blackwell.

Dunham, P., & Dunham, F. (1995). Developmental antecedents of taxonomic and thematic strategies at 3 years of age. *Developmental Psychology, 31,* 483–493.

Dweck, C. S. (1999). *Self-theories: Their role in motivation, personality, and development.* Philadelphia: Psychology Press.

Eimas, P. D., & Quinn, P. C. (1994). Studies on the formation of perceptually based basic-level categories in young infants. *Child Development, 65,* 903–917.

Elman, J., Bates, E., Johnson, M., Karmiloff-Smith, A., Parisi, D., & Plunkett, K. (1996). *Rethinking innateness: A connectionist perspective on development.* Cambridge, MA: MIT Press/Bradford Books.

Evans, E. M. (2000). Beyond scopes: Why creationism is here to stay. In K. S. Rosengren, C. N. Johnson, & P. L. Harris (Eds.), *Imagining the impossible* (pp. 305–333). New York: Cambridge University Press.

Fenson, L., Dale, P. S., Reznick, J. S., & Bates, E. (1994). Variability in early communicative development. *Monographs of the Society for Research in Child Development, 59*(173).

Flynn, E., O'Malley, C., & Wood, D. (2004). A longitudinal, microgenetic study of the emergence of false belief understanding and inhibition skills. *Developmental Science, 7,* 103–115.

Fodor, J. (1981). The present status of the innateness controversy. In *Representations: Philosophical essays on the foundations of cognitive science.* Cambridge, MA: MIT Press.

Fodor, J. (1998). *Concepts: Where cognitive science went wrong.* Oxford, England: Oxford University Press.

Gelman, R. (2002). Cognitive development. In H. Pashler & D. L. Medin (Eds.), *Stevens' handbook of experimental psychology* (3rd ed., Vol. 2, pp. 533–559). Hoboken, NJ: Wiley.

Gelman, R., & Baillargeon, R. (1983). A review of some Piagetian concepts. In J. H. Flavell & E. M. Markman (Eds.), *Handbook of child psychology* (Vol. 3, pp. 167–230). New York: Wiley.

Gelman, R., Durgin, F., & Kaufman, L. (1995). Distinguishing between animates and inanimates: Not by motion alone. In D. Sperber, D. Premack, & A. Premack (Eds.), *Causal cognition: A multidisciplinary debate* (pp. 150–184). New York: Clarendon Press.

Gelman, R., & Williams, E. (1998). Enabling constraints for cognitive development and learning: Domain specificity and epigenesis. In W. Damon (Editor-in-Chief) & D. Kuhn & R. Siegler (Vol. Eds.), *Handbook of child psychology: Vol. 2. Cognition, perception and language* (5th ed., pp. 575–630). New York: Wiley.

Gelman, S. A. (2003). *The essential child: Origins of essentialism in everyday thought.* New York: Oxford University Press.

Gelman, S. A., & Coley, J. D. (1990). The importance of knowing a dodo is a bird: Categories and inferences in 2-year-old children. *Developmental Psychology, 26,* 796–804.

Gelman, S. A., Coley, J. D., Rosengren, K., Hartman, E., & Pappas, T. (1998). Beyond labeling: The role of parental input in the acquisition of richly-structured categories. *Monographs of the Society for Research in Child Development, 63*(1, Serial No. 253).

Gelman, S. A., Croft, W., Fu, P., Clausner, T., & Gottfried, G. (1998). Why is a pomegranate an *apple*? The role of shape, taxonomic relatedness, and prior lexical knowledge in children's overextensions of *apple* and *dog. Journal of Child Language, 25,* 267–291.

Gelman, S. A., & Diesendruck, G. (1999). What's in a concept? Context, variability, and psychological essentialism. In I. E. Sigel (Ed.), *Development of mental representation: Theories and applications* (pp. 87–111). Mahwah, NJ: Erlbaum.

Gelman, S. A., & Ebeling, K. S. (1998). Shape and representational status in children's early naming. *Cognition, 66,* B35–B47.

Gelman, S. A., & Gottfried, G. (1996). Causal explanations of animate and inanimate motion. *Child Development, 67,* 1970–1987.

Gelman, S. A., & Heyman, G. D. (1999). Carrot-eaters and creature-believers: The effects of lexicalization on children's inferences about social categories. *Psychological Science, 10,* 489–493.

Gelman, S. A., & Hirschfeld, L. A. (1999). How biological is essentialism. In D. L. Medin & S. Atran (Eds.), *Folkbiology* (pp. 403–446). Cambridge, MA: MIT Press.

Gelman, S. A., & Kalish, C. W. (1993). Categories and causality. In R. Pasnak & M. L. Howe (Eds.), *Emerging themes in cognitive development: Vol. 2. Competencies* (pp. 3–32). New York: Springer-Verlag.

Gelman, S. A., & Koenig, M. A. (2001). The role of animacy in children's understanding of "move." *Journal of Child Language, 228,* 683–701.

Gelman, S. A., & Markman, E. M. (1986). Categories and induction in young children. *Cognition, 23,* 183–209.

Gelman, S. A., & Medin, D. L. (1993). What's so essential about essentialism? A different perspective on the interaction of perception, language, and conceptual knowledge. *Cognitive Development, 8,* 157–167.

Gelman, S. A., & Opfer, J. (2002). Development of the animate-inanimate distinction. In U. Goswami (Ed.), *Blackwell handbook of childhood cognitive development* (pp. 151–166). Malden, MA: Blackwell.

Gelman, S. A., & Raman, L. (2003). Preschool children use linguistic form class and pragmatic cues to interpret generics. *Child Development, 74,* 308–325.

Gelman, S. A., Star, J., & Flukes, J. (2002). Children's use of generics in inductive inferences. *Journal of Cognition and Development, 3,* 179–199.

Gelman, S. A., Taylor, M. G., & Nguyen, S. (2004). Mother-child conversations about gender: Understanding the acquisition of essentialist beliefs. *Monographs of the Society for Research in Child Development, 69*(1).

Gelman, S. A., & Wellman, H. M. (1991). Insides and essences: Early understandings of the nonobvious. *Cognition, 38,* 213–244.

Gentner, D. (1982). Why nouns are learned before verbs: Linguistic relativity versus natural partitioning. In S. A. Kuczaj (Ed.), *Language development: Vol. 2. Language, thought, and culture* (pp. 301–334). Hillsdale, NJ: Erlbaum.

Gentner, D., & Goldin-Meadow, S. (Eds.). (2003). *Language in mind: Advances in the study of language and thought.* Cambridge, MA: MIT Press.

Gentner, D., & Medina, J. (1998). Similarity and the development of rules. *Cognition, 65,* 263–297.

German, T. P., & Johnson, S. C. (2002). Function and the origins of the design stance. *Journal of Cognition and Development, 3,* 279–300.

Gershkoff-Stowe, L., & Smith, L. B. (2004). Shape and the first hundred nouns. *Child Development, 75,* 1098–1114.

Giles, J. W. (2003). Children's essentialist beliefs about aggression. *Developmental Review, 23,* 413–443.

Giles, J. W., & Heyman, G. D. (2003). Preschoolers' beliefs about the stability of antisocial behavior: Implications for navigating social challenges. *Social Development, 12,* 182–197.

Giles, J. W., & Heyman, G. D. (2004). When to cry over spilled milk: Young children's use of category information to guide inferences about ambiguous behavior. *Journal of Cognition and Development, 5,* 359–382.

Glymour, C. N. (2001). *The mind's arrow: Bayes nets and graphical causal models in psychology.* Cambridge, MA: MIT Press.

Gobbo, C., & Chi, M. (1986). How knowledge is structured and used by expert and novice children. *Cognitive Development, 1,* 221–237.

Goldin-Meadow, S. (2003). *The resilience of language: What gesture creation in deaf children can tell us about how all children learn language.* New York: Psychology Press.

Goldstone, R. L. (1998). Perceptual learning. *Annual Review of Psychology, 49,* 585–612.

Goldstone, R. L., & Johansen, M. K. (2003). Final commentary: Conceptual development from origins to asymptotes. In D. H. Rakison & L. M. Oakes (Eds.), *Early category and concept development: Making sense of the blooming, buzzing confusion* (pp. 403–418). New York: Oxford University Press.

Golinkoff, R. M., Harding, C. G., Carlson, V., & Sexton, M. E. (1984). The infant's perception of causal events: The distinction between animate and inanimate objects. In L. P. Lipsitt (Ed.), *Advances in infancy research* (Vol. 3, pp. 145–151). Norwood, NJ: Ablex.

Golinkoff, R. M., & Hirsh-Pasek, K. (2000). Word learning: Icon, index, or symbol. In *Becoming a word learner: A debate on lexical acquisition* (pp. 3–18). New York: Oxford University Press.

Golinkoff, R. M., Shuff-Bailey, M., Olguin, R., & Ruan, W. (1995). Young children extend novel words at the basic level: Evidence for the principle of categorical scope. *Developmental Psychology, 31,* 494–507.

Goodman, N. (1955). *Fact, fiction, and forecast.* Cambridge, MA: Harvard.

Gopnik, A., Glymour, C., Sobel, D. M., Schulz, L. E., Kushnir, T., & Danks, D. (2004). A theory of causal learning in children: Causal maps and Bayes nets. *Psychological Review, 111,* 3–32.

Gopnik, A., Meltzoff, A. N., & Kuhl, P. K. (1999). *The scientist in the crib: Minds, brains, and how children learn.* New York: HarperCollins.

Gopnik, A., & Sobel, D. M. (2000). Detecting blickets: How young children use information about novel causal powers in categorization and induction. *Child Development, 71,* 1205–1222.

Gopnik, A., Sobel, D. M., Schultz, L. E., & Glymour, C. (2001). Causal learning mechanisms in very young children: Two-, three-, and four-year-olds infer causal relations from patterns of variation and covariation. *Developmental Psychology, 37,* 620–629.

Gopnik, A., & Wellman, H. (1994). The theory theory. In L. A. Hirschfeld & S. A. Gelman (Eds.), *Mapping the mind: Domain specificity in cognition and culture* (pp. 257–293). New York: Cambridge University Press.

Goswami, U. (1996). Analogical reasoning and cognitive development. In H. W. Reese (Ed.), *Advances in child development and behavior* (Vol. 26, pp. 92–138). San Diego, CA: Academic Press.

Gottfried, D. B., & Gelman, S. A. (in press). Developing domain-specific causal-explanatory frameworks: The role of insides and immanence. *Cognitive Development.*

Graham, S. A., Kilbreath, C. S., & Welder, A. N. (2004). Thirteen-month-olds rely on shared labels and shape similarity for inductive inferences. *Child Development, 75,* 409–427.

Greenfield, D. B., & Scott, M. S. (1986). Young children's preference for complementary paids: Evidence against a shift to a taxonomic preference. *Developmental Psychology, 22,* 19–21.

Gutheil, G., & Rosengren, K. S. (1996). A rose by any other name: Preschooolers' understanding of individual identity across name and appearance changes. *British Journal of Developmental Psychology, 14,* 477–498.

Hahn, U., & Ramscar, M. (2001). *Similarity and categorization.* New York: Oxford University Press.

Hall, D. G. (1998). Continuity and the persistence of objects: When the whole is greater than the sum of the parts. *Cognitive Psychology, 37,* 28–59.

Hall, D. G., Waxman, S. R., & Bredart, S. (2003). Preschoolers' use of form class cues to learn descriptive proper names. *Child Development, 74,* 1547–1560.

Hallett, G. L. (1991). *Essentialism: A Wittgensteinian critique.* Albany, NY: SUNY Press.

Haslam, N., Rothschild, L., & Ernst, D. (2000). Essentialist beliefs about social categories. *British Journal of Social Psychology, 39,* 113–127.

Heit, E., & Hahn, U. (2001). Diversity-based reasoning in children. *Cognitive Psychology, 43,* 243–273.

Hejmadi, A., Rozin, P., & Siegal, M. (2004). Once in contact, always in contact: Contagious essence and conceptions of purification in American and Hindu Indian children. *Developmental Psychology, 40,* 467–476.

Hespos, S. J., & Spelke, E. S. (2004). Conceptual precursors to language. *Nature, 430,* 453–456.

Heyman, G. D., Dweck, C. S., & Cain, K. M. (1992). Young children's vulnerability to self-blame and helplessness: Relationship to beliefs about goodness. *Child Development, 63,* 401–415.

Heyman, G., & Gelman, S. A. (1999). The use of trait labels in making psychological inferences. *Child Development, 70,* 604–619.

Heyman, G. D., & Gelman, S. A. (2000a). Beliefs about the origins of human psychological traits. *Developmental Psychology, 36,* 665–678.

Heyman, G. D., & Gelman, S. A. (2000b). Preschool children's use of traits labels to make inductive inferences. *Journal of Experimental Child Psychology, 77,* 1–19.

Hirsch, E. (1982). *The concept of identity.* New York: Oxford University Press.

Hirschfeld, L. A. (1996). *Race in the making: Cognition, culture, and the child's construction of human kinds.* Cambridge, MA: MIT Press.

Hirschfeld, L. A. (2002). Why don't anthropologists like children? *American Anthropologist, 104,* 611–627.

Hollander, M. A., Gelman, S. A., & Star, J. (2002). Children's interpretation of generic noun phrases. *Developmental Psychology, 38,* 883–894.

Hull, C. L. (1920). *Quantiative aspects of the evolution of concepts, an experimental study.* Princeton, NJ: Psychological Review Company.

Imai, M., & Gentner, D. (1997). A cross-linguistic study of early word meaning: Universal ontology and linguistic influence. *Cognition, 62,* 169–200.

Inagaki, K., & Hatano, G. (2002). *Young children's naïve thinking about the biological world.* New York: Psychology Press.

Inhelder, B., & Piaget, J. (1958). *The growth of logical thinking from childhood to adolescence.* New York: Basic Books.

Inhelder, B., & Piaget, J. (1964). *The early growth of logic in the child.* New York: Norton.

Jaswal, V. K. (2004). Don't believe everything you hear: Preschoolers' sensitivity to speaker intent in category induction. *Child Development, 75,* 1871–1885.

Jaswal, V. K., & Markman, E. M. (2002). Children's acceptance and use of unexpected category labels to draw non-obvious inferences. In W. Gray & C. Schunn (Eds.), *Proceedings of the twenty-fourth annual conference of the Cognitive Science Society* (pp. 500–505). Hillsdale, NJ: Erlbaum.

Jipson, J. L., & Callanan, M. A. (2003). Mother-child conversation and children's understanding of biological and nonbiological changes in size. *Child Development, 74,* 629–644.

Johnson, K. E., & Eilers, A. T. (1998). Effects of knowledge and development on subordinate level categorization. *Cognitive Development, 13,* 515–545.

Johnson, K., Mervis, C., & Boster, J. (1992). Developmental changes within the structure of the mammal domain. *Developmental Psychology, 28,* 74–83.

Johnson, K. E., Scott, P., & Mervis, C. B. (1997). Development of children's understanding of basic-subordinate inclusion relations. *Developmental Psychology, 33,* 745–763.

Johnson, S. C., & Carey, S. (1998). Knowledge enrichment and conceptual change in folkbiology: Evidence from Williams syndrome. *Cognitive Psychology, 37,* 156–200.

Johnson-Laird, P. N., & Byrne, R. M. J. (1991). *Deduction.* Hillsdale, NJ: Erlbaum.

Jones, S. S., & Smith, L. B. (2002). How children know the relevant properties for generalizing object names. *Developmental Science, 5,* 219–232.

Kahneman, D., Slovic, P., & Tversky, A. (Eds.). (1982). *Judgment under uncertainty: Heuristics and biases.* New York: Cambridge University Press.

Kalish, C. W. (1994). *A Study of Preschoolers' and Adults' Understandings of the Domain of Illness.* Unpublished doctoral dissertation, University of Michigan, Ann Arbor.

Kalish, C. W. (1995). Graded membership in animal and artifact categories. *Memory and Cognition, 23,* 335–353.

Kalish, C. W. (1996). Preschoolers' understanding of germs as invisible mechanisms. *Cognitive Development, 11,* 83–106.

Kalish, C. W. (1998). Natural and artificial kinds: Are children realists or relativists about categories? *Developmental Psychology, 34,* 376–391.

Kalish, C. (2002). Gold, jade, and emeruby: The value of naturalness for theories of concepts and categories. *Journal of Theoretical and Philosophical Psychology, 22,* 45–66.

Kalish, C. W., & Gelman, S. A. (1992). On wooden pillows: Young children's understanding of category implications. *Child Development, 63,* 1536–1557.

Keil, F. C. (1979). *Semantic and conceptual development: An ontological perspective.* Cambridge, MA: Harvard University Press.

Keil, F. C. (1981). Constraints on knowledge and cognitive development. *Psychological Review, 88,* 197–227.

Keil, F. (1989). *Concepts, kinds, and cognitive development.* Cambridge, MA: Bradford Book/MIT Press.

Keil, F. (1994). The birth and nurturance of concepts by domains: The origins of concepts of living things. In L. A. Hirschfeld & S. A. Gelman (Eds.), *Mapping the mind: Domain specificity in cognition and culture* (pp. 234–254). New York: Cambridge University Press.

Keil, F. C. (1995). The growth of causal understandings of natural kinds. In D. Sperber, D. Premack, & A. Premack (Eds.), *Causal cognition: A multidisciplinary debate* (pp. 234–262). Oxford, England: Oxford University Press.

Keil, F. C. (2003). Folkscience: Coarse interpretations of a complex reality. *Trends in Cognitive Science, 7,* 368–373.

Keil, F. C., Smith, W. C., Simons, D. J., & Levin, D. T. (1998). Two dogmas of conceptual empiricism: Implications for hybrid models of the structure of knowledge. *Cognition, 65,* 103–135.

Kelemen, D. (1999). The scope of teleological thinking in preschool children. *Cognition, 70,* 241–272.

Kelemen, D. (2004). Are children "intuitive theists"? Reasoning about purpose and design in nature. *Psychological Science, 15,* 295–301.

Kemler, D. G., & Smith, L. B. (1978). Is there a developmental trend from integrality to separability in perception? *Journal of Experimental Child Psychology, 26,* 498–507.

Kemler Nelson, D. G., Frankenfield, A., Morris, C., & Blair, E. (2000). Young children's use of functional information to categorize artifacts: Three factors that matter. *Cognition, 77,* 133–168.

Kemler Nelson, D. G., Russell, R., Duke, N., & Jones, K. (2000). Two-year-olds will name artifacts by their functions. *Child Development, 71,* 1271–1288.

Koenig, M. A., Clément, F., & Harris, P. L. (in press). Trust in testimony: Children's use of true and false statements. *Psychological Science.*

Koenig, M. A., & Echols, C. H. (2003). Infants' understanding of false labeling events: The referential roles of words and the speakers who use them. *Cognition, 87,* 179–208.

Kogan, N. (1983). Stylistic variation in childhood and adolescence: Creativity, metaphor, and cognitive styles. In P. H. Mussen (Series Ed.) & J. Flavell & E. M. Markman (Vol. Eds.), *Handbook of child psychology: Vol. 3. Cognitive development* (4th ed., pp. 630–706). New York: Wiley.

Kolstad, V., & Baillargeon, R. (1996). *Appearance- and knowledge-based responses of $10^1/_2$-month-old infants to containers.* Unpublished manuscript, University of Illinois at Chicago.

Krascum, R. M., & Andrews, S. (1998). The effects of theories on children's acquisition of family-resemblance categories. *Child Development, 69,* 333–346.

Kripke, S. (1972). Naming and necessity. In D. Davidson & G. Harman (Eds.), *Semantics of natural language.* Dordrecht, The Netherlands: Reidel.

Kuhn, D. (1989). Children and adults as intuitive scientists. *Psychological Review, 96,* 674–689.

Kuhn, T. (1962). *The structure of scientific revolutions.* Chicago: University of Chicago Press.

Lakoff, G. (1987). *Women, fire, and dangerous things.* Chicago: University of Chicago Press.

Landau, B., Smith, L. B., & Jones, S. S. (1988). The importance of shape in early lexical learning. *Cognitive Development, 3,* 299–321.

Landau, B., Smith, L., & Jones, S. (1998). Object shape, object function, and object name. *Journal of Memory and Language, 38,* 1–27.

Larkey, L. B., & Love, B. C. (2003). CAB: Connectionist Analogy Builder. *Cognitive Science, 27,* 781–794.

Lau, R. R., & Hartman, K. A. (1983). Common sense representations of common illnesses. *Health Psychology, 2,* 167–185.

Lavin, B., Gelman, R., & Galotti, K. (2001, June). *When children are the experts and adults the novices: The case of Pokémon.* Poster presented at the American Psychological Society, Toronto, Ontario, Canada.

Legerstee, M. (1992). A review of the animate-inanimate distinction in infancy: Implications for models of social and cognitive knowing. *Early Development and Parenting, 1,* 59–67.

Legerstee, M., Barna, J., & DiAdamo, C. (2000). Precursors to the development of intention at 6 months: Understanding people and their actions. *Developmental Psychology, 36,* 627–634.

Legerstee, M., Pomerleau, A., & Malcuit, G. (1987). The development of infants' responses to people and a doll: Implications for research in communication. *Infant Behavior and Development, 10,* 81–95.

Lempert, H. (1989). Animacy constraints on preschool children's acquisition of syntax. *Child Development, 60,* 327–245.

Lillard, A. (1999). Developing a cultural theory of mind: The CIAO approach. *Current Directions in Psychological Science, 8,* 57–61.

Lillard, A. S., & Witherington, D. C. (2004). Mothers' behavior modifications during pretense and their possible signal value for toddlers. *Developmental Psychology, 40,* 95–113.

Lin, E. L., & Murphy, G. L. (2001). Thematic relations in adults' concepts. *Journal of Experimental Psychology: General, 130,* 3–28.

Lindsay, D. S., Johnson, M. K., & Kwon, P. (1991). Developmental changes in memory source monitoring. *Journal of Experimental Child Psychology, 52,* 297–318.

Liu, J., Golinkoff, R. M., & Sak, K. (2001). One cow does not an animal make: Young children can extend novel words at the superordinate level. *Child Development, 72,* 1674–1694.

Lizotte, D. J., & Gelman, S. A. (1999, October). *Essentialism in children's categories.* Poster presented at the Cognitive Development Society, Chapel Hill, NC.

Lo, Y., Sides, A., Rozelle, J., & Osherson, D. (2002). Evidential diversity and premise probability in young children's inductive judgment. *Cognitive Science, 26,* 181–206.

Locke, J. (1959). *An essay concerning human understanding* (Vol. 2). New York: Dover. (Original work published 1671)

Lucy, J. A. (1996). *Grammatical categories and cognition.* New York: Cambridge University Press.

Lucy, J. A., & Gaskins, S. (2003). Interaction of language type and referent type in the development of nonverbal classification preferences. In D. Gentner & S. Goldin-Meadow (Eds.), *Language in mind: Advances in the Study of Language and Thought.* Cambridge, MA: MIT Press.

Lutz, D. J., & Keil, F. C. (2002). Early understanding of the division of cognitive labor. *Child Development, 73,* 1073–1084.

Maccoby, E. E. (1998). *The two sexes: Growing up apart, coming together.* Cambridge, MA: Belknap/Harvard University Press.

Macnamara, J. (1982). *Names for things: A study of human learning.* Cambridge, MA: MIT Press.

Macnamara, J. (1986). *A border dispute.* Cambridge, MA: MIT Press.

MacWhinney, B. (1987). The competition model. In B. MacWhinney (Ed.), *Mechanisms of language acquisition* (pp. 249–308). Hillsdale, NJ: Erlbaum.

Madole, K. L., & Oakes, L. M. (1999). Make sense of infant categorization: Stable processes and changing representations. *Developmental Review, 19,* 263–296.

Malt, B. C. (1990). Features and beliefs in the mental representation of categories. *Journal of Memory and Language, 29,* 289–315.

Malt, B. C. (1994). Water is not $H_2O$. *Cognitive Psychology, 27,* 41–70.

Mandler, J. M. (2004). *The foundations of mind.* New York: Oxford University Press.

Mandler, J. M., & McDonough, L. (1993). Concept formation in infancy. *Cognitive Development, 8,* 291–318.

Mandler, J. M., & McDonough, L. (1996). Drinking and driving don't mix: Inductive generalization in infancy. *Cognition, 59,* 307–335.

Mandler, J. M., & McDonough, L. (1998). Studies in inductive inference in infancy. *Cognitive Psychology, 37,* 60–96.

Mandler, J. M., & McDonough, L. (2000). Advancing downward to the basic level. *Journal of Cognition and Development, 1,* 379–403.

Mareschal, D. (2003). The acquisition and use of implicit categories in early development. In D. H. Rakison & L. M. Oakes (Ed.), *Early category and concept development: Making sense of the blooming, buzzing confusion* (pp. 360–383). New York: Oxford University Press.

Margolis, E. (1994). A reassessment of the shift from the classical theory of concepts to prototype theory. *Cognition, 51,* 73–89.

Margolis, E. (1998). How to acquire a concept. *Mind and Language, 13,* 347–369.

Markman, A., & Gentner, D. (2000). Structure mapping in the comparison process. *American Journal of Psychology, 113,* 501–538.

Markman, E. M. (1989). *Categorization and naming in children: Problems in induction.* Cambridge, MA: MIT Press.

Markman, E. M., & Hutchinson, J. E. (1984). Children's sensitivity to constraints on word meaning: Taxonomic versus thematic relations. *Cognitive Psychology, 16,* 1–27.

Markman, E. M., & Jaswal, V. K. (2003). Commentary on Part II: Abilities and assumptions underlying conceptual development. In D. H. Rakison & L. M. Oakes (Eds.), *Early category and concept development: Making sense of the blooming, buzzing confusion* (pp. 384–402). New York: Oxford University Press.

Marler, P. (1991). The instinct to learn. In S. Carey & R. Gelman (Eds.), *Epigenesis of mind: Essays on biology and cognition* (pp. 37–66). Hillsdale, NJ: Erlbaum.

Marr, D. (1982). *Vision: A computational investigation into the human representation and processing of visual information.* New York: Freeman.

Martin, C. L., & Ruble, D. (2004). Children's search for gender cues: Cognitive perspectives on gender development. *Current Directions in Psychological Science, 13,* 67–70.

Mayr, E. (1991). *One long argument: Charles Darwin and the genesis of modern evolutionary thought.* Cambridge, MA: Harvard University Press.

McCarrell, N., & Callanan, M. (1995). Form-function correspondences in children's inference. *Child Development, 66,* 532–546.

McCawley, J. D. (1981). *Everything that linguists have always wanted to know about logic.* Chicago: University of Chicago Press.

McDonough, L., Choi, S., & Mandler, J. M. (2003). Understanding spatial relations: Flexible infants, lexical adults. *Cognitive Psychology, 46,* 229–259.

Medin, D. (1989). Concepts and conceptual structure. *American Psychologist, 44,* 1469–1481.

Medin, D. L., Goldstone, R. L., & Gentner, D. (2000). Respects for similarity. *Psychological Review, 100,* 254–278.

Medin, D. L., Lynch, E. B., Coley, J. D., & Atran, S. (1997). Categorization and reasoning among tree experts: Do all roads lead to Rome? *Cognitive Psychology, 32,* 49–96.

Medin, D. L., & Shoben, E. J. (1988). Context and structure in conceptual combination. *Cognitive Psychology, 20,* 158–190.

Meltzoff, A. N. (1995). Understanding the intentions of others: Reenactment of intended acts by 18-month-old children. *Developmental Psychology, 31,* 838–850.

Mervis, C. B., & Crisafi, M. A. (1982). Order of acquisition of subordinate-, basic-, and superordinate-level categories. *Child Development, 53,* 258–266.

Mervis, C. B., Pani, J. R., & Pani, A. M. (2003). Transaction of child cognitive-linguistic abilities and adult input in the acquisition of lexical categories at the basic and subordinate levels. In D. H. Rakison & L. M. Oakes (Eds.), *Early category and concept development: Making sense of the blooming, buzzing confusion* (pp. 242–274). New York: Oxford University Press.

Mill, J. S. (1843). *A system of logic, ratiocinative and inductive.* London: Longmans.

Millikan, R. G. (1998). A common structure for concepts of individuals, stuffs, and real kinds: More mama, more milk, and more mouse. *Behavioral and Brain Sciences, 21,* 55–100.

Mills, C. M., & Keil, F. C. (2004). Knowing the limits of one's understanding: The development of an awareness of an illusion of explanatory depth. *Journal of Experimental Child Psychology, 87,* 1–32.

Morris, S. C., Taplin, J. E., & Gelman, S. A. (2000). Vitalism in naive biological thinking. *Developmental Psychology, 36,* 582–595.

Murphy, G. L. (1993). Theories and concept formation. In I. Van Mechelen, J. Hampton, R. Michalski, & P. Theuns (Eds.), *Categories and concepts: Theoretical views and inductive data analysis* (pp. 173–200). New York: Academic Press.

Murphy, G. L. (2002). *The big book of concepts.* Cambridge, MA: MIT Press.

Murphy, G. L., & Allopenna, P. D. (1994). The locus of knowledge effects in concept learning. *Journal of Experimental Psychology: Learning, Memory, and Cognition, 20,* 904–919.

Murphy, G. L., & Medin, D. L. (1985). The role of theories in conceptual coherence. *Psychological Review, 92,* 289–316.

Nelson, C. A. (2001). The development and neural bases of face recognition. *Infant and Child Development, 10,* 3–18.

Nelson, K. (1973). Structure and strategy in learning to talk. *Monographs of the Society for Research in Child Development, 38*(1/2, Serial No. 149).

Nisbett, R. E., & Ross, L. D. (1980). *Human inference: Strategies and shortcomings of social judgment.* Englewood Cliffs: NJ: Prentice-Hall.

Oakes, L. M., & Madole, K. L. (2003). Principles of developmental change in infants' category formation. In D. H. Rakison & L. M. Oakes (Eds.), *Early category and concept development: Making sense of the blooming, buzzing, confusion* (pp. 132–158). New York: Oxford University Press.

Oakes, L. M., & Rakison, D. H. (2003). Issues in the early development of concepts and categories: An introduction. In D. H. Rakison & L. M. Oakes (Eds.), *Early category and concept development: Making sense of the blooming, buzzing, confusion* (pp. 3–23). New York: Oxford University Press.

Opfer, J. E., & Siegler, R. S. (2004). Revisiting preschoolers' "living things" concept: A microgenetic analysis of conceptual change in basic biology. *Cognitive Psychology, 59,* 301–332.

Osherson, D. N., Smith, E. E., Wilkie, O., Lopez, A., & Shafir, E. (1990). Category-based induction. *Psychological Review, 97,* 185–200.

Pearl, J. (2000). *Causality.* New York: Cambridge University Press.

Perner, J., Lang, B., & Kloo, D. (2002). Theory of mind and self-control: More than a common problem of inhibition. *Child Development, 73,* 752–767.

Perner, J., Ruffman, T., & Leekam, S. R. (1994). Theory of mind is contagious: You catch it from your sibs. *Child Development, 65,* 1228–1238.

Peterson, C. C., & Siegal, M. (2000). Insights into theory of mind from deafness and autism. *Mind and Language, 15,* 123–145.

Peterson, C., & Slaughter, V. (2003). Opening windows into the mind: Mothers' preferences for mental state explanations and children's theory of mind. *Cognitive Development, 18,* 399–429.

Piaget, J. (1929). *The child's conception of the world.* London: Routledge & Kegan Paul.

Piaget, J. (1970). Piaget's theory. In P. H. Mussen (Ed.), *Carmichael's manual of child psychology* (Vol. 1, pp. 703–732). New York: Wiley.

Pinker, S. (1994). *The language instinct.* New York: Morrow.

Pinker, S. (2002). *The blank slate: The modern denial of human nature.* New York: Viking.

Prasada, S. (2000). Acquiring generic knowledge. *Trends in Cognitive Sciences, 4,* 66–72.

Prasada, S. (2003). Conceptual representation of animacy and its perceptual and linguistic reflections. *Developmental Science, 6,* 18–19.

Premack, D., & Premack, A. J. (1997). Infants attribute value ± to the goal-directed actions of self-propelled objects. *Journal of Cognitive Neuroscience, 9,* 848–856.

Putnam, H. (1975). The meaning of "meaning." In H. Putnam. *Mind, language, and reality* (pp. 215–271). New York: Cambridge University Press.

Quine, W. V. (1960). *Word and object.* Cambridge, MA: MIT Press.

Quine, W. V. (1977). Natural kinds. In S. P. Schwartz (Ed.), *Naming, necessity, and natural kinds* (pp. 155–175). Ithaca, NY: Cornell University Press.

Quinn, P. C., Bhatt, R. S., Brush, D., Grimes, A., & Sharpnack, H. (2002). Development of the use of form similarity as a Gestalt grouping principle in 3- to 7-month-old infants. *Psychological Science, 13,* 320–328.

Quinn, P. C., & Eimas, P. D. (2000). The emergence of category representations during infancy: Are separate and conceptual processes required? *Journal of Cognition and Development, 1,* 55–61.

Quinn, P. C., Eimas, P. D., & Tarr, M. J. (2001). Perceptual categorization of cat and dog silhouettes by 3- to 4-month-old infants. *Journal of Experimental Child Psychology, 79,* 78–94.

Rakison, D. H. (2003a). Free association? Why category development requires something more. *Developmental Science, 6,* 20–22.

Rakison, D. H. (2003b). Parts, motion, and the development of the animate-inanimate distinction in infancy. In D. H. Rakison & L. M. Oakes (Eds.), *Early category and concept development: Making sense of the blooming, buzzing, confusion* (pp. 159–192). New York: Oxford University Press.

Rakison, D. H., & Oakes, L. M. (2003). *Early category and concept development: Making sense of the blooming, buzzing, confusion.* New York: Oxford University Press.

Rakison, D. H., & Poulin-Dubois, D. (2001). The developmental origin of the animate-inanimate distinction. *Psychological Bulletin, 127,* 209–228.

Rehder, B. (2003). Categorization as causal reasoning. *Cognitive Science, 27,* 709–748.

Rips, L. J. (2001). Necessity and natural categories. *Psychological Bulletin, 127,* 827–852.

Rips, L. J., & Collins, A. (1993). Categories and resemblance. *Journal of Experimental Psychology: General, 122,* 468–486.

Rosch, E. (1978). Principles of categorization. In E. Rosch & B. B. Lloyd (Eds.), *Cognition and categorization* (pp. 27–48). Hillsdale, NJ: Erlbaum.

Rosengren, K., Gelman, S. A., Kalish, C., & McCormick, M. (1991). As time goes by: Children's early understanding of biological growth. *Child Development, 62,* 1302–1320.

Rothbart, M., & Taylor, M. (1990). Category labels and social reality: Do we view social categories as natural kinds. In G. Semin & K. Fiedler (Eds.), *Language and social cognition* (pp. 11–36). London: Sage.

Sabbagh, M. A., & Baldwin, D. A. (2001). Learning words from knowledgeable versus ignorant speakers: Links between preschoolers' theory of mind and semantic development. *Child Development, 72,* 1054–1070.

Sacks, O. (1985). *The man who mistook his wife for a hat and other clinical tales.* New York: Summit Books.

Saffran, J. R., Aslin, R. N., & Newport, E. L. (1996). Statistical learning by 8-month-old infants. *Science, 274,* 1926–1928.

Samuelson, L. K. (2002). Statistical regularities in vocabulary guide language acquisition in connectionist models and 15–20-month-olds. *Developmental Psychology, 38,* 1016–1037.

Sandhofer, C. (2002). Structure in parents' input: Effects of categorization versus comparison. *BUCLD, 25,* 657–667.

Sandhofer, C. M., Smith, L. B., & Luo, J. (2000). Counting nouns and verbs in the input: Differential frequencies, different kinds of learning? *Journal of Child Language, 27,* 561–585.

Schulz, L. E., & Gopnik, A. (2004). Causal learning across domains. *Developmental Psychology, 40,* 162–176.

Schwartz, S. P. (Ed.). (1977). *Naming, necessity, and natural kinds.* Ithaca, NY: Cornell University Press.

Shafto, P., & Coley, J. D. (2003). Development of categorization and reasoning in the natural world: Novices to experts, naïve similarity to ecological knowledge. *Journal of Experimental Psychology: Learning, Memory, and Cognition, 29,* 641–649.

Shanks, D. R., Holyoak, K., & Medin, D. L. (Eds.) (1996). *Causal learning.* San Diego, CA: Academic Press.

Shatz, M., & Backscheider, A. (2001, December). *The development of non-object categories in 2-year-olds.* Paper presented at the Conference on Early Lexicon Acquisition, Lyon, France.

Shipley, E. F. (1993). Categories, hierarchies, and induction. In D. Medin (Ed.), *The psychology of learning and motivation* (Vol. 30, pp. 265–301). New York: Academic Press.

Shipley, E. F., Kuhn, I. F., & Madden, E. (1983). Mothers' use of superordinate category terms. *Journal of Child Language, 10,* 571–588.

Siegal, M. (1988). Children's knowledge of contagion and contamination as causes of illness. *Child Development, 59,* 1353–1359.

Siegler, R. S. (1996). *Emerging minds: The process of change in children's thinking.* New York: Oxford University Press.

Siegler, R. S., & Crowley, K. (1991). The microgenetic method: A direct means for studying cognitive development. *American Psychologist, 46,* 606–620.

Silverstein, M. (1986). Cognitive implications of a referential hierarchy. In M. Hickmann (Ed.), *Social and functional approaches to language and thought* (pp. 125–164). New York: Academic Press.

Simcock, G., Macari, S., & DeLoache, J. (2002, April). *Blenders, brushes, and balls: Intense interests in very young children.* Thirteenth Biennial International Conference on Infant Studies, Toronto, Ontario, Canada.

Simons, D. J., & Keil, F. C. (1995). An abstract to concrete shift in the development of biological thought: The insides story. *Cognition, 56,* 129–163.

Slobin, D. I. (1985). Crosslinguistic evidence for the language-making capacity. In D. I. Slobin (Ed.), *The Crosslinguistic Study of Language Acquisition: Vol. 2. Theoretical issues* (pp. 1157–1256). Hillsdale, NJ: Erlbaum.

Slobin, D. I. (1996). From "thought and language" to "thinking for speaking." In J. J. Gumperz & S. C. Levinson (Eds.), *Rethinking linguistic relativity* (pp. 70–96). New York: Cambridge University Press.

Slobin, D. I. (2001). Form-function relations: How do children find out what they are. In M. Bowerman & S. C. Levinson (Eds.), *Language acquisition and conceptual development* (pp. 406–449). New York: Cambridge University Press.

Sloman, S. A., & Malt, B. C. (2003). Artifacts are not ascribed essences, nor are they treated as belonging to kinds. *Language and Cognitive Processes, 18,* 563–582.

Slotta, J. D., Chi, M. T. H., & Joram, E. (1995). Assessing students' misclassifications of physics concepts: An ontological basis for conceptual change. *Cognition and Instruction, 13,* 373–400.

Sloutsky, V. M. (2003). The role of similarity in the development of categorization. *Trends in Cognitive Sciences, 7,* 246–251.

Sloutsky, V. M., & Fisher, A. V. (2004). Induction and categorization in young children: A similarity-based model. *Journal of Experimental Psychology: General, 133,* 166–188.

Sloutsky, V. M., & Lo, Y.-F. (1999). How much does a shared name make things similar? Pt. 1. Linguistic labels and the development of similarity judgment. *Developmental Psychology, 35,* 1478–1492.

Sloutsky, M., Lo, Y.-F., & Fisher, A. V. (2001). How much does a shared name make things similar? Linguistic labels, similarity, and the development of inductive inference. *Child Development, 72,* 1695–1709.

Smiley, S. S., & Brown, A. L. (1979). Conceptual preference for thematic or taxonomic relations: A nonmonotonic age trend from preschool to old age. *Journal of Experimental Child Psychology, 28,* 249–257.

Smith, C., Carey, S., & Wiser, M. (1985). On differentiation: A Case Study of the Development of the Concepts of Size, Weight, and Density. *Cognition, 21,* 177–237.

Smith, E. E. (1989). Concepts and induction. In M. I. Posner (Ed.), *Foundations of cognitive science* (pp. 501–526). Cambridge, MA: MIT Press.

Smith, E. E., & Medin, D. (1981). *Categories and concepts.* Cambridge, MA: Harvard University Press.

Smith, E. E., Patalano, A. L., & Jonides, J. (1998). Alternative strategies of categorization. *Cognition, 65,* 167–196.

Smith, L. B. (2000). Avoiding association when its behaviorism you really hate. In R. Golinkoff & K. Hirsh-Pasek (Eds.), *Breaking the word learning barrier* (pp. 169–174). New York: Oxford University Press.

Smith, L. B., Colunga, E., & Yoshida, H. (2003). Making an ontology: Cross-linguistic evidence. In D. H. Rakison & L. M. Oakes (Eds.), *Early category and concept development: Making sense of the blooming, buzzing, confusion* (pp. 275–302). New York: Oxford University Press.

Smith, L. B., Jones, S. S., & Landau, B. (1996). Naming in young children: A dumb attentional mechanism? *Cognition, 60,* 143–171.

Soja, N. N., Carey, S., & Spelke, E. S. (1991). Ontological categories guide young children's inductions of word meaning: Object terms and substance terms. *Cognition, 38,* 179–211.

Soja, N. N., Carey, S., & Spelke, E. S. (1992). Perception, ontology, and word meaning. *Cognition, 45,* 101–107.

Solomon, G. E. A., Johnson, S. C., Zaitchik, D., & Carey, S. (1996). Like father, like son: Young children's understanding of how and why offspring resemble their parents. *Child Development, 67,* 151–171.

Sorrentino, C. M. (2001). Children and adults represent proper names as referring to unique individuals. *Developmental Science, 4,* 399–407.

Spelke, E. (1994). Initial knowledge: Six suggestions. *Cognition, 50,* 431–445.

Spelke, E. S. (2003). What makes us smart? Core knowledge and natural language. In D. Gentner & S. Goldin-Meadow (Eds.), *Advances in the investigation of language and thought* (pp. 277–311). Cambridge, MA: MIT Press.

Spelke, E. S., Phillips, A., & Woodward, A. L. (1995). In D. Sperber, D. Premack, & A. Premack (Eds.), *Causal cognition: A multidisciplinary debate* (pp. 44–78). New York: Clarendon Press/Oxford University Press.

Sperber, D. (1994). The modularity of thought and the epidemiology of representations. In L. A. Hirschfeld & S. A. Gelman (Eds.), *Mapping the mind: Domain specificity in cognition and culture* (pp. 39–67). New York: Cambridge University Press.

Sperber, D. (1996). *Explaining culture: A naturalistic approach.* Oxford, England: Blackwell.

Springer, K. (1996). Young children's understanding of a biological basis of parent-offspring relations. *Child Development, 67,* 2841–2856.

Springer, K., & Keil, F. C. (1991). Early differentiation of causal mechanisms appropriate to biological and nonbiological kinds. *Child Development, 62,* 767–781.

Sternberg, R. J. (1987). Most vocabulary is learned from context. In J. G. McKeown & M. E. Curtis (Eds.), *Nature of vocabulary acquisition* (pp. 89–105). Hillsdale, NJ: Erlbaum.

Stevenson, H., & Stigler, J. (1992). *The learning gap: Why our schools are railing and what we can learn from Japanese and Chinese education.* New York: Summit Books.

Strevens, M. (2000). The naïve aspect of essentialist theories. *Cognition, 74,* 149–175.

Subrahmanyan, K., Gelman, R., & Lafosse, A. (in press). Animates and other separably moveable objects. In E. M. Forde & G. W. Humphreys (Ed.), *Category-specificity in brain and mind.* Hove, England: Psychology Press.

Tanaka, J. W., & Taylor, M. E. (1991). Object categories and expertise: Is the basic level in the eye of the beholder? *Cognitive Psychology, 23,* 457–482.

Tardif, T. (1996). Nouns are not always learned before verbs: Evidence from Mandarin speakers' early vocabularies. *Developmental Psychology, 32,* 492–504.

Tenenbaum, J. B., & Xu, F. (2000). Word learning as Bayesian inference. In L. R. Gleitman & A. K. Joshi (Eds.), *Proceedings of the 22nd annual conference of the Cognitive Science Society* (pp. 517–522). Mahwah, NJ: Erlbaum.

Tomasello, M. (1999). *The cultural origins of human cognition.* Cambridge, MA: Harvard University Press.

Tomasello, M., & Akhtar, N. (2000). Five questions for any theory of word learning. In R. Golinkoff & K. Hirsh-Pasek (Eds.), *Becoming a word learner: A debate on lexical acquisition* (pp. 179–186). New York: Oxford University Press.

Tomasello, M., & Barton, M. E. (1994). Learning words in nonostensive contexts. *Developmental Psychology, 30,* 639–650.

Troseth, G. L., & DeLoache, J. S. (1998). The medium can obscure the message: Young children's understanding of video. *Child Development, 69,* 950–965.

Uttal, D. H., Liu, L. L., & DeLoache, J. S. (1999). Taking a hard look at concreteness: Do concrete objects help young children learn symbolic relations. In L. Balter & C. S. Tamis-LeMonda (Eds.), *Child psychology: A handbook of contemporary issues* (pp. 177–192). Philadelphia: Psychology Press.

Vosniadou, S., Skopeliti, I., & Ikospentaki, K. (2004). Modes of knowing and ways of reasoning in elementary astronomy. *Cognitive Development, 19*, 203–222.

Vygotsky, L. S. (1962). *Thought and language.* Cambridge, MA: MIT Press. (Original work published 1934)

Wanner, E., & Gleitman, L. R. (Eds.). (1983). *Language acquisition: The state of the art.* New York: Cambridge University Press.

Waxman, S. R. (in press). The gift of curiosity. In W. Ahn, R. L. Goldstone, B. C. Love, A. B. Markman, & P. Wolff (Eds.), *Categorization inside and outside the lab: Essays in honor of Douglas L. Medin.* Washington, DC: American Psychological Association.

Waxman, S., & Gelman, R. (1986). Preschoolers' use of superordinate relations in classification and language. *Cognitive Development, 1*, 139–156.

Waxman, S. R., Lynch, E. B., Carey, K. L., & Baer, L. (1997). Setters and samoyeds: The emergence of subordinate level categories as a basis for inductive inference. *Developmental Psychology, 33*, 1074–1090.

Waxman, S. R., & Markow, D. B. (1995). Words as invitations to form categories: Evidence from 12- to 13-month-old infants. *Cognitive Psychology, 29*, 257–302.

Waxman, S. R., & Namy, L. L. (1997). Challenging the notion of a thematic preference in young children. *Developmental Psychology, 33*, 555–567.

Waxman, S. R., Shipley, E. F., & Shepperson, B. (1991). Establishing new subcategories: The role of category labels and existing knowledge. *Child Development, 62*, 127–138.

Weissman, M. D., & Kalish, C. W. (1999). The inheritance of desired characteristics: Children's view of the role of intention in parent-offspring resemblance. *Journal of Experimental Child Psychology, 73*, 245–265.

Welder, A. N., & Graham, S. A. (2001). The influence of shape similarity and shared labels on infants' inductive inferences about nonobvious object properties. *Child Development, 72*, 1653–1673.

Wellman, H. M. (1990). *The child's theory of mind.* Cambridge, MA: MIT Press.

Wellman, H. M. (2002). Understanding the psychological world: Developing a theory of mind. In U. Goswami (Ed.), *Blackwell handbook of childhood cognitive development* (pp. 167–187). Malden, MA: Blackwell.

Wellman, H. M., & Gelman, S. A. (1998). Knowledge acquisition. In W. Damon (Editor-in-Chief) & D. Kuhn & R. Siegler (Vol. Eds.), *Handbook of child psychology: Cognitive development* (4th ed., pp. 523–573). New York: Wiley.

Wellman, H. M., & Inagaki, K. (Eds.). (1997). *The emergence of core domains of thought: Children's reasoning about physical, psychological, and biological phenomena.* San Francisco: Jossey-Bass.

Werker, J. F., Cohen, L. B., Lloyd, V. L., Casasola, M., & Stager, C. L. (1998). Acquisition of word-object associations by 14-month-old infants. *Developmental Psychology, 34*, 1289–1309.

Werker, J. F., & Desjardins, R. N. (1995). Listening to speech in the 1st year of life: Experiential influences on phoneme perception. *Current Directions in Psychological Science, 4*, 76–81.

Werner, H., & Kaplan, B. (1963). *Symbol formation: An organismic-developmental approach to language and the expression of thought.* New York: Wiley.

Whorf, B. L. (1956). *Language, thought, and reality.* Cambridge, MA: MIT Press.

Wilcox, T., & Baillargeon, R. (1998). Object individuation in infancy: The use of featural information in reasoning about occlusion events. *Cognitive Psychology, 37*, 97–155.

Winnicott, D. W. (1969). *The child, the family, and the outside world.* Baltimore: Penguin Books.

Wisniewski, E. J. (1995). Prior knowledge and functionally relevant features in concept learning. *Journal of Experimental Psychology: Learning, Memory, and Cognition, 21*, 449–468.

Wisniewski, E. J., & Medin, D. L. (1994). On the interaction of theory and data in concept learning. *Cognitive Science, 18*, 221–281.

Woodward, A. L. (1998). Infants selectively encode the goal object of an actor's reach. *Cognition, 69*, 1–34.

Woodward, A. L. (2000). Constraining the problem space in early word learning. In R. Golinkoff & K. Hirsh-Pasek (Eds.), *Becoming a word learner: A debate on lexical acquisition* (pp. 81–114). New York: Oxford University Press.

Woodward, A. L., & Markman, E. M. (1998). Early word learning. In W. Damon (Editor-in-Chief) & D. Kuhn & R. Siegler (Vol. Eds.), *Handbook of child psychology: Vol. 2. Cognition, perception, and language* (pp. 371–420). New York: Wiley.

Xu, F. (1999). Object individuation and object identity in infancy: The role of spatiotemporal information, object property information, and language. *Acta Psychologica, 102*, 113–136.

Xu, F. (2002). The role of language in acquiring object kind concepts in infancy. *Cognition, 85*, 223–250.

Xu, F., & Carey, S. (1996). Infants' metaphysics: The case of numerical identity. *Cognitive Psychology, 30*, 111–153.

Yamauchi, T., & Markman, A. B. (1998). Category learning by inference and classification. *Journal of Memory and Language, 39*, 124–148.

Yoshida, H., & Smith, L. B. (2003). Shifting ontological boundaries: How Japanese- and English-speaking children generalize names for animals and artifacts. *Developmental Science, 6*, 1–34.

Younger, B. (1990). Infants' detection of correlations among feature categories. *Child Development, 61*, 614–620.

# CHAPTER 17

# *Development of Spatial Cognition*

NORA S. NEWCOMBE and JANELLEN HUTTENLOCHER

DEVELOPING TOWARD MATURE SPATIAL
   COMPETENCE   736
Do We Need Cognitive Constructs?   736
What Is the Nature of Mature Competence?   737
What Is the Nature of the Referent System?   740
What Does Symbolic Spatial Representation Add?   741
Summary   741
THE SPATIAL CAPABILITIES OF INFANTS   742
The A-not-B Error   742
Egocentric to Allocentric Shift   743
What Is an Object?   744
Summary   745
MODULARITY OR ADAPTIVE
   COMBINATION?   746
Modular Spatial Processing   746
The Development of Spatial Processing from an
   Adaptive Combination Point of View   749

REPRESENTING SPATIAL RELATIONS BETWEEN
   VIEWER AND ENVIRONMENT   755
Mental Rotation and Perspective Taking   755
Navigation   756
USING SYMBOLIC SPATIAL
   REPRESENTATIONS   758
Maps and Models   759
Spatial Language   760
INDIVIDUAL DIFFERENCES IN
   SPATIAL DEVELOPMENT   761
SPATIAL DEVELOPMENT IN NON-
   NORMATIVE CONTEXTS   765
Williams Syndrome   765
Visual Impairment   766
WHAT LIES AHEAD?   766
REFERENCES   768

For animate creatures, directed movements in space are critical for survival. Turtle hatchlings make their way to the sea, seed-caching birds hide and retrieve myriad tiny pieces of food, and human beings move around their houses, go to work or school, complete a variety of errands, and occasionally travel to distant and novel locations. Although these activities differ in many ways, they all involve using spatial information about the world to determine the direction of movement that permits obtaining a desired goal. Thus, the ability to deal with the spatial environment is a problem that evolutionary forces can be expected to have acted on in an important way. For developmental psychologists, this fact frames three vital issues about spatial knowledge and its development.

First, because spatial abilities are essential for survival and are found even in very humble organisms, spatial development provides an interesting arena in which to consider the question of the origins of human knowledge. Answers to this question in philosophy and in psychology have varied from extreme nativism to radical empiricism. On the face of it, spatial development is an excellent candidate for a domain with strong innate underpinnings, due to its adaptive significance for all mobile organisms. Piaget, however, offered a developmental theory in which innate underpinnings of spatial understanding were rather humble, hypothesizing that simple sensorimotor experiences such as reaching are the departure point for a gradually increasing spatial competence that emerges from the interaction of children with the world. His approach dominated developmental thinking about space for several decades, and inspired a great deal of research, some lines of which are still active. Recently, however, there has been a return of interest in a more strongly nativist theory in which infants come equipped with specific knowledge of the spatial world, along with similar specific understandings of domains such as language, physical causality, and number (e.g., Spelke & Newport, 1998).

The question of what capabilities are available at the start of life is obviously of central importance to understanding the origins of knowledge. However, debate about infant capabilities is only one aspect of research on this issue. Understanding the mature cognitive architecture to which the developing child is headed also has crucial implications for the origins debate. An important specific issue concerns the extent to which adults combine various kinds of spatial information. In a modular view, various sources of spatial information are processed independently in separable cognitive processing units (e.g., Wang & Spelke, 2002). In alternative models, information sources are combined, using mechanisms that weight sources based on their potential usefulness (e.g., Ernst & Banks, 2002; Huttenlocher, Hedges, & Duncan, 1991). Modularity is typically associated with nativist views, although this relation is by no means forced by logic (Fodor, 2001). Similarly, the adaptive combination view is often associated with empiricism because it seems natural to suppose that the weightings in an integrative process are affected by experience. However, it would also be possible to suggest that they are innately specified.

A second question that emerges from an evolutionary perspective regarding human spatial knowledge concerns development over evolutionary time. Understanding the ability of our species in full requires comparing our spatial capacities with the spatial capacities of other species. To what extent do humans share basic aspects of spatial adaptation with other species and in what ways might we be unique? Work on nonhuman animals has revealed many cross-species similarities, but also shows striking differences across species, with some distinctive characteristics of human spatial orientation (for reviews of the literature on spatial behavior in other species, see Jacobs, 2003; Jacobs & Schenk, 2003; Shettleworth, 1998). On the one hand, humans lack certain sensory mechanisms that other species rely on, such as a magnetic sense that would orient us directly to true north, or olfactory, tactile, and sonar sensitivities that could be used for spatial localization. On the other hand, humans also show certain spatial capabilities that other species do not possess. Most notably, our capability for complex internal processes allows us to represent entire spatial scenes from various perspectives and to visualize objects undergoing rotational transformation. Humans can utilize these symbolic abilities to communicate about the spatial environment in a flexible and powerful fashion and to carry out imagined activities in thought, as when reasoning about the behavior of gears or pulleys (Hegarty, 2004). In addition, these symbolic spatial mechanisms can be used to structure thought in

nonspatial domains. For example, people can imagine a set of items that vary along some dimension, such as intelligence or beauty, in terms of a spatial ordering that preserves information about order in that domain. The use of such orderings can support transitive reasoning (Huttenlocher, 1968) and has been shown to engage areas of the brain used for spatial processing (Goel & Dolan, 2001; Knauff, Mulack, Kassubek, Salih, & Greenlee, 2002). Further, communicative devices such as graphs or flowcharts can be valuable in discovering relations among nonspatial entities (e.g., the relation of poverty with premature birth) (Gattis, 2001; Gattis & Holyoak, 1996). The use of spatial reasoning and spatial symbolism in many kinds of human cognition that are not intrinsically spatial underlines the centrality of spatial processes to wider aspects of human cognitive adaptation.

A third important aspect of spatial development concerns individual differences in spatial skills, and here again, placing our thinking in an evolutionary context raises interesting questions. Since the ability to store and retrieve information about location is critically important, spatial competence might be expected to be a capability that would be under strong selective pressure and thus "canalized," showing a high degree of uniformity in development and eventual outcome. This appears to be true in some but not all cases. On the one hand, for example, although babies differ slightly in the age at which they exhibit certain spatial achievements (e.g., being able to find a hidden object), this variation is relatively small and generally assumed to be unimportant, in part because all normally developing children eventually acquire such understanding. On the other hand, certain lines of spatial development that seem adaptively important show considerable divergence across individuals. For example, the speed and efficiency of mental rotation show large individual differences. Yet mental rotation underlies adaptive functions such as finding desired objects from new vantage points or making tools.

Why do some adaptive spatial abilities show marked individual differences? The answer to this question is not yet clear. Some individual variation may be due to biological mechanisms, variation in which is perpetuated for adaptive reasons we do not yet appreciate, or merely because evolution does not ensure perfect adaptation. Alternatively, variation may reflect differences in the importance of certain spatial activities in the lives of different people, so that common biological potential is realized to variable extents. A challenge for researchers in cognitive development is to integrate understanding of normative development with understanding of the development of individual differences. Defining the sources of individual differences is basic both to comprehensive theoretical understanding and to the applied goal of maximizing performance in many spatial skills, ranging from basic tasks such as finding one's way to a store or office, to more complex ones such as assembling an electronic device, to even higher-level challenges such as reasoning in mathematics and the physical sciences.

In short, there are many reasons why the development of spatial skill is a central problem in cognitive and developmental science. A goal in the study of spatial development is to answer, with regard to this domain, some of the classic questions in the history of psychology, biology, and philosophy: the extent to which adaptation rests on innately available representations or represents emergent knowledge based on interaction with the world, the uniqueness of our species and the course of comparative evolution, the interplay of symbolic and more basic spatial processes, and the nature of individual differences. In addition, spatial development is an important research area because understanding how it occurs is likely to have considerable practical relevance for devising educational curricula that support optimal acquisition of skills that underlie many essential real-world activities.

This chapter is divided into eight major sections. We begin by describing current views of the nature of mature spatial competence, as well as issues concerning how to assess children's progress toward this adult state. The next two sections concern the two issues we have identified as relevant to the debate concerning the origins of knowledge: what we know about the spatial capabilities that exist in infancy and whether early spatial skills are modular. The fourth and fifth sections deal with capabilities that seem to be distinctively human aspects of spatial adaptation, namely, the capacity for mental transformation of spatial information and the capacity for symbolic representation of spatial information. In the sixth and seventh sections, we examine the development and causes of individual differences, including gender differences, and also consider what we can learn about the nature and mechanisms of spatial development from cases in which children have abnormal bases for learning based on genetic differences (Williams syndrome) or abnormal environmental contexts based on sensory limitations (impaired vision). Finally, we try to delineate the challenges to be addressed in the next years of research.

## DEVELOPING TOWARD MATURE SPATIAL COMPETENCE

Any consideration of how human beings come to develop adult levels of cognitive functioning would seem to begin most naturally with a consideration of the nature of mature competence, which would establish the standard against which to assess the developing capabilities of children. Such a goal is not easily attained, however, because investigation of adult functioning is an ongoing enterprise with its own uncertainties and controversies. (For overviews of research on adult spatial functioning, see Landau, 2003; Newcombe, 2002b; B. Tversky, 2000.) In this section, we concentrate on several key issues in characterizing how human adults process information about their spatial environment. However, we begin with a prior overarching issue involving the conceptual tools we should use, not only in describing mature competence but also in evaluating development.

### Do We Need Cognitive Constructs?

In general, cognitive theories posit internal states in explaining intelligent behavior, but questions have been raised about the scientific necessity of doing so (e.g., Brooks, 1991). Those who take a Gibsonian perspective emphasize the role of environmental "affordances" (e.g., Warren, 2005). Investigators working within the dynamic-systems perspective have also argued that we should avoid notions of representation (e.g., Thelen & Smith, 1994). The qualms expressed by these theorists involve the homunculus issue (nothing is explained if a mysterious entity must interpret representations) and the problem of falsifiability (unobservable entities can proliferate in some representational theories). However, representations seem to be needed as principles to explain behavior in various cognitive tasks (Huttenlocher, 2005). While some users of the term *representation* may be guilty of using a plethora of unobservable entities in complex theories that are not easily testable, such problems are not inevitable outcomes of using the construct. Careful work can tie explanations involving the idea of representation to multiple converging operations that can test implications derived from them.

In developmental work, the notion of mental representation can seem especially ill founded because very different results are obtained when small changes are made in test situations, especially with young children. For example, some developmental milestones in infancy seem to be achieved at earlier ages when assessed with regard to looking rather than reaching (e.g., Ahmed & Ruffman, 1998; Hofstadter & Reznick, 1996; Kaufman & Needham, 1999). Similarly, young infants seem to grasp that solid objects cannot pass through other solid objects when studied using habituation-of-looking or violation-of-expectancy techniques (e.g., Spelke, Breinlinger, Macomber, & Jacobson, 1992), but even 2-year-olds have difficulty in using solidity principles in the context of a seemingly simple task involving judging where to search for a rolling ball (Berthier et al., 2001; Hood, Cole-Davies & Dias, 2003; Keen, 2003; Mash, Keen, & Berthier, 2003). Yet another striking example of variations in children's apparent competence, in this case within a single action sequence, occurs when toddlers interact with small objects as if they were much larger (e.g., attempting to enter a toy car), yet as they do so, adjust their actions to the size of the object by, for example, using a precise grip to open the small door of the miniature vehicle (DeLoache, Uttal, & Rosengren, 2004).

Such facts lead certain investigators to reject the notions of representation and of competence as misleading reifications (Thelen & Smith, 1994). However, there are other ways to approach development that recognize the existence of task-specific variability but retain notions of representation and competence. First, in some cases, we can regard the age at first emergence of the simplest version of a competence in the most supportive circumstance as one bracketing date for a developmental process, and the age at which a competence is robustly evident in the most challenging circumstance as a second bracketing date. Along similar lines, we can define competence relative to an ecological standard of what is normally required in everyday life or what is typically possible for normally functioning adults (Newcombe & Huttenlocher, 2000). For example, we regard a digit span of approximately seven numbers as representing mature competence, despite the fact that fewer numbers can be retained when attention is divided or the fact that more numbers can be retained when special strategies are utilized. We do so because we view both distraction and the application of focused chunking strategies as exceptional circumstances.

Second, findings of this kind can be construed as invitations to explore the processes and mechanisms that underlie them, rather than as indicating that cognitive constructs have no utility at all. An example of such an approach comes from research on adults' susceptibility to the horizontal-vertical illusion, in which a horizontal line and a vertical line of equal length are in contact so as to make a capital T or an inverted capital T. Adults judge the horizontal line to be shorter than the vertical line in this display, even though the lines are equal. However, when they are asked to grasp the lines, their hand configurations suggest that they regard the lines as equal (Vishton, Rea, Cutting, & Nunez, 1999). Patterns such as these are often interpreted as indicating the existence of separable systems of thought and of action, or else as suggesting a need to analyze particular situations without positing any abstract competencies. However, exploring further, Vishton et al. (1999) showed that the different behavior patterns depended, not on the contrast between conscious judgment and physical action, but on the fact that the judgment task required a comparison between lines (a relative judgment) while the grasping task focused on a single line at a time (an absolute judgment). Absolute *judgments* do not show the illusion. Thus, a puzzling dissociation gave way, when probed analytically, to an interesting rule-governed generalization about cognitive functioning, namely that tasks requiring quantitative comparisons can lead to illusions not seen when we deal with quantities one at a time.

Overall then, judicious and careful use of cognitive constructs such as representation and competence are important in both cognitive and developmental psychology. Given this prologue, we proceed to a discussion of the nature of mature spatial competence that revolves around three issues: To what extent are spatial representations accurate and integrated? What spatial referent systems are used in constructing such representations? And, what do external symbolic representations such as maps and spatial language add as compared with internal spatial representations taken alone?

## What Is the Nature of Mature Competence?

Piaget and Inhelder (1948/1967) suggested that mature spatial competence is accurate, metric, and well-structured, involving a Euclidean system of spatial representation. They portrayed adults as easily able to remember and reconstruct spatial layouts, to take the perspective of others, and to perform a variety of other spatial tasks that children find difficult, using spatial representations that code location with respect to X and Y coordinates. This characterization of human capability has long been questioned, however, by researchers focused on spatial cognition in adults. Several alternative models currently claim to capture the nature of human spatial knowledge.

Some cognitive psychologists have asserted that adults' spatial representations are inevitably erroneous, biased, and fragmentary (e.g., Byrne, 1979; Kuipers, 1982; McNamara, 1991; B. Tversky, 1981). Such conclusions are based on well-known studies indicating that adults estimate spatial location in ways that create surprising errors, such as the judgment that Reno is east of San Diego (Stevens & Coupe, 1978) or the judgment that the distance from location A to location B is different from the distance from location B to location A (McNamara & Diwadkar, 1997; A. Tversky, 1977). Errors of this kind have been taken to indicate that adults do not encode metric information about precise spatial location. Rather, these judgments have seemed most compatible with models in which people remember location imprecisely or in terms of larger categories. For example, one can explain Stevens and Coupe's findings as arising from a spatial memory that encodes only qualitative categorical information regarding the location of cities in states (such as that Reno is located in Nevada) together with rough pointers about the relative arrangement of the states (that Nevada is east of California).

Other investigators of spatial functioning have focused less on the content and accuracy of spatial representations and more on the cognitive architecture that supports acquisition of spatial knowledge. Specifically, Gallistel (1990) and Spelke and her associates (Hermer & Spelke, 1996; Wang & Spelke, 2002) proposed that various features of space may form distinct modules, with one important example being a *geometric module* that encodes information about the relative length of environmental surfaces and the relation of these surfaces to each other (e.g., that a longer surface is to the left of a shorter surface). These authors argued that geometric sensitivity is modular in nature because there is evidence that featural information, such as knowledge of the color of surrounding surfaces, is not used to disambiguate two geometrically congruent locations. These capabilities are said to form separate and noninteracting cognitive units, that is, to be mutually impenetrable. Since these different aspects of spatial information have no direct contact with one another in a modular architec-

ture, extra principles are needed to explain how the information might become combined. One hypothesis is that language allows for communication among these modules (Spelke & Hermer, 1996).

An alternative to modularity proposals for conceptualizing how various sources of spatial information are used is a family of models that can be termed *adaptive combination models* (which are modular only in the relatively modest sense that initial perceptual processing of the various kinds of information relevant to spatial location may occur using physiologically distinct pathways or specific cortical regions). These approaches share a focus on combination of various sources of spatial information in a weighted fashion. One such model was proposed by Huttenlocher and Hedges and their associates (Crawford, Huttenlocher, & Engebretson, 2000; Huttenlocher, Hedges, & Duncan, 1991; Huttenlocher, Hedges, Corrigan, & Crawford, 2004). They have hypothesized that adult spatial coding involves such adaptive combination. Their work stems from the observation that spaces are typically encoded into units of different sizes that are hierarchically organized. Larger units (such as states or nations) encompass smaller ones (such as cities or states). Huttenlocher and Hedges suggest that coding of spatial location occurs at both a fine-grained and a categorical level, and is unbiased at both levels. However, combination of fine-grained coding with information from a categorical level typically leads to the appearance of bias in estimation. These biases are adaptive; they capitalize on use of category information in a Bayesian fashion to reduce variability in estimating location. This *hierarchical combination model* can explain a variety of estimation patterns that otherwise seem to be evidence for nonmetric spatial processing. For example, asymmetries in judging the distance between location A and location B, as found by A. Tversky (1977) and McNamara and Diwadkar (1997), can be explained (and are in fact predicted) by the hierarchical coding model (Newcombe, Huttenlocher, Sandberg, Lie, & Johnson, 1999).

There are other adaptive combination models in the literature on spatial functioning (as well as in the wider perceptual literature; see Ernst & Banks, 2002). For example, in Cheng's (1989) *vector-sum model* of the use of landmark cues by pigeons, vectors based on near landmarks are weighted more heavily than vectors based on far landmarks, presumably because they are encoded with less variability. Similarly, Hartley, Trinkler, and Burgess (2004) have developed a *boundary proximity model* of human memory for location within enclosed spaces that uses a mixture of absolute and relative distance information. Encoding of absolute distance from a wall is more accurate and less variable when the distance is short, while encoding of relative distances (ratios of distances from various walls) is less dependent on how close a location is to a wall. Hence, absolute information is weighted more heavily when encoding locations close to walls, while relative information is weighted more heavily when walls are distant (when a location is in the middle of the enclosure). The vector-sum model and the boundary-proximity model share a fundamental insight with the hierarchical combination model, namely, that it is adaptive to weight uncertain and variable information less heavily than more certain and less variable information. Such an approach may also serve to understand the conditions under which featural and geometric information are both used to determine location and the circumstances when one is used alone (Newcombe, 2005). In short, in all of the adaptive combination models, various sources of information about the spatial environment are combined in a way that weights an information source that is exact more heavily than one that is variable, and that therefore leads to maximal accuracy.[1]

The developmental origins of adaptive combination are not known. It might be that the system derives from prior experience; it is also possible that at least certain aspects of these coding mechanisms are innately specified. Cross-species convergence in mechanisms of spatial memory may suggest the possibility of hardwired adaptive mechanisms, and it is, therefore, interesting that adaptive combination models are useful in considering the behavior of a variety of nonhuman species. For instance, the Hartley et al. model captures the behavior of place cells in the hippocampus of rats as well as human behavior, and the Huttenlocher-Hedges model has recently been shown to characterize location coding in the rhesus monkey as well as in humans (Merchant, Fortes, & Georgopoulos, 2004). A great deal of further research will be needed, however, to specify exactly what aspects of spatial coding mechanisms are hardwired, because some part of cross-species convergence

may arise from similar tuning of starting-point mechanisms by common environmental demands. For example, absolute distance from a landmark will inevitably be more precisely estimated when the distance is shorter than when it is longer, for psychophysical reasons, and hence weightings of information that depend on distance would be expected to arise naturally through expectable interactions with the environment. On this view, what is innate, hardwired, and shared across species is the capacity for learning that reflects these statistical principles. However, in all instantiations of this family of models, development consists in the acquisition of maximally informative and useful combinatorial rules.

There are some similarities between adaptive combination models and other recent ways of thinking about cognitive development. In particular, dynamic systems theory (Thelen & Smith, 1994) and overlapping waves theory (Siegler, 1996) also emphasize the interacting impact of a variety of data on behavior. However, there are also differences in emphasis and focus between the approaches. To take dynamic systems thinking first, theorizing in this tradition has been less specific than an adaptive combination approach about what determines the weighting of the various influences. Additionally, dynamic systems theorists eschew the use of terms such as representation and competence even though these constructs can support productive theorizing when used carefully.

An overlapping waves approach focuses on the co-occurrence in developmental time of different strategies for approaching problems, and the waxing and waning of these strategies as a function of factors such as how a situation is encoded and feedback about success. The similarity to adaptive combination approaches is in the recognition that behavior emerges from the interaction of different bases for action, and an interest in variability as grist for the mill of development. However, overlapping waves theory has focused on variability in strategies or procedures rather than on the variability with which different kinds of stimulus information are encoded, and tends to think of competing influences as racing to determine action rather than as being combined. These contrasts are at least partially due to the different kinds of cognitive development under consideration. Adaptive combination theory analyzes representations in memory and their use for behavior, while the overlapping waves metaphor has mainly been applied to the acquisition of cognitive skills (such as addition) or

[1] Similar models have recently been proposed for other problems in adaptive combination, such as combining data derived from vision and from touch (Backus, Banks, van Ee, & Crowell, 1999; Ernst & Banks, 2002; Gepshtein & Banks, 2003).

rule-based judgments about dynamic problems (such as the balance beam problem).

## What Is the Nature of the Referent System?

Spatial coding requires a set of referents, or frameworks, to specify location. In recent years, investigators have arrived at a rough consensus about the nature of such frameworks (Gallistel, 1990; Newcombe & Huttenlocher, 2000; Sholl, 1995). There is agreement that spatial location can be coded with respect to either external frameworks or with respect to viewers. The first way of coding location can sometimes entail the simple and direct use of external landmarks as markers, especially when such landmarks are contiguous with a desired location (e.g., when a flag marks the place to aim for on a putting green). Such landmarks have been called *beacons,* and such spatial learning has been called *cue learning.* But such beacons are not always available. Thus, a more important function of external features of the environment (such as the shapes of enclosing spaces, or sets of separated landmarks) is to provide a set of fixed reference points for noting distance and direction, and mapping desired locations. This kind of spatial learning has been called *place learning.* It is limited by the availability of fixed features, so that it does not work well on the open sea or in the dark.

The second way to code location is with respect to the viewer. One simple way of doing so is to remember actions required to get to a desired location, such as how to move one's hand to reach the alarm clock from bed, or how to walk to get to school in the morning. Such coding can be called *response learning;* Piaget termed it *egocentric.* It works only when the initial starting point is maintained, but fails when movement must be taken into account, for example, when one reaches for the alarm clock after having rolled to the other side of the bed than the one usually slept on. Another kind of viewer-centered coding results from adjusting an initial location memory by taking the direction and distance of one's own movement into account. Location coding of this kind has been termed either *dead reckoning* or *inertial navigation.* The viewer's position is continually tracked in this kind of spatial memory, which is invaluable in situations where external frameworks are unavailable. However, ultimately, dead reckoning must be referenced to external frameworks, both because otherwise drift in memory for direction and distance causes accumulating error, and also because it is the external environment that is ultimately of interest.[2]

To what extent is the viewer's position bound up in all spatial representations that utilize the external environment? The issue of orientation-free versus orientation-specific representation is central to understanding of the processes of mental rotation, perspective taking, and navigation. It has sometimes been proposed that extensive experience in a particular environment could lead to the formation of orientation-free survey knowledge of the area (Presson, 1987; Presson & Hazelrigg, 1984; Siegel & White, 1975); it would incorporate the viewer as needed in a flexible manner without the viewer being an integral part of the representation. There has been long-standing debate about this claim, however. Many studies have found evidence that representations are primarily orientation-specific (for recent examples, see McNamara, Rump, & Werner, 2003; Mou, McNamara, Valiquette, & Rump, 2004; Shelton & McNamara, 2004; Sholl & Bartels, 2002). In addition, recent work on children's use of geometric information suggests that the viewer is represented in relation to the space rather than the space being represented in isolation (Huttenlocher & Vasilyeva, 2003; Lourenco, Huttenlocher, & Vasilyeva, 2005).

It is possible, however, that, in some circumstances or for some people, orientation-free representations may be possible attainments, even though orientation-specific representations are more common. For example, Sholl and Nolin (1997) found that people could point with equal facility to various locations in a space, independent of original viewing position and current location, when asked using certain specific spaces and acquisition and testing conditions. In addition, there may be individual differences, such that viewers with certain profiles of cognitive skill might be more likely than others to be able to form orientation-free representations. In terms of a different debate concerning the formation of situation models while reading text, inclusion of spa-

---

[2] One kind of spatial coding that may be considered viewer-centered is to retain the look of a particular area surrounding the target location, which makes it possible to locate the target again by matching the remembered and the current views (Wang & Spelke, 2002). This system is basically similar to cue learning, with the only difference, aside from terminological variations, being that the cues are multiple ones whose relations are taken into account, rather than simply being single beacons.

tial information has turned out to vary with spatial ability (Emerson, Miyake, & Rettinger, 1999; Friedman & Miyake, 2000). Perhaps the most interesting possibility is that the two kinds of representations coexist making it hard to find evidence of orientation-free representations because the coexisting orientation-specific representations will always exert some effect. Burgund and Marsolek (2000), for example, found viewpoint-independent processing in the left hemisphere and viewpoint-dependent processing in the right hemisphere. This effect may be dependent on the left hemisphere's ability to encode semantic information about objects (Curby, Hayward, & Gauthier, 2004).

Another fact worth keeping in mind is that, even if computing interpolated views that lie between actually experienced ones is difficult and time-consuming, humans appear to be able to perform the task, whereas other species, such as pigeons, do not (Spetch & Friedman, 2003). In fact, we are able to mix perspectives in describing environments (Taylor & Tversky, 1992a), to form similar spatial representations from descriptions of environments from different vantage points (Taylor & Tversky, 1992b) and, once representations are formed, to switch perspectives with rapidly diminishing costs (Tversky, Lee, & Mainwaring, 1999). Thus, while humans may show orientation specificity, we also appear to have considerable resources for coping with it.

## What Does Symbolic Spatial Representation Add?

One of the distinctive characteristics of our species is the capacity for symbolic spatial representation. Language is the leading example of a powerful human symbolic system, but in the spatial domain, models, maps, diagrams, and graphs are also of focal interest. Symbolic devices greatly enhance the scope of spatial competence in several ways. They allow individuals to communicate information, so that we can gain spatial knowledge of areas we have never personally visited, and they allow us to store information so that it can be reliably retrieved later. In addition, constructing and viewing linguistic or nonlinguistic spatial representations is a powerful support for reflection, integration, and inference (Liben, Kastens, & Stevenson, 2002; Uttal, 2000). For example, drawing a sketch map of a city may lead to the discovery of a useful shortcut; giving someone directions to one's home may reveal a lack of knowledge concerning certain crucial distances; and

viewing an aerial photograph of a polluted marsh may reveal a pattern to the distribution of pollutants that tells us its cause.

There are interesting and important differences between nonlinguistic and linguistic communication about space. In many ways, language is not well suited for communicating spatial knowledge. Spatial relations can only be described in a linear and serial fashion using language, rather than apprehended in a simultaneous and integrated fashion. Spatial relations in language also need to be expressed with reference to a spatial framework agreed on by speaker and listener, and the framework can end up being ambiguous (Levinson, 2003). For example, if the ball is said to be "in front of the car," it could be at the car's intrinsic front, that is by the headlights. But it could also be located in front of a speaker looking at a side door of the car or even in front of a listener looking at the side of the car. Metric aspects of space are generally reduced to categorical descriptions; communicating them exactly requires the use of technical measurement language. On the other hand, spatial language has advantages. For example, it is always available, because it does not require access to drawing or modeling materials. In addition, it is easily used to highlight a crucial aspect of a spatial scene, directing attention to a particular relation and making it memorable (Gentner & Loewenstein, 2002).

## Summary

This initial section has been devoted to an overview of some complex issues that are difficult to treat fully here, and yet which frame our approach to the development of spatial cognition. In brief, we believe that the concept of representation is essential in investigating the spatial capabilities of both adults and children; we think that mature spatial representation is neither fragmented and incomplete nor modularly separable, but rather consists of the adaptive combination of a number of different sources of spatial information; we adopt what is now close to a consensus view that both external frames of reference and viewer-centered ones are central components of an exploration of spatial cognition; and, we subscribe with many others to the view that symbolic spatial representations, both visual and verbal, are strikingly powerful augmentations of nonsymbolic spatial capabilities, whose adoption is one of our species' most distinctive spatial adaptations. These choices structure the treatment of spatial development that follows. In addition, some of the matters discussed in this section, notably the value of an adaptive combination approach, receive fuller consideration in the following sections.

## THE SPATIAL CAPABILITIES OF INFANTS

The classic approach to thinking about spatial development in infancy comes from Piaget, whose views structured much of the empirical work on the topic until relatively recently. Piaget suggested that infants initially interact with their world in a sensorimotor fashion, so that objects are located in terms of the physical actions required to make contact with them. Such egocentric coding was said to give way gradually over the 1st year of life to the notion of an object as having a permanent existence independent of action and to the associated ability to locate objects in relation to external landmarks. Piaget based these conclusions on his observations that, in the first 6 months or so, infants failed to search at all for completely occluded objects, and that, during the next 6 months or so, they searched in a fashion dominated by their memories of physical actions that had been successful in retrieving hidden objects in the past, ignoring more recent visual information about the objects' location.

Subsequent work has questioned this picture of the 1st year of life, but has not yet succeeded in replacing it with a coherent and consensually endorsed view. One possibility is that infants possess the idea of a permanent object early and even from birth, but lack specific abilities, such as perceptual sensitivities, inhibitory capabilities, or means-ends reasoning skills, to manifest this competence in every situation. An alternative account is that behaviors allowing for a mature conception of permanent objects and their location emerge gradually and as a result of interactions with the world. While basically constructivist, this account describes a sequence of developmental transitions different both in timing and in kind from the specific theory that Piaget offered. In this section, we examine these possibilities with regard to three phenomena: the A-not-B error, the egocentric-to-allocentric shift, and the infant's conception of an object.

### The A-not-B Error

Hundreds and possibly thousand of studies have been done that are relevant to the A-not-B error, which Piaget

originally conceptualized as an interim step in the progression toward a concept of the permanent object, the hallmark of "Stage IV object permanence." Over the years, investigation of the error has taken on a life of its own. The error has been regarded as informative about a wide variety of constructs, including memory, inhibition, and means-ends reasoning. Currently, the main contenders for explanation of the error are dynamic systems theory (Smith, Thelen, Titzer, & McLin, 1999; Thelen, Schoener, Scheier, & Smith, 2001), connectionist approaches that emphasize strength of representations (Munakata, 2000, 2001; Munakata, McClelland, Johnson, & Siegler, 1997), and a memory-plus-inhibition model that emphasizes the brain bases of inhibition (Diamond, 1991). From the point of view of thinking about spatial development, however, these approaches share a common flaw, namely inadequate analysis of what kinds of spatial memory the task involves (Newcombe & Huttenlocher, 2000). Dynamic systems models describe competing action tendencies rather than discussing ways of coding location, although it may be possible to translate from one mode of description to the other (see Newcombe, 2001); Munakata's connectionist model uses the constructs of active and latent memory traces, and although they may also map onto an analysis in terms of modes of coding spatial location, "the network represents space in a very limited way" (Munakata, 2000, p. 181).

What are the possible kinds of spatial memory involved in the A-not-B task? One important kind of memory is response learning, or the tendency to regard an object as obtainable in a location defined by previous action. Although response learning figures in the A-not-B literature, discussed by Piaget as the sensorimotor definition of an object and by Diamond as a prepotent response, there has been relatively little discussion of just what response is involved or what aspect of the response history is given weight. Considering the A-not-B situation, we see that there are four such responses. First, because infants watch objects hidden and also reach for them, there are two response systems on which they could base their search: looking and reaching. Second, they could base searches on either of two kinds of information about prior looks or reaches: frequency or recency. Of course, only the most recent look actually provides relevant evidence about location. Search at the location that has been most frequently looked at, or most frequently reached for, will lead to A-not-B errors, as will search at the location most recently reached for.

In interacting with the environment, infants inevitably find that searches based on some kinds of information work, whereas others don't. Infants who experiment with a variety of bases for their decisions will eventually settle on the most useful option. This analysis suggests an explanation for recent findings that looking behavior is more advanced than reaching behavior in the A-not-B situation (Ahmed & Ruffman, 1998; Hofstadter & Reznick, 1996). Visual memory provides a correct answer to where the hidden object is located (i.e., where the infant most recently saw the object), whereas reaching correctly requires relying on a memory of a response in a different system.

Various forms of response learning are not the only possibilities for spatial coding in the A-not-B testing situation, and memory for where they most recently looked is not the only way to succeed. While cue learning is impossible because the search locations typically have identical covers, and dead reckoning is irrelevant because infants do not move, infants can potentially base a correct response on coding of the distance of the correct hiding location from an environmental referent such as the edges of the testing surface. Experiments using looking time to anomalous events indicate that they have the ability to remember such information by 5 months of age (Newcombe, Huttenlocher, & Learmonth, 1999; Newcombe, Sluzenski, & Huttenlocher, 2005). However, they may not base their searches in an A-not-B situation on this information until a few months later, for several reasons. First, the A-not-B testing situation pits competing response options against each other, so the sorting out of which evidential basis is most reliable may well take longer to emerge than simply the ability to use a certain kind of information when there is no conflict. Second, reacting with increased looking time to objects emerging from the wrong location involves recognizing an anomaly, not actively retrieving a location. Hence, it provides a much less stringent assessment of coding distance in continuous space than recall of a location of a hidden object.

In summary, to search successfully for hidden objects whose location is variable, infants have to learn to reach to the location at which they most recently saw the object, rather than to reach to the locations they have most frequently looked at, or the locations they have most recently or frequently reached to. (To the extent that these other tendencies are strong, they may need to be inhibited, so Diamond's analysis of the A-not-B error may be an important aspect of a complete explanation of

errors.) Because the infant does not move, reliance on a response memory of the most recent look can be successful. However, coding location in terms of an external framework provided by the surrounding environment provides a more widely useful form of spatial memory, and it may possibly come to be relied on to an increasing extent in the second half of the 1st year.

This analysis leaves open the question of whether, in coming to rely on the location of the most recent look, infants are guided simply by reinforcement contingencies or whether at some point, they realize that the object must necessarily, not merely contingently, be in this location. The latter kind of knowledge was what Piaget was interested in, but we have as yet no definitive means of assessing it. One speculative approach would be to suggest that response memories are more likely to be contingent, while reliance on location memory that uses external frameworks reflects a more deeply conceptual network of knowledge about how the world works.

Assessing whether there is a fundamental transition from success at searching for objects in B locations in a way guided by contingency to one guided by a feeling of necessity is an interesting agenda, we think, for future studies. At present, however, one contribution of thinking about the A-not B error as the product of shifting reliance on different spatial coding methods is that this framework serves also to integrate the numerous studies that have been done on another developmental transition in infancy—the egocentric-to-allocentric shift.

## Egocentric to Allocentric Shift

Our account of the A-not-B error uses the idea that a variety of kinds of spatial coding compete for use during infancy, with development consisting in working out the best adaptive combination of these information sources. Such an account also provides a framework for thinking about a different line of research on infant spatial development, concerning a phenomenon that has been called the egocentric-to-allocentric shift. Acredolo (1978) and Bremner and Bryant (1977) showed infants objects or events located to their left or their right, and then moved them to the opposite side of the array or the room so that the positions were reversed. Through most of the 1st year, infants continued to search on the side on which they had originally seen the objects or events, without taking account of their movement. In the first half of the 2nd year, they began to take account of movement and to use external landmarks to track location.

Subsequent work suggested, however, that the transition to use of external landmarks does not occur as a single qualitative shift in infant functioning. Very salient external cues are useful as early as 6 months, especially in situations where they do not compete with other location cues (Acredolo & Evans, 1980; Bremner, 1978b; Lew, Foster, Crowther, & Green, 2004; McDonough, 1999; Rieser, 1979). Infants are fairly successful at looking in the right direction for objects when the motions that alter infants' relation to a location are familiar ones in their repertoires, such as twisting one's trunk when in a sitting position (Landau & Spelke, 1988; Lepecq & Lafaite, 1989; McKenzie, Day, & Ihsen, 1984; Rieser, 1979). They succeed more often when initial searches are few or are not reinforced, so that memory for motor responses is less powerful (Acredolo, 1979, 1982; Bremner 1978a). They also do better when emotional stress is minimized (Acredolo, 1982). Finally, infants who can crawl show less egocentric responding than infants of the same age who cannot (Bai & Bertenthal, 1992; Bertenthal, Campos, & Barrett, 1984; see review by Campos, Anderson, Barbu-Roth, Hubbard, Hertenstein, & Witherington, 2000).

Overall, the data on the shift from egocentric to allocentric coding suggest that a variety of bases for spatial location coding are present early in life, including use of visual beacons and compensation for the infant's own physical movement, as well as simple memory for action. As suggested by an adaptive combination approach to development, reliance on each kind of information shifts as a function of factors such as salience and cue competition as well as, most importantly, accumulating evidence on the relative validity of different sources of information. That is, experience in interacting with the physical world provides feedback on the usefulness of the various methods of coding. The effect of crawling provides one notable class of experience, in which infants learn to appreciate that, after they change position, repeating an action (such as reaching with the left hand) is unlikely to produce the same result as it did before. However, crawling is probably not the only source of such instructive experiences. For example, sitting while twisting one's trunk will affect what the infant sees with a certain degree of head turn, or what a grasp in a certain direction will lead to touching, and these experiences may in turn affect weighting of various sources of information in an adaptive combination process. Further research may show that each new class of spatial experience that infants become motorically capable of has its own specific effect on their spatial memory and spatial actions.

## What Is an Object?

Research has modified other aspects of our understanding of the development of the object concept in addition to the particular issues associated with Piaget's Stage IV and the A-not-B error. A series of widely cited experiments have provided evidence that by the middle of the 1st year, babies look longer at events that suggest that an occluded object does not continue to exist than at events in which they do (e.g., Baillargeon, 1986; Luo, Baillargeon, Brueckner, & Munakata, 2003). Initially, such data were seen as indicating that babies have a mature concept of objects and their permanence from the start of life. However, in the past few years, evidence has emerged that infants' treatment of objects may be different in the first few months from that emerging toward the end of the 1st year of life. Specifically, young infants may regard objects as defined by spatiotemporal tracking of their movement and may have difficulty in coordinating such information with information about the objects' static perceptual attributes (Leslie, Xu, Tremoulet, & Scholl, 1998; Xu & Carey, 1996).

Researchers have found that young infants react to violations of where objects are expected to be or how many objects are expected to exist, in situations where they do *not* react to changes in attributes such as size, shape, and color (Kaldy & Leslie, 2003; Newcombe, Huttenlocher, & Learmonth, 1999; Xu & Carey, 1996). Infants' ability to bind auditory and visual stimuli together based on perceived location, and to track such information dynamically, supports the hypothesis that location could play a primary role in coordinating across modalities and hence structuring the infant's perceptual world (Fenwick & Morrongiello, 1998; Richardson & Kirkham, 2004). The hypothesis of spatiotemporal primacy initially appears contradictory to data indicating that infants can use perceptual characteristics such as size, shape, and color to identify objects in certain tasks (Needham, 2001; Wilcox, 1999; Wilcox & Baillargeon, 1998a, b). However, young infants may concentrate on static perceptual characteristics primarily when objects do not move, or when their trajectory is a simple one, or when displays are very simple (Mareschal & Johnson, 2003).

Is there then an innate ability to track location over occlusion, and hence to represent the existence of an object based on its spatiotemporal trajectory? Apparently not—this ability appears to undergo development in the first months of life. This conclusion is based on several lines of evidence. First, before 6 months of age, infants seem to represent location in retinocentric coordinates centered on the eye itself, rather than egocentrically in relation to the body as a whole (Gilmore & Johnson, 1997). The emergence of egocentric coding is an achievement that allows for coordinated spatiotemporal tracking. Second, a series of studies by von Hoftsten and his associates have shown that infants' ability to represent the trajectories of moving objects develops considerably in the first 6 months and shows strong learning effects (e.g., Rosander & von Hofsten, 2004). The importance of learning is further supported by an intriguing study that demonstrated that infant reaching is less inhibited by blackout of the room lights than tracking is, whereas movement of an object behind an occluder affects reaching more than tracking (Jonsson & von Hoftsen, 2003). In the real world, a person can of course reach to an object in the dark, but not to an object behind a solid screen, whereas one can track an object as it emerges from behind a solid object but cannot visually track in the dark. Thus, the Jonsson and Von Hofsten findings suggest the importance of interactive experience with the world to development. Along similar lines, Shinskey and Munakata (2003) have found that 6.5-month-old infants will search in the dark for hidden objects, that is, at an age at which they do not search, in an otherwise comparable task, for objects hidden under an occluder in a lighted environment. Third, work by Scott Johnson and his associates provides a different kind of evidence for the hypothesis that perceptual completion of simple object trajectories develops over the first 6 months (e.g., Johnson, 2004; Johnson, Bremner, et al., 2003). In particular, his group has recently shown that learning effects can be seen in the laboratory (Johnson, Amso, & Slemmer, 2003). Infants who were taught to anticipate the emergence of a horizontally moving ball from behind an occluder later showed the ability to anticipate the emergence of a ball moving vertically.

In sum, there is an emerging case that infants acquire various aspects of a mature approach to defining an object and tracking its existence, building on innate departure points but changing in important ways with accrued experience. A model of the development of object under-standing along these lines has recently been proposed by Andrew Meltzoff and Keith Moore (Meltzoff & Moore, 1998; Moore & Meltzoff, 1999, 2004). In their account, the early basis of object understanding is termed object identity (i.e., "that's the same thing again"). Object identity is said to depend initially on spatial characteristics (e.g., "that's the same thing again because it's in the same place"). Object permanence is said to arise from object identity, as linkages are made among various appearances of the same object.

## Summary

An adaptive-combination approach to spatial development is helpful in explaining the A-not-B error, the egocentric to allocentric shift, and developing abilities to track and define objects in terms of changes in the use of various information sources. Infants have early ability to code location in a variety of ways, and their task in the 1st year of life is to determine which methods are most likely to succeed in which situations. In the A-not-B task, they come to rely on most recent look or on a memory of distance from external landmarks, learning that frequency is completely the wrong principle to use and that most recent grasp is often misleading as well. Similarly, in the egocentric-allocentric paradigm, they come to rely on either memory in terms of distance from external landmarks or a dead reckoning that can correct for their rotational and translational movement, rather than using a simple response memory. In tracking objects, infants begin by relying heavily on spatiotemporal parameters in setting up and maintaining object files. While they separately code the static perceptual attributes of objects, they find it challenging to combine information about these attributes with spatiotemporal trajectory information, and sometimes they rely on the latter in tasks where an older child or adult would rely on the former.

Changes in the sorts of spatial activities that children can engage in are important in creating changed opportunities for feedback. The best-examined milestone is crawling, which allows infants for the first time to experience a continuous and actively produced change in their spatial location. Crawling is associated with a variety of cognitive and emotional changes, including the egocentric-to-allocentric shift and the A-not-B error (Campos et al., 2000). A reduced probability of making the A-not-B error is especially interesting because the infant does not move during the search task. The improvement in search ability while remaining in the same position is plausibly related to increases in the reliance on most recent look or on distance from landmarks, created by the fact that these are useful information sources when one moves.

There may well be other spatial changes associated with locomotion. For instance, infants from 3 to 6 months show a very imprecise ability to determine their direction of motion from optic flow, and it is possible that improvement occurs only after the onset of crawling (Gilmore, Baker, & Grobman, 2004; Gilmore & Rettke, 2003). In addition, changes in motor abilities other than crawling may have important effects. The onset of walking may be associated with improvements in location coding (Clearfield, 2004); the onset of grasping is associated with improvements in object exploration and processing (Needham, Barrett, & Peterman, 2002).

In this section, we have briefly reviewed what is known about infant spatial ability, focusing on the A-not-B error, the egocentric-to-allocentric shift, and changing ways of treating objects. In each case, we analyzed existing findings as understandable on an adaptive combination view, in which a variety of possible bases for action and conceptualization compete, and in which the most useful ones eventually win. In the next section, we take a closer look at whether the adaptive combination approach can structure our knowledge about the spatial capabilities of somewhat older children. We begin with an examination of developmental findings that have been taken to support a competing modularity view, and go on to a review of work that examines development as viewed through the lens of the Huttenlocher-Hedges model of spatial coding.

## MODULARITY OR ADAPTIVE COMBINATION?

Research over the past 2 decades has revealed a remarkable fact about spatial functioning in a wide variety of animal species, including fish, birds, nonhuman mammals, and humans: All these mobile organisms share a powerful sensitivity to geometric properties of enclosing spaces (e.g., the relative length of walls defining enclosures), using such information to reestablish spatial orientation after being disoriented (Cheng, 1986; Hermer & Spelke, 1996; for a review, see Cheng & Newcombe, 2005). Based on findings that both rats and

human children fail to use nongeometric (or featural) information (e.g., colors or markings on surfaces), even when use of featural information would be adaptive because it would disambiguate geometrically congruent locations, it has been suggested that such geometric processing constitutes a specialized cognitive module that is impenetrable to nongeometric information, even when that information has been processed (Gallistel, 1990; Hermer & Spelke, 1996). The fact that adults and children of 6 years and older *do* integrate featural and geometric information has led to the suggestion, working within the modularity framework, that language is necessary for combining the output of cognitive modules (Spelke & Hermer, 1996). These findings have been exciting both to researchers interested in spatial functioning and also to a wider audience focused on cognitive architecture, comparative cognition, cognitive development, and the role of language in behavior. However, there is debate about the data and how to interpret them. In addition, the adaptive combination approach to spatial processing and development provides an alternative framework to modular architecture for considering the phenomena in this domain of research. Specifically, three models of how spatial information from various sources is used are outlined schematically in Figure 17.1 (from Cheng and Newcombe, 2005). Model A postulates impenetrable modules, across which information combination relies on the use of complex spatial language available only to school-age children and adults. In the absence of a linguistic link, useful sources of information may be ignored, as special-purpose modules dominate behavior in particular situations. By contrast, both Models B and C utilize an adaptive combination approach where a continually changing mix of spatial information sources is utilized, with the exact mix responsive to factors such as the sources' reliability, variability and usefulness, and the certainty with which it has been encoded.

### Modular Spatial Processing

Evaluating Model A requires a sharp differentiation between two aspects of the research on geometry. On the one hand, there is considerable evidence favoring early geometric sensitivity. These findings are, however, not directly germane to the modularity debate, although they are fascinating and important in their own right. After all, awareness of the relative length of extended surfaces and of the angles at which they connect is a sur-

(a)  Impenetrable Module

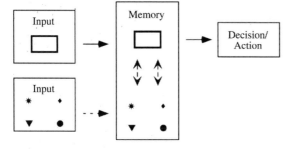

(b)  Modular Memorial Subsystems

(c)  Modular Input Systems Only

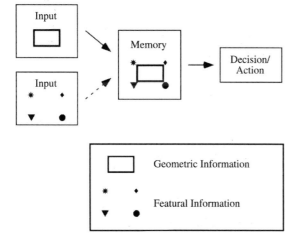

**Figure 17.1**  Views of modularity in reorientation. The input systems consist of perceptual and learning processes. Some modularity in processing geometric and featural information is assumed. (a) In the impenetrable module, featural information does not enter into the memorial system used for reorientation. If featural information is used at all, it goes through other central modules, one of which does view-based matching. (b) In a system with modular components, a metric frame (box inside of the memory box) contains only geometric information. Featural information may be pasted onto the frame in addition (represented by arrows inside the memory box). (c) An integrated system in which featural and geometric information are put together for reorientation. In both panels B and C, featural information may fail to be input into memory. This failure can cause systematic rotational errors. See the text for further details.

prising early competence that likely contributes in important ways to spatial behavior. On the other hand, whether this geometric sensitivity constitutes a cognitive module is controversial. We begin with the findings on geometric sensitivity, and only later proceed to discuss the question of whether such sensitivity constitutes a modular ability.

### Geometric Sensitivity

A good place to begin reviewing this body of research is by describing the basic experimental paradigm that led to the detection of the sensitivity. Cheng (1986) placed rats in an unmarked rectangular enclosure, with food hidden in one corner. They were disoriented to eliminate their use of the dead reckoning system and necessitate their reliance only on environment-centered spatial systems; they were then replaced in the chamber. The rats went to both of the two geometrically identical corners to search for the food, but avoided the two corners in which the relation of the long wall and the short wall was different from that of the correct corner. This kind of search pattern shows coding of the geometric features of the environment: some aspect of the lengths of the walls (either relative length or absolute length) and the handedness, or *sense*, of the relation at the corners (e.g., the fact that the long wall is to the left or the right of the short wall). Very similar results have been reported for human children aged 18 to 24 months (Hermer & Spelke, 1994, 1996).

The hypothesis that children have an early sensitivity to the geometry of enclosing spaces has held up well in subsequent research. For example, Huttenlocher and Vasilyeva (2003) found that toddlers can locate a hidden object after disorientation in a triangular as well as in a rectangular space, thus demonstrating the generality of geometric sensitivity. Huttenlocher and Vasilyeva's studies also explored the nature of early geometric sensitivity. They found that children rarely surveyed the various locations before going to the corner where they believed the object was hidden. Thus, it seems likely that toddlers represent the entire space rather than the appearance of a particular corner where a toy is hidden. This overall representation allows them to know their relation to the hiding corner, no matter where they face after disorientation. In addition, children were not restricted to dealing only with spaces that surround them (as was suggested by Wang and Spelke, 2002), but rather could locate a hidden object when they were outside as well as when they were inside a space. Finally, although children could use geometry when outside as well as when enclosed by a space, performance was better when children were inside the space. This finding suggests that the distinctiveness of the critical information about the enclosed space is important. For a viewer who faces the space from outside, all potential hiding corners lie in a frontal plane; these positions are similar and hence potentially confusable. In contrast, for a viewer who is inside, the potential hiding corners are not all in the frontal plane; these positions are more differentiated than in the outside condition (see Figure 17.2 for a visual illustration of how the corners are more distinct when a viewer is inside the space).

The data on better performance when inside the space argue for the hypothesis that the viewer is represented in relation to the entire space, rather than the space being represented in isolation. Further evidence for this hypothesis comes from work by Lourenco, Huttenlocher, and Vasilyeva (2005) examining situations in which children see a toy hidden while they are inside a space and are then translated outside it (or vice versa). Disorientation can occur either before or after the translation. If the translation occurs first, performance is not impaired, presumably because the tie between the viewer and the space can be maintained. However, when disorientation occurs first, children's performance falls to chance.

Existing data are conflicted on whether geometric processing occurs when separated objects are placed so as to define a rectangle or a triangle. Some studies have found that 3- and 4-year-old children could not use isolated elements to define geometric information (Gouteux & Spelke, 2001), to locate the middle of an array (MacDonald, Spetch, Kelly, & Cheng, 2004), or to locate one of the elements in terms of relations to the others (Uttal, Gregg, Tan, Chamberlin, & Sines, 2001). Other studies have shown that younger children do abstract geometry from separated objects (Garrad-Cole,

Lew, Bremner, & Whitaker, 2001) and also that rats and pigeons are able to do so (Benhamou & Poucet, 1998; Spetch, Cheng, & MacDonald, 1996). This contradiction is important to resolve in future research because the natural environment does not contain many continuously enclosed spaces. The usefulness of the geometric module in the natural environment (which was, after all, the environment of adaptation within which the module is supposed to have evolved) depends on showing its activation in such situations.

## Modularity

Sensitivity to geometry is a remarkable finding. Having established the existence of this capability and elucidated some aspects of its nature, we can now evaluate whether such sensitivity necessarily depends on modular processing. Postulating modularity is based on a very surprising finding in the rectangular room experiments, seen when features of various kinds, such as a colored wall, were added to the unmarked rectangular enclosure. Rats and human children continued to divide their searches evenly between the two geometrically correct corners, as they had in unfeatured rooms, ignoring the additional data that would have allowed them to search successfully on all trials. Children do this even though it is easy to show that they can notice and remember information about the colored wall. Evidence of this kind points to encapsulation or impenetrability, a crucial attribute of modularity in Fodor's (1983, 2001) treatment (although note that Fodor doubted the existence of central modules, which a geometric module would arguably be).

Although the findings of geometric sensitivity have held up well, there has been a good deal of controversy about the claim that such sensitivity forms a module. One challenge to the modular hypothesis, especially to a version where language plays an important role in using information from different modules, is that nonhuman animals (other than rats) have been found to integrate featural and geometric information. Vallortigara, Zanforlin, and Pasti (1990) have found such evidence in experiments with chickens, Kelly, Spetch, and Heth (1998) have found such evidence in pigeons and perhaps most dramatically, Sovrano, Bisazza, and Vallortigara (2002) found such evidence in fish, specifically *Xenotoca eiseni*. Similarly, Gouteux, Thinus-Blanc, and Vauclair (2001) found that monkeys did not show encapsulation of geometric knowledge; they used a colored wall to reorient and find a reward after disorientation in a rectan-

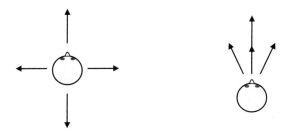

**Figure 17.2** Corners are more distinct when a viewer is inside a space as shown on the left, than when outside it.

gular room. Interestingly, monkeys did not use small cues to differentiate the geometry, but they did use larger cues. This result supports an adaptive combination interpretation of when features will be used to disambiguate geometry, because small objects are likely to move, and hence would not often provide a good cue to spatial location. By contrast, larger objects are much more likely to be stable, and thus to be useful in building a spatial framework.

Although the results with various nonhuman animal species are impressive, Hermer-Vazquez, Moffett, and Munkholm (2001) suggested that they might reflect the extensive training that was used in these experiments, which used a reference memory technique rather than the working memory design that had most clearly suggested modularity in Cheng's original experiments. They argued that only human adults, and children older than 5 years, have been shown to use nongeometric landmarks *flexibly* and *easily,* with minimal training. Evaluating the claims of a geometric module requires work either with working-memory paradigms or with paradigms in which training can be minimal, as is possible in studies of human children. Thus, evidence regarding circumstances in which very young children succeed in using nongeometric landmarks as well as geometric information to reorient is vital to the modularity debate. In fact, there is evidence that young children do use both kinds of information. In moderately large spaces, children as young as 18 months use features such as a colored wall to reorient, as well as coding geometric information (Learmonth, Newcombe, & Huttenlocher, 2001). The encapsulation result is restricted to the extremely small room used in the original Hermer-Spelke studies (Learmonth, Nadel, & Newcombe, 2002).

There are a fairly large number of data sets on children's use of featural and geometric information, at various ages and in rooms of various sizes. Cheng and Newcombe (2005) compared the available data, revealing several interesting patterns. First, although even very young children do make above-chance use of featural information in large rooms, they are not perfect users of such information. Children's performance improves with age in large as well as small rooms. Specifically, the ability to use the colored wall to choose between the geometrically identical corners in the larger space appears to improve at 5 years and then again at 6 years of age (the same age range at which the ability to use the colored wall at all appears in the small room). Second, performance in using featural information in

the larger room is better than performance in the smaller one, even at the older ages. Thus, two facts about the data need to be explained: the consistently greater difficulty of the small room, and the age-related changes that occur in each context. In addition, the age-related change in using featural information appears to be much more abrupt in the small room than in the larger one.

Newcombe (2005) has proposed that the existing data on integration of featural and geometric information can be best explained by an adaptive combination approach in which the likelihood of using the two kinds of information varies depending on factors such as uncertainty or history of cue validity. Being in a larger room may increase the likelihood of using a feature, because it increases its validity—in the real world, more distal features are more typically useful as landmarks. Alternatively or in addition, being in a room that affords more opportunities for movement may activate modes of processing that involve cue combinations not typically used in a more motorically passive situation, just as movement facilitates access to remembered spatial layouts (Rieser, Garing, & Young, 1994). Studies exploring the room-size effect, as well as directly manipulating the salience, certainty, variability, and usefulness of featural and geometric information, hold the promise of specifying how geometric and featural information are used and combined in different circumstances, and the developmental mechanisms that underlie behavioral changes in feature use in enclosed geometric spaces as well as in more naturalistic ones.

## The Development of Spatial Processing from an Adaptive Combination Point of View

We have examined studies of early spatial memory and action inspired by Piaget's thinking, and others inspired by theorizing about modular cognitive architecture, arguing in each case that an adaptive combination interpretation of the findings was possible and even preferable. In this section, we examine directly how spatial development occurs from the point of view of an adaptive combination theory, specifically, the Huttenlocher-Hedges hierarchical coding approach. Because this model postulates the combination of fine-grained and categorical information, it suggests the need to investigate the starting points and development of three kinds of processing: first, encoding of fine-grained (or distance) information, second, encoding of categorical information, and third, the hierarchical combination process itself. While all these lines of development are related, the development of spatial categorization and of hierarchical combination are especially intertwined, because the systematic biases that are evidence for combination of information also provide clues about the nature of categorical coding.

### Distance Coding

Recent evidence indicates that toddlers and even infants can use extent to code location and can retain that information after movement. Huttenlocher, Newcombe, and Sandberg (1994) found that 18- to 24-month-olds used distance information to locate an object hidden in a 5-foot-long sandbox; use of such information by toddlers is also supported by the findings of geometric sensitivity just reviewed (Hermer & Spelke, 1996; Learmonth et al., 2001). Newcombe, Huttenlocher, and Learmonth (1999) found that even 5-month-old infants may code distance; after familiarization to a hiding event, infants looked longer when an object emerged from a new location in a 3-foot-long sandbox. These reactions seem to reflect knowledge infants bring with them to the laboratory rather than online learning from familiarization events (Newcombe et al., 2005). In addition, Gao, Levine, and Huttenlocher (2000) found that 9-month-old infants could encode extent in a different setting involving the length (height) of an object. After being familiarized to a beaker filled with liquid to a particular height, infants looked longer when the height of liquid in a beaker was changed.

Comparing the paradigms used by Newcombe, Huttenlocher, and Learmonth (1999) and Gao et al. (2000) is interesting. In the first situation, an infant must encode a horizontal extent between the edge of a box and the place where an object disappeared. In the second situation, an infant must encode the vertical extent from the bottom (or the top) of a beaker to a liquid surface. In the first case, we speak of encoding distance, and in the second case, we speak of encoding either height or liquid quantity, but the situations are closely comparable. In other words, along with time and quantity, distance involves the registration of magnitudes along a dimension. General notions of extent are present across species and may be fundamental to several domains of human thought (Walsh, 2003). Tasks involving extent have been shown to have a common neural basis in humans in regions in and around the intraparietal sulcus (Dehaene, Dehaene-Lambertz, & Cohen, 1998; Fias, Lammertyn, Reynvoet, Dupont, & Orban, 2003), per-

haps based on common action principles (Rossetti et al., 2004). There are close relations between visuospatial competence and understanding of number in normally developing children (Ansari et al., 2003). Children with Williams syndrome, who have pronounced spatial deficits, also show delayed understanding of counting and cardinality (Ansari et al., 2003).

The linkage between the spatial notion of distance and the mathematical notion of quantity raises the possibility of a close connection between spatial and mathematical thinking based on sharing a developmental starting point. If true, this linkage undercuts claims of domain-specific innate representations and early modularity. Humans may build on this starting point, one shared with other species, in various ways that ultimately demarcate the spatial and mathematical domains. Many of the mechanisms that lead to separate lines of development revolve around human symbolic abilities, including the use of measuring instruments for relatively exact evaluation of distance and the use of numerical notation for exact specification of quantity.

One possible interpretation of these data is that young infants possess mature spatial (and quantitative) competence. However, another possibility is that, while the starting points for spatial development are stronger than those posited by Piaget, the abilities of young children are still limited. There is in fact evidence of several specific transitions in the development of extent coding. One change, which we have already discussed, is that during the 1st year of life, location may often not be coordinated with the static perceptual characteristics of objects, but rather be taken as definitional of objecthood (e.g., Leslie et al., 1998).

Other changes occur after infancy, particularly in the period between 18 and 24 months, when there are several changes in distance coding. Prior work with infants and toddlers had involved distance coding in the context of locating a single object, hidden for a relatively brief period, located in a surrounding container. Newcombe, Huttenlocher, Drummey, and Wiley (1998) examined the development of the use of distal landmarks located at the edges of a room in which there was a centrally located sandbox. Children ages 16 to 36 months observed a toy being hidden in the rectangular sandbox, moved to the opposite side, and then searched for the toy. Half the children performed this search with visible landmarks in the room and half without visible landmarks (because a circular white curtain surrounded the sandbox). Children 22 months and older performed better when the landmarks were visible, whereas the presence or absence of a curtain made no difference to the accuracy of children younger than 22 months. They did not seem to use the distance from surrounding objects to locate objects after movement, that is, did not exhibit what has been called place learning. These results are consistent with earlier work (Bushnell, McKenzie, Lawrence, & Connell, 1995; DeLoache, & Brown, 1983).

Sluzenski, Newcombe, and Satlow (2004) examined the ability of children aged 18 to 42 months to perform three other tasks that are basic to mature spatial functioning. In prior work with the sandbox paradigm, we had examined memory for only a single object, hidden for less than a minute. To be useful, however, spatial location memory needs to allow for representing multiple locations to support the learning of spatial relations among objects. We also need to exhibit recall after a substantial filled delay. When children from 18 to 42 months were tested on sandbox search tasks involving recall of two locations, learning a spatial relation, or retaining even the location of a single object over a filled delay, results indicated a transition from 18 to 24 months in all three abilities. A similar transition was found by Russell and Thompson (2003). Although Moore and Meltzoff (2004) found good performance by 14-month-olds after a 24-hour delay, their hiding situation involved very distinctive locations and a very highly marked hiding procedure, and they did not examine age-related change. Thus, the existing evidence, though still sparse, suggests the possibility of a general transition in spatial coding toward the end of infancy, in which a capability emerges for durable and complex memory that can support action and reasoning.

To say that this capability may emerge toward the end of the 2nd year is not to be equated with saying what we see by 2 years is mature competence. On the contrary, there is evidence that development of the capacity to construct spatial relations may continue for some time. In particular, place learning is not complete until well into the school years, perhaps not until the age of 10 years (Laurance, Learmonth, Nadel, & Jacobs, 2003; Leplow et al., 2003; Overman, Pate, Moore, & Peuster, 1996; see review by Learmonth and Newcombe, in press). In addition, there may be earlier roots of this capability in simpler situations (Clearfield, 2004; Lew, Bremner, & Lefkovich, 2000; Lew et al., 2004).

Another change in distance coding (or coding of extent) that occurs after infancy concerns the use of a surrounding container that can serve as a standard against

which to assess extent. Such a standard was present in all the sandbox or beaker studies reviewed so far. Without a perceptually present standard, a mental standard must be imposed, and applied uniformly across a wide range of situations, to determine extent. Huttenlocher, Duffy, and Levine (2002) found that infants and 2-year-olds could judge extent only as long as a target was aligned with a perceptually available standard. They could *not* do so when a target was presented in isolation (see Figure 17.3). It was not until the age of 4 years that children could determine extent without a perceptually available standard. Beginning at about 5 years of age, children show a mixed pattern of performance in extent coding tasks. On the one hand, they can determine extent without a perceptually available standard, indicating some independence from perceptual context. On the other hand, their judgment can be affected by a misleading standard. For example, if a target object is presented in a container of a particular height, and then children are given a choice task involving containers of a different height, they do not recognize the target since it has a changed relation to the container (Duffy, Huttenlocher, & Levine, 2005). If the foil in the choice task shows the same relation to the container as the target had to its container in the original presentation, they

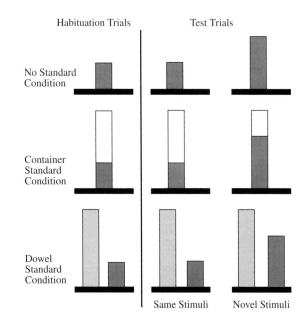

**Figure 17.3** Examples of the stimuli presented in habituation and test trials in three conditions. *Source:* From "Infants and Toddlers Discriminate Amount: Are They Measuring?" by J. Huttenlocher, S. Duffy, and S. Levine, 2002, *Psychological Science, 13*(3), pp. 244–249. Reprinted with permission.

choose the foil. Thus, it appears that children initially code extent only relative to a present standard ("relative extent"). Later, they become able to represent extent relative to a constant standard ("absolute extent"), but in ambiguous situations, the present context still affects their judgments.

### Development of Categorical Coding

Besides fine-grained coding of distance, the other kind of information used in spatial estimation, according to the hierarchical coding model, is categorical information. The earliest signs of categorical coding of location are evident by at least 3 months of age, in the ability of infants to dishabituate when stimuli presented in various positions above a bar are presented below the bar (or vice versa) (Quinn, 1994). A similar pattern is evident for switches from left to right of a bar (or vice versa), although, interestingly, there are no reactions to changes from one side to the other of a diagonal bar (Quinn, 2004). At 6 months, there are indications of understanding of an abstract notion of containment (Casasola, Cohen, & Chiarello, 2003).

Despite these indications of early spatial categorization, it is also clear that there is a developmental progression in the ability to categorize spatially. Categories of above and below are not formed without a bar to demarcate them (Quinn, 1994) and are not formed until 6 months of age when the stimuli shown during habituation vary in shape as well as in position (Quinn, Cummins, Kase, Martin, & Weissman, 1996). At 3 and 4 months, there is no category of between at all, and when it appears at 6 months, it is only evident with uniform habituation stimuli (Quinn, Norris, Pasko, Schmader, & Mash, 1999). This limitation is overcome by 9 to 10 months (Quinn, Adams, Kennedy, Shettler, & Wasnik, 2003). In sum, although only a few spatial categories have been examined so far, there may be gradual and protracted development in spatial categorization. The factors and mechanisms that underlie this development remain to be determined.

### Development of Hierarchical Combination

In the preceding sections, we reviewed the development of the two components of the Huttenlocher-Hedges hierarchical combination model of spatial coding: fine-grained coding of distance, and coding of spatial categories. We are now in a position to take up the issue of the development of hierarchical combination of these information sources. Evidence of such combination comes from systematic patterns of bias in spatial estimation toward category prototypes, bias patterns that in turn provide information on what categories are being used. Thus, for example, the fact that spatial estimations of the locations of dots in a circle are biased toward the centers of quadrants defined by horizontal and vertical axes suggests that those quadrants constitute spatial categories (Huttenlocher et al., 1991). The earliest evidence of hierarchical combination comes from children of 16 to 24 months, who show bias toward the center of the rectangular sandbox (Huttenlocher et al., 1994). This bias cannot be explained on perceptual or motoric grounds, as it is evident even when children move laterally along the box between hiding and search, or observe hiding and then search from an extreme end of the box. Whether hierarchical combination is evident before 16 months is unknown. The development of categorization ability in the 1st year of life may set some lower limit on the possibility of such adaptive combination. However, the process of hierarchical combination could potentially be available in principle or as a potential even before specific constituents appear.

Even if hierarchical combination is a basic cognitive process, it might be expected to change developmentally in various ways. First, the accuracy of fine-grained coding might improve, as well as its durability. Such change would be expected to reduce the weighting of category information and hence reduce the extent of bias. The research on this topic concentrates on the issue of durability, studied by manipulating the length of the delay between encoding information and being asked to estimate it. Research with adults has shown that longer delays lead to increased bias, as would be expected because categorical information should be more strongly weighted as the certainty of fine-grained information declines (Engebretson & Huttenlocher, 1996; Huttenlocher et al., 1991). Thus, one might expect that delay-related increases in bias would be more marked for younger children, if they experience more marked forgetting of fine-grained information (although whether there actually are such age differences in forgetting rates is controversial; see Brainerd, Kingma, & Howe, 1985). So far, delay-related increases in bias have been shown to be fairly constant from the age of 7 years on (Hund & Plumert, 2002).[3] However, if there are in fact age-related

---

[3] There is, however, a puzzling decline in delay-related bias at age 11 in these data.

changes in forgetting, they may exist at younger ages, so this question deserves examination in children between the ages of 2 and 7 years.

Second, categorical coding might change in any one of several ways. One possible change is that categories might become more conceptual and more likely to be based on functional groupings (e.g., "the playground area"). From the age of 7 years on, children and adults show increased systematic biases when objects in a certain spatial area also belong to the same conceptual category, with the effects constant across age (Hund & Plumert, 2003). However, the effect of conceptual categories might not be present for younger children whose categories are less firmly entrenched. Relatedly, spatial categories might become less dependent on the presence of physically present boundaries. For example, a rectangular space could be divided categorically into two halves by imposition of an imaginary line down the center. Indication of such a division appears to be more likely in smaller spaces, perhaps because they can be apprehended at a single glance: children's bias patterns showed evidence of dividing a rectangle into halves by 4 years for small spaces, although not until much later for larger ones (Huttenlocher et al., 1994). In addition, categories might not be formed in the most difficult circumstances until older ages. Hund, Plumert, and Benney (2002) found that only adults were capable of using categorical information when the locations of objects in four spatial regions were learned in a random order, so that the spatial categories were far less evident than when there was no temporal scrambling.

Third, hierarchical combination might change as information-processing capabilities strengthen. In fact, hierarchical combination seems initially to be limited to one dimension at a time. When children are asked to encode the location of a dot in a circle, they encode fine-grained location in the same two dimensions used by adults—distance from the center of the circle and angle—and they adjust the coding of distance from the center using category information. However, they do not also show categorical adjustment of angular information until 10 years of age (Sandberg, Huttenlocher, & Newcombe, 1996). This lack was not basic to encoding of angle because categorical coding and adjustment was demonstrated by children as young as 7 years when no coding of distance was also required (Sandberg, 2000). Thus, it seems likely that children have capacity limitations that prevent them from noticing or using the

central tendency of variation in two dimensions at the same time.

In summary, the principle of hierarchical combination seems to be in evidence as early as we have been able to examine it, by 16 months of age. It may well be a basic aspect of information processing, as arguably suggested by the fact that it is also shown by rhesus monkeys (Merchant et al., 2004). However, precise patterns of hierarchical combination may be expected to change with age. For instance, the components may change, as distance coding becomes more exact and/or categorical coding becomes more systematic, more conceptual, or more differentiated. Very little research has studied those questions. What we do know is that there is a basic change in late childhood in the ability to perform hierarchical combination along two dimensions at once. Acquisition of this capability may affect many other aspects of spatial functioning and is interestingly reminiscent of some of Piaget and Inhelder's proposals about the advent of mature spatial functioning in the same time period.

### Effects of Experience on Hierarchical Combination

Developmental change in hierarchical combination ought to be related to experience in the shorter run, as well as to age-related change in information-processing capacity or estimation ability. That is, when certain locations in a space are routinely clustered or more frequently occupied, categories may be formed based on these probabilities of occurrence (Huttenlocher, Hedges, & Vevea, 2000; Spencer & Hund, 2002, 2003). Formation of such ad hoc spatial categories is difficult to find in situations in which there are strongly engrained bases of organization, as in the case of the circle where it is difficult to override a vertical axis based on gravitation and a horizontal axis organized at right angles to the vertical and in parallel with the symmetry of the human body (Huttenlocher et al., 2004), or in cases where one basis of organization is around the midline of a person's body (Spencer & Hund, 2002, 2003). In fact, forming categories based on regions of high density of occurrence may not be adaptive in cases where other boundaries can be known with greater precision. However, dynamic alteration of spatial categories has been found in certain contexts.

One situation for studying the extent to which participants alter their categorical organization of a spatial array is when the sequential order of display of the various objects in the array initially suggests a certain organization and this order of display is then altered to suggest a different organization. Hund and Plumert (2005) displayed 20 objects in a large square box in an order that either emphasized organizing the objects by quadrant or by their relation to the sides of the box (see Figure 17.4). They found that adults could flexibly reorganize as a function of the most recent temporal structuring of the display. This finding is interesting because it indicates that the use of horizontal and vertical boundaries (Huttenlocher et al., 2004) is not inevitable; the availability of horizontal and vertical lines defining the edge of the space provides an alternative organization of some precision. However, Hund and Plumert found that children as old as 11 years displayed limited flexibility. The reasons for this limitation are unknown at present.

Another situation in which to study dynamic restructuring of spatial estimation occurs when a single location is repeatedly utilized in a spatial search situation, and then search is switched to a second location, as in the classic A-not-B task. Of course, if the A-not-B error is conceptualized as the result of a basic limitation in understanding of object permanence, as it was by Piaget, no such effects would be evident, but recent data show convincingly that biases toward location A when searching for location B can be found in children of 2, 3, 4, and even 6 years of age, under certain circumstances (Schutte & Spencer, 2002; Schutte, Spencer, & Schöner, 2003; Spencer & Schutte, 2004; Spencer, Smith, & Thelen, 2001). The tendency is a function of the number of A trials and the number of B trials (Spencer et al., 2001), as well as the separation between the A and the B locations (Schutte et al., 2003). It does not depend on active search to location A, being evident also when children simply observe hiding at location A (Spencer & Schutte, 2004).

An interesting kind of developmental change may depend on the relative use of prototypes based on intrinsic geometry, such as that defined by the vertical and horizontal lines that divide a circle into quadrants, and the prototypes of frequency-based spatial categories formed around groups of locations that are frequently occupied in a particular situation. Hund and Spencer (2003) found that 6-year-olds were more affected than 11-year-olds by such frequency-based categories. In fact, they exhibited biases toward a frequency-based prototype that ignored categories based on intrinsic geometry. These biases involved crossing the vertical boundary that defined categories of right and left of their bodies. This kind of flexibility might be important in forming categories early in life and may be lost as experience informs about the relative advantage of using a boundary that can be known with precision (Huttenlocher et al., 2004). However, the question of developmental change in flexibility is not yet clear, as Hund and Plumert (2005) found that adults were more, not less, flexible than children in reorganizing categorical structure on the basis of changes in temporal ordering.

### Summary

Fine-grained metric coding of distance and categorical groupings of spatial locations are both evident within the 1st year of life, although neither is present in its mature form. Coding of distance evolves over the toddler and preschool years by taking more account of distal objects, becoming more complex and enduring, and beginning to encompass absolute as well as relative extent. Categorical coding evolves in the 1st year to be less dependent on perceptually available demarcations and more able to encompass perceptually varied stimuli, and likely changes over the next few years as well. Hierarchical combination of these two kinds of information is evident as early as it has been assessed, at 16 months, but it too changes devel-

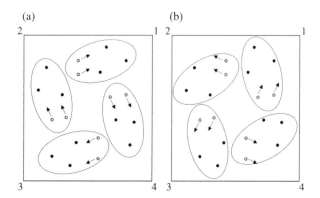

**Figure 17.4** Diagram of the experimental apparatus and locations. Open circles mark the eight target locations. Arrows show the predicted pattern of displacement for the target locations. (a) The locations experienced together in the side experience condition. (b) The locations experienced together in the quadrant experience condition. The arrows, ovals, and numbers are for illustration only. *Source:* From "The Stability and Flexibility of Spatial Categories," by A. M. Hund and J. M. Plumert, 2005, *Cognitive Psychology, 50,* pp. 1–44. Reprinted with permission.

opmentally, over the span of a decade or so. Some of these changes likely depend on increases in information-processing capabilities, whereas others may involve decreased sensitivity to frequency-based prototypes and increasing use of preset category boundaries that can be known with great precision.

## REPRESENTING SPATIAL RELATIONS BETWEEN VIEWER AND ENVIRONMENT

We have, so far, examined the development of human capability to encode spatial location. While such abilities likely differ to some extent between humans and other species (e.g., MacDonald et al., 2004), the fundamental capacity to encode location in some fashion is widely shared. The ability to manipulate such information may be more distinctively human. Although this issue has not been extensively studied, nonhuman primates have difficulty with mental rotation (Hopkins, Fagot, & Vauclair, 1993; Vauclair, Fagot, & Hopkins, 1993), and pigeons do not compute interpolated views in the same way that humans do in what amounts to a simple assessment of perspective-taking ability (Spetch & Friedman, 2003). These observations suggest limitations on the capacity of nonhuman animals to mentally transform spatial relations.

In this section, we discuss the development of mental rotation and perspective taking. We also examine the development of navigation, which in many species of nonhuman animal can be very sophisticated. Yet, there is no secure evidence that other species are capable of the kind of spatial inference that allows humans to devise new routes, that is, to get from location B to location C when they have previously traveled only between locations A and B and locations A and C (Shettleworth, 1998). Spatial inference of the sort that allows for way finding along novel routes may share with mental rotation and perspective taking the need to construct and manipulate relations between viewer and environment.

### Mental Rotation and Perspective Taking

Research over the past few decades has shown that mental rotation and perspective taking, while formally equivalent, are in fact very different psychologically. The formal equivalence is easy to appreciate; any computing machine that could move an object (or array) on its axis with respect to a viewer could also perform the computations required to move the viewer around the object (or array), and the output of (say) a 90-degree rotation of either kind would be identical. The psychological difference was implicitly appreciated by Piaget, who discussed mental rotation and perspective taking in different books (*Mental Imagery in the Child* and *The Child's Conception of Space*), conceptualizing them as part of different lines of development and as occurring at different ages. The fact that mental rotation and perspective taking differ psychologically though not logically was first demonstrated empirically by Huttenlocher and Presson (1973). They found that it is easier to select a picture showing the appearance of an object or array after imagining it rotating on its axis than after imagining moving oneself to take a different perspective on the same object or array. However, mental rotation is not invariably simpler than perspective taking (Huttenlocher & Presson, 1979). When people are asked what object in an array would be in a certain position relative to themselves following a transformation (e.g., what would be closest? on the left?), perspective taking is easier than mental rotation. In fact, with item-focused questions of this kind, children as young as 3 years show an impressive ability to work out the results of moving to take a different perspective on an array (Newcombe & Huttenlocher, 1992), although if asked to choose what picture shows the results of such movement, they do not succeed until 9 or 10 years.

Subsequent studies have confirmed these difficulty orderings (Presson, 1982), using change detection paradigms as well as more specific queries (Simons & Wang, 1998), in contexts where people are standing inside or outside an array (Wraga, Creem, & Proffitt, 2000), and with displays varying in complexity (Wraga, Creem-Regehr, & Proffitt, 2004). It has also been shown that perspective taking and mental rotation differ in terms of their neural substrates, with perspective transformations associated with increased activity in left temporal cortex and mental rotation associated with changes in activity in parietal cortex (Zacks, Vettel, & Michelon, 2003), and that perspective taking and mental rotation are separable abilities when analyzed in terms of patterns of individual differences (Kozhevnikov & Hegarty, 2001). Other work has decomposed the action of moving around the perimeter of an array, as one does in a perspective-taking task, into its rotational and translational components. It appears that rotation is much more difficult to imagine than translation (May, 2004; Presson & Montello, 1994; Rieser, 1989).

The explanation of these complex patterns turns on understanding the frames of reference involved in each task. For example, the classic Piagetian task of selecting a picture that shows the view of an array from a different perspective is difficult because the correct picture shows the elements of the array in the currently available external framework, not the framework as it would be transformed by actual physical movement. Physically moving to a new vantage point makes this task much easier, both because the movement transforms the framework and because dead reckoning mechanisms support the computation of new views. Asking a specific question about the viewer-array relation is easier because it isolates the relation of central interest, reducing the conflict between actual and imagined framework. Imaging the array rotating on its axis involves transforming the relations of the array to the external framework, so that there is no conflict between frameworks. In addition, people often concentrate on one element of the array in performing such a mental rotation, thus simplifying the task.

The developmental sequence from 3 to 10 years has been exhaustively investigated; for more complete reviews, see Newcombe (1989, 2002a) and Newcombe and Huttenlocher (2000). In brief, perspective taking can be seen in incipient form as early as 3 years of age (Newcombe & Huttenlocher, 1992), with mental rotation appearing a year or two afterward. However, variant forms of the task remain difficult at these ages and develop slowly, with good performance on some versions not being evident until 10 years or so. Sequences of this kind leave a powerful impression that the emergence of capabilities follows a complexity ordering, so that tasks that adults perform more slowly and on which they make more errors appear later in children's repertoires. By 3 years, there may be no fundamental lack in understanding the possibility of mentally transforming relations between the viewer and the environment, yet there may be important limitations on the ability to do so in particular performance situations, with the idea of conflict in frames of reference a key aspect of determining when tasks are easier versus harder.[4]

Thinking in terms of the conflict among frames of reference also allows us to explain certain problems children have with spatial tasks other than mental rotation and perspective taking. A prominent example is that children have great difficulty copying the arrangement of elements on a tableau, when the two arrays are not aligned (Laurendeau & Pinard, 1970; Piaget & Inhelder, 1948/1967; Pufall & Shaw, 1973), in finding hidden objects in misaligned models (Blades, 1991), or in indicating positions on misaligned maps (Liben & Downs, 1993). Vasilyeva (2002) showed that 4-year-old children could utilize objective frames of reference when the temptation to use egocentric frames was reduced, but that they failed when there was conflict between the objective and the egocentric frames.

## Navigation

We treat navigation after mental rotation and perspective taking, despite the fact that navigation is relatively unproblematic when a visible beacon marks the spot one wishes to reach, as when a church's spire is visible above the surrounding houses. However, reaching an unseen location is more challenging and may sometimes depend on spatial inference of the same kind that occurs in mental rotation and perspective: the construction and manipulation of relations between viewer and environment. Such operations are important in many settings, although they are not always necessary because it is sometimes possible to reach unseen locations by engaging in sequential beacon following. That is, one can go first to one visible landmark that marks an interim step on the journey, then to a second beacon visible from the first beacon, and so on. Such a system is generally called route learning, and seems to be available even to young children, although improvements in noticing landmarks and constructing routes occur with age through the elementary school years (Siegel, Kirasic, & Kail, 1979; Siegel & White, 1975).

Returning to the ability to navigate to unseen points when no route is known and where it may be necessary to conduct inference based on constructions of multiple spatial relations, it has been claimed that children gradually develop a knowledge base that allows for such inference. This knowledge base is often called *survey knowledge* of the environment and has also been termed a *cognitive map* (Siegel & White, 1975). However, the existence of such representations has been controversial, at least in nonhuman animals, and has been more assumed

---

[4] Such limitations should not be dismissed as uninteresting in the face of early basic ability; they are very functionally relevant and determine children's capacity to take on everyday tasks (Newcombe, 2002a). Thus, they deserve concentrated study with a view to maximizing competence and minimizing the extent to which some children develop less than optimal ability to perform these tasks.

than extensively studied in children. The most basic indication of integrated spatial knowledge is the ability to go from one point to another, without having previously traveled this route, based on navigation involving a third point. For example, if you can go from your home to school, and also from your home to the park, going directly from the school to the park would indicate spatial inference. Studying this ability in the situation depicted in Figure 17.5, in a blind child of 2.5 years, Landau, Spelke, and Gleitman (1984) argued that human spatial inference is a basic capacity that is evident early in life and is not dependent on visual input. Although this study has been criticized on methodological grounds (Liben, 1988; Millar, 1994), and a replication with a larger sample of blind children and with sighted children wearing blindfolds indicated that one must be skeptical about very early ability for spatial inference (Morrongiello, Timney, Humphrey, Anderson, & Skory, 1995), the data from the Morrongiello study did show that spatial inference is possible by the age of 4 years, with accuracy in-

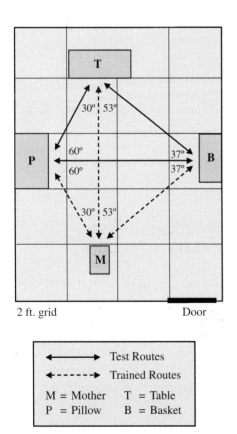

**Figure 17.5** Layout for task. *Source:* From "Spatial Knowledge in a Young Blind Child," by B. Landau, E. S. Spelke, and H. Gleitman, 1984, *Cognition, 16*(3), pp. 225–260. Reprinted with permission.

creasing with age to 8 years. Using a somewhat more complicated situation, Hazen, Lockman, and Pick (1978) found that 3- and 4-year-olds had a very limited ability to draw spatial inferences, but 5- and 6-year-olds did appreciably better.

We should consider further the bases of spatial inference in these paradigms. In the Landau et al. and Morrongiello et al. work, children cannot see the environment, either because they are blind or because they are blindfolded. In the Hazen et al. work, children are sighted and not blindfolded, but because the rooms have doors and roofs, they cannot relate their locations visually to each other or to an external framework. Thus, in these studies, spatial inference has to be based on dead reckoning—on memory for distances traveled and on the angles of turns. Studies of blindfolded adults doing simple integration tasks based only on dead reckoning (e.g., traveling outward from a home base, taking a turn and traveling further, and then being asked to point to home base) show that performance is reasonably accurate, but that even adults show at least a small amount of error in such simple tasks (Fukusima, Loomis, & Da Silva, 1997; Rieser, Guth, & Hill, 1986). Furthermore, the ability to perform such tasks improves from the preschool period to adulthood (Rieser & Rider, 1988, 1991). Thus, it is not surprising that spatial inference based on dead reckoning is difficult for young children and develops over the school years.

What about spatial inference in situations in which external frameworks are available? In the home-school-park example, if neither park nor home is visible from the school, then walking or pointing to the park from the school would be evidence of a spatial inference, arising from an integrated representation created by the availability of common external landmarks during travel of previous routes. Although there have been many studies in which children and adults have been asked to point to unseen locations in a neighborhood or on a campus from a particular vantage point (e.g., Anooshian & Kromer, 1986; Anooshian & Young, 1981; Cousins, Siegel, & Maxwell, 1983), none of these studies included a means of assessing whether the relations queried had ever been directly experienced. Thus, it is unknown to what extent they probed spatial inference. After several years spent living in a certain environment, it is possible that all possible pairs of locations have been traversed directly. Research on spatial inference in novel environments is oddly rare. In one of the few such studies, Heth, Cornell, and Flood (2002) found that 6-year-old children were able to point to where they started a 1-km hike across an unfamiliar campus after completing it. The performance is impressive given that they had not been told to keep track of their movements, and that the route was very long and traversed only once. However, the children's error, while better than chance, was still substantial at 54 degrees. Adults' error was 30 degrees. In addition, because children were not disoriented, their success could have been based on dead reckoning as well as on spatial inference.

Though sparse, the data suggest that the origins of spatial inference lie in the preschool period, with considerable refinement in the accuracy of inference over the school years. It is possible that spatial inference follows a similar developmental trajectory to transitive inference. After all, transitive inference has been shown to depend on the construction of an ordered spatial array from verbal statements (Huttenlocher, 1968), so spatial inference and traditional transitive inference seem quite similar. A considerable body of evidence on transitive inference suggests that, while it may first be evident in the preschool years, it appears more clearly and reliably as children move into the elementary school years (Chapman & Lindenberger, 1992; Halford & Kelly, 1984). In turn, transitive inference from verbal statements appears to depend on working memory (Oakhill, 1984; Perner & Aebi, 1985), which also develops considerably across the school years (e.g., Gathercole, Pickering, Ambridge, & Wearing, 2004). The same reliance on working memory is likely to be true for specifically spatial inference.

Navigation based on spatial inference may also improve in ways that are linked to the changes in hierarchical coding that we noted in a prior section. Children do not use categorical coding to correct fine-grained coding on two dimensions simultaneously until 9 years of age (Sandberg et al., 1996), and they do not divide even a 5-foot-long sandbox into halves for categorical coding until about the same age (Huttenlocher et al., 1994). These changes increase the accuracy with which spatial information is coded and therefore could affect the extent to which a set of spatial locations can be sensibly combined.

The fact that children's ability to navigate improves in many ways over the first 12 years or so of life (e.g., Cornell, Heth, & Alberts, 1994) is associated with an increase in the home range that they are allowed to travel without supervision (Hart, 1979). Causality here may run in both directions; parents allow children to

travel further when they appear competent to do so, while further travel may foster navigational ability. In addition to the age-related changes in spatial inference that we have been stressing, navigational prowess may increase as children develop specific strategies such as looking around at turns to note the view that will be seen on a return trip (Cornell, Heth, & Rowat, 1992) or selecting salient landmarks for rehearsal, especially landmarks located at turns (Allen, Kirasic, Siegel, & Herman, 1979).

In summary, spatial inference based in integrating dead reckoning information is likely first evident in the preschool years; inference based on integrating information using common external landmarks is little studied, but was perhaps seen at 6 years (the youngest age tested) in one study. However, we do not know what allows for the emergence of these abilities. Improvement in spatial inference and in navigation is considerable over the school years, and is likely linked to multiple lines of development, including reasoning in general, the accuracy of spatial coding, and the use of strategies such as looking around at turns. It is striking that there is much that remains unknown about navigation, an area of spatial functioning of considerable practical importance that has been intensively studied in nonhuman animals. Although navigation was the focus of a great deal of research a few decades ago, attention to it declined, in part because of the focus on infancy and the origins of knowledge question. It may now be time to return to its examination, which can be richly informed by recent advances in allied fields.

## USING SYMBOLIC SPATIAL REPRESENTATIONS

Our species may be unique, or at least very distinctive, in our capacities for mental rotation, perspective taking, and spatial inference. Another distinctive kind of human spatial competence rests on our ability to represent situations symbolically and to communicate with each other using language and nonlinguistic symbolic systems such as maps. In this section, we begin by addressing the development of nonlinguistic spatial communication, and then proceed to discuss spatial language. These two varieties of spatial communication present very different patterns of advantages and disadvantages, and very different challenges in acquisition.

## Maps and Models

As a device for communicating about spatial relations, maps and models differ from language in two ways. They must necessarily incorporate metric relations, which are optional in language, and they must show all depicted relations simultaneously, which is impossible in language. However, while maps and models have similarities, there are distinctions between them. Although there are many unclear cases and exceptions, generally speaking, maps are flat and models are three-dimensional; maps use arbitrary symbol-referent relations and models are more iconic; and maps deal with larger spaces and models with smaller ones.

Research on the development of understanding and using models and maps has been marked by the same kind of controversy evident in other research on spatial development, with some investigators arguing that mapping abilities emerge slowly in a fashion tied to the construction of spatial understanding as described by Piaget (Liben & Downs, 1993) and other investigators suggesting that mapping has an innate basis (Blaut, 1997; Landau, 1986). However, in this research area, a third tradition has been prominent. Investigators using a Vygotskyan perspective have analyzed maps and models, as well as other culturally transmitted tools such as navigation systems, as artifacts that build on distinctively human capabilities, either innate or constructed ones, in a fashion that is heavily dependent on social interaction. Newcombe and Huttenlocher (2000) pointed out that, while the Vygotskyan perspective fits the existing data reasonably well, a notable lack in the literature is investigation of the sporadic and variable exposure to mapping systems that is common in our culture. This situation has yet to be remedied, although a pioneering investigation by Szechter and Liben (2004) has shown that investigation of spatial input is feasible and valuable. These investigators observed parents explaining a graphically challenging book called *Zoom* to their 3- and 5-year-old children. They found substantial variability, even in a small middle-class sample, in the extent to which parents used helpful strategies, and found cross-sectional correlations of parental explanation strategies with children's spatial comprehension.

Although we are just beginning to get data on how symbolic spatial abilities are transmitted to children, we have a reasonably good, and continuously strengthening, body of descriptive data on the typical ages and sequences of emergence of mapping competence in children growing up in the cultural conditions of modern industrialized societies. The sequence begins at about the second birthday and involves appreciation of two aspects of maps and models: that elements in them stand for objects in the world (element-to-element correspondence) and that distances in them stand for distances in the world, although subject to a scaling factor (relational correspondence). Element-to-element correspondence has been the focus of a well-known research program (e.g., DeLoache, 1987, 1995) in which children are asked to find an object they have seen hidden in a model in a larger room (or vice versa). These studies have shown that in the use of information acquired in a model to guide search in a room, there are typically abrupt transitions that are not linked to memory for the location, which is always high. Rather, children seem to have (or not have) a representational insight that one element can stand for another (DeLoache, Miller, Rosengren, & Bryant, 1997). The exact age of this transition is somewhat variable and depends on factors such as iconic resemblance and the extent of differences in scale, but children younger than 2 years typically have great difficulty with even the easiest versions of the task, whereas children of 3.5 years and older succeed even in difficult contexts. Element-to-element correspondence of a completely arbitrary kind (e.g., X marks the spot) may appear slightly later. There is some evidence of success in children as young as 3 years (Dalke, 1998), but the ability strengthens from 3 to 6 years (Newcombe & Huttenlocher, 2000).

Relational correspondence seems, on the face of it, to be more difficult than element-to-element correspondence. Indeed, from a Piagetian perspective, scaling depends on proportionality and hence should not be evident until well into the elementary school years. However, Huttenlocher, Newcombe, and Vasilyeva (1999) have shown that 4-year-olds, and some 3-year-olds, can use a small map of a five-foot-long sandbox, in which a dot represents a hidden toy, to find the toy with great accuracy. Of course, this is a simple situation involving only one object and a single dimension. In the two-dimensional case, still with only a single location at issue, 5-year-olds succeed and 4-year-olds show the same kind of bimodal performance exhibited by 3-year-olds in the one-dimensional context (Vasilyeva & Huttenlocher, 2004). Children's performance was affected by the degree of rescaling required, with higher accuracy when the referent space was closer in size to the map. This fact may partially explain why 4- and 5-, and even

6- and 7-year-olds, show difficulty with scaling when dealing with maps or models of large spaces (Liben & Yekel, 1996; Uttal, 1996). These more difficult situations also involve the need to locate many objects at once, and hence to rescale many distances.

Overall, the data suggest that the ability to comprehend the relation between distance in a map or model and distance in a real-world space may be present earlier than proportional reasoning of a formal kind, but that there is only gradual emergence of the ability to use this insight in complex situations. The basis for early relational correspondence is not yet clear. Huttenlocher et al. (1999) suggested that relative coding of distance might be involved, but in this case, degree of rescaling should not be important, or at least not more marked than it is in simple memory for location in smaller versus larger spaces. However, Vasilyeva and Huttenlocher (2004) found that performance on a scaling task could not be completely accounted for by the difficulty of a nonscaling task. It is possible that early rescaling is based instead on a simple stretching of encoded distances and that error increases as more stretching is required.

Element-to-element and relational correspondence are not all that is required for map and model use. Other requirements include the ability to relate aerial or oblique views to eye-level views, the ability to align maps physically or mentally, and the ability to use maps to guide navigation. The first ability appears at a younger age than one might expect. By the age of 25 months, children lifted up so as to be able to view a barrier arrangement that separated them from their mothers could use this information to head for their mothers in the direction that was open (Rieser, Doxsey, McCarrell, & Brooks, 1982). They could do this even after having viewed the apparatus from a side perspective different from the view they had from the ground in direction as well as elevation. However, 21-month-olds failed to use information gained from an overhead view. The reason for this remarkable developmental transition is still unknown.

Alignment of maps is notoriously difficult, at least when it must be done mentally. Even adults struggle to answer questions that involve dealing with misalignment (Levine, Jankovic, & Palij, 1982). One reason for the problem may be that alignment of map and world involves mental rotation of the map (Scholnick, Fein, & Campbell, 1990; Shepard & Hurwitz, 1984). Children begin to show some success in simple situations involv-

ing misaligned maps by the age of 5 years (Blades, 1991; Bluestein & Acredolo, 1979) but difficulties persist into the school years (Presson, 1982).

Using maps for navigation involves the combination of all the skills discussed so far. Children as young as 4 years can use maps to guide navigation in simple situations (Scholnick et al., 1990; Uttal & Wellman, 1989), but have difficulty dealing with misalignment (Bremner & Andreasen, 1998). Children of 6 years can use maps in larger and more complex spaces, where there are many alternative ways to go and where rescaled distance information must be used (Sandberg & Huttenlocher, 2001). However, children of 5 and 6 years rarely turn the map into physical alignment with the space (Vosmik & Presson, 2004). Instead, they succeed when they can "look ahead," planning what they will do for several turns, while looking at an aligned map (Sandberg & Huttenlocher, 2001; Vosmik & Presson, 2004).

## Spatial Language

There are at least three ways in which human language is not particularly well suited to the communication of spatial information. First, it is difficult to capture metric knowledge without using technical terms. Instead, language naturally groups space into categories, such as "front" and "back." Second, ambiguity can arise in speaking about space because various frames of reference are possible for many spatial terms, so that "front" can mean two different locations depending on the system in use. Third, language is sequential, so that speakers must select a specific order in which to mention the spatial relations in a scene. Fortunately, although these issues are potential impediments to effective communication, adult speakers and listeners generally cope well with spatial description, in part through the use of various strategies and linguistic devices. For example, spatial-linguistic categories, like other categories, are structured so that terms refer to areas that have prototypic centers, albeit unclear boundaries (e.g., Crawford, Regier, & Huttenlocher, 2000; Franklin, Henkel, & Zangas, 1995; Munnich, Landau, & Dosher, 2001). Thus, while from a logical point of view, describing a location as in "front" may only communicate spatial information approximately, there is a general assumption that one means the prototypical front unless otherwise specified. When necessary, speakers supplement their use of a term such as *front* by saying things like "in front but a bit to the left" or "the hole is three yards in front of you." In the first case, they gradate the category; in the second case, they add metric specification in a case where it may be crucial. In another example of adroit use of strategies to use language to communicate about space, speakers often specify which of the different possible frames of reference they are using, in ways that are structured by politeness rules and conventions (Carlson-Radvansky & Radvansky, 1996; Schober, 1993, 1995). Sometimes speakers even mix frames of reference to maximize the chances of comprehension (Taylor & Tversky, 1992b). The comprehension of spatial layouts from verbal description is often, though not always, as good as that obtained from visual experience such as viewing environments and maps (e.g., Avraamides, Loomis, Klatzky, & Golledge, 2004; Taylor & Tversky, 1992a, 1992b, 1996).

Given this picture of mature competence, the developmental issue is how children acquire terms for spatial categories, conventions regarding frames of reference, and rules for structuring sequential linguistic description of spatial scenes. The first problem has generated the most controversy, as it involves the classic question of the relation of language and thought. One answer to the question is that the way a particular language carves up the spatial world into categories influences children's developing spatial understanding (Bowerman, 1996; Choi & Bowerman, 1991). For example, because Korean has special language that denotes to the relation of "tight fit," children search for a referent for the term and construct the corresponding category. An alternative answer is that children have already acquired an understanding of the spatial categories that may potentially be linguistically marked by the time they begin to acquire the corresponding linguistic terms (Mandler, 1996). In this view, children in all linguistic communities know about tight fit before they learn language, although only some of them will be exposed to a linguistic means of referring to this concept.

Research suggests that an intermediate position may be most appropriate. Infants of 9 to 14 months apparently categorize both contrasts that are lexicalized in their language and contrasts that are not, suggesting the prior existence of spatial understanding and favoring Mandler's point of view (Hespos & Spelke, 2004; McDonough, Choi, & Mandler, 2003). However, adults seem to pay little attention to contrasts that they do not routinely lexicalize (McDonough et al., 2003), suggesting that language may ultimately influence spatial conceptualization, leading to the atrophy of concepts that

are not used in language. Although this phenomenon is analogous to the loss of phonemic contrasts not used in one's native language, it may be easier to overcome; simple manipulations of context have been found to lead people to pay attention to spatial meanings that they do not linguistically code (Li & Gleitman, 2002; see also Levinson, 2003, and Levinson, Kita, Haun, & Rasch, 2002, for an opposing view).

We know a good deal about our second and third questions: how children learn to select frames of reference and how they learn to structure their spatial descriptions and direction giving. In both cases, there is a fairly protracted developmental course, so that children as old as 8 years or so may not be effective users of the conventions adopted by adults (Allen, Kirasic, & Beard, 1989; Craton, Elicker, Plumert, & Pick, 1990; Gauvain & Rogoff, 1989; Plumert, Ewert, & Spear, 1995; Plumert & Strahan, 1997). Children in elementary school may also have difficulty in constructing spatial knowledge from verbal descriptions (Ondracek & Allen, 2000). These abilities may appear late because of the social skills that are required: taking the listener's point of view and recognizing communication failures. Efficient referential communication about nonspatial matters is also rare in the early school years, although explicit training can help overcome the difficulties (Sonnenschein & Whitehurst, 1984). Another reason for protracted development of these skills may be the demands these tasks make on working memory capacity (Ondracek & Allen, 2000).

## INDIVIDUAL DIFFERENCES IN SPATIAL DEVELOPMENT

People often talk about how they are good (or bad) at fitting objects into the trunks of their cars, putting together electronic equipment, or finding their way in strange cities. Such matters have a strange fascination, for example, gender differences in tasks such as these are a staple of cartoons and comedy routines. But individual and gender differences in spatial ability are not trivial curiosities. They have real-world importance because they predict interest and success in occupations such as engineering, drafting, piloting, surgery, computer science, mathematics, and the physical sciences (Shea, Lubinski, & Benbow, 2001; for an overview, see Hegarty & Waller, 2005). Given these relations, understanding how children develop a range of abilities in spatial tasks becomes a crucial goal. Knowledge about the mechanisms involved could help us devise methods to maximize the availability of a set of cognitive skills that is more and more important in an increasingly technological society. Variability in spatial performance is theoretically as well as practically important. For example, an adaptive combination model of spatial development uses variability in its description of development, as do other contemporary approaches to developmental change (Siegler, 1996). As another example, some of the debates over the nature of mature spatial competence, such as whether representations are orientation-specific or orientation-free, may be clarified by considering individual differences (Friedman & Miyake, 2000). However, despite the practical and theoretical importance of understanding the development of individual differences in spatial skill, research on this topic has been peripheral to the study of cognitive development, and it has been pursued primarily as a branch of psychometrics, using correlational rather than experimental techniques.

There are several reasons for this state of affairs. Within the cognitive development community, there has been intense interest in constructing a dense and detailed account of normative development. This concentration leads to the neglect of individual differences for reasons both theoretical and practical. On the theoretical side, there is the assumption that much of spatial development is canalized and that variability in performance is truly error variance rather than meaningful information. This assumption is very common when investigators consider very early developments in infancy and preschool, and research on this period has been especially fascinating for cognitive developmentalists over the past few decades. Although the proposition may be correct, it is also possible that children who develop earlier ability to retain spatial information over delays or to rescale information from maps are in fact displaying meaningful strengths. Recently, there have been demonstrations of such linkages in other domains of cognitive development, for example, findings that variations in habituation to human intentional action at 14 months are related to the development of theory of mind in preschool (Wellman, Phillips, Dunphy-Lelii, & LaLonde, 2004) and that variations in speech perception at 6 months of age are linked to language development at 2 years (Tsao, Liu, & Kuhl, 2004). On the practical side, it has been difficult to assess the assumption of canalization and to integrate the study of normative development and individual differences because the

techniques used in studies of normative spatial development have never been adapted for use in the study of individual differences. Experiments often involve a small number of trials, and hence would have uncertain reliability and be difficult to use with confidence in longitudinal analyses.

The difficulty in uniting the two disciplines of psychology (Cronbach, 1957) does not derive only from the disinterest in individual differences in the cognitive development community. In addition, there are difficult problems within the psychometric tradition that has established the methods and agenda for the study of individual differences over the past century (Hegarty & Waller, 2005). Paper-and-pencil tests, especially those suitable for group administration, do not do a good job of assessing skills that involve three-dimensional objects or navigation in large-scale environments. For example, the Guilford-Zimmerman Test of Spatial Orientation attempts to simulate being in various positions in a moving boat using only small thumbnail sketches of the prow. Factor analysis, especially exploratory rather than confirmatory factor analysis, gives an unclear and ever-changing picture of the structure of spatial abilities, in part because it is at the mercy of the characteristics of the tests included in the battery under examination and in part because it ignores the fact that people may vary in the strategies they use to solve different items on the same test. Recent efforts to use virtual reality for testing and to study strategy directly are encouraging, but have not yet progressed far enough to provide techniques that can be relied on.

In summary, the study of individual differences seems poised to begin a mutually productive interaction with cognitive psychology and cognitive development, although there are currently only a few harbingers of what can be accomplished. Some promising methodologies and strategies are beginning to emerge, including virtual reality techniques, the adaptation of developmental research paradigms to the assessment of individual differences, and the close analysis of strategies as well as performance levels.

Given these problems, it is tempting to conclude this section simply with the hope that future research can address these issues. However, there has been enough interesting study of the development of sex-related differences in spatial ability that it seems important to review this topic, if only briefly (for fuller reviews, see Halpern & Collaer, 2005; Newcombe, Mathason, & Terlecki,

2002). We should begin by examining the state of the descriptive facts regarding the nature and development of sex-related differences.

First, looking at sex-related differences in adults, it has long been clear that there are large male advantages on many spatial tests, most notably, tests of mental rotation and tests that require defining a horizontal or vertical line while ignoring distracting cues (Linn & Petersen, 1985; Voyer, Voyer, & Bryden, 1995). These differences are diminishing with historical time for some tests (Feingold, 1988), but are maintaining or even increasing their size in the case of mental rotation (Voyer et al., 1995). As well as showing higher means, males also often show greater variability (Hedges & Nowell, 1995), which increases the predominance of men at very high performance levels. More recently, there have been findings indicating that males may also be more skilled at using geometric information regarding distance and direction in navigation, and in using maps to gain geographical knowledge (Halpern & Collaer, 2005).

Second, in terms of development, it is likely that sex differences exist by the age of 4 years, the earliest age at which it has been possible to devise a test that taps the areas in which sex-related differences are found in adults (Levine, Huttenlocher, Taylor, & Langrock, 1999). Other investigations have only found clear evidence of sex-related differences emerging at around the age of 9 or 10 years (Johnson & Meade, 1987; Kerns & Berenbaum, 1991), and meta-analyses consistently show that sex-related differences increase in size over childhood and adolescence (Linn & Petersen, 1985; Voyer et al., 1995). However, the question of earliest appearance and developmental course is difficult to address with current assessment instruments. New assessments taking advantage of recent work in normative cognitive development might be very helpful in addressing these issues.

Sex-related differences in spatial skill, especially in mental rotation, are among the largest gender differences we know. There have been many efforts to explain why they occur, and the area has been a contentious one for biology versus environment debate. Several hypotheses emphasizing biological factors have waxed and then waned in popularity over the past few decades. For example, Waber's (1976) hypothesis that higher spatial ability is related to later timing of puberty has not been substantiated by subsequent research (see

meta-analysis by Newcombe & Dubas, 1987). Hypotheses involving sex-related differences in lateralization of brain function have received only weak support from studies using behavioral techniques to assess lateralization (Voyer, 1996). More direct assessment of neural substrates of spatial tasks using imaging techniques may allow better evaluation of the lateralization hypothesis. Current studies of this kind have sometimes shown sex-related differences (Roberts & Bell, 2000), but many studies have not assessed the question, and samples so far have tended to be small and unrepresentative. Possibly the strongest evidence exists for the hypothesis that sex steroid hormones are the proximate cause of sex-related differences in spatial abilities, although even there the evidence is mixed, precisely which hormones are important is unknown, and the shape of the curve relating hormone levels to performance is not yet defined (Collaer & Hines, 1995; Halpern & Collaer, 2005).

Although the proximate biological mechanisms that may underlie sex-related differences are not yet known, sociobiology has provided a ready explanation for the ultimate reason for this sex difference. Actually, there are two explanations, both focusing on the reproductive advantage that might accrue to men for having higher spatial ability. One explanation focuses on the fact that men are generally the hunters in hunting-gathering societies, and hunting seems to require spatial skill in several of its component activities, including tracking animals, aiming at them, and fashioning the weapons with which to take aim. The protein obtained from hunting helps to ensure the survival of a man's children, and prowess in hunting may also enhance a man's access to women (who wish to have their children provisioned by a skilled hunter). In addition, aiming may come in handy in any struggles for dominance with other males over sexual access to females.

The other explanation for sex differences derives from elegant observational and experimental evidence of voles, a small mammal that comes in two varieties. One species, the prairie vole, is pair-bonded while a very similar species, the meadow vole, has a mating system in which females occupy territories, and during the mating season, males make the rounds of females, attempting to reach as many as possible in time to impregnate them. Strikingly, spatial ability (assessed by the ability to navigate mazes) is equal for males and females in the pair-bonded prairie vole, but male meadow voles surpass females at spatial tasks—during the mating season only, when the part of their brain that supports navigation (the hippocampus) actually enlarges to meet the reproductive challenge (Gaulin & Fitzgerald, 1989).

There are, however, problems with both kinds of sociobiological explanations (see also Jones, Braithwaite, & Healy, 2003). Looking first at hunting and gathering, gathering may require quite long trips away from home base to find various kinds of edible vegetation in their respective ripening seasons. While it is true that animals move while vegetation sits still, humans are unsuited to swift pursuit of most game animals, and much hunting by our ancestors may have consisted of setting traps, or waiting at waterholes, rather than tracking animals over meandering paths. In terms of manufacturing artifacts to use in hunting and gathering, spatial skill is required to weave or make baskets or pottery, as much as for fashioning arrows and spearheads. Lastly, while the aiming component of hunting success is a kind of action in space, it does not appear to be a spatial skill—success in hitting a target may not be related to success at mental rotation (Hines et al., 2003). In terms of extrapolating to humans from the vole studies, a major problem for a sociobiological approach is that human females, unlike female meadow voles, live in social groups rather than occupying widely separated home territories. Impregnating many females probably depends more on abilities such as charm or stealth than on the ability to find one's way among a cluster of huts.

We should also ask why, from an evolutionary point of view, sex differences would exist in a trait that has adaptive significance for both sexes when there is no obvious metabolic cost for that trait. Most sex-specific traits that enhance reproduction are for attributes such as growing antlers or ornamental tails, physical features that are cumbersome and costly for the body to produce. Males have these features only because they enhance their ability to do combat with other males and/or attract females. There is no reason both sexes should not have a trait that is useful in a wide variety of settings unless its possession exacts costs. Of course, developing high levels of spatial ability might exact some kind of cost; however, we currently have very little idea of what the trade-offs might be.

So far, we have not discussed environmental factors that may contribute to sex-related differences in spatial ability. Correlational analyses show that there are small but reliable relations between participation in spatial activities, many of which are sex-typed masculine, and

spatial ability (Baenninger & Newcombe, 1989). However, these correlations could be the product of self-selection of activities based on ability, rather than arising from the activities causing increases in ability. Some spatial sex differences are decreasing over historical time (Feingold, 1988), presumably for environmental reasons, but differences in mental rotation seem to be increasing (Voyer et al., 1995). Increasing as well as decreasing size in sex-related differences may indicate environmental causation. Although it is commonly assumed that society is becoming more egalitarian, there has been little direct examination of change in social factors that may affect mental rotation ability. Increasing computer usage in the past decades may influence increasing sex-related differences, as males are more likely to use computers in general and to engage in spatially demanding computer activities, including games, than females (De Lisi & Cammarano, 1996; Funk & Buchman, 1996). Approximately 75% to 80% of video game sales are generated by males (Natale, 2002). Computer use is related to spatial skill (De Lisi & Cammarano, 1996; De Lisi & Wolford, 2002; Okagaki & Frensch, 1994; Roberts & Bell, 2000; Saccuzzo, Craig, Johnson, & Larson, 1996; Sims & Mayer, 2002; Waller, Knapp, & Hunt, 2001).

Malleability of spatial skill is a central issue that is often overlooked in the fascination with sex differences (as well as overlooked more generally in the fascination with individual differences in intelligence, Ceci, 1991). Even though sex differences are substantial, levels of spatial ability do not seem to be biologically fixed. Several sorts of training can enhance spatial performance (Baenninger & Newcombe, 1989, 1995; Loewenstein & Gentner, 2001; Newcombe et al., 2002), including input during schooling (Huttenlocher, Levine, & Vevea, 1998). Like other intellectual abilities, and possibly more so, spatial ability has increased in the past century faster than the gene can change, in what has been called the *Flynn effect* (Flynn, 1987). It is true that training effects are often equivalent for males and females, so that sex differences do not disappear (Baenninger & Newcombe, 1989). However, the training effects are also substantial in size, often larger than the sex-related differences themselves, so that trained females do as well as or better than untrained males. If we want to maximize the human capital available for occupations that draw in spatial skill, such as mathematics, engineering, architecture, physical science, and computer science, it is vital to understand how to educate for spatial skill, rather than focusing solely on the explanation of sex differences.

## SPATIAL DEVELOPMENT IN NON-NORMATIVE CONTEXTS

Spatial development is the product of the interaction of biological and environmental factors that affect it. Some researchers have focused on genetic variations, which can sometimes lead to specific patterns of cognitive impact in which spatial ability seems particularly affected (e.g., Williams syndrome, Turner syndrome).[5] Studying syndromes of this kind has been based in part on the hope that we can gain information about the mechanisms and architecture of cognitive development from the fractionation that occurs when normal development goes awry. Other researchers have examined sensory impairments that can limit spatially relevant input, most notably visual impairments. Studying the effects of sensory limitations is potentially useful in elucidating what environmental input normal development rests on, and it can help resolve the issue of whether critical or sensitive periods exist during which input is essential for normal spatial development.[6] In this section, we concentrate on Williams syndrome and visual impairment as examples of research that can have considerable relevance for understanding spatial development in normally developing children.

---

[5] There are also two other interesting classes of syndromes. One category is diagnoses where there is diffuse slowing of cognitive progress but with indications of differentially larger spatial problems that may depend on hippocampal dysfunction. Syndromes in this category include genetic problems such as Down syndrome (Pennington, Moon, Edgin, Stedron, & Nadel, 2003) and environmental effects on prenatal development such as fetal alcohol syndrome (Uecker & Nadel, 1996). A second interesting diagnostic category is children with problems in cognitive development presumed to have a strong genetic basis, where spatial skills are relatively spared, for example, autism (Caron, Mottron, Rainville, & Chouinard, 2004).

[6] Not all sensory impairments have deleterious effects on spatial ability; in particular, there is reason to think that children with deafness may develop enhanced spatial competence, perhaps as a consequence of signing (Emmorey, Kosslyn, & Bellugi, 1993).

## Williams Syndrome

Williams syndrome (WS) is a rare genetic defect occurring about once in 20,000 births. People with WS have certain distinctive physical characteristics and also have an unusual cognitive profile. When cognitive research on WS began, investigators were impressed with the extent to which language and face processing were spared in WS, despite severe impairments in spatial ability (Bellugi, Marks, Bihrle, & Sabo, 1998; Bellugi, Wang, & Jernigan, 1994). More recently, evidence has emerged suggesting that there are actually a variety of deficits in language acquisition and processing in WS individuals (e.g., Grant, Valian, & Karmiloff-Smith, 2002; Thomas & Karmiloff-Smith, 2003), as well as some abnormalities in categorization and conceptual understanding (Johnson & Carey, 1998). Such data have led to the recognition that WS does not provide a strong example of modularity in development, as initially seemed possible (Mervis, 2003; Paterson, Brown, Gsodl, Johnson, & Karmiloff-Smith, 1999).

As with language, careful analysis of the spatial deficits in WS is revealing a complex picture of just what kinds of spatial ability are affected. Severe problems are evident when WS individuals are asked to copy designs by drawing or using blocks (Bellugi, Bihrle, Neville, Doherty, & Jerigan, 1992; Hoffman, Landau, & Pagani, 2003; Mervis, Morris, Bertrand, & Robinson, 1999). In addition, it has been shown that WS children show an intriguing early difficulty in guiding saccades using extraretinal information, a limitation that may impair their exploration of the visual environment (Brown et al., 2003). However, face recognition, which certainly requires spatial analysis, appears to be normal, although there is some controversy about the issue (Tager-Flusberg, Plesa-Skwerer, Faja, & Joseph, 2003). Similarly, WS individuals show an intact ability to perceive biological motion (Jordan, Reiss, Hoffman, & Landau, 2002). For spatial language, which is an interesting area given relative strengths in language and selective deficits in spatial skill, there are conflicting reports. Landau and Zukowski (2003) argue that there are limited effects of WS on spatial language, on the basis of data about how children with WS described motion events. They found that encoding of figure and ground objects and manner of motion was excellent in WS individuals, and their command of path information was surprisingly spared if somewhat fragile. However, Phillips, Jarrold, Baddeley, Grant, and Karmiloff-Smith (2004) report that WS individuals perform poorly when asked to comprehend sentences that involve spatial prepositions.

Most of the spatial skills discussed in this chapter are still unstudied in WS, including encoding of distance, use of spatial categories, hierarchical combination, mental rotation, perspective taking, navigation, and the use of maps and models. This surprising lack likely stems from the initial use of psychometrically derived and clinical batteries to study cognition in these children, as well as from the focus on the language development of these children and the language-space interface. Research on this population holds promise, however, for helping to understand the structure of spatial skill and for helping us analyze the various strands in spatial development.

## Visual Impairment

The spatial capacities of blind individuals appear to be central to two intertwined questions about spatial development: the extent to which it depends on innate capacities, and the ways in which it may depend on crucial input at certain periods in development. In an early philosophical argument for an innate basis for human spatial knowledge, Descartes proposed that a blind person who sequentially explores shapes and their interrelations would unify the impressions gained in this manner within a spatial framework that utilized metric properties derived from Euclidean geometry. Many years later, experiments with animals showed that visual experience is essential to normal development of visual cortex and visual perception (e.g., Wiesel & Hubel, 1965). Subsequent work with infants born with congenital cataracts has confirmed the existence of such sensitive periods in humans, and has clarified their duration and nature (e.g., Le Grand, Mondloch, Maurer, & Brent, 2001, 2003; Maurer, Lewis, Brent, & Levin, 1999).

Neither Descartes' speculations nor the experimental work on the effects of deprivation on the development of visual processes directly address the role played by an innate spatial framework versus the role played by visual experience in spatial development. While it might not appear difficult to address this topic, efforts to date have not resulted in a clear answer to the question of how, and how well, people born blind or with visual impairment develop spatial representation and navigation (see reviews by Millar, 1994 and Thinus-Blanc & Gaunet, 1997). In part, uncertainty arises because the causes and timing of vision loss may vary, large samples of individuals who are similar in these variables are difficult to assemble, and, even within apparently homogeneous groups, there appear to be large individual differences in spatial skill.

One of the most debated topics within the literature on vision loss is the capacity for spatial inference. We have already examined the report that a young blind child can, as predicted by Descartes, unify her spatial experience so as to permit inference (Landau et al., 1984) and subsequent findings that, contrary to this hypothesis, spatial inference develops slowly in both blind and sighted children (Morrongiello et al., 1995). Some studies of adults with blindness suggest that people who suffered vision loss early have limited capabilities for spatial inference, compared both with sighted people and with people who suffered late vision loss (Rieser, Guth, & Hill, 1986). Rieser et al. argued that vision provides the best means of learning to calibrate optic flow with the experience of walking. Support for this hypothesis was found in data showing that early loss of broad field vision produced effects on spatial inference comparable to the effects of early blindness (Rieser, Hill, Talor, Bradfield, & Rosen, 1992). By contrast, early acuity loss did not have such detrimental effects, nor did late field loss. Such a pattern is compatible with the view that calibration of kinesthetic cues and optic flow in the first 3 years of life is crucial for normal spatial inference ability. Work of this kind that is developmental in nature holds great promise for understanding the starting points and key inputs for spatial development in much more analytic detail than we possess at present.

## WHAT LIES AHEAD?

There is no better testimony to the current richness and excitement of research on spatial development than that this review has had to be selective in the topics covered and has only scratched the surface of many important issues in the developmental literature and, especially, in the research traditions of allied fields. We have touched only briefly on research about adult spatial cognition, individual differences, and the development of children with genetic or sensory impairments. Also, we have said almost nothing about research on nonhuman animals, research using neuroscientific techniques, or computational modeling of spatial skills. In general, our impression is that focus on the content area of spatial adaptation has led to a burst of interdisciplinary interchange of ideas and techniques that bodes extremely well for the development of rich theoretical understanding of this domain.

Although we have addressed a multitude of specific research questions in this chapter, we have emphasized a few major themes. First, we have suggested that the nativism-empiricism debate should be reconceptualized as the search to understand the starting points for cognitive development, the nature and timing of crucial environmental input, and the precise specification of how children use environmental input at specific points in their development from their initial starting points. Second, we have argued that an adaptive combination approach to spatial development is a powerful tool for understanding its nature and that a modular architecture is not necessary to explain the basic phenomena in this area. Third, we have attempted to highlight the distinctiveness and power of human abilities to transform and symbolically represent spatial information, and have suggested that culturally transmitted tools may be especially crucial to optimal development in this area. Fourth, we have noted that research on individual differences is crucial to a full understanding of spatial development, but that it is still very poorly integrated into most work on cognitive development. Similarly, and lastly, we have noted the enormous promise of research on spatial development in children with abnormal genetic inheritances or whose environmental stimulation is limited by sensory deprivation, especially to the extent that common conceptual and methodological tools can be used in research on normative and abnormal development.

A few research areas have not yet attracted the attention they deserve. An issue that is largely unexplored is the contribution to spatial development of various kinds of experience, many of them ubiquitous and expectable, but some of them variable and even rare. For ubiquitous and expectable input, the problem is that deprivation experiments cannot be conducted with humans. The need for more research on the effects of various kinds of visual and exploratory experiences on spatial development can often be filled through research with nonhuman animals. For example, there have been experiments evaluating the effects of rearing in the dark (Tees, Buhrmann, & Hanley, 1990) or with deprivation of social interaction (Pryce, Bettschen, Nanz-Bahr, & Feldon, 2003) on spatial development. We should use research with nonhuman animals when possible to investigate the interplay of spatial learning, activity, and exploration in

human development. In addition, we can more vigorously pursue research with human children who have naturally occurring cases of limited sensory input, such as various kinds of visual loss. This line of work needs to occur in closer contact than has often been true so far with the literature on normative spatial development.

With respect to variable and rare kinds of spatial input, we have an opposite kind of problem—long hours of naturalistic observation may yield very few interesting instances of spatial input. In contrast, studies of input to language acquisition are relatively easy, because talk is common and can be easily recorded for later transcription and analysis. One promising line of attack on this problem is to construct contexts that elicit spatial discussion in at least some parent-child dyads (Szechter & Liben, 2004). Another possibility is to train parents to record relevant examples of spatial interactions with their children, as recently done for quantitative development by Mix (2002).

Another area that we need to know much more about is individual differences in the normal range. One question here is whether the variation we see in studies focused on normative development is meaningful or represents true error variance. Researchers in cognitive development often assume that the variability in their studies is error variance, but this assumption has rarely been tested and may be false, as suggested by recent longitudinal findings in other domains (Tsao et al., 2004; Wellman & Liu, 2004). Insofar as the variability in cognitive-developmental experiments represents meaningful information about differences among children, we have the opportunity to develop more sensitive and more analytic assessment instruments for use in tracing early individual differences than has been possible from psychometrically derived tests that are not ideal for adults and that are even less well suited to developmental work in the downward extensions that have been made of them. A focus on assessment is hard and sometimes boring work that has historically been difficult to fund, but it is essential to progress on understanding why some children develop much greater spatial abilities than others.

Although these issues are important and difficult, our dominant mood is optimistic and our forecast is that the coming decade will see great advances in our understanding of spatial development. In particular, this progress will come to the extent that we can sensibly utilize techniques and concepts from allied fields to support our common goals.

# REFERENCES

Acredolo, L. P. (1978). Development of spatial orientation in infancy. *Developmental Psychology, 14,* 224–234.

Acredolo, L. P. (1979). Laboratory versus home: The effect of environment on the 9-month-old infant's choice of spatial reference system. *Developmental Psychology, 15,* 666–667.

Acredolo, L. P. (1982). The familiarity factor in spatial research. *New Directions for Child Development, 15,* 19–30.

Acredolo, L. P., & Evans, D. (1980). Developmental changes in the effects of landmarks on infant spatial behavior. *Developmental Psychology, 16,* 312–318.

Ahmed, A., & Ruffman, T. (1998). Why do infants make A not B errors in a search task, yet show memory for the location of hidden objects in a nonsearch task? *Developmental Psychology, 34*(3), 441–453.

Allen, G. L., Kirasic, K. C., & Beard, R. L. (1989). Children's expressions of spatial knowledge. *Journal of Experimental Child Psychology, 48*(1), 114–130.

Allen, G. L., Kirasic, K. C., Siegel, A. W., & Herman, J. F. (1979). Developmental issues in cognitive mapping: The selection and utilization of environmental landmarks. *Child Development, 50*(4), 1062–1070.

Anooshian, A., & Yong, D. (1981). Developmental changes in cognitive maps of a familiar neighborhood. *Child Development, 52*(1), 341–348.

Anooshian, L. J., & Kromer, M. K. (1986). Children's spatial knowledge of their school campus. *Developmental Psychology, 22*(6), 854–860.

Ansari, D., Donlan, C., Thomas, M. S. C., Ewing, S. A., Peen, T., & Karmiloff-Smith, A. (2003). What makes counting count? Verbal and visuo-spatial contributions to typical and atypical number development. *Journal of Experimental Child Psychology, 85*(1), 50–62.

Avraamides, M. N., Loomis, J. M., Klatzky, R. L., & Golledge, R. G. (2004). Functional equivalence of spatial representations derived from vision and language: Evidence from allocentric judgments. *Journal of Experimental Psychology: Learning, Memory and Cognition, 30,* 801–814.

Backus, B. T., Banks, M. S., van Ee, R., & Crowell, J. A. (1999). Horizontal and vertical disparity, eye position, and stereoscopic slant perception. *Vision Research, 39*(6), 1143–1170.

Baenninger, M., & Newcombe, N. (1989). The role of experience in spatial test performance: A meta-analysis. *Sex Roles, 20*(5/6), 327–344.

Baenninger, M., & Newcombe, N. (1995). Environmental input to the development of sex-related differences in spatial and mathematical ability. *Learning and Individual Differences, 7,* 363–379.

Bai, D. L., & Bertenthal, B. I. (1992). Locomotor status and the development of spatial search skills. *Child Development, 63,* 215–226.

Baillargeon, R. (1986). Representing the existence and the location of hidden objects: Object permanence in 6- and 8-month-old infants. *Cognition, 23,* 21–41.

Bellugi, U., Bihrle, A., Neville, H., Doherty, S., & Jernigan, T. (1992). Language, cognition, and brain organization in a neurodevelopmental disorder. In M. R. Gunnar & C. A. Nelson (Eds.), *Developmental behavioral neuroscience* (pp. 201–232). Hillsdale, NJ: Erlbaum.

Bellugi, U., Marks, S., Bihrle, A., & Sabo, H. (1988). Dissociation between language and cognitive functions in Williams syndrome. In D. Bishop & K. Mogford (Eds.), *Language development in exceptional circumstances* (pp. 177–189). Hillsdale, NJ: Erlbaum.

Bellugi, U., Wang, P. P., & Jernigan, T. L. (1994). Williams syndrome: An unusual neuropsychological profile. In H. Broman & J. Grafman (Eds.), *Atypical cognitive deficits in developmental disorders: Implications for brain function* (pp. 23–56). Hillsdale, NJ: Erlbaum.

Benhamou, S., & Poucet, B. (1998). Landmark use by navigating rats (Rattus norvegicus) contrasting geometric and featural information. *Journal of Comparative Psychology, 112*(3), 317–322.

Bertenthal, B. I., Campos, J., & Barrett, K. (1984). Self-produced locomotion: An organizer of emotional, cognitive and social development in infancy. In R. Emde & R. Harmon (Eds.), *Continuities and discontinuities in development* (pp. 175–210). New York: Plenum Press.

Berthier, N. E., Bertenthal, B. I., Seaks, J. D., Sylvia, M. R., Johnson, R. L., & Clifton, R. K. (2001). Using object knowledge in visual tracking and reaching. *Infancy, 2*(2), 257–284.

Blades, M. (1991). The development of the abilities required to understand spatial representations. In D. M. Mark & A. V. Frank (Eds.), *Cognitive and linguistic aspects of geographic space* (pp. 81–115). Dordrecht, The Netherlands: Kluwer Academic Press.

Blaut, J. M. (1997). Piagetian pessimism and the mapping abilities of young children: A rejoinder to Liben and Downs. *Annals of the Association of American Geographers, 87,* 168–177.

Bluestein, N., & Acredolo, P. (1979). Developmental changes in map-reading skills. *Child Development, 50*(3), 691–697.

Bowerman, M. (1996). Learning how to structure space for language: A crosslinguistic perspective. In P. Bloom & M. A. Peterson (Eds.), *Language and space* (pp. 385–436). Cambridge, MA: MIT Press.

Brainerd, C. J., Kingma, J., & Howe, M. L. (1985). On the development of forgetting. *Child Development, 56*(5), 1103–1119.

Bremner, J. G. (1978a). Egocentric versus allocentric spatial coding in 9-month-old infants: Factors influencing the choice of code. *Developmental Psychology, 14,* 346–355.

Bremner, J. G. (1978b). Spatial errors made by infants: Inadequate spatial cues or evidence of egocentrism? *British Journal of Psychology, 69,* 77–84.

Bremner, J. G., & Andreasen, G. (1998). Young children's ability to use maps and models to find ways in novel spaces. *British Journal of Developmental Psychology, 16*(2), 197–218.

Bremner, J. G., & Bryant, P. E. (1977). Place versus responses as the basis of spatial errors made by young infants. *Journal of Experimental Child Psychology, 23,* 167–171.

Brooks, R. A. (1991). How to build complete creatures rather than isolated cognitive simulators. In VanLehn, K. (Ed.), *Architectures for intelligence: The 22nd Carnegie-Mellon Symposium on Cognition* (pp. 225–239). Hillsdale, NJ: Erlbaum.

Brown, J. H., Johnson, M. H., Paterson, S. J., Gilmore, R., Longhi, E., & Karmiloff-Smith, A. (2003). Spatial representation and attention in toddlers with Williams syndrome and Down syndrome. *Neuropsychologia, 41*(8), 1037–1046.

Burgund, E. D., & Marsolek, C. J. (2000). Viewpoint-invariant and viewpoint-dependent object recognition in dissociable neural subsystems. *Psychonomic Bulletin and Review, 7*(3), 480–489.

Bushnell, E. W., McKenzie, B. E., Lawrence, D. A., & Connell, S. (1995). The spatial coding strategies of 1-year-old infants in a locomotor search task. *Child Development, 66*(4), 937–958.

Byrne, R. W. (1979). Memory for urban geography. *Quarterly Journal of Experimental Psychology, 31*(1), 147–154.

Campos, J. J., Anderson, D. I., Barbu-Roth, M. A., Hubbard, E. M., Hertenstein, M. J., & Witherington, D. (2000). Travel broadens the mind. *Infancy, 1,* 149–219.

Carlson-Radvansky, L. A., & Radvansky, G. A. (1996). The influence of functional relations on spatial term selection. *Psychological Science, 7*(1), 56–60.

Caron, M.-J., Mottron, L., Rainville, C., & Chouinard, S. (2004). Do high functioning persons with autism present superior spatial abilities? *Neuropsychologia, 42*(4), 467–481.

Casasola, M., Cohen, L. B., & Chiarello, E. (2003). Six-month-old infants' categorization of containment spatial relations. *Child Development, 74*(3), 679–693.

Ceci, S. J. (1991). How much does schooling influence general intelligence and its cognitive components? A reassessment of the evidence. *Developmental Psychology, 27*(5), 703–722.

Chapman, M., & Lindenberger, U. (1992). Transitivity judgments, memory for premises, and models of children's reasoning. *Developmental Review, 12*(2), 124–163.

Cheng, K. (1986). A purely geometric module in the rat's spatial representation. *Cognition, 23*(2), 149–178.

Cheng, K. (1989). The vector sum model of pigeon landmark use. *Journal of Experimental Psychology: Animal Behavior Presses, 15*(4), 366–375.

Cheng, K., & Newcombe, N. S. (2005). Is there a geometric module for spatial orientation? Squaring theory and evidence. *Psychonomic Bulletin and Review, 12,* 1–23.

Choi, S., & Bowerman, M. (1991). Learning to express motion events in English and Korean: The influence of language-specific lexicalization patterns [Special issue]. *Cognition, 41*(1/3), 83–121.

Clearfield, M. W. (2004). The role of crawling and walking experience in infant spatial memory. *Journal of Experimental Child Psychology, 89,* 214–241.

Collaer, M. L., & Hines, M. (1995). Human behavioral sex differences: A role for gonadal hormones during early development? *Psychological Bulletin, 118*(1), 55–107.

Cornell, E. H., Heth, C. D., & Alberts, D. M. (1994). Place recognition and way finding by children and adults. *Memory and Cognition, 22*(6), 633–643.

Cornell, E. H., Heth, C. D., & Rowat, W. L. (1992). Wayfinding by children and adults: Response to instructions to use look-back and retrace strategies. *Developmental Psychology, 28*(2), 328–336.

Cousins, J. H., Siegel, A. W., & Maxwell, S. E. (1983). Way finding and cognitive mapping in large-scale environments: A test of a developmental model. *Journal of Experimental Child Psychology, 35*(1), 1–20.

Craton, L. G., Elicker, J., Plumert, J. M., & Pick, H. L. (1990). Children's use of frames of reference in communication of spatial location. *Child Development, 61,* 1528–1543.

Crawford, L. E., Huttenlocher, J., & Engebretson, P. H. (2000). Category effects on estimates of stimuli: Perception or reconstruction? *Psychological Science, 11*(4), 280–284.

Crawford, L. E., Regier, T., & Huttenlocher, J. (2000). Linguistic and non-linguistic spatial categorization. *Cognition, 75*(3), 209–235.

Cronbach, L. J. (1957). The two disciplines of scientific psychology. *American Psychologist, 12,* 671–684.

Curby, K. M., Hayward, W. G., & Gauthier, I. (2004). Laterality effects in the recognition of depth-rotated objects. *Cognitive, Affective and Behavioral Neuroscience, 4,* 100–111.

Dalke, D. E. (1998). Charting the development of representational skills: When do children know that maps can lead and mislead? *Cognitive Development, 13*(1), 53–72.

Dehaene, S., Dehaene-Lambertz, G., & Cohen, L. (1998). Abstract representations of numbers in the animal and human brain. *Trends in Neurosciences, 21*(8), 355–361.

De Lisi, R., & Cammarano, D. M. (1996). Computer experience and gender differences in undergraduate mental rotation performance. *Computers in Human Behavior, 12*(3), 351–361.

De Lisi, R., & Wolford, J. L. (2002). Improving children's mental rotation accuracy with computer game playing. *Journal of Genetic Psychology, 163*(3), 272–282.

DeLoache, J. S. (1987). Rapid change in the symbolic functioning of very young children. *Science, 238*(4833), 1156–1557.

DeLoache, J. S. (1995). Early understanding and use of symbols: The model model. *Current Directions in Psychological Science, 4*(4), 109–113.

DeLoache, J. S., & Brown, A. L. (1983). Very young children's memory for the location of objects in a large-scale environment. *Child Development, 54*(4), 888–897.

DeLoache, J. S., Miller, K. F., & Rosengren, K. S. (1997). The credible shrinking room: Very young children's performance with symbolic and nonsymbolic relations. *Psychological Science, 8*(4), 308–313.

DeLoache, J. S., Uttal, D. H., & Rosengren, K. S. (2004). Scale errors offer evidence for a perception-action dissociation early in life. *Science, 304,* 1027–1029.

Diamond, A. (1991). Neuropsychological insights into the meaning of object concept development. In S. Carey & R. Gelman (Eds.), *Epigenesis of mind: Essays on biology and cognition* (pp. 67–110). Hillsdale, NJ: Erlbaum.

Duffy, S., Huttenlocher, J., & Levine, S. (2005). It is all relative: How young children encode extent. *Journal of Cognition and Development, 6,* 51–63.

Emerson, M. J., Miyake, A., & Rettinger, D. A. (1999). Individual differences in integrating and coordinating multiple sources of information. *Journal of Experimental Psychology: Learning, Memory, and Cognition, 25*(5), 1300–1312.

Emmorey, K., Kosslyn, S. M., & Bellugi, U. (1993). Visual imagery and visual-spatial language: Enhanced imagery abilities in deaf and hearing ASL signers. *Cognition, 46,* 139–181.

Engebretson, P. H., & Huttenlocher, J. (1996). Bias in spatial location due to categorization: Comment on Tversky and Schiano. *Journal of Experimental Psychology: General, 125*(1), 96–108.

Ernst, M. O., & Banks, M. S. (2002). Humans integrate visual and haptic information in a statistically optimal way. *Nature, 415,* 429–433.

Feingold, A. (1988). Cognitive gender differences are disappearing. *American Psychologist, 43*(2), 95–103.

Fenwick, K. D., & Morrongiello, B. A. (1998). Spatial co-location and infants' learning of auditory-visual associations. *Infant Behavior and Development, 21*(4), 745–759.

Fias, W., Lammertyn, J., Reynvoet, B., Dupont, P., & Orban, G. A. (2003). Parietal representation of symbolic and nonsymbolic magnitude. *Journal of Cognitive Neuroscience, 15*(1), 47–56.

Flynn, J. R. (1987). Massive IQ gains in 14 nations: What IQ tests really measure. *Psychological Bulletin, 101*(2), 171–191.

Fodor, J. A. (1983). *Modularity of mind: An essay on faculty psychology.* Cambridge, MA: MIT Press.

Fodor, J. A. (2001). *The mind doesn't work that way: The scope and limits of computational psychology.* Cambridge, MA: MIT Press.

Franklin, N., Henkel, L. A., & Zangas, T. (1995). Parsing surrounding space into regions. *Memory and Cognition, 23*(4), 397–407.

Friedman, N. P., & Miyake, A. (2000). Differential roles for visuospatial and verbal working memory in situation model construction. *Journal of Experimental Psychology: General, 129*(1), 61–83.

Fukusima, S. S., Loomis, J. M., & Da Silva, J. A. (1997). Visual perception of egocentric distance as assessed by triangulation. *Journal of Experimental Psychology: Human Perception and Performance, 23*(1), 86–100.

Funk, J. B., & Buchman, D. D. (1996). Children's perceptions of gender differences in social approval for playing electronic games. *Sex Roles, 35*(3/4), 219–232.

Gallistel, C. R. (1990). *The organization of learning.* Cambridge, MA: MIT Press.

Gao, F., Levine, S. C., & Huttenlocher, J. (2000). What do infants know about continuous quantity? *Journal of Experimental Child Psychology, 77*(1), 20–29.

Garrad-Cole, F., Lew, A. R., Bremner, J. G., & Whitaker, C. J. (2001). Use of cue configuration geometry for spatial orientation in human infants (homo sapiens). *Journal of Comparative Psychology, 115*(3), 317–320.

Gathercole, S. E., Pickering, S. J., Ambridge, B., & Wearing, H. (2004). The structure of working memory from 4 to 15 years of age. *Developmental Psychology, 40*(2), 177–190.

Gattis, M. (2001). Reading pictures: Constraints on mapping conceptual and spatial schemas. In M. Gattis (Ed.), *Spatial schemas and abstract thought* (pp. 223–245). Cambridge, MA: MIT Press.

Gattis, M., & Holyoak, K. J. (1996). Mapping conceptual to spatial relations in visual reasoning. *Journal of Experimental Psychology: Learning, Memory, and Cognition, 22*(1), 231–239.

Gaulin, S. J., & Fitzgerald, R. W. (1989). Sexual selection for spatial-learning ability. *Animal Behaviour, 37*(2), 322–331.

Gauvain, M., & Rogoff, B. (1989). Ways of speaking about space: The development of children's skill in communicating spatial knowledge. *Cognitive Development, 4*(3), 295–307.

Gentner, D., & Loewenstein, J. (2002). Relational language and relational thought. In E. Amsel & J. P. Byrnes (Eds.), *Language, literacy, and cognitive development: The development and consequences of symbolic communication* (pp. 87–120). Mahwah, NJ: Erlbaum.

Gepshtein, S., & Banks, M. S. (2003). Viewing geometry determines how vision and haptics combine in size perception. *Current Biology, 13*(6), 483–488.

Gilmore, R. O., Baker, T. J., & Grobman, K. H. (2004). Stability in young infants' discrimination of optic flow. *Developmental Psychology, 40*(2), 259–270.

Gilmore, R. O., & Johnson, M. H. (1997). Body-centered representations for visually-guided action emerge during early infancy. *Cognition, 65*(1), B1–B9.

Gilmore, R. O., & Rettke, H. J. (2003). Four-month-olds' discrimination of optic flow patterns depicting different directions of observer motion. *Infancy, 4*(2), 177–200.

Goel, V., & Dolan, R. J. (2001). Functional neuroanatomy of 3-term relational reasoning. *Neuropsychologia, 39*, 901–909.

Gouteux, S., & Spelke, E. S. (2001). Children's use of geometry and landmarks to reorient in an open space. *Cognition, 81*(2), 119–148.

Gouteux, S., Thinus-Blanc, C., & Vauclair, J. (2001). Rhesus monkeys use geometric and nongeometric information during a reorientation task. *Journal of Experimental Psychology: General, 130*(3), 505–519.

Grant, J., Valian, V., & Karmiloff-Smith, A. (2002). A study of relative clauses in Williams syndrome. *Journal of Child Language, 29*(2), 403–416.

Halford, G. S., & Kelly, M. E. (1984). On the basis of early transitivity judgments. *Journal of Experimental Child Psychology, 38*(1), 42–63.

Halpern, D. F., & Collaer, M. L. (2005). Sex differences in visuospatial abilities: More than meets the eye. In P. Shah & A. Miyake (Eds.), *Handbook of visuospatial thinking* (pp. 170–212). New York: Cambridge University Press.

Hart, R. (1979). *Children's experience of place.* Oxford, England: Irvington.

Hartley, T., Trinkler, I., & Burgess, N. (2004). Geometric determinants of human spatial memory. *Cognition, 94*, 39–75.

Hazen, N. L., Lockman, J. J., & Pick, H. L. (1978). The development of children's representations of large-scale environments. *Child Development, 49*(3), 623–636.

Hedges, L. V., & Nowell, A. (1995). Sex differences in mental test scores, variability, and numbers of high-scoring individuals. *Science, 269*(5220), 41–45.

Hegarty, M. (2004). Mechanical reasoning by mental simulation. *Trends in Cognitive Sciences, 8*, 280–285.

Hegarty, M., & Waller, D. (2005). Individual differences in spatial abilities. In P. Shah & A. Miyake (Eds.), *Handbook of visuospatial thinking* (pp. 121–169). New York: Cambridge University Press.

Hermer, L., & Spelke, E. S. (1994). A geometric process for spatial reorientation in young children. *Nature, 370*(6484), 57–59.

Hermer, L., & Spelke, E. S. (1996). Modularity and development: The case of spatial reorientation. *Cognition, 61*(3), 195–232.

Hermer-Vazquez, L., Moffet, A., & Munkholm, P. (2001). Language, space, and the development of cognitive flexibility in humans: The case of two spatial memory tasks. *Cognition, 79*(3), 263–299.

Hespos, S. J., & Spelke, E. S. (2004). Conceptual precursors to language. *Nature, 430*, 453–456.

Heth, C. D., Cornell, E. H., & Flood, T. L. (2002). Self-ratings of sense of direction and route reversal performance. *Applied Cognitive Psychology, 16*(3), 309–324.

Hines, M., Fane, B. A., Pasterski, V. L., Matthews, G. A., Conway, G. S., & Brook, C. (2003). Spatial abilities following prenatal androgen abnormality: Targeting and mental rotations performance in individuals with congenital adrenal hyperplasia. *Psychoneuroendocrinology, 28*, 1010–1026.

Hoffman, J. E., Landau, B., & Pagani, B. (2003). Spatial breakdown in spatial construction: Evidence from eye fixations in children with Williams syndrome. *Cognitive Psychology, 46*(3), 260–301.

Hofstadter, M., & Reznick, J. S. (1996). Response modality affects human infant delayed-response performance. *Child Development, 67*(2), 646–658.

Hood, B., Cole-Davies, V., & Dias, M. (2003). Looking and search measures of object knowledge in preschool children. *Developmental Psychology, 39*(1), 61–70.

Hopkins, W. D., Fagot, J., & Vauclair, J. (1993). Mirror-image matching and mental rotation problem solving by baboons (Papio papio): Unilateral input enhances performance. *Journal of Experimental Psychology: General, 122*(1), 61–72.

Hund, A. M., & Plumert, J. M. (2002). Delay-induced bias in children's memory for location. *Child Development, 73*(3), 829–840.

Hund, A. M., & Plumert, J. M. (2003). Does information about what things are influence children's memory for where things are? *Developmental Psychology, 39*(6), 939–948.

Hund, A. M., & Plumert, J. M. (2005). The stability and flexibility of spatial categories. *Cognitive Psychology, 50*, 1–44.

Hund, A. M., Plumert, J. M., & Benney, C. J. (2002). Experiencing nearby locations together in time: The role of spatiotemporal contiguity in children's memory for location. *Journal of Experimental Child Psychology, 82*(3), 200–225.

Hund, A. M., & Spencer, J. P. (2003). Developmental changes in the relative weighting of geometric and experience-dependent location cues. *Journal of Cognition and Development, 4*(1), 3–38.

Huttenlocher, J. (1968). Constructing spatial images: A strategy in reasoning. *Psychological Review, 75*(6), 550–560.

Huttenlocher, J. (2005). Mental representation. In J. Rieser, J. Lockman, & C. Nelson (Eds.), *Minnesota Symposium on Child Development Series: Action as an organizer of learning and development.* Mahwah, NJ: Erlbaum.

Huttenlocher, J., Duffy, S., & Levine, S. (2002). Infants and toddlers discriminate amount: Are they measuring? *Psychological Science, 13*(3), 244–249.

Huttenlocher, J., Hedges, L. V., Corrigan, B., & Crawford, E. L. (2004). Spatial categories and the estimation of location. *Cognition, 93*, 75–97.

Huttenlocher, J., Hedges, L. V., & Duncan, S. (1991). Categories and particulars: Prototype effects in estimating spatial location. *Psychological Review, 98*(3), 352–376.

Huttenlocher, J., Hedges, L. V., & Vevea, J. L. (2000). Why do categories affect stimulus judgment? *Journal of Experimental Psychology: General, 129*(2), 220–241.

Huttenlocher, J., Levine, S., & Vevea, J. (1998). Environmental input and cognitive growth: A Study Using Time-Period Comparisons. *Child Development, 69*(4), 1012–1029.

Huttenlocher, J., Newcombe, N., & Sandberg, E. H. (1994). The coding of spatial location in young children. *Cognitive Psychology, 27*(2), 115–148.

Huttenlocher, J., Newcombe, N., & Vasilyeva, M. (1999). Spatial scaling in young children. *Psychological Science, 10*(5), 393–398.

Huttenlocher, J., & Presson, C. C. (1973). Mental rotation and the perspective problem. *Cognitive Psychology, 4*(2), 277–299.

Huttenlocher, J., & Presson, C. C. (1979). The coding and transformation of spatial information. *Cognitive Psychology, 11*(3), 375–394.

Huttenlocher, J., & Vasilyeva, M. (2003). How toddlers represent enclosed spaces. *Cognitive Science, 27*(5), 749–766.

Jacobs, L. (2003). The evolution of the cognitive map. *Brain, Behavior and Evolution, 62*, 128–139.

Jacobs, L. F., & Schenk, F. (2003). Unpacking the cognitive map: The parallel map theory of hippocampal function. *Psychological Review, 110*(2), 285–315.

Johnson, E. S., & Meade, A. C. (1987). Developmental patterns of spatial ability: An early sex difference. *Child Development, 58*(3), 725–740.

Johnson, S. C., & Carey, S. (1998). Knowledge enrichment and conceptual change in folkbiology: Evidence from Williams syndrome. *Cognitive Psychology, 37*(2), 156–200.

Johnson, S. P. (2004). Development of perceptual completion in infancy. *Psychological Science, 15*, 769–775.

Johnson, S. P., Amso, D., & Slemmer, J. A. (2003). Development of object concepts in infancy: Evidence for early learning in an eye tracking paradigm. *Proceedings of the National Academy of Sciences, 100*, 10568–10573.

Johnson, S. P., Bremner, J. G., Slater, A., Mason, U., Foster, K., & Cheshire, A. (2003). Infants' perception of object trajectories. *Child Development, 74*(1), 94–108.

Jones, C. M., Braithwaite, V. A., & Healy, S. D. (2003). The evolution of sex differences in spatial ability. *Behavioral Neuroscience, 117*(3), 403–411.

Jonsson, B., & von Hofsten, C. (2003). Infants' ability to track and reach for temporarily occluded objects. *Developmental Science, 6*(1), 86–99.

Jordan, H., Reiss, J. E., Hoffman, J. E., & Landau, B. (2002). Intact perception of biological motion in the face of profound spatial deficits: Williams syndrome. *Psychological Science, 13*(2), 162–167.

Kaldy, Z., & Leslie, A. M. (2003). Identification of objects in 9-month-old infants: Integrating "what" and "where" information. *Developmental Science, 6*(3), 360–373.

Kaufman, J., & Needham, A. (1999). Objective spatial coding by 6½-month-old infants in a visual dishabituation task. *Developmental Science, 2*(4), 432–441.

Keen, R. (2003). Representation of objects and events: Why do infants look so smart and toddlers look so dumb? *Current Directions in Psychological Science, 12*(3), 79–83.

Kelly, D. M., Spetch, M. L., & Heth, C. D. (1998). Pigeons' (Columba livia) encoding of geometric and featural properties of a spatial environment. *Journal of Comparative Psychology, 112*(3), 259–269.

Kerns, K. A., & Berenbaum, S. A. (1991). Sex differences in spatial ability in children. *Behavior Genetics, 21*(4), 383–396.

Knauff, M., Mulack, T., Kassubek, J., Salih, H. R., & Greenlee, M. W. (2002). Spatial imagery in deductive reasoning: A functional MRI study. *Cognitive Brain Research, 13*, 203–212.

Kozhevnikov, M., & Hegarty, M. (2001). A dissociation between object manipulation spatial ability and spatial orientation ability. *Memory and Cognition, 29*(5), 745–756.

Kuipers, B. (1982). The "Map in the Head" metaphor. *Environment and Behavior, 14*(2), 202–220.

Landau, B. (1986). Early map use as an unlearned ability. *Cognition, 22*(3), 201–223.

Landau, B. (2003). Spatial cognition. In V. Ramachandran (Ed.), *Encyclopedia of the human brain* (p. 395–418). San Diego, CA: Academic Press.

Landau, B., & Spelke, E. (1988). Geometric complexity and object search in infancy. *Developmental Psychology, 24*, 512–521.

Landau, B., Spelke, E. S., & Gleitman, H. (1984). Spatial knowledge in a young blind child. *Cognition, 16*(3), 225–260.

Landau, B., & Zukowski, A. (2003). Objects, motions, and paths: Spatial language in children with Williams syndrome [Special issue]. *Developmental Neuropsychology, 23*(1/2), 105–137.

Laurance, H. E., Learmonth, A. E., Nadel, L., & Jacobs, W. J. (2003). Maturation of spatial navigation strategies: Convergent findings from computerized spatial environments and self-report. *Journal of Cognition and Development, 4*(2), 211–238.

Laurendeau, M., & Pinard, A. (1970). *The development of the concept of space in the child.* Oxford, England: International Universities Press.

Learmonth, A. E., Nadel, L., & Newcombe, N. S. (2002). Children's use of landmarks: Implications for modularity theory. *Psychological Science, 13*(4), 337–341.

Learmonth, A. E., & Newcombe, N. S. (in press). The development of place learning in comparative perspective. In F. Dolins & R. Mitchell (Eds.), *Spatial cognition: Mapping the self and space.* New York: Cambridge University Press.

Learmonth, A. E., Newcombe, N. S., & Huttenlocher, J. (2001). Toddlers' use of metric information and landmarks to reorient. *Journal of Experimental Child Psychology, 80*(3), 225–244.

Le Grand, R., Mondloch, C. J., Maurer, D., & Brent, H. P. (2001). Early visual experience and face processing. *Nature, 410*(6831), 890.

Le Grand, R., Mondloch, C. J., Maurer, D., & Brent, H. P. (2003). Expert face processing requires visual input to the right hemisphere during infancy. *Nature Neuroscience, 6,* 1108–1112.

Lepecq, J. C., & Lafaite, M. (1989). The early development of position constancy in a non-landmark environment. *British Journal of Developmental Psychology, 7,* 289–306.

Leplow, B., Lehnung, M., Pohl, J., Herzog, A., Ferstl, R., & Mehdorn, M. (2003). Navigational place learning in children and young adults as assessed with a standardized locomotor search task. *British Journal of Psychology, 94*(3), 299–317.

Leslie, A. M., Xu, F., Tremoulet, P., & Scholl, B. J. (1998). Indexing and the object concept: Developing "what" and "where" systems. *Trends in Cognitive Science, 2,* 10–18.

Levine, M., Jankovic, I. N., & Palij, M. (1982). Principles of spatial problem solving. *Journal of Experimental Psychology: General, 111*(2), 157–175.

Levine, S. C., Huttenlocher, J., Taylor, A., & Langrock, A. (1999). Early sex differences in spatial skill. *Developmental Psychology, 35*(4), 940–949.

Levinson, S. C. (2003). *Space in language and cognition: Explorations in cognitive diversity.* Cambridge, England: Cambridge University Press.

Levinson, S. C., Kita, S., Haun, D. B. M., & Rasch, B. H. (2002). Returning the tables: Language affects spatial reasoning. *Cognition, 84*(2), 155–188.

Lew, A. R., Bremner, J. G., & Lefkovich, L. P. (2000). The development of relational landmark use in 6- to 12-month-old infants in a spatial orientation task. *Child Development, 71,* 1179–1190.

Lew, A. R., Foster, K. A., Crowther, H. L., & Green, M. (2004). Indirect landmark use at 6 months of age in a spatial orientation task. *Infant Behavior and Development, 27,* 81–90.

Li, P., & Gleitman, L. (2002). Turning the tables: Language and spatial reasoning. *Cognition, 83*(3), 265–294.

Liben, L. S. (1988). Conceptual issues in the development of spatial cognition. In Stiles-Davis, J., & Kritchevsky, M. (Eds.), *Spatial cognition: Brain bases and development* (pp. 167–194). Hillsdale, NJ: Erlbaum.

Liben, L. S., & Downs, R. M. (1993). Understanding person-space-map relations: Cartographic and developmental perspectives. *Developmental Psychology, 29*(4), 739–752.

Liben, L. S., Kastens, K. A., & Stevenson, L. M. (2002). Real-world knowledge through real-world maps: A developmental guide for navigating the educational terrain. *Developmental Review, 22*(2), 267–322.

Liben, L. S., & Yekel, C. A. (1996). Preschoolers' understanding of plan and oblique maps: The role of geometric and representational correspondence. *Child Development, 67*(6), 2780–2796.

Linn, M. C., & Petersen, A. C. (1985). Emergence and characterization of sex differences in spatial ability: A meta-analysis. *Child Development, 56*(6), 1479–1498.

Loewenstein, J., & Gentner, D. (2001). Spatial mapping in preschoolers: Close comparisons facilitate far mappings. *Journal of Cognition and Development, 2,* 189–219.

Lourenco, S. F., Huttenlocher, J., & Vasilyeva, M. (2005). Toddlers' representations of space: The role of viewer perspective. *Psychological Science, 16,* 255–259.

Luo, Y., Baillargeon, R., Brueckner, L., & Munakata, Y. (2003). Reasoning about a hidden object after a delay: Evidence for robust representations in 5-month-old infants. *Cognition, 88,* B23–B32.

MacDonald, S. E., Spetch, M. L., Kelly, D. M., & Cheng, K. (2004). Strategies for landmark use by children, adults, and marmoset monkeys. *Learning and Motivation, 35,* 322–347.

Mandler, J. M. (1996). Preverbal representation and language. In P. Bloom & M. A. Peterson (Eds.), *Language and space* (pp. 365–384). Cambridge, MA: MIT Press.

Mareschal, D., & Johnson, M. H. (2003). The "what" and "where" of object representations in infancy. *Cognition, 88*(3), 259–276.

Mash, C., Keen, R., & Berthier, N. E. (2003). Visual access and attention in 2-year-olds' event reasoning and object search. *Infancy, 4*(3), 371–388.

Maurer, D., Lewis, T. L., Brent, H. P., & Levin, A. V. (1999). Rapid improvement in the acuity of infants after visual input. *Science, 286*(5437), 108–110.

May, M. (2004). Imaginal perspective switches in remembered environments: Transformation versus interference accounts. *Cognitive Psychology, 48*(2), 163–206.

McDonough, L. (1999). Early declarative memory for location. *British Journal of Developmental Psychology, 17,* 381–402.

McDonough, L., Choi, S., & Mandler, J. M. (2003). Understanding spatial relations: Flexible infants, lexical adults. *Cognitive Psychology, 46*(3), 229–259.

McKenzie, B. E., Day, R. H., & Ihsen, E. (1984). Localization of events in space: Young infants are not always egocentric. *British Journal of Developmental Psychology, 2,* 1–9.

McNamara, T. P. (1991). Memory's view of space. In G. H. Bower (Ed.), *Psychology of learning and motivation: Vol. 27. Advances in research and theory* (pp. 147–186). San Diego, CA: Academic Press.

McNamara, T. P., & Diwadkar, V. (1997). Symmetry and asymmetry in human spatial memory. *Cognitive Psychology, 34,* 160–190.

McNamara, T. P., Rump, B., & Werner, S. (2003). Egocentric and geocentric frames of reference in memory of large-scale space. *Psychonomic Bulletin and Review, 10*(3), 589–595.

Meltzoff, A. N., & Moore, M. K. (1998). Object representation, identity, and the paradox of early permanence: Steps toward a new framework. *Infant Behavior and Development, 21,* 201–235.

Merchant, H., Fortes, A. F., & Georgopoulos, A. P. (2004). Short-term memory effects on the representation of two-dimensional space in the rhesus monkey. *Animal Cognition, 7,* 133–143.

Mervis, C. B. (2003). Williams syndrome: 15 years of psychological research [Special issue]. *Developmental Neuropsychology, 23*(1/2), 1–12.

Mervis, C. B., Morris, C. A., Bertrand, J., & Robinson, B. F. (1999). Williams syndrome: Findings from an integrated program of research. In H. Tager-Flusberg (Ed.), *Neurodevelopmental disorders* (pp. 65–110). Cambridge, MA: MIT Press.

Millar, S. (1994). *Understanding and representing space: Theory and evidence from studies with blind and sighted children.* New York: Clarendon Press/Oxford University Press.

Mix, K. S. (2002). The construction of number concepts. *Cognitive Development, 17,* 1345–1363.

Moore, M. K., & Meltzoff, A. N. (1999). New findings on object permanence: A developmental difference between two types of occlusion. *British Journal of Developmental Psychology, 17,* 563–584.

Moore, M. K., & Meltzoff, A. N. (2004). Object permanence after a 24-hr delay and leaving the locale of disappearance: The role of memory, space, and identity. *Developmental Psychology, 40,* 606–620.

Morrongiello, B. A., Timney, B., Humphrey, G. K., Anderson, S., & Skory, C. (1995). Spatial knowledge in blind and sighted children. *Journal of Experimental Child Psychology, 59*(2), 211–233.

Mou, W., McNamara, T. P., Valiquette, C. M., & Rump, B. (2004). Allocentric and egocentric updating of spatial memories. *Journal of Experimental Psychology: Learning, Memory, and Cognition, 30*(1), 142–157.

Munakata, Y. (2000). Infant perseveration and implications for object permanence theories: A PDP model of the A-not B task. *Developmental Science, 1,* 161–211.

Munakata, Y. (2001). Graded representations in behavioral dissociations. *Trends in Cognitive Sciences, 5*(7), 309–315.

Munakata, Y., McClelland, J. L., Johnson, M. H., & Siegler, R. S. (1997). Rethinking infant knowledge: Toward an adaptive process account of successes and failures in object permanence tasks. *Psychological Review, 104*(4), 686–713.

Munnich, E., Landau, B., & Dosher, B. A. (2001). Spatial language and spatial representation: A cross-linguistic comparison. *Cognition, 81*(3), 171–207.

Natale, M. (2002). The effect of male-oriented computer gaming culture on careers in the computer industry. *Computers and Society, 32,* 24–31.

Needham, A. (2001). Object recognition and object segregation in 4½-month-old infants. *Journal of Experimental Child Psychology, 78*(1), 3–24.

Needham, A., Barrett, T., & Peterman, K. (2002). A pick me up for infants' exploratory skills: Early simulated experiences reaching for objects using "sticky" mittens enhances young infants' object exploration skills. *Infant Behavior and Development, 25*(3), 279–295.

Newcombe, N. S. (1989). The development of spatial perspective taking. In H. W. Reese (Ed.), *Advances in child development and behavior* (Vol. 22, pp. 203–247). New York: Academic Press.

Newcombe, N. S. (2001). A spatial coding analysis of the A-not-B error: What IS "location at A"? (Commentary on Thelen et al.) *Behavioral and Brain Sciences, 24,* 57–58.

Newcombe, N. S. (2002a). The nativist-empiricist controversy in the context of recent research on spatial and quantitative development. *Psychological Science, 13,* 395–401.

Newcombe, N. S. (2002b). Spatial cognition. In H. Pashler & D. Medin (Eds.), *Steven's handbook of experimental psychology: Vol. 2. Memory and cognitive processes* (3rd ed., pp. 113–163). Hoboken, NJ: Wiley.

Newcombe, N. S. (2005). Evidence for and against a geometric module: The roles of language and action. In J. Rieser, J. Lockman, & C. Nelson (Eds.), *Minnesota Symposium on Child Development Series: Action as an organizer of learning and development* (pp. 221–241). Mahwah, NJ: Erlbaum.

Newcombe, N. S., & Dubas, J. S. (1987). Individual differences in cognitive ability: Are they related to timing of puberty. In R. M. Lerner & T. T. Foch (Eds.), *Biological-psychosocial interactions in early adolescence* (pp. 249–302). Hillsdale, NJ: Erlbaum.

Newcombe, N. S., & Huttenlocher, J. (1992). Children's early ability to solve perspective-taking problems. *Developmental Psychology, 28*(4), 635–643.

Newcombe, N. S., & Huttenlocher, J. (2000). *Making space: The development of spatial representation and reasoning.* Cambridge, MA: MIT Press.

Newcombe, N. S., Huttenlocher, J., Drummey, A. B., & Wiley, J. G. (1998). The development of spatial location coding: Place learning and dead reckoning in the second and third years. *Cognitive Development, 13*(2), 185–200.

Newcombe, N. S., Huttenlocher, J., & Learmonth, A. (1999). Infants' coding of location in continuous space. *Infant Behavior and Development, 22*(4), 483–510.

Newcombe, N. S., Huttenlocher, J., Sandberg, E., Lie, E., & Johnson, S. (1999). What do misestimations and asymmetries in spatial judgment indicate about spatial representation? *Journal of Experimental Psychology: Learning, Memory, and Cognition, 25*(4), 986–996.

Newcombe, N. S., Sluzenski, J., & Huttenlocher, J. (2005). Pre-existing knowledge versus on-line learning: What do young infants really know about spatial location? *Psychological Science, 16,* 222–227.

Oakhill, J. (1984). Inferential and memory skills in children's comprehension of stories. *British Journal of Educational Psychology, 54*(1), 31–39.

Ondracek, P. J., & Allen, G. L. (2000). Children's acquisition of spatial knowledge from verbal descriptions. *Spatial Cognition and Computation, 2*(1), 1–30.

Okagaki, L., & Frensch, P. A. (1994). Effects of video game playing on measures of spatial performance: Gender effects in late adolescence. *Journal of Applied Developmental Psychology, 15*(1), 33–58.

Overman, W. H., Pate, B. J., Moore, K., & Peuster, A. (1996). Ontogeny of place learning in children as measured in the Radial Arm Maze, Morris Search Task, and Open Field Task. *Behavioral Neuroscience, 110*(6), 1205–1228.

Paterson, S. J., Brown, J. H., Gsodl, M. K., Johnson, M. H., & Karmiloff-Smith, A. (1999). Cognitive modularity and genetic disorders. *Science, 286*(5448), 2355–2358.

Pennington, B. F., Moon, J., Edgin, J., Stedron, J., & Nadel, L. (2003). The neuropsychology of Down syndrome: Evidence for hippocampal dysfunction. *Child Development, 74*(1), 75–93.

Perner, J., & Aebi, J. (1985). Feedback-dependent encoding of length series. *British Journal of Developmental Psychology, 3*(2), 133–141.

Phillips, C. E., Jarrold, C., Baddeley, A. D., Grant, J., & Karmiloff-Smith, A. (2004). Comprehension of spatial language terms in Williams syndrome: Evidence for an interaction between domains of strength and weakness. *Cortex, 40*(1), 85–101.

Piaget, J., & Inhelder, B. (1967). *The child's conception of space* (F. J. Langdon & J. L. Lunzer, Trans.). New York: Norton. (Original work published 1948)

Plumert, J. M., Ewert, K., & Spear, S. J. (1995). The early development of children's communication about nested spatial relations. *Child Development, 66,* 959–969.

Plumert, J. M., & Strahan, D. (1997). Relations between task structure and developmental changes in children's use of spatial clustering strategies. *British Journal of Developmental Psychology, 15,* 495–514.

Presson, C. C. (1982). Strategies in spatial reasoning. *Journal of Experimental Psychology: Learning, Memory, and Cognition, 8*(3), 243–251.

Presson, C. C. (1987). The development of landmarks in spatial memory: The role of differential experience. *Journal of Experimental Child Psychology, 44*(3), 317–334.

Presson, C. C., & Hazelrigg, M. D. (1984). Building spatial representations through primary and secondary learning. *Journal of Experimental Psychology: Learning, Memory, and Cognition, 10*(4), 716–722.

Presson, C. C., & Montello, D. R. (1994). Updating after rotational and translational body movements: Coordinate structure of perspective space. *Perception, 23*(12), 1447–1455.

Pryce, C. R., Bettschen, D., Nanz-Bahr, N. I., & Feldon, J. (2003). Comparison of the effects of early handling and early deprivation on conditioned stimulus, context, and spatial learning and memory in adult rats. *Behavioral Neuroscience, 117*(5), 883–893.

Pufall, P. B., & Shaw, R. E. (1973). Analysis of the development of children's spatial reference systems. *Cognitive Psychology, 5*(2), 151–175.

Quinn, P. C. (1994). The categorization of above and below spatial relations by young infants. *Child Development, 65*(1), 58–69.

Quinn, P. C. (2004). Spatial representation by young infants: Categorization of spatial relations or sensitivity to a crossing primitive? *Memory and Cognition, 32,* 852–861.

Quinn, P. C., Adams, A., Kennedy, E., Shettler, L., & Wasnik, A. (2003). Development of an abstract category representation for the spatial relation between in 6- to 10-month-old infants. *Developmental Psychology, 39*(1), 151–163.

Quinn, P. C., Cummins, M., Kase, J., Martin, E., & Weissman, S. (1996). Development of categorical representations for above and below spatial relations in 3- to 7-month-old infants. *Developmental Psychology, 32*(5), 942–950.

Quinn, P. C., Norris, C. M., Pasko, R. N., Schmader, T. M., & Mash, C. (1999). Formation of categorical representation for the spatial relation between by 6- to 7-month-old infants. *Visual Cognition, 6*(5), 569–585.

Richardson, D. C., & Kirkham, N. Z. (2004). Multimodal events and moving locations: Eye movements of adults and 6-month-olds reveal dynamic spatial indexing. *Journal of Experimental Psychology: General, 133*(1), 46–62.

Rieser, J. J. (1979). Spatial orientation in 6-month-old infants. *Child Development, 50,* 1078–1087.

Rieser, J. J. (1989). Access to knowledge of spatial structure at novel points of observation. *Journal of Experimental Psychology: Learning, Memory, and Cognition, 15*(6), 1157–1165.

Rieser, J. J., Doxsey, P. A., McCarrell, N. S., & Brooks, P. H. (1982, September). Wayfinding and toddlers' use of information from an aerial view of a maze. *Developmental Psychology, 18*(5), 714–720.

Rieser, J. J., Garing, A. E., & Young, M. F. (1994). Imagery, action, and young children's spatial orientation: It's not being there that counts, it's what one has in mind. *Child Development, 65,* 1262–1278.

Rieser, J. J., Guth, D. A., & Hill, E. W. (1986). Sensitivity to perspective structure while walking without vision. *Perception, 15*(2), 173–188.

Rieser, J. J., Hill, E. W., Talor, C. R., Bradfield, A., & Rosen, S. (1992). Visual experience, visual field size, and the development of nonvisual sensitivity to the spatial structure of outdoor neighborhoods explored by walking. *Journal of Experimental Psychology: General, 121*(2), 210–221.

Rieser, J. J., & Rider, E. A. (1988). Pointing at objects in other rooms: Young children's sensitivity to perspective after walking with and without vision. *Child Development, 59*(2), 480–494.

Rieser, J. J., & Rider, E. A. (1991). Young children's spatial orientation with respect to multiple targets when walking without vision. *Developmental Psychology, 27*(1), 97–107.

Roberts, J. E., & Bell, M. A. (2000). Sex differences on a mental rotation task: Variations in electroencephalogram hemispheric activation between children and college students. *Developmental Neuropsychology, 17*(2), 199–223.

Rosander, K., & von Hofsten, C. (2004). Infants' emerging ability to represent occluded object motion. *Cognition, 91*(1), 1–22.

Rossetti, Y., Jacquin-Courtois, S., Rode, G., Otta, H., Michel, C., & Boisson, D. (2004). Does action make the link between number and space representation? *Psychological Science, 15*(6), 426–430.

Russell, J., & Thompson, D. (2003). Memory development in the second year: For events or locations? *Cognition, 87,* B97–B105.

Saccuzzo, D. P., Craig, A. S., Johnson, N. E., & Larson, G. E. (1996). Gender differences in dynamic spatial abilities. *Personality and Individual Differences, 21*(4), 599–607.

Sandberg, E. H. (2000). Cognitive constraints on the development of hierarchical spatial organization skills. *Cognitive Development, 14*(4), 597–619.

Sandberg, E. H., & Huttenlocher, J. (2001). Advanced spatial skills and advance planning: Components of 6-year-olds' navigational map use. *Journal of Cognition and Development, 2*(1), 51–70.

Sandberg, E. H., Huttenlocher, J., & Newcombe, N. (1996). The development of hierarchical representation of two-dimensional space. *Child Development, 67*(3), 721–739.

Schober, M. F. (1993). Spatial perspective-taking in conversation. *Cognition, 47*(1), 1–24.

Schober, M. F. (1995). Speakers, addressees, and frames of reference: Whose effort is minimized in conversations about locations? *Discourse Processes, 20*(2), 219–247.

Scholnick, E. K., Fein, G. G., & Campbell, P. F. (1990). Changing predictors of map use in wayfinding. *Developmental Psychology, 26*(2), 188–193.

Schutte, A. R., & Spencer, J. P. (2002). Generalizing the dynamic field theory of the A-not-B error beyond infancy: Three-year-olds' delay- and experience-dependent location memory biases. *Child Development, 73*(2), 377–404.

Schutte, A. R., Spencer, J. P., & Schöner, G. (2003). Testing the dynamic field theory: Working memory for locations becomes more spatially precise over development. *Child Development, 74*(5), 1393–1417.

Shea, D. L., Lubinski, D., & Benbow, C. P. (2001). Importance of assessing spatial ability in intellectually talented young adolescents: A 20-year Longitudinal Study. *Journal of Educational Psychology, 93*(3), 604–614.

Shelton, A. L., & McNamara, T. P. (2004). Orientation and perspective dependence in route and survey learning. *Journal of Experimental Psychology: Learning, Memory, and Cognition, 30*(1), 158–170.

Shepard, R. N., & Hurwitz, S. (1984). Upward direction, mental rotation, and discrimination of left and right turns in maps [Special issue]. *Cognition, 18*(1/3), 161–193.

Shettleworth, S. J. (1998). *Cognition, evolution, and behavior.* London: Oxford University Press.

Shinskey, J. L., & Munakata, Y. (2003). Are infants in the dark about hidden objects? *Developmental Science, 6*(3), 273–282.

Sholl, M. J. (1995). The representation and retrieval of map and environment knowledge. *Geographical Systems, 2,* 177–195.

Sholl, M. J., & Bartels, G. P. (2002). The role of self-to-object updating in orientation-free performance on spatial-memory tasks. *Journal of Experimental Psychology: Learning, Memory, and Cognition, 28*(3), 422–436.

Sholl, M. J., & Nolin, T. L. (1997). Orientation specificity in representations of place. *Journal of Experimental Psychology: Learning, Memory, and Cognition, 23*(6), 1494–1507.

Siegel, A. W., Kirasic, K. C., & Kail, R. V. (1979). Stalking the elusive cognitive map: The development of children's representations of geographic space. In J. F. Wohlwill & I. Altman (Eds.), *Human behavior and environment: Vol. 3. Children and the environment* (pp. 223–258). New York: Plenum Press.

Siegel, A. W., & White, S. H. (1975). The development of spatial representations of large-scale environments. In H. W. Reese (Ed.), *Advances in child development and behavior* (Vol. 10, pp. 9–55). New York: Academic Press.

Siegler, R. S. (1996). *Emerging minds: The process of change in children's thinking.* London: Oxford University Press.

Simons, D. J., & Wang, R. F. (1998). Perceiving real-world viewpoint changes. *Psychological Science, 9*(4), 315–320.

Sims, V. K., & Mayer, R. E. (2002). Domain specificity of spatial expertise: The case of video game players. *Applied Cognitive Psychology, 16*(1), 97–115.

Sluzenski, J., Newcombe, N. S., & Satlow, E. (2004). Knowing where things are in the second year of life: Implications for hippocampal development. *Journal of Cognitive Neuroscience, 16,* 1443–1451.

Smith, L. B., Thelen, E., Titzer, R., & McLin, D. (1999). Knowing in the context of acting: The task dynamics of the A-not-B error. *Psychological Review, 106*(2), 235–260.

Sonnenschein, S., & Whitehurst, G. J. (1984). Developing referential communication: A hierarchy of skills. *Child Development, 55,* 1936–1945.

Sovrano, V. A., Bisazza, A., & Vallortigara, G. (2002). Modularity and spatial reorientation in a simple mind: Encoding of geometric and nongeometric properties of a spatial environment by fish. *Cognition, 85,* B51–B59.

Spelke, E. S., Breinlinger, K., Macomber, J., & Jacobson, K. (1992). Origins of knowledge. *Psychological Review, 99,* 605–632.

Spelke, E. S., & Hermer, L. (1996). Early cognitive development: Objects and space. In R. Gelman & T. Kit-Fong (Eds.), *Perceptual and cognitive development* (pp. 71–114). San Diego, CA: Academic Press.

Spelke, E. S., & Newport, E. (1998). Nativism, empiricism, and the development of knowledge. In W. Damon (Editor-in-Chief) & R. M. Lerner (Vol. Ed.), *Handbook of child psychology: Vol. 1. Theoretical models of human development* (5th ed., pp. 165–179). New York: Wiley.

Spencer, J. P., & Hund, A. M. (2002). Prototypes and particulars: Geometric and experience-dependent spatial categories. *Journal of Experimental Psychology: General, 131*(1), 16–37.

Spencer, J. P., & Hund, A. M. (2003). Developmental continuity in the processes that underlie spatial recall. *Cognitive Psychology, 47*(4), 432–480.

Spencer, J. P., & Schutte, A. R. (2004). Unifying representations and responses: Perseverative biases arise from a single behavioral system. *Psychological Science, 15*(3), 187–193.

Spencer, J. P., Smith, L. B., & Thelen, E. (2001). Tests of a dynamic systems account of the A-not-B error: The influence of prior experience on the spatial memory abilities of 2-year-olds. *Child Development, 72*(5), 1327–1346.

Spetch, M. L., Cheng, K., & MacDonald, S. E. (1996). Learning the configuration of a landmark array: Vol. 1. Touch-screen studies with pigeons and humans. *Journal of Comparative Psychology, 110*(1), 55–68.

Spetch, M. L., & Friedman, A. (2003). Recognizing rotated views of objects: Interpolation versus generalization by humans and pigeons. *Psychonomic Bulletin and Review, 10*(1), 135–140.

Stevens, A., & Coupe, P. (1978). Distortions in judged spatial relations. *Cognitive Psychology, 10*(4), 422–437.

Szechter, L. E., & Liben, L. S. (2004). Parental guidance in preschoolers' understanding of spatial-graphic representations. *Child Development, 75,* 869–885.

Tager-Flusberg, H., Plesa-Skwerer, D., Faja, S., & Joseph, R. M. (2003). People with Williams syndrome process faces holistically. *Cognition, 89*(1), 11–24.

Taylor, H. A., & Tversky, B. (1992a). Descriptions and depictions of environments. *Memory and Cognition, 20*(5), 483–496.

Taylor, H. A., & Tversky, B. (1992b). Spatial mental models derived from survey and route descriptions. *Journal of Memory and Language, 31*(2), 261–292.

Taylor, H. A., & Tversky, B. (1996). Perspective in spatial descriptions. *Journal of Memory and Language, 35*(3), 371–391.

Tees, R. C., Buhrmann, K., & Hanley, J. (1990). The effect of early experience on water maze spatial learning and memory in rats. *Developmental Psychobiology, 23*(5), 427–439.

Thelen, E., Schoener, G., Scheier, C., & Smith, L. B. (2001). The dynamics of embodiment: A field theory of infant perseverative reaching. *Behavioral and Brain Sciences, 24*(1), 1–86.

Thelen, E., & Smith, L. B. (1994). *A dynamic systems approach to the development of cognition and action.* Cambridge, MA: MIT Press.

Thinus-Blanc, C., & Gaunet, F. (1997). Representation of space in blind persons: Vision as a spatial sense? *Psychological Bulletin, 121*(1), 20–42.

Thomas, M. S. C., & Karmiloff-Smith, A. (2003). Modeling language and acquisition in atypical phenotypes. *Psychological Review, 110,* 647–682.

Tsao, F., Liu, H., & Kuhl, P. (2004). Speech perception in infancy predicts language development in the second year of life: A Longitudinal Study. *Child Development, 75,* 1067–1084.

Tversky, A. (1977). Features of similarity. *Psychological Review, 84,* 327–352.

Tversky, B. (1981). Distortions in memory for maps. *Cognitive Psychology, 13*(3), 407–433.

Tversky, B. (2000). Remembering spaces. In E. Tulving & F. I. M. Craik (Eds.), *Oxford handbook of memory* (pp. 363–378). London: Oxford University Press.

Tversky, B., Lee, P., & Mainwaring, S. (1999). Why do speakers mix perspectives? *Spatial Cognition and Computation, 1,* 399–412.

Uecker, A., & Nadel, L. (1996). Spatial locations gone awry: Object and spatial memory deficits in children with fetal alcohol syndrome. *Neuropsychologia, 34*(3), 209–223.

Uttal, D. H. (1996). Angles and distances: Children's and adults' reconstruction and scaling of spatial configurations. *Child Development, 67*(6), 2763–2779.

Uttal, D. H. (2000). Seeing the big picture: Map use and the development of spatial cognition. *Developmental Science, 3*(3), 247–286.

Uttal, D. H., Gregg, V. H., Tan, L. S., Chamberlin, M. H., & Sines, A. (2001). Connecting the dots: Children's use of a systematic figure to facilitate mapping and search. *Developmental Psychology, 37*(3), 338–350.

Uttal, D. H., & Wellman, H. W. (1989). Young children's representation of spatial information acquired from maps. *Developmental Psychology, 25,* 128–138.

Vallortigara, G., Zanforlin, M., & Pasti, G. (1990). Geometric modules in animals' spatial representations: A test with chicks (Gallus gallus domesticus). *Journal of Comparative Psychology, 104*(3), 248–254.

Vauclair, J., Fagot, J., & Hopkins, D. (1993). Rotation of mental images in baboons when the visual input is directed to the left cerebral hemisphere. *Psychological Science, 4*(2), 99–103.

Vasilyeva, M. (2002). Solving spatial tasks with unaligned layouts: The difficulty of dealing with conflicting information. *Journal of Experimental Child Psychology, 83*(4), 291–303.

Vasilyeva, M., & Huttenlocher, J. (2004). Early development of scaling ability. *Developmental Psychology, 40,* 682–690.

Vishton, P. M., Rea, J. G., Cutting, J. E., & Nunez, L. N. (1999). Comparing effects of the horizontal-vertical illusion on grip scaling and judgment: Relative versus absolute, not perception versus action. *Journal of Experimental Psychology: Human Perception and Performance, 25*(6), 1659–1672.

Vosmik, J. R., & Presson, C. C. (2004). Children's response to natural map misalignment during wayfinding. *Journal of Cognition and Development, 5,* 317–336.

Voyer, D. (1996). On the magnitude of laterality effects and sex differences in functional lateralities. *Laterality: Asymmetries of Body, Brain and Cognition, 1*(1), 51–83.

Voyer, D., Voyer, S., & Bryden, M. P. (1995). Magnitude of sex differences in spatial abilities: A meta-analysis and consideration of critical variables. *Psychological Bulletin, 117*(2), 250–270.

Waber, D. P. (1976). Sex differences in cognition: A function of maturation rate? *Science, 192*(4239), 572–573.

Walsh, V. (2003). A theory of magnitude: Common cortical metrics of time, space and quantity. *Trends in Cognitive Science, 7*(11), 483–488.

Waller, D., Knapp, D., & Hunt, E. (2001). Spatial representations of virtual mazes: The role of visual fidelity and individual differences. *Human Factors, 43*(1), 147–158.

Wang, R. F., & Spelke, E. S. (2002). Human spatial representation: Insights from animals. *Trends in Cognitive Sciences, 6*(9), 376–382.

Warren, W. H. (2005). Information, representation, and dynamics: A discussion of the chapters by Lee, von Hofsten, and Adolph. In J. Rieser, J. Lockman, & C. Nelson (Eds.), *Minnesota Symposium on Child Development Series: Action as an organizer of learning and development.* Mahwah, NJ: Erlbaum.

Wellman, H. M., Phillips, A. T., Dunphy-Lelii, S., & Lahande, N. (2004). Infant social attention predicts preschool social cognition. *Developmental Science, 7,* 283–288.

Wiesel, T. N., & Hubel, D. H. (1965). Comparison of the effects of unilateral and bilateral eye closure on cortical unit responses in kittens. *Journal of Neurophysiology, 28,* 1029–1040.

Wilcox, T. (1999). Object individuation: Infants' use of shape, size, pattern, and color. *Cognition, 72*(2), 125–166.

Wilcox, T., & Baillargeon, R. (1998a). Object individuation in infancy: The use of featural information in reasoning about occlusion events. *Cognitive Psychology, 37*(2), 97–155.

Wilcox, T., & Baillargeon, R. (1998b). Object individuation in young infants: Further evidence with an event-monitoring paradigm. *Developmental Science, 1*(1), 127–142.

Wraga, M., Creem, S. H., & Proffitt, D. R. (2000). Perception-action dissociations of a walkable Mueller-Lyer configuration. *Psychological Science, 11*(3), 239–243.

Wraga, M., Creem-Regehr, S. H., & Proffitt, D. R. (2004). Spatial updating of virtual displays during self- and display rotation. *Memory and Cognition, 32,* 399–415.

Xu, F., & Carey, S. (1996). Infants' metaphysics: The case of numerical identity. *Cognitive Psychology, 30,* 111–153.

Zacks, J. M., Vettel, J. M., & Michelon, P. (2003). Imagined viewer and object rotations dissociated with event-related fMRI. *Journal of Cognitive Neuroscience, 15*(7), 1002–1018.

CHAPTER 18

# Development of Mathematical Understanding

DAVID C. GEARY

**HISTORY**  778
**Early Learning Theory**  778
**Psychometric Studies**  778
**Constructivism**  778
**Information Processing**  779
**Neonativist Perspective**  780
**RESEARCH**  780

**Early Quantitative Abilities**  780
**Arithmetic in School**  789
**Mechanisms of Change**  799
**CONCLUSIONS AND FUTURE DIRECTIONS**  803
**REFERENCES**  804

The nature of children's numerical, arithmetical, and mathematical understanding and the mechanisms that underlie the development of this knowledge are at the center of an array of scientific, political, and educational debates. Scientific issues range from infants' understanding of quantity and arithmetic (Cohen & Marks, 2002; Starkey, 1992; Wynn, 1992a) to the processes that enable middle-school and high-school students to solve multistep arithmetical and algebraic word problems (Tronsky & Royer, 2002). The proposed mechanisms that underlie quantitative and mathematical knowledge range from inherent systems that have been designed through evolution to represent and process quantitative information (Geary, 1995; Spelke, 2000; Wynn, 1995) to general learning mechanisms that can operate on and generate arithmetical and mathematical knowledge but are not inherently quantitative (Newcombe, 2002). The wide range of competencies covered under the umbrella of children's mathematical understanding and the intense scientific debate about the nature of this knowledge and how it changes with experience and development make this a vibrant research area. The empirical research and theoretical debate also have implications for educational policy issues (Hirsch, 1996).

The chapter begins with a brief history of the more than 100 years of research and educational debate related to children's mathematics. The focus, however, is on contemporary research on the number, counting, and arithmetical competencies that emerge during infancy and the preschool years; elementary-school children's conceptual knowledge of arithmetic and how they solve formal arithmetic problems (e.g., $6 + 9$); and how adolescents understand and solve complex word problems. Where possible, I provide discussion of the mechanisms that support knowledge representation, problem solving, and corresponding developmental change. In the final section of the chapter, I discuss the potential mechanisms that may contribute to developmental and experience-based change in mathematical domains across a continuum, ranging from inherent, evolved abilities to abilities that are culturally specific. The discussion is meant to provide a broad outline for future scientific research on children's mathematical understanding and for thinking about how mathematics might be taught in school.

Preparation of this chapter was supported, in part, by grants R01 HD38283 from the National Institute of Child Health and Human Development (NICHD), and R37 HD045914 cofunded by NICHD and the Office of Special Education and Rehabilitation Services.

## HISTORY

The study of arithmetical and mathematical competencies and their development has occupied psychologists and educators for more than 100 years. The approaches include experimental studies of learning, child-centered approaches to early education (constructivism), psychometric studies of individual differences in test performance, and more recently the neonativist perspective.

### Early Learning Theory

Experimental psychologists have been studying children's understanding and learning of number, arithmetic, and mathematics since the early decades of the 20th century (e.g., Brownell, 1928; O'Shea, 1901; Starch, 1911; Thorndike, 1922). The topics these researchers explored were similar to those being studied today, including the speed and accuracy with which children apprehend the quantity of sets of objects (Brownell, 1928); the strategies children use to solve arithmetic problems (Brownell, 1928); the relative difficulty of different problems (Washburne & Vogel, 1928); and the factors that influence the learning of algebra (Taylor, 1918) and geometry (Metzler, 1912). A common theme was the study of the effects of practice on the acquisition of specific mathematical competencies (Hahn & Thorndike, 1914), the factors that influence the effectiveness of practice (Thorndike, 1922), and the extent to which these competencies transferred to other domains (Starch, 1911). Practice distributed across time results in substantive improvement in the specific domain that is practiced and sometimes results in transfer to related domains. Winch (1910) found practice-related improvements in basic arithmetic were, under some conditions (e.g., student ability), associated with improved accuracy in solving arithmetical reasoning problems (multistep word problems) that involved basic arithmetic. It was also found that transfer did not typically occur across unrelated domains (Thorndike & Woodworth, 1901).

### Psychometric Studies

Psychometric studies focus on individual differences in performance on paper-and-pencil ability tests and are useful for determining whether different types of cognitive abilities exist (Thurstone, 1938), and for making inferences about the source of individual differences (Spearman, 1927). Numerical, arithmetical, and mathematical tests have been included in these studies for more than 100 years (Cattell, 1890; Spearman, 1904), and they continue to be used to this day (Carroll, 1993). One of the most useful techniques is factor analysis, which allows correlations among ability tests to be grouped into clusters that reflect common sources of individual differences. The use of factor analysis has consistently revealed two mathematical domains, numerical facility and mathematical reasoning (e.g., Chein, 1939; Coombs, 1941; Dye & Very, 1968; French, 1951; Thurstone & Thurstone, 1941). Other relatively distinct quantitative skills, such as estimation, were also identified in some but not all psychometric studies (Canisia, 1962). Across studies, the Numerical Facility factor is defined by arithmetic computation tests (e.g., tests that require the solving of complex multiplication problems), and by tests that involve a conceptual understanding of number relationships and arithmetical concepts (Thurstone, 1938; Thurstone & Thurstone, 1941). Basically, the Numerical Facility factor appears to encompass most of the basic arithmetic skills described in the "Arithmetic in School" section. Tests that define the Mathematical Reasoning factor typically require the ability to find and evaluate quantitative relationships, and to draw conclusions based on quantitative information (French, 1951; Goodman, 1943; Thurstone, 1938).

Developmentally, Osborne and Lindsey (1967) found a distinct Numerical Facility factor for a sample of kindergarten children. The factor was defined by tests that encompassed counting, simple arithmetic, working memory for numbers, and general knowledge about quantitative relationships. Meyers and Dingman (1960) also argued that relatively distinct numerical skills are identifiable by 5 to 7 years of age. The most important developmental change in numerical facility is that it becomes more distinctly arithmetical with schooling. Mathematical reasoning ability is related to numerical facility in the elementary and middle-school years, and gradually emerges as a distinct ability factor with continued schooling (Dye & Very, 1968; Thurstone & Thurstone, 1941; Very, 1967). The pattern suggests mathematical reasoning emerges from the skills represented by the Numerical Facility factor, general reasoning abilities, and schooling.

### Constructivism

The constructivist approach to children's learning and understanding of mathematics also has a long history

(McLellan & Dewey, 1895), and continues to be influential (Ginsburg, Klein, & Starkey, 1998). There is variation in the details of this approach from one theorist to the next, but the common theme is that children's learning should be self-directed and emerge from their interactions with the physical world. McLellan and Dewey argued that children's learning of number and later of arithmetic should emerge through their manipulation of objects (e.g., grouping sets of objects). They argued their approach was better suited for children than teacher-directed instruction, and better than the emphasis on practice espoused by learning theorists (Thorndike, 1922). The most influential constructivist theory is that of Jean Piaget. Although his focus was on understanding general cognitive mechanisms (Piaget, 1950)—those applied to all domains such as number, mass, and volume—Piaget and his colleagues conducted influential studies of how children understand number (Piaget, 1965) and geometry (Piaget, Inhelder, & Szeminska, 1960).

For example, to assess the child's conception of number, two rows of seven marbles are presented and the child is asked which row has more. If the marbles in the two rows are aligned in a one-to-one fashion, then 4- to 5-year-old children almost always state that there are the same number of marbles in each row. If one of the rows is spread out such that the one-to-one correspondence is not obvious, children of this age almost always state that the longer row has more marbles. This type of justification led Piaget to argue that the child's understanding of quantitative equivalence was based on how the rows looked, rather than on a conceptual understanding of number. An understanding of number would require the child to state that, after the transformation, the number in each row was the same, even though they now looked different from one another. Children do not typically provide this type of justification until they are 7 or 8 years old, leading Piaget to argue that younger children do not possess a conceptual understanding of number. Mehler and Bever (1967) challenged this conclusion by modifying the way children's understanding was assessed and demonstrated that, under some circumstances, 2.5-year-olds use quantitative, rather than perceptual, information to make judgments about more than or less than (R. Gelman, 1972). With the use of increasingly sensitive assessment techniques, it now appears that preschool children and infants have a more sophisticated understanding of quantity than predicted by Piaget's theory (see "Early Quantitative Abilities" section).

## Information Processing

With the emergence of computer technologies and conceptual advances in information systems in the 1960s, reaction time (RT) reemerged as a method to study cognitive processes. Groen and Parkman (1972) and later Ashcraft and his colleagues (Ashcraft, 1982; Ashcraft & Battaglia, 1978) introduced these methods to the study of arithmetical processes (for a review, see Ashcraft, 1995). As an example, simple arithmetic problems, such as $3 + 2 = 4$ or $9 + 5 = 14$, are presented on a computer monitor, and the child indicates by button push whether the presented answer is correct. The resulting RTs are then analyzed by means of regression equations, whereby statistical models representing the approaches potentially used to solve the problems, such as counting or memory retrieval, are fitted to RT patterns. If children count both addends in the problem, starting from one, then RTs will increase linearly with the sum of the problem, and the value of the raw regression weight will provide an estimate of the speed with which children count implicitly. These methods suggest adults typically retrieve the answer directly from long-term memory and young children typically count.

Siegler and his colleagues merged RT techniques with direct observation of children's problem solving (Carpenter & Moser, 1984) to produce a method that enables researchers to determine how children solve each and every problem; make inferences about the temporal dynamics of strategy execution; and make inferences about the mechanisms of strategy discovery and developmental change (Siegler, 1987; Siegler & Crowley, 1991; Siegler & Shrager, 1984). The results revealed that children use a mix of strategies to solve many types of quantitative problem (Siegler, 1996). Improvement in quantitative abilities across age and experience is conceptualized as overlapping waves. The waves represent the strategy mix, with the crest representing the most commonly used problem-solving approach. Change occurs as once dominant strategies, such as finger counting, decrease in frequency, and more efficient strategies, such as memory retrieval, increase in frequency.

The use of observational, RT, and other methods has expanded to the study of quantitative abilities in infancy (Antell & Keating, 1983; Wynn, 1992a) and, in fact, across the life span (Geary, Frensch, & Wiley, 1993). These methods have also been applied to the study of how children and adolescents solve arithmetical and algebraic word problems (Mayer, 1985; Riley, Greeno, & Heller, 1983), and to more applied issues such as mathematics anxiety (Ashcraft, 2002) and learning disabilities (Geary, 2004b).

## Neonativist Perspective

Scientific discussion of evolved mental traits arose in the latter half of the nineteenth century, following the discovery of the principles of natural section (Darwin & Wallace, 1858). In 1871, Darwin (p. 55) noted, "[M]an has an instinctive tendency to speak, as we see in the babble of our young children; whilst no child has an instinctive tendency to . . . write." The distinction between evolved and learned cognitive competencies was overshadowed for much of the twentieth century by psychometric, constructivist, and information-processing approaches to cognition. Neonativist approaches emerged in the waning decades of the twentieth century with the discovery that infants have an implicit, although not fully developed, understanding of some features of the physical, biological, and social worlds (e.g., Freedman, 1974; R. Gelman, 1990; R. Gelman & Williams, 1998; S. Gelman, 2003; Keil, 1992; Rozin, 1976; Spelke, Breinlinger, Macomber, & Jacobson, 1992). The neonativist emphasis on modularized competencies (e.g., language) distinguishes the approach from the general cognitive structures emphasized by Piaget.

A neonativist perspective on children's knowledge of quantity was stimulated by R. Gelman's and Gallistel's (1978) *The Child's Understanding of Number.* The gist is that children's knowledge of counting is captured by a set of implicit principles that guide their early counting behavior and that provide the skeletal frame for learning about counting and quantity. Later, Wynn (1992a) discovered that infants have an implicit understanding of the effects of adding or subtracting one item from a small set of items, and others proposed that children's inherent understanding of quantity could be understood in terms of a system of number-counting-arithmetic knowledge (Geary, 1994, 1995; R. Gelman, 1990; Spelke, 2000). The system was thought to be limited to an implicit ability to organize objects into sets of four or less; an ability to manipulate these sets by means of counting; and an implicit understanding of the effects of adding or subtracting from these sets. This inherent or biologically primary system was contrasted with culturally specific or biologically secondary arithmetical and

mathematical knowledge (e.g., the Base-10 system) that was learned as a result of formal or informal instruction. Although the utility of the neonativist approach is debated (Newcombe, 2002), it continues to guide theoretical and empirical research on mathematical knowledge, its development, and cross-cultural expression (Butterworth, 1999; Dehaene, Spelke, Pinel, Stanescu, & Tsivkin, 1999; Gordon, 2004; Pica, Lemer, Izard, & Dehaene, 2004).

## RESEARCH

My review of empirical and theoretical research is organized in terms of early quantitative abilities (number, counting and arithmetic before formal schooling); arithmetic learned in school; and mechanisms of change.

### Early Quantitative Abilities

My review of the quantitative abilities that emerge before formal schooling is focused on infants' understanding of number and arithmetic; preschoolers' understanding of number and counting; and preschoolers' emerging arithmetic skills and conceptual knowledge of the properties of arithmetic.

#### Number and Arithmetic in Infancy

The study of infants' numerical prowess has focused on three specific competencies. The first concerns the infant's understanding of numerosity, that is, the ability to discriminate arrays of objects based on the quantity of presented items. The second and third respective competencies concern an awareness of ordinality, for example, that three items are more than two items, and the infants' awareness of the effects of adding and subtracting small amounts from a set. I provide an overview of research on each of these competencies and then discuss underlying mechanisms.

**Numerosity.**  Starkey and R. Cooper (1980) conducted one of the first contemporary investigations of the numerical competencies of infants. The procedure involved the presentation of an array of 2 to 6 dots. When an array of say three dots is first presented, the information is novel and thus the infant will orient toward the array, that is, look at it. With repeated presentations, the time spent looking at the array declines, or habituates. If the infant again orients to the array when the number of presented dots changes (dishabituation), then it is assumed that the infant discriminated the two quantities. However, if the infant's viewing time does not change, then it is assumed the infant cannot discriminate the two quantities. With the use of this procedure, Starkey and R. Cooper found that infants between the ages of 4 and 7.5 months discriminated two items from three items but not four items from six items. Working independently, Strauss and Curtis (1984) found that 10- to 12-month-old infants discriminated two items from three items, and some of them discriminated three items from four items.

The infants' sensitivity to the numerosity of arrays of one to three, and sometimes four, items has been replicated many times and under various conditions, such as homogeneous versus heterogeneous collections of objects (Antell & Keating, 1983; Starkey, 1992; Starkey, Spelke, & Gelman, 1983, 1990; van Loosbroek & Smitsman, 1990). Among the most notable of these findings is that infants show a sensitivity to differences in the numerosity of small sets in the 1st week of life (Antell & Keating, 1983), with displays in motion (van Loosbroek & Smitsman, 1990), and intermodally (Starkey et al., 1990). In the first intermodal study, Starkey et al., presented 7-month-old infants with two photographs, one consisting of two items and the other consisting of three items, and simultaneously presented either two or three drumbeats. Infants looked longer at the photograph with the number of items that matched the number of drumbeats, suggesting that the infants somehow extracted quantity from the visual information (the photographs) and matched this with the quantity extracted from the auditory information (the drumbeats). This result suggested infants have a cognitive system that abstractly codes for numerosities up to three or four items that is neither visually nor auditorily based.

In contrast with the matching of visual and auditory quantity found by Starkey et al. (1990), infants in later studies looked at visual displays that contained a number of objects that mismatched the number of sounds or showed no preference either way (Mix, Levine, & Huttenlocher, 1997; Moore, Benenson, Reznick, Peterson, & Kagan, 1987). The former results might be interpreted as evidence for an ability to discriminate a small number of objects from a sequence of sounds, but the mixed pattern of results leaves the issue unresolved. Other investigators have questioned whether infants' numerosity discriminations are based on an implicit understanding of quantity or other factors that are correlated with quantity in the experimental procedures

(Clearfield & Mix, 1999; Newcombe, 2002; Simon, 1997). As an example, as the number of items increases, so does total surface area, overall duration of tones, and so forth. Clearfield and Mix confirmed that infants can discriminate small sets of squares that differ in quantity, but the discriminations are more strongly influenced by the length of the perimeter of the squares than by number of squares (see also Feigenson, Carey, & Spelke, 2002).

To control for some of these perceptual-spatial and other confounds, Wynn and Sharon (Sharon & Wynn, 1998; Wynn, 1996) presented 6-month-old infants with a puppet that engaged in a series of two or three actions (see also Wynn, Bloom, & Chiang, 2002). In a two-action sequence, an infant might first see the puppet jump, stop briefly, and then jump again. Evidence for infants' ability to enumerate small numbers of items was provided by their ability to discriminate between two- and three-action sequences. In a series of related studies, Spelke and her colleagues found that 6-month-old infants can discriminate visually and auditorily presented sets of larger quantities from smaller quantities, but only if the number of items in the larger set is double that in the smaller set (e.g., 16 versus 8; Brannon, Abbott, & Lutz, 2004; Lipton & Spelke, 2003; Xu & Spelke, 2000). The results were interpreted as supporting the hypothesis that people, including infants, have an intuitive sense of approximate magnitudes (Dehaene, 1997; Gallistel & Gelman, 1992), but the mechanisms underlying infants' performance in Spelke's studies may differ from those underlying infants' discrimination of sets of two items, sounds, or actions, from sets of three items, sounds, or actions, as described in the "Representational Mechanisms" section.

**Ordinality.**  Even though infants are able to detect and represent small quantities, this does not mean they are necessarily sensitive to which set has *more* or *less* items. Initial research suggested that infants' sensitivity to these ordinal relationships, that is somehow knowing that 3 is more than 2 and 2 is more than 1, was evident by 18 months (R. Cooper, 1984; Sophian & Adams, 1987; Strauss & Curtis, 1984), although more recent studies suggest a sensitivity to ordinality may emerge by 10 months (Brannon, 2002; Feigenson, Carey, & Hauser, 2002). In an early study, Strauss and Curtis taught infants, by means of operant conditioning, to touch the side of a panel that contained the smaller or larger number of two arrays of dots. For the smaller-reward condition, the smaller array might contain three dots and the larger array four dots; infants would then be rewarded for touching the panel associated with the smaller array. The infants might next be presented with arrays of two and three dots. If infants were simply responding to the rewarded value, they should touch the panel associated with three. In contrast, if infants respond based on the ordinal relationship (responding to the smaller array in this example), then they would touch the panel associated with two. In this study, 16-month-olds responded to the two, suggesting a sensitivity to less than (Strauss & Curtis, 1984). Ten- to 12-month-olds seemed to notice that the numerosities in the arrays had changed, but they did not discriminate less than and more than; it was simply different than (R. Cooper, 1984).

Feigenson, Carey, and Hauser (2002) adopted a procedure used to study rhesus monkeys' (*Macaca mulatta*) sensitivity to ordinality (Hauser, Carey, & Hauser, 2000). In their first experiment, crackers of various size and number were placed, one at a time, in two opaque containers and the infant was allowed to crawl to the container of their preference. Groups of 10- and 12-month-old infants consistently chose the container with the larger number of crackers when the comparison involved 1 versus 2 and 2 versus 3. When four or more crackers were placed in one of the containers, performance dropped to chance levels. Another experiment pitted number against total amount (i.e., surface area) of cracker. In this experiment, 3 out of 4 infants chose the container with the greater amount of cracker (1 large cracker) as opposed to the container with the greater number of crackers (2 smaller crackers). Brannon (2002) demonstrated that 11-month-old, but not 9-month-old, infants could discriminate ordinally arranged sets that increased (e.g., 2, 4, 8 items) or decreased (e.g., 8, 4, 2 items) in quantity. A variety of experimental controls suggested that the discriminations were based on the change in number of items in the sets, and not change in surface area or perimeter.

**Arithmetic.**    Wynn (1992a) provided the first evidence that infants may implicitly understand simple arithmetic. In one experiment, 5-month-olds were shown a Mickey Mouse doll in a display area. A screen was then raised and blocked the infant's view of the doll. Next, the infant watched the experimenter place a second doll behind the screen. The screen was lowered and showed either one or two dolls. Infants tend to look longer at unexpected events (but see Cohen & Marks,

2002). Thus, if infants are aware that adding a doll to the original doll will result in more dolls, then, when the screen is lowered, they should look longer at one doll than at two doll displays. This is exactly the pattern that was found. Another procedure involved subtracting one doll from a set of two dolls and, again, infants looked longer at the unexpected (two dolls) than expected (one doll) outcome. The combination of results was interpreted as evidence that infants have an implicit understanding of imprecise addition and subtraction; they understand addition increases quantity and subtraction decreases quantity. Another experiment suggested infants may also have an implicit understanding of "precise" addition; specifically, that one item + one item = exactly two items.

Wynn's (1992a) empirical results and the claim they provide evidence for arithmetical competencies in infancy have been the focus of intense scientific study and theoretical debate (Carey, 2002; Cohen, 2002; Cohen & Marks, 2002; Kobayashi, Hiraki, Mugitani, & Hasegawa, 2004; Koechlin, Dehaene, & Mehler, 1997; McCrink & Wynn, 2004; Simon, Hespos, & Rochat, 1995; Uller, Carey, Huntley-Fenner, & Klatt 1999; Wakeley, Rivera, & Langer, 2000; Wynn, 1995, 2000, 2002; Wynn & Chiang, 1998). The findings for imprecise addition and (or) subtraction have been replicated several times (Cohen & Marks, 2002; Simon et al., 1995; Wynn & Chiang, 1998). In an innovative cross-modality assessment, Kobayashi et al., demonstrated that 5-month-olds can add one object and one tone or one object and two tones. In contrast, Koechlin et al., replicated Wynn's finding for imprecise subtraction but not addition, and Wakeley et al. failed to replicate the findings for imprecise or precise addition or subtraction. Wakeley et al. suggested that if infants do have implicit knowledge of arithmetic, then it is expressed only under some conditions. Other scientists have suggested that the phenomenon, that is, infants' looking patterns described in Wynn's original study, is robust but due to factors other than arithmetic competency (Cohen & Marks, 2002; Simon et al., 1995).

**Representational Mechanisms.**    The proposed perceptual and cognitive mechanisms that underlie infants' performance on the tasks previously described range from a system that encodes and can operate on abstract representations of numerosity (Starkey et al., 1990; Wynn, 1995) to mechanisms that result in performance that appears to be based on an implicit understanding of numerosity but in fact tap systems that are designed for other purposes. Included among these alternatives are mechanisms that function for object identification and individuation (Simon et al., 1995), and mechanisms that are sensitive to the contour and length of the presented objects (Clearfield & Mix, 1999; Feigenson, Carey, & Spelke, 2002). Cohen and Marks (2002) argued that an attentional preference for an optimal mix of familiarity and complexity explained Wynn's (1992a) findings. To illustrate, in Wynn's original 1 + 1 = 2 manipulation, the expected result is two dolls and the unexpected result is one doll. However, the unexpected result is also the original condition—one doll—viewed by the infants, and thus their looking preference might have been based on familiarity, not an expectation of two dolls. Kobayashi et al.'s (2004) cross-modality study controlled for familiarity and still provided evidence that infants can add small quantities, an object and one or two tones.

Figure 18.1 provides an illustration of the mechanisms that have been proposed as potentially underlying infants' performance on quantitative tasks. On the basis of Meck's and Church's (1983) studies of the numerosity and time-estimation skills in animals, Gallistel and Gelman (1992) proposed the existence of an innate preverbal counting mechanism in humans. There are two ways in which preverbal counting might operate. The

first is represented by the numerosity accumulator. The gist is that infants have a mechanism that accumulates representations of up to three or four objects, sounds, or events and then compares the accumulated representation (e.g., one, or two) to abstract and inherent knowledge of the numerosity of one, two, three, and perhaps four items. The second is an analog mechanism that can represent various types of magnitudes (e.g., surface area), including numerosities of any size, but with increases in magnitude size the precision of the estimate decreases. Object file and object representation mechanisms (e.g., Kahneman, Treisman, & Gibbs, 1992) function to individuate and represent whole objects rather than numerosity. The object file generates a marker for each object in the display, whereas the object representation mechanism adds object-specific information (e.g., area, contours) to each object marker. The number of object markers that can be simultaneously held in short-term memory is three or four (Trick, 1992). Thus, these object individuation mechanisms incidentally provide numerical information.

Starkey et al. (1990), Wynn (1992a, 1995), and Gallistel and Gelman (1992), among others (e.g., Spelke, 2000), have interpreted the numerosity, ordinality, and arithmetic performance of infants as being consistent with the existence of a numerosity accumulator and an analog magnitude mechanism that has evolved specifically to represent quantity. Simon et al. (1995) and Newcombe (2002), among others (e.g., Uller et al., 1999), have argued that the same pattern of results can be explained by the object file or object representation mechanisms. A set of one item can be discriminated from a set of two items because object files representing the two sets look different, not because of an inherent understanding of the "oneness" and "twoness" of the sets. It is also possible the object file systems evolved for individuating whole objects, and that numerosity mechanisms evolved later but are dependent on information generated by the object file mechanisms; specifically, the object file information might be fed into the numerosity accumulator. The best evidence to date for an independent numerosity accumulator comes from Kobayashi et al.'s (2004) cross-modality results, given that the tones were not likely to have been represented by object file mechanisms.

At this point, a definitive conclusion cannot be drawn regarding these alternative mechanisms. Whatever mechanisms may be operating, it is clear that infants can make discriminations based on the numerosity of sets of

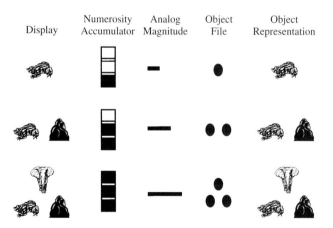

| Display | Numerosity Accumulator | Analog Magnitude | Object File | Object Representation |

**Figure 18.1** Potential mechanisms underlying infants' and young children's implicit understanding of the number. The numerosity accumulator exactly represents the number of one to three or four objects. The analog magnitude mechanism represents quantity, including number and area, but inexactly. The object file mechanism differentiates from one to three or four objects represented in visual short-term memory, and only incidentally provides information on number. The object representation mechanism is the same as the object file but in addition represents features of each object (e.g., color, shape).

three to four items (Starkey et al., 1990) and can later make simple ordinality judgments (Straus & Curtis, 1984), although their understanding of simple arithmetic is less certain. Spelke's recent studies suggest that infants can also make discriminations among larger sets of items, but only when the sets differ by a magnitude of 2 to 1 (e.g., 16 versus 8; Lipton & Spelke, 2003; Xu & Spelke, 2000). These findings support the existence of an inherent mechanism that represents analog magnitudes, but it is not known if the evolved function of the system is to represent numerosity per se or other forms of magnitude, such as area or distance. A recent neuroimaging study suggests that the brain regions that represent numerical magnitude also represent spatial magnitude (related size of objects) and thus these regions may not be specifically numerical in function (Pinel, Piazza, Le Bihan, & Dehaene, 2004).

### Number and Counting during Preschool

Counting and number-related activities are common in industrialized and traditional societies (Crump, 1990), although the extent and form of formal number-counting systems (e.g., number words) varies considerably from one culture to the next (Gordon, 2004). Saxe studied the representational and counting systems of the Oksapmin, a horticultural society in Papua New Guinea (Saxe, 1981, 1982). Here, counting and numerical representations are mapped onto 27 body parts. "To count as Oksapmins do, one begins with the thumb on one hand and enumerates 27 places around the upper periphery of the body, ending on the little finger of the opposite hand" (Saxe, 1982, pp. 159–160). This system is used not only for counting, but also for representing ordinal position and for making basic measurements. In many cultures, there are common activities, such as parent-child play, during the preschool years and childhood that facilitate children's understanding of counting and number, and their learning the specific representational systems (e.g., number words) of the culture (Saxe, Guberman, & Gearhart, 1987; Zaslavsky, 1973).

Although these patterns suggest that children's interest in understanding the rudiments of counting and number may be inherent (Geary, 1995; R. Gelman & Gallistel, 1978), achieving a mature understanding of these concepts and their use in culturally appropriate ways spans extends into early childhood (Fuson, 1988; Piaget, 1965). In the following sections, I provide an overview of how children's understanding of number and counting skills change during the preschool years.

These changes include the acquisition of number concepts, number words, counting procedures, and an understanding of the use of numbers and counting for representing cardinality, ordinality, and for making measurements.

**Number Concepts.**   To use number knowledge explicitly (e.g., to count) and to extend number concepts beyond small quantities, children must map their culture's number words and other representational systems (e.g., Arabic numerals) onto the numerosity and analog magnitude systems (Spelke, 2000). The process begins sometime between 2 and 3 years when children begin to use number words during the act of counting (R. Gelman & Gallistel, 1978), although young children do not always use the standard order of word tags (one, two, three). The child might state "three, five" to count two items, and "three, five, six" to count three items. Despite these apparent errors, this pattern has two important aspects; each number word is used only once during each count, and the sequence is stable across counted sets. For children who show this type of pattern, the implication is they implicitly understand that different number words represent different quantities and that the sequence with which the words are stated is important (R. Gelman & Gallistel, 1978). Many children as young as 2.5 years also understand that number words are different from other descriptive words. When children are asked to count a row of three red toy soldiers, they often use number words to count the set. The children understand that red describes an attribute of the counted items, but the number assigned to each soldier does not describe an attribute of the soldier but somehow refers to the collection of soldiers (Markman, 1979).

R. Gelman and Gallistel (1978; Gallistel & Gelman, 1992) argued regularities in the use of counting and number words emerge because children implicitly and automatically map counting onto representations of quantity, although the mechanisms that support this mapping are not fully understood (Sarnecka & Gelman, 2004). In any case, most 2-year-olds have not yet mapped specific quantities onto specific number words (Wynn, 1992b). Many 2.5-year-olds can discriminate four-item sets from three-item sets, and often know that the Arabic numeral 4 represents more than the numeral 3 (Bullock & Gelman, 1977), but might not be able to correctly label the sets as containing "four" and "three" items, respectively. Wynn argued that it requires as long as a year of counting experience, from 2 to 3 years of age, for children to begin to associate specific number words with their mental representations of specific quantities and then to use this knowledge in counting tasks. It is likely that many 3-year-olds are beginning to associate specific number words with specific quantities, but this knowledge appears to extend only to the quantities that can be represented by the numerosity accumulator or object file systems.

The learning of specific quantities beyond four and mapping number words onto the representations of these quantities is a difficult task, because the analog magnitude system that must be adapted for this purpose functions to represent general amounts, not specific quantities (Gallistel & Gelman, 1992). Children's conception of the quantities represented by larger numbers is thus dependent to an important degree on their learning of the standard counting sequence (1, 2, 3, . . .) and properties of this sequence (e.g., successive number words represent an increase of exactly one). The conception of number also appears to be related to an ability to generate a mental number line (Dehaene, 1997), which involves mapping the Arabic numeral sequence onto the analog magnitude system. However, the ability to use the mental number line to represent specific quantities only emerges with formal schooling (Siegler & Opfer, 2003), as described in the "Arithmetic in School" section.

**Number Words.**   Learning the culture's number words is an essential step in children's mathematical development. As noted, knowledge of the sequence of number words enables children to develop more precise representations of numbers greater than three or four, and contributes to knowledge of cardinality and ordinality described in the next section (Fuson, 1988; R. Gelman & Gallistel, 1978; Wynn, 1990). Most 3- to 4-year-olds know the correct sequence of number words from one to ten (Fuson, 1988; Siegler & Robinson, 1982). For children speaking most European-derived languages, including English, learning number words greater than ten is difficult (Fuson & Kwon, 1991; Miller & Stigler, 1987). This is because the number words for values up to the hundreds are often irregular; they do not map onto the underlying base-10 structure of the number system. For example, *twelve* is another number word in a continuous string of number words. Its special status—repetition of basic unit values—within the base-10 system is not evident from the

word itself. These irregularities slow the learning of number words and the understanding of the corresponding quantity the word represents, and result in word tagging errors, such as writing 51 when hearing 15 (Ginsburg, 1977).

Many of these confusions are avoided in East Asian languages, because of a direct one-to-one relation between number words greater than ten and the underlying base-10 values represented by the words (Fuson & Kwon, 1991; I. Miura, Kim, Chang, & Okamoto, 1988; I. Miura, Okamoto, Kim, Steere, & Fayol, 1993). The Chinese word for twelve is translated as "ten two." Using ten two to represent 12 has two advantages. First, children do not need to memorize additional word tags, such as eleven and twelve. Second, the fact that twelve is composed of a single tens value and two units values is obvious. As might be expected, the irregular structure of European-derived number words is not associated with cross-national differences in children's learning of number words less than 10, their ability to solve simple arithmetical word problems that involve manipulating quantities less than 10, or their understanding of the counting principles to be described (Miller, Smith, Zhu, & Zhang, 1995). However, differences in the structure of number words between 10 and 100 appear to contribute to later cross-national differences in ease of learning the base-10 structure of the number system and to use associated arithmetical procedures and problem-solving strategies (Geary, Bow-Thomas, Liu, & Siegler, 1996; Fuson & Kwon, 1992a).

**Counting Procedures and Errors.**   The conceptual principles that guide counting behavior emerge during the preschool years, but it is debated as to whether these principles have an inherent basis (R. Gelman & Gallistel, 1978), or emerge through observation of the counting behavior of others and regularities in this behavior (Briars & Siegler, 1984; Fuson, 1988). And, of course, counting principles may emerge from a combination of inherent constraints and counting experience (Geary, 1995; R. Gelman, 1990). R. Gelman and Gallistel proposed children's counting behavior is guided by five inherent and implicit principles that mature during the preschool years. During those years, children's counting behavior and their description of counting suggest knowledge of these implicit rules can become more explicit and the application of these principles during the act of counting becomes more stable and accurate.

The principles are one-one correspondence (one and only one word tag, e.g., "one," "two," is assigned to each counted object); stable order (the order of the word tags must be invariant across counted sets); cardinality (the value of the final word tag represents the quantity of items in the counted set); abstraction (objects of any kind can be collected together and counted); and order-irrelevance (items within a given set can be tagged in any sequence). The principles of one-one correspondence, stable order, and cardinality define the initial "how to count" rules, which, in turn, provide the skeletal structure for children's emerging knowledge of counting (R. Gelman & Meck, 1983).

Children make inductions about the basic characteristics of counting by observing standard counting behavior and associated outcomes (Briars & Siegler, 1984; Fuson, 1988). These inductions may elaborate and add to R. Gelman and Gallistel's (1978) counting rules. One result is a belief that certain unessential features of counting are essential. These unessential features include standard direction (counting must start at one of the end points of a set of objects), and adjacency. The latter is the incorrect belief that items must be counted consecutively and from one contiguous item to the next; "jumping around" during the act of counting results in an incorrect count. By 5 years of age, many children know most of the essential features of counting described by R. Gelman and Gallistel but also believe that adjacency and start at an end are essential features of counting. The latter beliefs indicate that young children's understanding of counting is influenced by observation of standard counting procedures and is not fully mature.

An implicit conceptual understanding of counting does not mean that children will not make counting errors; they do. Fuson (1988) has extensively documented the many different types of error committed by children while they count. A common error involves the child pointing to each item once, but speaking two or more word tags with each point. Sometimes children correctly assign one word tag to each counted object, but speak additional word tags, without pointing, in between counted objects. Sometimes children point and tag items with each syllable of a number word, and at other times they might tag and point to each item two or more times. Despite all the different types of errors that can be made during the act of counting, kindergarten children are typically proficient counters, especially for smaller set sizes.

**Cardinality and Ordinality.**    Although an implicit understanding of cardinality and ordinality appears to emerge before children learn the sequence of number words (Bermejo, 1996; Brainerd, 1979; Brannon & Van de Walle, 2001; R. Cooper, 1984; Huntley-Fenner & Cannon, 2000; Ta'ir, Brezner, & Ariel, 1997; Wynn, 1990, 1992b), the mapping of these concepts onto the counting sequence is an essential step in the development of arithmetical competencies. Children must learn that the number word assigned to the last counted object can be used to represent the total number of counted objects—*cardinality*—and that successive number words represent successively larger quantities—*ordinality.*

One way to assess children's understanding of cardinality is to ask them to count their fingers and then ask "how many fingers do you have?" Children who do not understand the significance of the last word tag, *five* in this example, will recount their fingers, rather than restating "five" (Fuson, 1991). Although some 3- and many 4- and 5-year-olds perform well on such cardinality tasks suggesting a developing sense of the concept, most preschoolers' understanding of cardinality is not yet mature. Their performance is inconsistent and often influenced by factors other than cardinality. For small set sizes (e.g., less then 10), most children have a good grasp of cardinal value by 5 years (Bermejo, 1996; Freeman, Antonucci, & Lewis, 2000), but generalization to larger sets and a consistent focus on cardinality information over other information (e.g., perceptual cues) may not emerge for several more years (Piaget, 1965).

As with infants, the demonstration of preschool children's knowledge of ordinal relationships requires special techniques. Bullock and Gelman (1977) assessed the ordinal knowledge of 2- to 5-year-old children, by using a "magic" game. In the first of two phases, the children were shown two plates of toys, one contained a single toy animal and the other contained two toy animals. The children were either told that the two-toy plate was the winner (more condition) or that the one-toy plate was the winner (less condition). The child was then shown a series of one- and two-toy plates, and asked to pick the winner. In Phase II, "the experimenter surreptitiously added one animal to the two-toy plate and three animals to the one-toy plate" (p. 429). The critical question was whether the children would choose the winner based on the relation, that is, more or less, that was reinforced in the first phase. The majority of 3- and 4-year-olds responded based on the relational information, but less than 50% of the 2-year-olds did. When the memory demands of the task were reduced, more than 90% of the 2 year olds responded based on the relational information. More recent studies suggest that some 2-year-olds can make ordinal judgments comparing sets as high as five objects versus six objects, independent of perceptual factors (e.g., total surface area of the objects) or verbal counting (Brannon & Van de Walle, 2001; Huntley-Fenner & Cannon, 2000).

These results suggest children as young as 2 years may have an understanding of ordinal relationships that extend to larger set sizes than found in the infancy studies. The mechanisms underlying this knowledge are not yet known, but Huntley-Fenner and Cannon (2000) argued that the analog magnitude mechanism shown in Figure 18.1 is the source of preschool children's ordinality judgments. This is a reasonable conclusion, given that knowledge of ordinal relations for larger numbers is based on knowledge of the counting-word sequence and that this sequence is likely mapped onto the analog system (Gallistel & Gelman, 1992).

### Arithmetic during Preschool

As I overview in the first section, research on preschooler's emerging arithmetic skills has focused on their implicit understanding of the effects of addition and subtraction on number; their implicit understanding of some properties of arithmetic (e.g., that addition and subtraction are inverse operations); and their integration of counting and arithmetic knowledge to develop procedures for solving formal arithmetic problems (e.g., $3 + 2 = ?$). As I note in the second section, there is vigorous debate regarding the relation between these emerging skills and the representational mechanisms that were described in Figure 18.1.

**Arithmetical Competencies.** Some of the earliest evidence of preschoolers' implicit knowledge of arithmetic was provided by Starkey (1992; see also Sophian & Adams, 1987; Starkey & Gelman, 1982). Here, a searchbox task was designed to determine if 1.5- to 4-year-olds understand how addition and subtraction affects numerosity without using verbal counting. The searchbox "consisted of a lidded box with an opening in its top, a false floor, and a hidden trap-door in its back. This opening in the top of the box was covered by pieces of elastic fabric such that a person's hand could be inserted through pieces of the fabric and into the chamber of the searchbox without visually revealing the chamber's contents" (Starkey, 1992, p. 102). In the first of

two experiments, children placed between one and five table-tennis balls, one at a time, into the searchbox. Immediately after the child placed the last ball, she was told to take out all the balls. An assistant had removed the balls and then replaced them one at a time, as the child searched for the balls. If a child placed three balls in the searchbox and then stopped searching once three balls were removed, then it could be argued that this child was able to represent and remember the number of balls deposited, and used this representation to guide the search. The results showed that 2-year-olds can mentally represent and remember numerosities of one, two, and sometimes three; 2.5-year-olds can represent and remember numerosities up to and including three; and 3- to 3.5-year-olds can sometimes represent numerosities as high as four.

The second experiment addressed whether the children could add or subtract from these quantities without verbally counting. The same general procedure was followed, except that once all the original balls were placed in the searchbox, the experimenter placed an additional 1 to 3 balls in the box, or removed from 1 to 3 balls. If children understand the effect of addition, then they should search for more balls than they originally placed in the searchbox, or for subtraction they should stop searching before this point. Nearly all 2- to 4-year-olds responded in this manner, as did many, but not all, of the 1.5-year-olds. Examination of the accuracy data indicated that many of the 1.5-year-olds were accurate for addition and subtraction with sums or minuends (the first number in a subtraction problem) less than or equal to two (e.g., $1 + 1$ or $2 - 1$), but were not accurate for problems with larger numbers. Most 2-year-olds were accurate with values up to and including three (e.g., $2 + 1$), and there was no indication (e.g., vocalizing number words) they used verbal counting to solve the problems. None of the children were accurate with sums or minuends of four or five.

Using a different form of nonverbal calculation task, Huttenlocher, Jordan, and Levine (1994) found that 2- to 2.5-year-olds understand that addition increases quantity and subtraction decreases it, but only a small percentage of them could solve simple 1 object + 1 object or 2 objects – 1 object problems. The ability to calculate exact answers improved for 2.5- to 3-year-olds such that more than 50% of them could mentally perform simple additions ($1 + 1$) and subtractions ($2 - 1$) of objects. Some 4-year-olds correctly solved nonverbal problems that involved 4 objects + 1 object, or 4 objects – 3 objects.

Klein and Bisanz (2000) used the same procedure to assess 4-year-olds but also administered three-step problems (e.g., 2 objects + 1 object − 1 object) and assessed potential predictors of problem difficulty as measured by error rate. The three-step problems assessed children's understanding of the inverse relation between addition and subtraction; 5 objects − 1 object + 1 object = 5 objects, because 1 object − 1 object results in no change in quantity. The indices of problem difficulty included the value of numbers in the problem, the answer, and the largest of these numbers, which was termed representational set size. So, for 5 objects + 1 object − 1 object, the representational set size is five, whereas for 3 + 1, the size is four. Representational set size provided an index of the working memory demands of the problem and thus provided an estimate of the capacity of the underlying mechanism for representing object sets (e.g., object file or numerosity accumulator).

The results revealed that error rates increased with increases in representational set size. Holding an object file or numerosity-accumulator file of four or five items in working memory and adding or subtracting from this representation was more difficult than holding an object file or numerosity-accumulator file of two or three in working memory. Thus, errors are due to a lack of ability to apply arithmetical knowledge to larger sets or (and) to working memory failures. The strategies children used to solve the inversion problems suggested that some of these children had a nascent and implicit understanding of the associative property of addition [(a + b) − c = a + (b − c)], and the inverse relation between addition and subtraction. Knowledge of the former was inferred "when children overtly subtracted the $c$ term from the $a$ term and then added the $b$ term, thus transforming $(a + b) − c$ to $(a − c) + b$" (Klein & Bisanz, 2000, p. 110).

Vilette (2002) administered a variant of Wynn's (1992a) task to 2.5-, 3.5-, and 4.5-year-olds; the problems involved 2 + 1, 3 − 1, and an inversion problem, 2 + 1 − 1. For these latter problems, the children first saw two dolls on a puppet theater stage. Next, a screen rotated up and the experimenter placed another doll, in full view of the child, behind the screen, and then placed his hand back behind the screen and removed a doll. The screen was then lowered and revealed two (expected) or three (unexpected) dolls. The children were instructed to respond "normal" (correct) to the expected result and "not normal" to the unexpected result. As a group, 2.5-year-olds solved 64% of the 1 + 1 problems, but failed

nearly all the 3 − 1 and inversion problems. The 4.5-year-olds solved all the problems with greater than 90% accuracy, in keeping with Klein's and Bisanz's (2000) findings that some 4-year-olds have an implicit understanding of the inverse relation between addition and subtraction. The negative findings for younger children need to be interpreted with caution, because poor performance could be due to the working memory demands of the task or to lack of arithmetical knowledge.

In any event, by 4 to 5 years, children have coordinated their counting skills, number concepts, and number words with their implicit arithmetical knowledge. The result is an ability to use number words to solve simple addition and subtraction problems (Baroody & Ginsburg, 1986; Groen & Resnick, 1977; Saxe, 1985; Siegler & Jenkins, 1989). The specific strategies used by children for solving these problems may vary somewhat from one culture to the next, but typically involve the use of concrete objects to aid the counting process. When young children in the United States are presented with verbal problems, such as "how much is 3 + 4," they will typically represent each addend with a corresponding number of objects, and then count all the objects starting with one; counting out three blocks and then four blocks, and then counting all the blocks. If objects are not available, then fingers are often used as a substitute (Siegler & Shrager, 1984). Korean and Japanese children apparently use a similar strategy (Hatano, 1982; Song & Ginsburg, 1987). Somewhat older Oksapmin use an analogous strategy based on their body-part counting system (Saxe, 1982).

**Mechanisms.**  There is debate whether the mechanisms underlying preschoolers' arithmetic competencies are inherently numerical (Butterworth, 1999; Dehaene, 1997; Gallistel & Gelman, 1992; Geary, 1995) or emerge from nonnumerical mechanisms (Houdé, 1997; Huttenlocher et al., 1994; Jordan, Huttenlocher, & Levine, 1992; Vilette, 2002). Inherent mechanisms would involve some combination of the numerosity accumulator and analog magnitude system (Spelke, 2000), with the assumption that the latter automatically results in at least imprecise representations of the quantities being processed (Dehaene, 1997; Gallistel & Gelman, 1992). Integrated with these systems for representing numerosity would be an inherent understanding of at least basic principles of addition (increases quantity) and subtraction (decreases quantity), and a later integration with counting competencies to provide a procedural system for solving arithmetic problems. These inherent biases are thought to provide the core knowledge that initially guides children's attention to numerical (e.g., seeing a group of objects as sets) and arithmetical (e.g., combining sets of objects) aspects of their experiences. These biases interact with these experiences to flesh out their conceptual knowledge and procedural competencies (Geary, 1995; R. Gelman, 1990). The fleshing out would involve extension of this knowledge and procedures to larger and larger quantities as well as making inductions about regularities in arithmetical processes and outcomes (e.g., inverse relation between addition and subtraction). In contrast, Huttenlocher et al. argued that preschoolers' arithmetical competencies emerge from a combination of a domain-general ability to mentally represent symbols—objects in the object file (as was shown in Figure 18.1)—and general intelligence, whereby children learn to manipulate representations of these symbols based on the rules of arithmetic they induce by engaging in arithmetical activities.

## Arithmetic in School

As children move into formal schooling, the breadth and complexity of the mathematics they are expected to learn increases substantially. The task of understanding children's development in these areas has become daunting, and our understanding of this development is thus only in the beginning stages. In the first section, I make a distinction between potentially inherent and culturally-universal quantitative competencies and culturally-specific and school-dependent competencies, which I return to in "Mechanisms of Change." In the remaining sections, I provide an overview of children's conceptual knowledge of arithmetic in the elementary school years; how children solve formal arithmetic problems (e.g., $16 - 7$); and the processes involved in solving word problems.

### Primary and Secondary Competencies

Most of the competencies reviewed in the "Early Quantitative Abilities" section emerge with little if any instruction, and some may be in place in the first days or weeks of life. As far as we know, most of these competencies are found across human cultures, and many are evident in other species of primate (Beran & Beran, 2004; Boysen & Berntson, 1989; Brannon & Terrace, 1998; Gordon, 2004; Hauser et al., 2000) and in at least

a few nonmammalian species (Lyon, 2003; Pepperberg, 1987). The combination of early emergence, cross-cultural ubiquity, and similar competencies in other species is consistent with the position that some of these competencies are inherent (Geary, 1995, R. Gelman, 1990; R. Gelman & Gallistel, 1978), no matter whether the evolved function is specifically quantitative. In contrast, much of the research on older children's development is focused on school-taught mathematics. It is thus useful to distinguish between inherent and school-taught competencies, because it is likely that some of the mechanisms involved in their acquisition differ, as discussed in the "Mechanisms of Change" section. Geary (1994, 1995; see also Rozin, 1976) referred to inherent forms of cognition, such as language and early quantitative competencies, as *biologically primary abilities,* and skills that build on these abilities but are principally cultural inventions, such base-10 arithmetic, as *biologically secondary abilities.*

### Conceptual Knowledge

**Properties of Arithmetic.**    The commutativity and associativity properties of addition and multiplication have been understood by mathematicians since the time of the ancient Greeks. The commutativity property concerns the addition or multiplication of two numbers and states that the order in which the numbers are added or multiplied does not affect the sum or product ($a + b = b + a$; $a \times b = b \times a$). The associativity property concerns the addition or multiplication of three numbers and again states that the order in which the numbers are added or multiplied does not affect the sum or product [$(a + b) + c = a + (b + c)$; $(a \times b) \times c = a \times (b \times c)$]. Both commutativity and associativity involve the decomposition (e.g., of the sum) and recombination (e.g., addition) of number sets; specifically, an understanding that numbers are sets composed of smaller-valued numbers that can be manipulated in principled ways. Research on children's understanding of these properties has focused largely on addition and commutativity (Baroody, Ginsburg, & Waxman, 1983; Resnick, 1992), although some research has also been conducted on children's understanding of associativity (Canobi, Reeve, & Pattison, 1998, 2002).

One approach has been to study when and how children acquire an understanding of commutativity and associativity as related to school-taught arithmetic (Baroody et al., 1983). The other approach has focused on the more basic and potentially biologically primary numerical and relational knowledge that allows children to later understand commutativity in formal arithmetical contexts (R. Gelman & Gallistel, 1978; Resnick, 1992; Sophian, Harley, & Martin, 1995). The latter approach meshes with the ability of infants and preschool children to mentally represent and manipulate sets of small quantities of objects.

Resnick (1992) proposed that aspects of these competencies provide the foundational knowledge for children's emerging understanding of commutativity as an arithmetical principle. The first conceptual step toward building an explicit understanding of commutativity is prenumerical and emerges as children physically combine sets of objects. One example would involve the physical merging of sets of toy cars and sets of toy trucks, and the understanding (whether inherent or induced) that the same group of cars and trucks is obtained whether the cars are added to the trucks or the trucks are added to the cars. The next step in Resnick's model involves mapping specific quantities onto this knowledge, as in understanding that 5 cars + 3 trucks = 3 trucks + 5 cars. At this step, children only understand commutativity with the addition of sets of physical objects. The third step involves replacing physical sets with numerals, as in knowing that 5 + 3 = 3 + 5, and the final step is formal knowledge of commutativity as an arithmetical principle, that is, understanding a + b = b + a. Empirical studies of children's emerging knowledge of commutativity are consistent with some but not all aspects of Resnick's model (Baroody, Wilkins, & Tiilikainen, 2003).

An implicit understanding that sets of physical objects can be decomposed and recombined emerges at about 4 years of age (Canobi et al., 2002; Klein & Bisanz, 2000; Sophian & McCorgray, 1994; Sophian et al., 1995). Most children of this age understand, for instance, that the group of toy vehicles includes smaller subsets of cars and trucks. Between 4 and 5 years, an implicit understanding of commutativity as related to Resnick's (1992) second step is evident for many children (Canobi et al., 2002; Sophian et al., 1995). As an example, Canobi et al. presented children with two different colored containers that held a known number of pieces of candy. The two containers were then given in varying orders to two toy bears and the children were asked to determine if the bears had the same number of candy pieces. The task was to determine if, for example, a container of 3 candies + a container of 4 candies was equal to a container of 4 candies + a container of 3 can-

dies, and was therefore a commutativity problem. In a variant of this task, a third set of candies was added to one of the two containers. For one trial, four green candies were poured into a container of three red candies, a manipulation that is analogous to (4 + 3). When presented with the second container of candy, the task represented a physical associativity problem; (a container of 3 candies + 4 candies) + a container of 4 candies. In keeping with Resnick's (1992) model, most of the 4-year-olds implicitly understood commutativity with these physical sets (see also Sophian et al., 1995), but many of them did not grasp the concept of associativity (Canobi et al., 2002).

Inconsistent with Resnick's (1992) model was the finding that performance on the commutativity task was not well integrated with their knowledge of addition. In other words, many of the children solved the task correctly because both bears received a *collection* of red candies and a *collection* of green candies and they understood that the order in which the bears received the containers of candy did not matter. Many of the children did not, however, approach the task as the addition of specific quantities.

Baroody et al. (1983) assessed children's understanding of commutativity as expressed during the actual solving of addition problems in a formal context (e.g., 3 + 4 = 4 + 3)—Resnick's third step—in first, second, and third graders. The children were presented with a series of formal addition problems, in the context of a game. Across some of the trials, the same addends were presented but with their positions reversed. For example, the children were asked to solve 13 + 6 on one trial and 6 + 13 on the next trial. If the children understood that addition was commutative, then they might count "thirteen, fourteen, . . . nineteen" to solve 13 + 6, but then state, without counting, "19" for 6 + 13, and argue "it has the same numbers, it's always the same answer" (p. 160). In this study, 72% of the first graders, and 83% of the second and third graders consistently showed this type of pattern. Using this and a related task, Baroody and Gannon (1984) demonstrated that about 40% of kindergartners recognized commutative relations across formal addition problems. For these kindergarten children and the first graders in the Baroody et al. study, commutative relations were implicitly understood before formal instruction on the topic. Many of the older children explicitly understood that, for example, 3 + 2 = 2 + 3, but it is not clear when and under what conditions (e.g., whether formal instruction is needed) children come to explicitly understand commutativity as a formal arithmetic principle; that a + b = b + a.

With respect to associativity, several studies by Canobi and her colleagues (Canobi et al., 1998, 2002) suggest that some kindergarten children recognize associative relations when presented with sets of physical objects, as described, and many first and second graders implicitly understand associative relations when they are presented as addition problems. These studies are also clear in demonstrating that an implicit understanding of associativity does not emerge until after children implicitly understand commutativity, suggesting that implicit knowledge of the latter is the foundation for implicitly understanding the former.

In summary, the conceptual foundation for commutativity emerges from or is reflected in children's manipulation of physical collections of objects and either an inherent or induced understanding that the order in which sets of objects are combined to form a larger collection is irrelevant (R. Gelman & Gallistel, 1978; Resnick, 1992). When presented with sets of physical collections that conform to commutativity, 4- to 5-year-olds recognize the equivalence; that is, they implicitly understand commutativity but they do not explicitly understand commutativity as a formal principle nor do all of the children implicitly understand that commutativity is related to addition at all. Some kindergarteners and most first graders recognize commutative relations in an addition context, but it is not clear when children explicitly understand commutativity as a formal arithmetical principle. Recognition of associative relations with physical sets emerges in some children in kindergarten but only for children who implicitly understand commutativity; an implicit understanding of associativity in an addition context is found for many first and second graders, but it is not known when and under what conditions children come to explicitly understand associativity as a formal arithmetical principle. Even less is known about children's implicit and explicit knowledge of commutativity and associativity as related to multiplication.

**Base-10 Knowledge.** The Hindu-Arabic base-10 system is foundational to modern arithmetic, and thus knowledge of this system is a crucial component of children's developing mathematical competencies. As an example, children's understanding of the conceptual meaning of spoken and written multidigit numerals,

among other features of arithmetic, is dependent on knowledge of the base-10 system (Blöte, Klein, & Beishuizen, 2000; Fuson & Kwon, 1992a). The word *twenty-three* does not simply refer to a collection of 23 objects, it also represents two sets of ten and a set of three unit values. Similarly, the position of the individual numerals (e.g., 1, 2, 3 . . .) in multidigit numerals has a specific mathematical meaning, such that the "2" in "23" represents two sets of 10. Without an appreciation of these features of the base-10 system, children's conceptual understanding of modern arithmetic is compromised.

The base-10 system is almost certainly a biologically secondary competency, the learning of which is not predicted to come easily to children (Geary, 1995, 2002). The more inherent mechanisms that might support learning of the base-10 system are discussed in the "Mechanisms of Change" section. For now, consider that studies conducted in the United States have repeatedly demonstrated that many elementary-school children do not fully understand the base-10 structure of multidigit written numerals (e.g., understanding the positional meaning of the numeral) or number words (Fuson, 1990; Geary, 1994), and thus are unable to effectively use this system when attempting to solve complex arithmetic problems (Fuson & Kwon, 1992a). The situation is similar, though perhaps less extreme, in many European nations (I. Miura et al., 1993). Many of these children have at least an implicit understanding that number-word sequences can be repeated (e.g., counting from 1 to 10 in different contexts) and can of course learn the base-10 system and how to use it in their problem solving. Nonetheless, it appears that many children require instructional techniques that explicitly focus on the specifics of the repeating decade structure of the base-10 system and that clarify often confusing features of the associated notational system (Fuson & Briars, 1990; Varelas & Becker, 1997). An example of the latter is the fact that sometimes 2 represents two units; other times it represents two tens; and still other times it represents two hundreds (Varelas & Becker, 1997).

East Asian students, in contrast, tend to have a better grasp of the base-10 system. I. Miura and her colleagues (I. Miura et al., 1988, 1993) provided evidence supporting their prediction that the earlier described transparent nature of East Asian number words (e.g., "two ten three" instead of "twenty three") facilitates East Asian children's understanding of the structure of the base-10 system and makes it easier to teach in school (but see Towse & Saxton, 1997). Using a design that enabled the separation of the influence of age and schooling on quantitative and arithmetical competencies, Naito and H. Miura (2001) demonstrated that Japanese children's understanding of the base-10 structure of numerals and their ability to use this knowledge to solve arithmetic problems was largely related to schooling. Because all the children had an advantage of transparent number words, the results suggest teacher-guided instruction on base-10 concepts also facilitates their acquisition (Fuson & Briars, 1990; Varelas & Becker, 1997).

**Fractions.** Fractions are ratios (or part-whole relations) of two or more values and an essential component of arithmetic. They can be represented as proper fractions (e.g., $\frac{1}{2}$, $\frac{1}{3}$, $\frac{7}{8}$), mixed numbers (e.g., $2\frac{1}{3}$, $6\frac{2}{3}$), or in decimal form (e.g., 0.5), although they are often represented pictorially during early instruction. As with the base-10 system, research in this area has focused on children's conceptual understanding of fractions, their procedural skills, as in multiplying fractions (Clements & Del Campo, 1990; Hecht, 1998; Hecht, Close, & Santisi, 2003), and the mechanisms that influence the acquisition of these competencies (I. Miura, Okamoto, Vlahovic-Stetic, Kim, & Han, 1999; Rittle-Johnson, Siegler, & Alibali, 2001). When used in a formal mathematical context (e.g., as a decimal), fractions are biologically secondary, although children's experiences with and understanding of part/whole relations among sets of physical objects, such as receiving $\frac{1}{2}$ of a cookie or having to share one of their two toys, may contribute to a nascent understanding of simple ratios (Mix, Levine, & Huttenlocher, 1999).

In a study of implicit knowledge of simple part-whole relations, Mix et al. (1999) administered a nonverbal task that assessed children's ability to mentally represent and manipulate $\frac{1}{4}$ segments of a whole circle, and demonstrated that many 4-year-olds recognize fractional manipulations. For example, if $\frac{3}{4}$ of a circle was placed under a mat and $\frac{1}{4}$ of the circle was removed, the children recognized that $\frac{1}{2}$ of a circle remained under the mat. However, it was not until 6 years when children began to understand manipulations that were analogous to mixed numbers; for instance, placing $1\frac{3}{4}$ circles under the mat and removing $\frac{1}{2}$ a circle. The results suggest that about the time children begin to show an understanding of part-whole relations in other contexts, as described earlier (Resnick, 1992; Sophian et al., 1995),

they demonstrate a rudimentary understanding of fractional relations. Further, Mix et al., argued these results contradicted predictions based on the numerosity and analog magnitude mechanisms shown in Figure 18.1. This is because R. Gelman (1991) and Wynn (1995) argued these mechanisms only represent whole quantities, and their operation should in fact interfere with children's ability to represent fractions. In this view, fractional representations such as $\frac{1}{4}$ of a circle can only be understood in terms of discrete numbers, such as 1 and 4, and it is possible that the children in the Mix et al. study represented the $\frac{1}{4}$ sections of the circles as single units and not as parts of a whole. At this point, the mechanisms underlying children's intuitive understanding of simple fractions, as assessed by Mix et al., remain to be resolved.

Nonetheless, children have considerable difficulty in learning the formal, biologically secondary conceptual and procedural aspects of fractions. During the initial learning of the formal features, such as the meaning of the numerator/denominator notational system, most children treat fractions in terms of their knowledge of counting and arithmetic (Gallistel & Gelman, 1992). A common error when asked to solve, for example, $\frac{1}{2} + \frac{1}{4}$ is to add the numerators and denominators, yielding an answer of $\frac{2}{6}$ instead of $\frac{3}{4}$. As another example, elementary-school children often will conclude that since 3 > 2, $\frac{1}{3} > \frac{1}{2}$. The names for fractions may also influence children's early conceptual understanding. In East Asian languages, the part-whole relation of fractions is reflected in the corresponding names; "one-fourth" is "of four parts, one" in Korean. I. Miura et al. (1999) showed these differences in word structure result in East Asian children grasping the part-whole relations represented by simple fractions (e.g., $\frac{1}{2}$, $\frac{1}{4}$) before formal instruction (in first and second grade) and before children whose native language does not have transparent word names for fractions (Croatian and English in this study). Paik and Mix (2003) demonstrated that first- and second-grade children in the United States perform as well as or better than the same-grade Korean children in the Miura et al. study, when fractions such as $\frac{1}{4}$ were worded as "one of four parts."

Studies of older elementary-school children and middle-school children have focused on the acquisition of computational skills (e.g., to solve $\frac{3}{4} \times \frac{1}{2}$), conceptual understanding (e.g., that $\frac{21}{18} > 1$), and the ability to solve word problems involving fractional quantities (Byrnes & Wasik, 1991; Rittle-Johnson et al., 2001). Hecht (1998) assessed the relation between children's accuracy at recognizing formal procedural rules for fractions (e.g., when multiplying, the numerators are multiplied and the denominators are multiplied), their conceptual understanding of fractions (e.g., of part-whole relations), their basic arithmetic skills and their ability to solve computational fraction problems, word problems that include fractions, and to estimate fractional quantities. Among other findings, the results demonstrated that scores on the procedure-recognition test predicted computational skills (i.e., accuracy in adding, multiplying, and dividing proper and mixed fractions), above and beyond the influence of IQ, reading skills, and conceptual knowledge. And, conceptual knowledge predicted accuracy at solving word problems that involved fractions and especially accuracy in the estimation task, above and beyond these other influences.

In a follow-up study, Hecht et al. (2003) demonstrated the acquisition of conceptual knowledge of fractions and basic arithmetic skills were related to children's working memory capacity and their on-task time in math class. Conceptual knowledge and basic arithmetic skills, in turn, predicted accuracy at solving computational problems involving fractions; conceptual knowledge and working memory predicted accuracy at setting up word problems that included fractions; and conceptual knowledge predicted fraction estimation skills. Rittle-Johnson et al. (2001) demonstrated that children's skill at solving decimal fractions was related to both their procedural and their conceptual knowledge of fractions and that learning procedural and conceptual knowledge occurred iteratively. Good procedural skills predicted gains in conceptual knowledge and vice versa (Sophian, 1997). The mechanism linking procedural and conceptual knowledge appeared to be the children's ability to represent the decimal fraction on a mental number line.

In all, these studies suggest that preschool and early elementary-school children have a rudimentary understanding of simple fractional relationships, but the mechanism underlying this knowledge is not yet known. It might be the case that the ability to visualize simple part-whole relations (e.g., $\frac{1}{2}$ of natural objects that can be decomposed, as in eating an apple) is biologically primary. Difficulties arise when children are introduced to biologically secondary features of fractions, specifically, as formal mathematical principles and as formal procedures that can be used in problem-solving contexts.

A source of difficulty is the misapplication of counting knowledge and arithmetic with whole numbers to fractions. Children's conceptual understanding of fractions and their knowledge of associated procedures emerges slowly, sometimes not at all, during the elementary and middle school years. The mechanisms that contribute to the emergence of these biologically secondary competencies are not fully understood, but involve instruction, working memory, and the bidirectional influences of procedural knowledge on the acquisition of conceptual knowledge and conceptual knowledge on the skilled use of procedures.

**Estimation.** Although not a formal content domain, the ability to estimate enables individuals to assess the reasonableness of solutions to mathematical problems and thus it is an important competency within many mathematical domains. Estimation typically involves some type of procedure to generate an approximate answer to a problem when calculation of an exact answer is too difficult or is unnecessary. The study of children's ability to estimate in school-taught domains and the development of these skills has focused on computational arithmetic (Case & Okamoto, 1996; Dowker, 1997, 2003; LeFevre, Greenham, & Waheed, 1993; Lemaire & Lecacheur, 2002b) and the number line (Siegler & Booth, 2004, 2005; Siegler & Opfer, 2003). Studies in both of these areas indicate that the ability to generate reasonable estimates is difficult for children and some adults and only appears with formal schooling.

Dowker (1997, 2003) demonstrated that elementary-school children's ability to generate reasonable estimates to arithmetic problems (e.g., 34 + 45) is linked to their computational skills. More specifically, children can estimate within a zone of partial knowledge that extends just beyond their ability to mentally calculate exact answers. Children who can solve addition problems with sums less than 11 (e.g., 3 + 5) can estimate answers to problems with sums less than about 20 (e.g., 9 + 7), but guess for larger-valued problems (e.g., 13 + 24). Children who can solve multidigit problems without carries (e.g., 13 + 24) can estimate answers to problems of the same magnitude with carries (e.g., 16 + 29), but guess for larger-valued problems (e.g., 598 + 634). Studies of how children and adults estimate have revealed that, as with most cognitive domains (Siegler, 1996), they use a variety of strategies (LeFevre et al., 1993; Lemaire & Lecacheur, 2002b). For younger children, a common strategy for addition is to round the units or decades segments down to the nearest decade or hundreds value and then add, as in 30 + 50 = 80 to estimate 32 + 53, or 200 + 600 = 800 to estimate 213 + 632. Older children and adults use more sophisticated strategies than younger children, and may for instance compensate for the initial rounding to adjust their first estimate. An example would involve adding 10 + 30 = 40 to the initial estimate of 800 for the 213 + 632 problem.

Siegler and his colleagues (Siegler & Booth, 2004; Siegler & Opfer, 2003) have studied how children estimate magnitude on a number line, as in estimating the position of 83 on a 1 to 100 number line. As with arithmetic, young children are not skilled at making these estimates but improve considerably during the elementary school years, and come to use a variety of strategies for making reasonable estimates. The most intriguing finding is that young children's performance suggests their estimates are supported by the analog magnitude mechanism described in the "Early Quantitative Abilities" section. Figure 18.2 provides an illustration of how this mechanism would map onto the number line. The top number line illustrates the values across the first 9 integers as defined by the formal mathematical system. The distance between successive numbers and the quantity represented by this distance are precisely the same at any position in the number line (e.g., 2 3, versus 6 7, or versus 123 124). The bottom number line illustrates perceived distances predicted to result from estimates based on the analog magnitude mechanism (Dehaene, 1997; Gallistel & Gelman, 1992). As magnitude increases, the number line is "compressed" such that distances between smaller-valued integers, such as 2 to 3, are more salient and more easily discriminated than distances associated with larger-valued integers.

When kindergarten children are asked to place numbers on a 1 and 100 number line, they place 10 too far to the right and compress the placement of larger-valued

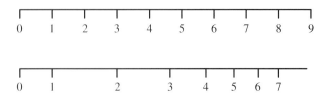

**Figure 18.2**   Spatial representations of number-line magnitudes. The top is the standard mathematical number line, and the bottom is the number line generated when numbers are mapped onto the analog magnitude mechanism.

numbers (Siegler & Booth, 2004), in keeping with the view that their initial understanding of Arabic numerals maps onto the analog magnitude mechanism (Spelke, 2000). By the end of elementary school, most children develop the correct mathematical representation of number placement and the meaning of this placement (Siegler & Opfer, 2003). Dehaene (1997), Gallistel and Gelman (1992), and Siegler and Booth (2005) proposed the analog magnitude mechanism onto which the mathematical number line is mapped is spatial. Indeed, Zorzi, Priftis, and Umilta (2002) found that individuals with injury to the right-parietal cortex showed deficits in spatial orientation and number line estimation. Dehaene et al. (1999) showed adults' computational estimation may also be dependent on a similar spatial system, that is, a mental number line.

### Arithmetic Operations

Research in this area is focused on children's explicit and goal-directed solving of arithmetic problems, as contrasted with an implicit understanding of the effects of addition and subtraction on the quantity of small sets. In the first section, I provide an overview of arithmetical development across cultures and in the second focus on addition to more fully illustrate developmental and schooling-based changes in how children solve arithmetic problems. In the third section, I provide a few examples of how children solve subtraction, multiplication, and division problems (for a more thorough discussion, see Geary, 1994); and in the final section I discuss the relation between conceptual knowledge and procedural skills in arithmetic.

**Arithmetic across Cultures.**   Even before formal instruction, there are important cross-cultural similarities in children's arithmetical development. Within all cultural groups that have been studied and across all four arithmetic operations, development is not simply a matter of switching from a less mature problem-solving strategy to a more adult-like strategy. Rather, at any given time most children use a variety of strategies to solve arithmetic problems (Siegler, 1996). They might count on their fingers to solve one problem, retrieve the answer to the next problem, and count verbally to solve still other problems. Arithmetic development involves a change in the mix of strategies, as well as changes in the accuracy and speed with which each strategy can be executed. A more intriguing finding is that children do not randomly choose one strategy, such as counting to solve one problem, and then retrieval to solve the next problem. Rather, children "often choose among strategies in ways that result in each strategy's being used most often on problems where the strategy's speed and accuracy are advantageous, relative to those of other available procedures" (Siegler, 1989, p. 497).

With instruction, a similar pattern of developmental change in strategy usage emerges for children in different cultures, although the rate with which the mix of strategies changes varies from one culture to the next (Geary et al., 1996; Ginsburg, Posner, & Russell, 1981; Saxe, 1985; Svenson & Sjöberg, 1983). Children in China shift from one favored strategy to the next at a younger age than do children in the United States, whereas the Oksapmin appear to shift at later ages (Geary et al., 1996; Saxe, 1982). These cultural differences appear to reflect differences in the amount of experience with solving arithmetic problems (Stevenson, Lee, Chen, Stigler, Hsu, & Kitamura, 1990), and to a lesser extent the earlier described language differences in number words. As an example, Ilg and Ames (1951) provided a normative study of arithmetic development for American children between the ages of 5 and 9 years. These children received their elementary-school education at a time when basic skills were emphasized much more than today. The types of skills and problem-solving strategies they described for American children at that time was very similar to arithmetic skills we see in present day same-age East Asian children (Fuson & Kwon, 1992b; Geary et al., 1996). Today, however, the arithmetic skills of East Asian children are much better developed than those of their same-age American peers (see also Geary et al., 1997).

**Addition Strategies.** The most thoroughly studied developmental and schooling-based improvement in arithmetical competency is change in the distribution of procedures, or strategies, children use during problem solving (e.g., Ashcraft, 1982; Carpenter & Moser, 1984; Geary, 1994; Lemaire & Siegler, 1995; Siegler & Shrager, 1984). Some 3-year-olds can explicitly solve simple addition problems and do so based on their counting skills (Fuson, 1982; Saxe et al., 1987). A common approach is to use objects or manipulatives. If the child is asked "how much is one cookie and two cookies," she will typically count out two objects, then one object, and finally all of the objects are counted starting from one.

The child states, while pointing at each object in succession, "one, two, three." The use of manipulatives serves at least two purposes. First, the sets of objects represent the numbers to be counted. The meaning of the abstract numeral, "three" in this example, is literally represented by the objects. Second, pointing to the objects during counting helps the child to keep track of the counting process (Carpenter & Moser, 1983; R. Gelman & Gallistel, 1978). The use of manipulatives is even seen in some 4- and 5-year-olds, depending on the complexity of the problem (Fuson, 1982).

By the time children enter kindergarten, a common strategy for solving simple addition problems is to count both addends. These counting procedures are sometimes executed with the aid of fingers, the finger-counting strategy, and sometimes without them, the verbal counting strategy (Siegler & Shrager, 1984). The two most commonly used counting procedures, whether children use their fingers or not, are called *min* (or counting on) and *sum* (or counting all; Fuson, 1982; Groen & Parkman, 1972). The min procedure involves stating the larger-valued addend and then counting a number of times equal to the value of the smaller addend, such as counting 5, 6, 7, 8 to solve 5 + 3. With the max procedure, children start with the smaller addend and count the larger addend. The sum procedure involves counting both addends starting from 1. The development of procedural competencies is related, in part, to improvements in children's conceptual understanding of counting and is reflected in a gradual shift from frequent use of the sum procedure to the min procedure (Geary, Bow-Thomas, & Yao, 1992; Siegler, 1987).

The use of counting also results in the development of memory representations of basic facts (Siegler & Shrager, 1984). Once formed, these long-term memory representations support the use of memory-based problem-solving processes. The most common of these are direct retrieval of arithmetic facts and decomposition. With direct retrieval, children state an answer that is associated in long-term memory with the presented problem, such as stating "eight" when asked to solve 5 + 3. Decomposition involves reconstructing the answer based on the retrieval of a partial sum. The problem 6 + 7 might be solved by retrieving the answer to 6 + 6 and then adding 1 to this partial sum. With the fingers strategy, children raise a number of fingers to represent the addends, which appears to trigger retrieval of the answer. The use of retrieval-based processes is moderated by a confidence criterion that represents an internal standard against which the child gauges confidence in the correctness of the retrieved answer. Children with a rigorous criterion only state answers that they are certain are correct, whereas children with a lenient criterion state any retrieved answer, correct or not (Siegler, 1988a). The transition to memory-based processes results in the quick solution of individual problems and reductions in the working memory demands that appear to accompany the use of counting procedures (Delaney, Reder, Staszewski, & Ritter, 1998; Geary et al., 1996; Lemaire & Siegler, 1995).

The general pattern of change is from use of the least sophisticated problem-solving procedures, such as sum counting, to the most efficient retrieval-based processes. The relatively unsophisticated counting-fingers strategy, especially with use of the sum procedure, is heavily dependent on working memory resources and takes the most time to execute, whereas direct retrieval requires little of working memory and is executed quickly, and with practice accurately and automatically (Geary, Hoard, Byrd-Craven, & DeSoto, 2004). However, as noted, development is not simply a switch from use of a less sophisticated strategy to use of a more sophisticated strategy. Rather, the change is best captured by Siegler's (1996) overlapping waves metaphor of cognitive development, as noted earlier. An example is provided by Geary et al.'s (1996) assessment of the strategies used by first-, second-, and third-grade children in China and the United States to solve simple addition problems. In the fall of first grade, the Chinese and American children, as groups and as individuals, used a mix of counting and retrieval to solve these problems. The American children used finger counting and verbal counting, but the Chinese children rarely used finger counting, although they did use this strategy in kindergarten. Across grades, there is an increase in use of direct retrieval and a decrease in counting for both groups, but a much more rapid (within and across school years) change in the strategy mix for the Chinese children.

When solving more complex addition problems, children initially rely on the knowledge and skills acquired for solving simple addition problems (Siegler, 1983). Strategies for solving more complex problems include counting, decomposition or regrouping, as well as the formally taught columnar procedure (Fuson, Stigler, & Bartsch, 1988; Ginsburg, 1977). Counting strategies typically involve counting on from the larger number (Siegler & Jenkins, 1989). For instance, $23 + 4$ would be

solved by counting "twenty-three, twenty-four, twenty-five, twenty-six, twenty-seven." The decomposition or regrouping strategy involves adding the tens values and the units values separately. So the problem $23 + 45$ would involve the steps $20 + 40$, $3 + 5$, and then $60 + 8$ (Fuson & Kwon, 1992a). The most difficult process involves carrying or trading, as in the problem $46 + 58$. These problems are difficult because of the working memory demands of trading (Hamann & Ashcraft, 1985; Hitch, 1978; Widaman, Geary, Cormier, & Little, 1989), and because trading requires an understanding of place value and the base-10 system.

**Subtraction, Multiplication, and Division Strategies.** Many of the same strategic and development trends described for children's addition apply to children's subtraction (Carpenter & Moser, 1983, 1984). Early on, children use a mix of strategies but largely count, often using manipulatives and fingers to help them represent the problem and keep track of the counting (Saxe, 1985). With experience and improvements in working memory, children are better able to mentally keep track of the counting process, and thus gradually abandon the use of manipulatives and fingers for verbal counting. There are two common counting procedures, counting up or counting down. Counting up involves stating the value of the subtrahend (bottom number), and then counting until the value of the minuend (top number) is reached. For example, $9 - 7$ is solved by counting "eight, nine." Since two numbers were counted, the answer is two. Counting down is often used to solve more complex subtraction problems, such as $23 - 4$ (Siegler, 1989), and involves counting backward from the minuend a number of times represented by the value of the subtrahend. Children also rely on their knowledge of addition facts to solve subtraction problems, which is called addition reference ($9 - 7 = 2$, because $7 + 2 = 9$). The most sophisticated procedures involve decomposing the problems into a series of simpler problems (Fuson & Kwon, 1992a), or solving the problem using the school-taught columnar approach.

Developmental trends in children's simple multiplication mirror the trends described for children's addition and subtraction, although formal skill acquisition begins in the second or third grade, at least in the United States (Geary, 1994). The initial mix of multiplication strategies is grounded in children's knowledge of addition and counting (Campbell & Graham, 1985; Siegler, 1988b). These strategies include repeated addition and counting by *n*. Repeated addition involves representing the multiplicand a number of times represented by the multiplier, and then successively adding these values; for example, adding $2 + 2 + 2$ to solve $2 \times 3$. The counting by *n* strategy is based on the child's ability to count by 2s, 3s, 5s, and so on. Somewhat more sophisticated strategies involve rules, such as $n \times 0 = 0$, and decomposition (e.g., $12 \times 2 = 10 \times 2 + 2 \times 2$). Use of these procedures results in the formation of problem/answer associations such that most children are able to retrieve most multiplication facts from long-term memory by the end of the elementary school years (Miller & Paredes, 1990). Considerably less research has been conducted on children's strategies for solving complex multiplication problems, but the studies that have been conducted with adults suggest that many individuals eventually adopt the formally taught columnar procedure (Geary, Widaman, & Little, 1986).

The first of two classes of strategy used for solving division problems are based on the child's knowledge of multiplication (Ilg & Ames, 1951; Vergnaud, 1983). For example, the solving of 20/4 (20 is the dividend, and 4 is the divisor) is based on the child's knowledge that $5 \times 4 = 20$, which is called multiplication reference (see also Campbell, 1999). For children who have not yet mastered the multiplication table, a derivative of this strategy is sometimes used. Here, the child multiplies the divisor by a succession of numbers until she finds the combination that equals the dividend. To solve 20/4, the sequence for this strategy might be $4 \times 2 = 8$, $4 \times 3 = 12$, $4 \times 4 = 16$, $4 \times 5 = 20$. The second class of strategies is based on the child's knowledge of addition. The first involves a form of repeated addition. To solve 20/4, the child would produce the sequence $4 + 4 + 4 + 4 + 4 = 20$, and then count the fours. The number of counted fours represents the quotient. Sometimes children try to solve division problems based directly on their knowledge of addition facts. For instance, to solve the problem 12/2, the child might base her answer on the knowledge that $6 + 6 = 12$; thus 12 is composed of two 6s.

**Conceptual Knowledge.** The progression in the mix of problem-solving strategies described in the preceding sections is related to frequency of exposure to the problems, instruction, and to children's understanding of related concepts (Blöte et al., 2000; Geary et al., 1996; Klein & Bisanz, 2000; Siegler & Stern, 1998). For example, children's use of min counting, as contrasted with sum counting, as well as their use of decomposition

to solve simple and complex addition problems is related to their understanding of commutativity (Canobi et al., 1998; R. Cowan & Renton, 1996) and to their understanding of counting principles (Geary et al., 2004). Children's understanding of the base-10 system facilitates their understanding of place value and is related to the ease with which they learn to trade from one column to the next when solving complex addition and subtraction problems (e.g., $234 + 589$; $82 - 49$) and to the frequency with which they commit trading errors (Fuson & Kwon, 1992a). For trading in the problem $34 + 29$, children must understand that the 1 traded from the units- to the tens-column represents 10 and not 1. Failure to understand this contributes to common trading errors, as in $34 + 29 = 513$ where $4 + 9$ is written as 13 without the trade (Fuson & Briars, 1990).

### Arithmetical Problem Solving

The study of children's and adolescents' mathematical problem solving typically focuses on competence in solving arithmetical or algebraic word problems, and the cognitive processes (Hegarty & Kozhevnikov, 1999; Mayer, 1985) and instructional factors (Fuchs et al., 2003a; Sweller, Mawer, & Ward, 1983) that drive the development of this competence. The ability to solve all but the most simple arithmetical and algebraic word problems does not come easily to children or many adults, and represents an important biologically secondary mathematical competence. A full review is beyond the scope of this chapter (see Geary, 1994; Mayer, 1985; Tronsky & Royer, 2002), but I illustrate some of the core issues as related to the solving of arithmetical word problems.

**Problem Schema.**   Word problems can be placed in categories based on the relations among objects, persons, or events described in the problem and the types of procedures needed to solve the problem (G. Cooper & Sweller, 1987; Mayer, 1985). The relations and procedures that define each category compose the schema for the problem type. As shown in Table 18.1, most simple word problems that involve addition or subtraction can be classified into four general categories: change, combine, compare, and equalize (Carpenter & Moser, 1983; De Corte & Verschaffel, 1987; Riley et al., 1983). Change problems imply some type of action be performed by the child, and are solved using the same procedures children use to solve standard arithmetic problems (e.g., $3 + 5$; Jordan & Montani, 1997). Most

**TABLE 18.1    Classification of Arithmetic Word Problems**

Change

1. Andy had two marbles. Nick gave him three more marbles. How many marbles does Andy have now?
2. Andy had five marbles. Then he gave three marbles to Nick. How many marbles does Andy have now?
3. Andy had two marbles. Nick gave him some more marbles. Now Andy has five marbles. How many marbles did Nick give him?
4. Nick had some marbles. Then he gave two marbles to Andy. Now Nick has three marbles. How many marbles did Nick have in the beginning?

Combine

1. Andy has two marbles. Nick has three marbles. How many marbles do they have altogether?
2. Andy has five marbles. Three are red marbles and the rest are blue marbles. How many blue marbles does Andy have?

Compare

1. Nick has three marbles. Andy has two marbles. How many fewer marbles does Andy have than Nick?
2. Nick has five marbles. Andy has two marbles. How many more marbles does Nick have than Andy?
3. Andy has two marbles. Nick has one more marble than Andy. How many marbles does Nick have?
4. Andy has two marbles. He has one marble less than Nick. How many marbles does Nick have?

Equalize

1. Nick has five marbles. Andy has two marbles. How many marbles does Andy have to buy to have as many marbles as Nick?
2. Nick has five marbles. Andy has two marbles. How many marbles does Nick have to give away to have as many marbles as Andy?
3. Nick has five marbles. If he gives away three marbles, then he will have as many marbles as Andy. How many marbles does Andy have?
4. Andy has two marbles. If he buys one more marble, then he will have the same number of marbles as Nick. How many marbles does Nick have?
5. Andy has two marbles. If Nick gives away one of his marbles, then he will have the same number of marbles as Andy. How many marbles does Nick have?

kindergarten and first-grade children can easily solve the first type of change problem shown in the table. Children typically represent the meaning of the first term, "Andy had two marbles," through the use of two blocks or uplifted fingers. The meaning of the next term, "Nick gave him three more marbles," is represented by three blocks or uplifted fingers. Some children then answer the "how many" question by literally moving the two sets of blocks together and then counting them or counting the total number of uplifted fingers (Riley & Greeno, 1988).

The change and combine problems are conceptually different, even though the basic arithmetic is the same

(Briars & Larkin, 1984; Carpenter & Moser, 1983; Riley et al., 1983). Combine problems involve a static relationship, rather than the implied action found with change problems. The first examples under the change and combine categories presented in Table 18.1 illustrate the point. Both problems require the child to add 2 + 3. In the change problem, the quantities in Andy's and Nick's sets differ after the action (addition) has been performed. In the combine example, however, the status—the quantity of owned marbles—of Andy's set and Nick's set is not altered by the addition. Compare problems involve the same types of static relationships found in combine problems. The quantity of the sets does not change. Rather, the arithmetic operation results in determining the exact quantity of one of the sets by reference to the other set, as illustrated with the third and fourth compare examples in Table 18.1. The first and second compare examples involve a more straightforward greater than/less than comparison. Examination of the equalize problems presented in Table 18.1 reveals that they are conceptually similar to change problems. The action, or arithmetic, performed results in a change in the quantity of one of the sets. The change is constrained such that the result is equal sets once the action has been completed, whereas there is no such constraint with change problems.

Across categories, the complexity of word problems increases with increases in the number of steps or procedures needed to solve the problem; the complexity of these procedures (e.g., differentiation in calculus versus simple addition); and the complexity of the relations among persons, objects, or events (e.g., timing of two events) conveyed in the problem. These more complex problems can still be categorized in terms of schemas, that is, the specific nature of the relations among these persons, objects, or events and the types of procedures needed to solve the problem (Mayer, 1981; Sweller et al., 1983).

**Problem-Solving Processes.**    The processes involved in solving word problems include translating each sentence into numerical or mathematical information, integrating the relations among this information, and executing the necessary procedure or procedures (Briars & Larkin, 1984; Kintsch & Greeno, 1985; Mayer, 1985; Riley et al., 1983; Riley & Greeno, 1988). For complex, multistep problems and especially unfamiliar problems, an additional step is solution planning—making explicit metacognitive decisions about problem type and potential procedural steps for solving the problem

(Fuchs, Fuchs, Prentice, Burch, Hamlett, Owen, & Schroeter, 2003; Mayer, 1985; Schoenfeld, 1987). The latter is important, because the number of potential ways a problem can be solved (e.g., sequence in which procedures are executed) increases with increases in problem complexity. The translation process is straightforward for most of the problems shown in Table 18.1, but integrating this information across sentences can be more difficult. Consider the second compare problem. Here, the key word "more" will often prompt children to add the quantities. These types of error can often be avoided if, for example, the relations between the quantities held by Nick and Andy are concretely represented on a visuospatial number line. Once represented in this way, the child can easily count from 2 to 5 on the number line and correctly determine that Nick has three more than Andy.

Improvement in the ability to execute these problem-solving processes and thus the ability to solve complex word problems is related to intraindividual and extraindividual factors. The latter include the quantity (e.g., amount of practice) and form of instruction (Fuchs, Fuchs, Prentice, Burch, Hamlett, Owen, & Schroeter, 2003; Sweller et al., 1983), and more general curricular factors, such as the grade in which multistep problems are introduced and the quality of textbooks (Fuson et al., 1988). One of the more difficult competencies to teach is the ability to transfer knowledge from familiar to novel problems. Teaching of this competence often requires explicit instruction on how to make links (e.g., based on problem type) between familiar and novel problems (Fuchs et al., 2003). For children and adults, intraindividual factors include working memory capacity (Geary & Widaman, 1992; Tronsky & Royer, 2002), basic computational skills (Sweller et al., 1983), knowledge of problem type and schema (G. Cooper & Sweller, 1987), the ability to form visuospatial representations of relations among problem features (Hegarty & Kozhevnikov, 1999; Lewis & Mayer, 1987), as well as self-efficacy and the resultant tendency to persist with problem-solving efforts (Fuchs, Fuchs, Prentice, Burch, Hamlett, Owen, & Schroeter, 2003).

## Mechanisms of Change

The processes that result in variability, competition, and selection drive change at all levels, ranging from gene frequency in populations to the pattern of corporate successes and failures. The combination of variability, competition, and selection is thus a useful organizing framework for studying the mechanisms underlying the development of children's mathematical competence and for understanding cognitive development in general (Siegler, 1996). Developmental or experience-related improvements in cognitive competence in turn are indexed by efficiency in achieving goals, such as solving an arithmetic problem or generating plans for the weekend, with efficiency typically measured in terms of the speed and accuracy with which the goal or subgoals are achieved. From this perspective, developmental or experience-related improvement in goal achievement will be related, in part, to (a) variability in the procedures or concepts that can be employed to achieve the goal; (b) underlying brain and cognitive mechanisms that generate this variability; and (c) contextual as well as brain and cognitive feedback mechanisms that select the most efficient procedures or concepts.

In the first section, I outline some basic mechanisms related to variability, competition, and selection among different problem-solving approaches; more detailed discussion of associated brain (Edelman, 1987) and cognitive (Shrager & Siegler, 1998; Siegler, 1996) mechanisms can be found elsewhere. In the second section, I conjecture about developmental change in these mechanisms, as related to biologically primary and biologically secondary competencies (Geary, 2004a, 2005). The discussion in both sections is necessarily preliminary but should provide an outline for conceptualizing how change might occur in mathematical and other domains.

### Darwinian Competition

**Variability and Competition.**    Siegler and his colleagues have demonstrated that children use a variety of procedures and concepts to solve problems in nearly all cognitive domains, and that with development and experience they become more efficient in achieving problem-solving goals (Shrager & Siegler, 1998; Siegler, 1996; Siegler & Shipley, 1995). The issue at this point is not whether variability in problem-solving approaches is an integral feature of cognitive development, but rather the mechanisms that result in variability and competition among these approaches. In Figure 18.3, I provide a skeletal framework for conceptualizing the mechanisms that might contribute to variability in, and competition among, problem-solving approaches at the level of cognitive and brain systems.

First, goal achievement requires an attentional focus on features of the external context that are either related

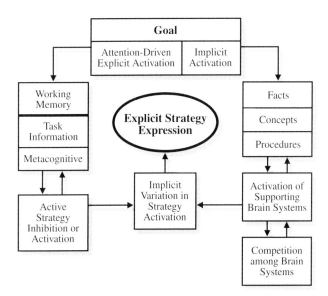

**Figure 18.3** Outline of explicit and implicit mechanisms that appear to contribute to the explicit use of one problem-solving strategy or another (see text for detailed description).

to the goal (e.g., a sheet of arithmetic problems to solve) or to an internally generated mental model of an anticipated goal-related context (Geary, 2005). Goal generation and a narrowing of attention onto the features of the external or internally represented context will result in the implicit activation—above baseline levels of activation but outside conscious awareness—of goal-related facts, concepts, and procedures (Anderson, 1982). These can be learned facts, concepts, and procedures associated with previous problem solving (Shrager & Siegler, 1998; Siegler, 1996) or inherent but rudimentary concepts and procedures (R. Gelman, 1990, 1991). The implicit activation of goal-related information means that existing conceptual knowledge and memorized facts and procedures may influence where attention is allocated and thus influence problem solving. Knowledge of the base-10 system and memorized procedures for solving complex arithmetic problems should influence the temporal pattern of attentional focus, from the units-column numbers to the tens-column numbers, and so on. More generally, conceptual knowledge can be understood at multiple levels, ranging from explicit descriptors of categorical features (e.g., sets of ten) to patterns of brain activity that direct attention toward specific goal-related features of the environment (e.g., columnar numbers, eyes on a human face; Schyns, Bonnar, & Gosselin, 2002).

The implicit activation of goal-related information will often mean that multiple facts, concepts, or proce-

dures are simultaneously activated and, as indicated by the bidirectional arrows in the right-hand side of Figure 18.3, multiple underlying systems of brain regions will be simultaneously activated. Edelman (1987) proposed these activated populations of neurons compete, as integrated groups, for downstream explicit, behavioral expression. As is also shown in the right-hand side of Figure 18.3, competition at the level of brain systems— relative activation of neuronal groups and inhibition of competing groups—creates variation in the level of implicit activation of corresponding facts, concepts, and procedures associated with goal-related behavioral strategies and thus variation in the probability of the expression of one strategy or another. Edelman also proposed that normal neurodevelopmental processes create a pattern of brain organization that will necessarily result in variation and competition at the level of neuronal groups and thus variation and competition at the levels of perception, cognition, and behavioral expression. The resulting systems of neuronal groups are well understood for only a few restricted perceptual or cognitive phenomena related to classical and operant conditioning (e.g., McDonald & White, 1993; Thompson & Krupa, 1994), although they are beginning to be explored in mathematical domains (Dehaene et al., 1999; Pinel et al., 2004). The point is that competition among neuronal groups activated by goal-related contextual features creates variation at the level of activation of cognitive representations (e.g., long-term memories of goal-related facts) and thus variation in the probability that one strategy or another will be expressed.

It is also clear that attentional focus can result in an explicit and conscious representation of the goal and goal-related facts, concepts, and procedures in working memory (N. Cowan, 1995; Dehaene & Naccache, 2001; Engle, 2002; Shrager & Siegler, 1998), as shown in the left-hand side of Figure 18.3. The working memory system provides at least two strategy-selection mechanisms. The first is composed of explicitly represented task or metacognitive knowledge that can guide the strategy execution and enable inferences to be drawn about goal-related concepts or procedures based on observation of problem-solving processes and outcomes. A task-relevant inference was provided by Briars' and Siegler's (1984) finding that preschool children's knowledge of counting is derived, in part, through observation of culture-specific procedures, such as counting from left to right. Metacognitive mechanisms operate across tasks and represent the ability to monitor problem solving for ways to improve efficiency. An example is children's discovery of min counting (Siegler & Jenkins, 1989). Although many children switch from sum counting to min counting before they are explicitly aware they have done so, others correctly infer that you do not have to count both addends to solve the problem and adjust their problem solving accordingly. In other words, explicit monitoring of goal-related problem solving can result in the identification and elimination of unnecessary problem-solving steps.

The second way in which explicit attentional control can influence problem solving is through active strategy inhibition or activation. An example is provided by choice/no choice problem-solving instructions (Siegler & Lemaire, 1997). Here, participants are instructed to solve one set of problems (e.g., arithmetic problems, spelling items) using any strategy they choose (e.g., finger counting, or retrieval), and are instructed to solve a comparable set of problems using only a single strategy, such as direct retrieval. Problem solving is more accurate under choice conditions, in keeping with the prediction that strategy variability is adaptive (Siegler, 1996). Equally important, the ability to explicitly inhibit the expression of all but one problem-solving strategy is easily achieved by most elementary-school children (Geary, Hamson, & Hoard, 2000; Jordan & Montani, 1997; Lemaire & Lecacheur, 2002a). Brain-imaging studies suggest that the dorsolateral prefrontal cortex is involved in attentional control, monitoring of explicit problem-solving, and the inhibition of task-irrelevant brain regions (Kane & Engle, 2002); maturation of these brain regions may contribute to developmental change in the ability to consciously influence strategy choices (Welsh & Pennington, 1988). As shown in the bottom left-hand side of Figure 18.3, these brain regions can amplify or inhibit the implicitly activated brain regions represented at the right-hand side of the figure. The combination of bottom-up competition and top-down mechanisms that amplify or inhibit these competing systems results in the expression of one behavioral strategy or another.

**Selection.** Variability and competition at levels of brain and cognition result in the execution of one problem-solving strategy or another. Over time, adaptive goal-related adjustments lead to the most efficient strategies being used more often and less efficient strategies becoming extinct (see Siegler, 1996 for review). Given this pattern, the *consequence* (e.g., successful problem solving) and *process* of strategy execution must be among the selection mechanisms acting on individual strategies. The specific means through which these selection processes operate are not well understood, but must involve changes in the pattern of memory and concept representation at both the brain (Edelman, 1987) and cognitive (Siegler, 1996) levels. Just as natural selection results in changes in gene frequencies across generations, selection processes that act on strategic variability result in a form of inheritance: changes in memory patterns, strategy knowledge, and physical changes in the underlying neuronal groups.

At a behavioral level, the most fundamental selective mechanisms are classical and operant conditioning (Timberlake, 1994), as illustrated by the learning of simple addition (Siegler & Robinson, 1982). As noted, early in skill development, children rely on finger and verbal counting. The repeated execution of these procedures has at least two effects. First, the procedures themselves are executed more quickly and with greater accuracy (Delaney et al., 1998), indicating the formation and strengthening of procedural memories. Second, the act of counting out the addends creates an associative link between the addend pair and the generated answer, that is, the formation of a declarative memory (Siegler & Shrager, 1984; see also Campbell, 1995). The neural changes that result in the formation and strengthening of these procedural and declarative memories are not known, but may require a simultaneous and synchronized firing of neurons within the associated neuronal group (e.g., Damasio, 1989). At a cognitive level, the formation of the associative memory results in greater variation in the number of processes (e.g., counting and retrieval) that can be used to achieve the goal and thus increases competition among these processes for expression.

Empirically, it is known that direct retrieval of arithmetic facts eventually obtains a selective advantage over the execution of counting procedures. Speed of retrieval (Siegler & Shrager, 1984) and the lower working memory demands of direct retrieval versus procedural execution (Geary et al., 2004) almost certainly contribute to this selective advantage. With sufficient experience, the speed of retrieval increases and the generated answer tends to be as accurate or more accurate than that generated by counting procedures. In effect, the greater efficiency of retrieval means that the goal is achieved before the execution of alternative processes can be completed. Goal achievement in turn may act—in ways not yet understood—to inhibit the expression of these alternative processes and may further enhance the competitive advantage of direct retrieval. At the level of brain systems, Edelman (1987) predicted that these selection mechanisms will strengthen connections among neurons within the selected neuronal group supporting retrieval in this example, and result in the death of neurons or at least fewer connections among the neurons within the neuronal groups supporting strategies that are not expressed (counting in this example).

### Primary and Secondary Domains

**Primary.**   Primary competencies are composed of an inherent, though often not fully developed, system of implicit concepts, procedures, and supporting brain systems represented at the right-hand side of Figure 18.3. The result is attentional, affective, and information-processing biases that orient the child toward the features of the ecology that were of significance during human evolution (Geary & Bjorklund, 2000). Coupled with these biases are self-initiated behavioral engagements of the ecology (Bjorklund & Pellegrini, 2002; Scarr, 1992). The latter generate evolutionarily expectant experiences that provide the feedback needed to adjust the architecture of primary brain and cognitive systems to nuances in evolutionarily significant domains (Greenough, Black, & Wallace, 1987), such as allowing the individual to discriminate one face from another. These behavioral biases are expressed as common childhood activities, such as social play and exploration of the environment.

Proposed biologically primary mathematical competencies include an implicit understanding of the quantity of small sets (Starkey et al., 1990); the effects of addition and subtraction on quantity (Wynn, 1992a); counting concepts and how to execute counting procedures (R. Gelman & Gallistel, 1978); and relative quantity (Lipton & Spelke, 2003). There is little developmental change in some of these primary competencies, such as the ability to estimate the quantity of small sets (Geary, 1994; Temple & Posner, 1998), and substantive developmental improvement in other competencies, such as skill at executing counting procedures and the emergence of an explicit understanding of some counting concepts (R. Gelman & Gallistel, 1978). Developmental change in these latter competencies is predicted to emerge from an interaction between early attentional biases and related activities such as counting sets of objects (R. Gelman, 1990). These activities allow inherent biases to be integrated with culturally specific practices, such as the culture's number words or manner of representing counts (e.g., on fin-

gers or other body parts, as with the Oksapmin). By the end of the preschool years, all these competencies appear to be well integrated and allow children to perform basic measurements, count, and do simple arithmetic (Geary, 1995).

**Secondary.**   Biologically secondary, academic development involves the modification of primary brain and cognitive systems for the creation of culturally specific competencies (Geary, 1995). Some of these competencies are more similar to primary abilities than others. Spelke (2000) proposed that learning the Arabic numeral system involves integrating primary knowledge of small numbers and counting with the analog magnitude system. In this way, the primary understanding of small sets and the understanding that successive counts increase quantity by one can be extended beyond the small number sizes of the primary system. Siegler's and Opfer's (2003) research on children's number-line estimation is consistent with this proposal. Recall, Figure 18.2 shows children's number-line estimates that conform to predictions of the analog magnitude system (bottom) and estimates that conform to the Arabic, mathematical system (top). With experience across numerical ranges (e.g., 1 to 100 or 1 to 1,000), children's representation of the number line based on the biologically primary analog-magnitude system is gradually transformed into the secondary mathematical representation (Siegler & Booth, 2004).

Other features of academic mathematics, such as the base-10 system, are more remote from the supporting primary systems (Geary, 2002). Competency in base-10 arithmetic requires a conceptual understanding of the mathematical number line, and an ability to decompose this system into sets of ten and then to organize these sets into clusters of 100 (10, 20, 30 . . .), 1,000, and so forth. Whereas an implicit understanding of number sets is likely to be primary knowledge, the creation of sets around 10 and the superordinate organization of these sets is not. This conceptual knowledge must also be mapped onto a number-word system (McCloskey, Sokol, & Goodman, 1986), and integrated with school-taught procedures for solving complex arithmetic problems (Fuson & Kwon, 1992a). The development of base-10 knowledge thus requires the extension of primary number knowledge to very large numbers, the organization of these number representations in ways that differ from primary knowledge, and the learning of procedural rules for applying this knowledge to the secondary domain of complex, mathematical arithmetic (e.g., to solve 234 + 697). In other words, multiple primary systems must be modified and integrated during children's learning of base-10 arithmetic.

Little is known about the mechanisms involved in modifying primary systems for learning secondary mathematics, but research on learning in other evolutionarily novel domains suggests the explicit attentional and inhibitory control mechanisms of the working memory system shown in Figure 18.3 are crucial (e.g., Ackerman & Cianciolo, 2002). It is known that some secondary mathematical learning, such as arithmetic facts or simple arithmetical relations, can occur implicitly but only with attentional focus and the repeated presentation of the same or similar arithmetical patterns (e.g., Siegler & Stern, 1998). In theory, the implicitly represented facts, concepts, and procedures (right-hand side of Figure 18.3) that result from this repetition will only emerge through modification underlying primary systems. There is no inherent understanding that 9 + 7 = 16, but the repeated solving of this problem results in the development of a language-based (primary system) declarative fact (Dehaene & Cohen, 1991).

The explicit and conscious representation of information in working memory and through this the ability to make inferences about school-taught mathematics appears to require the synchronized activity of the dorsolateral prefrontal cortex and the activity of the brain regions that implicitly represent goal-related facts, concepts, or procedures (Dehaene & Naccache, 2001; Posner, 1994). The details of how this might occur as related to academic learning are presented elsewhere (Geary, 2005), but there are several basic points. First, repetition of mathematical problems in school should result in the formation of implicitly represented facts, concepts, or procedures in long-term memory (e.g., Siegler & Stern, 1998). This knowledge will influence problem solving and remain implicit unless the activity of the underlying brain regions becomes synchronized with activity of the dorsolateral prefrontal cortex, as will often happen when attention is focused on achieving a specific goal. When this occurs, the fact, concept, or procedural pattern will "pop" into conscious awareness, and thus be made available for drawing inferences about the information, forming metacognitive knowledge, and so forth. Second, an explicit representation of goal-related features in working memory (e.g., through direct instruction) should, in theory, result in a top-down influence on the pattern of activation and inhibi-

tion of brain regions that might support problem solving. These top-down processes may bias which implicitly represented facts, concepts, or procedures are used to approach the problem and may direct changes in the associated implicit knowledge.

In this view, change occurs through the repeated processing of a mathematical problem or pattern. The result is the repeated activation of a set of brain regions that process the pattern and through competition and selection at the level of corresponding neuronal groups (Edelman, 1987) form implicit biologically secondary facts, concepts, or procedures. Developmental change can occur with the maturation of the brain systems (e.g., dorsolateral prefrontal cortex) that support the explicit, working memory mechanisms shown in Figure 18.3. These regions appear to mature slowly through childhood and early adolescence (Giedd et al., 1999; Welsh & Pennington, 1988), and result in an improved ability to focus attention on goal-related problem solving, inhibit irrelevant information from interfering with problem solving, make explicit inferences about the goal and problem-solving processes, and form metacognitive knowledge.

## CONCLUSIONS AND FUTURE DIRECTIONS

During the past 2 decades and especially in recent years, the study of children's mathematical development has emerged as a vibrant and exciting area. Although there is much to be learned, we now have considerable knowledge of infants', preschoolers' and young children's understanding of number, counting, arithmetic, and some aspects of more complex arithmetical and algebraic problem solving (Brannon & Van de Walle, 2001; Briars & Larkin, 1984; Siegler, 1996; Starkey, 1992; Wynn, 1992a). As a sign of a maturing field, the empirical findings in most of these areas are no longer contested, but the underlying cognitive mechanisms and the mechanisms of developmental change are the foci of vigorous theoretical debate (Cohen & Marks, 2002; Newcombe, 2002). Much of the debate centers on the extent to which the most basic quantitative abilities emerge from inherent and potentially evolved brain and cognitive systems that are designed to attend to and process numerical features of the environment (Gallistel & Gelman, 1992; Wynn, 1995), or whether brain and cognitive systems designed for other functions (e.g., object identification) are the source of these abilities (Mix et al., 1997).

Future research in this field will undoubtedly be focused on addressing this issue. In fact, recent behavioral (Brannon, 2002; Kobayashi et al., 2004) and brain-imaging (Pinel et al., 2004) studies have used sophisticated techniques to determine if the cognitive systems that support quantitative judgments are uniquely numerical, and whether the underlying brain regions are uniquely designed to process numerical information. The overall results are mixed, and thus a firm conclusion must await further studies. An equally important area of current debate and future study concerns the mechanisms that underlie children's cognitive development in the domain of mathematics and more generally (Siegler, 1996). We now have some understanding of the cognitive mechanisms (e.g., working memory, attention) that contribute to developmental change (Shrager & Siegler, 1998), and we are beginning to understand the operation of the supporting brain systems (Geary, 2005), but there is much to be learned about how these systems operate and change from one area of mathematics to another. A final direction is to apply knowledge derived from the scientific study of children's mathematical development to the study of how children learn mathematics in school.

# REFERENCES

Ackerman, P. L., & Cianciolo, A. T. (2002). Ability and task constraint determinants of complex task performance. *Journal of Experimental Psychology: Applied, 8,* 194–208.

Anderson, J. R. (1982). Acquisition of cognitive skill. *Psychological Review, 89,* 369–406.

Antell, S. E., & Keating, D. P. (1983). Perception of numerical invariance in neonates. *Child Development, 54,* 695–701.

Ashcraft, M. H. (1982). The development of mental arithmetic: A chronometric approach. *Developmental Review, 2,* 213–236.

Ashcraft, M. H. (1995). Cognitive psychology and simple arithmetic: A review and summary of new directions. *Mathematical Cognition, 1,* 3–34.

Ashcraft, M. H. (2002). Math anxiety: Personal, educational, and cognitive consequences. *Current Directions in Psychological Science, 11,* 181–185.

Ashcraft, M. H., & Battaglia, J. (1978). Cognitive arithmetic: Evidence for retrieval and decision processes in mental addition. *Journal of Experimental Psychology: Human Learning and Memory, 4,* 527–538.

Baroody, A. J., & Gannon, K. E. (1984). The development of the commutativity principle and economical addition strategies. *Cognition and Instruction, 1,* 321–339.

Baroody, A. J., & Ginsburg, H. P. (1986). The relationship between initial meaningful and mechanical knowledge of arithmetic. In J. Hiebert (Ed.), *Conceptual and procedural knowledge: The case of mathematics* (pp. 75–112). Hillsdale, NJ: Erlbaum.

Baroody, A. J., Ginsburg, H. P., & Waxman, B. (1983). Children's use of mathematical structure. *Journal for Research in Mathematics Education, 14,* 156–168.

Baroody, A. J., Wilkins, J. L. M., & Tiilikainen, S. H. (2003). The development of children's understanding of additive commutativity: From protoquantitative concept to general concept. In A. J. Baroody & A. Dowker (Eds.), *The development of arithmetic concepts and skills: Constructing adaptive expertise* (pp. 127–160). Mahwah, NJ: Erlbaum.

Beran, M. J., & Beran, M. M. (2004). Chimpanzees remember the results of one-by-one addition of food items to sets over extended time periods. *Psychological Science, 15,* 94–99.

Bermejo, V. (1996). Cardinality development and counting. *Developmental Psychology, 32,* 263–268.

Bjorklund, D. F., & Pellegrini, A. D. (2002). *The origins of human nature: Evolutionary developmental psychology.* Washington, DC: American Psychological Association.

Blöte, A. W., Klein, A. S., & Beishuizen, M. (2000). Mental computation and conceptual understanding. *Learning and Instruction, 10,* 221–247.

Boysen, S. T., & Berntson, G. G. (1989). Numerical competence in a chimpanzee (pan troglodytes). *Journal of Comparative Psychology, 103,* 23–31.

Brainerd, C. J. (1979). *The origins of the number concept.* New York: Praeger.

Brannon, E. M. (2002). The development of ordinal numerical knowledge in infancy. *Cognition, 83,* 223–240.

Brannon, E. M., Abbott, S., & Lutz, D. J. (2004). Number bias for the discrimination of large visual sets in infancy. *Cognition, 93,* B59–B68.

Brannon, E. M., & Terrace, H. S. (1998, October 23). Ordering of the numerosities 1 to 9 by monkeys. *Science, 282,* 746–749.

Brannon, E. M., & Van de Walle, G. A. (2001). The development of ordinal numerical competence in young children. *Cognitive Psychology, 43,* 53–81.

Briars, D. J., & Larkin, J. H. (1984). An integrated model of skill in solving elementary word problems. *Cognition and Instruction, 1,* 245–296.

Briars, D. J., & Siegler, R. S. (1984). A featural analysis of preschoolers' counting knowledge. *Developmental Psychology, 20,* 607–618.

Brownell, W. A. (1928). *The development of children's number ideas in the primary grades.* Chicago: University of Chicago.

Bullock, M., & Gelman, R. (1977). Numerical reasoning in young children: The ordering principle. *Child Development, 48,* 427–434.

Butterworth, B. (1999). *The mathematical brain.* London: Macmillan.

Byrnes, J. P., & Wasik, B. A. (1991). Role of conceptual knowledge in mathematical procedural learning. *Developmental Psychology, 27,* 777–786.

Campbell, J. I. D. (1995). Mechanisms of simple addition and multiplication: A modified network-interference theory and simulation. *Mathematical Cognition, 1,* 121–164.

Campbell, J. I. D. (1999). Division by multiplication. *Memory and Cognition, 27,* 791–802.

Campbell, J. I. D., & Graham, D. J. (1985). Mental multiplication skill: Structure, process, and acquisition. *Canadian Journal of Psychology, 39,* 338–366.

Canisia, M. (1962). Mathematical ability as related to reasoning and use of symbols. *Educational and Psychological Measurement, 22,* 105–127.

Canobi, K. H., Reeve, R. A., & Pattison, P. E. (1998). The role of conceptual understanding in children's addition problem solving. *Developmental Psychology, 34,* 882–891.

Canobi, K. H., Reeve, R. A., & Pattison, P. E. (2002). Young children's understanding of addition. *Educational Psychology, 22,* 513–532.

Carey, S. (2002). Evidence for numerical abilities in young infants: A fatal flaw? *Developmental Science, 5,* 202–205.

Carpenter, T. P., & Moser, J. M. (1983). The acquisition of addition and subtraction concepts. In R. Lesh & M. Landau (Eds.), *Acquisition of mathematical concepts and processes* (pp. 7–44). New York: Academic Press.

Carpenter, T. P., & Moser, J. M. (1984). The acquisition of addition and subtraction concepts in grades 1 through 3. *Journal for Research in Mathematics Education, 15,* 179–202.

Carroll, J. B. (1993). *Human cognitive abilities: A survey of factor-analytic studies.* New York: Cambridge University Press.

Case, R., & Okamoto, Y. (1996). The role of conceptual structures in the development of children's thought. *Monographs of the Society for Research in Child Development, 61*(1/2, Serial No. 246).

Cattell, J. M. (1890). Mental tests and measurements. *Mind, 15,* 373–381.

Chein, I. (1939). Factors in mental organization. *Psychological Record, 3,* 71–94.

Clearfield, M. W., & Mix, K. S. (1999). Number versus contour length in infants' discrimination of small visual sets. *Psychological Science, 10,* 408–411.

Clements, M. A., & Del Campo, G. (1990). How natural is fraction knowledge. In L. P. Steffe & T. Wood (Eds.), *Transforming children's mathematics education: International perspectives* (pp. 181–188). Hillsdale, NJ: Erlbaum.

Cohen, L. B. (2002). Extraordinary claims require extraordinary controls. *Developmental Science, 5,* 211–212.

Cohen, L. B., & Marks, K. S. (2002). How infants process addition and subtraction events. *Developmental Science, 5,* 186–212.

Coombs, C. H. (1941). A factorial study of number ability. *Psychometrika, 6,* 161–189.

Cooper, G., & Sweller, J. (1987). Effects of schema acquisition and rule automation on mathematical problem-solving transfer. *Journal of Educational Psychology, 79,* 347–362.

Cooper, R. G., Jr. (1984). Early number development: Discovering number space with addition and subtraction. In C. Sophian (Ed.), *The 18th Annual Carnegie Symposium on Cognition: Origins of cognitive skills* (pp. 157–192). Hillsdale, NJ: Erlbaum.

Cowan, N. (1995). *Attention and memory: An integrated framework.* New York: Oxford University Press.

Cowan, R., & Renton, M. (1996). Do they know what they are doing? Children's use of economical addition strategies and knowledge of commutativity. *Educational Psychology, 16,* 407–420.

Crump, T. (1990). *The anthropology of numbers.* New York: Cambridge University Press.

Damasio, A. R. (1989). Time-locked multiregional retroactivation: A systems-level proposal for the neural substrates of recall and recognition. *Cognition, 33,* 25–62.

Darwin, C. (1871). *The descent of man, and selection in relation to sex.* London: John Murray.

Darwin, C., & Wallace, A. (1858). On the tendency of species to form varieties, and on the perpetuation of varieties and species by natural means of selection. *Journal of the Linnean Society of London, Zoology, 3,* 45–62.

De Corte, E., & Verschaffel, L. (1987). The effect of semantic structure on first graders' strategies for solving addition and subtraction word problems. *Journal for Research in Mathematics Education, 18,* 363–381.

Dehaene, S. (1997). *The number sense: How the mind creates mathematics.* New York: Oxford University Press.

Dehaene, S., & Cohen, L. (1991). Two mental calculation systems: A Case Study of Severe Acalculia with Preserved Approximation. *Neuropsychologia, 29,* 1045–1074.

Dehaene, S., & Naccache, L. (2001). Towards a cognitive neuroscience of consciousness: Basic evidence and a workspace framework. *Cognition, 79,* 1–37.

Dehaene, S., Spelke, E., Pinel, P., Stanescu, R., & Tsivkin, S. (1999, May 7). Sources of mathematical thinking: Behavioral and brain-imaging evidence. *Science, 284,* 970–974.

Delaney, P. F., Reder, L. M., Staszewski, J. J., & Ritter, F. E. (1998). The strategy-specific nature of improvement: The power law applies by strategy within task. *Psychological Science, 9,* 1–7.

Dowker, A. (1997). Young children's addition estimates. *Mathematical Cognition, 3,* 141–154.

Dowker, A. (2003). Younger children's estimates for addition: The zone of partial knowledge and understanding. In A. J. Baroody & A. Dowker (Eds.), *The development of arithmetic concepts and skills: Constructing adaptive expertise* (pp. 243–265). Mahwah, NJ: Erlbaum.

Dye, N. W., & Very, P. S. (1968). Growth changes in factorial structure by age and sex. *Genetic Psychology Monographs, 78,* 55–88.

Edelman, G. M. (1987). *Neural Darwinism: The theory of neuronal group selection.* New York: Basic Books.

Engle, R. W. (2002). Working memory capacity as executive attention. *Current Directions in Psychological Science, 11,* 19–23.

Feigenson, L., Carey, S., & Hauser, M. (2002). The representations underlying infants' choice of more: Object files versus analog magnitudes. *Psychological Science, 13,* 150–156.

Feigenson, L., Carey, S., & Spelke, E. (2002). Infants' discrimination of number versus continuous extent. *Cognitive Psychology, 44,* 33–66.

Freedman, D. G. (1974). *Human infancy: An evolutionary perspective.* New York: Wiley.

Freeman, N. H., Antonucci, C., & Lewis, C. (2000). Representation of the cardinality principle: Early conception of error in a counterfactual test. *Cognition, 74,* 71–89.

French, J. W. (1951). The description of aptitude and achievement tests in terms of rotated factors. *Psychometric Monographs*(5).

Fuchs, L. S., Fuchs, D., Prentice, K., Burch, M., Hamlett, C. L., Owen, R., et al. (2003). Explicitly teaching for transfer: Effects on third-grade students' mathematical problem solving. *Journal of Educational Psychology, 95,* 293–305.

Fuchs, L. S., Fuchs, D., Prentice, K., Burch, M., Hamlett, C. L., Owen, R., & Schroeter, K. (2003). Enhancing third-grade students' mathematical problem solving with self-regulated learning strategies. *Journal of Educational Psychology, 95,* 306–315.

Fuson, K. C. (1982). An analysis of the counting-on solution procedure in addition. In T. P. Carpenter, J. M. Moser, & T. A. Romberg (Eds.), *Addition and subtraction: A cognitive perspective* (pp. 67–81). Hillsdale, NJ: Erlbaum.

Fuson, K. C. (1988). *Children's counting and concepts of number.* New York: Springer-Verlag.

Fuson, K. C. (1990). Conceptual structures for multiunit numbers: Implications for learning and teaching multidigit addition, subtraction, and place value. *Cognition and Instruction, 7,* 343–403.

Fuson, K. C. (1991). Children's early counting: Saying the number-word sequence, counting objects, and understanding cardinality. In K. Durkin & B. Shire (Eds.), *Language in mathematical education: Research and practice* (pp. 27–39). Milton Keynes, PA: Open University Press.

Fuson, K. C., & Briars, D. J. (1990). Using a base-10 blocks learning/teaching approach for first- and second-grade place-value and multidigit addition and subtraction. *Journal for Research in Mathematics Education, 21,* 180–206.

Fuson, K. C., & Kwon, Y. (1991). Chinese-based regular and European irregular systems of number words: The disadvantages for English-speaking children. In K. Durkin & B. Shire (Eds.), *Language in mathematical education: Research and practice* (pp. 211–226). Milton Keynes, PA: Open University Press.

Fuson, K. C., & Kwon, Y. (1992a). Korean children's understanding of multidigit addition and subtraction. *Child Development, 63,* 491–506.

Fuson, K. C., & Kwon, Y. (1992b). Korean children's single-digit addition and subtraction: Numbers structured by 10. *Journal for Research in Mathematics Education, 23,* 148–165.

Fuson, K. C., Stigler, J. W., & Bartsch, K. (1988). Grade placement of addition and subtraction topics in Japan, Mainland China, the Soviet Union, Taiwan, and the United States. *Journal for Research in Mathematics Education, 19,* 449–456.

Gallistel, C. R., & Gelman, R. (1992). Preverbal and verbal counting and computation. *Cognition, 44,* 43–74.

Geary, D. C. (1994). *Children's mathematical development: Research and practical applications.* Washington, DC: American Psychological Association.

Geary, D. C. (1995). Reflections of evolution and culture in children's cognition: Implications for mathematical development and instruction. *American Psychologist, 50,* 24–37.

Geary, D. C. (2002). Principles of evolutionary educational psychology. *Learning and Individual Differences, 12,* 317–345.

Geary, D. C. (2004a). Evolution and cognitive development. In R. Burgess & K. MacDonald (Eds.), *Evolutionary perspectives on human development* (pp. 99–133). Thousand Oaks, CA: Sage.

Geary, D. C. (2004b). Mathematics and learning disabilities. *Journal of Learning Disabilities, 37,* 4–15.

Geary, D. C. (2005). *The origin of mind: Evolution of brain, cognition, and general intelligence.* Washington, DC: American Psychological Association.

Geary, D. C., & Bjorklund, D. F. (2000). Evolutionary developmental psychology. *Child Development, 71,* 57–65.

Geary, D. C., Bow-Thomas, C. C., Liu, F., & Siegler, R. S. (1996). Development of arithmetic competencies in Chinese and American children: Influence of age, language, and schooling. *Child Development, 67,* 2022–2044.

Geary, D. C., Bow-Thomas, C. C., & Yao, Y. (1992). Counting knowledge and skill in cognitive addition: A comparison of normal and mathematically disabled children. *Journal of Experimental Child Psychology, 54,* 372–391.

Geary, D. C., Frensch, P. A., & Wiley, J. G. (1993). Simple and complex mental subtraction: Strategy choice and speed-of-processing differences in younger and older adults. *Psychology and Aging, 8,* 242–256.

Geary, D. C., Hamson, C. O., Chen, G. P., Liu, F., Hoard, M. K., & Salthouse, T. A. (1997). Computational and reasoning abilities in arithmetic: Cross-generational change in China and the United States. *Psychonomic Bulletin and Review, 4,* 425–430.

Geary, D. C., Hamson, C. O., & Hoard, M. K. (2000). Numerical and arithmetical cognition: A longitudinal study of process and concept deficits in children with learning disability. *Journal of Experimental Child Psychology, 77,* 236–263.

Geary, D. C., Hoard, M. K., Byrd-Craven, J., & DeSoto, M. C. (2004). Strategy choices in simple and complex addition: Contributions of working memory and counting knowledge for children with mathematical disability. *Journal of Experimental Child Psychology, 88,* 121–151.

Geary, D. C., & Widaman, K. F. (1992). Numerical cognition: On the convergence of componential and psychometric models. *Intelligence, 16,* 47–80.

Geary, D. C., Widaman, K. F., & Little, T. D. (1986). Cognitive addition and multiplication: Evidence for a single memory network. *Memory and Cognition, 14,* 478–487.

Gelman, R. (1972). Logical capacity of very young children: Number invariance rules. *Child Development, 43,* 75–90.

Gelman, R. (1990). First principles organize attention to and learning about relevant data: Number and animate-inanimate distinction as examples. *Cognitive Science, 14,* 79–106.

Gelman, R. (1991). Epigenetic foundations of knowledge structures: Initial and transcendent constructions. In S. Carey & R. Gelman (Eds.), *Epigenesis of mind: Essays on biology and cognition* (pp. 293–322). Hillsdale, NJ: Erlbaum.

Gelman, R., & Gallistel, C. R. (1978). *The child's understanding of number.* Cambridge, MA: Harvard University Press.

Gelman, R., & Meck, E. (1983). Preschooler's counting: Principles before skill. *Cognition, 13,* 343–359.

Gelman, R., & Williams, E. M. (1998). Enabling constraints for cognitive development and learning: Domain-specificity and epigenesis. In W. Damon (Editor-in-Chief) & D. Kuhn & R. S. Siegler (Vol. Eds.), *Handbook of child psychology: Vol. 2. Cognition, perception, and language* (5th ed., pp. 575–630). New York: Wiley.

Gelman, S. A. (2003). *The essential child: Origins of essentialism in everyday thought.* New York: Oxford University Press.

Giedd, J. N., Blumenthal, J., Jeffries, N. O., Castellanos, F. X., Liu, H., Zijdenbos, A., et al. (1999). Brain development during childhood and adolescence: A longitudinal MRI study. *Nature Neuroscience, 2,* 861–863.

Ginsburg, H. (1977). *Children's arithmetic: The learning process.* New York: Van Nostrand.

Ginsburg, H. P., Klein, A., & Starkey, P. (1998). The development of children's mathematical thinking: Connecting research with practice. In W. Damon (Editor-in-Chief) & I. E. Sigel & K. A. Renninger (Vol. Eds.), *Handbook of child psychology: Vol. 4. Child psychology in practice* (5th ed., pp. 401–476). New York: Wiley.

Ginsburg, H. P., Posner, J. K., & Russell, R. L. (1981). The development of mental addition as a function of schooling and culture. *Journal of Cross-Cultural Psychology, 12,* 163–178.

Goodman, C. H. (1943). A factorial analysis of Thurstone's sixteen primary mental ability tests. *Psychometrika, 8,* 141–151.

Gordon, P. (2004, October 15). Numerical cognition without words: Evidence from Amazonia. *Science, 306,* 496–499.

Greenough, W. T., Black, J. E., & Wallace, C. S. (1987). Experience and brain development. *Child Development, 58,* 539–559.

Groen, G. J., & Parkman, J. M. (1972). A chronometric analysis of simple addition. *Psychological Review, 79,* 329–343.

Groen, G., & Resnick, L. B. (1977). Can preschool children invent addition algorithms? *Journal of Educational Psychology, 69,* 645–652.

Hahn, H. H., & Thorndike, E. L. (1914). Some results of practice in addition under school conditions. *Journal of Educational Psychology, 5,* 65–83.

Hamann, M. S., & Ashcraft, M. H. (1985). Simple and complex mental addition across development. *Journal of Experimental Child Psychology, 40,* 49–72.

Hatano, G. (1982). Learning to add and subtract: A Japanese perspective. In T. P. Carpenter, J. M. Moser, & T. A. Romberg (Eds.), *Addition and subtraction: A cognitive perspective* (pp. 211–223). Hillsdale, NJ: Erlbaum.

Hauser, M. D., Carey, S., & Hauser, L. B. (2000). Spontaneous number representation in semi-free-ranging rhesus monkeys. *Proceedings of the Royal Society, B, 267,* 829–833.

Hecht, S. A. (1998). Toward an information-processing account of individual differences in fraction skills. *Journal of Educational Psychology, 90,* 545–559.

Hecht, S. A., Close, L., & Santisi, M. (2003). Sources of individual differences in fraction skills. *Journal of Experimental Child Psychology, 86,* 277–302.

Hegarty, M., & Kozhevnikov, M. (1999). Types of visual-spatial representations and mathematical problem solving. *Journal of Educational Psychology, 91,* 684–689.

Hirsch, E. D., Jr. (1996). *The schools we need and why we don't have them.* New York: Doubleday.

Hitch, G. J. (1978). The role of short-term working memory in mental arithmetic. *Cognitive Psychology, 10,* 302–323.

Houdé, O. (1997). Numerical development: From the infant to the child—Wynn's (1992) paradigm in 2- and 3-year olds. *Cognitive Development, 12,* 373–391.

Huntley-Fenner, G., & Cannon, E. (2000). Preschoolers' magnitude comparisons are mediated by a preverbal analog mechanism. *Psychological Science, 11,* 147–152.

Huttenlocher, J., Jordan, N. C., & Levine, S. C. (1994). A mental model for early arithmetic. *Journal of Experimental Psychology: General, 123,* 284–296.

Ilg, F., & Ames, L. B. (1951). Developmental trends in arithmetic. *Journal of Genetic Psychology, 79,* 3–28.

Jordan, N. C., Huttenlocher, J., & Levine, S. C. (1992). Differential calculation abilities in young children from middle- and low-income families. *Developmental Psychology, 28,* 644–653.

Jordan, N. C., & Montani, T. O. (1997). Cognitive arithmetic and problem solving: A comparison of children with specific and general mathematics difficulties. *Journal of Learning Disabilities, 30,* 624–634.

Kahneman, D., Treisman, A., & Gibbs, S. (1992). The reviewing of object-files: Object specific integration of information. *Cognitive Psychology, 24,* 175–219.

Kane, M. J., & Engle, R. W. (2002). The role of prefrontal cortex in working-memory capacity, executive attention, and general fluid intelligence: An individual-differences perspective. *Psychonomic Bulletin and Review, 9,* 637–671.

Keil, F. C. (1992). The origins of an autonomous biology. In M. R. Gunnar & M. Maratsos (Eds.), *The Minnesota Symposia on Child Psychology: Vol. 25. Modularity and constraints in language and cognition* (pp. 103–137). Hillsdale, NJ: Erlbaum.

Kintsch, W., & Greeno, J. G. (1985). Understanding and solving arithmetic word problems. *Psychological Review, 92,* 109–129.

Klein, J. S., & Bisanz, J. (2000). Preschoolers doing arithmetic: The concepts are willing but the working memory is weak. *Canadian Journal of Experimental Psychology, 54,* 105–115.

Kobayashi, T., Hiraki, K., Mugitani, R., & Hasegawa, T. (2004). Baby arithmetic: One object plus one tone. *Cognition, 91,* B23–B34.

Koechlin, E., Dehaene, S., & Mehler, J. (1997). Numerical transformations in 5-month-old human infants. *Mathematical Cognition, 3,* 89–104.

LeFevre, J.-A., Greenham, S. L., & Waheed, N. (1993). The development of procedural and conceptual knowledge in computational estimation. *Cognition and Instruction, 11,* 95–132.

Lemaire, P., & Lecacheur, M. (2002a). Applying the choice/no-choice methodology: The case of children's strategy use in spelling. *Developmental Science, 5,* 43–48.

Lemaire, P., & Lecacheur, M. (2002b). Children's strategies in computational estimation. *Journal of Experimental Child Psychology, 82,* 281–304.

Lemaire, P., & Siegler, R. S. (1995). Four aspects of strategic change: Contributions to children's learning of multiplication. *Journal of Experimental Psychology: General, 124,* 83–97.

Lewis, A. B., & Mayer, R. E. (1987). Students' miscomprehension of relational statements in arithmetic word problems. *Journal of Educational Psychology, 79,* 363–371.

Lipton, J. S., & Spelke, E. S. (2003). Origins of number sense: Large-number discrimination in human infants. *Psychological Science, 14,* 396–401.

Lyon, B. E. (2003, April 3). Egg recognition and counting reduce costs of avian conspecific brood parasitism. *Nature, 422,* 495–499.

Markman, E. M. (1979). Classes and collections: Conceptual organization and numerical abilities. *Cognitive Psychology, 11,* 395–411.

Mayer, R. E. (1981). Frequency norms and structural analysis of algebra story problems into families, categories, and templates. *Instructional Science, 10,* 135–175.

Mayer, R. E. (1985). Mathematical ability. In R. J. Sternberg (Ed.), *Human abilities: An information processing approach* (pp. 127–150). San Francisco: Freeman.

McCloskey, M., Sokol, S. M., & Goodman, R. A. (1986). Cognitive processes in verbal-number production: Inferences from the performance of brain-damaged subjects. *Journal of Experimental Psychology: General, 115,* 307–330.

McCrink, K., & Wynn, K. (2004). Large-number addition and subtraction by 9-month-old infants. *Psychological Science, 15,* 776–781.

McDonald, R. J., & White, N. M. (1993). A triple dissociation of memory systems: Hippocampus, amygdala, and dorsal striatum. *Behavioral Neuroscience, 107,* 3–22.

McLellan, J. A., & Dewey, J. (1895). *The psychology of number and its applications to methods of teaching arithmetic.* New York: Appleton.

Meck, W. H., & Church, R. M. (1983). A mode control model of counting and timing processes. *Journal of Experimental Psychology: Animal Behavior Processes, 9,* 320–334.

Mehler, J., & Bever, T. G. (1967, October 6). Cognitive capacity of very young children. *Science, 158,* 141–142.

Metzler, W. H. (1912). Problems in the experimental pedagogy of geometry. *Journal of Educational Psychology, 3*, 545–560.

Meyers, C. E., & Dingman, H. F. (1960). The structure of abilities at the preschool ages: Hypothesized domains. *Psychological Bulletin, 57*, 514–532.

Miller, K. F., & Paredes, D. R. (1990). Starting to add worse: Effects of learning to multiply on children's addition. *Cognition, 37*, 213–242.

Miller, K. F., Smith, C. M., Zhu, J., & Zhang, H. (1995). Preschool origins of cross-national differences in mathematical competence: The role of number-naming systems. *Psychological Science, 6*, 56–60.

Miller, K. F., & Stigler, J. W. (1987). Counting in Chinese: Cultural variation in a basic cognitive skill. *Cognitive Development, 2*, 279–305.

Miura, I. T., Kim, C. C., Chang, C. M., & Okamoto, Y. (1988). Effects of language characteristics on children's cognitive representation of number: Cross-national comparisons. *Child Development, 59*, 1445–1450.

Miura, I. T., Okamoto, Y., Kim, C. C., Steere, M., & Fayol, M. (1993). First graders' cognitive representation of number and understanding of place value: Cross-national comparisons—France, Japan, Korea, Sweden, and the United States. *Journal of Educational Psychology, 85*, 24–30.

Miura, I. T., Okamoto, Y., Vlahovic-Stetic, V., Kim, C. C., & Han, J. H. (1999). Language supports for children's understanding of numerical fractions: Cross-national comparisons. *Journal of Experimental Child Psychology, 74*, 356–365.

Mix, K. S., Levine, S. C., & Huttenlocher, J. (1997). Numerical abstraction in infants: Another look. *Developmental Psychology, 33*, 423–428.

Mix, K. S., Levine, S. C., & Huttenlocher, J. (1999). Early fraction calculation ability. *Developmental Psychology, 35*, 164–174.

Moore, D., Benenson, J., Reznick, J. S., Peterson, M., & Kagan, J. (1987). Effect of auditory numerical information on infants' looking behavior: Contradictory evidence. *Developmental Psychology, 23*, 665–670.

Naito, M., & Miura, H. (2001). Japanese children's numerical competencies: Age- and schooling-related influences on the development of number concepts and addition skills. *Developmental Psychology, 37*, 217–230.

Newcombe, N. S. (2002). The nativist-empiricist controversy in the context of recent research on spatial and quantitative development. *Psychological Science, 13*, 395–401.

Osborne, R. T., & Lindsey, J. M. (1967). A longitudinal investigation of change in the factorial composition of intelligence with age in young school children. *Journal of Genetic Psychology, 110*, 49–58.

O'Shea, M. V. (1901). The psychology of number: A genetic view. *Psychological Review, 8*, 371–383.

Paik, J. H., & Mix, K. S. (2003). United States and Korean children's comprehension of fraction names: A reexamination of cross-national differences. *Child Development, 74*, 144–154.

Pepperberg, I. M. (1987). Evidence for conceptual quantitative abilities in the African grey parrot: Labeling of cardinal sets. *Ethology, 75*, 37–61.

Piaget, J. (1950). *The psychology of intelligence*. London: Routledge & Kegan Paul.

Piaget, J. (1965). *The child's conception of number*. New York: Norton.

Piaget, J., Inhelder, I., & Szeminska, A. (1960). *The child's conception of geometry*. London: Routledge & Kegan Paul.

Pica, P., Lemer, C., Izard, V., & Dehaene, S. (2004, October 15). Exact and approximate arithmetic in an Amazonian indigene group. *Science, 306*, 499–503.

Pinel, P., Piazza, D., Le Bihan, D., & Dehaene, S. (2004). Distributed and overlapping cerebral representations of number, size, and luminance during comparative judgments. *Neuron, 41*, 1–20.

Posner, M. I. (1994). Attention: The mechanisms of consciousness. *Proceedings of the National Academy of Sciences, USA, 91*, 7398–7403.

Resnick, L. B. (1992). From protoquantities to operators: Building mathematical competence on a foundation of everyday knowledge. In G. Leinhardt, R. Putnam, & R. A. Hattrup (Eds.), *Analysis of arithmetic for mathematics teaching* (pp. 373–425). Hillsdale, NJ: Erlbaum.

Riley, M. S., & Greeno, J. G. (1988). Developmental analysis of understanding language about quantities and of solving problems. *Cognition and Instruction, 5*, 49–101.

Riley, M. S., Greeno, J. G., & Heller, J. I. (1983). Development of children's problem-solving ability in arithmetic. In H. P. Ginsburg (Ed.), *The development of mathematical thinking* (pp. 153–196). New York: Academic Press.

Rittle-Johnson, B., Siegler, R. S., & Alibali, M. W. (2001). Developing conceptual understanding and procedural skill in mathematics: An iterative process. *Journal of Educational Psychology, 93*, 346–362.

Rozin, P. (1976). The evolution of intelligence and access to the cognitive unconscious. In J. M. Sprague & A. N. Epstein (Eds.), *Progress in psychobiology and physiological psychology* (Vol. 6, pp. 245–280). New York: Academic Press.

Sarnecka, B. W., & Gelman, S. A. (2004). Six does not just mean a lot: Preschoolers see number words as specific. *Cognition, 92*, 329–352.

Saxe, G. B. (1981). Body parts as numerals: A developmental analysis of numeration among the Oksapmin of Papua, New Guinea. *Child Development, 52*, 306–316.

Saxe, G. B. (1982). Culture and the development of numerical cognition: Studies among the Oksapmin of Papua, New Guinea. In C. J. Brainerd (Ed.), *Children's logical and mathematical cognition: Progress in cognitive development research* (pp. 157–176). New York: Springer-Verlag.

Saxe, G. B. (1985). Effects of schooling on arithmetical understandings: Studies with Oksapmin Children in Papua, New Guinea. *Journal of Educational Psychology, 77*, 503–513.

Saxe, G. B., Guberman, S. R., & Gearhart, M. (1987). Social processes in early number development. *Monographs of the Society for Research in Child Development, 52*(2, Serial No. 216).

Scarr, S. (1992). Developmental theories of the 1990s: Developmental and individual differences. *Child Development, 63*, 1–19.

Schoenfeld, A. H. (1987). What's all the fuss about metacognition. In A. H. Schoenfeld (Ed.), *Cognitive science and mathematics education* (pp. 189–215). Hillsdale, NJ: Erlbaum.

Schyns, P. G., Bonnar, L., & Gosselin, F. (2002). Show me the features! Understanding recognition from the use of visual information. *Psychological Science, 13*, 402–409.

Sharon, T., & Wynn, K. (1998). Individuation of actions from continuous motion. *Psychological Science, 9*, 357–362.

Shrager, J., & Siegler, R. S. (1998). SCADS: A model of children's strategy choices and strategy discoveries. *Psychological Science, 9*, 405–410.

Siegler, R. S. (1983). Five generalizations about cognitive development. *American Psychologist, 38*, 263–277.

Siegler, R. S. (1987). The perils of averaging data over strategies: An example from children's addition. *Journal of Experimental Psychology: General, 116,* 250–264.

Siegler, R. S. (1988a). Individual differences in strategy choices: Good students, not-so-good students, and perfectionists. *Child Development, 59,* 833–851.

Siegler, R. S. (1988b). Strategy choice procedures and the development of multiplication skill. *Journal of Experimental Psychology: General, 117,* 258–275.

Siegler, R. S. (1989). Hazards of mental chronometry: An example from children's subtraction. *Journal of Educational Psychology, 81,* 497–506.

Siegler, R. S. (1996). *Emerging minds: The process of change in children's thinking.* New York: Oxford University Press.

Siegler, R. S., & Booth, J. L. (2004). Development of numerical estimation in young children. *Child Development, 75,* 428–444.

Siegler, R. S., & Booth, J. L. (2005). Development of numerical estimation: A review. In J. I. D. Campbell (Ed.), *Handbook of mathematical cognition* (pp. 197–212). New York: Psychology Press.

Siegler, R. S., & Crowley, K. (1991). The microgenetic method: A direct means for studying cognitive development. *American Psychologist, 46,* 606–620.

Siegler, R. S., & Jenkins, E. (1989). *How children discover new strategies.* Hillsdale, NJ: Erlbaum.

Siegler, R. S., & Lemaire, P. (1997). Older and younger adults' strategy choices in multiplication: Testing predictions of ASCM using the choice/no-choice method. *Journal of Experimental Psychology: General, 126,* 71–92.

Siegler, R. S., & Opfer, J. (2003). The development of numerical estimation: Evidence for multiple representations of numerical quantity. *Psychological Science, 14,* 237–243.

Siegler, R. S., & Robinson, M. (1982). The development of numerical understandings. In H. Reese & L. P. Lipsitt (Eds.), *Advances in child development and behavior* (Vol. 16, pp. 241–312). New York: Academic Press.

Siegler, R. S., & Shipley, C. (1995). Variation, selection, and cognitive change. In T. Simon & G. Halford (Eds.), *Developing cognitive competence: New approaches to process modeling* (pp. 31–76). Hillsdale, NJ: Erlbaum.

Siegler, R. S., & Shrager, J. (1984). Strategy choice in addition and subtraction: How do children know what to do. In C. Sophian (Ed.), *Origins of cognitive skills* (pp. 229–293). Hillsdale, NJ: Erlbaum.

Siegler, R. S., & Stern, E. (1998). Conscious and unconscious strategy discoveries: A microgenetic analysis. *Journal of Experimental Psychology: General, 127,* 377–397.

Simon, T. J. (1997). Reconceptualizing the origins of number knowledge: A "non-numerical" account. *Cognitive Development, 12,* 349–372.

Simon, T. J., Hespos, S. J., & Rochat, P. (1995). Do infants understand simple arithmetic? A replication of Wynn (1992). *Cognitive Development, 10,* 253–269.

Song, M. J., & Ginsburg, H. P. (1987). The development of informal and formal mathematical thinking in Korean and U.S. children. *Child Development, 58,* 1286–1296.

Sophian, C. (1997). Beyond competence: The significance of performance for conceptual development. *Cognitive Development, 12,* 281–303.

Sophian, C., & Adams, N. (1987). Infants' understanding of numerical transformations. *British Journal of Developmental Psychology, 5,* 257–264.

Sophian, C., Harley, H., & Martin, C. S. M. (1995). Relational and representational aspects of early number development. *Cognition and Instruction, 13,* 253–268.

Sophian, C., & McCorgray, P. (1994). Part-whole knowledge and early arithmetic problem solving. *Cognition and Instruction, 12,* 3–33.

Spearman, C. (1904). General intelligence, objectively determined and measured. *American Journal of Psychology, 15,* 201–293.

Spearman, C. (1927). *The abilities of man.* London: Macmillan.

Spelke, E. S. (2000). Core knowledge. *American Psychologist, 55,* 1233–1243.

Spelke, E. S., Breinlinger, K., Macomber, J., & Jacobson, K. (1992). Origins of knowledge. *Psychological Review, 99,* 605–632.

Starch, D. (1911). Transfer of training in arithmetical operations. *Journal of Educational Psychology, 2,* 306–310.

Starkey, P. (1992). The early development of numerical reasoning. *Cognition, 43,* 93–126.

Starkey, P., & Cooper, R. G., Jr. (1980, November 28). Perception of numbers by human infants. *Science, 210,* 1033–1035.

Starkey, P., & Gelman, R. (1982). The development of addition and subtraction abilities prior to formal schooling in arithmetic. In T. P. Carpenter, J. M. Moser, & T. A. Romberg (Eds.), *Addition and subtraction: A cognitive perspective* (pp. 99-116). Hillsdale, NJ: Erlbaum.

Starkey, P., Spelke, E. S., & Gelman, R. (1983, October 14). Detection of intermodal numerical correspondences by human infants. *Science, 222,* 179–181.

Starkey, P., Spelke, E. S., & Gelman, R. (1990). Numerical abstraction by human infants. *Cognition, 36,* 97–127.

Stevenson, H. W., Lee, S. Y., Chen, C., Stigler, J. W., Hsu, C. C., & Kitamura, S. (1990). Contexts of achievement: A study of American, Chinese and Japanese children. *Monographs of the Society for Research in Child Development, 55*(Serial No. 221).

Strauss, M. S., & Curtis, L. E. (1984). Development of numerical concepts in infancy. In C. Sophian (Ed.), *The 18th Annual Carnegie Symposium on Cognition: Origins of cognitive skills* (pp. 131–155). Hillsdale, NJ: Erlbaum.

Svenson, O., & Sjöberg, K. (1983). Evolution of cognitive processes for solving simple additions during the first 3 school years. *Scandinavian Journal of Psychology, 24,* 117–124.

Sweller, J., Mawer, R. F., & Ward, M. R. (1983). Development of expertise in mathematical problem solving. *Journal of Experimental Psychology: General, 112,* 639–661.

Ta'ir, J., Brezner, A., & Ariel, R. (1997). Profound developmental dyscalculia: Evidence for a cardinal/ordinal skills acquisition device. *Brain and Cognition, 35,* 184–206.

Taylor, J. F. (1918). The classification of pupils in elementary algebra. *Journal of Educational Psychology, 9,* 361–380.

Temple, E., & Posner, M. I. (1998). Brain mechanisms of quantity are similar in 5-year-old children and adults. *Proceedings of the National Academy of Sciences, USA, 95,* 7836–7841.

Thompson, R. F., & Krupa, D. J. (1994). Organization of memory traces in the mammalian brain. *Annual Review of Neuroscience, 17,* 519–549.

Thorndike, E. L. (1922). *The psychology of arithmetic.* New York: Macmillan.

Thorndike, E. L., & Woodworth, R. S. (1901). The influence of improvement in one mental function upon the efficiency of other functions: Vol. 2. Estimation of magnitudes. *Psychological Review, 8,* 384–394.

Thurstone, L. L. (1938). Primary mental abilities. *Psychometric Monographs*(1).

Thurstone, L. L., & Thurstone, T. G. (1941). Factorial studies of intelligence. *Psychometric Monographs*(2).

Timberlake, W. (1994). Behavior systems, associationism, and Pavlovian conditioning. *Psychonomic Bulletin and Review, 1,* 405–420.

Towse, J., & Saxton, M. (1997). Linguistic influences on children's number concepts: Methodological and theoretical considerations. *Journal of Experimental Child Psychology, 66,* 362–375.

Trick, L. M. (1992). A theory of enumeration that grows out of a general theory of vision: Subitizing, counting, and FINSTs. In J. I. D. Campbell (Ed.), *The nature and origins of mathematical skills* (pp. 257–299). Amsterdam: North-Holland.

Tronsky, L. N., & Royer, J. M. (2002). Relationships among basic computational automaticity, working memory, and complex mathematical problem solving. In J. M. Royer (Ed.), *Mathematical cognition* (pp. 117–146). Greenwich, CT: Information Age Publishing.

Uller, C., Carey, S., Huntley-Fenner, G., & Klatt, L. (1999). What representations might underlie infant numerical knowledge? *Cognitive Development, 14,* 1–36.

van Loosbroek, E., & Smitsman, A. W. (1990). Visual perception of numerosity in infancy. *Developmental Psychology, 26,* 916–922.

Varelas, M., & Becker, J. (1997). Children's developing understanding of place value: Semiotic aspects. *Cognition and Instruction, 15,* 265–286.

Vergnaud, G. (1983). Multiplicative structures. In R. Lesh & M. Landau (Eds.), *Acquisition of mathematics concepts and processes* (pp. 127–174). New York: Academic Press.

Very, P. S. (1967). Differential factor structures in mathematical ability. *Genetic Psychology Monographs, 75,* 169–207.

Vilette, B. (2002). Do young children grasp the inverse relationship between addition and subtraction? Evidence against early arithmetic. *Cognitive Development, 17,* 1365–1383.

Wakeley, A., Rivera, S., & Langer, J. (2000). Can young infants add and subtract? *Child Development, 71,* 1525–1534.

Washburne, C., & Vogel, M. (1928). Are any number combinations inherently difficult? *Journal of Educational Research, 17,* 235–255.

Welsh, M. C., & Pennington, B. F. (1988). Assessing frontal lobe functioning in children: Views from developmental psychology. *Developmental Neuropsychology, 4,* 199–230.

Widaman, K. F., Geary, D. C., Cormier, P., & Little, T. D. (1989). A componential model for mental addition. *Journal of Experimental Psychology: Learning, Memory, and Cognition, 15,* 898–919.

Winch, W. H. (1910). Accuracy in school children: Does improvement in numerical accuracy "transfer"? *Journal of Educational Psychology, 1,* 557–589.

Wynn, K. (1990). Children's understanding of counting. *Cognition, 36,* 155–193.

Wynn, K. (1992a, August 27). Addition and subtraction by human infants. *Nature, 358,* 749–750.

Wynn, K. (1992b). Children's acquisition of the number words and the counting system. *Cognitive Psychology, 24,* 220–251.

Wynn, K. (1995). Origins of numerical knowledge. *Mathematical Cognition, 1,* 35–60.

Wynn, K. (1996). Infants' individuation and enumeration of actions. *Psychological Science, 7,* 164–169.

Wynn, K. (2000). Findings of addition and subtraction in infants are robust and consistent: Reply to Wakeley, Rivera, and Langer. *Child Development, 71,* 1535–1536.

Wynn, K. (2002). Do infants have numerical expectations or just perceptual preferences? *Developmental Science, 5,* 207–209.

Wynn, K., Bloom, P., & Chiang, W.-C. (2002). Enumeration of collective entities by 5-month-old infants. *Cognition, 83,* B55–B62.

Wynn, K., & Chiang, W.-C. (1998). Limits to infants' knowledge of objects: The case of magical appearance. *Psychological Science, 9,* 448–455.

Xu, F., & Spelke, E. S. (2000). Large number discrimination in 6-month-old infants. *Cognition, 74,* B1–B11.

Zaslavsky, C. (1973). *Africa counts: Number and pattern in African culture.* Boston: Prindle, Weber, & Schmidt.

Zorzi, M., Priftis, K., & Umilta, C. (2002, May 9). Neglect disrupts the mental number line. *Nature, 417,* 138.

# CHAPTER 19

# *Social Cognition*

PAUL L. HARRIS

HISTORICAL BACKGROUND (1920–1980)  811
A FRESH START  812
INFANT SOCIAL COGNITION  813
The Detection of Goal-Directed Agency  813
Emotion and Preverbal Dialogue  816
Gaze Following and Social Referencing  817
Comforting and Helping  818
Offering Help and Cooperation  820
Hurting and Teasing  821
MENTAL STATE UNDERSTANDING IN
    EARLY CHILDHOOD  822
Goals, Desires, and Intentions  822
Beliefs  823
Perception, Knowledge, and Source Monitoring  826
Emotion  828
Thoughts, Memories, and the Stream
    of Consciousness  832
LATER DEVELOPMENTS AND MATURE
    FUNCTIONING  834
Understanding Doubt and Uncertainty  834

Understanding Second-Order Beliefs and
    Nonliteral Utterances  836
Measures of Reflective Functioning among Adults  837
HOW DO HUMANS DIFFER FROM OTHER
    NONHUMAN PRIMATES IN THEIR THEORY
    OF MIND?  839
IS THERE A UNIVERSAL CORE TO THE HUMAN
    THEORY OF MIND?  841
CHILDREN WITH AUTISM  842
INDIVIDUAL DIFFERENCES IN PRETEND PLAY
    AND THEORY OF MIND  844
THE RELATIONSHIP BETWEEN LANGUAGE AND
    THEORY OF MIND  845
TAKING STOCK  847
Social Cognition and Peer Relations  847
Social Cognition and Trust  848
Emerging Contours in the Child's Theory of Mind  850
REFERENCES  851

## HISTORICAL BACKGROUND (1920–1980)

A debate over the nature of social cognition was engaged very early in the history of developmental psychology. Piaget assumed that the child is naturally egocentric. Thus, even when the child uses a social tool such as language, it is put to egocentric use rather than to communicate. By contrast, Vygotsky assumed that the child is naturally social so that any nonsocial, egocentric use of language comes later in development. Despite this early debate—and the compelling arguments advanced by Vygotsky for acknowledging the very young child's capacity for social engagement—it was Piagetian theory that dominated the study of cognitive development throughout most of the 1960s and 1970s. Against that backdrop, it is not surprising that the development of social cognition was largely construed as the gradual breakdown of egocentrism—or the slow emergence of the capacity for role taking. On this view, the child's

task was to increasingly recognize and make allowances for differences between self and other. Two influential texts that emerged from that era are *The Development of Role-Taking and Communication Skills in Children* by Flavell and his colleagues (Flavell, Botkin, Fry, Wright, & Jarvis, 1968) and Kohlberg's (1969) chapter offering a cognitive-developmental approach to social cognition and to key issues in socialization.

In the following decade, a flurry of research with young infants gave pause to those wedded to the classic, Piagetian view of the young infant as egocentric. Several studies produced results that strongly suggested a capacity for sharing and mutuality from the earliest months. For example, Meltzoff demonstrated—albeit not without controversy—an early, imitative sensitivity to the facial and manual gestures of a partner (Meltzoff, 1976; Meltzoff & Moore, 1977). Trevarthen laid out a theory of early intersubjectivity (Trevarthen & Hubley, 1978). Scaife and Bruner (1975) published a pioneering paper showing that infants can engage in joint attention with an adult partner before the age of 12 months. These various demonstrations showed that the young infant is nicely attuned to other people. At the same time, they did not in themselves lead to any radically new theorizing in the larger study of social cognitive development. Rather, they added to the growing list of findings showing that the young infant was much more competent than standard Piagetian theory might lead us to believe. They also showed quite clearly that experimental analysis of the infant's social cognition was a feasible and potentially fruitful avenue to explore.

## A FRESH START

Vygotsky's developmental account had woven together two different strands. First, as a developmental psychologist, he emphasized functional changes that emerged in the course of development. In particular, he stressed the way that thought and language coalesce to form a new functional whole in the child's mind. At the same time, Vygotsky took a comparative approach to development. The available findings in primatology suggested to him that no such coalescence took place in the course of chimpanzee development. Oddly enough, despite his strong interest in evolution and a biological approach to the genesis of knowledge, Piaget rarely adopted a comparative approach to cognitive development, and—given the dominance of Piagetian theory—no such comparative approach was taken to the study of social cognition.

A landmark paper by two primatologists—David Premack and Guy Woodruff (1978)—showed that the study of social cognition can benefit greatly from a comparative flavor. They asked if the chimpanzee has a theory of mind, by which they meant does the chimpanzee go beyond the observation of overt behavior to infer the goals and plans that guide behavior. To answer that question, they showed their chimpanzee subject, Sarah, film clips of a human agent struggling unsuccessfully with a practical problem—for example, trying to reach some bananas overhead. After seeing each clip, Sarah was invited to indicate what the agent would do next by choosing from among several possible illustrated continuations to the film clip. Sarah was quite successful in selecting likely continuations. For example, she judged that the agent trying to reach the bananas would pile boxes underneath the bananas rather than push boxes aside. Premack and Woodruff concluded that

Sarah must have been able to figure out what the agent was trying to do and indicated his or her next steps appropriately in the light of that goal.

Commentaries on the results homed in on one further point. Ever since Kohler's famous experiments on the problem-solving abilities of chimpanzees, we have known that they can solve practical problems such as those with the bananas: They can search for boxes, pile them up, and climb on them in order to reach up. So, said the commentators, maybe the chimpanzee is not such a sophisticated psychologist after all. Maybe the chimpanzee is simply projecting onto the human agent what it would do in similar circumstances.

To counter this possibility, various commentators suggested an alternative experimental setup in which the observing subject is invited to make a prediction about a mistaken or misinformed protagonist. Such a setup would oblige the subject to differentiate between what he or she would do in the circumstances and what the mistaken protagonist would do. In other words, a simple strategy of projection would be wrong—it would not make appropriate allowance for the subjective stance of the protagonist. Prompted by this challenge, Wimmer and Perner (1983) reported a set of studies in which children were invited to make predictions about a doll protagonist that was mistaken about the current location of an object. For example, the protagonist put his chocolate in one cupboard and then left the scene; his brother moved the chocolate to another hiding-place in his absence. Wimmer and Perner (1983) found that 4- and 5-year-olds could accurately anticipate where the protagonist would search for the chocolate on his return (i.e., in the cupboard where he had first put it) but younger children could not (i.e., they assumed he would search at its new hiding-place).

This clever experiment triggered an avalanche of replications and challenges. Some who had been raised on the Piagetian notion of egocentrism—such as myself—were impressed and surprised that 4-year-olds could solve the problem at all. Others, by contrast, were dubious about the failure of 3-year-olds and attempted various experimental manipulations in an effort to uncover greater competence at that age. Alongside this program of research in developmental psychology, two other related research programs rapidly got underway. First, Baron-Cohen, Leslie, and Frith (1985) discovered that autistic children, even those with a relatively advanced mental age, frequently fail a variant of Wimmer and Perner's false-belief task. This led to a series of studies aimed at assessing the extent to which the various symptoms of the autistic syndrome can be understood as an innate deficit in the normal development of a theory of mind. Second, Bryne and Whiten asked whether detailed field observations of nonhuman primates might reveal mind-reading skills similar to those found in human children (Byrne & Whiten, 1988; Whiten, 1991). For example, does a chimpanzee realize that another member of the group might hold a false belief, and might even be led to such a false belief by a deliberate act of deception? This comparative perspective—fueled by dialog with developmental psychology and by debate in primatology among experimentalists—has kept the question of the biological origin of the child's theory of mind in focus. Arguably, key aspects of the child's theory of mind might be the result of some dedicated module, peculiar to the human species. Alternatively—as Vygotsky might have speculated—they might be better seen as the elaboration of an intuitive psychology found in the higher apes but transformed by their fusion with language and conversation. I return to these contentious issues later.

The three-pronged research program that emerged in the 1980s—comprising human development, developmental psychopathology, and comparative primatology—has increasingly assimilated a variety of older concepts and research traditions in social cognition. For example, studies of the development of metacognition (Flavell, Green, & Flavell, 1995) and of emotion understanding (Harris, 1989; Harris, Olthof, & Meerum Terwogt, 1981) have been transported into the capacious tent of theory-of-mind research. At the same time, other concepts and traditions have been mostly swept aside. For better or worse, few contemporary researchers debate the extent to which the young child is egocentric. Moreover, few look—as they once did (Graham & Weiner, 1986)—to social psychology or more specifically to attribution theory for an understanding of the development of social cognition.

What does this lively and relatively ecumenical program ignore? Most theory-of-mind research assumes that the child is equipped with categories for decomposing and explaining the workings of the prototypical human mind: timeless and universal. However, beneath that level of analysis, the child surely faces questions about what particular people are like as opposed to people in general—questions about the personality, skills, and reliability of specific individuals, especially those individuals whom he or she encounters firsthand in the

context of the family or community. Some of those individual differences will occasionally boil down to differences in the very categories emphasized by theory-of-mind research: This individual is misinformed but that individual is not. However, there are other individual differences that have to do with enduring traits. For example, this individual is trustworthy but that individual is not. Attachment theory has long called attention to the fact that infants, even in the 1st year of life, are quite sensitive to individual differences among their caregivers—for example, they may be securely attached to their father but display an avoidant attachment to their mother. It would be hard to deny that such sensitivity is part of the child's early social cognition. Yet, theory-of-mind researchers mostly ignore it. In a concluding section, I explore ways in which research on theory-of-mind might advance our understanding of children's sensitivity to individual differences in trustworthiness.

## INFANT SOCIAL COGNITION

Recent work on infant social cognition has been inspired both by the striking experimental results that began to appear in the 1970s and by the question of what precursors there might be to the relatively sophisticated understanding of false beliefs shown by 4- and 5-year-olds.

### The Detection of Goal-Directed Agency

To the extent that human beings move autonomously, infants are in a position to distinguish them from inanimate objects. Indeed, from about 7 months of age, infants are puzzled by the spontaneous motion of inanimate objects but not that of people (Golinkoff, Harding, Carlson, & Sexton, 1984; Spelke, Phillips, & Woodward, 1995). However, human beings also engage in a particular class of movements—their movements are autonomous and directed at some goal or target. This is particularly obvious in the case of hand and arm movements. Human agents do not simply wave a hand; they reach out and grasp objects. Recent research has actively focused on such targeted movements with a view to diagnosing the extent to which infants interpret them as goal-directed.

A study by Woodward (1998) offers an illustrative example. Infants of 5 and 9 months were habituated to the sight of a human hand and arm reaching toward and grasping one of two objects. Subsequently, infants saw an alteration in the reach: It was either directed to the same object along a different path; alternatively, it was directed to a different object along the same path. Infants treated the change of target object as more novel—as indexed by an increase in looking times. By implication, when infants watched the initial reach during habituation trials, they were more likely to encode the goal object that it was directed toward rather than the precise trajectory of the reach. As a result, they were more "surprised" by the change of target object than the change of trajectory.

At the same time, it is also clear that young infants do display some sensitivity to the trajectory of an object-directed movement: They expect it to be direct and efficient rather than unnecessarily circuitous. This fact has emerged in a series of experiments by Gergely and his colleagues (Csibra, Gergely, Biró, Koós, & Brockbank, 1999; Gergely, Nádasdy, Csibra, & Biró, 1995). Infants watched a film in which a "baby" circle went toward a larger, "mother" circle by moving up and over a barrier that separated them. After habituation, infants saw trials in which the barrier had been removed and the baby circle now either took the shorter, direct route toward mother or continued to follow the same up-and-over route—even in the absence of the barrier. Infants of 9 and 12 months looked longer at—and by implication were surprised by—the adoption of the indirect up-and-over route even though it corresponded exactly to the route taken during the previous habituation trials. Apparently, they expected the more direct route to be taken once the barrier was removed.

Summarizing across these studies on goal-directed movement, it appears that toward the end of the 1st year, infants encode the object that a movement is directed toward and generally anticipate that a movement will be direct and efficient rather than circuitous. How do infants establish such expectations? One possibility is that they learn a great deal from first-person experience. After all, by the end of the 1st year, infants will have engaged in countless deliberate, goal-directed behaviors. They will have reached for, and crawled toward, all sorts of objects. Arguably, such firsthand experience of efficient, targeted action leads infants to assume that a similar interpretation can be placed on many of the actions that they see others engaged in.

Three-month-old infants do not show the type of goal encoding that is evident among older infants. However, infants of this age are quite poor at reaching out to grasp an object themselves. If first-person experience is a vital ingredient in the interpretation of others' actions, this early lack of goal encoding is just what we might expect. Sommerville, Woodward, and Needham (2005) examined the potential role of first-person experience. When 3-month-old infants were fitted out with Velcro mittens that enabled them to grasp objects more successfully, they were subsequently able to encode the goal structure of reaching and grasping actions. So, should we conclude that infants are attributing goals on the basis of their own experience of goal-directed actions with the Velcro mittens? Possibly, but not necessarily. When the infants wore the mittens, they had the experience of being an agent. However, they could also watch—spectatorlike—as they executed such successful reaches. Arguably, the psychological experience of being an agent is critical, but it is also possible that sustained visual monitoring of reaching is sufficient to teach infants to encode action in terms of its goals.

These various findings demonstrate that the simple act of reaching can serve as an informative vehicle for figuring out how infants encode goal-directed action—and on what basis they do so. Nevertheless, a focus on such simple, and discrete, actions does not do full justice to the interpretive problems facing the infant. Consider the 12-month-old seated in a highchair. He watches as his mother goes to the refrigerator, opens the door, removes a carton of juice, pours juice into a cup, and hands him the cup. As Lashley pointed out more than 50 years ago (Lashley, 1951), such actions can scarcely be produced as a set of moment-by-moment responses to a serially ordered set of stimuli in the environment. Rather, they depend on some internal organization enabling the agent to control his or her own behavior. Miller, Galanter, and Pribram (1960) argued that the production of action is best construed as a problem of hierarchical organization, in which subordinate goal-oriented sequences are organized into a larger, overall sequence. Because it has been difficult for psychologists to understand the production of a planned sequence of actions, we might assume that infants have virtually no understanding of such a sequence. Yet, in contrast to Lashley and his contemporaries, there is no sign that young infants initially approach the problem with any predilection for stimulus-response explanations. Arguably, some form of hierarchical, goal-based analysis comes naturally to them.

In a pioneering effort to understand whether and how infants parse the stream of action, Baldwin, Baird, Saylor, and Clark (2001) showed 10- to 11-month-old infants a video of an adult engaging in an everyday action sequence. For example, in one video a woman notices a towel on the floor, reaches for the towel and picks it up, then moves toward a towel rack and places the towel on the rack. After being familiarized with this sequence, infants were given two test sequences. In the *completing* video, a still-frame pause was inserted at the point where the woman had just grasped the towel. In the *interrupting* video, by contrast, a still-frame was inserted as the woman reached down to pick up the towel. Infants spent longer looking at the interrupting video than the completing video. Baldwin et al. (2001) plausibly interpret this differential reaction as evidence that infants recognize that within a normally continuous action sequence there are subunits. Hence, a pause inserted between two identifiable subunits is less disconcerting than a pause inserted in a subunit. As the authors acknowledge, however, it is not clear how far infants' parsing into subunits is guided by a "top-down" appreciation of the subgoals that are completed in a larger hierarchy (e.g., in the case just described, an appreciation that the goal of grasping the towel has been completed) or by a "bottom-up" processing of cues that are correlates of such subdivisions. For example, if infants keep track of the direction in which an agent is moving, they might spot marked changes of direction and parse accordingly. Thus, in the case of the towel retrieval, they might parse a downward reach as one unit and an upward lift as another with little insight into the agent's intended goals.

Such theoretical issues might seem a little arcane but from an infant's point of view, they are likely to be quite practical. Consider a 12-month-old who is watching her father dip a spoon into a bowl of vegetables and then lift the spoon to her mouth. After attentively watching, the infant seeks to imitate—more or less—what he has done. On the top-down reading, she realizes that there are two goal-directed subunits: (1) lowering the spoon in order to fill it with food and (2) transporting this spoonful of food to her mouth. She tries to do the same. On the bottom-up reading, by contrast, she simply notes that the spoon is moved downward and then raised upward. She imitates her father by plunging the spoon into the bowl and lifting it up again. Whether the food is lifted to her mouth—or splattered over the table—is regarded as incidental.

Evidence for top-down processing has emerged from studies by Woodward and Somerville (2000). When 11-month-olds watched an agent produce a single ambigu-

ous single action—touching a box—they (understandably) showed no signs during a test phase of being able to decide whether the reach was aimed at the box itself or the toy inside the box. However, if they had previously seen the agent not simply touch the box lid but go on to extract the toy, they interpreted subsequent reaches to the box lid as directed at the contents of the box and not just at the box itself. By implication, watching the agent first touch the lid and then extract the toy led infants to interpret the action of touching the lid in light of the goal that it was ultimately directed at—recovery of the object. Further evidence of early top-down processing was reported by Sommerville and Woodward (2005). Infants watched an agent pull a cloth to retrieve a distant toy placed on the cloth. Subsequently, when they saw the agent simply pull a cloth they were likely to construe that action as aimed at retrieving the toy. A follow-up study with 10-month-olds revealed that this interpretation was only made by infants who could successfully retrieve objects with a cloth-pulling strategy, again suggesting—in line with the findings on 3-month-olds reported by Sommerville, Woodward, and Needham (2005)—that action production facilitates action interpretation.

Studies of imitation have also provided evidence of top-down processing. Carpenter, Call, and Tomasello (2002) invited 2-year-olds to open a box after watching an adult demonstrate the right technique—namely to pull at a wooden pin at the side of the box which enabled the front of the box to be lifted in a flaplike fashion. Most 2-year-olds failed to open the box after this demonstration. Why? Almost certainly, because when they watched the adult tug at the pin, they had no idea what she was trying to do—after all tugging at a protrusion is not standard operating procedure for getting inside a box. Support for this interpretation came from several other conditions in which children were first made aware of the adult's goal and then copied her much more successfully. For example, in one condition, the adult first tugged at the front of the box, failed to lift it, and only then pulled at the pin to release the door. Similar results, albeit with slightly older children, emerged in a study of imitation by Want and Harris (2001). If 3-year-olds saw an adult try to extract a toy from a tube by first poking a stick into the wrong end of the tube, withdrawing it, and then poking it into the correct end, they were much more likely to select the correct end when it was their turn to retrieve the toy than were children who saw the adult select the correct end straightaway. Again, it looks as if unsuccessful attempts highlight what an agent is aiming at so that the niceties of a successful attempt can be more easily encoded and reproduced.

In summary, recent evidence shows that infants rapidly come to see actions as goal-directed, and they generally expect such acts to be carried out efficiently. Two year-olds, and arguably even younger children, also recognize that any given action can be embedded in an organized hierarchy; it is aimed at a subgoal, which in turn serves a superordinate goal. Toddlers are not equipped to understand complex, long-term plans such as building a house or a railroad. Nevertheless, it looks as if they have an intuitive grasp of the hierarchical structure of human action from an early age. It is somewhat ironic that this insight emerges so early—albeit at a tacit level. That same insight is regarded as a major turning point in cognitive science (Boden, 2006).

### Emotion and Preverbal Dialogue

The understanding of emotion is, arguably, just one part of the child's more general understanding of mental states. Nevertheless, we might expect to find that sensitivity to other people's emotional states is one of the more precocious aspects of early mental state understanding. After all, except on rare occasions, people's beliefs cannot be read from their faces and even their desires are not so legible. Their emotional states, however, come with an expressive signature that might be read even by infants during the 1st year of life.

Darwin's writings on facial expression (Darwin, 1872/1998) have led to a systematic research program endorsing his claim that there is a universal, innate basis to the production of a small set of facial expressions (Ekman, 1973). However, Darwin made a nativist claim about the interpretation of facial expressions as well as their production. His argument was based on probabilistic reasoning and on analogy with other species: "Do our children acquire their knowledge of expression solely by experience through the power of association and reason? As most of the movements of expression must have been gradually acquired, afterwards becoming instinctive, there seems to be some degree of *a priori* probability that their recognition would likewise have become instinctive" (Darwin, 1872/1998, p. 353). With this hypothesis in mind, Darwin studied the emotional development of his own son and concluded that some degree of unlearned recognition was probably present. Thus, when his son's nurse deliberately pretended to

cry, his son—then aged 6 months—assumed "a melancholy expression." Given the infant's lack of experience of other people crying, Darwin reasoned that "an innate feeling must have told him that the pretended crying of his nurse expressed grief: and this, through the instinct of sympathy, excited grief in him" (Darwin, 1872/1998, p. 354).

Darwin's bold but plausible assertion of instinctive recognition has proved difficult to either verify or refute. What has emerged in the past 20 years is a small number of studies showing that young infants do respond appropriately to adults' facial expressions. For example, Termine and Izard (1988) observed a differentiated reaction by 9-month-olds to their mothers' displays of happiness versus sadness. Indeed, Haviland and Lelwica (1987) observed that babies of 10 weeks responded differently and for the most part appropriately to their mothers' displays of happiness, sadness, and anger. Yet, even by the age of 10 weeks, it could be argued that infants have had some opportunities for learning.

A related but different research theme concerns the way in which infants come to expect their caregivers to be responsive and expressive. If infants are confronted by someone who deliberately remains still and unresponsive, they become upset (for a review of this so-called still-face paradigm, see Muir & Hains, 1993). By the age of 2 to 3 months, infants show considerable sensitivity to the contingent relationship between their own expressive movements and those of an adult partner. Although they interact normally with a live image of their mother via closed-circuit television they show signs of distress if they are shown a video rather than a live image of their mother (Murray & Trevarthen, 1985; Nadel, Carchon, Kervella, Marcelli, & Réservat-Plantey, 1999). Indeed, by 3 months, infants are sensitive to the exact timing of the relationship between their own expressive movements and those of an adult partner—if a very subtle delay of 1 second is introduced into the live relay of their caretaker's image, they become less attentive (Henning & Striano, 2004; Striano, Henning, & Stahl, 2005).

There is also credible evidence that infants do not simply acquire a global expectation—that caregivers are likely to be contingently responsive. Rather, they appear to acquire a more specific expectation that is guided by the expressive style of their primary caregiver. Thus, 3- to 6-month-old infants of mothers suffering from depression are likely to adopt a less expressive style than infants with nondepressed mothers. Indeed, there is some evidence that infants of depressed mothers "overgeneralize" this flat, interactive style, adopting it even when interacting with a stranger (Field, 1984; Field, Healy, Goldstein, 1988).

Such sensitivity to the expressive style of a caretaker should not, however, be surprising. Attachment theorists have long argued that infants are sensitive to the responsiveness and availability of a caregiver. By the age of 12 months, characteristic modes of interacting with a caretaker can be identified and these characteristic modes tend to remain stable. The research on early dyadic interaction simply alerts us to the possibility that these distinctive modes can probably be discerned well before the infant is 12 months of age and well before the infant is capable of the kind of active locomotion and distal contact that is generally studied by attachment theorists in the context of the Strange Situation.

In summary, even if it is still not clear whether Darwin was right to postulate an innate, interpretive mechanism for decoding the expression of emotion, there is evidence that infants rapidly come to distinguish positive from negative emotional expressions and respond appropriately to each. They also come to expect a caregiver to be expressive and indeed to respond in a very brief time frame to their own expressive movements. Finally, infants appear to discern the emotional styles of their caregivers and to attune their own expressive behaviors to that style.

## Gaze Following and Social Referencing

At around 9 months, infants start to follow and direct the attention of a caregiver. As noted earlier, the phenomenon was first identified by Scaife and Bruner (1975). They found that when an adult turned to look either to the right or to the left, there was an increasing tendency with age for the infant to turn to look in the same direction (66% at 8 to10 months, 100% at 11 to14 months). Since this pioneering investigation, a variety of studies have described and analyzed the basic phenomenon in some detail. By 15 months, babies are able to differentiate not only one side from another but also the adult's direction of gaze within a side (Morissette, Ricard, & Decarie, 1995). Carpenter, Nagell, and Tomasello (1998) studied infants' ability to both follow and direct attention. In the study of following, an adult called the baby by name, then looked toward an object on the left or right with an excited vocalization, and then looked back and forth from object to baby. In a related condition, the adult added a pointing gesture to these various indicative behaviors. Gaze following increased in frequency between 9 and 13 months; point following also increased during the same age period and was generally somewhat more frequent.

In the study of directing, a stuffed animal was made to dance in midair or a puppet emerged from a partition. Adults pretended not to notice. A pointing gesture was credited if the child stretched toward the object and alternated gaze between object and adult's face. Give/show was credited if the infant gave or showed the object, gazed between the object and the adult's face, and vocalized as if to comment on the object. Both pointing and give/show increased markedly between 9 and 13 months with give/show being more frequent throughout. Taken together, these findings underscore the infant's emerging ability to engage in a triadic relationship comprising the self, another person, and an object of (potentially) mutual attention.

Infants capitalize on such triadic relationships in the context of what has come to be called social referencing. They receive emotional information from a caregiver and regulate their behavior toward a given object in the light of that information. An illustrative—and influential—study was reported by Sorce, Emde, Campos, and Klinnert (1985). They looked at the influence of the mother's emotional expression on whether babies would crawl over what they took to be a sharp drop (the so-called visual cliff). When the cliff was of intermediate height, such that babies hesitated to cross, most of them did cross if their mother smiled, whereas none of them did so if she produced a fearful facial expression.

Since identification of the basic phenomenon of social referencing, subsequent research has sought to analyze the exact mechanism involved. Two interpretations have seemed plausible. The caregiver's facial expression might serve as a mood-changing signal that shifts the baby toward either confident exploration or wariness. On this argument, the baby need not draw any conclusions about what object or situation has provoked the mother's emotion; rather, the baby simply resonates to the mother's expressive signals—and ends up acting appropriately—proceeding forward if she smiles but coming to a halt or retreating if she looks fearful. The second interpretation builds on the gaze-following competence just described. Suppose that the infant notices not only the caregiver's expression but also notes the object that she is attending to. The infant might treat the expression as a predicate or comment that refers to the object in question. On this account, the mother's emotional signal would not produce a broad shift toward either exploration or wariness; rather, it would produce a narrow shift in the infant's emotional stance toward a particular object.

The study reported by Sorce et al. (1985) is open to either interpretation. Various follow-up studies, however, allow us to distinguish between them. These studies indicate that although mood effects cannot be completely ruled out, infants of 12 months and upward are indeed sensitive to the referential specificity of the emotional signal (Hornik, Risenhoover, & Gunnar, 1987; Mumme, Won, & Fernald, 1994; Repacholi, 1998). For example, in a study by Repacholi (1998) infants of 14 and 18 months watched as an adult, by means of her gaze direction and actions, expressed pleasure at the (hidden) contents of one box and disgust at the (hidden) contents of another. Although infants touched both boxes, they preferred to search for the pleasurable rather than the disgusting object. Moreover, infants remained loath to retrieve the disgusting object throughout the trial period of 45 seconds. Thus, infants appropriately interpreted the adult's emotional signals as commentaries on the contents of the boxes and appropriately distinguished between the signals directed at each. This pattern of findings indicates referential specificity rather than a more global mood switch. Additional support for the claim that infants can understand referential specificity has emerged using techniques other than social referencing. Phillips, Wellman, and Spelke (2002) found that 12-month-olds, but not 8-month-olds, expected that an actor was likely to grasp the object that she had looked at with positive affect and were surprised when she did not.

Finally, it is worth underlining the limits on social referencing. As Baldwin and Moses (1996) have noted in a thoughtful commentary, it is tempting to conclude that infants *seek out* information from others. For example, when the infant approaches the visual cliff, comes to a halt, and looks up at his or her mother, it is tempting to assume that the infant is seeking information and guidance from the caregiver in the face of uncertainty. However, an equally plausible, indeed more plausible, interpretation is that infants are displaying an attachment-based strategy rather than an epistemic one. More specifically, infants who feel uncertain or apprehensive may check back to their mother in anticipation of reassurance. They are not looking to their mother in antici-

pation of information. Thus, it is reasonable to suppose that infants seek reassurance and are then offered guidance, including referentially specific guidance; we have no need to presume that infants are tacitly posing a question of the mother regarding the situation that has provoked their uncertainty. That said, it is obviously reasonable to raise the possibility that infants at some point—either in the second year or later—do come to regard other people as sources of information—sources who can identify and name unknown objects, demonstrate how to use an unfamiliar tool, or bring a means-end sequence to fruition. I return to the question of when and how infants come to regard other people as potential informants in a later section.

## Comforting and Helping

Among chimpanzees, acts of comforting and consolation are readily identifiable—especially in the aftermath of a conflict. De Waal and Aureli (1996) recorded affiliative contacts (kissing, embracing, grooming, gentle touching, and mounting) directed by bystanders toward victims of aggression. The frequency of such contacts was compared after severe aggression, mild aggression, and during randomly chosen baseline periods. In the minutes immediately following a bout of aggression, victims were much more likely to receive affiliative contact than during a baseline period, especially if the aggression had been severe rather than mild. By contrast, approaches to the aggressor were much less frequent. Were bystanders making a moral judgment and siding with victims? Conceivably, but more likely, they were simply sensitive to the higher level of distress expressed by the victims. Such selective comforting is not found throughout the primate order. For example, de Waal and Aureli (1996) found no postconflict elevation of contact among long-tailed macaques. Finally, it is worth noting that acts of consolation do not appear to be triggered by overt distress in the animal who is offering consolation. Visual records of such acts indicate that the victim may well be screaming but the consoler is not. By implication, consolers appear to grasp the distress displayed by a victim, not via some form of low-level contagion, but via some form of sympathy.

Do we find a similar set of consolation behaviors among human infants? In my view, the evidence points to a considerable continuity. To anticipate, human infants offer consolation, they do so in response to overt distress, and they do so based on sympathy rather than low-level contagion. Consider the following episode reported by Wolf (1982):

> When we came home this afternoon, I slipped and fell and came down really hard whacking my nose. I was in real pain and sat down on the rocker in J.'s room, holding and rubbing my nose. J. (14 months) was very sympathetic. He acted for me the way I do when he hurts himself. He hugged and patted me and even offered me his blanket that he uses when he's hurt or tired.

Or consider the following reported by Hoffman (1976, pp. 129–130):

> Michael, 15 months, is struggling with his friend Paul over a toy. Paul starts to cry. Michael appears concerned and lets go of the toy so Paul has it. But Paul continues to cry. Michael pauses, then gives his own teddy bear to Paul; Paul continues crying. Michael pauses again, runs to the next room, gets Paul's security blanket, and gives it to him. Paul stops crying.

Finally, here is the following favorite of mine, reported by Dunn and Kendrick (1982, pp. 115–116):

> Fifteen-month-old Len, was a stocky boy with a fine round tummy, and he played at this time a particular game with his parents that always made them laugh. His game was to come toward them, walking in an odd way, pulling up his T-shirt and showing his big stomach. One day his elder brother fell off the climbing frame in the garden and cried vigorously. Len watched solemnly. Then he approached his brother, pulling up his T-shirt and showing his tummy, vocalizing, and looking at his brother.

These apparent acts of consolation are difficult to explain as mere contagion. The child offers consolation but does not cry. The child makes obvious efforts to reduce the distress of the other person (e.g., via hugs, pats, comfort objects, and parlor tricks). Such efforts do not appear to be simply aimed at minimizing aversive expressions of distress—after all, the child will sometimes leave the scene (thereby escaping the distress altogether) but nevertheless comes back (e.g., with the victim's security blanket).

Zahn-Waxler, Radke-Yarrow, Wagner, and Chapman (1992) carried out a longitudinal study of such comforting behaviors in the 2nd year of life. They recorded naturally occurring instances of physical comforting (e.g., hugs, pats, or kisses), verbal comforting (e.g., "You be okay"), verbal advice (e.g., "Be careful"), helping (e.g., putting on a bandage or giving a bottle) and miscellaneous interventions (e.g., getting mother to retrieve a rattle for a baby, sharing food, attempting distraction, and trying to prevent further injury). Up to the age of 15 months, acts of comforting were mostly physical, but beyond 18 months, the entire repertoire was displayed across the sample. The investigators also looked at the frequency with which distress elicited concerned behavior and observed a marked increment from the beginning of the 2nd year, when only about 10% of distress episodes elicited concern, to the end of the 2nd year, when about 50% of distress episodes did so. Moreover, this increment was stable across various contexts—it was found for naturally occurring episodes of distress, for simulated episodes (e.g., where the mother deliberately feigned hurt and distress), and for distress that children had caused themselves (e.g., by taking another child's toy).

Recall that the chimpanzee data suggest that the act of comforting is not necessarily accompanied by any obvious distress on the part of the comforter. Much the same can be said of the human toddler. Zahn-Waxler et al. (1992) compared how often toddlers responded to another's distress by getting distressed themselves and by offering comfort. The frequency of both types of behavior was comparably low at the beginning of the 2nd year; toward the end, however, comforting behaviors were much more common than distress reactions. In other words, older toddlers frequently offer comfort in the absence of any overt signs of distress. This is especially true when toddlers have not been the cause of the other person's distress and are innocent bystanders.

In summary, concern for other people's distress appears to emerge in the 2nd year of life. It is displayed whether or not children have caused the distress, and when they show concern for another's distress, children are not necessarily distressed themselves. This emerging pattern of concern strongly suggests that toddlers appreciate the emotional state of the other person, and feel concern, even if they are not yet engaging in any sophisticated form of mind reading (Nichols, 2001).

Looking forward to developments in the 3rd and 4th year of life, it seems highly likely that this capacity for concern feeds into young children's moral judgment. A solid body of evidence indicates that 3- and 4-year-olds regard various moral breaches (e.g., hitting another child or taking another child's toy) as more serious than conventional breaches (e.g., putting toys away in the wrong place; Smetana, 1981). How do they come to that conclusion? One possibility is that they are guided by adult feedback. For example, Hetherington and Parke (1999, p. 635) emphasize that mothers and other family members respond to social-conventional violations by focusing on the disorder that the act created ("Look at the mess you made!"), whereas they respond to moral transgressions by focusing on the consequences of the acts for others' rights and welfare or by making pleas for perspective-taking requests ("Think about how you would feel if you were hit"). However, to the extent that mothers effectively respond to both types of violation—conventional as well as moral—it is far from clear that they thereby alert children to their differential gravity. A more probable explanation can be traced back to the capacity for concern at another's distress that has just been described as emerging in the 2nd year of life. It is plausible to suppose that children will soon observe that certain types of misdemeanor, such as hitting another child or taking another child's toy, cause distress, whereas other types of misdemeanor are met with indifference—at least by other children. For example, other children are likely to be indifferent if someone puts toys away in the wrong place. By implication, peers are likely to be excellent tutors, or, more precisely, the distress reactions of peers are likely to be an excellent cue to the serious nature of moral breaches as compared to the less serious nature of conventional breaches.

Consistent with this argument, preschoolers who are told about an unfamiliar action (e.g., "mibbing" another child) in a story context will conclude that it is akin to a moral breach if they are also told that the action in question causes distress (Smetana, 1985). Finally, it is worth dwelling on one further striking result reported by Smetana and her colleagues (Smetana, Kelly, & Twentyman, 1984): Preschool children with abusive and neglecting parents show no obvious difficulty in distinguishing between moral and conventional rules. This result is paradoxical if one assumes that parental feedback is a key element in making the distinction—as implied by Hetherington and Parke (1999). On the other hand, the result is quite plausible if one focuses on the role of peers and specifically of peer distress. The children were all attending preschools. Hence, irrespective of their home background they had an opportunity to discover how peers respond with distress to moral breaches but remain unmoved by conventional violations.

In conclusion, there is a fascinating continuity between the sensitivity that toddlers display to distress

and hurt in other people and the relatively sophisticated moral judgments that they come to make at the age of 3 and 4 years. However, this is not to say that preschool children are constantly behaving like good Samaritans and always do what is right. We soon take a look at the dark side of early social cognition. First, however, it is useful to examine one further prosocial behavior: helping.

## Offering Help and Cooperation

Although helping is obviously a benevolent form of behavior there are reasonable grounds for expecting that it might display a different ontogenetic and phylogenetic pattern when compared to comforting. As I emphasized earlier, comforting—whether among human toddlers or among chimpanzees—appears to be triggered by evident distress on the part of the comforted. The trigger for an act of helping is obviously different, more variable, and probably more complex. Recall the earlier discussion of toddlers' ability to analyze an agent's goal-directed action. Toddlers imitate an action sequence more effectively if the goal of that action sequence is made salient to them (Carpenter et al., 2002; Want & Harris, 2001). By implication, at least in certain circumstances, toddlers are well able to analyze the goal not only of a discrete movement or displacement but also of an action sequence with subgoals. When and how do toddlers start to offer assistance to someone whose action sequence goes awry or needs a helping hand?

Rheingold (1982) carried out a pioneering investigation into toddlers' inclination to help an adult engaged in various household tasks. Children aged 18, 24, and 30 months were observed in a domestic setting as an adult (the child's mother, father, or an unfamiliar adult) carried out various household chores such as laying the table or gathering up books. Even 18-month-olds offered help for more than half of the tasks. By 30 months, this figure rose to almost 90% of the tasks. Thus, toddlers were remarkably willing to offer assistance. Indeed, as Rheingold (1982) comments the children helped with alacrity: "They carried out their efforts with quick and energetic movements, excited vocal intonations, animated facial expressions, and with delight in the finished task" (p. 119).

How should this cooperative attitude be construed? On one interpretation, children may have been engaged in relatively low-level, albeit enjoyable, imitation of the adult's actions. Seeing the adult carry a book and stack it on the table, perhaps they did likewise. An alternative, richer interpretation is that children figured out the adult's overall goal and saw themselves as contributing to that goal. Various pieces of evidence favor the latter interpretation. Children sometimes started to provide help when the adult announced their intention but had not yet begun to act. They also stated their intention to perform a task, appeared to know when the task was complete, and supplied elements that were neither suggested nor modeled by the adults.

Dunn and Munn (1986) provide complementary data on children's willingness to help and cooperate with a sibling rather than an adult. They found that on average 18-month-olds cooperate with an older sibling 6 to 7 times each hour and by the age of 24 months that figure climbs to 10 to 11 times per hour. Not surprisingly, some of the collaborative acts are carried out in the context of pretend play but the majority are not. Moreover, as observed in the context of adult-child cooperation, collaborative acts cannot be reduced to imitation: Children take on complementary activities in pursuit of a common goal.

The capacity for such complementary activity was highlighted by Brownell and Carriger (1990) in a study of peer cooperation. Children ranging from 12 to 33 months were given various novel, practical problems that depended on their adoption of complementary roles for their solution. For example, to retrieve some toy animals, one child needed to stand away from and opposite to another child who rotated a handle that transported the animals in a cup toward the first child. Cooperation at 18 months was rare and possibly accidental. By 24 months, however, cooperation was generally rapid and effective.

Summarizing across these studies, it is clear that toddlers are disposed to cooperate. They spontaneously offer help to a parent, an unfamiliar adult, a sibling, or a peer. Sometimes they provide help to someone whose plan of action is already underway or established—they temporarily adopt the other's goal as their own. Sometimes, they cooperate in a more symmetrical fashion as when they adopt complementary roles to further a game of pretend or a practical activity. In either case, it is apparent that children can adjust their goals to those of another person. It is tempting to take such cooperative activity for granted given its familiarity and spontaneity. However, it is worth underlining the possibility that it is a uniquely human trait. Indeed, Tomasello, Carpenter, Call, Behne, and Moll (2005) conclude that there are no published experimental studies showing that chimpanzees collaborate by playing different and complementary roles in an activity. If they are right, their conclusion underlines the importance of distinguishing between prosocial acts of comforting and prosocial acts of cooperation. Whereas chimpanzees may be capable of the former, the latter looks as if it is a powerful but unique human disposition.

## Hurting and Teasing

In an earlier section, we saw that young children recognize others' distress and that in the 2nd year of life they acquire a repertoire of strategies for alleviating that distress. The ability to recognize distress and some of its causal elicitors can be put to other uses. Children can deliberately seek to tease, upset, frustrate, and provoke. As one might expect, given the increased frequency of comforting in the 2nd year, there is a parallel increase in acts of teasing (Dunn & Munn, 1985). By the middle of the 2nd year, many incidents between siblings involve the removal of the sibling's comfort object or an attack on some favorite possession. By 24 months, however—again in line with the pattern for comforting—the child's repertoire becomes more elaborate. For example, one child teased her older sister by pretending to be her imaginary companion.

Sibling relationships are often characterized by an admixture of teasing and comforting (Dunn, Kendrick, & MacNamee, 1981). Moreover, it is often the older sibling who is the prime instigator of hostile interactions (Abramovitch, Corter, & Lando, 1979; Abramovitch, Corter, & Pepler, 1980; Dunn & Kendrick, 1982). Despite these overall tendencies, investigators also note huge variation across sibling pairs in the proportion of mutually hostile and mutually friendly encounters. For example, in some sibling pairs, there are virtually no mutually hostile interactions; in others, they occur about half the time.

Some children display a pattern of social interaction that seems to lie outside the range of behaviors observed in the hurly-burly of everyday family life. When children who have been subjected to physical abuse by their parents are observed in a preschool setting, they often display a bias toward hostile as opposed to cooperative interaction. More specifically, as compared to children from the same social class background but with no known history of abuse, abused children are likely to display more aggression and less helping and sharing

(Hoffman-Plotkin & Twentyman, 1984; Trickett & Kuczynski, 1986). The response of abused children to the distress of other children is especially noteworthy because the pattern of concern described earlier appears to be disrupted. When abused toddlers were confronted by another's distress in a day-care setting, they never responded with obvious concern. At most, they patted or attempted to quiet the crying child. Their more frequent response was to respond in a negative fashion, with hostile or fearful gestures or sometimes with direct physical attacks on the crying child (George & Main, 1979). A similar pattern of results emerged among abused preschoolers aged 3 to 5 years even though they had had the opportunity to interact with nonabusive caregivers and peers for 1 or 2 years in their day-care setting (Klimes-Dougan & Kistner, 1990).

These observations underline the fact that the gestures of comfort and concern described in the previous section, and identified as part of our primate heritage, are not irreversibly wired into the young child's social cognitive repertoire. Whatever sensitivity infants and toddlers display to another's distress, it is likely that active and benevolent concern for that distress is a relational mode that abused children experience with their abusive parents much less often than nonabused children.

## MENTAL STATE UNDERSTANDING IN EARLY CHILDHOOD

When children move beyond infancy and begin to talk, it becomes somewhat easier to study the development of social cognition. We can analyze their spontaneous remarks and probe their understanding with a rich set of story formats. This shift in technique is especially evident in the study of children's understanding of goals and desires.

### Goals, Desires, and Intentions

Recall that Premack and Woodruff (1978) found that their chimpanzee subject was able to figure out what the actor in the film clip was aiming to do. We have also seen that infants are able to diagnose the goal that a human action is directed toward. Indeed, as discussed in the section on helping, toddlers will sometimes offer help or comfort by fetching an object that someone is

trying to get or needs. Should we not assume that chimpanzees as well as human infants and toddlers realize that other people have wants? A somewhat leaner interpretation is plausible. Chimpanzees or young humans might be good at diagnosing the direction or goal that an ongoing action, or even a sequence of actions, is aimed at—its external, perceptible target—without an understanding of the mental state of desire that initiates and guides such actions or states.

Under what circumstances might we be prepared to attribute a more mentalistic concept of desire to young children? My guess is that there is no straightforward, acid test. However, what does emerge from approximately 18 months upward is the competence to talk about desires and to articulate various contrasts using the key concept of desire. Bartsch and Wellman (1995) analyzed the spontaneous utterances of a small group of children regularly observed and recorded between the ages of 18 months and 5 years. Bartsch and Wellman searched through approximately 200,000 utterances and identified about 12,000 that included mental state terms that they divided into two broad categories—thought and belief terms such as *think* and *know* and desire terms such as *want, wish,* and *hope.* They found that children begin to use desire terms from about 18 to 24 months. In addition, when children are between 24 and 30 months, they begin to produce various contrastive utterances. For example, they begin to contrast what they want with what they actually get or are about to get (e.g., "I want a turtle, but I can't have one"). They also contrast what one person wants with what another person wants. Bartsch and Wellman (1995) plausibly conclude that children's references to "wants" are not references to actions-tending-toward-goals. Rather, they are references to internal states that are different from, albeit linked to, the actions that they motivate and the goals that they are directed toward.

The available data from children's spontaneous utterances also underline the fact that the concept of desire plays a central, organizing role in children's emerging understanding of mental states. First, children refer to desires earlier, and more often, than they refer to cognitive states such as thinking and knowing. Second, they do so despite the fact that their parents talk about cognitive states as often as they talk about desires. Third, the early discussion of desires is not confined to English-speaking children. It appears also in studies of Mandarin- and Cantonese-speaking children (Tardif & Wellman, 2000). Finally, children with autism—who show various problems in the understanding of belief—are relatively competent at talking about desires (Tager-Flusberg, 1993; Tan & Harris, 1991).

Experimental studies support the idea that 2- and 3-year-olds understand the way that desires are linked to actions and indeed to various simple emotions. For example, they understand that people will search for what they want and that if they obtain it, they will feel happy and that if they do not obtain it, they will persist in searching and feel sad or angry (Hadwin & Perner, 1991; Stein & Levine, 1987; Wellman & Woolley, 1990). Moreover, when invited to account for a story character's actions 3-year-olds also offer explanations couched in terms of desires (Bartsch & Wellman, 1989).

How does children's early understanding of desire connect with their understanding of intention? Recall that a long Piagetian tradition examined children's understanding of intentions in the context of moral judgment (Piaget, 1932). The standard conclusion was that young children are relatively slow to acknowledge the relevance of intention to moral judgment, focusing instead on the gravity of the consequences as the primary index of the seriousness of the misdemeanor. More recent research, especially in the context of theory of mind, has sought to assess children's understanding of intention in its own right. The link with moral judgment and moral responsibility has not been forgotten, but it is no longer so evidently center stage.

One important finding is that, contrary to the impression that might be gained from the older Piagetian literature, preschool children are able to distinguish between acts that are deliberate as compared to acts that are intentional. More specifically, when 3-year-olds engage in actions that go wrong; for example, if they inadvertently mispronounce a word in trying to repeat a tongue twister, they appropriately judge that the actions were not done "on purpose" (Shultz, 1980). However, it is also likely that 3-year-olds get by with a relatively simple, desire-based notion of unintended action, judging outcomes that are desirable as intended and outcomes that are undesirable as unintended (Astington, 1991). Thus, it is important to probe the extent to which young children realize that desires and intentions do not always coincide. For example, I can intend to do many chores that I do not want to do, and I can want to visit far-off places that I have no current intention of visiting.

To explore children's ability to make this distinction, Feinfeld, Lee, Flavell, Green, and Flavell (1999) presented 3- and 4-year-olds with stories in which the pro-

tagonist's desire and intention were different. For example, in one story, the protagonist wants to go to one place (e.g., to the mountain) but, on mother's instructions, intends to go to a different place (e.g., to the football field). However, because of a mistake by the bus driver, the protagonist ends up where he wanted to go and not where he intended. Four-year-olds performed quite systematically—they realized that the protagonist was trying and expecting to get to one place (e.g., the football field in the example just given) but wanted to go to a different place (e.g., the mountain). By contrast, 3-year-olds were much less systematic. Although they were generally accurate in identifying the protagonist's preference, they were much less accurate in indicating what he was trying and expecting to do. Moreover, even when they did identify the protagonist's intention correctly, they often added that the protagonist also intended to reach the other, more desirable goal. As Feinfeld et al. (1999) point out, one conceivable interpretation of these findings is that 3-year-olds have some difficulty in acknowledging the role that thinking and believing plays in the formulation of an intention. More specifically, intentions are generally formed with the belief—sometimes false—that one's plan can be executed (Moses, 1993). In the next section, we look in detail at children's understanding of belief.

## Beliefs

A great deal of research effort has been devoted to documenting and probing children's developing understanding of belief, and notably false belief. Indeed, the false-belief task has been the favored task for the refinement and testing of various competing accounts of the child's theory of mind. For that reason, I use this section to serve a double purpose—to review the extent to which there is an emerging empirical consensus regarding the major landmarks in the child's understanding of belief, and to provide an initial evaluation of those competing theories.

Three main tasks have played a role in the effort to assess children's understanding of belief. First, in the unexpected displacement task, a protagonist, having put an object in one place, is unaware of its transfer to a new place during a brief absence, and on his or her return, expects it to be where it was originally put. Children are asked to say where the protagonist will look for the object—in the new or the old place (Wimmer & Perner, 1983). Second, in the deceptive container task, children discover that a familiar container (e.g., a Band-Aid box) contains some unexpected content (e.g., stamps), and are asked—in the face of this unexpected discovery—to indicate (a) what they originally thought to be inside the container and (b) what someone looking at it for the first time would think is inside it (Gopnik & Astington, 1988; Perner, Leekam, & Wimmer, 1987). Finally, in the appearance-reality task, children are shown a misleading object—for example, a sponge shaped and painted to look like a rock; they examine it, discover its true identity, and are then asked both about its real and apparent identity (Flavell, 1986). As will be clear from this brief description, all three tasks turn on the fact that a protagonist, lacking full perceptual access to the object or situation in question, comes to, or might come to, an erroneous conclusion. Children are asked to diagnose the protagonist's erroneous conclusion, despite their current knowledge of the true facts.

Wellman, Cross, and Watson (2001) recently carried out a helpful meta-analysis of a large number of different studies covering all three types of task. They asked how performance changed with age and how it varied as a function of various potentially influential factors such as whether the child was actively involved in the displacement or switch or just a spectator. They obtained support for a very robust age-change between 3 and 5 years. At 30 months, children are more the 80% incorrect; at 44 months, they are 50% correct; and by 56 months, they are approximately 75% correct. Thus, children's performance shifts from being systematically below chance (at 41 months and younger) to systematically above chance (at 48 months and older). Moreover, the age change is quite stable across various conditions of testing. It is unaffected by whether children are questioned about what a protagonist thinks or asked to predict the protagonist's belief-based behavior. It emerges whether the target person is a story character, a puppet, or a real adult. It emerges whether the protagonist holds a false belief about an object's location or its identity. Finally, it is unaffected by whether children are asked about their own false belief or that of another person.

Wellman et al. (2001) did find that certain factors help or hinder accurate performance. For example, an explicit indication that the protagonist is being tricked or deceived, active participation by the child in performing the critical object switch or change of location, or an explicit cue (verbal or pictorial) regarding the protagonist's belief are all factors that help children to diagnose belief more accurately. Finally, the elimination

of the target object (e.g., in the unexpected displacement task, the removal of the desired chocolate from the old location together with its consumption—as opposed to its transfer to a new location) helps children diagnose the protagonist's search accurately. Nevertheless, as Wellman and his colleagues underline, each of these factors tends to help (or hinder) younger children and older children alike. There was no indication, for example, that younger children solve the false-belief task when it involves deception, whereas older children solve it irrespective of whether deception is involved. Rather, deception was a helpful factor across the entire age range. Similarly, the presence of the target object proved a hindrance across the entire age range. Thus, none of these factors do much to alter the observed gradient of improvement with age. In particular, there is no factor—or set of factors—that serves to unmask the competence of 3-year-olds and enables them to perform like 5-year-olds—or even to perform at above chance levels.

Armed with these empirical conclusions, Wellman et al. (2001) spell out plausible implications for theory. First, they note that the consistent age change, together with the failure to uncover a set of conditions under which 3-year-olds perform systematically above chance, undermines a family of theories implying that children have an innate, or early, capacity to understand false belief (Fodor, 1992; German & Leslie, 2000; Leslie, 2000). Such accounts have generally implied that such early understanding can be unmasked provided the child is tested under optimal conditions, notably conditions that minimize or eliminate various information-processing constraints. Yet, the meta-analysis failed to identify such conditions.

Second, they argue that even if room is made for the impact of information-processing constraints—particularly those identified by various executive function accounts (Carlson & Moses, 2001)—the fact that a consistent age change appears whether such constraints are maximized or minimized strongly suggests that some kind of conceptual change takes place between 3 and 5 years. The improvement that they consistently note cannot be exclusively attributed to the lifting of information-processing restrictions but probably implies the attainment of some type of conceptual insight.

Let us pause to consider each of these two claims in turn. Is it—as Wellman et al. (2001) conclude—time to abandon a nativist, modular stance toward the understanding of belief in the wake of overwhelming empirical evidence for conceptual change? As Moses (2001) points out in a level-headed commentary, such a move might be a bit premature. First, as Wellman et al. (2001) concede, there are no studies of 3-year-olds in which all of the four optimizing conditions that they themselves identify have been brought together. It is feasible that such an optimal conjunction would lift the performance of 3-year-olds above chance. Second, it is important to keep in mind the fact that research on false-belief understanding has—need it be said?—focused on the understanding of false belief. Yet, there are many cases where we are called on to understand someone's belief without knowing whether the belief is true or false because an accurate reading of reality is simply unavailable. Beliefs about the future fall into this category, as do many beliefs about the past. As an experimental illustration, consider a fascinating study conducted by Wellman and Bartsch (1988). They asked children to predict where the protagonist would look for his or her lost dog given that (a) the protagonist thought it was in place X; (b) the child participating in the study thought it was in place Y; and (c) the actual location of the lost dog was yet to be determined. Three-year-olds did very well in this task—much better than in a variety of closely matched conditions in which the nature of reality was not indeterminate. Thus, 3-year-olds predicted that the protagonist would be guided by his belief. Arguably, these findings need further confirmation. Can we be certain, for example, that 3-year-olds are not simply eliding the distinction between where the protagonist wants the dog to be—and where the protagonist thinks the dog is? Future studies might be aimed at setting up a clearer contrast between the protagonist's desire (or hope) and the protagonist's belief (or expectation). For example, the protagonist might hope that his dog has run off toward the park rather than the (dangerous) highway but nonetheless believe that the dog has actually gone toward the highway rather than the park. Still, the findings of Wellman and Bartsch (1988) definitely point to a way of escaping from the vast edifice of false-belief studies toward the less explored territory of what might be called indeterminate beliefs. Such an escape might ultimately offer succor to the nativists by showing that 3-year-olds do possess a useful, working notion of belief, even if they undeniably have trouble in understanding false beliefs.

What of the second conclusion reached by Wellman et al. (2001) that a conceptual change takes place between 3 and 5 years? This is a reasonable conclusion at this point in the research program. Still, it is worth un-

derlining three important caveats. The first caveat is that even if a conceptual change is involved, the meta-analysis is not much help in deciding among various different candidates for the nature of that conceptual change, as Wellman and his colleagues concede. Thus, each of the following three candidates remains viable. First, it could be argued that what is emerging is a concept of belief—no more and no less. This is essentially the position adopted by Wellman himself (Bartsch & Wellman, 1995) together with various like-minded colleagues (Gopnik & Wellman, 1994). On this account, the period between 3 and 5 years marks the construction of a second major pillar of our everyday theory of mind. Children below the age of 3 years have a good understanding of desires and by the age of 5 years they have an understanding of desires, beliefs, and their relationship. Second, it could be argued that the emerging concept of belief is actually better seen as an insight into the way in which beliefs are formed on the basis of access to particular sources (Wimmer & Hartl, 1991; Wimmer & Weichbold, 1994). This focus on children's understanding of the sources of belief is plausible because—as noted earlier in describing the three classic tasks used in false-belief research—the protagonist's incomplete perceptual access is critical to his or her false belief. Third, it is feasible to claim that the child's emerging insight into the nature of belief is part of a larger conceptual insight into various representational media, of which the mind is only one example, albeit a prominent one. In setting out this claim, Perner (1991, 1995) underlines the following puzzle—which he takes to be a major conceptual hurdle for the child. Consider an out of-date road map; it shows a forest beside Highway 1. You know that the forest has long disappeared and a large housing estate has been built in its place. Nevertheless, you also appreciate that someone to whom you lend the map might mistakenly drive along Highway 1 expecting to see the forest. You understand, therefore, that the map—despite its misrepresentation of reality—can nonetheless be read as an accurate representation of reality. According to Perner, it is this conflicting function—misrepresenting while being taken to accurately represent—that stymies the 3-year-old in thinking about beliefs—or any medium, be it a map, a photograph, or a signpost that purports to represent reality accurately while not actually doing so.

The second caveat concerning the claim that a conceptual change occurs between 3 and 5 years is that even if any one of the three types of conceptual change just described were to emerge as the most convincing account, we still need to understand the underlying engine of development. To make this point more explicit, let us suppose that the belief-focused account advocated by Wellman and his colleagues turns out to be the most convincing. This would still leave entirely open the question of how children come to construct such a concept. For example, is it by virtue of their firsthand experience of holding a belief, of acting, thinking, and talking in accord with that belief, and then discovering that the belief can still turn out to be false? Alternatively, is it explicable in terms of the modification of an increasingly untidy and nonpredictive desire-based theory? Or is it by virtue of hearing people's (false) beliefs articulated in language? The meta-analysis gives very few clues to help resolve these questions—although it is worth noting that one factor—the provision of an explicit cue, such as a verbal statement of the protagonist's belief—was one of the factors that boosted performance.

The third and final caveat concerns the future of research on the false-belief task. Consider the problem of conservation. Few, looking back at the various conflicting interpretations of that age change, would claim that we now have a definitive understanding of why or how it takes place. One plausible conclusion from the plethora of inconclusive research is that cross-sectional experimental analysis is just not potent enough to uncover the dynamics of developmental change. Moreover, in the case of conservation, it was far from clear what experiences in the child's everyday environment might promote development. Hence, even when training studies were conducted and were effective, their relevance to conceptual change in everyday life, outside of the laboratory, was unclear. Does this mean that research on false belief will fade away, in much the same way as has research on conservation? One optimistic sign is that investigators are turning much more actively to a consideration of the type of variation in children's everyday life that promotes understanding. The child's language ability and the conversational environment to which the child is exposed are emerging as very important factors. I return to the role that language might play in promoting the understanding of belief in the context of an analysis of individual differences.

## Perception, Knowledge, and Source Monitoring

False-belief tasks, and the conceptually related appearance-reality task, it was noted, turn on the child's real-

ization that perceptual access is a key to accurate knowledge. In the standard unexpected displacement task, the story protagonist ends up with a false belief because he or she was not present to witness the displacement. In the deceptive container task, the child (or some other person) has not witnessed the surreptitious replacement of the standard contents. In the appearance-reality task, the child has to identify what someone might conclude about the properties or identity of an object, in the absence of comprehensive perceptual access; for example, someone who has just looked at, but not touched, a sponge painted to resemble a rock, might take it to be a genuine rock—until they poke it.

Alongside this focus on what children understand about the consequences of blocked or restricted perceptual access, it is important to ask whether children also appreciate the consequences of appropriate perceptual access. A variety of related but distinct questions present themselves. Do children realize that appropriate perceptual access usually leads to knowledge? Can they distinguish among the various different sources of perceptual knowledge—seeing, hearing, touching, and so on? Do they differentiate between such perceptual sources and learning via the testimony of others? Finally, when do they realize that the judgment of someone with appropriate perceptual access should generally be trusted? As we shall see, these questions all speak to the wider issue of when and how children come to be insightful seekers and gatherers of information.

Three- and 4-year-olds are well able to report when someone can and cannot see an object (Flavell, Shipstead, & Croft, 1978) and they can position a doll so that it will not be seen by two doll policemen (Hughes & Donaldson, 1979). Young children also realize that seeing yields knowledge. For example, several experiments have established that 3- and 4-year-olds realize that someone who has looked into a box will know its contents, whereas someone who has picked it up but not looked inside will not know its contents (Pillow, 1989; Pratt & Bryant, 1990).

Children might conceptualize perceptual contact in an all-or-none fashion. Thus, they might assume that any kind of perceptual contact yields knowledge. Alternatively, they might have a more refined notion of perceptual contact, realizing, for example, that visual inspection is needed to identify an object's color but manual inspection is needed to identify its hardness. O'Neill, Astington, and Flavell (1992) found a shift with age from a more global to a more refined understanding of perceptual input. Thus, 3-year-olds were poor at judging that color has to be judged by looking, whereas hardness is best gauged by manual inspection. Five-year-olds, by contrast, were much more accurate at realizing that our senses can provide modality specific information. O'Neill and Chong (2001) extended this conclusion to all five senses: Three-year-olds were quite inaccurate in both saying and showing how they had determined, for example, the smell of a bubble bath—even when they had just copied the experimenter and smelled the liquid in question. Four-year-olds were much more accurate.

A similar development appears to occur with respect to children's differentiation between perceptual and nonperceptual sources of information. Gopnik and Graf (1988) informed 3-, 4-, and 5-year-olds about the contents of a drawer in three different ways: Children looked in the drawer, were told about the contents, or were given a clue. They were then asked how they knew the contents. Although 3-year-olds performed above chance, the performance of 5-year-olds was almost perfect. Moreover, even if 3-year-olds were correct on an immediate test, they were prone to forget their source in a delayed test.

Nevertheless, 4- and 5-year-olds do display a certain degree of amnesia about how they have come to know various facts (Taylor, Esbensen, & Bennett, 1994). Thus, whether they are reminded of a fact that they already know (e.g., that tigers have black stripes) or introduced to a fact that they do not know (e.g., tigers' stripes provide camouflage) both age groups, especially the 4-year-olds, often claim immediately afterward that they have known both facts "for a long time." Control procedures have established that children can judge time intervals in other contexts, for example, in assessing whether they have received a gift that day or "a long time ago."

Summarizing these various studies, it appears that 3-year-olds can differentiate between those who have been supplied with information about an object—for example by looking into a box—and those who have no information about it at all. At the same time, they are poor at distinguishing among different sources of information. Thus, they are prone to confuse perceptual and nonperceptual routes (such as being told or making an inference), and they often fail to differentiate among particular perceptual routes, such as touching, looking, and smelling. Five-year-olds perform much more accurately on all these source-monitoring tasks—but, as noted, they have some difficulty in pinpointing the time of the learning experience.

It is important to note that all of these tasks call for children to reenact, to verbally identify, or to pinpoint in time their reliance on some particular source such as looking or telling. Whitcombe and Robinson (2000) showed that 3- and 4-year-olds are better at what might be described as procedural or online source monitoring. In their study, children were given limited or inappropriate perceptual access to an object—for example, they could only see a small red patch of a larger picture, or they could only feel an object inside a tunnel, and therefore not properly identify its color. Having ventured nonetheless to state the identity of the object, an adult with fuller or more appropriate access to the object proposed a different identity. When children were asked for a final judgment, they tended to yield to the better-informed adult. Moreover, when the roles were switched—so that the children were better informed than the adult—they tended not to yield. By implication, children were tracking who had better perceptual access and they either revised—or retained—their initial judgment in an appropriate fashion. Despite this accurate source monitoring at a procedural level, the familiar pattern of inaccuracy reappeared when children were asked to indicate the source of their final judgment. For example, children who had appropriately revised their initial judgment when the adult was better informed often made the mistake of saying that they knew the object's identity because they had seen or felt it.

One interpretation of this type of accurate procedural source monitoring is that children follow a simple stay or shift rule. Specifically, they might stay with their own judgment if they have had a vivid and determinate perceptual encounter with the object but shift to the informant's judgment if they have not. Thus, if they have been able to inspect a whole picture and establish that it is a strawberry—or look inside a tunnel and establish the identity of an object located inside it, children stay with their own judgment. If, however, they have only glimpsed part of the object or tried to identify its color by feel alone—and ended up by making a guess—they revise their judgment if another is offered.

On this argument, procedural monitoring would involve, at best, some sensitivity to the determinacy or certainty of one's own perceptual encounters but it would not call for any monitoring of another informant. Robinson and Whitcombe (2003) tested this skeptical interpretation in a follow-up study. Children made an essentially uncertain judgment about an object, given their restricted perceptual access. They then heard an adult make a different judgment—sometimes on the basis of better access but sometimes on the basis of equally restricted access. If children yield to another judgment whenever they are uncertain, they should have yielded just as often whether or not the adult was better informed. They did not. Children were much more likely to adopt the adult's counterclaim when he or she was well-informed. In the future, we may expect to see more research intended to tease out the differences between "explicit" and procedural source monitoring. When children are uncertain, it is a useful strategy for them to seek and rely on information from someone else. Still, their reliance ought to be tempered by some sensitivity to how well-informed their interlocutor is. The findings of Robinson and Whitcombe (2003) suggest that even 3-year-olds have some competence at this type of fine-tuning.

Reviewing these diverse studies, it is evident that children's accuracy in identifying the source of a piece of information improves with age. Between 3 and 5 years, children improve in their identification of one perceptual channel as compared to another, and they improve in identifying information based on perception versus testimony. At the same time, 3- and 4-year-olds appear to keep a surprisingly watchful eye on their informants. They defer to an informant who is better informed but resist one who is not.

### Emotion

A great deal of research on emotional development has adopted what we might think of as the "continuity" position. Guided by Darwin's emphasis on the similarities between human beings and animals in the origins and function of the expression of the emotions, this research tradition has approached emotional development in terms of the key issues of the production and comprehension of nonverbal signs of emotion—especially in the face. I reviewed some of the key findings from this research tradition earlier.

However, there is an important aspect of emotional development that this approach ignores. First, young children can communicate about emotion in language. No other species has that capacity—and there is good reason to keep in mind the possibility that that capacity transforms the emotional lives of human beings as compared to other species. Second, as I describe later, young children increasingly interpret both their own emotional experiences and those of other people in the light of their larger theory of mind. Again, that capacity calls

into question the Darwinian "continuity" project, at the very least if it is taken to offer a comprehensive analysis of emotional development.

When do children start to put feelings into words and when do they begin to interpret emotions in relation to other mental states? Two and 3-year-olds already make references to basic emotions such as feeling happy, sad, and scared (Wellman, Harris, Banerjee, & Sinclair, 1995). They tend to talk mainly about their own emotions but references to those of other people, as well as those of stuffed animals and dolls, are also apparent. Moreover, they refer to likely future emotions and to emotions felt in the past. Thus, they talk about emotion in a referential and descriptive mode rather than an expressive mode. To clarify this distinction, consider the expressive terms: "Ouch," "Yuck," or "Oh!" These terms can be used to express a current emotion of the self but they cannot be readily used to identify a non-current emotion or one belonging to another person. Wittgenstein (1953) proposed that children's early emotion talk is acquired and used in the expressive mode. However, close analysis of children's comments on other people and their references to noncurrent emotion shows that that is not the case. More generally, it would be wrong to see children's early emotion talk as a supplement to some preexisting nonverbal system for the expression of emotion. The evidence suggests that it is an altogether different mode of communication—it is descriptive, discursive, and referential.

When children refer to an emotion what do they have in mind? They might be referring only to the outward signs of the emotion—the tears or the smiles—or they might be referring to the experiential changes that an emotion generally entails. Wellman et al. (1995) found some indications that preschoolers differentiate between the experience of emotion and the actions and expressions that frequently accompany emotion. They also found that children think of emotions—unlike pains—as intentional states directed at an object or target. They realize that people are sad *about* something, afraid *of* something, or mad *at* someone. Here, we do see an important continuity with children's interpretation of facial expressions. Recall that experiments on social referencing have established that toddlers in the 2nd year realize that an adult's emotion is directed at a particular target—they do not treat it as a diffuse mood change.

Granted that young children talk about emotion with apparent sophistication, do they do so in an accurate and appropriate fashion? More specifically, does the way in which they would describe an emotionally charged episode coincide with the description that an adult might supply of the same event? To explore this issue, Fabes, Eisenberg, Nyman, and Michealieu (1991) observed preschoolers aged 3 to 5 years in their daycare centers, and they approached bystanders following an emotional incident to ask for a description of what had happened. Three-year-olds gave an account of the target child's emotion that matched an adult observer's about two-thirds of the time and 5-year-olds did so about three-quarters of the time. For example, "She's sad because she misses her Mom," or "She's mad because she thought it was her turn."

How do children come to provide such accurate descriptions? One explanation that has appealed to various investigators (Lewis, 1989; Russell, 1989) is that children learn the typical script for any given emotion. They come to realize that there is some kind of standard elicitor (e.g., frustration in the case of anger; the unexpected in the case of surprise) together with an accompanying expressive and gestural pattern. When they see key features of the script, they identify the emotion accurately. The script-based analysis is consistent with the fact that preschoolers are quite good at describing the elicitors that would provoke various basic emotions such as sadness and fear (Trabasso, Stein, & Johnson, 1981). Such situational knowledge becomes richer and more differentiated as children get older so that they can describe situations likely to evoke more complicated emotions such as disappointment, relief, and jealousy (Harris et al., 1987).

There is, however, one important limitation of the script concept. It focuses on the external circumstances and observable behaviors that make up an emotional episode but it ignores the subjective appraisal that is frequently involved. What any given individual deems to be a frustration or surprise depends on the desires and beliefs that they bring to a situation. Are children sensitive to the crucial role played by these subjective appraisals? With this question in mind, Harris, Johnson, Hutton, Andrews, and Cooke (1989) asked 4-, 5-, and 6-year-olds to watch a naughty monkey who offered various animals either a nasty surprise (e.g., he gave the elephant whose favorite drink was coke a coke can with milk inside) or a nice surprise (e.g., he gave the horse whose favorite snack was peanuts a chewing gum packet with peanuts inside). Children were asked to say how the recipient of these gifts would feel both before and after

discovering the contents of the container. As might be expected, all three age groups understood the role of desires: They judged that the recipient would feel happy if he eventually found his favorite drink or snack but sad otherwise. For the question about how the animal would feel *before* discovering the surprise contents, there was a marked age change. The youngest children mostly attributed to the animal an emotion based on the actual contents of the container—ignoring the animal's mistaken belief about those contents. By contrast, the oldest children mostly did the reverse—they attributed an emotion based on the animal's mistaken belief—ignoring the actual contents. By implication, all the children realized that the animal's emotion would depend on his desires—as indexed by their answer to the question about how the animal would feel on discovering the actual contents—but their appreciation of the role of beliefs underwent a steep improvement with age.

At first sight, these results fit the pattern that has repeatedly emerged in other analyses. Children understand the role of desires well before they understand the role of beliefs. There is, however, a major deviation. The youngest group, with a mean age of 4 years, was quite poor at diagnosing the animals' emotions with reference to their (mistaken) beliefs. Moreover, only about half the 5-year-olds were correct. It was only among the oldest group of children, with a mean age of 6 years, that the majority was correct. Yet, as we noted in the discussion of children's understanding of belief, children generally understand a variety of false-belief tasks at around 4 to 5 years of age. Thus, even if 4- and 5-year-olds accurately predict a person's thoughts, actions and utterances on the basis of his or her beliefs, they continue to have difficulty in predicting a person's emotions on the basis of his or her beliefs.

Several subsequent studies have supported this intriguing conclusion. In a series of four experiments, Hadwin and Perner (1991) showed that children could appreciate a story character's mistaken belief before they made use of this knowledge to make attributions of surprise. For example, 5-year-olds were at chance in attributing surprise, whereas all but one child correctly judged the protagonist's false belief. Only by 6 years of age did a significant majority of children make correct belief-based attributions of surprise. A similar lag emerged for the attribution of happiness.

Bradmetz and Schneider (1999) replicated the same lag across five experiments and across two emotions (fear and happiness). Almost half the children ranging from 3 to 8 years appreciated the false belief held by the protagonist but still made the incorrect emotion attribution. For example, when given a version of the story of Little Red Riding Hood, children frequently realized that Little Red Riding Hood mistakenly thinks it is her grandmother in the bed but then went on to say that she was afraid—and invoked the wolf to explain her fear, for example, "Because it is a wolf!" or "Because the wolf wants to eat her." However, no child made a correct emotion attribution but failed the false-belief test. Thus, Bradmetz and Schneider (1999) document a robust lag between understanding belief and understanding the emotion that would be caused by that belief.

Finally, de Rosnay and Harris (2002) compared children's performance on a story version of the nasty-surprise task (involving an animal puppet mistakenly expecting his favorite food) with their performance on a filmed version (involving a child mistakenly expecting to be reunited with his or her mother after an absence but actually encountering a stranger). In two experiments, children frequently erred on both the story and the film task by incorrectly identifying the protagonist's emotion, despite correctly identifying the protagonist's belief.

These various studies indicate that an appreciation of the role of beliefs in the elicitation of emotion is consolidated at around 6 years of age. This is not because 4- and 5-year-olds fail to understand beliefs, including false beliefs. There is a large body of evidence to show that they do—as described earlier. Indeed, as just stated, even in the same study, children will accurately diagnose a protagonist's belief but fail to diagnose the concomitant emotion.

It is tempting to argue that such a lag is not surprising—children frequently grasp a concept without realizing all its implications. However, the puzzle is actually more acute. As described earlier, once children understand false beliefs, they immediately appreciate the implications for action. Thus, we do not find 3- and 4-year-olds who say that Maxi thinks his chocolate is where he left it but proceed to claim that he will search in the place to which it has been moved. Stated differently, recall that the meta-analysis reported by Wellman et al. (2001) showed that children solve the false-belief problem at approximately the same age whether they are quizzed about a protagonist's thoughts or actions.

To summarize, the two central pillars of children's theory of mind—desires and beliefs—are each relevant

to their understanding of emotion. Moreover, in line with a large number of other findings, children acknowledge the key role of desires before they acknowledge the role of beliefs. An important unanswered question is why they are so slow to acknowledge the role of beliefs in causing emotion. No existing account of the child's theory of mind offers a satisfactory explanation of this puzzle.

So far, I have discussed children's attribution of so-called basic emotions: fear, anger, sadness, and so forth. Can the same focus on children's understanding of beliefs and desires also explain children's attribution of more complex emotions, notably those emotions that are frequently designated as social, such as guilt and pride? My reading of the evidence is that children need to consider not only a person's desires and beliefs but also the way in which they assess themselves, and assume that others will assess them, in relation to various standards. Children who neglect these social considerations will fail to attribute guilt, pride, shame, and so forth in an appropriate fashion.

Earlier research on moral judgment by Piaget (1932) and by Kohlberg and his colleagues (Colby, Kohlberg, Gibbs, & Lieberman, 1983) analyzed children's developing conception of why such standards should be upheld. However, these analyses did not focus directly on children's attribution of guilt as a consequence of any failure to live up to those standards, the issue examined by Nunner-Winkler and Sodian (1988). They found that 4- and 5-year-olds consistently claimed that a story protagonist who had deliberately lied, attacked, or stolen from another child would feel happy. They justified this attribution by noting that the outcome—as seen from the point of view of the perpetrator, at any rate, was positive. He or she had, for example, stolen something desirable or successfully pushed another child off the swing. By contrast, children around the age of 8 years claimed that the protagonist would feel bad or sad and they explained their attribution by reference to the misdeed or the protagonist's bad conscience. By implication, young children are oblivious to feelings of guilt—this insouciance has come to be known as the "happy victimizer" phenomenon. It warrants analysis because, as Arsenio and Kramer (1992) point out, most adults would not have expected such a stance (Zelco, Duncan, Barden, Garber, & Masters, 1986) and it raises the possibility that attempts to prompt children to be guided by their conscience may be fruitless, at least in the preschool years.

Various explanations of this marked age change can be ruled out. First, there is no evidence that young children think of hitting, stealing, and lying as acceptable. They judge them as bad—and they maintain that these actions would still be bad in hypothetical communities with no rules or punishment for such actions (Smetana, 1981). Indeed, Keller, Lourenco, Malti, and Saalbach (2003) confirmed that younger children are just as likely as older children to judge the protagonist's actions to be wrong. More generally, these findings underline the fact that developmental changes in children's moral judgment—the focus of the earlier research by Piaget and Kohlberg—do not offer an adequate explanation for age changes in the attribution of guilt.

Second, it might be that older children are more inclined than younger children to focus on the likelihood of punishment for such a misdeed. Indeed, being older, they might reasonably expect more chastisement. Analysis of children's justifications lends no support to this interpretation either. When older children attribute bad feelings to the protagonist they scarcely ever explain that attribution by reference to punishment (Keller et al., 2003; Nunner-Winkler & Sodian, 1988).

A third possibility is that older children are more aware than younger children of the distress of the victim. Again, this seems unlikely because, as noted earlier, harm and distress are important factors leading preschoolers to judge certain actions as wrong (Davidson, Turiel, & Black, 1983; Smetana, 1985). Indeed, Arsenio and Kramer (1992) obtained direct evidence to rule out this interpretation. They asked children to comment on how the victim as well as the wrongdoer felt after a misdeed. The familiar age change emerged for attributions to the wrongdoer—whereas children in all age groups acknowledged that the victim would feel bad.

A fourth possibility is that children vary with age in their interpretation of the question. Maybe younger children assume that they are being asked to say how someone performing such a misdeed would *actually* feel—and conclude reasonably enough that a delinquent who hits and steals from other children would feel no remorse. By contrast, older children may assume that they are being asked to say how someone *ought* to feel. If this argument is correct, we might expect younger children to refer to bad feelings more often if they were asked how they themselves would feel. Keller et al. (2003) examined this prediction but found little support. Younger children were more likely to claim that they themselves

would feel bad as compared to a story protagonist. However, the same effect emerged for older children—so that the greater overall tendency of older children to attribute more guilt remained.

The most plausible explanation of the happy victimizer findings is that there is a major shift in how children conceive of actors—including themselves. Preschoolers typically see people as agents who aim to get what they want and feel happy or sad depending on whether they have done so. Older children are more likely to see people as agents who assess actions, including their own, against normative and moral standards; if their actions meet those standards, they may feel proud but if they fall short they may—and indeed should—feel guilty or ashamed (Harris, 1989). Indeed, we may push this analysis a little further. Arguably, older children see everyone—victims as well as wrongdoers—as part of a moral order. In line with that proposal, Arsenio and Kramer (1992) found that older children are more likely to explain the feelings of victims and wrongdoers in relation to moral considerations. Making the same point differently, younger children—as we have seen—know that misdeeds cause a victim distress; what older children may appreciate, in addition, is that such distress is compounded by a sense of injustice on the victim's part.

One reasonable yet troublesome objection to this general line of argument runs as follows. It might be argued that young children do feel guilt. To the extent that they feel guilt, they must appraise their actions in relation to normative standards, including moral standards. Some recent evidence appears to point firmly in that direction. Kochanska, Gross, Lin, and Nichols (2002) found that through the preschool years, preschoolers show a relatively stable tendency toward nonverbal displays of discomfort following a mishap; mothers' ratings of their child's proneness to guilt showed moderate correlations with such displays; and children who displayed more discomfort were more likely to abide by adult-imposed rules. If preschoolers actually do feel guilt, why are they prone to claim that wrongdoers will feel good rather than bad?

I think the most plausible answer to this question is a familiar one. The fact that children enter into a given mental state is no guarantee that they can diagnose that state in themselves or attribute it to others. We have already seen that this is the case for belief. Young children hold beliefs, including false beliefs. Nevertheless, it takes some time for them to recognize and attribute such beliefs. Young children can also display emotions that are based on a mistaken appraisal of a situation—alarm at an intruder when there is none or surprise at an unexpected outcome. Again, it takes time for them to recognize and attribute such belief-based emotions. In the same way, children can feel guilt but may take time to recognize and attribute it. More specifically, children may know that they have done something wrong, and feel badly as a result, but in the absence of an interpretation of why they feel as they do, they may not recognize themselves as feeling guilty—even though observers would reasonably do so. This lag between the emergence of a psychological process in the child and the child's capacity to recognize and attribute such a process is not confined to guilt. For example, children may hesitate as they read an anomalous sentence but when subsequently asked about whether there was something they did not understand, they will fail to recognize their comprehension problem (Harris, Kruithof, Meerum Terwogt, & Visser, 1981). Thus, we need not postulate an active process of repression or denial to explain children's lack of insight and awareness. It is a normal developmental process.

In conclusion, the fact that preschool children display overt signs of guilt is no guarantee that they can make sense of what they feel after a wrongdoing or accurately attribute guilty feelings to another person. In future research, it will be fascinating to examine this claim in more detail. It will be important not only to observe displays of emotion in young children but also to ask them what they feel. If the preceding analysis is correct, preschoolers will often display emotions but deny any such feelings, whereas older children will be better placed to recognize how they feel.

## Thoughts, Memories, and the Stream of Consciousness

Most adults share a variety of assumptions about the waking mind. We accept that it spontaneously generates a ceaseless flow of thoughts and feelings—what William James (1890) referred to as the "stream of consciousness." This flow is deemed to be partly controllable—we can turn our mind to a particular plan or problem that we need to finalize—but there are also intrusive thoughts that come unbidden. Emotional concerns can have an especially dramatic influence on the stream of consciousness. Guilty ruminations over what we might have done differently, apprehension in the face

of uncertainty, excitement about a potential success can all serve as attractors that redirect the flow of thought for varying lengths of time. Finally, we recognize that the contents of consciousness are limited—we cannot concentrate on two conversations at once or think concurrently about two unrelated problems. This limited capacity of consciousness is in some ways problematic—it means that when an emotionally charged thought intrudes, it is likely to interrupt, and even redirect the stream of consciousness. At the same time, it is a balm; in times of distress or anxiety, we can find solace by temporarily focusing on, and becoming absorbed in, some alternative activity, whether it is a book, a film, or an interesting conversation.

What do young children understand about these various aspects of our mental lives? Do they share adult assumptions about the ceaseless and partially controllable nature of the stream of consciousness? Research on this topic was spasmodic in the 1980s but is beginning to gather momentum—with important implications for the use of introspective self-reports from children in clinical settings. In a series of studies, Flavell and his colleagues have shown that preschoolers have a radically different view of our inner life from adults (Flavell, Green, & Flavell, 1993, 1995). For example, preschoolers do not consistently attribute any mental activity at all to someone sitting quietly or even to someone engaged in an activity such as reading or talking. This is not simply a problem in attributing mental activity to other people. Preschoolers are generally poor at acknowledging that they themselves have just been thinking and poor at saying what they have been thinking (Flavell et al., 1995). For example, after 5-year-olds had been asked by the interviewer to think about where they kept their toothbrush, they often denied that they had been thinking or acknowledged thinking but failed to mention either a toothbrush or a bathroom. Consistent with these findings, preschoolers are also often unaware of their ongoing inner speech (Flavell, Green, Flavell, & Grossman, 1997). In addition, when 5-year-olds were asked to try to have no thoughts at all for about 20 seconds, the majority claimed that they had succeeded. By contrast, the majority of 8-year-olds not only reported some mental activity but also reported specific thoughts (Flavell, Green, & Flavell, 2000).

How should this limitation be interpreted? Arguably, preschool children are providing accurate reports on their inner life but this does not seem likely. Especially when they have been prompted to reflect on a given topic (e.g., where their toothbrush is kept) it seems plausible to assume that they have actually done so; it also seems unlikely that they can keep their minds empty for 20 seconds at a stretch. An alternative interpretation is that preschoolers have a faulty theory of the way that the mind works. They do not yet subscribe to the folk theory adopted by adults. Rather than thinking of the mind as a homunculus or processing device that is constantly active, they construe the mind as a container that may or may not house thoughts and ideas at any given moment. Although this explanation seems plausible, it is probably not the whole story. After all, older children are not only more likely than younger children to acknowledge that thinking is continuous but also to identify particular thoughts that they have had. By implication, children improve in their recognition skills. As the stream of consciousness goes by, they can increasingly identify specific mental contents borne along by that stream.

When stated in this manner, it is reasonable to ask whether certain mental contents might be more easily spotted than others. For example, despite their limited introspective ability, preschoolers might be better at picking out those mental states that have an especially vivid or intrusive aspect. Some findings lend support to this idea. For example, preschoolers can report with apparent accuracy on their ability to imagine an object in motion (Estes, 1998; Estes, Wellman, & Woolley, 1989). Indeed, the report by Estes et al. (1989) points to the intriguing possibility that preschoolers might be able to discover the way that their mind functions—and come to more accurate conclusions—in the context of a dialogue with adults. They found that 3- and 4-year-olds, who had at first balked at imagining a pair of scissors open and close, reported that they had successfully done so, when further prompted by the experimenter.

Preschoolers also show some appreciation of the quality of our mental life when asked about emotion. For example, even 4-year-olds acknowledge that an intense emotional reaction will wane over time. They make that claim whether the initial emotion is positive or negative and with respect to their own emotional experience as well as that of story characters. Moreover, children make the same claim in different cultures—for example, whether they are growing up in the West or in China (Harris, Guz, Lipian, & Man-Shu, 1985). Children might be simply espousing a folk theory and not accurately reporting on their own phenomenology but a plausible conclusion from these systematic findings is that the waning of intense emotion is a universal experience, acknowledged and understood by young children everywhere.

However, as adults we realize that our emotions do not always dissipate in a steady fashion. We are vulnerable to flashbacks and reminders that override, however temporarily, the underlying pattern of dissipation. Do young children understand such intrusive flashbacks? In an initial investigation of this question, children were asked about a story character who woke up on the day after an emotionally charged experience, and either started thinking about the experience again, or alternatively had forgotten about it (Harris et al., 1985). Six-year-olds claimed that the character would feel happier thinking about a positive experience rather than forgetting about it, but would feel happier forgetting about a negative experience rather than thinking about it. Four-year-olds were less systematic. They reached similar conclusions to the 6-year-olds for the positive experience but did not appear to grasp the benefits of forgetting a negative experience.

In a more extensive investigation of the same issue, Lagattuta, Wellman, and Flavell (1997) asked 3- to 6-year-olds to listen to stories in which the protagonist experienced a sad event and, subsequently, encountered a reminder. Children were told that the story character felt sad in the presence of a reminder and questioned to check if they were able to explain that the reminder had led the protagonist to think back to the earlier, sad event. The majority of 5- and 6-year-olds were able to articulate such explanations; but this was rare among 4-year-olds. Nonetheless, in a follow-up study in which the cues were identical to (and not just associated with) items involved in the initial event some 3-year-olds also provided such explanations, especially after they were explicitly asked whether the character was thinking back to the past event.

Finally, we may ask whether children have any appreciation of the limited capacity of consciousness. In an interview study with 8- and 13-year-old boys who had newly entered a boarding school and were sometimes feeling homesick, some tacit appreciation of that limit often emerged in their discussion of coping strategies (Harris, 1989). More specifically, boys often talked about the way in which absorbing activities helped them to stop thinking about home. For example, one 8-year-old explained: "I would try and forget all about it (home) or try and get my mind off it with going to play with my friends . . . or getting stuck into work or something like that." Another explained: "Well if you were in the dorms, you could read a book; if the lights were out you could try and get to sleep; if you were in the middle of a lesson just occupy yourself. [*Interviewer:* What does that do?] Well, once you get started and you're really doing it, then you forget about being homesick and don't really think about it."

In summary, it is evident that children make rapid progress during the early school years in understanding the flow of consciousness. Whereas preschoolers seem to have little insight into the continuous nature of that stream, older children realize that the stream is more or less ceaseless. They also increasingly understand the way in which one type of mental content intrudes on—and for better or worse may displace—another. Such findings raise interesting questions about children's grasp of the complicated nature of mental control. At some level, we adults assume that we can control our mental processes—for example, we can choose to concentrate on this or that topic. At another level, we also recognize that our self-control is partial—even as we concentrate, we cannot dictate the ideas that we generate and we cannot suppress intrusive and irrelevant thoughts. What children understand about this delicate issue remains to be explored.

## LATER DEVELOPMENTS AND MATURE FUNCTIONING

Research on the child's theory of mind has focused mainly on young children. The way in which that theory is carried forward or radically revised in later years has been much less studied. However, there are some issues that have attracted attention. In this section, I discuss three notable examples.

### Understanding Doubt and Uncertainty

To the extent that 4- and 5-year-olds appreciate that someone with a mistaken belief effectively holds, and will act on, an inaccurate representation of reality, it is tempting to assume that children of this age appreciate that our everyday construal of reality is a question of interpretation: What one person represents as true, another person may deny. Indeed, some theorists have proposed that the onset of false-belief understanding marks the onset of what might be called an interpretive theory of mind.

Early dissent from this position was voiced by Michael Chandler (1988). He argued that such a conclusion overstates the young child's achievement. The false-belief task—and its close cousins such as the appearance-reality task or the level 2 visual-perspective-taking task—calls for the child to understand that the belief formed by a given protagonist depends critically on the history of his or her perceptual access to the situation under consideration. More generally, granted knowledge of that history, it is possible to predict what belief the person will arrive at. For example, knowing that the protagonist in the false-belief task failed to observe an object's unexpected displacement, it is possible to predict his or her mistaken belief that the object remains in its earlier location. Similarly, knowing that someone has only looked at—and not yet touched—a piece of sponge that has been fashioned and painted to resemble a rock, it is possible to understand that he or she will be misled by its visual appearance.

As Chandler emphasizes (Carpendale & Chandler, 1996; Chandler, 1988), however, there are many cases in which knowledge of a person's perceptual history does not fully constrain the predictions that can be made about his or her beliefs. Consider a familiar ambiguous stimulus, such as the illustration of a duck-rabbit that is found in introductory psychology textbooks. Two observers looking at this picture may draw different conclusions about what is depicted. To that extent, the setup resembles the standard false-belief or appearance-reality setup. However, knowing the person's perceptual history does not yield a prediction of which interpretation he or she will reach regarding the ambiguous figure. Similar remarks are applicable to ambiguous utterances. If there are three blocks, one blue and two red, children who are told to look under the red block might differ about which of the two red blocks they think is intended. Yet, knowledge of their individual perceptual histories will be of no assistance in deciding which child will opt for which block.

Carpendale and Chandler (1996) found that children's understanding of the impact of such perceptually ambiguous information emerged more slowly than their understanding of perceptually inaccessible information. More specifically, 5-year-olds who did well on a standard false-belief task, and could explain why the central protagonist had a different belief from the other story character (given his or her lack of perceptual access to the unexpected displacement), could rarely explain why two children looked at an ambiguous picture or hearing an ambiguous message would reach different conclusions. Eight-year-olds, however, performed much better. They explained the belief divergence in terms of the ambiguous nature of the stimulus. They realized that it was hard to predict which of the two interpretations any given observer would adopt although they also realized that other, more deviant interpretations—for example, that the ambiguous duck-rabbit illustration depicted an elephant—were unlikely. Chandler and his colleagues make a good case for distinguishing between children's understanding of information that is inaccessible and their understanding of information that is ambiguous. Even if 5-year-olds understand that some information is inaccessible, they are puzzled by the fact that some information is ambiguous.

Indeed, the cautionary conclusion reached by Carpendale and Chandler (1996) can be extended further. Some beliefs are relatively straightforward judgments about observable objects or events and such beliefs may well go wrong when perceptual access is blocked, but it is clear that we hold many different kinds of belief and we form those beliefs in various ways. For example, we also hold beliefs about what is right and wrong, about the past and the future, and about a large number of theoretical and metaphysical entities. In none of these cases, do we arrive at our beliefs by a simple act of perceptual observation. Given this "disunity" of belief, it is appropriate to ask whether children's sensitivity to disagreement among individuals varies from one belief domain to another.

Evidence in support of this variation has been reported by Wainryb and her colleagues (Wainryb, Shaw, Langley, Cottam, & Lewis, 2004). They found that 9-year-olds show considerable sensitivity to the type of belief that they were invited to consider. For example, with respect to relatively straightforward moral beliefs—such as whether it is acceptable to hit or steal—9-year-olds generally insist that only one stance is right and they also insist that dissent is not acceptable. However, with respect to factual matters, although they again insist that only one stance is right, they are more tolerant of dissent. Finally, with respect to uncertain issues whether in the realm of fact or taste, they acknowledge that more than one stance could be right and that more than one stance is acceptable. Even 5-year-olds show some emerging sensitivity to these various domains of belief but, in line with the results of Carpendale and Chandler (1996), they are less sensitive to the potential ambiguity or uncertainty of certain issues.

Thus, instead of allowing that opposing judgments might both be right, they tend to claim that only one belief can be right.

The acknowledgment that more than one stance toward a given issue could be right is a clear recognition of uncertainty. However, children might adopt two different attitudes toward uncertainty. On the one hand, they might conclude that competing claims are equally valid and that there is no way to adjudicate between them. For example, in the case of ambiguous figures or taste preferences, one individual's subjective appraisal is as good as another's. On the other hand, children might recognize that in some domains competing claims are not equally meritorious. Insofar as they come to acknowledge ambiguity and uncertainty, do children generally adopt the first stance—treating all competing claims as more or less equal? Alternatively, do they show some appreciation of the second stance—recognizing that rational adjudication among competing claims is possible? The answer to this question is obviously important from an educational point of view. Any genuine understanding of debate—whether in science, politics, morality, or history—critically depends on the realization that competing claims are *not* equally valid and there are various criteria for their adjudication, depending on the domain in question.

Some evidence points to a pessimistic conclusion. When preadolescents have been assessed for their understanding of competing knowledge claims, they rarely acknowledge that such claims can be compared and evaluated. For example, Kuhn, Cheney, and Weinstock (2000) presented children, ranging from 10 to 17 years, and adults with competing claims in various domains and asked participants to say whether only one claim was right—and in those cases where each claim was acknowledged as having some merit to say whether it was possible to judge one as superior. Across all participants, the most frequent response pattern was to acknowledge that more than one claim might be right but to deny that adjudication was possible. Even when the claims pertained to the physical world (e.g., the structure of atoms or the functioning of the brain), less than half of the adult participants acknowledged that one could be judged superior; among the youngest age group interviewed (10-year-olds), only 20% acknowledged that adjudication is possible. Only among a specialist group of adults (all doctoral students in philosophy) was there universal acknowledgment that competing claims about the physical and social world are open to adjudication.

More encouraging results have emerged from studies in which children have been invited to consider the type of evidence that might resolve a given empirical question. For example, Sodian, Zaitchik, and Carey (1991) told children aged 6 to 9 years a story about two brothers who were trying to figure out whether a mouse in their house—which they had not been able to see—was big or small. Children were shown two boxes, one with a large opening, the other with a small opening and asked what the brothers could conclude if either one or the other box was baited with cheese, left out during the night, and checked in the morning to see if the cheese had been eaten. More than half of the 6- to 7-year-olds and the large majority of the 7- to 9-year-olds (a) suggested leaving out the box with the small opening, (b) understood the implications of the cheese being either gone or still there in the morning, and (c) realized that leaving out the box with the big opening would be inconclusive. Similar results emerged in a parallel study. Most children judged that inviting an aardvark to find buried mild-smelling food would test the sensitivity of its sense of smell but burying strong-smelling food would produce only inconclusive results. Indeed, children of this age understand how evidence bears not only on the properties of a given individual but also on the properties of a class or set. Six- and 7-year-olds realized that different patterns of evidence about how hard various tennis rackets (differing in size, shape, and strings) could hit the ball could be used to evaluate not only the rackets that were tested but also what type of racket to buy in the future (Ruffman, Perner, Olson, & Doherty, 1993). Note, however, that these are all questions that have definite answers, once the necessary observations have been made. For example, the mouse is big or small, not both. Similarly, size of tennis racket either does or does not affect how hard the ball can be hit. If the issue is acknowledged as one where each of the competing views may have some validity (e.g., competing views about how the brain functions), children, as well as many adolescents and adults, are unlikely to report any possibility of determining their relative merits.

Although children in their study did well in understanding the implications of various sorts of evidential test suggested by the interviewer, Sodian et al. (1991) also observed that few children were able to generate a conclusive test themselves. More generally, it is almost certainly easier to recognize the implications of evidence once it is provided than to think about what evidence would be informative and ways to gather it. This gap between evidence evaluation and evidence seeking may explain, at least in part, why preadolescents often conclude that empirical claims cannot be adjudicated. They have difficulty in conceiving of the type of evidence that would be decisive. For example, when asked whether it is possible to adjudicate between different accounts of the way that the brain works, many children—and indeed many adults—may not know what type of evidence would be informative.

In summary, young children understand that beliefs may diverge when observers differ in their perceptual access. They do not, however, immediately appreciate all the various ways in which beliefs may diverge. In particular, they are slower to understand the way that ambiguous or uncertain information may be differentially interpreted. Moreover, when the existence of uncertainty is acknowledged, children—and even some adults—show some signs of being overwhelmed. They are likely to conclude that it is impossible to adjudicate among beliefs. Still, elementary school children can often differentiate between decisive and inconclusive evidence when such evidence is explicitly presented to them. Further analysis of adolescents' sensitivity to this central issue in epistemology is presented by Kuhn and Franklin (Chapter 22, this *Handbook,* this volume).

## Understanding Second-Order Beliefs and Nonliteral Utterances

An old idea in social cognition is that development is marked by an increasing ability not simply to take the perspective of another person, as exemplified by the standard false-belief task, but to contemplate multiple, potentially intersecting perspectives. For example, Selman (1980) claimed that it was not until approximately 10 years of age that children began to articulate not only the distinct perspectives of particular actors in a given social situation but also the perspective that one actor might have toward the perspectives of other actors. In theory-of-mind research, the most direct analysis of this developmental trend has focused on the second-order false-belief task. Extending their pioneering studies of the standard false-belief task, Perner and Wimmer (1985) introduced a more complex, second-order task in which children were called on to assess what one actor would believe about the beliefs of another actor. For example, children heard a story in which one actor did not realize that a second actor knew about an unexpected change of location; their task was to diagnose the first actor's mistaken belief about the second actor's belief. Perner and Wimmer (1985) found that children could solve the problem at around 6 to 7 years of age, well beyond the age at which the standard false-belief task is mastered but still in advance of what might have been expected on Selman's role-taking theory.

Subsequent research by Sullivan, Zaitchik, and Tager-Flusberg (1994), showed that most kindergarteners are able to manage the second-order task if simpler stories with a deceptive context are used. Still, as we saw with the standard task, even if thematic changes alter the absolute level of difficulty, this need not compromise the claim that there is a developmental improvement in the ability to handle the second-order task.

The difficulty of the second-order task is especially evident among children with autism. Recall that most children with autism, even those with a relatively advanced mental age, fail the standard false-belief task. Baron-Cohen (1989) focused on the minority of children with autism who pass that standard task. When such children were tested on the second-order task—Baron-Cohen found a severe impairment even among those who were in their teens.

In an interesting analysis, Happé (1993) proposed that success on the second-order task might be connected to the understanding of figurative speech, particularly irony. She went on to show that subjects with autism and with mild learning disabilities who failed the second-order task did indeed have difficulty understanding ironic remarks. For example, when presented with a vignette in which a parent said "Nice job!" to a child who had made a mess while doing a household chore, children with autism were inclined to focus on the literal meaning of the remark and to interpret it as a compliment.

Follow-up work by Happé (1994) showed that the interpretation of stories containing nonliteral utterances was a sensitive diagnostic tool in assessing the social cognitive impairments of mature subjects with autism. Performance on the stories was closely related to performance on theory-of-mind tasks, although even those subjects who managed to pass all the theory-of-mind tasks showed impairments on the more naturalistic story materials relative to normal controls.

In summary, research on the child's theory of mind has concentrated on the establishment of basic building blocks: children's developing understanding of desire, belief, and emotion. Some investigators, however, have taken up a more traditional theme of research on social cognition: the ability to take multiple perspectives. Various studies show that the understanding of beliefs about beliefs is mastered at around 6 years of age by normal children—but considerably later, if at all, by children with autism. Competence on these so-called second-order tasks turns out to be linked in an intriguing fashion to another aspect of social cognition—the ability to appropriately interpret nonliteral utterances, notably irony. That said, difficulty in interpreting such remarks turns out to be a persistent impairment of subjects with autism, even among those who do well on both first- and second-order tasks.

## Measures of Reflective Functioning among Adults

A great deal of research on the social cognition of adults has been conducted with little reference to developmental theory. Research on so-called reflective functioning among adults constitutes an important exception to that generalization. Both in its conceptualization and in its empirical yield, this line of research retains important links to developmental research. I briefly review some of the key findings.

In an influential study, Main, Kaplan, and Cassidy (1985) administered an adult attachment interview (AAI) in which they asked 40 middle-class mothers to reflect on, and describe, their relationships with their mothers during infancy and childhood. Memories of rejection, illness, and separation were probed as well as reasons for the parents' behavior. A link emerged between maternal reflections on their childhood attachments and the type of relationship that mothers had with their own children. "Autonomous" mothers offered a balanced and consistent account of their childhood relationships; they tended to have securely attached children. "Dismissing" mothers often devalued their childhood relationships, had difficulty in recalling them, and seemed unaware of inconsistencies in their account; they tended to have insecure-avoidant children. "Preoccupied" mothers were often caught up in their childhood memories, recalled conflictual relationships, and had difficulty in providing a coherent, integrated account; these mothers tended to have insecure-ambivalent children.

Subsequent research has lent considerable support to the claim that such reflections predict the kind of relationship that parents establish with their children. In a meta-analysis, Van Ijzendoorn (1995) found a strong relationship between the parents' attachment, as measured by the AAI, and the nature of their children's attachment, as measured by standard instruments such as the Strange Situation or the Attachment Q-sort (AQS). This relationship emerged for fathers but more strongly for mothers. As noted by Van Ijzendoorn (1995), the findings are impressive in that the two measures are quite different—reflective discourse for the AAI and the coding of behavioral responses for the Strange Situation and the Attachment Q-sort.

Several other findings are worth stressing. First, although performance on the AAI calls for a good deal of reflective discourse, classification appears to be independent of verbal IQ (Bakermans-Kranenburg & Van Ijzendoorn, 1993). Second, in line with the assumption that it is the parent who influences the child rather than the reverse, a similar predictive relationship emerges even if parents are interviewed prior to the birth of the child (Benoit & Parker, 1994; Fonagy, Steele, & Steele, 1991).

How exactly should we interpret this intriguing link? One possibility is that the nature of mother's early experience is critical. According to this "early experience" interpretation, mothers vary during their childhood in the way that they are mothered; that differential early experience eventually affects the way that they come to reflect on the past during the AAI, and it also affects the way that they relate to and nurture their own children. An alternative possibility is that the AAI is an index not so much of what mothers actually experienced as children but of their current capacity to reflect in a coherent fashion about intimate relationships. According to this "current reflective capacity" interpretation, mother's psychological sensitivity—as indexed by her discourse during the AAI—is linked to the way that she construes—and mothers—her child.

It is too early to adjudicate between these two alternatives. Still, it is worth noting that we may be able to do so in the future. Recent longitudinal research indicates that attachment in infancy can be a good predictor of performance on the AAI during late adolescence (Hamilton, 2000) or early adulthood (Waters, Merrick, Treboux, Crowell, & Albersheim, 2000). Nevertheless, in a sample of disadvantaged families who experienced high rates of stressful life events, no such predictive link

from infancy to late adolescence was found (Weinfeld, Sroufe, & Egeland, 2000). Similarly, disruptive effects of stressful life events, notably divorce, on continuity from infancy to late adolescence were also reported by Lewis, Feiring, and Rosenthal (2000). With respect to the latter two samples—where no relationship between early attachment and current performance on the AAI was found—it is possible to ask which measure is the more important for the prediction of later parenting—particularly the type of attachment that such adolescents will form with their own children. The early experience interpretation implies that early attachment would be the stronger predictor, whereas the reflective capacity interpretation implies that performance on the AAI would be the stronger predictor.

Beyond the question of whether it is the mother's past experience or her current reflective capacity that is important, it is worth noting that we continue to have a relatively weak understanding of how exactly characteristics of the mother influence the child's attachment. Maternal sensitivity has traditionally been emphasized by attachment theorists, but existing measures of such nonverbal responsiveness probably fail to capture the entire spectrum of transmission from mother to infant (Van Ijzendoorn, 1995). Recent research by Meins and her colleagues offers a way to broaden our assessment of that spectrum and promises to make connections with the concept of reflective functioning (Meins, Fernyhough, Fradley, & Tuckey, 2001). These investigators assessed maternal sensitivity in the usual fashion using the scale devised by Ainsworth, Bell, and Stayton (1971), but they also assessed maternal "mind-mindedness"—mothers' tendency to comment appropriately on the ongoing mental states of their infant. As expected, maternal sensitivity was correlated with infants' attachment security, as measured at 12 months but mind-mindedness proved to have an independent and somewhat stronger relationship to attachment security.

In summary, parents' comments on their own intimate relationships are a good predictor of the type of relationship that parents form with their infants. In particular, mothers who offer a psychologically coherent and balanced account of their childhood relationship with their own mother as well as mothers who comment appropriately and accurately on their infants' current mental states are likely to have infants who display a secure attachment. This striking relationship between psychological discourse on the part of the mother and emotional security on the part of the infant should encourage continuing collaboration and dialogue between two relatively distinct research communities—those who focus on social cognition especially as indexed by psychological discourse and those who focus on early attachment.

## HOW DO HUMANS DIFFER FROM OTHER NONHUMAN PRIMATES IN THEIR THEORY OF MIND?

As noted earlier, the initial impetus for research on theory of mind came from research on primatology. In that context, the possible role of language was not highlighted in any obvious way. Indeed, if we think about the classic false-belief task, it is not inconceivable that a languageless creature such as a chimpanzee could solve it. After all, it calls for an appreciation of the way in which an observer might have incomplete perceptual access to the true state of affairs. That appreciation does not necessarily call for any linguistic ability. It could be based on observation of an agent's lack of perceptual access at some given moment. As it happens, subsequent research with primates, notably chimpanzees, has mostly produced negative results when they have been tested on variants of the false-belief task (Call & Tomasello, 1999). In addition, despite an initially enthusiastic compilation of case notes from the field, suggesting deliberate deception among chimpanzees, doubts surfaced about the extent to which such ploys, deceptive though they might be, really did depend on a calculation of just what the dupe would falsely believe (Heyes, 1998). Perhaps, for example, they were guided by some past experience of the risks associated with acting in particular ways in full view of a rival or competitor.

In addition, three other streams of experimental research have suggested that chimpanzees are quite restricted in their psychological inferences. First, they seem to have a limited understanding of the link between seeing and knowing. They generally beg for food indiscriminately from humans who either can or cannot see them (Povinelli & Eddy, 1996), and they fail to realize that someone who has seen an event is likely to know more about it than someone who has not (Povinelli, Rulf, & Bierschwale, 1994). Second, chimpanzees do not seem to interpret fairly simple gestures or cues indicating a source of food. For example, if they know that food has been hidden in one of two boxes, and a trainer either gazes at, points to, or places a marker on the baited box,

chimpanzees typically choose randomly as if unable to "read" the trainer's action as a helpful communicative act (Call & Tomasello, 2005). Third, although chimpanzees appear to transmit tool-using techniques from one to another, so as to engender a form of local "culture" (Whiten, Goodall, McGrew, et al., 1999), this form of social transmission might not involve any systematic analysis of the intentions that underlie the model's actions (Tomasello, 1996)—it might rest instead on a more superficial observation of motor actions or of ensuing outcomes.

Nevertheless, the most recent evidence has led to a more positive assessment of the chimpanzee's mind-reading capacity. First, chimpanzees do display an ability to monitor one another's orientation and intended actions, at least in competitive contexts. For example, Tomasello, Call, and Hare (2003) have tested chimpanzees in the following situation. A subordinate and a dominant watch from separate rooms as food is placed in each of two locations, one open and one partially screened, in a central area. The subordinate can see where each piece of food is placed. The subordinate is also able to observe the range of the dominant's visual access and can observe that the dominant has seen the food at the open location but not at the screened location. The two animals are released into the central area, with the subordinate being given a brief head start. Under these circumstances, the subordinate appears to nicely calculate what the dominant has and has not seen. The subordinate heads for the food location that is visible only to her, thereby avoiding the risk of head-on competition with the dominant at the other food location. A variety of more pedestrian interpretations can be ruled out. For example, the subordinate is not reacting to the dominant's overt behavioral choice because the subordinate's food preference is manifest before the dominant's door has been lifted. Nor do subordinates show a generalized preference for food at a partially screened location: When tested in the absence of a dominant, they show no such preference.

In a series of follow-up studies, the subordinate's analysis of the dominant's history of perceptual access was analyzed. There were two partially screened locations. When both the subordinate and the dominant watched food hidden at one of these locations, the subordinate approached that location less often than when only the subordinate had seen the hiding. By implication, the subordinate remembered what the dominant had and had not seen and avoided the food source if the dominant knew about it. Again, plausible alternative interpretations can be ruled out. For example, it is not the case that subordinates steer clear of a food source that any dominant has monitored. Thus, if one dominant saw the hiding but a different dominant is present when an opportunity to retrieve the food arises, the subordinate shows less avoidance. By implication, the subordinate not only realizes and remembers that a food source has been spotted by a dominant but also realizes that such privileged access is available to one individual and not others. Summing up, these experiments indicate that chimpanzees realize that conspecifics have a particular field of vision, can see things in that field, and will act on what they have seen.

Tomasello et al. (2003) suggest that the more flexible, psychological analysis that they have uncovered is probably tied to larger features of chimpanzee social behavior. In their natural habitat, chimpanzees do compete for food, but they rarely, if ever, indicate food to another that they themselves could take. Thus, their ordinary living conditions promote sensitivity to the states and intentions of a competitor rather than the states and intentions of a collaborator or benefactor.

It is interesting to note that dogs do display such sensitivity to a benefactor. For example, unlike chimpanzees, domesticated dogs take advantage of communicative acts by their trainers when searching for food (Hare, Brown, Williamson, & Tomasello, 2002). This proclivity appears to be the product of selective breeding practices. It is not found among all members of the canine order—for example, wolves show no such sensitivity. Nor is early socialization in the company of human beings a critical factor. Puppies that have had little contact with human beings are also sensitive to human signals. Overall, the evidence is consistent with the claim that selection pressures operating over successive generations of domestic dogs have led to a robust island of social cognition. Needless to say, no such selection pressures have operated on chimpanzees, despite the fact that they are receptive to human domestication in certain respects.

Should we conclude then that chimpanzees' sensitivity to the knowledge state and likely future actions of a dominant is a very local awareness, tied quite narrowly to contexts in which there is competition for food between conspecifics? Such a conclusion would be premature. In an ongoing series of experiments, Call and his colleagues find that chimpanzees differentiate between a human trainer who is ostensibly unable to hand over some food (e.g., he cannot extract it from a tube or accidentally drops it) as compared to a human trainer who is unwilling to hand over food (e.g., he proffers the food but teasingly withdraws it). Faced with the unwilling as opposed to the incompetent trainer, they are more likely to display signs of impatience by banging on the cage or quitting the test area (Call, Hare, Carpenter, & Tomasello, 2004). Thus, chimpanzees do have some ability to read intentions in noncompetitive contexts.

How then should the strengths and limitations of chimpanzee social cognition be described? Tomasello and his colleagues propose that chimpanzees can "go a bit below the surface" of ongoing action. They grasp the fact that bodily and head orientation toward a given target can predict subsequent approach to that target. Similarly, they grasp the fact that ongoing signs of goal-directed behavior—including unsuccessful attempts—are good clues to subsequent actions (Tomasello et al., 2003). At the same time, they emphasize that there are currently no clear indications that chimpanzees can penetrate deeper—to understand, for example, the way in which an agent might deliberate and plan before acting, especially in collaboration with a group member (Tomasello, Carpenter, Call, Behne, & Moll, 2005). Thus, even if chimpanzees do read one another's perceptual states and intentions in noncompetitive as well as competitive situations, there is little or no evidence that they have the capacity to engage in planned cooperation. In line with this conclusion, Hare and Tomasello (2004) report that chimpanzees performed much more skillfully in a food-finding task if the task is structured as competition rather than cooperation. On this view, the divide between chimpanzee and human child has to do with both the depth and richness of psychological understanding in the two species and the differential capacity for cooperative endeavors.

Povinelli and Vonk (2003) are skeptical that any analysis in terms of merely gradualistic or quantitative differences captures the full extent of the gap between chimpanzee and child. They propose instead that at some point in human evolution the capacity that we share with our primate cousins—to go below the surface features of particular actions—was ramped up to a qualitatively different mode of apprehension. Specifically, they argue that we human beings have an almost ineluctable tendency to assume that actions are caused by internal mental states. In turn, we regard mental states as having an ontologically distinct status from the actions that they guide. On this view, chimpanzees may "go below the surface" but never conceptualize a genuinely mental substrate, whereas human beings invariably go much below the surface and infer a qualitatively distinct set of states. Indeed, so powerful is that inferential tendency that we human beings are prone to apply it—mistakenly—to our otherwise similar primate cousins, particularly chimpanzees. Povinelli and Vonk (2003) go on to argue that the food competition experiments reported by Tomasello and his colleagues do not allow us to decide between a lean and a rich interpretation of the strategies displayed by the chimpanzee subordinate. Maybe the subordinate is attributing visual experience and knowledge to the dominant but maybe the subordinate is using a much less sophisticated form of behavioral extrapolation: "Don't go after food if D was present and oriented toward it when it was placed in position; such an orientation is a good cue that D will go after the food."

The resolution of this debate in primatology is not likely to be rapid or straightforward (Povinelli & Vonk, 2004). Meantime, developmental psychologists may rejoice that the testing of human children is made a great deal easier by the fact that it is possible to talk to them about mental states, to ask them to make predictions about mental states, and to assess the degree to which they voice explanations in terms of mental states. In a later section, I explore the extent to which language is not only a means for the more sensitive assessment of the child's social cognition but also an intrinsic part of human social cognition.

## IS THERE A UNIVERSAL CORE TO THE HUMAN THEORY OF MIND?

In arguing for a universal core to the human theory of mind, stable across diverse cultures, Fodor (1987) observed, "There is, so far as I know, no human group that doesn't explain behavior by imputing beliefs and desires to the behavior. (And if an anthropologist claimed to have found such a group, I wouldn't believe him.)" As Avis and Harris (1991) noted, Fodor might have couched his incredulity in less hypothetical terms. In a classic monograph on the Dinka of southern Sudan, the Oxford social anthropologist Godfrey Lienhardt (1961) asserted just such an absence of mentalistic explanation: "The Dinka have no conception which at all corresponds to our popular conception of the 'mind' as mediating and, as it were, storing up the experiences of the self. . . . What we should

call the 'memories' of experiences, and regard therefore as in some way intrinsic to the person . . . appear to the Dinka as exteriorly acting upon him" (p. 149).

The available evidence tends to bear out at least part of Fodor's proposition. First, Wierzbicka (1992) has suggested that all human languages contain terms that roughly refer to wanting, thinking, and knowing. Second, cross-cultural studies have shown that children from radically different cultural backgrounds understand false beliefs even if the age of mastery is variable. Children growing up in industrialized centers of Western Europe, North America, and Asia solve the false-belief task at around 4 to 5 years of age (Wellman et al., 2001). Much the same age of mastery emerged in a more wide-ranging comparison of children attending urban preschools in India, Thailand, Canada, and Peru as well as a village preschool in Samoa (Callaghan et al., 2004). On the other hand, Vinden (1999) found that Mofu children from Northern Cameroon and Tolai children from Papua New Guinea could generally solve false-belief tasks only at around 7 years of age. Vinden also tested Tainae children in Papua New Guinea, but a variety of problems—including the reluctance of young children and females to be tested and difficulties in formulating one of the key test questions in the vernacular—render the results hard to interpret. The potentially crucial role of language was highlighted in another study reported by Vinden (1996). She tested 4- to 8-year-old Junín Quechua children growing up in a remote Quechua village in Peru. Most children passed an appearance-reality task—although there was a clear improvement with age. However, most children failed to solve false-belief tasks even when the same materials were used as for the appearance-reality task. They could usually say that an object that looked like a rock was really a sponge, but they often erred in saying what they had thought the object was before they touched it and what a newcomer would think it was before touching it. However, in Junín Quechua, "What would he think" is rendered by a phrase meaning (roughly) "What would he say." Thus, Junín Quechua children may have been unfamiliar or uncomfortable with the phrasing of the false-belief questions.

Summing across these studies, there is persuasive evidence from many different settings that children come to an understanding of false belief by about 5 years of age. Nevertheless, some reports indicate that children do not master the standard task until about 7 years of age—or persist in failure even beyond that age. For the moment, caution is needed in interpreting delayed mastery.

As acknowledged by Vinden (1996), language difficulties may play an important role. Studies of Western children provide convergent evidence of the critical role of language and there is every reason to expect that language will be equally important in non-Western settings.

How do children from different cultures fare on other mental-state tasks? With respect to emotion, we saw in an earlier section that children readily link particular situations with particular emotions and then gradually realize that individual desires and eventually beliefs may modulate a given individual's reactions to a situation. Only a limited amount of research has examined this claim in a cross-cultural context, but the scattered findings lend some support to the universality thesis. For example, Harris et al. (1987) asked children in Europe and a remote village of Nepal to describe what situations would be provoked by various emotions. Children in both settings suggested appropriate elicitors for various basic emotions. Vinden (1999) found that Mofu and Tolai children could predict from about 5- or 6-years that someone would be upset by an unexpected loss—not finding some fruit where it had been left.

Avis and Harris (1991) showed that most Baka 5-year-olds growing up in the rain-forests of Southeast Cameroon understood that someone approaching a pot and wrongly believing it contained food would be happy before lifting the lid but sad afterward. Tenenbaum, Visscher, Pons, and Harris (2004) observed a similar understanding of belief-based emotion among Quechua children ranging from 8 to 11 years. However, Vinden (1999) found little evidence for the understanding of belief-based emotions among the Mofu or Tolai.

Harris and Gross (1988) reported that children in Western Europe, North America, and Japan all come to differentiate felt and expressed emotion at around 6 years of age. Sissons Joshi and MacLean (1994) obtained similar findings among children in India. For the time being, we do not know whether and how children from a preliterate community come to make that distinction but like the concept of false belief, the concept of hidden, unexpressed emotion seems a good candidate for universality.

In sum, although linguistic obstacles have sometimes led to inconclusive results, children growing up in non-Western settings, including traditional rural villages, acquire an understanding of belief at roughly the same age as Western children. They can also identify what situations will provoke particular emotions and use that knowledge to anticipate how someone will feel. Some children in these setting also understand belief-based emotion. Regarding various other aspects of mental state understanding, we have, as yet, no evidence. In particular, there has been very little exploration of the possibility that certain basic concepts—for example the distinction between expressed and experienced emotion and the incessant flow of consciousness—are elaborated in culture-specific ways. Certainly, the existing evidence for some degree of cross-cultural stability in the acquisition of key concepts should not be taken to mean that there is no cultural variation in the way that these concepts are put to work and elaborated (Harris, 1990; Lillard, 1998, 1999).

## CHILDREN WITH AUTISM

Research on the normal development of a theory of mind was given an important boost in the United Kingdom by a related program of research on children with autism. In 1985, Baron-Cohen, Leslie, and Frith reported that only 20% of a group of children with autism passed a variant of the false-belief task compared to approximately 80% of normal children and children with Downs syndrome of comparable mental age. Leslie (1987) proposed a theoretical explanation by arguing that the well-known limitations in pretend play that are one of the diagnostic signs of autism reflect an innate, modular deficit in the conceptualization of various mental states including belief as well as pretence. My aim here is not to provide a comprehensive review of the syndrome of autism but rather to describe ways in which children with autism depart from—and thereby highlight—the standard pattern of development.

Subsequent research moved rapidly ahead in confirming that children with autism do have a wide-ranging difficulty in grasping false beliefs. First, even if some children with autism succeed in passing variants of the standard task, they frequently fail more complex versions that call for an understanding of beliefs about beliefs (Baron-Cohen, 1989). Second, children with autism are poor at deliberately creating a false belief by lying. For example, even if prompted to mislead a thief but help a friend, they tend to naively help both. This is not due to any insurmountable tendency to be cooperative. When prompted, they are able to act selectively by physically blocking the thief but helping the friend (Sodian & Frith, 1992). Third, children with autism show just the type of problems with emotion understanding that would flow from a difficulty in understanding beliefs. Whereas they perform quite well in grasping familiar links between situations and emotions (realizing, for example, that a birthday generally provokes happiness but a loss provokes sadness), they perform much less well than controls matched for verbal ability in understanding belief-based emotions (Baron-Cohen, 1991).

Nevertheless, the temptation to conclude that children with autism provide an instance of cognitive development with the theory-of-mind module neatly excised should be resisted. First, in line with normal children, the degree of difficulty that children with autism display on standard false-belief tasks is correlated with their language ability. Thus, autistic children with a verbal mental age of 6 to 7 years have approximately a 20% probability of passing the false-belief task, whereas those with a verbal mental age of 11 to 12 years have approximately an 80% probability of passing (Happé, 1995). Indeed, children with autism could be said to need a greater verbal ability than normal children to achieve the same theory-of-mind result. After all, among normal children a verbal mental age of 4 to 5 years is sufficient to yield a high probability of passing the standard false-belief task.

Second, the apparently clear-cut difference between children with autism and children with some other mental handicap such as Down's syndrome in performance on the false-belief task turns out to be less clear than it originally appeared. More specifically, mentally handicapped children also display a lag, albeit one that is less marked, than that shown by children with autism (Yirmiya, Osnat, Shaked, & Solomonica-Levi, 1998).

Third, there is increasing evidence that children with autism perform quite well on tasks that call for an understanding of other allegedly central concepts for a theory of mind: desire and perception. Tan and Harris (1991) showed that children with autism assert, and reassert, their desires—even in the face of an interlocutor who initially thwarts them. In addition, longitudinal studies of the spontaneous language production of children with autism show that despite a paucity of references to the cognitive states of knowing and thinking, they do often refer to desires and perceptions (Tager-Flusberg, 1993). Finally, children with autism perform quite well on visual perspective-taking tasks (Hobson, 1984; Reed & Peterson, 1990).

One potential interpretation of these findings is that children with autism follow the same developmental road map as normal children but at a much slower pace—a proposal made by Baron-Cohen (1989). By implication, their problems do not reveal a modular excision but rather an abnormally slow rate of growth in such a module. This interpretation is consistent with the fact that many children with autism do eventually pass the false-belief landmark and with the fact that a minority even comes to an understanding of beliefs about beliefs. It is also consistent with the observation that children with autism have no particular difficulty in talking about their own desires or those of other people. After all, there is solid evidence that the understanding and discussion of desires emerges early in the course of normal development (Bartsch & Wellman, 1995; Harris, 1996; Tardif & Wellman, 2000)—before an understanding and discussion of beliefs. Arguably, children with autism show no obvious delay on the earliest landmarks of a theory of mind but do so increasingly—as their slowed rate of development dictates.

However, this simple delay-based account runs into difficulties if we take a look at so-called precursors or early indices of a theory of mind. If children with autism perform more or less normally with respect to desires, we might expect them to perform without difficulty on all co-occurring or antecedent indices of a theory of mind. Yet, they display clear limitations in three areas: (1) the development of joint attention, (2) engagement in pretend play, and (3) concern for others in distress. I briefly take up each of these in turn.

As discussed earlier, normal infants start to show joint attention behaviors in the 1st year of life. By either following or directing the attention and gaze of another person, they establish a triadic relationship comprising the self, the other person and an object of mutual attention. Children with autism show important restrictions in joint attention (Mundy, Sigman, & Kasari, 1993). Indeed, longitudinal research has suggested that deficits in joint attention are an important early marker for a likely later diagnosis of autism. Baron-Cohen, Allen, and Gillberg (1992) targeted a group of 18-month-olds who had an older sibling with autism and who on genetic grounds therefore were at risk themselves. A small number of these children showed deficits in both joint attention and pretend play; follow-up studies confirmed that these children did go on to receive a diagnosis of autism. Finally, there is no evidence that these difficulties with joint attention are eventually overcome, as one might expect on a developmental delay hypothesis (Klin, Jones, Schultz, & Volkmar, 2004).

One of the defining features of autism—ever since Kanner's original description of the syndrome—has been a limitation in pretend play. Later experimental analysis has revealed that children with autism are not completely deficient at pretend play. First, with prompting, they engage in simple object-directed pretence (Lewis & Boucher, 1988). Second, if asked to watch an adult engage in object-directed pretence—for example, a pretend pouring or pretend squeezing—they perform competently in working out the likely pretend consequences (Kavanaugh & Harris, 1994). Nevertheless, even if the findings indicate a basic competence for both the production and comprehension of pretense, they also indicate persistent restrictions on fertility and generativity (Harris & Leevers, 2000; Jarrold, Boucher, & Smith, 1996; Lewis & Boucher, 1995). Moreover, as noted earlier, a delay in the onset of pretense, in combination with deficits in joint attention, appears to be an early marker for autism (Baron-Cohen et al., 1992).

Finally, children with autism differ from normal children and mentally retarded children in their responses to the distress of others. When an adult feigns distress or pain, children with autism are less likely to attend to the distressed person, more likely to remain engaged in toy play, and less likely to display concern. This finding has emerged among toddlers with autism (Sigman, Kasari, Kwon, & Yirmiya, 1992) and persists into adolescence (Sigman & Ruskin, 1999).

Taken together, these findings indicate that children with autism do not simply exhibit a delay in the acquisition or onset of an otherwise normal theory of mind. They show early difficulties with joint attention, pretend play, and empathic concern that appear to be quite persistent. Yet, they also show relatively normal progress on an aspect of a theory of mind (notably the understanding of desires) that is generally taken to emerge after the onset of joint attention, pretend play, and empathic concern. These findings imply that the gradual confluence that we see in normal children, more specifically the joint recourse to beliefs and desires in explaining behavior, may bring together two initially separate ontogenetic streams. Stated differently, the findings from autism suggest that the acquisition of a theory of mind is not a single, indivisible process. Children with autism understand some parts of the puzzle but not others.

## INDIVIDUAL DIFFERENCES IN PRETEND PLAY AND THEORY OF MIND

As noted in the discussion of autism, Leslie (1987) argued that children's ability to engage appropriately in pretend play, either alone or with a partner, implies that they understand the mentalistic nature of pretense. He further argued that this alleged capacity for metarepresentation sets the stage for an understanding of belief. Various commentators have concluded that Leslie's rich analysis of early pretense is wrong (Currie, 1998; Harris & Kavanaugh, 1993, pp. 75–76; Jarrold, Carruthers, Smith, & Boucher, 1994; Nichols & Stich, 2000; Perner, 1993).

Two persuasive objections have emerged: one conceptual and the other empirical. First, contrary to Leslie's analysis, young children could surely engage in pretense even if they did not possess any insight into the mental state of pretending. After all, there is a great deal of evidence that children can hold a belief—including a false belief—well before they show any signs of understanding beliefs as mental states. Toddlers might construe pretense play as a special form of action rather than a special mental state. So, they might think of the pretend action of pouring tea (e.g., the lifting and tilting of an empty teapot) as a special type of action—one that resembles genuine pouring in the motor gesture involved but which is also different in being directed at make-believe tea as opposed to real tea. To see the thrust of this alternative analysis, consider our appreciation of what a mime artist is doing. We see him peel an invisible banana, lift it to his mouth, and bite it. We readily conclude that he is now eating the banana but we do not need to consider the process of mental representation that might be taking place in his mind. It is enough for us to see him directing familiar gestures at an imaginary banana. Similarly, toddlers might construe pretend gestures as familiar actions directed at imaginary props.

The second objection is empirical. Studies indicate that even 4-year-olds, let alone toddlers who are just starting to engage in pretense, do not systematically appreciate that certain mental states are a necessary condition for particular pretend acts. For example, they do not realize that knowing that a kangaroo hops is a necessary condition for pretending to hop like a kangaroo (Joseph, 1998; Lillard, 1993; Sobel, 2004).

However, even if we accept these two arguments against the particular theoretical analysis advanced by

Leslie, it is still plausible that a relationship does exist between the capacity for pretend play and the eventual understanding of belief. One supportive point, noted by Leslie (1987) and corroborated by a good deal of subsequent research, is that even if children with autism are not incapable of pretend play they do show restrictions in generativity and they often show a marked delay in their understanding of false beliefs. It is tempting to see some connection between these two problems. Further evidence for such a connection has emerged more recently from the study of normal children. For example, the frequency of joint proposals (e.g., "You have to stay in my arms" or "Let's make cookies") and of role assignments in the course of pretend play (e.g., "You be mommy") are correlated with children's performance on theory-of-mind tasks (Astington & Jenkins, 1995; Jenkins & Astington, 2000). Similar findings have emerged from other studies (Schwebel, Rosen, & Singer, 1999; Taylor & Carlson, 1997; Youngblade & Dunn, 1995).

It is worth emphasizing, however, that in these various studies, although measures of joint pretend play or role-play correlate with measures of performance on theory-of-mind tasks (typically false-belief and/or appearance-reality tasks), the same does not hold for other aspects of pretense. For example, there is no consistent evidence that the amount of pretense, the diversity of pretend themes, the impersonation of a machine, or engagement in solitary pretend play correlates with performance on theory-of-mind tasks. Thus, role-play, but not pretend play in general, is associated with the understanding of belief (Harris, 2000).

In the next section, the evidence for a strong link between language ability and theory of mind will be reviewed. Granted that relationship, it is appropriate to ask if the relationship between pretend play and theory-of-mind understanding holds up if we take into account the possible contribution of children's language ability. As it happens, this possibility was examined in all the studies cited earlier. In each case, the relationship between pretend play and theory of mind was maintained even when language ability was controlled for, with language ability variously measured in terms of vocabulary, mean length of utterance (MLU), or syntax (Harris, 2005).

In summary, there is a good deal of evidence showing a correlation between children's pretend role-play and their performance on standard theory-of-mind tasks.

That correlation holds up when another potent predictor of children's theory-of-mind performance—their language ability—is taken into account. How should we explain this relationship? Given the objections raised earlier against Leslie's analysis, we need to look elsewhere. Indeed, Leslie's analysis would predict the understanding of belief to be correlated with pretense in general rather than role-play in particular. The findings just reviewed suggest instead that pretend role-play is linked to children's performance on standard theory-of-mind tasks. This link can be interpreted as support for simulation theory, which assumes that the solution to classic theory-of-mind tasks can be reached via a form of role play, in which one's own current situation and knowledge are temporarily set to one side (Harris, 2000). Still, it must be acknowledged that the link between role-play and theory-of-mind performance rests for the moment on correlational data only. Indeed, in one recent correlational study, there was some indication that earlier false-belief understanding predicts later role assignment and joint proposals rather than the reverse (Jenkins & Astington, 2000). Moreover, there have been no intervention studies to assess whether training in role-play leads to better performance on standard theory-of-mind tasks. Nonetheless, we do have the suggestive findings of an earlier research tradition (Smilansky, 1968) showing that educational programs in dramatic play have beneficial effects on children's social cognition in general.

## THE RELATIONSHIP BETWEEN LANGUAGE AND THEORY OF MIND

As discussed at various points throughout this chapter, human beings can observe other people's facial expressions and bodily posture for clues to their future intentions. Nonetheless, human beings, unlike any other species, can also talk to each other about their thoughts and feelings. A probable hypothesis is that children's understanding of thoughts and feelings varies with their opportunities to engage in such conversation (Harris, 1996, 1999). There are now four lines of evidence that converge on that claim. First, children's language ability has proved to be a consistent and potent predictor of their performance on assessments of mental-state understanding. Second, children deprived of ordinary access to everyday conversation, notably deaf children, exhibit a marked delay in their understanding of mental states. Third, parental language that is rich in references to mental states appears to improve children's performance on standard theory-of-mind tasks. Finally, intervention studies that make heavy use of language and explanation produce clear gains in understanding. I discuss key findings from each of these four areas and then ask in more detail about the theoretical implications.

Accuracy in the attribution of beliefs and emotions is strongly correlated with language skill among both normal children and children with autism (Cutting & Dunn, 1999; Happé, 1995; Pons, Lawson, Harris, & de Rosnay, 2003). One possible interpretation of that correlation is that children's early understanding of mental states facilitates the development of language. Recent investigations of early word learning have shown that young children notice what their conversation partner is attending to, or has in mind, when he or she introduces a new word and they use that information to decode the intended referent (Baldwin & Moses, 2001; Waxman & Lidz, Chapter 7, this *Handbook,* this volume). Arguably, children who are particularly sensitive to their interlocutor's thoughts and attitudes might be at an advantage in building their vocabularies or in decoding complicated utterances.

However, longitudinal research does not support this line of interpretation. Astington and Jenkins (1999) assessed the language ability and theory-of-mind performance of a group of preschool children on three successive occasions over a period of 7 months. Theory-of-mind performance was not a predictor of subsequent gains in language. However, language ability at the initial assessment proved to be a good predictor of subsequent improvement in theory-of-mind performance. Thus, children who had superior language skills at the beginning of the study—particularly in the domain of syntax—made more progress in their subsequent conceptualization of mental states. Similar findings were reported by Watson, Painter, and Bornstein (2001) over a longer period of time. Children's language ability at 24 months was a good predictor of their theory-of-mind performance at 48 months.

Further strong evidence that language facilitates the acquisition of a theory of mind has emerged from the study of deaf children. Deaf children perform poorly on standard theory-of-mind tasks compared to hearing controls. This difficulty is not attributable to deafness per se. Deaf children who learn to sign fluently in early childhood—typically deaf children born into a family

with a deaf adult who is a fluent signer—perform at a level similar to that of hearing controls. By implication, it is the delayed access to language and communication—which is typical of deaf children of hearing parents—that impairs performance (Peterson & Siegal, 2000).

Still, two different interpretations of that impairment are feasible. Arguably, those deaf children who are slow to enter into conversation and communication are at a disadvantage in processing the narrative that is normally used to pose a theory-of-mind problem. Alternatively, deaf children do understand the test narrative well enough. Their difficulty arises because they have a genuine difficulty in understanding mental states and notably beliefs. Support for the second alternative was obtained by Figueras-Costa and Harris (2001). Even when deaf children were given a nonverbal test of false belief, one that made minimal demands on their verbal comprehension, they still performed poorly. Moreover, Woolfe, Want, and Siegal (2002) found a delay among late-signing deaf children when they used a pictorial rather than a verbal test of false-belief understanding. Thus, late-signing children appear to be genuinely delayed in their conceptualization of beliefs. It is not that they have difficulty in grasping a verbal test procedure.

Families vary in terms of the conversational environment that they offer a young child. Three recent studies indicate the contribution that the mother's language style makes to children's mental-state understanding. Meins, Fernyhough, Wainwright, Das Gupta, Fradley, and Tuckey (2002) asked whether mothers' *mind-mindedness*—the proclivity to treat their infant as an individual with a mind of its own influences later theory-of-mind understanding. To assess mind-mindedness, they identified comments by mothers that were appropriately geared to their 6-month-infants' current focus of attention and demeanor—for example "You *know* what that is, it's a ball" or "You're just *teasing* me." The frequency of these mind-minded comments predicted children's success on a composite theory-of-mind measure more than 3.5 years later. Ruffman, Slade, and Crowe (2002) found that mothers' mental state language during picture-book sessions at earlier time points in the child's 4th year predicted children's later theory-of-mind performance at later points in that same year. The reverse pattern did not hold—thus, earlier theory-of-mind performance by the child did not predict mother's later pattern of discourse. Finally, in an assessment of 5- to 6-year-olds, de Rosnay, Pons,

Harris, and Morrell (2004) found that mothers' mentalistic descriptions of their child and the child's own verbal ability were positively associated both with correct false-belief attributions and with correct belief-based emotion attributions. Moreover, mothers' mentalistic descriptions predicted children's correct emotion attributions even when the sample was restricted to those who had mastered the simpler false-belief task.

Taken together, these correlational studies suggest that mothers whose conversation is rich in psychological references promote their children's mental state understanding; there is little evidence for the reverse direction of influence. It also looks as if mere loquacity on the part of the mother is not sufficient to promote mental state understanding. Ruffman et al. (2002) found that it was specifically mothers' mental state discourse rather than other aspects of their conversation (e.g., descriptive or causal talk) that predicted children's theory-of-mind performance. Moreover, aspects of the mother-child relationship that might be thought to play a role proved to have little independent impact on mental-state understanding. In particular, the nature of the child's attachment proves to have no predictive significance—once the mother's discourse is taken into account (de Rosnay, Harris, & Pons, in press; Meins et al., 2002). Finally, mothers' psychological orientation has a sustained influence. It is evident not only among 3-year-olds but also among 6-year-olds. Her influence definitely reaches beyond the standard index of children's developing theory of mind, namely false-belief understanding.

Confidence in correlational findings is always boosted when they can be supplemented by intervention studies. Two recent interventions are especially informative. Lohmann and Tomasello (2003) gave 3-year-olds who failed a standard test of false belief various types of training. The most effective combined two factors: (1) the presentation of a series of objects—some of which had a misleading appearance (e.g., an object that looked initially like a flower but turned out to be a pen); and (2) verbal comments on what people would *say, think, and know* about the perceptible properties and the actual identity of these objects. Hale and Tager-Flusberg (2003) obtained similar results. In one intervention, children discussed story protagonists who held false beliefs; in a second, they discussed story protagonists who made false claims. In each case, children were given corrective verbal feedback if they misstated what the protagonists thought or said. Both interventions

proved very effective in promoting 3-year-olds' grasp of false belief.

These two studies confirm that conversation about people's thoughts or claims has a powerful effect on children's understanding of belief. One additional finding underlines the critical role of conversation. When Lohmann and Tomasello (2003) gave children a series of misleading objects but offered minimal verbal comment, the impact on children's mental state understanding was negligible.

These four lines of research, from different laboratories using diverse techniques on a heterogeneous sample of children all confirm a reasonable intuition: Children's own language competence and their access to conversation, especially conversation that deals explicitly with mental states, promotes their theory of mind. This convergence is one of the most exciting developments in recent research on theory of mind and confirms the vigor of the field (Harris, de Rosnay, & Pons, 2005).

## TAKING STOCK

Research on the child's theory of mind has been conducted primarily in the cognitive-developmental tradition: the child is seen as a thinker trying to explain, predict, and understand people's thoughts, feelings, and utterances. Less attention has been paid to the consequences of such social cognitive skill for the child's social and intellectual relationships. Below, I briefly review research that begins to address these two lacunae. I discuss the way in which children's understanding of mental states affects their peer relations and their trust in the claims made by other people. I then attempt to take stock of how—after more than 25 years of intense investigation—we should conceptualize the understanding of mind that we see emerging in young children.

### Social Cognition and Peer Relations

Insofar as children gradually acquire a theory of mind, it is reasonable to ask about the implications of these conceptual changes for children's wider social behavior. Investigators who have examined this issue have focused on the possibility that children with more advanced social cognition will perform better on various measures of social interaction, particularly with peers.

This predicted link has emerged in several studies of preschool children. Denham, McKinley, Couchoud, and Holt (1990) examined the relationship between preschoolers' accuracy on an emotion-attribution task and their popularity amongst peers. Children with a better understanding of the causes of emotion were more popular with peers, even when the effects of age and gender were controlled. In a study of "hard-to-manage" children, aged 3 and 4 years, Hughes, Dunn, and White (1998) found that poor understanding of emotion was linked to various interpersonal difficulties (e.g., antisocial behavior, aggressiveness, restricted empathy, and limited prosocial behavior), whereas Dunn and Cutting (1999) found that 4-year-olds' with a good understanding of emotion cooperated and communicated more effectively with a close friend during play. Finally, in a longitudinal study of 4- and 5-year-olds, Edwards, Manstead, and MacDonald (1984) found that accuracy in identifying the expression of emotion was correlated with popularity one or 2 years later, even when initial popularity was taken into account.

A similar link between emotion understanding and peer relationships has emerged among school-aged children. Dunn and Herrera (1997) found that 6-year-olds' ability to solve interpersonal conflicts with their friends at school was predicted by their emotion understanding at the age of 3 years. Cassidy, Parke, Butkovsky, and Braungart (1992) reported a positive relationship between children's emotion understanding and their popularity with peers during the 1st year of obligatory schooling. Finally, in a study of 11- to 13-year-olds, Bosacki and Astington (1999) found a positive relation between emotion understanding and social skills as judged by teachers.

These various findings strongly suggest that the understanding of mental states and notably the understanding of emotion facilitates children's interactions with peers both before and during the school years. These are correlational findings, and short of proving the link by means of an intervention study, we cannot be certain of the exact causal relationship. Nevertheless, the link between competence at the identification and analysis of emotion and later peer relationships is encouraging.

On a more cautionary note, Cutting and Dunn (2002) found that there are costs as well as benefits to superior social cognition. Five-year-olds were assessed during their 1st year at school for their sensitivity to teacher criticism. Children's understanding of false belief and mixed emotions measured 1 year earlier—when they were in preschool—proved to be a good predictor of their sensitivity. More specifically, children who showed a better understanding of thoughts and feelings in preschool were likely to derogate their ability, when asked to imagine receiving criticism from a teacher for a minor error. As Cutting and Dunn (2002) point out, these findings raise important questions about the longer-term impact of social cognitive skills. On the positive side, they may indeed help children to navigate the playground and peer relationships more effectively. At the same time, they may render children more vulnerable to the inevitable slings and arrows of social life, including interactions with teachers.

## Social Cognition and Trust

For the most part, investigators have neglected a domain in which children's social cognition is likely to have far-reaching implications: their credulity with respect to other people's claims. Consider the dictum of the Scottish Enlightenment philosopher, Thomas Reid (1764/1970): "In a word, if credulity were the effect of reasoning and experience, it must grow up and gather strength, in the same proportion as reason and experience do. But if it is a gift of nature, it will be the strongest in childhood, and limited and restrained by experience; and the most superficial view of human life shows, that the last is really the case, and not the first" (pp. 240–241). Is there evidence that children become less credulous with age? One of the central findings in theory-of-mind research is that most normal children beyond the age of 4 years realize that sincere claims and beliefs may be false. It would be reasonable to expect that insight to render children less credulous.

Indeed, recent findings confirm that preschoolers do increasingly display selective trust and doubt in the claims made by particular people (Clément, Koenig, & Harris, 2004; Harris & Koenig, in press; Koenig, Clément, & Harris, 2004). When preschoolers are presented with two informants, one of whom makes various claims that the child knows to be true but the other makes either false claims or confesses ignorance, they subsequently trust the hitherto reliable informant but doubt the hitherto unreliable informant. For example when shown an unfamiliar object and offered different names for it by the two informants, children trust the hitherto reliable informant.

Two developmental phases are apparent in children's selective trust (Koenig & Harris, 2005a). Three-year-olds trust a hitherto reliable informant—by seeking information from her and endorsing her claims—and doubt a self-confessedly ignorant informant. They are less selective when invited to choose between a reliable informant and an inaccurate informant. Four-year-olds are selective in both cases: They trust a reliable informant and they doubt not only an ignorant informant but also an inaccurate informant. Arguably, 4-year-olds, attribute inaccurate claims to an informant's mistaken beliefs and adopt an appropriately skeptical stance toward that person's later assertions.

Beyond the particularities of the age change in trust and doubt, these findings call attention to the way that children use their emerging theory of mind to make trait attributions in the cognitive sphere. After a brief exposure to a distinctive pattern of reliability on the part of particular informants, preschoolers anticipate that those informants will continue to differ in terms of their future epistemic reliability. In some ways, there is nothing remarkable about this result. Attachment theory has long insisted, and provided evidence for, the claim that infants can gather and retain information about a caregiver's past emotional availability and use that to forecast how he or she will respond in the future. However, attachment theory has generally emphasized the infant's ability to anticipate a class of overt behaviors on the part of a caregiver—particularly, the caregiver's physical availability and emotional responsiveness. The findings on selective epistemic trust suggest that preschoolers are capable of a deeper type of attribution. They do not base their trait attributions on particular regularities in the overt behavior of their informants—at the behavioral level, mistaken claims have nothing in common with one another. Rather, they base their predictions on regularities in the psychological status and more specifically the epistemic reliability, of their informants (Koenig & Harris, 2005b).

Further evidence that preschoolers are able to assess the epistemic reliability of their informants and do not just focus on behavioral regularities emerged in a study that examined the scope of children's attributions. As in prior experiments, 3- and 4-year-olds were presented with two informants. One proved reliable in that she named a set of familiar objects accurately; the other informant, by contrast, proved unreliable in that she admitting to not knowing the names of any of the objects.

Subsequently, children were shown various novel objects and asked if they knew what they were for. Once they had acknowledged not knowing, children were prompted to seek help from either of the informants. In addition, each informant then offered a different demonstration of what to do with the object. Finally, children were asked to provide their own demonstration. As in previous studies, children were selective: They tended to ask for help from, and trust the help supplied by, the reliable as opposed to the unreliable informant. Thus, after witnessing the differential reliability of the informants in the verbal sphere, children made a relatively global assessment of their epistemic reliability. They displayed selective trust in the information that the two informants provided in the nonverbal sphere of object use (Koenig & Harris, 2005a).

Granted that children increasingly display selective trust and doubt in particular informants how exactly is that selectivity established? We may envisage two different mechanisms. In line with the thrust of Reid's dictum, children might start off by trusting every informant on first encounter. To the extent that informants continue to prove reliable (e.g., say nothing that contradicts what the child knows already and respond appropriately to questions) children would retain—but not add to—their initial stock of trust in that informant. However, whenever informants prove unreliable—by acknowledging ignorance in response to questions or by saying something the child knows to be false—children would accumulate doubt. On this account, selectivity is brought about by growing doubt with regard to unreliable informants rather than by any increment in trust.

Consider, however, a reasonable alternative. Arguably, children add to their stock of trust in an informant whenever he or she makes a claim that the child knows to be correct. Thus, children would be much more likely to believe the claims of familiar as compared to unfamiliar informants. Familiar informants—unlike unfamiliar informants—would generally have ample opportunities to prove themselves trustworthy. On this account, selectivity is brought about by cumulative trust in reliable informants rather than by any increment in doubt.

The first model fits the intuition that a person's false assertions are more distinctive—and make a deeper impression on us—than their true assertions. For example, an evidently false statement by a politician can dramatically undermine their reputation for probity. The second model fits a different intuition, namely that young children are especially likely to trust the claims of familiar caregivers more than those of relative strangers. Whichever model ultimately proves correct, it is clear that the development of children's epistemic trust is a tractable but neglected domain of research in social cognition. To the extent that theory-of-mind research has shown how young children attribute mental states, the stage is set for understanding how they make different attributions to different individuals depending on their past history.

## Emerging Contours in the Child's Theory of Mind

In this final section, I highlight selected major findings and draw them together into a larger conceptualization of the child's theory of mind. Four such findings stand out. First, if we study the progressive steps that children take in understanding mental states, there is now ample evidence that certain mental states are mastered more easily and in advance of others. One particularly robust finding from normal children is that they can conceptualize and talk about individuals' goals and preferences before they can conceptualize and talk about individuals' epistemic states of knowledge and belief (Bartsch & Wellman, 1995; Tardif & Wellman, 2000). A second, emerging finding from the primate literature is that chimpanzees are able to monitor the perceptual states and the associated goals of conspecifics (Tomasello, Call, & Hare, 2003), yet we have no comparable evidence showing that chimpanzees are capable of understanding beliefs (Call & Tomasello, 1999). A third finding from the study of autism is that despite their well-established difficulty in understanding beliefs (Happé, 1995; Yirmiya, Osnat, Shaked, & Solomonica-Levi, 1998), children with autism show no major impairment in understanding perceptual states (Reed & Peterson, 1990) or desires (Tager-Flusberg, 1993; Tan & Harris, 1991). A fourth finding from the study of deaf children echoes the pattern established for children with autism: Deaf children born into a nonsigning family display a marked lag in the understanding of beliefs (Peterson & Siegal, 2000) but no detectable lag in understanding perceptual states (Peterson, 2003) and frequent references to desires (Rieffe & Meerum Terwogt, 2000).

A plausible implication of these various findings is that even if investigators often talk in terms of having—

or lacking—a theory of mind, it is more appropriate to acknowledge a bifurcation: The understanding of perceptual states and goals can be achieved despite the handicaps of autism, despite restricted access to language as in the case of deaf children—and indeed despite the absence of any access to language, as in the case of nonhuman primates. By contrast, as discussed in an earlier section, the understanding of beliefs varies with language ability and with access to conversation. Why should there be this schism? My own speculation, set out elsewhere (Harris, 1996, 1999, 2005) and briefly elaborated here, is that among normal children, there are various mind-reading abilities that are probably part of our primate heritage: The ability to detect goals and to monitor perceptual states is part of that heritage, even if we have not yet fully established the degree of variation in the primate order. However, from approximately 2 to 3 years of age, a uniquely human capacity begins to emerge, notably the capacity to enter into conversations that are primarily aimed at the exchange of information. Broadly speaking, in the earliest stage of language acquisition, a great deal of early conversation by young children is instrumental. It is aimed at extralinguistic goals such as the regulation of the interlocutor's attention, perceptual states, and goals. Thus, the interlocutor is invited to pay attention to particular objects and events and to help with particular projects. The topic of conversation is closely tied to objects, events, and possibilities embedded in the immediate situation and there is minimal displacement from the here and now.

However, in the 3rd year of life, there are various signs that the exchange of information via conversation becomes an end in itself rather than a way to regulate ongoing action and to achieve instrumental goals. Children increasingly talk about absent entities and past events (Fivush, Gray, & Fromhoff, 1987; Morford & Goldin-Meadow, 1997; Snow, Pan, Imbens-Bailey, & Herman, 1996). They increasingly seek information by posing questions—not only to facilitate an ongoing plan—but also to gather information about things that they happen to see and hear (Lewis, 1938; Przetacznik-Gierowska & Likeze, 1990; Snow et al., 1996). Finally, when a request is misunderstood, they offer clarification even in circumstances where the request has been granted and clarification serves only an epistemic purpose rather than an instrumental goal (Shwe & Markman, 1997).

In conversations where information is exchanged about absent objects and noncurrent events, any two interlocutors will rarely share exactly the same knowledge base or perspective. Effective conversation therefore depends on the ability of each interlocutor to acknowledge that divergence and to allow for it in conveying what they know, think, and feel about the topic in question. Indeed, many of the speech acts of ordinary conversation—conveying information, asking a question, querying an assertion, or issuing a denial—all turn on the fact that different interlocutors have different perspectives. Studies of nonegocentric communication by preschoolers suggest that they display an early sensitivity to such variation (Menig-Peterson, 1976; O'Neill, 1996; Sachs, & Devin, 1976; Shatz & Gelman, 1973; Wellman & Lempers, 1977).

These comments underline the fact that cooperation that is directed at some practical goal typically has a different set of ground rules from conversation. In the context of pragmatic cooperation, partners can frequently act on the assumption that they share a common goal and a common set of beliefs about how to attain that goal. In the context of conversation, by contrast, differences in perspective and belief, and the acknowledgment and articulation of such differences, are of vital importance for the success and coherence of the conversation. Indeed, the voicing of shared beliefs and common knowledge scarcely amounts to a conversation at all. This key feature of conversation leads to the reasonable expectation that children who often participate in conversation—especially conversation that involves an exchange of viewpoints rather than the negotiation of a pragmatic goal—are likely to perform better on those theory-of-mind tasks that call for an understanding of differences in knowledge and belief. As discussed in an earlier section, there is now ample evidence for this prediction. Deaf children who have access to a native signer in their home perform better on standard false-belief tasks than deaf children who lack such access (Peterson & Siegal, 2000). Children with caregivers who frequently talk about what particular individuals think and know also do well on standard false-belief tasks (Ruffman et al., 2002). Finally, experimental interventions in which such viewpoints are articulated serve to promote false-belief understanding (Hale & Tager-Flusberg, 2003; Lohmann & Tomasello, 2003).

In conclusion, an intriguing irony emerges as we look back over the past 25 years. A major inspiration for research on theory-of-mind was an experiment not with children but with a chimpanzee, Sarah (Premack & Woodruff, 1978). If my analysis is correct, however, cumulative research increasingly reveals that the type of goal understanding that Sarah displayed has a very different phylogenesis and ontogenesis from the belief understanding that human children display. Goal understanding is connected to the analysis and pursuit of practical activities. Belief understanding is intimately connected with the ability to engage in conversation with no practical end in sight.

My guess is that we have yet to appreciate just how far children live in different conversational worlds. Not only do families vary in the extent to which they enunciate and discuss conflicting psychological reactions, they also vary in the extent to which they enunciate and discuss conflicting moral, scientific, religious, and historical claims. Moreover, just as family discourse has an impact on children psychological understanding, so it is plausible that family discourse has an impact on children's epistemological understanding. In any given domain, some children will be sensitized to the way that divergent claims can be adjudicated but others will scarcely recognize that alternative claims exist.

# REFERENCES

Abramovitch, R., Corter C., & Lando, B. (1979). Sibling interaction in the home. *Child Development, 50,* 997–1003.

Abramovitch, R., Corter, C., & Pepler, D. (1980). Observations of mixed-sex sibling dyads. *Child Development, 51,* 1268–1271.

Ainsworth, M. D. S., Bell, S. M., & Stayton, D. J. (1971). Individual differences in Strange Situation behavior of one-year-olds. In H. R. Schaffer (Ed.), *The origins of human social relations* (pp. 17–52). New York: Academic Press.

Arsenio, W. F., & Kramer, R. (1992). Victimizers and their victims: Children's conceptions of the mixed emotional consequences of moral transgressions. *Child Development, 63,* 915–927.

Astington, J. W. (1991). Intention in the child's theory of mind. In D. Frye & C. Moore (Eds.), *Children's theories of mind* (pp. 157–172). Hillsdale, NJ: Erlbaum.

Astington, J. W., & Jenkins, J. M. (1995). Theory-of-mind development and social understanding. *Cognition and Emotion, 9,* 151–165.

Astington, J. W., & Jenkins, J. M. (1999). A longitudinal study of the relation between language and theory-of-mind development. *Developmental Psychology, 35,* 1311–1320.

Avis, J., & Harris, P. L. (1991). Belief-desire reasoning among Baka children: Evidence for a universal conception of mind. *Child Development, 62,* 460–467.

Bakermans-Kranenburg, M. J., & Van Ijzendoorn, M. H. (1993). A psychometric study of the Adult Attachment Interview: Reliability and discriminant validity. *Developmental Psychology, 29,* 870–880.

Baldwin, D. A., Baird, J. A., Saylor, M. A., & Clark, M. A. (2001). Infants parse dynamic action. *Child Development, 72,* 708–717.

Baldwin, D. A., & Moses, L. J. (2001). Links between social understanding and early word learning: Challenges to current accounts. *Social Development, 10,* 309–329.

Baron-Cohen, S. (1989). The autistic child's theory of mind: A case of specific developmental delay. *Journal of Child Psychology and Psychiatry, 30,* 285–297.

Baron-Cohen, S. (1991). Do people with autism understand what causes emotion? *Child Development, 62,* 385–395.

Baron-Cohen, S., Allen, J., & Gillberg, C. (1992). Can autism be detected at 18 months? The needle, the haystack and the CHAT. *British Journal of Psychiatry, 161,* 839–843.

Baron-Cohen, S., Leslie, A. M., & Frith, U. (1985). Does the autistic child have a "theory of mind"? *Cognition, 21,* 37–46.

Bartsch, K., & Wellman, H. M. (1989). Young children's attribution of action to beliefs and desires. *Child Development, 60,* 946–964.

Bartsch, K., & Wellman, H. M. (1995). *Children talk about the mind.* New York: Oxford University Press.

Benoit, D., & Parker, K. C. H. (1994). Stability and transmission of attachment across three generations. *Child Development, 65,* 1444–1457.

Boden, M. (2006). *Mind as machine: A history of cognitive science.* Oxford, England: Oxford University Press.

Bosacki, S., & Astington, J. (1999). Theory of mind in preadolescence: Relations between social understanding and social competence. *Social Development, 8,* 237–255.

Bradmetz, J., & Schneider, R. (1999). Is Little Red Riding Hood afraid of her grandmother? Cognitive versus emotional response to a false belief. *British Journal of Developmental Psychology, 17,* 501–514.

Brownell, C. A., & Carriger, M. S. (1990). Changes in cooperation and self-other differentiation during the second year. *Child Development, 61,* 1164–1174.

Byrne, R. W., & Whiten, A. (1988). Toward the next generation in data quality: A new survey of primate tactical deception. *Behavioral and Brain Sciences, 11,* 267–283.

Call, J., Hare, B., Carpenter, M., & Tomasello, M. (2004). Unwilling or unable: Chimpanzees' understanding of human intentional action. *Developmental Science, 7,* 488–498.

Call, J., & Tomasello, M. (1999). A nonverbal false-belief task: The performance of children and great apes. *Child Development, 70,* 381–395.

Call, J., & Tomasello, M. (2005). What do chimpanzees know about seeing revisited: An explanation of the third kind. In N. Eilan et al. (Eds.), *Issues in joint attention.* Oxford, England: Oxford University Press.

Callaghan, T., Rochat, P., Lillard, A., Claux, M. C., Odden, H., Itakura, S., et al. (2005). Synchrony in the onset of mental state reasoning: Evidence from five cultures. *Psychological Science, 16,* 378–384.

Carlson, S. M., & & Moses, L. (2001). Individual differences in inhibitory control and children's theory of mind. *Child Development, 72,* 1032–1053.

Carpendale, J., & Chandler, M. (1996). On the distinction between false-belief understanding and subscribing to an interpretive theory of mind. *Child Development, 67,* 1686–1706.

Carpenter, M., Call, J., & Tomasello, M. (2002). Understanding "prior intentions" enables 2-year-olds to imitatively learn a complex task. *Child Development, 73,* 1431–1441.

Carpenter, M., Nagell, K., & Tomasello, M. (1998). Social cognition, joint attention, and communicative competence from 9–15 months of age. *Monographs of the Society for Research in Child Development, 63*(4, Serial No. 255).

Cassidy, J., Parke, R., Butkovsky, L., & Braungart, J. (1992). Family-peer connections: The roles of emotional expressiveness within the family and children's understanding of emotions. *Child Development, 63,* 603–618.

Chandler, M. (1988). Doubt and developing theories of mind. In J. W. Astington, P. L. Harris, & D. R. Olson (Eds.), *Developing theories of mind* (pp. 387–413). Cambridge, England: Cambridge University Press.

Clément, F., Koenig, M., & Harris, P. L. (2004). The ontogenesis of trust. *Mind and Language, 19,* 360–379.

Colby, A., Kohlberg, L., Gibbs, J., & Liberman, M. (1983). A longitudinal study of moral judgment. *Monographs of the Society for Research in Child Development, 48*(1/2, Serial No. 200).

Csibra, G., Gergely, G., Biro, S., Koos, O., & Brockbank, M. (1999). Goal attribution without agency cues: The perception of "pure reason" in infancy. *Cognition, 72,* 237–267.

Currie, G. (1998). Pretence, pretending and metarepresenting. *Mind and Language, 13,* 35–55.

Cutting, A. L., & Dunn, J. (1999). Theory of mind, emotion understanding, language, and family background: Individual differences and interrelations. *Child Development, 70,* 853–865.

Cutting, A. L., & Dunn, J. (2002). The cost of understanding other people: Social cognition predicts young children's sensitivity to criticism. *Journal of Child Psychology and Psychiatry, 43,* 849–860.

Darwin, C. (1998). *The expression of the emotions in man and animals.* New York: Oxford University Press. (Original work published 1872)

Davidson, P., Turiel, E., & Black, A. (1983). The effects of stimulus familiarity on the use of criteria and justifications in children's social reasoning. *British Journal of Developmental Psychology, 1,* 49–65.

Denham, S., McKinley, M., Couchoud, E., & Holt, R. (1990). Emotional and behavioral predictors of preschool peer ratings. *Child Development, 61,* 1145–1152.

de Rosnay, M., & Harris, P. L. (2002). Individual differences in children's understanding of emotion: The roles of attachment and language. *Attachment and Human Development, 4*(1), 39–54.

de Rosnay, M., Pons, F., Harris, P. L., & Morrell, J. (2004). A lag between understanding false belief and emotion attribution in young children: Relationships with linguistic ability and mothers' mental state language. *British Journal of Developmental Psychology, 22,* 197–218.

de Waal, F. B. M., & Aureli, F. (1996). Consolation, reconciliation, and a possible cognitive difference between macaques and chimpanzees. In A. E. Russon, K. A. Bard, & S. T., Parker (Eds.), *Reaching into thought: The minds of the great apes* (pp. 80–110). Cambridge, England: Cambridge University Press.

Dunn, J., & Cutting, A. L. (1999). Understanding others, and individual differences in friendship interactions in young children. *Social Development, 8,* 201–209.

Dunn, J., & Herrera, C. (1997). Conflict resolution with friends, siblings, and mothers: A developmental perspective. *Aggressive Behavior, 23,* 343–357.

Dunn, J., & Kendrick, C. (1982). *Siblings: Love, envy and understanding.* Cambridge, MA: Harvard University Press.

Dunn, J., Kendrick, C., & MacNamee, R. (1981). The reaction of first-born children to the birth of a sibling: Mother's reports. *Journal of Child Psychology and Psychiatry, 22,* 1–18.

Dunn, J., & Munn, P. (1985). Becoming a family member: Family conflict and the development of social understanding in the first year. *Child Development, 50,* 306–318.

Dunn, J., & Munn, P. (1986). Siblings and the development of prosocial behaviour. *International Journal of Behavioral Development, 9,* 265–284.

Edwards, R., Manstead, A. S., & MacDonald, C. J. (1984). The relationship between children's sociometric status and ability to recognize facial expression. *European Journal of Social Psychology, 14,* 235–238.

Ekman, P. (1973). Cross-cultural studies of facial expression. In P. Ekman (Ed.), *Darwin and facial expression* (pp. 11–98). New York: Academic Press.

Estes, D. (1998). Young children's awareness of their mental activity: The case of mental rotation. *Child Development, 69,* 1345–1360.

Estes, D., Wellman, H. M., & Woolley, J. D. (1989). Children's understanding of mental phenomena. In H. W. Reese (Ed.), *Advances in child development and behavior* (pp. 41–87). San Diego, CA: Academic Press.

Fabes, R. A., Eisenberg, N., Nyman, M., & Michealieu, Q. (1991). Young children's appraisals of others' spontaneous emotional reactions. *Developmental Psychology, 27,* 858–866.

Feinfeld, K. A., Lee, P. P., Flavell, E. R., Green, F. L., & Flavell, J. H. (1999). Young children's understanding of intention. *Child Development, 14,* 463–486.

Field, T. (1984). Early interactions between infants and their postpartum depressed mothers. *Infant Behavior and Development, 7,* 517–522.

Field, T., Healy, B., & Goldstein, S. (1988). Infants of depressed mothers show "depressed" behavior even with nondepressed adults. *Child Development, 59,* 1569–1579.

Figueras-Costa, B., & Harris, P. L. (2001). Theory of mind in deaf children: A non-verbal test of false-belief understanding. *Journal of Deaf Studies and Deaf Education, 6,* 92–102.

Fivush, R., Gray, J. T., & Fromhoff, F. A. (1987). Two-year-olds talk about the past. *Cognitive Development, 2,* 393–409.

Flavell, J. H. (1986). The development of children's knowledge about the appearance-reality distinction. *American Psychologist, 41,* 418–425.

Flavell, J. H., Botkin, P. T., Fry, C. L., Wright, J. W., & Jarvis, P. E. (1968). *The development of role-taking and communication skills in children.* New York: Wiley.

Flavell, J. H., Green, F. L., & Flavell, E. R. (1993). Children's understanding of the stream of consciousness. *Child Development, 64,* 387–398.

Flavell, J. H., Green, F. L., & Flavell, E. R. (1995). Young children's knowledge about thinking. *Monographs of the Society for Research in Child Development, 60*(1, Serial No. 243).

Flavell, J. H., Green, F. L., & Flavell, E. R. (2000). Development of children's awareness of their own thoughts. *Journal of Cognition and Development, 1,* 97–112.

Flavell, J. H., Green, F. L., Flavell, E. R., & Grossman, J. B. (1997). The development of children's knowledge about inner speech. *Child Development, 68,* 39–47.

Flavell, J. H., Shipstead, S. G., & Croft, K. (1978). Young children's knowledge about visual perception: Hiding objects from others. *Child Development, 49,* 1208–1211.

Fodor, J. (1987). *Psychosemantics.* Cambridge, MA: MIT Press.

Fodor, J. (1992). A theory of the child's theory of mind. *Cognition, 44,* 283–296.

Fonagy, P., Steele, H., & Steele, M. (1991). Maternal representations of attachment during pregnancy predict the organization of infant-mother attachment at 1 year of age. *Child Development, 62,* 891–905.

George, C., & Main, M. (1979). Social interaction of young abused children: Approach, avoidance and aggression. *Child Development, 50,* 306–318.

Gergely, G., Nádasdy, Z., Csibra, G., & Biró, S. (1995). Taking the intentional stance at 12 months of age. *Cognition, 56,* 165–193.

German, T., & Leslie, A. (2000). Attending to and learning about mental states. In P. Mitchell & K. Riggs (Eds.), *Children's reasoning and the mind* (pp. 229–252). Hove, England: Psychology Press.

Golinkoff, R. M., Harding, C. G., Carlson, V., & Sexton, M. E. (1984). The infant's perception of causal events: The distinction between animate and inanimate objects. In L. L. Lipsitt & C. Rovee-Collier (Eds.), *Advances in infancy research* (Vol. 3, pp. 145–165). Norwood, NJ: Ablex.

Gopnik, A., & Astington, J. W. (1988). Children's understanding of representational change and its relation to the understanding of false belief and the appearance reality distinction. *Child Development, 59,* 26–37.

Gopnik, A., & Graf, P. (1988). Knowing how you know: Young children's ability to identify and remember the sources of their beliefs. *Child Development, 59,* 1366–1371.

Gopnik, A., & Wellman, H. M. (1994). The theory theory. In L. Hirschfeld & S. Gelman (Eds.), *Domain specificity in cognition and culture* (pp. 257–293). New York: Cambridge University Press.

Graham, S., & Weiner, B. (1986). From an attributional theory of emotion to developmental psychology: A round-trip ticket? *Social Cognition, 4,* 152–179.

Hadwin, J., & Perner, J. (1991). Pleased and surprised: Children's cognitive theory of emotion. *British Journal of Developmental Psychology, 9,* 215–234.

Hale, C. M., & Tager-Flusberg, H. (2003). The influence of language on theory of mind: A training study. *Developmental Science, 6,* 346–359.

Hamilton, C. E. (2000). Continuity and discontinuity of attachment from infancy through adolescence. *Child Development, 71,* 690–694.

Happé, F. G. E. (1993). Communicative competence and theory of mind in autism: A test of relevance theory. *Cognition, 48,* 101–119.

Happé, F. G. E. (1994). An advanced test of theory of mind: Understanding of story characters' thoughts and feelings by able autistic, mentally handicapped and normal children and adults. *Journal of Autism and Developmental Disorders, 24,* 129–154.

Happé, F. G. E. (1995). The role of age and verbal ability in the theory-of-mind task performance of subjects with autism. *Child Development, 66,* 843–855.

Hare, B., Brown, M., Williamson, C., & Tomasello, M. (2002). The domestication of social cognition in dogs. *Science, 298,* 1634–1636.

Hare, B., & Tomasello, M. (2004). Chimpanzees are more skillful in competitive than in cooperative cognitive tasks. *Animal Behaviour, 68,* 571–581.

Harris, P. L. (1989). *Children and emotion.* Oxford, England: Blackwell.

Harris, P. L. (1990). The child's theory of mind and its cultural context. In G. E. Butterworth & P. E. Bryant (Eds.), *The causes of development* (pp. 215–237). London: Harvester Wheatsheaf.

Harris, P. L. (1996). Desires, beliefs and language. In P. Carruthers & P. K. Smith (Eds.), *Theories of theories of mind* (pp. 200–220). Cambridge, England: Cambridge University Press.

Harris, P. L. (1999). Acquiring the art of conversation: Children's developing conception of their conversation partner. In M. Bennett (Ed.), *Developmental psychology: Achievements and prospects* (pp. 89–105). London: Psychology Press.

Harris, P. L. (2000). *The work of the imagination.* Oxford, England: Blackwell.

Harris, P. L. (2005). Conversation, pretence, and theory of mind. In J. W. Astington & J. Baird (Eds.), *Why language matters for theory of mind.* New York: Oxford University Press.

Harris, P. L., (in press). Use your words. *British Journal of Developmental Psychology.*

Harris, P. L., de Rosnay, M., & Pons, F. (in press). Language and children's understanding of mental states. *Current Directions in Psychological Science, 14,* 69–73.

Harris, P. L., & Gross, D. (1988). Children's understanding of real and apparent emotion. In J. Astington, P. L. Harris, & D. R. Olson (Eds.), *Developing theories of mind.* Cambridge: Cambridge University Press.

Harris, P. L., Guz, G. R., Lipian, M. S., & Man-Shu, Z. (1985). Insight into the time course of emotion among Western and Chinese children. *Child Development, 56,* 972–988.

Harris, P. L., Johnson, C. N., Hutton, D., Andrews, G., & Cooke, T. (1989). Young children's theory-of-mind and emotion. *Cognition and Emotion, 3*(4), 379–400.

Harris, P. L., & Kavanaugh, R. D. (1993). Young children's understanding of pretense. *Monographs of the Society for Research in Child Development, 58*(1, Serial No. 231).

Harris, P. L., & Koenig, M. (in press). Imagination and testimony in cognitive development: The cautious disciple. In I. Roth (Ed.), *Imaginative minds.* Oxford, England: Oxford University Press.

Harris, P. L., Kruithof, A., Meerum Terwogt, M., & Visser, T. (1981). Children's detection and awareness of textual anomaly. *Journal of Experimental Child Psychology, 31,* 212–230.

Harris, P. L., & Leevers, H. (2000). Pretending, imagery and self-awareness in autism. In S. Baron-Cohen, H. Tager-Flusberg, & D. Cohen (Eds.), *Understanding other minds: Perspectives from autism and developmental cognitive neuroscience* (2nd ed., pp. 182–202). Oxford, England: Oxford University Press.

Harris, P. L., Olthof, T., & Meerum Terwogt, M. (1981). Children's knowledge of emotion. *Journal of Child Psychology and Psychiatry, 22,* 247–261.

Harris, P. L., Olthof, T., Meerum Terwogt, M., & Hardman, C. E. (1987). Children's knowledge of the situations that provoke emotion. *International Journal of Behavioral Development, 10,* 319–344.

Haviland, J. M., & Lelwica, M. (1987). The induced affect response: 10-week-old infants' responses to three emotional expressions. *Developmental Psychology, 23,* 97–104.

Henning, A., & Striano, A. (2004). Early sensitivity to interpersonal timing. In L. Berthouze, H. Kozima, C. G. Prince, G. Sandini, G., Stojanow, G. Metta, et al. (Eds.), *Proceedings of the fourth international workshop on epigenetic robotics: Modeling cognitive development in robotic systems* (pp. 145–146). Sweden: Lund University, Cognitive Studies, 117.

Hetherington, E. M., & Parke, R. D. (1999). *Child psychology: A contemporary viewpoint* (5th ed.). New York: McGraw-Hill.

Heyes, C. M. (1998). Theory of mind in nonhuman primates. *Behavioral and Brain Sciences, 21,* 101–148.

Hobson, R. P. (1984). Early childhood autism and the question of egocentrism. *Journal of Autism and Developmental Disorders, 14,* 85–104.

Hoffman, M. L. (1976). Empathy, role-taking, guilt and development of altruistic motives. In T. Lickona (Ed.), *Moral development and behavior: Theory, research and social issues*(pp. 124–143). New York: Holt, Rinehart and Winston.

Hoffman-Plotkin, D., & Twentyman, C. T. (1984). A multimodal assessment of behavioral and cognitive deficits in abused and neglected preschoolers. *Child Development, 55,* 795–702.

Hornik, R., Risenhoover, N., & Gunnar, M. (1987). The effects of maternal positive, neutral and negative affective communications on infant responses to new toys. *Child Development, 58,* 937–944.

Hughes, C., Dunn, J., & White, A. (1998). Trick or treat? Uneven understanding of mind and emotion and executive dysfunction in "hard-to-manage" preschoolers. *Journal of Child Psychology and Psychiatry and Allied Disciplines, 39,* 981–994.

Hughes, M., & Donaldson, M. (1979). The use of hiding games for studying the coordination of perspectives. *Educational Review, 31,* 133–140.

James, W. (1890). *The principles of psychology* (Vol. 1). New York: Henry Holt.

Jarrold, C. R., Boucher, J. J., & Smith, P. K. (1996). Generativity defects in pretend play in autism. *British Journal of Developmental Psychology, 14,* 275–300.

Jarrold, C. R., Carruthers, P., Smith, P. K., & Boucher, J. (1994). Pretend play: Is it metarepresentational? *Mind and Language, 9,* 445–468.

Jenkins, J. M., & Astington, J. W. (2000). Theory of mind and social behavior: Causal models tested in a longitudinal study. *Merrill-Palmer Quarterly, 46,* 203–220.

Joseph, R. M. (1998). Intention and knowledge in preschoolers' conception of pretend. *Child Development, 69,* 966–980.

Joshi, M. S., & MacLean, M. (1994). Indian and English children's understanding of the distinction between real and apparent emotion. *Child Development, 65,* 1372–1384.

Kavanaugh, R. D., & Harris, P. L. (1994). Imagining the outcome of pretend transformations: Assessing the competence of normal and autistic children. *Developmental Psychology, 30,* 847–854.

Keller, M., Lourenco, O., Malti, T., & Saalbach, H. (2003). The multifaceted phenomenon of "happy victimizers": A cross-cultural comparison of moral emotions. *British Journal of Developmental Psychology, 21,* 1–18.

Klimes-Dougan, B., & Kistner, J. (1990). Physically abused preschoolers' responses to peer distress. *Developmental Psychology, 26,* 599–602.

Klin, A., Jones, W., Schultz, R., & Volkmar, F. (2004). The enactive mind, or from actions to cognition: Lessons from autism. In U. Frith & E. Hill (Eds.), *Autism: Mind and brain* (pp. 127–160). Oxford, England: Oxford University Press.

Kochanska, G., Gross, J. N., Lin, M.-H., & Nichols, K. E. (2002). Guilt in young children: Development, determinants, and relations with a broader system of standards. *Child Development, 73,* 461–482.

Koenig, M. A., Clément, F., & Harris, P. L. (2004). Trust in testimony: Children's use of true and false statements. *Psychological Science, 10,* 694–698.

Koenig, M. A., & Harris, P. L. (2005a). Preschoolers mistrust ignorant and inaccurate speakers. *Child Development, 76,*1261–1277.

Koenig, M. A., & Harris, P. L. (2005b). The role of social cognition in early trust. *Trends in Cognitive Sciences, 9,*457–459.

Kohlberg, L. (1969). Stage and sequence: The cognitive-developmental approach to socialization. In D. A. Goslin (Ed.), *Handbook of socialization theory and research* (pp. 247–480). Chicago: Rand McNally.

Kuhn, D., Cheney, R., & Weinstock, M. (2000). The development of epistemological understanding. *Cognitive Development, 15,* 309–328.

Lagattuta, K. H., Wellman, H. M., & Flavell, J. H. (1997). Preschoolers' understanding of the link between thinking and feeling: Cognitive cuing and emotional change. *Child Development, 68,* 1081–1104.

Lashley, K. S. (1951). The problem of serial order in behavior. In L. A. Jeffress (Ed.), *Hixon Symposium: Cerebral mechanisms in behavior* (pp. 112–146). New York: Wiley.

Leslie, A. M. (1987). Pretense and representation: The origins of "theory of mind." *Psychological Review, 94,* 412–426.

Leslie, A. M. (2000). How to acquire a "representational theory of mind." In D. Sperber (Ed.), *Metarepresentations: A multidisciplinary perspective* (pp. 197–223). Oxford, England: Oxford University Press.

Lewis, M. M. (1938). The beginning and early function of questions in a child's speech. *British Journal of Educational Psychology, 8,* 150–171.

Lewis, M. (1989). Cultural differences in children's knowledge of emotion scripts. In C. Saarni & P. L. Harris (Eds.), *Children's understanding of emotion.* Cambridge, England: Cambridge University Press.

Lewis, M., Feiring, C., & Rosenthal, S. (2000). Attachment over time. *Child Development, 71,* 707–720.

Lewis, V., & Boucher, J. (1988). Spontaneous, instructed and elicited play in relatively able autistic children. *British Journal of Developmental Psychology, 6,* 325–339.

Lewis, V., & Boucher, J. (1995). Generativity in the play of young people with autism. *Journal of Autism and Developmental Disorders, 25,* 105–121.

Lienhardt, G. (1961). *Divinity and experience: The religion of the Dinka.* Oxford, England: Clarendon Press.

Lillard, A. (1993). Young children's conceptualization of pretend: Action or mental representational state? *Child Development, 64,* 372–386.

Lillard, A. S. (1998). Ethnopsychologies: Cultural variations in theory of mind. *Psychological Bulletin, 123,* 3–33.

Lillard, A. (1999). Developing a cultural theory of mind: The CIAO approach. *Current Directions in Psychological Science, 8,* 57–61.

Lohmann, H., & Tomasello, M. (2003). The role of language in the development of false-belief understanding: A training study. *Child Development, 74,* 1130–1144.

Main, M., Kaplan, A., & Cassidy, J. (1985). Security in infancy, childhood, and adulthood: A move to the level of representation. *Monographs of the Society for Research in Child Development, 50*(1/2, Serial No. 209), 66–104.

Meins, E., Fernyhough, C., Fradley, E., & Tuckey, M. (2001). Rethinking maternal sensitivity: Mothers' comments on infants' mental processes predict security of attachment at 12 months. *Journal of Child Psychology and Psychiatry, 42,* 637–648.

Meins, E., Fernyhough, C., Wainwright, R., Das Gupta, M., Fradley, E., & Tuckey, M. (2002). Maternal mind-mindedness and attachment security as predictors of theory of mind understanding. *Child Development, 73,* 1715–1726.

Meltzoff, A. N. (1976). *Imitation in early infancy.* Unpublished doctoral dissertation. University of Oxford, England, Department of Experimental Psychology.

Meltzoff, A. N., & Moore, M. K. (1977). Imitation of facial and manual gestures by human neonates. *Science, 198,* 75–78.

Menig-Peterson, C. L. (1976). The modification of communicative behavior in preschool-aged children as a function of a listener's perspective. *Child Development, 46,* 1015–1018.

Miller, G. A., Galanter, E., & Pribram, K. H. (1960). *Plans and the structure of behavior.* New York: Holt, Rinehart & Winston.

Morford, J. P., & Goldin-Meadow, S. (1997). From here and now to there and then: The development of displaced reference in Homesign and English. *Child Development, 68,* 420–435.

Morissette, P., Ricard, M., & Decarie, T. G. (1995). Joint visual attention and pointing in infancy: A longitudinal study of comprehension. *British Journal of Developmental Psychology, 13,* 163–175.

Moses, L. (1993). Young children's understanding of belief constraints on intention. *Cognitive Development, 8,* 1–25.

Moses, L. J. (2001). Executive accounts of theory-of-mind development. *Child Development, 72,* 688–690.

Muir, D. W., & Hains, S. M. J. (1993). Infant sensitivity to perturbations in adult facial, vocal, tactile, and contingent stimulation during face-to-face interactions. In B. de Boysson-Bardies, S. de Schonen, P. Jusczyk, P. MacNeilage & J. Morton (Eds.), *Developmental neurocognition: Speech and face processing in the first year of life* (pp. 171–185). Amsterdam: Kluwer Adadmic.

Mumme, D. L., Won, D., & Fernald, A. (1994, June). *Do 1 year old infants show referent specific responding to emotional signals?* Poster presented at the meeting of the International Conference on Infant Studies, Paris, France.

Mundy, P., Sigman, M., & Kasari, C. (1993). Theory of mind and joint attention deficits in autism. In S. Baron-Cohen, H. Tager-Flusberg, & D. J. Cohen (Eds.), *Understanding other minds: Perspectives from autism* (pp. 181–203). Oxford, England: Oxford University Press.

Murray, L., & Trevarthen, C. (1985). Emotional regulation of interaction between 2-month-olds and their mothers. In T. Field & N. Fox (Eds.), *Social perception in infants* (pp. 101–125). Norwood, NJ: Ablex.

Nadel, J., Carchon, I., Kervella, C., Marcelli, D., & Réservat-Plantey, D. (1999). Expectancies for social contingency in 2-month-olds. *Developmental Science, 2,* 164–173.

Nichols, S. (2001). Mind reading and the cognitive architecture of altruistic motivation. *Mind and Language, 16,* 425–455.

Nichols, S., & Stich, S. (2000). A cognitive theory of pretense. *Cognition, 74,* 115–147.

Nunner-Winkler, G., & Sodian, B. (1988). Children's understanding of moral emotions. *Child Development, 59,* 1323–1338.

O'Neill, D. K. (1996). Two-year-old children's sensitivity to a parent's knowledge state when making requests. *Child Development, 67,* 659–677.

O'Neill, D. K., Astington, J. W., & Flavell, J. H. (1992). Young children's understanding of the role that sensory experiences play in knowledge acquisition. *Child Development, 63,* 474–490.

O'Neill, D. K., & Chong, S. C. F. (2001). Preschool children's difficulty understanding the types of information obtained through the five senses. *Child Development, 72,* 803–815.

Perner, J. (1991). *Understanding the representational mind.* Cambridge, MA: MIT Press.

Perner, J. (1993). The theory-of-mind deficit in autism: Rethinking the metarepresentation theory. In S. Baron-Cohen, H. Tager-Flusberg, & D. Cohen (Eds.), *Understanding other minds; perspectives from autism* (pp. 112–137). Oxford, England: Oxford University Press.

Perner, J. (1995). The many faces of belief: Reflections on Fodor's and the child's theory of mind. *Cognition, 57,* 241–269.

Perner, J., Leekam, S., & Wimmer, H. (1987). Three-year-olds' difficulty with false belief: The case for a conceptual deficit. *British Journal of Developmental Psychology, 5,* 125–137.

Perner, J., & Wimmer, H. (1985). "John thinks that Mary thinks that . . .": Attribution of second-order beliefs by 5- to 10-year-old children. *Journal of Experimental Child Psychology, 39,* 437–471.

Peterson, C. (2003). The social face of theory-of-mind: The development of concepts of emotion, desire, visual perspective and false belief in deaf and hearing children. In B. Repacholi & V. Slaughter (Eds.), *Individual differences in theory of mind: Implications for typical and atypical development* (pp. 171–196). New York: Psychology Press.

Peterson, C. C., & Siegal, M. (2000). Insights into theory of mind from deafness and autism. *Mind and Language, 15,* 123–145.

Phillips, A., Wellman, H. M., & Spelke, E. (2002). Infants' ability to connect gaze and emotional expression to intentional action. *Cognition, 85,* 53–78.

Piaget, M. (1932). *The moral judgment of the child.* London: Routledge & Kegan Paul.

Pillow, B. H. (1989). Early understanding of perception as a source of knowledge. *Journal of Experimental Child Psychology, 47,* 116–129.

Pons, F., Lawson, J., Harris, P. L., & de Rosnay, M. (2003). Individual differences in children's emotion understanding: Effects of age and language. *Scandinavian Journal of Psychology, 44,* 347–353.

Povinelli, D. J., & Eddy, T. J. (1996). What young chimpanzees know about seeing. *Monographs of the Society for Research on Child Development, 61.*

Povinelli, D. J., Rulf, A. B., & Bierschwale, D. T. (1994). Absence of knowledge attribution and self-recognition in young chimpanzees (Pan troglodytes). *Journal of Comparative Psychology, 108,* 74–80.

Povinelli, D. J., & Vonk, J. (2003). Chimpanzee minds: Suspiciously human? *Trends in Cognitive Science, 7,* 157–160.

Povinelli, D. J., & Vonk, J. (2004). We don't need a microscope to explore the chimpanzee's mind. *Mind and Language, 19,* 1–28.

Pratt, C., & Bryant, P. (1990). Young children understand that looking leads to knowledge (so long as they are looking into a single barrel). *Child Development, 61,* 973–982.

Premack, D., & Woodruf, G. (1978). Does the chimpanzee have a theory of mind? *Behavioral and Brain Sciences, 1,* 515–526.

Przetacznik-Gierowsk, M., & Likeza, M. (1990). Cognitive and interpersonal functions of children's questions. In G. Conti-Ramsden & C. E. Snow (Eds.), *Children's Language* (Vol. 7, pp. 69–101). Hillsdale, NJ: Erlbaum.

Reed, T., & Peterson, C. (1990). A comparative study of autistic subjects' performance at two levels of visual and cognitive perspective-taking. *Journal of Autism and Developmental Disorders, 20,* 555–567.

Reid, T. (1970). *An enquiry into the human mind on the principles of common sense* (T. Duggan, Ed.). Chicago: Chicago University Press. (Original work published 1764)

Repacholi, B. (1998). Infants' use of attentional cues to identify the referent of another person's emotional expression. *Developmental Psychology, 34,* 1017–1025.

Rheingold, H. L. (1982). Little children's participation in the work of adults, a nascent prosocial behavior. *Child Development, 53,* 114–125.

Rieffe, C., & Meerum Terwogt, M. (2000). Deaf children's understanding of emotions: Desires take precedence. *Journal of Child Psychology and Psychiatry, 42,* 601–608.

Robinson, E. J., & Whitcombe, E. L. (2003). Children's suggestibility in relation to their understanding about sources of knowledge. *Child Development, 74,* 48–62.

Ruffman, T., Perner, J., Olson, D. R., & Doherty, M. (1993). Reflecting on scientific thinking: Children's understanding of the hypothesis-evidence relation. *Child Development, 64,* 1617–1636.

Ruffman, T., Slade, L., & Crowe, E. (2002). The relation between children's and mothers' mental state language and theory-of-mind. *Child Development, 73,* 734–751.

Russell, J. A. (1989). Culture, scripts, and children's understanding of emotion. In C. Saarni & P. L. Harris (Eds.), *Children's understanding of emotion* (pp. 293–318). Cambridge, England: Cambridge University Press.

Sachs, J., & Devin, J. (1976). Young children's use of age-appropriate speech styles in social interaction and role-playing. *Journal of Child Language, 3,* 81–98.

Scaife, M., & Bruner, J. S. (1975). The capacity for joint attention. *Nature, 253,* 265–266.

Schwebel, D. C., Rosen, C. S., & Singer, J. L. (1999). Preschoolers' pretend play and theory of mind: The role of jointly constructed pretence. *British Journal of Developmental Psychology, 17,* 333–348.

Selman, R. L. (1980). *The growth of interpersonal understanding.* New York: Academic Press.

Shatz, M., & Gelman, R. (1973). The development of communication skills: Modification in the speech of young children as a function of listener. *Monographs of the Society for Research in Child Development, 38*(5, Serial No. 152).

Shultz, T. R. (1980). Development of the concept of intention. In W. A. Collins (Ed.), *Minnesota Symposia on Child Psychology: Vol. 13. Development of cognition, affect, and social relations* (pp. 131–164). Hillsdale, NJ: Erlbaum.

Shwe, H. I., & Markman, E. M. (1997). Young children's appreciation of the mental impact of their communicative signals. *Developmental Psychology, 33*, pp. 630–636.

Sigman, M., Kasari, C., Kwon, J., & Yirmiya, N. (1992). Responses to the negative emotions of others by autistic, mentally retarded, and normal children. *Child Development, 63*, 796–807.

Sigman, M., & Ruskin, E. (1999). Continuity and change in the social competence of children with autism, Down syndrome, and developmental delays. *Monographs of the Society for Research in Child Development, 64*(1, Serial No. 256).

Smetana, J. G. (1981). Preschool children's conception of moral and social rules. *Child Development, 52*, 1333–1336.

Smetana, J. G. (1985). Preschool children's conceptions of transgressions: Effects of varying moral and conventional domain-related attributes. *Developmental Psychology, 2*, 18–29.

Smetana, J. G., Kelly, M., & Twentyman, C. T. (1984). Abused, neglected and nonmaltreated children's conceptions of socio-conventional transgressions. *Child Development, 55*, 277–287.

Smilansky, S. (1968). *The effects of sociodramatic play on disadvantaged preschool children.* New York: Wiley.

Snow, C. E., Pan, B. A., Imbens-Bailey, A., & Herman, J. (1996). Learning how to say what one means: A longitudinal study of children's speech act use. *Social Development, 5*, 56–84.

Sobel, D. M. (2004). Children's developing knowledge of the relationship between mental awareness and pretense. *Child Development, 75*, 704–729.

Sodian, B., & Frith, U. (1992). Deception and sabotage in autistic, retarded and normal children. *Journal of Child Psychology and Psychiatry, 33*, 591–605.

Sodian, B., Zaitchik, D., & Carey, S. (1991). Young children's differentiation of hypothetical beliefs from evidence. *Child Development, 62*, 753–766.

Sommerville, J. A., & Woodward, A. L. (2005). Pulling out the intentional structure of action: The relation between action processing and action production in infancy. *Cognition, 95*, 1–30.

Sommerville, J. A., Woodward, A. L., & Needham, A. (2005). Action experience alters 3-month-old infants' perception of others' actions. *Cognition, 96*, B1–B11.

Sorce, J. F., Emde, R. N., Campos, J. J., & Klinnert, M. D. (1985). Maternal emotional signalling: Its effects on the visual cliff behavior of 1-year-olds. *Developmental Psychology, 21*, 195–200.

Spelke, E. S., Phillips, A. T., & Woodward, A. L. (1995). Infants' knowledge of object motion and human action. In A. Premack (Ed.), *Causal understanding in cognition and culture.* Oxford, England: Clarendon press.

Stein, N. L., & Levine, L. J. (1989). The causal organization of emotional knowledge: A developmental study. *Cognition and Emotion, 3*, 343–378.

Striano, T., Henning, A., & Stahl, D. (2005). *Infant sensitivity to interpersonal timing.* Manuscript submitted for publication.

Sullivan, K., Zaitchik, D., & Tager-Flusberg, H. (1994). Preschoolers can attribute second-order beliefs. *Developmental Psychology, 30*, 395–402.

Tager-Flusberg, H. (1993). What language reveals about the understanding of minds in children with autism. In S. Baron-Cohen, H. Tager-Flusberg, & D. J. Cohen (Eds.), *Understanding other minds: Perspectives from autism* (pp. 138–157). Oxford, England: Oxford University Press.

Tan, J., & Harris, P. L. (1991). Autistic children understand seeing and wanting. *Development and Psychopathology, 3*, 163–174.

Tardif, T., & Wellman, H. M. (2000). Acquisition of mental state language in Mandarin- and Cantonese-speaking children. *Developmental Psychology, 36*, 25–43.

Taylor, M., & Carlson, S. M. (1997). The relation between individual differences in fantasy and theory of mind. *Child Development, 68*, 436–455.

Taylor, M., Esbensen, B. M., & Bennett, R. T. (1994). Children's understanding of knowledge acquisition: The tendency for children to report that they have always known what they have just learned. *Child Development, 65*, 1581–1604.

Tenenbaum, H. R., Visscher, P., Pons, F., & Harris, P. L. (2004). Emotional Understanding in Quechua children from an agro-pastoralist village. *International Journal of Behavioral Development, 28*, 471–478.

Termine, N. T., & Izard, C. E. (1988). Infants' responses to their mothers' expressions of joy and sadness. *Developmental Psychology, 2*(4), 223–229.

Tomasello, M. (1996). Do apes ape. In J. Galef & C. Heyes (Eds.), *Social learning in animals: The roots of culture* (pp. 319–343). New York: Academic Press.

Tomasello, M., Call, J., & Hare, B. (2003). Chimpanzees understand psychological states: The question is which ones and to what extent. *Trends in Cognitive Sciences, 7*, 153–156.

Tomasello, M., Carpenter, M., Call, J., Behne, T., & Moll, H. (2005). Understanding and sharing intentions: The origins of cultural cognition. *Behavioral and Brain Sciences, 28*, 675–691.

Trabasso, T., Stein, N. L., & Johnson, L. R. (1981). Children's knowledge of events: A causal analysis of story structure. In G. Bower (Ed.), *Learning and motivation* (Vol. 15, pp. 237–282). New York: Academic Press.

Trevarthen, C., & Hubley, P. (1978). Secondary intersubjectivity: Confidence, confiding and acts of meaning in the first year. In A. Lock (Ed.), *Action, gesture, and symbol* (pp. 183–229). London: Academic Press.

Trickett, P. K., & Kuczynski, L. (1986). Children's misbehaviors and parental discipline strategies in abusive and nonabusive families. *Developmental Psychology, 22*, 115–123.

Van Ijzendoorn, M. H. (1995). Adult attachment representations, parental responsiveness, and infant attachment: A meta-analysis on the predictive validity of the Adult Attachment Interview. *Psychological Bulletin, 117*, 387–403.

Vinden, P. G. (1996). Junín Quechua children's understanding of mind. *Child Development, 67*, 1707–1716.

Vinden, P. G. (1999). Children's understanding of mind and emotion. *Cognition and Emotion, 13*, 19–48.

Wainryb, C., Shaw, L., Langley, M., Cottam, K., & Lewis, R. (2004). Children's thinking about diversity of belief in the early school years: Judgments of relativism, tolerance and disagreeing persons. *Child Development, 75*, 687–703.

Want, S., & Harris, P. L. (2001). Learning from other people's mistakes: Causal understanding in learning to use a tool. *Child Development, 72*, 431–443.

Waters, E., Merrick, S., Terboux, D., Crowell, J., & Albersheim, L. (2000). Attachment security in infancy and early adulthood: A 20-year longitudinal study. *Child Development, 71*, 684–689.

Watson, A. C., Painter, K. M., & Bornstein, M. H. (2001). Longitudinal relations between 2-year-olds' language and 4-year-olds' theory of mind. *Journal of Cognition and Development, 2*, 449–457.

Weinfield, N. S., Sroufe, L. A., & Egeland, B. (2000). Attachment from infancy to early adulthood on a high-risk sample: Continuity, discontinuity, and their correlates. *Child Development, 71*, 695–702.

Wellman, H. M., & Bartsch, K. (1988). Young children's reasoning about beliefs. *Cognition, 30*, 239–277.

Wellman, H. M., Cross, D. D., & Watson, J. (2001). Meta-analysis of theory-of-mind development: The truth about false belief. *Child Development, 72*, 655–684.

Wellman, H. M., Harris, P. L., Banerjee, M., & Sinclair, A. (1995). Early understandings of emotion: Evidence from natural language. *Cognition and Emotion, 9*, 117–149.

Wellman, H. M., & Lempers, J. D. (1977). The naturalistic communicative abilities of 2-year-olds. *Child Development, 48*, 1052–1057.

Wellman, H. M., & Woolley, J. D. (1990). From simple desires to ordinary beliefs: The early development of everyday psychology. *Cognition, 35*, 245–275.

Whitcombe, E. L., & Robinson, E. J. (2000). Children's decisions about what to believe and their ability to report the sources of their belief. *Cognitive Development, 15*, 329–346.

Whiten, A. (Ed.). (1991). *Natural theories of mind: Evolution, development and simulation in everyday mindreading*. Oxford, England: Blackwell.

Whiten, A., Goodall, J., McGrew, W. C., Nishida, T., Reynolds, V., Sugiyama, Y., et al. (1999). Cultures in chimpanzees. *Nature, 399*, 682–685.

Wierzbicka, A. (1992). *Semantics, culture and cognition: Universal human concepts in culture-specific configurations*. New York: Oxford University Press.

Wimmer, H., & Hartl, M. (1991). Against the Cartesian view on mind: Young children's difficulty with own false beliefs. *British Journal of Developmental Psychology, 9*, 15–138.

Wimmer, H., & Perner, J. (1983). Beliefs about beliefs: Representation and constraining function of wrong beliefs in young children's understanding of deception. *Cognition, 13*, 103–128.

Wimmer, H., & Weichbold, V. (1994). Children's theory of mind; Fodor's heuristics or understanding informational causation. *Cognition, 53*, 45–57.

Wittgenstein, L. (1953). *Philosophical Investigations*. Oxford, England: Blackwell.

Wolf, D. (1982). Understanding others: A longitudinal case study of the concept of independent agency. In G. E. Forman (Ed.), *Action and thought* (pp. 297–327). New York: Academic Press.

Woodward, A. L. (1998). Infants selectively encode the goal object of an actor's reach. *Cognition, 69*, 1–34.

Woodward, A. L., & Sommerville, J. A. (2000). Twelve-month infants interpret action in context. *Psychological Science, 11*, 73–77.

Woolfe, T., Want, S. C., & Siegal, M. (2002). Signposts to development: Theory of mind in deaf children. *Child Development, 73*, 768–778.

Yirmiya, N., Osnat, E., Shaked, M., & Solomonica-Levi, D. (1998). Meta-analyses comparing theory-of-mind abilities of individuals with autism, individuals with mental retardation, and normally developing individuals. *Psychological Bulletin, 124*, 283–307.

Youngblade, L. M., & Dunn, J. (1995). Individual differences in young children's pretend play with mother and sibling: Links to relationships and understanding of other people's feelings and beliefs. *Child Development, 66*, 1472–1492.

Zahn-Waxler, C., Radke-Yarrow, M., Wagner, E., & Chapman, M. (1992). Development of concern for others. *Developmental Psychology, 28*, 126–136.

Zelco, F. A., Duncan, S. W., Barden, R. C., Garber, J., & Masters, J. C. (1986). Adults' expectancies about children's emotional responsiveness: Implications for the development of implicit theories of affect. *Developmental Psychology, 22*, 109–114.

CHAPTER 20

# Development in the Arts: Drawing and Music

ELLEN WINNER

DRAWING 859
Evolutionary Base 860
Historical and Theoretical Approaches 860
Picture Recognition, Comprehension, and Preference:
    Major Milestones in Development 863
Drawing: Major Milestones in Development 869
Universality versus Cultural Specificity of
    Drawing Schemas 879
Does Drawing Skill Improve Linearly with Age? 880
MUSIC 881

Evolutionary Base 882
Historical and Theoretical Approaches 883
Music Perception and Comprehension: Major
    Milestones in Development 884
Producing Music through Song: Major Milestones
    in Development 891
Does Musical Skill Improve Linearly with Age? 893
CONCLUSIONS 895
REFERENCES 895

Participation in the arts is central to human behavior. The earliest humans made art and traces of artistic ability can be seen in nonhuman animals. The arts are critical to the development of cognitive, social, and affective capacities in children and are included in the *Handbook* for the first time in the present edition.

I review the developmental course of the comprehension and production of two major nonverbal art forms, drawing and music, focusing on typical development in the absence of formal training. Research on individual differences and on giftedness in the arts is not covered (but see Moran & Gardner, Chapter 21, this *Handbook,* this volume for a discussion of giftedness). Unfortunately, almost all of the research on drawing and music has been conducted in Western settings, with a few exceptions (reviewed here).

Research on drawing has focused on production whereas research on music has focused on perception. This asymmetry, reflected here, may be due to the fact that the earliest music children produce is song rather than notated compositions. Songs are fleeting, while drawings are permanent and thus perhaps more amenable to study.

For each art form, I consider the following questions:

- What does an investigation into the evolutionary roots of this art form tell us?

- What historical, theoretical, and methodological approaches have been taken in the study of this art form?

- What are the major milestones in the development of comprehension and production of this art form?

For both drawing and music, I also consider one of the most enduring and provocative questions in the developmental study of the arts—whether development improves linearly with age, or whether some artistic abilities decline with age or are U-shaped, with young children responding more like adult artists than older children. This question is far more acute with respect to the arts than for logical, mathematical, scientific, or moral reasoning, where linear development is the normal expectation.

## DRAWING

Drawing is a complex activity that involves motoric, perceptual, and conceptual skills, including the use of schemas and rules specific to pictures (Gombrich, 1977; Thomas, 1995). Adults with no special training in drawing are able to translate a three-dimensional scene into a recognizable two-dimensional representation. While their drawings may not look highly skilled or accurate, their accomplishment is impressive: They can represent objects in a recognizable manner even though there is little actual similarity between a real-world scene and its small two-dimensional representation.

Pictures pervade our lives—we see them not only in art museums but also in magazines, billboards, cereal boxes, and so on. Pictures can be nonrepresentational (as in designs, abstractions) or representational, and, if the latter, they can be either realistic or nonrealistic. Nonrealistic representations are as easily recognized as realistic ones (witness cartoons, caricatures, and children's drawings). When we read a picture as a work of art (e.g., rather than as a diagram or scientific illustration), we attend to aesthetic properties—specifically we attend to what the picture expresses (properties not literally present such as sadness, agitation, loudness), the style of the work (the artist's individual handprint), and its composition (the organization of its parts and its balance or lack thereof; Arnheim, 1974; Goodman, 1976).

We can speculate about the evolutionary base of the visual arts from what we know about early human art as well as nonhuman capacities in picture-making and picture-responding.

## Evolutionary Base

The drawings of the earliest humans, from over 30,000 years ago, are extraordinarily realistic, capturing the fluid contours of the animals they hunted. Cave paintings have been likened in skill to the most highly prized human drawings (e.g., to drawings by Picasso). Cave art testifies to the drive to create art in humans: The earliest humans crawled through tunnels into deep recesses in caves to paint. The function of cave art has been debated (was it to encourage hunters? was it religious?) and we will only be able to speculate on this question. Perhaps the function was purely aesthetic, perhaps it was ritualistic, most likely it was polyfunctional. We also will never know what proportion of the population was able to draw in this way.

The visual arts extend to the nonhuman realm but only in a very limited manner. Apes and monkeys can recognize two-dimensional depictions of objects (Davenport & Rogers, 1971; Zimmerman & Hochberg, 1970; but see Winner & Ettlinger, 1979). Chimps have shown a sense of visual balance: Given a page with a small figure off-center, chimps added marks in a location that balanced the marks (Schiller, 1951). Morris (1967) gave painting materials to Congo, a laboratory chimp, and

noted certain resemblances between Congo's spontaneous paintings and those by very young children. Paintings by chimps in the laboratory have been confused with abstract expressionist paintings, though surely the intentions behind the chimp and adult works were not comparable (Hussain, 1965). Chimps trained in sign language have shown the ability to make a rudimentary drawing and then, using sign language, label the object drawn, revealing an understanding that a mark on a page can stand for something in the three-dimensional world (R. Gardner & Gardner, 1978; Patterson, 1978). And when Premack (1975) gave three chimps a photograph of a chimpanzee head with the face blanked out and offered them the cut out eyes, nose, and mouth, one of the three chimps was able to place these parts in correct position. But the fact remains that no nonhuman animals draw spontaneously, and even when given drawing and painting materials, chimps make only nonrepresentational marks (with the possible exception of those trained in sign language). The achievements of humans in the realm of visual arts are far more impressive, even in infancy.

## Historical and Theoretical Approaches

Psychologists have long been fascinated by the oddities of children's drawings when compared to those of even untrained adults. Why do children act out their scribbles as they draw and then give the resulting lines a name that looks nothing like what is drawn? Why do children all over the world today draw humans as "tadpole" figures (a circle with arms and legs radiating out of it, and two eyes) when they know that people don't look like this? Why were two-eyed profiles, such as that in Figure 20.1a drawn by nineteenth-century but not twentieth-century children? Why do they show one object behind another as if the object in front were transparent, as in the "transparent" boat in Figure 20.1b? Why do they draw objects in the same scene from mixed viewpoints, showing, for example, trees "folded out" from both sides of a street, as in Figure 20.1c?

The study of children's drawings began at the end of the nineteenth century with the rise of the field of child development. Early investigators include Barnes (1894), Hall (1892), Kerschensteiner (1905), Lukens (1896), Luquet (1913, 1927), Maitland (1895), Ricci (1887), Rouma (1913), and Sully (1895); for reviews, see H. Gardner (1980), Golomb (2002, chap. 2), and Strommen (1988). Drawings (like language) were seen as a reflection of de-

(a)                    (b)                    (c)

**Figure 20.1** Odd features of children's drawings. (a) Two-eyed profile. *Source:* From the Viktor Lowenfeld Papers, Penn State University Archives, Special Collections, Pennsylvania State University Libraries. Reprinted with permission. (b) Transparent boat. *Source:* From *L'arte dei bambini* [The art of children], by C. Ricci, 1887, Bologna, Italy: Zanichelli. (c) Trees folded out from a street and drawn from mixed viewpoints. *Source:* From *Die Entwicklung der zeichnerischen,* by G. Kerschensteiner, 1905, Begabung, Munich: Gerber.

velopmental stages, and parents, psychologists, and educators began to collect children's markings and to create descriptive taxonomies of drawing stages. The many oddities of children's drawings were seen as deficiencies reflective of children's immaturity and indicative of their incomplete or oversimplified concepts of the objects they were drawing.

The French art historian Luquet (1913, 1927) proposed three phases in the development of realism—a claim that remains influential yet controversial. At ages 3 to 4, Luquet theorized, children are in the phase of synthetic incapacity, or failed realism, in which they are unable to capture the spatial relationships among objects. From 5 to 8, children are in the phase of intellectual realism in which objects are depicted in canonical (stereotypical) position rather than from the particular viewpoint of the child drawing. At this phase, he argued, children draw what they know rather than what they see. Drawings are based on children's internal models (i.e., a table top is drawn as a rectangle because the child *knows* it to be rectangular; a near object appears transparent because the child shows what she knows to be behind it; a cup is always shown with handle even if the handle is not visible because the child knows cups have handles).

After age 9, according to Luquet, children enter the phase of visual realism. Now they draw what they see, basing their drawings on how things look from a single viewpoint, even if this means distorting an object by making it partially occluded or by altering its shape (e.g., drawing a table-top as a parallelogram despite knowing it is in reality a rectangle).

Piaget and Inhelder's (1956) studies of children's drawings were influenced by Luquet (1913, 1927), and exemplify this "deficiency/progressing toward realism" tradition. They saw the development of drawing as guided by the child's developing understanding of space. Following Luquet, they described a progression characterized at age 3 to 4 by synthetic incapacity in which children draw bounded objects (e.g., a closed circle) but ignore size and shape. Children at this age draw the human figure as a tadpole, and this figure was understood by Piaget and Inhelder to reflect not deficient perception but deficiencies in spatial representation. From age 4 to about 7 or 8, children were said to enter the stage of intellectual realism where they draw what they know not what they see. At the concrete operational stage, children were said to be able to draw in a realistic way, reflecting their understanding of Euclidean geometry and their emergence from spatial egocentrism. Piaget and Inhelder argued that at this stage the child could represent the third dimension (through occlusion and perspective). Thus, they saw drawing stages as progressive and assumed the desired endpoint to be visual realism. However, few concrete operational age children are able to draw in correct perspective (Willats, 1977), making it difficult to assume a close tie between concrete operational reasoning and realism in drawing (see Golomb, 2004, chap. 4, for further discussion of this issue).

The assumption that children's drawings become increasingly realistic with development led to the use of children's drawings as measures of intelligence, with higher scores for more detail and more accurate alignment of parts and proportion (Goodenough, 1926; Harris, 1963). Piaget and Inhelder's (1956) description of the shift from intellectual to visual realism, and their assumption that the oddities in children's drawings reflect what children *know* about an object rather than what they *see,* pervaded theories of children's drawings for many years. But as will be shown later, the assumption that the errors children make in their drawings are direct windows into their level of conceptual understanding is wrong. Even adults know far more about an object that they can show in a drawing: We can recognize our errors but simply have not acquired the rules for drawing complex objects or scenes (Golomb, 1973; Morra, 1995; Thomas, 1995). Such a view also reveals a Western-centric assumption of realism as the end state in the history of art. This assumption is misguided because the earliest human art (the art in the caves) is exceptionally realistic and because many cultures did not develop realistic art.

Although the study of children's drawings began with the emergence of the study of child development, this topic was gradually relegated to a minor area of developmental psychology. Just compare the number of developmental psychologists who study memory, language, and number versus those who study drawing. By the 1970s, children's drawings went unmentioned in many developmental textbooks (Thomas & Silk, 1990).

Freeman's (1980) experimental approach to children's drawings helped to revive the study of child art and to bring this study into the arena of cognitive developmental research. Freeman argued that children's drawings reflect production problems rather than conceptual limitations. For example, he argued that tadpole figures, which appear to have no body, stem from the strategy of drawing in linear fashion from head to legs. This causes children to fall prey to the serial order effect, remembering the first and last items of a list (head, legs) but forgetting the middle (trunk). Hence, his "production deficit" hypothesis of children's drawings diverges from Piaget and Inhelder's (1956) view that drawings reflect deficiencies of spatial representation.

Willats's (1995) information-processing theory of picture production (based on Marr's, 1982, theories of the visual system) also brought the study of child art into the arena of experimental cognitive development. Both Willats and Freeman (1980) distinguished between object-centered descriptions (in which shapes are not distorted) and viewer-centered descriptions (in which shapes are distorted to show how they look rather than how they actually are). What develops, for Willats, is a set of different drawing systems, from topological relations to various kinds of projection systems, with the final one being linear perspective. He also argued that denotation systems develop with two-dimensional regions first standing for volumes and later for surfaces of objects, and with one-dimensional lines ultimately standing for edges and contours. Willats's and Freeman's view that drawings develop from object-centered to viewer-centered descriptions parallels Piaget's view of the movement from intellectual to visual realism. Willats stands out however in his focus on the acquisition of drawing-specific rules for the emergence of visual realism.

In striking contrast to the deficit models of children's drawings was a more positive view put forth by artists and art educators at the beginning of the twentieth century. These artists and educators championed the striking resemblance between child art and emerging styles of Western art—impressionism, cubism, abstract expressionism—and organized exhibitions of child art (Fineberg, 1997; Golomb, 2002; Viola, 1936). Artists such as Kandinsky, Klee, and Picasso used child art as sources of inspiration for their own art (H. Gardner, 1980; Golomb, 2002). Arnheim (1974), the leading spokesperson for the aesthetic view, argued that children's art had its own aesthetics and was not just a sign of children's underdevelopment. He pointed out that many of the distortions and oddities found in children's drawings (e.g., fold-out drawings, lack of depth, transparencies) can be found in non-Western art (Paleolithic, Egyptian, South Sea Island, Kwakiutl Indian art, or pre-Renaissance Western art), showing us how many ways there are to represent and how much tolerance we have for lack of realism (cf. Deregowski, 1984, pp. 120–122). Arnheim (1974) argued that children's drawings are not failed attempts at realism but instead are intelligent solutions to the problem of depicting a three-dimensional world on paper. Arnheim interpreted children's drawings as graphic "equivalents" that are clear and readable and no more "deficient" than nonrealistic art produced by adult artist throughout the centuries.

A serious limitation of much of the experimental research on children's drawing to be reviewed later is the focus on how children represent geometric forms (e.g., copying cubes). Moreover, experimental studies have often used artificial tasks instead of analyzing properties of children's spontaneous drawings. Hence, many studies yield drawings very different from ones that children produce on their own. For instance, asking children to draw a cup positioned so that the handle is not visible may test whether they incorrectly make the occluded handle visible, but children probably would not choose to draw a cup from observation in their spontaneous drawing. These experimental approaches typically ignore the "aesthetics" of children's drawings and their ecological validity has been challenged (Costall, 1995). As is discussed later, studies of the development of music comprehension have also been criticized for using artificial stimuli rather than real pieces of music. However, studies using artificial tasks are useful because they test hypotheses about the limits of the child's capacities.

We turn now to a consideration of how children develop the ability to make sense of pictures, followed by a consideration of how they develop the ability to produce pictures.

## Picture Recognition, Comprehension, and Preference: Major Milestones in Development

Understanding pictures requires that one recognize pictures as representations. Understanding pictures also requires the ability to perceive the illusion of the third dimension in a two-dimensional picture, as well as the ability to perceive aesthetic properties of pictures. The development of these abilities is reviewed here, followed by a consideration of children's aesthetic sense—as measured by the kinds of pictures preferred at different ages.

### Understanding the Representational Nature of Pictures: Four Components

The representational information carried by pictures is far more impoverished than information available in the ordinary environment: Objects are smaller than in real life, color is frequently lacking, and edges of objects are often represented by lines despite the fact that objects in the real world do not come with outlines. In addition, pictorial information is contradictory: Certain depth cues suggest the third dimension, while other information (e.g., from binocular and motion parallax) shows the surface of the picture to be flat.

Understanding the representational nature of pictures is four-part: A person must recognize (1) the *similarity* between a picture and what it represents, (2) the

*difference* between a picture and what it represents, (3) the *dual reality* of a picture as both a flat object and a representation of the three-dimensional world, and (4) the fact that pictures are made with intentionality and are to be interpreted. Infants are excellent at the first two understandings while the third and fourth kinds develop later.

**Recognizing the Similarity between a Picture and What It Represents.**    Infants need no special instruction in reading pictures, even when these are small black-and-white line drawings (Hochberg & Brooks, 1962), which is a finding consistent with Gibson's (1979) view that pictures convey the critical information available from the world. Hochberg and Brooks kept their child from seeing any representational images until the age of 2, and then presented him with pictures of familiar objects such as a shoe or key (drawings, then black-and-white photos). The child labeled the pictures correctly, showing that no one needed to teach him to recognize objects represented in pictures. Later research with infants has confirmed this finding (Daehler, Perlmutter, & Myers, 1976; DeLoache, Strauss, & Maynard, 1979; Dirks & Gibson, 1977; Fagan, 1970; Fantz, Fagan, & Miranda, 1975; Field, 1976; Rose, 1977; Ruff, Kohler, & Haupt, 1976). Twelve-month-olds can even recognize line drawings of common objects when much of their contour has been deleted (Rose, Jankowski, & Senior, 1997). Thus, understanding what a picture represents is an untutored skill, in contrast to understanding what a word stands for—an understanding that must be learned because words have an arbitrary rather than iconic relationship to their referents.

The fact that adults in cultures without pictures can, with some effort, read what pictures represent helps to confirm the conclusion from infant research that all one needs to recognize what a picture represents is experience with the actual objects represented (Deregowski, 1989; Deregowski, Muldrow, & Muldrow, 1972; Jahoda, Deregowski, Ampene, & Williams, 1977; Kennedy & Ross, 1975). The exception are those pictorial schemas that are highly conventional (such as the depiction of a flying bird by a W-type shape), and thus, like words, require learning (Nye, Thomas, & Robinson, 1995).

**Recognizing the Difference between a Picture and What It Represents.**    Are young children realists when it comes to pictures? Piaget argued that children confuse the sign with the thing signified, referring to this trait as "realism" (Piaget, 1929). If children are re-alists, they should succeed at recognizing what a picture represents but fail to distinguish a picture from its refer-ent. In one sense, children are *not* realists about pic-tures. Infants discriminate between photographs and their referents between 3 to 6 months of age (Beilin, 1991; DeLoache, Pierroutsakos, & Uttal, 2003; De-Loache, Strauss, & Maynard, 1979); and 3- to 4-year-olds can readily sort pictures from objects (Thomas, Nye, & Robinson, 1994). For a review of such early pic-torial competence, see DeLoache, Pierroutsakos, and Troseth (1996).

But in another sense, children *are* realists about pic-tures. Despite their ability to discriminate pictures from objects, they sometimes see pictures as "substandard" versions of real objects possessing some of the proper-ties that only the real objects possess (Thomas, Nye, & Robinson, 1994). Ninio and Bruner (1978) described one child who, between 8 to 18 months of age, tried to ma-nipulate pictured objects. Pierroutsakos and DeLoache (2003) described 9-month-olds manually exploring pic-tures of objects as if they were the real thing. This be-havior occurred despite infants' ability to select the actual object when given a choice between the pictured versus real object (DeLoache, Pierroutsakos, & Uttal, 2003). By 19 months, the infants had stopped grasping at pictures and now pointed to them.

But even preschoolers can become confused. Beilin and Pearlman (1991) gave 3- and 5-year-olds pictures of objects such as a rattle along with life-size photos of the same objects and asked them about the physical and functional properties. Three-year-olds had some diffi-culty with these questions, especially those about phys-ical properties, sometimes believing, for example, that a picture of a rattle makes a noise when shaken. They had less difficulty with functional properties, usually real-izing that one cannot eat a picture of an ice cream cone, for example. Five-year-olds had no trouble with either type of question, and among the 3-year-olds, errors were made only by some. From this study it would ap-pear that by the age of 3, most children are no longer pictorial realists.

Still, young children are not completely clear about the relationship between a picture and what it repre-sents. They believe that a picture shares the fate of its referent, showing that they have not completely sepa-rated picture from referent. Beilin and Pearlman (1991) asked the same 3- and 5-year-olds what would happen to a picture of a flower if the real flower it de-picted were altered and found that children think that

the picture would change too (though this kind of re-sponse was more prominent among the 3- than the 5-year-olds). Zaitchik (1990) reported similar results when she showed 3- and 4-year-olds a toy duck on a bed and took a Polaroid photograph of the duck. Chil-dren then saw the toy duck go into a bath and were asked to predict what the photograph would show. Forty percent said that the photograph would show the duck in the bath. The finding that an already completed picture changes to match a subsequent change in its ref-erent was replicated by Charman and Baron-Cohen (1992), Leekam and Perner (1991), Leslie and Thaiss (1992), and Robinson, Nye, and Thomas (1994), though it is not clear whether children believe that the picture actually changes as the referent changes or whether they simply confuse the properties of picture and refer-ent due to forgetting. Thus, there remains support in the domain of picture perception for Piaget's claim that young children are realists.

**Recognizing the Representational Status of Pic-tures.**    Children under 2.5 years of age do not grasp that a picture *stands for* its referent. Callaghan (1999) showed 2-, 3-, and 4-year-olds several balls differing in size and features. The experimenter held up a picture to show which ball should be dropped down a tunnel. Two-year-olds could not use the pictures as symbolic objects and thus selected balls randomly rather than selecting the one that matched the picture. Sometimes they even put the picture down the tunnel instead of the object, showing that they treated the pictures as objects.

By 2.5 years, children can understand the representa-tional status of pictures. DeLoache (1987) showed chil-dren color photos of a room, each indicating where a toy was hidden in the actual room. The experimenter pointed to one of the photos to show the child where to search for a toy hidden in the room. Children aged 2.5 years could use the photos to find the toys, showing that they recognized the photos as representational objects. However, they could not find the hidden toy in the actual room when their cue was a scale model of the room with a hidden toy in the model. The contrast in findings led to the conclusion that children cannot treat a scale model as both an object and a symbol because they can't stop thinking of the model as an object. In contrast, they can treat a picture as a symbol because a picture is primarily only a representation and not an object.

However, Callaghan (2000a) has found that children do not fully understand the symbolic nature of pictures until age 3: Under age 3, children rely on verbal labels to mediate the matching of picture with referent. Further evidence for incomplete understanding comes from DeLoache (1991) who showed that 2.5-year-olds can be fooled into treating pictures as objects and hence fail to see them as symbols. When a miniature dog was hidden behind a photo of a chair (to indicate where the dog could be found in the room), children failed to retrieve the dog from behind the chair. In this condition, they treated the photograph as an object and could not use it as a clue to the location of the toy (see also Dow & Pick, 1992).

Children can actually succeed on DeLoache's (1991) task simply by attending to what the picture represents. Attending to the dual identity of a picture (i.e., recognizing that a picture of a flower is both a flower and a flat piece of paper) is not tested by her task and remains more difficult for children. Thomas, Nye, and Robinson (1994) showed children an actual flower, a color photo of a flower, and a plastic replica of a flower and asked them to label and handle each one. The alternative identity of the plastic and pictured flower was then explained (e.g., it does not really grow in the ground), and children were then asked an appearance question (Does it look like a flower?) and a reality question (Is it really a flower?). Four-year-olds made some errors when asked about the plastic and pictured flower, and most errors were realist ones in which they confused the representation with the referent (saying it both looked like a flower and was a flower).

Thus, while infants recognize pictures, it is not until at least 4 years of age that children fully understand the symbolic nature of pictures and grasp the dual identity of a picture. Some children under age 4 believe that a picture has some of the nonvisual properties of its referent and that a pictures changes as its referent changes; some also confuse the picture with its referent when asked to consider both of the picture's identities. These errors could be due to a difficulty holding in mind two interpretations of the same input (Flavell, 1988) or to being confused by the experimenter's questions. Errors might also be the result of how adults talk to children about pictures: We assume an understanding of (and gloss over) the dual identity of pictures, referring to a picture of a horse, for example, as simply "a horse" (Nye, Thomas, & Robinson, 1995). The way out of this confusion may be simply through learning—through experience with pictures.

**Acquisition of an Intentional Theory of Pictures.**
Full understanding of pictures requires the realization

that pictures are made by someone with a mind. The "artist" interprets what is seen and puts it on paper. Thus, beauty is not directly transferred from world to paper but is a matter of the artist's interpretation of what he or she sees. Moreover, the beholder too has a mind, and this affects how the picture is perceived (Freeman, 1995; Gardner, Winner, & Kircher, 1975).

Snippets of understanding the intentional basis of pictures can be seen in 3-year-olds. Bloom and Markson (1998) asked 3- and 4-year-olds to draw a lollipop and a balloon and both drawings looked the same. Later children were asked to label each, and they used their prior intentions to label each picture. Similarly, 3-year-olds were more likely to label a drawing as a picture of something if told that the picture was drawn intentionally rather than as a result of spilled paint.

Richert and Lillard (2002) found that children under age 8 are easily confused about the role of the artist's intention in determining what a picture represents. Even if they are told that an artist had no knowledge of a certain object, if the drawing produced looks like that object, children say that this is what the artist was drawing. Parallel findings were reported by Richert and Lillard in another representational domain—that of pretense: Children under age 8 did not realize that one cannot pretend to be a rabbit if one has never heard of a rabbit.

Studies have not pinpointed what causes the emergence of understanding of the role of intention in drawing. However, one likely catalyst is the experience of having one's own drawings misinterpreted, which could lead children to reflect about how their intentions determine the meaning of their drawings. Another possible mechanism of change is children's developing general ability to introspect (Flavell, Green, Flavell, & Grossman, 1997).

Freeman and Sanger (1993) found that subtle misunderstandings about the role of the artist in picture making persist until adolescence. When children were asked whether an ugly thing would make a worse picture than a pretty thing, most 11-year-olds said yes (revealing a belief that beauty flows directly from the world to the picture), but most 14-year-olds said no (they said that whether the picture is pretty or not depends on the artist's skill). Thus, the older children recognized that the artist determines whether a picture is beautiful. These findings about pictures are but one of many manifestations of a developmental progression in epistemological understanding by which children gradually come to understand that knowledge has its origin not only in the external world but also in the mind (see Kuhn & Franklin, Chapter 22, this *Handbook,* this volume).

### Perceiving Depth in Pictures

To perceive depth in a picture, one must overlook three kinds of cues that indicate that the picture is flat. First, binocular disparity is a cue resulting from small differences in how a scene looks to each eye. The farther away an object, the less disparity between the two views. In a picture, objects meant to appear far away are the same distance from our eyes as objects meant to appear near, which is why binocular disparity tells us that the two objects are on the same plane. Second, binocular convergence is a cue given by the fact that our eyes converge on what we focus on. For near objects, the angle of convergence is greater than for distant objects. This angle of convergence is interpreted by the brain as information about distance. But when we look at a picture, the angle of convergence is identical for images meant to be near and far in the picture because all of the objects are on the same flat picture plane. Third, motion parallax is a cue yielded by moving our head as we view a scene. When we do so, nearer objects are displaced faster than farther ones. But when we move our head in front of a picture, near and far represented objects move at the same rate, declaring the surface to be flat.

These three cues tell us that a three-dimensional scene is three-dimensional, and that a picture is only two-dimensional. How then do we perceive depth in two-dimensional pictures? We do so by ignoring these cues in favor of pictorial depth cues. These include occlusion (near objects partially occlude far ones), linear perspective (receding lines converge toward a vanishing point), size diminution (distant objects are smaller than near ones of the same absolute size), relative height (distant objects are drawn farther up on the picture plane), and texture gradients (textures get denser in the distance).

Infants perceive depth in the three-dimensional world when the nonpictorial cues of motion parallax and binocular cues are available, but they fail to read depth in pictures (Bower, 1965, 1966; Campos, Langer, & Krowitz, 1970). Children between the ages of 2 and 3, however, can judge which of two houses in a picture is farther away using either occlusion cues or the cue of relative height (Olson & Boswell, 1976). The addition of the linear perspective cue of converging lines did not result in improvement in children's pictorial depth perception for 3- to 5-year-olds, who still relied on occlusion and relative height (Olson, 1975). Some studies have

shown that children as old as age 5 can use relative height as a depth cue only in combination with other depth cues, such as partial occlusion (M. Hagen, 1976), or in a context showing the position of the objects with respect to the vanishing point in the picture (Perara & Cox, 2000). For other studies on pictorial depth perception in children, see Olson, Pearl, Mayfield, and Millar (1976); Wohlwill (1965); and Yonas, Goldsmith, and Hallstrom (1978).

While children as young as age 3 can use certain cues to judge whether one object is farther than another in a picture (relative depth judgment), the ability to determine precisely how far away a pictured object is meant to be relative to others develops later. Children as old as age 7 are less accurate than adults on such tasks (Yonas & Hagen, 1973). Even adults fail to make precisely accurate metric judgments about pictures: We read pictures as flatter than they should be read given the pictorial cues (Hagen, 1978). Perhaps the binocular and motion parallax cues that show the picture to be two-dimensional dilute the pictorial cues that yield the three-dimensional illusion.

Cross-cultural evidence suggests that the ability to read depth in pictures is not a skill that requires prior exposure to pictures. Children and adults in cultures with little or no exposure to pictures representing depth can read pictures as representations of three-dimensional scenes (Hagen & Jones, 1978; McGurk & Jahoda, 1975), despite Hudson's (1960) earlier claims that they could not. Like the ability to recognize what is represented in a picture, the ability to perceive depth in a picture may develop simply as a function of experience perceiving the actual world.

### Perceiving Aesthetic Properties of Pictures: Expression, Style, and Composition

Most research on the perception of pictures has focused on the perception of representation (the same is true of research on drawing, as is shown later, where researchers focus on the development of the ability to represent). However, a few studies have examined sensitivity to nonrepresentational, aesthetic aspects of pictures—in particular to expression, style, and composition. Detection of these features calls on skills quite different from those required to perceive representational properties of pictures.

**Expression.**  Pictures can express properties they do not literally possess. They can express nonvisual properties (loudness) and moods, doing so via representational content (a dying tree expresses sadness) or formal properties (dark colors express sadness; note that the depiction of a sad face is a literal rather than an expressive way to depict sadness). Because expressive properties are not literally present in pictures, reading expression in pictures can be considered a form of metaphorical thinking, and expression in art has been referred to as "metaphorical exemplification" (Goodman, 1976).

On very basic tasks, identification of expression in visual forms has been shown to emerge very early and may rely on universal, innate sensitivities. Even babies (age 11 months) have some capacity to perceive crossmodal (visual-auditory) similarities that might underlie metaphors: They can match a dotted line to an intermittent tone (both broken), and a continuous line to a continuous tone (both smooth; Wagner, Winner, Cicchetti, & Gardner, 1981). Preschoolers are sensitive to the expressive properties of abstract (nonrepresentational) stimuli, such as angular lines versus softly curving lines and bright colors versus dark colors (H. Gardner, 1974; Lawler & Lawler, 1965; Winston, Kenyon, Stewardson, & Lepine, 1995), and to expressive properties of certain kinds of representational content (e.g., a dying tree as sad; Winston et al., 1995). Shown abstract paintings, 5-year-olds respond with the same mood labels as do adults (Blank, Massey, Gardner, & Winner, 1984; Callaghan, 1997; Jolley & Thomas, 1994) though studies conflict in their reports of which emotions are best recognized in pictures by young children. When directly questioned about the mood in a drawing, children (including non-Western ones) as young as age 4 are typically correct (Jolley & Thomas, 1995; Jolley, Zhi, & Thomas, 1998a). While children may incorrectly match a "happy" painting (as judged by adults) with an excited face, they do not match it with a sad face, thereby showing a sensitivity to the positive or negative valence expressed by the picture even if they miss the precise mood (Callaghan, 1997). Children make the same kinds of errors when perceiving emotions in faces (Russell & Bullock, 1985). And even 3-year-olds can reliably select paintings that express happy, sad, excited, and calm, but only after first seeing adults modeling these judgments in other paintings (Callaghan, 2000b).

On more challenging expression tasks, young children do not succeed. When simply asked to select an appropriate completion for a picture, one of which matched the mood in the picture (e.g., a wilted tree versus a blooming tree to complete a sad picture), children did not succeed until 10 to 11 years of age (Carothers &

Gardner, 1979; Jolley & Thomas, 1995). Here, no mention was made of mood. When Winner, Rosenblatt, Windmueller, Davidson, and Gardner (1986) asked 7-, 9-, and 12-year-olds to pair abstract and representational paintings on the basis of their expressive property, only the two older age groups performed above chance. This latter task was a challenge because the abstract painting was not labeled for the child as sad, happy, excited, or calm; instead, children had to discern the mood expressed in the abstract picture and then match it to the mood conveyed by the representational picture.

**Style.** Features that distinguish one artist's style from another are hard to define and include a wide variety of properties such as level of abstraction, texture, brush stroke, color, and light. Children's ability to detect style in works of art has been studied through paradigms in which children are asked to match works by the same artist. Whenever it is possible to match on the basis of representational content, representation trumps style (H. Gardner, 1970). Jolley, Zhi, and Thomas (1998b) showed Chinese and English children triads of pictures and asked them to match two of them. Matches could be made on the basis of color, subject matter, or what was referred to as visual metaphor (e.g., two different objects both broken). Both Chinese and English children matched on color at age 4 and on subject matter by age 7. Though metaphorical matches increased between 7 and 10, subject matter remained predominant at age 10.

In matching tasks in which the choices vary in style but not subject matter, preschoolers and even 3-year-olds can perceive which paintings are by the same artist, though they justify such matches only in global terms such as looking alike (H. Gardner, 1970; Hardiman & Zernich, 1985; O'Hare & Westwood, 1984; Steinberg & DeLoache, 1986; Walk, Karusitis, Lebowitz, & Falbo, 1971). When asked to pick out their own drawing from drawings by a range of children (all of the same subject matter and 3 months after having made the drawing), even 3- to 4-year-olds succeeded, showing that they recognized their own style. Five- and 6-year-olds even recognized their own drawings after a 1-year delay (Gross & Hayne, 1999).

In a more difficult style perception task, children were asked to complete a drawing by adding a person the way the artist would have done it (Carothers & Gardner, 1979). They were given a choice of two drawings of people, one of which used the same line quality as the target drawing. Six-year-olds chose at random, but 9-year-olds selected the completion in the appropriate style of line.

Thus, when only line quality was varied, 6-year-olds failed to match by style. This was a difficult task, however, because children were not directly asked to match by line quality.

**Composition.**    Infants pay attention to the external contour of a pattern but not to the internal organization of its parts (Bond, 1972); sensitivity to the internal structure of a pattern develops gradually between the ages of 4 and 8 (Chipman & Mendelson, 1975). This was demonstrated by asking children to judge which of two patterns identical in external contour was simpler. The ability to look through the content of a painting to perceive its structure develops only by late childhood and early adolescence: When asked to sort groups of four paintings two of which had similar composition and two of which had similar content, classification by subject matter decreased with age with the main decline between ages 11 to 14, and classification by composition increased, with the main increase between ages 7 to 11 (H. Gardner & J. Gardner, 1973).

Taken together, studies of children's perception of aesthetic properties of pictures show that by age 3 or 4, children have the ability to perceive aspects of expression, style, and composition. However, when representational content is pitted against one of these nonrepresentational properties and competes for the child's attention, representation wins out and children ignore the aesthetic property.

### Aesthetic Responses

Aesthetic responses to pictures depend on what is perceived in pictures. Little research has examined aesthetic reactions to pictures, and the research that has been carried out has been limited to the study of the kinds of pictures children *prefer.*

**The Appeal of Realism.**    Parsons (1987) documented developmental changes in the bases of children's aesthetic preferences by interviewing children about their responses to different works of art. The 4- to 7-year-olds he interviewed liked abstract works as much as realistic ones. Between ages 7 to 10, children judged paintings as good only if they were realistic in form and color. In early adolescence (ages 10 to 14), expressive properties become more important than realism. By later adolescence, individuals begin to judge works by their social and historical context.

Parsons' (1987) study was carried out on only eight paintings and contained no statistical demonstration of a stage theory of aesthetic judgment. A more quantitative study by Linn and Thomas (2002) failed to find evidence for a stagelike progression in aesthetic preferences: From age 4 to adulthood, individuals used subject matter more often than any other property of a painting in explaining why they like it. Only for art students (who focused on the medium) was subject matter not the dominant criterion invoked, but even for them content was the second most often cited reason for liking a work. Even 2- and 3-year-olds show a preference for realism (McGhee & Dziuban, 1993). For other studies showing the appeal of realism for children, see Machotka (1966) and Rosenstiel, Morison, Silverman, and Gardner (1978).

Children prefer more realistic drawings of the human figure than they themselves can produce, and this finding holds for children at the scribbling stage on up to adolescence (Jolley, Knox, & Foster, 2000). Children also prefer perspective drawings that are more advanced than they themselves can produce (Kosslyn, Heldmeyer, & Locklear, 1977; H. Lewis, 1963). Thus, production lags behind preference (but see Brooks, Glenn, & Crozier, 1988, who found that preschoolers preferred drawings at their own level to drawings that were more complex).

**The Appeal of Regularity.**    Two studies have examined preference for regularity and have shown that children respond positively to balance. Infants (12-month-olds) show a preference for vertical symmetry (symmetry across a vertical axis) over both asymmetry and horizontal symmetry (Bornstein, Ferdinandsen, & Gross, 1981). The preference for vertical symmetry could be due to experience in a visual environment dominated by such symmetry, especially the vertical symmetry of the face and body. And children ages 4, 6, and 10 prefer balanced drawings to unbalanced ones (Winner, Mendelsohn, & Garfunkel, 1981).

Eysenck and his colleagues also reported studies claiming to show a preference for regularity in childhood as well as adulthood, but what he studied was the ability to *distinguish* regular from irregular forms (Eysenck, Götz, Long, Nias, & Ross, 1984; Götz, Borisy, Lynn, & Eysenck, 1979; Iwawaki, Eysenck, & Götz, 1979). Eysenck devised a test consisting of pairs of nonrepresentational forms identical except for the fact that one member had been changed so that eight artists considered the original to be superior in harmony, design, and "good gestalt." People taking this test were told that one member of each pair had been deemed more harmonious by art experts. They were told to pick out the less harmonious design and were explicitly told that this was not the same as being asked to pick out the one they found more pleasant. Children from 10 to 17 were tested along with art students over 17 years of age, and no relation was found between "visual aesthetic sensitivity" and age or education. No effect of culture was found when children and adults from Japan, Honk Kong, and Singapore were compared to Westerners.

The work of Eysenck demonstrates that children at least after age 11 are near adultlike in their judgments of what counts as harmonious. However, had the instructions asked for preference, the results might have differed. Perhaps older children or those trained in art would show a greater preference for the irregular forms because they are more surprising.

**Telling a Good Painting from a Less Good One.** Children often prefer works other than those considered "great" by experts in art. Child (1965) showed 6- to 18-year-olds pairs of pictures similar in style and content but in each case one member of the pair had been judged aesthetically superior by art experts. Participants were asked which one they preferred. Between the ages of 6 and 11, children agreed with the experts only about a third of the time. Between 12 to 18 years, agreement with experts rose, but peaked only at 50% by the oldest age. That agreement never rose above 50% shows that young adults (age 18) do not hold the same aesthetic preferences as do experts in the arts, conflicting with Eysenck et al.'s (1984) claims for universality. These findings suggest either that training in the arts shifts the bases of aesthetic preferences, or that those who go into the arts have different preferences to begin with.

**Conceptualizing Aesthetic Preference.** Neither children nor adults believe that in the case of conflicting aesthetic preferences only one can be right (Kuhn, Cheney, & Weinstock, 2000). This finding was determined by asking children (8-, 10-, 13-, and 17-year-olds) and adults of various education levels to react to pairs of statements about aesthetic preference: one about paintings, one about music, and one about literature (e.g., Robin thinks the first painting they look at is better. Chris thinks the second painting they look at is better.

Can only one of their views be right, or could both have some rightness?). Those who said only one could be right were classified as absolutists; at no age, did absolutist views predominate (though these views were more common among 7- to 8-year-olds than among older children). Those who said both could be right were then asked whether one view could be better or more right than the other. Those who replied no were classified as multiplists in the aesthetic domain; those who said yes were classified as evaluativists. Most children and adults were multiplists, believing that two conflicting aesthetic preferences were equally right, thereby failing to distinguish aesthetic judgments from matters of personal taste. Only adults with expertise in the study of epistemology were evaluativists, believing that while both aesthetic preferences could be "right," one could have more merit than another. Adolescents and adults were more likely to have become evaluativists in other domains than in the domain of aesthetic judgment and taste. Thus, they were more likely to respond as evaluativists when asked about conflicting value judgments (how bad lying is), conflicting judgments of truth about the social world (causes of crime), and conflicting judgments of truth about the physical world (composition of atoms). Yet, this finding could be a Western phenomenon. If children from a traditional society, such as China, were assessed, perhaps we would find them more likely to believe that one work of art can legitimately be judged as better than another.

## Drawing: Major Milestones in Development

The milestones in the development of picture production are striking, and the oddities of children's drawings have been characterized by some as indications of immaturity, but by others as indications that in some ways children are like artists.

### Action Representations

The first milestone in drawing is the emergence, sometime between the ages of 1 to 2, of the kind of mark making we call scribbling. Using a large sample of preschool drawings, Kellogg (1969) described 20 basic kinds of scribbles (e.g., single curved line, roving open line, multiple loop line, and zigzag) as the building blocks of later representational drawings (but see Golomb, 1981, who was able to identify only two kinds of scribbles—circular loop and whirls, and repeated parallel lines). According to Kellogg, children use the basic elements of scribbles to make progressively more controlled and complex forms. For example, a vertical and horizontal line together create a cross, which, when enclosed by a circle, becomes a "mandala"; when lines are drawn radiating out from the circle, the mandala becomes a sun or a tadpole human. Kellogg believed that representation emerges only after extensive practice with mark-making and only when adults respond to the child's "meaningless" forms by pointing out a resemblance to objects in the world (e.g., showing the child how the circle with lines radiating out looks like a person). But studies show that children and adults with no previous drawing experience can, after one or two trials, arrive at drawings of humans that children in our culture achieve only after much practice with scribbling (Alland, 1983; Harris, 1971; Kennedy, 1993; Millar, 1975). Thus, scribbling may not be a necessary precursor to graphic representation (for a review of these claims, see Golomb, 2004, chap. 1). Figure 20.2 shows the first drawings of a 5-year-old boy from the South American Andes who progressed rapidly to human figures (Harris, 1971).

There is also reason to believe that scribbling itself has representational meaning. According to early views, scribbling (the very name suggests something messy and lacking in purpose) is a nonrepresentational activity that children carry out primarily for rhythmic, kinesthetic pleasure rather than for an interest in the marks their motor activity leaves (Kellogg, 1969; Lowenfeld & Brittain, 1964/1987; Piaget & Inhelder, 1956). Evidence that scribbling children are not just carrying out a pleasurable motor activity but are also interested in the marks comes from Tarr (1990), who showed that children pay close visual attention to the marks they make, and from Gibson and Yonas (1968), who showed that when children are given a pencil without lead (and thus with no mark-making capacity), scribbling comes to an abrupt halt.

In scribbles, the act of representation is sometimes carried out through symbolic action and language (Matthews, 1984, 1997, 1999; Wolf & Perry, 1988). Children symbolize an object's motion as they draw (mimicking the action of a rabbit hopping; e.g., by making the marker hop along the page leaving dots and labeling each dot by saying "hop"; Wolf & Perry, 1988), but the resultant static marks do not capture the action and thus do not reveal to the naive eye what the child has intended to symbolize. Figure 20.3 on page 872 shows an action painting by a 2-year-old who moved the brush in circular motions while labeling his painting an airplane. Matthews refers to these kinds of early representations as "action representations," in contrast to later graphic representations where the final marks themselves reveal what they are intended to represent.

Action representations show us that even 2-year-olds grasp the concept that their own drawings are representational (this understanding emerges at about the same time as their understanding that pictures by *others* are representational, as reviewed earlier). A second indication of such representational awareness occurs when children give their scribbles names (called "romancing" or "fortuitous realism"; Gardner, 1980; Golomb, 2004; Gross & Hayne, 1999; Luquet, 1913, 1927). When asked what they have drawn, children ages 2 to 3 are more likely to give representational meanings to broken (angular) curves but to call smooth lines just "lines" (Adi-Japha, Levin, & Solomon, 1998). This finding may be due to a combination of two factors: (1) Broken curves create somewhat more closed forms; and (2) children may pay more attention to these kinds of lines because as they draw them they have to change direction intentionally. When children were asked to interpret scribbles by peers or their own scribbles produced several weeks earlier, they did not differentiate between types of line in this way. A third indication that 2-year-olds grasp the concept that drawings are representational is that they are able to draw recognizable representations of a human figure when the parts of the figure are dictated to them (called "guided elicitation") and when asked to complete a partially drawn figure (Bassett, 1977; Cox & Parkin, 1986).

### Graphic Representations

The first spontaneous graphic representations (ones that depict recognizable objects) emerge in typical children between 3 to 4 years of age (Golomb, 2004). Unlike action representations, graphic representations actually *look like* what they stand for. Even in cultures with almost no pictorial tradition, children make graphic representational drawings when asked by researchers to draw (Alland, 1983). Thus, children do not need to be instructed to arrive at graphic representation, nor do they first need models of representational drawings to do so.

**Representing the Human Form.**    One of the first graphic representations children attempt is the human figure (Golomb, 2004). Children's early attempts to represent the human figure have been described as "tadpoles" because these representations consist of a circle

**Figure 20.2** First drawings by a 5-year-old from the South American Andes who had never drawn before. *Source:* From "The Case Method in Art Education" (pp. 29–49), by D. B. Harris, in *A Report on Preconference Education Research Training Program for Descriptive Research in Art Education,* G. Kensler (Ed.), 1971, Reston, VA: National Art Education Association.

**Figure 20.3**   Action representation of an airplane by a child ages two years and two months. *Source:* From *The Art of Childhood and Adolescence: The Construction of Meaning* (p. 34, figure 11), by J. Matthews, 1999, London: Falmer Press. Reprinted with permission of Taylor and Francis Books.

with arms and legs (or just legs) emanating from it, as shown in Figures 20.4a and 20.4b. These figures appear to have heads but no trunks (Luquet, 1913, 1927; Piaget & Inhelder, 1956; Ricci, 1887), though Arnheim (1974) argued that the circle represented both head and body.

Children typically draw their first tadpole around 3 years of age (Cox & Parkin, 1986). Some remain in this phase for months, while others pass through this phase rapidly, moving on to more differentiated figures (Cox, 1993, 1997). Though tadpoles appear to have no trunks, Golomb (2004) showed that tadpoles do not reflect a limited understanding of the human body. For instance, when asked to construct a person out of given geometric shapes, only 2 out of 27 3-year-olds made tadpoles; when asked to complete a drawing consisting of a head with facial features, or when asked to model a person

out of Play-Doh, many of the same children who drew tadpoles included a trunk. Figure 20.5 shows drawings by a 4-year-old: When asked just to draw a person she drew an armless tadpole (the two figures on the left); when asked to draw a person with a tummy she drew a body (third figure from the left); and when asked to draw a person with a flower, she included a body and an arm. Thus, the task and the medium influence what is drawn. Tadpoles are not a printout of what the child knows about the human body; when it comes to the tadpole, the old adage that children draw what they know and not what they see has no support. They may not draw what they see, but their drawings do not tell us all that they know about what they draw.

According to Freeman's (1980) production deficit view of children's drawings, tadpoles are defective not because of the child's limited knowledge of the human form but rather because of children's planning and memory deficits. Freeman argues that drawing is a serially ordered performance. When children draw the figure, they begin with the head and end with the legs, forgetting what comes in the middle (trunk and arms), just as when remembering verbal lists we are more likely to remember the first and last word than those in the middle. But there are problems with this performance explanation. Experiments by Golomb and Farmer (1983) show that while children do draw the human starting at the top and moving down, 40% of the 3-year-olds also moved back up, adding arms, facial features, and so on. When asked to list the parts needed to draw a person, children were far more likely to include arms and a trunk than they were when asked to draw a person. As mentioned, when given global instructions (draw a person), 3- to 5-year-olds pro-

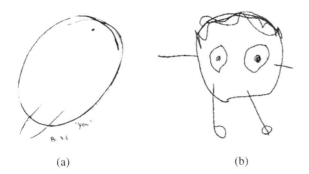

(a)                              (b)

**Figure 20.4**   (a) Armless tadpole by a child aged three years and three months. (b) Tadpole with legs and arms by a three and a half year old. *Source:* From *The Child's Creation of a Pictorial World,* second edition, p. 29, figures 16a and 16b, by C. Golomb, 2004, Mahwah, NJ: Erlbaum. Reprinted with permission.

**Figure 20.5**   Drawings by a 4-year-old showing the effect of instructions on presence/absence of arms in tadpoles. *Source:* From *The Child's Creation of a Pictorial World,* second edition, p. 46, figure 25a, by C. Golomb, 2004, Mahwah, NJ: Erlbaum. Reprinted with permission.

duced tadpoles, but when given more specific instructions (e.g., draw a person with a tummy, with a flower), these same children were able to add a torso and an arm (Golomb, 1981, 2004). And when children who spontaneously draw tadpoles were asked to construct a person out of cut out pieces of paper such as circles and rectangles, they often included a torso, showing that they are aware of the torso but just did not know how to include it in their spontaneous drawings (see also Bassett, 1977; Cox & Mason, 1998). Golomb (2004, p. 55) reports cases in which tadpole drawers scrutinized their drawings and criticized them, saying, for example, "The arms are wrong! They go here (points to the shoulders)." These findings fail to support Freeman's position that failure to remember the trunk and the arms explains why these are omitted from tadpole humans.

Taken together, the evidence shows that defects of knowledge, memory, or understanding do not explain tadpoles. The tadpole is a simple, undifferentiated form that is, in Arnheim's (1974) terms, a clear structural equivalent for a human reflecting the difficulty of the drawing task, but not reflecting all that the child can do when pushed, prodded, and stimulated by clever tasks and instructions.

Between the ages of 3 to 4.5, as children move from the tadpole to a "conventional" figure with a body differentiated from the head (Cox, 1993), they sometimes draw transitional figures in which the arms are attached to the legs (as in Figure 20.6) and with body features, such as buttons or stomach, sometimes placed between the legs (Cox & Parkin, 1986). The transition from tadpole to conventional figure is variable, with some children passing through a very short tadpole

phase, and others spending many months in this phase. Cox and Parkin found that children often produce tadpoles and conventional figures at the same time. While the mechanism of change from tadpole to conventional figure is not clear, it seems likely that children change when they want to make their drawings fit the model more accurately, and not as a function of seeing models by older children or of explicit instruction (Cox, 1993, 1997).

Early conventional figures are sometimes produced by adding a cross-line between the legs of a tadpole, thereby creating a body (Goodnow, 1977). More often, children draw two vertical lines from the head and join them with a horizontal line at the bottom, and then add two legs under this (Cox, 1997). Most, however, draw a rounded body stuck to the head by starting a line from the head and then bringing it back up again, as the 4-year-old did in Figure 20.7.

At first, children add features such as fingers or feet in a segmented manner, giving each body part its own space with no overlapping (Goodnow, 1977). However, after the age of 5 or 6, children become able to draw with a continuous contour line, as illustrated in Figure 20.8, a method referred to by Goodnow (1977) as "threading." Cox (1993) found in her sample that 26% of 5- and 6-year-olds, 81% of 7- and 8-year-olds, and 96% of 9- and 10-year-olds drew figures with a continuous outline.

Typically, children (at least in the modern West) draw figures in frontal view but when given specific instructions that call for other orientations (e.g., draw a

**Figure 20.6**   Transitional figure with arms attached to legs. *Source:* From *The Child's Creation of a Pictorial World,* second edition, p. 46, figure 25b, by C. Golomb, 2004, Mahwah, NJ: Erlbaum. Reprinted with permission.

**Figure 20.7**   Conventional figure with head and body differentiated drawn by child aged five years and eight months who started a line from the head and made a loop for the body. *Source:* From *The Child's Creation of a Pictorial World,* second edition, p. 52, figure 33, by C. Golomb, 2004, Mahwah, NJ: Erlbaum. Reprinted with permission.

**Figure 20.8**   Human drawn by 9-year-old using continuous outline. *Source:* From *The Child's Creation of a Pictorial World,* second edition, p. 69, figure 51), by C. Golomb, 2004, Mahwah, NJ: Erlbaum. Reprinted with permission.

man running), many children over five can draw people in profile (Cox, 1993). Figure 20.9 shows a profile drawing by my son at 5 years, 8 months when asked to draw from observation in an art class—he had only a side view of the person he was asked to draw. But even 4-

**Figure 20.9**   Profile by 5-year-old drawn from observation. From the the author's collection.

year-olds make clumsy attempts (e.g., simply leaving out one eye) to alter their figure when asked to draw people from the back or side (Cox & Lambon Ralph, 1996; Cox & Moore, 1994; Pinto & Bombi, 1996).

*Realism*

Because of the assumption of a universal trajectory from object-centered representation toward viewer-centered optical realism, the dominant question in the study of children's drawings has been how realism develops. Some researchers have asked why children do not at first draw realistically, using perspective (Costall, 1995). Such a question assumes that perspectival drawings are simply tracings of what we see if we could only look with an "innocent eye," and that something prevents children from drawing what they see. According to Sully (1895), an early student of child art, "the child's eye at a surprisingly early period loses its primal 'innocence,' grows 'sophisticated' in the sense that instead of seeing what is really presented it sees, or pretends to see, what knowledge and logic tell it is there. In other words his sense-perceptions have for artistic purposes become corrupted by a too large admixture of intelligence" (p. 396, cited in Costall, 1995, p. 18). A similar analysis was proposed by Bühler (1930), who believed that verbal labels interfere with the innocent eye. "As soon as objects have received their names, the formation of concepts begins, and these take the place of concrete images. Conceptual knowledge, which is formulated in language, dominates the memory of the child" (p. 114, cited in Costall, 1995, p. 18).

More recently, Freeman (1987) proposed a similar view, based on Marr's (1982) theory that the initial stages of visual processing give viewer-centered information about the perspectivally distorted projected retinal image, followed by a translation into an object-centered description without the distortion. According to Freeman (1987) it is difficult to move from an object- to a viewer-centered description, because this requires "actively curbing normal perceptual habits" (p. 147, cited in Costall, 1995, p. 21). In short, knowledge gets in the way.

There is however no good reason to believe that children initially see the world in perspective. According to optical scientist Charles Falco, perspective is an unnatural consequence of a fixed lens locked into position pointing in a fixed direction and projecting an image onto a surface. We do not see in this way. Our eyes are constantly scanning a scene, providing our brains with anything but a fixed perspective (Falco, personal communication, July 7, 2003). It is difficult to draw in perspective, and perspective was a late development in the history of Western art, made possible by the discovery of rules as well as inventions of external devices (e.g., looking at a scene with one eye through an aperture; viewing a scene with one eye through a plane of glass and tracing the scene on the glass) that help the artist adopt a single vantage point from which to draw (Gombrich, 1977; Radkey & Enns, 1987).

Also mistaken is the assumption that perspectively correct pictures are clearer than any other kind. Many nonperspectival pictures, such as cartoons, caricatures, and children's drawings, are highly informative because they capture perceptual invariants such as straightness, bentness, perpendicularity, convergence, symmetry, and so on (Costall, 1995; Gibson, 1973, 1979).

**The Trajectory from Intellectual to Visual Realism.** Luquet's (1913, 1927) and Piaget and Inhelder's (1956) claim that children do not draw what they see (visual realism) but instead what they know (intellectual realism), is consistent with a nineteenth-century demonstration by Clark (1897) who showed that 6-year-olds drew an apple with a pin stuck in it so that the pin (which the child knew was inside the apple) was visible inside the apple, which thus appeared transparent. Piaget and Inhelder (1956) demonstrated the same phenomenon by asking children to draw a stick shown either from a side view or a foreshortened end view. Children under ages 7 to 8 drew a line or long region for both orientations. It would have been correct to depict the foreshortened stick as a circle, and circles are just as easy for the child to draw as a straight line, but children's depictions of the foreshortened stick were presumed to reflect their knowledge that the stick was long.

Do children draw in an intellectually realistic way because their knowledge interferes or because they can't figure out how to translate a three-dimensional object into a two-dimensional representation? Evidence for the first of these explanations comes from a study showing that when children copied drawings of cubes, they drew much less accurately than when they copied designs, which were matched to the cubes in number of lines and regions (Phillips, Hobbs, & Pratt, 1978). When children knew they were copying a cube, their knowledge that a cube has square faces interfered with realism and they did not distort the faces of the cube by drawing them as parallelograms. Figure 20.10 shows the two models chil-

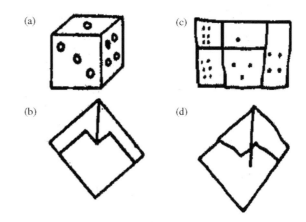

**Figure 20.10** Children copy pictures of cubes more accurately than they copy designs. (a) Cube model that children copied. (b) Design that children copied. (c) Intellectually realistic copy of cube. (d) Visually realistic correct copy of design. *Source:* From "Intellectual Realism in Children's Drawings of Cubes," by W. A. Phillips, S. B. Hobbs, and F. R. Pratt, 1978, *Cognition, 6*(1), pp. 15–33, Copyright © 1978 by Elsevier. Reprinted with permission from Elsevier.

dren were given to copy, and an example of an intellectually realistic copy of the cube and a fairly correct copy of the design. The fact that they were copying pictures of cubes rather than drawing from a three-dimensional model shows that in this case intellectual realism was not due to the difficulty of translating a three-dimensional image into a two-dimensional one because the drawing they were copying solved that problem for them. Presumably, their knowledge of a cube's actual shape interfered. Phillips, Hobbs, and Pratt (1978) suggest that young children have graphic-motor schemata for specific objects (e.g., when drawing a cube, they draw square faces). When they begin to draw a particular object, they select its corresponding schema; the observation of the object being copied then no longer influences the drawing.

There have been many demonstrations consistent with Luquet's (1913, 1927) original claim of a phase of intellectual realism followed by visual realism. One of the most often cited kinds of examples are X-ray or transparency drawings (Crook, 1984). For other research on children's development toward visual realism, see Barrett and Light (1976); Beyer and Nodine (1985); Bremner and Batten (1991); Bremner and Moore (1984); Chen (1985); Chen and Cook (1984); Colbert and Taunton (1988); Cox (1978, 1981, 1986); Crook (1985); A. Davis (1985); Freeman (1980); Ingram and Butterworth (1989); H. Lewis (1963); Light (1985);

Light and Humphreys (1981); Mitchelmore (1980); Nicholls and Kennedy (1992); Sutton and Rose (1998); Taylor and Bacharach (1982); Willats (1985); see Park and I (1995), for a review.

While there is ample evidence for intellectual realism in young children's drawings, we need not conclude that such drawings show us *all* that children know about the objects they draw. Young children are quite capable of producing viewer-centered drawings under certain conditions. For example, 6-year-olds who did not typically show occlusion were able to do so when they were asked to draw a toy policeman "hiding" behind a wall (Cox, 1981). Light and MacIntosh (1980) showed that when asked to draw a toy behind a glass, children drew the toy and glass side-by-side; when asked to draw a toy inside the glass, children drew realistically. While children under 7 to 8 draw cups with handles even when the handles are not visible (Freeman & Janikoun, 1972), they draw more accurately when asked to draw the cup exactly as it looks (Barrett, Beaumont, & Jennett, 1985; Barrett & Bridson, 1983; Beal & Arnold, 1990; Cox, 1978, 1981; C. Lewis, Russell, & Berridge, 1993; see also Cox & Martin, 1988). For a review of the conditions under which young children can produce viewer-centered drawings, see Sutton and Rose (1998). Thus, intellectual realism is best seen as a typical strategy rather than a full-blown stage.

Luquet (1927) argued that the shift to visual realism occurs because children recognize their drawings as failed in terms of realism and are therefore motivated to invent better methods. Piaget and Inhelder (1956, p. 178) argued, more plausibly, that the shift to visual realism occurred as a result of children becoming more aware of their own viewpoint. But Willats (1992, 1995) offers another explanation. He showed 4- to 12-year-olds a wooden figure holding a plate and asked them to draw it from both a foreshortened and nonforeshortened view. Four-year-olds made the same drawing from both views (showing that they were using object-centered descriptions that could be called examples of intellectual realism). But two-thirds of the 7-year-olds and almost all of the 12-year-olds changed their drawings in some way to show foreshortening, basing their drawings at least in part on what they saw. Willats reasoned that the foreshortened drawings were not a function of seeing more accurately but rather due to learning rules about line, rules specific to the graphic domain. His 4-year-olds drew single lines for arms (using lines to stand for linear objects) and round regions for plates (using regions to stand for round objects); a third of the 7-year-olds used regions rather than lines for both arms and plates; 12-year-olds used lines to stand for the edges of both arms and plates (using line to stand for edge rather than object). Only when they used lines to stand for edges were children also able to foreshorten. Willats argues that it is wrong to describe this sequence as moving from drawing what one knows to drawing what one sees because there is no reason to think that 12-year-olds see edges more clearly than do younger children. Rather, children have learned the rule (specific to the graphic domain) of using lines rather than regions as scene primitives, and this rule allows them to foreshorten.

Further evidence that drawing development does not progress by increasingly careful observation of the natural world comes from B. Wilson and Wilson (1977, 1984), who argue that realism is gained when children acquire pictorial schemata. They showed that children are more apt to copy each other's pictures than to draw from life. They reported that drawings by children and adolescents in their samples were always derived from another picture the drawer had seen. Moreover children in different cultures use different formulae for drawing trees, suggesting that they are using different pictures as models (Wilson & Ligtvoet, 1992). These views are consistent with those of Gombrich (1977), who argued that even the most "realistic" artists use pictorial schemata derived from other pictures. All pictures are schematic, but schemata are more obvious in children's drawings because they have fewer schemes and are less able to modify them (Thomas, 1995).

In considering the development of realistic depiction, it is important to remember that even the most realistic picture contains infinitely less information than does the actual scene (Gombrich, 1977), and thus the creation and perception of pictures both always require the ability to infer. Our knowledge of what we are drawing plays some role in allowing us to represent an object pictorially; our knowledge of what is represented in a picture also plays a role in helping us recognize what is represented. As Phillips, Hobbs, and Pratt (1978) point out, recognizing a realistic line drawing of a cube as a solid object requires some measure of what might be called intellectual realism. Our knowledge of what is depicted helps us see the drawing as a cube. There is no pure visual realism operating independently of knowledge.

**Representing Depth.**    Some of the studies reported earlier on the transition from intellectual to visual realism have shown children's difficulty in representing depth. Willats (1977, 1995) uncovered a series of stages that children go through as they acquire the graphic rules for creating the illusion of depth in a drawing. He asked children ages 5 to 17 to draw, from observation, a table with objects resting on it (Figure 20.11a). Five kinds of projective systems and five different sets of drawing rules for mapping objects onto the page were found. Drawings with no projection system were more common among the 5- to 7-year-olds than at older ages (Figure 20.11b). The most common strategy for 7- to 12-year-olds was to draw the table in orthographic projec-

tion, in which the tabletop was drawn as a line with objects resting on it, with the third dimension completely ignored (Figure 20.11c). This is a visually realistic way of depicting a table, and captures the view from eye level. The most common strategy for 12- to 13-year-olds was to use vertical oblique projection (Figure 20.11d), which is a system used in Indian, Islamic, and Byzantine art and never taught in Western art classes. Here the vertical dimension on the page represents the third dimension in the scene (vertical lines represent edges receding into depth). Vertical oblique projection allows children to show their knowledge that a table top is rectangular, but the drawing is no longer visually realistic. Moreover, this system results in ambiguity because it does not

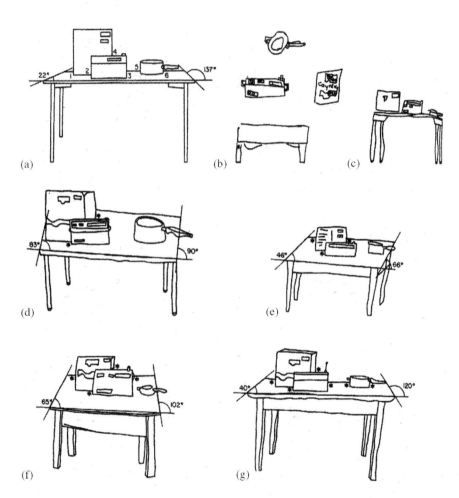

**Figure 20.11**    Drawings showing varying ways of depicting depth. (a) The tabletop children drew. (b) No projection system and objects float. (c) Orthographic projection with no indication of depth. (d) Vertical oblique projection where depth is ambiguously represented by vertical lines. (e) Oblique projection where depth is unambiguously represented by diagonal lines. (f) Naive perspective where lines converge but not at the correct angles. (g) Correct perspective. *Source:* From "How Children Learn to Draw Realistic Pictures," by J. Willats, 1977, *Quarterly Journal of Experimental Psychology, 29,* pp. 367–382. Reprinted with permission from the Experimental Psychology Society, http://www.psypress.co.uk/journals.asp.

disambiguate between high up versus receding into depth in the actual scene.

Only a minority of 13- to 14-year-olds figured out that one can resolve this ambiguity by using diagonal lines to indicate depth (Figure 20.11e; called oblique perspective—a system used in Asian art for centuries). Children using this system drew the tabletop as a parallelogram with diagonal lines representing edges receding into depth. The price they paid for creating a less ambiguous drawing is that they had to distort the rectangular shape of the table into a parallelogram. Forty percent of the drawings were in oblique projection, despite the fact that children rarely see drawings of this sort in illustrations.

The lines of true perspective drawings converge on a vanishing point; those of naive perspective do not converge sufficiently. Only a few children, between fifteen and a half and seventeen and a half, drew in naive perspective (Figure 20.11f); even fewer at this age drew in true perspective (Figure 20.11g). Consistent with Willats's findings, early collections of children's drawings included few perspective drawings even at adolescence (e.g., Kerschesteiner, 1905). Children in our culture do not naturally begin to draw in perspective, even though perspectival images are everywhere. Those who do draw in perspective have probably had training, or they are gifted in the visual arts (for descriptions of children gifted in drawing who figure out perspective early and essentially on their own, see Golomb, 2004, and Winner, 1996). Other studies of children learning to depict depth include Freeman, Eiser, and Sayers (1977); Light and MacIntosh (1980); Phillips, Innall, and Lauder (1985); Radkey and Enns (1987); and Reith and Dominin (1997).

Willats's stages show the complexity of the development of the ability to represent depth. The stages do not increase linearly in visual realism because the orthographic projections of stage 2 are actually more realistic than the vertical oblique projections that come next. Willats (1977) argued that perspective drawing develops not as a function of increasingly accurate observation of the world or of pictures, but rather due to the desire to reduce ambiguity. This view is consistent with Karmiloff-Smith's (1992) studies of children's overmarking in various domains (including drawing) to reduce ambiguity, and would explain the shift from vertical oblique to oblique perspective. Willats (1984, 1995) goes on to argue, in a manner that echoes Luquet (1927), that development away from object- to viewer-centered descriptions occurs as children begin to notice that their drawings do not fully capture how the scene really looks and begin to judge their drawings self-consciously in these terms. Children invent increasingly complex systems when they become aware of the limitations of the system they are using.

### Aesthetic Properties: Expression, Composition, Style, and Color

We know far less about aesthetic properties of children's drawings (e.g., expression, composition, style, color) than about representational properties, an imbalance that may reflect the assumption that the end state of visual art is realism.

**Expression.** While preschoolers' drawings appear expressive to adults, we cannot tell from spontaneous drawings whether the expressive properties are intentional. Some intervention is called for. When children were asked to draw a tree to complete a picture that was either gloomy (e.g., picturing a hunched-over figure with dark clouds overhead) or cheery (e.g., picturing a skipping person on a sunny day), they were unable to add expressively appropriate trees (e.g., drooping or dying tree versus blooming tree) until the age of about 11 (Carothers & Gardner, 1979). This finding would suggest that young children cannot intentionally express moods in their drawings. However, when instructions make it clear that children are to attend to expression, children succeed at a much younger age. This was shown in three studies. Asked directly to make a sad, happy, and angry tree, and a sad, happy, and angry line, even 4-year-olds succeed 37% of the time (Ives, 1984). In a study using equally explicit instructions, Winston et al. (1995) asked children ages 6, 9, and 12 to make a drawing of a tree that showed happiness, and one that showed sadness, adding that it did not matter if the tree looked like a real tree. Half of the children were given only a restricted set of colors (none of which could be used to represent a tree realistically), but all of which had been judged by young children to be either happy (e.g., yellow or orange) or sad (e.g., blue or purple). Children in this restricted condition were also told to make the tree without leaves or flowers, to maximize the chances they would use abstract properties to depict mood (e.g., color, line direction, size, or shape) rather than representational ones (e.g., a dying tree for sadness). Every child was able to use at least one strategy for expression. Older children were more likely than younger ones to use abstract properties expressively, though in the restricted condition, 6-year-olds used color expressively as often as did the 12-year-olds. Finally, when asked to look at a representational picture showing a person in either a happy, sad, calm, or excited mood, to think about the mood shown (but without being given any verbal labels for the moods), and to select from two abstract pictures the one that was most similar in mood (e.g., happy versus sad for the happy or sad target; calm versus excited for the calm or excited target), children performed above chance by age 4 or 7 (but not by age 3 or 8; Winner et al., 1986).

Thus, we can conclude that when directly asked to show certain very basic moods in their drawings, preschoolers show some ability to do so; by age 6, children reliably show moods in their drawings when asked to do so; and when their color choice is restricted to colors that cannot be used representationally to depict certain objects, 6-year-olds can use the abstract property of color to express moods. These findings are consistent with ones reported earlier showing that preschoolers can, under certain conditions, *perceive* expressive properties.

**Composition.** Studies of compositional principles in children's drawings show a development toward order and balance (Golomb, 1987, 2004; Golomb & Dunnington, 1985). Golomb and Farmer (1983) analyzed compositional principles found in over 1000 drawings of about 600 children ranging from 3 to 13 years of age. The most primitive compositional strategy, seen only infrequently in the drawings of 3-year-olds, was an aspatial one in which figures were placed arbitrarily across the page. This strategy was followed by a proximity strategy in which objects were clustered together. Both of these strategies gave way to alignment and centering.

The alignment principle was seen as young as age 3, with objects partially aligned side by side along an imaginary horizontal axis. The alignment is only partial because objects still appear to float about in space. Partial alignment was used by 3-year-olds 55% of the time in Golomb's (2004) samples. By age 4, figures were aligned carefully and evenly across the horizontal axis. Five- and 6-year-olds continued this strategy, but clearly located the figures at the bottom of the page, with the empty space on top representing the sky, thus defining up and down (see also Eng, 1931).

The centering principle can be seen in drawings of 3-year-olds. The earliest use of centering consists of a single figure placed in the middle of the page. This results in symmetry (recall that by 12 months of age children prefer vertical symmetry over asymmetry; Bornstein, Ferdinandsen, & Gross, 1981). Golomb (2004) found this kind of simple centering in 15% of 3-year-olds' drawings. By age 4, several figures may be balanced around the center (36% of 4-year-olds' drawings were centered). By age 5 and 6, symmetry was created by equal spacing of figures and repetition of elements. An increase in symmetry with age was also reported by Winner, Mendelsohn, and Garfunkel (1981).

Balance can also be achieved without symmetry, when different qualities counterbalance each other (e.g., a small bright form may be balanced by a larger pale form because brightness lends weight; Arnheim, 1974). This kind of "dynamic balance" was found by Winner et al. (1981) in 25% of drawings by children aged 4, 6, and 10. In contrast, dynamic balance was seen rarely by Golomb (2004), who found little change in compositional strategies after the ages of 9 to 13, perhaps due to children's competing interest in realistic depiction.

**Style.** Some children have recognizable drawing styles by age 5. This was demonstrated in a study in which adults judged the similarity relationships among pairs of drawings by three 5-year-old children (Hartley, Somerville, Jenson, & Eliefja, 1982). Their judgments showed that drawings by two of these children were cohesive, meaning they had a distinctive style. Judges were also able to recognize new drawings by the same two children drawn at the same time as well as 9 months later. An even stronger demonstration that children have persistent drawing styles was reported by Pufall and Pesonen (2000) who found that adults who learned to recognize the style of three 5-year-olds could identify drawings by these children done 4 years later. But Watson and Schwartz (2000) showed that only about a third of the children in their sample showed a distinctive style, with younger ones (5- to 8-year-olds) showing greater distinctiveness than older children (9- to 10-year-olds). Perhaps this decline is due to drawings in middle childhood becoming conventional, stereotyped, and less playful than those in the preschool years, as is discussed later.

### Universality versus Cultural Specificity of Drawing Schemas

Many aspects of drawing development appear to be universal and to emerge independently of culture and formal training (Alland, 1983; Anati, 1967; Belo, 1955; Dennis, 1957; Fortes, 1981; Golomb, 2004; Havighurst, Gunther, & Pratt, 1946; Jahoda, 1981; Kellogg, 1969; Kerschensteiner, 1905; McBride, 1986; Paget, 1932; Ricci, 1887; Sundberg & Ballinger, 1968; B. Wilson & Wilson, 1984). Yet, strong cultural differences in children's drawings also exist. For example, perspective is rarely found in the art of children (or adults) who are not exposed to realistic graphic representations (Golomb, 2002, chap. 4). And schemas for representing particular objects vary across cultures. For example, B. Wilson and Wilson (1981) report that many schemas in children's figure drawings common in the nineteenth century are rarely seen today, a finding which they attribute to the importance of models for children to copy. One such feature is the two-eyed profile. Ricci (1887) found that 70% of Italian children's profiles had two eyes, and half of Sully's (1895) English children's drawings were two-eyed profiles. In the Florence Goodenough "Draw a Man" collection of children's drawings amassed between 1917 to 1923 and housed at Pennsylvania State University, only about 5% were two-eyed profiles. By the 1950s, these figures were nowhere to be seen in American children's drawings. The demise of the two-eyed profile has been attributed to the decline of the profile as the culture's most characteristic pictorial view of the face and the rise of the daily comic strip with figures in every possible orientation (B. Wilson & Wilson, 1981). Wilson and Wilson note many other features that used to be found in children's drawings but are no longer: For example, ladder mouths (where the mouth looks like a horizontal ladder, with the rungs being the teeth), hands like garden rakes, and milk-bottle shaped bodies. Wilson and Wilson predict that future investigators may wonder about the origin and decline of figures with big biceps and capes flying through the air. Children's drawings, Wilson and Wilson remind us, do not emerge from some kind of innate program but instead are heavily influenced by the cultural models available to the child to copy.

The powerful effect of the pictorial culture was also demonstrated by B. Wilson and Wilson (1987) in a comparison between drawings by 12-year-olds from Egypt versus Japan. The Egyptian children were exposed to few pictures and had little arts instruction in school. Their drawings of human figures were static, figures floated in space, and there were only primitive attempts to depict depth. In contrast, the Japanese children were heavily exposed to images in Japanese comic books (and also had a richer arts education). Their drawings of humans looked very much like the images in the comic books that they read: The drawings were dynamic (the figures were depicted in motion), complex (there were many figures), the figures were grounded, and depth was represented through occlusion and size diminution.

Winner (1989) noticed the strong influence on Chinese children's drawings of cartoonlike images published in children's magazines. Wilson (1997) made the same observation about Japanese children who now draw humans with heart-shaped faces and huge eyes, images copied from popular comic books called *Manga*. Moreover sequential graphic narratives are far more common among Japanese children (showing the influence of *Manga*) than they are among Egyptian children (B. Wilson & Wilson, 1987; for other work on cultural influences on drawing, see Andersson, 1995a, 1995b; Court, 1989; Cox, 1998; Cox, Koyasu, Hiranumu, & Perara, 2001; Martlew & Connolly, 1996; Piaget, 1932; Stratford & Au, 1988; B. Wilson & Wilson, 1977, 1984).

## Does Drawing Skill Improve Linearly with Age?

While all would agree that technical drawing skills improve steadily with age, including the ability to draw realistically, researchers disagree about whether aesthetic properties of children's drawings improve linearly with age. Some aspects of drawing ability have been shown to be U-shaped, declining after the preschool years, only to return again in those children with talent and interest in drawing. Resemblances between the art of twentieth-century masters and drawings by young children (in terms of playfulness, simplicity, expressivity, and aesthetic appeal) have been noted (Arnheim, 1974; Gardner, 1980; Hagen, 1986; Schaeffer-Simmern, 1948; Winner & Gardner, 1981).

Children draw less frequently as they grow older (Cox, 1992; S. Dennis, 1991; Golomb, 2002) and drawings become conventional and lose their playfulness by age 9 or 10 (Gardner, 1980). A similar decline has been reported in the domain of metaphor (Winner & Gardner, 1981): Understanding of metaphor improves linearly with age, but the willingness to play with language and create metaphors dips in the middle school years, giving way to a desire to use words in a literally correct manner.

Support for the observation that the playful aspects of drawing decline with age during the literal stage, but emerge again in adolescence, comes from a study showing that young children are more willing to violate realism than are older children (Winner, Blank, Massey, & Gardner, 1983). Children ages 6 through 12 were given copies of black-and-white line drawings by artists varying in level of realism (e.g., a realistic Picasso versus a nonrealistic Picasso) and each with a small portion of the drawing deleted. Children were asked to finish the drawings the way the artist would have done. When the drawings were representational, children were told to add the "hair" or the "arm" and were shown where the drawing was incomplete. Responses were scored by whether the level of realism in the drawing was matched in the completion. Six-year-olds performed better than both 8- and 10-year-olds and did as well as the 12-year-olds. Thus, for example, 6-year-olds completed a schematic, nonrealistic Picasso drawing with a missing arm by adding an arm with a nonrealistic, schematic hand; they completed a realistic Picasso, also with a missing hand, with a far more realistic hand. In contrast, 8- and 10-year-olds completed all works in an equally realistic way. They were preoccupied with trying to draw realistically and thus were unable or unwilling to draw nonrealistically even when this tactic was called for by the criterion of stylistic consistency. Because the 6- to 12-year-olds performed equally well and better than the 8- to 10-year-olds, the willingness to violate realism was found to be U-shaped.

J. Davis (1997) provided the strongest evidence for U-shaped development in drawing. She elicited drawings by the following groups: Those presumed to be at the high end of the U-curve in aesthetic dimensions of their drawings (5-year-olds), those presumed to be in the depths of the literal, conventional stage (8-, 11-, 14-year-olds and adults, all nonartists), and those presumed to have moved beyond the literal stage (14-year-old self-declared artists and professional adult artists). Participants were asked to make three drawings under the following instructions: Draw happy, draw sad, and draw angry. Judges blind to group scored the drawings for overall expression, overall balance, appropriate use of line as a means of expression (e.g., sharp angled lines to express anger), and appropriate use of composition as a means of expression (e.g., asymmetrical composition as more expressive of sadness than a symmetrical composition). The results were clear: Scores for the adult artists' drawings were significantly higher than scores for the works of children ages 8, 11, 14 (nonartists) and adults (nonartists), but did not differ from the scores of two other groups—the youngest children (age 5) and the

adolescents who saw themselves as artists. Thus, only the 5-year-olds' drawings were similar to those by adult and adolescent artists, revealing a U-shaped developmental curve for aesthetic dimensions of drawing. While the adult artists often depicted a mood through nonrepresentational drawings, all but one of the 5-year-olds drew representational works. Thus, artists and young children used different means to achieve equally clear expression.

Pariser and van den Berg (1997) countered that the U-shaped curve is culturally determined—a product of the Western expressionist aesthetic. They found that while Westerners judged preschool art as more aesthetic than that of older children, Chinese American judges, influenced by their own more traditional, nonmodernist artistic tradition, awarded higher scores to older than younger children's art. This finding, if replicated in other studies, shows that the U-curve is a manifestation of how we judge children's art, and could be a product a Western modernist expressionist aesthetic.

The loss of interest in drawing, and the loss of expressiveness in drawing (as perceived by Westerners) in the middle childhood years, may not be inevitable. Arts education plays a very small role in our schools. It is certainly possible (though yet untested) that if the visual arts were taught seriously throughout the school years, no decline in interest or expressiveness would be found.

## MUSIC

Music is a near-constant presence in our lives, whether on the radio, TV, elevator, or concert hall, and almost all people love some kind of music. While we may not be able to talk explicitly about what it is that we hear when we listen to music, we have a great deal of implicit knowledge about music, based on certain innate sensitivities (to be discussed later) and years of exposure to the music of our culture.

Because almost all of the developmental research on music has been conducted on Western children exposed to Western tonal music, we know little about development in non-Western musical traditions. However, many musical universals exist. For example, all cultures have a systematic way of organizing pitches that repeat over octaves, and all scales have a limit of about seven pitches within an octave (Dowling & Harwood, 1986). Individuals from different musical traditions share the ability to perceive notes separated by octaves as equivalent (octave equivalence); and there is a weaker tendency to perceive the perfect fifth as having a special status (Dowling, 1991). Almost all scales divide the octave into five to seven pitches with unequal steps between them (A to A sharp is a half step, A to B is a whole step; the Western diatonic major scale is made up of seven notes; Sloboda, 1985). This property, which leads to a sense of motion and rest or tension and resolution is not found in the regularity of chromatic scales, which have 12 equally spaced notes (and in which, therefore, every tone has equal status), and might account for why chromatic scales have never been widespread (Shepard, 1982).

Although musical universals exist (as do universals in drawing), we also know that exposure to the music of one's culture has a profound effect on musical development. Western music, whether folk, rock, classical, or songs sung to infants, consists of a fairly small set of musical relationships, which form the basis of all of our music, and from which composers often deliberately deviate to create tension and affect (Lerdahl & Jackendoff, 1983; Meyer, 1956, 1973). How we hear music is constrained by our years of exposure to these basic relationships. Adults in Western culture have internalized tonal structure and tonality organizes our perception of music (D. Bartlett, 1996; Dewar, Cuddy, & Mewhort, 1977; Frances, 1988; Krumhansl, 1979; Lipscomb, 1996). For example, the major scale is the most common structure found in Western European music, and Western listeners find it easier to recall melodies in the major scale than in any other kind of scale (Cuddy, Cohen, & Mewhort, 1981).

## Evolutionary Base

Evidence of music making exists in every known human culture, from hunter-gatherers to industrial cultures (Miller, 2000). Evidence that Neanderthals had music comes from the discovery of a flute carved out of the bone of a bear and dated between 42,000 and 82,000 years ago (Wallin, Merker, & Brown, 2001). This bone had three holes, with the distance between the second and third hole twice that of the distance between the third and fourth, indicating that this flute played music based on the Western diatonic scale. We should not be too quick to conclude from this discovery that the diatonic scale is the most "natural," however, because other scales may also certainly have been used by Neanderthals or early humans.

Some have argued that music evolved for mate selection (Miller, 2000) or for group cohesion (Hagen & Bryant, 2003). Scholars may never resolve the question of whether music is a complex adaptation that occurred during evolution (Miller, 2000) or a by-product of other abilities that themselves evolved for adaptive purposes (Hauser & McDermott, 2003).

Comparative studies of musical abilities in nonhumans can help to clarify the evolutionary history of music. Here we must make a clear distinction between music production (either singing or with instruments) and music perception. No nonhuman primates sing (Hauser & McDermott, 2003), although one (Kanzi, a bonobo) showed controlled drumming on an object and bobbed his head rhythmically as he drummed (Kugler & Savage-Rumbaugh, 2002). Aside from Kanzi, the only nonhumans known to produce music are birds and birdsong is far more constrained than is human music (Hauser & McDermott, 2003).

With respect to music perception, some striking similarities have been found between human and nonhuman primate abilities. Wright, Rivera, Hulse, Shyan, and Neiworth (2000) trained rhesus monkeys to make same/different judgments of melodies and found that they treated a melody as the same when it was transposed by 1 to 2 octaves in the same key. However, if the transposition was only half or one and a half octaves from the original, the transposition (which was then in a new key) was not heard as the same as the original. This finding shows that monkeys hear two Cs as the same, even though they are separated by eight notes (octave generalization), but they hear a C and a G as different even though they are closer on the scale. Wright et al. also found that the perception of similarity between two notes an octave or two apart occurred only when the notes were part of melodies based on the diatonic scale, and not when atonal melodies were used (melodies whose notes are chosen from the 12 tones of the chromatic scale). We can conclude that nonhuman primates are sensitive to tonality and octave relationships (and we will see that human infants are as well).

Although monkeys show a humanlike sensitivity to musical structure, they do not create music. Hauser and McDermott (2003) argue that this frees us from the burden of explaining the evolutionary function of music. Human musical capacities (or at least some of them) may not have evolved as a special music faculty but instead may have drawn on auditory sensitivities that evolved for other purposes. Domain-general auditory capacities likely evolved before humans began to make music, and at least some basic human musical capacities depend on these more general auditory capacities. The same kind of argument holds for speech perception: Chinchillas perceive some speech sounds categorically, as do human infants, and from this it has been argued that the mechanisms underlying speech perception originally evolved for auditory perception and were later co-opted for speech perception (Hauser, Chomsky, & Fitch, 2002).

Hauser and McDermott (2003) suggest that the human music faculty may also have co-opted another mechanism for music—the mechanism by which human and nonhuman animals express emotion via vocalization, and the sensitivity that young children have to the emotional message in others' voices. Sensitivity to rhythm may also have evolved for nonmusical reasons. Ramus, Hauser, Miller, Morris, and Mehler (2000) showed that human infants and cotton-top tamarin monkeys could discriminate Dutch from Japanese sentences (languages that have different rhythmic properties). Thus, the ability to perceive rhythm may initially have served purposes other than musical or linguistic ones (given that monkeys have neither music nor language).

## Historical and Theoretical Approaches

After von Helmholtz published *On the Sensations of Tone as a Physiological Basis for the Theory of Music* (1877), interest in the acoustics of music was sparked. Perhaps the most influential early music psychologist in the United States was Seashore (1919, 1938). Other early music psychologists included Farnsworth (1928), Mursell (1937), Révész (1954), Stumpf (1883), Valentine (1962), and Wing (1968).

Early music psychologists conflated music perception with acoustics. They focused on the measurement of individual differences in musical aptitude, and numerous tests of musical aptitude were developed (for a review, see Shuter, 1968, chap. 2). The publication of the *Seashore Measures of Musical Talent* (Seashore, 1919) was a seminal event in the psychology of music, offering the possibility of assessing musical ability in children and adults primarily through degrees of acoustical discrimination (e.g., determining which of two tones is higher or louder, or which note in a melody has been altered). Seashore assumed musical ability to

be unaffected by training and to be adequately measured by acoustical tests, views criticized by Farnsworth (1928) and Mursell (1937).

Validity problems with the Seashore measures were noted by Mursell (1937), who found that they did not correlate highly with independent measures of musicality (defined as being in the advanced orchestra in school). This lack of validity did not surprise Mursell because he reasoned that people with good pitch discrimination skill are not necessarily musical. He criticized the atomistic approach underlying these measures. For example, it is quite possible for an individual to hear a melody as changed yet be unable to say which note was altered. Mursell also criticized the Seashore measures for focusing primarily on acoustic properties of music and on sensory capacities, ignoring important musical concepts such as the feeling of resolution when a piece ends. "Music . . . depends on the mind and not on the ear," Musell wrote (p. 57). Mursell called for the development of tests of musical aptitude that assessed judgments of rhythmic and tonal *relationships* (rather than sensory response to isolated elements) as well as affective responsiveness to music. Révész (1954) also pointed out that musical aptitude is not simply an aggregation of acoustical skills.

Since the cognitive revolution in psychology, with its focus on universal mental structures, music psychologists have turned their attention away from tests of individual differences to the search for universal principles of music perception. Psychologists of music have also begun to connect their work closely to the work of music theorists. Cook (1994) links the relationship between music theory and psychological studies of music to the work of music theorist Meyer (1956). Music theorists have developed models of musical grammar, which offer predictions for cognitive psychologists to test, with perhaps the most influential model being the grammar of music initially proposed by Lerdahl and Jackendoff (1983). For reviews of theory driven research in the cognitive psychology of music with the goal of determining the mental structures involved in the perception and interpretation of music, see Deutsch (1982) and Sloboda (1985).

Early developmental research in music consisted primarily of descriptive studies including case studies (e.g., Gesell & Ilg, 1946; Moorhead & Pond, 1978). For example, describing age norms in responses to music, Shinn (1907) reported that children show pleasure at music at around 6 weeks, and Shirley (1933) noted that children are calmed by music between 12 to 32 weeks of age. For a review of early studies, see chapters 5 and 6 in Shuter (1968).

One of the earliest theory-driven approaches to the developmental psychology of music analyzed children's music perception in the framework of Piagetian theory (e.g., Pflederer, 1964; Serafine, 1980). These researchers tried to equate the perception of invariance in music with conservation and hence with concrete operations. In the past few decades, research in the developmental psychology of music has become motivated less by developmental theory than by theories in the cognitive psychology of music.

The new cognitively driven research in the psychology of music (including developmental music research) has not been immune from controversy (see Cook, 1994, and Sloboda, 1985, pp. 151–154). Some have argued that psychologists have too quickly assumed psychological reality for abstract grammars proposed by music theorists in their analysis of music. For example, Cook (1994) argues against the idea of music grammars analogous to linguistic grammars, pointing to evidence that music is more "fluid" than language, and less rule-bound.

Another controversy concerns the use of experimental materials that are short, artificial, and musically impoverished. Sloboda (1985) reminds researchers that in real pieces of music, musical events distant from one another in time may still be closely related. Just as the linguistic study of isolated sentences cannot tell us how we respond to conversations or stories, so the study of short musical fragments (e.g., an interval or a phrase) or isolated musical elements (e.g., pitches or rhythms without melody) cannot tell us about mental activity as we listen to an actual piece of music. The use of short fragments leads us to conclude that music perception is more precisely and analytically rule-governed and less fluid and holistic than it actually is (Cook, 1994). For example, short fragments that do not return to the tonic or the home key sound unfinished; but long pieces of music may well not return to the home key and yet do not sound unfinished Cook (1994). Aiello (1994) calls for more naturalistic studies of how we perceive entire pieces of music as the music unfolds, and reviews several recent studies that do just this. Developmental studies of music perception that are more naturalistic will likely be the wave of the future.

Much of the research reviewed later is subject to the criticisms that the materials on which its conclusions

are based are far from real pieces of music. Similar criticisms—that the stimuli and tasks used are too artificial—have been leveled at studies of children's drawings (Golomb, 2004, p. 40). Yet, hypothesis testing often requires the use of somewhat impoverished stimuli. The tension between those who do experimental versus naturalistic studies can be found in all areas of psychology.

## Music Perception and Comprehension: Major Milestones in Development

While the ability to produce music shows wide variation, with some individuals demonstrating more talent than others, all normal humans have a considerable implicit understanding of music. And infants show an impressive perhaps inborn ability to process some (but not all) of the complexities of music.

The lullabies that adults sing to babies have universal properties across cultures, and these may influence early music perception skills. Infants show certain kinds of very early sensitivities to music. These include sensitivity to relational rather than absolute properties of melody and rhythm; sensitivity to unequal step structure in scales, a property that characterizes all scales whether Western or non-Western; sensitivity to certain prototypical structures of Western music; and preference for consonance over dissonance.

Other aspects of music perception develop only in the preschool years or later. These include sensitivity to diatonic tonal structure, sensitivity to key changes, sensitivity to the hierarchy of notes within a key, sensitivity to mode (major versus minor and the emotional connotations of each); and sensitivity to invariant structure. These later developments all involve the ability to go beyond the information given to infer a structure that is not literally present. Western children's sensitivity to these higher order properties of music very likely depends on years of exposure to Western music. Whether we are universally predisposed to acquire the structures used in Western tonal music, or whether we could as easily become acculturated to atonal music, is a question for future research.

### *Infant Music Perception: Sensitivity to Simple Musical Structures*

In many ways, infants process music in an adultlike fashion, suggesting that the ways in which music is processed is biologically constrained and innate. These findings, reviewed here, provide support for Meyer's

(1994) view that "the central nervous system . . . predisposes us to perceive certain pitch relationships, temporal proportions, and melodic structures as well shaped and stable" (p. 289, cited in Trehub, Schellenberg, & Hill, 1997, p. 122). However, because infants are exposed to music in utero and from the 1st day they are born, experience may play a role. Even studies that examine primate musical predispositions are not immune from this possibility because primates may be exposed to music in the lab from radios (Hauser & McDermott, 2003). Only if we can demonstrate humanlike musical predispositions in primates in the wild (not exposed to music) or identical musical predispositions in infants in cultures with entirely different musical traditions can we make the strong argument that certain musical predispositions are inborn and require no musical experience for them to become manifest. This research remains to be carried out.

Music processing in infancy is analogous to speech processing in several ways: (a) Infants must process complex sound patterns with affective rather than referential meaning; (b) there are special forms of music and speech directed to infants; and (c) infants' lack of acculturation allows them to make certain discriminations in music and speech that adults fail to make, as shown later (Trehub, Trainor, & Unyk, 1993).

**Universals in Songs Sung to Infants.** In all known cultures, children are exposed to music from early on, particularly in the form of songs sung to them by adults (Trehub & Schellenberg, 1995). Just as infants are exposed to child-directed-speech with certain universal properties, they are also exposed to child-directed-songs with universal properties. The types of songs infants hear are lullabies and "play songs" (Trehub & Trainor, 1998). Much like infant-directed speech, songs directed to infants in Western and non-Western cultures have certain characteristic and universal features that cut across musical traditions. These features are seen when the songs are sung by mothers, fathers, and even preschoolers.

Songs directed to infants are soothing: They are repetitive and have simple, descending contours. Unlike classical Western music or adult Western folk songs, Western nursery songs almost all remain in the same key. Dowling (1988) demonstrated this by coding 223 nursery songs, 317 folk songs, and 44 of Schubert's songs in terms of whether they contained a key shift. Almost none of the nursery songs, almost half of the adult

folk songs, and almost all of Shubert's songs contained a key shift. Nursery songs repeat strongly tonal patterns and thus may be particularly helpful for Western children's learning of the Western tonal scale system (Dowling, 1988). Songs directed to infants are higher in pitch, slower in tempo, and more emotionally expressive than songs directed to older children or to adults (Bergeson & Trehub, 1999; Trainor, Clark, Huntley, & Adams, 1997; Trehub, Unyk, & Henderson, 1994; Trehub, Unyk, Kamenetsky, Trainor, Henderson, & Saraza, 1997; Trehub, Unyk, & Trainor, 1993a, 1993b). Mothers' singing is stable, almost ritualized: When they sing the same song to their infants, the pitch level, and tempo remain practically unchanged (Bergeson & Trehub, 2002).

These aspects of infant-directed songs are perceivable by adults. Adults can distinguish lullabies from nonlullabies matched in tempo even when these come from unfamiliar cultures (Trehub, Unyk, & Trainor, 1993a). Adults can even distinguish songs *actually* sung to infants from the same songs sung by the same singers *pretending* to sing to an infant. This finding holds for musically untrained as well as foreign adults, suggesting the existence of universal features of songs sung to infants (Trehub, Unyk, Kamenetsky, et al., 1997).

The universal aspects of songs sung to babies capture babies' attention. Infants listen longer to songs in the maternal style than to songs sung by the same singers in their usual style (Masataka, 1999; Trainor, 1996) and prefer higher to lower pitched versions of songs (Trainor & Zacharias, 1998). Infants also pay more attention to videotapes of their mothers singing than tapes of them speaking (Nakata & Trehub, 2000). These attention-getting universal aspects of songs sung to infants probably help to mold infants' musical sensitivities.

**Relational Processing of Rhythm and Melody.** Like adults, infants perceive rhythms and melodies as coherent patterns rather than sequences of unrelated sounds (Dowling, 1978; Trehub, Schellenberg, et al., 1997). For instance, 7- to 9-month-olds perceive simple rhythmic patterns differing in speed as the same rhythm—they recognize the rhythm despite the change in speed (Trehub & Thorpe, 1989). Chang and Trehub (1977b) demonstrated a similar capacity in 5-month-olds.

Relational processing also occurs for melodies. Contours—the pattern of ups and downs in a melody—are defining properties of melodies for adults (Dowling & Fugitani, 1971) and for infants (Dowling, 1999; Trehub,

2001; Trehub, Schellenberg, et al., 1997). Infants perceive two melodies as the same when one is transposed to a new octave, as long as the relations among tones (and hence the melodic contour) are maintained. For example, 6-month-olds were habituated to a 6-note melody and then exposed to a key transposition either with or without the contour maintained (Chang & Trehub, 1977a). In both cases, the transposition contained all new notes. Infants dishabituated only to the contour-altered transpositions. Because the initial and transposed tune shared contour but not notes, the infants must have "recognized" the melody. Infants are sensitive to alterations in contour, noticing them even when the task is made difficult by inserting distractor tones in between the target and comparison melody (Trehub, Bull, & Thorpe, 1984). Thus, in both rhythm and melody, infants perceive simple musical gestalts, whether these be rhythmic groupings or melodic contours.

Infants are sometimes able to recall absolute rather than relative information when it comes to pitch (Saffran, 2003; Saffran & Griepentrog, 2001). When presented with a target and comparison melody that have the same key or same initial pitch, infants react to pitch changes (Lynch, Eilers, Oller, & Urbano, 1990). For example, when they hear a melody containing a G sharp and then a comparison melody identical except that the G sharp has been replaced by G, infants note the change (Trehub, Cohen, Thorpe, & Morrongiello, 1986). But such sensitivity is found only when all other pitches are unchanged. If the comparison melody is transposed, infants do not notice the change from G sharp to G and revert back to focusing on relational aspects of the melody (Cohen, Thorpe, & Trehub, 1987).

Studies claiming a dominance of absolute over relative pitch processing in infancy are based on short-term memory. When 6-month-olds listened to melodies over a period of days they could not tell when the melodies were transposed to a new key and thus recalled relative rather than absolute pitch intervals (Platinga & Trainor, 2002, cited in Trehub, 2003a, 2003b). Storing the relational information is a far more manageable feat of long-term memory than storing separate pitches.

Infants grasp other kinds of structures in music as well as rhythmic and melodic ones, as shown by their greater reaction to structure-violating changes than to structure-preserving changes. For example, when infants repeatedly heard a six-note sequence (e.g., AAAEEE, with A and E one fifth apart), and then heard the same sequence with a temporal gap, they noticed the gap only

when it occurred within (AAAE [gap] EE) but not between (AAA [gap] EEE) groups (Thorpe & Trehub, 1989; see Dowling, 1973, for this finding in adults). And infants also perceive phrases as wholes, as shown by Krumhansl and Jusczyk (1990) who reported the finding that 4- and 6-month-olds prefer to listen to Mozart when pauses are inserted *between* rather than *within* musical phrases. Parallels to speech processing are clear, because infants notice pauses within rather than between sentential clauses (Kemler Nelson, Hirsh-Pasek, Jusczyk, & Wright Cassidy, 1989) and are sensitive to melodic contours of speech (Fernald, 1989).

**Sensitivity to the Unequal-Step Structure of Musical Scales.** As mentioned, almost all music has scales with unequal steps between pitches. Can infants distinguish between scales with unequal steps and artificial scales with equal steps? Trehub, Schellenberg, and Kamenetsky (1999) played one of three types of scales to adults and 9-month-olds: (1) the familiar (unequal step) major scale; (2) an artificial major scale with unequal steps, created by dividing the octave into 11 equal units and selecting seven tones separated either by one or two units; and (3) an artificial equal-step scale created by dividing the octave into seven equal steps. The task was to detect a note that was out of tune. Adults had no difficulty with the major scale, but performed equally poorly on the two artificial scales. Infants did as well on the familiar as the artificial major scale (both have unequal steps). These findings show that unequal step scales are easier to process than are equal step scales. The fact that infants did as well on the artificial major scale shows that their performance with the familiar major scale was not due to familiarity but rather to its unequal step property. The fact that adults performed poorly on the artificial unequal step scale suggests that their initial predispositions were overridden by years of listening to the scales of their culture.

**Sensitivity to "Good" Melody Structure or "Good" Intervals.** Infants show better processing for melodies that Western music theory considers well-structured. Cohen et al. (1987) showed that 7- to 11-month-olds were better able to detect a semitone change in a transposition of a melody if the transposition resulted in a well-structured melody based on the major triad (CEGEC) than if it resulted in a less well-structured melody based on the augmented triad (CEGsharp EC). Similarly, Trehub, Thorpe, and Trainor (1990) found that

7- to 10-month-olds detected a semitone change (in a transposition) only when the original melody was a "good" Western melody in which all the notes belonged to a major scale (in contrast to a "bad" Western melody with notes not in any scale or to a non-Western melody with intervals less than one semitone apart). And Trainor and Trehub (1993) showed that infants have a processing advantage for transpositions related by a perfect fifth. The most likely explanation for infants' better performance with certain types of melodies and intervals that are privileged in Western music is that these infants have already acquired a sensitivity to Western musical structure. Yet, we cannot rule out the possibility that certain structures in Western music are intrinsically easier to process than are violations of these structures. To test this, we need to administer these same tasks to infants from a culture whose music does not follow these structures.

**Preference for Consonance.** Intervals separated by one semitone (e.g., a "second" such as A and B) sound dissonant; those separated by two semitones (e.g., a "third" such as A and C) sound consonant. Pythagoras showed that consonant combinations of tones have different frequency ratios than do dissonant combinations (e.g., the consonant octave has a frequency ratio of 2:1; the dissonant tritone has a frequency ratio of 45:32; Plomp & Levelt, 1965). Intervals related by simple ratios have more overtones in commons than do intervals related by complex ratios. Consonant intervals such as octaves and perfect fifths have a special status in much of the world's music (Frances, 1988; Schellenberg & Trehub, 1996; Trehub, Schellenberg, & Hill, 1997), and studies show a preference for consonance over dissonance in early infancy.

Zentner and Kagan (1996, 1998) played 4-month-olds two unfamiliar melodies in both a consonant and a dissonant version. The consonant version was played in parallel thirds (the third is the interval that adults judge as consonant); the dissonant version was played in parallel minor seconds (the interval judged by adults as most dissonant). Infants looked significantly longer at the source of the music and showed significantly less motor activity when they heard the consonant version, showing that they distinguished consonance from dissonance. Zentner and Kagan speculate that the findings also show that infants *prefer* consonance to dissonance because the dissonant version promoted more motor activity (including more fretting and turning away) and less fixation time, indicating a distressed state of arousal.

Zentner and Kagan's (1996, 1998) research confounded consonance with pitch distance (the consonant intervals were wider), but a study by Trainor and Heinmiller (1998) kept interval size constant and again reported a preference for consonance. Six-month-olds heard consonant intervals (e.g., perfect fifths or octaves) and dissonant intervals (e.g., tritones or minor ninths). The infants controlled listening time by their looking behavior, and they looked longer to the consonant intervals. In a second experiment, 5- and 6-month-olds heard a Mozart minuet played as Mozart had composed it as well as a dissonant version of the minuet in which the Gs and Ds were changed to G flat and D flat. Again infants listened longer to the consonant versions.

Preference for consonant over dissonant intervals has been shown in even younger infants though the results were not clear-cut. As in the study by Trainor and Heinmiller (1998), Trainor, Tsang, and Cheung (2002) played consonant chords (perfect fifths and octaves) and dissonant chords (tritones and minor ninths) to 2- and 4-month-olds who could control how long the sound lasted by looking behavior. When infants heard consonant chords first, there was a near-significant tendency for them to look longer to the consonant trials. But when they heard the dissonant chords first, they did not look longer at consonant trials. Trainor, Tsang, and Cheung (2002) suggest that perhaps the dissonant chords displeased the infants so much that they did not resume interest when the consonant chords were played next (see also Trainor & Trehub, 1993; Trehub, Thorpe, & Trainor, 1990).

Numerous other studies have also shown a preference for consonant over dissonant intervals in infancy. For example, infants as young as 6 months detect quarter semitone changes in intervals when the first interval heard is an octave, a "perfect fifth," and a perfect fourth (Schellenberg & Trehub, 1996), but they cannot detect such subtle changes when the first interval heard is a tritone, a chord considered to be unpleasing and nonharmonious. And octave intervals, the most consonant of all intervals, are clearly perceived by infants. Like adults, infants perceive octave equivalence of pitch: They can tell the difference between a pair of tones separated precisely by one octave versus a pair separated by almost an octave (Demany & Armand, 1984).

Whether perception of consonance as more pleasant than dissonance is inborn and a function of the human auditory system, as von Helmholtz (1877) believed (see also Plomp & Levelt, 1965; Tramo, Cariani, Delgutte, & Braida, 2001), or whether such judgments are due only to the greater familiarity of consonance given its special status, could be determined by examining infants' judgments prior to any music exposure. However, because infants hear music in utero, this study would be difficult to carry out and has not been done. Instead, we must make inferences from studies of infants several months old and we cannot rule out the effects of exposure on any kind of outcome. We can also look to animal studies. One study showed that rats develop a preference for consonance over 3 weeks (Borchgrevink, 1975, reviewed in Zentner & Kagan, 1998). However, this preference emerged only after exposure and thus cannot illuminate the question of whether a preference for consonance is innate in rats, much less in humans.

Researchers should be careful not to draw the conclusion that infants' preference for consonance explains why adults have difficulty making sense of atonal music (e.g., the music of Schoenberg) in which dissonance is prominent. The kind of dissonance in atonal music is far more subtle and complex than that which is created by simply playing two adjacent notes at the same time, and the perception of dissonance in atonal music results from the context in which the interval is heard (Cazden, 1980). In addition, experience may be able to override the perception of dissonance as unpleasant: In one part of Bulgaria, singing in parallel seconds (which sounds dissonant to Western ears) is common in songs with two voices, with the lead singer remaining above the other (Sadie, 1980).

### Post-Infancy: Sensitivity to Higher-Level Musical Structures

Although infants display an impressively adultlike response to simple musical structures, there are developmental changes still to occur. Whether these changes are a function of age or of years of exposure to Western music cannot be determined because we lack developmental studies of Western children's perception of music from cultures with nonwestern musical traditions.

**Sensitivity to Diatonic Structure.** Almost all Western tonal music (e.g., not only classical but also folk, jazz, and rock) is written within a particular key. Though Western music typically modulates from one key to another over time, at any point in time tonal music is made up primarily of the notes of a particular scale. In the context of a given key, the notes of a scale are perceived as closely related and tones outside of this key sound less related. The relationship among the seven notes of a key is referred to as "diatonic structure."

In tonal music, the notes in a key have varying functions. The first note of the scale is called the tonic (e.g., in the key of G, the tonic is G). The tonic is heard as the most stable note in a tune and as the central tone toward which the others are drawn (Krumhansl, 1979). Melodies often end on the tonic, resulting in a feeling of stability. If the tune ends on the second note of the scale, it feels incomplete, hanging in midair and unresolved.

As a piece modulates from one key to another, the tonic or tonal center also shifts. In twentieth-century Western atonal music, there is neither key nor tonal center. Atonal music lacks the organizing framework provided by a key because the notes are not limited to one scale (Krumhansl, 1979).

The importance of tonality in organizing adults' perception of music has been demonstrated. Adults can distinguish tonal from atonal music (Dowling, 1982), and they recall tonal melodies better than atonal ones (Cuddy, Cohen, & Miller, 1979; Dewar, Cuddy, & Mewhort, 1977; Krumhansl, 1979). The ability to hear tonal structure (which is an abstraction) is critically important to understanding music, but the ability to distinguish tonal from atonal music is not present in infancy. Zenatti (1969) showed that by age 6 (but not before), children recall tonal sequences better than atonal ones. Children heard tonal and atonal melodies of three, four, and six notes followed by a comparison melody with one of the notes altered by one or two semitones. The task was to indicate which note had been changed. When the melodies had only three notes, 5-year-olds performed the same (and above chance) for both tonal and atonal melodies. By age 6, children performed better on tonal melodies, showing that they had acquired Western scale structure. By age 12, performance on atonal melodies improved and the tonal melodies did not facilitate performance. However, when the melodies were four or six notes long, the tonal framework remained easier even for adults.

Support for the claim that sensitivity to tonality is a late development (and one that is enhanced by formal training) comes from Morrongiello and Roes (1990). In their study, 5- and 9-year-olds heard brief (nine note) tonal and atonal melodies and then selected the line drawing that matched each melody's contour. Superior performance for tonal over atonal melodies was found only for 9-year-olds. Those 9-year-olds who had formal music training (on average, 3 years) distinguished more strongly between tonal and atonal melodies than did those without formal training. Nonetheless, even those with no formal training performed better on the tonal melodies.

In a related study, Trehub et al. (1986) compared children's discrimination of pitch changes within diatonic melodies (e.g., C-E-G-E-C) versus nondiatonic melodies (e.g., C-E-Gsharp-E-C). Performance of 4- to 6-year-olds was better in the diatonic condition, but infants performed the same in both conditions. Thus, by the age of 4, familiarity with Western music has heightened children's sensitivity to tonality. Another study suggests that glimmerings of sensitivity to the Western diatonic scale may occur by 12 months of age. Lynch and Eilers (1992) tested the ability to detect changes in intervals in the same simple diatonic and nondiatonic melodies used by Trehub et al. (1986). Infants heard the melodies and their transpositions, some of which contained altered intervals. At 6 months, detection of interval changes was identical across conditions (but above chance). By 12 months, performance was better in the diatonic melodies.

**Sensitivity to Key Changes.**   Perception of key is also late to develop. Trainor and Trehub (1992) investigated the ability to detect changes in melodies when the altered pitch was either within or outside the key of the melody. Adults found changes that violated key much easier to detect than ones that remained within key. But 8-month-olds not only performed identically in both conditions (showing a lack of sensitivity to key) but also performed *better* than adults in detecting within-key changes. Thus, years of listening to Western music impose a structure on what adults hear, such that note changes that remain in key are not heard as changes.

By age 5, children can distinguish keys that are tonally near versus far, a distinction that is independent of geographical distance, because geographically near keys (e.g., C and D) are more remote than tonally near keys (e.g., C and G). J. Bartlett and Dowling (1980, Experiment 4) played children and adults a melody followed by either a transposition or a same-contour imitation, either in a key near to the original melody (and hence sharing many pitches) or in a key far from the original melody (sharing few pitches). Adults heard the transpositions as the same as the original melody, and the same-contour imitations as different. Five-year-olds responded in terms of key: Near key changes (whether transpositions or same-contour imitations) were heard as the same as the original melody, far key changes as different. Thus, 5-year-olds could distinguish near from far keys but could not detect interval size changes when the contour was preserved. By age 8, children were more likely to hear a far-key transposition as the same, and a near-key imitation as different, showing that, like adults, they attend both to key distance and interval changes.

**Sensitivity to the Hierarchy of Notes within a Key.**   Children show a growing awareness of the proper structure of melodies (in Western tonal music), recognizing the importance of the tonic note for the ending of a melody. Krumhansl and Keil (1982) asked children to judge the goodness of six-note melodies that began with the tonic triad (C-E-G) and ended on a randomly chosen pitch. When adults were asked to judge the goodness of the final note, notes that are part of the tonic triad (C-E-G) were more highly rated than notes that are outside this triad (Krumhansl, 1990). However, 6- and 7-year-olds only distinguished between endings that were within key versus outside of key. Only by ages 8 to 9 did children begin to distinguish among the pitches of the key, ranking those in the tonic triad as better endings than other notes. When the task was simplified by using five- rather than six-note melodies, sensitivity to this hierarchy of notes within the scale was found by ages 6 to 7 (Cuddy & Badertscher, 1987; see also Sloboda, 1985, pp. 211–212).

The diatonic tonal scale, with its key structure and its hierarchy of notes, is specific to Western tonal music. Thus, it is not surprising that sensitivity to tonality is a late development. Acquisition of sensitivity to tonality occurs implicitly: Such acquisition depends on exposure to Western music but not on formal music instruction.

**Recognizing Invariant Structure ("Music Conservation").**   Intelligent musical listening requires that we hear invariant structure underneath superficial transformations (e.g., hearing a melody played in different keys, at different speeds, or with different instruments as the same melody). Such recognition of underlying structure despite surface changes has been likened to Piagetian conservation tasks (Pflederer,

1964). Children succeed on musical "conservation" tasks between the ages of 5 and 8 (and hence at the same age as they succeed on some Piagetian conservation tasks). Thus, children under age 5 are unable to identify a melody if its rhythm or harmonic accompaniments are altered, but by age 8 they have no difficulty with this task. The same findings hold for tasks in which children are asked to recognize meter despite a change in the duration of notes or to recognize rhythm despite a change in pitch (Pflederer, 1964; Serafine, 1980). But the analogy to conservation may be flawed. Children grasp conservation through logic, realizing that nothing has been added or taken away. There is no way to recognize invariance in music through logic. Instead, these studies are simply studies of perception and memory (Wolhwill, 1981).

### Perceiving Aesthetic Properties of Music

**Expression.**  More than any other art form, music has been described as the language of the emotions. According to philosopher Langer (1953), music mirrors the structure of emotional life: Music sounds the way moods feel. Music is structured in terms of tension and release, motion and rest, and fulfillment and change. These alterations mirror how our moods fluctuate.

Whether or not they are musically trained, adults agree in general on the emotions expressed by music. We hear music in the major mode as expressing positive affect—in the minor mode as expressing negative affect; we hear dissonant chords as expressing agitation, excitement, or sorrow—consonant ones as expressing happiness and calm (Crowder, 1984; Hevner, 1936).

Does the experience of the major mode as happy, and the minor mode as sad depend on learning, or might this perception be universal and unlearned, a function of the acoustics of the major and minor modes? The ability to distinguish between major and minor modes is prerequisite to the ability to hear major as happier than minor, and Costa-Giomi (1996) showed that with brief training in learning to attend to mode, 5-year-olds can hear changes in mode.

Young children agree with adults in their interpretation of musical passages of happy or sad (Dolgin & Adelson, 1990; Kratus, 1993), though there is mixed evidence about how early the ability to recognize emotion in music emerges. Cunningham and Sterling (1988) found that children aged 5 (but not 4) agreed with adults about which pieces are happy, sad, or angry. Gentile,

Pick, Flom, and Campos (1994) found that 3-year-olds agreed with adults on which pieces communicated happiness and which sadness, but only for five out of eight musical passages. Because these studies used actual segments of music, they do not allow us to determine which aspects of the music (e.g., mode, tempo, pitch, and volume) contributed to the emotion attribution.

Kastner and Crowder (1990) played 3- to 12-year-olds tunes in minor and major modes and asked them to point to the face that went with the tune (choosing among a happy, content, sad, and angry face). Even 3-year-olds matched positive faces to pieces played in the major mode (though performance improved with age). It is possible that children actually heard the major/minor distinction as a happy/sad one. But it is equally possible that children heard the major/minor distinction as a familiar/unfamiliar one, and gave positive choices when they heard something familiar. It is also possible that correct scores for the major mode were inflated by the selection of the "content" face which looked neutral (and children called it "plain"). A similar study used only a happy versus sad face, and found that 5-year-olds could not reliably match the minor melodies with the sad face and the major melodies with the happy face (Gerardi & Gerken, 1995). Thus, it may be that the perception of the minor mode as negative in affect and the major mode as positive emerges only with experience—perhaps the experience of hearing songs that pair sad lyrics or sad movies with the minor mode.

**Style.**  A few studies have examined children's ability to attend to the style of musical passages. Gardner (1973) asked children ages 6 to 19 to decide whether two passages from classical music came from the same piece and found that all children could succeed on this task though accuracy increased with age. When popular music was used along with classical music and children were asked to decide whether two passages came from the same piece of music, Castell (1982) found that 8-year-olds succeeded remarkably well, confirming Gardner's findings. Both studies however showed that correct perceptual choices emerged earlier than the ability to verbalize what two passages deemed to be from the same piece had in common. Hargreaves (1982) documented the development of the ability to verbalize how two pieces are alike or different, and found that even 7- to 8-year-olds (the youngest he studied) were able to offer what he called "objective-analytic" responses describing the properties of the music.

## Producing Music through Song: Major Milestones in Development

Children's first musical productions are vocal, and thus in what follows the focus is on the development of the ability to sing (both invented and standard songs). Singing is a complex task: Western rules of music dictate that songs consist of intervals sung an exact (rather than approximate) distance apart, melodies consist of diatonic notes and have a tonal center, and there is a consistent underlying metric organization. Children do not master these rules until the age of 6. Existing studies of the production of music through song are primarily descriptive rather than experimental.

### Infant Song

Infants possess the rudimentary ability needed to make music: They vocalize and vary and imitate pitch. This early "singing" is much like scribbling and babbling.

**Pitch Matching.**   Newborn cries have musical qualities and involve a wide range of pitches (Ostwald, 1973), but there is no reason to consider these cries as evidence of intentional music making. Kessen, Levine, and Wendrich (1979) provided evidence of intentional music making in infancy by showing that 3- to 6-month-olds could match isolated pitches sung to them on a pitch pipe. The ability to imitate sequences of two notes did not emerge prior to 1 year of age. See also Révész (1954) and Platt (1933) for earlier studies showing infants' ability to match pitches.

**Babbled Songs.**   Even though 9- to 12-month-olds can imitate discrete pitches, when children this age sing they do so in continuous pitches on a single breath (sometimes called song babbling). This results in an undulating siren-like sound in which pitches are blurred. This kind of sound is rarely heard in Western adult music. Babbled songs are not based on the diatonic system and have no clear rhythmic organization (McKernon, 1979; Moog, 1976; Moorhead & Pond, 1978).

**Rhythm.**   In striking contrast to the evidence that children can imitate pitches, there is no evidence of intentional production of rhythm in the 1st year of life (Sloboda, 1985). To count as evidence of production of rhythm, it is not enough to see a child bang something over and over. One must look for subdivision of a beat so that there are two or more events within a regular superordinate pulse; omission of a beat with the picking up of the pulse at the correct time after a pause; imitation of a rhythmic pattern; and moving or beating in time to music (Sloboda, 1985).

### Post-Infancy: Invented Songs

When it comes to language, children reach the level of the typical adult by age 5 or 6, with no explicit training; similarly, children sing at the level of the untrained adult by age 6. They have overcome three hurdles: (1) pitch has become discrete, (2) intervals have widened, and (3) their songs now have a metric and tonal organization.

**Pitch Becomes Discrete.**   The undulating pitches of babbled song give way, at around 18 months, to an essential element of Western music—discrete pitches and discrete pitch intervals (Davidson, McKernon, & Gardner, 1981; McKernon, 1979; Werner, 1961). When children first begin to sing in discrete pitches, they do not yet use adult pitch categories—children do not yet sing in a diatonic scale (Dowling, 1988). In addition, pitches wander in and out of tune, interval sizes are not precise, and there is no tonal center (Dowling, 1984). At this age, children are not trying to imitate songs that they have heard; rather, they are inventing their own songs (Davidson et al., 1981; Moog, 1976).

**Intervals Widen.**   The first intervals that children sing are very small, and development is characterized by a gradual expansion of interval size (Jersild & Bienstock, 1934; McKernon, 1979; Nettl, 1956a; Werner, 1961). McKernon found that major seconds were the most commonly produced intervals between 17 to 23 months. A third of the intervals sung at this age were of this type, and major seconds are among the most common intervals in songs across cultures (Nettl, 1956b). Between 1.5 to 2.5 years, the kinds of intervals increased and widened.

Children first expand their intervals and later fill them in a step-wise fashion (Davidson, 1985). Davidson refers to these early tonal structures as contour schemes—they are the stable intervals that the child possesses. These schemes are imposed on any song that a child acquires, reducing the range of a song's contour if necessary, and sometimes expanding the range to match the size of a new contour scheme just being constructed.

**Melodies Gain Rhythmic and Tonal Organization.** Rather than following a primarily rising or falling pattern, the contours of early songs undulate up and down (McKernon, 1979). Adult songs do this, too: Undulating contours are the most common types in adult songs across cultures (Nettl, 1956b). In this respect, as with the most common intervals produced, early songs resemble adult songs. But in their lack of either rhythmic or tonal organization, early songs are qualitatively different from adult songs (McKernon, 1979; Moorhead & Pond, 1978).

The melodic contours of children's early songs are narrow despite the fact that children can vocalize across a wide range (Fox, 1990): And almost all contours range between middle C and the B seven notes above it. Early songs consist of atonal groups of pitches: They are chromatic rather than diatonic, based on any or all of the notes in an octave rather than on the notes of a particular scale, and thus they lack the tonal center heard in Western music (McKernon, 1979; Moorhead & Pond, 1978). The lack of melodic and rhythmic structure in children's first invented songs makes these songs very different from the songs (written by adults) to which they are constantly exposed. By age 3, children are able to sing songs in a single key, though they do not do so reliably at first (McKernon, 1979).

Dowling (1984) described the invented songs his two daughters produced over a 5-year period, beginning in infancy. These children produced an average of 2.23 songs a week. The phrases of the songs had steady beats, but the beat did not always carry across phrases, consistent with findings by Moorhead and Pond (1978) and Moog (1976). Between ages 1 to 2, these two children produced songs with one repeated contour. By age 3, their songs had two to three different contours and often had a "coda," a contour that occurs only at the end of the song. The use of a coda may well have been due to having heard nursery rhymes because this form is found more often in nursery rhymes than in other kinds of songs.

### Post-Infancy: Conventional Songs

**Imitated Songs.** At around the age of 2, children attempt to sing the songs of their culture (Davidson, 1985; Davidson et al., 1981; McKernon, 1979). These early attempts to reproduce conventional songs sound very much like spontaneous songs in their lack of a metric and tonal organization. In both spontaneous songs and early renditions of standard songs, a narrow range of pitches and contours undulates in groups of two or three notes. The first property of a standard song imitated successfully is the lyrics—and these are simply imported into the child's spontaneous musical repertoire without their accompanying tonal and rhythmic structure (McKernon, 1979; Moog, 1976). Next to be reproduced is a song's rhythm. By 28 months, children studied by Davidson et al. (1981) could imitate the rhythmic structure of the alphabet song and fit the words appropriately into the rhythm. Last to develop is the ability to reproduce correct intervals and remain within a key. Adults pass through a similar sequence when learning a new song (Davidson et al., 1981).

By 29 months, children's spontaneous tunes have diverged in sophistication from invented tunes (McKernon, 1979). By the age of 3 or 4, children's standard songs have a clear underlying Western metric structure, even though their invented songs at this age lack this structure (McKernon, 1979). By age 5, spontaneous invented songs have declined and children become self-conscious and concerned with singing "correctly" according to the culture's norms (Gardner & Wolf, 1983; Moog, 1976).

Children are able to reproduce rhythm before pitch. Five- to 7-year-olds were followed over 3 years as they learned the song, *Row, Row, Row Your Boat* (Davidson & Scripp, 1988). Accurate rhythm production requires that a person match the number of units, keep a steady underlying pulse, capture the surface grouping, and coordinate the underlying pulse with the surface notes. Accurate pitch production requires matching the initial pitch, the melodic contour, the interval boundary (highest and lowest notes), and the key. Most (85%) of the 5-year-olds got the rhythm right, but only about half got the pitch right. The ability to reproduce pitch developed rapidly so that by age 7 the gap between rhythm and pitch had narrowed considerably.

We can conclude that musically untrained children show quite sophisticated singing abilities. By the age of 2 or 3, they can reproduce the general contour of a melody even though they cannot reproduce pitches exactly. By age 4, they can maintain intervals but cannot sing in a stable key (because they shift keys at phrase boundaries; McKernon, 1979). They are sensitive to melodic contours very early but the acquisition of a stable tonal center is not present until age 5 or 6, when they can maintain a key. Thus, in both perception and production of music, tonality is a late-developing structure.

**Intentional Expression in Singing.**   Children as young as age 4 can intentionally vary how they sing a song to convey emotion. Adachi and Trehub (1998) asked 4- to 12-year-olds to sing a familiar song (e.g., *Twinkle, Twinkle, Little Star*) once to make a listener happy and once to make her sad. Children at all ages primarily used devices that express emotion in both speech and music—they sang faster, louder, and at a higher pitch for happy and slower, softer, and lower for sad. Devices for emotion expression that are specific to music (e.g., mode or articulation) were infrequent at all ages studied. Not surprisingly, some age trends were seen: Adults are better able to interpret the happy versus sad expression in the songs of children ages 8 to 10 than in those of children ages 6 to 7 (Adachi & Trehub, 2000).

### Post-Infancy: Invented Notations

By asking children to invent ways of notating music that they hear, we can learn whether children understand that music cannot be captured by words or pictures and requires its own system of representation. This understanding emerges at least at early as age 5. In the longitudinal study mentioned earlier in which 5- to 7-year-olds without musical training heard *Row, Row, Row Your Boat*, children were asked to write down "the song" so that another person could sing it back (Davidson & Scripp, 1988a). The most common kind of notation system at age 5 was one in which abstract symbols were used to represent the notes (e.g., increasingly long lines used to represent increasingly low notes). Forty-three percent of the 5-year-olds used some kind of invented abstract system. The second most common solution at age 5 (26%) was simply to draw a representational picture that captured nothing of the musical information (e.g., a picture of a boat in water). By age 7, 56% of the children still used an invented abstract notation, though half of these combined the abstract notations with words (and almost no children used representational pictures).

The task of notating music is one that these children have probably never encountered before. What is notable is that 5-year-olds did not all rely on pictures; many invented abstract symbols. By age 5, children have learned to write letters, and also know quite a bit about pictorial representation (as shown earlier in the discussion of drawing). When asked to represent music, they invent a symbol system that is independent of both language and pictorial representation. This finding shows that young children are not only inventive when it comes to symbol-

izing but also recognize that neither words nor pictures do an adequate job of representing music, and that music needs its own form of representational system.

## Does Musical Skill Improve Linearly with Age?

In two areas, development in music does not steadily improve: (1) Absolute pitch capacity may decline with age and (2) young children demonstrate a "figural" understanding of music—a kind of understanding as sophisticated as that of adult musicians.

### Absolute Pitch

Absolute pitch refers to the ability to recognize pitches when heard in isolation. This skill is typically assessed by asking people to name the pitch, but naming of the pitch is only one indication that the person recognizes the pitch. Other measures that have been used include the ability to sing back a pitch and the ability to say that this was the pitch they heard before. This incidence of absolute pitch is estimated at 1/1,500 to 1/10,000 (Bachem, 1955; Miyazaki, 1988; Profita & Bidder, 1988; Takeuchi & Hulse, 1993) though it is difficult to test for absolute pitch in nonmusicians because they have not learned about the names of musical notes. Among musicians the incidence is considerably higher, estimated to be between 5/100 and 50/100 (Chouard & Sposetti, 1991; Gregersen, Kowalsky, Kohn, & Marvin, 1999). Absolute pitch cannot be trained in adults. Many experiments have attempted to teach it (Crozier, 1997; Cuddy, 1968; Takeuchi & Hulse, 1993), but all that has been shown is that people can memorize a few tones with much practice. Genuine absolute pitch is not learnable.

However, some have argued for the role of learning in early childhood because an early start to music training (before age 7) is associated with absolute pitch (Gregersen et al., 1999; Schlaug, Jäncke, Huang, & Steinmetz, 1995; Sergeant, 1969). But these data come from retrospective studies and it is possible that children with absolute pitch start music lessons earlier because their parents perceive them to be more musical. Not all musicians with absolute pitch began training early, and thus early training is not necessary for the development of absolute pitch. Moreover, only a minority of those who receive early training develop absolute pitch (Brown, Sachs, Cammuso, & Folstein, 2002).

Crozier (1997) and Takeuchi and Hulse (1993) reported greater trainability of absolute pitch in preschoolers than at older ages. There is also evidence that the incidence of absolute pitch declines with age. Sergeant and Roche (1973) found that absolute pitch is more common in 3- than 6-year-olds. Children were taught to sing three tunes over the course of six sessions over 3 weeks. One week after the last lesson, they were asked to sing the tunes. While the older children were able to sing back the song with the correct contour and precise intervals, it was the younger children who sang back the pitches most precisely. Saffran and Griepentrog (2001) showed that when only one kind of pitch cue (absolute or relative) is available, 8-month-olds discriminate tone patterns on the basis of absolute but not relative pitch. Adults responded in opposite fashion, succeeding only on the relative pitch task. Thus, the ability to store and reproduce pitches precisely may decline with age, giving way to the ability to grasp the overall gestalt of a tune. It is possible that absolute pitch becomes "unlearned" with age as children begin to focus on the distance between tones rather than the tones themselves. Without the ability to represent relative distance, we could not grasp musical structure (but see Plantinga & Trainor, 2004).

There is some debate about whether absolute pitch (as measured by pitch memory) really does decline with age. Trehub (2003a) reports research in progress showing no age-related decline in remembering the absolute pitch level of familiar melodies. Trehub (2003b) argues that both absolute and relative pitch processing exists from infancy onward, but with age, different triggers elicit one or the other mode of processing. She suggests that absolute pitch processing is universal if we measure it by testing whether individuals can remember the precise pitch level of music (Schellenberg & Trehub, 2003). Absolute pitch is considered to be rare, she argues, because we have insisted that to count as having absolute pitch one must be able to name individual notes heard in isolation. However, some researchers feel that we should reserve the term *absolute pitch* for the ability to classify pitch according to pitch class and not extend it to heightened pitch memory (Schlaug, 2003).

Schlaug et al. (1995) have shown that adult musicians with absolute pitch have a larger than normal left-sided asymmetry in the planum temporale. The planum temporale is involved in auditory processing and is related to language (its left-sided asymmetry is considered a marker of left-hemisphere language dominance in right-handers; Geschwind & Levitzky, 1968). Whether this atypical brain structure is inborn in those with perfect pitch, or develops as a function of intensive musical

training begun at an early age, is not known. However, current longitudinal research in our lab in which children's brains are imaged prior to and during music training may yield an answer to that question (Norton et al., 2005). If the atypical brain structure is inborn, research will need to determine whether some children with this brain structure lose absolute pitch and whether the maintenance of absolute pitch requires formal musical training and continuous exposure.

### Figural Understanding

Children's invented notations of music demonstrate that they hear music in an intuitive "figural" manner akin to how adult musicians are able to hear music. Bamberger (1991) asked a classroom of 8- and 9-year-olds to make drawings of a clapped rhythm so that someone else could clap back the rhythm. The rhythm had been invented by one of the children in the class and matched the rhythm of the familiar nursery tune, "Three, four, shut the door; five, six, pick up sticks; seven, eight, shut the gate." Eight- and 9-year-olds invented two kinds of notations, which Bamberger refers to as figural and metric (or formal).

In the figural notation in Figure 20.12, claps 3-4-5 are shown to be alike. Clap 5 is like the two previous ones because all three form one rapidly clapped bounded figure. Figural drawings reveal that children are classifying claps in terms of gestures—the three small circles feel like they are all part of one gesture. In the formal notation in Figure 20.12, claps 5-6-7 are shown to be alike. Clap 5 is like 6 and 7, revealing that these children are classifying each clap in terms of duration from one clap to the next. To do this they must step back from the performance of clapping and compare claps.

Children who drew one kind of drawing could not understand how the other kind could be right. However,

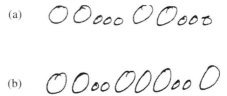

**Figure 20.12**  (a) Figural Notation of Rhythm. (b) Metric Notation of Rhythm. *Source:* From *The Mind behind the Musical Ear: How Children Develop Musical Intelligence* (p. 24), by J. Bamberger, 1991, Cambridge, MA: Harvard University Press. Copyright © 1991 by the President and Fellows of Harvard College. Reprinted with permission.

both can be considered right because each captures a different aspect of the rhythm (Bamberger, 1991). Metric notations capture the relative durations of claps—just what standard music notation captures. Figural notations are intuitive phrasings of what the rhythm sounds like—and they capture what musicians refer to as phrasing. For example, a musical performance of the previously mentioned rhythm might involve making claps 3, 4, and 5 louder or softer than the first two to indicate that they form a unit. Children who invented metric notations had managed to transform the continuous flow of the physical act of clapping into static and discrete symbols. These symbols are qualitatively different from the figural ones that capture the bodily flow of making music. In a further study with a large number of 7- to 12-year-olds, Upitas (1987) found that even with formal music training, children favor figural notations (though once they were shown the metric form, children with training were more able to switch to this form than were musically untrained children).

Musicians are able to perceive music both metrically and figurally: They would not be able to impose phrasing on a score without figural understanding. Musical scores often do not contain phrase markings, leaving phrasing up to the musician's interpretation. Thus, children's early and untrained understanding of rhythms as figures is an understanding that is not discarded by experts but instead is maintained. Figural drawings are too often considered less developed than metric ones. Yet, figural drawings capture what is important for musical expression—playing musically and achieving musical coherence (Bamberger, 1982). Thus, the child's earliest intuitive understanding of rhythm represents a way of knowing that remains important and ought to be retained even after more formal modes have been achieved. The challenge is for formal understanding to exist alongside figural understanding rather than have the formal replace the intuitive figural understanding.

## CONCLUSIONS

A basic premise of developmental psychology holds that one can only study a developmental process of an implicitly or explicitly defined end state (Kaplan, 1967). Freud assumed the normal healthy personality; along with most cognitive-developmentalists, Piaget presupposed the full-blown logical scientific formal-operational thinker. But norms of mental health differ across groups and cultures, and the kind of scientific thought valued by Piaget has only emerged in recent centuries.

In this chapter, by focusing on two prevalent art forms, I have viewed cognitive development through a set of different and, I hope, freshly illuminating lenses. The arts address and sometimes answer issues that are less visible in other spheres. Among these issues are why humans persist in activities with nonobvious survival value, to what extent skills develop and even flower in the absence of formal training, and in which ways development may proceed in nonlinear and even regressive directions. In addition, it is particularly in the arts that links between early and adult end states can be seen: Both child and adult artist are experimenters. Artists deliberately violate rules they have mastered; children have not yet mastered the rules and are therefore willing to be playful.

Visual arts and music are distinctly separate domains—it makes little sense to conceive of artistic development as a single entity (just as there is no single course of scientific development that encompasses the biologist and the theoretical physicist). Issues of tonal accuracy or the privileged fifth in music have little direct analogy with the emergence of the tadpole or the horizon line in children's drawings. And yet there may be certain intriguing parallels—children's inventions of their own notations may involve some of the same processes as children's attempts to master linear perspective (cf. Karmiloff-Smith, 1992). Even though the arts are universal in the way that science is not, I would not go so far as to claim that development perceived from a musical or visual artistic perspective provides the more important perspective. But I confidently assert that our understanding of development is enhanced if we can probe and synthesize findings from these various prized developmental end states.

## REFERENCES

Adachi, M., & Trehub, S. E. (1998). Children's expression of emotion in song. *Psychology of Music, 26*(2), 133–153.

Adachi, M., & Trehub, S. E. (2000). Decoding the expressive intentions in children's songs. *Music Perception, 18*(2), 213–224.

Adi-Japha, E., Levin, I., & Solomon, S. (1998). Emergence of representation in drawing: The relation between kinematic and referential aspects. *Cognitive Development, 13*, 25–51.

Aiello, R. (1994). Can listening to music be experimentally studied. In R. Aiello, with J. Sloboda (Eds.), *Musical perception* (pp. 273–282). New York: Oxford University Press.

Alland, A. (1983). *Playing with form.* New York: Columbia University Press.

Anati, E. (1967). *Evolution and style in Camonican rock art.* Brescia, Italy: Edizione Banca Populare di Sondrio.

Andersson, S. B. (1995a). Local conventions in children's drawings: A comparative study in three cultures. *Journal of Multicultural and Cross-Cultural Research in Art Education, 13,* 101–111.

Andersson, S. B. (1995b). Projection systems and X-ray strategies in children's drawings: Comparative study in three cultures. *British Journal of Educational Psychology, 65,* 455–464.

Arnheim, R. (1974). *Art and visual perception: A psychology of the creative eye.* Berkeley: University of California Press.

Bachem, A. (1955). Absolute pitch. *Journal of Acoustical Society of America, 27,* 1180–1185.

Bamberger, J. (1982). Revisiting children's drawings of simple rhythms: A function for reflection in action. In S. Strauss (Ed.), *U-shaped behavioral growth* (pp. 191–226). New York: Academic Press.

Bamberger, J. (1991). *The mind behind the musical ear.* Cambridge, MA: Harvard University Press.

Barnes, E. (1894). A study of children's drawings. *Pedagogical Seminary, 2,* 455–463.

Barrett, M. D., Beaumont, A., & Jennett, M. (1985). Some children sometimes do what they have been told to do: Task demands and verbal instructions in children's drawing In N. H. Freeman & M. V. Cox (Eds.), *Visual order: The nature and development of pictorial representation* (pp. 176–187). Cambridge, UK: Cambridge University Press.

Barrett, M. D., & Bridson, A. (1983). The effect of instructions upon children's drawings. *British Journal of Developmental Psychology, 1,* 175–178.

Barrett, M. D., & Light, P. H. (1976). Symbolism and intellectual realism in children's drawings. *British Journal of Educational Psychology, 46,* 198–202.

Bartlett, D. L. (1996). Tonal and musical memory. In D. A. Hodges (Ed.), *Handbook of music psychology* (pp. 177–195). San Antonio, TX: IMR Press.

Bartlett, J. C., & Dowling, W. J. (1980). The recognition of transposed melodies: A key distance effect in developmental perspective. *Journal of Experimental Psychology: Human Perception and Performance, 6,* 501–515.

Bassett, E. M. (1977). Production strategies in the child's drawing. In G. Butterworth (Ed.), *The child's representation of the world* (pp. 49–59). New York: Plenum Press.

Beal, C. R., & Arnold, D. S. (1990). The effect of instructions on view-specific representations in young children's drawing and picture selection. *British Journal of Developmental Psychology, 8,* 393–400.

Beilin, H. (1991). Developmental aesthetics and the psychology of photography. In R. M. Downs, L. S. Liben, & D. S. Palermo (Eds.), *Visions of aesthetics, the environment, and development: The legacy of Joachim F. Wohlwill* (pp. 45–86). Hillsdale, NJ: Erlbaum.

Beilin, H., & Pearlman, E. G. (1991). Children's iconic realism: Object versus property realism. In H. W. Reese (Ed.), *Advances in child development and behavior* (Vol. 2, pp. 73–111). San Diego, CA: Academic Press.

Belo, J. (1955). Balinese children's drawings. In M. Mead & M. Wolfenstein (Eds.), *Childhood in contemporary cultures* (pp. 52–69). Chicago: University of Chicago Press.

Bergeson, T. R., & Trehub, S. E. (1999). Mothers: Singing to infants and preschool children. *Infant Behavior and Development, 22I,* 51–64.

Bergeson, T. R., & Trehub, S. E. (2002). Absolute pitch and tempo in mothers' songs to infants. *Psychological Science, 13,* 71–74.

Beyer, F. S., & Nodine, C. F. (1985). Familiarity influences how children draw what they see. *Visual Arts Research, 11*(2), 60–68.

Blank, P., Massey, C., Gardner, H., & Winner, E. (1984). Perceiving what paintings express. In W. R. Crozier & A. J. Chapman (Eds.), *Cognitive processes in the perception of art* (pp. 127–143). Amsterdam: Elsevier.

Bloom, P., & Markson, L. (1998). Intention and analogy in children's naming of pictorial representations. *Psychological Science, 9,* 200–204.

Bond, E. (1972). Perception of form by the human infant. *Psychological Bulletin, 77,* 225–245.

Borchgrevink, H. M. (1975). Musikalske akkord-preferanser hos mennesket belyst ved dyredforsok [Musical chord preferences in humans as demonstrated through animal experiments]. *Tidskrift for den Norske Laegeforening, 95,* 356–358.

Bornstein, M. H., Ferdinandsen, K., & Gross, C. G. (1981). Perception of symmetry in infancy. *Developmental Psychology, 17,* 82–86.

Bower, T. G. R. (1965). Stimulus variables determining space perception in infants. *Science, 149,* 88–89.

Bower, T. G. R. (1966). The visual world of infants. *Scientific American, 215,* 80–92.

Bremner, J. G., & Batten, A. (1991). Sensitivity to viewpoint in children's drawings of objects and relations between objects. *Journal of Experimental Child Psychology, 2,* 371–376.

Bremner, J. G., & Moore, S. (1984). Prior visual inspection and object naming: Two factors that enhance hidden feature inclusion in young children's drawings. *British Journal of Developmental Psychology, 2,* 371–376.

Brooks, M. R., Glenn, S. M., & Crozier, W. R. (1988). Pre-school children's preferences for drawings of similar complexity to their own. *British Journal of Educational Psychology, 58*(2), 165–171.

Brown, W. A., Sachs, H., Cammuso, K., & Folstein, S. E. (2002). Early music training and absolute pitch. *Music Perception, 19*(4), 595–597.

Buhler, K. (1930). *The mental development of the child.* London: Kegan Paul.

Callaghan, T. C. (1997). Children's judgments of emotions portrayed in museum art. *British Journal of Developmental Psychology, 15,* 515–529.

Callaghan, T. C. (1999). Early understanding and production of graphic symbols. *Child Development, 70,* 1314–1324.

Callaghan, T. C. (2000a). Factors affecting children's graphic symbol use in the third year: Language, similarity and iconicity. *Cognitive Development, 15,* 185–214.

Callaghan, T. C. (2000b). The role of context in preschoolers' judgments of emotion in art. *British Journal of Developmental Psychology, 18,* 465–474.

Campos, J. J., Langer, A., & Korwitz, A. (1970). Cardiac responses on the visual cliff in prelocomotor human infants. *Science, 170,* 196.

Carothers, T., & Gardner, H. (1979). When children's drawings become art: The emergence of aesthetic production and perception. *Developmental Psychology, 15,* 570–580.

Castell, K. C. (1982). Children's sensitivity to stylistic differences in "classical" and "popular" music [Special issue]. *Psychology of Music, 22*–25.

Cazden, N. (1980). The definition of consonance and dissonance. *International Review of the Aesthetics and Sociology of Music, 2*, 23–168.

Chang, H. W., & Trehub, S. E. (1977a). Auditory processing of relational information by young infants. *Journal of Experimental Child Psychology, 24*, 324–331.

Chang, H. W., & Trehub, S. E. (1977b). Infants' perception of temporal grouping in auditory patterns. *Child Development, 48*, 1666–1670.

Charman, T., & Baron-Cohen, S. (1992, September). Understanding drawings and beliefs: A further test of the metarepresentation theory of autism: A research note. *Journal of Child Psychology and Psychiatry, 33*(6), 1105–1112.

Chen, M. J. (1985). Young children's representational drawings of solid objects: A comparison of drawing and copying. In N. H. Freeman & M. V. Cox (Eds.), *Visual order: The nature and development of pictorial representation* (pp. 157–175). Cambridge, UK: Cambridge University Press.

Chen, M. J., & Cook, M. (1984). Representational drawings of solid objects by young children. *Perception, 13*, 377–385.

Child, I. (1965). Personality correlates of esthetic judgment in college students. *Journal of Personality, 33*(3), 476–511.

Chipman, S., & Mendelson, M. (1975). The development of sensitivity to visual structure. *Journal of Experimental Child Psychology, 20*, 411–429.

Chouard, C. H., & Sposetti, R. (1991). Environmental and electrophysiological study of absolute pitch. *Acta Otolaryngol, 111*, 225–230.

Clark, A. B. (1897). The child's attitude towards perspective problems. In E. Barnes (Ed.), *Studies in education* (Vol. 1). Stanford, CA: Stanford University Press.

Cohen, A. J., Thorpe, L. A., & Trehub, S. E. (1987). Infants' perception of musical relations in short transposed tone sequences. *Canadian Journal of Psychology, 41*, 33–47.

Colbert, C. B., & Taunton, M. (1988). Problems of representation: Preschool and third grade children's observational drawings of a three dimensional model. *Studies in Art Education, 29*, 103–114.

Cook, N. (1994). Perception: A perspective from music theory. In R. Aiello, with J. Sloboda (Eds.), *Musical perception* (pp. 64–95). New York: Oxford University Press.

Costa-Giomi, E. (1996). Mode discrimination abilities of pre-school children. *Psychology of Music, 24*(2), 184–198.

Costall, A. P. (1995). The myth of the sensory core: The traditional versus the ecological approach to children's drawings. In C. Lange-Kuttner & G. V. Thomas (Eds.), *Drawing and looking: Theoretical approaches to pictorial representation in children* (pp. 16–26). New York: Harvester Wheatsheaf.

Court, E. (1989). Drawing on culture: The influence of culture on children's drawing performance in rural Kenya. *Journal of Art and Design Education, 8*, 65–88.

Cox, M. V. (1978). Spatial depth relationships in young children's drawings. *Journal of Experimental Child Psychology, 26*, 551–554.

Cox, M. V. (1981). One thing behind another: Problems of representation in children's drawings. *Educational Psychology, 1*(4), 275–287.

Cox, M. V. (1986). Cubes are difficult things to draw. *British Journal of Developmental Psychology, 4*, 341–345.

Cox, M. V. (1992). *Children's drawings.* London: Penguin.

Cox, M. V. (1993). *Children's drawings of the human figure.* Hove, England: Erlbaum.

Cox, M. V. (1997). *Drawings of people by the under-5s.* London: Falmer Press.

Cox, M. V. (1998). Drawings of people by Australian Aboriginal children: Intermixing of cultural styles. *Journal of Art and Design Education, 17*, 71–79.

Cox, M. V., & Lambon Ralph, M. (1996). Young children's ability to adapt their drawings of the human figure. *Educational Psychology, 16*(3), 245–255.

Cox, M. V., & Martin, A. (1988). Young children's viewer-centered representations: Drawings of a cube placed inside or behind a transparent or opaque beaker. *International Journal of Behavioral Development, 11*(2), 233–245.

Cox, M. V., & Mason, S. (1998). The young child's pictorial representation of the human figure. *International Journal of Early Years Education, 6*(1), 31–38.

Cox, M. V., & Moore, R. (1994). Children's depictions of different views of the human figure. *Educational Psychology, 14*, 427–436.

Cox, M. V., & Parkin, C. E. (1986). Young children's human figure drawings: Cross sectional and longitudinal studies. *Educational Psychology, 6*, 353–368.

Cox, M. V., Koyasu, M., Hiranuma, H., & Perara, J. (2001). Children's human figure drawings in the UK and Japan: The effects of age, sex and culture. *British Journal of Developmental Psychology, 19*, 275–292.

Crook, C. (1984). Factors influencing the use of transparency in children's drawing. *British Journal of Developmental Psychology, 2*, 213–221.

Crook, C. (1985). Knowledge and appearance. In N. H. Freeman & M. V. Cox (Eds.), *Visual order* (pp. 248–265). Cambridge, UK: Cambridge University Press.

Crowder, R. G. (1984). Perception of the major/minor distinction: Pt. 1. Historical and theoretical foundations. *Psychomusicology, 4*, 3–10.

Crozier, J. B. (1997). Absolute pitch: Practice makes perfect, the earlier the better. *Psychology of Music, 25*(2), 110–119.

Cuddy, L. L. (1968). Practice effects in the absolute judgment of pitch. *Journal of Acoustical Society of America, 43*, 1069–1076.

Cuddy, L. L., & Badertscher, B. (1987). Recovery of the tonal hierarchy: Some comparisons across age and levels of musical experience. *Perception and Psychophysics, 41*, 609–620.

Cuddy, L. L., Cohen, A. J., & Mewhort, D. J. K. (1981). Perception of structure in short melodic sequences. *Journal of Experimental Psychology: Human Perception and Performance, 7*, 869–883.

Cuddy, L., Cohen, A., & Miller, J. (1979). Melody recognition: The experimental application of musical rules. *Canadian Journal of Psychology, 33*, 148–157.

Cunningham, J. G., & Sterling, R. S. (1988). Developmental change in the understanding of affective meaning of music. *Motivation and Emotion, 12*, 399–413.

Daehler, M. W., Perlmutter, M., & Myers, N. A. (1976). Equivalence of pictures and objects for very young children. *Child Development, 47*(1), 96–102.

Davenport, R. K., & Rogers, C. M. (1971). Perception of photographs by apes. *Behavior, 39*, 318–320.

Davidson, L. (1985). Tonal structures of children's early songs. *Music Perception, 2*(3), 361–373.

Davidson, L., McKernon, P., & Gardner, H. (1981). *The acquisition of song: A developmental approach* (Documentary report of the Ann Arbor Symposium: Applications of psychology to the teaching and learning of music). Reston, VA: Music Educators National Conference.

Davidson, L., & Scripp, L. (1988). Young children's musical representations: Windows on music cognition. In J. Sloboda (Ed.), *Generative processes in music* (pp. 195–230). Oxford, England: Oxford University Press.

Davis, A. M. (1985). The canonical bias: Young children's drawings of familiar objects. In N. H. Freeman & M. V. Cox (Eds.), *Visual order: The nature and development of pictorial representation* (pp. 202–213). London: Cambridge University Press.

Davis, J. H. (1997). The what and the whether of the U: Cultural implications of understanding development in graphic symbolization. *Human Development, 40,* 145–154.

DeLoache, J. S. (1987). Rapid change in the symbolic functioning of very young children. *Science, 238,* 1556–1557.

DeLoache, J. S. (1991). Symbolic functioning in very young children: Understanding of pictures and models. *Child Development, 62,* 736–752.

DeLoache, J. S., Pierroutsakos, S. L., & Troseth, G. L. (1996). The three 'R's of pictorial competence. In R. Vasta (Ed.), *Annals of child development* (Vol. 12, pp. 1–48). Bristol, PA: Jessica Kingsley.

DeLoache, J. S., Pierroutsakos, S. L., & Uttal, D. H. (2003). The origins of pictorial competence. *Current Directions in Psychological Science, 12*(4), 114–117.

DeLoache, J. S., Strauss, M. S., & Maynard, J. (1979). Picture perception in infancy. *Infant Behavior and Development, 2,* 77–89.

Demany, L., & Armand, F. (1984). The perceptual reality of tone chroma in early infancy. *Journal of the Acoustical Society of America, 76,* 57–66.

Dennis, S. (1991). Stage and structure in children's spatial representations. In R. Case (Ed.), *The mind's staircase* (pp. 229–245). Hillsdale, NJ: Erlbaum.

Dennis, W. (1957). Performance of Near-Eastern children on the Draw-a-Man Test. *Child Development, 28,* 427–430.

Deregowski, J. B. (1984). *Distortion in art: The eye and the mind.* London: Routledge & Kegan Paul.

Deregowski, J. B. (1989). Real space and represented space. *Behavioral and Brain Sciences, 12,* 317–335.

Deregowski, J. E., Muldrow, E. S., & Muldrow, W. F. (1972). Pictorial recognition in a remote Ethiopian population. *Perception, 1,* 417–425.

Deutsch, D. (Ed.). (1982). *The psychology of music.* New York: Academic Press.

Dewar, K. M., Cuddy, L. L., & Mewhort, D. J. K. (1977). Recognition memory for single tones with and without context. *Journal of Experimental Psychology: Human Learning and Memory, 3,* 60–69.

Dirks, J., & Gibson, E. (1977). Infants' perception of similarity between live people and their photographs. *Child Development, 48*(1), 124–130.

Dolgin, K. G., & Adelson, E. H. (1990). Age changes in the ability to interpret affect in sung and instrumentally-presented melodies. *Psychology of Music, 18,* 87–98.

Dow, G. A., & Pick, H. L. (1992). Young children's use of models and photographs as spatial representations. *Cognitive Development, 7,* 351–363.

Dowling, W. J. (1973). The perception of interleaved melodies. *Cognitive Psychology, 5,* 322–337.

Dowling, W. J. (1978). Scale and contour: Two components of a theory of memory for melodies. *Psychological Review, 85,* 341–354.

Dowling, W. J. (1982). Melodic information processing and its development. In D. Deutsch (Ed.), *The psychology of music* (pp. 413–429). New York: Academic Press.

Dowling, W. J. (1984). Development of musical schemata in children's spontaneous singing. In W. R. Crozier & A. J. Chapman (Eds.), *Cognitive processes in the perception of art* (pp. 145–163). Amsterdam: Elsevier.

Dowling, W. J. (1988). Tonal structure and children's early learning of music. In J. Sloboda (Ed.), *Generative processes in music* (pp. 113–128). Oxford, England: Oxford University Press.

Dowling, W. J. (1991). Tonal strength and melody recognition after long and short delays. *Perception and Psychophysics, 50,* 305–313.

Dowling, W. J. (1999). The development of music perception and cognition. In D. Deutsch (Ed.), *The psychology of music* (pp. 603–625). San Diego, CA: Academic Press.

Dowling, W. J., & Fujitani, D. S. (1971). Contour, interval, and pitch recognition in memory for melodies. *Journal of the Acoustical Society of America, 49,* 524–431.

Dowling, W. J., & Harwood, D. L. (1986). *Music cognition.* New York: Academic Press.

Eng, H. (1931). *The psychology of children's drawings.* New York: Harcourt, Brace.

Eysenck, H. J., Götz, K. O., Long, H. L., Nias, D. K. B., & Ross, M. (1984). A new Visual Aesthetic Sensitivity Test-IV: Cross-cultural comparisons between a Chinese sample from Singapore and an English sample. *Personality and Individual Differences, 5*(5), 599–600.

Fagan, J. (1970). Memory in the infant. *Journal of Experimental Child Psychology, 9,* 218–226.

Fantz, R., Fagan, J., & Miranda, S. (1975). Early visual selectivity. In L. Cohen & P. Salapatek (Eds.), *Infant perception* (Vol. 1, pp. 249–345). New York: Academic Press.

Farnsworth, P. R. (1928). The effects of nature and nurture on musicality. In *The 27th yearbook of the National Society for the Study of Education* (Pt. 2, pp. 233–247). Chicago: NSSE.

Fernald, A. (1989). Intonation and communicative intent in mothers' speech to infants: Is the melody the message. *Child Development, 60,* 1597–1510.

Field, J. (1976). Relation of young infants' reaching behavior to stimulus distance and solidity. *Developmental Psychology, 12,* 444–448.

Fineberg, J. (1997). *The innocent eye.* Princeton, NJ: Princeton University Press.

Flavell, J. H. (1988). The development of children's knowledge about the mind: From cognitive connections to mental representations. In J. W. Astington, P. L. Harris, & D. R. Olson (Eds.), *Developing theories of mind* (pp. 244–271). New York: Cambridge University Press.

Flavell, J. H., Green, F. L., Flavell, E. R., & Grossman, J. B. (1997). The development of children's knowledge about inner speech. *Child Development, 68,* 39–47.

Fortes, M. (1981). Tallensi children's drawings. In B. B. Lloyd & J. Gay (Eds.), *Universals of human thought* (pp. 46–70). Cambridge, England: Cambridge University Press.

Fox, D. B. (1990). An analysis of the pitch characteristics of infant vocalizations. *Psychomusicology, 9,* 21–30.

Frances, R. (1988). *The perception of music.* Hillsdale, NJ: Erlbaum.

Freeman, N. H. (1980). *Strategies of representation in young children: Analysis of spatial skills and drawing processes.* London: Academic Press.

Freeman, N. H. (1987). Current problems in the development of representational picture-production. *Archives de Psychologie, 55,* 127–152.

Freeman, N. H. (1995). The emergence of a framework theory of pictorial reasoning. In C. Lange-Kuttner & G. V. Thomas (Eds.), *Drawing and looking: Theoretical approaches to pictorial representation in children* (pp. 135–146). New York: Harvester Wheatsheaf.

Freeman, N., Eiser, C., & Sayers, J. (1977). Children's strategies in producing three-dimensional relationships on a two-dimensional surface. *Journal of Experimental Child Psychology, 23,* 305–314.

Freeman, N. H., & Janikoun, R. (1972). Intellectual realism in children's drawings of a familiar object with distinctive features. *Child Development, 43,* 1116–1121.

Freeman, N. H., & Sanger, D. (1993). Language and belief in critical thinking: Emerging explanations of pictures. *Exceptionality Education Canada, 3,* 43–58.

Gardner, H. (1970). Children's sensitivity to painting styles. *Child Development, 41,* 813–821.

Gardner, H. (1973). Children's sensitivity to musical style. *Merrill-Palmer Quarterly, 19,* 67–77.

Gardner, H. (1974). Metaphors and modalities: How children project polar adjectives onto diverse domains. *Child Development, 45,* 84–91.

Gardner, H. (1980). *Artful scribbles: The significance of children's drawings.* New York: Basic Books.

Gardner, H., & Gardner, J. K. (1973). Developmental trends in sensitivity to form and subject matter in paintings. *Studies in Art Education, 14,* 52–56.

Gardner, H., Winner, E., & Kircher, M. (1975). Children's conceptions of the arts. *Journal of Aesthetic Education, 9,* 60–77.

Gardner, H., & Wolf, D. (1983). Waves and streams of symbolization. In D. R. Rogers & J. A. Sloboda (Eds.), *The acquisition of symbolic skills* (pp. 19–42). London: Plenum Press.

Gardner, R., & Gardner, B. (1978). Comparative psychology and language acquisition. *Annals of the New York Academy of Sciences, 309,* 37–76.

Gentile, D. A., Pick, A. D., Flom, R. A., & Campos, J. J. (1994, April). *Adults' and preschoolers' perception of emotional meaning in music.* Poster presented at the 13th Biennial Conference on Human Development, Pittsburgh, PA.

Gerardi, G. M., & Gerken, L. (1995). The development of affective responses to modality and melodic contour. *Music Perception, 12,* 279–290.

Gesell, A., & Ilg, F. (1946). *The child from 5 to 10.* London: Hamilton.

Geschwind, N., & Levitzky, W. (1968). Human brain: Left-right asymmetries in temporal speech region. *Science, 161,* 186–187.

Gibson, J. J. (1973). On the concept of "formless invariants" in visual perception. *Leonardo, 6,* 43–45.

Gibson, J. J. (1979). *The ecological approach to visual perception.* Boston: Houghton Mifflin.

Gibson, J. J., & Yonas, P. M. (1968). A new theory of scribbling and drawing in children. In H. Levin, E. G. Gibson, & J. J. Gibson (Eds.), *The analysis of reading skill.* Washington, DC: Department of Health, Education, and Welfare, Office of Education.

Golomb, C. (1973). Children's representation of the human figure: The effects of models, media and instructions. *Genetic Psychology Monographs, 87,* 197–251.

Golomb, C. (1981). Representation and reality: The origins and determinants of young children's drawings. *Review of Research in Visual Art Education, 14,* 36–48.

Golomb, C. (1987). The development of compositional strategies in drawing. *Visual Arts Research, 13*(2), 42–52.

Golomb, C. (2002). *Child art in context: A cultural and comparative perspective.* Washington, DC: American Psychological Association.

Golomb, C. (2004). *The child's creation of a pictorial world* (2nd ed.). Mahwah, NJ: Erlbaum.

Golomb, C., & Dunnington, G. (1985, June). *Compositional development in children's drawings.* Paper presented at the annual symposium of the Jean Piaget Society, Philadelphia, PA.

Golomb, C., & Farmer, D. (1983). Children's graphic planning strategies and early principles of spatial organization in drawing. *Studies in Art Education, 24*(2), 87–100.

Gombrich, E. H. (1977). *Art and illusion: A study in the psychology of pictorial representation* (5th ed.). London: Phaidon Press.

Goodenough, F. L. (1926). *Measurement of intelligence by drawing.* Yonkers, NY: World Books.

Goodman, N. (1976). *Languages of art* (2nd ed.). Indianapolis, IN: Hackett.

Goodnow, J. J. (1977). *Children's drawings.* Cambridge, MA: Harvard University Press.

Götz, K., Borisy, A., Lynn, R., & Eysenck, H. (1979). A new visual aesthetic sensitivity test: Pt. 1. Construction and psychometric properties. *Perceptual and Motor Skills, 49,* 795–802.

Gregersen, P. K., Kowalsky, E., Kohn, N., & Marvin, E. W. (1999). Absolute pitch: Prevalence, ethnic variation, and estimation of the genetic component. *American Journal of Human Genetics, 65,* 911–913.

Gross, J., & Hayne, H. (1999). Young children's recognition and description of their own and others' drawings. *Developmental Science, 2*(4), 476–489.

Hagen, E. H., & Bryant, G. A. (2003). Music and dance as a coalition signaling system. *Human Nature, 14*(1), 21–51.

Hagen, M. A. (1976). Development of ability to perceive and produce pictorial depth cue of overlapping. *Perceptual and Motor Skills, 42,* 1007–1014.

Hagen, M. A. (1978). An outline of an investigation into the special character of pictures. In H. Pick & E. Saltsman (Eds.), *Modes of perceiving and processing information.* Hillsdale, NJ: Erlbaum.

Hagen, M. A. (1986). *The varieties of realism.* Cambridge, UK: Cambridge University Press.

Hagen, M. A., & Jones, R. (1978). Cultural effects on pictorial perception: How many words is one picture really worth. In R. Walk & H. Pick Jr. (Eds.), *Perception and experience* (pp. 171–212). New York: Plenum Press.

Hall, S. (1892). Notes on children's drawings: Literature and notes. *Pedagogical Seminary, 1,* 445–447.

Hardiman, G., & Zernich, T. (1985). Discrimination of style in painting: A developmental study. *Studies in Art Education, 26,* 157–162.

Hargreaves, D. J. (1982). The development of aesthetic reactions to music [Special issue]. *Psychology of Music,* 51–54.

Harris, D. B. (1963). *Children's drawings as measures of intellectual maturity: A revision and extension of the Goodenough Draw-a-Man Test.* New York: Harcourt, Brace & World.

Harris, D. B. (1971). The case method in art education. In G. Kensler (Ed.), *A report on preconference education research training program for descriptive research in art education* (pp. 29–49). Restow, VA: National Art Education Association.

Hartley, J. L., Somerville, S. C., Jensen, D. C., & Eliefjua, C. C. (1982). Abstraction of individual styles from the drawings of 5-year-old children. *Child Development, 53,* 1193–1214.

Hauser, M. D., Chomsky, N., & Fitch, W. T. (2002). The faculty of language: What is it, who has it, and how did it evolve? *Science, 298,* 1569–1579.

Hauser, M. D., & McDermott, J. (2003). The evolution of the music faculty: A comparative perspective. *Nature Neuroscience, 6*(7), 663–668.

Havighurst, R. J., Gunther, M. K., & Pratt, I. E. (1946). Environment and the Draw-a-Man Test: The performance of Indian children. *Journal of Abnormal and Social Psychology, 41,* 50–63.

Hevner, K. (1936). Experimental studies of the elements of expression in music. *American Journal of Psychology, 48,* 246–268.

Hochberg, J., & Brooks, V. (1962). Pictorial recognition as an unlearned ability: A study of one child's performance. *American Journal of Psychology, 73,* 624–628.

Hudson, W. (1960). Pictorial depth perception in sub-cultural groups in Africa. *Journal of Social Psychology, 52,* 183–208.

Hussain, F. (1965). Quelques problèmes d'esthetique experimentale. *Sciences de l'Art, 2,* 103–114.

Imberty, M. (1969). *L'acquisition des structures tonales chez l'enfant.* Paris: Klincksieck.

Ingram, N., & Butterworth, G. (1989). The young child's representation of depth in drawing: Process and product. *Journal of Experimental Child Psychology, 47,* 356–369.

Ives, S. W. (1984). The development of expressivity in drawing. *British Journal of Educational Psychology, 54,* 152–159.

Iwawaki, S., Eysenck, H. J., & Götz, K. O. (1979). A new Visual Aesthetic Sensitivity Test (VAST)-II: Cross-cultural comparison between England and Japan. *Perceptual and Motor Skills, 49,* 859–862.

Jahoda, G. (1981). Drawing styles of schooled and unschooled adults: A study in Ghana. *Quarterly Journal of Experimental Psychology, 33A,* 133–143.

Jahoda, G., Deregowski, J. B., Ampene, E., & Williams, N. (1977). Pictorial recognition as an unlearned ability: A replication with children from pictorially deprived environments. In G. Butterworth (Ed.), *The child's representation of the world* (pp. 203–213). New York: Plenum Press.

Jersild, A., & Bienstock, S. (1934). A study of the development of children's ability to sing. *Journal of Educational Psychology, 25,* 481–503.

Jolley, R. P., Knox, E. L., & Foster, S. G. (2000). The relationship between children's production and comprehension of realism in drawing. *British Journal of Developmental Psychology, 18,* 557–582.

Jolley, R. P., & Thomas, G. V. (1994). The development of sensitivity to metaphorical expression of moods in abstract art. *Educational Psychology, 14,* 437–450.

Jolley, R. P., & Thomas, G. V. (1995). Children's sensitivity to metaphorical expression of mood in line drawings. *British Journal of Developmental Psychology, 12,* 335–346.

Jolley, R. P., Zhi, C., & Thomas, G. V. (1998a). The development of understanding moods metaphorically expressed in pictures: A cross-cultural comparison. *Journal of Cross-Cultural Psychology, 29*(2), 358–376.

Jolley, R. P., Zhi, C., & Thomas, G. V. (1998b). How focus of interest in pictures changes with age: A cross-cultural comparison. *International Journal of Behavioural Development, 22,* 127–149.

Kaplan, B. (1967). Meditations on genesis. *Human Development, 10,* 65–87.

Karmiloff-Smith, A. (1992). *Beyond modularity: A developmental perspective on cognitive science.* Cambridge, MA: MIT Press.

Kastner, M. P., & Crowder, R. G. (1990). Perception of major/minor: Pt. 4. Emotional connotations in young children. *Music Perception, 8,* 189–202.

Kellogg, R. (1969). *Analyzing children's art.* Palo Alto, CA: National Press Books.

Kemler Nelson, D. G., Hirsh-Pasek, K., Jusczyk, P. W., & Wright Cassidy, K. (1989). How the prosodic cues in motherese might assist language learning. *Journal of Child Language, 16,* 66–68.

Kennedy, J. M. (1993). *Drawing and the blind.* New Haven, CT: Yale University Press.

Kennedy, J. M., & Ross, A. S. (1975). Outline picture perception by the Songe of Papua. *Perception, 4,* 391–406.

Kerschensteiner, G. (1905). *Die Entwicklung der zeichnerischen Begabung.* Munich, Germany: Gerber.

Kessen, W., Levine, J., & Wendrich, K. A. (1979). The imitation of pitch in infants. *Infant Behavior and Development, 2,* 93–99.

Kosslyn, S. M., Heldmeyer, K. H., & Locklear, E. P. (1977). Children's drawings as data about internal representations. *Journal of Experimental Child Psychology, 23,* 191–211.

Kratus, J. (1993). A developmental study of children's interpretation of emotion in music. *Psychology of Music, 21,* 3–19.

Krumhansl, C. L. (1979). The psychological representation of musical pitch in a tonal context. *Cognitive Psychology, 11,* 325–334.

Krumhansl, C. L. (1990). *Cognitive foundations of musical pitch.* New York: Oxford University Press.

Krumhansl, C. L., & Jusczyk, P. W. (1990). Infants' perception of phrase structure in music. *Psychological Science, 1,* 70–73.

Krumhansl, C. L., & Keil, F. C. (1982). Acquisition of the hierarchy of tonal functions in music. *Memory and Cognition, 10,* 243–251.

Kugler, K., & Savage-Rumbaugh, S. (2002, June). *Rhythmic drumming by Kanzi and adult male bonobo (Pan Paniscus) at the Language Research Center.* Poster presented at the 25th Meeting of the American Society of Primatologists, Oklahoma City, OK.

Kuhn, D., Cheney, R., & Weinstock, M. (2000). The development of epistemological understanding. *Cognitive Development, 15,* 309–328.

Langer, S. (1953). *Feeling and form.* New York: Scribner.

Lawler, C., & Lawler, E. (1965). Color-mood associations in young children. *Journal of Genetic Psychology, 107,* 29–32.

Leekam, S. R., & Perner, J. (1991). Does the autistic child have a metarepresentational deficit? *Cognition, 40,* 203–218.

Lerdahl, F., & Jackendoff, R. (1983). *A generative theory of tonal music.* Cambridge, MA: MIT Press.

Leslie, A. M., & Thaiss, L. (1992). Domain specificity in conceptual development: Neuropsychological evidence from autism. *Cognition, 43,* 225–251.

Lewis, C., Russell, C., & Berridge, D. (1993). When is a mug not a mug: Effects of content, naming, and instructions on children's drawings. *Journal of Experimental Child Psychology, 56,* 291–302.

Lewis, H. P. (1963). Spatial representation in drawing as a correlate of development and a basis for picture preference. *Journal of Genetic Psychology, 102,* 95–107.

Light, P. H. (1985). The development of view-specific representations considered from a socio-cognitive standpoint. In N. H. Freeman & M. V. Cox (Eds.), *Visual order* (pp. 214–230). Cambridge, UK: Cambridge University Press.

Light, P. H., & Humphreys, J. (1981). Internal spatial relationships in young children's drawings. *Journal of Experimental Child Psychology, 31*(3), 521–530.

Light, P. H., & MacIntosh, E. (1980). Depth relationships in young children's drawings. *Journal of Experimental Child Psychology, 30,* 79–87.

Linn, S. F., & Thomas, G. V. (2002). Development of understanding of popular graphic art: A study of everyday aesthetics in children, adolescents, and young adults. *International Journal of Behavioral Development, 26*(3), 278–287.

Lipscomb, S. D. (1996). The cognitive organization of musical sound. In D. A. Hodges (Ed.), *Handbook of music psychology* (pp. 133–175). San Antonio, TX: IMR Press.

Löwenfeld, V., & Brittain, W. L. (1987). *Creative and mental growth.* Englewood Cliffs, NJ: Prentice-Hall. (Original work published 1964)

Lukens, H. T. (1896). A study of children's drawings in the early years. *Pedagogical Seminary, 4,* 79–109.

Luquet, G. H. (1913). *Le dessin d'un enfant.* Paris: Alcan.

Luquet, G. H. (1927). *Le dessin enfantin.* Paris: Alcan.

Lynch, M. P., & Eilers, R. E. (1992). A study of perceptual development for musical tuning. *Perception and Psychophysics, 52,* 599–608.

Lynch, M. P., Eilers, R. E., Oller, D. K., & Urbano, R. C. (1990). Innateness, experience, and music perception. *Psychological Science, 1,* 272–276.

Machotka, P. (1966). Aesthetic criteria in childhood: Justifications of preference. *Child Development, 37,* 877–885.

Maitland, L. (1895). What children draw to please themselves. *Inland Educator, 1,* 77–81.

Marr, D. (1982). *Vision: A computational investigation into the human representation and processing of visual information.* San Francisco: Freeman.

Martlew, M., & Connolly, K. J. (1996). Human figure drawings by schooled and unschooled children in Papua, New Guinea. *Child Development, 67,* 2750–2751.

Masataka, N. (1999). Preference for infant-directed singing in 2-day-old hearing infants of deaf parents. *Developmental Psychology, 35,* 1001–1005.

Matthews, J. (1984). Children drawing: Are young children really scribbling? *Early Child Development and Care, 18,* 1–39.

Matthews, J. (1997). How children learn to draw the human figure: Studies from Singapore. *European Early Childhood Education Research Journal, 5*(1), 29–58.

Matthews, J. (1999). *The art of childhood and adolescence: The construction of meaning.* London: Falmer Press.

McBride, L. R. (1986). *Petroglyphs of Hawaii.* Hilo: Hawaii Petroglyph Press.

McGhee, K., & Dziuban, C. D. (1993). Visual preferences of preschool children for abstract and realistic paintings. *Perceptual and Motor Skills, 76,* 155–158.

McGurk, H., & Jahoda, G. (1975). Pictorial depth perception by children in Scotland and Ghana. *Journal of Cross-Cultural Psychology, 6*(3), 279–296.

McKernon, P. (1979). The development of first songs in young children. *New Directions for Child Development, 3,* 43–58.

Meyer, L. B. (1956). *Emotion and meaning in music.* Chicago: University of Chicago Press.

Meyer, L. B. (1973). *Explaining music: Essays and explorations.* Berkeley: University of California Press.

Meyer, L. B. (1994). *Music, the arts and ideas: Patterns and predictions in twentieth-century culture.* Chicago: University of Chicago Press.

Millar, S. (1975). Visual experience or translation rules? Drawing the human figure by blind and sighted children. *Perception, 4,* 363–371.

Miller, G. F. (2000). *The mating mind.* New York: Doubleday.

Mitchelmore, M. C. (1980). Prediction of developmental stages in the representation of regular space figures. *Journal for Research in Mathematics Education, 11*(2), 83–93.

Miyazaki, K. (1988). Musical pitch identification by absolute pitch possessors. *Perception and Psychophysics, 44,* 501–512.

Moog, H. (1976). *The musical experience of the preschool child.* London: Schott.

Moorhead, G. E., & Pond, D. (1978). *Music of young children.* Santa Barbara, CA: Pillsbury Foundation.

Morra, S. (1995). A neo-Piagetian approach to children's drawings. In C. Lange-Kuttner & G. V. Thomas (Eds.), *Drawing and looking: Theoretical approaches to pictorial representation in children* (pp. 93–106). New York: Harvester Wheatsheaf.

Morris, D. (1967). *The biology of art.* Chicago: Aldine-Atherton.

Morrongiello, B. A., & Roes, C. L. (1990). Developmental changes in children's perception of musical sequences: Effects of musical training. *Developmental Psychology, 26,* 814–820.

Mursell, J. L. (1937). *The psychology of music.* New York: Norton.

Nakata, T., & Trehub, S. E. (2000, November). *Maternal speech and singing to infants.* Paper presented at the Society for Music Perception and Cognition, Toronto, Ontario, Canada.

Nettl, B. (1956a). Infant musical development and primitive music. *Southwestern Journal of Anthropology, 12,* 87–91.

Nettl, B. (1956b). *Music in primitive culture.* Cambridge, MA: Harvard University Press.

Nicholls, A. L., & Kennedy, J. M. (1992). Drawing development: From similarity of features to direction. *Child Development, 63,* 227–241.

Ninio, A., & Bruner, J. (1978). The achievement and antecedents of labeling. *Journal of Child Language, 5,* 1–15.

Norton, A., Winner, E., Cronin, K., Overy, K., Lee, D. J., & Schlaug, G. (2005). Are there pre-existing neural, cognitive, or motoric markers for musical ability? *Brain and Cognition, 59,* 124–134.

Nye, R., Thomas, G. V., & Robinson, E. (1995). Children's understanding about pictures. In C. Lange-Kuttner & G. V. Thomas (Eds.), *Drawing and looking: Theoretical approaches to pictorial representation in children* (pp. 123–134). New York: Harvester Wheatsheaf.

O'Hare, D., & Westwood, H. (1984). Features of style classification: A multivariate experimental analysis of children's response to drawing. *Developmental Psychology, 20,* 150–158.

Olson, R. K. (1975). Children's sensitivity to pictorial depth information. *Perception and Psychophysics, 17*(1), 59–64.

Olson, R. K., & Boswell, S. L. (1976). Pictorial depth sensitivity in 2-year-old children. *Child Development, 47,* 1175–1178.

Olson, R. K., Pearl, M., Mayfield, N., & Millar, D. (1976). Sensitivity to pictorial shape perspective in 5-year-old children and adults. *Perception and Psychophysics, 20*(3), 173–178.

Ostwald, P. F. (1973). Musical behavior in early childhood. *Developmental Medicine and Child Neurology, 15*(3), 367–375.

Paget, G. W. (1932). Some drawings of men and women made by children of certain non-European races. *Journal of the Royal Anthropological Institute, 62,* 127–144.

Pariser, D., & van den Berg, A. (1997). Beholder beware: A reply to Jessica Davis. *Studies in Art Education, 38*(3), 186–192.

Park, E., & I, B. (1995). Children's representation systems in drawing three-dimensional objects: A review of empirical studies. *Visual Arts Research, 21*(2), 42–56.

Parsons, M. J. (1987). *How we understand art.* Cambridge: Cambridge University Press.

Patterson, F. G. (1978). The gesture of a gorilla: Language acquisition in another pongid. *Brain and Language, 5*(1), 72–97.

Perara, J., & Cox, M. V. (2000). The effect of background context on children's understanding of the spatial depth arrangement of objects in a drawing. *Psychologia, 34,* 144–153.

Pflederer, M. R. (1964). The responses of children to musical tasks embodying Piaget's principle of conservation. *Journal of Research in Music Education, 13*(4), 251–268.

Phillips, W. A., Hobbs, S. B., & Pratt, F. R. (1978). Intellectual realism in children's drawings of cubes. *Cognition, 6,* 1, 15–33.

Phillips, W. A., Inall, M., & Lauder, E. (1985). On the discovery, storage and use of graphic descriptions. In N. H. Freeman & M. V. Cox (Eds.), *Visual order* (pp. 122–134). Cambridge, UK: Cambridge University Press.

Piaget, J. (1929). *The child's conception of the world.* New York: Harcourt Brace.

Piaget, J., & Inhelder, B. (1956). *The child's conception of space.* London: Routledge & Kegan Paul.

Pierroutsakos, S. L., & DeLoache, J. S. (2003). Infants' manual investigation of pictures objects varying in realism. *Infancy, 4,* 141–156.

Pinto, G., & Bombi, A. S. (1996). Drawing human figures in profile: A study of the development of representative strategies. *Journal of Genetic Psychology, 157*(3), 303–321.

Platinga, J., & Trainor, L. J. (2002, October). *Long-term memory for pitch in 6-month-old infants.* Poster presented at the Neurosciences and Music Conference, Venice, Italy.

Platinga, J., & Trainor, L. J. (2004, August). *Are infants relative or absolute pitch processors?* Poster session presented at the proceedings of the 8th International Conference on Music Perception and Cognition, Evanston, IL.

Platt, W. (1933). Temperament and disposition revealed in young children's music. *Character and Personality, 2,* 246–251.

Plomp, R., & Levelt, W. J. (1965). Tonal consonance and critical bandwidth. *Journal of the Acoustical Society of America, 38,* 518–560.

Premack, D. (1975). Putting a face together. *Science, 188,* 228–236.

Profita, J., & Bidder, T. G. (1988). Perfect pitch. *American Journal of Medical Genetics, 29,* 763–771.

Pufall, P. B., & Pesonen, T. (2000). Looking for the development of artistic style in children's artworlds. *New Directions for Child and Adolescent Development, 90,* 81–98.

Radkey, A. L., & Enns, J. T. (1987). De Vinci's window facilitates drawings of total and partial occlusion in young children. *Journal of Experimental Child Psychology, 44,* 222–235.

Ramus, F., Hauser, M. D., Miller, C. T., Morris, D., & Mehler, J. (2000). Language discrimination by human newborns and cotton-top tamarins. *Science, 288,* 349–351.

Reith, E., & Dominin, D. (1997). The development of children's ability to attend to the visual projection of objects. *British Journal of Developmental Psychology, 151,* 77–196.

Révész, G. (1954). *Introduction to the psychology of music.* Norman: University of Oklahoma Press.

Ricci, C. (1887). *L'arte dei bambini* [The art of children]. Bologna, Italy: Zanichelli.

Richert, R. A., & Lillard, A. A. (2002). Children's understanding of the knowledge prerequisites of drawing and pretending. *Developmental Psychology, 38*(6), 1004–1015.

Robinson, E. J., Nye, R., & Thomas, G. V. (1994). Children's conceptions of the relationship between pictures and their referents. *Cognitive Development, 9,* 165–191.

Rose, S. (1977). Infants' transfer of response between two-dimensional and three-dimensional stimuli. *Child Development, 48,* 1086–1091.

Rose, S. A., Jankowski, J. J., & Senior, G. J. (1997). Infants' recognition of contour-deleted figures. *Journal of Experimental Psychology: Human Perception and Performance, 23*(4), 1206–1216.

Rosenstiel, A. K., Morison, P., Silverman, J., & Gardner, H. (1978). Critical judgment: A developmental study. *Journal of Aesthetic Education, 12,* 95–107.

Rouma, G. (1913). *Le langage graphique de l'enfant.* Bruxelles, Belgium: Misch & Throw.

Ruff, H., Kohler, C., & Haupt, D. (1976). Infant recognition of two- and three-dimensional stimuli. *Developmental Psychology, 12,* 455–459.

Russell, J. A., & Bullock, M. (1985). Multidimensional scaling of emotional facial expressions: Similarities from preschoolers to adults. *Journal of Personality and Social Psychology, 48,* 1290–1298.

Sadie, S. (Ed.). (1980). *The new Grove dictionary of music and musicians.* Washington, DC: Grove's Dictionaries of Music.

Saffran, J. R. (2003). Absolute pitch in infancy and adulthood: The role of tonal structure. *Developmental Science, 6,* 35–43.

Saffran, J. R., & Griepentrog, G. J. (2001). Absolute pitch in infant auditory learning: Evidence for developmental reorganization. *Developmental Psychology, 37,* 74–85.

Schaefer-Simmern, H. (1948). *The unfolding of artistic activity.* Berkeley: University of California Press.

Schellenberg, E. G., & Trehub, S. E. (1996). Natural musical intervals: Evidence from infant listeners. *Psychological Science, 7,* 272–277.

Schellenberg, E. G., & Trehub, S. E. (2003). Good pitch memory is widespread. *Psychological Science, 14,* 262–266.

Schiller, P. (1951). Figural preferences in the drawings of a chimpanzee. *Journal of Comparative and Physiological Psychology, 44,* 101–111.

Schlaug, G. (2003, August). *Absolute pitch: Nature or/and nurture.* Paper presented at Annual Meeting of the American Psychological Association, Toronto, Ontario, Canada.

Schlaug, G., Jäncke, L., Huang, Y., & Steinmetz, H. (1995). *In vivo* evidence of structural brain asymmetry in musicians. *Science, 267,* 699–701.

Seashore, C. E. (1919). *Psychology of musical talent.* New York: Silver Burdett.

Seashore, C. E. (1938). *Psychology of music.* New York: McGraw-Hill.

Serafine, M. L. (1980). Piagetian research in music. *Bulletin of the Council for Research in Music Education, 62,* 1–21.

Sergeant, D. (1969). Experimental investigation of absolute pitch. *Journal of Research in Music Education, 17,* 135–143.

Sergeant, D., & Roche, S. (1973). Perceptual shifts in the auditory information processing of young children. *Psychology of Music, 1*(2), 39–48.

Shepard, R. N. (1982). Structural representations of musical pitch. In D. Deutsch (Ed.), *The psychology of music* (pp. 343–390). New York: Academic Press.

Shinn, M. W. (1907). *The development of the senses in the first 3 years of childhood* (Vol. 4). San Diego: University of California, Publications in Education.

Shirley, M. M. (1933). *The first 2 years: Pt. 2. Intellectual development.* Minneapolis: University of Minnesota Press.

Shuter, R. (1968). *The psychology of musical ability.* London: Methuen.

Sloboda, J. A. (1985). *The musical mind: The cognitive psychology of music.* Oxford, England: Clarendon Press.

Steinberg, D., & DeLoache, J. S. (1986). Preschool children's sensitivity to artistic style in paintings. *Visual Arts Research, 12,* 1–10.

Stratford, B., & Au, M.-L. (1988). The development of drawing in Chinese and English children. *Chinese University of Hong Kong Education Journal, 16*(1), 36–52.

Strommen, E. (1988). A century of children's drawing: The evolution of theory and research concerning the drawings of children. *Visual Arts Research, 14*(2), 13–24.

Stumpf, C. (1883). *Tonpsychologie.* Leipzig, Germany: S. Hirzel.

Sully, J. (1895). *Studies of childhood.* London: Longman, Green.

Sundberg, N., & Ballinger, R. (1968). Nepalese children's cognitive development as revealed by drawings of man, woman, and self. *Child Development, 39,* 969–985.

Sutton, P. J., & Rose, D. H. (1998). The role of strategic visual attention in children's drawing development. *Journal of Experimental Child Psychology, 68,* 87–107.

Takeuchi, A. H., & Hulse, S. H. (1993). Absolute pitch. *Psychological Bulletin, 113,* 345–361.

Tarr, P. (1990). More than movement: Scribbling reassessed. *Visual Arts Research, 16,* 83–89.

Taylor, M., & Bacharach, V. R. (1982). Constraints on the visual accuracy of drawings produced by young children. *Journal of Experimental Child Psychology, 34,* 311–329.

Thomas, G. V. (1995). The role of drawing strategies and skills. In C. Lange-Kuttner & G. V. Thomas (Eds.), *Drawing and looking: Theoretical approaches to pictorial representation in children* (pp. 107–122). New York: Harvester Wheatsheaf.

Thomas, G. V., Nye, R., & Robinson, E. J. (1994). How children view pictures: Children's responses to pictures as things in themselves and as representations of something else. *Cognitive Development, 9,* 141–144.

Thomas, G. V., & Silk, A. M. J. (1990). *An introduction to the psychology of children's drawings.* London: Harvester Wheatsheaf.

Thorpe, L. A., & Trehub, S. E. (1989). Duration illusion and auditory grouping in infancy. *Developmental Psychology, 25,* 122–127.

Trainor, L. J. (1996). Infant preferences for infant-directed versus non-infant-directed play songs and lullabies. *Infant Behavior and Development, 19,* 83–92.

Trainor, L. J., Clark, E. D., Huntley, A., & Adams, B. A. (1997). The acoustic basis of preferences for infant-directed singing. *Infant Behavior and Development, 20*(3), 383–396.

Trainor, L. J., & Heinmiller, B. M. (1998). The development of evaluative responses to music: Infants prefer to listen to consonance over dissonance. *Infant Behavior and Development, 21,* 77–88.

Trainor, L. J., & Trehub, S. E. (1992). A comparison of infants' and adults' sensitivity to Western tonal structure. *Journal of Experimental Psychology: Human Perception and Performance, 19,* 615–626.

Trainor, L. J., & Trehub, S. E. (1993). What mediates infants' and adults' superior processing of the major over the augmented triad? *Music Perception, 11,* 185–196.

Trainor, L. J., Tsang, C. D., & Cheung, V. H. W. (2002). Preference for sensory consonance in 2- and 4-month-old infants. *Music Perception, 20,* 187–194.

Trainor, L. J., & Zacharias, C. A. (1998). Infants prefer higher-pitched singing. *Infant Behavior and Development, 21*(4), 799–805.

Tramo, M., Cariani, P. A., Delgutte, B., & Braida, L. D. (2001). Neurobiological foundations for the theory of harmony in Western tonal music. In R. J. Zatorre & I. Peretz (Eds.), *The biological foundations of music* (pp. 92–116). New York: New York Academy of Sciences.

Trehub, S. E. (2001). Musical predispositions in infancy. *Annals of the New York Academy of Sciences, 930,* 1–16.

Trehub, S. E. (2003a). Absolute and relative pitch processing in tone learning tasks. *Developmental Science, 6*(1), 44–45.

Trehub, S. E. (2003b). Toward a developmental psychology of music. *Annals of the New York Academy of Sciences, 999,* 402–413.

Trehub, S. E., Bull, D., & Thorpe, L. A. (1984). Infants' perception of melodies: The role of melodic contour. *Child Development, 55,* 821–830.

Trehub, S. E., Cohen, A. J., Thorpe, L. A., & Morrongiello, B. A. (1986). Development of the perception of musical relations: Semitone and diatonic structure. *Journal of Experimental Psychology: Human Perception and Performance, 12,* 295–301.

Trehub, S. E., & Schellenberg, E. (1995). Music: Its relevance to infants. *Annals of Child Development, 11,* 1–24.

Trehub, S. E., Schellenberg, E., & Hill, D. (1997). The origins of music perception and cognition: A developmental perspective. In I. Deliege & J. Sloboda (Eds.), *Perception and cognition of music* (Vol. 1, pp. 103–128). East Sussex, England: Psychology Press.

Trehub, S. E., Schellenberg, E., & Kamenetsky, S. B. (1999). Infants' and adults' perception of scale structure. *Journal of Experimental Psychology: Human Perception and Performance, 25*(4), 965–975.

Trehub, S. E., & Thorpe, L. A. (1989). Infants' perception of rhythm: Categorization of auditory sequences by temporal structure. *Canadian Journal of Psychology, 43,* 217–229.

Trehub, S. E., Thorpe, L. A., & Trainor, L. J. (1990). Infants' perception of *good* and *bad* melodies. *Psychomusicology, 9,* 5–19.

Trehub, S. E., & Trainor, L. J. (1998). Singing to infants: Lullabies and play songs. In C. Rovee-Collier, L. Lipsitt, & H. Hayne (Eds.), *Advances in infancy research* (pp. 43–77). Stamford, CT: Ablex.

Trehub, S. E., Trainor, L. J., & Unyk, A. M. (1993). Music and speech processing in the first year of life. In H. W. Reese (Ed.), *Advances in child development and behavior* (Vol. 24, pp. 1–35). New York: Academic Press.

Trehub, S. E., Unyk, A. M., & Henderson, J. L. (1994). Children's songs to infant siblings: Parallels with speech. *Journal of Child Language, 21,* 735–744.

Trehub, S. E., Unyk, A. M., Kamenetsky, S. B., Hill, D. S., Trainor, L. J., Henderson, J. L., et al. (1997). Mothers' and fathers' singing to infants. *Developmental Psychology, 33,* 500–507.

Trehub, S. E., Unyk, A. M., & Trainor, L. J. (1993a). Adults identify infant-directed music across cultures. *Infant Behavior and Development, 16,* 193–211.

Trehub, S. E., Unyk, A. M., & Trainor, L. J. (1993b). Maternal singing in cross-cultural perspective. *Infant Behavior and Development, 16,* 193–211.

Upitas, R. (1987). Children's understanding of rhythm: The relationship between development and music training. *Psychomusicology, 7*(1), 41–60.

Valentine, C. W. (1962). *The experimental psychology of beauty.* London: Methuen.

Viola, W. (1936). *Child art and Franz Cizek.* Vienna: Austrian Red Cross.

von Helmholtz, H. (1954). *On the sensations of tone as a physiological basis for the theory of music.* New York: Dover. (Original work published 1877)

Wagner, S., Winner, E., Cicchetti, D., & Gardner, H. (1981). "Metaphorical" mapping in human infants. *Child Development, 52,* 728–731.

Walk, R. D., Karusitis, K., Lebowitz, C., & Falbo, T. (1971). Artistic style as concept formation for children and adults. *Merrill-Palmer Quarterly of Behavior and Development, 17,* 347–356.

Wallin, N. L., Merker, B., & Brown, S. (2001). *The origins of music.* Cambridge, MA: Bradford Books.

Watson, M. W., & Schwartz, S. N. (2000). The development of individual styles in children's drawing. *New Directions for Child and Adolescent Development, 90,* 49–63.

Werner, H. (1961). *Comparative psychology of mental development.* New York: Wiley.

Willats, J. (1977). How children learn to draw realistic pictures. *Quarterly Journal of Experimental Psychology, 29,* 3, 367–382.

Willats, J. (1984). Getting the drawing to look right as well as to be right. In W. R. Crozier & A. J. Chapman (Eds.), *Cognitive processes in the perception of art* (pp. 111–125). Amsterdam: North Holland.

Willats, J. (1985). Drawing systems revisited: The role of denotation systems in children's figure drawings. In N. H. Freeman & M. V. Cox (Eds.), *Visual order* (pp. 78–100). Cambridge, UK: Cambridge University Press.

Willats, J. (1992). The representation of extendedness in children's drawings of sticks and discs. *Child Development, 63,* 692–710.

Willats, J. (1995). An information-processing approach to drawing development. In C. Lange-Kuttner & G. V. Thomas (Eds.), *Drawing and looking: Theoretical approaches to pictorial representation in children* (pp. 27–43). New York: Harvester Wheatsheaf.

Wilson, B. (1997). Types of child art and alternative developmental accounts: Interpreting the interpreters. *Human Development, 40,* 155–168.

Wilson, B., & Ligtvoet, J. (1992). Across time and cultures: Stylistic changes in the drawings of Dutch children. In D. Thistlewood (Ed.), *Drawing research and development* (pp. 75–88). London: Longman.

Wilson, B., & Wilson, M. (1977). An iconoclastic view of the imagery sources in the drawings of young people. *Art Education, 30,* 5–11.

Wilson, B., & Wilson, M. (1981). The case of the disappearing two-eyed profile: Or how little children influence the drawings of little children. *Review of Research in visual Arts Education, 15,* 1–18.

Wilson, B., & Wilson, M. (1984). Children's drawings in Egypt: Cultural style acquisition as graphic development. *Visual Arts Research, 10,* 13–26.

Wilson, B., & Wilson, M. (1987). Pictorial composition and narrative structure: Themes and the creation of meaning in the draw-

ings of Egyptian and Japanese children. *Visual Arts Research, 13*(2), 10–21.

Wing, H. D. (1968). Tests of musical ability and appreciation (2nd ed.). *British Journal of Psychology* (Monograph Suppl. No. 27).

Winner, E. (1989). How can Chinese children draw so well. *Journal of Aesthetic Education, 23*(1), 41–63.

Winner, E. (1996). *Gifted children: Myths and reality.* New York: Basic Books.

Winner, E., Blank, P., Massey, C., & Gardner, H. (1983). Children's sensitivity to aesthetic properties of line drawings. In D. Rogers & J. A. Sloboda (Eds.), *The acquisition of symbolic skills.* London: Plenum Press.

Winner, E., & Ettlinger, G. (1979). Do chimpanzees recognize photographs as representations of objects? *Neuropsychologia, 17,* 413–420.

Winner, E., & Gardner, H. (1981). First intimations of artistry. In S. Strauss (Ed.), *U-shaped behavioral growth* (pp. 147–168). New York: Academic Press.

Winner, E., Mendelsohn, E., & Garfunkel, G. (1981, April). *Are children's drawings balanced?* Paper presented at the Symposium of the Society for Research in Child Development: A New Look at Drawing: Aesthetic Aspects, Boston, MA.

Winner, E., Rosenblatt, E., Windmueller, G., Davidson, L., & Gardner, H. (1986). Children's perception of "aesthetic" properties of the arts: Domain-specific or pan-artistic? *British Journal of Developmental Psychology, 4,* 149–160.

Winston, A. S., Kenyon, B., Stewardson, J., & Lepine, T. (1995). Children's sensitivity to expression of emotion in drawings. *Visual Arts Research, 21*(1), 1–14.

Wolf, D., & Perry, M. D. (1988). From endpoints to repertoires: Some new conclusions about drawing development. *Journal of Aesthetic Education, 22,* 17–34.

Wohlwill, J. F. (1965). Texture of the stimulus field and age as variables in the perception of relative distance in photographic slides. *Journal of Experimental Child Psychology, 2,* 166.

Wohlwill, J. F. (1981, August). *Music and Piaget: Spinning a slender thread.* Paper presented at the annual meeting of the American Psychological Association, Los Angeles, CA.

Wright, A. A., Rivera, J. J., Hulse, S. H., Shyan, M., & Neiworth, J. J. (2000). Music perception and octave generalization in rhesus monkeys. *Journal of Experimental Psychology: General, 129,* 291–307.

Yonas, A., Goldsmith, L., & Hallstrom, J. (1978). Development of sensitivity to information provided by cast shadows in pictures. In *Perception, 7*(3), 333–341.

Yonas, A., & Hagen, M. A. (1973). Effects of static and motion parallax depth information on the perception of size in children and adults. *Journal of Experimental Child Psychology, 15,* 254–265.

Zaitchik, D. (1990). When representations conflict with reality: The preschooler's problem with false beliefs and "false" photographs. *Cognition, 35,* 41–68.

Zenatti, A. (1969). Le développement génétique de la perception musicale. *Monographies Francaises de Psychologie, 17.*

Zentner, M. R., & Kagan, J. (1996). Perception of music by infants. *Nature, 383,* 29.

Zentner, M. R., & Kagan, J. (1998). Infants' perception of consonance and dissonance in music. *Infant Behavior and Development, 21,* 483–492.

Zimmerman, R., & Hochberg, J. (1970). Responses of infant monkeys to pictorial representations of a learned discrimination. *Psychonomic Science, 18,* 307–308.

# CHAPTER 21

# *Extraordinary Achievements:*
# *A Developmental and Systems Analysis*

SEANA MORAN and HOWARD GARDNER

HISTORY   906
Intelligence   906
Beyond General Intelligence   907
Expertise   907
Creativity   908
Leadership and Morality   908
Personality   909
CURRENT ISSUES   909
Definitional Issues   909
Developmental Issues   910
Domain Issues   911
Methodological Issues   912
A DEVELOPMENTAL-
   SYSTEMIC FRAMEWORK   913
ART   915
Ordinary Development   916
Markers of Extraordinariness   916

SCIENCE   920
Ordinary Development   921
Markers of Extraordinariness   921
POLITICAL LEADERSHIP   925
Ordinary Development   926
Markers of Extraordinariness   927
MORALITY   929
Ordinary Development   930
Markers of Extraordinariness   931
Varieties of Extraordinariness   933
CONCLUSION   936
Domain Differences   936
Domain Similarities   938
Further Research   940
REFERENCES   940

By the age of 4, Wang Yani had produced more than 4,000 Chinese ink and brush paintings (Ho, 1989). American Michael Kearney reportedly could read before his first birthday and earned a college degree by age 10 (Winner, 1996a). Violinist Midori toured internationally starting at age 11. With no formal education, Virginia Woolf became a novelist, essayist, and literary critic with incomparable influence in her lifetime and afterwards. Apprenticed to a bookbinder at age 14, Michael Faraday educated himself by reading the books he was making, published his own scientific papers by age 25, and helped launch modern physics with his field theory (Tweney, 1989). Alexander the Great became king of Macedonia at age 20, immediately showed his

leadership ability by quelling unrest in Greek cities, and conquered most of the civilized world by age 30. Nelson Mandela dedicated his life to the achievement of equality among the races; confined to prison for 27 years, he displayed no bitterness on release and instead effected a remarkably smooth transition from apartheid to a democratic South Africa.

What are we to make of these artists, scientists, political, and moral leaders who do surprising, unprecedented, *extraordinary* things? Through their actions, their words, and/or their works, they influence other people, organizations, bodies of knowledge, and worldviews, irreversibly changing domains, ranging from ballet to biology to business (Csikszentmihalyi, 1988; Gardner, 1993a).

On some accounts, extraordinariness is a quantitative difference, such as being more than two standard deviations from the norm for a certain criterion—for example, psychometric intelligence or running speed.

The authors would like to thank William Damon, Deanna Kuhn, and Anne Colby for their comments on earlier drafts of this chapter. With gratitude, the first author dedicates this chapter to Vera John-Steiner and the second author to William Damon.

Extraordinariness is represented by outliers around a supposedly universal average. Although both tails of the normal curve might be considered extraordinary from this perspective, we do not subscribe to the global categorization of "high end" giftedness versus "low end" learning disabled. Studies of disabilities tend to use a deficit framework, focusing on diagnosing errors and how children can adapt to be more "normal." Rarely do they consider a disabled individual's way of thinking or acting as influential on others. In addition, there has been little research on individuals with jagged profiles of abilities and disabilities (cf. L. Miller, 1989; for summaries of the low-end literature, see Brown & Campione, 1986; Robinson, Zigler, & Gallagher, 2000).

On other accounts, extraordinariness is a qualitative difference—for example, having innate talents or unique experiences, or using cognitive processes unavailable to ordinary achievers. Extraordinariness is represented by a different cluster of skills altogether. We aim to synthesize the quantitative and qualitative views developmentally, suggesting that extraordinariness arises from repeated, cumulative deviations from a norm. These cumulative deviations eventually put a person on a qualitatively different path that may lead to acts or works influencing others to an unexpected degree.

Is extraordinariness all of a kind, or are there many varieties? Is its path set at birth or early in life, or is it emergent over the life span? How similar is its expression or development in different domains? What contributes to and constrains its development? In this chapter, we first review how extraordinariness has been studied in psychology. Then, we present a developmental-systemic framework for distinguishing end states and developmental pathways of extraordinariness in various domains. We focus on four domains—visual art, science, political leadership, and moral excellence—expounding differences as well as similarities across these domains.

## HISTORY

The earliest scientific examination of extraordinariness entailed taxonomies and biographical studies of "men of genius" (Cattell, 1903; Cox, 1926; Ellis, 1926). Galton (1869) is generally regarded as the first student of individual differences, as his development of correlational and regression statistical methods made genius measurable. Arguing that abilities are hereditary and naturally lead to eminence, Galton calculated the odds of someone in a particular generation becoming a genius based on how many eminent men were in his family tree. Yet, Galton did not distinguish the abilities or qualities critical for eminence nor did he disentangle inherited from environmental factors.

## Intelligence

For most of the twentieth century, psychologists focused on intelligence as the individual quality that drives eminence. When Spearman (1904) first isolated g, the general intelligence factor, he conceived IQ as representing general mental energy, abstract thinking, and the ability to form and work with concepts. Other psychometricians devised hierarchical models of abilities subsidiary or additional to g (Thorndike, 1921; Thurstone, 1938; Vernon, 1950). Binet and Simon (1909/1976), Terman (1925), and Wechsler (1958) created simple clinical or paper-and-pencil tests to measure the "amount" of intelligence that each person had; these instruments foregrounded the linguistic, logical, and mnemonic capacities crucial for success in school. For most investigators in this tradition, which continues today, intelligence is considered an inborn trait stable across the life span and across different contexts (Eysenck, 1998; Herrnstein & Murray, 1994; Jensen, 1980; see Neisser, Boodoo, & Bouchard, 1996, for a critical discussion).

In the eyes of some, IQ, creativity, leadership, moral goodness, and eminence were expected to be of a piece. People with high IQs were likely to be the most exemplary, productive, innovative individuals in their communities (Terman, 1954). Most psychometric studies found that IQ did correlate, up to a point, with indices of creativity (Torrance, 1974), leadership (Terman, 1954), moral behavior (Thorndike, 1936), and moral reasoning (Hollingworth, 1942; Terman, 1925). Cox (1926) tried to tie IQ more directly to extraordinary achievements by estimating posthumous IQ scores for 510 eminent historical figures. She concluded that their genius could have been identified psychometrically during adolescence. However, her methods circularly calculate intellectual potential retrospectively based on achievement; she confound interests and motivation with ability; and she does not account for differences in what constituted eminence or genius across historical periods or cultural divides.

The most ambitious psychometric study of extraordinariness is Terman's longitudinal research (Holahan, Sears, & Cronbach, 1995; Sears & Barbee, 1977; Terman, 1925, 1954; Terman & Oden, 1947). More than

90% of elementary students in California in 1921 with IQs higher than 140 agreed to provide intellectual, physical, personality, behavioral, and social data; remarkably, some have participated for more than 70 years. Far from being maladjusted bookworms, Terman's subjects were described as healthy, socially competent, and productive. Yet, if IQ is the singular most important predictor of extraordinariness, the lack of *extraordinary* achievements among these high-IQ individuals was glaring. By age 40, many subjects in the Terman sample had earned graduate degrees, worked in professional fields, and published writings (Subotnik & Arnold, 1994). But none reached a level of influence on contemporary or future generations as President Richard Nixon or scientist William Shockley—California schoolchildren of the same cohort who were not selected for the Terman sample—and few pursued the arts or other primarily creative activities like Californians Martha Graham, Yehudi Menuhin, or John Steinbeck. In addition, not all studies support the rosy life picture that Terman portrayed: Hollingworth's (1942) population of children with IQs over 180 endured neuroses, loneliness, and unhappiness as their high IQs alienated them from their less intelligent peers; Sears's studies showed that women in the Terman sample led more frustrated and less fulfilled lives than the men (Holahan et al., 1995; Sears & Barbee, 1977).

## Beyond General Intelligence

The IQ approach to extraordinariness has failed to account for why some people change the course of history (see Gardner, Kornhaber, & Wake, 1996, for review). Starting in the 1950s, researchers recognized that IQ did not well predict extraordinary real-world achievement after the school years (Wallach & Kogan, 1965). In addition, complicating factors show that IQ may not be as straightforward, hereditary, or context-free as first conceptualized (Neisser, Boodoo, & Bouchard, 1996). For example, IQ scores rose steadily over the twentieth century (Flynn, 1999), but school performance and extraordinary achievement did not increase in tandem.

In addition, more recent psychometricians have construed intelligence as more than one cognitive ability—such as Cattell's (1971) difference between culturally acquired crystallized intelligence and more flexible fluid intelligence, or Sternberg's (1985) triarchic theory splitting academically oriented analytic intelligence from practical and creative intelligences. Intelligence also has been construed as a measure of metacognitive

control rather than the cognitive abilities themselves (Alexander, Carr, & Schwanenflugel, 1995; Sternberg, 1985), beliefs about one's own competence and its malleability (Dweck, 2000), and properties of the brain, from processing speed (Ceci, 1991) to dopamine system functioning (Fried, Wilson, Morrow, Cameron, Behnke, Ackerson, & Maidment, 2001; Previc, 1999).

Gardner's (1983, 1999) multiple intelligences theory synthesized findings from previously disparate research traditions, including the study of: cultural symbol systems, isolation of neurological functions, the highly skewed abilities of prodigies and/or savants, as well as experimental and psychometric findings. He concluded that each individual possesses a profile of linguistic, logical-mathematical, spatial, bodily kinesthetic, musical, interpersonal, intrapersonal, naturalistic, and possibly existential intelligences that can develop or stagnate based on experience with different cultural domains of performance.

All individuals possess this spectrum of intelligences, but in light of hereditary and experiential considerations, individuals differ from one another in their respective intellectual profiles at any given time. Highlighting this distinction, Gardner distinguishes between *intelligences* as computational capacities and *domains* as socially valued activities in which individuals can participate and eventually excel (Connell, Sheridan, & Gardner, 2003). The domains present in a society, the training resources available, and the individual's own computing powers and motivations combine to determine how, and to what extent, various intelligences are expressed (Gardner, 1983, 1999).

Specific intelligences are linked to different forms of extraordinariness. Spatial intelligence plays a role in visual art, logical-mathematical and sometimes spatial intelligences in science, interpersonal and linguistic intelligences in political leadership, and the personal and existential intelligences in moral excellence. Still, such generalizations should be tempered; case studies suggest that, in regards to career trajectories and contributions, an *unusual* profile of intelligences may be as important as sheer intellectual power. The asynchrony of Freud's enormous linguistic and personal capacities, in the context of unremarkable mathematical and poor spatial skills, may have contributed to his innovative approach to science.

## Expertise

Other researchers, including Gestalt and cognitive psychologists, stressed not mental ability per se but the strategic use of such abilities (Davidson & Sternberg, 1984; Perkins, 1981). How does a person interact with constraints of a problem (Wertheimer, 1954), use information simultaneously or sequentially to organize actions (Luria, 1976), or change mental representations to build more complex understandings of phenomena (Piaget, 1972)? Differences in these processes lead toward more or less expertise, which is defined as the highest level of performance in a specific domain (Bereiter & Scardamalia, 1993). In contrast to novices, experts not only have more knowledge but also use qualitatively different strategies. They think ahead further, chunk knowledge more flexibly, use resources more strategically, are more efficient, and base decisions on the deep rather than surface features of the problem (Bereiter & Scardamalia, 1993; Chi, Glaser, & Rees, 1982; DeGroot, 1965; Ericsson, 1998; Newell & Simon, 1972). This line of research emphasized experience over genetic endowment. For example, mastery of a domain requires 10 years of deliberate practice (Ericsson, 1998) and includes sensitivity to environmental conditions and affordances (Perkins, Tishman, Ritchhart, Donis, & Andrade, 2000). Crucially, however, the expertise approach does not distinguish between individuals who achieve competence and those who come to stand out in some way from other expert peers.

## Creativity

Since the 1950s, creativity has been studied psychometrically as a trait separate from IQ; the two traits do not correlate above an IQ of 120 (Getzels & Jackson, 1962). Guilford (1950, 1967) developed paper-and-pencil tests to measure ideational fluency, flexibility, and elaboration, and Mednick and Mednick (1967) devised a test to assess associational power. Guilford differentiated between convergent and divergent thinking traits. Experts and high-IQ individuals excelled at converging to one best answer for well-structured problems, whereas creative people diverged along multiple lines of thinking for relatively ill-defined problems. Getzels and Csikszentmihalyi (1976) went a step further, suggesting creativity involved problem formulation itself. Torrance (1963, 1974) determined that creative potential could be measured even in children; but in the American educational system, creative students were much less valued than high IQ students (Getzels & Jackson, 1962; Torrance, 1963). Follow-up studies of Torrance's students showed that those who scored high on creativity tests

did not necessarily achieve extraordinary ends as adults, although a few demonstrated more modest accomplishments (Millar, 2002; Plucker, 1999).

Building on influential earlier work on complex problem solving (Wallas, 1926; Wertheimer, 1954), theorists in the 1980s and 1990s emphasized how creativity can emerge from ordinary information processing (Finke, Ward, & Smith, 1992; Mumford, Baughman, Supinski, & Maher, 1996; Mumford, Baughman, Threlfall, Supinski, & Costanza, 1996; Mumford, Baughman, Maher, Costanza, & Supinski, 1997; Mumford, Supinski, Baughman, Costanza, & Threlfall, 1997; Perkins, 1981) and systemic interaction of emotional, cognitive, conative, and social factors (Csikszentmihalyi, 1988; Gruber, 1989). Researchers in artificial intelligence designed computer programs that recreated historically creative acts such as Kepler's discovery of the laws of motion (Boden, 1990; Hofstadter, 1995; Langley, Simon, Bradshaw, & Zytkow, 1987). Although these computer models have been criticized for programming in far too much already organized data, the models suggest how ordinary information processing can bring about extraordinary results. Dynamic computer models of creativity emphasize rate of change and interaction of abilities rather than a singular ability (Eckstein, 2000; Goertzel, 1997; Martindale, 1995).

As with intelligence, there has been a shift from investigating general creativity to processes of creativity as they unfold in specific domains and under specific conditions (Amabile, 1996; Csikszentmihalyi, 1996; Gardner, 1993a; Simonton, 1994). Idiographic case studies (Bloom, 1985; Feldman, 1986; Gardner, 1993a; John-Steiner, 2000; Wallace & Gruber, 1989) provide a way to understand how the affordances of the domain and individual characteristics interact over time to yield creative outcomes. Researchers are building a cumulative database that can serve to establish general principles of creativity (Policastro & Gardner, 1999; Simonton, 1994).

## Leadership and Morality

Leadership and morality have been studied separately from intelligence and creativity for most of the twentieth century, yet their study has followed a similar path—first conceived as a stable trait, later more as a process. Early, hereditary "great man" theories (Ellis, 1926; Galton, 1869) gave way to stable personality and motivational trait approaches (Cox, 1926; McClelland, 1967) then to interactionist theories involving cognitive "transactions of minds" (Gardner, 1995) and social-cognitive systems of leaders, followers, and situations (Burns, 1978; Gergen, 2000; Hunt, 1999; Jacobsen & House, 2001). Although high-IQ individuals often displayed leadership qualities (Terman, 1954), Thorndike (1921) suggested independence between social and academic intelligence. Extraordinary leaders tended to have above average rather than exceptionally high IQs (Cox, 1926; Thorndike, 1950), and too high an IQ could prove detrimental to leadership (Mann, 1959). In the same vein, social and moral thought became differentiated from behavior. Making perceptive moral judgments, knowing when to act appropriately, and acting morally did not always coincide (Jarecky, 1959; Walker, 2003).

Morality was first conceived psychologically as a set of character traits (Hartshorne & May, 1928–1930) acquired from society through membership in a collectivity (Durkheim, 1961), internalization (Freud, 1923/1961b, 1930/1961a), or reinforcement (Skinner, 1971). These theoretical foundations reverberated through the 1960s in psychoanalytically tinged studies relating child-rearing practices to defense mechanisms (Sears, Maccoby, & Levin, 1957) and social learning theory's research on reinforcement's contribution to guilt and internalization of norms (Bandura & Walters, 1963). Still, scholars and laymen noticed individual differences in moral maturity, which were attributed variously to heredity (Galton, 1869), gender (Freud, 1930/1961a), or stable intelligence (Terman, 1954; Thorndike, 1936). Piaget (1932) focused on the development of judgments about social relationships and documented how, with experience, these judgments become more complex, abstract, and flexible. Morality was constructed, not imposed. Kohlberg (1984) further developed Piaget's ideas, incorporating extraordinariness in his highest stages of moral reasoning.

## Personality

In contrast to the psychometric and cognitive traditions, researchers at IPAR, the Institute for Personality Assessment and Research (e.g., Barron, 1972; Helson, 1996; MacKinnon, 1975; see also Cattell & Drevdahl, 1955; Cross, Cattell, & Butcher, 1967), construed personality traits as key contributors to extraordinariness. These researchers found that creative individuals in various domains shared several personality characteristics: independence, unconventionality, openness, flexibility, and risk taking. Csikszentmihalyi (1996) synthesized these findings through his concept of complexity, with

creative individuals demonstrating integration of seemingly opposite traits such as being both energetic *and* quiet, or childlike *and* serious.

Another personality-oriented line of research continued the nineteenth-century fascination with the genius-insanity connection. The path to extraordinary achievement may be psychologically treacherous, as argued in Freud's (1910/1957) case study of Leonardo da Vinci, Erikson's (1958) case study of Martin Luther, Geschwind and Galaburda's (1987) studies of left-brain deficits and immune disorders in gifted children, and other studies of eminent creators, especially artists and poets (Andreason, 1987; Gedo, 1996; Jamison, 1989). However, Rothenberg (1990) suggests that productivity only occurs during times when the mental illness is under control. Furthermore, Storr (1988) argues that a craving for solitude or other putatively antisocial behaviors associated with extraordinariness need not stem from psychopathology.

Our survey of the literature reveals that the study of extraordinariness originally was rooted in the study of intelligence as a measurable quantity of competence leading to expertise. This competence, at first, was believed to be global in application. However, it increasingly came to be seen as domain-specific, context-dependent, and differentiated from creativity, leadership, morality, and personality factors. Interest has shifted from an all-encompassing IQ number as a predictor of extraordinariness per se to the properties, conditions, and interactions of person and setting that bring about or thwart extraordinary results.

## CURRENT ISSUES

The issues involved in the study of extraordinariness revolve around four foci:

1. *Definitional:* What is extraordinariness?
2. *Developmental:* How does extraordinariness arise?
3. *Domain specific:* What are the characteristics of various forms of extraordinariness?
4. *Methodological:* How can extraordinariness be studied?

## Definitional Issues

End-state extraordinariness includes expertise, creativity, leadership, and moral excellence. Researchers often intermingle these different forms of extraordinariness. Are these forms on the same continuum, or are they qualitatively different? Expertise comprises the highest performance in a domain without changing the domain. Examples include chess masters who can play better than anyone else but do not come up with innovative moves or new rules (De Groot, 1965) and map readers who understand the curvature of the Earth in two dimensions but do not conceive of a better representation (Anderson & Leinhardt, 2002). Expertise has been shown to extend beyond *more* knowledge to include qualitative differences in the complexity of interconnections among chunks of knowledge and in the strategies used to deploy those chunks. Expertise emerges as the most common form of end-state extraordinariness—the artists who can draw realistically, scientists who can reason rigorously, leaders who can garner a small group of followers, and everyday moral heroes.

Transformative end states, alternatively, only emerge for a handful of people per domain per century. Compared to experts, these end states of creativity, leadership, and moral excellence lead to novel configurations of symbolic resources, social organizations, or cultural values. They influence others' minds sufficiently to change the domain.

Creators engage in "conversations" with their materials or media—mathematical symbols, scientific theories, paint and canvas, and so on—that ultimately redirect or change the structure of a domain (Gardner, 1993a). Einstein reconceived Newton's mechanical universe in relativistic terms. Thomas Edison ushered in the twentieth-century, electronics-dominated, modern lifestyle. Creators influence others indirectly through their products. For example, other artists or patrons thought differently after seeing Cubist paintings by Picasso and Braque. Depending on the number, intensity, and timing of people influenced, creators' achievements can range from everyday, little-c creativity to historical, big-C creativity. We emphasize individuals whose innovations are historically important. For example, Newton and Leibnitz invented calculus in the late seventeenth century; it is now standard fare for high school and college students.

In contrast, leadership is a more direct form of influence, customarily achieved through person-to-person contacts or organizationally role-mediated interaction (Gardner, 1995). Leaders affect members of a society directly through their words or actions. They also attempt to influence through the power bases of organizations—such as legislatures, funding organizations, and regulatory agencies—that garner and dispense important resources. Like creativity, leadership forms a continuum, from little-l forms such as a child taking initiative to organize a playground game or a parent who organizes a bake sale, to middle-l forms such as local politicians or small-business presidents, to big-L forms such as revolutionaries, key national political figures, and executives of multinational organizations. The less ambitious forms of leadership tend to involve basic exchange processes to satisfy current needs, whereas the higher forms are transformative, impacting future, foreseen (and perhaps also unforeseen) needs (Burns, 1978).

Like the political and corporate forms of leadership, moral influence typically proceeds in a direct manner, through language, imagery, and social interaction. But in contrast, moral excellence dwells in the realm of values and is as much a conversation with oneself as with others. The outcomes can be far-reaching and symbolic; like the most impressive forms of creativity, moral excellence can change the value structure of a domain or society (Gardner, 1993a, 1997; Gardner, Csikszentmihalyi, & Damon, 2001). For example, like other leaders, Gandhi conveyed his message of India home rule through speeches, writings, and peaceful demonstrations. But his philosophical principles of *satyagraha* (a composite of the Hindu words for "truth" and "holding firmly"), which featured nonviolent resistance to injustice, continues to affect religious and legal/political domains around the world (Erikson, 1969; Gardner, 1993a). Moral excellence also forms a continuum, from little-m such as individual altruistic or heroic acts, to middle-m such as leading others in a moral way, to big-M which mobilizes groups to build a more socially just society.

At the start of the twenty-first century, the growing complexity and variety of forms of extraordinariness call for an integration of individual differences research with developmental research. *Genius* no longer suffices as an all-encompassing term. Extraordinariness can vary by form (expertise, creativity, leadership, moral leadership), degree (everyday acts as contrasted with transformative movements), interaction (direct and social as in leadership versus indirect and symbolic as in creativity and morality), and scope (influence within a domain versus crossing domain or national boundaries).

## Developmental Issues

Although extraordinariness is viewed increasingly as a life-span phenomenon, developmental research has focused primarily on children. Extraordinariness at early ages includes giftedness, talent, and prodigiousness. Compared to adult end-state forms of extraordinariness that emphasize achievement, developmental forms aim to identify children with potential; often, efforts are undertaken to accelerate or enrich the early experiences of select youngsters. *Giftedness* generally reflects an unusually high capacity for, proclivity toward, or faster rate of learning in a domain, mostly in scholastic domains such as language and logic or mathematics (Lubinski & Benbow, 2000; Winner, 1996a). *Talent* is used to designate high capacity or faster development in nonscholastic domains such as the arts, athletics, or social graces (Winner, 1996b). Although intelligence is still mostly conceived of and measured as a singular, global, abstract, problem-solving ability, trends suggest a construal of intelligence as a complex profile of domain-specific, biopsychological potentials. The issue changes from a determination of whether a person *is* gifted to an identification of domains in which a person *displays* gifts. Identification is based usually on comparative performance evaluations by teachers and coaches. *Giftedness* or *talent* is no longer "being smarter"; rather, these terms can be invoked to describe people of all ages and profiles who master a domain or situation with unusual facility.

*Prodigiousness* represents an interesting cross between an end-state and a developmental form of extraordinariness. The term describes adult, expert-level performance in a domain by a child younger than 10—for example, performing complicated pieces, calculating quickly, vying with chess masters, and drawing realistically or with personal style (Feldman, 1986; Winner, 1996b). Found most often in domains that have clear performance standards, such as mathematics, chess, and music, and less often in more ill-defined or integrative fields, such as politics, business or morality, these *Wunderkinder* reach the pinnacle of the culture's current standard at a phenomenal rate. They demonstrate an uncanny affinity for and agile skill in a particular domain's tasks and requirements, and they are well supported by parents, teachers, and structured practice (Bloom, 1985). Although prodigies might seem more likely to become adult extraordinary achievers, prodigiousness actually can constitute an obstacle. Young people may become stuck in the expert position, having received such acclaim for their early performances that they do not develop the independence or rebelliousness entailed in the most impressive, transformative achievements (Gardner, 1997).

Accordingly, developmental researchers have distinguished between potential and achievement, with potential an early precursor or capacity that influences and supports, but is not sufficient to determine, later work outcomes (Bloom, 1985; Gardner, 1993b; Helson & Pais, 2000). Many studies have examined antecedents of extraordinariness, such as birth order, family environment, and apprenticeships (Bloom, 1985; Goertzel & Goertzel, 1962, 1978; Simonton, 1994; Sulloway, 1996). Researchers who study extraordinariness through its products (Martindale, 1990; Simonton, 2000) or its most powerful exemplars (Gardner, 1993a; Wallace & Gruber, 1989) emphasize the interaction of individual differences and expected developmental trajectories (Gardner, 1993a; Helson & Pais, 2000).

**Domain Issues**

Extraordinariness has become viewed increasingly as a domain-specific phenomenon. Domains were invisible to earlier researchers (Piaget, 1937/1995, 1955/1995; Terman, 1925). The discovery of Vygotsky's work (1935/1994, 1934/1962, 1978) called attention to media and tools as mediators of performance. Several perspectives—cognitive science (Fodor, 1983), artificial intelligence (Boden, 1990; Hofstadter, 1995; Langley et al., 1987), and developmental psychology (Feldman, 1986; Gardner, 1983, 1988; John-Steiner, 1985)—have directed attention to the importance of the particular sphere in which an individual works. To understand extraordinariness, one must understand its contexts—the socially valued activities and corresponding symbol systems that afford extraordinary performance. As a result, researchers have called for ecologically valid studies of people working in situ (Dunbar, 1996; Gardner, 1993a; Hutchins, 1996; John-Steiner, 2000). Context, in turn, entails two aspects: (1) the symbolic and (2) the social.

The symbolic context involves the domain itself as a body of knowledge, symbol systems, and notations associated with a certain type of work or activity (Csikszentmihalyi 1996; Gardner, Phelps, & Wolf, 1990). For example, in the United States, the Constitution, federal and local laws, and legal terminology are all aspects of the law domain. Domains exist in individuals' minds and in artifacts produced by individuals, such as books, files, artworks, and inventions. No one individual "holds" all of a domain in his or her mind; rather, a domain is parceled out differentially among minds and media (Hutchins, 1996; Mieg, 2001).

This dispersion in any domain creates an important tension that stimulates extraordinary efforts. To be sure, much of an established domain is agreed on by people who have mastered it through schooling or a formal or informal apprenticeship; that is what makes it a domain. But surrounding this agreed-on core are idiosyncratic perspectives—old conceptions, misunderstandings, or yet-to-be-accepted, potentially innovative approaches (Merton, 1949/1967; Moran & John-Steiner, 2003; Vygotsky, 1934/1962). As such idiosyncratic perspectives are explored and found promising, what is initially unique or idiosyncratic ultimately becomes domainwide, culturewide, and possibly even universal (Feldman, 1994; Martindale, 1990). In addition, domains can change in their importance to the wider society and culture; some, such as science and business, have become increasingly more central in America, whereas arts, crafts, and civil debate to some extent have been marginalized (Bourdieu, 1993; Feldman, 1994; Gardner, 2001; Sorokin, 1947/1969).

The social context involves the field, a social organization for controlling practices in the domain. For example, law schools, the Bar, and the court system comprise institutions in the law field. Individuals who know something of the domain may be inside (professionals) or outside the field (amateurs or eccentrics). Based on abilities, interests, and opportunities, individuals take on roles defined by the field, such as trial lawyer, law school professor, or paralegal aide. With respect to extraordinary achievement, the function of the field is to determine which individual contributions are worthy to incorporate into the domain and preserve for future generations. Usually this judgment is based on the criteria of "novel and appropriate" (Amabile, 1996). Even in domains in which individuals seem to work in solitude, such as painting or writing, social institutions enable, disseminate, and give value to their contributions—consider the roles of teachers and mentors, materials suppliers, developers of technical improvements, critics, preservers (such as libraries and museums), and audiences (Becker, 1982; Bourdieu, 1993; Gardner, 1973).

The first societal activities to be researched from a domain-specific perspective were art and science: Bamberger's (1982) studies in music, Gardner's (1982) and Winner's (1982) studies in the visual and literary arts, and studies in math and science by Gruber (1981), Helson and Crutchfield (1970), Roe (1946, 1952), and Zuckerman (1977). In contrast to other spheres of activity, such as business or law, art and science tend to be more isolated from quotidian interactions and to require more specific, focused skills and dispositions, which we might call "laserlike" intelligences (Gardner, 2006). Artists and scientists keep to themselves, and their work depends less on consumers other than fellow artists and scientists (Bourdieu, 1993; Martindale, 1990).

Other domains, including leadership and morality, are murkier to formulate. Although leadership is found in many occupational domains, from business to sports, it also constitutes a form of expertise in itself. Similarly, any domain—art, science, politics, medicine, and so on—involves moral dimensions, but morality is also a domain organized, studied, and reproduced in its own right. Forms of extraordinariness that cross traditional domain boundaries emphasize "searchlight" intelligences that integrate information and skills from a variety of sources and that allow for communication to an audience much broader than one's fellow practitioners (Gardner, 2006).

## Methodological Issues

The end-state and developmental forms of extraordinariness typically have been studied by different methods. Experimental or observational studies with children or savants compare potential in abilities and dispositions (Milbraith, 1998; Selfe, 1995; Siegler, 1978). Experimental and microgenetic problem-solving designs examine differences between strong and weak performers' cognitive processing mechanisms and environmental constraints (Chi et al., 1982; Ericsson, 1998; D. Kuhn, Garcia-Mila, Zohar, & Andersen, 1995). Antecedents and concomitants of extraordinary achievement are ascertained through case studies (Colby & Damon, 1994; Gardner, 1993a; Gergen, 2000; Wallace & Gruber, 1989), interview studies (Csikszentmihalyi, 1996; John-Steiner, 1985), document analyses (Gruber, 1974; Holmes, 1989; A. Miller, 1989; Tweney, 1989), and historiometric surveys (Cox, 1926; Murray, 2003; Simonton, 1994).

Solid developmental or longitudinal evidence is in short supply. Most studies have been correlational and cross-sectional, documenting numerous differences between novices and experts, experts and creators, creators and leaders, followers and leaders, and children with low or high potential. Less is known about how a novice becomes an expert or creator. Retrospective and historiometric studies start with individuals known to be extraordinary; but often a collection of their childhood work or experiences is lacking. Longitudinal studies provide a richer base of developmental material, but there is no guarantee that childhood potential will develop into adult extraordinariness. More recent microgenetic studies have illuminated the detailed processes of thinking, discovery, or creation at a small scale but often do not connect these thinking patterns with real-life, domain-transforming events. The few longitudinal and case studies show that extraordinariness takes decades to develop. Its particular form is epigenetically determined as genetic endowment and environment change affect each other in different ways over the life span (Lykken, McGue, Tellegen, & Bouchard, 1992; Spinath, Ronald, Harlaar, Price, & Plomin, 2003).

A common criticism of the extraordinariness literature is its overreliance of samples of White, middle-class males (e.g., Murray, 2003). A few researchers, however, have looked at how gender, race, and culture affect interaction, performance, and assessment (Jensen, 1980; Simonton, 1998). For example, women's paths to extraordinary achievements seem to be more complex, less integrated, and less culturally supported than men's (Benbow & Stanley, 1983; Helson, 1999; Holahan et al., 1995; Sears & Barbee, 1977). Similarly, studies in non-middle-class or non-Western cultures suggest a disjunct between real-life and scholastic performance: Brazilian street children can run a business and Kenyan students can do sophisticated mathematical manipulations at home, but they do not perform well on SAT or IQ tests (Ceci, 1996; Sternberg et al., 2001). In addition, cultural and historical contexts affect which qualities are deemed desirable and which work is innovative—consider the different criteria obtained from China in the Ming dynasty, Florence in the Renaissance, or Silicon Valley circa 1990 (Csikszentmihalyi, 1996; Gardner, 1989; Schneider, 1999; Simonton, 1994).

## A DEVELOPMENTAL-SYSTEMIC FRAMEWORK

To capture the contemporary pull toward a multidimensional, interactive, developmental perspective, we expand a model originally developed for creativity (Csikszentmihalyi, 1988, 1996). Extraordinariness emerges in a three-component system composed of *individuals* working in a particular *domain* that is under partial control by the

*field*. The role of the individual is to generate variation in the domain—to come up with new ideas, procedures, arrangements, or products that may stimulate domain growth or newly position the domain relative to other domains (Simonton, 1999). The role of the domain is to provide a fount of past knowledge and practices against which to judge new contributions, cross-generational storage of past contributions, and symbolic materials on which future extraordinary contributions draw (Feldman, 1994; T. Kuhn, 1962; Martindale, 1990). For example, researchers in genetics must learn what is already known from past researchers, methods that are currently acceptable scientific practice, and scientific discourses (e.g., publication formats, conference formats). The role of the field is to allocate resources and determine which variations are worthy to incorporate into the domain and preserve for future generations. For example, researchers in genetics must work in one or another institution where research is carried out, such as universities, hospitals, or for-profit companies; submit papers to journal editors, who will determine whether they merit publication; and abide by regulations relating to conflicts-of-interest. Extraordinariness requires all three components. Without individual variation, the domain stagnates. Without the domain, there is only social interaction with no collective memory. Without the field, there is no informed way to evaluate new contributions.

This systems model freshly illuminates extraordinariness. It shifts extraordinariness from being a property of an individual—be it IQ score or personality trait—to being a property of a constantly evolving and interacting set of components. Experts are individuals (typically with laserlike intelligence) who understand the domain well and hold established positions of power in the field. Prodigies are similar except they rarely hold positions of power. Thus, experts stabilize both the domain and the field, and serve as the primary gatekeepers of distribution channels—be they artistic galleries or scientific journals—to which an individual's contribution must be submitted to garner field support. Expertise represents a relatively unproblematic alignment among individual, domain, and field.

Creators also command the domain but often stand in significant misalignment to the standardized concepts presented by the field (i.e., the concepts as presented in textbooks). Creators may also exhibit laserlike intelligence, but the laser pinpoints different, less well-known aspects of the domain. Whereas experts seem to fall into a career based on fit between the person and the environment, creators select a domain with an eye toward making an original contribution (Gardner, 1993a; Gardner & Nemirovsky, 1991; Rank, 1932; Shekerjian, 1990). Creators may, but need not, work their way up the career ladder of a field. Innovative contributions may be accepted by a field early or late in one's career (Galenson, 2001; Lehman, 1953; Simonton, 1994; Zuckerman, 1977). Creativity stems from a fruitful misalignment within or among individual, domain, and field, at least during key stages of career development.

Like ordinary leaders, who tend to function similar to experts and are often termed "managers," extraordinary leaders need to understand relevant domains. Thus, J. Robert Oppenheimer was knowledgeable about physics; Alfred Sloan mastered the automobile industry (Gardner, 1995). To effect significant change, however, leaders need a big-picture, generalist knowledge base and searchlight intelligence (Gardner, 2004a; Gergen, 2000). Unlike the scholastically gifted, leaders rarely are recognized in childhood; they need to spend significant time in real-world interactions. Leaders tend to emerge from the ranks—CEOs have held lower-management jobs, presidents held local political positions, generals were once privates or sergeants. Initially, leadership arises from a power alignment between individual and field—others follow the leader. But a transformative leader demonstrates his or her skill by navigating a misalignment between the current field composition and the ideal resolution of the situation or aspirations of the followers.

By changing values, moral extraordinariness can result in dramatic transformation of all parts of the system. For example, both indirectly, through his writings and speeches, and directly, through his nonviolent protests, Martin Luther King Jr. changed the status of the African-American community in America in the 1960s. His influence continues to be felt today. In its most extraordinary form, moral excellence takes the longest, faces the most resistance from current domain and field forces, and is the most difficult to accomplish. Moral excellence results from a misalignment of assumptions and values among individual, domain, and field. For example, Gandhi overcame the entrenched imperial notions of the British nation (Gardner, 1993a), while French economist Jean Monnet overcame nationalistic and jingoistic predispositions to lay the foundation for the European Union (Gardner, 1997).

The systems model also alters the construal of how extraordinariness develops. Extraordinariness is no longer an unfolding of inborn talents nor the consequence of well-timed environmental supports or challenges. It is manifested differently at different ages, can be impacted differentially by the same experience depending on age or circumstance, and it must respond to the continuing evolution of the domain and field (e.g., Feldman, 1986; Gardner, 1993a; Lykken et al., 1992; Sawyer, 1999). For example, with age, individual genetic contribution goes up (Plomin, DeFries, McClearn, & McGuffin, 2001) but general intelligence's contribution goes down (Ceci, 1996) in relation to cognitive performance. Adults may be better able to choose and tailor their environments—both social and symbolic—to their inborn sensitivities and dispositions (Changeux & Ricouer, 2000; Granott & Gardner, 1994; Moran & John-Steiner, 2003).

Several new tensions arise in this framework. For example, experts work to maintain the status quo or make only controllable, small, incremental, quantitative changes to the system, whereas transformers work to effect riskier, qualitative leaps. Should creators and leaders succeed in transforming the system, they render the experts' expertise less valuable and experts' power less palpable. For example, the Impressionists and the Cubists made the works of nineteenth-century Academicians look staid and less collectable. Yet, experts hold the strings to the primary resources and outlets for these innovators' efforts and often are the mentors of future transformers. So creators and leaders must change the minds of enough experts to secure social support needed to make a difference.

Issues of timing are also crucial for the aspiring transformer. If someone else publishes a breakthrough scientific finding or artistic technique first—as Einstein and Woolf did—a person working along the same lines is thwarted from earning the label of "creative" and citation in future textbooks (Kasof, 1995; Merton, 1957; Simonton, 1994). This timing is partially under the power of current experts in the field regarding to whom they pay attention and provide support. Therefore, individuals in different field roles battle for influence over the domain, thereby facilitating or thwarting development for themselves, contemporaries, and successors.

A second tension involves the differential influence of domain and field across an individual's life-span development. Domains and fields come to the fore and occupy specific niches at different periods of a person's life. Children first learn about many domains—such as science, drawing, music, and storytelling—through play or informal social interaction. Most people (except prodigies) do not encounter the field until adolescence, when they come to realize and experiment with the social manifestations—roles, positions, institutions—associated with different domains. For example, a child scribbles as a preschooler, learns drawing conventions in school, and starts to pursue a career in art after winning the high school art prize. Established requirements of roles, jobs, and social propriety can eclipse opportunities for more direct interaction with the domain through play or leisure. It may be easier for people who hold marginal positions in the field to make transformative breakthroughs—consider Einstein as a patent office clerk in Bern or Gandhi as a young expatriate Indian lawyer in South Africa. Such outliers have the time and space to play in the domain and explore its latent opportunities without the responsibilities and the obligations of field roles. For these individuals, field influences came into play chiefly after they had developed key ideas and practices.

Third is the interdependence of the individual and domain (Moran & John-Steiner, 2003). We focus on individual development, but it is important to note that cultural domains develop as well (Freud, 1930/1961a; Vygotsky, 1960/1997). As individuals create, their variations slowly change the norm for their domains (Martindale, 1990). Individual development proceeds at a much faster pace than domain development, but the two dialectically affect each other. For example, artists first work with domain elements in accordance with socially accepted standards and aesthetic tastes of their times (Getzels & Csikszentmihalyi, 1976; Simonton, 1994; Vygotsky, 1965/1971). Certain innovations cannot occur until the supporting tools are available—whether those tools be new graphic, perceptual, or conceptual instruments (John-Steiner, 1995; Vygotsky, 1935/1994). The power structures of the field can limit or enable the person's awareness of and access to these domain elements (Bourdieu, 1993).

Furthermore, the current state of a domain determines whether a particular individual's contribution will have a ripple effect. Domains follow a trajectory similar to individuals: from amorphous and general forms through increasing differentiation and integration to more complex forms. A new, relatively undifferenti-

ated domain, such as computer software in the 1980s or Internet journalism recently, can be a fertile ground for new ideas to grow as there are few social or symbolic constraints. However, the primitive state of the domain makes it difficult to separate the good ideas from the bad. A well-developed, cohesive domain, such as mathematics, makes it easier to notice useful novelties because a broader base of knowledge for judgment exists, assessment criteria are clearer, and a hierarchical field structure is in place.

A fragmented domain, such as visual art, may prove especially conducive to the development of individual creative potential (Simonton, 1975). Such a domain provides a complex environment to stimulate individual development toward transformative ends. As a "horizontal" environment, it is less restrictive than traditional "vertical" domains with more stable career paths (Keinanen & Gardner, 2004; Li, 1997). Such fragmentation and complexity at the societal level also may enhance individual potential. For example, splintered politics, cultures that interact via trade or immigration, and rebellion against oppression can increase the likelihood of extraordinary achievements from individuals in these milieus (Simonton, 1975; Sorokin, 1947/1969; Wolfe, 2001). One need only think of Florence in the Renaissance or Vienna in 1900 (Csikszentmihalyi 1996; Schorske, 1979).

We now turn to an analysis of these developmental processes and trajectories in four domain systems: (1) visual art, (2) biological and physical sciences, (3) political leadership, and (4) moral excellence. We organize findings from the literature to show how each domain presents a particular end state, developmental trajectory, and individual-domain interaction pattern for ordinary (usually deemed universal) and extraordinary achievements. The ordinary development trajectory, at its extreme, leads to expertise. The treatment of extraordinary development highlights key developmental points or processes culminating in domain or field transformation.

## ART

Art involves giving symbolic form to individual or collective thoughts, emotions, or ideas (Arnheim, 1966; Gardner, 1973; Goodman, 1976; Langer, 1957). The most valued artworks often play in surprising ways with the cultural or social expectations of the artist and/or audience (Bruner, 1962; Meyer, 1956). Extraordinary artists must master the techniques of the domain through independent work and/or working with masters from the field; they also feel free to reconfigure the media. In some historical periods, the art field has been more supportive of technical mastery—as with the portraitists in the seventeenth and eighteenth centuries; at other times, the field has been more oriented toward innovation—as in the twentieth century. Therefore, the time in which an artist enters the field greatly influences the expected developmental end state. Unlike other fields, where the expert is the expected end state, the expected end state for artistic development currently is the creator, although most artists only become technically proficient professionals. The expert designation in the field tends to be relegated to the supporting roles of art historian, critic, or curator—people who know a lot *about* art but do not necessarily produce it (Becker, 1982; Gardner, 1973).

We have chosen to focus our analysis largely, though not exclusively, on the role of the visual artist. Drawing and painting are accessible to children at a very young age, and children's visual artistry has been studied extensively (see Winner, Chapter 20, this *Handbook,* this volume). Art production is a nearly universal practice of young children as they scribble on paper, associate those marks with objects in the world, and increasingly portray those objects realistically. Yet, few children become professional artists as adults—much less artists who change the way people see and represent the world. Longitudinal studies show no more than one-third of young artists continue their artistry past college, and very few achieve lasting influence (Getzels & Csikszentmihalyi, 1976; Milbraith, 1998).

## Ordinary Development

Children tend to be conservative in their initial artistic efforts, using a circle to represent many different objects, or changing peripheral but not core features (Arnheim, 1974; Goodnow, 1977). Over time, young scribblers learn to differentiate, coordinate, and vary the shape, size, quantity, and position of pictorial elements into an integrated whole (Goodnow, 1977; Karmiloff-Smith, 1990). Children go through a less expressive, so-called "literal period" in middle childhood, when they accept realistic cultural norms, such as those found in comic books. Many never develop their artistic skills beyond this stage of stereotypical representation (Winner, 1982).

In adolescence, those who continue in art become more sensitive to expressive and aesthetic qualities of pictures. They experiment with subject matter, media properties, and cultural conventions in accordance with their budding artistic purposes (Gardner, 1980; Winner, 1996b). Depending on their individual values and available social opportunities, some start to orient more toward fine art and others toward applied art, such as advertising or design (Getzels & Csikszentmihalyi, 1976). Those who identify themselves as artists, find appropriate social outlets for expressing their talents, and manage to eke out a living may go on to become adult artists (Csikszentmihalyi, Rathunde, & Whalen, 1993).

As adults, artists attempt to become recognized in the field. Because the art field is more loosely organized than many others (Becker, 1982; Csikszentmihalyi, 1996), the developmental trajectory for an art vocation is not so age—or stage—graded. Many, including extraordinary achievers like Van Gogh, try other careers first (Brower, 2000; Sloane & Sosniak, 1985). Artists do not need institutionalized credentials; they can create art, sell their works, and earn awards without a formal field position, although such a position can help secure resources and opportunities (McCall, 1978). Most artists' productivity peaks in their 40s, a later age than that characterizing most other fields (Lindauer, 1993; Simonton, 1994). Moreover, as long as they remain healthy, artists can produce well into old age—Picasso and Titian being two well-known examples.

## Markers of Extraordinariness

When young, extraordinary achievers' works may not stray far from the ordinary. Knowledgeable contemporary judges could not distinguish the childhood drawings of Klee, Toulouse-Lautrec, Calder, Miro, Munch, O'Keeffe, and Wyeth from those of schoolchildren (Rostan, Pariser, & Gruber 2002). Though later extraordinary artists may stand out by learning more quickly, they apparently did not go through different stages that distinguished them from many other children (Gardner, 1980; Milbraith, 1998; Pariser, 1995; Winner, 1982).

Nonetheless, the literature documents five facets relevant to extraordinariness: (1) innate talent, (2) precocity, (3) conceptual versus perceptual orientation, (4) realistic versus stylistic goals, and (5) identification with the field. These approaches roughly coincide with developmental ages through the samples used to study them—precocity and orientation with young children, realism and style in early adolescence, and identification with late adolescence and adulthood—but they should not be considered strictly age-graded. Studies of younger children focus more on individual attributes, the domain becomes a factor in middle childhood, and the field becomes increasingly important thereafter.

### Talent

More than other domains, art seems to call for special talent. Even though everyone draws as a child, not everyone draws well. Many who do draw well seem to learn it on their own with little coaching or coaxing. Even the earliest drawings of talented children stand out—portraying a scene from an unusual angle or with remarkably more detail (Winner, 1996b). Historically, artistic ability seemed to run in families: Picasso's father was a painter; Marcel Duchamp had three siblings who were also artists; and the Wyeth family name has long been associated with visual artistry. Talented artists often show a pattern of strengths and weaknesses characteristic of dominance of the brain's right hemisphere: tendencies toward left-handedness; strong pattern recognition, mental rotation, and visual memory abilities; language deficits such as dyslexia; simultaneous/spatial rather than sequential/categorical information processing strategies; detail orientation; and heightened emotionality (Geschwind, 1984; Winner, 1996b). Striking evidence for innate talent comes from artistic savants, who may be found in both visual art and music (L. Miller, 1989; Sacks, 1995). Selfe (1977, 1995) documented the artworks of Nadia, an autistic child with severely curtailed linguistic and social abilities who, without instruction, could draw with photographic realism and conventional perspective when but 4 or 5 years old.

The talent approach suggests that those who achieve extraordinary ends are unusual from the beginning. With mere exposure to the domain, they easily and enjoyably learn by themselves the skills to draw realistically, an achievement that presumably creates momentum. Although such ease in learning might suggest a role for general intelligence, artistically inclined individuals tend to score poorly on traditional, scholastic-oriented IQ tests (Getzels & Jackson, 1962; Hudson, 1966). Artistic talent coincides more with a jagged profile of intelligences. Extraordinary drawing ability often coincides with weak intelligences—perhaps, interpersonal or scholastic—as well as expectedly strong spatial and

bodily kinesthetic intelligences. For example, Picasso had difficulty learning to read, write, add, and subtract (Gardner, 1993a), as did several other precocious children artists (Milbraith, 1995). Alternatively—at least in our era—it may be that children who are both artistically and academically gifted are less likely to become artists because they have available careers that are more valued, such as science or business. Artistic extraordinariness in today's economic and cultural conditions may *require* a jagged profile, which narrows vocational choice.

No one intelligence is artistic in and of itself; all can be mobilized for aesthetic purposes (Gardner, 1983). However, exceptional spatial intelligence, in particular, can help the visual artist with observation, orientation and perspective taking, sensitivity to form, and fine motor control (Golomb, 1995). Still, spatial intelligence need not be focal for an artist; other intellectual strengths such as the geometric facet of mathematical intelligence or the sensual movement of bodily kinesthetic intelligence may also catalyze breakthrough artworks. For example, Maurits Escher's optical artistry reflects keen mathematical skills, and Jackson Pollock's action paintings were as much created by his whole-body movement with the paint as by his eyes or his hands. Such diversity challenges a neat formulation of artistic talent. The biopsychological potential to render one's experience graphically may be less important than the aesthetic (or nonaesthetic) ends to which that potential is mobilized (Goodman, 1976; Winner, 1996b).

### Precocity

Studies that focus on young children emphasize differences in the timing of milestones. Extraordinariness stems not from a different path or skipping stages but rather from an easier and speedier journey—for example, drawing recognizable shapes and increasing one's repertoire of forms, details, orientations, and strategies 1 to 2 years ahead of others (Golomb, 1995; Milbraith, 1998; Winner, 1996b). Picasso, whom many consider to have been a prodigy, could draw with near adult skill at age 9 (Gardner, 1993a). Klee and Toulouse-Lautrec also tackled the common childhood drawing problems well ahead of their age-mates (Pariser, 1987).

In a landmark comparative study, Milbraith (1998) observed that more talented children, as nominated by teachers, draw recognizable shapes at age 2 rather than the expected ages 3 to 4. Precocious artists start pictures in unusual places (such as with the ear instead of the head); present noncanonical views of a subject (such as from the back or side rather than the full frontal view); and may pick up geometric perspective without instruction. Overall they are more confident and less likely to erase lines. Their strategies and products are unusually varied. The more talented tend to show less stable, nonlinear trajectories, whereas the less talented exhibit steady, linear growth. Still, the less talented rarely catch up to the skill level of the more talented. Although models of art might be available, the more talented have been playing in the domain largely on their own and developing idiosyncratic strategies for dealing with common art problems.

Early excellence does not always translate into later artistic extraordinariness. For example, Eitan, who first drew at age 2 and could depict with perspective around age 3½, as a young adult considered architecture or automobile design rather than fine art as a career (Golomb, 1995). One reason for the disjunct may be a chasm that needs to be leapt in middle childhood or adolescence. The precocious child must reconcile idiosyncratically derived, motor-based strategies with the culturally derived strategies favored in academic settings—a battle between individual and field-approved approaches to the domain. Bamberger (1982) described such a "midlife crisis" for early achievers in music as the bridge from figural to formal musical knowledge structuring. Milbraith (1995) extended this argument to the visual arts: later representation strategies that use linear perspective may prove hard to assimilate for precocious artists who somehow contrived their own ways to render depth.

### Conceptual versus Perceptual Orientation

By age 3, most children categorize an entity as a chair, an apple, or an elephant. They draw on these general schemas and have no reason to inspect the object further (Arnheim, 1974; Gombrich, 1960; Goodnow, 1977). Milbraith's (1998) comparative study found this conceptual predominance among the less talented. This overreliance on standardized knowledge impoverishes these children's visual sensitivity, limiting what they can later draw.

In contrast, the more talented children approach their subject matter with a different kind of mental eye. They tend to draw what they see, even if it counters the conventional models. These students draw categorically only briefly before switching to visually oriented rendering. More sensitive to visual discrepancies and patterns, their drawings include more elaboration. Talented

young artists may not necessarily need to *know* how to draw in perspective; their drawings may simulate perspective simply because the children can see that certain lines of an object approximate a particular diagonal angle. A strong perceptual faculty also may inoculate these children during the literal stage of artistic development. Rather than taking cultural norms as given, they construe them as one more variable to manipulate in their drawings; they trust what they personally observe, in the process developing their own visual vocabularies (Radford, 1990).

Observations of autistic youth support the argument of differences in orientation. Alex exhibited low conceptual abilities but high spatial abilities. He could draw "in perspective" at age 6. In the absence of input from the field via schooling, he was dominated by the properties of the domain. But as he developed more field-influenced conceptual knowledge by age 8, his drawings became less realistic and more like those of his agemates (Milbraith, 1998). Similarly, as Nadia grew older and developed a few more language skills, she began drawing in the more canonical, conceptual way of young children (Selfe, 1995).

An overreliance on perception can harbor its own problems. For instance, young Picasso wanted to treat numbers as visual patterns not quantity symbols, a proclivity that held him back in school (Gardner, 1993a). Milbraith (1998) concludes that neither conception nor perception is intrinsically better. Rather, the integration of the two perspectives leads to advanced artistic skill by providing children with flexible control for experimenting with subjects and medium properties. Extraordinariness seems to arise from the individual's purposeful manipulation and integration of both more field-influenced conventions and more idiosyncratic understandings of the domain.

### Realistic versus Stylistic Goals

Most studies of childhood drawing assume an end state of realism. However, at least since the invention of photography, which undermined the mission of preserving experience graphically, a newer end state of expressiveness has emerged—the domain and its attendant field expectations changed. The capacity to produce expressive works may prove crucial in determining whether an artist becomes creative and not just proficient and professional. Whereas a child may be heralded as a prodigy for nearly photographic reproduction, an adult artist is expected to create a deeper stratum of feeling, understanding, or meaning (Gardner, 1980). Creativity extends beyond technical proficiency to the emergence of a distinctive style. Despite impressive achievements, savants rarely go beyond photographic realism to improvise and, therefore, their products are rarely considered creative (Gardner, 1982). As a result, researchers who study artistic development in adolescence or adulthood now emphasize the emergence of style and expression (Csikszentmihalyi et al., 1993; Hudson, 1966; Radford, 1990).

Although individual differences in style can appear as early as age 7, they do not fully blossom until adolescence (Winner, 1996b). Children first imitate others' styles. Even eminent artists at first studied and appropriated the styles of historical masters or contemporary artists in their quest for opportunities inherent in their artistic media (Brower, 2000; Gardner, 1973, 1993a; Pariser, 1987; Vendler, 2003). Superceding standard technical expectations, some eventually develop a personal aesthetic that guides their decision making (Kay, 2000). Klee's whimsical sketches as a child, for example, seemed to support his later mature style, and Toulouse-Lautrec's intense concentration on the emotional impact of certain graphic approaches led to his highly stylized posters and other works (Pariser, 1987, 1995).

Some researchers suggest that style does not develop linearly but follows a U-shaped trajectory, at least in Western culture. Preschool children's drawings have personal style, which tends to decrease during elementary school when stereotypes predominate. Style reemerges in adolescence for a few, who now have gained more control over their graphic repertoire (Davis, 1997; Gardner & Wolf, 1988; Rosenblatt & Winner, 1988). Perhaps those who emerge on the upward swing of the U-curve—who survive the literal period—are those who establish a trust in their own viewpoint at a very young age, thus achieving a resilience that others lack. Young children can produce (but not perceive in others' artworks) stylistic elements without knowing why they are important, whereas adolescents and adults—more metacognitively aware—can perceive and produce stylistic elements intentionally (Carothers & Gardner, 1979). Their ability to manipulate the artistic medium subtly becomes focal to their artistry.

Precocious young artists may develop their first style as young as age 10; they do so by increasing details or providing variations on canonical themes or methods (Gardner, 1980; Winner, 1996b). Golomb and Haas's (1995) longitudinal case study of Varda from age 2 to her adult vocation as a sculptor shows such a shift. Early styles rarely are innovative. Even Picasso's Blue and Rose periods in his 20s stray little from the realistic norms of Western art at the time.

Vendler (2003) conducted a detailed study of four major English-language poets "coming into their own." She documented how each, with increasing intention, played aesthetically with the affordances of language: Milton with mystical imagery, Keats with the sonnet form, T. S. Eliot with middle-class mores, and Plath with the constraints of domesticity and family relations. Brower (2000) conducted a similar study of Van Gogh. After years of experimenting with lighting, drawing, painting, multiple media, and Japanese techniques, Van Gogh matured his own style of pulsating lines, thickly applied paint, and vibrant coloring. These artists learn to manipulate, manage, and integrate many aspects of their ideas, media, and practices until they become able purposefully to vary cultural or domain conventions. Once field norms have been internalized but no longer dominate one's thinking, style emerges from the ongoing interaction of individual interests and domain properties.

### Identity as an Artist

A final approach to extraordinariness in art, typically focused on late adolescence and early adulthood, emphasizes the social dimension: how a person identifies as an artist, is accepted by others as an artist, and finds a congenial position in the art field. Construing the determination of creativity as a social process, some researchers analyze how a person navigates interactions with other people, groups, and institutions, thereby garnering psychological and economic resources (Becker, 1982; Bourdieu, 1993; Csikszentmihalyi & Robinson, 1988). In part, this process depends on the state of the field. For example, the current modern art field demands innovation, whereas the pre-nineteenth-century Western academy-dominated field and the traditional Chinese painting field preferred works that were imitative of great masters (Li, 1997).

As adults, artists go through the same challenges of identity as others (Erikson, 1959; Marcia, 1966), but art plays a pivotal role in helping them define their unique contribution to the world, build relations with and receive praise (and criticism) from peers and family, and explore less popular vocational options (Getzels & Csikszentmihalyi, 1976; Rank, 1932; Sloane &

Sosniak, 1985). Despite their compulsions to draw as children, individuals do not necessarily experience a calling to an art career (Wrzesniewski, McCauley, Rozin, & Schwartz, 1997). Instead, their choice to become an artist evolves through accumulated and interacting decisions and happenstances with field elements—for example, attending art school, finding a mentor, envisioning a career, and becoming acculturated to art historical and critical stances (Getzels & Csikszentmihalyi, 1976).

Those who become eminent, such as Pablo Picasso or Andrew Wyeth, may benefit from a parent already in the field, so they have earlier exposure to authentic—as opposed to standardized or generic—role models, current controversies, emotional support, and exacting professional-level standards (Bloom, 1985; Gardner, 1993a). For most, however, parents and teachers either provide minimal direction or steer children away from risky artistic careers (Getzels & Csikszentmihalyi, 1976; Ochse, 1991; Sloane & Sosniak, 1985). Social obstacles or challenges also may play a role in defining one's place in the field; they may prove even more important than support in taking on a creative position that challenges the field's status quo (Gardner & Wolf, 1988).

Despite the Romantic notion of the artist as independent and free-spirited—a portrayal often perpetuated by artists themselves (Rank, 1932)—artists must develop social skills to gain attention from others (Gardner, 1993a; Getzels & Csikszentmihalyi, 1976; Kasof, 1995). Sometimes these contradictory notions of marginality and connectedness can come together when artists—such as Warhol, Toulouse-Lautrec, and Picasso—intentionally cultivate an image as an eccentric talent. Still, the artist's social interactions are often complex and sometimes antagonistic to those in powerful positions, who may themselves have been the innovators the generation before (Bloom, 1997; Bourdieu, 1993).

With no singular, culturally accepted end state for art beyond the realism of middle childhood, artists develop "against" what has come before—Impressionists reacted against academic painting, Abstract Expressionism against Cubism. So artists must learn to deal with anxiety and rejection, as well as to watch their artworks take on lives of their own in the world of art criticism and history (Jaques, 1990). It also may take considerable time for their work to be recognized. For example, concept-driven artists tend to be recognized as innovative at a younger age and their earlier paintings are worth more in the field, whereas experimental artists tend to be rec-

ognized and their work worth more later in their careers (Galenson, 2001).

### Summary

In the opening years of life, extraordinariness involves innate talent announcing itself in first drawings. The individual is preeminent. In preschool and elementary school, extraordinariness involves precocity in reaching the milestones of recognizable shapes, realism, and perspective, as well as better integration, flexibility, and control of conceptual and perceptual abilities. The individual and domain gradually begin to be affected by the field. In adolescence and adulthood, extraordinariness involves going beyond realism to develop a distinct style and finding one's place in the art field. Both constitute interactions of individual and field, somewhat paradoxically: the first in overcoming field conventions of the domain and the second in settling into (or perhaps helping to reformulate) the field's power structure. Although most of us rarely develop artistically beyond the production of stereotypical images appropriated from our culture, those who become extraordinary seem to "march to their own drummer"—trust their own vision, develop their own style, make their own mark(s) on the art world (Winner, 1996b).

## SCIENCE

Science involves the cumulative process of theorizing, testing ideas, and interpreting evidence to explain and predict how the world works. Despite science's usual steady march of small steps toward more sophisticated understanding, occasionally conditions in the domain occur in which a particular step, move, or reorientation produces an extraordinary leap in understanding (T. Kuhn, 1962). Familiar examples include Copernicus and the heliocentric solar system, Newton and his mechanical universe, and Darwin and evolution.

As with art, the most memorable or extraordinary discoveries reorient cultural or social understanding of a phenomenon. But unlike contemporary art, science includes both experts and creators as important end states. Experts deepen and extend our current understanding of a phenomenon through replication studies, use of current methodologies, and support of current theories. Creators reformulate understandings of a phenomenon through innovative methodologies, unexpected findings, or new theoretical frameworks. Because of the trajectory of science, in which ideas build on one another, once a creator's idea or discovery becomes accepted by the field and transforms the domain, he or she tends to hold an expert position in the transformed field. Very few scientists make more than one large-scale, transformative discovery. They spend their later years solidifying their breakthrough idea and training those who, they hope, will perpetuate and deepen it but who may ultimately overthrow it (Gardner, 1993a; Nakamura & Csikszentmihalyi, 2003).

This linear trajectory also creates differences across domains. Although the initial appearance in children of scientific thinking remains a subject of controversy (cf. Carruthers, 2002; Gopnik & Meltzoff, 1997), researchers agree that scientists *must* spend at least 10 years in school or apprenticeships mastering domain knowledge, such as molecular biology or theoretical physics (Ericsson, 1998). One cannot contribute new knowledge to a scientific domain one has not fully mastered. As these domains become increasingly complex and specialized (Leach, 1999), the young scientist may choose or even need to spend additional years in postdoctoral positions. Groundbreaking discoveries rarely occur without such intense years of training and collaboration.

## Ordinary Development

Ordinary development in science has been a staple of cognitive development and educational research (see D. Kuhn & Franklin, Chapter 22, this *Handbook,* this volume). Most studies emphasize problem solving and use either a Piagetian (1937/1995, 1955/1995) or a think-aloud (Chi et al., 1982; Newell & Simon, 1972) approach to illuminate how novices or younger children differ in their thought processes compared to experts or older children. Despite studies that challenge particular Piagetian claims (Fischer & Pipp, 1984; Gardner, 1973), Piaget's general approach underpins most work on the development of skills and concepts in mathematics and science (Fischer, Kenny, & Pipp, 1990; D. Kuhn, Garcia-Mila, Zohar, & Andersen, 1995; Tytler & Peterson, 2004). Recent work has turned attention to how analogies (Goswami, 1996), metacognitive processes (D. Kuhn, Katz, & Dean, 2004), and biases (Klahr, 2000) affect children's scientific reasoning.

Less work has been done on the development of scientific thinking beyond the school years. Newer lines of research have examined scientific thinking as a social discourse by studying scientists at work (Dunbar, 1996) or science as a form of argument or persuasion (Kelly & Bazerman, 2003; D. Kuhn, 1993). Adolescents and young adults who continue scientific pursuits come to understand that science is not simply a collection of facts but rather a process of recursively testing hypotheses and devising explanations (D. Kuhn et al., 2004; Leach, 1999; Schauble, 1996; Smith, Maclin, Houghton, & Hennessey, 2000). Without explicit instruction and practice, most people never go beyond considering science as the accumulation of absolute, incontrovertible facts. Indeed, they become increasingly entrenched in their biases, confirming what they already believe, and stumbling when they encounter the norms of inquiry and exploration underlying the scientific domain (Gardner, 2000; Greenhoot, Sembe, Columbo, & Schreiber, 2004; Klaczynski & Robinson, 2000).

## Markers of Extraordinariness

Some possible early flags of extraordinariness include: (a) innate, domain-relevant abilities evident as early as age 2, (b) unusual and independent curiosity in early childhood that is maintained over decades, (c) stronger skills for approaching problems encountered during training, and (d) social connections and circumstances that catalyze extreme productivity in one's adult career. As with art, these markers roughly follow an age profile, starting first with individual characteristics and expanding to include the domain and field.

### *Innate Ability*

Science is often associated with computational ability, high IQ, and analogical thinking, which may have biological roots. Computational ability often (Feist & Gorman, 1998) but not always (Radford, 1990) arises early in life, perhaps even in infancy (Gopnik & Meltzoff, 1997; cf. Carruthers, 2002). Unusual abilities can be demonstrated well before formal instruction (Bloom, 1985). Prodigies, such as Blaise Pascal, Carl Friedrich Gauss, and Norbert Wiener (Radford, 1990), as well as savants (Sacks, 1985), demonstrate near-miraculous abilities to add large numbers in their heads, determine the day of the week for a particular historical date, and recall complicated numerical series such as timetables or financial columns. Mathematical ability, at least below the genius level, runs in families, as with the Bernoulli brothers and Pascal and his father. Higher correlation in monozygotic twins points to a heritable component (Feist & Gorman, 1998). However, as Einstein's story attests, computational ability is not a prerequisite for extraordinary achievement in science, and extraordinary scientists can emerge in ordinary settings.

IQ is another supposedly innate ability that is proposed to underpin scientific achievement. Many well-known scientists are believed to have high IQs (Cox, 1926). Children with high IQs are quicker and more flexible in problem solving (Radford, 1990), pass through Piaget's stages of scientific reasoning more rapidly (Carter & Ormrod, 1982), and benefit from accelerated and enriched school activities (Lubinski & Benbow, 2000). IQ correlates more with scientific achievement, at least while in school, than with artistic achievement (Lubinski & Benbow, 2000), presumably because logical and mathematical skills are foregrounded in these measures (Gardner, 1983). However, as in art, prodigious behavior in science does not necessarily predict adult professional contributions. Lubinski and Benbow (2000) reported that only 25% of gifted young scientists persevere into a scientific vocation, a statistic that still does not implicate creativity or extraordinary achievement.

Standard IQ scores denote a child's overall ability to solve problems, whereas most children show uneven ability between the math and verbal sections of IQ, SAT, or other aptitude tests (Hudson 1966; Radford, 1990; Winner, 2000). The higher the IQ, the more jagged the intelligence profile is likely to be (Detterman & Daniel, 1989). In addition, correlations among verbal, mathematical and spatial abilities tests prove to be somewhat discipline specific. In Roe's (1952) studies, theoretical physicists scored the best on all tests, and psychologists tended to do relatively well across the board. But anthropologists scored well only on verbal sections, and applied physicists scored well on spatial but not verbal tests. Logical-mathematical intelligence is not the only intelligence on which scientific breakthroughs draw (Cox, 1926; Gardner, 1983). Spatial intelligence also seems to play a leading role in scientific breakthroughs, at least in physics and biology (Gardner, 1993a; Root-Bernstein, Bernstein, & Garnier, 1995). Darwin, Feynman, Faraday, Einstein, as well as Watson and Crick, all relied on images, diagrams, or other spatial tools to help them construct and organize their thoughts (Anderson & Leinhardt, 2002; Gooding, 1996; A. Miller, 1989; Watson, 1968).

Analogical thinking—the ability to effect connections among disparate things—is believed to underpin scientific achievement (Goswami, 1996). Such reasoning by analogy may be present from infancy as babies try to make sense of their world. Later deductive reasoning might be undermined by these early connections

because it is often difficult for people to set aside the "truth value" of a premise based on their own experience and adopt a premise as an abstracted given. Consequently, analogical thinking may be both a support and a challenge to scientific achievement—extraordinary scientists often rely on analogy to create fruitful frames for problem solving (Gruber, 1989) but they also must overcome the biases that such analogies might entail (Klahr, 2000).

### Curiosity

When asked what set them apart as children, eminent scientists and their parents and teachers most often mention unusual curiosity—an emotional and intellectual resonance between individual and domain (Feist & Gorman, 1998; Gustin, 1985; Sosniak, 1985). Pascal was fascinated with making charcoal drawings of perfect circles or equilateral triangles, Pierre Curie with ponds. In a post hoc analysis of 100 of Cox's (1926) sample of eminent achievers, Terman (1954) found a predictive childhood interest in half the cases. He also found significant differences in the childhood interests of his subjects who eventually became natural scientists, social scientists, and nonscientists (Terman, 1955). Lubinski and Benbow (2000) reported that interests are both differentiated and stable by age 12; moreover, with age, interests surpass ability as a predictor for a scientific career.

Future mathematicians or scientists love to learn, count, and make logical connections for their own sake—science is intellectual play for them (John-Steiner, 1985; Radford, 1990; Roe, 1952). They develop precise or sophisticated ways to arrange their toys; they enjoy jigsaw puzzles, model-building, and other manipulables (Bloom, 1985; Sosniak, 1985). Although some may have trouble learning to read (Gardner, 1993a; Gustin, 1985), once they master the skill, they devour texts to expand their scope of knowledge and solidify their interests in the domain (John-Steiner, 1985; Walters & Gardner, 1986).

Like artists, future eminent scientists tend to be loners (Roe, 1952; Storr, 1988). Rather than joining existing groups as most children do, they develop independent projects (Gustin, 1985; Sosniak, 1985). Einstein conducted thought experiments during his youth (Gardner, 1993a), and the biologist E. O. Wilson preferred designing his own Boy Scout projects (Csikszentmihalyi, 1996). Future mathematicians and scientists tend to see other people as something to study (e.g., social scientists) or ignore (e.g., natural scientists) rather than re-late to, help, or dominate (Gardner, 1993a, 2004b; Gustin, 1985; Hudson, 1966; Roe, 1952).

Such isolation may catalyze flexibility in classification skills by distancing nascent scientists from the normal categories of their culture (Gardner, 1983; Radford, 1990). It helps them overcome the obstacles of bias, confusion between theory and evidence, and lack of counterargument typically found with ordinary development (Gardner, 1991; Greenhoot et al., 2004; Klaczynski & Robinson, 2000; Klahr, 2000; D. Kuhn et al., 2004). Einstein spoke of the scientist's need to be "rendered independent of the customs, opinions and prejudices of others" (Gardner, 1983, p. 131). Time to develop one's own ideas and personality also may prepare future scientists for a life of scientific challenge, argument, and criticism (Feist, 1993; John-Steiner, 1985; Watson, 1968). Independent projects may keep students, who otherwise are bored in school, interested in scientific pursuits. One reason adolescents may not continue in the sciences is that schoolwork is too didactic and not sufficiently investigative to pique their interest (Feist, 1991; Lubinski & Benbow, 2000; Subotnik & Arnold, 1994). Most who do pursue scientific careers do not remember their school years favorably (Gustin, 1985; Shekerjian 1990; Sosniak, 1985). Without the early blossoming of interest, field constraints and prescribed educational paths may support technical mastery of existing knowledge while inhibiting the exploratory behavior that can lead to new knowledge creation (Amabile, 1996; Berlyne, 1950).

### Approaches to Problems

In adolescence and adulthood, what one knows becomes less important than how one knows. Process supercedes memory as a marker of extraordinariness. Most studies of problem-solving strategies compare responses to current field standards (e.g., Chi et al., 1982); accordingly, these investigations do not account for qualitative differences in solutions or approaches that attempt to change what the "right" response is. These studies do not differentiate creators from experts but rather provide additional support for how creators in science must first become experts and for what differentiates experts from novices. Beyond expertise, though, extraordinary scientists have a knack for finding good problems to work on, which often are not yet recognized by the field as important. They may even risk their entire career on one potentially fertile but still risky problem (Bereiter

& Scardamalia, 1993; Gruber, 1974). Whereas most people don't notice anomalies or explain them away (Chinn & Brewer, 1993), extraordinary scientists are drawn toward, rather than ignorant of or afraid of, anomalies (Csikszentmihalyi, 1996; Gardner, 2004b; Gardner & Nemirovsky, 1991). Those who do better in science—first as experts, then as creators for a select few—display several salient characteristics. They keep an open mind, persevere to make nuanced distinctions, create fruitful problem representations, coordinate theory and evidence, and are relentlessly meta-cognitive.

First, rather than favoring perceptual or conceptual information, experts stay open to both (Gooding, 1996; Langley et al., 1987). In contrast, novices rely excessively on their early perceptions, biases, or concepts learned didactically (Grotzer & Bell, 1999; Klahr, 2000; Perkins & Simmons, 1988); this reliance limits their ability to complexify their problem representations (Anderson & Leinhardt, 2002). Creative scientists go a step further to develop highly tuned observational mechanisms to perceive what others blinded by conventional conceptions fail to notice (Langley et al., 1987); moreover, to guard against their own conceptual inertias, they often work on more than one problem or project (Gruber, 1989). Individuals who believe that knowledge is mutable and uncertain, and who have faith that their curiosity and investigative efforts will be fruitful, are more likely to engage in scientific and other knowledge creation pursuits (De Corte, Op't Eynde, & Verschaffel, 2002; Dweck, 2002; Klaczynski & Robinson, 2000).

Second, whereas novices jump quickly to formulating solutions that coincide with their current beliefs, experts spend more time and attention setting up and revising problem representations (Klahr, 2000; D. Kuhn et al., 1995; Rostan, 1994; Schaffner, 1994; Smith et al., 2000). If children or novices learn scientific concepts by rote, they may become technicians without understanding clearly the opportunities lurking in the deeper structure of problems (Perkins & Simmons, 1988; Zuckerman & Cole, 1994). These individuals also do not learn how to separate and coordinate theory and evidence, nor do they come to appreciate the extent to which knowledge is uncertain, provisional, and constructed by a scientific field (Kuhn, Cheney, & Weinstock, 2000; Leach, 1999). Once a focus on anomalies or assumptions arises, it is not necessarily used consistently; many adults continue to exhibit confirmation bias and snap judgments that inhibit their creativity (Greenhoot et al., 2004; Klahr, 2000; D. Kuhn, 1989).

Creators are more tenacious than experts about going beyond the "right" answer currently accepted in the field. Notebooks of famous scientists show multiple problem representations based on imagery or analogy (Dunbar, 1996; A. Miller, 1989; Tweney, 1996). These representations help scientists to break free of conventional conceptions (Gardner, 1993a; Gruber, 1974), develop new methods and theories (Rostan, 1994), and maintain mental openness (Holmes, 1996). Whereas most people argue what they know, breakthrough thinkers focus on what they don't know (Qian & Pan, 2002). They orient to the gaps, anomalies, and counterfactuals of a situation. Yet, even acclaimed scientists acknowledge the difficulty in facing contradictions and maintaining a skeptical yet open-minded perspective (Wertheimer, 1945/1959; Zuckerman & Cole, 1994).

Third, whereas novices have less conscious control over their mental processing, experts are more metacognitive and metastrategic. High-IQ children show consistently better awareness of their knowledge and mental activities. Better science students exert more control over their strategy use in problem solving and thus become more conscious of not only *what* they learn but *how* (Alexander et al., 1995; Radford, 1990). Their coordination of theory and evidence, the transformation of their mental models with new information, and their understanding of the scientific process improves (Kuhn et al., 2004; Schauble, 1996; Sinatra & Pintrich, 2003; Tytler & Robinson, 2004; Zimmerman, 2000). Skilled scientists pay more attention to cues in the problem space (Klahr, 2000; Newell & Simon, 1972) as well as the aesthetic qualities of possible solutions (A. Miller, 1989; Polya, 1973; Radford, 1990). Experts tend to control their cognition based on correctness, creating a feedback loop to reduce variation. Creators control their cognition based on novelty, creating a feedback loop to enhance variation (Gruber & Davis, 1988).

### The Scientific Career

Although studies of scientific process often focus on cognition and problem solving, much interest has arisen in the social aspects of scientific achievement (Latour, 1987). Focus has shifted from problem solving to argumentation (D. Kuhn, 1993). Science is viewed as a discourse in which people try to persuade each other to accept one concept or theory over a rival account (Bell & Linn, 2002; Leach, 1999). People must understand the general discourse of science before they can make sense of scientific methods and findings (Lehrer, Schauble, &

Petrosino, 2001). Scholarly journals are a market or battlefield for dominance by those who are most persuasive (Kelly & Bazerman, 2003). From this perspective, a scientific career entails not only knowledge creation but also political and communicational savvy amidst a field of other scientists.

This discourse "game" has time constraints—scientists' work must connect with the flow of the field. If he or she is too early, eccentricity results; too late, ordinary science results. The timing must be right for a contribution to be considered creative. The normative scientific career trajectory peaks early and tends to follow an inverted-U arc over one's lifetime (Lehman, 1953; Simonton, 1988). One's first valuable contribution usually occurs in one's 20s, the biggest breakthrough in one's late 30s or 40s, and a final, important contribution in one's 50s (Simonton, 1991a). Mathematics and physics tend to show earlier peaks—in terms of seminal contributions—than biology or earth sciences (Gardner, 1983; Simonton, 1988, 1991a; Zuckerman, 1977).

Nowadays, these age trends are likely to have later peaks, given increasing complexity in scientific domains and fields that lead to longer training periods and delayed launching of one's official career—and possibly also better health in later life (Gardner et al., 2001; Simonton, 1991a). Although the field has long played a background role, budding scientists only become part of the field proper in college or graduate school. They start working alongside other scientists on problems that lack known solutions (P. Davis & Hersh, 1980; Gustin, 1985; Sosniak, 1985) and must learn to communicate in a scientific community (Kelly & Bazerman, 2003; Leach, 1999).

Despite the lengthy apprenticeship period, many extraordinary scientific breakthroughs have been made early in careers. The examples of Einstein, Newton, and Krebs are well known (Gardner, 1993a; Holmes, 1989). Although transformative scientists independently have studied the domain and are familiar with the field, often having been mentored by a more advanced scientist, at the time of their breakthroughs, they are often marginal to the field. They do not hold traditional expert positions of power that may inundate them with administrative work and reduce the time available for creative work (Nakamura & Csikszentmihalyi, 2003; Perry-Smith & Shalley, 2003).

Still, social support heralds a higher likelihood of making a breakthrough contribution, as it aids the acquisition of scientific cultural capital (Bourdieu, 1993). Even though science has often been viewed as solitary thinking (Gruber, 1989), collaboration skills are extremely important (Gardner, 1999; John-Steiner, 2000). More likely to continue and excel in science are those students who participate in talent searches and science fairs (Lubinski & Benbow, 2000), work in another scientist's lab at a young age (Fischman, Solomon, Greenspan, & Gardner, 2004; Gardner, 1993a; John-Steiner, 1985), and find (or are found by) influential and supportive mentors (Gardner, 2004b; John-Steiner, 1985, 2000; Noble, Subotnik, & Arnold, 1996; Zuckerman, 1977).

Furthermore, collaborations with other strong thinkers often continue throughout a scientific career. Einstein and his mathematician friend Marcel Grossman, physicists Richard Feynman and Freeman Dyson, and Marie and Pierre Curie, for example, established long-lived, joint productivity based on complementarity of skills and perspectives (John-Steiner, 2000). The Human Genome Project, the culmination of a century of work in biology, resulted from the cross-historical and contemporary collaborative efforts of hundreds of scientists (Keller, 2000). However, women scientists' careers tend to follow a more complex pattern, with fewer supports, different kinds of mentors, and less recognition. They produce fewer publications that tend to be longer, more discursive, and more synthetic (Holton, 1973). This scientific pattern of required credentialing, long training arcs, institutional affiliation, and collaboration differs from that found in less "vertical" domains (Li, 1997).

The most striking marker of extraordinariness as an adult is prolific productivity. A few scientists produce the most publications. Nobel laureates average more than three papers a year, whereas *American Men and Women of Science* scientists average only about 1.5, and most ordinary scientists publish only once or twice in a lifetime (Simonton, 1988). Mathematicians considered most creative by colleagues published three times more papers than the less creative (Helson & Crutchfield, 1970). Early productivity predicts later productivity, creating a cumulative advantage in both publication and citation rates (Merton, 1968; Zuckerman, 1977).

By middle age, the odds of making a transformative contribution diminish (Simonton, 1988). Even for those who become domain-transformers, their role in the field often changes afterward (Csikszentmihalyi, 1996; Nakamura & Csikszentmihalyi, 2003). Most likely, sci-

entists focus on integrating their own work (Gardner, 1993a), synthesizing others' work in the field (Csikszentmihalyi, 1996), institutionalizing their work in labs or writings (Holmes, 1996), becoming administrators or gatekeepers of field resources (Gardner, 1993a; Holmes, 1996), or philosophizing and critiquing the field and domain (Csikszentmihalyi, 1996; Gardner, 1993a). The attention garnered from a creative breakthrough may make it difficult for the scientist to devote the time and effort, or evince the risk taking needed for another breakthrough (Holmes, 1996).

### *Summary*

Extraordinariness in science comprises a fruitful "co-incidence" (Feldman, 1986) of ability, curiosity, training, opportunity, and support. Some, but not all, groundbreaking scientists display natural ability, either high IQs or more specific computational, logical, or spatial intelligences. Many exhibit a strong drive to learn the domain even before school starts. Through independent projects, schooling, and practice, budding scientists develop strategies, mechanisms, and epistemological beliefs to help them build, and navigate in, anomalous yet promising problems. Once launched on a scientific career, they develop networks of intellectual projects, social relations, and scientific discourse skills to garner resources, stimulate productivity, and continually feed their minds. Although many people acquire the basics of observing, hypothesizing, examining evidence, and drawing conclusions, those who become extraordinary in science also learn the importance of framing questions from a perspective independent of the field's conventional wisdom and/or their own biases; they persist systematically despite the uncertainty of scientific pursuits, and combine both collaborative and competitive aspects of breakthrough thinking. The field plays a major role, often as an antagonistic force in early schooling that focuses on more canonical methods and knowledge, but later as a supportive force in providing resources and opportunities for one's career.

## POLITICAL LEADERSHIP

Leadership consists of the role assumed by one person (or a small group) who garners resources and power to guide and align the beliefs and actions of others toward a goal, vision, or mission (Burns, 1978; Gardner, 1995, 2004a; J. Gardner, 1984; Simonton, 1991b). At one time based on presumed divine magic power, leadership evolved into an inherited right of royalty, a paternalistic autocracy of rulers and owners, or most recently the group most expert in a field. Now, in treating leadership, researchers de-emphasize the command-and-control aspects while stressing the importance of getting often antagonistic constituents to work together (Heifetz, 1994; Zander & Zander, 2000). Leadership occurs across domains; the domain of leadership—including general techniques and strategies—has been studied in itself (see Kellerman & Webster, 2001 for review). However, leadership is also situated in more traditional domains, such as art, science, law, and business. Leadership has been most studied in the business and political domains. In these realms, searchlight intelligences are more prevalent in field and domain dynamics than in arts and sciences, where expertise, creativity, and laserlike intelligences are foregrounded. Leadership does arise in the arts and sciences. Picasso was a leader of Cubist painters and Oppenheimer led scientists in the Manhattan Project. But their power stemmed more from their expertise than from the field-oriented, social skills and qualities we emphasize.

In business and politics, the creation of a social organization with purposeful momentum is often the main point, not just a side effect of one's primary expertise. Whereas in art and science, the medium of transformation is usually symbolic—through images, words, or mathematical formulae—in business and politics, the field structure with its current power relations is the medium to be transformed. The transformation is social. We focus chiefly on political leaders because they influence a wide circle of diverse people and have been most studied.

## Ordinary Development

As is true for the other domains surveyed, rudimentary sociopolitical activity can be observed even in young children. Except for individuals with severe disorders, everyone develops social skills for understanding, communicating with, and influencing others. The foundation for leadership—social dominance, or the variance in ability to compete for resources with, from, or through others—starts in preschool (Hawley, 1999). In early pretend play, children can symbolize the self and others, enact different roles, understand that people have different perspectives, and learn the consequences of different stances and actions (Gardner, 1983; Harris,

2000; Vygotsky, 1978). As with art and science, one's first encounter with leadership is through play with the domain—in this case, role playing. However, as the play medium is social interaction itself, such play is rarely unmediated by field forces; from their first years, children learn "good behavior" and tactics of influence just by operating in the family.

By kindergarten, some children display exceptional abilities to coerce, persuade, help, cooperate with, and command their peers to get their needs met; youngsters may also display a preference for either coercive/instrumental or prosocial/empathic strategies (Hawley, 1999). During elementary school, children's understandings of roles become more complex, starting with definitions based on specific actions, then incorporating motivations and intentions, and finally coordinating multiple roles and perspectives across situations (Fischer, Hand, Watson, Van Parys, & Tucker, 1984; Flavell, Botkin, & Fry, 1968; Selman, 1980).

In American society, adolescents take on institutionalized leadership roles such as student council representative, cheerleader, band drum major, or babysitter. Typically, they first become amateurs in the leadership domain, occupying "pretend" or "shadow" versions of generic roles that occur in many fields. Such early experiences can help form the values—such as left- or right-wing political activism—that may continue into adult leadership (Braumgart & Braumgart, 1990; Flacks, 1990). Those elected to leadership positions also learn to value and exhibit dependability (Mason, 1952), integrity, and knowledge (Morris, 1991), even as they explore potential vocations (Govindarajan, 1964). Traditionally, Scouts organizations, churches, the European *grands-ecoles*, the American armed services and their academies, and scholarship programs offer ladders that train youth in leadership skills. Evaluations of these and other programs rarely take a developmental perspective or separate leadership qualities from the demands of stipulated roles (Furr & Lutz, 1987; Hohmann, Hawker, & Hohmann, 1982; Kielsmeier, 1982).

As adults, most people are followers. Instead of taking initiative or responsibility for others, they work for others in an already established organization geared toward someone else's vision (Berg, 1998). Those oriented toward leadership typically are managers, rising up their organizations' hierarchies, taking on roles with increasing responsibility, maintaining efficient operations, but for the most part, still contributing to another person's or institution's vision (Kotter, 1990). As was the case in comparing experts and creators, leadership studies that use managers as subjects may not be useful—or even germane—for understanding the development of extraordinary leadership (Hunt, 1999; Lowe & Gardner, 2001). Moreover, exceptional leaders may arise from outside normal institutions, and such individuals may use their newly acquired authority for ends that are benign (e.g., Martin Luther King Jr. or Mahatma Gandhi) or malevolent (e.g., Adolf Hitler or Joseph Stalin; see Bullock, 1998). Compared to adolescents, adults tend to define leadership more by sense of purpose rather than by activities (Morris, 1991); yet, most forms in which adults engage tend to be transactional, based on exchange of resources for mutual benefit, rather than transformational toward a new, higher purpose (Burns, 1978).

## Markers of Extraordinariness

Goertzel et al.'s (1978) sample of eminent politicians, including Robert Kennedy, Lyndon Johnson, Cesar Chavez, and Adolf Hitler, depict a fairly normal childhood. The most effective leaders seem to have not the *extremes* of certain psychological abilities, such as a super high IQ or the most charismatic personality, but a better *balance* or relatively flatter profile of intelligences or traits. As a result, the individual can adapt to various situations; even though the person may not necessarily stand out from the crowd on any one attribute, he or she may well rise above others as the leader. Although neither necessary nor sufficient for leadership to arise, several identified features correspond with later eminence in leadership: (a) "high enough" general intelligence, (b) skills in connecting to others, (c) unusual drive, and (d) adversity in early life that is somehow addressed, plus (e) an opportunity to perform on a wide stage in adulthood—granted or seized—correspond with later eminence in leadership (Burns, 1978; Gardner, 1995; Simonton 1994; Wills, 1994).

### Intelligence

Compared to students with average IQs, students with high psychometric intelligence tend to show leadership potential (Terman, 1954). But too high an IQ can create difficulties in relating to others (Fischer, Hand, Watson, Van Parys, & Tucker, 1984; Hollingworth, 1942). IQ studies of historical leaders give mixed results, sometimes and sometimes not correlating with the measure of

leadership (Cox, 1926; Simonton, 1976, 1981, 1986, 1991b). The most eminent leaders tend to have above average—but not too high—intelligence and a moderate level of schooling (Cox, 1926; Mann, 1959; Simonton, 1976; Thorndike, 1950).

Unlike creators, leaders tend to be well rounded and versatile (Simonton, 1976). Most exhibit strengths in linguistic and possibly bodily kinesthetic intelligences for communication and embodiment of one's ideals and in the personal intelligences related to self-mastery and social competence (Gardner, 1983, 1995, 1999). This generalist, body-conscious (often including impressive stature), social-oriented intelligence profile helps leaders be good problem solvers, adapt to changing circumstances, and communicate with people of diverse abilities and interests (Connell et al., 2003). With this searchlight intelligence profile, such individuals can see the big picture—the gestalt of the situation—before others can, and they do not become distracted by the accumulation of details as might scientists, artists, or other specialists with more laserlike intelligence (J. Gardner, 1990).

### Connecting to Others

Although most management models adhere to a rational decision-making model emphasizing technical and administrative tasks, extraordinary leaders tap into the emotional energy of their followers (Burns, 1978; Goleman, 2002; Jacobsen & House, 2001). Some may effect this emotional connection simply to have and wield the power; others to use the power instrumentally to achieve a goal that can be constructive or destructive (McClelland, 1967). The most eminent seem to be able to blend the dual purposes of potency and instrumentalism, as Huey Long did (Williams, 1981). Therefore, interpersonal intelligence—the potential for empathy, perspective taking, and distinguishing crucial aspects of personality—underpins leadership effectiveness (Gardner, 1983, 1995). Such social facility has been shown to be independent of general IQ as well as prosocial behavior (Abroms & Gollin, 1980; Walker & Foley, 1973). Interpersonal giftedness can become apparent as early as kindergarten. In enacting the roles of friend, negotiator, and leader (Hatch, 1997), some young children are more flexible and theatrical in their performance (Fischer & Pipp, 1984), pick up more quickly on the key aspects of different roles (Bruchkowsky, 1992), and better coordinate potentially competing social values such as honesty and kindness (Lamborn, Fischer, & Pipp, 1994).

Several psychoanalytically based studies suggest that leaders reduce followers' anxiety in uncertain situations (Jaques, 1955), primarily through the leader's clear vision and personal example (Gardner, 1995). Followers, in turn, contribute their resources to the leader's cause (Berg, 1998; Jacobsen & House, 2001; Lawrence, 1998). Over time, the leader's vision and exemplary behaviors can become routinized, institutionalized, and depersonalized (Jacobsen & House, 2001; Weber, 1947), creating a "long shadow" on which others can stand (Gergen, 2000). Change cannot be too jolting, so leaders must stay one step ahead—not three or four. Such sensitivities to anxiety and timing seem to arise by adolescence. Compared to nonleaders, adolescent leaders exhibit superior emotional stability, coping mechanisms, and temporal perspective (Morris, 1991).

According to recent analyses, leaders typically articulate their vision through dramatic stories that stir the hearts and minds of others (Gardner, 1995, 2004a; Gergen, 2000; Hirschhorn, 1998). Franklin Roosevelt's story featured renewed economic stability through strategic government intervention; Reagan's and Thatcher's was prosperity based on individual initiative, a story that deliberately countered the entrenched narrative of Rooseveltian governmental hegemony (Gardner, 1995; Gergen, 2000). The ability to create such compelling stories commences around age 4, when children tell single, action-oriented episodes. During middle childhood, children add and integrate plot twists and internal motivations (Bruchkowsky, 1992; McKeough, 1992). Better storytellers exhibit more detail, flexibility, and expression in their stories (Faulkner, 1996; Porath, 1996); the most successful leaders tell stories that give meaning to the lives of their followers and embody those stories in their own daily actions.

### Drive

In contrast to the less eminent and the less successful, extraordinary leaders start and stick with their chosen missions (Bennis & Thomas, 2002; Bogardus, 1934). Besides intelligence, initiative emerged as the key predictor of leadership quality among 48 political leaders (Simonton, 1991b) and successful outcomes among generals in battle (Simonton, 1980). Years of experience predict presidential eminence (Simonton, 1981) and the perceived competence and trustworthiness of U.S. presidents as assessed by historians (Simonton, 1986). Although normal development of leadership focuses on taking already established roles, extraordinary leaders often do not wait for a role to make their presence felt (Burns, 1978). With unusual confidence in themselves, such leaders—even as children—present themselves as equals to others in leadership roles, challenge authority, negotiate or take power, and organize groups from scratch, manipulating and persuading others to join their team (Gardner, 1995; Goertzels et al., 1978; Kotter, 1990; Winter, 1987).

### Early Adversity

Facing a steep challenge, tapping into one's personal strengths to feel useful, and dealing with frustration in one's early years may prepare future leaders for the ups and downs of life in the limelight (Goertzels et al., 1978; Kotter, 1990; McClelland, 1967). Early adversity—such as sickness or poverty, the loss of or intense conflict with one's father, or early failure—can create tension and dissatisfaction that spur the future leader to act more independently (Bennis & Thomas, 2002; Bullock, 1998; Gergen, 2000; McClelland, 1967). Early career challenges—such as the sinking of John F. Kennedy's PT boat or the failure of Winston Churchill's plans at Gallipoli—can also create "awakening moments" that disembed the person from the conventional view of a situation and sow the seeds of personal, and perhaps later social or political, transformation (Burns, 1978; Kotter, 1990; Lukacs, 2002). To test their mettle, many future leaders intentionally choose difficult, risky assignments (Bennis & Thomas, 2002). If leaders have the most of any one quality, it is perhaps a robust temperament or the ability to bounce back from failures and try again despite the odds (Schwartz, Wright, Shin, Kagan, & Rauch, 2003). Such resilience makes it possible to be responsive to events in a timely fashion—a pattern that contrasts with that exhibited by scientists, artists, and moral leaders who dwell in longer mental time frames.

### Opportunity to Act

Once working in their fields as adults, leaders require a situation or issue conducive to their abilities and preparation to manifest their greatness. It is misleading to name leaders in isolation. It is not just Franklin D. Roosevelt but FDR and the Depression that made him extraordinary; not Lee Iacocca but Iacocca and the turnaround of Chrysler during a time when American automobile manufacturers were under assault from East Asian and European competition.

This need for opportunity may help explain why there are fewer women than men leaders in the history books. Except for hereditary power, social structure has precluded women from powerful roles or even being present in situations that presented leadership opportunities (such as battle, political voting bodies, or the boardroom). As in the sciences, where roles and opportunities are highly field-controlled, leadership roles have tended to be given to or taken by men. This situation, however, has changed in recent decades as women—and increasingly non-White populations—start companies, gain board seats, win elected positions, and voice their political views in mainstream venues. As a result, exemplary women leaders such as Indira Gandhi, Margaret Thatcher, Golda Meir, and Sandra Day O'Connor are emerging.

Whereas creativity is assessed in relation to a certain structure of the domain at a given time, leadership is assessed in relation to a certain structure of the field. Perhaps that is why some studies suggest situational factors, rather than personal qualities, predict leader accomplishments (Simonton, 1976, 1984). War, assassination, scandal—regardless of whether the leader had any control over them—can tend to increase one's historic memorability (Simonton, 1984; Winter, 1987). Whereas the medium for art is the canvas or marble, and for science is the experiment or hypothesis, the medium for leadership is the issue or social situation that calls for vision, organization, and action.

The world in which leaders grow up also influences their values and actions. For example, young "geek" leaders of the current technological age—who grew up in the 1980s of economic abundance, distrust in institutions, blended families, and globalization—prefer a leadership style of collaboration and experimentation. The older "geezer" generation—who grew up during the uncertainty and fear of the Depression and World War II—alternatively, prefers to lead in stable, structured organizations (Bennis & Thomas, 2002). Still, what places someone in a leadership position may be different than what makes others later perceive him or her as outstanding. People tend to vote for individuals with motivations similar to their own, but the presidents ranked the greatest—Washington, Lincoln, Theodore Roosevelt—tended to have motivations at odds with (and typically ahead of) the current Zeitgeist of their time (Winter, 1987).

When a situation presents itself, extraordinary leaders are ready to rise to the occasion. What others might consider a stressful problem, they view as an opportunity to make a difference. They are better able to act in the moment—whether on the battlefield or in a televised debate or in a tense cabinet meeting. They are more prepared to take on such high stakes performances (Gardner, 1993a, 1997) with less notice, perhaps because almost every problem is learned from and integrated into their later repertoire of experiences and skills. Possibly stemming from their searchlight intellect, they can simultaneously be fully present in the moment yet also be able to stand back mentally, see themselves as others see them, and place the moment in social and historical context (Gardner, 1995, 2004a; Klein, Gabelnick, & Herr, 1998).

*Summary*

In contrast to the domain-specific, targeted extraordinariness typical of the arts and sciences, leadership features extraordinariness as horizontal and integrative (Connell et al., 2003). The development of a leader stems from a convergence of multiple developing capacities that interact in nonlinear fashion. The field's social forces play a strong role from the beginning, more indirectly in childhood through parenting and schooling, then more directly in adolescence and adulthood through training and opportunities to act. A person's innate potentials foreshadow a versatile generalist profile. During childhood and throughout life, the future extraordinary leader learns to handle social adversity without losing equilibrium; develops self-control and social competence; and becomes able to tap into unconscious sources of energy and affect, tell compelling stories, and embody one's ideals in one's person. The leader takes initiative when opportunities arise or in making one's own opportunities, and stays the course. These actions, in turn, develop a disposition to behave in leaderly ways, tapping into the power of others toward transformational change in world view, organization, or action.

# MORALITY

Traditional philosophers and religious leaders pondered the nature of a virtuous life. This classical concern with moral excellence has reappeared in recent years. One impetus emanates from the disastrous bloodshed and genocidal episodes of the twentieth century. Scholarly direction has come from important philosophical tracts (e.g., Rawls, 1971) and empirical studies in developmental psychology. Included are pathbreaking works on moral judgment by Piaget (1932) and Kohlberg (1984); cross-cultural studies by Shweder, Mahapatra, and Miller (1987), and studies of particular moral traits like empathy, altruism, a sense of justice, or willingness to act on principle.

In contrast to social rules and roles that consist of manners, conventions, or other interpersonal routines, morality involves human relations governed specifically by deeply felt principles of right and wrong. The honorific term *moral* is usually reserved for individuals who behave in prosocial, honest, and fair ways that benefit more than themselves (and may at times be inimical or even dangerous to themselves). The psychological study of morality encompasses understanding how children and adults construe often ill-defined situations, formulate arguments, reach decisions, and take action in circumstances where issues of good-bad or right-wrong are salient (Damon, 1988). Such circumstances might include individuals with respect to their own standards (i.e., Freud's superego) as well as individuals' relationships with one another, with institutions, with one's professional domain, or with the wider society (Fischman et al., 2004).

The purview of morality has changed over history, becoming less divinely mandated and entailing choice among competing perspectives (Wolfe, 2001). Moral issues arise across domains. However, some domains, such as law, religion, psychotherapy, medicine, and politics, are rife with moral dilemmas. Other domains, such as art, science, and much of commerce, are less morally inflected. In psychology, morality has been mostly studied as its own domain—analogous to memory, personality, or leadership. With respect to the moral compass of the individual, the influence of the field derives from peers, colleagues, constituents, and competitors who expect one to live up to—or to violate—one's own or the community's moral standards.

We distinguish three varieties of moral excellence, roughly yoked to the three nodes of the system's model:

1. Individual acts of caring, courage, or heroism (whether or not lives are at risk). Included here are the actions of individuals who hid Jews and others during World War II as well as individuals who devote a significant part of their lives to helping the less fortunate.

2. Leadership in the moral sphere. Examples are individuals like Martin Luther King Jr. or Nelson Mandela, who assume direct leadership of a moral

crusade and confirm or alter long-standing values of a domain.

3. The creation of an organization dedicated to a moral issue. Our focus is directed to individuals who alter the field by launching or nurturing an institution that is dedicated to moral ends.

After describing the general markers of moral extraordinariness, we show which developmental features and combinations of features most clearly distinguish these three forms of moral excellence.

## Ordinary Development

The lines of ordinary moral development have been extensively documented (see Eisenberg, Chapter 11, this *Handbook*, Volume 3; Turiel, Chapter 13, this *Handbook*, Volume 3). Infants exhibit biological predispositions to be fearful of, curious about, or aggressive toward stimuli (Kagan, 1989; Schwartz et al., 2003); to understand emotional facial expressions; and to make movements and noises that draw others to help them (Trevarthen & Logothet, 1989). Through play and social interaction, infants and toddlers—unless they are autistic—quickly develop capacities to differentiate themselves from others (Piaget, 1932), understand intentions (Tomasello, 1999), appreciate how others see the world differently (Astington, 1993), empathize with others' distress (Hoffman, 2000; Zahn-Waxler, Radke-Yarrow, Wagner, & Chapman, 1992), share resources and take turns (Damon, 1988; Hay, Castle, Stimson, & Davies, 1995), distinguish universally applicable moral rules from context-specific social rules (Glassman & Zan, 1995; Turiel, 1983), perceive deviations from standards (Kagan, 1989), and learn to regulate their own behavior (Freud, 1930/1961a; Kagan, 1989).

Preschool is a period when children increase aggressive behaviors (Dunn, 1987) but also evolve from an egocentric to a more sympathetic form of empathy, becoming able to take on various perspectives and roles (Hoffman, 2000). They can separate their own distress from that of others—an important constituent of prosocial behavior (Astington, 1993; Miller, Eisenberg, Fabes, & Shell, 1996). Still, children's understandings of moral situations link to self-interest, obedience, and avoiding punishment (Kohlberg, 1984). Although children of kindergarten age can share their toys and help others, they base their decisions primarily on their own wants (Damon, 1988; Eisenberg & Fabes, 1992).

During the school years, children still judge moral situations based on authority, but apply the rules more flexibly and autonomously, with less need for external reinforcements (Piaget, 1932). By age 10, intentions, rather than consequences or rules, come to ground moral judgments (Helwig, 1995). At this time, children can better direct their attention and delay gratification (Metcalfe & Mischel, 1999), take initiative to comfort or get help (Zahn-Waxler et al., 1992a), consider cultural good-bad stereotypes (Eisenberg & Fabes, 1992), and empathize beyond specific situations to wider general life conditions (Hoffman, 2000). Sharing is based increasingly on fairness in elementary school and on merit in middle school (Damon, 1988).

Although adolescents share on the basis of who has the greatest need (Damon, 1988), self-centeredness may also increase temporarily at this time (Eisenberg & Fabes, 1992). As they become more aware of cultural conventions, adolescents tend to make moral judgments based on maintaining social order through cooperation or abiding by established rules (Eisenberg & Fabes, 1992; Kohlberg, 1984). They start to think ideologically, can envision utopias and dystopias, and consider social interaction apart from its current manifestations (Fischman et al., 2004; Michaelson, 2001). Adolescents often can make clear decisions in the abstract—be "for" free speech—but have difficulty coordinating the details of the case to take an unequivocal position regarding specifics—such as the Ku Klux Klan holding meetings at a community center (Helwig, 1995).

In adulthood, most people peak at the conventional rules-and-roles stages of moral judgment. A few adults reach postconventional stages where decisions are made based on contracts, justice, and rights (Kohlberg, 1984), and those who do reach these higher stages almost always are college educated (Shweder, Mahaptra, & Miller, 1987; Simpson, 1973). However, in a consideration crucial for the study of moral extraordinariness, judgment level does not correlate strongly with moral behavior (Damon, 1988; Hart & Fegley, 1995). Professional moral exemplar is not a recognized ambition, there are no credentials required, and anybody from any walk of life may rise to the occasion to become an exemplary figure.

## Markers of Extraordinariness

Although some have speculated about signs of early moral excellence, as manifest in the selection of the Dalai Lama, moral prodigies or savants have yet to be found (Hart, Yates, Fegley, & Wilson, 1995). Still, precursors to exceptional morality may occur in childhood: marked helpfulness, compassion, generosity, responsibility, and, with age, participation and leadership toward humanitarian ends. The most studied qualities associated with moral extraordinariness are: (a) precocity in moral judgment, (b) emotional sensitivity in childhood, (c) self-knowledge, (d) integrity, and (e) a disposition to act in adolescence and adulthood. Certain of these markers may be particularly associated with specific varieties of moral excellence.

### Precocity in Judgment

Early psychology studies tied moral extraordinariness to intelligence. Psychometric researchers found that intelligence was positively correlated with European royalty's moral behaviors (Thorndike, 1936) and the moral reasoning of children (Hollingworth, 1942; Terman, 1925). Such children tend to score higher than their age-mates on Kohlberg's stages of moral judgment (Howard-Hamilton, 1994; Simmons & Zumpf, 1986). But precocious use of abstract reasoning may not be conducive to precocious moral behavior. Average-IQ students tend to base their thinking on emotion-laden humanitarian ideals; high-IQ children may inhibit their empathic feelings for the sake of logical coherence in their moral arguments, with a resulting detachment from action (Andreani & Pagnin, 1993; Dentici & Pagnin, 1997). Additionally, high-IQ, logic-oriented children often feel compelled to follow a chain of reasoning to its bitter end, whereas those with less imposing IQs take a more nuanced position (Erikson, 1959).

Individuals who display extraordinary caring or heroism are not distinguished by high levels of moral reasoning or educational accomplishment. In contrast, of the 14 men who approved the "final solution" at the January 1942 Wannsee Conference, eight had doctorates from Central European universities. Nonetheless, we believe that the most impressive moral leaders are marked by the high—and sometimes, the highest—levels of moral judgment (e.g., Kohlberg, 1974).

### Unusual Sensitivity

From a very young age, some children display an instinctive knack for understanding themselves and reaching out to others in a caring way (Eisenberg & Fabes, 1992; Greenacre, 1956; Hoffman, 2000; Kagan, 1989). For example, as a child, Gandhi was keenly interested in the notions of right and wrong, tended to play peacemaker in schoolyard games, and felt extreme guilt at his transgressions of his own moral standards (Gandhi, 1993a). Twin studies suggest that perhaps as much as half of a person's abilities for empathy, nurturance, and altruism may be heritable (Davis, Luce, & Kraus, 1994; Zahn-Waxler et al., 1992b). Strong relationships further cultivate this innate sense (Aitken & Trevarthen, 1997), providing the support and sometimes motivation for moral action in adolescence and adulthood (Fischman et al., 2001; Michaelson, 2001; Youniss & Yates, 1999).

Sensitive children seem more easily to internalize moral expectations (Kagan, 1989), understand the role of intentions (Fischer & Pipp, 1984; Goldberg-Reitman, 1992), have a longer-term outlook in coordinating group moral efforts (Hart et al., 1995; Silverman, 1994), and act in a moral way (Arsenio & Lover, 1995). But there may be costs to hypersensitivity. Such young persons may become emotionally distraught at too much stimulation (Dabrowski, 1979/1994; Silverman, 1994), have trouble making straightforward decisions or become destabilized because they can see the exceptions and subtleties of situations (Lovecky, 1997), worry over potential consequences invisible to others (Silverman, 1994), and tend to question the rules (Erikson, 1958; Gross, 1993).

### Self-Awareness and Control

Self-awareness and self-control are important components of a moral orientation. Self-regulation is required if one is not to become inhibited (Kagan, 1989), overwhelmed (Silverman, 1994), or isolated (Getzels & Jackson, 1962). Moral exemplars are marked by strong intrapersonal intelligence as well as keen abilities to distinguish their own feelings and intentions, interpret their mental and physical states, draw on a vivid imagination, and/or express their inner states (Gardner, 1983; Parks, 1986). These emerging strengths aid them in imaginatively empathizing with people different from themselves (Zahn-Waxler et al., 1992a), determining their personal goals in a clear and comprehensive manner (Colby & Damon, 1994; Walker & Pitts, 1998), regulating their own needs (Colby & Damon, 1994; Eisenberg & Fabes, 1992), and having faith in their pursuits (Colby & Damon, 1994; J. Freedman, 1996; Parks, 1986).

Understanding options and consciously choosing one's personal values may provide the strongest moral

foundation (Perry, 1968/1999; Wolfe, 2001). Youths who become more reflective about their field and its moral stances are in a better position to stand apart from the status quo and aspire to deeper understanding of moral dimensions. Adolescent inner-city social activists, for example, do a better job than their peers in forming a coherent set of beliefs about themselves that not only situates them socially in relation to others but also temporally in relation to their past and future selves (Hart et al., 1995). Strong intrapersonal intelligence helps individuals to know who they are, yet pursue goals that transcend themselves and affect a wider sphere (Colby & Damon, 1994). Such self-awareness and control is particularly important for those who seek to lead a moral enterprise (Erikson, 1958).

Self-awareness may be catalyzed in early life by a crystallizing experience, such as the death of a loved one or a special mentoring partnership, that challenges values previously absorbed from family and culture (Colby & Damon, 1994; Fischman et al., 2001, 2003; Gardner, 1993a; Walters & Gardner, 1986). Such experiences may shift an individual from a general leadership or entrepreneurship orientation toward a particular focus on morally tinged missions.

### Integration

Moral extraordinariness results from an unusual integration of the domain and the person's identity—morality becomes the foundation of who the person is (Colby & Damon, 1994; Gardner, 1993a; Walker, 2003). For Martin Luther, nailing the *95 Theses* on the church door in Wittenberg was the culminating act of his identifying with personal, direct faith in opposition to absolute, institutional dogma (Erikson, 1958). Moral extraordinariness incorporates both thoughts and feelings (Haste, 1990), justice and care principles (Colby & Damon, 1994; Walker, 2003), a complex level of thinking regarding good and evil (Parks, 1986), a sensitivity to others' specific perspectives as well as more global issues (Dabrowski, 1979/1994), immediate and future consequences (Hart et al., 1995), faith in self and something greater (Colby & Damon, 1994; Walker, 2003), and principles and practices (Gardner et al., 2001). Integration, however, does not necessarily mean "the most of." As with leadership, too much of one facet—hyper-rationality, caring to the point of self-sacrifice, blinding honesty—can be detrimental (Dentici & Pagnin, 1997; Lamborn, Fischer, & Pipp, 1994; Walker, 2003). Although a sense of integration is important for all in the moral sphere, it is particularly salient for those who would devote their lifetimes to moral pursuits, less crucial for those who commit singular acts of courage.

### Disposition to Act

Moral exemplars act on their feelings and beliefs (Colby & Damon, 1994; Michaelson, 2001). Such agency begins young as children learn that their requests and demands influence adult behavior (Kagan, 1989). The more initiatives the person takes, the more habitual helping others becomes (Colby & Damon, 1994); over time, the person may develop an altruistic personality (Krebs & Van Hesteren, 1992). Compared to people who merely planned to go on Freedom Rides in the 1960s, those who actually went defined themselves as activists and needed tangible confirmation of that identity (McAdams, 1988).

This disposition can collectivize into professional codes of ethics that regulate how whole groups of people behave, in effect institutionalizing the preferred actions into professional or societal "shoulds." A doctor or therapist should do no harm and should intervene whenever a need arises. A scientist or journalist should seek the truth. These professional codes stabilize the foundational principles—utilitarianism, duty, virtue—as well as the moral conflicts, motives, intentions, and standards that arise in a particular professional domain (Beabout & Wenneman, 1994; B. Freedman, 1983; Tirri & Pehkonen, 2002). These codes also can draw people who resonate to certain values toward particular occupations, such as a sensitivity for fairness toward law, health toward medicine, or safety toward firefighting (Gardner et al., 2001). When the individual, field, and domain elements are in alignment working toward positive values, ethical judgments and behavior are less problematic; in contrast, when misalignments occur, more of the responsibility falls on the individual to decipher and decide what would lead to good work (Gardner et al., 2001; Gardner, 2005). Moral exemplars are at a particular premium when fields or cultures are in transition, and normative values have broken down or become so rigid that people are alienated from them (Gardner et al., 2001; Merton, 1957).

### Summary

Most of us do our best to do what is right, to be individually moral. But few of us risk creature comforts or personal safety to come to another's aid or change others' minds about what is good—to address morality at the field or domain level. Although individuals are rarely considered exemplary in the moral domain before adulthood, individual differences at various ages correspond to different emphases for extraordinariness: unusual sensitivity in young children, precocity in making moral arguments in school-age children, notable self-knowledge and initiative in adolescence, and self-defining altruism or social activism in adulthood. Learning when young how to cope constructively with difficult situations is an important marker as well. When these abilities, skills, experiences, and dispositions interweave and meet an opportunity to act courageously, moral extraordinariness may emerge.

## Varieties of Extraordinariness

A person can show moral extraordinariness in three ways: individual acts of caring, courage, and heroism; moral leadership; or the creation of an organization dedicated to a moral issue. All three types highlight an initial moral orientation, but leadership and institution building entail additional features. In most cases, an individual will emerge as outstanding in one of these respects. Only rarely does an individual—like Mahatma Gandhi—stand out as a person of courage, a leader, and the architect of a social organization.

We note that individuals may put their gifts to immoral or amoral ends. Individuals who are personally courageous may carry out terrorist acts; leaders who see themselves as moral agents (like Lenin) may condone immoral acts; and gifted organizational leaders may create crime syndicates. Judgments about moral excellence must be rendered by a field of knowledgeable observers. In the case of morality, the criteria for judgment include a coherent set of principles about human relations and justice; action based on these principles, even when one's own self-interest is sacrificed; and respect for the interests and sanctity of other human beings (Colby & Damon, 1994; Fischman et al., 2001; Gardner et al., 2001; Lawrence-Lightfoot, 1999; Oliner & Oliner, 1988).

### Individual Acts of Caring or Heroism

Every year, a number of individuals are recognized for acts of unusual caring or courage. In general, these acts are carried out without any expectation of reward or recognition. Sometimes these acts are one-time occurrences, as when a passerby jumps into a river or rushes into a burning house to rescue a stranger. The decisions are made instantaneously. At other times, these acts are recurring, as when a person without considerable resources regularly takes in foster children. Occasionally, individuals risk themselves and their families, as when individuals shielded Jews from the Nazis by allowing them to live in their homes.

Contrary to what might have been predicted, these individual moral agents rarely have high levels of education, let alone special training in morality. They do not perform at high levels on measures of moral judgment. They are more accurately described as seemingly quite ordinary individuals who, when faced with a morally tinged decision, act directly, in a forthright matter, and without obsession. Found in the same situation, such individuals typically expect that others would do likewise.

Three recent lines of research have enriched our understanding of moral commitment at the individual level. Oliner and Oliner (1988; see also Oliner, 2003) carried out extensive studies of individuals who hid Jews during World War II. In contrast with those who were mere bystanders, the rescuers stand out in terms of their benevolent view of their parents, the strong religious and personal values that they absorbed at home, their sense of personal agency, and especially, their inclusive and generous view of other human beings. During the rescuers' childhoods, parents exhibited caring, avoided physical punishment, offered explanations for preferred courses of action, and modeled high standards of conduct toward others. The rescuers did not see how one can simply segment human beings into two exclusive groups, let alone consider one group nonhuman, subhuman, or inhuman. In addition, norms of the surrounding culture and features of the physical environment (i.e., areas where Jews could be hidden) also were factors in determining whether an individual became a rescuer or a bystander.

Colby and Damon (1994) studied a small group of individuals who devoted their lives to aiding others. Many of these individuals were highly religious. They had a sustained commitment to high ideals, the capacity to act in terms of these ideals, a positive and optimistic orientation, and a willingness to suspend self-interest in favor of the needs of others. Once again, these individuals did not view themselves as special, even though their accomplishments would have seemed heroic to most others. Colby and Damon view this caring orientation as the outcome of a lengthy developmental process. Once the requisite behaviors and attitudes had coalesced, the individuals came to speak and behave instinctively in prosocial ways (cf. Youniss & Yates, 1997).

Fischman et al. (2001) studied Schweitzer Fellows, a group of young medical workers who devote themselves to treating underserved populations. Frequently these young persons drew their motivation from the combination of a traumatic personal loss early in life—such as the loss of a parent to AIDS—and a strong religious faith. Rather than becoming depressed or bitter at their loss, they selected a profession in which they could alleviate the disease or social pathology that occasioned their early trauma (see also Kidder, 2003). Learning to deal with adversity early helped them take in stride later obstacles—or "boulders" as they called them. The Fellows trace their choice of calling to a desire to prevent such tragedies in the future.

### Moral Leadership

Earlier in this chapter, we identified the principal features of leaders in business and politics: the capacity for creating compelling narratives, the ability to embody these narratives, the tenacity to remain committed to one's mission despite inevitable setbacks, and the capacity to recognize an opportunity and to make the most of it. These features also characterize individuals who provide leadership with a moral dimension.

Accordingly the question arises: Are there special characteristics of individuals who employ their leadership skills to promote missions deemed moral? Case studies of the lives of individuals who go on to become moral leaders—Martin Luther King Jr., Nelson Mandela, and Mahatma Gandhi—reveal many of the early markers found in highly caring individuals as well as certain distinctive patterns (Gardner, 1993, 1997, 2004a). In a number of cases, these individuals come from families that are personally secure but that represent a marginal or at least a nonmajority part of the population. The young individual feels both a part of the broader society but also—because of unusual demographic characteristics—alienated from that mainstream. At critical points in their young lives, such individuals witness examples of injustice. Either they themselves elect—or those around them encourage them—to protest this injustice. Such protest can, of course, lead to disaster or to null results. The future moral leader, however, discovers that he or she is able to influence other people and, in the happiest case, the course of events. Thus, in a way similar to, but broader than, the prototypical caring individual, the person is launched on a pathway of moral leadership. Skills of leadership sharpen and combine with personal courage. The moral leader realizes that, at any time, he may be assassinated by enemies or—as in the case of Gandhi and Israeli Prime Minister Yitzhak Rabin—by members of his own group who feel that the moral leader has been insufficiently faithful to his own core beliefs.

Gardner, Csikszentmihalyi, and Damon (2001) studied individuals whom they term *good workers*—professionals who are both excellent in a technical sense and who seek to act in ways that are socially responsible. Although their subjects did not reach the level of a Mother Teresa or Abraham Lincoln, many of them would qualify as moral leaders. These extraordinary individuals tend to come from homes where there are strong values and principles, often of a religious nature. These foundational values endure, even when the religious origins diminish in importance. Future good workers are inspired by mentors, peers, and paragons who are themselves oriented to good work. These inspirational colleagues do not emerge by chance; rather, the workers search for morally oriented colleagues who, in turn, are also seeking individuals with a moral orientation. Importantly, good workers do not select their occupations for strictly instrumental purposes. They reach out to do good work in their professions and they gain pleasure from that work. When purely financial or utilitarian considerations threaten to override the core of a profession, the good worker speaks out about and acts on her beliefs. And in the ultimate case, good workers are prepared to leave their organizations and to join in the creation of new institutions that more faithfully capture their moral values (Hirschman, 1970).

### Building Organizations with a Moral Mission

In recent years, an additional form of moral extraordinariness has been recognized. The social entrepreneur is an individual or group who recognizes and tackles a significant problem in the community, region, or even the world at large (Barendsen, 2004; Barendsen & Gardner, 2004; Bornstein, 2004; Drucker, 1992). Examples include Ashoka Fellows and Schwab Fellows—individuals from developing countries who devote their energies to the improvement of health, the reduction of poverty, the creation of new sources of energy, and other imperatives. On the American scene, exemplars range from Wendy Kopp, who began Teach for America immediately after graduating from college, to the social architect John Gardner, who launched a series of organizations including Common Cause, Independent Sector, the White House Fellows, and The Urban Coalition. Perhaps the most remarkable example, in a *Handbook of Child Psychology,* is the 12-year-old Canadian youth,

Craig Kielburger. Learning from the media about deplorable child labor practices in southern Asia, Kielburger launched Free the Children which soon grew into an internationally known organization with 100,000 organizers in 30 countries.

Such social entrepreneurs frequently exhibit leadership traits: they may be articulate and charismatic. But they stand out in two other respects. First, they have a strong moral orientation, typically a deeply felt concern about one or more vexing issues in their community or region. Second, they have an entrepreneurial bent, and they develop the skills requisite for building up an effective organization. Unlike designated moral leaders, they are prepared to remain in the background and give primary credit to their associates. The concatenation of these capacities is the distinguishing feature of a social entrepreneur. Without a caring mission, these individuals would simply be individual entrepreneurs. Without the entrepreneurial skill, these individuals could provide care only on a local, person-to-person scale.

In a study of 15 outstanding social entrepreneurs in their teen years, Michaelson (2001) found that the young persons were precociously sensitive to examples of suffering or injustice. Intriguingly, several of the subjects were raised by highly engaged single mothers who themselves were social activists. Examining social entrepreneurs in their 20s and 30s, Barendsen (2004) discerned early tragedies that had given a sense of mission to these individuals. What separated these subjects from individual caregivers or moral leaders was their interest in and capacity for building an organization. The social entrepreneurs thought more broadly about the problem, marshaled human and financial resources, inspired others to join them, and derived pleasure from steering the organization's growth. Indeed, once the organization had coalesced, these founders sometimes moved on to new challenges. Though often competing for limited resources, they nonetheless made common cause with other young social entrepreneurs. They have been recognized in the media and by organizations like the World Economic Forum as a distinctive moral agent for our time (Bornstein, 2004).

### Summary

Three distinct types of moral extraordinariness can be distinguished: (1) caring individuals, (2) moral leaders, and (3) social entrepreneurs. From their early years, all exhibit concern with issues of fairness, social justice, human rights, and social relations. Often they come from religious and ethically oriented families and have had to deal personally with traumatic events. Caring individuals stand out as adults in light of their virtually instinctive capacity to aid others. Moral leaders are distinguished by their capacity to mobilize members with often heterogeneous backgrounds to pursue an ethical agenda. Often content to remain in the background, social entrepreneurs have the capacity and inclination to build an organization that pursues a positive moral agenda.

Extraordinariness in the moral sphere does not yet occupy as well-delineated a place in the research literature or the popular consciousness as does artistic excellence, scientific excellence, or excellence in political or business leadership. Its dimensions are more controversial; its judgments are less secure. Indeed, Colby and Damon report that some experts refused to nominate moral exemplars, citing their dubiety about the very existence of the category (personal communication, August, 2004). We do not yet know at what point, or in what manner, moral precocity trifurcates into the varieties of caring, leadership, and entrepreneurship. Although moral judgment has been extensively studied, much less is known about capacities of integration and dispositions to act that mark the three principal varieties of moral excellence. We submit, however, that it is foolhardy to ignore the importance of moral excellence, particularly at a time when the very survival of our species and our planet may be in jeopardy. If we can understand better the origins of a caring orientation, of moral leadership, and of social entrepreneurship, our science may make a contribution to the society that supports our research.

## CONCLUSION

Extraordinary achievements demonstrate that people are makers of their destinies—both personal and, through their ultimate impact on others, historical. However, a long road—often unpaved and full of obstacles and sharp turns—extends from potential to realization of creativity in art or science, leadership in politics, or moral excellence. Furthermore, the end state of extraordinariness is a moving target because an extraordinary achievement by one person changes the playing field for everyone in the domain. Virginia Woolf made nonlinear, psychological novels with female protagonists a viable option for contemporary and later authors. Pierre Omidyar, founder of E-bay, created a viable, na-

tionwide market without middlemen. Such changes are not always for the better, as Hitler's, Napoleon's, or Osama bin Laden's extraordinary performances attest. Still, extraordinary achievements show that progress can happen. Individuals, fields, and domains are changed by their occurrence, often irreversibly. Table 21.1 summarizes our analysis of the four domains of art, science, political leadership, and morality in terms of their differences and commonalities.

## Domain Differences

Extraordinariness exhibits different features across domains. First, the relative importance of different forms of extraordinariness varies by domain. Creativity is most associated with art, science, or invention; leadership in politics and business; and moral excellence in religion, law, politics, and clinically, educationally, or public-service oriented professions. Some might say leadership and moral excellence are relatively marginal forms of extraordinariness in art. Perhaps Alfred Barr, founding director of the Museum of Modern Art, or Peggy Guggenheim, who helped launch the careers of mid-twentieth-century American artists, might be considered individuals who transformed the art institutions of New York. Likewise, creativity is often not wanted in many professions, such as accounting or engineering, and might even be considered immoral in light of these fields' ethical codes. Nonetheless, leaders (e.g., opinion leader collectors or gallery owners) and experts (e.g., art critics and historians) do exist in art, and doctors and lawyers have been known to devise innovative techniques to save their patients or clients.

Second, domains build on different intelligences. People with the most jagged profiles—an extreme strength in one or two intelligences and weaknesses in the others—are most often found in creative domains like art and science. Artists may use a variety of intelligences, depending on whether their media are canvas or clay (where spatial intelligence may be strong) to sound (where musical intelligence predominates) to their own hands and torso (where bodily kinesthetic intelligence comes to the fore). Science tends to build on logical-mathematical and spatial intelligence. Leadership-oriented domains prefer generalist profiles, with moderate ability across intelligences. Leadership particularly draws on linguistic and interpersonal intelligences, and moral excellence also tends to reward those with intrapersonal or existential strengths. However,

**TABLE 21.1 Summary of Domain Similarities and Differences**

| Domain | Art | Science | Political Leadership | Moral Excellence |
|---|---|---|---|---|
| *Between-Domain Differences* | | | | |
| Examples | Pablo Picasso<br>Igor Stravinsky<br>Virginia Woolf | Charles Darwin<br>Marie Curie<br>Albert Einstein | Franklin Roosevelt<br>Margaret Thatcher<br>Charles de Gaulle | Mahatma Gandhi<br>M. L. King, Jr.<br>Rescuers |
| Forms of extraordinariness | Mostly creator | Expert or creator | Transformative leader<br>Cross-domain generalist rather than domain expert | Caring individual<br>Moral leader<br>Social entrepreneur |
| Intelligences | Jagged Profile/Laserlike | | Flat Profile/Searchlight | |
|  | Any intelligence used aesthetically<br>Spatial<br>Musical<br>Bodily-kinesthetic | Logical-mathematical<br>Spatial | Linguistic<br>Interpersonal<br>Intrapersonal | Interpersonal<br>Intrapersonal<br>Existential |
| Principal entities | Objects/media<br>People affected through work | Objects | People<br>Organizations | People<br>Principles<br>Organizations |
| Personal qualities | Risk work but not self<br>May have an advocate/spokesperson | | Risk self<br>Resilience<br>Charisma<br>Caring | |
| Career arcs | Gradual<br>Peak early or late | Peak early and decline | Peak in middle or later life | Peak late |
| Early markers | Talent<br>Perceptual orientation<br>Personal style<br>Identification as artist<br>Immersion in one's own emotional life | Computational ability<br>Curiosity<br>Deeper problem structuring<br>Problem finding<br>Early productivity | Social graces<br>Drive/initiative<br>Early adversity<br>Leadership opportunities and mentoring | Judgment precocity<br>Emotional sensitivity<br>Self-awareness and reflectivity<br>Action orientation<br>Constructive reaction to trauma |
| Turning point | Distinctive personal style | Breakthrough discovery | Position of power + problematic situation | Personal action in problematic situation of wide scope |
| Influential researchers | Arnheim<br>Milbraith<br>Winner | Gruber<br>Roe<br>Zuckerman | Burns<br>Simonton | Colby and Damon<br>Kohlberg<br>Oliner and Oliner |
| *Cross-Domain Similarities* | Ordinary to expert to extraordinary/transformation continuum of influence<br>10-year rule of domain mastery<br>Developmental sensitive periods<br>Integration of individual, field, and domain at highest levels<br>Confidence, perseverance, and risk taking | | | |

those saints who lead in moral ways should not be considered more interpersonally intelligent than those knaves who are bent on power or destructiveness; rather, these individuals are using their interpersonal (and other) intelligences in the service of different values (Gardner, 2005).

Third, domains emphasize different objects of interest (Gardner, 1993a; Prediger, 1976). Idea-oriented domains manipulate symbolic objects and are more domain-sensitive; people-oriented domains manipulate people and are more field-sensitive. In our analysis, science is the domain most oriented toward ideas or objects, as scientists focus on stars, cells, corn, and so on and often ignore the personal dimensions or consequences of their work. Art also orients toward ideas and objects; it tends to affect people's emotions indirectly through crafted objects. Politics and morality are more people oriented, with politics the most people oriented, directly influencing others through communication and embodiment of goals. Moral leadership and social entrepreneurship tend to be principle based, whereas moral caring necessarily entails person-to-person interaction.

Fourth, domains differ in the motivations and qualities required of members in the field. Some domains that emphasize creativity are less time-pressured and reward laserlike intelligence, solitude, and time-on-task (Ericsson, 1996; Galenson, 2001; Storr, 1988). In leaping into the unknowns of their domains, such innovators risk their ideas and products, but their selves remain in the background. Other domains that emphasize leadership reward searchlight intelligence, versatility, in-the-moment thinking, resiliency, and charisma to respond to social changes in a timely way (Burns, 1978; Simonton, 1984). As their extraordinary products *are* their personal actions and embodiments, they risk themselves as well as their ideas when going beyond what is currently accepted. Even more subtle differences exist. For example, some sciences, such as genetics, are becoming less solitary, collaborative, and more influenced by quotidian market forces (Gardner et al., 2001). Similarly, moral leaders and social entrepreneurs navigate in longer time frames than political leaders; and their reasons for controlling events and effecting social change demonstrate a "universal intent" of personal ideals (Polanyi, 1958) as opposed to a "seize the day" mentality that characterizes most politicians today.

Fifth, domains present different career arcs. Some peak early, whereas others offer a slow, steady climb. Extraordinariness is most likely in math and physics to come early, in one's 20s and 30s, but can come later in biology or natural history (Simonton, 1988). The apex often depends on the versatility or specialization of the scientist (Sulloway, 1996). Artists can either peak early with more conceptual art or have their work recognized later with more experimental efforts (Galenson, 2001). The longest career arcs are shown by political leaders and moral exemplars, perhaps because they require less task-specific and more situational competence (Connell et al., 2003) and, therefore, more real-world experience. These individuals may seem rather undirected and drifting early in their careers before they find a group of people, institution, or situation that draws on their capacities and values. However, eminence may accrue not only to those with the longest lives and careers but also to those who have been stopped dramatically in their

prime—a pattern associated with Alexander the Great, Abraham Lincoln, and the Kennedy brothers (Simonton, 1994).

## Domain Similarities

Common ground in extraordinariness also can be found across domains. These similarities seem to be both developmental and systemic. Despite differences in end state and career arc steepness, the general path for most domains extends from novice to experts, who often are considered the pinnacle of normal development, to transformers (e.g., creators, leaders, and moral exemplars), who change the symbolic meanings, social structures, or values of their domains. Experts and more ordinary performers tend to have a more balanced ensemble of activities across several domains (i.e., have relatively separate work, leisure, and family lives), aim to satisfy requirements or standards, and depend on existing institutions to provide both a foundation and direction for their careers. They accept the field as currently constituted. Creators and leaders, alternatively, show a more integrated (though not a more balanced) identity stemming from an internally driven compulsion to master a specific domain, push its institutional boundaries, often with little institutional support, in a manner that encompasses almost all aspects of their lives. Their mates, friends, and hobbies tend to tie into their work. At the time of their breakthroughs, these individuals identify principally with the core mission of the domain and only marginally with the field. They continue to learn and reach beyond standards, maintain a lingering sense of dissatisfaction and incompleteness in all they do, and utilize the elements of the domain (i.e., symbol systems, task properties, or ideas) rather than field institutions as a foundation for their careers (Gardner, 1997).

Extraordinariness arises epigenetically, usually requiring at least 10 years of cultivation to show itself (Ericsson, 1998; Shekerjian, 1990). It may be thought of like a swinging pendulum that picks up speed based on its own momentum. It starts with individuals who engage in extraordinariness on the littlest (little-c, little-l, little-m) scale—for creativity, attempting slight modifications of conventional ways of doing things; for leadership, attempting to organize small groups of friends or events; for morality, eking out individual acts of courage and noting their consequences. Over time, some of these individuals continue on to midscale extraordinariness, which influences some people but not enough of a critical mass to transform the domain in a noticeable way. Examples include showing one's artwork in a regional show or running for local office or starting a nonprofit organization. This midlevel is often an important point for garnering recognition or more field resources, such as the MacArthur "Genius" Prize (Shekerjian, 1990), that can catalyze the continued transformation of one's potential into extraordinary performance—and hence one's personal development into domain development. Finally, a few jump to historically important creativity, leadership, or morality with corresponding far-reaching influence and implications.

Although these scales form a continuum of influence, the psychological factors contributing to them seem to involve nonlinearity. There is a jump in kind, not just in degree, from ordinariness, which mostly involves being a consumer of culture, to expertise, which involves being a reproducer of culture, to extraordinariness, which involves being a producer of culture (Bourdieu, 1993). Extraordinariness breaks free of the constraints of what already exists, using cultural heritage as a tool rather than a limit, and focuses on possibility—what could be.

Because extraordinariness arises from the particulars of a person's history in interaction with a domain and field, it is possible that certain moments in development present sensitive periods (Rostan, 1998; Winner, 2000). Society often posits expertise, which reproduces culture as is, as the main end state in development. Perhaps one reason is that expertise is safer, more common, more understood, or easier to achieve. But what if extraordinariness were the end goal of a career? Then the question becomes: Why, except in the most remarkable historical epochs, do so few people make transformations? There may be critical points when many people seem to slip off the path toward extraordinariness: when they do not demonstrate biological dispositions or talents in the earliest years of life (Winner, 1996a); when they fail to gain access to a domain, such as living in a culturally isolated location or coming from a family without resources that allow cultural exposure (Gardner, 1993a); when the enforcement of domain conventions in middle childhood may hinder children's independent exploration of the domain or fail to be integrated with their idiosyncratic styles (Bamberger, 1982); when adolescents find no appropriate or rewarded societal outlet for their efforts (Csikszentmihalyi et al., 1993); when young adults encounter the constraining forces of the field during their first jobs (Allmendinger, Hackman, &

Lehman, 1996; Gardner et al., 2001); when the work of young adults fails to be accepted by the field and they seek more regular forms of work to pay the bills (Stohs, 1991); or when would-be innovators become successful—for example, acclaimed prodigies—and may slip into a "formula" that works in the field but inhibits the development of a rebellious and robust personality (Gardner, 1993a; Rank, 1932).

The earlier childhood sensitive periods stem more from individual-domain interactions, whereas the later adolescence and adulthood sensitive periods involve more individual-field interactions. Individuals who become the most extraordinary appear ultimately to integrate in a personal manner all three nodes—individual, domain, and field. Although, historically, extraordinariness has been studied as an individual trait, the developmental-systemic perspective highlights the fact that rarely do extraordinary achievers go it alone. For those who reach the highest echelons and have the most influence, involving others and being mentored by others is crucial (Gardner, 1993a, 1995; John-Steiner, 1985, 2000). Future great leaders are often taken under the wing of current leaders. Mentorships provide field-supported stepping stones that include both emotional and career-building support—from a romantic view of the domain via early nurturing mentors, to a skill-oriented view of the domain via later technical mentors, to an integrated and innovative view of the domain as individuals move beyond mentors' direct influence to create their own approach (Bloom, 1985).

In a sense, the domain and field operate behind the scenes even before the individual is born. The Zeitgeist (e.g., individualistic versus collectivistic, progress versus tradition oriented), the state of the domain (e.g., organized versus chaotic, central versus marginal to the culture's values), and the state of the field (e.g., harmonious versus fragmented, resourceful versus poor) while the child grows up and into which she is socialized determines whether a developmental trajectory toward extraordinariness is even relevant. It is surely no accident that Athens in the fifth century A.D., or the T'ang Dynasty in China at the end of the first millennium A.D., produced a disproportionate number of extraordinary individuals and contributions (Csikszentmihalyi, 1996; Sorokin, 1947/1969). Such periods may have enjoyed a particularly fruitful combination of alignments and misalignments that led to an unusual blossoming of creativity and influence. If the culture is overly conservative, or the domain and field are toxically misaligned or disorganized, extraordinariness is less likely even if the individual leaps all of the above developmental hurdles. Extraordinariness does arise from tension and asynchronies among system elements, but too much tension may thwart even the most talented, resilient, ambitious individual.

## Further Research

Extraordinary achievements are never guaranteed by following a formula, including a stair-step, "universal" developmental path. Too many factors regarding individual, field, and domain characteristics must coincide for them to arise. Therefore, uncertainty underpins extraordinariness; it is probabilistic not deterministic.

How does this situation affect the outlook for extraordinariness research? In our view, researchers need to move conceptually beyond traits, categories, and linear prediction to models of interactions and emergence; and from direct, cross-sectional cause-effect toward recursive, reciprocal causal models with an explicit temporal dimension that allow for new end states and domain configurations to be formed. In addition to the general or universal mechanisms classically favored by developmentalists, we must look more closely at domain-specific contributions to extraordinariness and at domains not considered in this survey. And we must further integrate the cognitive with motivational, social, and historical factors, including their interactions at critical developmental junctures.

Methodologically, extraordinariness shows the limits of a laserlike or reductionist science isolated from other perspectives. This phenomenon calls for collaboration among social scientific and humanistic approaches. So few truly extraordinary individuals come along that it is difficult—and perhaps inappropriate—to apply traditional psychological research designs (Gardner, 1988; Simonton, 1999; Wallace & Gruber, 1989). Many methods have been used to explore different forms and factors of extraordinariness, from statistical analyses of large databases in an effort to ferret out general laws to in-depth, qualitative analyses of particular individuals that illuminate the life-span contours of an extraordinary life. A developmental-systemic approach calls for more longitudinal research. Given what we know now, if we could redo Terman's 70-plus-year study, what would we examine? Possibilities include using domain-specific sample selection criteria, such as curiosity in science, rather than a universal measure like IQ score; incorporating descriptions or assessments of the state of various

domains and fields, which define supports and constraints that operate on the individual; securing data on commitment (Moran, 2004) and other motivational-cognitive interactions; incorporating information about neural structure and functioning as well as genetic profile; tracking the individuals' relationships with and positioning in their respective domains and fields over time—perhaps via computer modeling—to see how intelligences become competences, performances, expertise, and perhaps move "beyond the given" (Bruner, 1962); and focusing our data collection points on the sensitive periods described earlier, when individual, domain, and field critically interact. Such a complex design may make us wish for the simpler days of searching for a test or gene for extraordinariness.

Finally, we need to expand the forms of extraordinariness about which we draw our conclusions. What are the extraordinary forms of parenting, social networking, and caring for the environment—just to name a few pursuits—that may have made a crucial difference but were ignored by researchers in the grip of a *Britannica* view of extraordinariness (cf. Murray, 2003)? What do the different forms of extraordinariness look like, and how do they develop among the working class, women, other ethnic groups, or third-world cultures (cf. Helson, 1999; Nisbett, 2003; Richie, Fassinger, Linn, Johnson, Prosser, & Robinson, 1997; Simonton, 1998)? This analysis could be expanded to include historical time period: As Fish (1999) and Bourdieu (1993) argued, the conceptions of "merit"—of which extraordinariness is a form—change over time as different ideas and people come to power. Therefore, what extraordinariness looks like now in early-twenty-first-century America differs from twentieth-century China, fourteenth-century Florence, or a twenty-fourth-century Star Trek-type scenario. As study of extraordinariness examines the borders of human possibility, it has a special obligation to encompass the widest definition of "human."

## REFERENCES

Abroms, K. I., & Gollin, J. B. (1980). Developmental study of gifted preschool children and measures of psychosocial giftedness. *Exceptional Children, 46*(5), 334–341.

Aitken, K. J., & Trevarthen, C. (1997). Self/other organization in human psychological development. *Development and Psychopathology, 9*(4), 653–677.

Alexander, J. M., Carr, M., & Schwanenflugel, P. J. (1995). Development of meta-cognition in gifted children: Directions for future research. *Developmental Review, 15*, 1–37.

Allmendinger, J., Hackman, J. R., & Lehman, E. V. (1996). Life and work in symphony orchestras. *Musical Quarterly, 80*(2), 194–219.

Amabile, T. (1996). *Creativity in context.* Boulder, CO: Westview Press.

Anderson, K. C., & Leinhardt, G. (2002). Maps as representations: Expert-novice comparison of projection understanding. *Cognition and Instruction, 20*(3), 283–321.

Andreani, O. D., & Pagnin, A. (1993). Moral judgment in creative and talented adolescence. *Creativity Research Journal, 6*(1/2), 45–63.

Andreasen, N. C. (1987). Creativity and mental illness: Prevalence rates in writers and their first-degree relatives. *American Journal of Psychiatry, 144*(10), 1288–1292.

Arnheim, R. (1966). *Toward a psychology of art.* Berkeley: University of California Press.

Arsenio, W. F., & Lover, A. (1995). Children's conceptions of sociomoral affect: Happy victimizers, mixed emotions, and other expectancies. In D. Hart & M. Killen (Eds.), *Morality in everyday life* (pp. 87–128). New York: Cambridge University Press.

Astington, J. W. (1993). *The child's discovery of the mind.* Cambridge, MA: Harvard University Press.

Bamberger, J. (1982). Growing up prodigies: The midlife crisis. *New Directions for Child Development, 17,* 61–78.

Bandura, A., & Walters, R. (1963). *Social learning and personality development.* New York: Holt, Rinehart and Winston.

Barendsen, L. (2004, April). *The business of caring: A study of young social entrepreneurs.* Retrieved November 10, 2005, from www.goodworkproject.org.

Barendsen, L., & Gardner, H. (2004, Fall). Is the social entrepreneur a new type of leader? *Leader to Leader, 34.*

Barron, F. (1972). *Artists in the making.* New York: Seminar Press.

Beabout, G. R., & Wennemann, D. J. (1994). *Applied professional ethics: A developmental approach for use with case studies.* Lanham, MD: University Press of America.

Becker, H. (1982). *Art worlds.* Berkeley: University of California Press.

Bell, P., & Linn, M. C. (2002). Beliefs about science: How does science instruction contribute. In B. K. Hofer & P. R. Pintrich (Eds.), *Personal epistemology: The psychology of beliefs about knowledge and knowing* (pp. 321–346). Mahwah, NJ: Erlbaum.

Benbow, C. P., & Stanley, J. C. (1983). Sex differences in mathematical reasoning ability: More facts. *Science, 212,* 1029–1031.

Bennis, W. G., & Thomas, R. J. (2002). *Geeks and geezers: How era, values, and defining moments shape leaders.* Boston: Harvard Business School Press.

Bereiter, C., & Scardamalia, M. (1993). *Surpassing ourselves: An inquiry into the nature and implications of expertise.* Chicago: Open Court.

Berg, D. N. (1998). Resurrecting the muse: Followership in organizations. In E. B. Klein, F. Gabelnick, & P. Herr (Eds.), *The psychodynamics of leadership* (pp. 27–52). Madison, CT: Psychosocial Press.

Berlyne, D. E. (1950). Novelty and curiosity as determinants of exploratory behavior. *British Journal of Psychology, 41,* 68–80.

Binet, A., & Simon, T. (1976). The development of intelligence in the child. In W. Dennis & M. W. Dennis (Eds.), *The intellectually gifted* (pp. 13–16). New York: Grune & Stratton. (Original work published 1909)

Bloom, B. (1985). *Developing talent in young people.* New York: Ballantine Books.

Boden, M. A. (1990). *The creative mind: Myths and mechanisms.* New York: Basic Books.

Bogardus, E. S. (1934). *Leaders and leadership.* New York: Appleton-Century-Crofts.

Bornstein, D. (2004). *How to change the world: Social entrepreneurs and the power of new ideas.* New York: Oxford University Press.

Bourdieu, P. (1993). *The field of cultural production.* New York: Columbia University Press.

Braumgart, M. M., & Braumgart, R. G. (1990). The life-course development of left-and right-wing young activist leaders from the 1960s. *Political Psychology, 11*(2), 283–292.

Brower, R. (2000). To reach a star: The creativity of Vincent Van Gogh. *High Ability Studies, 11*(2), 179–206.

Brown, A. L., & Campione, J. C. (1986). Psychological theory and the study of learning disabilities. *American Psychologist, 41*(10), 1059–1068.

Bruchkowsky, M. (1992). The development of empathic cognition in middle and early childhood. In R. Case (Ed.), *The mind's staircase: Exploring the conceptual underpinnings of children's thought and knowledge* (pp. 153–170). Hillsdale, NJ: Erlbaum.

Bruner, J. S. (1962). The conditions of creativity. In J. S. Bruner. *On knowing: Essays for the left hand.* Cambridge, MA: Belknap Press.

Bullock, A. (1998). *Hitler & Stalin: Parallel lives* (2nd ed.). London: Fontana.

Burns, J. M. (1978). *Leadership.* New York: Harper & Row.

Carothers, T., & Gardner, H. (1979). When children's drawings become art. *Developmental Psychology, 15*(5), 570–580.

Carruthers, P. (2002). The roots of scientific reasoning: Infancy, modularity and the art of tracking. In P. Carruthers, S. Stich, & M. Siegal (Eds.), *The cognitive basis of science* (pp. 73–95). New York: Cambridge University Press.

Carter, K. R., & Ormrod, J. E. (1982). Acquisition of formal operations by intellectual gifted children. *Gifted Child Quarterly, 26*(3), 110–115.

Cattell, J. M. (1903). A statistical study of eminent men. *Popular Science Monthly,* 359–377.

Cattell, R. B. (1971). *Abilities: Their structure, growth and action.* Boston: Houghton Mifflin.

Cattell, R. B., & Drevdahl, J. E. (1955). A comparison of the personality profile of eminent researchers with that of eminent teachers and administrators. *British Journal of Psychology, 46,* 248–261.

Ceci, S. (1991). *On intelligence . . . more or less.* Englewood Cliffs, NJ: Prentice-Hall.

Ceci, S. J. (1996). *On intelligence: A bioecological treatise on intellectual development.* Cambridge, MA: Harvard University Press.

Changeux, J.-P., & Ricouer, P. (2000). *What makes us think?* (M. B. DeBevoise, Trans.). Princeton, NJ: Princeton University Press.

Chi, M. T. H., Glaser, R., & Rees, E. (1982). Expertise in problem solving. In R. J. Sternberg (Ed.), *Advances in the psychology of human intelligence* (pp. 7–75). Hillsdale, NJ: Erlbaum.

Chinn, C. A., & Brewer, W. F. (1993). The role of anomalous data in knowledge acquisition: A theoretical framework and implications for science instruction. *Review of Educational Research, 63*(1), 1–49.

Colby, A., & Damon, W. (1994). *Some do care: Contemporary lives of moral commitment.* New York: Free Press-Macmillan.

Colby, A., Ehrlich, T., Beaumont, E., & Stephens, J. (2003). *Educating citizens.* San Francisco: Jossey-Bass.

Connell, M. W., Sheridan, K., & Gardner, H. (2003). On abilities and domains. In R. J. Sternberg & E. Grigorenko (Eds.), *Perspectives on the psychology of abilities, competencies and expertise* (pp. 126–155). New York: Cambridge University Press.

Cox, C. (1926). *Genetic studies of genius: Vol. 2. The early mental traits of three hundred geniuses.* Stanford, CA: Stanford University Press.

Cross, P. G., Cattell, R. B., & Butcher, H. J. (1967). The personality pattern of creative artists. *British Journal of Educational Psychology, 37,* 292–299.

Csikszentmihalyi, M. (1988). Society, culture, and person: A systems view of creativity. In R. J. Sternberg (Ed.), *The nature of creativity* (pp. 325–339). New York: Cambridge University Press.

Csikszentmihalyi, M. (1996). *Creativity.* New York: HarperCollins.

Csikszentmihalyi, M., Rathunde, K., & Whalen, S. (1993). *Talented teenagers: The roots of success and failure.* New York: Cambridge University Press.

Csikszentmihalyi, M., & Robinson, R. E. (1988). Culture, time and the development of talent. In R. J. Sternberg & J. E. Davidson (Eds.), *Conceptions of giftedness* (pp. 264–284). New York: Cambridge University Press.

Dabrowski, K. (1994). The heroism of sensitivity (E. Hyzy-Strzelecka, Trans.). *Advanced Development, 5,* 87–92. (Original work published 1979)

Damon, W. (1988). *The moral child: Nurturing children's natural moral growth.* New York: Free Press.

Davidson, J. E., & Sternberg, R. J. (1984). The role of insight in intellectual giftedness. *Gifted Child Quarterly, 28,* 58–64.

Davis, J. (1997). Drawing's demise: U-shaped development in graphic symbolization. *Studies in Art Education, 38*(3), 132–157.

Davis, M. H., Luce, C., & Kraus, S. J. (1994). The heritability characteristics associated with dispositional empathy. *Journal of Personality, 62,* 369–391.

Davis, P. J., & Hersh, R. (1980). *The mathematical experience.* Boston: Birkhauser.

De Corte, E., Op't Eynde, P., & Verschaffel, L. (2002). "Knowing what to believe": The relevance of students' mathematical beliefs for mathematics education. In B. K. Hofer & P. R. Pintrich (Eds.), *Personal epistemology: The psychology of beliefs about knowledge and knowing* (pp. 297–320). Mahwah, NJ: Erlbaum.

DeGroot, A. D. (1965). *Thought and choice in chess.* The Hague, The Netherlands: Mouton.

Dentici, O. A., & Pagnin, A. (1997). Moral reasoning in gifted adolescence: Cognitive level and social values. *European Journal for High Ability, 3*(1), 105–114.

Detterman, D. K., & Daniel, M. H. (1989). Correlations of mental tests with each other and with cognitive variables are highest for low IQ groups. *Intelligence, 13*(4), 349–359.

Drucker, P. (1992). *Managing the future.* New York: Plume.

Dunbar, K. (1996). How scientists really reason: Scientific reasoning in real world laboratories. In R. J. Sternberg & J. E. Davidson (Eds.), *The nature of insight* (pp. 365–395). Cambridge, MA: MIT Press.

Dunn, J. (1987). The beginnings of moral understanding: Development in the second year. In J. Kagan & S. Lamb (Eds.), *The emergence of morality in young children* (pp. 91–112). Chicago: University of Chicago Press.

Durkheim, E. (1961). *Moral education.* Glencoe, IL: Free Press.

Dweck, C. S. (2000). *Self-theories.* Philadelphia: Taylor & Francis.

Dweck, C. S. (2002). Beliefs that make smart people dumb. In R. J. Sternberg (Ed.), *Why smart people can be so stupid* (pp. 24–41). New Haven, CT: Yale University Press.

Eckstein, S. G. (2000). Growth of cognitive abilities: Dynamic models and scaling. *Developmental Review, 20,* 1–28.

Eisenberg, N., & Fabes, R. A. (1992). Emotion, regulation and development of social competence. In M. S. Clark (Ed.), *Review of personality and social psychology: Vol. 14. Emotion and social behavior* (pp. 119–150). Newbury Park, CA: Sage.

Ellis, H. (1926). *A study of British genius.* Boston: Houghton Mifflin.

Ericsson, K. A. (1998). The scientific study of expert levels of performance: General implications for optimal learning and creativity. *High Ability Studies, 9*(1), 75–98.

Erikson, E. (1958). *Young man Luther: A study in psychoanalysis and history.* New York: Norton.

Erikson, E. (1959). *Identity and the life cycle.* New York: International Universities Press.

Erikson, E. (1969). *Gandhi's truth on the origins of nonmilitant violence.* New York: Norton,

Eysenck, H. (1998). *Intelligence: A new look.* New Brunswick, NJ: Transaction.

Faulkner, J. (1996). *Talking about William Faulkner: Interviews with Jimmy Faulkner and others.* Baton Rouge: Louisiana State University Press.

Feist, G. J. (1993). A structural model of scientific eminence. *Psychological Science, 6*(4), 366–371.

Feist, G. J., & Gorman, M. E. (1998). The psychology of science: Review and integration of a nascent discipline. *Review of General Psychology, 2*(1), 3–47.

Feldman, D. H. (1986). *Nature's gambit: Child prodigies and the development of human potential.* New York: Basic Books.

Feldman, D. H. (1994). *Beyond the universals of cognitive development* (2nd ed.). Norwood, NJ: Ablex.

Finke, R. A., Ward, T. B., & Smith, S. M. (1992). *Creative cognition: Theory, research, and applications.* Cambridge, MA: MIT Press.

Fischer, K. W., Hand, H. H., Watson, M. W., Van Parys, M., & Tucker, J. (1984). Putting the child into socialization: The development of social categories in preschool. In L. Katz (Ed.), *Current topics in early childhood education* (Vol. 5, pp. 27–72). Norwood, NJ: Ablex.

Fischer, K. W., Kenny, S. L., & Pipp, S. L. (1990). How cognitive processes and environmental conditions organize discontinuities in the development of abstractions. In C. N. Alexander & E. J. Langer (Eds.), *Higher stages of human development: Perspectives on adult growth* (pp. 162–187). New York: Oxford University Press.

Fischer, K. W., & Pipp, S. L. (1984). Processes of cognitive development: Optimal level and skill acquisition. In R. J. Sternberg (Ed.), *Mechanisms of cognitive development* (pp. 45–80). New York: Freeman.

Fischman, W., Schutte, D., Solomon, B., & Lam, G. W. (2001). The development of an enduring commitment to service work. In M. Michaelson & J. Nakamura (Eds.), *Supportive frameworks for youth engagement* (pp. 33–44). San Francisco: Jossey-Bass.

Fischman, W., Solomon, B., Greenspan, D., & Gardner, H. (2004). *Making good: How young people cope with moral dilemmas at work.* Cambridge, MA: Harvard University Press.

Fish, S. (1999). *The trouble with principle.* Cambridge, MA: Harvard University Press.

Flacks, R. (1990). Social bases of activist identity: Comment on Braumgart article. *Political Psychology, 11*(2), 283–292.

Flavell, J. H., Botkin, P. J., & Fry, C. L. (1968). *The development of role-taking and communication skills in children.* New York: Wiley.

Flynn, J. R. (1999). Searching for justice: The discovery of IQ gains over time. *American Psychologist, 54*(1), 5–20.

Fodor, J. A. (1983). *The modularity of mind.* Cambridge, MA: MIT Press.

Freedman, B. (1983). A meta-ethics for a professional morality. In B. Baumrin & B. Freedman (Eds.), *Moral responsibility and the professions* (pp. 61–78). New York: Haven Publications.

Freedman, J. O. (1996). *Idealism and liberal education.* Ann Arbor: University of Michigan Press.

Freud, S. (1957). Leonardo da Vinci and a memory of his childhood. In J. Strachey, A. Freud, A. Strachey, & A. Tyson (Eds.), *The standard edition of the complete psychological works of Sigmund Freud* (Vol. 11, pp. 3–55). London: Hogarth Press. (Original work published 1910)

Freud, S. (1961a). Civilization and its discontents. In J. Strachey, A. Freud, A. Strachey, & A. Tyson (Eds.), *The standard edition of the complete psychological works of Sigmund Freud* (Vol. 21, pp. 64–145). London: Hogarth Press. (Original work published 1930)

Freud, S. (1961b). The ego and the id. In J. Strachey, A. Freud, A. Strachey, & A. Tyson (Eds.), *The standard edition of the complete psychological works of Sigmund Freud* (Vol. 19, pp. 3–66). London: Hogarth Press. (Original work published 1923)

Fried, I., Wilson, C. L., Morrow, J. W., Cameron, K. A., Behnke, E. D., Ackerson, L. C., et al. (2001). Increased dopamine release in the human amygdala during performance of cognitive tasks. *Nature Neuroscience, 4*(2), 201–206.

Furr, S. R., & Lutz, J. R. (1987). Emerging leaders: Developing leadership potential. *Journal of College Student Personnel, 28*(1), 86–87.

Galenson, D. (2001). *Painting outside the lines.* Cambridge, MA: Harvard University Press.

Galton, F. (1869). *Hereditary genius.* London: Macmillan.

Gardner, H. (1973). *The arts and human development.* New York: Wiley.

Gardner, H. (1980). *Artful scribbles: The significance of children's drawings.* New York: Basic Books.

Gardner, H. (1982). *Art, mind, and brain: A cognitive approach to creativity.* New York: Basic Books.

Gardner, H. (1983). *Frames of mind: The theory of multiple intelligences.* New York: Basic Books.

Gardner, H. (1988). Creativity: An interdisciplinary perspective. *Creativity Research Journal, 1,* 8–26.

Gardner, H. (1989). *To open minds: Chinese clues to the dilemma of contemporary education.* New York: Basic Books.

Gardner, H. (1991). *The unschooled mind: How children think and how schools should teach.* New York: Basic Books.

Gardner, H. (1993a). *Creating minds: An anatomy of creativity seen through the lives of Freud, Einstein, Picasso, Stravinsky, Eliot, Graham, and Gandhi.* New York: Basic Books.

Gardner, H. (1993b). The relationship between early giftedness and later achievement. In B. R. Bock & K. Ackrill (Eds.), *The origins and development of high ability* (pp. 175–182). New York: Wiley.

Gardner, H. (1995). *Leading minds.* New York: Basic Books.

Gardner, H. (1997). *Extraordinary minds.* New York: Basic Books.

Gardner, H. (1999). *Intelligence reframed: Multiple intelligences for the 21st century.* New York: Basic Books.

Gardner, H. (2000). *The disciplined mind.* New York: Penguin Putnam.

Gardner, H. (2001, September 19). *The return of good work in journalism.* Retrieved November 10, 2005, from www.goodworkproject.org.

Gardner, H. (2004a). *Changing minds.* Boston: Harvard Business School Press.

Gardner, H. (2004b). The making of a social scientist. In J. Brockman (Ed.), *When we were kids* (pp. 131–139). New York: Simon & Schuster.

Gardner, H. (2005, Summer). Compromised work. *Daedalus, 134*(3), 42–51.

Gardner, H. (2006). *Multiple intelligences: New horizons.* New York: Basic Books.

Gardner, H., Csikszentmihalyi, M., & Damon, W. (2001). *Good work: When excellence and ethics meet.* New York: Basic Books.

Gardner, H., Kornhaber, M., & Wake, W. L. (1996). *Intelligence: Multiple perspectives.* Fort Worth, TX: Harcourt Brace.

Gardner, H., & Nemirovsky, R. (1991). From private intuitions to public symbol systems: An examination of the creative process in Georg Cantor and Sigmund Freud. *Creativity Research Journal, 4*(1), 1–21.

Gardner, H., Phelps, E., & Wolf, D. (1990). The roots of adult creativity in children's symbolic products. In C. N. Alexander & E. J. Langer (Eds.), *Higher stages of human development: Perspectives on adult growth* (pp. 79–96). New York: Oxford University Press.

Gardner, H., & Wolf, C. (1988). The fruits of asynchrony: A psychological examination of creativity. *Adolescent Psychiatry, 15,* 106–123.

Gardner, J. W. (1984). *Excellence: Can we be equal and excellent too?* New York: Norton.

Gardner, J. W. (1990). *On leadership.* New York: Free Press.

Gedo, J. (1996). *The artist and the emotional world.* New York: Columbia University Press.

Gergen, D. (2000). *Eyewitness to power: The essence of leadership Nixon to Clinton.* New York: Simon & Schuster.

Geschwind, N. (1984). The biology of cerebral dominance: Implications for cognition. *Cognition, 17,* 193–208.

Geschwind, N., & Galaburda, A. (1987). *Cerebral lateralization.* Cambridge, MA: MIT Press.

Getzels, J. W., & Csikszentmihalyi, M. (1976). *The creative vision: A longitudinal study of problem finding in art.* New York: Wiley.

Getzels, J. W., & Jackson, P. W. (1962). *Creativity and intelligence: Explorations with gifted students.* New York: Wiley.

Glassman, M., & Zan, B. (1995). Moral activity and domain theory: An alternative interpretation of research with young children. *Developmental Review, 15,* 434–457.

Goertzel, B. (1997). *From complexity to creativity.* New York: Plenum Press.

Goertzel, M. G., Goertzel, V., & Goertzel, T. G. (1978). *Three hundred eminent personalities.* San Francisco: Jossey-Bass.

Goertzel, V., & Goertzel, M. G. (1962). *Cradles of eminence.* Boston: Little, Brown.

Goldberg-Reitman, J. (1992). Young girls' conceptions of their mother's role: A neo-structural analysis. In R. Case (Ed.), *The mind's staircase: Exploring the conceptual underpinnings of children's thought and knowledge* (pp. 135–151). Hillsdale, NJ: Erlbaum.

Goleman, D. (2002). *Primal leadership: Realizing the power of emotional intelligence.* Boston: Harvard Business School Press.

Golomb, C. (1995). Eitan: The artistic development of a child prodigy. In C. Golomb (Ed.), *The development of artistically gifted children: Selected case studies* (pp. 171–196). Hillsdale, NJ: Erlbaum.

Golomb, C., & Haas, M. (1995). Varda: The development of a young artist. In C. Golomb (Ed.), *The development of artistically gifted children: Selected case studies* (pp. 71–100). Hillsdale, NJ: Erlbaum.

Gombrich, E. (1960). *Art and illusion: A study in the psychology of pictorial representation.* Princeton, NJ: Princeton University Press.

Gooding, D. C. (1996). Scientific discovery as creative exploration: Faraday's experiments. *Creativity Research Journal, 9*(2/3), 189–205.

Goodman, N. (1976). *Languages of art.* Indianapolis, IN: Hackett.

Goodnow, J. (1977). *Children drawing.* Cambridge, MA: Harvard University Press.

Gopnik, A., & Meltzoff, A. N. (1997). *Words, thoughts and theories.* Cambridge, MA: MIT Press.

Goswami, U. (1996). Analogical reasoning and cognitive development. In H.W. Reese (Ed.), *Advances in child development and behavior* (Vol. 26, pp. 91–138). San Diego: Academic Press.

Govindarajan, T. N. (1964). Vocational interests of leaders and nonleaders among adolescent school boys. *Journal of Psychological Researches, 8*(3), 124–130.

Granott, N., & Gardner, H. (1994). When minds meet: Interactions, coincidence, and development in domains of ability. In R. J. Sternberg & R. K. Wagner (Eds.), *Mind in context: Interactionist perspectives on human intelligence* (pp. 171–201). New York: Cambridge University Press.

Greenacre, P. (1956). Experiences of awe in childhood. *Psychoanalytic Study of the Child, 11,* 9–30.

Greenhoot, A. F., Semb, G., Colombo, J., & Schreiber, T. (2004). Prior beliefs and methodological concepts in scientific reasoning. *Applied Cognitive Psychology, 18*(2), 203–221.

Grotzer, T., & Bell, B. (1999). Negotiating the funnel: Guiding students toward understanding elusive generative concepts. In L. Hetland & S. Veema (Eds.), *The project zero classroom: Views on understanding* (pp. 59–76). Cambridge, MA: Fellows and Trustees of Harvard College, Project Zero, Harvard Graduate School of Education.

Gruber, H. E. (1974). *Darwin on man: A psychological study of scientific creativity.* New York: Dutton.

Gruber, H. E. (1989). The evolving systems approach to creative work. In D. B. Wallace & H. E. Gruber (Eds.), *Creative people at work* (pp. 3–24). New York: Oxford University Press.

Guilford, J. P. (1950). Creativity. *American Psychologist, 5,* 444–454.

Guilford, J. P. (1967). *The nature of human intelligence.* New York: McGraw-Hill.

Gustin, W. C. (1985). The development of exceptional research mathematicians. In B. S. Bloom (Ed.), *Developing talent in young people* (pp. 270–331). New York: Ballantine Books.

Harris, P. L. (2000). *The work of the imagination.* Malden, MA: Blackwell.

Hart, D., & Fegley, S. (1995). Prosocial behavior and caring in adolescence: Relations to self-understanding and social judgment. *Child Development, 66*(5), 1346–1359.

Hart, D., Yates, M., Fegley, S., & Wilson, G. (1995). Moral commitment in inner-city adolescents. In D. Hart & M. Killen (Eds.), *Morality in everyday life* (pp. 317–341). New York: Cambridge University Press.

Hartshorne, H., & May, M. A. (1928–1930). *Studies in the nature of character.* New York: Macmillan.

Haste, H. (1990). Moral responsibility and moral commitment: The integration of affect and cognition. In T. E. Wren (Ed.), *The moral domain: Essays in the ongoing discussion between philosophy and the social sciences* (pp. 315–359). Cambridge, MA: MIT Press.

Hatch, T. (1997). Friends, diplomats, and leaders in kindergarten: Interpersonal intelligence in play. In P. Salovey & D. J. Sluyter (Eds.), *Emotional development and emotional intelligence: Educational implications* (pp. 70–89). New York: Basic Books.

Hawley, P. H. (1999). The ontogenesis of social dominance: A strategy-based evolutionary perspective. *Developmental Review, 19,* 97–132.

Hay, D. F., Castle, J., Stimson, C. A., & Davies, L. (1995). The social construction of character in toddlerhood. In D. Hart & M. Killen (Eds.), *Morality in everyday life* (pp. 23–51). New York: Cambridge University Press.

Heifetz, R. A. (1994). *Leadership without easy answers.* Boston: Belknap Press.

Helson, R. (1996). In search of the creative personality. *Creativity Research Journal, 9*(4), 295–306.

Helson, R. (1999). A longitudinal study of creative personality in women. *Creativity Research Journal, 12*(2), 89–101.

Helson, R., & Crutchfield, R. S. (1970). Mathematicians: The creative researcher and average PhD. *Journal of Consulting and Clinical Psychology, 34,* 250–257.

Helson, R., & Pais, J. L. (2000). Creativity potential, creative achievement, and personal growth. *Journal of Personality, 68*(1), 1–27.

Helwig, C. C. (1995). Social context and social cognition: Psychological harm and civil liberties. In D. Hart & M. Killen (Eds.), *Morality in everyday life* (pp. 166–200). New York: Cambridge University Press.

Herrnstein, R. J., & Murray, C. (1994). *The bell curve.* New York: Free Press.

Hirschhorn, L. (1998). The psychology of vision. In E. B. Klein, F. Gabelnick, & P. Herr (Eds.), *The psychodynamics of leadership* (pp. 109–125). Madison, CT: Psychosocial Press.

Hirschman, A. O. (1970). *Exit, voice, and loyalty.* Cambridge, MA: Harvard University Press.

Ho, W.-C. (1989). *Yani: The brush of innocence.* New York: Hudson Hills Press.

Hoffman, M. L. (2000). *Empathy and moral development.* New York: Cambridge University Press.

Hofstadter, D. R. (1995). *Fluid concepts and creative analogies: Computer models of the fundamental mechanisms of thought.* New York: Basic Books.

Hohmann, M., Hawker, D., & Hohmann, C. (1982). Group process and adolescent leadership development. *Adolescence, 17*(67), 613–620.

Holahan, C. K., Sears, R. R., & Cronbach, L. J. (1995). *The gifted group in later maturity.* Stanford, CA: Stanford University Press.

Hollingworth, L. S. (1942). *Children above 180 IQ.* New York: World Books.

Holmes, F. L. (1989). Antoine Lavoisier and Hans Krebs: Two styles of scientific creativity. In D. B. Wallace & H. E. Gruber (Eds.), *Creative people at work* (pp. 44–68). New York: Oxford University Press.

Holmes, F. L. (1996). Expert performance and the history of science. In K. A. Ericcson (Ed.), *The road to excellence: The acquisition of expert performance in the arts, sciences, sports and games* (pp. 313–319). Mahwah, NJ: Erlbaum.

Holton, G. (1973). *Thematic origins of scientific thought: Kepler to Einstein.* Cambridge, MA: Harvard University Press.

Howard-Hamilton, M. F. (1994). An assessment of moral development in gifted adolescents. *Roeper Review, 17*(1), 57–59.

Hudson, L. (1966). *Contrary imaginations: A psychological study of the English schoolboy.* London: Methuen.

Hunt, J. G. (1999). Transformational/charismatic leadership's transformation of the field: An historical essay. *Leadership Quarterly, 10*(2), 129–144.

Hutchins, E. (1996). *Cognition in the wild.* Cambridge, MA: MIT Press.

Jacobsen, C., & House, R. J. (2001). Dynamics of charismatic leadership: A process theory, simulation model, and tests. *Leadership Quarterly, 12,* 75–112.

Jamison, K. R. (1989). Mood disorders and patterns of creativity in British writers and artists. *Psychiatry, 52,* 125–134.

Jaques, E. (1955). Social systems as a defense against persecutory and depressive anxiety. In M. Klein, P. Heimann, & R. E. Money-Kyrle (Eds.), *New directions in psychoanalysis* (pp. 478–498). London: Tavistock.

Jaques, E. (1990). *Creativity and work.* Madison, WI: International Universities Press.

Jarecky, R. K. (1959). Identification of the socially gifted. *Exceptional Children, 25,* 415–419.

Jensen, A. (1980). *Bias in mental testing.* New York: Free Press.

John-Steiner, V. (1985). *Notebooks of the mind: Explorations of thinking.* Albuquerque: University of New Mexico Press.

John-Steiner, V. (1995). Cognitive pluralism: A sociocultural approach. *Mind, Culture and Activity, 2*(1), 2–11.

John-Steiner, V. (2000). *Creative collaboration.* New York: Oxford University Press.

Kagan, J. (1989). *Unstable ideas.* Cambridge, MA: Harvard University Press.

Karmiloff-Smith, A. (1990). Constraints on representational change: Evidence from children's drawings. *Cognition, 34,* 57–83.

Kasof, J. (1995). Explaining creativity: The attributional perspective. *Creativity Research Journal, 8*(4), 311–366.

Kay, S. I. (2000). On the nature of expertise in visual art. In R. C. Friedman & B. M. Shore (Eds.), *Talents unfolding: Cognition and development* (pp. 217–232). Washington, DC: American Psychological Association.

Keinanen, M., & Gardner, H. (2004). Vertical and horizontal mentoring for creativity. In R. J. Sternberg, E. L. Grigorenko, & J. L. Singer (Eds.), *Creativity: From potential to realization* (pp. 169–193). Washington, DC: American Psychological Association.

Keller, E. F. (2000). *The century of the gene.* Cambridge, MA: Harvard University Press.

Kellerman, B., & Webster, S. W. (2001). The recent literature on public leadership: Reviewed and considered. *The Leadership Quarterly, 12*(4), 485–514.

Kelly, G. J., & Bazerman, C. (2003). How students argue scientific claims: A rhetorical-semantic analysis. *Applied Linguistics, 24*(1), 28–55.

Kidder, T. (2003). *Mountains beyond mountains: The quest of Dr. Paul Farmer.* New York: Random House.

Kielsmeier, J. (1982). The National Leadership Conference. *Child and Youth Service, 4*(3/4), 145–154.

Klaczynski, A. A., & Robinson, B. (2000). Personal theories, intellectual ability, and epistemological beliefs: Adult age differences in everyday reasoning biases. *Psychology and Aging, 15*(3), 400–416.

Klahr, D. (2000). *Exploring science: The cognition and development of discovery processes.* Cambridge, MA: MIT Press.

Klein, E. B., Gabelnick, F., & Herr, P. (Eds.). (1998). *The psychodynamics of leadership.* Madison, CT: Psychosocial Press.

Kohlberg, L. (1984). *Essays on moral development: The psychology of moral development.* San Francisco: Harper & Row.

Kotter, J. P. (1990). *A force for change: How leadership differs from management.* New York: Free Press.

Krebs, D. L., & Van Hesteren, F. (1992). The altruistic personality. In P. M. Oliner, S. P. Oliner, L. Baron, L. A. Blum, D. L. Krebs, & M. Z. Smolenska (Eds.), *Embracing the other* (pp. 142–169). New York: New York University Press.

Kuhn, D. (1989). Children and adults as intuitive scientists. *Psychological Review, 96*(4), 674–689.

Kuhn, D. (1993). Science as argument: Implications for teaching and learning scientific thinking. *Science Education, 77*(3), 319–337.

Kuhn, D., Cheney, R., & Weinstock, M. (2000). The development of epistemological understanding. *Cognitive Development, 15*(3), 309–328.

Kuhn, D., Garcia-Mila, M., Zohar, A., & Andersen, C. (1995). Strategies of knowledge acquisition. *Monographs of the Society for Research in Child Development, 60*(4, Serial No. 245).

Kuhn, D., Katz, J. B., & Dean, D. (2004). Developing reason. *Thinking and Reasoning, 10*(2), 197–219.

Kuhn, T. (1962). *The structure of scientific revolutions.* Chicago: University of Chicago Press.

Lamborn, S. D., Fischer, K. W., & Pipp, S. (1994). Constructive criticism and social lies: A developmental sequence for understanding honesty and kindness in social interactions. *Developmental Psychology, 30*(4), 495–508.

Langer, S. (1957). *Problems of art.* New York: Scribners.

Langley, P. W., Simon, H. A., Bradshaw, G. L., & Zytkow, J. M. (1987). *Scientific discovery: Computational explorations of the creative processes.* Cambridge, MA: MIT Press.

Latour, B. (1987). *Science in action.* Milton Keynes: Open University Press.

Lawrence, W. G. (1998). Unconscious social pressures on leaders. In E. B. Klein, F. Gabelnick, & P. Herr (Eds.), *The psychodynamics of leadership* (pp. 53–75). Madison, CT: Psychosocial Press.

Lawrence-Lightfoot, S. (1999). *Respect.* Reading, MA: Perseus Books.

Leach, J. (1999). Students' understanding of the co-ordination of theory and evidence in science. *International Journal of Science Education, 21,* 789–806.

Lehman, H. C. (1953). *Age and achievement.* Princeton, NJ: Princeton University Press.

Lehrer, R., Schauble, L., & Petrosino, A. J. (2001). Reconsidering the role of experiment in science education. In K. Crowley, C. Schunn, & T. Okada (Eds.), *Designing for science: Implications from everyday, classroom, and professional settings* (pp. 251–277). Mahwah, NJ: Erlbaum.

Li, J. (1997). Creativity in horizontal and vertical domains. *Creativity Research Journal, 10*(2/3), 107–132.

Lindauer, M. S. (1993). The span of creativity among long-lived historical artists. *Creativity Research Journal, 6*(3), 221–239.

Lovecky, D. V. (1997). Identity development in gifted children: Moral sensitivity. *Roeper Review, 20*(2), 90–94.

Lowe, K. B., & Gardner, W. L. (2001). Ten years of The Leadership Quarterly: Contributions and challenges for the future. *Leadership Quarterly, 11*(4), 459–514.

Lubinski, D., & Benbow, C. P. (2000). States of excellence. *American Psychologist, 55*(1), 137–150.

Lukacs, J. (2002). *Churchill: Visionary, statesman, historian.* New Haven, CT: Yale University Press.

Luria, A. R. (1976). *Cognitive development: Its cultural and social foundations.* Cambridge, MA: Harvard University Press.

Lykken, D. T., McGue, M., Tellegen, A., & Bouchard, T. J., Jr. (1992). Emergenesis: Genetic traits that may not run in families. *American Psychologist, 47*(12), 1565–1577.

MacKinnon, D. W. (1975). IPAR's contribution to the conceptualization and study of creativity. In I. A. Taylor & J. W. Getzels (Eds.), *Perspectives on creativity* (pp. 37–59). Chicago: Aldine.

Mann, R. D. (1959). A review of the relationships between personality and performance in small groups. *Psychological Bulletin, 56,* 241–270.

Marcia, J. E. (1966). Development and validation of ego identity status. *Journal of Personality and Social Psychology, 3,* 551–558.

Martindale, C. (1990). *The clockwork muse: The predictability of artistic styles.* New York: Basic Books.

Martindale, C. (1995). Creativity and connectionism. In S. M. Smith, T. B. Ward, & R. A. Finke (Eds.), *The creative cognition approach* (pp. 249–268). Cambridge, MA: MIT Press.

Mason, B. D. (1952). Leadership in the fourth grade. *Sociology and Social Research, 36,* 239–243.

McAdams, D. (1988). *Freedom summer.* New York: Oxford University Press.

McCall, M. (1978). The sociology of female artists. *Studies in Symbolic Interaction, 1,* 289–318.

McClelland, D. (1967). *The achieving society.* New York: Free Press.

McKeough, A. (1992). A neo-structural analysis of children's narrative and its development. In R. Case (Ed.), *The mind's staircase: Exploring the conceptual underpinnings of children's thought and knowledge* (pp. 171–188). Hillsdale, NJ: Erlbaum.

Mednick, S. A., & Mednick, M. (1967). *Remote associates test.* Chicago: Riverside.

Merton, R. K. (1957). Priorities in scientific discovery: A chapter in the sociology of science. *American Sociological Review, 22,* 635–659.

Merton, R. K. (1967). *Social theory and social structure.* New York: Free Press. (Original work published 1949)

Merton, R. K. (1968). The Matthew effect in science. *Science, 159,* 56–63.

Metcalfe, J., & Mischel, W. (1999). A hot/cool system analysis of delay of gratification: Dynamics of willpower. *Psychological Review, 106*(1), 3–19.

Meyer, L. (1956). *Emotion and meaning in music.* Chicago: University of Chicago Press.

Michaelson, M. (2001). A model of extraordinary social engagement, or "moral giftedness." In M. Michaelson & J. Nakamura (Eds.), *Supportive frameworks for youth engagement* (pp. 19–32). San Francisco: Jossey-Bass.

Mieg, H. A. (2001). *The social psychology of expertise.* Mahwah, NJ: Erlbaum.

Milbraith, C. (1995). Germinal motifs in the work of a gifted child artist. In C. Golomb (Ed.), *The development of artistically gifted children: Selected case studies* (pp. 101–134). Hillsdale, NJ: Erlbaum.

Milbraith, C. (1998). *Patterns of artistic development in children: Comparative studies of talent.* Cambridge, England: Cambridge University Press.

Millar, G. (2002). *The Torrance kids at mid-life: Selected case studies of creative behavior.* Westport, CT: Ablex.

Miller, A. I. (1989). Imagery and intuition in creative scientific thinking: Albert Einstein's invention of the special theory of relativity. In D. B. Wallace & H. E. Gruber (Eds.), *Creative people at work* (pp. 171–188). New York: Oxford University Press.

Miller, L. K. (1989). *Musical savants: Exceptional skill in the mentally retarded.* Hillsdale, NJ: Erlbaum.

Miller, P. A., Eisenberg, N., Fabes, R. A., & Shell, R. (1996). Relations of moral reasoning and vicarious emotion to young children's prosocial behavior toward peers and adults. *Developmental Psychology, 32,* 210–219.

Moran, S. (2004). *Commitment: A theory of differences between conventional and creative work.* Unpublished qualifying paper, Harvard Graduate School of Education, Cambridge, MA.

Moran, S., & John-Steiner, V. (2003). Creativity in the making: Vygotsky's contribution to the dialectic of creativity and development. In R. K. Sawyer & V. John-Steiner (Eds.), *Creativity and development* (pp. 61–90). New York: Oxford University Press.

Morris, G. B. (1991). Perceptions of leadership traits: Comparison of adolescent and adult school leaders. *Psychological Reports, 61*(3), 723–727.

Mumford, M. D., Baughman, W. A., Maher, M. A., Costanza, D. P., & Supinski, E. P. (1997). Process-based measures of creative problem-solving skills: Pt. 4. Category combination. *Creativity Research Journal, 10*(1), 59–71.

Mumford, M. D., Baughman, W. A., Supinski, E. P., & Maher, M. A. (1996). Process-based measures of creative problem-solving skills: Pt. 2. Information encoding. *Creativity Research Journal, 9*(1), 77–88.

Mumford, M. D., Baughman, W. A., Threlfall, K. V., Supinski, E. P., & Costanza, D. P. (1996). Process-based measures of creative problem-solving skills: Pt. 1. Problem construction. *Creativity Research Journal, 9*(1), 63–76.

Mumford, M. D., Supinski, E. P., Baughman, W. A., Costanza, D. P., & Threlfall, K. V. (1997). Process-based measures of creative problem-solving skills: Pt. 5. Overall prediction. *Creativity Research Journal, 10*(1), 73–85.

Mumford, M. D., Supinski, E. P., Threlfall, K. V., & Baughman, W. A. (1996). Process-based measures of creative problem-solving skills: Pt. 3. Category selection. *Creativity Research Journal, 9*(4), 395–406.

Murray, C. (2003). *Human accomplishment: The pursuit of excellence in the arts and sciences, 800 B.C. to 1950.* New York: HarperCollins.

Nakamura, J., & Csikszentmihalyi, M. (2003). Creativity in later life. In R. K. Sawyer & V. John-Steiner (Eds.), *Creativity and development* (pp. 186–216). New York: Oxford University Press.

Neisser, U., Boodoo, G., & Bouchard, Jr., T. J. (1996). Intelligence: Knowns and unknowns. *American Psychologist, 51*(2), 77–101.

Newell, A., & Simon, H. A. (1972). *Human problem solving.* Englewood Cliffs, NJ: Prentice-Hall.

Nisbett, R. E. (2003). *The geography of thought: How Asians and Westerners think differently—And why.* New York: Free Press.

Noble, K. D., Subotnik, R. F., & Arnold, K. D. (Eds.). (1996). *Remarkable women: New perspectives on female talent development.* Cresskill, NJ: Hampton Press.

Ochse, R. (1991). Why there were relatively few eminent women creators. *Journal of Creative Behavior, 25*(4), 334–343.

Oliner, S. (2003). *Do unto others.* Boulder, CO: Westview.

Oliner, S. P., & Oliner, P. M. (1988). *The altruistic personality: Rescue of Jews in Nazi Europe.* New York: Free Press.

Pariser, D. (1987). The juvenile drawings of Klee, Toulouse-Lautrec and Picasso. *Visual Arts Research, 13*(2), 16.

Pariser, D. (1995). Lautrec: Gifted child artist and artistic monument—Connections between juvenile and mature work. In C. Golomb (Ed.), *The development of artistically gifted children: Selected case studies* (pp. 31–70). Hillsdale, NJ: Erlbaum.

Parks, S. (1986). *The critical years: The young adult search for a faith to live by.* New York: Harper & Row.

Perkins, D. N. (1981). *The mind's best work.* Cambridge, MA: Harvard University Press.

Perkins, D. N., & Simmons, R. (1988). Patterns of misunderstanding: An integrative model for science, math, and programming. *Review of Educational Research, 58*(3), 303–326.

Perkins, D., Tishman, S., Ritchhart, R., Donis, K., & Andrade, A. (2000). Intelligence in the wild: A dispositional view of intellectual traits. *Educational Psychology Review, 12*(3), 269–293.

Perry, W. G., Jr. (1999). *Forms of ethical and intellectual development in the college years: A scheme.* San Francisco: Jossey-Bass. (Original work published 1968)

Perry-Smith, J. E., & Shalley, C. E. (2003). The social side of creativity. *Academy of Management Review, 28*(1), 89–106.

Piaget, J. (1932). *The moral judgment of the child.* London: Routledge & Kegan Paul.

Piaget, J. (1972). *The psychology of intelligence.* Totowa, NJ: Littlefield, Adams.

Piaget, J. (1995). The construction of reality in the child. In H. E. Gruber & J. J. Voneche (Eds.), *The essential Piaget* (pp. 250–294). Northvale, NJ: Aronson. (Original work published 1937)

Piaget, J. (1995). The growth of logical thinking from childhood to adolescence. In H. E. Gruber & J. J. Voneche (Eds.), *The essential Piaget* (pp. 405–444). Northvale, NJ: Aronson. (Original work published 1955)

Plomin, R., DeFries, J. C., McClearn, J. E., & McGuffin, P. (2001). *Behavioral genetics* (4th ed.). New York: Worth.

Plucker, J. A. (1999). Is the proof in the pudding? Reanalyses of Torrance's (1958 to present) longitudinal data. *Creativity Research Journal, 12*(2), 103–114.

Policastro, E., & Gardner, H. (1999). From case studies to robust generalizations. In R. J. Sternberg (Ed.), *Handbook of creativity* (pp. 213–225). New York: Cambridge University Press.

Polya, G. (1973). *How to solve it.* Princeton, NJ: Princeton University Press.

Porath, M. (1996). Narrative performance in verbally gifted children. *Journal of Education of the Gifted, 19*(3), 276–292.

Prediger, D. J. (1976). A world-of-work map for career exploration. *Vocational Guidance Quarterly, 24,* 198–208.

Previc, F. H. (1999). Dopamine and the origins of human intelligence. *Brain and Cognition, 41*(3), 299–350.

Qian, G., & Pan, J. (2002). A comparison of epistemological beliefs and learning form science text between American and Chinese high school students. In B. K. Hofer & P. R. Pintrich (Eds.), *Personal epistemology: The psychology of beliefs about knowledge and knowing* (pp. 365–385). Mahwah, NJ: Erlbaum.

Radford, J. (1990). *Child prodigies and exceptional early achievers.* New York: Free Press.

Rank, O. (1932). *Art and artist: Creative urge and personality development.* New York: Knopf.

Rawls, J. (1971.) *A theory of justice.* Cambridge, MA: Harvard University Press.

Richie, B. S., Fassinger, R. E., Linn, S. G., & Johnson, J., Prosser, J., & Robinson, S. (1997). Persistence, connection, and passion: A qualitative study of the career development of highly achieving African American-Black and White women. *Journal of Counseling Psychology, 44*(2), 133–148.

Robinson, N. M., Zigler, E., & Gallagher, J. J. (2000). Two tails of the normal curve: Similarities and differences in the study of mental retardation and giftedness. *American Psychologist, 55*(12), 1413–1424.

Roe, A. (1946). Artists and their work. *Journal of Personality, 15*(1), 1–40.

Roe, A. (1952). *The making of a scientist.* New York: Dodd, Mead.

Root-Bernstein, R. S., Bernstein, M., & Garnier, H. (1995). Correlations between avocations, scientific style, work habits, and professional impact of scientists. *Creativity Research Journal, 8*(2), 115–137.

Rosenblatt, E., & Winner, E. (1988). Is superior visual memory a component of superior drawing ability. In L. Ober & D. Fein (Eds.), *The exceptional brain: Neuropsychology of talent and superior abilities* (pp. 341–363). New York: Guilford Press.

Rostan, S. (1994). Problem finding, problem solving, and cognitive controls: An empirical investigation of critically acclaimed productivity. *Creativity Research Journal, 7*(2), 97–110.

Rostan, S. (1998). A study of the development of young artists: The emergence of an artistic and creative identity. *Creativity Research Journal, 32*(4), 278–301.

Rostan, S., Pariser, D., & Gruber, H. (2002). A cross-cultural study of the development of artistic talent, creativity and giftedness. *High Ability Studies, 13*(2), 125–155.

Rothenberg, A. (1990). *Creativity and madness.* Baltimore: Johns Hopkins University Press.

Sacks, O. (1985). *The man who mistook his wife for a hat.* New York: HarperCollins.

Sacks, O. (1995). *An anthropologist on Mars: Seven paradoxical tales.* New York: Alfred A. Knopf.

Sawyer, R. K. (1999). The emergence of creativity. *Philosophical Psychology, 12*(4), 447–469.

Schaffner, K. (1994). Discovery in biomedical sciences: Logic or intuitive genius? *Creativity Research Journal, 7*(3/4), 351–363.

Schauble, L. (1996). The development of scientific reasoning in knowledge rich contexts. *Developmental Psychology, 32,* 109–119.

Schneider, B. H. (1999). Cultural perspectives on children's social competence. In M. Woodhead, D. Faulkner, & K. Littleton (Eds.), *Making sense of social development* (pp. 72–97). London: Routledge.

Schorske, C. E. (1979). *Fin-de-siecle Vienna: Politics and culture.* New York: Knopf.

Schwartz, C. E., Wright, C. I., Shin, L. M., Kagan, J., & Rauch, S. L. (2003). Inhibited and uninhibited infants "grown up": Adult amygdalar response to novelty. *Science, 300*(5627), 1952–1953.

Sears, P. S., & Barbee, A. H. (1977). Career and life satisfactions among Terman's gifted women. In J. C. Stanley, W. C. George, & C. H. Solano (Eds.), *The gifted and the creative: A 50 year perspective* (pp. 28–65). Baltimore: Johns Hopkins University.

Sears, R. R., Maccoby, E. E., & Levin, H. (1957). *Patterns of child rearing.* Evanston, IL: Row, Peterson.

Selfe, L. (1977). *Nadia: A case of extraordinary drawing ability in an autistic child.* New York: Academic Press.

Selfe, L. (1995). Nadia reconsidered. In C. Golomb (Ed.), *The development of artistically gifted children: Selected case studies* (pp. 197–236). Hillsdale, NJ: Erlbaum.

Selman, R. L. (1980). *The growth of interpersonal understanding.* New York: Academic Press.

Shekerjian, D. (1990). *Uncommon genius: How great ideas are born.* New York: Viking.

Shweder, R. A., Mahapatra, M., & Miller, J. G. (1987). Culture and moral development. In J. Kagan & S. Lamb (Eds.), *The emergence of morality in young children* (pp. 1–83). Chicago: University of Chicago Press.

Siegler, R. S. (1978). The origins of scientific reasoning. In R. S. Siegler (Ed.), *Children's thinking: What develops?* (pp. 109–149). Hillsdale, NJ: Erlbaum.

Silverman, L. K. (1994). The moral sensitivity of gifted children and the evolution of society. *Roeper Review, 17*(2), 110–116.

Simmons, C. H., & Zumph, C. (1986). The gifted child: Perceived competence, prosocial moral reasoning, and charitable donations. *Journal of Genetic Psychology, 147*(1), 97–105.

Simonton, D. K. (1975). Sociocultural context of individual creativity: A transhistorical time-series analysis. *Journal of Personality and Social Psychology, 32,* 1119–1133.

Simonton, D. K. (1976). Biographical determinants of achieved eminence: A multivariate approach to the Cox data. *Journal of Personality and Social Psychology, 33*(2), 218–226.

Simonton, D. K. (1980). Land battles, generals, and armies: Individual and situational determinants of victory and casualties. *Journal of Personality and Social Psychology, 38*(1), 110–119.

Simonton, D. K. (1981). Presidential greatness and performance: Can we predict leadership in the White House? *Journal of Personality, 49*(3), 306–323.

Simonton, D. K. (1984). Leaders as eponyms: Individual and situational determinants of ruler eminence. *Journal of Personality, 52*(1), 1–21.

Simonton, D. K. (1986). Dispositional attributions of presidential leadership: An experimental simulation of historiometric results. *Journal of Experimental Social Psychology, 22,* 389–418.

Simonton, D. K. (1988). *Scientific genius: A psychology of science.* New York: Cambridge University Press.

Simonton, D. K. (1991a). Career landmarks in science: Individual differences and interdisciplinary contrasts. *Developmental Psychology, 27,* 119–130.

Simonton, D. K. (1991b). Personality correlates of exceptional personal influence: A note on Thorndike's (1950) creators and leaders. *Creativity Research Journal, 4*(1), 67–78.

Simonton, D. K. (1994). *Greatness: Who makes history and why.* New York: Guilford Press.

Simonton, D. K. (1998). Achieved eminence in minority and majority cultures: Convergence versus divergence in the assessments of 294 African Americans. *Journal of Personality and Social Psychology, 74,* 804–817.

Simonton, D. K. (1999). *Origins of genius: Darwinian perspectives on creativity.* New York: Oxford University Press.

Simonton, D. K. (2000). Creative development as acquired expertise: Theoretical issues and an empirical test. *Developmental Review, 20,* 283–318.

Simpson, E. L. (1973). Moral development research: A case study of scientific cultural bias. *Human Development, 17,* 81–106.

Sinatra, G. M., & Pintrich, P. R. (Eds.). (2003). *Intentional conceptual change.* Mahwah, NJ: Erlbaum.

Skinner, B. F. (1971). *Beyond freedom and dignity.* New York: Knopf.

Sloane, K. D., & Sosniak, L. A. (1985). The development of accomplished sculptors. In B. S. Bloom (Ed.), *Developing talent in young people* (pp. 90–138). New York: Ballantine Books.

Smith, C. L., Maclin, D., Houghton, C., & Hennessey, M. G. (2000). Sixth-grade students' epistemologies of science: The impact of school science experiences on epistemological development. *Cognition and Instruction, 18*(3), 349–422.

Sorokin, P. A. (1969). *Society, culture, and personality.* New York: Cooper Square. (Original work published 1947)

Sosniak, L. A. (1985). Becoming an outstanding research neurologist. In B.S. Bloom (Ed.), *Developing talent in young people* (pp. 348–408). New York: Ballantine Books.

Spearman, C. (1904). 'General intelligence,' objectively determined and measured. *American Journal of Psychology, 15*(2), 201–293.

Spinath, F. M., Ronald, A., Harlaar, N., Price, T. S., & Plomin, R. (2003). Phenotypic g early in life: On the etiology of general cognitive ability in a large population sample of twin children aged 2 to 4 years. *Intelligence, 31*(2), 195–210.

Sternberg, R. J. (1985). *Beyond IQ: A triarchic theory of human intelligence.* New York: Cambridge University Press.

Sternberg, R. J., Nokes, C., Geissler, P. W., Prince, R., Okiatcha, F., Bundy, D. A., et al. (2001). The relationship between academic and practical intelligence: A case study in Kenya. *Intelligence, 29*(5), 401–418.

Stohs, J. M. (1991). Young adult predictors and midlife outcomes of "starving artists" careers: A longitudinal study of male fine artists. *Creativity Research Journal, 25*(2), 92–105.

Storr, A. (1988). *Solitude: A return to the self.* New York: Free Press.

Subotnik, R., & Arnold, A. (Eds.). (1994). *Beyond Terman: Contemporary longitudinal studies of giftedness and talent.* Norwood, NJ: Ablex.

Sulloway, F. (1996). *Born to rebel: Birth order, family dynamics, and creative lives.* New York: Pantheon.

Terman, L. M. (1925). Mental and physical traits of a thousand gifted children. In L. M. Terman (Ed.), *Genetic studies of genius* (Vol. 1). Stanford, CA: Stanford University Press.

Terman, L. M. (1954). The discovery and encouragement of exceptional talent. *American Psychologist, 9,* 221–230.

Terman, L. M. (1955). Are scientists different? *Scientific American, 192,* 25–29.

Terman, L. W., & Oden, M. H. (1947). The gifted child grows up. In L. M. Terman (Ed.), *Genetic studies of genius* (Vol. 4). Stanford, CA: Stanford University Press.

Thorndike, E. L. (1921). Intelligence and its measurement. *Journal of Educational Psychology, 12,* 124–127.

Thorndike, E. L. (1936). The relation between intellect and morality in rulers. *American Journal of Sociology, 42*(3), 321–334.

Thorndike, E. L. (1950). Traits of personality and their intercorrelations as shown in biographies. *Journal of Educational Psychology, 41*(4), 193–216.

Thurstone, L. L. (1938). *Primary mental abilities.* Chicago: University of Chicago Press.

Tirri, K., & Pehkonen, L. (2002). The moral reasoning and scientific argumentation of gifted adolescents. *Journal of Secondary Gifted Education, 13*(3), 120–129.

Tomasello, M. (1999). Having intentions, understanding intentions, and understanding communicative intentions. In P. D. Zelazo, J. W. Astington, & D. R. Olson (Eds.), *Developing theories of intention: Social understanding and self-control* (pp. 63–75). Mahwah, NJ: Erlbaum.

Torrance, E. P. (1963). *Education and the creative potential.* Minneapolis: University of Minnesota Press.

Torrance, E. P. (1974). *The Torrance Tests of Creative Thinking: Norms-technical manual.* Bensenville, IL: Scholastic Testing Service.

Trevarthen, C., & Logothet, K. (1989). Child in society and society in children: The nature of basic trust. In S. Howell & R. Willis (Eds.), *Societies at peace: Anthropological perspectives* (pp. 165–186). London: Routledge.

Turiel, E. (1983). *The development of social knowledge: Morality and convention.* New York: Cambridge University Press.

Tweney, R. D. (1989). Fields of enterprise: On Michael Faraday's thought. In D. B. Wallace & H. E. Gruber (Eds.), *Creative people at work* (pp. 91–106). New York: Oxford University Press.

Tweney, R. D. (1996). Presymbolic processes in scientific creativity. *Creativity Research Journal, 9*(2/3), 163–172.

Tytler, R., & Peterson, S. (2004). From "try it and see" to strategic exploration: Characterizing young children's scientific reasoning. *Journal of Research in Science Teaching, 41*(1), 94–118.

Vendler, H. (2003). *Coming of age as a poet.* Cambridge, MA: Harvard University Press.

Vernon, P. E. (1950). *The structure of human abilities.* New York: Wiley.

Vygotsky, L. S. (1962). *Thought and language* (E. Hanfmann & G. Vakar, Eds. & Trans.). Cambridge, MA: MIT Press. (Original work published 1934)

Vygotsky, L. S. (1971). *The psychology of art* (Scripta Technica, Inc., Trans.). Cambridge, MA: MIT Press. (Original work published 1965)

Vygotsky, L. S. (1978). *Mind in society: The development of higher psychological processes* (M. Cole, V. John-Steiner, S. Scribner, & E. Souberman, Eds.). Cambridge, MA: Harvard University Press.

Vygotsky, L. S. (1994). The problem of the environment (T. Prout, Trans.). In R. Van der Veer & J. Valsiner (Eds.), *The Vygotsky reader* (pp. 338–354). Malden, MA: Blackwell. (Original work published 1935)

Vygotsky, L. S. (1997). The history of the development of higher mental functions (M. J. Hall, Trans.). In R. W. Rieber (Ed.), *The collected works of L. S. Vygotsky* (Vol. 4, pp. 1–251). New York: Plenum Press. (Original work published 1960)

Walker, L. J. (2003). Moral exemplarity. In W. Damon (Ed.), *Bringing in a new era of character development* (pp. 65–83). Stanford, CA: Hoover Institute Press.

Walker, L. J., & Pitts, R. C. (1998). Naturalistic conceptions of moral maturity. *Developmental Psychology, 34*(3), 403–419.

Wallace, D. B., & Gruber, H. E. (1989). *Creative people at work.* New York: Oxford University Press.

Wallach, M. A., & Kogan, N. (1965). *Modes of thinking in young children.* New York: Holt, Rinehart and Winston.

Wallas, G. (1926). *The art of thought.* New York: Harcourt.

Walters, J., & Gardner, H. (1986). The crystallizing experience: Discovering an intellectual gift. In R. J. Sternberg & J. E. Davidson (Eds.), *Conceptions of giftedness* (pp. 306–331). New York: Cambridge University Press.

Watson, J. D. (1968). *The double helix: A personal account of the discovery of the structure of DNA.* New York: New American Library.

Weber, M. (1947). *The theory of social and economic organizations* (T. Parsons, Trans.). New York: Free Press.

Wechsler, D. (1958). *The measurement and appraisal of adult intelligence.* Baltimore: Williams & Wilkins.

Wertheimer, M. (1954). *Productive thinking.* New York: Harper.

Williams, T. H. (1981). *Huey Long.* New York: Random House.

Wills, G. (1994). *Certain trumpets.* New York: Simon & Schuster.

Winner, E. (1982). *Invented worlds: The psychology of the arts.* Cambridge, MA: Harvard University Press.

Winner, E. (1996a). *Gifted children: Myths and realities.* New York: Basic Books.

Winner, E. (1996b). The rage to master: The decisive role of talent in the visual arts. In K. A. Ericcson (Ed.), *The road to excellence: The acquisition of expert performance in the arts, sciences, sports and games* (pp. 271–301). Mahwah, NJ: Erlbaum.

Winner, E. (2000). The origins and ends of giftedness. *American Psychologist, 55*(1), 159–169.

Winter, D. G. (1987). Leader appeal, leader performance, and the motive profiles of leaders and followers: A study of American presidents and elections. *Journal of Personality and Social Psychology, 52*(1), 196–202.

Wolfe, A. (2001). *Moral freedom.* New York: Norton.

Wrzesniewski, A., McCauley, C., Rozin, P., & Schwartz, B. (1997). Jobs, careers, and callings: People's relations to their work. *Journal of Research in Personality, 31,* 21–33.

Youniss, J., & Yates, M. (1997). *Community service and social responsibility in youth.* Chicago: University of Chicago Press.

Youniss, J., & Yates, M. (1999). Youth service and moral-civic identity: A case for everyday morality. *Educational Psychology Review, 11*(4), 361–376.

Zahn-Waxler, C., Radke-Yarrow, M., Wagner, E., & Chapman, M. (1992). Development of concern for others. *Developmental Psychology, 28*(1), 126–136.

Zander, R. S., & Zander, B. (2000). *The art of possibility.* Boston: Harvard Business School Press.

Zimmerman, C. (2000). The development of scientific reasoning skills. *Developmental Review, 20,* 99–149.

Zuckerman, H. (1977). *Scientific elite.* New York: Free Press.

Zuckerman, H., & Cole, J. R. (1994). Research strategies in science: A preliminary inquiry. *Creativity Research Journal, 7*(3/4), 391–405.

# SECTION FIVE

# The Perspective beyond Childhood

# CHAPTER 22

# *The Second Decade: What Develops (and How)*

DEANNA KUHN and SAM FRANKLIN

WHY STUDY OLDER CHILDREN?  953
RECOGNIZING COMPLEXITY AND THE VALUE OF
  DEVELOPMENTAL ANALYSIS  954
Why Is Younger Children's Thinking Easier to Study
  than Older Children's Thinking?  954
What Develops? Abandoning the Singular Answer  955
BRAIN AND PROCESSING GROWTH  957
The Developing Brain  957
Processing Speed  957
Inhibition  957
Processing Capacity  958
Information Processing and Reasoning  959
DEDUCTIVE INFERENCE  960
The Critical Role of Meaning  961
What Develops?  961
When Knowledge and Reasoning Conflict  962
Deduction and Thinking  963
INDUCTIVE AND CAUSAL INFERENCE  964
Evidence for Early Competence  964
Coordinating Theory and Evidence  965
Interpreting Covariation Evidence  966
Coordinating Effects of Multiple Variables: Mental
  Models of Causality  967
LEARNING AND KNOWLEDGE ACQUISITION  968
Cross-Sectional Age Comparisons  969
The Development of Learning  970

INQUIRY AND SCIENTIFIC THINKING  971
Does Children's Thinking Need to
  Become "Scientific?"  971
The Process of Inquiry  972
Supporting the Development of Inquiry Skills  974
DECISION MAKING  975
Preference Judgments  976
Decision-Making Judgments  976
Dual-Process Theory  977
ARGUMENT  978
Individual Arguments  979
Argumentive Discourse  980
Supporting the Development of Argument Skills  981
UNDERSTANDING AND VALUING KNOWING  982
Epistemological Understanding and
  Scientific Thinking  982
Coordinating Objective and Subjective Elements
  of Knowing  984
What Difference Does Epistemological
  Understanding Make?  985
CONCLUSIONS: LEARNING TO MANAGE
  ONE'S MIND  986
Early Adolescence as a Second Critical Period  988
Understanding Development by Studying Both Origins
  and Endpoints  988
REFERENCES  989

## WHY STUDY OLDER CHILDREN?

A look at the table of contents of this volume reveals three chapters devoted exclusively to the period of infancy. Inclusion of the present chapter yields a total of four chapters that address specific periods in the life cycle. Human development texts typically adopt either a topical or an age-level organization, with the topical approach generally considered preferable for higher-level, research-based treatments. Why, then, does this volume include these chapters that are exceptions? Justification

for chapters dedicated to infancy is perhaps clearer. It is critical to identify and examine as closely as possible the earliest origins of cognitive achievements, with the goal of better understanding the process of evolution into their later, more complex forms. But why the present chapter? Aren't the remaining chapters exhaustive in elucidating the spectrum of developmental phenomena, from brain growth, perception, and action to information processing, learning, and thinking?

It happens that these chapters focus largely on the early years of the life cycle—a majority on the very early years, well before a child is of school age. The life-span perspective of Moran and Gardner's chapter is a notable exception. This focus should perhaps not be surprising in topic-based chapters. Again, to best understand how a capability emerges and further evolves, current thinking suggests, one should seek to identify and examine it in its earliest, most rudimentary forms. Since one set of research studies typically gives rise to others on the same topic, it is easy for such trends to assume a life of their own. In this light, statistics from the 2003 meeting of the Society for Research in Child Development become less surprising. Of 3,483 submissions to the meeting, only 222 fell under the primary topic heading of adolescence, and only 14 to 26 of these (depending on inclusion of topics such as moral reasoning and school achievement) were concerned with adolescents' cognition (Moshman, personal communication).

Are these numbers a cause for concern? A possible answer is no. If the authors of the topic-based chapters in this volume have done a good job of elucidating the patterns and processes that characterize development of the dimensions they address, this knowledge should be sufficient to explain any development that continues to occur in the years beyond early childhood. The argument is a reasonable one. If we understand the fundamentals of children's perception, information processing, learning, or memory in their early years, can we not assume that these processes continue to operate in much the same way as children develop through childhood and adolescence and into adulthood? This is exactly the question we address in the present chapter. Does any evidence exist for changes in the nature of children's cognitive functioning as they progress beyond the early childhood years and through later childhood and adolescence, into adulthood?

It is instructive to look at how textbooks answer this question. Developmental texts organized by age level typically include at least one chapter devoted to adolescence (and, if the text covers the life span, one or more chapters devoted to the adult years). The section on adolescent cognition invariably centers on the claim that adolescent cognition has important new features absent in children's cognition. The reader is left with the impression that these changes are a matter of established fact, far more than they in truth are.

But don't all textbooks smooth over controversies and present what is known as more certain than it actually is? Our examination of textbook chapters on adolescent cognition highlights two differences worth noting. First, they have undergone little change in the past several decades, in contrast to chapters on just about every other topic. Just about the same things are being said about adolescent cognition in early twenty-first century texts as were said in texts from the 1970s or 1980s. Second, the gap between what is presented in current texts and what is being claimed in current research literature appears greater in the case of adolescent cognition than in the case of other topics. In a word, the emergence of Piaget's stage of formal operations at adolescence remains the centerpiece of textbook chapters, often with accompanying portrayals of adolescent thought as more abstract and less egocentric than childhood thought, perhaps followed by a section on the adolescent personality (Elkind, 1994; Inhelder & Piaget, 1958). In stark contrast, in current scholarly literature the idea of thought developing toward greater abstraction has been largely dismissed as either incoherent or wrong (Keil, 1998), and no contemporary scholarly reviewer of research evidence endorses the emergence of a discrete new cognitive structure at adolescence that closely resembles Inhelder and Piaget's description of formal operations (Keating, 2004; Klaczynski, 2004; Kuhn, 1999a, 1999b; Moshman, 1998, 2005).

This striking divergence suggests the need for a chapter like the present one. The research literature on cognitive development in the years beginning in middle childhood, and extending through adolescence and into adulthood, is not huge, compared to research devoted to the early years of life. But it is substantial enough to have begun yielding some converging evidence, some tentative conclusions, and some coherent directions in which to proceed. This chapter hopefully will contribute toward reducing the significant gap between what we know in this area and what textbooks tell readers we know. In addition, we reflect on the topic itself, suggesting why it is worthwhile to look beyond early childhood, at least well into the 2nd decade of life, in seeking to achieve a fuller understanding of the developmental process itself.

## RECOGNIZING COMPLEXITY AND THE VALUE OF DEVELOPMENTAL ANALYSIS

### Why Is Younger Children's Thinking Easier to Study Than Older Children's Thinking?

One explanation for cognitive development researchers' focus on young children's cognition, we have suggested, is their desire to examine the earliest origins of later forms. If we can understand how something simple develops, we are arguably in the best position to understand the later development of its more complex instances. There may be another reason, however, and that is that cognition in older children and adolescents is more complex and problematic to study than is the cognition of young children. This is true in a practical respect—it is generally easier to gain access for research purposes to preschoolers than to high school students—but also in a theoretical respect. The cognition itself is more complex, having been longer in developing and subject to many more kinds of influences. A large number of researchers study adult cognition, but if one's interest lies in development, a focus on early origins seems a prudent choice.

Beyond the complexity of the cognition itself, there is another source of complexity that makes the study of older children's and adolescents' cognition challenging. The skills and understanding that develop during the early childhood years develop in more or less all children of the appropriate age level who fall within the broadly defined range of normal development. Researchers seek to understand the patterns and perhaps the mechanisms involved. The developmental phenomena themselves, in any case, are fairly regular and predictable.

By middle childhood, in contrast, researchers commonly encounter cognitive achievements that may or may not develop, depending on a child's experience. Indeed, many of the cognitive achievements we consider in this chapter are ones that are not universal. Some children will have attained them by the time they reach early adolescence; others will never do so throughout their adult lives. These attainments range from highly specific ones that appear only under particular conditions to those that develop given sufficient general experience of any of a wide variety of types. The result is enormous variability in cognitive functioning among normal adolescents, with some performing no better than third graders on many reasoning tasks and others performing as well or better than most adults. We probe in this chapter the factors that contribute to this great variability, among them not just environmental diversity but the greater role that older children and adolescents play in choosing what they will do, hence assuming a role as producers of their own development (Lerner, 2002).

But none of this variability implies that developmental analysis ceases to be useful. Wherever attainments lie on the individual/universal spectrum, it is useful to see them as building on a foundation of what has come before and proceeding along paths and toward endpoints that can be identified and examined, with the mechanisms of this progress amenable to investigation. It is not that developmental analysis becomes any less useful, only that it becomes more complex. In part reflecting this complexity, the distinctions between development, learning, and acquisition of expertise become less clear. Also, the concerns of the developmentalist and the educator converge to a greater extent than they do during earlier periods of the life cycle. If many of the important cognitive skills we examine here do not inevitably develop, the educator becomes concerned with identifying the conditions that will increase likelihood of attainment. Yet, it remains the developmentalist who stands to contribute essential knowledge about the paths, patterns, and mechanisms of development.

Yet another element of complexity is introduced by the fact that developmentalists studying older children and adolescents must compare them to younger children in two respects, not one. First, what new capabilities or understandings have they acquired? Second, are the mechanisms of acquisition different from those in operation during the earlier period? Researchers studying young children, in contrast, assess their abilities and may seek to identify mechanisms of acquisition, but they do not concern themselves with the possibility that the mechanisms themselves may undergo change. In this chapter, we are as interested in developmental changes in mechanisms of acquisition as we are in new acquisitions themselves.

If the response to all of this complexity is not to abandon developmental analysis but to recognize and appreciate the developmental complexity of the phenomena we examine, the first step, we suggest, is to recognize the need to reject simple answers. We begin, then, with that as our initial task.

## What Develops? Abandoning the Singular Answer

Widespread interest in adolescent cognition as having unique characteristics absent in children's thinking began in the context of Piaget's stage theory. Inhelder and Piaget (1958) proposed a final stage of formal operations as supported by a unique logical structure emerging at adolescence and manifesting itself in a number of different capabilities, most notably systematic combination and isolation of variables. What is important about formal operations from the perspective of Piagetian stage theory is that they are taken as reflections of the emergence of an underlying stage structure, which Piaget identified as composed of operations on operations. With the attainment of this stage, according to Piaget, thought becomes able to take itself as its own object—adolescents become able to think about their own thinking, hence the term "operations on operations," or, more precisely, mental operations on the elementary operations of classification and relation characteristic of the preceding stage of concrete operations. The formal operational thinker becomes able, for example, not only to categorize animals according to physical characteristics and according to habitats but also to operate on these categorizations, that is, to put them into categories and on this basis to draw inferences regarding relations that hold among animals' physical characteristics and habitats. The formal operational thinker is thus said to reason at the level of *propositions* that specify relations between one category (or relation) and another. As aspects of this second-order operatory structure, according to the theory, there emerge the other reasoning capabilities noted above—systematic combination and isolation of variables—and several others such as proportional and correlational reasoning, also thought to involve second-order operations.

Subsequent cross-sectional research generally upheld Inhelder and Piaget's (1958) claim that adolescents on average do better than children in tasks purported to assess these competencies (Keating, 1980, 2004; Neimark, 1975). Piaget, however, hypothesized these capabilities to appear in early adolescence as a tightly linked, integrated whole, a manifestation of the emergence of the formal operational thought structure. In this respect, subsequent research has been less supportive, yielding little evidence for a singular or abrupt transition from a childhood stage of concrete operations to an adolescent stage of formal operations.

Three kinds of variability contribute to this conclusion. One is inter-individual variability in the age of emergence of the different alleged behavioral manifestations of the formal operational structure, for example, combinatorial and isolation-of-variables reasoning. A second is intra-individual variability in the emergence of formal operations skills. There is little evidence to support the claim that these skills emerge synchronously within a single individual. Third, and most serious, is task variability. As is the case with respect to virtually all reasoning skills, whether an individual is judged to possess or not possess the skill is very much a function of the manner in which it is assessed, in particular the amount of contextual support provided (Fischer &

Bidell, 1991). Indeed, task variance is so pronounced that we confront in this chapter the phenomenon we shall call the paradox of early competence and later failures of competence. In other words, there are some tasks in which a particular form of reasoning can be identified as present in children as young as preschool age. In other forms of the same task, however, even adults appear deficient in exhibiting the skill.

These findings make it doubtful that emergence of a singular cognitive structure at a specific point in time—whether Piaget's formal operational structure or some different structure—can account adequately for the progress along multiple fronts that we examine in this chapter. Nonetheless, to anticipate our conclusions, we shall end up maintaining that Piaget was very much on the right track in identifying thinking about one's own thought as a hallmark of cognitive development in the 2nd decade of life. We can assign such a capability a modern-sounding name, like metacognition or executive control. But what needs to be abandoned is the idea that we can pinpoint its emergence to some narrow window of months or years in late childhood or early adolescence, or indeed any time. Even preschoolers can be metacognitive when, for example, they recognize an earlier false belief that they no longer hold (Harris, Chapter 19, this *Handbook*, this volume), while examples of adults' failures to be sufficiently metacognitive are myriad.

In what has perhaps been a final blow to any "immaculate transition" (Siegler & Munakata, 1993) model of developmental change, microgenetic research (Kuhn, 1995; Kuhn & Phelps, 1982; Siegler & Crowley, 1991; Siegler, Chapter 11, this *Handbook*, this volume) revealed that individuals simultaneously have available not just one but multiple potential cognitive strategies they might apply to a problem. Some of these are more and others less advanced. Development, then, entails gradual shifts in the frequency of usage of various strategies, with better strategies being used more frequently and weaker strategies less frequently. The microgenetic model of change, note, implicates some meta-level executive that manages strategy selection. We return to it in more detail later. For now, the implication is that we must forego any simple account of emergence of a singular structure that drives all of cognitive development, in favor of examining multiple strands of development that may have commonalities as well as unique characteristics.

Before we can abandon singular accounts in favor of multidimensional ones, however, we must consider another very different kind of singular account—one that explains developmental change not in terms of emergence of a qualitatively new structure but rather in terms of quantitative change in the cognitive system, specifically quantitative increase in its processing ability. How far do hypotheses of this kind take us in accounting for cognitive development, and what evidence exists with respect to them? We address this question in the next section.

## BRAIN AND PROCESSING GROWTH

The evidence likely to be most influential in stimulating interest in adolescent cognition in the next decade is not evidence about cognition itself but rather evidence about development of the brain.

### The Developing Brain

Neuroimaging techniques have become available in recent years that allow precise longitudinal examination of changes in brain structure in the years from middle childhood into middle adulthood. These studies have made it clear that the brain continues to develop into and through the adolescent years. The area of greatest change after puberty is the prefrontal cortex. It is implicated in what have come to be called "executive" functions (Nelson, Thomas, & de Haan, Chapter 1, this *Handbook,* this volume), which include monitoring, organizing, planning, strategizing—indeed any mental activity that entails managing one's own mental processes—and is also associated with increase in impulse control.

Modern longitudinal neuroimaging research reports two kinds of change, one in the so-called "gray matter," which undergoes a wave of overproduction (paralleling one occurring in the early years) at puberty, followed by a reduction, or "pruning," of those neuronal connections that do not continue to be used. A second change, in so-called "white matter," is enhanced myelination, that is, increased insulation of established neuronal connections, improving their efficiency (Giedd et al., 1999). By the end of adolescence, this evidence suggests, teens have fewer, more selective, but stronger, more effective neuronal connections than they did as children.

Notable about this neurological development is the fact that it is at least in part experience driven. It cannot be viewed in the traditional unidirectional manner simply as a necessary or enabling condition for cognitive or behavioral change. Instead, the activities a young adolescent chooses to engage in, and not to engage in, affect which neuronal connections will be strengthened and which will wither. These neurological changes in turn further support the activity specialization, in a genuinely interactive process that helps to explain the widening individual variation, already noted, that appears in the 2nd decade of life. We have more to say about this later.

### Processing Speed

What developments in cognitive function might these neurological advances support? Improvements in information processing may be of three major kinds. The clearest of the three is increase in processing speed. The most common measures of processing speed require naming a series of numbers or familiar words. Processing speed can also be measured simply as reaction time to a stimulus (Luna, Garver, Urban, Lazar, & Sweeney, 2004). In each of these cases, the pattern is clear. Response time has been found to decrease on measures of processing speed from early childhood roughly through mid-adolescence (Demetriou, Christou, Spanoudis, & Platsidou, 2002; Kail, 1991, 1993; Luna et al., 2004).

### Inhibition

While reaction time is a measure of how rapidly one can make a response, another cognitive function that is at least as important is the ability to inhibit a response. Although they are related, it is useful to make a distinction between two types of inhibition, especially as different research paradigms have been employed to investigate them.

In the first type, emphasis is on irrelevant stimuli that have the potential to interfere with processing and the challenge is to ignore them, that is, inhibit any attention to them, in favor of attending to stimuli relevant to the task at hand. This type of inhibition is typically referred to under the headings of selective attention or resistance to interference. In an early classic study, Maccoby and Hagen (1965) demonstrated that the superior performance of adolescents over children on a learning task was attributable not only to their greater attention to the stimuli that were to be remembered but also to their reduced attention to irrelevant stimuli that were also present. Older participants actually performed more poorly than younger ones on a test of memory for the irrelevant stimuli. Increasing ability to ignore attention to irrelevant stimuli during the childhood years has also been reported in other studies (Hagen & Hale, 1973; Schiff & Knopf, 1985). Included are studies based on the most common test of the ability to screen out irrelevant stimuli, the Stroop (1935) color-naming test, in which color names are printed on nonmatch color swatches and the task is to report either the names while ignoring the actual colors or the colors while ignoring names (Demetriou, Efklides, & Platsidou, 1993; Tipper, Bourque, Anderson, & Brehaut, 1989). A different kind of interference from competing stimuli arises not from simultaneous but from previously presented material. Kail (2002) reports a decline between middle childhood and adulthood in proactive interference—the interference of previously presented material in present recall. Adolescents and adults are better able than children to screen out and disregard the previous material.

A second type of inhibition has received less attention, despite its potential importance. It is the ability to inhibit an already established response in contexts where it is not appropriate to exhibit it. For example, an individual may be instructed to inhibit a response that has become routine whenever a particular signal is given. Performance on these tasks improves until mid-adolescence (Luna et al., 2004; Williams, Ponesse, Schacher, Logan, & Tannock, 1999). In another paradigm designed to assess response inhibition, a "directed forgetting" technique has been used in studies of memorization of word lists. In this paradigm, the individual is instructed to forget words that have already been presented and hence to inhibit them in subsequent free recall. During recall, improvement occurs across childhood in the ability to inhibit words under "forget" instructions, as well as to withhold production of incidentally learned words (Harnishfeger, 1995). Young children, in contrast, typically display no difference in frequencies of production of words they were instructed to forget and those they were instructed to remember.

In sum, the evidence is ample that both resistance to interfering stimuli and inhibition of undesired responses develop across the childhood years and into adolescence. It has even been suggested that they may play a role in the developmental improvement observed in basic memory tasks, notably digit span, that have been employed as measures of processing capacity (Bjorklund & Harnishfeger, 1993; Harnishfeger, 1995). It should be noted, however, that the evidence regarding inhibition of inappropriate responses comes from paradigms in which the individual is instructed to inhibit the undesirable response. We have less information about response inhibition in the important condition in which individuals must make their own decisions regarding the desirability of a response and hence which responses to exhibit and which to inhibit. We have more to say about this form of inhibition in examining the topic of executive control.

## Processing Capacity

In addition to speed and inhibition, a third processing dimension which may undergo developmental change is processing capacity. Here things become decidedly less clear, the primary reason being that different researchers operationalize this construct in different ways. At least two different components are involved. One, emphasized by Pascual-Leone (1970), is short-term storage space. The other, emphasized by Case (1992) in his revision of Pascual-Leone's theory, is operating space, which arises when the individual must manipulate the information rather than only store and reproduce it. The familiar construct "working memory" in some contexts has been used in the operating space sense and in others in the storage sense.

Developmentally increasing processing speed, as Case and his colleagues have proposed (Case, 1992; Case, Kurland, & Goldberg, 1982; Case & Okamoto, 1996), reduces the space required for operations, leaving more space available for short-term storage. The net result is greater processing efficiency, rather than any absolute increase in capacity. Others (Cowan, 1997; Demetriou et al., 2002), however, dispute Case's claim that processing speed and processing capacity are causally related, as opposed to independently increasing or mediated by a third variable such as increasing knowledge.

Whether processing capacity increases in an absolute sense or only as a by-product of increased efficiency, there remains the question of how to measure it. Pascual-Leone (1970), Case (1992, 1998; Case & Okamoto, 1996), and, more recently Halford (Halford & Andrews, Chapter 13, this *Handbook*, this volume; Halford, Wilson, & Phillips, 1998), have all proposed systems to identify the processing demands of a task, and, by implication, the processing capacity of an individual based on his or her performance on the task. Case, for example, identified progress from tasks requiring attention to a single dimension to tasks requiring the coordination of two dimensions (Case & Okamoto, 1996). In a parallel but not identical approach, Halford and his colleagues define the processing capacity required by a task by invoking the concept of structural complexity, indexed by the number of dimensions that must be simultaneously represented if their relations are to be understood. They present data for a number of tasks suggesting that this number increases developmentally from early childhood to early adolescence (Halford & Andrews, Chapter 13, this *Handbook,* this volume).

In sum, there is general agreement across studies that processing continues to improve in the 2nd decade of life, but there is little agreement about the particulars. There are several distinct components of processing ability and there is no universal agreement as to how they are related. Do speed and capacity develop independently or do they influence one another? The same question can be asked with respect to speed and inhibition (Luna et al., 2004). Do processing improvements take place in a domain-general manner, as some researchers maintain (Gathercole, Pickering, Ambridge, & Wearing, 2004; Swanson, 1999), or do improvements differ across domains, as others claim (Demetriou et al., 2002)? Perhaps most importantly, the challenge of achieving widely agreed upon measures of processing capacity remains. Tasks involving capacities to represent versus store versus manipulate mental symbols are likely to produce divergent capacity estimates. Moreover, the goal of producing "pure" measures of capacity remains elusive. Supporting this conclusion is the fact that we have yet to identify conclusively the set of factors that contribute to developmentally increasing performance on what might appear to be the simplest, most straightforward measure of capacity of all—digit span. Indeed, all the factors we have noted—capacity, efficiency, speed, inhibition—as well as several others—familiarity, knowledge, strategy—have been implicated (Bjorklund & Harnishfeger, 1990; Case et al., 1982; Harnishfeger, 1995).

### Information Processing and Reasoning

In turning to the question of how processing improvement figures in the development of thinking and reasoning, it is hardly surprising that we encounter a similar degree of uncertainty. The claim is rarely made that development at the neurological level or an increase in the number of pieces of information that can be simultaneously processed is the direct and sole cause of a qualitatively new form of reasoning. The

emergence and development of the new form must be accounted for at the psychological level. Still, processing increases may function as necessary conditions that create the potential for the emergence of new capabilities, allowing a child, for example, to solve a problem she was previously unable to or to devise a new approach to a familiar problem.

Demetriou et al. (2002) have undertaken the most wide-ranging empirical investigation to date of the relations between developing information-processing capacities and developing reasoning skills in a cross-sequential design in which children 8 to 14 years of age were assessed initially and again at two subsequent yearly intervals. Assessments included processing speed, capacity, and inhibition, as well as several kinds of reasoning; each skill was examined in three domains—verbal, numerical, and spatial. The authors' conclusion is that of a necessary-but-not-sufficient relation. Processing improvements, they say, "open possibilities for growth in other abilities. In other words, changes in these functions may be necessary but not sufficient for changes in functions residing at other levels of the mental architecture" (p. 97).

Unfortunately, however, the measurement uncertainties we have alluded to make it difficult for the authors to definitively rule out any directions of causality. Performance improves with age on all of the various tasks they administer. But even the sophisticated analytic methods they use do not allow them to conclude with certainty what causal relations may exist, due to measurement uncertainties. The reasoning tasks in particular are necessarily brief and arbitrarily chosen, for example, four syllogisms and four analogies in the verbal domain, and even the authors acknowledge in their discussion that an improved "yardstick for specifying differences between concepts or problems" is needed. With respect to the numerical reasoning problems, for example, they conclude, "the four levels of difficulty in the numerical operations task (each defined by 1 to 4 unknown operations) are not equally spaced in terms of attainment age" (p. 132). A further complication is the varying patterns the authors obtain in the three content domains, leading them to conclude that processing capabilities are specific to the kind of information being processed.

Demetriou et al. (2002) make it clear that processing capabilities can be no more than necessary conditions for thinking, and they stress the importance of what they label "top-down" as well as "bottom-up" influences. In particular they emphasize the role of a "hypercognitive" or executive operator which "may participate and contribute to the relations between all other processes and abilities" (p. 127). This top-down direction of influence, note, extends not just to thinking but to the processing capabilities themselves. In addition to bottom-up processing capacity, performance on a short-term memory task may be affected not just by top-down application of strategies but by skill and knowledge with respect to what strategies are useful, how to implement them, and facility in doing so (Cowan, 1997). These multiple possibilities contribute further to the challenge of obtaining any definitive measure of capacity.

Demetriou et al. (2002) conclude finally that all of "the various processes interact dynamically during development, so that change in each process is shaped both by its own internal dynamics and contributions originating from other processes" (p. 128). Few are likely to disagree with the general conclusion, but leaving all possibilities open does not help define a path toward the understanding of developing higher-order thinking. It also leaves the door open to the likelihood of individual developmental pathways, assuming one's individual experiences affect how information-processing capabilities and higher-order cognitive activities interact. Thus, in turning now to an examination of these high-order forms of thinking, we must keep in mind developing information-processing capabilities without expecting that they will by themselves explain what is observed to develop in the higher-order realm.

## DEDUCTIVE INFERENCE

In the remaining sections of this chapter, we examine kinds of thinking with respect to which there exists evidence of development during the 2nd decade of life. We begin with deductive inference not because it is the most important, either in children's intellectual development or in the research literature. Rather, we adopt a loosely historical approach, beginning with deductive inference because it was the first form of higher-order reasoning to be the topic of extensive systematic developmental research. The historical reason is in large part its connection to Inhelder and Piaget's theory of formal operations. Their theory was interpreted as claiming the formal operational stage to mark the advent of propositional reasoning, and drawing inferences from the propositions that make up formal syllogisms was taken as an index of this ability.

Most extensively studied have been classical syllogisms that assert conditional relations between cate-

gories, that is, *if p, then q.* In the traditional syllogistic reasoning task, the initial major premise—*if p, then q*—is presented, followed by one of four secondary premises, either *p* (known as the *modus ponens* form), *q, not-p,* or *not-q* (known as the *modus tollens* form). The respondent is asked if a conclusion follows. The *modus ponens* form allows the conclusion *q:* If *p* is asserted to be the case and it is known that *if p, then q,* it follows that *q* must be the case. Similarly, the *modus tollens* form allows the conclusion *not-p:* If *not-q* is asserted and it is known that *if p, then q,* it follows that *p* cannot be the case (because if it were, *q* would be the case and we know it is not). The other two forms, however, having *q* or *not-p* as secondary premises, allow no definite conclusion. Another extensively researched task is the selection task (Wason, 1966). In this case, instead of a secondary premise, the reasoner is asked to indicate which of the four cases (*p, not-p, q,* and *not-q*) would need to be examined in order to verify the truth of the major premise (*if p, then q*). (Here the answer is the two determinate cases—*p,* to verify that *q* follows, and *not-q,* to verify that *p* is not the case.)

The empirical data on children and adults' performance on these kinds of deductive inference tasks have been reviewed periodically by a number of authors (Braine & Rumain, 1983; Klaczynski, 2004; Markovits & Barrouillet, 2002; O'Brien, 1987). Two conclusions have emerged consistently. One reflects what we have referred to earlier as the paradox of early competence and later lack of competence. Provided the content and context are facilitative, even quite young children are able to respond correctly at least to the two determinate syllogism forms (Dias & Harris, 1988; Hawkins, Pea, Glick, & Scribner, 1984; Kuhn, 1977; Rumain, Connell, & Braine, 1983). The majority of adults, in contrast, do not respond correctly in the standard form of the selection task (Wason, 1966). The evidence, then, does not support any sudden onset, or even marked transition, in competence to engage in propositional reasoning.

The other consistent conclusion is the sizable effect of proposition content on performance. In short, what it is that is being reasoned about makes a great deal of difference (Klaczynski & Narasimham, 1998; Klaczynski, Schuneman, & Daniel, 2004; Markovits & Barrouillet, 2002). These consistent findings have led investigators to reject as implausible the acquisition of a general, content-free set of rules applicable across any content. In the words of Markovits and Barrouillet (2002), "The idea that most reasoners are able to use content-free reasoning procedures in any systematic way appears highly unlikely given the very large sources of variation in inferential performance observed" (p. 33).

## The Critical Role of Meaning

Contemporary investigators of deductive inference have turned their efforts to proposing models of how reasoning with conditional propositions does take place. There is general agreement that representation of the problem content is critical and mediates performance. Cheng and Holyoak (1985) emphasized semantic form, rather than specific content. If p, q, for example, may be interpreted causally, as in "p makes q happen," or as a statement of permission, as in "You must have q to do p." Adults, they found, performed significantly better in the selection task when the proposition was stated in the latter form, rather than the neutral if p, q form. This was so even when the content was not spelled out and remained simply the letters p and q.

Although semantic meanings such as permission, obligation, and causality facilitate representation of propositions and reasoning about them, Klaczynski and Narasimham (1998) question the claim that each of these semantic concepts (e.g., permission, obligation, causality) has its own concept-specific reasoning scheme. Rather, inference rules appear isomorphic across schemes (Braine, 1990). Markovits and Barrouillet (2002) developed a model based on Johnson-Laird's (1983) mental model theory to predict the difficulty of various syllogistic forms. Their model attributes developmental improvements in deductive reasoning tasks to increased capacity to manipulate multiple mental models and greater availability of such models (see Halford & Andrews, Chapter 13, this *Handbook,* this volume, for further description). Their model, however, is also consistent with the simpler attribution that Klaczynski (1998) concludes accounts for most of the performance variance, namely, the availability of mental representations of alternatives.

Consider, for example, the two propositions, "If Tom studies, he'll pass the exam," and "If Tom cheats, he'll pass the exam." Respondents of all ages are more likely to respond correctly to the two indeterminate syllogism forms when they occur in an example like the second proposition, compared to the first. For affirming the consequent, $q$ (Tom passed the exam), respondents may correctly note in the second example that it is indeterminate whether Tom cheated. In the example of the first

proposition, by contrast, they are more likely to falsely conclude that Tom studied hard. The likely reason is that in the case of the cheating proposition they can readily represent alternative antecedents, that is, possible causes of Tom's success other than cheating, leading to recognition that the antecedent does not follow from the consequent and that the true antecedent remains indeterminate. In the first (Tom studies) proposition, these alternatives come to mind less readily. Similarly for the other indeterminate syllogism form, denying the antecedent (*not-p*)—Tom didn't study hard or Tom didn't cheat—respondents are more likely to recognize that no conclusion follows when presented the second proposition (because not cheating leaves open multiple alternative consequents). Semantic content, or meaning, we must conclude, then, significantly enhances or impedes deductive reasoning.

## What Develops?

An account of the factors determining success on indeterminate syllogism forms assumes the bulk of researchers' attention since it is performance on the indeterminate forms that shows the only clear developmental change. On the two determinate forms (*modus ponens* and *modus tollens*), performance is very good (75% correct) by late childhood (and in many studies by an even earlier age) and at near ceiling level by late adolescence, indicating little developmental change (Klaczynski et al., 2004; Klaczynski & Narasimham, 1998). These forms are correctly answered by use of a simple biconditional (or mutual implication)—*if p, q* and *if q, p*—that is mastered even by young children: $p$ and $q$ simply "go together," such that if one is present so is the other and if one is absent so is the other. At the other end of the complexity continuum, performance in the standard selection task similarly shows no clear developmental change (Foltz, Overton, & Ricco, 1995; Klaczynski & Narasimham, 1998). Performance improves modestly in some respects and declines in others, remaining poor through adulthood and strongly content-dependent (Cheng & Holyoak, 1985; Klaczynski & Narasimham, 1998).

On the indeterminate syllogism forms, in contrast, a low level of correctness in childhood and early adolescence increases modestly by late adolescence, although content effects remain strong and performance remains far from ceiling (Barrouillet, Markovits, & Quinn, 2001; Klaczynski et al., 2004; Klaczynski & Narasimham,

1998). To what should this improvement be attributed? One possibility is willingness to make an indeterminacy judgment. However, in contexts in which children have been assured that "it's okay not to be sure," school-aged children (Kuhn, Schauble, & Garcia-Mila, 1992) and even preschoolers (Fay & Klahr, 1996) have been shown to be willing to suspend judgment, so it does not appear to be the acknowledgment of indeterminacy itself that is the stumbling block.

Another possibility is increased availability of alternatives due to an expanding knowledge base (Klaczynski et al., 2004), which leads to the correct recognition of indeterminacy. This remains a potential contributor that cannot be excluded but, again, seems not to tell the whole story. It is worthy of note in this respect that content familiarity itself does not predict performance on syllogistic reasoning problems. Klaczynski (2004) offers the example of the two propositions, "If a person eats too much, she'll gain weight" and "If a person grows taller, she'll gain weight." The former is more familiar, but performance on the indeterminate syllogistic forms of the latter is superior, due to the greater availability of alternatives, as elaborated earlier.

While task context and knowledge play a significant role, the determining factor must be the nature of the mental processing that occurs. One simple hypothesis is that incorrect responders terminate processing prematurely, with the tendency to do so diminishing into and through adolescence. Fay and Klahr (1996) explained failures to make correct indeterminacy judgments among preschoolers in exactly this way, although the tasks they examine are much simpler ones. In what they termed a "positive capture" strategy, children often made a determinate selection among alternatives and declared the problem solved as soon as they encountered one that met the stipulated criterion, ignoring the existence of other alternatives that also met the criterion. Similarly, we shall see in turning to inductive reasoning in the next section, children (and sometimes adults) are likely to rely on a "co-occurrence" inference strategy (Kuhn, Garcia-Mila, Zohar, & Andersen, 1995), judging that two co-occurring events are related as cause and effect without considering other alternatives that also co-occur with the events. In the conditional reasoning context considered here, children rely first on the inference rule that is simplest and most readily available in their repertoires, the biconditional—$p$ and $q$ "go together"—and consider the problem no further.

Klaczynski (2004) points to more developed metacognitive skills as key in the adolescent's increasing likelihood of inhibiting premature termination and continuing processing long enough to consider alternatives and recognize their implications with respect to indeterminacy. Ready availability of such alternatives of course supports doing so, as we have noted. We return through the remainder of this chapter to accounts of development in which the ability to inhibit initial responses figures prominently.

## When Knowledge and Reasoning Conflict

Before concluding our examination of deductive reasoning, it remains to highlight another important factor that significantly affects deductive reasoning performance—the truth status of the premises (Markovits & Vachon, 1989; Morris & Sloutsky, 2002; Moshman & Franks, 1986). Children become increasingly able into and during adolescence to reason deductively irrespective of their belief in the truth or falsity of the premises being reasoned about. This capability extends beyond syllogistic reasoning and indeed was identified by Inhelder and Piaget (1958) as a foundation of the stage of formal operations. Consider an 8-year-old, for example, who is well able to perform a standard task assessing mastery of hierarchical classification, judging that in a vase containing roses and other flowers, all the roses are flowers. Now imagine asking this child to solve the following deductive inference problem:

All wrestlers are police officers.

All police officers are women.

Assume the two previous statements are true; is the following statement true or false?

All wrestlers are women.

Children rarely are able to judge such conclusions as valid deductions from the premises, despite their empirical falsity, and fail to see their logical necessity (Moshman & Franks, 1986; Pillow, 2002). By early adolescence, the distinction between truth and validity begins to appear. But even older adolescents and adults continue to make errors in deductive reasoning when the premises are counterfactual (Markovits & Vachon, 1989).

Inhelder and Piaget (1958) maintained categorically that children, having not reached the stage of formal operations, are unable to reason about the hypothetical and are confined to mental operations on the empirical world. But the distinction is not as clear-cut as they implied. Children are able to exercise their imaginative capabilities in creative ways: "Imagine a world in which . . ." and simple counterfactuals are a routine part of the school curriculum, for example, "Suppose you had 9 marbles and gave 4 to a friend." As the deductive operations get more complex, however, as in the above example, a conflict arises between trusting the deductive operations (which seem trustworthy enough when content is neutral) or trusting your own knowledge.

Overcoming this conflict implicates the executive, or metacognitive, processes that have been suggested play a role in improvements in performance on deductive reasoning problems involving indeterminacy. In the present case, two meta-level components may be involved. One is increasing meta-level understanding of the deductive inference form, that is, its validity, dependability, independence from content, and utility. The other is increasing meta-level awareness and management of one's own system of beliefs, making it possible to "bracket," that is, temporarily inhibit, these beliefs, in order to allow the deductive system to operate, with the understanding that this suspension of belief is only temporary. Response inhibition capacities are implicated here (Handley, Capon, Beveridge, Dennis, & Evans, 2004; Simoneau & Markovits, 2003), a fact we return to in further examination of executive processes.

The importance of belief inhibition is also supported by findings that deductive reasoning performance is susceptible to improvement in children by introducing a fantasy context (Dias & Harris, 1988; Kuhn, 1977; Leevers & Harris, 1999; Morris, 2000). If belief is suspended by the fantasy context, it can't conflict with the conclusions reached through deductive reasoning, and the practice in suspending belief stands to benefit the reasoning process once the fantasy context is withdrawn. From each of these perspectives, then, belief inhibition appears key.

## Deduction and Thinking

Throughout this chapter, we consider meta-level understanding *about* reasoning strategies—their purpose, power, limitations, range of applications—as at least as important as performance-level knowledge of how to execute these strategies (Kuhn, 2001a). In the case of de-

ductive inference, this meta-level competence involves understanding of the purpose and value of deductive inference itself. This brings us to the final question we must address in this section. Is the development of deductive reasoning competence central to the development of mature, effective thinking? Does logic govern thought? The role of the deduction paradigm in research on thinking has been debated in recent years, leading one prominent researcher in the field of deductive reasoning to speculate that deductive tasks may involve simply the "application of strategic problem solving in which logic forms part of the problem definition" (Evans, 2002). Evans recommends that the deduction paradigm be supplemented with other methods of studying reasoning.

While Evans's recommendation seems sound, indeed hard to quarrel with, the extensive research literature on the development of deductive reasoning does point in several useful directions. One is toward the necessity of abandoning any view of deductive reasoning capability as a singular competence or one that emerges at a discrete point in the life cycle. As we observed, some forms of deductive reasoning are within the grasp of preschoolers while others elude even adults. The other direction is toward the role of executive processes that deploy, monitor, and manage inference rules, rather than simply execute them. These meta-level operators are implicated in the response inhibition that appears critical to deductive reasoning, allowing the temporary suspension of belief that permits the deductive system to operate and avoiding premature termination of processing that enables alternatives to be considered and indeterminacy recognized.

As for the specific findings from developmental research on deductive reasoning, we propose that mastery of the indeterminate syllogistic forms is secondary to development of ability to reason independently of the truth status of the premises—a broad, flexible, and powerful mental skill that allows us to disembed a representation of meaning from its context. With respect to mastery of the indeterminate syllogistic forms, adolescents and adults have learned to use these forms in practical, if not strictly logical, ways, drawing on their real-world knowledge to decide which interpretation applies. Thus, "If you drive too fast, you'll have an accident" readily invokes alternative antecedents and hence interpretation as the formal logical conditional. "If you drink too much, you'll have a hangover," in contrast, invokes the simpler (logically incorrect) biconditional. Little confusion arises over this difference in everyday reasoning.

When knowledge and deduction conflict, on the other hand, real-world knowledge does not scaffold reasoning. To the contrary it must itself be managed and controlled, enabling the deductive system to function. Weak executive control, we see through the remainder of this chapter, makes it difficult to temporarily inhibit one's beliefs, so as to enable the reasoning process to operate independently of them, causing a number of different kinds of limitations. This skill does show improvement in the years between late childhood and late adolescence, but its absence remains an obstacle to good thinking throughout adolescence and adulthood. We turn now to inductive reasoning, where we find its role is crucial.

## INDUCTIVE AND CAUSAL INFERENCE

One of the final issues we addressed in examining deductive reasoning—its relevance in everyday thinking—is one we can bypass entirely in examining inductive reasoning. There is simply no question about the fundamental role that inductive reasoning plays in thinking and in cognitive development. Children (and adults) confront enormous amounts of data, some consistent and some inconsistent over time, and they must construct meaning out of this wealth of information. An extended, and we will argue ultimately unproductive, debate has existed as to whether children approach this task as empiricists or theorists. In other words, do they rely strictly on observed frequencies of associations to determine "what goes with what" as an indication of how the world is organized, or do they impose theoretical constructions on their encounters with data?

These are the same questions that Gelman and Kalish (Chapter 16, this *Handbook,* this volume) confront in asking how young children form their early concepts. The field has seen some evolution in this respect. Keil (1991), for example, at one time proposed that young children were initially empiricists, forming their concepts on an entirely associationist basis, and later overlaid a theoretical structure on this associational base. Subsequently, however, Keil rejected this view in favor of the position that children's thinking is from the very

beginning theoretical. In other words, children try to make sense of a concept, rather than simply accept it as a statistical compilation of the features whose frequency associations define it. This sense-making effort influences the features they see as central versus peripheral to the concept, as much or more than statistical frequency of association. In Keil's (1998) words, "a system of covariation detection procedures must interact with a framework of expectations about causal patterns" (p. 378).

This is exactly the position we take here with respect to the formation of the more complex forms of understanding being constructed by older children, adolescents, and adults. Most often, their concern is with relations between concepts, relations that are commonly construed as causal. Does alcohol affect a person's judgment? Does this clothing style make one popular? A set of existing ideas is brought to contemplation of the topic, and the task becomes one of achieving coordination between these ideas and new information that becomes available. It is not a matter of identifying one or the other as more important (Koslowski, 1996).

There are thus two potentially problematic questions in examining inductive reasoning that we can set aside— Is it relevant? Does explanation *or* evidence govern it? Another question, however, that must be confronted squarely is the question of competence, and it appears to be a formidable one. Is the child on the cusp of adolescence a competent inductive reasoner? Here we face two strikingly disparate literatures. One, focused on infancy and early childhood, emphasizes the impressive causal inference skills evident in early childhood. The other, focused on adolescents and adults, highlights limitations in causal inference skills that remain characteristic into and throughout adulthood. Our task in this section, then, is to take account of both of these literatures and formulate a portrayal of the development of inductive inference skills in the years in between.

### Evidence for Early Competence

We begin our task with an examination of research on early competence. A wealth of evidence exists that even young infants make causal inferences, recognizing an association for example, between one of their own actions (e.g., moving an arm) and an external event (Cohen & Cashon, Chapter 5, this *Handbook,* this volume). We focus here on the more advanced inference skills displayed by preschool children who are asked to identify causes in a multivariable context. Multivariable contexts (ones in which multiple events co-occur with an outcome and are potential causes) are the ones people of all ages most often face in everyday experience and therefore are the ones we focus attention on here.

Schulz and Gopnik (2004) present evidence of 4-year-olds' ability to isolate causes in a multivariable context. Children observed a monkey handpuppet sniff varying sets of three plastic flowers, one red, one yellow, and one blue. An adult first placed the red and blue flowers in a vase and brought the monkey up to sniff them. The monkey sneezed. The monkey backed away, returned to sniff again, and again sneezed. The adult then removed the red flower and replaced it with the yellow one, leaving the yellow and blue flowers together in the vase. The monkey came up to smell the flowers twice and each time sneezed. The adult then removed the blue flower and replaced it with the yellow flower, leaving the red and yellow flowers together in the vase. The monkey came up to smell the flowers and this time did not sneeze. The child was then asked, "Can you give me the flower that makes Monkey sneeze?" Seventy-nine percent of 4-year-olds correctly chose the blue flower.

Our task is one of reconciling findings such as these with a sizable body of data on multivariable causal inference in older children, adolescents, and adults that portrays a more complex picture of causal reasoning skill. When individuals coordinate prior expectations with new information, as is usually the case, causal inference becomes more challenging and we see quite different patterns of performance. Here the findings of numerous investigators show the influence of theoretical expectation on the interpretation of data and the ubiquity of faulty causal inference (Ahn, Kalish, Medin, & Gelman, 1995; Amsel & Brock, 1996; Cheng & Novick, 1992; Chinn & Brewer, 2001; Klaczynski, 2000; Klahr, 2000; Klahr, Fay, & Dunbar, 1993; Koslowski, 1996; Kuhn, Amsel, & O'Loughlin, 1988; Kuhn et al., 1992, 1995; Lien & Cheng, 2000; Schauble, 1990, 1996; Stanovich & West, 1997). When theoretical expectations are strong, individuals may ignore the evidence entirely and base inferences exclusively on theory. Or they may make reference to the evidence but represent it in a distorted manner, characterizing it as consistent with their theoretical expectations when it in fact is not. Or they may engage in "local interpretation" of the data (Klahr et al., 1993; Kuhn et al., 1992), recognizing only

those pieces of data that fit their theory and failing to acknowledge the rest.[1]

## Coordinating Theory and Evidence

This biased processing of information about the world remains commonplace into and through adulthood. At the time of the 2004 presidential election, for example, three-fourths of Bush supporters, but less than a third of Kerry supporters, reported believing that Iraq provides substantial support to Al Qaeda, despite the findings of the 9/11 Commission that there was no evidence of significant support from Iraq ("When No Fact Goes Unchecked," 2004).

Should it be assumed that people engage in intentional misrepresentation of the information they are exposed to? Most of the time, it appears, this is not the most likely explanation. A more likely one is insufficient control over the interaction of theory and evidence in one's thinking (Kuhn, 1989). Under such conditions of weak control, thinking is based on a singular representation of "the way things are" with respect to the phenomena being contemplated, and new information is seen only as supporting—or, more aptly, "illustrating"—this reality. New information is not encoded as distinct from what is already known.

Under such conditions, new information can still modify understanding, but the individual may not be aware that this has taken place. A consequence is that individuals remain largely unaware regarding the source of their knowledge. When asked, "How do you know (that A is the cause of O)?" they make mistakes in attributing the inference to the new information they are contemplating, versus their own prior understanding

---

[1] In a subsequent experiment Schulz and Gopnik (2004) show that young children similarly behave less consistently when the causal effect portrayed conflicts with their prior knowledge, for example, presentation of an adult making a machine operate by saying "Machine, please go." Most children (75%) imitated the adult when asked to make the machine go. They were unlikely to generalize this learning (that people can cause machines to operate by speaking to them) to a new context, however. The authors conclude that there exists a tension "between children's prior beliefs and their assimilation of novel information" (Schulz & Gopnik, 2004) and that additional research is needed to determine how the two interact—a position in fact very similar to the one taken here.

(Kuhn et al., 1988, 1992, 1995; Schauble, 1990, 1996). This uncertainty regarding the source of one's knowledge parallels that observed on the part of preschool children who exhibit confusion regarding the source of their knowledge about simple events (Harris, Chapter 19, this *Handbook,* this volume). Thus, preschoolers answer the question of how they know a runner has won the race not with evidence ("He's holding the trophy") but with an explanation of why this state of affairs makes sense (e.g., "Because he has fast sneakers") (Kuhn & Pearsall, 2000).

Is there evidence of developmental progress in this respect? Kuhn et al. (1988, 1995) compared children, early adolescents, and adults with respect to evidence evaluation and inference skills and found some improvement in the years between middle childhood and early adulthood, despite the far from ideal performance of adults. Among sixth graders, the proportion of evidence-based inferences was about 25%, compared to roughly 50% for noncollege young adults. Following an evidence-focus probe ("Do these results here tell you anything about whether X has an effect?"), these percentages rose to 60% and 80%, respectively (Kuhn et al., 1988).

Once the evidence is attended to, are younger individuals more likely to exhibit biased interpretation than older ones? Here, improvement with age appears more fragile. Individual variation, however, is high, a fact we return to. Individuals were regarded as showing belief bias if they were more likely to interpret the evidence when it was consistent with their previously assessed theories, and/or they interpreted identical evidence differently as a function of its consistency with their theories. Roughly half of sixth graders exhibited one or both forms of bias in their interpretations of both covariation and noncovariation evidence (Kuhn et al., 1988). Among adults, this percentage dropped to 35%, although only for covariation evidence. (For noncovariation evidence, it remained at the sixth-graders' level of 50%.)

## Interpreting Covariation Evidence

The challenge of sound inductive inference is far from met simply by attending to the data. Even if the data are faithfully registered, the opportunity for inferential error remains strong, a major contributor continuing to be the potentially biasing effects of theoretical expectation. Much evidence exists of unjustified inductive inferences of a relation, usually causal, between two

variables, based on minimal evidence, notably as minimal as a single co-occurrence of two events (Klahr et al., 1993; Kuhn et al., 1988, 1992, 1995; Schauble, 1990, 1996). Because the events occurred together in time and/or space, one is taken to be the cause of the other, despite the presence of other covariates. This "false inclusion" is of course common in everyday thought at all ages. Thus, when community college students were told about an effort to improve student performance in which a new curriculum, teacher aides, and reduced class size were all introduced in various combinations (Kuhn et al., 2004), they sometimes relied on as little as a single instance in which multiple factors were introduced as potential evidence for the role that one or more of the factors had played in the outcome. The following is a typical inference, "Yes, a new curriculum is beneficial, because here where they had it the class did well."

False inclusion based on a single instance shows some decline in frequency in the years from late childhood to early adulthood (Kuhn et al., 1988, 1995, 2004). Adults are more likely than children to base their causal inferences on a comparison of two instances, rather than a single instance of co-occurrence of antecedent and outcome. Also showing developmental decline are instances of false exclusion, in which a variable is inferred to be noncausal (i.e., have played no role in the outcome) based on no, or a single instance of, evidence.

Even inferences based on comparisons of multiple instances can be fallacious if additional covariates are not controlled and causality is attributed to the wrong variable. These kinds of errors are ubiquitous in everyday life. A personal example that stands out in the first author's mind is one of her teen-aged son needing to be picked up late one night from a party that had gotten out of hand and listening to his frustrated father lament, "Drinking and trouble—haven't you figured out the connection?" Despite the late hour and his shaky state, the teenager advanced a lengthy argument to the effect that his father had the causality all wrong and the trouble should be attributed to other covariates, among them bad luck.

When presented with two or more multiple-covariate instances for possible inferences, performance in inhibiting unwarranted inferences and drawing warranted ones does improve between late childhood and adulthood in this "natural experiment" context (Kuhn & Brannock, 1977; Kuhn & Dean, 2004). We postpone further discussion of this improvement, however, to a later section in which we examine the more common research design in which individuals are given the opportunity to select their own instances for investigation and, hence, conduct controlled experimentation.[2]

What is notable and bears emphasis with respect to performance in the "natural-experiment" context of inductive inference is the extent to which the factors we have identified as important are similar to those we identified as important in the case of deductive inference. Both involve inhibition. One is the ability to inhibit the premature responding that terminates processing and prevents one from considering alternatives (in this case, additional covariates). The other is the ability to "bracket," that is, temporarily inhibit, one's beliefs, in order to accurately represent evidence and enable the inference system to operate. Both of these abilities, in turn, involve meta-level, or executive, control of mental processes, which we can accordingly hypothesize is increasing during the age period in which we see improvements in reasoning performance.

## Coordinating Effects of Multiple Variables: Mental Models of Causality

We have focused on the cognitive challenges encountered in isolating the relation between an individual variable and outcome embedded in a multivariable context. What happens when more than one causal factor has been identified and the task becomes one of identifying how they operate in conjunction, either additively or interactively? Kuhn and colleagues (Keselman, 2003; Kuhn, Black, Keselman, & Kaplan, 2000; Kuhn & Dean, 2004; Kuhn et al., 2004) identify an inadequate mental

model of multivariable causality as a further source of error affecting inductive causal inference in this case. Here we use the "mental model" terminology in this more generic sense, rather than its typical usage referring to mental representations of particular physical phenomena.

The implicit assumption underlying research in the adult causal inference literature is that people's understanding of multiple causality reflects a standard scientific model: Multiple effects contribute to an outcome in an *additive* manner; as long as background conditions remain constant, these effects are expected to be *consistent*, that is, the same antecedent does not affect an outcome on one occasion and fail to do so on another, or affect the same outcome differently on one occasion than another. A more complex model, encompassing *interactive* effects, presumes understanding of the simpler main effects of an additive model. Indeed, all of science is predicated on such a model. It is not clear how the world would operate in the absence of these assumptions, and hence it is not surprising that research on causal inference (Cheng, 1997) assumes such a model.

Data from the reasoning of both children and adults, however, bring that assumption into question (Kuhn & Dean, 2004; Kuhn et al., 2004). Least likely to be present is the recognition of potential interactivity and its distinction from additivity of multiple causes. When provided the amounts of pollution caused by each of three individual pollutants in a factory, for example, and asked what the pollution level would be if all three pollutants were present, no sixth graders and only 12% of college adults recognized the potential interactivity and hence indeterminacy; others simply added the individual effects, identical to what they had done in a parallel problem of how many logs three boys together would chop based on knowledge of their individual chopping outputs (Kuhn et al., 2004). These results are consistent with findings that even young children are able to add or average outcomes based on the joint effects of two variables when asked explicitly to do so (Dixon & Moore, 1996; Dixon & Tuccillo, 2001; Wilkening & Anderson, 1982). Yet, even adults tend not to differentiate additive and interactive causes when thinking about multiple factors affecting an outcome. This lack of differentiation is not surprising when we note that there exist no natural language equivalents to distinguish the two cases. If we say for example, "Get a good night's sleep and eat a good breakfast and you'll do really well," we are neither required nor encouraged to distinguish

---

[2] Still another form of reasoning that shows a similar developmental pattern is correlational reasoning, in which the pattern of relation between two variables is probabilistic rather than absolute. In the case of two binary variables, errors in assessing their relation arise from failure to consider all four cells in the resulting cross-tabulation. For example, in assessing whether lawyers are rich, the reasoner may take into account only his or her knowledge of positive cases (of rich lawyers), neglecting to compare them to poor lawyers or to rich and poor nonlawyers. Again, performance on these kinds of problems, which entail proportional reasoning (specifically, comparing two proportions), improves from childhood through adolescence but remains far from perfect among adults (Arkes & Harkness, 1983; Klaczynski, 2001b; Kuhn, Phelps, & Walters, 1985; Schustack & Sternberg, 1981).

between an additive and interactive model as applying in this situation.

When we turn to the simpler case of variables that are additive in their effects, however, limitations in intuitive mental models of causality appear equally severe. In the absence of explicit instruction to add or average effects, neither additivity nor consistency across instances can be assumed. Keselman (2003) asked sixth graders to investigate and make inferences regarding the causal role of five variables on an outcome (earthquake risk), as well as asking them to make outcome predictions for two new cases representing unique combinations of levels of the variables. Three of the five variables had additive effects on the outcome and the remaining two had no influence. After each prediction, the question was asked, "Why did you predict this level of risk?" All five variables were listed and children were instructed to indicate as many of them as had influenced their prediction judgment. The variables indicated were regarded as ones *implicitly* judged to be causal, as the respondent did not explicitly state them to be causal, saying only that they had entered into the prediction judgment. The variables named as causal in response to direct questions as to whether or not the variable played a causal role were taken as *explicit* causal judgments.

Consistency between explicit and implicit causal judgments was low. Over half of the children justified one or both of their predictions by implicating a variable they had explicitly judged to be noncausal. More than 80% failed to implicate as contributing to the outcome one or more variables they had previously explicitly judged to be causal. Overall, fewer features were implicated as contributory in the implicit attributions than were explicitly stated to be causal. Consistency was low not only between explicit and implicit causal attributions, but also across predictions. Almost three quarters of children failed to implicate the same variable(s) as having causal power across the two prediction instances. Finally, and most directly relevant to the additive model, roughly half of the students justified each of their predictions by appealing to the effect of only a single (usually shifting) variable. This behavior is consistent with the phenomenon known as discounting in the social psychology literature, in which identification of one cause of an outcome leads to the discounting of others, a phenomenon that has been observed by age 8 or 9 and throughout adulthood (Sedlak & Kurtz, 1981).

Adults do better in each of these respects (Kuhn & Dean, 2004), but their performance remains far from the normative scientific model of multivariable causality. About half of the members of a community choral group, representative of a broad cross-section of the adult population, showed inconsistency between implicit and explicit causal judgments. Almost half were inconsistent in causal attributions across three prediction questions. Like the sixth graders, these adults failed to implicate as causal in their implicit attributions as many variables as they needed to in order to yield correct predictions. Over a quarter appealed to the effect of only a single variable in their prediction judgments, and over half appealed to the effect of only two variables.[3]

We can thus point to an inadequate mental model of multivariable causality as a constraint on children's and even many adults' ability to reason about the simultaneous, additive effects of multiple variables. Additional challenges, we have seen, come into play when individuals bring new evidence to bear on their causal models and to coordinate them with theoretical expectations. Does experience in coordinating effects of multiple variables improve this mental model? This question is one part of the more general question to which we now turn. As children grow older and progress into and through adolescence, do they improve in their ability to integrate the new information they encounter with their existing understandings? In other words, do children become better learners?

## LEARNING AND KNOWLEDGE ACQUISITION

Although the study of children's learning has only recently come back into style (Siegler, 2000; Chapter 11, this *Handbook,* this volume), learning clearly plays a central role in the lives of children of all ages. Moreover, older children and adolescents have had more time and opportunities to learn, and as a result they clearly know more than younger children. Differences in knowledge, then, are certainly a large part of what makes children and adolescents different from one another. The question addressed in this section, and indeed throughout the

---

[3] A further challenge arises in detecting an inverse relation between a variable and outcome and integrating that relation with others that may be present (Kuhn et al., 1988; Lafon, Chasseigne, & Mullet, 2004). Children commonly confuse an inverse relation with independence (Kuhn et al., 1988).

chapter, is whether this is the only difference. What else may contribute to the difference between younger and older individuals? In particular, in this section, we ask whether the learning process itself differs with age.

## Cross-Sectional Age Comparisons

Two studies (Kuhn et al., 1995; Kuhn & Pease, in press) we review here have the objective of examining exactly this question. We focus on the simpler Kuhn and Pease study first. Young adults and 12-year-olds were presented the teddy bear shown in Figure 22.1a. The participant assisted the interviewer in outfitting the bear with seven accessories, producing a bear that now appeared as shown in Figure 22.1b. The interviewer presented the situation of a charity group raising funds and having the bears to give to donors as token gifts. In an effort to improve donations, it was explained, the charity wanted to try dressing the bear up a bit. They could afford to add a

few accessories and had to choose which ones. Participants were asked to choose two accessories they thought most likely to increase donations and the two least likely to do so. This content domain was selected to make it unlikely that either age group could be regarded as more knowledgeable in making these choices.

The participant was then presented results of some "test runs" involving these four accessories. A sequence of five instances, presented cumulatively, involving different combinations of the accessories, established that two accessories (one the participant believed effective and one the participant believed ineffective) increased donations and the other two did not. The most successful combination was presented as the fifth instance, such that the correct answer could simply be "read off" from this instance and no complex inferential reasoning was required. Nonetheless, neither group was entirely successful in learning the information presented. Adults, however, showed a higher rate of success than

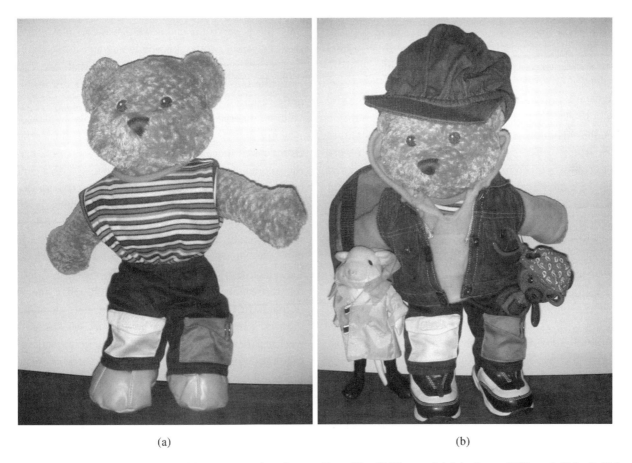

(a)                                          (b)

**Figure 22.1**   Teddy bear, with and without accessories. *Source:* From "Do Children and Adults Learn Differently?" by D. Kuhn and M. Pease, in press, *Journal of Cognition and Development.* Reprinted with permission.

the 12-year-olds: 75% reported the correct answer, versus 35% of the younger group.

How should one account for superior learning on the part of the adult group? Conceptualizing learning as change in understanding (Schoenfeld, 1999) and ruling out a number of alternative explanations, Kuhn and Pease (in press) proposed that the older participants made better use of a meta-level executive to monitor and manage learning. This executive allowed them to maintain dual representations, one of their own understanding (of the relations they expect or see as most plausible) and the other of new information to be registered. It is this executive control that enables one to temporarily set aside or "bracket" existing beliefs and thereby effectively inhibit their influence on the interpretation of new data. In the absence of this executive, there exists only a singular experience—of "the way things are"—as a framework for understanding the world. This executive control, manifested in response inhibition and bracketing, is of course exactly what we encountered earlier as a central factor in the development of deductive and inductive inference.

Kuhn and Pease's (in press) findings of less effective learning by preadolescents compared to adults were substantiated in a more extensive microgenetic study (Kuhn, 1995; Siegler, Chapter 11, this *Handbook,* this volume) of learning at these two age levels (Kuhn et al., 1995). Participants were observed over multiple sessions spanning several months as they sought to learn which variables were effective and which were not in contexts involving both physical content (e.g., the speed of model boats down a canal) and social content (e.g., the popularity of children's TV programs). Again, in both physical and social domains, the adult group was more effective in acquiring the new information.

Because participants conducted their own investigations within these domains, the context allowed them great explanatory freedom. If an outcome appeared to conflict with expectations with respect to one feature, these implications could be avoided simply by shifting to other features to do the explanatory work. What the results made most clear is what the process of knowledge acquisition is not, and that is a process of accessing and accumulating evidence until one feels one has enough to draw a conclusion. Instead, theoretical belief shapes the process at each point—in the evidence that is chosen for examination, the way in which the evidence is interpreted, and the conclusions that are drawn. The

challenge, then, is not simply one of correctly "reading" the data, but of coordinating theories and evidence. New knowledge does not simply add to or displace existing knowledge; the new and old must be coordinated and reconciled. Both children and adults, Kuhn et al. (1995) found, drew conclusions virtually from the outset, on the basis of minimal or no data, and then changed their minds repeatedly. But the children remained more strongly wedded to their initial theories, and drew on them more than on the new evidence they accessed, as a basis for their conclusions.

Both age groups did less well when the content was social rather than physical. To the extent theories in the social domain are more detailed, vivid, and/or affectively potent, a weak executive operator may make it more difficult to maintain dual representations (of theory and evidence). Less potent representations on the theory side, in the case of physical phenomena, may give the two representations a better chance to co-exist, while an executive seeks to coordinate them.

Microgenetic analysis in the Kuhn et al. (1995) research made possible the dual objectives of tracing not only the acquisition of knowledge over time but, also, the evolution of the knowledge-acquisition strategies that were responsible for generating that knowledge. Here the now widely observed findings from microgenetic research (Siegler, Chapter 11, this *Handbook,* this volume) emerge. At both ages, individuals displayed not just one but a variety of different strategies, ranging from less to more effective. Over time, what changes is the frequency of usage of these strategies, with a general decline over time in the usage of less effective strategies and increase in the use of more powerful ones. It is this process of change that Siegler terms his "overlapping waves" model. Our interest has been in the meta-level operators that execute this strategy selection and how they may develop in a way that has positive effects on the performance level (Kuhn, 2001a, 2001b). Since participants in the Kuhn et al. (1995) research conducted their own investigations of the domain, we discuss this work further in the next section on inquiry and scientific reasoning. Here, we return to the question of what it can tell us about how the learning process changes developmentally.

## The Development of Learning

Should it be concluded, then, that the learning process undergoes developmental change? Some years ago,

Carey (1985) answered this question with a categorical no, claiming there was no reason to believe that the learning process operated any differently in children than in adults. The findings described here suggest that Carey's sweeping claim, while likely true with respect to some kinds of learning, is not categorically correct. A great deal of the learning children and adults engage in, both in and out of school, is simple associative learning. It is not mindful learning, and there is no evidence to indicate that the nature of associative learning processes undergoes developmental change. Learning that is conceptual, in contrast—that is, involves change in understanding—requires cognitive engagement on the part of the learner, and hence an executive that must allocate, monitor, and otherwise manage the mental resources involved. These executive functions, and the learning that requires them, do show evidence of developing.

At the same time, Kuhn and Pease's (in press) findings show that developmental change of this sort is highly variable. Some 12-year-olds performed as well as the typical adult, and some adults performed no better than most 12-year-olds. The pattern in this respect is quite different from that observed in the case of the many childhood cognitive attainments described in this volume that are closely age linked. When, as here, progress is more variable, microgenetic research is especially valuable in affording insight into the kinds of experience that foster change and the nature of the process. We look further at the insights offered by microgenetic research in the next section.

The microgenetic method has been held responsible for blurring the distinction between development and learning (Kuhn, 1995, 2001b). While the distinction between the two may not be as rigid as theorists of the Piagetian era in the 1960s and 1970s held it to be, it does not follow that there remain no useful distinctions at all. Learning what recordings are on this week's "Top 100" List and learning that conflicting ideas can both be right are different kinds of learning in numerous important respects (among them generalizabilty, reversibility, and universality of occurrence). What is important is recognizing the process of change as one that has multiple parameters. When the process is examined microgenetically, it becomes possible to begin to characterize it in terms of many such parameters. It is more research of this sort that is required to support the claim that these change processes themselves undergo change as individuals mature.

## INQUIRY AND SCIENTIFIC THINKING

Modern research in developmental psychology on the development of scientific thinking began very narrowly, in the form of replication studies seeking to confirm the findings reported by Inhelder and Piaget (1958) in their volume *The Growth of Logical Thinking from Childhood to Adolescence.* The bulk of these replication studies focused even more narrowly on the "control of variables" or "controlled comparison" investigative strategy, which Inhelder and Piaget reported did not appear until the early adolescent years. Using Piagetian tasks in which participants were required to investigate simple physical phenomena such as a pendulum or the flexibility of rods, Inhelder and Piaget's findings were upheld with respect to children's difficulty with these tasks and evidence of improvement from childhood to adolescence, but it was also found that even older adolescents and adults did not always perform successfully (Keating, 1980; Neimark, 1975). Relatively little discussion occurred, however, regarding the broader educational or practical significance of these findings. Assuming these tasks were valid indicators of the ability to engage in scientific thinking, was it important for most people to be able to think scientifically?

### Does Children's Thinking Need to Become "Scientific"?

In the early twenty-first century, the picture could not be more different. What has come to be called "inquiry" has found its way into the American national curriculum standards for science (National Research Council, 1996) for every grade beginning with 2nd or 3rd through 12th and appears in a large majority of state standards as well. Inquiry often appears in social studies and even language arts standards as well (Levstik & Barton, 2001). In the national science standards, the goals of inquiry learning for Grades 5 to 8, for example, are the following (National Research Council, 1996):

- Identify questions that can be answered through scientific investigations.
- Design and conduct a scientific investigation.
- Use appropriate tools and techniques to gather, analyze, and interpret data.
- Develop descriptions, explanations, predictions, and models using evidence.

- Think critically and logically to make the relationships between evidence and explanations.

Under "Design and conduct a scientific investigation," subskills identified include "systematic observation, making accurate measurements, and identifying and controlling variables."

It is worth asking, then, what scientific thinking is and why it is so important, such that, within a few decades, it has come to be so widely embraced as an educational goal. Defining scientific thinking as "what scientists do" does not work very well, since very few children will grow up to become professional scientists, few enough certainly that educating all children toward this end in elementary school seems scarcely appropriate or worth the effort involved. Nor is defining scientific thinking operationally in terms of the control-of-variables strategy satisfactory, since few people, children or adults, have the opportunities or inclination to conduct controlled experiments in the course of their everyday activities.

The position we take here is to regard scientific thinking as central to science but not specific to it (Kuhn, 1996, 2002). The definition of scientific thinking we adopt is *intentional knowledge seeking* (Kuhn, 2002). This definition encompasses any instance of purposeful thinking that has the goal of enhancing the seeker's knowledge. As such, scientific thinking is a human activity engaged in by most people, rather than a rarefied few. It connects to other forms of thinking studied by psychologists, such as inference and problem-solving. We characterize its goals and purposes as more closely aligned with argument than with experimentation (Kuhn, 1993; Lehrer, Schauble, & Petrosino, 2001). Scientific thinking is frequently social in nature, rather than a phenomenon that occurs only inside people's heads.

From their earliest years, children construct implicit theories that enable them to make sense of and organize their experiences. In a process that has come to be referred to as *conceptual change,* these theories are revised as new evidence is encountered bearing on them. Unlike scientific thinking, early theory revision occurs implicitly and effortlessly, with little indication of conscious awareness or intent. Young children think *with* their theories, rather than about them. In the course of so doing they may revise these theories, but they are unlikely to be aware that they are doing so. As a result, as we noted earlier in the discussion of inductive reasoning, they are typically uncertain regarding the source of their knowledge.

It is the intention to seek knowledge that transforms implicit theory revision into scientific thinking. Theory revision becomes something one *does,* rather than something that happens to one outside of conscious awareness. To seek knowledge is to recognize that one's existing knowledge is incomplete, possibly incorrect—that there is something new to know. The process of theory-evidence coordination accordingly becomes explicit and intentional. Newly available evidence is examined with regard to its implications for a theory, with awareness that the theory is susceptible to revision and that its modification may be an outcome of the process.

In this framework, it becomes possible to reconcile the shortcomings in scientific thinking identified in this chapter with the "child as scientist" perspective adopted by authors such as Gelman and Kalish (Chapter 16, this *Handbook,* this volume) and Gopnik, Meltzoff, and Kuhl (1999). As theory builders, children are indeed young scientists (or scientists big children) virtually from the beginning. There is no evidence to indicate that children's construction and elaboration of theories as means of understanding the world take place in a qualitatively different way than they do for lay adults or scientists (although this is not a question that has been thoroughly researched). Where the difference arises is in the intentional, consciously controlled coordination of these theories with new evidence. Here the research evidence is plentiful that children execute this process less skillfully than most adults and certainly less skillfully than professional scientists.

## The Process of Inquiry

As Klahr (2000) notes, very few studies of scientific thinking encompass the entire cycle of scientific investigation, a cycle we characterize as consisting of four major phases: inquiry, analysis, inference, and argument. A number of researchers have confined their studies to only a portion of the cycle, most often the evaluation of evidence (Amsel & Brock, 1996; Klaczynski, 2000; Koslowski, 1996), a research design that links the study of scientific reasoning to research on inductive causal inference. We postpone discussion of argument to a later section, and we focus here on studies in which participants direct their own investigations and seek their own data as a basis for their inferences, hence involving at least the first three phases of the cycle (Keselman, 2003; Klahr, 2000; Klahr et al., 1993; Kuhn et al., 1992, 1995, 2000; Kuhn & Phelps, 1982; Penner & Klahr, 1996; Schauble, 1990, 1996). These studies offer a picture of how the strategies associated with each phase of scientific investigation are situated within a context of all the others and how they influence one another.

Studies of individuals engaged in scientific inquiry, or intentional knowledge seeking, have been at the same time both cross-sectional and microgenetic. In other words, initial strategies of individuals of different age levels can be compared cross-sectionally. If the individuals continue to engage in investigative activity over multiple sessions, change can be observed at two levels—in the products of their inquiry, that is, the knowledge they acquire, and in the strategies of inquiry, analysis, and inference used to generate that knowledge.

The studies by Klahr and his associates (Klahr, 2000; Klahr et al., 1993) have followed children and adults asked to conduct investigations of the function of a particular key in controlling the behavior of an electronic robot toy, or, in another version, the behavior of a dancer who performs various movements in a computer simulation. To do this, individuals need to coordinate hypotheses about this function with data they generate, or, in Klahr's (2000) terminology, to coordinate searches of an hypothesis space and an experiment space.

The microgenetic studies by Kuhn and associates, as well as those by Schauble (1990, 1996), Keselman (2003), and Penner and Klahr (1996) examine what we regard as a prototypical form of scientific inquiry—the situation in which a number of variables have potential causal connections to an outcome and the investigative task is to choose instances for examination and on this basis to identify causal and noncausal variables, with the goals of predicting and explaining variations in outcome. Examined in these studies in their simplest, most generic form, at the same time these are common objectives of professional scientists engaged in authentic scientific inquiry.

Studies originating in both Klahr's and Kuhn's laboratories have portrayed very similar overall pictures. Adults on average exhibit more skill than children or young adolescents at each stage of the process. The younger group is more likely to seek to investigate all factors at once, to focus on producing outcomes rather than analysis of effects, to fail to control variables and, hence, to choose uninformative data for examination, and to engage in what Klahr refers to as "local interpre-

tation" of fragments of data, ignoring other data that may be contradictory. Klahr (2000) concludes that, "adult superiority appears to come from a set of domain-general skills that . . . deal with the coordination of search in two spaces" (p. 119).

Kuhn et al. (1995) compared the progress of children and adults as they continued their investigations in multiple content domains over a period of months. Adults both started at a slightly higher level and progressed further. Although the strategies of both groups improved, the investigations of the older group overall yielded more valid conclusions and fewer invalid conclusions than those of the younger group. Unsurprisingly, as a result, they learned more about the causal structure of the domain they were investigating. Yet, microgenetic analysis of the change process confirmed the now common finding that individuals of both ages displayed not just one but a variety of different strategies ranging from less to more effective. Kuhn et al. (1995) concluded, "Rather than a unidimensional transition from a to b, the change process must be conceptualized in terms of multiple components following individual (although not independent) paths" (p. vi). This was the case with respect to *inquiry* strategies, which range from "generate outcomes" to "assess the effect of X on outcome"; with respect to *analysis* strategies, which range from "ignore evidence" to "choose instances that allow an informative comparison"; and with respect to *inference* strategies, which range from "unsupported claims" to "representations in relation to both consistent and inconsistent evidence" (Kuhn, 2002).

Consistent with other microgenetic research (Siegler, Chapter 11, this *Handbook,* this volume), over time the frequency of usage of less effective strategies diminished and the frequency of more effective strategies increased. If we accept that the density of exercise accelerates developmental change without altering its essential characteristics (Kuhn, 1995), the question of interest becomes one of identifying the mechanisms underlying this change process. In postulating mechanisms, Siegler (this volume) emphasizes the need for associations with the more frequent, less effective strategies to be weakened. While similarly emphasizing the relinquishment of less effective strategies as a more formidable obstacle than strengthening new ones, Kuhn (2001a, 2001b) proposed that knowledge at the meta-level is as important as that at the performance level and plays a major role in what happens there. Portrayed in the right side of Figure 22.2 (Kuhn, 2001b) are the strategies

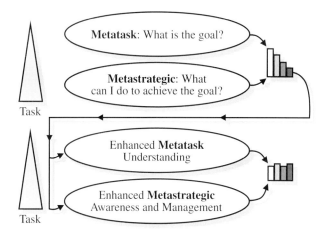

**Figure 22.2** Diagram of shifting distribution of strategy usage. *Source:* From "Why Development Does (and Doesn't) Occur: Evidence from the Domain of Inductive Reasoning," by D. Kuhn, in *Mechanisms of Cognitive Development: Neural and Behavioral Perspectives,* R. Siegler and J. McClelland (Eds.), 2001, Mahwah, NJ, Erlbaum. Reprinted with permission.

that coexist and are available for use (comparable to Siegler's "overlapping waves" model, this volume). In the progress depicted from the upper to the lower half of the diagram in Figure 22.2, the less effective strategies to the left become less frequent and the more effective strategies to the right more frequent (in this case, yielding a temporary, transitional result of all strategies of roughly equal strategy). Implicated in this change are the meta-level operators that appear in the center of the diagram, representing the individual's understanding of the task goal, understanding of the strategies he or she has available to apply, and awareness of the need to coordinate the two in selecting a strategy. Feedback from the performance level should enhance meta-level understanding, further enhancing performance, in a continuous process.

Strategic progress with continued engagement not only occurred in both age groups, Kuhn et al. (1995) found, but was maintained when new problem content was introduced midway through the sessions. A further indication that strategies were not confined to specific content was the emergence of new strategies at about the same time in the social and physical domains, even though performance in the social domain overall lagged behind. No simple predictors of change emerged, such as feedback discrepant from expectations, and it was hypothesized that the sense of effectiveness produced by good strategies may be as potent a source of change (Pressley & Hilden, Chapter 12; Siegler, Chapter 11,

this *Handbook,* this volume). Finally, and importantly, the most prevalent change to occur overall was not the emergence of any new strategies but the decline of ineffective ones, in particular the inhibition of invalid causal inference.

### Supporting the Development of Inquiry Skills

We have noted that the intellectual skills examined in this chapter, unlike the large majority of those addressed in the other chapters in this volume, cannot be counted on to routinely develop. In the case of deductive inference, this has not been an issue of wide concern. In the case of inductive inference, it has received somewhat wider attention, to a large extent in the context of discussions of critical thinking. As we noted at the outset of this section, inquiry skills have become a focus of very wide concern to educators. As a result, considerable attention has been devoted to how these skills might be most effectively promoted in young preadolescents or adolescents.

Studies dating back to the 1970s (Case, 1974; Kuhn & Angelev, 1976) established that the isolation- and control-of-variables strategy could be taught. But that evidence by no means resolves the matter of identifying the most effective educational interventions, an objective that goes beyond the scope of the present chapter. Most recently, Chen and Klahr (1999) and Klahr and Nigam (2004) present data that brief direct instruction effectively teaches control of variables and on this basis they advocate it as the most efficient, desirable method. At the same time, studies already described here by Kuhn et al. (1992, 1995, 2000) and by Schauble (1990, 1996) document that preadolescents develop this skill and others when they engage in dense exercise in problem-solving situations that require them. Preadolescents are unlikely to show much progress in the brief single session of self-directed activity that Klahr and Nigam (2004) employ as a control condition, but over time and sustained engagement, microgenetic studies show predictable patterns of advancement, as we have noted.

What strengths might this labor intensive, time inefficient means of fostering the development of inquiry skills have over the efficiency of simple, brief direct instruction? The most important in our view has to do with the metastrategic level of understanding that may accompany strategic learning (Kuhn, 2001a, 2001b). If we exclude unconscious strategy usage, when an individual voluntarily initiates use of a strategy to address a problem, the individual presumably does so with some degree of intention and hence belief that the strategy will serve his or her objectives. This metastrategic understanding is not necessarily present or of the same quality when one is following an instruction to use the strategy. The implications are significant with respect to how the individual may act when the instructional context is withdrawn and the individual resumes voluntary control of his or her own behavior. Intent underlying use of the strategy will remain difficult to identify with any certainty.

The second strength has to do with the fact that inquiry is a complex, multifaceted activity. It is more than a single strategy that we want to see young students of science acquire. If we are to achieve the much desired objective of involving students in "authentic" science (Chinn & Malhotra, 2001), the integrity of the whole must be respected. As we have noted, weaknesses in the inquiry process arise long before one gets to the phase of designing and interpreting experiments. A first, critical phase is formulating a question to be asked. Unless the student understands the purpose of the activity as seeking information that will bear on a question whose answer is not already known, inquiry often degenerates into an empty activity of students securing observations for the purpose of illustrating what they already take to be true (Kuhn, 2002). In the context of multiple variables potentially affecting an outcome, students who have developed an understanding of the need to access an available data base as a source of information may nonetheless initially pose ineffective questions, in particular by intending to discover the effects of all variables at once. And it may be this ineffective intention that then leads them to simultaneously manipulate multiple variables (in effect overattending to them, rather than underattending by failing to control them, as is often assumed).

Kuhn and Dean (2005) in the context of an extended intervention otherwise confined to exercise, added the simple suggestion to students that they choose a single variable to try to find out about. This simple intervention had a pronounced effect on their investigation and inference strategies, greatly enhancing the frequency of controlled comparison and valid inference, relative to a control group, in both the original and a new context. This finding documents, certainly, the complex multifaceted nature of inquiry. But it also highlights that more is involved in mastery than the ability to execute effective strategies.

The understanding associated with the initial phase of the inquiry process is most critical because it gives meaning and direction to what follows. If a question is identified that seems worth asking and the ensuing activity seems capable of answering, the stage is set for what is to follow. In the multivariable context of isolation of variables and controlled comparison, the individual may cease to vary other variables across two-instance comparisons because of an increasing sense that they are not relevant to the comparison being made. Once they are left alone, and thereby "neutralized" as Inhelder and Piaget (1958) described it, the way is prepared for increased usage and increasing metastrategic understanding of the power of controlled comparison. But the most important message here is that we need to look beyond the control-of-variables strategy as a narrow procedure to teach students to execute. Rather, it should be conveyed as a tool that serves as a resource for them to draw on in seeking answers to the questions that they may pose.

## DECISION MAKING

Are adolescents more competent decision-makers than children? Are they less competent decision makers than adults? The developmental changes in inference and reasoning noted thus far in this chapter would lead to a hypothesis of age differences in judgment and decision making, which presumably are the result of exercise of reasoning processes. Unfortunately, the research evidence regarding children's and adolescents' decision-making is limited.[4] To date, it consists almost entirely of administering to children and adolescents a number of the decision scenarios that have been used in research with adults and in which many adults have been found to make decisions that violate sound decision-making principles (Kahneman & Tversky, 1996; Stanovich & West, 1998, 1999, 2000). We report here how children and adolescents perform on these tasks, relative to the levels of performance observed among adults. We begin, however, with several studies of a different mold, having to do with simple judgments of preference.

---

[4] We do not review here programs that have been devised to teach good decision-making to adolescents. These programs are largely based on work with adults, and evidence regarding their effectiveness is limited (Beyth-Marom, Fischhoff, Jacobs, & Furby, 1991).

## Preference Judgments

Consider the following kind of problem, presented to 8-year-old and 12-year-old children by Bereby-Meyer, Assor, and Katz (2004).

In a computer store, Ron is offered four computer games that he can afford:

- The first one is interesting, has not-so-good voice quality, and comes with an option to add players.
- The second is not interesting, has not-so-good voice quality, and comes with an option to add players.
- The third one is not interesting, has good voice quality, and lacks an option to add players.
- The fourth one is interesting, has not-so-good voice quality, and lacks an option to add players.

Which computer game is the best choice for Ron?

In a parallel study (Capon & Kuhn, 1980), preferences of kindergarteners, fourth graders, eighth graders, and young adults were solicited regarding real, physically present objects—pocket-sized notebooks of two colors, binding types (side or top), shapes, and surfaces. At the end of the study, they were given their most preferred notebook to keep. They were also asked for separate preference judgments regarding the four dimensions themselves.

Results of the two studies are similar in many respects. Bereby-Meyer et al. (2004) observed some improvement with age, but they found frequent use at both ages of what they term the lexicographic error, in which judgment is based on a single dimension. Similarly, Capon and Kuhn (1980) found that rarely before adulthood did participants take more than a single dimension into account in making preference judgments for the notebooks, despite the fact that at all ages the majority indicated preferences on at least three of the four dimensions in making dimension preference judgments.

The data from these studies are notable in particular as they parallel the findings by Keselman (2003) and by Kuhn and Dean (2004) noted earlier in the section on inductive inference. A large majority of sixth graders failed to implicate as contributing to an outcome one or more variables they had previously explicitly claimed to be causal. Fewer variables were implicated as contributory in implicit attributions (associated with prediction judgments) than were explicitly attributed as causal, and half of the participants justified their predictions by appealing to the effect of only a single variable. It is difficult to attribute such patterns in the preference judgment study to capacity limitations, versus dispositional factors. The requested preference judgment regarding the dimension (e.g., color) is elicited, but it does not follow that a respondent cares enough about it to integrate status on this dimension into his or her object preference judgments. Still, the fact that in the inductive inference context, where it is clearly normative to do so, sixth graders (and even older individuals) do not attend to all dimensions they implicate as causal suggests that individuals may experience difficulty in attending to and integrating all of the multiple dimensions they would in fact wish to enter into preference judgments of objects, and that developmental factors may be relevant.

## Decision-Making Judgments

Klaczynski (2001a, 2001b) has collected the most comprehensive age-comparative data on children's and adolescents' decision-making judgments. He administered to young adolescents (average age 12) and older adolescents (average age 16) several of the most widely known decision scenarios in which adult errors have been documented. He reports improved rates of correct responding with age (see Table 22.1) in each of the following four scenarios. Two other scenarios that did not show clear age improvement were the conjunction fallacy (in which the conjunction of A and B is judged more likely than A alone) and hindsight bias (Kahneman & Tversky, 1996).

1. *Contingency:* A doctor has been working on a cure for a mysterious disease. Many people are getting sick from the disease, so the doctor has been working very hard. Finally, he created a drug that he thinks will cure people of the disease. Before he can begin to sell it, he has to test the drug. He selected 14 people for his test and compared how sick these people were after getting the drug to 7 people who did not get the drug. Of those who got the drug, 8 were cured and 6 were still sick. Of those who did not get the drug, 4

TABLE 22.1    Proportion of Correct Responses in Decision Scenarios by Age Group

|  | Young | Older |
| --- | --- | --- |
| Contingency | .35 | .52 |
| Statistically-based decision | .18 | .42 |
| Gambler compensation fallacy | .24 | .41 |

Adapted with permission from "The Influence of Analytic and Heuristic Processing on Adolescent Reasoning and Decision Making," by P. Klaczynski, 2001b, *Child Development, 72,* pp. 844–861.

were cured and 3 were still sick. What effect did the drug have? (5-point choice scale ranges from −2 to +2.)[5]

2. *Statistically-based (versus anecdotally based) decision:* Ken and Toni are teachers who are arguing over whether students enjoy the new computer-based teaching method used in some math classes. Ken's argument is, "Each of the 3 years that we've had the computer class, about 60 students have taken it. They have written essays on why they liked or didn't like the class. Over 85% of the students say they have liked it. That's more than 130 of 150 students." Toni's argument is, "Stephanie and John (the two best students in the school, both high-honors students) have complained about how much they hate the computer-based class and how much more they like regular math classes. They say a computer can't replace a good teacher" (4-point choice scale offered as to which course to take).

3. *Gambler compensation fallacy:* When playing video poker, the average person beats the computer one in every four tries (25% of the time). Julie, however, has just beaten the computer six out of eight times (75% of the time). What are her chances of winning the next time she plays? A range of response options is offered. The compensation fallacy is identified when the respondent indicates a likelihood lower than the objective probability.

4. *Outcome bias:* In these problems, a high-failure likelihood that has a favorable outcome is compared with a low-failure likelihood with an unfavorable outcome. The quality of each decision is rated on a 7-point scale. Outcome bias is calculated by subtracting ratings for the high-failure-likelihood event from those for the low-failure-likelihood event.

The fourth scenario, outcome bias, was scored based on the degree of bias shown. The quality of the decision was rated on a 7-point scale (7 = high). Outcome bias was determined by subtracting ratings on the high probability with negative outcome problems from ratings on the low probability with positive outcome problems. Summed across two problem domains, bias scores could range from −12 to +12, with positive scores indicating bias. Mean score for the young adolescents was 4.21 and

for the older adolescents 2.78, thus indicating a decline in outcome bias with age.

Klaczynski did not include adults in this study, so we cannot say with certainty whether the older teens performed any less well than would have adults from an equivalent population. The adult literature has reported these to be common judgment errors, however, so older teens did not perform substantially worse, if at all inferior to, adults. In a further study, Klaczynski (2001a) did compare the performance of young and older adolescents to that of young adults, but he employed different problems, notably the well-known sunk-cost fallacy:

A. You are staying in a hotel room on vacation. You paid $10.95 to see a movie on Pay TV. After 5 minutes, you are bored and the movie seems pretty bad. How much longer would you continue to watch the movie?

B. You are staying in a hotel room on vacation. You turn on the TV and there is a movie on. After 5 minutes, you are bored and the movie seems pretty bad. How much longer would you continue to watch the movie?

Because sunk costs are irretrievable, they should be ignored and decisions in the two situations should be the same. Here, Klaczynski found, all age groups were susceptible to the sunk-cost fallacy (choosing to watch longer in situation A than in situation B), with only 16% of young adolescents (average age 12), 27% of older adolescents (average age 16), and 37% of adults responding correctly.

In sum, then, the picture is one of modest improvement during the teen years toward an asymptote characteristic of the adult population—an asymptote itself of a very modest level, with the average adult at least as likely to make an incorrect judgment as a correct one in response to most of the scenarios.

**Dual-Process Theory**

Drawing on theories of Sloman (1996), Evans (2002) and others, Klaczynski (2004, 2005) proposes a "dual-process" theory to account for the development of decision-making skills. Cognitive development, Klaczynski proposes, is not in fact unidimensional, proceeding along a singular course as traditional theories espouse, but rather occurs along two trajectories. One is an experiential system and the other an analytic system. The major contrasting characteristics of the two systems appear in Table 22.2. The two systems are thought to be

---

[5] This problem is in fact equivalent to the earlier discussed correlation problem.

**TABLE 22.2   Contrasting Attributes of Two Cognitive Systems in Dual-Process Theories of Cognitive Development**

| Experiential System | Analytic System |
| --- | --- |
| Unconscious | Consciously controlled |
| Effortless | Effortful |
| Automatic | Volitional |
| Fast | Deliberate |
| Holistic | Analytic |
| Intuitive | Reflective |
| Contextualized | Decontextualized |

in competition with one another, especially in contexts like the decision scenarios considered here, in which they yield opposing judgments.

Developmentally, Klaczynski (2004, 2005) proposes, the experiential system is always present and remains the predominant system. It is useful and adaptive; were it not for its rapidity and automaticity, information processing would be overburdened. Developmental change may occur, however, in the degree to which the experiential system predominates. The potential to respond experientially increases with age, Klaczynski suggests, but also in the process of becoming more prominent with age are increasingly powerful metacognitive operators. These metacognitive operators have the potential to invoke the analytic system. Once invoked, the analytic system has the dual tasks of inhibiting the experiential system and doing its own primary work, which entails extracting the decontextualized representations that will lead to correct judgments.

The major limitation of this dual-process model of cognitive development is that there at present is little direct empirical evidence available to substantiate it. The model does fit the developmental decision-making data, however, and a number of Klaczynski's secondary findings are also consistent with it. He accounts, for example, for the finding that a "logical person" cue ("Think about this situation from the perspective of a perfectly logical person") enhances performance on the grounds that it induces uncertainty about whether to use one's normal experiential processing mode. On the other hand, there is no consistent evidence for developmental change occurring separately in two distinct systems. Despite two earlier reports of increased susceptibility to certain of the fallacies during adolescence (Davidson, 1995; Jacobs & Potenza, 1991), Klaczynski did not replicate these findings and found no evidence of increased reliance on experiential processing with age on any task.

At the same time, at a broader level, a dual-process model fits well with the data on deductive and inductive inference examined thus far in this chapter. Two factors that figure prominently in both kinds of inference were, first, response inhibition capability, particularly the premature termination of processing that precludes consideration of alternatives, and, second, the ability to bracket, or temporarily inhibit, one's beliefs, in order to accurately represent data and allow the inference system to operate. Both of these involve competing systems, one effortless and intuitive and the other deliberate and reflective. And both point to the importance of a meta-level executive that mediates selection of the more reflective, less contextualized alternative.

It is worth keeping the dual-process model in mind as a model that may come to have considerable utility as a framework for understanding a wide range of phenomena in the study of reasoning and cognitive development. Ultimately, however, the utility of the dual-process model as a framework for understanding cognitive development can only be established when efforts are made to relate a broader range of phenomena to it. The forced-choice judgments that children make to the well-known decision-making scenarios do not reveal a great deal about the thinking that underlies their choices or how that thinking may change with age. In this respect, research on children's decision making follows the model established by the adult decision-making literature, in which the reasoning associated with judgments is viewed with suspicion and only the judgments themselves are regarded as valid data (Janis & Klaczynski, 2002; Shafir, Simonson, & Tversky, 1993). In the next section, we turn to a very different line of inquiry—research on argument skills—in which the reasoning that underlies a judgment becomes the major focus of interest.

## ARGUMENT

In turning to the topic of argument, we encounter a paradox. Educators seeking to develop students' intellectual skills would consider it a great achievement if students became proficient in generating, evaluating, and engaging collaboratively in reasoned argument. Yet, the study of reasoning by cognitive psychologists has been devoted almost entirely to solitary problem solving, and there has been comparatively little interest in empirical research on argument skills and their development. Until fairly recently, most of what we know about children's and adolescents' argument skills has come from educators rather than psychologists.

The terms *argument* and *argumentation* reflect the two senses in which the term *argument* is used, as both product and process. An individual constructs an argument to support a claim. The dialogic process in which two or more people engage in debate of opposing claims can be referred to as *argumentation* or *argumentive discourse* to distinguish it from argument as product. Nonetheless, implicit in argument as product is the advancement of a claim in a framework of evidence and counterclaims that is characteristic of argumentive discourse, and the two kinds of argument are intricately related (Billig, 1987; Kuhn, 1991).

## Individual Arguments

Most of the empirical research on argument has been devoted to individual argument as product and we begin with it.

### *Producing Arguments*

Educators at all levels have long lamented students' weaknesses in producing a cogent argument in support of a claim in their expository writing. By asking adolescents and adults to generate arguments in individual verbal interviews, Kuhn (1991) probed whether these weaknesses reflect poorly developed writing skills or deficits that are more cognitive in nature. Individual argument skills remained poor among adolescents even when the possibly inhibiting factor of producing written text was removed. Only on average about one-third of a teen sample was able to offer a valid supporting argument for their claim regarding an everyday topic (e.g., why prisoners return to crime when they're released), a percentage that increased only very modestly to near one half among adults. Unsuccessful participants tended to offer pseudoevidence for their claims, in the form of an example or script (e.g., of a prisoner returning to crime), rather than any genuine evidence to support a claim as to the cause of the outcome in question. Similarly in the minority were those adolescents or adults who were able to envision counterarguments or rebuttals to their claims. Although chronological age (from adolescence through the sixties) was not a strong predictor of skill, education level was a significant predictor.

Other empirical research is consistent with a picture of poorly developed argument skills (Brem & Rips, 2000; Glassner, Weinstock, & Neuman, 2005; Knudson, 1992; Means & Voss, 1996; Perkins, 1985; Voss & Means, 1991). In particular there is a consistent picture of arguments that are confined to the merits of one's

own position, without attention to alternatives or opposing arguments. Kuhn, Shaw, and Felton (1997) compared the performance of young teens (seventh and eighth graders) and young adults (community college students) in producing arguments in favor of or opposing capital punishment. The two groups were equally likely to address both sides of the argument (31% of teens and 34% of adults did so); the remainder confined their arguments to supporting their own position. Adults, however, were somewhat more likely to present these arguments in a framework of alternatives. (For example, they might argue that life imprisonment is a better alternative than capital punishment, or, equally well, that life imprisonment is not a viable alternative and capital punishment is therefore necessary.) Only 6% (3 individuals) of the teens, versus 23% of the adults, offered such arguments (Kuhn et al., 1997). Overall, however, the available research indicates only slight improvement during the adolescent years in the ability to produce sound arguments.

### *Evaluating Arguments*

In other studies, participants have been asked to evaluate the strength or soundness of an argument presented to them in support of a claim (Kuhn, 2001a; Neuman, 2002; Weinstock, Neuman, & Tabak, 2004). Kuhn (2001a) reported a tendency on the part of eighth graders to focus on the content of the claim rather than the nature of the argument supporting it, hence producing the typical justification, "This is a good argument because it [the claim] is true." A comparison group of community college students were better able to separate their belief in the truth or falsity of the claim from their evaluation of the strength of the argument.

Several authors have examined the influence of one's belief regarding the claim on the evaluation of arguments supporting or opposing it (Klaczynski, 2000; Koslowski, 1996; Stanovich & West, 1997). These studies report that the same arguments are scrutinized more thoroughly and evaluated more stringently if they contradict the evaluator's beliefs than if they are supportive of these beliefs, paralleling findings from the scientific reasoning literature that individuals evaluate identical evidence differently if it is belief-supportive versus belief-contradictory (Kuhn et al., 1988, 1995; Schauble, 1990, 1996). Klaczynski (2000), for example, studied early adolescents (mean age 13.4) and middle adolescents (mean age 16.8) classified by self-reported social class and religion. They were asked to evaluate fictitious research studies in which it was concluded that one social class or one religion was superior to the other on some variable. At least one major and several minor validity threats were present in each study. Participants indicated the strength of the conclusion on a scale from 1 (very weak) to 9 (extremely well-conducted) and wrote accompanying justifications. The performance of the older group was superior in critiquing the studies. Both age groups, however, exhibited a positive bias toward studies that portrayed their group favorably, critiquing these studies less severely, although only for the religion grouping. Moreover, the extent of this bias did not diminish with age; on one indicator it in fact increased.

In another study, Klaczynski and Cottrell (2004) asked children of 9, 12, and 15 years of age to evaluate normative arguments against the sunk-cost decision-making fallacy described in the preceding section, as well as nonnormative ("waste not") arguments supporting the fallacy. Overall, at all ages, the normative arguments against the fallacy were rated as better than the nonnormative ones. When individuals were exposed to both kinds of arguments in conjunction, however, only the 15-year-olds showed significant improvement in subsequent decisions in sunk-cost kinds of problems. The authors explain these results in terms of the dual-process theory. Only the adolescents, they claim, engage in the "metacognitive intercession" that enables them to inhibit the more primitive experientially based heuristic, even though the more advanced analytic solution is understood by and potentially available to many of the younger children as well.

## Argumentive Discourse

The preceding research presents a consistent picture. There may be slight improvement along some dimensions during the adolescent years, but skills in producing or identifying sound arguments generally remain poor. Identifying more precisely the potential sources of difficulty and distinguishing among them remains a task for further research, although indications are that the meta-level skills involved in bracketing one's own beliefs figure importantly. We turn shortly to the question of primary interest to educators—how these skills can be improved. Graff (2003) makes the claim that developing arguments to support a thesis in expository writing is difficult for students because the task fails to reproduce the conditions of real-world argument, which is dialogic. In the absence of a physically present interlocutor, the student takes the writing task to be one of

stringing together a sequence of true statements, avoiding the complication of stating anything that might not be true. The result is often a communication in which both reader and writer are left uncertain as to why the argument needs to be made at all. Who would want to claim otherwise? If students plant a "naysayer"—an imaginary opponent—in their written arguments, Graff suggests, as a scaffold for the missing interlocutor, their essays become more like authentic arguments and hence more meaningful.

Graff's idea implies that individuals may exhibit stronger argument skills in the dialogic context of argumentive discourse than they do in producing their own individual arguments in support of a claim. Some research has been done observing the argumentive discourse of groups of young children in naturalistic settings (Anderson et al., 2001; Pontecorvo & Girardet, 1993). But, as noted earlier, there has until recently been relatively little systematic analysis of dyadic argumentive discourse at different age levels, to examine its characteristics compared to those of individually generated arguments.

Felton and Kuhn (2001) asked junior high school and community college students to engage in a discussion of the merits of capital punishment with a peer whose view opposed theirs. The pair was asked to talk for 10 minutes and to try to come to agreement if they could. Each of the utterances in the dialog was classified according to whether its function was (a) to advance exposition of the speaker's claims or arguments or (b) in some way to address the partner's claims or arguments. Among teens, an average of 11% of utterances were in the latter, other-focused category. Among adults, this percentage rose to 24%. Thus, while some improvement appears during adolescence, the weaknesses observed in dialogic argument in some ways resemble those observed in individual arguments, with only a minority of arguers going beyond exposition of their own position. Only infrequently do we see the genuine exchange that is the mark of authentic discourse. Why might this be? Felton and Kuhn (2001) suggest that attention to the other person's ideas and their merits may create cognitive overload, or it simply may not be recognized as part of the task. Most likely, both factors are at work—both procedural and meta-level limitations constrain performance.

As a result, dialogic argument is reduced to an activity curiously like that of individual argument. The objective is the same in both cases—to make the most compelling case possible as to the merits of one's position. If I do a good enough job, my position will prevail due to its merits, outshining any competitors, whose arguments will merely fade away into oblivion. In the case of individual argument, the task is taken on as a solitary endeavor. In the case of dialogic argument, the task is similarly individual but two people engage in it simultaneously, juxtaposing their respective efforts in a turn-taking format.

If the demands of participating in discourse create cognitive overload, and individual argument production is itself demanding, as suggested earlier, what would happen if we removed both of these demands? Kuhn and Udell (in press) explored this question by presenting participants with the following kind of simple forced-choice item:

You are told to drink fruit juice instead of soda. You like soda better. Which is the best argument for you to make?
Fruit juice is too sweet.
Soda keeps you alert.

On 10 such items, middle-school, high-school, and adult participants all showed a preference for alternatives supporting the preferred action over those arguing against the nonpreferred action. Mean number of choices arguing against the nonpreferred action showed a marginally significant increase (from 2.48 to 3.04) between middle school and high school groups and a nonsignificant difference between high school and adult groups. In a second study, however, in which participants were allowed to generate their own arguments with no constraints, both community and university adults substantially increased the extent to which these arguments included ones addressing the opposing position, while younger participants improved only slightly. Yet, in a final study, it was established that middle school students had no difficulty producing arguments against the opposing position when these were explicitly solicited. Thus, younger individuals had the cognitive competence to address opposing positions, but did not see a need to do so.

## Supporting the Development of Argument Skills

The preceding findings suggest that when argument tasks are stripped of both social role demands and ver-

bal production demands, the tendency to leave the opposing side of an argument unaddressed largely remains, despite presence of the requisite competence. This result points to the likelihood of meta-level factors constraining performance. In other words, the arguer does not understand the dual goals of argument—to identify and challenge the opponent's unwarranted claims, and to secure commitments in support of one's own claims (Walton, 1989). We return to this likelihood in examining epistemological understanding in the next section.

First, we summarize studies that have been conducted with the objective of enhancing argument skills, where these can be distinguished and assessed apart from students' broader academic skills in verbal and written expression and communication. Following Billig (1987), Graff (2003), and Kuhn (1991), the dialogic context of argumentation, which is implicit as well in individual expository arguments, seems the surest ground on which to base such efforts. The now large body of research employing the microgenetic method (Kuhn, 1995; Siegler, Chapter 11, this *Handbook*, this volume), in which cognitive skills have been shown to develop as a result of frequent engagement with problems that require them, provides a rationale for engaging students in dense practice of argument. The intent is that this practice will allow them to see its benefits at the same time that they are exercising and gradually developing the skills needed to execute it well.

Kuhn et al. (1997) observed junior-high-school students engaged in dialogic arguments over a period of weeks with a series of different classmates who held opposing (or, in some cases, agreeing) positions on capital punishment. Students were paired with a different partner each week, and the pair was asked to talk for 10 minutes and to try to come to agreement if they could. They later repeated this same activity with a new partner, until each participant had engaged in a total of five dialogs. In a later study (Felton, 2004), the design was similar except this time students alternated in roles of participants and peer advisors, the latter role intended to heighten students' reflective awareness of their argumentive discourse. After a dialog, the two participants met with their respective peer advisors (who had observed the dialog). Participants and advisors together reviewed the dialog (scaffolded by a checklist that encouraged them to identify what were termed "reasons," "criticism," and "defense"), examining the quality of what each participant had offered within each category, and considering what the participant might have done better and why. Pre-post differences following this experience were encouraging, especially as they mirrored the cross-sectional differences between teens and adults observed by Felton and Kuhn (2001), suggesting that the induced development was of the same character as naturally occurring development (Kuhn, 1995). Specifically, students decreased the proportion of utterances devoted to exposition of their own views and increased the proportion devoted to arguments against the other's position (counterargument). These gains transferred to students' dialogs on a new topic that had not been discussed previously. Hence, students had not simply learned more about the topic they were discussing. Rather, there was reason to think that they had increased their skill in argumentive discourse itself. Moreover, students who participated in the reflective activity with peer advisors showed greater gains than those in a comparison group who only engaged in the dialogs (Felton, 2004). And finally, participation in dialogic argumentation led to improvement in students' individual arguments as well (Felton, 2004; Kuhn et al., 1997), a finding also reported by Reznitskaya et al. (2001) in a study of group discourse among younger children.

One limitation of this method is that it engages young people in the relevant activity without offering them a reason to be engaged in it. Kuhn and Udell (2003) and Udell (2004) thus devised a more structured intervention in which students were organized into pro and con teams (based on their initial opinions) and engaged in various activities over a 10-week period toward a goal of a "showdown" debate with the opposing team. After several sessions devoted to developing and evaluating their own arguments, the teams exchanged arguments and then generated counterarguments to the opposing team's arguments, related evidence to both their own and the opposing team's arguments, and, finally, generated rebuttals to the opposing team's counterarguments. Progress occurred in the same directions as observed in the preceding studies, particularly a sizeable increase in counterargument. A comparison group who participated only in the initial phase of developing their own arguments showed some, but more limited, progress. Udell (2004) extended this design to a topic of personal relevance (teen pregnancy) as well as a more impersonal one (capital punishment) and found that gains following the pregnancy-topic intervention transferred to the capital punishment topic, but transfer did not occur in the reverse direction.

At the beginning of this intervention, students clearly wanted to win. By the end, they still wanted to win, but by now they cared deeply about their topic and had developed a richer understanding surrounding it, even though none of the participants had much initial knowledge. But had students learned anything about argument itself? Had they come to see a point to arguing, beyond prevailing, being the winner? Had they progressed from winning to knowing as a conceptual justification for their activity? Had they constructed an understanding of argument itself? The only possible answer is incompletely, at best. But to address the question more fully, we turn to our final topic—young people's developing understanding of knowledge and knowing.

## UNDERSTANDING AND VALUING KNOWING

In this section, we turn to the question of what children come to understand about their own and others' thinking and knowing as they enter and progress through the second decade of life. Here we encounter another striking disconnect, for young children's understanding and awareness of their mental functions, particularly memory, has been the topic of pioneering work by Flavell and others (see Pressley & Hilden, Chapter 12, this *Handbook,* this volume); more recently, the study of young children's "theory of mind," as it has come to be called, has assumed a prominent place in the field of cognitive development (see Harris, Chapter 19, this *Handbook,* this volume). Another entirely distinct body of work on epistemological understanding originated with the pioneering study of college students by Perry (1970) and, until recently, has been confined largely to the period of late adolescence and young adulthood (Hofer & Pintrich, 1997, 2002). Largely ignored has been the decade between middle childhood and late adolescence, the study of which has the potential to connect these two disparate literatures.

### Epistemological Understanding and Scientific Thinking

We begin our summary of developing understanding of knowing and knowledge with preschoolers' attainment of false belief understanding because we claim this early development is fundamental to the developments that follow (Table 22.3). Three-year-olds regard beliefs

**Table 22.3    Levels of Epistemological Understanding**

| Level | Assertions | Knowledge | Critical Thinking |
|---|---|---|---|
| Realist | Assertions are *copies* of an external reality. | Knowledge comes from an external source and is certain. | Critical thinking is unnecessary. |
| Absolutist | Assertions are *facts* that are correct or incorrect in their representation of reality. | Knowledge comes from an external source and is certain but not directly accessible, producing false beliefs. | Critical thinking is a vehicle for comparing assertions to reality and determining their truth or falsehood. |
| Multiplist | Assertions are *opinions* freely chosen by and accountable only to their owners. | Knowledge is generated by human minds and therefore uncertain. | Critical thinking is irrelevant. |
| Evaluativist | Assertions are *judgments* that can be evaluated and compared according to criteria of argument and evidence. | Knowledge is generated by human minds and is uncertain but susceptible to evaluation. | Critical thinking is valued as a vehicle that promotes sound assertions and enhances understanding. |

as faithful copies of reality; they are received directly from the external world, rather than constructed by the knower. Hence, there are no inaccurate renderings of events, nor any possibility of conflicting beliefs, since everyone perceives the same external reality. Thus, children of this age make the classic false-belief error of unwillingness to attribute to another person a belief they themselves know to be false (Perner, 1991).

Not often noted about the development of false-belief understanding is its foundational status in the development of scientific thinking, which we have examined as the coordination of theory and evidence. Three criteria must be met if it is to be claimed that one is engaged in the coordination of theory and evidence. First, the theoretical claim must be recognized as falsifiable. Second, evidence must be recognized as the means of falsification, and third, theoretical claim and evidence must be recognized as distinct epistemological categories—evidence must be distinguishable from the theory itself and bear on its correctness.

The 3-year-old who fails to recognize the possibility of a false belief meets none of these criteria. A single, true state of affairs is directly apprehended. Hence, theory and evidence do not exist as distinct epistemological categories. Thus, when asked for justification for a knowledge claim (that an event occurred), preschoolers are likely to respond with a theory as to why occurrence of the event is plausible rather than with evidence that it did in fact occur (Kuhn & Pearsall, 2000). (Thus, as noted earlier, preschool children respond with the explanation "because he has fast sneakers" rather than the evidence "because he's holding the trophy" as how they know that the boy pictured won the race.) Their error parallels the one made by older individuals justifying

more complex claims, typically causal relations between two variables, who confuse a theoretical explanation that a claim is plausible with evidence that it is true (Kuhn, 1991; Kuhn et al., 1995). Critics of the claim that children especially and even adults confuse theory and evidence have often failed to recognize the claim as one about epistemological understanding, that is, about the failure to recognize theory and evidence as distinct epistemological categories.[6]

---

[6] Thus, Ruffman, Perner, Olson, and Doherty (1993), for example, show that children can coordinate theory and evidence in the sense of drawing appropriate inferences from evidence (e.g., dolls who choose red food over green food) to theory (the dolls prefer red food to green) or from theory to evidence (in the form of a prediction of the dolls' food choice). The correspondences between theories and patterns of evidence that a child is able to identify increase in complexity with development. The one thing identification of correspondences between theories and patterns of evidence does not entail, however, is a firm differentiation between the two. Theory and evidence can "fit together," in the sense of being consistent with and implying one another, in the absence of a recognition of their differing epistemological status. Similarly, Sodian, Zaitchik, and Carey (1991) asked children to choose the more informative of two tests to find out if a mouse was large or small by placing food in a box overnight. The child was asked to choose between a box with a large opening (able to accommodate either size mouse) or one with a small opening (which only the small mouse could pass through). The task thus required the child to make a strategic choice of the more informative of two potential forms of evidence. Confusion between the theory (big mouse or small mouse) and the evidence (big or small opening) is not at issue.

## Coordinating Objective and Subjective Elements of Knowing

Later in the preschool years, the human knower, and knowledge as mental representations produced by knowers, finally come to life. Once it is recognized that assertions are produced by human minds and need not necessarily correspond to reality, assertions become susceptible to evaluation vis-à-vis the reality from which they are now distinguished. Here the potential for scientific thinking emerges.

The products of knowing, however, for a time still remain more firmly attached to the known object than to the knower. Hence, while inadequate or incorrect information can produce false beliefs, these errors are easily correctable by reference to an external reality—the known object. To be wrong is simply to be misinformed, mistaken, in a way that is readily correctable once the appropriate information is revealed. At this *absolutist* level of epistemological understanding, knowledge is thus regarded as an accumulating set of certain facts (Table 22.3).

Researchers studying the development of epistemological understanding have characterized childhood as a period in which the absolutist level of thought prevails. Although details vary across different researchers, there is general agreement that further development proceeds toward transition to a broad level of multiplism or relativism, as early as the beginning and by at least the end of adolescence, followed by, in at least some individuals, an evaluativist level (Hofer & Pintrich, 1997, 2002; see Table 22.3 for summary).

This further progress in epistemological understanding can be characterized as an extended task of coordinating the subjective and the objective elements of knowing (Kuhn, Cheney, & Weinstock, 2000). At the realist and absolutist levels, the objective dominates. Typically, with adolescence comes the likelihood of a radical change in epistemological understanding. The discovery that reasonable people—even experts—disagree is the likely source of recognizing the uncertain, subjective aspect of knowing. This recognition initially assumes such proportions, however, that it eclipses recognition of any objective standard that could serve as a basis for evaluating conflicting claims. Adolescents commonly fall into "a poisoned well of doubt" (Chandler & Lalonde, 2003), and they fall hard and deep. At this *multiplist* (sometimes called *relativist*) level, knowledge consists not of facts but of opinions, freely chosen by their holders as personal possessions and accordingly not open to challenge.

Knowledge is now clearly seen as emanating from the knower, rather than the known, but at the significant cost of any discriminability among competing knowledge claims. This lack of discriminability may be confused with tolerance. Because everyone has a right to their opinion, all opinions are equally right. That ubiquitous slogan of adolescence—"whatever"—holds sway. Hoisting oneself out of the "whatever" well of multiplicity and indiscriminability is much harder than the quick and easy fall into its depths. By adulthood, many, though by no means all, adolescents will have reintegrated the objective dimension of knowing and achieved the understanding that while everyone has a right to their opinion, some opinions are in fact more right than others, to the extent they are better supported by argument and evidence. Justification for a belief becomes more than personal preference. "Whatever" is no longer the automatic response to any assertion—there are now legitimate discriminations to be made. Rather than facts or opinions, knowledge at this *evaluativist* level of epistemological understanding consists of judgments, which require support in a framework of alternatives, evidence, and argument.

Beginning with King and Kitchener (1994), a trend in this area has been to assess epistemological thinking with detailed coding schemes of extended interview material.[7] The broad sequence from absolutist to multiplist to evaluativist can be captured fairly well, however, with just two simple questions. Kuhn et al. (2000) portrayed numerous scenarios in which two neutral characters, Robin and Chris, disagreed about something, for example which of two authors is the better one. For each scenario, respondents were asked first whether only one was right or whether both Robin and Chris could "have some rightness." If they answered that both could have some rightness, they were then asked the second question of whether one person's view could be better or more right than the other's. The response that only one person could be right was classified absolutist. The re-

---

[7] We address only that literature on epistemological understanding that is developmental in nature, that is, that regards this understanding as undergoing some systematic developmental change. Another set of researchers not reviewed here has treated the construct primarily as an individual-difference variable of a cognitive-style nature and focused empirical study largely on adults.

sponse that both could be right but one view could be no more right than the other was classified multiplist, and the response that both could have some rightness but one could be more right was classified evaluativist.

Kuhn et al. (2000) found that progression to the multiplist and evaluativist levels occurred in a domain-specific, rather than uniform, manner. Progression to the multiplist level occurred most readily in domains of personal taste and aesthetic judgments, while individuals were more likely to remain absolutist in their thinking in the domains of values and factual claims. In progression to the evaluativist level, however, this order was reversed. Here, although the subjective element of knowing that underlies the transition to multiplism was most readily acknowledged in the domains of tastes and aesthetic judgments, it proved easier to reintegrate the objective element of knowing required for the transition to evaluativist thinking in the domain of factual judgments (e.g., explanations of how the brain works) and harder to do so in the domain of aesthetic judgments— exactly the reverse. (Value judgments proved difficult for both transitions.) Developmentally, progress (from absolutist to multiplist to evaluativist) appeared in comparisons of 5th graders to 8th graders and 8th graders to 12th graders; 12th-grade respondents had reached levels equal to those of community college adults. Performance differences across domains were largely replicated in a study (Wainryb, Shaw, Langley, Cottam, & Lewis, 2004) assessing a younger sample with respect to the earlier phases of the progression, lending further support to the conclusion that epistemological understanding develops in a domain-specific manner.

## What Difference Does Epistemological Understanding Make?

In examining the development of epistemological understanding, we encounter a domain in which development is far from universal. The single most common pattern among adolescents and adults, Kuhn et al. (2000) found, was the solidly multiplist one. Absolutist thinking continued to be shown by some 12th graders in all domains but that of personal taste, and less than half of 12th graders or adults had achieved evaluativist thinking in any domain.

This same lack of universality appeared in dimensions of cognitive development examined in previous sections—the development of skills of argument, certainly, and even those of inquiry and decision-making. It is in

areas such as these, then, that the interests of developmentalists and those of educators converge, reflected in the fact that literature we have cited comes from educational as well as developmental psychology. Attention turns naturally to what conditions can be identified that might support the development in question, given its less than frequent occurrence. The interests of developmentalists have also converged to a degree with those of differential psychologists, who conceptualize developmental variation more in terms of individual differences in intellectual traits or styles that may predict performance (Stanovich & West, 1997, 1998, 1999).

Epistemological understanding is one variable that has been treated in this manner. Kokis, Macpherson, Toplak, West, and Stanovich (2002), for example, administered to 10-, 11-, and 13-year-olds a range of cognitive tasks similar to those administered to adults in previous work (Stanovich & West, 1997, 1998). They included inductive, deductive, and probabilistic reasoning, as well as an IQ measure and a composite measure of various "cognitive style" traits that included aspects of epistemological understanding. Replicating findings for adults, the style measure, it was found, accounted for additional variance in performance beyond IQ (which was a better predictor of performance than age). The conclusion these authors draw is that dispositional factors, not just competence factors, figure importantly in performance.

Several authors have focused more specifically on the relation between level of epistemological understanding and argument skill, reporting a relation between the two (Kardash & Scholes, 1996; Kuhn, 1991; Mason & Boscolo, 2004; Weinstock & Cronin, 2003; Weinstock et al., 2004). Kuhn (2005) makes a conceptual case for this relation: If facts can be ascertained with certainty and are readily available to anyone who seeks them, as the absolutist understands, or, alternatively, if any claim is as valid as any other, as the multiplist understands, there is little reason to expend the intellectual effort that argument entails. One must see the point of arguing to engage in it. This connection extends well beyond but certainly includes science, and in the field of science education a number of authors have made the case for the connection between productive science learning and a mature epistemological understanding of science as more than the empirical verification of facts (Carey & Smith, 1993; Metz, 2004; Smith, Maclin, Houghton, & Hennessey, 2000). For scientific inquiry to be valued as a worthwhile enterprise, it must be understood to occupy an epistemological ground other than the accumulation of undisputed facts dictated by absolutism or the suspension of judgment dictated by multiplism.

In their recent empirical work, Mason and Boscolo (2004) assessed the level of epistemological understanding of 10th and 11th graders. Using the Kuhn et al. (2000) instrument, they found students on average to be at the multiplist level. Students were divided into three groups—those who scored lower than average (hence, showing at least some absolutist thinking), those at the average level, and those above average (hence, showing at least some evaluativist thinking). On a separate occasion, argument skill was assessed by asking students to write a concluding paragraph to an essay that presented two opposing views regarding genetically modified food. The authors also assessed students' level of interest, degree of knowledge, and beliefs regarding the topic. Only epistemological level was predictive of the quality of the concluding paragraph the student produced. Only students in the highest epistemological group were likely to undertake any sort of reconciliation of the two positions, even the minimal one of suggesting that more information was needed. Students at the lower epistemological levels were likely to refer to only one position or to simply consecutively list the two contrasting positions in their summary.

Kuhn (2005; Kuhn & Park, in press) has gone on to predict that advancement in epistemological understanding supports the development of intellectual values, specifically the commitment to intellectual discussion and debate as the soundest basis for choosing between competing claims and resolving conflicts. Across cultural and subcultural groups of children and parents, level of epistemological understanding was (inversely) related to endorsement of items like this one:

> Many social issues, like the death penalty, gun control, or medical care, are pretty much matters of personal opinion, and there is no basis for saying that one person's opinion is any better than another's. So there's not much point in people having discussions about these kinds of issues.

In sum, after years of relative orphan status, the study of epistemological understanding has undergone a surge of attention and interest, prompted by Hofer and Pintrich's (1997) review, and the indications are that this attention is well deserved. The child's or adolescent's understanding of the intellectual activities of thinking and knowing is not an isolated epiphenomenon of interest only in a philosophical vein. To the contrary, it may provide a foundation that is critical in influencing what both adolescents and adults are disposed to do intellectually, as opposed to what they

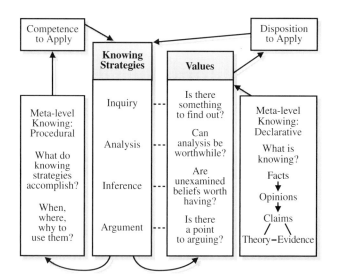

**Figure 22.3**   Components of knowing. *Source:* From "How Do People Know?" by D. Kuhn, 2001, *Psychological Science, 12,* pp. 1–8. Reprinted with permission.

are competent to do—a distinction that has itself begun to receive broader attention (Kuhn, 2001a; Perkins, Jay, & Tishman, 1993; Stanovich & West, 1999, 2000). A diagram proposing a summary of these relations appears in Figure 22.3 (from Kuhn, 2001a). The implication is that, by the second decade of life, disposition becomes a construct that cannot be ignored.

## CONCLUSIONS: LEARNING TO MANAGE ONE'S MIND

During the second decade of life, individuals continue to learn and to develop, in universal but also increasingly individual directions. The conceptual distinction between development and learning remains problematic, although the microgenetic method has made a contribution in highlighting their commonalities. In this chapter, we have taken the position that although the boundaries have become blurred, there remain real and significant distinctions between the two kinds of change. Development is generally progressive, irreversible, and generalizable, while learning need have none of these characteristics. The distinction has remained salient, for example, within our own research on inquiry, in which students will tell us that they have been finding out about what affects the speed of boats or risk of earthquakes, which indeed they have, while at the same time our microgenetic observations document that they have been developing skills that have to do with how one finds out about anything.

Where development and learning come together is in similarities in process, and hence the microgenetic method is useful in studying both. This is so largely because earlier conceptions of learning as formation of S-R bonds or strengthening of habits have been replaced by contemporary models in which learning is more likely to be defined as "change in understanding" (Schoenfeld, 1999). We thus need models more like those of development to characterize the process—that is, models that characterize change in terms of reorganization of patterns of thought, rather than strengthening of associations or habits.

What do we know about the nature of the change process? The phenomena reviewed in this chapter are consistent with a process in which multiple forms (of varying strengths and hence probabilities of occurrence) coexist over extended periods of time. Over time this distribution of probabilities shifts, as less effective forms are exercised less often and more effective ones more frequently (Kuhn, 1995, 2001b; Kuhn et al., 1995; Siegler, 2000; Chapter 11, this *Handbook,* this volume). Although new forms do emerge, first emergence rarely indicates the beginning of consistent usage, and the majority of change is of this shifting-frequency variety.

Two other features of this change process are of particular significance during the years of transition from childhood to adulthood. One is the fact that exercise (of existing forms) may be a sufficient condition for change (Kuhn, 1995). An implication, which we return to, is that adolescents are likely to get even better at what they are already good at, thus increasing the range and diversity of developmental pathways. The other is the importance of abandoning old, less effective forms, a challenge that in many cases exceeds that of adopting new, more effective ones. Interestingly, in a psychotherapeutic context, when a client finally abandons a self-limiting behavior, we do not hesitate to regard this event as an instance of positive change. In the case of cognitive development, however, we tend to focus only on attainment of new forms as markers of progressive change.

Finally, of greatest relevance in the present context is any age-related change that may occur in the change process itself. Evidence we have examined in this chapter suggests that as children enter their second decade, an increasingly strong executive may begin to develop. This executive assumes a role of monitoring and managing the deployment of cognitive resources as a function of task demands. As a result, cognitive functioning, and learning itself, become more effective (Kuhn & Pease, in press).

Emergence and strengthening of this executive is arguably the single most important and consequential intellectual development to occur in the second decade of life. Although he largely did not address its significance beyond the narrow confines of logic, in this respect we must grant that Piaget was on the right track in pointing to "thinking about one's own thought" as the major cognitive advance of the adolescent years. Today we are more likely to refer to metacognition or executive function as nascent functions in the early years that have the potential to come to full flower in the second decade, although they by no means always do so.

Broadly speaking, we know, young adolescents begin to acquire much more control over their activities and lives than they experienced as children. Hence, they have more discretion over how and where their cognitive resources will be deployed. Modern culture has introduced them to the art of dividing attention among multiple kinds of input. The executive thus fills a much needed role in determining how that attention will be allocated.

The developing executive also affords increasing ability to inhibit initial responses (generated by the experiential component in the dual-process model) and to process further, when one judges doing so to be worth the effort. And finally, and critically, it affords a level of metacognitive awareness that makes it possible to temporarily "bracket" the perspective dictated by one's own beliefs or understanding, in order to extract decontextualized representations, disembedded from a particular context, and to determine their implications. Without this skill, deductive, inductive, and argumentive reasoning are all severely impaired.

A stronger executive implies that development is increasingly governed from the "top down." This is not to say that most adults, as well as children and teens, don't apply "bottom-up" habitual patterns of thinking and behaving much of the time. But during the second decade of life young people, we have claimed, increasingly develop the potential to manage and deploy their cognitive resources in consciously controlled and purposefully chosen ways. A major implication is that disposition—to do or not to do x or y—becomes increasingly important (Kuhn, 2001a; Perkins, Jay, & Tishman, 1993; Stanovich & West, 1997, 1998, 2000). And disposition is governed by more than the competence to execute procedures. For these reasons, we have emphasized the larger picture that includes meta-level *understanding* of strategies—what they do or do not buy one—in relation to task *goals,* as well as *values* as a critical link mediating understanding and disposition. This larger structure presents a considerably more complex picture of what it is that needs to develop. Unsurprisingly, no simple change mechanism exists that can assume the entire explanatory burden.

**Early Adolescence as a Second Critical Period**

Stronger executive control of intellectual processes, we have suggested, differentiates the second decade of life from the first. Another difference is the extent and range of individual variability. In the second decade, individual variation becomes much more pronounced. All children within the normal intellectual range can be counted on to have exhibited certain universal developmental progressions in their thinking by age ten. They will also have learned a great deal about the world, much of it universally shared; many, however, will also have acquired expertise within domains of individual interest, although even here there are certain asymptotes—10-year-olds very rarely master calculus or advanced physics.

After the first decade of life, however, development along universal pathways, as we have seen, does not continue to the most advanced levels for everyone. Many adults cease to show any development beyond the level achieved by the typical early adolescent. Variation in positions along developmental pathways becomes pronounced. In addition, within specific content domains the range and depth of individually acquired expertise becomes much greater than it was in childhood. The processes involved in learning in "core domains," which all people encounter, and "noncore domains," which only some individuals choose to explore, may nonetheless be the same (Gelman, 2002).

How should we explain this heightened variability, and what are its implications? One level of explanation lies in the brain. Early adolescence, we noted, is a second developmental period during which a sequence of overproduction and pruning of neuronal connections occurs. This pruning of unused connections is guided by the activities in which the young teen engages. Both brain and behavior, then, together begin to become more specialized. To this evolution we add teens' increasing freedom and personal control—on the one hand in managing and deploying their intellectual resources to accomplish a task, and, on the other, more broadly, in choosing the activities in which they will invest themselves and in managing their lives.

As we have noted, simply through concentrated engagement in the activities they choose, adolescents get even better at what they are already good at, thus increasing the range and diversity of individual pathways. By early adolescence, individuals are indeed producers of their own development (Lerner, 2002). One consequence of these choices is an increasingly firm sense of personal identity—"this is who I am"—and, particularly, "this is what I'm good at" (and its even more potent complement, "this is what I'm no good at"). Evidence suggests that what happens at this age may be as influential as what happens in the first years of life (Feinstein & Bynner, 2004). Potential attainment in both core and noncore domains—in both universal and individual directions—can be encouraged and supported or left to wither, with enormously disparate results.

As we suggested in the section on epistemological understanding, during this second critical period it is disposition, as much or more than competence, that ought to be the focus of those concerned with supporting adolescents' intellectual development. To a greater extent than children, teens attribute meaning and value (both positive and negative) to what they do and draw on this meaning to define a self. Positively valued activities lead to behavioral investment which leads to greater expertise and hence greater valuing, in a circular process that has taken hold by early adolescence. The selfless curiosity and exploration characteristic of the early childhood critical period have likely gone underground and are difficult to detect. An implication is that the valuing of intellectual engagement can certainly be supported by those who work with young adolescents, but better results can be expected to the extent the way has been laid by activities involving genuine intellectual engagement in the years leading up to the second decade (Kuhn, 2005).

**Understanding Development by Studying Both Origins and Endpoints**

What are the implications for those seeking to investigate intellectual development during the second decade of life? One that follows fairly directly from what has just been said is the need to conduct more studies of adolescent cognition in the situated contexts of the activities in which teens choose to invest their intellectual resources. We are certainly taking a risk in drawing conclusions from investigations confined to artificial problems, constructed for research purposes, that bear no clear relation to the kinds of thinking that adolescents do in their daily lives. At the same time, the ability to decontextualize—to extract a generalized representation distinct from its specific context—remains a critical developmental achievement that needs to be studied further, especially across different reasoning contexts.

The emphasis we have placed on disposition, in addition to competence, suggests the importance of continued study of mechanism. We are dealing with a decade of life in which not everything that has the potential to develop does. Yet, continued development is more likely in this second decade than in the decades thereafter. The "good enough" intellectual environment that suffices to support the basic transitions characteristic of childhood cognitive development is apparently not good enough to support universal attainment of the cognitive capabilities that have the potential to develop during the second decade of life. The implications are strong ones in terms of both social policy and research. With respect to policy, investment of resources may have dividends at this life stage greater than at any other. With respect to research, the need to understand mechanism is, at this level, arguably even more urgent. Developmental research has a fundamental role to play in identifying developmental pathways. But its role is equally critical in identifying the factors that make this development more likely to occur.

We noted early in this chapter that the current focus in cognitive development research is on earliest origins in the first years of life. In time, the pendulum may well swing back toward greater interest in older children and adolescents and what they have to tell us about development. Diamond and Kirkham (2005), noting that early modes of responding are not outgrown or discarded but rather need to be overcome and managed, assert that we need to study the extremes of early childhood to fully understand adults. Arguably, the reverse is fully as true. We need to study its entire path and endpoint—to know where it's headed—in order to fully understand the significance of an early form. Indeed, that is exactly what developmental analysis is all about. We hope here to have illustrated to readers that it can be worthwhile to look beyond the earliest years in seeking to understand the what and how of cognitive development.

## REFERENCES

Ahn, W., Kalish, C., Medin, D., & Gelman, S. (1995). The role of covariation versus mechanism information in causal attribution. *Cognition, 54,* 299–352.

Amsel, E., & Brock, S. (1996). Developmental changes in children's evaluation of evidence. *Cognitive Development, 11,* 523–550.

Anderson, R., Nguyen-Jahiel, K., McNurlen, B., Archodidou, A., Kim, S., Reznitskaya, A., et al. (2001). The snowball phenomenon: Spread of ways of talking and ways of thinking across groups of children. *Cognition and Instruction, 19*(1), 1–46.

Arkes, H., & Harkness, A. (1983). Estimates of contingency between two dichotomous variables. *Journal of Experimental Psychology: General, 112,* 117–135.

Barrouillet, P., Markovits, H., & Quinn, S. (2001). Developmental and content effects in reasoning with causal conditionals. *Journal of Experimental Child Psychology, 81,* 235–248.

Bereby-Meyer, Y., Assor, A., & Katz, I. (2004). Children's choice strategies: The effects of age and task demands. *Cognitive Development, 19,* 127–146.

Beyth-Marom, R., Fischhoff, B., Jacobs, M., & Furby, L. (1991). Teaching decision making to adolescents: A critical review. In J. Baron (Ed.), *Teaching decision making to adolescents* (pp. 19–60). Hillsdale, NJ: Erlbaum.

Billig, M. (1987). *Arguing and thinking: A rhetorical approach to social psychology.* Cambridge, England: Cambridge University Press.

Bjorklund, D., & Harnishfeger, K. (1990). The resources construct in cognitive development: Diverse sources of evidence and a theory of inefficient inhibition. *Developmental Review, 10,* 48–71.

Braine, M. (1990). The "natural logic" approach to reasoning. In W. Overton (Ed.), *Reasoning, necessity, and logic: Developmental perspectives* (pp. 133–157). Hillsdale, NJ: Erlbaum.

Braine, M., & Rumain, B. (1983). Logical reasoning. In J. Flavell & E. Markman (Eds.), *Handbook of child psychology: Vol. 3. Cognitive development* (4th ed.). New York: Wiley.

Brem, S., & Rips, L. (2000). Explanation and evidence in informal argument. *Cognitive Science, 24,* 573–604.

Capon, N., & Kuhn, D. (1980). A developmental study of consumer information-processing strategies. *Journal of Consumer Research, 7*(3), 225–233.

Carey, S. (1985). Are children fundamentally different kinds of thinkers and learners than adults. In S. Chipman, J. Segal, & R. Glaser (Eds.), *Thinking and learning skills* (Vol. 2). Hillsdale, NJ: Erlbaum.

Carey, S., & Smith, C. (1993). On understanding the nature of scientific knowledge. *Educational Psychologist, 28,* 235–251.

Case, R. (1974). Structures and strictures: Some functional limitations on the course of cognitive growth. *Cognitive Psychology, 6,* 544–573.

Case, R. (1992). *The mind's staircase: Exploring the conceptual underpinnings of children's thought and knowledge.* Hillsdale, NJ: Erlbaum.

Case, R. (1998). The development of conceptual structures. In W. Damon (Editor-in-Chief) & D. Kuhn & R. Siegler (Vol. Eds.), *Handbook of child psychology: Vol. 2. Cognition, perception, and language* (5th ed., pp. 745–800). New York: Wiley.

Case, R., Kurland, D., & Goldberg, J. (1982). Operational efficiency and the growth of short-term memory span. *Journal of Experimental Child Psychology, 33*(3), 386–404.

Case, R., & Okamoto, Y. (1996). The role of central conceptual structures in the development of children's thought. *Monographs of the Society for Research in Child Development, 61*(Whole No. 246).

Chandler, M., & Lalonde, C. (2003, April). *Representational diversity redux.* Paper presented at the biennial conference of the Society for Research in Child Development, Tampa, FL.

Chen, Z., & Klahr, D. (1999). All other things being equal: Acquisition and transfer of the control of variables strategy. *Child Development, 70*(5), 1098–1120.

Cheng, P. (1997). From covariation to causation: A causal power theory. *Psychological Review, 104*(2), 367–405.

Cheng, P., & Holyoak, K. (1985). Pragmatic reasoning schemas. *Cognitive Psychology, 17*(4), 391–416.

Cheng, P., & Novick, L. (1992). Covariation in natural causal induction. *Psychological Review, 99,* 365–382.

Chinn, C., & Brewer, W. (2001). Models of data: A theory of how people evaluate data. *Cognition and Instruction, 19,* 323–393.

Chinn, C., & Malhotra, B. (2001). Epistemologically authentic scientific reasoning. In K. Crowley & C. Schunn (Eds.), *Designing for science: Implications from everyday, classroom, and professional settings* (pp. 351–392). Mahwah, NJ: Erlbaum.

Cowan, N. (1997). The development of working memory. In N. Cowan (Ed.), *The development of memory in childhood.* East Sussex, England: Psychology Press.

Davidson, D. (1995). The representativeness heuristic and the conjunction fallacy in children's decision-making. *Merrill-Palmer Quarterly, 41,* 328–346.

Demetriou, A., Christou, C., Spanoudis, G., & Platsidou, M. (2002). The development of mental processing: Efficiency, working memory, and thinking. *Monographs of the Society for Research in Child Development, 67*(Serial No. 268).

Demetriou, A., Efklides, A., & Platsidou, M. (1993). The architecture and dynamics of developing mind: Experiential structuralism as a frame for unifying cognitive developmental theories. *Monographs of the Society for Research in Child Development, 58*(5/6, Serial No. 234).

Diamond, A., & Kirkham, N. (2005). Not quite as grown-up as we like to think: Parallels between cognition in childhood and adulthood. *Psychological Science, 16,* 291–297.

Dias, M., & Harris, P. (1988). The effect of make-believe play on deductive reasoning. *British Journal of Developmental Psychology, 6,* 207–221.

Dixon, J., & Moore, C. (1996). The developmental role of intuitive principles in choosing mathematical strategies. *Developmental Psychology, 32,* 241–253.

Dixon, J., & Tuccillo, F. (2001). Generating initial models for reasoning. *Journal of Experimental Child Psychology, 78,* 178–212.

Elkind, D. (1994). *A sympathetic understanding of the child: Birth to sixteen.* Boston: Allyn & Bacon.

Evans, J., St. (1984). Heuristic and analytic processes in reasoning. *British Journal of Psychology, 75,* 451–468.

Evans, J., St. (2002). Logic and human reasoning: An assessment of the deduction paradigm. *Psychological Bulletin, 128*(6), 978–996.

Fay, A., & Klahr, D. (1996). Knowing about guessing and guessing about knowing: Preschoolers' understanding of indeterminacy. *Child Development, 67*(2), 689–716.

Feinstein, L., & Bynner, J. (2004). The importance of cognitive development in middle childhood for adulthood socioeconomic status, mental health, and problem behavior. *Child Development, 75,* 1329–1339.

Felton, M. (2004). The development of discourse strategies in adolescent argumentation. *Cognitive Development, 19,* 35–52.

Felton, M., & Kuhn, D. (2001). The development of argumentive discourse skills. *Discourse Processes, 32,* 135–153.

Fischer, K., & Bidell, T. (1991). Constraining nativist inferences about cognitive capacities. In S. Carey & R. Gelman (Eds.), *The epigenesis of mind: Essays on biology and cognition* (pp. 199–235). Hillsdale, NJ: Erlbaum.

Foltz, C., Overton, W., & Ricco, R. (1995). Proof construction: Adolescent development from inductive to deductive problem-solving strategies. *Journal of Experimental Child Psychology, 59,* 179–195.

Gathercole, S., Pickering, S., Ambridge, B., & Wearing, H. (2004). The structure of working memory from 4 to 15 years of age. *Developmental Psychology, 40*(2), 177–190.

Gelman, R. (2002). Cognitive development. In H. Pashler & D. Medin (Eds.), *Stevens' handbook of experimental psychology* (3rd ed., Vol. 2). Hoboken, NJ: Wiley.

Giedd, J., Blumenthal, J., Jeffries, N., Castellanos, F., Lui, H., Zijdenbos, A., et al. (1999). Brain development during childhood and adolescence: A longitudinal MRI study. *Nature Neuroscience, 2,* 861–863.

Glassner, A., Weinstock, M., & Neuman, Y. (2005). Pupils' evaluation and generation of evidence and explanation in argumentation. *British Journal of Educational Psychology, 75,* 105–118.

Gopnik, A., Meltzoff, A., & Kuhl, P. (1999). *The scientist in the crib: Minds, brains, and how children learn.* New York: HarperCollins.

Graff, G. (2003). *Clueless in academe: How schooling obscures the life of the mind.* New Haven, CT: Yale University Press.

Hagen, J., & Hale, G. (1973). The development of attention in children. In A. Pick (Ed.), *Minnesota Symposium on Child Psychology* (Vol. 7, pp. 117–139). Minneapolis: University of Minnesota Press.

Halford, G. S., Wilson, W. H., & Phillips, S. (1998). Processing capacity defined by relational complexity: Implications for comparative, developmental, and cognitive psychology. *Behavioral and Brain Sciences, 21,* 803–864.

Handley, S., Capon, A., Beveridge, M., Dennis, I., & Evans, J. (2004). Working memory, inhibitory control and the development of children's reasoning. *Thinking and Reasoning, 10,* 175–196.

Harnishfeger, K. (1995). The development of cognitive inhibition: Theories, definition, and research evidence. In F. Dempster & C. Brainerd (Eds.), *Interference and inhibition in cognition.* San Diego, CA: Academic Press.

Harnishfeger, K., & Bjorklund, D. (1993). The ontogeny of inhibition mechanisms: A renewed approach to cognitive development. In M. Howe & R. Pasnak (Eds.), *Emerging themes in cognitive development: Vol. 1. Foundations* (pp. 28–49). New York: Springer-Verlag.

Hawkins, J., Pea, R., Glick, J., & Scribner, S. (1984). Merds that laugh don't like mushrooms: Evidence for deductive reasoning by preschoolers. *Developmental Psychology, 20*(4), 584–594.

Hofer, B., & Pintrich, P. (1997). The development of epistemological theories: Beliefs about knowledge and knowing and their relation to learning. *Review of Educational Research, 67,* 88–140.

Hofer, B., & Pintrich, P. (2002). *Epistemology: The psychology of beliefs about knowledge and knowing.* Mahwah, NJ: Erlbaum.

Inhelder, B., & Piaget, J. (1958). *The development of logical thinking from childhood to adolescence.* New York: Basic Books.

Jacobs, J., & Potenza, M. (1991). The use of judgment heuristics to make social and object decisions: A developmental perspective. *Child Development, 62,* 166–178.

Janis, J., & Klaczynski, P. (2002). The development of judgment and decision making during childhood and adolescence. *Current Directions in Psychological Science, 11*(4), 145–149.

Johnson-Laird, P. (1983). *Mental models.* Cambridge, England: Cambridge University Press.

Kahneman, D., & Tversky, A. (1996). On the reality of cognitive illusions. *Psychological Review, 103,* 582–591.

Kail, R. (1991). Development of processing speed in childhood and adolescence. In R. Hayne (Ed.), *Advances in child development and behavior* (Vol. 23). San Diego, CA: Academic Press.

Kail, R. (1993). Processing time decreases globally at an exponential rate during childhood and adolescence. *Journal of Experimental Child Psychology, 56,* 254–265.

Kail, R. (2002). Developmental change in proactive interference. *Child Development, 73*(6), 1703–1714.

Kardash, C., & Scholes, R. (1996). Effects of pre-existing beliefs, epistemological beliefs, and need for cognition on interpretation of controversial issues. *Journal of Educational Psychology, 88,* 260–271.

Keating, D. (1980). Thinking processes in adolescence. In J. Adelson (Ed.), *Handbook of adolescent psychology* (pp. 211–246). New York: Wiley.

Keating, D. (2004). Cognitive and brain development. In R. Lerner & L. Steinberg (Eds.), *Handbook of adolescent psychology* (pp. 45–84). Chichester, England: Wiley.

Keil, F. (1991). The emergence of theoretical beliefs as constraints on concepts. In S. Carey & R. Gelman (Eds.), *The epigenesis of mind: Essays on biology and cognition* (pp. 237–256). Hillsdale, NJ: Erlbaum.

Keil, F. (1998). Cognitive science and the origins of thought and knowledge. In W. Damon (Editor-in-Chief) & R. Lerner (Vol. Ed.), *Handbook of child psychology: Vol. 1. Theoretical models of human development* (5th ed., pp. 341–413). New York: Wiley.

Keselman, A. (2003). Supporting inquiry learning by promoting normative understanding of multivariable causality. *Journal of Research in Science Teaching, 40*(9), 898–921.

King, P., & Kitchener, K. (1994). *Developing reflective judgment.* San Francisco: Jossey-Bass.

Klaczynski, P. (2000). Motivated scientific reasoning biases, epistemological beliefs, and theory polarization: A two-process approach to adolescent cognition. *Child Development, 71*(5), 1347–1366.

Klaczynski, P. (2001a). Framing effects on adolescent task representations, analytic and heuristic processing, and decision making: Implications for the normative-descriptive gap. *Journal of Applied Developmental Psychology, 22,* 289–309.

Klaczynski, P. (2001b). The influence of analytic and heuristic processing on adolescent reasoning and decision making. *Child Development, 72,* 844–861.

Klaczynski, P. (2004). A dual-process model of adolescent development: Implications for decision making, reasoning, and identity. In R. Kail (Ed.), *Advances in child development and behavior* (Vol. 31). San Diego, CA: Academic Press.

Klaczynski, P. (2005). Metacognition and cognitive variability: A two-process model of decision making and its development. In J. Jacobs & P. Klaczynski (Eds.), *The development of decision making: Cognitive, sociocultural, and legal perspectives.* Mahwah, NJ: Erlbaum.

Klaczynski, P., & Cottrell, J. (2004). A dual-processs approach to cognitive development: The case of children's understanding of sunk cost decisions. *Thinking and Reasoning, 10,* 147–174.

Klaczynski, P. A., & Narasimham, G. (1998). Representations as mediators of adolescent deductive reasoning. *Developmental Psychology, 5,* 865–881.

Klaczynski, P., Schuneman, M., & Daniel, D. (2004). Theories of conditional reasoning: A developmental examination of competing hypotheses. *Developmental Psychology, 40,* 559–571.

Klahr, D. (2000). *Exploring science: The cognition and development of discovery processes.* Cambridge, MA: MIT Press.

Klahr, D., Fay, A., & Dunbar, K. (1993). Heuristics for scientific experimentation: A developmental study. *Cognitive Psychology, 25*(1), 111–146.

Klahr, D., & Nigam, M. (2004). The equivalence of learning paths in early science instruction: Effects of direct instruction and discovery learning. *Psychological Science, 15*(10), 661–667.

Knudson, R. (1992). Analysis of argumentative writing at two grade levels. *Journal of Educational Research, 85,* 169–179.

Kokis, J., Macpherson, R., Toplak, M., West, R., & Stanovich, K. (2002). Heuristic and analytic processing: Age trends and associations with cognitive ability and cognitive styles. *Journal of Experimental Child Psychology, 83*(1), 26–52.

Koslowski, B. (1996). *Theory and evidence: The development of scientific reasoning.* Cambridge, MA: MIT Press.

Kuhn, D. (1977). Conditional reasoning in children. *Developmental Psychology, 13*(4), 342–353.

Kuhn, D. (1989). Children and adults as intuitive scientists. *Psychological Review, 96,* 674–689.

Kuhn, D. (1991). *The skills of argument.* Cambridge, England: Cambridge University Press.

Kuhn, D. (1993). Science as argument: Implications for teaching and learning scientific thinking. *Science Education, 77*(3), 319–337.

Kuhn, D. (1995). Microgenetic study of change: What has it told us? *Psychological Science, 6,* 133–139.

Kuhn, D. (1996). Is good thinking scientific thinking. In D. Olson & N. Torrance (Eds.), *Modes of thought: Explorations in culture and cognition* (pp. 261–281). New York: Cambridge University Press.

Kuhn, D. (1999a). Adolescent thought processes. In A. Kazdin (Ed.), *Encyclopedia of psychology* (pp. 52–59). New York: American Psychological Association.

Kuhn, D. (1999b). Metacognitive development. In L. Balter & C. Tamis-LeMonda (Eds.), *Child psychology: A handbook of contemporary issues* (pp. 259–286). Philadelphia: Psychology Press.

Kuhn, D. (2001a). How do people know? *Psychological Science, 12,* 1–8.

Kuhn, D. (2001b). Why development does (and doesn't) occur: Evidence from the domain of inductive reasoning. In R. Siegler & J. McClelland (Eds.), *Mechanisms of cognitive development: Neural and behavioral perspectives* (pp. 221–249). Mahwah, NJ: Erlbaum.

Kuhn, D. (2002). What is scientific thinking and how does it develop. In U. Goswami (Ed.), *Handbook of childhood cognitive development* (pp. 371–393). Oxford, England: Blackwell.

Kuhn, D. (2005). *Education for thinking.* Cambridge, MA: Harvard University Press.

Kuhn, D., Amsel, E., & O'Loughlin, M. (1988). *The development of scientific thinking skills.* San Diego, CA: Academic Press.

Kuhn, D., & Angelev, J. (1976). An experimental study of the development of formal operational thought. *Child Development, 47*(3), 697–706.

Kuhn, D., Black, J., Keselman, A., & Kaplan, D. (2000). The development of cognitive skills to support inquiry learning. *Cognition and Instruction, 18,* 495–523.

Kuhn, D., & Brannock, J. (1977). Development of the isolation of variables scheme in experimental and "natural experiment" contexts. *Developmental Psychology, 13*(1), 9–14.

Kuhn, D., Cheney, R., & Weinstock, M. (2000). The development of epistemological understanding. *Cognitive Development, 15,* 309–328.

Kuhn, D., & Dean, D. (2004). Connecting scientific reasoning and causal inference. *Journal of Cognition and Development, 5*(2), 261–288.

Kuhn, D., & Dean, D. (2005). Is developing scientific thinking all about learning to control variables? *Psychological Science, 16,* 866–870.

Kuhn, D., Garcia-Mila, M., Zohar, A., & Andersen, C. (1995). Strategies of knowledge acquisition. *Monographs of the Society for Research in Child Development, 60*(4, Serial No. 245).

Kuhn, D., Katz, J., & Dean, D. (2004). Developing reason. *Thinking and Reasoning, 10*(2), 197–219.

Kuhn, D., & Parks, S. (in press). Epistemological understanding and the development of intellectual values. *International Journal of Educational Research.*

Kuhn, D., & Pearsall, S. (2000). Developmental origins of scientific thinking. *Journal of Cognition and Development, 1,* 113–129.

Kuhn, D., & Pease, M. (in press). Do children and adults learn differently? *Journal of Cognition and Development.*

Kuhn, D., & Phelps, E. (1982). The development of problem-solving strategies. In H. Reese (Ed.), *Advances in child development and behavior* (Vol. 17, pp. 1–44). New York: Academic Press.

Kuhn, D., Phelps, E., & Walters, J. (1985). Correlational reasoning in an everyday context. *Journal of Applied Developmental Psychology, 6,* 85–97.

Kuhn, D., Schauble, L., & Garcia-Mila, M. (1992). Cross-domain development of scientific reasoning. *Cognition and Instruction, 9,* 285–332.

Kuhn, D., Shaw, V., & Felton, M. (1997). Effects of dyadic interaction on argumentive reasoning. *Cognition and Instruction, 15,* 287–315.

Kuhn, D., & Udell, W. (2003). The development of argument skills. *Child Development, 74*(5), 1245–1260.

Kuhn, D., & Udell, W. (in press). Coordinating own and other perspectives in argument. *Thinking & Reasoning.*

Lafon, P., Chasseigne, G., & Mullet, E. (2004). Functional learning among children, adolescents, and young adults. *Journal of Experimental Child Psychology, 88,* 334–347.

Leevers, H., & Harris, P. (1999). Transient and persisting effects of instruction on young children's syllogistic reasoning with incongruent and abstract premises. *Thinking and Reasoning, 5,* 145–174.

Lehrer, R., Schauble, L., & Petrosino, A. J. (2001). Reconsidering the role of experiment in science education. In K. Crowley, C. Schunn, & T. Okada (Eds.), *Designing for science: Implications from everyday, classroom, and professional settings* (pp. 251–277). Mahwah, NJ: Erlbaum.

Lerner, R. (2002). *Concepts and theories of human development* (3rd ed.). Mahwah, NJ: Erlbaum.

Levstik, L., & Barton, K. (2001). *Doing history: Investigating with children in elementary and middle schools.* Mahwah, NJ: Erlbaum.

Lien, Y., & Cheng, P. (2000). Distinguishing genuine from spurious causes: A coherence hypothesis. *Cognitive Psychology, 40,* 87–137.

Luna, B., Garver, K., Urban, T., Lazar, N., & Sweeney, J. (2004). Maturation of cognitive processes from late childhood to adulthood. *Child Development, 75*(5), 1357–1372.

Maccoby, E., & Hagen, J. (1965). Effects of distraction upon central versus incidental recall: Developmental trends. *Journal of Experimental Child Psychology, 2*(3), 280–289.

Markovits, H., & Barrouillet, P. (2002). The development of conditional reasoning: A mental model account. *Developmental Review, 22,* 5–36.

Markovits, H., & Vachon, R. (1989). Reasoning with contrary-to-fact propositions. *Journal of Experimental Child Psychology, 47*(3), 398–412.

Mason, L., & Boscolo, P. (2004). Role of epistemological understanding and interest in interpreting a controversy and in topic-specific belief change. *Contemporary Educational Psychology, 29*(2), 103–128.

Means, M., & Voss, J. (1996). Who reasons well? Two studies of informal reasoning among students of different grade, ability, and knowledge levels. *Cognition and Instruction, 14,* 139–178.

Metz, K. (2004). Children's understanding of scientific inquiry: Their conceptualization of uncertainty in investigations of their own design. *Cognition and Instruction, 22,* 219–290.

Morris, A. (2000). Development of logical reasoning: Children's ability to verbally explain the nature of the distinction between logical and nonlogical forms of argument. *Developmental Psychology, 36,* 741–758.

Morris, B., & Sloutsky, V. (2002). Children's solutions of logical versus empirical problems: What's missing and what develops? *Cognitive Development, 116,* 907–928.

Moshman, D. (1998). Cognitive development beyond childhood. In W. Damon (Editor-in-Chief), D. Kuhn & R. Siegler (Vol. Eds.), *Handbook of child psychology: Vol 2. Cognition, perception, and language* (5th ed., pp. 947–978). New York: Wiley.

Moshman, D. (2005). *Adolescent psychological development: Rationality, morality, and identity* (2nd ed.). Mahwah, NJ: Erlbaum.

Moshman, D., & Franks, B. A. (1986). Development of the concept of inferential validity. *Child Development, 57*(1), 153–165.

Moshman, D., & Geil, M. (1998). Collaborative reasoning: Evidence for collective rationality. *Thinking and Reasoning, 4,* 231–248.

National Research Council. (1996). *The national science education standards.* Washington, DC: National Academy Press.

Neimark, E. (1975). Intellectual development during adolescence. In F. Horowitz (Ed.), *Review of child development research* (Vol. 4, pp. 541–594). Chicago: Chicago University Press.

Neuman, Y. (2002). Go ahead, prove that God does not exist! On students' ability to deal with fallacious arguments. *Learning and Instruction, 13,* 367–380.

O'Brien, D. (1987). The development of conditional reasoning: An iffy proposition. In H. Reese (Ed.), *Advances in child development and behavior* (Vol. 20, pp. 61–90). Orlando, FL: Academic Press.

Pascual-Leone, J. (1970). A mathematical model for transition in Piaget's developmental stages. *Acta Psychologica, 32,* 301–345.

Penner, D., & Klahr, D. (1996). The interaction of domain-specific knowledge and domain-general discovery strategies: A study with sinking objects. *Child Development, 67*(6), 2709–2727.

Perkins, D. (1985). Postprimary education has little impact on informal reasoning. *Journal of Educational Psychology, 77*(5), 562–571.

Perkins, D., Jay, E., & Tishman, S. (1993). Beyond abilities: A dispositional theory of thinking. *Merrill-Palmer Quarterly, 39*, 1–21.

Perner, J. (1991). *Understanding the representational mind.* Cambridge, MA: MIT Press.

Perry, W. (1970). *Forms of intellectual and ethical development in the college years.* New York: Holt, Rinehart and Winston.

Pillow, B. (2002). Children's and adults' evaluation of the certainty of deductive inferences, inductive inferences, and guesses. *Child Development, 73*, 779–792.

Pontecorvo, C., & Girardet, H. (1993). Arguing and reasoning in understanding historical topics. *Cognition and Instruction, 11*(3/4), 365–395.

Reznitskaya, A., Anderson, R., McNurlen, B., Nguyen-Jahiel, K., Archodidou, A., & Kim, S. (2001). Influence of oral discussion on written argument. *Discourse Processes, 32*, 155–175.

Ruffman, T., Perner, J., Olson, D., & Doherty, M. (1993). Reflecting on scientific thinking: Children's understanding of the hypothesis-evidence relation. *Child Development, 64*, 1617–1636.

Rumain, B., Connell, J., & Braine, M. (1983). Conversational comprehension processes are responsible for reasoning fallacies in children as well as adults: It is not the biconditional. *Developmental Psychology, 19*(4), 471–481.

Schauble, L. (1990). Belief revision in children: The role of prior knowledge and strategies for generating evidence. *Journal of Experimental Child Psychology, 49*, 31–57.

Schauble, L. (1996). The development of scientific reasoning in knowledge-rich contexts. *Developmental Psychology, 32*, 102–119.

Schiff, A., & Knopf, I. (1985). The effect of task demands on attention allocation in children of different ages. *Child Development, 56*, 621–630.

Schoenfeld, A. (1999). Looking toward the 21st century: Challenges of educational theory and practice. *Educational Researcher, 28*, 4–14.

Schulz, L., & Gopnik, A. (2004). Causal learning across domains. *Developmental Psychology, 40*(2), 162–176.

Schustack, M., & Sternberg, R. (1981). Evaluation of evidence in causal inference. *Journal of Experimental Psychology: General, 110*, 101–120.

Sedlak, A., & Kurtz, S. (1981). A review of children's use of causal inference principles. *Child Development, 52*, 759–784.

Shafir, E., Simonson, I., & Tversky, A. (1993). Reason-based choice. *Cognition, 49*, 11–36.

Siegler, R. (2000). The rebirth of children's learning. *Child Development, 71*, 26–35.

Siegler, R., & Crowley, K. (1991). The microgenetic method: A direct means for studying cognitive development. *American Psychologist, 46*(6), 606–620.

Siegler, R. S., & Munakata, Y. (1993, Winter). Beyond the immaculate transition: Advances in the understanding of change. *Society for Research in Child Development Newsletter*, pp. 3, 10, 11, 13.

Simoneau, M., & Markovits, H. (2003). Reasoning with premises that are not empirically true: Evidence for the role of inhibition and retrieval. *Developmental Psychology, 39*(6), 964–975.

Sloman, S. (1996). The empirical case for two systems of reasoning. *Psychological Bulletin, 119*, 3–22.

Smith, C., Maclin, D., Houghton, C., & Hennessey, M. (2000). Sixth-grade students' epistemologies of science: The impact of school science experiences on epistemological development. *Cognition and Instruction, 18*, 349–422.

Sodian, B., Zaitchik, D., & Carey, S. (1991). Young children's differentiation of hypothetical beliefs from evidence. *Child Development, 62*, 753–766.

Stanovich, K., & West, R. (1997). Reasoning independently of prior belief and individual differences in actively open-minded thinking. *Journal of Educational Psychology, 89*, 342–357.

Stanovich, K., & West, R. (1998). Individual differences in rational thought. *Journal of Experimental Psychology: General, 127*, 161–188.

Stanovich, K., & West, R. (1999). Individual differences in reasoning and the heuristics and biases debate. In P. Ackerman & P. Kyllonen (Eds.), *Learning and individual differences: Process, trait, and content determinants* (pp. 389–411). Washington, DC: American Psychological Association.

Stanovich, K., & West, R. (2000). Individual differences in reasoning: Implications for the rationality debate? *Behavioral and Brain Sciences, 23*, 645–665.

Stroop, J. (1935). Studies of interference in serial verbal reactions. *Journal of Experimental Psychology, 18*, 643–662.

Swanson, H. L. (1999). What develops in working memory? A life span perspective. *Developmental Psychology, 35*(4), 986–1000.

Tipper, S., Bourque, T., Anderson, S., & Brehaut, J. (1989). Mechanisms of attention: A developmental study. *Journal of Experimental Child Psychology, 48*, 353–378.

Udell, W. (2004). *Enhancing urban girls' argumentive reasoning about personal and non-personal decisions.* Unpublished doctoral dissertation, Columbia University Teachers College, New York, NY.

Voss, J., & Means, M. (1991). Learning to reason via instruction in argumentation. *Learning and Instruction, 1*, 337–350.

Wainryb, C., Shaw, L., Langley, M., Cottam, K., & Lewis, R. (2004). Children's thinking about diversity of belief in the early school years: Judgments of relativism, tolerance, and disagreeing persons. *Child Development, 75*, 687–703.

Walton, D. N. (1989). Dialogue theory for critical thinking. *Argumentation, 3*, 169–184.

Wason, P. (1966). Reasoning. In B. Foss (Ed.), *New horizons in psychology* (Vol. 1, pp. 135–151). Hammondsworth, England: Penguin.

Weinstock, M., & Cronin, M. (2003). The everyday production of knowledge: Individual differences in epistemological understanding and juror-reasoning skill. *Applied Cognitive Psychology, 17*(2), 161–181.

Weinstock, M., Neuman, Y., & Tabak, I. (2004). Missing the point or missing the norms? Epistemological norms as predictors of students' ability to identify fallacious arguments. *Contemporary Educational Psychology, 29*, 77–94.

When no fact goes unchecked. (2004, October 31). *New York Times* [Week in review], Sec. 4, p. 5.

Wilkening, F., & Anderson, N. (1982). Comparison of two rule-assessment methodologies for studying cognitive development and knowledge structure. *Psychological Bulletin, 92*(1), 215–237.

Williams, B., Ponesse, J., Schacher, R., Logan, G., & Tannock, R. (1999). Development of inhibitory control across the life span. *Developmental Psychology, 35*, 205–213.

# Author Index

Aaron, F., 31
Abbot-Smith, K., 266
Abbott, S., 781
Abdala, C., 60, 61, 62, 66
Abdi, H., 150, 705
Abelson, R. P., 373, 378
Abercrombie, D., 77
Ablin, D. S., 395
Abney, S., 302
Abrahams, S., 35
Abrahamsen, A., 609
Abramov, I., 131, 146
Abramovitch, R., 821
Abramson, A. S., 73
Abroms, K. I., 927
Achard, B., 201
Achten, E., 31
Ackerman, P. L., 803
Ackerson, L. C., 907
Ackil, J. K., 398, 415
Acredolo, C., 350, 578
Acredolo, L., 338, 339, 340, 344, 345, 578, 743, 744
Acredolo, P., 760
Adachi, M., 893
Adams, A., 240, 289, 290, 752
Adams, B., 613, 885
Adams, C. D., 195
Adams, D. R., 84
Adams, G., 545
Adams, J. A., 196
Adams, M. J., 587
Adams, N., 781, 787
Adams, R. J., 123, 124
Adams, S., 407
Adelson, E. H., 890
Adi-Japha, E., 870
Adlam, A., 25, 380
Adlard, A., 68
Adleman, N., 31
Adler, S. A., 186
Adolph, K. E., 164, 165, 166, 172, 173, 174, 175, 176, 177, 178, 179, 180, 181, 189, 190, 191, 192, 193, 194, 195, 196, 198, 199, 200, 201, 436, 469, 474, 479, 480, 486, 487, 494, 496
Adolphs, R., 35, 38
Aebi, J., 758
Afflerbach, P., 526, 533, 537, 545
Aggarwal, J. K., 144
Aggleton, J. P., 35
Agre, P., 472
Agster, K. L., 25
Aguiar, A., 426

Ahmed, A., 449, 737, 743
Ahn, W., 705, 708, 722, 965
Aicardi, J., 26, 27
Aiello, R., 884
Ainsworth, M. D. S., 838
Aitken, K. J., 932
Aitsebaomo, A. P., 120
Aivano, S., 516
Aizawa, H., 10
Akhtar, N., 262, 265, 266, 270, 286, 306, 308, 311, 312, 380, 713, 714
Akiyama, M., 182
Akshoomoff, N. A., 32, 33
Albersheim, L., 838
Alberti, P. W., 67
Alberts, D. M., 758
Aldag, J. M., 19
Aleven, V. A. W. M. M., 498
Alexander, A. W., 531
Alexander, G., 25, 40
Alexander, J., 526, 907, 924
Alexander, K. R., 123
Alexander, M. P., 27
Alexander, P. A., 545
Alho, K., 73, 74
Alibali, M. W., 176, 195, 199, 342, 345, 346, 350, 351, 352, 353, 355, 357, 361, 363, 364, 427, 431, 470, 473, 474, 480, 481, 482, 483, 484, 485, 486, 489, 492, 493, 494, 495, 496, 498, 500, 501, 792, 793
Alland, A., 870, 880
Allen, C., 645
Allen, D., 116, 119, 123, 124
Allen, E., 722
Allen, G., 38, 758, 761
Allen, J., 83, 87, 115, 407, 843, 844
Allen, P., 61, 62, 65, 66, 67, 71
Allen, R., 343
Allen, S., 263
Allen, S. E. M., 273
Allen, S. W., 702
Allik, J., 73, 516
Allington, R., 542
Allison, P. D., 475, 476
Allison, T., 35, 37
Allmendinger, J., 939
Allopenna, P., 79, 91, 305, 317, 692
Almasi, J., 535, 537
Aloise-Young, P. A., 469, 470, 474, 480, 483, 487, 493, 494, 501
Altmann, G. T. M., 82, 568
Alvarado, M. C., 22, 24
Alvarez, E. D., 67

Alvarez-Buylla, A., 18
Amabile, T., 908, 912, 923
Amaral, D. G., 392
Amblard, B., 174, 178, 189
Ambridge, B., 758, 959
Ambrose, J., 38
Ames, E. W., 218, 219
Ames, L. B., 162, 165, 173, 176, 795, 797
Amiel-Tison, C., 77, 185, 301, 305
Amigues, R., 541
Ampene, E., 863
Amsel, E., 495, 497, 540, 965, 966, 968, 972, 979
Amsel, G., 228, 229, 230
Amso, D., 43, 181, 186, 202, 745
Amsterlaw, J., 470, 487, 491, 705, 708
Anati, E., 880
Anceschi, M. M., 182
Andersen, A. H., 36
Andersen, C., 542, 912, 921, 923, 962, 966, 969, 970, 973, 974, 979, 983, 987
Andersen, E. S., 345
Andersen, G. J., 128, 137
Andersen, R. W., 281
Anderson, A. K., 31
Anderson, A. W., 33, 36, 38
Anderson, C., 124, 470, 481, 483, 485, 489, 491, 492, 493, 494, 495, 496, 497, 498
Anderson, D. E., 200
Anderson, D. I., 164, 176, 178, 180, 191, 194, 195, 198, 200, 202, 617, 744, 745
Anderson, J. L., 82
Anderson, J. R., 196, 428, 429, 430, 437, 438, 444, 445, 446, 447, 448, 457, 521, 558, 617, 621, 800
Anderson, K. C., 910, 922, 923
Anderson, L. M., 538
Anderson, M., 292, 521
Anderson, N., 559, 596, 967
Anderson, P., 40
Anderson, R., 317, 542, 545, 980, 982
Anderson, S., 41, 116, 757, 766, 958
Anderson, T. H., 533
Anderson, V., 40, 536
Andersson, S. B., 880
Andrade, A., 908
Andreani, O. D., 931
Andreasen, G., 760
Andreasen, N. C., 909
Andre-Thomas, 168
Andrews, G., 559, 565, 575, 576, 583, 585, 588, 589, 598, 829
Andrews, S., 562, 705
Andruski, J. E., 80, 94

Angelev, J., 974
Angelillo, C., 661, 662
Angell, A. L., 525
Angelopoulos, M., 306
Anglin, J., 403
Angulo-Barroso, R., 170
Angulo-Kinzler, R. M., 169, 170
Anisfeld, M., 220
Ankrum, C., 123, 124
Anokhina, R., 625
Anooshian, A., 757
Anooshian, L. J., 757
Ansari, D., 750
Antell, S. E., 779, 781
Anthony, H. M., 538
Antinucci, F., 280
Antonucci, C., 786
Anzai, Y., 468, 469
Anzil, A. P., 8
Applebaum, M. I., 202
Arauz, R., 662
Araya, R., 503
Arbib, M. A., 433
Arcavi, A., 472
Archodidou, A., 542, 980, 982
Arduini, D., 182
Arehart, K. H., 60, 65, 66
Arendt, R. E., 117
Argyle, M., 336, 356
Ariel, M., 278
Ariel, R., 786
Ariew, A., 613
Ark, W. S., 31
Arkes, H., 967
Armand, F., 887
Armbruster, B. B., 533
Arnheim, R., 860, 862, 872, 873, 879, 880, 915,
    916, 918
Arnold, A., 907, 923
Arnold, D. S., 876
Arnold, K. D., 925
Aron, M., 169
Aronen, H. J., 33
Aronson, E., 197
Arsenio, W. F., 830, 831, 932
Arterberry, M., 111, 114, 120, 121, 127, 128,
    131, 132, 133, 137, 140, 143, 144, 148, 149,
    150, 152, 199, 244, 245, 704
Asarnow, J., 532
Asgari, M., 35
Ashburner, J., 17
Ashcraft, M. H., 475, 516, 779, 780, 795, 796
Ashizawa, K., 174
Ashmead, D. H., 60, 64, 69, 172, 186, 187
Aslin, R., 270, 435, 436
Aslin, R. M., 64
Aslin, R. N., 62, 64, 73, 75, 78, 79, 80, 81, 82, 83,
    85, 87, 88, 90, 91, 93, 94, 118, 125, 126, 130,
    131, 139, 146, 185, 226, 271, 301, 304, 305,
    314, 468, 469, 692, 710
Aslund, A., 622
Assaiante, C., 174, 178, 189
Assor, A., 976
Astington, J., 402, 823, 824, 826, 845, 846, 848,
    930
Astur, R. S., 35
Astuti, R., 664, 669, 724
Atanassova, M., 280
Atherton, C., 31

Atkinson, J., 44, 116, 118, 119, 120, 130
Atkinson, R. C., 515, 520
Atran, S., 613, 614, 619, 628, 638, 664, 668, 669,
    688, 715, 716, 720
Attermeier, S. M., 526
Au, M.-L., 880
Au, T. K., 312, 317, 705, 724
Auerbach, J., 382
Aujard, Y., 36
Aureli, F., 818
Aurenty, R., 178
Austin, G., 30, 41, 429, 701
Autgaerden, S., 168
Avan, P., 66
Avery, P., 89
Avis, J., 841, 842
Avison, M. J., 36
Avolio, A. M., 180, 189, 190, 193, 194, 195, 196,
    198, 199, 200
Avraamides, M. N., 761
Aydede, M., 624
Ayman-Nolley, S., 342, 361

Bacharach, V. R., 876
Bachem, A., 893
Bachevalier, J., 22, 24, 386, 417
Bachnan, H. J., 655
Backscheider, A., 715
Backus, B. T., 739
Badcock, D. R., 120
Baddeley, A., 26, 33, 291, 292, 520, 559, 765
Badenoch, M., 139, 140, 148, 149, 226
Badertscher, B., 889
Badgaiyan, R., 42
Baenninger, M., 764
Baer, D. M., 466
Baer, L., 696
Bagger-Sjoback, D., 66
Bahrick, L., 76, 148, 306, 308, 397, 414
Bai, D. L., 197, 198, 744
Bailenson, J. N., 614, 619
Baillargeon, R., 4, 215, 219, 222, 223, 227, 304,
    305, 306, 313, 315, 426, 428, 448, 497, 663,
    689, 700, 704, 744
Baillet, S., 74
Bailystok, E., 564
Bain, J. D., 559, 563, 565, 587, 588, 589
Baird, J. A., 234, 306, 692, 724, 814, 815
Bak, S. J., 537
Baker, C. L., 257
Baker, M., 302
Baker, R., 306, 563, 565
Baker, S., 537, 538
Baker, T. J., 197, 746
Bakermans-Kranenburg, M. J., 838
Baker-Ward, L., 406, 513, 517, 519
Balaban, M. T., 38, 306, 308, 309, 690, 715
Balakrishnan, K., 10
Baldwin, D. A., 234, 306, 384, 692, 697, 713,
    714, 723, 724, 814, 815, 818, 846
Baldwin, G., 263
Baldwin, J. M., 619
Bale, A. C., 237, 239
Bales, D., 303
Ball, D. W., 530
Ball, W., 129, 228
Balling, R., 7
Ballinger, R., 880
Balota, D., 29
Baltes, P. B., 470

Bamberger, J., 894, 895, 912, 918, 939
Band, G., 41
Bandi Rao, S., 270, 568
Bandura, A., 466, 909
Banerjee, M., 828
Bangert, A. S., 474, 477, 485, 495
Bangston, S. K., 382, 383, 390
Banks, M., 36, 114, 116, 117, 118, 120, 121, 122,
    123, 124, 616, 735, 738, 739
Barajas, J. J., 67
Barbee, A. H., 906, 907, 913
Barbieri, A., 531
Barbu-Roth, M. A., 164, 176, 178, 180, 191, 194,
    195, 198, 200, 202, 617, 744, 745
Barch, D., 41
Barclay, C. R., 516
Barden, R. C., 830
Bardy, B. G., 187
Barela, J. A., 197, 198
Barendsen, L., 935
Bargones, J. Y., 60, 61, 65, 66, 69, 71, 92
Barinaga, M., 9
Barlow, M., 286
Barna, J., 704
Barnard, P. H., 637, 645
Barnat, S. B., 383
Barndon, R., 31
Barnes, E., 860
Baron, J. B., 540
Baron-Cohen, S., 616, 704, 812, 837, 842, 843,
    844, 864, 968
Baroody, A. J., 585, 788, 789, 790
Barr, R., 25, 220, 234, 381, 382, 383, 384, 389
Barrash, J., 41
Barrett, K., 191, 744
Barrett, M., 261, 875, 876
Barrett, S. E., 705
Barrett, T., 197, 200, 202, 746
Barron, B., 76
Barron, F., 909
Barron, R. W., 531, 532
Barrouillet, P., 523, 576, 593, 594, 599, 960, 961
Barrow, H. G., 136
Barsalou, L., 309, 352, 626
Barsoum-Homsy, M., 611
Bartels, G. P., 740
Bartlett, D. L., 882
Bartlett, F. C., 373, 672
Bartlett, J. C., 889
Barto, A. G., 166, 177, 187
Barton, J. J., 35
Barton, K., 971
Barton, M., 262, 291, 713
Bartrip, J., 148
Bartsch, K., 448, 449, 451, 796, 799, 822, 823,
    825, 843, 850
Bartsch, U., 10
Bashore, T., 41
Basili, P. A., 541
Bassano, D., 312
Bassett, E. M., 870, 873
Bassok, M., 342, 497
Batchelder, E. O., 87
Batchelder, W. H., 638
Bates, E., 119, 152, 183, 201, 237, 241, 262, 263,
    265, 267, 268, 269, 275, 277, 282, 286, 289,
    290, 291, 301, 312, 316, 338, 391, 427, 430,
    433, 437, 499, 558, 616, 663, 664, 691, 700
Bates, J. E., 408
Bates, K. E., 14

Bateson, G., 675
Battaglia, J., 779
Batten, A., 875
Batterman-Faunce, J. M., 406
Batth, R., 12
Battro, A., 677
Bauer, H., 31
Bauer, J., 69, 470, 472, 473, 496
Bauer, P., 25, 220, 234, 240, 264, 379, 380, 381,
  382, 383, 384, 385, 386, 387, 388, 389, 390,
  391, 392, 394, 398, 399, 400, 401, 404, 405,
  406, 407, 408, 409, 412, 413, 414, 415, 417,
  524, 571
Bauer, R. H., 529, 530
Baughman, W. A., 908, 946
Baulac, M., 35
Baumann, A., 79, 81, 83, 86
Baumberger, T., 292, 312
Baumgartner, G., 130, 142
Bausano, M., 191
Bavelas, J. B., 352, 357
Bavelier, D., 15
Bayley, N., 163
Baylis, G. C., 149
Baylor, G. W., 429
Bazerman, C., 921, 924
Beabout, G. R., 933
Beach, D. H., 514, 515
Beach, D. R., 377
Beach, K., 649
Beach, R. W., 533
Beal, C. R., 519, 876
Beard, J. L., 392
Beard, R. L., 761
Beasley, D. S., 66
Beattie, G., 342, 356, 357, 363
Beauchaine, K. A., 60
Beauchaine, K. L., 60, 66
Beaumont, A., 876
Beaumont, E., 941
Bebko, J. M., 531
Bechtel, W., 609
Bechtold, A., 129
Beckel-Mitchener, A., 12
Becker, H., 912, 916, 919
Becker, J., 791, 792
Beckman, M. E., 89
Bédard, A., 8, 9
Bednar, J. A., 149, 241
Begun, D. R., 646
Behl-Chadha, G., 305
Behne, T., 644, 724, 821, 840
Behnke, E. D., 907
Behrend, D., 316
Behrens, H., 263, 289
Behrmann, M., 35
Beilin, H., 558, 864
Beishuizen, M., 791, 797
Bekken, K., 344
Bekoff, M., 645
Belanger, J., 312, 316, 318
Belanger, N. D., 230
Bell, B., 923
Bell, M. A., 31, 32, 180, 531, 763, 764
Bell, N., 497
Bell, P., 924
Bell, S. M., 838
Bell, T. S., 516
Bellanca, K. J., 195, 199
Bellgowan, P. S. F., 76

Bellinger, D., 30
Bellugi, U., 274, 291, 765
Belmont, J. C., 516
Belmont, J. M., 529
Belmonte-de-Abreu, P., 642
Belo, J., 880
Benbow, C. P., 761, 911, 913, 922, 923, 925
Benenson, J., 781
Benes, F., 12, 386, 399
Benhamou, S., 748
Benigni, L., 338
Bennett, D., 531
Bennett, P., 116, 117, 118, 120, 123, 124, 306
Bennett, R. T., 402, 827
Benney, C. J., 753
Bennis, W. G., 928, 929
Benoit, D., 838
Benoit, J., 611
Bensen, A. S., 133
Benson, J., 186, 187, 214, 216, 217, 219, 221,
  222, 223, 235, 239, 240, 374, 467
Benson, N. J., 531, 532
Benson, P. J., 148
Benson, R. R., 76
Benuzzi, F., 38
Benveniste, S., 318, 319
Beran, M. J., 789
Beran, M. M., 789
Berch, D., 361
Bereby-Meyer, Y., 976
Bereiter, C., 535, 538, 908, 923
Berenbaum, S. A., 763
Berg, D. N., 926, 928
Berg, K. M., 60, 64, 65, 69
Berg, W. K., 473
Berger, K. W., 356
Berger, S. E., 164, 166, 189, 192, 194, 195, 196,
  198, 199, 200, 201
Bergeson, T. R., 885
Bergman, J. L., 537
Berk, L. E., 167
Berkeley, G., 109, 111, 127, 140
Berkowitz, A., 34, 41
Berkowitz, S. J., 533
Berlim, M. T., 642
Berlin, B., 311
Berlin, L. J., 407, 408
Berlyne, D. E., 923
Berman, R., 263, 267
Bermejo, V., 786
Bernard, C., 37
Bernier, P. J., 8, 9
Berns, G., 29
Bernstein, E., 44
Bernstein, M., 922
Bernstein, N., 169, 187
Berntson, G. G., 589, 789
Berquin, P., 30
Berridge, D., 407, 876
Berridge, K. C., 171
Berry, J. W., 639, 677
Berthenthal, B. I., 139, 142, 144, 145, 164, 165,
  172, 173, 176, 177, 178, 180, 188, 191, 197,
  198, 224, 226, 244, 245, 360, 704, 737, 744
Berthier, N. E., 166, 177, 186, 187, 224, 737
Bertin, E., 133, 137
Bertoncini, J., 70, 72, 74, 77, 78, 79, 80, 83, 86,
  92, 301, 305, 611
Bertrand, J., 39, 291, 765
Best, C. T., 73, 74

Bettinardi, V., 15
Bettschen, D., 767
Bever, T., 87, 267, 311, 580, 581, 779
Beveridge, M., 963
Beyer, F. S., 875
Beylin, A., 8, 9
Beyth-Marom, R., 975
Bhatt, R., 31, 133, 137, 142, 236, 309, 380, 697
Bialystok, E., 622
Biancaniello, R., 181
Bibrose, S., 395
Bickerton, D., 641
Bidder, T. G., 893
Biddle, K. R., 34
Bidell, T., 956
Bidell, T. R., 435, 482, 483, 485, 493
Bidell, T. T., 217, 222, 224
Bieber, M. L., 122
Biederman, I., 136, 197
Biemiller, A., 528
Bienstock, S., 891
Bierschwale, D. T., 839
Bigelow, L. J., 363, 364
Bihrle, A., 291, 765
Bijeljac-Babic, R., 72, 74, 79, 83, 92
Bijou, S., 466
Billig, M., 979, 981
Binder, J. R., 76
Binet, A., 906
Binns, K. E., 70
Birch, E. E., 115, 130, 131
Bird, M., 535
Biringen, Z., 202
Birlen, D., 616
Biro, S., 619, 814
Bisanz, J., 788, 790, 797
Bisazza, A., 748
Bischoff-Grethe, A., 29
Bishop, D., 282, 283, 292
Bishop, J., 540
Biswas, A. K., 67
Bitterman, M. E., 590
Bixby, J. L., 10
Bjorklund, D., 374, 380, 406, 473, 474, 480,
  481, 482, 484, 491, 492, 493, 495, 496, 513,
  517, 524, 530, 558, 615, 637, 802, 958, 959,
  990
Blachowicz, C., 537
Black, A., 831
Black, J., 14, 17, 223, 428, 802, 967, 973, 974
Black, M. M., 516
Blackman, L. S., 529
Blades, M., 756, 760
Blair, E., 571, 670, 671, 707, 708
Blakemore, C., 70, 117
Blanchet, N., 690, 721
Blank, P., 867, 881
Blasey, C., 38
Blaut, J. M., 759
Blaye, A., 599
Blewitt, P., 572
Bloch, M. N., 662
Block, C. C., 535, 537, 542
Block, N., 618
Bloedel, S. L., 74
Blok, S. V., 668
Bloom, B., 908, 911, 920, 921, 922, 939
Bloom, F. E., 4, 14, 16
Bloom, L., 256, 261, 262, 265, 283, 284, 303,
  306, 311, 312

Bloom, P., 4, 299, 302, 304, 307, 311, 312, 526, 610, 614, 618, 629, 690, 700, 707, 708, 713, 714, 715, 781, 865

Blöte, A. W., 473, 474, 480, 483, 490, 493, 501, 791, 797

Blue, S., 85

Bluestein, N., 760

Blumberg, M. S., 199

Blumenthal, J., 12, 31, 34, 803, 957

Blumstein, S., 72

Bly, L., 188

Boag, C., 598

Bobb, K., 10

Boden, M., 816, 908, 911

Boesch, C., 644, 675, 676

Boesch, H., 644

Bogardus, E. S., 928

Bogartz, R. S., 222, 223, 224

Bogdahn, U., 16

Bogin, B., 660

Bogner, K., 542

Bohannon, N., 277

Bohn, O. S., 73

Boike, K., 64, 66, 92

Boisson, D., 750

Bojczyk, K. E., 172, 178, 180

Boker, S. M., 198

Boland, A. M., 405

Bolte, S., 38

Bombi, A. S., 874

Bond, B., 65

Bond, E., 868

Bonde, S., 9

Bone, R. A., 117

Bonfils, P., 66

Bongers, R. M., 200

Boniface, J., 25, 383, 389

Bonnar, L., 800

Boodoo, G., 906, 907

Book, C., 535

Boom, J., 598

Boone, K. B., 588

Booth, A. E., 144, 145, 306, 307, 308, 309, 310, 312, 314, 316, 317, 711

Booth, J. L., 793, 794, 802

Booth, J. R., 31, 32

Borchert, J., 122

Borchgrevink, H. M., 888

Borden, S. L., 532

Borgo, F., 616

Boring, E. G., 145

Borisy, A., 868

Borisy, G., 10

Borkowski, J. G., 512, 516, 521, 522, 523, 529, 544, 545

Bornstein, D., 935

Bornstein, M. H., 122, 144, 148, 149, 244, 245, 303, 312, 316, 694, 704, 846, 868, 879

Boroditsky, L., 312, 695

Bortfeld, H., 85, 88, 90

Borton, R., 225

Bos, C. S., 538

Bosacki, S., 848

Bosch, L., 78, 81, 305

Boscolo, P., 986

Boster, J., 704

Boswell, A. E., 64, 65, 69

Boswell, S. L., 866

Bothell, D., 428

Botkin, P. J., 926

Botkin, P. T., 811

Botvinick, M., 41

Bouchard, T. J., Jr., 906, 907, 913, 914

Boucher, J., 844

Boudreau, J. P., 164

Bouisset, S., 173

Bouman, M. A., 116

Bouquet, F., 76, 82, 93, 305

Bourcier, A., 229

Bourdieu, P., 912, 915, 919, 920, 925, 939, 940

Bourgeois, J.-P., 11, 34, 386, 399

Bourque, T., 958

Bousfield, W. A., 515

Bowden, D., 565

Bowen, E., 657

Bower, T. G., 76, 129, 221, 866

Bowerman, M., 256, 272, 273, 276, 281, 303, 311, 325, 495, 694, 695, 761

Bowman, E., 44

Bowman, S., 565, 566

Bow-Thomas, C. C., 785, 795, 796, 797

Boyer, P., 628

Boyes-Braem, P., 311

Boyle, F. M., 581

Boyle, P. A., 407

Boysen, S. T., 589, 643, 644, 664, 789

Braddick, O., 44, 116, 118, 119, 120, 130

Bradfield, A., 766

Bradley, M. M., 38

Bradmetz, J., 829, 830

Bradshaw, G., 168, 908, 911, 923

Braida, L. D., 888

Brainard, D. H., 116

Braine, M., 256, 262, 265, 267, 273, 277, 586, 595, 960, 961

Brainerd, C. J., 387, 389, 399, 400, 418, 573, 575, 576, 579, 589, 752, 786

Braisby, N., 583, 585, 708

Braithwaite, V. A., 764

Brakke, K. E., 644

Bramble, D. M., 642

Brand, J., 574

Brannock, J., 966

Brannon, E. M., 432, 568, 583, 584, 781, 782, 786, 787, 789, 803, 804

Bransford, J. D., 466, 468, 494, 513, 562, 621

Braswell, G. S., 484

Braten, I., 524

Braumgart, M. M., 926

Braumgart, R. G., 926

Braun, A., 66

Braun, I. E., 313

Braungart, J., 848

Braver, T., 40, 41, 437, 438, 449, 457

Bray, N. W., 66, 474, 475, 489, 493, 531

Breazeal, C., 613

Bredart, S., 318, 700

Bredberg, G., 60, 61, 66

Breedlove, D. E., 311

Breeze, K. W., 178

Bregman, A. S., 59

Brehaut, J., 958

Breinlinger, K., 136, 166, 222, 224, 428, 448, 617, 737, 780

Breiter, H. C., 31

Brem, S., 979

Bremner, J. G., 451, 743, 744, 745, 748, 751, 760, 875

Breniere, Y., 166, 172, 173, 174, 178, 179, 180

Brennan, C., 44

Brennan, P. A., 149

Brent, H., 15, 38, 150, 766

Brent, M. R., 83, 86, 88, 305, 311

Breslow, L., 586

Bresnan, J., 617

Bresson, C., 34

Bretherton, I., 201, 262, 289, 290, 291, 338, 409

Brewer, W., 597, 635, 923, 965

Brezner, A., 786

Brezsnyak, M., 29

Briars, D., 559, 785, 786, 791, 792, 797, 798, 800, 803

Briassoulis, G., 66

Bridger, W. H., 387

Bridges, A., 266

Bridson, A., 876

Bril, B., 166, 167, 172, 173, 174, 176, 178, 179, 180, 200

Briscoe, E., 620

Brittain, W. L., 870

Britton, B. K., 541

Brivanfou, A. H., 6

Brizzolara, D., 27

Broadbent, D. E., 515

Broaders, S., 361, 364

Brock, S., 965, 972

Brockbank, M., 814

Broks, P., 38

Bronner-Fraser, M., 7

Brook, C., 764

Brooks, A. S., 642

Brooks, L. R., 702

Brooks, M. R., 868

Brooks, P., 277, 288

Brooks, P. H., 760

Brooks, P. J., 273, 564

Brooks, R., 163, 306, 612, 613, 736

Brooks, T. E. W., 123

Brooks, V., 863

Brooks-Gunn, J., 407

Brose, K., 10

Broughton, J. M., 129

Brower, R., 916, 919

Brown, A., 201, 264, 630

Brown, A. L., 430, 466, 468, 494, 495, 513, 518, 519, 529, 533, 534, 536, 541, 543, 560, 621, 720, 751, 906

Brown, A. M., 66, 117, 118, 120, 123, 124

Brown, C., 89, 345, 559

Brown, D. A., 415

Brown, E., 79, 135, 139, 140, 141, 145, 146, 148, 149, 152, 226

Brown, J., 39, 407, 765

Brown, L. G., 537

Brown, L. Y., 7

Brown, M., 7, 9, 840

Brown, N., 314, 406

Brown, R., 85, 256, 265, 277, 279, 301, 302, 307, 414, 535, 621

Brown, S., 882

Brown, S. A., 7

Brown, S. C., 530

Brown, S. D., 74

Brown, T., 415

Brown, W. A., 893

Brownell, C. A., 821

Brownell, W. A., 778

Bruce, C., 40

Bruce, D., 513

Bruce, K., 191
Bruce, V., 148
Bruchkowsky, M., 927, 928
Brudkowska, J., 8
Brueckner, L., 744
Brumley, M. R., 169
Bruner, J., 267, 429, 535, 541, 578, 617, 623,
    624, 653, 660, 675, 688, 689, 701, 811, 817,
    864, 915, 940
Brunswik, E., 142
Brush, D., 697
Bruyer, R., 37
Bryant, G. A., 882
Bryant, P., 558, 578, 580, 581, 586, 587, 588,
    657, 743, 826
Bryden, M. P., 763, 764
Bryk, A., 303
Buchman, D. D., 764
Buchsbaum, M. S., 501
Buckingham, D., 438, 596
Buckner, J. P., 408
Buckner, R., 28, 375
Buczowska, E., 280
Budreau, D. R., 147
Budwig, N., 273
Buffalo, E. A., 23, 24
Buhler, C., xii
Buhler, K., 896
Buhrmann, K., 767
Buitelaar, J. K., 12
Bulen, J. C., 60, 65
Bull, D., 64, 78, 886
Bullemer, P., 28
Bullier, J., 36
Bullinger, A., 69
Bullock, A., 927, 928
Bullock, M., 784, 786, 867
Bunce, D. M., 541
Bunch, K. M., 565
Bundy, D. A., 913
Bundy, R. S., 75
Bunge, S., 41
Bunger, A., 321, 322
Burack, J. A., 563
Burch, M., 539, 540, 797, 799
Burch, M. C., 303
Burch, M. M., 234, 391, 400, 404, 405, 408
    409, 413
Bures, J., 386
Burger-Judisch, L. M., 74
Burgess, N., 35, 738
Burgess, P., 42
Burghardt, G. M., 645
Burgund, E. D., 741
Burkell, J., 538
Burnett, C. N., 178
Burnett, R. C., 668
Burnham, D., 77, 80
Burns, E. M., 60, 61, 65, 66
Burns, J. M., 909, 910, 925, 927, 928, 938
Burns, T., 107, 318
Burnside, L. H., 165
Burock, M., 28
Burr, D. C., 124
Burridge, K., 10
Burrone, J., 12
Burrows, J. J., 31
Burton, A. M., 37, 148
Burzio, L., 322
Busch, V., 16

Bush, G., 41
Bush, R. R., 590
Bushnell, E. W., 164, 186, 218, 751
Bushnell, I. W. R., 147, 148, 149, 152
Busnel, M.-C., 60
Buss, D. M., 614
Buss, E., 68
Bussiere, J. R., 37
Butcher, C., 339, 340, 341, 342, 345, 347, 348
Butcher, H. J., 909
Butkovsky, L., 848
Butler, D. L., 530
Butler, S., 401, 408
Butt, S. J. B., 168
Butterfield, E. C., 516, 529, 530
Butters, M. A., 26
Butters, N., 29
Butterworth, B., 363, 780, 788
Butterworth, E., 616
Butterworth, G., 148, 149, 197, 220, 235, 240,
    342, 597, 875
Buus, S., 66
Buxton, R., 32, 37
Bybee, J., 257
Bynner, J., 988
Byrd, D. L., 473
Byrd-Craven, J., 796, 797, 801
Byrne, M. D., 428
Byrne, R., 646
Byrne, R. M. J., 558, 560, 591, 593, 718
Byrne, R. W., 637, 645, 738, 813
Byrnes, J. P., 792

Cahill, L. F., 20
Cain, K. M., 721
Cairns, P., 86
Calabresi, P., 44
Calabretta, R., 614
Calder, A. J., 38
Calkins, S., 292
Call, J., 66, 644, 667, 724, 815, 820, 821, 839,
    840, 850
Callaghan, B. P., 71
Callaghan, T., 666, 841, 864, 867
Callahan, M. R., 71
Callanan, M., 483, 485, 572, 696, 712, 722
Camaioni, L., 312, 338
Cameron, K. A., 907
Cameron-Faulkner, T., 260
Camilli, G., 531
Cammarano, D. M., 764
Cammuso, K., 893
Campa-Muller, M., 526
Campbell, A., 308
Campbell, B. A., 379
Campbell, F. W., 116, 118, 120
Campbell, G., 13
Campbell, J. I. D., 796, 797, 801
Campbell, M. R., 200
Campbell, P. F., 760
Campbell, R., 148
Campbell, S. L., 60, 65, 66
Campbell, T., 561
Campione, J. C., 466, 468, 513, 529, 541, 621,
    906
Campos, J., 142, 164, 176, 178, 180, 191, 193,
    194, 195, 197, 198, 199, 200, 202, 617, 744,
    745, 817, 818, 866, 890
Candela, A., 597
Canfield, R., 29

Canisia, M., 778
Cannizzo, S. R., 516
Cannon, E., 786, 787
Canobi, K. H., 789, 790, 791, 797
Canoune, H., 33
Cant, J. G. H., 184
Cantalupo, G., 38
Capirci, O., 338, 339, 340, 344
Capitani, E., 619
Capon, A., 963
Capon, N., 976
Cappa, S., 616
Caramazza, A., 619, 688
Carchon, I., 816
Carey, D. P., 624
Carey, K. L., 696
Carey, S., 36, 37, 148, 166, 215, 227, 230, 300,
    306, 313, 431, 558, 563, 569, 570, 571, 620,
    626, 664, 667, 669, 688, 689, 690, 692, 693,
    697, 700, 704, 705, 709, 711, 712, 715, 719,
    720, 724, 744, 765, 781, 782, 783, 789, 836,
    971, 983, 985
Cariani, P. A., 888
Cariglia-Bull, T., 520
Carleton, A., 18
Carlson, D., 31
Carlson, S., 33, 718, 824, 845
Carlson, V., 703, 813
Carlson-Luden, V., 201
Carlson-Radvansky, L. A., 761
Carmichael, L., xiii
Carnine, D., 545
Caroff, X., 579
Caron, J., 482
Caron, M.-J., 765
Caron-Pargue, J., 482
Carothers, T., 867, 878, 919
Carpendale, J., 834, 835
Carpenter, M., 286, 306, 380, 644, 724, 815, 817,
    820, 821, 840
Carpenter, P., 430, 437, 455, 469
Carpenter, T. P., 779, 795, 796, 797, 798
Carr, M., 512, 522, 907, 924
Carraher, D., 657, 671
Carrell, T. D., 75
Carrico, R. L., 186
Carriger, M. S., 821
Carroll, J. B., 778
Carroll, J. J., 137
Carroll, J. M., 149
Carruthers, P., 613, 844, 921
Carson, R. G., 201
Carter, C., 41, 438
Carter, D. M., 80
Carter, E. A., 62, 64
Carter, K. R., 922
Cartwright, T. A., 83, 86, 88, 305, 311
Carver, L. J., 25, 26, 34, 41, 220, 234, 379, 382,
    383, 386, 387, 388, 389, 390, 399, 524
Cary, L., 77
Cary, M. S., 388, 400, 413
Casadio, P., 312
Casalini, C., 27
Casasola, M., 89, 228, 236, 240, 311, 315, 710,
    752
Case, R., 426, 438, 442, 470, 499, 563, 793, 958,
    959, 974
Caselli, C., 263
Caselli, M. C., 263, 312, 338, 344, 345
Caselli, M. S., 338, 339

Casey, B., 12, 30, 34, 39, 40, 41, 42, 43, 417, 449, 469
Cashon, C. H., 142, 148, 215, 216, 228, 229, 230, 231, 232, 236, 237, 239, 242, 246, 567
Cassell, J., 357
Casse-Perrot, C., 39
Cassia, V. M., 147, 242
Cassidy, D. J., 519, 543
Cassidy, J., 407, 408, 837, 848
Cassidy, K., 304
Castelfranco, A. M., 174
Castell, K. C., 890
Castellanos, F., 30, 31, 803, 957
Castle, J., 930
Castle, R., 124
Catala, M., 16
Catan, L., 471
Catroppa, C., 40
Cattell, J. M., 778, 906
Cattell, R. B., 907, 909
Cavanaugh, J. C., 529
Caviness, V. S., 8
Cazden, N., 888
Ce, S., 29
Ceci, S., 361, 513, 563, 671, 764, 907, 913, 914
Cenedella, C., 195, 199
Ceponiene, R., 73
Cezayirli, E., 35
Chadwick-Dias, A., 292
Chall, J. S., 531
Chalmers, D. J., 625, 626
Chalmers, M., 589, 590
Chamberlin, M. H., 748
Chambers, C. K., 90
Chambers, K. E., 84, 90, 91, 301, 304, 305
Champagne, A. B., 541
Chan, M. Y., 181
Chance, G., 69
Chandler, C. R., 63, 64
Chandler, M., 834, 835, 984
Chang, C., 357, 785, 791
Chang, H. W., 885, 886
Chang, K. D., 31
Changeux, J.-P., 12, 449, 914
Chapa, C., 227, 228
Chapman, M., 563, 587, 758, 819, 930, 931, 932
Chapman, R. S., 291
Chaput, H. H., 215, 216, 229, 230, 237, 239, 246
Charest, M., 292
Charles, R. I., 538
Charles-Luce, J., 81, 82, 87
Charman, T., 864
Chasseigne, G., 968
Chater, N., 86, 305, 457, 620
Chatkupt, S., 7
Chatterjee, M., 66
Chavajay, P., 658, 662
Cheatham, C. L., 388, 391, 413
Chechik, G., 11
Chein, I., 778
Chen, C., 795
Chen, G. P., 795
Chen, M. J., 875
Chen, Y., 342, 352, 356, 363
Chen, Z., 201, 442, 443, 469, 473, 474, 480, 483, 484, 485, 486, 487, 489, 491, 492, 493, 495, 498, 500, 559, 560, 561, 595, 598, 663, 974
Cheney, R., 835, 869, 923, 973, 974, 984, 985
Cheng, E. F., 14
Cheng, K., 738, 746, 747, 748, 749, 755

Cheng, P., 558, 560, 717, 961, 965, 967
Chenn, A., 8
Cheour, M., 73
Cheour-Luhtanen, M., 74
Chescheir, N. C., 182
Cheshire, A., 745
Cheung, V. H. W., 887
Cheyne, J. A., 647
Chi, M., 378, 406, 497, 498, 517, 545, 621, 628, 630, 689, 719, 720, 908, 912, 921, 923
Chiang, W.-C., 4, 781, 782
Chiarello, E., 240, 752
Chierchia, G., 312
Child, I., 869
Childers, J., 85, 244, 275, 287, 290, 326, 484
Childs, C. P., 650, 671
Chinn, C., 470, 923, 965, 975
Chinsky, J. H., 377
Chinsky, J. M., 514, 515
Chipman, S., 541, 868
Chistovich, I. A., 80, 94
Chistovich, L. A., 80, 94
Chiu, J., 195, 198
Chiu, M.-H., 497, 498
Chiu, M. M., 488
Chletos, P. N., 486, 495, 500
Choi, S., 261, 312, 410, 695, 761
Chomsky, N., 93, 94, 151, 257, 301, 304, 429, 611, 614, 617, 623, 663, 693, 883
Chong, S. C. F., 149, 827
Chouard, C. H., 893
Chouinard, S., 765
Chovil, N., 352
Christian, K., 655
Christiansen, M. H., 82, 83, 85, 87, 287, 438, 443, 620
Christianson, S.-A., 414
Christoff, K., 31
Christophe, A., 77, 81, 86, 88, 304
Christou, C., 563, 957, 958, 959, 960
Chu, T. K., 167
Chugani, H. T., 34, 44, 385, 386
Chun, M. M., 35, 149
Church, B., 90, 91, 301, 304
Church, K. W., 86
Church, R. B., 176, 340, 341, 342, 344, 350, 359, 361, 473, 481, 482, 484, 485, 489, 493, 501
Church, R. M., 568, 783
Churchill, J. D., 12, 14, 47
Churchland, P. M., 624
Churchland, P. S., 623
Cianciolo, A. T., 803
Cicchetti, D., 39, 867
Cioni, G., 182
Claasen, J.-H., 9
Clancy, P., 271
Clark, A., 163, 561
Clark, A. B., 875
Clark, A. M., 542
Clark, E., 273, 277
Clark, E. D., 885
Clark, E. V., 273, 277, 710, 723
Clark, H., 280
Clark, J. E., 167, 176, 178, 180, 197
Clark, K., 29, 537
Clark, L., 42
Clark, M., 234, 814, 815
Clark, R. E., 23, 24
Clark, V. P., 76
Clarke, P. G., 130

Clarkson, M., 63, 65, 69, 172, 186
Clasen, L., 30
Clausner, T., 704
Claux, M. C., 841
Claux, M. L., 666
Clavadetscher, J. E., 123, 124
Claverie, B., 34
Claxton, L. J., 184
Clearfield, M. W., 195, 200, 432, 452, 569, 746, 751, 781, 783
Clément, F., 722, 848
Clements, M. A., 792
Clements, W. A., 667
Clifford, B. R., 597
Clifton, R., 63, 65, 69, 164, 165, 172, 177, 186, 187, 201, 224, 428, 448, 737
Cline, H., 14
Clohessy, A., 29, 44
Close, L., 792, 793
Clower, R. P., 392
Clower, W. T., 25
Clubb, P. A., 393
Coady, J. A., 81, 91
Cocking, R. R., 494
Coffey, P. J., 38
Coffey-Corina, S. A., 315
Coghill, G. E., 162, 163
Cohen, A., 888
Cohen, A. A., 352, 355
Cohen, A. J., 882, 886, 889
Cohen, D., 616
Cohen, J., 34, 40, 41, 437, 438, 449, 455, 457
Cohen, K. M., 170, 171
Cohen, L., 15, 76, 750, 803
Cohen, L. B., 89, 142, 148, 215, 216, 217, 218, 220, 223, 224, 226, 228, 229, 230, 231, 232, 233, 235, 236, 237, 239, 240, 242, 246, 306, 309, 311, 315, 432, 567, 710, 752, 777, 782, 783, 803
Cohen, L. J., 558
Cohen, M., 592
Cohen, M. H., 141
Cohen, M. M., 8, 76
Cohen, M. S., 31
Cohen, N. J., 17, 385, 396
Cohen, S. B., 530
Colamarino, S. A., 9
Colantonio, C., 73
Colasante, C., 356
Colbert, C. B., 875
Colby, A., 830, 912, 932, 933, 934, 941
Colcombe, S. J., 17
Cole, J. R., 923, 924
Cole, M., 516, 541, 619, 637, 639, 652, 656, 657, 658, 663, 667, 672
Cole, R., 84
Cole, S., 639
Cole-Davies, V., 737
Coleman, M., 148
Coley, J., 299, 571, 614, 619, 668, 699, 704, 713, 715, 716, 720, 721, 722, 724
Collaer, M. L., 762, 763
Collard, R. R., 201
Collie, R., 47, 382
Collins, A., 690, 693, 702
Collins, A. A., 65
Collins, A. M., 701
Collins, C., 536
Collins, D., 12, 34, 616
Collins, L. M., 475

Collins, P. F., 23
Collins, W. A., 409
Collyer, C. E., 586
Colombo, J., 75, 78, 390, 921, 923
Colunga, E., 306, 710
Comrie, B., 280, 324
Condron, B., 10
Cone-Wesson, B., 60, 66
Connell, J., 960
Connell, M. W., 907, 927, 929, 938
Connell, S., 751
Connelly, A., 26
Connolly, K. J., 880
Connor, J. R., 392
Connor, L., 29
Conrad, R., 346
Content, A., 77
Conti-Ramsden, G., 292
Conway, C. M., 287
Conway, G. S., 764
Cook, J. E., 123, 124
Cook, M., 875
Cook, N., 883, 884
Cook, S., 564
Cooke, D. W., 168
Cooke, T., 829
Coolen, R., 85
Cools, R., 42
Coombes, A., 148
Coombs, C. H., 778
Coombs, S., 69
Cooney, J. B., 474
Cooper, F. S., 72
Cooper, G., 797, 799
Cooper, L., 178
Cooper, R. G., 639
Cooper, R., Jr., 780, 781, 782, 786
Cooper, R. P., 75, 77, 78, 80, 94, 611
Copan, H., 72
Coppage, D., 216, 240
Coppola, M., 348
Corballis, M. C., 74
Corbetta, D., 172, 177, 178, 180, 186, 187, 189,
    464, 470, 473, 474, 484, 485, 486, 499
Corbetta, M., 44
Corcoran, K. M., 89, 94
Corina, D., 15, 76
Corkin, S., 20, 27, 624
Cormier, P., 796
Cornell, E. H., 757, 758
Cornia, C., 28
Cornia, G., 622
Cornoldi, C., 34, 531
Cornsweet, T., 116, 189
Correa-Chávez, M., 652, 655, 662
Corrigan, B., 738, 753, 754
Corrigan, R., 704
Corter, C., 821
Cortese, J. M., 128, 137
Coser, S., 531
Cosmi, E., 182
Cosmides, L., 558, 614, 615, 691
Costa-Giomi, E., 890
Costall, A. P., 863, 874, 875
Costanza, D. P., 908
Cote, L. R., 303, 694
Cottam, K., 835, 985
Cottrell, G. W., 614
Cottrell, J., 980
Couchoud, E., 848

Couet, A. M., 195, 199
Coughlan, J., 363
Coulter, D. K., 60
Coupe, P., 738
Coupland, S. G., 66
Courage, M. L., 123, 124, 381, 387, 399, 401
Courchesne, E., 38, 43
Court, E., 880
Courtney, S. M., 33
Cousins, J. H., 757
Couturier-Fagan, D. A., 220
Couvillon, P. A., 590
Cowan, N., 520, 563, 800, 958, 960
Cowan, R., 797
Cowburn, C. A., 67
Cowie, F., 613
Cox, B. D., 470, 497, 498
Cox, C., 906, 908, 909, 912, 922, 927
Cox, D., 619
Cox, M. V., 866, 870, 872, 873, 874, 875, 876,
    880
Cox, R. W., 76
Coyle, T. R., 470, 473, 474, 479, 480, 481, 482,
    484, 488, 491, 493, 496, 499, 500, 517, 524,
    530
Crabbe, G., 306
Crago, M. B., 273
Craig, A. S., 764
Craig, C. M., 183
Craik, F. E., 23
Crain, S., 304
Crain-Thoreson, C., 291
Craton, L. G., 128, 141, 761
Craw, S., 395, 415
Crawford, E. L., 738, 753, 754
Crawford, L. E., 738, 760
Creem, S. H., 755
Creem-Regehr, S. H., 755
Cremer, J. F., 193
Cress, E. M., 190
Crisafi, M. A., 696
Critchfield, T. S., 563
Crivello, F., 36
Croft, K., 826
Croft, W., 257, 302, 704
Crognale, M. A., 122, 123
Cronbach, L. J., 762, 906, 907, 913
Crone, D. A., 525
Cronin, K., 894
Cronin, M., 985
Crook, C., 875
Cross, A., 448, 449, 451
Cross, D. D., 824, 825, 830, 841
Cross, D. R., 534
Cross, P. G., 909
Crow, T. J., 642
Crowder, E. M., 342
Crowder, R. G., 890
Crowe, E., 846, 847, 851
Crowell, J., 117, 118, 739, 838
Crowhurst, M. J., 85
Crowley, K., 350, 479, 480, 495, 497, 498, 502,
    521, 722, 779, 956
Crowther, C., 92, 611
Crowther, H. L., 744, 751
Crozier, J. B., 893
Crozier, W. R., 868
Cruess, L., 564
Cruickshank, M., 80, 82

Crump, T., 784
Crutcher, R. J., 475
Crutchfield, R. S., 912, 925
Csibra, G., 39, 619, 814
Csikszentmihalyi, M., 905, 908, 909, 910, 911,
    912, 913, 915, 916, 919, 920, 921, 922, 923,
    924, 925, 932, 933, 935, 938, 939
Cuddy, L., 882, 888, 889, 893
Culicover, P., 611
Cummins, D. D., 593
Cummins, M., 752
Cummins, R., 618
Cuneo, D. O., 559, 596
Cunningham, A. E., 531
Cunningham, C. C., 75
Cunningham, J., 66, 890
Curby, K. M., 616, 741
Curcio, F., 579
Curran, T., 616
Currie, G., 844
Curtin, S., 74, 79, 82, 83, 85, 87, 89, 90, 438
Curtis, L. E., 781, 782, 784
Curtis, W. J., 24
Cushman, F., 94
Cuthbert, B. N., 38
Cutler, A., 77, 79, 80, 82, 83, 85, 86, 305
Cutting, A. L., 846, 848
Cutting, J. E., 144, 737
Cuvo, A. J., 516
Cycowicz, Y. M., 20
Cymerman, E., 290, 303
Czéh, B., 386
Czurkó, A., 386

Dabholkar, A. S., 11, 386
Dabrowska, E., 274
Dabrowski, K., 932
Daehler, M. W., 518, 863
Dahan, D., 88
Dahl, R. E., 39
Dai, H., 66
Dailey, M. N., 614
Dale, A. M., 32
Dale, K. E., 507
Dale, P., 290, 291, 316, 391, 700
Daley, T. C., 658, 659
Dalke, D. E., 759
Dallago, M. L. L., 530
Dalton, C., 598
Daly, B. P., 384, 390
Damasio, A., 38, 41, 801
Damasio, H., 38, 41
Damerow, P., 638, 648
Damiano, D. L., 168
Damon, W., 541, 910, 912, 924, 930, 931, 932,
    933, 934, 935, 938, 939
Danchin, A., 12
D'Andrade, R., 637
Danemiller, J. L., 147
Daniel, B. M., 187
Daniel, D., 960, 961, 962
Daniel, M. H., 922
Danks, D., 623, 717
Dannemiller, J. D., 147
Dannemiller, J. L., 125, 126
Danovitch, J. H., 625
Danziger, S., 44
Dapretto, M., 312
Darby, B. L., 225
Darwin, C., 146, 614, 780, 816

Das Gupta, M., 846, 847
Da Silva, J. A., 757
Daugherty, K., 444, 448
Davenport, R. K., 860
Davidson, B., 29
Davidson, D., 623, 978
Davidson, I., 637, 640, 645
Davidson, J. E., 908
Davidson, L., 867, 879, 891, 892, 893
Davidson, M., 41, 42
Davidson, N. S., 696
Davidson, P., 831
Davies, K. I., 407, 410, 411
Davies, L., 930
Davies, M., 291, 625
Davis, A. M., 875
Davis, B. E., 200
Davis, C. E., 36
Davis, D., 69
Davis, H., 302
Davis, J., 881, 919
Davis, L., 470
Davis, M., 38, 67, 932
Davis, P., 144, 407, 924
Day, J. D., 533
Day, R. H., 145, 188, 744
Deacon, T. W., 641
Deák, G. O., 564, 571, 720
Dean, A. L., 31
Dean, D., 921, 924, 966, 967, 968, 975, 976
Deane, S., 520
DeBaryshe, B. D., 525
Deblaere, K., 31
de Boer, B., 73
DeBoer, T., 25, 28, 381, 392
de Boysson-Bardies, B., 89, 90
de Cani, J. S., 537
Decarie, T. G., 817
DeCasper, A. J., 60, 80, 524, 611
de Castro, F., 10
De Corte, E., 797, 923
de Courten, C., 11
Deecke, L., 16
Deevy, P., 292
Deffenbacher, K. A., 150
DeForest, M., 377, 657
DeFries, J. C., 914
de Gelder, B., 77
Degiovanni, E., 37
DeGroot, A. D., 908, 910
de Haan, M., 4, 14, 19, 25, 33, 36, 37, 39, 150,
    241, 242, 243, 380, 383, 388, 392
Dehaene, S., 15, 74, 76, 449, 610, 664, 665, 750,
    780, 781, 782, 784, 785, 788, 794, 800, 803,
    804
Dehaene-Lambertz, G., 74, 76, 82, 93, 305, 750
DeHart, G., 265, 639
Dehay, C., 36
Deiber, M. P., 16
Deisenhammer, E. A., 31
de Laguna, G., 339
Delaney, P. F., 796, 801
de Lange, F. P., 31
De La Paz, S., 538
Del Campo, G., 792
del Castillo Pintado, J., 303
de Leeuw, N., 497, 498
Delery, D. B., 199
Delgutte, B., 888
D'Elia, A., 182

Deliagina, T. G., 168
Delis, D. C., 32
De Lisi, R., 486, 495, 500, 764
Delius, J. D., 589, 590
Dell, G. S., 84
DeLoache, J., 168, 518, 519, 543, 560, 630, 690,
    721, 722, 737, 751, 759, 863, 864, 865, 867
Delorme, A., 198
Del Savio, M., 531
Demany, L., 62, 70, 77, 887
DeMarie, D., 526
de Menezes Santos, M., 588
Demetriou, A., 563, 957, 958, 959, 960
Demirdache, H., 302
deMornay-Davies, P., 625
Dempster, F. N., 520
Demuth, K., 81, 273, 301, 305
DeNeys, W., 594
Denham, S., 848
Dennis, I., 963
Dennis, S., 880
Dennis, W., 880
Dennis-Rounds, J., 521
Denny, M. A., 172, 173, 176, 177, 178
Denos, M., 35
Dentici, O. A., 931, 932
De Palma, M., 532
dePaolis, R., 81
DeRegnier, R.-A., 48
Deregowski, J. B., 862, 863
Deregowski, J. E., 863
DeRose, T. M., 521
de Rosnay, M., 830, 846, 847
Derrah, C., 83
Deruelle, C., 33, 39, 147, 148, 150
De Ruiter, J.-P., 355
de Schonen, S., 32, 33, 36, 38, 39, 147, 148, 150
Deshler, D. D., 530, 545
Desimone, R., 17, 39, 449
Desjardins, R., 76, 77, 695
Desmond, J., 30, 41
DeSoto, M. C., 796, 797, 801
Despland, P., 37
Desrochers, S., 229, 230
Detterman, D. K., 922
Deutsch, D., 883
Deutsch, W., 317
Dev, M. B., 68, 71
Devenpeck, G., 527
DeVilliers, J., 263, 265
DeVilliers, P., 263, 265
Devin, J., 851
Devoe, S., 340
DeVos, J., 223, 428
Devoscovi, A., 263
deVries, J. I. P., 163, 172, 182
de Vries, L., 66
de Waal, F., 642, 645, 818
Dewar, K. M., 882, 888
Dewey, C., 200
Dewey, J., 779
Dewson, J. H., 74
DiAdamo, C., 704
Diamond, A., 24, 40, 42, 43, 221, 223, 428, 449,
    564, 742, 989
Diamond, J., 647
Diamond, R., 36, 37, 148
Dias, M., 737, 960, 963
Diaz, I., 76
Diaz, R. M., 500

DiBella, J., 542
Dick, F., 32, 282
Dickson, J. C., 589
Diedrich, F. J., 169, 172, 182, 188, 470, 472, 484,
    490, 496
Diehl, R. L., 74
Dienes, K., 31
Dienes, Z., 82, 351, 568
Diesendruck, G., 306, 311, 314, 573, 693, 699,
    707, 708, 711, 714, 715
Diessel, H., 283, 284
Di Ferdinando, A., 614
DiGirolamo, G. J., 31
Dilley, L., 85
Dimitropoulou, K. A., 195, 199
Dimyan, M. A., 677
Dingel, A., 216, 240
Dingle, K., 616
Dingman, H. F., 778
Dinwiddy, L. S., 581
Dirks, J., 863
DiRusso, A. A., 363
diSessa, A. A., 714
Diwadkar, V., 738
Dixon, J., 474, 477, 485, 495, 967
Dixon, R. M. W., 302, 316
Dixon, W., 29
Do, M. C., 173
Dobkins, K. R., 16, 124
Dobmeyer, S., 76
Dobson, M. V., 125
Dobson, V., 117, 118, 155
Dodd, B., 77
Dodds, J. B., 163, 176, 178, 191
Dodge, M., 347, 348
Dodow, S. M., 404
Dodson, J. D., 414
Dodson, K., 262, 270, 276, 277, 288
Doesbergh, S., 148
Dogtrop, A. P., 182
Doherty, M., 836, 983
Doherty, S., 765
Dolan, R. J., 23, 735
Dolan, T., 61, 67
Dolezal, S. E., 542
Dolgin, K. G., 890
Dollard, J., 466
Domakonda, K. V., 180
Dominin, D., 878
Dommergues, J., 77
Don, M., 66
Donald, M., 641, 642, 647, 648, 676
Donaldson, M., 578, 580, 581, 826
Donis, K., 908
Donlan, C., 292, 750
D'Onofrio, B., 13
Dooling, R. J., 74
Dosher, B. A., 760
Dostie, D., 15
Douglass, S., 428
Dove, H., 661
Dow, G. A., 383, 384, 865
Dowd, J. M., 69
Dowden, A., 234, 382, 383
Dow-Ehrensberger, M., 655
Dowker, A., 484, 793
Dowling, K., 124
Dowling, W. J., 881, 882, 885, 886, 888, 889, 891,
    892
Downs, R. M., 756, 758

Dowty, D., 321
Doxsey, P. A., 760
Draganski, B., 16
Drain, H. M., 242
Dresner Barnes, H., 271
Drevdahl, J. E., 909
Drevets, W. C., 39
Drew, J., 24
Dromi, E., 435, 488
Dronkers, N., 282
Dropik, P., 25, 381, 382, 383, 384, 387, 389, 390,
    391, 399, 412, 524
Drucker, P., 935
Drummey, A., 28, 402, 750
Druss, B., 81
Druyan, S., 595
Dubas, J. S., 763
Dubois, F., 356
Dubowitz, L. M. S., 66
Dubowitz, V., 66
Duchaine, B., 615, 616
Dudukovic, N., 41
Duffy, G. G., 454, 535
Duffy, S., 751
Duhe, D. A., 31
Duit, R., 541
Duke, N., 706, 707
Dumais, S. T., 130, 131
Dumas, C., 588, 590
Dunbar, C., 193
Dunbar, K., 449, 560, 911, 921, 924, 965, 966,
    973
Dunbar, R. I., 641
Duncan, J., 39, 41
Duncan, R. M., 470
Duncan, S., 735, 738, 752, 830
Duncker, K., 126
Dunham, F., 690, 721
Dunham, P., 690, 721
Dunlea, A., 345
Dunn, D., 519
Dunn, J., 407, 819, 821, 845, 846, 848, 930
Dunning, D., 521
Dunnington, G., 879
Dunphy-Lelii, S., 762, 767
Dupont, P., 750
Dupoux, E., 15, 76, 77, 86
Durgin, F., 704
Durieux-Smith, A., 63
Durkheim, E., 909
Durston, S., 12, 29, 39, 40, 41, 42, 449
Dushay, R. A., 352, 356
Dweck, C. S., 689, 721, 907, 923
d'Ydewalle, G., 594
Dye, N. W., 778
Dyer-Friedman, J., 34
Dziuban, C. D., 868
Dziurawiec, S., 36, 146, 147, 241

Easterbrook, J. A., 414
Easterbrook, M. A., 146
Ebbinghaus, H., 377, 389
Ebeling, K. S., 316, 711
Eberhard, K. M., 91
Eccard, C., 30, 39, 42
Echevarria, M., 537
Echols, C., 81, 85, 244, 304, 305, 306, 310, 312,
    713
Echols, K., 495
Eckenhoff, M., 385, 386, 399

Eckenrode, J., 526
Eckerman, C. O., 404
Eckstein, S. G., 908
Eddins, D. A., 67
Eddy, T. J., 839
Edelman, G. M., 799, 800, 801, 802, 803
Edgin, J., 765
Edman, M., 60
Edmonds, G. E., 37
Edward, V., 16
Edwards, C. G., 63
Edwards, C. P., 660
Edwards, J., 89
Edwards, R., 848
Efklides, A., 958
Efron, R., 32
Egeland, B., 838
Eggermont, J. J., 60, 66
Ehrle, N., 35
Ehrlich, T., 941
Ehrlinger, J., 521
Eichenbaum, H., 20, 21, 25, 385
Eidelman, A., 382
Eifuku, S., 37
Eigsti, I., 41, 42
Eilers, A. T., 697
Eilers, R. E., 886, 889
Eilers, R. J., 78
Eimas, P. D., 72, 73, 74, 79, 83, 238, 240, 301,
    303, 305, 570, 689, 697, 710
Eimer, M., 37
Eisenberg, N., 168, 829, 930, 931, 932
Eiser, C., 878
Eizenman, D. R., 139, 226
Ejiri, K., 340
Ek, E. U., 669
Ekdahl, C. T., 9
Ekman, P., 337, 816
Elbert, T., 16
Elder, A. D., 342, 360, 481
El-Dinary, P. B., 537
Elfenbein, J. L., 67
Elicker, J., 761
Elieff, C., 133, 303
Eliefjua, C. C., 879
Eliez, S., 34, 38
Elkind, D., 954
Elliot, E. M., 563
Elliott-Faust, D. J., 545
Elliott-Faust, D. L., 512, 513
Ellis, E. S., 545
Ellis, H., 36, 146, 147, 241, 906, 908
Ellis, N. R., 528
Ellis, R., 622
Ellis, S., 474, 497
Ellis Weismer, S., 345
Ellsworth, P., 337
Elman, J., 82, 119, 152, 237, 241, 286, 427, 430,
    433, 438, 444, 448, 452, 499, 558, 568, 616,
    663, 664, 691
Elvevåg, B., 10
Emde, R. N., 174, 193, 199, 202, 817, 818
Emerson, M. J., 741
Emmons, Y. D., 345
Emmorey, K., 765
Emslie, H., 279
Endman, M. W., 65
Endo, S., 37
Eng, H., 879
Eng, P., 169

Engebretson, P. H., 738, 752
Engle, R. A., 482, 489, 496
Engle, R. W., 800, 801
Englert, C., 538
English, L. D., 560, 583, 584, 591, 595
Enns, J. T., 875, 878
Enright, M. K., 169
Enright, R. D., 541
Enwere, E., 9
Eppler, M. A., 164, 189, 190, 191, 193, 196, 197,
    198, 200
Epstein, J. N., 525
Erickson, C. A., 17, 449
Erickson, L. G., 533
Ericsson, K. A., 474, 475, 621, 912, 921, 938
Erikson, E., 908, 909, 910, 919, 931, 932, 938
Erikson, K. I., 17
Erikson, K. M., 392
Erkinjuntti, M., 181
Ernst, D., 721
Ernst, M. O., 735, 738, 739
Erreich, A., 274
Erskine, L., 10
Ersland, L., 31
Erteschik-Shir, N., 272
Ervinslow, J. T., 19
Esbensen, B., 402, 827
Eslinger, P. J., 26, 34
Esmonde, I., 652
Espinosa, M. P., 658, 659
Estes, D., 833
Estrada, J., 361
Etcoff, N. L., 38, 149
Ettayne, H., 47
Ettlinger, G., 860
Evans, A., 15, 76
Evans, D., 311, 744
Evans, E. M., 689, 724
Evans, J., 963
Evans, J., St., 960, 963
Evans, J. L., 345, 346
Evans, J. S. B. T., 558
Evans, M. A., 342
Ewart, A. K., 39
Ewert, K., 761
Ewing, S. A., 750
Exposito, M., 67
Eymard, L. A., 591
Eysenck, H., 868, 869, 906

Fabes, R. A., 829, 930, 931, 932
Fabre-Grenet, M., 147, 148
Fagan, J., 135, 863
Fagan, M. K., 340
Fagard, J., 172, 187
Fagen, J. W., 169
Fagot, B. I., 148
Fagot, J., 755
Faja, S., 765
Falbo, T., 867
Falco, F. L., 525
Falk, D., 640
Falkenhainer, B., 622
Fan, J., 41, 42
Fane, B. A., 764
Fanselow, M. S., 387
Fant, L. J., 346
Fantz, R., 115, 120, 124, 135, 146, 218, 379, 524,
    863
Farah, M. J., 4, 242, 455, 616, 619, 626

Farmer, D., 872, 879
Farnsworth, P. R., 883
Farnum, C. E., 175
Farol, P., 12
Farrant, K., 404, 408, 418
Farrar, J., 277, 283, 290
Fassbender, C., 70
Fassinger, R. E., 940
Faulkner, J., 928
Favilla, M., 451
Fay, A., 595, 962, 965, 966, 973
Fay, R. R., 69
Fayol, M., 523, 785, 791
Fearing, D. D., 216, 235, 569
Federspiel, A., 38
Fegley, S., 931, 932
Feigenson, L., 431, 664, 781, 782, 783
Fein, G. G., 760
Feineis-Matthews, S., 38
Feinfeld, K. A., 823
Feingold, A., 763, 764
Feinman, G. M., 638, 647
Feinstein, L., 988
Feiring, C., 409, 838
Feist, G. J., 921, 922, 923
Feldman, D. H., 530, 908, 911, 912, 913, 914, 925
Feldman, H. M., 31, 32
Feldman, J. F., 390, 611
Feldon, J., 767
Felton, M., 541, 979, 980, 981, 982
Feng, L. Y., 67
Feng, Q., 187, 624
Fennell, C., 89, 90, 94, 304, 315
Fenson, L., 290, 312, 316, 391, 700
Fenwick, K., 69, 744
Ferdinandsen, K., 868, 879
Ferguson, C. A., 260
Ferguson, J. N., 19
Ferland, D., 244
Fernald, A., 67, 78, 80, 91, 94, 305, 312, 314, 611, 818, 886
Fernandez, L., 117
Fernandez-Dols, J. M., 149
Fernyhough, C., 838, 846, 847
Ferrara, R. A., 466, 468, 513, 529, 621
Ferrari, F., 182
Ferraro, F., 29
Ferretti, R. P., 529
Ferron, J., 526
Ferstl, R., 751
Feyereisen, P., 354, 356
Fias, W., 750
Field, D., 119, 579, 582
Field, J., 863
Field, T., 817
Fields, W. M., 643, 646
Fiez, J. A., 76
Fifer, W. P., 60, 77, 80, 611
Figueras-Costa, B., 846
Fillmore, C., 258
Finch, S., 305
Fincham, J. M., 438
Findlay, J. M., 146
Fine, I., 16
Fineberg, J., 862
Finke, R. A., 908
Finney, E. M., 16
Finoccio, D. V., 185
Fiorentini, A., 116, 124
Fireman, G., 470, 592

Firtel, R. A., 10
Fischel, J. E., 525
Fischer, K., 217, 222, 224, 435, 470, 474, 481, 482, 483, 485, 493, 497, 500, 563, 921, 926, 927, 932, 956
Fischhoff, B., 975
Fischl, B., 32
Fischman, W., 925, 930, 931, 932, 933, 934
Fiser, J., 93
Fish, S., 940
Fishell, G., 8
Fisher, A. V., 562, 692, 711, 712, 713
Fisher, C., 81, 84, 90, 91, 266, 267, 301, 302, 304, 312, 315, 320, 321, 322
Fisher, C. H., 90
Fisher, C. L., 305
Fisher, D. M., 167, 168, 169, 170, 171, 177
Fisher, H., 38
Fisk, J. D., 451
Fitch, W. T., 93, 94, 614, 883
Fitneva, S. A., 513
Fitzgerald, R. W., 764
Fitzsimmons, C. M., 89, 309
Fivush, R., 378, 380, 383, 384, 393, 394, 395, 396, 397, 398, 401, 402, 403, 404, 405, 406, 407, 408, 409, 410, 412, 414, 415, 417, 524, 525, 673, 850
Flacks, R., 926
Flavell, E. R., 812, 823, 832, 865
Flavell, J., 26, 279, 377, 402, 427, 467, 511, 514, 515, 516, 521, 529, 624, 811, 812, 823, 824, 826, 832, 833, 865, 926
Fleischchmann, T. B., 17
Fleisig, W. E., 519
Fleming, P., 200
Fletcher, K. L., 474, 475, 489, 493, 531
Fletcher, P., 23, 274
Flevares, L., 357
Flinchbaugh, B. E., 144
Floccia, C., 78, 80
Flock, H. R., 129
Flom, R. A., 890
Flombaum, J., 41, 42
Flood, T. L., 757
Flower, L., 537, 545
Flukes, J., 701
Flynn, E., 470, 484, 485, 487, 491, 494, 496, 500, 718
Flynn, J. R., 658, 764, 907
Fodor, J., 558, 562, 691, 719, 824, 841
Fodor, J. A., 113, 561, 618, 619, 620, 623, 624, 627, 628, 631, 663, 735, 748, 911
Fodor, J. D., 611
Fogel, A., 435, 470, 489
Foley, J. M., 119
Foley, R. A., 641, 642
Folsom, R. C., 60, 62, 65, 66
Folstein, S. E., 893
Foltz, C., 961
Fonagy, P., 838
Fontaine, R., 174
Foorman, B. R., 531
Foos, P. W., 587, 588
Forbes, J., 244, 303, 311
Forbes, P., 30
Forbus, K. D., 622
Forde, E. M. E., 616
Forgeron, N., 470
Forman, E. A., 497
Forman, S., 40, 41

Forrest-Pressley, D., 512, 513
Forssberg, H., 34, 166, 167, 168, 170, 171
Fortes, A. F., 739, 753
Fortes, M., 653, 880
Fortier, L., 594
Fortin, N. J., 25
Fossella, J., 39, 40, 41, 42, 449
Foster, J. C., 376
Foster, K., 744, 745, 751
Foster, S. G., 868
Fowler, A., 291, 292, 322, 325
Fowler, C. A., 77
Fox, D. B., 892
Fox, N. A., 180
Fox, R., 130, 131, 145
Frackowiak, R. S. J., 17
Fradley, E., 838, 846, 847
Fraisse, F. E., 195, 199
Frambach, M., 27
Frances, R., 882, 887
Francis, D. D., 13
Francis, W. N., 446
Francis, W. S., 483, 497
Francois, M., 66
Frangiskakis, J. M., 39
Frank, L., 32
Frank, R., 41, 302
Frankel, D., 129
Frankel, F., 516
Frankenburg, W. K., 163, 176, 178, 191
Frankenfield, A., 571, 670, 671, 707, 708
Franklin, A., 348
Franklin, N., 760
Franks, B., 594, 708, 962
Franks, J. J., 562
Franzen, P., 16, 34, 41
Fraser, B. J., 541
Frauenfelder, U., 77
Frawley, W., 302
Frazier, J., 41
Fredenburg, K. A., 531
Freedland, R. L., 125, 126, 172, 173, 176, 177
Freedman, B., 933
Freedman, D. G., 780
Freedman, J., 304, 932
Freeman, N., 407, 786, 862, 865, 872, 874, 875, 876, 878
Freitas, P. B., 198
French, B. F., 531
French, J., 118, 778
French, L. A., 583
French, R., 237, 238, 239, 433
Frensch, P. A., 764, 779
Freud, S., 394, 524, 624, 909, 915, 930
Fried, I., 907
Friederici, A., 81, 305
Friedman, A., 741, 755
Friedman, J., 44
Friedman, L., 43
Friedman, N. P., 741, 762
Friedman, W. J., 402, 595, 596
Friedrich, F., 43, 44
Friesen, W., 337
Frigon, J. Y., 198
Frijters, J. C., 532
Friston, K. J., 23, 27
Frith, C. D., 38
Frith, U., 16, 812, 842, 843
Fromhoff, F., 394, 404, 412, 850
Frongillo, E. A., 172, 174

Frost, J. A., 76
Frost, P. E., 76
Fry, C. L., 811, 926
Frye, D., 42, 563, 564, 567, 583, 585, 600, 622
Fu, P., 704
Fuchs, A. F., 185
Fuchs, D., 539, 540, 797, 799
Fuchs, L. S., 537, 539, 540, 797, 799
Fujikawa, H., 9
Fujikawa, S. M., 67
Fujimoto, S., 66
Fujimura, N., 482, 492
Fujita, A., 67
Fujitani, D. S., 885
Fukumoto, K., 181
Fukura, K., 181
Fukusima, S. S., 757
Fulbright, K. A., 38
Fuligni, A., 659
Fulkerson, A. L., 306, 307, 308, 309
Funahashi, S., 40
Funai, H., 65
Fung, T., 470
Funk, J. B., 764
Funnell, E., 523, 524
Furby, L., 975
Furey, M. L., 36
Furr, S. R., 926
Furrer, S. D., 240
Furtado, E., 406
Furth, H., 541
Furumoto, S., 40
Fuson, K. C., 502, 583, 784, 785, 786, 791, 792,
    795, 796, 797, 799, 802
Fuster, J., 40, 449
Fyer, A., 30

Gabelnick, F., 929
Gabrieli, J., 31, 41
Gadian, D. G., 17, 26, 27
Gage, F. H., 8, 9
Gahery, Y., 188
Gaiani, C., 531
Galaburda, A., 41, 909
Galanter, E., 814
Galco, J., 722
Galenson, D., 914, 920, 938
Galizio, M., 563
Gallagher, D., 542
Gallagher, J. J., 906
Gallagher, J. M., 705
Galles, N. S., 15
Gallimore, R., 639
Gallistel, C. R., 354, 568, 582, 615, 623, 664,
    738, 740, 746, 780, 781, 783, 784, 785, 786,
    787, 788, 789, 790, 791, 792, 794, 795, 802,
    803
Gallogly, D. P., 142
Galloway, C., 260
Galloway, J. C., 187
Galotti, K., 720
Galton, F., 906, 908, 909
Galvez, R., 47
Gambrell, L., 537
Ganel, T., 37
Ganger, S., 537
Gannon, K. E., 790
Gao, F., 750
Gapenne, O., 197
Garber, J., 830

Garber, P., 342, 351, 359, 501
Garciaguirre, J. S., 172, 179, 180, 181
Garcia-Mila, M., 470, 472, 480, 481, 483, 485,
    489, 491, 492, 493, 494, 495, 496, 497, 498,
    542, 559, 912, 921, 923, 962, 965, 966, 969,
    970, 973, 974, 979, 983, 987
Gardner, B., 890
Gardner, H., 482, 615, 860, 862, 865, 867, 868,
    870, 878, 879, 880, 881, 890, 891, 892, 905,
    907, 908, 909, 910, 911, 912, 913, 914, 915,
    916, 917, 918, 919, 920, 921, 922, 923, 924,
    925, 926, 927, 928, 929, 930, 931, 932, 933,
    934, 935, 937, 938, 939, 940
Gardner, J. K., 868
Gardner, J. W., 925, 927
Gardner, R., 860
Gardner, W. L., 927
Garfunkel, G., 868, 879
Garing, A. E., 749
Garnett, P. J., 541
Garnier, H., 922
Garrad-Cole, F., 748
Garrigan, P., 138
Gartner, B., 283, 284
Garton, A., 279
Gartus, A., 16
Garver, K., 41, 957, 958, 959
Gascon, J., 429
Gaser, C., 16
Gaskins, I., 537
Gaskins, S., 312, 651, 661, 695
Gasser, M., 316, 317
Gatenby, J., 30
Gathercole, S., 289, 290, 292, 758, 959
Gathercole, V., 263, 311, 319
Gati, J. S., 31
Gattis, M., 560, 735
Gaulin, S. J., 764
Gaultney, J. F., 474, 482, 493, 517, 518, 524, 530
Gauna, K., 15
Gaunet, F., 766
Gauthier, I., 33, 36, 37, 38, 149, 241, 616, 741
Gauvain, M., 761
Gay, J., 656, 667
Gayford, C., 541
Gayl, I. E., 116
Gazdar, G., 617
Gearhart, M., 665, 784, 795
Geary, C., 9
Geary, D. C., 485, 529, 530, 585, 777, 779, 780,
    784, 785, 788, 789, 791, 794, 795, 796, 797,
    799, 800, 801, 802, 803, 804
Gedo, J., 909
Geertz, C., 639, 669, 675
Geil, M., 992
Geisler, W. S., 116, 142
Geissler, P. W., 913
Gekoski, M., 169
Gelber, E. R., 218
Geldart, S., 32, 38, 150
Gellner, E., 647
Gelman, R., 244, 301, 303, 354, 468, 470, 483,
    497, 558, 563, 568, 578, 580, 582, 619, 639,
    663, 664, 665, 670, 671, 689, 690, 691, 692,
    697, 704, 705, 706, 720, 723, 779, 780, 781,
    782, 783, 784, 785, 786, 787, 788, 789, 790,
    791, 792, 794, 795, 800, 802, 803, 851, 988
Gelman, S., 299, 309, 311, 312, 316, 470, 571,
    572, 619, 627, 628, 663, 671, 688, 690, 691,
    692, 693, 695, 696, 699, 700, 701, 703, 704,

705, 706, 708, 709, 711, 712, 713, 715, 716,
    719, 721, 722, 780, 784, 965
Genesee, F., 78
Gentile, A. M., 181
Gentile, D. A., 890
Gentner, D., 236, 274, 275, 301, 303, 311, 312,
    559, 560, 562, 566, 622, 694, 695, 709, 711,
    714, 718, 741, 764
George, C., 822
Georgieff, M., 25, 48, 392, 531
Georgopoulos, A., 31, 451, 739, 753
Gepshtein, S., 739
Geraldi-Caulton, G., 42
Gerardi, G. M., 890
Gerard-Ngo, P., 265
Gergely, G., 619, 664, 814
Gergen, D., 909, 912, 914, 928
Gerhardstein, P., 31, 379, 380, 518
Gerhardt, J., 280, 283
Gerhardt, K. J., 60
Gerken, L., 79, 80, 81, 82, 83, 84, 91, 92, 271,
    305, 890
German, T., 708, 824
Gernsbacher, M. A., 282
Gershkoff-Stowe, L., 342, 484, 488, 711
Gersten, R., 537, 538
Gescheider, G. A., 65
Geschwind, N., 894, 909, 917
Gesell, A., 162, 163, 165, 172, 173, 176, 182, 883
Getzels, J. W., 908, 915, 916, 917, 919, 920, 932
Geurds, M. P., 7
Ghahramani, Z., 618
Ghatala, E. S., 522, 544
Ghazanfar, A. A., 77
Ghez, C., 451
Gholson, B., 591
Ghysselinckx, A., 363, 364
Gibbs, C., 70
Gibbs, J., 830
Gibbs, S., 783
Gibertoni, M., 28
Gibson, E., 111, 112, 127, 129, 137, 163, 164,
    177, 183, 187, 189, 190, 191, 192, 193, 195,
    196, 197, 198, 200, 202, 215, 570, 863
Gibson, J. J., 112, 113, 114, 124, 126, 127, 128,
    129, 132, 137, 143, 145, 151, 163, 164, 189,
    196, 863, 870, 875
Gibson, K., 640
Gick, M. L., 539, 591
Giedd, J., 12, 30, 31, 34, 803, 957
Gielen, C. C. A. M., 198
Giere, R. N., 493
Gifford, G. W., 19
Gilbert, J. H., 73
Gilchrist, L., 173
Giles, J. W., 708, 712, 721
Gill, C. B., 531
Gill-Alvarez, F., 175, 176, 181
Gill-Alvarez, S. V., 180
Gillan, J., 597
Gillberg, C., 843, 844
Gillenwater, J. M., 64, 67
Gillette, J., 312, 320
Gilliam, F., 33
Gilmore, R., 167, 186, 197, 202, 745, 746, 765
Gilovich, T., 485
Gilstrap, L. L., 513
Ginsberg, M. H., 10
Ginsburg, A. P., 36, 116
Ginsburg, H., 779, 785, 788, 789, 790, 795, 796

Girardet, H., 980
Givón, T., 257, 278
Gjedde, A., 76
Glachen, M., 497
Glanville, B. B., 74
Glasberg, B. R., 67
Glaser, R., 497, 541, 908, 912, 921, 923
Glassman, M., 930
Glassner, A., 979
Gleeson, J. G., 10
Gleitman, H., 126, 139, 312, 320, 323, 324, 757, 766
Gleitman, L., 81, 85, 301, 304, 305, 312, 315, 316, 317, 318, 320, 321, 322, 323, 324, 345, 610, 690, 761
Glenberg, A. M., 352, 363
Glenn, C. G., 373, 377
Glenn, S. M., 75, 868
Glick, J., 656, 667, 960
Glicksman, M. L., 128, 137
Glisky, E. L., 26
Glock, H. J., 623
Glover, G., 30, 34, 41
Gluck, M. A., 20
Glymour, C., 307, 623, 717
Glynn, S. M., 541
Gobbini, M. I., 35, 36
Gobbo, C., 720
Gobet, F., 621
Godoi, D., 198
Goel, V., 735
Goertzel, B., 908
Goertzel, M. G., 911, 927, 928
Goertzel, T. G., 911, 927, 928
Goertzel, V., 911, 927, 928
Gogate, L., 199, 306, 308
Gold, E. M., 611
Goldberg, A., 257, 258, 271, 277, 397, 414
Goldberg, J., 958, 959
Goldberg, R., 325
Goldberg-Reitman, J., 932
Goldenberg, C. N., 639
Goldfield, B. A., 312
Goldfield, E. C., 164, 173, 177, 183
Golding, J., 200
Goldinger, S. D., 90
Goldin-Meadow, S., 176, 338, 339, 340, 341, 342, 343, 344, 345, 346, 347, 348, 349, 350, 351, 353, 355, 357, 358, 359, 360, 361, 362, 363, 364, 473, 474, 481, 482, 483, 484, 485, 486, 489, 492, 493, 495, 500, 501, 694, 850
Goldman, A., 625
Goldman, P., 40
Goldman, T., 530
Goldman-Rakic, P., 4, 40, 386, 399
Goldsmith, L., 866
Goldstein, D., 530
Goldstein, S., 817
Goldstone, R. L., 618, 710, 711
Goldvarg-Steingold, E. G., 318
Goleman, D., 927
Golinkoff, R., 85, 88, 263, 299, 302, 304, 306, 308, 311, 312, 696, 703, 714, 813
Golledge, R. G., 761
Gollin, J. B., 927
Golomb, C., 860, 861, 862, 869, 870, 872, 873, 874, 878, 879, 880, 884, 917, 918, 919
Gombrich, E., 859, 875, 876, 918
Gómez, R., 83, 91, 92, 271, 305
Göncü, A., 661

Good, C. D., 17
Goodale, M. A., 451, 624
Goodall, J., 643, 839
Goode, S., 292
Goodenough, F. L., 862
Goodhew, A., 597
Gooding, D. C., 922, 923
Goodman, C. H., 778
Goodman, C. S., 10
Goodman, G., 29, 181, 393, 395, 406, 414, 415
Goodman, J., 28, 301, 314, 528
Goodman, M. B., 79, 81, 83
Goodman, N., 304, 342, 611, 716, 860, 867, 915, 917
Goodman, R. A., 802
Goodnow, J., 429, 636, 638, 701, 873, 916, 918
Goodrich, W., 355
Goodsitt, J. V., 85
Goodwyn, S., 338, 339, 340, 344, 345
Goody, J., 654
Gopnik, A., 240, 261, 306, 307, 312, 314, 457, 558, 623, 628, 664, 691, 692, 708, 715, 717, 718, 824, 825, 827, 921, 965, 972
Gordon, B. N., 406, 513
Gordon, F., 129
Gordon, P., 665, 780, 784, 789
Gore, J., 30, 33, 35, 36
Goren, C., 146, 241
Gorga, M. P., 60, 65, 66
Gorman, M. E., 921, 922
Goshen-Gottstein, Y., 37, 562
Goss, C. M., 182
Gosselin, F., 800
Goswami, U., 560, 566, 709, 921, 922
Goto, Y., 178
Gotowiec, A., 69
Gottesman, I. I., 13
Gottfried, A. W., 387
Gottfried, D. B., 706
Gottfried, G., 704
Gottlieb, G., 73
Gottlob, I., 611
Gotts, S. J., 448
Gottschaldt, K., 110
Götz, K., 868, 869
Götz, M., 10
Goubet, N., 187, 188, 428, 448
Goudvis, A., 535, 537
Gould, E., 8, 9, 18, 398
Gould, S. J., 177, 617
Gout, A., 88
Gouteux, S., 748
Govindarajan, T. N., 926
Graber, M., 222, 223, 428
Grabowski, T., 41
Graf, E. W., 122
Graf, P., 513, 827
Graf Estes, K. M., 94
Graff, D., 317
Graff, G., 980, 981
Grafman, J., 16, 29, 33
Grafton, S., 29
Graham, D. J., 796
Graham, G., 609
Graham, J. A., 356
Graham, S., 306, 307, 309, 313, 314, 530, 538, 545, 546, 695, 696, 699, 715, 716, 813
Graham, T., 342, 350, 354, 473, 481, 482
Granier-Deferre, C., 60

Granott, N., 474, 480, 483, 493, 497, 500, 550, 914
Granrud, C. E., 128, 131, 132, 133, 137, 142, 143, 144, 145
Grant, J., 765
Grant-Webster, K. S., 133, 142
Gray, B., 558, 563, 572
Gray, J. T., 394, 412, 850
Gray, L., 70
Gray, W., 311
Greco, C., 518
Green, D. A., 31
Green, D. G., 116, 118
Green, D. M., 67, 71
Green, F. L., 812, 823, 832, 865
Green, K. P., 76
Green, M., 527, 744, 751
Greenacre, P., 931
Greenberg, G. Z., 66
Greene, T. R., 574
Greenfield, D. B., 721
Greenfield, P., 261, 339, 340, 578, 650, 659, 671, 688, 689
Greenham, S. L., 793
Greenhoot, A. F., 390, 406, 921, 923
Greenlee, M. W., 735
Greeno, J. G., 780, 797, 798
Greenough, W. T., 12, 14, 17, 802
Greenspan, D., 925, 930, 931
Greenstein, D., 30
Greer, T., 201
Gregersen, P. K., 893
Gregg, C., 9
Gregg, K., 622
Gregg, S., 538
Gregg, V. H., 748
Greif, M., 616, 619
Grenier, A., 185
Grice, H. P., 558, 595
Grice, S. J., 39
Griepentrog, G., 93, 886, 894
Grieser, D., 72
Grieve, R., 574, 575
Griffin, G. R., 19
Griffin, N. J., 171
Griffin, P., 541
Griffith, S. B., 516
Griffiths, S. K., 60
Griffiths, T. L., 623
Grill, H. J., 171
Grillner, S., 168
Grimes, A., 697
Grobman, K. H., 197, 746
Grocki, J. J., 187
Groen, G., 779, 788, 795
Gropen, J., 325
Grose, J. H., 61, 68, 70, 71
Grose-Fifer, J., 131, 146
Gross, C. G., 9, 868, 879
Gross, D., 842
Gross, J., 831, 867, 870
Grossberg, S., 138, 623
Grossman, A. W., 14, 47
Grossman, J. B., 832, 865
Grotoh, R., 40
Grotzer, T., 923
Grover, L., 342
Gruber, D. B., 42
Gruber, H., 908, 912, 916, 922, 923, 924, 925, 940

Gruendel, J., 378, 393, 394
Gruenenfelder, T. M., 516
Grun, J., 30
Grupe, L., 474, 489, 493, 500, 531
Gsodl, M. K., 39, 765
Guajardo, J. J., 306
Guan, Y. L., 66
Guasti, M. T., 77, 304, 305
Guberman, S. R., 665, 784, 795
Gudeman, R., 265
Gugga, S. S., 537
Guilford, J. P., 908
Guillaume, P., 339
Guitterez, F., 619
Gulberg, M., 354
Gundel, J., 278
Gunderson, V. M., 133, 142
Gunn, D., 291
Gunnar, M., 392, 818
Gunstone, R. F., 620
Gunther, M. K., 880
Gureckis, T. M., 239
Gurevich, I., 10
Gustin, W. C., 922, 923, 924
Gutfreund, Y., 612, 632
Guth, D. A., 757, 766
Gutheil, G., 571, 621, 700
Guthrie, D., 622
Gutstein, J., 364
Guttentag, R. E., 493, 520
Guz, G. R., 833
Güzeldere, G., 624
Gwiazda, J., 69, 115, 130, 131
Gwinner, E., 19
Gyoba, J., 140, 141
Gzesh, S. M., 559, 597, 599

Haaf, R. A., 236, 306, 307, 308, 309
Haake, R. J., 133, 519
Haarmann, H. J., 455
Haas, M., 911
Haberecht, M. F., 34
Habib, R., 23
Hacker, B., 526
Hackman, J. R., 939
Hadar, U., 363
Hadders-Algra, M., 182, 188
Haden, C. A., 397, 398, 404, 405, 408, 673
Hadijkhani, M., 32
Hadwin, J., 823, 829
Hafitz, J., 283, 284
Hagen, E. H., 882
Hagen, J., 516, 656, 957, 958
Hagen, M. A., 866, 880
Hager, L., 449
Hahn, H. H., 778
Hahn, U., 609, 691, 701, 711
Haidt, J., 621
Haier, R. J., 501
Haight, J. C., 381, 387, 399, 407, 408
Haight, W., 303
Haine, R., 404
Hainline, L., 131, 146
Hains, S. M. J., 816
Haith, M., 29, 121, 124, 142, 181, 186, 187, 214,
    216, 217, 219, 221, 222, 223, 224, 235, 239,
    240, 374, 467
Hakuta, K., 267, 622
Hale, C. M., 847, 851
Hale, G., 958

Hale, K., 321
Haley, A., 13
Halff, H. M., 317
Halford, G. S., 427, 431, 457, 558, 559, 560, 561,
    563, 565, 566, 570, 572, 573, 574, 575, 576,
    577, 579, 581, 582, 583, 584, 585, 586, 587,
    588, 589, 592, 598, 758, 958
Halit, H., 36, 37, 39
Hall, D. G., 300, 301, 308, 311, 312, 315, 316,
    317, 318, 700
Hall, G., 312, 320, 321, 322
Hall, J. W., 61, 68, 70, 71
Hall, K. M., 537
Hall, L. K., 520
Hall, S., 860
Hallahan, D. P., 530
Hallberg, K. I., 643, 664
Hallé, P., 81, 89, 90
Hallett, G. L., 695
Hallett, M., 16, 677
Hallpike, C. R., 638, 648
Hallstrom, J., 866
Halparin, J. D., 42
Halpern, D. F., 762, 763
Halpin, C. F., 62, 64, 67
Halsted, N., 77, 301, 305
Halverson, H. M., 165, 172
Halwes, T., 74, 516
Hamada, H., 65
Hamann, M. S., 796
Hamann, S., 38
Hamberger, L., 182
Hamburger, S. D., 12
Hamer, D. R., 123
Hamilton, C. E., 838
Hamilton, R., 16
Hamilton, Z., 563
Hamlett, C. L., 539, 540, 797, 799
Hammeke, T. A., 76
Hammer, R. D., 117
Hamner, A., 183
Hamond, N. R., 394, 395, 396
Hampson, J., 270
Hampton, J. A., 708
Hamsher, J. H., 407
Hamson, C. O., 795, 801
Han, J. H., 792
Han, J. J., 407, 410, 411
Hanakawa, T., 677
Hanashima, C., 8
Hanauer, J. B., 564
Hand, H. H., 926, 927
Handley, S., 963
Hanley, J., 767
Hanlon, C., 277
Hanna, E., 148, 383, 384
Hans, L. L., 74
Happé, F. G. E., 837, 843, 846, 850
Hardiman, G., 867
Harding, C. G., 703, 813
Hardman, C. E., 829, 842
Hare, B., 66, 667, 839, 840, 850
Hare, M., 444, 448
Hargrave, S., 516
Hargreaves, D. J., 890
Hari, R., 25
Harkness, A., 967
Harkness, S., 661
Harlaar, N., 913
Harley, H., 302, 790, 792

Harley, K., 401, 405
Harlow, H. F., 196
Harm, M. W., 434
Harnishfeger, K., 958, 959, 990
Harre, R., 618
Harris, D. B., 862, 870
Harris, I. M., 32
Harris, K. R., 530, 538, 545
Harris, M. R., 590
Harris, P., 217, 220, 221, 240, 315, 433, 454, 594,
    722, 813, 815, 820, 823, 828, 829, 830, 831,
    832, 833, 841, 842, 843, 844, 845, 846, 847,
    848, 849, 850, 926, 960, 963
Harris, W. A., 10
Harris, Z., 85
Harrison, H. M., 469
Harrison, R. P., 352, 355
Hart, B., 525
Hart, D., 931, 932
Hart, R., 758
Hartl, M., 825
Hartley, D. E. H., 68
Hartley, J. L., 879
Hartley, T., 35, 738
Hartman, B., 188
Hartman, E., 299, 699, 716, 721, 722
Hartman, K. A., 716
Hartmann, E. E., 123
Hartshorn, K., 31, 380
Hartshorne, H., 909
Hartup, W. W., 376
Harvey, S., 535, 537
Harwood, D. L., 881
Haryu, E., 302, 311, 312, 316, 317, 318
Hasboun, D., 35
Hasegawa, T., 782, 783, 804
Hashtroudi, S., 29
Haslam, N., 721
Haspelmath, M., 324
Hassam, R., 9
Hasselmo, M. E., 20
Haste, H., 932
Hastings, N. B., 398
Hata, T., 182
Hatano, G., 77, 488, 541, 559, 618, 620, 636, 638,
    652, 654, 655, 663, 665, 667, 668, 704, 706,
    716, 788
Hatch, T., 927
Hatten, M. B., 7
Hatten, M. E., 10
Haun, D. B. M., 761
Haupt, D., 863
Hauser, L. B., 782, 789
Hauser, M., 78, 93, 94, 271, 614, 664, 781, 782,
    789, 882, 883, 885
Havighurst, R. J., 880
Haviland, J. M., 816
Hawker, D., 926
Hawkins, J., 960
Hawley, P. H., 926
Haxby, J. V., 35, 36
Hay, D. F., 930
Hayabuchi, I., 66
Hayes, B., 28, 570, 597
Hayes, J., 537
Hayes, K. C., 166
Hayes, R., 79, 148, 149
Hayne, H., 22, 25, 220, 234, 380, 381, 382, 383,
    384, 389, 410, 412, 413, 674, 867, 870
Haynes, H., 118

Hayward, W. G., 741
Hazan, C., 29, 181
Hazelrigg, M. D., 740
Hazeltine, E., 29
Hazen, N. L., 757
Hazzard, A., 415
Healey, P., 148
Healy, B., 817
Healy, S. D., 764
Hearn, E. F., 19
Heath, D. C., 352, 353
Hebb, D. O., 430
Hecht, S. A., 792, 793
Hedberg, N., 278
Hedges, L. V., 735, 738, 752, 753, 754, 763
Hegarty, M., 735, 755, 761, 762, 797, 799
Heibeck, T. H., 317
Heifetz, R. A., 926
Heim, I., 312
Hein, A., 191
Heindel, W., 29
Heinmiller, B. M., 887
Heinze, H. J., 31
Heit, E., 309, 597, 609, 701
Heitger, F., 136
Hejmadi, A., 708
Held, R., 69, 115, 116, 118, 124, 130, 131, 191,
    470, 472, 473, 496
Heldmeyer, K. H., 868
Heller, J. I., 780, 797, 798
Helm, A., 322, 325
Helmholtz, H. von, 110, 112, 127, 139, 142
Helson, R., 909, 911, 912, 913, 925, 940
Heltne, P. G., 645
Helwig, C. C., 931
Hembree, R., 539
Henderson, C., 191, 193
Henderson, J., 67, 885
Hendrickson, A., 118
Hening, W., 451
Henkel, L. A., 760
Hennessey, M., 921, 923, 985
Hennessy, B. L., 73
Hennessy, R., 28
Henning, A., 816
Henninghausen, K. H., 409
Hennon, E. A., 304, 311
Hennson, R. N. A., 23
Henry, B., 243
Henson, A. M., 65
Henson, R., 16, 37
Hepper, P. G., 60, 182
Hepps, D., 415
Hepworth, S., 34, 35
Herbert, J., 381, 383, 384
Hering, E., 112, 113
Herman, J., 758, 850
Hermer, L., 738, 746, 747, 750
Hermer-Vazquez, L., 749
Hernandez-Reif, M., 148
Heron, C., 449
Herr, P., 929
Herrera, C., 848
Herrmann, D. J., 513
Herrnstein, R. J., 906
Hersh, R., 924
Hershberger, S. L., 475
Hertenstein, M. J., 164, 176, 178, 180, 191, 194,
    195, 198, 200, 202, 617, 744, 745
Hertsgaard, L. A., 234, 381, 384, 390

Hertwig, R., 457
Hertz-Pannier, L., 76
Herzog, A., 751
Hesketh, L. J., 345
Hespos, S. J., 568, 695, 761, 782, 783
Hesse, J., 355
Hesselink, J. R., 12
Heth, C. D., 748, 757, 758
Hetherington, E. M., 820
Hevner, K., 890
Hewitt, K. L., 69
Hewlett, B. S., 661
Heyes, C. M., 839
Heyman, G., 696, 699, 708, 712, 721
Heywood, S., 356
Hiatt, S., 191, 193
Hickey, T. L., 118, 131
Hickmann, M., 470, 471, 474, 497
Hicks, J., 360
Hicks, L., 197
Higgins, C. I., 198
Hill, D., 697, 885, 886, 887
Hill, E. W., 757, 766
Hillenbrand, J. A., 72
Hillier, L., 69
Hines, M., 763, 764
Hinton, G. E., 433, 618, 625
Hiraki, K., 782, 783, 804
Hirano, S., 117
Hiranuma, H., 880
Hirsch, E., 700
Hirsch, E., Jr., 777
Hirschfeld, L., 613, 614, 663, 688, 705, 706, 708
Hirschhorn, L., 928
Hirschman, A. O., 935
Hirschman, J. E., 415
Hirsh-Pasek, K., 81, 87, 263, 299, 302, 304, 306,
    308, 311, 312, 714, 886
Hiscock, K., 507
Hitch, G. J., 33, 796
Ho, V., 497
Ho, W.-C., 905
Hoard, M. K., 795, 796, 797, 801
Hobbes, T., 109
Hobbs, S. B., 875, 876
Hobson, R. P., 843
Hochberg, I., 62, 64, 69
Hochberg, J., 860, 863
Hockett, C. F., 347
Hockley, N. S., 76
Hodges, J., 38, 42
Hodges, R. M., 583
Hodkin, B., 574
Hoeffner, J. H., 447, 448
Hof, F. A., 7
Hofer, A., 31
Hofer, B., 982, 984, 986
Hoff, E., 300, 303
Hoff-Ginsberg, E., 303, 326
Hoffman, D. D., 144
Hoffman, E., 35
Hoffman, H., 74
Hoffman, J. E., 765
Hoffman, M. L., 819, 930, 931
Hoffman-Plotkin, D., 822
Hoffmeister, R., 346
Hofstadter, D. R., 560, 908, 911
Hofstadter, M., 162, 449, 737, 743
Hogan, D. M., 497
Hogan, K., 541

Hogan, S. C., 68
Hohenstein, J., 705, 708
Höhle, B., 79
Hohmann, C., 926
Hohmann, M., 526, 926
Hohne, E. A., 79, 86, 88
Hoijtink, H., 598
Holahan, C. K., 906, 907, 913
Holcomb, W. L., 590
Holden, D. J., 519
Holden, G., 183
Holdstock, J. S., 22, 35
Hollander, M., 281, 282, 325, 444, 445, 446, 448,
    701
Holley, F. B., 185, 186
Hollich, G., 94, 299, 302, 306, 308, 315
Hollingworth, L. S., 906, 907, 927, 931
Holmes, C. J., 12
Holmes, F. L., 912, 924, 925
Holroyd, C., 174
Holstege, G., 38
Holt, L. L., 72, 74
Holt, R., 848
Holton, G., 925
Holway, A. H., 145
Holyoak, K., 457, 539, 558, 560, 588, 591, 717,
    735, 961
Honda, M., 16, 677
Hood, B., 44, 119, 224, 428, 737
Hood, R., 186
Hopkins, B., 170, 180, 182, 200
Hopkins, D., 755
Hopkins, W. D., 755
Hopper, P., 269, 302
Hoptman, M. J., 31
Horn, C. L., 170
Horner, J. S., 63, 64
Hornik, R., 818
Hornstein, D., 257
Hornung, K., 39
Horobin, K., 350
Horowitz, F. D., 78, 217
Horrobin, K. D., 345
Horton, J. J., 574
Hosenfeld, B., 482, 484, 486, 496, 561
Hoshino, T., 66
Houdé, O., 599, 788
Houghton, C., 921, 923, 985
Houle, S., 23
House, B. J., 466
House, R. J., 909, 927, 928
Houston, D. M., 85, 86, 89, 90, 94
Houston-Price, C. M. T., 564
Howard, D., 76
Howard-Hamilton, M. F., 931
Howe, C., 257
Howe, M. J., 563
Howe, M. L., 381, 387, 389, 399, 400, 401, 418,
    575, 576, 591, 752
Howell, S., 666
Howland, H. C., 118
Howlin, P., 292
Hoyer, E., 62
Hoyne, K. L., 308
Hsiao, H. S., 613
Hsu, C. C., 795
Hu, S.-C., 10
Huang, E. J., 12
Huang, J. Q., 66
Huang, X., 60

Huang, Y., 894
Hubbard, E. M., 164, 176, 178, 180, 191, 194, 195, 198, 200, 202, 617, 744, 745
Hubel, D. H., 119, 130, 766
Hubl, D., 38
Hubley, P., 811
Hudson, J. A., 384, 385, 397, 400, 404, 413, 524
Hudson, L., 917, 919, 922, 923
Hudson, W., 866
Huffman, L. F., 474, 475, 489, 493, 531
Hugdahl, K., 31
Hughes, C., 848
Hughes, M., 574, 575, 826
Huizenga, H. M., 558
Hull, C. L., 466, 701
Hulse, S. H., 882, 893
Hulshoff Pol, H. E., 12
Hume, D., 109, 228, 625
Hummel, J. E., 136, 457
Humphrey, G. K., 757, 766
Humphrey, K., 73
Humphrey, T., 183
Humphreys, G. W., 616
Humphreys, J., 876
Humphreys, K., 241, 242
Hund, A. M., 752, 753, 754
Hung, C. P., 623
Hunkin, N. M., 22
Hünnerkopf, M., 473
Hunt, C. M., 90
Hunt, E., 764
Hunt, J. G., 909, 927
Hunt, J. M., 221
Hunt, R., 29
Hunter, M. A., 218, 219
Hunter, S. K., 219
Huntington, K., 531
Huntley, A., 885
Huntley-Fenner, G., 782, 783, 786, 787
Hupet, M., 363, 364
Hurwitz, S., 760
Hurwitz, W. M., 316
Hussain, F., 860
Hutchings, M. E., 70
Hutchins, E., 638, 911
Hutchins, G., 76, 642
Hutchinson, J. E., 311, 316, 630, 696, 719, 720
Hutt, C., 390
Huttenlocher, J., 290, 303, 312, 432, 569, 582, 735, 737, 738, 739, 740, 742, 743, 744, 747, 748, 749, 750, 751, 752, 753, 754, 755, 756, 758, 759, 760, 763, 764, 781, 787, 788, 792, 803
Huttenlocher, P. R., 11, 14, 386
Hutton, D., 829
Hutton, J., 292
Hyde, M. L., 67
Hynd, G. W., 530
Hynes, R. O., 10

Ibanez, V., 16
Iga, N., 19
Igarashi, Y., 66
Iglesias, J., 149
Ihsen, E., 744
Ikospentaki, K., 597, 724
Ilari, B., 89
Ilg, F., 795, 797, 883
Imai, M., 302, 303, 311, 312, 316, 317, 318, 695, 714

Imbens-Bailey, A., 850
Imberty, M., 900
Immisch, I., 677
Inagaki, K., 488, 541, 559, 618, 620, 665, 667, 668, 704, 706, 716
Inall, M., 878
Ince, G., 10
Incisa della Rocchetta, A., 35
Ingram, D., 274, 621
Ingram, N., 875
Inhelder, B., 438, 470, 471, 500, 540, 558, 573, 586, 596, 617, 625, 672, 689, 699, 709, 737, 756, 862, 870, 872, 875, 876, 954, 955, 962, 971, 975
Inhelder, I., 779
Inhoff, A., 44
Inman, K., 303, 319
Inoue, H., 140, 141
Insel, T. R., 13, 19
Irwin, R. J., 61
Irwin, S. A., 47
Isaac, C. L., 22, 35, 38
Isaacs, E. B., 27, 33
Ishac, M. G., 173
Ishai, A., 36
Ishak, S., 194
Ishihara, K., 181
Ishii, T., 66
Israel, M., 273
Itakura, S., 666, 841
Itier, R. J., 37
Itoh, H., 40
Ittleson, W. H., 133
Iverson, J. M., 338, 339, 340, 341, 342, 344, 345, 353, 355
Ives, S. W., 878
Ivry, R., 29, 30
Iwawaki, S., 868
Izard, C. E., 816
Izard, V., 665, 780
Izzo, C., 526

Jackendoff, R., 321, 882, 883
Jacklin, C. N., 406
Jackson, A., 31
Jackson, N. E., 530
Jackson, P. W., 908, 917, 932
Jacobs, D. S., 117
Jacobs, J., 534, 978
Jacobs, L., 735
Jacobs, M., 975
Jacobs, R., 40, 614
Jacobs, W. J., 751
Jacobsen, C., 909, 927, 928
Jacobson, K., 136, 166, 222, 224, 428, 448, 617, 737, 780
Jacobson, S. W., 382, 411
Jacoby, L. L., 513
Jacquin-Courtois, S., 750
Jagadeesh, B., 17
Jahoda, G., 863, 866, 880
Jahrsdorfer, R., 70
Jain, S., 611
Jakimik, J., 84
Jakobson, L. S., 624
James, D., 182
James, W., 109, 139, 398, 832
Jamieson, D., 61, 67
Jamison, K. R., 909
Jäncke, L., 31, 894

Jancovic, M. A., 340
Janik, V. M., 637, 645
Janikoun, R., 876
Janis, J., 978
Jankovic, I. N., 760
Jankowski, J. J., 390, 611, 863
Janos, P. M., 482
Janowsky, J. S., 25
Jansen, B. R. J., 442, 443, 598
Janveau-Brenman, G., 593
Jaques, E., 920, 928
Jaramasz, M., 31
Jarecky, R. K., 909
Jarrold, C., 291, 765, 844
Jarvis, P. E., 811
Jaswal, V. K., 300, 301, 306, 311, 315, 317, 699, 702, 713, 715, 716, 724
Jay, E., 986, 987
Jeanty, P., 174
Jeffries, N., 30, 31, 803, 957
Jeka, J. J., 164, 173, 177, 197
Jenike, M., 41, 149
Jenkins, E., 472, 473, 474, 480, 482, 483, 487, 488, 489, 490, 491, 492, 493, 494, 501, 502, 559, 788, 801
Jenkins, J. J., 73
Jenkins, J. M., 845, 846
Jenkins, W. M., 68
Jennett, M., 876
Jennings, J., 42
Jensen, A., 906, 913
Jensen, D. C., 879
Jensen, I., 559
Jensen, J. K., 62, 67
Jensen, J. L., 164, 167, 169, 178, 180
Jentzsch, I., 37
Jerison, H., 640
Jernigan, T., 12, 765
Jersild, A., 891
Jessell, T. M., 10
Jesteadt, W., 60, 66
Jezzard, P., 15, 34, 41
Jian, W., 173
Jiang, Z. D., 63, 67
Jipson, J. L., 722
Joanisse, M. F., 434, 445
Joh, A. S., 190, 194, 200
Johansen, M. K., 710
Johansson, G., 114, 124, 127, 138, 143, 144, 145
Johnson, A., 376, 521
Johnson, C., 273
Johnson, C. J., 533
Johnson, C. N., 829
Johnson, D., 311, 392
Johnson, E. J., 474
Johnson, E. K., 78, 86, 87, 93, 271, 305
Johnson, E. S., 763
Johnson, E. W., 178
Johnson, J., 940
Johnson, J. A., 77
Johnson, J. E., 10
Johnson, J. S., 622
Johnson, J. W., 521
Johnson, K., 187, 189, 521, 704
Johnson, K. E., 240, 472, 486, 492, 574, 575, 576, 689, 697
Johnson, K. L., 226
Johnson, L. R., 829

Johnson, M., 286, 691
Johnson, M. H., 4, 14, 19, 33, 36, 37, 39, 44, 119, 146, 147, 150, 152, 167, 181, 186, 202, 237, 241, 242, 243, 286, 306, 427, 430, 433, 434, 450, 454, 468, 499, 558, 562, 613, 614, 615, 616, 623, 663, 664, 742, 744, 745, 765
Johnson, M. K., 723
Johnson, M. L., 172, 174, 175
Johnson, N. E., 764
Johnson, N. S., 373, 377, 516
Johnson, R., Jr., 33
Johnson, R. L., 224, 737
Johnson, S., 139, 140, 271, 738
Johnson, S. C., 632, 705, 708, 709, 765
Johnson, S. P., 93, 128, 139, 140, 181, 186, 202, 226, 237, 239, 558, 745
Johnson-Laird, P., 560, 586, 591, 593, 594, 718, 961
Johnsrude, I. S., 17
John-Steiner, V., 908, 911, 912, 914, 915, 922, 923, 925, 939
Johnston, S., 31
Jolley, R. P., 867, 868
Jones, C. M., 764
Jones, G., 431
Jones, I., 470, 473, 474, 486, 497
Jones, K., 706, 707
Jones, R., 62, 866
Jones, R. M., 436
Jones, R. S., 529
Jones, S. S., 691, 701, 706, 707, 708
Jones, T., 14, 17, 565
Jones, W., 844
Jonides, J., 33, 449, 701, 702
Jonsson, B., 187, 745
Joram, E., 689
Jordan, H., 765
Jordan, K., 31
Jordan, N. C., 582, 787, 788, 797, 801
Joseph, R. M., 765, 844
Joshi, M. S., 842
Jouen, F., 197
Joulian, F., 642
Joyce, P. F., 75
Judge, P., 64
Juel, C., 531
Julesz, B., 130
Jungers, M. K., 89
Juola, P., 444, 445, 447
Juraska, J. M., 17
Jusczyk, A. M., 81, 85
Jusczyk, P., 67, 72, 74, 77, 78, 79, 80, 81, 82, 83, 85, 86, 87, 88, 89, 90, 91, 92, 94, 301, 303, 304, 305, 315, 468, 886
Just, M., 430, 437, 455, 469

Kaga, K., 63
Kagan, J., 389, 781, 887, 888, 928, 930, 931, 932, 933
Kahneman, D., 89, 457, 520, 558, 568, 586, 718, 783, 975, 976
Kail, R., 516, 520, 756, 957, 958
Kaitz, M., 382
Kako, E., 321, 322
Kalakanis, L., 148
Kaldy, Z., 227, 229, 744
Kalish, C., 309, 571, 693, 698, 699, 700, 705, 706, 708, 712, 716, 722, 965
Kallio, K. D., 587
Kamenetsky, S. B., 885, 886

Kameyama, M., 40, 41
Kamhi, A. G., 591
Kaminaga, T., 677
Kaminski, J. R., 60, 66
Kamm, K., 172, 177, 186
Kampe, K., 16
Kanani, P. H., 175, 176
Kane, M., 264, 495, 801
Kane, S., 541
Kant, I., 126, 228
Kanwisher, N., 35, 149, 241, 616
Kapfhamer, J., 94
Kaplan, A., 837
Kaplan, B., 689, 895
Kaplan, D., 967, 973, 974
Kaplan, G. A., 128, 137
Kaplan, H., 661
Kaplan, P. S., 117
Kaplan, R., 354
Karasik, L. B., 195, 199
Kardar, M., 612
Kardash, C., 985
Karmiloff-Smith, A., 39, 119, 152, 237, 241, 286, 291, 351, 427, 430, 433, 434, 455, 457, 468, 470, 471, 472, 480, 483, 488, 496, 499, 500, 501, 558, 561, 616, 620, 624, 628, 663, 664, 691, 750, 765, 878, 895, 916
Karusitis, K., 867
Karzon, R. G., 78, 80
Kasari, C., 843, 844
Kaschak, M., 352
Kase, J., 752
Kasof, J., 914, 920
Kass, J., 72
Kassubek, J., 735
Kastens, K. A., 741
Kastner, M. P., 890
Kastner, S. B., 530
Kaszniak, A. W., 26
Kattef, E., 579
Katz, I., 976
Katz, J., 921, 924, 966, 967
Katz, W., 76
Kauffman, J. M., 530
Kaufman, J., 76, 737
Kaufman, L., 125, 704
Kaufmann, F., 125, 128, 137, 142
Kaufmann, J. M., 37
Kaufmann-Hayoz, R., 125, 128, 137, 142
Kavanaugh, R. D., 844
Kavsek, M. J., 133
Kawabata, H., 140, 141
Kawabata, M., 174
Kawahara, S., 387
Kawashima, R., 40
Kay, B. A., 177, 198
Kay, D., 119
Kay, S. I., 919
Kaye, P., 258
Kay-Raining Bird, E., 291
Kazmi, H., 15
Kearney, J. K., 193
Keating, D., 779, 781, 954, 956, 971
Keating, M. J., 70
Keckley, C., 183
Kee, D. W., 516, 520
Keeble, S., 229, 230, 245, 306, 567
Keefe, D. H., 60, 65
Keele, S., 42, 562
Keen, R., 162, 184, 186, 187, 201, 570, 737

Keenan, J. P., 16
Keene, E. O., 537
Keeney, F. J., 516
Kegl, J., 348
Keil, F., 20, 306, 309, 470, 497, 558, 563, 571, 609, 610, 616, 618, 619, 620, 621, 625, 626, 627, 628, 632, 669, 670, 671, 690, 692, 693, 699, 701, 702, 703, 705, 706, 708, 711, 712, 714, 715, 716, 717, 718, 780, 889, 954, 964
Keinanen, M., 915
Keislar, E. R., 545
Keith, A., 6
Kekelis, L. S., 345
Kelemen, D., 717
Kellas, G., 516
Keller, A., 30
Keller, E. F., 925
Keller, H., 170, 200, 299, 659
Keller, M., 831
Kellerman, B., 926
Kellman, P., 111, 114, 120, 121, 125, 126, 127, 128, 129, 130, 132, 134, 136, 137, 138, 139, 140, 141, 142, 143, 144, 146, 150, 152, 199, 226, 616
Kellogg, R., 869, 870, 880
Kelly, D. M., 748, 755
Kelly, G. J., 921, 924
Kelly, J., 122, 123, 124
Kelly, M., 521, 820
Kelly, M. E., 587, 589, 758
Kelly, M. H., 79, 632
Kelly, S. D., 342, 343, 344, 360, 362
Kelso, J. A. S., 164, 169, 173, 177, 430, 435
Kemler, D. G., 711
Kemler Nelson, D. G., 81, 87, 571, 619, 670, 671, 706, 707, 708, 886
Kemmer, S., 273, 286
Kemmerer, D., 81
Kendler, H. H., 466, 499
Kendler, T. S., 466, 499
Kendon, A., 336, 337, 339, 349, 356
Kendrick, C., 819, 821
Kennedy, C., 317
Kennedy, E., 240, 752
Kennedy, H., 36
Kennedy, J. M., 863, 870, 876
Kennedy, L., 81, 83, 92
Kenny, S. L., 921
Kenrick, D. T., 559
Kenyon, B., 867, 878
Kermoian, R., 178, 180, 191, 198
Kerns, K. A., 763
Kerschensteiner, G., 860, 861, 878, 880
Kertzman, C., 44
Kervella, C., 816
Kerwin, K., 516
Keselman, A., 967, 968, 973, 974, 976
Kesler-West, M. L., 36
Kessel, C., 488
Kessen, W., 121, 316, 891
Kestenbaum, R., 148, 149, 227
Kester, E., 319
Keubli, J., 393
Keutmann, D., 355
Keynes, R., 7, 9
Keyser, S. J., 321
Khan, Y., 12
Kidd, G., Jr., 71
Kidd, T., 10
Kidder, T., 934

Kiehl, K. A., 75, 76
Kiehn, O., 168
Kielsmeier, J., 926
Kikuchi-Yorioka, Y., 33
Kikyo, H., 40, 41
Kilbreath, C. S., 313, 314, 715, 716
Killeen, P. R., 74
Kim, C. C., 785, 791, 792
Kim, I. H., 542
Kim, J. J., 387
Kim, M., 312, 325
Kim, N. S., 616, 619
Kim, S., 31, 339, 344, 980, 982
Kimberg, D. Y., 455
Kincade, J., 44
Kind, C., 611
King, A., 70, 537
King, P., 984
King, S. W., 34, 41
King, W. M., 68
Kingma, J., 400, 418, 589, 752
Kingsley, M. E., 530
Kingsley, P. R., 516
Kingsnorth, S., 180, 190
Kinsley, C. H., 19
Kintner, C., 6
Kintsch, W., 373, 798
Kirasic, K. C., 756, 758, 761
Kircher, M., 865
Kirino, Y., 387
Kirk, E. P., 475
Kirk, K. I., 94
Kirkham, N., 43, 93, 271, 564, 744, 989
Kirkorian, G., 30, 41
Kisilevsky, B. S., 146
Kistler, D., 39, 61, 67, 71
Kistner, J., 822
Kita, S., 354, 355, 363, 364, 761
Kitamura, C., 80
Kitamura, S., 795
Kitayama, S., 674
Kitchener, K., 984
Kitcher, P., 620, 624
Klaczynski, A. A., 921, 923
Klaczynski, P., 625, 626, 954, 960, 961, 962, 965,
    967, 972, 976, 977, 978, 979, 980
Klahr, D., 426, 427, 428, 429, 430, 431, 436, 439,
    440, 443, 457, 467, 468, 473, 492, 495, 497,
    498, 558, 582, 592, 595, 620, 921, 922, 923,
    924, 962, 965, 966, 972, 973, 974
Klatt, L., 782, 783
Klatzky, R., 361, 761
Klecan-Aker, J., 531
Kleim, J., 14
Klein, A., 779
Klein, A. J., 67
Klein, A. S., 791, 797
Klein, E., 617, 929
Klein, J. S., 788, 790, 797
Klein, P., 31, 380, 383, 384
Klein, R. E., 73
Klein, S., 43
Klein, S. A., 115, 120
Klein, S. M., 363, 364
Klein, W., 282
Kleiner, K. A., 120, 146, 147
Kleinknecht, E. E., 234, 391
Kleven, G. A., 163, 169
Klibanoff, R. S., 301, 316, 317, 318, 320
Kliener, K. A., 120

Klima, E., 274
Klimes-Dougan, B., 822
Klin, A., 38, 616, 844
Klingberg, T., 34
Klingner, J. K., 536
Klinnert, M. D., 193, 199, 817, 818
Klintsova, A. Y., 47
Klip, A. W. J., 188
Klip-Van den Nieuwendijk, A. W. J., 182
Kloo, D., 718
Kluckhohn, C., 638
Kluender, K. R., 72, 74
Knapp, D., 764
Knapp, M. L., 336
Knauff, M., 735
Knoblauch, K., 122
Knopf, I., 958
Knopman, D., 29, 381
Knowlton, B., 27, 375, 380, 588
Knox, E. L., 868
Knudsen, E. I., 5, 14, 612, 632
Knudson, R., 979
Kobasigawa, A., 518
Kobayashi, T., 782, 783, 804
Koch, E. G., 62, 64
Kochanska, G., 831
Koda, V., 30
Koechlin, E., 782
Koedinger, K. R., 498
Koenderink, J. J., 127
Koenig, M., 704, 713, 722, 848, 849
Koeske, R., 719, 720
Koffka, K., 112, 137
Kogan, N., 720, 907
Kohlberg, L., 545, 811, 830, 909, 930, 931
Kohler, C., 863
Köhler, S., 376
Köhler, W., 201
Kohn, N., 893
Kohno, M., 73
Koizumi, H., 76, 82, 93, 305
Kokaia, Z., 9
Kokinov, B., 560
Kokis, J., 985
Kolb, B., 17
Kolb, S., 170
Kolinsky, R., 657
Kolstad, V., 704
Konczak, K., 190
Konieczna, E., 280
Konishi, S., 40, 41
Konner, M., 170
Koos, O., 619, 814
Kopyar, B. A., 64
Kornack, D. R., 8
Kornhaber, M., 907
Korvenoja, A., 33
Korwitz, A., 866
Koseff, P., 27
Koslowski, B., 964, 965, 972
Kosslyn, S. M., 31, 765, 868
Kostovic, I., 11
Kotovsky, L., 497
Kotter, J. P., 926, 928
Koutstaal, W., 28
Kovacic, D., 76, 82, 93, 305
Kowalksy, E., 893
Koyasu, M., 880
Kozhevnikov, M., 755, 797, 799
Kozhevnikova, E. V., 80, 94

Kozlowski, P. B., 8
Kozuch, P., 12
Krajewski, K., 473
Kramer, A. F., 17
Kramer, R., 830, 831
Kramer, S. J., 144
Krascum, R. M., 562, 705
Kraszpulski, M., 8
Kratus, J., 890
Kratzer, A., 312
Kraus, S. J., 932
Krauss, R. M., 342, 352, 356, 363
Krebs, D. L., 933
Kremenitzer, J. P., 124
Kremser, C., 31
Krentz, U. C., 76
Kreuzer, J. A., 74
Kriegstein, A. R., 10
Kripke, S., 698
Kroch, A., 302
Kroeber, A. L., 638
Kromer, M. K., 757
Kron, V., 473
Kropfl, W., 130
Kroupina, M. G., 380, 382, 391, 392, 412, 413
Krowitz, A., 197
Kruetzer, M. A., 514
Kruger, A., 286, 541
Kruger, J., 521
Kruithof, A., 832
Krumhansl, C. L., 81, 882, 886, 888, 889
Krupa, D. J., 800
Kruse, A., 470
Kryscio, R. J., 36
Kübler, O., 136
Kucan, L., 527
Kucera, H., 446
Kuchuk, A., 149
Kuczaj, S., 281
Kuczynski, L., 822
Kuebli, J., 401, 407, 408
Kugler, K., 882
Kugler, P. N., 435
Kuhl, P., 15, 72, 73, 74, 76, 80, 85, 91, 94, 305,
    691, 692, 715, 762, 767, 972
Kuhlmeier, V., 619, 644
Kuhn, A., 149
Kuhn, D., 470, 471, 472, 479, 480, 481, 483, 485,
    488, 489, 491, 492, 493, 494, 495, 496, 497,
    498, 500, 512, 513, 522, 540, 541, 542, 544,
    545, 546, 559, 624, 718, 835, 869, 912, 921,
    923, 924, 954, 956, 960, 962, 963, 965, 966,
    967, 968, 969, 970, 971, 972, 973, 974, 975,
    976, 979, 980, 981, 982, 983, 984, 985, 986,
    987, 988
Kuhn, I. F., 696
Kuhn, J., 406
Kuhn, T., 619, 626, 703, 913, 920
Kuijala, T., 74
Kuijpers, C., 85
Kuipers, B., 738
Kulig, J. W., 69
Kulik, J., 414
Kuniyoshi, Y., 163
Kunnen, S., 598
Kuno, A., 182
Kuo, L. J., 542
Kuo, Z., 430
Kupersmidt, J., 169
Kurita, J. A., 533

Kurland, D., 958, 959
Kurtz, B. E., 516, 529
Kurtz, R., 292
Kurtz, S., 968
Kurtzberg, D., 74, 124
Kushnir, T., 623, 717
Kusunoki, M., 614
Kutas, M., 381
Kwon, H., 34
Kwon, J., 844
Kwon, P., 723
Kwon, Y., 785, 791, 795, 796, 797, 802
Kwong, B., 66
Kwong, T. E., 480
Kyriakidou, C., 407

LaBar, K., 30
Lacasse, M. A., 531
Lacerda, F., 73, 305
Lacerenza, L., 532
Lacey, J. F., 563
Ladd, S. F., 474
Ladhar, N., 89
Lafaite, M., 744
LaFleur, R., 73
Lafon, P., 968
Lafosse, A., 704
Lagace, C., 198
Lagattuta, K. H., 833
Lahande, N., 762, 767
Lahey, M., 283
Lahr, M. M., 641, 642
Lai, E., 8
Lai, S., 76
Laiacona, M., 619
Lakoff, G., 302, 723
Lalonde, C., 73, 984
Lalonde, R., 37
Lam, G. W., 932, 933, 934
LaMantia, A. S., 34
Lambertz, G., 77, 301, 305
Lambon Ralph, M., 874
Lamborn, S. D., 927, 932
LaMendola, N. P., 87
Lamm, C., 31
Lammertyn, J., 750
Lampl, M., 172, 174, 175
Landau, B., 316, 325, 345, 691, 701, 706, 707, 708, 736, 744, 757, 759, 760, 765, 766
Lander, A. D., 10
Lando, B., 821
Landrum, J. T., 117
Lanfermann, H., 38
Lang, B., 564, 718
Lang, P. J., 38
Lang, W., 16
Langacker, R., 258, 269, 278, 280
Lange, G., 516, 519, 521
Lange, N., 12
Langer, A., 197, 866
Langer, J., 222, 643, 782
Langer, S., 890, 915
Langley, M., 835, 985
Langley, P., 430, 438, 620, 908, 911, 923
Langois, J. H., 148
Langrock, A., 763
Lansford, R., 18
Lany, J., 338, 345, 353
Lanzenberger, R., 16
Laplante, D. P., 146

Lapsley, D. K., 541
Laren, E., 76
Larkey, L. B., 718
Larkin, J., 621, 798, 803
Larsen, J. S., 117
Larsen, M. T., 653
Larson, G. E., 764
Lary, S., 66
Lashley, K. S., 814
Lasky, R. E., 67, 73
La Torre, R., 182
Latour, B., 924
Lau, R. R., 716
Laudan, L., 620
Lauder, E., 878
Lauer, K. D., 537
Laurance, H. E., 751
Laurence, S., 611
Laurendeau, M., 756
LaVancher, C., 497, 498
Lave, C. A., 656, 658
Lave, J., 494, 671
Lavelli, M., 470, 489
Lavigne-Rebillard, M., 66
Lavin, B., 720
Lavin, T. A., 300, 301, 311, 312, 315, 317, 318
Lawler, C., 867
Lawler, E., 867
Lawler, R. W., 472
Lawrence, D. A., 751
Lawrence, J. A., 575, 576
Lawrence, W. G., 928
Lawrence-Lightfoot, S., 933
Lawrie, D. A., 352
Laws, G., 291
Lawson, J., 846
Lazar, N., 957, 958, 959
Lea, S. E. G., 139
Leach, J., 921, 923, 924
Leadbeater, B., 540
Leamey, C. A., 14
Learmonth, A., 743, 744, 749, 750, 751
Leavitt, L. A., 72
Lebiere, C., 428, 429, 430, 437, 457
Le Bihan, D., 784, 800, 804
Lebowitz, C., 867
Lebowitz, K., 311
Lecacheur, M., 793, 801
Lecanuet, J.-P., 60
Lecas, J., 593
Lechuga, M. T., 383
Lecuyer, R., 229
Ledebt, A., 167, 172, 173, 174, 176, 178, 179, 180
Lederer, A., 312, 320
LeDoux, J., 30
Lee, D., 127
Lee, D. J., 894
Lee, D. N., 183, 185, 186, 187, 193, 197
Lee, K., 183, 480, 483
Lee, M. B., 149
Lee, P., 30, 187, 741, 823
Lee, S. Y., 795
Lee, T. D., 180, 181
Leek, E. C., 31
Leekam, S., 720, 824, 864
Leeuwen, C. V., 201
Leeuwen, L. V., 201
Leevers, H., 594, 844, 963
LeFevre, J., 507, 793

Lefkovich, L. P., 751
Legerstee, M., 704
Legge, G. E., 119
Le Grand, R., 15, 38, 243, 766
Lehmann, E. V., 939
Lehman, H. C., 914, 924
Lehnung, M., 751
Lehrer, R., 545, 924, 972
Lehrman, D. S., 430
Lehtokoski, A., 73
Leibold, L., 65, 71, 92
Leichtman, M. D., 407, 410, 411, 674
Leiferman, E. M., 175
Leinbach, J., 444, 445, 448
Leinbach, M. D., 148
Leinhardt, G., 910, 922, 923
Leitch, E., 574
Lejeune, L., 191
Lelwica, M., 816
Lemaire, P., 474, 482, 793, 795, 796, 801
Lemer, C., 780
Lemire, R. J., 8
Lempers, J. D., 851
Lempert, H., 704
Lenneberg, E. H., 346
Lenz, B. K., 545
Leo, A. J., 195, 198
Leonard, C., 68, 514
Leonard, E., 167, 170
Leonard, L., 282, 283, 292
Leopold, W., 339
Lepage, A., 244
Lepage, M., 25
Lepecq, J. C., 197, 744
Lepine, T., 867, 878
Leplow, B., 751
Lercari, L. P., 42
Lerdahl, F., 882, 883
Lerner, C., 665
Lerner, R., 955, 988
Leslie, A., 215, 227, 229, 230, 231, 245, 306, 567, 610, 614, 616, 627, 664, 666, 744, 750, 812, 824, 842, 844, 845, 864
Lespinet, V., 34
Lester, F. K., Jr., 538
Leung, E., 342
Levelt, W. J., 887, 888
Levenson, R., 74
Lévesque, M., 8, 9
Levi, D. M., 120
Levi, E. C., 65, 68
Levin, A. V., 15, 766
Levin, B., 321, 322, 325
Levin, D. T., 618, 626, 692, 693, 699, 701, 702, 705, 712
Levin, H., 40, 909
Levin, I., 595, 870
Levin, J. R., 518, 521, 522, 523, 543, 544
Levine, D., 579
Levine, J., 891
Levine, L. J., 823
Levine, M., 466, 760
LeVine, R., 636, 638, 654, 658
Levine, S., 290, 303, 432, 569, 582, 750, 751, 763, 764, 781, 787, 788, 792, 803
LeVine, S. E., 654, 658
Levinson, S. C., 303, 311, 694, 741, 761
Levitt, P., 6, 11
Levitzky, W., 894
Levstik, L., 971

Levy, G. D., 236
Levy, J., 86
Levy, R., 40
Levy, V. M., 541
Lew, A. R., 744, 748, 751
Lewens, T., 615
Lewicki, P., 29
Lewin, J., 43
Lewin, K., 430, 435
Lewin, R., 641
Lewis, A. B., 799
Lewis, C., 407, 786, 876
Lewis, H. P., 868, 875
Lewis, J. L., 474, 481, 482, 491
Lewis, K. D., 404, 408, 409
Lewis, L., 277, 288
Lewis, M., 407, 409, 497, 838
Lewis, M. D., 435, 470
Lewis, M. M., 829, 850
Lewis, R., 835, 985
Lewis, T., 15, 117, 119, 147, 766
Lewis, V., 844
Lewis, W., 92
Lewontin, R., 617
Li, J., 915, 919, 925
Li, N. S., 197
Li, P., 280, 761
Li, S., 8, 19
Lia, B., 124
Liben, L. S., 741, 756, 757, 758, 759, 760, 767
Liberman, A. M., 72, 74
Liberman, M., 830
Liberty, C., 516
Lichtman, J. W., 11
Lickiss, K. P., 352
Liddle, P. F., 75, 76
Lidz, J., 304, 321, 322, 323, 324
Lie, D. C., 9
Lie, E., 738
Lieberman, D. E., 642
Lieberman, P., 641
Lien, Y., 965
Lienhardt, G., 841
Lieven, E., 260, 262, 263, 266, 271, 285, 289, 291
Light, P., 497, 875, 876, 878
Lightfoot, C., 639
Lightfoot, D., 610, 617, 621
Lightfoot, N., 257
Ligtvoet, J., 876
Likeza, M., 850
Lillard, A., 666, 724, 841, 842, 844
Lillard, A. A., 865
Lillard, A. S., 666, 667, 723
Lillo-Martin, D., 346
Lim, J. S., 120
Limber, J., 283, 284
Lin, A., 529
Lin, E. L., 690, 702, 721
Lin, J., 34, 41
Lin, M.-H., 831
Lindauer, M. S., 916
Lindblom, B., 73, 305
Lindeke, L., 531
Lindenberger, U., 470, 563, 587, 758
Lindhagen, K., 186
Lindinger, G., 16
Lindner, K., 269
Lindsay, D. S., 723
Lindsey, D. T., 123, 124
Lindsey, J. M., 778

Lindvall, O., 9
Ling, C. X., 438, 447
Linn, M. C., 763, 924
Linn, S. F., 868
Linn, S. G., 940
Linotte, S., 37
Linsker, R., 119
Lipian, M. S., 833
Lipscomb, S. D., 882
Lipsitt, L. P., 466
Lipson, M. Y., 534
Lipton, J. S., 781, 784, 802
Lishman, J. R., 197
Lisker, L., 73
Liston, C., 389
Litovsky, R. Y., 69, 224
Little, T. D., 796, 797
Liu, A. K., 32
Liu, F., 785, 795, 796, 797
Liu, G. T., 4
Liu, H., 15, 31, 73, 80, 94, 305, 762, 767, 803
Liu, J., 696
Liu, L. L., 690
Liu, X. Y., 67
Livet, M. O., 39
Lizotte, D. J., 706
Lledo, P.-M., 18
Lloyd, V. L., 89, 236, 315, 710
Lo, T., 190, 200
Lo, Y., 308, 701, 712, 713
Lobo, S. A., 194, 195, 199, 201
Loboschefski, T., 29
Lochhead, J., 540
Lock, E., 15
Locke, J., 109, 315, 698, 708
Locklear, E. P., 868
Lockman, J. J., 129, 195, 201, 757
Loeches, A., 149
Loewenstein, J., 741, 764
Logan, C., 30
Logan, G., 958
Logan, J. S., 73
Logie, R. H., 33, 520
Logothet, K., 930
Logothetis, N. K., 77
Lohmann, H., 847, 851
Loman, M. M., 89
Lombardino, L. J., 68
Lombroso, P. J., 8, 10
Londero, A., 66
Long, H. L., 868, 869
Long, L., 572
Longhi, E., 765
Longobardi, E., 312, 338, 344, 345
Longworth, C., 625
Lonigan, C. J., 525
Loomis, J. M., 757, 761
Lopez, A., 571, 701
Lord, K. M., 537
Lottenberg, S., 501
Lotto, A. J., 72, 74
Lotto, R. B., 112, 152
Lou, J.-S., 29
Lourenco, O., 558, 831
Lourenco, S. F., 740, 748
Love, B. C., 239, 718
Lovecky, D. V., 932
Lover, A., 932
Lovett, M. W., 531, 532
Lowe, J., 583, 585

Lowe, K. B., 927
Löwenfeld, V., 870
Lowry, C., 19
Lu, Y., 19, 181
Luberoff, A., 80
Lubinski, D., 761, 911, 922, 923, 925
Lucariello, J., 639, 663, 670, 671
Lucas, A., 27
Lucas, D., 169
Luce, C., 932
Luce, P., 81, 82, 86, 87, 94, 305, 315
Luciana, M., 4, 19, 26, 33, 40, 42, 531
Luck, S. J., 563
Lucksinger, K. L., 228
Lucy, J. A., 312, 695
Ludemann, P. M., 149
Lufkin, N., 342, 350
Lui, H., 957
Lukacs, J., 928
Lukens, H. T., 860
Lukowski, A. F., 381, 387, 399, 415
Lumsden, A., 6, 7, 9
Luna, B., 41, 957, 958, 959
Lundervold, A., 31
Luo, J., 312, 722
Luo, Y., 744
Luquet, G. H., 860, 861, 870, 872, 875, 876, 878
Luria, A. R., 639, 648, 908
Lust, B., 617
Lutfi, R. A., 71, 93
Lutz, D. J., 715, 781
Lutz, D. R., 625
Lutz, J. R., 926
Luu, P., 41
Luuk, A., 73
Lycan, W., 618
Lykken, D. T., 913, 914
Lynch, E., 669, 696, 715, 720
Lynch, M. P., 886, 889
Lynn, R., 868
Lyon, B. E., 789
Lyon, T. D., 554
Lyons, T., 303
Lytle, S., 527
Lyytinen, P., 280

Mabbott, D. J., 35
Macari, S., 721
Macario, J. F., 316
Maccoby, E., 406, 688, 909, 957
MacDonald, A., 41
MacDonald, C. J., 848
MacDonald, J., 76
MacDonald, K. B., 615
MacDonald, M. C., 83, 443, 617
MacDonald, S., 383, 410, 674, 748, 755
Macedonia, C., 182, 183
MacFadyen, J., 512, 518
Machado, A., 558
Machotka, P., 868
MacIntosh, E., 876, 878
MacKain, K., 76
Mackay, H. A., 590
MacKinnon, C. E., 519
MacKinnon, D. W., 530, 909
MacLachlan, A., 501
MacLean, M., 842
Maclin, D., 921, 923, 985
Macnamara, J., 300, 301, 302, 309, 313, 343, 700
MacNamee, R., 821

Macomber, J., 166, 222, 224, 428, 448, 617, 737, 780
MacPhail, J., 497
Macpherson, R., 985
MacWhinney, B., 31, 32, 263, 265, 267, 268, 269, 277, 303, 319, 426, 429, 430, 436, 440, 444, 445, 448, 468, 610, 709
Madden, E., 618, 696
Madden, T. C., 17
Madole, K. L., 216, 217, 220, 228, 235, 236, 237, 240, 246, 710
Madonia, L., 19
Madsen, S. D., 409
Maffei, L., 116
Magnani, L., 633
Magnuson, J. S., 91, 317
Maguire, E. A., 17, 27
Maguire, M. J., 304, 311
Mahapatra, M., 621, 930, 931
Maher, M. A., 908
Mahootian, S., 342
Maia, T. V., 448
Maier, J., 117, 118
Maier-Brueckner, W., 517
Maikranz, J. M., 390
Main, M., 822, 837
Mainwaring, S., 741
Maital, S., 303, 694
Maitland, L., 860
Maki, A., 76, 82, 93, 305
Malcuit, G., 704
Malfait, N., 588, 593
Malhotra, B., 975
Málková, L., 24
Malt, B. C., 708, 716
Malti, T., 831
Mamelak, A. N., 35
Mancini, J., 39
Mancl, L. R., 64, 66
Mandel, D., 81, 88, 305
Mandernach, T., 531
Manders, K., 318
Mandler, J., 25, 215, 216, 220, 230, 234, 235, 239, 240, 244, 246, 270, 305, 373, 374, 377, 379, 380, 382, 384, 405, 412, 562, 563, 567, 569, 570, 618, 626, 657, 689, 690, 695, 697, 704, 761
Manganari, E., 68
Mann, M., 31
Mann, R. D., 909, 927
Manning, C., 617
Manns, J. R., 22, 23, 27
Manny, R. E., 115
Man-Shu, Z., 833
Manstead, A. S., 848
Manzo, A. V., 533
Mao, H., 29
Marantz, A., 74
Marata, A., 614
Maratos, E. J., 38
Maratsos, M., 265, 269, 279, 282, 303, 307, 311, 315, 468
Marcelli, D., 816
Marchman, V., 275, 433, 444, 445, 447, 448
Marcia, J. E., 919
Marconi, F., 34
Marcos, L. R., 354
Marcos-Ruiz, R., 383
Marcovitch, S., 448, 451, 563, 564, 567, 622
Marcus, D., 30

Marcus, G., 82, 91, 93, 239, 270, 271, 281, 282, 305, 438, 444, 445, 446, 448, 558, 561, 568, 599, 612, 618, 623, 626
Marean, G. C., 65, 66, 67, 69, 92
Mareschal, D., 237, 238, 239, 433, 438, 454, 620, 624, 711, 744
Margetts, S., 183
Margolis, E., 611, 687, 699
Margulis, C., 261, 312
Maridaki-Kassotaki, K., 407
Marieb, E. N., 182
Marigold, D. S., 200
Marin, L., 181, 200
Marini, A., 470
Marinov, M., 447
Marin-Padilla, M., 9
Mark, L. S., 189, 193
Markel, M. D., 175
Markman, A., 274, 702, 718
Markman, E., 89, 299, 300, 301, 306, 309, 311, 312, 315, 316, 317, 384, 521, 533, 571, 572, 592, 594, 689, 690, 694, 695, 696, 697, 699, 701, 702, 710, 711, 713, 715, 716, 724, 784, 850
Markovits, H., 588, 590, 592, 593, 594, 599, 960, 961, 962, 963
Markow, D. B., 301, 302, 307, 312, 316, 570, 696, 697, 715
Markowitsch, H. J., 23, 385
Marks, J., 643
Marks, K. S., 223, 226, 233, 432, 777, 782, 783, 803
Marks, S., 291, 765
Markson, L., 306, 707, 708, 714, 865
Markus, H., 636, 638, 674
Marler, P., 723
Maroudas, C., 583, 585
Marr, D., 112, 113, 150, 151, 691, 862, 874
Marrett, S., 32
Marslen-Wilson, M., 625
Marslen-Wilson, W. D., 625
Marsolek, C. J., 741
Marti, C. N., 304, 305, 306, 310, 312
Martin, A., 36, 619, 876
Martin, A. E., 597
Martin, A. J., 20
Martin, C. L., 688
Martin, C. S. M., 790, 792
Martin, E., 752
Martin, M., 29, 564
Martin, V., 523, 537
Martin, W. D., 13
Martindale, C., 908, 911, 912, 913, 915
Martinez, A., 32
Martinez, S. L., 117
Martinez-Pons, M., 530
Martin-Johnson, N. M., 526
Martlew, M., 340, 880
Marvin, E. W., 893
Marzocchi, G. M., 531
Masataka, N., 340, 885
Mash, C., 737, 752
Mason, B. D., 926
Mason, C. R., 71
Mason, L., 986
Mason, O., 148
Mason, S., 873
Mason, U., 128, 745
Massaquoi, S., 29

Massaro, D., 76, 356
Massey, C., 312, 867, 881
Massion, J., 188
Massop, S. A., 190, 200
Masters, J. C., 830
Mastropieri, M. A., 531
Masur, E. F., 340
Mathivet, E., 33
Matsen, D., 12
Matsuda, F., 595, 596
Matsuo, K., 117
Matsuzawa, T., 645
Mattevi, B. S., 642
Matthews, G. A., 764
Matthews, J., 89, 574, 870, 872
Matthewson, L., 302
Mattingly, I. G., 74
Mattock, A., 135, 139, 141, 145, 146, 152, 226
Mattys, S. L., 82, 86, 87
Matushita, M., 19
Matzuk, M. M., 19
Mauk, M., 30, 457
Maurer, D., 15, 32, 38, 117, 119, 146, 147, 150, 241, 243, 766
Mawer, R. F., 797, 798, 799
Maxon, A. B., 62, 64, 69
Maxwell, S. E., 757
May, A., 16
May, M., 755, 909
Mayberry, R. I., 15, 346
Maybery, M., 29, 559, 587, 588, 589
Maye, J., 82, 92
Mayer, D., 117
Mayer, R., 539, 545, 764, 780, 797, 798, 799
Mayes, A. R., 22, 35
Mayfield, N., 866
Maynard, A. E., 650, 659, 662, 671
Maynard, J., 863, 864
Mayr, E., 689, 695
Mazer, P., 473, 474, 483, 493, 501
Mazoyer, B., 36
Mazziotta, J., 44, 386
McAdams, D., 933
McAdams, S., 70, 74
McAuley, E., 17
McAvoy, M., 44
McBrearty, S., 642
McBride, L. R., 880
McCabe, A., 404, 405, 574
McCall, D. D., 186
McCall, M., 916
McCandliss, B., 41, 42, 417
McCarrell, N., 712, 760
McCarthy, G., 35, 37
McCarthy, J. J., 257
McCarty, M. E., 184, 187, 201
McCauley, C., 920
McCawley, J., 321, 701
McClearn, J. E., 914
McClelland, D., 908, 927, 928
McClelland, J. L., 82, 181, 202, 237, 286, 428, 430, 433, 434, 437, 440, 441, 443, 444, 445, 447, 448, 449, 450, 452, 454, 455, 491, 558, 562, 598, 612, 615, 616, 618, 623, 625, 742
McCloskey, M., 396, 802
McCollum, G., 174
McConnell, S. K., 8
McConnell-Ginet, S., 312
McCorgray, P., 790
McCormick, C. B., 521

McCormick, M., 700, 705
McCoy, G. S., 63, 64
McCredden, J. E., 563, 565
McCrink, K., 782
McCulloch, W. S., 430
McCullough, K.-E., 357
McCune, L., 199, 261
McCutchen, D., 538
McDaniel, C., 145
McDermott, J., 35, 149, 621, 882, 883, 885
McDonald, C. A., 473
McDonald, M. A., 123, 124
McDonald, R. J., 800
McDonough, L., 25, 220, 235, 240, 305, 314, 380, 382, 384, 569, 570, 689, 690, 695, 697, 704, 744, 761
McGarrigle, J., 574, 575, 578, 580, 581
McGhee, K., 868
McGilly, K., 475, 481
McGoldrick, J. A., 533
McGonigle, B., 589, 590, 591
McGraw, M. B., 163, 165, 167, 170, 171, 172, 173, 174, 176, 178, 179, 180, 182, 188, 201
McGregor, K. K., 312
McGrew, W. C., 637, 644, 645, 648, 839
McGue, M., 913, 914
McGuffin, P., 914
McGurk, H., 76, 866
McInerney, S. C., 38, 149
McIntosh, B. J., 79
McKee, R., 22, 25, 27, 380
McKee, S. P., 130, 131
McKenzie, B., 77, 145, 188, 744, 751
McKeough, A., 470, 474, 491, 928
McKernon, P., 891, 892
McKinley, M., 848
McKinney, M. L., 642, 643, 644, 646
McKinnon, E., 531
McKone, E., 513
McLaughlin, G. H., 563
McLellan, J. A., 779
McLeod, P. J., 78
McLin, D., 451, 468, 742
McMurray, B., 63, 78, 79
McNally, L., 317
McNamara, J. P. H., 473
McNamara, T. P., 738, 740
McNaughton, B. L., 455
McNeil, N. M., 345, 346
McNeill, D., 267, 336, 337, 338, 339, 340, 341, 342, 349, 353, 354, 357, 358
McNurlen, B., 980, 982
McRoberts, G., 73, 91, 129, 305, 314
McShane, J., 280, 519
McVey, K. A., 495, 497
McWhorter, J. H., 282
Meacham, J. A., 656
Mead, M., xiii, 660
Meade, A. C., 763
Meadow, K., 346
Means, B., 619
Means, M., 979
Meck, E., 244, 786
Meck, W. H., 568, 783
Medin, D., 309, 317, 562, 613, 614, 619, 638, 668, 669, 690, 692, 693, 699, 708, 709, 711, 713, 715, 717, 720, 965
Medina, J., 274, 275, 457, 562, 709
Mednick, M., 908
Mednick, S. A., 908

Meerum Terwogt, M., 813, 829, 832, 842, 850
Meeuwson, H. J., 190
Mehdorn, M., 751
Mehl, A. L., 60
Mehler, J., 15, 72, 74, 76, 77, 78, 79, 81, 83, 86, 88, 92, 271, 301, 304, 305, 580, 581, 611, 779, 782, 883
Meichenbaum, D., 521, 528, 529, 532
Meier, R. P., 81, 83, 346
Meilijson, I., 11
Meins, E., 838, 846, 847
Meister, C., 534
Mejia-Arauz, R., 662
Melartin, R. L., 384, 697
Meletti, S., 38
Melinger, A., 354
Mellers, B., 457
Melloy-Carminar, P., 387
Meloth, M., 535
Melrose, R., 29
Meltzoff, A., 25, 76, 166, 220, 224, 225, 234, 286, 306, 378, 379, 380, 381, 382, 383, 384, 391, 411, 646, 664, 691, 692, 704, 715, 745, 751, 811, 921, 972
Mendelsohn, E., 868, 879
Mendelson, M., 868
Menig-Peterson, C. L., 851
Menke, D., 537
Mennuti-Washburn, J., 407, 408
Menon, R. S., 31
Menon, V., 31, 34, 38
Menyuk, P., 73
Menzel, E. W., Jr., 644
Menzel, R. C., 644
Mercer, M. E., 123
Merchant, H., 739, 753
Merker, B., 882
Merriam, E., 41
Merrick, S., 838
Merriman, W. E., 302
Merritt, K., 406, 414
Merton, R. K., 912, 914, 925, 933
Mertz, K., 497
Mervis, C., 39, 240, 291, 311, 470, 472, 473, 486, 492, 501, 574, 575, 576, 689, 696, 704, 716, 720, 765
Merzenich, M. M., 14, 68
Meschulach-Sarfaty, O., 382
Mesibov, G., 656
Messer, D., 342, 350, 486, 498
Metcalfe, J., 197, 514, 931
Metcalfe-Haggert, A., 531
Mettke-Hofmann, C., 19
Metz, K., 470, 985
Metzler, W. H., 778
Meulemans, T., 29
Meuter, R. F., 531
Mewhort, D. J. K., 882, 888
Meyer, A. S., 84
Meyer, E., 76
Meyer, L., 882, 883, 884, 915
Meyers, C. E., 778
Meyers, J., 527
Mezey, J., 614
Michaels, C. F., 200
Michaelson, M., 931, 932, 933, 935
Michealieu, Q., 829
Michel, C., 750
Michelon, P., 755
Michimata, D., 677

Michotte, A., 228, 306
Mieg, H. A., 911
Mierkiewicz, D., 583
Miesegaes, G., 16
Miezin, F., 28, 76
Miikkulainen, R., 149, 241
Miklósi, Á, 637, 645
Milani, I., 36
Milbraith, C., 912, 916, 917, 918
Mill, J. S., 111, 142, 698, 710
Millar, D., 866
Millar, G., 908
Millar, S., 757, 766, 870
Miller, A. I., 912, 922, 924
Miller, C., 78, 271, 292
Miller, C. J., 530
Miller, C. T., 883
Miller, D., 43
Miller, E. K., 449
Miller, G. A., 515, 520, 814
Miller, G. E., 512, 513
Miller, G. F., 882
Miller, J., 888
Miller, J. D., 74
Miller, J. G., 930, 931
Miller, J. L., 72, 79, 83, 182, 183
Miller, K. F., 560, 759, 785, 797
Miller, L. K., 906, 917
Miller, M. E., 92
Miller, N. E., 466
Miller, P., 521, 636, 638
Miller, P. A., 910
Miller, P. H., 26, 173, 469, 470, 474, 479, 480, 483, 487, 488, 493, 494, 499, 500, 501, 517, 519, 544
Miller, P. J., 347
Miller, R., 280
Miller, S. A., 26, 582, 586
Miller, S. L., 68
Millikan, R. G., 699
Mills, C. M., 718
Mills, D. L., 89, 315
Mills, M., 531
Milner, A. D., 624
Milner, B., 20, 25, 27, 624
Min, H., 311, 319
Minard, K. L., 567, 568
Ming, G.-I., 9
Mingolla, E., 138
Miniussi, C., 32
Minksy, M., 623
Minshew, N., 41
Mintz, T. H., 85, 87, 301, 305, 311, 312, 316, 317, 318, 320
Miranda, S., 135, 863
Mirescu, C., 9
Mischel, W., 931
Mishkin, F. S., 588
Mishkin, M., 24, 25, 26, 27, 380
Mistretta, J., 537
Mitchelmore, M. C., 876
Mitroff, S. R., 614
Mitsui, T., 66
Miura, H., 792
Miura, I. T., 785, 791, 792
Miura, T., 65
Mix, K. S., 432, 569, 583, 584, 767, 781, 783, 792, 803
Miyake, A., 741, 762
Miyamoto, K., 37

Miyamoto, R. T., 76, 94
Miyashita, Y., 40, 41
Miyazaki, K., 893
Mizuno, K., 183
Moar, K., 116
Moccia, G., 182
Mochizuki, N., 181
Modloch, C. J., 243
Moely, B. E., 516, 530
Moffet, A., 749
Moffit, A. R., 72
Mohagheghi, A. A., 200
Mohay, H., 346
Molenaar, P. C. M., 435, 442, 443, 484, 558
Molfese, D. L., 74
Molfese, V., 74
Moll, H., 644, 821, 840
Molliver, M., 11
Moltmann, F., 312
Mondloch, C., 15, 32, 38, 147, 150, 766
Mondschein, E. R., 189, 194
Monk, C. S., 11, 24, 28, 34, 41, 243, 417
Monnier, M., 168
Monroe, E. K., 521
Montague, D. P. F., 149
Montague, M., 538
Montanari, S., 338, 340
Montanaro, D., 27
Montani, T. O., 797, 801
Montello, D. R., 755
Montero, I., 500
Montgomery, C. R., 63
Monting, J. S., 611
Mon-Williams, M., 198
Moog, H., 891, 892
Moon, C., 77, 611
Moon, E., 107
Moon, J., 765
Moon, R. Y., 200
Moore, B. C. J., 62, 67
Moore, C., 76, 306, 638, 967
Moore, D., 781
Moore, D. G., 597
Moore, D. R., 68, 70
Moore, J. K., 60, 66
Moore, K., 163, 182, 751
Moore, M., 129, 166, 220, 224, 225, 382, 411,
    745, 751, 811
Moore, R., 874
Moore, S., 875
Moores, D. F., 346
Moorhead, G. E., 883, 891, 892
Moorman, K., 620
Mora, J. A., 67
Moraes, R., 200
Morais, J., 74, 77, 657
Moran, S., 912, 914, 915, 940
Morelli, G. A., 661
Morford, J. P., 347, 348, 850
Morford, M., 340, 343, 347
Morgan, D., 591
Morgan, J., 79, 81, 82, 83, 84, 85, 86, 87, 88, 89,
    90, 301, 305
Morikawa, H., 312
Morison, P., 868
Morison, V., 139, 141, 145, 152, 197, 226
Morissette, P., 817
Moriwaki, A., 19
Morra, S., 862
Morrell, J., 846, 847

Morrel-Samuels, P., 342, 356
Morrengiello, B. A., 64
Morris, A., 595, 963
Morris, B., 595, 962
Morris, C., 39, 291, 571, 670, 671, 707, 708, 765
Morris, D., 78, 271, 860, 883
Morris, G. B., 926, 927, 928
Morris, J., 38, 507
Morris, R. G., 35
Morris, S. C., 706, 716
Morrison, D., 345
Morrison, F. J., 655
Morrison, V., 119
Morrone, M. C., 124
Morrongiello, B. A., 61, 63, 64, 67, 69, 169, 744,
    757, 766, 886, 888, 889
Morrow, J. W., 907
Morrow, L. M., 542
Morse, P. A., 72, 74
Morton, J., 36, 146, 147, 148, 150, 241, 433, 449,
    452, 616
Moschovich, J., 488
Moscovitch, M., 35, 376, 562
Moser, E., 31
Moser, J. M., 779, 795, 796, 797, 798
Moses, L., 306, 718, 818, 823, 824, 846
Moses, P., 32, 33
Moshman, D., 594, 954, 962, 992
Moskowitz, D. S., 475
Mosteller, F., 590
Mottron, L., 765
Mou, W., 740
Mrzljak, L., 11
Much, N. C., 621
Mugitani, R., 782, 783, 804
Muir, D. W., 146, 172, 186, 816
Muir, G. D., 166, 167, 168
Muir-Broaddus, J. E., 517
Mulack, T., 735
Muldrow, E. S., 863
Muldrow, W. F., 863
Mullen, M. K., 410, 411, 674
Muller, J., 112
Muller, R. A., 38
Muller, U., 563, 564, 567, 576, 577, 622
Mullet, E., 968
Mullin, J. T., 147, 152
Mumford, M. D., 908, 946
Mumme, D. L., 818
Munakata, Y., 167, 176, 181, 183, 202, 224, 225,
    237, 239, 286, 417, 427, 428, 433, 438, 448,
    449, 450, 452, 454, 455, 456, 610, 615, 623,
    742, 744, 745, 956
Mundy, P., 843
Munkholm, P., 749
Munn, N. L., 465, 466
Munn, P., 821
Munnich, E., 760
Munoz, D., 41
Munoz-Nunez, A., 488
Murchison, C., xi, xii, xiii, xiv
Murloz-Sanjuan, I., 6
Murphy, C. M., 342
Murphy, G. L., 301, 309, 690, 692, 693, 699, 702,
    705, 707, 709, 721
Murphy, J., 644
Murphy, K., 513
Murray, C., 906, 912, 913, 940
Murray, J., 74
Murray, L., 816

Mursell, J. L., 883
Murthy, V. N., 12
Musen, G., 27, 375, 380
Mussen, P., xv, xvi
Myers, H. J., 352, 353
Myers, J., 87
Myers, M., 67
Myers, N. A., 412, 516, 863
Mylander, C., 344, 347, 348
Mynatt, B. T., 587, 588

Nabakubo, A., 163
Naccache, L., 800, 803
Nadarajah, B., 10
Nádasdy, Z., 619, 814
Nadel, J., 816
Nadel, L., 386, 749, 751, 765
Naegele, J. R., 8, 10
Nagell, K., 817
Naglieri, J., 560
Nagy, Z., 34
Naigles, L., 91, 267, 302, 303, 312, 320, 321,
    322, 325, 326
Naito, M., 667, 792
Nakai, S., 81
Nakai, Y., 66
Nakajima, K., 10, 40, 41
Nakamura, J., 921, 924, 925
Nakata, T., 885
Nakayama, K., 616
Namy, L., 308, 312, 339, 344, 690, 697, 702, 721
Nanez, J. E., 129, 139, 226
Nanz-Bahr, N. I., 767
Nappa, R., 304
Narasimham, G., 960, 961
Narcy, P., 66
Nashner, L. M., 166
Nastasi, B. K., 541
Natale, F., 263
Natale, M., 764
Nathan, M. J., 497
Naus, M. J., 516, 517
Navichoc Cotuc, M., 652, 655
Nazzi, T., 78, 80, 85, 240, 305, 306, 307, 314,
    611
Neches, R., 430, 436, 488, 620
Needham, A., 136, 142, 197, 200, 202, 215, 315,
    737, 744, 746, 814, 815
Neely, S. T., 60, 66
Neff, D. L., 62, 67, 71
Neimark, E., 516, 956, 971
Neisser, U., 414, 625, 659, 906, 907
Neiworth, J. J., 882
Nelson, C., 4, 11, 14, 16, 17, 19, 20, 21, 22, 23,
    24, 25, 26, 28, 29, 33, 34, 36, 37, 38, 41, 42,
    48, 148, 149, 150, 220, 242, 243, 381, 382,
    385, 386, 388, 389, 392, 399, 412, 417, 531,
    673, 704
Nelson, D. G. K., 81
Nelson, K., 264, 270, 283, 287, 290, 373, 374,
    378, 380, 384, 393, 394, 396, 398, 401, 402,
    403, 404, 410, 412, 417, 524, 525, 570, 674,
    697
Nemanic, S., 22, 24
Nemirovsky, R., 914, 923
Nersessian, N. J., 633
Nespor, M., 77
Nesselroade, J. R., 558
Nettelbeck, T., 658
Nettl, B., 891, 892

Netto, D., 148
Neufeld, J., 200
Neuman, Y., 979, 985
Neumann, C., 658, 659
Neville, H., 15, 89, 315, 765
Nevis, S., 120, 124
Newcombe, N., 28, 402, 736, 737, 738, 739, 740, 742, 743, 744, 746, 749, 750, 751, 753, 755, 756, 758, 759, 760, 763, 764, 777, 780, 781, 783, 803
Newcombe, R., 409
Newell, A., 428, 429, 430, 438, 454, 457, 491, 582, 620, 908, 921, 924
Newell, K. M., 176
Newman, A. J., 15
Newman, D., 342, 541
Newman, G. E., 619
Newman, L., 183, 519
Newman, R. S., 495, 497
Newport, E., 81, 82, 83, 85, 93, 94, 166, 167, 168, 171, 270, 271, 301, 304, 305, 306, 311, 346, 348, 467, 468, 469, 622, 692, 710, 734
Newsome, M., 85, 86
Newstead, S. E., 558
Nguyen, S., 722
Nguyen-Jahiel, K., 542, 980, 982
Nias, D. K. B., 868, 869
Nichelli, P., 28, 38
Nicholas, J. G., 78
Nicholls, A. L., 876
Nicholls, J., 583, 585
Nichols, K. E., 831
Nichols, S., 819, 844
Nicolay, A.-C., 318
Nida, R. E., 519
Niehbur, A., 93
Nigam, M., 974
Nijhuis, J. G., 182
Nikeiski, E. J., 15
Niklasson, L., 561
Niles, D., 170
Nilsson, L., 182
Ninio, A., 261, 864
Nisbett, R. E., 718, 940
Nishi, K., 73
Nishida, T., 839
Nishijo, H., 37
Nishitani, N., 25
Nissen, M., 28, 29, 381
Nittrouer, S., 92
N'Kaoua, B., 34
Nobes, G., 597
Noble, K. D., 925
Noble, W., 640
Nodine, C. F., 875
Noël, M.-P., 583, 584
Noelle, D., 437, 438, 457
Nokes, C., 913
Nolin, T. L., 740
Nolin, Z., 292
Noll, D., 34, 40, 41, 449
Nomura, Y., 181
Noonan, K. J., 175
Norcia, A., 115, 116, 117, 119, 123, 124, 129
Norgren, R., 171
Norman, D. A., 515
Norris, C. M., 752
Norris, D., 77, 80, 83, 86, 305
North, T., 292
Northam, E., 40

Norton, A., 894
Norton, S. J., 60, 65
Nortz, M. J., 531
Novak, G. P., 74
Noveck, I. A., 594
Novick, L., 717, 965
Nowakowski, R. S., 8
Nowell, A., 763
Noyer, R., 302
Nozza, R. J., 60, 64, 65, 70
Nunes, T., 657
Nunes, Y., 657
Nunez, L. N., 737
Nunn, J. A., 35
Nunner-Winkler, G., 830, 831
Nusbaum, H., 359, 362, 363, 501
Nye, R., 863, 864, 865
Nygaard, L. C., 83
Nyman, M., 829
Nystrom, L., 40, 41, 449

Oakes, L. M., 216, 219, 220, 228, 229, 231, 235, 236, 237, 240, 246, 306, 687, 688, 691, 710
Oakhill, J., 587, 758
Oaksford, M., 457
O'Brien, C., 273
O'Brien, D., 595, 960
O'Brien-Malone, A., 29
O'Byrne, M., 12
Ochs, E., 300
Ochse, R., 920
O'Connell, D. N., 143
O'Connell, K. M., 470, 472, 473, 496
O'Conner, M., 258
O'Connor, J., 350
Odden, H., 666, 841
Oden, D. L., 563
Oden, M. H., 906
Odom, R., 69
Ofenloch, I. T., 24
Ogle, D., 537
Oh, E., 71
O'Hare, D., 867
Ohmura, Y., 163
Ohtsubo, H., 140, 141
Oja, E., 433
Ojemann, J., 28, 33
Oka, E. R., 534, 535
Okabe, K. S., 65
Okada, T., 16
Okagaki, L., 764
Okamoto, T., 178
Okamoto, Y., 470, 563, 785, 791, 792, 793, 958
O'Keefe, J., 35
Okiatcha, F., 913
O'Laughlin, M., 495, 497
Olesen, P. J., 34
Olguin, R., 306, 696
Oliner, P. M., 933, 934
Oliner, S., 933, 934
Oliver, A., 434
Olivier, D. C., 85
Oller, D. K., 78, 886
Ollinger, J., 44
O'Loughlin, M., 540, 965, 966, 968, 979
Olseth, K. L., 342
Olshausen, B. A., 119
Olshen, R., 178
Olsho, L. W., 61, 62, 63, 64
Olson, D., 657, 836, 983

Olson, F. A., 516
Olson, R. K., 866
Olthof, T., 813, 829, 842
Olver, R. R., 578, 688, 689
Olzak, L. A., 115
O'Malley, C., 470, 484, 485, 487, 491, 494, 500, 718
Ondracek, P. J., 761
O'Neill, D. K., 402, 826, 827, 851
Ong, L., 185
Onishi, K. H., 84, 305
Ono, S., 40
Opfer, J., 485, 488, 490, 492, 495, 496, 500, 671, 688, 722, 785, 793, 794, 802
Oppenheim, A. V., 120
Oppenheim, R. W., 10
Op't Eynde, P., 923
Orban, G. A., 750
Ordy, J. M., 115
O'Reilly, A. W., 571
O'Reilly, R. C., 427, 433, 434, 437, 438, 445, 447, 448, 455, 456, 457
Orendi, J., 40, 41
Orlich, E., 30
Orlovsky, G. N., 168
Ormrod, J. E., 922
Ornstein, P. A., 404, 405, 406, 415, 513, 516, 517, 519
Orquin, J., 611
Ortony, A., 317, 619
Osborne, R. T., 778
O'Shea, M. V., 778
Osherson, D., 594, 611, 701
Osnat, E., 843, 850
Ostad, S. A., 474
Oster, H. E., 122
Ostertag, J., 533
Ostwald, P. F., 891
O'Sullivan, J. T., 389, 399, 400, 521, 523, 544, 545
Otake, T., 77
Otani, T., 163
O'Toole, A. J., 150
Otta, H., 750
Otten, E., 188
Otten, L. J., 37
Ottolini, M. C., 200
Overman, W. H., 24, 417, 751
Overton, W., 576, 577, 961
Overy, K., 894
Owen, A., 41, 42
Owen, R., 539, 540, 797, 799
Owen, V., 44
Owsley, C., 127, 129, 132, 144
Oyama, S., 172
Oyen, A. S., 531
Ozcaliskan, S., 340, 344

Paccanaro, A., 625
Packer, O., 123
Padden, D. M., 74
Padowska, B., 564
Pagani, B., 765
Paget, G. W., 880
Pagnin, A., 931, 932
Pagulayan, R. J., 187
Paik, J. H., 792
Painter, K., 303, 694, 846
Pais, J. L., 911
Palij, M., 760

Palincsar, A. S., 533, 534, 536
Palladino, A., 527
Palmer, C., 89
Palmer, E. M., 141
Palmer, J., 123, 124
Palmer, S., 137, 561
Palmers, E., 583, 584
Pan, B. A., 850
Pan, J., 924
Panagiotaki, G., 597
Pandey, J., 677
Pang, M. Y. C., 170
Pani, A. M., 240, 716, 720
Pani, J. R., 240, 716, 720
Pantev, C., 16
Paour, J., 599
Papafragou, A., 304, 312
Papert, S., 623
Papka, M., 30
Pappas, A., 299
Pappas, T., 699, 716, 721, 722
Paradise, R., 662
Paredes, D. R., 797
Parent, A., 8, 9
Paris, S. G., 495, 497, 521, 534, 535
Pariser, D., 881, 916, 917, 919
Parisi, D., 119, 152, 237, 241, 286, 427, 430, 433,
    457, 499, 558, 614, 616, 663, 664, 691
Park, E. I. B., 876
Park, L., 621
Park, S., 303, 694
Parke, R., 820, 848
Parker, J., 397, 414
Parker, K. C. H., 838
Parker, S., 642, 643, 644, 646
Parkin, A., 28
Parkin, C. E., 870, 873
Parkin, L., 667
Parkman, J. M., 779, 795
Parks, S., 932
Parsons, M. J., 868
Parsons, S., 148, 149
Parvavelas, J. G., 10
Parziale, J., 474, 483, 493, 497, 550
Pascalis, O., 22, 24, 36, 37, 147, 148, 149, 150,
    242, 243
Pascual, L., 303, 694
Pascual-Leone, A., 16, 29
Pascual-Leone, J., 563, 958
Pashler, H., 454
Pasko, R. N., 752
Passarotti, A., 32, 37
Passingham, R., 640
Pasterski, V. L., 764
Pasti, G., 748
Patalano, A. L., 701, 702
Pate, B. J., 751
Pater, J., 89
Paterson, S. J., 39, 765
Patla, A. E., 199, 200
Patterson, F. G., 860
Patterson, K., 76, 444, 448, 623, 625
Patterson, M. L., 76
Pattison, P. E., 789, 790, 791, 797
Pauen, S., 560, 569
Paul, B. M., 37
Paul, R. A., 666
Paulesu, D., 76
Paulesu, E., 15
Paus, T., 12, 34
Pawley, A., 259

Pawluski, J., 318
Payne, A. C., 525
Payne, D. G., 513
Pea, R., 960
Pearl, J., 717
Pearl, M., 866
Pearlman, E. G., 864
Pears, R., 587, 588
Pearsall, S., 497, 544, 966, 983
Pearson, K., 169
Pearson, P. D., 537, 545
Pease, M., 969, 970, 971, 987
Pechmann, T., 317
Pedersen, A. V., 180
Peduzzi, J. D., 118, 131
Peen, T., 750
Peeples, D. R., 122, 123
Pegg, J. E., 73, 79, 86
Pehkonen, L., 933
Peiper, A., 168
Pelisari, K. B., 31
Pellathy, T., 74
Pellegrini, A. D., 474, 486, 497, 615, 637, 802
Pelli, D., 116
Pellis, S. M., 171
Pellis, V. C., 171
Pena, M., 74, 76, 82, 93, 305
Penner, D., 973
Pennington, B., 434, 765, 801, 803
Peperkamp, S., 88
Pepler, D., 821
Pepperberg, I. M., 789
Perani, D., 15, 76
Perara, J., 866, 880
Perazzo, L. M., 66
Percy, A. J., 73
Perdue, C., 282
Perett, D. I., 38
Peretz, I., 74
Perfetti, C. A., 531
Perkins, D., 540, 908, 923, 979, 986, 987
Perkins, S. A., 621
Perlmutter, D., 322
Perlmutter, M., 378, 396, 516, 863
Perlstein, W. M., 449
Perner, J., 351, 402, 564, 667, 718, 720, 758, 812,
    823, 824, 825, 829, 836, 837, 844, 864, 983
Perret, J.-F., 497
Perret, M. A., 486
Perret, P., 599
Perret-Clermont, A.-N., 497
Perrett, K. I., 38
Perris, E. E., 65, 69, 224, 412
Perruchet, P., 29
Perry, J. S., 142
Perry, M., 73, 342, 350, 360, 361, 474, 481, 482,
    489, 491, 870
Perry, W., 982
Perry, W., Jr., 932
Perry-Smith, J. E., 924
Persaud, K. L., 163, 182
Persoage, K., 316
Pesetsky, D., 531
Pesheva, P., 10
Pesonen, T., 879
Peteres, M., 31
Peterhans, E., 136, 142
Peterman, K., 197, 200, 202, 746
Peters, J. D., 9
Petersen, A. C., 763
Petersen, S., 28, 41

Peterson, C., 395, 404, 405, 412, 413, 414, 415,
    524, 720, 722, 843, 846, 850, 851
Peterson, M., 183, 781
Peterson, S., 921, 924
Peterzell, D. H., 117
Pethick, S., 290, 316, 391
Petitto, L. A., 15, 338
Petreanu, L. T., 18
Petrig, B., 130
Petrosino, A. J., 924, 972
Pettersen, L., 129, 133
Pettigrew, J. D., 130, 131
Peuster, A., 751
Pflederer, M. R., 884, 889, 890
Phelps, E., 22, 25, 30, 38, 471, 480, 483, 493,
    494, 495, 540, 559, 911, 956, 967, 973
Phelps, M., 34, 44, 385, 386
Phill, C., 400, 413
Phillips, A., 136, 228, 666, 688, 762, 767, 813,
    818
Phillips, C., 74, 291, 325, 765
Phillips, J. O., 185
Phillips, L. M., 527
Phillips, S., 558, 560, 561, 565, 566, 570, 572,
    575, 592, 598, 958
Phillips, S. B., 347
Phillips, S. J., 167, 176, 178, 180
Phillips, W. A., 875, 876, 878
Philpott, L., 35
Piaget, J., 109, 111, 136, 140, 142, 166, 182, 201,
    221, 222, 223, 228, 245, 256, 264, 376, 377,
    379, 381, 411, 428, 429, 430, 438, 448, 449,
    467, 470, 484, 488, 499, 500, 524, 540, 558,
    573, 577, 578, 586, 596, 617, 619, 624, 625,
    672, 689, 699, 709, 737, 756, 779, 784, 786,
    861, 862, 864, 870, 872, 875, 876, 880, 908,
    909, 911, 921, 930, 931, 954, 955, 962, 971,
    975
Piaget, M., 823, 830
Piazza, D., 784, 800, 804
Piazze, J. J., 182
Pica, P., 665, 780
Picariello, M. L., 395
Pick, A. D., 163, 164, 177, 190, 191, 564, 890
Pick, H. L., 184, 757, 761, 865
Pickering, A., 35
Pickering, E. C., 37
Pickering, S., 33, 758, 959
Picton, T. W., 63
Pierce, K., 38
Piercy, M., 68
Pierroutsakos, S. L., 560, 864
Pietrini, P., 36
Pighetti, M., 182
Pike, K. L., 77
Pillai, M., 182
Pillemer, D. B., 394, 395, 412, 674
Pillow, B., 826, 962
Pinard, A., 756
Pine, D., 30
Pine, J., 262, 263, 271, 274
Pine, K. J., 342, 350, 486, 498
Pinel, P., 780, 784, 794, 800, 804
Pinero, D. J., 392
Pinker, S., 82, 94, 257, 265, 267, 276, 277, 281,
    282, 302, 325, 444, 445, 446, 448, 611, 614,
    615, 617, 621, 625, 628, 691, 712
Pinto, G., 874
Pinto, J., 91, 144, 145, 314
Pintrich, P., 924, 982, 984, 986
Pion, N., 593

Piotrowski, L. N., 120
Pipe, M.-E., 395, 415
Pipp, S., 921, 927, 932
Pirchio, M., 116
Pisoni, D., 305
Pisoni, D. B., 64, 67, 73, 74, 75, 76, 83, 88, 94
Pisoni, D. P., 468
Pitts, R. C., 932
Pitts, W., 430
Piwoz, J., 81
Pizzini, E. L., 541
Pizzuto, E., 263
Plack, C. J., 67
Platinga, J., 886, 894
Platsidou, M., 563, 957, 958, 959, 960
Platt, W., 891
Plaut, D. C., 444, 448, 455, 616
Plesa-Skwerer, D., 765
Plessinger, M. A., 67
Plomin, R., 913, 914
Plomp, R., 887, 888
Plotkin, H., 642
Plucker, J. A., 908
Plumert, J. M., 193, 752, 753, 754, 761
Plunkett, K., 89, 119, 152, 237, 241, 286, 311,
    315, 427, 430, 433, 444, 445, 447, 448, 454,
    499, 558, 616, 663, 664, 691
Pohl, J., 751
Poirier, C. R., 224
Poirier, L., 576
Poiroux, S., 37
Polastri, P. F., 198
Policastro, E., 908
Polka, L., 73, 76, 85, 89
Polkey, C., 35, 42
Pollack, I., 71
Pollak, S. D., 39
Polya, G., 538, 560, 924
Pomerleau, A., 704
Pond, D., 883, 891, 892
Ponesse, J., 958
Pons, F., 74, 842, 846, 847
Pontecorvo, C., 980
Ponton, C. W., 60, 66
Poo, M. M., 612
Poortinga, W. H., 677
Popelka, G. R., 356
Popov, V., 622
Porath, M., 928
Porter, D. A., 26, 27
Posner, J. K., 665, 795
Posner, M., 29, 41, 42, 43, 44, 562, 802, 803
Postal, P., 322
Posteraro, F., 27
Potenza, M., 978
Pothos, E. M., 625
Poucet, B., 748
Poulin-Dubois, D., 244, 245, 303, 306, 307, 311,
    688, 703, 704
Povinelli, D. J., 184, 401, 839, 840, 841
Prasad, A., 565
Prasada, S., 301, 306, 311, 316, 690, 701, 704
Prat, C., 89
Pratt, C., 826
Pratt, F. R., 875, 876
Pratt, I. E., 880
Pratt, M. W., 470
Prechtl, H. F. R., 163, 168, 172, 182
Prediger, D. J., 937
Premack, A. J., 704
Premack, D., 244, 563, 704, 812, 822, 851, 860

Prentice, K., 539, 540, 797, 799
Prentice, S. D., 200
Prescott, P., 80
Pressley, M., 473, 499, 512, 513, 517, 518, 520,
    521, 522, 523, 526, 528, 531, 533, 535, 537,
    538, 541, 542, 543, 544, 545
Presson, C. C., 740, 755, 760
Previc, F. H., 907
Prevor, M., 313
Pribram, K. H., 814
Price, C., 76
Price, D. W. W., 393
Price, T. S., 913
Prieto, T., 76
Priftis, K., 794
Prince, A., 444, 445
Prince, R., 913
Principe, G., 406
Prinz, J., 626
Prinz, W., 646
Proffitt, D. R., 144, 704, 755
Proffitt, J. B., 715
Profita, J., 893
Prosser, J., 940
Pruett, J. C., 395
Pryce, C. R., 767
Przetacznik-Gierowsk, M., 850
Puce, A., 35
Pufall, P. B., 193, 756, 879
Pujol, R., 66
Pullum, G., 611, 617
Puranik, C. S., 68
Purves, D., 112, 152
Putaansuu, J., 125, 129, 130
Putnam, H., 698, 719
Pye, C., 273
Pylyshyn, Z., 113, 561, 627, 631

Qian, G., 924
Qin, Y., 428
Quantz, D., 316
Quartz, S. R., 558, 563, 567, 675
Quas, J. A., 395, 406, 415
Quayle, A., 37
Quigley, K. S., 589
Quillian, M. R., 701
Quine, W. V., 301, 304, 306, 311, 690, 699
Quinlan, P., 433
Quinn, G. E., 4
Quinn, P. C., 142, 148, 149, 235, 237, 238, 240,
    301, 303, 305, 306, 562, 569, 570, 689, 697,
    710, 752
Quinn, S., 961
Quixtan Poz, P., 273

Rabinowitz, C., 4, 619, 626
Rabinowitz, F. M., 575, 576, 591
Rabinowitz, M., 517
Rachel, R. A., 10
Rackliffe, G., 535
Rademacher, J., 415
Rader, N., 191, 193, 199
Radford, J., 918, 919, 921, 922, 923, 924
Radkey, A. L., 875, 878
Radke-Yarrow, M., 819, 930, 931, 932
Radvansky, G. A., 761
Rafal, D., 44
Rafal, R., 42, 43, 44
Raglioni, S. S., 76
Raijmakers, M. E. J., 442, 443

Rainville, C., 765
Rajapakse, J., 12
Rajaram, S., 375
Rakic, P., 6, 8, 9, 11, 34, 385, 386, 399
Rakison, D. H., 220, 235, 236, 237, 240, 244,
    245, 246, 687, 688, 691, 693, 702, 703, 704,
    710, 714, 715, 724
Rakoczy, H., 643, 646
Rakowitz, S., 312, 320, 321, 322
Ram, A., 620
Rama, P., 33
Ramachandran, V. S., 130
Raman, L., 701
Ramsay, D., 191, 193
Ramscar, M., 691, 711
Ramsden, B. M., 623
Ramus, F., 77, 78, 271, 883
Randall, B., 625
Rank, O., 914, 919, 920, 939
Rao, S. B., 82, 91, 93, 305
Rao, S. M., 76
Raper, J. A., 10
Raphael, L., 542
Raphael, T. E., 538
Rapoport, J. L., 30
Rappaport, M., 325
Rappaport-Hovav, M., 321, 322
Rapus, T., 42, 563, 564
Rasch, B. H., 761
Rashotte, C. A., 531
Raskind, W. H., 529
Rathbun, K., 85, 88
Rathunde, K., 916, 919, 939
Ratner, H., 286
Ratner, N. B., 80
Rattermann, M. J., 566
Rauch, S., 38, 41, 149, 928, 930
Rauf, L., 292
Rauscher, F., 342, 352, 356, 363
Raven, P. H., 311
Rawls, J., 929
Ray, S. D., 564
Rayner, K., 531
Rea, J. G., 737
Read, J. D., 513
Read, L. E., 482, 524, 530
Reagan, T., 652, 653
Rebai, M., 37
Reber, A., 27, 28, 29
Reboff, P. J., 11
Redanz, N. J., 80
Redbond, J., 564
Reder, L. M., 796, 801
Redford, M. A., 228
Redington, M., 305
Reeck, K., 93
Reed, A., 39
Reed, E. S., 113, 164, 184, 187, 200
Reed, J. M., 392
Reed, K. D., 84
Reed, M. A., 67
Reed, T., 843, 850
Rees, E., 908, 912, 921, 923
Reese, E., 401, 404, 405, 406, 408, 409, 418
Reese, H. W., 517
Reeve, R. A., 789, 790, 791, 797
Reeves, A., 8, 9
Regier, T., 760
Rehder, B., 705
Reichardt, L. F., 12
Reid, A. J., 38

Reid, T., 848
Reiland, J. K., 60
Reimann, P., 497
Reinikainen, K., 74
Reinisch, J. M., 390
Reiss, A., 31, 34
Reiss, J. E., 765
Reitan, R. M., 560
Reith, E., 878
Rekau, L., 262, 270
Rellinger, E. A., 512, 522
Remez, R. E., 75
Rempel, N. L., 392
Renfrew, C., 642
Renkl, A., 498
Renton, M., 797
Rentschler, I., 120
Repacholi, B., 306, 818
Repp, B. H., 72
Rescorla, L. R., 292
Rescorla, R. A., 590
Réservat-Plantey, D., 816
Resing, W. C. M., 473, 474, 480, 483, 491, 493,
    496, 501
Resnick, L. B., 585, 788, 789, 790, 791, 792
Restle, R., 466
Rettinger, D. A., 741
Rettke, H. J., 197, 746
Reudor, A., 306, 714
Reutter, B., 36
Révész, G., 883, 891
Reyna, V. F., 399, 400, 418, 573, 575, 576, 589
Reynolds, H. N., Jr., 128, 137
Reynolds, V., 839
Reynvoet, B., 750
Reznick, J. S., 162, 290, 316, 391, 449, 570, 700,
    737, 743, 781
Reznitskaya, A., 980, 982
Rheingold, H., 342, 820
Riach, C. L., 166
Ricard, M., 817
Ricci, C., 860, 861, 872, 880
Riccio, G., 193, 195, 198, 200
Ricciuti, C., 531
Ricco, R., 961
Rice, K., 89
Rice, M., 316
Richards, B. J., 260
Richards, C. A., 592, 594
Richards, D. D., 488, 595
Richards, J., 43, 185, 186, 191, 193, 199, 219
Richardson, D. C., 744
Richardson, J. J., 183
Richardson, M., 76
Richardson, P., 26
Richer, F., 25
Richert, R. A., 865
Richie, B. S., 940
Richman, W. A., 390
Richter, W., 31
Rickards, C., 530
Ricouer, P., 914
Riddell, P., 131, 146
Ridderinkhof, K., 41
Riddlesberger, M., 406
Rideout, R., 412, 413, 414, 524
Rider, E. A., 757
Ridgeway, D., 409
Ridlehuber, H., 30, 41
Ridley, A. J., 10
Ridley, M., 643

Ridley-Johnson, R., 168, 170, 171
Rieffe, C., 850
Riesen, A. H., 110
Rieser, J. J., 744, 749, 755, 757, 760, 766
Riley, C. A., 586
Riley, M. A., 187
Riley, M. S., 780, 797, 798
Rimé, B., 352, 363, 364
Rinehart, S. D., 533
Ringach, D. L., 138
Rips, L., 690, 693, 702, 708, 979
Riseborough, M. G., 356
Risenhoover, N., 818
Risley, T. R., 525
Rispoli, M., 267, 270, 283, 284
Ritchhart, R., 908
Ritter, F. E., 431, 796, 801
Ritter, K. G., 518, 519
Ritter, W., 33
Rittle-Johnson, B., 486, 492, 498, 523, 792, 793
Rivera, J. J., 882
Rivera, S., 222, 782
Rivera-Gaxiola, M., 73, 91
Rizzo, G., 182
Robbins, O., 579
Robbins, T., 42
Roberston, L. C., 32
Roberts, A., 42
Roberts, J. E., 31, 32, 763, 764
Roberts, J. O., 116
Roberts, K., 263
Roberts, N., 35
Roberts, R., 449
Roberts, S., 454
Roberts, T., 531
Robertson, D. A., 352, 363
Robertson, R. R. W., 89
Robertson, S. S., 172
Robin, A. F., 630, 719, 720
Robin, D. J., 186, 187
Robinette, A., 178, 188
Robinson, A. J., 22
Robinson, B., 39, 291, 470, 472, 473, 501, 765,
    921, 923
Robinson, C., 200
Robinson, D., 44
Robinson, E., 827, 828, 863, 864, 865
Robinson, F. P., 533
Robinson, J. A., 530
Robinson, K. M., 475
Robinson, M., 543, 592, 785, 801
Robinson, N. M., 482, 906
Robinson, R. E., 919
Robinson, S., 163, 168, 169, 171, 172, 175, 176,
    181, 486, 940
Rocca, P. T., 69
Rochat, P., 149, 188, 224, 568, 666, 782, 783,
    841
Roche, S., 894
Rock, I., 113, 137
Rockstroh, B., 16
Rode, G., 750
Roder, B. J., 218
Rodriguez, L. M., 409
Rodriguez, T., 666
Rodriguez, W., 303
Roe, A., 623, 912, 922, 923
Roe, K., 32, 33
Roeder, E. R., 7
Roediger, H. L., 375
Roehler, L. R., 535

Roehrig, A. D., 542
Roes, C. L., 888
Rogers, C. M., 860
Rogers, E. C., 63
Rogers, J., 76
Rogers, T. T., 433, 448, 612, 616, 618, 623
Rogoff, B., 468, 541, 545, 637, 639, 652, 655,
    656, 657, 658, 661, 662, 671, 761
Rohwer, W. D., Jr., 515, 530
Roisman, G. I., 409
Roit, M., 536
Rollins, H. A., 516
Rolls, E. T., 149
Romanini, C., 182
Romero, R. D., 455
Romney, A., 638
Romo, L., 483, 497, 705, 724
Ronald, A., 913
Roncesvalles, M. N. C., 167, 178, 180
Ronnqvist, L., 187
Root-Bernstein, R. S., 922
Rosander, K., 173, 178, 185, 186, 187, 188, 624,
    745
Rosch, E., 311, 562, 688, 690, 693, 696, 698
Roschelle, J., 620
Rose, D. H., 876
Rose, J. L., 198
Rose, S., 220, 387, 390, 611, 863
Rosen, C. S., 845
Rosen, J. T., 444, 445, 446, 448
Rosen, S., 68, 766
Rosen, T. J., 281, 282
Rosenberg, D., 193, 195, 198, 200
Rosenberg, F. R., 220
Rosenblatt, E., 867, 879, 919
Rosenblatt, F., 430
Rosenblatt, L. M., 535
Rosenblith, J. F., 466
Rosenblum, L. A., 390
Rosenblum, L. D., 77
Rosengren, K., 699, 700, 705, 716, 721, 722
Rosengren, K. K., 484
Rosengren, K. S., 299, 700, 737, 759
Rosenkrantz, S. L., 238
Rosenshine, B., 534
Rosenstein, M. T., 166, 177, 187
Rosenstiel, A. K., 868
Rosenthal, S., 409, 838
Rosenthaler, L., 136
Rosman, H., 564
Ross, A. S., 863
Ross, G., 412, 535, 541
Ross, L., 30, 718
Ross, M., 868, 869
Ross, N., 619, 668
Ross, W., 516
Rossetti, Y., 750
Rossi, S., 516
Rossion, B., 37
Rostan, S., 916, 923, 924, 939
Rosvold, H., 40
Rothbart, M., 29, 44, 219, 408, 708
Rothenberg, A., 909
Rothschild, L., 721
Rotstein, C., 317
Rotte, M., 28
Roug-Hellichius, L., 199
Rougier, A., 34
Rougier, N. P., 437, 438, 457
Rouma, G., 860
Rousselle, L., 583, 584

Rovee, C. K., 169
Rovee, D. T., 169
Rovee-Collier, C., 30, 31, 169, 236, 309, 375, 379, 380, 518
Rowat, W. L., 758
Rowland, C., 274
Rowland, D., 38
Rowland, G., 263
Roy, M. S., 611
Royer, J., 611, 777, 797, 799
Rozelle, J., 701
Rozenblit, L., 497
Rozin, P., 620, 708, 780, 789, 920
Ruan, W., 696
Rubboli, G., 38
Rubenstein, A. J., 148
Rubin, D. B., 390
Rubin, E., 135
Rubin, K. H., 342
Rubin, P. E., 75
Rubino, R., 263
Ruble, D., 688
Ruchkin, D. S., 33
Rudy, J. W., 438, 445
Rudy, L., 415
Rueda, M. R., 42
Ruff, H., 144, 219, 220, 863
Ruffman, T., 402, 449, 594, 667, 720, 737, 743, 836, 846, 847, 851, 983
Rugg, M. D., 37
Rulf, A. B., 839
Rumain, B., 960
Rumbaugh, D. M., 643
Rumelhart, D. E., 82, 373, 428, 430, 433, 437, 444, 445, 447, 448, 562
Rumiati, R. I., 531
Rump, B., 740
Rundell, L. J., 231, 232
Rupert, A., 67
Ruppin, E., 11
Rushton, K., 198
Ruskin, E., 844
Russell, C., 876
Russell, J., 149, 751, 829, 867
Russell, P., 66
Russell, R., 706, 707, 795
Russo, J. E., 474
Russo, R., 28
Russon, A., 646
Ruth, R. A., 63, 64
Rutishauser, U., 10
Rutter, M., 292, 415
Ryan, B., 497
Ryan, C. M. E., 139
Ryan, N. D., 39
Ryskina, V. L., 80, 94

Saada-Robert, M., 470, 472
Saalbach, H., 831
Sabatier, C., 200
Sabbagh, M. A., 713
Sabo, H., 291, 765
Sabol, M. A., 587, 588
Sacco, K., 31, 32
Saccuzzo, D. P., 764
Sachs, H., 200, 893
Sachs, J., 851
Sacks, O., 688, 917, 921
Sadato, N., 16, 677
Sadie, S., 888
Sáez, L., 530

Saffran, J., 82, 83, 84, 85, 86, 87, 89, 92, 93, 94, 270, 271, 301, 304, 305, 468, 469, 692, 710, 886, 894
Sag, I. A., 617
Sage, S., 438
Sahni, S. D., 449, 452
Sai, F., 147, 148, 152
Sainio, K., 74
Saint-Anne Dargassies, S., 168
Sak, K., 696
Sakai, R., 62
Sakata, H., 614
Sala, J. B., 33
Salapatek, P., 36, 116, 117, 118, 121, 185
Sales, J., 397, 407, 408, 414, 415
Saliba, E., 37
Salih, H. R., 735
Salmon, D., 29
Salmon, K., 415
Salmond, C. H., 27
Salthouse, T. A., 795
Saltzman, E., 183
Saltzman, J., 344
Samarapungavan, A., 597
Samson, S., 35
Samuels, R., 613
Samuelson, L. K., 303, 452, 710, 715
Samuelstuen, M. S., 524
Sanchez, J., 530
Sanchez, R. P., 561
Sandberg, E., 738, 750, 753, 758, 760
Sanderl, L., 312
Sanderson, A., 470, 474, 491
Sanderson, J. A., 592, 594
Sandhofer, C., 312, 316, 318, 358, 722
Sanes, D. H., 63, 67
Sanford, J. P., 541
Sanger, D., 865
Sanjana, N., 623
Santangelo, N., 182
Santelmann, L., 85, 91
Santisi, M., 792, 793
Sarfati, D., 415
Sargent, P. L., 133, 142
Sarnecka, B. W., 784
Sarty, M., 146, 241
Sasaki, M., 73
Sasaki, Y., 32
Sasseville, A. M., 218
Satlow, E., 751
Satoh, K., 40
Satterwhite, T., 191
Sauer, E., 355
Saults, J. S., 563
Saunders, C., 24
Saunders, R. C., 26
Savage, C., 285
Savage-Rumbaugh, S., 643, 644, 646, 882
Savelsbergh, G. J. P., 178, 187, 188
Sawaguchi, T., 33
Sawyer, R. K., 914
Saxe, G. B., 354, 651, 652, 657, 665, 784, 788, 795, 796
Saxton, M., 792
Sayer, A. G., 475
Sayers, J., 878
Saylor, M. A., 814, 815
Saylor, M. M., 234, 692, 724
Saywitz, K. J., 554
Scaife, M., 811, 817
Scalf, P., 17

Scarborough, H. S., 292
Scardamalia, M., 538, 908, 923
Scarr, S., 615, 802
Scarre, C., 642
Scassellati, B., 613
Schacher, R., 958
Schachner, M., 10
Schacter, D., 26, 28, 375, 513
Schade, A., 61
Schaefer-Simmern, H., 880
Schaeken, W., 594
Schafer, G., 89, 311, 315
Schaffner, K., 923
Scharf, B., 66
Schauble, L., 469, 472, 480, 481, 483, 485, 492, 493, 495, 496, 497, 498, 540, 545, 559, 921, 924, 962, 965, 966, 972, 973, 974, 979
Schefrin, B., 123, 124
Scheier, C., 164, 183, 435, 451, 452, 453, 742
Schellenberg, E., 885, 886, 887, 894
Schendan, H., 29
Schenk, F., 735
Schiaratura, L., 363, 364
Schick, K., 642
Schieffelin, B., 300
Schiff, A., 958
Schiff, W., 128
Schiller, P., 860
Schlagmüller, M., 470, 472, 473, 474, 481, 482, 483, 486, 492, 500, 524
Schlauch, R. S., 66
Schlaug, G., 893, 894
Schleifer, M., 594
Schlesinger, I., 256
Schlesinger, M., 457
Schliemann, A., 657, 671
Schlottmann, A., 245
Schmader, T. M., 752
Schmandt-Besserat, D., 653
Schmidt, R. A., 180, 181
Schmidt, R. C., 183
Schmidt, W., 438, 620
Schmuckler, M. A., 77, 164, 180, 189, 190, 193, 195, 197, 198, 200
Schneck, M. E., 123, 124
Schneider, B., 538
Schneider, B. A., 60, 61, 63, 64, 67, 69
Schneider, B. H., 913
Schneider, K., 169, 172, 177, 186
Schneider, R., 829, 830
Schneider, W., 374, 380, 406, 470, 472, 473, 474, 481, 482, 483, 486, 492, 500, 512, 513, 516, 517, 518, 520, 521, 523, 524, 545
Schnell, B., 654, 658
Schober, M. F., 761
Schoener, G., 742
Schoenfeld, A., 472, 545, 799, 970, 987
Scholes, R., 985
Scholl, B., 227, 610, 614, 627, 744, 750
Scholnick, E. K., 521, 760
Scholz, B. C., 611
Schöner, G., 164, 172, 177, 183, 202, 435, 437, 451, 452, 453, 754
Schonert-Reichl, K., 342
Schoon, C., 62
Schoppik, D., 26
Schorske, C. E., 915
Schouten, J. L., 36
Schrander-Stumpel, C. T., 7

Schreiber, T., 921, 923
Schroeter, K., 797, 799
Schubert, A., 40, 41
Schuder, T., 535, 537
Schuierer, G., 16
Schulsinger, M. F., 390
Schultz, R., 38, 844
Schulz, L., 307, 623, 717, 718, 965
Schumaker, J. B., 530
Schumm, J. S., 536
Schuneman, M., 960, 961, 962
Schunk, D. H., 523
Schunn, C. D., 621
Schustack, M., 967
Schutte, A., 452, 468, 754
Schutte, D., 932, 933, 934
Schwade, J. A., 382, 391, 412
Schwanenflugel, P. J., 526, 907, 924
Schwartz, B., 29, 920
Schwartz, C. E., 928, 930
Schwartz, M. A., 10
Schwartz, S. E., 291
Schwartz, S. N., 879
Schwartz, S. P., 698, 708
Schwartz, T., 638
Schwarzer, G., 33
Schwebel, D. C., 845
Schweinberger, S. R., 37
Schweinle, A., 227, 228
Schyns, P. G., 800
Scioloto, T., 44
Scott, L., 28
Scott, M. S., 721
Scott, P., 574, 575, 576, 689
Scoville, W. B., 20, 624
Scribner, S., 656, 657, 663, 960
Scripp, L., 892, 893
Scruggs, T. E., 531
Seah, E., 191
Seaks, J. D., 224, 737
Searl, M., 29
Sears, P. S., 906, 907, 913
Sears, R. R., 906, 907, 909, 913
Seashore, C. E., 883
Sebastián, E., 263
Sebastián-Gallés, N., 77, 78, 81, 88, 304, 305
Sedey, A. L., 60
Sedivy, J. E., 91
Sedlak, A., 968
Segal, J. W., 541
Segal, N. L., 615
Segawa, M., 181
Seger, C., 27
Segui, J., 77, 83
Sehgal, M., 76
Seibel, R., 94
Seidenberg, M., 82, 83, 87, 433, 434, 438, 444, 445, 448, 531, 568, 617
Seidl, A., 81
Seidman, L., 41
Seier, W., 173, 517, 519, 544
Sejnowski, T., 558, 563, 567, 623, 675
Sekel, M., 122, 123
Sekiguchi, N., 116
Sekuler, A. B., 116
Selfe, L., 912, 917, 918
Selman, R. L., 836, 926
Seltzer, M., 303
Semb, G., 921, 923
Senders, S. J., 188

Senghas, A., 303, 311, 318, 319, 348
Senior, G. J., 863
Senkfor, A. J., 381
Senn, M. J. E., 166
Sera, M., 303
Serafine, M. L., 884, 890
Seress, L., 385, 386
Sergeant, D., 893, 894
Sergent, J., 148
Serpell, R., 652, 654, 655
Serrano, J. M., 149
Serrat, E., 263
Serres, L., 22
Sersen, E. A., 8
Servan-Schreiber, D., 40, 449, 455
Sevcik, R., 643, 644
Sewell, F., 24
Sexton, M. E., 703, 813
Shaddy, D. J., 390
Shady, M., 80, 305
Shafer, V. L., 79
Shafir, E., 701, 978
Shafto, P., 720
Shahidullah, S., 60, 182
Shaked, M., 843, 850
Shalley, C. E., 924
Shallice, T., 39, 42, 531, 592, 616
Shanks, D. R., 717
Shankweiler, D. P., 72, 74
Shannon, E. S., 123, 124
Shapley, R., 138
Sharma, A., 611
Sharon, T., 781
Sharp, D., 516, 656, 658, 667
Sharp, W., 30
Sharpnack, H., 697
Shastri, L., 568
Shattuck-Hufnagel, S., 85
Shatz, M., 311, 312, 316, 343, 344, 573, 715, 851
Shaw, L., 270, 835, 985
Shaw, R. E., 113, 756
Shaw, V., 541, 979, 981, 982
Shaywitz, B. A., 529
Shaywitz, S. E., 529
Shea, D. L., 761
Shea, S. L., 125, 126, 130, 131
Sheffield, E. G., 385, 400
Sheiber, F. J., 220
Sheingold, K., 394
Shekerjian, D., 914, 923, 938, 939
Shell, R., 930
Shelton, A. L., 31, 740
Shelton, J. R., 688
Shen, L., 8
Shengel-Rutkowski, S., 7
Shepard, R. N., 114, 127, 143, 145, 760, 882
Shepardson, D. P., 541
Shepherd, G. M., 430
Sheppard, S. L., 66
Shepperson, B., 697
Sheridan, K., 907, 927, 929, 938
Shettler, L., 240, 752
Shettleworth, S. J., 735, 755
Shi, R., 79, 80, 82, 305
Shi, S. R., 66
Shibata, T., 37
Shiffrar, M. M., 197
Shiffrin, R. M., 515, 520
Shillcock, R., 86
Shilling, T. H., 218

Shimamura, A., 25, 27, 514
Shimojo, S., 115, 116, 470, 472, 473, 496
Shin, L. M., 38, 928, 930
Shingo, T., 9
Shinn, M. W., 883
Shinskey, J., 202, 222, 223, 224, 428, 448, 745
Shipley, C., 436, 483, 799
Shipley, E. F., 696, 697, 701, 716
Shipley, T. F., 128, 132, 136, 137, 138, 141, 142, 226
Shipstead, S. G., 826
Shirai, Y., 280, 281
Shiraki, S., 73
Shirley, M. M., 163, 165, 166, 167, 172, 173, 178, 180, 884
Shoben, E. J., 317, 692
Sholl, M. J., 740
Shore, C. M., 379
Shors, T. J., 8, 9, 16
Short, K. R., 138, 139, 143, 144
Shovelton, H., 342, 356, 357
Shrager, J., 173, 436, 472, 481, 483, 485, 502, 503, 722, 779, 788, 795, 799, 800, 801, 804
Shreyer, T. A., 589
Shrout, P. E., 174, 176, 178, 179, 180, 181, 190, 200
Shucard, D. W., 79
Shucard, J. L., 79
Shuff-Bailey, M., 696
Shugart, Y. Y., 7
Shulman, G., 44
Shulman, L. S., 545
Shults, C., 29
Shultz, T., 237, 239, 433, 438, 580, 596, 620, 823
Shum, M. S., 614, 619
Shumway-Cooke, A., 166
Shuter, R., 883, 884
Shvachkin, N. K., 89
Shwe, H. I., 850
Shweder, R., 621, 636, 638, 930, 931
Shyan, M., 882
Sides, A., 701
Sidman, R., 6
Siedentopf, C. M., 31
Siegal, M., 581, 701, 706, 708, 722, 846, 850, 851
Siegel, A. W., 516, 740, 756, 757, 758
Siegel, B. V., Jr., 501
Siegel, L. S., 529, 574
Siegler, R., 26, 168, 173, 176, 181, 183, 201, 202, 237, 286, 350, 360, 426, 427, 431, 433, 436, 438, 439, 440, 442, 443, 450, 454, 469, 470, 472, 473, 474, 475, 476, 477, 478, 479, 480, 481, 482, 483, 484, 485, 486, 487, 488, 489, 490, 491, 492, 493, 494, 495, 496, 497, 498, 499, 500, 501, 502, 503, 512, 521, 522, 523, 543, 545, 559, 560, 579, 595, 597, 598, 615, 620, 623, 663, 709, 722, 739, 742, 762, 779, 785, 786, 788, 792, 793, 794, 795, 796, 797, 799, 800, 801, 802, 803, 804, 912, 956, 968, 987
Sigman, M., 658, 659, 843, 844
Silk, A. M. J., 862
Silva-Pereyra, J., 73, 91
Silver Isenstadt, J., 73
Silverman, A. K., 537
Silverman, I. W., 596
Silverman, J., 868
Silverman, L. K., 932

Silverstein, M., 703
Simcock, G., 412, 413, 721
Simion, F., 36, 147, 242
Simmons, C. H., 931
Simmons, R., 923
Simon, D. P., 621
Simon, H., 429, 430, 467, 468, 469, 474, 475, 620, 621, 908, 911, 921, 923, 924
Simon, T., 427, 431, 432, 457, 558, 568, 569, 582, 781, 782, 783, 906
Simoneau, M., 592, 593, 594, 963
Simons, D., 227, 571, 618, 626, 692, 693, 699, 701, 702, 705, 706, 712, 755
Simonson, I., 978
Simonton, D. K., 908, 911, 912, 913, 914, 915, 916, 924, 925, 927, 928, 929, 938, 940
Simpson, E. L., 931
Sims, K., 291
Sims, V. K., 764
Sinatra, G. M., 924
Sinclair, A., 828
Sinclair, J., 512
Sines, A., 748
Singer, J. D., 475, 476
Singer, J. L., 845
Singer, M., 339, 344
Singer, M. A., 344, 358, 359, 360
Singh, L., 89, 90, 305
Singleton, J., 347, 348, 361
Singley, M. K., 196
Sinha, P., 39
Sininger, Y., 60, 66
Sinnott, J. M., 62, 64, 74
Sippola, L., 306, 307
Siqueland, E. R., 72, 74, 466
Siri, S., 616
Siskind, J. M., 86
Sithole, N. M., 73
Sivan, E., 535
Sjöberg, K., 795
Skala, K., 169
Skibbe, L., 666
Skinner, B. F., 429, 466, 663, 909
Skoczenski, A. M., 115, 116, 118, 119
Skopeliti, I., 597, 724
Skory, C., 757, 766
Skouteris, H., 188
Skudlarski, P., 33, 36
Slackman, E., 378, 393, 396
Slade, L., 846, 847, 851
Sladewski-Awig, L. J., 521
Slaney, P., 62
Slater, A., 79, 119, 135, 139, 140, 141, 145, 146, 148, 149, 152, 197, 226, 745
Slaughter, V., 720
Slawinski, J. L., 517
Slee, J., 513
Slemmer, J., 93, 181, 186, 202, 271, 745
Sloane, K. D., 916, 919, 920
Slobin, D., 81, 244, 256, 261, 267, 268, 281, 312, 695, 703, 720
Sloboda, J. A., 882, 883, 884, 889, 891
Sloman, S., 625, 635, 708, 977
Slomkowski, C., 407
Slotnick, N. S., 516
Slotta, J. D., 689
Sloutsky, M., 712, 713
Sloutsky, V., 308, 562, 571, 595, 691, 692, 711, 712, 713, 962
Slovic, P., 586, 718

Sluzenski, J., 739, 743, 750, 751
Small, A. M., 67
Smart, L. J., 187
Smedslund, J., 586
Smeele, P. M. T., 76
Smetana, J. G., 819, 820, 831
Smievoll, A. I., 31
Smilansky, S., 845
Smiley, P., 303
Smiley, S. S., 720
Smith, C., 618, 620, 626, 692, 719, 985
Smith, C. D., 36
Smith, C. L., 921, 923
Smith, C. M., 785
Smith, C. S., 280
Smith, E., 29, 33, 571, 635, 687, 688, 693, 701, 702
Smith, I. M., 128, 137
Smith, J., 339, 340
Smith, J. H., 261
Smith, J. P., III, 472
Smith, K. H., 587, 588
Smith, L., 164, 166, 168, 169, 171, 177, 183, 239, 303, 306, 311, 312, 316, 317, 318, 342, 430, 435, 451, 452, 453, 468, 484, 488, 558, 655, 691, 692, 695, 701, 704, 706, 707, 708, 710, 711, 712, 714, 722, 736, 737, 739, 742, 754
Smith, M., 34, 35
Smith, M. C., 60, 64
Smith, M. L., 25, 35
Smith, M. R., 77
Smith, O. W., 129
Smith, P., 29, 844
Smith, S. B., 589
Smith, S. L., 60
Smith, S. M., 908
Smith, W. C., 692, 693, 699, 701, 702, 705, 712
Smith-Chant, B. L., 507
Smitsman, A., 200, 201, 781
Smoleniec, J., 182
Smolensky, P., 561, 623, 625
Smotherman, W. P., 168, 171, 172
Snedeker, J., 315, 320, 326
Snell, J., 12
Snow, C., 260, 319, 850
Snow, K., 29
Snowdon, C. T., 74
Snyder, L., 262, 289, 290, 291
Snyder, W., 303, 319
Sobel, D. M., 307, 314, 623, 708, 717, 844
Soderling, E., 501
Soderstrom, M., 81
Sodian, B., 402, 516, 518, 830, 831, 836, 843, 983
Soja, N. N., 316, 704, 711
Sokol, B., 576, 577
Sokol, S., 115, 802
Sokoloff, G., 199
Sokolov, E. N., 237
Solis, C., 67
Solomon, B., 925, 930, 931, 932, 933, 934
Solomon, G. E. A., 664, 669, 705, 724
Solomon, S., 870
Solomonica-Levi, D., 843, 850
Somers, M., 119, 139, 141, 152, 226
Somerville, S. C., 519, 879
Sommer, T., 29
Sommerville, J. A., 202, 814, 815
Somorjai, R., 31
Son, J. Y., 618

Song, H., 9
Song, M. J., 788
Song, Y. K., 312
Sonies, B. C., 182, 183
Sonnenschein, S., 761
Sophian, C., 221, 581, 781, 787, 790, 792, 793
Sorce, J. F., 193, 199, 817, 818
Sorensen, L., 30
Sorknes, A., 128, 137
Sorokin, P. A., 912, 915, 939
Sorrentino, C. M., 700
Sosniak, L. A., 916, 919, 920, 922, 923, 924
Soto, P., 263
Soursa, P., 669
Sovrano, V. A., 748
Sowell, E. R., 12
Spaepen, G., 94
Spanoudis, G., 563, 957, 958, 959, 960
Sparling, J. W., 182
Sparrow, S., 616
Speaker, C. J., 222, 412
Spear, N. E., 400
Spear, S. J., 761
Speares, J., 289
Spearman, C., 778, 906
Spelke, E., 4, 126, 136, 138, 139, 140, 141, 142, 166, 167, 168, 171, 187, 202, 215, 219, 222, 224, 226, 227, 244, 304, 305, 306, 428, 431, 448, 467, 568, 617, 620, 624, 664, 688, 691, 693, 695, 696, 704, 711, 720, 734, 735, 737, 738, 740, 744, 746, 747, 748, 750, 757, 761, 766, 777, 780, 781, 782, 783, 784, 788, 794, 800, 802, 813, 818
Spellman, B. A., 231, 232
Spence, K. W., 466
Spence, M. J., 60, 524, 611
Spencer, J., 164, 169, 172, 177, 182, 186, 187, 188, 202, 435, 437, 452, 457, 468, 470, 472, 484, 490, 496, 753, 754
Sperber, D., 613, 614, 621, 628, 716, 722
Sperduto, V., 62
Spetch, M. L., 741, 748, 755
Spetner, N. B., 61, 63, 64, 67, 144, 704
Spieker, S., 76
Spiers, H. J., 35
Spinath, F. M., 913
Spinelli, D., 116
Spivey-Knowlton, M. J., 91
Sposetti, R., 893
Spratling, M. W., 39
Springer, J. A., 76
Springer, K., 664, 705, 706
Squire, L., 22, 23, 24, 25, 27, 28, 375, 380, 385, 392
Srinivas, K., 375
Sroufe, L. A., 409, 639, 838
Staddon, J. E. R., 589, 590
Stager, C. L., 88, 89, 90, 94, 236, 315, 710
Stahl, D., 816
Stahl, S. A., 533
Stanescu, R., 780, 794, 800
Stanley, J. C., 913
Stanovich, K., 965, 975, 979, 985, 986, 987
Stanovich, K. E., 531
Stanovich, K. G., 516
Stanowicz, L., 277
Stanzani Maserati, M., 38
Star, J., 701
Starch, D., 778
Stark, C. E., 22, 23

Stark, E. N., 415
Starkey, P., 568, 777, 779, 780, 781, 782, 783, 784, 787, 802, 803
Staszewski, J. J., 469, 796, 801
Stauffer, R. G., 533
Stavy, R., 488
Stayton, D. J., 838
Stedron, J., 225, 239, 417, 449, 765
Steel, S., 523, 524
Steele, H., 838
Steele, M., 838
Steenbergen, B., 201
Steere, M., 785, 791
Stefanacci, L., 23, 24
Stein, N. L., 373, 377, 823, 829
Stein, S., 273
Steinbach, K. A., 532
Steinberg, D., 867
Steinberg, E., 529
Steiner, R. D., 531
Steinmetz, H., 894
Stellmack, M. A., 71, 93
Stenger, V., 41, 438
Stennes, L., 407, 408
Stephens, B. R., 120, 147
Stephens, D. L., 474
Stephens, J., 941
Stephens, M. J., 168, 170
Stergiou, C. S., 195, 199
Sterling, R. S., 890
Stern, C., 566
Stern, D., 76
Stern, E., 473, 476, 477, 488, 490, 493, 495, 503, 797, 803
Sternberg, R., 540, 586, 589, 715, 907, 908, 913, 967
Stevens, A., 738
Stevens, C. E., 9
Stevens, D. D., 538
Stevens, K. N., 73, 305
Stevens, S. S., 65
Stevenson, C., 74, 480, 490, 501, 704
Stevenson, H., 465, 466, 468, 689, 795
Stevenson, L. M., 741
Stevenson, R., 279
Stewardson, J., 867, 878
Stewart, L., 16
Stewart, M., 29
Stich, S., 844
Stigler, J., 689, 785, 795, 796, 799
Stiles, J., 32, 33, 37, 566
Stillman, J. A., 61
Stimson, C. A., 930
Stocking, G., 637
Stoffregen, T. A., 187, 193, 195, 198, 200
Stohs, J. M., 939
Stokes, P. D., 469, 482, 486, 487
Stoll, S., 263
Stone, A., 342
Storkel, H. L., 81
Storksen, J. H., 180
Storr, A., 909, 922, 938
Stout, D., 642
Stout, J., 642
Strahan, D., 761
Strange, B. A., 23
Strange, W., 73
Stratford, B., 880
Strauss, M. S., 148, 569, 781, 782, 784, 863, 864
Streete, S., 28
Streeter, L. A., 73

Streibl, B., 16
Strevens, M., 708
Striano, A., 816
Striano, T., 149, 816
Strik, W., 38
Stromer, R., 590
Strommen, E., 860
Stromso, H. I., 524
Stroop, J., 958
Stucki, M., 125, 128, 137
Studdert-Kennedy, M., 72, 74, 76, 92
Stumpf, C., 883
Subotnik, R., 907, 923, 925
Subrahmanyam, K., 704
Sudhalter, V., 273, 292
Sugata, Y., 117
Sugiyama, Y., 839
Sullivan, J., 42
Sullivan, K., 837
Sullivan, M., 169
Sulloway, F., 911, 938
Sully, J., 860, 874, 880
Sumi, S., 144
Summers, B., 42
Summers, R., 31
Sun, D. K., 67
Sun, R., 626
Sundara, M., 73, 85
Sundberg, N., 880
Sundermier, L., 178, 180
Supalla, T., 348
Super, B. J., 142
Super, C. M., 170, 180, 200, 660, 661
Supinski, E. P., 908, 946
Suppes, P., 561
Sur, M., 14
Surber, C. F., 559, 597, 599
Surian, L., 245
Sutherland, D. H., 178
Sutherland, R. J., 35
Suttle, C. M., 122
Sutton, P. J., 876
Suzman, S. M., 273
Svejda, M., 191, 193
Svenkerud, V. Y., 81
Svenson, O., 795
Svetina, M., 470, 481, 483, 484, 485, 486, 490, 492, 493, 500
Swainson, B., 76
Swanson, H. L., 513, 530, 959
Swanson, P., 538
Sweda, J., 531
Sweeney, J., 957, 958, 959
Sweller, J., 797, 798, 799
Swingley, D., 82, 86, 90, 91, 94, 314
Swoboda, P., 72
Swoyer, C., 113
Syc, S. E., 342
Syder, F., 259
Sylvia, M. R., 186, 224, 737
Symons, S., 533
Syrdal, A. K., 74
Syrdal-Lasky, A., 73
Szechter, L. E., 759, 767
Szegda, K., 13
Szeminska, A., 586, 779
Szesko, P., 30

Taatgen, N. A., 437, 444, 445, 446, 447, 448
Tabak, I., 979, 985
Tabata, H., 10

Tackeff, J., 283
Tager-Flusberg, H., 291, 292, 765, 823, 837, 843, 847, 850, 851
Taglialatela, J. P., 643, 646
Ta'ir, J., 786
Taira, M., 614
Takahashi, T., 8
Takayama, H., 117
Takehara, K., 387
Takeichi, M., 10
Takeshi, M., 181
Takeuchi, A. H., 893
Tallal, P., 12, 68, 76, 292
Talmy, L., 315
Talor, C. R., 766
Tamis-LeMonda, C. S., 189, 194, 195, 199, 200
Tamura, R., 37
Tan, J., 38, 823, 843, 850
Tan, L. S., 748
Tanaka, H., 182
Tanaka, J. W., 242, 697, 720
Tanaka, S., 65, 677
Tanaka, T., 10
Tanaka, Y., 63, 614
Tanapat, P., 8, 9, 398
Tanenhaus, M. K., 91, 317
Tanner, J. M., 174
Tannock, R., 958
Tao, P. K., 620
Taormina, J., 193, 195, 198, 200
Taplin, J. E., 570, 706, 716
Taraban, R., 484, 485
Tardif, T., 261, 312, 694, 822, 843, 850
Tarquinio, N., 64
Tarr, M. J., 33, 36, 37, 241, 697
Tarr, P., 870
Tarver, S. G., 530
Tassinary, L. G., 77
Taub, E., 16
Taunton, M., 875
Taylor, A., 529, 763
Taylor, B., 415, 533, 537
Taylor, D., 139, 141, 152, 226
Taylor, H. A., 741, 761
Taylor, J., 10, 470, 497, 498, 778
Taylor, L. B., 35
Taylor, M., 29, 402, 708, 827, 845, 876
Taylor, M. B., 537
Taylor, M. E., 697, 720
Taylor, M. G., 722
Taylor, M. J., 37
Team, A. S., 200
Tees, R. C., 73, 242, 305, 767
Teitelbaum, P., 171, 456
Tellegen, A., 913, 914
Teller, D. Y., 60, 122, 123, 124
Tellinghuisen, D. J., 219
Temple, C. M., 26
Temple, E., 802
Tencer, H. L., 338, 345, 353
Tenenbaum, H. R., 722, 842
Tenenbaum, J. B., 623, 696
Tenenbaum, J. M., 136
Teng, E., 23, 24
Tenney, Y. J., 394
Terada, K., 163
Terboux, D., 838
Terman, L. M., 906, 909, 911, 922, 927, 931
Terman, L. W., 906
Termine, N. T., 816
Terrace, H. S., 590, 591, 789

Tervoort, B. T., 346
Tesla, C., 407
Tessier-Lavigne, M., 10
Tessler, M., 404
Teuber, H., 27
Teylan, M., 30
Thacker, N., 31
Thagard, P., 560, 620
Thaiss, L., 616, 864
Tharpe, A. M., 60, 64
Thayer, E. S., 586
Theakston, A., 285
Thelen, E., 162, 164, 165, 166, 167, 168, 169,
   170, 171, 172, 173, 177, 178, 179, 181, 182,
   183, 186, 187, 188, 189, 340, 360, 430, 435,
   437, 451, 452, 453, 457, 464, 468, 470, 472,
   473, 474, 484, 485, 486, 490, 496, 499, 613,
   736, 737, 739, 742, 754
Therriault, D., 521
Theuring, C. F., 200, 201
Thiede, K. W., 521
Thiessen, E. D., 84, 85, 86, 87, 94
Thines, G., 306
Thinus-Blanc, C., 748, 766
Thomachot, B., 178
Thomas, C., 538
Thomas, E. M., 311
Thomas, G. V., 859, 862, 863, 864, 865, 867, 868,
   876
Thomas, H., 574
Thomas, J. P., 115
Thomas, K., 29, 30, 34, 38, 39, 41, 42, 48, 417
Thomas, M., 434, 455
Thomas, M. A., 704
Thomas, M. S. C., 750, 765
Thomas, R. J., 928, 929
Thomas, T. D., 200
Thomason, M., 41
Thomasson, M. A., 124
Thompson, C. K., 312
Thompson, C. P., 513
Thompson, D., 751
Thompson, E., 72
Thompson, H., 163, 165, 172, 182
Thompson, L., 43, 76, 356
Thompson, N. C., 62
Thompson, P. M., 12
Thompson, R., 30
Thompson, R. F., 800
Thompson, R. K. R., 563
Thompson, R. M., 559
Thompson, S., 269, 302
Thompson, W. L., 31
Thomsen, T., 31
Thomson, J. B., 529
Thorndike, E. L., 196, 778, 779, 906, 909, 927,
   931
Thornton, S., 474, 484, 492, 496, 497, 498
Thorpe, L. A., 64, 65, 69, 885, 886, 887, 889
Threlfall, K. V., 908, 946
Thulborn, K., 31, 32, 41
Thurstone, L. L., 778, 906
Thurstone, T. G., 778
Tighe, T. J., 191
Tiilikainen, S. H., 790
Timberlake, W., 801
Timney, B., 131, 757, 766
Tincoff, R., 88, 305
Tinker, E., 261, 306, 312
Tipper, S., 958

Tirri, K., 933
Tishman, S., 908, 986, 987
Titchener, E. B., 109, 110, 127
Titzer, B., 451
Titzer, R., 191, 468, 742
Tjebkes, T. L., 219
Tobias, S., 345
Tobin, K., 541
Todd, C. M., 378, 396
Toga, A. W., 12
Toglia, M. P., 513
Togo, M., 174
Togo, T., 174
Tokura, H., 81, 301, 302, 312, 320, 322
Toma, K., 677
Tomasello, M., 255, 258, 260, 262, 263, 264, 265,
   266, 267, 270, 272, 274, 275, 276, 277, 279,
   281, 284, 285, 286, 287, 288, 289, 290, 291,
   302, 303, 306, 308, 326, 380, 484, 643, 644,
   646, 666, 667, 675, 676, 694, 713, 714, 721,
   724, 815, 817, 820, 821, 839, 840, 847, 850,
   851, 930
Tomizawa, K., 19
Tooby, J., 558, 614, 615, 691
Toolan, M., 985
Topping, K., 722
Torgesen, J. K., 530, 531
Toro, J. M., 93
Torrance, E. P., 906, 908
Toth, N., 642
Tottenham, N., 24, 41, 42
Touwen, B. C., 168
Towse, J., 563, 564, 792
Trabasso, T., 586, 587, 829
Trainor, L. J., 89, 885, 886, 887, 889, 894
Trainor, R., 34, 40, 41
Tramo, M., 888
Tran, T., 30
Tranel, D., 38, 41
Trask, L., 279
Trauner, D. A., 12
Trauner, D. J., 32, 33
Travers, S. H., 521
Travis, L. L., 380, 384
Treagust, D. F., 541
Trehub, S. E., 60, 61, 63, 64, 65, 67, 72, 73, 94,
   885, 886, 887, 889, 893, 894
Treisman, A., 568, 783
Tremoulet, P., 227, 610, 744, 750
Treutwein, B., 120
Trevarthen, C., 166, 811, 816, 930, 932
Triano, L., 498
Trick, L. M., 783
Trickett, P. K., 822
Trinkler, I., 738
Trobalón, J. B., 93
Tronick, E., 129
Tronsky, L. N., 777, 797, 799
Troseth, G. L., 722, 864
Trotoux, J., 66
Trueswell, J., 304, 326
Truwit, C. L., 34, 41
Tsang, C. D., 89, 887
Tsao, F., 15, 73, 80, 94, 305, 762, 767
Tsivkin, S., 780, 794, 800
Tsushima, T. T. O., 73
Tuccillo, F., 967
Tucker, J., 926, 927
Tuckey, M., 838, 846, 847
Tudge, J., 497
Tulving, E., 19, 23, 398, 400, 402

Tulviste, P., 656
Tunteler, E., 480, 491, 496
Turati, C., 36, 147, 241, 242
Tureski, K., 19
Turiel, E., 621, 831, 930
Turk, A. E., 80
Turk, H., 531
Turkewitz, G., 220
Turkheimer, E., 13
Turner, R., 16, 34, 41
Turnure, J. E., 529
Turpin, R., 62
Turtle, M., 12
Turvey, M. T., 113, 187, 435
Tversky, A., 485, 558, 586, 718, 736, 738, 975,
   976, 978
Tversky, B., 736, 738, 741, 761
Tweney, R. D., 905, 912, 924
Twentyman, C. T., 820, 822
Tyack, D., 274
Tyler, C. W., 116, 117, 119
Tyler, L. K., 291, 625
Tyrrell, D. J., 567, 568
Tytler, R., 921, 924
Tzourio-Mazoyer, N., 34, 36

Ubels, R., 182
Uchida, I., 40, 41
Uchida, N., 303
Uchiyama, I., 200
Udelf, M. S., 115
Udell, W., 542, 981, 982
Udwin, O., 291
Uecker, A., 765
Ueda, A., 183
Uesiliana, K., 410
Ugurbil, K., 31
Uhl, F., 16
Uller, C., 782, 783
Ullman, M., 281, 282, 444, 445, 446, 448, 625
Ullman, S., 113, 127, 143
Ulrich, B., 162, 168, 170, 172, 183, 435, 472,
   496
Ulrich, D. A., 170
Ulrich, T., 516
Umilta, C., 36, 242
Umiltá, C., 794
Ungerleider, L. G., 36
Unyk, A. M., 885
Upitas, R., 895
Urban, T., 957, 958, 959
Urbano, R. C., 886
Utman, J., 282
Uttal, D. H., 690, 737, 741, 748, 760, 864
Uylings, H. B. M., 11
Uzgiris, I., 221

Vachon, R., 962
Vadeboncoeur, I., 593
Vaidya, C., 30, 41
Vail, N., 9
Vaituzis, A. C., 30
Valdez-Menchaca, M. C., 525
Valentin, D., 150
Valentine, C. W., 883
Valenza, E., 147, 242
Valenzeno, L., 361
Valian, V., 765
Valiquette, C. M., 740
Vallone, R., 485
Vallortigara, G., 748

Van Abbema, D. L., 383, 388, 392, 398, 400, 413, 415
van Asten, W. N. J. C., 198
Vandemaele, P., 31
van den Berg, A., 881
van den Boom, D. C., 482, 484, 486, 496, 561
van der Fits, I. B. M., 188
van der Gon, J. J. D., 198
van der Kamp, J., 187, 188, 201
van der Lely, H., 68
van der Linden, M., 29
Van der Loos, H., 11
van der Maas, H., 431, 435, 440, 441, 442, 443, 482, 484, 486, 496, 561, 598
van der Meer, A. L. H., 183, 185, 186, 187, 190, 193
van der Molen, M., 41
van der Weel, F. R., 183, 185, 186, 187, 193
Van de Walle, G., 142, 228, 313, 583, 584, 786, 787, 803
van de Wiele, M., 356
VanEden, C., 11
van Ee, R., 739
van Emmerick, R. E. A., 176
van Engeland, H., 12
van Eykern, L. A., 182, 188
van Geert, P., 435, 438, 481, 484, 499, 501, 558
Van Gelder, T., 561
van Gelderen, P., 677
van Ham, J. J., 38
Van Hesteren, F., 933
van Hof, P., 187
Van Ijzendoorn, M. H., 838
van Koten, S., 442, 443
VanLehn, K., 436, 592
van Loosbroek, E., 781
Vanmann, E. J., 149
Van Meter, P., 535
van Nes, F. L., 116
Van Noort, D. A., 473, 474, 483, 493, 501
Van Otterloo, S. G., 74, 480, 490, 501
Van Paesschen, W., 26
Van Parys, M., 926, 927
Van Pettern, C., 381
van Rijn, H., 431, 440, 441, 442, 443
van Someren, M., 431, 440, 441, 442, 443
van Tol, J., 182
VanVeen, V., 438
van Wieringen, P. C., 178
van Zon, M., 77
Vapnarsky, V., 669
Varelas, M., 791, 792
Vargas, S., 531
Vargha-Khadem, F., 25, 26, 27, 33, 35, 74, 380
Varner, D., 123, 124
Varnhagen, C. K., 480
Vasilyeva, M., 290, 303, 740, 747, 748, 756, 759, 760
Vasudeva, A., 409, 410
Vatuzis, A. C., 12
Vauclair, J., 748, 755
Vaughan, H. G., 74, 124
Vaughn, S., 536
Vecchi, T., 34
Vecera, S., 44, 455
Veenman, M. V. J., 74, 480, 490, 501
Veldhuis, J. D., 174, 175
Vellutino, F. R., 529
Vendler, H., 919
Venet, M., 593

Venezky, R. L., 525
Venza, V., 263
Vera, A., 621
Vereijken, B., 164, 169, 170, 172, 173, 174, 176, 177, 178, 179, 180, 181, 182, 188, 470, 472, 474, 484, 490, 496
Verfaellie, M., 27
Vergnaud, G., 797
Vernon, P. E., 906
Verschaffel, L., 797, 923
Very, P. S., 778
Vettel, J. M., 755
Vevea, J., 753, 764
Vhiman, M. M., 199
Vibbert, M., 149
Videen, T., 28
Viemeister, N. F., 66, 67, 68
Vigliocco, G., 616
Vigorito, J., 72, 74
Vihman, M., 81
Vijayan, S., 82, 91, 93, 270, 305, 568
Vilette, B., 788
Vinden, P. G., 666, 667, 841, 842
Vinet, J., 8, 9
Vingerhoets, G., 31
Vinson, D. P., 616
Viola, W., 862
Vishram, R., 168, 170
Vishton, P., 82, 91, 93, 187, 270, 305, 448, 568, 624, 737
Visscher, P., 842
Visser, G. H. A., 163, 172, 182
Visser, T., 832
Vitevitch, M. S., 81, 86
Vizueta, N., 29, 30
Vlahovic-Stetic, V., 792
Vogel, E. K., 563
Vogel, M., 778
Vogele, D., 189
Vohr, B. R., 60, 65
Voice, K., 291
Volkmann, F. C., 125
Volkmar, F., 17, 38, 616, 844
Vollmer-Conna, U., 80
Volpe, J. J., 7, 8, 10, 11
Volterra, V., 338, 340
von Bertalanffy, L., 430, 435, 456
von der Heydt, R., 136, 142
von der Malsburg, C., 119
Von der Schulenburg, C., 148, 149
von Fersen, L., 589, 590
von Helmholtz, H., 883, 887
von Hofsten, C., 125, 126, 129, 130, 136, 164, 166, 172, 173, 177, 178, 184, 185, 186, 187, 188, 196, 197, 201, 202, 448, 624, 745
von Holst, E., 126
Vonk, J., 840, 841
Vosmik, J. R., 760
Vosniadou, S., 560, 597, 635, 724
Voss, J., 979
Vouloumanos, A., 15, 75, 76, 305
Voyer, D., 763, 764
Voyer, S., 763, 764
Voyvodic, J., 31, 32
Vrba, E. S., 177
Vriezen, E., 562
Vroomen, J., 77
Vurpillot, E., 77
Vygotsky, L. S., 467, 468, 471, 499, 541, 560, 617, 619, 626, 637, 639, 689, 694, 911, 912, 915, 926

Waber, D., 30, 31, 763
Wachtel, G. F., 592
Waddell, K., 657
Waddington, C. H., 430
Wade, A., 352
Wagers, M., 9
Wagner, A. D., 375
Wagner, A. R., 590
Wagner, D. A., 654, 656
Wagner, E., 819, 930, 931, 932
Wagner, G. P., 614
Wagner, L., 280, 306
Wagner, S., 362, 363, 867
Waheed, N., 793
Wainryb, C., 835, 985
Wainwright, R., 846, 847
Wakaua, H. J., 619
Wake, W. L., 907
Wakefield, G. H., 67
Wakeley, A., 222, 782
Waldron, M., 13
Walicke, P., 29
Walk, R. D., 111, 129, 187, 191, 192, 867
Walkenfeld, F. F., 406
Walker, A. S., 191, 193, 197
Walker, J., 43, 44
Walker, L. J., 909, 932
Walker-Andrews, A. S., 76, 149, 306, 308
Wallace, A., 780
Wallace, C. S., 802
Wallace, D. B., 908, 912, 940
Wallace, J. G., 429, 430, 431, 467, 558, 582
Wallace, S. B., 148
Wallach, H., 110, 126, 143
Wallach, M. A., 907
Wallas, G., 908
Wallberg, H., 167, 168, 170
Wallen, P., 168
Waller, D., 761, 762, 764
Walley, A., 74
Wallin, N. L., 882
Walpole, S., 537
Walsh, E. J., 63, 67
Walsh, V., 16, 750
Walter, J., 30
Walters, J., 922, 932, 967
Walters, R., 466, 909
Walther, D., 142
Walton, D. N., 981
Walton, G. E., 76
Waltz, D., 136
Waltz, J. A., 588
Wang, P. P., 765
Wang, Q., 407, 410, 411, 674
Wang, R. F., 735, 738, 740, 747, 755
Wang, X.-L., 344
Wann, J. P., 198
Wanner, E., 81, 85, 690
Want, S., 815, 820, 846
Warburton, D., 7
Warburton, E., 76
Ward, J. A., 168
Ward, M. R., 797, 798, 799
Ward, R., 44
Ward, T. B., 908
Waring, M. D., 66
Warkany, J., 8
Warren, W. H., 189, 190, 193, 198, 736
Warren, W., Jr., 177
Warsofsky, I. S., 34
Washburn, D. A., 643

Washburne, C., 778
Wasik, B. A., 792
Wasnik, A., 240, 752
Wason, P., 960
Wasserman, S., 4, 219, 222
Waters, E., 838
Waters, H. S., 409, 511, 517, 518
Waters, J. M., 25, 220, 382, 383, 386, 387, 388, 389, 390, 399
Waters, L. J., 581
Waters, R. A., 74
Waters, S. E., 133
Watkins, K. E., 26, 27
Watson, A. C., 846
Watson, J., 824, 825, 830, 841
Watson, J. B., 429
Watson, J. D., 922, 923
Watson, M. W., 879, 926, 927
Wattam-Bell, J., 119, 120, 124, 125, 141
Waugh, N. C., 515
Wax, N., 488
Waxman, B., 789, 790
Waxman, S., 240, 299, 301, 302, 304, 306, 307, 308, 309, 310, 311, 312, 313, 314, 316, 317, 318, 319, 320, 339, 570, 690, 694, 696, 697, 700, 702, 711, 715, 721
Wearing, H., 758, 959
Webb, J. A., 144
Webb, R., 342
Webb, S. J., 11, 21, 22, 25, 28
Weber, B. A., 67
Weber, M., 928
Webster, S. W., 926
Webster, T. W., 175, 176
Wechsler, D., 906
Wechsler, M. A., 480
Wegener, A., 493
Weichbold, V., 825
Weikart, D. P., 526
Weikum, W. M., 78
Weiler, I. J., 12, 47
Weiler, M., 30
Wein, D., 227, 357
Weinacht, S., 611
Weinberg, A., 91, 314
Weinberg, R. A., 376
Weinberger, D. R., 10
Weiner, B., 521, 813
Weinfield, N. S., 838
Weinstock, M., 835, 869, 923, 973, 974, 979, 984, 985
Weir, C., 63
Weir, J., 312
Weisberg, J., 619
Weise, I. B., 200
Weiskopf, S., 316
Weiskrantz, L., 619
Weisner, T. S., 638, 639
Weiss, A. H., 122, 123
Weiss, D., 93, 271
Weiss, E., 31
Weiss, M. J., 64, 167, 170
Weissenborn, J., 79
Weissman, M. D., 705
Weissman, S., 752
Weist, R., 267, 280
Welch, J., 300
Welch, L., 572
Welch-Ross, M. K., 401, 402, 406, 407
Welder, A. N., 309, 313, 314, 695, 696, 699, 715, 716

Wellens, A. R., 352
Weller, S. C., 638
Wellman, H., 692
Wellman, H. M., 221, 448, 449, 451, 470, 487, 491, 519, 571, 624, 627, 628, 666, 690, 691, 703, 705, 706, 709, 719, 723, 762, 767, 818, 822, 823, 824, 825, 828, 830, 833, 841, 843, 850, 851
Wellman, H. W., 760
Wells, G., 260
Welsh, L. M., 542
Welsh, M. C., 801, 803
Welsh, T., 34, 41, 42
Wendrich, K. A., 891
Wendt, J., 191
Wennemann, D. J., 933
Wenner, J. A., 25, 380, 381, 382, 383, 384, 387, 389, 390, 391, 399, 412, 413, 524
Wentworth, N., 186, 187
Werker, J. F., 15, 73, 74, 75, 76, 77, 78, 79, 80, 82, 83, 86, 88, 89, 90, 94, 107, 149, 150, 236, 242, 304, 305, 315, 695, 710
Werner, H., 467, 468, 471, 499, 617, 689, 891
Werner, J. S., 116, 117, 122
Werner, L. A., 60, 64, 65, 66, 67, 68, 69, 71, 92
Werner, S., 740
Wertheimer, M., 112, 137, 138, 908, 924
Wertsch, J., 470, 471, 474, 497, 637, 639
Wesp, R., 355
Wessels, J., 81, 305
West, R., 965, 975, 979, 985, 986, 987
Westerberg, H., 34
Westermann, G., 239
Westheimer, G., 115, 130, 131
Westra, T., 170, 180, 200
Westwood, H., 867
Wetzer, H., 316
Wewerka, S., 25, 48, 234, 381, 382, 383, 384, 387, 389, 390, 391, 392, 399, 406, 412, 524
Wexler, K., 611
Whalen, D. H., 72, 76
Whalen, J., 568
Whalen, N., 395
Whalen, P., 38, 39, 41, 149
Whalen, S., 916, 919, 939
Whalen, T., 69
Whaley, S. E., 658, 659
Whang, S., 189, 190, 193
Wharton-McDonald, R., 537, 542
Wheaton, K., 355
Wheeler, K., 128, 137
Whewell, W., 609
Whishaw, I. Q., 17
Whitaker, C. J., 748
Whitall, J., 167, 176, 178, 180
Whitcombe, E. L., 827, 828
White, A., 848
White, B., 118, 124
White, C. D., 34, 38
White, D. A., 531
White, K., 82, 89, 305
White, M. I., 654, 658
White, N. M., 800
White, R., 182
White, S., 394, 412, 465, 740, 756
Whitehurst, G. J., 525, 761
Whiten, A., 287, 813, 839
Whiting, B. B., 660
Whiting, H. T. A., 176
Whitman, T. L., 529

Whittaker, S., 280, 519
Whitten, A., 637, 645, 646
Whitteridge, D., 130
Whorf, B. L., 694
Wible, C. G., 396
Widaman, K. F., 796, 797, 799
Widen, J. E., 60
Wiebe, S. A., 25, 220, 381, 382, 383, 386, 387, 388, 389, 390, 399, 400, 413
Wienbruch, C., 16
Wiener, M., 340
Wiener-Vacher, S., 178, 180
Wierzbicka, A., 312, 315, 841
Wiesel, T. N., 119, 130, 766
Wightman, F., 61, 65, 66, 67, 71, 93
Wilbur, R., 346
Wilcox, T., 227, 228, 313, 315, 700, 744
Wilder, A. A., 537
Wiley, J. G., 750, 779
Wilhelm, I. J., 182
Wilk, A., 697
Wilkening, F., 559, 560, 595, 596, 967
Wilkie, O., 701
Wilkins, J. L. M., 790
Willats, J., 861, 862, 876, 877, 878
Willatts, P., 201, 224, 428
Willett, J. B., 475, 476
Williams, B., 958
Williams, D. R., 116, 118
Williams, E., 303, 468, 470, 663, 664, 665, 690, 691, 704, 705, 706, 780
Williams, J. P., 537
Williams, K. A., 73, 305
Williams, N., 863
Williams, R. J., 433
Williams, S. E., 10
Williams, T. H., 927
Williamson, C., 840
Willihnganz, M. S., 71, 93
Willner, J., 386
Wills, G., 927
Wilmington, D., 70
Wilsman, N. J., 175
Wilson, B., 876, 880
Wilson, C., 658, 907
Wilson, D., 92, 93, 621
Wilson, G., 931, 932
Wilson, H. R., 117, 118
Wilson, M., 876, 880
Wilson, R., 92
Wilson, W. A., Jr., 74
Wilson, W. H., 558, 560, 561, 565, 566, 570, 572, 575, 592, 598, 958
Wilson, W. R., 60, 64, 65
Wimmer, H., 402, 812, 823, 824, 825, 836, 837
Winch, W. H., 778
Windischberger, C., 16, 31
Windmueller, G., 867, 879
Winer, G. A., 573
Wing, H. D., 883
Winkelaar, R., 66
Winner, E., 860, 865, 867, 868, 878, 879, 880, 881, 894, 905, 911, 912, 916, 917, 919, 920, 922, 939
Winnicott, D. W., 700
Winocur, G., 35
Winograd, E., 414
Winograd, P., 521
Winsler, A., 500, 560
Winston, A. S., 867, 878
Winston, P. H., 136

Winter, D. A., 169, 173
Winter, D. G., 928, 929
Winter, Y., 317
Winterhoff, P. A., 497
Wise, R., 76
Wiser, M., 620, 692, 719
Wishart, J. G., 221
Wisniewski, E. J., 692
Witherington, D., 164, 176, 178, 180, 187, 188,
    191, 194, 195, 198, 200, 202, 617, 723, 744,
    745
Withington, D. J., 70
Witkowska-Stadnik, K., 280
Wittek, A., 263, 267
Wittgenstein, L., 562, 828
Wittrock, M. C., 516
Wohlwill, J. F., 866, 890
Wohlwill, J. P., 177, 180
Wojdak, R., 302
Wolf, C., 919, 920
Wolf, D., 819, 870, 892, 911
Wolfe, A., 915, 930, 932
Wolff, P., 183, 364
Wolfman, C. M., 363, 364
Wolford, J. L., 764
Woloshyn, V. E., 523, 537
Won, D., 818
Wondoloski, T. L., 380
Wong, B. Y. L., 530
Wong, D., 76
Wong, E., 32
Wong, E. C., 32, 37
Wong, E. L. R., 32, 33
Wong, R. O., 11
Woo, S., 178
Wood, D., 431, 470, 484, 485, 487, 491, 494, 500,
    718
Wood, E., 537
Wood, S. S., 535, 541
Woodruf, G., 812, 822, 851
Woodruff-Pak, D., 30
Woods, J. R., 67
Woodward, A., 81, 87, 89, 202, 228, 244, 299,
    301, 306, 308, 309, 311, 312, 688, 690, 704,
    710, 711, 714, 723, 813, 814, 815
Woodward, J. Z., 87
Woodworth, R. S., 196, 778
Woody-Dorning, J., 521
Woolfe, T., 846
Woollacott, M. H., 164, 166, 167, 169, 174, 178,
    180, 188
Woolley, J. D., 666, 823, 833
Worden, P. E., 521
Worsley, K., 12, 34
Worthington, D. W., 60
Wraga, M., 755
Wrangham, R. W., 645
Wright, A. A., 22, 882
Wright, B. A., 68
Wright, B. C., 589
Wright, C. I., 38, 928, 930
Wright, J. W., 811
Wright Cassidy, K., 81, 886
Wrzesniewski, A., 920
Wrzolek, M. A., 8
Wu, B. J., 66
Wu, D., 43

Wu, L., 89
Wu, P., 146, 241
Wu, Y. Y., 63, 67
Wulfeck, B., 282
Wundt, W., 109, 336
Wustenberg, T., 31
Wynn, K., 4, 223, 233, 354, 431, 568, 569, 582,
    583, 610, 614, 617, 619, 777, 779, 780, 781,
    782, 783, 784, 785, 786, 788, 792, 802, 803
Wynn, T. G., 642
Wynne, C. D. L., 589, 590
Wynne, M. K., 62
Wysocka, H., 280
Wysocka, J., 280

Xu, F., 227, 228, 281, 282, 300, 307, 312, 313,
    444, 445, 446, 448, 568, 569, 610, 696, 697,
    700, 715, 744, 750, 781, 784
Xu, M., 198

Yahr, J., 149
Yamamoto, K., 66
Yamamoto, Y., 117
Yamashiro, C., 182
Yamauchi, T., 702
Yamazaki, H., 66
Yan, Z., 470, 481
Yanagihara, T., 182
Yancey, S. W., 22, 25
Yanez, B. R., 180
Yang, C., 610, 617, 618
Yang, J. F., 168, 170
Yang, T. T., 38
Yang, Y., 29, 41, 42
Yao, Y., 795
Yates, M., 931, 932, 934
Yeany, R. H., 541
Yekel, C. A., 760
Yerkes, R. M., 414
Yerys, B. E., 452
Yi, S., 410, 411, 674
Yilmaz, E. H., 198
Yin, C., 138, 142
Ying, E. A., 94
Yirmiya, N., 843, 844, 850
Yonas, A., 127, 128, 129, 131, 132, 133, 137, 142,
    143, 144, 188, 866
Yonas, P. M., 870
Yonekura, Y., 16
Yong, D., 757
York, K., 596
Yorozu, Y., 163
Yoshida, H., 306, 692, 695, 704, 710, 714
Yoshida, K. A., 78
Yoshinaga-Itano, C., 60
Yoshizuka, M., 66
Yotive, W., 540
Young, A. J., 355, 363
Young, A. W., 38
Young, J. W., 175, 176, 181, 486
Young, L. J., 19
Young, M. F., 749
Young, R., 241, 429
Youngblade, L., 407, 845
Younger, B., 216, 235, 236, 237, 238, 239, 240,
    309, 569, 697
Youniss, J., 541, 932, 934

Yu, C. Y., 7
Yun, J. K., 170
Yuodelis, C., 118
Yurecko, M., 531
Yussen, S. R., 521

Zacharias, C. A., 885
Zacharski, R., 278
Zack, E. A., 195, 199
Zacks, J. M., 33, 755
Zago, L., 34
Zahn-Waxler, C., 819, 930, 931, 932
Zaitchik, D., 705, 836, 837, 864, 983
Zan, B., 930
Zander, B., 926
Zander, R. S., 926
Zanforlin, M., 748
Zangas, T., 760
Zangl, R., 80, 89
Zanone, P. G., 164, 173, 177
Zaslavsky, C., 784
Zatorre, R. J., 15, 76
Zauner, N., 33
Zeaman, D., 466
Zee, A., 612
Zelazo, N. A., 170, 171
Zelazo, P. D., 42, 170, 171, 444, 448, 451, 563,
    564, 567, 600, 622
Zelazo, P. R., 64, 167, 170, 171
Zelco, F. A., 830
Zenatti, A., 888
Zentall, S. S., 531
Zentall, T. R., 563
Zentner, M. R., 887, 888
Zernich, T., 867
Zernicke, R. F., 169, 172, 177, 186
Zhang, H., 785
Zhang, L., 63, 67, 612
Zhang, Y., 73
Zheng, W., 67, 612
Zhi, C., 867
Zhu, J., 785
Zhuang, J., 24
Zielinski, T., 598
Zigler, E., 906
Zijdenbos, A., 12, 31, 34, 803, 957
Zimmerman, B. J., 523, 530
Zimmerman, C., 924
Zimmerman, R., 860
Zimmermann, S., 537
Zingaro, M. C., 567, 568
Zinnes, J. L., 561
Zinober, B., 340
Zocchi, S., 531
Zohar, A., 470, 481, 483, 485, 489, 491, 492,
    493, 494, 495, 496, 497, 498, 542, 912, 921,
    923, 962, 966, 969, 970, 973, 974, 979, 983,
    987
Zola, S. M., 23, 24, 385
Zola-Morgan, S., 392
Zorzi, M., 794
Zuckerman, H., 912, 914, 923, 924, 925
Zuidema, N., 596
Zukowski, A., 765
Zumph, C., 931
Zur, O., 664
Zytkow, J. M., 908, 911, 923

# Subject Index

Absolutist level of epistemological understanding, 983

Abstract/concrete development, 617–619

Abstract constructions. *See* Linguistic constructions

Accessible models, information processing and, 457–458

Achromatic discriminations, 121

Action representations in drawings, 869–870

Active intermodal matching, 220

Actor-environment fit, 189–190

Acuity, visual, 114–116

Adapted mind, 614–617

Adaptive combination perspective on spatial processing development, 749–755
    categorical coding, 752
    distance coding, 750–752
    effect of experience, 753–754
    hierarchical combination, 752–753

Adaptors (gesture), 337

ADHD. *See* Attention deficit hyperactivity (ADHD)

Ad hoc models, information processing, 436–437

Adjectives, acquisition of, 315–320
    basic level categories as an entry point, 317
    cross-linguistic work, 318–320
    developmental work, 316–318
    linking adjectives to object properties, 316–317
    moving beyond the basic level, 317–318

Adolescent development, 953–989
    argument, 978–982
    brain and processing growth, 957–960
    complexity and value of developmental analysis, 954–957
    critical period, early adolescence as second, 988
    decision making, 975–978
    deductive inference, 960–964
    inductive and causal inference, 964–968
    knowing, understanding/valuing, 982–986
    learning and knowledge acquisition, 968–971
    mind, learning to manage, 986–989
    scientific thinking and inquiry, 971
    what develops, 955–957

Adult attachment interview (AAI), 837–838

Adult plasticity, 16–17

Adult work, primacy of, 662

Affect displays, gesture as, 337

Affordances, 189–196, 200–201
    actor-environment fit, 189–190
    creating, 200–201
    parents' role in promoting action, 200
    perceiving, 189–196
    specificity of learning, 193–195
    tools expanding possibilities for action, 200–201

Alerting/vigilance/arousal, 43

Ambiguity argument, 111, 112–113

Amygdala, 38

Analogy, schematization and; linguistic constructions, 287

Anatomical/cultural change, chronology of, 641

Animacy:
    conceptual development of, 703–704
    infant cognition, animate-inanimate distinction, 244–245

Animals. *See also* Primates, nonhuman:
    culture and, 637, 642–647
    human linguistic communication versus that of other species, 255–256

A-not-B task:
    information processing example, comparing models, 448–454
        dynamic systems model, 451–452, 453
        neural network model, 449–451
    spatial cognition, 742–743

Area, concept of, 596

Argument(s), 978–982
    argumentive discourse, 980–981
    evaluating, 979–980
    individual, 979–980
    producing, 979
    supporting development of skills in, 981–982

Arithmetic:
    development of (*see* Mathematical understanding)
    New Guinea, cultural evolution of in, 651–652

Arts, 859–895, 915–920
    domain similarities/differences, 936–940
    drawing, 859–881, 895
        evolutionary base, 860
        historical and theoretical approaches, 860–863
        overview/introduction, 859
        picture production: major milestones in development, 869–879
        picture recognition/comprehension/preference: major milestones in development, 863–869
        skill improvement and age, 880–881
        universality versus cultural specificity of drawing schemas, 879–880
    extraordinary achievement in, 915–920
        conceptual versus perceptual orientation, 918
        identity as an artist, 919–920
        markers of extraordinariness, 916–920
        versus ordinary development, 916
        precocity, 917–918
        realistic versus stylistic goals, 918–919
        talent, 917
    music, 839, 881–895
        absolute pitch, 893–894
        evolutionary base, 882–883
        figural understanding, 894–895
        historical and theoretical approaches, 883–884
        perception, infant, 884–888
        perception/comprehension, post-infancy, 888–890
        production through song, infancy, 891–893

Arts *(Continued)*
    production through song, post-infancy, 891–893
        skill improvement and age, 893–895
    overview/introduction, 859, 895
Association and rules, role of in cognitive development, 625–626
Associationism, 110
Associative learning:
    conceptual development, 710–711
    limits of similarity and associations, 712–715
    neural bases of cognitive development, 30–31
Attachment history, narrative/event memory and, 409–410
Attachment Q-sort (AQS), 838
Attention:
    alerting, vigilance, or arousal, 43
    nonexecutive aspects of, 43–44
    orienting, 43–44
Attentional control, 41–43
Attention deficit hyperactivity (ADHD):
    basal ganglia circuitry, 30
    strategies instruction and Meichenbaum's analyses, 528
Auditory function, developmental plasticity, and neural bases of, 14–15
Auditory world of infant, 58–95
    building from input during the first year, 83–92
        beginnings of grammar, 91–92
        beginnings of word recognition, 88–89
        learning phonology and phonotactics, 84
        listening for meaning, 89–91
        word segmentation, 84–88
    future directions, 92–95
        constraints on learning, 93
        domain specificity and species specificity, 93–94
        relationship between auditory processing and speech perception, 92–93
    implicit discovery of cues in the input, 80–81
        higher-level units, 81
        stress and phonotactic cues, 80–81
    infant audition, 59–72
        development of auditory apparatus, 59–60
        development of auditory scene analysis, 70–71
        frequency coding, 60–63
        implications for development of speech perception, 71–72
        intensity coding, 63–67
        measuring auditory development, 60–61
        perception of loudness, 65–67
        perception of pitch, 62–63
        perception of timbre, 65
        spatial resolution, 69–70
        temporal coding, 67–69
    infant speech perception and word learning, 72–80
        perception of prosodic attributes of the speech signal, 77–78
        perception of speech signal, 78–80
        perception of visible information in speech, 76–77
        phonetic perception, first studies, 72–75
        preference for speech, 75–76
    learning mechanisms, 81–83
    overview/introduction, 58–59, 94–95
    units for computations, 83
Autism:
    linguistic constructions, 291–292
    social cognition, 842–844
    theory of mind, 842–844
Autonoetic awareness, 402
Axons:
    development of, 10
    disorders of, 11

Balance scale:
    comparison of models, 438–444
    reasoning and problem solving, 597–599
Base-10 knowledge, 791–792

Behavioral flexibility, 169–170
Behaviorism, 4
Beliefs:
    social cognition, 823–826
    understanding second-order, 836–837
Biological domain, culture, 663–670
Biology. *See* Neural bases of cognitive development
Blindness, gesturing and, 353–354
Boundary assignment, visual perception, 134, 137
Brain development. *See* Neural bases of cognitive development

Calcium-regulated transcriptional activator (CREST), 10–11
Capability argument, 111, 113
Case and agreement, linguistic constructions, 267–268
Case Grammar, 256
Categorization:
    conceptual development, 696–701
    individuals versus categories, 700–701
    infant, 234–240, 569–570
        categorization paradigms, 235
        connectionist models, 237–239
        feature correlations and categorization, 235–237
        perceptual versus conceptual categories, 239–240
        reasoning and problem solving, 569–570
    levels of, 562–563, 696–698
    natural kinds versus arbitrary groupings, 698–700
    prototypes and family resemblance, 562
    reasoning and problem solving, and changed theories of, 561–563
    spatial cognition, and development of categorical coding, 752
    theory-based, 562
Causation:
    causal learning, 717–718
    conceptual development, 705–706
    inductive and causal inference, 964–968
    infants' understanding of events:
        complex causal chains, 231–233
        complex event sequences, 233–234
        simple causal events, 228–231
    recognition of cause in infancy, 567
    universals in expression of causativity, 324–325
CCC (cognitive complexity and control) theory, 563–564
Cell adhesion molecules (CAMs), 10
Cell migration, 9–10
Change, dimensions of cognitive, 479
    breadth of change, 479, 494–496
        basic phenomena, 494–495
        influences of child and environment, 495
        theoretical questions and implications, 495–496
    path of change, 479, 487–490
        basic phenomena, 487–489
        influences of child and environment, 489–490
        theoretical questions and implications, 490
    rate of change, 479, 490–494
        basic phenomena, 491–492
        influences of child and environment, 492–493
        theoretical questions and implications, 493–494
    source of change, 479, 496–499
        basic phenomena, 496–498
        influences of child and environment, 498
        theoretical questions and implications, 498–499
    variability of change, 479, 480–487
        basic empirical phenomena, 480–484
        between-child, 485–486
        influences of child and environment, 484–486
        significance for analyzing change, 482–483
        significance for identifying change mechanisms, 483–484
        significance for predicting change, 481–482
        significance of within-child, 481–484
        theoretical implications and questions, 486–487
Child-directed-speech (CDS), 260

Chomskian generative grammar, 257
Chromatic/achromatic attributes, 121. *See also* Color vision
Chromatic deficiency hypothesis, 123
Chromatic discriminations, 121
Cognition, infant. *See* Infant cognition
Cognitive domains, 627–629
Cognitive science and cognitive development, 609–629. *See also* Neural
   bases of cognitive development
   adapted mind, 614–617
   developmental universals, 626–627
   domains, 627–629
   earliest periods of cognitive development, 610–617
   generality/specificity, 626–629
   initial state, 611–614
   overview/introduction, 609–610, 629
   patterns of change, 617–622
      development from concrete to abstract, 617–619
      difference between learning and development, 621–622
      nature of conceptual change, 619–621
      representational formats underlying developmental change, 622–624
      role of association and rules, 625–626
      role of implicit and explicit thought in cognitive development,
         624–625
Cognitive strategies. *See* Strategies, cognitive
Collaborative strategic reading, 536
Color vision, 120–124
   assessing, 122–123
   brightness, 120–121
   chromatic/achromatic attributes, 121
   hue, 120–122
   origins of hue discrimination, 121–122
   psychological attributes, 120–121
   saturation, 120–121
Comforting/helping, in infancy, 818–820
Complexity, reasoning and, 563–567
   relational complexity (RC) metric, 565–567
   summary of research, 567
Composition, drawing, 868, 879
Comprehension strategies instruction, 532–537
   collaborative strategic reading, 536
   1980s-era studies, 534–535
   reciprocal teaching, 533–534
   transactional strategies instruction, 535–536
Computational models/approaches. *See* Information processing
Conceptual development, 687–724
   animacy, 703–704
   causation, 705–706
   competing metaphors of dictionary/encyclopedia, 702
   conceptual diversity, 693–702
      categories versus individuals, 700–701
      concepts encoded in language versus those that are not, 694–696
      implications for children's concepts, 701–702
      levels of categorization, 696–698
      natural kinds versus arbitrary groupings, 698–700
   current approaches to children's concepts, 690–693
      empiricist approaches, 691–692
      naive theory approaches, 692–693
      nativist approaches, 690–691
   essence, 708
   experience and individual variation, 718–723
   function, 706–708
   historical background, 689–690
   individual variation, 719–721
      cognitive style, 720–721
      expertise, 719–720
   mechanisms of conceptual acquisition and change, 709–718
      associative mechanisms, 710–711
      causal learning, 717–718
      conceptual placeholders, 715–717
      conceptual variation, 714–715

      constraints, 714
      context-sensitivity, 712
      interleaving, 723–724
      labels, 712–714
      limits of similarity and associations, 712–715
      modes of construal, 716–717
      similarity, 711–712
      words as pointers, 715–716
   nonobvious properties, 706–708
   ontology, 703–705
   overview/introduction, 687, 693, 723–724
   relevance/importance of, 688–689
   theories, concepts embedded in, 702–709
Concrete/abstract development, 617–619
Conditional reasoning, mental models in, 592–594
Conditioning or associative learning, 30–31
CONLERN, 147, 150, 241
Conservation and quantification, 577–585
   age of attainment of conservation, 580–582
   compensation and, 578–580
   number, 582–585
   perceptual factors and, 578–580
Consolidation and storage, event memory, 387–388, 399–400
CONSPEC, 147, 150, 241
Constructions, linguistic. *See* Linguistic constructions
Constructive Learning Architecture (CLA), 230
Constructivism/constructivist perspective:
   information-processing account of infant face processing, 242–244
   information-processing approach, infant cognition, 216–217
   information processing models, 456–457
   mathematical understanding, 778–779
   theory of perceptual development, 110–112
   visual perception, 110–112
Content-independent cognition, 567–568
Contour junctions, detection/classification of, 136–137
Contrast sensitivity, 116–119
Crawling, 176–177
Creativity, 908
Culture, 636–678
   animals and, 637, 642–647
   arithmetic across cultures, 794–795
   chronology of anatomical and cultural change, 641
   cognition and, synthetic framework for, 639–640
   cultural history, 637–638, 647–659
      cross-sectional comparisons, 648–650
      IQ scores, change in, 658–659
      long-distance transport of raw materials, 647
      longitudinal studies, 650–652
      production of second-order tools, 647
      production/use of simple machines, 647
      semeiosis, 647
      social differentiation, and education, 652–658
      spatial structural organization of living sites, 647
   defined, 637–639
   development, 637–638, 639
   drawing schemas, universality versus cultural specificity of, 879–880
   hominization and, 640–642
   ideal and material in, 638–639
   linguistic constructions, and intention-reading and cultural, 286–287
   living primates, 637, 642–647
   narrative differences, event memory, 410–411
   ontogeny, 659–674
      importance of parental beliefs, 662
      independence of children's motivation, 662
      intertwining of biology and cultural practices in conceptual
         development, 663–670
      number, 664–666
      primacy of adult work, 662
      proximal locus of development: activity settings and cultural
         practices, 660–663

Culture *(Continued)*
  overview/introduction, 636–637
  patterns, shared/distributed, 638
  phylogenetic development and, 640
  word learning, cross-linguistic evidence, 303, 318–320

Darwinian competition, 799–802
  selection, 801–802
  variability and competition, 799–801
Data analysis issues, 475–477
  graphical techniques, 475–476
  inferential statistical techniques, 476–477
Deafness, and gesture, 346–349
Decision making in adolescence, 975–978
  contingency, 976–977
  decision-making judgments, 976–977
  dual-process theory, 977–978
  gambler compensation fallacy, 977
  outcome bias, 977
  preference judgments, 976
  statistically-based (versus anecdotally-based) decisions, 977
Deduction:
  critical role of meaning, 961
  thinking and, 963–964
  indeterminate syllogisms, 961–962
  induction and, 592
  inference, 960–964
  relational problems of, 591–592
  what develops, 961–962
  when knowledge and reasoning conflict, 962–963
Delayed non-match-to-sample (DNMS) task, 24
Dendrites:
  development of, 10–11
  disorders of, 11
Depth in drawings:
  perceiving, 866
  representing, 877–878
Depth perception:
  familiar size, 133
  interposition cues, 132–133
  pictorial, 131–134
  stereoscopic, 129–131
Determinacy, logical and empirical, 594–595
Developmental universals, 626–627
Development versus plasticity and, 17–19
Development in second decade. *See* Adolescent development
Dialogue, function and preverbal, 816–817
Dictionary versus encyclopedia metaphor, 702
Dimensional Change Sort (DCCS) task, 563–565
Directional selectivity, motion perception, 124–125
Distance:
  coding (spatial cognition), 750–752
  reasoning and problem solving; time, speed, and, 595–596
Doubt/uncertainty, understanding, 834–836
Down syndrome:
  autism versus, 843
  false-belief task, 843
  linguistic constructions, 291
Drawing, 859–881, 895
  evolutionary base, 860
  historical and theoretical approaches, 860–863
  overview/introduction, 859
  picture production: major milestones in development, 869–879
    action representations, 869–870
    aesthetic properties, 878–879
    composition, 879
    depth representation, 877–878
    expression, 878–879
    graphic representations, 870–874
    human form representation, 870–874
    realism, 874–878
    style, 879
    trajectory from intellectual to visual realism, 875–876
  picture recognition/comprehension/preference: major milestones in development, 863–869
    acquisition of an intentional theory of pictures, 865–866
    aesthetic perception, 866–868
    aesthetic responses, 868–869
    components (four) of understanding representational nature of pictures, 863–866
    composition, 868
    depth perception, 866
    evaluating quality, 869
    expression, 866–867
    realism, appeal of, 868
    recognizing difference between a picture and what it represents, 863–864
    recognizing representational status of pictures, 864–865
    recognizing similarity between a picture and what it represents, 863
    regularity, appeal of, 868–869
    style, 867–868
  skill improvement and age, 880–881
  universality versus cultural specificity of drawing schemas, 879–880
Dynamic systems:
  A-not-B task, 448–454
  applications to development, 435–436
  basics, 435
  comparison of models, 451–454
  described, 435–436

Earth, concept of, 596–597
Ecological view, theories of perceptual development, 112–113
  ambiguity and, 112–113
  capability and, 113
Edge, visual perception and:
  classification, 134, 135–136
  detection, 135–136
  process, edge-insensitive/edge-sensitive, 138
  unity based on edge orientations and relations, 141–142
Education/schooling, culture and, 652–658
  comparing schooled and nonschooled children, 655–656
    metacognitive skills, 656
    organization of word meaning, 655–656
    spatio-temporal memory, 656
  intergenerational studies of impact of schooling, 657–658
  questioning validity of evidence, 656–657
  rudimentary forms of separation between enculturation and schooling, 653
  school-cutoff strategy, 655
  small, face-to-face societies, 653
  social accumulation, differentiation, and the advent of, 653–655
Egocentric to allocentric shift, spatial cognition, 743–744
Elaboration strategy, 517
Elicited imitation, 220
Emblems, gestures as, 337
Emotion, social cognition and, 828–832
Empiricism, 110, 691–692
Encoding, event memory and, 386–387, 399
Encyclopedia versus dictionary metaphors, 702
Environment, brain development/function and enriched, 17
Episodic memory, 19–20
Epistemological understanding, 982–983
  absolutist, 983
  components of knowing, 986
  coordinating objective and subjective elements of knowing, 984–986
  levels of, 983, 986
  multiplist, 983
  realist, 983
  relevance of, 985–986
Essence, 708

Essentialism, 571–572
Event(s), infants' understanding of, 228–234
    complex causal chains, 231–233
    complex event sequences, 233–234
    simple causal events, 228–231
Event memory, 373–418. *See also* Memory
    assessing nonverbally, 378–380
    changing the course of research, 377–380
    continuities and discontinuities in development of, 411–414
    defining, 374
    future directions in research, 416–418
    importance of, 374
    importance of familiarity, 378
    importance of organization or structure, 377–378
    overview/introduction, 373–376
    stressful or traumatic events, 414–416
    traditional accounts of development of, 376–380
Event memory development in infancy and early childhood, 380–392,
    412–413
    assessing using elicited and deferred imitation, 381–382
    changes in basic mnemonic processes, 386–390
    consolidation and storing, 387–388
    developmental trends, 382–385
        changes in efficacy of different types of reminder, 384–385
        changes in length of time that infants remember, 382–383
        changes in robustness of memory, 383–384
        changes in sensitivity to the temporal structure of events, 384
    encoding, 386–387
    group and individual differences, 390–392
        gender, 390–391
        language, 391
        special populations, 391–392
    neural substrate, 385–386
    retrieval, 388–389
    transition from infancy to early childhood, 412–413
Event memory development in/after preschool years, 392–411
    age-related changes in how long children remember, 394–395
    age-related changes in how much children report, 397
    age-related changes in productivity of external cues to recall, 395–396
    age-related changes in recall of past events, 394–397
    age-related changes in what children report, 396–397
    attachment history of the dyad, 409–410
    background knowledge, 406
    conceptual developments, 401–402
    consolidation and storage, 399–400
    culture group differences, 410–411
    developmental changes in basic mnemonic processes, 398–401
    developments in autonoetic awareness, 402
    emergence of autobiographical or personal memory, 397–398
    encoding, 399
    family constellation variables, 407
    gender differences, 406, 407–408
    group and individual differences, 405–411
        in basic mnemonic processes, 405–406
        in conceptual developments, 406–407
        in narrative socialization, 407–411
    information processing variables, 406
    language ability and, 406, 408
    placing events in a specific time and place, 402
    retrieval, 400–401
    routine events, 393
    self-concept, 401–402
    socialization/narrative production, 402–405, 407
    temperament and, 408–409
    unique events, 393–394
Executive functions, 39–43
    attentional control, 41–43
    domains, 40
    inhibitory control, 41
    working memory and, 40–41

Experience:
    conceptual development, and individual variation in, 718–723
    neural bases of cognitive development, 38–39
Expertise:
    conceptual development, 719–720
    research on, 907–908
Explicit memory. *See* Memory
Expression:
    drawing, 866–867, 878–879
    music, 890
Extraordinary achievements, 905–940
    in art, 915–920
        conceptual versus perceptual orientation, 918
        identity as an artist, 919–920
        markers of extraordinariness, 916–920
        ordinary development, 916
        precocity, 917–918
        realistic versus stylistic goals, 918–919
        talent, 917
    definitional issues, 909–910
    developmental issues, 910–911
    domains:
        differences, 938–940
        issues, 911–912
        similarities, 936–938
    framework, developmental-systemic, 913–915
    future research, 940
    history, 906–909
        beyond general intelligence, 907
        creativity, 908
        expertise, 907–908
        intelligence, 906–907
        leadership and morality, 908–909
        personality, 909
    methodological issues, 912–913
    in moral excellence, 929–936
        building organizations with moral mission, 935
        disposition to act, 933
        individual acts of caring or heroism, 933–934
        integration, 932–933
        markers of extraordinariness, 931–933
        moral leadership, 934–935
        ordinary development, 930–931
        precocity in judgment, 931
        self-awareness and control, 932
        unusual sensitivity, 931–932
        varieties of extraordinariness, 933–936
    overview/introduction, 905–906, 936–940
    in political leadership, 925–929
        connecting to others, 927–928
        drive, 928
        early adversity, 928
        intelligence, 927
        markers of extraordinariness, 927–929
        opportunity to act, 928–929
        ordinary development, 926–927
    in science, 920–925
        approaches to problems, 923–924
        career, 924–925
        curiosity, 922–923
        innate ability, 921–922
        markers of extraordinariness, 921–925
        ordinary development, 921
    strategies used by gifted students, 530

Face processing/perception, infant, 35, 146–150, 240–245
    animate-inanimate distinction, 244–245
    cognition and, 240–244
    constructivist information-processing account, 242–244
    development of, 242

Face processing/perception, infant (Continued)
  mechanisms, 149–150
  neural bases of cognitive development, 35
  perceiving information about people through faces, 148–149
  preference for facelike stimuli, 146–148, 241–242, 244
  visual perception, 146–150
Facial wiping, motor development and, 171
Familiarity, 133, 378, 562
Family:
  constellation variables, event memory and, 407
  parents:
    culture and importance of parental beliefs, 662
    deaf children's gestures versus parental gestures, 348–349
    event memory, and styles of conversation, 403–405
    motor development, and role in promoting action, 200
  resemblance and prototypes, reasoning problem solving, 562
Fast mapping and exclusivity, 592
Filopodia, 10
Forced-choice preferential looking (FPL), 115
Form perception, 142–146. See also Object perception/understanding
  nonrigid unity, 144–145
  optical transformations, infancy, 143
  perception of size, 145–146
  static, 143–144
Fragile X syndrome, 12
Frequency coding, 60–63
  discrimination, 62
  perception of pitch, 62–63
  resolution, 61–62
Frequency memory, 25
Frontal cortex, 25–26
Function, conceptual development, 706–708
Functionally based distributional analysis, 288

Gambler compensation fallacy, 977
Gaze following in infancy, 817–818
Gender:
  event memory and, 390–391, 406
  narrative and, 407–408
Generality and specificity, 626–629
Generalized imitation, 220
Generative Semantics, 256
Genome, human, 4
Geometric sensitivity, 747–748
Gestures, 336–365
  blind speakers, 353–354
  functions, 355–365
  language-learning children, development in, 338–345
    becoming a gesture comprehender, 342–344
    becoming a gesture producer, 338–342
    gestural input children receive, 344–346
  language-learning problems, 345–349
    deaf children, 346–349
    delayed language development, 345–346
  motivation for, 352–355
  overview/introduction, 336–337, 365
  role in communication (conveying information to listener), 355–358
    adult reactions to children gesturing "live," 358
    context of speech, 356–357
    mismatching speech, 357–358
  role in communication (influencing listeners' reaction to speaker), 358–361
    children's gestures shaping learning environment, 359
    teachers use of gestures, 359–361
  role in thinking (influence on speaker's cognition), 361–365
    creating ideas, 363–365
    direct impact on learner, 363–365
    lighten the speaker's cognitive load, 361–363
  situating within realm of nonverbal behavior, 337–338
  types of nonverbal behavior:

    adaptors, 337
    affect displays, 337
    emblems, 337
    illustrators, 337
    regulators, 337
  when conversing, 352–354
  when describing from memory, 354–355
  when listeners are present, 352–353
  when number of items in a task increases, 354
  when reasoning rather than describing, 355
  when speaking is difficult, 354
  when thinking and, 354–355
  as window on the mind, 349–352
    offering insight into child's knowledge, 350–352
    revealing thoughts not found in speech, 349–350
Giftedness. See also Extraordinary achievements:
  defined, 911
  strategies used by gifted students, 530
Goal-directed agency, infancy, 813–816
Goals/desires/intentions, social cognition and, 822–823
Government and Binding theory, 256
Grammar, beginnings of, 91–92. See also Language
Grammaticalization, 255
Graphical techniques, data analysis, 475–476
Graphic representations, drawing, 870–874
Grating acuity, 114, 115
Growth cones, 10

Habituation, 218–220
Hand gestures. See Gestures
Helping/comforting, in infancy, 818–822
Hierarchical combination, spatial cognition:
  development of, 752–753
  effect of experience on, 753–754
Hominization, culture and, 640–642
Hue discrimination, origins of, 121–122
Human form, drawing, 870–874
Hurting and teasing, infant social cognition, 821–822
Hyperacuity, 115

Illustrators, gestures as, 337
Imitation:
  deferred, 220, 381–382
  elicited, 24–25, 220, 381–382
  event memory and, 381–382
  generalized, 220
  infant cognition and, 220
  neural bases of cognitive development, 24–25
  of songs, 892
Implicit/explicit process, 561
Implicit sequence learning, 28–30
Induction:
  causal inference, 964–968
  coordinating effects of multiple variables: mental models of causality, 967–968
  coordinating theory and evidence, 965–966
  evidence for early competence, 964–965
  interpreting covariation evidence, 966–967
  reasoning and problem solving, 592
  word learning; conceptual consequences, 313–314
Infant cognition, 214–246
  animate-inanimate distinction, 244–245
  audition (see Auditory world of infant)
  categorization, 234–240, 569–570
    categorization paradigms, 235
    connectionist models of, 237–239
    feature correlations and categorization, 235–237
    perceptual versus conceptual categories, 239–240
  constructivist information-processing perspective, 216–217
  content-independent cognition, 567–568

defined, 214–217
events, understanding of, 228–234
   complex causal chains, 231–233
   complex event sequences, 233–234
   simple causal events, 228–231
face processing, 240–244
   constructivist information-processing account, 242–244
   development of, 242
   newborns' preferences for faces, 146–148, 241–242, 244
methodological issues, 218–220
   deferred imitation, 220
   habituation and related paradigms, 218–220
   object exploration and sequential touching, 220
   violation-of-expectation paradigm, 219
music:
   babbled songs, 891
   perception, 884–888
   pitch matching, 891
   rhythm, 891
number/arithmetic in, 780–784
objects, understanding of, 221–228 (see also Object
   perception/understanding)
overview/introduction, 245–246
quantitative reasoning, 568–569
recognition of cause, 567
representational mechanisms, 782–784
social cognition, 813–822
   detection of goal-directed agency, 813–816
   function and preverbal dialogue, 816–817
   gaze following and social referencing, 817–818
   hurting/teasing, 821–822
   offering help and cooperation, 818–821
spatial capabilities, 742–746
thinking, 567–570
Infinitival complement constructions, 283–284
Information processing, 426–458, 515–527
   accessible models, 457–458
   all-purpose models, 457
   benefits of computational models, 427–429
   constructivist models, 456–457
   criticisms of models, 454–456
      indeterminacy problem, 454–455
      reductionistic, 456
      too complex, 455
      too simple, 455–456
   event memory, variables, 406
   frameworks (four), overviews and examples, 430–438
      ad hoc models, 436–437
      dynamic systems, 435–436
      neural networks, 432–435
      production systems, 430–432
   frameworks compared, 437–454
      language: the past tense, 444–448
      memory: the A-not-B task, 448–454
      problem solving: the balance scale task, 438–444
      relative strengths and weaknesses, 437–438
      representations, 437
      strongest track record, 438
   future directions, 456–458
   general issues, 454–458
   historical context, 429–430
   mathematical understanding, 779–780
   multiple models, 457
   overview/introduction, 426–427, 458
   reasoning in adolescence, 959–960
   strategies, cognitive, 515–527
      development of children's verbal list learning strategies, 515–518
      elaboration, 517
      intentional, strategic memory model, 519–526
      metacognition, 521–523

      organizational strategies, 516–517
      rehearsal strategies, 515–516
      strategy knowledge as procedural knowledge, 521
      strategy use as coordination of information-processing components,
         526–527
      working/short-term memory, 519–521
      world knowledge, 523–525
Inhibition, 957–958
Inhibitory control, 41
Initial state, 611–614
Inquiry. See Scientific and technological thinking
Intelligence:
   extraordinary achievement, 906–907
   IQ scores, cultural-historical change in, 658–659
Intensity coding, 63–67
   intensity resolution, 63–65
   perception of loudness, 65–67
   perception of timbre, 65
Intentional expression in singing, 893
Intention-reading and cultural learning, 286–287
Interposition depth cue, 132–133
IQ scores, cultural-historical change in, 658–659
Item-based constructions, 263–264

Kinematic information, space perception, 127–129
Knowing:
   components of, 986
   coordinating objective and subjective elements of, 984–986
   epistemological understanding, 982–983
      absolutist, 983
      levels of, 983, 986
      multiplist, 983
      realist, 983
      relevance of, 985–986
   scientific thinking, 982–983
   understanding/valuing, 982–986
Knowledge:
   conflicting with reasoning, 962–963
   social cognition, and perception/source monitoring, 826–828
   strategy/procedural, 521

Labels, role of, 712–714
Lamellipodia, 10
Language. See also Linguistic constructions; Word learning:
   concepts encoded in, 694–696
   cultural history, nonhuman primates, 643–644
   past tense (example comparing models), 444–448
      analogy, 446
      comparison of models, 447–448
      neural network, 444–445
      production system, 445–447
      retrieval, 446
      zero strategy, 446
   spatial, 760–761
   theory of mind and, 845–847
Language abilities:
   event memory/narrative, 391, 406, 408
   gesture, and deafness, 346–349
   gesture, and inability, 345–346
Leadership and morality, 908–909
Learning:
   in adolescence, 968–971
   children's (see Microgenetic analyses of children's learning)
   development versus, 621–622
   mechanisms, and infant auditory world, 81–83
   morphology, linguistic constructions, 281–283
   neural bases of cognitive development:
      adult plasticity, 17
      developmental plasticity, 16
Learning disabilities, strategy instruction with students with, 529–530

Leg movements, alternating, 167
Lexical categories, 269–271
Lexical Functional Grammar, 256
Linear perspective, 132
Linguistic constructions, 253–293
    abstract constructions, 271–276
        analogy, 274–276
        ditransitives, datives, and benefactives, 272
        identificationals, attributives, and possessives, 271
        locatives, resultatives,and causatives, 272–273
        passives, middles, and reflexives, 273–274
        questions, 274
        simple transitives, simple intransitives, and imperatives, 271–272
    complex constructions, 283–285
        infinitival complement constructions, 283–284
        relative clause constructions, 284–285
        sentential complement constructions, 284
    constraining generalizations, 276–278
    constructing lexical categories, 269–271
    earliest language, 261–262
    history and theory, 256–259
        Chomskian generative grammar is a FORMAL theory, 257
        Cognitive-Functional Linguistics, 257–258
        constructions, 258–259
        dual approach (words/rules approach), 257
        two theories/strands, 257
    human versus animal linguistic communication, 255–256
    item-based constructions, 262–265
        item-based constructions, 263–264
        pivot schemas, 262–263
        processes of schematization, 264–265
        word combinations, 262
    language children hear, 260–261
    learning morphology, 281–283
    marking syntactic roles, 265–269
        case and agreement, 267–268
        cue coalition and competition, 268–269
        word order, 265–267
    nominal constructions, 278–279
    ontogeny:
        early, 259–271
        later, 271–285
    overview/introduction, 255–256, 292–293
    processes of language acquisition, 285–292
        atypical development, 291–292
        autism, 291–292
        Down syndrome, 291
        entrenchment and preemption, 287–288
        functionally based distributional analysis, 288
        growing abstractness of constructions, 285–286
        individual differences, 289–291
        intention-reading and cultural learning, 286–287
        production, 288–289
        psycholinguistic processes, 286–289
        rate, 289–290
        schematization and analogy, 287
        specific language impairment (SLI), 292
        style, 290–291
        Williams syndrome, 291
    verbal constructions, 279–281
Linguistic function, developmental plasticity; neural bases of cognitive development, 15
    Locative verbs, 325
Locomotion, type of radial migration, 10
Loudness, perception of, 65–67

Machines production/use, culture and, 647
Maps and models, 759–760
Mathematical understanding, 538–540, 777–804
    future directions, 803–804
    history, 778–780

        constructivism, 778–779
        early learning theory, 778
        information processing, 779–780
        neonativist perspective, 780
        psychometric studies, 778
    mechanisms of change, 799–803
        Darwinian competition, 799–802
        primary and secondary domains, 802–803
        selection, 801–802
        variability and competition, 799–801
    overview/introduction, 777, 803–804
    strategies instruction, and problem solving, 538–540
Mathematical understanding in infants, 780–784
    arithmetic, 782
    numerosity, 780–781
    ordinality, 781–782
    representational mechanisms, 782–784
Mathematical understanding in preschoolers, 784–789
    arithmetic, 787–789
        competencies, 787–788
        mechanisms, 788–789
    number and counting, 784–787
        cardinality and ordinality, 786–787
        counting procedures and errors, 785–786
        number concepts, 784–785
        number words, 785
Mathematical understanding in school-age children, 789–799
    arithmetical problem solving, 797–799
        classification of arithmetic word problems, 798
        problem schema, 797–798
        problem-solving processes, 798–799
    arithmetic operations, 794–797
        addition strategies, 795–796
        arithmetic across cultures, 794–795
        conceptual knowledge, 797
        subtraction, multiplication, and division strategies, 796–797
    conceptual knowledge, 789–794
        base-10 knowledge, 791–792
        estimation, 793–794
        fractions, 792–793
        properties of arithmetic, 789–791
    primary and secondary competencies, 789
Meaning:
    critical role of, 961
    listening for, 89–91
Memory, 19–31. *See also* Event memory
    A-not-B task, and information processing models, 448–454
        dynamic systems model, 451–452, 453
        neural network model, 449–451
    culture and ontogeny of autobiographical memory, 672–674
    delayed non-match-to-sample (DNMS) task, 24
    disorders of, 26–27
    elicited imitation, 24–25
    episodic, 19–20
    explicit:
        in the developing brain, 22–23, 411–412
        in the mature brain, 21–22
        role of frontal cortex in, 25–26
    frequency, 25
    gesturing when describing from, 354–355
    importance of, 19
    neural bases of cognitive development, 19–31
    nondeclarative, 27–31
        conditioning or associative learning, 30–31
        diagram of medial temporal lobe memory system, 28
        implicit sequence learning, 28–30
        visual priming, 28
    novelty preferences, 23–24
    overview table, 21
    semantic, 19–20
    social cognition; thoughts and stream of consciousness, 832–834

source, 25
strategies:
    classical research on development of, 513–515
    remembering instructions, 519
    strategies instruction, 519–521
systems, 19–20
for temporal order, 25–26
working:
    executive functions, 40–41
    production systems, 430
    strategies instruction, 519–521
Mental models, reasoning and problem solving:
    analogy, 561
    conditional reasoning, 592–594
Mental retardation, strategy instruction with students with, 528–529
Mental rotation:
    neural bases of cognitive development, 31–32
    perspective taking, spatial cognition and, 755–756
Mental state understanding in early childhood, 822–834
    beliefs, 823–826
    emotion, 828–832
    goals, desires, and intentions, 822–823
    perception, knowledge, and source monitoring, 826–828
    thoughts, memories, and the stream of consciousness, 832–834
Metacognition, 521–523
Microgenetic analyses of children's learning, 464–504
    breadth of change, 479, 494–496
    centrality of learning to children's development, 464–469
    change mechanisms, 501–504
    dimensions of cognitive change, 479
    history, 465–469
    list of twenty major findings, 471
    methodological issues, 472–477
        data analysis, 475–477
        experimental design, 472–473
        graphical techniques, 475–476
        inferential statistical techniques, 476–477
        reactivity of self-reports, 475
        strategy assessment, 473–475
    microgenetic methods, 469–477
        applicability, 469–471
        essential properties, 469
        history, 471–472
    new field of children's learning, 480–499
    overlapping waves theory, 477–479
    overview/introduction, 503–504
    path of change, 479, 487–490
    rate of change, 479, 490–494
    relations between learning and development, 499–501
    source of change, 479, 496–499
    variability of change, 479, 480–487
Mind, adapted, 614–617
Mind-mindedness, 846
Modularity, spatial cognition, 746–749
Morality/moral excellence, 908–909, 929–936
    domain similarities/differences, 936–940
    historical perspective, 908–909
    markers of extraordinariness, 931–933
        disposition to act, 933
        integration, 932–933
        precocity in judgment, 931
        self-awareness and control, 932
        unusual sensitivity, 931–932
    ordinary development, 930–931
    varieties of extraordinariness, 933–936
        building organizations with a moral mission, 935
        individual acts of caring or heroism, 933–934
        moral leadership, 934–935
Motion, infant perception of:
    animate-inanimate distinction, 244
    directional selectivity, 124–125

flicker, 125–126
mechanisms, 125–126
object unity, 138–141
position, 125–126
space perception, 129
velocity sensitivity, 125–126
Motivation, independence of children's, 662
Motor development, 16, 161–202
    adult plasticity, 16
    formal structure of movements, 161–163
    neural bases of cognitive development, 16
    overview/introduction, 164–165
    perceptual control of motor actions, 163–164
Motor development as a model system, 165–184
    developmental trajectories, 172–176
        evidence for developmental stages, 175–176
        fits and starts, 174–175
        one step backward, two steps forward, 173–174
    emergent developments, 166–172
        alternating leg movements, 167
        behavioral flexibility, 169–170
        brain-based explanations, 166–167
        contextual factors, 170–171
        facial wiping, 171
        pattern generators, 168–169
        rate-limiting factors, 171–172
        reflexes, 167–168
        regressions, 170
    qualitative changes, 165–166
        developmental stages, 165–166
        what's new, 166
    summary: models of change, 183–184
    time, age, and experience, 177–181
        empty time, 180
        improvements in walking skill, 178–180
        what infants experience, 180–181
    ubiquity of movement, 181–183
        epochs of movement, 181–182
        movement is fundamental, 182–183
        movement is pervasive in development, 182
    variability, 176–177
        crawling, 176–177
        reasons for variability, 177
Motor development as a perception-action system, 184–202
    affordances, creating, 200–201
        parents' role in promoting action, 200
        tools expanding possibilities for action, 200–201
    affordances, perceiving, 189–196
        actor-environment fit, 189–190
        learning to perceive affordances, 190–193
        specificity of learning, 193–195
        what infants learn, 195–196
    centrality of posture, 187–189
        anticipatory postural adjustments, 188–189
        nested actions, 187–188
    overview/introduction, 199–202
    perception-action loop, 196–200
        information-generating behaviors, 198–199
        real-time loop, 199–200
        sensitivity to perceptual information, 197–198
    prospective control, 184–187
        common paths to prospectivity, 185–187
        divergent developments in prospective looking and prehension, 187
        early action systems, 185
Movement. See Motor development
Multiplist level of epistemological understanding, 983
Music, 839, 881–895
    absolute pitch, 893–894
    evolutionary base, 882–883
    figural understanding, 894–895

Music (*Continued*)
    historical and theoretical approaches, 883–884
    perception, infant, 884–888
        preference for consonance, 887–888
        relational processing of rhythm and melody, 885–886
        sensitivity to "good" melody structure or intervals, 886–887
        sensitivity to unequal-step structure of musical scales, 886
        universals in songs sung to infants, 885
    perception/comprehension, post-infancy, 888–890
        aesthetic properties, 890
        expression, 890
        recognizing invariant structure ("music conservation"), 889–890
        sensitivity to diatonic structure, 888–889
        sensitivity to key changes, 889
        sensitivity to the hierarchy of notes within a key, 889
        style, 890
    production through song, infancy, 891–893
        babbled songs, 891
        pitch matching, 891
        rhythm, 891
    production through song, post-infancy:
        conventional songs, 892–893
        imitated songs, 892
        intentional expression in singing, 893
        intervals widening, 891–892
        invented notations, 893
        invented songs, 891–892
        pitch becoming discrete, 891
        rhythmic and tonal organization, 892
    skill improvement and age, 893–895
Myelination, 12

Naive psychology:
    conceptual development, 692–693
    culture, 666–667
    theory of mind, 666–667
Narrative, 402–405, 407–411
    culture and, 410–411
    developmental changes in and socialization of, 402–405
    event memory and, 402–405, 407–411
    gender, 407–408
    group and individual differences, 407–411
    language abilities, 408
    socialization, 403
    temperament, 408–409
Nativism, 4, 690–691, 780
Navigation, 35, 756–758
Neural bases of cognitive development, 19–31
    attention, nonexecutive aspects of, 43–44
        alerting, vigilance, or arousal, 43
        orienting, 43–44
    brain development and neural plasticity, 5–13, 957–960
        adolescence, and processing growth, 957–960
        axons, 10, 11
        cell migration, 9–10
        dendrites, 10–11
        growth and development of processes, 10–11
        myelination, 12
        neural induction and neurulation, 6–8
        neurodevelopmental timeline, from conception through adolescence, 7
        neurogenesis, disorders of, 8
        neurogenesis, postnatal, 8–9
        synaptic plasticity, 12
        synaptic pruning, 11–12
        synaptogenesis, 11–12
    developmental psychologists and neuroscience, 4–5
    executive functions, 39–43
        attentional control, 41–43
        domains, 40

        inhibitory control, 41
        working memory, 40–41
    future of developmental cognitive neuroscience, 44–45
    memory, 19–31, 385–386 (*see also* Memory)
    motor development, brain-based explanations, 166–167
    neural plasticity, 13–19
        adult plasticity, 16–17
        auditory function, 14–15
        developmental plasticity, 14–16
        development versus plasticity, 17–19
        effects of enriched environments on brain development and function, 17
        learning and memory function, 16, 17
        linguistic function, 15
        motor learning, 16
        visual and auditory function, 15–17
    object recognition, 35–39
        amygdala, 38
        experience's role, 38–39
        face/object recognition, 35
        occipito-temporal cortex, 35–38
        visuospatial module, 39
    overview/introduction, 3–4
    spatial cognition, 31–35
Neural networks, 432–435
    applications to development, 433–435
    basics, 433
    comparisons to other models, 437–454
        language: the past tense, 444–448
        memory: the A-not-B task, 448–454
        problem solving, balance scale task, 438–444
        relative strength/weakness, 437–438
        representations, 437
        strongest track record, 437, 438
New Guinea, cultural evolution of arithmetic in, 651–652
Nominal constructions, 278–279
Nondeclarative memory, 27–31
Nonverbal:
    assessing event memory, 378–380
    communication (*see* Gestures)
Nouns, 309–315
    advantage, 312–313
    consequences of early noun learning, 313–315
    evolution of link between object categories and, 309–311
    individuation, 313
    induction, 313–314
    informational differences between nouns and verbs, 320–321
    privileged position of, 303
    processing consequences, 314–315
Novelty preferences, 23–24
Number. *See also* Mathematical understanding:
    conservation and, 582–585
    culture and, 664–666

Object categories/properties, and word learning:
    broadening range of concepts, 308–309
    evolution of link between nouns and object categories, 309–311
    linking adjectives to object properties, 316–317
Object perception/understanding, 220–228, 744–745
    infant cognition, 220–228
        exploration and sequential touching, 220
        object individuation, 227–228
        object permanence, 221–225
        object unity, 226–227
        phase 1: demonstration and modification, 221
        phase 2: refutation and rejection, 221–222
        phase 3: rebuttal and recent evidence, 222–225
        recent empirical evidence, 222–224
        recent theoretical proposals, 224–225

neural bases of cognitive development, 35–39
  amygdala, 38
  experience's role, 38–39
  face/object recognition, 35
  occipito-temporal cortex, 35–38
  visuospatial module, 39
spatial cognition, 744–745
unity, 137–142, 226–227
visual perception, 134–146
  boundary assignment, 137
  common motion, 138–141
  contour junctions, detection/classification of, 136–137
  edge detection and edge classification, 135–136
  edge-insensitive process, 138
  edge-sensitive process, 138
  multiple processes, 137–138
  multiple tasks in, 134–135
  object unity, 137–142
Occipito-temporal cortex, 35–38
Ontogeny, cultural variation in, 659–674, 676–678. *See also* Culture
Ontology, 703–705
Optical development. *See* Visual perception, infant
Optical expansion/contraction, space perception, 128–129
Optokinetic nystagmus (OKN), 115
Organizational strategies, 516–517
Orientation sensitivity, visual perception, 119
Orienting, neural bases of cognitive development, 43–44
Overlapping waves theory, 477–479

Parents. *See* Family
Pattern discrimination, visual perception, 119–120
Pattern generators, motor development and, 168–169
Pattern processing, spatial, 32–33
Peer relations, 847–848
Perception-action system. *See* Motor development as a perception-action system
Perception/knowledge, and source monitoring, social cognition, 826–828
Perceptual development, theories of, 110–114
Personality, 909
Perspective:
  mental rotation and, 755–756
  linear, 132
Phenylketonuria (PKU), 42
Phonetic perception, 72–75. *See also* Auditory world of infant; Speech perception, infant
Phonology, 84
Photoreceptors (rods/cones), 121
Phylogenetic development, culture and, 640, 675–676
Piagetian developmental milestones, nonhuman primates, 644
Pictorial depth perception, 131–134
Pitch:
  absolute, 893–894
  discrete, 891
  perception of, 62–63
Pivot Grammar, 256–257
Pivot schemas, linguistic constructions, 262–263
Placeholders, conceptual, 715–717
Political leadership, 925–929
  connecting to others, 927–928
  domain similarities/differences, 936–940
  drive, 928
  early adversity, 928
  intelligence, 927
  markers of extraordinariness, 927–929
  opportunity to act, 928–929
  ordinary development, 926–927
Posture, 187–189
  anticipatory adjustments, 188–189
  nested actions, 187–188

Preference judgments, 976
Preschoolers:
  mathematical understanding, 784–789
  memory (*see* Event memory development in/after preschool years)
  strategies-productive, 518–519
Pretend play: and theory of mind, 844–845
Primates, nonhuman, 642–647, 839–841
  cognition and, 645–647
  cognitive achievements, 643
  culture, 642–647
  language, 643–644
  Piagetian developmental milestones, 644
  theory of mind, 644–645, 839–841
  tools use, 644
Problem solving:
  balance scale task, 438–444
    comparison of models, 443–444
    early production system model, 440
    neural network model, 440–441
    recent production system model, 441–443
  reasoning and (*see* Reasoning)
Processing capacity, older children, 958–959
Processing speed, older children, 957
Prodigiousness, defined, 911. *See also* Extraordinary achievements
Production systems:
  act process, 431
  applications to development, 431–432
  balance scale task and, 438–444
  basics, 430–431
  comparisons with other models, 437–444
  conflict resolution process, 431
  defined/described, 430–432
  production memory, 430
  recognition or matching process, 431
  structures, two interacting, 430–432
  working memory, 430
Prototypes, 562, 570–571

Quantitative reasoning:
  abilities (*see* Mathematical understanding)
  infant, 568–569

Raw materials, cultural history and transport of, 647
Rayleigh discrimination tests, 123
Realist level of epistemological understanding, 983
Real-time loop, motor development, 199–200
Reasoning, 557–600
  categorization, 561–563
    levels of categorization, 562–563
    prototypes and family resemblance, 562
    theory-based categorization, 562
  childhood, concepts and categories in, 569–577
    class inclusion and hierarchical classification, 572–577
    essentialism, 571–572
    prototype categories, 570–571
    theory-based categories, 571
  complexity, 563–567
  conservation and quantification, 577–585
    age of attainment of conservation, 580–582
    number, 582–585
    perceptual factors, compensation, and conservation, 578–580
  domain specificity versus generality, 558–559
  gesturing and, 355
  infancy, origin of thinking in, 567–570
    category formation, 569–570
    content-independent cognition, 567–568
    quantitative reasoning, 568–569
    recognition of cause, 567
  knowledge conflicting with, 962–963

Reasoning (Continued)
  methods of analysis of cognitive processes, 559
  origins of current conceptions of reasoning, 558
  relational, 585–595
    fast mapping and exclusivity, 592
    logical and empirical determinacy, 594–595
    logical deduction and induction, 592
    mental models in conditional reasoning, 592–594
    relational problems of deduction, 591–592
    relational problem solving, 592
    transitive inference, 585–589
    transitivity of choice and learning of order, 589–591
  scientific and technological thinking, 595–599
    area, 596
    balance scale, 597–599
    earth, 596–597
    time, speed, and distance, 595–596
  strategies, 559–561
    implicit versus explicit process, 561
    mental models and analogy, 561
    verbal, 560–561
  symbolic processes in, 561
Reciprocal teaching, 533–534
Reflective functioning among adults, measures of, 837–839
Reflexes, 167–168
Regressions (motor development), 170
Regulators, gestures as, 337
Rehearsal strategies, 515–516
Relational complexity (RC), 563, 565–567
Relational reasoning, 585–595
  fast mapping and exclusivity, 592
  logical and empirical determinacy, 594–595
  logical deduction and induction, 592
  mental models in conditional reasoning, 592–594
  relational problems of deduction, 591–592
  relational problem solving, 592
  transitive inference, 585–589
  transitivity of choice and learning of order, 589–591
Relative clause constructions, 284–285
Representational formats underlying developmental change, 622–626
Representational nature of pictures, understanding, 863–866
Representation of patterns, mental; culture and changing modes of, 651
Retrieval (event memory), 388–389, 400–401
Retrieving hidden objects, 518–519
Rods/cones, 121
Rules, association and, 625–626

SCADS model of strategy choice and strategy discovery, 503
Schematization, linguistic constructions and:
  analogy and, 287
  processes, 264–265
School, arithmetic in, 789–799. See also Mathematical understanding
  arithmetical problem solving, 797–799
    classification of arithmetic word problems, 798
    problem schema, 797–798
    problem-solving processes, 798–799
  arithmetic operations, 794–797
    addition strategies, 795–796
    conceptual knowledge, 797
    subtraction, multiplication, and division strategies, 796–797
  conceptual knowledge, 789–794
    base-10 knowledge, 791–792
    estimation, 793–794
    fractions, 792–793
    properties of arithmetic, 789–791
  primary and secondary competencies, 789
Schooling and culture. See Education/schooling, culture and
Scientific and technological thinking:
  children's thinking as "scientific," 971–972
  development in adolescence, 971–975

extraordinary achievement in, 920–925
  approaches to problems, 923–924
  career, 924–925
  curiosity, 922–923
  domain similarities/differences, 936–940
  innate ability, 921–922
  markers of extraordinariness, 921–925
  ordinary development, 921
inquiry process/skills, 972–975
reasoning and problem solving, 595–599
  area, concept of, 596
  balance scale problem, 597–599
  earth, concept of, 596–597
  time/speed/distance, 595–596
strategies instruction, 540–542
Self-concept, 401–402
Semantic memory, 19–20
Semantic Relations approach, 256
Semeiosis, 647
Sentential complement constructions, 284
Shading, depth cue of, 132
Similarity, conceptual development, 711–715
Size, perception of, 145–146
Social cognition, 811–851
  historical background (1920–1980), 811–812
  infant, 813–822
    comforting and helping, 818–820
    detection of goal-directed agency, 813–816
    function and preverbal dialogue, 816–817
    gaze following and social referencing, 817–818
    hurting and teasing, 821–822
    offering help and cooperation, 820–821
  mature understanding/functioning, 834–839
    doubt and uncertainty, 834–836
    measures of reflective functioning among adults, 837–839
    second-order beliefs and nonliteral utterances, 836–837
  mental state understanding in early childhood, 822–834
    beliefs, 823–826
    emotion, 828–832
    goals, desires, and intentions, 822–823
    perception, knowledge, and source monitoring, 826–828
    thoughts, memories, and the stream of consciousness, 832–834
  overview/introduction, 847–851
  peer relations and, 847–848
  theory of mind:
    autism and, 842–844
    emerging contours in children, 850–851
    language and, 845–847
    nonhuman primates, 839–841
    pretend play, individual differences, 844–845
    universal core, 841–842
  trust and, 848–850
Socialization, 402–405, 407–411, 650–651
Somal translocation, 10
Songs. See Music
Sounds:
  infant audition (see Auditory world of infant)
  song (see Music)
  words versus, 308
Source memory, 25
Source monitoring, perception, knowledge, and, 826–828
Spatial perception/cognition, 31–35, 126–134, 734–767
  adaptive combination point of view, 749–755
  categorical coding, development of, 752
  cognitive constructs, 736–737
  distance coding, 750–752
  future directions, 766–767
  geometric sensitivity, 747–748
  hierarchical combination, development of, 752–754
  individual differences, 761–765

infant audition, and spatial resolution, 69–70
infant capabilities, 742–746
  A-not-B error, 742–743
  egocentric to allocentric shift, 743–744
  objects, 744–745
infant visual perception, 126–134
  accretion/deletion of texture, 128
  familiar size, 133
  interposition depth cue, 132–133
  kinematic information, 127–129
  motion perspective, 129
  optical expansion/contraction, 128–129
  pictorial depth perception, 131–134
  stereoscopic depth perception, 129–131
maps and models, 759–760
mature competence, 737–740
mental rotation, 31–32, 755–756
modularity, 746–749
navigation, 35, 756–758
neural bases of cognitive development, 31–35
nonnormative contexts, 765–766
overview/introduction, 734–735
pattern processing, 32–33
perspective taking, 755–756
referent system, 740–741
representing spatial relations between viewer and environment, 755–758
spatial language, 760–761
symbolic representations, 741, 758–761
visual impairment, 766
visuospatial recognition and recall memory, 34–35
visuospatial working memory, 33–34
Williams syndrome, 765–766
Spatial structural organization of living sites, cultural history, 647
Specific Language Impairment (SLI):
  information processing approaches, 434
  linguistic constructions, 292
Speech perception, infant, 72–80. See also Auditory world of infant
  implications of infant audition for development of, 71–72
  perception of prosodic attributes of speech signal, 77–78
  perception of visible information in speech, 76–77
  phonetic perception, first studies, 72–75
  preference for speech, 75–76
  relationship between auditory processing and, 92–93
Speed/time/distance, reasoning and, 595–596
SRT (serial reaction time) task, 27–31
Stability, perceiving motion and, 126
Static form perception, 143–144
Statistical techniques, inferential, 476–477
Stereoscopic depth perception, 129–131
Strange Situation, 838
Strategies, cognitive, 511–547
  definition of strategy, 512–513
  elaboration, 517
  future directions, 545–547
  information-processing model of intentional, strategic memory, 519–526
    metacognition, 521–523
    strategy knowledge as procedural knowledge, 521
    working/short-term memory, 519–521
    world knowledge, 523–525
  information-processing theory (1960s), 515–518
  instructional applications, 531–543
    collaborative strategic reading, 536
    comprehension strategies instruction, 532–537
    mathematical problem solving, 538–540
    reciprocal teaching, 533–534
    scientific reasoning, argument skills, and strategies, 540–542
    transactional strategies instruction, 535–536
    word recognition, 531–532
    writing strategies instruction, 537–538

instruction with exceptional children, 527–531
  Meichenbaum's analyses of attention deficit hyperactivity, 528
  strategies use by gifted students, 530
  students with learning disabilities, 529–530
  students with mental retardation, 528–529
memory strategies, classical research on development of, 513–515
organizational strategies, 516–517
overview/introduction, 511–512, 543–545
preschoolers, strategies-productive, 518–519
  remembering instructions, 519
  retrieving hidden objects, 518–519
reasoning, 559–561
  implicit versus explicit process, 561
  mental models and analogy, 561
  verbal strategies, 560–561
rehearsal strategies, 515–516
strategy use as coordination of information-processing components, 526–527
verbal list learning strategies, 515–518
Stream of consciousness, 832–834
Stress and phonotactic cues, infant audition, 80–81
Structuralism, 110
Style:
  artistic:
    drawing, 867–868, 879
    music, 890
  cognitive, 720–721
Syllogisms, 961–962
Symbolic processes in reasoning, 561
Symbolic spatial representations, 741, 758–761
Synaptogenesis, 11–12
  background, 11
  development, 11
  disorders, 12
  synaptic plasticity, 12
  synaptic pruning, 11–12
Syntactic roles, marking, 265–269

Talent, defined, 911
Teachers and gesture, 359–361
Teasing/hurting, infant social cognition, 821–822
Teddy bear illustration, 969
Temperament, event memory, narrative, and, 408–409
Temporal coding, infant audition, 67–69
Temporal order, memory for, 25–26
Texture, 128, 132
Theory of mind:
  autism, 842–844
  culture, 644–645, 666–667
  emerging contours in children's, 850–851
  individual differences in pretend play, 844–845
  language and, 845–847
  naive psychology and, 666–667
  nonhuman primates, 644–645, 839–841
  universal core, 841–842
Thinking:
  gesture's role in, 361–365
  problem solving (see Reasoning)
  social cognition, and thoughts, memories, and the stream of consciousness, 832–834
Timbre, perception of, 65
Time/speed/distance, reasoning and, 595–596
Tools:
  culture and, 644, 647
  motor development and, 200–201
Transactional strategies instruction, 535–536
Transformational Generative Grammar, 256
Transitive inference, 585–589
Transitivity of choice and learning of order, 589–591
Traumatic events, memory for, 414–416

Tritan test, 123
Trust, social cognition and, 848–850

Uncertainty/doubt, understanding, 834–836
Uniform loss hypothesis, color vision, 123
Unity, object, 137–142, 226–227
Universals, 324–325, 626–627
Up-down symmetry, 242
Usage-Based Linguistics, 257–258

"Value added" thinking, 4–5
Velocity sensitivity, visual perception, 125–126
Verbal constructions, 279–281
Verbal strategies, reasoning and problem solving, 560–561
Verb learning, 320–326
    children's use of syntax, 321–323
    cross-linguistic evidence and constraints on, 323–325
    informational differences between nouns and verbs, 320–321
    role of input in, 325–326
    syntactic and semantic types of arguments, 323–324
    universals and constraints on locative verbs, 325
    universals in expression of causativity, 324–325
Verbal list learning strategies, 515–518
Veridicality, 474–475
Vernier acuity, 115
Vigilance/alerting/arousal, 43
Violation of expectation paradigm, 219, 222
Visual arts. See Drawing
Visual efficiency hypothesis, 123
Visual evoked potential (VEP), 115–116
Visual function, neural bases of cognitive development:
    adult plasticity, 16–17
    developmental plasticity, 15–16
    memory and visual priming, 28
    visuospatial module, 39
    visuospatial recognition and recall memory, 34–35
    visuospatial working memory, 33–34
Visual impairment, spatial cognition and, 766
Visual perception, infant, 109–152
    basic visual sensitivities in infancy, 114–126
        color vision, 120–124
        contrast sensitivity, 116–119
        motion perception, 124–126
        orientation sensitivity, 119
        pattern discrimination, 119–120
        space perception, 126–134
        visual acuity, 114–116
    face perception, 146–150
    future directions, 152
    hardwiring versus construction, 151–152
    levels of analysis, 150–151
    object perception, 134–146
        boundary assignment, 137
        contour junctions, detection/classification of, 136–137
        edge detection and edge classification, 135–136
        multiple tasks in, 134–135
        nonrigid unity and form, 144–145
        object unity, 137–142

        optical transformations, 143
        size perception, 145–146
        static form perception, 143–144
        three-dimensional form, 142–145
    overview/introduction, 150–152
    space perception, 126–134 (see also Spatial perception/cognition)
    theories of perceptual development, 110–114
        constructivist view, 110–112
        contemporary situation, 113–114
        ecological view, 112–113

Walking skill, 178–180. See also Motor development
Waves theory, overlapping, 477–479
Williams syndrome:
    linguistic constructions, 291
    spatial cognition, 765–766
Wisconsin Card Sorting Task (WCST), 42
Word(s):
    combinations, 262
    open- and closed-class, 305
    order, 265–267
    as pointers, 715–716
    recognition:
        beginnings of, 88–89
        strategies instruction, 531–532
    segmentation, first year, 84–88
Word learning, 299–327
    cross-linguistic evidence, 303
    first steps into (broad initial link between words and concepts),
        306–309
        advantages of broad initial link, 309
        familiarization phase, 307
        object categories or a broader range of concepts, 308–309
        specificity of initial link, 307–309
        test phase, 307
        words or sounds, 308
    foundational capacities, 304–306
        discovering words and word-sized units, 304–305
        identifying relevant concepts, 305–306
        interpreting intentions of others, 306
    future research, 326–327
    gateway between linguistic and conceptual organization, 299–302
    later steps into (more specific links between kinds of words and kinds of
        concepts), 309–326
        adjectives, 315–320
        nouns, 303, 309–315
        verbs, 320–326
    overview/introduction, 302–304
    puzzle of, 300–302
    structure, input versus mind, 303–304
Working memory:
    executive functions, 40–41
    production systems, 430
    strategies instruction, 519–521
World knowledge, 523–525
Writing strategies instruction, 537–538

Zinacantan, historical change and cognitive change in, 650